AN

ARABIC-ENGLISH LEXICON

AN

ARABIC-ENGLISH LEXICON

BY

EDWARD WILLIAM LANE

IN EIGHT PARTS

PART 4 س - ص

القَامُوسُ

AN

ARABIC-ENGLISH LEXICON,

DERIVED FROM THE BEST AND THE MOST COPIOUS EASTERN SOURCES;

COMPRISING A VERY LARGE COLLECTION
OF WORDS AND SIGNIFICATIONS OMITTED IN THE ḲÁMOOS,
WITH SUPPLEMENTS TO ITS ABRIDGED AND DEFECTIVE EXPLANATIONS,
AMPLE GRAMMATICAL AND CRITICAL COMMENTS,
AND EXAMPLES IN PROSE AND VERSE:

COMPOSED BY MEANS OF THE MUNIFICENCE OF THE MOST NOBLE
ALGERNON,
DUKE OF NORTHUMBERLAND, K. G.,
ETC. ETC. ETC.,
AND THE BOUNTY OF
THE BRITISH GOVERNMENT:

BY EDWARD WILLIAM LANE,
CORRESPONDENT OF THE INSTITUTE OF FRANCE, ETC.

IN TWO BOOKS:

THE FIRST CONTAINING ALL THE CLASSICAL WORDS AND SIGNIFICATIONS COMMONLY KNOWN
TO THE LEARNED AMONG THE ARABS:
THE SECOND, THOSE THAT ARE OF RARE OCCURRENCE AND NOT COMMONLY KNOWN

BOOK I.—PART 4.

س — ص

KALPAZ

ISBN: 978-93-5128-814-5(Set)
ISBN: 978-93-5128-826-8(PB)

First Published in 1872
Indian Reprint in 2017

Published by

Kalpaz Publications
C-30, Satyawati Nagar,
Delhi – 110052
E-mail: kalpaz@hotmail.com
Website: kalpazpublications.com
Ph.: +91-9212142040

Cataloging in Publication Data—DK

Courtesy: D.K. Agencies (P) Ltd. <docinfo@dkagencies.com>

Lane, Edward William, 1801-1876, **author.**

Madd al-qa˜mu˜s = An Arabic-English lexicon : derived from the best and the most copious eastern sources, comprising a very large collection of words and significations omitted in the Kamoos, with supplements to its abridged and defective explanations, ample grammatical and critical comments, and examples in prose and verse : composed by means of the munificence of the most noble algernon, Duke of Northumberland, K. G., etc. etc. etc., and the bounty of the British Government / by Edward William Lane.

volumes cm

English and Arabic.

Parts 6-8 edited with a memoir by Stanley Lane Poole.

"First published in 1863"—Title page verso.

"In two books: the first containing all the words and significations commonly known to the learned among the Arabs : the second, those that are of rare occurrence and not communly known."
ISBN 9789351288145 (set :

1. Arabic language—Dictionaries—English. 2. English language—Dictionaries—Arabic. I. Lane-Poole, Stanley, 1854-1931, editor. II. Title. III. Title: Arabic-English lexicon.

PJ6640.L36 2017 DDC 492.7321 23

س

The twelfth letter of the alphabet; called سِينٌ. It is one of the letters termed مَهْمُوسَة [or non-vocal, i. e. pronounced with the breath only, without the voice]; and of the letters termed أَسَلِيَّة, as also ص and ز, because proceeding from the tip of the tongue: its place of utterance is between that of ص and that of ز: and Az says that it is never conjoined with either of these two letters in any Arabic word: (TA:) it is a sibilant letter; and is distinguished from ص by the raising of the tongue to the palate [in the utterance of the latter], and from ز by the suppression of the voice [in the utterance of the former]. (Ḳ in art. سين.) It is one of the letters of augmentation [occurring in the form اِسْتَفْعَلَ and its derivatives]. (Ṣ and L in art. سين.) [See also سِينٌ in art. سين. It is sometimes substituted for ص; as in سَقْر, for صَقْر: and for ش, as in سِطْرَنْج, for شِطْرَنْج: (see De Sacy's Chrest. Arabe, sec. ed., ii. 230-233: and iii. 530-532:)] and AZ says that some of the Arabs substitute for it ت, (Ṣ and L and Ḳ* in art. سين,) as in the saying (Ṣ and L in art. سين) of 'Alyà Ibn-Arḳam, (L ib.,)

يَا قَبَحَ ٱللّٰهُ بَنِي السِّعْلَاتِ
عَمْرَو بْنَ يَرْبُوعٍ شِرَارَ النَّاتِ
لَيْسُوا أَعِفَّآءَ وَلَا أَكْيَاتِ

[*O, may God remove far from good,* or *from prosperity, the sons of the Sialáh, 'Amr Ibn-Yarbooa, the worst of mankind: they are not chaste, nor sharp in intellect*]: he means النَّاس and بِأَكْيَاس: (Ṣ and L ib.:) and in like manner one says طَسْتٌ for طَسّ. (TA in art. كيت.) — يٰسٓ in the Ḳur [commencing ch. xxxvi.] is like الٓر and حمٓ at the commencement of chapters of the same; and is said by 'Ikrimeh to mean يَا إِنْسَانُ [*O man*]; because it is followed by the words إِنَّكَ لَمِنَ الْمُرْسَلِينَ: (Ṣ and L in art. سين:) or it means either thus, or يَا سَيِّدُ [*O man of dignity*]. (Ḳ in art. سين.) ═ سَ is a particle peculiarly prefixed to the aor., rendering it clearly denotative of the future, (Mughnee, and Ṣ* and L* in art. سين,) as in سَيَفْعَلُ [*He will do* such a thing], (Ṣ and L ib.,) and considered as forming a part thereof, for which reason it does not exercise any government upon it: it is not contracted from سَوْفَ, contrary to what the Koofees hold: nor is the extent of the future with it shorter than it is with سَوْفَ, contrary to what the Baṣrees hold: the analytical grammarians term it حَرْفُ تَنْفِيسٍ, by which is meant a particle of amplification; because it changes the aor. from the strait time, which is the present, to the ample time, which is the future: but plainer than their expression is the saying of Z and others, [that it is] a particle denoting the future. (Mughnee.) Kh asserts that it corresponds [as an affirmative] to [the negative] لَنْ. (Ṣ and L in art. سين.) Some assert that it sometimes denotes continuance, not futurity: this is mentioned in relation to the saying in the Ḳur [iv. 93], سَتَجِدُونَ آخَرِينَ [as though meaning *Ye continually find others*]; and they adduce as an evidence thereof the saying in the same [ii. 136], سَيَقُولُ ٱلسُّفَهَآءُ مِنَ ٱلنَّاسِ مَا وَلَّاهُمْ عَنْ قِبْلَتِهِمْ [as meaning *The light-witted of the people continually say, What hath turned them away,* or *back, from their ḳibleh?*]; affirming that this was revealed after their saying مَا وَلَّاهُمْ: but this the grammarians know not; and that this verse was revealed after their saying ما ولّاهم is not a fact agreed upon: moreover, if it be conceded, still continuance is inferred from the aor.; like as when you say, فُلَانٌ يَقْرِى الضَّيْفَ and يَصْنَعُ الجَمِيلَ, you mean that it is his custom to do thus. (Mughnee.) Z asserts that when it is prefixed to a verb signifying what is liked or disliked, it denotes that the event will inevitably happen: i. e., when it is prefixed to a verb signifying a promise or a threat, it corroborates and confirms its meaning. (Mughnee.) ═ [As a numeral, س denotes *Sixty.*]

سا

سَا *i. q.* سَوْفَ, q. v.

سأب

1\. سَأَبَهُ, (Ṣ, M, Ḳ,) aor. َ, (M, Ḳ,) inf. n. سَأْبٌ, (Ṣ, M,) *He throttled him,* syn. خَنَقَهُ; (Ṣ, M, IAth, Ḳ;) i. e., *squeezed his throat:* (IAth:) or, *so that he died,* (Ṣ,) or *so that he killed him.* (M, Ḳ.) — And سَأَبَهُ *He widened it;* namely, a سِقَآء [or skin for water or milk]. (Ṣ, Ḳ.) ═ سَأَبَ مِنَ الشَّرَابِ, (M, Ḳ,) aor. and inf. n. as above; (M;) and سَئِبَ, (M, Ḳ,) aor. َ, (Ḳ,) inf. n. سَأَبٌ; (M;) *He was satisfied with drinking of wine* or *beverage.* (M, Ḳ.)

سَأْبٌ and ↓ مِسْأَبٌ *A* [*skin such as is termed*] زِقّ, (Ṣ, M, Ḳ,) *for wine:* (M:) or *such as is large:* (M, Ḳ:) or *a* زِقّ *of any kind:* (M:) or *a receptacle of skin,* or *leather, in which the* زِقّ *is put:* (M, Ḳ:) the former also occurs in a verse in which it is read without ء, for the sake of the rhyme: (M:) and its pl. is سُؤُوبٌ: (Ṣ, M, Ḳ:) and (so in the Ṣ, but in the Ḳ "or,") the latter (مسأب) signifies *a skin for honey;* (Ṣ, Ḳ;) and in a verse of Aboo-Dhu-eyb, (Ṣ, M, K,) cited voce خَافَة, (Ṣ, M,) it is written مِسَابٌ, (Ṣ, M, Ḳ,) without ء: (Ṣ, M:) and it signifies also *a skin in which clarified butter is put.* (Ṣ and L voce مِسْأَد.)

إِنَّهُ لَسُؤْبَانُ, in the following saying, (IJ, M,) إِنَّهُ لَسُؤْبَانُ مَالٍ, meaning *Verily he is one who pastures,* or *tends, the cattle, and takes care of them, and manages them, well,* (IJ, M, Ḳ,*) is from سَأْبٌ signifying "a زِقّ," because the زِقّ is made only for the preservation of its contents. (IJ, M.)

مِسْأَبٌ: see سَأْبٌ. — Also, (Ḳ,) applied to a man, (TA), *Who drinks much water.* (Ḳ.)

سأد

1\. سَئِدَ: see 1 in art. سود.

4\. إِسْآدٌ signifies The *hastening,* or *being quick, in journeying;* (Ṣ, Ḳ;) and is mostly used in relation to journeying by night: (Ṣ:) or the *journeying all the night;* (M;) or the *journeying in the night without alighting to rest;* (Mbr, Ṣ, Ḳ;) and تَأْوِيبٌ signifies the "journeying in the day without alighting to rest:" (Mbr, Ṣ:) or the *journeying* of camels *night and day* (AA, Ṣ, M, Ḳ) *together.* (M, Ḳ.) And ↓ سَأْدٌ occurs [as an inf. n. in the sense of إِسْآدٌ]; but [ISd says] I know not any verb [properly] belonging to it. (M.) — You say also, اسأد السَّيْرَ *He prosecuted the journey with energy,* (M,) or *persistently,* or *continually.* (MA.) [See an ex. in a verse of Aboo-Duwád cited voce مُرْدُونٌ.]

سَأْدٌ [an inf. n. of which the verb is not mentioned,] The act of *walking,* or *going any pace on foot.* (M.)

سَأْدٌ: see 4, above.

سُؤْدَةٌ *Somewhat remaining of youthfulness* (Ṣ, Ḳ) *and strength* (Ṣ) in a woman. (Ṣ, Ḳ.* [See also سُؤْرَةٌ.])

مِسْآدٌ *A skin for clarified butter,* (Ṣ, Ḳ, [see بَدْرَةٌ,]) or *for honey;* as also مِسَادٌ, without ء; the former of the measure مِفْعَلٌ, and the latter of the measure فِعَالٌ: or a [*skin of the kind called*] زِقّ, *smaller than the* حَمِيت [which is similarly described as a skin, or small skin, of the kind called زِقّ]: (El-Aḥmar, L:) but Sh says, what we have heard is مِسْأَبٌ, meaning *a large* [*skin of the kind called*] زِقّ. (L.)

مَسْؤُودٌ: see art. سود.

سادج

سَاذَجٌ (O, Ḳ, TA) and سَاذِجٌ (TA) arabicized from [the Pers.] سَادَهْ: (O, Ḳ: [in some copies of the Ḳ سَاذَهْ:]) this is the only explanation in some of the copies of the Ḳ: (TA:) *Plain;* i. e. *without variegation, decoration, embellishment,* or *engraved* or *sculptured work:* (O, TA:) or *without any hair upon it:* or *of one unmixed colour:* this last is [said to be] the correct meaning [in many instances]; but the sheykh Welee-ed-Deen El-'Irákee says, in the Expos. of the "Sunan" of Aboo-Dáwood, respecting a pair of boots of the Prophet, described as خُفَّانِ أَسْوَدَانِ سَاذَجَانِ or سَاذِجَانِ, that this phrase seems to mean *A pair of black boots of one unmixed colour;* the last word being used in this sense in the common conventional language; though he had not found it with this meaning in the lexicons, nor in the books of authors on the strange words occurring in traditions. (TA.) — Also *Free from self-constraint:* and one *who knows not badness, wickedness, deceit,* or *guile; in whom is no latent rancour, malevolence, malice,* or *spite, nor cunning:* (O:) or *free in intellect;* and *easy* [or *simple* or *artless*] *in nature or disposition.* (TA in art. سدج.) — حُجَّةٌ سَاذَجَةٌ, also written سَاذِجَةٌ, is used by authors on the scholastic theology of the Muslims as meaning *An argument, a plea, an allegation, an evidence,* or *a testimony, that is undecisive:* and sometimes the same epithet is used [in like manner] in other cases. (L.) ═ In some copies of the Ḳ, it is said to be [the name of] *Certain roots and shoots, that grow in waters, useful for such and such things;* arabicized from سادِه [or سَادَهْ]: (TA:) or *certain leaves and shoots,* (O, CḲ,) *used as a medicine, having a flower; one sort thereof called* رُومِىّ; *and another,* هِنْدِىّ; [the latter name, i. e. سَاذَجٌ هِنْدِىّ, as well as سَاذَجٌ alone, applied in the present day to *malabathrum,* or *Indian spikenard;*] *growing in waters that collect and stagnate in black muddy lands,* (O,) *standing up on the surface of the water,* (O, CḲ,) *like the plant called* عَدَسُ المَآءِ, (O,) *without attachment to a root;* (O, CḲ;) *beneficial for swellings of the eye.* (CḲ.)

سأر

1. سَأَرَ: see 4, in two places. ═ سَئِرَ, aor. ـَ, (Mṣb, Ḳ,) inf. n. سُؤْرٌ, (Mṣb,) *It remained; became left, as a residue.* (Mṣb, Ḳ.)

4. *He left a remainder,* or *somewhat remaining;* (IAṭr, M, Ḳ;) as also ▼ سَأَرَ, (IAṭr, Ḳ,) or سَأَرَ سُؤْرًا, (A,) inf. n. سَأْرٌ: (TḲ:) or *he left somewhat of the beverage in the bottom of the vessel from which he had drunk;* (Ṣ, TA;) as also اسأر فِى الإِنَاءِ سُؤْرًا: (A:) the doing of which is prescribed in a trad. (TA.) You say also اسأرهُ *He left it remaining.* (Mṣb.) And اسأر سُؤْرًا and سُؤْرَةً *He left a remainder,* or *residue.* (T, TA.) And اسأر مِنْهُ شَيْئًا *He left somewhat of it remaining.* (M.) And أَسْأَرَتِ الإِبِلُ فِى الحَوْضِ; and ▼ سَأَرَتْ سُؤْرًا; *The camels left some water remaining in the trough,* or *tank.* (A.) Also اسأر مِنَ الطَّعَامِ سُؤْرَةً ‡ *He left somewhat remaining of the food.* (A.) And اسأر مِنْ حِسَابِهِ ‡ *He left somewhat of his calculation unreckoned.* (M,* TA.)

5. تَسَأَّرَ (so in the Tekmileh and M and CḲ, and in a MS. copy of the Ḳ; but in some copies of the Ḳ, and in a copy of the A, ▼ تَسَاءَرَ;) *He drank the remains:* (A:) or *the remainder of the* نَبِيذ; (Ḳ;) or so تسأر النَّبِيذَ. (Lḥ, M.)

6: see what next precedes.

سُؤْرٌ *A remainder,* or *residue;* (T, M, Mṣb, Ḳ;) of a thing, (M,) or of anything; (TA;) as also ▼ سُؤْرَةٌ: (T:) or *a remainder of beverage in the bottom of a vessel after one has drunk;* (Ṣ,* A;) *such as is left by a rat or mouse &c. after drinking:* (Ṣ:) properly applied to *a remainder of water left by the drinker in a vessel or watering-trough:* and tropically to ‡ *a remainder of food, &c.:* (Mgh:) and ▼ سُؤْرَةٌ signifies likewise ‡ *a remainder* of food: (A:) pl. of the former أَسْآرٌ, (Ṣ, M, Mgh, Mṣb,) and, by transposition, آسَارٌ, like آبَارٌ and آرَامٌ, pls. of بِئْرٌ and رِئْمٌ. (M.) [See also سَائِرٌ, below.] — سُؤْرَةُ ▼ الصَّقْرِ means ‡ *What remains of the portion of the flesh of the game that is given to the hawk which has captured it.* (A.) — *And* ▼ سُؤْرَةٌ also signifies ‡ *A remainder of youthful vigour* in a man, (M, Ḳ,) or in a woman who has passed the prime of youth, (Lth,) or in a woman who has passed the period of youth but not been rendered decrepit by old age. (A.) [See also سُؤْدَةٌ.] — And † *What is good,* or *excellent,* of property, or of camels or the like: pl. سُؤَرٌ. (L.) [App. because such is left when one has parted with the bad.] — ▼ سُؤْرَةٌ مِنَ القُرْآنِ ‡ [means *A chapter of the Ḳur-án;*] so called because it is a portion, (A,) or a remainder: (TA:) or it may be from the signification immediately preceding: (L:) or it is a dial. var. of سُورَةٌ: (Ḳ:) pl. سُؤَرٌ. (A, TA.) — فُلَانٌ سُؤْرُ شَرٍّ means *Such a one is very evil* or *mischievous.* (A.)

سُؤْرَةٌ: see the next preceding paragraph, in five places.

سَآرٌ One *who leaves a remainder,* or *residue,* (Ṣ, M, Ḳ,) *of beverage in the bottom of the vessel from which he has drunk:* (Ṣ, M:) [and ‡ *of food in a dish; &c.:*] deviating from rule, (Ṣ, M,) like جَبَّارٌ from أَجْبَرَ: (Ṣ:) [see دَرَّاكٌ, which is said to be the only other instance of the kind:] by rule it should be ▼ مُسْئِرٌ; (Ṣ, Ḳ;) which is [said to be] also allowable: (Ḳ:) but MF denies this; (TA;) or it may be [regular] from سَأَرَ or [irregular] from أَسْأَرَ. (T, TA.)

سَائِرٌ *The rest,* or *remainder,* (T, and M in art. سير, and Mṣb and Ḳ,) of a thing, (Z, M, Mṣb,) whether little or much; (T, Mṣb;) and of men, or people: (Ṣgh, Mṣb:) not the *whole,* or *all,* as many imagine it to mean, (Ṣgh, Mṣb, Ḳ,) though people use it in this latter sense, (IAth,) which Ṣgh asserts to be a vulgar error: (Mṣb:) it occurs repeatedly in trads., and always in the former sense: (IAth:) or it is sometimes used [in chaste Arabic] in the latter sense: (Ḳ:) and is correctly so used accord. to AAF and J and IJ and El-Jawáleeḳee and IB, the last of whom confirms this signification by many examples and evident proofs: but whether, in this sense, it is derived from السَّيْرُ, as AAF and J and others hold, or from سُورٌ the "wall which surrounds a town or city," as others hold, is disputed: (TA:) and سَارُ الشَّىْءِ is a dial. var. of سَائِرُهُ. (Ṣ in art. سير.) — An Arab of the desert became the guest of a party, and they ordered the female slave to perfume him; whereupon he said, بَطْنِى عَطِّرِى وَسَائِرِى ذَرِى [*My belly perfume thou, and the rest of me leave thou*]: (Ḳ:) but in other lexicons than the Ḳ, we find أَعْطِرِى. (TA in art. عطر.) This saying is a well-known prov. (TA.) [In the TA it is added that سائرى here signifies *the whole of me,* or *all of me:* but this is an evident mistake.] You say this to a man who gives you what you do not want, and refuses you what you want. (Ṣgh, TA in art. عطر.) — It is related, also, that a hostile attack was made upon a people, and they cried out for aid to the sons of their uncle; but these held back from them until they had been made captives and taken away; then they came inquiring respecting them; and the person asked replied, أَسَائِرَ اليَوْمِ وَقَدْ زَالَ الظُّهْرُ [*What, all the day, when the noon has passed?*] (Ḳ:) i.e., Dost thou covet what is remote, (مَا بَعُدَ, (Ṣ, Ḳ, TA, in a copy of the Ṣ and in one of the Ḳ and in the CḲ مَا بَعْدَ,) when [reason for] despair hath become manifest to thee: for when one wants the whole day, and the noon has passed, he must despair like as he despairs of accomplishing his want at sunset. (Ṣ in art. سير, and Ḳ.) This saying is a prov.; (Ṣ, A;) and is used with reference to a thing which one hopes to attain when its time has passed. (A.)

[أَسَائِرُ expl. by Golius as a pl. meaning "Partes reliquæ" is an evident mistake, app. caused by a misunderstanding of the latter prov. mentioned above.]

مُسْئِرٌ: see سَآرٌ.

سأسم

سَأْسَمٌ a dial. var. of سَاسَمٌ without ء; *A certain tree;* [accord. to some,] *i. q.* شِيزَى. (TA.) [See art. سسم.]

سأل

1. سَأَلَهُ, (Ṣ, M, Ḳ) with كَذَا following it, and سَأَلَهُ عَنْ كَذَا and بِكَذَا, (Ṣ,* Ḳ,) aor. يَسْأَلُ, (M,)

inf. n. سُؤَالٌ and مَسْأَلَةٌ, (Ṣ, M, Ḳ,) which latter is also pronounced مَسَلَةٌ, without the hemzeh, (TA,) and تَسْآلٌ and سَآلَةٌ, (M, Ḳ,) and سَأَلَةٌ or سَآلَةٌ, (accord. to different copies of the Ḳ, the former of these two accord. to the TA, [and it appears from a statement that will be found below, voce سُؤْلٌ, that one of these is correct, but in an excellent copy of the M, in the place thereof, I find, and ▾ سَآءَلَهُ, as a verb, doubly trans., first thus by itself, and secondly by means of عَنْ, as shown by an ex. in a verse cited below, (see 3,) and this also is correct,]) all [sometimes] signify the same, (Ṣ,* Ḳ,) i. e. *He asked him such a thing*; or *asked him, interrogated him, questioned him*, or *inquired of him, respecting such a thing*: but عن كذا is more common than بكذا: when سَأَلَ means the asking, or demanding, of property, it is trans. [only] by itself or by means of مِنْ [so that you say سَأَلَ مِنْهُ كَذَا and سَأَلَهُ كَذَا meaning *he asked*, or *demanded, of him such a thing*]: (Er-Rághib, TA:) and one says also سَالَ, aor. يَسَالُ, (Akh, Ṣ, M, Mṣb, Ḳ,) like خَافَ, aor. يَخَافُ; (Mṣb, Ḳ;) which is of the dial. of Hudheyl; the medial letter of this being originally و, as is shown by the phrase, mentioned by AZ, هُمَا يَتَسَاوَلَانِ: (TA:) [respecting this dial. var., see what follows:] the imperative (Ṣ, Mṣb, Ḳ, TA) of سَأَلَ (Ṣ, Mṣb, TA) is اِسْأَلْ; (Ṣ, M, Mṣb, Ḳ, TA;) and (Ṣ, Ḳ, &c.) that of سَالَ, (Ṣ, Mṣb, TA,) سَلْ, (Ṣ, Mṣb, Ḳ, TA,) dual. سَلَا, and pl. سَلُوا, [these two being] irregular; (Mṣb;) and AAF mentions that Aboo-'Othmán heard one say اِسَلْ, [a form omitted in some copies of the Ḳ, but mentioned in the CḲ,] meaning اِسْأَلْ, suppressing the ء, and transferring its vowel to the preceding letter, like as some of the Arabs said لَحْمَر for الأَحْمَر [as many do in the present day]: (M:) accord. to ISd, (TA,) the Arabs universally suppress the ء in the imperative except when they prefix to it وَ or فَ; (M, TA;) saying فَاسْأَلْ and وَاسْأَلْ: (TA:) or when وَ [or فَ] is prefixed, it is allowable to pronounce the ء and also to suppress it, as in saying وَاسْأَلُوا and وَسَلُوا: (Mṣb:) and for the pass. سُئِلَ, one may say سِيلَ, and سُيِلَ, in this instance making the kesreh to partake of the sound of dammeh, and سُولَ; and also سُيِلَ, in which the middle letter is pronounced with a sound between that of ء and that of ى, or resembling that of و. (IJ, TA.) As Er-Rághib says, سُؤَالٌ signifies The *asking*, or *demanding, knowledge*, or *information*, or *what leads thereto*: and the *asking*, or *demanding, property*, or *what leads thereto*. (TA.) سَأَلْتُهُ عَنِ الشَّىْءِ means *I asked of him information respecting the thing*: (IB, TA: [and the like is said in the Mṣb:]) and سَأَلْتُهُ الشَّىْءَ [is sometimes used in the same sense, as has been shown above, but generally] means *I asked him to give me the thing*: (IB, TA:) you say, سَأَلَهُ مَالًا *He asked, demanded, or begged, of him property*, and in like manner, سَأَلَ مِنْهُ and سَأَلَ إِلَيْهِ [followed by مَالًا]: (MA:) and سَأَلْتُ ٱللّٰهَ العَافِيَةَ, inf. n. سُؤَالٌ and مَسْأَلَةٌ, *I begged, or sought, of God health*, or *freedom from disease*, &c. (Mṣb.) The saying in the Ḳur [lxx. 1], سَأَلَ سَائِلٌ بِعَذَابٍ وَاقِعٍ means عَنْ عَذَابٍ [i. e. *An asker asked respecting a falling punishment*]: (S:) [for] one says, خَرَجْنَا نَسْأَلُ عَنْ فُلَانٍ and بِفُلَانٍ [meaning *We went forth asking respecting such a one*]: (Akh, Ṣ:) or the phrase in the Ḳur means *a caller called* [*for a falling punishment*]: (TA:) and some read سَالَ سَائِلٌ بعذاب واقع, (Bḍ, TA,) [likewise] from السُّؤَال: (Bḍ:) or this means سَالَ وَادٍ بعذاب واقع [i. e. *a valley flowed with a falling punishment*]; (Bḍ, TA;) so some say; (TA;) from السَّيَلَانُ. (Bḍ.) The saying, in a trad., نَهَى عَنْ كَثْرَةِ السُّؤَالِ [*He* (Mohammad) *forbade much questioning* or *inquiring*] is said to relate to subtile questions or inquiries, that are needless; like another trad., mentioned below, voce, مَسْأَلَةٌ: or to the begging, of men, their property needlessly. (TA.)

3. سَآءَلَهُ, (M, TA,) inf. n. مُسَآءَلَةٌ: (TA:) see 1, first sentence. Aboo-Dhu-eyb says,

* أَسَآءَلْتَ رَسْمَ الدَّارِ أَمْ لَمْ تُسَائِلِ *

* عَنِ السَّكْنِ أَمْ عَنْ عَهْدِهِ بِالأَوَائِلِ *

[*Didst thou ask the remains of the dwelling*, or *didst thou not ask, respecting the inhabitants*, or *respecting their knowledge of the former occupants?*]. (M, TA.) — In the saying of Bilál Ibn-Jereer,

* إِذَا ضِفْتَهُمْ أَوْ سَايَلْتَهُمْ * وَجَدْتَ بِهِمْ عِلَّةً حَاضِرَهْ *

[*When thou becomest their guest, or askest of them, thou findest with them a ready excuse*], سَايَلْتَهُمْ is a combination of two dial. vars.; the ء being in the original phrase سَآءَلْتُ زَيْدًا, and the ى being a substitute in the phrase سَايَلْتُ زَيْدًا; the measure of سَايَلْتَهُمْ being فَعَايَلْتَهُمْ: (M, Ḳ:*) so said Aḥmad Ibn-Yaḥyà, [i. e. Th,] who had at first ignored the expression: (M:) and it is an instance of which we know not a parallel in the language. (M, Ḳ.*) — [Accord. to analogy, سَآءَلَهُ also signifies *He asked him*, &c., *being asked by him*, &c. — And Freytag states that Reiske has explained سَآءَلَ as meaning *He always demanded that another should express wishes for his health*: but I know not any instance of its being used in this sense.]

4. ▾ أَسْأَلَهُ سُؤْلَهُ, (Ḳ,) or ▾ سُؤْلَتَهُ, (Ṣ,) and ▾ مَسْأَلَتَهُ, (Ṣ, Ḳ,) *He accomplished for him his want*. (Ṣ, Ḳ.)

[5. تَسَأَّلَ, in the modern language, signifies *He begged*, or *asked alms*; as also تَسَوَّلَ: both probably post-classical.]

6. تَسَآءَلُوا *They asked*, or *begged, one another*. (Ṣ, Mṣb, Ḳ.) You say, هُمَا يَتَسَآءَلَانِ, (M,) and also يَتَسَاوَلَانِ, (M, Mṣb, Ḳ,) and يَتَسَايَلَانِ. (TA.) In the Ḳur [iv. 1], some read وَٱتَّقُوا ٱللّٰهَ ٱلَّذِى تَسَّآءَلُونَ بِهِ; and others, تَسَآءَلُونَ بِهِ: in each case, originally تَتَسَآءَلُونَ: the meaning is, [*And fear ye God*,] *by Whom ye demand* [*one of another*] *your rights*, or *dues*: (M:) or *by Whom ye ask*, or *demand, one of another*; (Bḍ, Jel;) *saying, I ask thee*, or *beg thee, by God*; and *I beseech thee*, or *adjure thee, by God*. (Jel.) — One says also تَسَآءَلُوا القَوْمَ, meaning *They* [*together*] *asked*, or *begged, the people*. (Mgh in art. نقض.)

سُؤْلٌ, (Ṣ, M, Ḳ,) also pronounced سُولٌ, without ء, (Ṣ, Ḳ,) [*A petition*; or *a request*; meaning] *a thing that people ask* or *beg*; (Ṣ;) or *a thing that one has asked* or *begged*; (M, Ḳ;) as also ▾ سُؤْلَةٌ, (IJ, M, Ḳ,) which is likewise pronounced سُولَةٌ, without ء; (Ḳ;) and ▾ سُؤُولٌ; (Ḥar p. 422; [or this is app. pl. of سُؤْلٌ, like as بُرُوجٌ is of بُرْجٌ, and بُرُودٌ of بُرْدٌ, &c.;]) [and ▾ سَأَلَةٌ or سَآلَةٌ, as will be shown by what follows;] and ▾ مَسْؤُولٌ; (Mṣb;) [and ▾ مَسْأَلَةٌ:] see 4: the first of these said by Z to be of the measure فُعْلٌ in the sense of the measure مَفْعُولٌ; like عُرْفٌ and نُكْرٌ. (TA.) Thus in the Ḳur [xx. 36], قَدْ أُوتِيتَ سُؤْلَكَ يَا مُوسَى *Thou hast been granted thy petition*, or *the thing that thou hast asked, O Moses*. (Ṣ, M, TA.) In the saying ▾ اَللّٰهُمَّ أَعْطِنَا سَأَلَاتِنَا [*O God, grant Thou us our petitions*], mentioned by Aboo-'Alee on the authority of AZ, the inf. n. is used as a subst., properly so termed, and is therefore pluralized. (M.)

سَأَلَةٌ or سَآلَةٌ; pl. سَأَلَاتٌ: see the next preceding paragraph, in two places.

سُؤْلَةٌ: see 4: and see also سُؤْلٌ.

سُؤَلَةٌ, (Ṣ, Ḳ,) also pronounced سُوَلَةٌ, (TA,) *A man* (Ṣ) *who asks, or begs, much*; (Ṣ, Ḳ;) as also ▾ سَآلٌ, and ▾ سَؤُولٌ: (TA:) such is improperly termed ▾ سَائِلٌ. (Durrat el-Ghowwás, in De Sacy's Anthol. Gramm. Ar., p. 47 of the Ar. text.)

سُؤَالٌ an inf. n. of 1. (Ṣ, M, Ḳ, &c.) — [It is often used as a subst. properly so called; like مَسْأَلَةٌ; meaning *A question*; *an interrogation*; correlative of جَوَابٌ: and *a demand*, or *petition*: and as such has a pl., سُؤَالَاتٌ; perhaps post-classical.]

سَؤُولٌ: see سُؤَلَةٌ.

سُؤُولٌ: see سُؤْلٌ [of which it is app. pl.].

سَآلٌ: see سُؤَلَةٌ.

سَائِلٌ [i. e. *Asking*; meaning *interrogating, questioning, or inquiring*; and *demanding*, or *begging*;] has for its pl. سَأَلَةٌ and سُؤَّالٌ. (TA.) See سُؤَلَةٌ. — It also means [*A beggar*; i. e.] *a poor man asking, or begging, a thing*. (Er-Rághib, TA.) So it has been expl. as used in the Ḳur [xciii. 10], where it is said, وَأَمَّا ٱلسَّائِلَ فَلَا تَنْهَرْ [*And as for the beggar, thou shalt not chide* him, or *address* him *with rough speech*]: or, accord. to El-Ḥasan, it here means *the seeker of knowledge*. (TA.)

مَسْأَلَةٌ, an inf. n. of 1, is tropically used in the sense of a pass. part. n. [with the noun qualified by it understood; meaning ‡ *A thing asked*; i. e. *a question*; *a problem*, or *proposition*; *a matter*, or *an affair, proposed for decision* or *determination*]: (TA:) and the pl. is مَسَائِلُ. (Mṣb, TA.) So in the saying, تَعَلَّمْتُ مَسْأَلَةً ‡ [*I learned a question*, or *problem*, &c.]. (TA.) The saying, in a trad., كَرِهَ المَسَائِلَ وَعَابَهَا means † [*He* (Mohammad) *disliked and discommended*] *subtile questions, such as are needless.* (TA.) —— See also سُؤْلٌ: —— and see 4.

مَسْؤُولٌ [pass. part. n. of 1: and used as a subst.]: see سُؤْلٌ.

سأم

1. سَئِمَ مِنْهُ, (Ṣ, M, Mṣb, Ḳ,) and سَئِمَهُ, (M, Mṣb, Ḳ,) aor. َ, (Ṣ, Mṣb, Ḳ,) inf. n. سَأْمٌ (Ṣ, M, Ḳ) and سَأَمٌ (Ḳ) and سَآمَةٌ (Ṣ, M) and سَآمٌ and سَأْمَةٌ, (Ṣ, Mṣb, Ḳ,) *He turned away with disgust from it; was averse from it; was disgusted at it or with it; loathed,* or *nauseated, it;* (Ṣ, M, Mṣb, Ḳ;) namely, a thing; (Ṣ, M, Ḳ;) syn. مَلَّ, (Ṣ, M, Mṣb, Ḳ,) and ضَجِرَ: (Mṣb:) سَآمَةٌ exceeds مَلَالٌ. (Ḥam pp. 775-6.) It is said in the Ḳur [xli. 49], لَا يَسْأَمُ الإِنْسَانُ مِنْ دُعَآءِ الخَيْرِ [*Man will not turn away with disgust from,* or *will not be weary of, praying for good,* or *wealth,* or *prosperity*]. (Mṣb.) And in a trad., إِنَّ اللّٰهَ لَا يَسْأَمُ حَتَّى تَسْأَمُوا *Verily God will not turn away with disgust until ye turn away with disgust;* like لَا يَمَلُّ حَتَّى تَمَلُّوا, and thus the trad. is commonly related. (TA.) And it is related in a trad. of 'Áisheh that she used to say to the Jews, عَلَيْكُمُ السَّأْمُ وَالذَّامُ وَاللَّعْنَةُ [*Disgust,* or *loathing, and contempt, and cursing,* rest *upon you*]: thus related with ء, meaning ye shall turn away with disgust from your religion: but commonly related without ء [and with a different meaning], as will be stated hereafter [in art. سوم]. (IAth, TA in this art. and in art. سوم.)

4. اسأمهُ *He,* or *it, made him to turn away with disgust, to be averse, to be disgusted, to loathe,* or *to nauseate.* (M, Ḳ.)

سَؤُومٌ an [intensive] epithet from 1 [meaning *Wont,* or *much disposed, to turn away with disgust, to be averse, to be disgusted, to loathe,* or *to nauseate*]: (Ṣ, M, Ḳ:) or *much affected with vexation,* or *disgust; having little patience.* (Ḥam p. 532.)

سأو

1. سَآهُ, (Ṣ, M, Ḳ,) like رَعَاهُ, [or rather like دَعَاهُ,] incorrectly [and differently] written in copies of the Ḳ, (TA,) i. q. سَآءَهُ, (Ṣ, M, Ḳ, TA,) formed from the latter by transposition; (Ṣ, M;) mentioned by Sb: you say, سَآهُ الأَمْرُ, like سَآءَهُ, [*The affair displeased, grieved,* or *vexed, him*]: (M:) and سَأَوْتُهُ, meaning سُؤْتُهُ [*I displeased, grieved,* or *vexed, him*]. (Ṣ, TA.) —— And سَأَا بَيْنَهُمْ, (Ḳ, TA,) inf. n. سَأْوٌ, (TA,) *He created,* or *excited, disorder,* or *discord, between them,* or *among them; made,* or *did, mischief between them,* or *among them:* (Ḳ, TA:) mentioned by Az: app. a dial. var. of سَعَى. (TA.)

4. أَسْأَيْتُ القَوْسَ *I made a* سِئَةٌ [q. v.] *to the bow.* (Ḳ, TA.)

سَآةٌ: } see what next follows.
سُؤَةٌ: }

سِئَةٌ of a bow, and † سُؤَةٌ, (Ibn-Málik, Az, ISd, Ḳ, TA,) and † سَآةٌ, (Ibn-Málik, Ḳ, TA,) [in the CḲ erroneously written سَاةٌ, and it is there implied that the other vars. are سِيئَةٌ and سُوْءَةٌ,] dial. vars. of سِيَةٌ, (Ḳ, &c.,) i. e. *The curved extremity* thereof. (TA.) [See also art. سو.]

مَسَآةٌ, like مَسْعَاةٌ, is a dial. var. of مَسَآءَةٌ, [or] formed from the latter by transposition; and has for its pl. مَسَاءٍ: whence the saying, أَكْرَهُ مَسَائِيَكَ [*I dislike,* or *hate, thy vices, faults,* or *acts of disobedience*]: (TA:) Sb mentions this saying; (M, TA;) and says, مَسَآءَةٌ is pluralized, and then the pl. is transformed, so that it is as though it were pl. of مَسْآةٌ, like مَسْعَاةٌ. (M.)

سب

1. سَبَّهُ, (Ṣ, M, Ḳ,) [aor. ُ,] inf. n. سَبٌّ, (M,) *He cut him,* or *it.* (Ṣ, M, Ḳ.) —— And i. q. عَقَرَهُ [i. e. *He wounded him;* or *hocked, houghed,* or *hamstrung, him;* &c.]. (Ṣ,* Ḳ.) —— And, (Ṣ, M, Ḳ,) aor. as above, (Ṣ, TA,) and so the inf. n., (M, TA,) ‡ *He pierced him in the* سُبَّة, i. e. the اِسْت. (Ṣ, M, Ḳ, TA.) [See an ex. in a verse cited in the first paragraph of art. سر.] —— Also سَبَّهُ, (Ṣ, M, A, Mṣb, Ḳ,) aor. as above, (Ṣ, M,) inf. n. سَبٌّ (Ṣ, M, Mṣb, Ḳ) and سِبِّيبَى, (Ḳ,) [but the latter, accord. to analogy, has an intensive signification,] *He reviled him, vilified him, upbraided him, reproached him, defamed him,* or *gave a bad name to him;* (Ṣ, M, A, MA, Ḳ, Bḍ in vi. 108, &c.;) from the same verb in the first of the senses expl. in this art.; (M;) as also † سَبَّبَهُ; (Ḳ;) or the latter signifies *he reviled him, vilified him,* &c., *much;* syn. أَكْثَرَ سَبَّهُ; (M;) or is more than سَبَّهُ (أَكْثَرُ مِنْ سَبَّهُ). (TA.)

2: see what next precedes. —— سَبَّبَ لِلْأَمْرِ, (MA,) inf. n. تَسْبِيبٌ, (KL, PṢ,) † *He made,* or *appointed,* or *prepared, a means,* or *cause,* (MA, KL, PṢ,) *of attaining,* or *accomplishing, the thing,* or *affair.* (MA.) [And سَبَّبَ, alone, † *He,* or *it, caused* or, *occasioned.*] You say, سَبَّبَ اللّٰهُ لَكَ سَبَبَ خَيْرٍ ‡ [*May God make,* or *appoint,* or *prepare, for thee a means of attaining good,* or *prosperity*]. (A, TA.) And سَبَّبَ لِلْمَآءِ مَجْرًى ‡ *He made,* or *prepared, a channel for the water.* (A, TA.)

3. سَابَّهُ, inf. n. سِبَابٌ (Ṣ,* M, A, Mṣb, Ḳ*) and مُسَابَّةٌ, (M, Mṣb, KL, TA,) *He reviled him, vilified him, upbraided him, reproached him, defamed him,* or *gave a bad name to him,* (M, A, KL, TA,) *being reviled,* &c., *by him.* (M, A, TA.) You say, بَيْنَهُمَا سِبَابٌ *Between them two is mutual reviling,* &c. (A.) And المِزَاحُ سِبَابُ النَّوْكَى [*Jesting is the mutual reviling,* &c., *of those that are foolish,* or *stupid*]. (A, TA.) And it is said in a trad., سِبَابُ المُسْلِمِ فُسُوقٌ (TA) *The mutual reviling of the Muslim is a departure from obedience to God.* (El-Munáwee in his Expos. of the Jámi' eṣ-Ṣagheer of Es-Suyootee.)

5. تَسَبَّبَ [as quasi-pass. of 2, † *It was,* or *became, made,* or *appointed,* or *prepared, as a means,* or *cause, of attaining,* or *accomplishing* a thing, or an affair; followed by لِأَمْرٍ. And *It was,* or *became, caused,* or *occasioned*]. You say, تَسَبَّبَ مَالُ الفَىْءِ † [*The property of the spoil,* or *acquisition,* or *tribute, termed* فَىْء *was caused,* or *occasioned, to accrue*]: for that whereby the property is caused, or occasioned, [to be obtained, as the abandonment of their abodes by unbelievers, or their making peace with Muslim invaders on the condition of paying a poll-tax or the like,] is made a means, or cause, of the accruing of the property to those to whom it is due of the recipients of the فَىْء. (Az, TA.) [See also 10.] —— تَسَبَّبَ بِهِ إِلَى شَىْءٍ † *He made use of it as a means,* or *cause, of attaining,* or *accomplishing, a thing.* (M.) And أَتَسَبَّبُ بِفُلَانٍ إِلَيْكَ † [*I make use of such a one as a means of access to thee*]. (TA in art. درع.) —— [Hence, in the present day, تَسَبَّبَ is used as meaning † *He trafficked;* because trafficking is a using means to procure subsistence.]

6. تَسَابَّا, (Ḳ,) [or تَسَابُّوا,] inf. n. تَسَابٌّ, (Ṣ,) *They two cut each other,* (Ṣ,* Ḳ,) [or *they* (i. e. more than two persons) *cut one another.*] —— [Hence, (see 1, last sentence,)] تَسَابُّوا, (Ṣ, M, A, MA, Ḳ,) inf. n. as above; (Ṣ;) and † اِسْتَبُّوا; (A, MA;) *They reviled, vilified, upbraided, reproached, defamed,* or *gave bad names to, one another.* (Ṣ, M, A, MA.) And بَيْنَهُمْ أُسْبُوبَةٌ يَتَسَابُّونَ بِهَا (Ṣ, M, A,* TA) *Between them is a thing* [meaning *reviling* or *vilifying speech*] *with which they revile,* or *vilify,* &c., *one another.* (M, TA.)

8: see the next preceding paragraph.

10. اِسْتَسَبَّ لِأَبَوَيْهِ [*He invited,* or *attracted, reviling,* or *vilifying, to his two parents*]. (A.) It is said in a trad. of Aboo-Hureyreh, لَا تَمْشِيَنَّ أَمَامَ أَبِيكَ وَلَا تَجْلِسْ قَبْلَهُ وَلَا تَدْعُهُ بِاسْمِهِ وَلَا تَسْتَسِبَّ لَهُ, i. e. [*By no means walk thou before thy father, nor sit down before him, nor call him by his name,*] *nor expose him to reviling,* or *attract reviling to him,* by reviling another's father, for in that case he may revile thy father in requital to thee. (TA.) —— اِسْتَسَبَّ لَهُ الأَمْرُ ‡ (A, TA) [*The thing,* or *affair,* or *event, became caused,* or *prepared, for him:* thus expl. by IbrD: see also 5].

R. Q. 1. سَبْسَبَ † *He severed his tie,* or *ties, of relationship, by unkind behaviour to his kindred.* (AA.) —— *He went a gentle pace.* (AA. [Freytag, on the authority of "Hamak. Waked.," assigns this meaning to † تَسَبْسَبَ.]) —— *He smelt a foul smell.* (AA.) —— *He discharged* his *urine.* (M, Ḳ.) *He made water to flow.* (Ḳ.)

R. Q. 2. تَسَبْسَبَ *It* (water) *ran,* or *flowed.* (Ḳ.) —— See also R. Q. 1.

سِبٌّ *One who reviles, vilifies, upbraids, reproaches,* or *defames, much, being reviled,* &c.; (A'Obeyd, Ṣ, M, Mṣb,* Ḳ;) as also † مِسَبٌّ. (Ṣ, Ḳ.) And [simply] *One's mutual reviler* or *vilifier* &c.; (A'Obeyd, Ṣ, M, Ḳ;) as also † سَبِيبٌ.

(M, Ḳ.) A poet, (Ṣ,) namely, 'Abd-Er-Raḥmán Ibn-Ḥassán, satirizing Miskeen Ed-Dárimee, (TA,) says,

لَا تَسُبَّنَّنِى فَلَسْتَ بِسِبِّى •
إِنَّ سِبِّى مِنَ الرِّجَالِ الكَرِيمُ •

[*Thou shalt by no means revile me; for thou art not my mutual reviler: verily he, of men, who is my mutual reviler is the generous*]. (Ṣ, TA.) [See also مُسَبِّبٌ: and سِبَابٌ.] — *A veil, or the like; syn.* سِتْرٌ. (M.) — *A woman's muffler, or head-covering; syn.* خِمَارٌ. (Ṣ, M, Mṣb, Ḳ.) — *A turban.* (Ṣ, M, Mgh, Mṣb, Ḳ.) El-Mukhabbal Es-Saadee says, (Ṣ, M, Mgh,) using it in this sense, (M, Mgh,)

وَأَشْهَدُ مِنْ عَوْفٍ حُلُولًا كَثِيرَةً •
يَحُجُّونَ سِبَّ الزِّبْرِقَانِ المُزَعْفَرَا •

[*And I witness many persons of 'Owf, alighting during their journeys, going repeatedly to and fro to see Ez-Zibrikán's turban dyed with saffron*]: (Ṣ, M, Mgh:) for it was a custom of the chiefs of the Arabs to dye their turbans with saffron: or, as some say, the meaning is his اسْت; [but this is correctly, or more commonly, termed سَبَّة;] and Ḳṭr asserts that he was suspected: (M:) he says that Ez-Zibriḳán used to tinge his است yellow; but this is a strange saying. (TA in art. زبرق.) — Also, and ▼سَبِيبَةٌ, *An oblong piece* (Ṣ, M, Ḳ) *of cloth*, (M,) or *of thin cloth*, (Ḳ,) or *of thin linen cloth*, (Ṣ,) or *of white cloth*: (M:) or *a thin garment*: (Aboo-'Omar, TA:) or so the latter word: (M:) or this signifies *a linen stuff that is brought from the region of the Nile, of a kind commonly known among the merchants by* [*the name of*] كرخ, *some of which are made in Miṣr, and their length is eight by six* [*cubits*: cubits being meant because the ns. of number here are fem., and ذِرَاعٌ is fem.]: (Sh, TA:) or this same word signifies *an oblong piece of cloth of any kind*, or, as some say, *of linen*: (TA:) the pl. of the former is سُبُوبٌ; (Ṣ, Ḳ, TA;) and of the latter, سَبَائِبُ: (Ṣ, M, Ḳ, TA:) in a verse of 'Alḳameh Ibn-'Abadeh, the phrase بِسَبَائِبِ الكَتَّانِ is used for بِسَبَا الكَتَّانِ. (M.) — See also سَبَبٌ, first signification.

سَبَّةٌ *i. q.* اسْتٌ ‡ [The *podex*, or the *anus*]: (Ṣ, M, A, Ḳ:) because it is discommended. (A.) [See also سنب.] — مَضَتْ سَبَّةٌ مِنَ الدَّهْرِ ‡ *A space, or long space, of time passed*; (Ṣ, M, A;) [thus termed] because time is always complained of; (A;) and so سَنْبَةٌ, in which the ن is [said to be] a substitute for the [former] ب of سَبَّة, in like manner as it is substituted in the case of إِجَّاصٌ and إِنْجَاصٌ; because [it is asserted, though this is contradicted, that] there is no word of which the radical letters are سنب. (M.) And مَا رَأَيْتُهُ مُنْذُ سَبَّةٍ † *I have not seen him for, or during, a space, or long space, of time*; (Ṣ, Ḳ;*) like as you say مُنْذُ سَنْبَةٍ. (Ṣ.) And عِشْنَا بِهَا سَبَّةً and سَنْبَةً † *We lived in it a space, or long space, of time.* (Ks, TA.) And أَصَابَتْنَا سَبَّةٌ مِنَ الحَرِّ, and البَرْدِ, and الصَّحْوِ, (Ḳ,* TA,) and الرَّوْحِ, (TA,) ‡ *A period of some days' continuance* [*of heat*, and *of cold* and *of serene weather*, and *of gentle wind, betided us*]. (Ḳ, TA.) [The pl. is سِبَابٌ.] One says, الدَّهْرُ سِبَابٌ † *Time consists of vicissitudes*; one turn is thus, and one is thus. (ISh, TA.)

سُبَّةٌ *A disgrace; a shame; a thing that occasions one's being reviled.* (Ṣ, M, A, Ḳ.) One says, صَارَ هٰذَا الأَمْرُ سُبَّةً عَلَيْهِ *This thing became a disgrace to him, occasioning his being reviled.* (Ṣ.) And أَنْتَ سُبَّةٌ عَلَى قَوْمِكَ [*Thou art a disgrace to thy people*]. (A.) [And ▼مَسَبَّةٌ, in like manner, (a word of the class of مَبْخَلَةٌ and مَجْبَنَةٌ, being originally مَسْبَبَةٌ,) signifies *A cause of reviling*, or *of being reviled*; as is shown by the saying of Ṭufeyl El-Ghanawee, cited in the TA in art. عقب,

فَلَمْ يَجِدِ الأَقْوَامُ فِينَا مَسَبَّةً •

And the people did not find in us a cause of reviling, or of being reviled: pl. مَسَابٌّ.] One says, ▼إِيَّاكَ وَالمَسَبَّةَ and المَسَابَّ [*Beware thou of*, or *avoid thou, the cause of reviling* or *of being reviled*, and *the causes thereof*]. (A.) — Also *One whom people revile* (Ṣ, Ḳ) *much*. (Ḳ.) See also سُبَبَةٌ.

السُّبَّابَةُ: see السَّبَّةُ.

سَبَبٌ *A rope, or cord*; (Ṣ, M, A, Mṣb, Ḳ;) as also ▼سِبٌّ; (Ṣ, M, Ḳ;) the latter of the dial. of Hudheyl, (Ṣ,) and occurring in this sense in a verse of Aboo-Dhu-eyb cited voce خَيْطَةٌ; (Ṣ, M;) accord. to some, as there meaning *a wooden peg*, [a meaning assigned to it in the Ḳ,] but the former is the correct meaning: (M:) the pl. of both words is أَسْبَابٌ, (M, TA,*) [and] the pl. of the latter word is سُبُوبٌ (Ṣ, TA) also: (TA:) or سَبَبٌ signifies *any rope let down, or made to descend, from above*: (AO, TA:) or *a strong and long rope*, but no rope is so called except one *by means of which one ascends and descends*: (Khálid Ibn-Jembeh, TA:) or this appellation is only given to *a rope of which one end is attached to a roof or ceiling or the like*: (TA:) or *one by means of which one ascends palm-trees*: (Er-Rághib, TA:) [and] *a rope by means of which one reaches, or gains access to, water.* (TA.) فَلْيَمْدُدْ بِسَبَبٍ إِلَى السَّمَآءِ ثُمَّ لْيَقْطَعْ, in the Ḳur [xxii. 15], means *Let him stretch a rope to the roof*, or *ceiling*, of his dwelling; *then let him die strangled*: i. e. let him die of rage: (M, TA:) or, as some say, *let him stretch a rope to* the lowest *heaven*; *then let him traverse* the intervening space until he reach the highest part thereof. (Bḍ.) The saying

جُبَّتْ نِسَاءَ العَالَمِينَ بِالسَّبَبْ •

has been expl. in art. جب: in this instance, a *rope* or *cord*, may be meant; or a *string*, or *thread*. (M, TA.) — Hence, (Mṣb,) ‡ *A thing* (Ṣ, M, Mṣb, Ḳ) *of any kind* (Ṣ, Mṣb, Ḳ) *by means of which one attains, reaches, or gains access to another thing*: (Ṣ, M, Mṣb, Ḳ:) pl. as above. (M.) One says, جَعَلْتُ فُلَانًا لِى سَبَبًا إِلَى فُلَانٍ فِى حَاجَتِى, i. e. † [*I made such a one*] *a means of access* [*to such a one in the case of my want*]. (TA.) Hence, (M,) أَسْبَابُ السَّمَآءِ † *The places of ascent of the heaven, or sky*: (M, Ḳ:) or *the tracts*, or *regions, thereof*: (Ṣ, Ḳ:) or *the gates thereof.* (Ibn-Es-Seed, Ḳ. [See an ex. in a verse cited voce ثَمَانُونَ.]) And the saying, اِرْتَقَى فِى الأَسْبَابِ, meaning † *He excelled* [or *attained to excellence*] *in religion.* (M.) — † *A road, or way.* (A. [There mentioned among proper, not tropical, significations.]) So in the saying, in the Ḳur xviii. 88 and 91, ثُمَّ أَتْبَعَ سَبَبًا † [*Then he followed a road*, or *way*]. (Bḍ.) [And] so in the saying, مَا لِى إِلَيْهِ سَبَبٌ † [*There is not for me any road, or way, to him*, or *it*]. (A.) So too ▼سَبِيبَةٌ: pl. سَبَائِبُ. (Ḥam p. 347.) — [† *A mean, or means, used in order to any end*: *a means by which a thing is brought about*: *a cause*; but more properly only *a second cause*: *an occasion*, or *accidental cause*: and *a reason*, or *motive*.] One says, هٰذَا سَبَبُ هٰذَا † [*This is the cause*, or *occasion, of this*]. (Mṣb.) And بِسَبَبِهِ كَانَ كَذَا † [*Because of him*, or *it, it was thus*, or *such a thing was*]. (Mṣb in art أجل.) And سَبَّبَ ٱللّٰهُ لَكَ سَبَبَ خَيْرٍ ‡ [*May God appoint*, or *prepare, for thee a means*, or *cause, of good*, or *prosperity*]. (A.) — ‡ *A connexion*, or *tie*, (Ṣ, A, Ḳ, TA,) *of relationship* (Ṣ, Ḳ, TA) *by marriage*; distinguished from نَسَبٌ, which is by birth: from the same word as signifying "a rope by means of which one reaches, or gains access to, water." (TA.) One says, اِنْقَطَعَ بَيْنَهُمُ السَّبَبُ i. e. ‡ *The connexion*, or *tie*, [*of affinity between them was severed*,] and الأَسْبَابُ *the connexions*, or *ties*. (A) وَتَقَطَّعَتْ بِهِمُ الأَسْبَابُ [in the Ḳur ii. 161] means, accord. to I 'Ab, † *And their ties and affections* [*shall be dissundered*]: or, accord. to AZ, † *and their places of abode* [*shall be divided asunder*]. (TA.) [But] قَطَعَ ٱللّٰهُ بِهِ السَّبَبَ means † [*God cut short, or may God cut short*,] *his life.* (M, Ḳ.) — Also, [from the same word as signifying the "cord, or rope, of a بَيْت," properly meaning "tent," and tropically "verse,"] † *A portion*, or *division, of a foot of a verse, consisting of a movent letter and a quiescent letter*; and also *one consisting of two movent letters*: pl. أَسْبَابٌ. (M, Ḳ. [In some of the copies of the Ḳ, the latter kind is not mentioned.]) سَبَبٌ خَفِيفٌ † [*A light cord*] means *a movent letter followed by a quiescent letter*; as قَدْ and مِنْ: and سَبَبٌ ثَقِيلٌ † [*A heavy cord*], *two movent letters*; as لَكَ and لِمَ. (KT.) سَبَبَانِ مَقْرُونَانِ † [*Two conjoined cords*] means *two portions in which are three successive short vowels followed by a quiescent letter*; as مُتَفَا in مُتَفَاعِلُنْ, and عَلَتُن in مُفَاعَلَتُنْ: and سَبَبَانِ مَفْرُوقَانِ † [*Two disjoined cords*], *two portions of which each consists of a movent letter and a quiescent letter, and which is followed by a movent letter*; as مُسْتَفْ in مُسْتَفْعِلُنْ, and عِيلُنْ in مَفَاعِيلُنْ. (M, TA.)

سُبَبَةٌ *One who reviles people*; (Ṣ, Ḳ;) as also

▼ مُسَبَّةٌ. (Ḳ.) One says, ▼ لَا تَكُنْ سُبَبَةً وَلَا سُبَّةً [*Be not thou a reviler of others, nor one whom others revile*]. (A.)

[سَبَبِىٌّ *Causative.*]

[سَبَبِيَّةٌ *Causality.*]

سَبِيبٌ: see سِبٌّ, second sentence. ═ Also *The hair of the forelock,* (AO, Ṣ, M, A, Ḳ,) and *of the tail,* (Ṣ, M, A, Ḳ,) the latter meaning [only] assigned to it by Er-Riyáshee, (TA,) and *of the mane,* (Ṣ, M, Ḳ,) of a horse: (M, A, Ḳ:) pl. أَسَابِيبُ and سَبَائِبُ. (A, TA.) — And † *A lock* (خُصْلَة) *of hair;* as also ▼ سَبِيبَةٌ: (M, Ḳ:) pl. سَبَائِبُ: which is also expl. as ‡ *syn. with* ذَوَائِب [app. as meaning *pendent locks,* or *pendent plaits, of hair*]: (TA:) thus in the phrase اِمْرَأَةٌ طَوِيلَةُ السَّبَائِبِ ‡ *A woman having the* ذوائب *long.* (A, TA.)

سَبِيبَةٌ: see سِبٌّ: — and سَبِيبٌ: — and سَبَبٌ. — عَلَيْهِ سَبَائِبُ الدَّمِ means ‡ *Upon him are,* or *were, streaks of blood:* (A, TA:) the sing. of سبائب in this sense is سَبِيبَةٌ. (Ḥam p. 347.) ═ Also [*Trees of the kind called*] عِضَاه *abounding in a place.* (M, Ḳ.)

سَبَّابٌ [*That cuts much, or sharply*]. سَبَّابُ العَرَاقِيبِ means *The sword:* (Ḳ, TA:) or is an epithet applied to the sword: (A:) because it cuts the عراقيب [or hock-tendons]: (TA:) [but Z holds it to be tropical, from the signification following; for] it is added in the A, as though it were hostile to the عراقيب, and reviled them. (TA.) — [One *who reviles much* or *frequently;* or *a great reviler:* a meaning indicated in the Mṣb, and of frequent occurrence.]

السَّبَّابَةُ, an epithet in which the quality of a subst. is predominant, (M,) ‡ [*The index,* or *fore finger;*] *the finger that is next to the thumb* (Ṣ, M, A,* Mṣb, Ḳ, TA) *and middle-finger;* (M, TA;) *between these two;* (TA;) as also ▼ السُّبَّةُ: (Ḳ:) so called because one [often] points with it in reviling: (Mṣb:) called by persons praying المُسَبِّحَةُ and السَّبَّاحَةُ [because it is raised in asserting the unity of God]. (TA in the present art. and in art. سبح.)

سَبْسَبٌ *A desert;* or *a desert in which is no water,* or *in which is neither water nor herbage;* syn. مَفَازَةٌ (Ṣ, Ḳ) and قَفْرٌ: (TA:) or *a tract of land level and far-extending:* (M, Ḳ:) or *a* [*desert such as is termed*] قفر *that is far-extending, whether level or not level, rugged or not rugged, without water and without any one to cheer by his presence:* (ISh, TA:) or *a land affected with drought, barrenness,* or *dearth:* (Aboo-Kheyreh, TA:) and بَسْبَسٌ signifies the same: (TA:) pl. سَبَاسِبُ: (M, TA:) A'Obeyd explains سَبَاسِبُ and بَسَابِسُ as *syn. with* قِفَارٌ, [pl. of قَفْرٌ]. (TA.) One says also بَلَدٌ سَبْسَبٌ, (Ṣ, Ḳ,) [using the latter word as an epithet;] and بَلَدٌ سَبَاسِبُ, (Lḥ, Ṣ, M, Ḳ,) thus using the pl. as though he termed every part of the بَلَد a سَبْسَب; (Lḥ, M;) or the pl. is added to give intensiveness to the meaning: (IAth, TA voce بَلْقَعٌ, q. v.:) but some say ▼ سُبَاسِبٌ, with ḍamm; and this is more common, because it is a sing. epithet. (MF, TA.) ═ Also *i. q.* سَاسَبٌ [or سَيْسَبٌ (q. v. in art. سسب)], if not a mistranscription for this last], i. e. *A kind of tree, from which arrows,* or, as in the book of AḤn, *camels' saddles* (رِحَال), *are made:* Ru-beh says, [accord. to one reading, another being given in art. سسب, q. v.,]

وَاحَتْ وَرَاحَ كَعَصَا السَّبْسَابِ ▼

[*She went, and he went, like the rod of the sebsáb,* meaning, the arrow]; in which the last word is a dial. var. of السَّبْسَب, or the ا is inserted by poetic license. (TA.) — [Hence, perhaps,] السَّبَاسِبُ, (M, Ḳ,) or يَوْمُ السَّبَاسِبِ, (Ṣ, TA,) *A certain festival of the Christians;* (Ṣ,* TA;) *i. q.* أَيَّامُ السَّعَانِينِ, (Abu-l-'Alà, M, Ḳ,) or يَوْمُ السَّعَانِينِ [*Palm-Sunday;* now commonly called أَحَدُ الشَّعَانِين or عِيدُ الشَّعَانِين, with ش]. (TA.)

سَبْسَابٌ: } see the next preceding paragraph.
سُبَاسِبٌ: }

أُسْبُوبَةٌ [like أُهْجُوَّةٌ, contr. of أُمْدُوحَةٌ,] *A thing* [meaning *reviling speech*] *with which persons revile one another:* (M, TA:) pl. أَسَابِيبُ. (A, TA.) Using it in this sense, (M, TA,) one says, بَيْنَهُمْ أُسْبُوبَةٌ يَتَسَابُّونَ بِهَا [*Between them is reviling speech*] (Ṣ, M, A,* Ḳ) *with which they revile one another.* (M, TA.)

أَسَابِيبُ pl. of سَبِيبٌ: ═ and also of أُسْبُوبَةٌ. ═ أَسَابِيبُ الوَجْهِ *The beauties of the face.* (TA in art. سر.)

مِسَبٌّ: see سِبٌّ, first signification.

مَسَبَّةٌ: see سُبَّةٌ, in two places: — and سُبَبَةٌ.

مَسْبُوبٌ [*Much reviled:* see its verb]. — مَسْبُوبَةٌ, as an epithet applied to camels, (Ṣ, Ḳ, TA,) or to horses, (A,) and to wild asses, (TA,) means ‡ *Goodly,* or *excellent:* (Ṣ, A,* Ḳ, TA:) because (Ṣ, TA) they are such that one says of them, (Ṣ, A, TA,) when admiring them, (Ṣ, TA,) or when deeming them goodly, or excellent, (A,) May God curse them, (قَاتَلَهَا ٱللّٰهُ, Ṣ, A, TA,) and abase them: (أَخْزَاهَا: A, TA:) how goodly, or excellent, are they! (TA.) ═ [Also *Made, appointed,* or *prepared, as a means,* or *cause, of attainment* or *accomplishment,* لِأَمْرٍ *for a thing, or an affair.* And *Caused,* or *occasioned:* and *a thing caused* or *occasioned; an effect.*] One says, هٰذَا مُسَبَّبٌ عَنْ هٰذَا [*This is caused,* or *occasioned, by that: this is an effect of,* or *arising from, that*]. (Mṣb.)

مِسَبٌّ [*Reviling much:* see its verb. ═ And *Making, appointing,* or *preparing, a means,* or *cause:* and *causing,* or *occasioning:* and *a causer*]. مُسَبِّبُ الأَسْبَابِ [*The Appointer,* or *Preparer, of means or causes;* or *the Causer of causes;*] is an epithet applied to God. (Ṣ.)

مُسْتَبٌّ [act. and pass. part. n. of 8]. It is said in a trad., المُسْتَبَّانِ شَيْطَانَانِ (A, TA) *The two mutual revilers are two devils.* (El-Munáwee in his Expos. of the Jámi' eṣ-Ṣagheer of Es-Suyooṭee.)

سبأ

1. سَبَأَ الخَمْرَ, (Ṣ, M, Ḳ,) aor. ـَ, (M, Ḳ,) inf. n. سَبْءٌ (Ṣ, M, Ḳ) and سِبَآءٌ, (M, Ḳ, TA,) like كِتَابٌ, (TA, in the CḲ سَبَاء,) [but see سِبَآءٌ below,] and مَسْبَأٌ; (Ṣ, Ḳ;) and ▼ اِسْتَبَأَهَا; (Ṣ, M, Ḳ;) *He bought wine,* syn. شَرَاهَا, (M, Ḳ,) which mostly means "he sold it," (TA,) or اِشْتَرَاهَا, (Ṣ, O,) which is well known as meaning "he bought it," wherefore it is here used in the Ṣ and O, (TA,) *in order that he might drink it:* (Ṣ, O:) accord. to Ks, (TA,) when you buy wine to carry it to a place, you say, سَبَيْتُ الخَمْرَ, without ء; (Ṣ, TA;) and so say the [other] celebrated lexicologists, except Fei, accord. to whom you say in this case [as in others], سَبَأْتُهَا; and it is itself called سَبِيئَةٌ: (TA:) the verbs are only used, in the sense of buying, in relation to wine. (Ṣ, Mṣb, TA.) [See also art. سبى.] — And سَبَأَ الشَّرَابَ *He collected the wine* in vessels: occurring in this sense in a trad. (Aboo-Moosà, TA.) ═ سَبَأَتْهُ, (M,) or سَبَأَتِ الجِلْدَ, (Ḳ,) said of fire, (M, Ḳ,) and of whips, (M,) *It,* or *they, burned,* or *hurt,* (M, Ḳ,) or, as some say, (M, but in the Ḳ "and,") *altered,* (M, Ḳ,) *him,* (M,) or *the skin:* (Ḳ:) and in like manner one says of the sun, and of fever, and of journeying. (M.) — And سَبَأْتُهُ بِالنَّارِ *I burned him with fire:* (AZ, Ṣ:) or سَبَأَ جِلْدَهُ, inf. n. سَبْءٌ, *He burned his skin;* or, as some say, *stripped it off:* (M:) or سَبَأَ الجِلْدَ *he burned the skin:* and سَبَأَ signifies also *he stripped off* [skin], or *he skinned.* (Ḳ.) — And سَبَأْتُ الرَّجُلَ, (inf. n. سَبْءٌ, TA,) *I flogged the man.* (Ṣ, Ḳ.*) ═ سَبَأَ عَلَى يَمِينٍ كَاذِبَةٍ, (Ṣ, M,) aor. ـَ, inf. n. سَبْءٌ, (M,) *He passed over a false oath* [that he had sworn], *not caring for it:* (Ṣ): or *he swore a false oath:* and some say, سَبَأَ عَلَى يَمِينٍ, aor. and inf. n. as above, meaning *he passed over an oath* [that he had sworn], *lying.* (M.) ═ سَبَأَ is also syn. with صَافَحَ [*He took by the hand:* &c.]: (O, Ḳ:) deemed by MF a strange meaning. (TA.)

4. اسبأ *He* (a man) *was,* or *became, silent.* (Sh, TA in art. وطر.) — اسبأ لِأَمْرِ ٱللّٰهِ *He,* (M, Ḳ,) or *his heart,* (L,) *was,* or *became, submissive to the decree of God.* (M, L, Ḳ.) — And اسبأ عَلَى الشَّىْءِ *His heart became in a bad state,* or *heavy,* (خَبُثَ, [so in the M and in a copy of the Ḳ, in the CḲ and TA خَبُتَ, and thus in my MS. copy of the Ḳ, but there altered from خَبُثَ, app. on the authority of the TA, and I think it a mistranscription, although expl. in the TA as meaning اِنْخَضَعَ, which is a signification of أَخْبَتَ, the explanation of اسبأ in the next preceding sentence,]) *at the thing.* (M, Ḳ.)

7. انسبأ *It* (the skin) *was,* or *became, stripped*

off. (Ṣ, M.) —— And It (a person's skin) *peeled off*, or *became abraded*. (TA.)

8: see 1, first sentence.

سَبَأٌ: see سَبِيْئَةٌ = تَفَرَّقُوا أَيْدِى سَبَا, and أَيَادِى سَبَا, (M, Ḳ,) and with ذَهَبُوا in the place of تفرّقوا, (T, TA,) *They became scattered*, or *dispersed*, (Ḳ, TA,) and *they went away* in a state of dispersion, *in the ways of Seba*, (T, TA,) a people of El-Yemen, who were dispersed in consequence of the inundation of their lands by the bursting of their [famous] dam, (TA,) and who became proverbial on that account: (M, Ḳ, TA:) سَبَا is here made indecl., (M, Ḳ, TA, [بَنُوهُ in the CḲ being a mistranscription for بَنَوْهُ, wherefore كما تَبَدَّد has been there interpolated, immediately before بَنَوْهُ,]) with the last letter quiescent, and forms, with the preceding word, a compound like خَمْسَةَ عَشَرَ [which implies that we should read أَيَادِىَ سَبَا and أَيْدِىَ سَبَا, but I have never found it thus written]: (TA:) it is not formed from سَبَأ by suppression of the ء, but is a substitute for that word, (M, Ḳ, TA,) on account of the frequent use of this phrase. (M, TA.) [See also art. سبى.]

سُبْأَةٌ *A long*, or *far, journey*, (IAạr, T, M, Ḳ,) *that alters one*: (IAạr, M, TA:) so termed because the sun alters him who makes a long journey. (T, TA. [See 1.]) You say, إِنَّكَ تُرِيدُ سُبْأَةً *Verily thou desirest a long journey*, (IAạr, M, Ḳ,*) *that will alter thee*. (IAạr, M.) In the case of a short journey, you say, تُرِيدُ سُرْبَةً. (T, TA.)

السَّبَئِيَّةُ, (Ṣ, and so in a copy of the Ḳ,) or ▼السَّبَائِيَّةُ; (so in another copy of the Ḳ and accord. to the CḲ;) MF says that the former is the correct term, but both are correct; (TA;) *Certain of the* غُلَاة, (Ṣ, Ḳ, TA,) i. e. *extravagant zealots of the class of innovators; a party of the* غُلَاة *of the* شِيعَة [q. v.]; *who are divided into eighteen sects*: (TA:) they are so called in relation to Seba (سَبَأ) the father of 'Abd-Allah, (Ḳ,) or in relation to 'Abd-Allah Ibn-Seba. (Ṣ.)

سِبَآءٌ [The *purchase of wine*;] a subst. from سَبَأَ الخَمْرَ; (Ṣ;) or an inf. n. (M, Ḳ, TA.) = See also سَبِيْئَةٌ, in two places.

سَبِىءٌ The *skin*, or *slough*, of a serpent; (Ḳ;) as also سَبِىٌّ; for it is with, and without, ء. (TA.)

سَبِيْئَةٌ (Ṣ, M, Ḳ) and ▼سِبَآءٌ (M, Ḳ) and, accord. to Ks, ▼سَبَأٌ, but the form commonly known is ▼سِبَآءٌ, with kesr to the س, and with medd, (IAmb, TA,) *Wine*, (Ṣ, M, Ḳ,) *in an absolute sense*; (TA;) or, [as is perhaps meant in the Ṣ,] *wine that is bought to be drunk, not for merchandise*. (Ḥar p. 409, in explanation of the first word.) [See an ex. of the second in a verse of Lebeed cited in art. وكن: and see also سَبِيئَةٌ, in art. سبى.]

السَّبَائِيَّةُ: see السَّبَئِيَّةُ, above.

سَبَّآءٌ *A vintner*, or *seller of wine*. (Ṣ, M, Ḳ.) —— [It is said in a marginal note in my MS. copy of the Ḳ that it signifies also *A seller of grave-clothes*: but this is evidently a mistake, app. occasioned by a mistranscription, for سَبَّاءٌ, with ى.]

مَسْبَأٌ *A road* (Ṣ, Ḳ) *in a mountain*. (Ṣ.)

سبت

1. سَبَتَ, (Ṣ, M, Mṣb,) aor. ـُ (Ṣ, Mṣb) only, (Ṣ,) or ـِ, (so written in a copy of the M,) [both of which are said by MF to be indicated, or implied, in the Ḳ, but this is not clearly the case,] inf. n. سَبْتٌ, (M, Ḳ,* TA,) *He rested*: (Ṣ, M, Mṣb, Ḳ:*) and *ceased*, or *abstained, from works*: (TA:) and *was*, or *became, quiet, still*, or *motionless*: (M, TA:) and ▼اسبت signifies [the same, or] *he was*, or *became, motionless*: (Ṣ, TA:) Az says that سَبَتَ in the first of these senses is not known in the language of the Arabs: (TA:) [but J says that] the primary signification of سُبَاتٌ is "rest:" and hence the former of these verbs signifies *he slept*. (Ṣ.) —— And سَبَتَتِ اليَهُودُ, (Ṣ,* A, Ḳ,) aor. ـِ (Ṣ, Ḳ) and ـُ, (Ḳ,) inf. n. سَبْتٌ, (Ṣ, Ḳ,) *The Jews kept*, or *performed, the ordinances of their* سَبْت [or *sabbath*]: (Ṣ, Ḳ:*) or سَبَتُوا, aor. ـِ (M, Mṣb) and ـُ, (M,) inf. n. سَبْتٌ; (Mṣb;) and ▼اسبتوا; (Ṣ, M, Mṣb;) *they entered upon the* سَبْت [or *sabbath*]: (Ṣ, M:) or *they* (the Jews) *ceased from seeking the means of subsistence, and the labouring to acquire gain*. (Mṣb.) It is said in the Ḳur [vii. 163], وَيَوْمَ لَا يَسْبِتُونَ *And on the day when they were not keeping the ordinances of their* سَبْت: (Ṣ:) where some read ▼لا يُسْبِتُونَ, from أَسْبَتَ; and some, ▼لا يُسْبَتُونَ, in the pass. form, meaning *when they were not made to enter upon* [*the observance of*] *the* سَبْت. (Bḍ.) = سَبَتَتْ, aor. ـِ, inf. n. سَبْتٌ, *She* (a camel) *went the pace termed* سَبْت meaning as expl. below. (M.) —— And سَبْتٌ signifies also The *outstripping in running*. (M.) = And as inf. n. of سَبَتَ said of a man, (TḲ,) سَبْتٌ also signifies The *being confounded*, or *perplexed, unable to see one's right course*, (Ḳ, TA,) *and being* [*therefore*] *silent*, or *lowering the eyes, looking towards the ground*. (TA.) = سَبَتَ الشَّىْءَ, (M, TA,) inf. n. سَبْتٌ, (M, A, Mgh, Ḳ,) i. q. قَطَعَهُ [meaning *He cut the thing*; or *cut it off*; *severed it*; and *intercepted*, or *interrupted, it*; *put a stop*, or *an end, to it*; or *made it to cease*; relating to ideal as well as real objects; for instance, to work, or action, as is shown in the TA]; (M, A, Mgh, Ḳ, TA;) as also ▼سَبَّتَهُ: expl. by Lḥ as relating particularly to necks. (M, TA.) [Hence,] سَبَتَ عِلَاوَتَهُ, (Ṣ, M,) inf. n. سَبْتٌ, (Ṣ, Ḳ,) *He smote his neck* [*so as to decapitate him*]: (Ṣ, M, Ḳ:) and سُبِتَتْ عِلَاوَتُهُ, *His head was cut off*. (A. [This is there said to be tropical; but why, I do not see.]) —— And سَبَتَتِ اللُّقْمَةُ حَلْقِى, and ▼سَبَّتَتْهُ, i. q. قَطَعَتْهُ [i. e. *The morsel*, or *gobbet, obstructed*, or *stopped, my fauces*]: but the verb without teshdeed is the more usual. (M, TA.) —— And سَبَتَ رَأْسَهُ, (M, A, Mgh, Mṣb,) aor. ـِ, (M, Mṣb, TA,) inf. n. سَبْتٌ, (Ṣ, M, A, Mṣb, Ḳ,) *He shaved his head*: (Ṣ, M, A, Mgh, Mṣb, Ḳ:) and in like manner, سَبَتَ شَعْرَهُ, *he shaved off his hair*; (TA;) as also ▼سَبَّتَهُ and ▼اسبتهُ. (AA, TA in art. سبد.) —— And سَبْتٌ also signifies The *letting down* the hair, or *letting* it *fall* or *hang down, after* (lit. *from*, عَن,) [*the twisting*, or *plaiting, termed*] العَقْص. (Ṣ, Ḳ.) = سُبِتَ *He* (a man) *was*, or *became, affected with* [the *kind*, or *degree*, or *semblance, of sleep termed*] سُبَات [q. v.]: (IAạr, M, TA:) and (TA) *he swooned*: (Mṣb, TA:) and *he became prostrated like him who is sleeping, generally closing his eyes*; said of a sick man: (TA:) and also *he died*. (Mṣb, TA.)

2: see 4: = and see also 1, latter half, in three places.

4: see 1, former half, in four places. —— اسبتت الحَيَّةُ, inf. n. إِسْبَاتٌ *The serpent was*, or *became, silent*; or *bent down its head*, or *lowered its eyes, looking towards the ground*. (TA.) = [اسبت *It* (a drug) *produced the kind*, or *degree*, or *semblance, of sleep termed* سُبَات: and hence, *it torpified*, or *benumbed*: often used in this sense in medical works: and ▼سبّت is also used in this sense in the present day.] = See also 1, near the end of the paragraph.

7. انسبت [*It became cut off, interrupted, put a stop to*, or *put an end to*, or *it ceased*: meanings indicated in this art. in the M and TA.] —— *It became extended*: (Ḳ:) or *long and extended, together with softness*. (TA.) It is said in a description of the countenance of the Prophet, (TA,) كَانَ فِى وَجْهِهِ ٱنْسِبَاتٌ *There was, in his face, length, and extension*. (Ḳ,* TA.) —— *It* (a hide) *became soft* by the process of tanning. (IAạr, TA.) —— انسبتت الرُّطَبَةُ *The date became wholly pervaded by ripeness*: (M, TA:) and *became soft*. (TA.) And انسبت الرُّطَبُ *The dates became all ripe*, or *ripe throughout*. (M, TA.)

سَبْتٌ *Rest*: (Ṣ, Ḳ:) and *quiet, stillness*, or *freedom from motion*. (TA.) [See 1, of which it is an inf. n.] See also سُبَاتٌ. —— السَّبْتُ, (M, Ḳ,) or يَوْمُ السَّبْتِ, (Ṣ, Mṣb,) [*The sabbath*, or *Saturday*;] *one of the days of the week*; (M, Ḳ;) *the seventh of those days*: (M:) so called because the creation commenced on the first day of the week and continued to [the end of] Friday, and on the سبت there was no creation, the work having ceased thereon: or, as some say, because the Jews ceased thereon from work, and the management of affairs: (M, TA:) or because the days [of the week] end thereon: (Ṣ, TA:) Az says that he errs who asserts it to have been so called because God commanded the Children of Israel to rest thereon, and that God created the heavens and the earth in six days, whereof the last was Friday, then rested, and the work ceased, and therefore He named the seventh day يوم السبت: this, he says, is an error, because [he affirms that] سَبَتَ as meaning "he rested" is not known in the language of the Arabs, but signifies قَطَعَ; and rest cannot be attributed to God, because He knows not fatigue, and rest is only after fatigue and work: (TA:) the pl. [of pauc.] is أَسْبُتٌ and [of mult.] سُبُوتٌ: (Ṣ, M, Mṣb, Ḳ:)

it has no dim. (Sb, Ṣ in art. امس.) — سَبْتٌ also means *A week; from the* سَبْت *to the* سَبْت [i. e. *from the sabbath to the sabbath*]: so in the saying, in a trad., فَمَا رَأَيْنَا الشَّمْسَ سَبْتًا [*And we saw not the sun for a week*]: as when one says "twenty autumns" meaning "twenty years:" or it means in this instance *a space of time, whether short or long.* (TA.) — *I. q.* بُرْهَةٌ [i. e. *A space, or period, or a long space or period,*] (M, Ḳ, TA) مِنَ الدَّهْرِ [*of time*]: (TA:) so in the saying, أَقَمْتُ سَبْتًا [*I remained, staid, dwelt,* or *abode, a space,* or *a long space, of time*]; as also ↓ سَبْتَةً and ↓ سَنْبَتًا and ↓ سَنْبَتَةً. (M, Ḳ.) — And *i. q.* دَهْرٌ [meaning *Time; or a long time;* or *a space,* or *period, of time, whether long or short;* &c.]; as also ↓ سُبَاتٌ. (Ṣ, M, Ḳ.) And [hence] ↓ اِبْنَا سُبَاتٍ means † *The night and the day:* (Ṣ, M, Ḳ:) Ibn Aḥmar says,

* وَكُنَّا وَهُمْ كَٱبْنَىْ سُبَاتٍ تَفَرَّقَا *
* سِوًى ثُمَّ كَانَا مُنْجِدًا وَتِهَامِيَا *

[*And we were, with them, like the night and the day that parted asunder alike, then became one going towards Nejd and one going towards Tihámeh*]: (Ṣ, Ḳ:) such, they say, is the meaning: (Ṣ:) or, as IB says, on the authority of Aboo-Jaafar Mohammad Ibn-Ḥabeeb, ابنا سبات were two men, one of whom saw the other in a dream, and then one of them awoke in Nejd, and the other in Tihámeh: or they were two brothers, one of whom went to the east to see where the sun rose, and the other to the west to see where it set. (L, TA.) ═ Also *A certain pace* (Ṣ, M, Ḳ) *of camels:* (Ṣ, Ḳ:) or *a quick pace:* (TA:) or *i. q.* عَنَقٌ [q. v.]: (AA, Ṣ:) or *a pace exceeding that termed* العَنَق. (M.) ═ *A swift,* or *an excellent,* horse; (Ḳ, TA;) *that runs much.* (TA.) — A boy, or young man, *of bad disposition,* or *illnatured, and bold,* or *daring.* (Ḳ) — A man *cunning,* i. e. *possessing intelligence,* or *sagacity,* or *intelligence mixed with craft and forecast; and excellent in judgment;* or *very cunning* &c.; (K, TA;) *silent,* or *lowering his eyes, looking towards the ground;* (TA;) and ↓ سُبَاتٌ signifies the same. (Ḳ, TA.) — A man *who sleeps much;* (Ḳ;) i. e. كَثِيرُ السُّبَاتِ. (TA.) See also مَسْبُوتٌ. ═ See also what next follows.

سَبْتٌ *A certain plant, resembling the* خِطْمِىّ [or *marsh-mallow*]; (Kr, M, Ḳ;) as also ↓ سَبَتٌ, (Ḳ [there expressly said to be with fet-ḥ],) or ↓ سُبْتٌ: (M [so written in a copy of that work]:) said to be *a certain plant used for tanning.* (MF.) See the next paragraph.

سِبْتٌ The *hides,* or *skins, of oxen;* (M, Ḳ;) *whether tanned or not tanned:* so some say: (M:) or (so accord. to the M, in the Ḳ and TA "and," but the و is omitted in the CḲ,) *any tanned hide;* (Aṣ, AA, M, Ḳ;) said to be so called [because the tanning removes the hair,] from السَّبْتُ, "the act of shaving:" (AA, TA:) or *such as is tanned with* قَرَظ [q. v.]: (M, Ḳ:) or only *ox-hides tanned:* so says AḤn on the authority of Aṣ and AZ: (TA:) or *ox-hides tanned with* قَرَظ, (Ṣ, Mgh,) *whereof are made* [*the sandals called*] ↓ نِعَالٌ سِبْتِيَّةٌ: (Ṣ) these are hence thus called: (Mgh:) they are *sandals having no hair upon them:* (M, Mṣb:) or *sandals tanned with* قرظ: (AA, TA:) accord. to Az, they are thus called because their hair has been shaven off (سُبِتَ, i. e. حُلِقَ,) and removed by a well-known process in tanning, (Mgh,* TA,) so that they are soft; and they are of the sandals of people that lead a life of ease and softness: (Mgh:) IAạr says that they are thus called because of their having become soft by the tanning: accord. to this, they should be called ↓ سَبْتِيَّة; and so accord. to a saying of Ed-Dáwoodee, that they are called in relation to سُوقُ السَّبْتِ ["the Market of the Sabbath"]: it is also said that they are called in relation to the ↓ سُبْت, with ḍamm, which is a plant used for tanning therewith; so that they should be called ↓ سُبْتِيَّة, unless the appellation be an instance of a rel. n. deviating from its source of derivation [or unless this plant be also termed سِبْت, as it is accord. to a copy of the M]: (TA:) see سُبْتٌ. It is related of the Prophet, that he saw a man walking among the graves wearing his sandals, and said, يَا صَاحِبَ السِّبْتَيْنِ ٱخْلَعْ سِبْتَيْكَ [meaning ‡ *O wearer of the pair of sandals of* سِبْت, *pull off thy pair of sandals of* سِبْت]: (Ṣ,* TA:) and accord. to the A, they are thus termed tropically: it is like the saying "Such a one wears wool, and cotton, and silk;" meaning "garments made thereof;" as is said in the Nh: but, as some relate it, what he said was, ↓ يَا صَاحِبَ السِّبْتِيَّتَيْنِ, the last of these words being a rel. n.; and thus it is found in the handwriting of Az, in his book. (TA.)

سُبْتٌ, (M, L, Ḳ,) like قُفْلٌ, (TA,) [in a copy of the M erroneously written سَبْت,] *A certain plant;* [*anethum graveolens,* or *dill, of the common garden-species;*] an arabicized word, from [the Pers.] شِبِتّ [or شِبْت]: (AḤn, M, L:) or *i. q.* شِبِتٌّ; both words arabicized from شِوِذْ [or شُوذ]: (Ḳ:) asserted by some to be *the same as* سَنُّوتٌ [q. v.]: (M, L:) Az says that شُبْت, the name of *a well-known herb,* or *leguminous plant,* is an arabicized word; that he had heard the people of El-Baḥreyn call it سُبْت, with the unpointed س, and with ت; that it is originally, in Pers., شِوِذْ; and that it has another dial. var., namely, سبط [i. e. سُبِطّ]. (El-Jawáleeḳee, TA.)

سَبْتَةٌ: see سَبْتٌ, in the middle of the paragraph. ═ Also *Goats,* collectively. (Ḳ.)

سَبْتَاةٌ *A* [*desert such as is termed*] صَحْرَاء: (AZ, Ḳ:) or أَرْضٌ سَبْتَاةٌ *is like* صَحْرَاء: or *a land in which are no trees:* (M:) and *i. q.* ↓ مَسْبُوتَة [i. e. *a bare* land; as though shorn of its herbage]: (TA:) pl. سَبَاتِى. (M.) — Also, [in like manner] a fem. epithet, *Having spreading,* or *expanded, ears, whether long or short.* (Ḳ.)

سَبْتِىٌّ *One who fasts alone on the* سَبْت [i. e. *sabbath,* or *Saturday*]: thus in the saying mentioned by Th, on the authority of IAạr, لَا تَكُ سَبْتِيًّا [*Be not thou one who fasts* &c.]. (M.)

سِبْتِيَّةٌ, نِعَالٌ سِبْتِيَّةٌ, and سَبْتِيَّةٌ, and سُبْتِيَّةٌ; and the dual of سِبْتِىّ, applied to a pair of sandals: see سِبْتٌ, in four places.

سِبْتَانٌ, with kesr, *Foolish, stupid,* or *of little sense;* (Ḳ, TA;) *confounded,* or *perplexed, and unable to see his right course; without understanding.* (TA.)

سُبَاتٌ primarily signifies *Rest* [like سَبْتٌ]: (Ṣ, Mṣb:) and hence, *sleep:* (Ṣ, Ḳ:) or *heavy sleep:* (Mṣb:) or *sleep that is hardly perceptible* (خَفِىٌّ, M, Ḳ, [in some copies of the Ḳ, as mentioned by Freytag, خفيف, i. e. *light,*]), *like a swoon:* (M:) or the *commencement of sleep in the head* [*and its continuance*] *until it reaches the heart:* (Th, M, Ḳ:) or the *sleep of one who is sick;* i. e. *light sleep:* (TA:) and ↓ سَبْتٌ signifies the same as سُبَاتٌ. (T, TA.) Hence, in the Ḳur [lxxviii. 9, and in like manner the word is used in xxv. 49], وَجَعَلْنَا نَوْمَكُمْ سُبَاتًا; (Ṣ;) i. e. قَطْعًا; as though a man, when he slept, were cut off from [the rest of] mankind: (IAạr, TA:) or سبات is when one is cut off, or ceases, from motion, while the soul still remains in the body; i. e., the text means, *And we have made your sleep to be rest unto you:* (Zj, TA:) or *we have made your sleep to be a cutting off from sensation and motion, for rest to the animal forces, and for causing their weariness to cease:* or, *to be death:* (Bḍ:) or, *to be rest unto your bodies by the interruption of labour,* or *work.* (Jel.) ═ See also سَبْتٌ, latter half, in three places.

سَبُوتٌ A she-camel *that goes the pace termed* سَبْت: or *constantly going the pace termed* عَنَق. (M.)

سِبَنْتًى, (Ṣ, M, Ḳ,) as also سِبَنْدًى, (Ṣ,) *Bold,* or *daring;* (Ṣ, M, Ḳ;) as an epithet applied to anything [i. e. man or brute]: the ى is added to render it quasi-coordinate to the class of quinqueliteral-radical words, not to denote the fem. gender, for it receives ة as a termination [to denote the fem.], becoming سِبَنْتَاةٌ; (Ṣ;) and has tenween. (TA.) A poet applies the fem. epithet to a she-camel. (Ṣ.) — Also *The leopard;* (Ṣ, M, Ḳ;) so too with ة; (AHeyth, L in art. سبد;) and so سِبَنْدًى: probably thus called because of his boldness, or daringness: (Ṣ:) or, as some say, the *lion:* fem. with ة: or the fem. signifies *a bold,* or *daring, lioness:* or *a she-camel of bold,* or *daring, breast;* but this last is not of valid authority: (M:) and *a beast of prey* [absolutely]: (L in art. سبد:) pl. سَبَانِتُ; (Ḳ, TA;) and some of the Arabs make سَبَانِى [or rather سَبَانٍ] to be its pl. (TA.) — The fem. also, applied to a woman, signifies *Sharp in tongue;* or *clamorous;* or *clamorous and foul-tongued;* or *long-tongued and vehemently clamorous.* (TA.)

سَبْتَةٌ : } see سَبْتٌ, in the middle of the paragraph.
سُبْتَةٌ :

مُسْبِتٌ *Motionless; not moving.* (Ṣ, Ḳ.) — And, accord. to the L and Ḳ, *Entering upon the day called* السَّبْتُ [i. e. *the sabbath*]: but correctly, *entering upon the observance of the* سَبْت [or *sabbath*]. (TA.)

مَسْبُوتٌ *Affected with* [*the kind,* or *degree,* or *semblance, of sleep termed*] سُبَات [q. v.]: (IAạr, M:) or *affected with a swoon:* and, applied to a sick man, *prostrated like him who is sleeping, generally closing his eyes:* (Ṣ:) or *confounded,* or *perplexed, and unable to see his right course:* (Mṣb:) and ▼ سَبِتٌ signifies the same as مَسْبُوتٌ; as in the saying, cited by Aṣ,

يُصْبِحُ مَخْمُورًا وَيُمْسِى سَبِتَا

[*He is in the morning affected with the remains of intoxication, and he is in the evening affected with sleep,* or *heavy sleep,* &c.]. (T, TA.) — Also *Dead.* (Ṣ, Ḳ.) = رَأْسٌ مَسْبُوتٌ [*A head cut off.*] (A.) — أَرْضٌ مَسْبُوتَةٌ : see سَبْتَاةٌ.

رُطَبٌ مُنْسَبِتٌ *Dates that have become all ripe,* or *ripe throughout.* (Ṣ, Ḳ.) And رُطَبَةٌ مُنْسَبِتَةٌ [*A date that is ripe throughout:* and also] *a soft date.* (TA.)

سبح

1. سَبَحَ, aor. ـَ , inf. n. سَبْحٌ (Mṣb, Ḳ) and سِبَاحَةٌ, (Ṣ,* Ḳ,) or the latter is a simple subst., (Mṣb,) *He swam,* syn. عَامَ, (Ṣ,* Ḳ,) بِالنَّهْرِ and فِيهِ [*in the river*], (Ḳ,) or rather بِالمَآءِ (MF, TA) or فِى المَآءِ (Mṣb) [i. e. *in the water*], for it is likewise in the sea, and in a pool, and also in any expanse: (MF, TA:) [or *he swam upon the surface, without immersing himself;* for,] accord. to Z, there is a difference between عَوْمٌ and سِبَاحَةٌ; the former signifying the "coursing along in water with immersion of oneself;" and the latter, the *coursing along upon water without immersion of oneself.* (MF, TA.) — [Hence,] النُّجُومُ تَسْبَحُ فِى الفَلَكِ (A, TA) ‡ *The stars* [*swim,* or *glide along,* or] *pass along, in the firmament, with a spreading forth.* (TA.) It is said in the Ḳur xxi. 34 and xxxvi. 40, with reference to the sun and the moon, (Bḍ and Jel in xxi. 34,) with which the stars are meant to be included, (Jel ibid.,) كُلٌّ فِى فَلَكٍ يَسْبَحُونَ, i. e. † *All* [*glide* or] *travel along swiftly,* [*in a firmament,*] *like the swimmer* (Bḍ and Jel ibid.) *upon the surface of the water,* (Bḍ ibid.,) or *in the water;* (Jel ibid.;) wherefore the form of the verb used is that which is appropriate to rational beings, (Bḍ and Jel ibid.,) swimming being the act of such beings. (Bḍ ibid.) — And [hence] one says, سَبَحَ ذِكْرُكَ مَسَابِحَ ▼ الشَّمْسِ وَالقَمَرِ ‡ [*Thy fame has travelled as far as the sun and the moon;* lit., *swum along the tracts along which swim the sun and the moon*]. (A, TA.) — [Hence, likewise, as inf. n. of سَبَحَ, aor. as above,] سَبْحٌ also signifies ‡ The *running* of a horse (Ṣ, L, Ḳ,* TA) *in which the fore legs are stretched forth well* [*like as are the arms of a man in swimming*]. (L, Ḳ,* TA.) — And † The *being quick,* or *swift.* (MF.) — And † The *being,* or *becoming, remote.* (MF.) — And † The *travelling far.* (Ḳ.) You say, سَبَحَ فِى الأَرْضِ † *He went,* or *travelled, far, in,* or *into, the land,* or *country:* (O, TA:) and سَبَّحَ: both thus expl. by Abu-l-Jahm El-Jaạfaree. (TA.) — And † The *journeying for the purpose of traffic* (تَقَلُّب [q. v.]); and [a people's] *becoming scattered,* or *dispersed, in the land,* or *earth.* (Ḳ.) And † The *busying oneself in going to and fro,* or *seeking gain,* (IAạr, TA,) and *occupying oneself according to his own judgment* or *discretion, in the disposal* or *management of affairs, in respect of the means of subsistence.* (IAạr, Ṣ, Ḳ, TA.) You say, فُلَانٌ يَسْبَحُ النَّهَارَ كُلَّهُ فِى طَلَبِ المَعَاشِ ‡ [*Such a one busies himself in going to and fro,* or *occupies himself according to his own judgment* or *discretion, in seeking the means of subsistence*]. (A, TA.) And سَبَحَ فِى حَوَائِجِهِ † *He occupied himself according to his own judgment* or *discretion in the accomplishment of his needful affairs.* (Mṣb.) — As used in the Ḳur [lxxiii. 7], where it is said, إِنَّ لَكَ فِى النَّهَارِ سَبْحًا طَوِيلًا, it is variously explained: (Ṣ, TA:) accord. to Ḳatádeh (Ṣ) and El-Muärrij, (Ṣ, TA,) the meaning is, † [*Verily thou hast in the day-time*] *long freedom from occupation;* (Ṣ, Ḳ,* TA;) and in this sense, also, its verb is سَبَحَ, aor. ـَ: (JM:) [thus it has two contr. significations:] or, accord. to Lth, † *leisure for sleep:* (TA:) accord. to AO, the meaning is, † *long-continued scope,* or *room, for free action;* syn. مُتَقَلَّبًا طَوِيلًا: and accord. to El-Muärrij, it means also † *coming and going:* (Ṣ, TA:) accord. to Fr, the meaning is, † *thou hast in the day-time the accomplishment of thy needful affairs:* (TA:) or the meaning is, † [*long*] *occupation of thyself in thy affairs of business;* not being free from occupation therein for the reciting of the Ḳur-án. (Jel.) Some read سَبْخًا, which has nearly the same meaning as سَبْحًا. (Zj, TA.) — As inf. n. of سَبَحَ, (TḲ,) it signifies also † The state of *sleeping.* (Ḳ.) And as such also, (TḲ,) † The *being still, quiet,* or *motionless.* (Ḳ.) — [Also † The *glistening* of the mirage.] You say, سَبَحَ السَّرَابُ, or الآلُ, meaning لَمَعَ [i. e. † *The mirage glistened*]. (O.) — And † The *digging,* or *burrowing,* in the earth, or ground. (Ḳ,* TA.) You say of the jerboa, سَبَحَ فِى الأَرْضِ † *He dug,* or *burrowed, in the earth,* or *ground.* (O, TA.) — And † The *being profuse* in speech. (Ḳ.) You say, سَبَحَ فِى الكَلَامِ † *He was profuse in speech.* (O, TA.) — See also the next paragraph, in two places.

2. تَسْبِيحٌ signifies The *declaring* [God] *to be far removed,* or *free, from every imperfection* or *impurity,* or *from everything derogatory from* [his] *glory;* syn. تَنْزِيهٌ, (Ṣ, O, Mṣb, TA,) and تَقْدِيسٌ: (Mṣb:) the *magnifying, celebrating, lauding,* or *praising,* and *glorifying,* God; and *declaring* Him *to be far removed,* or *free, from everything evil.* (TA.) You say, سَبَّحَ ٱللّٰهَ, (T, A, Mgh, Mṣb, TA,) and سَبَّحَ لِلّٰهِ, (Ḳur lvii. 1 &c., and A,) in which the لِ is redundant, (Jel in lvii. 1 &c.,) inf. n. تَسْبِيحٌ, and سُبْحَانٌ is a subst. that [sometimes] stands in the place of the inf. n., (T, TA,) or it is an inf. n. of which the verb is سَبَّحَ, (Ḳ, TA,) *He declared God to be far removed,* or *free, from every imperfection* or *impurity* &c., (A, Mgh, TA,) or *from what they say* [*of Him*] *who disacknowledge* [*his attributes*]; (Mṣb;) [i. e. *he declared,* or *celebrated,* or *extolled, the perfection* or *purity,* or *absolute glory, of God;*] and *he magnified, celebrated, lauded,* or *praised, God, by the mention of his names, saying* سُبْحَانَ ٱللّٰهِ and *the like:* (Mṣb:) and سَبَّحَ [alone], (Mgh, Ḳ,) inf. n. تَسْبِيحٌ, (Ḳ,) *he said* سُبْحَانَ ٱللّٰهِ; (Mgh, Ḳ;) as also ▼ سَبَحَ, inf. n. سُبْحَانٌ: (Ḳ, TA;) the latter, which is like شَكَرَ, inf. n. شُكْرَانٌ, a dial. var. mentioned by ISd; and no regard should be paid to the saying of Ibn-Ya'eesh and others, that سبحان is an inf. n. of which the verb is obsolete: accord to El-Mufaḍḍal, سُبْحَانٌ is the inf. n. of ▼ سَبَحَ signifying *he raised his voice with supplication,* or *prayer, and magnification* or *celebration* or *praise* [*of God, as when one says* سُبْحَانَ ٱللّٰهِ or *the like*]; and he cites as an ex.,

قَبَحَ الإِلٰهُ وُجُوهَ تَغْلِبَ كُلَّمَا
سَبَحَ الحَجِيجُ وَكَبَّرُوا إِهْلَالَا

[*May God remove far from good,* or *prosperity,* or *success, the persons* (وُجُوه here meaning نُفُوس) *of the tribe of Teghlib, whenever the pilgrims raise their voices with supplication,* &c., *and say* لَبَّيْكَ ٱللّٰهُ أَكْبَرُ, *ejaculating*]. (MF, TA.) وَنَحْنُ نُسَبِّحُ بِحَمْدِكَ, in the Ḳur ii. 28, is a phrase denotative of state, (Ksh, Bḍ, Jel,) meaning *While we declare thy remoteness from evil* [*of every kind*], (Ksh, Bḍ,) or *while we say* سُبْحَانَ ٱللّٰهِ, (Jel,) *praising Thee,* (Ksh,) [or *with the praising of Thee,* i. e.] *making the praising of Thee to be an accompaniment,* or *adjunct, to our doing that:* (Ksh, Bḍ, Jel:) so that we are the more worthy to be appointed thy vice-agents. (Ksh,* Bḍ,* Jel.) فَسَبِّحْ بِٱسْمِ رَبِّكَ العَظِيمِ, in the Ḳur lvi. 73 and last verse, means *Therefore declare thou the remoteness from what is unsuitable to his majesty by mentioning the name of thy Lord,* or *by mentioning the Lord,* for the pronouncing of the name of a thing is the mentioning of it, [i. e., of the thing itself,] *the great name,* or *the great Lord:* (Bḍ:) or it means *therefore pray thou commencing with,* or *uttering, the name of thy Lord* [*the great name* or *Lord*]: (Kull p. 211:) [for] — تَسْبِيحٌ also signifies The act of *praying.* (Ḳ, Mṣb.) You say, سَبَّحَ meaning *He prayed.* (A, Mgh.) And [particularly] *He performed the* [*supererogatory*] *prayer of* [*the period termed*] الضُّحَى. (TA.) And فُلَانٌ يُسَبِّحُ ٱللّٰهَ, i. e. ▼ يُصَلِّى السُّبْحَةَ, meaning *Such a one performs prayer to God,* either *obligatory* or *supererogatory:* [but generally the latter: (see

سُبْحَةً :)] and يُسَبِّحُ عَلَى رَاحِلَتِهِ *performs supererogatory prayer* [*upon his camel that he is riding*]. (Mṣb.) It is said in the Ḳur [iii. 36], وَسَبِّحْ بِٱلْعَشِيِّ وَٱلْإِبْكَارِ, i. e. *And pray thou* [*in the evening, or the afternoon, and the early morning*]. (TA.) And it is related of 'Omar, أَنَّهُ جَلَدَ رَجُلَيْنِ سَبَّحَا بَعْدَ العَصْرِ, meaning [*That he flogged two men*] *who prayed* [*after the prescribed time of the afternoon-prayer*]. (Ṣ, TA.) You say also, بِيَدِهِ سُبْحَةٌ يُسَبِّحُ بِهَا [i.e. *In his hand is a string of beads by the help of which he repeats the praises of God*: see سُبْحَةٌ, below]. (A, Mṣb.*) — Also *The making an exception, by saying* إِنْ شَآءَ ٱللّٰهُ [*If God will*]: because, by so saying, one magnifies God, and acknowledges that one should not will unless God will: and thus is expl. the saying in the Ḳur [lxviii. 28], أَلَمْ أَقُلْ لَكُمْ لَوْلَا تُسَبِّحُونَ [*Did I not say to you, Wherefore will ye not make an exception?* addressed to the owners of a garden, who "swore that they would certainly cut its fruit when they should be entering upon the time of morning, they not making an exception"]. (TA.)

3. سَابَحَهُ, [inf. n. مُسَابَحَةٌ,] *i. q.* رَاسَاهُ, (T and Ḳ in art. رسو,) i. e. *He swam with him.* (TḲ in that art.) [And app. also *He vied*, or *contended, with him in swimming.*]

4. اسبحهُ *He made him to swim* (Ḳ, TA) فِى ٱلْمَآءِ [*in the water*] or فَوْقَ ٱلْمَآءِ [*upon the water*]. (TA.)

سُبْحَةٌ *Garments of skins*: (Ḳ:) or, accord. to Sh, سِبَاحٌ, which is the pl., signifies *shirts of skins, for boys*: AO corrupted the word, relating it as written سُبْجَةٌ, *with* ج, and with ḍamm to the س; whereas this signifies "a black [garment of the kind called] كِسَآء:" and a verse cited by him as presenting an ex. of its pl., in its last word, is from a poem of which each verse has for its fundamental rhyme-letter the unpointed ح: ISd, in art. سبج, mentions سِبَاجٌ as signifying "garments of skin," and having سبجة for its sing.; but says that the word with the unpointed ح is of higher authority; though he also states it, in the same art., to have been corrupted by AO. (TA.) — [A meaning belonging to سَبْحَةٌ (q. v.) is assigned in some copies of the Ḳ to سُبْحَةٌ.] — السُّبْحَةُ, (Ḳ,) or سَبْحَةُ, from سَابِحٌ as an epithet applied to a horse, or mare, (IAth, TA,) is a proper name of *A horse*, or *mare, belonging to the Prophet*: (IAth, Ḳ, TA:) and of *another belonging to Jaafar the son of Aboo-Ṭálib*; (Ḳ;) or this was *a mare named* سُبْحَةُ: (O:) and of *another belonging to another.* (Ḳ.)

سُبْحَةٌ *Beads* (Ṣ, Mṣb, Ḳ, TA) *strung* (Mṣb, TA) *upon a string* or *thread*, (TA,) [*ninety-nine in number, and having a mark after each thirty-three*,] *with which* (by counting them, Ḳ) *one performs the act termed* التَّسْبِيح [meaning *the repetition of the praises of God*, generally consisting in repeating the words سُبْحَانَ ٱللّٰهِ thirty-three times, ٱلْحَمْدُ لِلّٰهِ thirty-three times, and ٱللّٰهُ أَكْبَرُ thirty-three times, which is done by many persons after the ordinary prayers, as a supererogatory act]: (Ṣ, A, Mṣb, Ḳ:) its appellation implies that it is an Arabic word; but Az says that it is post-classical: its pl. is سُبَحٌ (Mṣb) and سُبُحَاتٌ also. (Ḥar p. 133.) See 2, last sentence but one. — Also *Invocation of God*; or *supplication*: (Ḳ:) and *prayer*, (A, Mṣb,) *whether obligatory* or *supererogatory*: (Mṣb:) or *supererogatory praise*; (Ṣ;) and *supererogatory prayer*; (Ṣ, A, Mgh, Ḳ;) because of the تَسْبِيح therein. (Mgh.) You say, فُلَانٌ يُصَلِّى السُّبْحَةَ, expl. above; see 2, in the latter part of the paragraph. (Mṣb.) And قَضَى سُبْحَتَهُ *He performed*, or *finished, his prayer*: (A:) or قَضَيْتُ سُبْحَتِى means *I performed*, or *finished, my supererogatory praise* and *such prayer.* (Ṣ.) And صَلَّى السُّبْحَةَ *He performed the supererogatory prayer*: (A:) and سُبْحَةَ الضُّحَى [*the supererogatory prayer of the period termed* الضُّحَى]. (Mṣb.) سُبْحَةُ ٱللّٰهِ, (IAth, Ḳ, TA,) with ḍamm, (TA, [but in my MS. copy of the Ḳ written سَبْحَة, and so in the CḲ,]) means † *The greatness*, or *majesty, of God*: (IAth, Ḳ, TA:) or [the pl.] السُّبُحَاتُ, occurring in a trad., means † *the greatness*, or *majesty, and the light* [or *splendour*], *of God*: (Mṣb:) or by the saying سُبُحَاتُ وَجْهِ رَبِّنَا, with ḍamm to the س and ب, is meant † *the greatness*, or *majesty, of the face of our Lord*: (Ṣ:) or سُبُحَاتُ وَجْهِ ٱللّٰهِ means † *the lights* [or *splendours*], (Ḳ,) or, accord. to ISh, *the light* [or *splendour*], (TA,) *of the face of God*: (ISh, Ḳ, TA:) some say that سُبُحَاتُ الوَجْهِ means † *the beauties of the face*; because, when you see a person of beautiful face, you say, سُبْحَانَ ٱللّٰهِ [to express your admiration]: and some, that [when it relates to God] it denotes a declaration of his being far removed from every imperfection; meaning سُبْحَانَ وَجْهِهِ. (TA. [See سُبْحَان.]) One says, [addressing God,] أَسْأَلُكَ بِسُبُحَاتِ وَجْهِكَ الكَرِيمِ, with two ḍammehs, meaning ‡ [*I ask Thee*] *by the evidences of thy greatness*, or *majesty*, [or *of the greatness*, or *majesty, of thy glorious face*,] *by the acknowledgement whereof thy praise is celebrated.* (A.) — السُّبُحَاتُ also signifies † *The places of prostration* [probably meaning *in the reciting of the Kur-án*]. (Ḳ.) — Also, i. e. [the sing.,] سُبْحَةٌ, *A piece of cotton.* (TA.)

سُبْحَانٌ is the inf. n. of سَبَحَ as syn. with سَبَّحَ [q. v.]; (Ḳ, TA;) and is a subst. that [sometimes] stands in the place of the inf. n. of the latter of these verbs, i. e. in the sense of تَسْبِيح. (T, TA.) — سُبْحَانَ is a proper name in the sense of التَّسْبِيح, and [for this reason, and also because it ends with ا and ن,] it is imperfectly decl., and is also invariable; being put in the accus. case in the manner of an inf. n. (Mgh.) You say سُبْحَانَ ٱللّٰهِ, meaning *I declare* [or *celebrate* or *extol*] *the remoteness*, or *freedom, of God* [*from every imperfection* or *impurity*, or *from everything derogatory from his glory*, i. e.] *from the imputation of there being any equal to Him, or any companion, or anything like unto Him, or anything contrary to Him*; or *from everything that should not be imputed to Him*: (L:) [*I declare*, or *celebrate*, or *extol, his absolute perfection* or *glory* or *purity*: or *extolled be his absolute perfection* &c.:] or *I declare the remoteness of God*, or *his freedom* (بَرَآءَة), *from evil*, (Zj,* Ṣ, Ḳ, TA,) or *from every evil*; (TA;) and [especially] *from the imputation of his having a female companion, and offspring*: (Ḳ:) or *I declare God's being very far removed from all the foul imputations of those who assert a plurality of gods*: (MF:) [it sometimes implies wonder, and may well be rendered *how far is God from every imperfection!* &c.:] in this case, سبحان is a determinate noun; (Ḳ;) i. e., a generic proper name, for التَّسْبِيح, like as بَرَّةُ is for البِرُّ. (MF:) Zj says, (TA,) it is put in the accus. case in the manner of an inf. n.; (Ṣ, Ḳ;) i. e., as the absolute complement of a verb understood; the phrase with the verb supplied being أُسَبِّحُ ٱللّٰهَ سُبْحَانَهُ; (MF;) meaning أُبَرِّئُ ٱللّٰهَ مِنَ ٱلسُّوْءِ بَرَآءَةً; (Ṣ, Ḳ, MF;) سبحان thus supplying the place of the verb: accord. to Ibn-El-Ḥájib and others, when it is prefixed to another noun or pronoun, governing it in the gen. case, it is a quasi-inf. n.; and when not so prefixed, it is a proper name, imperfectly decl.: but to this it is objected that a proper name may be thus prefixed for the purpose of distinction, as in the instances of زَيْدُ الفَوَارِسِ and حَاتِمُ طَيِّئٍ: some say that it is an inf. n. of an obsolete verb; but this assertion is not to be regarded; for, as an inf. n., its verb is سَبَّحَ, like شَكَرَ of which the inf. n. is شُكْرَانٌ: others say that it may be an inf. n. of سَبَحَ, though far from being agreeable with analogy: and some derive it from السَّبْحُ as signifying "the act of swimming," or "the being quick, or swift," or "the being, or becoming, remote," &c.: (MF:) [hence F adds,] or the phrase above-mentioned denotes quickness in betaking oneself to God, and agility in serving, or obeying, Him; [and therefore may be rendered *I betake myself quickly to the service of God, and am prompt in obeying Him*;] (Ḳ;) so accord. to ISh, to whom a man presented himself in a dream, and indicated this explanation of the phrase, deriving it from سَبَحَ الفَرَسُ ["the horse ran stretching forth his fore legs, as one does with his arms in swimming"]. (L.) فَسُبْحَانَ ٱللّٰهِ حِينَ تُمْسُونَ وَحِينَ تُصْبِحُونَ, [in which سبحان is used in the place of the inf. n. of سَبِّحْ, and سَبِّحُوا is understood before it,] in the Ḳur [xxx. 16], means *Therefore perform ye prayer to God* [or *declare ye the remoteness of God from every imperfection* &c.] *when ye enter upon the time of evening and when ye enter upon the time of daybreak.* (Fr, TA.) And سُبْحَانَ ٱللّٰهِ عَمَّا يَصِفُونَ, in the Ḳur xxiii. 93, means *Far* [or *how far*] *is God from that by which they describe* Him! (Jel.) One says also, سُبْحَانَكَ ٱللّٰهُمَّ وَبِحَمْدِكَ, meaning سَبَّحْتُكَ بِجَمِيعِ آلَائِكَ وَبِحَمْدِكَ سَبَّحْتُكَ [i. e. *I glorify Thee by* enumerating *all thy benefits, and by the praising of Thee I glorify Thee*]. (Mgh. [See also the prep. ب.]) — سُبْحَانَ مِنْ كَذَا, (Mṣb, Ḳ,) or سُبْحَانَ ٱللّٰهِ مِنْ كَذَا, سُبْحَانَ مِنْ فُلَانٍ, (Ṣ,) and (A,) are ‡ phrases expressive of wonder (Ṣ, A, Mṣb, Ḳ) at a thing (Ṣ, Mṣb, Ḳ) and a person; (A;) originating from God's being glorified (أَنْ يُسَبَّحَ ٱللّٰهُ) at the sight of what is wonderful of his works, and afterwards, by reason of its being frequently said, employed in relation to anything at which one wonders; (Er-Raḍee, TA;) meaning † [*I wonder greatly* (lit., *with wondering*) *at such a thing* and *such a person*; as is shown by what follows; or] *how extraordinary*, or *strange, is such a thing!* [and *such a person!*]. (Mṣb.) El-Aạshà says,

أَقُولُ لَمَّا جَآءَنِى فَخْرُهُ *
سُبْحَانَ مِنْ عَلْقَمَةَ ٱلْفَاخِرِ *

(Ṣ, Mṣb*) † [*I saying, when his boasting reached me, I wonder greatly at 'Alḳameh the boasting*]; i. e. العَجَبُ مِنْهُ, (Ṣ,) or [rather] عَجَبًا لَهُ [for أَعْجَبُ عَجَبًا لَهُ], lit. *I wonder with wondering at him*; (Mṣb;) [or *how extraordinary a person is 'Alḳameh the boasting!*:] سبحان being without tenween because it is regarded by them as a determinate noun, and having a resemblance to a fem. noun: (Ṣ:) [though in what quality it resembles a fem. noun, except in its being of one of the measures of broken pls., I do not know:] or it is imperfectly decl. because it is a determinate noun, being a proper name for البَرَآءَةُ (IJ, IB) and التَّنْزِيه, (IJ,) and because of the addition of the ا and ن: (IJ, IB:) this is the true reason: but some hold that it is rendered determinate by its being prefixed to a noun understood, governing it in the gen. case; the complete phrase being سُبْحَانَ ٱللّٰهِ مِنْ عَلْقَمَةَ. (MF.) — سُبْحَانًا, thus with tenween, as an indeterminate noun, occurs in the phrase سُبْحَانَهُ ثُمَّ سُبْحَانًا, in a poem of Umeiyeh. (IB.) — سُبْحَان is also used in the sense of نَفْس, in the saying أَنْتَ أَعْلَمُ بِمَا فِى سُبْحَانِكَ [*Thou art possessed of more*, or *most, knowledge of that which is in thine own mind*]. (Ḳ.)

سُبُوحٌ: see سَابِحٌ, in three places.

سِبَاحَةٌ an inf. n., (Ḳ,) or a simple subst., (Mṣb,) from سَبَحَ; (Mṣb, Ḳ;) *Natation*; or the *act* [or *art*] *of swimming*: (Ṣ, A, Mṣb,* Ḳ:) or the *coursing along upon water without immersion of oneself*. (MF, TA. [See 1, first sentence.])

سَبَّاحٌ: see سَابِحٌ, in two places.

سُبُّوحٌ, also pronounced سَبُّوحٌ, (T, Ṣ, Mṣb, Ḳ, &c.,) the latter the more agreeable with analogy, but the former the more common, (Th, T, Ṣ, Mṣb,*) one of the epithets applied to God, (T, Ṣ, A, Mṣb,* Ḳ,) because He is an object of تَسْبِيح, (Ḳ,) and [often] immediately followed by قُدُّوس, (A, Mṣb, Ḳ,) which is likewise also pronounced قَدُّوس, though the former pronunciation is the more common: (Th, T, Ṣ, Mṣb:*) it signifies [*All-perfect, all-pure*, or *all-glorious*; i. e.] *far removed*, or *free, from everything evil*, (Zj, Mgh, Mṣb, TA,) *and from every imperfection* [*and the like*]. (Mṣb. [See 2, and see also سُبْحَانَ ٱللّٰهِ.]) It is said (Ṣ, Mṣb) by Th (Ṣ) that there is no word like the two epithets above, of the measure فُعُّول with ḍamm as well as with fet-ḥ to the first letter, except ذَرُّوح: (Ṣ, Mṣb:) but the following similar instances have been pointed out: سُتُّوق among epithets, and فَرُّوج and ذُرُّوح and شُبُّوط and سُفُّود and كَلُّوب among substs. (TA.) Sb says, لَيْسَ فِى ٱلْكَلَامِ فُعُّولٌ بِوَاحِدَةٍ [expl. voce ذَرَّاحٌ]: (Ṣ:) [or] accord. to AḤei, Sb said that there is no epithet of the measure فُعُّول except سُبُّوح and قُدُّوس: Lḥ mentions سُتُّوق also, as an epithet applied to a دِرْهَم, as well as سَتُّوق. (TA.)

السُّبَّاحَةُ: see المُسَبِّحَةُ, in two places.

سَابِحٌ and ▼ سَبَّاحٌ (Mṣb, Ḳ) and ▼ سَبُوحٌ (Ḳ) are part. ns., or epithets, from سَبَحَ in the first of the senses assigned to it above: (Mṣb, Ḳ:) [the first signifies *Swimming*, or *a swimmer*:] the second has an intensive signification [i. e. one *who swims much*, or *a great swimmer*; as also the third]: (Mṣb:) the pl. of the first, accord. to IAạr, not of the first and last as it appears to be accord. to the Ḳ, is سُبَّحَآءُ: (MF:) that of the second is سَبَّاحُونَ: (Ḳ:) and that of the third is سُبُحٌ or سُبَّحٌ, the former reg., and the latter irreg. (MF.) — السَّابِحَات, (Ḳ, &c.,) in the Ḳur [lxxix. 3], accord. to Az, (TA,) means *The ships*: (Ḳ:) or † *the souls of the believers* (أَرْوَاحُ المُؤْمِنِينَ [for which Golius seems to have found in a copy of the Ḳ أَزْوَاجُ المُؤْمِنِينَ, for he gives as an explanation *piæ et fidelium uxores*,]) (Ḳ, TA) *which go forth with ease*: or † *the angels that swim*, or *glide*, (تَسْبَحُ,) *from* (من [app. a mistranscription for بَيْنَ *between*]) *the heaven and the earth*: (TA:) or † *the stars*, (Ḳ,) *which swim*, or *glide along*, (تَسْبَحُ,) *in the firmament, like the* سَابِح *in water*. (TA.) [The meanings *fœminæ jejunantes* and *veloces equi* and *planetæ*, assigned to this word by Golius as on the authority of the KL, are in that work assigned to سَائِحَات; the first of them as the meaning of this word in the Ḳur lxvi. 5.] And you say نُجُومٌ سَوَابِحُ ‡ [*Stars gliding along* in the firmament: سوابح being a pl. of سَابِح applied to an irrational thing, and of سَابِحَة]. (A.) — سَابِحٌ is also applied as an epithet to a horse, (Ṣ, IAth, A, L,) meaning ‡ *That stretches forth his fore legs well in running* [*like as one does the arms in swimming*]; (Ṣ,* IAth, L;) and in like manner ▼ سَبُوحٌ [but in an intensive sense]: (A, L:) the pl. [of the former] is سَوَابِحُ and سُبَّحٌ. (A.) And سَوَابِحُ also signifies ‡ *Horses*; (Ḳ, TA;) as an epithet in which the quality of a subst. is predominant; (TA;) because they thus stretch forth their fore legs in running. (Ḳ,* TA.) Hence, (TA,) ▼ السَّبُوحُ is the name of *A horse of Rabeeạ Ibn-Jusham*. (Ḳ, TA.) And in like manner, ▼ السَّبَّاحُ is the name of *A celebrated courser*: (TA:) and of *A certain camel*. (Ḳ, TA.)

تَسَابِيحُ and تَسْبِيحَاتٌ [pls. of تَسْبِيحَةٌ *A single act of* تَسْبِيح: see 2]. (A.)

[مَسْبَحٌ *A place of swimming*, &c.: pl. مَسَابِحُ.] — See an ex. of the pl. in the first paragraph of this art.

مُسَبَّحٌ, accord. to AA and the Ḳ, applied as an epithet to a [garment of the kind called] كِسَآء, means *Strong*: and accord. to the former, مُسَبَّحٌ, so applied, means "made wide." (TA.)

مُسَبِّحٌ [act. part. n. of 2]. فَلَوْلَا أَنَّهُ كَانَ مِنَ ٱلْمُسَبِّحِينَ, in the Ḳur [xxxvii. 143], means *And had he not been of the performers of prayer*, (A,* Mgh, Mṣb, Ḳ,*) as some say. (Mgh.)

المُسَبِّحَةُ (A, Mṣb, TA) and ▼ السَّبَّاحَةُ (A, TA) ‡ [*The index*, or *fore finger*;] *the finger that is next the thumb*: (Mṣb, TA:) so called because it is like the glorifier when one makes a sign with it [by raising it] when declaring [the unity of] the divine essence. (Mṣb, TA.*) One says, أَشَارَ إِلَيْهِ بِالمُسَبِّحَةِ and ▼ بِالسَّبَّاحَةِ ‡ [*He pointed towards him*, or *it, with the fore finger*]. (A, TA.)

سبخ

1. سَبِخَتِ ٱلْأَرْضُ, (JK, A, Mṣb,) aor. ـَ, inf. n. سَبَخٌ; (Mṣb;) and ▼ اسبخت; (JK, A, Mṣb, Ḳ;) *The land*, or *earth, exuded water and produced salt*: (JK, Ḳ:) or *was*, or *became, salt; had in it salt*. (A, Mṣb.) And سَبِخَ المَكَانُ, inf. n. as above, *The place produced salt, and was such that the feet sank in it*. (TA.) — See also 2. — سَبْخٌ, an inf. n. of which the verb is سَبَخَ, aor. ـُ, (TḲ,) means also † *The being in a state of sleep*: (AA, Ṣ:) and ▼ تَسْبِيخٌ † *The sleeping soundly*: (Ṣ:) or both have this meaning: (Ḳ:) or the former signifies † *the being in a state of rest, and easing the body by sleep*: (IAạr, L:) and ▼ the latter, † *the sleeping every hour*: (TA:) and the former signifies also † *the being unoccupied, at leisure*, or *free from work* or *business*; (AA, Ṣ, Ḳ;) and so ▼ the latter. (Ḳ.) In the Ḳur lxxiii. 7, some read سَبْخًا [instead of سَبْحًا, q. v.]; (Ṣ, Ḳ;) meaning † *rest, and easing of the body by sleep*; (IAạr, L;) and said by Fr to be from تَسْبِيخ, in the first of the senses expl. in the next paragraph: (L:) or † *freedom from occupation* or *work* or *business*. (Ṣ.) Accord to Zj, السَّبْخ and السَّبْح are nearly the same in meaning. (TA.) You say also سَبْخٌ مِنْ نَوْمٍ and مَشْىٍ and حَرٍّ [app. meaning † *A ceasing from sleeping* and *from walking* or *journeying* and *of heat*]. (JK.) — And سَبَخْتُ ٱلنَّوْمَ, inf. n. سَبْخٌ, † [*I slept long*; or] *I lengthened sleeping*. (JK.) — And سَبَخْتُ فِى ٱلْأَرْضِ † *I went*, or *travelled, far, in*, or *into*,

the land, or *country;* (JK, Ḳ,* TA;) like سَبْخَتْ. (TA.)

2. تَسْبِيخٌ [inf. n. of سَبَّخَ] The *separating,* or *plucking asunder, and loosening,* of cotton, *and making* it [or *spreading* it *out*] *wide.* (Fr, L.) — And The *winding* of cotton and the like, (Ḳ, TA,) such as wool, and soft hair (وَبَر), *after the separating and loosening, for a woman to spin it;* (TA;) [as also سَبْخٌ, inf. n. of ▼ سَبَخَ; see سَبِيخٌ.] — [Hence,] ‡ The act of *lightening,* or *alleviating.* (Ṣ, A, Ḳ.) It is related in a trad. that the Prophet said to 'Áisheh, when she had cursed a thief, (Ṣ, A, TA,) who had stolen something from her, (Ṣ, TA,) لَا تُسَبِّخِى عَنْهُ بِدُعَائِكِ عَلَيْهِ, (Ṣ, A,* TA,) meaning ‡ *Do not thou alleviate* (Ṣ, A, TA) *the merited punishment of his crime by thy cursing him.* (Ṣ,* TA.) And a poet says,

فَسَبِّخْ عَلَيْكَ الهَمَّ وَٱعْلَمْ بِأَنَّهُ
إِذَا قَدَّرَ الرَّحْمٰنُ شَيْئًا فَكَائِنُ

[*Then alleviate thou the disquietude of thy mind; and know that, when the Compassionate decreeth a thing, it happeneth*]. (Ṣ.) One says also, سَبَّخَ ٱللّٰهُ عَنْكَ الحُمَّى *May God alleviate thy fever.* (Ṣ.) And ٱللّٰهُمَّ سَبِّخْ عَنَّا الأَذَى *O God, remove from us,* or *alleviate to us, that which harms,* or *hurts.* (TA.) — And † The act of *stilling, quieting, rendering motionless, appeasing, tranquillizing, calming, allaying, assuaging,* or *quelling.* (Ḳ.) — Also † The *becoming* [*alleviated,* or *lightened,*] *still, quiet, motionless, appeased, tranquil, calm, allayed, assuaged,* or *quelled.* (Ḳ,* TA.) One says of heat, (Ṣ, Ḳ,) and of anger, (TA,) سَبَّخَ, (Ṣ, Ḳ,) inf. n. as above; and ▼ تَسَبَّخَ; (Ḳ;) † *It became abated,* or *allayed,* (Ṣ, Ḳ, TA,) and *alleviated.* (Ṣ.) — Also † The *ceasing* of veins *from the throbbing occasioned by pain* therein. (IAṭr, L, Ḳ.*) — See also **1**, in three places.

[**3.** سَابَخَ expl. by Freytag as meaning *He contended* with another *in swimming* is a mistake for سَابَحَ.]

4. أَسْبَخَ *He reached salt earth* in digging (Ṣ, Ḳ) a well. (TA.) — See also **1**, first sentence.

5: see **2**, near the end of the paragraph.

[سَبْخٌ is expl. by Freytag as applied in the Deewán of Jereer to *A dense cloud that is seen suspended apart from other clouds.*]

سَبَخٌ; and its fem., with ة: see سَبِخَةٌ, in three places.

سَبْخَةٌ: see the next paragraph, in three places.

سَبَخَةٌ and ▼ سَبْخَةٌ [*A piece, or tract, of*] *land that exudes water and produces salt:* (Ḳ:) pl. (of the former, Ṣ, or of the latter, Mṣb) سِبَاخٌ: (Ṣ, A, Mṣb, Ḳ:) ▼ أَرْضٌ سَبِخَةٌ [also] signifies as above; (JK;) or *land containing* سِبَاخ, (Ṣ, A,) i. e. [*places that exude water and produce salt,* or simply] *salt;* (A;) or *salt land* or *earth,* as also ▼ أَرْضٌ سَبَخَةٌ, in which the latter word is a contraction of سَبِخَةٌ, and أَرْضٌ سَبْخَةٌ also: (Mṣb:) and ▼ سَبَخٌ signifies a place *producing salt,* (Mṣb,* TA,) *and in which the feet sink:* (TA:) the pl. of ▼ سَبِخَةٌ is سَبِخَاتٌ. (Mṣb.) The Prophet said to Anas, on his mentioning El-Baṣrah, إِنْ مَرَرْتَ بِهَا وَدَخَلْتَهَا فَإِيَّاكَ وَسِبَاخَهَا, meaning [*If thou pass by it and enter it, then beware thou of*] *its tracts of land overspread with saltness, that seldom,* or *never, give growth to anything but some trees,* or *shrubs.* (L.) — Also, (Ḳ,) or the latter, i. e. ▼ سَبْخَةٌ, (JK,) *A thing that overspreads water* (JK, Ḳ, TA) *in consequence of its having been long left,* (TA,) *resembling* [*the green substance called*] طُحْلُب, (JK, Ḳ,) or *such as* طحلب *and the like.* (TA.)

سَبِيخٌ Cotton, and wool, and soft hair (وَبَر), *separated,* or *plucked asunder, and loosened;* as also ▼ مُسَبَّخٌ: (TA:) [and ▼ سَبِيخَةٌ, in which the ة is added to convert the epithet into a subst., signifies *a portion,* i. e. *a loose flock, thereof;* and its pl. is سَبَائِخُ, whence] one says, طَارَتْ سَبَائِخُ القُطْنِ [*The loose flocks of the cotton flew about*]. (A.) — [Hence,] ‡ Feathers (رِيش) *that fall off* (Ṣ, A, Ḳ) *and become scattered:* (Ḳ:) as also ▼ مُسَبَّخٌ: (TA:) the pl. of the former (Ḳ, TA) [used as a subst.], in this and in the following senses, (TA,) [or rather of ▼ سَبِيخَةٌ as a n. un. thus used,] is سَبَائِخُ. (Ḳ, TA.) One says, وَرَدْتُ مَآءً حَوْلَهُ سَبِيخُ الطَّيْرِ, and ▼ سَبَائِخُهُ, i. e. ‡ [*I came to water around which were*] *the feathers that had fallen off* [*and become scattered*] *of birds.* (A.) — Also Cotton *made wide for a medicament to be put upon it* (Ḳ, TA) *and for it to be applied upon a wound:* (TA:) and ▼ سَبِيخَةٌ signifies *a portion of cotton thus prepared for this purpose.* (JK, Ḳ.*) — And Cotton, (Ṣ, Ḳ,) and wool, and soft hair (وَبَر), (Ṣ,) *wound, after the separating and loosening,* (Ṣ, Ḳ, in the former ▼ يُسَبَّخُ بَعْدَ النَّدْفِ i. e. يُلَفُّ,) *to be spun* (Ṣ, Ḳ) *by a woman:* (Ṣ:) and ▼ سَبِيخَةٌ signifies *a portion thereof.* (Ṣ.)

سَبِيخَةٌ; and its pl., سَبَائِخُ: see the next preceding paragraph, in five places.

مُسَبَّخٌ: see سَبِيخٌ, in two places.

سبد

1: see what next follows.

2. سَبَّدَ شَعَرَهُ, (AA, TA,) inf. n. تَسْبِيدٌ, (Ḳ, TA,) *He shaved off his hair;* (AA, Ḳ, TA;) as also ▼ سَبَدَهُ, (AA, Ḳ,) inf. n. سَبْدٌ; (Ḳ, TA;) and ▼ اسبدهُ, (AA, TA,) inf. n. إِسْبَادٌ: (Ḳ, TA:) or all signify *he shaved off his hair and* [so] *removed it utterly:* and سَبَتَ شَعَرَهُ and سَبَتَهُ and اسبتهُ also have the former signification accord. to AA: (TA:) [and] تَسْبِيدُ الرَّأْسِ signifies the *removing utterly the hair of the head* [*by shaving*]: (Ṣ:) or سَبَّدَ شَعَرَهُ signifies *he shaved off his hair and then left it until it had grown a little:* (A'Obeyd, L:) or *he removed utterly his hair, making it to be* [*shaven*] *close to the skin;* (A'Obeyd, M, L;) as also سَبَدَهُ. (A'Obeyd, L.) — And *He let the whole of his hair grow ample and long:* thus it has two contr. significations. (M.) — And تَسْبِيدٌ signifies also The *combing,* or *combing down,* or *letting down and loosing, and then moistening, and leaving,* the hair of the head. (Suleymán Ibn-El-Mugheyreh, L, Ḳ.*) — And The *rendering* [one's hair] *matted,* or *compacted, and dusty.* (M, L.) — And [hence, app., the objective complement being meant to be understood,] The *leaving off,* or *neglecting, the anointing of oneself* [or *of one's hair*], (A'Obeyd, Ṣ, Ḳ, TA,) *and washing:* and some say تَسْبِيدٌ, which signifies the same. (A'Obeyd, TA.) — تَسْبِيدٌ is also used [intransitively,] as signifying The *appearing* of the hair of the head: (Ḳ:) or the *growing after some days:* (M:) or سَبَّدَ الشَّعَرُ means *The hair grew so that its blackness appeared* after the shaving. (Ṣ, M.) — And The *coming forth of the down* [of a young bird]: (M:) or the *appearing of the feathers* of a young bird. (Ḳ.) You say, سَبَّدَ الفَرْخُ *The young bird began to show its feathers,* or *to become fledged.* (Ṣ.) — And The *growing of fresh shoots upon,* or *among, the old portions* of the [plant called] نَصِىّ; as also ▼ إِسْبَادٌ: (Ḳ:) you say [of that plant], سَبَّدَ and ▼ اسبد: (TA:) or سَبَّدَ النَّبَاتُ *The plant had heads coming forth, before the spreading thereof.* (M.)

4: see **2**, in three places; first and last sentences.

سِبْدٌ i. q. دَاهِيَةٌ [as meaning *Cunning,* or *very cunning:* and perhaps also as meaning *a calamity:* pl. أَسْبَادٌ]. (Ṣ, M, Ḳ.) You say, هُوَ سِبْدُ أَسْبَادٍ *He is cunning,* or *very cunning,* (دَاهٍ, Ṣ, M, or دَاهِيَةٌ, Ḳ,) *in theft,* or *robbery.* (Ṣ, M, Ḳ.) — And [hence, perhaps, or the reverse may be the case,] *A wolf:* (Ḳ:) it occurs, in the accus. case, in a verse, in this sense, (TA,) or in the former sense; (Ṣ;) or, as some relate it, the word in this instance is سِيدًا [which has the latter meaning]. (Ṣ, TA.)

سَبَدٌ *Hair* [*of goats*]; syn. شَعَرٌ; (Aṣ, Ṣ, M;) as also ▼ سُبُودٌ: (M:) or *a small quantity thereof:* (Ḳ:) or *fur* [*of camels*]; syn. وَبَرٌ. (M.) One says, مَا لَهُ سَبَدٌ وَلَا لَبَدٌ (Aṣ, Ṣ, M, Ḳ) *He has neither goats' hair nor wool:* (Aṣ,* Ṣ,* M:) or *neither camels' fur nor wool:* or *neither camels' fur nor goats' hair:* meaning ‡ *he has neither goats nor sheep:* or ‡ *neither camels nor sheep:* or ‡ *neither camels nor goats:* (M:) or ‡ *neither little nor much;* (Aṣ, Ṣ, Ḳ, TA;) i. e. *he has not anything.* (TA.) [See also لَبَدٌ.] Hence سَبَدٌ is an appellation for † *Cattle* (مَال). (TA.) Hence also the saying of 'Átikeh Bint-Zeyd,

لَمْ يَدَعْهُ ٱللّٰهُ يَمْشِى بِسَبَدْ

[i. e. † *God let him not walk with goats, &c.*]; meaning † *God reduced him to poverty, so that He left not* [*to him*] *anything.* (Ḥam p. 495.) — Also sing. of أَسْبَادٌ (TA) which signifies *Black garments* or *cloths* [app. *of goats' hair* or *of* camels' fur]. (Ḳ, TA.) — أَسْبَادٌ, (Ḳ, TA,) as pl. of سَبَدٌ, (TA,) signifies also The *heads* of the [plant called] نَصِىّ *when they first come forth:* (Ḳ, TA:) or, as pl. of سَبَدٌ, the *heads* of plants *coming forth, before spreading.* (M.) — And, likewise as pl. of سَبَدٌ, *Remains of plants* or *herbage* in a land. (TA.) [See also سَبَدٌ.] = سَبَدٌ also signifies *Unluckiness, ill luck,* or *evil fortune:* (M:) or so ✝ سُبَدٌ: (Ḳ, TA:) so says Lth, on the authority of ADḳ. (TA.)

سُبَدٌ *A remnant of herbage* or *pasturage.* (Ḳ.) [See also سَبَدٌ, last sentence but one.]

سُبَدٌ *A certain bird,* (Ṣ, M, Ḳ,) *having plumage so soft,* or *smooth, that when two drops of water drop upon it,* (Ṣ, M,* Ḳ,) *upon its back,* (Ṣ, M,) *they run off from it;* (Ṣ,* M, K,* TA;) or *such that when a drop of water drops upon its back, it runs* [*off*]: (M:) the Arabs liken to it a horse when he sweats: (Ṣ:) or *a certain bird like the eagle:* (TA:) or the *male eagle:* (M, TA:) or the *swallow of the desert* (خُطَّافٌ بَرِّىّ): (Aṣ, TA:) or *a bird like the* خُطَّاف; *when water falls upon it, it runs off from it quickly:* so says Aboo-Naṣr; and so Skr in his Expos. of the poetry of Hudheyl, on the authority of Aṣ: (TA:) said by Aṣ to be *a certain black bird:* (so in a marg. note in one of my copies of the Ṣ:) pl. سِبْدَانٌ. (Ṣ, M.) — Also *A piece of cloth with which the watering-trough* (Ḳ, TA) *such as is termed* مَرْكُوّ [q. v.] (TA) *is rendered close,* or *firm,* [*in its bottom and sides,*] (يُسَدُّ, [in the L يُسْبَدُ, but I know not any apposite meaning of this verb,]) *in order that the water may not become turbid:* (Ḳ:) *it is spread therein; and the camels are made to drink* [*the water*] *above it.* (L.) — See also سِبْدَةٌ. = And see سَبَدٌ, last sentence.

سِبْدَةٌ, (M, L,) or ✝ سُبَدٌ, (Ḳ,) or both, (TA,) The *pubes.* (M, L, K.)

سُبُودٌ: see سَبَدٌ, first sentence.

سِبَنْدَى *Tall,* or *long;* (Ḳ;) in the dial. of Hudheyl: (TA:) and also *bold,* or *daring;* (Ṣ, M, Ḳ;) applied to anything [i. e. to any creature]; (Ṣ, Ḳ;) of the dial. of Hudheyl: (M:) as also سِبَنْتَى: (Ṣ, TA:) or, so applied, *bold,* or *daring, to undertake anything:* and the fem. [سِبَنْدَاةٌ, like سِبَنْتَاةٌ,] is said to signify *a bold lioness:* and *a bold-breasted she-camel:* and in like manner [the masc. signifies] *a bold-breasted he-camel:* (M, L:) and, (Ṣ, M, L, K,) as also بِسِنْدَى, (M, L,) the *leopard;* (Aṣ, Ṣ, M, L, Ḳ;) and so سِبَنْتَى, (Aṣ, Ṣ, L,) or سِبَنْتَاةٌ, which is also applied to *a beast of prey* [absolutely]: (A Heyth:) or the *lion:* (M, L:) pl. سَبَانِدُ and سَبَانِدَةٌ: or the meaning of this, or these, [i. e. of the latter pl. or of both, for the pronoun (هى) may relate to the latter or to both,] is *idle,* and *sportful,* and *vain,* or *frivolous, persons;* (Ḳ, TA;) like سَبَادِرَةٌ. (TA.)

مُسْبَدٌ, like مُعْظَمٌ, (TA,) or ✝ مُسْبِدٌ, (accord. to a copy of the M,) as meaning † *Consummate,* (M,* TA,) is applied as an epithet to a calamity, دَاهِيَة, (M, TA,) which a poet terms, for the sake of the measure, أُمُّ فَأْرٍ, because it is termed أُمُّ أَدْرَاصٍ, and دِرْصٌ is applied to a young one of a bitch, and of a she-wolf, and of a she-cat, and of the [species of فَأْر called] جُرَذ, and of the jerboa. (M.)

مُسَبِّدٌ [act. part. n. of 2]. It is said of Ibn-'Abbás, قَدِمَ مَكَّةَ مُسَبِّدًا رَأْسَهُ, meaning *He came to Mekkeh having his head unanointed and unwashed.* (A'Obeyd, Ṣ.) = See also the next preceding paragraph.

سبر

1. سَبَرَ الجُرْحَ, (Ṣ, M, A, &c.,) aor. ـُ (Ṣ, M, Mṣb) and ـِ, (M, TA,) inf. n. سَبْرٌ; (Ṣ, M, Mṣb, Ḳ;) and ✝ اِسْتَبَرَهُ; (Ḳ;) *He probed the wound; measured its depth* with the مِسْبَار, i. e., with an iron or other instrument; (A, Mgh;) *tried,* (Ḳ,) or *examined,* (Ṣ,) or *endeavoured to learn,* (Mṣb,) *its depth;* (Ṣ, Mṣb, Ḳ;) *examined its extent.* (M.) — سَبَرَهُ † *He determined,* or *computed by conjecture* or *by the eye, its measure, quantity, size,* or *bulk.* (M, Ḳ,* TA.) — † *He tried, proved,* or *tested, it; proved it by experiment* or *experience;* (Ṣ, M, TA;) namely, anything; as also ✝ اِسْتَبَرَهُ. (Ṣ.) — † *He elicited its true,* or *real, condition.* (TA.) — It is related in the trad. of the cave, that Aboo-Bekr said to Moḥammad, لَا تَدْخُلْهُ حَتَّى أَسْبُرَهُ قَبْلَكَ † *Do not thou enter it until I explore it before thee, and see if there be in it any one,* or *anything that may hurt.* (TA.) — مَفَازَةٌ لَا تُسْبَرُ ‡ *A desert of which the extent cannot be known.* (A.) — سَبَرْتُ فُلَانًا ‡ [*I searched into such a one*]. (A.) — فِيهِ خَيْرٌ كَثِيرٌ لَا يُسْبَرُ ‡ [*In him is much good, the extent of which cannot be known*]. (A.) — أَمْرٌ عَظِيمٌ لَا يُسْبَرُ ‡ [*A great affair, of which the uttermost cannot be known*]. (A.) — اُسْبُرْ لِى مَا عِنْدَهُ † *Learn thou for me what he has* [*in his mind,* or *in his possession*]. (M.) — سَبَرْتُ القَوْمَ, aor. ـُ and ـِ, inf. n. سَبْرٌ, † *I observed the people attentively, with investigation, one after another, that I might know their number.* (Mṣb.)

8: see 1, in two places.

سَبْرٌ: see سِبْرٌ. = Also The *lion.* (El-Muärrij, Ḳ.)

سِبْرٌ (Ṣ, M, Ḳ) and ✝ سَبْرٌ (M, Ḳ) The *source,* or *origin,* [of a thing,] syn. أَصْلٌ: (M, Ḳ:) pl. of both أَسْبَارٌ. (M.) — ‡ *Form,* or *appearance; figure, feature,* or *lineaments; external state* or *condition; state with regard to apparel and the like;* (Ṣ, M, K;) or *goodly form* or *appearance* &c.; (Ḳ;) *aspect; garb,* or *habit;* (TA;) *colour,* or *complexion;* (M, Ḳ;) *beauty;* (Ḳ;) *brightness of countenance:* (M:) pl. of both as above. (M.) — IAạr says, I heard Aboo-Ziyád El-Kilábee say, I returned from Marw to the desert, and one of its people said to me, أَمَّا السِّبْرُ فَحَضَرِىٌّ وَأَمَّا اللِّسَانُ فَبَدَوِىٌّ ‡ *As to garb and appearance,* [thou art like] *an inhabitant of a town; but as to tongue, an inhabitant of the desert.* (Ṣ,* TA.) — You say, فُلَانٌ حَسَنُ الحِبْرِ وَالسِّبْرِ ‡ *Such a one is beautiful and of goodly appearance.* (Ṣ.) [See also حِبْرٌ.] — A woman of the desert said, أَعْجَبَنِى سِبْرُ فُلَانٍ ‡ *The good condition, and flourishing state of body, of such a one pleased me:* and رَأَيْتُهُ سَيِّئَ السِّبْرِ ‡ *I saw him to have an altered and ill appearance of body:* thus she assigned to سبر two significations. (TA.) — One says also, إِنَّهُ لَحَسَنُ السِّبْرِ ‡ *Verily he is goodly in complexion and appearance.* (TA.) — سِبْرٌ also signifies ‡ *A characteristic by which one knows the generousness or ungenerousness of a beast.* (AZ, M.) — And † *One's knowledge of the fruitfulness or unfruitfulness* [or *the good or bad condition*] *of a beast.* (AZ, TA.) — Also † *Likeness;* syn. شَبَهٌ. (Ḳ, TA. [In some copies of the Ḳ, شُبْهَةٌ, which is an evident mistake.]) So in the phrase, occurring in a trad., غَلَبَ عَلَيْهِمْ سِبْرُ أَبِى بَكْرٍ † *The likeness* (شَبَه) *of Aboo-Bekr predominated in them.* (IAạr, TA.) One says also, عَرَفَهُ بِسِبْرِ أَبِيهِ † *He knew him by the appearance and likeness of his father.* (TA.) — Also the former (سِبْرٌ), *Enmity,* (Ḳ,) accord. to El-Muärrij; but Az says that this is strange. (TA.)

سُبْرَةٌ *A cold morning, between daybreak and sunrise:* (Ṣ, M, A, Mgh, Ḳ:) or *from the time a little before daybreak to daybreak:* or *from daybreak to sunrise:* (M:) or *a cold morning during the period next after sunrise:* (Mṣb:) pl. سَبَرَاتٌ: (Ṣ, M, Mgh, Mṣb, Ḳ:) which latter is also expl. as signifying the *intenseness of the cold of winter,* and *of the year.* (TA.)

سُبْرُتٌ and سِبْرَاتٌ and سُبْرُوتٌ and سِبْرِيتٌ: &c.: see art. سبرت.

سُبْرُورٌ *Poor;* (Ḳ, TA;) *possessing no property:* like سُبْرُوتٌ, in this sense, and in that following. (TA.) — ‡ Land *in which is no herbage.* (Ḳ, TA.)

سِبَارٌ and ✝ مِسْبَارٌ *A probe; an instrument with which a wound is probed;* (Ṣ, M, Ḳ;) as also ✝ مِسْبَرٌ: (Ḥam p. 818:) *a twist like a wick,* (T, Mṣb,) or *a similar thing,* (Mṣb,) *which is put into a wound* (T, Mṣb) *to ascertain its depth;* (Mṣb;) *an iron or other instrument with which the depth of a wound is measured:* (A, Mgh:) pl. of the first, سُبُرٌ; and of ✝ the second, مَسَابِيرُ. (Mṣb.) It is said in a prov., لَوْلَا المِسْبَارُ مَا عُرِفَ غَوْرُ الجُرْحِ [*Were it not for the probe, the depth of the wound would not be known*]. (A.) And ✝ بَعِيدُ المِسْبَارِ is applied as an epithet to a woman's vulva [or vagina, in an obvious sense,] by Ibn-Ḥabeeb: and accord. to the Ḳ, to a woman [in allusion to her vagina]. (TA in art. عجى.)

سَبَارٍ an irreg. pl. of سُبْرُوتٌ: see the latter in art. سبرت.

سَابِرِىٌّ *A coat of mail made of slender rings, and strongly:* (Ḳ:) so called in relation to the king Sáboor. (TA.) — Hence, (TA,) or from

Sáboor, a province of Persia, (Mgh, Mṣb,) *A thin, or delicate, kind of garment* or *cloth,* (IDrd, Ṣ, M, Mgh, Mṣb, Ḳ,) *of excellent quality:* (Ḳ:) and *anything thin,* or *delicate.* (M.) Whence the prov., عَرْضٌ سَابِرِىٌّ (Ṣ, M,* Ḳ*) *A slight exhibition:* (M:) [see variations of this phrase in art. عرض, under عَرَضَ الشَّىْءَ:] said to him to whom a thing is shown in a slight manner: (Ṣ:) because the garment or cloth called سابرىّ, (Ṣ, Ḳ,) being of the best of qualities, (Ṣ,) is desired when exhibited in the slightest manner. (Ṣ, Ḳ. [See the first paragraph in art. عرض; and see also عَرْضٌ عَلَىَّ سَوْمَ عَالَّةٍ in the first paragraph of art. سوم.]) — *A certain sort of dates,* (Ṣ, Mṣb, Ḳ,) *of good quality.* (Mṣb, Ḳ.) It is said that the best of the dates in El-Koofeh are the نِرْسِيَان and the سابرىّ. (Ṣ.) — نَخْلَةٌ سَابِرِيَّةٌ *A palm-tree of which the unripe dates are yellow and somewhat long.* (AḤát, Mṣb.)

مَسْبَرٌ † [The *internal state* or *condition* of a man]. You say, حَمِدْتُ مَسْبَرَهُ and مَسْبُرَهُ † [*I praised his internal state or condition*]: (Ṣ:) and ▼ مَسْبُرَةٌ also signifies † The *internal state* or *condition; an internal,* or *intrinsic, quality;* or the *intrinsic,* or *real, as opposed to the apparent, state, or aspect.* (TA.)

مِسْبَرٌ: see سِبَارٌ.

مَسْبَرَةٌ The *utmost point* of a wound. (M.) — See also مَسْبَرٌ.

مِسْبَارٌ: see سِبَارٌ, in four places. — It may also be applied to † *A man who probes a wound.* (Ḥam p. 818.)

مَسْبُورٌ *Goodly in form or appearance; in figure, feature,* or *lineaments; in external state* or *condition; in state of apparel* or *the like.* (Ḳ, TA.)

سبرت

Q. 1. سَبْرَتَ *He begged;* and *became lowly, humble,* or *submissive;* or *affected to be like the* مَسَاكِين [or *destitute,* or *needy,* &c.]; syn. قَنِعَ; (Ḳ, TA; [omitted in the CḲ, and in my MS. copy of the Ḳ erroneously written قَنَعَ;]) and تَمَسْكَنَ. (TA.)

سُبْرُوتٌ: see سُبْرُوتٌ.

سِبْرَاتٌ: see the next paragraph, in two places.

سُبْرُوتٌ *A desert,* syn. قَفْرٌ, (Ṣ, Ḳ,) or *a plain,* syn. قَاعٌ, (M,) *in which is no herbage:* (M, Ḳ:) or *weak land:* (TA:) and أَرْضٌ سُبْرُوتٌ and ▼ سِبْرِيتٌ (Aṣ, Lḥ, M) and ▼ سِبْرَاتٌ (M) *Land in which is no herbage;* (M;) or *land in which is nothing:* (Aṣ, Lḥ, M:) pl. سَبَارِيتُ and سَبَارٌ, the latter anomalous, mentioned by Lḥ: (M:) accord. to A'Obeyd, the pl. سَبَارِيتُ signifies *deserts,* or *waterless deserts,* (فَلَوَاتٌ,) *in which is nothing:* and accord. to Aṣ, *land* [or *lands*] *in which nothing grows:* (TA:) and one says also أَرْضٌ سَبَارِيتُ, (M, Ḳ,) a phrase of the same class as ثَوْبٌ أَخْلَاقٌ, (Ḳ,) as though the sing. سُبْرُوتٌ or سِبْرِيتٌ were applied to every portion thereof. (M.) — Hence, (TA,) applied to a man, (AZ, Ṣ, TA,) *Needy, in want, indigent,* (AZ, Aṣ, Ṣ, M, Ḳ, TA,) *poor,* (AZ, Aṣ, Ḳ, TA,) *possessing little,* (M, TA,) or, as some say, *possessing nothing;* (Ṣ,* M, TA;) and ▼ سِبْرِيتٌ signifies the same, (AZ, Ṣ, M, Ḳ,) as also ▼ سِبْرَاتٌ, and ▼ سُبْرُتٌ: (M, Ḳ:) also *bankrupt,* or *insolvent;* syn. مُفْلِسٌ: (TA in explanation of the first [but equally applying to all]:) the epithet applied to a woman is سُبْرُوتَةٌ and ▼ سِبْرِيتَةٌ; (AZ, Ṣ;) the latter of which is applied to a man [app. in intensive sense, agreeably with analogy,] as well as to a woman: (M:) and the pl. is سَبَارِيتُ, applied to men and to women. (AZ, Ṣ.) — [Hence, also,] applied to a youth, or young man, *Beardless;* or *having no hair upon the sides of his face.* (M, Ḳ, TA. [In the Ḳ, this signification is immediately followed by the mention of the pls. سَبَارِيتُ and سَبَارٌ.]) — And *Little,* or *small, in quantity* or *number;* (Ṣ, M, Ḳ;) *paltry,* or *inconsiderable:* (Ḳ:) applied to a thing, (Ṣ, Ḳ,) and (Ṣ) to property, or cattle. (Ṣ, M.) — Also *Tall,* or *long.* (M, TA.) — And *A skilful,* or *an expert, guide, well acquainted with the lands.* (TA.) It is mentioned by Sb, who says that it is of the measure فُعْلُولٌ, like زُنْبُورٌ and عُصْفُورٌ; and most hold him to be right: but some of the authors on inflection assert that it is of the measure فُعْلُوتٌ, from سَبَرْتُ الشَّىْءَ meaning "I tried, proved, or tested, the thing, or proved it by experiment or experience;" and that the ت is added to give intensiveness to the signification; which several deny: (MF, TA:) سُبْرُورٌ, however, is mentioned in the Ḳ, in art. سبر, as meaning "poor," and land "in which is no herbage." (TA.)

سِبْرِيتٌ and سِبْرِيتَةٌ: see the next preceding paragraph, in three places.

سَنْبَرِيتٌ A man (TA) *of evil disposition* or *nature.* (Ḳ, TA: but omitted in the CḲ.)

مُسْبَرَتٌ *Bald,* or *bare of hair.* (Ḳ, TA: but omitted in the CḲ.)

سبط

1. سَبِطَ, aor. ـَ; (Sb, Ṣ, M, Mṣb, Ḳ;) and سَبُطَ, aor. ـُ; (M, Mṣb, Ḳ;) inf. n. سَبَطٌ, of the former verb, (Ṣ, Mṣb,) or سَبْطٌ, (so in the Ḳ, as is remarked in the TA,) and سُبُوطَةٌ, (M, Mṣb, Ḳ,) which is of the latter verb, (M, Mṣb,) and سَبَاطَةٌ and سُبُوطٌ, (M, Ḳ,) which are also of the latter verb; (M;) *It* (hair, Ṣ, M) *was,* or *became, lank, not crisp:* (Ṣ, M,* Mṣb, Ḳ:*) or the former verb is used in this sense, said of hair; and the latter is said of a man, signifying *he was,* or *became, lank, not crisp, in his hair.* (TA.) — سَبَاطَةٌ, relating to a man, also signifies The *being tall:* (M:) or the *being long in the* [*bones called*] أَلْوَاح [pl. of لَوْحٌ], *and even therein.* (TA.) — Also سَبُطَ, inf. n. سَبَاطَةٌ; (M, TA;) and سَبِطَ, inf. n. سَبَطٌ; (M;) ‡ *He* (a man) *was,* or *became, easy,* or *facile,* بِالْمَعْرُوفِ *in beneficence.* (M, TA.) And سُبُوطَةٌ is likewise expl. as signifying ‡ The *being liberal, bountiful,* or *munificent.* (M, TA.) — And سَبَاطَةٌ, relating to rain, ‡ The *being abundant and extensive.* (Sh, Ḳ, TA.) [— See also the part. n. سَبِطٌ.] — سَبَطَ عَلَيْهِ الْعَطَآءَ ‡ *He gave to him successive and large gifts.* (Ṣgh, TA.) — سُبِطَ *He was affected with fever.* (Ṣgh, Ḳ.) [See سُبَاطٌ.]

2. سَبَّطَتْ, (M, Ḳ, &c.,) inf. n. تَسْبِيطٌ, (Ṣ, Ḳ,) *She* (a camel, AZ, Aṣ, M, Ḳ, and a ewe, Ḳ) *cast her young one,* or *fœtus, in an incomplete state:* (M, Ḳ:) or *before its form was apparent;* (AZ, Ḳ;) like أَجْهَضَتْ and رَجَعَتْ: (AZ:) or *when its fur had grown, before completion;* as also سَبَّغَتْ: (Aṣ, TA:) or سَبَّطَتْ بِوَلَدِهَا *she* (a camel) *cast her young one when its hair had grown:* and سَبَّطَتْ *she* (a ewe) *cast her young one,* or *fœtus, abortively.* (Ṣ.) The epithet applied to her in this case is ▼ مُسَبِّطٌ [without ة]. (M, Ḳ.)

4. اسبط *He* (a man, Ṣ, M) *extended himself,* or *became extended* or *stretched,* (Ṣ, M, Ḳ, TA,) *upon the ground,* (Ṣ, TA), *in consequence of being beaten,* (M, Ḳ, TA,) &c.: (TA:) *he fell* (M, Ḳ, TA) *upon the ground,* (TA,) *and was unable to move,* (M, Ḳ, TA,) *by reason of weakness,* (M, TA,) or *from drinking medicine,* or *some other cause;* on the authority of AZ: (M:) *he fell upon the ground, and became extended* or *stretched, in consequence of being beaten,* or *from disease,* and in like manner *from drinking medicine.* (TA.) And اسبط بالأَرْضِ *He clave to the ground.* (Ibn-Jebeleh, M, Ḳ.) — *He was silent, by reason of fear,* or *fright:* (M, L, Ḳ:) *he was silent and still;* or *he lowered his eyes, looking towards the ground, and was still.* (O.) — اسبط فِى نَوْمِهِ *He shut,* or *closed, his eyes,* or *eyelids, in his sleep.* (Ṣgh, Ḳ.) — اسبط عَنِ الأَمْرِ *He feigned himself negligent of the thing* or *affair, inattentive to it,* or *heedless of it.* (Ṣgh, Ḳ.)

سَبْطٌ: see سَبِطٌ, throughout.

سِبْطٌ *A grandchild;* (Ṣ, Mṣb, Ḳ;) *a son's child,* and *a daughter's child:* (M, TA:) pl. أَسْبَاطٌ; (Ṣ, Mṣb, TA;) which is commonly used by the vulgar as signifying *daughters' children;* distinguished by them from أَحْفَاد [which they apply to son's children, pl. of حَفِيد]; but the leading lexicologists expressly declare that it includes sons' children and daughters' children, as it is said to do by ISd: IAạr explained سِبْطٌ and سِبْطَانِ and أَسْبَاطٌ as signifying the *particularly distinguished,* and *choicest, of children.* (TA.) It is said in a trad., (TA,) الحَسَنُ وَالحُسَيْنُ سِبْطَا رَسُولِ اللّٰهِ *El-Ḥasan, and El-Ḥoseyn are the two grandsons of the Apostle of God.* (M, TA.*) — *A tribe of the Jews:* pl. أَسْبَاطٌ: (M, Mṣb, Ḳ:) سِبْطٌ (M) and أَسْبَاطٌ (Ṣ, Mṣb) in relation to the Jews, (M, Mṣb,) or [rather] the Children of Israel, (Ṣ,) being like قَبِيلَةٌ (M) and قَبَائِلُ (Ṣ, Mṣb) in relation to the Arabs: (Ṣ, M, Mṣb:) and the former are thus called to distinguish them from the children of Ishmael. (M, TA.) In the phrase, وَقَطَّعْنَاهُمُ ٱثْنَتَىْ عَشْرَةَ أَسْبَاطًا [*And we divided them into twelve* divisions, *tribes*], (Ṣ, M, Ḳ,) in the Ḳur [vii. 160], (Ṣ, M,) اسباطا is a substitute (Ṣ, M, Ḳ) for اثنتى عشرة, (Ṣ, M,) not a specificative, (Ṣ, M, Ḳ,) because the specificative may only be a sing.; (Ṣ, M;) the meaning being وقطّعناهم اثنتى عشرة فِرْقَةً اسباطًا, (Akh, Zj, Ṣ,) and therefore the numeral is fem.; (Akh, Ṣ;) or this is a mistake; for it should be فِرَقًا اثنتى عشرة; and therefore the numeral is fem. (Abu-l-'Abbás, TA.) Accord. to Ḳṭr, you say, هٰذَا سِبْطٌ and هٰذِهِ سِبْطٌ, and هٰؤُلَآءِ سِبْطٌ using سبط as a pl., meaning فِرْقَةٌ. (TA.) The saying

كَأَنَّهُ سِبْطٌ مِنَ الأَسْبَاطِ

is [asserted to be] a mistake, inasmuch as its author imagined that سِبْطٌ meant *a man*: (M:) IDrd ascribes it to El-'Ajjáj or Ru-beh: it occurs in an أُرْجُوزَة by the latter. (Ṣgh, TA.) [But it is applied to a single man: for] it is said in a trad., (TA,) حُسَيْنٌ سِبْطٌ مِنَ الأَسْبَاطِ, i. e. *Ḥoseyn is* [as though he were] *a nation of the nations* (أُمَّةٌ مِنَ الأُمَمِ Ḳ) *in goodness*; so expl. by Aboo-Bekr: (TA:) or *one of the fathers of tribes*; because of the multitude of his descendants: or *one of the sons of daughters*. (So in a marginal note in a copy of the "Jámi' eṣ-Ṣagheer" of Es-Suyooṭee.) — Also *A generation* (قَرْن) *that comes after another*. (Zj, TA.) ═ And سِبْطٌ رِبْعِيَّةٌ, (TA in the present art. and in art. ربع,) or ↓ سَبِطٌ رِبْعِيَّةٌ, (so accord. to a copy of the M, in the present art.,) *A palm-tree of which the fruit ripens in the end of the summer*, or *hot-season*. (M, TA.)

سَبَطٌ: see the next paragraph, first sentence. ═ Also *Such as is fresh of the* [*plant called*] حَلِىّ; *one of the plants of the sands*; (M;) [i. e.] the [*plant called*] نَصِىّ, *while fresh*; (A'Obeyd, Ṣ, O, Ḳ;) *when it has dried up, called* حَلِىّ; (A'Obeyd, Ṣ, O;) *a plant like the* ثِيل [q. v.], *except that it becomes tall; growing in the sands*: (Lth, TA:) n. un. with ة: (Lth, Ṣ:) it is *one of those that, when they dry up, become white*, [as is said of the حَلِىّ,] *resembling hoariness, like the* ثُمَام [or *panic grass*]: (AḤn, O: in the TA, the ثُمَام:) it is asserted that the Arabs say, "The صِلِّيَان is the bread of the camels, and the سَبَط is their خَبِيص:" (AḤn, O:) *its manner of growth is like* [*that of*] دُخْن [q. v.]; *and it is a good pasture*: (Ḳ:) AḤn says, a desert-Arab, of 'Anazeh, told me that *its manner of growth is like that of large* دُخْن, *falling short of* [so I render دُونَ, but this also signifies *exceeding*,] ذُرَة [q. v.], *and it has grain like the grain termed* بُزُر [q. v.], *which will not come forth from its envelopes but by bruising*, or *pounding*, *and men extract it and eat it, made into bread, and cooked*: (M, O:) the n. un. is with ة: and the pl. is أَسْبَاطٌ. (M.) Also The *tree that has many branches and one* أَصْل [meaning *stem*]: (Ḳ:) so says Az.; adding that hence is derived أَسْبَاطٌ [pl. of سِبْطٌ]; as though the father represented the tree and the children represented the branches: (TA: [but this is questionable:]) accord. to Abu-Ziyád, *a certain tree*, (AḤn, M, O,) *growing in the sands*, (AḤn, O,) *tall, having slender branches, eaten by the camels and the sheep or goats*, (AḤn, M, O,) *and collected by men, who sell it upon the roads* (عَلَى الطُّرُقِ), (AḤn, O,) or *with the tamarisk* (مَعَ الطَّرْفَآءِ); (so in the TA;) *without blossom and without thorns, having thin leaves of the size of* [*those of*] *the* كُرَّاث [or *leek*] (AḤn, M, O) *when this first comes forth*. (AḤn, O.) — See also the last sentence of the next preceding paragraph.

سَبْطٌ and ↓ سَبِطٌ and ↓ سَبَطٌ, (the first and third of these in one copy of the Ṣ, and the second alone in another copy of the Ṣ, and all in the M and Mṣb and Ḳ,) the first of the dial. of El-Ḥijáz, (TA,) from سَبُطَ, and the second from سَبِطَ, the last being an inf. n. used as an epithet, (Mṣb,) *Lank, not crisp*; (Ṣ, M,* Mṣb, Ḳ;*) applied to hair: (Ṣ, Mṣb:) pl. سِبَاطٌ, which is said by Sb to be of the measure most common for a pl. of an epithet of the measure فَعْلٌ, (M,) or فَعِلٌ. (TA.) — سَبِطُ الشَّعَرِ, (Ṣ, M,) and ↓ سَبْطُهُ, (M,) A man *having lank hair*: (Ṣ, M:) and in like manner سِبَاطٌ, alone, applied to a number of persons. (TA.) ↓ سَبْطٌ is also metonymically applied to ‡ *A foreigner*, like as [its contr.] جَعْدٌ is to an Arab. (TA.) — سَبْطٌ also signifies *Tall*; (M, Ḳ;) applied to a man: (M:) or, as also ↓ سَبِطٌ, (TA,) or سَبِطُ الجِسْمِ, (M,) so applied, *long in the* [*bones called*] أَلْوَاح [pl. of لَوْح], (M, TA,] *and even therein*: (TA:) or سَبْطُ الجِسْمِ or ↓ سَبِطُهُ, (accord. to different copies of the Ḳ,) or both, (Ṣ, TA,) *goodly in stature*, or *person*, or *proportion*, (Ṣ, Ḳ,) *and evenness*. (Ṣ.) Also *Having extended limbs, and perfect in make*. (TA.) And سَبْطُ القَصَبِ, and ↓ سَبِطُهَا, A man [*long and even*, or] *extended, and without protuberances, in the bones of the fore arms and the shanks*. (TA.) And سَبْطُ البَنَانِ and سَبِطُهَا, ‡ *Long in the fingers*. (TA.) And سَبْطُ الخَلْقِ A man *lank in make*: (L in art. رد:) and سَبْطَةُ الخَلْقِ, and ↓ سَبِطَتُهُ, ‡ a woman *lank*, or *soft*, or *tender, in make*. (M, Z, TA.) And سَبْطُ السَّاقَيْنِ A man *soft*, or *flaccid*, or *uncompact, in the shanks*. (Ḥam p. 238.) — ↓ سَبِطُ اليَدَيْنِ, (M, Ḳ, TA,) and سَبْطُهُمَا, (TA, and so in the CḲ,) and سَبْطُ الكَفَّيْنِ, (TA,) ‡ A man who is *liberal, bountiful*, or *munificent*. (M, Ḳ, TA.) And سَبْطٌ بِالمَعْرُوفِ ‡ A man *easy*, or *facile, in beneficence*. (M, TA.) — مَطَرٌ سَبْطٌ, (Sh, TA,) and ↓ سَبِطٌ, (Sh, Ḳ,) ‡ *Rain pouring abundantly and extensively*, (Sh, Ḳ,) *and consecutively*. (Ṣh, TA.)

سِبْطَةٌ: see سِبْتَةٌ.

سُبَاطٌ *Fever*: (M, O, Ḳ:) so called because the man attacked by it extends himself, and becomes relaxed: (Skr, O:) or *fever attended with shivering*, or *trembling*. (O.)

سُبَاطٌ (AA, Ṣ, M, Ḳ) and سُبَاطُ, being perfectly and imperfectly decl., (AA, Ḳ,) and also written with ش, (TA, and Ḳ in art. شبط,) *The name of a month in Greek*; (Ṣ;) *a certain month*, [*next*] *before* آذَار; (Ḳ;) *the month that is between the winter and the spring*; (M;) [*the fifth month of the Syrian year, corresponding with February O. S.*;] *it is in the winter-quarters, and in it is the completion of the day whereof the fractions circulate in the years*: when the said day is complete in that month, the people of Syria call that year عَامُ الكَبِيسِ; and when a child is born, or a person arrives from a country, in that year, they consider it fortunate. (Az, TA.) [See كَبِيس.]

سُبَاطَةٌ *Sweepings*, syn. كُنَاسَةٌ, (Ṣ, M, Mgh, Mṣb, Ḳ,) *which are thrown every day in the courts of houses*. (Ḳ.) — Also *A place in which sweepings* (Mgh, TA) *and dirt* (TA) *are thrown*: occuring in a trad., (Mgh, TA,) and so expl. by El-Khaṭṭábee: (Mgh:) but some assign to it there the former meaning. (TA.) [It should be observed that كُنَاسَةٌ also is said to have both these meanings.] — Also *What falls from*, or *of, hair when it is combed*. (M, TA.) ═ *A raceme of a palm-tree, with its fruit-stalks* (عَرَاجِين) *and its fresh ripe dates*: of the dial. of Egypt. (TA.)

سَابَاطٌ *A roof* (Ṣ, M, Mgh, Mṣb, Ḳ) *between two walls*, (Ṣ,) or *between two houses*, (M, Ḳ,) *having beneath it a road*, or *way*, or *passage*, (Ṣ, Mgh, Mṣb, Ḳ,) *which is a thoroughfare*: (Mgh:) pl. سَوَابِيطُ (Ṣ, Mṣb, Ḳ) and سَابَاطَاتٌ. (Ṣ, Ḳ.)

مَا لِى أَرَاكَ مُسْبِطًا *Wherefore do I see thee hanging down thy head like one in grief, or anxiety, lax in body?* (Ṣ.) And تَرَكْتُهُ مُسْبِطًا *I left him* (meaning a sick person) *not moving nor speaking*. (TA.) ═ أَرْضٌ مُسْبِطَةٌ, (M, and so in some copies of the Ṣ,) or ↓ مَسْبَطَةٌ, (thus in other copies of the Ṣ, and in the O,) *Land abounding with* سَبَط [q. v.]. (Ṣ, M,* O.)

مَسْبَطَةٌ: see what next precedes.

مُسَبَّطٌ: see 2.

سبطر

Q. 4. اِسْبَطَرَّ *He stretched himself*: (M:) *he lay upon his side, and stretched himself*. (Ṣ, Ḳ.) — *He* (a slaughtered beast) *stretched himself to die*. (TA.) — اسبطرّت الإِبِلُ فِى سَيْرِهَا *The camels hastened*, (M,* Ḳ,* TA,) *and stretched themselves, in their march*, or *course*. (TA.) — اسبطرّت لَهُ البِلَادُ *The provinces became rightly disposed to him*. (Fr, Ḳ.*)

سِبَطْرٌ A lion *stretching himself when about to spring* or *leap*. (Ṣ, Ḳ.) — A *quick* camel: pl. سِبَطْرَاتٌ: it has no broken pl. (Sb, M.) — Also, the pl. above mentioned, Camels *long, upon the surface of the ground* [or *horizontally*]. (Ṣ, Ḳ.) The ت [says J] is not the denotative of the fem. gender: (Ṣ:) it is like that in رِجَالَاتٌ (Ṣ, Ḳ) and حَمَّامَاتٌ, as masc. pls.: (Ṣ:) but IB says, the ت in this word is the denotative of the fem. gender; for it is an epithet applied to جِمَالٌ, which is fem. as a [broken] pl.; as is shown by the saying الجِمَالُ سَارَتْ, and رَعَتْ, &c.: and he adds, J's saying that it is like رجالات and حمّامات

is a mistake, inasmuch as he confounds رجالات with حمّامات; for رِجَال is a fem. pl., as is shown by one's saying الرِّجَالُ خَرَجَتْ, and سَارَتْ; but حَمَّام is masc., and should not regularly have a pl. with ا and ت, but, as Sb says, it has this pl. form, like some other masc. words, in lieu of a broken pl., and would not have it if it had a broken pl. (TA.) —— Also the sing., *Penetrating; effective;* (Lth, M, Ḳ;) [as though *stretching far;*] *sharp in intellect; clever; acute:* (Ḳ: [in the CḲ, الماضى الشِّبر is put by mistake for الماضى الشَّهْم:]) or *sharp in intellect, and very bold* or *daring* or *courageous.* (TA.) —— *Lank* hair. (M.) —— A man (Sh) *lank and tall.* (Sh, Ḳ.) —— And with ة, *A corpulent* woman. (M.)

سِبَطْرَى *A proud and self-conceited gait, with an affected inclining of the body from side to side.* (M, Ḳ.)

سُبَاطِرٌ: see what next follows.

سِبَطْرٌ and ↑ سُبَاطِرٌ *Tall,* or *long.* (M, Ḳ.) —— Also the former, *A certain bird having a very long neck,* (Ṣ, Ḳ,) *which one sees always in shallow water; surnamed* أَبُو العَيْزَارِ. (Ṣ.) [Freytag says, on the authority of Dmr, that it is also called مالك الحزين. See art. ملك.]

سبع

1. سَبَعَهُمْ, aor. ـَ (Ṣ, Mṣb, Ḳ) and ـُ (Yoo, Mṣb, Ḳ) and ـِ, (Yoo, Mṣb,) inf. n. سَبْعٌ, (Mṣb,) *He was,* or *became, the seventh of them:* (Ṣ, Mṣb, Ḳ:) or *he made them, with himself, seven:* (Ṣ in art. ثلث:) or it signifies, (Ṣ, and so in some copies of the Ḳ,) or signifies also, (Mṣb, and so in some copies of the Ḳ,) *he took the seventh part of their property,* or *possessions.* (Ṣ, Mṣb, Ḳ.) And *He made them,* they being sixty-nine, *to be seventy with himself.* (A'Obeyd, Ṣ in art. ثلث.) And سَبَعَ also signifies *He made* sixteen *to be seventeen.* (T in art. ثلث.) —— سَبَعْتُ لَهُ الأَيَّامَ, aor. ـَ, inf. n. as above, *I completed to him the days by making them seven:* and ↑ سَبَّعْتُهَا signifies the same in an emphatic manner. (Mṣb.) [See also 2.] —— سَبَعَ الحَبْلَ, (Ḳ,) aor. ـَ, inf. n. as above, (TA,) *He made the rope,* or *cord, of seven strands.* (Ḳ, TA.) —— سُبِعَ المَوْلُودُ *The infant had its head shaven, and an animal* [generally a goat] *sacrificed by way of expiation for it, on the seventh day* [*after its birth,* (commonly called يَوْمُ السُّبُوعِ,) agreeably with an ordinance of Moḥammad; the sacrifice being for the expiation of original sin]. (IDrd.) ═ سَبَعَ الغَنَمَ *He* (a wolf) *seized the sheep,* or *goats, and broke their necks,* or *killed them,* or *made them his prey,* (Ṣ, Ḳ, TA,) *and ate them.* (TA.) —— سُبِعَتِ الوَحْشِيَّةُ *The female wild animal had her young,* or *young one, eaten by the* سَبُع [or *beast,* or *bird, of prey*]. (TA.) —— سَبَعَهُ *He stole it;* [as though, like a سَبُع, he made it his prey;] as also ↑ اسْتَبْعَهُ. (AA, Ḳ.) —— *He shot him* [with an arrow or the like], or *hurled at him and struck him* [with a lance, or a missile of any kind]; namely, a wolf: or *he frightened him;* namely, a wolf; (Ḳ;) and also, a man. (TA.) —— † *He reviled, vilified,* or *vituperated, him; charged him with a vice* or *fault* or *the like;* (Ṣ, Ḳ, TA;) *assailed him with foul language, such as displeased him:* (TA:) or *he bit him* (Ḳ, TA) *with his teeth, like as does the* سَبُع. (TA.)

2. سَبَّعَهُ, inf. n. تَسْبِيعٌ, *He made it seven;* or *called it seven;* (Ṣ, Ḳ;) as also ↑ اسبعهُ. (TA.) See also 1. —— *He made it to have seven angles,* or *corners; to be heptagonal.* (Ḳ.) —— *He* (God) *gave him his reward,* or *recompense, seven times,* or *seven fold.* (Ḳ.) An Arab of the desert said to a man who had done a good act to him, (TA,) سَبَّعَ اللّٰهُ لَكَ *May God give thee thy reward,* or *recompense, seven times,* or *seven fold.* (Ḳ, TA.) The Arabs also said, سَبَّعَ اللّٰهُ لَكَ أَجْرَهَا *May God multiply to thee the reward,* or *recompense, for it;* meaning, for this good act: (Aboo-Sa'eed:) [for] تَسْبِيع is used by them to signify the act of *multiplying,* though it be more than seven fold. (TA.) And سَبَّعَ اللّٰهُ لِفُلَانٍ is used as meaning *May God make a thing to be followed by another thing to such a one;* in relation to good and to evil; as also تَبَّعَ لَهُ. (TA.) And سَبَّعَ اللّٰهُ لَكَ meaning *May God bless thee with seven children.* (TA.) —— *He washed it* (namely, a vessel,) *seven times.* (Ḳ.) Hence the saying of Aboo-Dhu-eyb,

كَنَعْتِ ٱلَّتِى قَامَتْ تُسَبِّعُ سُؤْرَهَا *

[*Like her who has arisen to wash out seven times her remains of beverage in the bottom of a vessel, left by a drinker;* that drinker, as is said in a marginal note in my copy of the TA, being her dog]: or, accord. to Es-Sukkaree, the meaning is, *to give as alms her* سُؤْر [*remains of beverage in the bottom of a vessel after one had drunk,* or *remains of food &c.*], *thereby seeking to have her reward,* or *recompense, multiplied;* بِسُؤْرِهَا being used by the poet for سُؤْرَهَا. (TA.) —— سَبَّعَ القُرْآنَ [app. followed by لَهُ or عَلَيْهِ] *He appointed him the reading,* or *recitation, of the Ḳur-án* [*in seven portions so that he should complete the whole*] *in every seven nights.* (O, L, Ḳ.) —— سَبَّعَ لِامْرَأَتِهِ, (Ḳ, TA,) or عِنْدَهَا and ↑ أَسْبَعَ لَهَا, (TA,) *He remained with his wife seven nights.* (Ḳ, TA.) In like manner one says ثَلَّثَ; and thus of every number from one to ten; in relation to any saying or action. (TA.) —— سَبَّعَت *She* (a woman) *brought forth at seven months.* (TA.) —— سَبَّعَ دَرَاهِمَهُ *He made his dirhems to be seventy complete;* but this is post-classical; (Ḳ;) and in like manner, ↑ سَبْعَنَ دراهمه, meaning the same, and also post-classical, and not allowable; the proper phrase to express the meaning "I made it to be seventy" being كَمَّلْتُهُ سَبْعِينَ. (TA.) —— سَبَّعَتِ القَوْمُ *The people,* or *company of men, completed the number of seven hundred men:* (Ḳ, TA:) occurring in a trad. (TA.)

3. سِبَاعٌ, (Ḳ,) inf. n. of سابع, (TḲ,) *The performing of the act of coïtus,* (IAạr, Th, Ḳ,) with a woman. (TḲ.) —— *The vying with another in the endeavour to surpass him in obscene, or lewd, language, and in frequency of coïtus, and in speaking plainly of such subjects as should only be alluded to, in relation to women:* (IAạr, Ḳ:*) such seems to be its meaning in a trad. in which the doing this is forbidden. (IAạr.) —— † *Mutual reviling, vilifying,* or *vituperating;* (Ḳ, TA;) *when each of two men assails the other with foul language, such as displeases him:* (TA:) this is said by some to be its meaning in the trad. in which it is forbidden. (TA.)

4. اسبع, said of a party of men, *It became seven:* (Ṣ, Ḳ:) also, *it became seventy.* (M and L in art. ثلث.) —— Said of a man, it signifies *He was,* or *became, one whose camels came to the water on the seventh day* [*counting the day of the next preceding watering as the first*]. (Ṣ, Ḳ.) —— اسبع لِامْرَأَتِهِ: see 2. —— أَسْبَعَتْ *She brought forth her seventh offspring.* (TA in art. بكر.) —— اسبعهُ: see 2, first signification. ═ *It* (a road) *abounded with* سِبَاع [or *animals of prey*]. (TA.) —— اسبع الرُّعْيَانُ *The pastors had their beasts fallen upon by the* سَبُع [or *animal of prey*]. (Yaạḳoob, Ṣ, Ḳ.) ═ اسبعهُ i. q. أَطْعَمَهُ السَّبُعَ [which may be rendered *He gave him as food the animal of prey,* or *he gave him as food to the animal of prey;* but it seems from what here follows that the former is meant]: (Ṣ, Ḳ:) in the "Mufradát," [*he gave him as food*] *the flesh of the* سَبُع. (TA.) ═ *He gave him,* or *delivered him,* (namely, his son,) *to the* ظُؤُورَة [which means both *nurse* and *nurses*]. (Ṣ, Ḳ.) —— *He left him to himself;* or *left him without work,* or *occupation;* namely, his slave; syn. أَهْمَلَهُ. (Ṣ, Ḳ.) [See مُسْبَع.]

8: see 1.

Q. Q. 1; سَبْعَنَ: see 2, last sentence but one.

سَبْعٌ fem. of سَبْعَةٌ, q. v. ═ See also سَبُعٌ in two places. ═ السَّبْعُ *The place to which mankind shall be congregated* (Ḳ, TA) *on the day of resurrection.* (TA.) Hence the trad., (Ḳ, TA,) which relates that while a pastor was among his sheep, or goats, the wolf rushed upon him, and took from them a sheep, or goat, and the pastor pursued him until he rescued it from him; whereupon the wolf looked aside towards him, and said to him, (TA,) مَنْ لَهَا يَوْمَ السَّبْعِ, meaning *Who will be for it* [namely, the sheep, or goat, *as aider,* or *defender,*] *on the day of resurrection?* (Ḳ, TA:) thus expl. by IAạr, and mentioned by Ṣgh and the author of the L: (TA:) but to this is contradictory, or repugnant, يُعَكِّرُ, [in the CḲ erroneously written يَعْكُرُ,]) the saying of the wolf, (Ḳ, TA,) after the words mentioned above, (TA,) "the day when it shall have no pastor but me;" for the wolf will not be a pastor on the day of resurrection: or the meaning is, *who shall be for it on the occasion of trials, when it shall be left to itself, without pastor, a spoil to the animals of prey:* the animal of prey being thus made to be a pastor to it: (Ḳ, TA:) this is in the way of a trope: and accord. to this explanation, it may be [↑ يَوْمُ السُّبْعِ] with ḍamm to the ب:

(TA:) or يَوْمُ السُّبْعِ was *a festival of their's in the Time of Ignorance, on which they were diverted from everything by their sport:* (AO, Ḳ, TA:) and accord. to one relation [of the trad.] it is with ḍamm to the ب. (L, Ḳ.)

سُبْعٌ (Ṣ, Mṣb, Ḳ) and ▼ سُبُعٌ, (Mgh, Mṣb,) of which the former is a contraction, (Mṣb,) *A seventh part; one of seven parts;* (Ṣ, Mgh, Mṣb, Ḳ;) as also ▼ سَبِيعٌ; (Ṣ, Mṣb, Ḳ;) the last not heard by Sh on any authority beside that of AZ: (TA:) pl. of the first (Mṣb) and second (Mgh, Mṣb) أَسْبَاعٌ. (Mgh, Mṣb, TA.) Hence, أَسْبَاعُ القُرْآنِ [*The seven sections,* or *volumes, of the Ḳur-an,*] in which one reads: said to be post-classical. (Mgh.) ═ See also أُسْبُوعٌ, in three places.

سِبْعٌ *A certain* ظِمْء *of the* أَظْمَاء *of camels;* (T, Ṣ, Ḳ;) i. e. *their coming to the water on the seventh day* [*counting the day of the next preceding watering as the first*]; (Ḳ;) or [in other words, which have virtually the same meaning,] *their remaining in their places of pasturing five complete days, and coming to the water on the sixth day, not reckoning the day of the* [*next preceding*] *return from the water.* (Az, TA.) You say, وَرَدَتْ إِبِلُهُ سِبْعًا *His camels came to the water* &c. (Ṣ, Ḳ.) — Also *The seventh young one,* or *offspring.* (A in art. ثلث.)

سَبْعٌ: see what next follows.

سَبُعٌ (Ṣ, Ṣgh, Mṣb, Ḳ) and ▼ سَبْعٌ, (Ṣgh, Mṣb, Ḳ,) a dial. var., (Ṣgh, Mṣb,) and the form in common use with the vulgar, (Mṣb,) adopted also by several readers of the Ḳur in v. 4, (Mṣb, TA,) and often occurring in the poems of the Arabs, (TA,) and ▼ سَبِعٌ, (Ṣgh, Ḳ,) a form adopted by two readers of the Ḳur in the place above mentioned, and perhaps a dial. var., (Ṣgh, TA,) *The animal of prey; the rapacious animal;* (Ḳ;) [*whether beast or bird;* being sometimes applied to the latter, as, for instance, in the Ḳ, voce مِخْلَبٌ; but generally to the former:] or *whatsoever has a fang,* or *canine tooth, with which it makes hostile attacks, and seizes its prey;* (Mṣb;) *such as the lion,* [to which it is particularly applied by most of the Arabs in the present day,] *and also* (TA) *such as the wolf and the lynx and the leopard,* (Mṣb, TA,) *and the like of these, that has a fang, and attacks men and beasts and makes them its prey:* (TA:) the fox, however, is not thus called, though having a fang, (Mṣb, TA,) because he does not attack with it nor take prey, (Mṣb,) or because he does not attack small beasts, nor seize with his fang any animal; (TA;) and in like manner the hyena (Mṣb, TA) is not reckoned among the hostile animals thus called, wherefore the Sunneh allows that its flesh may be eaten, and requires that a compensation be made for it [by the sacrifice of a ram] if it be smitten [and killed] in the sacred territory or by a person in the state of iḥrám: but *as to the jackal, it is a noxious* سبع, and its flesh is unlawful, because it is of the same kind as wolves, except that it is smaller in size and weaker in body: thus says Az: but some others say that the سبع is *any hostile beast having a* مِخْلَب [or *tearing claw*]: and it is said in the Mufradát to be thus called because of the perfectness of its strength; for السَّبْعُ [seven] is one of the perfect numbers: (TA:) the pl. is سِبَاعٌ, (Sb, Ṣ, Mṣb, Ḳ,) i. e., of سَبُعٌ, which has no other pl.; (Sb, Mṣb;) أَسْبُعٌ is also a pl., (Ṣgh, Mṣb, Ḳ,) but this is pl. of pauc. of ▼ سَبْعٌ, (Ṣgh, Mṣb,) which, not being a contraction [of سَبُعٌ, but a dial. var. thereof], has also for its pls. [of mult.] سُبُوعٌ and سُبُوعَةٌ, like صُقُورٌ and صُقُورَةٌ, pls. of صَقْرٌ. (TA.) See also سَبْعٌ: [and see سَبُعَةٌ.] You say of him who is very injurious, or mischievous, مَا هُوَ إِلَّا سَبُعٌ مِنَ السِّبَاعِ ‡ [*He is none other than one of the animals of prey*]. (TA.) — السَّبُعُ is also the name of † *The constellation* [*Lupus*] *behind* [i. e. *on the east of*] *Centaurus, containing nineteen stars in the figure.* (Ḳzw.)

سَبِعٌ: see سَبُعٌ.

سَبْعَةٌ, (Ṣ, Ḳ,) sometimes pronounced ▼ سَبَعَةٌ but some disallow this latter, and say that it is pl. of سَابِعٌ, (Ḳ,) [*Seven;*] *a well-known number; and called one of the perfect numbers:* (TA:) fem. سَبْعٌ. (Ṣ, Ḳ.) You say, سَبْعَةُ رِجَالٍ [*Seven men*]: and سَبْعُ نِسْوَةٍ [*seven women*]. (Ṣ, Ḳ.) — أَخَذَهُ أَخْذَ سَبْعَةٍ: see سَبُعَةٌ. — وَزْنَ سَبْعَةٍ means *Of the weight of seven* مَثَاقِيل: (Ṣ, Ḳ:) one says, أَخَذْتُ مِنْهُ مِائَةَ دِرْهَمٍ وَزْنَ سَبْعَةٍ, meaning [*I took,* or *received, from him a hundred dirhems*] every ten whereof were *of the weight of seven* mithḳáls. (TA.) [But see دِرْهَمٌ.] — إِحْدَى مِنْ سَبْعٍ [lit. *One of seven;*] means † *a great, momentous,* or *difficult, thing,* or *affair:* (Sh, Ḳ:*) *an affair difficult to decide:* perhaps as being likened to one of the seven nights in which God sent the punishment upon [the tribe of] 'Ád: or, as some say, the seven years [of famine in the days] of Joseph. (Sh, TA.) — السَّبْعُ المَثَانِي *The Fátiḥah;* [or *first chapter of the Ḳur-án;*] because it consists of seven verses: or *the long chapters from* البَقَرَة to الأَعْرَاف [a mistake for الأَنْفَال]; as in the Mufradát: or, as in the L, *to* التَّوْبَة, reckoning التوبة and الانفال as one chapter, for which reason they are not separated by the بَسْمَلَة. (TA.) [See also مَثْنًى.] — El-Farezdaḳ says,

وَكَيْفَ أَخَافُ النَّاسَ وَاللّٰهُ قَابِضٌ ✱
عَلَى النَّاسِ وَالسَّبْعَيْنِ فِي رَاحَةِ اليَدِ ✱

meaning [*And how should I fear men when God is comprehending mankind and*] *the seven heavens and seven earths* [*in the palm of the hand?*]. (Ḳ.) — See also أُسْبُوعٌ; last sentence. — [سَبْعَةٌ is also used in a vague manner, as meaning *Seven or more;* or *several;* or *many;* as Bḍ says, in ix. 81, and as is indicated, though not plainly declared, in the TA. See 2: and see also سَبْعُونَ. — Respecting a peculiar pronunciation of the people of El-Ḥijáz, and a case in which سَبْعَة is imperfectly decl., see ثَلَاثَةٌ. See also سِتَّةٌ.] — سَبْعَةَ عَشَرَ [indecl. in every case, meaning *Seventeen,*] is pronounced by some of the Arabs سَبْعَةَ عْشَرَ: and [the fem.] سَبْعَ عَشْرَةَ, thus in the dial. of El-Ḥijáz [and of most of the Arabs], is pronounced سَبْعَ عَشِرَةَ in the dial. of Nejd. (Ṣ in art. عشر.) ═ See also سَبُعَةٌ, in two places.

سَبَعَةٌ: see سَبْعَةٌ.

سَبُعَةٌ and ▼ سَبْعَةٌ, the latter a contraction of the former, *The lioness.* (ISk, Ṣ, Mṣb, Ḳ.) Hence the saying, ▼ أَخَذَهُ أَخْذَ سَبْعَةٍ, (ISk, Ṣ, Ḳ,) or السَّبُعَةِ, (Mṣb,) *He seized him with the seizing of a lioness,* (ISk, Ṣ, Ḳ,) or *of the lioness,* (Mṣb,) which is more impetuous (أَنْزَقُ) than the lion, (ISk, Ṣ,) or more bold than the lion: (Mṣb:) or the saying is, أَخَذَهُ أَخْذَ سَبْعَةَ (Ṣ, Ḳ) *he seized him with the seizing of Seb'ah,* who was a certain strong man, (Ibn-El-Kelbee, Ṣ,) or a certain insolent and audacious rebel, (Ibn-El-Kelbee, Lth, Ḳ,) of the Arabs, (TA,) whom one of the kings of El-Yemen seized, and, after having cut off his hands and feet, or arms and legs, crucified; [so that the meaning is, *he punished him with the punishment of Seb'ah;*] and hence it was said, لَأُعَذِّبَنَّكَ عَذَابَ سَبْعَةَ [*I will assuredly punish thee with the punishment of Seb'ah*]; (El-Kelbee, Lth, Ḳ;*) and لَأَعْمَلَنَّ بِكَ عَمَلَ سَبْعَةَ *I will assuredly do with thee as was done with Seb'ah:* (O:) or the man's name was سَبُعٌ, and it was contracted, and made fem. by way of contempt: or the meaning of the first saying is, *he seized him with the seizing of seven* men: (Ḳ:) and in like manner the last saying is expl. by some [who say سَبْعَة instead of سَبْعَةَ]. (TA.) The dim. is ▼ سُبَيْعَةٌ. (Mṣb.) [See also سَبُعٌ.]

[سَبُعِيٌّ *Of,* or *relating to, an animal of prey.*]

سَبْعُونَ [*Seventy;*] *a well-known number;* (Ḳ;) the *round number that is between* سِتُّونَ *and* ثَمَانُونَ. (TA.) — The Arabs also use it as meaning [*Seventy or more;* or] *many.* (TA.) Thus it is used in the Ḳur [ix. 81], where it is said, إِنْ تَسْتَغْفِرْ لَهُمْ سَبْعِينَ مَرَّةً فَلَنْ يَغْفِرَ اللّٰهُ لَهُمْ, meaning *If thou beg forgiveness for them many times, even then God will not forgive them;* not that God would forgive them if forgiveness were begged more than seventy times: (Bḍ,* TA:) and سَبْعَة and سَبْعُمِائَة and the like are used in the same manner. (Bḍ.) — [Also *Seventieth.*]

[سُبَاعَ as meaning *Seven and seven,* or *seven and seven together,* or *seven at a time and seven at a time,* seems not to have been used; for] A'Obeyd says that more than أُحَادَ and ثُنَاءَ and ثُلَاثَ and رُبَاعَ has not been heard, excepting عُشَارَ. (TA in art. عشر.)

سَبُوعٌ [app. *Wont to frighten*]: (TA: [in which the meaning here given seems to be indicated.])

سُبُوعٌ: see أُسْبُوعٌ, in four places.

سَبِيعٌ: see سُبْعٌ: — and سَابِعٌ.

سُبَيْعَةٌ dim. of سَبْعَةٌ, q. v.

سُبَاعِيٌّ A garment, or piece of cloth, *seven cubits*, or *seven spans, in length*. (TA.) — A *great and tall* camel; (En-Naḍr, Ḳ;) [as though *seven cubits in height*:] fem. with ة. (Ḳ.) And سُبَاعِيُّ البَدَنِ, (Ṣ, Ḳ,) applied to a man, has the like meaning; (Ḳ;) *complete*, or *full-grown, in body*; (Ṣ, TA;) [or *seven spans in height*; for] when a boy has attained seven spans, he is a man. (Ṣ, voce خُمَاسِيٌّ, q. v.)

سَابِعٌ [act. part. n. of 1: generally meaning *Seventh*]: pl. سَبَعَةٌ. (Ḳ.) You say, كُنْتُ سَابِعَهُمْ [*I was the seventh of them*]. (Ṣ, Ḳ.) And هٰذَا سَبِيعُ ↓ هٰذَا, meaning سَابِعُهُ [*This is the seventh of this*: not the seventh part; though the former has also this latter meaning]. (TA.) And هُوَ سَابِعُ سَبْعَةٍ [*He is the seventh of seven*]. (TA.) And هُوَ سَابِعُ سِتَّةٍ [*He is making six to become seven*]. (TA.) — إِبِلٌ سَوَابِعُ [pl. of سَابِعَةٌ] *Camels coming to the water on the seventh day* [*counting the day of the next preceding watering as the first*]. (TA.) [See سِبْعٌ — سَابِعَ عَشَرَ] and سَابِعَةَ عَشْرَةَ, the former masc. and the latter fem., meaning *Seventeenth*, are subject to the same rules as ثَالِثَ عَشَرَ and its fem., expl. in art. ثلث, q. v.]

أُسْبُوعٌ *A certain number of days*; (Ṣ,* Mṣb, Ḳ;*) i. e. *seven days*; *a week*; (Mṣb;) also termed ↓ سُبُوعٌ, (Lth, Mṣb, Ḳ,) by some of the Arabs; (Lth, Mṣb;) [and ↓ سُبْعٌ, as shown by what follows:] pl. of the first أَسَابِيعُ. (Mṣb, TA.) One says, أَقَمْتُ عِنْدَهُ سُبْعَيْنِ ↓ [in the sense of أُسْبُوعَيْنِ, which is more common,] i. e. *I remained at his abode two weeks*. (TA.) — Also *The seventh day*; and so ↓ سُبُوعٌ; as in a trad., where it is said, إِذَا كَانَ يَوْمُ سُبُوعِهِ, meaning *When his seventh day after the celebration of his marriage is come*. (TA.) [↓ يَوْمُ السُّبُوعِ is used in this sense in the present day: and also as meaning *The seventh day after childbirth*; in which sense it is generally to be understood when used unrestrictedly; as this day is celebrated with more rejoicing than the former: also as meaning *the seventh day after the return from pilgrimage*.] — And *Seven circuitings* [round the House of God, meaning the Kaabeh]: (Lth, Mgh, Mṣb:) pl. أَسَابِيعُ (Ṣ, Mgh, Mṣb) and أُسْبُوعَاتٌ. (Lth, Mgh, Mṣb.) You say, طَافَ بِالْبَيْتِ أُسْبُوعًا, (Ṣ, Mgh,* Ḳ,) and ↓ سُبُوعًا, (Lth, IDrd, Ḳ,) but Aboo Sa'eed says, I know not any one who has said this except IDrd, and the former is the word commonly known, (TA,) and ↓ سَبْعًا, (Ḳ,) and ↓ سُبْعًا, (TA,) *He circuited round the House* [of God] *seven times*, (Ṣ, TA,) or *seven circuitings*; (Mgh;) and ثَلَاثَةَ أَسَابِيعَ [*thrice seven times*, or *thrice seven circuitings*]. (Ṣ.)

مُسْبَعٌ *Given*, or *delivered, to the* ظُؤُورَة [which means both *nurse* and *nurses*]: (Skr, Ṣ, TA:) this is the primary signification: (Skr:) or *whose mother dies, and who is therefore suckled by another*; (Ḳ; in which the next following signification may be regarded as implied, TA;) *left to himself*; or *left without work*, or *occupation*; applied to a slave; syn. مُهْمَلٌ: (Skr, Ṣ:) or مُتْرَفٌ, (Ṣgh, Ḳ,) [which has the same and other significations; or] which is [here] nearly the same as مُهْمَلٌ, for he who is مُهْمَل is usually مُتْرَف: (TA:) or one who is *left to himself with the* سِبَاع [or *animals of prey*] *so that he becomes like one of them in mischievousness*, or *noxiousness*, or *evilness*: (AO, Ḳ:) or who is *left to himself and not restrained from his daringness, so that he remains daring*: and a slave *left to himself, and daring*; *left until he has become like the* سَبُع: (TA:) or one *whose origin is suspected*; (Ḳ;) *whose father is not known*: (Er-Rághib, Ṣgh:) or *a bastard*: (Ḳ:) or one *whose lineage is of slaves*, (Ḳ, TA,) or *ignoble*, (TA,) *up to seven male ancestors*, (Ḳ, TA,) or, *to seven female ancestors*; (TA;) or, *to four male ancestors*; (En-Naḍr, Ḳ;) or *whose lineage is traced up to four female ancestors all of them slaves*: (TA:) or *born at seven months*; (Ḳ, TA;) *not matured by the womb, his months not being completed*. (Az, IF, TA.)

مُسْبِعٌ One *whose camels come to the water on the seventh day* [*counting the day of the next preceding watering as the first*]. (TA.) = A slave *finding a* سَبُع [or *rapacious animal*] *among his sheep, or goats*. (Aboo-Sa'eed Eḍ-Ḍareer, Ṣ.)

أَرْضٌ مَسْبَعَةٌ, (Ṣ, Mgh, Mṣb, Ḳ,) with fet-ḥ (Ṣ, Mṣb) to the first and third letters, (Mṣb,) like مَرْحَلَةٌ, (Ḳ,) and مَذْأَبَةٌ, with an inseparable ة, (Sb,) *A land containing*, (Ṣ,) or *abounding with*, (Mgh, Mṣb, Ḳ,) سِبَاع [or *animals of prey*]. (Ṣ, Mgh, Mṣb, Ḳ.)

مُسَبَّعٌ *A verse consisting of seven feet*. (TA.) — A camel *having, in the middle part of his back, between the withers and the rump, seven vertebræ redundant* [app. meaning *in size*]. (TA.) — [See also مُثَلَّثٌ.]

مَسْبُوعٌ A rope *consisting of seven strands*. (M, voce مَثْلُوثٌ.) = With ة, A cow, (Ṣ, TA,) [app. meaning a wild cow,] or [other] female wild animal, (TA,) *whose offspring has been eaten by the* سَبُع [or *beast, or bird, of prey*]. (Ṣ, TA.)

مَسْبَعٌ The *place of a* سَبُع [or *beast, or bird, of prey*]. (TA.)

سبغ

1. سَبَغَ, (Mṣb, Ḳ, &c.,) aor. ُ (MA, Mṣb) and َ, (MA,) inf. n. سُبُوغٌ, (Mṣb, Ḳ, &c.,) *It* (a garment [&c.]) *was complete, full, ample*, or *without deficiency*: (MA, Mṣb:) *it* (a thing, Lth, Mṣb, of any kind, JK, Mṣb, such as a garment, TA, a coat of mail, JK, Mṣb, TA, and the like, TA, and hair, JK, TA) *was long*, (JK, Mṣb, Ḳ,) *from above to below*, (Mṣb,) or *reaching to*, or *towards, the ground*. (Lth, Ḳ.) [Hence,] ذُو سُبُوغ [*The ample, or long*, &c.,] was the name of a coat of mail belonging to the Prophet. (TA.) — [Hence also] سَبَغَتْ قُصْرَى الفَرَسِ *The* قصرى [app. here meaning the *rib next the flank*] *of the horse was of full length*. (TA.) — And سَبَغَ المَطَرُ ‡ *The rain approached the earth, and extended*. (TA.) — And سَبَغَتِ النِّعْمَةُ, (Ṣ, Mṣb, Ḳ,) inf. n. as above, (Ṣ, Mṣb,) ‡ *The benefit*, or *boon, was*, or *became, ample*. (Ṣ, Mṣb, Ḳ, TA.) One says, الحَمْدُ لِلّٰهِ عَلَى سُبُوغِ النِّعْمَةِ *Praise be to God for the ampleness of the benefit*, or *boon*. (TA.) — And سَبَغَ لِبَلَدِهِ † *He tended towards, and reached, his town*, or *country*; (AA,* Ḳ;) inf. n. as above. (TA.)

2. سَبَّغَتْ, inf. n. تَسْبِيغٌ, *She* (a camel, Aṣ, JK, Ṣ, or a pregnant female, Ḳ) *cast her young one*, or *fœtus*, (Aṣ, JK, Ṣ, Ḳ,) *in an incomplete state*, (TA,) or *when its hair had grown*, (Aṣ, Ṣ, Ḳ,) or *when its fur had grown*; (JK;) accord. to the T, (TA,) *i. q.* أَجْهَضَتْ: (JK, TA:) or, accord. to AA, سَبَّغَتِ الإِبِلُ بِأَوْلَادِهَا *the camels cast their young abortively*; and, in like manner, accord. to Lth, one says of all pregnant females: (TA:) [see also سَبَّقَتْ:] the epithet applied to her is ↓ مُسَبِّغٌ, without ة. (Aṣ, Ḳ, TA.)

4. اسبغهُ *He made it complete, full, ample*, or *without deficiency*; (Mṣb;) *he made it wide*; namely, his garment [&c.]: and *he made it long*; namely, [his garment, and the like, and] his hair. (TA.) — [Hence,] اسبغ اللّٰهُ عَلَيْهِ النِّعْمَةَ (Ṣ, Mṣb,* Ḳ*) ‡ *God made the benefit*, or *boon, complete, full*, or *ample, to him*. (Ṣ,* Mṣb,* Ḳ,* TA.) And اسبغ لَهُ فِى النَّفَقَةِ † *He expended upon him what was completely sufficient for his wants; bestowed upon him amply*. (TA.) — And اسبغ الوُضُوْءَ, (Ḳ,) inf. n. إِسْبَاغٌ, (Ṣ,) ‡ *He performed completely the* [*ablution termed*] وضوء, (Ṣ, Ḳ, TA,) *making it to reach to the proper places thereof, and giving fully to every member its due*. (Ḳ, TA.) = And اسبغ *He put on a wide*, or *an ample*, [or *a long*,] *coat of mail*. (KL.)

سُبْغٌ: see مُسْبَغٌ.

سَبْغَةٌ ‡ *Plentifulness*, and *pleasantness* or *easiness*, and *softness* or *delicacy*, of life. (Ḳ, TA.) One says, إِنَّهُمْ لَفِى سَبْغَةٍ مِنَ العَيْشِ ‡ *Verily they are in a state of plentifulness*, &c., *of life*. (TA.)

سَابِغٌ, applied to a thing (JK, Ṣ) of any kind, (JK,) *Complete, full, ample*, or *without deficiency*: (Ṣ, TA:) [and] *long*. (JK.) You say, دِرْعٌ سَابِغَةٌ *A coat of mail that is wide, or ample*, (Ṣ, Ḳ,* TA,) and *long*: (Ḳ, TA:) or *such that one drags it upon the ground*, or [*that falls*] *against one's ankles, by reason of length and ampleness*: pl. سَوَابِغُ. (TA.) And ذَنَبٌ سَابِغٌ *A complete, a full*, or *an ample, tail*. (TA.) And دَلْوٌ سَابِغَةٌ ‡ *A long* دلو [or *leathern bucket*]. (TA.) And نَاقَةٌ سَابِغَةُ الضَّرْعِ ‡ *A she-camel full*, or *without lack* or *defect, in the udder*: (Lth, and so in the Ḳ accord. to the TA:) or سَابِغَةُ الضُّلُوعِ *without lack or defect, and long, in the ribs*. (So in copies of the Ḳ.) And عَجِيزَةٌ سَابِغَةٌ and أَلْيَةٌ سَابِغَةٌ (Mṣb, Ḳ) signify in like manner, (Ḳ,) [or] ‡ *A long buttock.* (Mṣb, TA.*) And رَجُلٌ سَابِغُ الأَلْيَتَيْنِ † *A man large in the buttocks.* (TA.) And فَحْلٌ سَابِغٌ ‡ *A stallion long in the veretrum:* (Ṣ, Ḳ, TA:) the contr. thereof is termed كَمِشٌ. (Ṣ, TA.) And لِثَةٌ سَابِغَةٌ ‡ *A foul,* or *an ugly, gum.* (Lth, Ḳ, TA.) — And مَطْرَةٌ سَابِغَةٌ ‡ *A copious rain.* (Ḳ,* TA.) — And نِعْمَةٌ سَابِغَةٌ ‡ *A complete, a full,* or *an ample, benefit,* or *boon.* (Ḳ,* TA.) — See also تَسْبِغَةٌ.

أَسْبَغُ *More* [and *most*] *complete, full, ample,* or *free from deficiency* [*in breadth* and *in length*]: occurring in this sense in a trad., relating to a coat of mail. (TA.)

تَسْبَغٌ: see what next follows.

تَسْبِغَةٌ (JK, Ṣ, Ḳ) and تَسْبُغَةٌ and ▼ تَسْبِغٌ and تَسْبَغٌ, (JK, Ḳ,) the first of which is the most chaste, (TA,) *I. q.* مِغْفَرٌ [q. v.]: (JK:) or *a portion of the mail of the coat of mail, that is conjoined to the helmet, and protects the neck:* (JK, Ṣ, Ḳ:) for the helmet becomes lengthened (تَسْبُغُ) thereby; and but for it, there would be between it and the opening at the neck of the coat of mail an intervening space: (Ṣ:) or the *mail composing the* رَفْرَف *of the helmet, at the bottom thereof, with which the man protects his neck, and which is also called the* مِغْفَر: or, accord. to "the Book of the Coat of Mail and the Helmet," by AO, the رَفْرَف of the helmet is other than its تَسْبِغَة; for he says that, of helmets, there is that which has a رَفْرَف, [consisting of] rings [or mail] encompassing the bottom thereof, so as to surround the back and other parts of the neck, and the two cheeks, and to reach to the مَحْجِرَانِ [q. v.] of the two eyes; and he afterwards says, but when it [the helmet] is not of plate, or expanded metal, but is [*a head-covering*] *of mail,* it is called مِغْفَر and غِفَارَة and تَسْبِغَة: (TA:) [the pl. is تَسَابِغُ:] and the helmet [that has a تَسْبِغَة attached to it, accord. to those who mean by this term the mail attached to the bottom thereof,] is called ▼ سَابِغٌ: (JK:) or, accord. to Aṣ, one says بَيْضَةٌ لَهَا سَابِغٌ, (Ṣ,) or لَهَا تَسَابِغُ. (Ḳ, TA: in the CḲ [erroneously] تَسَابُغ.)

مُسْبِغٌ, (Ṣ, A, L, TA,) in the O and Ḳ ▼ سُبُغٌ, like عُنُقٌ, which seems to be a mistranscription, copied by the author of the Ḳ, accord. to his usual practice, from the O, (TA,) A man *having upon him a coat of mail such as is termed* سَابِغَة. (Ṣ, A, O, L, Ḳ.)

مُسَبَّغٌ is expl. by Kr as meaning The *young that is cast by its mother after the soul has been blown into it.* (TA. [But see its verb, 2.])

مُسَبِّغٌ: see 2.

مِسْبَاغٌ A she-camel *that usually casts her young abortively:* but a term not well known. (IDrd, TA.)

سبق

1. سَبَقَهُ, (Ṣ, O, Mṣb, Ḳ, &c.,) aor. ـِ (O, Mṣb, Ḳ) and ـُ, (O, Ḳ,) but the former is of higher authority, or more usual, (O, TA,) inf. n. سَبْقٌ, (Ṣ, Mṣb,) *He preceded him; he was,* or *became, got, went,* or *came, before him,* or *ahead of him; he outwent,* or *outstripped, him; he had, got,* or *took, precedence of him;* syn. تَقَدَّمَهُ; (Ḳ, TA;) in running, and in everything. (TA.) Some read, in the Ḳur [xxi. 27], لَا يَسْبُقُونَهُ بِالقَوْلِ, thus, with ḍamm, meaning *They say not* [anything] *without his having taught them:* (O, TA:) or *they say not* anything *until He has said* it: originally, لَا يَسْبِقُ قَوْلُهُمْ قَوْلَهُ [*their saying does not precede his saying*]: this reading is from the phrase سَابَقْتُهُ فَسَبَقْتُهُ, [expl. below,] aor. of the latter أَسْبُقُهُ. (Bḍ.) See 3. — سَبَقَ الفَرَسُ فِى الحَلْبَةِ *The horse outstripped,* or *came in first, among those started together for a wager,* or *in the race-ground.* (O, Ḳ.) Hence the trad. of 'Alee, سَبَقَ رَسُولُ ٱللّٰهِ وَصَلَّى أَبُو بَكْرٍ وَثَلَّثَ عُمَرُ † [*The Apostle of God came in first in the race, and Aboo-Bekr came in next, and 'Omar came in third*]. (O, TA.) [And سَبَقَ used in like manner with the objective complement understood means *He preceded,* &c., as above; and hence, *he was,* or *became, first, foremost,* or *beforehand; he had,* or *got, the priority,* or *precedence.* And *He was,* or *became, one of the first* or *foremost:* see سَابِقٌ. See also قَصَبُ السَّبْقِ in art. قصب.] — سَبَقَ النَّاسَ إِلَى الأَمْرِ [*He preceded the other people; was,* or *became, before them;* or *had, got,* or *took, precedence of them; in betaking,* or *applying, himself to the affair*]. (Ṣ, Ḳ.) And in like manner one says, لَهُ سَبْقٌ فِى هٰذَا الأَمْرِ *To him belongs priority,* or *precedence, in this affair;* like سَابِقَةٌ; syn. قُدْمَةٌ. (A, TA.) — [Hence,] سَبَقَ وَهْمُهُ إِلَى شَىْءٍ فَغَلِطَ فِيهِ † [*He preconceived a thing, and therefore made a mistake,* or *erred, respecting it*]. (Mṣb, in explanation of دُخِلَ عَلَيْهِ.) [And سَبَقَ ذِهْنُهُ إِلَى الشَّىْءِ means in like manner † *He preconceived the thing:* or *his mind adverted hastily, before reflection,* or *without premeditation, to the thing;* from what next follows.] — سَبَقَ إِلَيْهِمْ *He went,* or *passed, hastily,* or *quickly, to them.* (TA.) — [And hence,] سَبَقَ إِلَيْهِ مِنِّى قَوْلٌ † *A saying proceeded hastily, before reflection,* or *without premeditation, to him from me;* syn. فَرَطَ: (Ṣ in art. فرط:) and سَبَقَ مِنْهُ كَلَامٌ † *speech proceeded hastily,* &c., *from him;* syn. فَرَطَ: (Mṣb in that art.:) [but this phrase also means, more agreeably with the primary signification of the verb, † *speech proceeded previously from him;* (see the Ḳur x. 20, &c.;) and in like manner the former phrase.] See also 8. And سَبَقَهُ القَىْءُ, (Ṣ, Mṣb, Ḳ, all in art. ذرع,) i. e. سَبَقَهُ فِى الخُرُوجِ إِلَى فِيهِ [meaning † *The vomit came forth to his mouth before he was aware*]. (TA in that art.) [And سَبَقَ القَلَمُ † *The pen anticipated, skipping over something,* in transcribing.] — One says also, سَبَقْتُ عَلَيْهِ, meaning ‡ *I overcame him.* (TA.) And سَبَقَ عَلَى قَوْمِهِ † *He overcame his people in generosity.* (TA.) And سَبَقَهُ فِى الكَرَمِ † *He exceeded him in generosity.* (TA.)

2. سبّق, (inf. n. تَسْبِيقٌ, Mgh,) *He took,* or *received, the* سَبَق [i. e. *stake,* or *wager, laid at a race or a shooting-match, to be taken by the successful competitor*]: (IAạr, O, Ḳ:) or سَبَّقْتُهُ *I took,* or *received, the* سَبَق, *from him.* (Az, Mgh, Mṣb.) — And *He gave the* سَبَق: (IAạr, O, Ḳ:) or سَبَّقْتُهُ *I gave him the* سَبَق. (Az, Mgh, Mṣb.) Thus it has two contr. significations. (IAạr, Az, Mgh, O, Mṣb, Ḳ.) Hence, in the trad. of Rukáneh the wrestler, مَا تُسَبِّقُنِى, i. e. *What wilt thou give me* [if I overcome]? and he said, The third of my sheep, or goats. (Mgh.) And سَبَّقَ البَدْرَةَ بَيْنَ الشُّعَرَاءِ ‡ *He made the* [*sum of money termed*] بدرة *to be a* سَبَق [i. e. *stake,* or *wager,*] *among the poets,* to be taken by him who should overcome. (Z, TA.) And it is said in a trad., أَمَرَ بِإِجْرَاءِ الخَيْلِ وَسَبَّقَهَا ثَلَاثَةَ أَعْذُقٍ مِنْ ثَلَاثِ نَخَلَاتٍ, meaning [*He ordered the making of the horses to run, and*] *gave them as a* سَبَق [*three racemes of dates from three palm-trees*]: or it may mean, *he took,* or *received, as their* سَبَق: or it [i. e. سبقها] may be without teshdeed, [as a subst. with its affixed pronoun,] meaning *the property assigned* [*as their* سَبَق]. (L, TA.) — One says also, سَبَّقْتُ بَيْنَ الخَيْلِ [app. meaning *I gave a* سَبَق *among the horses*]: (O:) or سَبَّقْتُ الخَيْلَ, and ▼ سابقت بَيْنَهَا, meaning *I sent forth the horses with their riders upon them, to see which of them would outstrip.* (TA.) — And سَبَّقَتِ الشَّاةُ, inf. n. as above, *The ewe,* or *she-goat, cast her young one,* or *fœtus, in an incomplete state:* (Ibn-'Abbád, O, Ḳ:) but سَبَّغَتْ, with غ, is better known. (Ibn-'Abbád, O.) — سَبَّقْتُ الطَّائِرَ ‡ *I put the* سِبَاقَانِ [or *pair of jesses*] *upon the legs of the bird, and* [so] *shackled it.* (TA.)

3. سَابَقْتُهُ, inf. n. مُسَابَقَةٌ and سِبَاقٌ, [*I strove,* or *contended, with him to precede him; to be,* or *become, get, go,* or *come, before him,* or *ahead of him; to outgo,* or *outstrip, him; to have, get,* or *take, precedence of him;* in running (i. e. *I raced,* or *ran a race, with him*); and in everything.] (Mṣb, TA.) You say, ▼ سَابَقْتُهُ فَسَبَقْتُهُ [*I strove,* or *contended, with him to precede him,* &c., *and I surpassed him,* or *overcame him, in doing so*]: (Ṣ:) the aor. of the latter verb in this case is أَسْبُقُهُ, (Bḍ in xxi. 27,) and the inf. n. is سَبْقٌ. (Ṣ.) — See also 6. — And see 2.

4. اسبق القَوْمُ إِلَى الأَمْرِ [perhaps a mistranscription for ▼ استبق] *The people,* or *party, hastened to the thing,* or *affair;* or *employed the fulness of their power,* or *force, to hasten to it;* syn. بَادَرُوا. (TA.)

6. تسابقا and ▼ استبقا signify the same: (Ḳ, TA:) thus the saying [in the Ḳur xii. 25] وَٱسْتَبَقَا ▼ البَابَ, means تَسَابَقَا إِلَيْهِ, i. e. *And they strove,* or *contended, each with the other, to precede,* or *get before, to the door.* (TA.) [And

both are trans. by means of إِلَى:] you say, تسابقوا إِلَى كَذَا and استبقوا ▼ إِلَيْهِ [They strove, or contended, together, to precede, or be first, in attaining to such a thing: and so ▼ سَابِقُوا: see the Kur lvii. 21, where سَابِقُوا إِلَى مَغْفِرَةٍ is expl. by Bd as meaning سَارِعُوا مُسَارَعَةَ المُسَابِقِينَ فِى المِضْمَارِ i. e. Strive ye, one with another, in hastening, with the striving of those that contend to outstrip in the hippodrome, to obtain forgiveness]. (Msb.) And you say, ▼ اِسْتَبَقْنَا فِى العَدْوِ, meaning تَسَابَقْنَا [i. e. We strove, or contended, one with another, to precede, get before or ahead, or outstrip, in running: and in like manner each of these verbs is used in relation to any object of contention for precedence]. (S.) — And تسابقوا and ▼ استبقوا ‡ They competed, or contended, together in shooting. (TA.) ▼ ذَهَبْنَا نَسْتَبِقُ, in the Kur [xii. 17], means † We went to compete, or contend, together in shooting: (S, Bd:) or in running. (Bd.) — And ▼ the latter of these verbs, as well as the former, signifies also They laid bets, wagers, or stakes, one with another. (TA.)

8. [استبقهُ and استبق إِلَيْهِ i. q. بَادَرَ إِلَيْهِ. Thus] فَاسْتَبِقُوا الخَيْرَاتِ, in the Kur [ii. 143 and v. 53], means Therefore hasten ye to good acts, &c.; or employ the fulness of your power, or force, in hastening thereto; syn. بَادِرُوا إِلَيْهَا. (O.) See also 4. — You say also, استبق إِلَيْهِ الأَمْرُ, (K in art. بدر,) or ▼ سَبَقَ, (M in that art.,) The thing, or event, came to him, or happened to him, hastily, quickly, or speedily; and beforehand [or before he expected it]; syn. بَدَرَهُ, and بَدَرَ إِلَيْهِ. (M and K in that art.) — فَاسْتَبَقُوا الصِّرَاطَ, in the Kur xxxvi. 66, in which الصراط is in the accus. case because of إِلَى suppressed before it, or by making الاِسْتِبَاق to imply the meaning of الاِبْتِدَار, (Bd,) means And they would hasten, make haste, or strive to get first or beforehand, to the road that they were wont to travel: (Bd, Jel:) or ‡ they would go along the road and leave it behind them, (Bd,* O, K, TA,) so that they would wander from the right way. (O, K, TA.) — See also 6, throughout.

سِبْقٌ A competitor of another in striving to precede, to be before or ahead, to outgo or outstrip, or to have precedence: [pl. أَسْبَاقٌ; and the sing. is also used as a pl.:] you say, هُمْ سِبْقِى and أَسْبَاقِى: (L:) and هُمَا سِبْقَانِ They are two that compete &c. (El-Moheet, O, K.)

سَبَقٌ A stake, or wager, that is laid between the persons concerned in a race, (T, S, O, Mgh,* Msb,* K,) and in a shooting-match; in the former case taken by [the owner of] the one that outstrips; (T, TA;) and ▼ سُبْقَةٌ signifies the same: (K:) pl. of the former أَسْبَاقٌ. (O, K.) It is said in a trad., لَا سَبَقَ إِلَّا فِى خُفٍّ أَوْ حَافِرٍ أَوْ نَصْلٍ meaning There shall be no stake, or wager, except in the case of the racing of camels, or of horses or mules or asses, or in the case of [the arrowhead or lance-head, i. e.] shooting or casting [the lance]: for all these affairs are preparations for engaging in fight with the enemy; and mules and asses are included because they carry the baggage of the army. (O, TA.) — Also † The lesson of a boy, that is learned each day in the school; also called إِمَامٌ. (TA in art. ام.)

سُبْقَةٌ: see the next preceding paragraph.

سِبَاقٌ an inf. n. of 3 [q. v.]. (Msb, TA.) — [As a simple subst., A race, or contest in running. — And The preceding part of a discourse &c. You say سِبَاقُ الكَلَامِ وَسِيَاقُهُ The preceding and following parts of the discourse; the context, before and after.] — سِبَاقَا البَازِى قَيْدَانِ The [or pair of shackles, i. e. jesses,] of the hawk or falcon, of leathern thongs or straps, or of other material. (S, O, K.)

سَبُوقٌ: see سَابِقٌ.

هُوَ سَبَّاقُ غَايَاتٍ ‡ He is one who [often] obtains the winning canes (قَصَبَاتُ السَّبْقِ [see art. قصب]). (O, K, TA.)

سَابِقٌ [act. part. n. of 1, Preceding, &c.: and sometimes it means one of the first or foremost: as is shown by what here follows]: sometimes what is thus termed has one coming up with it; as [sometimes happens] in the case of the سابق of horses: and sometimes it is like him who obtains the winning-cane (قَصَبَةُ السَّبْقِ [see art. قصب]); for he outstrips to it and has none to share with him in it, there being none coming up with him. (Msb.) It is applied to a horse That outstrips; as also ▼ سَبُوقٌ: (T, Msb, TA:*) and the pl. [masc., i. e. pl. of the former,] applied to horses is سُبَّقٌ and [fem., i. e. pl. of سَابِقَةٌ,] سَوَابِقُ: (TA:) [or] سَوَابِقُ may be pl. of سَابِقٌ regarded as a subst. like كَاهِلٌ and غَارِبٌ of which the pls. are كَوَاهِلُ and غَوَارِبُ. (Ham p. 46.) — By the سَابِقَات mentioned in the Kur lxxix. 4 are meant The angels that precede the devils with the revelation [that they convey] to the prophets: (TA:) or the angels that precede the jinn, or genii, in listening to the revelation: (T, K, TA:) or the angels that precede with the souls of the believers to Paradise (Bd, Jel) and with the souls of the unbelievers to Hell: (Bd:) or the horses [that precede in battle]: (Zj, TA:) or the souls of the believers, that go forth with ease: or the stars [that precede other stars]. (TA. [See more in the Expositions of Bd and others.]) — [The pl.] سُبَّقٌ, applied to palm-trees, means † That produce their fruit early. (TA.)

سَابِقَةٌ [fem. of سَابِقٌ, q. v.: and also a subst. formed from the latter by the affix ة, signifying Priority, or precedence]. One says, لَهُ سَابِقَةٌ فِى هٰذَا الأَمْرِ ‡ [To him belongs priority, or precedence, in this affair,] when he has preceded the [other] people [in betaking, or applying, himself] to the affair: (S, K, TA:) like as you say, لَهُ سَبْقٌ [mentioned above: see 1]. (TA.) — [Also, as used by physicians, A predisposition to disease.]

سَابِقِيَّةٌ [The state, or condition, of preceding]. (De Sacy's Anthol. Gramm. Ar. p. 302.)

أَسْبَقُ [More, and most, preceding or prevenient; more, and most outgoing or outstripping; &c.]. أَسْبَقُ مِنَ الأَجَلِ and مِنَ الأَفْكَارِ are provs. [meaning More prevenient than the period of death and than the thoughts]. (Meyd.)

مُسَبَّقٌ A horse much, or often, outstripped. (Msb.)

مَسْبُوقِيَّةٌ [The state, or conditon, of being preceded]. (De Sacy's Anthol. Gramm. Ar. p. 302.)

سبك

1. سَبَكَ, (S, Mgh, Msb, K,) aor. ـُ, (S, K,) so says El-Fárábee, and so in the Jm, and in the handwriting of Aboo-Sahl El-Harawee, (TA,) or ـِ, (Msb,) thus in the handwriting of Az, (TA,) inf. n. سَبْكٌ, (S, Mgh, Msb,) He melted, (S, Mgh, Msb, K, TA,) and cleared of its dross, (Mgh,) and poured forth (K, TA) into a mould, (TA,) gold, (Mgh, Msb, TA,) or silver, (S, Mgh, TA,) &c.; (S, TA;) and ▼ سبّك signifies the same, (K,) inf. n. تَسْبِيكٌ; (TA;) this inf. n. and سَبْكٌ both signifying the melting of gold and silver, and pouring it forth into a مِسْبَكَة [or mould] of iron, like the half of a cane divided lengthwise. (Lth, TA.) — Hence, سَبْكٌ is metaphorically used in the sense of تَجْرِبَةٌ. (Har pp. 140 and 211.) One says, فُلَانٌ سَبَكَتْهُ التَّجَارِبُ ‡ [Such a one, tryings tried, or have tried, him]. (TA.) And كَلَامٌ لَا يَثْبُتُ عَلَى السَّبْكِ is another tropical phrase [app. meaning ‡ Speech or language, that does not stand good, or is not sound, or valid, when tried, or tested; that will not stand trying, or testing]. (TA.)

2: see the preceding paragraph.

7. انسبك said of تِبْر [i. e. native, or unwrought, gold or silver or the like], It melted. (TA.)

سَبِيكٌ, applied to تِبْر [i. e. native, or unwrought gold or silver or the like, Melted and cleared of its dross, and poured forth into a mould], i. q. ▼ مَسْبُوكٌ. (TA.)

سَبِيكَةٌ [a subst. formed from the epithet سَبِيكٌ by the affix ة, An ingot, i. e.] a piece (Lth, Mgh, Msb, K) of gold, (Lth, Mgh, Msb, TA,) or of silver, (Lth, S, Mgh, TA,) &c., (Mgh,) [i. e.,] sometimes, of any metal, (Msb,) of an oblong form, (Mgh, Msb,) that has been melted, (Lth, S, Mgh, Msb, K, TA,) and cleared of its dross, (Mgh,) and poured forth (K, TA) into a mould, (TA,) [i. e.,] into a مِسْبَكَة of iron like the half of a cane divided lengthwise: (Lth, TA:) pl. سَبَائِكُ. (Lth, S, Msb.) An Arab of the desert likened to it a difficult mountain that he desired to ascend, because of its smoothness; saying, أَىُّ سَبِيكَةٍ هٰذِهِ [What an ingot is this!]. (A, TA.) — The pl. is also applied to رُقَاق [i. e. † Thin, flat, bread]; this being so called because it is made of choice, or pure, flour; and is as though it were prepared therefrom by being melted and poured into a mould (كَأَنَّهُ سُبِكَ مِنْهُ), and cleared from the bran. (TA.)

[سَبَّاكٌ *A melter and purifier and caster*, or *one who makes* سَبَائِك, *of gold*, or *silver*, or *the like*. — Hence,] هُوَ سَبَّاكٌ لِلْكَلَامِ a tropical phrase [app. meaning ‡ *He is a trier*, or *tester*, or *a purifier, of speech*, or *language*: see 1]. (TA.)

سُنْبُكٌ: see art. سنبك.

مِسْبَكَةٌ *A mould of iron like the half of a cane divided lengthwise, into which molten gold and silver* (Lth, TA) *and the like* (TA) *are poured*: (Lth, TA:) pl. مَسَابِكُ. (TA.)

مَسْبُوكٌ: see سَبِيكٌ.

سبكر

Q. 4. اِسْبَكَرَّ *i. q.* اِسْبَطَرَّ in its several significations: (Ḳ:) i. e. (TA) — *He stretched himself*: (TA:) *he lay upon his side, and stretched himself*: (AA, Ṣ, TA:) [&c.] — *He* (a youth, or young man,) *became tall*: (Lḥ:) and اسبكرّت *She* (a girl) *became of erect and justly-proportioned stature*. (Ṣ, Ḳ.) An ex. occurs in a verse of Imra-el-Ḳeys, cited voce مَجُولٌ. (Ṣ.) — *It* (a plant) *became tall and full-grown*: (TA:) *and it* (anything) *became extended, and long*, or *tall*. (Lḥ.) — *He went at random*, or *heedlessly; without consideration, or certain aim*. (Lḥ.) — *It* (a river) *flowed*. (TA.) — اسبكرّت عَيْنُهُ *His eye shed tears*. (Lḥ.) But ISd says that this is not known in classical Arabic. (TA.)

مُسْبَكِرٌّ [act. part. n. of the verb above]. — A youth, or young man, *of just proportion, and full grown*. (Aboo-Ziyád El-Kilábee, Ṣ, Ḳ.) — *Hair that hangs down; lank; not crisp*: (Ṣ, Ḳ:) or *of just length*: or *full-grown, and standing out*. (TA.) — And Anything *extended, and long*, or *tall*. (Lḥ.)

سبل

2. سَبَّلَهُ, inf. n. تَسْبِيلٌ, means جَعَلَهُ فِى سَبِيلِ ٱللّٰهِ [*He assigned it*, or *the profit*, or *revenue*, or *usufruct, thereof, to be employed in the way*, meaning *cause, of God*, or *of religion*; or *in the doing of anything*, or *all, that God has commanded*, or *of the works whereby one pursues the way that leads to advancement in the favour of God; he dedicated it to pious*, or *charitable, uses* or *purposes*]; (Ḳ, TA;) as though [meaning] *he made it a trodden way* [*whereby to advance*] *to* [*the favour of*] *God*. (TA.) You say, سَبَّلَ ضَيْعَتَهُ, using the verb in this sense [i. e. *He assigned the profit*, or *revenue*, or *usufruct, of his estate to be employed in the cause of God*, or *of religion*]; (Ṣ;) *to be given to the wayfarer, and the poor, and the warrior against unbelievers, and others*. (TA voce سَبِيل.) And سَبَّلَ الثَّمَرَةَ *He assigned the profit to be employed in the ways of good works* (Mgh, Mṣb) *and the various kinds of pious deeds*: (Mṣb:) or *he made the profit to be allowable*, or *free, to those for whose benefit the property itself was made unalienable in perpetuity*. (TA. [See an ex. in the first paragraph of art. حبس, relating to some palm-trees which 'Omar desired to give in charity.]) — سَبِلَ, [either سَبَلَ or, سَبِلَ both app. allowable, (see the part. ns., below,)] *He* (a man) *was*, or *became, long in the* سَبَلَة [q. v.]; *as though he had a long* سبلة *given to him*. (TA.) — See also 4.

4. أَسْبَلَتِ الطَّرِيقُ *The road had many passengers following*, or *succeeding, one another*, or *going repeatedly to and fro, upon it*. (M, Ḳ.) — اسبل إِزَارَهُ, (Ṣ, M, Ḳ,) inf. n. إِسْبَالٌ, (TA,) *He let loose, let down*, or *lowered, his waist-wrapper*; (Ṣ, M, Ḳ;) and so السِّتْرَ *the veil*, or *curtain*, (Mṣb,) or *he let down, let fall*, or *made to hang down, the veil*, or *curtain*: (Mgh:) the former act is forbidden in a trad. (TA.) And اسبلت ذَيْلَهَا [*She made her skirt to hang down*; or *to hang down low, so that she dragged it on the ground*]; said of a woman. (M.) And اسبل ثَوْبَهُ *He dragged his garment* [*on the ground*]; (O;) and ▼ سَبَّلَهُ signifies the same, (O, TA,) inf. n. تَسْبِيلٌ. (TA.) And اسبل ذَنَبَهُ *He made his tail to hang down; he hung down his tail*; said of a horse. (M.) — [Hence,] اسبل المَآءَ † *He* (a man) *poured forth the water*. (Mṣb.) And اسبل دَمْعَهُ (M, Ḳ, TA) ‡ *He shed*, or *let fall, his tears*. (Ḳ, TA.) — The verb is also similarly used intransitively. (TA.) You say, of a part of the beard, اسبل عَلَى الصَّدْرِ [*It fell*, or *hung down, upon the breast*]. (Az, O, TA.) — And اسبل المَطَرُ ‡ *The rain let fall a shower, and became dense*; as though it let down a curtain: (A, TA: [but accord. to this explanation, the verb is app. trans.; and the phrase, elliptical:]) or *the rain fell continuously*, or *in consecutive showers, and in large drops*: and in like manner, الدَّمْعُ *the tears*. (Ṣ, Ḳ.) — And اسبلت السَّمَآءُ (AZ, Ṣ, M, Ḳ) † *The sky let fall its rain issuing from the clouds and not as yet having reached the earth*: (AZ, Ṣ, TA:) or [simply] *the sky rained*. (Ḳ.) And اسبلت أَرْوَاقُ العَيْنِ ‡ *The sides of the eye shed tears*. (O, Ḳ,* TA, all in art. روق.) — And اسبل عَلَيْهِ ‡ *He poured forth his speech against him abundantly*, [or *in torrents*,] (A, Ḳ,* TA,) *like as rain pours*. (A. TA.) — اسبل الزَّرْعُ *The seed-produce put forth its* سُنْبُل [or *ears*]; (Ṣ;) and so ▼ سَنْبَلَ; (Ṣ, Mgh, Mṣb;) or *put forth its* سَبَل, (Mṣb in explanation of the former,) which is syn. with سُنْبُل, (Ṣ, M, Mṣb, Ḳ,) or *its* سُبُولَة: (Ḳ in explanation of the former:) [Mṭr says,] ▼ تَسَنْبَلَ I have not found. (Mgh.)

Q. Q. 1. سَنْبَلَ: see 4, last sentence: — and art. سنبل.

Q. Q. 2. تَسَنْبَلَ: see 4, last sentence.

سَبَلٌ *A thing that one has let loose, let down, let fall*, or *made to hang down, and to drag* [*on the ground*]; like as نَشَرٌ signifies "a thing that one has spread" &c.: whence the trad., مَنْ جَرَّ سَبَلَهُ مِنَ الخُيَلَآءِ لَا يَنْظُرُ ٱللّٰهُ إِلَيْهِ يَوْمَ القِيٰمَةِ [*He who drags what he has made to hang down* of his garment *from pride*, or *self-conceit, God will not look towards him on the day of resurrection*]: (O:) or سَبَلٌ means *garments made to hang down* [*so as to drag*]; and is pl. of ▼ سَبَلَةٌ; [or rather a coll. gen. n. of which سَبَلَةٌ is the n. un.;] whence جَرَّ سَبَلَتَهُ, (TA,) which means [*He dragged his garment*; though said to mean,] *his garments*. (Ḳ, TA.) — Also ‡ *Rain*: (Ṣ, M, Ḳ:) or *rain issuing from the clouds and not as yet having reached the earth*: (AZ, Ṣ, TA:) or *flowing rain*: and likewise *flowing blood*. (Ḥam p. 359.) — [Hence, app., as indicating swiftness,] سَبَلٌ is the name of † *A certain mare*, (Ṣ, Ḳ,) *an excellent mare, said by Aṣ to have been the mother of* أَعْوَج, *and to have belonged to* [*the tribe of*] *Ghanee*. (Ṣ, TA.) — And سَبَلُ [or سَبَلٌ as a fem. proper name] is a name for † *A ewe*, or *she-goat*: and such is called to be milked by saying سَبَلْ سَبَلْ. (Ibn-'Abbád, TA.) — Also *i. q.* ▼ سُنْبُلٌ, (Ṣ, M, Mṣb, Ḳ,) which signifies The *ears of corn*: (MA:. [and in like manner both are expl. in the KL, but as singulars, app. because used as gen. ns.:]) n. un. of the former with ▼ ة, and so of ▼ the latter: and the pl. of ▼ سُنْبُل, which is of the measure فُنْعُل, is سَنَابِل: (Mṣb:) or this is pl. of سُنْبُلَة, (Ṣ,) as also سُنْبُلَات: (Ḳur xii. 43 and 46:) or سُنْبُلَة [in the CḲ (erroneously) سُبْلَة] signifies *an ear of corn* [so I render زَرْعَة (in the CḲ زُرْعَة)] *that is bending*, or *inclining*, as also ▼ سُبُولَة [mentioned in one of my two copies of the Ṣ as syn. with سُنْبُلَة but not in the other copy] and ▼ سُبُولَة (M, Ḳ) and ▼ سَبَلَة; (Ḳ;) or, accord. to Lth, ▼ سُبُولَة signifies *an ear* (سُنْبُلَة) *of millet* (ذُرَة), and *of rice*, and *the like, when bending*, or *inclining*: (O, TA:) and some say that سَبَل signifies *spreading*, or *expanding, awn of the* سُنْبُل [or *ears of corn*]; (M, TA;) or the *extremities thereof*; (TA;) and the pl. is سُبُول; (M;) or سبول is *syn. with* سُنْبُل, in the dial. of بنو هميان [?]. (TA.) ▼ السُّنْبُلَة is also the name of *A certain sign of the Zodiac* [i. e. *Virgo*]: (Ṣ in the present art., and Ḳ in art. سنبل:) [or *Spica Virginis*;] *a star in Virgo; thus called by astrologers; also called* السِّمَاكُ الأَعْزَلُ. (Ḳzw. [See art. سمك.]) ▼ سُنْبُلُ الطِّيبِ is *A well-known plant*, [*spikenard*, which is called in the present day السُّنْبُل الهِنْدِى,] *brought from India*. (O. [See also art. سنبل.]) — Also sing. of أَسْبَال, which signifies † The *uppermost parts of a bucket*, (O,) or the *lips* thereof: (Ṣ:) or ▼ سَبَلَة is the sing. of أَسْبَال in these senses; and signifies ‡ the *head* of a vessel [like as it signifies the "ear," which is the "head," of a culm of wheat &c.]. (TA.) You say, مَلَأَهَا إِلَى أَسْبَالِهَا ‡ *He filled it* (i. e. the wine-cup, الكَأْس, M, TA, or the bucket, الدَّلْو, O) *to its edges*, (M, Ḳ, TA,) and *to its lips*. (Ḳ.) And a poet says, (Ṣ,) namely Bá'ith Ibn-Ṣureym El-Yeshkuree, (TA,)

إِذْ أَرْسَلُونِى مَاتِحًا بِدِلَائِهِمْ

فَمَلَأْتُهَا عَلَقًا إِلَى أَسْبَالِهَا

[*When they sent me drawing with their buckets, and I filled them with blood to their brims*]: he says, they sent me seeking to execute their blood-revenges, and I slew many: العَلَق meaning "blood." (Ṣ, TA. [See also Ḥam p. 268, where some different readings are mentioned; and it is said that the اسبال may mean the *knots that are connected with the cross-pieces of wood* of the bucket.]) — And † *A number of spears, few* or *many*. (Ḳ. [Perhaps because their heads are likened to the heads of corn.]) — Also The *nose*: (Ḳ:) pl. سِبَال: so in the Moḥeeṭ. (TA.) One says, أَرْغَمَ ٱللّٰهُ سَبَلَتَهُ [*May God make his nose to cleave to the earth, or dust*: or † *abase, or humble, him*]. (TA.) — And *Garments made of the hards*, or *hurds, of flax of the coarsest of qualities*: and so ▾ سَبَلَةٌ [if one of these words be not a mistranscription for the other]. (TA.) — And *A certain disease in the eye*, [thus رِيحُ السَّبَلِ is expl. in the M,] *resembling a film, as though it were the web of a spider, with red veins*: (Ṣ:) or *a film of the eye, from the swelling*, or *inflation, of its external veins upon the surface of the* مُلْتَحِمَة, (Ḳ,) which is one of the layers of the eye, (TA,) [namely, the *tunica albuginea*, or *white of the eye*, so called in the present day,] *and the appearance of a web*, or *thing woven, between the two*, [i. e. *between those veins and the white tunic*,] *like smoke*: (Ḳ:) or *a film covering the eye*; as though from إِسْبَال meaning the "letting down" of a veil, or curtain. (Mgh.) — Also *A reviling*, or *vilifying*. (Ḳ.) One says, بَيْنِى وَبَيْنَهُ سَبَلٌ *Between me and him is a reviling*, or *vilifying*: so in the Moḥeeṭ. (TA.)

سَبِلٌ [is app. a possessive epithet, meaning *Having length and flaccidity*]. خُصْيَةٌ سَبِلَةٌ means [*A scrotum*] *that is long* (M, Ḳ, TA) *and flaccid*. (TA.)

سُبْلَةٌ † *A rain of wide extent*. (IAạr, O, Ḳ.)

سَبَلَةٌ: see سَبَلٌ, in five places. — Also † The شَارِب [or *mustache*]: (Ṣ:) or the دَائِرَة [or *small protuberance termed* حِتْرِمَة, q. v.,] *in the middle of the upper lip*: or the *hair that is upon* [app. meaning *of*] *the* شَارِب; (M, Ḳ;) whence the saying, طَالَتْ سَبَلَتُكَ فَقُصَّهَا [*thy hair of the mustache has become long, therefore clip it*]; and it is tropical: (TA:) or the *extremity of that hair*: (M, Ḳ:) or the *two mustaches together*: (M, Ḳ:*) or *what is upon the chin, to the extremity of the beard*: or the *fore part of the beard*: (M, Ḳ:) or *what hangs down, of, or from, the fore part of the beard*: (Zj, in his "Khalḳ el-Insán:") or, accord. to Az, it signifies, with the Arabs, the *fore part of the beard, and what hangs down thereof*, or *therefrom, upon the breast*: or, accord. to IDrd, some of them apply it to the *extremity of the beard*; and some, to the *hair of the mustache that hangs down on the beard*: in a trad., in which it is said that he [Moḥammad] was full in the سَبَلَة, Az says that it means the *hairs beneath the lower jaw*: accord. to AZ, it is *what appears, of the fore part of the beard, after* [or *exclusive of*] *the hair of the side of each cheek and the* عُثْنُون [here app. meaning the *portion of the beard next the front of the throat*], *and what is concealed* [*thereof*]: (TA:) or, accord. to Th, the *beard altogether*: (M:) the pl. is سِبَال, (Ṣ, Ḳ,) [to which ة is sometimes added, agreeably with a common license, as appears from an ex. in what follows,] and سَبَلَاتٌ, occurring in the saying, إِنَّهُ لَذُو سَبَلَاتٍ, mentioned by Lḥ, in which the term سَبَلَة is made to apply to every separate portion [so that the meaning is, *Verily he has a* سَبَلَة]. (M.) One says, of enemies, هُمْ صُهْبُ ٱلسِّبَالِ † [*They are red*, or *reddish, in respect of the mustaches*, &c.: see art. صهب]. (TA.) And of a man who has come threatening, one says, جَآءَ فُلَانٌ وَقَدْ نَشَرَ سَبَلَتَهُ ‡ [*Such a one came having spread out his mustache*, &c.]. (Ḳ,* TA.) And in a trad. respecting Dhu-th-Thudeiyeh, [see art. ثدى,] it is said, عَلَيْهِ شُعَيْرَاتٌ مِثْلُ سِبَالَةِ ٱلسِّنَّوْرِ [app. meaning † *Having upon him small hairs like the whiskers of the cat*]. (TA.) — سَبَلَةُ ٱلبَعِيرِ means † The *part of the camel, in which he is stabbed*, or *stuck, in the uppermost part of the breast*; (T, M;) called also the ثُرْبَة: (T:) or the *fur that flows down upon that part of the camel*. (M, Ḳ. [In the CḲ, مَنْخَرِه is erroneously put for مَنْحَرِه.]) You say لَتَبَ فِى سَبَلَةِ ٱلنَّاقَةِ, meaning † *He stabbed*, or *stuck, the she-camel in the part above mentioned*: (M in art. لتب: [in the Ḳ, in the present art., كَتَبَ is erroneously put, in this phrase, in the place of لَتَبَ:]) Az heard an Arab of the desert say لَنَتَمَرَ فِى سَبَلَةِ بَعِيرِهِ, [which means the same as لَتَبَ,] and he supposes the سَبَلَة to be *hairs in the part above mentioned*. (TA.) You say also, بَعِيرٌ حَسَنُ ٱلسَّبَلَةِ, meaning † [*A camel goodly in respect of*] *the thinness of his skin* (جِلْدِه): so in the O and K: but accord. to the T, *of his cheek* (خَدِّه); and this is probably the right explanation. (TA.)

سَبَلَانِىٌّ: see أَسْبَلُ.

سَبِيلٌ *A way, road*, or *path*; (Ṣ, M, Mṣb, Ḳ;) and *what is open*, or *conspicuous, thereof*: (M, Ḳ;) and Er-Rághib adds, *wherein is easiness*: (TA:) and ▾ سَبِيلَةٌ signifies the same: (Ibn-'Abbád, Ḳ:) the former is masc. and fem.; (Ṣ, M, Mgh, Mṣb, Ḳ;) like زُقَاق; (Mṣb;) made fem. by the people of El-Ḥijáz, and masc. by Temeem; (Akh, Ṣ voce زقاق;) but mostly fem.; (IAth, TA;) in the Ḳur it is made masc. in vii. 143, and fem. in xii. 108: (Ṣ, M, TA:) pl. سُبُلٌ, (M, Ḳ,) or, accord. to ISk, it has this pl. when masc., and سُبُولٌ, like عُنُوق when fem., (Mṣb, [but this distinction and the latter pl. are both strange,]) and it has also as a pl. [of pauc.] أَسْبِلَةٌ. (TA.) In the saying, وَعَلَى ٱللّٰهِ قَصْدُ ٱلسَّبِيلِ [*And upon God it rests to show the right way* (see art. قصد)], (M, Ḳ,) in the Ḳur [xvi. 9], (M,) it is used as a gen. n., because it is added, وَمِنْهَا جَائِرٌ. (M, Ḳ.) — اِبْنُ ٱلسَّبِيلِ means † *The son of the road*; (M, Ḳ;) *he whom the road has brought*, or [*as it were*] *brought forth*; (IB;) *the wayfarer*, or *traveller*: (Mgh, Mṣb:) or *he who travels much* or *often*: (TA:) or *the traveller who is far from his place of abode*: (Er-Rághib:) as used in the verse of the Ḳur, (M, Mgh, Mṣb,) ix. 60, (M,) it means *the person to whom the way has become cut short* [*so that he is unable to continue his journey*]; (M, Ḳ;) to which has been added, *who desires to return to his country*, or *town, and finds not what will suffice him*: (TA:) or *the traveller who is cut off from his property*: (Mgh, Mṣb:) or *the person who desires to go to a country*, or *town, other than his own, for a necessary affair*: or, accord. to Ibn-'Arafeh, *the guest who has become disabled from proceeding in his journey, his means having failed him*: to such should be given as much as will suffice him to his home. (TA.) — وَتَقْطَعُونَ ٱلسَّبِيلَ, in the Ḳur [xxix. 28], means † [*And ye cut off*] *the way of offspring* [by your unnatural practices]: or *and ye oppose yourselves to men in the roads* [or *road*] *for the purpose of that which is excessively*, or *enormously, foul or abominable*. (TA.) — [سَبِيلُ ٱللّٰهِ means † *The way*, or *cause, of God*, or *of religion*; or *the way whereby one seeks approach to God*, or *advancement in his favour*.] It is said in the Ḳur [ii. 191], وَأَنْفِقُوا فِى سَبِيلِ ٱللّٰهِ, meaning † *And expend ye in warring against unbelievers and the like*, and *in every good work commanded by God*; (M, Ḳ;) such being of the ways [that lead] to God: (M:) mostly used in relation to warring against unbelievers and the like. (M, Ḳ.) And in the same, iii. 163, ٱلَّذِينَ قُتِلُوا فِى سَبِيلِ ٱللّٰهِ, meaning [*Who have been slain in the cause of God*, or *of his religion*, i. e.,] *for the sake of the religion of God*. (Jel.) And you say, جَعَلَ ضَيْعَتَهُ فِى سَبِيلِ ٱللّٰهِ † [*He made his estate to have its profit*, or *revenue*, or *usufruct, employed in the cause of God*, or *of religion*]. (Ṣ.) — سَبِيلٌ also signifies † *A means of access*; *a connexion*, or *a tie*: so in the saying, in the Ḳur [xxv. 29], يَا لَيْتَنِى ٱتَّخَذْتُ مَعَ ٱلرَّسُولِ سَبِيلًا † [*O would that I had obtained, with the Apostle, a means of access to* Paradise]: (Ṣ, Mṣb, TA:) thus it has been explained: (TA:) or the meaning is, [*O would that I had taken, with the Apostle*,] *a way to safety*: or *one way*, the way of truth. (Bd.) — [Also, in the present day, applied to *A public drinking-fountain*.]

سَبُولٌ and سَبُولَةٌ: see سَبَلٌ, in three places.

سَبِيلَةٌ: see سَبِيلٌ, first sentence.

سَابِلٌ *Travelling upon a road*: pl. سَوَابِلُ and [coll. gen. n.] ▾ سَابِلَةٌ: (TA:) this last signifies *travellers*, (Ṣ, M,*) or *a company of people*, (Mgh, Ḳ,) *following*, or *succeeding, one another*, or *going repeatedly to and fro*, (Ṣ, M, Mgh, Ḳ,) *upon the roads*, (Ṣ, Mgh,) or *upon the road*, (M, Ḳ,) *for the accomplishment of their wants*: it is made fem. as denoting a جَمَاعَة. (Mgh.) — Also, ▾ سَابِلَةٌ, (TA in art. شغر,) or سَبِيلٌ سَابِلَةٌ, (M, Ḳ,* TA,) *A travelled road*; (M, Ḳ, TA;) *a beaten road*. (TA in art. شغر.) — غَيْثٌ سَابِلٌ † *Rain falling continuously*, or *in successive showers, and in large drops, and copiously*. (TA.)

سَابِلَةٌ: see the next preceding paragraph, in two places.

سُنْبُلٌ and سُنْبُلَةٌ: see سَبَلٌ, in five places: and see also art. سنبل.

سَلْسَبِيلٌ the name of *A certain fountain in Paradise:* determinate; [without tenween;] but occurring at the end of a verse of the Kur [lxxvi. 18], (Akh, Ṣ, Ḳ,) and being with fet-ḥ, (Akh, Ṣ,) ا is added to it, (Akh, Ṣ, Ḳ,) for the sake of conformity [with the endings of other verses before and after it]. (Ḳ.) See also art. سلسبل.

أَسْبَلُ ‡ A man *long in the* سَبَلَة [q. v., here said in the TA to mean the *beard*, but this is questionable], as also ▼ سَبَلَانِىٌّ and ▼ مُسْبِلٌ and ▼ مُسْبَلٌ and ▼ مُسَبَّلٌ and ▼ مُسْبِلٌ. (M, Ḳ, TA.) —— And the fem., سَبْلَآءُ, † A woman *having hair in the place of the mustache.* (TA.) —— And † An eye *having long lashes.* (M, Ḳ.)

مُسْبِلٌ: see the next preceding paragraph.

مُسْبِلٌ A man *lengthening his garment, and making it to hang down to the ground.* (IAạr, TA.) [And in like manner,] applied to a woman, [though without ة,] *Who has made her skirt to hang down* [app. *to the ground*]. (M.) —— See also أَسْبَلُ. —— And المُسْبِلُ signifies ‡ *The penis:* (M, Ḳ, TA:) because of its pendulousness. (TA.) —— And † *The* [*lizard called*] ضَبّ. (Ḳ.) —— And *the fifth of the arrows used in the game called* المَيْسِر: (M, Ḳ:) or *the sixth of those arrows,* (Lḥ, Ṣ, M, Ḳ,) also called المُصْفَحُ, (Ṣ,) in which are six notches, and to which are assigned six shares [of the slaughtered camel] if it win, and six fines if it do not win: (M:) pl. المَسَابِلُ. (TA.) —— And مُسْبِلٌ is one of the names of *Dhu-l-Ḥijjeh;* (M, Ḳ;*) of the time of 'Ád. (M.)

مُسْبَلٌ: see أَسْبَلُ. —— Also *An ugly old man:* (Ḳ:) app. because of the length of his beard. (TA.)

مُسَبَّلٌ: see أَسْبَلُ.

سبى

1. سَبَى العَدُوَّ, (Ṣ, M, Mṣb, Ḳ,) وَغَيْرَهُ, (M,) aor. يَسْبِى, (Mṣb, TA,) inf. n. سَبْىٌ (Ṣ, M, Mṣb, Ḳ) and سِبَآءٌ, (Ṣ, M, Ḳ,) or ▼ the latter is a simple subst., as also ▼ سَبًا or سِبًى, (Mṣb,) *He made captive, captived,* or *took prisoner,* [*the enemy,* and *other than an enemy;*] (Ṣ, Ḳ;) as also ▼ اِسْتَبَاهُ. (Ṣ, Mṣb, Ḳ.) —— [Hence,] تَسْبِى قَلْبَ الرَّجُلِ † [*She captivates the heart of the man*], said of a woman. (Ṣ.) —— And سَبَيْتُ قَلْبَهُ and ▼ اِسْتَبَيْتُهُ † *I captivated his heart.* (M.) And ▼ اِسْتَبَتْ قَلْبَ الفَتَى, said of a girl, or young woman, *i. q.* سَبَتْهُ [i. e. † *She captivated the heart of the youth,* or *young man.*] (TA.) —— One says also, إِنَّ اللَّيْلَ طَوِيلٌ وَلَا أُسْبَ لَهُ and لا أُسْبَى له, the latter on the authority of Lḥ, who says that it means a prayer, (M, TA,) for which reason the verb [in the former instance] is in the mejzoom form, (TA,) i. e. [*Verily the night is long, and*] *may I not be made as the captive* [*to it*]. (M, TA.) —— سَبَى الخَمْرَ, (Ṣ, M, Ḳ,) aor. as above, (M,) inf. n. سَبْىٌ and سِبَآءٌ, (T, M, Ḳ,) though J says only the latter, (Ḳ,) *He conveyed wine from one town,* or *country, to another;* (Ṣ, Ḳ;) or *he brought wine from one land to another;* as also ▼ اِسْتَبَاهَا: (M:) [and] so سَبَأَهَا, with hemz: (Mṣb:) or سَبَأْتُ, with hemz, means "I bought" (Ṣ, M) wine, to drink it. (Ṣ. [See art. سبأ.]) —— سَبَاهُ اللّٰهُ, (ISk, Ṣ, M, Ḳ,) aor. as above, (Ṣ,) inf. n. سَبْىٌ, (Ṣ, M,) *God estranged him;* (ISk, Ṣ, M, Ḳ;) *removed him far away;* (Ṣ, Ḳ;) and *cursed him:* (M:) or it is like the saying لَعَنَهُ اللّٰهُ: (Ṣ:) [or *may God estrange him;* &c.:] one says, مَا لَهُ سَبَاهُ اللّٰهُ [*What ails him? May God estrange him;* &c.]. (TA.) —— سَبَى المَآءَ, (M, Ḳ,) aor. as above, (M,) inf. n. سَبْىٌ, (TA,) *He dug until he reached the water.* (M, Ḳ.)

5. تَسَبَّى لَهُ † *He manifested,* or *showed, love,* or *affection, to him;* and *became inclined to him.* (TA.)

6. تَسَابَوْا *They made one another captive.* (Az, Ḳ.)

8: see 1, in four places.

سَبْىٌ *i. q.* ▼ مَسْبِىٌّ [i. e. *Made captive*]; (M;) or السَّبْىُ signifies مَا يُسْبَى [i. e. *what is made captive;* but I rather think that the right explanation is مَنْ يُسْبَى i. e *the person who is made captive;* agreeably with what follows]: pl. سُبِىٌّ: (M, Ḳ:) one says قَوْمٌ سَبْىٌ [*a company,* or *party, of men made captive*]; the latter word in this case being an inf. n. used as an epithet; [therefore, as such, it is applicable to a single person, male or female, as well as to a pl. number;] and accord. to Aṣ, one says not otherwise than thus in speaking of a company, or party, of men: (Mṣb, TA:) [but] ▼ سَبِىٌّ is [also] applied to a single person, to the male and the female, (M, Ḳ,) i. e. to the latter, as to the former, without ة, (M;) as meaning *made captive:* (Ḳ:) or سَبِىٌّ is applied to a boy, or young man, or male slave, as also ▼ مَسْبِىٌّ; and سَبِيَّةٌ to a girl, or young woman, or female slave, as also ▼ مَسْبِيَّةٌ; (Mṣb;) or to a woman, in this sense: (Ṣ:) and the pl. of ▼ سَبِىٌّ, (M, Ḳ,) or of سَبِيَّةٌ, (Mṣb,) is سَبَايَا, (M, Mṣb, Ḳ,) applied to women. (M.) —— Also *Women,* (IAạr, M, Ḳ,) universally; (IAạr, M;) because they captivate the hearts; or because they are made captive, and possessed as property. (M, Ḳ.)

سَبًا: see سَبْىٌ. —— Also *A tribe of El-Yemen;* regarded as a حَىّ, perfectly decl.; and regarded as a قَبِيلَة, [and therefore a fem. proper name,] imperfectly decl. [and written سَبَا]: (M, TA:) or, as is said in the Mṣb, it is the name of *a town,* or *province, in El-Yemen;* masc., and therefore perfectly decl.; and fem., and therefore imperfectly decl.; called by the name of its builder: (TA:) [hence,] one says, ذَهَبُوا أَيْدِى سَبَا and أَيَادِى سَبَا, [making the last word to be without tenween either as a fem. proper name or because of pausing after it,] i. e. *They went away scattered,* or *dispersed:* (Ṣ, M, Ḳ:) J says, (TA,) they are two nouns made one, like مَعْدِى كَرِبَ, perfectly decl. because not occurring otherwise than as a denotative of state, [and therefore indeterminate,] whether you make the former to be a prefixed noun governing the latter in the gen. case, or do not so. (Ṣ, TA. [See also art. سبأ.]) In a verse of 'Alḳameh Ibn-'Abadeh, the phrase بِسَبَا الكَتَّانِ is used for بِسَبَائِبِ الكَتَّانِ. (M in art. سب: see سِبٌّ.)

سِبًى or سِبًا: see 1, first sentence.

سَبِىٌّ: see سَبْىٌ.

سِبَآءٌ: see 1, first sentence.

سَبِىٌّ: see سَبْىٌ, in two places. —— Also, (Ḳ,) or عُودٌ سَبِىٌّ, (M,) *A branch,* or *piece of stick* or *wood, brought by a torrent from one tract,* or *region, to another,* (M, Ḳ,) or *from a distant place;* (M;) and ▼ سَبِيَّةٌ and ▼ سَبًا signify the same. (Ḳ.) —— سَبِىُّ الحَيَّةِ *The slough of the serpent;* (M,* Ḳ;) as also سِبْؤُهَا. (Ḳ in art. سبأ. [Accord. to different copies of the Ḳ in the present art., سَبْىٌ or سِبْىٌ or سَبِىٌّ, all of which are wrong.]) —— سَبِيَّةٌ [or دُرَّةٌ سَبِيَّةٌ] *A pearl,* or *large pearl, brought out by the diver* (Ḳ, TA,) *from the sea.* (TA.) —— Also, [or خَمْرٌ سَبِيَّةٌ,] *Wine brought from one town,* or *country, to another:* (Ṣ, M, Ḳ:) if bought to be drunk, it is termed سَبِيْئَةٌ, with ء: (Ṣ, M:) or, perhaps, the former may be an instance of the alleviation of ء. (M. [See also سَبِيْئَةٌ in art. سبأ.])

سَابِيَآءُ The مَشِيمَة [or *membrane enclosing the fœtus in the womb*], *which comes forth with the young:* (Ṣ, Ḳ:) or *a thin pellicle over the nose of the fœtus, which dies if it be not removed from it at the birth:* (Ḳ:) or *the water that comes forth upon the head of the fœtus,* (T, M,) [i. e.] *at the birth:* (T:) pl. سَوَابِى [or سَوَابٍ]. (Ṣ.) —— Hence, as being likened thereto, because of its fineness, (M,) † The *dust of the burrows,* or *holes, of the jerboa;* (Ḳ;) or *fine dust which the jerboa extracts from its burrow,* or *hole:* said by Abu-l-'Abbás to be [*one*] *of the burrows,* or *holes, of the jerboa;* but this saying of his has been rebutted. (M.) —— Hence also, (M,) ‡ *Increase* or *offspring* [*of camels* or *the like*]; (Ṣ, M, Ḳ, TA;) called by the name of that from which they come: (M, TA:) or (so accord. to the M, but accord. to the Ḳ "and") *camels for breeding:* and *numerous cattle:* (M, Ḳ:) or also *sheep,* or *goats, having numerous offspring:* (T, Ṣ, Ḳ:) and it is also applied to denote *a large number* [app. of animals &c.]. (TA.) One says, لِآلِ فُلَانٍ سَابِيَآءُ, meaning ‡ [*To such a one belong*] *numerous cattle.* (TA.)

إِسْبَآءَةٌ *A streak* of blood; (AO, Ṣ, M, Ḳ;) as also ▼ أُسْبِيَّةٌ: (M, TA:) pl. أَسَابِىُّ. (AO, Ṣ, M, Ḳ.) —— And *An extended thread* or *string of* [*goats'*] *hair.* (TA.) —— And [the pl.] أَسَابِىُّ signifies The *conspicuous tracks* of a road. (TA.)

أُسْبِيَّةٌ: see the next preceding paragraph.

مَسْبِىٌّ; and its fem., with ة: see سَبْىٌ, in three places.

ست

1. سَتَّهُ, [aor. ـُ, accord to rule, and inf. n. app. سَتٌّ, q. v.,] *He attributed* or *imputed to him,* or *charged him with,* or *accused him of, a fault,* or *defect,* or *the like;* as also سَدَّهُ; syn. عَابَهُ. (TA. [The sense in which عابه is there used is indicated by the context.])

سِتٌّ a dial. var. of اِسْتٌ: see the latter word in art. سته, in two places.

سَتٌّ *Foul,* or *evil, speech* or *language.* (IAạr, Ḳ.) — And also, [like سَدٌّ,] *A fault,* or *defect,* or *the like;* syn. عَيْبٌ. (Ḳ.)

سِتٌّ: see سِتَّةٌ, of which it is the fem. — سِتِّى said to a woman means, (Ḳ, TA,) accord. to the explanation of IAmb, (TA,) يَا سِتُّ جِهَاتِى [*O thou who occupiest the six places in relation to me; or, who art above me, below me, before me, behind me, on my right, and on my left*]: (Ḳ, TA:) as though alluding to her holding the speaker in her possession: (TA:) or it is an incorrect expression; (Ḳ;) or it is vulgar, and held in low estimation; (IAạr, TA;) and is correctly سَيِّدَتِى [*my lady,* or *my mistress*]: (Ḳ:) it may be regarded as a contraction of سَيِّدَتِى, accord. to Esh-Shihláb El-Ḳásimee: (TA:) and Es-seyyid 'Eesà Eṣ-Ṣafawee says that it should not be restricted to the class of expressions used as vocatives. (MF, TA.)

سِتَّةٌ (Lth, T, Ṣ, M) and ▾ سِتٌّ, (Lth, T, Ṣ, M, Ḳ,) the former masc. and the latter fem., (Ṣ,) [signifying *Six,*] are originally سِدْسَةٌ (Lth, T, M) and سِدْسٌ; (Lth, T, Ṣ, M, Ḳ;) the latter س is changed into ت, and the د is incorporated into it; (Lth, T, Ṣ, M, Ḳ;) for the dim. of سِتَّةٌ is سُدَيْسَةٌ [and that of سِتٌّ is سُدَيْسٌ], and the pl. is أَسْدَاسٌ. (Lth, T, Ṣ.) You say, عِنْدِى سِتَّةُ رِجَالٍ وَنِسْوَةٍ [*I have with me,* or *at my abode, six men and women*], i. e., *three men and three women:* and you may say, عِنْدِى سِتَّةُ رِجَالٍ وَنِسْوَةٌ, meaning, *six men, and also women:* and in like manner you do in the case of any number that can be divided so as to apply to two plurals, as six and seven and the higher numbers: but in the case of a number that cannot be divided so as to apply to two plurals, as five and four and three, you put the latter noun in the nom. case only, saying, for ex., عِنْدِى خَمْسَةُ رِجَالٍ وَنِسْوَةٌ. (ISk, Ṣ.) [Respecting a peculiar pronunciation of the people of El-Ḥijáz, and a case in which سِتَّة is imperfectly decl., see ثَلَاثَةٌ and تِسْعَةٌ.] — سِتَّةَ عَشَرَ [indecl. in every case, meaning *Sixteen,*] is pronounced by some of the Arabs سِتَّةَ عْشَرَ: and [the fem.] سِتَّ عَشْرَةَ, thus in the dial. of El-Ḥijáz [and of most of the Arabs], is pronounced سِتَّ عَشِرَةَ in the dial. of Nejd. (Ṣ in art. عشر.) — سِتُّمِائَةٍ [meaning *Six hundred*] should be written thus, without separating the two words; because سِتٌّ is originally سِدْسٌ, and the union of the two words is to compensate for the incorporation of the د into the ت. (El-Ḥareeree, in De Sacy's Anthol. Gramm. Ar., p. 72 of the Arabic text.)

سِتُّونَ [*Sixty,*] *one of the tenfold numbers,* (M, TA,) namely, that between خَمْسُونَ and سَبْعُونَ, (TA,) is derived from سِتٌّ. (M, TA.) — [Also *Sixtieth.*]

سَاتٌّ [*Sixth*]. You say, جَآءَ فُلَانٌ سَادِسًا and سادسا and سَاتًّا and سَادِيًا [*Such a one came sixth*]; سادسا being formed from سِدْسٌ; and سَاتًّا, from سِتَّةٌ and سِتٌّ: in سَادِيًا, the [latter] س [of سادسا] is changed into ى; for certain letters in other cases are sometimes so changed; as in أَمَّا and أَيْمَا and تَسَنَّنَ and تَسَنَّى, and تَقَضَّضَ and تَقَضَّى, and تَلَعَّعَ and تَلَعَّى, and تَسَرَّرَ and تَسَرَّى. (ISk, Ṣ.)

اِسْتٌ: see arts. است and سته: it is properly mentioned in the latter art., being originally سَتَهٌ. (Ṣ, TA.)

ستر

1. سَتَرَهُ, aor. ـُ (Ṣ, M) and ـِ, (M,) inf. n. سَتْرٌ (Ṣ, M) and سَتَرٌ, (M,) *He,* or *it, veiled, concealed,* or *hid,* a thing; (M;) *covered it:* (Ṣ:) and ▾ ستّرهُ signifies the same, (M,) [or has an intensive sense, or denotes frequency or repetition of the action, or its application to many objects: accord. to Golius, "*sub velo, obtenso eo* [sic], *ne quis vir intueretur eam, custodivit* puellam: et *clam asservavit habuitque* eam:" as on the authority of the KL: in which I find nothing of the kind but تَسْتِير expl. by the words در پرده داشتن (*to have* or *hold, within a curtain.*] — † *He protected* another. (The Lexicons passim.) ═ سَتُرَتْ, inf. n. سَتَارَةٌ, سِتَارَةٌ, ‡ *She* (a woman) *was,* or *became,* (A,) i. e., *modest,* or *bashful.* (M.) — And سَتُرَ, inf. n. سِتْرٌ, † *He was,* or *became, intelligent.* (M.)

2: see the preceding paragraph.

3. سَاتَرَهُ العَدَاوَةَ, inf. n. مُسَاتَرَةٌ, ‡ [*He concealed enmity with him*]. (A.) [See also the act. part. n., below.]

5 and 7: see the next paragraph.

8. استتر and ▾ تستّر (Ṣ, M, Ḳ) and ▾ انستر (IAạr, M) *It became veiled, concealed,* or *hidden;* or *it veiled, concealed,* or *hid, itself:* (M:) *it became covered;* or *it covered itself.* (Ṣ, Ḳ.) — [Hence,] فُلَانٌ لَا يَسْتَتِرُ مِنَ اللّٰهِ بِسِتْرٍ ‡ [*Such a one does not protect himself from* the displeasure *of God by piety;* i. e.,] *such a one does not fear God.* (A, TA.)

سِتْرٌ and ▾ سُتْرَةٌ [which latter see also below] and ▾ سِتَارَةٌ (Ṣ, M, Ḳ) and ▾ سِتَارٌ (Ḳ) and ▾ سَتَرَةٌ and ▾ إِسْتَارٌ (TA) and ▾ إِسْتَارَةٌ, (M, Ḳ,) which last is only known to occur in one instance, in a trad., (M, TA,) and ▾ مِسْتَرٌ, (M, Ḳ,) *Anything by which a person or thing is veiled, concealed, hidden, or covered; a veil; a curtain; a screen; a cover; a covering; a covert:* (Ṣ, M, Ḳ:) [and the first and second, *anything by which one is protected,* or *sheltered:*] the pl. of سِتْرٌ is سُتُورٌ and أَسْتَارٌ (Ṣ, M, Ḳ) [the latter a pl. of pauc.] and سُتُرٌ; (M, TA;) which last is also pl. of ▾ سِتَارٌ, (Ḳ,) like as كُتُبٌ is of كِتَابٌ; (TA;) and the pl. of ▾ سِتَارَةٌ is سَتَائِرُ. (Ṣ, Ḳ.) — [Hence the phrase] هَتَكَ اللّٰهُ سِتْرَهُ [lit., *God rent open,* or *may God rend open, his veil,* or *covering;* meaning,] ‡ *God manifested,* or *made known,* or *may God manifest,* or *make known, his vices,* or *faults:* (A:) [or *God disgraced,* or *dishonoured, him,* or *exposed him to disgrace,* or *dishonour,* or *may God disgrace* or *dishonour him* &c.] And مَدَّ اللَّيْلُ أَسْتَارَهُ ‡ [*Night spread its curtains*]. (A.) And أَمُدُّ إِلَى اللّٰهِ يَدَىَّ تَحْتَ سِتَارِ ▾ اللَّيْلِ ‡ [*I stretch forth my hands* in supplication *to God beneath the veil of night*]. (A.) — سِتْرٌ also signifies ‡ *Fear.* (Ḳ.) [Because by it one protects himself from the displeasure of God. See 8.] And ‡ *Modesty,* or *bashfulness.* (Ḳ.) One says, مَا لِفُلَانٍ سِتْرٌ وَلَا حِجْرٌ ‡ *Such a one has not modesty nor intelligence.* (TA.) — And *Intelligence;* syn. عَقْلٌ. (M.) In the Ḳ it is explained by عَمَلٌ; but this appears to be a mistranscription, for عَقْلٌ. (TA.)

سَتْرٌ *A shield.* (M, Ḳ.)

سُتْرَةٌ: see سِتْرٌ. — Its predominant application is to *A thing which a person praying sets up before him;* [*sticking it in the ground,* or *laying it down if the ground be hard, in order that no living being or image may be the object next before him;*] *such as a whip, and a staff having a pointed iron at its lower extremity.* (Mgh.) [See عَنَزَةٌ: and see my "Modern Egyptians," 5th ed., p. 72.] — Also *A parapet,* or *surrounding wall,* of a flat house-top. (Mgh.) — And i. q. ظُلَّةٌ [q. v.]. (Mgh.)

سَتَرَةٌ: see سِتْرٌ.

سَتِيرَةٌ: see سَتِيرٌ, in two places.

سِتَارٌ: see سِتْرٌ, in three places.

سَتِيرٌ (Ṣ, M, Ḳ) and ▾ مَسْتُورٌ, (Ṣ, A, Ḳ,) applied to a man, (Ṣ, A, &c.,) and سَتِيرَةٌ (Ṣ, M, A, Ḳ) and سَتِيرٌ and ▾ سَتِرَةٌ, (M,) applied to a girl (Ṣ) or female, (M, &c.,) [properly *Veiled, concealed,* or *covered.* — And hence,] ‡ *Modest; bashful;* (M;) *chaste:* (Ṣ, Ḳ:) pl. of سَتِيرٌ, as masc., سُتَرَاءُ; (M;) and of ▾ مَسْتُورٌ, مَسْتُورُونَ, [and مَسَاتِيرُ]; (A;) and, app. of سَتِيرٌ [as fem.] and سَتِيرَةٌ and also, سَتَائِرُ; and the pl. of ▾ سَتِرَةٌ is سَتِرَاتٌ only, accord. to a rule laid down by Sb. (M.) — شَجَرٌ سَتِيرٌ ‡ *Trees having many boughs or branches.* (A.) — سَتِيرٌ applied to God is of the measure فَعِيلٌ in the sense of the measure فَاعِلٌ, meaning † *Veiling, or protecting; a veiler, or protector.* (TA.)

سِتَارَةٌ: see سِتْرٌ, in two places. — Also *The piece of skin that is upon the nail.* (Ḳ.)

سَتَّارٌ *One who veils,* or *conceals,* [*much,* or *often;* or *who does so*] *well.* (KL.) [Hence,] اَللّٰهُ سَتَّارُ العُيُوبِ ‡ *God is He who is wont to veil vices*, or *faults*]. (A.) — And The *keeper of the curtain* [*that hangs over, and closes, the door of a chamber*]. (MA.)

إِسْتَارٌ : see سِتْرٌ. ═ Also *Four*: (Ṣ, M, A, Ḳ:) said by Aboo-Sa'eed and Az to be arabicized, from the Pers. چَهَارْ : pl. أَسَاتِيرُ and أَسَاتِرُ. (TA.) It is applied to men: (Ṣ, M:) and you also say, أَكَلْتُ إِسْتَارًا مِنَ الخُبْزِ meaning *I have eaten four cakes of bread*. (TA.) — And The *fourth* of a party of people. (TA.) — And The *weight of four mith-kháls* (مَثَاقِيل) *and a half*: (Ṣ, Ḳ:) [see رِطْلٌ :]) likewise arabicized: (Az:) [app. from the Greek στατήρ:] pl. أَسَاتِيرُ. (Ṣ.)

إِسْتَارَةٌ : } see سِتْرٌ.
مِسْتَرٌ : }

مَسْتُورٌ : see سَتِيرٌ, in two places. — حِجَابًا مَسْتُورًا, in the Ḳur xvii. 47, means *A veil covered by another veil*; implying the thickness of the veil: (Ṣ:) or مستورا is here of the measure مَفْعُولٌ in the sense of the measure فَاعِلٌ, like مَأْتِيًّا in the Ḳur xix. 62, (Ṣ, M,) which some say is the only other instance of the kind; (TA;) and Th explains it as signifying *preventing*, or *hindering*, or *obstructing*; and says that it is of the measure مَفْعُولٌ because the veil itself is hidden from man. (M.)

جَارِيَةٌ مُسَتَّرَةٌ *A girl kept behind*, or *within, the curtain*. (Ṣ.)

هُوَ مُدَاجٍ مُسَاتِرٌ ‡ [*He is a wheedler*, or *cajoler, who conceals enmity*]. (A.)

ستق

سُتُّوقٌ (Ṣ, Mgh, Ḳ) and سَتُّوقٌ, (Ṣ, Ḳ,) [said to be] the only instances of the kind except سُبُّوحٌ and قُدُّوسٌ and ذُرُّوحٌ, all of which are with ḍamm and with fet-ḥ, (Ṣ,) [but see سُبُّوحٌ,] as also ▼ تُسْتُوقٌ, (Ḳ,) this last mentioned by Lḥ on the authority of a desert-Arab of Kelb, (TA,) applied to a dirhem, *Such as is termed* زَيْفٌ (Ṣ, Ḳ) *and* نَبَهْرَجٌ (Ṣ) or بَهْرَجٌ (Ḳ) [i. e. *bad*, &c.]; *worthless*; (TA;) *coated with silver*: (Ḳ:) accord. to El-Karkhee, *such as consists for the most part of brass* or *of copper*: and it is said in the "Risáleh Yoosufeeyeh" that the ▼ سَتُّوقَة it is *unlawful to take, as being* فُلُوس [which means certain small *coins of copper*; whence it seems that سَتُّوقة has a pl. meaning, though otherwise it would seem to be a sing. subst.]: it is said to be arabicized, from سِهْ تُو, (Mgh, TA,) which is Pers., meaning "three fold;" as is [thought to be] indicated by its being said to be coated with silver. (TA.)

سَتُّوقَةٌ : } see the preceding paragraph.
تُسْتُوقٌ : }

مُسْتُقَةٌ (Ṣ, O, Ḳ) and مُسْتَقَةٌ, (O, Ḳ,) the latter allowed by Ibn-'Abbád, (O,) *A fur-garment*, (فَرْوَة, Ḳ,) or *one of what are termed* فِرَاء, (Ṣ, O,) *with long sleeves*: (Ṣ, O, Ḳ:) accord. to A'Obeyd, (Ṣ, O,) arabicized, from the Pers. مُشْتَهْ: [or app., in the sense above expl., from the Pers. مُشْتِي; and in the sense following, from the former Pers. word:] pl. مَسَاتِقُ. (Ṣ, O.) — Also *An instrument with which the* صَنْج [q. v.] *and the like are beaten*. (Ḳ.)

سته

1. سَتَهَهُ, (Ṣ, Ḳ,) aor. ـَ, (Ḳ,) inf. n. سَتْهٌ, (Ṣ,) *He struck his* اِسْت; (Ṣ, Ḳ;) i. e. a man's. (Ṣ. [See اِسْتٌ below.]) — And, (Ḳ,) inf. n. as above, (TA,) *He followed him from behind*, (Ḳ, TA,) *not quitting him*; because following his اِسْت. (TA.)

4. أَسْتَهَ *He* (a man) *was*, or *became, large in the buttocks*. (TA.)

سَتْهٌ and سُتْهٌ : see اِسْتٌ, below.

سِتْهٌ : see اِسْتٌ, below, in two places.

سَتَهٌ : see اِسْتٌ, below, in two places. ═ Also *Largeness of the* اِسْت. (Ṣ, Ḳ.)

سَتِهٌ ; and its fem., with ة : see أَسْتَهُ, in two places: and see what next follows.

سَتَهِيٌّ *Of*, or *relating to, the* اِسْت; and in the same sense, if you will, you may say ▼ اِسْتِيٌّ; and ▼ سَتِهٌ also, with kesr to the ت, like as they said حَرِحٌ. (Ṣ.)

سُتْهُمٌ : see أَسْتَهُ, in three places.

سُتَيْهَةٌ dim. of اِسْتٌ, from the original of the latter, i. e. سَتَهٌ. (TA.)

سُتَاهِيٌّ : see أَسْتَهُ, in two places.

سُتْهِيٌّ : see what next follows.

سُتَّهِيٌّ, thus correctly, in the handwriting of Ṣgh, on the authority of Fr; in the Ḳ, ▼ سُتْهِيٌّ; (TA;) One *who always walks*, or *goes, at the rear of a people*, or *party*, (IB, Ḳ, TA,) *remaining behind them, and looking to their goods*. (IB, TA.)

اِسْتٌ (Ṣ, Mgh, Ḳ, written with the conjunctive hemzeh, Mṣb in art. است) and ▼ سَتَهٌ (Ṣ, Mgh, Ḳ) and ▼ سَتْهٌ (Ḳ) and ▼ سِتْهٌ (CḲ [but not in my MS. copy of the Ḳ nor in the TA, and of doubtful authority, as will be seen from what follows,]) signify the same, (Ṣ,* Mgh,* Ḳ,) i. e. The *podex*, *buttock* or *buttocks*, *posteriors*, *rump*, or *croup*; and sometimes the *anus*; (Ṣ;) ▼ سَتَهٌ being the original form, as is shown by the pl., (Ṣ, Mgh,) which is أَسْتَاهٌ; (Ṣ, Mgh, Ḳ;) like جَمَلٌ and أَجْمَالٌ: it may not be [▼ سِتْهٌ and ▼ سُتْهٌ] like جِذْعٌ and قُفْلٌ, of which the pls. are also of the measure أَفْعَالٌ, because, when you restore the ه which is the final radical, and reject the medial radical [which is ت], you say سَهٌ, with fet-ḥ, (Ṣ, Mgh,*) which has both of the meanings expl. above, as also سُهٌ, (Ḳ,) but [SM says,] this last, mentioned by the author of the Ḳ, is strange, and I have not seen it on the authority of any one [else]: (TA:) and some say سَتٌ, (IKh, Ṣ, Mgh, TA,) suppressing the final radical [of سَتَهٌ], (Ṣ,) i. e., without ه at the end and without hemzeh [or ا] at the beginning. (TA.) [All are of the fem. gender.] It is said in a trad., العَيْنُ وِكَآءُ السَّهِ, or, as some relate it, السَّتِ, (Ṣ, Mgh, TA,) [*The eye is the tie of the anus*,] meaning that when one [closes the eye and] sleeps, the tie of the سه becomes loosed, and the excrement and wind issue. (TA.) And أَبُو الأَسْتَاهِ means *He who has large posteriors*. (Az, TA.) بِاسْتِ فُلَانٍ is a phrase of the Arabs significant of reviling; (Ṣ;) said when holding one in contempt; meaning لَصِقَ العَارُ بِاسْتِ فُلَانٍ † [*May disgrace cleave to the* است *of such a one*]. (Mgh.) And يَا ٱبْنَ ٱسْتِهَا ‡ [*O son of her* است], (Ḳ, TA,) a prov. of the Arabs, (TA,) is an allusion to one's father's إِحْمَاض [see 2 in art. حمض] of the former's mother; (Z, TA;) and is said to mean أَنَّهُ وُلِدَ مِنِ ٱسْتِهَا : (TA:) and the Arabs called the sons of the female slave بَنُو ٱسْتِهَا. (Sh, TA.) And one says to a man who is deemed abject and weak, اِسْتُ أُمِّكَ أَضْيَقُ [lit. *Thy mother's* است *is too contracted*], and اِسْتُكَ أَضْيَقُ مِنْ أَنْ تَفْعَلَ كَذَا وَكَذَا [*Thine* است *is too contracted*, meaning † *thine ability is too small, for thy doing such and such things*]: (TA: [see also Freytag's Arab. Prov., i. 607:]) and أَنْتُمْ أَضْيَقُ أَسْتَاهًا مِنْ أَنْ تَفْعَلُوهُ [in like manner] is an allusion to inability [meaning † *Ye are unable to do it*]. (Ḳ.) The saying of a poet,

• وَأَنْتَ مَكَانُكَ مِنْ وَائِلٍ •
• مَكَانُ القُرَادِ مِنِ ٱسْتِ الجَمَلْ •

‡ [*And thou, thy place in the tribe of Wáïl is like the place of the tick in the rump of the camel*,] is tropical; for they do not [properly] say اِسْتُ الجَمَلِ, but عَجُزُ الجَمَلِ. (Ṣ.) One says also to a man who is deemed low, or base, أَنْتَ الاِسْتُ السُّفْلَى, (TA,) and انت السَّهُ السُّفْلَى, meaning † *Thou art among others in the condition of the* است of mankind: (Ṣ, TA:) and of low, or base, men, one says, هٰؤُلَآءِ الأَسْتَاهُ ; and of such as are excellent, هٰؤُلَآءِ الأَعْيَانُ, and الوُجُوهُ. (TA.) And one says, لَقِيتُ مِنْهُ ٱسْتَ الكَلْبَةِ, (A, Ḳ,) a prov., (TA,) meaning † *I experienced from him*, or *it, what I disliked*, or *hated*. (A, Ḳ, TA. [See also Freytag's Arab. Prov., ii. 445.]) And اِسْتُ البَائِنِ أَعْرَفُ, or أَعْلَمُ : see art. بين. And مَا لَكَ ٱسْتٌ مَعَ ٱسْتِكَ † *Thou hast no one* [*with thee*] *to assist thee*: (A, Ḳ, TA:) another prov., related on the authority of AZ as said to one who has no large amount of property, nor number of men. (Ṣgh, TA.) And تَرَكْتُهُ بِٱسْتِ الأَرْضِ, another prov., (TA,) meaning † *I left him destitute, poor*, (Ḳ, TA,) *possessing nothing*: (TA:) or تَرَكْتُهُ بِٱسْتِ المَتْنِ † *I left him on the hard ground, alone*. (Meyd.) And مَا لَكَ فِى هٰذَا الأَمْرِ ٱسْتٌ وَلَا فَمٌ † *Thou hast not in this thing*, or *affair, root nor branch*: Jereer says,

• فَمَا لَكُمُ ٱسْتٌ فِى العَلَاءِ وَلَا فَمٌ •

[*And ye have not any root in eminence, nor branch*]. (TA.) And كَانَ ذٰلِكَ عَلَى آسْتِ الدَّهْرِ ‡ *That was in the beginning of time:* (A, Ḳ, TA:) or *in the olden time;* (AO, Ṣ, TA;) as also عَلَى إِسْتِ الدَّهْرِ. (AO, TA.) See also art. است. [And see other exs. in Freytag's Arab. Prov. i. 355 and 378 (a variation of a prov. mentioned in the preceding page) and 607 and 622 and 729-730.]

أَسْتَهُ, applied to a man, (ISk, Ṣ, Mgh,) *Large in the* اِست, (ISk, Ṣ, Mgh, Ḳ,) or عَجُز; (Ṣ;) as also ▼ سُتَاهِىٌّ, (ISk, Ṣ, Mgh, Ḳ,) and ▼ سُتْهُمٌ: (Ṣ:) and so, applied to a woman, سَتْهَآءُ [fem. of the first], and ▼ سُتْهُمٌ, in which the م is augmentative, (ISk, Ṣ,) and ▼ سَتِهَةٌ: (TA:) pl. [of the first] سُتْهٌ, like كُتْبٌ, and سُتْهَانٌ: (Ḳ:) and ▼ مُسْتَهٌ, applied to a man, signifies *large in the buttocks.* (TA.) —— And, as also ▼ سُتَاهِىٌّ and ▼ سَتِهٌ and ▼ سُتْهُمٌ, *A seeker,* or *desirer, of the* اِست; (Ḳ;) or one *addicted thereto;* (TA;) *i. q.* لُوطِىٌّ [one *addicted to the crime of the people of Lot*]. (TḲ.)

إِسْتِىٌّ: see سَتْهِىٌّ, with which it is syn.

مُسْتَهٌ: see [its syn.] أَسْتَهُ.

ستهم

سُتْهُمٌ *Large in the posteriors:* (Ḳ:) accord. to the Ṣ, *syn. with* أَسْتَهُ; [see this latter, in art. سته, in three places;] and the م is augmentative: (TA:) some explain it as *syn. with* اِسْتٌ: the author of the Ḳ [a mistake for the Ṣ], in art. سته, as meaning *large in the* اِست. (MF, TA.)

ستى

1. سَتَى, (Ḳ,) aor. يَسْتِى, said of a camel, (TA,) *He hastened, made haste,* or *went quickly;* (Ḳ, TA;) as also سَدَى: mentioned by Az. (TA.)

2: see 4, in two places.

3: سَاتَاهُ, (Ḳ,) inf. n. مُسَاتَاةٌ, (TA,) *He played with him the* [*game called*] شَفَلَّقَة [expl. in art. شفلق in the Ḳ as consisting in one's striking with the hand, or with the fore part of the foot, the hinder part, or backside, of a man, from behind him, and so throwing him down prostrate: whence it seems that the verb is perhaps irregularly derived from the سَتْهُ, q. v.]. (Ḳ.)

4. استى الثَّوْبَ (Ṣ, Ḳ) and ▼ سَتَّاهُ (M, TA) are syn. with اسداه (Ṣ, Ḳ) and سَدَّاهُ, (M, TA,) [i. e. *He set,* or *disposed, the warp of the garment,* or *piece of cloth,*] said of a weaver; *contr. of* أَلْحَمَهُ; except that ▼ سَتَّى means he did so for himself and for another, whereas سَدَّى means he did so for another, تسدّى meaning he did so for himself. (TA.)

12 [accord. to the Ṣ and Ḳ]. اِسْتَاتَتْ, inf. n. اِسْتِيتَآءٌ, said of a she-camel, *She became relaxed by reason of lust:* (Ṣ, Ḳ:) thus mentioned here by J and in the Ḳ; but its proper place, as is evident, is art. اتى, in which it has been explained. (TA: see 10 in art. اتى.)

سَتًى is *syn. with* سَدًى, (Ṣ, M, Ḳ,) relating to a garment, or piece of cloth; (Ṣ, M;) as also ▼ أُسْتِىٌّ; (Ḳ;) both signify [The *warp* thereof;] the *contr. of* لُحْمَةٌ; like سَدًى and أُسْدِىٌّ: (M:) and ▼ سَتَاةٌ is [the n. un. of the former, or] *syn. with* سَدَاةٌ, relating to a garment, or piece of cloth: (AZ, Ṣ:) [whence,] one says to him who neither harms nor profits, مَا أَنْتَ لُحْمَةٌ وَلَا ▼ سَتَاةٌ [lit. *Thou art neither a woof nor a warp:* see also a similar saying voce نير]: (TA: [see also سَدًى:]) and ▼ أُسْتِىٌّ signifies also ثَوْبٌ مُسْدًى or مُسَدًّى (accord. to different copies of the Ḳ) [lit. *a garment,* or *piece of cloth, having its warp set* or *disposed;* perhaps meaning *having a good,* or *strong, warp;* in art. اسد written, as from the L, مُسَدًّى, for which I find no other authority]; so expl. by AHeyth: but accord. to others, it is what the weavers term سَتًى, as mentioned above, i. e. the *warp.* (TA. [See also أُسْتِىٌّ in art. است, and أُسْدِىٌّ in art. اسد and in art. سدو and سدى.]) —— Also *i. q.* مَعْرُوفٌ [as meaning *A favour, benefit, benefaction,* or *the like*]; (Ḳ;) in this sense also a dial. var. of سَدًى. (TA.) —— Also a dial. var. of سَدًى signifying *Dates while continuing green and small;* syn. بَلَحٌ. (TA.)

سَتَاةٌ: see the next preceding paragraph, in two places.

أُسْتِىٌّ: see سَتًى, above, in two places.

سجح

1. سَجِحَ, aor. ـَ, inf. n. سَجَحٌ, (so accord. to the L, and the text of the Ḳ followed in the TA,) or سُجُحٌ, (so accord. to the CK and my MS. copy of the Ḳ,) and سَجَاحَةٌ, [which last suggests that سَجُحَ also may be used in the sense here following,] said of a cheek, *It was even, and soft, and long, in moderation, with little flesh,* (M, TA,) *and wide:* (TA:) or *was smooth, and long, with little flesh, and wide.* (L. [See سَجِحٌ, below.]) —— سَجُحَ, inf. n. سَجَاحَةٌ, is said of a man's natural disposition, [meaning *It was,* or *became, gentle,* or *easy:* (see سَجِيحٌ, voce سُجُحٌ, below:)] and one says, فِى عَقْلِهِ رَجَاحَةٌ وَفِى خُلُقِهِ سَجَاحَةٌ [*In his intellect is gravity, and in his natural disposition is gentleness,* or *easiness*]. (A.) —— سَجَعَتْ *i. q.* سَجَحَتِ الحَمَامَةُ [i. e. *The pigeon cooed;* or *reiterated its voice* or *cry;* &c.]: (Lth, Ḳ:) but said by some to be a mispronunciation, and disallowed by IDrd. (MF.) —— سَجَحَ لَهُ بِكَلَامٍ *He expressed a meaning to him obliquely, indirectly, obscurely,* or *allusively, by speech;* as also ▼ سَجَّحَ: (Az, Ḳ:) so in the "Nawádir." (Az, TA.)

2: see what next precedes.

4. إِسْجَاحٌ signifies The *pardoning,* or *forgiving, with goodness.* (Ṣ, O, Ḳ.) One says, مَلَكْتَ فَأَسْجِحْ; (Ṣ, A, O, TA;) a prov., relating to pardoning, or forgiving, when having power [to punish or to take vengeance]; (TA;) meaning [*Thou hast become possessed of power, then pardon,* or *forgive, with goodness;* or] *thou hast attained thine object, then act with goodness;* (A,* TA;) and *thou hast obtained power, then pardon,* or *forgive, in an easy and a good manner:* (TA:) it was said by the Prophet to Ibn-El-Akwa', and by 'Áisheh to 'Alee on the "Day of the Camel." (O.) And one says also, إِذَا سَأَلْتَ فَأَسْجِحْ *When thou askest,* or *beggest, then make thy words,* or *expressions, easy, and be gentle.* (Ṣ.)

7. انسجح لِى بِكَذَا *i. q.* اِنْسَمَحَ [app. syn. with أَسْمَحَ, or perhaps a mistranscription for this last word, meaning *He was liberal,* or *generous, to me with such a thing;* or *he complied with my desire in such a thing*]. (Ḳ.)

سَجْحٌ: see سُجُحٌ, in five places.

سَجَحٌ *Beauty, and justness of proportion,* (T, Ṣ, L,) of the make, (T,) or of the face, (Ṣ,) or of a man. (L.) [See also 1, first sentence.]

سُجُحٌ *Soft,* or *gentle,* and *even,* or *easy;* as also ▼ سَجِيحٌ. (Ḳ.) You say مِشْيَةٌ سُجُحٌ *An easy* (Ṣ, A) *and a direct,* or *right,* (A,) *gait,* or *manner of going.* (Ṣ, A.) And مَشَى فُلَانٌ مَشْيًا سُجُحًا and ▼ سَجِيحًا, and مِشْيَةً سُجُحًا, *Such a one walked,* or *went, with an easy gait* or *manner of going:* (L:) or *with an equable gait, without inclining the body from side to side in pride.* (T.) And ▼ خُلُقٌ سَجِيحٌ *A gentle,* or *an easy, natural disposition.* (L.) And رَجُلٌ سُجُحٌ *A man easy and good in natural disposition:* (Ḥar p. 314:) and ▼ سَجِيحُ الخُلُقِ [which means the same]. (A.) —— Also The *middle* of a road, (Ṣ, A, Ḳ,) or its *main part,* or *beaten track;* (A, Ḳ;) and so ▼ سَجْحٌ: (Ṣ, A, Ḳ:) because of its evenness. (TA.) One says, ▼ خَلِّ لَهُ عَنْ سَجْحِ الطريق or سُجُحِ الطَّرِيقِ [*Leave thou for him the middle of the road*]. (Ṣ, accord. to different copies.) And ▼ مَنْ طَلَبَ بِالحَقِّ وَمَشَى فِى سَجْحِهِ أَوْصَلَهُ اللّٰهُ إِلَى نُجْحِهِ [*He who seeks, demands, or sues for, that which is a right, or due, and goes in the beaten track thereof, God will conduct him to the attainment of his object*]. (A, TA.) —— And *Measure, size,* or *proportion;* (Ṣ, Ḳ;) as also ▼ سَجْحٌ, (Ṣ,) and ▼ سَجِيحَةٌ: (Ṣ, A, Ḳ:) so in the saying, بَنَى القَوْمُ بُيُوتَهُمْ عَلَى سُجُحٍ سَجِيحَةٍ (Ṣ, Ḳ*) and ▼ سَجْحٍ وَاحِدٍ (Ṣ) and وَاحِدَةٍ (Ṣ, A) [*The people,* or *party, constructed their tents,* or *houses, of one uniform measure* &c.].

سَجِيحَةٌ: see سُجُحٌ.

سُجَاخٌ The *air.* (O, Ḳ.) [Perhaps a mistranscription for سُخَاخٌ.]

سَجَاحِ *i. q.* تُجَاهَ: (Fr, O, Ḳ:*) so in the saying, قَعَدْتُ سَجَاحَ وَجْهِهِ [*I sat over against,* or *fronting, his face*]. (Fr, O.)

سَجِيعٌ: see سُجْعَةٌ, in four places.

سَجِيعَةٌ: see سُجْعَةٌ, in two places. —— Also *Natural disposition;* (Ṣ, A, Ḳ;) and so ↑سُجْعَةٌ (Ḳ, in the TA سجع,) and ↑مَسْجُوعَةٌ and ↑مَسْجُوعٌ (Ḳ,) the last an inf. n., though having no verb. (Abu-l-Ḥasan, TA.) You say, هُوَ كَرِيمُ السَّجِيعَةِ *He is generous in respect of the natural disposition.* (A.) And رَكِبَ فُلَانٌ سَجِيعَةَ رَأْسِهِ *Such a one followed his own opinion.* (AZ, TA.)

أَسْجَعُ *Beautiful, and of just proportion;* (T, Ṣ, L, Ḳ;) applied to the make, (T,) or to the face, (Ṣ,) or to a man: (L:) or a face *equable in form.* (A.) And رَجُلٌ أَسْجَعُ الخَدَّيْنِ (A, L, TA) *A man even, and soft, and long, in moderation, with little flesh, and wide, in the cheeks:* (TA:) or *smooth, and long, with little flesh, and wide, in the cheeks.* (L.) —— Also A camel *thin in the lip.* (Ḥam p. 283.) —— And the fem., سَجْعَآءُ, A she-camel *perfect,* or *complete,* (L, Ḳ,) in *length,* or *tallness,* and *in largeness:* (L:) and a she-camel *long in the back.* (Ḳ.)

مَسْجُوعٌ: see سَجِيعَةٌ. —— Also *i. q.* جِهَةٌ [The *place,* or *point, towards which a person,* or *thing goes, tends,* or *is directed*]. (O, Ḳ.)

مَسْجُوعَةٌ: see سَجِيعَةٌ.

سجد

1. سَجَدَ, (Ṣ, A, Mṣb, Ḳ, &c.,) [aor. ُ,] inf. n. سُجُودٌ, (Mṣb,) *He was,* or *became, lowly, humble,* or *submissive;* syn. خَضَعَ, (Ṣ, A, Ḳ, TA,) or تَطَامَنَ, and ذَلَّ: (Mṣb:) or *he bent himself down towards the ground:* (Aboo-Bekr, TA: [and such is often meant by خَضَعَ and by تَطَامَنَ:]) [or it has both of these significations combined; i. e. *he was,* or *became, lowly, humble,* or *submissive, bending himself down;* for] the primary signification of السُّجُودُ is تَذَلُّلٌ together with تَطَامُنٌ [or تَطَامُنٌ]. (Bḍ in ii. 32.) And ↑اسجد *He lowered his head, and bent himself;* (AA, Ṣ, Mgh, Ḳ;) said of a man; (AA, Ṣ, Mgh;) *and put his forehead on the ground:* (Mgh:) and likewise said of a camel; (Ṣ, A;) in the latter case tropical; (A;) as also سَجَدَ; (A, Mgh, Mṣb;) meaning ‡ *he lowered his head* (Ṣ, A, Mgh, Mṣb,) *to be ridden,* (Ṣ, Mgh,) or *to his rider,* (A,) or *on the occasion of his being ridden,* or *mounted.* (Mṣb.) —— The سُجُود of prayer is from سَجَدَ in the first of the senses expl. above; (Ṣ;) and means The [*prostrating oneself;*] *putting the forehead on the ground:* (Ṣ, Mgh:) سَجَدَ, (ISd, Mṣb, TA,) aor. and inf. n. as above, (ISd, TA,) signifies *he put his forehead on the ground:* (ISd, Mṣb, TA:) but سُجُود to God denotes a particular manner [of doing this; i. e. the *prostrating oneself* in prayer *by dropping gently upon the knees, placing the palms of the hands on the ground, a little before the place of the knees, and then putting the nose and forehead on the ground, the former first, between the two hands*]. (Mṣb.) —— It is said of Kisrà, in a trad., كَانَ يَسْجُدُ لِلطَّالِعِ, i. e. *He used to lower himself,* or *bend himself down, to the arrow passing beyond the butt, going over it;* which they used to reckon like that which hit the butt; meaning that he used to concede to the shooter thereof: or, accord. to Az, it means that he used to lower his head when his arrow was elevated [too high] above the object shot at, in order that the arrow might be rightly directed, and might hit the circle. (TA.) —— And [as salutation is often accompanied with a bending of the body,] سُجُودٌ also signifies † The act of *saluting.* (L, TA.) [You say, سَجَدَ لَهُ † *He saluted him.* And also † *He paid respect,* or *honour, to him;* or *magnified him;* see Ḥam p. 294.] —— You say also, سَجَدَتِ النَّخْلَةُ ‡ *The palm-tree bent,* or *inclined,* (AḤn, Mgh, TA,) by reason of the abundance of its fruit. (Mgh.) And السَّفِينَةُ تَسْجُدُ لِلرِّيحِ ‡ *The ship bends,* or *inclines, by the influence of the wind.* (A, TA.) —— وَالنَّجْمُ وَالشَّجَرُ يَسْجُدَانِ, in the Ḳur [lv. 5], means, accord. to Fr, † [*And the herbs and the trees*] *turn towards the sun and incline with it until the afternoon-shade becomes broken:* (TA:) or *the herbs and the trees humbly submit to his will.* (Bḍ, Jel.) The سُجُود of inanimate things to God we understand, in the Ḳur, as denoting obedience to that whereto they are made subservient, and as a fact to be believed without inquiry into the manner thereof. (I'Ab, L.) ═ Also *He stood erect:* (Lth, Mṣb, Ḳ:) so in the dial. of Ṭeiyi. (Mṣb.) It is said in the Ḳ, immediately after the mention of the first signification and this last, that thus the verb has two contr. meanings: but it may be said that there is no [necessary, or absolute,] contrariety between الخُضُوع and الاِنْتِصَاب. (MF.) ═ سَجِدَت رِجْلُهُ, aor. َ, ‡ *His leg became inflated,* or *swollen.* (Ḳ, TA.)

4. اسجد: see 1, second sentence. —— Also, (Ḳ,) inf. n. إِسْجَادٌ, (Ṣ,) ‡ *He looked continuedly and tranquilly:* (TA:) or *he looked continuedly,* (Ṣ, Ḳ,) *and lowered the eyelids in a languid,* or *languishing, manner,* (Ṣ, [the inf. n. being there expl. by إِدَامَةُ النَّظَرِ وَإِمْرَاضُ الأَجْفَانِ,]) or *lowering the eyelids* [&c.], (Ḳ,* TḲ,) *with a look indicative of* [*amorousness, and feigned coyness* or *opposition,* or] *confidence in one's love, and consequent presumptuousness:* (TA:) or *he had a languid,* or *languishing, eye.* (L.) —— And اسجدت عَيْنَهَا ‡ *She lowered her eye.* (A, TA.)

سَجْدَةٌ *A single act of* سُجُود [as meaning *prostrating oneself* in prayer or the like: pl. سَجَدَاتٌ]: so in the phrase سَجَدْتُ سَجْدَةً [*I performed a prostration of myself*]: (Mṣb:) and قَرَأْتُ سُورَةَ السَّجْدَةِ [*I recited,* or *read, the chapter of the prostration;* which is the thirty-second chapter of the Ḳur-án]. (Ṣ,* Mṣb.)

سِجْدَةٌ a subst. from سَجَدَ; (Ṣ;) *A species,* or *sort,* [or *kind,*] *of* سُجُود [as meaning *prostration of oneself* in prayer or the like]: so in the phrase سَجَدْتُ سِجْدَةً طَوِيلَةً [*I performed a long kind of prostration of myself*]. (Mṣb.)

رَجُلٌ سَجَّادٌ [*A man who prostrates himself much,* or *frequently,* in prayer or the like]. (A, TA.)

سَجَّادَةٌ A [*small mat, such as is termed*] خُمْرَة, (Ṣ, Mgh, L, TA,) [*of an oblong shape,* and *a small oblong carpet,*] *upon which one prostrates himself* [*and stands and sits in prayer*]; (L, TA;) also called ↑سُجَّادَةٌ, (A, TA,) and ↑مَسْجَدَةٌ. (A, L, TA.) You say, بَسَطَ سَجَّادَتَهُ &c. [*He spread his prayer-mat,* or *prayer-carpet*]. (A.) —— And The *mark of* سُجُود [or *prostration* in prayer] *upon the forehead* [when dust adheres to it]. (Ṣ, A, Mgh.)

سُجَّادَةٌ: see the next preceding paragraph.

سَاجِدٌ act. part. n. of سَجَدَ: (L:) [*Being lowly, humble,* or *submissive: bending himself down towards the ground:* &c.: and hence, *prostrating himself in prayer; putting his forehead on the ground:* &c.:] pl. سُجَّدٌ (Ṣ, A, L) and سُجُودٌ. (L.) —— وَادْخُلُوا البَابَ سُجَّدًا, in the Ḳur [ii. 55 and vii. 161], means *And enter ye the gate bending down your heads:* (I'Ab, Ḳ:) it was a narrow [or low] gate. (I'Ab.) —— And سُجَّدًا لِلّٰهِ, in the Ḳur xvi. 50, means ‡ *Humbling themselves to God, with subserviency.* (TA.) —— You say also شَجَرَةٌ سَاجِدَةٌ, and شَجَرٌ سَاجِدٌ and سَوَاجِدُ, [this last word being pl. of سَاجِدَةٌ,] ‡ *A tree, and trees, bending,* or *inclining:* (A:) and نَخْلٌ سَوَاجِدُ † *palm-trees bending,* or *inclining:* (AḤn:) and نَخْلَةٌ سَاجِدَةٌ † *a palm-tree bent by its fruit.* (Ḳ.) [But it is said that] غُلْبٌ سَوَاجِدُ, occurring in a verse of Lebeed, means † *Firmly-rooted* [*tall*] *palm-trees.* (IAạr.) —— And فُلَانٌ سَاجِدُ المَنْخِرِ ‡ *Such a one is abject, low, humble,* or *submissive.* (A, TA.) —— And عَيْنٌ سَاجِدَةٌ ‡ *A languid,* or *languishing, eye.* (A, Ḳ.)

أَسْجَدُ ‡ *Having his leg inflated,* or *swollen:* (Ḳ, TA:) applied to a man. (TA.)

دَرَاهِمُ الأَسْجَادِ, (O, Ḳ,) or الإِسْجَادِ, (Ṣ, O, Ḳ,) thus some relate it, with kesr to the ء, (O, Ḳ,) in the saying of El-Aswad Ibn-Yaạfur,

* مِنْ خَمْرِ ذِي نُطَفٍ أَغَنَّ مُنَطَّقٍ *
* وَافَى بِهَا لِدَرَاهِمِ الأَسْجَادِ *

[*Of the wine of one with earrings, having a nasal twang, girded with a waist-belt,* i. e., of a foreigner: *he brought it for what are termed* دراهم الاسجاد], (Ṣ,* O, Ḳ, but in the copies of the Ḳ كَدَرَاهِمِ, [which I think a mistranscription,]) means *dirhems whereon were effigies to which people performed the act of* سُجُود: (Ṣ, O, Ḳ:) it is said that *upon them was the effigy of Kisrà, and he who beheld them lowered his head to them and showed humility* [as the Persians in the present day do to the picture of their King]: (IAmb, TA:) or الأَسْجَاد means *the tax called* جِزْيَة: (O, Ḳ:) so says AO, (O,) or A'Obeyd: (TA:) or *the Jews* and *the Christians:* (O, Ḳ:) some say the former and some say the latter: (O:) and it is read with kesr to the ء, and expl. as meaning *the Jews,* (O, Ḳ,) by IAạr. (O.) [Whatever be the signification of the last word, the verse plainly means, "of wine of a foreigner, sold by him for foreign money."]

مَسْجَدٌ The *forehead,* (Ṣ, Ḳ,) *where is the*

mark made by the سُجُود [or *prostration* in prayer]. (Ṣ.) [Said in the TA to be tropical; but not so accord. to the A.] And sing. of مَسَاجِد which signifies The *parts* of a man *that are the places of* سُجُود; (Lth, Mgh, Mṣb, L;) المَسَاجِد meaning *the forehead, the nose, the hands, the knees, and the feet:* (Mgh, L:) or *the forehead, the hands, and the knees:* (Mgh:) or *the seven* آرَاب; (Ṣ, Ḳ;) namely, *the forehead, the hands, the knees, and the feet:* (TA in art. ارب:) such, accord. to some, is its meaning in the Ḳur lxxii. 18. (L.) — See also the next paragraph, in two places.

مَسْجِد [*Any place in which one performs the act of* سُجُود, or *acts of worship* or *devotion*; and particularly *a mosque*; *a Muslim temple*; *an oratory*;] *a house in which one performs the act of* سُجُود; (IB;) *a house of prayer*; (Mgh, Mṣb;) *any place in which one performs acts of worship* or *devotion*: (Zj:) a word of well-known meaning; (Ḳ;) sing. of مَسَاجِد; (Ṣ, Mgh, Ḳ;) and also pronounced ▾ مَسْجَد: (Ṣ, Ḳ:) this latter word signifies, accord. to IAạr, the مِحْرَاب [here meaning *oratory*, or *place of private prayer*,] *of a house*; and the *place of prayer of the congregations*; (TA;) or it signifies *any of the parts of the ground, as well as of the body, that are the places of* سُجُود: (Lth, L:) or the *place of the forehead* [*on the ground in the act of prostration in prayer*]. (IB.) Fr says, (Ṣ,) the مَفْعَل of every verb of the class of فَعَلَ having its aor. of the measure يَفْعُلُ is with fet-ḥ to the medial radical letter, whether it be a subst, or an inf. n., (Ṣ, Ḳ,) without any difference, so that you say, دَخَلَ مَدْخَلًا, and هٰذَا مَدْخَلُهُ; (Ṣ;) except some words (Ṣ, Ḳ) among substs., (Ṣ,) as مَسْجِد and مَطْلِع (Ṣ, Ḳ) and مَشْرِق and مَغْرِب (Ṣ) and مَسْقِط and مَفْرِق and مَجْزِر and مَسْكِن and مَرْفِق (Ṣ, Ḳ) from رَفَقَ, aor. يَرْفُقُ, (Ṣ,) and مَنْبِت and مَنْسِك (Ṣ, Ḳ) from نَسَكَ, aor. يَنْسُكُ; (Ṣ;) these being with kesr (Ṣ, Ḳ) to the medial radical letter (Ḳ) as a sign of their being substs.; but sometimes some of the Arabs pronounce it with fet-ḥ in the subst.: مَسْكَن and مَسْكِن have been transmitted; and we have heard المَسْجَد and ▾ المَسْجِد, and المَطْلَع and المَطْلِع: and he further says, (Ṣ,) fet-ḥ is allowable, (Ṣ, Ḳ,) in all of these, (Ṣ,) even if we have not heard it: but when the verb is of the class of فَعَلَ having its aor. of the measure يَفْعِلُ, the n. of place [or time] is with kesr, and the inf. n. is with fet-ḥ, to distinguish the one from the other; so that you say, نَزَلَ مَنْزَلًا, meaning نُزُولًا, and هٰذَا مَنْزِلُهُ, meaning دَارُهُ. (Ṣ, Ḳ.*) — [Hence مَسْجِدٌ جَامِعٌ *A congregational mosque*; i. e. *a mosque in which a congregation assembles to perform the Friday-prayers.*] المَسْجِدُ الحَرَامُ [*The sacred mosque* of Mekkeh]. (Mṣb in art. حرم.) المَسْجِدُ الأَقْصَى *The furthest mosque* [which is in Jerusalem]. (Mṣb in art. قصو.) مَسْجِدُ الخَيْفِ *The mosque of the* خَيْف [q. v.] in Minè. (Ṣ &c. in art. خيف.) And المَسْجِدَانِ *The two mosques*; that of Mekkeh and that of El-Medeeneh: (Ṣ, Mgh:) so in a verse cited in the first paragraph of art. ثرو. (Ṣ.)

مَسْجَدَةٌ: see سَجَّادَةٌ.

سجر

1. سَجَرَهُ, (Ṣ, A, Mṣb, Ḳ,) aor. ـُ, (Mṣb,) inf. n. سَجْرٌ (Mṣb, TA) and سُجُورٌ; (TA;) and ▾ سجّرهُ, inf. n. تَسْجِيرٌ; (TA;) *He filled it*; (Ṣ, A, Mṣb, Ḳ;) namely, a river, or channel for water; (Ṣ, A, Ḳ;) and a vessel; as also سَكَرَهُ; (TA;) *with water*. (Ṣ.) You say, سَجَرَ السَّيْلُ الآبَارَ [*The torrent filled the wells*]. (A.) And سَجَرَتِ الثِّمَادُ *The* ثماد [see its sing. ثَمْدٌ] *became filled by the rain*. (Ṣ.) In the Ḳur [lxxxi. 6], وَإِذَا البِحَارُ سُجِرَتْ, some read thus; and others, ▾ سُجِّرَتْ; (Zj;) and Th explains it, and so Zj the former reading, as signifying, *And when the seas shall be filled*: but ISd says that there is no way of understanding this unless it mean *filled with fire*: or it means *and when the seas shall overflow*: or *shall meet together and become one sea*: (TA:) or ▾ سُجِّرَتْ signifies *shall flow forth, one into another, and thus become one sea*, (Zj, Bḍ,) *and so be filled*: (Bd:) and there are other explanations of the above-mentioned words of the Ḳur, which see below. — سَجَرَ المَآءَ فِى حَلْقِهِ *He poured the water into his throat*. (Ḳ.) — سَجَرَ التَّنُّورَ, (Ṣ, A, Mṣb, Ḳ,) aor. ـُ, inf. n. سَجْرٌ; (Ṣ;) and ▾ سجّرهُ; (Bḍ in lxxxi. 6;) or the latter has an intensive signification; (Mgh;) *He heated the oven*; (Ṣ, A, Ḳ;) *kindled fire in it*: (Mṣb:) or *filled it with firewood, to heat it*: (Mgh Bḍ:) or *he heated it fully with fuel*. (TA.) The words of the Ḳur quoted above, واذا البحار سُجِّرَتْ, are said to signify *And when the seas shall be set on fire*: (El-Ḥasan El-Baṣree:) or *shall become without water*, (Ḳatádeh,) or *shall be dried up, by the kindling of fire therein*: (B:) or *shall be kindled, and become fire*: (Jel:) or *shall be mixed together, and dry up, and become fire*; (El-Ubbee;) an explanation founded upon the license to employ a homonym in its several significations together: (MF:) or by "sea" is meant hell. (Kaạb.) You say also, سَجَرَ الوَقُودَ بِالمِسْجَرَةِ [*He stirred the fuel with the* مسجرة]. (A.) — سَجَرَتِ النَّاقَةُ, (Ṣ, A, Ḳ,) aor. ـِ, (Ṣ,) inf. n. سَجْرٌ (Ṣ, A, Ḳ) and سُجُورٌ; (Ṣ, Ḳ;) and ▾ سجّرت, inf. n. تَسْجِيرٌ; (A;) ‡ *The she-camel prolonged her yearning cry* (حَنِين, Ṣ, A, Ḳ) *after her young one*, (Aṣ, A,) *and filled her mouth with it*. (A.) — سَجَرَهُ, inf. n. سَجْرٌ; [and ▾ سجّرهُ, and ▾ سَوْجَرَهُ; (see the pass. part. ns., below;)] *He made it* [namely hair or the like] *to hang down*. (TA. [See also سُجِّرَتْ شَعْرُهَا.]) — سَجَرَهُ; (A, Ḳ;) and ▾ سجّرهُ, (A,) inf. n. تَسْجِيرٌ; (TA;) and ▾ سَوْجَرَهُ; (IJ, A, Ḳ;) *He put a* سَاجُور *upon*, or *around, his* (a dog's) *neck*: (A:) or *he bound him* (a dog) *with a* سَاجُور. (Ḳ.)

2. سجّر المَآءَ, inf. n. تَسْجِيرٌ, *He opened a way to the water; made it to flow forth*, (Aboo-Sa'eed, Ḳ,) *whithersoever he would*. (Aboo-Sa'eed.) — See also 1, throughout.

3. سَاجَرَهُ, (A,) inf. n. مُسَاجَرَةٌ, (A, Ḳ,) ‡ *He acted* or *associated with him as a friend*, or *as a true friend*; (A,* Ḳ,* TA;) *mixed*, or *held intercourse, with him*: from سَجَرَتِ النَّاقَةُ. (A.)

7. انسجر *It* (a vessel) *became full*. (TA.) — [*It* (hair) *hung down*. (See the part. n., voce مُسْجُور.)] — انسجرت الإِبِلُ *The camels followed one another in a continuous series*, or *uninterruptedly*, in their march, or progress: (Ṣ, Ḳ:* [but in some copies of the Ḳ, for انسجر فى السَّيْرِ, is put أَسْجَرَ:]) or *they advanced and hastened*; as also انشجر. (TA.)

Q. Q. 1. سَوْجَرَهُ: see 1, last two sentences.

سَجَرٌ (T, Ṣ, M, Ḳ, &c.) and ▾ سُجْرَةٌ (T, M, Ḳ) *Turbidness*, or *dinginess*: this is the primary signification: and hence, (TA,) ‡ *an intermixture of redness in the white of the eye*: (Ṣ, Ḳ:) or *redness in the white of the eye*: (T:) or *redness inclining to whiteness*: or *redness inclining to blueness*: or *redness in the black of the eye*: or *an intermixture*, or *a tinge, of redness in the black of the eye*: or *a slight redness mixing with the blackness*: or *an inclining of the black to redness*: or *a slight whiteness in the black of the eye*: or *a dinginess in the interior of the eye, arising from neglecting*, or *leaving off, the use of collyrium*. (TA.)

سُجْرَةٌ: see سَجَرٌ. — Also [*A full of*] *rainwater which fills what are called* ثِمَاد [pl. of ثَمْدٌ, q. v.]: pl. سُجَرٌ. (Ṣ.)

بِئْرٌ سَجْرٌ *A full well*. (TA.)

سَجُورٌ *Fuel with which an oven* (تَنُّور) *is heated*; (Ṣ, A, Mgh, Ḳ;) as also ▾ مِسْجَرٌ (Ḳ) and ▾ مِسْجَرَةٌ. (TA). [See also مِسْجَرَةٌ below.]

سَجِيرٌ ‡ A man's *friend*, or *true* or *sincere friend*: pl. سُجَرَآءُ: (Ṣ, A, Ḳ:) from سَجَرَتِ النَّاقَةُ; because each of two friends yearns towards the other. (A.) — And hence, † *A sword*. (Ḥam p. 265.)

سَاجِرٌ A torrent *that fills everything*. (TA.) — *A place upon which a torrent comes and which it fills*: (Ṣ, A, Ḳ:) a possessive epithet, or of the measure فَاعِل in the sense of the measure مَفْعُول. (TA.) — See also مَسْجُور.

سَاجُورٌ *A wooden thing*, or *piece of wood*, (Ṣ, Ḳ,) *that is put*, (Ṣ,) or *hung*, (Ḳ,) *upon the neck of a dog*: (Ṣ, Ḳ:) or *a collar*, (TA,) or *ring* or *collar of iron*, (A,) *that is put upon the neck of a dog*: (A, TA:) [pl. سَوَاجِرُ or سَوَاجِيرُ.] One says, فِى أَعْنَاقِهِمْ سَوَاجِرُ ‡ *Upon their necks are iron collars*. (A.)

أَسْجَرُ, applied to a pool of water left by a torrent (غَدِير), † *Having mud unmixed with sand*; or *having good mud*: (Ṣ, Ḳ:) or † *of which the water inclines to a red colour*; which is the case when its rain-water is recent, before it has become clear: (TA:) and ‡ rain-water *intermixed with turbidness and redness*. (A.) — ‡ A man *having what is termed* سَجَر or سُجْرَة *in the eye or eyes*: fem. سَجْرَآءُ. (TA.) — عَيْنٌ بَسْجْرَآءُ

‡ *An eye of which the white is intermixed with redness:* (Ṣ, A, Ḳ:) *an eye in which is what is termed* سُجْرَة [q. v.]. (TA.) —— قَطْرَةٌ سَجْرَآءُ ‡ *A turbid drop:* (A,* TA:) and in like manner نُطْفَةٌ. (TA.)

سَجُورٌ: see مَسْجُورٌ: and also what here follows.

مِسْجَرَةٌ: see سَجُورٌ. —— Also [and app. ▼ مِسْجَرٌ] *A piece of wood, or stick, with which the fuel in an oven* (تَنُّور) *is stirred.* (A, L, TA.)

مَسْجُورٌ *Filled:* (AZ:) applied to the sea in this sense: (Ṣ:) or the sea [*itself*]: (Ḳ: [in the TA, by the omission of وَاللَّبَنُ after البَحْرُ, it is made to signify "a sea of which the water is more than it is itself;" a meaning which, as there remarked, is not found in other lexicons:]) and مَسْجُورٌ بِالنَّارِ *filled with fire:* ('Alee:) and عَيْنٌ مَسْجُورَةٌ, and ▼ مُسْجَرَةٌ, *a full eye* or *source;* syn. مُفْعَمَةٌ. (A, TA.) —— Milk *of which the water is more than it is itself.* (Fr, Ṣ, Ḳ.) —— *Made to flow forth.* (TA.) —— *Empty.* (AZ, Aboo-'Alee.) Thus it bears two contr. significations. (TA.) —— *Kindled.* (Ḳ.) —— *Still,* or *quiet;* (Ḳ;) as also ▼ سَاجِرٌ: (TA:) or *still,* or *quiet, and full at the same time.* (A'Obeyd, TA.) —— لُؤْلُؤٌ مَسْجُورٌ *Pearls strung and hanging down:* (A'Obeyd, Ṣ, Ḳ:) or *that have fallen and become scattered from their string:* and لُؤْلُؤَةٌ مَسْجُورَةٌ is said to signify *a pearl of much brilliancy.* (TA.) —— شَعَرٌ مَسْجُورٌ, (TA,) and ▼ مُسَجَّرٌ, and ▼ مُسْجَرٌ, (Ḳ,) and ▼ مُنْسَجِرٌ, (Ṣ, Ḳ,) *Hair made to hang down;* (Ḳ;) *hanging down.* (Ṣ, Ḳ.) —— كَلْبٌ مَسْجُورٌ, (AZ, A,) and ▼ مُسَجَّرٌ, (A,) and ▼ مُسَوْجَرٌ, (Ṣ, A,) *A dog having a* سَاجُور (q. v.) *upon his neck.* (AZ, Ṣ, A.)

مُسَجَّرٌ: see مَسْجُورٌ, in three places. —— Also, *Dried up; of which the water has sunk into the ground.* (TA.)

مُسَوْجَرٌ: see مَسْجُورٌ, in two places.

مُنْسَجِرٌ: see مَسْجُورٌ.

سجس

1. سَجِسَ, (Ṣ, A, Ḳ,) aor. ـَ, (Ḳ,) inf. n. سَجَسٌ, (TA,) *It* (water) *became altered, changed in odour, or stinking;* syn. تَغَيَّرَ: (IAạr, A'Obeyd, Ṣ, A, Ḳ:) *it became turbid, thick,* or *muddy:* (ISk, A, Ḳ:) or *it became corrupted, and stirred up.* (TA.)

2. سَجَّسَهُ, inf. n. تَسْجِيسٌ, *He made it* (namely, water,) *turbid, thick,* or *muddy.* (Ḳ, TA.)

سَجْسٌ:
سَجَسٌ:
سَجِسٌ:
} see the next paragraph, in five places.

مَآءٌ سَجِيسٌ *Water that is altered, changed in odour,* or *stinking;* syn. مُتَغَيِّرٌ: *turbid, thick,* or *muddy:* as also ▼ سَجِسٌ, (Ḳ, TA,) and ▼ سَجْسٌ: (TA:) or *corrupted, and stirred up;* as also ▼ مُسَجَّسٌ: or the last signifies *made turbid, thick,* or *muddy, and stirred up:* the [only] form mentioned in the Ṣ is ▼ سَجْسٌ: but Aboo-Sahl says that ▼ سَجِسٌ is the form learned by him in reading under Aboo-Usámeh in the Muṣannaf; and as to ▼ سَجَسٌ, it is only an inf. n. (TA, from a note in the handwriting of Aboo-Zekereeyà.) —— Hence the saying, (TA,) لَا آتِيكَ سَجِيسَ ٱللَّيَالِى *I will not come to thee to the end of nights:* (TA:) or *ever;* (Ṣ, Ḳ;) as also سَجِيسَ اللَّيَالِى وَالأَيَّامِ, (TA,) and سَجِيسَ الأَوْجَسِ, (Ṣ, Ḳ,) and سَجِيسَ عُجَيْسٍ, (Ḳ,) and سَجِيسَ الأَوْجَسِ: (Ṣ, Ḳ:) or *while time lasts;* as also سَجِيسَ الدَّهْرِ, and سَجِيسَ الأَوْجَسِ: (A:) it is from سَجِيسٌ meaning "turbid," because water thus termed is the last that remains: عُجَيْسٌ is a corroborative; and عَجْسُ اللَّيْلِ signifies "the last part of the night:" (TA:) or سَجِيسَ اللَّيَالِى means *while the nights glide along continuously.* (Ḥam p. 243.)

سَاجِسِىٌّ A ram *having much wool:* fem. with ة: (A:) or a ram *having white wool, good for tupping,* or *covering, and of excellent breed.* (Ḳ,* TA.) And *Certain sheep* [i. e. *a breed of sheep*] *belonging to the Benoo-Teghlib,* (Ḳ,* TA,) *in El-Jezeereh.* (TA.)

مُسَجَّسٌ: see سَجِيسٌ.

سجع

1. سَجَعَ, aor. ـَ, inf. n. سَجْعٌ, *He pursued an even, uniform course; he pursued an even course, following one order:* this is the primary signification. (TA.) [It seems to be properly intrans.; but is sometimes used as a trans. verb, لِ or إِلَى being perhaps understood; as in the following phrase;] سَجَعَ ذٰلِكَ المَسْجَعَ *He pursued,* or *aimed at, that object of pursuit* or *aim;* (Ḳ, TA;) occurring in a trad. (TA.) —— And *It was even and uniform, one part thereof being like another.* (TA.) —— [Hence,] سَجَعَتِ الحَمَامَةُ, (IDrd, Ṣ, Mṣb, Ḳ,) aor. ـَ, (Mṣb, Ḳ,) inf. n. سَجْعٌ, (Mbr, TA,) and quasi-inf. n. ▼ سُجُوعٌ, (TA,) *The pigeon continued its cry uninterruptedly in one uniform way* or *manner;* or *called, and prolonged its voice* or *cry, modulating it sweetly:* (Mbr, in the "Kámil;" and TA:) or *cooed:* or *reiterated its voice* or *cry:* syn. هَدَرَتْ: (Ṣ, Mṣb:) and صَوَّتَتْ: (Mṣb:) or رَدَّدَتْ صَوْتَهَا. (IDrd, Ḳ.) It is said in a prov., لَا آتِيكَ مَا سَجَعَ الحَمَامُ [*I will not come to thee as long as the pigeon cooes;*] meaning *I will never come to thee.* (Lḥ.) —— You say also, سَجَعَتِ النَّاقَةُ, (Ṣ, TA,) inf. n. سَجْعٌ, (TA,) *The she-camel prolonged her yearning cry in one uniform manner.* (Ṣ, TA.) —— And سَجَعَتِ القَوْسُ ‡ *The bow prolonged its twang in one uniform manner, monotonously.* (TA.) —— And hence by way of comparison to the سَجْع of the pigeon, سَجَعَ كَلَامَهُ ‡ *He* (a man) *made his speech,* or *language,* [*to be rhyming prose,* i. e.,] *to have* فَوَاصِل *like the rhymes of verse, without its being measured.* (Mṣb.) And سَجَعَ [alone], (Ṣ, Ḳ,) aor. ـَ, (Ḳ,) inf. n. سَجْعٌ; (Ṣ, TA;) and ▼ سَجَّعَ, inf. n. تَسْجِيعٌ; (Ṣ, TA;) ‡ *He* (a man, Ṣ) *spoke,* or *uttered,* [or *composed,*] (Ṣ,* Ḳ, TA,) *rhyming speech* or *language,* (Ṣ,) [i. e., *rhyming prose,* i. e.,] *speech,* or *language, having* فَوَاصِل (Ḳ, TA) *like the* فَوَاصِل *of verse, without measure:* as is said in a description of Sijistán, مَاؤُهَا وَشَلٌ • وَلِصُّهَا بَطَلٌ • وَتَمْرُهَا دَقَلٌ • إِنْ كَثُرَ الجَيْشُ بِهَا جَاعُوا • وَإِنْ قَلُّوا ضَاعُوا • [Its water is such as scantily distils, in interrupted drops, from mountains or rocks, and its robber is a man of courage, and its dates are of the worst kind: if the army be numerous in it, they hunger; and if they be few, they perish]: so says Lth. (TA.) You say also, سَجَعَ بِالشَّىْءِ, meaning ‡ *He uttered the thing in the manner above described.* (TA.) [See also سَجْعٌ, below.]

2: see the preceding paragraph.

سَجْعٌ; [originally inf. n. of سَجَعَ, q. v.;] (Ṣ, Mṣb, Ḳ, &c.;) or, as some say, ▼ سِجْعٌ, but the former is that which commonly obtains, the latter being said to be a subst. like ذِبْحٌ meaning "what is slaughtered," unknown, however, in the lexicons, and probably one of the instances of the elicitations of the foreigners, (MF, TA,) the object of him who says that it is سِجْع being app. to make a distinction between the simple subst. and the inf. n., as in the case of the simple subst. and the inf. n. of سَجَعَ said of the pigeon; [see سَجَعَتِ الحَمَامَةُ;] (TA;) and ▼ أُسْجُوعَةٌ; (Ṣ,* Ḳ;) ‡ *Rhyming speech* or *language;* (Ṣ, Ḳ, TA;) [i. e. *rhyming prose;* i. e.] *speech,* or *language, having* فَوَاصِل *like the rhymes of verse, without being measured;* so called as being likened to the سَجْع of the pigeon; (Mṣb;) or because of its uniformity, (TA,) and the mutual resemblance and agreement of the words which end its clauses: (IJ, TA:) or *a consecution* [*of clauses*] *of speech* or *language, with one* رَوِىّ [which is the *principal, or only, rhyme-letter*]: (Jm, Ḳ:*) or *it consists in the agreement of the endings of words* [or *clauses*], *in a certain order, like the agreement of the rhymes* (قَوَاف) [*of verses*]: (Mbr, in the "Kámil;" TA:) *each clause ends with a quiescent letter; and consists of at least two words:* (Kull p. 208:) [see an ex. in the first paragraph of this art.:] you say also ▼ كَلَامٌ مُسَجَّعٌ (Ṣ) and ▼ كَلَامٌ مَسْجُوعٌ, meaning the same as سَجْعٌ: (TA:) the pl. of سَجْعٌ is أَسْجَاعٌ (Ṣ, Ḳ) and, accord. to IJ, سُجُوعٌ, but ISd says, I know not whether he have related this from another or coined it, (TA,) and أَسَاجِيعُ, (Ṣ,) or this last is pl. of ▼ أُسْجُوعَةٌ (Ḳ) [and is also a pl. pl., i. e. pl. of أَسْجَاعٌ, like as أَزَاهِيرُ is pl. of أَزْهَارٌ which is pl. of زَهْرٌ, and many similar instances might be added, such instances being numerous app. because أَفْعَالٌ is properly a measure of a pl. of paucity]. السَّجْعُ المُطَرَّفُ is *That* [*rhyming prose*] *in which the two words* [*that end two corresponding clauses*] *agree in the letter of the* سَجْع *but not in measure;* as الأَمَمُ and الرِّمَمُ: and السَّجْعُ المُتَوَازِى is *that in which the measure is observed in the two words as well as the letter of the*

سَجْع ; القَمَرُ and القَمَرُ. (KT.) It is said in a trad., that Moḥammad forbade سَجْع in prayer: [but many of the forms of prayer which he himself prescribed, and many others commonly used by Muslims in every age to the present time, are سَجْع, and the Ḳur-án is a composition of the same kind, though some do not allow this term to be applied to it, because سَجْع is *a highly artificial style of prose-language, characterized by a kind of rhythm as well as rhyme*, and it is obviously not proper to ascribe such artificial language to God, nor is it proper to use it in prayer, wherefore] Az says that سَجْع is disapproved in prayer because it resembles the language of the diviners, or soothsayers, but that other kinds of rhyming styles are allowable in خُطَب and رَسَائِل. (TA.) He is also related to have said, إِيَّاكُمْ وَسَجْعَ الكُهَّانِ ‡ [*Avoid ye the rhyming prose of the diviners*, or *soothsayers*]. (TA.) One says also, بَيْنَهُمْ أُسْجُوعَةٌ ▾ [*Between them is a discourse*, or *colloquy*, oral or written, *in rhyming prose*]. (Ṣ.)

سِجْع : see سَجَعَتِ الحَمَامَةُ : — and see سَجْع.

سَجُوعٌ : } see سَاجِعٌ.
سَجَّاعٌ :
سَجَّاعَةٌ :

سَاجِعٌ *Pursuing* [*an even, uniform, course*, or] *a direct*, or *right, course*, (AZ, Ṣ, Ḳ, TA,) in going, or journeying, (AZ, Ṣ, TA,) [and] ‡ in speech, &c. (Ḳ, TA.) Dhu-r-Rummeh says,

قَطَعْتُ بِهَا أَرْضًا تَرَى وَجْهَ رَكْبِهَا
إِذَا مَا عَلَوْهَا مُكْفَأً غَيْرَ سَاجِعِ

i. e. [*I traversed*, or *have traversed, with her a land* in which *thou wouldst see the face* of every one *of the company of travellers riding over it, when they get upon it*,] جَائِرًا غَيْرَ قَاصِدٍ [*turning aside from the right course*, (or rather *turned aside*, unless, which is not improbable, the right reading be مُكْفَتًا,) *not direct*], (AZ, Ṣ, TA,) or *not direct towards one point*: (TA:) but in the O we find, as on the authority of AZ, غَيْرَ سَاجِعٍ غير جَائِرٍ عَنِ القَصْدِ [which is evidently a mistranscription; the right reading being غَيْرَ سَاجِعٍ أَىْ جَائِرًا عَنِ القَصْدِ, or the like]. (TA.) — [Hence,] A face *justly proportioned*; [*symmetrical*;] *well*, or *beautifully, formed*. (Ḳ.) — [Hence also,] حَمَامَةٌ سَاجِعَةٌ, and ▾ سَجُوعٌ, (Ḳ,) without ة, (TA,) [*A pigeon continuing its cry uninterruptedly in one uniform way* or *manner*; or *calling, and prolonging its voice* or *cry, modulating it sweetly*: or *cooing*: (see 1:) or] *reiterating its voice* or *cry*: pl. [of the former or of both] سُجَّعٌ and [of the former] سَوَاجِعُ. (Ḳ.) — And نَاقَةٌ سَاجِعٌ *A she-camel prolonging her yearning cry in one uniform manner*: (TA:) or *quavering, and prolonging her voice*, [in the copies of the Ḳ مُطَرِّبَةٌ, but correctly مُطْرِبَةٌ,] *in her yearning cry*: (Ḳ:) or *tall*; (AA, Ḳ;) but Az says, I have not heard this on any authority beside that of AA. (TA.) — [And hence,] سَاجِعٌ also signifies ‡ [*A rhyming-proser*, or *rhyming-prosaist*;] one *who speaks*, or *utters*, [or *composes*,] سَجْع: and in like manner, [▾ سَجَّاعٌ (mentioned by Golius, and by Freytag as on the authority of the Ḳ, in no copy of which do I find it,) meaning one *who speaks*, or *utters*, or *composes*, سَجْع *much*: and] ▾ سَجَّاعَةٌ [meaning one *who does so very much*: the three epithets being similar to رَاجِزٌ and رَجَّازٌ and رَجَّازَةٌ]. (Ḳ, TA.)

أُسْجُوعَةٌ : see سَجْع, in three places.

مَسْجَعٌ *A place*, or *an object*, [to which latter it is applied in a phrase mentioned in the second sentence of this art.,] *of pursuit* or *aim*; syn. مَقْصِدٌ. (Ḳ.)

مُسَجَّعٌ : } see سَجْع.
مَسْجُوعٌ :

سجف

1. سَجَفَ البَيْتَ : see 2. — سَجِفَتْ, aor. ـَ, inf. n. سَجَفٌ, *She* (a woman) *was*, or *became, slender in the waist*: and *lank in the belly*. (TḲ.) [See also سَجَفٌ, below.]

2. سَجَّفَ البَيْتَ, (Ḳ,) inf. n. تَسْجِيفٌ, (TA,) *He let down the curtain* (السِّجْف) *upon* [*the entrance of*] *the tent*, or *chamber*; as also ▾ سَجَفَهُ, and ▾ اسجفه : (Ḳ, TA:) accord. to the T, التَّسْجِيفُ signifies *the letting down of the* سِجْفَانِ [or *two separate halves, that hang side by side, of a curtain*]: accord. to the M, *the letting down of the curtain*. (TA. [See also what next follows.])

4. اسجف السِّتْرَ *He let down the curtain*. (Ṣ, Ḳ, TA.) — [Hence,] اسجف اللَّيْلُ ‡ *i. q.* أَسْدَفَ, (Ṣ, Ḳ, TA,) i. e. *The night became dark*. (TA.) — See also 2.

سَجَفٌ : see the next paragraph.

سِجْفٌ and ▾ سَجْفٌ [of which the former is the more common] *A curtain*; *a veil*; or *a thing that veils, conceals, hides, covers*, or *protects*; (Ṣ, Ḳ;) as also ▾ سِجَافٌ, and ▾ سِجَافَةٌ : (TA:) or *a pair of curtains having an opening between them*: (IDrd, Ḳ:) or *each half of a pair of curtains*, (Lth, Ḳ, TA,) *divided in the midst*, (Lth, TA,) *by which any door*, or *entrance, is veiled*; (Lth, Ḳ, TA;) as also ▾ سِجَافٌ : (Ḳ, TA:) this last is not a pl. of سِجْفٌ : (TA:) thus السِّجْفَانِ signifies *the two separate halves* [*that hang side by side, so as to meet together*,] *of the curtain* of a tent, (Lth, Ṣ, TA,) in the fore part thereof: (Ṣ:) so in a verse of En-Nábighah Edh-Dhubyánee cited in the second paragraph of art. رفع : (Ṣ, TA:) the pl. of سِجْفٌ and سَجْفٌ is أَسْجَافٌ and سُجُوفٌ ; and the pl. of ▾ سِجَافٌ is سُجُفٌ. (TA.) [Hence] one says, أَرْخَى اللَّيْلُ سُجُوفَهُ ‡ *The night let down its curtains*. (TA.) — سِجْفٌ also signifies The *part that is behind a door* or *an entrance*. (O, TA.)

سَجَفٌ *Slenderness of the waist*: and *lankness of the belly*. (Ḳ.) One says فِى خَصْرِهِ سَجَفٌ *In his waist is slenderness*: and فِى بَطْنِهِ سَجَفٌ *In his belly is lankness*. (TA.) [See also سَجِفَتْ, in the first paragraph.]

سُجْفَةٌ *A period* (سَاعَةٌ) of the night; (Ḳ;) like سُدْفَةٌ. (TA.)

سِجَافٌ : see سِجْفٌ, in three places. — Hence, The *thing* [i. e. *edging*, such as a *fringe*, &c., (thus applied in the present day,)] *that is affixed to the borders of a garment*, or *piece of cloth*. (TA.)

سِجَافَةٌ : see سِجْفٌ. — Hence the saying of Umm-Selemeh to 'Áïsheh, وَجَّهْتِ سِجَافَتَهُ i. e. وَجْهَ سِجَافَتِهِ أَخَذْتِ وَجْهَهَا ‡ [i.e. هَتَكْتِ سِتْرَهُ and (as in the JM in art. وجه in explanation of وَجَّهْتِ سِدَافَتَهُ) *Thou hast rent open his veil*, or *covering*; both of these explanations meaning the same, as is said in the O and Ḳ in art. سدف]: but it is also related otherwise, i. e. وَجَّهْتِ سِدَافَتَهُ, which has the same meaning. (TA. [See art. سدف.])

بَيْتٌ مُسَجَّفٌ [*A tent*, or *chamber*,] *having a pair of curtains* (سِجْفَانِ) *upon its entrance*, or *door*. (Aṣ, TA.) El-Farezdaḳ applies this masc. sing. epithet to a pl. n., saying الحِجَالُ المُسَجَّفُ. (TA.)

سجل

1. سَجَلَ المَآءَ, (Ṣ, Ḳ,) inf. n. سَجْلٌ, (TA,) *He poured out*, or *forth, the water*, (Ṣ, Ḳ, JM, TA,) *continuously*. (JM, TA.) — Hence, سَجَلَ القُرْآنَ *He read*, or *recited, the Ḳur-án continuously*. (JM. [See also سَجْل.]) — See also 2: — and 4.

2. سَجَّلَ, inf. n. تَسْجِيلٌ, (Ṣ, Mṣb, Ḳ,) said of a judge, (Ṣ,) or ḳádee, (Mṣb,) *He wrote a* سِجِلّ [q. v.]: (Ṣ,* Ḳ:) or *he decided judicially, and recorded his sentence in the* سِجِلّ : (Mṣb:) and Mṭr says that ▾ إِسْجَال may be syn. with تَسْجِيل, signifying the *writing of* سِجِلَّات [pl. of سِجِلّ], though not found by him in the lexicons: (Ḥar p. 473:) [but I have found it, for Ṣgh says,] the إِسْجَال of the ḳádee and his تَسْجِيل are one [in meaning]. (O.) You say, سَجَّلَ بِهِ *He decided it judicially*, [*and recorded it in the* سِجِلّ;] or *he decreed it decisively*; so expl. by the Shereef: or, as in the 'Ináyeh, *he established it and recorded it* [*in the* سِجِلّ]. (TA.) And سَجَّلَ القَاضِى لِفُلَانٍ بِمَالِهِ *The ḳádee secured to such a one his property* [*by a judicial decision recorded in the* سِجِلّ]. (TA.) And سَجَّلَ عَلَيْهِ القَاضِى [*The ḳádee decided judicially against him, and recorded his sentence in the* سِجِلّ]. (Mgh.) — And سَجَّلَ عَلَيْهِ بِكَذَا † *He rendered him notorious by reason of such a thing, and stigmatized him with it*. (Z, TA.) — And سَجَلَ بِهِ *He threw it from above*; as also ▾ سَجَّلَ, inf. n. سَجْلٌ. (Ḳ.) — And سَجِلَ, inf. n. as above, *He* (a man, TA) *became affected with carnal appetite*. (Ḳ.)

3. ساجله, (Ḳ,) inf. n. مُسَاجَلَةٌ, (Ṣ, IB, TA,) [and app. سِجَالٌ also, (see سَجْلٌ,)] *He vied, competed*, or *contended for superiority, with him; emulated*, or *rivalled, him*; or *imitated him*; (Ṣ, IB,* Ḳ;) *doing like as he did*; (Ṣ, IB;) originally *in the drawing of water*; (Ṣ,* IB;) *each of them bringing forth in his* سَجْل [or *bucket*] *the like of what the other brought forth* [or *endeavouring to do so*]; *the one, of them, that desisted being overcome*: (IB:) and also, † *in running*: or *in watering*. (Ṣ.) Hence, فُلَانٌ يُسَاجِلُ فُلَانًا ‡ *Such a one vies with such a one, each of them producing*, [*of the evidences*] *of nobility, the like of what the other produces; the one, of them, that desists being overcome*. (IB.) El-Faḍl Ibn-'Abbás Ibn-'Otbeh Ibn-Abee-Lahab says,

مَنْ يُسَاجِلْنِى يُسَاجِلْ مَاجِدًا
يَمْلَأُ الدَّلْوَ إِلَى عَقْدِ الكَرَبْ

[*He who contends for superiority with me contends for superiority with one possessing glory, who fills the bucket to the tying of the rope that is attached to the middle of its cross-bars*]: and hence the saying, الحَرْبُ سِجَالٌ. (Ṣ. [See سَجْلٌ.])

4. اسجلهُ *He gave him a bucketful* (سَجْلًا) or *two bucketfuls* (سَجْلَيْنِ): (Ḳ:) or, as some say, † *he gave him much*. (TA.) — And اسجل الحَوْضَ *He filled the watering-trough, or tank*; (Ṣ, Ḳ;) as also † سَجَلَهُ. (JM.) — أُسْجِلَتِ البَهِيمَةُ مَعَ أُمِّهَا *The beast was sent forth, or set loose or free, with its mother*. (TA.) It is said in a trad., لَا تُسْجِلُوا أَنْعَامَكُمْ, meaning *Set not loose your cattle in men's fields of seed-produce*. (TA.) — And you say, اسجل النَّاسَ *He left*, or *left alone, the people*. (Ḳ.) — And اسجل لَهُمُ الأَمْرَ † *He made the affair free, or allowable, to them*. (Ḳ.) — And أَسْجَلْتُ الكَلَامَ † *I made the speech*, or *language, to be unrestricted*. (Ṣ.) = اسجل *He* (a man, TA) *abounded in goodness*, (Ḳ, TA,) *and beneficence, and gifts to men*. (TA.) = أَسْجَلْتُ لِلرَّجُلِ, inf. n. إِسْجَالٌ, *I wrote a writing for the man*. (Mṣb.) — See also 2.

6. تساجلوا *They vied, competed*, or *contended for superiority, one with another; emulated*, or *rivalled, one another*; or *imitated one another*; [originally, *in the drawing of water*: and hence, † *in other things*: (see 3:)] (Ṣ, TA:) and هُمَا يَتَسَاجَلَانِ *They two vie*, &c., *each with the other*. (Ḳ.)

7. انسجل *It* (water) *poured out*, or *forth*; or *became poured out*, or *forth*; (Ṣ, Ḳ;) [app., *continuously*: see 1.]

سَجْلٌ *A full bucket*: so accord. to Az and El-Fárábee and others: (MṢ:) or *a bucket containing water*, whether *little* or *much*: such as is empty is not called سَجْل nor ذَنُوب: (Ṣ:) or *a great bucket*: (Mṣb: [see also سَجِيل:]) or *a great bucket that is full* (Ḳ, TA) *of water*: (TA:) and *a bucketful*; *the quantity that fills a bucket*: (Ḳ:) it is of the masc. gender [though دَلْو (the most common word for "a bucket") is generally fem.]: (Ṣ, Ḳ:) pl. سِجَالٌ. (Ṣ.) — And [hence,] † *A share*, or *portion*; (Mṣb;) like دَلَاةٌ [which likewise originally signifies "a bucket"]. (Ṣ in art. دلو. [See also سَجِيل.]) And hence is derived the saying, الحَرْبُ سِجَالٌ, [as though meaning † *War is an affair of shares, or portions*;] i. e. *the victory in war is shared by turns* among the people [engaged therein]: (Mṣb:) [but it is implied in the Ṣ that it is from المُسَاجَلَةُ, and that سِجَال is here an inf. n. like مُسَاجَلَة, agreeably with analogy; and if so, the saying may be rendered *war is a contention for superiority*: (see 3:)] or the saying الحَرْبُ بَيْنَهُمْ سِجَالٌ means † [*War between them consists of portions, in such a manner that*] *a* سَجْل [or *portion*] *thereof is against these, and another is against these*: (Ḳ:) originating from the act of two men drawing water with two buckets from a well, each of them having [in his turn] a full bucket. (TA.) You say also, أَعْطَاهُ سَجْلَهُ مِنْ كَذَا ‡ *He gave him his share, or portion, of such a thing*; like as one says, ذَنُوبَهُ. (Ḥar p. 19.) The phrase لَهُمْ مِنَ المَجْدِ سَجْلٌ سَجِيلٌ † سَجِيل in the saying سَجْلٌ (Ḳ,* TA) has an intensive signification; (Ḳ, TA;) [the saying app. meaning † *They have, of glory, a large share*.] — Hence likewise, metaphorically applied to signify ‡ *A gift*: one says جَوَادٌ عَظِيمُ السَّجْلِ ‡ [*A bountiful man who is large in gift*]. (Ḥar ibid. [The first word in this saying is there written جَوَّاد.]) One says also, لَهُ بِرٌّ فَائِضُ السِّجَالِ † [*He has overflowing goodness* or *beneficence*]. (TA.) — Also † *A bountiful man*. (Abu-l-'Omeythil, Ḳ.) — And † *A great udder*: pl. سِجَالٌ and سُجُولٌ. (Ḳ.) = See also سِجِلٌّ, in two places.

سِجْلٌ: see the next paragraph.

سِجِلٌّ *A writing*; or *paper*, or *piece of skin, written upon*; (Ḳ,* TA;) as also سُجُلٌّ (TA) and † سِجْلٌ (Ḳ, TA) [and † سَجْلٌ, as appears from what follows]: or *a* طُومَار [meaning *a roll*, or *scroll*, or *the like*,] *for writing upon* or *written upon*: (Bḍ in xxi. 104:) and *a written statement of a contract* and *the like*; (Ḳ, TA;) i. e. (TA) i. q. صَكٌّ: (Ṣ, TA: [but see this word, which has also other meanings, and among them that here following, which is the most common meaning of سِجِلّ:]) the *record of a ḳádee*, or *judge, in which his sentence is written*; (Mṣb;) *a judicial record*: (Mgh:) [see also مَحْضَرٌ:] pl. سِجِلَّاتٌ. (Mṣb, Ḳ.) كَطَيِّ السِّجِلِّ لِلْكِتَابِ, in the Ḳur xxi. 104, means *Like the folding of the* طُومَار [expl. above] *for the purpose of writing* [thereon]: or *for what is to be written*: (Bḍ:) or *upon what is written*; (Bḍ,* Jel;) i. e., upon the written record [of the works] of the son of Adam at his death: (Jel:) or السِّجِلّ here has the third of the meanings here following: (Bḍ, Jel:) or the second thereof. (Bḍ.) — And *A writer*, or *scribe*: (Ḳ:) and so some explain it in the verse above cited. (TA.) — And السِّجِلُّ *A certain scribe of the Prophet*. (Ḳ.) — And *A certain angel*, (Ḳ,) *who folds the written statements of* [*men's*] *works*. (Bḍ ubi suprà.) — And, without the article, *A man*, in the Abyssinian language. (Ḳ.) In the verse cited above, I 'Ab read † السُّجُلّ, and explained it as meaning *A certain man*: but it is also said to mean *a certain angel*: and another reading is السُّجْلّ, a dial. var. mentioned above. (TA.)

السَّجَالُ a name for *The ewe*. (Ibn-'Abbád, O.) — And سَجَالِ سَجَالِ [i. e. سَجَالِ سَجَالِ, so in my MS. copy of the Ḳ, but in the CK سَجَالِ سَجَالِ,] is *A call to the ewe to be milked*. (Ibn-'Abbád, O, Ḳ.)

سَجُولٌ A she-goat *abounding in milk*: thus correctly, as in the O: in the copies of the Ḳ, in the place of عَنْز is put عَيْن [making the meaning to be a spring *abounding in water* or an eye *abounding in tears*]. (TA.)

سَجِيلٌ, applied to a bucket (دَلْو), *Large*, or *big*; as also with ة: (Ḳ:) or † سَجِيلَةٌ [alone, i. e. as a subst., rendered such by the affix ة,] signifies *a large*, or *big, bucket*. (Ṣ.) — And, applied to an udder (ضَرْع), *Long*: (Ṣ:) or *pendent and wide*; as also † أَسْجَلُ: (Ḳ:) or this latter, applied to an udder, but only of a sheep or goat, *wide, flaccid, and tossing about; striking the animal's hind legs, from behind*. (ISh, TA.) — And, with ة, applied to a testicle (خُصْيَة), *Flaccid and wide in the scrotum*. (Ḳ.) — See also سَجْل. — Also *Hard*, and *strong*. (Ḳ.) = And *A share*, or *portion*: (Ḳ:) IAạr says, it is of the measure فَعِيل from سَجْل meaning "a full bucket" [and likewise "a share, or portion"]; but, he adds, it does not please me. (TA.)

سَجَالَةٌ, in a testicle, *Flaccidity and wideness in the scrotum*. (K.)

سَجِيلَةٌ: see سَجِيل.

سِجِّيلٌ *Stones like lumps of dry*, or *tough, clay*: arabicized from سَنْگ وَگِل; (Ḳ, TA;) which are Pers. words, meaning "stone and clay;" the conjunction falling out in the arabicizing: (TA:) or *baked clay*: (Jel in xi. 84 and xv. 74 and cv. 4:) or *stones* (Ṣ, Ḳ) *of clay* (Ṣ) *baked by the fire of Hell, whereon were inscribed the names of the people* [*for whom they were destined*]: (Ṣ, Ḳ:) so in the Ḳur; as is indicated therein, in li. 33 and 34: (Ṣ:) or مِنْ سِجِّيلٍ in the Ḳur means مِنْ سِجِلٍّ, i. e. *of what had been written* [or *decreed*] *for them, that they should be punished therewith*; and سِجِّين means the *same as* سِجِّين, mentioned and expl. in the Ḳur lxxxiii. 8 and 9: (Ḳ:) AO says that مِنْ سِجِّيلٍ means *many and hard*; and that سِجِّين is syn. with سِجِّيل in this sense: (TA:) it is also said to be from سِجِّين meaning *Hell*; the ن being changed into ل: (Bḍ in xi. 84:) also, to be from أَسْجَلْتُهُ meaning "I sent forth him or it:" or from أَسْجَلْتُ meaning "I gave;" and to be from السَّجْل. (TA.) = Also *i. q.* دَائِمٌ; and so سِجِّينٌ [q. v.]. (L in art. سجن.)

سَجَنْجَلٌ *A mirror*: (Ṣ, Ḳ:) or *a Chinese mirror*: (MA:) [said to be] a Greek word (رُومِىّ),

(Ṣ, Ḳ,) arabicized: (Ṣ:) and some say زَجَنْجَل. (Az, TA.) [Pl., accord. to Freytag, سَنَاجِل.] — And † *Pieces such as are termed* سَبَائِك, *of silver;* (Ḳ,* TA;) as being likened to the mirror. (TA.) — And *Gold.* (Ḳ.) — And *Saffron.* (Ḳ.)

أَسْجَل: see سَجِيل. — سَجْلَآءُ, [the fem.,] applied to a she-camel, (Ṣ, Ḳ,) means † *Long in the udder:* (Ṣ:) or *big in the udder:* pl. سُجْل. (Ḳ.) — And, applied to a woman, † *Big in the posteriors:* (Ḳ:) pl. as above. (TA.)

مُسْجَل *Allowed,* or *made allowable, to every one;* (Ṣ, Ḳ;) *not denied to any one.* (Ṣ.) — Mohammad Ibn-El-Ḥanafeeyeh said, in explaining the words of the Ḳur [lv. 60], هَلْ جَزَآءُ ٱلْإِحْسَانِ إِلَّا ٱلْإِحْسَانُ [Shall the recompense of doing good be other than doing good?], هِىَ مُسْجَلَةٌ لِلْبَرِّ وَالفَاجِرِ, meaning † *It is unrestricted in its relation to the righteous and the unrighteous:* a righteous person is not made to be conditionally intended thereby, exclusively of an unrighteous. (Aṣ, Ṣ, TA.) — And one says, فَعَلْنَاهُ وَالدَّهْرُ مُسْجَلٌ † [*We did it when fortune was unrestricted*], i. e., *when no one feared any one.* (Ḳ.)

سجم

1. سَجَمَ الدَّمْعُ, (Ṣ, Ḳ, JM,) aor. ـُ, (JM,) inf. n. سُجُومٌ and سِجَامٌ; (Ṣ, Ḳ;) and ▼انسجم; (Ṣ, JM;) *The tears flowed:* (JM:) or *poured forth;* (TA in explanation of the latter verb;) and so the latter verb said of water. (TA.) — And سَجَمَ عَنِ الأَمْرِ ‡ *He held back from the thing,* or *affair, delaying to do it;* (A, Ḳ, TA;) and *shrank from it.* (A, TA.) ═ سَجَمَتِ العَيْنُ دَمْعَهَا, (Ṣ, Ḳ,*) aor. ـُ and ـِ inf. n. سَجْمٌ and سُجُومٌ and سَجَمَانٌ, *The eye shed its tears in drops:* or *shed its tears, little or much:* (Ḳ:) or *poured forth its tears.* (TA.) And in like manner, سَجَمَتِ السَّحَابَةُ المَآءَ ‡ *The cloud poured forth the water,* (Ḳ, TA,) *little or much:* (Ḳ:) and ▼اسجمت السحابة † *The cloud rained continually;* as also انْجمت: (IAạr, TA:) and اسجمت السَّمَآءُ *The sky poured forth* [rain]; as also انْجمت. (Ṣ.) And سَجَمَهُ [*He poured it forth,* app. meaning either دَمْعَهُ or المَآءَ]; and [so] ▼اسجمهُ; and [app. in an intensive sense] ▼سَجَّمَهُ, inf. n. تَسْجِيمٌ and تَسْجَامٌ. (Ḳ: omitted in the TA.)

2: see the last sentence above.

4: see **1**, last two sentences.

7: see **1**, first sentence. — انسجم الكَلَامُ ‡ *The language was,* or *became, rightly,* or *regularly, ordered, arranged,* or *disposed.* (TA.)

دَمْعٌ سَجْمٌ and ▼سِجَامٌ and ▼سُجُومٌ (TA) [are instances of inf. ns. used as epithets, (as is said in the TA of the first and second, to which the third is obviously similar,) meaning *Tears flowing,* or *pouring forth:* or the first may be more correctly rendered *tears shed in drops,* or simply *shed,* or *poured forth*].

سَجْمٌ *Tears:* (Ḳ:) or *flowing tears.* (TA.) — And *Water:* (so in copies of the Ḳ:) i. e. the *water of the sky:* (TA:) or *water that is apparent,* or *manifest.* (CḲ.) ═ Also The *leaves of the* [*tree called*] خِلَاف [q. v.]; (Ḳ;) to which broad and long arrow-heads are likened. (TA.)

سِجَامٌ an inf. n. used as an epithet: see سَجْمٌ. (TA.)

عَيْنٌ سَجُومٌ [*An eye shedding many tears*]. (Ṣ, TA.) — And سَحَابٌ سَجُومٌ † [*Clouds pouring forth much rain;* like سَجَّامٌ]. (TA.) — And نَاقَةٌ سَجُومٌ ‡ *A she-camel yielding much milk:* (A, TA:) or *that parts her hind legs on being milked, and raises her head:* (Ḳ, TA: [in the CḲ, سَعَطَتْ is erroneously put for سَعْعَتْ:]) as also ▼مِسْجَامٌ. (Ḳ.) — رَجُلٌ سَجُومٌ عَنِ المَكَارِمِ ‡ *A man who shrinks from generous actions.* (TA.)

سُجُومٌ: see سَجْمٌ. [As it is originally an inf. n., used as an epithet,] you say also أَعْيُنٌ سُجُومٌ *Eyes shedding tears in drops,* or simply *shedding tears,* or *pouring forth tears;* i. q. سَوَاجِمُ [pl. of ▼سَاجِمَةٌ fem. of ▼سَاجِمٌ, of which last, accord. to Freytag, سُجُومٌ is a pl.]. (TA.)

سَحَابٌ سَجَّامٌ † *Clouds pouring forth much rain.* (TA. [See also سَجُومٌ.])

سَاجِمٌ; and its fem., with ة: see سُجُومٌ.

سَاجُومٌ *A certain dye.* (Ḳ.)

أَسْجَمُ A camel *that does not utter the grumbling cry termed* رُغَآء: (Ṣ, TA:) or *that does not bray clearly:* (TA:) i. q. أَزْيَمُ. (Ḳ.)

مِسْجَامٌ: see سَجُومٌ.

أَرْضٌ مَسْجُومَةٌ ‡ *Land watered by rain.* (Ṣ, TA.)

سجن

1. سَجَنَهُ, (Ṣ, Mṣb, Ḳ,) aor. ـُ, inf. n. سَجْنٌ, (Ṣ, Mṣb,) *He imprisoned him.* (Ṣ, Mṣb, Ḳ.) — [Hence,] it is said in a trad., مَا شَىْءٌ أَحَقُّ بِطُولِ السَّجْنِ مِنْ لِسَانٍ † [*There is not anything more deserving of long restraint than a tongue*]. (L.) — And سَجَنَ الهَمَّ ‡ *He secreted anxiety; did not reveal it.* (L, Ḳ.) A poet says,

وَلَا تَسْجُنَنَّ الهَمَّ إِنَّ لِسَجْنِهِ
عَنَآءً وَحَمِّلْهُ المَهَارَى النَّوَاجِيَا

‡ [*And by no means secrete thou anxiety: verily to the secreting thereof pertains embarrassment: but load with it fleet camels of Mahreh*]. (L.)

2. سَجَّنَهُ, inf. n. تَسْجِينٌ, i. q. شَقَّقَهُ [*He cut it, or divided it, lengthwise; clave it; split it;* &c.]. (Ḳ.) — And سَجَّنَ النَّخْلَ *He made the palm-trees to be such as are termed* سِلْتِين [or سِجِين; i. e. *he dug at their feet trenches to conduct the water to them when it did not reach to them*]. (Ḳ.)

سِجْنٌ *A prison;* (Ṣ, L, Mṣb, Ḳ;) as also ▼سِجِّينٌ: (L:) pl. of the former سُجُونٌ. (Mgh, Mṣb.)

سَجِينٌ is syn. with ▼مَسْجُونٌ [*Imprisoned*]; pl. سُجَنَآءُ and سَجْنَى: and is applied to a female likewise, as also سَجِينَةٌ; pl. سَجْنَى and سَجَائِنُ. (Ḳ.)

سَجَّانٌ The *keeper of a prison.* (Ḳ.)

سِجِّينٌ: see سِجْنٌ. — [In the Ḳur lxxxiii. 7,] *A certain place in which is the record* [*of the deeds*] *of the wicked;* (Ṣ, L, Ḳ;) or, as I'Ab says, *in which are their registers:* AO says, it is of the measure فِعِّيل from السِّجْن, like الفِسِّيق from الفِسْق: (Ṣ, L:) or *a certain valley in Hell:* or *a certain stone,* [or *rock,*] (L, Ḳ,) *beneath,* (L,) or *in,* (Ḳ,) *the seventh earth:* (L, Ḳ:) [these explanations are given by those who hold that مَا سِجِّينٌ in the next verse is for مَا كِتَابُ سِجِّينٍ:] or it there means *a register comprising the deeds of the wicked,* (Bḍ, Jel,*) *of the jinn,* or *genii, and of mankind,* (Bḍ,) or *of the devils and the unbelievers:* (Jel:) or ما سجين in the next verse is for ما كتاب سجين, and the meaning is the *place,* (Bḍ, Jel,) *which is beneath the seventh earth, the abode of Iblees and his forces:* (Jel:) IAth says, it occurs in a trad. with the article ال; and without that article it is a proper name for *the fire* [*of Hell*], and hence the mention of it in the Ḳur lxxxiii. 7. (L.) [See also سِجِّيل.] ═ Also Anything *hard:* (L:) and *hard, vehement,* or *severe;* (Ṣ, L, Ḳ;) applied to a beating. (Ṣ, L.) — And *Continuing, lasting,* or *everlasting;* syn. دَائِمٌ; (L, Ḳ;) as also سِجِّيل: so accord. to El-Muärrij. (L. [See, again, سِجِّيل.]) ═ And i. q. عَلَانِيَةٌ: (L, Ḳ:) so in the saying, عَمِلَ ذٰلِكَ سِجِّينًا [*He did that openly,* or *publicly*]. (L.) ═ Also *Palm-trees* (نَخْل) *such as are termed* سِلْتِين (Aṣ, L, Ḳ) in the dial. of the people of El-Baḥreyn; (Aṣ, L;) [app. meaning that the latter word is of that dial.; for it is said that] the Arabs [app. the Arabs in general] say سِجِّين in the place of سِلْتِين, which is not Arabic: (L:) the palm-trees thus termed are *such as have trenches dug at their feet to conduct the water to them when it has not reached to them.* (L, and Ḳ in art. سلتن.)

أَنِيثٌ سَاجُونٌ *Iron such as is termed* أنيث [i. e. *female,* meaning *soft*]. (L.)

[مَسْجَنَةٌ, accord. to Freytag, The *act of imprisoning:* but it seems rather to be a word of the class of مَبْخَلَةٌ and مَجْبَنَةٌ &c., and to signify *a cause of imprisonment.*]

مَسْجُونٌ: see سَجِينٌ.

سجو

1. سَجَا, (Ṣ, Mṣb, Ḳ, &c.,) aor. يَسْجُو, (Ṣ, Mṣb,) inf. n. سُجُوٌّ (Ṣ, Ḳ, TA) and سَجْوٌ, (TA,) said of the night, (Fr, IAạr, Mṣb, TA,) &c., (TA,) *It was,* or *became, silent, quiet,* or *still:* (Fr, IAạr, Ṣ, Ḳ, TA:) and *dark:* (Fr, TA:) or *its darkness became extended:* (IAạr, TA:) or *it covered,* or *concealed, by its darkness.* (Mṣb, TA.) وَٱللَّيْلِ إِذَا سَجَا, in the Ḳur [xciii. 2], means *And the night when it becomes still, silent,* or *quiet*

(IAar, Zj, Ṣ, Jel:) or *when it covers with its darkness:* (Jel:) or *when its people become silent:* or *when its darkness becomes still:* from سَجَا البَحْرُ, inf. n. سُجُوٌّ, *The sea became calm.* (Bḍ.) And one says, سَجَتِ الرِّيحُ *The wind became still.* (TA.) — سَجَتِ النَّاقَةُ *The she-camel prolonged her* حَنِين [or *cry of yearning towards her young one*]. (Ḳ.) — See also 2.

2. سَجَّى *He covered* anything; as also ▼ اسجى, and ▼ سَجَا. (IAar, TA.) You say, سَجَّى المَيِّتَ, (Ṣ, Mgh, Mṣb,) inf. n. تَسْجِيَةٌ, (Ṣ, Mgh, Ḳ,) *He covered the dead person* (Mgh, Mṣb, Ḳ) with a garment, or piece of cloth, (Mgh, Mṣb,) and the like. (Mṣb.)

3. ساجاهُ, (Ḳ,) inf. n. مُسَاجَاةٌ, (TA,) *He touched it.* (Ḳ.) One says, أَتَانَا بِطَعَامٍ فَمَا سَاجَيْنَاهُ i. e. [*He brought us food, and*] *we did not touch it.* (AZ, TA.) — And *i. q.* عَالَجَهُ [meaning *He worked,* or *laboured, upon it,* or *at it;* &c.]. (Ḳ.) One says, هَلْ تُسَاجِي ضَيْعَةً تُعَالِجُهَا i. e. [meaning *Dost thou work,* or *labour, upon a landed estate?* or, probably, *dost thou cultivate a landed estate by the work,* or *labour, of others?*]. (Aboo-Málik, TA.)

4: see 2. — اسجت النَّاقَةُ *The she-camel had much milk.* (Ṣgh, Ḳ.)

[سِجْيٌ *A sincere companion* and *friend.* (Golius, from Meyd.)]

سَجِيَّةٌ *A nature;* or *a natural, a native,* or *an innate, disposition* or *temper* or *the like;* syn. خُلُقٌ, and طَبِيعَةٌ, (Ṣ,) or غَرِيزَةٌ: (Mṣb:) or *a faculty,* or *quality, firmly rooted in the mind, not easy of removal:* (MF:) pl. سَجَايَا. (Mṣb.)

نَاقَةٌ سَجْوَاءُ *A she-camel still,* or *quiet, when being milked.* (M, Ḳ.) — And *A she-camel whose fur is unruffled:* and شَاةٌ سَجْوَاءُ *a sheep whose wool is unruffled.* (TA.) — And رِيحٌ سَجْوَاءُ *A gentle wind.* (TA.) — And امْرَأَةٌ سَجْوَاءُ الطَّرْفِ i. e. ▼ سَاجِيَتُهُ, (Ḳ,) meaning *A woman languid,* or *languishing, in the eye.* (TA.)

سَاجٍ *Still, silent,* or *quiet:* thus applied to the sea [as meaning *calm,* or *unruffled*]. (Ṣ, Ḳ.) And لَيْلَةٌ سَاجِيَةٌ *A calm night, in which the wind is still, and such as is not dark:* (T, TA:) or *a night in which the cold has become allayed, and in which the wind and the clouds have become still, and which is not dark.* (M, TA.) And طَرْفٌ سَاجٍ *A still,* or *motionless, eye:* (Ṣ, Ḳ:) [or] عَيْنٌ سَاجِيَةٌ, accord. to IAar, means *an eye that has a languid,* or *languishing, look;* which is an accessory to beauty in women. (TA.) See also the next preceding paragraph.

سح

1. سَحَّ, (Ṣ, A, TA,) aor. ـُ, (Ṣ, TA,) inf. n. سَحٌّ, (Ṣ, Ḳ, &c.,) *He poured out,* or *forth,* (Ṣ, A, Ḳ,) water, (Ṣ, A,) &c.: (Ṣ:) or, accord. to IDrd, سَحٌّ signifies the *pouring out,* or *forth, in consecutive quantities:* or, accord. to the Mṣb, [but this art. is not in my copy of that work,] the *pouring forth much,* or *abundantly;* and the like is said in the Jámi' of Ḳz. (TA.) You say also, سَحَّتِ السَّمَآءُ مَطَرَهَا [*The sky poured forth its rain*]. (A, TA.) See also an ex. of the inf. n. voce سَحَّآءُ, below. — [Hence,] one says, اسْتَنْشَدْتُهُ قَصِيدَةً فَسَحَّهَا عَلَىَّ ‡ [*I asked him to recite an ode, and he poured it forth to me;* lit., *upon me*], inf. n. as above. (A.) — [Hence likewise,] سَحٌّ signifies also † The act of *flogging.* (Ḳ, TA.) One says, سَحَّهُ مِائَةَ سَوْطٍ, (Ṣ, TA,) aor. and inf. n. as above, (TA,) † *He inflicted upon him a hundred stripes of a whip.* (Ṣ, TA.) — And † The act of *beating, striking,* or *smiting.* (Ḳ.) — And † The act of *thrusting* or *piercing* [with a spear or the like]. (TA.) — سَحَّ, (Ṣ, A,) aor. ـِ, (Ṣ,) so says Fei, or, accord. to some, ـُ, agreeably with analogy, (TA,) inf. n. سَحٌّ (Ṣ, Ḳ) and سُحُوحٌ, (Ḳ,) or the former is the inf. n. of the trans. verb, and the latter is that of the intrans., (MF,) *It flowed from above;* (Ṣ, Ḳ;) [i. e. *it flowed down;*] said of water, (Ṣ,) and of rain, and of tears; (Ṣ, A;) as also ▼ تَسَحْسَحَ and ▼ تَسَحَّحَ: (Ḳ:) or سَحَّ signifies, or signifies also, *it poured out,* or *forth, vehemently:* (TA:) and ▼ تَسَحْسَحَ, *it flowed;* said of water, (Ṣ, TA,) and of a thing. (TA.) — [Hence,] سَحَّتِ الشَّاةُ, (Ṣ, A, TA,) and البَقَرَةُ, (TA,) aor. تَسِحُّ, (Ṣ, TA,) or, accord. to Lḥ and Z, تَسُحُّ, (TA,) inf. n. سَحٌّ, (Ḳ,) or سُحُوحٌ, (Ṣ, A,) or both, (TA,) and سُحُوحَةٌ, (Ṣ, Ibn-Et-Teiyánee, TA,) ‡ *The sheep* or *goat, and the animal of the ox-kind, became fat:* (AZ, AḤn, Ṣ, TA:) or *became fat to the utmost degree:* (Ḳ:) or *became fat so as to flow with grease:* (A:) or *became fat, but not to the utmost degree.* (TA.)

5: see 1, in the latter half of the paragraph.

7. انسحّ عَرَقًا *It* (a camel's arm-pit) *poured with sweat.* (TA.)

R. Q. 2. تَسَحْسَحَ: see 1, latter half, in two places.

سَحٌّ Rain *pouring abundantly and extensively:* (Ḳ in art. سبط:) and ▼ سَحْسَاحٌ (Ṣ, Ḳ) and ▼ سَحْسَحٌ (Ḳ) rain *pouring vehemently,* (Ṣ, Ḳ,* TA,) *paring the surface of the earth:* (TA:) and ▼ سَحُوحٌ, applied to rain that falls in large drops, *pouring much,* or *abundantly;* and also applied to a thundering cloud, (حَنَّانَةٌ, i. e. سَحَابَةٌ فِيهَا رَعْدٌ, [or, accord. to the Ṣ and A, to any cloud, سَحَابَةٌ,]) *pouring forth much rain:* (Ḥam p. 391: [in which it is said that in the latter case it may be proper; and in the former case, tropical:]) and ▼ عَيْنٌ سَحْسَاحَةٌ, so in a copy of the Ḳ, [and thus in my MS. copy of it,] in other copies ▼ سَحَّاحَةٌ, but the former is the right, (TA,) *an eye pouring forth tears abundantly,* or *much:* (Ḳ, TA:) and ▼ طَعْنَةٌ مُسَحْسِحَةٌ (Ṣ, TA) [*a spear-wound, or the like,*] *flowing* [*with blood*]. (TA.) — [Hence,] حَلِفٌ سَحٌّ † *A swearing in which oaths pour forth consecutively.* (L.) — Also † *i. q.* قَسْبٌ [i. e. *Dry,* or *tough, dates, that crumble in the mouth and have hard stones*]; (Ḳ:) Az relates his having heard the Baḥránees thus term a certain kind of قَسْب: (TA:) or ‡ *scattered dates:* (A:) or ‡ *dry,* or *tough, dates,* (Ḳ, TA,) *not sprinkled with water* [in order that they may stick together, for thus they do for this purpose, or they sprinkle the palm-leaf-receptacle of the dates for this purpose], (TA,) *scattered* (Ḳ, TA) *upon the ground, not collected in a receptacle, and not packed;* (TA;) as also ▼ سُحٌّ, (IDrd, Ḳ,) which is of the dial. of El-Yemen. (IDrd.)

سُحٌّ: see what next precedes.

سَحَاحٌ The *air.* (Fr, T, O, Ḳ.) [See also سُخَاخٌ, which is perhaps a mistranscription.]

سَحُوحٌ: see سَحٌّ.

سَحَّآءُ a fem. epithet, an instance of فَعْلَآءُ having no أَفْعَلُ, [i. e. not having أَسَحُّ for the masc. form], occurring in a trad., in which it is said, يَمِينُ ٱللّٰهِ سَحَّآءُ لَا يَغِيضُهَا شَىْءٌ ٱللَّيْلَ وَٱلنَّهَارَ (TA,) (A, TA) i. e. ‡ *The right hand of God is continually pouring with gifts, nothing will render it deficient, night and day:* or, as some relate it, the phrase is ▼ يَمِينُ ٱللّٰهِ مَلْأَى سَحًّا [*the right hand of God is full, with pouring forth*]; the last word being with tenween, as an inf. n.: it is thus likened to the abundant source that is not diminished by drawing from it, nor by descending into it and filling the bucket. (TA.) — You say also غَارَةٌ سَحَّآءُ (A, TA) ‡ [*An incursion into the territory of an enemy*] *that pours calamity upon people with sudden impetuosity.* (TA.) — [Golius explains سَحَّآءُ, on the authority of Meyd, as signifying † *A hot wind:* it is probably a mistranscription for سَخْنَآءُ.]

سَحَّاحَةٌ: see سَحٌّ.

سَحْسَحٌ: see سَحٌّ. — Also, applied to land (أَرْض), † *Wide,* or *spacious:* but IDrd says, I know not the truth of this. (TA.) — Also, and ▼ سَحْسَحَةٌ, *A court,* or *a spacious portion in which is no building* or *that is vacant,* of a house, (Ṣ, Ḳ, TA,) and of a place of alighting, or of a settlement, or of a collection of houses or tents: the former expl. by IAar as meaning a man's *quarter,* or *tract,* in which he alights. (TA.)

سَحْسَحَةٌ: see what next precedes.

سَحْسَاحٌ; and its fem., with ة: see سَحٌّ: — and see also the fem. in what here follows.

شَاةٌ سَاحٌّ, (A, Ḳ,) after the manner of a possessive noun, (TA,) and سَاحَّةٌ, (Ḳ,) the latter occurring in a trad., or, as some relate it, ▼ سَحْسَاحَةٌ, which means the same, (TA,) ‡ *A sheep,* or *goat, that is fat:* (Ṣ, TA: but in the former, only a pl., as applied to sheep or goats, is mentioned; namely, the first of the pls. below:) or *that flows with grease by reason of its fatness:* (A:) or *full of fat:* (TA:) or *fat in the utmost degree:* (Ḳ:) [or *fat, but not in the utmost degree;* for] one says مَهْزُولٌ; then مُنْقٍ when it has become a little fat: then شَنُونٌ; then سَمِينٌ; then سَاحٌّ; and then مُتْرَطِمٌ, which means fat in the utmost degree: (Aboo-Ma'add El-Kilábee, TA:) pl. سُحَّاحٌ, (Th, Ṣ, L,) thus in the handwriting of J, and mentioned by Aboo-Mis-ḥal, (TA,) or سِحَاحٌ (IḲṭṭ, Ḳ) and سُحَّاحٌ, which is extr. [in form]. (Ḳ.) And لَحْمٌ سَاحٌّ † *Fat flesh-meat; as though, by reason of its fatness, it poured forth grease.* (Aṣ, Ṣ, TA.)

فَرَسٌ مِسَحٌّ ‡ *A swift horse;* (Ḳz, Ḳ, TA;) *as though it poured forth running;* (Ṣ, Ḳz, TA;) likened to rain in swiftness. (TA.)

طَعْنَةٌ مُسْحَسِحَةٌ: see سَحٌّ.

سحب

1. سَحَبَهُ, (Ṣ, A, Mṣb, Ḳ,) aor. َ, (Mṣb, Ḳ,) inf. n. سَحْبٌ, (Mṣb, TA,) *He dragged it,* or *drew it along,* (Ṣ, A, Mṣb, Ḳ,) namely, his ذَيْل [or skirt], (Ṣ,) or a thing, such as a garment &c., (TA,) upon the ground. (Mṣb, Ḳ, TA.) One says of a woman, تَسْحَبُ ذَيْلَهَا [*She drags,* or *draws along, her skirt* upon the ground]. (TA.) And سَحَبَتِ الرِّيحُ التُّرَابَ [*The wind drew along the dust* upon the ground]. (TA.) — [Hence,] سَحَبَتِ الرِّيَاحُ أَذْيَالَهَا ‡ [*The winds dragged their skirts* upon the ground; i. e., *blew so as to efface the traces upon the ground*]. (A: in the TA, الرِّيحُ.) And اِسْحَبْ ذَيْلَكَ عَلَى مَا كَانَ مِنِّى ‡ [*Drag thy skirt over that which has proceeded from me;* i. e. *efface what has proceeded from me,* as when a person dragging his skirt effaces the traces upon the sand or dust over which he walks]. (A, TA.) And مَا اسْتَبْقَى رَجُلٌ وُدَّ صَاحِبِهِ بِمِثْلِ مَا سَحَبَ الذَّيْلَ عَلَى مَعَايِبِهِ ‡ [*A man has not preserved,* or *kept alive, the love,* or *affection, of his companion with anything that is* in its effect *like his dragging the skirt over his vices,* or *faults*]. (A, TA.) — [Hence likewise, as will be shown by what next follows,] سَحِبَ, aor. َ, (Ḳ, TA,) inf. n. as above, (Ṣ, TA,) means also ‡ *He ate and drank vehemently.* (Ṣ, Ḳ, TA.)

4. أَسْحَبْتُ مِنَ الطَّعَامِ وَالشَّرَابِ ‡ *I took,* or *ate and drank, much of the food and beverage;* as also ▼ تَسَحَّبْتُ: because it is the habit of the glutton to draw and appropriate to himself the victuals [and beverages]. (A, TA.)

5: see 4. — تسحّب عَلَيْهِ † *He acted,* or *behaved, towards him with boldness,* or *presumptuousness;* or *did so confiding in his love,* or *affection:* (Az, Ṣ, MA, TA:) or *with coquettishness, and feigned opposition.* (Az,* MA, TA.*) — تَسَحَّبَتْ فِى حَقِّهِ, occurring in a trad. of Sa'eed and [a woman named] Arwà, means † *She took his right,* or *rightful property, by force, and annexed it to her own, and to her land.* (TA.)

7. انسحب *It was,* or *became, dragged,* or *drawn along,* (Ṣ, A, Mṣb, Ḳ,) upon the ground: (Mṣb, Ḳ:) said of one's skirt, (Ṣ,) or of a thing, such as a garment &c. (TA.) — [Hence,] اِنْسَحَبَتْ فِيهَا ذَلَاذِلُ الرِّيحِ ‡ [*The skirts of the wind were,* or *became, dragged upon it,* i. e., upon the ground (الأَرْض), so as to efface the traces upon it]. (A, TA.)

سُحْبَةٌ i. q. غِشَاوَةٌ [app. as meaning particularly *A covering,* or *film,* upon the eye: expl. by Freytag, from the Deewán el-Hudhaleeyeen, as meaning *oculorum caligo*]. (Ḳ.) — And *Remains of water in a pool left by a torrent;* as also ▼ سُحَابَةٌ: (Ḳ, TA:) dim. of the former ▼ سُحَيْبَةٌ. (TA.)

رَجُلٌ سَحْبَانُ *A man who takes,* or *carries,* or *sweeps, away everything by which he passes.* (Ḳ.) — [Golius explains سَحْبَانُ, as on the authority of Meyd, as meaning *A portion of water remaining in a skin or other thing:* but I think that this is a mistranscription for سُحْبَةٌ.]

سَحَابٌ [termed in the Ṣ and Ḳ pl. of سَحَابَةٌ, as also سُحُبٌ and سَحَائِبُ,] is, accord. to Aṣ, [correctly,] a coll. gen. n., used alike as masc. and fem. and sing. and pl.; (MF, TA;) and سَحَابَةٌ is its n. un.; (MF, Mṣb,* TA;) and سُحُبٌ is pl. of سَحَابٌ or of سَحَابَةٌ; (L, Mṣb,* MF, TA;) it may be pl. of either of these; (L, MF, TA;) and سَحَائِبُ is pl. of سَحَابَةٌ absolutely, and of سَحَابٌ when used as fem.: (MF, TA:) it signifies *Clouds* [or *a collection of clouds*]; (Ṣ, Ḳ, KL, TA, &c.;) and [*clouds*] *from which the rain comes:* (TA:) so called because drawn along in the air; (Mṣb, TA;) or because they draw along one another; or because the winds draw them along; (TA;) or because they draw along their fringes. (TA in art. حبو.) One says, مَطَرَتْهُمُ السَّحَابَةُ [*The cloud rained upon them*]. (A.) — [Hence,] أَقَمْتُ عِنْدَهُ سَحَابَةَ نَهَارِى ‡ *I remained at his abode the whole of my day:* originally said in relation to a cloudy day; and then proverbially used in relation to any day. (A, TA.) And مَا زِلْتُ أَفْعَلُهُ سَحَابَةَ يَوْمِى ‡ *I ceased not to do it the whole of my day.* (Ḳ,* TA.) — مَآءُ السَّحَابِ [properly *The water of the clouds*] is a term for † *wine.* (TA in art. جفن.) — السَّحَابُ is a name of † *The Prophet's turban;* (Mgh, TA:) it was thus called as being likened to the سحاب of the rain because of its being drawn along in the air. (TA.) — Also the name of *A sword of Ḍirar Ibn-El-Khaṭṭáb.* (Ḳ.)

سَحَابَةٌ n. un. of سَحَابٌ [q. v.]. (Aṣ, Mṣb, &c.)

سُحَابَةٌ: see سُحْبَةٌ.

سُحَيْبَةٌ dim. of سُحْبَةٌ, q. v. (TA.)

أُسْحُوبٌ ‡ A man *who eats and drinks much,* (Ṣ, A,) or *vehemently:* (Ḳ:) Az says that the word known to him in the former sense is أُسْحُوتٌ, with ت; but that perhaps اسحوب is allowable. (L, TA.)

[مَسْحَبٌ *A place of dragging,* or *drawing along,* of a skirt, or garment, &c., upon the ground: pl. مَسَاحِبُ: see Ḥar p. 78.]

سحت

1. سَحَتَهُ, [aor. َ, inf. n. سَحْتٌ,] *He extirpated it, eradicated it, exterminated it,* or *destroyed it utterly;* as also ▼ اسحتهُ: (Ṣ, Ḳ, TA:) both signify *he,* or *it, made it to go, go away, pass away,* or *depart; made away with it, did away with it, made an end of it,* or *destroyed it;* namely, a man's property: and the latter, *he destroyed utterly what he* (a man) *possessed.* (TA.) You say, سَحَتَ الخِتَانَ, inf. n. as above; and ▼ اسحتهُ; *He performed the circumcision so as to remove the prepuce utterly.* (TA.) And سَحَتَ شَعَرَهُ *He removed his hair utterly* in shaving and cutting: (A:) and سَحَتَ رَأْسَهُ, inf. n. as above; and ▼ اسحتهُ; *He shaved his head so as to remove the hair utterly.* (Lḥ, TA.) And سَحَتَ الشَّحْمَ عَنِ اللَّحْمِ, (aor. as above, Ḳ,) *He peeled off the fat from the flesh;* (Ṣ, A, Ḳ;) as also سَحَفَهُ. (Ṣ.) And سَحَتَ شَيْئًا, aor. and inf. n. as above, *He peeled,* or *peeled off, a thing by little and little.* (L, TA.) And سَحَتَ وَجْهَ الأَرْضِ *He,* or *it, effaced the traces,* or *the like, upon the surface of the earth.* (A, TA.) فَيَسْحَتَكُمْ بِعَذَابٍ, in the Ḳur xx. 64, means *Lest He destroy you* [*by a punishment*], (Bḍ, Jel,) or *utterly destroy you;* (Bḍ;) and some read ▼ فَيُسْحِتَكُمْ, (Ṣ, Bḍ, Jel,) which means the same; (Bḍ, Jel;) this being of the dial. of Nejd and Temeem; and the former, of the dial. of El-Ḥijáz: (Bḍ:) or ‡ *lest He harass,* or *distress,* or *afflict, you* [*by a punishment*]: (A, TA:) or † *lest He pare you* [*from the surface of the earth thereby*]. (TA.) سَحَتْنَاهُمْ and ▼ أَسْحَتْنَاهُمْ both signify ‡ *We harassed,* or *distressed,* or *afflicted, them:* and سَحَتَهُمْ [and ▼ أَسْحَتَهُمْ], *He slaughtered them.* (TA.) — See also the next paragraph, in two places.

4: see above, in six places. — [Hence,] أَسْحَتَ, said of a man, † *His property went away.* (Lḥ, TA.) — اسحت *He gained,* or *earned, what is termed* سُحْتٌ [i. e. *gain that was unlawful,* &c.]; (Ṣ, A, Ḳ;) as also ▼ سَحَتَ: (Ḳ:) or *he earned little.* (Mṣb.) You say, اسحت فِى تِجَارَتِهِ *He earned such gain in his traffic;* (Ṣ, A;) as also ▼ سَحَتَ فِيهَا: (TA:) or *he earned little therein;* and so اسحت تِجَارَتَهُ. (Mṣb.) And اسحتت تِجَارَتُهُ *His traffic was,* or *became, disapproved, abominable,* or *foul, and unlawful.* (Ḳ.)

سَحْتٌ inf. n. of 1 [q. v.]. (L, TA.) — Also † *Vehemence of eating and drinking.* (TA.) — And † *Punishment, castigation,* or *chastisement.* (TA.) — بَرْدٌ سَحْتٌ, (Ḳ,) [as also سَخْتٌ, q. v.,] and صَادِقٌ, i. q. بَحْتٌ, and نَحْتٌ, (TA,) [and نَخْتٌ,] [i. e. † *Vehement,* or *intense, cold:* see بَحْتٌ &c.]. (Ḳ.) — See also سُحُوتٌ: — and مَسْحُوتٌ: — and see the paragraph here following, in two places.

سُحْتٌ (Ṣ, A, Mṣb, Ḳ) and ▼ سُحُتٌ, (Ṣ, Mṣb, Ḳ,) the former a contraction of the latter, (Mṣb,) *A thing that is forbidden, prohibited,* or *unlawful;* (Ṣ, A, Ḳ;) and (so in the A, but in the Ḳ "or") *what is disapproved, abominable,* or *foul, of gains,* (A, Ḳ, TA,) *that occasions disgrace* (Ḳ, TA) *and bad repute;* as the price of a dog, and of wine, and of a pig; (TA;) *any pro-*

perty that is forbidden, not lawful to be gained (Mṣb, TA) *nor to be eaten;* (Mṣb;) *anything forbidden,* or *unlawful, and of bad repute:* sometimes it means what is disapproved; and sometimes, what is unlawful; the context showing in which sense it is used: and it is also applied to signify *a bribe that is given to a judge* or *the like:* so called because it cuts off blessing: (TA:) in the Ḳur v. 46, some read لِلسُّحْتِ; and some, لِلسُّحُتِ; (Bḍ, TA;) and it has also been read as the inf. n., ▼ لِلسَّحْتِ: (Bḍ:) the pl. is أَسْحَاتٌ. (Ḳ.) — Also *Little,* or *small, in quantity* or *number; paltry, mean,* or *inconsiderable.* (Mṣb.) — مَالُهُ سُحْتٌ or ▼ سَحْتٌ (accord. to different copies of the Ḳ [the former the better known]) *His property may be taken and destroyed with impunity:* and in like manner, دَمُهُ سُحْتٌ *His blood may be shed with impunity.* (Ḳ,* TA.) — See also مَسْحُوتٌ.

سُحُتٌ: see the next preceding paragraph.

سَحْتِىٌّ: see what next follows.

سُحْتُوتٌ An *old and worn-out* garment or piece of cloth; as also ▼ سَحْتٌ and ▼ سَحْتِىٌّ. (Ḳ.) — [A mess of] سَوِيق [or meal of parched barley, &c.,] *having little grease* or *gravy* [*mixed with it*]; as also ▼ سِحْتِيتٌ; (Ḳ;) the latter a dial. var. of سِخْتِيتٌ [q. v.]. (TA.) — And A desert (مَفَازَةٌ) *of which the earth is soft.* (Ḳ.)

سِحْتِيتٌ: see the next preceding paragraph.

سَحِيتٌ: see مَسْحُوتٌ, in two places. — سَحَابَةٌ سَحِيتَةٌ *A cloud that carries away,* or *sweeps away, that by which it passes.* (TA.)

عَامٌ أَسْحَتُ, and أَرْضٌ سَحْتَاةٌ, † *A year,* and *a land, in which is no pasture.* (Ḳ.)

أُسْحُوتٌ: } see the following paragraph.
مُسْحَتٌ: }

مَسْحُوتٌ † *Property* (مَالٌ) *made to go away,* or *depart; made away with, made an end of,* or *destroyed;* as also ▼ مُسْحَتٌ, (Ṣ, Ḳ,) as in a verse cited voce مُجَلَّفٌ, (Ṣ,) and ▼ سُحْتٌ and ▼ سَحِيتٌ. (Ḳ.) — † A man *who eats and drinks vehemently;* as also ▼ سُحْتٌ and ▼ سَحِيتٌ: (TA in the present art.:) and ▼ أُسْحُوتٌ signifies [the same, or] a man *who eats and drinks much.* (Az, TA voce أُسْخُوبٌ, q. v.) And مَسْحُوتُ الجَوْفِ † A man (Ṣ) *who does not become satiated:* (Ṣ, Ḳ:) *having a capacious belly,* (Ḳ, TA,) *and who does not become satiated with food:* (TA:) and as some say, *hungry:* (TA:) and one *who suffers much from indigestion.* (Ḳ, TA.) And مَسْحُوتُ المَعِدَةِ ‡ A man *having a greedy,* or *gluttonous, stomach.* (A, TA.)

سحج

1. سَحَجَهُ, (Ṣ, A, Ḳ, TA,) aor. ـَ, (Ḳ, TA,) inf. n. سَحْجٌ, (TA,) *He abraded,* or *otherwise removed, its outer integument,* or *superficial part;* (Ṣ, A, Ḳ, TA;) relating to one's skin; (Ṣ, A, TA:) and *he scratched him;* or *wounded him in the outer skin:* also *he rubbed it,* namely, a thing, with another thing, *so as to abrade,* or *remove, its superficial part:* and *it,* namely, a thing, hitting another thing, *abraded from it a little of its superficial part;* as when a thing hits the solid hoof previously to [that state of attenuation and abrasion which is termed] الوَجَى. (TA.) You say, سَحَجْتُ جِلْدَهُ *I abraded,* or *removed, the outer integument* [i. e. *the cuticle*] *of his skin.* (Ṣ.) And أَصَابَهُ شَىْءٌ فَسَحَجَ وَجْهَهُ [*A thing hit him, and abraded the cuticle of his face*]. (Ṣ.) And سَحَجَ العُودَ بِالمِبْرَدِ *He abraded the outer part of the wood,* or *piece of wood,* or *stick, with the file.* (TA.) And يَسْحَجُ الأَرْضَ بِخُفِّهِ, referring to a camel, (Ṣ, Ḳ, TA,) *He pares the surface of the ground with his foot, so that he is not slow in becoming attenuated and abraded in the sole.* (TA.) And سَحَجَتِ الرِّيَاحُ الأَرْضَ [*The winds pared the surface of the earth, removing the dust and pebbles:* like سَهَجَت]. (A.) — Also *He bit him so as to make a mark,* or *marks, upon him;* [or *so as to lacerate his skin;*] used especially in relation to wild asses; and so ▼ سَحَّجَهُ, [but in an intensive sense, i. e. *he so bit him much,* or *many times,* (see مُسَحَّجٌ,)] inf. n. تَسْحِيجٌ and مُسَحَّجٌ [of which latter see an ex. in the next paragraph]. (TA.) — سَحْجٌ also signifies The *combing gently upon the skin of the head:* (Ḳ, TA:) [*combing* the hair *with a gentle pressure upon the skin of the head:*] one says, سَحَجَ شَعَرَهُ بِالمُشْطِ, inf. n. سَحْجٌ, *He combed his hair* [*pressing the comb*] *gently* [*upon the skin of his head*]. (TA.) — And The *going quickly* [as though paring the surface of the earth with the feet, or making marks upon it]. (O, Ḳ.) You say, مَرَّ يَسْحَجُ *He passed along going quickly:* and [so] يَسْحَجُ السَّيْرَ. (O, TA.) — And *A running* of beasts *falling short of such as is vehement.* (Ḳ.) — And [hence, app.,] سَحَجَ الأَيْمَانَ, (TA,) aor. as above, (Ḳ, TA,) † *He made the oaths to follow one another with little,* or *no, interruption.* (Ḳ,* TA.) = See also 7.

2. سَحَّجَهُ, (Ṣ, Ḳ,) inf. n. تَسْحِيجٌ and مُسَحَّجٌ, [of which latter, see an ex. in what follows,] (TA,) *He abraded,* or *otherwise removed, its outer integument,* or *superficial part, much,* or *often.* (Ṣ, Ḳ.) — See also 1. An ex. of the latter inf. n. occurs in the following hemistich of the "Jeemeeyeh" of El-'Ajjáj:

جَأْبًا تَرَى بِلِيتِهِ مُسَحَّجَا

[*A bulky,* or *strong, wild ass, in the side of whose neck thou seest much biting,* or *lacerating of the skin, that has made marks upon it*]: thus heard by AḤát from the mouth of AZ, and thus recited by the former to Aṣ, who disallowed it, and said, تَلِيلَهُ [i. e. *whose neck,* or *cheek,* thou seest to be much bitten, &c., instead of بِلِيتِهِ], but abstained from objecting after AḤát had adduced other exs. [of similar inf. ns.], and among them the saying in the Ḳur [xxxiv. 18], وَمَزَّقْنَاهُمْ كُلَّ مُمَزَّقٍ: Az says that مُسَحَّجًا is here made an inf. n., like تَسْحِيجًا. (TA.)

5. تَسَحَّجَ *It had its outer integument,* or *superficial part, abraded,* or *otherwise removed, much,* or *often:* (Ṣ, Ḳ:) said of the skin [&c.]. (Ṣ.)

7. انسحج *It had its outer integument,* or *superficial part, abraded,* or *otherwise removed:* (Ṣ, Ḳ:) said of the skin: (Ṣ:) [and it seems from the phrase سَحَجَ الفَخِذَيْنِ occurring in the O and Ḳ in art. بذح, that ▼ سَحِجَ, inf. n. سَحَجٌ, may signify the same: but سَحَجَ may there be a mistranscription for سَحْجُ.] One says, انْسَحَجَ جِلْدُهُ مِنْ شَىْءٍ مَرَّ بِهِ *His skin had its cuticle abraded in consequence of a thing that passed by him.* (TA.)

سَحْجٌ inf. n. of سَحَجَ. (TA.) — And [hence, *Dysentery,* or *the like;* because attended by abrasion, or excoriation, of the colon;] *a certain disease of the bowels;* (PṢ;) *an abrading disease in the belly.* (TA.) You say, بِهِ سَحْجٌ (Ṣ) i. e. *In him is the disease above mentioned.* (PṢ.)

سَحَّاجٌ: see سَحُوجٌ.

سَحِيجٌ *Having its outer integument,* or *superficial part, abraded,* or *otherwise removed;* as also ▼ مَسْحُوجٌ. (TA.)

سَحُوجٌ A camel *that pares the surface of the ground with his foot,* (Ṣ,* Ḳ,* TA,) *so that he is not slow in becoming attenuated and abraded in the sole.* (TA.) — Also † A man *who makes oaths to follow one another with little,* or *no, interruption:* (TA:) and so ▼ مِسْحَاجٌ and ▼ سَحَّاجٌ applied to a woman. (Ḳ,* TA.) And حَلِفٌ سَحَّاجٌ † *A swearing in which the oaths are made so to follow one another.* (TA.)

[سَاحِجٌ act. part. n. of سَحَجَ: fem. with ة: pl. of the fem. سَوَاحِجُ. Hence,] رِيَاحٌ سَوَاحِجُ [*Winds paring,* or *that pare, the surface of the earth, removing the dust and pebbles*]. (A, TA.)

[مَسْحَجٌ *A place of abrasion,* &c.: pl. مَسَاحِجُ. — Hence,] one says, of an ass, (A,) i. e. a wild ass, (TA,) عَلَيْهِ المَسَاحِجُ *Upon him are the marks,* or *scars, of the biting of other asses.* (A, TA.)

مِسْحَجٌ The [*instrument called*] مِبْرَاة *with which one pares,* or *shapes, wood.* (O, Ḳ.) — [And hence, app., A rain *that is as though it pared the surface of the earth.* Accord. to Freytag, مَسْحَجٌ occurs in this sense in the Deewán of Jereer: pl. مَسَاحِجُ: but the correct word is evidently مِسْحَجٌ.] — Also, and ▼ مِسْحَاجٌ, (O, Ḳ, TA,) A wild ass *that bites* [*other asses*] *much,* or *frequently:* (TA:) [or each signifies, though not so expl. in the TA,] an ass [i. e. a wild ass] *that runs a pace falling short of such as is vehement.* (O, Ḳ.)

مُسَحَّجٌ An ass [i. e. a wild ass] *much bitten.* (Ṣ, A, Ḳ.) — [See also 2.]

سَحَّاج : see مِسْحَج :— and see also مِسْحَاج.

سَحِيج : see مَسْحُوج.

سحر

1. سَحَرَهُ *He, or it, hit, or hurt, his* سَحْر [or *lungs*, &c.], (Mgh, TA,) or *his* سُحْرَة [i. e. *heart*]. (TA.) —— And the same, aor. ـَ , inf. n. سَحْر, (T, TA,) [said to be] the only instance of a pret. and aor. and inf. n. of these measures except the verb فَعَلَ, aor. يَفْعَلُ, inf. n. فَعْل, (MF,) ‡ *He turned it,* (T,) or *him,* (TA,) عَنْ وَجْهِهِ [*from its,* or *his, course,* or *way,* or *manner of being*]: and hence other significations here following. (T, TA. [Accord. to the T, this seems to be proper; but accord. to the A, tropical.]) In this sense the verb is used in the Ḳur xxiii. 91. (Fr.) The Arabs say to a man, مَا سَحَرَكَ عَنْ وَجْهِ كَذَا وَكَذَا ‡ *What has turned thee from such and such a course?* (Yoo.) أُفِكَ and سُحِرَ are syn. [as meaning ‡ *He was turned* from his course &c.]. (TA.) —— And ‡ *He turned him from hatred to love.* (TA.) —— Hence, (TA,) aor. and inf. n. as above, (T, Ṣ, TA,) and inf. n. also سِحْر, (KL, TA,) ‡ *He enchanted,* or *fascinated, him,* or *it;* (Ṣ,* Ḳ,* KL, PṢ;) and so ↓ سَحَّرَهُ (MA, TA) [in an intensive or a frequentative sense, meaning *he enchanted,* or *fascinated, him,* or *it, much,* or (as shown by an explanation of its pass. part. n.) *time after time*]: and سَحَرَ عَيْنَهُ *He enchanted,* or *fascinated, his eye.* (MA.) You say, سَحَرَ الشَّىْءَ عَنْ وَجْهِهِ, meaning ‡ *He* (an enchanter, سَاحِر) *apparently turned the thing from its proper manner of being, making what was false to appear in the form of the true, or real; causing the thing to be imagined different from what it really was.* (T, TA. [See سِحْر, below.]) And المَرْأَةُ تَسْحَرُ النَّاسَ بِعَيْنِهَا ‡ [*The woman enchants,* or *fascinates, men by her eye*]. (A.) And سَحَرَهُ بِكَلَامِهِ † *He caused him,* or *enticed him, to incline to him by his soft,* or *elegant, speech, and by the beauty of its composition.* (Mṣb.) —— ‡ *He deceived, deluded, beguiled, circumvented,* or *outwitted, him;* (Ṣ, Mgh, Ḳ;*) as also ↓ سَحَّرَهُ, [but app. in an intensive or a frequentative sense,] (Ḳ, TA,) inf. n. تَسْحِير. (TA. [Accord. to the Mgh, the former verb in this sense seems to be derived from the same verb in the first of the senses expl. in this art.]) —— And in like manner, † *He diverted him* [with a thing], *as one diverts a child with food, that he may be contented, and not want milk;* syn. عَلَّلَهُ; as also ↓ سَحَّرَهُ, inf. n. تَسْحِير. (Ṣ, TA.) One says, سَحَرَهُ بِالطَّعَامِ وَالشَّرَابِ, and ↓ سَحَّرَهُ, † *He fed him, and diverted him* [*from the feeling of want*], *with meat and drink.* (TA.) —— And سَحَرْتُ الفِضَّةَ † *I gilded the silver.* (Ḥam p. 601.) —— سَحْر is also *syn. with* فَسَادٌ [as quasi-inf. n. of أَفْسَدَ, as is indicated in the TA; thus signifying The act of *corrupting, marring, spoiling,* &c.: see the pass. part. n. مَسْحُور]. (TA.) [Hence,] one says, سَحَرَ المَطَرُ الطِّينَ and التُّرَابَ, † *The rain spoiled the clay, and the earth,* or *dust, so that it was not fit for use.* (TA.) —— And one says of the adhesion of the lungs to the side by reason of thirst, يَسْحَرُ أَلْبَانَ الغَنَمِ, meaning † *It causes the milk of the sheep,* or *goats, to descend before bringing forth.* (TA.) ═══ سَحَرَ also signifies *He went, or removed, to a distance,* or *far away;* syn. تَبَاعَدَ; (T, Ḳ;) said of a man. (T, TA.) ═══ سَحِرَ, aor. ـَ , † *He went forth early in the morning, in the first part of the day;* or *between the time of the prayer of daybreak and sunrise;* syn. بَكَّرَ. (O, Ḳ. [See also 4.])

2. سَحَّرَ, inf. n. تَسْحِير: see 1, in four places. —— Also ‡ *He fed* another, or others, *with the food,* or *meal, called the* سَحُور: (M, Mgh, TA:) or سَحَّرَهُمْ signifies *he gave to them the meal so called.* (Mgh.)

4. اسحر ‡ *He was,* or *became, in the time called the* سَحَر; (Ṣ, A, Ḳ;) as also ↓ استحر. (TA.) And ‡ *He went,* or *journeyed, in the time so called:* (Ṣ, Ḳ, TA:) or *he rose to go,* or *journey, in that time;* and so ↓ استحر: (TA:) or this latter signifies *he went forth in that time.* (A. [See also 1, last sentence.])

5. تسحّر (A, Mgh, Mṣb) and تسحّر السَّحُورَ (Az, TA) ‡ *He ate the food,* or *meal,* [or *drank the draught of milk,*] *called the* سَحُور. (Az, A, Mgh, Mṣb, TA.) —— And تسحّر بِهِ ‡ *He ate it,* (Ṣ,* Ḳ,* TA,) namely, food, or سَوِيق [q. v.], [or *drank it,* namely, milk,] *at the time called the* سَحَر. (TA.)

8. استحر: see 4, in two places. —— Also † *He* (a cock) *crowed at the time called the* سَحَر: (Ṣ, Ḳ:) and *he* (a bird) *sang, warbled,* or *uttered his voice, at that time.* (TA.)

سَحْر, and ↓ سَحَر, (Ṣ, Mgh, Mṣb, Ḳ,) sometimes thus because of the faucial letter, (Ṣ,) and ↓ سُحْر, (Ṣ, Mṣb, Ḳ,) and, accord. to El-Khafájee, in the 'Ináyeh, ↓ سِحْر, but this is not mentioned by any other, and therefore requires confirmation, (TA,) The *lungs,* or *lights:* (Ṣ, A, Mgh, Mṣb, Ḳ:) or *what adheres to the gullet and the windpipe, of* [*the contents of*] *the upper part of the belly:* or *all that hangs to the gullet, consisting of the heart and liver and lungs:* (Mṣb, TA:) and the *part of the exterior of the body corresponding to the place of the lungs:* (Mgh, TA:*) and سَحْر signifies also the *liver; and the core,* or *black* or *inner part,* (سَوَاد,) and *sides,* or *regions, of the heart:* (TA:) and ↓ سُحْر, the *heart;* (El-Jarmee, Ḳ;) as also ↓ سُحْرَة: (TA:) the pl. (of سَحْر, Ṣ, Mṣb) is سُحُور, and (of ↓ سُحْر, Ṣ, Mṣb, and of ↓ سَحَر, Mṣb) أَسْحَار. (Ṣ, Mṣb, Ḳ.) —— Hence, اِنْتَفَخَ سَحْرُهُ, (Ṣ, A, Ḳ,) and اِنْتَفَخَتْ مَسَاحِرُهُ ↓, (A, Ḳ,) ‡ *His lungs became inflated,* or *swollen, by reason of timidity and cowardice:* (A:) said of a coward: (Ṣ:) and of one who has exceeded his due bounds: Lth says that, when repletion arises in a man, one says انتفخ سحره, and that the meaning is, [as given also in the Ḳ,] *he exceeded his due bounds:* but Az says that this is a mistake, and that this phrase is only said of a coward, whose inside is filled with fear, and whose lungs are inflated, or swollen, so that the heart is raised to the gullet: and of the same kind is the phrase in the Ḳur [xxxiii. 10] وَبَلَغَتِ القُلُوبُ الحَنَاجِرَ. (TA.) —— And المُقَطَّعَةُ السُّحُورِ, and الأَسْحَارِ, † [*She that has her lungs burst asunder*], an appellation given to *the* أَرْنَب [i. e. *hare,* or *female hare*], (Ṣ, Ḳ,) or to *the swift* ارنب, (TA in art. قطع,) by way of good omen, meaning that her lungs will burst asunder; like المُقَطَّعَةُ النِّيَاطِ: (Ṣ:) and some (of those of later times, Ṣ) say المُقَطِّعَةُ, with kesr to the ط; (Ṣ, Ḳ;) as though, by her speed and vehemence of running, she would burst asunder her lungs; (Ṣ;) or because she bursts the lungs of the dogs by the vehemence of her running, and the lungs of him who pursues her. (ISh, Ṣgh.) —— And اِنْقَطَعَ مِنْهُ سَحْرِى ‡ *I despaired of him,* or *it.* (A, Ḳ.) And أَنَا مِنْهُ غَيْرُ صَرِيمِ سَحْرٍ ‡ *I am not in despair of him,* or *it.* (A, B.) صَرِيمُ سَحْرٍ is also expl. as signifying ‡ *Having his hope cut off:* and ‡ anything *despaired of.* (TA.) And صُرِمَ سَحْرُهُ means ‡ *His hope was cut off.* (TA.) ═══ Also The *scar of a gall on the back of a camel,* (Ḳ, TA,) *when it has healed, and the place thereof has become white.* (TA.) ═══ And The *upper,* or *highest, part* of a valley. (TA.) ═══ See also سُحَارَة. ═══ And see سَحَر, in two places.

سُحْر: see the next preceding paragraph, in three places.

سِحْر: see سَحْر, first sentence. ═══ [Also] an inf. n. of سَحَرَهُ, meaning ‡ The *turning* a thing *from its proper manner of being to another manner:* (T, TA: [accord. to the T, this seems to be proper; but accord. to the A, tropical:]) and hence, (T, TA,) ‡ *enchantment,* or *fascination:* (T,* Ṣ,* MA, KL, PṢ:) for when the enchanter (السَّاحِر) makes what is false to appear in the form of truth, and causes a thing to be imagined different from what it really is, it is as though he turned it from its proper manner of being: (T, TA:) the *producing what is false in the form of truth:* (IF, Mṣb:) or, in the common conventional language of the law, *any event of which the cause is hidden, and which is imagined to be different from what it really is:* and *embellishment by falsification, and deceit:* (Fakhr-ed-Deen, Mṣb:) or *a performance in which one allies himself to the devil, and which is effected by his aid:* (TA:) *i. q.* أُخْذَة [meaning *a kind of enchantment,* or *fascination, which captivates the eye and the like, and by which enchantresses withhold their husbands from other women*]: (Ṣ:) and *anything of which the way of proceeding* or *operation* (مَأْخَذُهُ) *is subtile:* (Ṣ, Ḳ:) accord. to Ibn-Abee-'Áïsheh, سِحْر is thus called by the Arabs because it changes health, or soundness, to disease: (Sh:) [and in like manner it is said to change hatred to love: (see 1:)] pl. أَسْحَار and سُحُور. (TA.) —— Also ‡ *Skilful eloquence:* (TA:) or used absolutely, it is applied to that for which the agent is blamed: and when restricted, to that which is praiseworthy. (Mṣb.) Thus it is in the saying of Moḥammad, إِنَّ مِنَ البَيَانِ لَسِحْرًا

‡ [*Verily there is a kind of eloquence that is enchantment*]: because the speaker propounds an obscure matter, and discloses its true meaning by the beauty of his eloquence, inclining the hearts [of his hearers] in like manner as they are inclined by سِحْر: or because there is in eloquence a novelty and strangeness of composition which attracts the hearer and brings him to such a pass as almost diverts him from other things; therefore it is likened to سِحْر properly so called: and it is said to be السِّحْرُ الحَلَالُ [or *lawful enchantment*]. (Mṣb.) The saying of Moḥammad mentioned above was uttered on the following occasion: Ḳeys Ibn-'Áṣim El-Minḳaree and Ez-Zibriḳán Ibn-Bedr and 'Amr Ibn-El-Ahtam came to the Prophet, who asked 'Amr respecting Ez-Zibriḳán; whereupon he spoke well of him: but Ez-Zibriḳán was not content with this, and said, "By God, O apostle of God, he knows that I am more excellent than he has said; but he envies the place that I have in thine estimation:" and thereupon 'Amr spoke ill of him; and then said, "By God, I did not lie of him in the first saying nor in the other; but he pleased me, and I spoke as pleased; then he angered me, and I spoke as angered:" then Moḥammad uttered the above-mentioned words. (TA.) Their meaning is, but God knows best, he praises the man, speaking truth respecting him, so as to turn the hearts of the hearers to him, (Ḳ,) or to what he says; (TA;) and he dispraises him, speaking truth respecting him, so as to turn their hearts also to him, (Ḳ,) or to what he says after. (TA.) A'Obeyd says nearly the same. Or, as some say, the meaning is, that there is an eloquence that is sinful like سِحْر. (TA.) — Also ‡ *Skill; science:* Moḥammad said, مَنْ تَعَلَّمَ بَابًا مِنَ النُّجُومِ فَقَدْ تَعَلَّمَ بَابًا مِنَ السِّحْرِ ‡ [*He who learneth a process of the science of the stars* (meaning *astrology* or *astronomy*) *learneth a process of enchantment*], which may mean that the science of the stars is forbidden to be learned, like the science of enchantment, and that the learning of it is an act of infidelity: or it may mean that it is *skill*, and *science*; referring to what is acquired thereof by way of calculation; as the knowledge of eclipses of the sun or moon, and the like. (ISd, TA.) — Also ‡ *Food; aliment; nutriment:* so called because its effect is subtile. (TA.) — غَيْثٌ ذُو سِحْرٍ means † *Superabundant rain.* (TA.)

سُحْرٌ: see سَحْرٌ, in two places. ═ Also, (Ṣ, A, Mgh, Mṣb, Ḳ, &c.,) and ▼ سُحُرٌ, (TA,) and ▼ سَحَرٌ, (Mṣb,) and ▼ سَحَرِىٌّ, and ▼ سَحَرِيَّةٌ, (Ḳ,) ‡ The *time a little before daybreak:* (Ṣ, Ḳ:) or [simply] *before daybreak:* (Mṣb:) or the *last part of the night:* (Lth, Mgh:) or the *last sixth of the night:* (Mgh:) the pl. of سَحَرٌ (Mṣb) and of ▼ سُحْرٌ (TA) and of ▼ سُحُرٌ, (Mṣb,) is أَسْحَارٌ: (Mṣb, Ḳ, TA:) the سَحَر is thus met. called because it is the time of the departure of the night and the coming of the day; so that it is the مُتَنَفَّس [lit. the "time of the breathing," by which is meant the "shining forth,"] of the dawn: (A:) there are two times of which each is thus called; one, which is [specially] called السَّحَرُ الأَعْلَى, [or *the earlier* سَحَر,] (A, Mgh,) is *before daybreak;* (Mgh;) or *a little before daybreak:* (A:) and the other, *at daybreak:* (A, Mgh:) like as one says "the false dawn" and "the true:" (A:) the earlier سَحَر is also called ▼ سُحْرَةٌ: (Ṣ, Ḳ:) or the سُحْرَة is the *same as the* سَحَر: or it is the *last third of the night, to daybreak.* (TA.) Using سَحَر indeterminately, you make it perfectly decl., and say, أَتَيْتُهُ بِسَحَرٍ [*I came to him a little before daybreak*], agreeably with the phrase in the Ḳur liv. 34; (Ṣ;) and in like manner, ▼ بِسُحْرَةٍ [*in the earlier* سَحَر]: (Ṣ, Ḳ:) you also say سَحَرًا, and ▼ سُحْرَةً, (A,) and مَا زَالَ سَحَرًا مِنَ الأَسْحَارِ: and عِنْدَنَا مُنْذُ السَّحَرِ [*He ceased not to be with us*, or *at our abode, from a little before daybreak*]: and لَقِيتُهُ بِالسَّحَرِ الأَعْلَى, and بِأَعْلَى سَحَرَيْنِ, and فِى أَعْلَى السَّحَرَيْنِ, (TA,) and بِأَعْلَى السَّحَرَيْنِ, (A, TA,) [*I met him in the earlier* سَحَر;] but بِأَعْلَى سَحَرٍ, a phrase used by El-'Ajjáj, is erroneous: (TA:) and لَقِيتُهُ سَحَرِىَّ ▼ هٰذِهِ اللَّيْلَةِ and ▼ سَحَرِيَّتَهَا [*I met him in the time a little before daybreak of this last night*]. (TA.) When, by سَحَر alone, you mean the سَحَر of the night immediately preceding, you say, لَقِيتُهُ سَحَرَ يَا هٰذَا [*I met him a little before daybreak this last night, O thou* man], (Ṣ, Ḳ,) making it imperfectly decl. because it is altered from السَّحَر, (Ṣ,) or because it is for بِالسَّحَرِ; (TA;) and it is thus determinate by itself, (Ṣ, Ḳ,) without its being prefixed to another noun and without ال: (Ṣ:) and in the same sense you say بِسَحَرَ: (TA:) and you say, سِرْ عَلَى فَرَسِكَ سَحَرَ يَا فَتَى [*Go thou on thy horse a little before daybreak this night, O youth:* so in the TA; but in two copies of the Ṣ, for سِرْ I find سِيرَ]: you do not make it to terminate with ḍamm, [like قَبْلُ and بَعْدُ &c.,] because it is an adv. n. which, in a place where it is fitting to be such, may not be used otherwise than as such: (Ṣ:) and [in like manner] you say, ▼ لَقِيتُهُ سُحْرَةَ يَا هٰذَا [*I met him in the earlier* سَحَر *of this last night, O thou* man]. (TA.) If you make سَحَر the proper name of a man, it is perfectly decl.: and so is the dim.; for it is not of the measure of a noun made to deviate from its original form, like أُخَرُ: you say, ▼ سِرْ عَلَى فَرَسِكَ سُحَيْرًا [*Go thou on thy horse a very little before daybreak:* so in the TA; but here again, in two copies of the Ṣ, for سِرْ I find سِيرَ]: you do not make it to terminate with ḍamm, [like قَبْلُ &c.,] because its being made of the dim. form does not bring it into the class of adv. ns. which may also be used as nouns absolutely, though it does bring it into the class of nouns which are perfectly declinable. (Ṣ, TA.) — سَحَرٌ also signifies ‡ *Whiteness overspreading blackness;* (Ḳ;) like صُحْرَةٌ; except that the former is mostly used in relation to the time so called, of daybreak; and the latter, in relation to colours, as when one says حِمَارٌ أَصْحَرُ; (TA;) and ▼ سُحْرَةٌ signifies the same; (TA;) *i. q.* صُحْرَةٌ. (Ḳ.) — And ‡ The *extremity* (T, A, Ḳ) of a desert, (T,) and of the earth or a land, (A,) or of anything: (Ḳ:) from the time of night so called: (A:) pl. أَسْحَارٌ. (T, A, Ḳ.)

سُحُرٌ: see سَحِيرٌ.

سَحَرٌ: see سَحْرٌ, first sentence, in two places.

سُحْرَةٌ: see سَحْرٌ: ═ and سَحَرٌ, in five places.

سَحَرِىٌّ and سَحَرِيَّةٌ: see سَحَرٌ; each in two places.

سَحُورٌ *A meal*, or *food*, (Mgh, Mṣb, TA,) or [particularly] سَوِيق [generally meaning *meal of parched barley*], *that is eaten at the time called the* سَحَر; (Ṣ,* Mgh, Mṣb, Ḳ,* TA;) or *a draught of milk that is drunk at that time.* (TA.) It is repeatedly mentioned in trads. [relating to Ramaḍán, when the Muslim is required to be exact in the time of this meal], and mostly as above; but some say that it is correctly [in these cases] with ḍamm, [i. e. سُحُور, which see below,] because the blessing and recompense have respect to the action, and not to the food. (TA.)

سُحُورٌ, an inf. n. [without a verb properly belonging to it, or rather a quasi-inf. n., for its verb is تَسَحَّرَ], (TA,) The act of *eating the meal*, or *food*, [or *drinking the draught of milk*,] *called the* سَحُور [q. v.]. (Mṣb, TA.)

سَحِيرٌ: see مَسْحُورٌ. — Also A man *having his lungs* (سَحْرُهُ) *ruptured;* and so ▼ سَحِرٌ. (TA.) — And *Having a complaint of the belly*, (Ḳ, TA,) *from pain of the lungs.* (TA.) — And A horse *large in the belly*, (Ḳ,) or *in the* جَوْف [which often means the *chest*]. (TA.) ═ [And An arrow *wounding the lungs:* so accord. to Freytag in the "Deewán el-Hudhaleeyeen."]

سُحَيْرًا: see سَحَرٌ, in the latter half of the paragraph.

سُحَارَةٌ The *parts, of a sheep* or *goat, that the butcher plucks out* (Ḳ, TA) *and throws away*, (TA,) *consisting of the lungs*, or *lights*, (سَحْر,) *and the windpipe*, (Ḳ, TA,) *and the appendages of these.* (TA.)

سَحَّارٌ: see سَاحِرٌ, in two places.

سَحَّارَةٌ ‡ *A certain plaything of children;* (A, Ḳ, TA;) *having a string attached to it;* (A;) *which, when extended in one direction, turns out to be of one colour; and when extended in another direction, turns out to be of another colour:* (A,* TA:) it is also called ▼ سَحَّارٌ: and whatever resembles it is called by the former appellation: so says Lth. (TA.)

سَاحِرٌ ‡ [*An enchanter;*] a man *who practises* سِحْر; as also ▼ سَحَّارٌ [in an intensive sense, or denoting habit or frequency]: pl. of the former سَحَرَةٌ and سُحَّارٌ; and of ▼ the latter, سَحَّارُونَ only, for it has no broken pl. (TA.) [Hence,] one says, لَهَا عَيْنٌ سَاحِرَةٌ ‡ [*She has an enchanting*, or *a fascinating, eye*], and عُيُونٌ سَوَاحِرُ [*enchanting*, or *fascinating, eyes*]. (A, TA.) And أَرْضٌ سَاحِرَةُ السَّرَابِ ‡ [*A land of delusive mirage*]. (A, TA.) — And † *Knowing, skilful*, or *intelligent.* (Ṣ,* TA.)

مُسَحَّر, of which the pl. occurs in the Ḳur xxvi. 153 and 185, means *Having* سَحْر or سُحْر [i. e. *lungs*]; (Bḍ, TA;) or *created with* سَحْر [or *lungs*]; (Ṣ;) i. e. a human being: (Bḍ:) or *diverted* [*from want*] *with food and drink*: (Ṣ,* TA:) and this seems to be implied by the explanation in the Ḳ; which is *hollow*; from Fr: (TA:) or *enchanted time after time, so that his intellect is disordered*, or *rendered unsound*: (A, TA:) or *enchanted much, so that his reason is overcome*: (Bḍ, Jel:) [see also مَسْحُور:] or *deceived, deluded, beguiled, circumvented*, or *outwitted*. (TA.)

مَسْحُورٌ *Having his lungs* (سَحْرُهُ), or *his heart* (سُحْرَتُهُ), *hit*, or *hurt*; as also ▼ سَحِيرٌ [q. v.]. (TA.) — [‡ *Enchanted*, or *fascinated*.] — † *Deprived of his reason* or *intellect; corrupted* or *disordered* [*in his intellect*]. (IAạr, Sh.) [See also مُسَحَّر.] — † *Food* (طَعَام) *marred*, or *spoilt*, (Ḳ, TA,) *in the making thereof*. (TA.) † *Herbage marred*, or *spoilt*. (TA.) † *A place marred*, or *spoilt, by much rain*, or *by scantiness of herbage*. (Ḳ.) The fem., with ة, accord. to Az, signifies † *Land* (أَرْض) *marred*, or *spoilt, by superabundant rain*, or *by scantiness of herbage*: accord. to ISh, † *land in which is little milk*; i. e. [because] *without herbage*: accord. to Z, [in the A,] ‡ *land that produces no herbage*. (TA.) — And the fem., applied to a she-goat, ‡ *Having little milk*: (A, TA:) or *large in her udder, but having little milk*. (Ḥam p. 26.)

مَسَاحِرُ: see سَحْر, second sentence.

سحف

1. سَحَفَهُ, (Ṣ, Ḳ, TA,) aor. َ, (Ḳ, TA,) inf. n. سَحْفٌ, (Ṣ, TA,) *He pared it*, or *peeled it, off*; (Ṣ, Ḳ, TA;) namely, a thing; (TA;) and [particularly] the fat from the back (Ṣ, Ḳ) of the sheep or goat, (Ṣ, TA,) not of the she-camel, as is indicated by the context in the Ḳ, (TA,) by reason of its abundance, after which he roasted it, (Ṣ, TA,) i. e., accord. to the Ṣ, the fat, but correctly the sheep or goat: (TA:) so says ISk. (Ṣ, TA.) — And سَحَفَهُ, (Lth, TA,) inf. n. as above, (Lth, Ḳ, TA,) *He removed it*, or *stripped it off*, namely, hair from skin, *so that none of it remained*. (Lth, Ḳ, TA.) — Hence, (TA,) سَحَفَتِ الإِبِلُ ‡ *The camels ate what they would*. (Ḳ, TA.) — And سَحَفَتِ الرِّيحُ السَّحَابَ † *The wind removed the clouds*; (Lth, Ḳ;) as also ▼ أَسْحَفَتْهُ. (Zj, Ḳ, TA: in the CḲ اسْتَحَفَتْهُ.) — سَحَفَ رَأْسَهُ, (Ṣ, Ḳ,) inf. n. as above, (TA,) *He shaved his head* (Ṣ, Ḳ, TA) *so as to remove the hair utterly*. (TA.) — سَحَفَ الشَّىْءَ, and النَّخْلَةَ وَغَيْرَهَا, (Ḳ,) aor. and inf. n. as above, (TA,) *He burned the thing*, and *the palm-tree &c.*; (Ḳ, TA;) *in the case of the palm-tree, by kindling fire at the stumps of the branches, being unable to strip them off*. (Aboo-Naṣr, TA.) — And سَحَفَهُ *He* (i. e. God) *caused him to be affected with* سُحَاف, i. e. *consumption*, or *ulceration of the lungs*. (TA.)

4. اسحف *He sold the fat termed* سَحْفَة. (Ḳ.) — See also 1.

سَحْفٌ *Fat*, as a subst.: pl. سِحَافٌ. (TA.) An Arab of the desert said, أَتَوْنَا بِصِحَافٍ فِيهَا لِحَامٌ وَسِحَافٌ *They brought us bowls in which were sorts of flesh-meat and of fat*. (IAạr, Ḳ,* TA.)

سَحْفَةٌ *A piece*, or *portion, of fat*; in a general sense: (TA:) or the *portion of fat that is upon the back*, (Ṣ, Ḳ, TA,) *sticking to the skin, in the part between the two shoulder-blades, extending to the haunches*: so says ISk: (Ṣ, TA:) or *that is upon the two sides and the back*: and it is never but from fatness: accord. to IKh, it is in all beasts except the camel: ISd says that, accord. to some, it is in the camel [also]. (TA.) — And [the dual] سَحْفَتَانِ The *two sides of the tuft of hair that is between the lower lip and the chin*: (Aboo-Sa'eed, Ḳ:) pl. سَحَفَاتٌ. (TA.) — See also سَحِيفٌ. — [Freytag makes it to be also syn. with مُسْحَف, as on the authority of the Ḳ, in which I do not find it in this sense.]

سُحْفَةٌ: see what next follows.

سُحْفُنِيَةٌ (in which the ن is augmentative, TA) A man *having the head shaven*; (IB, Ḳ, TA;) as also ▼ سُحْفَةٌ. (IB, TA.) — And with the article ال, *What one has shaven off*: thus it is sometimes a subst.; and sometimes, [i. e. in the former sense,] an epithet. (IB, TA.) — Also *A certain beast*, or *creeping thing*: (Seer, TA:) [SM says,] I think it is the سُلَحْفِيَة [or *tortoise*]. (TA.)

سُحَافٌ *Consumption*; or *ulceration of the lungs*; syn. سِلٌّ. (Ṣ, Ḳ.)

سَحُوفٌ A bucket (دَلْو) *that takes, and bears away, the water that is in a well*. (Seer, Ḳ.) — Also, applied to a she-camel, *Of which the fat has gone away*. (ISd, TA.) — And, applied to a sheep or goat, or to a ewe or she-goat, (شَاة,) *Having a portion of fat such as is termed* سَحْفَة, or *two such portions of fat*; as also ▼ أَسْحُوفٌ: (TA:) or, so applied, (Ṣ,) and applied to a she-camel, (Ṣ, Ḳ,) and to a he-camel, (Ḳ,) *having abundance of* سَحَائِف, (Ṣ,* Ḳ, TA,) pl. of سَحِيفَة [q. v.]; or *having abundance of the fat termed* سَحْفَة. (TA.) — Also A she-camel *long in the teats*. (IDrd, Ḳ.) — And A she-camel *narrow in the orifices of the teats*. (IDrd, Ḳ.) — And A she-camel *that drags her feet*, or *the extremities of her feet, upon the ground, in going along*; (Ḳ, TA;) so say some; i. e., by reason of fatigue: a dial. var. of زَحُوف. (TA.) — And A sheep, or ewe, *thin in the wool of the belly*. (Ḳ.) — In the Ḳ, three other meanings are erroneously assigned to this word; one of them belonging to سَحِيفَة, and each of the others to سَحِيف. (TA.)

سَحِيفٌ, (ISk, Ṣ, Ṣgh, TA,) accord. to the context in the Ḳ سَحُوفٌ, which is wrong, in this and the next sense, (TA,) The *sound* of the mill *when one grinds*. (ISk, Ṣ, Ṣgh, Ḳ.*) And The *sound of the streaming* of milk from the udder; (O, Ḳ,* TA;) as also ▼ سَحْفَةٌ. (Ḳ,* TA.)

سَحِيفَةٌ The *fat called* سَحْفَة *that one has pared off from the back of a sheep or goat*. (ISk, Ṣ.) — And sing. of سَحَائِف, (Lth, TA,) which signifies The *layers of fat between the layers* [*of flesh*] *of the flanks*: and *similar wide portions of fat that are seen adhering to the skin*. (Lth, Ḳ, TA.) — Also *A rain* (مَطْرَة) *that sweeps away that along which it passes*: (Ṣ, O, L, TA:) in the Ḳ, by the omission of كَسُفَيْنَة, this meaning is erroneously assigned to سَحُوف: accord. to Aṣ, *a sharp rain, that sweeps away everything*: and سَحِيقَة, with ق, a vehement rain, consisting of large drops, but of little width: pls. سَحَائِف and سَحَائِق. (TA.)

أُسْحُوفٌ: see سَحُوف. — أُسْحُوفُ الأَحَالِيلِ, (Ḳ,) mentioned by ISh, on the authority of Aboo-Aslam, (TA,) and إِسْحُوفُ الاحاليل, (Ḳ,) thus accord. to Sb, (TA,) A she-camel *wide in the orifices of the teats*: (Aboo-Aslam, Ḳ:) or *having much milk, the streaming of which causes a sound to be heard*. (Aboo-Málik, Ḳ,* TA.)

مَسْحَفٌ The *mark*, or *track*, of a serpent, *upon the ground*; (Ibn-'Abbád, Ḳ;) as also مَزْحَف. (TA.)

أَرْضٌ مُسْحَفَةٌ, with fet-ḥ [to the ح, or perhaps to the م and ح], *A land of which the herbage is thin* [or *scanty*]: mentioned in the Ḳ in art. سخف, as being [written مُسْخِفَة,] like مُحْسِنَة. (TA.)

مِسْحَفَةٌ *A thing with which flesh*, or *flesh-meat, is pared*. (Ibn-'Abbád, Ḳ.)

مَسْحُوفٌ A man *affected with* سُحَاف, i. e. *consumption*, or *ulceration of the lungs*; (Ṣ;) syn. مَسْلُول. (Ḳ.)

سحق

1. سَحَقَهُ, (Ṣ, Mgh, Mṣb, Ḳ,) aor. َ, (Mṣb, Ḳ,) inf. n. سَحْقٌ, (Mṣb,) *He bruised, brayed*, or *pounded, it*; syn. دَقَّهُ; (Mgh, Ḳ;) namely, a thing, (Ṣ, TA,) or medicine: (Mgh, Mṣb:) or i. q. سَهَكَهُ [app. as meaning *he bruised, brayed*, or *pounded, it coarsely*; but see this latter verb]: (Ṣ, Ḳ:) or it signifies [*he did so in a degree*] *less than what is meant by* دَقَّهُ: (Lth, Ḳ:) or [*he powdered*, or *pulverized, it*; i. e.] *he bruised, brayed*, or *pounded, it finely*: or *he bruised, brayed*, or *pounded, it time after time*. (TA.) — [Hence,] سَحَقَتِ الرِّيحُ الأَرْضَ, (Ḳ,) aor. and inf. n. as above, (TA,) ‡ *The wind effaced the traces of the ground*, (Ḳ, TA,) *and carried away the broken particles* [*that were upon it*]: (M, TA:) or *passed along as though it were bruising*, or *braying*, or *pounding*, (كَأَنَّهَا تَسْحَقُ,) *the dust*: (O, Ḳ:) or *pared*, or *abraded, the surface of the earth by its vehement blowing*; as also سَهَكَتْهَا [q. v.]. (T, A, TA.) — And سَحَقَهُ, (Ḳ, TA,) aor. and inf. n. as above, (TA,) ‡ *He wore it out*; namely, a garment. (Ḳ, TA.) And سَحَقَهُ مَرُّ الزَّمَانِ † *The course of time rendered it* (a garment) *thin and worn out*. (O, TA.) And سَحَقَهُ البِلَى † [*Wear wasted it*]; namely, a garment. (TA.) — Also *He*, or *it, rendered it soft*, or

smooth; namely, a hard thing. (Ḳ.) —— And † *He destroyed it*; and so ▼ اسحقهُ. (Ḥar p. 257-8.) —— سَحَقَ القَمْلَةَ *He killed the louse.* (Ḳ.) —— سَحَقَ رَأْسَهُ *He shaved his head.* (Ḳ.) —— سَحَقَتِ العَيْنُ دَمْعَهَا *The eye spent its tears*; (Ḳ, TA;) *shed them*, or *let them fall.* (TA.) —— See also 4. ═ سَحُقَ, aor. ـُ, inf. n. سُحُوقَةٌ, † *It* (a garment) *was*, or *became, old, and worn out*; (Ḳ;) [and so, app., سَحَقَ, inf. n. سَحْقٌ, accord. to a usage of this noun, in the Deewán el-Hudhaleeyeen, mentioned by Freytag, and agreeably with the phrase ثَوْبٌ سَحْقٌ, mentioned below;] as also ▼ اسحق, (Yaạḳoob, Ṣ, Mṣb, Ḳ,) inf. n. إِسْحَاقٌ. (Mṣb.) ═ سَحُقَ, (Ṣ, Mṣb, Ḳ,) aor. ـُ; and سَحِقَ, aor. ـَ; (Ḳ;) inf. n. سُحْقٌ (Ṣ,* Mṣb,* Ḳ) [and app. سُحُقٌ also]; *It* (a thing, Ṣ, or a place, Mṣb) *was*, or *became, distant*, or *remote*; (Ṣ, Mṣb, Ḳ;) as also ▼ اسحق, and ▼ انسحق. (TA.) سُحْقٌ and سُحُقٌ are both syn. with بُعْدٌ. (Ṣ, Ḳ.) One says, سُحْقًا لَهُ, (Ṣ, Mṣb,) a form of imprecation, (Mṣb,) meaning *May God alienate him*, or *estrange him, from good*, or *prosperity!* or *curse him!* i. e. may he not be pitied with respect to that which has befallen him! like بُعْدًا لَهُ: the most approved way is to put the noun thus in the accus. case as an inf. n.; but the tribe of Temeem say, بُعْدٌ لَهُ, and سُحْقٌ. (TA in art. بعد.) —— سَحَقَتِ النَّخْلَةُ *The palm-tree became tall*: (Ḳ:) or *tall with smoothness* [*of its trunk*]. (TA.) ═ سَحَقَتِ الدَّابَّةُ, [inf. n. سَحْقٌ,] *The beast ran vehemently*: or *ran a pace above that termed* مَشْىٌ *and below that termed* حُضْرٌ, (Ḳ, TA,) agreeably with what is said in explanation of السَّحْقُ in the Ṣ: or *below that termed* حُضْرٌ *and above that termed* سَحْجٌ. (TA.)

3. مُسَاحَقَةُ النِّسَآءِ [meaning ‡ *The mutual act, of women, indicated by the epithet* سَحَّاقَةٌ (q. v.), as also ▼ تَسَاحُقٌ,] is post-classical: (T, TA:) such it is said to be. (Mgh.)

4. اسحقهُ: see 1. —— Said of God, (Ṣ, TA,) *He removed him far away*, or *alienated him*, or *estranged him, in a general sense*, or *from good*, or *prosperity*; syn. أَبْعَدَهُ; (Ṣ, O, Ḳ, TA; [accord. to the CḲ انسحقهُ, which is wrong;]) as also ▼ سَحَقَهُ: or, *from his mercy.* (TA.) ═ اسحق as intrans.: see 1, in two places. —— Also, [in the CḲ, erroneously, انسحق,] said of a camel's foot, *It was*, or *became, smooth, with a degree of hardness*; syn. مَرَنَ. (ISk, Ṣ, O, Ḳ.) —— And said of an udder, *It lost its milk, and became wasted, and clave to the belly*: (ISk, Ṣ, O, Ḳ:) or *it dried up*: (Aṣ, TA:) or *it went away*; and *wasted.* (A'Obeyd, TA.) —— And اسحقت الدَّلْوُ *The bucket became empty of what was in it.* (TA.)

6. تَسَاحُقٌ The act of *rubbing together.* (KL.) See also 3.

7. انسحق [*It was*, or *became, bruised, brayed*, or *pounded*: &c.:] quasi-pass. of سَحَقَهُ as expl. in the first sentence of this art. (Ṣ, O, Ḳ.) —— Said of a garment, *It was*, or *became*, [*worn out*; or *thin and worn out*; (see 1;) or] *threadbare*, or *napless, while new.* (TA.) —— And [said of a place,] *It was wide*, or *ample.* (O, Ḳ.) —— See also 1. —— انسحق الدَّمْعُ *The tears were shed.* (TA.)

سَحْقٌ *An old and worn-out garment*, (Ṣ, Mgh, O, Mṣb, Ḳ,) *that has become thin*, (O,) *and threadbare*; (Ḥam p. 591;) also used as a prefixed noun, (Mgh, Mṣb,) so that you say سَحْقُ ثَوْبٍ [meaning as above], (Mgh,) and سَحْقُ بُرْدٍ [*an old and worn-out* بُرْد], and سَحْقُ عِمَامَةٍ [*an old and worn-out turban*]: (Mgh, Mṣb:) and one says ثَوْبٌ سَحْقٌ, [using it as an epithet,] (O, TA,) and ▼ ثَوْبٌ سَحِقٌ, (Ḥar p. 258, [but for this I have found no other authority, and it may be a mistranscription,]) and ▼ ثَوْبٌ مُنْسَحِقٌ likewise signifies *an old and worn-out garment*: (TA:) سَحْقٌ applied to a garment is an inf. n. used as a subst.: (O, TA:) the pl. is سُحُوقٌ. (TA.) Hence one says دِرْهَمٌ سَحْقٌ, meaning ‡ *A* [*bad*] *dirhem* [or] *such as is termed* زَائِفٌ. (Mgh.) —— Also *A pastor's bag* (كِنْفٌ): so in a verse cited voce خُفٌّ. (Ṣ in art. خف.) —— And ‡ *Thin clouds*: (Ḳ:) likened to an old and worn-out garment. (TA.) —— And The *mark*, or *scar, of a gall*, or *sore, on the back of a camel, when it has healed, and the place thereof has become white*: (TA:) [like سَلْقٌ and سَلَقٌ.]

سَحَقٌ: see the next preceding paragraph.

[سُحْقَةٌ *Baldness*: of the dial. of El-Yemen. (Freytag, from IDrd.)]

سَحُوقٌ *Tall*; applied to a palm-tree; (Ṣ, Mṣb, Ḳ;) as also ▼ سُحُوقٌ; (Ṣ;) and to a he-ass and to a she-ass; (Ṣ, Ḳ;) and by some, metaphorically, to a woman; (TA;) and ▼ سَوْحَقٌ signifies the same, (Ḳ,) applied to a man; (TA;) and ▼ سَوْحَقُ الرِّجْلَيْنِ *long in respect of the legs*: (IB:) or سَحُوقٌ applied to a palm-tree signifies *tall so that its fruit is far above the gatherer*; Aṣ says, I know not whether that be with a bending: or, accord. to Sh, so applied, *smooth and tall, having no stumps of the branches remaining* [*upon the trunk*]; and to such the neck of a horse is likened by a poet: and applied to a he-ass and to a she-ass, *tall, and advanced in age*: (TA:) pl. سُحُقٌ, (Ṣ, O, Mṣb,) like رُسُلٌ, (Mṣb,) or سُحْقٌ. (So in the Ḳ.) One says also جَنَّةٌ سُحُقٌ, meaning *A garden of tall palm-trees.* (TA.)

سَحِيقٌ *Bruised, brayed*, or *pounded*: (Mgh:) [&c.: (see 1, first sentence:)] *i. q.* ▼ مَسْحُوقٌ: (O:) applied to musk; (Mgh, O;) and to saffron. (Mgh in art. ورس.) —— And *Distant*; *remote*; (Ṣ, Mṣb, Ḳ;) applied to a thing, (Ṣ,) or to a place; (Mṣb, Ḳ;) as also ▼ أَسْحَقُ; (IB, TA;) and ▼ سَاحِقٌ in the same sense, applied to a place, is allowed in poetry. (TA.) One says, إِنَّهُ لَبَعِيدٌ سَحِيقٌ [app. meaning *Verily he*, or *it, is very distant* or *remote*]. (TA.)

سَحِيقَةٌ *A great rain that sweeps away that along which it passes*: (Ḳ:) or, accord. to Aṣ, سَحِيفَةٌ, with ف, has this meaning; and the former word signifies *a vehement rain, consisting of large drops*, (TA in the present art.,) *but of little width*: pls. سَحَائِقُ and سَحَائِفُ. (TA in art. سحف.)

سَحَّاقَةٌ [*Fricatrix; quæ confrictu libidinem alterius explet*: (Golius, from Meyd:)] an epithet of evil import, applied to a woman: (O, Ḳ:) pl. سَحَّاقَاتٌ: of such it is said that they are cursed by God. (Mgh.)

سَاحِقٌ: see سَحِيقٌ. —— You say also سُحْقٌ سَاحِقٌ, meaning *Great distance* or *remoteness.* (TA.)

سَوْحَقٌ: see سَحُوقٌ, in two places.

أَسْحَقُ: see سَحِيقٌ. —— [Also *Bald*: of the dial. of El-Yemen. (Freytag, from IDrd.)]

مِسْحَقٌ *An instrument with which one bruises, brays*, or *pounds*: &c.: (يُسْحَقُ بِهِ:) [see 1, first sentence.] (TA.)

مَسْحُوقٌ: see سَحِيقٌ.

مُنْسَحِقٌ: see سَحْقٌ. —— Also *Wide*, or *ample.* (TA.) —— دَمْعٌ مُنْسَحِقٌ *Tears pouring forth*; syn. مُنْدَفِقٌ: (Lth, Az, TA:) in the Ḳ, مُنْدَفِعٌ: (TA:) pl. مَسَاحِيقُ, which is extr.; (Ḳ;) like مَكَاسِيرُ, pl. of مُنْكَسِرٌ. (TA.)

سحل

1. سَحَلَهُ, aor. ـَ, (Ḳ,) inf. n. سَحْلٌ, (Ṣ, TA,) *He pared it*; *peeled it*; or *stripped off, scraped off, rubbed off, abraded*, or *otherwise removed, its outer covering* or *integument*, or *superficial part*: or *he pared, peeled*, or *stripped, it off*: (Ṣ, Ḳ, TA:) this is the primary signification: (Ṣ:) and *he filed it.* (TA.) It is said in a trad., فَجَعَلَتْ تَسْحَلُهَا لَهُ, i. e. *And she betook herself to paring off from it the flesh that was upon it for him*: or, as some relate it, تَسْحَاهَا, which means the same. (TA.) —— [Hence,] الرِّيَاحُ تَسْحَلُ الأَرْضَ ‡ *The winds strip off what is upon the earth*, (Ḳ, TA,) or *the surface of the earth.* (TA: and the like is said in the Ṣ.) —— And سَحَلَهُ مِائَةَ سَوْطٍ, (Ṣ, Ḳ,) inf. n. as above, (TA,) † *He struck him a hundred lashes*, or *strokes of a whip*, (Ṣ, Ḳ, TA,) *and pared off his skin*, (TA,) or *as though he pared off his skin.* (Ṣ.) —— And سَحَلَ فُلَانٌ † *Such a one reviled* [another], *and blamed* [him: like as you say, قَشَرَ بِاللِّسَانِ]. (Ḳ. [See مِسْحَلٌ as meaning "a tongue."]) One says, وَجَدَ النَّاسَ يَسْحَلُونَهُ † *He found the people reviling him*, (Ḳ, TA,) *and blaming him, and speaking evil of him behind his back*, or *in his absence*, or *otherwise.* (TA.) —— سَحَلْتُ الشَّىْءَ *i. q.* سَحَقْتُهُ [*I bruised, brayed*, or *pounded, the thing*: or *pulverized it*: &c.]. (Ṣ.) —— سَحَلَ الثِّيَابَ *He washed the clothes*, [*beating them in doing so*,] *and removed* [or *rubbed off*] *from them the soils.* (TA.) —— سَحَلْتُ الدَّرَاهِمَ *I made the pieces of money smooth.* (Ṣ.) Accord. to ISk,

I poured out, or *forth*, *the pieces of money; as though I rubbed them, one against another*. (Ṣ.) [Or] سَحَلَ الدَّرَاهِمَ, aor. as above, (Ḳ,) and so the inf. n., (TA,) *i. q.* انْتَقَدَهَا [which signifies *He picked the pieces of money, separating the good from the bad;* or *examined them to do so:* and also *he received the pieces of money*]. (Ḳ.) And سَحَلْتُهُ مِائَةَ دِرْهَمٍ *I paid him a hundred dirhems in ready money*. (Ṣ.) [Or] سَحَلَ الغَرِيمَ مِائَةَ دِرْهَمٍ *He paid the creditor a hundred dirhems in ready money*. (Ḳ.) ═ سَحَلَ الثَّوْبَ, (Ḳ,) aor. and inf. n. as above, (TA,) *He wove the garment*, or *piece of cloth, of spun thread not formed of two twists:* (Ḳ:) or *he wove it without having twisted its warp* [i. e. *without having made its warp to consist of threads of two twists*]. (TA.) — And سَحَلْتُ الحَبْلَ *I formed the rope of a single twist;* (Ṣ, TA;) and accord. to some, one says also ↓ أَسْحَلْتُهُ, but the former is the chaste expression. (TA.) [Hence,] سُحِلَتْ مَرِيرَةُ فُلَانٍ is said of one whose strength has become weakened; meaning ‡ *His well-twisted rope, or rope of two twists, has become a rope of a single twist*. (TA.) — سَحَلَ القِرَآءَةَ, inf. n. سَحْلٌ, *He performed the reading*, or *recitation, in consecutive portions, continuously:* and some relate it with ج [i. e. سَجَلَ]: سَحْلٌ is *syn. with* سَرْدٌ, signifying the *making* [a thing] *to be consecutive in its parts*, or *portions*. (TA.) — بَاتَتِ السَّمَآءُ تَسْحَلُ لَيْلَتَهَا ‡ *The sky continued pouring forth water that night:* (Aṣ, Ṣ, TA:) inf. n. as above. (TA.) — And سَحَلَتِ العَيْنُ, (Ḳ,) aor. as above, (TA,) inf. n. سَحْلٌ and سُحُولٌ, ‡ *The eye wept;* (Ḳ;) *poured forth tears*. (TA.) ═ سَحَلَ, aor. ـَ (Ṣ, Ḳ) and ـِ, (Ḳ,) inf. n. سَحِيلٌ and سُحَالٌ, (Ṣ,* Ḳ, [the latter inf. n. erroneously written in the CḲ سِحال,]) *He* (an ass) *made a rolling sound in his chest;* whence the ass of the desert is called ↓ مِسْحَلٌ: (Ṣ: [see also سَحِيلٌ below:]) *he* (a mule, Ḳ, and an ass, TA) *brayed*. (Ḳ, TA.)

3. ساحلوا, (Ṣ, Ḳ,) inf. n. مُسَاحَلَةٌ, (TA,) ‡ *They took*, (Ṣ,) or *came*, (Ḳ,) *to the* سَاحِل [or *shore*, &c., of the sea]. (Ṣ, Ḳ, TA.) Hence, in a trad. respecting Bedr, فَسَاحَلَ بِالعِيرِ *And he brought the caravan to the* سَاحِل *of the sea*. (TA.) ═ هُوَ يُسَاحِلُهُ, inf. n. سِحَالٌ and مُسَاحَلَةٌ, *He contends, disputes*, or *litigates, with him*. (TA.)

4. اسحل فُلَانًا † *He found the people reviling such a one*, (Ḳ, TA,) *and blaming him, and speaking evil of him behind his back*, or *in his absence*, or *otherwise*. (TA.) ═ See also 1, in the latter half of the paragraph.

7. انسحل *It became pared*, or *peeled;* or *had its outer covering* or *integument*, or *its superficial part, stripped off, scraped off, rubbed off, abraded*, or *otherwise removed:* or *it became pared, peeled*, or *stripped, off*. (Ḳ.) It is said, in this sense, of the surface of the earth [as meaning † *It was stripped of what was upon it* by the wind: see 1, third sentence]. (TA.) — انسحلت الدَّرَاهِمُ *The pieces of money became smooth*. (Ṣ.) ═ *It poured out*, or *forth;* or *became poured out*, or *forth*. (TA.) — انسحلت النَّاقَةُ † *The she-camel was*, or *became, quick*, or *swift, in her going*, or *pace*. (Aṣ, TA.) — انسحل بِالكَلَامِ ‡ *He* (an orator, Ṣ, TA) *ran on with speech:* (Ṣ, Ḳ, TA:) or *was fluent, and diffuse*, or *without pause*, or *hesitation, therein*. (TA.)

سَحْلٌ *A white garment* or *piece of cloth:* (Mṣb:) or *a white, thin garment* or *piece of cloth:* (TA:) or *a white garment* or *piece of cloth, of cotton*, (Ṣ, Ḳ,) *of those of El-Yemen:* (Ṣ:) pl. [of mult.] سُحُولٌ and سُحْلٌ (Ṣ, Mṣb, Ḳ) and [of pauc.] أَسْحَالٌ. (Ḳ. [See also ثِيَابٌ سَحُولِيَّةٌ, below.]) — And *A garment*, or *piece of cloth, of which the spun thread is not composed of two twists;* as also ↓ سَحِيلٌ: (Ḳ:) or, as some say, the latter is not applied to a garment, or piece of cloth; but to thread, in a sense expl. below: (TA:) or, accord. to Aboo-Naṣr, it (the latter) is applied also to a garment, or piece of cloth, *of which the spun thread is a single yarn:* the مُبْرَم is that of which the spun thread is twisted of two yarns: and the مُتْآم is that of which the warp and the woof are each of two yarns. (Ṣ, TA.) — Also, (Ḳ,) or ↓ سَحِيلٌ, (Ṣ,) or both, (TA,) *A rope that is of a single strand;* (Ḳ, TA;) or the latter, a rope *that is twisted of one twist*, like as the tailor twists his thread: the مُبْرَم is that which is composed of two twists twisted together into one: (Aboo-Naṣr, Ṣ, TA:) such a rope is also termed ↓ مَسْحُولٌ; but not ↓ مُسْحَلٌ, for the sake of [analogy to] مُبْرَم; (Ṣ, TA;) or the latter epithet is sometimes applied to it: (Ṣ, TA: [see also مُسْحَلٌ:]) ↓ سَحِيلٌ likewise signifies thread *not twisted;* (Aboo-Naṣr, Ṣ, TA;) or spun thread *not composed of two twists*. (TA.) ═ Also *Ready money:* (Ṣ, TA:) an inf. n. used as a subst. [properly so termed]. (TA.)

سَحِيلٌ: see سُحَالٌ.

مِسْحَلٌ: see سِحَالٌ.

سَحُولٌ *One who beats and washes and whitens clothes:* hence, accord. to some, ثِيَابٌ سَحُولِيَّةٌ [q. v.]. (TA.)

سَحِيلٌ: see سَحْلٌ, in three places. ═ Also, and ↓ سُحَالٌ, [both mentioned above as inf. ns., (see 1, last sentence,)] The *rolling sound in the chest of the ass:* (Ṣ, Ḳ:) or the former, [and probably the latter also,] the *most vehement braying* of the wild ass. (TA.)

سُحَالَةٌ *Filings* of gold and of silver (Ṣ, Ḳ) and the like, (Ṣ,) or of anything. (TA.) — The *husks* of wheat and of barley and the like (Ḳ, TA) *when stripped off* therefrom, and so of other grains, as rice and [the species of millet called] دُخْن: accord. to Az, the *particles that fall off* of rice and of millet (ذُرَة) *in the process of bruising*, or *braying*, or *pounding, like bran*. (TA.) — And [hence,] ‡ The *refuse*, or *lowest* or *basest* or *meanest sort*, of a people or party of men. (IAạr, Ḳ, TA.)

ثِيَابٌ سَحُولِيَّةٌ *Certain garments*, or *pieces of cloth*, (Ṣ, Mgh, Mṣb, Ḳ, TA,) *of cotton*, (Ṣ, TA,) *white*, (Mgh, TA,) *so called in relation to* سَحُول, (Ṣ, Mgh, Mṣb,) *a place*, (Ṣ, Ḳ,) or *town*, (Mgh, Mṣb,) *of El-Yemen*, (Ṣ, Mgh, Mṣb, Ḳ,) *where they are woven*, (Ḳ,) or *whence they are brought:* (Mṣb:) some say سُحُولِيَّةٌ, with ḍamm; (Mgh, Mṣb, TA;) so say Az and El-Ḳutabee; (Mgh;) a rel. n. from سُحُول, pl. of سَحْل, (Mgh, Mṣb,* TA,) meaning "a white garment or piece of cloth (Mgh, TA) of cotton;" (TA;) but this is [said to be] a mistake; (Mṣb;) or it is allowable because فُعُول sometimes occurs as the measure of a sing., to which this pl. is likened; as is said in the O: (TA:) or the former appellation is applied, as some say, *to garments*, or *pieces of cloth, beaten and washed and whitened;* so called in relation to سَحُول meaning "one who beats and washes and whitens clothes." (TA.)

سَاحِلٌ ‡ *A shore of a sea* or *great river* (Ṣ, Mṣb, Ḳ, TA) [and] *of a river* (نَهْر) like جُدٌّ; (Mgh in art. جد;) [generally, *a sea-shore, sea-coast*, or *seaboard;*] and *a tract of cultivated land, with towns* or *villages, adjacent to a sea* or *great river:* (Ḳ:) a reversed word, (IDrd, Ṣ, Ḳ,) by rule مَسْحُولٌ, (IDrd, Ḳ,) of the measure فَاعِلٌ in the sense of the measure مَفْعُولٌ, (TA,) because the water abrades it, (IDrd, Ṣ, Ḳ, TA,) or comes upon it: (TA:) or [it is a possessive epithet, like تَامِرٌ and لَابِنٌ,] meaning *having abrading water* (ذُو سَاحِلٍ مِنَ المَآءِ) when the tide flows and ebbs and so sweeps away what is upon it. (Ḳ.) And The *side* (سِيف) of a valley. (Ḳ in art. سيف.) Pl. سَوَاحِلُ. (Mṣb.)

إِسْحِلٌ *A kind of trees*, (AḤn, Ṣ, Ḳ,) *resembling the* [*species of tamarisk called*] أَثْل, *and growing in the places where the* [*trees called*] أَرَاك *grow, in plain*, or *soft, tracts:* (AḤn, TA:) *its twigs are used for cleaning the teeth:* (AḤn, Ḳ,* TA:) and Imra-el-Ḳeys likens the fingers of a woman to tooth-sticks (مَسَاوِيك) thereof. (Ṣ, TA. [See EM p. 30.]) It is [said to be] a word that has no parallel in form except إِجْرِدٌ and إِذْخِرٌ and إِبْلِمٌ and إِثْمِدٌ. (TA.)

أَسَاحِلُ [a pl. of which the sing. is not mentioned] *Water-courses*, or *places in which water flows*. (Ibn-'Abbád, Ḳ.)

مُسْحَلٌ: see سَحْلٌ.

مِسْحَلٌ *An implement for cutting, hewing*, or *paring*, (Lth, Ḳ, TA,) *of wood*. (Lth, TA.) — *A file*. (Ṣ, Ḳ.) — [Hence,] † The *tongue, in an absolute sense:* (Ḳ, TA:) [see مِبْرَدٌ: or as being an instrument of reviling,] from سَحَلَ "he reviled." (TA.) J explains المِسْحَل as meaning اللِّسَانُ الخَطِيبُ, (Ḳ, TA,) and MF defends this as meaning *The tongue that speaks well:* (TA:) [and it is said in the Ḥam p. 683 to signify اللِّسَانُ الَّذِى لَا يَتَأَتَّى لِلْكَلَامِ, app. meaning *the tongue that does not prepare itself for speech;* i. e. *the ready tongue:*] but [F says that] the right reading is اللِّسَانُ وَالخَطِيبُ (Ḳ) [i. e.] —

مِسْحَلٌ also signifies i. q. خَطِيبٌ † [*A speaker, an orator*, or *a preacher*; or *a good speaker* &c.]: and *an eloquent* خَطِيب; (Ḳ, TA;) *one who scarcely*, or *never, stops short in his speech; excelling such as is termed* مِصْقَع. (TA.) — † *One who is skilled in the reading*, or *reciting, of the Ḳur-án*: (Ḳ:) from سَحْلٌ meaning the "making" [a thing] "to be consecutive in its parts, or portions;" and the "pouring forth" [water &c.]. (TA.) — *A copious rain*: (Ḳ:) from سَحْلٌ meaning the act of "pouring forth." (TA.) — *A water-spout* (مِيزَاب) *of which the water is not to be withstood* [so I render لَا يُطَاقُ مَاؤُهُ, app. meaning, *that pours forth its water with such violence that no obstruction will resist it*]. (O, Ḳ.) — The *mouth of a* مَزَادَة [or *leathern water-bag*]. (O, Ḳ.) — *A brisk, lively, sprightly*, or *active, waterer*, or *cup-bearer*. (O, Ḳ.) — *Extreme* (نِهَايَة) *in bounty*, or *munificence*. (O, Ḳ.) — *A courageous man, who acts*, (يَعْمَلُ, so in the M and Ḳ, TA,) or *charges*, or *makes an assault* or *attack*, (يَحْمِلُ, so in the O, TA,) *alone*, or *by himself*. (M, O, Ḳ.) — The *flogger who inflicts the castigations appointed by the law* (O, Ḳ) *before*, or *in the presence of, the Sultán*. (O.) — *I. q.* لِجَام [as meaning The *bridle*, or *headstall and reins with the bit and other appertenances*]; as also ▼ سِحَالٌ; (Ḳ;) like as you say مِنْطَقٌ and نِطَاقٌ, and مِئْزَرٌ and إِزَارٌ: (TA:) or *its* فَأْس; (Ḳ;) which is the *piece of iron that stands up in the mouth* [*from the middle of the bit-mouth*]; as IDrd says in the "Book of the Saddle and Bridle:" (TA:) and *two rings*, (Ḳ, TA,) *one of which is inserted into the other*, (TA,) *at the two extremities of the* شَكِيم *of the bridle*, (Ḳ, TA,) *which is* [generally applied to *the bit-mouth*, but is here said by SM to be] *the piece of iron that is beneath the lower lip*: or, accord. to IDrd, the مِسْحَل of the bridle is *a piece of iron which is beneath the lower jaw*; and the فَأْس is the piece of iron that stands up in the شَكِيمَة; and the شَكِيمَة is the piece of iron that lies crosswise in the mouth: and the pl. is مَسَاحِلُ: (TA:) or the مِسْحَلَانِ are *two rings at the two extremities of the* شَكِيم [or *bit-mouth*] *of the bridle, one of which is inserted into the other* [*so that they occupy the place of our curb-chain*]: (Ṣ:) they are [also said to be] the خَدَّانِ [lit. *two cheeks*] of the bridle: (TA:) the مِسْحَل is beneath the part in which is the bridle, and upon it flow the foam and blood of the horse. (Az, TA voce قَيْقَب. [See also فَأْس and لِجَام.]) One says of a horse when exerting himself, and being quick, in his going, and thrusting forward therein his head, رَكِبَ مِسْحَلَهُ [*He bore upon his bridle*, &c.]. (O, TA.) And hence, (TA,) this phrase means [also] † *He* (a man, TA) *followed his error, not desisting from it*: (Ḳ, TA:) مِسْحَل signifying † *error*: (Ḳ:) and [in like manner] طَعَنَ فِى مِسْحَلِ ضَلَالَتِهِ means † *He hastened, and strove in his error*. (TA.) Also, the former of these two phrases, † *He resolved*, or *determined, upon the* [or *his*] *affair, and strove*, or *exerted himself therein*: (O, TA:) [for] مِسْحَل signifies also † *decisive resolution* or *determination*. (O, Ḳ, TA.) And † *He went on with energy in his discourse, sermon, speech, oration*, or *harangue*: (Ṣ, TA:) and so *in his poetry*. (A, TA.) — Also, [from the same word as meaning the "bridle," or "headstall &c.,"] ‡ The *side of the beard*: [like as it is called عِذَار because it is in the place corresponding to that of the عِذَار of a horse or the like: (جانب in the CḲ is a mistake for جَانِبُ:)] or the *lower part of each* عِذَار [or *side of the beard*], *to the fore part of the beard*; both together being called مِسْحَلَانِ: (Ḳ, TA: [اسفل in the CḲ is a mistake for أَسْفَلُ:]) or the *place of the* عِذَار: (Az, TA:) or the *temple*; مِسْحَلَانِ meaning the *two temples*: (TA:) and (Ḳ) the عَارِض [or *side of the cheek*] of a man. (Ibn-'Abbád, O, Ḳ.) One says, شَابَ مِسْحَلُهُ, meaning ‡ *The side of his beard became white*, or *hoary*. (TA.) — *A clean* (O, Ḳ, TA) *thin* (TA) *garment*, or *piece of cloth, of cotton*. (O, Ḳ, TA. [See also سَحْلٌ.]) — *A rope*, (Ḳ,) or *string*, or *thread*, (M, TA,) *that is twisted alone*: (Ḳ:) if with another, [i. e. with another strand,] it is termed مُبْرَم, and مُغَار. (TA. [See, again, سَحْلٌ.]) — *A sieve*. (O, Ḳ.) — The *wild ass*: (Ṣ, TA:) [because of his braying:] see 1, last sentence: an epithet in which the quality of a subst. predominates. (TA.) — *A brisk, lively, sprightly*, or *active, ass*. (O.) — *A low, vile, mean*, or *sordid, man*. (O, TA.) — *A devil*. (O, TA.) — The name of *The* تَابِعَة (Ṣ, O) or [*familiar*] *jinnee* or *genie* (Ḳ) *of* [*the poet*] *El-Aashà*. (Ṣ, O, Ḳ. [In the Ḳ it is implied that it is with the article ال: but accord. to the Ṣ and O and TA, it is without ال.])

مِسْحَلَةٌ *A ball of spun thread*. (AA, TA.)

مَسْحُولٌ [*Pared, peeled*, &c.: see 1. — And hence, because abraded by the feet of men and beasts,] *A road*. (TA in art. رفع.) — And *An even, wide place*. (O, Ḳ.) — See also سَحْلٌ. — As an epithet applied to a man, *Small and contemptible*. (O, Ḳ.) — And the name of *A camel belonging to* [*the poet*] *El-'Ajjáj*. (O, Ḳ.)

سحم

1. سَحِمَ, aor. ـَ, inf. n. سَحَمٌ; and سَحُمَ; *He, or it, was*, or *became, black*. (Mṣb.)

2. سَحَّمُوا وَجْهَهُ *They blackened his face*; syn. حَمَّمُوهُ; as also سَخَّمُوهُ. (A, TA.)

4. اسحمت السَّمَآءُ *The sky poured forth its water*: (Ḳ:) mentioned as on the authority of IAạr: but it has been mentioned before, on his authority, as with ج. (TA.)

سَحَمٌ: see سُحْمَةٌ. — *A sort of tree*; (Ṣ, Ḳ;) like ▼ سَحَمَةٌ: (Ṣ:) the latter also signifies a sort of tree: (Ḳ:) the former is said by ISk to be *a certain plant*: and by AḤn, to be *a plant that grows like the* نَصِىّ *and* صِلِّيَان *and* عَنَكَث, *except that it is taller*; *the* سَحَمَة [i. e. the *single plant of this species*] *being sometimes as tall as a man, and larger*. (TA.) — Also *Iron*: (IAạr, Ḳ:) n. un. with ة; meaning *a lump*, or *piece, of iron*. (IAạr, TA.)

سُحُمٌ [a pl. of which the sing. is not mentioned,] The *blacksmith's hammers*. (IAạr, Ḳ.)

سُحْمَةٌ *Blackness*; (Ṣ, Mṣb, Ḳ;) as also ▼ سَحَمٌ, [mentioned above as inf. n. of سَحِمَ,] and ▼ سُحَامٌ; (Ḳ;) like [سُخْمَة and] سُخَامٌ: (TA in art. سخم:) *a blackness like the colour of the crow to which the epithet* ▼ أَسْحَمُ *is applied*. (Lth, TA.)

سُحَامٌ: see the next preceding paragraph.

سُحَيْمٌ: see the next following paragraph.

أَسْحَمُ *Black*; (Ṣ, Mṣb, Ḳ;) like أَسْخَمُ; (TA in art. سخم;) applied to the crow; see سُحْمَةٌ: (Lth, TA:) fem. سَحْمَآءُ; (Mṣb, TA;) applied to a plant of that colour; (ISk, TA;) and particularly to the نَصِىّ when it is of that colour, and thus applied as an intensive epithet; and to a woman in the same sense: (TA:) and ▼ إِسْحِمَانٌ signifies anything *black* (ISd, Ḳ) accord. to some; but this is a mistake, for it is only أَسْحَمُ. (ISd, TA.) — [Hence,] الأَسْحَمُ is the name of *A certain idol*, (Ḳ, TA,) *which was black*. (TA.) — And *The night*. (TA.) — [Hence likewise,] أَسْحَمُ signifies also *Clouds* (سَحَاب): (Ṣ, Ḳ:) or, as some say, *black clouds*: and سَحْمَآءُ signifies *a black cloud*. (TA.) — Also *Blood into which are dipped the hands of persons swearing, one to another*; (Ḳ;) or *blood into which the hand is dipped on the occasion of swearing with another* or *others*: said to have this meaning in the saying of El-Aạshà,

* رَضِيعَىْ لِبَانٍ ثَدْىَ أُمٍّ تَحَالَفَا *
* بِأَسْحَمَ دَاجٍ عَوْضُ لَا نَتَفَرَّقُ *

[*Two foster-brothers by the sucking of the breast of one mother swore together, by dark blood into which they dipped their hands, that you*, or *they*, i. e. a tribe (قَبِيلَة) or a company of men (جَمَاعَة), for, without the context, the meaning is doubtful, *should not ever become separated*]: or it has here one, or another, of three meanings here following. (Ṣ.) — The *womb*. (Ṣ.) — The *nipple of a woman's breast*: (Ḳ:) or the *blackness of the nipple of a woman's breast*. (Ṣ.) — *A skin such as is termed* زِقّ, *for wine*: (Ṣ, Ḳ:) because of its blackness: and ▼ سُحَيْمٌ also signifies *a* زِقّ. (TA.) — Also *A horn*: (Ṣ, Ḳ:) thus in the saying of Zuheyr,

* وَتَذْبِيبُهَا عَنْهُ بِأَسْحَمَ مِذْوَدِ *

[*And the frequent repelling of her*, or *them, from him with a horn*; so that مذود is merely an explicative adjunct, for it also means a horn, or it may be rendered here *an instrument for repelling*]: (Ṣ,* TA:) or [اسحم is here an epithet, and] the meaning is, *with a black horn*. (TA.) Another poet uses the phrase تَذُبُّ بِسَحْمَاوَيْنِ, [so in the TA, app. a mistranscription for تُذَبِّبُ,] i. e., [reading تَذُبُّ, *She repels*] *with a pair of horns*; using the fem. as meaning بِصِيصَتَيْنِ;

as though he said بِعِصِيَّتَيْنِ سَحْمَاوَيْنِ [*with two black horns*]. (IAar, TA.) — The fem., السَّحْمَآءُ also signifies *The* دُبُر [here meaning *anus*]: (K:) because of its colour. (TA.) — For another signification of the fem., see سَحْم.

أُسْحُمَانٌ *Of the colour termed* أُدْمَة [here app. meaning *tawniness*] *in an intense degree.* (TA.) — Also *A sort of tree.* (M, K.) A poet uses the phrase الأُسْحُمَانُ الأَسْحَمُ [*The black, or dark,* اسحمان]. (M, TA.)

إِسْحِمَانٌ: see أَسْحَمُ, first sentence.

سحن

1. سَحَنَ, (S, L, K,) aor. ـَ, (K,) inf. n. سَحْنٌ, (L,) *He broke* a stone. (S, L, K.) And *He crushed, bruised, brayed,* or *pounded,* a thing. (L.) — Also *He rubbed* [in the CK ذَلَكَ is erroneously put for دَلَكَ] a piece of wood *so as to make it smooth,* (L, K,) *with an instrument called* مِسْحَن, *without taking anything from it.* (L.)

3. سَاحَنَ المَالَ: see 5. — The inf. n. مُسَاحَنَةٌ signifies also The *meeting* [another] *face to face.* (L, K.) — And you say, سَاحَنْتُكَ, (L,) inf. n. مُسَاحَنَةٌ, (S, L, K,) *I mixed with thee in familiar,* or *social, intercourse:* (L:) and *did so in a good manner.* (S, L, K.) And سَاحَنَهُ الشَّىْءَ *He joined,* or *took part, with him in the thing.* (L.)

5. تَسَحَّنَ المَالَ *He looked at the* سَحْنَآء [or *aspect* &c.] *of the* مَال [i. e. *cattle,* or other *property*]; as also ▼ سَاحنه. (L, K.) You say, تَسَحَّنْتُ المَالَ فَرَأَيْتُ سَحْنَآءَهُ حَسَنَةً [*I looked at the aspect of the cattle,* or other *property, and saw the aspect thereof to be goodly*]. (S, L.)

سَحْنٌ *A numerous congregation:* so in the phrase يَوْمُ سَحْنٍ [*A day of a numerous congregation*]. (K.)

سِحْنٌ *Quarter, shelter,* or *protection;* syn. كَنَفٌ: so in the saying, هُوَ فِى سِحْنِهِ [*He is in his quarter* or *shelter* or *protection*]. (K.)

سَحْنَةٌ and ▼ سِحْنَةٌ, (L, K,) or the latter, and, as sometimes pronounced, سَحَنَةٌ, (S,) and ▼ سَحْنَآءُ and ▼ سَحْنَاءُ, (S, L, K,) pronounced سَحَنَآءُ by Fr, the only person heard by A'Obeyd to pronounce it thus, and said by Ibn-Keysán to be thus pronounced because of the faucial letter, (S, L,) but ▼ سَحْنَآءُ is better, (L,) *Aspect, appearance,* or *external state* or *condition:* (S, L, K:) and simply *state,* or *condition:* (L:) and *colour:* and *softness,* or *smoothness, of the external skin:* and *i. q.* نَعْمَةٌ [as meaning *softness,* or *delicateness:* in the CK, النَّغْمَةُ is erroneously put for النَّعْمَةُ]. (L, K.) You say, إِنَّهُ لَحَسَنُ السَّحْنَةِ (L) and ▼ السَّحْنَآءِ (S, L) [*Verily he is goodly in aspect,* &c.]: and ▼ هٰؤُلَآءِ قَوْمٌ حَسَنٌ سَحْنَتُهُمْ [*These are a people,* or *party, whose aspect,* &c., *is goodly*]. (S, L.) And سَحْنَةٌ is also expl. as signifying The *beauty of the hair, and of the complexion, and of the external skin,* of a man. (L.) And it occurs in a trad. as meaning The *external skin of the face;* and is sometimes pronounced ▼ سِحَنَة, and is also called the ▼ سَحْنَآء. (L.)

سِحَنَةٌ: see what next precedes.

سَحَنَةٌ: see سَحْنَةٌ, in two places.

سَحْنَآءُ and سَحَنَآءُ: see سَحْنَةٌ; the former in four places.

مُسْحَنٌ A horse *goodly in condition;* as in the saying, جَآءَ الفَرَسُ مُسْحَنًا [*The horse came goodly in condition*]: fem. with ة: (L, K:) you say فَرَسٌ مُسْحَنَةٌ, (L,) or ▼ مُسْتَحْنَةٌ, (S, [so in my copies,]) *a mare goodly in condition and in aspect,* (L,) or *goodly in aspect.* (S.)

مِسْحَنٌ *An instrument with which wood is rubbed so as to make it smooth without taking anything from it.* (L.)

مِسْحَنَةٌ *A thing with which stones are broken.* (S, L, K.) *I. q.* صُلَّآءَة [i. e. *A stone such as fills the hand:* or *a stone with which,* or *on which, one brays,* or *powders, perfumes* or *other things*]. (L, K. [In the CK, الصَّلَابَةُ is erroneously put for الصُّلَّآءَةُ or its var. الصَّلَايَةُ.]) *A thing with which gold is rubbed so that it becomes smooth and glistening.* (Skr pp. 154 and 155.) And its pl. مَسَاحِنُ is said to signify *Stones with which are crushed,* or *brayed, the stones of* [i. e. *containing*] *silver.* (Skr, L.) And *Mill-stones with which one grinds.* (Skr.) And *Thin stones with which iron is made thin,* (L,* K, [in the former of which يُبْنَى is erroneously put for يُرَقَّقُ,]) *like* [*as is done with*] *the* مِسَنّ. (L.) And *Stones of* [i. e. *containing*] *gold and silver:* (Skr, K:) so says Ibn-Habeeb. (Skr.)

مُسْحَنٌ: فَرَسٌ مُسْتَحْنَةٌ: see

سحو and سحى

1. سَحَا الطِّينَ, (K,) first pers. سَحَوْتُ (S, Msb) and سَحَيْتُ, (S,) aor. يَسْحُو, (S, Msb, K,) and يَسْحَى, and يَسْحِى, (S, K,) inf. n. سَحْوٌ (Msb, TA) and سَحْىٌ, (K, TA,) *He scraped off,* (S, K,) or *cleared away,* (Msb, K,) [*the clay, soil,* or *mud,*] عَنْ وَجْهِ الأَرْضِ [*from the surface of the earth*], (S, Msb,) *with the* مِسْحَاة [q. v.]. (Msb.) — سَحَا الجَمْرَ *He cleared,* or *swept, away the live,* or *burning, coals:* (K:) ISd says, I think that Lh has mentioned this; but the verb well known in this sense is with خ. (TA. [See سَخَا.]) — سَحَا الشَّحْمَ عَنِ الإِهَابِ, inf. n. سَحْوٌ, *He scraped,* or *pared, off the fat from the skin,* or *hide.* (TA.) It is said in a trad., as some relate it, فَجَعَلَتْ تَسْحَاهَا, or, as others relate it, تَسْحَلُهَا, both meaning the same, i. e. *And she betook herself to paring,* or *stripping, off from it the flesh that was upon it.* (TA in art. سحل.) And ▼ استحى اللَّحْمَ signifies *He pared,* or *stripped, off the flesh.* (TA.) — سَحَا الشَّعَرَ, (K,) aor. يَسْحَى and يَسْحُو, inf. n. [app. سَحْوٌ and] سَحْىٌ (TA,) *He shaved off the hair;* as also ▼ استحاه.

(K.) — سَحَوْتُ القِرْطَاسَ, and سَحَيْتُهُ, aor. أَسْحَى, *I scraped off,* or *otherwise removed, the superficial part of the paper.* (S.) [And] سَحَا مِنَ القِرْطَاسِ *He took a little from the paper.* (K,* TA. [See سِحَاءَةٌ, second sentence.]) — سَحَا الكِتَابَ, (K,) first pers. سَحَيْتُ and سَحَوْتُ, (S,) aor. يَسْحَى and يَسْحُو, (TA,) *He bound the writing* (S, K) *with a* سِحَاءَة (K) or *with the* سِحَآء [q. v.]; (S;) and so ▼ سَحَّاهُ, (K,) inf. n. تَسْحِيَةٌ; (TA;) and ▼ اسحاه; (K;) as in the M. (TA.)

2: see the next preceding sentence.

4. اسحى *He* (a man S) *had many* أَسْحِيَة [pl. of سِحَاءَة, (q. v.,) n. un. of سِحَآء]. (S, K.) — See also 1, last sentence.

7. انسحى *It was,* or *became, pared;* or *pared off.* (TA.)

8: see 1, in two places.

سَحًا: see the next paragraph, in two places.

سَحَاةٌ The قِشْر [or *covering, integument, peel,* or *the like,*] of anything: pl. [or rather coll. gen. n.] ▼ سَحًا. (S.) See also سِحَاءَةٌ. — *A certain thorny tree;* (K, TA;) *the fruit thereof is white: it is a herb in the spring-season, as long as it remains green: when it dries up in the hot season, it is a tree.* (TA.) — *A bat:* (ISh, S, K:) pl. ▼ سَحًا; (K;) or [rather] it is the n. un. of سَحًا, which is syn. with خُفَّاش [used as a gen. n.]: (ISh, S:) and ▼ سَحَآء is a dial. var. of سَحًا used in this sense, accord. to Az. (TA.) — *I. q.* سَاحَة [i. e. The *court,* or *open area,* of a house]: (S, K:) formed from the latter word by transposition: (TA:) one says, لَا أَرَيَنَّكَ بِسَحْسَحِى وَسَحَاتِى [*I will assuredly not see thee in my quarter,* or *tract, and my court*]. (S.) And *I. q.* نَاحِيَة [*A side, region, quarter,* or *tract,* &c.]. (K.)

سَحَآء: see سِحَاءَة, in two places. — Also *A certain plant,* (S, K,) *having thorns,* (K,) *and having a blossom of a red hue inclining to whiteness, called the* بهرنة [app. a mistranscription for بُهْرُمَة]: (TA:) *the bees feed upon it,* (S, K,) *and their honey in consequence thereof becomes sweet* (S, K*) *in the utmost degree.* (K.) — See also سَحَاة.

سِحَاءَةٌ, of a writing, (S, K, TA, [in the CK and in my MS. copy of the K, written, سَحَاءَة,]) and ▼ سِحَآء, (TA,) or [rather] the former is the n. un. of the latter, (S,) *A certain thing with which a writing is bound;* (S, K, TA;) *called in Pers.* بَنْد نَامه, (PS,) or مُهْر نَامه; (Adillet el-Asmà of Meyd, cited by Golius;) *and in Turkish* نَامه بَاغِى; (Mirkát el-Loghah, cited by the same;) [*a sealed strip of paper with which a letter,* or *the like, is bound:*] the letter of a kádee to another kádee is perforated for the سِحَاءَة, and is then sealed [upon this strip:] (Mgh in art. خزم:) pl. أَسْحِيَة. (S.) [The same seems to be meant by what here follows:] سِحَاءَةُ القِرْطَاسِ, (K, TA,) with ء, (TA,) and ▼ سِحَاوَةٌ, (K, TA,) with و [and ء],

(TA,) or ↑ سُحَاتَةٌ, (so in the CḲ,) or this last also, like حَصَاةٌ, is a dial. var. of the first, (TA,) and ↑ سِحَايَةٌ, (Ḳ, TA, [in the CḲ written with fet-ḥ to the س, but it is]) like كِتَابَةٌ, with ى, (TA,) *What is taken from paper;* (Ḳ;) *the small portion* [or *strip,* app.,] *that is taken from paper:* (TA:) pl. أَسْحِيَةٌ [as above]. (Ḳ.) — Also, (Ṣ, M,) or ↑ سِحَايَةٌ, (Ḳ,) *A portion* (Ḳ) of cloud. (Ṣ, Ḳ.) One says, مَا فِى السَّمَآءِ سِحَاةٌ مِنْ سَحَابٍ [*There is not in the sky a portion of cloud*]. (Ṣ.) — السِّحَاةُ [in the CḲ السَّحَاةُ] also signifies أُمُّ الرَّأْسِ [q. v.], (Ḳ, TA,) [app. here meaning The *meninx;* for SM adds,] *in which is the brain;* (TA;) as also ↑ السِّحَايَةُ, with kesr [to the س]. (Ḳ.)

سِحَايَةٌ, (Ḳ, TA,) [in the CḲ سَحَايَةٌ, but it is] with kesr, (TA,) *Anything that is pared,* or *peeled, from a thing.* (Ḳ, TA.) — See also سِحَاةٌ, in three places. ═ Also The *art,* or *craft, of making the kind of implement called* مِسْحَاةٌ: (Ḳ, TA:) in this sense, likewise, with kesr, agreeably with analogy. (TA.)

سَحَّآءٌ *A maker of the kind of implement called* مِسْحَاةٌ. (T, Ḳ.)

سَاحٍ, applied to a [lizard of the species called] ضَبٌّ, *That feeds upon the plant called* سِحَآءٌ. (Ṣ.)

سَاحِيَةٌ, (Ṣ, Ḳ,) [from سَاحٍ, the ة denoting intensiveness, (TA,) A torrent *that carries away everything;* (Ḳ;) *that pares and sweeps away everything.* (TA.) — And A rain *that falls with vehemence,* (Ṣ, Ḳ,) *paring the surface of the earth.* (Ṣ.)

أُسْحِيَّةٌ (with ḍamm, TA) *Any integument of skin upon the portions of flesh that are on bones.* (Az, Ḳ.)

أُسْحُوَانٌ, with ḍamm, (Ṣ, Ḳ,) A man (Ṣ) *that eats much.* (Ṣ, Ḳ.) — And (Ḳ) *Beautiful,* or *comely,* (Ḳ,) so expl. by AO, (TA,) [and] *tall,* (Ḳ,) thus expl. by Fr, likewise applied to a man. (TA.)

مِسْحَاةٌ *A shovel,* or *spade, of iron;* (MA, PṢ;) *an implement* (Ṣ, Mṣb, Ḳ) *like the* مِجْرَفَة, *except that it is of iron,* (Ṣ, Mṣb,) *with which clay, soil,* or *mud, is cleared away* (Mṣb, Ḳ) *from the surface of the earth:* (Mṣb:) a مِسْحَاةٌ [*for digging,* i. e. *a spade,*] *has a cross piece of wood upon which the digger presses his foot:* (Ḳ, voce عَتَلٌ:) and there is *a curved kind,* [app. *a sort of hoe,*] *such as is called in Pers.* كَلَنْد: (Ṣ:) pl. مَسَاحٍ. (Ṣ, Mṣb.) Ru-beh likens the toes, or extremities of the fore parts of the hoofs, of horses, to مَسَاحٍ; because with them they pare the ground: so in the T: or, accord. to the M, he likens thereto the hoofs of asses. (TA.) — مِسْحَاةُ النَّارِ means [*The fire-shovel;*] *a thing with which the fire is stirred.* (TA voce مِحْرَاثٌ.)

سخب

1. سَخَبٌ [inf. n. of سَخِبَ] *i. q.* صَخَبٌ [inf. n. of صَخِبَ], (A, Ḳ,) signifying The *raising a loud cry,* or *a clamour:* (TA:) or it [is used as a subst., and] signifies *a confusion of sounds.* (Mgh, MF, TA.) The substitution of س for ص is allowable in every word containing خ: [for instance,] in a trad. [cited voce خُشُبٌ, q. v., as some relate it], the hypocrites are described as خُشُبٌ بِاللَّيْلِ سُخُبٌ بِالنَّهَارِ. (TA.)

سِخَابٌ *A necklace* (قِلَادَةٌ) *made of* [*the composition termed*] سُكّ *and of other things, without any jewels:* (Ṣ:) or *a* قِلَادَة *of cloves and* سُكّ *and* مَحْلَب [q. v.], *without jewels,* (A, Ḳ, TA,) *and without pearls:* and likewise, *of gold:* and *of silver:* or, accord. to Az, it is, with the Arabs, *any* قِلَادَة, whether *with jewels* or *without:* accord. to IAth, *a string on which are strung beads, worn by boys and by girls:* (TA:) it is thus called because of the sound of its beads when in motion: (MF, TA:) pl. سُخُبٌ. (Ṣ, Ḳ.) [Hence] one says, وَجَدْتُكَ وَارِثَ السِّخَابِ [*I have found thee to be the inheritor of the* سِخَاب], meaning, ‡ *like the boy that has no knowledge.* (A, TA.)

سخبر

سَخْبَرٌ *A certain kind of trees,* (Ṣ, Ḳ,) *the heads of which, when it grows tall, bend and hang down;* [a coll. gen. n.;] n. un. with ة: (TA:) *it resembles the* إِذْخِر; (Ḳ;) *or it is like the* ثُمَام [or *panic grass*], *and has a* [*root such as is termed*] جُرْثُومَة; *its branches,* or *twigs, are, in abundance, like the* كُرَاث [app. كَرَاث, a certain large tree, growing on the mountains]; *and its fruits resemble brooms of reeds,* or *are more slender:* (AḤn:) *serpents make their abodes at its roots.* (TA.) It is related in a trad. of Ibn-Ez-Zubeyr, that he said to Mo'áwiyeh, لَا تُطْرِقْ إِطْرَاقَ الْأُفْعُوَانِ فِى أُصُولِ السَّخْبَرِ [*Do not thou look down upon the ground like as does the male viper at the roots of the sakhbar*]; meaning † *do not thou affect heedlessness of the state in which we are,* or *of the affair in which we are engaged.* (TA.) One says also, رَكِبَ فُلَانٌ السَّخْبَرَ, meaning, † *Such a one acted perfidiously, treacherously,* or *unfaithfully.* (Ṣ.) And a poet says,

* وَالْغَدْرُ يَنْبُتُ فِى أُصُولِ السَّخْبَرِ *

† [*And perfidy grows at the roots of the sakhbar*]: (Ṣ:) [because the viper lives there: or] the poet means, that the people of whom he speaks dwelt in places where the sakhbar grow; and they are thought to have been of the tribe of Hudheyl: IB says that he likens the perfidious to this tree because, when it is full-grown, its head hangs down, not remaining erect; and that he means, ye do not remain faithful, like as this tree does not remain in one state. (TA.)

سخت

سَخْتٌ, (Ṣ, Ḳ,) originally Pers., (TA,) *Vehement,* or *intense;* (Ṣ, Ḳ;) as also ↑ سَخِّيتٌ (Ḳ) and ↑ سِخْتِيتٌ. (Ṣ, Ḳ.) One says, هٰذَا حَرٌّ سَخْتٌ, (Lḥ, Ṣ,) or سَخْتٌ لَخْتٌ, (TA,) *This is vehement,* or *intense, heat;* a phrase well known in the language of the Arabs, who use certain Pers., or foreign, words, as, for instance, بَلَاس for مِسْح (Lḥ, Ṣ, TA. [See also سَخْتٌ.]) And حَلِفٌ ↑ سِخْتِيتٌ *Vehement swearing.* (Ṣ.) And كَذِبٌ ↑ سِخْتِيتٌ *A vehement lie:* and *a pure,* or *an unmixed, lie.* (TA.) — Also, from the Pers., Anything *hard and thin* or *fine.* (TA.)

سَخِّيتٌ: see the preceding paragraph: — and that here following.

سِخْتِيتٌ: see the first paragraph, in three places. — Also Dust *rising very high:* (Ṣ, Ḳ:) and ↑ سَخِّيتٌ likewise signifies [the same, or] dust *rising high;* (TA in art. شخت;) as also شِخْتِيتٌ and شَخِّيتٌ and شُخْتُوتٌ; (Ḳ in that art.;) said to be arabicized words from the Pers. سَخْت: (TA in that art.:) and the first (سِخْتِيت [and app. the others also]), *fine* dust. (TA in the present art.) And Anything *fine;* as, for instance, flour, or meal. (AA, TA.) *Fine* سَوِيق [or meal of parched barley, &c.]: (Aṣ, TA:) or سويق *that is not moistened with any seasoning,* or *savoury admixture:* (Ṣ:) or سويق *having little grease* or *gravy* [*mixed with it*]; as also سِخْتِيت and سُخْتُوت. (Ḳ and TA in the present art. and in art. سحت.) And *Fine* حُوَّارَى [or white flour]. (Aṣ, Ḳ.)

سِخْتِيَانٌ and سَخْتِيَانٌ (Ḳ, TA) and accord. to some سُخْتِيَانٌ; the second of which is asserted by the expositors of Bkh to be the most common and most chaste; but Esh-Shiháb [El-Khafájee], in the "Sharḥ esh-Shifà," mentions only the form with kesr to the س and fet-ḥ and kesr to the ت; and Ibn-Et-Tilimsánee mentions only the form with ḍamm to the س and fet-ḥ and kesr to the ت, adding that it is also written with ج; MF, however, deems what this last says to be very strange, and more especially with respect to the word's being written with ج, which he affirms to be unknown; (TA;) [*Morocco-leather;* so in the present day;] *tanned goat's skin;* an arabicized word, (Ḳ,) from the Pers.: expl. by IAth as *jujube-coloured* [or *dark dull red*] *skins* (جُلُودٌ عُنَّابِيَّةٌ); *not* [*such as from their red colour are termed*] أُدْم. (TA.)

سِخْتِيَانِىٌّ *A preparer and seller of* سِخْتِيَان. (Ḳ,* TA.)

سخد

سُخْدٌ [The *matter contained in the secundines;*] *a yellow, thick water* [or *fluid*], *that comes forth with the fœtus;* (Ṣ, M, Ḳ;) as also سُخْتٌ: (M, TA:) hence, in a trad., the appearance upon the face produced by excitement from remaining awake during the night is termed, by way of comparison, سُخْد upon the face: (Ṣ,* L:) or *blood and water in the membrane that envelops the fœtus of a beast:* or *what comes forth with the membrane that envelops the fœtus:* said to be peculiar to the human species: or common to the human species and beasts: (L:) or the *water* [or *fluid*] *in that membrane*; as also سُخْتٌ and نُخْطٌ and فَقْءٌ: (IAạr, TA in art. فقأ:) or [the *placenta*; i. e.] *a thing like the liver*, or *like the spleen, compact, which is in the membrane that envelops the fœtus of a beast*: sometimes children play with it: or *that membrane itself*: and i. q. رَهَلٌ [which is expl. as meaning *yellow water in the* سُخْد, and it is also the inf. n. of رَهِلَ, q. v.]: and صُخْدٌ is a dial. var. thereof in all its senses, those above mentioned and those following. (L.) — Also The *urine of a camel's fœtus* (فَصِيل) *in its mother's belly*. (L.) — And † *Yellowness in the face* [as in the trad. above mentioned]. (L.)

مُسَخَّدٌ † *Having the stomach in a heaving state, agitated by a tendency to vomit, or disordered*; (Ḳ;) *yellow*, (Ṣ, Ḳ,) *heavy*, (Ṣ,) *and swollen*, (Ṣ, Ḳ,) *by disease or by some other cause*. (TA.)

سخر

1. سَخِرَ مِنْهُ, (Fr, Akh, Ṣ, A, Mṣb, Ḳ,) and بِهِ, (AZ, Akh, Ṣ, Mṣb, Ḳ,) like as one says ضَحِكَ مِنْهُ and بِهِ, and هَزِئَ مِنْهُ and بِهِ, (Akh, Ṣ,) but the former is the more chaste, (En-Nawawee, TA,) and is that which occurs in the Ḳur ix. 80, and xi. 40, [&c.,] (TA,) and J says that the latter is the worse of the two, (Ṣ,) and Fr disallows it absolutely, (TA,) aor. ـَ, (Ṣ, Mṣb, Ḳ,) inf. n. سَخَرٌ (Ṣ, Mṣb, Ḳ) and سَخْرٌ (Ḳ) and سُخْرٌ and سُخُرٌ (Ṣ, Ḳ) and سُخْرَةٌ (Ḳ) and مَسْخَرٌ, (Ṣ, Ḳ,) *He mocked at, scoffed at, laughed at, derided, or ridiculed, him*; (Ṣ,* A, Mṣb, Ḳ, &c.;) as also ▾ استسخر: (A,* Ḳ:) and ▾ يَسْتَسْخِرُونَ, in the Ḳur xxxvii. 14, signifies, accord. to Ibn-Er-Rummánee, *they invite one another to mock, scoff, deride, or ridicule*. (TA.) — It is said in a trad., أَتَسْخَرُ مِنِّى وَأَنَا المَلِكُ *Dost thou mock at me, or deride me, when I am the king?* or, as some say, it is tropical, and means, ‡ *dost thou put me in a place which I do not regard as my right?* so that it seems to denote a species of mockery. (TA.) — And in another trad. it is said, ‡ أَنَا أَقُولُ كَذَا وَلَا أَسْخَرُ [*I say so, and I do not jest*]; meaning I say not aught but the truth. (A,* TA.) — The words (of the Ḳur [xi. 40] TA) إِنْ تَسْخَرُوا مِنَّا فَإِنَّا نَسْخَرُ مِنْكُمْ كَمَا تَسْخَرُونَ are said to signify *If ye deem us ignorant, we also deem you ignorant like as ye deem us ignorant*. (Ḳ.) — سَخَرَهُ: see 2. — سَخَرَتِ السَّفِينَةُ, aor. ـَ, ‡ *The ship had a good wind and voyage*; (Ḳ;) [as though it made the wind subservient, or submissive, to it; (see 2;)] *it obeyed, and ran its course*. (TA.)

2. سَخَّرَهُ, inf. n. تَسْخِيرٌ, *He constrained him, or compelled him*, (JK, Ṣ, Ḳ,) namely, a servant, or a beast, *to do what he* [the latter] *did not desire*, (JK, TA,) or *to work, without recompense, or hire, or wages*, (Ṣ, Ḳ,) *and without price*; (TA;) as also ▾ تسخّرهُ: (Ṣ, Mgh,* Ḳ:) and [in like manner,] ▾ سَخَرَهُ, aor. ـَ, inf. n. سِخْرِىٌّ and سُخْرِىٌّ, *he constrained him to do what he did not desire; compelled him*: (Ḳ:) or سخّرهُ, *he made use of him without compensation*, (A, Mṣb,) فِى العَمَلِ [*in work*]. (Mṣb.) You say, ▾ تَسَخَّرْتُ دَابَّةً لِفُلَانٍ *I rode a beast belonging to such a one without recompense*. (TA.) — *He brought him under, or into subjection; rendered him subservient, submissive, tractable, or manageable*. (Ṣ, Ḳ.) You say, سَخَّرَ ٱللّٰهُ الإِبِلَ *God hath made the camels subservient, or submissive, and manageable*. (Mṣb.) And in the Ḳur [xiv. 37], it is said, وَسَخَّرَ لَكُمُ ٱلشَّمْسَ وَٱلْقَمَرَ † *And He hath made subservient to you, or submissive for you, the sun and the moon* [to run their appointed courses]. (TA.) سُخِّرَ لَهُ [as also ▾ تَسَخَّرَ له] signifies † *It* (anything) *was rendered submissive or manageable or practicable, to him, or prepared or disposed for him agreeably with his desire*. (TA.) You say also, سَخَّرَ ٱللّٰهُ السَّفِينَةَ, inf. n. تَسْخِيرٌ, ‡ *God made the ship to obey and to run its course; to have a good wind and voyage*. (TA.) سَخَّرَهَا عَلَيْهِمْ, in the Ḳur lxix. 7, means † *He sent it upon them by force*; namely, the wind: (Jel:) or *made it to prevail against them by his power*. (Bḍ.)

5: see 2, in three places.

10: see 1, in two places.

سُخْرَةٌ *One who is mocked at, scoffed at, laughed at, derided, or ridiculed; a laughingstock*; (Ṣ, A, Ḳ;) as also ▾ سِخْرِىٌّ and سُخْرِىٌّ; (Az, A;) which are used as sing., as in the phrase ٱتَّخَذُوهُ سُخْرِيًّا *they made him a laughingstock*; (A;) and as pl., as in هُمْ لَكَ سُخْرِىٌّ, and also ▾ سُخْرِيَّةٌ, the former being masc. and the latter fem., *they are to thee laughingstocks*; the former occurring in the Ḳur [see xxiii. 112, and xxxviii. 63, and xliii. 31,] with ḍamm and with kesr accord. to different readings. (Az, TA.) — Also *One who is constrained, or compelled, to do what he does not desire, or to work, without recompense, or hire, or wages*; (JK, Ṣ,* Mgh,* Mṣb,* Ḳ,* TA;) applied to a servant, (JK, Ṣ, Mṣb,) and to a beast; (JK, Mṣb;) as also ▾ سُخْرِىٌّ (Mṣb, Ḳ) and سِخْرِىٌّ; (Ḳ;) or the former of these, only, is used in this sense; and the latter, and sometimes the former also, in the sense immediately preceding: (TA:) and سُخْرَةٌ is also used as a pl., (JK, A,) as in the phrase هٰؤُلَآءِ سُخْرَةٌ لِلسُّلْطَانِ *these are persons made use of without compensation for the Sultán*: (JK,* A:) it also signifies *one who employs any person*, (Ḳ, TA,) or *beast*, (TA,) *that he has subjected, or compelled to obey him, without recompense, or hire, or wages*: (Ḳ, TA:) [or this is a mistake, and the correct signification is] *one who is so employed by him who has subjected him*. (L.) — It is also *syn. with* تَسْخِيرٌ [inf. n. of 2]. (TA in art. سمع.)

سُخَرَةٌ *One who mocks at, scoffs at, laughs at, derides, or ridicules, others*, (Ṣ, Ḳ,) *much*. (Ṣ.) [See also مَسْخَرَةٌ.]

سُخْرِىٌّ and سِخْرِىٌّ (T, Ṣ, Mṣb, Ḳ) and سُخْرِيَّةٌ (T, Ṣ, Ḳ) *Mockery; scoff; derision; ridicule*. (T, Ṣ, Mṣb, Ḳ.) — See also سُخْرَةٌ, in three places.

سُخَّرٌ *A certain herb, or leguminous plant*, (Ṣgh, Ḳ,) *in Khurásán*; (Ḳ;) accord. to AḤn, i. q. سَيْكُرَانٌ [q. v.]. (TA.)

سُفُنٌ سَوَاخِرُ [pl. of سَفِينَةٌ سَاخِرَةٌ] ‡ *Ships obeying, and having a good wind*. (Ṣ.)

مَسْخَرَةٌ [*An occasion, or a cause, of mockery, scoffing, derision, or ridicule*]: pl. مَسَاخِرُ. (A.) You say رُبَّ مَسَاخِرَ يَعُدُّهَا النَّاسُ مَفَاخِرَ [*Many occasions of mockery, &c., men reckon occasions of boasting, or glorying*]. (A.) And هُوَ مَسْخَرَةٌ [*He is a cause of mockery, &c.*]. (A.) [See also مَسْخُرَةٌ.] — Also *One who mocks at, scoffs at, laughs at, derides, or ridicules, others*. (A.) [See also سُخَرَةٌ.]

مُسَخَّرٌ Any one *that is constrained, or compelled*, [*brought into subjection, or made subservient or submissive*,] *and managed, unable to free himself from constraint*. (TA.) — وَٱلنُّجُومُ مُسَخَّرَاتٌ بِأَمْرِهِ [in the Ḳur xvi. 12 means *And the stars are made subservient, or submissive*,] *running their courses*. (Az, TA.)

سخط

1. سَخِطَ, aor. ـَ, inf. n. سَخَطٌ (Ṣ,* Mṣb, Ḳ*) [and مَسْخَطٌ, (see سُخْطٌ, below,)] *He was, or became, displeased, or discontented*; (Ṣ,* Ḳ, TA;) as also ▾ تسخّط; (Ḳ, TA;) syns. كَرِهَ and تَكَرَّهَ [the latter of which, app. referring particularly to ▾ تسخّط, properly and generally signifies, when intrans., *he expressed, or showed, dislike, displeasure, disapprobation, discontent, or hatred*]: (TA:) *he was, or became, angry*; (Ṣ, Mṣb, TA;) and ▾ تسخّط signifies *the same*; or *he became angered*; syn. تَغَضَّبَ. (TA.) You say, سَخِطَ عَلَيْهِ [*He was, or became, displeased, or discontented, or angry, with him*]. (Ḳur v. 83.) And سَخِطَهُ *He was, or became, displeased, or discontented, with him*; as also ▾ تَسَخَّطَهُ; both expl. by لَمْ يَرْضَ بِهِ; (Ḥam p. 502;) and the latter by تَكَرَّهَهُ, which signifies as above, like كَرِهَهُ, and also [which signifies as above, like كَرِهَهُ, and also *he expressed, or showed, dislike of it, displeasure with it, disapprobation of it, discontent with it, or hatred of it*]; (Ḳ, TA;) and لَمْ يَرْضَهُ; (TA;) as in the saying, ▾ كُلَّمَا عَمِلْتُ لَهُ عَمَلًا تَسَخَّطَهُ [*Every time that I did for him a deed, he expressed, or showed, dislike of it, &c.*]; and in like manner, ▾ أَعْطَاهُ قَلِيلًا فَتَسَخَّطَهُ [*He gave him little and he expressed, or showed, dislike of it, &c.*]: (TA:) and [hence,] ▾ تَسَخَّطَ عَطَآءَهُ *He deemed his gift little, and it did not stand with him in any stead*; expl. by ٱسْتَقَلَّهُ وَلَمْ يَقَعْ مِنْهُ مَوْقِعًا. (Ṣ, Ḳ.) You say also, ٱللّٰهُ يَسْخَطُ لَكُمْ كَذَا, meaning *God forbiddeth you such a thing*: or *will punish you for such a thing*: or it may refer to the desire of punishing for it. (TA.)

4. اسخطهُ [*He displeased, or discontented, him*:] *he angered him; made him angry*. (Ṣ, Mṣb, Ḳ.)

5: see 1, in seven places.

سُخْطٌ, (Ṣ, Mṣb, Ḳ,) a subst. from سَخِطَ, (Mṣb,) *Dislike, displeasure, disapprobation,* or *discontent;* (TA;) contr. of رِضًى; (Ṣ, Ḳ, TA;) as also ↓ سُخُطٌ (Ṣgh, Ḳ) and ↓ سَخَطٌ (Ṣ, Ḳ) and ↓ مَسْخَطٌ: (Ṣgh, Ḳ:) [the last two of which are inf. ns.:] *anger;* (Mṣb;) as also ↓ سَخَطٌ. (TA.)

سَخَطٌ: see سُخْطٌ, in two places.

سُخُطٌ: see سُخْطٌ.

سَاخِطٌ [*Displeased; discontented:*] *angry.* (Ṣ.)

مَسْخَطٌ: see سُخْطٌ.

مَسْخَطَةٌ [*A cause,* or *means,* or *an occasion, of dislike, displeasure, disapprobation,* or *discontent:* and, *of anger:* or *a cause,* &c., *of procuring dislike,* &c.: pl., app., مَسَاخِطُ and مَسَاخِطَةٌ. Hence the saying,] البِرُّ مَرْضَاةٌ لِلرَّبِّ مَسْخَطَةٌ لِلشَّيْطَانِ [*Piety is a cause of approbation to the Lord; a cause of disapprobation,* or *anger, to the devil*]. (TA.)

مَسْخُوطٌ *Disliked, disapproved,* or *hated:* (A, Ḳ:) in this sense applied to a gift. (A, TA.) You say also, هُوَ مَسْخُوطٌ عَلَيْهِ *He is an object of anger.* (TA.) — [Hence,] *Transformed,* or *metamorphosed, into a worse,* or *more foul,* or *more ugly, shape:* [and hence applied by the Arabs in the present day to any idol or other image of ancient workmanship; such being regarded by them as metamorphosed in consequence of having incurred the wrath of God:] and *short:* but thus applied, it is a vulgar term. (TA.)

سخف

1. سَخُفَ, [aor. ـُ,] inf. n. سَخَافَةٌ (Mgh, Mṣb, TA) and سُخْفٌ, or, accord. to Kh, the former only, (Mṣb,) said of a garment, or piece of cloth, (Mgh, Mṣb, TA,) *It was,* or *became, thin, flimsy,* or *unsubstantial;* (Mṣb;) *scanty in the yarn;* (Mgh, Mṣb;) or *thin in texture.* (TA.) And سَخُفَ, (TA,) inf. n. سَخَافَةٌ, said of anything, *It was,* or *became, thin, slender,* or *unsubstantial.* (Mṣb,* TA. [See سَخَافَةٌ below, voce سُخْفٌ.]) And سَخُفَ, inf. n. سُخْفٌ, (Ḳ,) or rather سَخَافَةٌ, accord. to what is said below of a distinction between these two ns., (TA,) said of a skin for water or milk, *It was,* or *became, unsound,* (Ḳ, TA,) *altered for the worse, old, and worn out.* (TA.) — سَخُفَ, aor. سَخَافَةٌ, [or سُخْفٌ, q. v. infrà,] is also said of a man, meaning *He was,* or *became, slender,* or *shallow,* or *weak, in intellect.* (Ṣ, Ḳ.*) And it is also said of the intellect, meaning *It was,* or *became, slender,* &c. (Ḳ,* TḲ.)

2. سَخَّفَهُ, inf. n. تَسْخِيفٌ, [*It rendered him thin, lean,* or *emaciated,*] said of hunger. (A, TA.)

3. سَاخَفَهُ, (Ṣ, Ḳ,) inf. n. مُسَاخَفَةٌ, (TA,) *i. q.* حَامَقَهُ [*He aided him in his foolishness,* or *stupidity*]. (Ṣ, Ḳ.) — مُسَاخَفَةٌ signifies [also] *The showing,* or *making a show of, foolishness* or *stupidity.* (KL.)

4. اسخف, inf. n. إِسْخَافٌ, said of a man, *His property became little,* or *scanty.* (TA.) — مَا أَسْخَفَهُ *How* [*slender, shallow, weak,*] *deficient,* or *defective, is he in intellect!* (Sb, TA.)

[10. استسخفهُ *He deemed him slender, shallow,* or *weak, in intellect:* but this is perhaps post-classical.]

سَخْفٌ *Slenderness of the means of subsistence.* (AA, Ḳ.) — See also the next paragraph.

سُخْفٌ (AA, JK, Ṣ, Mgh, Mṣb, Ḳ) and ↓ سَخْفٌ (JK, K) and ↓ سُخْفَةٌ and ↓ سَخَافَةٌ (Ḳ) *Slenderness, shallowness,* or *weakness, of intellect,* (AA, JK, Ṣ, Mgh, Mṣb, Ḳ,) *&c.:* (Ḳ:) or, as some say, *a lightness* [*of body*] *incident to a man when he is hungry:* [but it is not clearly shown whether this refer to all of the foregoing words or only to the last, or last two, of them: (see سَخْفَةٌ, below:)] and some say that ↓ سُخْفَةٌ signifies *weakness of intellect;* or *deficiency thereof:* (TA:) or سُخْفٌ is in the intellect; and ↓ سَخَافَةٌ is [*thinness,* &c., (see 1,)] in everything; (Kh, Mṣb, Ḳ, TA;) as, for instance, in clouds, and in a skin for water or milk, and in herbage, and in a garment, or piece of cloth, &c. (TA.)

سَخْفَةُ الجُوعِ, (Ṣ, Ḳ,) and ↓ سُخْفَتُهُ, (JK, Ḳ,) *The thinness,* and *leanness,* or *emaciation, consequent upon hunger.* (JK, Ṣ, Ḳ.) One says, بِهِ سَخْفَةٌ مِنَ الجُوعِ *In him is thinness,* &c., *consequent upon hunger.* (Ṣ, TA.)

سُخْفَةٌ: see سُخْفٌ, in two places: — and see the paragraph here next preceding.

سَخِيفٌ, applied to a garment, or piece of cloth, (JK, Mgh, Mṣb, Ḳ, TA,) *Thin, flimsy,* or *unsubstantial;* (Mṣb;) *scanty in the yarn;* (Mgh, Mṣb;) or *thin in texture.* (JḲ, TA.) It is also applied to anything, as, for instance, clouds (سَحَاب), and herbage, (JK,) in both of these cases meaning *Thin;* (TA;) and to a skin for water or milk [as meaning *unsound, altered for the worse, old, and worn out;* see 1]: (JK:) and to the iron head or blade of an arrow or a spear or the like as meaning *long and broad* [*and* app. *thin*]. (AḤn, TA.) — Also, applied to a man, *Slender,* or *shallow,* or *weak, in intellect:* (JK, Ṣ, Mgh, Mṣb, Ḳ:*) and, thus applied, (Ḳ,) or سَخِيفُ العَقْلِ, (TA,) *lightwitted;* or *light,* or *unsteady, in intellect:* (Ḳ, TA:) from the same epithet applied to a garment, or piece of cloth. (Mgh, Mṣb.)

سَخَافَةٌ: see سُخْفٌ, in two places. [And see also 1, of which it is an inf. n.]

أَرْضٌ مَسْخَفَةٌ *A land in which is little herbage:* (ISh, Ḳ:) from سَخِيفٌ as an epithet applied to a garment, or piece of cloth. (TA.) [See also ارض مَسْحَفَةٌ, in art. سحف.]

سخل

1. سَخَلَهُمْ, aor. ـَ, (Ḳ,) inf. n. سَخْلٌ, (TA,) *He drove away, repelled,* or *banished, them:* (Ḳ, TA: [in the CḲ, نَفَاهُمْ is erroneously put for نَفَاهُمْ:]) and خَسَلَهُمْ signifies the same. (TA.) — And سَخَلَ الشَّىْءَ *He took the thing by deceit* (Ḳ, TA) *and by seizure:* but not known to Az except on the authority of Lth; and its correctness is doubted by him, unless it be formed by transposition from خَلَسَ, like as they said جَذَبَ and جَبَذَ, and بَضَّ and ضَبَّ. (TA.)

2. سَخَّلَتِ النَّخْلَةُ, inf. n. تَسْخِيلٌ, *The palm-tree bore dates such as are termed* [سُخَّل, i. e.] شِيص: (Ṣ, TA:) so in the dial. of El-Ḥijáz: (TA:) or *it was weak in its date-stones and its dates:* or *it shook off its dates.* (Ḳ, TA.) — And سَخَّل, (Ḳ,) or سَخَّلَ النَّخْلَةَ, (TA,) said of a man, *He shook the palm-tree in order that its dates might fall off.* (Ḳ, TA.) — And سَخَّلَهُ, (Ṣ,) or سَخَّلَهُمْ, inf. n. as above, (Ḳ,) *He attributed,* or *imputed, to him,* or *them, a vice, fault,* or *defect,* (Ṣ, Ḳ, TA,) *and reckoned him,* or *them, weak:* of the dial. of Hudheyl. (Ṣ, TA.)

4. اسخلهُ *It* (an affair, or event, TA) *kept him,* or *held him, back; delayed him,* or *retarded him.* (Ḳ, TA.)

سَخْلٌ: see سَخْلَةٌ. — Also † *An infant that is an object of love to his parents:* (IAạr, O, TA:) originally, the "offspring of the sheep or goat" [app. as a sing. as well as a coll. gen. n.]. (TA.) — See also سُخَّلٌ, in two places.

سَخْلَةٌ *A lamb,* or *kid, in whatever state it be;* (Ḳ;) *male* or *female:* (TA:) or *a lamb,* or *kid, when just born; male* or *female:* (Ṣ, M, O, Mṣb, Ḳ:) or, accord. to some, peculiarly applied to a *lamb;* and this is affirmed by 'Iyáḍ and Er-Ráfi'ee: accord. to some, peculiarly to *a kid;* and so affirms IAth: (TA:) [see also بَهْمٌ, in three places:] pl. ↓ سَخْلٌ, (Ṣ, O, Mṣb, Ḳ,) [or rather this is a coll. gen. n.] like as تَمْرٌ is of تَمْرَةٌ, (Mṣb,) [and is app. also used as a sing., (see the next preceding paragraph,)] and [the pl. properly so termed is] سِخَالٌ (Ṣ, O, Mṣb, Ḳ) and سِخَلَةٌ, which is extr. [as a pl. form, so much so that Sh holds it to be a quasi-pl. measure, not a broken pl. measure, as is said in the TA voce جِبَاةٌ]. (Ḳ.)

سُخَّلٌ (Az, Ṣ, O, Ḳ) and ↓ سُخَّالٌ, (Az, O, Ḳ,) applied to men, *Weak;* (Ṣ, O, Ḳ;) *bad, vile,* or *base;* (Ḳ;) or *low, ignoble, mean,* or *sordid:* (Az, O:) a pl. having no sing.: (Az, Ṣ, O:) or its sing. is ↓ سَخْلٌ: (Ḳ, TA: in the CḲ سُخَّلٌ [like the former pl.]:) so says Khálid. (IJ, TA.) — Also سُخَّلٌ, (CḲ,) or ↓ سَخْلٌ, (TḲ,) [in the TA without any syll. signs,] Anything *not completed.* (IJ, Ḳ.) — Also the former, (Ṣ, O, Ḳ,) in the dial. of the people of El-Medeeneh, (Ṣ, O,) The *sort of dates termed* شِيص, (Ṣ, O, Ḳ,) i. e. *of which the stones do not become hard:* (TA:) or, accord. to 'Eesà Ibn-'Omar, *dates of which two or three grow together in one place, intermingling.* (O, TA.)

سُخَالَةٌ *Refuse;* syn. نُفَايَةٌ. (JK, O, Ḳ, TA: in the CḲ نَفَايَةٌ.)

سُخَّالٌ: see سُخَّلٌ.

مَسْخُولٌ *Pronounced to be low, base, vile, mean,* or *contemptible:* (Ḳ:) like مَخْسُولٌ. (TA.) —

Unknown: (Ṣ, O, Ḳ:) and so مَخْسُولٌ. (O.) A poet says,

* وَأَنْتُمْ كَوَاكِبُ مَسْخُولَةٌ * تُرَى فِى السَّمَآءِ وَلَا تُعْلَمُ *

[*And ye are stars unknown, that are seen in the sky but not known*]: or, as some relate it, مَخْسُولَةٌ. (Ṣ, O.)

سخم

2. سَخَّمَ وَجْهَهُ, [inf. n. تَسْخِيمٌ,] *He blackened his face* (Ṣ, Mgh, Mṣb, Ḳ) *with* سُخَام, i. e. *crock of the cooking-pot*, (Mṣb,) or it is from السُّخَامُ; (Mgh;) like سَحَّمَهُ, (Z, TA,) which is from الأَسْحَمُ. (Mgh.) 'Omar said of him who bears false witness, يُسَخَّمُ وَجْهُهُ [*His face shall be blackened*]. (TA.) And one says, سَخَّمَ ٱللّٰهُ وَجْهَهُ, i. e. *May God blacken his face*: (Ṣ:) [or † *may God disgrace him*:] or ‡ *may God hate him*, or *hate him in the utmost degree*; and *be angry with him*. (Mṣb.) — سَخَّمَ المَآءَ, *He heated the water*, (IAạr, Ḳ, TA,) and *made it to boil*. (IAạr, TA.) — And سَخَّمَ بِصَدْرِهِ, inf. n. as above, † *He angered him*. (Ḳ.) — سَخَّمَ اللَّحْمُ, (Ḳ,) inf. n. as above, (TA,) *The flesh-meat became stinking*; (Ḳ, TA;) *became altered* [*for the worse*]. (TA.)

5. تَسَخَّمَ عَلَيْهِ † *He became affected with rancour, malevolence, malice, or spite, against him*: (Ḳ:) or *he became angered against him*. (TA.)

سَخَمٌ: see what next follows.

سُخْمَةٌ, (Ṣ, TA, [so in both of my copies of the former, erroneously written by Golius and Freytag, in the first of the following senses, سَخْمَةٌ,]) with ḍamm, (TA,) *Blackness*; (Ṣ, TA;) as also ▾ سَخَمٌ, (Ḳ, TA,) and [سُخْمَةٌ and] سُخَمٌ. (TA.) — And † *Anger*. (TA.) See also سَخِيمَةٌ.

سُخَامٌ *Crock, or black matter*, [*that collects upon the outside*] *of a cooking-pot*. (Ṣ, Mgh, Mṣb, Ḳ.) — And *Charcoal*: (Ḳ:) heard in this sense from a man of Ḥimyer. (Aṣ, TA.) — [Hence,] *Black hair*. (TA.) And لَيْلٌ سُخَامٌ and ▾ سُخَامِىٌّ *Black night*. (Ḥam p. 38.) — Also *Soft feathers beneath the upper feathers of a bird*: (Ḳ,* TA:) n. un. with ة. (TA.) — And *Soft to the feel*, (Ḳ, TA,) and *goodly*; (TA;) applied to a garment, or piece of cloth; such as [the kind of cloth called] خَزّ; and cotton; and the like: (Ḳ, TA:) you say ثَوْبٌ سُخَامُ المَسِّ *a garment soft to the feel*; such as خَزّ: and رِيشٌ سُخَامٌ *feathers soft to the feel*: and قُطْنٌ سُخَامٌ [*cotton soft to the feel*]: it is not from the signification of "blackness." (Ṣ.) And hence, (Ṣ,) خَمْرٌ سُخَامٌ *Wine that descends smoothly and easily* [*down the throat*]; as also ▾ سُخَامِيَّةٌ (Ṣ, Ḳ) and ▾ سُخَامِىٌّ, (Ḳ,) or, accord. to 'Alee Ibn-Ḥamzeh, only the former of these two: (TA:) and [in like manner] طَعَامٌ سُخَامٌ *food that is soft, or smooth, and easy in descent*. (IAạr.)

سَخِيمٌ, applied to water, *Neither hot nor cold*; as also سَخِينٌ. (AA, L in art. سخن.)

سَخِيمَةٌ (Ṣ, Ḳ) and ▾ سُخْمَةٌ (Ḳ) *Rancour, malevolence, malice, or spite*; (Ṣ, Ḳ;) and *anger in the soul*: (Ṣ, TA:) pl. of the former سَخَائِمُ. (TA.) [See two exs. in the first paragraph of art. سل.] — And the former, by a metonymy, is used as meaning ‡ *Excrement*, or *dung*: so in the trad., مَنْ سَلَّ سَخِيمَتَهُ فِى طَرِيقِ المُسْلِمِينَ لَعْنَةُ ٱللّٰهِ ‡ [*Whoso voids his excrement in the road, or path, of the Muslims, him God curses*]. (TA.)

سُخَامِىٌّ, and سُخَامِيَّةٌ: see سُخَامٌ, in three places.

أَسْخَمُ *Black*; (Ṣ, Ḳ;) like أَسْحَمُ. (TA.) — [The fem.] سَخْمَآءُ is said to be applied to wine (خَمْر) as meaning *Inclining to blackness*: but what has been said above [app. as to the word and the meaning] is more approved. (TA.) — Also, applied to a [stony tract such as is termed] حَرَّة, *Of which what is smooth, or soft, or plain, thereof, is intermixed with what is rugged*. (Ḳ.)

مُسَخَّمٌ One in whom is سَخِيمَة, i. e. *rancour, malevolence, malice, or spite*. (Ḳ.)

سخن

1. سَخُنَ, (JK, Ṣ, MA, L, Mṣb, Ḳ,) aor. ـُ; (TA;) and سَخَنَ, (Ṣ, MA, L, Mṣb, Ḳ,) aor. ـُ; (TK;) and سَخِنَ, (L, Mṣb, Ḳ,) which is of the dial. of Benoo-'Ámir, (L,) aor. ـَ; (TK;) inf. n. سُخُونَةٌ, (JK, Ṣ, MA, L, Mṣb, Ḳ,) which is of the first [agreeably with analogy] (JK, Ṣ, MA) and of the second also, (Ṣ,) and سُخْنَةٌ, (JK, L, Ḳ,) which is of the first, (JK,) and سُخْنٌ, (MA, L, Ḳ, [accord. to some copies of the Ḳ, in which بِضَمَّتَيْنِ is put instead of بِضَمِّهِنَّ after these three inf. ns., سُخُنٌ,]) which is likewise of the first, (MA,) [or of the first and second,] and سَخَانَةٌ, (L, Mṣb, Ḳ,) [also of the first accord. to general analogy,] and سَخَنٌ, (Ḳ,) [which is of the third verb;] *It was*, or *became, hot*, or *warm*; (JK, Ṣ, MA, L, Ḳ;) said of water, (JK, Ṣ, L, Mṣb,) &c. (Ṣ, MA, L, Mṣb.) And سَخُنَتِ النَّارُ, and القِدْرُ, [and سَخِنَتْ,] aor. ـُ, inf. n. سُخْنٌ and سُخُونَةٌ, [*The fire, and the cooking-pot, became hot*.] (L.) And سَخُنَتِ الأَرْضُ and سَخَنَتْ and سَخِنَتْ [*The ground became hot*]. (L.) And سَخِنَتْ عَلَيْهِ الشَّمْسُ [*The sun became hot upon him*]: in the dial. of Benoo-'Ámir سَخَنَتْ. (L.) And سَخُنَ اليَوْمُ, (L, Mṣb,) and سَخَنَ, aor. ـُ, and some say سَخِنَ, aor. ـَ, inf. n. سُخْنٌ and سُخُنٌ, [*The day was*, or *became, hot*, or *warm*.] (L.) And سَخُنَتِ الدَّابَّةُ *The beast*, being made to run, *became hot in its bones, and light*, or *agile, in its running*; [or simply, *became hot*, or *heated*; (see EM pp. 172 and 173;)] as also سَخَنَتْ. (L.) And سَخِنَتْ عَيْنُهُ, with kesr, (JK,* Ṣ, MA, L, Ḳ,) and سَخُنَتْ, (JK, L,) or the former only, (L,) inf. n. سُخْنَةٌ (JK, Ṣ,* MA, L, Ḳ, [in the CḲ, erroneously, سَخْنَةٌ,]) and سُخُونٌ (JK, L, Ḳ) and سُخْنٌ, (L, Ḳ, [accord. to the CḲ سَخْنٌ, but this is a mistake,]) *contr. of* قَرَّتْ (Ṣ,* L, Ḳ*) [i. e.] *His eye was*, or *became, hot*, [or *heated*, or *inflamed, by weeping*, or *by grief* or *sorrow*; or *hot*] *in its tears*. (MA.)

2: see the next paragraph.

4. اسخنهُ; (L, Mṣb, Ḳ;) inf. n. إِسْخَانٌ, (Ṣ, L,) *He heated it*, or *warmed it*; *made it hot*, or *warm*; (Ṣ,* L, Mṣb,* Ḳ;) namely, water, (Ṣ, L, Mṣb,) &c.; (L, Mṣb;) as also ▾ سَخَّنَهُ, (L, Mṣb, Ḳ,) inf. n. تَسْخِينٌ. (Ṣ, L.) And اسخن ٱللّٰهُ عَيْنَهُ, (Ṣ, L, Ḳ,) and بِعَيْنِهِ, (L, Ḳ,) [*God made his eye to become hot*, or *heated*, or *inflamed, by weeping, or by grief* or *sorrow*; or, simply,] *made him to weep*. (Ṣ, L, Ḳ.)

سَخَنٌ: see سُخْنَةٌ. — [The signification of "calor aquæ aliarumve rerum," assigned to it by Freytag as on the authority of J, is a mistake, probably occasioned by a fault in his copy of the Ṣ.]

سُخْنٌ an inf. n. of 1 [q. v.]. (MA, L, Ḳ.) — Also *Hot*, or *warm*; (MA, PṢ;) *i. q.* حَارٌّ; (Ṣ, MA, Mgh, L, Ḳ;) *contr. of* بَارِدٌ; (JK, L;) an epithet applied to water, (JK, MA, Mgh, L,) &c.; (Mṣb;) as is also (in the same sense, JK, MA, Mgh, L) ▾ سَخِينٌ, (JK, Ṣ, MA, Mgh, L, Mṣb, Ḳ,) and ▾ مُسْخَنٌ, (Mṣb,) and ▾ سَاخِنٌ, syn. with سَخِينٌ like as مُبْرَمٌ is with بَرِيمٌ, &c., (IAạr, Ṣ, L,) or ▾ مُسَخَّنٌ, [which is syn. with مُسْخَن like مُسَخَّن as meaning *heated*, or *warmed*,] like مُعَظَّمٌ [in measure], (Ḳ,) and ▾ سِخِّينٌ, (L, Ḳ,) and ▾ سُخَاخِينٌ, which is the only instance of the measure, (Ṣ, L, Ḳ, [which measure is said in the Ṣ to be فُعَاعِيلٌ, but in the Ḳ فُعَالِيلٌ,]) and which is also applied to food; (L;) syn. حَارٌّ: (L, Ḳ:) or, accord. to AA, ▾ سَخِينٌ, applied to water, means *neither hot nor cold*; as also سَخِيمٌ. (L.) And يَوْمٌ سُخْنٌ and ▾ سَاخِنٌ (Ṣ, L, Mṣb, Ḳ) and ▾ سَخْنَانٌ or ▾ سُخْنَانٌ, (accord. to different copies of the Ṣ,) or both these, (Ḳ,) and ▾ سُخُنَّانٌ, (L, Ḳ,* [in the CḲ and in my MS. copy of the Ḳ written سُخْنَانٌ, which is incorrect, and in like manner سَخْنَانٌ is there written ▾ سُخْنَانٌ, but this, as well as سَخْنَانٌ, may be correct, for it appears that سَخْنَان has سَخْنَاةٌ for its fem. as well as سَخْنَانَةٌ,]) and ▾ سُخَاخِينٌ signifies the same, [i. e. *A hot*, or *warm, day*,] or, accord. to IAạr, ▾ يَوْمٌ سُخَاخِينٌ signifies *a day that is* [*so hot as to be*] *hurtful*, and *painful*: (L:) and لَيْلَةٌ سُخْنَةٌ (Ṣ, L, Mṣb, Ḳ) and ▾ سَاخِنَةٌ (L, Mṣb, Ḳ) and ▾ سَخْنَانَةٌ or ▾ سُخْنَانَةٌ, (Ṣ, accord. to different copies,) or both, (Ḳ,) and ▾ سُخُنَّانَةٌ, (L, Ḳ,) [i. e. *a hot*, or *warm, night*,] or ▾ يَوْمٌ سَخْنَانٌ signifies *a day intensely hot*, and ▾ لَيْلَةٌ سَخْنَاةٌ [the latter word being fem. of سَخْنَانٌ] *a sultry night*, or *intensely hot so that it takes away the breath*: (JK:) and it is said in a trad. of Mo'áwiyeh Ibn-Ḳurrah, ▾ شَرُّ الشِّتَآءِ السُّخَيْنُ, meaning [*The worst of winter is*] *the hot in which is no cold*; in the "Ghareeb" of El-Ḥarbee, ▾ السُّخَيْخِينُ, expl. as meaning the same, but this is probably a mistranscription. (L.)

سُخُنٌ an inf. n. of 1 [q. v., last sentence]. See also سُخْنَةٌ.

سُخَنَةٌ : see the next paragraph.

سُخْنَةٌ an inf. n. of 1 [q. v.]. (JK, Ṣ,* &c.) [Hence,] one says, إِنِّى لَأَجِدُ فِى نَفْسِى سُخْنَةً (L, Ḳ,*) as also ↑ سَخْنَةً (Ṣ, L, Ḳ, the only form mentioned in the Ṣ in this case) and ↑ سِخْنَةً (L, Ḳ) and ↑ سُخُنَةً and ↑ سُخْنًا, (Ḳ,) or ↑ سَخَنًا, (JK,) and ↑ سُخْنَاءَ (L) and ↑ سُخُونَةً (L, Ḳ) [and ↑ إِسْخِنَةً (in the JK erroneously written أُسْخِنَةً) contr. of إِبْرِدَةٌ], meaning [*Verily I find, or experience, in myself,*] *an excess of heat arising from pain:* (Ṣ, L:) or [simply] *heat:* or *fever.* (L, Ḳ.) [Hence also,] سُخْنَةُ العَيْنِ *contr. of* قُرَّتُهَا [i. e. it signifies *A hot,* or *heated,* or *an inflamed, state of the eye, by reason of weeping,* or *of grief* or *sorrow;* or *heat in the tears of the eye:* see 1, last sentence]. (Ṣ, L, Ḳ.)

سِخْنَةٌ : see the next preceding paragraph. — One says also, عَلَيْكَ بِالأَمْرِ عِنْدَ سِخْنَتِهِ, meaning † [*Keep thou to the affair*] *while it is in its first state, before it become cold* [i. e. unmanageable, like cold iron]. (L.)

سَخْنَةٌ : see سُخْنَةٌ.

سُخْنَاةٌ [as fem. of سُخْنَانٌ]: see سُخْنٌ, latter part. — See also سُخْنَةٌ.

سُخْنَانٌ and سَخْنَانٌ and سُخُنَّانٌ, and سُخَنَّانٌ in two places, and the same with ة : see سُخْنٌ.

سَخُونٌ Broth *heated,* or *made hot.* (Ṣ, L, Ḳ.)

سَخِينٌ : see سُخْنٌ, in three places. [See also a saying of 'Amr Ibn-Kulthoom cited in the first paragraph of art. سخو and سخى.] — Also, (Ḳ,) or سَخِينُ العَيْنِ, (Ṣ, MA, L,) A man *whose eye is* [*hot,* or *heated,* or *inflamed, by weeping,* or *by grief* or *sorrow;* or] *hot in its tears.* (Ṣ,* MA, L,* Ḳ.*) — And ضَرْبٌ سَخِينٌ, (Ḳ,) or ↑ سِخِّينٌ, (L,) † *A hot,* [i. e.] *painful, smiting.* (L, Ḳ. [Both are probably correct: that the latter is so is shown by what here follows.]) Ibn-Muḳbil says,

* ضَرْبًا تَرَامَتْ بِهِ الأَبْطَالُ سِخِّينَا ↑ *

[*A smiting which the brave* men *cast, one at another, burning,* or *painful:* the measure (بَسِيط) requires us to read the last word thus, with teshdeed to the خ]. (L.)

سَخِينَةٌ : see سُخُونَةٌ.

سُخُونَةٌ an inf. n. of 1 [q. v.]. (JK, Ṣ, &c.) See also سُخْنَةٌ.

سَخِينَةٌ *A certain thin food, made of flour;* (Ḳ;) *a kind of food made of flour, thinner than* [*the kind of gruel called*] عَصِيدَة *and thicker than* [*the soup called*] حَسَآء; like نَفِيتَة, it is eaten only in a time of straitness, and dearth, and leanness of the cattle; and Ḳureysh were taunted on account of their eating it; (Ṣ, L;) for they ate it much; and were called سَخِينَة: accord. to Az, it is also called ↑ سَخُونَة: accord. to AHeyth, on the authority of an Arab of the desert, it is *flour thrown upon water* or *upon milk, and cooked, and then eaten* [*with dates* (see خَزِيرٌ)], or *supped;* and this is what is called حَسَآء: [it is said in the Mgh to be the *same as* حَسَآء:] accord. to others, *hot food:* or *food made of flour and clarified butter:* or, *of flour and dates, thicker than* حَسَآء *and thinner than* عَصِيدَة. (L.)

سِخِّينٌ : see سُخْنٌ: and سَخِينٌ, in two places. — Also, (L, Ḳ,) in the Ṣ سَخِينٌ, which is a mistake, (Ḳ,) *A* مِسْحَاة [or *shovel,* or *spade*]: or *a curved* مِسْحَاة: of the dial. of 'Abd-El-Ḳeys: (Ṣ, L:) pl. سَخَاخِينُ. (L, Ḳ.) [And] The مَرّ [or *shovel,* or *spade,*] *with which one works in earth* or *mud:* (JK:) or the *handle of the* [*implement called*] مِحْرَاث [q. v.]; (L, Ḳ;) i. e., (L,) *its* مَرّ, which is also called مِعْزَق. (IAạr, L.) And *A knife:* or *a butcher's knife:* pl. as above. (IAạr, L, Ḳ.)

سُخَاخِينُ : see سُخْنٌ, in three places. Also Rain *coming in the intense heat of summer.* (JK.)

السُّخَيْخِينُ : see سُخْنٌ, last sentence.

سَاخِنٌ ; and its fem., with ة : see سُخْنٌ, in three places.

إِسْخِنَةٌ *contr. of* إِبْرِدَةٌ : (Ḳ:) [see the latter word: and] see سُخْنَةٌ.

تَسْخَنٌ and تَسْخَانٌ : see the next paragraph; the latter, in two places.

تَسَاخِينُ, accord. to Th, (Mgh, L, Mṣb,) a pl. having no sing., (Ṣ, Mgh, L, Mṣb, Ḳ,) like تَعَاشِيبُ; (Ṣ;) or its sing. is ↑ تَسْخَانٌ and ↑ تَسْخَنٌ, (Mgh, L, Mṣb, Ḳ,) *Boots;* syn. خِفَافٌ [pl. of خُفٌّ]: (JK, Ṣ, Mgh, L, Mṣb, Ḳ:) occurring in a trad., in which it is said, أَمَرَهُمْ أَنْ يَمْسَحُوا عَلَى المَشَاوِذِ وَالتَّسَاخِينِ, (Ṣ, L,) [expl. as] meaning [*He ordered them to wipe*] *the turbans and the boots.* (L.) [But see what here follows.] — Also *A kind of thing like the* طَيَالِس [pl. of طَيْلَسَان, q. v.]: (Ḳ:) Ḥamzeh El-Iṣbahánee says, ↑ تَسْخَان is an arabicized word from [the Pers.] تَشْكَن [?], the name of *a certain kind of head-covering, which the learned men, and the lawyers of the Persians,* or *the judges of the Magians, exclusively of other persons, used to put upon their heads;* and by such as knew not its Pers. original, it has been expl. as meaning *a boot.* (IAth, L.) — Also i. q. مَرَاجِل [i. e. *Cooking-pots,* or *copper cooking-pots,* &c.; pl. of مِرْجَل, q. v.]. (L, Ḳ. [In the CḲ, المَرَاجِلُ الخِفَافُ is erroneously put for المَرَاجِلُ وَالخِفَافُ. See also مِسْخَنَةٌ.])

مُسْخَنٌ : see سُخْنٌ, second sentence.

مَسْخَنَةٌ [*A cause of heat* or *warmth*]: see an ex. voce مَبْرَدَةٌ [which signifies the contrary].

مِسْخَنَةٌ *A cooking-pot* (قِدْرٌ, JK, Ṣ, L) *of the kind called* بِرَام [pl. of بُرْمَة, q. v.], (L, K,) *like the* [*vessel called*] تَوْر [q. v.], (JK, Ṣ, L, Ḳ,) *in which food is heated:* or accord. to ISh, *a small cooking-pot in which one cooks for a child.* (L.)

مُسَخَّنٌ : see سُخْنٌ, second sentence.

سخو and سخى

1. سَخَا, aor. يَسْخُو; (Ṣ, Mṣb, Ḳ;) and سَخِىَ, aor. يَسْخَى; (Ḳ;) and سَخُوَ, aor. يَسْخُو; (Ṣ, Mṣb, Ḳ;) inf. n. سَخَآءٌ, (Ṣ,* M, Mṣb,* Ḳ, TA,) of the first verb, (M, Mṣb,* TA,) and of the second, (TA,) and سُخُوٌّ, (M, Ḳ, TA, [in the CḲ سُخُو,]) of the first verb, (M, TA,) or of the last, (TA,) and سُخُوَّةٌ, (M, Ḳ, TA,) of the first verb, (M, TA,) or of the third, (TA,) and سَخًى, (Mṣb, Ḳ, TA,) of the third verb, (Mṣb, TA,) and سَخَاوَةٌ, of the last verb; (Ṣ, Mṣb, TA;) *He was,* or *became, liberal, bountiful, munificent,* or *generous;* or *he affected,* or *constrained himself, to be generous;* (Ṣ,* Mṣb,* Ḳ,* TA;) syn. جَادَ, and تَكَرَّمَ; (TA;) the inf. ns. signifying جُود (Ṣ, Mṣb) and كَرَم (Mṣb) [or تَكَرُّم]. And سَخَتْ نَفْسُهُ *His mind was,* or *became, liberal,* &c. (Mṣb.) [Accord. to J,] the saying of 'Amr Ibn-Kulthoom, [relating to wine,]

* إِذَا مَا المَآءُ خَالَطَهَا سَخِينَا *

means [*When the water mixes with it,* and *we drink it,*] *we are,* or *become, liberal,* or *bountiful, with our riches;* and the assertion that سخينا is from السُّخُونَة, in the accus. case as a denotative of state, is a mistake: (Ṣ:) the former is the saying of AA; and the latter, of Aṣ: but IB says, on the authority of IKṭṭ, that the right explanation is that which J disallows; and Eṣ-Ṣafadee says the like. (TA.) [See also 5.] — [Hence,] سَخِيتُ نَفْسِى عَنِ الشَّىْءِ *I left,* or *relinquished, the thing.* (Ṣ.) And سَخَا بِنَفْسِهِ عَنْهُ *He left,* or *relinquished, it:* (TA:) or *he held himself far from it;* or *withdrew his heart from it;* as also سَخِىَ بِنَفْسِهِ عَنْهُ and ↑ سَخَّى نَفْسَهُ عَنْهُ: (MA:) or سَخَّيْتُ ↑ نَفْسِى عَنْ هٰذَا الشَّىْءِ and سَخِيتُ بِنَفْسِى عَنْهُ *I left,* or *relinquished, this thing, and my soul did not strive with me to incline me to it.* (JK.) And سَخَا قَلْبِى عَلَيْكَ [perhaps a mistranscription for عَنْكَ] *I endured with patience the being debarred from thee.* (JK.) — سَخَا, (Ḳ,) aor. يَسْخُو, inf. n. سَخْوٌ, (TA,) *He* (a man) *rested from his state of motion:* (Ḳ:) from ISd. (TA.) — سَخَا النَّارَ, aor. يَسْخُو, inf. n. سَخْوٌ; (AA, Ṣ, Ḳ;) and سَخَاهَا, aor. يَسْخَى, inf. n. سَخْىٌ; (AA, Ṣ;) and سَخَاهَا, aor. يَسْخَى, inf. n. سَخْىٌ; (Ṣgh, Ḳ;) *He made an opening in the live and extinct coals of the fire which had become collected together after it had been kindled:* (T, Ṣ:) or *he made a way* [or *vent*] *for the fire, beneath the cooking-pot:* (M, Ḳ:) or سَخَا النَّارَ signifies فَتَحَ عَيْنَهَا [i. e. *he made an opening in the live coals of the fire, that had become collected together,* (as expl. in the TḲ in art. صخو,) i. e., *that had become compacted; in order that it might burn up well*]; as also صَخَاهَا: or, as some say, *he cleared,* or *swept, away the live*, or *burning, coals of the fire;* as also with ع : (TA: [see سَخَا :]) and سَخَيْتُ ▾ النَّارَ, inf. n. تَسْخِيَةٌ, *I opened the heart of the place where the fire was kindled, in order that it might burn up well.* (JK.) And one says, اِسْخِ نَارَكَ meaning *Make thou a place upon which to kindle thy fire.* (Ṣ.) — And سَخَا القِدْرَ, (Ḳ,) aor. يَسْخُو, inf. n. سَخْوٌ, (TA,) *He made a way* [or *vent*] *for the fire beneath the cooking-pot;* (Ḳ;) mentioned by ISd, who adds that one says also, سَخَا الجَمْرَ مِنْ تَحْتِ القِدْرِ: (TA:) or the former phrase, [and app. the latter also,] *he put aside the live coals from beneath the cooking-pot;* (JK, TA;) as also ▾ سَخَّاهَا. (JK.) = سَخِىَ, aor. يَسْخَى, inf. n. سَخًا, said of a camel, (Ṣ, Ḳ,) and of a young weaned camel, (Ṣ,) *He became affected with a limping,* or *halting,* (Ṣ, Ḳ,) *having leaped with a heavy load, in consequence of which a flatus had intervened between the skin and the shoulder-blade:* (Ṣ:) the epithet applied to the animal in this case is ▾ سَخٍ, (Ṣ, Ḳ,) mentioned by Yaạḳoob, (Ṣ,) and ▾ سَخِىٌّ, (JK, Ḳ,) this latter mentioned by Ṣgh, and anomalous, being of a measure proper to an epithet from a verb of the measure فَعُلَ, with ḍamm to the medial radical; (TA;) and the pl. of this latter epithet is سَخَايَا and سَخَاوَى. (JK.)

2: see above, in four places.

5. تَسَخَّى *He affected,* or *constrained himself, to be liberal, bountiful, munificent,* or *generous,* (Ṣ, Ḳ,) عَلَى أَصْحَابِهِ [*over and above his companions*]. (Ṣ.)

سَخْوٌ مِنْ كَلَامٍ *Somewhat of speech.* (JK.)

سَخٍ: see سَخِىٌّ: = and see also 1, last sentence.

سَخِىٌّ *Liberal, bountiful, munificent,* or *generous;* (Ṣ,* Mṣb, Ḳ;) as also ▾ سَاخٍ and ▾ سَخٍ. (Mṣb, TA:) fem. of the first with ة: pl. masc. أَسْخِيَآءُ and سُخَوَآءُ: and pl. fem. سَخِيَّاتٌ and سَخَايَا. (Ḳ.) — [Hence,] one says, إِنَّهُ لَسَخِىُّ النَّفْسِ عَنْهُ [*Verily he is content to leave,* or *relinquish, it*]. (TA.) = See also 1, last sentence.

سَخَآءٌ *A certain plant of the* [*season called*] رَبِيع: n. un. with ة: (JK:) the latter, of which the former is [said to be] the pl., signifies *a certain herb,* or *leguminous plant,* (Ḳ, TA,) *rising upon a stem, having what resembles in form an ear of wheat, in which are grains like those of the* يَنْبُوت [which is variously explained], *and a heart,* or *kernel,* (لُبَاب,) *the grain of which is a remedy for wounds:* it is also called صَخَآءَةٌ; but the more approved pronunciation is with س. (TA in art. صخو.)

سُخَوَآءُ: see the next paragraph.

سَخَاوِىٌّ applied to a place, and سَخَاوِيَّةٌ applied to a land (أَرْض), *Soft in the earth* [*thereof*]; (Ṣ, TA;) to which is added in the Ṣ, وَهِىَ مَنْسُوبَةٌ [and it is a rel. n.]; but in the handwriting of Aboo-Zekereeyà, وَهِىَ مُسْتَوِيَةٌ [i. e. *and such as is even,* or *level*]: (TA:) or the former is pl. [or rather coll. gen. n.] of the latter, which signifies *land soft in the earth* [*thereof*]: or *wide,* or *ample:* as also ▾ سُخَوَآءُ: (Ḳ:) or this last signifies a *soft,* or *plain, and wide,* or *ample,* land: (Ṣ:) and its pl. is سَخَاوِى and سَخَاوَى [or rather سَخَاوٍ, when indeterminate]: (Ṣ, Ḳ: [in the former, these two pls. are correctly written with the article السَّخَاوِى and السَّخَاوَى:]) or, accord. to AA, سَخَاوِىٌّ signifies *land,* or *lands,* [for the explanation is ambiguous, app. meaning the latter,] *in which is nothing;* and in like manner سَخَاوِيَّةٌ [but app. as a n. un.]: accord. to Aṣ and A'Obeyd, *land;* but correctly *lands:* (TA:) or *width,* or *wide extent,* (JK, TA,) so some say, (TA,) of a desert, or waterless desert, *and vehemence of heat* thereof. (JK.)

سَاخٍ: see سَخِىٌّ.

أَسْخَى [*More,* and *most, liberal, bountiful, munificent,* or *generous*]: see an ex. voce أَلَا.

مَسْخَى النَّارِ *The place that is widened* [or *hollowed*], *in the fire, beneath the cooking-pot, in order that it may be able to burn up well:* and hence, some say, is derived السَّخَآءُ meaning الجُودُ; because the bosom becomes expanded on the occasion of giving. (TA.)

سد

1. سَدَّ, (Ṣ, M, A, Mgh, Mṣb, Ḳ,) aor. ـُ, (Ṣ, M, Mṣb, Ḳ,) inf. n. سَدٌّ; (Ṣ, M, Mgh, Mṣb;) and ▾ سَدَّدَ; (M;) [but the latter has an intensive signification, or relates to several objects;] *He closed,* or *closed up,* an interstice, or intervening space: (M:) and *stopped,* or *stopped up,* (M,) or *repaired, and made firm* or *strong,* (Ṣ, A, Ḳ,) a breach, or gap, (Ṣ, M, A, Mgh, Mṣb, Ḳ,) and the like. (Ṣ, Mṣb.) — [Hence one says,] سُدَّتْ عَلَيْهِ الطَّرِيقُ † [*The road,* or *way, became closed,* or *stopped, against him*]. (Ḳ.) And سُدَّ طَرِيقُهُ مِنْ بَيْنِ يَدَيْهِ وَمِنْ خَلْفِهِ † [*His road,* or *way, became closed,* or *stopped, before him and behind him*]. (Zj, M.) And سَدَّ الأُفُقَ ‡ [*It obstructed the horizon*]; said of a multitudinous swarm of locusts. (Ṣ, A,* Ḳ.) And سَدَّ عَلَيْهِمْ, and ▾ أَسَدَّ, *It closed,* or *obstructed, against them, the horizon;* [الأُفُقَ being understood;] said of a collection of clouds rising. (M.) And سَدَّ مَا وَرَآءَهُ [*It barred,* or *excluded, what was behind it*]. (M.) — [Hence also,] سَدَدْتُ عَلَيْهِ بَابَ الكَلَامِ † [*I closed,* or *stopped, to him the door of speech;* i. e.] *I prevented him from speaking;* as though I closed, or stopped, his mouth. (Mṣb.) And مَا سَدَدْتُ عَلَى لَهَوَاتِ خَصْمٍ قَطُّ † *I never stopped the way of speech of an adversary, nor prevented his saying what was in his mind.* (Shureyḥ, Mgh.) And مَا سَدَدْتُ عَلَى خَصْمٍ قَطُّ † *I never stopped an adversary from speaking;* (El-Fáïḳ, Mgh, L;) on the authority of Esh-Shaạbee: (Mgh:) occurring in a trad. (L.) — And هُوَ يَسُدُّ مَسَدَّ ▾ أَبِيهِ ‡ [*He fills up,* or *supplies, the place of his father*]: and يَسُدُّونَ مَسَدَّ ▾ أَسْلَافِهِمْ ‡ [*They fill up,* or *supply, the place of their ancestors*]. (A, TA.) And يُسَدُّ بِهِ الحَاجَةُ ‡ *Want is supplied thereby:* (M,* TA:) [whence the saying,] تَصَدَّقُوا وَلَوْ بِتَمْرَةٍ فَإِنَّهَا تَسُدُّ مِنَ الجَائِعِ † [*Give ye something as alms, though it be but a date,* or *a dried date; for it will supply somewhat of the want of the hungry*]: a trad. (El-Jámi' eṣ-Ṣagheer.) And يَسُدُّ الرَّمَقَ † [*It stays,* or *arrests, the remains of life;* as though it stopped the passage of the last breath from the body; or] *it maintains, and preserves, the strength.* (Mṣb in art. رمق.) — And سَدَّهُ † *He attributed,* or *imputed, to him,* or *he charged him with,* or *accused him of, a fault;* [as though he thereby stopped his mouth; (see سَدٌّ;)] as also سَتَّهُ. (TA in art. ست.) = سَدَّ, aor. يَسِدُّ, (Ṣ, L, Ḳ,) with kesr, (Ṣ,) inf. n. سَدَادٌ and سُدُودٌ, (L, the former inf. n. expl. in the Ṣ and Ḳ as signifying اِسْتِقَامَةٌ,) said of a spear, and an arrow, (TA,) and a saying, (Ṣ,) and an action, (TA,) or a thing [absolutely]; (L;) or سَدَّ, [sec. pers. سَدِدْتَ,] aor. يَسَدُّ, with fet-ḥ to the س, (A,) inf. n. سَدَدٌ, (TḲ, expl. in the Ṣ and Ḳ as signifying اِسْتِقَامَةٌ like سَدَادٌ, of which it is said in the Ṣ to be a contraction,) said of a saying, and an affair; (A;) or سَدَّ, aor. يَسَدُّ and يَسِدُّ, inf. n. سَدَدٌ; (MA;) *i. q.* صَارَ سَدِيدًا [i. e. *It was,* or *became, right, direct,* or *in a right state; it had,* or *took, a right direction* or *tendency; it tended towards the right point* or *object*]: (Ṣ, A, L, Ḳ, TA:) and [in like manner] ▾ اسْتَدَّ is *syn. with* اِسْتَقَامَ [which signifies the same]; (Ṣ, Ḳ;) as also ▾ اسدّ and ▾ تَسَدَّدَ: (TA:) ▾ اِسْتَدَّ said of an affair signifies *it was,* or *became, rightly ordered* or *disposed; in a right state.* (Mṣb.) You say, ▾ اِسْتَدَّ and ▾ تَسَدَّدَ لَهُ *It was,* or *became, rightly directed towards it.* (M.) And ▾ اِسْتَدَّ سَاعِدُهُ and ▾ تَسَدَّدَ *His fore arm was,* or *became, in a right state,* or *rightly directed,* عَلَى الرَّمْىِ [*for shooting*]; syn. اِسْتَقَامَ. (A.) A poet says,

* أُعَلِّمُهُ الرِّمَايَةَ كُلَّ يَوْمٍ ۞ فَلَمَّا اسْتَدَّ سَاعِدُهُ رَمَانِى *

[*I teaching him the art of shooting every day; and when his fore arm became in a right state, he shot me*]: Aṣ says that [the reading] اشتدّ, with ش, is not to be regarded. (Ṣ, TA.) — And سَدَّ, aor. يَسِدُّ, with kesr to the س, (A, Mṣb, TA,) inf. n. سُدُودٌ (Mṣb) [and app. also, as above, سَدَادٌ, q. v. infrà], is said of a man, (A, Mṣb, TA,) in like manner meaning صَارَ سَدِيدًا [i. e. *He was,* or *became, in a right state; he had,* or *took, a right direction* or *tendency; he tended towards the right point* or *object*]: (A, TA:) or, (Mṣb,) as also ▾ اسدّ, (Ṣ, Ḳ, TA,) *he hit the right thing* (Ṣ, Mṣb, Ḳ, TA) in his saying (Ṣ, Mṣb, TA) and in his action: (Mṣb:) or ▾ اسدّ signifies *he said,* or *did, what was right:* (Mṣb:) or *he sought what was right;* (L, Ḳ;) as also ▾ سَدَّدَ; (L;) or it has this last meaning also. (Ṣ,* L.) You say, إِنَّهُ لَيُسِدُّ ▾ فِى القَوْلِ *Verily he hits the right thing in the saying.* (Ṣ, L.) And قَدْ

▼ أَسْدَدْتَ مَا شِئْتَ (Ṣ,* L) is said to a man when he seeks [or has sought] what is right, (Ṣ,) meaning *Thou hast sought what is right;* whether the person thus addressed have hit the right thing or not. (L.) One says also, سَدَّ عَلَيْكَ الرَّجُلُ, aor. يَسِدُّ, inf. n. سد [app. a mistranscription for سَدَاد or سُدُود], *The man said, or did, what was right* [*against thee*]: so in the handwriting of Sh. (Az, TA.)

2: see 1, first sentence. — [Hence,] سَدَّدَ مَلْأَهُ [*He filled it up*]; namely, a vessel, and a watering-trough. (Aboo-Sa'eed, TA in art. خنق.) — And سَدَّدَ عَلَيْهِمْ كُلَّ شَىْءٍ قَالُوهُ † *He annulled, in opposing them, everything that they said.* (Jábir, as related by Aboo-'Adnán.) — سَدَّدَهُ, (Ṣ, A, L, Mṣb, Ḳ,) inf. n. تَسْدِيدٌ, (Ḳ,) *He directed it,* (A,* L, Mṣb, Ḳ,) namely, an arrow, (A, Mṣb,) نَحْوَهُ *towards him* or *it,* (A,) or إِلَى الصَّيْدِ *towards the game;* (Mṣb;) and شَدَّدَهُ, with ش, is a dial. var. thereof: (Towsheeḥ, TA:) and [in like manner] his spear; contr. of عَرَّضَهُ, (Ṣ, Mṣb,) or عَرَضَهُ. (L.) — And *He taught him the art of shooting.* (TA.) — Also, (M, A, Ḳ,) inf. n. as above, (Ṣ,) *He directed, accommodated, adapted,* or *disposed, him* (Ṣ, M, A, Ḳ) *to that which was right,* of words and of actions: (Ṣ, Ḳ: [and the like is implied in the M and A:]) said of God. (M, A.) And you say, سَدِّدْ صَاحِبَكَ *Teach thou thy companion, and direct him to the right course.* (Sh, TA.) — And [hence,] سَدِّدْ مَالَكَ *Act thou well with thy property,* or *cattle.* (L.) And سَدَّدَ الإِبِلَ, inf. n. as above, *He gave the camels easy access to every pasturage, and to every place where the ground was soft and spacious.* (L.) — See also 1, near the end of the paragraph.

4: see 1, near the beginning: — and see also the latter half of the same paragraph, in five places.

5: see 1, in the latter half of the paragraph, in three places.

7. انسدّ, said of an interstice, or intervening space, *It became closed,* or *closed up;* as also ▼ استدّ: (M:) and both, said of a breach, or gap, (M, A,) *it became stopped,* or *stopped up,* (M,) or *repaired, and made firm* or *strong.* (A.) اِنْسَدَّتْ and ▼ اِسْتَدَّتْ عُيُونُ الخُرَزِ signify the same [i. e. *The punctures made in the sewing* of the skin *became closed*]; (Ṣ, Ḳ;) expressing a consequence of pouring water into a skin. (Ṣ.)

8: see the next preceding paragraph, in two places: — and see also 1, in the latter half of the paragraph, in five places.

سَدٌّ and ▼ سُدٌّ *Any building,* or *construction, with which a place is closed* or *closed up,* or *stopped* or *stopped up:* (M: [see also سِدَادٌ:]) *a dam:* (Mṣb:) *a thing intervening, as a separation, a partition, a fence, a barrier, a rampart,* or *an obstacle,* or *obstruction, between two other things:* (Ṣ, Mṣb, Ḳ:) and *a mountain:* (Ṣ, M, Ḳ: [in the last it seems that this meaning is restricted to the former word; but if restricted to either, it should be to the latter:]) or, as some say, *anything that faces one,* or *is over against one, and bars,* or *excludes,* (يَسُدُّ,) *what is behind it:* whence goats are said to be سُدٌّ يُرَى مِنْ وَرَائِهِ الفَقْرُ † [*a barrier behind which is seen poverty*]; meaning that they are not of great utility: (M:) or سَدٌّ signifies *what is made by man;* and سُدٌّ, *what is created by God,* (Zj, M, Mṣb, Ḳ,) as *a mountain:* (Mṣb:) in the Ḳur xviii. 92 and 93, and xxxvi. 8, some read with fet-ḥ, and some with ḍamm: (M, TA:) the pl. is أَسْدَادٌ, [a pl. of pauc.,] (A, Mṣb,) or أَسِدَّةٌ, [also a pl. of pauc.,] and سُدُودٌ, [a pl. of mult.,] the latter of these two agreeable with general analogy, and the former of them anomalous, or, [ISd says,] in my opinion, this (أَسِدَّةٌ) is pl. of سِدَادٌ. (M.) You say, ضُرِبَ بَيْنَهُمَا سَدٌّ and سُدٌّ [*A barrier, or an obstacle, was set between them two*]: and ضُرِبَتْ بَيْنَهُمَا الأَسْدَادُ [*Barriers,* or *obstacles, were set between them two*]. (A.) And ضَرَبَتْ عَلَيْهِ الأَرْضُ بِالأَسْدَادِ ‡ [*The earth,* or *land, set barriers,* or *obstacles, against him*]; meaning, *the ways became closed,* or *stopped, against him, and the courses that he should pursue became obscure to him:* (Ḳ: in the CḲ ضُرِبَتْ:) the sing. of أَسْدَادٌ [accord. to general analogy] is سَدٌّ. (TA.) — [Hence,] the former (سَدٌّ) also signifies, (Fr, Ṣ, M, L, Ḳ,) or ▼ سِدَادٌ, (A,) or the former and ▼ سَدَادَةٌ, (L,) ‡ *A fault,* or *defect,* (Fr, Ṣ, M, A, &c.,) *such as blindness* and *deafness* and *dumbness,* (Ṣ,) or *such as closes,* or *stops, one's mouth, so that he does not speak:* (A:) pl. of the first, (Ṣ, M, Ḳ,) or of the second, (A,) أَسِدَّةٌ, [a pl. of pauc.,] (Ṣ, M, A, Ḳ,) accord. to analogy سُدُودٌ, (Ṣ, M, Ḳ,) or أَسُدٌّ [which is a pl. of pauc.]. (M.) You say, ▼ مَا بِهِ سِدَادٌ ‡ *There is not in him any fault* &c.: and فُلَانٌ بَرِىْءٌ مِنَ الأَسِدَّةِ ‡ *Such a one is free from faults* &c. (A.) And مَا بِفُلَانٍ سَدَادَةٌ ▼ تَسُدُّ فَاهُ عَنِ الكَلَامِ † *There is not in such a one a fault that stops his mouth from speaking.* (Aboo-Sa'eed, L.) And لَا تَجْعَلَنَّ بِجَنْبِكَ الأَسِدَّةَ ‡ *By no means render thou thy bosom contracted so that thou shalt be unable to return an answer, like him who is deaf or dumb.* (Ṣ, Ḳ.) — See also سُدٌّ. — سد [so in the TA, i. e. either سَدٌّ or سُدٌّ,] also signifies † *A she-camel by which the sportsman conceals himself from the game;* also called دَرِيئَةٌ and دَرِيعَةٌ: whence the saying, رَمَاهُ فِى سَدِّ نَاقَتِهِ † [*He shot him, or shot at him, by his she-camel whereby he was concealing himself*]. (IAạr, TA.) — And سَدٌّ, (M,) or سُدٌّ, (O, Ḳ,) is also *syn.* with ظِلٌّ [as meaning ‡ *Shade,* or *shadow;* or *cover,* or *protection*]. (IAạr, M, O, Ḳ, TA.) A poet cited by IAạr says,

* قَعَدْتُ لَهُ فِى سَدِّ نِقْضٍ مُعَوَّدٍ *
* لِذٰلِكَ فِى صَحْرَاءَ جِذْمٍ دَرِينُهَا *

‡ [*I sat for him, i. e. lay in wait for him, in the shade,* or *cover, of a camel rendered lean by travel, accustomed to that, in a desert whereof the dry herbage was old*]: i. e. I made him a cover, or screen, to me, in order that he might not see me: and by جِذْم he means "old," because الجِذْمُ signifies الأَصْلُ, and there is nothing older than the أَصْل; and he uses it as an epithet because it implies the meaning of an epithet. (M.) — سَدٌّ also signifies *A thing,* (Ṣ, Ḳ,) [i. e.] *a* [*basket such as is called*] سَلَّة, (M, TA,) *made of twigs,* (Ṣ, M, Ḳ,) *and having covers* (أَطْبَاق): (Ṣ, Ḳ: [but this addition in the Ṣ and Ḳ seems properly to apply to the pl., as will be shown by what follows:]) pl. سِدَادٌ and سُدُودٌ: (M, TA:) or, accord. to Lth, سُدُودٌ signifies [*baskets such as are called*] سِلَالٌ, [pl. of سَلَّةٌ,] *made of twigs, and having covers* (أَطْبَاق); *one of which is called* [not سَدٌّ but] ▼ سَدَّةٌ: and it is said also on other authority that the سَلَّة is called سَدَّةٌ and طَبْلٌ. (L, TA.)

سُدٌّ: see the next preceding paragraph, passim. — Also † *A swarm of locusts obstructing the horizon:* (M:) or so سُدٌّ مِنْ جَرَادٍ: (TA:) and جَرَادٌ سُدٌّ ‡ *locusts* (Ṣ, M, A, Ḳ) *that have obstructed,* (Ṣ, Ḳ,) or *obstructing,* (M, A,) *the horizon,* (Ṣ, M, A, Ḳ,) *by their multitude:* (Ṣ, A, Ḳ:) in which case, سُدٌّ is either a substitute for جَرَادٌ and therefore a substantive, or it is pl. of ▼ سَدُودٌ signifying that *which obstructs the horizon* and therefore an epithet. (M.) — And ‡ *A black cloud,* (AZ, Ṣ, Ḳ, TA,) *that has risen in any tract of the sky:* (TA:) or *a collection of clouds rising, obstructing the horizon:* (M:) pl. سُدُودٌ: (Ṣ, M, Ḳ:) [or] ▼ سَدٌّ and صُدٌّ, but the former is the more approved, signify † *a cloud,* or *collection of clouds, rising high, and appearing like a mountain.* (M and L in art. صد.) — And *A valley:* (Ḳ:) so called because it becomes closed, or stopped up. (TA.) — And *A valley containing stones and masses of rock, in which water remains for some time,* or *a long time:* pl. سِدَدَةٌ: (Ṣ, L, Ḳ:) or you say, أَرْضٌ بِهَا سِدَدَةٌ [*a land in which are valleys containing stones and masses of rock,* &c.]; and the sing. is ▼ سُدَّةٌ. (L.) — And † The *departure* [or *loss*] *of sight:* (IAạr, M:) from the same word in the first of the senses expl. in the next preceding paragraph. (M.)

سِدٌّ: see سَدِيدٌ.

سَدَّةٌ: see سَدٌّ, last sentence.

سُدَّةٌ *A certain disease in the nose,* (Ṣ, M, L, Ḳ,) *which stops it up,* (M, L,) *attacking the passage of the breath,* (L,) *and preventing respiration;* (Ṣ, L;) as also ▼ سُدَادٌ. (Ṣ, M, L, Ḳ.) *A thing that obstructs the passage of the humours, and of the food, in the body.* (KL.) [And *Any obstruction in the body:* pl. سُدَدٌ.] — See also سُدٌّ. — Also [*A vestibule, or porch, for shade and shelter, before the door of a house:* this is a common signification of the word, and is app. what is meant by its being said that] the سُدَّة is *what is before the door of a house:* (M, A:) or, as some say, a سَقِيفَة [i. e. *roof,* or *covering, such as projects over the door of a house &c.;* or *a place roofed over*]: (M:) or a ظُلَّة [i. e. *roof,* or *cover-*

ing, for shade and shelter,] over a door: (Mgh:) or it is [a thing, or place,] like a صُفَّة [or سَقِيفَة] before a بَيْت [or house, or perhaps here meaning tent]: and a ظُلَّة at the door of a house (دَار): (AA, TA:) or, accord. to Aboo-Sa'eed, (TA,) in the language of the Arabs [of the desert] it signifies [a space such as is termed] a فِنَآء pertaining to a tent of hair-cloth and the like; and those who make it to be like a صُفَّة, or like a سَقِيفَة, explain the word accord. to the way in which it is used by the people of the towns and villages: (Mṣb, TA:) or it signifies the door [itself]: (Ṣ, A, Mgh, Ḳ:) or it has this meaning also: (Mṣb:) some thus apply it to the door itself: (A'Obeyd, L:) and the surrounding portico [of the interior court] of the largest, or larger, mosque: (M, TA:) pl. سُدَدٌ. (Ṣ, L, Mṣb, Ḳ.) You say, رَأَيْتُهُ قَاعِدًا بِسُدَّةِ بَابِهِ [I saw him sitting in the vestibule of his door]: (Ṣ, TA:) and بِسُدَّةِ دَارِهِ [in the vestibule before the door, or at the door, of his house]. (TA.) Abu-d-Dardà said, مَنْ يَغْشَ سُدَدَ السُّلْطَانِ يَقُمْ وَيَقْعُدْ, (Ṣ, L,) or مَنْ يَأْتِ السُّدَد, i. e. [He who comes to the vestibules, or gates, of the Sultán] experiences returns of recent and old griefs, disquieting him so that he is not able to remain at rest, but stands up and sits down: (Mgh in art. قدم:) this he said when he came to the gate of Mo'áwiyeh and did not receive permission to enter. (L.) And it is said in a trad., الشُّعْثُ الرُّؤُوسِ الَّذِينَ لَا تُفْتَحُ لَهُمُ السُّدَدُ, (Ṣ, A,) meaning الأَبْوَابُ [i. e. The shaggy, or dishevelled, and dusty, in the heads are those to whom the doors will not be opened]. (A.) — Hence, Umm-Selemeh, addressing 'Áïsheh, termed her a سُدَّة, i. e. a بَاب [meaning † A means of communication], between the Prophet and his people. (L, from a trad.) — Also Palm-sticks, i. e. palm-branches stripped of their leaves, bound together, [side by side,] upon which one sleeps. (M.)

سَدَدٌ: see the next paragraph, in four places: — and see also سَدِيدٌ.

سَدَادٌ [an inf. n. of the intrans. verb سَدَّ; as also ♦ سَدَدٌ]. [Hence,] one says, إِنَّهُ لَذُو سَدَادٍ Verily he has a faculty of hitting the right thing, or his object or aim, in speaking, and in the managing or disposing of affairs, and in shooting. (TA.) — [Hence also, as a subst.,] A thing that is right, syn. صَوَابٌ, (Ṣ, A, Mṣb, Ḳ,) and قَصْدٌ, (Ṣ,) of what is said and of what is done; (Ṣ, A,* Mṣb, Ḳ;) as also ♦ سَدَدٌ, (Ṣ, A,) which is a contraction of the former. (Ṣ.) One says, قَالَ سَدَادًا مِنَ القَوْلِ He said a right thing [lit. of what is said, i. e., a right saying]; (Ṣ, A;) as also ♦ سَدَدًا. (A.) And يُصِيبُ السَّدَادَ He hits the right thing in speech [or action]. (Ṣ.) And هُوَ عَلَى سَدَادٍ مِنْ أَمْرِهِ and ♦ سَدَدٍ [He is following a right course of action in respect of his affair]. (A.) And أَمْرُ فُلَانٍ يَجْرِى عَلَى السَّدَادِ The affair of such a one goes on according to that which is right. (Ṣ.) — [And hence the saying,] أَتَتْنَا رِيحٌ مِنْ سَدَادِ أَرْضِهِمْ ‡ A wind came to us from the direction of their land. (A, TA.) — It is also used as an epithet, syn. with سَدِيدٌ, q. v. (L.) — And السَّدَادُ [as though meaning The right projecter] is a name that was given to a bow belonging to the Prophet, as ominating the hitting of the object aimed at by that which was shot from it. (TA.) — See also سِدَادٌ, in three places.

سُدَادٌ: see سُدَّةٌ, first sentence.

سِدَادٌ A thing with which an interstice, or intervening space, is closed, or closed up: (AO, M, L: [see also سُدٌّ:]) and a thing with which a breach, or gap, (M, A,) is stopped, or stopped up, (M,) or repaired, and made firm or strong: (A:) pl. أَسِدَّةٌ. (M.) Primarily, accord. to ISh, (Meyd, in explanation of a prov. mentioned in what follows,) Somewhat of milk that dries up in the orifice of a she-camel's teat; (Meyd, Ḳ;) because it stops up the passage of the milk. (Meyd.) Also A stopper of a bottle (Ṣ,* Mgh,* Mṣb, Ḳ,* TA) &c.: (Mṣb:) in this sense [as well as in those before mentioned] with kesr (Ṣ, Mgh, Mṣb, Ḳ) only [to the س]: and so in the sense next following. (Ṣ, Ḳ.) A body of horse and foot serving as blockaders of the frontier of a hostile country. (S, Ḳ,* TA.) — سِدَادٌ مِنْ عَوَزٍ and ♦ سَدَادٌ, (ISk, Ṣ, M, Mṣb, Ḳ,) but the former is the more chaste, (Ṣ,) and it alone is mentioned by most authors in this saying, because it is from سداد as meaning the "stopper" of a bottle; (Mṣb;) and some say that ♦ سَدَاد, with fet-ḥ, is a corruption; (Mṣb, Ḳ;) expressly disallowed by Aṣ and ISh; (Mṣb;) a prov.; (Meyd;) meaning ‡ A thing by which want is supplied, (Ṣ, M, Mṣb, Ḳ,) and by which life is preserved; accord. to ISh, if incomplete; and accord. to Aṣ, a thing by which somewhat of the entire wants of one's case is supplied. (Mṣb.) One says also, أَصَبْتُ بِهِ سِدَادًا مِنَ العَيْشِ and ♦ سَدَادًا ‡ I attained thereby a thing by which want was supplied; (Ṣ, Ḳ,* TA;) or a means of sustaining life. (AO, L.) — See also سُدٌّ, in two places.

سُدُودٌ: see سُدٌّ.

سَدِيدٌ, applied to a spear, Seldom missing; and [to the same, and] to an arrow, that hits the mark; (TA;) and to a saying, (Ṣ, M, L,) as also ♦ سَدَادٌ (M, L) and ♦ سَدَدٌ; (L;) and an action; (TA;) and an affair, as also ♦ أَسَدُّ; (Ṣ, A, L;) right, direct, or in a right state; having, or taking, a right direction or tendency; tending towards the right point or object: (Ṣ, M, A, L, TA:) and ♦ سَدٌّ, applied to speech, signifies the same; (TA;) and true. (Ḳ, TA.) — And applied to a man, meaning Who pursues a right course; as also ♦ أَسَدُّ; (M;) and [in an intensive sense] ♦ سَدَّادٌ: (TA:) or, (Mṣb,) as also ♦ مُسِدٌّ, (Ṣ,) who hits the right thing in his saying (Ṣ, Mṣb) and in his action. (Mṣb.)

سَدَادَةٌ: see سَدٌّ, in two places.

سَدَّادٌ: see سَدِيدٌ.

سَادَّةٌ ‡ An eye (عَيْنٌ) of which the sight has gone; (A;) that has become white, and with which one does not see, but which has not yet burst: (Az, A,* L, Ḳ:) or that is open, but does not see strongly: (IAạr, L, Ḳ:) pl. سُدُودٌ, (IAạr, L,) or سُدَّدٌ. (Ḳ.) — Also † An old and weak she-camel. (IAạr, Ḳ.)

أَسَدُّ: see سَدِيدٌ, in two places.

مَسَدٌّ [properly A place of closing, or stopping, &c.]: see 1, in two places.

مُسِدٌّ: see سَدِيدٌ.

مُسَدَّدٌ Directed; pointed in a right direction. (Ṣ, TA.) — And A man directed, accommodated, adapted, or disposed, to that which is right [of words and of actions]; (L;) who does that which is right, (يَعْمَلُ بِالسَّدَادِ وَالقَصْدِ, Ṣ, L,) keeping to the right way; in which sense it is related by some with kesr, ♦ مُسَدِّدٌ. (L.) [Golius explains it as meaning, on the authority of the Ṣ, who executes his affairs with sure and good judgment, and with happy success: and Freytag thus explains ♦ مُسَدِّدٌ, as from the Ṣ.]

مُسَدِّدٌ: see the next preceding paragraph, in two places.

سدح

1. سَدَحَهُ بِشَىْءٍ, (O, Ḳ,) aor. ـَ, inf. n. سَدْحٌ, (TḲ,) He thought a thing to be in him; (O, Ḳ;) i. e. he suspected him of a thing: (TA:) or سَدَحَ بِشَىْءٍ he imagined, or thought, a thing. (L.) — See also what next follows, in two places.

5. تَسَدَّحَ; (Ṣ, L, Ḳ;) and ♦ سَدَحَ, inf. n. سَدْحٌ; (L;) He lied, affected lying, or lied purposely; and forged, or fabricated: (Ṣ, L, Ḳ: [in the CḲ, تَخَلَّقَ is erroneously put for تَخَلَّقَ:]) he forged and uttered false and vain tales: (L:) or ♦ سَدَحَ, aor. ـَ, signifies [simply] he lied; (O, in the present art. and in art. سرح;) like سَرَحَ. (O in art. سرح.) [See also تَسَرَّحَ.]

7. انسدح He fell prostrate; fell upon his face; (O, Ḳ, TA;) like him who is prostrating himself in prayer: (TA:) [it may perhaps be a mistranscription for انسدح; which seems to be better known in this sense: but it is said to be] formed by transposition from انسجد and [so] اندسح. (TA.)

سَدَاجَةٌ, used by Ibn-El-Khaṭeeb and others of the people of El-Andalus, [and by post-classical writers of other countries,] as meaning Easiness, and goodness of nature or disposition, [or rather simplicity, or plainness, of mind or manners,] is from سَاذَج, an arabicized word from [the Pers.] سَادَه, signifying, with them, "free in intellect," and "easy in nature or disposition:" frequent usage occasioned the change of the ذ into د. (TA. [See De Sacy's Chrest. Ar., 2nd ed., ii. 292.])

سَدَّاحٌ A great, or habitual, liar, (Ṣ, O, L, Ḳ,) who will not tell thee truly whence he comes, but will tell thee lyingly. (L.) [See also سَرَّاح.]

سدر

1. سَدِرَ, aor. ـَ, inf. n. سَدَرٌ and سَدَارَةٌ, (Ṣ, Ḳ,) *He became dazzled by a thing at which he looked, so that he turned away his face from it:* or *became confounded,* or *perplexed, and unable to see his right course:* syn. تَحَيَّرَ: (Ḳ:) and *he* (a camel) *became dazzled by a thing at which he looked, so that he turned away his face from it, by reason of intense heat:* (Ṣ,* Ḳ:) also, (TA,) or سَدِرَ بَصَرُهُ, (M,) *he* [app. a man or any animal] *was hardly able to see:* (M, TA:) or سَدِرَ بَصَرُهُ *he was dazzled,* or *confounded* or *perplexed, and did not see well;* as also ▼ اِسْمَدَرَّ. (A, TA.) [See also سَدِرٌ, below.] — سَدَرَ, (M, Ḳ,) or سَدَرَتْ, (Ṣ,) aor. ـُ, inf. n. سَدْرٌ, (M,) *He,* or *she, let down, let fall,* or *made to hang down,* his, or her, hair; (Ṣ, M, Ḳ;) and in like manner, a curtain, or veil, (M,) and a garment; (Lḥ;) a dial. var. of سَدَلَ. (Ṣ, Ḳ.*) — Also سَدَرَ, aor. ـِ, inf. n. سَدْرٌ and سُدُورٌ, *He rent* his garment. (Yaạkoob, M.)

4. اسدرت الشَّمْسُ عَيْنَهُ [*The sun dazzled his eye, and confused his sight*]. (Ḳ in art. جهر.)

5. تسدّر بِثَوْبِهِ *He covered himself with his garment.* (AA.)

7. انسدر *It* (hair, Ṣ, M, Ḳ, and a curtain or veil, M) *hung down;* (Ṣ, M, Ḳ;) a dial. var. of انسدل. (Ṣ, Ḳ.*) — انسدر يَعْدُو *He was somewhat quick,* or *made some haste, running:* (Ṣ, M:*) or *he went down,* or *downwards, and persevered* (A'Obeyd, Ḳ) *in his running, going quickly.* (A'Obeyd.) [In the CḲ, for يعدو, is put by mistake يَبْعُدُ.]

Q. Q. 4. اِسْمَدَرَّ بَصَرُهُ *His sight became weak, in the manner described below, voce* سَمَادِيرُ. (Ṣ in art. سدر, and M and Ḳ in art. سمدر.) It is of the measure اِفْمَعَلَّ, from السَّدَرُ; (IḲṭṭ;) the م being augmentative. (Ṣ.) See also سَدِرَ. — اسمدرّت عَيْنُهُ *His eye shed tears;* accord. to Lḥ; but this is not known in the classical language. (M in art. سمدر.)

سِدْرٌ [a coll. gen. n., The *species of lote-tree called by Linnæus rhamnus spina Christi; and by Forskål, rhamnus nabeca;*] the *tree,* or *trees, of which the fruit is called* نَبِق *and* نَبْق: (Ṣ, M, Mgh, Mṣb, Ḳ:) sing., (Mṣb,) or [rather] n. un., (Ṣ, M, Ḳ,) سِدْرَةٌ: (Ṣ, M, Mṣb, Ḳ:) and sometimes سِدْرٌ is used as meaning the smallest or smaller of numbers [generally denoting from three to ten inclusively]: (Ibn-Es-Sarráj, Mṣb:) AḤn says, accord. to Aboo-Ziyád, *the* سدر *is of the kind called* عِضَاه, *and is of two species,* عُبْرِىّ *and* ضَالّ: the عبرى *is that which has no thorns except such as do not hurt: the* ضال *has thorns* [*which hurt*]: *the* سدر *has a broad round leaf: and sometimes people alight and rest beneath a tree of this kind; but the* ضال *is small: the best* نبق *that is known in the land of the Arabs is in Hejer* (هَجَر), *in a single piece of land which is appropriated to the Sultán alone: it is the sweetest of all in taste and odour: the mouth of him who eats it, and the garments of him who has it upon him, diffuse an odour like that of perfume:* (M, TA:) *it is* [*also*] *said that the* سدر *is of two species; whereof one grows in the cultivated lands, and its leaves are used in the ablution termed* غُسْل, *and its fruit is sweet; and the other grows in the desert, and its leaves are not so used, and its fruit is juicy:* the زُعْرُور is so described that it may be supposed to be the wild نبق: (Mṣb:) when سِدْرٌ is used absolutely, with relation to the ablution termed غُسْل, it means the *ground leaves of the tree so called:* (Mgh,* Mṣb:) the pl. of سِدْرَةٌ is سِدْرَاتٌ and سِدَرَاتٌ and سِدِرَاتٌ (Ṣ, Ḳ) and سِدَرٌ (Ṣ, M, Ḳ) and سُدُورٌ, (M, Ḳ,) which last is extr. (M.) — سِدْرَةُ الْمُنْتَهَى is said to be *The lote-tree in the Seventh Heaven;* (Lth, Ḳ;*) *beyond which neither angel nor prophet passes, and which shades the water and Paradise:* (Lth:) in the Ṣaḥeeḥ it is said to be *in the Sixth Heaven:* 'Iyáḍ reconciles the two assertions by the supposition that *its root is in the Sixth,* and that *it rises over the Seventh:* accord. to IAth, it is *in the furthest part of Paradise to which, as its furthest limit, extends the knowledge of ancients and moderns.* (MF, TA.)

سَدَرٌ [see 1]. You say, فِى بَصَرِهِ سَدَرٌ, and ▼ سَمَادِيرُ, *In his sight is a confusedness, so that he does not see well.* (A.) — Some say that it signifies *An affection resembling vertigo, common to a voyager upon the sea:* or [simply] *vertigo.* (TA in art. بقل.)

سَدِرٌ *Having his eyes dazzled by a thing, so that he turns away his face from it:* or *in a state of confusion* or *perplexity, and unable to see his right course:* syn. مُتَحَيِّرٌ: (Ḳ:) as also ▼ سَادِرٌ: (Ṣ, Ḳ:) and the former, a camel *having his eyes dazzled by a thing, so that he turns away his face from it, by reason of intense heat:* (Ṣ:) and also one *having his eyes dazzled by snow;* as well as by intense heat. (IAạr.) — عَيْنُهُ سَدِرَةٌ *His eye is confused in its vision,* or *dazzled, so that he cannot see well.* (A.) — And سَدِرَةٌ means An *old and weak* she-camel. (IAạr, TA in art. سد.) — Also سَدِرٌ *The sea:* (Ṣ, M, Ḳ:) one of the [proper] names thereof; (Ṣ;) occurring only in a poem of Umeiyeh Ibn-Abi-ṣ-Ṣalt: (M:) he says,

• فَكَأَنَّ بِرْقِعَ وَالْمَلَائِكَ حَوْلَهُ •
• سَدِرٌ تَوَاكَلَهُ الْقَوَائِمُ أَجْرَدُ •

[*And as though the first heaven, with the angels around it, were the sea, the winds deserting it,* and *smooth*]: (Ṣ, M, TA: [but in the M and TA, for حَوْلَهُ, we find حَوْلَهَا; and in the Ṣ, for أَجْرَدُ, we find أَجْرَبُ, which is inconsistent with the rhyme of the poem:]) by القوائم he means the winds; and by تواكله, [for تَوَاكَلَتْهُ,] [or rather تَتَرَكَهُ]: he likens the sky to the sea when calm: (TA:) Th quotes thus:

• وَكَأَنَّ بِرْقِعَ وَالْمَلَائِكَ تَحْتَهَا •
• سَدِرٌ تَوَاكَلَهُ قَوَائِمُ أَرْبَعُ •

and says that the poet likens the angels, with respect to their fear of God, to a man affected with a vertigo [lit., turning round, though it would seem more appropriate had he said, the poet likens them to a camel so affected, whom his four legs failed: he prefaces this explanation with the words, سَدِرٌ يَدُورُ وَقَوَائِمُهُ أَرْبَعٌ هُمُ الْمَلَائِكَةُ; to which he or ISd adds, لَا يَدْرِى كَيْفَ خَلْقُهُمْ: but (using a common phrase of ISd) I can only say, لَا أَدْرِى كَيْفَ هٰذَا; unless there be some omission in the transcription]: (M, TA:) Ṣgh says that the correct reading is سِدْرٌ, meaning the kind of tree so called, not the sea; and the author of the Námoos adopts his opinion; but MF rejects it: (TA:) some read رَقْعًا [in the place of برقع] and explain it as meaning *the seventh heaven.* (TA in art. رقع.)

سِدْرِىٌّ *One who grinds and sells the leaves of the* سدر. (TA.) [See also سَدَّارٌ.]

سِدَارٌ *A thing resembling a* [*curtain of the kind called*] خِدْر: (Ḳ:) or *resembling a* كِلَّة, *which is put across a* [*tent of the kind called*] خِبَاء. (M.)

سَدَّارٌ *A seller of the leaves of the* سِدْر. (TA.) [See also سِدْرِىٌّ.]

سَادِرٌ: see سَدِرٌ. — Also *Losing his way:* you say, إِنَّهُ سَادِرٌ فِى الغَىِّ *Verily he is losing his way, in error.* (A.) And أَتَى أَمْرَهُ سَادِرًا i. e. [*He entered into, or did, his affair*] *in a wrong way.* (Ḥam p. 432.) — A man *without firmness,* or *deliberation.* (M.) You say, تَكَلَّمَ سَادِرًا *He spoke without deliberation.* (A.) — A man *who cares not for anything, nor minds what he does:* (Ṣ,* M, Ḳ:) or one *who occupies himself with vain* or *frivolous diversion.* (TA.)

سُمْدُورٌ* *A cloudiness of the eye;* (Ḳ;) *and weakness of sight:* (TA:) and سَمَادِيرُ [originally pl. of the preceding, app.,] *weakness of sight,* (Ṣ, M, Ḳ,) or *something appearing to a man by reason of weakness of his sight,* (M, Ḳ,) *on the occasion of,* (Ṣ, M,) or [*arising*] *from,* (Ḳ,) *intoxication* (Ṣ, M, Ḳ) *by drink &c.,* (M,) *and from* [or if the reading in the CḲ be correct this prep. should be omitted] *the insensibility arising from drowsiness and vertigo.* (Ṣ, Ḳ.) The م is augmentative. (Ṣ: but the word is mentioned in the M and Ḳ in art. سمدر.) See also سَدَرٌ. — Also *A king:* because the eyes become weak, or dazzled, in consequence of looking at him. (Ḳ in art. سمدر.)

الأَسْدَرَانِ *The shoulder-joints,* (Ṣ, M, A, Ḳ,) *and the sides:* (Ṣ, Ḳ:) or (so in the M, but accord. to the Ḳ "and") *two veins* (M, Ḳ) *in the eye,* (M,) or *in the two eyes:* (Ḳ:) or *beneath the temples.* (M.) Hence the saying جَآءَ يَضْرِبُ أَسْدَرَيْهِ *He came beating* (with his hands, TA) *his shoulder-joints* (Ṣ, A, Ḳ) *and his sides;* (Ṣ, Ḳ;) meaning, ‡ *he came empty,* (Ṣ, A, Ḳ,) *having nothing in his hand,* (Ṣ,) or *having no occupation,* (M,) *and without having accomplished the object of his desire:* (Ṣ, Ḳ:) and in like manner, جَآءَ يَنْفُضُ أَسْدَرَيْهِ and أَصْدَرَيْهِ: (Ṣ:)

(AZ,) and أَصْدَرِيْهِ, (TA,) and ,أَزْدَرِيْهِ, (ISk,) *he came shaking his shoulder-joints*: (AZ:) or *his sides*: meaning as above. (TA.)

مُسْدُورٌ Hair [*let down*, or *made to hang down*, or] *hanging down*; like مُسْدُولٌ. (TA.)

مُسْمَدِرٌ A *dazzled* eye. (TA in art. سمدر.) — A *long and direct* road. (Ḳ ibid.) — And hence, (TA ibid.,) † *Right* speech or language. (Ḳ and TA ibid.)

سدس

1. سَدَسَ القَوْمَ, (Ṣ, M, Mṣb, Ḳ,*) aor. ـُ, (Ṣ, M, Mṣb,) inf. n. سَدْسٌ, (M, Mṣb, TA,) *He took the sixth part of the possessions of the people*. (M, Mṣb, Ḳ.) — And سَدَسَ القَوْمَ, aor. ـِ, (Ṣ, M, Mṣb, Ḳ,) inf. n. سَدْسٌ, (Mṣb, TA,) *He was*, or *became, the sixth of the people*: (M, Mṣb, Ḳ:) or *he made them, with himself, six*. (Ṣ in art. ثلث.) And *He made the people*, they being fifty-nine, *to be sixty with himself*. (A'Obeyd, Ṣ in art. ثلث.) And سَدَسَ also signifies *He made* fifteen *to be sixteen*. (T in art. ثلث.)

2. سَدَّسَهُ, inf. n. تَسْدِيسٌ, *He made it six*. (Esh-Sheybánee, and Ḳ voce وَحَّدَهُ.) — *He made it to be six-cornered; six-angled; hexagonal*: or *six-ribbed*. (Ṣgh, TA.) — سدّس لِٱمْرَأَتِهِ, or عِنْدَهَا, *He remained six nights with his wife*: and in like manner the verb is used in relation to any saying or action. (TA voce سَبَّعَ.)

4. اسدس القَوْمُ *The party of men became six*: (Ṣ, M, Mṣb:) also *the party of men became sixty*. (M and L in art. ثلث.) — اسدس البَعِيرُ *The camel cast the tooth after the* رَبَاعِيَة; (Ṣ, Mṣb, Ḳ;) *cast the tooth called* سَدِيس; (M, A;) *which he does in his eighth year*: (Ṣ, IF, A, Mṣb:) and in like manner one says of a sheep or goat. (M.) — اسدس الرَّجُلُ *The man was*, or *became, one whose camels came to water on the sixth day, counting the day of the next preceding drinking as the first*. (Ṣ,* Ḳ,* TA.) [See سِدْسٌ.]

سُدْسٌ: see سُدُسٌ.

سِدْسٌ is the original form of سِتٌّ, (M, Ḳ,) fem. of سِتَّةٌ, which is originally سِدْسَةٌ, (M,) [meaning *Six*; for] the dim. [of سِتٌّ is ▼ سُدَيْسٌ, and that] of سِتَّةٌ is ▼ سُدَيْسَةٌ; and the pl. is أَسْدَاسٌ. (Ṣ in art. ست, q. v.) — Also [The *drinking of camels on the sixth day, counting the day of the next preceding drinking as the first*; as will be seen from what here follows;] the *period of the drinking of camels* [next] *after that called* خِمْسٌ: or *after six days and five nights*: (M, TA:) or *their being kept from the water five days, and coming to it on the sixth*: (Ṣ:) but Ṣgh says that this is a mistake, and that the correct meaning of the term is, *their being kept from the water four days, and coming to it on the fifth*; and so it is explained in the [A and] Ḳ: (TA:) or *their drinking one day, then being kept from the water four days, then coming to it on the fifth day*; so [by the application of the term سِدْسٌ] they include in their reckoning the first day in which the camels drink: (Aboo-Sahl, TA:) or *their remaining in the place of pasture four days* [*after drinking*], *then coming to the water on the fifth*: (TA:) pl. أَسْدَاسٌ. (M, Ṣgh, TA.) You say, وَرَدَتْ إِبِلُهُ سِدْسًا [*His camels came to the water on the sixth day, counting the day of the next preceding drinking as the first*]. (Ṣ, A, Ḳ.) [Hence the saying,] ضَرَبَ أَخْمَاسًا لِأَسْدَاسٍ [which see expl. voce خِمْسٌ]. (A.) — Also The *sixth young one*, or *offspring*. (A in art. ثلث.)

سَدَسٌ: see سَدِيسٌ, in three places: — and, as an epithet applied to a calf, see عَضْبٌ.

سُدُسٌ (Ṣ, M, A, Mṣb, Ḳ) and ▼ سُدْسٌ (Ṣ, Mṣb, Ḳ) *A sixth part*; (Ṣ, M, A, Mṣb, Ḳ;) as also ▼ سَدِيسٌ, (Ṣ, Mṣb, Ḳ,) a form used by some, like as one says عَشِيرٌ and عُشْرٌ: (Ṣ:) pl. أَسْدَاسٌ. (M, Mṣb, TA.) — [Hence, app., the saying, ضَرَبَ أَخْمَاسَهُ فِى أَسْدَاسِهِ, which see expl. voce خِمْسٌ.]

[سُدَاسَ as meaning *Six and six together*, or *six at a time and six at a time*, seems not to have been heard: see عُشَارَ. But Freytag mentions سُدَاسٌ as used by El-Mutanebbee for سِتَّةٌ.]

سُدُوسٌ: see the next paragraph.

سُدُوسٌ (Sh, Ṣ, M, Ḳ) and ▼ سَدُوسٌ, (Sh, M, Ḳ,) Aṣ used to say the latter, (Ṣ,) *A* [*garment of the kind called*] طَيْلَسَان: (M:) or *a* طيلسان, (Ṣ, M, Ḳ,) or *any garment*, (Sh,) *of the colour termed* خُضْرَة [here app. meaning *a dark*, or *an ashy, dust-colour*]. (Sh, Ṣ, M, Ḳ.) — And the former, (Ḳ,) or the latter, (M,) *Smoke-black of fat*; or *lamp-black*; syn. نِيلَنْج. (M, Ḳ.)

سَدِيسٌ: see سُدُسٌ: — and see سُدَاسِىٌّ. — Also The *tooth that is before that called the* بَازِل; (Ṣ, Ḳ;) *after that called the* رَبَاعِيَة; (M, L, TA;) as also ▼ سَدَسٌ; (Ṣ, Ḳ;) masc. and fem., because the fem. names of teeth are all with ة, except سِنٌّ and سَدِيسٌ and بَازِلٌ: (Ṣ:) the pl. (of the former, Ṣ,) is سُدُسٌ and (of the latter, Ṣ) سُدْسٌ. (Ṣ, Ḳ.) You say, of a camel, أَلْقَى سَدِيسَهُ and ▼ سَدَسَهُ [*He cast his tooth called the* سديس *and* سدس]. (A.) — And hence, (Mgh,) A camel, (M, A, Mgh, Mṣb,) and a sheep or goat, (M, TA,) *casting his* سَدِيس, (M, A, TA,) or *his tooth that is after the* رَبَاعِيَة; (Mṣb;) i. e., *in the eighth year*; (A, Mgh, Mṣb;) as also ▼ سَدَسٌ: (A, Mgh, TA:) masc. and fem.: (M, TA:) or a sheep or goat *six years old*: (Ṣ, Ḳ:) pl. سُدُسٌ. (M.) A poet, (Ṣ,) namely, Manṣoor Ibn-Misjáḥ, speaking of a fine for homicide, taken from among selected camels, (TA,) says,

فَطَافَ كَمَا طَافَ المُصَدِّقُ وَسْطَهَا * يُخَيِّرُ مِنْهَا فِى البَوَازِلِ وَالسُّدْسِ

[*And he went round about, as the collector of the poor-rate went round about, amid them, preferring certain of them, among the nine-year-old and the eight-year-old camels*]. (Ṣ, TA.) — Also *A sort of measure*, or *a sort of* مَكُّوك, [in some copies of the Ḳ ضَرْبٌ مِنَ المَكَايِيلِ, and in others and in the O ضرب من المَكَاكِيك,] (O, Ḳ,) *with which dates are measured*. (O.) — سَدِيس in the saying لَا آتِيكَ سَدِيسَ عُجَيْسٍ is a dial. var. of سَجِيس, q. v. (Ṣ.)

سُدَيْسٌ and سُدَيْسَةٌ: see سِدْسٌ.

سُدَاسِىٌّ, applied to a garment of the kind called إِزَار, (Ṣ, A, Ḳ,) *Six cubits in length*; (A, Ḳ;) as also ▼ سَدِيسٌ. (Ṣ,* A, Mṣb, Ḳ.) — Also [as meaning *Six spans in height*, said to be] applied to a slave. (Mṣb in art. خمس.) [But see خُمَاسِىٌّ.] — [Also A word *composed of six letters, radical only*, or *radical and augmentative*.]

سَادِسٌ [*Sixth*]: fem. with ة. (Ṣ, Ḳ, &c.) See also سَاتٌّ, in art. ست. — [سَادِسَ عَشَرَ, and the fem. سَادِسَةَ عَشْرَةَ, meaning *Sixteenth*, are subject to the same rules as ثَالِثَ عَشَرَ and its fem., expl. in art. ثلث, q. v.]

سُنْدُسٌ: see art. سندس.

مُسَدَّسٌ A thing *composed of six layers* or *strata*, or *of six distinct fascicles* or *the like*. (TA in art. ثلث. [See also مَسْدُوسٌ, below.]) — [*Hexagonal*; *a hexagon*.] — A verse *composed of six feet*. (M.)

مَسْدُوسٌ A rope *composed of six strands*. (M in art. ثلث.)

سدغ

سُدْغٌ a dial. var. of صُدْغٌ, (Ḳ,) which is the more common. (TA. [See the latter.])

مِسْدَغٌ: see what follows.

مِسْدَغَةٌ a dial. var. of مِصْدَغَةٌ [q. v.]; (TA;) as also مِزْدَغَةٌ; (L and TA in art. زدغ;) and ▼ مِسْدَغٌ and مِزْدَغٌ signify the same [as dial. vars. of مِصْدَغٌ]. (TA.)

سدف

2. سَدَّفَهُ, (M, TA,) inf. n. تَسْدِيفٌ, (TA,) *He cut it in pieces*; namely, a camel's hump. (M, TA.)

4. اسدف *It* (the night) *became dark*; (Ṣ, M, Ḳ;) accord. to some, *after the* جِنْح [app. as meaning the *first part thereof*; or *about the half*; or *a great*, or *the greater, part*]: (M:) or *let down its curtains, and became dark*: and ازدف and اشدف signify the same. (AO, TA.) — And اسدف القَوْمُ *The people, or party, entered upon the* [*period of the night called*] سُدْفَة. (M.) — And اسدف *He slept*; (AA, Ḳ, TA;) as also ازدف. (AA, TA.) — And ‡ *His eyes became dark by reason of hunger or age*: (Ḳ, TA:) said of a man. (TA.) — Also, said of the daybreak, or dawn, *It shone*: (Ṣ, Ḳ, TA:) [thus,] as AO says, it has two contr. significations. (TA.) — And *He lighted the lamp*: (Ḳ:) or one says, in the dial. of Hawázin, أَسْدِفُوا, i. e. أَسْرِجُوا [*Light* ye a lamp, or with a lamp]; from السِّرَاجُ: (Ṣ, TA:) or one says in that dial., أَسْدِفُوا لَنَا, i. e. أَسْرِجُوا [They lighted for us a lamp, or with a lamp]. (M.) —— Also He moved away or aside [in order that the light might enter a place]. (Ḳ.) When a man is standing at a door or an entrance, one says to him, أَسْدِفْ, i. e. Move thou away or aside from the door, or entrance, in order that the chamber, or tent, may become light. (AA, TA. [See also the last sentence of this paragraph.]) —— [In all of these senses, perhaps excepting one, it is intrans.: in others, trans.] ══ You say of a woman, اسدفت القِنَاعَ, (Ṣ, TA,) and الحِجَابَ, (TA,) She let down [the head-covering, and the veil, or curtain]. (Ṣ, TA.) —— And اسدف السِّتْرَ He raised [the veil, or curtain]. (Ḳ.) —— One says also, أَسْدِفِ البَابَ Open thou the door, or entrance, in order that the chamber, or tent, may become light. (Ṣ.)

سَدَفٌ: see سُدْفَةٌ, in three places. —— Also The night. (Ṣ, TA.) —— And The daybreak, or dawn: (AA, Ṣ, Ḳ:) and the advent thereof: (Fr, Ṣ, Ḳ:) and the whiteness of day. (TA.) ══ Also A ewe: (Ibn-'Abbád, Ḳ:) or such as has a blackness like that of night. (TA.) —— And سَدَفْ سَدَفْ is A call to the ewe to be milked. (Ḳ.)

سَدْفَةٌ: see the next paragraph.

سُدْفَةٌ and ↓ سَدْفَةٌ i. q. ↓ سَدَفٌ, (Aṣ, Ṣ, M, Ḳ,) as meaning The darkness, (Aṣ, Ṣ, Ḳ,) in the dial. of Nejd, (Aṣ, Ṣ,) or of Temeem; (Ḳ;) or as meaning the darkness of night; or, as some say, after the جِنْح [which here app. means the first part of the night; or about the half; or a great, or the greater, part]: (M:) and also as meaning the light, (Aṣ, Ṣ, Ḳ, and M in explanation of the first word,) in the dial. of others, (Aṣ, Ṣ,) or of Ḳeys: (Ḳ:) thus having two contr. significations; (Ṣ, Ḳ;) or the darkness and the light are called by one and the same name because each of them comes upon the other: (Ḳ:) or the first, (Ṣ, M, Ḳ,) and second, (Ḳ,) the commingling of the light and the darkness, (Ṣ, M, Ḳ,) as in the time between the rising of the dawn, (Ṣ,) or as in the time between the prayer of the dawn, (M,) and that when the sun becomes white, (Ṣ, M,) accord. to some, as is said by A'Obeyd; (Ṣ;) or, as 'Omárah says, the first signifies darkness in which is light, of the former part of the night and of the latter part thereof, between the redness after sunset and the darkness and between the dawn and the prayer [of the dawn]; And Az says that this is the correct explanation: (TA:) and the first and second, a portion of the night: (M, Ḳ:) or the first, a remaining portion of the night: (Ibn-Ḥabeeb, TA:) or the first of five divisions of the night: (TA in art. خدر: see خُدْرَةٌ, voce خَدَرٌ:) and the first, (Ḳ, TA,) i. e. with damm, (TA,) or the second, (CḲ,) as also ↓ سَدَفٌ, the blackness of night: (Ḳ:) the pl. of the first is سُدَفٌ; as in the saying of 'Alee, كَشَفْتُ عَنْهُمْ سُدَفَ اللَّيْلِ I removed from over them the darknesses of night: (TA:) and the pl. of ↓ سَدَفٌ is أَسْدَافٌ. (M, TA.) You say also, رَأَيْتُ سُدْفَةَ شَخْصِهِ مِنْ بُعْدٍ ‡ I saw the blackness of his body, or form, from a distance. (TA.) ══ Also the first, A door, or an entrance: (M, Ḳ:) or its سُدَّة [i. e. vestibule, or porch, &c.]: (Ḳ:) and a sort of covering over a door to protect it from the rain. (Ḳ,* TA.)

سُدُوفٌ [a pl. of which the sing. is app. سَدَفٌ, like شَدَفٌ,] The corporeal forms or figures or substances of men or other things which one sees from a distance: (Ḳ:) accord. to Ṣgh, (TA,) correctly with ش: (Ḳ, TA:) but the truth is, that they are two dial. vars. (TA.)

سَدِيفٌ A camel's hump: (Ṣ:) or a camel's hump cut into pieces: (M, TA:) or pieces [or slices] of a camel's hump: (Ḥam p. 258:) or the fat of a camel's hump: (M, Ḳ, and Ḥam p. 257:) [or a very fat hump of a camel: (Freytag, from the Deewán of Jereer:)] pl. سَدَائِفُ and سِدَافٌ. (TA.)

سِدَافَةٌ A veil, or covering; a thing that veils, conceals, covers, or protects: whence the saying of Umm-Selemeh to 'Áisheh, (O, Ḳ, TA,) when she desired to go forth to El-Baṣrah, (TA,) قَدْ وَجَّهْتِ سِدَافَتَهُ i. e. هَتَكْتِ السِّتْرَ i. e. أَخَذْتِ وَجْهَهَا [i. e. وَجْهَ سِدَافَتِهِ (JM in art. وجه) Thou hast rent open his veil, or covering, meaning the Prophet's, as is shown in the TA]: (O, Ḳ, TA:) or thou hast removed his veil, or covering: (O, TA:) or thou hast removed his veil, or covering, from its place, to which thou wast commanded to keep, and hast placed it before thee: (O, Ḳ, TA:) but the saying is also related otherwise, i. e. وَجَّهْتِ سِجَافَتَهُ, mentioned before [in art. سجف]. (TA.) One says also, وَجَّهَ فُلَانٌ سِدَافَتَهُ, meaning Such a one quitted his veil, or covering, and came forth from [behind] it. (TA.)

أَسْدَفُ, as an epithet applied to night, Dark, (M, [as also مُسْدِفٌ,]) or black. (Ḳ.)

مُسْدِفٌ Dark: [like أَسْدَفُ:] and also light: having two contr. significations. (M, TA.) —— And Entering upon the [period called] سُدْفَة. (TA.)

سَنَامٌ مُسَدَّفٌ A camel's hump cut into pieces [or slices]. (M.)

حِجَابٌ مَسْدُوفٌ A veil, or curtain, let down. (TA.)

سدل

1. سَدَلَهُ, aor. ـُ, (Ṣ, M, Mgh, Mṣb, Ḳ,) and ـِ, (M, Ḳ,) inf. n. سَدْلٌ, (Ṣ, M, Mgh, Mṣb,) He let it loose, let it down, lowered it, or let it fall; (Ṣ, M, Ḳ;) namely, his garment, (Ṣ, M,) and hair, (Fr, M, Ḳ,) and a veil, or curtain; (M;) and ↓ سَدَّلَهُ signifies the same; (Fr, TA;) as also ↓ اسدلهُ; (M, Ḳ;) or this latter is a mistake; (Mgh; [but this the author asserts because, he says, he had searched through books without finding it except in the "Nahj-el-Balághah;"]) not allowable; (Mṣb;) and the former signifies he let it down, or let it fall, namely, the garment, without drawing together its two sides: (Mgh, Mṣb:) or, as some say, he threw it upon his head, and let it loose, let it down, or let it fall, upon his shoulders: (Mgh:) and he let it down, or let it fall, namely, hair, not مَعْقُوف [i. e. made recurvate at the extremities], nor tied in knots: (Lth, TA:) and one says also, يَزْدُلُ ثَوْبَهُ, changing the س into ز. (Sb, M.) The سَدْل that is forbidden in prayer is The letting down one's garment without drawing together its two sides: or the enveloping oneself with his garment, and putting his arms within, and bowing the head and body, and prostrating oneself, in that state; as the Jews used to do; and this applies uniformly to the shirt and other garments: or the putting the middle of the إِزَار [or waist-wrapper] upon the head, and letting fall its two ends upon one's right and left, without making it to be upon his two shoulder-blades. (TA.) سَدَلَ عِمَامَتَهُ بَيْنَ كَتِفَيْهِ is said in a trad. [as meaning He made the end of his turban to hang down between his two shoulder-blades]. (Mgh.) And one says also, سدّل ↓ شَعْرَهُ عَلَى عَاتِقَيْهِ وَعُنُقِهِ, [meaning He let his hair fall down abundant and long upon his shoulders and his neck,] inf. n. تَسْدِيلٌ. (ISh, TA. [See its pass. part. n., voce مُنْسَدِلٌ.]) —— Also, aor. ـُ, (M, Ḳ,) inf. n. as above, (TA,) He slit it, or rent it; namely, his garment. (M, Ḳ.) —— And سَدَلَ فِى البِلَادِ, (O, Ḳ,) inf. n. as above, (TA,) He went away into the countries, or provinces. (O, Ḳ.)

2: see 1, last sentence but two.

4: see 1, first sentence.

5: see the next paragraph.

7. انسدل [and accord. to Freytag ↓ تسدّل also, but he names no authority for this, and I have not found it in any MS. lexicon, but it is agreeable with analogy as quasi-pass. of 2,] It was let loose, let down, lowered, or let fall; said of hair [&c.]. (MA, KL.) —— And انسدل يَعْدُو He was somewhat quick, or made some haste, running; like انسدر; the ر and ل being app. interchangeable. (Ḥar p. 576.)

Q. Q. 1. سَوْدَلَ He (a man) had long mustaches, (IAạr, TA,) or he had a long mustache. (Aṣ, Ḳ.)

سُدْلٌ and ↓ سِدْلٌ [the former written in a copy of the M سَدْل, but said in the Ḳ to be with ḍamm,] A veil, or curtain: pl. [of mult.] سُدُولٌ and [of pauc.] أَسْدَالٌ (M, Ḳ) and أَسْدُلٌ. (Ḳ.) In a verse of Ḥomeyd Ibn-Thowr, as it is related by Yaạkoob, السُّدُول is used as a sing., because it is of a measure which is [in some instances] that of a sing., such as السُّدُوس, meaning a sort of garment: but others relate it differently, saying السَّدِيل, which is correctly a sing. (M.) [See also سِدْنٌ.]

سِدْلٌ A string of gems or jewels: (Ṣ:) or a string of pearls or large pearls, reaching to the breast: (M, Ḳ:) pl. سُدُولٌ. (Ṣ.) —— See also سُدْلٌ.

سَدْلٌ An inclining. (M, Ḳ.) [See أَسْدَلُ.]

سِدِلِّيٌّ, of the measure فِعِلِّيٌّ, an arabicized

word, originally, in Pers., سه دله ["three-hearted"], as though it were three chambers in one chamber (كَأَنَّهُ ثَلَاثَةُ بُيُوتٍ فِى بَيْتٍ), like the حَارِىّ بِكُمَّيْنِ [i. e., I suppose, "like the garment of El-Ḥeereh with two sleeves;" app. meaning that it signifies *An oblong chamber with a wide and deep recess on either hand at*, or *near*, *one extremity thereof*; so that its ground-plan resembles an expanded garment with a pair of very wide sleeves: in the present day, it is commonly applied to a single recess of the kind above mentioned, the floor of which is elevated about half a foot or somewhat more or less above the floor of the main chamber, and which has a mattress and cushions laid against one or two or each of its three sides]. (Ṣ.) [Golius explains it, as on the authority of the Ṣ, (in which is nothing relating to it but what I have given above,) thus: *Pers.* سِيدِلَّه *seu* سِدِرَه, *i. q.* سُدُر.]

سَدِيلٌ The *thing* [or *hanging*] *that is let down*, or *suspended*, *upon the* [*kind of camel-vehicle for women called*] هَوْدَج: (Ṣ, O, Ḳ:) pl. [of mult.] سُدُول and سَدَائِل and [of pauc.] أَسْدَال: (Ṣ, O:) the first of which pls. is expl. by Aṣ as meaning the *pieces of cloth with which the* هودج *is covered*; as also سُدُون. (TA.) — Also *A thing* [app. *a hanging* or *curtain*] *that is extended across*, or *sideways*, (يُعَرَّضُ,) *in the space from side to side of the* [*tent called*] خِبَآء (فِى سَعَةِ الخِبَآءِ): and (some say, M) the *curtain of the* حَجَلَة [or *bridal canopy*, &c.,] *of a woman*: (M, Ḳ:) pls. as above. (TA.)

سَنْدَلٌ, or سَمَنْدَلٌ, (accord. to different copies of the Ṣ,) *A certain bird, that eats* [*the poisonous plant called*] بيش [generally applied to the *common wolf's-bane, aconitum napellus*]: on the authority of El-Jáḥiḍh. (Ṣ.) [See also art. سمندل.]

سَوْدَلٌ The *mustache*. (Ṣ, IAạr, Ḳ.) You say, طَالَ سَوْدَلُهُ, (Aṣ, Ḳ,) or سَوْدَلَاهُ, (IAạr,) *His mustache*, or *mustaches*, *became long*. (Aṣ, IAạr, Ḳ.)

ذَكَرٌ أَسْدَلُ *An inclining penis*: (M, Ḳ:) pl. [by rule سُدْلٌ, but it is said to be] سُدُلٌ, i. e. like كُتُبٌ. (Ḳ.)

مُسْدَلٌ and مُسَدَّلٌ: see what follows.

مُنْسَدِلٌ Hair *let loose*, *let down*, *lowered*, or *let fall*: (Ṣ:) or *lank*, or *long*, *and pendent*; (M, Ḳ;) as also ▼ مُسْدَلٌ: (TA:) or *abundant and long*, (Lth, TA,) and so ▼ مُسَدَّلٌ, (ISh, TA,) *falling upon the back*. (Lth, TA.)

سدم

1. سَدِمَ, (Ṣ, M, Ḳ,) aor. ـَ, (Ḳ,) inf. n. سَدَمٌ, (Ṣ, M, Ḳ,) *He repented and grieved*: (Ṣ:) or *he was*, or *became*, *affected with anxiety*: or *with anxiety together with repentance*: or *with wrath*, or *rage*, *together with grief*. (M, Ḳ.) [Hence,] one says, مَا لَهُ هَمٌّ وَلَا سَدَمٌ إِلَّا ذَاكَ [*He has no object of anxiety nor of repentance and grief except that*: or this saying may be from what next follows]. (Ṣ.) — سَدِمَ بِالشَّىْءِ, aor. and inf. n. as above, *He desired the thing vehemently*, *eagerly*, *greedily*, *very greedily*, or *excessively*; *hankered after it*, or *coveted it*; and *he was*, or *became*, *devoted*, *addicted*, or *attached*, *to it*: (TḲ:) [but these meanings of the verb are perhaps only inferred from the saying that] السَّدَمُ is *syn.* with الحِرْصُ: and اللَّهَجُ بِالشَّىْءِ, (M, Ḳ, [in the CḲ اللَّهْجُ,]) and الوُلُوعُ. (TA.) Hence the trad., مَنْ كَانَتِ الدُّنْيَا هَمَّهُ وَسَدَمَهُ جَعَلَ اللّٰهُ فَقْرَهُ بَيْنَ عَيْنَيْهِ [*To whomsoever the present state of existence is the object of his anxiety and of his eager desire* &c., *God places his poverty before his eyes*]. (TA.) = And سدم, [i. e. سَدِمَ, as is indicated by the form of the part. n. سَدِمٌ, and by سَدَمٌ as an inf. n. used in the sense of that part. n.,] said of water, *It became altered* [*for the worse*] *by reason of long standing*, *and overspread with* [*the green substance termed*] طُحْلُب, *and choked with dust and other things that had fallen into it*. (A, TA.) = [And سَدِمَ said of a stallion, *He was withheld from covering*: so in the Deewán of Jereer, accord. to Freytag: it is said of a stallion-camel: see سَدِمٌ.] = سَدَمَ المَآءَ طُولُ العَهْدِ بِالشَّارِبَةِ [*The length of time that had elapsed since the coming thereto of the drinkers*] *altered the water* [*for the worse*]. (A, TA.) — And سَدَمَ البَابَ *He shut*, or *closed*, *the door*; syn. رَدَمَهُ; (IAạr, M, TA;) in the Ḳ, erroneously, رَدَّهُ: and so سَطَمَهُ. (TA.) = See also سَدِيمٌ.

2. تَسْدِيمٌ [inf. n. of سَدَّمَ] The *binding*, or *closing*, *the mouth* of a camel [*with a muzzle*; i. e. the *muzzling* of a camel: see the pass. part. n., below]. (KL.)

[4. أَسْدَمَ, said of water, *It was prevented from flowing by dust and wind*: so in the Deewán of Jereer, accord. to Freytag.]

7. انسدم دَبَرُ البَعِيرِ *The galls*, or *sores*, *on the back of the camel became healed*. (Ḳ, TA.)

سُدْمٌ, as a sing. epithet: see سَدِمٌ, last sentence. It is also a pl. of سَدُومٌ. (M, TA.)

سَدَمٌ inf. n. of سَدِمَ. (Ṣ, M, Ḳ. [See 1, first four sentences.]) — See also سَدِمٌ, in two places.

سُدُمٌ: see the latter half of the next paragraph.

سَدِمٌ [is a part. n. of سَدِمَ: and is also app. used as an imitative sequent to نَدِمٌ]. You say [سَدِمٌ and] ▼ سَادِمٌ and ▼ سَدْمَانُ (M, Ḳ, TA) meaning *Repenting and grieving*: (TA:) or *affected with anxiety*: or *with anxiety together with repentance*: or *with wrath*, or *rage*, *together with grief*: (M, Ḳ, TA:) and نَدِمٌ سَدِمٌ, in which one is used as an imitative sequent to the other; and ▼ سَدْمَانُ ▼ نَدْمَانُ, and ▼ سَادِمٌ نَادِمٌ, [app. in like manner,] السَّدَمُ being seldom used without النَّدَمُ: (TA:) or [نَدِمٌ سَدِمٌ, and] ▼ نَادِمٌ سَادِمٌ, and ▼ نَدْمَانُ سَدْمَانُ; in which one is said to be an imitative sequent to the other; (Ṣ:) or, accord. to IAmb, ▼ سَادِمٌ, in the phrase رَجُلٌ نَادِمٌ سَادِمٌ means, as some say, *altered* [*for the worse*] *in intellect in consequence of grief*; from مَآءٌ سُدُمٌ, i. e. "water that has become altered [for the worse]:" or, as others say, *grieving*, *not able to go nor to come*. (TA.) You say also رَجُلٌ سَدِمٌ *A man affected with wrath*, or *rage*. (Ṣ, TA.) — And عَاشِقٌ سَدِمٌ *Affected with amorous*, or *passionate*, *desire*, *in a vehement degree*. (AO, Ḳ.) — And in like manner, (TA,) فَحْلٌ سَدِمٌ (Ṣ, M, Ḳ) and ▼ سَدَمٌ [which is an inf. n. used as an epithet] and ▼ مَسْدُومٌ and ▼ مُسَدَّمٌ (M, Ḳ) *A stallion* [*camel*] *excited by lust for the female*: (Ṣ, M, Ḳ:) or *one that is sent among the she-camels*, *and that brays amidst them*, *and*, *when they have become excited by lust*, *is taken forth from them*, *because what he begets is disesteemed*; (M, Ḳ, TA;) *therefore*, *when he is excited by lust*, *he is shackled*, *and pastures around the dwelling*; *and if he attacks the she-camels*, *he is muzzled*: (TA:) or *one that is in any manner debarred from covering*; (Ḳ;) or the last two epithets have this last signification. (M.) — And نَاقَةٌ سَدِمَةٌ *An old and weak she-camel*. (AO, TA.) = مَآءٌ سَدِمٌ and ▼ سَدَمٌ and ▼ سُدُمٌ (M, Ḳ) and ▼ سَدُومٌ (Ḳ) and ▼ سُدْمٌ (M, TA) and ▼ سَدِيمٌ (TA) i. q. مُنْدَفِنٌ [i. e. *Water filled up*, *stopped up*, or *choked up*, *with earth* or *dust*; or *into which the dust has been swept by the wind*]: (M: [in the Ḳ and TA, erroneously, مُنْدَفِقٌ:]) pl. أَسْدَامٌ [a pl. of pauc.] and سِدَامٌ [a pl. of mult.]; or the sing. and pl. are alike; (M, Ḳ;) [i. e.] you say مَآءٌ أَسْدَامٌ and سِدَامٌ, applying pl. epithets to a sing. noun; (Z, TA;) as well as مِيَاهٌ أَسْدَامٌ (IAmb, TA, and Ḥam p. 102) and سِدَامٌ (IAmb, TA) meaning *waters altered* [*for the worse*] (IAmb, TA, and Ḥam ubi suprà) *in consequence of long standing*, and so سُدُمٌ: (Ḥam:) this last is pl. of ▼ سَدُومٌ, as also سُدْمٌ: (M, TA:) [and each of these two is also used as a sing.; i. e.] you say also ▼ رَكِيَّةٌ سُدُمٌ and ▼ سُدْمٌ meaning *a well filled up*, *stopped up*, or *choked up*, *with earth* or *dust*; or *into which the dust has been swept by the wind*: (Ṣ, Ḳ, TA: [in the CḲ, مُنْدَفِقَةٌ is erroneously put for مُنْدَفِنَةٌ:]) or *into which varieties of small rubbish*, *and dust*, or *small pebbles*, *whirled round by the wind*, *have fallen*, *so that it is nearly choked up*: (Lth, TA:) and ▼ مَآءٌ سُدُمٌ is expl. as meaning *water that has become altered* [*for the worse*]: (IAmb, TA:) ▼ مُسَدَّمٌ, also, applied to water, signifies the same as سَدِمٌ; (M, Ḳ;) and so does ▼ مَسْدُومٌ: (TA:) [or ▼ the former of these, so applied, *prevented from flowing by dust and wind*. (Freytag, from the Deewán of Jereer.)]

سُدْمٌ, as a sing. epithet: see the latter half of the next preceding paragraph, in three places. It is also a pl. of سَدُومٌ. (M, TA.)

سَدْمَانُ: see سَدِمٌ, second sentence, in three places.

سَدُومٌ and سُدُومٌ: see سَدِمٌ, in the latter half of the paragraph; the former word, in two places.

سَدِيمٌ: see سَدِمٌ, in the latter half of the paragraph. — Also *Mist;* syn. ضَبَابٌ: or *such as is thin.* (M, Ḳ.) — And i. q. كَثِيرُ الذِّكْرِ (Ḳ) [app. as meaning *Remembering* God, or *celebrating* Him, *much*, or *frequently:* for SM adds], hence the saying,

لَا يَذْكُرُونَ ٱللّٰهَ إِلَّا سَدِمًا

[app. *They remember not, or celebrate not, God, otherwise than doing so much,* or *frequently:* from which it seems that one says, سَدِمَ ▼ ٱللّٰهَ, inf. n. سَدْمٌ, meaning *He remembered,* or *celebrated, God,* &c.]. (TA.) — And i. q. تَعِبٌ [*Fatigue:* but I incline to think that this explanation is a mistranscription]. (TA.)

سَادِمٌ: see سَدِمٌ, second sentence, in four places.

مُسَدَّمٌ: see سَدِمٌ, in the former half of the paragraph. — Also A camel *left to pasture by itself* (Ḳ, TA) *around the dwelling.* (TA.) — And A [camel of generous race, such as is termed] فَنِيق *having a muzzle put upon his mouth.* (Ṣ.) — And A camel *having galls, or sores, upon his back, and therefore exempted from the saddle until his galls, or sores, have become healed.* (Ḳ.) — See also سَدِمٌ, last sentence, in two places.

مَسْدُومٌ: see سَدِمٌ, in the former half of the paragraph: — and again in the last sentence. — Also A door *shut,* or *closed.* (TA.)

سدن

1. سَدَنَ, (Ṣ, L, Ḳ,) aor. ِ, (Ṣ, L,) inf. n. سَدْنٌ and سِدَانَةٌ, [or the latter, accord. to the Mṣb, seems to be a simple subst.,] *He acted as minister,* or *servant, of the Kaabeh,* and [so in the Ṣ and L, but in the Ḳ "or"] *of the temple of idols;* (Ṣ, L, Ḳ;) and *performed the office of door-keeper,* or *chamberlain.* (Ḳ.) [And] سَدَنَ الكَعْبَةَ, aor. ِ, inf. n. سَدْنٌ, has the former meaning. (Mṣb.) A'Obeyd says, (L,) سِدَانَةُ الكَعْبَةِ signifies *The ministry,* or *service, of the Kaabeh,* (Mgh, L,) *and the superintendence thereof, and the opening and locking of its door.* (L.) The لِوَآء [q. v.] and the سِدَانَة belonged to [the family named] Benoo-'Abd-ed-Dár in the Time of Ignorance, and the Prophet confirmed it to them in El-Islám: (Ṣ, L:) [in the first age of El-Islám,] the سدانة of the Kaabeh belonged to the sons of 'Othmán Ibn-Ṭalhah [of the family of Benoo-'Abd-ed-Dár]. (Mgh.) السِّدَانَةُ signifies [also (L)] الحِجَابَةُ [which seems to be properly a subst., meaning *The office of door-keeper,* or *chamberlain,* but here seems, from the context, to be used as an inf. n., meaning *the performing that office*]: you say, سَدَنَهُ, aor. as above, [app. meaning *He acted as door-keeper,* or *chamberlain, to it,* namely a temple, or *for him:*] (M, L:) or سَدَّنَهُ, inf. n. سِدَانَةٌ, signifies *he served it,* or *him.* (MA.) — سَدَنَ ثَوْبَهُ, (Ṣ, L, Ḳ,) and السِّتْرَ, (Ṣ, L,) aor. ُ and ِ, (Ḳ,) *He* (a man, Ṣ, L) *let down,* or *lowered, his garment,* (Ṣ, L, Ḳ,) and *the curtain,* or *veil,* (Ṣ, L,) and الشَّعْرَ *the hair;* like سَدَلَهُ [which is held by some to be the original, the ن being held by them to be a substitute for ل: see سِدْنٌ]. (Fr, TA in art. سدل.)

سَدَنٌ: see what next follows, in two places.

سِدْنٌ, (L, Mṣb,) or ▼ سَدَنٌ, (so in a copy of the M,) or ▼ سَدَنٌ, and ▼ سَدَانٌ, (Ḳ,) as also ▼ سَدِينٌ, (AA, L, Ḳ,) *A curtain,* or *veil:* (AA, M, L, Mṣb, Ḳ:) [like سِدْلٌ and سَدْلٌ:] pl. of the first (L) or second (M) [and app. of the last also, like as أَسْدَالٌ is pl. of سِدْلٌ or سَدْلٌ and also of سَدِيلٌ,] أَسْدَانٌ; in which the ن is said by some to be a substitute for ل: (M, L:) or أَسْدَانٌ is a dial. var. of أَسْدَالٌ signifying the سُدُول *of the* [*kind of camel-vehicles for women called*] هَوَادِج; (Ṣ, L;) [i. e.,] accord. to ISk, it signifies the *pieces of cloth with which the* هَوْدَج *is covered;* (L;) as also سُدُونٌ; (Aṣ, TA voce سَدِيلٌ;) and its sing. is [سَدِينٌ, like سَدِيلٌ, or] ▼ سَدْنٌ. (L. [The last word is there thus written, in this instance, with fet-ḥ.])

سَدَنٌ: } see the next preceding paragraph.
سَدَانٌ: }

سَدِينٌ: see سِدْنٌ. — Also *Fat,* as a subst. (AA, L, Ḳ.) — And *Blood.* (Ḳ.) — And *Wool.* (Ḳ.)

سِدَانَةٌ *Ministry,* or *service.* (Mṣb.) [And particularly The *ministry,* or *service, and superintendence, of a temple of idols;* and afterwards, *of the Kaabeh:* see 1.]

سَادِنٌ *A minister,* or *servant, of the Kaabeh,* (Ṣ, Mgh, L, Mṣb, Ḳ,) and [so in the Ṣ and L, but in the Ḳ "or"] *of the temple of idols;* (Ṣ, L, Ḳ;) and *one who performs the office of door-keeper,* or *chamberlain:* (Ḳ:) pl. سَدَنَةٌ: (Ṣ, Mgh, L, Mṣb, Ḳ:) or سَدَنَةٌ signifies the *door-keepers,* or *chamberlains,* (حُجَّاب, [pl. of حَاجِب,]) *of the House* [*of God,* i. e. *the Kaabeh*]; and *the intendants of the idols in the Time of Ignorance;* the latter being the primary application: (M, L:) but IB says that there is this difference between the سَادِن and the حَاجِب; that the latter precludes, and his license to do so belongs to another; whereas the سادن precludes, and his license to do so belongs to himself. (L.)

سدى and سدو

1. سَدَا بِيَدَيْهِ, (M,) or بِيَدِهِ, (Ḳ,) [aor. يَسْدُو,] inf. n. سَدْوٌ, (Ṣ, M, Ḳ,) *He stretched forth* (Ṣ, M, Ḳ) *his arms* or *hands,* or, as when said of a camel, *his fore legs,* (M,) or *his arm* or *hand, or his fore leg,* (Ṣ, Ḳ, TA,) إِلَيْهِ [*towards him* or *it*], (CḲ,) or نَحْوَ ٱلشَّىْءِ [*towards the thing*], *like as do camels* (كَمَا تَسْدُو ٱلْإِبِلُ) *in their going along;* (TA;) as also ▼ استدى, (M, Ḳ, TA,) in [some of] the copies of the Ḳ اسدى, but the former is the right. (TA.) You say of a man, سَدَا, aor. يَسْدُو, *He stretched forth his arm,* or *hand, towards a thing:* and of a camel, سَدَا, inf. n. سَدْوٌ, *he stretched forth his fore leg in going along:* (Mṣb:) or of a she-camel, سَدَتْ, (Ṣ, Ḳ,) aor. تَسْدُو, inf. n. سَدْوٌ, (Ṣ,) *she went with wide steps;* (Ḳ;) or *she stretched forth her arms in going along, and went with wide steps:* and مَا أَحْسَنَ سَدْوَ رِجْلَيْهَا وَأَتْوَ يَدَيْهَا [*How good,* or *beautiful, is her stretching forth of her hind legs, and her returning of her fore legs in her going!*]. (Ṣ.) See also سَتَى. — سَدَا, (M,) or يَسْدُو, (Ṣ,) ▼ سَدْوَ كَذَا, (Ṣ, M,) *He went,* (M,) or *he goes,* (Ṣ,) *towards,* or *in the direction of, such a thing;* (Ṣ, M;) said of a man. (Ṣ.) — سَدْوٌ also signifies The *going at random, heedlessly,* or *in a headlong manner, without consideration,* or *without any certain aim,* or *object, not obeying a guide to the right course, in journeying;* (Ṣ, M;) said in relation to camels and horses. (M.) — Hence, (M,) سَدَا بِالجَوْزِ, (Ḳ,) aor. يَسْدُو, (TA,) inf. n. سَدْوٌ, (M, TA,) *He* (a boy, or child,) *played with walnuts,* (M, Ḳ, TA,) *throwing them into a hole;* (TA;) a dial. var. of زَدَا; (Ḳ;) or, accord. to the T, the latter is of the dial. of children; (TA;) as also ▼ استدى, (M, Ḳ, TA,) in [some of] the copies of the Ḳ, erroneously, اسدى. (TA.) See also مِدْحَاةٌ, in art. دحو. — See also 5. — سَدِيَتِ الأَرْضُ *The land was,* or *became, moistened by much dew,* (Ṣ, Mṣb,) either *from the sky* or *from the ground.* (Ṣ.) And سَدِيَتِ اللَّيْلَةُ *The night was,* or *became, moist with much dew.* (M,* TA.) — سَدِىَ البُسْرُ, (Ṣ, Ḳ,) or البَلَحُ, (M,) inf. n. سَدًى; (TA;) and ▼ أَسْدَى; (M;) *The dates in the state in which they are termed* بسر, or بلح, [see these words,] *were,* or *became, lax in their* ثَفَارِيق [or *bases,* so as to be easily detached therefrom], (Ṣ, M, Ḳ,) *and moist.* (M.)

2: see 4, first three sentences, in four places. — [Hence,] one says of honey, يُسَدِّيهِ ٱلنَّحْلُ † [*The bees make, prepare,* or *produce, it*]. (M.) — See 4, again, in two places. — See also 5.

4. اسدى الثَّوْبَ, (Ṣ, Mṣb, Ḳ,) and اسْتَاهُ; (Ṣ;) as also ▼ سَدَّاهُ, (Ḳ,) inf. n. تَسْدِيَةٌ; (TA;) and ▼ تَسَدَّاهُ; (Ḳ;) *He set,* or *disposed, the warp* (السَّدَى) *of the garment, or piece of cloth;* (Ṣ,* Mṣb, Ḳ,* TA;) *he made a warp* (سَدًى) *in the garment,* or *piece of cloth:* (Ḥar p. 241:) or ▼ سَدَّاهُ means *he did so for another;* and ▼ تَسَدَّاهُ, *he did so for himself.* (M, TA.) [Golius explains ▼ سَدَّى as signifying also "*Oblevit telam viscosiore aquâ, ut cui mistus fuerit panis, quod fit roboris conciliandi ergo;*" as on the authority of the KL; in my copy of which I find only its inf. n., تَسْدِيَة, expl. as meaning the weaver's *making a warp in a garment, or piece of cloth* (تار در جامه كردن جولاه): and Freytag adds, as a signification assigned to the same verb by Jac. Schultens, "*Cirris s. fimbriis ornavit vestem.*"] — [Hence,] one says, هُوَ يُسَدِّى ▼ الأُمُورَ وَيُنِيرُهَا (A in art. نير) or يُسْدِى (TA in that art.) [meaning † *He commences things,* or *affairs, and completes them*]. And أَلْحِمْ مَا أَسْدَيْتَ † *Complete what thou hast commenced* (Ṣ and Ḳ in art. لحم) *of beneficence.* (Ṣ in that art.) — Hence also, اسدى بَيْنَهُمْ حَدِيثًا i. q. نَسَجَهُ [i. e. ‡ *He wove,* or *composed,* or *he forged, a discourse between them*]. (M, TA.) — And اسدى بَيْنَهُمَا i. q. أَصْلَحَ [i. e. † *He effected a* *rectification of affairs, an agreement, a harmony,* or *a reconciliation, between them two*]. (AA, Az, Ḳ.) — And اسدى إِلَيْهِ † *He did a benefit to him;* as also ▼ سدّى, inf. n. تَسْدِيَةٌ: (Ḳ:) or اسدى إِلَيْهِ سُدًى, and ▼ سدّاه عَلَيْهِ, (M, TA, [thus in the latter case, عليه, not اليه,]) or اسدى إِلَيْهِ مَعْرُوفًا, (Mṣb,) *he did to him,* or *conferred upon him, a benefit, benefaction, favour,* or *the like:* (M,* Mṣb, TA:) [app. from اسدى الثَّوْبَ, and سدّاه; and accordingly mentioned in the M in art. سدى: or] it is from سدى [or rather سَدَا, inf. n. سَدْوٌ,] as meaning "he (a camel) put forward his fore legs in going along;" for he of whom one says أَسْدَاكَ خَيْرًا [*he did to thee good,* like أَسْدَى إِلَيْكَ خَيْرًا,] is as though he stretched forth to thee his arm, or hand, therewith, advancing: (Ḥam p. 696:) you say, اسدى نِعْمَةً, meaning اِصْطَنَعَ [i. e. *he did a benefit,* &c.]. (Idem p. 750.) — You say also, طَلَبْتُ أَمْرًا فَأَسْدَيْتُهُ i. e. † [*I sought a thing, and*] *I attained it,* or *obtained it:* [as though meaning I stretched forth my hand to it and reached it:] if you do not attain it, or obtain it, you say, أَعْمَيْتُهُ: (Ṣ:) or إِسْدَآءٌ signifies the *attaining quickly.* (KL. [There expl. by the words زود دريافتن: for which Golius seems to have found in his copy زود رفتن; for he has assigned to اسدى, as on the authority of the KL, the meaning of *cito incessit.*]) — اسداه also signifies *He left, let alone,* or *neglected, him,* or *it:* (Ḳ:) *he left him to himself, uncontrolled,* (M, Mṣb,) *neither commanded nor forbidden.* (M.) And you say, أَسْدَيْتُ إِبِلِى, (AZ, T, Ṣ,) inf. n. إِسْدَآءٌ, (AZ, T,) *I left my camels to pasture by themselves.* (AZ, T, Ṣ.) — اسدى النَّخْلُ: اسدى البَلَحُ: see 1, last sentence. — *The palm-trees had dates such as are termed* سَدٍ. (Aṣ, T, Ṣ, Ḳ.)

5. تسدّاه: see 4, first sentence, in two places. — Also *He mounted it,* or *mounted upon it;* (M, Ḳ;) *he was,* or *became,* or *got, upon it;* (Ṣ, M, Ḳ;) syn. رَكِبَهُ, (M, Ḳ,) and عَلَاهُ; (Ṣ, M, Ḳ;) namely, a thing. (M.) A poet says, (Ṣ, TA,) namely, Imra-el-Ḳeys, (TA,)

* فَلَمَّا دَنَوْتُ تَسَدَّيْتُهَا * فَثَوْبًا نَسِيتُ وَثَوْبًا أَجُرْ *

[*And when I drew near, I got upon her, and a garment I forgot,* or *neglected, and a garment I was dragging* upon the ground: أَجُرْ being for أَجُرُّ]. (Ṣ, TA.) And سدى جَارِيَتَهُ [or ▼ سَدَا (for تسدّاه meaning as expl. above is mentioned in the M in art. سدو), or it may be ▼ سدّى] signifies [in like manner] عَلَاهَا. (TA.) — And *He followed him,* (Ḳ, TA,) *and overtook him.* (TA.) — And *He overcame,* or *overpowered, him;* namely, a man. (TA.) And *He conquered,* or *mastered, it;* namely, an affair. (TA.)

8. استدى: see 1, in two places. — Also, said of a horse, *He sweated.* (Ḳ.)

سَدْوٌ inf. n. of سَدَا. (Ṣ, M, Ḳ.) Hence, سَدَا يَسْدُو سَدْوَ كَذَا or سَدْوَ كَذَا: see 1. And خَطَبَ الأَمِيرُ فَمَا زَالَ عَلَى سَدْوٍ وَاحِدٍ i. e. [*The prince,* or *commander, recited an oration,* or *a harangue,* &c., *and ceased not to keep to*] *one prose-rhyme.* (M.)

سَدًى of a garment, or piece of cloth, (Ṣ, M, Ḳ, &c.,) The *warp;* (MA, KL;) *contr. of* لُحْمَةٌ; (Ṣ, M, Mṣb;) i. e. (Mṣb [in the M "and it is said to mean"]) the *portion* [or *threads*] thereof *extended longitudinally* (M,* Mṣb, Ḳ*) *in the weaving:* (Mṣb:) and it is said to mean the *lower,* or *lowest, part* thereof: (M: [but this is a strange explanation, which I do not find elsewhere:]) it is [said to be] from السَّدْوُ [inf. n. of سَدَا] signifying "the stretching forth the arm, or hand, or the fore leg, towards a thing:" (Ḥar p. 241: [but it is mentioned in the M as belonging to art. سدى; and its dual, mentioned below, requires its being so:]) and ▼ أُسْدِىٌّ, (M, Ḳ,) also [and more commonly] written ▼ أُسْتِىٌّ, (Ḳ,) signifies the same; (M, Ḳ;) as also ▼ سَدَاةٌ; (Ṣ, Ḳ;) or this last is the n. un. of سَدًى, (M, TA,) having a more special signification, (Mṣb, TA,) [as though meaning *a warp,* or *a sort of warp;* or the ة may be affixed for the purpose of assimilating the word to its contr. لُحْمَةٌ, with which it is often coupled:] the dual [of سَدًى] is سَدَيَانِ: (Ṣ, Mṣb, TA:) and the pl. is أَسْدِيَةٌ (accord. to the Ṣ) or أَسْدَآءٌ. (Mṣb.) ▼ مَا أَنْتَ بِلُحْمَةٍ وَلَا سَدَاةٍ [lit. *Thou art neither a woof nor a warp*] is said to him who neither harms nor profits. (TA. [See also سَتًى.]) — Hence, as being likened thereto, (M, [see 2, second sentence,]) ‡ *Honey in its comb;* syn. شُهْدٌ or شَهْدٌ. (M, Ḳ, TA.) — And ‡ *A benefit, benefaction, favour,* or *the like.* (Ṣ, M, Ḳ, TA. [See also the next two sentences.]) — The *night-dew;* (Ṣ, M, Mṣb, Ḳ;) by means of which seed-produce lives: (Ṣ,* Mṣb:) or, as some say, سَدًى and نَدًى are syn. [and both applied to *dew in an absolute sense*]: and the pl. is أَسْدَآءٌ. (M.) — And ‡ *Liberality, bounty, munificence,* or *generosity;* as being likened thereto; and so نَدًى. (Ṣ in art. ندو and ندى.) [See an ex. in a verse cited voce رِقْبَةٌ.] — *Green dates,* (M, Ḳ,) *with their* شَمَارِيخ [or *fruit-stalks*]; (M;) as also ▼ سَدَآءٌ; (M, Ḳ;) of the dial of El-Yemen: n. un. ▼ سَدَاةٌ and ▼ سَدَآءَةٌ, (M, TA,) on the authority of AA, and of Sh also, who says that they are of the dial. of El-Medeeneh. (TA.) [See also the last sentence of the next paragraph: and see سَيَابٌ.] — Also sometimes used in the sense of سُدًى. (Ṣ, Ḳ.) See this latter word.

سَدٍ [originally سَدِىٌ] *Moist;* applied in this sense to anything. (AḤn, M.) — And [particularly] *Moist with dew,* [or *with night-dew,* or *with much thereof,*] applied to a place. (M.) And you say أَرْضٌ سَدِيَةٌ *A land moist with much night-dew.* (Ṣ, Mṣb.) And لَيْلَةٌ سَدِيَةٌ *A night moist with much dew:* (M,* TA:) the epithet [سَدٍ] is seldom applied to a day. (M, TA.) — And بَلَحٌ سَدٍ *Dates in the state in which they are termed* بَلَح, (Ṣ, M, Ḳ,) accord. to Aṣ, *when they have fallen,* (T, TA,) *that have become lax in their* تَفَارِيق [or *bases,* so as to be easily detached therefrom], (Aṣ, T, Ṣ, M, Ḳ,) *and moist:* (Aṣ, T, M:) one thereof [i. e. a بَلَحَة] is termed سَدِيَةٌ: (Aṣ, T, TA:) the تُفْرُوق is the قِمَع of the بُسْرَة [or بَلَحَة]. (TA.) You say also بُسْرٌ سَدٍ; and بُسْرَةٌ سَدِيَةٌ, which is the same as ▼ سَدَاةٌ [expl. above, voce سَدًى]. (Ṣ.)

سُدًى and ▼ سَدًى, (Ṣ, M, Ḳ,) the former the more common, (Ṣ, Ḳ,) used alike as sing. and pl., (Ṣ,* M, Ḳ,) *Left, let alone,* or *neglected;* or *left to pasture by itself* or *by themselves;* (Ṣ, M, Ḳ;) applied to a camel, (Ḳ, TA,) and to camels: (Ṣ, Ḳ, TA:) you say نَاقَةٌ سُدًى (TA) and إِبِلٌ سُدًى: (Ṣ, TA:) and ▼ سَادٍ signifies the same [as a sing. epithet]. (M, Ḳ.) أَيَحْسَبُ الْإِنْسَانُ أَنْ يُتْرَكَ سُدًى, in the Ḳur [lxxv. 36], means *Doth man think that he is to be left to himself, uncontrolled, neither commanded nor forbidden?* (M.)

سَدَاةٌ: see سَدًى, in three places: and see also سَدٍ.

سَدَآءٌ: } see سَدًى, last sentence but two.
سَدَآءَةٌ: }

سَدُوٌّ A she-camel *that stretches forth, and flings out, her fore legs in going along.* (M.) [See also سَادٍ.]

الرُّمَّانُ السَّدَوِىُّ *The pomegranate of* السَّدَا, *a town near Zebeed.* (Ḳ.)

سَادٍ *Stretching forth the arms,* or *fore legs, in going along,* (M,* TA,) *and wide in step;* (TA;) applied to a camel: (M, TA:) and so سَوَادٍ, [pl. of the fem. سَادِيَةٌ,] applied to she-camels: (Ṣ, Ḳ,* TA:) [see also سَدُوٌّ:] or, accord. to the T, the Arabs apply the term سَوَادٍ as a name for the *fore legs of camels,* because of their stretching them forth in going along; and then as a name for the camels themselves. (TA.) And سَادٍ signifies also *Good in pace* or *going;* applied to a camel; and so زَادٍ. (TA.) — See also سُدًى. — السَّادِى is also used for السَّادِسُ; (Ṣ, Ḳ, TA;) the س being changed into ى. (TA.) One says, جَآءَ فُلَانٌ سَادِسًا and سَادِيًا [*Such a one came sixth*]. (ISk, Ṣ voce سَاتٌّ, q. v.)

أُسْدِىٌّ and أُسْدِىٌّ: see سَدًى. — The former also signifies ثَوْبٌ مُسَدًّى [like أُسْتِىٌّ: see this last word, voce سَتًى]. (AHeyth, Ḳ.)

[مُسْدَاةٌ *A weaver's yarn-beam,* or *roller;* i. e., as expl. by Golius, on the authority of Meyd, the *implement on which the weaver rolls the warp.*]

المَسَادِى: see مِدْحَاةٌ, in art. دحو.

سذب

سُذْبَةٌ *A bag,* or *other receptacle, for travelling-provisions* or *for goods* or *utensils &c.;* syn. وِعَآءٌ. (Ḳ.)

سَذَابٌ, said to be an arabicized word, because [it is asserted that] س and ذ are not combined in any Arabic word; [and if so, سُذْبَةٌ also, mentioned above, is arabicized;] but in some of the books on plants it is written with the unpointed د; (TA;) *i. q.* فَيْجَن, (Ḳ,) which is an ancient Greek word, (TA,) [i. e. πήγανον, meaning *Rue;*] *a well-known* بَقْل [or *kind of herb*], (Ḳ,) *having properties described in the medical books.* (TA.)

سَذَابِىٌّ *A seller of* سَذَاب [or *rue*]. (Ḳ,* TA.)

سذج

سَاذَجٌ and سَاذِجٌ, mentioned under this head in the O and Ḳ: see art. ساذج.

سر

[1. سَرَّهُ, accord. to the TA, has two contr. significations: for it is there stated that "one says سَرَرْتُهُ meaning كَتَمْتُهُ and سَرَرْتُهُ meaning أَعْلَنْتُهُ:" and it is added that "it will occur again soon:" but it does not again occur in that work, nor have I found it in any other lexicon: I therefore think that it is a mistranscription, for أَسْرَرْتُهُ, first pers. of أَسَرَّهُ, q. v.] ═ سَرَّهُ, (Ṣ, O, Mṣb, Ḳ, &c.,) aor. ـُ, (MṢ,) inf. n. مَسَرَّةٌ (Ṣ, O, Ḳ) and سُرُورٌ [which latter, from the explanations of it which will be found below, seems to be generally, if not only, as an inf. n., that of سُرَّ,] and سُرٌّ [which is also syn. with سُرُورٌ in the senses assigned to the latter below] and تَسِرَّةٌ and سُرًى [which last may be also an inf. n. of ↓ سَرَّاهُ expl. by Freytag as syn. with سَرَّهُ in the sense here following, but without an indication of any authority], (O, Ḳ,) *He,* or *it, rejoiced him; gladdened him;* or *made him happy;* syn. أَفْرَحَهُ: (Mṣb, Ḳ:) [or *made him to experience a pleasure,* or *delight, and dilatation of the heart, of which there was no external sign:* see سُرُورٌ, below.] And سُرَّ, [inf. n. سُرُورٌ, (see above,)] *He rejoiced; was joyful,* or *glad;* or *was happy:* (Ṣ,* A,* Ḳ:) [or *he experienced a pleasure,* or *delight, and dilatation of the heart, of which there was no external sign;* accord. to an explanation of سُرُورٌ:] you say, سُرَّ بِهِ and ↓ اِسْتَسَرَّ [*He rejoiced, was joyful* or *glad,* or *was happy, by reason of him,* or *it*]. (A.) — سَرَّهُ, (Ḳ,) aor. as above, (TA,) also signifies *He saluted him with* [*the offering of what are termed*] المَسَرَّةُ, i. e. *the extremities of sweet-smelling plants.* (Ḳ.) ═ Also سَرَّهُ, (Ṣ, M,) aor. as above, inf. n. سَرٌّ, (Ṣ,) or سُرٌّ, (so in a copy of the M,) *He cut his* (a child's) سُرّ, or سِرَر, i. e. *navel-string.* (Ṣ, M.) And سُرَّ *He* (a child) *had his navel-string cut.* (Ḳ.) — And سَرَّهُ, aor. as above, *He pierced him,* or *thrust him,* [with a spear or the like,] *in his* سُرَّة [or *navel*]: a poet says,

* نَسُرُّهُمْ إِنْ هُمْ أَقْبَلُوا * وَإِنْ أَدْبَرُوا فَهُمْ مَنْ نَسُبّْ *

[*We pierce them in the navel if they advance; and if they retreat, they are those who are pierced in the podex;* نَسُبّْ being for نَسُبُّ]. (Ṣ.) ═ سَرَّ الزَّنْدَ, aor. as above, inf. n. سَرٌّ, *He put a piece of wood,* (M, Ḳ,) or *a little piece of wood,* (Ṣ,) *in the interior of the* زند [or *piece of stick,* or *wood, for producing fire*], (M,) or *in its extremity,* (Ṣ, Ḳ,) *inserting it in its interior,* (Ṣ,) *in order that he might produce fire with it.* (Ṣ, M, Ḳ.) One says, سُرَّ زَنْدَكَ فَإِنَّهُ أَسَرُّ *Fill up the interior of thy* زند, *that it may produce fire,* (AḤn, M,) *for it is* [*worn*] *hollow.* (Ṣ, Ḳ.) ═ سَرِرَ, [sec. pers. سَرِرْتَ,] aor. يَسَرُّ, (IAạr, Ṣgh, L, Ḳ,) inf. n. سَرَرٌ, remarked upon by MF as extr., [though it is agreeable with a general rule,] said of a man, (TA,) *He had a complaint of the* سُرَّة [or *navel*]. (IAạr, Ṣgh, L, Ḳ.) — Also, aor. and inf. n. as in the next preceding case, said of a camel, *He had the pain,* or *disorder, termed* سَرَرٌ [q. v.]. (IAạr, M.)

2: see 1, second sentence. ═ سَرَّرْتُهُ in the phrase سَرَّرْتُهُ سُرِّيَّةً *I gave him,* or *caused him to take, a concubine slave,* doubly trans., is [said to be] changed to سَرَّيْتُهُ for alleviation of the pronunciation. (Mṣb.) ═ سَرَّرَهُ, inf. n. تَسْرِيرٌ, said of water, *It reached his* سُرَّة [or *navel*]. (Ḳ.)

3. سَارَّهُ, inf. n. مُسَارَّةٌ and سِرَارٌ, (Ṣ, M,) [*He spoke,* or *discoursed, secretly to him* or *with him;*] *he acquainted him with a secret.* (M.) You say, سَارَّهُ فِى أُذُنِهِ *He spoke secretly to him in his ear.* (Ṣ,* Ḳ,* TḲ.) And كَانَ يُحَدِّثُهُ كَأَخِى السِّرَارِ occurs in a trad., meaning *He* (Moḥammad) *used to talk to him* ('Omar) *in a low voice, like him who is telling a secret.* (TA.) — بَيْعُ السِّرَارِ is *The selling in which one says, "I will put forth my hand and thou shalt put forth thy hand, and if I produce my signet-ring before thee, it is a sale for such a price; and if thou produce thy signet-ring before me, for such a price:"* if they produce together, or do not both produce, they do thus again. (Mgh.)

4. أَسَرَّهُ, (Ṣ, M, A, Mgh, Mṣb, Ḳ,) inf. n. إِسْرَارٌ; (Mṣb;) [and accord. to the TA سَرَّهُ; but see the first sentence of this art.;] *He concealed it; suppressed it; kept it secret;* (Ṣ, M, A, Mgh, Mṣb, Ḳ;) namely, a story, or the like: (A, Mgh, Mṣb:) and, contr., *he manifested it; revealed it; published it; made it known.* (Ṣ, M, Mṣb, Ḳ.) Both of these significations have been assigned to the verb in the phrase وَأَسَرُّوا النَّدَامَةَ, in the Ḳur [x. 55 and xxxiv. 32]: (Ṣ:) some say, that the meaning is *They will manifest repentance:* Th says, *they will conceal it* from their chiefs: the former [says ISd] is the more correct: (M:) the former meaning is also given on the authority of AO; but Sh says, I have not heard it on the authority of any other; and Az says that the lexicologists most strongly disapprove of the saying of AO; and it is said that the meaning is, *they,* the chiefs of the polytheists, *will conceal repentance* from the lower class of their people, whom they shall have caused to err; and in like manner say Zj and the [other] expositors. (TA.) In like manner also the two contr. significations are assigned to the verb in the saying of Imra-el-Ḳeys, [in his Mo'allaḳah,] لَوْ يُسِرُّونَ مَقْتَلِى, which Aṣ used to quote with ش, thus, لَوْ يُشِرُّونَ مَقْتَلِى, meaning *that they might publish,* or *make known, my slaughter.* (Ṣ.) You say also, أَسَرَّ إِلَيْهِ حَدِيثًا *He revealed unto him a story* (Ṣ, Ḳ) *secretly.* (TA.) An ex. occurs in the Ḳur lxvi. 3. (TA.) And أَسْرَرْتُ إِلَيْهِ المَوَدَّةَ, and بِالمَوَدَّةِ, *I showed,* or *manifested, to him love,* or *affection.* (Ṣ.) It is said in the Ḳur [lx. 1], تُسِرُّونَ إِلَيْهِمْ بِالْمَوَدَّةِ, meaning, *Ye reveal to them* the news of the Prophet *by reason of* the *love* that is between you and them; the objective complement of the verb being suppressed: or المودّة may be an objective complement, the ب being a redundant corroborative, as in أَخَذَ الخِطَامَ and أَخَذَ بِهِ: (Mṣb:) and this interpretation is correct; for إِسْرَار to a person necessarily implies revealing a secret to him and at the same time concealing it from another. (B.) — وَأَسَرُّوهُ بِضَاعَةً, in the Ḳur xii. 19, signifies *And they concealed,* or *kept secret, his case,* making him *as an article of merchandise:* (Jel:) or *they conjectured in their minds that they should obtain, by selling him, merchandise.* (TA.) [See also an ex. voce اِرْتَغَى, in art. رغو.] — أَسَرَّ الفَاتِحَةَ, and بِالفَاتِحَةِ, *He recited the Fátiḥah* [or First Chapter of the Ḳur-án] *secretly,* or *inaudibly:* (Mṣb:) or the latter form of expression is a mistake. (Mgh.) — أَسْرَرْتُهُ also signifies نَسَبْتُهُ إِلَى السِّرِّ [which may mean either *I attributed it to secrecy,* or, like many phrases of this kind, by inversion, *I attributed to him secrecy, or mystery*]. (Mṣb.)

5. تسرّر and تسرّى, (M, Ḳ,) and ↓ استسرّ, (Ḳ,) *He took to himself a concubine-slave.* (M,* Ḳ,* TA.) And تَسَرَّرْتُ جَارِيَةً, and تَسَرَّيْتُهَا, (Ṣ,) and ↓ اِسْتَسْرَرْتُهَا, (TA,) *I took to myself a girl,* or *young woman, as a concubine-slave.* (Ṣ,* TA.) تَسَرَّرْتُهَا is [said to be] thus changed to تَسَرَّيْتُهَا, (T, Ṣ, Mṣb,) for alleviation of the pronunciation, (Mṣb,) on account of the three ر following one another, (T,) being like تَظَنَّنْتُ and تَظَنَّيْتُ. (T,* Ṣ.) Lth says that تسرّيت is a mistake; but Az says that it is correct. (TA.) ↓ اِسْتَسَرَّنِى occurs in a trad. as signifying *He took me to himself as a concubine-slave;* but by rule one should say تَسَرَّرَنِى, or تَسَرَّانِى: as to ↓ اِسْتَسَرَّنِى, it [more properly] signifies "He revealed to me his secret." (TA.) — تَسَرَّرَ فُلَانٌ بِنْتَ فُلَانٍ [as though signifying *Such a one took to himself the daughter of such a one as a concubine-slave*] is said when a man of low birth takes as his wife a woman or girl of high birth because of the abundance of his property and the littleness of hers. (M.)

6. تسارّوا *They spoke,* or *discoursed, secretly together; acquainted one another with secrets.* (Ṣ, Ḳ.) [See also 3.] ═ تَسَارَّ إِلَى ذٰلِكَ ‡ *He experienced pleasure,* or *delight, at that:* as, for instance, at his scratching a part of his body, or pressing, or kneading, it; and at a thing disliked by another person. (A, TA.) [But I am in some doubt as to the correctness of this, and incline to think that it is a mistake for ↓ استسرّ.]

10. استسرّ *He,* or *it, became concealed;* or *he,*

or *it, concealed himself* or *itself:* (Ḳ:) *it* (a thing, or an affair,) *became hidden* or *concealed* or *secret:* (A, Mṣb:) *it* (the moon) *became concealed* (Ṣ, M, A, TA) *by the light of the sun,* (TA,) [i. e. *by its proximity to the sun,*] *for one night,* or *for two nights.* (AO, Ṣ.) —— استسرّه *He took extraordinary pains in concealing it,* or *keeping it secret.* (TA.) — See also 5, in four places. — استسرّني *He revealed to me his secret.* (TA.) —— See also 1; and see 6, last sentence.

سَرٌّ *A man who rejoices,* or *gladdens, another;* or *makes him happy;* (Ṣ, Ḳ;) [and so ▼ سَارٌّ:] fem. سَرَّةٌ; with which ▼ سَارَّةٌ is syn. (Lḥ, M, Ḳ.) You say رَجُلٌ بَرٌّ سَرٌّ *A man who treats with goodness and affection and gentleness, and rejoices* &c., (Ṣ, Ḳ, TA,) *his brethren:* (TA:) pl. بَرُّونَ سَرُّونَ. (Ṣ, Ḳ.)

سُرٌّ: see سُرُورٌ: —— and سِرٌّ, last sentence but one. —— It is also a contraction of سُرُرٌ, pl. of سَرِيرٌ. (Sb, M.) —— Also, and ▼ سُرَرٌ, (Ṣ, M, Ḳ,) and ▼ سِرَرٌ, (Ṣ, Ḳ, in the CḲ سُرَر,) The *navel-string* of a child; i. e. the *thing that the midwife cuts off from the navel* (سُرَّة) of a child; (Ṣ, Ḳ;) the *thing that hangs from the navel* (سُرَّة) of a newborn child, *and that is cut off:* or ▼ سِرَرٌ signifies the *part that is cut off thereof, and that goes away:* (M:) pl. (of سُرٌّ or سُرَرٌ, Ṣ, [or of سِرَرٌ,]) أَسِرَّةٌ, (Yaạḳoob, Ṣ, M, Ḳ,) which is extr. (M.) One says, عَرَفْتُ ذٰلِكَ قَبْلَ أَنْ يُقْطَعَ سُرُّكَ [*I knew that before thy navel-string was cut*]: one should not say سُرَّتُكَ; for the سُرَّة is not cut. (Ṣ.) And وَلَدَتْ ثَلَاثَةً فِى سِرَرٍ ▼ وَاحِدٍ *She brought forth three* [boys] *consecutively,* or *one at the heels of another.* (M.) [See also سِرٌّ, last sentence.]

سِرٌّ *A secret; a thing that is concealed,* or *suppressed,* (Ṣ, M, A, Mgh, Mṣb, Ḳ,) *in the mind;* (TA;) as also ▼ سَرِيرَةٌ: (Ṣ, M, A, Ḳ:) or the former has the above-mentioned signification, and the latter signifies *a secret action, whether good or evil:* (Lth:) [and the former, also, *a mystery:*] pl. of the former, أَسْرَارٌ; (Ṣ, M, A, Mgh, Mṣb, Ḳ;) and of the latter, سَرَائِرُ. (Ṣ, A, Ḳ.) It is said in a prov., مَا يَوْمُ حَلِيمَةَ بِسِرٍّ [*The day of Haleemeh is not a secret*]: applied to anything commonly known: alluding to Haleemeh the daughter of El-Hárith the son of Aboo-Shemir El-Ghassánee; for, when her father sent an army to El-Mundhir the son of Má-es-Semà, she took forth for the soldiers some perfume in a vessel (مِرْكَن), and perfumed them with it. (Ṣ.) [You say also, هُوَ مَوْضِعُ سِرِّى *He is the depositary of my secret, or secrets.*] The words of the Ḳur [lxxxvi. 9] يَوْمَ تُبْلَى ▼ السَّرَائِرُ signify *In the day wherein the secret tenets and intentions shall be tried and revealed:* (Jel:) or by السرائر is here meant *fasting, and prayer, and alms-giving, and ablution on account of the pollution termed* جَنَابَة. (TA.) [See also a verse cited in the third paragraph of art. عرض.] — *A thing that is revealed, appears,* or *is made manifest:* thus it has two contrary significations. (MF.) — السِّرُّ [for مَحَلُّ السِّرِّ, † *The heart; the mind; the recesses of the mind; the secret thoughts; the soul;*] is a syn. of الضَّمِيرُ. (Ḳ in art. ضمر. [See also سَرِيرَةٌ.]) [لَا تُتْعِبْ سِرَّكَ † *Weary not thy heart,* or *mind,* is a common modern phrase. And one says, of a deceased holy man, قَدَّسَ ٱللّٰهُ سِرَّهُ † *May God sanctify his soul.*] — سِرٌّ also signifies *Secrecy; privacy; contr. of* عَلَانِيَةٌ. (Ṣ in art. علن.) You say سِرًّا وَعَلَانِيَةً [*Secretly and openly;* or *privately and publickly*]. (Ḳur ii. 275, &c.) — *Concealment.* (Ṣ.) — *Suppression; contr. of* إِعْلَانٌ. (Mṣb.) [So in the phrase تَكَلَّمَ سِرًّا *He spoke with a suppressed,* or *low, voice; softly.*] — [*One having private knowledge* of a thing. You say,] فُلَانٌ سِرُّ هٰذَا الأَمْرِ † *Such a one has* [*private*] *knowledge of this thing.* (TA.) — ‡ The *penis* (T, Ṣ, M, Ḳ) of a man: (T:) and ‡ the *vulva,* or *external portion of the organs of generation,* of a woman. (Ḳ.) One says, ٱلْتَقَى السِّرَّانِ ‡ *The two pudenda met.* (A.) — ‡ *Concubitus.* (AHeyth, Ṣ, Mgh, Ḳ.) — ‡ *Marriage:* (M, A, Mṣb, Ḳ:) pl. أَسْرَارٌ. (TA.) You say, وَاعَدَهَا سِرًّا ‡ *He promised her marriage, she promising him the same.* (A.) So, accord. to some, in the Ḳur ii. 235. (TA.) — ‡ *Plain declaration of marriage:* (Ḳ:) i. e., *a man's offering himself in marriage to a woman during her* عِدَّة: so expl. as occurring in the Ḳur ubi suprà: (TA:) or *a man's demanding a woman in marriage during her* عِدَّة. (Mujáhid.) — ‡ *Adultery,* or *fornication:* (AHeyth, Ḳ:) so, accord. to Aboo-Mijlez and El-Hasan, in the Ḳur ubi suprà. (TA.) Hence the saying, لَا يُرْتَجَى مِنْ وَلَدِ السِّرِّ بِرٌّ ‡ *One does not hope for filial piety from the offspring of adultery,* or *fornication.* (TḲ.) — † *Origin;* syn. أَصْلٌ; (M, Ḳ;) as in the phrase هُوَ كَرِيمُ السِّرِّ كَثِيرُ البِرِّ *He is of generous origin, of much filial piety.* (TḲ.) — † The *commencement,* or *first night,* of a lunar month: (Ḳ, TA:) or its *middle;* (Ḳ;) app. meaning *what are called* الأَيَّامُ البِيضُ: (TA:) but Az says, I know it not in this sense. (IAth.) — † The *interior* of anything; its *heart.* (Ḳ.) Whence سِرُّ الشَّهْرِ and اللَّيْلِ † [*The middle of the lunar month* and *of the night*]. (TA.) — The *marrow* of anything. (TA.) — ‡ The *pure,* or *choice,* or *best, part* of anything. (Fr, M, Ḳ.) You say, أَعْطَيْتُكَ سِرَّهُ ‡ *I gave thee the pure,* or *choice,* or *best, part of it.* (A.) — ‡ The *pure,* or *genuine, quality* of race, or lineage: (Ṣ, A, Ḳ:) its *best quality:* (Ṣ, Ḳ:) and the *middle sort* thereof; (Ṣ;) and of rank, or quality, or the like: (M:) as also ▼ سَرَارٌ and ▼ سَرَارَةٌ. (M, Ḳ.) One says, هُوَ فِى سِرِّ قَوْمِهِ ‡ *He is of the best* [in race or family] *of his people:* (TA:) or *of the middle sort of them.* (Ṣ.) — ‡ The *low,* or *depressed, part* of a valley: (Ḳ:) the *best,* (Ṣ, Ḳ,) or *most fruitful,* (Aṣ, M, TA,) *part* thereof: (Aṣ, Ṣ, M, Ḳ:) as also ▼ سَرَارٌ (M, Ḳ) and ▼ سَرَارَةٌ (Aṣ, Ṣ, M, Ḳ) and ▼ سُرَّةٌ: (M, Ḳ:) or the last signifies the *middle* of a valley: (Ṣ:) the pl. of سِرٌّ is سُرُورٌ and سُرُورٌ (M) and أَسِرَّةٌ, like as أَقِنَّةٌ is of قِنٌّ, (Ṣ,) or the last is pl. of ▼ سَرَارٌ, like as أَقْذِلَةٌ is of قَذَالٌ; (M;) and that of ▼ سَرَارَةٌ is ▼ سَرَارٌ, (Ṣ,) or [this is a coll. gen. n., and the pl. is] سَرَائِرُ: (M:) also ▼ سُرَّةٌ † the *middle* of a city: and أَسِرَّةٌ the *middles* of meadows. (TA.) And أَرْضٌ سِرٌّ † *Fruitful, good, land;* (M, Ḳ;) as also ▼ سَرَاةٌ. (Ḳ,* TA.) — Also † *Goodness; excellence.* (Mṣb.) — Also, and ▼ سُرٌّ, (M, Ḳ,) and ▼ سِرَرٌ, (Ṣ, M, Ḳ,) and ▼ سُرَرٌ, (Ḳ,) and ▼ سِرَارٌ, (Ṣ, M, Ḳ,) *A line* of the palm of the hand, (M, Ḳ,*) and of the face, (M,) and of the forehead: (Ṣ, M, Mgh:) pl. (of سِرٌّ, TA, or of ▼ سِرَارٌ, Ṣ) أَسِرَّةٌ, (M, TA,) and (of the same, Ḳ, or of ▼ سِرَرٌ, Ṣ, Mgh) أَسْرَارٌ; (Ṣ, M, Mgh, Ḳ;) and pl. pl., [i. e. pl. of أَسْرَارٌ,] أَسَارِيرُ: (Ṣ, M, (Mgh, Ḳ:) this last, accord. to AA, signifies the *lines in the forehead, from the shrivelling of the skin;* and its sing. is ▼ سُرَرٌ: (TA:) some also apply the pl. أَسِرَّةٌ to ‡ *lines,* or *streaks, of herbage;* as being likened to the lines of the hand and of the face, but this is not of valid authority: (M:) and أَسَارِيرُ (as pl. of أَسْرَارٌ, which is pl. of سِرَرٌ, TA) also signifies the *beauties* of the face, and of the cheeks, and of the elevated parts of the cheeks. (Ḳ, TA.) — وُلِدَ لَهُ ثَلَاثَةٌ عَلَى سِرٍّ, (Ḳ,) and عَلَى سِرَرٍ ▼ وَاحِدٍ, (Ḳ,* TA,) means *Three children were born to him, whose navel-strings were cut in a similar manner, without any female among them.* (Ḳ. [See also سُرٌّ.])

سُرَّةٌ The *navel;* i. e. the *place from which the navel-string* (سُرّ) *has been cut off;* (Ṣ;) the *small cavity,* or *hollow, of the belly,* (M, TA,) *in the middle thereof;* (TA;) *what remains of the* سُرّ: (M:) [see سُرٌّ:] pl. سُرَرٌ [in the CḲ erroneously سِرَرٌ] and سُرَّاتٌ. (Ṣ, Ḳ.) — [Hence,] سُرَّةُ الفَرَسِ † [*The navel of the horse,*] *the star, of Pegasus, that is in the head of Andromeda.* (Ḳzw.) — [Hence likewise] سُرَّةٌ also signifies † *A perforation in the middle of a jar such as is termed* مُزَمَّلَة [q. v.], *in which is fixed a tube of silver or lead, whence one drinks.* (Ḥar p. 548.) — And † The *place where the water rests, in the furthest part,* of a watering-trough, or tank. (Ḳ, TA.) — See also سِرٌّ, in two places, in the latter part of the paragraph.

سَرَرٌ a subst. from سَارَّهُ [like its syn. نَجْوَى from نَاجَاهُ, signifying *Secret discourse,* or *a secret communication, between two persons or parties*]. (M.) —— See also سَرَارُ الشَّهْرِ: —— and سِرٌّ, last sentence but one: —— and سُرٌّ, in two places. —— Also *A pain which a camel suffers in his* كِرْكِرَة [or *callous projection upon the breast*], *arising from a gall,* or *sore:* (Ṣ,* Ḳ:) or *sores in the hinder part of the* كركرة *of a camel, nearly penetrating into his inside, but not mortal:* or *a disease that attacks the horse:* (M:) it is said by Lth to be *a pain in the navel;* but Az and others say that this is a mistake. (TA.) — Also *Hollowness* of a spear-shaft [&c.]. (Ṣ, Ḳ.) [See أَسَرُّ.]

سُرُورٌ : see سِرٌّ, last sentence but one : — and سُرُورٌ. — It is also a pl. of سَرِيرٌ [q. v.]. (Ṣ, M, Mṣb, Ḳ.)

سِرَرٌ : see سَرَارُ الشَّهْرِ : — and سِرٌّ, last two sentences, in three places : — and سِرٌّ, in two places. — Also The *coats*, or *coverings, and earth, that are upon truffles*; (Ṣ, Ḳ;) and ▼ سُرَيْرٌ signifies the same, (TA,) or the *sand* (Ḳ, TA) *and earth and coats* or *coverings* (TA) *upon truffles*: (Ḳ, TA:) here, and in some copies of the Tekmileh, for كَمْأَةٌ, is put أَكَمَةٌ : (TA:) or both signify the *earth that is upon truffles*: (M:) or the former signifies the *round clod of earth in which a truffle grows*: (ISh, TA:) pl. of the former, (ISh, Ṣ,) and of ▼ the latter, (TA,) أَسْرَارٌ. (ISh, Ṣ, TA.)

سَرَارُ الشَّهْرِ and ▼ سِرَارُهُ, (Ṣ, M, Ḳ,) but the latter is not approved by the lexicologists [in general], (Az,) and ▼ سَرَرُهُ (Ṣ, M, Ḳ) and ▼ سِرَرُهُ, (M,) and ▼ لَيْلَةُ السَّرَارِ (Ṣ) [or السِّرَارِ &c.], *The last night of the lunar month*: (Ṣ, Ḳ:) or *when the month is twenty-nine, it is the twenty-eighth night; and when the month is thirty, it is the twenty-ninth night*: (Fr:) or *the night in which the moon becomes concealed by the light of the sun*: (M:) sometimes this is the case one night, and sometimes it is two nights. (AO, Ṣ.) [See also الدَّعْجَآءُ, voce أَدْعَجُ.] — سَرَارٌ is also syn. with سِرٌّ, in two senses: see سِرٌّ, in the latter part of the paragraph, in four places. — It signifies also [*Dates in the unripe state in which they are termed*] سَيَابٌ [q. v.]. (Ḳ.)

سِرَارٌ : see the next preceding paragraph, in two places : — and سِرٌّ, last sentence but one, in two places : — and مَسَرَّةٌ.

سُرُورٌ : see what next follows.

سُرُورٌ, (Ṣ, M, A, Mṣb,) or ▼ سُرُورٌ, when used as a simple subst., (IAṭr, Ṣgh, Ḳ,) but this is strange, and, accord. to MF, unknown, whether as a simple subst. or as an inf. n., (TA,) and ▼ سُرٌّ (M, Mṣb) and ▼ سُرَّآءُ and ▼ تَسُرَّةٌ, (M,) *Happiness*, or *joy*, or *gladness*; syn. فَرَحٌ; (M, Ḳ;*) *contr. of* حُزْنٌ: (Ṣ:) or *dilatation of the bosom with delight*, or *pleasure, wherein is quiet* or *tranquillity* or *rest of mind, of short* or *of long continuance*; whereas فَرَحٌ is dilatation of the bosom with delight, or pleasure, of short continuance, transitory, or fleeting, not lasting, as is the case in bodily and worldly pleasures; but فَرَحٌ is sometimes called سُرُورٌ, and vice versâ: (Er-Rághib, TA in art. فرح:) or سُرُورٌ signifies *pleasure*, or *delight, and dilatation of the heart, of which there is no external sign*; distinguished from حُبُورٌ, which is cheerfulness, i. e., pleasure, or delight, or dilatation of the heart, which has a visible effect in the aspect. (TA.) — Also sing. of ▼ سُرُورٌ, (TA,) which signifies The *upper extremities of the stems* of plants. (Ḳ, TA.) See also مَسَرَّةٌ.

سَرِيرٌ [*A couch-frame; a bedstead: a raised couch*, or *couch upon a frame: a throne*:] *a thing upon which one lies*; syn. مُضْطَجَعٌ: (M, Ḳ:) or *a thing upon which one sits*: (TA:) pl. [of pauc.] أَسِرَّةٌ and [of mult.] سُرُرٌ, (Ṣ, M, Mṣb, Ḳ,) and some, for the latter, say سُرَرٌ, as more easy of pronunciation, (Ṣ, Mṣb,) and make the same change in other similar pls., (Ṣ,) and he who says صُيَدٌ [for صُيُدٌ, pl. of صَيُودٌ,] says سُرَرٌ for سُرُرٌ. (Sb, M.) It is said to be derived from سُرُورٌ, because it generally belongs to persons of ease and affluence and of authority, and to kings. (MF.) — Hence, and as an appellation of good omen, (Er-Rághib,) *A bier, before the corpse is carried upon it*: (Ḳ:) when the corpse is carried upon it, it is called [نَعْشٌ and] جَنَازَةٌ. (TA.) — [Hence,] سَرِيرُ بَنَاتِ نَعْشٍ † [*The bier of Benát-Naash*;] *the seven stars that are upon the neck and breast and two knees of the Greater Bear, resembling a semicircle*; [app. τ, h, υ, φ, θ, e, and f; (as in Freytag's Lex.;)] also called الحَوْضُ. (Ḳzw.) — [Hence likewise] سَرِيرٌ also signifies ‡ *Dominion, sovereignty, rule*, or *authority*: and *ease, comfort*, or *affluence*: (Ṣ,* Ḳ: [in some copies of each of which, we find النِّعْمَةُ in the place of النَّعْمَةُ:]) and *settled means of subsistence*. (M, TA.) You say, زَالَ عَنْ سَرِيرِهِ ‡ *He ceased to enjoy authority*, or *power, and ease, comfort*, or *affluence*. (A.) [See also an ex. in a verse cited in art. دغفل.] — And ‡ The *part where the head rests upon the neck*: (Ṣ, M, Ḳ, TA:) pl. أَسِرَّةٌ and سَرَائِرُ. (TA.) — See also سِرَرٌ, in two places : — and مَسَرَّةٌ.

سَرَارَةٌ : see سِرٌّ, in the latter part of the paragraph, in three places. It signifies also † The *best of the productive parts* of a meadow. (TA.) — And hence, (TA,) † *Pureness, choiceness*, or *excellence*, of anything: (M, Ḳ:) *pureness, and excellence*, of race, or lineage. (Ṣ.) It has no verb. (M.) You say, هُوَ فِى سَرَارَةٍ مِنْ عَيْشَةٍ ‡ [*He is in the best condition*, or *mode, of life*]. (A.) And لَهَا عَلَيْهَا سَرَارَةٌ † *She possesses superiority over her*. (Fr.)

سَرِيرَةٌ; and its pl. سَرَائِرُ : see سِرٌّ, first and fourth sentences, in three places. — Also The *heart*, or *mind*. (KL. [And so سِرٌّ, q. v.]) And One's *inner man*; syn. جَوَّانِىٌّ : opposed to عَلَانِيَةٌ and بَرَّانِىٌّ [q. v.]. (T in art. بر.)

سَرَّآءُ *Ampleness*, or *freedom from straitness, of the means*, or *circumstances, of life*; syn. رَخَآءٌ; [or *a happy state* or *condition*;] *contr. of* ضَرَّآءُ; (Ṣ;) *i. q.* ▼ مَسَرَّةٌ and ▼ سَارُورَآءُ [*contr. of* مَضَرَّةٌ and ضَارُورَآءُ]. (Ḳ.) — See also سُرُورٌ : — and see سِرٌّ, near the end of the paragraph. — Also *i. q.* بَطْحَآءُ [q. v.]. (TA.)

سِرِّىٌّ [rel. n. from سِرٌّ; *Of*, or *relating to, anything secret*: a *secret*, or *mysterious*, thing. — And] A man *who does things secretly*: pl. سِرِّيُّونَ. (M.)

سُرِّيَّةٌ *A concubine-slave; a female slave whom one takes as a possession and for concubitus*; (M;) *a female slave to whom one assigns a house*, or *chamber, in which he lodges her*, (Ṣ, Ḳ,) *and whom he takes as a possession and for concubitus*: (TA:) of the measure فُعْلِيَّةٌ, (Ṣ, M, Mgh, Mṣb,) from سِرٌّ as signifying "concubitus," (Ṣ, M,* Mgh, Mṣb, Ḳ,) or as signifying "concealment," because a man often conceals and protects her from his wife; (Ṣ;) altered from the regular form of a rel. n., (Ṣ, M, Mṣb, Ḳ,) by its having ḍamm [in the place of kesr]; (Ṣ, Mṣb;) for the rel. n. is sometimes thus altered, as in the instances of دُهْرِىٌّ from الدَّهْرُ and سُهْلِىٌّ from الأَرْضُ السَّهْلَةُ : (Ṣ:) or it is with ḍamm to distinguish it from سِرِّيَّةٌ, which is applied to "a free woman with whom one has sexual intercourse secretly," (Mṣb,) or "one who prostitutes herself:" (TA:) or it is from سُرٌّ in the sense of سُرُورٌ; because her owner rejoices in her; (Akh,* Ṣ,* Mṣb;) and if so, it is agreeable with analogy: (Mṣb:) so says AHeyth; and this is the best that has been said respecting it: (TA:) or it is of the measure فُعُّولَةٌ, from سَرْوٌ, (M, Mgh,) the latter و being changed into ى for euphony, and then the [other] و being incorporated into it and thus becoming ى like it, after which the ḍammeh is changed into a kesreh because the ى is next to it: (M:) the pl. is سَرَارِىُّ (ISk, Ṣ, TA) and سَرَارٍ; (ISk, TA;) the latter, by poetic license. (Ḥam p. 304.)

سِرِّيَّةٌ *A free woman with whom one has sexual intercourse secretly*, (Mṣb, TA,*) or *who prostitutes herself*: (TA:) distinguished from سُرِّيَّةٌ [q. v.]. (Mṣb, TA.)

سُرْسُورٌ *Intelligent; knowing; skilful*; (Ṣ, M, Ḳ;) *entering much into affairs*, (Ṣ, Ḳ,) *by means of his good artifices* or *artful contrivances*. (TA.) You say, هُوَ سُرْسُورُ مَالٍ *He is one who manages well*, or *takes good care of, property*, or *cattle*, (AA, M,* Ḳ,* TA,) *knowing what is conducive to the good thereof*. (AA, TA.) And هُوَ ٱبْنُ سُرْسُورِهَا *He is the knowing with respect to it*. (T in art. بنى.) — *A person beloved*, or *a friend*; *a special*, or *choice, companion*; (Ḳ;) as also ▼ سُرْسُورَةٌ. (TA.) — Also The نَصْل [or *spun thread, that has come forth*,] of the spindle. (Ḳ.)

سُرْسُورَةٌ : see the next preceding paragraph.

سَارٌّ; and its fem., with ة : see سِرٌّ.

سَارُورَآءُ : see سَرَّآءُ.

أَسَرُّ *An adventive; one abiding among a people to whom he is not related*; syn. دَخِيلٌ. (Ṣ, Ḳ.) Lebeed says,

وَجَدِّى فَارِسُ الرَّعْشَآءِ مِنْهُمْ
رَئِيسٌ لَا أَسَرُّ وَلَا سَنِيدُ

[*And my grandfather, the rider of Er-Raashà, was of them; a chief, not an adventive, nor of suspected origin*]. (Ṣ.) — Also a camel *having a gall*, or *sore, in the* كِرْكِرَة [or *callous projection upon the breast*]: (Ṣ:) or *having a pain therein, arising from a gall*, or *sore*: (Ḳ:) or *having sores in the hinder part thereof, nearly penetrating into his inside, but not mortal*: or *having the disorder termed* ضُبّ, *which is a tumour in the breast*: (M:) fem. سَرْآءُ. (M, Ḳ.) [See سُرُورٌ.] — زَنْدٌ أَسْرُ *A* زند [or *piece of stick*, or *wood, for producing fire,*] *that has become hollow* [*by wear*]. (AḤn, Ṣ, M, Ḳ. [See 1, near the end of the paragraph.]) And قَنَاةٌ سَرْآءُ *A hollow spear-shaft*. (Ṣ, M, Ḳ.)

تَسُرَّةٌ: see سُرُورٌ.

مَسَرَّةٌ an inf. n. of سَرَّهُ [q. v.] (Ṣ, O, Ḳ.) — [And *A cause of* سُرُور, i. e. *happiness*, or *joy*, or *gladness*;] *a thing whereby one is made happy*, or *joyful*, or *glad*: pl. مَسَارُّ. (Mṣb.) — See also سَرَارٌ. — Also, [perhaps as being a cause of pleasure,] The *extremities of sweet-smelling plants*; (M, O, Ḳ;) and so ▼ سُرُورٌ: (O, Ḳ:) or the latter, the *upper halves of the stems of plants*; (Lth, M, O; [but see سُرُورٌ;]) properly, the *parts* of a lotus-plant *that are concealed* [*by the water*] *and are consequently succulent and soft and beautiful*: and ▼ سَرِيرٌ, the *root*, or *lower part*, of a lotus-plant, *whereon it rests*: (O:) or this last, the *pith* of the lotus-plant; (M, Ḳ;) and so ▼ سِرَارٌ: (TA:) [accord. to Az,] اِبْنُ المَسَرَّةِ signifies the *branch* [or *sprig*] *of* رَيْحَان [or *of a sweet-smelling plant*]. (T in art بنى.)

مِسَرَّةٌ *An instrument in which one speaks secretly, like a* طُومَار [i. e. a *roll*, or *scroll*] (Ṣ, Ḳ) &c. (TA.)

مَسْرُورٌ *Happy*, or *joyful*, or *glad*; or *affected with* سُرُور [q. v.]. (Ṣ, TA.) ═ *Having the navel-string cut*. (TA, from a trad.) — And with ة, applied to the kind of jar termed مُزَمَّلَة, *Having a* سُرَّة, meaning a *perforation in the middle, in which is fixed a tube of silver or lead, whence one drinks*. (Ḥar p. 548.)

وَقَفْتُ عَلَى مُسْتَسَرِّهِ *I became acquainted with his hidden*, or *secret, affair*. (A,* TA.)

سرأ

1. سَرَأَتْ, (Ṣ, Ḳ,) aor. َ, inf. n. سَرْءٌ; (Ṣ, TA;) and ▼ سَرَّأَتْ, inf. n. تَسْرِئَةٌ; (Ḳ;) said of the female locust, (Ṣ, Ḳ,) and of the female of the [lizard called] ضَبّ, (TA,) [and of a fish, and the like, (see سِرْءٌ,)] *She laid eggs*: (Ṣ, Ḳ, TA:) and سَرَتْ, inf. n. سَرْوٌ, is a dial. var. thereof. (TA in art. سرو.) [And accord. to El-Ḳanánee, as cited in the TA, it seems that one says also, of locusts (جَرَاد), سَرَأَ البَيْضَ and سَرَأَ بِهِ.] — Also, each of these two verbs, (Ḳ,) the former mentioned by IDrd, and ▼ the latter by Fr, (TA,) said of a woman, *She bore many children*. (Ḳ.)

2: see above, in two places.

4. اسرأت, said of a female locust, [and app. of a female of the lizard called ضَبّ, and a fish, and the like, (see سِرْءٌ,)] *She attained the period of laying eggs*. (Ṣ, Ḳ.)

سَرْءٌ and ▼ سَرْأَةٌ (M, Ḳ) and ▼ سِرْأَةٌ (Ḳ [for وَيُكْسَرُ in the CḲ should be وَتُكْسَرُ, referring to the second form,]) and ▼ سِرْءٌ, (TA, [accord. to which وتكسر refers to the س in the first and second, but this I think improbable,]) or سرأة is with kesr [only, i. e. ▼ سِرْأَةٌ], (Ṣ, Ḳ, [supposing that in the latter the pronoun هِىَ refers to سرأة, but accord. to the TA it means الكَلِمَةُ, so as to refer to سرء also,]) and most hold this to be correct, (TA,) The *egg*, (Ṣ, Ḳ,) or *eggs*, (M,) *of the locust*, (Ṣ, M, Ḳ,) and *of the* [*lizard called*] ضَبّ, (M, TA,) and *of fish* (M, Ḳ, TA) and *the like*; (M, TA;) and سِرْوَةٌ signifies the same, but is originally with ء: (Ṣ:) accord. to 'Alee Ibn-Ḥamzeh El-Iṣbahánee, ▼ سِرْأَةٌ and سِرْوَةٌ signify the *eggs of the locust*; but some say, only *when laid*: accord. to Lth, سرء [app. سَرْءٌ] signifies the *eggs* of the fish and the like, as also سُرُوءٌ; [the former as a coll. gen. n., and the latter as its pl., agreeably with analogy;] and one is called سرأة [app. ▼ سَرْأَةٌ as a n. un., agreeably with analogy; or it may be ▼ سِرْأَةٌ]. (TA. [See also سِرْوَةٌ in art. سرو: and see دَبًى.])

سِرْءٌ: see the next preceding paragraph.

سَرْأَةٌ: see سَرْءٌ, in two places.

سِرْأَةٌ: see سَرْءٌ, in four places.

سِرْوَةٌ, originally سِرْأَةٌ [q. v., voce سَرْءٌ]. — Also *A dust-coloured arrow*: in this sense likewise originally with ء: thus expl. by 'Alee Ibn-Ḥamzeh. (TA.) [See also art. سرو.]

سَرَآءٌ *A species of tree, of which bows are made*: n. un. with ة. (TA.) [See art. سرى.]

سَرُوءٌ, applied to a female locust, (El-Iṣbahánee, Ḳ,) and to the female of the [lizard called] ضَبّ, (Lth, TA,) [and to a fish and the like, (see سَرْءٌ,)] *Laying eggs*: (El-Iṣbahánee, Ḳ,* TA:) or *having eggs in her belly; not yet laid*: (Lth, Ḳ,* TA:) pl. سُرُؤٌ (Lth, El-Iṣbahánee, Ḳ) and سُرَّأٌ, which latter is extr. in form as pl. of a sing. of the measure فَعُولٌ, (Ḳ,) and سُرُوءٌ [which is also extr., like هُجُودٌ as pl. accord. to some of هَجُودٌ]. (MF.)

أَرْضٌ مَسْرُوَةٌ, (Ṣ, Ḳ,) or مَسْرُوءَةٌ, (TA,) *A land containing* سِرْوَة [meaning *locusts' eggs*]: (El-Iṣbahánee, Ṣ:) or *abounding with locusts* (Ḳ,* TA) [or *with locusts' eggs*: for the explanation in the Ḳ is ambiguous].

Quasi سرأل and سرأن

إِسْرَائِيلُ a surname of [the patriarch] *Jacob*; (Ksh and Bḍ* and Jel* in ii. 38;) also pronounced إِسْرَائِلُ, (Ḳsh and Bḍ ibid.,) and إِسْرَائِلّ, (Ksh ibid.,) and إِسْرَالُ, and إِسْرَايِيلُ. (Bḍ ibid.) — And the name of *A certain angel*; also pronounced إِسْرَائِينُ; in which the ن is asserted by Yaạḳoob to be a substitute for the ل. (TA.) — [But the إ is more properly to be regarded as a radical letter.]

سرب

1. سَرَبَ aor. ُ, inf. n. سُرُوبٌ, *He went forth*: and *he went away*. (M.) You say, سَرَبَ فِى الأَرْضِ, (M, A, Mgh, Mṣb,) aor. as above, (M, Mṣb,) and so the inf. n., (M, A, Mṣb,) *He went away* [*into the country*, or *in the land*]. (M, A, Mgh, Mṣb.) And سَرَبَ فِى حَاجَتِهِ *He went*, or *went away*, (A'Obeyd, M,) or, as some say, *during the day*, (M,) *for the accomplishment of his want*. (A'Obeyd, M.) And هُوَ يَسْرُبُ النَّهَارَ كُلَّهُ فِى حَوَائِجِهِ [*He goes*, or *goes away, all the day, accomplishing his wants*]. (A.) — سَرَبَ [or rather سَرَبَ فِى الأَرْضِ] also signifies *He* (a man) *went away at random into the country*, or *in the land*. (Ḥar pp. 448 and 511.) A poet says, (Ṣ,) namely, Ḳeys Ibn-El-Khaṭeem, (TA,)

* أَنَّى سَرَبْتِ وَكُنْتِ غَيْرَ سَرُوبِ ▼ *

[i. e. *Whence hast thou gone away at random? for thou wast not one wont to go away at random*:] (Ṣ, TA:) thus, سربت, as related by IDrd: accord. to others, [سَرَيْتِ,] with ى. (TA.) — سَرَبَتِ الإِبِلُ, aor. and inf. n. as above, *The camels went away into the country*, or *in the land, going forth whithersoever they would*: and in like manner سَرَبَ is said of a stallion [camel]: (Az, TA:) or سَرَبَ, (Ṣ, Ḳ,) said of a stallion [camel], aor. as above, (Ṣ,) and so the inf. n., signifies *he repaired*, or *betook himself, to the place of pasture*: (Ṣ, A, Ḳ:) and سَرَبَ المَالُ, aor. ُ, inf. n. سَرْبٌ, *the camels*, or *cattle, pastured during the day without a pastor*. (Mṣb.) — سَرَبَ المَآءُ, (A, Mgh, Mṣb,) aor. as above, (Mṣb,) inf. n. سُرُوبٌ; (Mgh, Mṣb;) or سَرِبَ, [aor. َ,] inf. n. سَرَبٌ; (M;) *The water ran* (A, Mgh) upon the surface of the ground: (A:) or *flowed*; as also ▼ انسرب: (M:) [or the latter signifies *it ran swiftly*: (see Ḥar p. 586:)] and in like manner one says of the سَرَاب [or mirage], يَسْرُبُ, inf. n. سَرْبٌ, *it runs*. (AHeyth, TA.) And سَرِبَتِ العَيْنُ, inf. n. سَرَبٌ; and سَرَّبَتْ, aor. ُ, inf. n. سُرُوبٌ; *The* عين [or *source*, or perhaps † *eye*, (see مَسْرَبٌ,)] *flowed*; as also ▼ تسرّبت: so says Lḥ. (M.) And سَرِبَتِ المَزَادَةُ, aor. َ, (Ṣ, Ḳ,) inf. n. سَرَبٌ, (Ṣ,) *The* مزادة [or *leathern water-bag*] *flowed*. (Ṣ, Ḳ.) And خَرَجَ المَآءُ سَرَبًا *The water came forth from the punctures made in sewing the skin*. (TA.) [Or] سَرِبَتْ said of a new [water-skin such as is termed] قِرْبَة, or of a مَزَادَة, signifies *It had water poured into it in order that the thong* [*with which it was sewed*] *might become moistened, so as to swell, and fill up the holes made in the sewing*. (M.) — See also سَرَبَ, below. — [Golius explains سرب, inf. n. سَرَبَانٌ, as on the authority of the KL, as signifying "*Ingressus fuit in rem, totum subivit implevitve locum*:" but this is a mistake, evidently occasioned by his finding سَرَبَانٌ, explained in this sense, instead of سَرَيَانٌ, the reading in my copy of the KL.] ═ سَرْبٌ [as an inf. n.] is [also] *syn. with* خَرْزٌ [signifying The *sewing* of a skin or the like]. (Kr, Ḳ, TA. [In a copy of the M, I find السَّرَبُ الخَرَزُ erroneously written for السَّرْبُ الخَرْزُ.]) You say, سَرَبْتُ القِرْبَةَ, inf. n. سَرْبٌ, *I sewed the* قربة [i. e. *water-skin*, or *milk-skin*]. (TḲ.) ═

سُرِبَ, (M, Ḳ,) like عُنِىَ, [i. e. pass. in form but neuter in signification,] (Ḳ,) said of a man, (TA,) *He became affected with suppression of the feces*, or *constipation of the bowels*, (أَخَذَهُ حُصْرٌ or حُصُرٌ accord. to different copies of the Ḳ,) *by the entrance of the fume of* [molten] *silver* [see أُسْرُبٌ] *into the innermost parts of his nose, and other passages*, (Ḳ,) or *into his mouth, and the innermost parts of his nose, and his anus*, (M,* TA,) *and other passages:* (TA:) the epithet applied to a man thus affected is ▾ مَسْرُوبٌ: (Ḳ:) sometimes he recovers, and sometimes he dies. (TA.)

2. [سرّب app. signifies, primarily, *He sent camels in a herd* or *drove, together, to pasture.* And hence, —] سَرَّبَ عَلَىَّ الإِبِلَ † *He sent* [*against me*] *the camels* [app. with armed riders], *one detached number after another:* (Aṣ, Ṣ, A, Ḳ, TA:) and in like manner, الخَيْلَ † [*the horsemen*]. (Ṣ, A, Mgh, TA.) It is said in a trad. of 'Áïsheh, [referring to girls who were her playmates,] كَانَ يُسَرِّبُهُنَّ إِلَىَّ فَيَلْعَبْنَ مَعِى † *He used to send them to me* [app. *party after party, and they would play with me*]. (TA.) And one says, سَرَّبْتُ إِلَيْهِ الشَّىْءَ † *I sent to him the thing, one by one;* or rather, *portion by portion.* (L, TA.) And سَرَّبْتُ إِلَيْهِ الأَشْيَآءَ ‡ *I gave him the things, one after another.* (A, TA.) And سَرَّبَهُ *He sent him back in his* سرب [i. e. سَرْب], meaning *way* [by which he had come]. (Ḥar p. 20.) — See also 4. = سَرَّبَ سَرَبًا *He made a subterranean excavation.* (M, A.) — سَرَّبَ الحَافِرُ, (Aṣ, TA,) inf. n. تَسْرِيبٌ, (Ṣ, Ḳ,) *The digger* [of a well], *in digging, took* [i. e. *dug*] *towards the right and left:* (Aṣ, Ṣ,* Ḳ,* TA:) in some copies of the Ḳ, [and in the Ṣ,] *right or left:* but the former is the correct explanation. (TA.) = سَرَّبَ القِرْبَةَ, (Ṣ, M, A,) inf. n. as above, (Ḳ,) *He poured water into the* قربة [i. e. *water-skin*, or *milk-skin*], *in order that the holes made in the sewing might become filled up* (Ṣ, M, A, Ḳ) *by their being moistened*, (Ṣ, Ḳ,) or *by the moistening, and consequent swelling, of the thong* [*with which it was sewed*]; the قربة being new. (M.)

4. اسرب *He made* water *to flow;* as also ▾ سرّب. (M.)

5: see 1, near the middle of the paragraph. — [Hence, app.,] تَسَرَّبُوا فِيهِ † *They followed one another continuously in it;* namely, a road. (M.) — See also 7. = تَسَرَّبَ مِنَ المَآءِ *He became full of water.* (TA.)

7: see 1, near the middle of the paragraph. — انسرب فيه *He entered into it;* (Ṣ, M, Ḳ;) i. e., a wild animal, into his سَرَب, (Ṣ, M, Mṣb,) meaning his subterranean habitation, (Ṣ, Mṣb,) or his place of abode; (M;) and a fox, (Ṣ,) into his burrow; as also ▾ تسرّب. (Ṣ, Ḳ.)

سَرْبٌ *Pasturing* مَال, (M, A, TA,) i. e. *camels:* (M, TA:) or *camels*, and مَال [here meaning *cattle* in general], *that pasture:* (Ṣ:) or مَال [i. e. *camels or cattle*] *pasturing during the day without a pastor;* an inf. n. used as a subst. in this sense; and ▾ سَارِبٌ [meaning مَالٌ سَارِبٌ] signifies the same: (Mṣb:) or, accord. to IAạr, (M,) *any* مَاشِيَة [i. e. *camels* and *other cattle*]; (M, Ḳ;) thus say IJ and Ibn-Hishám El-Lakhmee: and accord. to Ḳz, ▾ سِرْبٌ also, [q. v.,] with kesr, signifies مَال [syn. with مَاشِيَة]; and IO says the like: (TA:) pl. of the former سُرُوبٌ, (M, TA,) and some say أَسْرَابٌ [which is a pl. of pauc.]. (TA.) Hence the saying, اِذْهَبْ فَلَا أَنْدَهُ سَرْبَكَ, i. e. *Go thou away, for I will not drive back thy* [*pasturing*] *camels;* (Ṣ, Mṣb;*) they shall go, (Ṣ,) or I will leave them to pasture, (Mṣb,) where they will; (Ṣ, Mṣb;) meaning, I have no need of thee: (Ṣ:) in the Time of Ignorance, they used to divorce by saying thus, (Ṣ, M, Mṣb,) اِذْهَبِى فَلَا أَنْدَهُ سَرْبَكِ. (Ṣ, M, A.) — [Freytag also explains it, from the Deewán el-Hudhaleeyeen, as meaning *A sheep-fold.*] = Also *A way*, or *road;* (AZ, Ṣ, M, A, Mgh, Mṣb, Ḳ;) and so ▾ سِرْبٌ, with kesr; (M, Ḳ;) the latter accord. to Aboo-'Omar and Th, but disallowed by Mbr, who knew only the former in this sense; said by Ibn-Es-Seed to have been pronounced by AZ with fet-ḥ, and by Aboo-'Omar with kesr: (TA:) and one's *way*, or *course;* (M, Ḳ,* TA;) the *way by which one goes.* (T, TA. [See also سُرْبَةٌ, and مَسْرَبٌ.]) One says, خَلِّ سَرْبَهُ *Leave thou free*, or *unobstructed, his way* (T, M, Mgh, Mṣb, TA) *by which he goes*, (T, TA,) and *his course;* (M, TA;) and so ▾ سِرْبَهُ, with kesr; (M, TA;) accord. to Aboo-'Omar: (TA:) or خَلِّ لَهُ سَرْبَهُ *leave thou free*, or *unobstructed, to him his way.* (Ṣ, A.) And أَطْلَقَ الأَسِيرَ وَخَلَّى سَرْبَهُ [*He loosed the captive and left free to him his way*]. (A.) Hence, in a trad., مَنْ أَصْبَحَ آمِنًا فِى سَرْبِهِ, meaning فِى مُتَصَرَّفِهِ and مُتَقَلَّبِهِ [i. e. *He who has become secure in his scope*, or *room, for free action*]: or, accord. to one reading, the last words are فِى ▾ سِرْبِهِ, meaning, ‡ *in respect of his wives*, or *women under covert*, and *his household*, or *family;* a metaphorical sense, from the سِرْب of gazelles &c. (A, and so in the Fáïḳ. [See also سِرْب.]) Hence also the saying, إِذَا كَانَ مُخَلًّى السَّرْبِ, meaning *When he is made to be in ample circumstances; not straitened.* (Mgh.) And you say وَاسِعُ السَّرْبِ, instead of السِّرْبِ; meaning *Whose way that he pursues is ample.* (TA. [But see what follows.]) = Also The *bosom*, or *breast;* or the *mind;* syn. صَدْرٌ. (Mbr, M, Ḳ.) إِنَّهُ لَوَاسِعُ السَّرْبِ means *Verily he is of ample bosom*, or *mind;* and *judgment;* and *love:* (M, TA:) or, as some say, *ample of bosom*, or *mind; slow of anger.* (M. [The latter meaning is assigned in the Mṣb and TA to وَاسِعُ السِّرْبِ: see the next paragraph.])

سِرْبٌ: see سَارِبٌ. — [Hence, app.,] *A* قَطِيع, (Ṣ, M, Ḳ,) or جَمَاعَة, (Mgh, Mṣb,) [i. e. *herd*,] of gazelles, (Ṣ, M, A, Mgh, Mṣb, Ḳ,) and of oxen, (M, Mgh, Mṣb,) [app. meaning wild oxen,] and of [wild] asses, (M,) and of wild animals [in general], (Ṣ, Mṣb,) and [*a flock* or *herd*] of sheep or goats, (M,) and [*a flock*] of the birds called قَطًا, (Ṣ, Mṣb,) and of birds [in general], (M,) and [*a party*, or *bevy*,] of women, (Ṣ, M, Mṣb, Ḳ,) &c.; (Ḳ;) and, as used by El-'Ajjáj, it is of men also: (Sh, TA:) and a poet of the Jinn, as they assert, used it metaphorically in speaking of a سِرْب of the [lizards called] عَظَآء: (M:) it signifies also † *a collection* of palm-trees; (M, Ḳ; in some copies of the latter of which النَّحْل is erroneously put for النَّخْل; TA;) so says AḤn; and Abu-l-Ḥasan thinks it to be by way of comparison: and ▾ سُرْبَةٌ is like it [in its meanings]: (M: [particularly mentioned in the Ḳ as used in the last of the senses above mentioned:]) each of these words is said to be applied to a قطيع of the birds called قَطًا, and of gazelles, and of sheep or goats, on the authority of Aṣ; and the latter [or each] of them is applied to a قطيع of women as being likened to gazelles: (TA:) the pl. of the former is أَسْرَابٌ; (Sh, M, Mṣb, TA;) and of ▾ the latter, سُرُبٌ, (Ḳ, accord. to the TA,) with two ḍammehs, (TA,) [in the CḲ سُرُوبٌ,] or سُرَبٌ, (so in my MS. copy of the Ḳ, [either a contraction of the former pl. or a coll. gen. n. of which سُرْبَةٌ is the n. un.,]) or both. (TA. [See also سُرْبَةٌ below, where the pl. is said to be سُرَبٌ.]) — [Hence, as some explain them, two phrases mentioned below in this paragraph.] — See also سَرْبٌ, first sentence. = It is also syn. with سَرْبٌ as meaning *A way*, or *road:* and *a course:* see سَرْبٌ in two places. — Also *i. q.* بَال [app. as syn. with حَال, i. e. *State*, or *condition*]. (Ṣ, Mṣb, Ḳ.) One says, فُلَانٌ وَاسِعُ السِّرْبِ, meaning رَخِىُّ البَالِ [i. e. *Such a one is in an ample*, or *unstraitened, state* or *condition:* or the meaning may be, *such a one is easy*, or *unstraitened, in mind:* see what follows, and see also بَال]: (Ṣ, Mṣb:) or, as some say, *ample of bosom*, or *mind; slow of anger:* (Mṣb, TA:) [see also وَاسِعُ السَّرْبِ, in two places near the end of the next preceding paragraph:] MF thinks that for بَال we should read مَال, agreeably with an explanation of a phrase in what here follows. (TA.) — Also The قَلْب [meaning *heart*, or *mind*]: (M, Ḳ:) and the نَفْس [meaning *self*]. (IAạr, M, Mṣb, Ḳ.) One says, هُوَ آمِنٌ فِى سِرْبِهِ *He is secure in*, or *in respect of, his heart*, or *mind:* or, *himself:* (M:) but IDrd disallows this latter explanation; and says that the meaning is, *his family*, and *his* مَال [or *camels*, or *cattle*, or *other property*], and *his children;* as though the phrase آمن فى سربه were originally used in relation to the pastor, and the stallion [camel], and then extended in its relation to others, metaphorically: (TA:) or the meaning is [simply], *his* مَال: or, *his people*, or *party:* (M, TA:) or as expl. above, voce سَرْبٌ, q. v.: or, accord. to Ḳz, *his way.* (TA.) The pl. is سِرَابٌ. (El-Hejeree, M, TA.) = See also مَسْرُبَةٌ.

سَرَبٌ *A subterranean excavation:* (M, Ḳ:) or *a habitation* (Ṣ, Mgh, Mṣb, TA) of a wild animal, (Ṣ,* Mṣb,) *in*, (Ṣ, Mgh, Mṣb,) or *beneath*, (TA,) *the earth*, or *ground*, (Ṣ, Mgh, Mṣb, TA,) *having no passage through it;* also called وَكْرٌ: (Mṣb:) such as has a passage through it is termed نَفَقٌ: (Mgh, Mṣb:) the *burrow*, or *hole*, (M, Ḳ,) of a wild animal, (Ḳ,) or of a fox, and likewise [the *den*] of a lion, and of a hyena, and of a wolf; and the *place into which a wild animal enters*: (M:) pl. أَسْرَابٌ. (M, A, Mṣb.) In the saying in the Ḳur [xviii. 60], فَٱتَّخَذَ سَبِيلَهُ فِى ٱلْبَحْرِ سَرَبًا [*And it* (the fish) *took its way into the sea* &c.], Fr says that when the fish was restored to life by the water that came upon it from the fountain [of life], and fell into the sea, its way became congealed, and like a سَرَب [or *subterranean excavation*, &c.]: Zj says that سربا may be considered as put in the accus. case in two ways; either as a second objective complement of the verb, or as an inf. n. [of ↓ سَرِبَ, q. v.]: and AḤát thinks that it here means ذَهَابًا [*going away*]: or, accord. to IAth, سَرَبٌ signifies *a secret*, or *hidden*, *place of passage*: or, as used by El-Moṣtariḍ Edh-Ḍhafaree, it means [simply] *a road*, or *way*. (TA.) It signifies also *A subterranean channel* or *conduit*, *by which water enters a* حَائِط [or *garden*, or *walled garden of palm-trees*]. (M, Ḳ.) And طَرِيقٌ سَرَبٌ means *A way*, or *road*, *in which people follow one another continuously*. (M.) — Also *Flowing water*: (M, Ḳ: [see also سَرِبٌ:]) or *water flowing from a* مَزَادَة [or *leathern water-bag*] *and the like*: (Ṣ:) or *water dropping from the punctures made in the sewing* of a water-skin. (A.) — And *Water that is poured into a* قِرْبَة [or *skin for water or milk*], (M, Ḳ,) *when it is new*, or *into a* مَزَادَة [or *leathern water-bag*], (M,) *in order that the thong* [*with which it is sewed*] *may become moistened*, (M, Ḳ,) *so as to swell, and fill up the holes made in the sewing*. (M.)

سَرِبٌ *Flowing* water. (Ṣ, M. [See also سَرَبٌ.]) You say also مَزَادَةٌ سَرِبَةٌ, i. e. [*A leathern-water-bag*] *flowing*. (Ṣ, Ḳ.)

سُرْبَةٌ: see the next paragraph. ═ *I. q.* خُرْزَة [*A single puncture*, or *stitch-hole*, *made in sewing a skin or the like*]. (Ḳ. [There expressly said to be, in this sense, with fet-ḥ; but I think that we should read سُرْبَة, and خُرْزَة: see, again, the next paragraph.])

سُرْبَةٌ *A short journey*; (IAạr, M;) or so ↓ سَرْبَةٌ. (Ḳ. [But I think that the former is the right.]) You say, إِنَّكَ لَتُرِيدُ سُرْبَةً *Verily thou desirest a short journey*. (IAạr, M.) A long journey is termed سُبْأَةٌ. (TA.) — And *i. q.* مَذْهَبٌ (Ṣ, M, A, Ḳ) and طَرِيقَةٌ (A, Ḳ) [i. e. *A way by which one goes* or *goes away*, a proper meaning of the former word; and *a way, course, mode*, or *manner, of acting* or *conduct* or *the like*, which is a meaning of both of these words]. One says, فُلَانٌ بَعِيدُ ٱلسُّرْبَةِ, (Ṣ, A, TA,) meaning [*Such a one is*] *one who takes a distant way into the country*, or *land*: (TA:) or meaning بَعِيدُ ٱلْمَذْهَبِ (Ṣ, A) and ٱلطَّرِيقَةِ (A) [i. e., *who follows a distant*, or *remote*, *way* in journeying, and *a long way, course, mode*, or *manner, of acting* or *conduct* or *the like*. See also سَرْبٌ, and مَسْرَبٌ]. Esh-Shenfarà says,

هَدَوْنَا مِنَ ٱلْوَادِى ٱلَّذِى بَيْنَ مِشْعَلٍ
وَبَيْنَ ٱلْحَشَا هَيْهَاتَ أَنْسَأْتُ سُرْبَتِى

[*We passed from the valley that is between Mish'al and El-Ḥashà: distant was it: I made my way to lead me far off*]; meaning, how distant was the place from which I commenced my journey! (TA.) And one says also, إِنَّهُ لَقَرِيبُ ٱلسُّرْبَةِ, meaning قَرِيبُ ٱلْمَذْهَبِ [i. e. *Verily he is one who pursues a near way*]; *who hastens*, or *is quick, in accomplishing his want*. (Th, M.) ═ Also *A portion*, or *detached number*, (Ṣ, Mgh, Mṣb,) *of what compose a* سِرْب, (Mgh, Mṣb,) i. e., of a *collection* [or *herd*] *of gazelles*, and *of* [*wild*] *oxen*, (Mgh,) or [*of a flock*] *of the birds called* قَطًا, and *of horses*, and *asses*, and *gazelles*: (Ṣ:) pl. سُرَبٌ, like غُرَفٌ pl. of غُرْفَةٌ. (Mṣb.) See also سِرْبٌ, in two places; in the latter of which the pl. is said to be سُرَبٌ and سُرْبٌ. — *A collection of* خَيْل [i. e. *horses*, or *horsemen*], *from twenty to thirty*, (M, Ḳ,) or *from ten to twenty*. (M.) — *A company of men who steal away from an army, and make a hostile incursion into the territory of a people, and return*. (IAạr, TA.) — *A row of grape-vines*: (M, Ḳ:) and *any* طَرِيقَة [meaning *row* or *line*]. (M.) — See also مَسْرُبَة. — Also *i. q.* خُرْزَة [i. e. *A seam*, or *a stitch*, or *a puncture*, or *stitch-hole*, of a skin or the like]. (M. [See also سَرْبَة.])

سَرَابٌ [The *mirage*;] *i. q.* آلٌ: (Aṣ, M, TA:) or the *semblance of water*, (Ṣ, M, A, Ḳ,) *of running water*, (M,) *at midday*, (Ṣ, M, A, Ḳ,) *cleaving to the ground*, (M,) *and* [*in appearance*] *lowering everything so that it becomes* [*as though it were*] *cleaving to the ground, having no* شَخْص; (TA;) whereas the آل is that which is in the ضُحًى [or early part of the day when the sun is yet low], raising figures seen from a distance, and making them to quiver: (M:) [several other distinctions between the سراب and the آل, mentioned here in the TA, see voce آلٌ:] سَرَابٌ has no pl. (Ṣ and Ḳ voce نَهَارٌ.) One says أَخْدَعُ مِنْ سَرَابٍ [*More deceitful than a midday-mirage*]. (A.) ═ سَرَابِ, like قَطَامِ, (A, Ḳ, TA,) i. e. indecl., with kesr for its termination, as also سَرَابُ, imperfectly decl., (TA,) determinate, (Ḳ, TA,) as a proper name, not having the article ال prefixed to it, (TA,) is the name of *The she-camel of El-Basoos* (ٱلْبَسُوس), (Ḳ,) or *the she-camel El-Basoos*, (A, TA,) for El-Basoos was her surname: (TA:) whence the saying أَشْأَمُ مِنْ سَرَابِ [*More inauspicious than Sarábi*]: (A, Ḳ, TA:) a celebrated prov.: for she was the cause of a famous war. (TA.)

سَرُوبٌ [*Wont to go away at random*]: see 1, near the beginning of the paragraph.

سَرِيبَةٌ *A sheep*, or *goat*, (شَاةٌ,) *which one drives back*, or *brings back, from the water, when the sheep*, or *goats, are satisfied with drinking, and which they follow*. (M, TA. [See also شَرِيبَةٌ.])

سَارِبٌ *Going forth*: and *going away*; as also ↓ سَرُوبٌ; the latter expl. by IAạr as *syn. with* ذَاهِبٌ and مَاضٍ: (M: [in one place in the TA the latter is erroneously written سروب:]) or *going away at random* into the country, or in the land. (Ṣ, Ḳ.) See also سَرْبٌ, first sentence. You say مَالٌ سَارِبٌ, (A,) and فَحْلٌ سَارِبٌ, (TA,) i. e. [*Camels, or cattle*, and *a stallion-camel*,] *repairing to the place of pasture*: (A, TA:) and ظَبْيَةٌ سَارِبٌ (M) or سَارِبَةٌ (TA) [*a she-gazelle*] *going away in her place of pasture*. (M, TA.) A poet says, (Ṣ, M,) namely, El-Akhnas Ibn-Shiháb Et-Teghlibee, (TA,)

وَكُلُّ أُنَاسٍ قَارَبُوا قَيْدَ فَحْلِهِمْ
وَنَحْنُ خَلَعْنَا قَيْدَهُ فَهْوَ سَارِبُ

[*And all* other *men have contracted the shackles of their stallion-camel; but we have pulled off his shackles, and he is going away whithersoever he will in his place of pasture*]: (Ṣ, M, TA: but in the last, حَلَلْنَا is put in the place of خَلَعْنَا: [in the Ḥam (p. 347) it begins thus: أَرَى كُلَّ قَوْمٍ:]) this, says Aṣ, is a prov.; meaning [other] men have abode in one place, not daring to remove to another, and have contracted the shackles of their stallion, that is, confined him, that he may not advance, and be followed by their [other] camels; fearing a hostile attack upon them: but we are people of might, wandering about the land, and going whithersoever we will; and we have pulled off the shackles of our stallion, that he may go whither he will; and whithersoever he hastes away to herbage produced by the rain, thither we follow him: (IB, TA:) or it may be that by the فحل he means the chief, whom, Abu-l-'Alà says, he likens to the stallion-camel. (Ḥam p. 347.) And hence the saying in the Ḳur [xiii. 11], مُسْتَخْفٍ بِٱللَّيْلِ وَسَارِبٌ بِٱلنَّهَارِ, (Ṣ, M, TA,) i. e. [*Hiding himself by night, and*] *appearing by day*: (Ṣ:) or *appearing by day in his way*, or *road*, or *in the roads*: or, as is related on the authority of Akh, *appearing by night, and hiding himself by day*; and Ḳṭr says the same of سارب. (TA.)

أُسْرُبٌ, (M, Ḳ,) and أُسْرُبٌّ, (M, Mṣb, Ḳ,) the former mentioned by Sh, (TA,) [the latter the more common,] a Pers. word, (M, TA,) arabicized, (Mṣb, TA,) originally أُسْرُبْ, (M,) [or أُسْرُبّ,] or أُسْرُفْ, (Mṣb, MF, TA,) [and in the TA سترب,] *i. q.* رَصَاصٌ [i. e. *Lead*], (M, Mṣb,) or آنُكٌ [which signifies the same, or *black lead*, or *tin*, or *pewter*]. (Ḳ.) — And the latter, The *fume of* [*molten*] *silver*. (M. [See 1, last sentence.])

مَسْرَبٌ *A way by which one goes*; [like سَرْبٌ and سُرْبَةٌ;] syn. مَذْهَبٌ: (Ḥar p. 448:) *a place in which the* مَال [i. e. *camels*, or *cattle*,] *go to pasture* (تَسْرُبُ); (Ḥam p. 99;) and ↓ مَسْرُبَةٌ signifies [the same, or] *a place of pasture*: (Ṣ, Ḳ:) pl. of the former مَسَارِبُ, (Ḥam ubi suprà,) and so of the latter. (Ṣ, Ḳ.) — And *A channel* of water. (A, and Ḥar ubi suprà.) [Hence,] one says, اِخْضَلَّتْ مَسَارِبُ عَيْنَيْهِ i. e. ‡ *The channels of the tears* [*of his eyes became moist so as to scatter drops*]. (A.)

مَسْرُبَةٌ : see the next preceding paragraph. — Also The *passage*, and *place of exit*, *of the dung*; (Mgh, Mṣb, TA;) in this sense with fet-ḥ (Mgh, Mṣb) only [i. e. to the ر]; or so and likewise ▼ مَسْرَبَةٌ : and both signify the *upper part of the anus.* (TA.) — See also the next following paragraph. — Also [*A sitting-place*] *like a* صُفَّة [q. v.], *before a* [*chamber such as is called*] غُرْفَة : not مشربة ; for this is a غُرْفَة [itself]. (TA.)

مَسْرُبَةٌ, (Ṣ, M, A, Mgh, Mṣb, Ḳ,) with ḍamm to the ر, (Ṣ, Mgh, Mṣb,) and ▼ مَسْرَبَةٌ, (M, Mṣb,) with fet-ḥ, (Mṣb,) i. e. to the ر, (TA,) and ▼ سُرْبَةٌ, (M, Ḳ,) The *narrow hair that extends from the breast to the navel:* (Ṣ:) or the *hair growing in the middle of the breast, extending to the belly:* (M, Ḳ:) or the *hair extending from the breast to the pubes:* (A, Mgh:) or the *hair of the breast, extending to the pubes:* (Mṣb:) and ▼ سُرْبٌ, also, signifies the *hair of the breast.* (TA.) [See an ex. in a verse cited voce جُلْمُ.] — The مَسَارِب of beasts are The *soft parts of their bellies:* (M, TA:) or the مسربة of any beast means the *upper parts, from the part next the neck to the root of the tail:* and the *soft parts of the belly*, and the *groins*, or *any similar parts.* (A 'Obeyd, TA.) — See also مَسْرَبَةٌ.

مَسْرُوبٌ : see 1, last sentence.

مُنْسَرِبٌ *Very tall;* (Ḳ, TA;) applied to a man: and *very long;* applied to hair. (TA.)

سربخ

Q. 1. سَرْبَخْتُ فِى ٱلْمَشْىِ, inf. n. سَرْبَخَةٌ, *I walked*, or *marched, an hour*, or *a while:* (JK:) [or *in the middle of the day:* and *gently*, or *in a leisurely manner:* for] — سَرْبَخَةٌ signifies The *walking*, or *marching, in the middle of the day.* (Ḳ.) And The *walking*, or *marching, gently*, or *in a leisurely manner.* (JK, Ḳ.) — And The *being light*, or *agile*, or *active; light in any work or action*, or *unsteady or lightwitted*, or *so on an occasion of anger*, or *hasty, with foolishness* or *ignorance;* syn. خِفَّةٌ and نَزَقٌ. (Ḳ.)

سَرْبَخٌ *A wide*, or *spacious, land:* (Ṣ, Ḳ:) or *one far extending:* (TA:) and *a land in which one cannot find his way.* (Ḳ,* TA.)

مَهْمَهٌ سَرْبَاخٌ *A desert*, or *waterless desert, wide*, or *spacious*, (Ḳ, TA,) *in the sides:* (TA:) and ▼ مَهْمَهٌ مُسَرْبَخٌ *a desert*, or *waterless desert, far extending*, (Ḳ,* TA,) *wide*, or *spacious:* so in a verse of Aboo-Duwád cited voce مُزْدَوِنٌ, q. v. (TA.)

مُسَرْبَخٌ : see what next precedes.

سربل

Q. 1. سَرْبَلَهُ, (Ṣ, Ḳ,) or سَرْبَلَهُ سِرْبَالًا, (M, Mṣb,) inf. n. سَرْبَلَةٌ, (KL,) *He clad him with a* سِرْبَال. (Ṣ, Mṣb, Ḳ.)

Q. 2. تَسَرْبَلَ, (Ṣ,) or تَسَرْبَلَ سِرْبَالًا (Mṣb) or بِسِرْبَالٍ, (M, Ḳ,) *He clad himself*, or *became clad, with a* سِرْبَال : (Ṣ, M, Mṣb, Ḳ:) and so تَسَرْبَنَ, in which, accord. to Yaḳoob, the ن is a substitute for the ل of the former. (M.)

سَرْبَلَةٌ *Broken*, or *crumbled, bread*, (ثَرِيدٌ, M, Ḳ,) or *a mess of broken*, or *crumbled, bread*, (ثَرِيدَةٌ, AA, TA,) *having*, (Ḳ,) or *moistened with*, (AA,) *grease*, or *dripping*, or *gravy*, (AA, Ḳ,) or *having much thereof.* (M.)

سِرْبَالٌ *A shirt:* (Ṣ, M, Mṣb, Ḳ:) and [so in the M, and in the Ḥam p. 65, but in the Mṣb and Ḳ "or"] *a coat of mail:* (M, Mṣb, Ḳ:) the former is the primary signification: (Ḥam p. 349:) or *anything that is worn:* (M, Ḳ:) pl. سَرَابِيلُ, (Mṣb, TA,) which occurs in the Ḳur xvi. 83 [in the first and also in the second of the senses mentioned above]: (TA:) and سِرْبَانٌ signifies the same as سِرْبَالٌ, the ن being, accord. to Yaḳoob, a substitute for the ل. (M.) — In the following words of a trad. of 'Othmán, لَا أَخْلَعُ سِرْبَالًا سَرْبَلَنِيهِ ٱللّٰهُ [*I will not pull off a garment with which God has invested me*], it is metonymically applied to the *office of Khaleefeh.* (TA.)

سربن

Q. 2. تَسَرْبَنَ : see تَسَرْبَلَ.

سِرْبَانٌ : see سِرْبَالٌ.

سرج

1. سَرَجَ, (O, Ḳ,) aor. ـُ, (Ḳ,) inf. n. سَرْجٌ, (TḲ,) † *He lied;* as also سَرِجَ, (O, Ḳ,) aor. ـَ; (Ḳ;) but the latter is outweighed [in authority]; (TA;) like سَدَجَ : (O:) and so ▼ سرّج : (TA:) and شَرَجَ. (O and Ḳ* in art. شرج.) You say, تَكَلَّمَ فُلَانٌ بِكَلِمَةٍ فَسَرَجَ عَلَيْهَا بِأُسْرُوجَةٍ ▼ † [*Such a one spoke a word, or sentence, and followed it with a lie*]. (O.) — And سَرَجَ ٱلْكَذِبَ, aor. ـُ, inf. n. سَرْجٌ, † *He forged the lie.* (TA.) [See also 2.] — سَرْجٌ, as an inf. n., signifies The *being bright*, or *shining.* (KL.) — [And hence,] سَرُجَ, (O, Ḳ,) aor. ـُ, (Ḳ,) inf. n. سُرُوجٌ, (TḲ,) said of one's face, † *It was*, or *became, beautiful:* (O:) or, said of a man, (TA,) ‡ *he was* or *became, beautiful in his face:* (Ḳ, TA:) but said by some, to be post-classical; and by some, to be strange. (TA.) — سَرَجَتْ شَعْرَهَا, (O, Ḳ, TA, but not in the CḲ,) and ▼ سرّجت, (Ḳ, TA, but not in the O,) [thought by SM to be a mistranscription for سَرَّحَتْ, with the unpointed ح,] *She* (a woman, O) *plaited her hair;* (O, Ḳ;) like سَجَرَتْهُ. (O.) — [سَرَجَ, aor. ـُ, expl. as signifying "*Ephippio instruxit instravitve* equum" by Golius and Freytag, by the latter as on the authority of the Ṣ and Ḳ, I do not find in either of those lexicons, nor in any other. The verb having this meaning is اسرج only.]

2. سَرَّجَهُ, (A, Ḳ,) inf. n. تَسْرِيجٌ, (Ḳ,) ‡ *He rendered it beautiful;* (A, Ḳ;) namely, a person's face; said of God: (A:) † *he adorned, ornamented, decorated*, or *embellished, it;* namely, a thing. (L.) The meaning given in the Ḳ [and A] has the authority of El-Beyhaḳee and IḲṭṭ and Es-Saraḳusṭee and IḲooṭ; but Aboo-'Abd-Allah Mohammad Ibn-Esh-Shádhilee thought it to be not of established authority as belonging to the ancient language. (TA.) [Hence,] one says, سَرِّجْ إِلَيْهِ أَمْرَكَ † *Embellish and elucidate thou to him thy affair*, or *case.* (Ḥam p. 326.) — And i. q. وَفَّقَهُ † [*He accommodated, adapted*, or *disposed, him, or it, to a right course*, or *issue*]. (TA.) — One says also, سرّج عَلَىَّ أُسْرُوجَةً ▼ ‡ [*He forged against me a lie*]. (A, TA.) And تسرّج ▼ عَلَىَّ ‡ *He lied*, or *lied purposely, against me.* (A, TA. [See also تسدّج.]) And إِنَّهُ يُسَرِّجُ ٱلْأَحَادِيثَ ‡ [*Verily he forges traditions*, or *stories*]. (A, TA.) — See also 1, first sentence. — سرّجت شَعْرَهَا : see 1.

4. أَسْرَجْتُ ٱلسِّرَاجَ, (O, Mṣb, TA) *I lighted the lamp*, or *wick.* (Mṣb, TA.) — [And اسرج signifies also *He lighted himself* or *another* with a lamp &c.; and so ▼ استسرج : or each of these, with بِهِ following it, *he employed it* (i. e. a lamp, or oil, &c.,) *as a means of light:* see اِصْطَبَحَ, in art. صبح.] — أَسْرَجْتُ ٱلدَّابَّةَ, (Ṣ, Ḳ,*) or ٱلْفَرَسَ, (Mṣb,) *I bound the saddle*, or *his saddle, upon the beast*, or *horse:* (Mṣb, Ḳ:) or *I made a saddle for the* [*beast*, or] *horse.* (Mṣb.)

5: see 2.

10: see 4.

Q. Q. 1. سَرْجَنَ ٱلْأَرْضَ *He manured the land with* سِرْجِين. (L in art. سرجن.)

سَرْجٌ *A certain appertenance of a horse* or similar beast, (Mṣb, Ḳ,*) *well known;* (Ṣ, Mṣb;) i. e., his رَحْل [or *saddle*]: (TA:) an Arabic word; or, accord. to the Shifá el-Ghaleel, arabicized from سرك [which is written by Freytag شرك, and said by him to be Pers., but I know not either of these two words in Pers. with an apposite meaning]: (TA:) dim. ▼ سُرَيْجٌ : (Mṣb:) and pl. سُرُوجٌ. (Mgh, Mṣb, TA.) [Hence,] مَالَ سَرْجُكَ † *Thy affair*, or *case, was*, or *has become, in a disordered*, or *an unsound, state:* a proverbial saying. (Ḥam p. 242.)

سَرْجَجٌ *Continuing*, or *lasting;* or *continuing*, or *lasting, long;* or, *for ever.* (O, Ḳ.)

سُرْجُوجٌ *Foolish*, or *stupid.* (O, Ḳ.)

سِرْجِينٌ i. q. زِبْلٌ [i. e. *dung of horses* or *other solid-hoofed animals*, or *fresh dung of camels, sheep and goats, wild oxen, and the like; used for manure*]: (Mṣb, and Ḳ in art. سرجن:) a foreign, or Pers., word, (Mṣb,) originally سَرْكِين, [meaning سَرْگِين,] (Mṣb, Ḳ) arabicized, (Mṣb, and Ṣ and Ḳ in art. سرجن,) by the conversion of the ك [or گ] into ج, and also into ق, so that one says also سِرْقِين [q. v.]: Aṣ is related to have said, I know not how to say it, and I only say رَوْثٌ : it is with kesr to the first letter in order to agree with Arabic words; fet-ḥ not being allowable, because there is no instance of the measure فَعْلِيل; though it is said in the M to be سِرْجِين and سَرْجِين: (Mṣb:) [the word being arabicized, all its letters should be regarded as radical; but] many assert the ن to be augmentative [and therefore mention the word, or the two words, in the present art., as does the author of the Mṣb]. (TA.)

سُرْجُوجَةٌ (Ṣ, O, Ḳ) and ▼ سِرْجِيجَةٌ (O, Ḳ) *Nature; or natural, native,* or *innate, disposition,* or *temper,* or *the like:* (Ṣ, O, Ḳ, TA:) and *a way, mode,* or *manner, of acting* or *conduct* or *the like.* (Ṣ, O, TA.) One says, هُمْ عَلَى سُرْجُوجَةٍ وَاحِدَةٍ *They are of one uniform nature* or *disposition.* (Aṣ, Ṣ, O.) And الكَرَمُ مِنْ سِرْجِيجَتِهِ and سُرْجُوجَتِهِ *Generosity is a quality of his nature* or *disposition.* (Lḥ, TA.) And إِنَّهُ لَكَرِيمُ السِّرْجِيجَةِ and السُّرْجُوجَةِ *Verily he is generous of nature* or *disposition.* (AZ, TA.)

سِرْجِيجَةٌ: see the next preceding paragraph.

سِرَاجٌ a word of well-known meaning; (Ṣ, O, Ḳ;) i. q. مِصْبَاحٌ [i. e. *A lamp,* or its *lighted wick,* (the latter of which meanings is assigned to both of these words by Jel in xxiv. 35,)] (L, Mṣb, TA) *that gives light by night:* (L, TA:) or, properly, *a lighted wick;* its employment to signify the *place thereof* [i. e. *a lamp,* generally *a vessel of glass having in its bottom a small glass tube into which the lower part of the wick is inserted,*] being a well-known tropical application: (MF, TA:) pl. سُرُجٌ. (O, Mṣb, TA.) [See also مِسْرَجَةٌ.] — [Hence,] the sun is called a سِرَاج [in the Ḳur lxxi. 15, and also xxv. 62, and lxxviii. 13], (Ṣ, O,) and السِّرَاجُ, (Ḳ,) and سِرَاجُ النَّهَارِ ‡ [*The lamp of day*]. (A, TA.) So too is the Prophet. (Ḳur xxxiii. 45.) 'Omar, also, is called in a trad. سِرَاجُ أَهْلِ الجَنَّةِ † [*The lamp of the people of Paradise*]. (TA.) And one says, الهُدَى سِرَاجُ المُؤْمِنِينَ ‡ [*The Ḳur-án is the lamp of the believers*], (A,) or سِرَاجُ المُؤْمِنِ [*the lamp of the believer*]. (TA.) — Also, metaphorically, ‡ The *eye;* because of its being often likened to a سِرَاج. (Ḥar p. 554.)

سُرَيْجٌ dim. of سَرْجٌ, q. v. (Mṣb.)

سِرَاجَةٌ The *craft,* or *occupation, of the* سَرَّاج [or *saddler*]. (O, Ḳ, TA.)

سُيُوفٌ سُرَيْجِيَّةٌ, (O, Ḳ,) or سُرَيْجِيَّاتٌ, (Aṣ, Ṣ,) *Certain swords so called in relation to a blacksmith named* سُرَيْج: (Aṣ, Ṣ, O, Ḳ:) or they may be so called because *having much water, and* [*glistening*] *wavy marks* or *streaks* or *grain.* (Ham p. 326.) [See also مُسَرَّجٌ.]

سَرَّاجٌ *A saddler;* i. e. *a maker of* سُرُوج [or *saddles*]: (O, Ḳ,* TA:) or *a seller thereof.* (TA.) — Also ‡ *A great,* or *habitual, liar,* (Ḳ, TA,) *who will not tell thee truly whence he comes, but will tell thee lyingly.* (TA.) One says, إِنَّهُ سَرَّاجٌ مَرَّاجٌ ‡ *Verily he is a lying person,* (A,) or *a great,* or *habitual, liar,* (TA,) *who adds,* or *exaggerates,* (يَزِيدُ,) *in his narration,* or *talk,* or *discourse.* (A, TA.) And it is used alone, [without مَرَّاج,] so that one says, رَجُلٌ سَرَّاجٌ ‡ [*A man who lies much,* or *habitually,* &c.]. (TA.) [See also سَدَّاجٌ.]

جَبِينٌ سَارِجٌ † [*A side of a forehead,* or *a forehead* itself,] *clear,* or *white,* [*and bright,*] *like the* سِرَاج [or *lamp*]. (Th, TA.)

سِيرَجٌ i. q. شَيْرَجٌ; (TA in the present art. and in art. شرج; [but in the present art., غير الشيرج is erroneously put for عَيْنُ الشَّيْرَجِ, meaning the same as الشيرج;]) but vulgar; (TA in art. شرج;) i. e. *Oil of sesame,* or *sesamum:* an arabicized word, from [the Pers.] شِيرَهْ. (TA in the present art.)

أُسْرُوجَةٌ ‡ *A lie.* (TA.) See 1 and 2.

مُسْرَجٌ, applied to a horse, (A,) or beast (دَابَّة), [or app., when applied to the latter, with ة,] *Saddled;* i. e. *having the* سَرْج *bound upon it.* (TA.)

مَسْرَجَةٌ, with fet-ḥ (Ṣ, Mgh, O, Mṣb) to the م and ر, (Mṣb,) [*A lamp;* i. e.] the *thing in which is the wick and the oil:* (Ṣ, Mgh, O, TA:) and also the *thing upon which the* سِرَاج [app. here meaning *lamp*] *is put:* (O:) or the *thing upon which the* ▼ مِسْرَجَة *is placed:* (Mṣb:) or ▼ مِسْرَجَةٌ, with kesr, has the last of these meanings: مَسْرَجَةٌ, with fet-ḥ, having the first thereof: or, as some say, the reverse is the case; (Mgh;) [i. e.] ▼ مِسْرَجَةٌ, with kesr, signifies the *thing in which is the wick* [*and the oil*]: and مَسْرَجَةٌ, with fet-ḥ, the *thing upon which that is put:* (A, TA:) the pl. (of either, Mgh) is مَسَارِجُ. (Mgh, Mṣb.) [See also سِرَاجٌ.]

مِسْرَجَةٌ: see the next preceding paragraph, in three places.

مُسَرَّجٌ ‡ A face *rendered beautiful* by God. (A.) — A nose *beautiful in thinness and evenness:* used in this sense by El-'Ajjáj; likened by him to the kind of sword called سُرَيْجِيّ. (Ṣ, O.)

سرجن

Q. 1. سَرْجَنَ: } see art. سرج.
سِرْجِين: }

سرح

1. سَرَحَ المَالُ, (TA,) or سَرَحَتِ المَاشِيَةُ, (Ṣ, TA,) or الإِبِلُ, (Mgh, Mṣb,) aor. ـَ, (Mṣb, TA,) inf. n. سُرُوحٌ (Ṣ, A, Mṣb, Ḳ) and سَرْحٌ, (Mgh, Mṣb, Ḳ,) *The cattle, or camels, pastured,* (Ṣ, Mgh, Mṣb, Ḳ, TA,) or *pastured where they pleased,* (Ṣ, Ḳ, TA,) *by themselves;* (Ṣ,* Mṣb, Ḳ,* TA;*) [or *in the morning;* for] you say, رَاحَتْ بِالعَشِيِّ and سَرَحَتْ بِالغَدَاةِ: (Ṣ:) or *pastured in the morning until the* ضُحًى [or *period of bright morning-sunshine*]. (AHeyth, TA.) — [Hence, app.,] هُوَ يَسْرَحُ فِى أَعْرَاضِ النَّاسِ [as though meaning *He feeds upon the reputations of men;*] i. e. ‡*he defames men;* or *defames men in their absence.* (A, TA.) — And سَرَحْتُ أَنَا, inf. n. سُرُوحٌ, *I went,* or *went away, in the morning.* (AHeyth, TA.) And أَسْرَحُ إِلَيْكَ *I go,* or *walk, to thee.* (Ḥar p. 44.) — And سَرَحَ السَّيْلُ, (A, TA,) aor. ـَ, inf. n. سَرْحٌ and سُرُوحٌ, (TA,) *The torrent ran,* or *flowed, easily:* (A, TA:) on the authority of Aboo-Sa'eed. (TA.) — And سَرِحَ البَوْلُ, (A, Ḳ,) aor. ـَ, inf. n. سَرَحٌ (Ḳ) and سُرُوحٌ, (TA,) *The urine had vent, poured out* or *forth, flowed,* or *streamed,* (A, Ḳ, TA,) after its having been suppressed. (A, TA.) = سَرَحَ المَاشِيَةَ, (AHeyth, Ṣ, A,* TA,) or الإِبِلَ, (Mgh, Mṣb,) aor. ـَ, (Mṣb,) inf. n. سَرْحٌ; (Ṣ, A, Mgh, Mṣb, TA;) and ▼ سَرَّحَهَا, (Mgh, Mṣb,) inf. n. تَسْرِيحٌ, (Mgh, Ḳ,) but the teshdeed in this verb denotes intensiveness, or muchness, or frequency, of the action, or its application to many objects; (Mṣb;) *He sent forth,* or *set free,* [or *drove,*] *the cattle,* or *camels, to pasture,* (Ṣ,* Mgh, Mṣb,* Ḳ,*) or *to pasture where they pleased,* (Ṣ, Ḳ, TA,) *by themselves:* (Ṣ,* Mṣb, Ḳ,* TA:) [or *he did so in the morning,* as is indicated in the Ṣ; i. e.] *he made them to go forth in the morning to the pasturage.* (AHeyth, TA.) You say, أَرَحْتُ المَاشِيَةَ and أَنْفَشْتُهَا and أَسَمْتُهَا and أَهْمَلْتُهَا and سَرَحْتُهَا; this last alone without ا. (Ṣ. [Yet Golius mentions the last also with ا, though without assigning any authority for it.]) And hence, in the Ḳur [xvi. 6], حِينَ تُرِيحُونَ وَحِينَ تَسْرَحُونَ [*When ye bring,* or *drive,* them *back in the evening, and when ye send,* or *drive,* them *forth in the morning*]. (AHeyth, Ṣ.) — [Hence also,] سَرَحَ, aor. ـَ, inf. n. سَرْحٌ; (Ḳ;) and ▼ سَرَّحَ, (Ṣ, A, L,) inf. n. تَسْرِيحٌ; (L;) *He sent* (Ṣ, L, Ḳ) a messenger to another person, (A, TA,) or such a one to such a place, (Ṣ, L,) or to accomplish some needful affair. (L.) — [And hence, app.,] سَرَحَهُ اللّٰهُ, and ▼ سَرَّحَهُ, ‡ *God disposed him* [to what was right or good], or *adapted him* [thereto]: mentioned by Az, on the authority of El-Iyádee, but as being strange. (TA.) One says, سَرَّحَكَ ▼ اللّٰهُ لِلْخَيْرِ ‡ *May God dispose thee,* or *adapt thee, to that which is good.* (A.) — And سَرَحَ, aor. ـَ, inf. n. سَرْحٌ, *He voided his excrement,* or *ordure;* or, *in a thin state;* [the objective complement being understood;] syn. سَلَحَ. (Ḳ.) — And سَرَحْتُ مَا فِى صَدْرِى, (Ḳ,* TA,) aor. ـَ, inf. n. سَرْحٌ, (Ḳ,) † *I manifested,* or *gave forth,* (أَخْرَجْتُ,) *what was in my bosom.* (Ḳ,* TA.) = سَرِحَ, aor. ـَ, *He set out easily in his affairs.* (Ḳ.)

2: see above, in four places. — تَسْرِيحٌ also signifies The *dismissing* a wife *by divorcement.* (Ṣ, Ḳ.) You say, سَرَّحَهَا *He dismissed her by divorcement:* (A, Mṣb:) from سَرَّحَ الإِبِلَ [expl. above]. (Mṣb.) And *He sent her forth from his abode;* (Bḍ in xxxiii. 48;) or *let her go free;* (Jel ibid.;) meaning one to whom he had not gone in. (Bḍ and Jel ibid.) [See also سَرَاحٌ, below; a subst. used as a quasi-inf. n. of this verb.] — [Also The *putting,* or *sending,* another *away, far away,* or *far off;* removing him *far away;* or *alienating,* or *estranging,* him: see Ḥar p. 44.] — And The act of *removing,* or *clearing away:* you say, سَرَّحَ عَنْهُ *He removed,* or *cleared away, from him* [grief or sorrow]; syn. فَرَّجَ. (L, TA.) — [And The *causing* water *to flow;* or *letting* it *flow.*] You say, سَرَّحُوا المَآءَ فِى الخَنْدَقِ [*They caused the water to flow,* or *let it flow, into the moat*]; from سَرَّحَ الإِبِلَ. (Mgh.) — And The *letting down, and loosing,* the hair, (Ṣ, Ḳ,) *before the combing:* (Ṣ:) or the *disentangling* the hair: or the *separating* it *with the comb:* or the *combing* it: (Mgh:) or the *combing down* the hair; and *disentangling* it *with the comb.* (Az, TA.) You say, سَرَّحَتْ شَعْرَهَا (A) or الشَّعْرَ, inf. n. as above, (Mṣb,) *She combed* [&c.] *her hair* (A) [or *the hair*]. — [And it is used also in relation to poetry, or verses.] You say also, سَرَّحَ الشَّاعِرُ الشِّعْرَ [app. meaning *The poet trimmed the poetry,* or *verses;* as seems to be indicated by the context; for it is mentioned by Z immediately after what here precedes it]. (A.) — And The act of *facilitating,* or *rendering easy.* (Ṣ, Ḳ.)

5. تسرّح *He* (a man) *went away,* and *went forth,* from a place. (TA.) — See also the next paragraph.

7. اِنْسِرَاحٌ The act of *running,* or *going along* [*quickly and easily*]. (ḲL.) You say of a she-camel, اِنْسَرَحَتْ فِى سَيْرِهَا *She was,* or *became, quick and easy in her pace.* (A.) — And انسرح *He lay upon his back, or lay as though thrown down or extended, and parted his legs.* (Ṣ.) — And *He was,* or *became, naked, bare,* or *without clothing.* (KL. [See also its part. n., مُنْسَرِحٌ.]) — And *It* (grief or sorrow) *became removed,* or *cleared away;* [syn. اِنْفَرَجَ;] as also ▼ تسرّح; quasi-pass. of سَرَّحَ signifying فَرَّجَ. (L, TA.)

سَرْحٌ *Cattle,* or *camels &c., pasturing,* (Ṣ, A, Mgh, Mṣb, Ḳ,) or *pasturing where they please, by themselves:* (Ṣ, A, Ḳ:) or only *such as are sent,* or *driven, forth* [*to pasture*] *in the morning, and brought,* or *driven, back in the evening to their nightly resting-place:* (L:) an inf. n. used as a subst. (Mgh, Mṣb.) A'Obeyd says that سَرْحٌ and ▼ سَارِحٌ and ▼ سَارِحَةٌ signify *Cattle,* or *camels &c.:* and Khálid Ibn-Jembeh says that ▼ سَارِحَةٌ means *camels* and *sheep* or *goats:* and *a single beast;* as well as *a collection* [*of beasts*]. (TA.) = Also *A certain kind of trees, of great size,* (Ṣ, Ḳ, TA,) *and tall,* (Ṣ, TA,) *not depastured,* or *seldom eaten by the camels &c., but used for their shade: they grow in Nejd, in plain,* or *soft, and in rugged ground, but not in sand nor upon a mountain; and have a yellow fruit:* (TA:) n. un. with ة: and it is said to be the *same as the* آء: (Ṣ:) but this is a mistake; the fact being that *it bears a kind of berry termed* آء, (Ḳ, TA,) *resembling the olive:* (TA:) or *any trees without thorns:* (Ḳ:) n. un. in this sense with ة: (Fr, Ḥam p. 603, TA:) or *any tall trees:* (Ḳ:) or [*trees*] *of the kind called* عِضَاه, *great, with spreading branches, beneath which men alight in the* صَيْف [*or summer*]: (Ḥam ubi suprà:) accord. to AḤn, the سَرْحَة is *a great tree with spreading branches, beneath which people often alight, widely extending; men alight beneath it in the* صَيْف [*or summer*], *and pitch tents,* or *build houses, beneath it; and its shade is good:* accord. to information given to Az by an Arab of the desert not known by him to have uttered a lie, *it has a dusty colour, is not so tall as the* أَثْل [a species of tamarisk], *has small leaves, and lank branches,* or *twigs, and always grows slanting, its inclination among all the trees being towards the south* (اليَمِين): Lth says that the سَرْح are *a kind of trees that have a fruit, and they are the* آلَآء [app. a mistranscription for الآء, i. e. the آء,]; but Az says that this is a mistake: Lth cites the saying of 'Antarah,

بَطَلٌ كَأَنَّ ثِيَابَهُ فِى سَرْحَةٍ • • تُحْذَى نِعَالَ السِّبْتِ لَيْسَ بِتَوْأَمِ

(L,) i. e. He is *a man of valour,* tall of stature, *as though his clothes were upon* a great tree such as is called سرحة; *sandals of* سبت [q. v.] *are cut and made* for him, such as are worn by the kings; and *he is not a twin;* so that he has been well suckled: (EM p. 245:) thus he describes this person as tall of stature, showing that the سرحة is a large tree: but the الآء [or آء] has no trunk nor tallness: IAạr says that the سَرْح are ذُكْوَان *that have become large;* and the ذكوان are certain trees having beautiful [shoots such as are termed] عَسَالِيج: the pl. is سِرَاحٌ. (L.) — The n. un., سَرْحَةٌ, is applied to signify ‡ A man's *wife,* (Ṣ, A,) by a metonymy. (Ṣ.) The Arabs are said by Az to term a woman, or wife, a سَرْحَة growing over water, because in this case it is in the most beautiful condition. (TA.) — [Accord. to Forskål, (Flora Aegypt. Arab. pp. cvi. and 68,) the name of سرح is applied to a plant of the class pentandria, which he terms *Cadaba farinosa,* (described by him in p. 68,) growing in the lower region of the mountains of Wádee-Surdud, in Tihámeh.] = Also The *exterior court* or *yard of a house,* (Ḳ,) or, as in the L, *of a gate,* or door. (TA.)

سَرْحٌ *Easy;* as also ▼ سَرِيحٌ. (L.) You say, وَلَدَتْهُ سَرْحًا *She brought him forth with ease.* (TA.) And تَخْرُجُ سَرْحًا *It passes forth easily and quickly:* occurring in a trad., describing a draught of water that satisfies thirst (شَرْبَةُ مَآءٍ). (TA.) And نَاقَةٌ سَرْحٌ and ▼ مُنْسَرِحَةٌ *A quick,* or *swift, she-camel;* (Ṣ;) as also ▼ سَرُوحٌ: (L:) or *a she-camel quick and easy in pace.* (A, MA, and Ḥar p. 481.) And فَرَسٌ سَرْحٌ and ▼ مُنْسَرِحٌ (Ḳ) and ▼ سِرْيَاحٌ, (TA,) or خَيْلٌ سَرْحٌ, (Ṣ,) *A horse,* or *horses, quick,* or *swift.* (Ṣ, Ḳ.) [See also سَرَاحٌ, and سُرَاحٌ.] And مِلَاطٌ سَرْحُ الجَنْبِ *A shoulder-blade,* (TA,) or *an upper arm-bone,* of a camel, (ISh, T, TA,) *quick to go and come* [or *move forwards and backwards*]. (Aṣ, Ṣ, TA.) And مِشْيَةٌ سَرْحٌ *An easy gait,* or *manner of going;* (Ṣ, Ḳ;) like سُجُحٌ. (TA.) And عَطَآءٌ سَرْحٌ † *A gift promptly given, without deferring:* (Ḳ:) or ‡ *a gift that is easy and quick;* a metaphorical phrase from نَاقَةٌ سَرْحٌ expl. above. (Ḥar p. 481.) = [See also سَرِيحَةٌ, of which, in two senses, it is a pl.]

سَرْحَةٌ *A single tree of the kind called* سَرْح [q. v.]. (Fr, Ṣ, TA.) = Also *A she-ass that has attained to maturity but has not become pregnant.* (O, Ḳ.) = And سَرْحَةُ, (O,) or السَّرْحَةُ, (Ḳ,) is the name of *A certain dog.* (O, Ḳ.)

سِرْحَانٌ, of the measure فِعْلَانٌ, the ن being an augmentative letter, (Sb, Ṣ,) from the verb سَرَحَ, (TA,) The *wolf;* (Ṣ, A, Mgh, Mṣb, Ḳ;) as also سِرْحَالٌ; (Yaḳoob, Ḳ;) fem. سِرْحَانَةٌ (Ks, Ṣ) and سِرْحَالَةٌ; (TA;) and the *lion,* (Ṣ, O, Mṣb, Ḳ,) in the dial. of Hudheyl: (Ṣ, O:) pl. سَرَاحِينُ (Ṣ, A, O, Mṣb, Ḳ) and سَرَاحٍ and سِرَاحٌ, (O, L, Ḳ,) but the last not remembered to have been heard by Az. (L.) It is said in a prov.,

سَقَطَ العَشَآءُ بِهِ عَلَى سِرْحَانٍ •

[*The evening-meal,* or *supper,* (i. e. the seeking for it,) *made him to fall,* or *light, upon a wolf*]: (Ṣ, Meyd:) accord. to A'Obeyd, it originated from a man's going forth to seek the evening-meal, and falling upon a wolf, which devoured him: accord. to Aṣ, from the like accident to a beast: accord. to IAạr, from a man's being slain by another man, named سِرْحَان: it is applied to the seeking an object of want that leads one to destruction. (Meyd. [See Freytag's Arab. Prov. i. 599: but the name there written "Hasahah" is هَزْلَة; accord. to Meyd, the father, but accord. to the O, the brother, of Sirḥán.]) — Hence, (Mgh, Mṣb,) i. e. from السِّرْحَان as meaning "the wolf," or, as some say, "the lion," (TA,) ذَنَبُ السِّرْحَانِ *The false dawn;* (Mgh, O, Ḳ, TA;) i. e. *the first* [*dawn*]. (TA. [A term nearly agreeing with the Greek λυκοφως.]) — السِّرْحَانُ, (O, Ḳ,) or سِرْحَانُ, (TA,) is also the name of *A certain dog:* and of *a certain horse:* and of *another horse.* (O, Ḳ.) = Also The *middle* of a watering-trough or tank: (O, Ḳ:) pl. as above. (Ḳ.)

سَرَاحٌ a subst. from تَسْرِيحُ المَرْأَةِ; (Ṣ, Mṣb, Ḳ;) [i. e., a subst.] signifying The *dismissal* of a wife *by divorcement:* (Bḍ in xxxiii. 28 [where it is used as a quasi-inf. n., as it is also in verse 48 of the same chap.]:) like طَلَاقٌ and فِرَاقٌ, it signifies *divorcement* explicitly. (L.) — [And *Dismissal* in a general sense. Hence,] it is said in a prov., السَّرَاحُ مِنَ النَّجَاحِ ‡ [i. e. *Dismissal is a part of the accomplishment of one's want*]; (Ṣ, A, L;) meaning, when thou canst not accomplish a man's want, make him to despair; for thy doing so will be in his estimation an act that will stand him in lieu of thy helping him to accomplish it: (Ṣ, L: [in some copies of the former, for فَأَيْئِسْهُ, we find فَآيِسْهُ:]) or it is applied to a man who does not desire to accomplish the want [of another]; and means, it behooves thee to make him to despair if thou accomplish not his want. (Meyd. [See a similar prov. voce سُرَاحٌ.]) — Also *Haste,* expedition, or promptness. (TA.) — And † Ease: so in the saying, اِفْعَلْ ذٰلِكَ فِى سَرَاحٍ وَرَوَاحٍ (TA) i. e. ‡ Do thou that in a state of ease (Ṣ and A and Ḳ in art. روح) and rest. (A in that art.) — سَرَاحِ [indecl.] like قَطَامِ, [app. as meaning The quick, or quick and easy in pace, like السُّرُحُ,] the name of a certain horse. (Ḳ.)

سُرُحٌ: see سَرُوحٌ.

سَرِيحٌ: see سُرُحٌ. — أَمْرٌ سَرِيحٌ An affair done quickly, expeditiously, or promptly; (TA;) in which is no deferring. (A.) You say also, لَا يَكُونُ ذٰلِكَ إِلَّا فِى سَرِيحٍ That will not be save with quickness, expedition, or promptness. (TA.) And اِنَّ خَيْرَكَ لَسَرِيحٌ and إِنَّ خَيْرَكَ لَفِى سَرِيحٍ Verily thy bounty is quick, expeditious, or prompt. (TA.) — فَرَسٌ سَرِيحٌ A horse without a saddle. (Ṣ, Ḳ.) — See also the next paragraph, in five places.

سَرِيحَةٌ A thong with which one sews soles or sandals or the like: (Ṣ, O, Ḳ:) pl. سَرَائِحُ (Ṣ, O, Ḳ*) and سُرُحٌ (TA) and [coll. gen. n.] ↓ سَرِيحٌ: (Ṣ, TA:) or, as some say, the thong wherewith is fastened, or tied, the خَدَمَة, which is a [thick plaited] thong that is fastened upon the pastern [of a camel, encircling it like a ring, for the attachment of a leathern shoe, or sandal]: (TA:) the pl. سُرُحٌ is also expl. as signifying the نِعَال [or leathern shoes, or sandals,] of camels: or, as some say, the thongs, or straps, of their نِعَال each thong, or strap, being called سَرِيحَةٌ: (L, TA:) Suh says, in the R, that ↓ سَرِيحٌ signifies a kind of thing like the نَعْل with which camels' feet are clad. (TA.) The سَرَائِح of an arrow are The sinews that are wound around it; sing. سَرِيحَةٌ: and also certain marks upon it, like those of fire. (TA.) — Also A piece of a garment (Ḳ, TA) that has been much torn: (TA:) pl. سَرَائِحُ (Ḳ, TA) and [coll. gen. n.] ↓ سَرِيحٌ. (TA.) — And A conspicuous elongated strip of ground, (O, Ḳ,) even, (O,) narrow, and having more trees, or shrubs, (O, Ḳ,) or, as Az says, having more plants, or herbage, and trees, or shrubs, (TA,) than what is around it, (O, Ḳ, TA,) and rising above what surrounds it; (TA;) so that one sees it to be oblong, abounding with trees, or shrubs, what is around it having few trees, or shrubs: and sometimes it is what is termed عَقَبَةٌ [app. as meaning a long mountain lying across the way, and over which one passes]: (O, TA:) pl. سَرَائِحُ (O, Ḳ,* TA) and [coll. gen. n.] ↓ سَرِيحٌ. (TA.) — And An oblong, or enlongated, tract of blood, (Ḳ, TA,) when flowing: (TA:) pl. سَرَائِحُ (Ḳ,* TA) and [coll. gen. n.] ↓ سَرِيحٌ. (TA.)

سِرْيَاحٌ: see سُرُحٌ. — Also Tall; (Ṣ, Ḳ;) as an epithet applied to a man. (TA.) — And Locusts, or the locust. (Ṣ, O, Ḳ, TA. [In the CḲ, and in my MS. copy of the Ḳ, الجَوَادُ is erroneously put for الجَرَادُ.]) And أُمُّ سِرْيَاحٍ The female locust: (Aboo-'Amr Ez-Záhid, IB:) and the name of A certain woman, (Ṣ, Ḳ,) in one instance only. (Aboo-'Amr Ez-Záhid, IB.) — السِّرْيَاحُ, (Ḳ,) or سِرْيَاحٌ, (O,) is the name of A certain dog. (O, Ḳ.)

سُرَّاحٌ [probably meaning Quick, or quick and easy in pace, like سُرُحٌ,] the name of a horse of El-Mohallak Ibn-Hantam. (O, Ḳ.)

سَارِحٌ and سَارِحَةٌ: see سَرْحٌ, second sentence, in three places. مَا لَهُ سَارِحَةٌ وَلَا رَائِحَةٌ [lit. He has not any camels, &c., that go away to pasture, nor any that return from pasture,] means † he has not anything: (Ṣ, TA:) and sometimes it means † he has not any people, or party. (Lḥ, TA.) — سَيْلٌ سَارِحٌ A torrent running, or flowing, easily. (Aboo-Sa'eed, A, TA.) — سَارِحٌ is also used as a subst., signifying A pastor who sends forth, or sets free, camels, or cattle, to pasture, or to pasture where they please, by themselves, or who sends them forth in the morning to the pasturage: and a people, or party, having camels, or cattle, pasturing, or pasturing where they please, by themselves, or sent forth in the morning to the pasturage. (TA.)

مَسْرَحٌ A place of pasturage: (Ḳ:) or a place into which beasts are sent forth, or sent forth in the morning, to pasture: (O:) pl. مَسَارِحُ. (TA.) لَهُ إِبِلٌ قَلِيلَاتُ المَسَارِحِ occurs in a trad., of Umm-Zara, meaning [He has camels whose places of pasturage are few; i. e.] his camels do not go forth into distant pasturages, but lie down in his outer court, or yard, in order that they may be near by to supply the guests with their milk and their flesh. (TA.)

مِسْرَحٌ A comb. (O, Ḳ.) — And [the dual] مِسْرَحَانِ Two wooden things, or two pieces of wood, [composing a yoke,] that are bound upon the neck of the bull with which one ploughs. (AḤn, TA.)

مِسْرَحَةٌ An instrument with which hair and flax or the like are separated and combed. (TA.)

مَسْرُوحٌ The سَرَاب [or mirage]: (Ḳ: [in some copies of which, الشَّرَابُ is put in the place of السَّرَابُ:]) mentioned on the authority of Th; but he was not sure of its correctness: (TA:) a dial. var. of مَشْرُوحٌ in this sense. (TA in art. شرح.)

مُنْسَرِحٌ; and its fem., with ة: see سُرُحٌ, in two places. — Also the former, (Ḳ, TA,) applied to a man, (TA,) Lying upon his back, or lying as though thrown down or extended, and parting his legs. (Ḳ, TA.) — And Denuded, or divested, of his clothes; or making himself to be so: or having few clothes; lightly clad: (TA:) or coming, or going, forth from his clothes; (Ṣ, O, Ḳ;) or so هُوَ مُنْسَرِحٌ مِنْ ثِيَابِهِ. (A.) [Hence,] one says, مُنْسَرِحٌ مِنْ أَثْوَابِ الكَرَمِ ‡ He is divested, or divesting himself, of the apparel of generosity. (A.) — And [applied to a camel as meaning] Divested of his وَبَر [i. e. fur, or soft hair]. (TA.) — المُنْسَرِحُ is also the name of A kind of verse; (Ṣ, O, Ḳ;) [namely, the tenth;] the [full] measure of which is

مُسْتَفْعِلُنْ مَفْعُولَاتُ مُسْتَفْعِلُنْ *

twice. (O.)

سرحب

سُرْحُوبٌ, applied to a mare, Long-bodied; (Ṣ, Ḳ;*) [said to be] applied only to a female: (Ṣ:) or, as some say, a mare that moves the fore legs quickly in running: and a horse of generous race, or excellent, and light, or active: said by Az to be mostly applied to the horse-kind, but restricted by some to the female. (TA.) And A she-camel swift, and long [in the body]. (TA.) It is also applied to a man, (Ḳ,) meaning Tall, and beautiful in body: and with ة, to a woman: but not known to the Kilábees as applied to a human being. (TA.) — السُّرْحُوبُ The jackal; syn. اِبْنُ آوَى. (Ḳ.) — And A certain blind devil, dwelling in the sea. (Ḳ.) — سُرْحُوبْ سُرْحُوبْ, (Ḳ, TA,) with the ب quiescent, (TA,) [in the CḲ with بُ,] A cry by which the ewe is called on the occasion of milking. (Ḳ.)

سرحل

سِرْحَالٌ; fem with ة: see سِرْحَانٌ, in art. سرح.

سرد

1. سَرَدَ, aor. ـُ, inf. n. سَرْدٌ, He carried on a thing, or put it forward from one stage to another, in regular order, consecutively, or one part immediately after another, uninterruptedly; he made it consecutive, successive, or uninterrupted, in its progressions, or gradations, or the like: (M, L:) [and so ↓ سرّد, inf. n. تَسْرِيدٌ; or this may have an intensive signification.] — You say, سَرَدَ الدِّرْعَ, (A,) [aor. and] inf. n. as above, (Ṣ, Ḳ,) He fabricated the coat of mail (Ṣ, A, Ḳ) by inserting the rings one into another: (Ṣ, A:) [and so (as appears from an explanation of its pass. part. n.) ↓ سرّدها; or this may have an intensive signification:] and زَرَدَهَا signifies the same. (Ḳ in art. زرد.) [See also سَرْدٌ below.] — And سَرَدَ الشَّىْءَ, (M,) inf. n. as above; (M, Ḳ;) and ↓ سرّده, (M,) inf. n. تَسْرِيدٌ; (Ḳ;) and ↓ اسرده, (M,) inf. n. إِسْرَادٌ; (TA;) He perforated the thing [as one does in fabricating a coat of mail, (see, again, سَرْدٌ, below,) and in sewing leather]: (M, Ḳ:) some say that سَرْدٌ signifies the act of perforating. (Ṣ.) — And سَرَدَ النَّعْلَ وَغَيْرَهَا, [inf. n. as above and سِرَادٌ,] He sewed the sandal &c.; (A;) [as also ↓ سرّد, for] سَرْدٌ (Ṣ, Ḳ) and سِرَادٌ (Ḳ) and ↓ تَسْرِيدٌ (Ṣ, Ḳ) signify the sewing of leather. (Ṣ, Ḳ.) — And سَرَدَ خُفَّ البَعِيرِ, inf. n. سَرْدٌ, i. q. خَصَفَهُ بِالقِدِّ [app. meaning He covered the camel's foot with thongs interwoven]. (M.) — And سَرَدَ الحَدِيثَ (M, A, Mṣb) وَنَحْوَهُ, (M,) aor. ـُ, (Ṣ, M, Mṣb,) inf. n. سَرْدٌ; (Ṣ, M, Mṣb, Ḳ;) and ↓ سرّده; (TA;) ‡ He carried on, or continued, uninterruptedly, (Ṣ,* M, A, Mṣb, Ḳ,*) and well, (Ṣ, Ḳ,) the narrative, or tradition, or discourse, (Ṣ, M, A, Mṣb, Ḳ,) and the like; (M;) and in

like manner, القِرَآءَةَ *the recitation*, or *reading:* (A:) from سَرَدَ الدِّرْعَ and النِّعَالَ [or النَّعْلَ, expl. above]: (Ḥar p. 307:) and سَرَدَ القُرْآنَ *He carried on, or continued, uninterruptedly and with rapidity the recitation, or reading, of the Ḳur-án.* (M, L.) And سَرَدَ الصَّوْمَ (Ṣ, Ḳ*) or الصِّيَامَ, (TA,) and صَوْمَهُ, aor. ُ, inf. n. سَرْدٌ, (Ḳ,) † *He continued uninterruptedly the fast,* (Ṣ, Ḳ,) and *his fast.* (Ḳ. [See also what next follows.]) ═ سَرِدَ, aor. َ, (Ḳ,) inf. n. سَرَدٌ, (TḲ,) *He* (a man, TA) *fasted uninterruptedly.* (Ḳ.)

2: see the preceding paragraph, in six places.

4: see 1. ═ اسرد النَّخْلُ *The palm-trees had hard green dates, which are termed* سَرَادٌ. (Ḳ.)

5. تسرّد الدُّرُّ ‡ *The pearls,* or *large pearls, followed one another,* or *did so uninterruptedly, upon the string.* (A.) And تسرّد دَمْعُهُ كَمَا يَتَسَرَّدُ اللُّؤْلُؤُ ‡ *His tears followed one another,* or *did so uninterruptedly, like as do pearls.* (A.) And تسرّد الحَدِيثُ, and, القِرَآءَةُ, ‡ *The narrative,* or *tradition,* and *the recitation,* or *reading, was carried on,* or *continued, uninterruptedly* [*and well:* see 1]. (A.)

Q. Q. 3. اِسْرَنْدَاهُ, (Ṣ, M, Ḳ,) inf. n. اِسْرِنْدَآءٌ, (Ṣ,) *It* (a thing, M) *prevailed against him,* or *overcame him;* (Ṣ,* M, Ḳ;*) like اِغْرَنْدَاهُ: (Ṣ,* Ḳ:) these two are said to be the only verbs of this measure: (TA:) [but several others should be added; as اِعْلَنْدَى and اِكْلَنْدَى and اِغْلَنْتَى:] the ى in اسرندى [and the like] is to render it quasi-coordinate to [quadriliteral-radical verbs of the measure] اِفْعَنْلَلَ. (Ṣ.) A rájiz says,

قَدْ جَعَلَ النُّعَاسُ يَغْرَنْدِينِى •
أَطْرُدُهُ عَنِّى وَيَسْرَنْدِينِى •

[*Drowsiness was beginning to prevail against me; I driving it from me, and it overcoming me*]. (Ṣ, M; but in the latter, with أَدْفَعُهُ in the place of أَطْرُدُهُ.)

سَرْدٌ inf. n. of 1 [q. v.]. (Ṣ, M, &c.) [Hence,] وَقَدِّرْ فِى السَّرْدِ, in the Ḳur xxxiv. 10, means *And do thou make a due adaptation* of the rings *in the fabrication* of the coats of mail: (Bḍ, Jel:) or *and do thou properly adapt* the nails, or pins, and the holes of the rings, [*in the fabrication,*] not making the former thick and the latter small, nor the reverse: (M, Bḍ,* L:) or السَّرْدُ means السَّمْرُ [i. e. *the nailing,* or *the making firm,* or *fast, with nails*], (Zj, M, L,) in this instance. (Zj, L.) ═ Also † *Coats of mail;* (Ṣ, M, L, Ḳ;) a gen. n. in this sense: (Ṣ, Ḳ:) [and *a single coat of mail;* like زَرْدٌ and زَرَدٌ:] and ‡ *any other* حَلَق [properly signifying *rings,* but here meaning *mail*]; (Ṣ, A, Ḳ;) [i. e.] it signifies also the *like of coats of mail, made of* حَلَق: (M, L:) [said to be] so called because the two extremities of each ring are perforated by the nail, or pin; and these rings are [termed] ▼ المَسْرُودُ: (L:) [if so, the word is an inf. n. used in the sense of a pass. part. n.,] see مَسْرُودٌ, [and then as a subst.; and, being originally an inf. n., it is used alike as sing. and pl.; or, as Z says,] it is an inf. n. used as a subst.: (A:) or السَّرْدُ, as some say, means السَّمْرُ, [as mentioned above,] and ▼ السَّرَدُ means الحَلَقُ [like الزَّرَدُ]. (M.) ═ Also ‡ *Consecutive,* or *following one another:* so in the phrase نُجُومٌ سَرْدٌ ‡ [*Stars that are consecutive:* the epithet retaining the masc. sing. form, though applied to a pl. subst., because originally an inf. n.; like عَدْلٌ in the phrase رِجَالٌ عَدْلٌ]. (A.) So too as an epithet applied to three of the sacred months, in the saying, ثَلَاثَةٌ سَرْدٌ وَوَاحِدٌ فَرْدٌ [*Three are consecutive and one is separate*]: (A:) thus an Arab of the desert answered when asked if he knew the sacred months: (Ṣ, M, Mṣb:) the سرد are Dhu-l-Ḳaadeh and Dhu-l-Ḥijjeh and El-Moḥarram, and the فرد is Rejeb. (Ṣ, M.)

سَرَدٌ: see السَّرْدُ in the next preceding paragraph.

سَرَادٌ *Hard green dates:* (Ḳ:) and *dates that are injured by want of water,* (Ḳ, TA,) *and consequently dry up before ripening:* (TA:) or *unripe dates that drop before attaining to maturity, while green:* n. un. with ة: (AḤn, M, TA:) or the latter signifies *a date that becomes sweet before it becomes coloured, being such as is termed a* بَلَحَة. (M, TA.) [See بُسْرٌ.] ═ See also مِسْرَدٌ. ═ [سَرَادٌ and سُرُودٌ said by Golius, and by Freytag after him, to signify the same as the "Pers. رَمِيدَن *Pavidum fugacemque esse,*" as on the authority of the KL, are mistranscriptions for شَرَادٌ and شُرُودٌ, which I find thus expl. in the KL.]

سِرَادٌ: see مِسْرَدٌ.

سَرِيدٌ: see مِسْرَدٌ in two places.

سِرَادَةٌ The *art of fabricating coats of mail;* as also زِرَادَةٌ. (TA in art. زرد.)

سَرَّادٌ *A fabricator of coats of mail;* (TA in art. زرد;) i. q. زَرَّادٌ. (M and TA in art. زرد.) — And *A sewer of leather;* (TA;) as also ▼ سَارِدٌ. (AA, L, TA.)

سَرْمَدٌ: and سَرْمَدِيٌّ: see art. سرمد.

سَرَنْدَى *Strong:* (Ṣ, M, Ḳ:) or *bold, daring, brave,* or *courageous:* (M:) and *quick in his affairs:* (Ḳ:) or a man *who goes on,* or *advances, boldly;* derived from السَّرْدُ: (Sb, TA:) [accord. to Sb, therefore, this is its proper art.; but accord. to the Ḳ, its proper art. is سرند, in which F mentions it again: it is perfectly decl., i. e., with tenween, for] the fem. is سَرَنْدَاةٌ. (Ṣ, TA.) — Also A sword *that penetrates the thing that it strikes.* (L.)

سَارِدٌ: see سَرَّادٌ.

مَسْرُودٌ: see السَّرْدُ.

مِسْرَدٌ (Ṣ, M, A, L, Mṣb) and ▼ سِرَادٌ (Ṣ, M, A, L) *An instrument for perforating:* (M, L, Mṣb:) and, (M,) or as some say, (Mṣb,) *an instrument with which leather is sewed;* (Ṣ;) syn. مِخْرَزٌ; (M, L, Mṣb;) or إِشْفًى; which is [said to be] the same thing as the مِخْرَز; (L;) as also ▼ سَرِيدٌ: (Ḳ:) or *an* [*instrument of the kind called*] إِشْفًى *that has a hole at its extremity;* (A;) and so ▼ سَرِيدٌ and ▼ سَرَادٌ. (TA: [but the last I think a mistake for سِرَاد.]) — [Hence,] one says, هُوَ ٱبْنُ أَمْ مِسْرَدٍ, (Ḳ,) or هُوَ ٱبْنُ أُمِّ مِسْرَدٍ, (A,) ‡ *He is the son of a female slave:* (A, Ḳ:) because she is a sewer of skins, or leather: (A:) an expression of vituperation. (Ḳ.) — [Hence, likewise,] مِسْرَدٌ also signifies ‡ The *tongue.* (M, A.) So in the saying, فُلَانٌ يَخْرِقُ الأَعْرَاضَ بِمِسْرَدِهِ ‡ [*Such a one wounds reputations with his tongue*]. (A.) ═ Also A sandal *having its* لِسَان [or *tongue,* i. e. the *thing projecting in its fore part,*] *faced with another piece sewed on.* (M, L.)

مَسْرَدٌ; and its fem., with ة: see the next paragraph, in three places.

خَرْزٌ مَسْرُودٌ and ▼ مُسَرَّدٌ [app. *A sewing* of leather or skin *carried on in regular and uninterrupted order*]. (Ṣ. [In one of my copies of the Ṣ, I find خَرَزٌ in the place of خَرْزٌ; and so in the L; but the latter appears from the context to be the right reading.]) — And likewise دِرْعٌ مَسْرُودٌ and ▼ مُسَرَّدَةٌ, (Ṣ,) or دِرْعٌ مَسْرُودَةٌ, and ▼ لَبُوسٌ مُسَرَّدٌ, [though دِرْع and لَبُوس are both generally fem.,] and ▼ لَأْمَةٌ سَرْدٌ, [in which the epithet retains the masc. form because originally an inf. n., like عَدْلٌ in the phrase اِمْرَأَةٌ عَدْلٌ,] *A coat of mail fabricated by inserting the rings one into another.* (A.) And مَسْرُودَةٌ signifies A coat of mail (دِرْع) *perforated* [in its rings]. (Ṣ.)

لُؤْلُؤٌ مُتَسَرِّدٌ ‡ *Pearls following one another,* or *doing so uninterruptedly.* (A.) And مَاشٍ مُتَسَرِّدٌ ‡ One *walking,* or *going, with consecutive,* or *uninterrupted, steps.* (A.)

مُسْرَنْدٍ [A thing] *that overcomes one.* (Ṣ.)

سرداب

سِرْدَابٌ, an arabicized word, (Ḳ,) from [the Pers.] سَرْد [i. e. "cold"] and آبْ ["water"], (TA,) *A subterranean structure, for the summer:* (El-Aḥmar, Ḳ:) or *a narrow place into which one enters:* (Mṣb:) [applied in the present day to *a cellar,* or *subterranean vault, in which anything is put to be kept cool:*] pl. سَرَادِبُ (Mṣb) [or سَرَادِيبُ].

السِّرْدَابِيَّةُ *A people of those who compose the extravagant zealots of the* [*sect called*] رَافِضَة [q. v.], *who expect El-Mahdee's coming forth from the* سِرْدَاب *that is in Rei, wherefore they bring a saddled and bridled horse every Friday, after the prayer* [*of the congregations at noon*], *saying,* "*O Imám: in the name of God:*" *three times.* (TA.)

سردق

[Q. 1. سَرْدَقَ, inf. n. سَرْدَقَةٌ, *He covered* a house *with an awning over its interior court,* as a protection from the heat of the sun: so accord. to Golius, as on the authority of the KL: and the same is indicated by the explanation of the pass. part. n. in the PṢ: but in the KL, I find only the inf. n. expl. by سَرَاپَرْدَهْ كَرْدَن: the verb may, however, be better expl. as signifying *he furnished with a* سُرَادِق, q. v.]

سُرَادِقٌ, said by El-Jawáleekee to be an arabicized word from [the Pers.] سَرَادَارْ or سَرَاطَاق, (MF,) *An awning extended over the interior court of a house:* (Ṣ, O, Mṣb, Ḳ:) [and the *cover of a tent:*] and *any tent of cotton:* (Ṣ, O, Ḳ, and mentioned in the Mṣb as on the authority of J:) or *a* [*tent of the kind called*] فُسْطَاط; (Bḍ in xviii. 28;) so says AO: (Mṣb:) also (Mṣb) *an enclosure around a* خَيْمَة [*or tent*], *consisting of pieces of cloth, without a roof:* (Mgh, Mṣb:) or *an enclosure* (حُجْرَة) *around a* فُسْطَاط: (Ksh and Bḍ ubi suprà:) or *what surrounds the* [*tent called*] خَيْمَة and *the* [*tent called*] قُبَّة: (Ḥam p. 772:) or *any wall or enclosure*, or [*tent such as is called*] مِضْرَب, or [*such as is called*] خِبَاء, *that surrounds a thing:* (IAth, TA:) pl. سُرَادِقَاتٌ: (Ṣ, O, Ḳ:) it has this pl., though it is masc., because it has no broken pl. (Sb, TA.) El-Kedhdháb El-Ḥirmázee says, not Ru-beh as in the "Book" of Sb [and in the Ṣ], addressing Ḥakam Ibn-El-Mundhir Ibn-El-Járood,

* سُرَادِقُ المَجْدِ عَلَيْكَ مَمْدُودْ *

† [*The canopy of glory is extended over thee*]. (O, TA.) — [Hence,] † *Dust rising; or spreading, or diffusing itself.* (Az, O, Ḳ.) — And † *Smoke rising high, and surrounding a thing.* (Az, O, Ḳ.) — In the Ḳur xviii. 28, it is applied to what will surround the unbelievers, of the fire of Hell, (Ksh, Bḍ,) as being likened to a فُسْطَاط, (Bḍ,) or to an enclosure around a فسطاط; or as meaning the *smoke* of the fire; or a *wall* thereof. (Ksh, Bḍ.)

بَيْتٌ مُسَرْدَقٌ (Lth, Ṣ, &c.) [*A house, or tent,*] *having a* سُرَادِق: (Ksh in xviii. 28, and PṢ:) or *having the whole of its upper part, and of its lower part,* مَشْدُود [accord. to the TḲ here meaning *curtained*, which seems to be the only apposite rendering, but I know not any authority for it], (Lth, JK, O, Ḳ, TA,) or مَسْدُود [i. e. *closed*, &c.]. (So in the CḲ.)

سرط

1. سَرِطَهُ, aor. ـَ, inf. n. سَرْطٌ (Ṣ, M, Mṣb, Ḳ) and سَرَطَانٌ; (M, Ḳ;) and سَرَطَهُ; (Ṣgh, Ḳ;) but the former is the more chaste, and is the form commonly known, and the latter is by some disallowed; (TA;) *He swallowed it:* (Ṣ, M, Mṣb, Ḳ:) or, as in some of the copies of the Ṣ, *without chewing:* or, accord. to the A, *by little and little:* (TA:) and ↓ استرطه signifies the same; (Ṣ, M, Mṣb, Ḳ;) and so ↓ تسرّطه: (Aṣ, Ḳ:) and in like manner, زَرِدَهُ and ازدرده (TA) [and تزرّده]. It is said in a prov., لَا تَكُنْ حُلْوًا فَتُسْتَرَطَ وَلَا مُرًّا فَتُعْقَى *Be not thou sweet, so that thou shouldest be swallowed; nor bitter, so that thou shouldest be put out of the mouth because of thy bitterness:* (Ṣ, TA:) or, accord. to one relation, فَتُعْقِى, i. e., *so that thou shouldest be disliked for being very bitter:* used in enjoining the taking of a middle course of conduct: so in the O. (TA.)

4. أَسْرَطْتُهُ ذِرَاعِى *I put my fore arm upon his throat* [*from behind him*], *to strangle him, or throttle him.* (TA in art. ذرع.)

5: see 1.

7. انسرط فِى حَلْقِهِ *It* (a thing, M) *passed easily in his throat.* (M, Ḳ.)

8: see 1.

Q. Q. 1. سَرْطَمَ: see art. سرطم.

سُرُطٌ A man *that swallows quickly;* (Ibn-'Abbád, O;) as also ↓ سُرَطَةٌ (Ibn-'Abbád, O) and ↓ سُرْطُوطٌ: (O:) or ↓ سُرَطْرِطٌ (so accord. to the TA) and ↓ مِسْرَطٌ and ↓ سَرَّاطٌ a man *that eats quickly:* (TA:) or the first, and ↓ سَرَطَانٌ and ↓ سِرْطِيطٌ, (M, Ḳ,) a man (M) *that swallows well,* (M,) or *largely.* (Ḳ.) [See also سُرَاطِىٌّ.] — Also, and ↓ سَرَطَانٌ, (M, Ḳ,) ‡ *A horse* (M, TA) *that runs vehemently.* (M,* Ḳ, TA.) [See again سُرَاطِىٌّ.]

سُرَطَةٌ: see the next preceding paragraph.

سِرْطِمٌ and سُرْطُمٌ: see سُرَاطِىٌّ, in three places. — Hence, (M,) the former also signifies † *An eloquent speaker;* (M, Ḳ;) as also ↓ سَرْطَانٌ. (TA.) [See also art. سرطم.]

سَرَطَانٌ: see سُرُطٌ, in two places: and سُرَيْطَى, and سِرْطِمٌ. — Also [*The crab;*] *a certain aquatic creature;* (Ṣ;) *a certain animal of the sea;* (Mṣb;) *a certain creeping thing* (دَابَّة), *of aquatic creatures;* (M;) *a certain fluvial creeping thing* (دابّة); and also *a marine kind, which is an animal that becomes hard like stone: the former kind is of much utility; the quantity of three* مَثَاقِيل *of its ashes, when burnt in a cooking-pot of copper* (نُحَاسٍ أَحْمَرَ) [for the latter of which words we find in the CḲ خُمَيْر]), *with water or wine, or with half its weight of gentian* (جِنْطِيَانَا), *is very good against the bite of the mad dog; if its eye be hung upon a person affected with a tertian fever, he is cured; and if its leg be hung upon a tree, its fruit falls spontaneously:* (Ḳ:) this is [said of] the سرطان that is bred in rivers: (TA:) *of the marine kind, what is burnt is an ingredient in collyriums,* (Ḳ,) *for removing whiteness,* (TA,) *and in dentifrices* (سُنُونَات, so in copies of the Ḳ and in the TA [but in the CḲ, erroneously, سُفُوفَات]), *and strengthens the gum:* (TA:) pl. سَرَطَانَاتٌ. (Mṣb.) — السَّرَطَانُ is also the name of † *A certain sign of the Zodiac;* (Ṣ, M, Ḳ;) [*Cancer;*] *the fourth sign;* so called because resembling the creature above mentioned in form. (TA.) — [*The disease called cancer;*] *a black-biliary tumour, which begins like an almond, and smaller, and when it becomes large, there appear upon it veins, red and green, resembling the legs of the* سَرَطَان: *there is no hope for its cure; and it is treated medicinally only in order that it may not increase:* (Ḳ:) *a certain disease that attacks men and beasts:* (M:) it is also (Ḳ) *a certain disease in the pastern of a beast, rendering it hard, or rigid, so that the animal inverts his hoof:* (Ṣ, Ḳ:) *a certain disease that appears in the legs of beasts:* (T, TA:) some say that it is *a disease which affects a man in his fauces, having relation to the blood, and resembling the* دُبَيْلَة [which is explained by ISh, in describing the disease termed ذَاتُ الجَنْبِ, as an ulcer that perforates the belly]: and some say, that it is [*the disease called*] دَآءُ الفِيلِ. (TA.)

سِرْطِيطٌ: see سُرُطٌ.

سُرَطْرِطٌ or سُرْطُوطٌ: see سُرُطٌ.

سِرِطْرَاطٌ (Lth, Lḥ, Ṣ, M, Ḳ) and سُرَطْرَاطٌ, (Lth, M, Ḳ,) the former said by Az to be a good form, like جِلِبَّابٌ and سِجِلَّاطٌ, but the latter to be the only instance of its form known to him, (TA,) and ↓ سُرَيْطٌ, like زُبَيْرٌ, (accord. to the Ḳ,) or ↓ سُرَّيْطٌ, (as in the M,) like قُبَّيْطٌ, (TA, [in which this is said to be the right form,]) [*The kind of sweet food called*] فَالُوذ, (Lḥ, Ṣ, M, Ḳ,) or فَالُوذَج; (as in some copies of the Ḳ and in the TA;) so called because very delicious to eat and swallow, from سَرْطٌ signifying the "act of swallowing;" (Az, TA;) of the dial. of Syria: (Lḥ, M:) or [*the kind of sweet food called*] خَبِيص. (M, Ḳ.)

سُرَاطٌ: see سُرَاطِىٌّ.

سِرَاطٌ *A road,* or *way:* (Mṣb:) or *a conspicuous road or way;* (M, Ḳ;) so called because he who goes away on it disappears like food that is swallowed; (Ḳ;) *i. q.* صِرَاطٌ, (Ṣ, M, Mṣb, Ḳ,) which is of the dial. of the early Ḳureysh, (Fr,) and is the more approved, on account of the mutual resemblance [of the ص and ط], (M, Ḳ,) though the former is the original; (M, Mṣb, Ḳ;) and زِرَاطٌ; for the saying that the pronunciation with the pure ز is a mistake, is [itself] a mistake: (Ḳ:) [ISd says,] Aṣ mentions the reading الزِّرَاطَ, with the pure ز; but this is a mistake; for he only heard the resemblance, and imagined it to be ز; and Aṣ was not a grammarian, that he should be trusted in this matter: (M:) this is [itself, however,] a mistake; for AA is related to have read الزِّرَاطَ, and the same is related of Ḥamzeh, by Ks. (TA.) One says also, هُوَ فِى دِينِهِ عَلَى سِرَاطٍ مُسْتَقِيمٍ ‡ [*He is, in respect of his religion, on, or in, a right way*]. (TA.) [It is fem. as well as masc.: see زُقَاقٌ.]

سِرْوَطٌ: see سُرَاطِىٌّ.

سُرَيْطٌ: see سِرِطْرَاطٌ: — and سُرَيْطَى.

سُرَيْطَى: see سُرَيْطَآءُ: — and سُرَّيْطَى.

سُرَاطِىٌّ *A great eater;* (Ḳ;) as also ↓ سِرْوَاطٌ

(Seer, M, Ḳ,) and ▼ سِرْطِرٌ: (Ḳ:) or one who swallows everything; as also ▼ سِرْوَاطٌ (M) and ▼ سِرْطِمٌ and ▼ سُرْطُمٌ; (Lḥ, M;) from الاِسْتِرَاطُ; the م, accord. to IJ, being augmentative; (M;) and so ▼ سُرْوُطٌ. (TA.) [See also سُرُطٌ.] — Also, (Ṣ, M, Ḳ,) and ▼ سُرَاطٌ, (M, Ḳ,) ‡ A sword that cuts (Ṣ, Ḳ, TA) much, or well; (Ḳ, TA;) that passes into the object that is struck with it; (M, TA;) that goes quickly into the flesh. (Ibn-Ḥabeeb, O, in explanation of the former word.) — سُرَاطِىُّ الجَرْىِ ‡ A horse that runs vehemently. (Ḳ, TA.) [See again سُرُطٌ.]

سُرَيْطَآءُ, (Jm, M, Ḳ, TA,) or ▼ سُرَيْطَى, (L,) A kind of soup, or food that is supped, (Jm, M, Ḳ, TA,) like خَزِيرَةٌ [q. v.]; (Jm, M, TA;) in the Ḳ, erroneously, like حَرِيرَةٌ: (TA:) or resembling خَزِيرَةٌ. (L in explanation of the latter word.) — See also سُرَيْطَى.

سِرْوَاطٌ: see سُرَاطِىٌّ, in two places.

سُرَاطٌ: see سُرُطٌ.

سُرَيْطٌ: see سِرِطْرَاطٌ: — and see also the paragraph here following.

سُرَيْطَى a word occurring in the following prov.: الأَخْذُ سُرَيْطَى وَالقَضَآءُ ضُرَيْطَى, (Ṣ, Ḳ,) or ▼ سُرَيْطَى and ضُرَيْطَى, (so in a copy of the M, without teshdeed,) and one says also ▼ سُرَّيْطَى and ضُرَّيْطَى, (O, Ḳ,) and ▼ سُرَيْطَآءُ and ضُرَيْطَآءُ, (O, Ḳ, TA, in the CḲ سُرَيْطا and ضُرَيْطا,) and ▼ سُرَيْطٌ and ضُرَيْطٌ, (Ḳ, and so in a copy of the Ṣ,) each like زُمَّيْرٌ, (TA,) or ▼ سُرَّيْطٌ and ضُرَّيْطٌ, (so in another copy of the Ṣ,) or both, (M,) [Taking, or receiving, is a swallowing, and paying is a making with the mouth a sound like that of the emission of wind from the anus; i. e.] one takes, or receives, a loan, or the like, (Ṣ, M, O, Ḳ,) and swallows it, (M, O, Ḳ,) and when payment is demanded of him he makes with his mouth a sound like that of the emission of wind from the anus: (Ṣ, M, O, Ḳ, TA:) meaning that taking, or receiving, is liked, and paying is disliked: (TA:) and ▼ الأَخْذُ سُرَّطَانٌ, (O, Ḳ,) or, as some relate it, سُلَّجَانٌ, (O,) وَالقَضَآءُ لَيَّانٌ. (O, Ḳ. [See 1 in art. سلج.])

سُرَّيْطَى: see the next preceding paragraph.

مَسْرَطٌ and ▼ مُسْتَرَطٌ The gullet: (M, Ḳ:) also written with ص. (M.)

مُسْتَرَطٌ: see what next precedes: — and see also سُرُطٌ.

سرطم

Q. 1. سَرْطَمَ He (a man) was, or became, silent. (Sh, TA in art. رطم.) — [From what follows, it would seem to signify also He was perspicuous in speech, or eloquent.]

سَرْطَمٌ Long, or tall; (Ṣ, Ḳ;) as also ▼ سِرْطِمٌ: (Ḳ:) in the latter sense, the former epithet is applied to a man; as also ▼ سُرْطُومٌ and ▼ سُرَاطِمٌ: (M:) and a poet (namely 'Adee Ibn-Zeyd, TA) uses the phrase سَرْطَمُ اللَّحْيَيْنِ [long in the two jaw-bones]. (Ṣ.) — And The gullet; because of its width. (M.) — And, as also ▼ سِرْطِمٌ, Wide in the fauces, quick in swallowing, (M, Ḳ,) or that swallows much, (TA,) with [largeness of] body and make: (M, Ḳ:) or that swallows everything: held by Kh to be of the triliteral-radical class; (M, TA;) and mentioned in art. سرط. (TA. [See سُرَاطِىٌّ.]) — And hence ▼ the latter, † An eloquent speaker: (M in art. سرط and in the present art., and Ḳ* in the former:) or perspicuous in speech; (M and Ḳ in the present art.;) as also سَرْطَمٌ. (Ḳ.) — سَرْطَمٌ is also expl. as meaning الذى يستوعب الزمام [which may be rendered That takes the whole of the nose-rein, or leading-rope; but the exact meaning must be determined from the context]; and so ▼ سَرْطَمَانٌ. (Freytag, from the Deewán of Jereer.)

سِرْطِمٌ: see سَرْطَمٌ, in three places.

سَرْطَمَانٌ: see سَرْطَمٌ, last sentence.

سُرْطُومٌ: } see سَرْطَمٌ, first sentence.
سُرَاطِمٌ: }

سرع

1. سَرُعَ, aor. ـُ, inf. n. سِرْعٌ (Ṣ, Mṣb, Ḳ) and سُرْعٌ (TA [and mentioned in the Ḳ, but app. as a simple subst.,]) and سِرَعٌ and سَرَعٌ and سَرَاعَةٌ (TA) and سُرْعَةٌ, (Ḳ,) or this last is a simple subst. from أَسْرَعَ, (Mṣb,) [but it is also generally used as syn. with the inf. ns. before mentioned when they are employed as simple substs., and is more common than any of them,] He, or it, was quick, expeditious, hasty, speedy, rapid, swift, or fleet: [in course, tendency, action, speech, &c.:] (Ṣ, Ḳ:) or, said of a man, i. q. أَسْرَعَ [which may mean as above, or he hastened, made haste, or sped,] in his speech and in his actions: (IAạr, TA:) but Sb makes a difference between سَرُعَ and أَسْرَعَ: see the latter below: (TA:) one says also سَرِعَ, aor. ـَ; a dial. var. of سَرُعَ: and ▼ تَسَرَّعَ, said of an affair, or event, signifies the same as سَرُعَ. (TA.) One says, السَّرَعَ السَّرَعَ الوَحَآءَ and like الوَحَآءَ, (Ṣ, Ḳ,) i. e. [Make thou] haste; or haste to be first, or before, or beforehand: haste; or haste to be first, &c. (Ṣ and TA in art. وحى.) And سَرُعَ مَا فَعَلْتَ ذَاكَ, (Ṣ,* TA,) and سَرْعَ, which is a contraction of the former; for the Arabs contract by the suppression of ḍammeh and kesreh because they are difficult of pronunciation, saying فَخْذٌ for فَخِذٌ and عَضْدٌ for عَضُدٌ, but one should not say حَجْرٌ for حَجَرٌ, (Ṣ, TA,) or the like, accord. to the Baṣrees, though the Koofees allow the contraction in the case of fet-ḥah also, as in سَلْفٌ for سَلَفٌ; (M in art. سلف;) and one says also سُرْعَ, as a contraction of سَرُعَ; all meaning سَرْعَانَ [i. e. Quick was thy doing that: or how quick was thy doing that! or, which is nearly the same, excellently quick was thy doing that; for سَرُعَ is similar to قَضُوَ and رَمُوَ, denoting excellence]. (TA.)

2: see 4.

3. مُسَارَعَةٌ signifies The hastening with another; or vying, or striving, with another, in hastening; or hastening to be, or get, before another or others; (Ṣ, Ḳ;) إِلَى شَىْءٍ to a thing; (Ṣ;) as also ▼ تَسَارُعٌ; syn. مُبَادَرَةٌ; (Ṣ, Ḳ;) with which, also, [not, however, as it is expl. above, but in the sense of بُدُورٌ, i. e. simply the hastening to a thing,] ▼ إِسْرَاعٌ is syn. (TA.) One says, سَارَعُوا إِلَى كَذَا and ▼ تَسَارَعُوا إِلَيْهِ, [They hastened, one with another, &c., to such a thing,] both signifying the same. (Ṣ.) And [of a single person,] سارع إِلَى الشَّىْءِ He hastened to the thing; syn. بَادَرَ. (Mṣb.) And it is said in the Ḳur [iii. 127], وَسَارِعُوا إِلَى مَغْفِرَةٍ مِنْ رَبِّكُمْ [And vie ye, one with another, in hastening to obtain forgiveness from your Lord]. (TA.) And again, [iii. 170,] الَّذِينَ يُسَارِعُونَ فِى الكُفْرِ Who fall into unbelief hastily, or quickly, (Bḍ, Jel,) and eagerly. (Bḍ.)

4. اسرع is originally trans.; (Ṣ, Ḳ;) [signifying He quickened, or hastened, himself, or his going, &c.;] and hence the saying, in a trad., إِذَا مَرَّ أَحَدُكُمْ بِطِرْبَالٍ مَائِلٍ فَلْيُسْرِعِ المَشْىَ [When any one of you passes by a high wall, or the like, that is inclining, let him quicken, or hasten, the pace, or going]. (Ḳ,* TA.) But [it is used also elliptically, as meaning He hastened, in an intrans. sense; he made haste; he sped; he went quickly; and hence] you say, اسرع فِى السَّيْرِ, (Ṣ, Ḳ,) like سَرُعَ [He was quick, expeditious, hasty, speedy, rapid, swift, or fleet, in going, journeying, or pace]: (Ḳ:) or [rather he hastened, made haste, or sped, therein; for] اسرع signifies he endeavoured, or sought, and affected, to be quick, &c., as though he hastened the pace, or going; but ▼ سَرُعَ denotes what is as it were an innate quality: (Sb:) the verb being originally trans., when you say of one اسرع فى السير it is as though [meaning] he urged himself forward with haste; or he quickened, or hastened, the pace, or going; and it is only because the meaning is understood by the persons addressing one another, that the objective complement is not expressed: (Lth, Ḳ:) or the verb may be trans. by means of a particle and without a particle: or when made immediately trans., the phrase may be meant to be understood as elliptical. (TA.) [Accord. to Fei,] اسرع فِى مَشْيِهِ, &c., inf. n. إِسْرَاعٌ, is originally اسرع مَشْيَهُ [He quickened, or hastened, his pace, or going]; فى being redundant; or اسرع الحَرَكَةَ فِى مَشْيِهِ [he quickened, or hastened, the motion in his going]: and اسرع إِلَيْهِ means اسرع المُضِىَّ إِلَيْهِ [he quickened, or hastened, the going to him]. (Mṣb.) ▼ سَرَّعَ is syn. with اسرع. (TA.) And you say, ▼ تَسَرَّعَ إِلَى الشَّرِّ, (Ṣ, Ḳ,) meaning He hastened, or made haste, to [do] evil, or mischief; (Ḳ;) as also تَزَرَّعَ. (Ṣgh and Ḳ in art. زرع.) And ▼ تَسَرَّعَ

بِالأَمْرِ *He hastened to do the thing, or affair;* syn. بَادَرَ بِهِ. (TA.) See also 3. —— اسرع إِلَيْهِ occurs in a trad. as meaning *He was quick, or hasty, in being angry with him, or in blaming him, or in reviling him.* (Mgh.) —— اسرع بِهِ: see [its contr.] بَطَّأَ بِهِ. —— أَسْرَعُوا signifies also, *Their beasts on which they rode were, or became, quick, swift, or fleet.* (AZ, Ṣ, Ḳ.) ═ مَا أَسْرَعَ مَا صَنَعْتَ هٰكَذَا [*How quick was thy doing that!*]. (Ṣ, Ḳ.)

5: see 1 and 4; the latter in two places.

6: see 3, in two places.

سَرْعٌ [originally an inf. n. of سَرُعَ, like سِرْعٌ and سَرَعٌ accord. to the TA]: see سَرِيعٌ, in two places.

سِرْعٌ: see [1 and] سُرْعَةٌ.

سَرِعٌ: see سَرِيعٌ.

سُرْعَةٌ *Quickness, expedition, haste, speed, rapidity, swiftness, or fleetness;* [of course, tendency, action, speech, &c.;] (Ṣ, Ḳ;) as also ▼سَرَعٌ; (Ḳ;) [the former said in the Ḳ, and the latter in the TA, to be an inf. n. of سَرُعَ:] and *a hastening, making haste, or speeding;* i. q. إِسْرَاعٌ [inf. n. of 4]; (TA;) or a subst. therefrom. (Mṣb.) You say, عَجِبْتُ مِنْ سُرْعَةِ ذٰلِكَ [*I wondered at the quickness, &c., of that*]. (Ṣ.)

سَرْعَانَ and سُرْعَانَ and سِرْعَانَ (Ṣ, Ḳ) and ▼سَرُعَانَ, the last with ḍamm to the ر, (IAạr,) occurring in the phrase سرعان ذَا خُرُوجًا, (IAạr, Ṣ, Ḳ,) meaning سَرُعَ ذَا خُرُوجًا [*Quick is this in coming forth:* or *how quick is this in coming forth!* or, which is nearly the same, *excellently quick* &c.], (Ṣ, Ḳ,) are dial. vars., changed from the original form, which is سَرُعَ, and, for this reason, (Ṣ,) made indecl., with the final vowel of سَرُعَ for their termination. (Ṣ, Ḳ.) The word سرعان is used as a simple enunciative [placed before its inchoative], and also as an enunciative denoting wonder: [see بُطْآنَ:] and hence the saying, (Ḳ,) سَرْعَانَ مَا صَنَعْتَ هٰكَذَا *How quick was thy doing that!* (Ṣ, Ḳ.) The saying سَرْعَانَ ذَا إِهَالَةً originated from the fact that a man had a lean ewe, her snivel running from her nostrils by reason of her leanness, and it being said to him "What is this?" he answered, "Her grease:" whereupon the asker said as above: the last word is in the accus. case as a denotative of state; and the meaning is, *Quick,* or *how quick, is this* snivel [coming forth] *in the state of melted grease!* or the last word is a specificative, under the supposition that the action is transferred [from its proper agent, which thus becomes a specificative], as in the phrase تَصَبَّبَ زَيْدٌ عَرَقًا; and the meaning to be understood is, *Quick,* or *how quick, is the melted grease of this!* the saying is applied to him who tells of a thing's coming to pass before its time: (O, Ḳ:) it is a prov. (TA.) ═ سَرْعَانُ; and its fem., سَرْعَى: see سَرِيعٌ, in two places: see also the paragraph here next following, in two places.

سَرَعَانٌ: سَرَعَانُ النَّاسِ, (Ṣ, Mgh, Mṣb, Ḳ,) and ▼سَرْعَانُ, (IAạr, Ḳ,) *The first,* or *foremost, of the men,* or *people,* (IAạr, Ṣ, Mgh, Mṣb, Ḳ,) *striving, one with another, to be the first to do a thing;* (Ḳ;) so says Aṣ, with reference to soldiers hastening: (TA:) the former word in this phrase is [distinguished from سَرْعَان in being] declinable in every case: (Ṣ:) in two trads. in which the phrase occurs, we find it differently related, سَرَعَان and سُرْعَان; the latter being pl. of سَرِيعٌ. (TA.) سَرَعَانُ الخَيْلِ, also, signifies *The first* or *foremost, of the horsemen,* and sometimes they said ▼سَرْعَانُ الخيل. (Ḳ.) Abu-l-'Abbás says that when سرعان is an epithet applied to men, it has both of the above-mentioned forms; but when applied to others, the former is the more chaste, though the latter is allowable. (TA.)

سُرْعَانٌ: see سَرَعَانٌ.

سُرَاعٌ; and its fem., with ة: see what next follows, in three places.

سَرِيعٌ *Quick, expeditious, hasty, speedy, rapid, swift,* or *fleet;* [in course, tendency, action, speech, &c.;] (Ṣ, Mṣb,* TA;) as also ▼سَرِعٌ [and ▼سَرْعٌ] and ▼سُرَاعٌ, of which the fem. is with ة, and ▼سَرْعَانُ, of which the fem. is سَرْعَى; (TA;) i. q. ▼مُسْرِعٌ, (Ḳ,) which signifies as above; (TA;) [and which also signifies *hastening, making haste,* or *speeding;*] and ▼مِسْرَعٌ, also, signifies *quick,* &c., (سَرِيع,) to [do] good or evil: (Ḳ:) the pl. of سريع is سُرْعَانٌ, (Ḳ,) and سِرَاعٌ is [also a pl. of the same,] syn. with مُسْرِعُونَ. (Mṣb.) You say, فَرَسٌ سَرِيعٌ and ▼سُرَاعٌ [*A quick, swift,* or *fleet, horse*]: (IB:) and ▼حِجْرٌ سُرَاعَةٌ meaning سَرِيعَةٌ [*a quick, swift,* or *fleet, mare*]. (Ḳ.) And ▼إِسْعَ عَلَى رِجْلِكَ السُّرْعَى [*Go thou quickly;* lit. *go thou,* or *walk thou,* or *run thou, upon thy quick,* or *swift, leg*]. (Fr.) And ▼جَآءَ سَرْعًا meaning سَرِيعًا [*He,* or *it, came quickly, hastily, speedily,* &c.]. (TA.) And God is said [in the Ḳur ii. 198, &c.] to be سَرِيعُ الحِسَابِ [*Quick in reckoning*], meaning that his reckoning will inevitably come to pass; or that one reckoning will not divert Him from another reckoning, nor one thing from another thing; or that his actions are quick, none of them being later than He desireth, because it is done without manual operation and without effort, so that He will reckon with mankind, after raising them from death and congregating them, in the twinkling of an eye, without numbering, or calculating: (Ḳ:) and [in like manner He is said in the same, chap. vi., last verse, to be] سَرِيعُ العِقَابِ [*quick in punishing*]. (El-Mufradát, B.) —— Also *A certain kind of going,* or *pace;* coupled with سُنْبُكٌ, which signifies another kind thereof. (Ibn-Ḥabeeb, TA.) —— السَّرِيعُ *The ninth metre* (بَحْر) *in prosody, in which each hemistich originally consisted of* مُسْتَفْعِلُنْ مُسْتَفْعِلُنْ مَفْعُولَاتُ.] —— And أَبُو سَرِيعٍ *The* [shrub called] عَرْفَج: or *the fire that is therein.* (Ḳ. [See زَحْفَةٌ.]) ═ Also *A shoot,* or *twig, that falls from the* بَشَام [or *tree of the balsam of Mekkeh*]: pl. سُرْعَانٌ and سِرْعَانٌ. (Ḳ.)

أَسْرَعُ [*More, and most, quick, expeditious, hasty, speedy, rapid, swift,* or *fleet,* of course, tendency, action, speech, &c.]. [It is said, of God, in the Ḳur vi. 62,] وَهُوَ أَسْرَعُ الحَاسِبِينَ [*And He is the quickest of the reckoners*]. (Ḳ.) [The fem.] سُرْعَى is applied to a she-camel by Ḥoneyf El-Ḥanátim [as meaning *Surpassingly quick* or *fleet*]. (IAạr, TA in art. سبى.)

مُسْرِعٌ: } see سَرِيعٌ.
مِسْرَعٌ: }

مِسْرَاعٌ *Very quick,* or *hasty,* (Ḳ, TA,) to [do] good or evil, (Ḳ,) or in affairs. (TA.)

سرف

1. سَرِفَ, aor. َ, inf. n. سَرَفٌ, *He was ignorant:* or *he was unmindful, negligent,* or *heedless.* (Mṣb.) [In these senses it is trans.: you say,] سَرِفَهُ, (Ṣ, M, Ḳ,) aor. َ, (Ḳ,) inf. n. سَرَفٌ, (Ṣ,* M, Ḳ,*) *He was unmindful, negligent,* or *heedless, of it;* (Ṣ, M, Ḳ;) namely, a thing: (Ṣ, M:) and *he was ignorant of it:* (Ṣ, Ḳ:) and *he missed it;* (Ṣ,* M, Ḳ;* [in the first and third of which, only the inf. n. of the verb in this sense is mentioned, and expl. as syn. with خَطَأ;]) syn. أَخْطَأَهُ. (M.) And طَلَبْتُهُمْ فَسَرِفْتُهُمْ *I sought them and missed them:* or *was ignorant of them.* (Mṣb.) And سَرِفَ القَوْمَ *He passed by the people,* or *party, and left them behind him.* (M.) Aṣ relates, of an Arab of the desert, with whom some companions of his made an appointment to meet him in a certain place of the mosque, and to whom he broke his promise, that, being asked respecting that, he said, مَرَرْتُ بِكُمْ فَسَرِفْتُكُمْ, meaning [*I passed by you and*] *I was unmindful of you.* (Ṣ.) And hence the saying of Jereer, (Ṣ, TA,) praising the Benoo-Umeiyeh, (TA,)

* أَعْطَوْا هُنَيْدَةَ يَحْدُوهَا ثَمَانِيَةٌ *
* مَا فِي عَطَائِهِمُ مَنٌّ وَلَا سَرَفُ *

meaning [*They gave a hundred camels, eight persons driving them,* or *urging them by singing to them: there was not in their gift reproach for a benefit conferred, nor*] *unmindfulness:* or the meaning is, *nor missing* (خَطَأ); that is, they did not miss the proper place of the gift by their giving it to such as did not deserve it and refusing it to the deserving. (Ṣ, TA.) You say also, سَرِفْتُ يَمِينَهُ *I was unacquainted with,* or *knew not, his oath.* (TA.) —— [سَرَفٌ is also, as expl. below, *syn. with* إِسْرَاف, but as a subst., having no verb properly belonging to it.] ═ سَرَفَتِ الشَّجَرَةَ, (ISk, Ṣ, Ḳ,) aor. ُ, inf. n. سَرْفٌ, (ISk, Ṣ,) said of the سُرْفَة [q. v.], *It ate the leaves of the tree:* (ISk, Ṣ, Ḳ:) and سَرَفَتِ الخَشَبَ is likewise said of the سُرْفَة [as meaning *it ate the wood*]. (Z, TA.) And سُرِفَتِ الشَّجَرَةُ, (ISk, Ṣ, M, TA,) inf. n. سَرْفٌ, (ISk,) *The tree had its leaves eaten by the* سُرْفَة: (Ṣ:) or *was smitten,* or *lighted on, by the* سُرْفَة: (ISk, M, TA:) and سُرِفَ الخَشَبُ [*the wood was eaten by the* سُرْفَة], the verb in this phrase being quasi-pass. of the verb in the phrase سَرَفَتِ السُّرْفَةُ الخَشَبَ, like as خَطِرَ and

صَعِقَ are quasi-passives of the verbs in the phrases صَعَقَتْهُ السَّمَآءُ and حَطَمَتْهُ السِّنُّ: (Z, TA:) and [hence] one says also, سُرِفَ الطَّعَامُ ‡ *The wheat, or food, was, or became, cankered, or eaten away;* as though smitten, or lighted on, by the سُرْفَة. (M, TA.) — [Hence also,] سُرِفَتْ أُذُنُ الشَّاةِ ‡ *The ear of the sheep, or goat, was entirely cut off.* (A, TA.) — And سَرِفَتْ وَلَدَهَا ‡ *She* (a mother) *injured her child by too much milk.* (A, Ḳ,* TA.)

4. اسرف, (Mṣb,) inf. n. إِسْرَافٌ, (M, Mṣb,) *He exceeded,* or *transgressed, the just,* or *right, bound,* or *limit,* or *measure; acted extravagantly, exorbitantly,* or *immoderately:* (M, Mṣb:) or إِسْرَافٌ signifies the *being extravagant in expenditure,* syn. تَبْذِيرٌ; (Ḳ;) or so إِسْرَافٌ فِى النَّفَقَةِ: (Ṣ, TA:) or, as some say, تبذير means the "exceeding in respect of the right objects of expenditure," which is ignorance of the [right] manner, and of things that should prevent it; and اسراف means the *exceeding with respect to quantity* [*in expenditure*], and is ignorance of the values of the right objects: (MF in art. بذر:) or the latter signifies the *expending otherwise than in obedience of God,* (Sufyán, Ḳ,* TA,) *whether little or much;* (TA;) as also ▼ سَرَفٌ: (M, TA:) it is also said to mean the *eating that which it is not lawful to eat;* and this is said to be meant in the Ḳur vi. 142 or vii. 29: and the *putting a thing in a wrong place* [as when one expends his money upon a wrong object]: and accord. to Iyás Ibn-Mo'áwiyeh, الإِسْرَافُ is *that* [*action*] *whereby one falls short of what is due to God.* (TA.) You say also, اسرف فِى مَالِهِ, meaning *He was hasty in respect of his property,* [i. e. *in expending it,*] *without pursuing the just course,* or *keeping within due bounds.* (M.) And اسرف فِى الكَلَامِ, and فِى القَتْلِ, *He exceeded the due bounds,* or *just limits, in speech,* and *in slaying.* (M.) الإِسْرَافُ فِى القَتْلِ, which is forbidden in the Ḳur xvii. 35, is said to mean *The slaying of another than the slayer of one's companion:* (Zj, M, Mgh:*) or *the slaying the slayer without the authority of the Sultán:* or *the not being content with slaying one, but slaying a number of persons, because of the high rank of the slain and the low condition of the slayer:* or *the slaying one higher in rank than the slayer:* (Zj, M:) or *the slaying two when the slayer is one:* or *the maiming* or *mutilating* [*before slaughter*]. (Mgh.) إِسْرَافٌ also signifies The *committing of many faults, offences,* or *crimes, and sins.* (TA.) And you say, أَكَلَهُ إِسْرَافًا (TA) and ▼ سَرَفًا, (M, TA,) meaning *He ate it hastily.* (M, TA.)

5. تسرّف *He sucked:* and *ate, gnawed,* or *devoured.* (KL. [App. from سُرْفَة, q. v. See also سُرِفَتِ الشَّجَرَةُ, &c., in the latter half of the first paragraph.])

سَرَفٌ inf. n. of سَرِفَ [q. v.]. (Ṣ,* M, Mṣb, Ḳ.*) — And also a subst. from أَسْرَفَ; (Mṣb;) *i. q.* إِسْرَافٌ; (M;) signifying *Excess,* or *transgression, of the just,* or *right, bound,* or *limit,* or *measure; extravagant, exorbitant,* or *immoderate, action* or *conduct;* (M, Mṣb, TA;) *contr. of* قَصْدٌ. (Ṣ, Ḳ.) See also 4, in two places. — [Hence,] ‡ The *overflowing* of water *from the sides* of a watering-trough, or tank; as in the saying, ذَهَبَ مَآءُ الحَوْضِ سَرَفًا ‡ *The water of the watering-trough,* or *tank,* [*went away running to waste,* or] *overflowed from its sides:* (Ḳ, TA:) or سَرَفُ المَآءِ means † *what goes, of water, without irrigating and without profit:* [or rather *its going for nought:*] you say, أَرْوَتِ البِئْرُ النَّخِيلَ وَذَهَبَ بَقِيَّةُ المَآءِ سَرَفًا † [*The well irrigated the palm-trees, and the rest of the water went for nought, in waste*]. (Sh, TA.) — And *Addictedness* (ضَرَاوَةٌ, Ṣ, Ḳ, or لَهَجٌ, M) to a thing, (M,) or in respect of wine. (Ḳ, TA.) It is said in a trad. (Ṣ, M) of 'Áïsheh, (TA,) إِنَّ لِلَّحْمِ سَرَفًا كَسَرَفِ الخَمْرِ [*Verily there is an addictedness to flesh-meat like the addictedness to wine*]: (Ṣ, M, TA:) i. e. he who is accustomed to it is addicted to the eating thereof, like as he who is constantly drinking wine is addicted thereto, having little self-restraint therefrom: or the meaning here is *unmindfulness* [*of consequences with respect to flesh-meat &c.*]: or *corruptness of conduct, arising from hardness of heart, and daringness to disobey, and self-impulsion to the gratification of appetite:* (TA:) or it may be [that the meaning is, *there is an extravagance with respect to flesh-meat &c.,*] from الإِسْرَافُ (Ṣ, TA) in expenditure for that which is not needed, or otherwise than in obedience [to the law of God]. (TA.) — It is also said in a trad., لَا يَنْتَهِبُ الرَّجُلُ نُهْبَةً ذَاتَ سَرَفٍ وَقَدْرٍ كَبِيرٍ, وَهُوَ مُؤْمِنٌ, meaning, [i. e. *The man shall not take a thing as spoil that is of high and great estimation, he being a believer*]: (Ḳ, TA:) [for] people disapprove of that: (TA:) and it is also related with ش [i. e. ذات شَرَفٍ]. (Ḳ.)

سَرِفٌ *Ignorant;* (IAạr, M, Mṣb, TA;) as also ▼ مُسْرِفٌ: (IAạr, TA:) or *unmindful, negligent,* or *heedless.* (Mṣb.) And رَجُلٌ سَرِفُ الفُؤَادِ ‡ *A man missing,* or *mistaking, in heart,* or *mind; negligent,* or *heedless, therein.* (Ṣ, Ḳ, TA.) And رَجُلٌ سَرِفُ العَقْلِ † *A man having little intellect,* or *intelligence:* or ‡ *corrupt in intellect;* accord. to Z, from سُرِفَتِ السُّرْفَةُ الخَشَبَ, of which the quasi-pass. is سَرِفَ [q. v.; meaning that it is from سَرِفٌ as a part. n. of this latter verb]. (TA.) — أَرْضٌ سَرِفَةٌ, (Ṣ, M, Ḳ,) and وَادٍ سَرِفٌ, (M, TA,) *A land,* and *a valley, abounding with the* [*worm,* or *caterpillar,* or *small creeping thing, called*] سُرْفَة. (Ṣ, M,* Ḳ, TA.)

سُرُفٌ *A certain white thing* [or *substance*] *resembling the web of the silkworm.* (Ibn-'Abbád, O, Ḳ.)

سُرْفَةٌ [*A certain worm,* or *caterpillar,* or *small creeping thing;*] *a small creeping thing that makes for itself a habitation,* (Ṣ, Ḳ,) *four-sided,* or *square,* (Ṣ,) *of fragments of wood,* (Ṣ, Ḳ,) *joining them together by means of its spittle, in the form of a* نَاوُوس [here meaning *coffin*], (Ṣ,) *which it then enters, and* [*therein it*] *dies:* (Ṣ, Ḳ:) or the *silkworm:* or *a certain small creeping thing, dust-coloured, that constructs a beautiful habitation in which it is:* or *a very small creeping thing, like the half of a lentil, that bores a tree, and then constructs therein a habitation of pieces of wood, which it conjoins by means of what resembles the web of the spider:* or *a very small dust-coloured creeping thing, that comes to a piece of wood and excavates it, and then brings a bit of wood and puts it therein, then another, then another, and then weaves what resembles the web of the spider:* or, accord. to AḤn, *a certain small creeping thing, like the worm, inclining in some degree to blackness, found upon the* [*plants called*] حَمْض, *that constructs a four-sided,* or *square, habitation, of pieces of wood, joining the extremities of these together by means of a thing* [or *substance*] *resembling the web of the spider:* or *the worm* [or *caterpillar*] *that weaves* [*a web*] *upon certain trees, and eats their leaves, and destroys the rest thereof by that weaving:* or *a certain worm* [or *caterpillar*] *like the finger, hairy, speckled with black or white, that eats the leaves of trees so as to make them bare:* or *a certain worm* [or *caterpillar*] *that weaves upon itself, of the size of the finger in length, a thing like the* قِرْطَاس [or *roll,* or *scroll, of paper*], *which it enters, so becoming unattainable:* or *a certain light, small creeping thing, like a spider:* (M:) pl. سُرَفٌ. (TA.) Hence the prov., أَصْنَعُ مِنْ سُرْفَةٍ [*More skilled in fabricating than a* سُرْفَة]. (Ṣ, M, Ḳ.) And one says also, أَخَفُّ مِنْ سُرْفَةٍ [*Lighter than a* سُرْفَة]. (M.)

[سُرَافٌ, accord. to Freytag, (but he has not named his authority,) The *erosion of a tree by wood-fretters* ("teredines," by which he means سُرَفٌ, pl. of سُرْفَةٌ).]

سَرُوفٌ *Hard, severe,* or *difficult; great, momentous,* or *formidable:* (O, Ḳ, TA:) an epithet applied to a day. (O, TA.)

سَرِيفٌ *A row of grape-vines.* (O, Ḳ.)

سَرَافِيلُ: see إِسْرَافِيلُ, below.

أُسْرُفٌ *i. q.* آنُكٌ [i. e. *Lead,* or *black lead,* or *tin,* or *pewter*]; (O, Ḳ;) of Pers. origin, (O,) arabicized, from سُرُبْ, (O, L, Ḳ,) or أُسْرُبْ. (CḲ.) [See also أُسْرُبٌ.]

إِسْرَافِيلُ, (Ṣ, M, O, Ḳ,) and El-Ḳanánee used to say ▼ سَرَافِيلُ, the name of *A certain angel;* (M; [in which it is mentioned among quadriliteral-radical words; but it is there said that the ا may be radical;]) *the angel who is to blow the horn on the day of resurrection:* (Jel in vi. 73, &c.:) [see رُوحَانِىٌّ:] a foreign word (Ṣ, O, Ḳ) prefixed, (Ḳ,) or as though prefixed, (Ṣ, O,) to إِيلُ: (Ṣ, O, Ḳ:) and إِسْرَافِينُ is a dial. var. of the same; (Kh, Ṣ, M, O, Ḳ;) like as they said جِبْرِينُ and إِسْمَاعِينُ and إِسْرَائِينُ. (Akh, Ṣ, O.)

مُسْرِفٌ [*Exceeding,* or *transgressing, the just,* or

right, bound, or limit, or measure; acting extravagantly, &c.: see its verb (4)]. — See also سَرِفٌ. — [Also] Denying, or disacknowledging, the favours, or benefits, or the unity, and the prophets and law, of God; a disbeliever, an unbeliever, or an infidel: it is said to be used in this sense in the Ḳur xl. 36. (TA.)

مَسْرُوفٌ Eaten by the سُرْفَة [q. v.]. (TA.) And شَجَرَةٌ مَسْرُوفَةٌ A tree of which the leaves have been eaten by the سُرْفَة; (Ṣ;) or smitten, or lighted on, by the سُرْفَة. (ISk, TA.) — شَاةٌ مَسْرُوفَةٌ ‡ A sheep, or goat, that has had its ear entirely cut off. (M, A.)

سرفل and سرفن

سَرَافِيلُ and إِسْرَافِيلُ and إِسْرَافِينُ: see the next preceding art.

سرق

1. سَرَقَ مِنْهُ مَالًا, (Ṣ, Mgh, O, Mṣb,) or الشَّىْءَ, (Ḳ,) and سَرَقَهُ مَالًا, (Ṣ, Mgh, O, Mṣb,) thus also they sometimes said, (Ṣ, O,) the prep. being suppressed for the sake of alleviation, but meant to be understood, (Ḥam p. 155,) aor. ـِ, inf. n. سَرَقٌ (Ṣ, Mgh, O, Mṣb, Ḳ) and سَرِقٌ and سَرِقَةٌ (Mgh, Ḳ) and سَرْقَةٌ and سَرْقٌ, (Ḳ,) He stole from him property, [or the thing,] i. e. he took it [from him] secretly, and by artifice; (Mgh;) or he came clandestinely to a place of custody, and took what belonged to him, namely, another person; (O, Ḳ;) as also ▼ استرقهُ [followed by مِنْهُ]. (IAar, Ḳ.) And سَرَقَهُمْ [alone, He stole from them; or robbed them]. (JK and Ḳ in art. بوق.) It is said in a prov., سُرِقَ السَّارِقُ فَٱنْتَحَرَ (Ṣ, O) The thief was robbed, and in consequence slew himself: applied to him who has a thing not belonging to him taken from him, and whose impatience consequently becomes excessive. (Meyd,* O.) And ▼ سرّقهُ, inf. n. تَسْرِيقٌ, signifies the same as سَرَقَهُ: El-Farezdaḳ says,

لَا تَحْسِبَنَّ دَرَاهِمًا سَرَقْتَهَا
تَمْحُو مَخَازِيَكَ الَّتِى بِعُمَانِ

[By no means reckon thou that dirhems which thou stolest will efface thy disgraceful practices that were committed in 'Omán]. (IB, TA.) And you say in selling a slave, بَرِئْتُ إِلَيْكَ مِنَ الإِبَاقِ وَالسَّرَقِ [I am irresponsible to thee for running away and stealing]. (TA.) — One says also, سَرَقَ السَّمْعَ, meaning استرقهُ. (Mṣb. See 3.) — And سُرِقَ صَوْتُهُ [lit. His voice was stolen], meaning ‡ he became hoarse. (Z, TA.) — And سرقت يا قوم [app. سُرِقْتُ يَا قَوْمِ], expl. as meaning سرقت عرفنى, which I think a mistranscription for سُرِقْتُ عِرْضِى, i. e. † I have been robbed of my honour, or reputation, O my people]. (TA.) — And سَرَقْنَا لَيْلَةً مِنَ الشَّهْرِ † We passed pleasantly, or with enjoyment, a night of the month. (TA.) — And سَرَقَتْنِى عَيْنِى ‡ My eye overcame me. (TA.) — سَرِقَ, aor. (Yoo, IDrd, Ḳ,) inf. n. سَرَقٌ, (TḲ,) said of a thing, (Yoo, IDrd,) i. q. خَفِىَ [It was, or became, unperceived, or imperceptible, or hardly perceived or perceptible, &c.]. (Yoo, IDrd, Ḳ.) — And سَرِقَتْ مَفَاصِلُهُ, aor. as above, (IDrd, Ḳ,) and so the inf. n., (TA,) His joints became weak, or feeble; (IDrd, Ḳ;) as also ▼ انسرقت. (Ḳ.)

2. سرّقهُ: see 1. — Also, (Ṣ,) inf. n. تَسْرِيقٌ, (Ḳ,) He attributed to him [or accused him of] theft. (Ṣ.) It is said in the Ḳur [xii. 81], accord. to one reading, إِنَّ ٱبْنَكَ سُرِّقَ [Verily thy son has been accused of theft]. (Ṣ.)

3. هُوَ يُسَارِقُ النَّظَرَ إِلَيْهِ ‡ He avails himself of, (Ṣ, O,) or seeks, (Ḳ,) his inadvertence, to look at him: (Ṣ, O, Ḳ:) [he takes an opportunity of looking at him by stealth:] and in like manner one uses the phrases ▼ تَسَرُّقُهُ and ▼ اِسْتِرَاقُ النَّظَرِ [as meaning ‡ the taking an opportunity of looking by stealth]: and ▼ التَّسَرُّقُ [alone] signifies † the taking an opportunity of looking and of hearing: (TA:) [and the hearing discourse by stealth; as is indicated in the TA:] and ▼ استرق السَّمْعَ [and استرق alone, as appears from an explanation of the part. n. مُسْتَرِقٌ, below,] ‡ He listened, (Ṣ, O,) or heard, (Mṣb,) by stealth; (Ṣ, O, Mṣb;) as also سَرَقَ ▼ السَّمْعَ. (Mṣb.)

5. تسرّق He stole [by degrees, or] one thing and then another. (O, Ḳ.) So in the phrase تسرّق شِعْرِى [He stole my poetry, bit by bit], used by Ru-beh. (O, TA.) — See also 3, in two places.

7. انسرق He went, drew, or shrank, back, in order to go away, عَنْهُمْ from them. (Ḳ, TA. [In this and the following sense, the verb is erroneously written in the CḲ أَسْرَقَ.]) — And He was, or became, languid, and weak, or feeble. (O, Ḳ, TA.) See also 1, last sentence.

8. استرق: see 1, first sentence: — and see 3, in two places. [See also كَبِيسٌ.] — Also ‡ He deceived, or circumvented, secretly, [or by stealth,] like him who [so] listens. (TA.) — And you say, استرق الكَاتِبُ بَعْضَ الْمُحَاسَبَاتِ ‡ The writer suppressed some of the items of the reckoning. (TA.)

Q. Q. 1. سَرْقَنَ الأَرْضَ He manured the land with سِرْقِين. (L in art. سرقن.)

سَرَقٌ Oblong pieces (Ṣ, O, Mṣb,* Ḳ) of silk; (Ṣ, O, Mṣb;) accord. to A'Obeyd, (Ṣ, O,) of white silk: (Ṣ, O, Ḳ:) or silk in general: (Ḳ:) said by A'Obeyd to be arabicized from the Pers. سَرَهْ, meaning "good:" (Ṣ, O:) n. un. with ة; (Ṣ, O, Mṣb;) which is expl. as meaning a piece of good silk. (TA.)

سَرِقٌ and ▼ سَرِقَةٌ [the former of which is said in the Mgh and Ḳ, and the latter in the Ḳ, to be an inf. n., are also said to be] substs. from سَرَقَ, [as such signifying Theft,] as also ▼ سَرْقَةٌ, (O, Ḳ,) or ▼ سِرْقَةٌ. (Mṣb.)

سَرْقَةٌ: } see what next precedes.
سِرْقَةٌ: }

سَرِقَةٌ: see سَرِقٌ. — Also, (Mṣb,) A thing stolen; (Mgh, Mṣb;) and so ▼ سُرَاقَةٌ; [pl. of the latter سُرَاقَاتٌ;] whence the saying عِنْدَهُ سُرَاقَاتُ الشِّعْرِ [He has stolen things of poetry or verse]. (TA.)

سِرْقِينٌ, (Ḳ, and Ṣ and Mṣb in art. سرج,) sometimes written سَرْقِينٌ, (Ḳ,) as also سِرْجِينٌ, (Mṣb, TA,) Dung of horses or other solid-hoofed animals, syn. رَوْثٌ, and زِبْلٌ, (Mṣb,) or fresh dung of camels, sheep and goats, wild oxen, and the like; (TA in art. ذأر;) a manure for land: (L:) arabicized from سركين [or سَرْكِينٌ], (Mṣb, Ḳ,) a Pers. word. (Mṣb.) [See سِرْجِينٌ, in art. سرج.]

سَرُوقٌ [Thievish; a great thief]; an epithet applied to a man, and to a dog: pl. سُرُقٌ. (TA.)

سُرَاقَةٌ: see سَرِقَةٌ. — Also A stealer of poetry or verses. (TA.)

سَرُوقَةٌ [Very thievish; a very great thief]: it has no pl. (TA.)

سَارِقٌ [Stealing; a thief; or] one who comes clandestinely to a place of custody, and takes what does not belong to him: (O:) pl. سَرَقَةٌ and سُرَّاقٌ (TA) and سُرَّقٌ. (Mgh.)

سُورَقٌ A certain disease in the members, or limbs. (Ibn-'Abbád, O.)

سَارِقَةٌ sing. of سَوَارِقُ, which signifies [Collars by means of which the two hands are confined together to the neck, called also] جَوَامِعُ, (O, Ḳ, TA,) of iron, attached to fetters or shackles. (TA.) — And the pl., سَوَارِقُ, signifies also The adjuncts (زَوَائِدُ) in the catches (فَرَاشٌ [q. v.]) of a lock. (Ibn-'Abbád, O, Ḳ.)

مَسْرُوقُ الصَّوْتِ [lit. Having the voice stolen,] means ‡ hoarse in voice. (Z, TA.) And hence, مَسْرُوقُ البُغَامِ ‡ [A young gazelle] having a nasal sound, or twang, in its cry; as though its voice were stolen: a phrase used by El-Aashà. (TA.)

مُسْتَرِقٌ ‡ Listening by stealth, (Ḳ, TA,) like the thief. (TA.) — † Defective, weak in make. (Ibn-'Abbád, O, Ḳ.) — مُسْتَرِقُ القَوْلِ ‡ Weak in speech or saying. (A, TA.) — مُسْتَرِقُ العُنُقِ ‡ Short in the neck; (Ibn-'Abbád, O, Ḳ, TA;) applied to a man; (Ibn-'Abbád, O, TA;) contracted therein. (A, TA.) [In the CḲ, المُسْرِقُ is erroneously put for المُسْتَرِقُ.]

سرقن

Q. 1. سَرْقَنَ: } see the next preceding art.
سِرْقِينٌ: }

سرم

سُرْمٌ The anus; (IAar, T;) the place of egress of the feces; i. e. the extremity of the rectum; (Ṣ, Ḳ;) a post-classical word: (Ṣ:) or the interior of the extremity of the rectum: (Lth, TA:) or the edge, or margin, of the rectum: accord. to some, peculiarly in beasts of prey that have claws: pl. أَسْرَامٌ. (M.) Hence the phrase رَجُلٌ وَاسِعُ السُّرْمِ ضَخْمُ البُلْعُومِ, occurring in a trad., meaning † *A man strong*, or *vehement, and violent*, or *wrongful* or *unjust* or *tyrannical in conduct: or a man prodigal of wealth and of blood*: and therefore described as wide in the places of egress and ingress. (TA in art. بلعم and in the present art.)

سَرَمٌ *Pain of the anus*. (Ḳ, TA.)

سرمد

سَرْمَدٌ [signifies, or implies,] *Continuance*, or *incessant continuance*, (دَوَام, Kh, M, L, and اِتِّصَال, Kh, L,) of time, (Kh, M, L,) either of night or of day. (Kh, L.) [I have said "or implies" because I have not found it used otherwise than as an epithet, in the following senses.] — *Continuing*; or *continuing incessantly*, or *endlessly*; syn. دَائِمٌ; (Zj, Ṣ, L, Ḳ;) or دَائِمٌ لَا يَنْقَطِعُ. (Nh, L.) It is applied in this sense to night (Nh, L) [and also to day: to each in the Ḳur xxviii. 71 and 72]: and to night as meaning *Long*. (L, Ḳ.) — Accord. to El-Fakhr Er-Rázee, it is derived from السَّرْدُ, which denotes consecutiveness and uninterruptedness, and the م is added to give intensiveness to the signification: if so, its proper place is in art. سرد; its measure being فَعْمَلٌ: (MF:) [thus] its م is augmentative like the م in دُلَامِصٌ. (Bḍ in xxviii. 71.) — One says also, هُوَ لَكَ سَرْمَدًا *He, or it, is thine ever*, or *for ever*. (Mgh in art. سمد.)

سَرْمَدِيٌّ *Having neither beginning nor end*. (KT.)

سرند

اِسْرَنْدَاهُ: and سَرَنْدَى: and مُسْرَنْدٍ: see art. سرد.

سرهد

Q. 1. سَرْهَدَ, (Ṣ, Ḳ,) inf. n. سَرْهَدَةٌ, (Ṣ,) *He fed*, or *nourished*, a child *well*. (Ṣ, L, Ḳ.) — And *He cut* a camel's hump [*in pieces*: see the pass. part. n., below]. (Ḳ.)

سَرْهَدٌ a term sometimes applied to The *fat of a camel's hump*. (Ṣ, L.) — And *Much water*. (L.)

مُسَرْهَدٌ A *fat* camel's hump: (Ṣ, L, Ḳ:) or a camel's hump *cut in pieces*. (L.) — *Supplied with the comforts and conveniences of life*, and *well fed*: and, with ة, a woman *fat, and well fed*. (L.) [Applied also to a young camel: see an ex. in a hemistich cited in the first paragraph of art. رجل.]

سرو

1. سَرُوَ, (Ṣ, M, Mgh, Ḳ,) aor. يَسْرُو; (Ṣ, Ḳ;) and سَرَا, (Ṣ, M, Ḳ,) aor. as above; (Ṣ, Ḳ;) and سَرِيَ, (Ṣ, M, Ḳ,) aor. يَسْرَى; (Ṣ, Ḳ;) inf. n. سَرَاوَةٌ, (Ṣ, M, Ḳ,) of the first verb, (Ṣ, M,) and سَرْوٌ, (Sb, Lḥ, Ṣ, M, Mgh, Ḳ,) of the same verb, (M, Mgh,) and of the second, (Ṣ, M,) and of the third, (Ṣ,) and سَرًا and سَرَآءٌ, (M, Ḳ,) both of the third, but سَرَآءٌ, and this only, is mentioned by Lḥ as inf. n. of the second verb; (M;) *He was*, or *became, possessed of liberality, bountifulness, munificence*, or *generosity, combined with manliness*, or *manly virtue*: (Ṣ, Mgh:) or *manliness*, or *manly virtue*, (M, Ḳ,) and (M,) or *combined with*, (Ḳ,) *high* or *elevated rank* or *condition, nobility, dignity, honour*, or *glory*. (M, Ḳ.) — سَرْوُ المَسَاقِى means *The cleaning out of what are termed* مَسَاقٍ [pl. of مَسْقَاةٌ or مِسْقَاةٌ, which see in art. سقى]. (TA.) — سَرْوٌ also signifies, like تَسْرِيَةٌ [inf. n. of ▼ سَرَّى], and إِسْرَآءٌ [inf. n. of ▼ اسرى], The *throwing off* a thing from oneself [or from another]; (Ḳ, TA;) and the *pulling off* a thing. (TA.) You say, سَرَوْتُ الثَّوْبَ عَنِّى, (ISk, Ṣ,) or عَنْهُ, aor. أَسْرُو, (Mgh,) inf. n. سَرْوٌ, *I threw off the garment from me*, (ISk, Ṣ,) or *I removed the garment from over him*; (Mgh;) and سَرَيْتُ is a dial. var. thereof; (Ṣ;) or سَرَا ثَوْبَهُ عَنْهُ, inf. n. سَرْوٌ; and ▼ سَرَّاهُ; *he pulled off his garment from him*: (M:) and سَرَوْتُ الجُلَّ عَنِ الفَرَسِ, (TA,) or عَنْ ظَهْرِ الفَرَسِ, (M,) and ▼ سَرَّيْتُهُ, and ▼ أَسْرَيْتُهُ, *I threw off* [*the horse-cloth from the horse*, or *from the back of the horse*]. (TA.) And سَرَوْتُ عَنِّى دِرْعِى [*I threw off from me my coat of mail*]: in this case the verb is only with و. (Ṣ.) [Hence,] ▼ سُرِّىَ عَنْهُ, (M,) or سُرِّىَ عَنْهُ الهَمُّ, (Ṣ, Ḳ,*) inf. n. تَسْرِيَةٌ, (TA,) ‡ *Anxiety became removed from him*; as also ▼ انسرى عَنْهُ الهَمُّ: (Ṣ, Ḳ,* TA:) or *his anxiety became removed*, or *cleared away*. (M, in explanation of the first of these phrases.) And ▼ سُرِّىَ عَنْهُ الخَوْفُ † *Fear was made to quit him*: the teshdeed denotes intensiveness. (TA.) And hence the phrase in a trad., فَلَمَّا سُرِّىَ ▼ عَنْهُ بُرَحَآءُ الوَحْيِ † [*And when the vehement distress of mind arising from the oppression caused by inspiration was made to quit him*]; referring to the Prophet. (Mgh.) — سَرَتْ, (Ḳ,) inf. n. سَرْوٌ, (TA,) said of the female locust, *She laid eggs*: (Ḳ:) a dial. var. of سَرَأَتْ. (TA.)

2. اليَوْمَ تُسَرَّوْنَ, said by the Prophet on the occasion of the expedition of Oḥod, means *To-day ye shall have your* سَرِىّ [*or that person, among you, who is distinguished by liberality and manliness, &c.,*] *slain*: and [accordingly] Ḥamzeh was then slain. (TA.) — See also 1, in six places.

3. سَارَاهُ, inf. n. مُسَارَاةٌ, *i. q.* فَاخَرَهُ [i. e. *He vied with him*, or *contended with him for superiority, in glory*, or rather *in liberality and manliness*, &c.: see 1, first sentence]. (TA.)

4. اسرى *He became in*, or *upon, land*, or *ground, such as is termed* سَرَاة: belonging to the present art., accord. to Er-Rághib: (TA:) or *he betook himself to the* سَرَاة [app. meaning *the mountainous tract so called*]: (Ḳ and TA in art. سرى:) it is like أَنْجَدَ and أَتْهَمَ. (TA in that art.) — See also 1, in two places.

5. تسرّى signifies تَكَلَّفَ السَّرْوَ, (Ṣ, Ḳ,* TA,) i. e. [*He affected*, or *constrained himself*, to *possess liberality and manliness*, &c., (see 1, first sentence,) or] *high* or *elevated rank* or *condition, nobility, dignity, honour*, or *glory*, and *manliness*, or *manly virtue*: (TA:) or it signifies أَخَذَ سُرِّيَّةً [*he took a concubine-slave*]: (Ḳ:) or — one says also, تسرّى الجَارِيَةَ [*He took the girl*, or *young woman, as a concubine-slave*], from السُّرِّيَّة; said by Yaạkoob to be originally تَسَرَّرَ, [which see in art. سر,] from السُّرُورُ. (Ṣ.) — And تسرّاه signifies ▼ أَخَذَ أَسْرَاهُ [i. e. *He took the best thereof*]. (M, TA. [See also 8.])

7: see 1, in the latter part of the paragraph.

8. استرى *He chose*, or *selected, as being the best*, (Ṣ, M, Ḳ,) a thing, (M,) or men, (Ṣ, Ḳ,) and camels, and sheep or goats. (Ṣ.) And اِسْتَرَيْتُهُ *I took the best of it*. (T, TA. [See also 5, last sentence.]) And اِسْتَارَ signifies the same as استرى, being formed from the latter by transposition. (TA.) One says, استرى المَوْتُ بَنِى فُلَانٍ, (Ṣ,) or الحَىَّ, (Ḳ,) i. e. *Death chose* [or *took*] *the best of the sons of such a one*, or *of the tribe*. (Ṣ,* Ḳ,* TA.)

سَرْوٌ an inf. n. of 1 [q. v.]. (Ṣ, M, Ḳ, &c.) [Used as a simple subst., *Liberality, bountifulness, munificence*, or *generosity, combined with manliness*, or *manly virtue*; &c.] — Hence, أَبُو السَّرْوِ † *Aloes-wood*, or *the like, that is used for fumigation*; syn. البَخُورُ. (Ḥar p. 228.) — Also *A part that rises from* [*the bottom of*] *a valley, and slopes down from the rugged portion of a mountain*: (M, Ḳ:) or *that rises from the channel in which the water flows, and slopes down from the rugged portion of a mountain*: (M:) it is *like a* خَيْف. (Ṣ.) السَّرْوُ, (Ṣ, Ḳ,) or سَرْوُ حِمْيَرَ, occurring in a trad., is said to mean مَحَلَّةُ حِمْيَرَ [*The settlement of Ḥimyer*]. (Ṣ, M, Ḳ.) — And *A certain kind of tree*, (Ṣ, M, Ḳ,) *well-known*; (Ḳ;) [the *common*, or *evergreen, cypress*; *cupressus sempervirens* of Linn.: applied thereto in the present day: (Delile's Floræ Aegypt. Illustr., no. 900:)] n. un. with ة. (Ṣ, M, Ḳ.) — And *Certain worms that light upon plants*, (M, Ḳ, TA,) *and eat them*: (M:) الثِّيَاب, in [some of] the copies of the Ḳ, is a mistranscription for النَّبَات: (TA:) sing. [or rather n. un.] with ة. (M.)

سَرَاةٌ The *back* (Ṣ, M, Ḳ) of anything: (Ṣ:) pl. سَرَوَاتٌ: (Ṣ, M, Ḳ:) it has no broken pl. (M.) And The *higher*, or *highest, part* of anything: (M in the present art., and Ḳ in art. سرى:) so [for instance] of a mountain. (TA in art. سرى.) [Hence,] سَرَاةُ اليَمَنِ, (M,) or السَّرَاةُ [by way of preeminence, for سَرَاة is prefixed to the names of a number of places and of tribes, as is said in the TA in art. سرى], *A certain mountain* [or *mountainous tract*] *commencing near 'Arafát and extending to Nejrán of El-Yemen*: (Mṣb:) pl. as above. (M.) — The *highest* [or *most advanced state*] of the day: (TA:) [or] the *state of advancement, when the sun has become somewhat high*, (syn. اِرْتِفَاع,) of the day, (M, Ḳ, TA,) and so of other things; by some said to mean the *middle* thereof; (M;) so in the Ṣ, in relation to the day; but this is [said to be] a mistake: (TA:)

in a verse of El-Bureyḳ El-Hudhalee, of the night: pl. as above: and the sing. also occurs used as a pl. (M.) —— The *middle* of anything: pl. as above. (Ṣ.) The *middle and main part* of a road; (Mgh, Mṣb;) the *hard and elevated part* thereof. (Ḳ.) It is said in a trad., لَيْسَ لِلنِّسَآءِ سَرَوَاتُ الطَّرِيقِ (Ṣ, Mgh) *The back and middle of the road,* (Ṣ,) or *the middle and main parts thereof,* (Mgh,) *are not for the women;* meaning that they should walk upon the side parts. (Ṣ.) —— Accord. to Er-Rághib, *A wide tract of land.* (TA in art. سرى.) ═ It is also a pl., of a rare form, (Ṣ, Mṣb,) or a quasi-pl. n., (M, Ḳ,) of سَرِىٌّ [which see in several places]. (Ṣ, M, Mṣb, Ḳ.)

سَرْوَةٌ n. un. of سَرْوٌ [q.v.] in two senses. ═ See also سِرْوَةٌ.

سُرْوَةٌ: see what next follows.

سِرْوَةٌ (Th, AḤn, T, Ṣ, M, Ḳ) and ▼ سُرْوَةٌ (Th, M, IAth, Ḳ) and ▼ سَرْوَةٌ (Kr, M, Ḳ) *A small arrow:* (Ṣ:) or *a small and short arrow:* or *an arrow broad and long in the head;* (M, Ḳ, TA;) *but therewithal slender and short; with which one shoots at the butt:* (TA:) or *such as is round and smooth, not broad;* the broad and long being termed مِعْبَلَةٌ: (M:) or the *very slenderest of arrow-heads, that penetrates into the coats of mail:* (Th, M:) or *it* [*is an arrow that*] *penetrates into the coats of mail, for which reason it is called* الدِّرْعِيَّةُ, *its head entering like the needle:* (T, TA:) or *an arrow-head resembling an ordinary needle or a large needle:* it is mentioned also in art. سرى, [as being *a small, short, round and smooth arrow-head, having no breadth,* and as being called سِرْوَةٌ and سِرْيَةٌ,] because the word belongs to that art. and to this: (M:) [see also مِرْمَاةٌ; and see سِرْوَةٌ in art. سرأ:] the pl. is سُرًى [or سِرًى?] accord. to the T, or سِرَآءٌ accord. to the Ṣ. (TA.) ═ The first (سِرْوَةٌ) also signifies The *locust in its first state, when it is a larva;* (Ṣ;) or *in its first state of growth, when it comes forth from its egg:* (M:) originally with hemz: (Ṣ:) [see سِرْءٌ, in two places:] and سِرْيَةٌ is a dial. var. thereof. (Ṣ.) [See also جَرَادٌ.]

سَرِىٌّ, as an epithet applied to a man, (Ṣ, M, Ḳ, &c.,) may be from اِسْتَرَيْتُ الشَّىْءَ "I chose, or selected, the thing," or from السَّرَاةُ "the higher, or highest, part" of a thing, (Ḥam p. 337,) or, accord. to Er-Rághib, from سَرَوْتُ الثَّوْبَ عَنِّى "I pulled off the garment from me," (TA, [in which this derivation is said to be good, but I think it far-fetched,]) *Possessing liberality, bountifulness, munificence,* or *generosity, combined with manliness,* or *manly virtue:* (Ṣ, Mgh:) or *possessing manliness,* or *manly virtue,* (M, Ḳ,) and, (M,) or *combined with,* (Ḳ,) *high* or *elevated rank* or *condition, nobility, dignity, honour,* or *glory:* (M, Ḳ:) or *i. q.* رَئِيسٌ [meaning a *chief,* or person *high in rank* or *condition*]: (Mṣb:) [or a *generous and manly* or *noble* person:] fem. with ة: (M, Ḳ:) and ▼ مَسْرُوَانٌ signifies the same, applied to a man; and ▼ مَسْرُوَانَةٌ applied to a woman: (M:) the pl. of سَرِىٌّ is أَسْرِيَآءُ and سُرَوَآءُ (Lḥ, M, Ḳ) and سُرًى, (Az, Ḳ,) which is anomalous, (TA,) and سَرَاةٌ, (T, Ṣ, Mgh,* Mṣb,) [originally سَرَوَةٌ,] which is [also] anomalous, (T, TA,) the only instance of فَعَلَةٌ as the measure of a pl. of a word of the measure فَعِيلٌ, (Ṣ, Mṣb,) or it is a quasi-pl. n., (Sb, M, Ḳ,) and its pl. is سَرَوَاتٌ; (Ṣ, M, Mgh,* Ḳ;) meaning سَادَاتٌ [or *chiefs,* &c.]; (Mgh); and سُرَاةٌ, with ḍamm, [originally سُرَوَةٌ,] is a dial. var. of سَرَاةٌ, as pl. [or quasi-pl. n.] of سَرِىٌّ: (IAth, TA:) the pl. of سَرِيَّةٌ is سَرِيَّاتٌ and سَرَايَا. (M, Ḳ.) Also *Chosen,* or *choice,* or *select:* (M:) what is *good* of anything; pl. [or quasi-pl. n.] سَرَاةٌ: (Ḥam p. 337:) the *best,* (Mṣb, TA, and Ḥar p. 56,) and in like manner سَرَاةٌ [as a pl.]; (M, Mṣb, TA, and Ḥam p. 57, and Ḥar ubi suprà;) the former, of men, (Ḥar ubi suprà,) and of camels; (Ṣ;) and the latter, of men, (Ṣ, TA, and Ḥam ubi suprà, and Ḥar,) and of cattle or camels and the like, (Ṣ, M, TA,) as also the former. (TA.) ═ See also art. سرى.

سُرِّيَّةٌ, said by some to be originally of the measure فُعْوَلَةٌ, from سَرْوٌ: see art. سر.

أَسْرَى is of the measure أَفْعَلُ [denoting the comparative and superlative degrees] from السَّرْوُ signifying "liberality, bountifulness, munificence, or generosity, combined with manliness, or manly virtue:" [&c.:] whence the phrase أَسْرَاهُمْ سُودَدًا, meaning *The best of them in respect of chiefdom* or *the like:* or it may be from السُّرَى; meaning in this instance that the fame of the chiefdom, or the like, of him to whom it relates has pervaded the countries and spread among mankind; and this is more worthy of regard in respect of the method of grammatical analysis; from Mṭr: (Ḥar p. 363: [see art. سرى:]) [ISd, however, assigns the word to the present art.:] see 5, last sentence.

أَرْضٌ مَسْرُوَةٌ *A land containing the* سِرْوَة, or *locust in its first state, when it is a larva.* (Ṣ.) [In a copy of the M, it is said to be from السُّرْوَةُ; and the context there indicates the meaning to be *A land infested by a worm of the kind termed* سَرْوٌ, of which سَرْوَةٌ is the n. un.: but probably السُّرْوَةُ, in this instance, is a mistranscription for السِّرْوَةُ, which is mentioned immediately after as meaning "the locust in its first state of growth, when it comes forth from its egg."]

مَسْرُوَانٌ; and its fem., with ة: see سَرِىٌّ.

سرول

Q. 1. سَرْوَلَهُ, (inf. n. سَرْوَلَةٌ, TA,) *He clad him with* سَرَاوِيل. (Ṣ, M, Ḳ.)

Q. 2. تَسَرْوَلَ *He clad himself,* or *became clad, with* سَرَاوِيل. (Ṣ, M, Ḳ.)

سِرْوَالٌ: see سَرَاوِيلُ, latter half, in two places.

سِرْوِيلٌ: see سَرَاوِيلُ, in the latter half.

سِرْوَالَةٌ: see the next paragraph, latter half, in two places.

سَرَاوِيلُ a Pers. word, (Ṣ,* M, Mṣb,* Ḳ,) originally شَلْوَار, (MA, KL, [in the former loosely expl. by the word إِزَار, and so in the PṢ,]) of well-known meaning, (Ṣ,) [*Drawers, trousers,* or *breeches;* originally applied to *such as are worn under other clothing;*] *a certain under-garment;* (MA;) [but now applied also to *such as are worn externally;*] is masc. [and perfectly decl., i. e. with tenween], and fem. [and imperfectly decl., i. e. without tenween]; (Ṣ, M, Mṣb, Ḳ;*) sometimes masc., (Mṣb, Ḳ,) but not known to Aṣ otherwise than as fem.; (M;) accord. to the usage most commonly obtaining, it is imperfectly decl. and fem.: (MF:) Sb says that it is a sing., and is a foreign, or Pers., word, arabicized; resembling, in their [the Arabs'] language, what is imperfectly decl. [as a pl. of the measure فَعَالِيلُ] when determinate and when indeterminate; but is perfectly decl. when indeterminate; and imperfectly decl. if applied as a proper name to a man, and so is its dim. if so applied, because it is fem. and of more than three letters: (Ṣ:) or it is imperfectly decl. as a proper name because it is also originally a foreign word; and its dim., ▼ سُرَيِّيلٌ, [for سُرَيْوِيل, the و being changed into ى, as in سُيَيِّد for سُيَيْوِد,] is perfectly decl. unless used as a proper name, in which latter case it is imperfectly decl. [for the reason above mentioned or] because it is fem. and determinate: (IB, TA:) it (i. e. سَرَاوِيل) is made, as a pl., imperfectly decl. when indeterminate by some of the grammarians; (Ṣ;) and it occurs in poetry imperfectly decl. [when indeterminate]: (Ṣ, M,* IB, TA:) [but this may be by poetic license:] thus in the saying of Ibn-Muḳbil,

* أَتَى دُونَهَا ذَبُّ الرِّيَادِ كَأَنَّهُ *
* فَتًى فَارِسِىٌّ فِى سَرَاوِيلَ رَامِحُ *

[*There came as an obstacle intervening in the way to her, or them, the wild bull, as though he were a Persian youth in drawers; one with a pair of horns*]: (Ṣ,* IB, TA:) the former [however] is the usual way, [contrary to what has been said on the authority of MF,] though the latter is more valid: (Ṣ:) the pl. is سَرَاوِيلَاتٌ: (Ṣ, M, Mṣb, Ḳ:) Sb says that it has no broken pl., because, if it had, it would be the same as the sing.: (M:) or, (Ḳ,) some say, (Ṣ, M, Mṣb,) namely those grammarians who make it imperfectly decl. when indeterminate, (Ṣ,) holding it to be [originally] an Arabic word, (Mṣb,) it is a pl. of which the sing. is ▼ سِرْوَالَةٌ (Ṣ, M, Mṣb, Ḳ) and ▼ سِرْوَالٌ (Ṣ, Ḳ) and ▼ سِرْوِيلٌ, which is [said to be] the only instance of a word of the measure فِعْوِيلٌ: (Ḳ:) [this, therefore, confirms the opinion that I hold, that the measure of this word is فِعْلِيلٌ, and that all the words of the present art. are quadriliteral-radical, agreeably with an assertion in the TA that سرول is not genuine Arabic: though it seems that all the lexicographers regard the و in the words of this art. as augmentative:] a poet says,

* عَلَيْهِ مِنَ اللُّؤْمِ سِرْوَالَةٌ * فَلَيْسَ يَرِقُّ لِمُسْتَعْطِفِ *

[*Upon him is an under-garment of ignobleness,* (i. e. ignobleness cleaves to him like a pair of drawers,) *so that he does not become tender-hearted to one who endeavours to conciliate* him]: (Ṣ,* M:) in the "Mujarrad," سَرَاوِيلُ is made fem., and ▼ سِرْوَالٌ masc.: (Mṣb:) سَرَاوِينُ is a dial. var.; (Ḳ;) or syn. with سَرَاوِيلُ; the ن in the former being asserted by Yaḳoob to be a substitute for the ل [in the latter]: (M:) and شِرْوَالٌ, with ش, is likewise a dial. var. [of سِرْوَالٌ], (Ḳ,) mentioned by Es-Sijistánee, on the authority of some one or more of the Arabs: (TA:) [the common modern pronunciation is شَرْوَالٌ: pl. شَرَاوِيل.]

سُرَيْيِيلٌ: dim. of سَرَاوِيلُ, q. v. (IB, TA.)

مُسَرْوَلٌ *Clad with* سَرَاوِيل; as also ▼ مُتَسَرْوِلٌ. (A, TA.) — [Hence,] طَائِرٌ مُسَرْوَلٌ ‡ *A bird whose plumage clothes its legs.* (M, L, TA.) And حَمَامَةٌ مُسَرْوَلَةٌ ‡ *A pigeon having feathers upon its legs.* (Ṣ, Ḳ, TA.) And فَرَسٌ مُسَرْوَلٌ, (Ḳ,) or فَرَسٌ أَبْلَقُ مُسَرْوَلٌ, (A'Obeyd, Ṣ, TA,) ‡ [*A horse, or a black and white horse,*] *whose whiteness of the legs extends* (A'Obeyd, Ṣ, Ḳ) *beyond,* (A'Obeyd, Ḳ, TA,) or *to,* (Ṣ,) *the arms and thighs:* (A'Obeyd, Ṣ, Ḳ:) or مُسَرْوَلٌ applied to a horse means *white in the hinder part,* [*and black,* or *of some other colour, in the hind legs,*] *the whiteness descending to the thighs.* (A, voce آزَرُ.) — And المُسَرْوَلُ signifies † *The wild bull:* because of the blackness that is in his legs. (Az, TA.)

مُتَسَرْوِلٌ: see the next preceding paragraph.

سرون

سَرَاوِينُ: see سَرَاوِيلُ, in art. سرول.

سرى

1. سَرَى, (Ṣ, M, Ḳ,) or سَرَى اللَّيْلَ (Mṣb) and بِاللَّيْلِ, (Mgh, Mṣb,) aor. يَسْرِى, (Ḳ,) inf. n. سُرًى (Ṣ, M, Mgh, Ḳ) and مَسْرًى (Ṣ, Ḳ) and سَرْيَةٌ and سُرْيَةٌ (M, Ḳ) and سِرَايَةٌ; (Ṣ,* and TA as from the Ḳ, but not in the CḲ nor in my MS. copy of the Ḳ;) the first of a form rare among inf. ns., because it is one of the forms of pls., as is shown by the fact that some of the Arabs make it and هُدًى fem., namely, Benoo-Asad, supposing them to be pls. of سُرْيَةٌ and هُدْيَةٌ, (Ṣ,) and Lḥ knew not سُرًى but as a fem. noun; (M;) or the inf. n. is سُرًى, and سُرْيَةٌ and سَرْيَةٌ are more special [in meaning, as will be shown below, voce سَرْيَةٌ], and سُرًى is pl. of سُرْيَةٌ; (Mṣb;) or سَرْيَةٌ is an inf. n. un., and سُرْيَةٌ is a simple subst., and so is سُرًى, (Ṣ, TA,) and so is سِرَايَةٌ (Mṣb, TA) also, as some say; (TA;) *He journeyed,* or *travelled, by night,* or *in the night,* (Ṣ, M, Mgh, Mṣb, Ḳ,) *in a general sense;* (M, Ḳ;) accord. to AZ, in the first part part of the night, and in the middle thereof, and in the last part thereof; (Mṣb, TA;) and ▼ اسرى signifies the same (Ṣ, M, Mgh, Mṣb, Ḳ) in the dial. of El-Ḥijáz, (Ṣ, Mṣb,) inf. n. إِسْرَآءٌ; (M;) as also ▼ استرى; (M, Ḳ;) and perhaps ▼ تسرّى likewise. (Mgh.) [See also سُرًى and سُرْيَةٌ below.] It is said in a prov., ذَهَبُوا إِسْرَآءَ ▼ قُنْفُذٍ [*They went away in the manner of a hedge-hog's night-travelling;* meaning *they went away by night*]; because the قنفذ goes all the night, not sleeping. (M.) — [Hence, as denoting unseen progress,] it is said also of the root of a tree, meaning *It crept along beneath the ground;* (Az, M, Ḳ;) aor. as above, (M,) inf. n. سَرْىٌ. (TA.) — And it is said of ideal things, as being likened to corporeal things; tropically, and by extension of the signification; (Mṣb, TA;) or metaphorically; [as, for instance,] of calamities, and wars, and anxieties: (M, TA:) and the predominant inf. ns. [in these cases] are سَرَيَانٌ and سِرَايَةٌ. (TA.) One says, سَرَى عِرْقُ السُّوْءِ فِى الإِنْسَانِ ‡ [*The root,* or *strain, of evil crept in the man*]. (Es-Saraḳustee, Mṣb, TA.) And سَرَى فِيهِ السَّمُّ ‡ [*The poison crept in him,* or *pervaded him*]; and similarly one says of wine; and of the like of these two things. (El-Fárábee, Mṣb, TA. [See also دَبَّ.]) And the lawyers say, سَرَى الجُرْحُ إِلَى النَّفْسِ ‡ [*The wound extended to the soul*], meaning that the pain of the wound continued until death ensued in consequence thereof: (Mgh,* Mṣb, TA:) and قُطِعَ كَفُّهُ فَسَرَى إِلَى سَاعِدِهِ ‡ [*His hand was cut off, and it extended to his upper arm*], meaning that the effect of the wound passed by transmission: and سَرَى العِتْقُ, and التَّحْرِيمُ, ‡ *The prohibition,* and *the emancipation,* [*extended,* or] *passed by transmission:* phrases current among the lawyers, but not mentioned in books of repute, though agreeable with others here preceding and following. (Mṣb, TA.) One says also, سَرَى عَلَيْهِ الهَمُّ ‡ *Anxiety came to him* [or *upon him*] *by night:* and سَرَى هَمُّهُ ‡ *His anxiety went away.* (Mṣb, TA.) And similar to these is the phrase in the Ḳur [lxxxix. 3], وَاللَّيْلِ إِذَا يَسْرِ ‡ *And by the night when it goes away:* (Mṣb, TA:) or, as some say, *when one journeys in it;* like as one says لَيْلٌ نَائِمٌ meaning "night in which one sleeps:" the [final] ى [of the verb] is elided because it terminates a verse. (TA.) — It is made trans. by means of ب: (Mṣb:) one says, سَرَى بِهِ [*He made him to journey,* or *travel,* or *he transported him, by night,* or *in the night;* or it may be rendered *he journeyed,* or *travelled, with him, by night,* or *in the night*]; (M, Mṣb, Ḳ;) and in like manner, [and more commonly,] ▼ أَسْرَى بِهِ; (Ṣ, M, Mṣb, Ḳ;) and ▼ أَسْرَاهُ; (Ṣ, M, Ḳ;) like as one says, أَخَذَ بِالخِطَامِ as well as اخذ الخطامَ. (Ṣ.) As to the saying in the Ḳur [xvii. 1], سُبْحَانَ الَّذِى أَسْرَى ▼ بِعَبْدِهِ لَيْلًا [*Extolled be the glory of Him who transported his servant by night!*], it is an instance of corroboration, (Ṣ, Ḳ,* TA,) like the saying, سِرْتُ أَمْسِ نَهَارًا and البَارِحَةَ لَيْلًا: (Ṣ, TA:) or the meaning is [simply] سَيَّرَهُ: (Ḳ, TA:) accord. to 'Alam-ed-Deen Es-Sakháwee, لَيْلًا is added, although الإِسْرَآء is not otherwise than by night, because the space over which he was transported is not to be traversed in less than forty days, but was traversed by him in one night; as though the meaning [intended] were, فِى لَيْلٍ وَاحِدٍ; and it denotes wonder: لَيْلًا is here used instead of لَيْلَةً because when they say سَرَى لَيْلَةً the meaning generally is *he occupied the whole of the night in journeying:* Er-Rághib holds the verb in this instance to be from سَرَاةٌ signifying "a wide tract of land," to belong to art. سرو, and to be like أَجْبَلَ and أَتْهَمَ; the meaning being, *who transported his servant over a wide tract of land:* but this is strange. (TA.) — سَرَى مَتَاعَهُ, (M, Ḳ,) aor. يَسْرِى, (M, TA,) inf. n. سَرْىٌ, (TA,) *He threw his goods,* or *utensils and furniture, upon the back of his beast.* (M, Ḳ.) — And سَرَى عَنِّى الثَّوْبَ, inf. n. سَرْىٌ, *He removed from over me the garment:* but و is more approved [as the final radical: see 1 in art. سرو]. (M, TA.) You say, سَرَيْتُ الثَّوْبَ and ▼ سَرَّيْتُهُ *I pulled off the garment:* and ▼ سُرِّىَ عَنْهُ *It was removed from over him,* and *removed from its place:* the teshdeed denotes intensiveness. (TA.)

2. سرّى, (Ḳ,) or سَرَّى سَرِيَّةً, (TA,) inf. n. تَسْرِيَةٌ, *He* (the leader of an army, TA) *detached a* سَرِيَّة [q.v.] (Ḳ, TA) *to the enemy by night.* (TA.) — سرّى العَرَقَ عَنْ بَدَنِهِ, inf. n. as above, *He exuded the sweat from his body.* (TA.) — See also 1, last sentence, in two places.

4: see 1, in the former half of the paragraph, in two places: — and again, in the latter half, in three places. — See also 4 in art. سرو.

5: } see 1, first sentence.
8: }

سُرًى, [said by some to be an inf. n., by some to be a simple subst., and by some to be pl. of سُرْيَةٌ, or supposed to be so, and therefore made fem., as mentioned in the first sentence of this art.,] meaning *A journeying,* or *travelling, by night,* or *in the night, in a general sense,* is masc. and fem., (M, Ḳ,) by some of the Arabs made fem., (Ṣ,) and not known to Lḥ but as a fem. noun. (M.) It is said in a prov.,

* عِنْدَ الصَّبَاحِ يَحْمَدُ القَوْمُ السُّرَى *

[*At daybreak, the party commend night-journeying*]: applied to the man who endures difficulty, or distress, or fatigue, hoping for rest, or ease: (Meyd:) and in inciting to labour for the accomplishment of an affair with patience, and to dispose and subject the mind, until one commends the result thereof. (Ḥar p. 555, q. v.)

سَرَاةٌ: see art. سرو.

سَرْيَةٌ and ▼ سُرْيَةٌ are inf. ns. of سَرَى: (M, Ḳ:) or have a more special signification than the inf. n. of that verb, which is سُرًى: one says, سَرَيْنَا سَرْيَةً مِنَ اللَّيْلِ and ▼ سُرْيَةً [*We journeyed by night a journey of the night*]: and the pl. of ▼ سُرْيَةٌ is [said to be] سُرًى: (Mṣb:) or one says,

سَرَيْنَا سُرْيَةً وَاحِدَةً [We journeyed by night a single night-journey]: and the subst. [signifying a journeying, or travelling, by night, or in the night,] is ▼ سُرْيَةٌ, and سُرًى. (Ṣ, TA.)

سُرْيَةٌ: see the next preceding paragraph, in four places.

سِرْيَةٌ meaning An arrow-head, (Aṣ, M, TA,) such as is small, short, round and smooth, having no breadth, (M, TA,) is a dial. var. of سِرْوَةٌ [q. v.], (Aṣ, TA,) or formed from the latter word by the substitution of ى for و because of the kesreh: (M, TA:) accord. to the Ḳ, ▼ سَرِيَّةٌ signifies a small round arrow-head; but this is a mistake; the correct word being سِرْيَةٌ, with kesr, and without teshdeed to the ى. (TA.) ═ It is also a dial. var. of سِرْوَةٌ signifying The locust in its first state, when it is a larva. (Ṣ in art. سرو.)

سَرَآءٌ A certain tree, (AḤn, Ṣ, M, Ḳ,) from which bows are made, (AḤn, Ṣ, M,) the wood whereof is of the best of woods, and which is of the trees of the mountains: (AḤn, M:) El-Ghanawee El-Aạrábee says, the شَوْحَط and نَبْع [q. v.] and سَرَآء are one: (TA in art. شحط:) [it is also mentioned in the TA in art. سرأ:] n. un. سَرَآءَةٌ. (M, Ḳ.)

سَرِىٌّ i. q. نَهْرٌ [A river, &c.]: (Th, M:) or a rivulet, or streamlet: (Ṣ, M, Mṣb:) or a rivulet running to palm-trees: (M, Ḳ:) pl. [of pauc.] أَسْرِيَةٌ (Ṣ, M, Ḳ) and [of mult.] سُرْيَانٌ: (Sb, Ṣ, M, Mṣb, Ḳ:) أَسْرِيَآءُ as its pl. has not been heard. (Ṣ.) Thus it has been expl. as occurring in the Ḳur xix. 24. (M, TA.) ═ See also art. سرو.

سَرِيَّةٌ A portion of an army: (Ṣ, Mṣb:) of the measure فَعِيلَةٌ in the sense of the measure فَاعِلَةٌ; because marching by night, privily; (Mgh, Mṣb;) thus originally, and afterwards applied also to such as march by day: (Ḥam p. 45:) or it may be from الإِسْتِرَآءُ "the act of choosing, or selecting;" because a company chosen from the army: (Mgh: [but if so, belonging to art. سرو:]) from five persons to three hundred: (M, Ḳ:) or four hundred: (Ḳ:) or, of horsemen, about four hundred: (M:) or the best thereof, (Ṣ,) or the utmost, (Nh,) consists of four hundred: (Ṣ, Nh:) or, accord. to the "Fet-ḥ el-Bári," from a hundred to five hundred: (TA:) or nine, and more than this; three, and four, and the like being termed طَلِيعَةٌ, not سَرِيَّةٌ: but it is related of the Prophet that he sent a single person as a سَرِيَّة: (Mgh:) the pl. is سَرَايَا (Ṣ, Mṣb) and سَرِيَّاتٌ. (Mṣb.) ═ See also سِرْيَةٌ.

سِرَايَةٌ A journeying, or travelling, by night, or in the night: (Ṣ, Mṣb, TA:) an inf. n.; (TA as from the Ḳ; [see 1, first sentence;]) or a simple subst. (Mṣb, TA.)

[سَرَيَانِىٌّ, from the inf. n. سَرَيَانٌ, Pervasive: occurring in philosophical works, and probably post-classical.]

[السُّرْيَانِيَّةُ The Syriac language.]

سَرَّآءٌ One who journeys much, or often, by night. (Ḳ.)

سَارٍ Journeying, or travelling, by night, or in the night, in a general sense: (M, TA:*) pl. سُرَاةٌ. (TA.) — Hence, because of his going [about] by night, (TA,) السَّارِى signifies The lion; as also ▼ المُسَارِى and ▼ المُسْتَرِى. (Ḳ, TA.)

سَارِيَةٌ A party, or company of men, journeying by night. (Er-Rághib, TA.) — And A cloud that comes by night: (Ṣ, Mṣb:) or clouds that travel by night: (Ḳ:) or a cloud that is between that which comes in the early morning and that which comes in the evening: [perhaps thus termed as having previously travelled in the night:] or, accord. to Lḥ, a rain that comes in the night: (M, TA:) pl. سَوَارِى [app. a mistranscription for سَوَارٍ, being indeterminate]. (Ḳ, TA.) — One says, جَآءَ صَبِيحَةَ سَارِيَةٍ He came in the morning of a night in which was rain. (TA.) — And the pl. السَّارِيَاتُ signifies The asses: (M:) or the wild asses: (TA:) because they rest not by night: (M:) or because they pasture by night. (TA.) ═ Also A column, syn. أُسْطُوَانَةٌ, (Ṣ, M, Mṣb, Ḳ,) of stone, or of baked bricks; so in the "Bári':" (TA:) pl. سَوَارٍ. (Mgh.) — [And A mast: see حَنٌّ and صَرٌّ: and see also صَارِيَةٌ.]

أَسْرَى [More, and most, used to night-journeying]. أَسْرَى مِنْ قُنْفُذٍ [More used to go about by night than a hedge-hog] is a prov. of the Arabs. (TA.) [See also the same word in art. سرو.]

مَسْرًى may be a n. of place and a n. of time, [signifying A place, and a time, of night-journeying,] as well as an inf. n. (Ḥam p. 23.) It is [used also in a larger sense, as] syn. with مَذْهَب [A place, and a time, of going &c.: a way by which one goes &c.]. (Ḥar p. 540.)

المُسَارِى: } see سَارٍ, above.
المُسْتَرِى: }

المُتَسَرِّى He who goes forth in, or among, the [company termed] سَرِيَّة. (IAth, TA.)

سسب

سَاسَبٌ and ▼ سَيْسَبٌ, (M, Ḳ,) i. q. سَبْسَبٌ, with two ب s, (L, TA,) the second of which is commonly pronounced بِيسب, and by some سيسم, (TA,) A kind of tree, (M, Ḳ,) a kind of lofty tree, (TA,) of which arrows are made, (M, Ḳ, TA,) and bows. (TA.) In the saying of Ru-beh,

• رَاحَتْ وَرَاحَ كَعِصِىِّ السَّيْسَابْ ▼ •

[She went, and he went, like the rods of the seysáb, (of which see another reading voce سَبْسَبٌ, in art. سب,) meaning, like arrows], it may be that السيساب is a dial. var. of السَّيْسَب, or it may be that the ا is added for the sake of the rhyme like as it is in العَقْرَاب in a verse cited in art. عقرب. (M. [Accord. to the Ḳ and TA, ▼ السَّيْسَاب is used by Ru-beh for السَّيْسَبَان: but this is evidently a mistake.])

سَيْسَبٌ: see the preceding paragraph: — and see also سَيْسَبَانٌ.

سَيْسَبًا, and سَيْسَبَى, and سِيسَبَى, and سَيْسَبَآءُ: see the paragraph that next follows.

سَيْسَبَانٌ and ▼ سَيْسَبَى, (Ḳ,) or the former and ▼ سَيْسَبَآءُ, which is mentioned by Th, (M,) A kind of tree; (M, Ḳ;) accord. to AḤn, it grows from its seeds, and becomes tall, but does not endure the winter; it has leaves like those of the دِفْلَى [q. v.], beautiful; people sow it in the gardens, desiring its beauty; and it has a produce like the oblong pericarps (خَرَائِط) of sesame, but thinner: (M, TA:) AḤn adds that, when its pericarps dry, it makes a rustling sound (a sound such as is termed خَشْخَشَةٌ) [in the wind], like the [species of cassia called] عِشْرِق: (TA:) [the sesbania Aegytiaca of Persoon; æschynomene sesban of Linn.; (Delile, Flor. Aegypt. Illustr., no. 682;) dolichos sesban of Forskål (in his Flora Aegypt. Arab, p. lxx., no. 362):] AḤn further says, وَحَكَى الفَرَّآءُ فِيهِ سَيْسَبًا: (M, TA:) [this may perhaps mean that Fr has mentioned, as a var. of this word, ▼ سَيْسَبٌ, as it is in the accus. case: but I think that the right reading is ▼ سَيْسَبَى, and also سِيسَبَى, (which last has been mentioned above on the authority of the Ḳ,) for it is immediately added in the TA, "it is masc. and fem.," app. indicating that it is with, and without, tenween: then it is there further and strangely added, "it is brought from India:"] a rájiz uses the form ▼ السَّيْسَبَا, at the end of a verse, for السَّيْسَبَانَ, necessarily eliding [the ن for the sake of the rhyme]. (M, TA.)

سَيْسَابٌ: see the first paragraph, in two places.

سسم

سَاسَمٌ, without ء, (AḤát, TA,) A kind of tree, of which arrows are made: (AḤát, M:) a kind of black tree: (Ṣ, Ḳ:) or a kind of tree (AḤn, M, Ḳ) of the mountains, of the [sort termed] عُتْق, (AḤn, M,) of which bows are made: (AḤn, M, Ḳ:) or, (Ḳ,) as some assert, (AḤn, M,) the [tree called] آبِنُوس [i. e. ebony]: (AḤn, M, Ḳ:) or, (Ḳ,) as others assert, (AḤn, M,) the [tree called] شِيز: (AḤn, M, Ḳ: [in some copies of the Ḳ شِيزَى, which means the same:]) but neither of these two is suitable for bows. (AḤn, M.)

سطب

أُسْطُبَّةٌ [an arabicized word, app. from the Greek στύππη or στύπη,] Tow; i. e. what falls from flax in the process of combing. (Ḳ. [See also art. صطب.])

مِسْطَبٌ and مِسْطَبَةٌ are sings. of مَسَاطِبُ, which signifies The [wide benches, of stone or brick &c., generally built against a wall, called] دَكَاكِين, upon which people sit: (AZ, Ḳ:) [and particularly such as surround the court of a mosque: for] one says, رَأَيْتُهُمْ قَاعِدِينَ عَلَى المَسَاطِبِ, meaning [*I saw them sitting upon*] the دَكَاكِين *around the court of the mosque.* (A. [See also art. صطب.]) — The pl. also signifies *Blacksmiths' anvils.* (IAar, K. [See, again, art. صطب.]) — And *Waters stopped up, or choked up, with earth or dust; or altered for the worse by long standing;* syn. مِيَاهٌ سُدُمٌ [q. v.]. (IAar, K.)

سطح

1. سَطَحَهُ, (A, K,) aor. ـَ, (K,) inf. n. سَطْحٌ, (Msb,) *He spread it, spread it out* or *forth*, or *expanded it:* (A, Msb, K:) this is the primary signification. (Msb.) You say, سَطَحَ اللّٰهُ الأَرْضَ, inf. n. as above, *God spread,* or *expanded, the earth.* (S.) And سَطَحَ التَّمْرَ, aor. and inf. n. as above, *He spread the dates* [to dry]. (Msb.) And سَطَحَ الثَّرِيدَ فِى الصَّحْفَةِ [*He spread evenly the crumbled, or broken, bread in the bowl*]. (A.) And سَطَحَ سُطُوحَهُ *He made even his* سُطُوح [or *flat roofs*]; as also ▾ سَطَّحَهَا, (K,) inf. n. تَسْطِيحٌ. (TA.) And سَطَحَ البَيْتَ, aor. and inf. n. as above; [*He made a flat roof to the house, or chamber;*] as also ▾ سَطَّحَهُ. (TA.) And ▾ سَطَّحْتُ القَبْرَ, inf. n. as above, *I made the top* [or *roof*] *of the grave* [*flat*] *like the* سَطْح [*of a house*]: (Msb:) تَسْطِيحُ القَبْرِ *is the contr. of* تَسْنِيمُهُ. (S, A.) — *He threw him down* (A, L, K) [*so that he lay*] *extended on the back of his neck,* (A,) or *spread upon the ground.* (L.) And *He threw him down on his side.* (K.) And سَطَحَ النَّاقَةَ *He made the she-camel to lie down on her breast.* (TA.) — And *He sent him with his mother;* namely, a lamb or kid, or a new-born lamb or kid. (O, K.)

2: see above, in three places.

5: see what next follows.

7. انسطح *It was,* or *became, spread, spread out* or *forth,* or *expanded;* as also ▾ تسطّح. (TA.) — Said of a man, *He became extended* [*lying*] *on the back of his neck,* (S, Msb,) *affected by a disease of long continuance,* or *crippled,* (Msb,) *and moved not:* (S, Msb:) or *he became thrown down* [*so that he lay*] *extended on the back of his neck.* (A.)

Q. Q. 3 [accord. to the S, but of an extr. form]. اِسْلَنْطَحَ *It* (a thing) *was,* or *became, long and wide.* (AA, S. [Mentioned in the S in this art., as though of the measure اِفْلَنْعَلَ: see also art. سلطح.])

سَطْحٌ a word of well-known meaning; (S;) *The upper,* or *uppermost, part* [or *surface*] of a house or chamber &c.; (Msb;) [the *flat top* or *roof* of a house &c.;] the *back* (ظَهْر) of a house or chamber (K, TA) *when it is flat, level,* or *even;* because of its expansion: (TA:) and the *upper,* or *uppermost, part* [or *surface*] of anything: (K:) or it has this last meaning [primarily]: and hence the سَطْح of a house or chamber: (A:) pl. سُطُوحٌ. (Msb, TA.) — [In geometry, *A plane;* i. e.] the سَطْح is *that which is divisible in length and breadth and is terminated by a line* [or *lines*]. (KT.)

سَطِيحٌ *Spread, spread out* or *forth,* or *expanded;* as also ▾ مَسْطُوحٌ. (TA.) — *Extended,* (Msb,) or *thrown down* [*so as to be lying*] *extended,* (A,) or *lying as though thrown down* or *extended,* (S,) *on the back of his neck,* (S, A, Msb,) *in consequence of disease of long continuance,* or *crippleness;* (S, Msb;) and ▾ مُنْسَطِحٌ signifies the same: (A:) or *spread* [*upon the ground*], *slow in rising, by reason of weakness,* (L, K,) or *disease of long continuance,* or *crippleness.* (K.) And One *born weak, unable to stand and to sit, so that he is always spread* [*upon the ground*]. (TA.) And *Slain, spread* [*upon the ground*]; as also ▾ مَسْطُوحٌ. (K.) — See also the next paragraph.

سَطِيحَةٌ *One of the vessels for water;* (TA;) *a* [*leathern water-bag of the kind called*] مَزَادَة, (S, A, Mgh, Msb, K, TA,) *made of two skins* (Mgh, TA) *placed opposite to each other;* it is *small,* and *large; but the* مزادة [*properly so called*] *is larger than it;* (TA;) and ▾ سَطِيحٌ signifies the same. (S, K, TA.)

سُطَّاحٌ *A certain kind of plant,* (As, AHn, S, O, K,) *of the plants that grow in plain,* or *soft, ground:* (AHn, O:) n. un. with ة: (As, AHn, S, O:) accord. to Az, the سُطَّاحَة is *a certain herb,* or *leguminous plant, upon which cattle pasture, and with the leaves of which the heads are washed:* (TA:) or it is *a certain plant growing in plain,* or *soft, tracts, and spreading upon the ground:* or *a certain tree,* or *shrub, that grows in the places where cattle recline around the waters, spreading, but scanty, and of no use.* (L.) And *Any kind of plant that spreads* (AHn, O, K) *upon the ground, and does not grow tall:* such as run and extend, as the melon or water-melon (بِطِّيخ), and the cucumber (قِثَّاء), and the colocynth, are all called شَرْىٌ: and such especially as are eaten [by men], like the gourd, and the cucumber (قِثَّاء and خِيَار), and the melon or water-melon (بِطِّيخ), are called يَقْطِين. (AHn, O.)

مَسْطَحٌ, (Msb,) or ▾ مِسْطَحٌ, (K,) or both, (S, O,) the former because it means a place, (O,) *A place* (S, R, O, Msb) *that is even,* or *level,* (R,) *in which,* (S, O, Msb,) or *upon which,* (R,) *dates are spread* (S, R, O, Msb) *and dried;* (S, R, O;) i. q. جَرِينٌ; (K;) of the dial. of El-Yemen: (TA:) [pl. مَسَاطِحُ.] — رَأَيْتُ الأَرْضَ مَسَاطِحَ means *I saw the land* [*bare, or*] *destitute of pasturage;* likened to بُيُوت مَسْطُوحَة [i. e. flat-topped houses]. (TA.)

مِسْطَحٌ *A rolling-pin;* i. e. the *implement with which bread* [or *dough*] *is expanded.* (O, K.) — The *pole,* (S, A, Mgh, O, Msb,) or *a pole,* (K,) *of a* [*tent such as is called*] خِبَآء, (S, A, O, Msb, K,) or *of a* [*tent such as is called*] فُسْطَاط. (Mgh.) — The *transverse piece of wood upon the two props of the grape-vine, with the hoops* [*that are affixed upon it*]. (K.) ISh says that when a grape-vine had a raised support made for its branches to lie thereon, recourse was had to props, for [the feet of] which holes were dug in the ground, each prop having two forking portions [at the head]; then a piece of wood (خَشَبَة, so in the O, in the TA [erroneously] شعبة,) is taken, and laid across two props, and this transverse piece of wood is called the مِسْطَح, [pl. مَسَاطِح,] and upon the مَسَاطِح are placed hoops, from the nearest part thereof to the furthest; (O, TA;) and the مساطح with the hoops are called مساطح. (O.) — *A smooth piece of rock* or *hard stone, surrounded with stones, in which water collects:* (S, O, K:) or *a wide slab of rock* or *hard stone, bordered round, for the rain-water* [*to collect therein*]: and sometimes God creates, at the mouth of the well, a smooth, even, piece of rock or hard stone, [thus called,] which is surrounded with stones, and from which the camels are watered, like the حَوْض. (T, TA.) [See also حَوْبَة.] — Also *i. q.* مَسْطَحٌ, q. v. (S, O.) — And *A mat* (S, O, K) *woven* (O) *of* خُوص (A, K) or مُقْل (O) [i. e. *leaves*] *of the* دَوْم [or *Theban palm*]; (O, K;) as also ▾ مِسْطَاحٌ. (A.) — *A large roasting-pan* (مِقْلًى) *for wheat,* (K, TA,) *which is roasted therein.* (TA.) — And *A mug* (كُوز) *that is used in travelling, having one* جَنْب [app. here meaning *flat side*]; (O, K, TA;) as also ▾ مِسْطَحَةٌ: it is *like the* مِطْهَرَة; *not four-sided.* (TA.)

مِسْطَحَةٌ: see what next precedes.

مُسَطَّحٌ [*Plane,* or *flat;* opposed to كُرِىٌّ &c.]. — A flat roof (سَطْح) *made even.* (A, TA.) — A nose *spreading very widely.* (S, K.)

مِسْطَاحٌ: see مِسْطَحٌ, last sentence but two.

مَسْطُوحٌ: see سَطِيحٌ, in two places. — بَيْتٌ مَسْطُوحٌ [*A house, or chamber, having a flat roof made to it*]. (TA.)

مُنْسَطِحٌ: see سَطِيحٌ.

سطر

1. سَطَرَ, (S, M, Msb, &c.,) aor. ـُ, (S, M, Msb,) inf. n. سَطْرٌ; (S, M, Msb, K;*) and ▾ سطّر; (M;) and ▾ استطر; (S, M, A, Msb, K;) *He wrote* (S, M,* A, Msb, K) a writing or book. (M, Msb.) — [And سَطَرَ *He ruled* a book. (See مِسْطَرَة.)] — Also سَطَرَ, (TA,) inf. n. as above, (K, TA,) ‡ *He cut* another man *with a sword.* (K,* TA.) — And سَطَرَهُ *He prostrated him; threw him down prostrate.* (S.)

2. سطّر: see 1. — Also, inf. n. تَسْطِيرٌ, *He composed* (M, K) lies, falsehoods, (TA,) or أَسَاطِير, i. e. stories having no foundation, &c. (M.) — Also, [not تسطّر as in Gol.,] *He said what was false:* and *he pretended a false thing.* (KL.) And سطّر عَلَيْنَا أَسَاطِير *He told us* أَسَاطِير, i. e. *stories having no foundation;* or *no right tendency* or *tenour:* (M, K:) or *he told us stories resembling falsehoods:* (Lth:) or *he embellished stories to us with lies:* (TA:) or *he related to us wonderful*

stories of the ancients. (A.) And سطّر فُلَانٌ فُلَانًا *Such a one told falsehoods to such a one.* (Mṣb.) — And سطّرهُ *He made him to form wishes,* or *desires.* (Ṣgh, TA.)

4. اسطر اسْمِى *He passed over the line in which was my name.* (Az, Ḳ.) — And اسطر ‡ *He committed a mistake,* or *an error,* (Ibn-Buzurj, Ḳ, TA,) *in his reading,* or *recitation.* (Ḳ.)

8: see 1, first sentence.

11. اسطارّ, aor. يَسْطَارُّ, [app. signifies *It* (beverage, or wine,) *became what is termed* مُسْطَار or مُسْطَارٌ, q. v.] (TA.)

Q. Q. 1. سَيْطَرَ عَلَيْنَا, (Ṣ, M, A, Ḳ,) inf. n. سَيْطَرَةٌ; (A;) and سَوْطَرَ; (Ḳ;) or سُوطِرَ; (so in a copy of the M; [but see what is said below respecting the pass. form of سَيْطَرَ;]) and † تَسَيْطَرَ; (A, Ḳ;) *He had,* or *exercised, absolute authority over us:* (M, A, Ḳ:) or *he was set in absolute authority over us, to oversee us, and to pay frequent attention to our various states* or *conditions, and to write down our manner of action:* (Ṣ:) or *he acted as a watcher and guardian over us,* (M, Ḳ, TA,) *paying frequent attention to us:* (TA:) also written with ص in the place of س; but originally it is with س, from السَّطْرُ: and every س immediately followed by ط may be changed into ص: (TA:) the pass. form of سَيْطَرَ is not used. (T.)

Q. Q. 2. تَسَيْطَرَ: see the next preceding paragraph.

سَطْرٌ, (Ṣ, M, A, Mṣb, Ḳ,) originally an inf. n., [see 1,] (Ṣ,) and † سَطَرٌ, (Ṣ, M, Mṣb, Ḳ,) *A line* (Ṣ, M, Ḳ) of a book or writing: (M, A, Ḳ:) and *a writing:* (Ṣ, Ḳ:) and ‡ *a line* or *row* (Ṣ, M, A, Mṣb, Ḳ) of buildings, (Ṣ, A,) and of trees, (Ṣ, M, A, Mṣb, Ḳ,) &c., (Mṣb, Ḳ,) and [particularly] of palm-trees, and the like, (M,) [and so, app., † مُسْطَار, q. v.:] pl. (of the former, Ṣ, Mṣb) أَسْطُرٌ (Ṣ, M, A, Mṣb, Ḳ) and (of the latter, Ṣ) أَسْطَارٌ (Ṣ, M, A, Ḳ) [both pls. of pauc.] and (of the former, Ṣ, Mṣb) سُطُورٌ, (Ṣ, M, A, Mṣb, Ḳ,) and أَسَاطِيرُ (Lḥ, Ṣ, M, Ḳ) is a pl. pl., (Ṣ, Ḳ,) i. e. pl. of أَسْطَارٌ. (Ṣ.) You say, كَتَبَ سَطْرًا مِنْ كِتَابَةٍ [*He wrote a line of writing*]: (A:) and بَنَى سَطْرًا ‡ *He built a row* (Ṣ, A) مِنْ بِنَائِهِ [*of his building*]: (A:) and غَرَسَ سَطْرًا ‡ *He planted a row* (Ṣ, A) مِنْ وَدِيِّهِ [*of his palm-shoots,* or *young palm-trees*]. (A.) — [Hence the saying,] اِجْعَلِ الأَمْرَ سَطْرًا وَاحِدًا † *Make thou the affair,* or *case,* [*uniform,* or] *one uniform thing.* (Fr, TA in art. بأج.) — Also the former, (سَطْرٌ,) *A yearling* (عَتُودٌ, T, M, Ḳ) *of goats,* (M,) or *of sheep* or *goats:* (T, Ḳ:) and صَطْرٌ is a dial. var. thereof. (IDrd, M.)

سَطَرٌ: see the next preceding paragraph.

سُطُرٌ: see أُسْطُورَةٌ.

سُطْرَةٌ ‡ *An object of wish* or *desire.* (Ḳ, TA.) You say, رَاجَعْتُ فُلَانًا وَلَمْ يُسَاعِدْ سُطْرَتِى ‡ [*I consulted such a one, and he did not aid in the accomplishment of the object of my wish* or *desire*]. (TḲ.)

سَطَّارٌ: see what next follows.

سَاطِرٌ ‡ *A butcher;* (Fr, O, Ḳ, TA;) as also † سَطَّارٌ. (Fr, O, TA.)

سَاطُورٌ *A butcher's cleaver;* (MA, O, Ḳ;*) i. e. the *great knife with which the butcher cuts* [*the slaughtered beast:* pl. سَوَاطِيرُ]. (O.)

أُسْطُورَةٌ [resembling the Greek ἱστορία] (Ṣ, M, A, Mṣb, Ḳ) and أُسْطُورٌ (M, Mṣb, Ḳ) and إِسْطَارَةٌ (Ṣ, M, Mṣb, Ḳ) and إِسْطَارٌ and إِسْطِيرَةٌ and إِسْطِيرٌ (M, Ḳ) sings. of أَسَاطِيرُ, (Ṣ, M, A, Mṣb, Ḳ,) which signifies *Lies;* or *falsehoods;* or *fictions:* (Ṣ, Mṣb, TA:) or *stories having no foundation,* or *no right tendency* or *tenour:* (لَا نِظَامَ لَهَا:) [such as we commonly term *legends:*] (M, Ḳ:) or *wonderful stories* of the ancients: (A:) or their *written stories:* (Bḍ in viii. 31:) or their *written tales:* (Jel in lxxxiii. 13:) or their *written lies:* (Bḍ in xxiii. 85, and Jel in xxvii. 70:) or *stories embellished with lies;* as also † سُطُرٌ: (TA:) or, accord. to some, أَسَاطِيرُ is pl. of أَسْطَارٌ which is pl. of سَطْرٌ: or, accord. to AO, اساطير is pl. of أَسْطُرٌ which is pl. of سَطْرٌ: or, accord. to Abu-l-Ḥasan, اساطير has no sing.: (M:) or the pl. of أَسْطُرٌ, accord. to AO, is أَسَاطِرُ, i. e., without ى: or, as some say, اساطير is an irreg. pl. of سَطْرٌ. (TA.)

مِسْطَرَةٌ *An instrument with which a book is ruled* (يُسْطَرُ) [*made of a piece of pasteboard with strings strained and glued across it, which is laid under the paper; the latter being ruled by being slightly pressed over each string*]. (TA.)

مَسْطُورٌ *Written.* (Ṣ, M.)

مُسَيْطِرٌ: see مُسَيْطَرٌ.

مُسْطَارٌ: see سَطْرٌ. — † *Dust rising into the sky:* (Ḳ, TA;) as being likened to a row of palm-trees or other things. (TA.) — Also, (thus in some copies of the Ḳ, and so correctly written accord. to Ṣgh, with ḍamm, TA,) or مِسْطَارٌ, (thus in the Ṣ, and in some copies of the Ḳ,) with kesr to the م, (Ṣ,) or with teshdeed, [مُسْطَارٌّ,] as written by Ks, and this also shows it to be with ḍamm, being in this case from إِسْطَارَّ, aor. يَسْطَارُّ, (Ṣgh, TA,) *A kind of wine in which is acidity;* (Ṣ;) *an acid kind of wine:* (A'Obeyd, Ḳ:) or *a kind of wine which prostrates its drinker:* (Ḳ:) or *new,* or *recently-made, wine,* (Ḳ,) *of which the taste and odour are altered:* (TA:) or *wine made of the earliest of grapes, recently:* (T, TA:) or *a wine in which is a taste between sweet and sour;* also termed † مُسْطَارَةٌ: (Ḥar p. 618:) Az says, it is of the dial. of the people of Syria; and I think that it is Greek, [or perhaps it is from the Latin "mustarius," which is from "mustum,"] because it does not resemble an Arabic form: it is with ص, or, as some say, with س; and [app. a mistake for "or"] I think it to be of the measure مُفْتَعَل from صَارَ, with the ت changed into ط. (TA.)

مُسْطَارَةٌ: see the next preceding paragraph.

مُسَيْطِرٌ (Ṣ, M, A, Mṣb, Ḳ) and † مُسَيْطَرٌ, (Ṣ, Ḳ,) as also مُصَيْطِرٌ, (Ṣ, A,) One *who has,* or *exercises, absolute authority* (M, A, Ḳ) *over others:* (M:) one *who is set in absolute authority over a thing* [or *people*], *to oversee it, and to pay frequent attention to its various states* or *conditions, and to write down its manner of action:* from السَّطْرُ: (Ṣ:) or *a watcher* and *guardian;* (M, Ḳ;) one *who pays frequent attention to a thing.* (Mṣb,* TA.)

سطرنج

سِطْرَنْج [commonly pronounced سِطْرَنْج] a dial. var. of شِطْرَنْج. (Ḳ in art. شطرنج, q. v.)

سطع

1. سَطَعَ, aor. ـَ, (Ṣ, Mgh,* Mṣb, Ḳ,) inf. n. سُطُوعٌ (Ṣ, Ḳ) and سَطْعٌ (TA) and سَطِيعٌ, which last is rare, (Ḳ,) *It rose:* (Ṣ, Mgh, Mṣb, Ḳ, TA:) or *it spread,* or *diffused itself:* (Mgh, TA:) said of dust, and of the dawn, (Ṣ, Mṣb, Ḳ,) [meaning as above, and *it radiated, gleamed,* or *shone,* (see سَاطِعٌ,)] and of light, (TA,) and of lightning, and of the rays of the sun, (Ḳ,) and ‡ of odour, (Ṣ, Mgh, Mṣb, Ḳ,) in relation to which last it is tropical, and signifies *it diffused itself, and rose:* or it was originally said only of light; and was then used absolutely, as meaning *it appeared,* or *became apparent.* (TA.) You say also سَطَعَ السَّهْمُ *The arrow,* being shot, *rose into the sky, glistening.* (TA.) And يَسْطَعُ, the aor. of سَطَعَ, is used by Dhu-r-Rummeh, in describing an ostrich, as meaning *He raises his head, and stretches his neck.* (TA.) And you say, سَطَعَ لِى أَمْرُكَ † *Thine affair became,* or *has become, apparent,* or *manifest, to me.* (Lḥ.) — سَطَعَتْنِى رَائِحَةُ المِسْكِ ‡ *The odour of the musk rose to my nose.* (Ḳ, TA.) — سَطَعْتُ الشَّىْءَ *I laid hold of the thing with the palm of the hand,* or *with the hand, striking* [*the thing*]. (Mṣb.) And سَطَعَ بِيَدَيْهِ, inf. n. سَطْعٌ, *He clapped with his hands:* whence the subst. سَطْعٌ [q. v.]. (IDrd, Ḳ.) — سَطِعَ, aor. ـَ, (Ḳ,) inf. n. سَطَعٌ, (TḲ,) *He was long-necked; he had a long neck.* (Ḳ.) [See أَسْطَعُ.]

2. سَطَّعَهُ, inf. n. تَسْطِيعٌ, *He marked him* (namely a camel) *with the mark called* سِطَاعٌ. (Ḳ.)

اِسْطَعْتُهُ (for اِسْتَطَعْتُهُ), aor. أَسْطِيعُهُ (for أَسْتَطِيعُهُ); or أَسْطَعْتُهُ (for أَطَعْتُهُ), aor. أُسْطِيعُهُ (for أُطِيعُهُ): see in art. طوع. (TA.)

سَطَعٌ *Length of neck.* (Ṣ.) It is said of Moḥammad, فِى عُنُقِهِ سَطَعٌ *In his neck was length.* (TA.) [See أَسْطَعُ.] — *A clapping with the hands,* or *striking with one hand upon the other,* or *upon the hand of another:* (Ḳ:) or *a striking a thing with the palm of the hand,* or *with the fingers.* (TA.) And The *sound of a striking* or *throwing:* as in the saying, سَمِعْتُ لِوَقْعِهِ سَطَعًا شَدِيدًا [*I heard, in consequence of its falling, a loud sound of a striking* or *throwing*]. (Ḳ.) It is with fet-ḥ to the medial radical because it is an onomatopœia, not an epithet nor an inf. n., for onomatopœias are sometimes made to differ [in form] from epithets. (Lth, Ḳ.)

سِطَاعٌ The *pole of the* [*tent called*] بَيْت: (Ṣ, Ḳ:) and the *longest of the poles of the* [*tent called*] خِبَآء: (Ḳ:) from سَاطِعٌ applied to the dawn: (Az, TA:) and *a pole that is set up in the middle of the* خباء and *of the* [*tent called*] رِوَاق: pl. [of pauc.] أَسْطِعَةٌ and [of mult.] سُطُعٌ. (TA.) — Hence, as being likened thereto, ‡ The *neck.* (TA.) — Hence also, (Az, TA,) ‡ *A tall, bulky, camel.* (Az, Ibn-'Abbád, Ḳ, TA.) — † *A mark made with a hot iron upon the neck of a camel,* (Az, Ṣ, Ḳ,) or *upon his side,* (TA,) *lengthwise:* (Az, Ṣ, Ḳ, TA:) in the R, it is said to be *upon the limbs,* or *members.* (TA.)

سَطِيعٌ *Tall,* or *long.* (Ḳ.) — See also سَاطِعٌ.

سَاطِعٌ *Rising:* or *spreading,* or *diffusing itself:* [and *radiating, gleaming,* or *shining:*] applied [to dust, (see 1,) and] to the dawn, and to light, and to fire [&c.]: applied to the dawn, it denotes that *extending lengthwise into the sky, and called* ذَنَبُ السِّرْحَانِ [q. v.]. (TA.) — Also The *dawn* [*itself*]; (TA;) and so ▼ سَطِيعٌ; (Ṣ, TA;) because of its shining, and spreading; *when it first breaks, extending lengthwise.* (TA.) — نَاقَةٌ سَاطِعَةٌ *A she-camel having the front of the neck,* and *the* [*whole*] *neck, extended.* (TA.)

أَسْطَعُ *Long-necked;* (Ḳ;) applied to a camel, and an ostrich: (TA:) fem. سَطْعَآءُ; applied to a she-camel, (TA,) and a she-ostrich. (Ṣ.) — عُنُقٌ أَسْطَعُ *A long, erect, neck:* (TA:) and عُنُقٌ سَطْعَآءُ *a neck that is long, and erect in its sinews.* (AO, in describing horses; and TA.)

مِسْطَعٌ *Chaste in speech;* or *eloquent;* (Lḥ, Ḳ, TA;) *fluent in speech.* (TA.)

مُسَطَّعٌ † A camel *marked with the mark called* سِطَاع; (Ṣ, TA;) fem. with ة: and ▼ مَسْطُوعَةٌ signifies the same, applied to a she-camel. (TA.) — And إِبِلٌ مُسَطَّعَةٌ † *Camels tall as the tent-poles called* سُطُع, pl. of سِطَاع. (TA.)

مَسْطُوعَةٌ: see مُسَطَّعٌ.

سطل

1. سَطَلَهُ, inf. n. سَطْلٌ, said of a medicine, *It intoxicated him:* but it is a vulgar word. (TA.) — [And hence, † *He,* or *it, charmed,* or *fascinated,* or *delighted, him.*]

7. انسطال *A state of intoxication* produced by the حَشِيش [or herb, or perhaps species of hemp,] known by the name of زيه; as also ▼ اِسْتِطَال. (De Sacy's Chrest. Ar., 2nd ed., i. 282; from the book entitled كتاب الكواكب السائرة فى اخبار مصر والقاهرة.) [Both app. post-classical: see 1, of which each is quasi-pass.]

8. اِسْتِطَال: see what next precedes.

Q. Q. 2. جَآءَ يَتَسَيْطَلُ *He came alone, having nothing with him.* (Ibn-'Abbád, Ḳ.)

سَطْلٌ A طُسَيْسَة [or *small vessel of the kind called* طَسّ, or طَسْت, q. v.], (M, Ḳ,) *like the* تَوْر [q. v.], (M,) *having a loop-shaped handle,* (M, Ḳ,) *like that of the* مِرْجَل; (TA;) *well known:* (Ṣ, Mṣb:) a genuine Arabic word: (M:) or an arabicized word: [said by Golius to be in Pers. سَطْل:] and صَطْل is a dial. var. thereof: (Mṣb:) *a vessel of copper, a large* [*vessel of the kind called*] طَاس [q. v.], *for the hot bath;* (MA;) the *thing* [i. e. *vessel*] *in which water is drawn from the hot bath:* (KL:) [in the present day applied to *a kind of pail, of tinned copper, which the women take with them to the hot bath, containing the water that they require for washing after the other operations of the bath; and also used for various other purposes;* as also ▼ سَطْلَةٌ:] and ▼ سَيْطَل signifies the same: (Ṣ, M, Ḳ, KL:) or this last signifies, (Ḳ,) or signifies also, (M,) *a* [*vessel of the kind called*] طَسْت; (M, Ḳ;) *not the well-known* [*vessel called*] سَطْل: (Ḳ:) the pl. [of mult.] of سَطْل is سُطُول (M, Mṣb, Ḳ) and [of pauc.] أَسْطَال. (Mṣb.)

سَطْلَةٌ: see the next preceding paragraph.

سَاطِلٌ Dust *rising,* or *rising high;* as also طَاسِلٌ. (Ḳ.)

سَيْطَلٌ: see سَطْلٌ. — Also *A tall* man: (Ḳ:) or سَيْطَلٌ نَيْطَلٌ a man *tall,* or *long, in body.* (Ibn-'Abbád, TA.)

أُسْطُولٌ *A ship of war, prepared for fighting with the unbelievers on the sea:* mentioned by El-Maḳreezee in the "Khiṭaṭ;" and he says, "I do not think this word to be [genuine] Arabic:" (TA:) [it is evidently from the Greek στόλος:] several writers mention it among arabicized words. (MF, TA.)

سطن

[2. سَطَّنَ a verb of which only the pass. part. n. (q. v. infrà) is mentioned: if used, app. signifying *He supported upon* أَسَاطِين, i. e. *columns:* — and hence, *upon long legs:* — and *he made firm.*]

سَاطِنٌ *i. q.* خَبِيثٌ [*Bad, corrupt,* &c.; like شَاطِنٌ]. (M, L, Ḳ.)

أُسْطَانٌ [a pl. of which the sing. is not mentioned] *Vessels of* صُفْر [or *brass*]. (L, Ḳ.)

أُسْطُوَانٌ, an arabicized word, (Az, L,) [app. from the Pers. أُسْتُون, like the word next following,] A man *long in the legs and back.* (M, L.) And A camel *long in the neck,* (M, L, Ḳ,) or (Ḳ) *high.* (Ṣ, M, L, Ḳ.) — What is termed أُسْتُوَانُ البَيْتِ is well known [app. meaning *The pole of the tent:* (see what next follows:) and this seems to be the primary signification]. (M, L.)

أُسْطُوَانَةٌ a word of well-known meaning, (Ṣ, L,) arabicized from [the Pers.] أُسْتُون [which signifies the same], (Ḳ,) *i. q.* سَارِيَةٌ [meaning *A column, of stone* or *of baked bricks*]: (Ṣ, M, L, Mṣb, Ḳ:) pl. أَسَاطِينُ (Ṣ, M,* L, Mṣb, Ḳ*) and أُسْطُوَانَاتٌ: (Mṣb:) it is of the measure أُفْعُوَالَةٌ, (Ṣ, L, Mṣb, Ḳ,) because its pl. is أَسَاطِينُ, the ن being radical, (L, Mṣb,) accord. to Kh (Mṣb) and Fr, who says that it is the only instance of this measure; (L;) or of the measure فُعْلُوَانَةٌ, (Ṣ, L, Ḳ,) accord. to Akh, but, (J says, L,) if so, the و is augmentative and has next to it two augmentative letters, and this is scarcely ever, or never, the case; (Ṣ, L;) IB, however, says that this is the true measure, as is shown by its pl., أَسَاطِينُ, and its dim., ▼ أُسَيْطِينَةٌ: (L:) accord. to some, it is of the measure أُفْعُلَانَةٌ, (Ṣ, L, Mṣb,) but, if it were so, it would not have for its pl. أَسَاطِينُ, as there is no instance of the measure أَفَاعِينُ. (Ṣ, L.) — [Also *A portico.* Hence, أَهْلُ الأُسْطُوَانَةِ *The Stoics.* — And *A cylinder.*] — And The *legs* of a beast: (Ḳ:) [or rather the pl.] أَسَاطِينُ has this meaning. (L.) — And The *penis.* (Ḳ.)

أُسَيْطِينَةٌ dim. of أُسْطُوَانَةٌ, q. v. (IB, L.)

مُسَطَّنٌ [app. *Supported upon* أَسَاطِين, i. e. *columns.* — And hence,] A man, and a beast, *having long legs.* (L.) — And أَسَاطِينُ مُسَطَّنَةٌ (Ṣ, M, L, Ḳ,) [*Columns*] *made firm.* (Ḳ.)

سطو

1. سَطَا بِهِ (Ṣ, M, Mṣb, Ḳ, &c.) and عَلَيْهِ (M, Mṣb, Ḳ,) aor. يَسْطُو, (Mṣb,) inf. n. سَطْوٌ (Ṣ, M, Mṣb, Ḳ) and سَطْوَةٌ, (M, Mṣb, Ḳ,) or the latter is an inf. n. un., (Ṣ,) *He sprang,* or *rushed, upon him; made an assault,* or *attack, upon him;* syn. صَالَ: (M, Ḳ:) *he sprang upon him and seized him violently* or *laid violent hands upon him:* (Bḍ in xxii. 71:) *he seized him violently with uplifted hand:* (Er-Rághib, TA:) *he overbore him, overpowered him,* or *subdued him,* (قَهَرَهُ, Lth, Ṣ, Mṣb, Ḳ, or تَطَاوَلَ عَلَيْهِ, T, TA,) *by seizing him violently,* or *laying violent hands upon him,* (Lth, Ṣ, Ḳ,) *and abased him;* or *he seized him with great violence:* (Mṣb:) or *he stretched forth his hand to him* [*to seize him*]. (Th, M, TA.) And in like manner, (M,) one says of a stallion [camel], يَسْطُو عَلَى طَرُوقَتِهِ [*He springs,* or *rushes, upon,* or *he overbears, the she-camel that he covers*]. (Ṣ, M.*) — سَطَا عَلَى النَّاقَةِ, (Ṣ, M, Ḳ,) and الفَرَسِ, inf. n. سَطْوٌ and سُطُوٌّ, (M,) *He* (the pastor) *put his hand into the* رَحِم [or *vulva*] *of the she-camel,* (Ṣ, M, Ḳ,) and *of the mare,* (M,) *to extract,* (Ṣ, Ḳ,) or *and extracted,* (M,) *the sperma of the stallion:* (Ṣ, M, Ḳ:) when this is not extracted, the she-camel

does not conceive: (Ṣ:) or this is done when she has been leaped by a stallion of low race; or when the sperma is bad, and she has not conceived in consequence of it. (M.) And *He extracted from her* (i. e. a she-camel, TA) *the fœtus, dead:* (M, TA:) and مَسَطَ signifies "he extracted the sperma of the stallion:" thus Az distinguishes between the two verbs. (TA.) Accord. to IAạr, one says, سَطَا عَلَى الحَامِلِ, and سَاطَ, which is formed by transposition, meaning *He extracted the fœtus,* or *young one, of the pregnant female.* (TA.) And A'Obeyd mentions السَّطْوُ as used in relation to a woman: it is said in a trad. of El-Ḥasan, لَا بَأْسَ أَنْ يَسْطُوَ الرَّجُلُ عَلَى المَرْأَةِ [*There is,* or *will be, no harm in the man's extracting the fœtus of the woman*]; (M, TA;) which Lth explains by saying, when her child sticks fast in her belly, dead, it may be extracted [by him] when fear is entertained for her and a woman is not found to do this. (TA.) — سَطَا said of a horse, (M, Ḳ,) inf. n. سَطْوٌ, (M,) *He went at random, heedlessly,* or *in a headlong manner, not obeying guidance.* (M, Ḳ.) — Also, said of a horse, *He went with wide step:* (Ṣ, M, Ḳ:) or *raised his tail in running;* the doing of which is approved. (M.) — Also ‡ *It was,* or *became, abundant,* or *copious;* said of water. (Ṣ, M, Mṣb, Ḳ, TA.) — And ‡ *He tasted* food; (Ḳ, TA;) and *took* it *with the hand,* or *with the extended hand.* (TA.) — And *i. q.* عَاقَبَ [app. as meaning *He punished:* see سَطْوَةٌ, below]. (M, TA.) — And سَطَاهَا *He compressed her;* [and so سَطَأَهَا and شَطَأَهَا;] on the authority of Aboo-Sa'eed. (TA.)

3. سَاطَاهُ, (Ḳ,) inf. n. مُسَاطَاةٌ, (TA,) *He treated him with hardness, severity,* or *rigour:* (Ḳ, TA:) so says Az, on the authority of IAạr. (TA.) — And *He treated him with gentleness,* or *tenderness.* (IAạr, T, TA.) Thus it has two contr. significations. (TA.)

سَطْوَةٌ [as a simple subst., or] as an inf. n. un., has for its pl. سَطَوَاتٌ. (Ṣ.) It signifies [*A spring,* or *rush;* or *an assault,* or *attack:* &c.: (see 1, first sentence:) *impetuosity* in war or battle:] *a reviling: a beating:* and *punishment,* or *chastisement;* as in the saying, اِتَّقِ سَطْوَتَهُ [*Guard thyself against his punishment,* or *chastisement;* or it may mean in this phrase, *his violence,* or *impetuosity*]. (TA.)

سَاطٍ [act. part. n. of 1, *Springing,* or *rushing; making an assault,* or *attack:* &c. — Hence,] applied to a horse, *That springs,* or *rushes, upon other horses, and stands upon his hind legs and attacks with his fore legs:* (T, TA: [in the Ḥam p. 383, *and raises his fore legs:*]) or a horse *wide in step:* (Aṣ, Ṣ, M, Ḳ:) or *that attacks other horses:* (Ṣ:) or *that raises his tail in his running;* (Ṣ, M, Ḳ;) the doing of which is approved. (M.) — And A stallion-camel *excited by lust, and going forth from camels to other camels* (Ṣ, Ḳ) *in consequence thereof.* (Ṣ.) — And What is *tall,* or *long,* (K, TA,) of camels &c. (TA.) — الأَيْدِى السَّوَاطِى *The hands that reach,* or *take,* or *take hold of, a thing.* (TA.)

سعب

5. تسعّب *It* (a thing, TA, [such as saliva, and any thick liquid,]) *roped;* i. e. *drew out, with a viscous, glutinous, cohesive, sticky, ropy,* or *slimy, continuity of parts;* or *was,* or *became, viscous, glutinous, cohesive, sticky, ropy,* or *slimy;* syn. تَمَطَّطَ. (Ḳ.)

7. انسعب *It* (water [&c.]) *flowed;* (Ḳ;) [or *flowed in a continuous stream;*] like انثعب (TA) [and انذعب].

سَعْبٌ Any kind of wine, or beverage, &c., *that ropes;* i. e. *that draws out, with a viscous, glutinous, cohesive, sticky, ropy,* or *slimy, continuity of parts;* or *that is viscous, glutinous,* &c. (Ḳ.)

سُعْبُوبٌ and سُعْبُوبَةٌ: see the next paragraph.

سَعَابِيبُ *What extend like threads,* or *strings, from honey* (A,* Ḳ) *and marsh-mallows,* (Ḳ,) *and the like:* (A, Ḳ:) pl. of ♦ سُعْبُوبٌ. (TA.) You say, سَالَ فَمُهُ سَعَابِيبَ *His slaver extended,* or *stretched out, like threads,* or *strings.* (A, Ḳ.) And فُوهُ يَجْرِى سَعَابِيبَ *His mouth runs with clear water, having an extended* [or *a ropy*] *flow;* like يجرى ثَعَابِيبَ. (Ṣ.) — And *What follow the hand in milking,* [*stretching out*] *like phlegm:* pl. of ♦ سُعْبُوبَةٌ. (ISh, TA.)

هُوَ مُسْعَبٌ لَهُ كَذَا وَكَذَا *To him are allowed,* or *permitted, such and such things:* (Ḳ:) like مُرْغَبٌ and مُسْغَبٌ. (TA.)

سعتر

سَعْتَرٌ *A certain plant,* (Ṣ, Mṣb, Ḳ,) *of the kind called* بَقْوْل, (Mgh,) *well known;* (Mṣb, Ḳ;) and applied also to the *grain,* or *seed, thereof:* (Mgh:) [*a species of origanum,* or *majoram:* so in the present day; and so says Golius, as on the authority of Ibn-Beyṭár, "*origani species,* sc. consonante voce, *satureia,* Hisp. *axedrea:*" accord. to Forskål, (Flora Aeg. Arab. p. cxiv.,) "*thymus serpyllum:*"] some write the word in books of medicine with ص, in order that [when written without the diacritical points] it may not be confounded with شَعِير: (Ṣ, Mgh:) in the T, it is with ص, on the authority of AA, only; and thus in the book of Lth: in the Jámi' of El-Ghooree, with س and ص: (Mgh:) or the س is changed into ص in the dial. of Bel'ambar [or Benu-l-'Ambar]; and some pronounced it only with ص: (Mṣb:) accord. to Abu-l-'Alà, the vulgar pronounce it with س, and the approved word is with ص. (Ḥam p. 462.) [In the present day, it is also written with ز.]

سَعْتَرِىٌّ *i. q.* شَاطِرٌ [q. v.], (Ḳ,) in the dial. of the people of El-'Irák. (TA.) — And *Generous, noble,* or *high-born, and courageous, brave,* or *strong-hearted.* (Ḳ.) The pronunciation with ص is of higher authority. (Ḳ. [This remark is probably there meant to relate to both of the words of this art.])

سعد

1. سَعَدَ, (Ṣ, A, Mṣb, Ḳ,) aor. ـَ; (Mṣb, Ḳ;) and سَعِدَ; (Ṣ, A, Mṣb, Ḳ;) inf. n. of the former, (Mṣb,) or of the latter, (MA,) or of both, (TA,) سَعْدٌ, (MA, Mṣb, TA,) and of the former, (MA,) or of both, (TA,) سَعَادَةٌ, (MA, TA,) or this latter is a simple subst.; (Mṣb;) *He* (a man, Ṣ, A, Mṣb) *was,* or *became, prosperous, fortunate, happy,* or *in a state of felicity;* (Ṣ, MA, Mṣb, TA;) *contr. of* شَقِىَ; (Ṣ,* Mṣb, Ḳ;*) with respect to religion and with respect to worldly things. (Mṣb.) You say, سَعِدْتُ بِهِ and سُعِدْتُ [*I was,* or *became, prosperous,* &c., *by means of him,* or *it*]. (A.) In the Ḳur xi. 110, Ks read سُعِدُوا [instead of the common reading سَعِدُوا]. (Ṣ.) [See also سَعَادَةٌ, below.] — And سَعَدَ يَوْمُنَا, aor. ـَ, inf. n. سُعُودٌ (Ṣ, Ḳ) and سَعْدٌ, (Ḳ,) *Our day was,* or *became, prosperous, fortunate, auspicious,* or *lucky;* (Ṣ, Ḳ;) [*contr. of* نَحِسَ; and in like manner the verb is used in relation to a star or an asterism &c.; and] سَعِدَ, inf. n. سَعْدٌ, signifies [likewise] the *contr. of* نُحِسَ. (Mgh.) [See also سُعُودَةٌ, below.] — سَعَدَ المَآءُ فِى الأَرْضِ means *The water came upon the land unsought;* i. e., *came flowing* [*naturally*] *upon the surface of the land, not requiring a machine to raise it for the purpose of irrigation.* (TA, from a trad.) — See also 4, in three places.

3. ساعدهُ, (A, L, Mṣb,) inf. n. مُسَاعَدَةٌ (Ṣ, L, Mṣb) and سِعَادٌ; (L;) and ♦ اسعدهُ, (Ḳ,) inf. n. إِسْعَادٌ; (Ṣ;) *He aided, assisted,* or *helped, him;* syn. of the former عَاوَنَهُ, (Ṣ,* L, Mṣb,) and of the latter أَعَانَهُ: (Ṣ,* Ḳ:) [like as is said of عَاوَنَهُ and أَعَانَهُ,] both signify the same: or مُسَاعَدَةٌ signifies the *aiding,* or *assisting,* or *helping, in any manner* or *case;* and is said to be from a man's putting his arm, or hand, upon the سَاعِد [or fore arm] of his companion when they walk together to accomplish some object of want, and aid each other to do a thing: [so that سَاعَدَهُ more properly signifies *he aided him, being aided by him:* but see سَاعِدٌ:] whereas ♦ إِسْعَادٌ signifies specially a woman's *aiding, assisting,* or *helping,* another *to wail* for a dead person: so says El-Khaṭṭábee: and this is what is meant in a trad. in which اسعاد is forbidden. (L.) One says, ساعدهُ عَلَيْهِ [*He aided, assisted,* or *helped him against him,* or *it,* or *to do it*]: and أَسْعَدَتِ ♦ النَّائِحَةُ الثَّكْلَى *The wailing-woman assisted the woman bereft of her child to weep and wail.* (A.) Accord. to Fr, [but this is questionable,] the primary signification of مُسَاعَدَةٌ and ♦ إِسْعَادٌ is A man's *performing diligently the command and good pleasure of God.* (L.)

4. اسعدهُ اللّٰهُ, [inf. n. إِسْعَادٌ,] *God rendered him prosperous, fortunate, happy,* or *in a state of felicity;* (Ṣ, Mṣb, Ḳ;) as also ♦ سَعَدَهُ, aor. ـَ; (T, Mṣb, TA;) but the former is the more common. (Mṣb.) And اسعد اللّٰهُ جَدَّهُ, (A, L,) *God made his good fortune to increase;* as also ♦ سَعَدَ جَدَّهُ. (L.) And accord. to Az, اسعدهُ اللّٰهُ and ♦ سَعَدَهُ signify *God aided, assisted,* or *helped, him;* and *accommodated, adapted,* or *disposed, him to the right course.* (L, TA.) See also 3, in four places.

5. تسعّد *He sought after the plant called* سُعْدَان. (Ḳ.)

10. استسعد به *He deemed it, or reckoned it, fortunate, auspicious, or lucky.* (Ḳ.) You say, استسعد بِرُؤْيَةِ فُلَانٍ *He deemed, or reckoned, the sight of such a one fortunate, auspicious, or lucky.* (Ṣ.) —— *He became fortunate by means of him, or it.* (MA.) —— *He sought good fortune by means of him, or it.* (MA.) —— [And استسعدهُ *He desired, or demanded, his aid or assistance:* for] اِسْتِسْعَادٌ also signifies the *desiring, or demanding, aid or assistance* [of another]. (KL.)

سَعْدٌ an inf. n. of سَعَدَ, (Mṣb,) or of سَعِدَ, (MA,) or of both: (TA:) and of سَعَدَ: (Ḳ, TA:) [and also used as a simple subst.:] see سَعَادَةٌ [with which it is syn.]: and see also سُعُودَةٌ [with which it is likewise syn.]; i. q. يُمْنٌ. (Ṣ, A.) —— It is also an inf. n. used as an epithet, i. e. *Prosperous, fortunate, auspicious, or lucky,* applied to a day, and to a star or an asterism [&c.: so that it may be used alike as masc. and fem. and sing. and pl.: but it is also used as originally an epithet, forming its fem. with ة; and in this case it has for pl. of mult. سُعُودٌ and pl. of pauc. أَسْعُدٌ]: you say يَوْمٌ سَعْدٌ, as well as يَوْمُ سَعْدٍ [in which it is used as a subst.]; and كَوْكَبٌ سَعْدٌ: and IJ mentions لَيْلَةٌ سَعْدَةٌ, in which سَعْدَةٌ is like جَعْدَةٌ as fem. of جَعْدٌ. (L.) —— [Hence,] السَّعْدَانِ is an appellation of *The two planets Venus and Mercury:* like as [the contr.] النَّحْسَانِ is applied to Saturn and Mars. (Ibn-'Abbád, TA in art. نحس.) —— And [hence, also,] سَعْدٌ is an appellation given to *Each of ten asterisms,* (Ṣ, L, Ḳ,) *four of which are in the signs of Capricornus and Aquarius,* (Ṣ, L,) *and are Mansions of the Moon:* pl. [of mult.] سُعُودٌ (Ṣ, L, Ḳ) and سُعْدٌ; but the former is the more known, and more agreeable with analogy; and pl. of pauc. أَسْعُدٌ: (L:) they are distinguished by the following names:—سَعْدُ الذَّابِحِ, (Ṣ, L, Ḳ,) [or سَعْدُ الذَّابِحِ, see art. ذبح,] *Two stars near together, one of which is called* الذابح *because with it is a small obscure star, almost close to it, and it seems as though the former were about to slaughter it; and* الذابح *is a little brighter than it;* (Ibn-Kunáseh;) they are *the two stars* [α and β] *which are in one of the horns of Capricornus;* so called because of the small adjacent star, which is said to be the sheep (شَاة) of الذابح, which he is about to slaughter; *the Twenty-second Mansion of the Moon:* (Ḳzw:) [see also art. ذبح:] —— سَعْدُ بُلَعَ (Ṣ, L, Ḳ) *Two obscure stars, lying obliquely,* of which Aboo-Yaḥyà says, the Arabs assert that they rose [at dawn] when God said, يَا أَرْضُ ٱبْلَعِى مَآءَكِ [Ḳur xi. 46]; and said to be thus called because one of them seems as though about to swallow the other, on account of its nearness to it: (Ibn-Kunáseh:) or *three stars* [app. ε and μ *with the star of the same magnitude next to them on the north*] on [or rather near] *the left hand of Aquarius;* [*the Twenty-third Mansion of the Moon:*] (Ḳzw, descr. of Aquarius:) [See also art. بلع:] —— سَعْدُ السُّعُودِ (Ṣ, L, Ḳ) *Two stars, the most approved of the* سُعُود, and therefore thus named, *resembling* سعد الذابح [app. a mistake for سَعْدُ البَارِعِ, or some other سعد, not of the Mansions of the Moon,] *in the time of their* [*auroral*] *rising;* (Ibn-Kunáseh;) *the star* [β] *which is on the left shoulder-joint of Aquarius, together with the star* [δ] *in the tail of Capricornus;* [*the Twenty-fourth Mansion of the Moon:*] (Ḳzw, descr. of Aquarius:) or *a certain solitary bright star:* (Ṣ:) —— سَعْدُ الأَخْبِيَةِ (Ṣ, L, Ḳ) [also called الأَخْبِيَةُ and الخِبَآءُ (see خِبَآءٌ in art. خبى)] *Three stars, not in the track of the other* سُعُود, *but declining from it* [*a little*], *in, or respecting, which there is a discordance;* they are *neither very obscure nor very bright;* and are thus called because, when they rise [aurorally], the venomous or noxious reptiles of the earth, such as scorpions and serpents, come forth fiom their holes; (Ibn-Kunáseh;) [and this observation is just; for this asterism, about the commencement of the era of the Flight, rose aurorally, in Central Arabia, on the 24th of February, O. S., after the end of the cold season: see مَنَازِلُ القَمَرِ, in art. نزل:] or it consists of *three stars, like the three stones upon which the cooking-pot is placed, with a fourth below one of them;* (Ṣ;) *the star* [γ] *that is on the right arm, together with the three stars* [ζ, η, *and* π,] *on the right hand of Aquarius:* so called because, when it rises [aurorally], the venomous or noxious reptiles that have hidden themselves beneath the ground by reason of the cold appear: (Ḳzw, descr. of Aquarius; [in some copies, incorrectly, for "that have hidden themselves," &c., "hide themselves beneath the ground by reason of the cold:"]) it is said that *the* سعد *is one star, the brightest of four, the other three of which are obscure;* and it is [correctly] said to be called thus because, when it rises [aurorally], the venomous or noxious reptiles that are hidden beneath the ground come forth: it is *the Twenty-fifth Mansion of the Moon:* (Ḳzw, descr. of the Mansions of the Moon:) —— the following are the other سعود, which are not Mansions of the Moon: (Ṣ, L, Ḳ:) —— سَعْدُ نَاشِرَةَ (Ṣ, L, Ḳ) [*Two stars,* situate, accord. to Ideler, as is said in Freytag's Lex., *in the tail of Capricornus*]: —— سَعْدُ المَلِكِ (Ṣ, L, Ḳ) *The two stars* [α and ο?] *on the right shoulder of Aquarius:* (Ḳzw:) —— سَعْدُ البِهَامِ (Ṣ, L, Ḳ) *The two stars* [ε and θ?] *on the head of Pegasus:* (Ḳzw: [but in the copies of his work the name is written سَعْدُ البَهَائِمِ:]) —— سَعْدُ الهُمَامِ (Ṣ, L, Ḳ) *The two stars* [ζ and 31?] *on the neck of Pegasus:* (Ḳzw:) —— سَعْدُ البَارِعِ (Ṣ, L, Ḳ) *The two stars near together* [μ and λ?] *in the breast of Pegasus:* (Ḳzw:) —— سَعْدُ مَطَرٍ (Ṣ, L, Ḳ) *The two stars* [η and ο?] *on the right* [or *left?*] *knee of Pegasus:* (Ḳzw: but there called سَعْدُ المَطَرِ:) —— each سعد of these six consists of two stars: between every two stars, as viewed by the eye, is [said to be] a distance of a cubit, (ذِرَاع,) (Ṣ, L,) or about a cubit; (Ḳ;) [but this is not correct;] and they are disposed in regular order. (Ṣ, L.) —— It is also the name of *A certain object of idolatrous worship that belonged to the sons of Milhán* (Ṣ, Ḳ) *the son of Kináneh,* (Ṣ,) *in a place on the shore of the sea, adjacent to Juddeh.* (TA.) A poet says,

* وَهَلْ سَعْدُ إِلَّا صَخْرَةٌ بِتَنُوفَةٍ *
* مِنَ الأَرْضِ لَا تَدْعُو لِغَيٍّ وَلَا رُشْدِ *

[*And is Saad aught but a mass of rock in a desert tract of the earth, not inviting to error nor to a right course?*]. (Ṣ, TA.) Hudheyl is said to have worshipped it in the Time of Ignorance. (TA.) —— بِنْتُ سَعْدٍ is metonymically used as meaning ‡ *The virginity,* or *hymen,* of a girl or woman. (TA.) —— أَسَعْدٌ أَمْ ▼ سُعَيْدٌ, meaning ‡ *Is it a thing liked or a thing disliked?* (Ṣ, A, Ḳ,) is a prov., (Ṣ, A,) which [is said to have] originated from the fact that Saad and So'eyd, [the latter name erroneously written in some copies of the Ṣ and Ḳ سَعِيد,] the two sons of Ḍabbeh the son of Udd, went forth (Ṣ, Ḳ, TA) to seek some camels belonging to them, (TA,) and Saad returned, but So'eyd was lost, and his name became regarded as unlucky: (Ṣ, Ḳ, TA:) Ḍabbeh used to say this when he saw a dark object in the night: and hence it is said in allusion to care for one's relation; and in inquiring whether a good or an evil event have happened. (TA.) [The saying may also be rendered, *Is it a fortunate thing or a little fortunate thing?*] —— سَعْدَيْكَ, in the saying لَبَّيْكَ وَسَعْدَيْكَ, signifies *Aiding Thee after aiding* [i. e. *time after time*]; syn. إِسْعَادًا لَكَ بَعْدَ إِسْعَادٍ: (ISk, T, Ṣ, L, Ḳ:) or *aiding Thee and then aiding:* (Aḥmad Ibn-Yaḥyà, L:) or *aiding thy cause after aiding* [i. e. *time after time*]: (T, L:) and hence it is in the dual number: (IAth, L:) El-Jarmee says that it has no sing.; and Fr says the same of it, and also of لَبَّيْكَ: it is in the accus. case as an inf. n. governed by a verb understood. (L.) It occurs in the form of words preceding the recitation of the Opening Chapter of the Ḳur-án in prayer, لَبَّيْكَ وَسَعْدَيْكَ وَالخَيْرُ بَيْنَ يَدَيْكَ وَالشَّرُّ لَيْسَ إِلَيْكَ [meaning *I wait intent upon thy service, or upon obedience to Thee, time after time, and upon aiding thy cause time after time; and good is before Thee, and evil is not imputable to Thee*]. (L, TA.) ═ Also *The third part of the* لَبِنَة [or *gore*] (Ḳ, TA) *of a shirt:* (TA:) [the dim.] ▼ سُعَيْدٌ signifies the *fourth part thereof.* (Ḳ, TA.)

سُعْدٌ and ▼ سُعَادَى *A certain kind of perfume,* (Ṣ, Ḳ,) *well known:* (Ḳ:) or the former is pl. of ▼ سُعْدَةٌ, [or rather a coll. gen. n. of which سُعْدَةٌ is the n. un.,] and this last is [the name of] *a certain kind of sweet-smelling root;* it is *a rhizoma* (أُرُومَة), *round, black, hard, like a knot; which forms an ingredient in perfumes and medicines:* (AḤn:) and ▼ سُعَادَى is the name of *its plant;* (Lth, AḤn;) and its pl. is سُعَادَيَاتٌ: (AḤn:) or the سُعْد is *a certain plant having a root* (أَصْل) *beneath the ground, black, and of sweet odour:* and the ▼ سُعَادَى is *another plant:* (Az:) [in the present day, the former of these two names (سُعْد) is applied to *a species of cyperus:* a species thereof is termed by Forskål (in his Flora Aegypt. Arab, pp. lx. and 14,) *cyperus* complanatus; and he writes its Arabic name "saad" and "sæd:"] it has a wonderful efficacy applied to ulcers, or sores, that heal with difficulty. (Ḳ.)

سُعْدٌ *A certain sort of dates.* (Ḳ, TA.)

سُعْدَةٌ: see سُعْدٌ [of which it is the n. un.].

دُرُوعٌ سُعْدِيَّةٌ *Coats of mail of the fabric of a town called* السُّعْدُ. (TA.)

سَعْدَانٌ, in which the ن is an augmentative letter, because there is not in the language any word of the measure فَعْلَال except خَزْعَال and قَهْقَار unless it is of the reduplicative class, (Ṣ,) *A certain plant,* (Ṣ, Ḳ,) *growing in the plain,* or *soft, tracts,* (TA,) *one of the best kinds of the pastures of camels,* (Ṣ, Ḳ,) *as long as it continues fresh;* (TA;) *having* [*a head of*] *prickles,* (T, Ṣ, Ḳ,) *called* حَسَكَةُ السَّعْدَانِ, (T, Ṣ,) *to which the nipple* [or *the areola*] *of a woman's breast is likened:* (Ṣ, Ḳ: [see سَعْدَانَةٌ, below:]) the Arabs say that the camels that yield the sweetest milk are those that eat this plant: (TA:) and they fatten upon it: (Az, TA:) *it is of the kind of plants called* أَحْرَار [pl. of حُرٌّ, meaning *slender, and succulent* or *soft* or *sweet*], *dust-coloured, and sweet, and eaten by everything that is not large,* [*as well as by camels,*] *and it is one of the most wholesome kinds of pasture:* (AḤn, TA:) it is a *herb,* or *leguminous plant, having a round fruit with a prickly face, which, when it dries, falls upon the ground on its back, and when a person walking treads upon it, the prickles wound his foot: it is one of the best of their pastures in the days of the* رَبِيع, *and sweetens the milk of the camels that feed upon it; for it is sweet as long as it continues fresh; and in this state men suck it and eat it:* (Az, L:) the n. un. is with ة. (TA.) Hence the prov., مَرْعًى وَلَا كَالسَّعْدَانِ [*Pasture, but not like the* سعدان]: (Ṣ, Ḳ:) said of a thing possessing excellence, but surpassed in excellence by another thing; or of a thing that excels other things of the like kind. (TA.) — Also The *prickles of the palm-tree.* (AḤn, TA.)

سَعْدَانَ, like سُبْحَانَ, is a name for الإِسْعَاد [inf. n. of 4, and, like سبحان, invariable, being put in the accus. case in the manner of an inf. n.]: one says, أُسَبِّحُهُ وَأُطِيعُهُ سُبْحَانَهُ وَسَعْدَانَهُ, meaning [i. e. *I declare,* or *celebrate,* or *extol, his* (i. e. God's) *remoteness,* or *freedom, from every imperfection,* or *impurity,* &c., (see art. سبح,) *and I render Him obedience,* or *aid his cause*]. (Ḳ, TA.)

سَعْدَانَةٌ n. un. of سَعْدَانٌ. (TA.) — سَعْدَانَةُ الثُّنْدُوَةِ *The nipple of a woman's breast;* as being likened to the [head of] prickles of the plant called سَعْدَان, as mentioned above: (Ṣ, Ḳ:) or سَعْدَانَةُ الثَّدْيِ, i. e. *the blackness* [or *areola*] *around the nipple:* (A:) or *the part surrounding the* ثَدْى [here meaning *nipple*], *like the whirl of a spindle.* (TA.) — [Hence likewise,] سَعْدَانَةٌ signifies also The *knot of the* شِسْع [or *appertenance that passes between two of the toes and through the sole*] of the sandal, (Ṣ, A, Ḳ,) *beneath,* (A, Ḳ,) *next the ground;* (Ṣ;) also called زُغْبَانَةٌ. (Ḳ in art. زغب.) — And The *knot beneath the scale* of a balance: (Ḳ,* TA:) the *knots beneath the scale* of a balance (Ṣ, A) are called its سَعْدَانَات. (A.) — And the pl., سَعْدَانَاتٌ, *Things in the lower parts of the* [*tendons,* or *sinews, called*] عُجَايَة, *resembling nails* (أَظْفَار). (Ṣ, Ḳ.) — Also the sing., The *callous protuberance upon the breast of the camel,* (Ṣ, A, Ḳ,) *upon which he rests when he lies down:* (A, TA:) so called because of its roundness. (TA.) — And The *anus:* (Ḳ:) or the *sphincter thereof.* (TA.) — And The *part of the vulva of a mare where the veretrum enters.* (TA.) = Also *A pigeon:* or السَّعْدَانَةُ is *the name of a certain pigeon.* (Ḳ,* TA.)

سَعِيدٌ, applied to a man, (Ṣ, Mṣb,) *Prosperous, fortunate, happy,* or *in a state of felicity;* (T, Ṣ, A, Mṣb, Ḳ;) with respect to religion and with respect to worldly things; (Mṣb;) as also ↓ مَسْعُودٌ: (A,* Ḳ:) or the latter signifies, (T, Ṣ, Mṣb,) or signifies also, (Ḳ,) and so may the former signify, (T, TA,) *rendered prosperous, fortunate, happy,* or *in a state of felicity,* by God; (T, Ṣ, Mṣb, Ḳ;) irregularly derived from أَسْعَدَهُ, (Ṣ,* Ḳ,* MF,) or regularly from سَعَدَهُ: (T, Mṣb:) one should not say مُسْعَدٌ: (Ṣ, Ḳ:) fem. of the former [and latter] with ة: (TA:) pl. of the former سُعَدَآءُ, (A, Mṣb, TA,) and, accord. to Lḥ, سَعِيدُونَ and أَسَاعِدُ; but ISd says, I know not whether he mean [of] the [proper] name or of the epithet; but أَسَاعِدُ as pl. of سَعِيدٌ is anomalous: (TA:) the pl. of ↓ مَسْعُودٌ is [مَسْعُودُونَ and] مَسَاعِيدُ. (A, TA.) = Also *A* نَهْر [i. e. *river,* or *rivulet,* or *canal of running water,*] (Ḳ, TA) *that irrigates the land in the parts adjacent to it, when it is appropriated thereto:* or *a small* نَهْر: the نَهْر *for irrigation* of a tract of seed-produce: pl. سُعُدٌ. (TA.)

سُعَيْدٌ: see سَعْدٌ, [of which it is the dim.,] in the last quarter of the paragraph, in two places.

سَعَادَةٌ an inf. n. of سَعِدَ (MA, TA) and of سُعِدَ, (TA,) or a simple subst., (Mṣb,) *Prosperity, good fortune, happiness,* or *felicity,* of a man; (Ṣ, Mṣb, Ḳ;) *contr. of* شَقَاوَةٌ; (Ṣ, Mṣb,* Ḳ;) with respect to religion and with respect to worldly things: (Mṣb:) [and so ↓ سَعْدٌ used as a simple subst.:] it is of two kinds; أُخْرَوِيَّةٌ [*relating to the world to come*] and دُنْيَاوِيَّةٌ [*relating to the present world*]: and the latter is of three kinds; نَفْسِيَّةٌ [*relating to the soul*] and بَدَنِيَّةٌ [*relating to the body*] and خَارِجِيَّةٌ [*relating to external circumstances*]. (Er-Rághib, TA in art. شقو.) [See also what next follows.]

سُعُودَةٌ *Prosperousness, fortunateness, auspiciousness,* or *luckiness,* (Ṣ, L,) of a day, and of a star or an asterism [&c.]; (L;) [as also ↓ سَعْدٌ used as a simple subst.;] *contr. of* نُحُوسَةٌ. (Ṣ, L.)

السَّعِيدَةُ *A temple to which the Arabs* (Ḳ, TA) *of the tribe of Rabeeạ* (TA) *used to perform pilgrimage,* (Ḳ, TA,) *at* [*Mount*] *Ohod, in the Time of Ignorance.* (TA.)

سَعَادَى: see سَعْدٌ, in three places.

سَعِيدِيَّةٌ *A sort of garments of the kind called* بُرُود, *of the fabric of El-Yemen:* (Ṣ, Ḳ:) app. so called in relation to the mountains of Benoo-Sa'eed. (TA.) — And حُلَّةٌ سَعِيدِيَّةٌ [*A certain kind of dress*]: so called in relation to Sa'eed Ibn-El-'Áṣ, whom, when a boy, or young man, the Prophet clad with a حُلَّة, the kind of which was thence thus named. (Ḥar. p. 596.)

سَاعِدٌ The *fore arm* (ذِرَاع) of a man; (Ḳ;) the *part of the arm from the wrist to the elbow;* (T, L;) or *from elbow to the hand:* (Mgh, Mṣb:) so called because it aids the hand in seizing a thing (T, Mṣb) or taking it (T) and in work: (Mṣb:) or it signifies, (Ṣ,) or signifies also, (Mṣb,) the *upper arm,* or *upper half of the arm, from the elbow to the shoulder-blade,* syn. عَضُدٌ, [q. v.,] (Ṣ, Mṣb,) of a man: (Ṣ:) [and in like manner, of a beast, both the *fore shank* and the *arm:*] in some one or more of the dialects, the *upper of the* زَنْدَانِ [which may mean either the *upper arm* or the *radius*]; the ذِرَاع being the lower of them [which may mean either the "fore arm" or the "ulna"]: (L, TA:) of the masc. gender: (Mṣb:) pl. سَوَاعِدُ. (T, Mgh, Mṣb, TA.) One says, شَدَّ اللّٰهُ عَلَى سَاعِدِكَ and سَوَاعِدِكُمْ [*May God strengthen thy fore arm and aid thee,* and *your fore arms and aid you*]. (A, TA.) — And hence, [*A kind of armlet;*] *a thing that is worn upon the fore arm, of iron* or *brass* or *gold.* (Mgh.) — [Hence also,] سَاعِدَا الطَّائِرِ † *The two wings of the bird.* (Ṣ, Ḳ.) — And السَّوَاعِدُ ‡ *The anterior,* or *primary, feathers of the wing:* so in the phrase, طَائِرٌ شَدِيدُ السَّوَاعِدِ ‡ [*A bird strong in the anterior,* or *primary, feathers of the wing*]. (A, TA.) — Also the sing., † *A chief, upon whom people rely.* (TA.) — And the pl., سَوَاعِدُ, ‡ The *channels in which water runs to a river* or *small river* (نَهْر), (Ṣ, A, Ḳ,) or *to a sea* or *large river* (بَحْر); (AA, Ṣ, Ḳ;) the sing. said by AA to be سَاعِدٌ, without ة: or this latter signifies *a channel in which water runs to a valley,* and *to a sea* or *large river* (بَحْر): or the *channel in which a large river* (بَحْر) *runs to small rivers* (أَنْهَار). (L.) And ‡ The *places from which issues the water of a well:* the *channels of the springs* thereof. (L.) — Also † The *medullary cavities;* the *ducts through which runs the marrow in a bone.* (Ṣ, Ḳ.) — And ‡ The *ducts* (AA, A, TA) *in the udder* (A, TA) *from which the milk comes* (AA, A, TA) *to the orifice of the teat;* as being likened to the سواعد of the بَحْر: (AA, TA:) the قَصَب *of the udder:* (Aṣ, TA:) or سَاعِدٌ signifies the *orifice of a she-camel's teat, from which the milk issues:* and سَاعِدُ الدَّرِّ, *a duct by which the milk descends to the she-camel's udder:* and in like manner سَاعِدٌ signifies *a duct that conveys the milk to a woman's breast* or *nipple.* (TA.) — أَمْرٌ ذُو سَوَاعِدَ means ‡ *An affair having several modes,* or *manners,* [*in which it may be per-*

formed,] and several ways of egress therefrom. (A, TA.)

سَاعِدَةٌ The bones of the shank. (TA.) — And A piece of wood, (Ḳ, TA,) set up, (TA,) that holds the pulley. (Ḳ, TA.) ═ سَاعِدَةُ is a name of The lion: (Ṣ, Ḳ:) imperfectly decl., like أُسَامَةُ. (TA.)

أَسْعَدُ [More, and most, prosperous or fortunate or happy; an epithet applied to a man:] masc. of سُعْدَى: (Ṣ, Ḳ:) but IJ says that سُعْدَى as an epithet has not been heard. (TA.) ═ Also A [cracking of the skin, such as is termed] شُقَاق, resembling mange, or scab, that happens to a camel, and in consequence of which he becomes decrepit, (Ḳ, TA,) and weak. (TA.)

مَسْعُودٌ: see سَعِيدٌ, in two places.

سعر

1. سَعَرَ النَّارَ, (Ṣ, A, Mṣb, Ḳ,) aor. ـَ, (Mṣb, Ḳ,) inf. n. سَعْرٌ; (Mṣb;) and ↓ اسعرها, (A, Mṣb, Ḳ,) inf. n. إِسْعَارٌ; (Mṣb;) and ↓ سعّرها, (A, Ḳ,) inf. n. تَسْعِيرٌ; (TA;) or the last has an intensive signification; (Ṣ;) He lighted, or kindled, the fire; or made it to burn, to burn up, to burn brightly or fiercely, to blaze, or to flame; syn. أَوْقَدَهَا, (Mṣb, Ḳ,) or هَيَّجَهَا and أَلْهَبَهَا. (Ṣ, A.) In the Ḳur lxxxi. 12, some read سُعِرَتْ; and others, ↓ سُعِّرَتْ, which latter has an intensive signification. (Ṣ.) And سَعَرَ النَّارَ He stirred the fire with a مِسْعَر. (TA.) — [Hence,] سَعَرَ الحَرْبَ, (Ṣ, Ḳ,) aor. as above, (Ḳ,) and so the inf. n.; (TA;) and ↓ اسعرها, and ↓ سعّرها; (Ḳ;) ‡ He kindled war; (Ḳ, TA;) excited, or provoked, it. (Ṣ, TA.) And سَعَرُوا نَارَ الحَرْبِ ‡ [They kindled, or excited, the fire of war]. (A.) — [Hence also,] سَعَرَهُمْ شَرٌّ ‡ [Evil, or mischief, excited them, or inflamed them]. (A.) And سَعَرَ عَلَى قَوْمِهِ ‡ [He excited, or inflamed, against his people]. (A.) — And سَعَرَهُمْ شَرًّا ‡ He did extensive evil, or mischief, to them: (ISk, Ṣ, TA:*) or he did evil, or mischief, to them generally, or in common; as also ↓ اسعرهم, and ↓ سعّرهم; (TA;) or one should not say ↓ اسعرهم. (ISk, Ṣ, TA.) — And سَعَرْنَاهُمْ بِالنَّبْلِ † We burned and pained them [or inflicted upon them burning pain] with arrows. (Ṣ.) — And سَعَرَ الإِبِلَ, aor. as above, (Ḳ,) and so the inf. n., (TA,) ‡ He (a camel, TḲ) communicated to the [other] camels his mange, or scab. (Ḳ, TA.) — And سُعِرَ, (Ṣ, A,) inf. n. سُعَارٌ, (TA,) ‡ He (a man) was smitten by the [hot wind called] سَمُوم. (Ṣ, A.) And ‡ He (a man) was, or became, vehemently hungry and thirsty. (TA.) And † He was, or became, mad, insane, or a demoniac. (MA.) — You say also, سَعَرْتُ اليَوْمَ فِى حَاجَتِى سَعْرَةً † I made a circuit during the day, or to-day, for the accomplishment of my want. (Ṣ.) And لَأَسْعَرَنَّ سَعْرَهُ, i. e. لَأَطُوفَنَّ طَوْفَهُ † [app. meaning I will assuredly practise circumvention like his practising thereof]. (Fr, O, Ḳ.) — And سَعَرَ اللَّيْلَ بِالمَطِىِّ, inf. n. as above, † He journeyed throughout the night with the camels, or beasts, used for riding. (ISk, TA.) — And سَعَرَتِ النَّاقَةُ † The she-camel was quick, or swift, in her going. (TA.) [See also سَعَرَان, below.]

2: see 1, in four places. ═ سعّره [from سِعْرٌ], (Ṣgh, Mṣb,) inf. n. تَسْعِيرٌ; (Mṣb;) and ↓ اسعره; (Ṣgh, Mṣb;) He assigned to it a known and fixed price: (Mṣb:) or he declared its current price, or the rate at which it should be sold. (Ṣgh.) And سعّر لَهُمْ, (A, TA,) inf. n. as above; (Ṣ;) and ↓ اسعر لهم; (A;) He (a governor, A) fixed the amount of the prices of provisions &c. for them; (Ṣ, TA;) the doing of which is not allowable. (TA.) — And سعّروا, inf. n. as above; and ↓ اسعروا; They agreed as to a price, or rate at which a thing should be sold. (Ḳ.)

[3. ساعره app. signifies † He acted with him, or it, like one mad, or like a mad dog; for, accord. to Et-Tebreezee, (Ḥam p. 785,) it is from مُسْعَرٌ as an epithet applied to a dog, meaning "mad."]

4: see 1, in four places. — أَسْعَرَنَا قَفْزًا, said of a wild animal, means † He excited and annoyed us by leaping, or bounding. (TA, from a trad.) ═ See also 2, in three places.

5: see the next paragraph.

8. استعرت النَّارُ, (Ṣ, A, Mṣb, Ḳ,) and ↓ تسعّرت, (Ṣ, A, Ḳ,) [but the latter, app., has an intensive signification,] The fire burned or burned up, burned brightly or fiercely, blazed, or flamed. (Ṣ, A, Mṣb, Ḳ.) — [Hence,] استعرت الحَرْبُ ‡ The war [raged like fire, or] spread. (Ḳ, TA.) And in like manner, (TA,) استعر الشَّرُّ ‡ The evil, or mischief, [raged, or] spread. (Ḳ, TA.) — And استعر اللُّصُوصُ, (Ṣ, A, Ḳ,) or استعرت, (TA,) ‡ The thieves, or robbers, put themselves in motion, (Ḳ, TA,) for mischief, (TA,) as though they were set on fire. (Ṣ, Ḳ, TA.) — And استعر الجَرَبُ فِى البَعِيرِ ‡ The mange, or scab, began in the armpits and the groins or similar parts (AA, Ṣ, A,* Ḳ) and the lips (Ṣ) of the camels. (AA, Ṣ, A, Ḳ.) — And استعر النَّاسُ فِى كُلِّ وَجْهٍ † The people ate the fresh ripe dates in every direction, and obtained them; like اِسْتَنْجَوْا. (Aboo-Yoosuf, TA.)

رَمْىٌ سَعْرٌ ‡ A vehement shooting or throwing: (A:) [or a burning, painful shooting; as is indicated in the Ṣ:] one says ضَرْبٌ هَبْرٌ وَطَعْنٌ نَتْرٌ وَرَمْىٌ سَعْرٌ † [a smiting that cleaves off a piece of flesh, and a piercing inflicted with extraordinary force, and a burning, painful shooting]. (Ṣ.) It is said in a trad. of 'Alee, اَضْرِبُوا هَبْرًا وَارْمُوا سَعْرًا † [Smite ye so as to cleave off a piece of flesh, and] shoot ye quickly: the shooting being thus likened to the burning of fire. (TA.)

سُعْرٌ: see سُعَارٌ. — [Hence,] † Madness, insanity, or demoniacal possession; (Ḳ;) as also ↓ سُعُرٌ: (Ṣ, Ḳ:) so ↓ the latter is expl. by AAF as used in the Ḳur liv. 47: and so it is expl. as used in verse 24 of the same chap.: (TA:) or it signifies in the former, (Ṣ,) or in the latter, (TA,) † fatigue, or weariness, or distress, or affliction, and punishment: (Fr, Ṣ, TA:) or, accord. to Az, إِنَّا إِذًا لَفِى ضَلَالٍ وَسُعُرٍ, in verse 24, may mean † verily we should in that case be in error, and in punishment arising from what would necessarily befall us: or, accord. to Ibn-'Arafeh, it means, in a state that would inflame and excite us. (TA.) — Also † Hunger; and so ↓ سُعَارٌ: (Fr, Ḳ, TA:) or the former signifies vehemence of desire for flesh-meat: (Ḳ, TA:) and ↓ the latter, vehemence of hunger: (Ṣ:) or the burning of hunger: (TA:) and the burning of thirst. (A.) — And † A disease, such as the mange, or scab, that is transitive from one to another; or the transition of the mange, or scab, or other disease, from one to another; syn. عَدْوَى. (Ḳ. [See 1.])

سِعْرٌ The current price, or rate, at which a thing is to be sold: (MA, Ḳ:) pl. أَسْعَارٌ. (Ṣ, A, Mṣb, Ḳ.) One says, لَهُ سِعْرٌ, meaning It is exceedingly valuable: and لَيْسَ لَهُ سِعْرٌ It is exceedingly cheap. (Mṣb.)

سَعَرٌ: see سُعْرَةٌ.

سَعِرٌ † Mad, insane, or possessed by a demon: (Ḳ:) and so ↓ مَسْعُورَةٌ applied to a she-camel: (Ṣ:) or the latter, so applied, that will not remain still; from سُعْرٌ meaning "madness, or insanity, or demoniacal possession:" (Ḥam p. 785:) [See also مِسْعَرٌ:] the pl. of سَعِرٌ is سَعْرَى. (Ḳ.)

سُعُرٌ: see سُعْرٌ, in two places.

سَعْرَةٌ † A cough: (O, Ḳ:) or a sharp cough; as also ↓ سَعِيرَةٌ. (IAạr, TA.) — And † The beginning of an affair or a case; and the newness thereof: (Ḳ, TA:) in some copies of the Ḳ, جِدَّتُهُ is erroneously put for حِدَّتُهُ. (TA.)

سُعْرَةٌ A colour inclining to blackness, (Ṣ, TA,) a little above what is termed أُدْمَةٌ; as also ↓ سَعَرٌ. (TA.)

سَعَرَانٌ [an inf. n.] Vehemence of running. (O, Ḳ.) [See 1, last signification.]

سُعَارَةٌ (Ṣ, Ḳ) and ↓ سُعْرُورَةٌ (Ḳ) † Daybreak. (Ḳ.) — And † The rays of the sun entering an aperture of a house or chamber: (Ḳ,* TA:) or the motes that are seen in the rays of the sun (Az, Ṣ, TA) when they fall into a chamber, moving to and fro. (Az, TA.)

سُعْرُورَةٌ: see the next preceding paragraph.

سُعَارٌ The heat (Ṣ, Ḳ) of fire; (Ṣ;) as also ↓ سُعْرٌ: (Ḳ:) and ‡ of night. (A.) — See also سُعْرٌ, in two places. — Also † Evil, or mischief: so in the saying, لَا يَنَامُ النَّاسُ مِنْ سُعَارِهِ [Men will not sleep by reason of his evil, or mischief], occurring in a trad. (TA.)

سَعُورٌ † A she-camel quick, or swift, in her going. (TA.) [See 1, last signification.]

سَعِيرٌ Lighted, or kindled; or made to burn, burn up, burn brightly or fiercely, blaze, or flame: (Ḳ, TA:) of the measure فَعِيلٌ in the sense of the measure مَفْعُولٌ: (TA:) [and thus] similar to دَهِينٌ and صَرِيعٌ; for you say نَارٌ

▼ مَسْعُورَةٌ: (Akh, Ṣ:) or نَارٌ سَعِيرٌ signifies *fire kindled, or made to burn &c., with other fire.* (Lḥ, TA.) — Also *Fire* (Ṣ, Ḳ) *itself;* (Ṣ;) and so ▼ سَاعُورَةٌ and ▼ سَاعُورٌ: (Ḳ:) or [so in the TA, but in the Ḳ "and,"] *its flame;* (Ḳ;) as also ▼ سَاعُورَةٌ and ▼ سَاعُورٌ. (TA.) = السَّعِيرُ: see what next follows.

السُّعَيْرُ, (O, Ḳ,) and ▼ السَّعِيرُ, (Ṣ,) or the latter is a mistake, (O, TA,) *A certain idol,* (Ṣ, Ḳ,) *belonging peculiarly to [the tribe of] 'Anazeh.* (Ibn-El-Kelbee, Ṣ.) [See an ex. in a verse cited in art. صور.]

سَعِيرَةٌ: see سُعْرَةٌ.

سَاعُورٌ: see سَعِيرٌ, in two places. — Also *A sort of fire-place, or oven,* (تَنُّورٌ, Ḳ, TA,) *dug in the ground, in which bread is baked.* (TA.) = And *The chief of the Christians in the knowledge of medicine* (Ḳ, TA) *and of the instruments thereof:* [said to be] originally سَاعُورَاء, a Syriac word, meaning the *investigator of the cases of the diseased.* (TA.)

سَاعُورَةٌ: see سَعِيرٌ, in two places.

أَسْعَرُ, applied to a man, *Of the colour termed* سُعْرَةٌ: fem. سَعْرَآءُ. (TA.) — And, so applied, (TA,) *Having little flesh,* (Ḳ, TA,) *lean,* or *lank in the belly,* (TA,) *having the sinews apparent, altered in colour* or *complexion,* or *emaciated,* (Ḳ, TA,) *and slender.* (TA.)

مَسْعَرٌ The *slender part of the tail* of a camel. (Ḳ.) — See also مَسَاعِرُ.

مِسْعَرٌ and ▼ مِسْعَارٌ (Ṣ, Ḳ) The *thing,* (Ḳ,) or *wood,* (Ṣ,) or *instrument of iron* or *of wood,* (TA,) *with which a fire is stirred* [or *made to burn* or *burn up* &c.]: (Ṣ,* Ḳ,* TA:) pl. (of the former, A) مَسَاعِرُ (A, TA) and [of the latter] مَسَاعِيرُ. (TA.) — Hence one says of a man, إِنَّهُ لَمِسْعَرُ حَرْبٍ ‡ *Verily he is one who makes the fire of war to rage;* (Ṣ, A,* Ḳ,* TA;) *a stirrer of the fire of war.* (TA.) — Also the former, (مِسْعَرٌ), † *Long;* (AA, Ṣ, Ḳ;) applied to a neck (Ḳ) or some other thing: (TA:) or *strong.* (Aṣ, Ḳ.) — And, applied to a dog, † *Mad.* (Ḥam p. 785.) [See also سَعِرٌ.] — المِسْعَرُ as an epithet applied to a horse means الَّذِى يُطِيحُ قَوَائِمَهُ مُتَفَرِّقَةً وَلَا ضَبْرَ لَهُ [i. e., app., *That makes his legs to fall spread apart, and that has no leaping with his legs put together*]: (Ḳ:) or, in the words of AO, [and so in the O,] الذى تُطِيحُ قَوَائِمَهُ [app. *whose legs thou makest to fall* &c.]: (TA:) [in the CḲ, ولا صَبْرَ لَهُ, which is, I doubt not, a mistake: and in the TA is added, وقيل وَثْبٌ مُجْتَمِعُ القَوَائِمِ, in which وقيل is evidently a mistranscription for وَهُوَ, referring to ضَبْرٌ, which is well known as meaning وَثْبٌ مُجْتَمِعُ القَوَائِمِ:] and ▼ مُسَاعِرٌ signifies the same. (AO.)

مِسْعَارٌ: see the next preceding paragraph.

مَسْعُورٌ: see its syn. سَعِيرٌ. — [Hence,] ‡ A man *smitten by the* [hot wind called] سَمُوم. (Ṣ, A.) — And ‡ *Vehemently hungry and thirsty:* (TA:) *eager for food,* even though his belly be full; (Ḳ;) and, it is said, *for drink* also. (TA.) — See also سَعِرٌ.

مَسَاعِرُ [a pl. of which the sing., if it have one, is probably ▼ مَسْعَرٌ,] † The *armpits,* and the *groins* or *similar parts,* (Ṣ, A,* Ḳ,) and the *lips,* (Ṣ,) of camels. (Ṣ, A, Ḳ.)

مُسَاعِرٌ: see مِسْعَرٌ, last sentence.

سعط

1: see what next follows.

4. اسعطهُ, (Ṣ,) or اسعطهُ دَوَآءً, (AA, IDrd, Mgh, Mṣb, Ḳ,) *He poured,* (Ṣ, Mgh, Mṣb,) or *introduced,* (Ḳ,) *medicine into his* (a man's, Ṣ) *nose;* (Ṣ, Mgh, Mṣb, Ḳ;) as also ▼ سَعَطَهُ, aor. ـُ and ـَ, (Ḳ,) the former of which, namely ـُ, is the more approved, inf. n. سَعْطٌ. (TA.) Both are also written with ص. (Ḳ and TA in art. صعط.) — [Hence,] اسعطهُ الرُّمْحَ ‡ *He pierced him in his nose with the spear:* ('Eyn, Ḳ:) or it is like أَوْجَرَهُ, meaning *he pierced him in his breast,* or *chest, with the spear.* (Ṣ.) — [Hence also,] اسعطهُ عِلْمًا ‡ *He took extraordinary pains in making him to understand science,* (K, TA,) *and in repeating to him what he taught him.* (TA.)

8. استعط *He* (a man, Ṣ) *poured medicine into his* (i. e. *his own*) *nose;* or *had it poured therein;* (Ṣ, Mgh;) or *introduced it,* or *had it introduced, therein:* (Ḳ:) the pass. form, أُسْتُعِطَ, is not allowable. (Mgh.)

10. استسعط † *He* (a camel, TA) *smelled the urine of the she-camel,* (Ḳ,) or *somewhat thereof,* (TA,) *and it,* (Ḳ,) or *some of it,* (TA,) *entered into his nose;* (Ḳ;) *then he covered her, and failed not to impregnate.* (TA.)

سَعْطَةٌ وَاحِدَةٌ *A single introduction of medicine into the nose;* as also ▼ إِسْعَاطَةٌ وَاحِدَةٌ. (Lth, Ḳ.)

سُعَاطٌ: see سَعِيطٌ, in four places.

سَعُوطٌ *Medicine that is poured,* (Ṣ, Mgh, Mṣb,) or *introduced,* (Ḳ,) *into the nose;* (Ṣ, Mgh, Mṣb, Ḳ;) [*an errhine;*] as also صَعُوطٌ; (Lḥ, Ḳ;) which is thought, by ISd, to be an instance of assimilation [like صِرَاطٌ for سِرَاطٌ] such as Sb mentions. (TA.) — Also *Sweat.* (TA.)

سُعُوطٌ: see the next paragraph, in two places.

سَعِيطٌ *Sweet,* or *pleasant, odour,* of wine and the like, or of anything: (A'Obeyd, Ḳ:) and *sharpness,* or *pungency, of odour;* as also ▼ سُعَاطٌ; (Ḳ;) the former, [for instance,] of mustard, (IṢk,) and so ▼ the latter, and likewise ▼ سُعُوطٌ: (TA:) and سُعَاطُ المِسْكِ signifies *the odour of musk.* (Fr.) A rájiz says, describing camels and their milk,

• حَمْضِيَّةٌ طَيِّبَةُ ▼ السُّعَاطِ •

[*That eat the plants called* حَمْض, *sweet in odour*]. (AḤn.) And you say, ▼ هُوَ طَيِّبُ السُّعُوطِ and ▼ الإِسْعَاطِ [*He, or it, is sweet in odour:* but the latter is perhaps a mistranscription, for السُّعَاطِ]. (TA.) — The *dregs, lees,* or *sediment, of wine.* (Ṣ, Ḳ.) — The بَان [or ben]: (Ḳ:) the *oil thereof:* (IB, Ḳ:) the *oil of mustard:* (Ḳ:) and the *oil of the* زَنْبَق [or jasmine]. (TA.) = *I. q.* مُسْعَطٌ [pass. part. n. of 4, q. v.]. (TA.)

إِسْعَاطٌ: see the next preceding paragraph.

إِسْعَاطَةٌ: see سَعْطَةٌ.

مُسْعُطٌ, (Ṣ, Mṣb, Ḳ,) and مِسْعَطٌ, (Lth, Ḳ,) the former an instance of the instr. n. with ḍamm, (Ṣ, Mṣb, TA,) which is extr., (Mṣb, TA,) like مُنْخُلٌ &c., (TA,) The *thing,* (Ḳ,) or *vessel,* or *receptacle,* (Ṣ, Mṣb,) *into which* سَعُوط *is put,* (Ṣ, Mṣb, Ḳ,) *and from which it is poured into the nose.* (Ḳ.)

سعف

1. سَعَفَهُ بِحَاجَتِهِ: see 4. = سَعِفَتْ يَدُهُ, (Ṣ, TA,) inf. n. سَعَفٌ, (Ṣ, Ḳ,) *His hand became cracked around the nails;* (Ṣ, Ḳ,* TA;) as also سُعِفَتْ. (Ṣ, TA.) — سَعِفَتِ النَّاقَةُ, in the Ḳ, erroneously, سُعِفَتْ, with ḍamm, (TA,) or سَعِفَ البَعِيرُ, (ISk, Ṣ,) *The she-camel,* (Ḳ, TA,) or *he-camel,* (ISk, Ṣ,) *became affected with what is termed* ▼ سُعَاف, meaning *a disease in the mouth, like mange,* or *scab, in consequence of which the hair of the* خُرْطُوم [i. e. *nose,* or *fore part of the nose,*] *falls off,* (ISk, Ṣ, Ḳ,) *and the hair of the eyes:* (ISk, Ṣ:) the like thereof in sheep or goats is termed غَرَبٌ: (Ṣ:) accord. to IAạr, it is not used in relation to he-camels; and A'Obeyd says the like: accord. to some, as AZ says, it is allowable to use it in relation to he-camels; (TA;) but it is rarely thus used. (Ḳ, TA.) — سُعِفَ, (Ṣ, Ḳ,) like عُنِىَ, (Ḳ,) said of a boy, *He became affected with the pustules termed* سَعْفَة [q. v.]. (Ṣ, Ḳ.)

2. تَسْعِيفٌ The *mixing* of musk and the like *with aromatic perfumes* (Ḳ, TA) *and sweet-scented oils.* (TA.) One says, سَعِّفْ لِى دُهْنِى [*Mix thou for me my oil with aromatic perfumes*]. (ISh, TA.)

3. ساعفهُ, (Ḳ, TA,) inf. n. مُسَاعَفَةٌ, (Ṣ, TA,) *He aided, assisted,* or *helped, him;* [like أَسْعَفَهُ;] or [so accord. to the Ḳ, but accord. to the Ṣ "and,"] *agreed,* or *complied, with him,* (Ṣ,* Ḳ, TA,) *to perform an affair,* (TA,) *acting towards him with reciprocal purity,* or *sincerity, of love,* or *affection, and aiding, assisting,* or *helping, with him,* (Ḳ, TA,) *well.* (TA.) — [Hence,] ساعفهُ جَدُّهُ ‡ *His fortune aided him:* and in like manner, ساعفتهُ الدُّنْيَا ‡ [*Worldly prosperity aided him*]. (A, TA.)

4. اسعف, (Ḳ,) inf. n. إِسْعَافٌ, (TA,) *It* (a thing, TA) *drew near,* or *approached:* (Ḳ, TA:) and اسعف بِهِ *it drew near,* or *approached, to him,* or *it.* (TA.) — اسعف لَهُ *It* (an object of the chase) *became within his power,* or *reach.* (Ḳ.) — اسعف إِلَيْهِ *He tended, repaired,* or *betook*

himself, to, or *towards, him,* or *it.* (TA.) — اسعف بأهْلِهِ *He came to his family;* syn. أَلَمَّ. (Ḳ.) [And in a similar sense the verb is trans. without a particle, as will be shown by the last sentence of this paragraph.] — أَسْعَفْتُهُ *I aided, assisted,* or *helped, him to perform his affair.* (Mṣb. [See also 3.]) — And اسعفهُ بِحَاجَتِهِ, (Ṣ, Mṣb, Ḳ,*) inf. n. إِسْعَافٌ, (Mṣb,) *He performed,* or *accomplished, for him the object of his want;* (Ṣ, Mṣb, Ḳ;) as also ↓ سَعَفَهُ بِهَا, (Ibn-'Abbád, Ḳ,* TA,) aor. ـَ, (Ḳ,) inf. n. سَعْفٌ. (TA.) — It is said in a trad., thus related, فَاطِمَةُ بَضْعَةٌ مِنِّى يُسْعِفُنِى مَا يُسْعِفُهَا, meaning [*Fátimeh is a part of me:*] *that betides,* or *happens to,* [or *affects,*] *me which betides,* or *happens to,* [or *affects,*] *her.* (TA. [See another reading in art. بضع.])

سَعْفٌ *A commodity; an article of merchandise.* (O, Ḳ, TA.) One says, إِنَّهُ سَعْفُ سَوْءٍ *Verily it is a bad commodity.* (O, TA.) — And *A man vile,* or *mean, and despised in all his circumstances.* (AHeyth, O, Ḳ.)

سَعَفٌ *Palm-branches,* (Az,* Ṣ, Mṣb, Ḳ,) *as long as they have the leaves upon them:* when these are removed from them, called جَرِيدٌ: (Mṣb:) or the *part* [or *parts*] *of palm-branches upon which leaves have grown:* (Ṣ voce ↓ عَسِيبٌ:) or the *leaves of palm-branches,* (Mgh, Ḳ, TA,) *of which are woven* [*baskets of the kind called*] زُبُل (Mgh) or زُبْلَان (TA) [pls. of زَبِيلٌ], *and* [*the similar receptacles called*] جِلَال [pl. of جُلَّةٌ], (TA,) *and fans* [which are made in the form of small flags], (Mgh, TA,) *and the like:* (TA:) and sometimes *palm-branches themselves* are thus called: (Mgh:) accord. to Lth, (Mgh, TA,) *such as have become dry* [*of palm-branches*] are mostly thus called; the fresh [palm-branch] being called شَطْبَةٌ: (Mgh, Ḳ, TA:) sing., (Ṣ,) or [rather] n. un., (Mgh, Mṣb,) with ة: (Ṣ, Mgh, Mṣb:) which also signifies *a palm-tree* itself; and its pl. is سَعَفَاتٌ. (TA.) — [Hence, as being likened to palm-leaves,] The *forelock* of a horse: so in the saying of Imra-el-Ḳeys,

وَأَرْكَبُ فِى الرَّوْعِ خَيْفَانَةً
كَسَا وَجْهَهَا سَعَفٌ مُنْتَشِرْ

[*And I ride, in war,* or *battle, a brisk,* or *an agile, leaving mare, whose face a spreading forelock has clad*]: which shows that سَعَفٌ [properly] signifies the leaves [of a palm-branch]. (Az, TA.) [Jac. Schultens, as mentioned by Freytag, explains it as meaning *A whiteness upon the forehead of a horse:* but this explanation is perhaps conjectural, from the verse cited above.] — The *paraphernalia* (جَهَاز) *of a bride:* pl. سُعُوفٌ. (IAạr, Ḳ.) — *Anything good, goodly,* or *excellent, and consummate, such as a slave,* or *any precious thing,* or *a house that one possesses.* (IAạr, Ḳ.) — *A species of fly:* mentioned by a poet as smiting a lion. (IB, TA.) — See also 1.

سُعْفَةٌ *A certain disease,* (Kr, TA,) or *pustules,* (Ṣ, Ḳ, TA,) *coming forth upon the head* (Kr, Ṣ, Ḳ, TA) *of a child,* (Ṣ, Ḳ, TA,) *and upon his face:* (Ḳ, TA:) said by AḤát to be دَآءُ الثَّعْلَبِ [i. e. *alopecia*], *which occasions baldness;* and ↓ سَعَفَةٌ is a dial. var. thereof in this last sense. (TA.)

سَعَفَةٌ n. un. of سَعَفٌ [q. v.]. (Ṣ,* Mgh, Mṣb.) — See also the next preceding paragraph.

سُعَافٌ *A cracking, and scaling off, around the nail:* (TA:) or *a cracking at the root of the nail.* (Ibn-'Abbád, O.) [See 1.]

سُعُوفٌ *Large* [*drinking-cups* or *bowls such as are called*] أَقْدَاح. (IAạr, Ḳ.) — And The *goods,* or *furniture and utensils, of a tent* or *house,* (Ṣ, TA,) *and its carpets* or *the like:* or, as some say, particularly *such as are held in little estimation, as the* [*drinking-vessel called*] تَوْر, *and the bucket, and the rope, and the like.* (TA.) — [See also سَعَفٌ, of which it is pl.] — Also The *natural dispositions,* (AA, IAạr, Ḳ, TA,) *generous* and *other, of men:* (IAạr, Ḳ, TA:) AA says, I have not heard any sing. thereof. (TA.)

أَسْعَفُ A camel *having the disease termed* سَعَفٌ (see 1): fem. سَعْفَآءُ, applied to a she-camel: (ISk, Ṣ, Ḳ:) A'Obeyd mentions only the fem. epithet. (TA.) — Also A horse *white,* (Ṣ,* Ḳ,) or *hoary,* (Ṣ,) *in the forelock,* (Ṣ, Ḳ,) *when there is some other colour in it, different from the white:* (TA:) when the whole of it is white, he is termed أَصْبَغُ: (Ṣ, TA:) so in the "Book of Horses" by AO. (TA.)

مَسْعُوفٌ A boy *affected with the pustules termed* سُعْفَةٌ [q. v.]. (Ṣ, Ḳ.)

مُسَاعِفٌ A place, (Ḳ,) and a place of alighting, (TA,) *near.* (Ḳ, TA.)

سعل

1. سَعَلَ, aor. ـُ, (Ṣ, O, Mṣb, Ḳ,) inf. n. سُعَالٌ (Ṣ, O, Ḳ) and سَعْلَةٌ, (Ḳ,) or the latter of these is the inf. n., and the former is a simple subst., (Mṣb,) [*He coughed:*] سَعْلَةٌ signifies [the *having*] *a motion whereby nature expels somewhat hurtful from the lungs and the organs connected therewith:* (Ibn-Seenà, Ḳ, TA:) wherefore the ducts of the lungs are called قَصَبُ السُّعَالِ [*the tubes of coughing,* meaning *the bronchial tubes,*] because it [i. e. what is hurtful in the lungs] has its exit by them. (TA.) One says, إِنَّهُ يَسْعُلُ سَعْلَةً مُنْكَرَةً [*Verily he coughs with an abominable coughing*]. (TA.) And بِهِ سَعْلَةٌ [*In him is a coughing;* i. e. *he has a coughing,* or *cough*]. (TA.) And أَغَصَّكَ السُّؤَالُ فَأَخَذَكَ السُّعَالُ [*The question,* or *petition, has choked thee, and consequently coughing has seized thee*]. (TA.) — Hence the saying, رَمَاهُ فَسَعَلَ الدَّمَ [*He shot him, and he consequently coughed up blood*]; i. e., *he threw* [*up*] *blood from his chest.* (TA.) — سَعِلَ, aor. ـَ, inf. n. سَعَلٌ; accord. to the Ḳ, app., سَعَلَ, aor. ـُ, inf. n. سَعْلٌ; [and thus the pret. and inf. n. are written in the copies of the Ḳ;] but the former is the right; (TA;) † *He was,* or *became, brisk, lively,* or *sprightly;* (Ḳ, TA;) like زَعِلَ, inf. n. زَعَلٌ. (TA. [See the part. n., سَعِلٌ, below.])

4. اسعلهُ *It* [*made him to cough,* or] *occasioned him a coughing.* (TA.) — And † *He,* or *it, made him,* or *pronounced him, to be like the* سِعْلَاة [q. v.]. (O, TA.) — And † *He,* (a man, Ḳ, TA,) and *it,* (pasture, or herbage, O, TA,) *rendered him* (a horse, TA) *brisk, lively,* or *sprightly;* (O, Ḳ, TA;) as also أَزْعَلَهُ. (O, TA.)

10. استسعلت ‡ *She* (a woman) *became a* سِعْلَاة, i. e., *very clamorous, and foul-tongued;* (Ṣ, O;) or *like a* سِعْلَاة, (Ḳ, TA,) *in badness, wickedness,* or *guile, and clamorousness, and foulness of tongue:* (TA:) similar to استكلبت, and to استأسد said of a man, &c. (AZ, TA.)

سَعَلٌ *Dry* [*dates of the bad sort termed*] شِيص. (IAạr, O, Ḳ.)

سَعِلٌ, applied to a horse, † *Brisk, lively,* or *sprightly;* like زَعِلٌ. (AO, O, TA.)

سِعْلَى: see the next paragraph.

سِعْلَاةٌ and ↓ سِعْلَاءُ (Ṣ, O, Ḳ [app. thus, without tenween, as a fem. noun, though فِعْلَاء without tenween is unusual,]) and ↓ سِعْلَى (Ṣ, O, TA) The [*kind of goblin, demon, devil,* or *jinnee, called*] غُول: (Ḳ:) or the *female of the* غُول: (Abu-l-Wefee El-Aạrábee, TA in art. غول; and Ḥar p. 76:) or the *worst, most wicked,* or *most guileful, of the* غِيلَان [pl. of غُول]: (Ṣ, O:) or *an enchantress of the jinn,* or *genii:* (Ḳ:) pl. [of the first] سَعَالٍ [written with the article السَّعَالِى] (Ṣ, O, Ḳ) [and of the second سَعَالِىُّ] and of the third سِعْلَيَاتٌ, which is said to signify the *females of the* غِيلَان. (TA.) — [Hence,] سِعْلَاةٌ signifies ‡ *A very clamorous, foul-tongued, woman:* (Ṣ, O, TA:) accord. to Aboo-'Adnán, *a woman foul in face, evil in disposition,* is likened to the سِعْلَاة: but some of the Arabs say that the Arabs do not apply the epithet سِعْلَاة to any but *an old woman.* (TA.) — And [the pl.] السَّعَالِى signifies ‡ *Horses;* as being likened to what are [properly] so termed. (TA.) — And [the same pl.] السَّعَالِى, (Ḳ, TA,) with kesr to the ل, (TA,) [in the TḲ ↓ السَّعَالِى, and in the CḲ ↓ السُّعَالِى,] signifies † *A certain plant, the leaves of which make* [*the ulcers termed*] دُبَيْلَات *to discharge their contents, and dissolves them; and the fresh thereof remove the mange,* or *scab: it is a most excellent remedy for the cough;* [wherefore it is also called حَشِيشَةُ السُّعَالِ; (TḲ;)] *and causes the erection of the* ذَكَر *to subside* (وَيَفُشُّ الإِنْتِصَابَ, Ḳ, TA, for which we find in some copies of the Ḳ وَيَنْفِى الإِنْتِصَابَ); *even the fumigating of oneself therewith.* (Ḳ.)

سِعْلَآءُ: see the next preceding paragraph.

سُعَالٌ an inf. n. of سَعَلَ [q. v.]: (Ṣ, O, Ḳ:) or a simple subst. [meaning *A cough*]. (Mṣb.)

السُّعَالِى: see سِعْلَاةٌ.

سَاعِلٌ [*Coughing*]. You say نَاقَةٌ سَاعِلٌ, (O,

Ḳ,) without ة, (O,) meaning *A she-camel having a cough.* (O, Ḳ.) — And إِنَّهُ لَذُو سُعَالٍ سَاعِلٍ [*Verily he has a violent cough*]: (O, Ḳ:*) a phrase having an intensive meaning: (Ḳ:) by rule one should say سُعَالٌ مُسْعِلٌ; but thus the Arabs said, like as they said شُغْلٌ شَاغِلٌ and شِعْرٌ شَاعِرٌ: and [in like manner] a poet cited by Lth says ذُو سَاعِلٍ. (O.) — See also what follows.

مَسْعَلٌ The *part of the fauces, or throat, which is the place of coughing:* (Ṣ, Mṣb:) or [simply] the *fauces,* or *throat;* as also ▼ سَاعِلٌ; (Ḳ;) which latter is expl. by Az as meaning The *mouth;* because with it one coughs. (TA.)

سعى and سعو

1. سَعَى, aor. يَسْعَى, inf. n. سَعْىٌ (Ṣ, Mṣb, Ḳ, &c.) [and مَسْعًى, agreeably with general analogy], *He walked, went,* or *went along,* (Er-Rághib, Mṣb, Ḳ, TA,) *quickly:* (Er-Rághib, Mgh, TA:) this, accord. to Er-Rághib, is the primary signification: and hence, اَلسَّعْىُ بَيْنَ الصَّفَا وَالمَرْوَةِ [*The tripping to and fro between Eṣ-Ṣafà and El-Marweh*]: (TA:) and سَعَى فِى مَشْيِهِ [app. meaning *He tripped along,* or *he trudged along, in his walking*]: (Mṣb:) [or] اَلسَّعْىُ signifies *the going along with vigorousness, and with lightness, activity,* or *quickness.* (Ḥam p. 665.) — *He* (a man, Ṣ) *ran;* syn. عَدَا; (IAạr, Ṣ, Ḳ, TA;) or جَرَى: by the former of which is meant [*he went*] *a pace below what is termed* اَلشَّدّ *and above what is termed* اَلْمَشْىُ. (IAạr, TA.) — *I. q.* قَصَدَ [as meaning *He repaired,* or *betook himself*]. (Ḳ.) The saying, in the Ḳur [lxii. 9], فَاسْعَوْا إِلَى ذِكْرِ اللّٰهِ is expl. as meaning فَاقْصِدُوا [*Then repair ye to prayer to God*]: (TA:) or *then go ye* (فَامْضُوا) *to prayer* [*to God*]: (Jel:) and Ibn-Mes'ood read فَامْضُوا. (TA.) Or سَعَى إِلَى الصَّلَاةِ means *He went to prayer, in any manner* [i. e. whether *quickly* or not]. (Mṣb.) — *He was active,* or *busy and bustling,* in procuring the means of subsistence: (TA:) *he strove, laboured,* or *exerted himself; employed himself vigorously, strenuously,* or *with energy;* in any affair, whether good or evil; but mostly used in relation to what is praiseworthy, or praised: (Er-Rághib, TA:) *he occupied himself according to his own judgment or discretion or free will,* in any work, or deed: (Mṣb:) *he worked,* or *wrought,* or *did,* (Ṣ, Mṣb, Ḳ, TA,) any work, or deed, good or evil: (TA:) *he earned,* or *gained.* (Ṣ, Ḳ, TA.) One says, هُوَ يَسْعَى عَلَى قَوْمِهِ *He manages, conducts, orders, regulates,* or *superintends, the affairs of his people,* or *party.* (Ḥam p. 771, Mṣb.*) And سَعَى لَهُمْ and عَلَيْهِمْ *He worked,* or *wrought, and earned,* or *gained, for them.* (TA.) And اَلْمَرْءُ يَسْعَى لِغَارَيْهِ, a prov., meaning *The man earns for his belly and his pudendum.* (TA.) And سَعَى الْمُكَاتَبُ فِى عِتْقِ رَقَبَتِهِ, (Ṣ,) or فِى فَكِّ رَقَبَتِهِ, i. e. [*The slave who had made a contract with his master to pay him a certain sum for his emancipation*] *laboured to earn the means of releasing himself:* (Mṣb:) the inf. n. of the verb thus used is سِعَايَةٌ: (Ṣ, Mṣb:) and this term is employed when a slave emancipated in part, and in part retained in slavery, labours and earns for the completion of his release. (IAth, TA.) The saying, in the Ḳur [liii. 40], لَيْسَ لِلْإِنْسَانِ إِلَّا مَا سَعَى means [*There is nothing* imputable *to the man*] *but what he hath wrought,* or *done.* (Mṣb.) And فَلَمَّا بَلَغَ مَعَهُ السَّعْىَ, in the same [xxxvii. 100], means *And when he attained to working with him:* or *and when he was able to assist him in his working.* (TA.) — Also *He superintended, managed,* or *conducted, in his own person, the collection of the poor-rates;* (Ḳ, TA;) *he went to exact them, and received them;* (TA;) and the inf. n. in this case also is سِعَايَةٌ: (Ḳ, TA:) or سَعَى عَلَى الصَّدَقَةِ, (Ṣ, Mṣb,) aor. يَسْعَى, inf. n. سَعْىٌ, (Mṣb,) *he officiated in the exacting,* or *receiving,* or *collecting, of the poor-rate.* (Ṣ,* Mṣb.) [And سَعَى is trans. without a prep. as meaning *He exacted* the poor-rate:] a poet says, (namely, 'Amr Ibn-'Addà, TA,)

* سَعَى عِقَالًا فَلَمْ يَتْرُكْ لَنَا سَبَدًا *
* فَكَيْفَ لَوْ قَدْ سَعَى عَمْرٌو عِقَالَيْنِ *

[*He exacted the poor-rate of a year, and left not to us camels' fur,* or *goats' hair: then how would be the case if 'Amr had exacted the poor-rate of two years?*]. (Ṣ.) — سَعَيْتُ فِى أَمْرِ فُلَانٍ is said when one rectifies, redresses, or reforms, the affair of such a one, or mars, vitiates, or perverts it, by his سَعْى [or striving, or labouring; and may be rendered *I strove,* or *laboured, in respect of the affair of such a one,* either *to rectify, redress,* or *reform, it,* or *to mar, vitiate,* or *pervert, it*]: and وَالَّذِينَ سَعَوْا فِى آيَاتِنَا, in the Ḳur xxii. 50 [and xxxiv. 5], means *And they who strive,* or *labour, in respect of our signs, to mar,* or *vitiate,* or *pervert, their meaning, by impugning their character;* seeing that they called them enchantment, and poetry, and tales, or legends, or fictions: (Ksh in xxii. 50:) or these words of the Ḳur mean *and they who strive,* or *labour, to falsify,* or *nullify, our signs;* i. e. the Ḳur-án. (Jel.) — سَعَى بَيْنَهُمْ means *He created,* or *excited, disorder,* or *discord, between them,* or *among them; made,* or *did, mischief between them,* or *among them;* as also سَأَّ, which is app., in this case, a dial. var. of سَعَى. (TA in art. سأو.) [Hence,] سَعَى بَيْنَ النَّاسِ بِالنَّمَائِمِ [*He created,* or *excited, disorder,* &c., *among the people by calumnies,* or *slanders:* or it may be well rendered *he busied himself among the people with propagating calumnies,* or *slanders*]. (Ṣ and O in art. اكل; &c.) — And سَعَى بِهِ ‡ *He calumniated him,* or *slandered him,* (Ṣ, Mṣb, Ḳ,* TA,) إِلَى الوَالِى [*to the ruler,* or *magistrate*]; (Ṣ, Mṣb, Ḳ;) inf. n. سِعَايَةٌ. (TA.) — سَعَتْ, said of a female slave, (Ḳ, TA,) aor. تَسْعَى, inf. n. سَعْىٌ, (TA,) *She committed fornication,* or *prostituted herself.* (Ḳ, TA.) [See also 3.] — سَاعَانِى فُلَانٌ فَسَعَيْتُهُ: see 3.

3. سَاعَانِى فُلَانٌ فَسَعَيْتُهُ ▼, aor. of the latter أَسْعِيهِ, means [*Such a one strove with me in walking,* or *going along, quickly,* &c.,] *and I overcame him* [*therein*]. (Ṣ, TA.) The inf. n. مُسَاعَاةٌ signifies The *walking,* or *going, quickly* [&c., or rather the *striving,* or *contending, in doing so,*] *with any one.* (KL.) Hence the trad. of 'Alee, in discommendation of worldly enjoyments, مَنْ سَاعَاهَا فَاتَتْهُ, meaning مَنْ سَابَقَهَا [i. e. *He who runs a race with them, they evade him,* or *escape his pursuit*]. (TA.) — مُسَاعَاةٌ also signifies One's *committing fornication with a female slave:* and a female slave's *committing fornication with any one:* (KL:) you say, of a man, زَنَى and عَهَرَ, and this is with a free woman and with a female slave; but one says in the case of a female slave, peculiarly, قَدْ سَاعَاهَا [*He has committed fornication with her*]; مُسَاعَاةٌ not being with any but with female slaves: thus in a trad., إِمَآءٌ سَاعَيْنَ فِى الجَاهِلِيَّةِ [*Female slaves that committed fornication in the Time of Ignorance*]: and أُتِىَ عُمَرُ بِرَجُلٍ سَاعَى أَمَةً [*There was brought to 'Omar a man who committed fornication with a female slave*]: (Ṣ, TA:*) [and hence, وَلَدُ المُسَاعَاةِ (occurring in the L, in art. بهث, as mentioned by IAạr on the authority of Abu-l-Mekárim), meaning *The offspring of fornication, begotten on a slave:*] or سَاعَاهَا, (Ḳ, TA,) inf. n. as above, (TA,) signifies [or rather signifies also] *He sought her for the purpose of fornication:* (Ḳ, [in which the context seems to indicate that it relates to a female slave,] and TA:) accord. to Th, relating to the free woman and the female slave: it is also said that مُسَاعَاةُ المَرْأَةِ signifies *The imposing upon the woman, by her owner, an impost which she is to pay by means of* [*the gain of*] *prostitution:* and it is said in a trad. that there shall be no مُسَاعَاةٌ in El-Islám. (TA.) — [It is said in the TA in art. ربع, that مُسَاعَاةٌ from السَّاعَةُ is like مُشَاهَرَةٌ from الشَّهْرُ and مُرَابَعَةٌ from الرَّبِيعُ &c.; but I think that مساعاة in this instance is a mistranscription for مُسَاوَعَةٌ: see art. سوع.]

4. اسعاهُ signifies جَعَلَهُ يَسْعَى, (Ḳ, TA,) i. e. *He made him to earn,* or *gain.* (TA.) — And اسعى عَلَى صَدَقَاتِهِمْ *He employed a collector of their poor-rates.* (TA.) [See also 10.] — And أَسْعَوْا بِهِ *They gave him,* or *performed* or *accomplished for him, what he desired,* or *sought,* or *needed.* (Ṣgh, Ḳ, TA.)

10. استسعى العَبْدَ (Ṣ, Mṣb, Ḳ) فِى قِيمَتِهِ (Ṣ, Mṣb) *He required of the slave that he should labour to earn the means of releasing himself:* (Mṣb:) or *he imposed upon the slave work by means of which he should pay for himself, when he had been emancipated in part, in order to his completing his emancipation:* and ▼ سِعَايَةٌ signifies *the work so imposed.* (Ḳ.) — And استسعاهُ *He employed him as collector of the poor-rate.* (JM; and the like is said in the TA, from a trad.) [See also 4.]

سَعْوٌ: see the next paragraph, in two places: — and see also سِعْوَةٌ.

سِعْوٌ, with kesr, (T, Ṣ, TA,) [and ▼ سَعْوٌ, with fet-ḥ, as shown by what follows,] or ▼ سِعْوَةٌ, with kesr, (Ḳ,) or ▼ سَعْوَةٌ, thus written in the M, with fet-ḥ, (TA,) and ▼سَعْوَآء, (T, Ṣ, ISd, Ḳ, [Freytag found this last written in a copy of the Ṣ سَعْواء, and in one of my copies of the Ṣ it is written سَعَاوَى,]) which is said to be masc., (TA,) [and therefore with tenween, accord. to a general rule applying to ns. of the measure فِعْلَآء,] and ▼سُعْوَآء, (IAạr, Ṣgh, Ḳ,) A [portion, or short portion, such as is termed] سَاعَة, (Ṣ, M, Ḳ, &c.,) of the night: (Ṣ, M, TA:) [like سِهْوَآء, q. v.:] one says, مَضَى مِنَ اللَّيْلِ سِعْوٌ, (Ṣ, TA,) and ▼سَعْوٌ, with fet-ḥ as well as with kesr, (TA, and thus in the Ḥam p. 708,) and ▼سَعْوَةٌ, with fet-ḥ, (TA,) [or ▼سِعْوَةٌ,] and ▼سِعْوَآءٌ, (Ṣ,) [and ▼سُعْوَآءٌ,] A portion (قِطْعَة) of the night passed; (TA;) [or a short portion:] and سِعْوٌ مِنَ اللَّيْلِ signifies the same: (Ḥam p. 708:) or, as some say, ▼سِعْواء signifies more than a ساعة, of the night, and likewise of the day; and one says, كُنَّا عِنْدَهُ فِى سِعْوَاوَاتٍ مِنَ اللَّيْلِ and النَّهَارِ [app. meaning We were with him, or at his abode, during some considerable portions of the night and of the day]: so in the T. (TA.)

سَعْىٌ inf. n. of 1 [in most of its senses]. (Ṣ, Mṣb, Ḳ, &c.) — See also سَعْيَة.

سَعَاةٌ The occupation of oneself according to his own judgment or discretion or free will (Ḳ, TA) in procuring the means of subsistence, and in earning, or gain. (TA.) Hence the prov., شَغَلَتْ سَعَاتِى جَدْوَاىَ [My occupation of myself in procuring the means of subsistence has diverted me from giving]: El-Mundhireo says that شِعَابِى, with ش, is a mistranscription: it is applied to him whose disposition is generous but who is in want. (TA. [See also art. شعب.])

سَعْوَةٌ: see سِعْوٌ, in two places. — Also i. q. شَمْعَةٌ or شَمَعَةٌ [i. e. A piece of wax, or a candle]: (IAạr, TA:) in the Ḳ, السمعة is erroneously put for الشمعة: [so in the TA; but it is omitted in the CḲ and in my MS. copy of the Ḳ:] pl. [or rather coll. gen. n.] ▼سَعْوٌ. (TA.)

سِعْوَةٌ: see سِعْوٌ, in two places. — Also, [accord. to the Ḳ, سِعْوَةُ, for it is there written with the article ال, but] accord. to IAạr without the article ال, [app. سِعْوَةُ, as a proper name,] (TA,) A woman foul, unseemly, or obscene, in tongue; having little, or no, shame or modesty: (IAạr, Ḳ,* TA:) الخَالِعَةُ in the Ḳ is a mistranscription for الجَالِعَةُ, with جيم. (TA.)

سَعْيَةُ a proper name for The she-goat. (Ḳ.) And she is called to be milked by the cry ▼سَعْىِ سَعْيَه. (TA.)

سِعْوَآءٌ and سُعْوَآءٌ: see سِعْوٌ, in five places.

سِعَايَةٌ an inf. n. of سَعَى, in three of its senses. — See also 10.

سُعَاوِىٌّ One who patiently endures sleeplessness and travel: (Ḳ:) very laborious, active, and bustling. (TA.)

سَاعٍ act. part. n. of 1. (Mṣb.) A messenger; a courier, or messenger that journeys with haste; or a messenger on a beast of the post; syn. بَرِيدٌ. (TA.) [See an ex. at the end of the first paragraph of art. ربم.] — Any manager, conductor, orderer, regulator, or superintendent, (Ṣ, Ḳ,) of a thing, over a people, or party, (Ṣ,) or of an affair, and of a people, or party, whatever it be: (Ḳ:) pl. سُعَاةٌ. (Ṣ,* TA.) Mostly, (Ṣ, TA,) or when used without restriction, (Mṣb,) applied to The intendant, or collector, of the poor-rate: pl. as above. (Ṣ, Mṣb, TA. [See رَكِيبٌ.]) And particularly The headman of the Jews and Christians, (Ḳ, TA,) from whose opinion, or judgment, they do not deviate, and without whom they do not decide an affair. (TA.) And [the pl.] سُعَاةٌ signifies Persons who take upon themselves responsibility for the prevention of the shedding of blood, and for the stilling of sedition, or discord, or the like; because they labour in the reforming, or amending, of the circumstances subsisting between parties. (TA.) — Also A calumniator, or slanderer; [and especially] to the ruler, or magistrate: whence the saying, in a trad., السَّاعِى لِغَيْرِ رِشْدَةٍ The calumniator is not trueborn: and in another trad., السَّاعِى مُثَلِّثٌ [The calumniator of another to the ruler is a trebler of evil]; meaning that he destroys, by his calumny, himself, and the calumniated, and the ruler. (TA.)

مَسْعًى, syn. with سَعْىٌ, [an inf. n. of سَعَى,] signifying The act of running, and working, and earning or gaining, [&c., when used as a simple subst.,] has for its pl. مَسَاعٍ. (Ḥar p. 384.)

مَسْعَاةٌ A means of attaining honour and eminence or elevation, in the various kinds of glory; (Ḳ;) a good, or laudable, act or endeavour; generosity: pl. مَسَاعٍ. (MA.) [See an ex. voce مَدْعَاةٌ, and another voce أَقْعَدُ.] J says, [in the Ṣ,] المَسْعَاةُ وَاحِدَةُ المَسَاعِى فِى الكَلَامِ وَالجُودِ, and the author of the Ḳ, following Ṣgh, says that he has committed a mistake in saying فِى الكَلَامِ instead of فِى الكَرَمِ: in some copies of the Ṣ is found فِى الكَرَمِ; but this is an emendation: the original reading is فِى الكَلَامِ: which, however, should be termed a slip of the pen [rather than a mistake, for it cannot be that J was ignorant of the meaning of so common a word as مَسْعَاةٌ]. (TA.)

مَسْعِىٌّ بِهِ Calumniated, or slandered, [and especially] to a ruler, or magistrate. (TA.)

سغب

1. سَغِبَ, aor. ـَ; (Ṣ, A, Mṣb, Ḳ;) and سَغَبَ, aor. ـُ; (A, Ḳ;) inf. n. سَغَبٌ, (Ṣ, A,* Mṣb, Ḳ,) which is of the former, (Ṣ, Mṣb, TA,) and سَغْبٌ, (Ḳ,) which is of the latter, (TA,) and سُغُوبٌ (Ḳ) and سَغَابَةٌ and مَسْغَبَةٌ, (A,* Ḳ,) the last syn. with مَجَاعَةٌ; (Ṣ, Mṣb;) He was, or became, hungry: (Ṣ, A, Mṣb, Ḳ:) or suffered hunger together with fatigue. (A, Mṣb, Ḳ.) You say, بِهِ سَغَبٌ and مَسْغَبَةٌ and سَغَابَةٌ, [using these ns. as simple substs.,] In him is hunger: or hunger together with fatigue. (A.) And يَتِيمٌ ذُو مَسْغَبَةٍ [An orphan] having hunger. (Ṣ.) And فِى يَوْمٍ ذِى مَسْغَبَةٍ, in the Ḳur [xc. 14], means In a day of hunger. (TA.) [See also سَغْبَةٌ and سَغْبٌ below.]

4. اسغب He (a man, TA) entered upon a state of hunger. (Ḳ.)

سَغْبٌ an inf. n. of سَغَبَ [q. v.]. (Ṣ, &c.) — It also signifies Thirst: but is unused: (Ḳ:) [or] thirst is sometimes thus termed. (Mṣb.)

سَاغِبٌ: see سَغِبٌ.

سَغْبَةٌ Hunger: or hunger combined with fatigue. (TA.) [See also 1.]

سَغْبَانُ; and its fem., سَغْبَى: see the next paragraph, in three places.

سَغِبٌ and ▼سَغْبَانُ (Ṣ, A, Mṣb, Ḳ) and ▼سَاغِبٌ (Ḳ) Hungry: (Ṣ, A, Mṣb, Ḳ, TA:) or suffering hunger together with fatigue: (A, Mṣb, Ḳ:) or thirsty: (TA:) fem. [of the second] ▼سَغْبَى, (Ṣ, Ḳ,) pl. سِغَابٌ. (Ḳ.) You say also, هُوَ سَاغِبٌ لَاغِبٌ (A, TA) and ▼سَغْبَانُ لَغْبَانُ (TA) [He is hungry and fatigued, or fatigued in the utmost degree]. And it is said in a trad., دَخَلَ خَيْبَرَ وَهُمْ ▼مُسْغِبُونَ, expl. as meaning [He entered Kheyber] they being hungry. (TA.)

مُسْغِبٌ: see its pl. in what next precedes.

هُوَ مُسْغَبٌ لَهُ كَذَا and مُسْغِبٌ [the latter written in the CḲ مُسْغَبٌ] To him is allowed, or permitted, such a thing. (Ḳ, TA.)

سف

1. سَفَّ, (A'Obeyd, Az, Ṣ, M, Ḳ,) aor. ـُ, inf. n. سَفٌّ; (Ṣ, TA;) and ▼اسفّ, (A'Obeyd, Ṣ, M, Ḳ,) inf. n. إِسْفَافٌ; (TA;) He wove (A'Obeyd, Az, Ṣ, M, Z, Ḳ) with his fingers (Z, TA) [or plaited] a mat, (A'Obeyd, TA,) or palm-leaves, (Az, Ṣ, M, Ḳ,) and any other thing that may be woven with the fingers; (TA;) like رَمَلَ and أَرْمَلَ. (A'Obeyd, TA.) — سَفَّ عَلَى وَجْهِ الأَرْضِ, (Lth, O, Ḳ) (Lth, O,) [aor. ـُ accord. to the TḲ, but more probably ـِ, agreeably with a general rule relating to intrans. verbs of this class,] inf. n. سَفِيفٌ, He (a bird) went along upon the surface of the earth. (Lth, O, Ḳ.) [See also 4.] — سَفِفْتُ, (Ṣ, M, Mgh,* Mṣb, Ḳ,) third pers. سَفَّ, (Mgh,) aor. أَسَفُّ, (Mṣb, TA,) inf. n. سَفٌّ; (M, Mṣb, Ḳ;) and ▼اِسْتَفَفْتُ; (Ṣ, M, Mṣb, Ḳ; [in one of my copies of the Ṣ, erroneously, أَسْفَفْتُ;]) I took [into my mouth], (Ṣ, Ḳ,) or ate, (Mgh, Mṣb,) medicine, (Ṣ, M, Mgh, Mṣb, Ḳ,) and meal of parched barley or wheat, (Ṣ, M, Mgh,) and the like of either of these, (M,) or anything dry, (Mgh, Mṣb,) not moistened, (Ṣ, Mṣb, Ḳ,) and not kneaded [with water &c.]; (Ṣ;) or i. q. قَمِحْتُ, (M, Ḳ, TA,) which signifies as above, (TA,) or I took it in the palm of my hand, (A and L in art. قمح,) and conveyed it to my mouth, (A in that art.,) or licked it up: (L in that art.:) and ▼سَفَّةٌ signifies the doing thus once. (TA.) And [hence,] سَفٌّ signifies also Camels' eating

dry herbage. (Ḳ.) Hence the saying of 'Amr Ibn-Kulthoom,

تَسُفُّ الجِلَّةُ الخُورُ الدَّرِينَا

The she-camels advanced in age, abounding with milk, eating the [dry and] old and wasted herbage. (Mgh. [See EM p. 208: and the same, p. 224.]) Hence also the phrase, لَأَنْ أُسِفَّ التُّرَابَ *Assuredly that I should eat the dust.* (Mgh.) — And سَفِفْتُ المَآءَ, (M, Ḳ,) aor. أَسَفُّ, inf. n. سَفٌّ, (TA,) *I drank much of the water without satisfying my thirst:* (M, Ḳ:) and so سَفَّهُ, aor. أَسُفُّهُ, inf. n. سَفٌّ. (TA.) — سُفَّ الرَّمَادُ فِى وَجْهِهِ: see 4.

4. اسفّ: see 1, first sentence. — [Hence,] أَسْفَفْتُ الشَّىْءَ, inf. n. إِسْفَافٌ, *I stuck one part of the thing to another.* (Yz, TA.) — [And from the same signification, as is indicated in the O and TA,] اسفّ النَّظَرَ ‡ *He looked sharply,* (Ṣ, M, A, O, Ḳ,) *and hardly,* (Ṣ, O,) *and minutely,* (A,) towards, or at, (إِلَى,) a person, (Ṣ, A, O,) and an affair, (A,) and AAF adds, *and inclined towards the ground.* (M.) — Also *He fed a camel with dry herbage.* (Ḳ.) — [Hence,] اسفّ الفَرَسَ اللِّجَامَ † *He put the bit into the mouth of the horse.* (Moḥeeṭ, L, Ḳ.) — And اسفّ الدَّوَآءَ † *He stuffed the wound with the medicament:* (M:) or اسفّ الجُرْحَ دَوَآءً ‡ *he put a medicament into the wound;* (Ḳ, TA;) as though he put سَفُوف to it. (TA.) — And اسفّ الوَشْمَ نَؤُورًا † *He filled in the tattoo with* نؤور [i. e. *smoke-black of fat*]. (M.) — And أُسِفَّ وَجْهُهُ النَّؤُورَ † *His face was sprinkled with* نؤور. (Ṣ.) It is said in a trad., فَكَأَنَّمَا أُسِفَّ وَجْهُهُ, meaning † *His face was altered,* (Ṣ, Ḳ,*) *as though something that altered it had been sprinkled upon it.* (Ṣ.) You say also, كَأَنَّ وَجْهَهُ أُسِفَّ رَمَادًا, meaning † *His face became of a blackish, or an ashy, hue, altered, as though ashes had been sprinkled upon it:* and ▼ سُفَّ الرَّمَادُ فِى وَجْهِهِ † [*Ashes were sprinkled upon his face*], meaning *his face became altered.* (Ḥar p. 626.) — Also *It approached the earth,* or *ground;* (Ṣ, M, Ḳ;) said of a bird in its flight; (Ṣ, Ḳ;) or of a bird &c.: (M:) or *it* (a bird) *flew over the ground so near that its feet almost reached it.* (A.) And اسفّت السَّحَابَةُ *The cloud approached the earth.* (Ṣ, Ḳ.) — Said of a stallion, *He stooped his head to bite.* (M, Ḳ.) And one says of a man, اسفّ مِنَ الأَرْضِ [and إِلَى الارض *He stooped towards the ground*]. (O in art. شب.) — And, said of a man, (Ṣ,) † *He pursued small, or little, things:* (Ṣ, Ḳ:) and † *he followed after low, or mean, things:* (Ḳ:) [† *he stooped to such things:*] or اسفّ إِلَى مَدَاقِّ الأُمُورِ وَالأَدَانِيهَا † *He approached* [or *pursued*] *small, or little, things, and the meanest,* or *most ignoble, thereof;* or *became mean,* or *ignoble:* (M,* TA:) and اسفّ إِلَيْهِ [and الدَّنِىْءَ, or correctly لِلْأَمْرِ الدَّنِىِّ,] † *He approached* [*the thing that was near, or that was low, or mean*]; from اسفّ said of a bird in its flight, meaning *It approached the ground so that its feet almost touched it.* (Ḥar p. 206.) [Hence the saying,] تَحَفَّظْ مِنَ العَمَلِ السَّفْسَافِ وَلَا تُسِفَّ لَهُ بَعْضَ الإِسْفَافِ ‡ [*Guard thyself from the bad action, and approach it not with any degree of approaching*]. (TA.) — You say also, مَا أَسَفَّ مِنْهُ بِتَافِهٍ *He obtained not* [*from him,* or *of it, a paltry acquisition*], (Ḳ, TA,) [or] *anything.* (TA.) — And اسفّ *He fled from his companion,* (Ḳ, TA,) *running most vehemently.* (TA.)

8: see 1.

R. Q. 1. سَفْسَفَ, (Ḳ,) inf. n. سَفْسَفَةٌ, (Ṣ, M,) *He cleared,* or *sifted,* (اِنْتَخَلَ,) flour, (Ṣ, M, Ḳ,) and the like, (Ṣ, Ḳ,) with the مُنْخُل [or sieve], and the like. (L, TA.) One says, سَمِعْتُ سَفْسَفَةَ المُنْخُلِ [*I heard the sifting of the sieve*]. (TA.) — And سَفْسَفَ عَمَلَهُ ‡ *He did his deed imperfectly,* or *not soundly.* (IDrd, M, Ḳ, TA.) — And سَفْسَفَتِ الرِّيحُ *The wind raised the fine dust, blowing a little above the surface of the earth.* (TA.)

R. Q. 2. لَا تَزَالُ تَتَسَفْسَفُ فِى هٰذَا الأَمْرِ a phrase mentioned by Ibn-'Abbád as meaning *Thou wilt not cease to destroy,* or *bring to nought, this thing,* or *affair.* (O, TA.)

سَفْ, with the ف quiescent, *i. q.* سَوْفَ; as in the phrase سَفْ تَفْعَلُ [*Thou wilt do* such a thing]: mentioned by Th. (M. [See art. سوف; and see also the letter س.])

سُفٌّ, accord. to the Ḳ, or ▼ سِفٌّ, with kesr, accord. to Ṣgh, [in the O,] (TA,) *A spadix,* or *a spathe,* (طَلْعَة) *of a male palm-tree.* (AA, O, Ḳ.) — See also سِفٌّ.

سِفٌّ: see what next follows.

سُفٌّ and ▼ سُفُّ, (O, Ḳ,) or the former and ▼ سِفٌّ, (so in a copy of the M,) The *serpent called* أُرْقَم: (AA, O, Ḳ:) or the *serpent that flies* (M, O, Ḳ) *in the air:* (M, O:) and sometimes peculiarly applied to the أُرْقَم: (M:) or the *male serpent.* (O.) And the Hudhalee poet Ed-Dákhil Ibn-Ḥarám uses the first of these words as meaning † *A man like a* سِفّ. (M.) — See also سُفّ.

سَفَّةٌ [an inf. n. un.]: see 1.

سُفَّةٌ *A plait of palm-leaves,* (M, Ḳ, TA,) i. e. a ▼ سَفِيفَة, (TA,) *made according to the measure of the* زَبِيل *or the* جُلَّة [*of which it is to form a part*]. (Ḳ, TA.) — And *A thing of the kind termed* قَرَامِل [pl. of قَرْمَل], (Ḳ, TA,) [i. e. *a plait*] *of* [*goat's*] *hair,* or *of wool,* (TA,) *which a woman attaches to her* [*plaits of*] *hair:* it was not disapproved by Ibráheem En-Nakha'ee; (Ḳ, TA;) though he disapproved of other things attached to the hair: IAth explains it as *a thing that a woman puts upon her head, and attaches to her hair in order that it may be lengthened* [*thereby*]. (TA.) — *A small portion,* (حَبَّة,) and (Ṣ) *a handful,* (Ṣ, Ḳ,) of meal of parched barley or wheat, (Ṣ,) or of wheat, and the like. (Ḳ.) — See also what next follows.

سَفُوفٌ *Medicine,* (Ṣ, M, Mṣb, Ḳ,) and *meal of parched barley or wheat,* (Ṣ, M,) and the *like of either of these,* (M,) or *anything dry,* (Mṣb,) *taken* [*into the mouth*], (Ṣ, M,* Ḳ,) or *eaten,* (Mṣb,) *not moistened,* (Ṣ, M,* Mṣb, Ḳ,) or *not kneaded* [*with water &c.*]; (Ṣ;) and ▼ سُفَّةٌ signifies the same; (M, Ḳ;) each a subst. from سَفِفْتُ السَّوِيقَ and الدَّوَآءَ &c. (M.) — Also *Blackness of the gum.* (M, TA.)

سَفِيفٌ *Woven* [*with the fingers,* or *plaited,*] *of palm-leaves.* (KL.) — [And hence,] The *girth of the* رَحْل [*or camel's saddle*], (Ṣ, M, Ḳ,) and *of the* [*women's vehicle called*] هَوْدَج: (M:) the *fore-girth of the* رَحْل; because made broad, like the سَفِيف of palm-leaves. (T, TA.) [See also the next paragraph.] — *A certain plant.* (IDrd, Ḳ.) — The *sharpness* of the ears of the wolf. (M, TA.) — And السَّفِيفُ is *A name of Iblees:* (O, Ḳ:) so says AA: (O:) in one or more of the copies of the "Nawádir," ▼ السَّفْسَفُ. (TA.)

سَفِيفَةٌ *A thing woven* [*with the fingers,* or *plaited,*] of palm-leaves: (Ṣ, O:) *a piece of woven* [or *plaited*] *work* of palm-leaves (Ḳ voce عَرَقٌ) &c.: (TA ibid.:) pl. سَفَائِفُ. (TA.) See سُفَّةٌ, first sentence. — *A wide belly-girth with which a* رَحْل [or *camel's saddle*] *is bound,* or *fastened.* (M.) [See also سَفِيفٌ.] — The *appertenance* [or *suspensory*] *of a water-skin* (قِرْبَة), *which the carrier of the* قربة *puts over his chest* [*when carrying the* قربة *on his back*]. (Ḳ voce عَرَقٌ.) — See also جُمَّانٌ. — *A* [*receptacle for dates, such as is called*] دَوْخَلَّة, [*made of palm-leaves,*] *before it is woven.* (M, TA.) — And [the pl.] سَفَائِفُ signifies *Wide ribs:* or, as some say, *all the ribs.* (M.)

سَفْسَفٌ *A certain plant;* (M, TA;) said by IDrd to be of the dial. of El-Yemen; *that which the people of Nejd call the* عَنْقَز, *which is the* مَرْزَنْجُوش [or *marjoram*]. (TA.) — See also سَفِيفٌ.

سَفْسَافٌ The *dust* of flour, *that rises,* (Ḳ,) or *flies and rises,* (TA,) *at the sifting.* (Ḳ, TA.) — The *fine particles* of dust: (Ṣ, Mgh, Ḳ:) or *such as rises,* or *spreads,* of dust. (M.) — Hence, (Mgh,) سَفْسَافُ الشِّعْرِ (Mgh, Ḳ) † *What is bad of poetry,* (Ḳ, TA,) *imperfectly,* or *unsoundly, done.* (TA. [In the CḲ, الشَّعْرِ is erroneously put for الشِّعْرِ; and Freytag appears to have read الشَّعِيرِ.]) سَفْسَافٌ signifies † *Bad* poetry: and † anything *imperfectly,* or *unsoundly, done.* (M.) Anything *bad.* (Ṣ, Ḳ. [Compare the Hebr. אֲסַפְסֻף, occurring with the article, and with the quiescent, in Numbers xi. 4.]) † *Such as is bad* of natural dispositions. (M.) And † *A contemptible,* or *despicable,* thing or affair. (Ṣ, Ḳ.) It is said in a trad., إِنَّ ٱللّٰهَ يُحِبُّ مَعَالِىَ الأُمُورِ وَيُبْغِضُ سَفْسَافَهَا, (Ṣ, M, Mgh, TA,) or يَكْرَهُ سَفْسَافَهَا, (Ṣ, TA,) i. e. † [*Verily God loves lofty things,* or *things whereby one acquires eminence or nobility,* and] *hates paltry, and mean, things.* (Mgh, Ṣgh, TA.)

سَفْسَافٌ signifies [also] † An action, and a saying, in which is no good. (Ḥam p. 232; where the foregoing trad. is cited as an ex.) And † Any bad wind: (TA:) [or] سَفْسَافَةٌ signifies a wind running a little above the ground; and so ▼ مُسَفْسِفَةٌ: (M:) or the latter, a wind that raises the fine dust, and runs a little above the ground. (Ṣ, Ḳ.) — حَلِفٌ سَفْسَافٌ ‡ A false, or lying, swearing, in which is no ratification. (TA.)

سُفَاسِفُ Vehement hunger. (Ibn-'Abbád, Ḳ.)

مُسِفٌّ [act. part. n. of 4, q. v.]. — Anything cleaving, or sticking, to another thing. (A'Obeyd, TA.) — مَرَّ مُسِفًّا He passed by fleeing from his companion, running most vehemently. (Ibn-'Abbád, TA.)

مُسَفْسِفَةٌ: see سَفْسَافٌ, last sentence but one. = Also, without the ة, ‡ Ungenerous, or mean, in giving. (Ṣ, M.)

سفح

1. سَفَحَ, (Ṣ, A, Mṣb, Ḳ,) aor. َ, (Mṣb, Ḳ,) inf. n. سَفْحٌ, (Mṣb,) [and app. سُفُوحٌ also, mentioned in what follows,] He poured out, or forth, water: (Ṣ, A:) and he shed blood, (Ṣ, A, Mṣb, Ḳ,) the blood of another; (Ṣ, A;) and tears; (Mṣb, Ḳ;) inf. n. as above, and سُفُوحٌ: (Ḳ:) or سَفَحَتِ العَيْنُ دَمْعَهَا [the eye shed its tears]. (A.) The saying, in a trad., فَقَتَلَ عَلَى رَأْسِ المَآءِ حَتَّى سَفَحَ الدَّمُ المَآءَ has been explained as meaning [And he slew at the head of the water so that] the blood covered the water: but IAth says that this is not consistent with the language; for سَفْحٌ signifies the act of "pouring out, or forth;" and that the meaning may therefore be, that the blood made the water to pour forth; like as when, into a full vessel, something heavier than what is in it is poured; for in this case there comes forth from it as much as has been poured into it. (TA.) — سُفِحَ فِى الأَرْضِ † [He was stretched, or extended, upon the ground], said of a camel. (Ḳ.) = The verb is also used intransitively; you say, سَفَحَ المَآءُ, (Mṣb,) and الدَّمْعُ, inf. n. سُفُوحٌ and سَفَحَانٌ (O, Ḳ) and سَفْحٌ, (Ḳ,) The water, (Mṣb,) and the tears, (O, Ḳ,) poured out, or forth. (O, Mṣb, Ḳ.)

2. سَفَّحَ, inf. n. تَسْفِيحٌ, † He did a deed that profited him not; (Ḳ;) likened to the arrow called السَّفِيحُ. (TA.)

3. [سَافَحَهُ, inf. n. سِفَاحٌ, and perhaps مُسَافَحَةٌ also, He contended with him in the shedding of blood.] You say, بَيْنَهُمْ سِفَاحٌ Between them is a shedding of blood. (TA.) — And [hence,] بَيْنَهُمَا سِفَاحٌ ‡ Between them two is a contending in fight: or, in hocking [of camels] (مُعَاقَرَة). (A, TA.) — And سِفَاحٌ and مُسَافَحَةٌ also signify ‡ The committing fornication with another; (Ṣ, A, Mṣb, Ḳ;) لِأَنَّ المَآءَ يُصَبُّ ضَائِعًا; (Mṣb;) as also ▼ تَسَافُحٌ [which is said of more than one pair]. (Ḳ.) You say, سَافَحَهَا ‡ He committed fornication with her. (A, Mṣb.) And سَافَحَتْهُ ‡ She committed fornication with him: (L:) or she abode with him in the practice of fornication. (TA.) [In all the copies of the Ṣ that I have been able to consult, three in number, I find سَافَحَهُ.] And فِى النِّكَاحِ غُنْيَةٌ عَنِ السِّفَاحِ ‡ [In marriage is that which renders one in no need of fornication]. (A, Mṣb.) In the Time of Ignorance, when a man demanded a woman in marriage, he said, إِنْكِحِينِى; and when he desired fornication, he said, سَافِحِينِى. (TA.)

4. أَجْرَوْا إِسْفَاحًا † They made [horses] to run without a wager. (Ḳ.) [App., like 2, from السَّفِيحُ, the arrow thus called.]

[5. تسفّح, accord. to Freytag, signifies It was, or became, poured out, or forth: but he names no authority for this.]

6. تَسَافَحُوا الدِّمَآءَ [They mutually shed blood; lit., bloods]. (A.) — See also 3.

سَفْحٌ The base, foot, bottom, or lowest or lower part, (أَصْلٌ, Ḳ, or أَسْفَلُ, Ṣ, A, Ḳ,) of a mountain, (Ṣ, A, Ḳ,) which is the part whereinto is poured (يُسْفَحُ) the water [from the parts above]; i. e. the part where the side thereof rests upon the ground: (Ṣ: [as also صَفْحٌ:]) or the [part called] عُرْض thereof, [see this word,] that rests its side upon the ground: or the حَضِيض [app. as meaning the low ground at, or by, the base, or foot,] thereof: (Ḳ:) or the spreading part thereof: (A: [there said to be in this sense tropical; but why, I see not:]) or the face thereof: (Mṣb:) or the lowest, or lower, part thereof, where it is rugged: (Ḥam p. 80:) pl. سُفُوحٌ. (Ḳ.) — [The pl.] سُفُوحٌ also signifies Rocks that are soft, or smooth, (Ḳ, TA,) and slippery. (TA.)

سَفُوحٌ: see سَافِحٌ. You say جَفْنٌ سَفُوحٌ [An eyelid shedding copious tears]. (A.)

سَفِيحٌ A sack; syn. جُوَالِقٌ: (Ḳ:) سَفِيحَانِ signifies a pair of sacks which are placed (Ṣ, L) upon a camel, (L,) like the خُرْج. (Ṣ, L.) — And A thick, or coarse, [garment of the kind called] كِسَآء. (O, Ḳ.) — السَّفِيحُ [incorrectly written by Freytag سَفِيحة, as on the authority of the Ṣ,] is the name of An arrow used in the game called المَيْسِر, to which no portion pertains: (Ṣ, A,* Ḳ:) it is the fourth of the arrows to which the term غُفْل is applied, which have no notches, and to which is assigned no portion and no fine; these being added only to give additional weight to the collection of arrows from fear of occasioning suspicion [of foul play]: the first of them is called المُصْدَرُ; the next, المُضَعَّفُ; the next, المَنِيحُ; and the next, السَّفِيحُ. (Lḥ, TA.) — See also مُسَافِحٌ.

سَفَّاحٌ A shedder of much blood. (A.) [Hence,] السَّفَّاحُ is the name of A sword of Ḥomeyd Ibn-Bahdal. (Ḳ.) — [Hence also,] † A giver of many gifts; or one who gives much. (Ḳ.) — And † Chaste [or rather fluent or eloquent] in speech; syn. فَصِيحٌ: (Ḳ:) or possessing ability for speech. (Ṣ.)

سَافِحٌ Pouring out, or forth; (O, L, Mṣb, Ḳ;) applied to water, (A, Mṣb,) [and blood,] and tears (دَمْعٌ): (O, L, Ḳ:) [accord. to some, unacquainted with the intrans. verb سَفَحَ, a possessive epithet, i. e.] meaning ذُو سَفْحٍ: (Ḥam p. 709:) syn. with ▼ سَفُوحٌ, [or rather this is an intensive epithet,] and ▼ مَسْفُوحٌ also is syn. with سَفُوحٌ; (TA;) or [rather] signifies poured out, or forth; (A,* L, Mṣb;) and is applied to water, (A, Mṣb,) and tears (دَمْعٌ). (L.)

أَسْفَحُ † Bald in the fore part of the head; (Ḳ;) as also أَسْقَحُ (TA) [and أَصْقَحُ].

مَسْفَحٌ A place where water is poured out, or forth; and where blood, and tears, are shed: pl. مَسَافِحُ. One says, لِلْوَادِى مَسَافِحُ The valley has places where it pours out, or forth. (A, TA.)

مُسَفِّحٌ † One who does a deed that profits him not. (Ḳ. [See 2.])

مَسْفُوحٌ: see سَافِحٌ. — [Hence,] applied to a camel, it means قَدْ سُفِحَ فِى الأَرْضِ وَمُدَّ † [Stretched, or extended, upon the ground; وَمُدَّ being an explicative adjunct]. (Ḳ.) — † Wide. (Ḳ.) You say نَاقَةٌ مَسْفُوحَةُ الإِبْطِ ‡ A she-camel wide in the arm-pit. (A, Ḳ.) And جَمَلٌ مَسْفُوحُ الضُّلُوعِ ‡ A camel [wide i. e.] not contracted in the ribs. (A, TA.) — † Thick, coarse, or big. (Ḳ.) — You say also, إِنَّهُ لَمَسْفُوحُ العُنُقِ, meaning † Verily he is long, and thick, coarse, or big, in the neck. (TA.) — And المَسْفُوحُ is the name of † A horse of Ṣakhr Ibn-'Amr Ibn-El-Ḥárith. (Ḳ.)

مُسَافِحٌ † A fornicator. (TA.) And مُسَافِحَةٌ † A fornicatress; (TA;) a woman who does not abstain from fornication. (Aboo-Is-ḥáḳ, TA.) اِبْنُ مُسَافِحَةٍ means † A son of a fornicatress; (TA;) and [in like manner] ▼ سَفِيحٌ a son who is the offspring of fornication. (Ṣgh, TA in art. عرض.)

سفد

1. سَفِدَ and سَفَدَ, (Ṣ,) or سَفِدَ عَلَى الأُنْثَى and سَفَدَهَا, (M, Mṣb) and سَفَدَ [عَلَيْهَا], (Ḳ,) or سَفِدَهَا (M, A,) aor. of the former َ, (Ṣ, M, Mṣb, Ḳ,) and of the latter ِ, (M, Ḳ,) inf. n. سِفَادٌ (Ṣ, M, Mṣb) and سَفْدٌ, which are of both the verbs; (M;) and ▼ سَافَدَهَا, inf. n. سِفَادٌ; (A;) He leaped the female: (Ṣ, Ḳ:) said of a bird, (A, Mṣb,) &c.; (Mṣb;) or of any beast or bird of prey; (Aṣ, TA;) or of a quadruped and of a bird; (M, TA;) or of a goat (Ṣ, TA) and of a camel (Aṣ, Ṣ, TA) and of a bull and of a beast of prey and of a bird; (Ṣ, TA;) and, in poetry, of a swimmer [app. meaning a fish]: (M, TA:) sometimes, also, it is used to convey an allusion to الجِمَاع [relating to human beings]. (A.)

2. تَسْفِيدُ اللَّحْمِ † The arranging of the flesh-

meat upon the سَفُّود, to roast: (Ḳ:) Z [app.] makes it tropical, by his derivation of سَفُّود [q. v.]. (TA.)

3: see 1: — and see also 6.

4. اسفدهُ *He made him to leap* [the female]. (Ṣ,* Ḳ,* PṢ, TḲ.) — أَسْفِدْنِى تَيْسَكَ, mentioned by Lḥ, means *Lend me thy he-goat in order that he may leap my she-goat:* and Umeiyeh Ibn-Abi-ṣ-Ṣalt uses its pass. part. n. metaphorically in relation to the زَنْد [or piece of stick used for producing fire]; saying,

وَالْأَرْضَ صَيَّرَهَا الْإِلٰهُ طَرُوقَةً ٭
لِلْمَآءِ حَتَّى كُلُّ زَنْدٍ مُسْفَدُ ٭

[*And the land, God made it to be soaked by the water, so that every* زند *was lent;* no man being able to go far enough to cut one for himself]. (M, TA.)

5. تسفّد فَرَسَهُ *He mounted his mare from behind;* (M;) as also ↓ استسفدها: (AAF, M:) or استسفد ↓ بَعِيرَهُ *he came to his camel from behind, and mounted him:* (IAạr, Ḳ:) and [in like manner] تسفّدهُ i. q. تَعَرَّقَبَهُ, (Ḳ,) i. e. *he mounted him from behind.* (TA.)

6. تسافدت السِّبَاعُ (Ṣ) and الطُّيُورُ, (A,) or تسافد السِّبَاعُ (Ḳ) and الطُّيُورُ, (TA,) and ↓ الشِّيَاهُ سافدت, (Mṣb, [perhaps a mistranscription for تسافدت,]) *The beasts of prey* [and *the birds* and *the sheep* or *goats*] *leaped one another.* (TḲ.)

10: see 5, in two places.

سَفْدُ اللِّقَاحِ *A certain game, in which boys arrange themselves one behind another, every one laying hold upon the* حُجْزَة [or *uppermost part of the waist-wrapper*] *of his fellow, from behind him.* (T in art. جعر, and TA.)

سَفُودٌ A mare *that is not allowed to be leaped* [*by the stallion*] *until she has completed her* مُنْيَة, which is a *period of twenty days.* (Kr, M.)

سَفُّودٌ (Ṣ, M, Mṣb, Ḳ) and سُفُّودٌ (M, TA) † *An iron instrument,* (Ṣ, M, Ḳ,) *with curved prongs,* (M, TA,) *with which flesh-meat is roasted:* (Ṣ, Ḳ:) Z makes is to be tropical, saying [in the A] that it is so called because of its adhering to that which is roasted upon it: (TA:) pl. سَفَافِيدُ. (Mṣb, TA.) [For instances of substs. similar to سَفُّودٌ and سُفُّودٌ, see سُبُّوحٌ.]

إِسْفِنْدٌ and إِسْفَنْدٌ *Wine:* (Ḳ:) the etymologists assert that its د is a substitute for the ط in إِسْفِنْطٌ, which is one of the names of wine. (TA.)

مُسْفَدٌ pass. part. n. of 4, q. v.

سفر

1. سَفَرَ, (Ṣ, M, A, Ḳ,) aor. ِ , inf. n. سَفْرٌ, (M, Ḳ,) *He swept* a house, or chamber, (Ṣ, M, A, Ḳ,) &c. (M.) — And *He,* or *it,* [*swept away;* or *took away,* or *carried off, in every direction:* and] *dispersed:* (M, Ḳ:) and *removed, took off,* or *stripped off,* a thing from a thing which it covered. (M,* A,* Ḳ.) You say, سَفَرَتِ الرِّيحُ التُّرَابَ, and الوَرَقَ, † *The wind swept away the dust,* and *the leaves:* or *took them away,* or *carried them off, in every direction.* (M.) And سَفَرَتِ الرِّيحُ الغَيْمَ † *The wind dispersed the clouds:* (M, TA:) or † *removed the clouds* from the face of the sky. (A,* TA.) And you say of a woman, سَفَرَتْ, (Ṣ, M, A, Mgh, Ḳ,) aor. ُ , (M,) inf. n. سُفُورٌ, (M, Mgh,) meaning *She removed* her veil (M, A, Mgh) عَنْ وَجْهِهَا *from her face:* (A, M:) and [elliptically] (M) *she uncovered her face:* (Ṣ, M, Ḳ:) [for] سَفَرْتُ الشَّىْءَ, [being for سفرت عَنِ الشَّىْءِ,] aor. ِ , inf. n. سَفْرٌ [or سُفُورٌ ?], signifies *I uncovered the thing; made it apparent,* or *manifest:* (Mgh:) [but accord. to Mṭr,] the phrase تُسْفِرُ وَجْهَهَا [meaning *she uncovers her face*] is of weak authority. (Mgh.) — Hence, i. e. from سَفَرَتْ meaning "she uncovered her face," (M,) سَفَرْتُ بَيْنَ القَوْمِ, (Ṣ, M, Mgh,* Mṣb, Ḳ,) aor. ِ , (Ṣ, Mṣb, Ḳ) and ُ , (Ḳ,) inf. n. سِفَارَةٌ (Ṣ, Mgh, Mṣb, Ḳ) and سَفَارَةٌ and سَفْرٌ, (Ḳ,) † *I made peace, effected a reconciliation,* or *adjusted a difference, between the people;* (Ṣ, Mgh, Mṣb, Ḳ;) because he who does so exposes what is in the mind of each party: (TA:) or *I exposed what was in the mind of this and the mind of this in order to make peace, &c., between the people.* (M.) [See also سِفَارَةٌ, below.] — [And likewise, perhaps, from سَفَرَتْ meaning "she uncovered her face,"] سَفَرَتِ الشَّمْسُ, aor. ِ , inf. n. سَفْرٌ, † *The sun rose.* (Mṣb.) — See also 4, in two places. — سَفَرَ, (Ṣ, Mṣb,) aor. ِ , (Ṣ,) or ُ , (Mṣb,) inf. n. سُفُورٌ, (Ṣ,) or سَفْرٌ, (Mṣb,) [the former of which inf. ns. perhaps indicates a radical relation to سَفَرَتْ said of a woman, and of the sun, expl. above,] *He went forth to journey:* (Ṣ, Mṣb:) this verb, however, in this sense, [which appears to have been unknown, or not acknowledged, by the authors of the M and Ḳ, (see مُسَافِرٌ,)] is obsolete; but its inf. n. سَفَرٌ is used as a simple subst. (Mṣb. [See 3, the verb commonly used in this sense.]) — [Hence, app.,] سَفَرَ شَحْمُهُ ‡ *His fat went away.* (A, TA.) — and سَفَرَتِ الحَرْبُ ‡ *The war declined;* syn. وَلَّتْ. (A, Ḳ.) = سَفَرَ الكِتَابَ, (Ṣ, A,) aor. ِ , inf. n. سَفْرٌ, (Ṣ,) *He wrote the book,* or *writing.* (A. [See سِفْرٌ.]) = سَفَرَ البَعِيرَ, (Ṣ, Ḳ,) or سَفَرَهُ بِالسِّفَارِ, (M,) aor. ِ , (M, Ḳ,) inf. n. سَفْرٌ; (M;) and ↓ اسفرهُ, (AZ, M, Ḳ,) inf. n. إِسْفَارٌ; (TA;) and ↓ سفّرهُ, (Kr, M, Ḳ,) inf. n. تَسْفِيرٌ; (TA;) *He put the* سِفَار [q. v.] *upon the nose of the camel.* (Ṣ, M, Ḳ.) = سَفَرَ الغَنَمَ *He sold the best of the sheep,* or *goats.* (Ḳ.)

2. سفّرهُ, inf. n. تَسْفِيرٌ, *He sent him to go a journey.* (Ḳ, TA.) — سفّر الإِبِلَ, (Ḳ,) inf. n. as above, (TA,) *He pastured the camels between sunset and nightfall,* and *in the* سُفَير, (Ḳ, TA,) i.e., the *whiteness* [*of the sky*] *before night:* (TA:) or *he fed the camels with* سَفِير [q. v.]: (so in the O:) and سفّر فَرَسَهُ, inf. n. تَسْفِيرٌ, *He fed his horse with* سَفِير: or *he kept him continually going, and trained him, in order that he might become strong to journey.* (JM.) — سفّر النَّارَ, (Ḳ,) inf. n. as above, (TA,) *He made the fire to flame,* or *blaze;* (Ḳ, TA;) *kindled it;* or *made it to burn, burn up,* or *burn brightly* or *fiercely.* (TA.) = See also 1, last sentence but one.

3. [سافر is trans. and intrans.] You say, الرِّيَاحُ يُسَافِرُ بَعْضُهَا بَعْضًا [*The winds vie, one with another, in sweeping the ground, effacing one another's traces*]: for the east wind removes and disperses the longitudinal traces made by the west wind, and the south wind makes traces across them. (Ṣ,* Ḳ,* TA.) = And سافر, inf. n. مُسَافَرَةٌ (Ṣ, Mṣb, Ḳ) and سِفَارٌ, (Ṣ, Ḳ,) *He journeyed,* or *went,* (Ḳ,) or *went forth to journey,* (Ṣ, Mṣb,) إِلَى بَلَدِ كَذَا [*to such a country,* or *town*]. (Ṣ, Ḳ.) And سَافَرَ سَفَرًا بَعِيدًا [*He journeyed,* or *went, a far journey*]. (A, Mgh.) [See also 1.] — [Hence,] † *He died.* (Ḳ.) — And سَافَرَتِ الشَّمْسُ عَنْ كَبِدِ السَّمَآءِ ‡ [*The sun declined from the middle of the sky*]. (A.) — And سَافَرَتْ عَنْهُ الحُمَّى ‡ [*The fever departed from him*]. (A.)

4. اسفرت الشَّجَرَةُ *The tree had its leaves blown off* [*and swept away*] *by the wind;* (Ḳ,* TA;) *they having become changed in colour, and white.* (TA.) — And اسفر, (inf. n. إِسْفَارٌ, Mgh, Mṣb,) *It* (the dawn, or daybreak,) *shone,* (T, Ṣ, M, A, Mgh, Mṣb, Ḳ,) *so that there was no doubt respecting it;* (T, TA;) as also ↓ سَفَرَ, (M, Ḳ,) aor. ِ , (Ḳ,) inf. n. سَفْرٌ: (TA:) it has a special relation to colour; meaning *it shone in colour.* (B, TA.) — *It* (the moon) *caused a shining* [*in the sky*] *before its rising.* (M.) — ‡ *It* (a man's face) *shone* (Ṣ, M) [*with happiness* (see مُسْفِرٌ)]; or with beauty; for you say, اسفر حُسْنًا; (Ṣ;) as also ↓ سَفَرَ: (M:) or *became overspread with beauty.* (Mṣb.) — And *He entered upon the time of dawn,* or *daybreak;* (M;) or *the time when the dawn became white.* (Ḳ.) The Prophet said, أَسْفِرُوا بِالفَجْرِ, meaning *Perform ye the prayer of daybreak when ye enter upon the time in which the dawn shines,* or *becomes white:* (Ṣ,* Mṣb:) or *when the dawn has become manifest, so that there is no doubt respecting it, every one knowing it to be the true dawn when he sees it;* accord. to Esh-Sháfi'ee and Ibn-Ḥambal and others: (T, TA:) or *prolong ye the prayer of daybreak until ye enter upon the time when the dawn becomes white:* (Ṣ, TA:) some say that it relates especially to nights in [the end of] which the moon shines, because in such the commencement of daybreak is not manifest: (TA:) or أَسْفَرَ بِالصَّلَاةِ means *he performed prayer in the shining of the dawn:* and the ب is for the purpose of making the verb transitive. (Mgh.) — اسفرت الحَرْبُ ‡ *The war became vehement.* (A, Ḳ.) = See also 1, last sentence but one.

5. تسفّر means أَتَى بِسُفْرٍ, (O, Ḳ,) i. e. *He came in* [*the time of*] *the whiteness of day* [either *before sunrise* or *after sunset*]. (TA.) — And تسفّرت الإِبِلُ *The camels pastured between sunset and nightfall,* (O, Ḳ,) and *in the* سُفَير, (Ḳ, TA,)

i. e. the *whiteness* [*of the sky*] *before night.* (TA. [But see 2, second sentence.]) ═ تسفّر النِّسَآءَ (O, Ḳ, TA) عَنْ وُجُوهِهِنَّ (O, TA) *i. q.* ↓ اِسْتَسْفَرَهُنَّ, (O, Ḳ, TA,) i. e. *He sought the brightest of the women in face and in beauty* (TA, TḲ*) for marriage. (TḲ.) — And تسفّر شَيْئًا مِنْ حَاجَتِهِ ‡ *He attained,* or *obtained, somewhat of the object of his want* (O, Ḳ, TA) *before its becoming beyond his reach.* (TA.) — And تسفّر فُلَانًا † *He sought to obtain of such a one the half* (النَّصَفَ, O, Ḳ, TA [in the CḲ النَّصَفَ, by which, if it be correct, may perhaps be meant *what was equitable,* and النَّصَف may bear the same interpretation,]) *of a claim* (تَبِعَة) *that he had upon him.* (O, Ḳ, TA.) ═ تسفّر الجِلْدُ *The skin received,* or *had, a mark,* or *an impression:* (O, Ḳ:) from سَفْرٌ meaning أَثَرٌ. (TA.)

7. انسفر الغَيْمُ † *The clouds became dispersed:* (M, TA:) [or] *became removed* from the face of the sky. (TA.) — انسفر مُقَدَّمُ رَأْسِهِ مِنَ الشَّعَرِ † *The fore part of his head became divested of the hair.* (Ṣ, Ḳ.*) — انسفرت الإِبِلُ فِى الأَرْضِ † *The camels went away into the country,* or *land.* (M, Ḳ.*)

9. [اِسْفَرَّتِ الشَّمْسُ, inf. n. اِسْفِرَارٌ, app. means *The sun became white,* previously to setting.] See سَفَرٌ.

10. استسفر النِّسَآءَ: see 5. ═ استسفرهُ *He sent him as a* سَفِير [q. v.]. (JM.)

سَفْرٌ: see مُسَافِرٌ, in two places. ═ Also *A mark, an impression, a trace,* or *a vestige,* (أَثَرٌ, Ḳ, TA,) *remaining:* (TA:) pl. سُفُورٌ. (Ḳ.) [Accord. to Freytag, it occurs in the Deewán El-Hudhaleeyeen as meaning The *track,* or *trace, of a surge,* or *torrent.*]

سِفْرٌ *A book,* or *writing:* (Ṣ, M:) or *a great,* or *large, book:* or *a section of the Book of the Law revealed to Moses:* (M, Ḳ:) or *a book that discovers,* or *reveals, truths:* (TA:) or a book is thus called because it discovers things, and makes them evident: (M:) pl. أَسْفَارٌ. (Ṣ, M.) — With respect to the saying of Aboo-Ṣakhr El-Hudhalee,

لِلَيْلَى بِذَاتِ البَيْنِ دَارٌ عَرَفْتُهَا •
وَأُخْرَى بِذَاتِ الجَيْشِ آيَاتُهَا سِفْرُ •

Skr says, [the poet means,] the marks, or traces, thereof had become effaced: [accordingly, the verse may be rendered, *To Leylà there was in Dhát-el-Beyn an abode that I knew, and another in Dhát-el-Jeysh whereof the marks,* or *traces, are effaced:*] IJ says, [app. holding the meaning to be, *the marks,* or *traces, whereof are* (*like those of*) *an ancient book,* such as a portion of the Mosaic Law,] the last word should be from the phrase سَفَرْتُ البَيْتَ, i. e. "I swept the house, or chamber;" as though the writing were swept off from the طِرْس [or "written paper" or the like, to which the poet seems to compare the site of the abode in Dhát-el-Jeysh]. (M, TA.)

سَفَرٌ *Journey,* or *travel;* the *act of journeying* or *travelling;* (Ṣ, A, Ḳ;) *contr. of* حَضَرٌ: (M, Ḳ:) thus called because of the going and coming in it, like the going and coming of the wind sweeping away fallen leaves: (M:) or the *act of going forth to journey;* an inf. n. used as a simple subst.: (Mṣb:) [therefore] the pl. is أَسْفَارٌ: (Ṣ, M, A, Mṣb, Ḳ:) [and therefore it is often used as a n. un.; but, properly speaking, the n. un. is ↓ سَفْرَةٌ:] you say, كَانَتْ سَفْرَتُهُ قَرِيبَةً [*His journey was near*]: and the pl. of سَفْرَةٌ, accord. to rule, is سَفَرَاتٌ. (Mṣb.) In law, [as relating to the obligation of fasting &c.,] The *going forth with the intention of performing a journey of three days and nights, or more.* (KT.) ═ Also The *whiteness of dawn* or *daybreak:* (A:) or the *whiteness of the day:* (Ṣ, M:) and *i. q.* صَبَاحٌ [*dawn,* or *morning,* or *forenoon;* but app. here used in the first of these senses]: (M:) and ↓ سَفِيرٌ, the *whiteness* [*of the sky*] *before night:* (A, TA:) or the former, the *remains of the whiteness of day after sunset.* (Ḳ.) You say سَفَرًا i. e. صَبَاحًا [app. as meaning *In the dawn*]. (A.) And the prose-rhymer says, إِذَا طَلَعَتِ الشِّعْرَى سَفَرَا لَمْ تَرَ فِيهَا مَطَرَا (Ṣ,* TA) i. e. *When Sirius rises in the whiteness of day* [meaning *in the clear twilight of morning, thou seest not then rain:* for Sirius rises aurorally, in Arabia, in the middle and the latter half of July, when rain scarcely ever falls there]. (Ṣ. [Accord. to the TA, the meaning, app. taken without consideration from one of the foregoing explanations of سَفَرٌ, is, *when Sirius rises at nightfall:* but this is during the usual winter-rains.]) You say also, لَقِيتُهُ سَفَرًا, and فِى سَفَرٍ, meaning ↓ عِنْدَ اَسْفِرَارِ الشَّمْسِ لِلْغُرُوبِ, thus related, with س [in the word اسفرار (not with ص), and app. meaning *I met him when the sun was becoming white, previously to the setting*]. (M.) And بَقِىَ سَفَرٌ مِنْ نَهَارٍ [*There remained a white gleam of daylight*]. (A.)

سَفْرَةٌ: see the next preceding paragraph.

سُفْرَةٌ The *food of the traveller;* (M, Ḳ;) the *food that is prepared for the traveller,* (Ṣ, Mṣb,) or *for a journey:* (TA:) pl. سُفَرٌ. (Mṣb.) This is the primary signification. (TA.) You say, أَكَلُوا السُّفْرَةَ *They ate the food for the journey.* (A.) — Hence, ‡ The *receptacle thereof;* (TA;) the *piece of skin in which it is put.* (Ṣ,* M,* Mṣb, Ḳ,* TA.) [This is commonly of a round form, with a running string; so that it is converted into a bag to contain the food, at one time, and at another time is spread flat upon the ground, when persons want to eat upon it.] — And hence, ‡ The *thing* [*whatever it be*] *upon which one eats:* (TA:) [in the desert, it is generally a round piece of skin, such as I have described above: in the towns, in the houses of the middle classes, a round tray of tinned copper, which is usually placed on a low stool; and in the dwellings of some of the highest classes, and the lowest, respectively, of silver and wood:] accord. to the T, سُفْرَةٌ has the last of the significations given before this, and the thing which it denotes is thus called because it is spread when one eats upon it. (TA.)

سِفَارٌ (Lḥ, Ṣ, M, Ḳ) and ↓ سِفَارَةٌ (Lḥ, M) *A piece of iron,* (Ṣ, M, Ḳ,) or *a cord,* (M,) or *a piece of skin,* (Ḳ,) *that is put over the nose* [*and jaws*] *of a camel, in the place of the* حَكَمَة [q. v.] (Lḥ, Ṣ, M, Ḳ) *of the horse:* (Ṣ, Ḳ:) or *a cord that is attached to the* خِطَام [q. v.] *of a camel, a part being twisted round it, and the rest being made a rein:* and *sometimes it is of iron:* (Lth:) pl. [of pauc., of the former,] أَسْفِرَةٌ (M, Ḳ) and [of mult.] سُفُرٌ (Ṣ, M, Ḳ) and [of either] سَفَائِرُ. (M, Ḳ.)

سَفِيرٌ *Leaves which the wind sweeps away;* (M;) *leaves which fall from trees* (Ṣ, A, Ḳ) *and which the wind sweeps away,* (A,) or because the wind sweeps them away: (Ṣ:) or *leaves of herbs;* because the wind sweeps them away: (T, TA:) or *what have fallen of the leaves of trees and of the lower portions of seed-produce.* (JM.) ═ Also *A messenger:* (Ṣ:) and † *a mediator;* or *a man who makes peace, effects a reconciliation,* or *adjusts a difference, between a people;* (Ṣ, M, Mṣb;) as also ↓ سَافِرٌ: (Mṣb:) or *a messenger who makes peace, &c.:* (T, Mgh, TA:) [see 1:] pl. of the former سُفَرَآءُ, (Ṣ, M, Mgh,) and of the latter سَفَرَةٌ. (Ḥar p. 255. [See also سِفَارَةٌ, below.]) — And † *A commissioned agent, a factor,* or *a deputy;* and *the like:* pl. as above: app. so called because he discovers, and makes manifest, the affair in which he acts as a substitute for another person. (Mṣb.) ═ See also سَفَرٌ.

سُفَارَةٌ *Sweepings.* (Ṣ, M, Ḳ.)

سِفَارَةٌ an inf. n. of سَفَرَ in the phrase سَفَرَ بَيْنَ القَوْمِ [q. v.]. (Ṣ, Mgh, Mṣb, Ḳ.) [And hence, The *office of the* سَفِير (q. v.). See also De Sacy's Chrest. Ar., sec. ed., i. 126 and 172: and Quatremère's Hist. des Sultans Mamlouks, i. 193.] ═ Also The *falling of one's hair from* [*above*] *his forehead.* (Ṣgh, TA.) ═ See also سِفَارٌ.

سَافِرٌ [act. part. n. of 1:] A woman *having her face uncovered:* (Ṣ, M, Mgh, Ḳ:) pl. سَوَافِرُ. (TA.) — And a horse † *having little flesh:* (Ḳ:) or so سَافِرُ النَّحْرِ, a phrase used by Ibn-Muḳbil. (TA.) — See also سَفِيرٌ. — And see مُسَافِرٌ, in two places. ═ Also *A writer;* *a scribe:* (Akh, Ṣ, M, Ḳ:) in the Nabathæan language سَافِرَا: (M:) pl. سَفَرَةٌ: (Akh, Ṣ, M, Ḳ:) which is also applied to the *angels who register actions.* (M, Ḳ.)

تَسْفِيرَةٌ: see مِسْفَرَةٌ.

مَسْفَرٌ sing. of مَسَافِرُ, (A,) which signifies The *part that appears* [or *parts that appear*] of the face. (Ṣ, A,* Ḳ.) — [Also, or مَسْفَرٌ, *A place of journeying* or *travelling:* in which sense, likewise, its pl. is مَسَافِرُ.] One says, بَيْنِى وَبَيْنَهُ مَسَافِرُ بَعِيدَةٌ [*Between me and him, or it, are far-extending tracts to be travelled*]. (A.)

مُسْفِرٌ [act. part. n. of 4, q. v.:] ‡ A face *shining* (A, TA) *with happiness.* (A.) — النَّاقَةُ المُسْفِرَةُ

الحَمْرَةُ [in the CḲ (erroneously) الحُمْرَةُ] means † [*The she-camel*] *that is somewhat above such as is termed* صَهْبَآء [*in respect of redness*]. (O, Ḳ, TA.)

مِسْفَرٌ : see مِسْفَرَةٌ. —— Also A man (TA) *that journeys*, or *travels, much*; (Ḳ;) and so ↓ مِسْفَارٌ : (A:) or *that journeys*, or *travels, much, and is strong for journeying*: (M:) and, applied to a camel, (Ṣ, M, A,) *strong for journeying*; (Ṣ, M, A, Ḳ;) fem. with ة, (Ṣ, M, Ḳ,) applied to a she-camel, (Ṣ, M,) as also ↓ مِسْفَارٌ, thus applied. (M.)

مِسْفَرَةٌ *A broom; a thing with which one sweeps*; (Ṣ, M, Ḳ;) as also ↓ مِسْفَرٌ, and ↓ تَسْفِيرَةٌ, of which last, (expl. by مَا يُسْفَرُ بِهِ,) the pl. is تَسَافِيرُ. (TA.)

مُسَفِّرٌ *i. q.* مُجَلِّدٌ [i. e. *One who binds books* (أَسْفَار, pl. of سِفْر), or *covers them with leather*]. (A, TA.)

مِسْفَارٌ : see مِسْفَرٌ, in two places.

مَسْفُورٌ *Distressed*, or *fatigued, by journeying* or *travel*. (TA.)

مُسَافِرٌ A man *journeying*, or *travelling; a traveller; a wayfarer*; (Ṣ, M, Ḳ;) as also ↓ سَافِرٌ ; (M,* Ḳ;) which latter is [said to be] not a part. n., but [a possessive epithet] meaning ذُو سَفَرٍ, (M,) having no verb belonging to it (M, Ḳ) that we have seen; (M;) or it is from سَفَرٌ, and signifies *going forth on a journey*: (Ṣ, Mṣb:) pl. of the former مُسَافِرُونَ, (Ṣ,) and of the latter سُفَّارٌ (Ṣ, M, A, Mṣb, Ḳ) and أَسْفَارٌ (M, Ḳ) and سَفْرٌ; (TA;) and you also say ↓ قَوْمٌ سَافِرَةٌ [fem. of سَافِرٌ], (Ṣ,* M, Mṣb, Ḳ,) and ↓ قَوْمٌ سَفْرٌ, (Ṣ, M, A, Mṣb, Ḳ,) [سَفْرٌ being a quasi-pl. n.,] like صَحْبٌ in relation to صَاحِبٌ : (Ṣ, Mgh, Mṣb:) and ↓ سَفْرٌ is also used as a sing., (M, Ḳ,) being originally an inf. n. (TA.) —— مُسَافِرَةٌ is used by Zuheyr as a name for *A* [*wild*] *cow*. (M, TA.)

سفرجل

سَفَرْجَلٌ [The *quince; pyrus cydonia* of Linn.;] *a certain fruit*, (Ḳ,) *well known*; (Ṣ, Ḳ;) *abundant in the land of the Arabs*: (AḤn, TA:) *it is astringent*, or *constipating; strengthening; diuretic; excites the appetite* (Ḳ, TA) *for food and venery*; (TA;) *allays thirst; and when eaten upon* [*other*] *food, loosens* [*the bowels*]; *and the most beneficial thereof is that which has been scooped out, and had its pips extracted, and honey put in the place thereof, and been plastered over with clay, and baked* (Ḳ, TA) *in the oven*: (TA:) [a coll. gen. n.:] n. un. with ة: (Ḳ:) and pl. سَفَارِجُ : (Ṣ, Ḳ:) the dim. is سُفَيْرِجٌ and سُفَيْرِجَلٌ, mentioned by Az. (TA.) —— [سَفَرْجَلٌ هِنْدِىٌّ *Annona glabra; a species of custard-apple*; mentioned by Forskål, Flora Aegypt. Arab., p. cxiv.] ▬ The saying of Sb, that there is not in the language the like of سفرجال does not mean that this word is applied to anything: and in like manner his saying that there is not in the language the like of اسفرجلت does not mean that this word is used. (TA.)

سفط

1. سَفُطَ, aor. ـُ, (M, Ḳ,) inf. n. سَفَاطَةٌ, (M, TA,) *He was*, or *became, cheerful, happy*, or *free from straitness, in mind: liberal, bountiful*, or *munificent*. (M, Ḳ, TA.)

4. مَا أَسْفَطَ نَفْسَهُ عَنْكَ *How pleased*, or *content, is his mind to give thee up*, or *relinquish thee!* syn. مَا أَطْيَبَهَا. (IAạr, Ḳ.)

5. تَسَفَّطَ الخَمْرَ *It* (a jar) *drank up*, or *absorbed, the greater part of the wine*. (Ḳ.)

8. اِسْتِفَاطٌ The *drinking up entirely* [what is in a vessel]; syn. اِشْتِفَافٌ. (Ḳ.)

سَفَطٌ *A thing* (M, Mgh, Mṣb, Ḳ) *like a* جُوَالِق [or *sack*], (M, Ḳ,) or *like a* قُفَّة [or *basket woven of palm-leaves*], (Ḳ,) *in which are stowed perfume and similar things*, (Mgh, Mṣb, TA,) *of the apparatus of women*: (Mgh, TA:) an Arabic word, well known: (TA:) pl. أَسْفَاطٌ. (Ṣ, M, Mgh, Mṣb, Ḳ.) —— And hence, ‡ *A casket*, or *small chest*. (Mgh.) It is related that an Arab of the desert, passing by at the burial of Moḥammad, asked why they had not placed the Apostle of God in a سَفَط of brown aloes-wood encased with gold. (TA.)

سَفِيطٌ *Cheerful, happy*, or *free from straitness, in mind: liberal, bountiful*, or *munificent*. (Ṣ, M, Ḳ.) You say, هُوَ سَفِيطُ النَّفْسِ *He is cheerful, happy*, or *free from straitness, and liberal, in mind*: (TA:) or *cheerful*, or *brisk, to do what is kind* or *beneficent*. (Aṣ.) And نَفْسُهُ سَفِيطَةٌ بِكَذَا [*His mind is pleased*, or *content, with such a thing*]. (TA.) ▬ *Vile*, or *mean, and despised in all his circumstances*: (M, Ḳ:) a man, (IAạr, M, Ḳ,) or thing, (IAạr, M,) *of no estimation*. (IAạr, M, Ḳ.) Thus it has two contr. significations. (Ḳ.) —— *What drop from the tree, of green unripe dates*. (M, L, Ḳ. [المُتَسَافِطُ in the CḲ is a mistake for المُتَسَاقِطُ.]) ▬ أَمْوَالُهُمْ سَفِيطَةٌ بَيْنَهُمْ *Their possessions are mixed among them*. (AZ, Ṣ.)

سَفَاطَةٌ The *goods*, or *utensils and furniture, of a house* or *tent*. (IDrd, Ṣ, [but wanting in one copy,] M, Ḳ.)

سَفَّاطٌ *A maker of what is called* سَفَط. (TA.)

إِسْفَنْطٌ, (Ṣ, M, Ḳ,) so in the handwriting of J, (TA,) and إِسْفِنْطٌ, (M, Ḳ,) also written with ص, (Aṣ, and Ḳ in art. صفط,) *Perfumed juice of grapes*: (M, L, Ḳ:) or *wine in which are aromatics*: (TA:) or the *upper part of wine*; (AO, M, Ḳ;) the *clear part thereof*; (AO, TA;) so called because the jars (دِنَان) have drunk up, or absorbed, the greater portion of it, (Ḳ, TA,) the clear part remaining; (TA;) or from سَفِيط in the first of the senses assigned to it above: (IAạr, Ḳ:) or *various wines mixed together*: (TA:) or it signifies *a certain sort of beverage* or *wine*: and is a Persian word, [originally إِسْفَنْد,] arabicized: (Ṣ, Ḳ:) or, accord. to Aṣ, a Greek word, (Ṣ, M,) signifying *wine*: (TA:) if not Arabic, all its letters are radicals: and Sb says that it is a quinqueliteral-radical word, like إِصْطَبْل. (TA.)

مُسَفَّطُ الرَّأْسِ A man *having a head like a* سَفَط. (IAạr, Ḳ.)

سفع

1. سَفَعَتْهُ السَّمُومُ, (Ṣ,) or سَفَعَ السَّمُومُ وَجْهَهُ, (Ḳ,) and النَّارُ, (Ṣ,) and الشَّمْسُ, (TA,) aor. ـَ, (Ḳ,) inf. n. سَفْعٌ, (TḲ,) *The hot wind*, (Ṣ, Ḳ,) and *the fire*, (Ṣ,) and *the sun*, (TA,) *smote*, or *burned*, (Ṣ, Ḳ,) *him*, (Ṣ,) or *his face*, (Ḳ,) *slightly*, (Ṣ, Ḳ,) *so that it altered the colour of the external skin*, (Ṣ,) *and*, as some add, *blackened it*; (TA;) as also ↓ سفّعهُ, (Ḳ,) inf. n. تَسْفِيعٌ. (TA.) [It is app. from سُفْعَةٌ signifying "blackness tinged with redness."] —— [And hence,] سَفَعَهُ, aor. as above, (Ḳ,) and so the inf. n., (TA,) *He made a mark upon it*: and *he made a mark upon it with a hot iron*, or *with fire*. (Ḳ,* TA.) —— Also, aor. as above, (L, Ḳ,) and so the inf. n., (L,) † *He slapped* (L, Ḳ) *it*, a man's face, (L,) or *him*, a man, (Ḳ,) with his hand. (L.) And † *He struck it* (a man's neck) *with his expanded hand*: in which sense it is also written with ص. (TA.) And † *He struck him*, or *beat him*, (Ḳ,) with a staff, or stick. (TA.) And † *He* (a bird) *slapped it*, (Ṣ, [in which only the inf. n. is mentioned,] and Ḳ,) namely, the object struck by him, (Ḳ,) *with his wing*, (Ṣ,) or *with his wings*. (Ḳ: and so [as is implied in the TA] in some copies of the Ṣ.) —— سَفَعَ بِنَاصِيَتِهِ, (Lth, Ṣ, Ḳ,) aor. and inf. n. as above, (TA,) *He laid hold upon*, or *seized*, (Lth, Ṣ, Ḳ,) *and dragged*, (Lth, Ḳ,) *his* نَاصِيَة, (Lth, Ṣ, Ḳ,) i. e. *the fore part of his head* (TA) [or *his forelock* or *the hair over his forehead*]: or سَفْعٌ signifies the *laying hold upon*, or *seizing, the* سُفْعَة *of the head*, i. e. *the black part of its* نَاصِيَة. (El-Mufradát, TA.) You say, سَفَعَ بِنَاصِيَةِ الفَرَسِ لِيَرْكَبَهُ [*He laid hold upon*, or *seized, the forelock of the horse, to mount him*]. (TA.) And سَفَعَ بِرِجْلِهِ *He laid hold upon*, or *seized, and dragged, his foot*. (TA.) And سَفَعَ بِيَدِهِ *He laid hold upon his hand*: (IAạr:) or *he laid hold upon his hand and raised him*: often used in this sense by 'Obeyd-Allah Ibn-Al-Ḥasan, Ḳádee of El-Baṣrah. (Ṣgh.) It is said in the Ḳur [xcvi. 15], لَنَسْفَعًا بِالنَّاصِيَةِ; (Ṣ, Ḳ, &c.;) [or لَنَسْفَعَنْ; (see أَلِفُ النُّونِ الخَفِيفَةِ in art. ا;)] the Arabs [sometimes] substituting ا for the quiescent ن [in a case of this kind]; (Ṣgh;) i. e. *We will assuredly take by the* نَاصِيَة (Az, Ṣ, TA) *to the fire* [*of hell*]: (Az, TA:) or *we will assuredly lay hold upon his* نَاصِيَة *and drag him thereby with violence to the fire*: (Bḍ:) or *we will assuredly drag him thereby to the fire*: (O, Ḳ:) or *we will assuredly blacken his face*; the نَاصِيَة being put for the face because it is the fore part thereof: (Fr, Az, Ḳ:) or *we will assuredly mark him with the mark of the people of the fire*, (O, Ḳ,) *making his face black, and his eyes blue*: (O:) or *we will assuredly abase him*: or, *render him despicable*:

(O, Ḳ:) or *we will assuredly abase him and make him to stand:* so in the L and other lexicons; for these, instead of أَوْ لَنُقِيمَنَّهُ in the O and Ḳ, have وَلَنُقِيمَنْهُ, and this is shown to be the right reading by the last explanation in the sentence next preceding. (TA.) —— سَفِعَ, aor. ـَ, inf. n. سَفَعٌ, *It* (a thing) *was,* or *became, of the colour termed* سُفْعَة, i. e. *black tinged,* or *intermixed, with red.* (Mṣb.)

2: see 1; first sentence.

3. سافعهُ, inf. n. مُسَافَعَةٌ, (Ṣ, TA,) ‡ *He slapped him, being slapped by him: he struck him,* or *beat him, being struck,* or *beaten, by him:* and *he fought with him;* namely his adversary: (TA:) [or *he charged upon,* or *assaulted,* or *attacked, him, the latter doing the same;* for] مُسَافَعَةٌ is like مُطَارَدَةٌ. (Ṣ.) —— † *He embraced him, being embraced by him.* (TA.)

5. تسفّع *He warmed himself,* (Ḳ, TA,) بِالنَّارِ *with the fire.* (TA.)

8. أُسْتُفِعَ لَوْنُهُ *His colour became altered* by reason of fear, or the like, (Ḳ, TA,) as, for instance, disease. (TA.) —— [اِسْتَفَعَ *He,* or *it, became swollen,* or *affected with a tumour;* for] اِسْتِفَاعٌ is like تَبَيُّحٌ, (Ḳ, TA,) with ب before the ج. (TA: [in the CḲ تَبَيُّج.]) —— اِسْتَفَعَ [from سَفْعٌ] *He* (a man) *put on,* or *clad himself with, his garment:* and اِسْتَفَعَتْ *She* (a woman) *put on her garments.* (TA.)

سَفْعٌ مِنَ النَّارِ *A mark, from fire, altering the colour of a man.* (TA.) —— سَفْعٌ also signifies *A garment of any kind:* (Ḳ:) but mostly *such as is dyed:* pl. سُفُوعٌ. (TA.) —— [And hence, perhaps,] The *spathe,* or *spadix,* (طَلْع,) *of a tree called* ظِلْمِخ. (AA, T in art. ظلمخ.)

سُفْعٌ: see أَسْفَعُ, of which it is pl., though sometimes used as a subst.

سَفَعٌ: see سُفْعَةٌ.

سَفْعَةٌ † *A stroke from a devil:* (TA:) or *a touch of madness* or *diabolical possession, in a person, as though a devil had laid hold upon his* نَاصِيَة: (Ṣ, TA:) [see سَفَعَ بِنَاصِيَتِهِ:] or *a stroke with the evil eye:* (TA:) or *a stroke of an* [*evil*] *eye by which one is affected from the jinn's looking at him;* as also نَظْرَةٌ: (T in art. نظر:) or *an evil eye.* (Ḳ, TA: [in the CḲ, for سَفْعَةٌ أَىْ عَيْنٌ, is put سَفْعَةٌ أَوْ عَيْنٌ.]) One says, بِهِ سَفْعَةٌ *In him is a touch of madness,* &c. (Ṣ.) And أَصَابَتْهُ سَفْعَةٌ *An evil eye smote him.* (Ḳ, TA.)

سُفْعَةٌ *Blackness tinged,* or *intermixed, with redness:* (Lth, Ṣ, Mṣb, Ḳ:) or *blackness that is not much:* or *blackness with another colour:* or *blackness with blueness;* or, *with yellowness;* accord. to the Towsheeḥ: but Lth says that, as meaning a colour, it has the first of all these meanings only: (TA:) or [simply] *blackness.* (Mgh.) In the face, it is *A blackness in the cheeks of a man, or haggard, woman:* (Ṣ:) and ▼ سَفَعٌ [which is properly the inf. n. of سَفِعَ, q. v.,] *a blackness tinged with redness in the cheeks of a man,* or *haggard, woman,* (O, Ḳ,) and *of a sheep,* or *goat.* (O.) One says also, أَرَى فِى وَجْهِهِ سُفْعَةً مِنْ غَضَبٍ ‡ *I see in his face a change to blackness in consequence of anger.* (TA.) The سُفْعَة of the head is The *blackness of its* نَاصِيَة [i. e. *fore part,* or *forelock,* or *hair over the forehead*]. (El-Mufradát, TA.) And سُفَعٌ [which is the pl.] signifies *Black spots,* or *specks, on the face of a bull.* (TA.) —— Also *A spot of ground, in the traces of a house, differing, in its blackness, from the rest of the colour of the ground:* (Ṣ, TA:) [i. e. *a black,* or *dark, patch of ground where a house has stood:*] or *dung of beasts,* (Ḳ, TA,) or *sand,* (TA,) or *ashes,* or *sweepings commingled and compacted together, in the traces left by the inhabitants of a house, differing in colour from the ground* [*around*]; (Ḳ, TA;) so says Lth. (TA.)

سَافِعٌ [act. part. n. of سَفَعَ,] A man *laying hold upon,* or *seizing, the* نَاصِيَة [or *forelock*] *of his horse* [*to mount him*]. (Ṣ,* and Ḥam p. 7.) —— سَوَافِعُ [pl. of سَافِعَةٌ,] *Burning blasts of the* [*wind called*] سَمُوم. (Ṣ, Ḳ.)

أَسْفَعُ *Of a black colour tinged,* or *intermixed, with redness:* (Ṣ, Mṣb:) or *black:* (Mgh:) applied to a man: (Ṣ:) fem سَفْعَآءُ: (Mgh, Mṣb:) and سُفْعٌ [is the pl., and] signifies *blacks inclining to redness.* (Ḳ.) Applied to an ostrich, *i. q.* أَرْبَدُ [which is variously explained, as signifying *Of a colour inclining to blackness,* or *of the colour of dust,* &c.]. (TA.) And the fem., applied to a ewe, *Having black cheeks, the rest of her being white.* (TA.) The masc. also signifies *A wild bull:* (Ḳ:) or, applied to a wild bull, it signifies *having in his cheeks a blackness inclining a little to redness.* (TA.) And The *hawk;* (Ḳ;) because it has spots of black: (Er-Rághib:) all hawks are سُفْعٌ: (Ṣ:) and the fem., *A pigeon* (حَمَامَةٌ); because of the سُفْعَة upon its neck: (Ṣ:) or, applied to a pigeon, it signifies *of which the* سُفْعَة *is upon its neck,* (Ḳ, TA,) *exclusively of the head,* (TA,) *in the part on each side of the neck above the ring.* (Ḳ,* TA.) It is also a name for *Sheep,* or *goats;* used when they are called to be milked: (Ḳ:) so in the O: but in some copies, and in the TṢ, for the *she-goat:* (TA:) thus in the phrase, أَشْلِ إِلَيْكَ الأَسْفَعَ [*Call thou to thee the sheep,* or *goats,* or *the she-goat, to be milked*]: (O, TṢ, Ḳ:) mentioned by Ibn-'Abbád. (TA.) —— Applied to a garment, or piece of cloth, *Black.* (Ḳ.) —— ▼ The pl. is also applied to The أَثَافِىّ, (Lth, Ṣ, Ḳ,) or *three stones upon which the cooking-pot is set up;* (TA;) because of their blackness: (Lth, Er-Rághib:) [see خَاصِن:] and a single one thereof is called سَفْعَآءُ: (Ḳ:) or *an iron* أُثْفِيَّة [meaning *trivet*], (Ḳ, TA,) *upon which the cooking-pot is set up;* and this is said to be the primary application. (TA.) —— سُفْعٌ also signifies The *seeds,* or *grain, of the colocynth;* (Ibn-'Abbád, Ḳ;) because of their blackness: (TA:) n. un. with ة. (Ḳ.)

مُسْفَعٌ applied to a man clad in armour, *Black from the rust of the iron.* (TA.) Applied to a bull, *Having black spots,* or *specks, on his face.* (TA.)

مَسْفُوعٌ A man (I'Ab) *smitten by an evil eye.* (I'Ab, Ḳ.) —— مَسْفُوعُ العَيْنِ A man *whose eye is sunk,* or *depressed, in his head.* (I'Ab, Ḳ.) —— [See also مُسْفَوعٌ.]

مُسَافِعٌ † *Striking,* or *beating, another, being struck,* or *beaten, by him.* (Ḳ.) † *Charging upon,* or *assaulting,* or *attacking, another who is doing the same.* (Ḳ.) —— [And hence,] † The *lion* (Ḳ, TA) *that prostrates his prey.* (TA.) —— † *Embracing.* (Ḳ.) —— ‡ *I. q.* مُسَافِحٌ; (Ibn-'Abbád, Ḳ;) i. e. *having sexual intercourse without marriage.* (TA.)

سفق

1. سَفَقَ البَابَ, (T, Ṣ, Mṣb, Ḳ,) aor. ـُ, inf. n. سَفْقٌ; (Mṣb;) and ▼ اسفقهُ; (T, Ṣ, Mṣb, Ḳ;) *He shut,* or *closed, the door;* (T, Ṣ, Mṣb, Ḳ;) or *locked it:* (Mṣb:) and in like manner with ص [in the place of the س]. (TA.) —— سَفَقَ وَجْهَهُ, (inf. n. as above, TA,) *He slapped his face.* (IDrd, Mṣb, Ḳ.) [See also صَفَقَ.] —— السَّفْقُ فِى الأَسْوَاقِ, occurring in a trad., means *The striking of the hands* [of the contracting parties] on the occasion of selling and buying [in token of the ratification thereof *in the markets*]: and so with ص. (TA.) —— سَفَقَ امْرَأَتَهُ, inf. n. as above, *i. q.* أَصَابَهَا [app. meaning *He compressed his wife;* like اصاب منها]. (TA.) —— سَفُقَ, (Ṣ, Mṣb, Ḳ,) aor. ـُ, (Ḳ,) inf. n. سَفَاقَةٌ, (Ṣ, Mṣb,) *It* (a garment, or piece of cloth,) *was thick, substantial, close,* or *compact, in texture;* (T, Ṣ, Mṣb, Ḳ;) *not* سَخِيف; (T;) *contr. of* سَخُفَ: (Mṣb:) [and so صَفُقَ.]

4: see above, first sentence. —— اسفق الغَنَمَ *He milked the sheep,* or *goats, but once in the day:* and so with ص. (TA.) —— اسفق الثَّوْبَ *He* (a weaver) *made the garment,* or *piece of cloth, thick, substantial, close,* or *compact, in texture.* (TA.)

7. انسفق *It* (a door) *became shut,* or *closed:* (Ṣ, TA:) and so with ص. (TA.)

أَعْطَاهُ سَفْقَةَ يَمِينِهِ *i. q.* بَايَعَهُ [*He sold and bought with him: he made a covenant, a compact, an engagement,* or *the like, with him:* or *he promised,* or *swore, allegiance to him*]: (O, Ḳ:) occurring in a trad., related thus and with ص. (TA.) —— And اِشْتَرَيْتُ الشَّيْئَيْنِ سَفْقَةً وَاحِدَةً, (O,) or فِى سَفْقَةٍ وَاحِدَةٍ, (Ḳ,) *I purchased the two things by a single act of purchasing.* (O, Ḳ.)

سَفِيقٌ, applied to a garment, or piece of cloth, *Thick, substantial, close,* or *compact, in texture.* (T, Ṣ, Mṣb, Ḳ.) —— And [hence,] سَفِيقُ الوَجْهِ † A man (Ṣ, O, TA) *having little shame.* (Ṣ, O, Ḳ, TA.)

سَفِيقَةٌ *A broad, thin, long piece of wood, which is put, or laid down, and upon which are then wound the* [*mats of reeds called*] بَوَارِىّ, (Lth, O, Ḳ,) *above the house-tops of the people of El-Baṣrah.* (Lth, O. [See also سَقِيفَةٌ.]) — And *Any piece of gold, and of silver, or other metal, that is beaten thin and long.* (Lth, O, Ḳ.* [See, again, سَقِيفَةٌ.])

سفك

1. سَفَكَهُ, aor. ـِ, (Ṣ, M, O, Mṣb, Ḳ) and ـُ, (O, Mṣb, TA, &c.,) inf. n. سَفْكٌ, (Ṣ, O, Mṣb,) *He shed, poured forth,* or *caused to run* or *flow,* blood, (Ṣ, O, Mṣb, Ḳ, TA,) and tears, (Ṣ, O, Mṣb, TA,) and water, and any fluid or liquid, but app. most especially blood. (TA.) — And [hence,] سَفَكَ الكَلَامَ, (Ḳ,) inf. n. as above, (TA,) ‡ *He poured forth speech profusely,* (Ḳ, TA,) *with haste,* or *quickly.* (TA.)

2. سَفَّكَهُ, inf. n. تَسْفِيكٌ, *He fed him* (i. e. his guest) *with something whereby to content,* or *satisfy, him,* [*so as to allay the craving of his stomach,*] *before the morning-meal;* i. q. لَهَّجَهُ. (O, TA.)

6. تَسَافَكُوا دِمَآءَهُمْ [*They contended together in the mutual shedding of blood*]. (TA in art. نجز.)

7. اِنْسَفَكَ, said of blood, (Ḳ, TA,) and tears, and water, and any fluid or liquid, (TA,) *It was,* or *became, shed, poured forth,* or *caused to run* or *flow;* or *it poured forth,* or *flowed.* (Ḳ, TA.)

سُفْكَةٌ *A portion of food that is presented to a guest, to content, or satisfy, him,* [*so as to allay the craving of his stomach,*] *before the morning-meal; like* لُهْجَةٌ. (IAar, O, Ḳ.*)

سَفُوكٌ : see سَفَّاكٌ, in two places. — Also † The *soul:* (Ḳ:) [like كَذُوبٌ: app. because of its proneness to lying.]

سَفِيكٌ Blood, (Ḳ, TA,) and tears, and water, and any fluid or liquid, (TA,) *Shed, poured forth,* or *caused to run* or *flow;* as also ▼ مَسْفُوكٌ. (Ḳ, TA.)

سَفَّاكٌ One who sheds blood, and tears, *much;* (Mṣb;) [as also ▼ سَفُوكٌ.] You say سَفَّاكٌ لِلدِّمَآءِ *A great shedder of blood.* (TA.) — And † *Eloquent;* (Kr, Ḳ;) *an able speaker.* (Ṣ, Ḳ.) — And ‡ *Mendacious; a great,* or *habitual, liar;* (TA;) as also ▼ سَفُوكٌ, (Ḳ,) or سَفُوكٌ بِالكَلَامِ. (TA.)

سَافِكٌ *Shedding,* or *pouring forth,* blood and tears [&c.]. (Mṣb.) You say عُيُونٌ سَوَافِكُ *Eyes shedding,* or *pouring forth, tears.* (TA.) — And دُمُوعٌ سَوَافِكُ [*Tears pouring forth;* properly] meaning ذَوَاتُ سَفْكٍ [*having a shedding* or *pouring forth*], the latter word being pl. of سَافِكَةٌ : so as used in a verse of Mutemmim Ibn-Nuweyreh: but the obviously-right expression is ▼ مَسْفُوكَةٌ. (Ḥam p. 370.)

مِسْفَكٌ † *Loquacious; garrulous.* (Ḳ,* TA.)

مَسْفُوكٌ : see سَافِكٌ and سَفِيكٌ.

سفل

1. سَفَلَ, aor. ـُ; (M, MA, Mgh, O,* Mṣb, Ḳ;) and سَفُلَ, aor. ـُ; (M, Mṣb, Ḳ;) and سَفِلَ, (O, Ḳ,) aor. ـَ; (Ḳ;) inf. n. (of the first, Mgh, Mṣb, TA, and of the last, TA) سُفُولٌ (M, MA, Mgh, Mṣb, Ḳ) and سَفَالٌ (M, MA, Ḳ, TA, in the CḲ [erroneously] سِفَالٌ,) and of the second سَفَالَةٌ; (TA;) and ▼ تَسَفَّلَ; (M, Ḳ;) *He,* or *it, was,* or *became, low;* (M,* Mgh, O, Ḳ;*) the first *contr. of* عَلَا; (Mgh, O;) and the third, of عَلِىَ; and † both are said of a man; (O;) سُفُولٌ and سَفَالٌ being the contr. of عُلُوٌّ and عَلَآءٌ: (Ṣ, Ḳ:) or *became lower than another:* (Mṣb:) [and] the first signifies *it descended, subsided,* or *sank downwards.* (MA.) Hence the phrase بِنْتُ بِنْتِ بِنْتٍ وَإِنْ سَفَلَتْ † [*A daughter of a daughter of a daughter, and if she be lower in descent*]: سَفُلَتْ, i. e. with ḍamm to the ف, in this case, is a mistake. (Mgh.) And سَفَلَتْ مَنْزِلَتُهُ عِنْدَ الأَمِيرِ † [*His station with,* or *in the estimation of, the commander, governor,* or *prince, was,* or *became, low,* or *lower*]. (TA.) And أَمْرُهُمْ فِى سَفَالٍ † [*Their case is in a low state*]. (TA.) And سَفَلَ فِى الشَّىْءِ, (Ḳ,* TA, [in the former of which the context implies that it is سَفُلَ, but it is]) like نَصَرَ, [aor. ـُ,] (TA,) inf. n. سُفُولٌ, [*It subsided in the thing;*] *it descended from the upper,* or *uppermost, part of the thing, to the lower,* or *lowest, part thereof.* (Ḳ.) — And سَفُلَ, [aor. ـُ,] inf. n. سَفَالَةٌ (Fr, Ṣ, MA, Mgh, O, Ḳ*) and سَفَالِيَةٌ (MA) and سُفْلٌ, (Fr, O,) † *He was,* or *became, low, base, vile, ignoble, mean,* or *sordid;* (Fr, Ṣ, MA, Mgh, O, Ḳ;*) as also سَفَلَ, with fet-ḥ, (Fr, O,) or سَفِلَ. (MA.) You say, سَفَلَ, like قَتَلَ, (Mṣb,) or سَفُلَ, like كَرُمَ, (Ḳ,) and فِى خُلُقِهِ, (Mṣb, Ḳ,) and نَسَبِهِ, (TA,) [aor. in either case ـُ,] inf. n. سَفْلٌ (Mṣb, Ḳ) and سُفْلٌ (Ḳ) and سَفَالٌ, (Mṣb,* Ḳ, [in the former without any indication of the syll. signs,]) the last like كِتَابٌ; (Ḳ;) [and app. سَفَلٌ also accord. to the MA, as shown above;] and ▼ تَسَفَّلَ, and ▼ اِسْتَفَلَ; (TA;) ‡ *He was low, base, vile, ignoble,* or *mean, in his lot,* [or, as seems to be indicated in the Mṣb, *inferior to others,*] *in respect of his disposition,* and *his deed,* and *his lineage:* (TA:) ▼ تَسَفَّلَ is the *contr. of* جَادَ. (Mṣb.)

2. تَسْفِيلٌ The act of *lowering,* or *depressing;* syn. تَصْوِيبٌ. (Ṣ, O.)

3. هُوَ يُسَافِلُ فُلَانًا † *He vies with,* or *imitates, such a one in his low, base, vile, ignoble, mean,* or *sordid, actions.* (TA.)

5. تَسَفُّلٌ [quasi-pass. of 2,] The *being lowered,* or *depressed;* syn. تَصَوُّبٌ; (Ṣ, O;) *contr. of* تَعَلٍّ. (TA.) — See also 1, first sentence: — and the same, last sentence, in two places.

8: see 1, last sentence.

سُفْلٌ and ▼ سِفْلٌ (Ṣ, M, Mgh, O, Mṣb, Ḳ) [but it is strangely added in the Mṣb that IKt disallowed the pronunciation with ḍamm] and ▼ سُفْلَةٌ (M, Ḳ) and ▼ سُفَالَةٌ (Ṣ, O, Ḳ) The *lowest,* or *lower, part* [of a thing]; *contr. of* عُلْوٌ (Ṣ, M, Mgh, O, Mṣb, Ḳ) and عِلْوٌ (Ṣ, Mgh, O, Mṣb, Ḳ) and عُلْوَةٌ (Ḳ) and عُلَاوَةٌ; (Ṣ, O, Ḳ;) [and so ▼ سُفَالَةٌ ▼ سَافِلَةٌ, *contr. of* عَالِيَةٌ:] ▼ كُلِّ شَىْءٍ signifies, (Ḳ,) or is said to signify, (M,) *the lowest,* or *lower, part of anything:* i. e. ▼ أَسْفَلُهُ; (M, Ḳ;) and عُلَاوَتُهُ, [the contr., i. e.] أَعْلَاهُ. (M.)

سِفْلٌ : see the next preceding paragraph.

سِفْلٌ from سَفَلَ, and ▼ سَفِيلٌ from سَفُلَ, † A *low, base, vile, ignoble, mean,* or *sordid,* man: (MA:) or ▼ سَفِيلٌ signifies *low* (▼ سَافِلٌ) [in *condition*], *deficient in lot,* or *fortune:* (TA:) and ▼ سَفِلَةٌ, (Ṣ, M, MA, Mgh, Mṣb, Ḳ,) said by some to be from this word as signifying the "legs" (Mgh, Mṣb) of a camel (Mgh) or of a beast, or quadruped, (Mṣb,) and ▼ سِفْلَةٌ, (Ṣ, M, MA, Mgh, Mṣb, Ḳ,) a contraction of سَفِلَةٌ, (Ṣ, Mgh, Mṣb,) or it may be pl. of ▼ سَفِيلٌ, like as عِلْيَةٌ is of عَلِىٌّ, (Mgh,) † *low, base, vile, ignoble, mean,* or *sordid, persons;* (Ṣ,* MA, Mgh, Mṣb;) or the *lowest,* or *lower, basest,* or *baser, vilest,* or *viler,* &c., of mankind, or of people; the *refuse,* or *rubble,* thereof: (Ṣ,* M, Ḳ:) and ▼ سِفِلَةٌ, with two kesrehs, is a dial. var. of سَفِلَةٌ and سِفْلَةٌ, mentioned by Ṣgh and IB on the authority of Yoo and IKh, and is said to mean the *lowest, basest,* &c., *of the low, base,* &c.: the pl. of ▼ سِفْلَةٌ is سِفَلٌ; (TA;) one should not say, ▼ هُوَ سَفِلَةٌ, because this is [used only as] a pl.: (Ṣ:) the vulgar say رَجُلٌ ▼ سِفْلَةٌ ▼ مِنْ قَوْمٍ سِفَلٍ; (Ṣ, Mgh;*) but this has been disallowed: (Mgh:) a man is related to have said to his wife, (Mgh, TA,) who had called him سِفْلَةٌ, (TA,) إِنْ كُنْتُ سِفْلَةً فَأَنْتِ طَالِقٌ, (Mgh, TA,) meaning *If I be low, base,* &c., *in my intellect and my religion* [*thou art divorced*]; (Mgh;) whence it seems that سِفْلَةٌ may be applied to a single person; but this requires consideration. (TA.) ▼ أَيْمَانُ السِّفْلَةِ means † [*The oaths*] *of the ignorant:* or accord. to Aboo-Ḥaneefeh, *of the heretics,* or *schismatics:* such [oaths] are said to be وَأَمَانَةِ ٱللّٰهِ and وَوَجْهِ ٱللّٰهِ. (Mgh.)

سُفْلَةٌ : see سُفْلٌ: — and see also سِفْلٌ, in three places.

سَفِلَةٌ The *legs* (Ṣ, M, Mgh, Mṣb, Ḳ) of a camel (Ṣ, M, Mgh, Ḳ) or of a beast, or quadruped: (Mṣb:) because they are lowest. (M.) — See also سَافِلَةٌ: — and see سِفْلٌ, in three places.

سِفِلَةٌ : see سِفْلٌ.

سُفْلِىٌّ [*Of,* or *relating to, the lowest,* or *lower, part* or *place;*] a rel. n. from سُفْلٌ. (TA.) [Hence, the pl.] سُفْلِيُّونَ means Persons *alighting,* or *abiding, in the lowest,* or *lower, parts of a country:* opposed to عَلِيُّونَ. (TA in art. علو.) — It is also opposed to عَلِىٌّ [in relation to condition]: whence the saying, مَنْ يَرْحَمِ السُّفْلِىَّ يَرْحَمْهُ العَلِىُّ † [*He who has mercy on the low in condition, on him will the high in condition have mercy*]. (TA.) سُفْلِيُّونَ, meaning † *Persons low in condition,* is opposed to عَلِيُّونَ, meaning "opulent persons." (TA in art. علو.)

سَفِيلٌ: see سَفِلٌ, in three places.

سُفَالَةٌ: see سُفْلٌ, in two places. — One says, قَعَدَ سُفَالَةَ الرِّيحِ, and فِى سُفَالَةِ الرِّيحِ (M, Ḳ,* TA,) or بِسُفَالَةِ الرِّيحِ, (Ṣ,) [*He sat in,* or *on, the leeward side;* like as one says in French, *sous le vent;*] *in,* or *on, the side,* or *quarter, towards which the wind blew;* (Ṣ, M, Ḳ,* TA;) and particularly with respect to the object or objects of the chase [in order that his smell might not be perceived thereby]: (TA in the present art. and in art. علو:) opposed to عُلَاوَتَهَا, and فِى عُلَاوَتِهَا (M, Ḳ,* TA,) or بِعُلَاوَتِهَا. (Ṣ.)

سَافِلٌ *Low; contr. of* عَالٍ. (Ṣ, Mṣb,* TA.) See also سَفِلٌ: and see an ex. voce أَسْفَلُ.

سَافِلَةٌ: see سُفْلٌ. — [Hence,] سَافِلَةُ الرُّمْحِ *The half that is next to the* زُجّ [or *pointed iron shoe,* or *foot,*] *of the spear:* (M, Ḳ:) [opposed to عَالِيَتُهُ.] — And السَّافِلَةُ *The bottom, podex, posteriors,* or *buttocks;* and *the anus;* syn. المَقْعَدَةُ, (Ṣ,) and الدُّبُرُ; (TA;) as also ▼ السَّفِلَةُ; syn. الدُّبُرُ. (L in art. حجر.)

أَسْفَلُ *Lower,* and *lowest;* contr. of أَعْلَى: (M, Mṣb, Ḳ:) fem. سُفْلَى: (TA:) and pl. أَسَافِلُ. (M, TA.) One says, صَارَ أَسْفَلَ مِنْ غَيْرِهِ [*He,* or *it, became lower than another*]. (Mṣb.) And it is said in the Ḳur [viii. 43], وَالرَّكْبُ أَسْفَلَ مِنْكُمْ *The caravan being in a place lower than ye;* اسفل being here an adv. n.: or, as some read, أَسْفَلُ مِنْكُمْ, i. e. *being lower than ye.* (M.) — ثُمَّ رَدَدْنَاهُ أَسْفَلَ سَافِلِينَ ▼, in the Ḳur [xcv. 5], means † [*Then we rendered him the lowest of low:* or] *we reduced him to extreme old age,* or *decrepitude:* or *to a state of perishing,* or *passing away:* or *to a state of error;* relating to him who has disbelieved; (M, Ḳ;) for every infant is born of the natural constitution with which he is created in his mother's womb, and he who disbelieves and errs is reduced to this state: (M:) or the meaning is, *we have made him to be of the people of the fire* [*of Hell*]: or [*we have made him to go down*] *to the fire* [*of Hell*]. (Bḍ.) — سُفْلَى مُضَرَ [*The lower of Muḍar*] is said to denote *those of Muḍar with the exception of Ḳureysh and Ḳeys:* opposed to عُلْيَا مُضَرَ. (TA in art. علو.) — See also سُفْلٌ. — The pl. أَسَافِلُ means The *lower,* or *lowest, parts* of valleys [&c.]. (TA.) The phrase كِلَابُ الأَسَافِلِ occurs in a verse of Aboo-Dhu-eyb as meaning [*The dogs*] *of the lower,* or *lowest, parts of the valleys.* (M.) — And † The *young ones* of camels. (Aṣ, Ṣ,* TA.)

سفن

1. سَفَنَهُ, (Ṣ, M, L, Ḳ,) aor. ـُ, (M, L, Ḳ,) inf. n. سَفْنٌ, (Ṣ, M, L,) i. q. قَشَرَهُ [i. e. *He divested* or *stripped it of,* or *he stripped off, scraped off, rubbed off, abraded,* or *otherwise removed, its outer covering* or *integument,* or *superficial part; he pared it, peeled it,* &c.: and *he,* or *it, pared, peeled, stripped,* or *rubbed, it off;* namely, anything superficial and generally a thing adhering to the surface of another thing]. (Ṣ, M, L, Ḳ.) Imra-el-Keys says,

• فَجَآءَ خَفِيًّا يَسْفِنُ الأَرْضَ بَطْنُهُ •
• تَرَى التُّرْبَ مِنْهُ لَاصِقًا كُلَّ مَلْصَقِ •

[*And he came clandestinely, his belly paring the ground, thou seeing the dust sticking to him with the utmost sticking*]; (Ṣ, M, L; but in the Ṣ, لَازِقًا and مَلْزَقِ;) meaning that he came cleaving to the ground in order that the objects of the chase might not see him and flee from him. (Ṣ, L.) — And *He pared and smoothed it;* as also ▼ سَفَّنَهُ [but app. in an intensive sense, or used in relation to several objects]. (M, L.) — And سَفَنَتِ الرِّيحُ التُّرَابَ, (M, L,) aor. as above, (L,) and so the inf. n., (M, L,) *The wind reduced the dust to a fine powder:* (M, L:) or سَفَنَتِ الرِّيحُ التُّرَابَ عَنْ وَجْهِ الأَرْضِ [*The wind pared off the dust from the surface of the earth*]. (Ṣ, L.) — And سَفَنَتِ الرِّيحُ, aor. ـِ, (Lḥ, M, L, Ḳ,) inf. n. سُفُونٌ, (Lḥ, M, L,) *The wind blew upon the surface of the earth* [app. *removing the dust*]; as also سَفِنَتْ, (Lḥ, M, L, Ḳ,) aor. ـَ. (Ḳ.) — And السَّفِينَةُ تَسْفِنُ عَلَى وَجْهِ الأَرْضِ *The ship,* or *boat, sticks upon the ground.* (L.)

2: see the preceding paragraph.

سَفَنٌ *A carpenter's adz,* or *axe,* (L,) or *a large adz* or *axe,* (M, L,) or *a thing* (Ṣ, L, Ḳ) *of any kind,* (Ḳ,) *with which one hews,* or *shapes out,* or *pares, a thing;* as also ▼ مِسْفَنٌ: (Ṣ, L, Ḳ:) or *an adz with which palm-trunks are pared;* as also سَفْرٌ and شَفْرٌ. (ISk, L.) — Also *Rough skin,* (Ṣ, M, L, Ḳ,) *thick,* or *coarse,* (M,) *such as the skins of crocodiles,* (Ṣ, L,) *which is put upon the hilts of swords:* (Ṣ, M, L:) or *the skin of the fish called* أُطُوم, *which is a rough skin, wherewith whips and arrows are rubbed* [*to smooth them*], *and which is upon the hilts of swords:* (Mgh, L:*) accord. to AḤn, (M, L,) *a rough piece of the skin of the* [*lizard called*] ضَبّ, *or of the skin of a fish, with which the arrow is rubbed so as to remove from it the marks of the paring-knife:* (M, L, Ḳ:) or, as some say, (M, L,) *a stone with which one shapes out,* or *pares, and smooths:* (M, L, Ḳ:) sometimes, accord. to Lth, *an iron implement with which one rubs wood so as to smooth it:* (L:) accord. to AHeyth, *a cane which is hollowed, and has some notches cut in it, through which an arrow is put and repeatedly drawn* [*to smooth it*]; also called طَرِيدَةٌ. (L in art. طرد.) See an ex. in a verse cited in art. خوف, conj. 5.

سَفُونٌ A wind *that blows upon the surface of the earth* [app. *removing the dust*]; (M, Ḳ;) as also ▼ سَافِنَةٌ: (Ḳ:) or the former, a wind *always blowing:* (L:) and ▼ the latter signifies a wind *as though wiping the surface of the earth;* (A'Obeyd, L;) or *paring it;* (L;) or [simply] *a wind;* (Ṣ;) and its pl. is سَوَافِنُ. (A'Obeyd, Ṣ, L, Ḳ.)

سَفِينٌ: see سَفِينَةٌ, in two places.

سِفَانَةٌ The *craft,* or *occupation, of constructing,* (M, L, Ḳ,) and *of navigating,* (M, L,) *ships* or *boats.* (M, L, Ḳ.)

سَفِينَةٌ *A ship,* or *boat;* (M, L;) of the measure فَعِيلَةٌ in the sense of the measure فَاعِلَةٌ; (IDrd, Ṣ, M, L, Mṣb;) as though it pared the surface of the water; (IDrd, Ṣ, L, Mṣb;) or so called because it pares [meaning skims] the surface of the water; (M, L;) or because it pares the sands [by running aground] when the water is little [in depth]; or because [in that case] it sticks upon the ground; or it may be from سَفَنٌ meaning "a carpenter's adz or axe with which he hews &c.," and, if so, having the meaning of the measure مَفْعُولَةٌ: (L:) the pl. is سَفَائِنُ and سُفُنٌ (M, L, Mṣb, Ḳ) and [coll. gen. n.] ▼ سَفِينٌ: (Ṣ, M, L, Mṣb, Ḳ:) the first of these is a regular pl.: (Sb, M, L:) the second is pl. of the third, (Mṣb,) or it is as though it were pl. of the third: (Sb, M, L:) ▼ the third is anomalous, being of a class proper to created things, as in the instances of تَمْرٌ and تَمْرَةٌ, and نَخْلَةٌ and نَخْلٌ, and only heard in a few instances in the cases of things made by art; and some say that it is a dial. var. of سَفِينَةٌ. (Mṣb.) [Hence,] السَّفِينَةُ † [*The constellation Argo;*] *one of the southern constellations, of which the stars are five and forty, the bright great star upon the southern oar being* سُهَيْل [i. e. *Canopus*], *accord. to Ptolemy, and it is the most remote star from the* سفينة, *in the south, and is marked on the astrolabe; but some of the Arabs say that the bright star at the extremity of the second oar* [but what star is meant thereby I know not] *is called* سُهَيْل, *without restriction.* (Ḳzw.) — [Also *An oblong book:* and *a commonplace book:* app. post-classical.]

سَفَّانٌ *A constructor,* or *builder, of ships* or *boats:* (M, L, Ḳ:) and *a navigator,* (M, L,) or *a master,* (Ṣ, Mṣb,) *of a ship* or *boat.* (Ṣ, M, L, Mṣb.)

سَفَّانَةٌ *A pearl.* (Ḳ.)

سَافِنَةٌ; pl. سَوَافِنُ: see سَفُونٌ, in two places.

السَّافِنُ *A certain vein in the inner side of the spine, extending lengthwise, with which is united the* نِيَاط [q. v.] *of the heart.* (Ḳ.) [Golius and Freytag explain it as meaning the "Saphæna;" but this is called الصَّافِنُ.]

سَيْفَنَةٌ *A certain bird* [*found*] *in Egypt, that*

does not alight upon a tree without eating all the leaves thereof. (K.)

سَفَنٌ : see مِسْفَنٌ.

سفند and سفنط.

إِسْفَنْطٌ and إِسْفَنْدٌ : see arts. سفد and سفط.

سفه

1. سَفِهَ, (S, MA, Msb,) aor. سَفَهَ ; (Msb;) and سَفُهَ, [aor. سَفُهَ ;] (S, Msb;) inf. n. سَفَهٌ and سَفَاهَةٌ (S, MA, Msb, K*) and سَفَاهٌ, (S, MA, K,*) [all mentioned in the MA as of the former verb, and so in the TA when that verb is trans., but properly] the first is of the former verb, and the second is of the latter verb, (S, Msb,) and so is the third; (S;) *He* (a man, S) *was,* or *became, such as is termed* سَفِيه ; (S, TA;) [i. e.] *he was,* or *became, unwise, witless,* or *destitute of wisdom* or *understanding,* or [rather] *lightwitted.* (MA.) — The phrase سَفِهَ نَفْسَهُ, [of which an instance occurs in the Kur ii. 124, and] to which وَفِقَ أَمْرَهُ and أَلِمَ بَطْنَهُ and بَطِرَ عَيْشَتَهُ and غَبِنَ رَأْيَهُ and رَشِدَ أَمْرَهُ are similar, was originally سَفِهَتْ نَفْسُ زَيْدٍ [or rather سَفِهَتْ نَفْسُهُ i. e. *Himself,* or *his mind, was,* or *became, lightwitted,* &c.]; but when [the dependence of] the verb became transferred [from the نفس] to the man, what followed the verb was put in the accus. case by being its objective complement, for the phrase became identical in meaning with سَفَّهَ ▼ نَفْسَهُ [*he made himself,* or *his mind, lightwitted,* &c.]: so say the Basrees and Ks; and it is allowable with them to make this accus. to precede [the verb]; like as it is allowable to say, غُلَامَهُ ضَرَبَ زَيْدٌ : (S, TA:) accord. to the K, the verb thus used has three forms; (TA;) you say سَفِهَ نَفْسَهُ and رَأْيَهُ, (K, TA,) and حِلْمَهُ, (TA,) and سَفَهَ, and سَفُهَ, meaning حَمَلَهُ عَلَى السَّفَهِ [which is virtually the same as سَفَّهَهُ i. e. *he made himself,* or *his mind, lightwitted,* or *unwise,* &c., and in like manner *his judgment,* or *opinion, and he made his gravity,* or *forbearance,* or *the like, to become levity,* or *hastiness,* &c.]: or *he attributed* سَفَه [i. e. *lightwittedness,* &c., *to himself,* or *his mind,* and *to his judgment,* or *opinion*]: or *he destroyed it;* (K, TA;) agreeably with the meaning assigned to سَفِهَ نَفْسَهُ by AO: (TA:) or this means *he held himself in mean,* or *light, estimation;* (MA, and Ksh and Bd in ii. 124;) and *rendered himself low, base,* or *contemptible:* (Bd ibid.:) but Lh says that سَفِهَ نَفْسَهُ, with kesr [to the ف], inf. n. سَفَهٌ and سَفَاهَةٌ and سَفَاهٌ, means حَمَلَهُ عَلَى السَّفَهِ [or حَمَّلَهَا], and is the approved form, and that some say سَفُهَ, which is rare: and accord. to J and others, (TA,) when they say سفه نَفْسَهُ, and رَأْيَهُ, they do not say it otherwise than with kesr [to the ف], because فَعُلَ is not trans.: (S, TA:) so that the three forms of the verb mentioned in the K require consideration: (TA:) accord. to Fr, when [the dependence of] the verb in the phrase سَفِهَ نَفْسَهُ became transferred from the نفس to the possessor thereof, what followed the verb became an explicative, to indicate that the سَفَه [or lightwittedness, &c.,] was therein; and by rule it should be سَفِهَ زَيْدٌ نَفْسًا, for the explicative should not be otherwise than indeterminate; but it was left in its state of a prefixed noun, and put in the accus. case in the manner of an indeterminate noun as being likened thereto; [the meaning, therefore, accord. to him, is *he was,* or *became, lightwitted,* &c., *as to his mind;*] it is not allowable, however, in his opinion, to make this accus. to precede [the verb], because the explicative may not precede; and similar to this is the phrase طِبْتُ بِهِ نَفْسًا, and ضِقْتُ بِهِ ذَرْعًا, meaning طَابَتْ نَفْسِى بِهِ and ضَاقَ ذَرْعِى بِهِ : (S, TA:) but this saying [of Fr] is disallowed by the grammarians; for they say that explicatives are indeterminate, and that determinate nouns may not be used as indeterminate: some of the grammarians say that إِلَّا مَنْ سَفِهَ نَفْسَهُ in the Kur [ii. 124] means الّا من سَفِهَ فى نَفْسِهِ [*but he who is lightwitted,* &c., *in his mind*], i. e., who becomes سَفِيه ; [the prep.] فى being suppressed [and the noun therefore put in the accus. case agreeably with a general rule]: Zj holds that the approvable saying is, that it means إِلَّا مَنْ جَهِلَ نَفْسَهُ i. e., *but he who is* [*ignorant* or *silly* or *foolish* or] *unreflecting in his mind:* and in like manner, سَفِهَ رَأْيَهُ means جَهِلَهُ [i. e. *he was ignorant,* &c., *in his judgment,* or *opinion*]; and *his judgment,* or *opinion, was unsound, without rectitude:* and سَفِهَ نَفْسَهُ signifies also *he lost himself,* or *his own soul.* (TA.) سَفِهَ الحَقَّ is likewise expl. as meaning سَفَّهَ ▼ الحَقَّ [*He made the truth,* or *right, to be foolishness,* or *the like*]; and Yoo held the one to be a dial. var. of the other, and the measure of the former verb to denote intensiveness; and accord. to this explanation one may say, سَفِهْتُ زَيْدًا meaning سَفَّهْتُ ▼ زَيْدًا [*I pronounced Zeyd lightwitted,* &c.]: or the meaning is جَهِلَ الحَقَّ [*he ignored the truth,* or *right*], and *he did not see it to be the truth,* or *right:* (TA:) or *he regarded the truth,* or *right, as foolishness,* or *ignorance.* (S and TA in art. غمط.) See also 2. — سَفِهَ عَلَيْهِ signifies جَهِلَ [i. e., when thus trans. by means of عَلَى, *He feigned ignorance to him*]; as also سَفُهَ, (K, TA,) and ▼ تسافه. (K.) — And سَفِهْتُ نَصِيبِى [and it is implied in the K that one says سَفَهْتُ نصيبى also, but only the former is authorized by the TA,] *I forgot my share,* or *portion.* (Th, K, TA.) — And سَفَهَ صَاحِبَهُ, aor. سَفَهَ, *He overcame his companion in what is termed* مُسَافَهَة [inf. n. of 3, q. v.]. (K.) You say, ▼ سَافَهَهُ فَسَفَهَهُ. (TA.) — سَفِهَتِ الطَّعْنَةُ, (JK, K, TA,) inf. n. سَفْهٌ, (TA,) ‡ *The spear-wound,* or *the like, emitted blood which came from it quickly* (JK, K, TA) *and dried up* (وَجَفَّ [in the TK وخف]): (K, TA:) so in the A. (TA.) — سَفِهَ الشَّرَابَ, (S, K,) inf. n. سَفْهٌ, (TA,) *He drank much of the beverage,* or *wine, without having his thirst satisfied thereby.* (S, K, TA.) See also 3. And سَفِهَ المَآءَ ‡ *He drank the water immoderately.* (TA.) — And سَفِهْتُ and سَفَهْتُ signify شُغِلْتُ, (so in the CK,) in [some of] the copies of the K, but the right reading is شُغِلْتُ [i. e. *I was occupied,* or *busied,* or *diverted* from a thing]: or, accord. to the copies of the K, تَشَغَّلْتُ ; but correctly, or شَغَلْتُ [i. e. *I occupied,* or *busied,* or *diverted* from a thing]. (TA.)

2. see 5. — [Hence,] سَفَّهَهُ, inf. n. تَسْفِيهٌ, (S, Msb, K,) signifies جَعَلَهُ سَفِيهًا [i. e. *He,* or *it, made him to be,* or *he pronounced him to be, lightwitted,* &c.]; as also ▼ سَفِهَهُ ; (K, TA;) on the authority of Akh and Yoo: (TA:) or *he attributed to him what is termed* سَفَه [i. e. *lightwittedness,* &c.]: (S, Msb:) or *he said to him that he was such as is termed* سَفِيه. (Msb.) And سَفَّهَ الجَهْلُ حِلْمَهُ *Ignorance made him light, inconstant, unsteady, irresolute,* or *fickle;* syn. أَخَفَّهُ and أَطَاشَهُ. (TA.) See also 1, in three places.

3. سَافَهَهُ, (S, MA, K,) inf. n. مُسَافَهَةٌ, (S, KL,) *He acted* [*in a lightwitted manner,*] *foolishly,* or *ignorantly, with him;* (MA, KL;) *showed lightness, levity, weakness of mind, and lack of* حِلْم [or *gravity,* &c.], *with him.* (KL.) You say, سَافَهَهُ فَسَفَهَهُ : see 1, near the end of the paragraph. [سافه in this instance may mean as above, or may have the meaning here next following.] — *He reviled him;* or *he reviled him, being reviled by him;* syn. شَاتَمَهُ : whence the prov., سَفِيهٌ لَمْ يَجِدْ مُسَافِهًا ▼ [*A lightwitted person found not a reviler,* or *mutual reviler*]; (K, TA;) mentioned in the S. (TA.) [See also 5.] — سَافَهَ الدَّنَّ, (S, K,) or الوَطْبَ, (S,) † *He sat with* (قَاعَدَ) *the* دن [or *wine-jar*], (S, K,) or *the* وطب [or *milk-skin*], (S,) *and drank from it while after while.* (S, K.) And سافه الشَّرَابَ ‡ *He exceeded the due bounds in respect of the beverage,* or *wine, drinking it without measure;* (K, TA;) as also ▼ سَفِهَهُ. (K.) And سَافَهْتُ المَآءَ ‡ *I drank the water immoderately,* (Lh, TA,) or *without measure.* (A, TA.) [See also 1, near the end of the paragraph.] — And سَافَهَتِ النَّاقَةُ الطَّرِيقَ ‡ *The she-camel kept to the road,* or *way,* (A, K, TA,) or *took to it,* (A, TA,) *with a vehement pace:* (A, K, TA:) or *was light,* or *agile, in her pace,* or *going.* (TA.)

4. أَسْفَهْتُهُ *I found him to be* سفيه [i. e. *lightwitted,* &c.]. (TA. [There said to be tropical; but I see not why.]) — أَسْفَهَكَ اللّٰهُ الشَّرَابَ † *May God make thee to drink of the beverage,* or *wine, without having thy thirst satisfied thereby:* or أَسْفَهَهُ اللّٰهُ *God made him,* or *may God make him, to drink without having his thirst satisfied:* (S, accord. to different copies:) or اسفه اللّٰهُ فُلَانًا المَآءَ *God made,* or *may God make, such a one to drink much water.* (TA.)

5. تسفّهت الرِّيَاحُ *The winds became in a state of commotion.* (TA.) — تسفّهت الرِّيحُ الشَّجَرَ, (S,) or الغُصُونَ, (K, TA,) and سَفَّهَتْ ▼ الرِّيحُ الغُصُونَ, (Ham p. 350,) *The wind made the trees,* (S,) or *the branches,* (K,) *to bend,* or *incline:* (S, K:) and *put the branches in motion:* (K,

and Ḥam ubi suprà:) or *ruffled, and put in motion, the branches.* (TA. [There said to be tropical: but see what is said of the primary signification of سَفَهٌ, below.]) — [Hence,] it is said in a prov., قُرَارَةٌ تَسَفَّهَتْ قُرَارَةً *A lamb,* or *kid, made a sheep,* or *goat, to incline* [to silly behaviour]: applied to the old whom the young incites to lightwittedness (السَّفَه) and levity. (Meyd. [See also a similar prov. in Freytag's Arab. Prov., ii. 253.]) — تَسَفَّهَهُ عَنْ مَالِهِ *He deluded him,* or *beguiled him, of his property.* (Ṣ, Ḳ.) — تسفّه عَلَيْهِ *He acted with* سَفَاهَة [i. e. *lightwittedness,* &c.], or *foolishly, towards him.* (MA.) — And تَسَفَّهْتُ عَلَيْهِ signifies أَسْمَعْتُهُ [as meaning *I reviled him*]. (Ṣ.) [See also 3.]

6. تَسَافَهَ عَلَيْهِ: see 1, in the last quarter of the paragraph. — [And تسافهوا *They behaved in a lightwitted, foolish,* or *ignorant, manner, one with another.* See also 3, which has a similar meaning. — And *They reviled one another:* as seems to be indicated in the TA. See also Ḥar p. 522: and see, again, 3.] — تَسَافَهُ أَشْدَاقُهَا, in a verse of Khalaf Ibn-Is-ḥáḳ El-Bahránee, [describing swift camels,] means *Their sides of the mouth casting forth their foam, one at another:* like the saying of El-Jarmee,

* تَسَافَهُ أَشْدَاقُهَا بِاللُّغَامِ *

[*Their sides of the mouth casting forth the foam, one at another*]. (TA. [تسافه, there written without any syll. signs, is app. thus, (for تَتَسَافَهُ,) not تَسَافَهُ.])

سَفَهٌ, (Ṣ, TA,) as also ↓ سَفَاهَةٌ and ↓ سَفَاهٌ, (TA,) [all mentioned as inf. ns. in the first paragraph of this art.,] primarily signifies خِفَّةٌ [in its proper sense of *Lightness*], and *motion, commotion,* or *agitation.* (Ṣ, TA.) — And hence (Ṣ, TA) the first, (Ṣ, K, TA,) like each of the others, (Ḳ, TA,) signifies [generally *Lightwittedness,* or *the like;*] the *contr. of* حِلْمٌ; (Ṣ, Ḳ, TA;) [i. e.] خِفَّةٌ [as meaning *lightness* or *levity, inconstancy, unsteadiness, irresoluteness;* or *lightness* or *levity, &c., and hastiness;* for, as is said in the TA in art. رجح, the contr. of حِلْم is described by the terms خِفَّة and عَجَل, like as حِلْم is described by the term ثِقَل]; *and slenderness, shallowness,* or *weakness, of judgment; qualities which deficiency of intellect,* or *understanding, necessarily involves:* (Bḍ in ii. 12, in explanation of سَفَهٌ:) or خِفَّةُ حِلْمٍ [i. e. *slightness of gravity* or *staidness* or *sedateness* or *calmness* &c.]: or جَهْلٌ [i. e. *ignorance,* or *silliness* or *foolishness*]: (Ḳ, TA:) all of which explanations are nearly alike: (TA:) or سَفَه is *a deficiency in intellect* or *understanding:* (Mṣb:) or *a lightness,* or *levity, accidental to a man, arising from joy* or *anger, inducing him to act unreasonably and unlawfully.* (KT.)

سَفَاهٌ: see the next preceding paragraph.

سَفِيهٌ [*Having the quality termed* سَفَهٌ; i. e., accord. to the explanation of the primary signification of the latter, above, *Light;* and *in a state of motion, commotion,* or *agitation:*] applied to a camel's nose-rein, (Ṣ, Ḳ,) *light:* (Ṣ:) or *quivering;* (Ḳ, TA;) because of the she-camel's shaking it, and contending in pulling it. (TA: but there said to be, when thus applied, tropical.) Dhu-r-Rummeh says,

* عَلَى ظَهْرِ مِقْلَاتٍ سَفِيهٍ جَدِيلُهَا *

i. e. [*Upon the back of a she-camel that had brought forth but once and not conceived after,*] *whose nose-rein was light.* (Ṣ. In the TA, زِمَامُهَا is here put in the place of جَدِيلُهَا.) And one says also نَاقَةٌ سَفِيهَةُ الزِّمَامِ, (Ḳ, TA,) meaning [*A she-camel whose nose-rein is light,* or *quivering:* or] *light,* or *agile, in pace* or *going.* (TA: in which this, also, is said to be tropical.) — Also *Lightwitted; light of intellect* or *understanding;* (TA;) *deficient in intellect* or *understanding;* (Mṣb;) *ignorant;* (Mujáhid, Ḳ, TA;) *weak; foolish, stupid, unsound in intellect* or *understanding, dull therein,* or *having little,* or *no, intellect,* or *understanding;* (Mujáhid, TA;) and ↓ سَافِهٌ, also, [which is syn. with سَفِيهٌ in all the senses mentioned above,] is expl. by IAạr as having this last meaning of *foolish, stupid, &c.:* (TA:) the fem. is سَفِيهَةٌ: (Mṣb, Ḳ:) and the pl. of the masc., (Ḳ,) or of the masc. and fem., (Mṣb, TA,) is سُفَهَآءُ, (Mṣb, Ḳ, TA,) and of both, سِفَاهٌ, and of the fem., سَفِيهَاتٌ also and سَفَائِهُ and سُفَّهٌ. (Ḳ, TA.) In the Ḳur ii. 282, سَفِيهًا means, accord. to Ibn-'Arafeh, *Ignorant of the ordinances,* or *statutes; one who does not dictate well, and knows not what dictation is;* for he who is ignorant in all his circumstances may not deal with another upon credit: accord. to ISd, *ignorant* or صَغِير [meaning *under the age of puberty*]; not ignorant of dictating, as Lḥ asserts it to mean, because it is added, "or not able to dictate, himself:" this, says Er-Rághib, denotes سفه in respect of worldly matters: in the Ḳur lxxii. 4, سَفِيهُنَا denotes سفه in religion. (TA.) In the Ḳur iv. 4, the pl. السُّفَهَآء is said to mean *Women, and young children;* because they are ignorant of the proper object of expense: and I'Ab is related to have said that women are termed السُّفَّه and السُّفَهَآء: (Lḥ, TA:) Az, also, says that a woman is termed سَفِيهَةٌ because of the weakness of her intellect, and because she does not manage well her property; and in like manner are termed children as long as they are not known to be characterized by maturity of intellect, and rectitude of actions, and good management of affairs. (TA.) — ثَوْبٌ سَفِيهٌ ‡ *A garment,* or *piece of cloth, badly woven; thin, flimsy, unsubstantial,* or *scanty in the yarn.* (Ḳ,* TA.)

سَفَاهَةٌ: see سَفَهٌ.

سَافِهٌ: see سَفِيهٌ. — Also, applied to a man, † *Vehemently thirsty:* and so سَاهِفٌ. (Az, TA.)

وَادٍ مُسْفَهٌ ‡ *A valley filled* [*with water*]: (Ḳ, TA:) as though it exceeded the due bounds, and became such as is termed سَفِيه: imagined to be from أَسْفَهْتُهُ signifying "I found him to be سَفِيه." (TA.)

طَعَامٌ مَسْفَهَةٌ, (Ḳ, TA, in the CḲ [erroneously] مُسْفِهَةٌ,) as also مُسْفِهَةٌ, (TA,) † *Food that incites* [in the CḲ يَتْعَبُ is erroneously put for يَبْعَثُ] *to the drinking of much water.* (IAạr,* Ḳ, TA.)

مُسَافِهٌ act. part. n. of 3, q. v.

سفو and سفى

1. سَفَا, (Ṣ, M,) aor. يَسْفُو, inf. n. سُفُوٌّ, (Ṣ, TA,) like عُلُوٌّ, (TA,) or سَفْوٌ, (so accord. to a copy of the M,) *He was quick,* or *swift, in walking,* or *going, and in flying.* (Ṣ, M.) ═ سَفَتِ الرِّيحُ التُّرَابَ, (Ṣ, M, Mgh, Ḳ,) aor. تَسْفِى, (Ṣ, Ḳ,) inf. n. سَفْىٌ, (Ṣ, M,) *The wind raised the dust,* or *made it to fly, and carried it away,* or *dispersed it;* (Ṣ, Mgh, Ḳ;) and *cast it:* (Mgh:) or *bore it, carried it,* or *carried it away;* (M, Ḳ;) as also ↓ أَسْفَتْهُ, (Ḳ,) a dial. var. of weak authority, mentioned by Ṣgh on the authority of Fr; (TA;) [or it may be thus expl. by a mistake originating from the fact that] IAạr mentions سَفَتِ الرِّيحُ and أَسْفَتْ, [as syn.,] but [in a sense to be expl. hereafter,] not making either of them trans.: (M:) [and ↓ سَافَتِ الرِّيحُ التُّرَابَ occurs in the M and L in art. سنف:] and تَسْفِى بِهِ, relating to the wind and the dust, also occurs; the ب being redundant, or added because the verb implies the meaning of رَمَتْ [which is trans. by means of ب]. (Mgh.) — And سَفَتِ الرِّيحُ *The wind blew;* as also ↓ أَسْفَتْ. (IAạr, TA.) And سَفَتْ عَلَيْهِ الرِّيَاحُ [*The winds blew upon him,* or *it*]. (Z, TA.) — And سَفَى التُّرَابُ, aor. يَسْفِى, [*The dust,* or *earth, poured down,*] the verb being intrans. as well as trans. (Ḥam p. 454. [It is there indicated that the meaning is إِنْهَالَ.]) ═ سَفِىَ: see سَفًا, below. ═ سَفِيَتْ يَدُهُ *His hand became much cracked,* or *chapped,* (Ḳ, TA,) in consequence of work. (TA.) ═ And سَفِىَ, [aor. يَسْفَى,] inf. n. سَفًا and سَفَآءٌ, *He was,* or *became, lightwitted;* or *unwise, witless,* or *destitute of wisdom* or *understanding;* i. q. سَفِهَ, inf. n. سَفَهٌ and سَفَاهٌ; (M, Ḳ;) as also ↓ اسفى. (Az, Ḳ.)

3. سافت الرِّيحُ التُّرَابَ: see 1. ═ سَافَاهُ, (Ṣ, Ḳ,) inf. n. مُسَافَاةٌ and سِفَآءٌ, i. q. سَافَهَهُ [*He acted in a lightwitted manner, foolishly,* or *ignorantly, with him*]. (Ṣ, Ḳ.) ═ And *He treated him medically,* or *curatively:* (Ḳ:) from سِفَآءٌ. (TA. [But see سِفَآءٌ, below.])

4. اسفى *He took for himself a mule such as is termed* سَفْوَآءُ, i. e. *quick* [&c.]. (Ḳ.) ═ أَسْفَتْ said of the wind, intrans. and trans.: see 1, in two places. ═ اسفى said of corn, *It became rough,* or *coarse, in the extremities* [or *awn*] *of its ears.* (Ṣ, Ḳ.) — اسفت said of بُهْمَى [or barley-grass], *It let fall its* سَفًا [or *prickles,* or *awn,* or *extremities*]. (M, Ḳ.) — And اسفى said of a man, *He took the prickles* [or *awn* or *extremities*] *of the* بُهْمَى [or *barley-grass*]. (TA.) ═ Also, said of a man, *He removed dust,* or *earth,* (سَفًا, TA) *from one place to another.*

(Az, Ḳ.) ═ And اسفت said of a she-camel, ‡ *She became lean*, or *emaciated*, (Ḳ,) *so that she was like the* سفا [or *prickles of barley-grass*]. (TA.) ═ See also 1, last sentence. ═ اسفاهُ *It* (an affair, or event, M) *incited him* (a man, Ḳ) *to unsteadiness, and levity*. (M, Ḳ.) — And hence, perhaps, (M,) اسفى بهِ *He did evil or ill*, or *acted ill, to him*, or *with him*, (M, Ḳ,) i. e., his companion. (M.)

8. استفى وَجْهَهُ *i. q.* اِصْطَرَفَهُ, (Ṣgh, Ḳ,) i. e. *He turned away his face*. (TḲ.)

سَفًا *Lightness, thinness*, or *scantiness, in the hair of the forelock*, (Ṣ, M, Mgh, Ḳ,) of the horse, in which it is discommended, (Ṣ,* Z, Mgh,) and of the mule and ass, in both of which it is commended: (Z, Mgh:) or *shortness, and scantiness, of the forelock*: accord. to Th, it is ▼ سَفَآءٌ, with medd: which is metaphorically used by a poet as meaning *scantiness* in milk. (M.) [Accord. to the TḲ, the former is an inf. n., of which the verb is ▼ سَفِىَ, said of a horse, as meaning *He was*, or *became, light, thin*, or *scanty, in the forelock*.] — And, accord. to IAạr, *A whiteness* [or *a tinge thereof*] *in the hair* [of a horse]: particularly said by him in one place to be such as is termed أَذْهَر, and such as is أَشْقَر. (M, in art. سفو.) ═ Also, [but more properly written سَفًى, the last radical in this case being ى,] *Dust*, or *earth*; (Ṣ, M, Ḳ;) and so ▼ سَافٍ: (TA:) or this is applied to earth, or dust, [as meaning *pouring down*,] from سَفَى التُّرَابَ [expl. above]: (Ḥam p. 454:) the former signifies *dust*, or *earth*, though not raised and carried away, or dispersed, by the wind: or, accord. to the T, *whatever is raised and carried away*, or *dispersed, by the wind*: (TA:) accord. to IAạr, *dust*, or *earth, taken forth from a grave or a well*: (M:) سَفَاةٌ is a more special term, (Ṣ,) the n. un., (M,) سَفَاةٌ مِنْ تُرَابٍ signifying *a collection* (كُثْبَةٌ) *of dust*, or *earth*. (Ḥam p. 810.) ═ Also *Any kind of tree having prickles*, or *thorns*: (Ḳ: [but this seems to have been erroneously taken from what here follows:]) the *prickles* [or *awn* or *beard*] *of* بُهْمَى [or *barley-grass*], (Ṣ, M,) and *of the ears of corn*, [*of wheat* or *barley*, (TA in art. خدش,)] and *of anything having prickles*: accord. to Th, the *extremities of* بُهْمَى: n. un. سَفَاةٌ, as above. (M.) ═ Also *Leanness*, or *emaciation*, (Ḳ, TA,) *in consequence of disease*. (TA.) ═ It is also an inf. n. of سَفِىَ as syn. with سَفِهَ, expl. above. (M, Ḳ.)

سَفَآءٌ: see the first sentence of the next preceding paragraph: it is expl. in the Ḳ [and also in the M] as signifying *A stopping, stopping short*, or *ceasing*, of the she-camel's milk: and ISd cites [in the M, after Th], from a poet, the phrase فِى أَلْبَانِهِنَّ سَفَآءٌ, [ending a verse,] referring to [she-camels such as are termed] قَلَائِص: but Az relates it differently, فِى أَلْبَابِهِنَّ, with ب [in the place of ن]; saying that سَفَآءٌ means *lightness*, or *levity*, in anything; and *ignorance*; and that the phrase, as he cites it, means *in whose faculties of understanding is lightness*. (TA.) [See 1, last sentence: and] see also what next follows.

سَفَآءٌ, accord. to the Ḳ, signifies *A medicine*, or *remedy*: [see 3, last signification:] but this requires consideration; for it is said in the M, [▼ السَّفَآءُ signifies *unsteadiness*, and *levity*; and IAạr says,] السَّفَآءُ from السَّفِىُّ is like الشَّقَآءُ from الشَّقِىُّ. (TA.)

سَفِىٌّ Dust *raised*, or *made to fly, and carried away*, or *dispersed, by the wind*; (Ṣ, Ḳ;) and (Ḳ) so ▼ سَافٍ, (M, Ḳ,) *i. q.* ▼ مَسْفِىٌّ; a possessive epithet, or of the measure فَاعِل in the sense of the measure مَفْعُول. (M. [See another explanation of سَافٍ voce سَفًا, from the Ḥamáseh. Freytag explains both سَفِىٌّ and سَافٍ, as on the authority of the Ḳ, as epithets applied to the wind, not to the dust.]) — Also *Clouds*; [app. as being driven by the wind;] syn. سَحَابٌ. (Ṣ.) ═ And *i. q.* سَفِيهٌ [*Lightwitted*, &c.: see 1, last sentence]. (M, Ḳ.) [And it seems to be indicated in the Ṣ that ▼ سَافٍ is *syn. with* سَافِهٌ, which is *syn. with* سَفِيهٌ.]

سَفَآءٌ: see مُسْفٍ.

سَافٍ: fem. سَافِيَةٌ, pl. سَوَافٍ: see this last in the next paragraph: — and for the first, see سَفًا: and سَفِىٌّ, first sentence. ═ See also سَفِىٌّ again, last sentence.

سَافِيَآءُ *Dust*, syn. غُبَارٌ: (M, Ḳ:) or *dust* (تُرَابٌ) and *dry herbage* or *the like*: (Ḥam p. 445:) or *dust* (تُرَابٌ) *with the wind*: (M:) or *wind that bears*, or *carries*, or *carries away, dust*, (M, Ḳ, TA,) *much, upon the surface of the earth, impelling it against men*: (TA, and in like manner in the Ḥam ubi suprà:) and ▼ رِيَاحٌ سَوَافٍ, (TA,) pl. of رِيحٌ سَافِيَةٌ, (Ḥam ubi suprà,) *winds that raise the dust*, or *make it to fly, and carry it away*, or *disperse it*: you say, لَعِبَتْ بِهِ السَّوَافِى [*The winds raising the dust, &c., made sport with him*, or *it*]. (TA.) — [Also *Tracks*, or *streaks, upon a pool put in motion by the wind*: so says Freytag; but he names not any authority for this.]

أَسْفَى applied to a horse, (Aṣ, Ṣ, M, Mgh,) *Light, thin*, or *scanty, in the hair of the forelock*: (Aṣ, Ṣ, M, Mgh, Ḳ:) or *short and scanty therein*: fem. سَفْوَآءُ: (M:) [and accord. to some, it seems to be in like manner applied to a mule and an ass: (see سَفًا:)] one says فَرَسٌ أَسْفَى and بَغْلَةٌ سَفْوَآءُ: (Mgh:) [or,] accord. to Aṣ, أَسْفَى in the sense first expl. above is not applied to anything but a horse: applied to a mule, it means † *quick*, or *swift*: (Ṣ:) or بَغْلَةٌ سَفْوَآءُ signifies ‡ *a she-mule that is quick*, or *swift*, (Ṣ, M, A, Ḳ, TA,) *like the wind*, (A, TA,) *active*, or *light*, (Ṣ,) *of middling make, compact and strong in the back*; (M, TA;) and in like manner سَفْوَآءُ is applied to a wild she-ass. (M.) — Accord. to IAạr, الأَسْفَى applied to the horse signifies الَّذِى تَنْزِعُهُ شَعْرَةٌ بَيْضَآءُ [app. meaning *Distinguished by some white hairs*, though I find no authority for thus rendering the verb here used] whether he be bay or of some other colour: or *having that whiteness of the hair which is termed* سَفًا [expl. above], which is particularly said by him in one place to be in such as is termed أَذْهَر, and such as is أَشْقَر: and the fem. in this sense also is as above. (M.) — One says also رِيحٌ سَفْوَآءُ, meaning ‡ *A swift wind*; like as one says رِيحٌ هَوْجَآءُ. (TA.)

مُسْفٍ [and, accord. to Golius, ▼ سَفَآءٌ, mentioned by him as on the authority of the Ḳ, in which, however, I do not find it, nor did Freytag,] *A calumniator*, or *slanderer*. (Ḳ.)

مَسْفِىٌّ: see سَفِىٌّ.

سقب

1. سَقِبَ, aor. ـَ, inf. n. سَقَبٌ, *He*, or *it, was*, or *became, near*. (Mṣb.) سَقِبَ is syn. with قَرُبَ. (Ṣ, A, Ḳ.) You say, سَقِبَتْ دَارُهُ, (Ṣ, and so in the Ḳ accord. to the TA,) with kesr [to the ق], (Ṣ,) [inf. n. as above;] or سَقُبَتْ, (so in the CḲ and in my MS. copy of the Ḳ and in my copy of the Mgh,) inf. n. سُقْبٌ, (so in my copy of the Mgh,) or سُقُوبٌ; (Ḳ;) [but I believe the verb to be correctly سَقَبَتْ, like its syn. صَقَبَتْ, and the inf. n. to be correctly سَقْبٌ, and perhaps also سُقُوبٌ;] *His house was near*; (Ṣ, Mgh, Ḳ;) as also ▼ أَسْقَبَتْ. (Ṣ, Ḳ.) It is said in a trad., الجَارُ أَحَقُّ بِسَقَبِهِ, meaning [*The neighbour has a better*, or *the best, claim* to pre-emption] *by reason of his being near*: (Ṣ,* A, Mṣb:) or the ب is a connective of احقّ with its complement, (Mgh, Mṣb,) not to denote a cause, (Mgh,) and بِسَقَبِهِ is expl. as meaning بِالشُّفْعَةِ; (Mgh, Mṣb;) i. e. *the neighbour has a better*, or *the best, claim to* الشُّفْعَة [or *pre-emption*], when his house is contiguous: (Mgh:) IAth says that it is adduced as an evidence that الشُّفْعَة belongs to the neighbour though not a sharer; i. e., that he has a better claim thereto than one who is not a neighbour: but some explain الجار as meaning *the partner*, or *sharer*: or the meaning of the trad. may be, the neighbour has a better, or the best, claim to kindness and assistance because of his being near. (L, TA. [See also another reading (بِصَقَبِهِ), and explanations thereof, in art. صقب.])

4. اسقبهُ *He made him*, or *it, to be near*: (Ḳ:) or اسقب دَارَهُ *he made his house to be near*. (Ṣ.) [And so with ص.] ═ See also the paragraph above. ═ أَسْقَبَتْ is also said of a she-camel, meaning *She brought forth mostly males*. (A,* TA.) [And اسقب *He got*, or *got mostly, male offspring*.] In the following saying, (Ṣ, TA,) of Ru-beh, describing the two parents of a man eulogized [by him], (TA,)

* وَكَانَتِ العِرْسُ الَّتِى تَنَخَّبَا *
* غَرَّآءَ مِسْقَابًا ▼ لِفَحْلٍ أَسْقَبَا *

[*And the wife whom he chose was generous*, or *noble*, or *fair, one that brought forth*, or *brought* *forth mostly, male offspring, to a male that begot*, or *begot mostly, such offspring*,] the last word is a verb, in the pret. tense, not an epithet applied to فحل. (Ṣ,* TA. [In the former, only the second hemistich is cited.])

[6. تساقبت أَبْيَاتُهُمْ was probably used as meaning *Their tents*, or *houses, were near together*: see the part. n. of this verb below.]

سَقْبٌ The *young one of a camel*: or, *when just brought forth*: (Ḳ:) or only the *male young one of a camel*: (Ṣ, Ḳ:) [see also صَقْبٌ:] when a she-camel has brought forth her young one, the latter, when just born, is called سَلِيلٌ, before it is known whether it is a male or a female; but when it is known, if it is a male, it is called سَقْبٌ: (Aṣ, TA:) the female is not called سَقْبَةٌ, (Ṣ, Ḳ,) but حَائِلٌ: (Ṣ:) or it is [sometimes] called by the former of these appellations: (Ḳ:) [see De Sacy's Chrest. Arabe, 2nd ed., ii. 358: and see سَقْبَةٌ below:] the pl. is أَسْقُبٌ [a pl. of pauc.] and سِقَابٌ and سُقُوبٌ and سُقْبَانٌ. (Ḳ.)

أَذَلُّ مِنَ السُّقْبَانِ بَيْنَ الحَلَائِبِ

[*More vile than the male young ones of camels among the milch camels*] is a prov. [from a verse of Ḳeys Ibn-El-Khaṭeem]. (TA.) — *Tall*: (Ḳ: [see also سَكْبٌ:]) or anything *tall, together with plumpness*; or *fatness, softness, thinness of the skin, and plumpness*. (Ṣ. [See also صَقْبٌ.]) Applied to a branch, *Juicy, thick, and long*: (Az, TA: [and so صَقْبٌ:]) or anything of the like kind *full and complete*. (ADḳ, TA.) In the following verse, cited by Sb,

وَسَاقِيَيْنِ مِثْلِ زَيْدٍ وَجُعَلْ
سَقْبَانِ مَمْشُوقَانِ مَكْنُوزَا العَضَلْ

سَقْبَانِ signifies طَوِيلَانِ [*tall*], and is also written صَقْبَانِ: (Sh, TA:) [so that the meaning may be, *And two waterers*, or *givers of drink, like Zeyd and Jo'al*: they being *two tall persons, light of flesh, compact in the muscles*: I suppose هُمَا to be understood before the latter hemistich; because of the ns. in the nom. case: and I have substituted مَكْنُوزَا for مَنْكُوزَا, the reading in the TA, doubtless a mistranscription:] or it is for مِثْلِ سَقْبَيْنِ [meaning *like two male young ones of camels*]. (L, TA.) — And The *pole of a* [*tent such as is called*] خِبَآء; (Ṣ, Ḳ;) as also ▼ سَقِيبَةٌ: and so صَقْبٌ: (Ṣ:) pl. of the first سِقْبَانٌ. (Ḳ.)

سَقْبٌ inf. n. of سَقِبَ [q. v.]. (Mṣb.) — See also سَاقِبٌ, in three places.

سَقْبَةٌ The *female foal of a wild ass*. (Ṣ, Ḳ,* TA.) — [See also سَقْبٌ, of which, in the first of the senses assigned to it above, it is said by some to be the fem.]

سِقَابٌ *A bit of cotton which a woman afflicted* (Ḳ, TA) *by the death of her husband, in the Time of Ignorance, after shaving her head, and scratching her face*, (TA,) *used to make red with her blood*, (Ḳ, TA,) i. e. *her own blood*, (TA,) *and put upon her head, making its extremity to protrude from a hole*, or *rent, of her* قِنَاع [or *head-covering*], *in order that people might know her to be so afflicted*. (Ḳ,* TA.)

سُقُوبٌ a pl. of سَقْبٌ [q. v.]. (Ḳ.) — Also The *hind legs* of camels: (IAạr, Ḳ:) pronounced also with ص. (IAạr, TA in art. صقب.)

سَقِيبٌ: see سَاقِبٌ.

سَقِيبَةٌ: see سَقْبٌ, last sentence. — Also *A baker's kneading-board*: or *his rolling-pin*. (MA.)

سَاقِبٌ [in the CḲ ثاقب] *Near*; (A, Mṣb, Ḳ;) and likewise with ص; (A;) as also ▼ سَقِيبٌ (Mṣb) and ▼ سَقْبٌ, [likewise pronounced with ص,] (Mgh, Ḳ,* TA,) for ذُو سَقْبٍ, or it may be an inf. n. used as a subst. or an epithet, (Mgh,) and ▼ مُسْقِبٌ. (Ḳ,* TA.) You say مَكَانٌ سَاقِبٌ *A near place*: (A:) and ▼ مَنْزِلٌ سَقْبٌ and ▼ مُسْقِبٌ *a near place of alighting* or *abode*: (Ḳ,* TA:) and دَارِى سَقْبٌ ▼ مِنْ دَارِهِ *My house is near his house*. (Mgh.) — Also *Distant*: (Mṣb, Ḳ:) this meaning is mentioned by some, as well as the former: (Mṣb:) thus it has two contr. meanings: (Ḳ:) the latter of these is mentioned in the Mj; and the following verse is cited as a proof thereof;

تَرَكْتَ أَبَاكَ بِأَرْضِ الحِجَازِ
وَرُحْتَ إِلَى بَلَدٍ سَاقِبِ

[*Thou leftest thy father in the land of El-Ḥijáz, and wentest to a distant country*]. (MF, TA.)

سَوْقَبٌ A man *tall and slender*. (Suh, TA.)

أَسْقَبُ or أَصْقَبُ, occurring in a trad., accord. to different relaters, *Nearer* [and *nearest*]. (TA in art. صقب.)

مُسْقِبٌ: see سَاقِبٌ, in two places.

مُسْقِبٌ The *dam of a* سَقْب [q. v.]; as also ▼ مِسْقَابٌ: (Ḳ:) [or] the latter signifies a she-camel *that usually brings forth males*. (Ṣ.)

مِسْقَابٌ: see what next precedes: and see a verse cited above, conj. 4.

أَبْيَاتُهُمْ مُتَسَاقِبَةٌ *Their tents*, or *houses, are near together*. (Ḳ.)

سقر

1. سَقَرَتْهُ الشَّمْسُ, (Ṣ,) aor. ـُ, inf. n. سَقْرٌ, (TA,) *The sun scorched*, or *burned, him, altering the colour of his complexion and skin*, (Ṣ,* TA,) *and pained him*, or *pained his brain by its heat*: (TA:) *melted and heated him*, or *it*. (TA.) And سَقَرَتْهُ النَّارُ *The fire altered the colour of his skin*; or *scorched his skin, and altered its colour*; as also صَقَرَتْهُ. (Bḍ in liv. 48.)

سَقْرٌ The *heat, and hurtful action, of the sun*. (Ḳ.)

سَقَرُ *Hell*: (Ṣ, Ḳ:) one of the [proper] names thereof: (Ṣ:) Aboo-Bekr says, There are two opinions respecting this word: some say, that *the fire of the world to come* is thus called, and that the derivation of the word is unknown, and that it is imperfectly decl. because it is determinate and a foreign word: others say that it is from سَقَرَتْهُ الشَّمْسُ, because it melts the bodies and souls, and that it is an Arabic word; and he who holds it to be such says that it is imperfectly decl. because it is determinate and of the fem. gender. (TA.)

سَقَرَاتٌ The *vehemence of the stroke* of the sun. (Ṣ.)

مُسْمَقِرٌّ A day *vehemently hot*. (Ṣ in this art., and Ḳ in art. سمقر.) This is its proper place. (TA.)

سقرقع

سُقُرْقَعٌ, an arabicized word from سُكُرْكَه, (Ṣ, Ḳ,) [or سُكُرْكَهْ, so written in Persian,] *A certain beverage*, (O, Ḳ,) *the wine of the Abyssinians*, (Ṣ,) *made from* ذُرَة [or *millet*]: (Ṣ, Ḳ:) or *a certain beverage of the people of El-Ḥijáz, from barley and* [*other*] *grains; to which they have become addicted*: (Lth, Ḳ:) Lth says, (TA,) it is an Abyssinian word, (Ḳ, TA,) not of the language of the Arabs, because (TA) there is not in the language a quinqueliteral-radical word having ḍamm to the first syllable and fet-ḥ to the last, (Ḳ, TA,) except such as is reduplicative, like ذُرَخْرَخٌ. (TA.) [See also سُكُرْكَةٌ, and مِزْرٌ, and غُبَيْرَآءُ.]

سقط

1. سَقَطَ, (Ṣ, M, &c.,) aor. ـُ, (M, MṢ,) inf. n. سُقُوطٌ (Ṣ, M, Mgh, Mṣb, Ḳ) and مَسْقَطٌ, (Ṣ, Ḳ,) *It fell; fell down; dropped; dropped down; tumbled down*; (M, Mgh, Mṣb, Ḳ;) *upon the ground*; (Mgh;) or *from a higher to a lower place*; (Mṣb;) namely, a thing from the hand; (Ṣ;) or from a high place, as a roof of a house; and from a low place, as when said of a person in an erect posture; (B;) also said of a building; (TA in art. هور;) and of a جُرُف [q. v.]: (Mṣb and TA in that art.:) [and often used by anatomists and physicians, as meaning *it delapsed; it slipped*, or *fell, down*:] and ▼ اِسَّاقَطَ [originally تَسَاقَطَ] signifies the same; (Ḳ;) as in the phrase in the Ḳur [xix. 25], تَسَّاقَطْ عَلَيْكِ رُطَبًا جَنِيًّا, or يَسَّاقَطْ, accord. to different readings, *It*, namely the palm-tree (نَخْلَة) accord. to the former reading, and the trunk (جِذْع) accord. to the latter reading, *shall drop upon thee with fresh ripe dates, plucked*; رطبا جنيا being transferred from its proper place, and used as a specificative; the meaning being, يَسَّاقَطْ رُطَبُ الجِذْعِ: so says Fr. (Az, TA.) [This phrase of the Ḳur, with the above-mentioned explanation, but less fully given, occurs in a copy of the Ṣ which, throughout this art., differs much from other copies.] You say also, سَقَطَ فُلَانٌ مَغْشِيًّا عَلَيْهِ [*Such a one fell down in a swoon*]. (TA.) And مَنْ نَازَعَ أَطْوَلَ مِنْهُ سَقَطَ الشَّغْزَبِيَّةَ [*He who contends with one taller than himself falls by the trick which consists in one's twisting his leg with the leg of the other*]. (TA.) سَقَطَ الوَلَدُ مِنْ بَطْنِ أُمِّهِ —, (Kh, Ṣ, Mṣb, Ḳ,)

inf. n. سُقُوطٌ, (Mṣb,) The child, or fœtus, came forth [or fell] from the belly of its mother (Mṣb, Ḳ) abortively, or in an immature, or imperfect, state, (Mṣb,) or dead, (A,) but having the form developed, or manifest: (Mṣb:) you do not say وَقَعَ (Kh, Ṣ, Mṣb, Ḳ) unless the child is born alive. (A, TA.) — سُقِطَ فِى يَدِهِ, and أُسْقِطَ ↓ فى يده, (Fr, Zj, Ṣ, M, Ḳ,) but the former is more common, and better, (Fr,) the latter allowed by Akh, but disallowed by AA and by Aḥmad Ibn-Yaḥyà [i. e. Th], (Ṣ,) [lit. There was a falling, and there was a making to fall, upon his hand; i. e., of his hand upon his hand, or of his teeth upon his hand, by reason of repentance, and grief, or regret; meaning] ‡ he repented, (Fr, Zj, Ṣ, M, Ḳ,) of what he had done; and grieved for, or regretted, an act of inadvertence; (Zj, M;) or, and became confounded, or perplexed, and unable to see his right course: (O, Ḳ:) or both signify, (TA,) or signify also, (Ḳ,) or the former signifies also, (M,) he slipped; fell into an error, or a fault; committed a mistake. (M, Ḳ.) Hence the saying in the Ḳur [vii. 148], وَلَمَّا سُقِطَ فِى أَيْدِيهِمْ ‡ And when they repented: (Ṣ:) or struck their hands upon their hands, by reason of repentance; accord. to AAF: (M:) or repented greatly; because he who repents, and grieves, or regrets, bites his hand in sorrow, so that his hand is fallen upon [by his teeth]: (Bḍ:) the phrase was not known to the Arabs before the time of the Ḳur-án: (O:) it has also been read سَقَطَ فى ايديهم, (Akh, Ṣ, M,) as though النَّدَمُ were understood; (Akh, Ṣ;) i. e. سَقَطَ النَّدَمُ; like as you say, قَدْ حَصَلَ فِى يَدِهِ مِنْ هٰذَا مَكْرُوهٌ, likening what comes into the heart, and into the mind, to what comes into the hand, and is seen with the eye: (M, TA:) and this, as well as the former, is tropical. (TA.) — سَقَطَ القَمَرُ ‡ The moon set: and in like manner النَّجْمُ [the star, or asterism; generally meaning the Pleiades; and when this is the case, the phrase in most instances means the Pleiades set at dawn: see مُسْقِطٌ]. (Mgh, TA.) — سَقَطَ الرَّجُلُ ‡ The man died. (TA.) — [And † The man tottered by reason of age.] You say of an old man, سَقَطَ مِنَ الكِبَرِ † [He tottered by reason of age]. (Ṣ in art. دوهر.) — سَقَطَ إِلَىَّ القَوْمُ, (M, Ḳ,) inf. n. سُقُوطٌ, (TA,) ‡ The people, or company of men, alighted at my abode: (M, Ḳ, TA:) they came to me. (TA.) سَقَطَ إِلَى جِيرَانٍ لَهُ, occurring in a trad., means ‡ He came to some neighbours of his, and they gave him refuge, and protected him. (M, TA.) And it is said in a post-classical prov., حَيْثُمَا سَقَطَ لَقَطَ [Wherever he alights he picks up something]: applied to him who practises evasions, shifts, artifices, or the like. (Meyd, and Ḥar p. 660.) — سَقَطَ عَلَى ضَالَّتِهِ ‡ He stumbled upon, lighted on, or became acquainted with, the place of his stray, or lost, beast; he lighted on his stray, or lost, beast. (TA.) Moḥammad said to El-Ḥárith Ibn-Ḥassán, on the latter's asking him respecting a thing, عَلَى الخَبِيرِ سَقَطْتَ ‡ On the possessor of knowledge thou hast lighted: and this is a prov. current among the Arabs. (TA.) And it is said in a prov.,

سَقَطَ العَشَآءُ بِهِ عَلَى سِرْحَانٍ

† [The evening-meal, or supper, (i. e. the seeking for it,) made him to fall, or light, upon a wolf: or سرحان, as is said in a copy of the Ṣ, is here the name of a certain man: see also art. سرح]: applied to him who seeks an object of desire, and falls into a thing that destroys him. (TA.) — سَقَطَ also signifies He descended [from the place which he occupied], and his place became vacant. (TA.) And you say, سَقَطَ فُلَانٌ مِنْ مَنْزِلَتِهِ ‡ [Such a one fell from his honourable station]. (TA.) And سَقَطَ فُلَانٌ مِنْ عَيْنِى ‡ [Such a one fell from the place which he held in my regard]. (TA.) سَقَاطَةٌ, as an inf. n., meaning † The being ignoble in respect of the deeds or qualities of one's ancestors, and of oneself, [as though its verb were سَقُطَ,] is a mistake, although it has been used, for the purpose of assimilation, coupled with وَقَاحَةٌ. (Mgh.) — [Also, † He dropped off; fell behind: he, or it, remained behind, or in the rear. See سَاقِطٌ.] — سَقَطَ عَنِ الطَّرِيقِ † [He deviated from the road]. (IAạr, TA in art. فجر.) — سَقَطَ فِى كَلَامِهِ, (M, Ḳ,) and بِكَلَامِهِ, (TA,) inf. n. سُقُوطٌ; (M, TA;) and أَسْقَطَ ↓ فى كلامه; (Ṣ, TA;) ‡ He committed a mistake in his speech. (M, Ḳ, TA.) And تَكَلَّمَ فَمَا سَقَطَ بِكَلِمَةٍ, (M, TA,) and فِى كَلِمَةٍ, and مَا أَسْقَطَ ↓ فِى كَلِمَةٍ, and مَا أَسْقَطَ ↓ كَلِمَةً, (M, Ḳ,) ‡ He spoke, and did not commit a mistake in a word. (M, Ḳ, TA.) And تَكَلَّمَ بِكَلَامٍ فَمَا سَقَطَ بِحَرْفٍ, and مَا أَسْقَطَ ↓ حَرْفًا, [held by him on whose authority it is mentioned to mean † He spoke speech, and did not drop a letter, or a word; for this is] said by Yaạḳoob to be like أَدْخَلْتُهُ and دَخَلْتُ بِهِ, &c. (Ṣ.) — سَقَطَ ذِكْرُهُ † [The mention of him, or it, was, or became, dropped, left out, or omitted]. (TA, passim.) And سَقَطَ الرَّجُلُ ‡ The man's name fell out, or became dropped, from the register of soldiers or pensioners. (TA.) — سَقَطَتْ قُوَّتُهُ دُونَ بُلُوغِ الأَمْرِ [His power fell short of the attainment or accomplishment, of the affair.] (TA in art. ذرع.) — [سَقَطَ, inf. n. سُقُوطٌ, likewise signifies † It (a claim or demand, a due, an argument or a plea, a condition, a law, a command or prohibition, a gift, a reward, a punishment, a good action, a sin, &c.,) became null, annulled, void, of no force, or of no account; as though it fell to the ground, or became dropped; whence سَقَطَ حُكْمُهُ, by which phrase بَطَلَ, q. v., is expl. in the Mṣb.] You say, سَقَطَ الفَرْضُ † [The assigned, or appointed, gift, or soldier's stipend or pay, became annulled], meaning سَقَطَ طَلَبُهُ وَالأَمْرُ بِهِ † [the demand for it and the order for it became dropped]. (Mṣb.) And إِذَا صَحَّتِ المَوَدَّةُ سَقَطَتْ شُرُوطُ الأَدَبِ وَالتَّكْلِيفِ † [When love, or affection, is free from imperfection, the conditions of politeness and constraint become annulled]. (TA.) And سَقَطَتْ خَطَايَاهُ † His sins fell [from him]; went away; or departed. (TA in art. خر.) — سَقَطَ الحَرُّ, (M, Ḳ,) aor. ـُ, inf. n. سُقُوطٌ, (M,) ‡ The heat fell [like as one says of rain]; (M, Ḳ;) it befell; (TA;) it came. (Ḳ.) But سَقَطَ عَنَّا الحَرُّ † The heat left us or quitted us: (IAạr, M, Ḳ:) as though the verb had two contr. significations. (M, Ḳ.*) — سَقَطَ الحَدِيثُ مِنْكَ إِلَيْهِ وَمِنْهُ إِلَيْكَ ‡ [Discourse fell from thee to him, and from him to thee]: (M:) or سَقَطَ مِنْ كُلٍّ عَلَى الآخَرِ ‡ [it fell from each to the other]. (Ḳ.)

3. ساقطهُ, (Ṣ, M, Ḳ,) inf. n. مُسَاقَطَةٌ and سِقَاطٌ, (M, Ḳ,) i. q. أَسْقَطَهُ ↓ [q. v.]: (Ḳ:) or he made it to fall, fall down, drop, drop down, or tumble down, in consecutive portions or quantities; syn. تَابَعَ إِسْقَاطَهُ [in the CḲ اَسْقاطَهُ]: (M, Ḳ:) or it has both of these significations. (So in the L, and in some copies of the Ṣ; but in one copy of the Ṣ, the former only is mentioned.) A poet says, (Ṣ, M,) namely Ḍábi Ibn-El-Ḥárith El-Burjumee, (TA,) describing a [wild] bull and the dogs, (Ṣ,)

يُسَاقِطُ عَنْهُ رَوْقُهُ ضَارِيَاتِهَا
سِقَاطَ حَدِيدِ القَيْنِ أَخْوَلَ أَخْوَلَا

[His horn makes to fall consecutively from him those of them that were trained for hunting, as the iron of the blacksmith makes sparks to fall consecutively, scattered about]. (Ṣ, M.) — ساقط الخَيْلَ ‡ He (a horse) outstripped the [other] horses: (TA:) [as though he made them to drop behind him, one after another.] — ساقطهُ الحَدِيثَ, (M, Ḳ,) inf. n. سِقَاطٌ (Ṣ, M, A) and مُسَاقَطَةٌ, (TA,) ‡ [He discoursed with him alternately;] discourse fell (سَقَطَ) from each of them to the other, (M, Ḳ,) so as that one discoursed, and the other listened to him, and when he became silent, he who had been silent discoursed: (Ṣ, Ḳ:) or he discoursed to him telling him thing after thing. (A, TA.) — كَانَ يُسَاقِطُ ذٰلِكَ عَنْ رَسُولِ اللّٰهِ † He used to relate that from the Apostle of God amid his discourse; as though he mixed his discourse therewith. (TA, from a trad.) — ساقط الفَرَسُ العَدْوَ, (M, Ḳ,) inf. n. سِقَاطٌ, (Ṣ, M, Ḳ,) ‡ The horse came [running] in a slack, or languid, manner: (Ṣ,* M, Ḳ, TA:) or سِقَاطٌ in a horse is the incessantly having the foot wounded and made to bleed by stones, or hurt thereby. (A, TA.) You say also فَرَسٌ بَيِّنُ السِّقَاطِ † A horse slow in running. (TA.) — ساقط الرَّجُلُ, inf. n. سِقَاطٌ, ‡ The man failed of attaining to the condition of the generous, or noble. (TA.)

4. اسقطهُ He made it to fall, fall down, drop, drop down, or tumble down; threw it down; dropped it; let it fall; (Ṣ,* M, Mgh, Mṣb;) upon the ground; (Mgh;) or from a higher to a lower place. (Mṣb.) See also 3, first sentence. — أَسْقَطَتْ, (Ṣ, Mgh, O, Mṣb, Ḳ,) or اسقطت وَلَدَهَا, (M, Ḳ,) or the latter is wrong, (MF,) for the Arabs disused, as some say, the objective complement after this verb, scarcely, or never, saying أَسْقَطَتْ سِقْطًا, nor do they say, أَسْقَطَ الوَلَدَ, (Mṣb, MF,) or the lawyers use these last two phrases, but they are not Arabic, (Mgh,) or a phrase like the last, i. e. أُسْقِطَتِ الأَجِنَّةُ, occurs in an Arabic verse, (TA,) She (a pregnant female, Mgh, Mṣb, or a woman, M, B, and so in a copy of the Ṣ, or a camel or other animal, as in some copies of the Ṣ and in the O, or, accord. to El-

Ḳálee, only said of a woman, like as اجهضت is only said of a she-camel, TA,) *cast her young one*, or *fœtus*, or *her young; brought forth her young one*, or *fœtus*, or *her young*, *abortively*, or *in an immature*, or *imperfect*, *state*, (Ṣ,* M, Mṣb, Ḳ, B,) or *dead*, (Mgh,) *but having the form developed*, or *manifest*. (Mgh, Mṣb.) — أَسْقَطَ فِى يَدِهِ: see 1. — اسقطهُ السُّلْطَانُ ‡ [*The Sultán made him to fall*, or *degraded him*, مِنْ مَنْزِلَتِهِ *from his honourable station*]. (TA.) — [اسقط also signifies † *He dropped, left out*, or *omitted*, a letter of a word, a word of a phrase, &c.] You say, اسقط حَرْفًا, and كَلِمَةً, and فِى كَلِمَةٍ, and فِى كَلَامِهِ: see 1. And اسقط الفَارِضُ اِسْمَهُ ‡ *The appointer*, or *registrar, of the stipends of soldiers or pensioners dropped, left out*, or *omitted, his name*. (TA.) — [Also † *He*, or *it*, *annulled; made*, or *rendered, null, void, of no force*, or *of no account; he rejected*; said in relation to a claim or demand, a due, an argument or a plea, a condition, a law, a command or prohibition, a gift, a reward, a punishment, a good action, a sin, &c.; of any of these you say, اسقطهُ, and اسقط حُكْمَهُ: see an ex. voce هَدَرَ: and see 1, near the end of the paragraph. Hence,] اسقط مِنَ الثَّمَنِ كَذَا † *He abated of the price so much*; syn. حَطَّ. (Mgh and Mṣb in art. حط.) — اسقطهُ is erroneously put in the Ḳ, in one instance, for استسقطهُ. (TA.) See 5. — أَسْقَطُوا لَهُ بِالكَلَامِ ‡ *They reviled him with evil speech*. (TA.)

5. تسقّطهُ ‡ *He sought his mistake*, or *error*: (Ṣ, Ḳ, TA:) ‡ *he strove*, or *laboured, to make him commit a mistake*, or *an error; or to make him lie; or to make him reveal what he had to tell*; (M, Ḳ, TA;) as also ▼ استسقطهُ; (M, TA;) in the copies of the Ḳ, ▼ أَسْقَطَهُ, which is a mistake. (TA.) — تسقّط الخَبَرَ ‡ *He took*, or *received, the news*, or *information, by little and little*; (Ḳ, TA;) *thing after thing*: mentioned by Aboo-Turáb, on the authority of Abu-l-Miḳdám Es-Sulamee. (TA.)

6. تساقط: see its variation إِسَّاقَطَ in 1; first sentence. — *It fell in consecutive portions* or *quantities* [like the leaves of a tree, &c.; *by degrees; gradually*]. (M, Ḳ.) A poet says,

• وَيَوْمٍ تَسَاقَطُ لَذَّاتُهُ • كَنَجْمِ الثُّرَيَّا وَأَمْطَارِهَا •

i. e. † [*Many a day*] *of which the pleasures come one thing after another*; [such a day being *like the asterism of the Pleiades, and* the pleasures thereof like *its rains*;] meaning the abounding of its pleasures. (TA.) And you say, تَسَاقَطَ إِلَىَّ خَيْرُ فُلَانٍ ‡ [*The wealth of such a one fell*, or *came, to me, one thing after another*]. (TA.) — تساقط عَلَى الشَّىْءِ *He threw himself upon the thing*. (Ṣ.) You say, تساقط عَلَى الرَّجُلِ يَقِيهِ بِنَفْسِهِ [*He threw himself upon the man, protecting him with his own person*]. (TA.)

10: see 5.

سَقْطٌ: see سِقْطٌ, in three places: — and سَقِيطٌ, in two places: — and سَاقِطٌ: — and سَقْطَةٌ.

سُقْطٌ: see سِقْطٌ, in three places.

سِقْطٌ and ▼ سُقْطٌ and ▼ سَقْطٌ *A child*, or *young one*, or *fœtus, that falls from the belly of the mother abortively*, or *in an immature*, or *imperfect, state*, (Ṣ, M, Mṣb, Ḳ,) or *dead*, (Mgh,) *but having the form developed*, or *manifest*; (Mgh, Mṣb;) for otherwise it is not so called; (Mgh;) *whether male or female*: (Mṣb, TA:) the first of these three forms is the most common: and the pl. is أَسْقَاطٌ. (TA.) The reward which a father will receive for such offspring is [held to be] more than that for adult offspring. (TA.) — Hence, (M, B, TA,) the same three words, (Ḳ,) or سِقْطُ النَّارِ and ▼ سُقْطُهَا and ▼ سَقْطُهَا, (Ṣ, M, Mṣb,) ‡ *What falls*, (Ṣ, M, Mṣb, Ḳ,) *of fire*, (Ṣ,) *from the* زَنْد, (Mṣb,) or *between the* زَنْدَانِ, (M, Ḳ,) *when one produces fire*, (Ṣ,) or *before the emission of the fire is thoroughly effected*: (M, Ḳ:) masc. and fem. (Fr, Ṣ, Ḳ.) — Also سِقْطُ رَمْلٍ and ▼ سُقْطُهُ and ▼ سَقْطُهُ (Ṣ, M, Mṣb, Ḳ) and ▼ مَسْقَطُهُ (M, Ḳ) and ▼ مَسْقِطُهُ (M, TA) [*The fall*, or *slope, of a tract*, or *quantity, of sand*;] *the place where sand* [*falls*, or *slopes, and*] *ends*: (Ṣ:) or *the place to which the extremity of sand extends*: (Mṣb:) or *the place where the main portion of sand ends, and where it* [*falls*, or *slopes, and*] *becomes thin*; (M, Ḳ;) for it is [derived] from سُقُوطٌ [inf. n. of 1]. (M.) — Also سِقْطٌ ‡ *The edge*, or *extremity, of a cloud*: (M, Ḳ:) or *the part of a cloud where the edge*, or *extremity, is seen as though it were falling upon the earth, in the horizon*. (Ṣ.) — And hence, or from the same word as used in relation to sand, (TA,) ‡ The *similar part* of a [tent of the kind called] خِبَآء: (Ṣ:) or the *lowest strip of cloth, that is next the ground, on either side of a* خباء: (A, TA:) or the *side of a* خباء: (Ḳ:) or [*each of*] *the two sides* thereof. (M.) — Also, (Ṣ, M, Ḳ,) and ▼ سِقَاطٌ and ▼ مَسْقَطٌ, (M, Ḳ,) ‡ The *wing*; (Ḳ;) *each of the two wings*; (Ṣ, M;) of a bird; (M, Ḳ;) or of a male ostrich. (Ṣ.) And سِقْطُ جَنَاحِ الطَّائِرِ ‡ *The part of the wing of the bird which it drags upon the ground*. (Ṣ, TA.) — [And hence,] سِقْطَا اللَّيْلِ ‡ *The two sides of the darkness of night*; (TA;) *the beginning and end thereof*; (Ṣ, TA;) as also ▼ سِقَاطَاهُ: (TA:) whence the saying of the poet, (Ṣ, TA,) namely Er-Rá'ee, (TA,)

• حَتَّى إِذَا مَا أَضَآءَ الصُّبْحُ وَٱنْبَعَثَتْ •
• عَنْهُ نَعَامَةُ ذِى سِقْطَيْنِ مُعْتَكِرِ •

‡ [*Until, when the dawn shone, and the blackness of confused night became dispelled from it*]: he means by نعامة the "blackness" of night: he says that the night, having its beginning and end, passed, and the dawn shone clearly. (Ṣ, TA.)

سَقَطٌ *What is made to fall, thrown down*, or *dropped*, of, or from, a thing, (M, Ḳ,) *and held in mean estimation*: (TA:) and [in like manner] ▼ سُقَاطَةٌ the *refuse* of anything; (IDrd;) or *what falls*, of, or from, a thing, (M, Ḳ,) *and is held in mean estimation*; (TA;) as also ▼ سُقَاطٌ; (Ḳ;) or, accord. to some, this last is a pl. [or rather a coll. gen. n.], and ▼ سُقَاطَةٌ is its sing. [or n. un.]; and سُقَاطَاتٌ is also a pl. of this last. (TA.) [Hence,] سَقَطُ الطَّعَامِ ‡ *What is worthless, of food*: (M, Ḳ:*) or *what falls from*, or *of, food*: (M:) and [in like manner] ▼ سُقَاطَةٌ and ▼ سُقَاطٌ *refuse that falls, and is held in mean estimation*, of, or from, food and beverage and the like: (TA:) the pl. of سَقَطٌ is أَسْقَاطٌ. (Ḳ.) And سَقَطُ المَتَاعِ ‡ *What is worthless, paltry, mean, vile*, or *held in little account, of the furniture or utensils of a house or tent*, or *of household goods*: (Ṣ, Mṣb, Ḳ:) or *the refuse thereof*; (Mgh;) and so ▼ سُقَاطَةُ المَتَاعِ: (TA:) and سَقَطُ البَيْتِ signifies the same; (M;) or *such articles of the tent or house as the needle and the axe and the cooking-pot and the like*: (Lth:) pl. as above. (M.) And hence, أَسْقَاطُ النَّاسِ (q. v. infrà, as also سَقَطُ النَّاسِ, voce سَاقِطٌ). (Lḥ, M.) سَقَطٌ also signifies † *Things of which the sale is held in mean estimation; such as the seeds that are used in cooking, for seasoning food; and the like*; (M, TA;) or *such as sugar and raisins*. (A, TA.) Also † The *parts of a slaughtered beast that are held in mean estimation; such as the legs and the stomach and the liver, and the like of these*: pl. as above. (TA.) — ‡ *A mistake*, or *an error*, (Ṣ, M, Mgh, Mṣb, Ḳ,) *in speech*, (M, Mṣb, Ḳ,) *in reckoning*, (Ṣ, M, Ḳ,) *in writing*, (Ṣ, M, Mgh, Ḳ,) and *in action*; (Mṣb;) as also ▼ سِقَاطٌ. (M, Ḳ.) [See also ▼ سَقْطَةٌ.] — ‡ *A disgraceful*, or *shameful, thing; a vice*, or *fault*, or *the like*. (M, Ḳ, TA.) — سَقَطُ الكَلَامِ ‡ *Evil speech*. (TA.)

سَقْطَةٌ [*A fall*: or] *a violent fall*. (M, TA.) — ‡ *A slip, lapse, fault*, or *wrong action*; as also ▼ سِقَاطٌ; (Ṣ, Ḳ;) and ▼ سَقْطٌ; which last is also used in a pl. sense: (TA:) or the second (سقاط) is pl. of سَقْطَةٌ: (Mṣb, Ḳ:) as sing., it is an inf. n. of سَاقَطَ: (TA:) and سَقْطَةٌ also signifies *a bad word or saying, that swerves from rectitude*: (TA in art. عور:) its pl., or one of its pls., is سَقَطَاتٌ. (TA.) You say, لَا يَخْلُو أَحَدٌ مِنْ سَقْطَةٍ ‡ [*No one will be free from a slip*]. (TA.) And الكَامِلُ مَنْ عُدَّتْ سَقَطَاتُهُ ‡ [*The perfect is he whose slips are so few that they may be counted*]. (TA.)

سَقَطِىٌّ (Mgh, Ḳ) and ▼ سَقَّاطٌ, (Ṣ, Mgh, Ḳ,) the latter disallowed by some, (Mgh, TA,) but occurring in a trad., (Ṣ, Mgh, TA,) *A seller of what is worthless*, or *mean*, or *vile, of the furniture or utensils of a house or tent*, or *of household goods*; (Ṣ, Ḳ;) or *of the refuse thereof*; (Mgh;) *of what are termed* سَقَطُ المَتَاعِ: (Ṣ, Mgh, Ḳ:) those who disallow the latter epithet term such a person صَاحِبُ سَقَطٍ: (TA:) or ▼ the latter epithet signifies *a seller of things of which the sale is held in mean estimation; such as the seeds that are used in cooking, for seasoning food; and the like; which are termed* سَقَطٌ. (M.) [See also أَسْقَاطِىٌّ.]

سُقَاطٌ: see سُقَاطَةٌ.

سِقَاطٌ: see سَقَطٌ, in two places.

سُقَاطٌ *What falls from palm-trees, of unripe dates:* (Ḳ:) or such are termed سُقَاطُ النَّخْلِ: (M:) سقاط, thus used, may be a sing., or pl. of سَاقِطٌ [q. v.]. (TA.) —— ‡ *Dates that are brought from El-Yemámeh by those who journey thither to procure them.* (M, Ḳ.) —— See also سَقَطَةٌ: and سَقَطٌ, near the end of the paragraph: —— and see سِقْطٌ, in two places, near the end of the paragraph.

سَقُوطٌ: see سَاقِطٌ.

سَقِيطٌ *Hoar-frost*, or *rime;* i. e. *dew that falls and congeals upon the ground;* (Ṣ, M, Ḳ;) also called جَلِيدٌ and ضَرِيبٌ; (Ṣ in art. جلد;) of the dial. of Ṭeiyi. (M.) —— *Snow;* (Ṣ, TA;) as also ▼ سَقَطٌ. (Ḳ, TA.) —— *Hail:* (Ḳ:) or this is called سَقِيطُ السَّحَابِ. (M, TA.) —— *What falls*, or *has fallen*, of dew, (M, Ḳ, TA,) *upon the ground;* (M, TA;) as also ▼ سَقَطٌ. (Ḳ, TA.) —— دُرٌّ سَقِيطٌ *Scattered pearls.* (TA.) And وَرَقٌ سِقَاطٌ [*Scattered leaves*]: the latter word is pl. of سَقِيطٌ, like as طِوَالٌ is pl. of طَوِيلٌ. (TA.) —— See also سَاقِطٌ. == *A whelp;* syn. جَرْوٌ. (TA.) == It is also said by some to signify *Baked pottery;* but the correct word in this sense is with ش. (TA.)

سُقَاطَةٌ: see سَقَطٌ, in four places.

سَقِيطَةٌ: see سَاقِطٌ, in two places.

سَقَّاطٌ (Ṣ, Ṣgh, L, Ḳ) and ▼ سُقَاطٌ, (Ḳ,) or سَقَّاطٌ وَرَاءَ الضَّرِيبَةِ, (M,) A sword *that falls behind the object struck therewith, cutting it so as to pass to the ground:* (Ṣ, Ḳ:) or *that cuts the object struck therewith, and then reaches to what is after it:* (M, Ḳ:) or *that cleaves so as to reach to the ground after cutting:* (IAạr, M:) or *that passes through the object struck therewith, and then falls.* (Expos. of the Deewán of the Hudhalees.) == See سَقَّطِىٌّ, in two places.

سُقَّيْطٌ i. q. حَبُّ العَزِيزِ [*The small tubercles that compose the root of the cyperus esculentus:* or *that plant itself*]. (TA.)

سُقَّاطَةٌ [*A door-latch;*] *a thing that is put over the upper part of a door, and that falls upon it, so that it becomes fastened.* (TA.)

سَاقِطٌ *Falling; falling down; dropping; dropping down; tumbling down;* as also ▼ سَقُوطٌ; (M, Ḳ;) which latter is both masc. and fem. (M, TA.) —— ▼ سَاقِطَةٌ [its fem., as an epithet in which the quality of a subst. predominates,] *A fruit that falls before maturity:* pl. سَوَاقِطُ: which also signifies *what falls from palm-trees:* or *branches that fall;* not fruits. (Mgh.) —— هُوَ سَاقِطٌ فِى يَدِهِ: see مَسْقُوطٌ. —— لِكُلِّ سَاقِطَةٍ ▼ لَاقِطَةٌ ‡ *For every saying that falls from one, there is a person who will take it up:* (Mṣb:) or *for every word that falls from the mouth of the speaker, there is a person who will hear it and pick it up and publish it:* a prov., relating to the guarding of the tongue: (TA:) the ة in لاقطة is either to give intensiveness to the meaning or for the purpose of assimilation. (Mṣb.) —— سَوَاقِطُ ▼ مِنْ حَرٍّ ‡ *Fallings of heat.* (M, TA.) [See 1, near the end of the paragraph.] —— سَاقِطٌ also signifies *Hanging down; pendent; pendulous:* and the pl. is سُقَّاطٌ. (TA.) —— [And *Tottering* by reason of age.] You say شَيْخٌ سَاقِطٌ كِبَرًا [*An old man tottering by reason of age*]. (Ḳ in art. دوهر.) —— Also † *Low, ignoble, base, vile,* or *mean, in respect of the deeds or qualities of his ancestors, and of himself;* (Ṣ, Mgh;) and so ▼ سَاقِطَةٌ: (Ṣ:) or, † *in respect of the deeds or qualities of his ancestors, and of his race;* and so ▼ سَاقِطَةٌ: (TA:) † one who is *not reckoned among the better,* or *best, class of young men;* as also ▼ سَقَطٌ: (Ḳ:) ‡ one *who is,* or *remains, behind,* or *in the rear of, other men:* (M, Ḳ:) [*obscure, unnoted, reputeless,* or *of no reputation:*] pl. سُقَّاطٌ (Ṣ, Mgh, TA) and سَقْطَى (Ṣ, TA) and سِقَاطٌ, which last is like نِيَامٌ as pl. of نَائِمٌ, and سُقَطَآءُ, [by rule a pl. of سَقِيطٌ, which see in what follows,] and ▼ سَوَاقِطُ [is pl. of سَاقِطَةٌ]. (TA.) The epithets سَاقِطٌ مَاقِطٌ لَاقِطٌ are used together, as signifying † *Low, ignoble, base, vile,* or *mean;* applied to a man; as is said in the L: or, accord. to the O, [and the Ṣ in art. مقط,] the Arabs say, in reviling, فُلَانٌ سَاقِطُ بْنُ مَاقِطِ بْنِ لَاقِطٍ, meaning *Such a one is a slave of a slave of a slave of a freedman, son of a slave of a slave of a freedman, son of a slave of a freedman;* the ساقط being the slave of the ماقط, and the ماقط being the slave of the لاقط, and the لاقط being the slave of the freedman. (TA.) سُقَّاطُ النَّاسِ signifies, accord. to IAạr, † *The refuse, rabble,* or *lowest* or *basest* or *meanest sort, of mankind,* or *of people;* (TA in art. خشر;) as also ▼ سَقَطُ النَّاسِ, (TA,) and ▼ أَسْقَاطُ النَّاسِ, as being likened to those articles of a tent or house which are termed سَقَطٌ, q. v.: (Lḥ, M:) and سُقَّاطُ الجُنْدِ † *Soldiers of whom no account is made.* (TA.) ▼ سَاقِطَةٌ, (M, L, TA,) in the Ḳ ▼ سَقِيطَةٌ, but this is a mistake, (TA,) or, applied to a man, only used when immediately followed by لَقِيطَةٌ, (TA in art. لقط,) also signifies † *Deficient in intellect,* or *intelligence,* or *understanding;* (M, L, Ḳ;) as also ▼ سَقِيطٌ; (Ez-Zejjájee, M, L, Ḳ;) and ▼ سَقِيطَةٌ is the fem. of the latter; (M, L, TA;) and signifies also, applied to a woman, † *Low, ignoble, base, vile,* or *mean,* (Ṣ, TA,) *and stupid.* (So in some copies of the Ṣ, and in the TA.) You say also, هُوَ سَاقِطَةٌ ▼ الفِعْلِ, † [*He is mean in conduct:* or *one of whose actions no account is made*]. (TA.) —— Also, [as signifying † *Vile, mean,* or *paltry,*] applied to a thing: (TA in art. لقط:) [a thing] † *falling short of the due,* or *just, mean.* (M in art. وسط.) —— سَاقِطُ الشَّدِّ † A horse *that runs interruptedly.* (A, TA.) —— ▼ سَوَاقِطُ ‡ *Persons who come to El-Yemámeh to bring thence for themselves provisions of dates.* (M, Ḳ, TA.) —— And ▼ this last word, † *Small, low mountains,* [*as though*] *cleaving to the ground.* (TA.)

سَاقِطَةٌ, and its pl. سَوَاقِطُ: see سَاقِطٌ, throughout.

أَسْقَاطِىٌّ † *One who sells the parts of a slaughtered beast that are called* سَقَطٌ [q. v.]. (TA.) [See also سَقَطِىٌّ.]

مَسْقَطٌ (Ṣ, M, Ḳ) and مَسْقِطٌ, (M, Ḳ,) the former extr. [with respect to rule, though the contr. with respect to usage], (M,) and the latter an inf. n. as well as a noun of place [and of time], (Ṣ, Ḳ,) *A place* [and *a time*] *of falling, falling down, dropping, dropping down,* or *tumbling down,* (Ṣ, M, Ḳ,) of a thing; (M, TA;) as, for instance, of a whip, and of rain: pl. مَسَاقِطُ. (TA.) —— مَسْقِطُ الرَّأْسِ, (Ḳ,) and مَسْقَطُهُ, (Aṣ,) and المسقط alone, (A, TA,) ‡ *The place of birth.* (Ḳ, TA.) You say, هٰذَا مَسْقِطُ رَأْسِى ‡ *This is my birth-place.* (Ṣ.) And البَصْرَةُ مَسْقِطُ رَأْسِى ‡ [*El-Basrah is my birth-place*]. (M.) And هُوَ يَحِنُّ إِلَى مَسْقِطِهِ ‡ *He yearns towards his birth-place.* (A, TA.) —— أَتَانَا فِى مَسْقِطِ النَّجْمِ ‡ *He came to us at the time of the setting of the star,* or *asterism;* (Ṣ, TA;) [meaning, *at the time of the auroral setting of the Pleiades:* see مَنَازِلُ القَمَرِ, in art. نزل.] —— مَسْقِطٌ also signifies The *place of the ending* of anything. (TA.) See سِقْطٌ, in three places.

مُسْقِطٌ *Casting her young one or fœtus; bringing it forth abortively,* or *in an immature,* or *imperfect, state,* (M, Ḳ,) [or *dead, but having the form developed,* or *manifest:* see 4.]

هٰذَا الفِعْلُ مَسْقَطَةٌ لِلْإِنْسَانِ مِنْ أَعْيُنِ النَّاسِ ‡ [*This deed is a cause of a man's falling from the place which he holds in the regard of people*]: (Ṣ, Ḳ:*) said when one does a thing that is not proper for him to do. (TA.)

مِسْقَاطٌ *Accustomed to cast her young; to bring them forth abortively,* or *in an immature,* or *imperfect, state,* (Ḳ,) [or *dead, but having the form developed,* or *manifest:* see 4.]

تَمْرَةٌ مَسْقُوطَةٌ [*A fallen date*]: some say that this means سَاقِطَةٌ: others, ذَاتُ سُقُوطٍ [*having a falling*]: it may be from أَسْقَطَهُ; like مَحْمُومٌ from أَحَمَّهُ اللّٰهُ. (TA.) —— هُوَ مَسْقُوطٌ فِى يَدِهِ ‡ *He is repenting, and abject;* as also سَاقِطٌ ▼ فِى يَدِهِ. (TA.)

مَشَى مُتَسَاقِطًا ‡ [*He walked,* or *went, in a slack,* or *languid, manner; as though repeatedly stumbling;* or *as though throwing himself down:* see 3, near the end; and see also 6]. (A in art. طرح.)

سقف

1. سَقَفَ البَيْتَ, (Ṣ, O, Mṣb, Ḳ,) aor. ـُ, (Ṣ, O, Mṣb,) or ـِ, (Ḳ, [but this is app. a mistake, being anomalous,]) inf. n. سَقْفٌ, (Ṣ, O, Mgh,) *He made a* سَقْف [i. e. *ceiling,* or *roof,*] *to the house* or *chamber* or *tent;* [*he ceiled it,* or *roofed it;*] (Ṣ,

O, Mṣb, Ḳ;) as also ▼ اسقفه; (Mṣb;) and ▼ سقّفه, inf. n. تَسْقِيفٌ; (O, Ḳ;) or this last has an intensive signification. (Mṣb.) — سَقِفَ, [aor. ـَ,] inf. n. سَقَفٌ, *He was*, or *became, tall, and bent*, or *bowed;* said of a man, and of an ostrich, &c. (TA.) — See also 5.

2: see 1. — سُقِّفَ, inf. n. تَسْقِيفٌ, *He was made an* أُسْقُفّ [i. e. *a bishop*]. (O, Ḳ.)

4: see 1.

5. تسقّف *He became an* أُسْقُفّ [i. e. *a bishop*]; (O, Ḳ;) as also ▼ سقف [app. سَقَّفَ], inf. n. سِقِّيفَى [like خِلِّيفَى inf. n. of خَلَفَ]. (TḲ.)

سَقْفٌ The *ceiling, roof*, or *covering*, (JK, MA, PṢ,) of a house or chamber or tent; (JK, Ṣ, MA, Ḳ, PṢ;) as also ▼ سَقِيفٌ; (Ḳ;) so called because of its height, and the tallness of its wall [or walls]: (TA:) pl. of the former سُقُوفٌ and سُقُفٌ, (Ṣ, Mṣb, Ḳ,) the latter pl. on the authority of Akh, (Ṣ,) extr., (Mṣb,) or, accord. to Fr, this is pl. of ▼ سَقِيفٌ, (Ṣ, Mṣb, TA,) or, accord. to Fr, it may be a pl. pl., i. e. you may say سَقْفٌ and سُقُوفٌ and [then] سُقُفٌ [as pl. of سُقُوفٌ], (TA,) and سُقْفٌ [also] is a pl. of سَقْفٌ. (Ḥam p. 227.) [In the Ḳur xliii. 32,] Aboo-Jaạfar read سَقْفًا مِنْ فِضَّةٍ; with fet-ḥ: (TA:) others read سُقُفًا: (Ṣ, TA:) in the former reading, it is a sing. denoting a pl. meaning; i. e., "we would have made to the house of every one of them a سَقْف of silver." (TA.) — [Hence,] The *sky*, or *heaven:* (Ṣ, Ḳ:) this is called سَقْفُ الأَرْضِ [*the ceiling*, or *roof, of the earth*]: of the masc. gender: occurring in the Ḳur xxi. 33 and lii. 5. (TA.) — Also, applied to the لَحْى [or part on which the beard grows] *Long, and flaccid*, or *pendulous;* syn. طَوِيلٌ مُسْتَرْخٍ. (Ṣ, Ḳ.) — See also أُسْقُفٌّ.

سُقْفٌ: see أُسْقُفٌّ. — Also a pl. of سَقْفٌ [q. v.: perhaps a contraction of سُقُفٌ]. (Ḥam p. 227.)

سَقَفٌ *Tallness, with a bending*, or *bowing:* (Ṣ, Ḳ:) it is in a man, (Ṣ,) [and] in an ostrich &c. (Ḳ.) [See 1, second sentence.]

السُّقَّفَآءُ in the saying of El-Ḥajjáj, إِيَّاىَ وَهٰذِهِ السُّقَّفَآءَ [Beware ye of *me with respect to these* سقفاء], (Ṣ, Ḳ,* TA,) is [said to be] a word of which the meaning is unknown: (Ṣ:) Ḳt says, "I have asked often respecting it, and no one knew it:" but accord. to Z, as is related by IAth, (TA,) it is said to be a mistranscription for الشُّفَعَآءُ, (Ḳ,* TA,) pl. of شَفِيعٌ; (TA;) for they used to assemble in the presence of the Sultán and intercede for him who was suspected, (Ḳ, TA,) and for criminals; and he [i. e. El-Ḥajjáj] forbade their doing that. (TA.)

سَقِيفٌ: see سَقْفٌ, in two places: — and see also the paragraph here following, in two places.

سَقِيفَةٌ *A* صُفَّة, (Ṣ, Mṣb, Ḳ, TA,) or *the like*, (TA,) [i. e. a *roof*, or *covering*,] *such as projects* [*over the door of a house*], (TA,) [or *of which the ends of the beams rest upon opposite houses;* i. e.] *a* ظُلَّة; [often applied in the present day to *a roofed*, or *covered, portion of a street* or *the like;*] and *any wing* or *porch* or *other thing* [*of a building*] *that is roofed over:* (Mṣb:) of the measure فَعِيلَةٌ in the sense of the measure مَفْعُولَةٌ: (TA:) pl. سَقَائِفُ (Mṣb) and [coll. gen. n.] ▼ سَقِيفٌ. (MA.) — *Any broad piece of wood, such as a plank*, or *a broad piece of stone, with which one may form a roof* (O, Ḳ, TA) *to the lurking-place of a hunter &c.* (O, TA.) And [the pl.] سَقَائِفُ signifies The طوايق [app. a mistranscription for طَوَابِقُ, and, if so, meaning, agreeably with a modern usage, *flat stones covering a hollow such as that*] *of the lurking-place of the hunter.* (TA.) [And The *pieces of wood which form the roof of the kind of vehicle called* مَحْمِل: see عَارِضَةٌ: and see also خُذْرُوفٌ.] — ‡ *A plank* [app. *of the deck*] *of a ship* or *boat:* (Ṣ, Ḳ, TA:) pl. as above. (Ṣ, TA.) — ‡ *A single cranial bone* of the head of the camel: (Ibn-'Abbád, Ḳ, TA:) the cranial bones being termed سَقَائِفُ الرَّأْسِ. (Ibn-'Abbád, TA.) — And ‡ *A single rib* of a camel: (Ḳ, TA:) its ribs being termed سَقَائِفُ (Az, Z, O, TA) and ▼ سَقِيفٌ. (O, TA.) One says, هَدَمَ السَّفَرُ سَقَائِفَ البَعِيرِ [*Travel disjointed*, or *luxated*,] *the ribs of the camel.* (Az, Z, TA.) — Also ‡ *A splint;* i. e. *a piece of wood with which a bone is set*, or *reduced from a fractured state:* (O, Ḳ, TA:) pl. as above. (O, TA.) — And *A broad and long piece of wood, which is put*, or *laid down, and upon which are wound the mats of reeds* (البَوَارِىّ) *above the house-tops of the people of El-Baṣrah.* (TA. [See also سَفِيفَةٌ.]) — And † *Any piece of gold*, and *of silver, that is beaten thin and long.* (TA. [See, again, سَفِيفَةٌ.])

سَقَّافٌ *One whose occupation is the construction of ceilings or roofs* (سُقُوف). (TA.)

سِقِّيفَى [and ▼ أُسْقُفِيَّةٌ or أُسْقُفِّيَّةٌ] The *office of an* أُسْقُفّ [i. e. *of a bishop*]. (Ḳ,* O, TA.) [See also 5.]

أَسْقَفُ *Tall, and bent*, or *bowed;* (Ṣ, Ḳ;) applied to a man, (Ṣ, TA,) and to an ostrich, &c.; (Ḳ, TA;) as also with ḍamm, (Ḳ,) i. e. ▼ أُسْقُفٌ: (TA:) fem. سَقْفَآءُ, (Ḳ,) mentioned by IB as an epithet applied to a female ostrich: (TA:) and hence the ▼ أُسْقُفّ of the Christians, (Ṣ, Ḳ,) accord. to ISk [and others ignorant of its true derivation], because he affects lowliness. (Ṣ.) And, applied to a man, [simply,] *Tall;* (Ḳ;) likened to the سَقْف [or ceiling, or roof,] in height; (TA;) and so ▼ مُسَقَّفٌ: (O, Ḳ:) or *thick and big in the bones:* (Ḳ:) and [simply] *bent*, or *bowed:* (TA:) and, applied to an ostrich, *crooked in the neck* (Ḳ, TA) *and the legs:* (TA:) fem. as above; (Ḳ;) which is applied to a female ostrich as meaning *long and crooked in the legs:* (O:) or to a she-camel as meaning *long in the hind legs*, and in like manner applied to a she-ostrich. (JK.) — And, applied to a camel, *Having no fur upon him.* (Ḳ.)

أُسْقُفٌ: see the next preceding paragraph: — and the next following also.

أُسْقُفّ and ▼ أُسْقُفٌ, (Ṣ, Mṣb, Ḳ,) as also ▼ سُقْفٌ (Ḳ) and ▼ سُقُفٌ, (TA,) [each a variation of] a foreign word used by the Arabs, (TA,) [from the Greek ἐπίσκοπος, *A bishop;* i. e.] *a headman of the Christians* (Ṣ, Mṣb, Ḳ) *in religion;* (Ṣ, Ḳ;) or [more exactly] *one who is above the* قِسِّيس [i. e. *presbyter*, or *priest*], *and below the* مَطْرَان [or *metropolitan*]: (Ḳ:) or *one who is learned* (Ḳ, TA) *in their religion:* (TA:) or *a king who affects lowliness in his gait:* (Ḳ: [a very strange explanation:]) pl. أَسَاقِفَةٌ (Mṣb, Ḳ) and أَسَاقِفُ. (Ḳ.) See also أَسْقَفُ.

أُسْقُفِيَّةٌ or أُسْقُفِّيَّةٌ: see سِقِّيفَى.

مُسَقَّفٌ *Wide in the bone* [or *bones*] *of the body.* (JK.) — See also أَسْقَفُ.

شَعَرٌ مُسْقَنْفِفٌ, (Ḳ accord. to the TA,) or ▼ مُسْتَقِفٌ, (so in several copies of the Ḳ,) or both, (TḲ,) *Hair that is raised, and shaggy*, or *dishevelled*, or *disordered.* (Ḳ.)

مُسْتَقِفٌ: see what next precedes.

سقم

1. سَقِمَ, aor. ـَ; (Ṣ, Mṣb, Ḳ;) and سَقُمَ, aor. ـُ; (Mṣb, Ḳ;) inf. n. سَقَمٌ, (Ṣ, Mṣb, TA,) of the former verb; (Ṣ, Mṣb;) and سُقْمٌ, of the latter verb, (Mṣb,) and سَقَامَةٌ and سَقَامٌ, (TA,) [also of the latter verb, the last like جَمَالٌ of جَمُلَ, &c.,] or the last is a simple subst.; (Mṣb;) *He was*, or *became, diseased, disordered, distempered, sick*, or *ill;* syn. مَرِضَ: (Ṣ, Ḳ, TA:) or *he was long diseased* &c. (Mṣb.) [See also سَقَمٌ below.]

2: see what next follows.

4. اسقمهُ, (Ṣ, Mṣb, TA,) inf. n. إِسْقَامٌ; (TA;) and ▼ سقّمهُ, (Mṣb, TA,) inf. n. تَسْقِيمٌ; (TA;) *He* (God) [or *it*] *caused him to be*, or *become, diseased, disordered, distempered, sick*, or *ill:* (Ṣ, TA:) or *caused him to be long diseased* &c. (Mṣb.) — And أَسْقَمَ الرَّجُلُ *The man had his family affected with diseases, and the diseases came afterwards upon him.* (TA.)

سُقْمٌ and ▼ سَقَمٌ and ▼ سَقَامٌ [are all inf. ns.; or the last, accord. to the Mṣb, is a simple subst.; and all are used as substs., signifying] *A disease, disorder, distemper, malady, sickness*, or *an illness;* syn. مَرَضٌ: (Ṣ, Ḳ, TA:) سُقْمٌ and مَرَضٌ are both said to be in the body, and also † in religion [&c., as is implied by phrases mentioned below, voce سَقِيمٌ]: (Aboo-Is-ḥák, TA in art. مرض:) pl. [of the first] أَسْقَامٌ. (TA.) ▼ سَقَمُ الجُفُونِ means † *Languidness, and slowness in motion, of the eyelids.* (Ḥar p. 113.)

سَقَمٌ: see the next preceding paragraph, in two places.

سَقِيمٌ: see سَقِمٌ.

سِقَامٌ : see سُقْمٌ.

سَقِيمٌ *Diseased, disordered, distempered, sick,* or *ill;* (Ṣ, Ḳ, TA;) as also ↓ سَقِمٌ: (TA:) or *long diseased* &c.: (Mṣb:) pl. of the former سِقَامٌ, (Mṣb, Ḳ,) like كِرَامٌ pl. of كَرِيمٌ. (Mṣb.) See also مِسْقَامٌ, and مُسْقِمٌ. The phrase إِنِّى سَقِيمٌ occurring in the Ḳur [xxxvii. 87], as a saying of Abraham, is expl. by some as meaning [*Verily I am*] *smitten with the* طَاعُون [or *pestilence*]: or the meaning is, *I shall be diseased* at a future time, when the period shall have come; and it is said that he inferred, from looking at the stars, the time of a fever's coming to him: or it means † *verily I am sick of your worshipping what is not God:* IAth says that, in truth, it is one of his three lies; all of which were for the sake of God and his religion. (TA.) You say also قَلْبٌ سَقِيمٌ ‡ [*A diseased, a sickly,* or *an unsound, heart*]: and فَهْمٌ سَقِيمٌ ‡ [*Diseased, unsound, faulty,* or *weak, understanding*]: and كَلَامٌ سَقِيمٌ ‡ [*Unsound, faulty,* or *weak, language*]. (TA.) And هُوَ سَقِيمُ الصَّدْرِ عَلَيْهِ ‡ *He is affected with rancour, malevolence, malice,* or *spite, against him.* (TA.)

سَوْقَمٌ *A kind of tree resembling the* خِلَاف [q. v.], *but not the same as this latter:* (TA:) or *a kind of large tree,* (AḤn, Ḳ, TA,) *exactly like the* أَثْأَب, (AḤn, TA,) *which is a tree of the fig-kind,* (TA in art. ثأب,) *except that it is taller than the latter, and less broad, having a fruit like the fig* (التِّين), *which, when green, is* [*like*] *stone in hardness, but when it ripens it becomes somewhat yellow, and soft, and very sweet, and of a pleasant odour, and people send it, one to another, as a present.* (AḤn, TA.) [Forskål, in his Flora Aegypt. Arab., p. cxxiv., mentions سقم, which is evidently a mistranscription for سوقم, and which he writes in Italic letters "sokam," as one of the names of the *ficus sycomorus;* and app. of another species or variety of fig which he terms *ficus sycomoroides.*]

رَجُلٌ سَقِيمٌ ↓ مُسْقِمٌ *A man who is diseased and whose family are diseased.* (TA.)

مَسْقَمَةٌ [*A cause of disease:* a word of the same class as مَجْبَنَةٌ and many others of the measure مَفْعَلَةٌ]: see an ex. voce كِظَّةٌ.

مِسْقَامٌ *i. q.* ↓ سَقِيمٌ [*Diseased, disordered,* &c.]: (TA:) or [rather, agreeably with analogy,] *much,* or *often, diseased* &c.: (Ṣ, TA:) and accord. to Lḥ it is also applied as an epithet to a female. (TA.)

سقمونيا

سَقَمُونِيَا, (so in copies of the Ḳ,) or سَقْمُونِيَا, (Mgh, Mṣb,) said to be an ancient Greek word, [Σκαμμωνία,] or, as some say, (Mṣb,) Syriac, (Mgh, Mṣb,) [*Scammony;*] *a certain plant, from the hollows of which is extracted a mucilage, which is dried, and is called by the name of its plant: it is more repugnant to the stomach and the bowels than all the laxatives; but it is rendered good by aromatic substances, such as pepper and ginger and aniseed: the weight of six barley-corns thereof to twenty eases the yellow bile, and noxious viscosities, from the most remote parts of the body; and a portion thereof with a portion of* تُرْبُد, or تَرْبَد, [so in different copies of the Ḳ, or تُرْبَذ, or تُرْبِد, i. e. *turpeth,*] *in fresh milk, taken fasting, will not leave a single worm in the belly: it is wonderful in that effect, and proved by experiment.* (Ḳ.)

سقى

1. سَقَاهُ, aor. يَسْقِيهِ, (Ḳ,) inf. n. سَقْىٌ; (TA; [see also سِقَايَةٌ, which is likewise said to be an inf. n. of the same verb;]) and ↓ سَقَّاهُ, (Ḳ,) with teshdeed; (TA;) and ↓ اسقاهُ; (Ḳ, TA; [in the CḲ, erroneously, اسْتَقَاهُ;]) all have one meaning; (TA;) [i. e. *He gave him to drink,* generally water, often milk, and sometimes poison or some other thing: and the first often signifies *he watered him,* namely, a beast; and in like manner seed produce &c., i. e. *irrigated it;* as will be shown by what follows:] or سَقَاهُ [is said when you mean *he gave him drink*] لِشَفَتِهِ [*to his lip*], (Ṣ,) or بِالشَّفَةِ [*by means of the lip*], as also ↓ سَقَّاهُ; and ↓ اسقاهُ means *he directed him to water,* (Ḳ,) or *he watered* (سَقَى) *his cattle* or *his land:* (Ṣ,* Ḳ:) or both of them, (Ḳ, TA,) i. e. سَقَاهُ and ↓ اسقاهُ, (TA,) signify *he assigned to him, or gave to him,* (جَعَلَ لَهُ,) *water,* (Ḳ, TA,) or *drink,* or *water for irrigation;* so that سَقَاهُ is like كَسَاهُ, and ↓ اسقى is like أَلْبَسَ, as Sb says: (TA:) or, as some say, سَقَيْتُهُ *I gave him water to his mouth;* and ↓ أَسْقَيْتُهُ, *I assigned to him,* or *gave to him,* (جَعَلْتُ لَهُ,) *drink,* or *water for irrigation, that he might do as he would;* and like them are كَسَوْتُهُ and أَكْسَيْتُهُ: (Ḥam p. 45:) Er-Rághib says that السَّقْىُ signifies *the giving* one *drink;* and ↓ الإِسْقَآءُ, *the giving* one *drink so that he may take it howsoever he will;* so that the latter is more ample in meaning than the former. (TA.) Both سَقَى and ↓ اسقى are sometimes used in relation to what is in the bellies of camels or other cattle; [meaning their milk;] as in the Ḳur [xxiii. 21], where it is said, نُسْقِيكُمْ ↓ مِمَّا فِى بُطُونِهَا, or نَسْقِيكُمْ, [i. e. *We give you to drink of what is in their bellies,*] accord. to different readings. (TA.) One says, سَقَاهُ المَآءَ, [*He gave him to drink water,* or *the water,*] inf. n. as above: (Mgh:) and سَقَّيْتُهُ ↓ المَآءَ [*I gave him to drink water,* or *the water, much,* or *often*]: the teshdeed denotes muchness, or frequency. (Ṣ.) [See also a tropical usage of the former verb in a verse cited in p. 85, col. 3: and another, from Ṭarafeh, in p. 134, col. 3. One says also, سَقَى المَآءَ, without a second objective complement, *He supplied,* or *gave, water,* or *the water.*] And سَقَيْتُ الزَّرْعَ, [*I watered,* or *irrigated, the seed-produce,*] inf. n. as above; as also ↓ أَسْقَيْتُهُ, (Mṣb.) And سَقَيْتُ فِى القِرْبَةِ and ↓ أَسْقَيْتُ فِيهَا [*I poured water into the water-skin*]: a poet says, [in one of my copies of the Ṣ, Dhu-r-Rummeh,]

وَمَا شَنَّتَا خَرْقَآءَ وَاهٍ كُلَاهُمَا •
سَقَى فِيهِمَا مُسْتَعْجِلٌ لَمْ تَبَلَّلَا •
بِأَضْيَعَ مِنْ عَيْنَيْكَ لِلدَّمْعِ كُلَّمَا •
تَعَرَّفْتَ دَارًا أَوْ تَوَهَّمْتَ مَنْزِلَا •

[*And two old and worn-out skins of an unskilful woman* who has not sewed them well, *each of them unsound, into which a person in haste has poured water, they not having been* previously *moistened,* (تَبَلَّلَا being for تَتَبَلَّلَا,) *are not more liable to the shedding of their water than are thine eyes* to the shedding *of tears whenever thou investigatest a dwelling or imaginest a place of alighting,* or *abode*]. (Ṣ.) [And hence, app.,] سَقَى فُلَانٌ فِى ذَكَرِهِ † *Such a one became vehemently affected by sexual appetite.* (JK.) One says also, سَقَاهُ ٱللّٰهُ الغَيْثَ and ↓ اسقاهُ (Ṣ, Mṣb,* Ḳ) *God sent down rain to him,* or *may God send* &c.: (Ḳ:) both of these verbs being used by Lebeed in his saying,

سَقَى قَوْمِى بَنِى مَجْدٍ وَأَسْقَى •
نُمَيْرًا وَالقَبَائِلَ مِنْ هِلَالِ •

[*May He send down rain to my people, the sons of Mejd, and may He send down rain to Numeyr, and the tribes of Hilál*]. (Ṣ.) [Hence,] one says, سَقَى ٱللّٰهُ عَصْرَ الشَّبِيبَةِ † [*May God freshen as with rain the times,* or *mornings,* or *afternoons, of youth,* or *young manhood*]. (A and TA in art. شب.) And سَقَيْتُ فُلَانًا, (Ṣ,) and ↓ أَسْقَيْتُهُ, and ↓ سَقَّيْتُهُ, (Ṣ, Ḳ,*) which last is the form in most repute as expressive of a prayer, (Ḥam p. 45,) and of which the inf. n. is تَسْقِيَةٌ, (Ḳ,) *I said to such a one* سَقَاكَ ٱللّٰهُ [*May God send down rain to thee*], (Ṣ and Ḳ in explanation of the second and third,) or سَقْيًا [which virtually means the same, for سَقَاكَ ٱللّٰهُ سَقْيًا]: (Ṣ in explanation of the first and second, and Ḳ in explanation of the second and third:) [or,] accord. to some, one says سَقَيْتُهُ when it [which he gives, i. e. water or the like,] is in his hand; [agreeably with the first explanation in this art.;] and ↓ أَسْقَيْتُهُ signifies *I prayed for him, saying* سَقْيًا لَكَ. (Mṣb.) — سَقَى بَطْنُهُ, (JK, Ṣ, MA, Ḳ,) inf. n. سَقْىٌ; (JK, Ṣ;) and سَقِىَ, (JK, IAth, TA,) or سُقِىَ, aor. يَسْقَى, inf. n. سَقًى or سِقًى; (MA;) and ↓ استسقى; (JK, Ṣ, Ḳ; [in my copy of the Mṣb استقى, which I doubt not to be a mistranscription, as the verb most commonly known in the sense here following is استسقى, and as this is not there mentioned;]) *His belly* [*was,* or *became, diseased with dropsy,* i. e.] *had yellow water* [meaning *serum*] (JK, Ṣ, Mṣb, Ḳ,* TA) *apparent in it,* (JK,) or *collected in it;* (Ṣ, Ḳ, TA;) for which there is scarcely, or never, any cure; (Mṣb, TA;) *his belly became swollen* [*with dropsy*]. (MA.) — [In the phrase written in the CḲ سَقَى قَلْبَهُ عَدَاوَةً, the verb is correctly سَقَّى: see 2.] — سَقَى العَرَقُ *The sweat flowed without stopping.* (TA.) — سَقَى الثَّوْبَ, and ↓ سَقَّاهُ, *He made the garment,* or *piece of cloth, to imbibe a dye.* (TA.) — [سَقَى also signifies *He tempered* steel; and is used in this sense in the present day: and accord. to a reading in one of my copies of the Ṣ, in art. شرخ, ▼ سقى also has this meaning.] —— See also 4, last sentence.

2: see 1, in six places. —— سُقِّىَ قَلْبُهُ عَدَاوَةً, (Ḳ, TA, [in the CḲ, erroneously, سُقِىَ,]) and بِالعَدَاوَةِ, (TA, and thus, and thus only, in the JK,) inf. n. تَسْقِيَةٌ, (JK, TA,) ‡ *His heart was made to imbibe enmity*, (Ḳ, TA,) is said of a man to whom a thing that he dislikes, or hates, has been repeatedly done. (TA.)

3. مُسَاقَاةٌ [*The giving to drink, one with another*. See a tropical usage of its verb in an ex. cited in art. شف, conj. 8. ——] *The drawing of water together.* (KL.) —— And a man's *employing a man to take upon himself*, or *manage, the culture* [or *watering* &c.] *of palm-trees* or *grape-vines* [or *the like*] *on the condition of his having a certain share of their produce*: (Ṣ, TA:) Az says that the people of El-'Irák term it مُعَامَلَةٌ. (TA.)

4: see 1, in thirteen places. —— One says also, أَسْقَيْتُهُ رَكِيَّتِى *I assigned to him my well* [*to draw water therefrom*]: and أَسْقَيْتُهُ جَدْوَلًا مِنْ نَهْرِى *I assigned to him* [*a streamlet as*] *a place*, or *source, of irrigation, from my river*, or *rivulet*; and أَسْقَيْتُ لَهُ مِنْهُ [which means the same]. (TA.) —— And اسقاهُ *It produced in him* [*dropsy*, or] *yellow water*. (JK. [See 1, near the end of the paragraph.]) —— And *He gave him a made* [*skin such as is termed*] سِقَآء: (Az, Ḳ, TA: [it is said in the TA that وَهَبَ مِنْهُ in the Ḳ should be وَهَبَ لَهُ, as in the explanation by Az: but see art. وهب, in which it is said that وهب منه is allowable, and occurs in several trads.:]) or *he gave him a hide to make of it a* سِقَآء: (Ḳ:) or اسقاه إِهَابًا has the latter meaning: (JK, TA:) and أَسْقِ إِهَابَهَا occurs in a trad. as meaning *Give thou its hide to him who will make of it a* سِقَآء, (TA,) or *make thou its hide to be a* سِقَآء *for thee*. (JK.) —— Also, (JK, Ṣ, Ḳ, TA,) and ▼ سَقَّاهُ, (Ḳ,) the latter mentioned as on the authority of IAạr, but disallowed by Sh, (TA,) *i. q.* اِغْتَابَهُ ‡ [*He spoke evil of him, or traduced him, in his absence or otherwise*], (JK, Ṣ, Ḳ, TA,) *in a foul manner*; (TA;) and *imputed to him a vice, fault, or the like*: (Ṣ, TA:) and J cites [in the Ṣ] a verse of Ibn-Aḥmar ending with the phrase أَسْقَى ▼ سِقَائِيَا [app. as meaning † *Who has spoken evil of me*, &c.]. (TA.)

5. تسقّى *It* (a thing) *received*, or *admitted, moisture*, (M, TA,) or *irrigation*; or *became plentifully irrigated*, or *succulent*, or *sappy*. (M, Ḳ, TA.) The Hudhalee (El-Mutanakhkhil, TA) says,

• مُجَدَّلٌ يَتَسَقَّى جِلْدُهُ دَمَهُ •
• كَمَا تَقَطَّرَ جِذْعُ الدَّوْمَةِ القُطُلُ •

meaning [*Thrown down upon the ground, his skin*] *becomes drenched with his blood* (يَتَشَرَّبُهُ) [*like as drips the severed trunk of the Theban palm-tree*]: or, as some relate the verse, يَتَكَسَّى [*becomes overspread*, here meaning *suffused*], from الكِسْوَةُ. (Ṣ, TA.) —— تَسَقَّتِ الإِبِلُ الحَوْذَانَ † *The camels ate the* حوذان (a certain plant, TA) *in its fresh and moist state, and became fat upon it*. (Ḳ.)

6. تَسَاقَوْا *They gave to drink, one to another*, (Ṣ, MA, TA,) *with the full measure of the vessel in which they were given to drink*. (Ṣ, TA.) [See also 3.]

8. استقى *He drew water* (TA) مِنَ البِئْرِ [*from the well*], (Ṣ, TA,) and مِنَ النَّهْرِ [*from the river*, or *rivulet*]. (TA. [Golius and Freytag make the verb in this sense, erroneously, استسقى; but the former mentions استقى also in the same sense.]) [And استقى عَلَى بَعِيرٍ *He drew water upon a camel* in a manner expl. voce سَانِيَةٌ, q. v.: often occurring in the Lexicons.] —— And ‡ *He was*, or *became, fat*, (Ḳ, TA,) *and satisfied with drinking of water* (TA.) —— See also 10, in two places.

10. استسقى *He sought*, or *demanded, drink* (سُقْيًا, Ḳ, TA, [in the CḲ سَقْيًا,] i. e. مَا يُشْرَبُ, TA); مِنْهُ [*from him*]; as also ▼ استقى. (Ḳ, TA. [In the CḲ is immediately added after this explanation, وسَقْيًا; but this is a mistranscription for وَتَقَيَّأَ; expressing another signification of these two verbs, which will be expl. below.]) And *He asked, begged*, or *prayed, for rain*; (Mṣb,* TA;) *i. q.* اِسْتَمْطَرَ. (Ṣ in art. مطر, and Mṣb.*) [Hence, صَلَاةُ الاِسْتِسْقَآءِ *The prayer of the petitioning for rain*. And استسقى لَنَا *He said* سَقَاهَا ٱللّٰهُ *May God send down rain upon it*, namely, a land: see Ḥar p. 300.] —— And *He constrained himself to vomit*; or *vomited intentionally*; syn. تَقَيَّأَ; [see a statement above, in this paragraph, respecting a mistranscription in the CḲ;] as also ▼ استقى; (Ḳ, TA;) mentioned by ISd. (TA.) —— See also 1, in the last quarter of the paragraph.

سَقْىٌ in the phrase سَقْىُ الفُرَاتِ, which means *The towns*, or *villages*, [or *lands*,] *watered by the Euphrates*, is said by Mṭr to be an inf. n. used as a subst. [properly so termed, and, being originally an inf. n., it may be used alike as sing. and pl.]; or, in this phrase, a noun that should be prefixed to it [such as ذَاتُ], is suppressed: or, accord. to some, it is سِقْىٌ [q. v.], an instance of the measure فِعْلٌ in the sense of the measure مَفْعُولٌ; and thus it is in the handwriting of El-Ḥareeree in his 22nd Maḳámeh. (Ḥar p. 246.) —— See also the next paragraph.

سِقْىٌ *Drink*; or *what is drunk*; (TA;) or *what is given to drink*; (Ḳ, TA;) a subst. from سَقَاهُ and أَسْقَاهُ; (Ṣ, TA; [in the former of which, this meaning is indicated, and also the meaning of *water given to drink to cattle*; and *water with which land is irrigated*;]) in the M, *drink given to camels*: (TA:) pl. أَسْقِيَةٌ. (Ṣ, TA.) And [particularly] *A share*, or *portion, of water* [*for irrigation*]: one says, كَمْ سِقْىُ أَرْضِكَ [*How many* bucketfuls or skinfuls, (the specificative being suppressed,) virtually meaning *how much, is the share*, or *portion, of water for the irrigation of thy land?*]. (Ṣ, TA.) —— And *Water*, (Ḳ, TA, [in the CḲ ما, a mistranscription for مَآء,]) i. e. *yellow water* [meaning *serum*, effused in dropsy], *incidental in the belly*, (Ḳ, TA,) scarcely, or never, curable; (TA;) as also ▼ سَقْىٌ: (Ḳ: [وَيُفْتَحُ being there added: and the word as meaning "yellow water" is written only with fet-ḥ in the JK: but in the TA, ويفتح forms part of the addition here following:]) or *it is in white* نَفَافِيخ [meaning *cells*] *in the fat of the belly*; [in which sense, also, the word is written only with fet-ḥ in the JK;] *and it* [app. meaning the belly] *is opened* (وَيُفْتَحُ) *on the occasion of its issuing*: so says ISd: (TA:) a subst. from سَقَى بَطْنُهُ [q. v.]. (Ṣ, TA.) And *A skin* [or *membrane*] *containing yellow water, which cleaves asunder from over the head of the young one* [*at the birth*]: (Ḳ, TA:) or, as in the T, *the water that is in the* [*membrane called*] مَشِيمَة, *that comes forth* عَلَى رَأْسِ الوَلَدِ [meaning *at the birth*]. (TA.) ═ Also *Land that is irrigated*; having the meaning of the measure مَفْعُولٌ, like نِقْضٌ [in the sense of مَنْقُوضٌ]: (Er-Rághib, TA: [see also ▼ سَقِىٌّ:]) or it signifies, (Ḳ,) or so ▼ سَقِىٌّ, of the same measure as شَقِىٌّ and صَبِىٌّ, (Mgh,) and ▼ مَسْقَوِىٌّ, (Ṣ, Mgh, Ḳ,) app. a rel. n. from مَسْقًى, not from مُسْقًى, for if it were from the latter it would be مُسْقَوِىٌّ, (M, TA,) [or, accord. to some, if from مُسْقًى, it may be either مُسْقَوِىٌّ or مُسْقِىٌّ, (see Lumsden's Arab. Gr. p. 630,)] *seed-produce irrigated* (Ṣ, Mgh, Ḳ) *by water running upon the surface of the earth*; (Ṣ, Mgh;) [i. e., not by rain only;] ▼ سَقِىٌّ being the contr. of بَخْسِىٌّ; (Mgh;) and ▼ مَسْقَوِىٌّ, *contr. of* مَظْمَئِىٌّ, (Mgh, TA,) which signifies "watered [only] by the rain;" and the vulgar say ▼ مِسْقَاوِى. (TA.)

بَطْنٌ سَقٍ *A belly swollen* [*with dropsy*]. (MA.)

سُقْيَا *A giving of drink*; [or *a giving to drink*;] like [the inf. n.] سَقْىٌ. (Er-Rághib, TA.) —— And *A sending down of rain* upon mankind and the lands: (TA:) a subst. from سَقَاهُ ٱللّٰهُ الغَيْثَ. (Ṣ, Ḳ,* TA.*) One says, دَعَوْتُ لَهُ بِالسُّقْيَا [*I prayed for him for the sending down of rain*]. (JK.) And it is said in a form of prayer, سُقْيَا رَحْمَةٍ وَلَا سُقْيَا عَذَابٍ [We ask of Thee *a sending down of a rain of mercy, and not a sending down of a rain of punishment*]; meaning, send Thou down upon us a rain in which shall be benefit, without injury, and without laying waste. (Mṣb.) One says also أَرْضٌ خَافِضَةُ السُّقْيَا *Land easy of irrigation* [either by the rain or otherwise]: (Ḳ in art. خفض:) and the contr. is termed رَافِعَةُ السُّقْيَا. (TA in that art.) —— Also i. q. شرب [i. e. شِرْبٌ, meaning *A beast's share*, or *portion, of water*]: so in the Ḳur xci. 13. (Jel.)

سِقَآءٌ *A skin*, (KL,) or *a* قِرْبَة, (JK,) [i. e.] *a skin of a young goat or sheep when it has entered its second year*, (M, Ḳ,) *used for water* and *for milk*, (ISk, JK, Ṣ, Mṣb, Ḳ, KL,) or, accord. to ISd, *only for water*: (TA:) it is termed اِبْنُ أَدِيمٍ [*made of one hide*; but there are larger sorts]; and if larger, it is termed اِبْنُ أَدِيمَيْنِ [*made of two hides*], and اِبْنُ ثَلَاثَةِ آدِمَةٍ [*made of three hides*]: (T and TA in art. بنى:) accord. to ISk, the وَطْب is peculiarly for milk; and the نِحْى for clarified butter; and the قِرْبَة, for water: (Ṣ:) the pl. (of pauc., Ṣ) is أَسْقِيَةٌ and أَسْقِيَاتٌ and (of mult., Ṣ) أَسَاقٍ, (Ṣ, Ḳ,) or this last is a pl. pl. (T, TA.) — See also 4, last sentence. — [And see a phrase voce حِذَآء, in art. حذو, where it is applied to † The *stomach* of a camel, in which water is stored.]

سَقِىٌّ: see سِقْىٌ, last sentence, in two places. — Also *A cloud having large drops* [*of rain*], (Ṣ, Ḳ,) *vehement in the falling* [*thereof*]: (Ṣ:) [like رَمِىٌّ and رَوِىٌّ:] pl. أَسْقِيَةٌ. (Ṣ, Ḳ.) — And *The papyrus* (بَرْدِىّ): (JK, Ṣ, Ḳ:) or *tender papyrus*: so called because of its growing in, or near to, water: (TA:) occurring in a verse of Imra-el-Ḳeys, cited voce مُذَلَّل: (Ṣ, TA: [but see what is said under this word, مذلّل: and see Ḥam p. 555:]) n. un. سَقِيَّةٌ. (Ṣ.) — And *Palm-trees*; (Ṣ, Ḳ;) and سَقِيَّةٌ signifies [the same, or] *palm-trees that are irrigated by means of water-wheels* (دَوَالٍ, [pl. of دَالِيَةٌ, q. v.]). (TA.)

سُقَايَةٌ: see what next follows.

سِقَايَةٌ and ▼ سُقَايَةٌ and ▼ مَسْقَاةٌ and ▼ مِسْقَاةٌ *A place for giving to drink* or *for watering*: (Ḳ,* TA:) what is termed سِقَايَةُ المَآءِ is well known: (Ṣ:) i. e. سِقَايَةٌ signifies *a place made*, or *prepared, for the giving to drink to people*: (Mṣb:) *a construction for water*: (Mgh:) or *a place in which beverage is made*, or *prepared, at the fairs*, or *festivals*, *&c.*: (JK, T, TA:) [and particularly *a place in which a beverage made of raisins steeped in water was given at the general assembly of the pilgrims*:] and ▼ مَسْقَاةٌ signifies *a drinking-place* [in a general sense]: and he who pronounces it with kesr to the م [▼ مِسْقَاةٌ] makes it to be like the utensil called مِسْقَاةُ الدِّيكِ [*the drinking-vessel of the cock*]: (Ṣ:) [see ثُرْثَةٌ:] and the pl. is مَسَاقٍ. (TA.) — سِقَايَةٌ also signifies *A vessel in which one is given to drink*: (Ḳ:) in the Ḳur [xii. 70], it means the king's *drinking-cup*; (Mgh;) his صُوَاع, *in* [or *from*] *which he drank*, (JK, Ṣ, TA,) *and with which they measured corn; and it was a vessel of silver*. (TA.) — And سِقَايَةُ الحَاجِّ means *The beverage made of raisins steeped in water which* [*the tribe of*] *Kureysh used to give to the pilgrims to drink*: it was under the superintendence of El-'Abbás in the Time of Ignorance and in El-Islám: (TA:) or سِقَايَةٌ in this phrase is an inf. n.; so in the Ḳur ix. 19; (Mgh;) where it is said, أَجَعَلْتُمْ سِقَايَةَ ٱلْحَاجِّ وَعِمَارَةَ ٱلْمَسْجِدِ ٱلْحَرَامِ كَمَنْ آمَنَ بِٱللّٰهِ وَٱلْيَوْمِ ٱلْآخِرِ; the two words سقاية and عمارة being inf. ns. of سَقَى and عَمَرَ; (Bḍ;) the meaning being أَجَعَلْتُمْ أَهْلَ سِقَايَةِ الحَاجِّ وَعِمَارَةِ المَسْجِدِ الحَرَامِ [i. e. *Have ye made*, or *pronounced, the authors of the giving to drink to the pilgrims, and of the keeping in repair of the sacred mosque, to be like him who has believed in God and the last day?*]; and this is confirmed by another reading, which is, سُقَاةَ الحَاجِّ وَعَمَرَةَ المَسْجِدِ: (Ksh, Bḍ:) or the meaning is, أَجَعَلْتُمْ سِقَايَةَ الحَاجِّ كَإِيمَانِ مَنْ آمَنَ [&c., i. e. *have ye made*, or *pronounced, the giving to drink to the pilgrims*, &c., *to be like the belief of him who has believed* &c.?]. (Bḍ.) [See also رِفَادَةٌ.]

سَقَّآءٌ; and the fem. سَقَّآءَةٌ and سَقَّايَةٌ: see سَاقٍ, in six places. — السَّقَّآءُ is also the appellation of *A certain intelligent bird, that draws water for itself*. (JK.) [It is applied in the present day, by some, to *The pelican*: and by some, to *the aquiline vulture; commonly called the* رَخَم.]

سَاقٍ and ▼ سَقَّآءٌ *Giving to drink*; or *one who gives to drink*: (Ḳ, TA:) the former signifies [generally as above, or *a cup-bearer*: and also] *watering* seed-produce; or *a waterer* of seed-produce: (Mṣb:) [and ▼ the latter generally signifies *a water-carrier*:] the pl. of the former is سُقًّى, (Ḳ, TA,) with ḍamm and then teshdeed, (TA,) [accord. to the CḲ سُقِّى, which is app. a mistranscription,] and سُقَّآءٌ, (Ḳ, TA,) like رُمَّانٌ, (TA,) or سُقَاةٌ: (CḲ: [this last is a well-known pl. of سَاقٍ, and as such has occurred above, voce سِقَايَةٌ:]) the pl. of ▼ سَقَّآءٌ is سَقَّآؤُونَ: (Ḳ:) and a woman is termed ▼ سَقَّآءَةٌ and ▼ سَقَّايَةٌ. (Ṣ, Ḳ.) It is said in a prov.,

• اِسْقِ رَقَاشِ إِنَّهَا سَقَّايَةٌ ▼ •

[*Give thou to drink to Raḳáshi: verily she is one who gives to drink*: رَقَاشِ being a woman's name]: it is applied to him who does good: meaning do thou good to him, because of his doing good. (A'Obeyd, Ṣ.) — [Hence,] سَاقِى العَيْنِ *A certain vein* [app. *the central artery of the retina*] *which passes from the interior of the head to the eye, and the severing of which occasions the loss of the sight*. (JḲ.) [See also the next paragraph.]

سَاقِيَةٌ [a subst. from سَاقٍ, made so by the affix ة,] *A rivulet*, or *streamlet*, (T, Ḳ, TA,) *for the irrigation of seed-produce*; (T, TA;) *a small channel for the irrigation of land*; (Mṣb;) it is *larger than a* جَدْوَل, *and than a* نَهْر: (Mgh:) pl. سَوَاقٍ. (Mgh, TA.) It is now vulgarly applied to designate The [*kind of water-wheel for irrigation termed*] دُولَاب [q. v.]. (TA in art. دولب.) — And [the pl.] السَّوَاقِى signifies *Certain veins which discharge into the* أَبْهَرَانِ [dual of أَبْهَر, q. v.]. (JK.)

مَسْقًى *A time* [and *a place*] *of giving to drink*. (JK, TA.)

مَسْقَاةٌ: see سِقَايَةٌ, in two places. One says when the Sulṭán has dealt gently with his subjects in his government of them, أَبْلَغَ السُّلْطَانُ الرَّاتِعَ مَسْقَاتَهُ † [*The Sulṭán has caused the beast pasturing at pleasure amid abundant herbage to come to his drinking-place*]. (TA.) [See also شَرْبَةٌ.]

مِسْقَاةٌ: see سِقَايَةٌ, in two places. — Also *A thing which is made for the* جِرَار [or *water-jars*], *and upon which the mugs are hung*. (JK, TA.)

مَسْقِىٌّ [*Given to drink*: and] *watered* seed-produce [&c.]. (Mṣb.) — [Hence,] إِنَّهُ لَمَسْقِىُّ الدَّمِ *Verily he is tinged with redness*. (JK.)

مَسْقَوِىٌّ and مِسْقَاوِىٌّ: see سِقْىٌ, last sentence, in three places.

سك

1\. سَكَّ الشَّىْءَ, aor. ـُ, (TA,) inf. n. سَكٌّ, (Ḳ, TA,) i. q. سَدَّهُ [i. e. *He closed* or *closed up*, or *he stopped* or *stopped up*, or *repaired, and made firm* or *strong, the thing*]. (Ḳ,* TA.) [In the place of سَدُّ الشَّىْءِ, the explanation of the inf. n. accord. to the reading in the TA, we find in the CḲ شَدُّ الشَّىْءِ: and it seems that شَدَّهُ is a correct meaning of سَكَّهُ; for it is said that] from مَسْكُوك as signifying مَشْدُود is the post-classical phrase سَكُّ الأَبْوَابِ [i. e. *The making fast of doors*]. (TA.) [In the present day, سَكَّ البَابَ, aor. and inf. n. as above, means *He locked*, and *he bolted, the door*.] — And سَكَّهُ, (TA,) inf. n. as above, (Ṣ, Ḳ, TA,) *He clamped it* (ضَبَّبَهُ) *with iron*; namely, a door, (Ṣ, Ḳ, TA,) and wood. (TA.) — Also سَكَّهُ, aor. as above, (Ṣ, TA,) and so the inf. n., (Ḳ, TA,) *He cut off his ears*. (Ṣ, Ḳ,* TA.) — سَكَّ بِمَا فِى بَطْنِهِ, (TA,) inf. n. as above, (Ḳ, TA,) *He cast forth what was in his belly*; (Ḳ,* TA;) *muted*, or *dunged*; (TA;) said of an ostrich: (Ḳ, TA:) and so سَجَّ. (TA.) And سَكَّ بِسَلْحِهِ, (AA, TA,) inf. n. as above, (Ḳ, TA,) *He cast forth his excrement*, or *ordure*, (AA, Ḳ, TA,) *in a thin state*; (AA,* Ḳ, TA;) as also زَكَّ, (AA, TA,) and هَكَّ. (TA.) And هُوَ يَسُكُّ, inf. n. as above, *He voids thin excrement* or *ordure*; (Aṣ, Ṣ, TA;) as also يَسُجُّ, inf. n. سَجٌّ. (Aṣ, TA.) And أَخَذَهُ سَكٌّ [*He was taken with a looseness of the bowels*;] *he had thin evacuations of the bowels*; expl. by قَعَدَ مَقَاعِدَ رِقَاقًا: and أَخَذَهُ سَكٌّ فِى بَطْنِهِ [signifies the same; or] *his bowels became loose*; as also سَجٌّ; so says Yaḳoob; and he asserts it to be formed by substitution; but which of the two is so formed is unknown. (TA.) — سَكَّ فِى الأَرْضِ *He went at random in the land*, or *country, not knowing whither to go, and was perplexed*. (Ibn-'Abbád, O. [See also 7.]) — One says also, أَيْنَ تَسُكُّ *Whither goest thou?* (Ibn-'Abbád, O.) — مَا سَكَّ سَمْعِى مِثْلُ ذٰلِكَ الكَلَامِ *The like of that speech has not entered my ear*, or *ears*: and مَا ٱسْتَكَّ ▼ فِى مَسَامِعِى مِثْلُهُ *The* *like of it has not entered my ears.* (TA.) ═ سَكَّ, [sec. pers., app., سَكُكْتَ,] aor. ُ, (TA,) inf. n. سُكٌّ, (Ḳ, TA,) *It* (one's nature, or disposition,) *was,* or *became, base, ignoble, mean,* or *sordid.* (Ḳ,* TA.) ═ سَكَّ, (Mṣb, TA,) sec. pers. سَكِكْتَ, (Mṣb, Ḳ, TA, [in the CḲ, erroneously, سَكَكْتَ,]) inf. n. سَكَكٌ, (Ṣ, Mgh, Mṣb, Ḳ, TA,) said of a man, &c., (Ḳ,) † *He was small in the ear,* (Ṣ, Mgh, Mṣb, Ḳ, TA,) *with a sticking thereof to the head, and small projection thereof:* (Ḳ, TA:) or *he was short in the ear, with a sticking thereof to the part behind it:* (TA:) or *he was small in the* قُوف [here meaning either the *upper part* or the *helix* (in the CḲ (قُوب)] *of the ear, and narrow in the ear-hole.* (Ḳ, TA.) And † *He was,* or *became, deaf.* (Ḳ, TA.)

7. انسكّت الإبلُ *The camels went at random.* (Ibn-'Abbád, O, TA. [See also سَكَّ فِى الأَرْضِ above.]) انْسِكَاكٌ in the case of the birds called قَطًا means Their *going at random, and depressing their breasts, after soaring in their flight and circling in the air.* (Ibn-'Abbád, O, Ḳ.)

8. استكّ *It* (a thing) *was,* or *became, closed* or *closed up,* or *stopped* or *stopped up,* or *repaired, and made firm* or *strong;* quasi pass. of 1 in the first of the senses assigned to it above; syn. انْسَدَّ. (TA.) — [Hence,] استكّت مَسَامِعُهُ ‡ *His ears became stopped up,* or *deaf,* (Ṣ, Mṣb, Ḳ,*) *and narrow* [*in the aperture*]. (Ṣ, Ḳ.) — And استكّ النَّبْتُ † *The herbage became luxuriant and dense,* (Ṣ, Ḳ,) *its interstices becoming closed up.* (Ṣ.) And استكّت الرِّيَاضُ † *The meadows became luxuriant and dense* [*in their herbage*]. (Aṣ, TA.) ═ See also 1.

سَكٌّ *A nail; a pin,* or *peg, of iron;* as also ▼ سَكِّىٌّ; (Ṣ, Ḳ;) like as one says دَوٌّ and دَوِّىٌّ: (Ṣ:) pl. سِكَاكٌ (Ṣ, Ḳ) and سُكُوكٌ. (Ḳ.) [A verse of Aboo-Dahbal El-Jumahee is cited as an ex. in the TA as follows:

دِرْعِى دِلَاصٌ سَكُّهَا سَكٌّ عَجَبْ
وَجَوْبُهَا القَاتِرُ مِنْ سَيْرِ اليَلَبْ

but see يَلَبٌ.] ═ *A straight,* or an *even,* building, and excavation, (O, Ḳ,) *like a wall, without curvity,* or *bending.* (O.) — A coat of mail *narrow in the rings;* (Ṣ, Ḳ;) as also ▼ سُكٌّ, and ▼ سُكَاكٌ: (Ḳ:) or, accord. to the O, *soft in the rings.* (TA.) — See also the next paragraph.

سُكٌّ A well *narrow* (Lth, AZ, Aṣ, Ṣ, O, Ḳ) *in its cavity,* or *interior,* (Lth, O,) or *from its top to its bottom,* (AZ, Ṣ, O,) or *in its aperture;* as also ▼ سَكٌّ, and ▼ سَكُوكٌ: (Ḳ:) or a well *even in its cavity,* or *interior, and in its casing:* or, accord. to Fr, one *well,* or *strongly,* or *compactly, cased, and narrow:* the pl. of سُكٌّ is سِكَاكٌ; and the pl. of ▼ سَكُوكٌ is سُكٌّ, so that the latter is both a sing. and a pl. (TA.) — And A *narrow* road: (I'Abbád, O:) or a road *stopped up:* (Ḳ:) or a road *narrow and stopped up.* (Lḥ, TA.) — See also سِكَّةٌ. — Also The *hole of the scorpion,* (Ibn-'Abbád, Ṣ, O, Ḳ,) in the dial. of the Benoo-Asad; (Ibn-'Abbád, O;) and *of the spider,* (O, Ḳ,) likewise, because of its narrowness. (TA.) ═ Also *A sort of perfume,* (Ṣ, Mgh, O, Mṣb, Ḳ,) *prepared from* رَامَك [q. v.], (Ḳ,) or *from musk and* رَامَك, (O,) *the former being bruised,* or *pounded, sifted, kneaded with water, and wrung hard, and wiped over with oil of the* خِيرِىّ [q. v.] *in order that it may not stick to the vessel, and left for a night; then musk is pounded,* or *powdered,* (يُسْحَقُ,) *and put into it by degrees, and it is* [*again*] *wrung hard, and cut into small, round, flat pieces, and left for two days, after which it is perforated with a large needle, and strung upon a hempen string, and left for a year; and as it becomes old, its odour becomes the more sweet.* (Ḳ.) ═ Also pl. of أَسَكُّ. (Ḳ.)

سِكَّةٌ *A ploughshare;* i. e. the *iron thing with which the ground is ploughed;* (Ṣ, TA;) the *iron appertenance of the plough.* (Ḳ.) Hence the trad., مَا دَخَلَتِ السِّكَّةُ دَارَ قَوْمٍ إِلَّا ذَلُّوا [*The ploughshare enters not the abode of a people,* or *party, but they become abased*]; meaning, in consequence of the violence and the demands that the agriculturists experience from the ruling power. (TA.) — And *A die,* i. e. *an engraved piece of iron,* (Ṣ,* Mṣb, Ḳ, TA,) *having an inscription upon it,* (TA,) *with which dirhems and deenárs are stamped,* (Ṣ,* Mṣb,) or *upon which pieces of money* (دَرَاهِم) *are struck:* (Ḳ:) pl. سِكَكٌ. (Mṣb.) — And, because stamped therewith, *A coined dirhem,* and *deenár;* (TA;) which latter is called [also] ▼ سِكِّىٌّ, (O, Ḳ, TA,) [in the CḲ سَكِّى, but it is] with kesr. (TA.) ═ Also *A row* (طَرِيقَةٌ مُصْطَفَّةٌ, Ṣ, O, Mṣb, or سَطْرٌ, Ḳ, or سَطْرٌ مُصْطَفٌّ, TA) *of palm-trees.* (Ṣ, O, Mṣb, Ḳ, TA.) Hence their saying, (Ṣ,) or the saying of the Prophet, (O,) خَيْرُ المَالِ مُهْرَةٌ مَأْمُورَةٌ أَوْ سِكَّةٌ مَأْبُورَةٌ (Ṣ, in the O سكة مأبورة او مهرة مأمورة,) meaning [*The best of property is*] *a prolific filly* (TA) *or a row of palm-trees fecundated:* (Ṣ, TA:) or, accord. to Aṣ, سكة مأبورة here signifies *a ploughshare properly prepared* [*for ploughing*]; and, he says, the meaning is, that the best of property is a brood [of a mare] or seed-produce. (Ṣ.) [It has been suggested to me that, if طريقة in the explanation above have the signification here assigned to it, the epithet مصطفّة is redundant; and therefore that طريقة alone may be the proper explanation, and may mean in this case, as it does in many others, *a tall palm-tree,* or the *tallest of palm-trees,* or *a smooth palm-tree,* or *a palm-tree the head of which is reached by the hand;* and that مصطفّة may have been added in consequence of misunderstanding, and سطر substituted for طريقة for the same reason: but I think it much more probable that the epithet has been added because طريقة is ambiguous; and this is confirmed by what here follows.] — Also *A* زُقَاق [meaning *street*]: (Ṣ, O,* Mṣb:) or [rather] *a wide* زُقَاق: (Mṣb:) or *an even road,* (Ḳ, TA,) [or *street,*] *of such as are termed* أَزِقَّة [pl. of زُقَاق]: (TA:) so called because the houses therein form a row or rows [on either side]; (O, TA;) being likened to a سِكَّة of palm-trees: (TA:) [in the present day, often applied to *a highway,* and to *any road:*] pl. سِكَكٌ [as above]: (O:) and ▼ سَكَائِكُ is *syn. with* [سِكَكٌ as meaning] أَزِقَّة. (TA.) — [Hence also, app., one says,] اِجْعَلِ الأَمْرَ سِكَّةً وَاحِدَةً † *Make thou the affair,* or *case,* [*uniform,* or] *one uniform thing.* (Fr, TA in art. بأج.) — And أَخَذَ الأَمْرَ بِسِكَّتِهِ, (Ḳ,) and أَدْرَكَهُ بِسِكَّتِهِ, (TA,) † [*He took the thing, and he attained it, in its proper way,* or] *when it was possible.* (Ḳ, TA.) — And فُلَانٌ صَعْبُ السِّكَّةِ ‡ *Such a one will not remain quiet,* or *still,* or *steady, by reason of hastiness of temper.* (Ibn-'Abbád, Z, O, TA.) ═ Also The *house* [or *station*] *of the* بَرِيد [or *messenger that journeys on a beast of the post,* or *messengers on beasts of the post:* it is likewise called سِكَّةُ البَرِيدِ: see بَرِيدٌ]: and أَصْحَابُ السِّكَكِ, occurring in a letter of 'Omar Ibn-'Abd-El-'Azeez, means *the* بُرُد [or *messengers on beasts of the post*] *who are stationed there to be sent on affairs of importance.* (Mgh.) سِكَّةُ البَرِيدِ is well known [as having the meaning assigned to it above: and also as meaning *The space,* or *distance, between each station of the messengers above mentioned and the station next to it:* see, again, بَرِيدٌ]. (Ibn-'Abbád, O.)

سَكَكٌ inf. n. of سَكَّ, sec. pers. سَكِكْتَ. (Mṣb, TA. [See 1, last sentence but one.])

سُكُكٌ [a pl. of which the sing. is not mentioned,] *Bustards;* syn. حُبَارَيَاتٌ. (TA.)

سُكَاكٌ The *air that is next to the clouds,* or *to the higher part,* (عَنَان,) *of the sky;* as also ▼ سُكَاكَةٌ: (Ṣ, Ḳ:) or both signify the *air,* or *atmosphere, between heaven and earth:* like لُوحٌ: the pl. of the second is سَكَائِكُ. (TA.) Hence the saying, لَا أَفْعَلُ ذٰلِكَ وَلَوْ نَزَوْتَ فِى السُّكَاكِ, meaning [*I will not do that even if thou leap*] *into the sky.* (Ṣ.) — Also The *part, of an arrow, which is the place of the feathers.* (Ibn-'Abbád, O, Ḳ.)

سَكُوكٌ: see سُكٌّ, in two places.

ضَرَبُوا بُيُوتَهُمْ سِكَاكًا [*They pitched their tents*] *in one row:* (Th, Ḳ:) and said with ش, [i. e. شِكَاكًا,] accord. to IAạr: (TA:) but Th says that it is only with س, deriving it from سِكَّةٌ signifying "a wide زُقَاق." (TA in art. شك.)

سُكَاكَةٌ *Small in the ear,* (M, Ḳ,) or *in the ears.* (IAạr, TA.) [See also أَسَكُّ.] — And † One who is *alone in his opinion, having none to share with him in it,* (AZ, Ḳ, TA,) *who acts without caring how his opinion happens to be:* pl. سُكَاكَاتٌ: it has no broken pl. (AZ, TA.) ═ See also سُكَاكٌ.

سَكَائِكُ pl. of سُكَاكَةٌ as syn. with سُكَاكٌ [q. v.]. (TA.) — See also سِكَّةٌ, in the latter half of the paragraph.

سِكِّىٌّ: see سَكٌّ:

سَكِّىٌّ : see سِكَّةٌ, in the former half of the paragraph. ═ Also i. q. بَرِيدٌ [meaning either *A beast of the post* or *a messenger who journeys on a beast of the post*]: a rel. n. from سِكَّةٌ. (Ibn-'Abbád, O, TA.)

سَكَّاكٌ [*A stamper of money;*] *one who strikes the* سِكَّة. (TA.) — [And said by Golius, as on the authority of Meyd, to signify *A maker of knives;* like سَكَّانٌ.]

سُكَّاكَةٌ [as a coll. gen. n., app. derived from سِكَّةٌ signifying "a road,"] *Wayfarers.* (TA.)

سِكِّينٌ, mentioned by Ibn-'Abbád in this art., and said in the Mgh to be of the measure فِعْلِينٌ from السَّكّ, or فِعِّيلٌ from السُّكُونُ : see art. سكن.

أَسَكُّ *Small in the ear,* (Mgh, Ḳ,) *with a sticking thereof to the head, and small projection thereof:* (Ḳ:) or *short in the ear, with a sticking thereof to the part behind it:* (TA:) or *small in the* قوف [meaning either the *upper part* or the *helix*] *of the ear, and narrow in the ear-hole:* (Ḳ:) applied to a man, (Mgh, Ḳ,) &c.: (Ḳ:) fem. سَكَّآءُ : (Ṣ, Mgh, O, Mṣb, Ḳ:) applied [to a woman, as is implied in the Ḳ, and to a female bird, and particularly to a female ostrich, and] to a single bird of the species called قَطًا, because having no ear [apparent or projecting], (TA,) and to a she-goat, meaning, with the lawyers, *having no ear except the ear-hole,* or, accord. to El-Ḳudooree, *naturally earless:* (Mgh:) and applied to an ear, as meaning *small:* (Ṣ, Mṣb:) pl. سُكٌّ : applied [to human beings, &c., more commonly to birds, and particularly] to ostriches, (Ḳ,) and to birds of the species called قَطًا : (TA:) it is said that every سَكَّآء is oviparous, and every شَرْفَآء is viviparous; the former meaning *a female that has no ear* (Ṣ, O) *apparent,* or *external;* (O;) and the latter, "a female that has an ear (Ṣ, O) apparent, or external, (O,) though it be slit." (Ṣ.) A rájiz says,

* لَيْلَةُ حَكٍّ لَيْسَ فِيهَا شَكُّ *
* أَحُكُّ حَتَّى سَاعِدِى مُنْفَكُّ *
* أَسْهَرَنِى الأُسَيْوِدُ الأَسَكُّ *

[*A night of scratching: there is no doubt respecting it: I scratch so that my fore arm,* or *my upper arm,* (for ساعد is used in both of these senses,) *is dislocated: the little black thing without ears having rendered me sleepless*]: he means the fleas, using the sing. as a gen. n. (TA.) — Also *Having the ears cut off.* (TA.) [This seems to be the primary, though not a usual, signification.] — And † [*Having the ears stopped up:* (see 8:) or] *deaf.* (Ḳ.) It is applied in this sense to the ostrich, because [they say that] he does not hear. (Lth, TA.) — And الأَسَكُّ was the name of *A certain horse.* (O, Ḳ.) — See also سَكٌّ.

مِنْبَرٌ مَسْكُوكٌ [*A pulpit*] *nailed with nails of iron:* but also said to be with ش, [i. e. مَشْكُوكٌ,] meaning مَشْدُودٌ [made firm or strong, &c.]. (TA.)

سكب

1. سَكَبَ, (Ṣ, A, Mṣb, Ḳ,) aor. ـُ, (A, TA,) inf. n. سُكُوبٌ (Ṣ, A, Mṣb, Ḳ) and سَكْبٌ (Mṣb) and تَسْكَابٌ, (Ṣ, [this last assigned in the Ḳ to the trans. verb,]) said of water, (Ṣ, A, Mṣb, Ḳ,) and a flow of tears (دَمْع), (A, TA,) and the like, (TA,) *It poured out* or *forth;* or *was,* or *became, poured out* or *forth;* (Ṣ, A, Mṣb, Ḳ;) as also ↓ انسكب. (Ṣ, Ḳ.) ═ And سَكَبَهُ, (Ṣ, A, Mgh, Mṣb, Ḳ,) aor. as above, (A, TA,) inf. n. سَكْبٌ (Ṣ, Mgh, Ḳ) and تَسْكَابٌ, (Ḳ, [the latter assigned in the Ṣ to the intrans. verb,]) *He poured it out* or *forth;* namely, water, (Ṣ, A, Mgh, Mṣb, Ḳ,) and a flow of tears, (A, TA,) and the like; (TA;) as also ↓ اسكبهُ. (A.) The people of El-Medeeneh say, أَسْكِبْ عَلَى يَدَىَّ *Pour thou out,* or *forth, upon my hands.* (A.) And it is said in a trad., هَاهُنَا تُسْكَبُ العَبَرَاتُ [*Here tears are to be poured forth*], meaning this is the place in which one should weep, seeking forgiveness. (Mgh.)

4: } see the next preceding paragraph.
7: }

سَيْكَبٌ ↓ and سَاكِبٌ ↓ and سَكُوبٌ ↓ and سَكْبٌ (Ḳ) and سَكِيبٌ ↓ (CḲ [omitted in the TA and in my MS. copy of the Ḳ]) and أُسْكُوبٌ ↓ (Ḳ) Water *poured out* or *forth,* or *being poured out* or *forth:* or *poured out* or *forth,* (Ḳ, TA,) *running upon the surface of the earth without any excavation:* (TA:) or the first signifies water *poured out* or *forth;* and is an inf. n. used as an epithet, like صَبٌّ and غَوْرٌ applied as epithets to water: and سَكُوبٌ ↓, water *running upon the surface of the earth without any excavation:* and أُسْكُوبٌ ↓, water *pouring out* or *forth,* or *being poured out* or *forth;* (Ṣ;) or, as some say, *pouring much:* (Ḥar pp. 469 et seq.:) and also this last, *running* water: (TA:) or this signifies دَائِمُ الهَطَلَانِ [i. e. *continually pouring,* or *continually pouring dispersedly and in large drops;* as also سَكْبٌ; for hence it appears evident that الهَطَلَانُ الدَّائِمُ as an explanation of السَّكْبُ and الأُسْكُوبُ in the Ḳ is a mistake for الدَّائِمُ الهَطَلَانِ]; and is applied as an epithet to water and to blood; (A;) and also [probably in this sense] to clouds (سَحَابٌ); and to a wound made with a spear or the like (طَعْنَةٌ): and سَاكِبٌ ↓ is applied as an epithet to tears (دَمْع). (TA.) — [Hence] سَكْبٌ applied to a horse means ‡ *Wide in step:* (Ṣ, A, Ḳ:) or *fleet,* or *swift,* or *excellent in running;* (A, Ḳ;) *that runs much:* (Mgh, TA:) or *light,* or *active:* and أُسْكُوبٌ ↓, so applied, has one or another of these meanings: (A:) or the former, thus applied, *that runs vehemently;* as also فَيْضٌ; likened to water pouring forth: (Eth-Thaạlebee, TA:) also, (Ḳ, TA,) applied to a horse and a man and a boy, (TA,) † *light of spirit;* and *brisk, lively,* or *sprightly,* (Ḳ, TA,) *in work,* or *action.* (TA.) السَّكْبُ was the name of the first horse possessed by the Prophet; (Mgh,* Ḳ;) as also السَّكْبُ ↓: and the name of a horse of Shebeeb Ibn-Mo'áwiyeh. (Ḳ.) — [Hence also,] † *A certain sort of clothes,* or *garments,* (T, Ṣ, Ḳ,) *thin so as to resemble dust, and as though resembling pouring water by reason of its thinness;* and so, accord. to IAạr, سَكَبٌ ↓. (T, TA.) — Applied to a man, † *Tall;* (Ḳ;) a dial. var. of شَقْبٌ [q. v.]. (TA.) — And ‡ A *necessary* thing or affair: (A, Ḳ, TA:) and ‡ a disgrace (سُبَّة) that is *necessary,* or *unavoidable.* (A, TA.) Laḳeeṭ Ibn-Zurárah said to his brother Maạbad, when he required him to ransom him with two hundred camels, he being a captive, نُمِيطُ عَنْكَ شَيْئًا يَكُونُ عَلَى أَهْلِ بَيْتِكَ سُبَّةً سَكْبًا, meaning ‡ [*We will put away from thee a thing that would be to the people of thy house*] *a necessary,* or *an unavoidable, disgrace.* (TA.) ═ Also *Copper,* or *brass;* syn. نُحَاسٌ : or *lead:* (IAạr, Ḳ:) and so سَكَبٌ ↓, (Ḳ,) in the latter sense, or in both senses, or in all the senses. (TA.)

سَكَبٌ : see the next preceding paragraph, latter half, in three places. ═ Also *A certain kind of tree,* (Ṣ, Ḳ,) *of sweet odour,* (Ṣ,) *as though its odour were that of* [*the perfume called*] خَلُوق [q. v.], *growing apart from others, upon a single root, having a downy substance, and leaves like those of the* صَعْتَر [*a species of origanum,* or *marjoram*], *except in being more green: it grows in the plains and the valleys; and what has dried up thereof is of no use to any one: it has a fruit which is eaten, and the people of El-Ḥijáz make of it a* [*beverage such as is termed*] نَبِيذ : *its fruit does not grow forth in one year, but only in several years:* AḤn says that the سَكَب *is a herb that rises to the height of a cubit, having dust-coloured leaves like those of the* هِنْدَبَآء [or *endive*], *and a blossom intensely white, of the form of that of the* فِرْسِك [i. e. *peach,* or *a species* or *variety thereof*]: (TA:) n. un. with ة: (Ṣ, TA:) Aṣ mentions the سَكَب *as one of the plants of the plain,* or *soft, tracts.* (TA.) — It is also said to be The [*plant called*] رِيح [app. رَيِّح or رِيَح, which seem to be coll. gen. ns. of each of which the n. un. is with ة (see رَيِّحَة)], *having a yellow blossom.* (TA.) — And The *anemone* (شَقَائِقُ النُّعْمَانِ). (Ḳ.) — And *One of the trees of the hot season.* (TA.)

سَكَابٌ and سَكَابِ, the latter [indecl., with kesr for its termination,] like قَطَامِ, and سَكَّابٌ ↓, [all app. meaning *The fleet,* or *swift,* like السَّكْبُ and الأُسْكُوبُ,] are names of certain horses. (Ḳ: the second only mentioned in the Ṣ.)

سَكُوبٌ : see سَكْبٌ, in two places.

سَكِيبٌ : see سَكْبٌ.

سَكَّابٌ : see سَكَابٌ.

سَاكِبٌ : see سَكْبٌ, in two places. ═ [And act. part. n. of سَكَبَهُ. Hence,] سَاكِبُ المَآءِ † [*The sign of Aquarius;*] *the eleventh of the signs of the Zodiac;* also called الدَّلْوُ. (Ḳzw.)

سَيْكَبٌ : see سَكْبٌ.

أُسْكُفَّةٌ The أُسْكُفَّة [i.e. *threshold*] of a door. (Ḳ.)

إِسْكَابٌ : see the next paragraph.

أُسْكُوبٌ : see سَكْبٌ, in three places. — Also Lightning *extending towards the earth.* (Ḳ.) So in the saying of Zuheyr El-Mázinee,

• بَرْقٌ يُضِىءُ أَمَامَ البَيْتِ أُسْكُوبُ •

[*Lightning shining*, or *shining brightly*, *before the tent*, or *house*, *extending towards the earth*]; as though it were pouring forth rain. (TA.) — And *A row* of palm-trees; (IAạr, Ḳ;) as also أُسْلُوبٌ : if of other than palm-trees, it is termed أُنْبُوبٌ, and مِدَادٌ. (IAạr, TA.) — Also *i. q.* إِسْكَافٌ [*A maker of shoes* or *boots*, or *a sewer of leather*, &c.]; like ▾ إِسْكَابٌ : or *a blacksmith*. (Ḳ.)

المِسْكَبَةُ [altered in a copy of the A from المَسْكَبَةُ, which may perhaps be the right word,] The *higher*, or *highest*, *rivulet*, or *small channel for irrigation*, *from which the other rivulets*, or *small channels*, *are supplied with water.* (A.) — [In a copy of the A (in art. سطب), المَسْطَبَةُ, which I believe to be in that instance a mistranscription for المسكبة, occurs expl. as meaning † *The Milky Way.*]

سكبج

Q. 1. سَكْبَجَ *He prepared* سِكْبَاج. (TA.)

سِكْبَاجٌ an arabicized word, (O, Mṣb, Ḳ,) with kesr (Mṣb, Ḳ) to the س, not with fet-ḥ, because there is no word of the measure فَعْلَال except of the reduplicate class [like زَلْزَال &c.], (Mṣb,) from سِكْ, meaning "vinegar," in Pers., and بَاج, [arabicized from the Pers. بَاهَا,] i. e. لَوْن [as meaning "a sort," or "species," of food or viands]; (O; [in which it is erroneously said that بَاج is in Pers. بَاوَا;]) or from [the Pers.] سِرْكَهٔ پَاچَه; [سِرْكَهٔ] meaning "vinegar;" and پَاچَه, "sheeps' feet," or "trotters;"] (TA;) [but the former derivation is evidently the more probable;] *A well-known kind of food*; (Mṣb;) *flesh-meat cooked with vinegar*: this is the best that is said [in explanation of the word]: (TA:) [in the present day, applied to *a sort of food composed of flesh-meat, wheat-flour, and vinegar*; and sometimes to other varieties of food, but vinegar, I believe, enters into the composition of them all: also called سِكْبَا; from the Pers. سِكْ "vinegar," and بَا "spoon-meat:" accord. to Golius, on the authority of the Loghat Niạmet-Allah Khaleel Ṣoofee, *a sort of food composed of flesh-meat cut in pieces*, (*to which are afterwards added raisins, a few figs, and some vetches*,) *with vinegar and honey, or acid syrop*: and سِكْبَاجُ البَقَرِ is a name given to *such food prepared with beef*:] سِكْبَاجٌ أَصْفَرُ is *a well-known sort of broth* [or *soup*] *in which is saffron*, wherefore it is termed اصفر. (Mgh.)

سكبنج

سَكْبِينَجٌ an arabicized word [from the Pers. سَكْبِينَه]; (O;) [*Sagapenum*;] *a certain medicine*, (O, Ḳ,) *well-known*; (Ḳ;) the *gum of a certain tree* (O, TA) *in Persia*, (TA,) [*supposed to be the ferula Persica*,] *in which is no useful property, but only in its gum*: some say that there is *a sort of* قِنَّة [or *galbanum*] *that changes from its original state and becomes* سكبينج. (O.)

سكت

1. سَكَتَ, (Ṣ, Mṣb, TA,) aor. ـُ, (Lth, TA,) inf. n. سُكُوتٌ and سَكْتٌ (Ṣ, A, Mṣb, Ḳ) and سُكَاتٌ (Ṣ, Ḳ) and سَاكُوتَةٌ, (Ḳ,) [all these ns. said in the Ḳ to signify the same, but this is not exactly the case, for the last is of an intensive form,] *He was*, or *became, silent, mute*, or *speechless*; *contr. of* نَطَقَ; (TA;) *i. q.* صَمَتَ: (Lth, Mṣb, TA:) or سَكَتَ is said of him who has the power, or faculty, of speech, but abstains from making use of it; whereas صَمَتَ is sometimes said of that which has not the power, or faculty, of speech: (Er-Rághib, MF, TA:) or سَكَتَ, aor. ـُ, inf. n. سُكُوتٌ and سَكْتٌ, signifies *he* (a man) *ceased*, or *stopped, speaking*; and سَكَتَ, aor. ـُ, inf. n. سَكْتٌ, † *he* (a man) *was*, or *became, still*, or *quiet*; syn. سَكَنَ: (Zj, TA:) [it is said that] ▾ اسكت, also, is *syn. with* صَمَتَ, like سَكَتَ; (Mṣb;) accord. to AZ, one says of a man, صَمَتَ and أَصْمَتَ and سَكَتَ and ▾ أَسْكَتَ: (TA:) or, as some say, ▾ اسكت signifies *he was*, or *became, silent*, or *he spoke not*; and *he ceased* [*from speech*], or *broke off* [*therefrom*], or *became cut short* [*therein*]: (Mṣb:) or سَكَتَ signifies *he was*, or *became, silent intentionally*; and ▾ اسكت, *he was*, or *became, silent by reason of thought* or *disease* or *fear*: (TA:) or you say تَكَلَّمَ ثُمَّ سَكَتَ without ا [when you mean *he spoke* and *then became silent*, i. e., *intentionally*]; (Ṣ;) but you say ▾ اسكت when you mean *his speech became broken off*, or *cut short, and so he spoke not.* (Ṣ, Ḳ.) It is said in a prov., سَكَتَ أَلْفًا وَنَطَقَ خَلْفًا *He held his tongue from a thousand words* (سَكَتَ عَنْ أَلْفِ كَلِمَةٍ), *and then uttered what was wrong.* (ISk, Ṣ and Mṣb in art. خلف.) And you say [of the quiescent ه that is sometimes added at the end of a word, after a vowel or a letter of prolongation, as in لَمْ يَرْضَهْ and وَا زَيْدَاهْ], هٰذِهِ هَاءُ السَّكْتِ [*This is the* هاء *of pausation*]. (A, TA.) One says also, of a she-camel, سَكَتَتْ, inf. n. سُكُوتٌ, meaning *She uttered not the* [*grumbling*] *cry termed* رُغَاء *when the saddle was put upon her.* (ISd, TA.) — [Hence سَكَتَ, aor. as above, inf. n. سَكْتٌ, as syn. with سَكَنَ, meaning as expl. above; and also † *It was*, or *became, still, quiet, motionless, at rest, stilled, quieted, appeased, tranquillized, calm, allayed, assuaged*, or *quelled*; *it remitted*; *it subsided*; and so ▾ اسكت.] You say, ضَرَبَهُ حَتَّى سَكَتَتْ حَرَكَتُهُ (A) or ▾ أَسْكَتَتْ حركته (TA) ‡ [*He beat him until his motion became stilled*]; and ▾ حَتَّى أَسْكَتَ † [*until he became still*]. (TA.) And سَكَتَ الغَضَبُ *i. q.* سَكَنَ, (Ṣ, Mṣb, TA,) meaning فَتَرَ [i. e. † *The anger remitted*; or *became stilled, appeased*, or *allayed*]; (TA:) as also ▾ اسكت: (Mṣb:) and سَكَتَ عَنْهُ الغَضَبُ ‡ [*Anger*, or *the anger, became stilled so that it departed from him*]. (A.) Hence, in the Ḳur [vii. 153], وَلَمَّا سَكَتَ عَنْ مُوسَى الغَضَبُ, (Ṣ,) meaning, accord. to Zj, سَكَنَ [i. e. † *And when the anger became stilled so that it departed from Moses*]: or, as some say, the phrase is inverted, the meaning being وَلَمَّا سَكَتَ مُوسَى عَنِ الغَضَبِ [*And when Moses was silent, ceasing from anger*]: but the former is the explanation of those skilled in the Arabic language. (TA. [See also 4.]) You say also, سَكَتَ الحَرُّ, meaning † *The heat became vehement*, or *intense, the wind being still.* (TA.) — [Hence also,] † *He died*: (Ḳ:) occurring in this sense in a trad. (TA.) — سَاكَتَنِى فَسَكَتُّ : see 3. — سَكَتَ said of a horse, [from السُّكَيْتُ,] *He came in tenth in a race.* (TA.)

2: see 4, in two places.

3. ▾ سَاكَتَنِى فَسَكَتُّ [may mean *He kept silence with me and I was silent*: or *he vied with me in keeping silence and I surpassed therein*: or it may have both of these meanings; both being agreeable with analogy]. (Ṣ, TA; in neither of which it is explained.)

4. اسكت as an intrans. verb: see 1, in nine places. — *He turned away, and spoke not*; occurring in this sense in a trad.: and اسكت عَنِ الشَّىْءِ *He turned away from the thing.* (TA.) — اسكتهُ and ▾ سكّتهُ (Ṣ, A, Mṣb) both signify the same, said of God (Ṣ) [and of a man]; *He made him*, or *rendered him, silent, mute*, or *speechless*; (Mṣb;) [*he silenced*, or *hushed, him*;] namely, a person speaking. (A.) And اسكتهُ عَنِّى [*He made him to abstain from speaking of*, or *to, me*]. (Aṣ, TA in art. نصت.) And اسكت الصَّبِىَّ بِسُكْتَةٍ [*He silenced*, or *hushed, the child with a* سُكْتَة]. (Lḥ, Ṣ, A, Ḳ.) And أُسْكِتَ means *He was silenced in a dispute* or *the like.* (A, TA.) — [And hence, † *He stilled, quieted, appeased, tranquillized, calmed, allayed, assuaged*, or *quelled, it.*] In the Ḳur vii. 153, some read, ▾ وَلَمَّا سُكِّتَ عَنْ مُوسَى الغَضَبُ and أُسْكِتَ [i. e. † *And when the anger was stilled so that it was made to depart from Moses*]. (Bḍ. [For the usual reading see 1, latter part.])

سَكْتٌ an inf. n. of 1 [q. v.]. (Ṣ, &c.) — And [hence,] *A division* [or *pause*] *between two musical sounds, or notes, without breathing*; (T, Ḳ, TA;) as also ▾ سَكْتَةٌ. (TA.) — See also سِكِّيتٌ, in two places.

سَكْتَةٌ *A single state of silence, muteness*, or *speechlessness.* (Mṣb.) One says, لِلْحُبْلَى صَرْخَةٌ ثُمَّ سَكْتَةٌ [*To the pregnant woman is attributable a vehement cry, then a silence*]. (A, TA.) — In prayer, *A silence* [or *pause*] *after the commencement*; [i. e. *after what precedes the first recitation of the Opening Chapter of the Ḳur-án*;] which is approved: and, in like manner, *after the ending of the recitation of the Opening Chapter of the Ḳur-án.* (T, TA.) — See also

سَكْتٌ. — Also *A certain disease* [*by which a person loses his powers of speech and motion*], (Ṣ, Ḳ, TA,) *well known among the physicians*; (TA;) [i. e. *apoplexy*; thus called in the present day:] accord. to some, the word in this sense should be written ↑ سُكْتَةٌ, because it denotes *a mode* [*of silence* or *stillness*]; but this is incorrect, being at variance with the authority of transmission. (TA.) — See also the next paragraph: = and see سِكِّيتٌ.

سُكْتَةٌ: see سَكْتَةٌ. — Also *A thing* (Ṣ, A, Mṣb, Ḳ) *of any kind* (Ṣ) *with which one silences*, or *hushes*, or *quiets*, *a child*, (Ṣ, A, Mṣb, Ḳ,) or *other person*; (Ṣ, Ḳ;) [generally meaning *a lullaby of any kind for a child*:] and *somewhat remaining in a bag or other receptacle*, (Ḳ, TA,) i. e., *of food*. (TA.) One says, مَا لَهُ سُكْتَةٌ لِعِيَالِهِ, and ↑ سُكَتَةٌ, meaning *He has not any food with which to silence*, or *quiet his family*, or *household*. (Lḥ, TA.)

سَكْتَةٌ is a subst. from سَكَتَ; [signifying *Silence*, &c.; like سُكُوتٌ used as a subst.;] as also ↑ سُكْتَةٌ. (Lḥ, TA.) — See also سُكْتَةٌ.

سُكَاتٌ *Constant*, or *continual*, *silence*. (Mṣb.) Hence, by way of comparison, one says, الإِفْحَامُ سُكَاتٌ [as though meaning *The state of being silenced in a dispute*, &c., *is a state of constant*, or *continual*, *silence*: but it seems to mean, more probably, الافحام (as an act. inf. n.) *is an act that silences*; agreeably with what here follows]. (Mṣb.) — رَمَاهُ بِسُكَاتٍ (AZ, M, Ḳ) and ↑ سُكَاتَةٍ, (AZ, Ṣ, M, A, Ḳ,) to which latter is generally added وَصُمَاتَةٍ, (M, TA,) *He* (a man, Ṣ, M, and God, TA) *smote him*, or *afflicted him*, *with a thing that silenced him*; (Ṣ, A, Ḳ;) thought by ISd to mean, *with anxiety*, or *grief*, *that silenced him*, or *a thing in consequence of which he became silent*: not expl. by AZ. (TA.) — [In like manner] one says also, ↑ رَمَاهُ بِالمُسْكِتَاتِ [*He smote him*, or *afflicted him*, *with the words*, or *acts*, *that silenced him*]. (T in art. رمو, from Aboo-Málik.) And بِهِ سُكَاتٌ [*He has in him that which makes him silent*]: said of one long silent in consequence of disease (A, TA) or of some evil in him. (TA.) And أَصَابَ سُكَاتًا *He met with*, or *experienced*, *a disease that prevented him from speaking*. (TA.) — هُوَ عَلَى سُكَاتِ الأَمْرِ *He is at the point of accomplishing the affair*. (Ḳ.) And كُنْتُ عَلَى سُكَاتِ هٰذِهِ الحَاجَةِ *I was at the point of attaining this want*, or *needful affair*. (Ṣ.) — حَيَّةٌ سُكَاتٌ ‡ *A serpent that bites before one has knowledge of it*; (Ṣ, A, Ḳ, TA;) as also ↑ سَكُوتٌ. (TA.)

سَكُوتٌ: see سِكِّيتٌ. — Applied to a she-camel, *That does not utter the* [*grumbling*] *cry termed* رُغَآء *when the saddle is put upon her*. (M, TA.) — See also سُكَاتٌ, last sentence.

سُكَيْتٌ: see سِكِّيتٌ. — السُّكَيْتُ and ↑ السُّكَّيْتُ, (Ṣ, Mṣb, Ḳ,) sometimes pronounced thus with teshdeed, (Ṣ,) the former being the more common, (Mṣb,) *The tenth horse in a race*; i. e. *the last of them*; (Mṣb;) *the last horse among those that start together in a race*, (Ṣ, Ḳ,) *of the ten that are reckoned*; (Ṣ;) also called الفِسْكِلُ (Ṣ, Mṣb) and القَاشُورُ; those that come in after this one not being reckoned. (Ṣ.) The other nine are thus called, beginning with the first of these: المُجَلِّى, المُصَلِّى, المُسَلِّى, التَّالِى, المُرْتَاحُ, العَاطِفُ, الحَظِىُّ, المُؤَمَّلُ, and اللَّطِيمُ. (TA.) Sb says that سُكَيْتٌ is a contracted dim. of سُكَّيْتٌ; the uncontracted dim. of which is سُكَيْكِيتٌ. (TA.) — [Hence,] one says, فُلَانٌ سُكَيْتُ الحَلْبَةِ [lit. *Such a one is the tenth horse of those that are started together for a wager*], meaning ‡ *such a one is scrupulously nice and exact*, or *neat*, [*and therefore deliberate*,] *in his handicraft*. (A, TA.)

سُكَاتَةٌ: see سُكَاتٌ.

سُكَّيْتٌ: see سِكِّيتٌ. — السُّكَّيْتُ: see السُّكَيْتُ.

سِكِّيتٌ (Ṣ, A, Mṣb, Ḳ) and ↑ سَاكُوتٌ (Ṣ, A, Ḳ) and ↑ سَكُوتٌ (A, TA) and ↑ سُكَيْتٌ and ↑ سُكَّيْتٌ and ↑ سِكِّيتٌ and ↑ سَاكُوتَةٌ, (Ḳ,) [all intensive epithets, and the last doubly intensive,] A man *constantly*, or *continually*, *silent*: (Ṣ in explanation of the first and second:) or *much*, or *often*, *silent*, (Mṣb in explanation of the first, and Ḳ in explanation of all above-cited therefrom,) *restraining himself from speech*; (Mṣb;) and ↑ سَكْتٌ signifies the same: (Ḳ:) and ↑ this last, [which is originally an inf. n., and therefore used as an intensive epithet, like عَدْلٌ &c.,] (AZ, Ḳ,) and ↑ سَاكُوتٌ and ↑ سَاكُوتَةٌ and ↑ سُكُتَةٌ, (TA,) [but the last, which is written in the TA without any syll. signs, is doubly intensive, as is also that next preceding it,] a man *who speaks little*, (AZ, Ḳ, TA,) *without inability to express his mind*, or *to express what he would say*, (AZ, TA,) *and, when he speaks, does so well*. (AZ, Ḳ, TA.)

سِكِّيتٌ: see the next preceding paragraph.

سَاكِتٌ [part. n. of 1; *Silent*, &c.: pl. سُكُوتٌ]. (TA.)

سَاكُوتٌ :
سَاكُوتَةٌ : } see سِكِّيتٌ; each in two places.

أُسْكَاتٌ The *temperate days in the latter*, or *last*, *part of the* صَيْف [app. here meaning *summer*]. (Ḳ.) — *Remains* of anything: (Ḳ:) as though pl. of سُكْتَةٌ, before mentioned. (TA.) — Also, (Ḳ,) or أُسْكَاتٌ مِنَ النَّاسِ, (IAạr, Lḥ,) *Sundry*, or *scattered*, *parties*, or *classes*, *of people*: (IAạr:) or i. q. أَوْبَاشٌ [i. e. *a medley*, or *mixed multitude*; or the *lowest* or *basest* or *meanest sort*, or *refuse*, or *riffraff*]: (Lḥ, Ḳ:) IAạr does not assign to it a sing.: some say that its sing. is سكت [app. سُكْتٌ]; but this demands consideration. (TA.)

إِسْكَاتَةٌ, of the measure إِفْعَالَةٌ from السُّكُوتُ; *A silence* [or *pause*] *of short duration, requiring something to be said or read or recited after it*: or *an abstaining from elevating the voice in speech*; not an absolute silence, in which one ceases, or abstains, from reading or reciting or speaking; for it occurs in a trad. in the words, مَا تَقُولُ فِى إِسْكَاتَتِكَ [*What dost thou say in thy* اسكاتة?]. (IAth, TA.)

مُسْكِتَاتٌ: see رَمَاهُ بِالمُسْكِتَاتِ.

المُسْكِتُ *The last of the* قِدَاح [or *arrows used in the game called* المَيْسِر]. (Ḳ.) This is omitted in some of the copies of the Ḳ. (MF.)

الحِكْمَةُ المَسْكُوتُ عَنْهَا *The secrets of the science of the Divine Essence*. (TA in art. حكم, q. v.)

سكر

1. سَكِرَ, aor. ـَ, inf. n. سَكَرٌ (Ṣ, Mgh, Mṣb, Ḳ) and سُكْرٌ, (A, Mgh, Ḳ,) or this is a simple subst., (Ṣ, Mṣb,) and سُكُرٌ and سَكْرٌ (Ḳ) and سِكْرٌ (Mṣb) and سَكَرَانٌ, (Ḳ,) *He was*, or *became*, *intoxicated*, *inebriated*, or *drunken*; (MA, KL, &c.;) contr. of صَحَا. (Ṣ, A, Ḳ.) [See also سُكْرٌ, below.] — [Hence,] سَكِرَ عَلَىَّ فُلَانٌ, (A,) inf. n. سَكَرٌ, (Ḳ,) ‡ *Such a one was*, or *became*, *violently angry with me*: (A:) or *angry*; or *enraged*. (Ḳ.) And لَهُ عَلَىَّ سَكَرٌ ‡ *He has violent anger against me*. (A.) — And سَكِرَتْ أَبْصَارُ القَوْمِ; and سُكِّرَتْ أَبْصَارُنَا; and سَكِرَتْ عَيْنُهُ: see 2. — Also, سَكِرَ, aor. ـَ, (TḲ,) inf. n. سَكَرٌ, (IAạr, Ḳ,) *It* (a watering-trough, or tank, TḲ) *was*, or *became*, *full*. (IAạr, Ḳ, TḲ.) — And سَكِرَتِ الرِّيحُ, (A, and so in my MS. copy of the Ḳ,) or سَكَرَتْ, (Ṣ, O, and so in the CḲ,) aor. ـُ, (Ṣ, O,) or, as some relate a verse of Jendel Ibn-El-Muthennà Eṭ-Ṭuhawee, in which it occurs, ـَ, (O,) [indicating that the pret. is سَكِرَتْ or that the aor. is irreg.,] inf. n. سُكُورٌ (Ṣ, O, Ḳ) and سَكَرَانٌ, (Ḳ,) ‡ *The wind became still*, (Ṣ, A, O, Ḳ,) *after blowing*. (Ṣ.) And سَكَرَ, [or سَكِرَ,] inf. n. سُكُورٌ, ‡ *It* (water) *became still, ceasing to run*: so says AZ: and ‡ *it* (the sea) *became calm*, or *motionless*: so says IAạr. (TA.) And سَكِرَ, (A,) or سَكَرَ, aor. ـُ, (TA,) ‡ *It* (food [in a cooking-pot], or hot water, A, or a hot thing, TA) *ceased to boil*, or *estuate*, (A, TA,) or *to burn*, or *be hot*: (TA:) and † *it* (heat) *became allayed*, or *it subsided*. (TA.) = سَكَرَهُ: see 4. — Also, (IAạr, TA,) aor. ـُ, (TḲ,) inf. n. سَكْرٌ, (Ḳ,) *He filled it*. (IAạr, Ḳ,* TA.) — Also, (Ṣ, Mgh, Mṣb,) aor. as above, (Ṣ, Mṣb,) and so the inf. n.; (Ṣ, Mgh, Mṣb, Ḳ;) and ↑ سَكَّرَهُ, inf. n. تَسْكِيرٌ; (MF;) *He stopped it up*, or *dammed it*; namely, a river, or rivulet. (Ṣ, Mgh, Mṣb, Ḳ, MF.) And hence, سَكَرَ البَابَ, and ↑ سَكَّرَهُ, † *He closed*, or *stopped up*, *the door*. (TA.) — سُكِّرَتْ أَبْصَارُنَا: see 2.

2. سَكَّرَهُ: see 4. — And see also 1, last two explanations. — سُكِّرَتْ أَبْصَارُنَا, in the Ḳur [xv. 15], means ‡ *Our eyes have been prevented from seeing, and dazzled*: (Ṣ, Ḳ:) or *have been covered over*: (Aboo-'Amr Ibn-El-'Alà, Ṣ, Ḳ:) and ↑ سُكِرَتْ, without teshdeed, *have been prevented from seeing*: (Fr, Ḳ:*) or this latter, which is the reading of El-Ḥasan, means, accord. to him, *have been enchanted*: (Ṣ:) or both mean, *have been covered*

and closed by enchantment, so that we imagined ourselves to behold things which we did not really see: (T, TA:) Mujáhid explains the latter reading as meaning, *have been stopped up;* i. e., *have been covered by that which prevented their seeing, like as water is prevented from flowing by a* سِكْر [or *dam*]: (A'Obeyd:) and another reading is ↓ سَكِرَتْ, meaning, *have become dazzled, like those of the intoxicated:* (Ksh, Bḍ:*) AO says that ↓ سَكِرَتْ أَبْصَارُ القَوْمِ means ‡ *The people became affected by a giddiness; and an affection like cloudiness of the eye, or weakness of the sight, came over them, so that they did not see;* and Aboo-'Amr Ibn-El-'Alà says that this signification is derived from سُكْر; as though their eyes were intoxicated: Zj says that ↓ سَكِرَتْ عَيْنُهُ means † *his eye became dazzled, and ceased to see.* (TA.) — سُكِّرَ لِلْحَاجَةِ, meaning † *His judgment,* or *opinion, was confused respecting the object of want,* is said of a man only before he has determined upon the thing alluded to. (TA.) — سَكَّرَهُ, inf. n. تَسْكِيرٌ, also signifies *He squeezed his throat,* or *throttled him.* (Ṣ, Ḳ.) One says, البَعِيرُ يُسَكِّرُ آخَرَ بِذِرَاعِهِ حَتَّى يَكَادُ يَقْتُلُهُ [*The camel throttles another with his arm so that he almost kills him*]. (Ṣ.)

4. اسكرهُ *It* (wine, or beverage,) *intoxicated,* or *inebriated, him;* (Ṣ, A;) or *deprived him of his reason;* (Mṣb;) as also, accord. to some, ↓ سَكَّرَهُ; (MF, TA;) but the former is that which commonly obtains; (TA;) [and ↓ سكّرهُ has the same signification; or its inf. n.] تَسْكِيرٌ signifies the *causing,* or *making, to be affected with the remains of intoxication.* (KL. [See the pass. part. n. of this last, below.]) The first is also said of قريض [app. a mistranscription for قريص, which may be syn. with قَارِصٌ, meaning "sour milk," for this has an effect like intoxication when too much of it has been drunk]; and thus applied it is tropical. (TA.)

6. تساكر *He feigned intoxication,* or *a state of drunkenness.* (Ṣ, A.*)

8. استكر الضَّرْعُ *The udder became full of milk.* (MA.) — And استكرت السَّمَآءُ *The sky rained vehemently.* (MA.)

سَكْرٌ: see سَكْرَانُ: = and سِكْرٌ. = Also *A certain herb,* or *leguminous plant,* (بَقْلَةٌ,) *of such as are termed* أَحْرَار [pl. of حُرٌّ], (Aboo-Naṣr, Ḳ,) *which is of the best of* بُقُول: (TA as from the Ḳ: [but not in my MS. copy of the Ḳ nor in the CḲ:]) AḤn says that no description of its general attributes or qualities had come to his knowledge. (TA.)

سُكْرٌ an inf. n., (A, Mgh, Ḳ,) or a simple subst., signifying *Intoxication, inebriation,* or *drunkenness;* i. e. the *state thereof;* (Ṣ, Mṣb;) *a state that intervenes as an obstruction between a man and his intellect;* mostly used in relation to intoxicating drinks: but sometimes as meaning † *such a state arising from anger,* or *from the passion of love:* a poet says,

* سُكْرَانِ سُكْرُ هَوًى وَسُكْرُ مُدَامَةٍ *

* أَنَّى يُفِيقُ فَتًى بِهِ سُكْرَانِ *

[*Two intoxications, the intoxication of love and the intoxication of wine: how shall a youth recover his senses in whom are two intoxications?*]. (Er-Rághib, TA.)

سِكْرٌ a subst. from السَّكْرُ (Mgh, Ḳ) as meaning "the stopping up, or damming," of the river, or rivulet; (Ḳ;) i. e. *A dam; a thing with which a river,* or *rivulet, is stopped up;* (Ṣ,* Mṣb, Ḳ, TA;) and ↓ سَكْرٌ, originally an inf. n., occurs in the same sense: (Mgh:) the pl. of the former is سُكُورٌ. (Ḳ.)

سَكَرٌ *Wine:* (Ḳ:) so, accord. to Fr and others in the Ḳur [xvi. 69], تَتَّخِذُونَ مِنْهُ سَكَرًا وَرِزْقًا حَسَنًا, meaning, *ye obtain therefrom wine, and raisins and dried dates and the like;* this being said before wine was prohibited: (TA:) and the [*beverage called*] نَبِيذ (Ṣ, A) *prepared from dried dates:* (Ṣ:) so in the Ḳur, ubi suprà: (Ṣ:) or the *expressed juice of fresh ripe dates when it has become strong;* (Mgh, Mṣb;) originally an inf. n.: (Mgh:) or *an infusion of dried dates, untouched by fire:* (A'Obeyd:) *a beverage,* (A,) or نَبِيذ, (Ḳ,) *made from dried dates and from* كَشُوث [*a species of cuscuta,* or *dodder*] (A, Ḳ) *and myrtle,* آس, (A,) which is the most bitter beverage in the world, (A,) and forbidden like wine; (TA;) or *made from dried dates and* كشوث, *disposed layer upon layer, upon which water is poured;* and some assert that *sometimes myrtle* (آس) *is mixed with it, and this increases its strength:* (AḤn:) also *anything that intoxicates:* (Ḳ:) and *what is forbidden* [*that is obtained*] *from fruit* (I'Ab, T, Ḳ) [*of the palm-tree and grape vine*], meaning wine, before its being forbidden; and الرِّزْقُ الحَسَنُ is what is lawful [that is obtained] from grapes and dates: (I'Ab, T, TA:) and *vinegar;* (Ḳ;) accord. to some of the expositors of the Ḳur, ubi suprà; but this is a meaning unknown to the leading lexicologists: (B, TA:) and *food:* (Ḳ:) so accord. to AO alone; as in the following saying of a poet;

* جَعَلْتَ أَعْرَاضَ الكِرَامِ سَكَرًا *

[*Thou hast made the reputations of the generous to be food:* or] *thou hast made the vituperation of the generous to be food to thee:* but the leading lexicologists disallow this; and Zj says that the more probable meaning here is *wine.* (TA.)

سَكِرٌ: see سَكْرَانُ: — and سِكِّيرٌ.

سَكْرَةٌ *A fit of intoxication:* (A, Mgh:) pl. سَكَرَاتٌ. (Mgh.) You say, ذَهَبَ بَيْنَ الصَّحْوَةِ وَالسَّكْرَةِ *He went away in state between that of sensibility and insensibility,* or *mental perception and inability thereof.* (TA.) — And ‡ *A fit of anger.* (TA.) — And ‡ *An overpowering sensation of delight, affecting youth.* (TA.) — سَكْرَةُ المَوْتِ ‡ [*The intoxication of death;* meaning] *the confusion of the intellect by reason of the severity of the agony of death:* (B, TA:) *the oppressive sensation attendant upon death, which deprives the sufferer of reason:* (Bḍ in l. 18:) the *oppressive sensation,* (Ṣ, A,* Mgh, Ḳ,) *and disturbance of the mind, and insensibility,* (Ḳ,) *attendant upon death.* (Ṣ,* A, Mgh, Ḳ.) And in like manner, سَكْرَةُ الهَمِّ, (Ḳ,) and النَّوْمِ, (TA,) ‡ *The oppressive sensation, &c., attendant upon anxiety,* (Ḳ,) and *upon sleep.* (TA.)

سَكْرَةٌ *I. q.* شَيْلَمٌ; (Ḳ;) [or *resembling the* شيلم; (see زُوَانٌ;) *a certain plant,* app. called by the former name because *a decoction thereof is used as an anæsthetic;* said to be] *the same that is called* مُوَيْزَاءُ, *that is* [*often found*] *in wheat.* (TA.)

سَكْرَانُ (Ṣ, A, Mgh, Mṣb, Ḳ) and سَكْرَانٌ, (TA,) which latter is seldom used, and is of the dial. of the Benoo-Asad, as is said in the Ṣ and Mṣb of its fem., (TA,) and ↓ سَكْرٌ; (Ḳ; [in the TA ↓ سَكِرٌ, but this is afterwards mentioned in the Ḳ as an intensive epithet;]) fem. [of the first,] سَكْرَى; (Ṣ, Mgh, Mṣb, Ḳ;) and [of the second,] سَكْرَانَةٌ; (Ṣ, Mṣb, Ḳ;) and [of the third,] سَكْرَةٌ; (Ḳ; [in the TA سَكِرَةٌ;]) *Intoxicated; inebriated; drunken:* (Ṣ, Mṣb, Ḳ:) [see سُكْرٌ:] pl. سُكَارَى [which is said in the TA to be also pl. of سَكِرٌ] and سَكَارَى, (Ṣ, Mṣb, Ḳ,) of which the former is the more common, or, as some say, the latter, and the former of which is said to be the only instance of the kind, except كُسَالَى and عُجَالَى and غُيَارَى, (TA,) [to which should be added حُيَارَى, and probably some other instances,] and سَكْرَى; (Ṣ, Ḳ;) or this is a fem. sing. applied as an epithet to a pl. n.; (Fr;) and in the Ḳur iv. 46, El-Aạmash read سُكْرَى, with ḍamm, which is very strange, since no pl. of the measure فُعْلَى is known. (TA.) Th says that the words of the Ḳur [iv. 46] لَا تَقْرَبُوا الصَّلَاةَ وَأَنْتُمْ سُكَارَى [*Engage ye not in prayer when ye are intoxicated*] was said before the prohibition of wine was revealed: others say that the meaning is, *when ye are intoxicated with sleep.* (TA.)

سُكُرْكَةٌ, written by Sh سُكْرُكَةٌ: see art. سكرك. (TA.)

سَكُورٌ: see سِكِّيرٌ.

سُكَّرٌ [*Sugar;*] *a certain sweet substance,* (TA,) *well known:* (Mṣb, TA:) a Pers. word, (Ṣ,) arabicized, (Ṣ, Ḳ,) from شَكَرْ: (Ḳ:) n. un. with ة [signifying *a piece of sugar*]: (Ṣ, Ḳ:) it is hot and moist, accord. to the most correct opinion; but some say, cold: and the best sort of it is the transparent, called طَبَرْزَذ; and the old is more delicate than the new: it is injurious to the stomach, engendering yellow bile; but the juice of the لَيْمُون and نَارَنْج counteract its noxiousness: it is said to be a word recently introduced; but some say that it occurs in one trad. (TA.) — Also *Like* سُكَّر [or *sugar*] *in sweetness:* so used by Aboo-Ziyád El-Kilábee. (TA.) — Also *A certain kind of sweet fresh ripe dates;* (Ḳ;) *a sort of fresh ripe dates, likened to sugar in sweetness:* (Mgh:) or *a kind of very sweet dates;* (AḤát, T, Mṣb;) *known to the people of El-Baḥreyn,* (T,) *and in Sijilmáseh and Dar'ah, and, as some say, in El-Medeeneh, where, how-*

ever, they require to be dried artificially. (MF.) —— A kind of grapes, which, being affected by what is termed مُرَق, fall off, (Ḳ,) for the most part: their bunches are of middling size; and they are white, juicy, and very sweet, (TA,) of the best kinds of grapes; (Ḳ;) and are made into raisins. (TA.)

سُكَّرِىٌّ [Sugary; saccharine. —— And] Cake containing sugar, or barley-sugar, with almonds, or pistachio-nuts. (MA.)

سَكَّارٌ One who makes, or sells, the beverage called نَبِيذ; syn. نَبَّاذٌ. (Ṣ, Ḳ.)

سِكِّيرٌ One who intoxicates himself much, or often; a drunkard; a tippler; (Ḳ;) as also ▼ مِسْكِيرٌ (Ṣ, Ḳ) and ▼ سَكُورٌ (IAạr, Ḳ) and ▼ سَكِرٌ: (Ḳ:) or constantly intoxicated: (Ṣ:) the pl. of سَكِرٌ is سَكَارَى, which is also pl. of سَكْرَانُ. (TA.)

رِيحٌ سَاكِرَةٌ ‡ Wind becoming still. (A.) And لَيْلَةٌ سَاكِرَةٌ ‡ A still night; a night in which the wind is still; (Ṣ,* A;) a night in which there is no wind. (TA.) And مَآءٌ سَاكِرٌ ‡ Still, not running, water. (AZ, TA.)

سَيْكَرَانٌ A certain plant, always green, the grain whereof is eaten: (Ḳ: [but this description seems to be an incorrect abstract of what here follows:]) Ed-Deenawaree [i. e. AḤn] says, it is of the plants that continue green throughout the whole of the summer: I asked a sheykh of the Arabs of Syria, and he said, it is the سُعْر, [correctly سُمْر,] and we eat it in its fresh state, with what an eating! and, he said, it has green grains, like the grain of the رَازِيَانِج [or fennel], except that they are round: (O:) [in the present day, it is applied to henbane, or a species thereof: accord. to Forskål, (Flora Aegypt. Arab., p. lxiii.,) hyoscyamus datora. See also شَيْكَرَان.]

مُسَكَّرٌ Affected with the remains of intoxication. (Ṣ, Ḳ.)

مِسْكِيرٌ: see سِكِّيرٌ.

سكرج

سُكُرُّجَةٌ, or سُكُرَّجَةٌ, accord. to different authorities, (TA,) or both, (MF,) not an Arabic word, but occurring in a trad.; [arabicized from the Pers. سُكُرُّجَهْ, meaning A saucer;] a sort of small bowl-shaped vessel, in [or out of] which one eats: it is of two sizes; the larger holding six ounces; and the smaller, three ounces, or four mithkáls, or between two thirds of an ounce [and some other quantity more or less (for there is an omission in this place in my original)]: in such vessels, placed upon the tables, around the meats, the Arabs used to put sauces and the like to excite the appetite and to aid digestion: expl. by Ed-Dáwoodee as a small, varnished, bowl-shaped vessel. (TA.)

سكرك

سُكُرْكَةٌ, (Mgh, and so in some copies of the Ḳ,) thus written by IAth, (TA,) [and thus in copies of the Ṣ and A voce مِزْرٌ, and of the Ṣ and Ḳ voce سُقُرْقَعٌ, and of the Mgh and Mṣb and Ḳ voce غُبَيْرَآءُ, &c.,] or سُكُرُّكَةٌ, thus written by Sh, (TA in art. سكر, and thus in a copy of the Ḳ,) an Abyssinian word, (TA,) arabicized, (Mgh, TA,) A certain beverage, (Mgh, Ḳ, TA,) of the Abyssinians, (Mgh,) prepared from ذُرَة [or millet], (Mgh, Ḳ, TA,) which intoxicates; the wine of the Abyssinians; also called سُقُرْقَعٌ [q. v.], (TA,) and غُبَيْرَآءُ, (Mgh and Mṣb and Ḳ in art. غبر, and TA in the present art.,) and مِزْرٌ [q. v.]. (A in art. مزر.)

سكف

1. مَا سَكَفْتُ البَابَ, (Ibn-'Abbád, Ḳ, TA,) and بَابَهُ, (TA in art. عتب,) aor. ـُ, (Ḳ,) I did not tread, or have not trodden, upon the threshold of the door, (Ibn-'Abbád, Ḳ, TA,) and of his door; (TA;) as also ▼ مَا تَسَكَّفْتُهُ: (Ḳ:) and لَا أَتَسَكَّفُ ▼ لَهُ بَابًا [I will not tread upon the threshold of a door of his; or] I will not enter a house, or chamber, of his. (Z, TA.)

4. اسكف, (inf. n. إِسْكَافٌ, Mṣb,) He was, or became, an إِسْكَاف [q. v. infrà]. (IAạr, T, Mṣb, Ḳ.)

5: see 1, in two places.

سِكَافَةٌ The craft, or handicraft, of the إِسْكَاف [q. v.]: (Ḳ:) termed by Lth an inf. n., the source of الإِسْكَاف, having no [unaugmented] verb. (TA.)

سَكَّافٌ: see إِسْكَافٌ.

سَاكِفٌ The lintel of a door, in which turns the صَائِر, (O, Ḳ, TA,) this latter word meaning [the upper and] the lower extremity of the door, the upper of which turns [in a socket in the lintel, and the lower in a socket in the threshold]: so says En-Naḍr. (O, TA. [The explanation of صَائِر in the O seems to have been mutilated by a copyist, and requires the additions which I have made, according to modern usage.])

سَيْكَفٌ: see إِسْكَافٌ.

أُسْكُفٌ: see إِسْكَافٌ, in two places.

أُسْكُفَّا العَيْنَيْنِ The parts on which grow the eyelashes of the two eyes: (IAạr, Ḳ:) or the lower eyelids. (Z, Ḳ.)

أُسْكُفَّةٌ The threshold of a door, (Ṣ, O, Ḳ,) upon which one treads; (O, Ḳ;) as also ▼ أُسْكُوفَةٌ: (TA:) or the lintel of a door: and sometimes [or rather almost universally] used in the former sense, which is the only meaning mentioned in the T [and] in the Abridgment of the 'Eyn [and in most other lexicons]: pl. اسكاف [app. أَسْكَافٌ, and, if so, anomalous]. (Mṣb.) = Also The خرقة [i. e. خِرْقَة, or rag, or ragged garment, or perhaps it is a mistranscription for حِرْفَة, i. e. craft, or handicraft, like سِكَافَةٌ,] of the إِسْكَاف: extr.: on the authority of Fr. (TA.)

إِسْكَافٌ (Sh, Ṣ, M, Mṣb, Ḳ, &c.) and ▼ أُسْكُوفٌ (Sh, Ṣ, M, Ḳ) and ▼ سَيْكَفٌ and ▼ أُسْكُفٌ and ▼ سَكَّافٌ (Ḳ) A maker of boots, (Sh, Mṣb, Ḳ,) or of shoes or sandals; (MA;) or a sewer of boots &c.: (Mṣb;) or the first word, (Mṣb, Ḳ, TA,) as used by the Arabs [of the desert], (Mṣb, TA,) any artificer, or artisan, (Mṣb, Ḳ, TA,) thus expl. in the M, and so its three [perhaps a mistake for four] dial. vars., but said by J [in the Ṣ] to be a meaning not known, (TA,) except the maker of boots, for he is called ▼ أُسْكُفٌ, (Ḳ, TA,) i. e. when they mean such as is called إِسْكَاف in the cities or towns or villages: (TA:) or a carpenter; (Ḳ;) in which sense it is used by Esh-Shemmákh, but J says, [in the Ṣ,] only on the ground of supposition; (TA;) and any handicraftsman who works with an iron tool: (AA, Ḳ,* TA:) pl. أَسَاكِفَةٌ (Ṣ, Mṣb, TA) [and أَسَاكِيفُ]. —— Also the first word, Skilful with an affair. (O, Ḳ.) Sh says, I heard El-Fak'asee say, إِنَّكَ لَإِسْكَافٌ بِهٰذَا الأَمْرِ, meaning Verily thou art skilful with this affair. (O.) = Accord. to Ibn-'Abbád, الإِسْكَافُ is also used (O, Ḳ) by Ibn-Mukbil (O) as meaning The redness of wine: but this is a mistranscription, (O, Ḳ,) and a perversion of the meaning: (O:) the right word is الإِسْكَابُ. (O, Ḳ.)

أُسْكُوفٌ: see the next preceding paragraph.

أُسْكُوفَةٌ: see أُسْكُفَّةٌ.

سكن

1. سَكَنَ, (Ṣ, Mgh, L, Mṣb, Ḳ,) aor. ـُ, (L,) inf. n. سُكُونٌ, (Ṣ, Mgh, L, Mṣb, Ḳ,) said of a thing, (Ṣ, L,) of a thing that moves, (Mgh, Mṣb,) It was, or became, still, motionless, stationary, in a state of rest, quiet, calm, or unruffled, (هَدَأَ, Abu-l-'Abbás, L, or قَرَّ, Ḳ,) after motion; (Abu-l-'Abbás, L;) its motion [ceased, or] went away; (L, Mṣb;) and in like manner said of a man, and of a beast: (Abu-l-'Abbás, L:) and said of anything such as wind and heat and cold and the like; of rain; [and of pain;] and of anger; [&c.;] it was, or became, still, calm, tranquillized, appeased, allayed, assuaged, or quelled; [it died away, passed away, or ceased to be: and it remitted, or subsided; became alleviated, light, slight, or gentle:] and said of a man [or beast or the like, and of a voice or sound], he [or it] was, or became, still, or silent. (L.) [Hence,] one says, سَكَنَ الدَّمْعُ, and الدَّمُ, meaning رَقَأَ [The tears, and the blood, stopped, or ceased to flow]. (Ṣ and Mgh in art. رقأ.) [And one says of heat, and cold, and pain, &c., سَكَنَ عَنْهُ It passed away from him; quitted him. And سَكَنَتِ النَّارُ The fire became extinguished; or became allayed or assuaged; subsided; or ceased to flame or blaze or burn fiercely.] —— [Hence also, It (a letter) was or became, quiescent; i. e., without a vowel immediately following it; contr. of تَحَرَّكَ.] —— And سَكَنَ إِلَيْهِ, (Mṣb, [where the aor. is said to be ـَ, but this is either a mistake or rare, for the aor. accord. to common usage is ـُ, as in the Ḳur vii. 189 and xxx. 20,]) inf. n. سُكُونٌ (Mgh, Mṣb) and سَكَنٌ, (Mṣb,) He trusted to it, or relied upon it, so as to be, or become, easy, or quiet, in mind; i. q. رَكَنَ إِلَيْهِ; (Ṣ and Ḳ &c. in art. ركن;) and

اِطْمَأَنَّ إِلَيْهِ; (TA in art. طمن;) [and اِعْتَمَدَ عَلَيْهِ; and وَثِقَ بِهِ; &c.; and *he inclined to it;* syn. مَالَ إِلَيْهِ; and *became familiar with it;* syn. اِسْتَأْنَسَ بِهِ, and أَلِفَ; agreeably with explanations here following;] namely, a thing: (Mṣb:) and سَكَنَ إِلَيْهَا, aor. ـُ, *he trusted to her,* or *relied upon her, so as to be,* or *become, easy,* or *quiet, in mind;* &c., as above; syn. اِطْمَأَنَّ إِلَيْهَا; (Ksh and Bḍ in vii. 189, and Ksh in xxx. 20;) and مَالَ إِلَيْهَا; (Ksh in vii. 189, and the same and Bḍ in xxx. 20;) and اِسْتَأْنَسَ بِهَا, and أَلِفَ; (Bḍ in the same two places;) namely, his wife. (Ksh and Bḍ.) — And سَكَنَ الدَّارَ, (Ṣ, MA, Mgh, L, Mṣb, Ḳ,) and فِى الدَّارِ, (Mgh, Mṣb,) and بِالْمَكَانِ, (L,) aor. ـُ, (L, Mṣb, JM,) inf. n. سُكْنَى (MA, Mgh, L, JM) and سُكُونٌ (MA, L) and سَكَنٌ, (MA,) or ▼ سُكْنَى is a simple subst., and the inf. n. is سكن, (Mṣb, [accord. to which the latter is app. سَكْنٌ, for it is there said that the verb in this case is like طَلَبَ, the unaugmented inf. n. of which is طَلْبٌ, but this inf. n. سَكْنٌ I have not found elsewhere, and what is generally used as the inf. n. or quasi-inf. n. of the verb in this case is ▼ سُكْنَى,]) or ▼ سُكْنَى is a subst. in the sense of إِسْكَانٌ, as expl. below, (Mgh,) [or rather it is also a subst. in this sense,] *He inhabited,* or *dwelt* or *abode in, the house* [and *the place*]. (MA, Mgh.) وَلَهُ مَا سَكَنَ فِى ٱللَّيْلِ وَٱلنَّهَارِ, in the Ḳur [vi. 13], is from السُّكْنَى (Ksh, Bḍ) or from السُّكُونُ: (Bḍ:) if from the former, (Ksh, Bḍ,) it signifies *To Him belongeth what taketh up its abode in the night and the day;* (IAạr, Ksh,* Bḍ,* L, Jel;) meaning, what the night and the day include within their limits: (Ksh,* Bḍ:) or, if from السُّكُونُ, (Bḍ,) *what is still,* or *motionless,* (Abu-l-'Abbás, Bḍ, L,) and what moves; one of the two contraries being mentioned as sufficient [to show what is intended] without the other; (Bḍ;) app. meaning the creation, collectively, or all created beings. (Abu-l-'Abbás, L.) — And سَكَنَ, (L, Ḳ,) aor. ـُ, (Ḳ,) *He became such as is termed* مِسْكِين [q. v.]; (L, Ḳ;) as also سَكُنَ, (Ḳ,) and ▼ اسكن, and ▼ تسكّن, and ▼ تَمَسْكَنَ: (L, Ḳ:) and [thus it means particularly] *he was,* or *became, lowly, humble,* or *submissive;* and *low, abject, abased, and weak;* as also ▼ اسكن, (L,) and ▼ تسكّن, and ▼ تَمَسْكَنَ; (Ṣ,* L;) the former of these being the regular form, (Ṣ, L,) and the more common and more chaste; (L;) the latter of them anomalous, [from المِسْكِينُ,] like تَمَنْدَلَ from المِنْدِيلُ, and تَمَدْرَعَ from المِدْرَعَةُ; (Ṣ, L;) and ▼ استكن, (L, Mṣb,) and ▼ اِسْتَكَانَ, of the measure اِفْتَعَلَ (L, Mṣb, Ḳ) from المَسْكَنَةُ (L, Ḳ) or from السُّكُونُ, (Mṣb,) with ا added, (L, Mṣb,) the vowel of the medial radical letter being thus rendered full in sound, (L, Mṣb, Ḳ,) or it is of the measure اِسْتَفْعَلَ from الكَيْنَةُ, signifying "evil state or condition," (Mṣb,) or from الكَيْنُ signifying "the [piece of] flesh in the interior of the vulva," because he who is lowly and abject is the most obscure of mankind. (L. [See also arts. كين and كون.])

2. سكّنهُ, (Ṣ, L, Mṣb, Ḳ,) inf. n. تَسْكِينٌ, (Ṣ, L, Ḳ,) *He,* or *it, caused it to be,* or *become, still, motionless, stationary, in a state of rest, quiet, calm,* or *unruffled;* (Ṣ,* L, Mṣb, Ḳ;) namely, a thing: (Ṣ, L, Mṣb:) [*and caused it,* namely, anything such as wind, and heat, and cold, and the like, as rain, and pain, and anger, *to be,* or *become, still,* or *calm; stilled, calmed, tranquillized, appeased, allayed, assuaged,* or *quelled, it; caused it to die away, pass away,* or *cease to be:* and *caused it to remit,* or *subside; to become alleviated, light, slight,* or *gentle:* and *caused him,* and *it,* namely, a man or beast or the like, and a voice or sound, *to become still,* or *silent:* (see 1, first sentence:)] and ▼ اسكنهُ signifies the same. (L.) [Hence,] one says of God, سَكَّنَ دَمْعَهُ, meaning أَرْقَأَهُ [*He caused his tears to stop,* or *cease flowing*]. (Ṣ and TA in art. رقأ.) — [And hence, *He made it* (a letter) *quiescent;* i. e., *made it to be without a vowel immediately following it; contr. of* حَرَّكَهُ.] = تَسْكِينٌ also signifies The *straightening* a cane, or spear, (صَعْدَة,) *with fire* [which is termed السَّكَن]. (IAạr, L, Ḳ.) = And The *constantly riding a light and swift ass* which is termed سُكَيْن. (IAạr, L, Ḳ.)

3. ساكنهُ, inf. n. مُسَاكَنَةٌ, i. q. جَاوَرَهُ [meaning *He lived in his neighbourhood,* or *near to him*]. (TA in art. جور.)

4. اسكن: see 1, near the end, in two places. = اسكنهُ: see 2, first sentence. — [Hence,] said of poverty, *It made him to be little,* or *seldom, in motion.* (Aboo-Is-ḥáḳ, L, Ḳ.) — And, said of God, *He made him to be such as is termed* مِسْكِين [q. v.]. (L, Ḳ.) — And اسكنهُ الدَّارَ, (Ṣ, L, Mṣb, Ḳ,) or المَنْزِلَ, (MA,) *He made him* [or *gave him*] *to inhabit the house,* or *abode;* (Ṣ,* MA, L,* Mṣb,* Ḳ;*) *he lodged him therein.* (MA.)

5. تسكّن, said of a man, is from السَّكِينَةُ [i. e. *He had,* or *possessed,* or *affected, the quality thus termed;* meaning *he was,* or *became,* or *affected to be, calm, tranquil, grave, staid, steady,* or *sedate;* &c.]. (L.) See also Q. Q. 2, below: and see 1, above, near the end, in two places.

8. استكن, and its var. or syn. اِسْتَكَانَ: see 1, near the end.

Q. Q. 2. تَمَسْكَنَ *He affected to be like,* or *he imitated, such as are termed* مَسَاكِين [pl. of مِسْكِين, q. v.]. (IAth, L.) — See also 1, near the end, in two places. You say, تَمَسْكَنَ لِرَبِّهِ *He humbled,* or *abased, himself to his Lord;* or *addressed himself with earnest,* or *energetic, supplication to Him:* and ▼ تسكّن is like تَمَسْكَنَ. (Lḥ, L.)

سَكْنٌ, a quasi-pl. n. of ▼ سَاكِنٌ, like as شَرْبٌ is of شَارِبٌ, called by Akh a pl., (L,) The *inhabitants, people,* or *family,* of a house or tent; (Ṣ, L, Ḳ;) *a household.* (L.) — And The *collective body of the people of a tribe:* one says, تَحَمَّلَ السَّكْنُ فَذَهَبُوا [*The collective body of the people of the tribe bound the loads,* or *burdens, upon their beasts, and went away*]. (Lḥ, L.) — See also سَكَنٌ. — And see the paragraph here next following.

سُكْنٌ: see سُكْنَى. — And see also مَسْكَنٌ, in three places. — Also, (L, JM, [thus written in both, and expressly said in the latter to be "with ḍamm,"]) or ▼ سَكْنٌ, (thus in copies of the Ḳ,) or ▼ سَكَنٌ, (thus in the CḲ,) [but the first is app. the right,] *Food, aliment,* or *victuals,* syn. قُوتٌ; (L, Ḳ, JM;) like نُزُلٌ meaning "food (طَعَام, L, JM) of a party alighting to partake of it," and said to be called سُكْن because by means of it a place is inhabited, like as the نُزُل of an army means the "appointed rations of an army alighting at a place." (L.)

سَكَنٌ *A thing,* (Ṣ, L, Mṣb, Ḳ,) *of any kind,* (Ṣ, L,) *to which one trusts,* or *upon which one relies, so as to be,* or *become, easy,* or *quiet, in mind;* (Ṣ, L, Mṣb, Ḳ;) and in like manner, *a person,* or *persons, to whom one trusts,* &c.: applied in this sense to a family, or wife, (L, Mṣb,) as well as to property, (Mṣb,) &c.: (L, Mṣb:) and hence [particularly] signifying *a wife.* (L.) One says, [app. using it in this sense, as seems to be indicated by the context in the Ṣ,] فُلَانٌ ٱبْنُ ٱلسَّكَنِ [*Such a one is the son of the* سَكَن]; and Aṣ used to say ▼ السَّكْنِ: (Ṣ, L:) accord. to Ibn-Ḥabeeb, one says سَكْن and سَكَن. (L.) And it is said in the Ḳur [vi. 96], جَعَلَ ٱللَّيْلَ سَكَنًا *He hath made,* or *appointed, the night to be a resource for ease,* or *quiet.* (L.) And in the same [ix. 104], إِنَّ صَلَوَاتَكَ سَكَنٌ لَهُمْ, i. e. [*Verily thy prayers for forgiveness are*] *a cause of ease,* or *quiet, to them.* (Zj, L.) [And ▼ سُكْنَةٌ seems to have a similar meaning: for] ISh says, تَغْطِيَةُ الوَجْهِ عِنْدَ النَّوْمِ سُكْنَةٌ, app. [*The covering of the face on the occasion of sleep is a cause of ease,* or *quiet,*] in the case of loneliness, or of fear arising therefrom. (L.) And it is said in a trad., اَللّٰهُمَّ أَنْزِلْ عَلَيْنَا فِى أَرْضِنَا سَكَنَهَا, meaning *O God, send down upon us, in our land, the succour,* or *relief, of its inhabitants,* [app. alluding to rain,] *to which they may trust so as to be easy,* or *quiet, in mind.* (L.) — Also i. q. مَسْكَنٌ. (Lḥ, L, and Ḥam p. 400.) See the latter word, in three places. — And *Fire;* [app. first applied thereto as being a cause of ease, or comfort;] (Ṣ, L, Ḳ;) as in the saying [of a rájiz],

• وَسَكَنٍ تُوقَدُ فِى مِظَلَّهْ •

[*And a fire kindled in a large tent of hair-cloth, or in a booth, or shed*], (Ṣ, L,) describing himself as driven to have recourse thereto by the night, and by a moist wind, or a wind cold with moisture; and [afterwards used without any allusion to its being a cause of ease, or comfort,] as in the saying of another, describing a cane,

• أَقَامَهَا بِسَكَنٍ وَأَدْهَانْ •

meaning *He straightened it with fire and oils.* (L.) — And *Mercy, pity,* or *compassion.* (Ḳ.

[See also سَكِينَةٌ.] — And i. q. بَرَكَةٌ [*A blessing; prosperity*, or *good fortune; increase*; &c.]. (Ḳ.) — See also سُكْنٌ: — and سُكْنَى: — and see سَاكِنٌ.

سَكْنَةٌ [*A quiescence* of a letter; its *having no vowel immediately following*; opposed to حَرَكَةٌ: pl. سَكَنَاتٌ.] — تَرَكْتُهُمْ عَلَى سَكَنَاتِهِمْ: see سَكِنَةٌ.

سُكْنَةٌ: see سَكَنٌ.

سَكِنَةٌ *A place*; [properly] *a place of habitation* or *abode*: pl. سَكِنَاتٌ. (L.) It is said in a trad., اِسْتَقِرُّوا عَلَى سَكِنَاتِكُمْ فَقَدِ ٱنْقَطَعَتِ الهِجْرَةُ, (Ṣ, L, Ḳ,*) i. e. *Rest ye*, or *remain ye, at your places*, (Ṣ, L,) or *in your places of habitation* or *abode*, (Ṣ, L, Ḳ,) *for emigration has* [ended, having] become no longer needful. (L.) And one says, النَّاسُ عَلَى سَكِنَاتِهِمْ, [virtually] meaning, accord. to Fr, *The people are in their right state*: (Ṣ, L:) and in like manner is expl. the saying, تَرَكْتُهُمْ عَلَى سَكِنَاتِهِمْ and ▼ سَكَنَاتِهِمْ and نَزِلَاتِهِمْ; but the approved explanation is, [*I left them*] *at their places of habitation*, which is that of Th; or, as in the M, *their places of alighting*, or *abode*. (L.) — Also The *part, of the neck, which is the resting-place of the head.* (Ṣ, L, Ḳ.) So in the saying, (Ṣ, L,) attributed to several poets, (L,)

بِضَرْبٍ يُزِيلُ الهَامَ عَنْ سَكِنَاتِهِ

[*With a smiting that removes the heads from their resting-places on the necks*]. (Ṣ, L.)

سُكْنَى is an inf. n. of سَكَنَ in the phrase سَكَنَ الدَّارَ: (MA, Mgh, L, JM:) or a simple subst. therefrom: (Mṣb:) or a subst. in the sense of إِسْكَانٌ, like رُقْبَى in the sense of إِرْقَابٌ: (Mgh:) see 1, in three places: or it is a subst. (Ṣ, L, Ḳ) also (L) from أَسْكَنَهُ الدَّارَ, (Ṣ, L, Ḳ,) like as عُتْبَى is from إِعْتَابٌ, (Ṣ, L,) and so is ▼ سَكَنٌ, (Lḥ, L, Ḳ,) [which is app. mentioned in the Mṣb as an inf. n. of the former verb,] signifying, as also ▼ سُكْنٌ, [so in one place, as on the authority of Lth, in the L, and said in the MA to be, like سُكْنَى, an inf. n. of the verb first mentioned above,] The *making* [or *giving*] a man *a place*, or *an abode, to inhabit, without rent*; (L, and Ḥam p. 400 in explanation of the first of these words;) the term سُكْنَى being similar to عُمْرَى. (L.) — See also مَسْكَنٌ, in five places.

سَكِينٌ An ass *light*, or *active, and quick*, or *swift*: and سَكِينَةٌ is applied to a she-ass (L, Ḳ) in the same sense. (L.) — Hence the latter is used as a name for † *A girl*, or *young woman*, or *a female slave, that is of a light*, or *an active, spirit*. (L.) — The former also signifies *A wild ass*. (L.) — And السَّكِينَةُ is the name of *The gnat that entered into the nose of Numrood* [or *Nimrod*]. (L, Ḳ.)

سَكِينَةٌ (Ṣ, L, Mṣb, Ḳ) and ▼ سِكِّينَةٌ (Ks, L, Ḳ) and ▼ سَكِّينَةٌ, (L, Mṣb,) mentioned in the "Nawádir," (Mṣb,) on the authority of AZ, (L,) but of a measure of which there is no [other] known instance, (L, Mṣb,) *Calmness*, or *tranquillity*; (Ṣ, L, Mṣb, Ḳ;) *gravity, staidness, steadiness*, or *sedateness*; (Ṣ, L, Mṣb;) and *a quality inspiring reverence* or *veneration*: (Mṣb:) and, as some say, *mercy, pity*, or *compassion*: [see also سَكَنٌ:] and *aid* or *assistance*; or *victory* or *conquest*: and *a thing whereby a man is calmed*, or *tranquillized*: (L:) pl. of the first word سَكَائِنُ. (Ḥar p. 62.) One says of a man who is calm or tranquil, or grave &c., عَلَيْهِ السَّكِينَةُ [*Upon him is resting*, or *abiding, calmness* &c.]. (L.) And it is said in a trad., respecting the Prophet, on the occasion of the coming down of revelation, فَغَشِيَتْهُ السَّكِينَةُ, meaning *And calmness*, or *tranquillity, and* غَيْبَة [i. e., as here used, *absence of mind from self and others by its being exclusively occupied by the contemplation of divine things*], *came upon him*. (L.) And in the Ḳur [ii. 249], it is said, [with reference to the coming of the ark of the covenant,] فِيهِ سَكِينَةٌ مِنْ رَبِّكُمْ, meaning [*In which shall be*] *a cause of your becoming tranquil*, [or *easy in your minds*,] when it cometh to you [*from your Lord*]: (Zj, L, Ḳ:) or, as some say, there was in it *a head like that of the cat; when it uttered a cry, victory betided the Children of Israel*: (L:) or *a thing having a head like that of the cat* [*and a tail like that of the cat* (Bḍ)], *of chrysolite and sapphire, and a pair of wings*: (L, Ḳ:) or *an image like the cat*, that was with them among their forces, *on the appearance of which their enemies were routed*: or *an animal having a face like that of a human being, compact* [*in substance*], *the rest thereof being unsubstantial like the wind and the air*: or *the images of the Prophets, from Adam to Mohammad*: (Bḍ:) or *the signs*, or *miracles, with the performance of which Moses was endowed, and to which they trusted so as to be easy*, or *quiet, in their minds*: (L:) or by the تَابُوت to which these words refer is meant the heart, [or rather the chest, i. e. bosom,] and the سكينة is the *knowledge, and purity*, or *sincerity, in the heart* [or *bosom*]. (Bḍ.) In a trad. of 'Alee, respecting the building of the Kaabeh, it is said, فَأَرْسَلَ ٱللّٰهُ إِلَيْهِ السَّكِينَةَ, meaning [*And God sent to him*] *the wind swift in its passage*. (L.)

سُكَيْنَةٌ fem. of سُكَيْنٌ [q. v.]. (L, Ḳ.*)

الطُّرَّةُ السُّكَيْنِيَّةُ [*The hair over the forehead* (of a girl or woman) *that is cut with a straight*, or *even, edge*, or *with two such edges one above the other, so as to form a kind of border, after the fashion of Sukeyneh*,] is so called in relation to Sukeyneh the daughter of El-Ḥoseyn. (Ṣ, L, Ḳ.)

سَكَّانٌ *A maker of* سَكَاكِين [or *knives*], (ISd, L, Ḳ,*) pl. of سِكِّينٌ; (ISd, L;) as also ▼ سَكَاكِينِيٌّ, (ISd, L, Ḳ,) which latter is held by ISd to be post-classical, being formed from the pl., whereas by rule it should be formed from the sing. (L.)

سُكَّانٌ The ذَنَب, (Lth, Ṣ, MA, Mgh, L,) [i. e.] the *rudder*, (MA, KL, PṢ,) *of a ship* or *boat*, (Lth, Ṣ, MA, Mgh, L,) *by means of which it is rightly directed*, (Lth, Mgh,* L,) *and made still*, or *steady*; (Mgh, L;) its خَذْف; (AA, L;) i. q. خَيْزُرَان and كَوْثَل [meaning the same, or *its tiller*]: (A'Obeyd, L:) it is an Arabic word. (L.) Hence the saying of Ṭarafeh, (L,) likening to it the elevated neck of a she-camel, as being long, and quick in motion, (EM p. 73,) [and thus app. applying it to the upper and narrow part of a rudder,]

كَسُكَّانِ بُوصِيٍّ بِدِجْلَةَ مُصْعِدِ

(L, EM,) i. e. *Like the* سُكَّان *of a vessel of the sort called* بُوصِىّ [*ascending the Tigris*]. (EM.) — Also pl. of سَاكِنٌ [q. v.]. (L, Mṣb.)

سِكِّينٌ a word of well-known meaning; (Ṣ, Mṣb, Ḳ;) i. e. *A knife*; (MA, PṢ;) i. q. مُدْيَةٌ; (L;) as also ▼ سِكِّينَةٌ, (ISd, L, Ḳ,) a dial. var., (ISd, L,) occurring in a trad., but the former is that which is commonly known: (L:) so called because it stills the animals slaughtered with it: (Az, L, Mṣb:) of the measure فِعِّيلٌ: (IDrd, L, Mṣb:) or, accord. to some, its ن is augmentative, so that it is of the measure فِعْلِينٌ: (Mṣb:) it is masc., and sometimes fem.: (Zj, IAmb,* L, Mṣb, Ḳ:*) not heard as fem. by IAar: (L:) held to be only masc. by AZ and Aṣ and some others: (Mṣb:) but sometimes it occurs in poetry as fem. on the ground of meaning [as being syn. with مُدْيَةٌ or شَفْرَةٌ], (Mṣb,) and as such it occurs in a trad.: (L:) the pl. is سَكَاكِينُ. (ISd, MA, L.) [See an ex. in a prov. cited voce سَلَى.]

سَكِّينَةٌ: see سَكِينَةٌ.

سِكِّينَةٌ: see سَكِينَةٌ: — and see also سِكِّينٌ.

سَكَاكِينِيٌّ: see سَكَّانٌ.

سَاكِنٌ *Still, motionless, stationary, in a state of rest, quiet, calm*, or *unruffled*: [applied to a letter, *quiescent*; i. e. *without a vowel immediately following it*:] *still, calm, tranquil, becoming appeased* or *allayed* or *assuaged* or *quelled*; [*dying away, passing away*, or *ceasing to be*: *remitting*, or *subsiding*; *becoming alleviated, light, slight*, or *gentle*:] *still*, or *silent*. (L. [See its verb, سَكَنَ, first sentence.]) — *Inhabiting, dwelling*, or *abiding*; *an inhabitant*, or *a lodger*: (L, Mṣb:) and ▼ سَكَنٌ signifies the same as سَاكِنٌ [app. thus used]: (L:) the pl. of سَاكِنٌ is سُكَّانٌ. (L, Mṣb.) You say, هُمْ سُكَّانُ فُلَانٍ [*They are the lodgers of such a one*]. (Ṣ, L.) And سُكَّانُ الدَّارِ signifies *The Jinn*, or *Genii, inhabiting the house*. (L. [Respecting the custom of sacrificing an animal to the Jinn on the occasion of buying a house, in order to prevent any injury from the Jinn thereof, see ذِبْحٌ. The belief that houses are inhabited by Jinn obtains among the Arabs in the present day.]) See also سَكَنٌ. — [Other meanings are indicated by explanations of its verb.]

[أَسْكَنُ *More*, and *most, still*, &c.]

مَسْكَنٌ and مَسْكِنٌ; (Ṣ, L, Mṣb, Ḳ;) the people of El-Ḥijáz say the former, (Ṣ, L,) and the latter is anomalous; (L;) [*A place of habitation*;] *a place of alighting, abiding, sojourning*, or *lodging*; *an abode*, or *a dwelling*; (Ṣ, L, Ḳ;) *a house*, or *a tent*; (Ṣ, L, Mṣb;) pl. مَسَاكِنُ: (Mṣb:) and ▼ سَكَنٌ signifies the same as مَسْكِنٌ, [thus in the

Ḳur xvi. 82,] (Lḥ, L, and Ḥam p. 400,) as also ▼ سُكْنَى, (Lḥ, L,) and ▼ سُكُنٌ: you say, دَارٌ فِيهَا ▼ سَكَنٌ and ▼ سُكُنٌ, i. e. ▼ سُكْنَى [or مَسْكَنٌ, meaning *A house in which is a place of habitation*, or *a lodging*]: (L: [▼ سَكَنٌ and ▼ سُكُنٌ are there mentioned as syn., each of them, with مَسْكَنٌ and سُكْنَى, but in different places; and I incline to think that سُكُنٌ thus mentioned may be a mistranscription for سَكَنٌ: I have not found it elsewhere in this sense:]) and دَارِى لَكَ ▼ سُكْنَى, in which the last word is [said to be] virtually in the accus. case, as a denotative of state, meaning [*My house is for thee,*] *as made* [or *given*] *to be inhabited*, or *as being inhabited*: (Mgh:) or لَكَ دَارِى هٰذِهِ ▼ سُكْنَى, meaning *To thee this my house is a lent dwelling-place*: and ▼ سُكْنَى المَرْأَةِ means *The wife's dwelling-place in which the husband lodges her*. (L.)

مَرْعًى مُسْكِنٌ *Abundant pasturage*, [*that causes people to abide in it*,] *not requiring to go away*; like مُرْبِعٌ and مُنْزِلٌ. (L.) —— أَصْبَحُوا مُسْكِنِينَ *They became in the state termed* مَسْكَنَةٌ. (L, Ḳ.)

مَسْكَنَةٌ (L, Mṣb, Ḳ) The *state of him who is termed* مِسْكِينٌ: primarily, *lowliness, humility*, or *submissiveness*: and meaning also *lowness, abjectness, ignominiousness, abasement*, or *humiliation*; and *paucity of property*; and *an evil state* or *condition*; also *poverty of mind*; and *weakness*: (IAth, L:) it is from السُّكُونُ [an inf. n. of سَكَنَ meaning as expl. in the first sentence of this art.]. (L.)

مُسْكَانٌ, meaning "an earnest," or "earnest money," and of which [as well as of مُسْكِينٌ] the pl. is مَسَاكِينُ, belongs to art. مسك. (TA.)

مِسْكِينٌ (Ṣ, Mgh, L, Mṣb, Ḳ, &c.) and مَسْكِينٌ, (L, Mṣb, Ḳ,) the latter anomalous, for there is no [other] instance of the measure مَفْعِيلٌ, (L,) of the dial. of Benoo-Asad, (L, Mṣb,) mentioned by Ks as heard by him from some one or more of that tribe, (L,) others saying مِسْكِينٌ, (Mṣb,) of the measure مِفْعِيلٌ (L) from السُّكُونُ, because the person to whom it is applied trusts to, or relies upon, others, so as to be, or become, easy, or quiet, in mind: (Mgh, L, Mṣb:) primarily, (L,) it signifies *Lowly, humble*, or *submissive*; (IAth, Mgh, L;) and therefore the Prophet said, اَللّٰهُمَّ أَحْيِنِى مِسْكِينًا وَأَمِتْنِى مِسْكِينًا وَاحْشُرْنِى فِى زُمْرَةِ المَسَاكِينِ [*O God, make me to live lowly, and make me to die lowly, and gather me among the congregation of the lowly*]: (Mgh,* L:) and hence it sometimes applies to him who possesses little and [sometimes] to him who possesses much: (L:) sometimes, (Ṣ,) it signifies (Ṣ, IAth, L, Mṣb, Ḳ) also (IAth, L) *low, abject, ignominious*, or *in a state of abasement* or *humiliation*; (Ṣ, IAth, L, Mṣb, Ḳ;) and *weak*; (Ṣ, L, Ḳ;) and *subdued*, or *oppressed*; though possessing riches or competence: (Mṣb:) [therefore] Sb says, it is one of the words expressive of pity, or compassion; [and as such may be rendered *poor*;] you say, مَرَرْتُ بِهِ المِسْكِينَ [*I passed by him*, I mean *the poor* man], putting it in the accus. case by the implication of أَعْنِى, though it may be in the genitive case as a substitute [for the pronoun], and in the nom. case by the suppression of هُوَ meant to be understood: (L:) in other cases, (Ṣ,) it is *syn. with* فَقِيرٌ, (Ṣ, L, Mṣb,) meaning (Mṣb) *destitute*, i. e. *possessing nothing*: (L, Mṣb, Ḳ:) or accord. to ISk, مسكين means thus; but the فقير is he who possesses a sufficiency of the means of subsistence: (Mṣb:) or the former means *possessing somewhat*; (L;) or [rather] *needy*, i. e. *possessing what is not sufficient* (L, Ḳ) *for him* (Ḳ) or *for his family*: (L:) or *caused by poverty to have little power of motion*; (L, Ḳ;) thus expl. by Aboo-Is-ḥáḳ; but this is improbable; for مسكين has the meaning of an active part. n., and his explanation [like one of the others mentioned above] makes it to have that of a pass. part. n.: (L:) Yoo says the like of ISk: (Mṣb:) he used to say that the مسكين is in a harder condition than the فقير: (Ṣ, L,* Mṣb:*) he says, I asked an Arab of the desert, Art thou فقير? and he answered, No, by God, but rather مسكين; (Ṣ, L,* Mṣb;) but 'Alee Ibn-Ḥamzeh says that this man may have meant that he was low, or abject, by reason of his distance from his people and his home; and that he does not think he meant anything but that: (L:) [J also adds,] it is said in a trad. that the مسكين is not he whom a mouthful or two mouthfuls will turn back, or away, but is only he who does not beg, and who is not known so that he may be given [anything]; (Ṣ;) but Ziyádet-Allah Ibn-Aḥmad says that the فقير is he who sits in his house, not begging, and the مسكين is he who begs and is given; and hence it is argued that the latter is in a better condition than the former; though it indicates that the former is more high-minded than the latter: (L:) accord. to Aṣ, the مسكين is better in condition than the فقير; and this is [said to be] the right assertion, (Mgh, L, Mṣb,) for the pl. of the former is applied in the Ḳur xviii. 78 to men possessing a ship, or boat, which is worth a considerable sum; (L, Mṣb;) but they may have been thus termed because they were humbled and abased by the tyranny of the king who took every ship, or boat, that he found upon the sea, by force; (L;) and it is said that these men were hirers, not owners, of the vessel: (TA voce فَقِيرٌ, q. v.:) 'Alee Ibn-Ḥamzeh says, that the مسكين is better in condition than the فقير is shown by a passage in the Ḳur [ix. 60], where it is said that the poor-rates are for the فُقَرَآء and the مَسَاكِين; for you will find the classes to be there mentioned in such an order that the second is better in condition than the first, and the third than the second, and in like manner the fourth and the fifth and the sixth and the seventh and the eighth: and he says that the same is shown by the fact that the Arabs sometimes used مسكين as a proper name, but not فقير: (L:) or when these two words are used together, they differ in signification; and when used separately, they [sometimes] signify the same: (El-Bedr El-Ḳaráfee, TA in art. فقر:) [see more voce فَقِيرٌ:] a woman is termed مِسْكِينَةٌ (Sb, Ṣ, L, Mṣb, Ḳ) and مِسْكِينٌ also; (Ṣ, L, Ḳ;) the former by way of assimilation to فَقِيرَةٌ; (Sb, Ṣ, L;) the latter being accord. to rule, for an epithet of the measure مِفْعِيلٌ is regularly applied alike to a male and a female; (Ṣ, Mṣb;) or, as Abu-l-Ḥasan says, this is only when it is an intensive epithet, which مِسْكِينَةٌ is not: (L:) the pl. is مَسَاكِينُ and مِسْكِينُونَ, (Ṣ, L, Ḳ,) applied to men, (Ḳ,) or to a company of people, (Ṣ, L,) and مِسْكِينَاتٌ applied to females. (Ṣ, L, Ḳ.)

سل

1. سَلَّ الشَّىْءَ, (Ṣ, M, Mgh,) aor. ـُ, (Ṣ, M,) inf. n. سَلٌّ; (Ṣ, M, Mgh, Ḳ;) and ▼ اِسْتَلَّهُ, (M,) inf. n. اِسْتِلَالٌ; (Ḳ; [in the CḲ, الإِسْلَال is put in the place of الإِسْتِلَال;]) *He drew the thing out* or *forth* from another thing: (Jel in xxiii. 12:) or *he pulled out the thing*, or *drew it forth, gently*: (M, Ḳ:*) or *he drew*, or *pulled, the thing out*, or *forth, as a sword from its scabbard, and a hair from dough*. (Mgh.) You say, سَلَّ السَّيْفَ, (Ṣ, Mṣb,) aor. and inf. n. as above; (Mṣb;) and ▼ اِسْتَلَّهُ, both signifying the same; (Ṣ;) [i. e. *He drew the sword*;] as also ▼ أَسَلَّهُ, inf. n. إِسْلَالٌ. (TA.) In the saying of El-Farezdaḳ,

• غَدَاةَ تَوَلَّيْتُمْ كَأَنَّ سُيُوفَكُمْ •
• ذَآنِينُ فِى أَعْنَاقِكُمْ لَمْ تُسْلَلِ ▼ •

[*In the morning when ye turned back, as though your swords were* ذَآنِين (pl. of ذُؤْنُونٌ a species of fungus) *upon your necks*, (for the sword was hung upon the shoulder, not by a waist-belt,) *not drawn forth*], he has separated the doubled letter: thus the verse is related by IAạr: but by Th, ▼ لَمْ تَسَلَّلِ [for تَتَسَلَّلِ]. (M.) It is said in a trad., لَأَسُلَّنَّكَ مِنْهُمْ كَمَا تُسَلُّ الشَّعْرَةُ مِنَ العَجِينِ [*I will assuredly draw thee forth from them like as the single hair is drawn forth from dough*]. (TA.) And in another trad., اَللّٰهُمَّ اسْلُلْ سَخِيمَةَ قَلْبِى ‡ [*O God, draw forth the rancour of my heart*]: and hence the saying الهَدَايَا تَسُلُّ السَّخَائِمَ وَتَحُلُّ الشَّكَائِمَ ‡ [*Presents draw away feelings of rancour, and loose*, or *melt, resistances*, or *incompliances*]. (TA.) And سُلَّ, said of a colt, means *He was drawn forth a* سَلِيل [q. v.]. (M, TA.) —— Also *He took the thing*. (Mṣb.) Hence one says, تُسَلُّ المَيِّتُ مِنْ قِبَلِ رَأْسِهِ إِلَى القَبْرِ, i. e. [*The dead body*] *is taken* [*head-foremost to the grave*]: (Mṣb:) [or *is drawn forth* &c.: for] it is said of the Apostle of God, سُلَّ مِنْ قِبَلِ رَأْسِهِ, meaning *He was drawn forth* [&c.] from the bier. (Mgh.) —— Also, aor. and inf. n. as above, *He stole the thing*: (Mṣb, TA:) or *he stole it covertly, secretly*, or *clandestinely*; (TA;) and so ▼ أَسَلَّهُ. (TḲ. [But see 4, below, where أَسَلَّ meaning "he stole" is mentioned only as intrans.]) You say, سَلَّ البَعِيرَ فِى جَوْفِ اللَّيْلِ *He drew away the camel from among the other camels in the middle of the night*: and in like manner you say of other things. (TA.) ═ سُلَّ, aor. ـُ, (Ḳ,) inf. n. سُلٌّ, (TḲ,) said of a man; (TA;) or سُلِلْتَ, aor. ـُ, [whence it would seem that the sec. pers. of the pret. is سُلِلْتَ, and the inf. n. سَلَلٌ,] said of a sheep or goat, شَاةٌ; (M;) *He, or it, lost his,* or *its, teeth:* (M, Ḳ:) on the authority of Lḥ. (M.) — سُلَّ, (M, Mṣb, Ḳ,) in the pass. form, (Mṣb,) with ḍamm, (Ḳ,) *He was,* or *became, affected with the disease termed* سِلّ [q. v.]. (M, Mṣb, Ḳ.)

4: see 1, second sentence. — اسلّ, (ISk, Ṣ, M, Mgh,) inf. n. إِسْلَالٌ, (ISk, Ṣ, Ḳ,) also signifies *He stole:* (ISk, Ṣ, Mgh:) or *he stole covertly, secretly,* or *clandestinely.* (M, Ḳ.) See also 1, in the latter half of the paragraph. You say, اسلّ مِنَ المَغْنَمِ *He stole of the spoil.* (Mgh.) — إِسْلَالٌ signifies also *An open raid* or *predatory incursion.* (TA.) — And اسلّ *He aided another to steal,* or *to steal covertly, secretly,* or *clandestinely.* (TA.) — [See also إِسْلَالٌ below. Accord. to Freytag, اسلّ signifies *He received a bribe:* but this requires consideration: he gives no authority but the Ḳ, which does not justify this explanation.] — اسلّهُ *He* (God) *caused him to be affected with the disease termed* سِلّ [q. v.]. (Ṣ, M, Mṣb, Ḳ.)

5. تسلّل: see 7: and see also 1, in the former half of the paragraph. — Also *i. q.* اِضْطَرَبَ [*It was,* or *became, in a state of commotion, agitation,* &c.]; said of a thing; as though it were imagined to be repeatedly drawn forth. (Er-Rághib, TA.)

7. انسلّ *It* (a thing) *became pulled out,* or *drawn forth, gently;* (M;) *it became drawn,* or *pulled out* or *forth, as a sword from its scabbard, and a hair from dough.* (Mgh.) You say, انسلّ السَّيْفُ مِنَ الغِمْدِ *The sword* [*became drawn from the scabbard:* or] *slipped out from the scabbard.* (TA.) And انسلّ قِيَادُ الفَرَسِ مِنْ يَدِهِ [*The leading-rope of the horse slipped out* or] *came forth* [*from his hand*]. (Mgh.) — And [hence], as also ↓ تسلّل, (Ṣ, M, Ḳ,) *He slipped away,* or *stole away;* i. e., *went away covertly, secretly,* or *clandestinely:* (M, Ḳ:) or *he went forth,* مِنْ بَيْنِهِمْ [*from among them*]. (Ṣ.) And اِنْسَلَلْتُ مِنْ بَيْنِ يَدَيْهِ *I went away,* and *went forth, deliberately,* or *leisurely,* and *by degrees, from before him.* (TA.) Sb says that اِنْسَلَلْتُ [used in this or a similar sense] is not a quasi-pass. verb; but is only like [a verb of the measure] فَعَلْتُ; like as افتقر is like ضَعُفَ. (M.) It is said in a prov., رَمَتْنِى بِدَائِهَا وَٱنْسَلَّتْ [*She reproached me with her own fault, and slipped away*]: (Ṣ, Meyd, TA:) [originally] said by one of the fellow-wives of Ruhm, daughter of El-Khazraj, wife of Saạd Ibn-Zeyd-Menáh, on Ruhm's reproaching her with a fault that was in herself. (Meyd, TA. [See also Freytag's Arab. Prov. cap. x. no. 2; and another prov. there referred to in cap. ii. no. 78.]) And one says also, استلّ ↓ بِكَذَا, meaning *He went away with such a thing covertly, secretly,* or *clandestinely.* (TA.)

8: see 1, first and second sentences: — and see also 7, last sentence.

10. استلّ النَّهْرُ جَدْوَلًا ‡ *The river had a rivulet,* or *streamlet, branching off from it.* (TA.)

R. Q. **1.** سَلْسَلَةٌ [as inf. n. of سَلْسَلَ (see مُسَلْسَلٌ below)] signifies A thing's *being connected* with another thing. (M, Ḳ.) [It is also inf. n. of سَلْسَلَ, as such signifying The *connecting* a thing with another thing.] — [Hence, or the reverse may be the case,] سَلْسَلْتُهُ *I bound him with the* سِلْسِلَة [or *chain*]. (O, TA.) — And سَلْسَلْتُ المَآءَ فِى الحَلْقِ *I poured the water into the throat,* or *fauces,* [app. *in a continuous stream.*] (Ṣ,* O.) — And مَا سَلْسَلَ طَعَامًا *He did not eat food:* (Ḳ:) as though he did not pour it into his throat, or fauces. (TA.) — Accord. to IAạr, سَلْسَلَ signifies *He ate a* سَلْسَلَة, i. e., *a long piece of a camel's hump.* (O.) — See also 1, third sentence.

R. Q. **2.** تَسَلْسَلَ, said of water, *It ran* into the throat, or fauces: (Ṣ, O:) or *it ran down a declivity,* or *declivous place:* (M, Ḳ:) or † *it became* [*fretted with a succession of ripples*] *like a chain, in running* [*in a shallow and rugged bed*], or *when smitten by the wind.* (Ṣ.) — And, said of lightning, † *It assumed the form of* سَلَاسِل, [i. e. *chains,* meaning *elongated streams,*] pl. of سِلْسِلَة [q. v.], in the clouds. (M.) — And تَسَلْسُلٌ signifies † The *glistening,* and [*apparent*] *creeping, of the diversified wavy marks, streaks,* or *grain,* [*resembling a chain,* (see مُسَلْسَلٌ,) and also *likened to the creeping of ants,* (see فِرِنْدٌ, and رُبَدٌ,)] of a sword. (TA. [See also أُثْرٌ.]) — And تَسَلْسَلَ said of a garment, † *It was worn until it became thin;* (O, Ḳ;) like تَخَلْخَلَ. (O.)

سُلٌّ, (M, Ḳ,) applied to a man, (M,) *Whose teeth are falling out;* (M;) *losing his teeth:* (Ḳ:) fem. with ة: (M, Ḳ:) likewise applied to a sheep or goat (شَاةٌ); on the authority of Lḥ; (M;) and to a she-camel *whose teeth have fallen out from extreme old age;* or one *extremely aged, having no tooth remaining;* on the authority of IAạr. (TA.) — See also سَلَّةٌ, in two places.

سُلٌّ: see what next follows.

سِلٌّ (Ṣ, M, Mṣb, Ḳ) and ↓ سُلَالٌ, (Ṣ, M, Ḳ,) the former [the more common, and] often occurring in the verses of chaste poets, though El-Ḥareeree says in the "Durrat el-Ghowwáṣ" that it is an erroneous term of the vulgar, and that the latter is the right term, (TA,) signify the same, (Ṣ, M, Ḳ,) as also ↓ سُلٌّ and ↓ سُلَّةٌ, (Ḳ,) [*Consumption:* or *phthisis:*] *an emaciating, oppressive, and fatal malady:* (T, TA:) *a certain disease, well known;* said in the medical books to be *one of the diseases of girls,* because of the abundance of blood in them: (Mṣb:) accord. to the physicians, (TA,) *an ulcer,* (Ḳ, TA,) or *ulcers,* (Mṣb,) [or *ulceration,*] *in the lungs;* (Mṣb, Ḳ, TA;) *succeeding* (تُعَقِّبُ [grammatically referring to سُلَّة]) *either* ذَاتَ الرِّئَةِ [i. e. *inflammation of the lungs*] *or* ذَاتَ الجَنْبِ [i. e. *pleurisy*]: (in the CḲ, يعقّب ذَاتِ الرِّئَةِ او ذاتِ الجَنْبِ is [erroneously] put in the place of تُعَقِّبُ ذَاتَ الرِّئَةِ أَوْ ذَاتَ الجَنْبِ: and in what here follows, the gen. case is put in the place of the nom. in four instances:) or *a rheum* (زُكَامٌ), *and defluxions* (نَوَازِلُ), or *a long cough, and attended with constant fever.* (Ḳ, TA.) — Hence the saying, in a trad., غُبَارُ ذَيْلِ المَرْأَةِ الفَاجِرَةِ يُورِثُ السِّلَّ † [*The dust of the skirt of the vitious woman occasions the loss of property*]; meaning that he who follows vitious women and acts vitiously, loses his property, and becomes poor: the diminution and departure of property being likened to the diminution and wasting away of the body when one has the disorder termed سِلّ. (TA.)

سَلَّةٌ The *drawing of swords;* (Ṣ, M, Ḳ;) as also ↓ سِلَّةٌ. (Ḳ.) So in the saying, أَتَيْنَاهُمْ عِنْدَ السَّلَّةِ [*We came to them on the occasion of the drawing of swords*]. (Ṣ, M, Ḳ.) — And *Theft:* (Ṣ, Mṣb:) or *covert, secret,* or *clandestine, theft;* (M, Ḳ;) like إِسْلَالٌ [except that the former is a simple subst., and the latter is an inf. n., i. e. of 4]: (Ḳ:) one says, فِى بَنِى فُلَانٍ سَلَّةٌ [*Among the sons of such a one is theft,* or *covert theft*]: (Ṣ:) and الخَلَّةُ تَدْعُو إِلَى السَّلَّةِ [*Want invites to theft,* or *covert theft*]. (TA.) — Also ‡ The *rush* (دُفْعَة) of a horse *among other horses, in running:* (TA:) or the *rush* (دُفْعَة) of a horse *in striving to outstrip:* (Ṣ, TA: [I read فِى سِبَاقِهِ, as in a copy of the Ṣ; instead of فِى سِيَاقِهِ, as in other copies of the Ṣ and in the TA:]) so in the saying, فَرَسٌ شَدِيدُ السَّلَّةِ ‡ [*A horse of which the rush* &c. *is vehement*]: (Ṣ, TA:) and خَرَجَتْ سَلَّتُهُ عَلَى الخَيْلِ (Ṣ) or عَلَى سَائِرِ الخَيْلِ (TA) ‡ [*His rush in striving to outstrip proceeded against the other horses*]. — And *A revulsion of shortness of breathing* (اِرْتِدَادُ رَبْوٍ) *in the chest of a horse, in consequence of his suppressing such shortness of breathing* [so I render مِنْ كَبْوَةٍ يَكْبُوهَا, but this phrase admits of other renderings, as will be seen in art. كبو]: (M, Ḳ:) when he is inflated thereby, one says, أَخْرَجَ سَلَّتَهُ [app. meaning *he has manifested his revulsion of shortness of breathing*]; and thereupon he is urged to run with vehemence, and made to sweat, and coverings are thrown upon him, and that shortness of breathing (ذٰلِكَ الرَّبْوُ) passes forth. (M.) — [In a sheep or goat, or a ewe or she-goat, it seems to mean *Power,* or *force, of long continuance:* see مَسْلُولٌ, voce مَسْلُولَةٌ.] — See also سِلٌّ. — Also *A* [*basket of the kind called*] جُونَة: (Ḳ:) or *a thing like the* جُونَة, (M,) or *like the covered* جُونَة, *which is also called* سَبَذَةٌ; so says Az: (TA:) *a receptacle in which fruit is carried:* (Mṣb:) [*sometimes covered with red skin:* (see حَوَرٌ:) in the present day commonly applied to *a basket made of twigs, oblong and deep, generally between a foot and a foot and a half in length:*] and ↓ سَلٌّ signifies the same: (M, Ḳ:) what is termed سَلَّةُ الخُبْزِ [*the bread-basket*] is well known: (Ṣ:) سَلَّةٌ meaning as expl. above is not thought by IDrd to be an Arabic word: (M:) [the dim. ↓ سُلَيْلَةٌ occurs in the Ḳ voce جُونَة, and in the Mgh voce رَبْعَةٌ, &c.:] the pl. is سِلَالٌ (M, Ḳ) and سَلَّاتٌ (Mṣb) and [coll. gen. n.] ↓ سَلٌّ, of which Abu-l-Ḥasan says that it is in his opinion a rare kind of pl. [or coll. gen. n.] because it denotes what is made by art, not created, and it should more properly be regarded as of the class of كَوْكَب and كَوْكَبَة [which are syn.] because this is more common than the class of سَفِينَة and سَفِين. (M.) — Also *A fault*, or *defect, in a watering-trough* or *tank*, or *in a* [*jar of the kind called*] خَابِيَة: (M, Ḳ:) or *a breach between the* أَنْصَاب, (Ḳ,) or [more properly] *between the* نَصَائِب, [i. e. the *stones set up, and cemented together with kneaded clay, around the interior*,] (M,) *of a watering-trough* or *tank*. (M, Ḳ.) — And *Fissures in the ground, that steal* [i. e. *imbibe*] *the water*. (TA.) — Also One's *sewing* [a skin, or hide, *with*] *two thongs in a single puncture*, or *stitch-hole*. (M, Ḳ.)

سِلَّة: see سَلَّة, first sentence.

سُلَال i. q. سِلّ, q. v. (Ṣ, M, Ḳ.)

سَلِيل A *drawn* sword; i. q. ↓ مَسْلُول. (M, Ḳ.) — † *A child*, or *male offspring*; [because drawn forth;] (Ṣ, M, Mṣb, Ḳ;) as also ↓ سُلَالَة; (M, Mgh, Mṣb, Ḳ;) metonymically so termed: (Mgh:) or, *when it comes forth from the belly of its mother*; as also ↓ the latter; the former so called because created from the [sperma genitalis, which is termed] سُلَالَة: (Akh, TA:) fem. of the former ↓ سَلِيلَة, (Ṣ, M, Mṣb, Ḳ,) applied to *a daughter*. (AA, Ḳ.) — *A colt*; (M, Ḳ;) and with ة *a filly*; (Ṣ,* M, TA;) the ة being affixed, though سليل is of the measure فَعِيل in the sense of the measure مَفْعُول, because the word is made a subst.: (Ḥam p. 102:) or, as some say, (M, in the Ḳ "and") the former signifies *a colt that is born not in a* [*membrane such as is called*] مَاسِكَة *nor* [*in one such as is called*] سَلًى: if in either of these, it is termed بَقِير [not بَقِيز as in the CḲ]. (M, Ḳ.) [See also دُعْمُوص.] — And *A young camel when just born, before it is known whether it is a male or a female*. (Aṣ, Ṣ, TA.) — *Clear*, or *pure, beverage* or *wine*; (Ḳ, TA;) as though gently drawn away from dust or motes or particles of rubbish or the like: such is said to be the beverage, or wine, of Paradise: or *cool beverage* or *wine*: or *such as is clear from dust* or *motes* or *particles of rubbish* or *the like, and from turbidness*; of the measure فَعِيل in the sense of the measure مَفْعُول: or *such as is easy* [*in its descent*] *in the throat*, or *fauces*. (TA.) [See also سُلَالَة, and سَلْسَال.] — The *channel of the water*, or *place in which the water flows, in a valley*: or the *middle of a valley*, (M, Ḳ,*) *where flows the main body of water*. (M.) And *A wide* (Ṣ, M, Ḳ) *and deep* (M, Ḳ) *valley*, (Ṣ, M, Ḳ,) *that gives growth to the* [*trees called*] سَلَم *and* سَمُر, (Ṣ, Ḳ,) or *that gives growth to the* سَلَم *and* ضَعَة *and* يَنَمَة *and* حَلَمَة; (M;) and ↓ سَالّ signifies the same: (M, Ḳ:) or this latter, *a place in which are trees*: (TA:) or *a narrow channel of a torrent in a valley*: (Aṣ, Ṣ, TA:) or *a low place surrounded by what is elevated, in which the water collects*: (En-Naḍr, TA:) pl. of both سُلَّان, (M, Ḳ,) or of the former accord. to Kr, (M, TA,) and of the latter accord. to Aṣ [and the Ṣ], (TA,) or that of the latter is سَوَالُّ. (En-Naḍr, Ḳ, TA.) One says سَلِيلٌ مِنْ سَمُرٍ like as one says غَالٌّ مِنْ سَلَمٍ. (Ṣ.) The phrase سَالَ السَّلِيلُ بِهِمْ [lit. *The wide*, or *wide and deep, valley*, &c., *flowed with them*] is used by the poet Zuheyr (Ṣ, IB) as meaning † *they journeyed swiftly*. (IB, TA.) — The *brain of the horse*. (M, Ḳ.) — The *hump of the camel*. (M, Ḳ.) — The نُخَاع [or *spinal cord*]. (M, Ḳ.) — And سَلِيلُ اللَّحْمِ *The* [*portions that are termed*] خَصِيل [q. v. voce خَصِيلَة] *of flesh*: [the former word in this case being app. a coll. gen. n., of which the n. un. is ↓ سَلِيلَة (q. v.); the more probably as it is added that] the pl. is سَلَائِل. (TA.)

سُلَالَة *What is*, or *becomes, drawn forth*, or *drawn forth gently, from*, or *of, a thing*: (M, Ḳ:) or so سُلَالَةُ شَىْءٍ: (Ṣ:) [*an extract* of a thing: and hence,] the *clear*, or *pure, part*, or the *choice, best*, or *most excellent, part* [of a thing]; (Mgh; and Ksh and Bḍ and Jel in xxiii. 12;) because drawn from the thick, or turbid, part. (Mgh.) It is said in the Ḳur [xxiii. 12], وَلَقَدْ خَلَقْنَا الْإِنْسَانَ مِنْ سُلَالَةٍ مِنْ طِينٍ, meaning [*And verily we created man from*] *what was drawn forth from every kind of dust*, or *earth*: (Fr, TA:) or *from a pure*, or *choice*, or *most excellent, sort of earth* or *clay*. (Ksh, Bḍ, Jel.) — And [hence,] The *sperma genitalis* of a man, or human being; (Ṣ, TA;) *what is drawn from the* صُلْب [app. here meaning *loins*] *of the man and from the* تَرَائِب [pl. of تَرِيبَة, q. v.,] *of the woman*: (AHeyth, TA:) the *water* (مَآء) *that is drawn from the back*. ('Ikrimeh, TA.) — See also سَلِيل, second sentence, in two places.

سَلِيلَة: see سَلِيل, second sentence. — Also *A sinew*, (عَصَبَة, (M, Ḳ, or عَقَبَة, Ḳ,) or *a portion of flesh having streaks*, or *strips*, (M, Ḳ,) *that separate, one from another*. (TA.) And The *oblong portion of flesh of the part on either side of the backbone*: (Ḳ:) or this is called سَلِيلَةُ الْمَتْنِ: (M:) [or] accord. to Aṣ, [the pl.] سَلَائِل signifies the *long streaks*, or *strips, of flesh extending with the backbone*. (TA.) See also سَلِيل, last sentence. [Also] *A small thin thing* [or *substance*] *resembling flesh*: pl. سَلَائِل. (TA in art. خشم.) And سَلَائِلُ السَّنَامِ *Long slices cut from the camel's hump*. (TA.) — And the pl., *Oblong* نَغَفَات [or *portions of dry mucus* or *the like*] *in the nose*. (M.) — Also [*Goats'*] *hair separated*, or *plucked asunder, with the fingers, then folded, and tied; then the woman draws from it one portion after another, which she spins*: (M:) or سَلِيلَةٌ مِنْ شَعَرٍ signifies *what is drawn forth from a* ضَرِيبَة *of* [*goats'*] *hair, which is a portion thereof separated*, or *plucked asunder, with the fingers, then folded, and rolled up into long portions, the length of each being about a cubit, and the thickness that of the half of the fore arm next the hand*: *this is tied, then the woman draws from it one portion after another, and spins it*. (Ṣ.) [See also عُمِيتَة.] — Also *A certain long fish*, (Ḳ, TA,) *having a long* مِنْقَار [app. meaning *beak-like snout*, or *nose*]. (TA.)

سُلَيْلَة: see سَلَّة (of which it is the dim.), in the latter half of the paragraph.

سَلَّآء; n. un. with ة; mentioned in the M and Ḳ in this art. as well as in art. سلأ: see the latter art.

سَلَّال: see سَالّ. — [And it seems to be somewhere mentioned in the Ṣ, though not in the present art., as meaning *A maker of the sort of baskets called* سِلَال (pl. of سَلَّة): for Golius explains it, as on the authority of J, as signifying *qui sportas qualesque contexit*.]

سَلْسَل and ↓ سَلْسَال and ↓ سُلَاسِل (Ṣ, M, Ḳ) *Sweet* water, (M, Ḳ,) *that descends easily in the throat*, or *fauces*; (M;) water *that enters easily into the throat*, or *fauces, by reason of its sweetness and clearness*: (Ṣ:) or *cold*, or *cool*, water: (M, Ḳ:) or water *that has fluctuated to and fro, in the place where it has continued, until it has become limpid*, or *clear*. (Er-Rághib, TA.) And the first and ↓ second, *Mellow* wine: (M, Ḳ:) the former is expl. by Lth as meaning *sweet and clear, that runs* [*easily*] *into the throat*, or *fauces, when drunk*. (TA.) — And غَدِيرٌ سَلْسَلٌ [*A pool of water left by a torrent*] *which, being smitten* [or *blown upon*] *by the wind, becomes* [*rippled so as to be*] *like the* سِلْسِلَة [or *chain*]. (TA.)

سُلْسُل A boy, or young man, *light*, or *active, in spirit*; as also نُشْنُش. (IAạr, O.)

سِلْسِل: see سِلْسِلَة, in two places.

سَلْسَلَة [as an inf. n.: see R. Q. 1. — Also] *A long piece of a camel's hump*: (IAạr, O, Ḳ:) accord. to AA, it is called نَشْنَشَة: accord. to Aṣ, بِلْسِنَة. (O.)

سِلْسِلَة *A chain*, i. q. زِنْجِير in Pers.; (KL;) *rings* دَائِر [app. used as a coll. gen. n., though I do not know any authority for such usage of it,] (Ḳ [in the M دَائِرَة]) *of iron* (Ṣ, M, Ḳ) or *the like* (M, Ḳ) *of metals*: derived from السَّلْسَلَة signifying "the being connected" with another thing: (M: [see R. Q. 1:]) pl. سَلَاسِل. (Ṣ, Mgh, TA.) It was a custom to extend a سِلْسِلَة over a river or a road, the ships or boats or the passengers being arrested thereby, for the purpose of the taking of the tithes from them by an officer set over it. (Mgh.) — [Hence,] سِلْسِلَةُ بَرْقٍ ‡ *An elongated stream of lightning* [*like a chain*] *in the midst of the clouds*: (Ṣ, TA:*) or سَلَاسِلُ الْبَرْقِ means *what have assumed the form of chains* (مَا تَسَلْسَلَ), *of lightning*, (M, Ḳ,) *in the clouds*; (M;) and السَّحَاب [i. e., *of the clouds* in like manner]: (Ḳ: [but I think that وَالسَّحَاب in the Ḳ is evidently a mistranscription for فِى السَّحَاب, the reading in the M:]) sing. سِلْسِلَة (M, Ḳ) and ↓ سِلْسِل, (Ḳ,) thus in the copies of the Ḳ, but in the L ↓ سِلْسِيل, which is [said to be] the correct word. (TA. [See, however, what follows.]) And in like manner, سَلَاسِلُ الرَّمْلِ † *What have assumed the form of chains* (مَا تَسَلْسَلَ) *of sands*: (M:) or سَلَاسِلُ signifies ‡ *sands that become accumulated*, or *congested*, (يَنْعَقِدُ,) *one upon another, and extended along*: (A'Obeyd, Ṣ, O, Ḳ, TA:) you say رَمْلٌ ذُو سَلَاسِلَ ‡ [*sands having portions accumulated*, or *congested*, &c.]: and ذَاتُ سَلَاسِلَ, which has been expl. as meaning † *elongated sands*: (TA:) sing. سِلْسِلَةٌ (M, TA) and ▼ سَلْسُولٌ, (M,) or ▼ سِلْسِيلٌ; and الرَّمْلِ, with fet-ḥ [to the first letter], is a dial. var. of سِلْسِلَةٌ. (TA.) —— And سَلَاسِلُ كِتَابٍ ‡ *The lines of a book* or *writing*. (O, Ḳ, TA.) —— And بِرْذَوْنٌ ذُو سَلَاسِلَ † [*A hackney*] *upon whose legs one sees what resemble* سَلَاسِل [or *chains*]. (M.) ═══ Also The وَحَرَة, (O, Ḳ,) which is *a small reptile*, [*a species of lizard, the same that is called* السِّلْسِلَةُ الرَّقْطَآءُ, (see أَرْقَطُ,)] *spotted, black and white, having a slender tail, which it moves about when running*. (TA.)

سَلْسَالٌ: see سَلْسَلٌ, in two places.

سَلْسُولٌ: see سِلْسِلَةٌ.

سِلْسِيلٌ: see سِلْسِلَةٌ, in two places.

سَلَاسِلُ: see سَلْسَلٌ.

سَالٌّ [act. part. n. of سَلَّ, *Drawing out*, or *forth*: &c. —— *Stealing*: or *stealing covertly*, *secretly*, or *clandestinely*:] *a thief*; as also ▼ سَلَّالٌ [which is commonly applied in the present day to *a horse-stealer* and *the like*] and ▼ أَسَلُّ. (TA.) ═══ See also سَلِيلٌ.

أَسَلُّ: see the next preceding paragraph.

إِسْلَالٌ *A bribe*. (Ṣ, M, Ḳ.) It is said in a trad., لَا إِغْلَالَ وَلَا إِسْلَالَ *There shall be no treachery*, or *perfidy*, *and no* [giving or receiving of a] *bribe*: or, *and no stealing*. (Ṣ in this art. and in art. غل. [See 4.])

مَسَلٌّ in the phrase مَضْجَعُهُ كَمَسَلِّ شَطْبَةٍ, in the trad. of Umm-Zarạ, meaning [*His sleeping-place is*] *like a green palm-stick drawn forth* from its skin [by reason of his slenderness], or, as some say, *a sword drawn forth* [from its scabbard], is [originally] an inf. n. used in the sense of a pass. part. n. (TA. [See also art. شطب.])

مِسَلَّةٌ *A large needle*: (Ṣ, M, Mgh, Mṣb, Ḳ:) [*a packing-needle*:] pl. مَسَالُّ. (Ṣ, Mgh, Mṣb.)

مُسِلٌّ *Subtle of machination in stealing*. (TA.)

مَسْلُولٌ: see سَلِيلٌ. —— [Hence, elliptically,] A man (Mṣb) *whose testicles have been extracted*. (Mgh, Mṣb.) ═══ Also *Affected with the disease termed* سُلّ: (Ṣ, M, Mṣb, Ḳ:) [regularly derived from سُلَّ, but] anomalous [as derived from أَسَلَّهُ]: (Ṣ, M, Mṣb:) Sb says, as though the سِلّ were put into him. (M.) ═══ AA says that the مَسْلُولَة of غَنَم [meaning sheep or goats, i. e., applied to a شَاة, meaning a sheep or goat, or a ewe or she-goat,] is One *whose powers*, or *forces*, *are of long continuance* (الَّتِى يَطُولُ قُوَاهَا): and that one says [of such] فِى فِيهَا سَلَّةٌ [in which phrase فى seems evidently to have been preposed by mistake: see سَلَّةٌ]. (O, TA.)

مُسَلْسَلٌ A thing *having its parts*, or *portions*, *connected*, *one with another*. (Ṣ, O.) —— And [hence, (see سِلْسِلَةٌ,)] *Chained*; *bound with the* سِلْسِلَة. (TA.) [الْمَرْأَةُ الْمُسَلْسَلَةُ is the name of *The constellation Andromeda*; described by Ḳzw and others.] —— † Lightning *that assumes the form of chains* (يَتَسَلْسَلُ) *in its upper portions*, *and seldom*, or *never*, *breaks its promise* [*of being followed by rain*]. (IAạr, TA.) —— Applied to hair, [as also ▼ مُتَسَلْسِلٌ, (Ḳ in art. حجن,)] † *Forming a succession of rimples*, *like water running in a shallow and rugged bed*, or *rippled by the wind*; (see R. Q. 2;) or] *crisp*, or *curly*, or *twisted*, *and contracted*; syn. جَعْدٌ. (Mgh.) —— † A sword *having in it*, or *upon it*, *diversified wavy marks*, *streaks*, or *grain*, *resembling the* سِلْسِلَة [or *chain*]. (TA.) [See also مُسَلْسَل.] —— † A garment, or piece of cloth, *figured with stripes*, or *lines*; (Ḳ;) as also مُلَسْلَس: as though formed by tranposition. (TA.) Also, and ▼ مُتَسَلْسِلٌ, † A garment, or piece of cloth, *woven badly* (M, Ḳ) *and thinly*. (M.) —— حَدِيثٌ مُسَلْسَلٌ † *A tradition* [*related by an uninterrupted chain of transmitters*,] *such as when one says*, *I met face to face such a one who said*, *I met face to face such a one*, *and so on*, *to the Apostle of God*. (O, TA.)

مُتَسَلْسِلٌ: see the next preceding paragraph, in two places. —— Also † A garment *worn until it has become thin*. (TA.)

سلأ

1. سَلَأَ السَّمْنَ, (Ṣ, M, Mgh, Mṣb, Ḳ,) aor. َ, (M, Mṣb, Ḳ,) inf. n. سَلْءٌ; (M, Mṣb;) and ▼ اسْتَلَأَهُ; (Ṣ, Ḳ;) *He cooked the* سَمْن [here meaning *butter*], (Ṣ, M, Mgh, Mṣb, Ḳ,) *and worked it together*, (Ṣ, Mgh, Ḳ,) *and melted its* زُبْد [or *fresh*, *unclarified*, *portion*], (M,) *until it became clear* (Mgh, Mṣb) *from the milk remaining in it*; (Mṣb;) *he cleared the* سمن [or *butter*] *from the* زبد [or *fresh*, *unclarified*, *portion*]; (Ḥam p. 2, in explanation of the former phrase; [i. e. *he clarified the butter*:] and سُلِئَ سَمْنًا, said of fresh butter, *it was made into* سَمْن [or *clarified butter*; i. e., *was clarified*]. (Mgh.) —— And سَلَأَ السِّمْسِمَ, (M, Ḳ,) [aor. and] inf. n. as above, (M,) *He pressed the sesame*, or *sesamum*, (M, Ḳ,) *and extracted its oil*. (M.) ═══ سَلَأَ النَّخْلَ, (AZ, Ṣ,) or النَّخْلَةَ, (AḤn, M,) or الجِذْعَ, (M, Ḳ,) and العَسِيبَ, [aor. and] inf. n. as above, (AZ, AḤn, Ṣ, M,) *He plucked off the prickles*, (AZ, Ṣ, M, Ḳ,) i. e. (Ḳ) *what are called the* سُلَّآء, (AḤn, M, Ḳ,) *of the palm-trees*, (AZ, Ṣ,) or *of the palm-tree*, (AḤn, M,) or *of the palm-trunk*, (M, Ḳ,) and *of the* [*part called*] عَسِيب [*of a palm-branch*]. (AZ, AḤn, Ṣ, M.) ═══ سَلَأَهُ مِائَةَ سَوْطٍ, (Aṣ, Ṣ, M, Ḳ,*) [aor. and] inf. n. as above, (M,) *He inflicted upon him a hundred lashes of the whip*. (M, Ḳ.*) —— And سَلَأَهُ مِائَةَ دِرْهَمٍ, (Aṣ, Ṣ, M, Ḳ,*) [aor. and] inf. n. as above, (M,) *He payed him*, or *payed him in ready money*, *a hundred dirhems*, (Aṣ, Ṣ, M, Ḳ,*) *promptly*, or *quickly*. (Ḳ.)

8: see above, first sentence. [See also 8 in art. سلى.]

سِلَآءٌ [*Clarified butter*;] the subst. from سَلَأَ السَّمْنَ: pl أَسْلِئَةٌ. (Ṣ, M, Ḳ.) El-Farezdaḳ says,

• كَانُوا كَسَالِئَةٍ حَمْقَآءَ إِذْ حَقَنَتْ •
• سِلَآءَهَا فِى أَدِيمٍ غَيْرِ مَرْبُوبِ •

[*They were like a stupid female clarifying butter*, *when she collected her clarified butter in a skin not seasoned with rob*]. (Ṣ.) ═══ See also what follows.

سُلَّآءٌ The *prickles of the palm-tree*: [a coll. gen. n.:] n. un. with ة. (Ṣ, M, Mṣb, Ḳ.) —— Also, (Ḳ,) or [correctly the n. un.] سُلَّآءَةٌ, (M,) *A sort of arrow-head*, or *spear-head*, (M, Ḳ,*) *in shape like the prickle of the palm-tree*: (M, Ḳ:) and سِلَاءَة, app. [سُلَاءَة] without teshdeed [and with kesr], occurs in a trad. in this sense; for it is said that its pl. is ▼ سِلَآءٌ, of the same measure as حِمَارٌ. (TA.) ═══ Also *A certain bird*, (M, Ḳ,) *dust-coloured*, *and long-legged*. (M.)

سلب

1. سَلَبَهُ, (Ṣ, A, Ḳ,) aor. ُ, (TA,) inf. n. سَلْبٌ (Ṣ, Ḳ) and سَلَبٌ, (Ḳ,) from the former of which the pl. سُلُوبٌ has been formed, on the authority of hearsay, (El-Jurjánee, Mṣb in art. قصد,) *He seized it*, or *carried it off*, *by force*; (Ṣ, A, Ḳ;) as also ▼ اسْتَلَبَهُ. (Ṣ, Ḳ.) You say, سَلَبَهُ الشَّىْءَ, aor. ُ, inf. n. سَلْبٌ and سَلَبٌ; and اسْتَلَبَهُ إِيَّاهُ; (M, TA;) *He seized*, or *carried off*, *by force* [*from him the thing*; or *he spoiled him*, *despoiled him*, *plundered him*, or *deprived him*, *of the thing*]. (TA.) And سَلَبْتُهُ ثَوْبَهُ, (Mgh,* Mṣb,) aor. ُ, (Mṣb,) inf. n. سَلْبٌ, (Mgh, Mṣb,) *I took away from him his garment*; (Mgh,* Mṣb;) as also ▼ أَسْلَبْتُهُ [perhaps a mistranscription for ▼ اسْتَلَبْتُهُ, but another instance of the former of these two verbs, in a similar sense, occurs in what follows]: originally, سَلَبْتُ ثَوْبَ زَيْدٍ [*I took away the garment of Zeyd*]; but the verb has been made to have زيد for its object, and the ثوب is postponed, and put in the accus. case as a specificative [though by rule the specificative should be indeterminate]; and it may be suppressed, [so that you may say simply, سَلَبْتُهُ, meaning *I took away from him what was upon him* or *with him*, *spoiled him*, or *plundered him*,] the meaning being understood. (Mṣb.) —— [Hence] one says also, سَلَبَهُ فُؤَادَهُ وَعَقْلَهُ ‡ [*He*, or *it*, *despoiled him*, or *deprived him*, *of his heart and his reason*], and ▼ أَسْلَبَهُ. (A, TA.) [The latter one might think to be a mistranscription for ▼ اسْتَلَبَهُ were it not for an instance of the same verb before men-

tioned, and for the fact that it is immediately followed in the A by وَهُوَ مُسْلَبُ العَقْلِ : perhaps, however, مُسْلَب may be here a mistake for مُسْلَب.] — And أَسْلُبْ هٰذِهِ القَصَبَةَ † *Peel thou this cane, or reed.* (TA.) — [In grammar and logic, سَلْبٌ is used to signify † *Privation*, or *deprivation*, in a general sense; and † *negation*; opposed to إِيجَابٌ and إِثْبَاتٌ.] = سَلْبٌ [as an inf. n. of which the verb (app. سَلَبَ) is not mentioned] † The *going*, or *journeying, lightly and quickly*. (M, K.) Ru-beh says,

• قَدْ قَنَحَتْ مِنْ سَلْبِهِنَّ سَلْبَا •
• قَارُورَةُ العَيْنِ فَصَارَتْ وَقْبَا •

† [*The black of the eye became depressed so that it became a hollow in consequence of their going with* much *lightness and quickness*: سَلْبًا, for سَلْبًا, being an absolute complement to the inf. n. in سَلْبِهِنَّ]. (M. [See also 7.]) = سَلِبَ [or سَلَبَتْ, as appears from what follows], aor. ـَ, † *He* [or *she*] *put on black garments* (K, TA) *which women wear at assemblies for the purpose of mourning.* (TA. [See also 5.])

2: see 5, in three places.

[3. سَالَبَهُ الشَّىْءَ, if used, means *He contended with him in a mutual endeavour to seize, or carry off, the thing by force.* See 6.]

4. اسلبت, said of a she-camel, (S, M, K,) ‡ *She became deprived of her young one by death* (M, K, TA) *or by some other means*: (M, TA:) or *she cast her young one in an imperfect state.* (S, M, K.) — اسلب الشَّجَرُ ‡ *The trees became bare of their fruit, and dropped their leaves.* (K, TA.) — اسلب الثُّمَامُ (S, TA) † *The* ثمام [or *panic grass*] *put forth its* خُوص [or *leaves*, so that *it became fit to be cut*: see سَلَبٌ]. (TA.) = See also 1, in two places.

5. تسلّبت, (S, K,) said of a woman, (S,) *i. q.* أَحَدَّتْ [i. e. † *She abstained from the wearing of ornaments, and the use of perfumes, and dye for the hands &c., and put on the garments of mourning*,] عَلَى زَوْجِهَا [*for her husband*]: (K:) or, as some say, إِحْدَادٌ is for the husband; (S, A;) but تَسَلُّبٌ is sometimes for another than the husband: (S, TA:) [therefore] تسلّبت signifies † *she put on the black garments of mourning*; (M, TA;) as also ↓ سلّبت: (M, A:) you say, ↓ تُسَلِّبُ عَلَى حَمِيمِهَا or زَوْجِهَا (Lh, M) † *She puts on the black garments of mourning* [*for her husband* or *her loved and loving relation or friend*]: (M:) and ↓ سَلَّبَتْ عَلَى مَيِّتِهَا † *She put on the black garments of mourning for her dead one*: تَسْلِيبٌ having a general application. (A.)

[6. تسالبا الشَّىْءَ *They both contended together, each endeavouring to seize, or carry off, the thing by force.* The inf. n. occurs in the S and K in art. خلس, as a syn. of تَخَالُسٌ.]

7. انسلب † *He went a very quick pace*: (K:) or *he went well*; said of a horse and of a camel: (KL:) but mostly (TA) one says, انسلبت النَّاقَةُ † *The she-camel went so quick a pace that she was as though she went forth from her skin*: (S, TA:) [or she *outstripped*: see an ex. voce عَابِسٌ.]

8: see 1, in four places.

سَلْبٌ The *longest* [*thing*] *of the apparatus of the plough*: (AHn, M, K:) or *a piece of wood that is joined to the base of the* لُؤْمَة [here meaning *ploughshare*], *its end being* [*inserted*] *in the hole, or perforation, of the latter.* (M, K.)

سَلَبٌ: see سَلِيبٌ. — *Spoil, plunder*, or *booty*; (TA;) *what is seized*, or *carried off, by force*, (M, Msb, K, TA,) *from a man, of spoils, whatever it be*; (TA;) *comprising all the clothing that is upon the man*; (Mgh, Msb, TA;) accord. to Lth and Az (Mgh) and the Bári'; (Msb;) or *whatever one of two antagonists in war takes from the other, of the things upon him and with him*, i. e. *of clothes and weapons, and his beast*: of the measure فَعَلٌ in the sense of the measure مَفْعُولٌ, i. e., (TA,) *i. q.* مَسْلُوبٌ [used in the manner of a subst., or as an epithet in which the quality of a subst. is predominant]: (Mgh, TA:) pl. أَسْلَابٌ. (M, A, Msb, K.) You say, أَخَذَ سَلَبَ القَتِيلِ [*He took the spoil of the slain* man], and أَسْلَابَ القَتْلَى [*the spoils of the slain* men]. (A.) — Also † The *hide and shanks and paunch* of a slaughtered animal. (K. [App. so called because given to the slaughterer, as though they were his spoil; or, in the case of an animal of the chase, to the dog or dogs: see the verses cited voce بَدَنٌ.]) — And † The *peel*, or *rind*, [or *skin*,] of a cane, or reed, (K, TA,) and of a tree. (TA.) And [particularly] The *bark*, or *rind, of a kind of tree* (S, K) *well known* (S) *in El-Yemen, of which ropes are made*, (S, K,) *and which is coarser and harder than the fibres of the Theban palm-tree*: (S:) hence it is that a well-known kind of [thick] rope [made of the fibres of the common palm-tree] is called by the vulgar ↓ سَلَبَة: (TA:) or the *bark of a kind of trees of which are made* [*baskets of the kind called*] سِلَال: (Sh, TA:) there is a market called ↓ سُوقُ السَّلَّابِينَ in El-Medeeneh, (Sh, S, K, TA,) and in Mekkeh also, as being the market [of the sellers, or manufacturers, of what are made] of سَلَب: (Sh, TA:) it is also [said to be] (K) *a certain kind of tall tree*, (M, K,) *growing symmetrically, which is taken and laid beneath hot ashes* (مَلّ), *and then split asunder, whereupon there comes forth from it a white* مُشَاقَة [or *coarse fibrous substance*] *like* [*the fibres of the palm-tree, called*] لِيف; and *it is one of the best of the materials of which ropes are made*: the n. un. is with ة: (M:) and (M, K) AHn says, (M,) it is *a certain plant* (M, K) *which grows in form like candles, except that it is larger and longer, and of which are made ropes of every sort*: (M:) and (M, K) some say, (M,) it is the *fibrous substance* (لِيف) *of the Theban palm-tree*, (M, K,) this Lth asserts it to be, (TA,) *which is brought from Mekkeh*, (M,) and Lth adds, *and it is white*; but Az says that Lth has erred respecting it: A'Obeyd says, I asked respecting it, and was told, it is not the fibrous substance of the Theban palm-tree, but is *a kind of tree well known in El-Yemen, of which ropes are made*: and some say that it is the خُوص [or *leaves*] *of the* ثُمَام [or *panic grass*]: and this [says SM] is what is commonly known among us in El-Yemen: (TA:) [accord. to Forskål, (Flor. Aegypt. Arab., p. cx.) this name is applied in El-Yemen to *a species of hyacinth*, which he terms *hyacinthus aporus*.] A poet says, (S,) namely, [Murrah] Ibn-Mahkán [El-Temeemee], (M,)

• فَنَشْنَشَ الجِلْدَ عَنْهَا وَهْىَ بَارِكَةٌ •
• كَمَا تُنَشْنِشُ كَفَّا فَاتِلٍ سَلَبَا •

(S, M,*) i. e. *And he stripped off quickly the skin* [*from her, while she was lying upon her breast, like as the two hands of the twister of* ropes *strips off quickly the seleb*]: (S in art. نش:) some read قَاتِلٍ, meaning [by the word following it] "what is seized, or carried off by force, from one slain:" (M:) As read فَاتِلٍ, with ف; IAar, with ق: Th says that the right reading is that of As. (S in the present art.)

سَلِبٌ *Light*, or *active*, (K, TA,) *and quick*. (TA.) You say, رَجُلٌ سَلِبُ اليَدَيْنِ بِالطَّعْنِ *A man light*, or *active, in the arms*, or *hands, in thrusting*, or *piercing*: and ثَوْرٌ سَلِبُ الطَّعْنِ بِالقَرْنِ *A bull light*, or *active, in thrusting*, or *piercing, with the horn.* (S, TA.) And فَرَسٌ سَلِبُ القَوَائِمِ *A horse light*, or *active*, (S, M, K,) *in the legs*, (M, K) [i. e.,] *in the shifting of the legs*: (S:) or, accord. to Az, the right meaning is, *long in the legs*: (TA:) [for] — سَلِبٌ signifies also *Long* or *tall*; (S, M, K;) applied to a spear, and to a man [&c.]: pl. سُلُبٌ. (M.)

سُلُبٌ, as a sing., see سَلِيبٌ, in three places. — It is also a pl. of سَلِبٌ [q. v., last sentence]: (M:) and of سِلَابٌ, as a subst.: (S, K:) and of سَلُوبٌ as an epithet applied to a spear: (Ham p. 171:) and of the same, (S, M,) or of سِلَابٌ, (M,) as an epithet applied to a she-camel (S, M) and to a woman: (M:) and of سَلِيبٌ as an epithet applied to a tree. (S.)

سُلْبَةٌ *i. q.* جُرْدَةٌ [i. e. The *denuded*, or *unclad, part*, or *parts, of the body*]: (IAar, K:) or *a state of nudity.* (TA.) One says, مَا أَحْسَنَ سُلْبَتَهَا [*How goodly is what is unclad of her person!* or, *her state of nudity!*]. (K.)

سَلَبَةٌ: see سَلَبٌ, in the former half of the paragraph: — and see also سِلَابٌ. = Also *A string*, or *cord, that is tied to the* خَطْم [i. e. *muzzle*, or *nose*,] *of the camel, exclusive of the* خِطَام [q. v.]. (M.) — And *A sinew that is bound upon an arrow*: accord. to AHn, the *sinew that is wound upon the* لِيط [or *skin of the reed, or cane*,] *of the arrow.* (M.)

سِلَابٌ sing. of سُلُبٌ, which signifies The *black garments of women at their assemblies for mourning*: (S:) MF says that the former is expl. in the K as meaning *black garments*, which necessarily implies that it is a pl.; and the latter is there said to be its pl., which necessarily implies that it is a sing.: (TA:) [but it may be replied that the author of the Ḳ regarded the former as a pl. without a sing.; and the latter, as a pl. pl.:] or both signify *black garments worn by women;* and the sing. is ▼ سَلَبَةٌ: (M:) accord. to the T, سِلَابٌ signifies *a black garment with which a woman mourning for the death of her husband covers her head:* accord. to the R, *a black* خِرْقَة [or *piece torn off from a garment* or *cloth*] *that is worn by a woman bereft of her child,* or *of a person beloved, by death.* (TA.) ═ See also سَلِيبٌ.

سَلُوبٌ: see سَلِيبٌ, in four places. ═ Also *A spear that takes away life:* pl. سُلُبٌ. (Ḥam p. 171.)

سَلِيبٌ i. q. ▼ مَسْلُوبٌ [as meaning *Seized,* or *carried off, by force:* — and more commonly *spoiled, despoiled, plundered,* or *deprived of what was upon one* or *with one*]: (Ṣ, A,* Mṣb:) as also ▼ سَلَبٌ [but app. in the former sense only]. (Ṣ.) [Hence] one says شَجَرَةٌ سَلِيبٌ ‡ *A tree despoiled,* or *deprived, of its leaves and its branches:* (M, Ḳ, TA:) or *of which the leaves and fruit have been taken:* (A:) pl. سُلُبٌ, as in the phrases نَخْلٌ سُلُبٌ *palm-trees upon which is no fruit,* and شَجَرٌ سُلُبٌ *trees upon which are no leaves;* the sing. being of the measure فَعِيلٌ in the sense of the measure مَفْعُولٌ: (Ṣ:) and one says also ▼ شَجَرَةٌ سُلُبٌ, [using سُلُبٌ as a sing., like other words of the same measure mentioned in what follows,] meaning *a tree of which the leaves have become scattered,* or *strewn.* (Az, TA.) And سَلِيبٌ is applied to a woman as meaning † *Whose husband has died,* or *her loved and loving relation* or *friend, and who puts on the black garments of mourning for him;* as also ▼ مُسَلِّبٌ and ▼ سَلُوبٌ: (Lḥ, M:) or ▼ مُسَلِّبٌ, so applied, signifies [simply] † *putting on,* or *wearing, the black garments of mourning.* (M. [See an ex. of this last word with the affix ة, used as a pl., in a verse cited voce خَطَبٌ; and an ex. of its pl., مُسَلِّبَاتٌ, in a verse cited voce ثَدْىٌ.]) Also, applied, to a she-camel, and so ▼ سَالِبٌ and ▼ سَلُوبٌ and ▼ مُسْلِبٌ, (Ḳ,) the last in one instance in the copies of the Ḳ erroneously written مُسَلِّبٌ, (TA,) and ▼ سُلُبٌ, (Ḳ, TA,) with ḍamm to the first and second letters, (TA,) [in the CḲ سُلْبٌ, and said to be with ḍamm,] or ▼ سَلُوبٌ thus applied, (Ṣ, M,) and ▼ سِلَابٌ, (M,) † *Whose young has died:* (M, Ḳ:) or *that has cast her young one in an imperfect state:* (Ṣ, M, Ḳ: and in this latter sense, as applied to a she-camel, ▼ مُسْلِبٌ is particularly mentioned in the M:) and in like manner applied to a woman: (M, Ḳ:) the pl. (of سَلُوبٌ, Ṣ, M, or سِلَابٌ, M) is سُلُبٌ (Ṣ, M, Ḳ, TA, in the last expressly stated to be like كُتُبٌ, but in the CḲ سُلْبٌ,) and سَلَائِبُ: (M, Ḳ:) and sometimes they said ▼ اِمْرَأَةٌ سُلُبٌ, like نَاقَةٌ عُلُطٌ and فَرَسٌ فُرُطٌ, and numerous other instances that have been enumerated by A'Obeyd, in which words of the measure فُعُلٌ, without ة, are used as fem. epithets: (M:) or ▼ سَلُوبٌ signifies ‡ *a she-camel whose young one has been taken;* and its pl. is سَلَائِبُ; (A:) and, applied to a she-camel, it signifies also ‡ اَلَّتِى يُرْمَى وَلَدُهَا [which may mean *whose young one is cast abortively;* or *cast away* because abortive; or *cast at,* or *shot at, and killed*]: (L, TA:) and is also applied to a she-gazelle, as meaning *despoiled,* or *deprived, of her young one:* and so ▼ سَالِبٌ. (M.) Applied to a man, (M,) it signifies also ▼ مُسْتَلَبُ العَقْلِ † [*Despoiled,* or *deprived, of reason*]; (M, Ḳ;) and you say [also] ▼ مُسْلَبُ العَقْلِ, [perhaps a mistranscription for ▼ مُسْلَبٌ, see 1,] a tropical expression: (A:) pl. سَلْبَى. (M, Ḳ.)

سَلَبُوتٌ, (Lḥ, M, Ḳ, TA, [in the CḲ, erroneously, سَلَبُوبٌ,]) of the measure فَعَلُوتٌ, from سَلَبَهُ الشَّىْءَ, (M,) and ▼ سَلَّابَةٌ, are [doubly intensive] epithets of which each is applied to a man and to a woman; (Lḥ, M, Ḳ;) meaning *Wont to spoil,* or *plunder, people* [*very often,* or] *constantly.* (TḲ.)

سَلَّابٌ [One *who spoils,* or *plunders, people much* or *often.* ═ And *A seller,* or *manufacturer, of ropes,* or *baskets, made of* سَلَب]: see its pl., voce سَلَبٌ.

سَلَّابَةٌ: see سَلَبُوتٌ.

سَالِبٌ: see سَلِيبٌ, in two places.

أُسْلُوبٌ *A row* of palm-trees; as also أُسْكُوبٌ. (IAạr, TA in the present art. and in art. سكب. [This is app. the primary signification; as seems to be indicated, by its occupying the first place, in the TA.]) — *A road,* or *way,* (M, Mṣb, Ḳ, TA,) *that one takes:* (M, TA:) *any extended road* or *way: a way* or *direction* [*in which one goes*]: (TA:) *a way, course, mode,* or *manner, of acting* or *conduct* or *the like:* (A, TA:) *a mode, manner, sort,* or *species;* syn. فَنٌّ: (Ṣ, M,* Mṣb, TA:) pl. أَسَالِيبُ. (Ṣ, M, A, Mṣb.) You say, هُوَ عَلَى أُسْلُوبٍ مِنْ أَسَالِيبِ القَوْمِ, i. e. [*He is following*] *a way of the ways of the people,* or *party.* (Mṣb.) And هُمْ فِى أُسْلُوبِ سُوْءٍ [*They are in a bad,* or *an evil, way*]. (TA.) And سَلَكَ أُسْلُوبَهُ *He pursued his way, course, mode,* or *manner, of acting* or *conduct* or *the like.* (A, TA.) And أَخَذَ فِى أَسَالِيبَ مِنَ القَوْلِ *He began,* or *entered upon, modes, manners, sorts,* or *species,* [meaning *varieties,* or *diversities,*] *of speech;* syn. فُنُونٍ, (Ṣ,) or أَفَانِينَ. (M.) And كَلَامُهُ عَلَى أَسَالِيبَ حَسَنَةٍ [*His speech,* or *language, is according to good,* or *beautiful, modes, manners, sorts,* or *species*]. (A, TA.) And one says of him who is proud, أَنْفُهُ فِى أُسْلُوبٍ (M, A) [*His nose is* kept *in one direction*], meaning ‡ *he looks not to the right nor to the left.* (A.) [Hence it is said that] أُسْلُوبٌ signifies also ‡ *Elevation in the nose, from pride.* (Ḳ, TA.) — Also The *aperture of a watering-trough,* or *tank, through which the water flows.* (IAạr, TA in art. بيب.) — And The *neck of the lion.* (Ḳ.)

أُسْلُوبَةٌ *A certain game of the Arabs of the desert:* or *some action that they perform among them:* one says, بَيْنَهُمْ أُسْلُوبَةٌ [*Among them is a performance of what is termed* اسلوبة]. (Lḥ, M.)

مُسْلَبُ العَقْلِ: see سَلِيبٌ, last sentence.

مُسْلِبٌ: see سَلِيبٌ, in three places.

مُسَلِّبٌ: see سَلِيبٌ, in two places. — مَا لِى أَرَاكَ مُسَلِّبًا i. e. [*What hath happened to me that I see thee*] *unfamiliar, not inclining to any one?* is a saying whereby a man is likened to a wild animal: one says also, إِنَّهُ لَوَحْشِىٌّ مُسَلِّبٌ, meaning *Verily he is unsociable and ungentle.* (AZ, L, TA.)

مَسْلُوبٌ: see سَلِيبٌ, first sentence.

مُسْتَلَبُ العَقْلِ: see سَلِيبٌ, last sentence.

المُسْتَلِبُ the name of *A sword of 'Amr Ibn Kulthoom:* and of *another, belonging to Aboo-Dahbal.* (Ḳ.)

سلت

1. سَلَتَ المِعَى, aor. ـُ, (M, Ḳ) and ـِ, (Ḳ,) inf. n. سَلْتٌ, (M, TA,) *He extracted,* or *made to come forth,* [*the contents of*] *the gut* [*by compressing it*] *with his hand.* (M, Ḳ. [In both it is expl. by أَخْرَجَهُ بِيَدِهِ: but it seems that a fault has been accidentally committed by a copyist in the former or in its original, and thence passed into the latter; and that the words which I have supplied are necessary to explain the true meaning. That such is the case, appears from what here follows.]) It is said in the L that السَّلْتُ signifies *The griping, with the hand, a thing that is contaminated by dirt,* or *filth, so that what is in it comes forth;* and thus is done with a gut. (TA.) It is also said to signify *The extracting,* or *causing to come forth, what is fluid,* or *moist, adhering to another thing.* (MF, TA.) [Hence,] سَلَتَ خَشْمَهُ i. e. مُخَاطَهُ عَنْ أَنْفِهِ [*He cleansed his nose of the mucus that was in it by compressing it with his fingers*]: occurring in two trads.; in one of which, the Prophet is related to have been in the habit of doing this to El-Ḥoseyn when he used to carry him upon his shoulder. (TA.) [Hence, likewise,] it is said in a trad., فَيَنْفُذُ الجَحِيمُ إِلَى جَوْفِهِ فَيَسْلُتُ مَا فِيهِ, i. e. [*And the fire of Hell shall penetrate to his inside, and*] *shall exscind and extirpate what is in it.* (TA.) — You say also, سَلَتَ القَصْعَةَ, (Ṣ, A, Ḳ,) aor. ـُ, inf. n. سَلْتٌ; (Ṣ;) and ▼ اِسْتَلَتَهَا; (Ḳ;) *He cleansed the bowl by taking off with his finger what remained upon its sides;* (Ṣ;) *he wiped the bowl* (A, Ḳ) *with his fingers* (A) or *with his finger.* (Ḳ.) And سَلَتَتْ خِضَابَهَا عَنْ يَدِهَا, (Ṣ, Mṣb, Ḳ,) aor. ـُ, inf. n. سَلْتٌ, (Mṣb,) *She cast from her,* or *from her hand, the remains of her stuff for dyeing the hands* or *hair:* (Ṣ, Ḳ:) or *she put away,* or *removed, that stuff from her hand:* (Mṣb:) or *she wiped off, and cast away, that stuff from her hand:* (TA:) or سَلَتَ الخِضَابَ, aor. ـُ, *he took away,* and *wiped off, the material for dyeing the hands* or *hair;* and in like manner, a similar thing; and sweat; and blood. (Mgh.) سَلَتَ الدَّمَ عَنْهَا occurs in a trad. as meaning *He*

removed the blood [from her or it]. (TA.) — سَلَتَ دَمَ البَدَنَةِ (M, Ḳ) means, accord. to Lḥ, *He scraped off the blood of the* بدنة [*or beast brought to Mekkeh for sacrifice*, or *there sacrificed*,] *with the knife*: but [ISd says, (and in like manner هَلَتَ دَمَ البَدَنَةِ is expl. in the L as on the authority of Lḥ,)] in my opinion the meaning is, *he scraped off the skin of the* بدنة *with the knife so that he made its blood to appear*. (M. [The explanation in the Ḳ is made up from the two different explanations in the M, being as follows: قَشَرَهُ حَتَّى أَظْهَرَ دَمَهَا, as though meaning *he scraped off the dried blood of the* بدنة *so that he made its fresh blood to appear*: but in the copy of the Ḳ followed in the TA, النَّدَبَة (i. e. *the scar*) is put in the place of البَدَنَة, and the former of these two (i. e. الندبة) I regard as the right word.]) — سَلَتَ also signifies † *He cut off* a thing. (Ḳ. [This is said in the TA to be the primary meaning: but accord. to the A, the phrase here following, in which it has this meaning, is tropical.]) You say, سَلَتَ أَنْفَهُ, (Ṣ, M, A, Ḳ,) aor. ـُ and ـِ, inf. n. سَلْتٌ, (M,) ‡ *He cut off his nose* (Ṣ, M, A, Ḳ) *entirely* (TA) with a sword. (Ṣ, A.) And سَلَتَ يَدَهُ بِالسَّيْفِ † *He cut off his hand*, or *arm*, *with the sword*. (M.) And سَلَتَ شَعْرَهُ † *He shaved off his hair*. (M, Ḳ.) And سَلَتَ رَأْسَهُ ‡ *He shaved his head*. (Aṣ, Ṣ, L.) — سَلَتَهُ † *He beat*, *struck*, or *smote*, *him*: (Ḳ, TA:) and *flogged him*. (TA.) You say, سَلَتُّهُ مِائَةَ سَوْطٍ † *I inflicted upon him a hundred strokes of the whip*. (Ṣ, TA.) — And سَلَتَ بِسَلْحِهِ † *He cast forth his excrement*, or *ordure*. (Ḳ.)

7. انسلت عَنَّا *He stole*, or *slipped*, *away from us without his being known to do so*. (M, Ḳ.)

8: see 1, in the former half of the paragraph.

سُلْتٌ *A species of* شعير [or *barley*], (Lth, Ṣ, M, Mgh, Mṣb, Ḳ,) *having no husk*, (Lth, Ṣ, Mgh, Mṣb,) أَجْرَدُ [which may mean either *beardless* or *smooth*], (Lth,) [*in appearance*] *as though it were wheat*, (Ṣ,) *growing in El-Ghowr and El-Ḥijáz*; (Mgh, Mṣb;) *the* سَوِيق [or *meal of the parched grain*] *whereof is employed as a cooling diet in the* صَيْف [or *summer*]: (TA:) or *i. q.* شَعِير [i. e. the *common barley*]; (M, Ḳ;) as some say: (M:) or the *sour* (حَامِض) *sort of* شعير: (M, Ḳ:) or *a white* شعير, *without husk*: or, as some say, *a species of wheat*; but the explanation next preceding this last is the more correct, for البَيْضَآءُ and السُّلْتُ are mentioned in a trad. as distinct, each from the other, and by the former is meant wheat: (TA:) or *a species of* شعير *with a thin husk and small grain*: (IF, Mṣb:) or *a grain between wheat and barley* (شعير), *not having a husk like that of the latter, and thus being like wheat in smoothness, and like barley* (شعير) *in its nature*, or *quality*, *and in its coolness*: (Az, Mṣb:) accord. to Eṣ-Ṣeydelánee, *like barley* (شعير) *in its form, and like wheat in its nature*, or *quality*; but this is a mistake: (Ibn-Eṣ-Ṣaláh, Mṣb:) [*gymnocrithon* (i. e. *hordeum nudum*) of Galen: *tragus* of Diosc. (Golius.)]

ذَهَبَ مِنِّى فَلْتَةً وَسَلْتَةً *It* (a thing, or an affair, TA) *escaped me*: (Ḳ, TA:) accord. to some, سلتة is here an imitative sequent. (TA.)

سَلْتَآءُ A woman *who does not make frequent use of* حِنَّآء [*for tinging*, or *dyeing*, *her hands*]; (Ṣ;) a woman *who does not frequently tinge her hands with* خِضَاب: (M:) or a woman *who does not make use of* خضاب *for herself* (M, A, Ḳ) *at all*: so some say. (M.) It is related of the Prophet, in a trad., that he cursed such a woman. (TA.)

سُلَاتَةٌ *What is extracted*, or *made to come forth*, (M, Ḳ,*) *from a gut* [*by compressing it*] *with the hand*. (M.) — *What is taken off with the finger from the sides of a bowl, to clean it*. (Ṣ, Ḳ.*)

أَسْلَتُ A man (Ṣ) *whose nose has been cut off* (Ṣ, M, Ḳ) *entirely*. (Ṣ, Ḳ.)

مِسْلَاتُ حِنَّآءٍ [app. *An instrument with which* حنّآء *is scraped off*, or *removed*, *from the hand*]. One says, أَعْطِنِى مِسْلَاتَ حِنَّائِكَ [*Give thou to me* &c.]. (A.)

مَسْلُوتٌ That *whereof the flesh that was upon it has been taken off* or *away*, or *removed*. (Ḳ.) — And *A shaven* head. (Aṣ, Ṣ, L.)

سلتم

سِلْتِمٌ *A calamity*, or *misfortune*. (Ṣ, M, Ḳ.) — *A hard*, or *severe*, *year*. (Ṣ, M, Ḳ.) — *A* [*goblin*, or *demon*, *such as is termed*] غُول. (Ṣ, M, Ḳ.) — A she-camel *having no tooth remaining, and whose lower lip has fallen and she is unable to raise it*. (Ḳ, TA. [The explanation in the CḲ is faulty: the last words should be لَا تَسْتَطِيعُ رَفْعَهَا.]) Some say that the م is augmentative. (TA.) — One says also مَا أَصَابَ سِلْتِمًا, [in the CḲ سَلْتَمًا,] meaning *He got not anything*. (Ḳ, TA.)

سلج

1. سَلِجَ, aor. ـَ, inf. n. سَلَجَانٌ (Ṣ, O, Mṣb, Ḳ) and سَلْجٌ, (Ṣ, O, Ḳ,) *He swallowed* (Ṣ, O, Mṣb, Ḳ) a morsel, or mouthful, or gobbet, (Ṣ, O, Ḳ,) and food, (TA,) or a thing; (Mṣb;) as also سَلَجَ, aor. ـُ; (Mṣb;) and ▼ تسلّج: (O, Ḳ:*) or سَلَجَانٌ signifies the *eating* quickly. (TA.) Hence the saying, الأَكْلُ سَلَجَانٌ وَالقَضَآءُ لَيَّانٌ [*Eating is a swallowing, and paying is a putting off*], (Ṣ, Meyd, O,) or الأَخْذُ سَلَجَانٌ الخ [*Taking*, or *receiving*, *is a swallowing*, &c.]: (Meyd, TA:) i. e., when a man receives a loan, or the like, he devours it [greedily]; but when he from whom he has received it demands his due, he puts him off by promising to pay it: (Ṣ, O:) a prov., (Meyd, O, TA,) applied to him who takes the property of others and to whom it is easy to do so; but when he is sued for payment, puts off, and it is difficult to him: (Meyd:) meaning that one loves to take, and hates to return, or restore. (L. [See also سُرَيْطَى.]) — سَلَجَ النَّاقَةَ, said of a young camel, *He sucked the she-camel*; (O, Ḳ;) as also مَلَجَهَا. (L, TA.) = سَلِجَتِ الإِبِلُ, aor. ـَ, (Ṣ, K, TA,) inf. n. سُلُوجٌ; (TA;) and سَلَجَت, aor. ـُ; (Ḳ, TA;) or the latter only accord. to AḤn; (TA;) or the latter is better than the former accord. to Sh; (O, TA;) *The camels had a looseness* (Ṣ, Ḳ) *of their bellies* (Ṣ) *from eating the plant called* سُلَّج. (Ṣ, Ḳ.)

5. تسلّج: see 1, first sentence. — Also *He persevered*, or *persisted*, *in drinking* (Lḥ, O, Ḳ) the beverage called نَبِيذ, (Lḥ,) or wine; (O, Ḳ;) like تَزَلَّجَ; (Lḥ;) meaning *he made it to enter his* سِلِّجَان; (O;) or *as though he filled with it his* سِلِّجَان, (Ḳ,) i. e. his حُلْقُوم: (TA:) and so ▼ استلج. (O, Ḳ.)

8: see what next precedes.

سَلِيجٌ: see سَلَجْلَجٌ, below.

سَاجَةٌ A سَلِيجَةٌ, (O, Ḳ,) i. e. *an oblong and squared piece of wood of the tree called* سَاج, *as brought from India*, (TA in art. سوج,) *from which a door is cloven, or divided off, lengthwise*: (O, Ḳ:) so says AḤn. (TA.) = See also what next follows.

سُلَّجٌ *A certain plant*, (Ṣ, Ḳ,) *upon which the camels pasture*, (Ṣ,) *soft*, *flaccid*, or *fragile*, *of the shrub-kind*; (TA;) also called ▼ سُلَّجَانٌ, (Ḳ, TA,) or ▼ سُلَّجَانٌ, (CḲ,) like قُمَّحَانٌ; (Ḳ;) and ▼ سَلِيجَةٌ: (TA:) or the ▼ سُلَّجَان, (O, TA,) i. e. سُلَّجَان, with ḍamm to the س, and teshdeed and fet-ḥ to the ل, (O,) is *a species of the* سُلَّج; (O, TA;) and this last is *one of the largest of the kind of trees called* حَمْض: (O:) accord. to AḤn, (TA,) or as is said by some one or more of the Arabs of the desert, (O,) the سُلَّج is *a large kind of trees, like the tails of the* [*lizards called*] ضِبَاب [pl. of ضَبٌّ], *green, and having thorns, and* [*of the kind termed*] حَمْض: (O, TA:) in the T it is said to be *a sort of* حَمْض *that ceases not to be green in the summer*, or *hot season*, *and in the* رَبِيع [app. here meaning *autumn*], *and is weak*, or *weak and soft*: Az also says that *it grows in the plains*, or *level tracts*, *has a fruit*, or *produce*, *with a sharpness in the extremities thereof, and is green in the* [*season called*] رَبِيع, *and then dries up, and becomes yellow*: and he adds, [contr. to what has been said above, from his work, the T,] it is *not reckoned among the trees called* حَمْض. (L, TA.)

سُلُّجَانٌ or سُلَّجَانٌ: see the next preceding paragraph, in three places.

سِلِّجَانٌ The حُلْقُوم [properly the *windpipe*, but here app. meaning the *gullet*: see 5]. (O, Ḳ.) One says, رَمَاهُ ٱللّٰهُ فِى سِلِّجَانِهِ [*May God smite him*, or *afflict him*, *in his* سلّجان]. (O.)

سَلَجْلَجٌ and طَعَامٌ سَلَجْلَجٌ and ▼ سَلِيجٌ *Good*,

or *pleasant, food,* (O, Ḳ, TA,) *that is swallowed* (Ḳ, TA) *with ease.* (TA.)

أَسْلَجُ *Bald in the fore part of the head;* like أَسْلَغُ; but the former is the more common. (TA in art. سلغ.)

سلجم

سَلْجَمٌ and ↓ سُلَاجِمٌ *Tall, or long;* (Ṣ, Ḳ;) as epithets applied to a horse, and to a man, and to the iron head or blade of an arrow &c.: (Ḳ:) or, applied to this last, the former word signifies *long and broad:* (AḤn, TA:) or *slender;* as also سَلْجَمٌ: and the pls. of these two words are سَلَاجِمُ and سَلَاجِمُ: which, applied to such iron heads or blades, signify [also] *sharpened,* or *pointed,* or *sharp-pointed:* (TA:) and سَلَاجِمُ applied to arrows signifies *long in the iron heads.* (Ṣ.) سَلْجَمٌ and ↓ سُلَاجِمٌ are also applied as epithets to a camel: (Ṣ, Ḳ: [in the former it is implied that in this case they have the first of the significations above; but see what follows:]) thus applied, they signify *Advanced in age, and strong:* (Ḳ:) or the former, so applied, signifies *strong:* (Ṣ voce صَلْخَدٌ:) the pl. of each is سَلَاجِمُ, with fet-ḥ [to the س]. (Ṣ, Ḳ.) — Also the former, applied to the لَحْىٌ [or jaw-bone], *Strong,* (Ḳ, TA,) *full-sized,* (TA,) *and thick,* or *compact.* (Ḳ, TA.) And, applied to a head, *Long in the* لَحْيَانِ [or *jaw-bones*]. (Ḳ, TA.) — Also A well *ancient* (عَادِيَّةٌ) *and having much water.* (Ḳ.) — سَلْجَمٌ is also the name of *A certain well-known plant;* (Ḳ, TA;) *of those termed* بُقُول; *which is eaten;* (TA;) [namely, *colza;* or *brassica napus oleifera:* so in the present day:] it is an arabicized word, [from the Pers. شَلْغَمْ,] originally with ش, but pronounced by the Arabs with س: (AḤn, TA:) one should not say ثَلْجَمٌ, nor شَلْجَمٌ, or this is a word of weak authority: (T, Ḳ, TA:) Az says that some pronounce it with ش, but that it is correctly with س. (TA.)

سُلَاجِمٌ: see the preceding paragraph, in two places.

سِهَامٌ مُسَلْجَمَاتٌ *Arrows made long and broad* [*in their iron heads*]. (TA.)

سلح

1. سَلَحَ, (Ṣ, Mgh, Ḳ,) aor. ـَ, (Mṣb, Ḳ,) inf. n. سَلْحٌ, (Ṣ, Mgh, Mṣb,) said of a man, (TA,) *He voided his excrement,* or *ordure;* (Ṣ, Ḳ;) [or *thin excrement:* see سَلْحٌ: and] said of a bird, *it muted,* or *dunged;* (Mṣb;) like تَغَوَّطَ (Mgh,* Mṣb) said of a man: (Mṣb:) and said also [of other animals, as, for instance,] of a camel, (Ṣ, Ḳ, TA,) and of a bull. (Ḳ in art. ثلط.)

2. سَلَّحَهُ *He armed him with a weapon* or *weapons.* (A.) And سَلَّحَهُ السَّيْفَ, (Ḳ, TA,) and القَوْسَ, (TA,) *He armed him with the sword,* (Ḳ, TA,) and *the bow.* (TA.) — سَلَّحَ الإِبِلَ, (A, TA,) inf. n. تَسْلِيحٌ, (TA,) *It caused the camels to void* سُلَاح [or *thin excrement;* i. e. *it purged them*]; said of a herb. (A, TA.) [See also 4.] — سَلَّحَ نِحْيَهُ, inf. n. as above, *He rubbed over his* نِحْى [or *skin for holding clarified butter*] *with* سَلْح, i. e. *rob,* or *inspissated juice.* (Ḳ, TA.)

4. اسلحهُ *He made him to void* سُلَاح [or *thin excrement*]. (Ṣ, Ḳ.) [See also 2.]

5. تسلّح *He wore,* or *put on,* [or *armed himself with,*] *a weapon,* or *weapons.* (Ṣ, A, L, Ḳ.) — [Hence,] تَسَلَّحَتِ الإِبِلُ بِأَسْلِحَتِهَا: see سِلَاحٌ.

سَلْحٌ *Excrement, ordure,* or *dung:* (L, TA: [and evidently so accord. to the Mṣb; in my copy of which, and so, app., in the copy used by SM, immediately after the mention and explanation of the verb سَلَحَ, is added, وهو سلحة تسمية بالمصدر; plainly showing, by what follows سلحة, that this word is a mistranscription for سَلْحُهُ; and that the meaning is, "and it is its سَلْح, an instance of the inf. n. used as a subst. properly so called;" i. e., the dung of a bird is called its سَلْح; for the verb is there said to relate to a bird; though in truth it has a general application:]) or *such as is thin, of any dung:* (L, TA: [and this is the sense in which it is commonly known:]) and ↓ سُلَاحٌ signifies [the same: i. e.] *excrement, ordure,* or *dung,* (Ṣ, A, MA, L, Ḳ, KL,) of a human being, (KL,) or of a bird (MA) [and of any animal]: or *thin excrement* or *dung:* (MA:) this latter is said to be the correct meaning in a marginal note in a copy of the Ṣ: (TA:) the pl. of the former is سُلُوحٌ and سُلْحَانٌ. (L, TA.) [رَمَى بِسَلْحِهِ frequently occurs in the Lexicons &c., meaning *He cast forth his excrement,* or *ordure;* or properly, *in a thin state.*] يَا سَلْحَ الغُرَابِ [lit. *O dung of the crow*], an expression used by 'Omar, means يَا خَبِيثُ † [*O foul,* or *filthy,* man]. (Mgh.)

سَلْحٌ signifies رُبٌّ [i. e. *Rob,* or *inspissated juice, generally of dates,*] *with which a skin for clarified butter is rubbed over,* (Ḳ, TA,) *for the purpose of seasoning it.* (TA.)

سِلْحٌ: see سِلَاحٌ.

سَلَحٌ *Rain-water in pools left by torrents:* (Ḳ:) so says ISh: but not heard by Az from the Arabs. (TA.)

سُلَحٌ The *young of the* حَجَل [or *partridge*]; (Ṣ, Ḳ;) like سُلَكٌ and سُلَفٌ: (Ṣ:) [a coll. gen. n.: n. un. with ة: for] it is said in the T that سُلَحَةٌ and سُلَكَةٌ signify the *young one of the* حَجَل: (TA:) pl. سِلْحَانٌ, (T, Ṣ, Ḳ,) like سِلْكَانٌ. (T, TA.)

سِلَحٌ: } see سِلَاحٌ.
سُلْحَانٌ: }

سُلَاحٌ: see سَلْحٌ. — [Also *A looseness,* or *flux of thin excrement from the bowels: diarrhœa.*]

سِلَاحٌ, (Ṣ, A, Mgh, Mṣb, Ḳ, &c.,) as also ↓ سِلْحٌ (accord. to the Ḳ) or ↓ سِلَحٌ (accord. to the Mṣb) and ↓ سُلْحَانٌ, (Ḳ,) [the last mentioned in the L as a pl.,] *A weapon,* or *weapons;* i. e. *an instrument,* or *instruments, of war;* (A, Ḳ;) the *thing* [or *things*] *with which one fights in war, and repels,* or *defends oneself;* (Mṣb;) *anything with which one repels the enemy, as a sword and spear &c.:* (Ḥam p. 73:) or *a weapon,* or *weapons, of iron:* (Lth, Mgh, Ḳ:) it is of the masc. gender, (Ṣ, Mṣb, TA,) accord. to the more approved usage, (TA,) or that which most prevails, (Mṣb,) because in the pl. it takes the form of أَسْلِحَةٌ, which is a pl. form of a masc. n., (Ṣ, Mṣb,*) as in the instances of أَحْمِرَةٌ, pl. of حِمَارٌ, and أَرْدِيَةٌ, pl. of رِدَآءٌ, (Ṣ,) but it is also fem., (Ṣ, Mṣb, Ḳ,) and has also for pls. سُلُحٌ and سُلْحَانٌ, (L,) and the pl. fem. is سِلَاحَاتٌ. (Mṣb.) You say رَجُلٌ ذُو سِلَاحٍ [*A man having a weapon* or *weapons*]. (Ḳ.) And قَوْمٌ ذَوُو سِلَاحٍ [*A people,* or *party, having weapons,* or *arms*]. (Ṣ, A, Ḳ.) And لَبِسَ السِّلَاحَ [*He wore,* or *put on, the weapon,* or *the weapons,* or *arms*]. (Ṣ, A, Ḳ.) And أَخَذَ القَوْمُ أَسْلِحَتَهُمْ *The people,* or *party, took their weapons,* or *arms, each taking his.* (Mṣb.) — *A sword* (Az, Mgh, Ḳ) alone is sometimes termed سِلَاحٌ. (Az, Mgh.) — And *A bow without a string* (Ḳ) is likewise thus termed. (TA.) — And *A staff,* or *stick.* (Ḳ.) — سِلَاحُ الثَّوْرِ means † *The horns of the bull.* (Ṣ,* TA.) — ذُو السِّلَاحِ is ‡ an appellation of السِّمَاكُ الرَّامِحُ [i. e. *The star Arcturus*]. (A, TA.) — And أَخَذَتِ الإِبِلُ سِلَاحَهَا and تَسَلَّحَتْ ↓ بِأَسْلِحَتِهَا mean ‡ *The camels became fat, and of goodly appearance;* (A, L, TA;) i. e. their fat became as though it were weapons with which they prevented their being slaughtered: (L, TA:) and the like has been mentioned before, [voce رُمْحٌ,] in art. رمح. (TA.)

سَالِحٌ A man *having,* (Ḳ,) or *having with him,* (Ṣ,) *a weapon,* or *weapons:* (Ṣ, Ḳ:) an epithet [of the possessive kind, having no verb,] similar to تَامِرٌ and لَابِنٌ. (TA.) — And A she-camel *that has voided excrement,* [or *thin excrement,*] *in consequence* [*of the eating*] *of herbs,* or *leguminous plants.* (Ṣ, Ḳ.)

أَسْلَحُ مِنْ حُبَارَى [*More wont to mute than a bustard*] (Meyd, A, Mgh) and مِنْ دَجَاجَةٍ [*than a domestic hen*]: the former mutes in the time of fear; and the latter, in the time of security: (Meyd:) a prov. (Meyd, Mgh.)

إِسْلِيحٌ *A certain plant, the pasturing upon which causes the milk* (Ṣ, Ḳ) *of the camels* (Ṣ) *to become abundant:* (Ṣ, Ḳ:) or *a certain kind of tree,* or *shrub, that has this effect:* (L:) [see also إِسْلِيخ:] it was said to an Arab woman of the desert, "What is thy father's tree?" and she answered, شَجَرَةُ أَبِى الإِسْلِيحُ رَغْوَةٌ وَصَرِيحٌ وَسَنَامٌ إِطْرِيحٌ [*The tree of my father is the isleeḥ: froth upon the milk, and milk free from froth; and a long,* or *tall, hump:* these are the consequences of pasturing upon it]: (Ṣ,* L:) or it is *a certain* *herb, or leguminous plant, of those that are slender and soft* (مِنْ أَحْرَارِ البُقُولِ), *growing in the winter, that causes the camels to void* سُلَاح [or *thin excrement*] *when they eat much of it:* or *a certain herb* (عُشْبَة), *resembling the* جَرْجِير [or *rocket*], *growing upon tracts of sand such as are termed* حُقُوف: or *a certain kind of plant, growing conspicuously in plain, or soft, tracts, having a thin and delicate leaf, and a pericarp* (سِنْفَة) *stuffed with grains, or seeds, like those of the poppy; which is one of the plants of the rain of the* صَيْف [here meaning *spring* (see زَمَن)], *and which causes the cattle to void* سُلَاح: n. un. with ة: Aboo-Ziyád says that the places in which the اسليح grows are sands. (L.)

مَسْلَحَةٌ *A* ثَغْر [or *frontier of a hostile country*]: (Ḳ:) or *a place of arms or weapons,* (Mgh,) *like a* ثغر *and a* مَرْقَب [which is *an elevated place of observation*], (Ṣ, Mgh, TA,) *wherein are parties that watch the enemy, lest they should make an incursion at unawares, and, when they see them, inform their companions, in order that they may prepare themselves for them:* (Nh, TA:) pl. مَسَالِحُ. (Ṣ, Mgh.) — Also, [in one of my copies of the Ṣ erroneously written مُسَلَّحَة,] *A people, or party, having arms, or weapons; an armed people or party;* (Ṣ, A, Ḳ, TA;) *composing a numerous body, in a place of observation, with the keeping of which they are entrusted, at the frontier of an enemy's country; a single person of whom is termed* ↓ مَسْلَحِىٌّ; (A,* L;) and مَسْلَحَةٌ [also] is thus applied to a single person in a saying of 'Omar: (Mgh:) they are thus called because of their having weapons, or because of their occupying the place called مَسْلَحَة: (Nh:) or the مسلحة of the army are *a party of capturers that go before the army, exploring for them the way, and searching as spies to learn news of the enemy, lest the enemy should make a sudden assault upon them; not suffering any one of the enemy to enter the territory of the Muslims, and warning the Muslims of the approach of an army.* (ISh.)

مَسْلَحِىٌّ: see the next preceding paragraph.

سلحب

Q. 4. اِسْلَحَبَّ *It was, or became, right, direct, rightly directed, straight, or even.* (Ṣ, Ḳ.) — *It* (a road) *was extended:* (Ṣ:) or *conspicuous and extended.* (Ḳ.) — [And app. *It was, or became, spread out,* or *expanded:* see the part n., below.]

سُلْحُوبٌ A woman *who cares not for what she does nor for what is said to her.* (AA, TA.)

مُسْلَحِبٌّ *Right, direct, rightly directed, straight, or even:* (Ṣ, Ḳ:) like مُتْلَئِبٌّ. (TA.) — *Extended:* (Ṣ:) or *conspicuous and extended:* (Ḳ:) applied to a road: (Ṣ, Ḳ:) like مُطْلَحِبٌّ. (L.) — *I. q.* مُنْبَطِحٌ [app. as meaning *Spread out,* or *expanded*]. (TA.) — ظَلَّ يَوْمُنَا مُسْلَحِبًّا means *Our day was,* or *became, one of protracted journeying.* (L, TA.)

سلحف

سُلَحْفَى (AZ, Mṣb, Ḳ) and سُلْحَفَى, (Fr, Ḳ,) pronounced by the vulgar سِلْحَفَى, (TA,) and سُلَحْفَاةٌ [which is the most common of the dial. vars.] (Ṣ, Mṣb, Ḳ) and سِلَحْفَاةٌ (Fr, Ḳ) and سُلَحْفَاةٌ, (Mṣb,) and سُلَحْفَآءُ, (AZ, Mṣb, Ḳ,) and سُلَحْفِيَةٌ, (Ṣ, Ḳ,) [*The tortoise, commonly so called;* and also *the turtle,* or *sea-tortoise;* applied to both in the present day;] *a certain well-known beast;* (Ḳ;) [and] *a certain aquatic animal;* (Mṣb;) called in Pers. بَاخَهْ and كَشَفْ (MA, PṢ) and سَنْگْ پُشْتْ; (MA;) applied to the *male* and the *female:* (Mṣb:) pl. سَلَاحِفُ: (Ṣ, Mṣb:) or, accord. to Fr, the male of the سلاحف is called غَيْلَمٌ; and the *female* is called سلحفاة in the dial. of Benoo-Asad: (Mṣb:) [it is said to be derived from the Pers. سولاخ پاى; because there is a hole in the body, into which the foot enters: (Freytag's Lex.:)] its blood and its gall-bladder are [asserted to be] beneficial to him who is affected with epilepsy; and the smearing with its blood, to the joints; (Ḳ, TA;) which thereby become strong: (TA:) and it is said that when the cold has become intense in a place, (Ḳ, TA,) and one fears for the seed-produce from it, (TA,) and this beast is placed upside-down, so that its fore and hind legs are towards the air, the cold will not alight upon that place. (Ḳ, TA.) — السُّلَحْفَاةُ or السُّلْحَفَاةُ is also a name of ‡ *The constellation Lyra;* commonly called الشَّلْيَاقُ.]

سلخ

1. سَلَخَ, (Ṣ, A, Mṣb, Ḳ, &c.,) aor. ِ, (Ṣ, Ḳ, [as in the Ḳur xxxvi. 37,]) or ُ, (Mṣb, [but this I find in no other lexicon,]) and َ, (Ṣ, Mṣb, Ḳ,) inf. n. سَلْخٌ, (Ṣ, Mṣb,) *He stripped off* (Ṣ, Ḳ) the hide, or skin, of a sheep or goat: (Ṣ:) or *he skinned* a sheep or goat. (A, Mṣb.) And سُلِخَ جِلْدُهَا [*Its skin was stripped off*]. (A.) One does not say of a camel, سَلَخْتُ جِلْدَهُ; but كَشَطْتُهُ, and نَجَوْتُهُ, and أَنْجَيْتُهُ. (Mṣb.) — [Hence,] † *He pulled off* or *stripped off* [a garment]. (Ḳ, TA.) You say of a woman, سَلَخَتْ دِرْعَهَا, (Ṣ, TA,) and سَلَخَتْ عَنْهَا دِرْعَهَا, (A, TA,) ‡ *She pulled off her shift; stripped it off.* (Ṣ, TA.) — And [hence,] سَلَخَ الشَّهْرَ, (Ṣ, A, Mṣb,) or شَهْرَهُ, (Ḳ,) aor. ِ (L, Mṣb) and ُ, (L,) inf. n. سَلْخٌ and سُلُوخٌ, (L, Mṣb,) ‡ *He passed the month,* or *his month;* (Ṣ, Ḳ, TA;) *came to the end of it.* (Ṣ, A, Mṣb, Ḳ.) سَلَخْنَا الشَّهْرَ means ‡ *We passed forth from the month; having pulled off from ourselves every night one thirtieth part until the nights were complete, when we pulled off from ourselves all of it:* and أَهْلَلْنَا هِلَالَ شَهْرِ كَذَا means "We entered upon [the period of the new moon of] such a month; clothing ourselves with it and increasing the clothing of ourselves therewith until the passing of the half of it:" then we pull off from ourselves [by degrees] the whole of it: hence a verse cited voce جُمَادَى. (T, TA.) And one says of God, سَلَخَ النَّهَارَ مِنَ اللَّيْلِ ‡ *He drew forth gently the day from the night:* (Ḳ, TA:) or *He separated the day from the night.* (Jel in xxxvi. 37.) — See also 7, in three places. — سَلَخَ الحَرُّ جِلْدَ الإِنْسَانِ and [in an intensive sense] ↓ سَلَّخَهُ † [*The heat made the skin of the man to peel off;* or *excoriated the man*]. (TA.) And سَلَخَ الجَرَبُ جِلْدَهُ ‡ [*The mange,* or *scab, excoriated him,* i. e., a camel]: (A, TA:) [and so سَلَخَهُ without the mention of the skin:] see سَالِخٌ. And سُلِخَ الظَّلِيمُ † *The ostrich had a disease in his feathers* [app. such as caused many of them to fall off]. (TA.) — سَلَخَ النَّبَاتُ † [*The plant shed its foliage, and then became altogether green again:* (see سَالِخٌ:) or] *the plant became green again after having dried up.* (M, Ḳ.) — فَسَلَخُوا مَوْضِعَ المَآءِ كَمَا يُسْلَخُ الإِهَابُ فَخَرَجَ المَآءُ, in a trad. respecting Solomon and the هُدْهُد [or hoopoe, i. e. † *And they stripped off the surface of the place of the water, like as the hide is stripped off, and thereupon the water came forth*], means that they dug until they found the water. (TA.) — سُلِخَ مِنْ بَطْنِ أُمِّهِ, said of a child, means † *He was drawn out from the belly of his mother.* (TA.) — سَلْخُ الشِّعْرِ is † *The substituting throughout the poetry, for the original words, other words synonymous therewith:* what falls short of this is termed مَسْخٌ. (TA. [See Ḥar p. 263.])

2: see 1, in the latter half of the paragraph.

5: see the next paragraph, first sentence.

7. انسلخ جِلْدُهُ and [in an intensive sense] ↓ تسلّخ [*His skin became stripped off:* — and † *he became excoriated* by heat]. (A, TA. [The latter meaning is indicated in the TA.]) — انسلخت الحَيَّةُ مِنْ قِشْرِهَا [*The serpent cast off,* or *divested itself of, its slough*]: (Ṣ:) and ↓ سَلَخَتِ الحَيَّةُ, (L, Ḳ,) aor. ُ, inf. n. سَلْخٌ, (L,) [signifies the same, or] *the serpent withdrew itself from its slough:* (L, Ḳ:) and in like manner one says of any creeping thing: (L:) and one says of the serpent termed السَّالِخ [q. v.], ↓ يَسْلَخُ جِلْدَهُ, [*He casts off his slough*]. (Ṣ.) — One says also of a man, انسلخ مِنْ ثِيَابِهِ † [*He became stripped,* or *divested,* or *he divested himself, of his clothes*]. (Ṣ.) — And انسلخ الشَّهْرُ مِنْ سَنَتِهِ (Ṣ, A, Mṣb, Ḳ) (Ṣ) ‡ *The month passed,* or *passed away* [*from its year*]; (Mṣb, Ḳ, TA;) as also ↓ سَلَخَ. (Ḳ.) And انسلخ النَّهَارُ مِنَ اللَّيْلِ (Ṣ, A, Ḳ) ‡ *The day became drawn forth gently from the night;* (Ḳ, TA;) *came forth from the night so as not to leave with it aught of its light.* (TA.) [As used in this phrase and in others,] انسلخ مِنْهُ means † *It became altogether separated from it; quitted it entirely.* (MF.)

9. اسلخّ, inf. n. اِسْلِخَاخٌ, *He lay upon his side.* (Ḳ.)

سَلْخٌ: see مِسْلَاخٌ, in two places. — سَلْخُ الشَّهْرِ † *The last,* or *end, of the month;* (Mṣb, Ḳ;) as also ▼ مُنْسَلَخَهُ: (Ḳ:) or *the last day thereof.* (MA.)

سِلْخ: see مِسْلَاخ, in two places.

سَلْخ The *spun thread that is upon the spindle.* (Ḳ.)

سَلْخَةٌ: see مِسْلَاخ.

سَلِيخ A *skinned* sheep or goat; (L;) as also ▼ مَسْلُوخ (Ṣ, Ḳ) and ▼ مَسْلُوخَةٌ: (TA:) or this last is an epithet in which the quality of a subst. is predominant, meaning *a skinned sheep* or *goat, without head and without legs and without belly:* (Mgh:) and the first is an epithet applied to a sheep or goat until some part of it has been eaten; after which, what remains is called شِلْو, whether much or little. (L.) ═ سَلِيخٌ مَلِيخٌ A thing, (JK,) accord. to the Ḳ a person, but this is not in the other lexicons, (TA,) *insipid; without taste.* (JK, Ḳ, TA.) — And A man (TA) *vehement in* جِمَاع, *without impregnating.* (Ḳ, TA.)

فِيهِ سَلَاخَةٌ وَمَلَاخَةٌ *In it* (accord. to the Ḳ *in him,* but see سَلِيخ, TA) *is insipidity,* or *tastelessness.* (Ḳ,* TA.)

سَلَاخَة [app. *A piece of skin,* or *hide, stripped off*]. (Ḳ voce جُوز.) ═ The *urine of the mountain-goat.* (KL.) [In Pers. سَلَاخَهْ: thus, with ح, and with fet-ḥ to the first letter, accord. to Johnson's Pers. Ar. and Engl. Dict. Golius adds, on the authority of Ibn-Beyṭár, that it is black and viscous like pitch, and is collected from the rocks.]

سَلِيخَة † *A certain perfume,* or *odoriferous substance, resembling bark stripped off,* (JK, Ḳ, TA,) *and having* شُعَب [or *forking projections*]. (TA.) — † Of the [plants called] رِمْث (JK, Ṣ, Ḳ) and عَرْفَج, (JK, Ṣ,) [*Such as has been stripped of what was good for pasture;*] the *portion that has in it nothing for pasture* (JK, Ṣ, Ḳ, TA) *remaining;* (TA;) *consisting only of dry wood:* (Ṣ, TA:) and of the عرفج, *such as is thick, of what has become dried up.* (TA.) — And † The *oil of the fruit,* or *produce, of the* بَان [or *ben-tree*] *before it has been seasoned* (Ḳ, TA) *with aromatics:* when it has been seasoned with musk and [other] perfume, and then expressed, it is termed مَنْشُوش; and one says of it, نُشَّ. (TA.) Also † *Offspring:* (JK, Ḳ, TA:) because it has been drawn out (نُزِعَ i. e. سُلِخَ) from the belly of its mother. (TA.)

سُلَّخَة an extr. pl. [or quasi-pl. n.] of سَالِخ, q. v. (TA.)

سَلَّاخ *A skinner,* or *flayer.* (KL.)

سَالِخ *Skinning,* or *flaying.* (KL.) — † *Mange,* or *scab, in consequence of which the camel is excoriated* (▼ يُسْلَخ). (Ḳ.) — [A serpent *casting off its slough.* And hence,] *A black serpent,* (JK, Ṣ, Ḳ,) *intensely black:* (JK, TA:) you say, أَسْوَدُ سَالِخٌ, (Ṣ, Ḳ,) not prefixing the former word so as to govern the latter in the gen. case: [so called] because it casts off its slough (يَسْلَخُ جِلْدَهُ) every year: (Ṣ:) the female is called أَسْوَدَةٌ, and is not qualified by the epithet سَالِخَةٌ: (Ṣ, Ḳ:) and you say أَسْوَدَانِ سَالِخٌ, (Ḳ,) not giving to the epithet the dual form, accord. to AZ and Aṣ; but IDrd authorizes its being in the dual form, though the former mode is the better known: (TA:) and أَسَاوِدُ سَالِخَةٌ and سَوَالِخُ and سُلَّخٌ and ▼ سُلَّخَةٌ, (Ḳ,) which last is extr. [i. e. anomalous]. (TA.) — Also † A plant of the kinds termed حَمْض &c. *that has shed its foliage* (سَلَخَ) *and then become altogether green again.* (TA.)

أَسْلَخُ, applied to a man, (JK,) † *Very red* [as though skinned]. (JK, Ḳ.) — And [its pl.] سُلْخٌ, applied to camels, † *Having mange,* or *scab, by which they are excoriated.* (JK.) — Also † *Bald in the fore part of the head:* (Ḳ:) but أَنْلَخ is more common in this sense. (TA.)

إِسْلِيخ *A certain plant.* (Ḳ.) [Perhaps a dial. var. of إِسْلِيح, or a mistranscription for this latter.]

مَسْلَخ *A place in which sheep or goats are skinned.* (Mṣb.)

مِسْلَاخ *A skin,* or *hide;* (JK, Ṣ, Ḳ;) as also ▼ سِلْخ: (TA:) or, of a sheep or goat; (A;) as also ▼ سَلْخ, i. e. its *skin,* or *hide, that is stripped off.* (Ḳ, TA.) [Hence,] one says, فُلَانٌ حِمَارٌ فِى مِسْلَاخِ إِنْسَانٍ ‡ [*Such a one is an ass in the skin of a man*]. (A, TA.) — And The *slough* of a serpent; (JK, Ṣ, A, L, Ḳ;) as also ▼ سِلْخ, (MA, KL, and so in the CḲ,) or ▼ سَلْخ, (TA,) and ▼ سَلْخَةٌ. (L, and so in copies of the Ḳ and in the TA.) — Also † *A palm-tree of which the unripe dates fall and become scattered about in a green state.* (Ṣ, Ḳ.)

مَسْلُوخ; and with ة: see سَلِيخ.

مُنْسَلَخُ الشَّهْرِ: see سَلْخ.

سلس

1. سَلِسَ, [aor. ـَ,] inf. n. سَلَسٌ and سَلَاسَةٌ and سُلُوسَةٌ, [*It was,* or *became, loose, not tight;* as meaning *slack;* the only signification indicated by ISd; (see سَلِس, below;) and also as meaning *unsteady:*] (M:) [in the Ḳ, سَلَس and سَلَاسَة are said to be simply substs.: see the former of these two words below.] — سَلِسَ, (Mṣb, TA,) aor. ـَ, inf. n. سَلَسٌ (Mṣb) [and app. سَلَاسَةٌ also, (see سَلَس below,)] said of a colt, (TA,) [and of a horse, and, tropically, of a man, (see سَلِس,)] *He was,* or *became, tractable, submissive, compliant, obsequious,* (TA,) or *easy,* (Mṣb, TA,) and *gentle.* (Mṣb.) You say, سَلِسَ لِى بِحَقِّى ‡ [*He was easy to me in giving me my due,* or *right*]. (A, TA.) And سَلِسَ بَوْلُهُ, (TA,) inf. n. سَلَسٌ, (Mṣb,) † *His urine flowed involuntarily; he was unable to retain his urine;* (Mṣb, TA;) *by reason of disease.* (Mṣb.) [The explanations of سَلِس and سَلِس &c. below will serve to give further illustrations of this verb.] — سَلِسَتِ النَّخْلَةُ, aor. ـَ, *The palm-tree lost the stumps,* or *lower ends, of its branches;* (Ibn-'Abbád, Ḳ;) as also ▼ أَسْلَسَتْ: and the epithet applied to the palm-tree in this case is ▼ مِسْلَاس; (Ḳ;) or, accord. to the Tekmileh and O and L, ▼ مُسْلِس; but it seems that ▼ نَخْلَةٌ مُسْلِسٌ means *a palm-tree that lets fall and strews its unripe dates;* and ▼ مِسْلَاس, *that usually does thus:* (TA:) and ▼ سَلَس means *what falls from the palm-tree.* (Ibn-Abbád, TA.) — سَلِسَتِ الخَشَبَةُ, (inf. n. سَلَس, TA,) *The piece of wood became old and crumbling and wasted.* (Ibn-'Abbád, Ḳ.) ═ سُلِسَ, (Ṣ, M, Ḳ,) inf. n. سَلْسٌ and سَلَسٌ, (IAạr, M,) *He became bereft of reason.* (Ṣ, M, Ḳ.)

2. سَلَّسَ, (Ibn-'Abbád,) inf. n. تَسْلِيس, (Ḳ,) *He set, fixed,* or *put together,* a composite ornament, of the ornaments worn by women, not consisting of خَرَز [or beads]. (Ibn-'Abbád, Ḳ,* TA.)

4. أَسْلَسَتْ *She* (a camel) *produced her young one before the completion of the days:* (T, Ḳ:) the epithet applied to her in this case is ▼ مُسْلِس; and to the young one, ▼ مُسْلَس, (TA,) and ▼ سَلَس. (Ibn-'Abbád, TA.) — See also 1.

سَلْس *A string upon which beads,* (M,) or *white beads worn by female slaves,* (Ṣ, Ḳ,) *are strung:* (Ṣ, M, Ḳ:) pl. سُلُوس: (Ṣ, M:) or [*a woman's ear-drop;* i. e.] the *woman's ornament called* قُرْط. (Ibn-'Abbád, Ḳ.) — And [the pl.] سُلُوس signifies also *Women's mufflers,* or *head-coverings;* syn. خُمُر [pl. of خِمَار]: so says IAạr; and he cites as an ex.,

قَدْ مَلَأَتْ مَرْكُوَّهَا رُؤُوسَا •
كَأَنَّ فِيهِ عُجُزًا جُلُوسَا •
شُمْطَ الرُّؤُوسِ أَلْقَتِ السُّلُوسَا •

[*They* (referring to camels) *had filled their watering-trough with heads, as though there were in it old women sitting, with grizzled heads, having thrown off the mufflers*]: they having eaten of [the kind of plants, or trees, called] حَمْض, so that their faces and heads had become white, he likens them to old women that had thrown off the mufflers. (M.)

سَلَس and ▼ سَلَاسَة [said in the M to be inf. ns. of سَلِسَ, (q. v.,) and in the Ḳ to be simply substs., signify, as substs., *Looseness;* as meaning *slackness;* and as meaning *unsteadiness:* — and also] *Easiness, gentleness, tractableness, submissiveness; compliance,* or *obsequiousness.* (Ṣ, Ḳ.) [Hence,] one says, ▼ فِى كَلَامِهِ سَلَاسَةٌ ‡ [*In his speech is easiness*]. (A.) ═ For the former, see also 1: — and 4.

سَلِس part. n. of سَلِسَ; as also ▼ سَالِس: (M:) *Loose, not tight;* meaning [*slack;* (see 1, first sentence;) and also] *unsteady;* applied to a nail, (A, TA,) and to any other thing. (TA.) A rájiz says,

مَمْكُورَةٌ غَرْثَى الوِشَاحِ السَّالِسِ ▼ •
تَضْحَكُ عَنْ ذِى أُشُرٍ غُضَارِسِ •

[*A female of slender make, whose loose* وِشَاح (q. v.) *required more than it had within it to fill it, laughing so as to discover cool and sweet serrated and sharp teeth*]. (M, TA.) — *Easy*; applied to a thing: (Ṣ:) *easy,* (Mṣb, Ḳ,) *gentle;* (Ṣ, Mṣb, Ḳ;) *tractable; submissive; compliant; obsequious;* (Ṣ, Ḳ;) applied [to a horse and the like, and, tropically,] to a man. (Ṣ.) You say, فَرَسٌ سَلِسُ القِيَادِ [*A horse easy to be led; tractable*]. (A.) And فُلَانٌ سَلِسُ القِيَادِ and ↓ مِسْلَاسُ القِيَادِ ‡[*Such a one is easy to be led,* or *persuaded; tractable, submissive,* or *compliant*]. (A.) — ‡A man *easy in private conference;* expl. by سَهْلُ الخَلْوَةِ. (Mṣb.) — Beverage, or wine, *that descends gently* or *easily* [*down the throat*]. (TA.) — سَلِسُ البَوْلِ A man *whose urine flows involuntarily; who is unable to retain his urine;* (Ṣ, A, Mṣb, Ḳ;) *by reason of disease.* (Mṣb.)

سَلِسَةٌ *A certain herb, bearing a near resemblance to the* نَصِىّ, (AḤn, M, Ḳ,* TA,) *except that it has a grain like that of the* [*species of barley called*] سُلْت; (AḤn, TA;) *and when it dries up, it has an awn that flies about, when it is put in motion, like arrows, sticking into the eyes and the nostrils, and often blinding the pasturing beasts:* (AḤn, M, TA:) *the places of its growth are the plain,* or *soft, tracts.* (AḤn, TA.)

سُلَاسٌ *Loss,* or *departure, of reason* or *intellect.* (Ṣ, M, Ḳ.)

سَلَاسَةٌ: see سَلِسٌ, in two places.

سَالِسٌ: see سَلِسٌ, in two places.

مُسْلَسٌ: see 4.

مُسْلِسٌ: see 1, in two places: — and see also 4.

مُسَلَّسٌ A sword *having wavy marks resembling a chain:* occurring in a verse of Ibn-Ḳilábeh El-Hudhalee, as some relate it; but accord. to others, مُلَسْلَس, formed by transposition from مُسَلْسَل. (TA.)

مِسْلَاسٌ: see سَلِسٌ: — and see also 1, latter part, in two places.

مَسْلُوسٌ *Bereft of reason,* or *intellect;* (Ṣ, M;) and [*of bulk*] *of body,* (M, TA,) as some say; but accord. to the T, one says رَجُلٌ مَسْلُوسٌ in respect of his reason, or intellect, but مَهْلُوسٌ in respect of his body: (TA:) *possessed,* or *insane.* (Ḳ.)

سلسبل

سَلْسَبِيلٌ, a quinqueliteral-radical word, (M,) *Easy* [*as a beverage*] *in the utmost degree:* (TA:) [applied as an epithet to milk, (لَبَن, so in a copy of the M, and so in the CḲ,) or signifying *smooth,* (لَيِّن, so in copies of the Ḳ,)] *in which is no roughness:* (M, Ḳ:) and sometimes applied as an epithet to water, (M, TA,) or beverage, meaning *easy of entrance into the throat,* or *fauces.* (TA.) — And *Wine:* (Ḳ:) so accord. to some, as in the saying of 'Abd-Allah Ibn-Rawáḥah, in which it is [said to be] used as a syn. adjunct to the preceding word:

إِنَّهُمْ عِنْدَ رَبِّهِمْ فِى جِنَانٍ
يَشْرَبُونَ الرَّحِيقَ وَالسَّلْسَبِيلَا

[as though meaning *Verily they are with their Lord, in gardens, drinking wine and fermented juice of the grape:* but the meaning may be, *the choicest of wine,* or *the sweetest thereof,* &c., (see رَحِيقٌ,) *and wine easy to swallow,* or *the like*]. (TA.) — And *A certain fountain in Paradise* [mentioned in art. سبل, q. v.]: (M, Ḳ:) Aboo-Bekr says that it may be a proper name of the fountain, and properly imperfectly decl. [i. e. without tenween] as being determinate and of the fem. gender, but made to be with tenween at the end of a verse in the Ḳur [lxxvi. 18] in order that it may be conformable with other endings of verses; or it may be an epithet applied to the fountain, and therefore perfectly decl.: (TA:) Sb mentions it as an ex. of an epithet: IAạr says that he had not heard it except in the Ḳur-án: (M, TA:) I'Ab says that سَلْسَبِيلًا [in the Ḳur] means *that slips,* or *steals,* (يَنْسَلُّ,) *into the throats,* or *fauces:* [as though the radical letters were only س and ل, which some assert to be the case:] accord. to Aboo-Jaạfar El-Báḳir, it means *soft in the part between the* حَنْجَرَة [or *head of the windpipe*] *and the* حَلْق [or *fauces*]: the explanation as meaning [سَلْ رَبَّكَ سَبِيلًا إِلَى هٰذِهِ i. e.] سَلْ سَبِيلًا العَيْنِ [*Ask of thy Lord a way of access to this fountain*] is a mistake, not allowable. (TA.) — The pl. is سَلَاسِبُ and سَلَاسِيبُ: and the pl. of [the fem.] سَلْسَبِيلَةٌ is سَلْسَبِيلَاتٌ. (TA.) — [In the present day it is applied to *An artificial fountain that throws up water.*]

سلط

1. سَلُطَ, aor. ـُ, (M,) inf. n. سَلَاطَةٌ, (Ṣ, M, B,) *He,* or *it, overcame, prevailed,* or *predominated:* (Ṣ, TA:) or *was,* or *became, firm,* or *established, in superior power* or *force:* (B, TA:) *he possessed power of dominion* or *sovereignty* or *rule.* (M.) — *It* (anything, as, for instance, a solid hoof, and a camel's foot,) *was,* or *became, strong,* or *hard.* (M.) — *He was,* or *became, sharp.* (TA.) And the same verb, (M, Mṣb, Ḳ,) inf. n. as above (Ṣ, M, Mṣb, Ḳ) and سُلُوطَةٌ, (Ṣ, M, Ḳ,) *He was,* or *became, chaste,* or *perspicuous, in speech,* or *eloquent, and sharp in tongue:* (Ṣ:) or *long-tongued;* (M, Ḳ;) as also سَلِطَ, aor. ـَ, (Ḳ,) inf. n. سَلَطٌ: (TṢ, TA:) or *clamorous and foul-tongued:* (Mṣb:) [or this verb, said of a man, has the first of these three significations; but] سَلُطَتْ, inf. n. سَلَاطَةٌ, signifies *she* (a woman) *was,* or *became, long-tongued, and vehemently clamorous.* (Lth.) [See سَلِيطٌ, below.]

2. سَلَّطَهُ عَلَيْهِ, (Ṣ, M, Mṣb,) inf. n. تَسْلِيطٌ, (M, Ḳ,) also written with ص, (Ibn-'Abbád, and Ḳ in art. صلط,) *He* (God, Ṣ) *made him to overcome him; to prevail,* or *predominate, over him;* or *to have,* or *exercise, superior power* or *force over him:* (Ṣ, Ḳ:) *he made him to have mastery, dominion,* or *authority, and power, over him:* (Mṣb:) *he made him to have,* or *exercise, absolute dominion* or *sovereignty* or *rule, over him;* (M;) or *absolute superiority of power* or *force:* (Ḳ:) *he gave him power over him,* and *superior power* or *force.* (TA.) [You say also, سَلَّطَ عَلَيْهِ الكِلَابَ *He set the dogs upon him.*]

5. تَسَلَّطَ عَلَيْهِمْ *He overcame them; prevailed* or *predominated, over them;* or *was made to do so; he had,* or *exercised,* or *was made to have* or *exercise, superior power* or *force over them:* (Ṣ:) *he had,* or *was made to have, mastery, dominion,* or *authority, and power,* or *absolute dominion* or *authority and power, over them:* (Mṣb:) *he had,* or *received, power over them;* and *superior power* or *force;* quasi-pass. of سَلَّطَهُ عَلَيْهِمْ. (TA.)

سَلْطٌ: } see سَلِيطٌ; for the former, in four
سَلِطٌ: } places; and for the latter, in seven.

سُلْطَةٌ: } see سُلْطَانٌ; for the latter, in three
سَلْطَنَةٌ: } places.

سُلْطَانٌ *Strength, might, force,* or *power;* (TA;) as also ↓ سَلْطَنَةٌ: (Bḍ in iii. 144:) *predominance;* the *possession,* or *exercise, of superior power* or *force,* or *of dominion,* or *authority,* and *power,* or *of absolute dominion* or *authority and power;* (Mgh;) as also ↓ سُلْطَةٌ; (Ṣ;) the former being *syn. with* تَسَلُّطٌ [used as a subst.]; (Mgh;) and the latter being the subst. from تَسَلَّطَ: (Ṣ:) *power of dominion; sovereign,* or *ruling, power;* (M;) [in this sense, as well as in the first,] *i. q.* ↓ سَلْطَنَةٌ; (Mṣb;) *power of a king;* (Lth, Mgh, Ḳ;) and *of a governor;* (Mgh, Mṣb;) [i. e.] *delegated power,* or *power given to one who is not a king;* (TA;) also written سُلُطَانٌ: (M, Mṣb, Ḳ;) which is the only instance of this form: (Mṣb:) it is masc. and fem.; (M, TA;) generally masc., in the opinion of the skilful; but sometimes fem.; so say IAmb and Zj and others: (Mṣb:) but ISk says that it is fem. (TA.) One says, (ISk,) or some say, (Mṣb,) قَضَتْ بِهِ السُّلْطَانُ (ISk, Mṣb) *The sovereign,* or *ruling, power* (↓ السَّلْطَنَةُ) *decreed it.* (Mṣb.) And Aboo-Zuheyr says, I heard one, in whose chasteness of speech I have confidence, say, أَتَتْنَا سُلْطَانٌ جَائِرَةٌ [*A tyrannical sovereign,* or *ruling, power, came to us*]. (Mṣb.) It is said in a trad., إِلَّا أَنْ تَسْأَلَ ذَا سُلْطَانٍ, meaning *Unless thou ask the ruler,* or *governor,* or *the king,* for thy due from the public treasury. (Mgh.) And you say, قَدْ جَعَلْتُ لَكَ سُلْطَانًا عَلَى أَخْذِ حَقِّى مِنْ فُلَانٍ *I have given thee power,* or *authority, to take,* or *receive, my due from such a one.* (TA.) And لَا يَؤُمُّ الرَّجُلُ الرَّجُلَ فِى سُلْطَانِهِ [*A man shall not take precedence of a man in his authority*]; meaning, in his house, and where he has predominance, or superior power, or authority; nor shall he sit upon his cushion; for in doing so he would show him contempt. (Mgh.) — *Strength,* or *hardness,* of anything: (M, Ḳ:) *sharpness* of anything: *force,* or *violence,* of anything. (TA.) The *vehemence* of winter. (TḲ.) *An excited and predominant state* of the blood; or *inflammation* thereof. (IDrd, M, Ḳ.) The *flaming,* or *blazing,* of fire. (IDrd.) — *A proof; an evidence; an argument;*

a plea; an allegation; syn. حُجَّةٌ, (Ṣ, M, Mgh, Mṣb, Ḳ,) and بُرْهَانٌ: (Ṣ, Mṣb:) a حُجَّة being thus called because of the force with which truth attacks the mind: (B:) or, accord. to Moḥammad Ibn-Yezeed, from سَلِيطٌ, (M, TA,) signifying "oil of olives," because it enlightens: (TA:) and in these senses it has no pl., because it is used in the place of an inf. n. (Ṣ, TA.) Accord. to I'Ab, it signifies حُجَّة wherever it occurs in the Ḳur. (TA.) But in the words of the Ḳur [xvii. 35], فَقَدْ جَعَلْنَا لِوَلِيِّهِ سُلْطَانًا, the meaning may be either [*We have given to his executor*, or *heir*,] *authority, and power*, or *absolute authority and power*, or *the like*; or *a plea*, or *the like*. (Mgh.) And again, in the Ḳur [lxix. 29], هَلَكَ عَنِّى سُلْطَانِيَهْ, the meaning may be *My dominion*, and *my authority and power over men, has perished from me*; or *my plea*. (Bḍ, B.) And sometimes it means *A miracle*; as in the words of the Ḳur [li. 38], إِذْ أَرْسَلْنَاهُ إِلَى فِرْعَوْنَ بِسُلْطَانٍ مُبِينٍ [*When we sent him to Pharaoh with a manifest miracle*]. (TA.) Az says that it is sometimes masc. because it has a masc. form; and thus it is in the last of the instances above. (TA.) — Also *A ruler*, or *governor*, or *the like*; *a king*; *a sovereign*; (Ṣ, Ḳ, TA;) *a khaleefeh*: (TA:) these are its most common applications [in the writings of post-classical times]: (TA:) thus applied because the person so called is made to predominate; to have, or exercise, superior power or force; to have dominion, or the like: or because he is one of the evidences of God: (Aboo-Bekr, TA:) or because he possesses proof or evidence [of his right]: or because by him pleas and rights are established: (TA:) or because he enlightens the earth, (Mṣb,* B,) and is of great usefulness; (B;) the word being derived from سَلِيطٌ [signifying "olive-oil"]: (Mṣb:) it is of the measure فُعْلَانٌ: (Ṣ:) and when [thus] applied to a person, it is masc.: (Mṣb:) or it is masc. and fem.: (Ṣ, TA:) accord. to Moḥammad Ibn-Yezeed, (TA,) fem. because it is [originally] pl. of سَلِيطٌ applied to "oil;" as though the kingdom shone by him; or because it has the signification of حُجَّة: and sometimes masc., because regarded as meaning a man; (Ḳ, TA;) or because regarded as a sing.: so says Moḥammad Ibn-Yezeed; but Az observes that none beside him says this: Fr says that he who makes it masc. regards it as meaning رَجُلٌ; and he who makes it fem. regards it as meaning حُجَّة: (TA:) the pl. is سَلَاطِينُ. (Ṣ, Mṣb.) It is also, itself, sometimes used as a pl.; as in the phrase سَيِّدُ السُّلْطَانِ, used by a poet, meaning سَيِّدُ السَّلَاطِينِ [*The lord of kings*]; i. e. *the khaleefeh*: [but this may be rendered *the lord of sovereign power*, &c.:] or, as some say, the latter word is here pl. of سَلِيطٌ, like as رُغْفَانٌ is pl. of رَغِيفٌ. (Mṣb.)

سَلَطَانَةٌ, and سِلِطَّانَةٌ, or سِلِطَّانَةٌ: see سَلِيطٌ.

سَلِيطٌ *Strong*, or *hard*; (M, Ḳ;) as also ▼ سَلِطٌ, (M,) or ▼ سَلْطٌ. (Ḳ.) You say, ▼ حَافِرٌ سَلِطٌ, (M,) or ▼ سَلْطٌ, (TA,) and سَلِيطٌ, (M, TA,) *A strong*, or *hard, solid hoof.* (M, TA.) And دَابَّةٌ سَلِطَةُ ▼ الحَافِرِ *A beast having a strong*, or *hard, hoof.* (M.) And بَعِيرٌ سَلِطُ ▼ الخُفِّ *A camel having a strong*, or *hard, foot.* (M.) — *Sharp*; applied to anything. (Ḳ.) You say also, ▼ سَنَابِكُ سَلِطَاتٌ *Sharp edges of the fore parts of hoofs.* (Ṣ, TA.) — *Chaste in speech*, or *eloquent*, (Ṣ, Ḳ,) *and sharp in tongue*: (Ṣ:) an epithet of praise when applied to the male, and of dispraise when [with ة] applied to the female: (IDrd, Ḳ:) also, (Ḳ,) *long-tongued*; (M, Ḳ;) and so ▼ سَلِطٌ, (M,) or ▼ سَلْطٌ; (Ḳ:) fem. سَلِيطَةٌ, and ▼ سَلَطَانَةٌ, (M, Ḳ,) and ▼ سِلِطَانَةٌ, (Ḳ,) or ▼ سِلِطَّانَةٌ; (M;) the last written [thus] with teshdeed to the ط in the Jm., and there explained as signifying *long-tongued and clamorous*: (TA:) or سَلِيطٌ signifies *clamorous and foul-tongued*; and so سَلِيطَةٌ applied to a woman: (Mṣb:) or the latter, applied to a woman, *clamorous*: (Ṣ:) or *long-tongued and vehemently clamorous*: (Lth:) or سَلِيطَةُ اللِّسَانِ is applied to a woman in two senses; signifying *sharp-tongued; and long-tongued.* (Az, TA.) You say also, لِسَانٌ سَلِيطٌ, (M, Ḳ,) and ▼ سَلِطٌ, (M,) or ▼ سَلْطٌ, (Ḳ,) *A long tongue.* (M, Ḳ.) = *Oil of olives*; (Ṣ, M, Mṣb, Ḳ;) so applied by the generality of the Arabs: but by the people of El-Yemen applied to *oil of sesame*, or *sesamum*: (Ṣ, M:) IDrd, in the Jm, says the reverse; and IF has followed him; but what J says is right, as Ṣgh, has observed in the O: (TA:) also, (Ḳ,) or as some say, (M,) *any oil expressed from grains* or *berries*: (M, Ḳ:) pl. سُلُطَانٌ. (Mṣb, Ḳ.)

أَسْلَطُ *More*, and *most, overcoming, prevailing, predominating*, or *superior in power* or *force.* (Ḥar p. 661.) — هُوَ أَسْلَطُهُمْ لِسَانًا *He is the most chaste*, or *eloquent, and the sharpest*, [&c., (see an ex. voce سَلِقٌ,)] *of them in tongue.* (Ṣ.)

سلطح

Q. 3. اِسْلَنْطَحَ *It* (a thing) *was*, or *became, long and wide.* (AA, O and L in this art.: mentioned in the Ṣ in art. سطح.) — *It* (a valley) *became wide*: (Ḳ:) accord. to IF, both the ل and ن are added to give intensiveness to the signification. (O.) — *He* (a man) *extended himself* or *became extended* [app. on the ground]; syn. اِنْبَسَطَ: (L:) or *he became thrown down upon his face*: or *he lay*, or *lay as though thrown down* or *extended*: or *he stretched himself*; or *lay, and stretched himself; upon his face, extended upon the ground*: syn. اِنْبَطَحَ: (O:) or *he lay as though thrown down or extended, upon the back of his neck*: (Ibn-'Abbád, O:) or *he* (a man, L) *fell upon his face*: (L, Ḳ:) and *upon his back.* (L.)

سُلَطِحٌ, (Ḳ,) or ▼ سُلْطُوحٌ, (O,) *A smooth mountain*: (O, Ḳ:) so says Ibn-'Abbád. (O.)

سَلَطْحَةٌ, applied to a girl, or young woman. *Broad.* (Ḳ.)

سُلْطُوحٌ: see سُلَطِحٌ.

سَلَاطِحٌ *Wide.* (Lth, T, O, Ḳ.) It is said of rain [as meaning *Wide-spreading*]. (O.)

سَلَنْطَحٌ *A wide open tract*; (IDrd, O, Ḳ;) as also ▼ مُسْلَنْطِحٌ. (Ḳ.)

مُسْلَنْطِحٌ: see what next precedes.

سلع

1. سَلَعَ رَأْسَهُ, aor. َ, (Ṣ, Mṣb,) inf. n. سَلْعٌ, (Ṣ, TA,) *He clave*, or *split, his head*, [i. e., *the skin thereof*, (see سَلْعَةٌ,)] (Ṣ, Mṣb, TA,) *by striking it*, with a staff, or stick. (TA.) = سَلِعَتْ قَدَمُهُ, (Ṣ, Ḳ,*) aor. َ, inf. n. سَلَعٌ, (Ṣ, Ḳ,) *His foot became chapped*, or *cracked*, (Ṣ, Ḳ,) *in its upper part* and *in its under*, like زَلِعَتْ. (Ṣ, TA.) [See also 5.] — سَلَعَ جِلْدُهُ بِالنَّارِ, [so in the L and TA, app. a mistranscription for سَلِعَ,] inf. n. سَلَعٌ, *His skin became burned by fire so that the mark thereof was seen upon it.* (L, TA.) — سَلِعَ, aor. َ, inf. n. سَلَعٌ, *He was*, or *became, affected with* بَرَص [i. e. *leprosy*, particularly *the white, malignant kind thereof*]. (IDrd, Ḳ.)

2. تَسْلِيعٌ [inf. n. of سَلَّعَ as used in the phrase سَلَّعَ البَقَرَ, or ثِيرَانَ الوَحْشِ, (see مُسَلَّعَةٌ,)] signifies a practice which was observed in the Time of Ignorance, when the people were afflicted with drought, or barrenness of the earth; which was The *hanging the* [*kind of tree, or plant, called*] سَلَع, *with the* [*species of swallow-wort called*] عُشَر, *to wild bulls, and sending them down from the mountains, having kindled fire in the* سلع *and* عشر; seeking thereby to obtain rain: (Ḳ, TA:) or the *loading the backs of those animals with the fire-wood of the* سلع *and* عشر, *then kindling fire therein*; seeking to obtain rain by the flame of the fire, which was likened to the gleaming of lightning. (TA.) [See also سَلَعٌ, where a meaning somewhat different from those above is indicated.])

4. اسلع *He* (a man, TA) *had a* [*wound in the head, such as is termed*] شَجَّة, (Ḳ, TA,) i. e., *a* سَلْعَة: (TA:) or *he had a* [*kind of ulcer in the belly, called*] دُبَيْلَة. (TA.)

5. تسلّع عَقِبُهُ *His heel became chapped*, or *cracked.* (Ṣgh, Ḳ.) [See also 1; and see 7.]

7. انسلع *It clave*, or *split*, or *slit, in an intrans. sense.* (Ṣ, Ḳ.) [See also 1, and 5.]

سَلْعٌ *A chap*, or *crack, in the human foot*: pl. سُلُوعٌ. (Ṣ, Ḳ.) — See also the next paragraph, in two places.

سِلْعٌ *A cleft*, or *fissure, in a mountain*, (Lḥ, IAạr, Yaạkoob, Ṣ, Ḳ,) *having the form of a crack*; (TA;) as also ▼ سَلْعٌ, (Ṣ, Ḳ,) accord. to some: (Ṣ, TA:) pl. [of either] أَسْلَاعٌ (Yaạkoob, Ṣ, Ḳ) and (of the latter, TA) سُلُوعٌ. (Ḳ.) = Also *A like*, or *fellow*; (AA, L, Ḳ;) and so ▼ سَلْعٌ: (L, TA:) pl. أَسْلَاعٌ. (IAạr, L, Ḳ.) You say, هٰذَا سِلْعُ هٰذَا *This is the like of this.* (TA.) And غُلَامَانِ سِلْعَانِ *Two boys,* or *young men, that are fellows,* or *equals in age:* and غِلْمَانٌ أَسْلَاعٌ. (Ibn-'Abbád, Ḳ.) And أَعْطَاهُ أَسْلَاعَ إِبِلِهِ *He gave him the likes,* or *fellows, of his camels.* (L.) ═ And the pl. أَسْلَاعٌ signifies also The *portions of flesh that cling to the* نَسَيَانِ [or *two sciatic veins*] of a mare when she is fat. (Ṣgh, Ḳ.)

سَلَعٌ [originally inf. n. of سَلِعَ, q. v.,] *Marks left by fire upon the skin.* (TA.) ═ *A certain kind of bitter tree;* (Ṣ, Ḳ;) which, in the Time of Ignorance, was used in one or the other of the manners described above in the explanations of تَسْلِيعٌ; (Ḳ, TA;) or they used, in the case of drought, or barrenness of the earth, to hang somewhat of this tree and of the عُشَر to the tails (ذُنَابَى [a sing. used as a pl.]) of [wild] bulls or cows, then to kindle fire therein, and make them to ascend upon the mountain; and thus, they assert, they used to obtain rain: (Ṣ, TA:) the author of the Ḳ says that J has made a mistake in saying ذنابى, in the above-cited passage; that he should have said أَذْنَاب; but others had made this remark before the author of the Ḳ; and 'Abd-El-Ḳádir Ibn-'Omar El-Baghdádee says that the mistake is to be imputed to these, and not to J, who has only used a sing. in the sense of a pl., like as الدُّبُر is used in the Ḳur [liv. 45], for الأَدْبَار: (MF, TA:) AḤn cites an Arab of the desert, of the سَرَاة, as saying that *the* سلع *grows near to a tree, and then clings to it, and climbs it, with long, green, leafless shoots, twining upon the branches and interweaving themselves, and having a fruit like bunches of grapes, which is small, and, when ripe, becomes black, and is eaten only by the monkeys,* or *apes, not by men, nor by the beasts that are left to pasture at their pleasure;* and adding, *I have not tasted it, but I think that it is bitter; and when it is broken, there flows from it a viscous fluid, clear, and having strings:* such is the description of the man of the سراة: (TA:) or it is *a certain poisonous plant,* (Ḳ, TA,) *not to be tasted, like* زَرْع [here meaning *wheat* or *barley*] *when it first comes forth, scantily scattered in the ground, and having a small, yellow, prickly leaf, its prickles being downy; it is a herb,* or *leguminous plant, which spreads itself upon the surface of the ground, like* [*the plant called*] رَاحَةُ الكَلْبِ, *having no root, and it is not improbable that the ostrich may feed upon it, notwithstanding its bitterness, for it sometimes feeds upon the colocynth:* (Aboo-Ziyád, TA:) or it is *a species of aloes:* (Ḳ:) or *a herb,* or *leguminous plant,* (Ḳ, TA,) *of those termed* ذُكُور [*that are hard and thick,* or *thick, and inclining to bitterness,* or *thick and rough*], (TA,) *of bad,* or *nauseous,* or *disgusting, taste:* (Ḳ, TA:) so says Aboo-Naṣr: (TA:) [Forskål found this name applied in El-Yemen to the *salasthus quadragonus:* (Flora Ægypt. Arab., pp. cv. and 33:) and the *cacalia sonchifolia:* (Ibid., p. cxix.:) and the name of سَلَع أَبْيَض, or سَلَع البَقَر, to the *senecio hadiensis.* (Ibid., pp. cxix. and 149.)]

سَلْعَةٌ *A wound by which the head is broken,* syn. شَجَّةٌ, (Ṣ, L, Mgh, Mṣb, Ḳ,) *of whatever kind it be;* as also ↓ سَلَعَةٌ: or *that* [*only*] *cleaves the skin:* (Ḳ:) pl. سَلَعَاتٌ (Mṣb, Ḳ, [in the CḲ, erroneously, سَلْعَاتٌ,]) and سِلَاعٌ, and quasi-pl. n. [or coll. gen. n.] سَلْعٌ. (Ḳ.) — See also what next follows.

سِلْعَةٌ [*A ganglion;*] *a thing like the* غُدَّة, *that comes forth upon the body,* or *person;* (Ḳ,* TA;) as also ↓ سَلْعَةٌ, (Ḳ,) which is the form of the word now commonly known, (TA,) and ↓ سَلَعَةٌ, (Ḳ,) and ↓ سِلَعَةٌ: (Ibn-'Abbád, Ḳ:) or *an excrescence* (Ṣ, Mgh, Ḳ) *of flesh,* (Mgh,) *that arises in the body,* (Ṣ, Mgh, Ḳ,) or *a* [*kind of spontaneous swelling that comes forth upon the body, such as is termed*] خُرَاج, (Mṣb,) *like the* غُدَّة, (Ṣ, Mgh, Mṣb, Ḳ,) *that moves about when moved,* (Ṣ, Mṣb, Ḳ,) or *moves to and fro between the skin and the flesh,* (Mgh,) *and varies from* [*the size of*] *a chick-pea to* [*that of*] *a melon;* (Ṣ, Ḳ;) also termed ضَوَاةٌ: (Ṣ:) the physicians say that it is *a thick tumour, not adhering to the flesh, moving about when moved, having a cyst,* or *case which encloses it, and capable of increase, because it is extrinsic to the flesh,* wherefore the doctors of practical law allow its being cut off, when it is safe to do so: (Mṣb:) or *a* خُرَاج [vide suprà] *in the neck:* (Ḳ:) or *a* غُدَّة *in the neck:* (Ibn-'Abbád, Ḳ:) pl. سِلَعٌ. (Mṣb.) — [Hence,] *A thing* [i. e. *a knob*] *that comes forth in a tree.* (AḤn, TA in art. بلط.) — [Hence also,] *A leech;* (Ḳ;) because it attaches itself to the body like the غُدَّة: (TA:) pl. سِلَعٌ. (Ḳ.) ═ *A commodity; an article of merchandise;* (Ṣ,* Mgh,* Mṣb, Ḳ;*) *a thing with which one trafficks:* (Ḳ:) pl. سِلَعٌ. (Mṣb, Ḳ.)

سَلَعَةٌ: see سَلْعَةٌ: — and سِلْعَةٌ.

سِلَعَةٌ: see سِلْعَةٌ.

سَلِيعَةٌ *Nature,* or *disposition:* so in the phrase إِنَّهُ لَكَرِيمُ السَّلِيعَةِ [*Verily he is generous in respect of nature,* or *disposition*]. (TA.) [But perhaps this may have originated from a mistranscription for سَلِيقَة.]

سُوَلَّعٌ The *bitter aloe.* (IAạr, Ṣgh, Ḳ.)

أَسْلَعُ A man *having the foot chapped,* or *cracked:* pl. سُلْعٌ. (Ḳ.) — A man *having his skin burned by fire so that the mark thereof is seen upon it.* (TA.) — A man *affected with* بَرَص [i. e. *leprosy,* particularly *the white, malignant kind thereof*]. (Mgh, Ḳ.) — And *Humpbacked.* (TA.)

مُسْلَعٌ [A man *having a wound in the head, such as is termed* سَلْعَة: (see 4; and see also مَسْلُوع:) or] *having a* [*kind of ulcer in the belly, called*] دُبَيْلَة. (TA.)

مِسْلَعٌ *A guide that directs aright:* (Lth, Ḳ:) so called because he cleaves the desert. (TA.)

بَقُورٌ مُسَلَّعَةٌ *A number of* [*wild*] *bulls* or *cows having some firewood of the* سَلَع *hung to their tails,* [*with* عُشَر, *and then set on fire,*] (Ṣ,* TA,) or *having their backs laden therewith.* (TA.) [See 2, and see also سَلَع.]

مَسْلُوعٌ A man *having* [*the skin of*] *his head cleft,* or *split;* (Mṣb;) *a man having* [*a* سَلْعَة, i. e.] *a* شَجَّة; as also ↓ مُنْسَلِعٌ. (TA.) [See also مُسْلَع.] — *Having a* سِلْعَة, i. e. [*ganglion,* or] *thing like the* غُدَّة, &c. (Ḳ.) — مَسْلُوعَةٌ The *main part,* or *middle, of a road;* the *part of a road along which one travels;* syn. مَحَجَّةٌ: (Ibn-'Abbád, L, Ḳ:) because it is cleft, or furrowed. (L.)

مُنْسَلِعٌ: see مَسْلُوعٌ.

سلغ

1. سَلَغَتِ البَقَرَةُ, and الشَّاةُ, aor. ـَ, inf. n. سُلُوغٌ, *The bovine animal,* and *the sheep* or *goat, shed the tooth* [*next*] *behind that called the* سَدِيس; (Ṣ, Ḳ;) as also صَلَغَتْ: (Ṣ:) this is in the sixth year; (Ṣ, Ḳ;) and سُلُوغ in cloven-hoofed animals is like بُزُول in camels: for it is the furthest of their teeth [that they then shed]: (Ṣ:) or *bred its* [*tooth called the*] نَاب: (Ḳ:) or *attained its full fatness:* (TA: [or more probably, I think, *its full age;* for I think that سمنها in the TA is a mistranscription for سِنَّهَا: see أَسَنَّ:]) the epithet is ↓ سَالِغٌ and صَالِغٌ, applied [to the male and] likewise to the female, without ة: (Ṣ:) you say نَعْجَةٌ سَالِغٌ and بَقَرَةٌ سَالِغٌ: (Lth, Ḳ:) the young one of the بَقَرَة in the first year being termed عِجْل, then تَبِيع, (Ṣ, Ṣgh, Ḳ,) or, correctly, accord. to IB, in the first year عِجْل and تَبِيع, (TA,) then جَذَع, then ثَنِىّ, then رَبَاع, then سَدِيس, then سَالِغ سَنَةٍ and سَالِغُ سَنَتَيْنِ, and so on; and the young one of the شَاة in the first year being termed حَمَل or جَدْى, then جَذَع, then ثَنِىّ, then رَبَاع, then سَدِيس, then سَالِغ: (Ṣ, Ṣgh, Ḳ:) and سُلَّغ is [the pl.,] applied to [bovine animals and] sheep or goats, like صُلَّغ. (TA.) — You say also, سَلَغَ الحِمَارُ, meaning قَرِحَ [i. e. *The ass finished teething*]. (TA.)

سَالِغٌ: see the preceding paragraph.

سلف

1. سَلَفَ, (Ṣ, M, Mṣb, Ḳ,) aor. ـُ, (Ṣ, M, Mṣb,) or, accord. to some, ـِ, and accord. to IḲṭṭ, ـُ and ـِ, (MF,) inf. n. سَلَفٌ, (Ṣ, Ḳ,) or سُلُوفٌ, (Mṣb,) [both app. correct,] *It* (a thing, Ḳ) [and also *he* (a man)] *passed; passed away;* (Ṣ, Mṣb, Ḳ;) *came to an end,* or *to nought;* or *became cut off:* (Mṣb:) and, (Ḳ,) inf. n. سَلْفٌ, (M, MF, and so in copies of the Ḳ,) or سَلَفٌ, (so in the CḲ,) and سُلُوفٌ, (M, Ḳ,) *he* (a man, Ḳ) [and also *it* (a thing)] *went before,* or *preceded;* (M, Ḳ;) and so ↓ سَالَف, said of a camel. (Ḳ.) In a verse cited voce رَدَاةٌ, سَلَفَ is used by poetic

license for سَلَفَ: but this kind of contraction is allowed by the Basrees only in verbs of which the medial radical letter is with kesr or damm, as in عَلْمَ for عَلِمَ, and كَرْمَ for كَرُمَ. (M. [See سَرْعَ.]) — You say also, سَلَفَ لَهُ عَمَلٌ صَالِحٌ, meaning *A good*, or *righteous, deed of his preceded* [*so as to prepare for him a future reward*]. (TA.) — And سَلَفَتِ النَّاقَةُ, inf. n. سُلُوفٌ, *The she-camel was*, or *became, among the foremost of the camels in arriving at the water.* (TA.) — [Golius and Freytag mention also سَلَفَ as a trans. verb; the former explaining it as signifying "*Præteriit, præcessit,* rem;" and the latter adding "*tempore,*" and assigning to it the inf. ns. سَلَفٌ and سُلُوفٌ; as on the authority of the Ḳ; in which I find no indication of such a usage of this verb.] ═ سَلَفَ الأَرْضَ, (Ṣ, M, Ḳ,) aor. ـُ, inf. n. سَلْفٌ; (Ṣ, M;) and ▼ اسلفها; (M, Ḳ;) *He turned over the land for sowing:* (M, Ḳ:) or (so in the Ḳ, but in the M "and") *he made it even with the* مِسْلَفَة [q. v.]. (Ṣ, M, Ḳ.) — سَلَفَ المَزَادَةَ, inf. n. سَلْفٌ, [in some copies of the Ḳ سَلَّفَ,] *He oiled*, or *greased, the* مزادة [or *leathern water-bag*]. (Ḳ.)

2. تَسْلِيفٌ signifies The *making* [a thing] *to go before*, or *precede*. (Ṣ, Ḳ.) — And *I. q.* إِسْلَافٌ. (Ḳ.) See 4, in six places. — And The *giving* to another *the portion of food termed* سُلْفَة [q. v.]. (Ṣ.) You say, سلّف الرَّجُلَ, (Ṣ,) or القَوْمَ, (M,) inf. n. as above, (Ṣ,) *He gave to the man*, (Ṣ,) or *to the people* or *party*, (M,) *the portion of food so called;* (Ṣ, M;) as also [سلّف لَهُ, or] سلّف لَهُمْ. (M.) — And The *eating of the* [*portion of food termed*] سُلْفَة. (Ḳ.) [See also 5.]

3. سالف: see 1, first sentence. ═ سالفهُ فِى الأَرْضِ, (Ibn-'Abbád, Ḳ,) inf. n. مُسَالَفَةٌ, (Ibn-'Abbád, TA,) *i. q.* سَايَرَهُ [i. e. *He went*, or *kept pace*, or *ran, with him*, or *he vied, contended*, or *competed, with him in going* or *running, in the land;* as though striving to be before him]. (Ibn-'Abbád, Ḳ.) — And سالفهُ *He equalled him* in an affair. (Ibn-'Abbád, Ḳ.)

4. اسلفهُ *He did it previously*, or *beforehand*. (O and TA in art. زلف.) — [Hence,] اسلف فِى كَذَا, (Ṣ, Mgh, Mṣb, TA,) inf. n. إِسْلَافٌ; (TA;) and ▼ سلّف فيه, (Mgh, Mṣb, TA,) inf. n. تَسْلِيفٌ; (Mṣb, TA;) *He paid in advance*, or *beforehand, for such a thing*, (Ṣ, Mgh, TA,) i. e. a commodity described to him, (Ṣ,) or wheat or the like, *for which the seller became responsible*, [*with something additional to the equivalent of the current price at the time of the payment*, (see سَلَفٌ,)] (TA,) *to be delivered at a certain period:* (Ṣ:) and أَسْلَمَ signifies the same. (TA.) You say, ▼ سَلَّفْتُ and أَسْلَفْتُ إِلَيْهِ فِى كَذَا [*I paid in advance to him for such a thing*, &c.]. (Mṣb.) Hence the saying in a trad., مَنْ سَلَّفَ فَلْيُسَلِّفْ فِى كَيْلٍ مَعْلُومٍ وَوَزْنٍ مَعْلُومٍ إِلَى أَجَلٍ مَعْلُومٍ i. e. *He who pays in advance* for a commodity for which the seller is responsible, *let him pay in advance for a certain measure, and a certain weight, to be delivered at a certain period.* (TA.) — And اسلفهُ مَالًا, (Ṣ, M, Mgh, TA,) and ▼ سلّفهُ, (M, Mgh, TA,) *He lent him property* [*to be repaid*, or *returned, without any profit*]. (M, Mgh, TA. [See, again, سَلَفٌ.]) [Whence one says, اسلفهُ إِحْسَانًا and إِسَاءَةً, and ▼ سلّفهُ, meaning † *He did to him, to be requited it, a good action* and *an evil action;* as is shown by the words مَا أَسْلَفْتَ مِنْ إِسَاءَةٍ أَوْ إِحْسَانٍ وَمَا تُعْطِيهِ لِتُقْضَاهُ in art. قرض in the Ḳ, and by the corresponding words مَا سَلَّفْتَ مِنْ إِحْسَانٍ وَمِنْ إِسَاءَةٍ in the same art. in the Ṣ: see also Bḍ in xxxvi. 11: and see زَلَّفَهُ. And hence,] a poet says,

تُسَلِّفُ ▼ الجَارَ شِرْبًا وَهْىَ حَائِمَةٌ

وَالمَآءُ لَزْنٌ بَكِىءُ العَيْنِ مُقْتَسَمُ

† [*They* (referring to camels) *yield promptly to the neighbour a draught* of milk, *while they are thirsty, and going round about the water, when the water is crowded upon, scanty in the source, divided by lot*]. (TA. [See also some verses of El-Akra' Ibn-Mo'ádh, in which the former hemistich occurs with a different latter hemistich, in the Ḥam p. 753.]) ═ See also 1, last sentence but one.

5. تسلّف *He received payment in advance:* and ▼ استسلف [perhaps a mistranscription for ▼ استلف] signifies [the same; or] *he took*, or *received, what is termed* سَلَف. (Mṣb.) — [And hence,] تسلّف مِنْهُ *He received from him a loan;* syn. اِقْتَرَضَ; as also ▼ استلف. (A in art. قرض.) And تسلّف مِنْهُ كَذَا *He received as a loan from him such a thing.* (TA.) — See also 10. — And تسلّف *He ate the* [*portion of food termed*] سُلْفَة. (MA.) [See also 2.]

6. تسالفا *They two took as their wives two sisters.* (M, Ḳ.)

8: see 5, in two places.

10. اِسْتَسْلَفْتُ مِنْهُ دَرَاهِمَ *I sought*, or *demanded, of him money as a loan;* as also ▼ تَسَلَّفْتُ. (Ṣ,* TA.) Hence, استسلف مِنْ أَعْرَابِىٍّ بَكْرًا *He sought*, or *demanded, as a loan, from an Arab of the desert, a* [*youthful he-camel such as is termed*] بَكْر. (TA.) — And استسلف ثَمَنَهُ *He sought*, or *demanded, its price in advance;* syn. اِسْتَقْرَضَهُ. (Ḥar p. 530.) — See also 5. ═ [And استسلف *He took as his wife the wife of his deceased brother:* so in a version of the Bible, in Deut. xxv. 5: mentioned by Golius.]

سَلْفٌ *A* [*bag for travelling-provisions &c., such as is termed*] جِرَاب, (M, Ḳ,) *of any sort:* (M:) or *a large* جِرَاب: (Ṣ, M, Ḳ:) [and the contr., i. e. *a small one:* (Freytag, from the Kitáb el-Aḍdád:)] or *a hide not well*, or *not thoroughly, tanned:* (M, Ḳ, TA:) pl. [of pauc.] أَسْلُفٌ and [of mult.] سُلُوفٌ. (M, Ḳ.)

سُلَفٌ [perhaps a mistranscription for سُلَكٌ, q. v.,] *A certain species of bird*, not particularized. (TA.) — See also مُسْلِف.

سِلْفٌ; and its fem., with ة; and their duals: see سِلْف, in five places: ═ and see سَلَفٌ, last sentence.

سَلَفٌ *Such as have gone before*, or *preceded;* (M, Mṣb;*) [i. e. the *preceding generations;*] as also ▼ سَلِيفٌ and ▼ سُلْفَةٌ and ▼ سُلُوفٌ; all quasi-pl. ns.; (M;) of which the sing. is ▼ سَالِفٌ: (M, Mṣb:*) or *such as have gone before*, or *preceded, of* a man's *ancestors* (Ṣ, Ḳ) *and of* his *relations*, (Ḳ,) *that are above* him *in age and in excellence;* [but this addition is not always agreeable with usage;] one of whom is termed ▼ سَالِفٌ: (TA:) the pl. of سَلَفٌ is أُسْلَافٌ and سُلَّافٌ, (Ṣ, Ḳ,) [the former a pl. of pauc. and the latter of mult.,] or the latter is pl. of ▼ سَالِفٌ, and so is سَلَفٌ [said to be, though this is more properly termed, as it is in the M, a quasi-pl. n.]: (IB, Mṣb, TA:) and, accord. to Zj, سُلُفٌ is pl. of ▼ سَلِيفٌ, and سُلَفٌ is pl. of ▼ سُلْفَةٌ, which means *a company* (عُصْبَةٌ) *that has passed away:* (M:) or ▼ سَالِفٌ and ▼ سَلِيفٌ signify the same; *going before; preceding;* syn. مُتَقَدِّمٌ. (Ṣ.) [Accord. to Abu-l-Maḥásin, السَّلَفُ is particularly applied to 'Áïsheh the wife of Moḥammad, the three Khaleefehs Aboo-Bekr and 'Omar and 'Othmán, Ṭalḥah and Ez-Zubeyr, the Khaleefeh Mo'áwiyeh, and 'Amr Ibn-El-Áṣ. (De Sacy's Chrest. Ar., sec. ed., i. 156.)] And السَّلَفُ الصَّالِحُ is applied to the first chief persons of the Tábi'ees. (TA.) And السَّلَفُ المُقَدَّمُ is an appellation of the prophet Moḥammad. (Ḥam p. 780.) [Hence, مَذَاهِبُ السَّلَفِ *The tenets of the early Muslims.*] — Also *A people*, or *party, going before*, or *preceding, in journeying.* (TA.) — And [simply] *A company* of men; as in the saying, جَآءَنِى سَلَفٌ مِنَ النَّاسِ [*A company of men came to me*]. (M.) — And *Any good*, or *righteous, deed, that one has done beforehand* [*by way of preparing a future reward*]: or *any* فَرَط [i. e. *cause of reward*, or *recompense, in the world to come, such as a child dying in infancy*], *that* [*as it were*] *goes before one.* (A'Obeyd, O, Ḳ.) — And *i. q.* سَلَمٌ; (T, Hr, Mgh, O, Ḳ, TA;) i. e. *Any money*, or *property, paid in advance*, or *beforehand, as the price of a commodity for which the seller has become responsible and which one has bought on description:* (T, TA:) or *payment for a commodity to be delivered at a certain* [*future*] *period with something additional to* [*the equivalent of*] *the current price at the time of such payment;* this [transaction] being a cause of profit to him who makes such payment; and سَلَمٌ also has this meaning: (TA:) or *a sort of sale in which the price is paid in advance, and the commodity is withheld, on the condition of description, to a certain* [*future*] *period:* (Ṣ, O:) it is a subst. from الإِسْلَافُ. (Mṣb,* Ḳ, TA.) — And *A loan* (قَرْض) *in which is no profit* (Hr, O, Mgh, Ḳ, TA) *to the lender* (Hr, O, Ḳ, TA) *except recompense* [*in the world to come*] *and thanks*, (TA,) *and which it is incumbent on the recipient thereof to return as he received it:* (Hr, O, Ḳ, TA:) thus the Arabs term it: (Hr, O, TA:) and in this sense also the word is a subst.

from الإِسْلَافُ. (TA.) ═ Also *A stallion-camel.* (IAạr, M, TA.) ═ Also, (M,) or ↑ سُلْفَةٌ, (O, TA,) The *prepuce of a boy;* (M, O, TA;) so says Lth; (O, TA;) and ↑ سَلْفٌ and ↑ سِلْفٌ signify the same; for this is meant by الجِلْدُ as an explanation of السُّلْفُ and السَّلْفُ in the Ḳ, in some copies of which الخُلْدُ is erroneously put for الجِلْدُ. (TA.)

سَلْفٌ and ↑ سِلْفٌ The *husband of the sister of the wife* of a man: (Ṣ, Ḳ:) and [the duals] سَلْفَانِ (M, TA) and ↑ سِلْفَانِ (M, Ḳ) signify the *two husbands of two sisters:* (M, Ḳ:) accord. to IAạr, the epithet سَلْفَةٌ [or ↑ سِلْفَةٌ] is not applied to a woman; (M;) one only uses the term سَلْفَانِ applied to two men: (M:) or, (M, Ḳ,) accord. to Kr, سَلْفَتَانِ, (M,) or ↑ سِلْفَتَانِ, (Ḳ,) is applied to the *two wives of two brothers:* (M, Ḳ:) [in the present day, ↑ سِلْفَةٌ is used as meaning a woman's *husband's sister,* and her *brother's wife:*] the pl. applied to men is أَسْلَافٌ, (M, Ḳ, TA,) and that applied to women is سَلَائِفُ. (TA.) ═ See also سَلَفٌ, last sentence.

سُلَفٌ The *young one of the* حَجَل [or *partridge*]: (Ṣ, M, Ḳ:) or, accord. to Kr, *of the* قَطَاة [n. un. of قَطًا, q. v.]: (M:) AA says that he had not heard سُلَفَةٌ, applied to the female; but if one said سُلَفَةٌ, like as one says سُلَكَةٌ as meaning a single female of what are termed سِلْكَان, it would be approvable: (Ṣ:) the pl. is سِلْفَانٌ (Ṣ, M, Ḳ) and سُلْفَانٌ: (M, Ḳ:) some say that سِلْفَانٌ signifies *a species of bird,* not particularized. (M.) [See also سُلَحٌ and سُلَكٌ.]

سُلْفَةٌ: see سَلَفٌ, first sentence, in two places. [Hence,] one says, جَاؤُوا سُلْفَةً سُلْفَةً, meaning *They came* [*one before another;* or, which is virtually the same,] *one after,* or *near after,* or *at the heels of, another.* (AZ, Ḳ.) — Also *A portion of food* (Ṣ, M, TA) *which a man takes betimes,* (Ṣ,) or *with which one contents,* or *satisfies, himself* [*so as to allay the craving of his stomach*], (M,) *before the* [*morning-meal called*] غَدَآء; (Ṣ, M, TA;) *i. q.* لُمْجَةٌ (Ḳ, TA) and لُهْنَةٌ: (TA:) or a لُهْنَة *that is supplied betimes for a guest, before the* غَدَآء. (TA.) — And السُّلْفَةُ also signifies *That which a woman reposits,* or *prepares,* or *provides,* [app. *of food,*] *to present to her visiter.* (M.) ═ Also *A piece,* or *portion, of land of seed-produce made even* [*with the* مِسْلَفَة, q. v.]: pl. سُلَفٌ. (Az, O, Ḳ.) ═ And *Thin skin* (M, O, Ḳ) *which is put as a lining to boots,* (O, Ḳ,) *sometimes red, and* [*sometimes*] *yellow.* (O.) — See also سَلْفٌ, last sentence.

سِلْفَةٌ; and its dual: see سِلْفٌ, in three places.

أَرْضٌ سَلْفَةٌ *Land in which are few trees.* (AA, Ḳ.) ═ [See also سَلِيفٌ.]

سُلَافٌ (T, Ṣ, M, Mgh) and ↑ سُلَافَةٌ (T, M, Mgh) The *portion that flows before its being expressed,* (Ṣ, Mgh,) of the juice of the grape; (Ṣ;) and this is the most excellent of wine: (Mgh:) or the *first that is expressed,* of wine: or the *portion that flows without its being expressed:* or the *first that descends,* thereof: (M:) or the *clearest,* or *purest, and most excellent,* of wine, *such as flows from the grapes without their being pressed, and without steeping,* or *maceration;* (T, TA;) and in like manner, *such as flows from dates,* (T, TA,) and *from raisins, before water has been added to it* (T, M,* TA) *after the exuding of the first thereof;* (T, TA:) or the latter signifies the *first that is expressed,* of anything: (M:) or it has this meaning also: and the former is a name for *wine* [absolutely]: (Ṣ:) or each has this meaning: (Ḳ:) or each signifies the *clear,* or *pure,* of wine, and of anything. (M.) — سُلَافُ العَسْكَرِ: see سَالِفٌ.

سَلُوفٌ: see سَلَفٌ, first sentence. — Also, applied to a she-camel, (Ṣ, M, Ḳ,) *That is among the foremost of the camels when they come to the water:* (Ṣ, Ḳ:) or *that precedes the* [*other*] *camels to the watering-trough* or *tank:* (M:) or *that precedes,* or *leads, the other camels;* opposed to عَنُودٌ. (El-Keysee, TA in art. عند.) — And *A swift,* or *fleet,* horse: (M, Ḳ:) pl. سُلُفٌ. (Ḳ.) — And An arrow *having a long head:* (M:) or a *long* arrow-head. (Ḳ.)

سَلِيفٌ: see سَلَفٌ, first sentence, in three places. ═ Also *A road,* or *way.* (TA.)

سُلَافَةٌ: see سُلَافٌ.

سَالِفٌ *Passing; passing away; coming to an end,* or *to nought; becoming cut off:* (Mṣb:) and *going before; preceding:* (Ṣ:) pl. سُلَّافٌ and [quasi-pl. n.] سَلَفٌ: (IB, Mṣb, TA:) see سَلَفٌ, first sentence, in four places. [Hence,] الأُمَمُ السَّالِفَةُ *The peoples going before,* or *preceding,* [or *that have gone,* or *passed away, before,*] *those remaining,* or *continuing:* (Ḳ,* TA:) pl. سَوَالِفُ. (TA.) One says, كَانَ ذٰلِكَ فِى الأُمَمِ السَّالِفَةِ وَالقُرُونِ السَّوَالِفِ [*That was in the* time of *the preceding peoples, and the preceding generations*]: the pl. in this instance being used because every portion of the قرون is termed سَالِفَة. (TA.) [Hence also,] سُلَّافُ العَسْكَرِ, in the Ḳ, by implication, سُلَافُ ↑ العسكر, the former word like غُرَّاب, whereas it is correctly like رُمَّان, *The van of the army,* as expl. in the Ḳ. (TA.)

سَالِفَةٌ [fem. of سَالِفٌ, q. v. — And hence, as a subst.,] The *side of the fore part of the neck, from the place of suspension of the ear-ring to the hollow* (قَلْت [in the CḲ erroneously قَلْب]) *of the collar-bone:* (Ṣ, Ḳ:) or the *upper,* or *uppermost, part of the neck:* (M:) or the *side of the neck,* (M, Mgh, TA,) *from the place of suspension of the ear-ring to the* حَاقِنَة [here meaning the *pit of the collar-bone*]: pl. سَوَالِفُ. (M.) In the saying إِنَّهَا لَوَضَّاحَةُ السَّوَالِفِ [*Verily she is fair in respect of the* سَالِفَة], mentioned by Lḥ, the term سالفة is made applicable to every part thereof, and then the pl. is used accordingly. (M.) It is said in a trad. respecting [the covenant at] El-Ḥodeybiyeh, لَأُقَاتِلَنَّهُمْ حَتَّى تَنْفَرِدَ سَالِفَتِى i. e. [*I will assuredly fight with them,* or *combat them,*] *until the side of my neck shall become separate* from what is next to it: an allusion to death. (TA.) — And [hence, i. e.] by the application of the name of the place to that which occupies the place, † The *locks of hair that are made to hang down upon the cheek* [or rather *upon the side of the fore part of the neck*]: said by MF to be metonymical, or tropical. (TA.) — Also The *fore part of the neck* of a horse (Ḳ, TA) &c.: so in the O and L. (TA.)

بَيْنَهُمَا أُسْلُوفَةٌ *Between them two is* صِهْر [i. e. *affinity,* app. *by their having married to sisters:* see سِلْفٌ]. (O, Ḳ.)

مُسْلِفٌ, (Ṣ, M, O, L,) thus in some copies of the Ḳ, as in the Ṣ &c., but in other copies of the Ḳ, erroneously, ↑ مُسْلَفٌ, (TA,) A woman *that has attained the age of five and forty years,* (Ṣ, M, O, Ḳ,) and *the like:* (Ṣ, M, O:) or *i. q.* نَصَفٌ [i. e. *middle-aged,* or *forty-five years old,* or *fifty years old*]: (M:) an epithet specially applied to a female. (Ṣ, O.) A poet says,

فِيهَا ثَلَاثٌ كَالدُّمَى * وَكَاعِبٌ وَمُسْلِفُ *

[*Among them three females like the images of ivory,* or *of marble,* &c., *and one with swelling breasts, and one of middle age,* &c.]. (Ṣ, M: in the O with إِلَى in the place of فِيهَا.)

مِسْلَفَةٌ *An instrument with which land is made even,* (Ṣ, M, O, Ḳ, TA,) *of stone:* A'Obeyd says, I think it is *a stone made round* [or *cylindrical,* i. e. *a stone roller,*] *which is rolled upon the land to make it even.* (TA.) [In the present day, applied to *A harrow.*]

أَرْضُ الجَنَّةِ مَسْلُوفَةٌ, occurring in a trad., *The ground of Paradise is made even:* (Aṣ, T, Ṣ, O, TA:) said by Aṣ to be of the dial. of El-Yemen and Eṭ-Ṭáïf: accord. to IAth, *smooth and soft.* (TA.)

سلق

1. سَلَقَهُ, (Ṣ, Ḳ,) [aor. ـُ,] inf. n. سَلْقٌ, (TḲ,) *He prostrated him on the back of his neck;* (Ḳ;) or *threw him down on his back;* (Ṣ;) as also ↑ سَلْقَاهُ, inf. n. سِلْقَآءٌ. (Ṣ, Ḳ.) You say, طَعَنْتُهُ فَسَلَقْتُهُ and ↑ سَلْقَيْتُهُ, i. e. [*I thrust him,* or *pierced him, and*] *threw him down on his back.* (Ṣ.) And سَلْقَانِى ↑ عَلَى قَفَاىَ and سَلَقَنِى لِحَلَاوَةِ القَفَا *He threw me down on my back:* and so with ص; but more commonly with س. (TA, from a trad.) And سَلَقَهُ الطَّبِيبُ عَلَى ظَهْرِهِ *The physician extended him on his back.* (TA.) And سَلَقَهَا, (Ṣ, Mṣb, Ḳ,) inf. n. as above, (TA,) *He threw her down on the back of her neck* [or *on her back*] *for the purpose of compressing her;* namely, his wife: (Mṣb:) or he *spread her, and then compressed her;* (Ṣ, Ḳ;) as also ↑ سَلْقَاهَا; (Ṣ;) namely, a girl, or young woman. (Ḳ.) — *He thrust him,* or *pierced him,* (Ḳ, TA,) with a spear; (TḲ;) and *pushed him,* or *repelled him;* and *dashed himself,* or *his body, against him;* (TA;) and ↑ سَلْقَاهُ signifies the same; (Ḳ, TA;) inf. n. سِلْقَآءٌ: (TA:) [and *he struck him,* or

smote him; for the inf. n.] سَلْقٌ signifies *the act of striking,* or *smiting.* (TA.) [Hence,] سَلَقَهُ بِالكَلَامِ, (Ṣ, Ḳ,) aor. ـُ, (TA,) inf. n. سَلْقٌ, (Ṣ, TA,) ‡ *He hurt him,* or *displeased him, with speech;* (Ṣ, Ḳ, TA;) *spoke strongly,* or *severely, to him;* (Ṣ, TA;) *made him to hear that which he disliked,* or *hated, and did so much:* (TA:) and سَلَقَهُ بِلِسَانِهِ † *he said to him that which he disliked,* or *hated.* (Mṣb.) سَلَقُوكُمْ بِأَلْسِنَةٍ حِدَادٍ, in the Ḳur xxxiii. 19, means ‡ *They hurt you,* or *displease you,* (Fr, Jel, TA,) *by what they say,* or *bite you,* (Fr, TA,) or *are extravagant,* or *vehement, in speech to you,* (AO, Ṣ, TA,) or *smite you,* (Bḍ, Jel,) *with sharp tongues:* (Fr, Bḍ, TA:) سَلْقٌ signifying *the act of assaulting,* and *smiting, with force,* with the hand, or arm, or † with the tongue: (Bḍ:) and the verb is also with ص; but this is not allowable in the reading [of the Ḳur]. (TA.) —— You say also, سَلَقَتِ الأَقْدَامُ وَالحَوَافِرُ الطَّرِيقَ, (TḲ,) inf. n. سَلْقٌ, (Ḳ,) *The feet of men, and the hoofs of horses or the like, marked,* or *made marks upon, the road.* (Ḳ, TḲ.) —— And سَلَقَهُ *He flayed him* with a whip. (Ḳ.) —— *He galled it;* namely, the back of his camel. (TA.) —— *He* (a beast) *abraded the inner side of his* (the rider's) *thigh.* (TA.) —— *He peeled it off;* namely, the flesh from the bone (عَنِ العَظْمِ); syn. اِنْتَحَاهُ; (O, Ḳ, TA;) *he removed it* therefrom. (TA.) —— *He removed its hair,* (Mṣb, Ḳ,) and *its fur,* (Ḳ,) *with hot water,* (Mṣb, Ḳ,) *leaving the traces thereof remaining;* (Ḳ;) aor. ـُ, inf. n. سَلْقٌ. (Mṣb.) —— *He boiled it with fire:* (Ḳ:) or *he boiled it slightly:* inf. n. as above. (TA.) You say, سَلَقْتُ البَقْلَ *I boiled the herbs,* or *leguminous plants, with fire, slightly:* (Ṣ:) or *I boiled them with water merely:* thus heard by Az from the Arabs: (Mṣb:) and in like manner, eggs, (Ṣ, Mṣb,) in their shells: so says Az. (Mṣb.) You say also, سَلَقْتُ شَيْئًا بِالمَآءِ الحَارِّ [*I cooked a thing with hot water*]. (Lth, TA.) And سُلِقَ is said of anything as meaning *It was* [*boiled,* i. e.] *cooked with hot water* (TA.) —— سَلَقَ البَرْدُ النَّبَاتَ *The cold nipped, shrunk, shrivelled,* or *blasted, the herbage,* or *plants;* syn. أَحْرَقَهُ [q. v.]. (Ḳ.) —— سَلَقَ المَزَادَةَ, (inf. n. as above, TA,) *He oiled,* or *greased, the leathern water-bag:* (Ṣ, Ḳ:) and in like manner, الأَدِيمَ [*the hide,* or *tanned hide*]. (TA.) And سَلَقَ البَعِيرَ (Ḳ, TA) بِالهِنَآءِ (TA) *He smeared the camel all over with tar:* (Ḳ, TA:) from Ibn-'Abbád. (TA.) ═ سَلَقَ الجُوَالِقَ, aor. ـِ, (TA,) inf. n. سَلْقٌ, (Ṣ, TA,) *He inserted one of the two loops of the* [*sack called*] جوالق *into the other:* (Ṣ, TA:) or سَلَقَ العُودَ فِى العُرْوَةِ *he inserted the stick into the loop* [of the جوالق]; as also ▼ اسلقهُ: (Ḳ:) accord. to AHeyth, سَلْقٌ signifies *the inserting the* [*stick called*] شِظَاظ *at once into the two loops of the* [*two sacks called*] جُوَالِقَانِ *when they are put and bound upon the camel.* (TA. [See also سَلْقٌ ═ ([.قَطَبَ الجُوَالِقَ سَلِقَتْ أَفْوَاهُنَا مِنْ أَكْلِ وَرَقِ الشَّجَرِ ═ السَّحَائِطَ: see 5. *Our mouths broke out with pimples,* or *small pustules, from the eating of the leaves of trees.* (TA. [See ▼ هٰذِهِ سَلِيقَتُهُ ═ ([.سُلَاقٌ الَّتِى سُلِقَ عَلَيْهَا and سُلِقَهَا [*This is his nature, to which he was constitutionally adapted* or *disposed*]: said by Sb. (TA.) ═ سَلَقَ, [intrans., aor. ـُ,] (Ṣ, Ḳ,) inf. n. سَلْقٌ, (TA,) *He called out, cried out,* or *shouted;* or *did so vehemently;* or *with his utmost force:* (Ṣ, Ḳ:) a dial. var. of صَلَقَ: (Ṣ:) *he raised the voice:* (Ibn-El-Mubárak, TA:) or *he raised his voice on the occasion of the death of a man,* or *on the occasion of a calamity:* (A'Obeyd, TA:) accord. to IDrd, the meaning [of the inf. n.] is a woman's *slapping and scratching her face:* but the first explanation is more correct. (TA.) —— Also *He ran.* (Ḳ.) You say سَلَقَ سَلْقَةً *He ran a run.* (Ibn-'Abbád, O.)

4. اسلق, said of a man, *His camel's back became white after the healing of galls.* (TA.) ═ And *He hunted, snared,* or *trapped, a she-wolf,* (IAạr, Ḳ,) which is called سِلْقَة. (IAạr.) ═ See also 1, in the latter half of the paragraph.

5: see Q. Q. 3. —— تسلّق عَلَى فِرَاشِهِ (IAạr, Ḳ, TA) ظَهْرًا لِبَطْنٍ (IAạr, TA) *He was,* or *became, restless, agitated,* or *in a state of commotion, upon his bed, by reason of anxiety* or *pain:* (IAạr, Ḳ, TA:) but Az says that the verb known in this sense is with ص. (TA.) ═ تَسَلَّقَ الجِدَارَ, (Ṣ, Ḳ,) or الحَائِطَ; and ▼ سَلَقَهُ, inf. n. سَلْقٌ, (TA; [comp. the Chald. סְלֵק;]) *He ascended, climbed,* or *scaled, the wall:* (Ṣ, Ḳ, TA:) or تَسَلُّقٌ signifies the *ascending a smooth wall:* or it is *like the* تَسَلُّق *of the Messiah to Heaven.* (TA.)

7. انسلق [app. signifies *It was,* or *became, affected with what is termed* سُلَاق; said of the tongue: and in like manner said of the eye: or,] said of the tongue, *it was,* or *became, affected with an excoriation:* and اِنْسِلَاقٌ in the eye is *a redness* incident thereto. (TA.)

Q. Q. 1. سَلْقَاهُ &c.: see 1, in five places.

Q. Q. 3. اِسْلَنْقَى, of the measure اِفْعَنْلَى, (Ṣ,) *He lay,* or *slept,* (نَامَ,) *on his back;* (Ṣeer, Ṣ, O, Ḳ;) like اِسْتَلْقَى [which belongs to art. لقى]; (O, Ḳ;) as also ▼ تسلّق. (TA.)

سَلَقٌ The *mark,* or *scar, of a gall,* or *sore, on the back of a camel, when it has healed, and the place thereof has become white;* (Ḳ;) [like سَحَقٌ;] as also ▼ سَلْقٌ. (Ṣ, Ḳ.) —— And The *mark made by the* [*plaited thong called*] نِسْع *upon the side of the camel,* (Ḳ, TA,) or *upon his belly, from which the fur becomes worn off;* (TA;) and so ▼ سَلِيقَةٌ: (Ṣ, Ḳ:*) سَلَائِق [is pl. of ▼ the latter word, and] signifies the *marks made by the feet of men and by the hoofs of horses or the like upon the road:* (Ḳ, TA:) and to these the marks made by the [plaited thongs called] أَنْسَاع upon the belly of the camel are likened. (TA.)

سِلْقٌ [*Bete;* and particularly *red garden-bete:* so called in the present day; and also called بَنْجَر and سَوَنْدَر and شَوَنْدَر] *a certain plant,* (Ṣ, Mṣb,) or *herb* (بَقْلَةٌ), (Ḳ,) *that is eaten,* (Ṣ,) *well known;* (Mṣb, Ḳ;) i. q. جغندر [or جُغُنْدُر, whence the vulgar name شَوَنْدَر, and hence سَوَنْدَر]; so says ISh; i. e. in Pers.; in some of the MSS. جلندر [a mistranscription for چُغُنْدُر]; *a plant having long leaves, and a root penetrating* [*deeply*] *into the earth, the leaves of which are tender, and are cooked:* (TA:) *it clears* [*the skin*], *acts as a dissolvent, and as a lenitive, and as an aperient,* or *a deobstruent; exhilarates, and is good for the* نِقْرِس [i. e. *gout,* or *podagra,*] *and the joints: its expressed juice, when poured upon wine, converts it into vinegar after two hours; and when poured upon vinegar, converts it into wine after four hours; and the expressed juice of its root, used as an errhine, is an antidote to toothache and earache and hemicrania.* (Ḳ.) [See also حُمَّاض, and كُرُنْب.] سِلْقُ البَرِّ and سِلْقُ المَآءِ, also, are the names of *Two plants.* (Ḳ.) ═ Also The *he-wolf:* (Ṣ, Mṣb, Ḳ:) and ▼ سِلْقَةٌ the *she-wolf:* (Ṣ, Ḳ:) or the latter signifies thus; but سِلْقٌ is not applied to the he-wolf: (Ḳ:) the pl. of سِلْقَةٌ is سِلْقَانٌ and سُلْقَانٌ: (JM, TA;) or these are pls. of سِلْقٌ; and the pl. of سِلْقَةٌ is سِلَقٌ and سِلْقٌ, (Ḳ,) or [rather] this last is a coll. gen. n. of which سِلْقَةٌ is the n. un. (Sb.) Hence the prov., ▼ أَسْلَطُ مِنْ سِلْقَةٍ (JK, Meyd) i. e. *More clamorous than a she-wolf:* or it may mean *more overpowering.* (Meyd.) —— And hence, (TA,) ▼ سِلْقَةٌ is applied to a woman as meaning ‡ *Clamorous;* or *long-tongued and vehemently clamorous,* (Ṣ, Ḳ, TA,) *foul, evil,* or *lewd;* (Ḳ, TA;) likened to the she-wolf in respect of her bad qualities: (TA:) pl. سُلْقَانٌ and سِلْقَانٌ. (Ḳ.) —— ▼ سِلْقَةٌ also signifies *A female lizard of the kind called* ضَبّ, (JK,) or *a female locust,* (TA,) *when she has laid her eggs.* (JK, TA.) ═ Also *A water-course,* or *channel in which water flows,* (Ḳ, TA,) *between two tracts of elevated,* or *elevated and rugged, ground:* or, accord. to Aṣ, *an even, depressed tract of ground:* (TA:) pl. سُلْقَانٌ (Ḳ) and أَسْلَاقٌ and أَسَالِقُ, which (i. e. the second and third of these pls.) are also said to be pls. of سَلَقٌ [q. v.]. (TA.)

سَلَقٌ *An even plain:* (Ṣ:) or *a smooth, even, tract, of good soil:* (O, Ḳ: [a meaning erroneously assigned in the CḲ to سَلَقَةٌ:]) or *a depressed, even, plain, in which are no trees:* (ISh:) or *a low tract,* or *portion, of land, that produces herbage:* (JK:) pl. [of mult.] سُلْقَانٌ (Ṣ, O, Ḳ) and سِلْقَانٌ (Ḳ) and [of pauc.] أَسْلَاقٌ, (JK, O, Ḳ,) and أَسَالِقُ is also a pl. of سَلَقٌ, or of its pl. أَسْلَاقٌ, as is likewise أَسَالِيقُ: (TA:) ▼ سَمْلَقٌ also, with an augmentative م, signifies the same, and its pl. is سَمَالِقُ: (Ṣ:) or the pl. سُلْقَانٌ signifies *meadows* (رِيَاض) *in the higher parts of* [*tracts such as are termed*] بِرَاق [pl. of بُرْقَةٌ] *and* قِفَاف [pl. of قُفّ]. (Az, TA in art. روض.) —— See also سِلْقٌ.

سِلْقَةٌ: see سِلْقٌ, in four places.

سَلْقَاةٌ *A certain mode of compressing, upon the back.* (Ibn-'Abbád, Ḳ, TA.) [See 1.]

سُلَاقٌ *Pimples,* or *small pustules, that come*

forth upon the root of the tongue: or *a scaling in the roots of the teeth:* (Ṣ, Ḳ:) sometimes it is in beasts (دَوَابّ). (TA.) —— And *A thickness,* or *roughness, in the eyelids, by reason of a corrosive matter which causes them to become red and occasions the falling off of the eyelashes and then the ulceration of the edges of the eyelids:* (Ḳ:) thus سلاق of the eye is expl. in the "Ḳánoon." (TA.)

سَلِيقٌ *What fall off* [app. *of the leaves*] (Ṣ, Ḳ) *from trees,* (Ṣ,) or *from shrubs,* or *small trees;* (Ḳ;) or *from trees which the cold has nipped,* or *blasted:* or, accord. to Aṣ, *trees which heat,* or *cold, has nipped,* or *blasted:* (TA:) pl. سُلُقٌ. (Ḳ.) —— And *What has dried up of* [*the plant called*] شِبْرِق, (Ibn-'Abbád, Ḳ,) *and become parched by the sun.* (Ibn-'Abbád.) —— Also *Honey which the bees build up* (Ibn-'Abbád, O, Ḳ) *along the length of their hive,* or *habitation:* (Ḳ:) or, accord. to the T, ↓ سَلِيقَةٌ signifies *a certain thing which the bees fabricate in their hive,* or *habitation, lengthwise:* (TA:) pl. سُلُقٌ. (Ḳ.) —— Also The *side* of a road. (Ḳ.) The two sides of the road are called سَلِيقَا الطَّرِيقِ. (Ibn-'Abbád, O.)

سَلِيقَةٌ *What is cooked with hot water* (مَا سُلِقَ), *of herbs,* or *leguminous plants,* and *the like:* (Ḳ:) or, accord. to Az, *what is cooked* (مَا طُبِخَ) *with water, of the herbs,* or *leguminous plants, of the* [*season called*] رَبِيع, *and eaten in times of famine:* pl. سَلَائِقُ, which occurs in a trad., and, as some relate it, with ص. (TA.) —— And *Millet* (ذُرَةٌ) *bruised,* (IAạr, IDrd, Z, Ḳ,) *and dressed,* (IAạr, IDrd, Ḳ,) *by being cooked with milk:* (IAạr:) or أَقِط [*a preparation of dried curd*] *with which are mixed* [*plants called*] طَرَاثِيث. (Ḳ.) —— Accord. to Lth, (TA,) The *place where the* [*plaited thong called*] نِسْع *comes forth* [*from the ropes that form the breast-girth*], (O, Ḳ, TA,) *in the side of the camel:* said by him to be derived from the phrase سَلَقْتُ شَيْئًا بِالمَآءِ الحَارِّ; because it is [as though it were] burnt by the ropes: or, accord. to another explanation, its pl., سَلَائِقُ, signifies the *strips of flesh between the two sides.* (TA.) —— See also سُلَق, in two places. —— And see سَلِيقٌ. —— And The *nature,* or *natural disposition* or *constitution,* (AZ, IAạr, Ṣ, Ḳ,) of a man. (IAạr, Ṣ.) See 1, in the last quarter of the paragraph. One says, إِنَّهُ لَكَرِيمُ السَّلِيقَةِ *Verily he is generous in respect of nature.* (AZ.) [See also سَلِيقِيَّةٌ.]

سَلُوقِىٌّ [applied in the present day to *A greyhound,* and *any hunting-dog;*] *a sort of dog:* (MA:) and *a sort of coat of mail:* (TA:) ↓ سَلُوقِيَّةٌ [as a coll. n.] is applied to *certain coats of mail:* (Ṣ, Ḳ:*) and *to certain dogs:* so called in relation to سَلُوق, [said by Freytag to be written in the Ḳ سُلُوقة, but it is there said to be like صَبُور,] a town in El-Yemen; (Ṣ, MA, Ḳ;*) or a town, or district, in the border of Armenia, (Ḳ,) called اللَّان [or لَان]: (TA:) or the coats of mail are so called in relation to the former سلوق; (so in a copy of the Ṣ;) and the dogs, in relation to سَلُوق which is the city of اللَّان [or لَان]: (Ṣ, TA:*) or both are so called in relation to سَلَقِيَة, a town in the Greek Empire, (IDrd as on the authority of Aṣ, and Ḳ,) said by El-Mes'oodee to have been on the shore of [the province of] Antioch, remains of which still exist; (TA;) and if so, it is a rel. n. altered from its proper form. (Ḳ, TA.) —— [It is also said in the TA to signify *A sword:* but a verse there cited, after Th, as an ex. of it in this sense, is mistranscribed, and casts doubt upon the orthography of the word, and upon this explanation.]

كَلَامٌ سَلِيقِىٌّ [*Natural,* or *untaught, speech;*] *speech whereof the desinential syntax is not much attended to, but which is chaste and eloquent in respect of what has been heard, though often tripping,* or *stumbling, in respect of grammar:* (Lth, L, TA:) or the *speech which the dweller in the desert utters according to his nature and his proper dialect, though his other speech be nobler and better.* (L, TA.) And ↓ سَلِيقِيَّةٌ [in like manner, the ة being affixed to the epithet سَلِيقِىٌّ to convert it into a subst.,] signifies The *dialect in which the speaker thereof proceeds loosely,* or *freely, according to his nature, without paying much attention to desinential syntax, and without avoiding incorrectness.* (O, TA.) You say, ↓ فُلَانٌ يَتَكَلَّمُ بِالسَّلِيقِيَّةِ, meaning *Such a one speaks according to his nature, not from having learned.* (Ṣ, Ḳ.) And ↓ فُلَانٌ يَقْرَأُ بِالسَّلِيقِيَّةِ *Such a one reads,* or *recites, according to the natural condition in which he has grown up, not as having been taught.* (TA.)

سَلُوقِيَّةٌ: see سَلُوقِىٌّ. —— Also The *sitting-place of the* رُبَّان [or *captain*] of a ship. (Ibn-'Abbád, O, Ḳ.)

سَلِيقِيَّةٌ: see سَلِيقِىٌّ, in three places.

سَلَّاقٌ: see مِسْلَقٌ, in two places.

السُّلَّاقُ *A certain festival of the Christians;* (Ḳ;) *that of the Ascension of Jesus into Heaven:* (TḲ:) derived from سَلَقَ الحَائِطَ [expl. above (see 5)]: said by IDrd to be a foreign word (أَعْجَمِىّ), and in one place said by him to be Syriac, arabicized. (TA.)

سَالِقَةٌ A woman *raising her voice, on the occasion of a calamity,* (Ḳ, TA,) or *on the occasion of the death of any one:* (TA:) or *slapping her face:* (Ḳ, TA:) thus says Ibn-El-Mubárak: but the former explanation is the more correct: it occurs in a trad., in which such is said to have been cursed by the Prophet; and, as some relate it, with ص. (TA.)

سَمْلَقٌ: see سَلَقٌ: and see also art. سملق.

سَيْلَقٌ *Quick,* or *swift;* a fem. epithet; (Ibn-'Abbád, O, Ḳ;) applied to a she-camel: (Ibn-'Abbád, O:) in the Tekmileh, سَلِيقٌ, which is a mistake: in the L, a she-camel *having a penetrative energy in her pace.* (TA.)

الأَسَالِقُ *What is next to the* لَهَوَات [app. here a pl. used as a sing., meaning the *uvula*] *of the mouth, internally:* (Ibn-'Abbád, O, Ḳ:) or *the upper parts of the interior of the mouth:* (TA:) or *the upper parts of the mouth,* (M, TA,) *those to which the tongue rises:* thus applied, it is a pl. having no sing. (TA.)

خَطِيبٌ مِسْلَقٌ and ↓ مِسْلَاقٌ and ↓ سَلَّاقٌ ‡ *An eloquent speaker* or *orator* or *preacher:* (Ṣ, Ḳ, TA:) because of the vehemence of his voice and his speech. (Ṣ, TA.) And لِسَانٌ مِسْلَقٌ and ↓ سَلَّاقٌ ‡ *A sharp, cutting,* or *eloquent, tongue.* (TA.)

مِسْلَاقٌ: see the next preceding paragraph.

مَسْلُوقَةٌ, meaning *A skinned fowl cooked* [i. e. *boiled*] *with water, by itself,* [and also *any boiled meat,* is agreeable with a classical usage of the verb from which it is derived, but] is [said to be] a vulgar term. (TA.)

سلك

1. سَلَكَ الطَّرِيقَ, (IAạr, MA, Mṣb,) or المَكَانَ, (Ḳ,) aor. ُ, (Mṣb, TA,) inf. n. سُلُوكٌ (MA, Mṣb, Ḳ) and سَلْكٌ, (Ḳ, [but I doubt this latter's being correctly used as an inf. n. of the verb in the sense here immediately following,]) *He travelled,* (MA,) or *went along in,* (Mṣb,) *the road,* (IAạr, MA, Mṣb,) or *the place:* (Ḳ:) or سَلَكَ المَكَانَ *he entered into the place.* (TḲ.) [In these and similar instances, it seems that the prep. فِى is suppressed, and the noun therefore put in the accus. case, as in دَخَلَ البَيْتَ &c.: for it is said that] سَلَكَ as meaning *He entered* (دَخَلَ) is intrans.: (Kull p. 206:) ↓ انسلك [likewise] has this meaning: (Ṣ:) ↓ اسلك as an intrans. verb [in the sense of سَلَكَ] is extr. (Mṣb.) [سَلَكَ طَرِيقًا is also often used tropically, as meaning ‡ *He pursued a course of conduct* or *the like.*] —— And سَلَكَهُ الطَّرِيقَ, (IAạr, Mṣb,) or المَكَانَ, and فِيهِ, (Ḳ,) [inf. n. سَلْكٌ;] and ↓ اسلكهُ إِيَّاهُ, (Mṣb, Ḳ,) this also is allowable, (IAạr, TA,) and فِيهِ, and عَلَيْهِ; (Ḳ;) *He made him* [*to travel or*] *to go along in* [or *to enter*] *the road,* (IAạr,* Mṣb,) or *the place:* (Ḳ:) and so سَلَكَ بِهِ الطَّرِيقَ: (Mṣb:) and ↓ سلّكهُ, inf. n. تَسْلِيكٌ, signifies the same as [سَلَكَهُ thus used, and] اسلكهُ. (TA.) And سَلَكْتُ الشَّىْءَ فِى الشَّىْءِ, (Ṣ, Mṣb,) inf. n. سَلْكٌ, (Ṣ,) *I made the thing to enter,* or *I inserted it,* or *introduced it, into the thing:* (Ṣ:) or *I made the thing to go,* or *pass, through the thing:* (Mṣb:) and ↓ أَسْلَكْتُهُ signifies the same. (Ṣ. [See an ex. of the latter verb in a verse of 'Abd-Menáf Ibn-Ribạ El-Hudhalee, voce إِذَا; cited there and here also in the Ṣ.]) You say, سَلَكَ الخَيْطَ فِى الإِبْرَةِ *He inserted the thread into the needle.* (MA.) And سَلَكَ يَدَهُ فِى الجَيْبِ *He inserted* [*his hand,* or *arm, into the opening at the neck and bosom of the shirt*]; as also ↓ أَسْلَكَهَا: (Ḳ:) and so into the skin for milk or water, and the like. (TA.) And it is said in the Ḳur [xxvi. 200], كَذٰلِكَ سَلَكْنَاهُ فِى قُلُوبِ المُجْرِمِينَ *Thus we have caused it to enter* [*into the hearts of the sinners*]. (Ṣ.) And in the same [xxxix. 22], فَسَلَكَهُ يَنَابِيعَ فِى الأَرْضِ [*And*

hath caused it to enter into springs in the earth]. (TA.)

2: see 1. — [In the present day, سلّك signifies *He cleared* a passage or way. And *He cleaned out* a pipe for smoking. — And, from سِلْك, *He wound* thread *upon a reel* or *into a skein.*]

4: see 1, in four places.

7: see 1, second sentence.

سِلْكٌ *Thread,* or *string,* (Ṣ, Mgh, Ḳ,) *with which one sews:* (Ḳ:) or *upon which beads are strung;* (Ḥam p. 42;) [*but*] *not having beads upon it;* for if it have, it is termed سِمْطٌ: (Ṣ and Mgh in art. سمط:) [in the present day it signifies *wire:*] a pl. [or rather a coll. gen. n.] of which the sing. [or n. un.] is ▼سِلْكَةٌ: the pl. [of pauc.] of سلك is أَسْلَاكٌ and [of mult.] سُلُوكٌ. (Ḳ.) — [Hence,] one says, هٰذَا كَلَامٌ رَقِيقُ السِّلْكِ ‡ *This is speech,* or *language,* [*subtile;* or] *abstruse in its course,* or *tenour;* i. e. ▼خَفِىُّ المَسْلَكِ. (TA.) — And مَا أَنْتَ بِمُنْجَرِدِ السِّلْكِ, (AZ, TA in art. جرد,) or بِمُتَجَرِّدِ السِّلْكِ, (so in a copy of the A in that art.,) said to one who is shy, or bashful, † meaning [*Thou art*] *not free from shyness in appearing* [*before others*]: (AZ, TA in that art.:) or ‡ *thou art not celebrated,* or *well-known.* (A and TA in that art.) — Also The *first of what is emitted by the she-camel* [*from her udder*], *before the* لِبَأ [or *biestings*]. (Ibn-'Abbád, Ḳ.)

سُلَكٌ The *young one of the* حَجَل [or *partridge*]; (Ṣ, Ḳ;) like سُلَحٌ: (Ṣ in art. سلح:) or *of the bird called* قَطًا: (Ḳ:) fem. سُلَكَةٌ, (Ṣ, Ḳ,) and ▼سُلَكَانَةٌ, but the latter is rare: (Ḳ:) pl. سِلْكَانٌ, (Ṣ, Ḳ,) like صِرْدَانٌ pl. of صُرَدٌ (Ṣ) [and سِلْحَانٌ pl. of سُلَحٌ].

سِلْكَةٌ: see سِلْكٌ.

طَعْنَةٌ سُلْكَى [*A thrust,* or *piercing thrust,*] *directed right towards the face.* (Ṣ, Ḳ.) And أَمْرٌ سُلْكَى [*An affair*] *rightly directed;* (Ḳ, TA;) and so رَأْىٌ [*an opinion*]: (TA:) or the former, [*an affair*] *following one uniform course.* (ISk, TA.) — In the saying of Ḳeys Ibn-'Eyzárah,

* غَدَاةَ تَنَادَوْا ثُمَّ قَامُوا فَأَجْمَعُوا *
* بِقَتْلِى سُلْكَى لَيْسَ فِيهَا تَنَازُعُ *

he means [*In the morning when they congregated, then arose and determined upon my slaughter*] *with a strong resolution in respect of which there was no contention.* (TA.)

سَلَكُوتٌ, like جَبَرُوتٌ [in measure], *A certain bird.* (Ḳ.)

سُلَكَانَةٌ: see سُلَكٌ.

مَسْلَكٌ [*A place of passage* of a man or beast and of anything;] *a way, road,* or *path:* pl. مَسَالِكُ. (TA.) — [Hence,] مَسْلَكَا المَرْأَةِ [*The vagina and rectum of the woman*]. (M in art. فيض. [See أَفَاضَ المَرْأَةَ in that art.]) — [Hence, also,] one says, خُذْ فِى مَسَالِكِ الحَقِّ ‡ [*Enter thou upon the ways of truth*]. (TA.) — See also سِلْكٌ.

مُسَلَّكَةٌ *A border* (طُرَّة) *slit from the side of a garment,* or *piece of cloth:* (Ḳ:) so called because extended, like the سِلْك. (TA.)

مُسَلَّكٌ *Slender,* or *lean,* (IDrd, Ḳ, TA,) *in body;* applied to a man and to a horse. (IDrd, TA.) And مُسَلَّكُ الذَّكَرِ *Sharp in the head of the penis:* and so مُسْمَلَكُ الذَّكَرِ. (AA, TA.)

سلم

1. سَلِمَ, [aor. سَ,] inf. n. سَلَامَةٌ (Ṣ, M, A, Mgh, Mṣb, Ḳ) and سَلَامٌ (A, TA) and سَلْمٌ and سِلْمٌ and, (Bḍ in xxxix. 30,) *He was,* or *became, safe,* or *secure;* or *he escaped;* (M, TA;) or *he was,* or *became, free;* (TA;) مِنَ الآفَاتِ [*from evils of any kind*], (Ṣ, Mgh,) or مِنَ الآفَةِ [*from evil of any kind*], (Ḳ,) or مِنَ البَلَآءِ [*from trial,* or *affliction*], (A, TA,) or مِنَ الأَمْرِ [*from the affair*]: (M:) *he* (a traveller) *was,* or *became, safe, secure,* or *free, from evils of any kind:* (Mṣb:) and سَلِمَ مِنَ العَيْبِ *he was,* or *became, free from fault, defect, imperfection, blemish,* or *vice;* syn. بَرِئَ. (Mṣb in art. برأ.) [Hence,] one says, لَا بِذِى تَسْلَمُ مَا كَانَ كَذَا وَكَذَا, (ISk, Ṣ, Ḳ,*) meaning *No, by God* [or *Him*] *who maketh thee to be in safety,* (ISk, Ṣ, Ḳ,) [*such and such things were not;*] and to two persons لا بذى تَسْلَمَانِ, and to a pl. number لا بذى تَسْلَمُونَ, and to a female لا بذى تَسْلَمِينَ, and to a pl. number [of females] لا بذى تَسْلَمْنَ. (ISk, Ṣ, Ḳ.*) And لَا أَفْعَلُ ذٰلِكَ بِذِى تَسْلَمُ, meaning, بِذِى سَلَامَتِكَ [i. e. *I will not do that, by the Author* (lit. *Lord* or *Master*) *of thy safety*]; and in like manner, بذى تَسْلَمَانِ, and بذى تَسْلَمُونَ. (Sb, M. [See also ذو.]) And اِذْهَبْ بِذِى تَسْلَمُ, i. e. اِذْهَبْ بِسَلَامَتِكَ [*Go thou with thy safety;* or, *with the Author of thy safety* to protect thee; meaning *go thou in safety*]; and [to two persons] اِذْهَبَا بِذِى تَسْلَمَانِ. (Ṣ, Ḳ.) ذى is thus prefixed to a verb [as virtually governing it in the gen. case] like as آيَة is in an instance mentioned under this latter word; but these are two extr. instances; for only a noun significant of time is [regularly] prefixed to a verb, as in the phrase هٰذَا يَوْمُ يَفْعَلُ, meaning يَفْعَلُ فِيهِ: (Akh, Ṣ:) it is not prefixed to any but this verb تَسْلَمُ [and its variations as above mentioned]. (Sb, M, Ḳ.) — And hence, (Mgh,) one says also, سَلِمَتْ لَهُ الضَّيْعَةُ, meaning [*The landed estate*] *was,* or *became, free from participation to him;* syn. خَلَصَتْ. (Mgh, TA.) — سلمهُ, [app. سَلَمَهُ, or perhaps سَلِمَهُ, for some verbs of this measure are trans., as حَسِبَ and وَرِثَ,] inf. n. سلم, [app. سَلْمٌ, q. v. infrà,] *He made him a captive.* (TA.) — سَلَمَتْهُ الحَيَّةُ, (TA,) inf. n. سَلْمٌ, (M, Ḳ, TA,) *The serpent bit him:* (M,* Ḳ,* TA:) mentioned by Az, but he adds that no one but Lth has said this. (TA.) — سَلَمَ الجِلْدَ, aor. سَ, (Ṣ, Ḳ,) inf. n. سَلْمٌ, (TA,) *He tanned the skin with* [قَرَظ, i. e. *leaves of*] *the* سَلَم [or *mimosa flava*]. (Ṣ, Ḳ, TA.) — سَلَمَ الدَّلْوَ, (M, Ḳ,) aor. سَ, inf. n. سَلْمٌ, (M,) *He finished making the leathern bucket;* and *made it firm, strong,* or *sound,* or *made it firmly, strongly,* or *soundly.* (M, Ḳ.)

2. سَلَّمَهُ, (Ṣ, M, Mṣb, Ḳ,) inf. n. تَسْلِيمٌ, (Ḳ,) *He* (God) *made him to be safe, secure,* or *free; saved, secured,* or *freed, him;* (M, Mṣb, TA;) مِنَ الآفَاتِ [*from evils of any kind*], (Ṣ, Mṣb,) or مِنَ الآفَةِ [*from evil of any kind*], (Ḳ,) or مِنَ الأَمْرِ [*from the affair*]. (M.) [Freytag assigns the same meaning to ▼اسلمهُ also, as on the authority of the Ḥam; in which I find no explanation of this verb except one which will be found later in this paragraph.] — [Hence,] التَّسْلِيمُ is also syn. with السَّلَامُ, (Ṣ, Ḳ, TA,) as meaning *The saluting,* or *greeting,* one *with a prayer* for his *safety,* or *security,* or *freedom, from evils of any kind in* his *religion and in* his *person;* and the interpretation thereof is [*the expressing a desire for*] التَّخْلِيصُ; (Mbr, TA;) or *the saluting,* or *greeting,* one *with a prayer for* his *life;* or, *by saying* سَلَامٌ عَلَيْكَ [q. v. infrà, voce سَلَامٌ]; syn. التَّحِيَّةُ. (TA.) You say, سَلَّمَ عَلَيْهِ [meaning *He so saluted,* or *greeted, him*]. (M, Mṣb.) [This, when said of God, virtually means سَلَّمَهُ, i. e. *He saved him;* and should be rendered agreeably with this explanation in the phrase commonly used after the mention of the Prophet, صَلَّى ٱللّٰهُ عَلَيْهِ وَسَلَّمَ *May God bless and save him.* You say also, سَلَّمَ عَلَيْهِ بِالخِلَافَةِ *He saluted him with the acknowledgment of his being Khaleefeh;* saying, سَلَامٌ عَلَيْكَ يَا أَمِيرَ المُؤْمِنِينَ *Salutation to thee, or peace be on thee,* &c., *O Prince of the Faithful.*] التَّسْلِيمَةُ signifies *The salutation that is pronounced on finishing every two rek'ahs in prayer:* (Ḥar p. 180:) [and also *that which is pronounced after the last rek'ah of each of the prayers* (i. e. after the sunneh prayers and the farḍ alike), addressed to the two guardian and recording angels: (see my "Modern Egyptians," ch. iii., p. 78 of the 5th ed.:) and سَلَّمَ means *He pronounced either of those salutations.*] — [Hence also,] سَلَّمَ إِلَيْهِ الشَّىْءَ, (Ṣ, Ḳ,*) inf. n. as above; (Ḳ;) and ▼اسلم اليه الشىء; (M;) *He gave to him the thing;* (Ṣ,* M, Ḳ;) or *delivered it to him:* (M:) [*he resigned it to him:*] and سَلَّمَ إِلَيْهِ الوَدِيعَةَ, (Mgh,) or سَلَّمَ الوَدِيعَةَ لِصَاحِبِهَا, *He delivered the deposit* [*to him,* or] *to its owner:* (Mṣb:) and ▼اسلم الثَّوْبَ إِلَى الخَيَّاطِ (Mgh) signifies the same as سَلَّمَهُ إِلَيْهِ [i. e. *He delivered the garment,* or *piece of cloth, to the tailor*]. (Ḥar p. 166.) — See also 4, in two places. — You say also, سَلَّمَ الأَجِيرُ نَفْسَهُ لِلْمُسْتَأْجِرِ *The hired man gave himself up,* or *gave authority over himself, to the hirer.* (Mṣb.) And ▼أَسْلَمْتُهُ and سَلَّمْتُهُ *I left him in the power of him who desired to kill him or to wound him.* (Ḥam p. 115.) And ▼اسلمهُ لِلْهَلَكَةِ [*He gave him up to destruction*]: in this case with [the prep.] ل only. (Ḥar p. 166.) And

اسلم الرَّجُلَ, (Ṣ,* M, Mṣb,*) or العَدُوَّ, (Ḳ,) *He left, forsook,* or *deserted,* (M, Ḳ,) *the man,* (Ṣ,* M, Mṣb,*) or *the enemy;* (Ḳ;) or *abstained from aiding,* or *assisting, him;* (Ṣ, M, Mṣb, Ḳ;) and *threw him into destruction.* (IAth, TA.) And ↓ اسلمهُ لِمَا بِهِ *He left him* [*to that bane which was in him:* app. referring to the bite of a serpent, or any evil affection: see سَلِيمٌ, third sentence]. (Ṣ,* M.) — And سلّم أَمْرَهُ إِلَى ٱللّٰهِ and ↓ اسلمهُ, both meaning the same, (Ṣ, Mṣb, Ḳ, TA,) i. e. *He committed his case to God.* (TA.) — And سلّم الدَّعْوَى *He acknowledged the truth* [or *justice*] *of the claim, demand,* or *suit;* [*he conceded its truth* or *justice;*] from سلّم الوَدِيعَةَ لِصَاحِبِهَا, expl. above; denoting an ideal delivering [or yielding of a thing to another person]. (Mṣb.) [Hence one says, سلّم أَنَّهُ كَذَا *He conceded that it was thus.*] — And التَّسْلِيمُ signifies also [*The assenting,* or] *the giving* [one's] *approval* (Ṣ, Ḳ, TA) *unreservedly,* (Ṣ,) to that which is ordained, or decreed, (Ṣ, Ḳ, TA,) by God; and *the submitting* to his commands; and *the abstaining from offering opposition in the case in which it is not becoming* [*to do so*]. (TA.) You say, سلّم لِأَمْرِ ٱللّٰهِ *He assented to the command of God:* [or *he gave his approval to it:*] or *he submitted to it;* as also ↓ اسلم. (MA.)

3. سالمهُ, (M, Mṣb,) inf. n. مُسَالَمَةٌ (Ṣ, M, Mṣb) and سِلَامٌ, (M, Mṣb,) *He made peace,* or *became at peace* or *reconciled, with him;* or *he reconciled himself with him:* [implying mutual concession, or a compromise:] (Ṣ,* M, Mṣb:) and سَالَمَا *They made peace,* or *became at peace* or *reconciled,* or *they reconciled themselves, each with the other.* (Ḳ.)

4: see 2, in nine places. [The first of the meanings there assigned to this verb is, in my opinion, more than doubtful. In all its senses, it seems to be properly trans.: when it is used as an intrans. verb, an objective complement is app. understood. Thus,] أَسْلَمَ is syn. with أَسْلَفَ [as meaning *He paid in advance,* or *beforehand*]; (Ṣ, M, Mgh, Mṣb;) الثَّمَنَ [*the price*] being suppressed, though sometimes it is expressed; (Mgh;) as also ↓ سلّم; (M;) and ↓ تسلّم, as occurring in a trad., where it is said, مَنْ تَسَلَّمَ فِى شَىْءٍ فَلَا يَصْرِفْهُ إِلَى غَيْرِهِ [*Whoso pays in advance for a thing, he shall not turn it over,* or *transfer it, to another than him*]; but Ḳt says that he had not heard this verb thus used except in this instance. (TA.) So the first of these verbs signifies in the saying, اسلم فِى الطَّعَامِ (Ṣ) or فِى البُرِّ (Mgh) [*He paid in advance for the wheat*], and فِى الشَّىْءِ [*for the thing*], as also ↓ سلّم. (M.) And hence the saying, إِذَا أَسْلَمَ صُوفًا فِى لِبْدٍ أَوْ شَعْرًا فِى مِسْحٍ لَمْ يَجُزْ [*If he give in advance wool for felt, or goats' hair for a garment,* or *piece, of hair-cloth, it will not be allowable*]. (Mgh.) And so in the phrase, أَسْلَمْتُ إِلَيْهِ [*I paid in advance to him*]. (Mṣb.) — Also [*He resigned,* or *submitted, himself;* نَفْسَهُ being understood: or] *he was,* or *became, resigned,* or *submissive;* (M, Ḳ;) and so ↓ استسلم: (Ṣ, M, Mṣb, Ḳ:) you say, اسلم لِلّٰهِ [*He resigned,* or *submitted, himself,* or *he was,* or *became, resigned,* or *submissive, to God:* see also an ex. (before referred to) in the last sentence of the second paragraph: or *he was,* or *became, sincere in his religion,* or *without hypocrisy, towards God:* see مُسْلِمٌ]: (Mṣb:) [or] اسلم signifies *he entered into* السَّلْمُ, (Ṣ, Mṣb,) which here means الاِسْتِسْلَامُ [i. e. *the state of resignation,* or *submission*]. (Ṣ.) — And *He became a Muslim;* as also ↓ تسلّم; (M,* Ḳ;) as in the saying, كَانَ كَافِرًا ثُمَّ تَسَلَّمَ, i. e. أَسْلَمَ [*He was an unbeliever,* or *a denier of the unity of God, &c.; then he became a Muslim*]: (M:) or *he entered* [*the pale,* or *communion, of*] *the religion of* الإِسْلَام. (Ṣ,* Mṣb.) الإِسْلَامُ as a principle of the law of God is *The manifesting of humility or submission, and outward conforming with the law of God, and the taking upon oneself to do or to say as the Prophet has done or said:* for this, the blood is to be spared, and one may demand the repelling of evil: (T,* M:) and if there is therewith firm belief with the heart, it is إِيمَانٌ: (T:) this is the doctrine of Esh-Sháfi'ee; but the doctrine of Aboo-Ḥaneefeh makes no difference between these two terms: (KT:) [agreeably with the former doctrine,] Th well and briefly says, الاسلام is with the tongue, and الايمان is with the heart: and he says, in explaining verse 48 of ch. v. of the Ḳur, that every prophet has been sent with الاسلام, though the ordinances differ. (M.) — One says also, أَسْلَمْتُ عَنْهُ, meaning *I left it* [app. an affair, as in an explanation in the TḲ,] *after I had been* [*engaged*] *in it.* (Ibn-Buzurj, Ḳ.) And اسلم occurs intransitively in the saying, كَانَ رَاعِىَ غَنَمٍ ثُمَّ أَسْلَمَ, meaning [*He was a pastor of sheep,* or *goats; then*] *he left them.* (M.) — [Freytag assigns to اسلم another signification "*Adscendere fecit* (vid. a سُلَّم)," as from the Ḥam, p. 39: but this is app. a mistake, into which he has been led by a saying, there cited, of Zuheyr, which I read thus:

هُوِىَّ الدَّلْوِ أَسْلَمَهَا الرِّشَاءُ

(meaning, *The descent,* or *as the descent, of the bucket that the well-rope has let go*): and by its being there said that "you should not prefer any reading of هوى to that with ḍamm, though it has been said otherwise:" whereas the correct reading is, in my opinion, هَوِىَّ, agreeably with what here follows:] Er-Riyáshee says, on the authority of AZ, that الهَوِىُّ, with fet-ḥ, is downwards; and with ḍamm, upwards; and he cites the saying above as an ex. of the word as meaning downwards. (TA in art. هوى.)

5. تسلّم مِنْهُ *He asserted,* or *declared, himself to be free from,* or *clear of,* or *quit of, it,* or *him.* (M.) — تسلّم is also syn. with أَسْلَمَ, in two senses: see the latter, in two places. = And تسلّمهُ signifies *He took it,* or *received it;* namely, a thing given, or delivered. (Ṣ, M, Mṣb, Ḳ.)

6. تسالموا, (M,) and تسالما, (Ḳ,) inf. n. تَسَالُمٌ, (Ṣ,) *They,* (M,) or *they two,* (Ḳ,) *made peace,* or *became at peace* or *reconciled,* (Ṣ,* M, Ḳ,) *one with another,* (Ṣ, M,) or *each with the other.* (Ṣ, Ḳ.) [See also 8.] — One says of a man, (M,) of a great, or frequent, liar, (TA,) لَا تَسَالَمُ خَيْلَاهُ, [for لَا تَتَسَالَمُ,] (M,) or لَا يَتَسَالَمُ خَيْلَاهُ, (Ḳ, TA,) [† *His two troops of horses will not agree in pace, each with the other;*] meaning ‡ [*his assertions will not be found to agree together;* or] *he will not say what is true, so that it may be accepted from him:* for تَسَالَمَتْ, said of horses, means † *they kept pace, one with another;* (تَسَايَرَتْ [q. v.];) *not exciting one another.* (M, Ḳ, TA.)

8. استلم *He became at peace,* or *reconciled.* (TA.) Hence the saying, (TA,) هُوَ لَا يَسْتَلِمُ عَلَى سَخَطِهِ *He will not become at peace,* or *reconciled, during his displeasure* at a thing. (Ḳ, TA.) [See also 6.] — استلم الزَّرْعُ *The seed-produce put forth its ears.* (Ḳ.) = استلم الحَجَرَ *He touched,* (Ṣ, Ḳ,) or *reached,* (Mgh,) *the stone,* [meaning the Black Stone of the Kaabeh,] *by kissing,* or *with the hand:* (Ṣ, Mgh, Ḳ:) or *he wiped it,* or *stroked it, with the hand:* (Mgh:) or *he kissed the stone:* or *he embraced it:* (M:) and اِسْتَلْأَمَهُ signifies the same; (M, Ḳ;) but is not the original: (M:) accord. to ISk, the Arabs pronounced it with hemz, contr. to analogy; (Mṣb;) or it should not be pronounced with hemz, though some thus pronounce it, (Ṣ,) the original being استلم, (ISk, Mṣb,) because it is from سِلَامٌ [pl. of سَلِمَةٌ] signifying "stones," (ISk, Ṣ,* M, Mṣb,* [in the Mgh, from سَلِمَةٌ signifying "a stone," and in the Mṣb the pl. of سَلِمَةٌ is said to be سِلَامٌ, like كِلَامٌ,]) accord. to Sb, who says that it does not denote the act of taking; (M;) or, accord. to Sb, it is from السَّلَامُ, with fet-ḥ, meaning "salutation," and it means the touching with the hand by way of salutation in order to obtain a blessing thereby: (TA:) but accord. to IAar, the original is with hemz, from المُلَاءَمَةُ, meaning الاِجْتِمَاعُ ["the coming together," &c., because denoting contact]. (Mṣb.) Abu-ṭ-Ṭufeyl is related to have said, رَأَيْتُ رَسُولَ ٱللّٰهِ صَلَّى ٱللّٰهُ عَلَيْهِ وَسَلَّمَ يَطُوفُ عَلَى رَاحِلَتِهِ يَسْتَلِمُ بِمِحْجَنِهِ وَيُقَبِّلُ المِحْجَنَ [i. e. *I saw the Apostle of God* (*may God bless and save him*) *circuiting* around the Kaabeh, *upon his camel, touching* the Black Stone *with his hooked staff, and kissing the hooked staff*]. (TA.) The primary signification of الاِسْتِلَامُ is [said to be] *The wiping,* or *stroking, the* سَلِمَة, i. e. the *stone:* afterwards it was used in relation to other things, and one said اِسْتَلَمْتُ يَدَهَا, meaning *I stroked,* or *kissed, her hand.* (Ḥar pp. 30 and 31.) — استلم الخُفُّ قَدَمَيْهِ means *The boot rendered his feet soft* [after he had been accustomed to walking barefoot]. (TA.)

10: see 4, in the former half of the paragraph. = استسلم ثَكَمَ الطَّرِيقِ *He went upon the middle of the road, not missing it.* (Ḳ,* TA. [In the CḲ, after وَاسْتَسْلَمَ انْقَادَ, for وَثَكَمَ الطَّرِيقِ, meaning وَاستسلم ثَكَمَ الطَّرِيقِ, is erroneously put وَتَسَلَّمَ

الطَّرِيقُ, assigning to تسلّم a meaning belonging to استسلم.])

Q. Q. 2. تَمَسْلَمَ [from مُسْلِمٌ] *He named, or called, himself a Muslim;* or *he named himself Muslim;* his name having before been Moḥammad: (M, Ḳ:) mentioned by Er-Ru-ásee. (M.)

سَلْمٌ: see the next paragraph, in six places. — Also *A leathern bucket* (دَلْو) *having one* عُرْوَة [or *loop-shaped handle*], (T, Ṣ, M, Ḳ,) *with which the waterer walks, like the buckets* (دِلَاء) *of the attendants of the camels or other beasts upon which water is drawn or which carry water,* (T, TA,) or *like the* دَلْو *of the water-carriers:* (Ṣ, Ḳ:) expl. in the Ṣ as above as on the authority of AA; but IB says that the correct explanation is, *having one* عَرْقُوَة [or *stick fixed across from one part of the brim to the opposite part, serving as a handle as well as to keep it from collapsing*]: (TA:) of the masc. gender [whereas دَلْو is fem.]: (M:) pl. [of pauc.] أَسْلُمٌ and [of mult.] سِلَامٌ, (M, Ḳ,) and Lḥ mentions as its pl. أَسَالِمُ, which is extr. [unless as a pl. pl., i. e. pl. of أَسْلُمٌ]. (M.)

سِلْمٌ *Peace,* or *reconciliation;* as also ▼سَلْمٌ; (Ṣ, M, Mṣb, Ḳ;) masc. and fem.; (Ṣ, Mṣb, Ḳ;*) and ▼سَلَمٌ and ▼سَلَامٌ are like سِلْمٌ [in signification]: (M: [the context there shows that the signification mentioned above is what is meant in this instance:]) or سِلْمٌ signifies the *making peace,* or *becoming at peace* or *reconciled,* with another or others; (Ḥam p. 80;) as also ▼سَلْمٌ; and both are sometimes fem. as being syn. with مُصَالَحَةٌ. (L voce جَنَحَ, q. v.) In the saying of El-Aạshà,

• أَذَاقَتْهُمُ الحَرْبُ أَنْفَاسَهَا •
• وَقَدْ تُكْرَهُ الحَرْبُ بَعْدَ السِّلِمْ •

[*War made them,* or *has made them, to taste its draughts, and verily war is disliked after peace*], he has transferred the vowel of the م to the ل, in pausing; or it may be that he has inserted a kesreh in imitation of the preceding kesreh: it is not an instance like إِبِلٌ, in the opinion of Sb; for in his opinion the latter is the only instance of its kind. (M.) It is said in a trad., respecting El-Ḥodeybiyeh, أَخَذَ ثَمَانِينَ مِنْ أَهْلِ مَكَّةَ سِلْمًا, or ▼سَلْمًا, or ▼سَلَمًا, accord. to different relations, meaning [*He took forty of the people of Mekkeh*] *peaceably:* thus expl. by El-Ḥomeydee, in his "Ghareeb." (TA. [See also سَلَمٌ below.]) — Also *i. q.* ▼إِسْلَامٌ, (Ṣ, Ḳ, TA,) as signifying *Self-resignation,* or *submission;* (TA; [and thus the latter is expl. in one place in the Ṣ;]) which is also a signification of ▼سَلَمٌ: (Ṣ, M, Ḳ, TA:) and this is meant in the Ḳur [iv. 96], where it is said, وَلَا تَقُولُوا لِمَنْ أَلْقَى إِلَيْكُمُ ٱلسِّلْمَ لَسْتَ مُؤْمِنًا, (Bḍ, TA,) or ▼السَّلَمَ, as some read, (Bḍ,) [i. e. *And say not ye to him who offers to you submission, Thou art not a believer:*] or ▼السَّلَامَ here means *the salutation of* الإِسْلَام [by saying سَلَامٌ عَلَيْكُمْ]: (Bḍ, TA:*) or *salutation, and submission by uttering the profession of* الإِسْلَام; and so ▼السَّلَمَ: (Jel:) [or the latter here means, simply, *salutation;* and this is app. what is meant by its being said that] السَّلَمُ is the subst. from التَّسْلِيمُ; (Ḳ;) [but accord. to SM,] this means *the unreserved approval of what is decreed;* and this is said to be meant by the reading السَّلَم mentioned above. (TA.) — And [hence] السِّلْمُ signifies also الإِسْلَامُ [as meaning *The religion of the Muslims;* because it is a religion of self-resignation, or submission]: (Ṣ, Ḳ:) this is meant in the Ḳur [ii. 204], where it is said, ٱدْخُلُوا فِي ٱلسِّلْمِ كَافَّةً [*Enter ye into the religion of El-Islám wholly*]; (Ṣ, Bḍ, Jel;) and so ▼السَّلْمِ, as some there read; (Bḍ, Jel;) or both there mean *submission and obedience* to God: (Bḍ:) [and] ▼السَّلْمُ [also] has the former meaning. (M.) — Also, (Ṣ, M, Ḳ,) and ▼سَلْمٌ, (M,) A man, (Ṣ, Ḳ, TA,) [and] a woman, (M,) *who makes peace,* or *is at peace,* with another; (Ṣ, M, Ḳ;) and in like manner, a company of men (قَوْمٌ). (M.) This is said to be meant in the Ḳur [xxxix. 30], where it is said, وَرَجُلًا سِلْمًا لِرَجُلٍ, as some read, i. e. *And a man who is at peace with respect to a man:* (TA:) or سِلْمًا and ▼سَلْمًا and ▼سَلَمًا, three different readings, in the place of [the more common reading] سَالِمًا, are all inf. ns. of سَلِمَ, used as epithets [syn. with سَالِمًا], or ذَا is suppressed before them. (Bḍ.) You say, أَنَا سِلْمٌ لِمَنْ سَالَمَنِي [*I am one who is at peace with respect to him who is at peace with me*]. (Ṣ, TA.) And a poet says, [using this word in two different senses, the latter of which has been mentioned above,]

• أَنَائِلُ إِنَّنِي سِلْمٌ • لِأَهْلِكِ فَٱقْبَلِي سِلْمِي •

[*O Náïleh,* (نَائِلُ being for نَائِلَةُ, a woman's name, apocopated,) *verily I am one who is at peace with respect to thy family, therefore accept thou my submission*]. (TA. [It seems to be there indicated by the context that سلمى here means *my peace,* or *reconciliation;* which is less appropriate than the meaning that I have assigned to it.])

سَلَمٌ: see سَلَامٌ: and see also سِلْمٌ, in seven places. — Also, in buying or selling, (Mṣb,) the subst. from سَلَّمَ and أَسْلَمَ فِي الشَّيْءِ signifying أَسْلَفَ, (M,) *i. q.* سَلَفٌ; (Ṣ, Mṣb, Ḳ;) i. e. *Any money,* or *property, paid in advance,* or *beforehand, as the price of a commodity for which the seller has become responsible and which one has bought on description:* (T and TA in art. سلف:) or *payment for a commodity to be delivered at a certain* [*future*] *period with something additional to* [*the equivalent of*] *the current price at the time of such payment;* this [transaction] being a cause of profit to him who makes such payment: (TA in that art.:) or *a sort of sale in which the price is paid in advance, and the commodity is withheld, on the condition of description, to a certain* [*future*] *period:* (Ṣ and O in that art., in explanation of سَلَفٌ:) but it is said in a trad. that the term سَلَمٌ as meaning سَلَفٌ was disliked; app. because the former is applied to obedience, and self-resignation, or submission, to God. (TA.) — And The *making* [one] *captive.* (Ḳ. [See 1, in the latter part of the paragraph.]) — And *A captive;* (Ḳ;) because he submits himself. (TA.) One says, أَخَذَهُ سَلَمًا, (M, TA, [in the TḲ بِالسَّلَمِ,]) *He took him* [*a captive*], (TA,) or *made him captive,* (M,) *without war:* (M, TA:) or *he brought him in a state of submission, not resisting;* and so, *if wounded:* (IAạr, M, TA:) and thus El-Khaṭṭábee has expl. the phrase in the trad. respecting El-Ḥodeybiyeh cited above, voce سِلْمٌ. (TA.) — Also *A sort of tree,* (Ṣ, M, Mṣb, Ḳ,) [the *mimosa flava* of Forskål, who writes its Arabic name in Italic characters *syllæm,* and in Arabic characters سليم, (Flora Aegypt. Arab., p. cxxiii.,)] *a species* (M) *of the* [*kind of thorny trees called*] عِضَاه, (Ṣ, M, Mgh, Mṣb, TA, [not غَضَاة, as in the Lexicons of Golius and Freytag,]) *the leaves whereof are the* قَرَظ, *with which skin is tanned:* (TA:) AḤn says, *its branches are long, like rods; and it has no wood such as is used in carpentry, even if it grows large: it has slender, long thorns, grievous when they wound the foot of a man; and a yellow* [*fruit such as is termed*] بَرَمَة [n. un. of بَرَمٌ, see this word, and see also حُبْلَةٌ,] *which is the sweetest of the* بَرَم *in odour; and they tan with its leaves:* and it is said, on the authority of the Arabs of the desert, that *it has a yellow flower, containing a green grain* (حَبَّة خَضْرَاء) [or this may mean *a grain of a dark,* or *an ashy, dust-colour*]), *of sweet odour, in which is somewhat of bitterness, and of which the gazelles are very fond:* (M:) the n. un. is with ة: (Ṣ, M, Mgh, Mṣb, Ḳ:) and pl. أَسْلَامٌ, (M,) and سِلَامٌ is said by IB to be pl. of the n. un., like as إِكَامٌ is of أَكَمَةٌ. (TA.) [Hence,] ذَاتُ أَسْلَامٍ *A land* (أَرْضٌ) *that gives growth to the* [*trees called*] سَلَم. (Ḳ.) See also سَلَمَان.

سَلِمٌ *Stones;* (Ṣ, M;) as also ▼سِلَامٌ: (M:) and ▼سَلِمَةٌ [as n. un. of the former and sing. of the latter, (incorrectly written by Freytag, in one place, سَلَمَةٌ, and incorrectly said by him to be of the dial. of the people of Ḥimyer,)] signifies *a stone:* (Ṣ, M, Mgh, Mṣb:) [or] the pl. [or quasi-pl. n.] of سَلِمَةٌ in this sense is ▼سِلَامٌ, like كِلَامٌ in measure: (Mṣb:) or ▼سَلِمَةٌ signifies *stones;* (Ḳ;) or *hard stones;* (TA;) and ▼سِلَامٌ is its pl.: (Ḳ:) [said to be] so called because of their freedom (سَلَامَة) from softness: (TA:) or this last signifies *stones,* the *small* thereof and the *large;* and they assign to it no sing.: (ISh, TA:) or سلام [probably meaning ▼سِلَامٌ] is a quasi-pl. n.: (Aboo-Kheyreh, TA:) and it is also said to be a name for *any broad stone.* (TA.) See also سَلْمَان. A poet says, (namely, Bujeyr Ibn-'Anameh, IB, TA,)

• يَرْمِي وَرَائِي بِٱمْسَهْمِ وَٱمْسَلِمَةْ •

[*He casts from behind me* (i.e. *defends me*) *with the arrow and the stone*]: this [usage of ام for ال] is of the dial. of [Ṭeiyi and] Ḥimyer. (Ṣ, TA.)

السَّلِمُ for السِّلْمُ: see سِلْمٌ, second sentence.

سَلِمَةٌ: see سَلِمٌ, in two places: and سَلْمَان. — Also A woman *soft,* or *tender, in the* أَطْرَاف [or *fingers,* or other *extremities*]. (Ḳ.) — And An *old and weak* she-camel. (IAạr, TA in art. سد.)

سَلْمَى *A certain plant* (Ḳ, TA) *which becomes green in the* [*season called*] صَيْف [app. here meaning *spring*]. (TA.) — أَبُو سَلْمَى *The* [*species of lizard called*] وَزَغ: (Ḳ:) or, some say, [as is said in the M,] ▼ أَبُو سَلْمَان. (TA.) — See also the next paragraph. — [In the CḲ, by a mistranscription, a meaning belonging to سُلَامَى is assigned to سَلْمَى.]

السَّلْمَآءُ, accord. to Aboo-Mis-ḥal, as meaning *The earth*, occurs in the prov., أَنْفٌ فِى المَآءِ وَٱسْتٌ فِى السَّلْمَآءِ [*A nose in the water and a rump on the earth*]: and if this be correct, it may be derived from سلام [i. e. سِلَام] meaning "stones:" and it may be originally ▼ السَّلْمَى, and lengthened for the sake of the rhyme. (Ḥam p. 214.) [But the reading commonly known is, أَنْفٌ فِى السَّمَآءِ وَٱسْتٌ فِى المَآءِ.]

هُوَ سَلْمَانُ بَيْتِهِ *He is the special*, or *particular, friend of his* [another's] *house; one who mixes with him much:* from the saying of the Prophet, سَلْمَانُ مِنَّا أَهْلَ البَيْتِ [*Selmán is of us, the people of the house*]; referring to Selmán El-Fárisee. (Ḥar p. 472.) — أَبُو سَلْمَان: see سَلْمَى. — Also *A species of the* [*black beetles called*] جِعْلَان [pl. of جُعَل, q. v.]: (M:) or *i. q.* جُعَل, (IAạr, Ḳ,) or أَبُو جَعْرَان, with fet-ḥ [app. a mistake for kesr] to the ج: (Kr, TA:) or *the largest of the* جِعْلَان: or *a certain insect like the* جُعَل, *having a pair of wings:* (TA:) or *the male of the* [*black beetles called*] خَنَافِس [pl. of خُنْفُسَآء, q. v.]. (IAạr, TA in art. فرض.)

سَلَمَان or سِلْمَان, accord. to different readings, occurs in a trad. of Ibn-'Omar, in which it is said, كَانَ يُصَلِّى عِنْدَ سَلَمَانٍ فِى طَرِيقِ مَكَّةَ [*He used to pray at certain selem-trees*, or *certain stones, in the road of Mekkeh*]: each may be a pl. [or rather a quasi-pl. n.]; the former, of ▼ سَلَمَةٌ, the "tree so called;" the latter, of ▼ سَلِمَةٌ, "stones" [or a "stone:" but both of these explanations are strange]. (TA.)

سَلَامٌ, (Ṣ, Ḳ, TA,) in its primary acceptation, (TA,) is *syn. with* ▼ سَلَامَةٌ, (Ṣ, Ḳ, TA,) as is also سَلْمٌ, (Ṣ, [so in one of my copies, but omitted in the other copy,]) and signifies *Safety, security, immunity*, or *freedom, from faults, defects, imperfections, blemishes*, or *vices*, (Ṣ,* [mentioned in one only of my two copies, and there as relating peculiarly to the third word,] Ḳ, [in which it ostensibly relates peculiarly to the first word, but in the CḲ, by the omission of a و before it, it is made to relate only to the second word,] and TA, [accord. to which it relates to the first and second words, as it is well known to do,]) *and from evils of any kind:* (TA:) or [simply] *safety, security, immunity*, or *freedom;* as also ▼ سَلَامَةٌ: (Sb, M:) IḲt says that these two words may be dial. vars. [syn. each with the other]; or the former may be pl. of the latter [or rather a coll. gen. n. of which the latter is the n. un.]: (M, TA:) and Suh says, in the R, that most of the lexicologists hold them to have one [and the same] meaning: but that if they considered the language of the Arabs, and the distinction, or limitation, denoted by the ة, they would see that between them is a great difference [inasmuch as the former has a large range of meaning which the latter has not, as will be seen from what follows]. (TA.) سَلَامٌ عَلَيْكُمْ is an announcement of the continuance of سَلَامَة [or safety, &c.]: (Bḍ in xiii. 24:) [it may therefore be rendered *Safety*, &c., *be*, or *light and abide, on you;* or, generally, *peace be*, or *light and abide, on you;* for] it means *nothing disliked*, or *evil, shall befall you henceforth:* (Bḍ in xvi. 34:) and سَلَامٌ عَلَيْكَ [may be rendered in like manner; for it virtually] means *I will not do to thee anything that is disliked*, or *evil;* (Bḍ and Jel in xix. 48;) *nor say to thee henceforward what would annoy thee*, or *be disagreeable*, or *evil, to thee.* (Bḍ ibid.) It may also be [rendered *May safety*, &c., or *peace, be*, or *light and abide, on you;* as] a prayer for سَلَامَة, to those to whom it is addressed, from the state in which they are at the time. (Bḍ in xxviii. 55.) [It is generally held that this salutation may not be used by, nor to, any but a Muslim.] In the beginning of an epistle, the approved practice is to write سَلَامٌ عَلَيْكَ, without the article ال; and in repeating it, at the end, to write it with that article. (Durrat el-Ghowwáṣ, in De Sacy's Anthol. Gramm. Arabe, p. 72 of the Arabic text. [In the latter case, the general practice in the present day is to write simply وَالسَّلَامُ, suppressing عَلَيْكَ.]) In saluting the dead, one puts عَلَيْكَ first, saying, عَلَيْكَ سَلَامُ ٱللّٰهِ. (Ḥam p. 307.) You also say, لَا بِسَلَامَتِكَ ▼ مَا كَانَ كَذَا وَكَذَا [*No, by thy safety, such and such things were not*]. (Ṣ.) السَّلَامُ is also a name of *God*, (Ṣ, M, Mṣb, Ḳ,) [applied to Him in the Ḳur lix. 23, accord. to some for ذُو السَّلَامِ, i. e. ذُو السَّلَامَةِ,] because of his safety, or freedom, from defect, and imperfection, and cessation of existence; (IḲt, M, TA;) or from variations, and as being the everlasting, who brings the creation to nought and will not come to nought; or, accord. to Suh in the R, He is so named [as being *the Author of Safety, Security*, &c.; i. e.] because He has rendered all his creatures safe, or free, from defectiveness, or unsoundness, and mankind and the jinn, or genii, from the betiding of injustice, or wrong, to them, from Him; and the expositors who assert that He is thus named because of his safety, or freedom, from imperfections, and evils of any kind, utter an unseemly saying, making سَلَامٌ to be syn. with ▼ سَالِمٌ, which latter applies only to him who is liable to evil of any kind, and who expects it, and then becomes safe, or free, from it. (TA.) دَارُ السَّلَامِ is an appellation of *Paradise*, (M, Ḳ,) [applied thereto in the Ḳur vi. 127 and x. 26,] as being *the abode of everlasting safety*, or *security;* (Zj, M, TA;) *the abode of safety*, or *security, from evils of any kind, from death and decrepitude and diseases* [*&c.*]: (TA:) or as being *the abode of God.* (M, TA.) — See also سِلْمٌ, in four places. — [As is there stated,] it signifies also *Salutation*, or *greeting;* (M, TA;) particularly the *salutation of* الإِسْلَام [*by saying* سَلَامٌ عَلَيْكُمْ or سَلَامٌ عَلَيْكَ, expl. above]; (Bḍ in iv. 96;) a subst. (Ṣ, Mgh, Mṣb, TA) from سَلَّمَ عَلَيْهِ, (Mṣb,) [i. e.] from التَّسْلِيمُ, (Ṣ, Mgh, TA,) like كَلَامٌ from التَّكْلِيمُ. (Mgh. [See 2, third sentence.]) — In the saying in the Ḳur [xxv. 64], وَإِذَا خَاطَبَهُمُ ٱلْجَاهِلُونَ قَالُوا سَلَامًا [*And when the ignorant speak to them, they say*, سَلَامًا], this last word signifies تَسَلُّمًا, (Sb, M,) or تَسَلُّمًا مِنْكُمْ [for تَتَسَلَّمُ مِنْكُمْ تَسَلُّمًا *We declare ourselves to be clear*, or *quit, of you*], and مُتَارَكَةً لَكُمْ [for نُتَارِكُكُمْ مُتَارَكَةً *we relinquish you*], (Bḍ,) [and means] *there shall be neither good nor evil between us* (Sb, M, Bḍ) *and you:* it is not the سلام that is used in salutation; for the verse was revealed at Mekkeh, and the Muslims had not then been commanded to salute the believers in a plurality of gods: (Sb, M:) [in iv. 88 of the Ḳur, which was promulgated afterwards, at El-Medeeneh, is a general command to return a salutation with a better or with the same; but the Sunneh prescribes that the salutation of سَلَامٌ عَلَيْكَ or سَلَامٌ عَلَيْكُمْ when addressed to a Muslim by one not a Muslim is to be returned only by saying وَعَلَيْكَ or وَعَلَيْكُمْ:] or the meaning in xxv. 64 is, *they say a right saying, in which they are secure from harming and sinning.* (Bḍ.) Sb asserts that Aboo-Rabee'ah used to say, إِذَا لَقِيتَ فُلَانًا فَقُلْ سَلَامًا, meaning أَتَسَلَّمُ مِنْكَ [for تَسَلُّمًا, تَسَلُّمًا], i. e. *When thou meetest such a one, say, I declare myself to be clear*, or *quit, of thee*]: and he says that some of them said سَلَامٌ, meaning *The case of me and thee is the* [*case of*] *being clear*, or *quit, each of the other; and the* [*case of*] *mutual relinquishing.* (M.) [It is usual, in the present day, to say, اِفْعَلْ كَذَا وَالسَّلَامُ, meaning *Do thou such a thing, and there will be an end of altercation* between us.] — See also سَلِمٌ. — Also *A kind of trees;* (Ṣ, M, Mṣb, Ḳ;) they assert that *they are evergreen; nothing eats them; but the gazelles keep to them, and protect themselves by their shade, but do not hide among them; and they are not great trees, nor of the kind called* عِضَاه: (AḤn, M:) they are also called ▼ سِلَامٌ; (Ḳ;) or this is pl. of سَلَمَةٌ [n. un. of سَلَمٌ], which is of another kind; like as إِكَامٌ is pl. of أَكَمَةٌ: (IB, TA:) n. un. with ة. (Ṣ, M.) السَّلَامُ عَلَيْكَ was said to an Arab of the desert; and he replied, الجَثْجَاثُ عَلَيْكَ: and being asked, "What is this reply?" he answered, "They are two bitter trees: thou hast put upon me one, so I have put upon thee the other." (Ḳ.) — See also سَلِمٌ, in two places.

سِلَامٌ: see سَلِمٌ, in two places: — and the paragraph here next preceding, last sentence but two.

سَلِيمٌ *i. q.* ▼ سَالِمٌ, (Ṣ, M, Ḳ,) which means *Safe, secure*, or *free*, (Mṣb,) *from evils of any kind;* (Ḳ, Mṣb, TA;) applied to a man: (M:) pl. سُلَمَآءُ; (M, Ḳ, TA;) in some copies of the Ḳ سَلْمَى, like جَرْحَى pl. of جَرِيحٌ; (TA;) [but this is probably its pl. only when it is used in the sense of جَرِيحٌ or the like, as seems to be the case from what follows.] Also, (M,) applied to a heart: (Ṣ, M:) بِقَلْبٍ سَلِيمٍ, in the Ḳur xxvi. 89, means *With a heart free from unbelief:* (M, TA:) or, *divested of corruptness,* or *unsoundness:* (Er-Rághib, TA:) in the Ḳur xxxvii. 82, some say that it means *with a grieving,* or *sorrowful, heart;* from سَلِيمٌ in the sense here next following. (Bḍ.) — Also *i. q.* لَدِيغٌ [meaning *Bitten by a serpent*]; (Ṣ, M, Ḳ;) as also ▼سَلَامٌ (Ṣ, Ḳ) and ▼مُسْلَمٌ: (Ḳ:) app., (Ṣ,) as implying a good omen, of safety; (Ṣ, M;) or because the person is left (مُسْلَمٌ) to that [bane] which is in him: (IAạr, Ṣ,* M:) and sometimes it is metaphorically used as meaning ‡ *wounded:* (M:) or it means *wounded, at the point of death,* (M, Ḳ,) as some say: (M:) pl. سَلْمَى. (M, and Ḥam p. 214.) = Also, (M, Ḳ,) of a horse, (M,) The *part, of the hoof, that is between the* أَشْعَر [or *hair,* or *extremity of the skin, next the hoof*], (M, TA,) or *that is between the* أَمْعَر [q. v.], (Ḳ,) but the former is the right, (TA,) *and the interior of the hoof.* (M, Ḳ, TA.)

سَلَامَةٌ [the most usual inf. n. of سَلِمَ]: see سَلَامٌ, in three places. = Also n. un. of سَلَامٌ applied to a kind of trees [described above]. (Ṣ, Ḳ.)

سُلَامَى, a noun of the fem. gender, (Mṣb,) *A certain bone that is in the* فِرْسِن [q. v., here meaning *foot*] *of the camel:* (Ṣ, Ḳ:) this is said by A'Obeyd to be the primary signification: (Ṣ:) or the سُلَامَى of the camel are the *bones of the* فِرْسِن [or *foot*]: (M:) [for] سُلَامَى is used alike as sing. and pl., and sometimes it has also a pl., (Ṣ,) which is سُلَامَيَاتٌ: (Ṣ, M, Ḳ:) or it is a pl. [or rather a coll. gen. n.], of which the sing. [or n. un.] is سُلَامِيَةٌ, signifying the أُنْمُلَة [q. v.] *of* [*any of*] *the fingers:* (IAth, TA:) [but this is a strange explanation:] it is said that the last parts in which مُخّ [here meaning marrow or pulp and the like] remains in a camel when he has become emaciated are the سُلَامَى and eye; and when it has gone from these, he has none remaining: (Ṣ:) the pl. سُلَامَيَاتٌ, (Ṣ, TA,) or سُلَامَى, (M, Mṣb,) also signifies the *bones of the* أَصَابِع, (Ṣ, M,) so says Kh, and Zj adds that they are also called the قَصَب, (Mṣb,) *of the hand* and *of the foot;* (M;) [i. e., *of the fingers* and *of the toes;* and this seems to be the most common meaning, in relation to a human being; namely, the *phalanges of the fingers* and *of the toes;*] *that are between every two joints* [*and what are beyond the extreme joints*] *of the* أَصَابِع: accord. to Lth, the سلامى are the *bones of the* أَصَابِع [or *fingers* and *toes*] *and the* أَشَاجِع *and the* أَكَارِع, *and are hard and compact bones like* كِعَاب [pl. of كَعْب]: (TA: [see the words that I have here left untranslated, for the senses in which they are here used are doubtful:]) accord. to IAạr, (M,) *certain small bones, of the length of the* إِصْبَع [or *finger*], (M, Ḳ,) or *nearly so,* (M,) or *less,* (Ḳ,) *of which there are four,* or *three,* (M,) [or app., *five,* for the meaning here seems to be the *metacarpal* and *metatarsal bones,* to which the terms سُلَامَى and سُلَامَيَاتٌ are sometimes applied, (see أَشْجَع and مُشْط,)] *in the hand* and *in the foot,* (Ḳ,) [i. e.] *in each hand* and *foot:* (M:) Ḳṭr says that the سلاميات are the عُرُوق [app. a mistake for عظام i. e. *bones*] *of the outer side of the hand* and *foot:* (Mṣb:) سلامى is also said to signify *any small hollow bone:* and *any bone of a human being:* and ISh says that in every horse are six سلاميات [app. in the fore legs and the same in the hind legs; for he seems to mean that the term سلامى is applied to *each of the pastern-bones* and to the *coffin-bone;* these three corresponding to the phalanges of a human being: see قُصّ]: (TA:) it is not allowable to write سلامى otherwise than with what is termed the short alif. (MF, TA.) = سُلَامَى, (M, Ḳ,) like سُكَارَى, (Ḳ, TA, [in the CḲ like سَكْرَى, which is shown to be wrong by a verse cited in the M and TA,]) signifies also The [*south,* or *southerly, wind called*] جَنُوب. (M, Ḳ.)

سَلَامَانٌ *A kind of tree,* (Ṣ, M, Ḳ,) *growing in soft,* or *plain, tracts:* (M:) AZ says, it is *like the* أَلَآء, which is a tree resembling the myrtle, which changes not in the midst of summer, and which has a produce resembling the head [or ear] of millet (ذُرَة), *except that it is smaller than the* الآء; *tooth-sticks* (مَسَاوِيك) *are made from it; and its produce is like that of the* الآء; *and it grows in the sands and the deserts:* (TA in art. الآ:) n. un. with ة. (M.)

نَمْلُ سُلَيْمَانَ *Red ants* [lit. *the ants of Solomon*]. (TA voce أُحْوَى, in art. حو.)

سُلَّمٌ *A ladder,* or *a series of stairs* or *steps,* syn. مِرْقَاةٌ, (M, Ḳ,) and دَرَجَةٌ, (M,) or مِعْرَاجٌ, (Mṣb,) *upon which one ascends;* (Ṣ, Mgh;) either *of wood* or *of clay* [*&c.*]: (Mgh:) said by Zj to be so called because it delivers thee (يُسَلِّمُكَ) to the place to which thou desirest to go, (Mgh, TA,) i. e., to some high place, and thou hopest for safety (السَّلَامَة) by means of it: (Er-Rághib, TA:) masc. and fem.; (Lth, M, Mgh;) [app., accord. to Lth and F, generally fem.; for] accord. to Lth, one says, هُوَ السُّلَّمُ and هِيَ السُّلَّمُ; (Mgh;) [and F says,] it is sometimes made masc.: (Ḳ:) pl. سَلَالِيمُ (Ṣ, Mgh, Ḳ) and سَلَالِمُ, (Ḳ,) [which latter is the original, for] the ى in سلاليم is added by poetic license. (M, TA.) [Hence,] السُّلَّمُ † *Certain stars, below* [*those called*] العَانَة, *on the right of them;* (Ḳ;) as being likened to the سُلَّم [above-mentioned]. (TA.) — And The غَرْز [or *stirrup of the camel's saddle*] (Ṣ, Ḳ) is sometimes thus called [as being a means of mounting]. (Ṣ.) — And ‡ *A means to a thing;* (Ḳ, TA;) because it leads to another thing like as does the سُلَّم upon which one ascends. (TA.) — And السُّلَّمُ is the name of *The horse of Zebbán* (in the CḲ Zeiyán) *Ibn-Seiyár.* (Ḳ.)

سَالِمٌ: see سَلِيمٌ; and see سَلَامٌ, near the middle of the paragraph. [See also an ex. voce شَاجِبٌ.] — [Hence,] كَلِمَةٌ سَالِمَةُ العَيْنَيْنِ ‡ *A good word* or *expression* or *sentence.* (TA.) = The saying of J [in the Ṣ], (Ḳ,) in which he has followed his maternal uncle El-Fárábee, (TA,) that it signifies The *portion of skin between the eye and the nose,* is a mistake; (IB, Ḳ;) and his citation, as an authority, of the verse of 'Abd-Allah Ibn-'Omar (Ḳ) in which he says,

* وَجِلْدَةُ بَيْنَ العَيْنِ وَالأَنْفِ سَالِمُ *

(TA,) is futile: (Ḳ:) for, as IB says, Sálim was the son of Ibn-'Omar, who, by reason of his love of him, thus makes him to be as the skin between his eyes and his nose: or, as MF says, the truth is, that the said verse is by Zuheyr, and Ibn-'Omar used it as a proverb: and [SM says], if this be correct, it strengthens the saying of J. (TA.)

أَسْلَمُ [*More,* and *most, safe* or *secure* or *free from evils of any kind*]. You say, هٰذَا أَسْلَمُ مِنْ هٰذَا [*This is more safe &c. than this*]: and هٰذِهِ الأَسْلَمُ [*This is the most safe &c.*]; and السُّلْمَى. (Ḥam p. 214.) = And الاسلم [app. الأَسْلَمُ] signifies, like الطلفى [i. e. الطُّلْفَى], *The leaves* (خُوص) *of the* دَوْم [or *Theban palm*]. (Ibn-Beyṭár, app. from AḤn, cited by De Sacy in his Chrest. Arabe, 2nd ed., iii. 480.)

الإِسْلَامُ [inf. n. of 4, q. v. — It is the general term for *The religion of Mohammad:* differing from الإِيمَان, as shown above: see 4. — And hence, for أَهْلُ الإِسْلَامِ, or the like,] *The Muslims, collectively.* (M in art. بيض, &c.)

إِسْلَامِيٌّ [*Of,* or *relating to,* الإسلام as meaning *the religion of Mohammad.* — And particularly] *A poet of the class next after the* مُخَضْرَمُونَ *and next before the* مُوَلَّدُونَ. (Mz 49th نوع.) [See the Preface to the present work, p. ix.] The most celebrated of the poets of this class, it seems, were Jereer, El-Farezdaḳ, El-Akhṭal, and Dhu-r-Rummeh, who were contemporaries, and flourished in the first and second centuries of the Flight. (Mz ubi suprà, and Ibn-Khillikán in art. جَرِير.) — لَفْظٌ إِسْلَامِيٌّ *A word,* or *phrase, introduced,* or *used in a new sense, on the occasion of the promulgation and establishment of the religion of* الإِسْلَام, by means of the Ḳur-án &c. (Mz 20th نوع.)

الأُسَيْلِمُ [*The vena salvatella;*] *a certain vein* (Ṣ, M, Ḳ) *in the hand,* (M,) *between the little finger and the finger next to this:* (Ṣ, Ḳ:) it occurs only [thus] in the dim. form. (M.)

مُسْلِمٌ act. part. n. of 4 [q. v.]. (Mṣb.) وَٱجْعَلْنَا مُسْلِمَيْنِ لَكَ, in the Ḳur ii. 122, means *And make both of us self-resigned,* or *submissive, to Thee:* (Bḍ, Jel:) or, *sincere in religion,* or *without hypocrisy, towards Thee;* syn. مُخْلِصَيْنِ: (M, Bḍ:) and therefore مسلمين is made trans. by means of لِ. (M.) — [It commonly means *One who holds,* or *professes, the religion of* الإِسْلَام.] And one says, كَانَ كَافِرًا ثُمَّ هُوَ اليَوْمَ مُسْلِمَةٌ ▼ [*He was an unbeliever: then, to day, he has become a Muslim*]. (M.)

مُسْلِمَةٌ: see what next precedes.

المُسَلَّمُ is said to be used in the sense of ▼ المُسْتَلَمُ in the saying of El-'Ajjáj,

• بَيْنَ الصَّفَا وَالكَعْبَةِ المُسَلَّمِ •

[*Between Eṣ-Ṣafà and the Kaạbeh of which the Black Stone is touched with the hand, or kissed:* see 8]. (M.)

مَسْلُومٌ: see سَلِيمٌ. —— Also *A hide, or skin, tanned with* [قَرَظ, or *leaves of*] *the* سَلَم. (Ṣ, M.)

أَرْضٌ مَسْلُومَآءُ *A land abounding with the trees called* سَلَم. (M, Ḳ.) —— Suh says, on the authority of AḤn, that مَسْلُومَآءُ is a name for *A collection of* سَلَم; like مَشْيُوخَآءُ applied to "many elders, or men advanced in age." (TA.)

مُسْتَلَمٌ: see المُسَلَّمُ. —— مُسْتَلَمُ القَدَمَيْنِ means *A man soft, or tender, in the feet.* (TA.)

سلهب

Q. 4. اِسْلَهَبَّ, said of a horse running, *He stretched himself forth; or extended, or elongated, himself:* (Ṣ: [the meaning is there indicated, and it is expressed by an interlinear explanation in one of my copies of that work:]) or *he pressed onward with a penetrative energy or force, or with sharpness of spirit.* (TA.) Some hold that the ه in the words of this art. is augmentative: others, [app. the greater number,] that it is radical. (MF.)

سَلْهَبٌ, sometimes pronounced with ص, (Ṣ, TA,) *Long, or tall;* (Ḳ, TA;) as an epithet of general application: (TA:) or a *tall* man: pl. سَلَاهِبَةٌ. (Ḳ.) —— Applied to a horse, *Long-bodied:* (Ṣ:) or, so applied, *large,* (Ḳ, TA,) *and long, or tall,* (TA,) *and long in the bones;* as also ▼ سَلْهَبَةٌ, (Ḳ, TA,) which is applied to the male: (TA:) and the former, likewise applied to a horse, *that presses onward with a penetrative energy or force, or with sharpness of spirit:* (TA:) or, so applied, *large and long or tall:* and likewise applied to a spear: and tropically, [but in what sense is not explained,] to a wind (رِيح). (A.) —— The fem. ▼ سَلْهَبَةٌ signifies *Corpulent, or large in body;* (Ḳ, TA;) not an epithet of commendation: (TA:) or, applied to a woman, it signifies *tall* or *beautiful.* (JK.) —— And سَلْهَبٌ is the name of *A certain dog.* (Ḳ,* TA.)

سَلْهَبَةٌ: see سَلْهَبٌ, in two places.

سِلْهَابٌ: see what follows.

سِلْهَابَةٌ and ▼ سِلْهَابٌ, each as a fem. epithet, (Ḳ, TA,) and each with kesr [to the س], (TA,) [but each in the CḲ is with fet-ḥ,] *Bold, daring, brave, or courageous.* (Ḳ.)

سلو

1. سَلَا عَنْهُ, (Ṣ, M, Mṣb, Ḳ,) first pers. سَلَوْتُ, (Ṣ, Mṣb,) aor. يَسْلُو, (Mṣb, Ḳ,) and يَسْلَا also, [or يَسْلَى,] though neither the second nor the third radical is a faucial letter; (Ḥam p. 568;) and سَلَاهُ, (M, Ḳ,) aor. يَسْلُوهُ; (Ḳ;) and سَلِىَ عَنْهُ, first pers. سَلِيتُ, (Ṣ, Mṣb,) aor. يَسْلَى; (Mṣb;) or سَلِيَهُ, (M, Ḳ,) aor. يَسْلَاهُ; (Ḳ;) and سَلَاهُ, first pers. سَلَيْتُهُ, aor. يَسْلِيهِ; (TA in art. سلى, on the authority of Esh-Shereeshee;) inf. n. سُلُوٌّ, (Ṣ, M, Mṣb, Ḳ,) of the first, (Ṣ, Mṣb, TA,) and سَلْوٌ, (M, Ḳ,) [app. of the second,] and سُلْوَانٌ, (M, MA, Ḳ,) of the first, as also سَلْوَةٌ, (MA,) or this last is a simple subst., (M,* Mṣb, Ḳ,) and سُلِىٌّ, (Ṣ, M, MA, Ḳ,) of the third, (Ṣ,) or of the first, (MA,) and سِلِىٌّ [with kesr substituted for ḍamm because of the kesr of the medial radical]; (M, TA;) *He was, or became, forgetful, unmindful,* or *neglectful,* (M, Ḳ, TA,) or *diverted from the remembrance,* (TA,) *of him, or it:* (M, Ḳ, TA:) *he endured with patience the loss, or want, of him, or it:* (Mṣb:) *he was, or became, content,* or *happy, without him, or it:* (PṢ:) [or *he experienced comfort,* or *consolation, for the loss, or want, of him, or it:*] accord to AZ, السُّلُوُّ [or rather سُلُوُّ الإِلْفِ عَنِ الإِلْفِ] signifies *the familiar's being content,* or *happy, without the familiar:* (Mṣb:) or السُّلُوُّ [or السُّلُوُّ عَنْ شَىْءٍ] signifies *the being content,* or *happy, without a thing.* (Ḥam p. 403.) One says also, سَلَا عَنِ الحُبِّ, meaning *He was* or *became, free from love,* or *affection.* (MA.) [And سَلَا عَنِ الهَمِّ *He was, or became, free from anxiety.* See also 5.] —— Also مَا سَلِيتُ أَنْ أَقُولَ ذَاكَ, meaning *I did not forget, but neglected, to say that:* and one does not say سَلِيتُ أَنْ أَقُولَهُ except as meaning مَا سَلِيتُ أَنْ أَقُولَهُ. (AZ, TA.)

2. سَلَّاهُ عَنْهُ, (M, TA,*) inf. n. تَسْلِيَةٌ; (TA;) and ▼ أَسْلَاهُ عَنْهُ; (M, Ḳ;) *He, or it, made him, or rendered him, forgetful, unmindful,* or *neglectful,* (M, Ḳ, TA,) or *made him to be diverted from the remembrance,* (TA,) *of him, or it:* (M, Ḳ, TA:) [*made him to endure with patience the loss, or want, of him, or it: made him to be content,* or *happy, without him, or it:* or *comforted him,* or *consoled him, for the loss, or want, of him or it:* see 1, first sentence:] and the former verb occurs, in a verse of Aboo-Dhu-eyb, followed by an accus. as a second objective complement, in the place of a gen. preceded by عَنْ. (M, TA.) And one says also, سَلَّانِى مِنْ هَمِّى, inf. n. as above; and ▼ أَسْلَانِى; meaning [*He freed me from my anxiety;* or] *he removed from me my anxiety.* (Ṣ.) And سَلَّاهُ [alone] *He, or it,* [*made him to be content,* or *happy; comforted,* or *consoled, him;* or] *freed him from grief* [or *anxiety*]. (MA.)

4: see 2, in two places. ═ Also اسلى القَوْمُ *The people, or party, were, or became, secure, or safe, from the beast of prey.* (Ḳ.)

5. تسلّى عَنْهُ quasi-pass. of سَلَّاهُ عَنْهُ (M) or of أَسْلَاهُ عَنْهُ (M, Ḳ) [and therefore signifying *He was made, or rendered, forgetful, unmindful,* or *neglectful,* or *was made to be diverted from the remembrance, of him, or it: was made to endure with patience the loss, or want, of him, or it: was made to be content,* or *happy, without him, or it:* or *was comforted,* or *consoled, for the loss,* or *want, of him, or it*]: or تسلّى signifies تَكَلَّفَ السُّلْوَانَ [*he affected the being forgetful,* &c., of a person, or thing]: (Ḥam p. 403:) [*he made himself content,* or *happy: comforted,* or *consoled, himself: diverted,* or *amused, himself:* and, like سَلَا, (with which it is said in the Ḥam p. 572 to be syn.,) or nearly so,] *he became free from,* or *he relinquished, anxiety.* (MA.) See also what next follows.

7. انسلى عَنْهُ الهَمُّ *Anxiety became removed,* or *cleared away, from him;* as also ▼ تسلّى. (Ṣ.)

8: see art. سلى.

سَلًا or سَلًى: see art. سلى.

سَلْوَةٌ, (M, Mṣb, Ḳ,) as also ▼ سُلْوَةٌ, (M, Ḳ,) a subst. from سَلَا عَنْهُ (M, Mṣb, Ḳ) [as such signifying *A state of forgetfulness, unmindfulness,* or *neglectfulness,* or *of diversion from remembrance,* of a person or thing: *patient endurance of a loss or want: content,* or *happiness, in a case of privation:* or *comfort,* or *consolation, for a loss or want:* accord. to the MA, the former is an inf. n.]. One says, سَقَيْتَنِى مِنْكَ سَلْوَةً and ▼ سُلْوَانًا *Thou hast made me content,* or *happy,* [or *hast infused into me content,* or *happiness,*] *without thee* [or *in thine absence*]. (Aṣ, Ṣ.) And هُوَ فِى سَلْوَةٍ مِنَ العَيْشِ *He is in a state of life ample in its means or circumstances, unstraitened,* or *plentiful, and pleasant.* (AZ, Ṣ.)

سُلْوَةٌ: see the next preceding paragraph.

سَلْوَى [accord. to those who make the alif to be a sign of the fem. gender] or سَلْوًى [accord. to those who make that letter to be one of quasi-coordination] *A certain bird,* (Ṣ, M, Mṣb, Ḳ,) [in the present day applied to the *quail,*] i. q. سُمَانَى [which is also applied in the present day to the quail], (Ksh and Bḍ and Jel in ii. 54,) [or] *white* [?], *resembling the* سُمَانَى, (M,) or *like the pigeon, but longer in the shank and neck than the latter, and of a colour resembling that of the* سُمَانَى, *quick in motion:* accord. to Akh, the word is used as sing. and pl.: (Mṣb:) [or] Akh says, I have not heard any sing. thereof, and it seems that the single one is thus called like the pl. number, in like manner as دِفْلَى is [said to be] applied to one and to the pl. number: (Ṣ:) or the n. un. is سَلْوَاةٌ; (M, Ḳ;) of which Lth cites as an ex. this saying, [in which بَلَّلَهُ should be بَلَّلَهَا,]

• كَمَا انْتَفَضَ السَّلْوَاةُ بَلَّلَهُ القَطْرُ •

[*Like as shakes the selwáh which the rain has much wetted*]. (TA.) ═ Also *Honey;* (Ṣ, M, Ḳ;) and so ▼ سُلْوَانَةٌ, with ḍamm: (Ḳ:) the former is used in this sense by a poet, (Ṣ, M,) namely, Khálid Ibn-Zuheyr; and Zj says that Khálid has made a mistake, the word سلوى signifying only a certain bird; but, accord. to AAF, (M,) —— السَّلْوَى signifies [also] *Whatever renders thee forgetful,* or *content,* or *happy, in a case of privation;* (كُلُّ مَا سَلَّاكَ, M, Ḳ;) and honey is thus called because it renders thee thus by its sweetness. (M.)

سُلْوَانٌ *A water which is drunk and which*

renders one forgetful, or *content*, or *happy*, *in a case of privation*; or *comforts*, or *consoles*, *for a loss* or *want*: (Lḥ, M, Ḳ:) or *a thing that is given to drink to the passionate lover in order that he may be forgetful*, or *content*, or *happy*, *without the woman*: (Lḥ, M:) or *it consists in one's taking some of the dust*, or *earth*, *of a grave, and sprinkling it upon water, and giving it to drink to the passionate lover*, (M, Ḳ,*) *whereupon his love dies*: (Ḳ:) or *rain-water poured upon a certain bead* (خَرَزَة) *called* ▾ سُلْوَانَة, *of which they used to say that when the passionate lover drank this water he became forgetful*, or *content*, or *happy*, *in his privation*: (Ṣ:) or *a certain medicine which is given to drink to him who is in grief and in consequence of which he becomes happy*; (Ṣ, Ḳ;) *called by the physicians* مُفَرِّح: (Ṣ:) or *a certain bead* (خَرَزَة) *for captivating*, or *fascinating*, also called ▾ سُلْوَانَة, (Lḥ, M, Ḳ,) and ▾ سَلْوَانَة, (Ṣgh, Ḳ,) *with which women captivate*, or *fascinate*, *men, restraining them from other women*: (Lḥ, M:) or ▾ سُلْوَانَة signifies [or, accord. to the Ḳ, signifies also] *a certain bead* (خَرَزَة, M, Ḳ,) *transparent*, (M,) *which, when one has buried it in the sand and then scraped the sand up from over it, is seen to be black, and is given* [*in water*] *to drink to a man, and renders him forgetful*, or *content*, or *happy*, *in a case of privation*: (M, Ḳ:*) or *a pebble upon which water is poured and given to drink to a man, who thereupon becomes forgetful*, or *content*, or *happy*, *in a case of privation*: (M:) Ru-beh says,

لَوْ أَشْرَبُ السُّلْوَانَ مَا سَلِيتُ
مَا بِي غِنًى عَنْكِ وَإِنْ غَنِيتُ

(Ṣ, M,*) and Nuṣeyr Ibn-Abee-Nuṣeyr, in answer to a question of Aṣ respecting the meaning of السلوان, said that it is *a bead* (خَرَزَة) *which is bruised*, or *pulverized*, [*and upon which water is then poured*,] *the water of which occasions in the drinker thereof forgetfulness*, or *content*, or *happiness*, *in a case of privation*: but Aṣ disallowed this, and said that it is an inf. n. of سَلَوْتُ, and that the meaning is لَوْ أَشْرَبُ السُّلُوَّ [i. e. † *Were I made to drink forgetfulness*, &c., *I should not become forgetful*, &c.: *there is not in me freedom from want of thee, though I be free from want of others*]. (TA.) See also سَلْوَةٌ.

سَلْوَانَةٌ: see the next preceding paragraph.

سُلْوَانَةٌ: see سَلْوَى: — and see also سُلْوَانٌ, in three places.

سُلَّى, [said to be] like رُبَّى, [but it may be سُلًّى, as there is no apparent cause for its being imperfectly decl.,] *A quality that renders forgetful of the objects of love* or *affection*, or *that renders content*, or *happy*, *without them*. (TA in art. سلى.)

سَالٍ [act. part. n. of 1: as such often signifying] *Having his heart free from love*, or *affection*. (Ḥar p. 41.)

مَسْلَاةٌ [a noun of the class of مَبْخَلَةٌ and مَجْبَنَةٌ &c., originally مَسْلَوَةٌ]. One says, فِيهِ مَسْلَاةٌ عَنِ الكُرَبِ [*In him is a cause of forgetfulness of*, or *freedom from, anxieties*]: like مَغْلَاةٌ [in form]. (TA.)

المُسَلِّى *The third* [*in arriving at the goal*] *of the ten horses that are started together for a race*: so called because he renders his owner content, or happy (يُسَلِّيهِ). (Ḥam p. 46.)

مُتَسَلًّى [a noun of place from 5]. One says, مَا عَنْهُ مُتَسَلًّى [*There is not any place in which one may be rendered forgetful*, &c., *of him*, or *it*; or *in which one may be rendered content*, or *happy*, *without him*, or *it*]. (TA.)

سلى

1. سَلِيَتْ, (M, Ḳ,) aor. ـَ, (Ḳ,) inf. n. سَلًى, said of a ewe, or she-goat, [and of a she-camel,] *Her secundine* (سَلَاهَا) *became disrupted* [*in her belly*]. (M, Ḳ.) — سَلَاهَا, inf. n. سَلْىٌ; (M;) or ▾ سَلَّاهَا, inf. n. تَسْلِيَةٌ; (Ṣ, Ḳ;) *He pulled out* or *off*, or *removed from its place, her secundine* (سَلَاهَا), namely, a ewe's, or she-goat's, (Ṣ, M, Ḳ,) or a she-camel's. (So in one of my copies of the Ṣ.) And سَلَيْتُ النَّاقَةَ *I drew* [*forth*] *the she-camel's secundine* (سَلَاهَا) *after the bringing forth without letting it fall* (بَعْدَ الوَحْمِ or الرَّحْمِ). (Lḥ, M.) — سَلَيْتُهُ a dial. var. of سَلَوْتُهُ, mentioned by Esh-Shereeshee. (TA.) See 1 in art. سلو, first sentence.

2: see the preceding paragraph.

8. اِسْتَلَتْ *She* (a camel, TA, [or a ewe or goat,]) *cast forth her secundine* (سَلَاهَا). (Ḳ, TA.) — *She* (a ewe, or goat,) *became fat*. (Ḳ in art. سلو, and TA in the present art.) — استلت سمنا [i. e. سَمْنًا] *She collected* سمن [or *clarified butter*]. (TA. [See also 8 in art. سلأ.])

سَلًى or سَلًا [thus differently written, the former the more correct, unless the word be derived from السَّلْوَةُ, as it is said to be in the Ḥam p. 656, but this is improbable,] The *secundine*; i. e. the *skin*, [or *membrane*,] (M, Ḳ,) or *thin skin*, (Ṣ,) *in which is the fœtus*, or *young*, [*in the womb*,] (Ṣ, M, Mṣb, Ḳ,) of human beings, and of horses and camels, (M,) or of human beings and of cattle, (Ḳ,) or [peculiarly] of cattle, (T, Ṣ,) that of human beings being termed مَشِيمَةٌ: (TA:) it is pulled off from the face of the young camel at the time of the birth, or else it kills it, like as it does when it becomes disrupted in the belly: when it comes forth, the she-camel is safe, and so is the young one; but if it becomes disrupted in the belly, she perishes, and so does the young one: (Ṣ:) pl. أَسْلَآءٌ. (M, Mṣb, Ḳ.) [Hence,] one says, اِنْقَطَعَ السَّلَى فِي البَطْنِ † [*The secundine became disrupted in the belly*]; (Ṣ, Meyd, Ḳ;) i. e. artifice departed [or came to an end]; (Ṣ;) a prov. applied in the case of an affair's becoming beyond one's power of accomplishment, and coming to an end; (Meyd;) like the saying, بَلَغَ السِّكِّينُ العَظْمَ [The knife reached to the bone]. (Ṣ, Ḳ.) And هُوَ آكِلُ الأَسْلَآءِ † [*He is the eater of secundines*]; meaning he is low, base, vile, or sordid. (TA.) And وَقَعَ القَوْمُ فِي سَلَى جَمَلٍ † [*The people*, or *party, fell into* the like of *the secundine of a he-camel*]; meaning they fell into a difficult affair or case; (Ṣ, Ḳ;*) or they fell into an unparalleled evil; (Meyd;) for the he-camel has no سلى. (Ṣ, Meyd.)

سَلْيَآءُ A ewe, or she-goat, (Ṣ, Ḳ,) and a she-camel, (Ṣ,) *whose secundine* (سَلَاهَا) *has become disrupted* [*in her belly*]. (Ṣ, Ḳ.) — And A ewe, or she-goat, [or she-camel,] *whose secundine* (سَلَاهَا) *has been pulled out* or *off*, or *removed from its place*. (TA.)

سُلَّى, [or سُلًّى,] mentioned in this art. in the TA: see art. سلو.

سمر

1. سَمَّهُ, (Ṣ, Mṣb, Ḳ,) aor. ـُ, inf. n. سَمٌّ, (Mṣb,) *He put poison into it*; [*poisoned it*; *infected it with poison*;] namely, food. (Ṣ, Mṣb, Ḳ.) And *He gave him to drink poison*. (Ṣ, Ḳ.) And سَمَّتْهُ الهَامَّةُ *The* هامّة [or *venomous reptile* or *the like*] *smote him with its poison*. (M.) — [Hence, perhaps, *He suggested it*, إِلَيْهِ *to him*: a signification mentioned by Freytag, but without any indication of the authority.] — [And, app., *It perforated it*; *transpierced it*; or *pierced*, or *passed, through it*: for it is said that] مَسَمٌّ may be an inf. n. of the verb [signifying نَفَذَ], and may also signify a place of نُفُوذ. (Mṣb.) — And, (Ḳ,) aor. ـُ, (Ṣ, TA,) inf. n. سَمٌّ, (TA,) ‡ *He probed it*; namely a case, or an affair; *and examined*, or *endeavoured to learn, its depth*. (Ṣ, Ḳ, TA.) — Also, inf. n. سَمٌّ, *i. q.* شَدَّهُ [*He made it firm, fast*, or *strong*; &c.]: (M:) [or this may be a mistranscription for سَدَّهُ; for] you say, سَمَمْتُ القَارُورَةَ وَنَحْوَهَا, (Ṣ, Ḳ,*) inf. n. as above, (TA,) meaning سَدَدْتُ [i. e. *I closed, stopped*, or *stopped up, the flask*, or *bottle, and the like*]. (Ṣ, Ḳ.*) — Also, (M, Ḳ,) aor. ـُ, inf. n. سَمٌّ, (TA,) *i. q.* أَصْلَحَهُ [*He rectified it*; or *put it into a good, sound, right*, or *proper, state*; &c.]; namely, a thing. (M, Ḳ.) And سَمَّ بَيْنَ القَوْمِ, (Ṣ, M,) or سَمَّ بَيْنَهُمَا, (Ḳ,) aor. ـُ, [for the verb is trans., الأَمْرَ being understood, or بَيْنَ meaning ذَاتَ البَيْنِ,] (M,) inf. n. سَمٌّ, (Ṣ, M,) *i. q.* أَصْلَحَ [*He rectified*, or *reformed*, or *amended, the circumstances subsisting between the people*, or *between them two*; or *he effected a rectification of affairs*, or *an agreement, a harmony*, or *a reconciliation, between the people*, or *between them two*]. (Ṣ, M, Ḳ.) — And سَمَّ الوَدَعَ *He strung the* وَدَع [or *cowries*]; which, when strung, are termed سَمَّة and سَمٌّ. (M.) — سَمَّهُ, inf. n. سَمٌّ, signifies also *He appropriated it to a particular, peculiar*, or *special, object*. (M.) You say, سَمَّ النِّعْمَةَ *He so appropriated the benefit*, or *bounty*. (Ḳ.) And سَمَّتِ النِّعْمَةُ *The benefit*, or *bounty, was*, or *became, particular, peculiar*, or *special, as to its object*: (Ṣ, Ḳ:) the verb being intrans. as well as trans. (Ḳ.) El-'Ajjáj says,

هُوَ الَّذِي أَنْعَمَ نُعْمَى عَمَّتْ
عَلَى الَّذِينَ أَسْلَمُوا وَسَمَّتْ

(Ṣ,) or the latter hemistich is

* عَلَى البِلَادِ رَبُّنَا وَسَمَّتْ

(M,) [*He is the Being who has bestowed bounty that has been general and that has been particular upon those who have become Muslims,* or *upon the countries,* namely, *our Lord*]: he means that it has reached all. (Ṣ.) — [And i. q. قَصَدَهُ:] you say, سَمَمْتُ سَمْتَكَ, i. e. قَصَدْتُ قَصْدَكَ [which means *I tended, repaired, betook myself,* or *directed my course, towards thee;* or *I have tended,* &c.: and also *I pursued,* or *have pursued, thy way,* or *course, doing like thee*]. (Ṣ.) == [سُمَّ *It was smitten by the wind called* سَمُوم; applied to a plant; and in like manner to a man: see its part. n., مَسْمُومٌ. And] سُمَّ يَوْمُنَا, with ḍamm [to the س], *Our day was,* or *became, attended with the wind called* سَمُوم. (Ṣ, Ḳ.)

2. تَسْمِيمٌ signifies The *making loops to the* [*girth called*] وَضِين. (TA.) [You say, سَمَّمَ الوَضِينَ *He made loops to the* وضين: see the pass. part. n., below. And also *He adorned the* وضين *with* سُمُوم, i. e. *strung cowries:* see, again, the pass. part. n.]

R. Q. 1. سَمْسَمَ *He* (a man) *walked,* or *went along, gently.* (IAạr, TA.) And *He* (a fox) *ran;* [or *ran in a certain manner;*] inf. n. سَمْسَمَةٌ: (TḲ:) the latter signifies the *running,* (Ḳ,) or *a sort of running,* (M,) of the fox. (M, Ḳ.)

سَمٌّ *Poison,* or *venom;* (PṢ, TḲ;) or *deadly poison* or *venom;* (KL;) or the *poison,* or *venom, of the serpent;* (MA;) *a certain deadly thing,* (Ṣ, M, Mṣb, Ḳ,) *well known;* (Ḳ;) as also ↓ سُمٌّ, (Ṣ, M, Mṣb, Ḳ,) which is of the dial. of the people of El-'Áliyeh, (Yoo, Mṣb, TA,) and is said to be the most chaste; (MF, TA;) and ↓ سِمٌّ, (Mṣb, Ḳ,) which is [said to be] of the dial. of Temeem, (Mṣb,) [but is thought by SM to be vulgar, and] accord. to Yoo, the first is of the dial. of Temeem, (TA,) and this is the most common of the three: (Mṣb:) pl. سِمَامٌ (Ṣ, M, Mṣb, Ḳ) and سُمُومٌ: (Ṣ, Mṣb, Ḳ:) and ↓ سَمْسَمٌ signifies the same, in the sing. sense. (ISk, Ḳ, TA.) [In some copies of the Ḳ, by a mistranscription (وَالسَّمْ or وَالسِّمْ for وَالسَّمُ or وَالسِّمُ) سَمٌّ or سُمٌّ is made to be syn. with سَمْسَم as signifying "a fox." That the right reading is that which I have followed is shown in the TA by an ex., in which سَمْسَم is spoken of as drunk.] — [Hence,] سَمُّ الفَأْرِ *Arsenic;* [in like manner called by us *ratsbane;*] syn. الشَّكُّ, (Ḳ, TA,) i. e. الرَّهْجُ [which is a modern word for arsenic]. (TA.) [Also applied in the present day to *The hyoscyamus muticus* of Linn. (Delile's Floræ Aegypt. Illustr., in the Descr. de l'Égypte, no. 242.)] — And سَمُّ الحِمَارِ *The* [*tree called*] دِفْلَى [q. v.]. (Ḳ.) — And سَمُّ السَّمَكِ *The tree called* مَاهِيزَهْرَه [or مَاهِي زَهْرَه], (Ḳ,) which latter appellation is Pers., meaning the same, [i. e. "fish-poison,"] (TA,) *and also known by the name of* البُوصِير: *it is beneficial for pains of the joints, and pain of the hip and the back, and the* نِقْرِس [i. e. *gout,* or specially *gout in the foot* or *feet*]; *but the only part of its tree that is beneficial is its* لِحَآء [or *bark*]: (Ḳ, TA:) *when somewhat thereof,* (Ḳ,* TA,) *kneaded with leaven,* (TA,) *is put into a pool of water, it intoxicates the fish thereof,* (Ḳ, TA,) *so that they float upon the surface of the water:* (TA:) *and its leaves burn in lamps in lieu of wicks,* (Ḳ, TA,) *by reason of their oleaginous property.* (TA.) — سَمُّ أَبْرَصَ: see سَامٌّ. == Also, and ↓ سُمٌّ, (Ṣ, M, Mṣb, Ḳ,) and ↓ سِمٌّ, (Mṣb, Ḳ,) [but the last is thought by SM to be vulgar, in this sense as well as in the first,] *A perforation, bore,* or *hole,* (Ṣ, M, Mṣb, Ḳ,) of anything; (M;) or *such as is narrow;* (TA;) for instance, (Ṣ, TA,) [the *eye*] of a needle; (Ṣ, Mṣb, TA;) as in the Ḳur vii. 38; [see جَمَلٌ;] and the *hole* of the nose, and of the ear: (TA:) pl. سُمُومٌ, (M,) or سِمَامٌ, (Mṣb,) or both. (Ṣ, Ḳ.) The سُمُوم and سِمَام of a human being are His *mouth and his nostril and his ear,* (Ṣ,) or his *mouth and his nostrils and his ears;* (Ḳ;) and the sing. is سَمٌّ and ↓ سُمٌّ: (Ṣ:) or the سُمُوم of a human being, and of a horse or the like, are the *clefts* (مَشَاقّ) *of the skin* thereof. (M.) And the سُمُوم of the horse are The *thin portions of the hard bone,* [*extending*] *from the two sides of the nasal bone to the channels of the tears:* sing. سَمٌّ: (M:) or, as some say, (M,) the سَمَّانِ, (Ṣ, M,) or the سَمّ, (Ḳ, [but this seems evidently to be a mistake for the dual,]) means *two veins in the nose* (أَنْف, M, or خَيْشُوم, Ṣ, Ḳ, [which latter often means the same as the former,]) of the horse: (Ṣ, M, Ḳ:) accord. to Lth, سُمُوم, as pl. of سَمّ, signifies the *channels of the tears* of the horse: AO says that in the face of the horse are سُمُوم; and the bareness of his سُمُوم is approved, and is regarded as indicative of generous breed. (TA.) By the سُمُوم of the horse are also meant *Any bone* [or rather *bones*] *in which is marrow.* (TA.) And the سُمُوم of a sword are *Notches* therein, whether new or old. (TA.) — أَصَابَ سَمَّ حَاجَتِهِ [is app. from سَمّ as signifying the "eye" of a needle, or the like, and] means † *He hit,* or *attained, the object of his aim* or *pursuit:* (M, Ḳ:) and in like manner, هُوَ بَصِيرٌ بِسَمِّ حَاجَتِهِ [*He is knowing,* or *skilful, in respect of the object of his aim* or *pursuit*]. (M.) — [And hence, perhaps, though another derivation is asserted in what follows,] one says also, مَا لَهُ سَمٌّ وَلَا حَمٌّ غَيْرُكَ and ↓ سُمٌّ وَلَا حُمٌّ, (Ṣ, M,) meaning † *He has no object in his mind except thee;* syn. هَمٌّ: (M:) and in like manner, مَا لَهُ سَمٌّ وَلَا حَمٌّ and ↓ سُمٌّ وَلَا حُمٌّ [alone]: or, accord. to Fr, it means *he has not any who hopes for him:* this is from [سَمَمْتُ سَمْتَكَ and] هَمَمْتُ هَمَّكَ and حَمَمْتُ حَمَّكَ meaning قَصَدْتُ قَصْدَكَ; سَمّ and حَمّ being the inf. ns., and ↓ سُمّ and حُمّ the simple substs.; and the meaning is, *he has not any who seeks after him;* i. e. *he has no good in him for which he is to be sought after:* (Meyd:) or it means *he has neither little nor much.* (Ḳ and TA in art. حم.) — سَمٌّ also signifies The *loop* (عُرْوَة) of the [girth called] وَضِين: pl. سُمُوم. (TA. [See مُسَمَّم.]) — And *Anything like* وَدَع [or *cowries*] *brought forth from the sea,* (Ṣ, K, TA,) *and strung for ornament.* (TA.) And also, (TA,) or ↓ سُمّ and ↓ سَمَّة, (M,) *Strung* وَدَع [or *cowries*]: (M, TA:) pl. سُمُوم. (TA.)

سُمٌّ: see the next preceding paragraph, in seven places.

سِمٌّ: see سَمٌّ, in two places.

سَمَّةٌ The *meatus of the vagina* of a woman; (Aṣ, TA;) as also ↓ سِمَام, [which is shown to be thus used as a sing., by a citation from a trad., though said to be] from سِمَام as signifying the "eyes" (ثُقَب) of the needle [or of needles]: or the *rima* of a woman, *with the parts that are next to it of the haunch and of the borders of the vulva,* i. e. *of the labia majora.* (TA.) — See also سُمَّة. == Also السَّمَّة, (AA, TA,) or سَمَّةُ القَلْبِ, (TA,) *The heart,* or *cerebrum, of the palm-tree:* pl. سمم [app. سِمَمٌ, or سُمَمٌ]. (TA.)

سُمَّةٌ: see سَمٌّ, last sentence. == Also *A mat,* (AḤn, M,) or *a* سُفْرَة [q. v.], (Ḳ,) or *a thing like a wide* سُفْرَة, (T, TA,) *made,* (AḤn, M,) [i. e.] *woven,* (T, TA,) *of* خُوص [or *leaves*] (AḤn, T, M, Ḳ) *of the* غَضَف [a tree resembling a dwarf-palm-tree]: (AḤn, M:) *it is spread beneath the palm-tree* (T, Ḳ, TA) *when the dates are cut off,* (T, TA,) *and upon it fall what become scattered* (T, Ḳ, TA) *of the dates:* (T, TA:) pl. سِمَامٌ, (AḤn, M, TA,) or سُمَمٌ, (Ḳ,) or, as in the T, سُمُومٌ. (TA.) == See also سَامٌّ, latter part, in two places.

سِمَّةٌ The اِسْت [here app. meaning *anus*]; as also ↓ سَمَّة [q. v.]. (Ḳ.)

سُمَامٌ *A sort of bird,* (T, Ṣ, M,) *less than the species called* قَطًا, *in make,* (T, TA,) *like the* سُمَانَى [or *quail*]: (M, TA:) [accord. to explanations of سُمَامَة in the MA, *mountain-swallows:* or, accord. to the same and Meyd, *birds like swallows:* accord. to Dmr, as stated by Golius, i. q. طير ابابيل: but this is app. said in relation to an assertion of 'Áisheh, mentioned in art. ابل in the Mṣb, that the birds termed أَبَابِيل in the Ḳur cv. 3 were most like to swallows:] the word is a pl., (Ṣ,) [or rather a coll. gen. n.,] and the sing. [or n. un.] is with ↓ ة, (Ṣ, M,) pl. سَمَائِمُ: (Meyd:) see سُمَامَة. — And hence, as being likened thereto, *A banner, an ensign,* or *a standard;* syn. لِوَآء: (M:) or so ↓ سُمَامَةٌ. (Ḳ.) — And [hence, also, perhaps, without ة, as in a verse cited by IB and in the TA, for the coll. gen. n. may be used as a sing.,] *A swift she-camel:* (Ṣ, IB, TA:) [pl. سَمَائِم, mentioned by Freytag, from Reiske, as signifying *swift she-camels.*] — Also, and ↓ سُمْسُمٌ, and ↓ سُمَاسِمٌ and ↓ سُمْسُمَانٌ and ↓ سُمْسُمَانِيٌّ, applied to anything, [of men and of beasts &c.,] *Light, active,* or *agile, and slender, and swift;* (M, Ḳ;)

and so ▼ سَمْسَمَةٌ : (M: [thus there written; not سَمْسَامَةٌ nor سُمْسَامَةٌ, though both of these are app. correct:]) or ▼ سُمْسَامٌ and ▼ سُمْسُمَانِىٌّ, applied to a man, signify *light*, or *active*, or *agile, and swift*, or *quick*; (Ṣ;) and ▼ سُمْسُمٌ so applied, and ▼ سُمْسُمَةٌ and ▼ سَمَامَةٌ, applied to a woman, signify *light*, or *active*, or *agile, and slender*: (TA:) or ▼ سُمْسُمٌ, applied to a man, signifies [simply] *light*, or *active*, or *agile*. (Ḳ.)

سِمَامٌ a pl. of سَمٌّ or سُمٌّ: (Ṣ, M, Mṣb, Ḳ:) — and also used as a sing.: see سَمَّةٌ. — [In one place, in the CḲ, erroneously put for سَمْسَامٌ as syn. with سَمْسَمٌ, q. v.]

سَمُومٌ, of the fem. gender, (Ṣ,) *A hot wind*, (Ṣ, M, Mṣb, Ḳ,) or, as some say, *a cold wind*, (M, [perhaps a mistake occasioned by a misunderstanding of the phrase سَمُومٌ بَارِدٌ, expl. below,]) *in the night* or *in the day*, (M,) or generally (Ḳ) *in the day*, (Mṣb, Ḳ,) but authorities differ respecting it, as has been shown voce حَرُورٌ; (Mṣb;) accord. to AO, it is *in the day*, and *sometimes in the night*; and the حَرُور is in the night, and sometimes in the day: (Ṣ:) but some say that the former is *in the night*, and the latter in the day: (Ibn-Es-Seed in the "Farḳ," TA:) [in the present day it is commonly applied to *a violent and intensely-hot wind, generally occurring in the spring or summer, in Egypt and the Egyptian deserts usually proceeding from the south-east or south-south-east, gradually darkening the air to a deep purple hue, whether or not (according to the nature of the tract over which it blows) accompanied by clouds of dust or sand, and at length entirely concealing the sun; but seldom lasting more than about a quarter of an hour or twenty minutes*:] the word is used as a subst. [i. e. alone], and also as an epithet [qualifying the subst. رِيحٌ]: (M:) pl. سَمَائِمُ. (Ṣ, M, Ḳ.) One says also سَمُومٌ بَارِدٌ, meaning *A* سَمُوم *that is constant, continual, permanent, settled*, or *incessant*. (Ṣ and L in art. برد.) [See also بَارِحٌ.]

سَمَامَةٌ : see سَمَامٌ, in three places: ═ and see سَمْسَمٌ. ═ Also *A certain feather*, (دَائِرَةٌ, M, Ḳ, TA,) *which is approved* (Ḳ, TA) *by the Arabs*, (TA,) *in the neck of the horse*, (Ḳ,) *in the middle of the neck of the horse*, (M,) or *in the side of his neck*. (TA.) ═ And The شَخْص [or *corporeal form* or *figure*, or *person*,] (M, Ḳ,) of a man: (Ḳ:) or, as some say, (M, but accord. to the Ḳ "and") the *aspect*; (M, Ḳ;) as in the saying, هُوَ بَهِىُّ السَّمَامَةِ [*He is beautiful*, or *pleasing, in aspect*]. (TA.) — And *A portion standing up of ruined dwellings*. (Ḳ.)

سَمَّاسٌ *A seller of* سِمْسِم [q. v.]; like لَآّلٌ signifying a seller of لُؤْلُؤ. (IKh, TA.)

سَمَّانٌ *A certain plant*. (Ḳ.) ═ [See سُمَّانٌ in art. سمن.]

سِمَّانٌ The *decorations*, or *embellishments*, (تَزَاوِيق,) *of a ceiling*: so says IAạr; and in like manner, Lḥ; and he says, I have not heard a sing. of it. (TA.) [See also سُمَّانٌ, in art. سمن.]

سَمْسَمٌ : see سَمٌّ, first sentence. ═ It is also an epithet, of which only the fem., with ة, is mentioned: see سَمَامٌ. — [Hence,] سَمْسَمٌ and ▼ سَمْسَامٌ, (M,) or السَّمْسَمُ and ▼ السَّمْسَامُ, (Ḳ, TA, [the latter erroneously written in the CḲ السَّمَامُ,]) *The wolf*; (M, Ḳ;) because of his lightness, or activity, or agility: (M:) or السَّمْسَمُ signifies *the wolf that is small in the body*. (M, Ḳ.) — And السَّمْسَمُ *The fox*; (Ṣ, M, Ḳ;) as also سَمْسَمٌ [without ال], (M,) and ▼ السُّمَاسِمُ. (Ḳ.)

سُمْسُمٌ; and its fem., with ة: see سَمَامٌ, last sentence, in three places. ═ Also, the former, and ▼ سِمْسِمٌ, or the latter is a mistake, [ascribed in the Ḳ to J,] *Red ants*: n. un. with ة: (Ḳ:) or سُمْسُمَةٌ (M) and سِمْسِمَةٌ (Ṣ, M) signify *a certain insect*, (M,) *a red ant*; (Ṣ, M;) as also ▼ سَمَامَةٌ: (M:) accord. to Lth, *an insect of the form of the* اكلة [app. a mistranscription for نَمْلَة, i. e. *ant*], *of a red colour*: Az says, I have seen it in the desert, and *it bites*, or *stings, painfully*: (TA:) pl. سَمَاسِمُ, (Ṣ, TA,) said by Aboo-Kheyreh to be *certain things found in El-Baṣrah, that bite vehemently, having longish heads, and the colours of which incline to redness*. (TA.) See سَمَاسِمُ below

سِمْسِمٌ [*Sesame*; *sesamum orientale* of Linn.; applied in the present day to the plant and its grain;] *a well-known grain*; (Mṣb;) it is called in Pers. كُنْجُدْ; (MA, KL;) *i. q.* جُلْجُلَانٌ, (M, Ḳ,) said by AḤn to be *abundant in the Saráh* (السَّرَاة), *and El-Yemen*, and to be *white*; (M;) [by this is evidently here meant *sesame*, or the *grain thereof*, or *both*; though it also signifies the "fruit of the coriander;" for otherwise, the most commonly-known meaning of سِمْسِمٌ would be unmentioned in the M;] the *grain of the* حَلّ; [i. e. the *grain from which the oil called* حَلّ *is expressed*;] (Ṣ, Ḳ; [by the author of the latter of which, this was evidently understood to be different from the جُلْجُلَان, which is mentioned by him after the description of properties here following;]) *it is glutinous, corruptive to the stomach and the mouth; but is rendered good by honey; and when it is digested, it fattens; and the washing of the hair with the water in which its leaves have been cooked lengthens and improves it: the wild sort thereof is known by the name of* جَلْبَهَنْك, (Ḳ, TA,) thus, with fet-ḥ to the ج and ب and ه, and sukoon to the ل and ن, [but written in the CḲ جُلْبُهُنْك,] a Pers. word, [originally جلبهنگ,] arabicized; (TA;) *its action is nearly like that of the* خَرْبَق [or *hellebore*]; *and sometimes from half a drachm to a drachm is administered to him who is affected with palsy, and he is cured thereby*, (Ḳ, TA,) *speedily*; (TA;) *but a drachm thereof is dangerous*, (Ḳ, TA,) *in a great degree*. (TA.) — السِّمْسِمُ الهِنْدِىُّ: see جِرْوَعٌ, in art. جرع. ═ Also The *serpent*: (Ḳ, TA:) or *a certain creeping thing resembling it*. (TA.) — See also the next preceding paragraph, where it and its n. un. with ة are mentioned.

سَمْسَمَانٌ : see سَمَامٌ.

سُمْسُمَانِىٌّ : see سَمَامٌ, in two places.

سَمْسَامٌ : see سَمَامٌ, in two places: — and see also سَمْسَمٌ, likewise in two places.

سَمَاسِمُ *A species of bird*, (M, Ḳ,) *resembling the swallow*; [but see what follows;] thus expl. by Th, who has not mentioned any sing. thereof; (M;) and Lḥ adds that *its eggs are unattainable*: (TA:) so in the prov., كَلَّفْتَنِى بَيْضَ السَّمَاسِمِ [*Thou hast imposed upon me the task of procuring the eggs of the* سَمَاسِم]; (M;) applied in the case of a man's being asked for that which he will not find, and which will not be: (TA:) or السَّمَاسِم is here pl. of ▼ السمسمة [i. e. السُّمْسُمَة or السِّمْسِمَة], and means *the red ants*: thus some relate the prov.: but others say, ▼ السَّمَائِمِ, pl. of سَمَامَةٌ, [n. un. of سَمَامٌ,] which means *a species of bird like the swallow, the eggs of which are unattainable*. (Meyd. [By Freytag, سَمَائِمُ is erroneously said, as on the authority of Meyd, to be pl. of سَامَّةٌ in this sense.]) In [some of] the copies of the Ḳ, السُّمَاسِمُ is here erroneously put for السَّمَاسِمُ. (TA.)

سُمَاسِمٌ : see سَمَامٌ: — and see also سَمْسَمٌ.

سَامٌّ [act. part. n. of سَمَّ; as such signifying *Poisoning*, or *infecting with poison*]. سَامَّةٌ, as an act. part. n. [in the fem. form because applied to things of the fem. gender (such as the عَقْرَب &c.), and to such as are denoted by gen. ns., which are used in a pl. sense], (Mṣb,) *Such as is*, or *are*, *venomous* (Ṣ, Mṣb, Ḳ) of animals, (Ḳ,) or of creeping things, [and insects,] *but of which the venom does not kill*; as the scorpion, and the hornet: (Mṣb:) and such things (Sh, Mṣb) and the like thereof (Sh) are termed سَوَامّ, (Sh, Mṣb,) which is the pl. of سَامَّةٌ. (Mṣb.) — [And hence,] سَامُّ أَبْرَصَ (Ṣ, M, Mgh, Ḳ) and سَامّ أَبْرَص, as one word, (Ṣ and Mṣb in art. برص, and the latter in the present art. also,) and ▼ سَمُّ أَبْرَصَ, (Ḳ,) *A species of the* [*lizard called*] وَزَغ: (M:) or *such as are large, of the* وَزَغ: (A in art. برص, and Mṣb:) or [*one*] *of the large* [*sorts*] *of the* وَزَغ: (Ṣ, Mgh, Ḳ:) also called السَّامُّ: (TA, from a trad.:) [see more in art. برص:] applied to the male and the female: (Zj, Mṣb:) dual سَامَّا أَبْرَصَ; (TA;) and pl. سَوَامُّ أَبْرَصَ. (M, Mgh, TA.) — And يَوْمٌ سَامٌّ [as though meaning "a poisoning day"] (M, Ḳ) and ▼ مُسِمٌّ, (IAạr, M, Ḳ,) the latter rare, (M,) [and anomalous, being from سَمَّ,] and ▼ مَسْمُومٌ, (Ṣ, M, Ḳ,) *A day attended with the wind called* سَمُوم. (Ṣ, M, Ḳ.) ═ سَامَّةٌ is also fem. of سَامّ as part. n. of the intrans. verb سَمَّ signifying "it was, or became, particular, peculiar, or special." And hence,] السَّامَّةُ signifies also ‡ *The* خَاصَّة [*or distinguished people, or people of distinction; and the particular, peculiar, or special, friends, intimates, familiars, or the like*] (Ṣ, M, IAth, Ḳ, TA) of a man; (IAth, TA;) and ♦ السُّمَّةُ, pl. سُمَمٌ, signifies the same; (M;) and so ♦ المَسَمَّةُ, like as المَعَمَّةُ signifies العَامَّةُ: (IAạr, TA:) or ♦ السُّمَّةُ signifies *the relations*, syn. القَرَابَةُ; (Ḳ;) or *the particular, or choice, relations*: (TA:) and ♦ أَهْلُ المَسَمَّةِ signifies *the relations*; syn. الأَقَارِبُ; (M;) or *the* خَاصَّة [expl. above], (El-Umawee, Ṣ, Ḳ,) and *the relations*. (Ḳ.) One says, كَيْفَ السَّامَّةُ وَالعَامَّةُ † [*How are the people of distinction, &c., and the common people, or people in general?*]. (Ṣ.) And عَرَفَهُ العَامَّةُ وَالسَّامَّةُ ‡ [*The people in general, or the vulgar, and the people of distinction, &c., knew it, or him*]. (TA.)

سَامَّةٌ [fem. of سَامٌّ: see the latter in several places]. — السَّامَّةُ also signifies *Death*: (M, Ḳ:) but this is extr.: (M, TA:) the word commonly known, (M,) or the correct word in this sense, (TA,) is السَّامُ, [belonging to art. سوم,] without teshdeed (M, TA) to the م, and without ة. (TA.)

أَسَمُّ A nose *narrow* (Ḳ, TA) *and fat* (TA) *in the nostrils*. (Ḳ, TA.)

مَسَمٌّ *A place of perforation, of transpiercing, or of passing through*: pl. مَسَامُّ. (Mṣb.) [Hence,] مَسَامُّ الجَسَدِ (Ṣ, Ḳ) or البَدَنِ (Mṣb) *The perforations* [or *pores*] *of the body* (Ṣ, Mṣb, Ḳ) *through which the sweat and the exhalation of the interior thereof pass forth*: (Mṣb:) المَسَامُّ [thus] applied to *the* مَنَافِذ [*of the body*] is a term of the physicians. (Mġh.)

مُسِمٌّ: see سَامٌّ.

مِسَمٌّ One *who eats what he is able to eat*. (Ḳ.)

المَسَمَّةُ and أَهْلُ المَسَمَّةِ: see سَامٌّ.

مُسَمَّمٌ, applied to a [girth such as is called] وَضِين, *Having three* سُمُوم, i. e. *loops* (عُرًى) [*attached to it*]. (TA.) And also, thus applied, *Adorned with* سُمُوم, i. e. *strung cowries*. (TA.)

مَسْمُومٌ [*Poisoned; infected with poison;*] *having had poison put into it*; applied to food. (TA.) And A man *having had poison given him to drink*. (TA.) — Also *Smitten by the wind called* سَمُوم; applied to a plant; and in like manner to a man. (TA.) See also سَامٌّ.

سمت

1. سَمْتٌ [as an inf. n.] is *syn. with* قَصْدٌ [in an intrans. sense], (Ṣ,* Mṣb,) and هُدًى [in the sense of رَشَادٌ], and اِسْتِقَامَةٌ: (Mṣb:) or حُسْنُ نَحْوٍ: (M, Ḳ:) you say, سَمَتَ, aor. ـُ, (Ṣ, M, Ḳ,) and ـِ, (Ḳ,) or in this case the former only, (TA,) inf. n. سَمْتٌ, (M, TA,) *He pursued a right course*; syn. قَصَدَ: (Ṣ, TA:) or † *he followed a good direction* (M, Ḳ,* TA*) *in the way of religion* [&c.]. (TA.) Accord. to Khálid Ibn-Ḍabbeh, it signifies † The *following the truth and the right way or direction, and being a good neighbour, and doing little harm*. (TA.) [But more commonly, or primarily, it relates to the course that one pursues in journeying.] An Arab of the desert, of [the tribe of] Ḳeys, says,

سَوْفَ تَجُوبِينَ بِغَيْرِ نَعْتِ ∗ تَعَسُّفًا أَوْ هٰكَذَا بِالسَّمْتِ

i. e. [*Thou shalt traverse* (addressing a woman), or, more probably, *ye shall traverse* (addressing camels or other beasts), a land *without a description*], *journeying without any sign of the way and without any track* [*for guidance*], such being the meaning of تَعَسُّفًا, *or thus, pursuing a right course*, السَّمْتُ meaning القَصْدُ. (TA.) Accord. to Sh, السَّمْتُ signifies *The seeking, searching, or inquiring, for, or after, the right way or direction*. (TA.) — السَّمْتُ also signifies قَصْدُ الطَّرِيقِ [i. e. سَمْتُ الطَّرِيقِ signifies *The road's having a right, or direct, tendency*]: (M:) or [سَمْتُ الشَّىْءِ] signifies قَصْدُ الشَّىْءِ [i. e. *The thing's having a right, or direct, tendency*]. (Ḳ.) [This last explanation has been misunderstood by the Turkish translator of the Ḳ; who has hence been led to assert that one says, سَمَتَ الشَّىْءَ, as well as سَمَتَ نَحْوَهُ, meaning قَصَدَهُ: it is تَسَمَّتَهُ that (like سَمَتَ نَحْوَهُ) signifies قَصَدَهُ; not سَمَتَهُ, for سَمَتَ is always intrans.] — Also *The journeying* (Ṣ, M, Ḳ) *upon the road* (M, Ḳ) [*guided only*] *by opinion* (Ṣ, M, Ḳ) *and conjecture*: (Ṣ:) or, as some say, *the journeying by conjecture and opinion, not upon a* [*known*] *road*. (TA.) A poet says,

لَيْسَ بِهَا رِيعٌ لِسَمْتِ السَّامِتِ ♦

[*There is not, or was not, in it, a road of any kind* (see رِيعٌ) *for the journeying by opinion and conjecture of him who so journeys*]. (Ṣ, TA.) — And *The pursuing a course, or direction*, [*of any kind*,] and [particularly] † *in religion and in worldly affairs*. (TA.) You say, هُوَ يَسْمُتُ سَمْتَهُ †*He pursues his* [another's] *way, or course, doing as he* [the latter] *does*. (TA.) [سَمْتَهُ is here an absolute (not an objective) complement of يَسْمُتُ; like سِيرَتَهُ in the phrase هُوَ يَسِيرُ سِيرَتَهُ. See also سَمْتٌ below.] — Also سَمَتَ, aor. ـُ, inf. n. سَمْتٌ, † *He* (a man) *was, or became, grave, staid, steady, sedate, or calm*. (Mṣb.) — And سَمَتَ لَهُمْ, aor. ـِ, (Fr, Ḳ,) inf. n. سَمْتٌ, (Fr, TA,) † *He prepared, arranged, or disposed, for them, the mode, or manner, of speech*, and *of judging, or forming an opinion*, (Fr, Ḳ, TA,) and *of work, or action*. (Fr, TA.)

2. تَسْمِيتٌ The *keeping to the* سَمْت [i. e. *road*, &c.]. (Ḳ.) It is said in a trad., فَانْطَلَقْتُ لَا أَدْرِى أَيْنَ أَذْهَبُ إِلَّا أَنِّى أُسَمِّتُ, meaning [*And I departed, not knowing whither I should go, but*] *I kept to the course, or direction, of the road*: or as some say, *I prayed to God*. (TA.) — Also † The *mentioning of God*, (Ṣ, M, A, Mṣb, Ḳ,) or, as in some copies of the Ṣ, the *mentioning of the name of God*, [like تَسْمِيَةٌ, inf. n. of سَمَّى,] (TA,) upon, or over, a thing, (Ṣ, M, A, Mṣb, Ḳ,) or in any case. (TA.) One says, سَمَّتَ عَلَى الطَّعَامِ † *He mentioned the name of God upon, or over, the food*. (TḲ.) — And سَمَّتَ لَهُ and عَلَيْهِ, inf. n. تَسْمِيتٌ, † *He prayed for what was good for him; prayed for a blessing upon him*; as also شَمَّتَ. (L and TA in art. شمت, q. v.) In a trad. respecting eating, it is said, سَمُّوا ٱللّٰهَ وَدَنُّوا وَسَمِّتُوا, meaning † [*Pronounce ye the name of God, and take what is next you* of the food, or *make your words to be near together*, (see 2 in arts. سمو and دنو,) *and*,] when ye have ended, *invoke a blessing* upon him at whose abode or table ye have eaten. (TA.) — التَّسْمِيتُ also signifies, (M, Ḳ,) or تَسْمِيتُ العَاطِسِ, (Ṣ, Mṣb,) † *The praying for the sneezer*; (M, Mṣb, Ḳ;) *saying*, هَدَاكَ ٱللّٰهُ إِلَى السَّمْتِ [*May God guide thee to the right, or good, course*]; because the person sneezing is disturbed and disquieted: so says AAF: (M, TA:) or *the saying to him*, يَرْحَمُكَ ٱللّٰهُ [*May God have mercy on thee*]: (Th, Ṣ, M:) or التَّسْمِيتُ signifies *the saying* بَارَكَ ٱللّٰهُ فِيكَ [*May God bless thee*]: (ISh, TA:) it is with س and with ش: (Ṣ, M, Mṣb:) one says سَمَّتَهُ, (T, M, Mṣb,) i. e. سَمَّتَ العَاطِسَ, meaning *He prayed for the sneezer*, [*saying as above*,] (A,) and شَمَّتَهُ: (T, M, Mṣb:) Th says that the former is preferred, (Ṣ,) or is the original, (Mṣb,) being from السَّمْتُ signifying القَصْدُ, (Ṣ, M, Mṣb,) and الهُدَى, and الاِسْتِقَامَةُ, (Mṣb,) and المَحَجَّةُ, (Ṣ,) or الطَّرِيقُ; (M;) as though one made a person his object by this prayer; (M;) and that the س is changed [by some] into ش: (TA:) but A'Obeyd says that the pronunciation with ش is of higher authority, and more common. (Ṣ, Mṣb.) The Prophet said, When any of you sneezes, let him say, الحَمْدُ لِلّٰهِ [*Praise be to God*]; and he who prays for him (الَّذِى يُسَمِّتُهُ [or يُشَمِّتُهُ]), يَرْحَمُكَ ٱللّٰهُ; and let him [i. e. the sneezer] say [in reply], يَهْدِيكُمُ ٱللّٰهُ وَيُصْلِحُ بَالَكُمْ [*May God direct you aright, and render good your state, or condition, or case*]. (Ḥar p. 250.)

3. سَامَتَهُ, inf. n. مُسَامَتَةٌ, *He, or it, faced, or fronted, or was opposite to or over against, him, or it*. (Mṣb, TA.)

5. تَسَمَّتَهُ, (Aṣ, Ṣ, A, TA,) [and] تَسَمَّتَ لَهُ, (M,) *He directed himself, or his course, or aim, to, or towards, him, or it*; syn. قَصَدَهُ, (Ṣ, M,) or قَصَدَ نَحْوَهُ, and تَعَمَّدَهُ. (Aṣ, A, TA.)

سَمْتٌ inf. n. of 1 [q. v.]. (M, TA.) — Also *A road, or way*; syn. طَرِيقٌ, (Ṣ, M, A, Mġh, Mṣb, Ḳ,) and مَحَجَّةٌ, (Th, Ṣ,) and نَحْوٌ: (A:) [pl. سُمُوتٌ.] One says, اِلْزَمْ هٰذَا السَّمْتَ *Keep thou to this road, or way*. (TA.) — And [hence,] † *The way, or course, that one pursues in his religion and his worldly affairs*: (TA:) † *a way, mode, or manner, of acting or conduct or the like*: (Ṣ, TA:) ‡ the *mode, or manner*, [of life,] syn. هَيْئَة, (Ṣ, A, Mġh, Mṣb, Ḳ, TA,) *of good people*, (Ṣ, A, Mġh, Ḳ, TA,) *in respect of religion*, not in respect of goodliness of person: (TA:) a metaphorical meaning, from the same word as signifying "a road," or "way." (Mgh.) One says, إِنَّهُ لَحَسَنُ السَّمْتِ † *Verily he is good in respect of the way, or course, that he pursues in his religion and his worldly affairs:* (TA:) or هُوَ حَسَنُ السَّمْتِ means † *he is good in his* هَيْئَة [i. e., as here used, *mode,* or *manner, of life*]. (Mṣb.) And مَا أَحْسَنَ سَمْتَهُ ‡ *How good is his way, mode,* or *manner, of acting* or *conduct* or *the like!* (Ṣ, A,* Mgh,* TA.) —— [Hence,] † *Gravity, staidness, steadiness, sedateness,* or *calmness.* (Mṣb.) —— السَّمْتُ also signifies *The region,* or *quarter, to which,* or *towards which, the course,* or *aim, is directed.* (M.) —— [And hence, *The bearing,* or *direction, of an object by the compass.* And more particularly, *The azimuth.* —— And سَمْتُ الرَّأْسِ *The zenith; or vertical point in the heavens.* ("Zenit" appears to have been, as Golius observes, a mistranscription for "zemt," or "semt.") —— سَمْتُ الشَّمْسِ *The path of the sun; the ecliptic:* from سَمْتٌ signifying "a road," or "way." —— سَمْتُ الاِعْتِدَالِ *The equinoctial colure.* And سَمْتُ الاِنْقِلَابِ *The solstitial colure.*]

سَامِتٌ [part. n. of 1]: see an ex. in the latter half of the first paragraph of this art.

مُسَمِّتٌ † Any one *praying,* or *who prays, for what is good,* (Ṣ and TA in art. شمت,) لِأَحَدٍ [*for any one*]; (TA in that art.;) as also مُشَمِّتٌ: (Ṣ and TA in that art.:) any one *praying,* or *who prays, for a return to the right,* or *good, way, and continuance therein.* (Mṣb.)

مُتَسَمَّتُ النَّعْلِ *The part of the sandal that is below its* مُخَصَّر [or *narrow part,* more commonly called its خَصْر, *extending thence*] *to its extremity.* (Ḳ.)

سمج

سَمُجَ, [aor. ـُ,] inf. n. سَمَاجَةٌ (Ṣ, O, Mṣb, Ḳ) and سُمُوجَةٌ; (L, TA;) and سَمِجَ, [aor. ـَ,] (Lḥ, TA, and so in a copy of the A,) inf. n. سَمَاجَةٌ; (A;) *It* (a thing, Ṣ, O, Mṣb) *was,* or *became, foul, unseemly,* or *ugly;* (Ṣ, A, O, Mṣb,* Ḳ;) or *devoid of beauty.* (A, L, Mṣb.)

2. سَمَّجَهُ, (A, O, L, Mṣb, Ḳ,) inf. n. تَسْمِيجٌ, (O, Ḳ,) *He,* or *it, rendered it foul, unseemly,* or *ugly;* (O, Mṣb,* Ḳ;) or *devoid of beauty.* (L, Mṣb.) One says, مَا سَمَّجَهُ عِنْدِى إِلَّا كَذَا [*Nothing rendered it foul, unseemly, &c., in my estimation, but such a thing*]. (A.)

4. مَا أَسْمَجَ فِعْلَهُ [*How foul,* or *unseemly, is his deed!*]. (A.)

10. اِسْتَسْمَجَهُ *He reckoned it,* or *esteemed it, foul, unseemly,* or *ugly;* (Ṣ, O;) or *devoid of beauty.* (L.) One says, أَنَا أَسْتَسْمِجُ فِعْلَكَ [*I reckon,* or *esteem, thy deed foul,* or *unseemly*]. (A, TA.)

سَمْجٌ, (Ṣ, O, Ḳ,) like ضَخْمٌ from ضَخُمَ, (Ṣ, O,) and ▼ سَمِجٌ, (Ṣ, A, O, Mṣb, Ḳ,) like خَشِنٌ (Ṣ, A, O, Mṣb) from خَشُنَ, (Ṣ, O,) and ▼ سَمِيجٌ, (Ṣ, A, O, Ḳ,) like قَبِيحٌ (Ṣ, A, O) from قَبُحَ, (Ṣ, O,) *Foul, unseemly,* or *ugly;* (Ṣ, A, O, Mṣb,* Ḳ;) or *devoid of beauty:* (A, L, Mṣb:) pl. سِمَاجٌ, (Ṣ, O, Ḳ,) [of سَمْجٌ,] like ضِخَامٌ [pl. of ضَخْمٌ, or of سَمِيجٌ, like قِبَاحٌ pl. of قَبِيحٌ], applied to a number of men, (Ṣ, O,) and, so applied, سَمَاجَى, [of سَمِجٌ, like حَذَارَى pl. of حَذِرٌ, or of سَمِيجٌ, like قَبَاحَى pl. of قَبِيحٌ,] (IF, O, L,) and سَمْجَاءُ, [of سَمِيجٌ,] and سَمِيجُونَ: (L:) ▼ سَمِيجٌ is of the dial. of Hudheyl; and is said by some to signify *possessing no good,* or *no good things.* (L.) One says also سَمِيجٌ ▼ لَمِيجٌ and سَمِجٌ ▼ لَمِجٌ and سَمْجٌ لَمْجٌ, using the latter word in each case as an imitative sequent [for the purpose of corroboration]. (AO, Ṣ and Ḳ in art. لمج, q. v.) —— سَمْجٌ applied to milk signifies *Greasy, and bad,* or *foul, in flavour;* as also ▼ سَمِيجٌ; (Ṣ, O, Ḳ;) and so سَمْهَجٌ and سَمَلَّجٌ: (Ṣ:) or *having no flavour;* (L;) or so ▼ سَمِيجٌ: (Mṣb:) and *bad,* or *foul, in odour.* (L.)

سَمِجٌ: see the next preceding paragraph, in three places.

سَمِيجٌ: see سَمْجٌ, in four places.

سمح

1. سَمَحَ, (Ṣ, Mṣb, Ḳ,) aor. ـَ, (Mṣb, Ḳ,) inf. n. سَمْحٌ and سَمَاحَةٌ and سُمُوحٌ and سُمُوحَةٌ and سَمَاحٌ and سِمَاحٌ, (Ḳ,) *He was,* or *became, liberal, bountiful, munificent,* or *generous;* (Ṣ,* Mṣb,* Ḳ;) as also ▼ أَسْمَحَ: (Mṣb, Ḳ:) but the unaugmented verb commonly known, but faultily omitted in the Ḳ, is سَمُحَ, aor. ـُ; and this is the only one mentioned by IḲṭṭ and IḲooṭ and a number of other authors: سَمُحَ, like كَرُمَ, means *he became of the people of* السَّمَاحَة [i. e. *liberality,* &c.]: (MF:) [but] سَمَحَ and ▼ أَسْمَحَ both signify as above; *he was, or became, liberal,* &c.; and *he gave from a motive of generosity and liberality:* this is the correct explanation of both; though some say that the former only is used in this sense; and the latter, in relation to compliance and submissiveness. (L.) You say, سَمَحَ بِهِ, (Ṣ, A, Mṣb,) aor. ـَ, inf. n. سَمَاحٌ and سَمَاحَةٌ (Ṣ,* A,* Mṣb) and سُمُوحٌ, (Mṣb,) *He was liberal, bountiful, munificent,* or *generous, with it;* (Ṣ, A, Mṣb;) and *gave it;* and *complied therein with that which was desired of him;* as also ▼ أَسْمَحَ. (Mṣb.) [And سَمَحَ لَهُ *He was liberal,* &c., *to him;* as also ▼ أَسْمَحَ; whence,] God is represented, in a trad., as saying, أَسْمِحُوا ▼ لِعَبْدِى كَإِسْمَاحِهِ إِلَى عِبَادِى *Be ye liberal, &c., to my servant,* [meaning Mohammad,] *like as he is liberal, &c., to my servants.* (L.) And سَمَحَ لِى, (Ṣ,) or لَهُ, (A,) *He gave* (Ṣ, A) *to me,* (Ṣ,) or *to him:* (A:) and ▼ سَامَحَهُ بِكَذَا *he gave him such a thing.* (Mṣb.) And سَمَحَ لِى بِذٰلِكَ, and ▼ أَسْمَحَ, and ▼ سَامَحَ, *He complied with my desire in that thing.* (L: see also a similar phrase below.) —— سَمَحَتْ, said of a she-camel, means *She became submissive, and went quickly:* (L:) and ▼ أَسْمَحَتْ said of a beast (دَابَّة), *it became gentle and submissive after being refractory:* (L, Ḳ:*) and in like manner ▼ أَسْمَحَ; (A;) and ▼ سَمَّحَ, inf. n. تَسْمِيحٌ; (L;) said of a camel: (A, L:) or تَسْمِيحٌ signifies the *going an easy pace:* (Ṣ, L, Ḳ:) and the *going quickly:* (L, Ḳ:) or (so in the L, but in the Ḳ "and") the act of *fleeing.* (L, Ḳ.) And ▼ أَسْمَحَ *It became easy and submissive.* (L.) You say, ▼ أَسْمَحَتْ قَرُونَتُهُ, (Ṣ, A, Ḳ,) and قَرِينَتُهُ, as also ▼ سَامَحَتْ, (L,) *His mind became submissive,* (Ṣ, A, L, Ḳ,) لِذٰلِكَ الأَمْرِ *to that thing.* (L.) —— سَمَحَ, inf. n. سَمَاحٌ; (L;) and ▼ سَمَّحَ, (Mgh, L,) inf. n. تَسْمِيحٌ; (L, Ḳ;) and ▼ سَامَحَ, (Mgh, L,) inf. n. مُسَامَحَةٌ; (Ṣ, A, L, Ḳ;) and ▼ أَسْمَحَ, (Mgh,) and ▼ تَسَمَّحَ; (L;) also signify *He acted in an easy,* or *a gentle, manner;* (Ṣ, A, Mgh, L, Ḳ;) and *he made easy,* or *facilitated;* (L;) فِى أَمْرٍ *in an affair:* (Mgh, L:) and ▼ مُسَامَحَةٌ signifies the *acting in an easy,* or *a gentle, manner* in a contest in thrusting, or piercing, with spears or the like, and smiting with swords, and running. (L.) It is said in a well-known trad., السَّمَاحُ رَبَاحٌ *The acting in an easy,* or *a gentle, manner, in affairs, is a means of gain,* or *profit, to the performer thereof.* (L.) And you say, ▼ سَامَحَهُ فِى الأَمْرِ *He acted in an easy,* or *a gentle, manner with him.* (TḲ.) And سَمَحَ لَهُ and بِهِ, and ▼ أَسْمَحَ, *He made* [a thing] *easy to him.* (L.) And اِسْمَحْ يُسْمَحْ لَكَ (Meyd, Mgh, L) and بِكَ, (L,) and ▼ أَسْمِحْ يُسْمَحْ لَكَ (Meyd, L) and بِكَ, (L,) a trad., (Mgh, L,) meaning *Facilitate thou, and facilitation shall be rendered to thee:* (Aṣ, Sh, L:) or *act thou in an easy,* or *a gentle, manner, and easy,* or *gentle, treatment, shall be rendered to thee:* (Mgh:) or *be thou compliant, and compliance shall be rendered to thee.* (Meyd.) And سَمَحَ لَهُ بِحَاجَتِهِ, and ▼ أَسْمَحَ, *He made easy to him the object of his want.* (IAạr, L: see also a similar phrase above.) —— سَمَاحَةٌ (A, TA) and سُمُوحَةٌ, (TA,) [app. inf. ns. of which the verb is سَمُحَ,] in a branch, or rod, signify ‡ The *being even and smooth, without any knots* [or *inequality of thickness:* see سَمْحٌ]. (A, TA.)

2: see 1, in two places. —— تَسْمِيحُ الرُّمْحِ means † *The straightening,* or *making even, of the spear,* (Ṣ, Ḳ, TA,) *so as to render it smooth.* (TA. [See 1, last sentence.])

3: see 1, in six places.

4: see 1, in all but four sentences.

5: see 1, in the latter half of the paragraph: —— and see also the paragraph here following, in two places.

6. تَسَامَحُوا *They acted in an easy, or a gentle, manner, one with another.* (Ṣ, A, Ḳ.) — [Hence] تَسَامُحٌ [as a conventional term in lexicology, or in relation to language,] is [*A careless, or defective, manner of expression,*] *when the meaning of a sentence is not known, and, in order to its being understood, requires another word or phrase to be supplied:* (KT:) [or the *using a careless mode of expression, relying upon the understanding of the reader* or *hearer;* as also ▼ تَسَمُّحٌ: or] *a deficiency in what a speaker says, relying upon* [*the knowledge of*] *the person addressed.* (Marginal note in a copy of the KT, subsigned سمع [app. to denote that the authority is Isma'eel Ḥaḳḳee].) [See also تَسَاهُلٌ, which is often used as though it were syn. with تَسَامُحٌ.] — The primary meaning of تَسَامُحٌ and ▼ تَسَمُّحٌ is [said to be] The *being wide,* or *ample:* whence the phrase فِى الحَقِّ مُسْمَحٌ [expl. below]. (Mṣb.)

7. انسمح [app. syn. with أَسْمَحَ, or perhaps a mistranscription for the latter word]: see اِسْتَمَحَ.

سَمْحٌ (T, Ṣ, A, Mgh, Mṣb, Ḳ) and ▼ سَمِحٌ, of which the former is a contraction, (Mṣb,) [but which is seldom used,] as also ▼ سَمِيحٌ and [in an intensive sense] ▼ مِسْمَحٌ (T, M, TA) and ▼ مِسْمَاحٌ (T, Ṣ,* M, A,* Ḳ,* TA) [and ▼ سَمُوحٌ, occurring in the Ḳ voce نَعُوسٌ, the last three fem. as well as masc.], *Liberal, bountiful, munificent,* or *generous:* (T, Ṣ, M, A, Mgh, Mṣb, Ḳ, TA:) fem. سَمْحَةٌ: (T, Ṣ, M, A, Ḳ:) pl. سِمَاحٌ, (Th, T, Ṣ, M, A, Mṣb, Ḳ,) applied to women (Th, Ṣ, Mṣb, Ḳ) only, (Th, Ṣ, Ḳ,) or to men and to women, (T, M, TA,) and سُمَحَاءُ, (T, Ṣ, M, A, Mṣb, Ḳ,) applied to a party of people, (Ṣ, A,) [i. e.] to men and to women, (T, M, TA,) as though pl. of سَمِيحٌ, (Ṣ, Ḳ,) and مَسَامِيحُ, (T, Ṣ, M, A, Ḳ,) applied to men and to women, (T, M, A,*) pl. of مِسْمَاحٌ, (A,) or as though pl. of مِسْمَاحٌ. (Ṣ, Ḳ.) The dim. of سَمْحٌ is ▼ سُمَيْحٌ and ▼ سُمَيِّحٌ; (Ḳ;) but the latter is by some disallowed. (TA.) You say also, فُلَانٌ سَمْحٌ لَمْحٌ and سَمِيحٌ ▼ لَمِيحٌ [app. meaning *Such a one is very liberal, &c.;* for in each case the latter epithet is probably an imitative sequent, and therefore a corroborative]. (L.) — دَابَّةٌ سَمْحَةٌ [*A beast that is submissive,* or *easy,* or *gentle:* and probably also *quick:* see 1]. (A, voce جَمْحَةٌ, q. v.) — [Hence, app.,] سَمْحَةٌ is the name of *A mare of Jaafar the son of Aboo-Ṭálib.* (Ḳ. [See also سَبْحَةٌ.]) — And أُمُّ سَمْحَةَ *The she-goat.* (T in art. امر.) — And قَوْسٌ سَمْحَةٌ † *A pliant bow.* (Ḳ,* TA.) — And عُودٌ سَمْحٌ ‡ *A branch,* or *rod, that is even and smooth,* (A,* Mṣb,* TA,) *without any knot:* (A, Ḳ, TA:) or *of even growth, so that what is between its two extremities is not more slender than its two extremities or than one of them.* (AḤn, TA.) One says also سَاجَةٌ سَمْحَةٌ ‡ [*An oblong squared piece,* or *a board* or *tablet, of the wood of the* سَاج (q. v.), *that is even and smooth*]. (TA.) — And مِلَّةٌ سَمْحَةٌ † *A religion in which is no straitness* (Ḳ, TA) *nor difficulty.* (TA.) — The saying of 'Omar Ibn-'Abd-El-'Azeez أَذِّنْ أَذَانًا سَمْحًا means † [*Recite thou a call to prayer*] *without a prolonging of the voice, and trilling,* and *without modulation.* (Mgh.)

سَمِحٌ: see the next preceding paragraph.

سِمَاخٌ *Tents* (بُيُوتٌ) *made of skins.* (Ibn-El-Faraj, Ḳ.)

سَمُوحٌ: see سَمْحٌ, first sentence.

سَمِيحٌ: see سَمْحٌ, in two places.

سُمَيْحٌ and سُمَيِّحٌ dims. of سَمْحٌ, q. v. (Ḳ.)

أَسْمَحُ [*More,* and *most, liberal, bountiful, munificent,* or *generous*]. See an ex. voce أَرْفَقُ.

عَلَيْكَ بِالحَقِّ فَإِنَّ فِيهِ لَمَسْمَحًا, (A, Mṣb,* Ḳ,*) *Keep thou to the truth, for verily in it is ample scope* for avoiding falsity; expl. by مُتَّسَعًا, (A, Mṣb, Ḳ,) and مَنْدُوحَةً عَنِ البَاطِلِ. (A, Mṣb.)

مِسْمَحٌ: } see سَمْحٌ, first sentence.
مِسْمَاحٌ: }

سمحج

سَمْحَجٌ, applied to a she-ass and to a mare, (Ṣ, O, Ḳ,) but not to a male, (AO, Ṣ, O,) and sometimes to a she-camel, (TA,) *Long in the back;* (Ṣ, O, Ḳ;) as also ▼ سِمْحَاجٌ (O, Ḳ) and ▼ سَمْحُوجٌ: (O:) [see an ex. in a verse cited voce شَغَبَ:] pl. of the last but one, or of the last, not of the first as it is asserted to be by A'Obeyd and by Kr, سَمَاحِيجُ: (TA:) and the first, a mare *slender in the body,* or *lean in the belly, but thick in the part between the shoulder and shoulder-blade,* (O, Ḳ, TA,) *having thick and strong flesh:* (TA:) applied only to females. (Ḳ.) — Also, applied to a bow, *Long.* (O, Ḳ.)

سَمْحَجَةٌ *Length* in anything. (T, O, Ḳ.)

سِمْحَاجٌ: see سَمْحَجٌ.

سَمْحُوجٌ: see سَمْحَجٌ. — Also *Tall and hateful* or *hated;* (O, Ḳ;) applied in this sense to a man. (O.)

سمحق

سِمْحَاقٌ [The *pericranium;* i. e.] the *thin skin,* (T, Mgh, Mṣb,) or *thin integument,* (Ṣ, Mgh, Ḳ,) *above the skull:* (T, Ṣ, Mgh, Mṣb, Ḳ:) and *any thin skin resembling that;* (Mṣb;) or [the *periosteum* of any bone; i. e.] the *skin that is between the bone and the flesh, above the bone and beneath the flesh;* every bone having what is thus termed: (TA:) [pl. سَمَاحِيقُ. — Hence,] one says, عَلَى ثَرْبِ الشَّاةِ سَمَاحِيقُ مِنْ شَحْمٍ, (Ṣ, Ḳ, TA,) i. e. ‡ [*Upon the fat that covers the stomach and bowels of the sheep* or *goat is* or *are*] *a thin integument* [or *thin integuments of fat*]. (TA.) — And سَمَاحِيقُ السَّمَآءِ ‡ *The* [*strata* or] *thin portions of cloud.* (Ṣ, Ḳ, TA.) — سِمْحَاقٌ also signifies [The *cicatrix which is*] the *mark of circumcision.* (TA.) — And *A wound by which the head is broken* (شَجَّةٌ [q. v.]) *reaching to the thin skin,* or *integument, thus called.* (T, Ṣ, Mṣb, Ḳ.)

سَمْحُوقٌ *Tall;* applied to a palm-tree; (Ṣ, O, Ḳ;) as also سُمْحُوقٌ: (Ṣ:) or *tall and thin:* (Lth, TA:) not known to Az on any other authority than that of Lth. (TA.)

[J held the م in each of these words, as he says, to be augmentative; and has therefore mentioned them in art. سحق.]

سمد

1. سَمَدَ, (Ṣ, M, &c.,) aor. ـُ, (M, L,) inf. n. سُمُودٌ, *He* (a man, IAạr) *was,* or *became, high,* or *elevated.* (IAạr, Ṣ, M, L, Ḳ. [عَلَاءٌ in the CḲ is a mistake for عَلَا.]) — *He raised his head;* (L; [and the same is implied in the Ṣ; see سَامِدٌ;]) and so سَمَّدَ: (M, L:) [and] *he raised his head in pride.* (Ṣ, L, Ḳ.) And in the former sense it is said of a camel, in his going along. (Bḍ in liii. 61.) — Also *He* (a man) *stood, raising his head, and with his breast erect;* like as the stallion [camel] does when excited by lust: (A:) [for] it is said of a stallion [camel] when thus excited. (L.) — And hence, (A,) ‡ *He sang:* (M, A, L:) because the singer raises his head and erects his breast: (A:) but Th says that this is rare: (M:) accord. to I'Ab, سُمُودٌ signifies the act of *singing* in the dial. of Ḥimyer. (L.) — Also, (M, Ḳ,) aor. as above, (TA,) and so the inf. n., (Ṣ, M,) † *He diverted himself, sported,* or *played.* (Ṣ, M, Ḳ, TA. [For لَهِىَ in the CḲ, I read لَهَا, as in the M, and in MS. copies of the Ḳ, and in the TA; and agreeably with the Ṣ, in which the inf. n. is expl. as syn. with لَهْوٌ.]) — *He was,* or *became, negligent, inattentive, inadvertent, inconsiderate,* or *heedless;* and *went away from,* or *relinquished,* or *left, a thing.* (L.) — *He was,* or *became, confounded, perplexed,* or *amazed, and unable to see his right course;* or *affected with wonder;* or *cut short,* or *silent, being confounded,* or *perplexed, and unable to see his right course;* syn. بُهِتَ: inf. n. as above: (M:) [or] *he stood confounded,* or *perplexed, and unable to see his right course;* syn. قَامَ مُتَحَيِّرًا. (Ḳ. [After this explanation and لَهَا immediately following it, it is said in the Ḳ, وَالسُّمُودُ يَكُونُ حُزْنًا وَسُرُورًا: meaning that it is by reason of grieving, or mourning, as signifying the "standing confounded" &c.; and by reason of rejoicing, or being happy, as signifying the "diverting oneself" &c. See as an ex. of its usage in a case of grief the verses which I have cited at the close of the first paragraph of art. رود, and which are cited in the present art. in the L and TA.]) — Also *He kept constantly,* or *continually,* (M, L,) *to an affair,* (M,) or *upon the ground,* or *in the land.* (L.) — *He strove, laboured,* or *exerted himself,* or *he wearied himself, in work,* (Ḳ, TA,) and *in journeying.* (TA.) And سَمَدَتِ الإِبِلُ فِى سَيْرِهَا (Ṣ, M, Ḳ) (Ṣ,) aor. and inf. n. as above, (M,) *The camels strove, laboured,* or *exerted themselves, in their journeying:* (Ṣ, Ḳ:) or *knew not fatigue,* or *weariness.* (M.) [See also سَمَّدَ, (which is likewise, perhaps,

an inf. n. of the same verb,) below.] — سَمَدَهُ, inf. n. سَمْدٌ, i. q. قَصَدَهُ [*He tended, repaired, betook himself*, or *directed himself* or *his course* or *aim, to*, or *towards, him*, or *it*; or *endeavoured to reach*, or *attain*, or *obtain, him*, or *it*; &c.]; like صَمَدَهُ. (M.) — And سَمَدَ الأَرْضَ, inf. n. سَمْدٌ, *He made the land*, or *ground, plain*, or *smooth*, or *soft*. (M.)

2. سَمَّدَهُ, (M, TA,) inf. n. تَسْمِيدٌ, (TA,) † *He diverted him*: (M, TA:) [and in like manner, ↓ اسمدهُ; for] one says to a slave-songstress, أَسْمِدِينَا, [in one of my copies of the Ṣ, erroneously, اِسْمُدِينَا,] meaning *Divert thou us by singing*. (Ṣ, O, L, TA.) — سَمَّدَ الأَرْضَ, (M, Mṣb, Ḳ,) inf. n. as above, (Ṣ, Mṣb, Ḳ,) *He manured the land with* سَمَاد [q. v.]: (Ṣ, Mṣb, Ḳ:) *he dunged*, or *manured, the land*; syn. زَبَّلَهَا. (M. [So in a copy of the M: in the TA زبلها, without teshdeed; and thus only, I believe, correctly; though it is commonly pronounced with teshdeed in the present day.]) — سَمَّدَ شَعْرَهُ, (M,) or الشَّعْرَ, (Ḳ,) inf. n. as above, (TA,) *He removed utterly his hair*, or *the hair*; (M, Ḳ, TA;) *taking the whole of it* [*in shaving*]: a dial. var. of سبّد. (TA.) تَسْمِيدُ الرَّأْسِ is *The removing utterly the hair of the head* [*by shaving*]: a dial. var. of تَسْبِيدٌ. (Ṣ.) — And تَسْمِيدٌ is also used [alone, the objective complement being app. meant to be understood,] as meaning The *leaving off*, or *neglecting, the anointing of oneself* [or *of one's hair*], *and washing*: and so تَسْبِيدٌ. (A'Obeyd, TA in art. سبد.)

4: see 2, first sentence.

9: see Q. Q. 4, in two places.

11: see what next follows.

Q. Q. 4. اِسْمَأَدَّ, (Ṣ, M, L,) inf. n. اِسْمِئْدَادٌ, (Ṣ,) *He*, or *it, became swollen*: (M, L:) or *became much swollen*: (AZ, M, L:) or *he* (a man) *became swollen with anger*; (Ṣ, L;) or so ↓ اِسْمَادَّ, inf. n. اِسْمِيدَادٌ; and ↓ اِسْمَدَّ, inf. n. اِسْمِدَادٌ. (Ḳ.) One says, اسمأدّت يَدُهُ *His arm*, or *hand, became swollen*: and اسمأدّت رِجْلُهَا *Her leg*, or *foot, became inflated and swollen*. (L, TA.) — Also, said of anything, *It went*, or *passed, away*: or *perished*; and so ↓ اسمدّ. (L, TA.) And اسمأدّ مِنَ الغَضَبِ *He perished by reason of anger*. (L.)

سَمْدٌ *Continuing*, or *unceasing, journeying*. (M, L.) [Perhaps an inf. n.: see سَمَدَتِ الإِبِلُ, and what next precedes it, in the latter part of the first paragraph.] — هُوَ لَكَ سَمْدًا, (Ḳ, TA,) or ↓ سَمَدًا, (M,) [in my copy of the Mgh سمدا, and in the O سَمدًا,] *He*, or *it, is thine ever*, or *for ever*; syn. سَرْمَدًا, (Th, M, Mgh, O, Ḳ,) and أَبَدًا. (Th, M, Mgh.) And لَا أَفْعَلُ ذٰلِكَ سَمْدًا, or ↓ سَمَدًا, (M,) *I will not do that ever*. (M, TA.)

سَمَدًا: see the next preceding paragraph, in two places.

سَمَادٌ *A compost*, or *manure, consisting of* سِرْجِين, (Ṣ, Mgh, Mṣb,) or سِرْقِين, (Ḳ,) [both meaning *dung of beasts, such as horses, camels, sheep and goats, wild oxen, and the like*,] *with ashes*, (Ṣ, Ḳ,) or *with earth* or *dust*: (Mgh, Mṣb:) or *a manure consisting of strong earth*. (M.)

سَمِيدٌ i. q. حُوَّارَى (A, Ḳ) [app. as meaning *White*, or *whitened, flour*: but said in the TḲ to mean *fine bread*]: accord. to Kr, i. q. طَعَام [app. as meaning *wheat*]; and said by him to be with the unpointed د: (Ḳ:) but more chastely, (Ḳ,) and better known, (TA,) with ذ. (Ḳ, TA.) [In the present day, applied to *Semoulia*; *a kind of paste made of very fine wheat-flour, reduced to small grains*. See also إِسْمِيذٌ, below.]

سَامِدٌ Any [man or animal] *raising his head* [in pride or otherwise]. (Ṣ, M, L.) — A man *standing*: (IAạr; and so in a copy of the Ṣ:) or *standing, raising his head, and with his breast erect*; (A, IAth;) as the stallion [camel] does when excited by lust. (A.) — [And hence, as is indicated in the A, (see 1,)] † *A singer*; or *singing*. (M, L; and so in two copies of the Ṣ.) And the latter is said to be the meaning of the pl. in the Ḳur liii. 61. (M, L.) — [Hence also,] *Behaving proudly*. (I'Ab in explanation of the pl. in the Ḳur liii. 61; and IAạr.) — *Diverting himself*; *playing*; or *sporting*. (IAạr, Ṣ, M; and Bḍ in liii. 61,) — *Negligent, inattentive, inadvertent, inconsiderate*, or *heedless*. (Lth, IAạr A.) Thus the pl. is said by Lth to mean in the Ḳur liii. 61. (TA.) — *Standing in a state of confusion, perplexity*, or *amazement*: (Mgh:) and so the pl. is said to mean in the Ḳur liii. 61: (TA:) or *confounded, perplexed*, or *amazed, by reason of inordinate exultation*. (IAạr.) — And *Silent*. (So in a copy of the Ṣ.) — And *Grieving*, or *mourning, and lowly, humble*, or *submissive*. (So, too, in a copy of the Ṣ.) — In the saying of Ru-beh, (Ḳ,) describing camels, (TA,)

سَوَامِدُ اللَّيْلِ خِفَافُ الأَزْوَادْ

the meaning is, *Continuing journeying*, (Ḳ,) or *striving, labouring*, or *exerting themselves*, or *wearying themselves*, [*during the night*,] *having no fodder in their bellies*: (L:) F says that J has erred in saying that the meaning is, "having no fodder in their bellies:" but this is the explanation of the words خفاف الازواد, as IM and others have expressly stated; and this necessarily indicates that سوامد has the meaning assigned to it in the Ḳ; so that no error is attributable to J in this case: or, as some say, خفاف الازواد means *not having upon their backs* [*much*] *provision* for the riders. (TA.) — سَامِدٌ as an epithet applied to a وَطْب [or skin in which milk is put] means ‡ *Full*, [*so as to be*] *standing upright*. (A, TA.)

إِسْمِيذٌ *What is called in Persian* سِمِيذ [app. a mistranscription for شَمِيذ, i. e. *white bread*]; an arabicized word: [so says ISd; and he adds,] I know not whether it be the same as سَمِيذ expl. by Kr as signifying طَعَام, or not. (M.)

مِسْمَدٌ i. q. زِبِّيل [i. e. *A basket of palm-leaves*; probably one *used for carrying* سَمَاد, or *manure*]: so says Lḥ; adding that one should not say مِسْمَدَةٌ. (M.)

سمدر

Q. 4, accord. to the M and Ḳ, اِسْمَدَرَّ: and سُمْدُورٌ and سَمَادِيرُ: and مُسْمَدِرٌّ: see art. سدر.

سمدع

سَمَيْدَعٌ, (Ṣ, Ḳ, &c.,) of the measure فَعَيْلَلٌ, (Sb, TA,) so accord. to the grammarians, but Aboo-Usámeh Junádeh El-Azdee says that it is of the measure فَمَيْعَل, from سَدَعَ as syn. with ذَبَحَ and بَسَطَ, (Ṣgh, TA,) pronounced by the vulgar سُمَيْدَع, with ḍamm to the س, (IDrst, TA,) which is a mistake, (Th, IDrst, Ṣ, Ḳ, &c.,) for there is not in the language of the Arabs a noun of the measure فُعَيْلَل, (IDrst, TA,) *A lord, master, chief, prince*, or *man of rank* or *quality*; ('Eyn, Ṣ, O, Ḳ;) to which Et-Teiyánee adds, from Aṣ, on the authority of Munteji' Ibn-Nebhán, (TA,) *of easy nature* or *disposition, generous, and very hospitable*, or *in whose vicinity his companion has power* or *authority* or *dignity, not being harmed nor inconvenienced*; (Ṣ, Ḳ, TA;) and thus expl. by AHát also; (TA;) *generous*; *noble*, or *elevated in rank*; *liberal, bountiful*, or *munificent*: (O, Ḳ:) and also (Ḳ) *courageous*: (Lth, Ḳ:) and *goodly, and stout, bulky*, or *corpulent*: (AZ, Et-Teiyánee:) pl. سَمَادِعُ. (IJ.) — The *lion*. (Ibn-Ed-Dahhán, T, Ṣ, O.) — And hence, [accord. to SM, but the reverse I think more probable,] ‡ *A chief*, or *person of authority*. (TA.) — The *wolf*; (En-Naḍr, Ḳ;) because of his swiftness. (En-Naḍr.) — And hence, (TA,) † A man *active, agile*, or *prompt, in accomplishing his wants*. (Ḳ, TA.) — And *A sword*. (Ḳ.)

سمذ

سَمِيذٌ i. q. سَمِيدٌ [q. v.]; (Ḳ:) [said to be] more chaste than the latter: (Ḳ in art. سمد:) [but] accord. to Kr, it is with the unpointed د. (M in that art.)

سمر

1. سَمَرَ, (Ṣ, M, Ḳ,) aor. ـُ, (Ṣ, M,) inf. n. سَمْرٌ and سُمُورٌ, (M, Ḳ,) *He held a conversation*, or *discourse, by night*: (Ṣ:) or *he waked*; *continued awake*; *did not sleep*: (M, Ḳ:) and ↓ اسمر may signify the same; or may be of the same class as أَهْزَلَ and أَسْمَنَ, and thus signify *he had*, or *came to have, a* سَمَر [or *conversation*, or *discourse, by night*]. (M.) [See also 3.] — سَمَرَتِ المَاشِيَةُ, aor. ـُ, inf. n. سُمُورٌ, † *The cattle pastured by night without a pastor*; or *dispersed themselves by night*: (M, TA:) [or simply *pastured by night*; for] one says, إِنَّ إِبِلَنَا تَسْمُرُ, meaning † *Verily our camels pasture by night*: (TA:) and سَمَرَتِ الإِبِلُ لَيْلَتَهَا كُلَّهَا ‡ *The camels pastured during their night, the whole of it*. (A.) And سَمَرَتِ المَاشِيَةُ النَّبَاتَ † *The cattle pastured upon the herbage*; (M, Ḳ;) aor. as above: (M:) [or *pastured upon the herbage by night*: like as one says,] سَمَرَ الخَمْرَ † *He drank wine*, or *the wine*, (Ḳ, TA,) *by night*: (TA:) and بَاتُوا يَسْمُرُونَ

الخَمْرَ ‡ They passed, or spent, their night drinking wine, or the wine. (A.) — See also سَمِيرٌ, in three places. ═ سَمُرَ, (Ṣ, M, Mṣb, Ḳ,) aor. ـُ ; (Ḳ;) and سَمِرَ, (Ṣ, Ḳ, in a copy of the M سَمَرَ,) aor. ـَ ; inf. n. of each سُمْرَةٌ; (Ḳ;) and ↓ اسمارّ, (Ṣ, M, Ḳ,) inf. n. اِسْمِيرَارٌ; (Ṣ;) He, or it, was, or became, [tawny, brownish, dusky, or dark in complexion or colour; i. e.,] of the colour termed سُمْرَة [expl. below]. (Ṣ, M, Mṣb, Ḳ.) ═ سَمَرَهُ: see 2, first signification. — [Hence,] سَمَرَ عَيْنَهُ i. q. سَمَلَهَا, (M, Ḳ,) which signifies He put out, or blinded, (فَقَأَ,) his eye with a heated iron instrument: (Ṣ and Mṣb in art. سمل:) or he put out, or blinded, (كَحَلَ,) his eye with a مِسْمَار [or nail] (Mgh, Mṣb, TA) of iron (TA) made hot (Mgh, Mṣb, TA) in fire: (Mṣb:) or [simply] he put out, or blinded, his eye; syn. فَقَأَهَا. (Ḳ.) ═ سَمَرَ اللَّبَنَ: ═ and سَمَرَ سَهْمَهُ: see 2.

2. سَمَّرَهُ, (Ṣ, M, Mgh, Mṣb, Ḳ,) inf. n. تَسْمِيرٌ; (Ṣ;) and ↓ سَمَرَهُ, (Ṣ, M, Mgh, &c.,) aor. ـُ (M, Mṣb, Ḳ) and ـِ, (M, Ḳ,) inf. n. سَمْرٌ; (M, Mṣb;) or the former has an intensive signification; (Mṣb;) [He nailed it; i. e.] he made it fast, firm, or strong, (M, Mgh, Ḳ,) with a nail [or nails]; (Ṣ,* M,* Mgh, Mṣb, Ḳ;*) namely, a door [&c.]. (Mgh, Mṣb.) [See also سَرَدَ.] ═ سَمَّرَ اللَّبَنَ, (M, TA,) inf. n. تَسْمِيرٌ; (Ṣ;) and ↓ سَمَرَهُ, (Ḳ, TA,) aor. ـُ ; (TA;) He made the milk thin with water; (Ṣ;) made it to be what is termed سَمَار [q. v.]. (M, Ḳ.) ═ سَمَّرَ, inf. n. as above, is also syn. with شَمَّرَ (Ṣ, M, Ḳ) and أَرْسَلَ. (M, Ḳ.) You say, سَمَّرَ سَهْمَهُ He discharged, or shot, his arrow; (M, TA;) as also ↓ سَمَرَهُ: (Ḳ, TA:) or the former, he discharged it, or shot it, hastily; (Ḳ;) opposed to غَرْقَلَ; for one says, سَمِّرْ فَقَدْ أَخْطَبَكَ الصَّيْدُ [Discharge, or shoot, thine arrow quickly, for the game has become within thy power], and غَرْقِلْ حَتَّى يُخْطِبَكَ [Discharge, or shoot, deliberately, in order that it may become within thy power]. (IAạr, TA.) One says also, سَمَّرَ جَارِيَتَهُ He dismissed his female slave, or let her go free. (Ṣ and M, from a trad.) A'Obeyd says that this is the only instance in which سَمَّرَ, with س, has been heard [in this sense: but several other instances have been mentioned]. (TA.) You also say, سَمَّرَ الإِبِلَ He let the camels go, or left them: and he hastened them; syn. كَمَّشَهَا; as also ↓ أَسْمَرَهَا; originally with ش: (TA:) or he sent them, or left them, to pasture by themselves, without a pastor, by night [which is perhaps the more proper meaning (see 1)] or by day; syn. أَهْمَلَهَا. (M, TA.) And سَمَّرَ السَّفِينَةَ He sent off, or launched forth, the ship; let it go; or let it take its course. (M, TA.)

3. سَامَرَهُ, (M,) inf. n. مُسَامَرَةٌ, (Ṣ, A,) He held a conversation, or discourse, with him by night. (Ṣ, M.) [See also 1, first sentence.]

4: see 1: — and سَمِيرٌ, in four places: ═ and see also 2.

11. اسمارّ: see 1, in the latter half of the paragraph.

سَمَرٌ Conversation, or discourse, by night; (Ṣ, M, Ḳ;) as also مُسَامَرَةٌ. (Ṣ, A.*) It is said in a trad., السَّمَرُ بَعْدَ العِشَآءِ, or, accord. to one relation, السَّمْرُ, Conversation or discourse by night is after nightfall. (TA.) And you say, لَا أَفْعَلُهُ السَّمَرَ وَالقَمَرَ I will not do it as long as men hold conversation or discourse in a night when the moon shines: (Ṣ:) or as long as men hold conversation or discourse by night, and as long as the moon rises: (Lḥ, M:) or ever. (M.) [See also below. The pl., أَسْمَار, is often used as meaning Tales related in the night, for amusement: but this usage is probably post-classical.] — ‡ Conversation, or discourse, by day. (TA.) — A place in which people hold conversation or discourse by night; or in which they wake, or remain awake; (M, Ḳ;) as also ↓ سَامِرٌ; (Ṣ,* M, Ḳ;) which latter is expl. by Lth as signifying a place in which people assemble for conversation or discourse by night. (TA.) — A people's assembling and holding conversation or discourse in the dark. (TA.) — And hence, (TA,) The dark; or darkness. (Aṣ, M, Ḳ, TA.) So in the saying حَلَفَ بِالسَّمَرِ وَالقَمَرِ He swore by the darkness and the moon. (Aṣ.) — Night: (M, Ḳ:) you say, أَتَيْتُهُ سَمَرًا I came to him in the night. (A.) — A night in which there is no moon: hence the saying لَا أَفْعَلُ ذٰلِكَ السَّمَرَ وَالقَمَرَ I will not do that when the moon does not rise nor when it does rise. (Fr.) [See also above.] — The shade of the moon. (M, Ḳ.) — The light of the moon; moonlight; accord. to some, the primary signification; because they used to converse, or discourse, in it. (TA.) — The time of daybreak: you say, طُرِقَ القَوْمُ سَمَرًا The people were come to at daybreak. (AḤn, M.) — See also سَمِيرٌ.

سَمُرٌ A certain kind of tree, (M, Ḳ,) well known; (Ḳ;) i. q. طَلْحٌ [the gum-acacia-tree; acacia, or mimosa, gummifera]; (Mṣb;) or [a species] of the طَلْح, (Ṣ,) of the kind called عِضَاه, (Mgh, Mṣb,) having small leaves, short thorns, and a yellow fruit (بَرَمَة) which men eat: there is no kind of عضاه better in wood: it is transported to the towns and villages, and houses are covered with it: (M:) its produce is [a pod] termed حُبْلَة [q. v.]: (TA in art. حبل:) [the mimosa unguis cati of Forskål (Flora Aegypt. Arab., pp. cxxiii. and 176:)] n. un. سَمُرَةٌ: (M, Mgh, Mṣb, Ḳ:) [in the Ṣ, سَمُر is said to be pl. of سَمُرَة: but it is a coll. gen. n.:] the pl. of سَمُرَة is سَمُرَات, and أَسْمُر, a pl. of pauc., of which the dim. is ↓ أُسَيْمِر. (Ṣ.) It is said in a prov., أَشْبَهَ شَرْجٌ شَرْجًا لَوْ أَنَّ ↓ أُسَيْمِرًا [Sharj would resemble Sharj if a few gum-acacia-trees were found there: Sharj is a certain valley of El-Yemen: for the origin of this prov., see Freytag's Arab. Prov., i. 662]. (Ṣ.) يَا أَصْحَابَ السَّمُرَةِ [O people of the gum-acacia-tree], in a saying of the Prophet, was addressed to the persons meant in the Ḳur xlviii. 18. (Mgh.)

سُمْرَةٌ [A tawny, or brownish, colour, of various shades, like the various hues of wheat; (see أَسْمَر;) duskiness; darkness of complexion or colour;] a certain colour, (Ṣ, Mṣb,) well known, (Mṣb,) between white and black, (M, Ḳ,) in men and in camels and in other things that admit of having it, but in camels the term أُدْمَة is more common, and accord. to IAạr it is in water also; (M;) in men, the same as وُرْقَة [in camels]; (IAạr, TA;) a colour inclining to a faint blackness; (T, TA;) the colour of what is exposed to the sun, of a person of whom what is concealed by the clothes is white: (IAth:) from سَمَر signifying the "shade of the moon." (TA.)

السَّمَرَةُ: see السَّامِرَةُ.

إِبِلٌ سَمُرِيَّةٌ Camels that eat the tree called سَمُر. (AḤn, M, Ḳ.)

سَمَرْمَرَةٌ The [demon called] غُول. (Ṣgh, Ḳ.)

سَمَارٌ Thin milk: (Ṣ:) milk containing much water: (Th, M, Ḳ:) or [diluted] milk of which water composes two thirds: n. un. with ة, signifying some thereof. (M.) — [See also a tropical usage of this word in a prov. cited voce رَبَض.] ═ [In the present day it is also applied to A species of rush, growing in the deserts of Lower and Upper Egypt, of which mats are made for covering the floors of rooms; the juncus spinosus of Forskål, (Flora Aegypt. Arab., p. 75,) who writes its Arabic name "sammar;" the juncus acutus β of Linn.]

سُمُورٌ, applied to a she-camel, (Ḳ, TA,) Swift: (Ḳ:) or generous, excellent, or strong and light, and swift. (TA.)

سَمِيرٌ i. q. ↓ مُسَامِرٌ; (M, A, Ḳ;) i. e. A partner in conversation, or discourse, by night. (TA.) You say, أَنَا سَمِيرُهُ and ↓ مُسَامِرُهُ [I am his partner &c.]. (A.) — Afterwards used unrestrictedly [as signifying † A partner in conversation, or discourse, at any time]. (TA.) — [Golius and Freytag add the meaning of A place of nocturnal confabulation; as from the Ḳ; a sense in which this word is not there found.] — اِبْنُ سَمِيرٍ The night in which is no moon: [contr. of اِبْنُ ثَمِيرٍ:] a poet uses the phrase مَا أَسْمَرَ ↓ اِبْنُ سَمِيرٍ, meaning As long as the moonless night allows the holding conversation, or discourse, in it. (M. [See also another explanation of this phrase in what follows.]) — سَمِيرٌ is also syn. with دَهْرٌ [as meaning Unlimited time, or time without end]; (Lḥ, Ṣ, M, Ḳ;) as also ↓ سَمَرٌ, (Fr, M, Ḳ,) whence the saying فُلَانٌ عِنْدَ فُلَانٍ السَّمَرَ Such a one is with, or at the abode of, such a one ever, or always. (M.) Hence, or because people hold conversation, or discourse, in them, (Ṣ,) اِبْنَا سَمِيرٍ means The night and the day. (Ṣ, M, Ḳ.) You say, لَا آتِيكَ السَّمِيرَ, (Ṣ, Ḳ,) and لَا أَفْعَلُهُ مَا سَمَرَ ↓ اِبْنَا سَمِيرٍ, (M,) and مَا سَمَرَ ↓ اِبْنُ سَمِيرٍ, and مَا سَمَرَ السَّمِيرُ, (M, Ḳ,) and مَا أَسْمَرَ ↓ اِبْنَا سَمِيرٍ, and مَا أَسْمَرَ ↓ اِبْنُ سَمِيرٍ, (Lḥ, M, Ḳ,) and مَا أَسْمَرَ ↓ السَّمِيرُ, (Ḳ,) i. e. [I will not do it, and I will not come to thee,] ever, (Ṣ,) or in all time, (M,) or while night and day alternate. (Ḳ.) And لَا أَفْعَلُهُ سَمِيرَ اللَّيَالِي (Ṣ, M) [I will not do it] to the end of the nights. (M.) — اِبْنَا جَالِسٍ وَسَمِيرٍ is expl. by AHeyth, in his handwriting, as meaning *Two roads that differ, each from the other.* (Az, TA.)

سُمَيْرِيَّةٌ *A certain kind of ships.* (Ṣ.) [سُمَيْرِىٌّ signifies the same, (Golius on the authority of Meyd.,) applied to *A single ship of that kind.*] — IAạr mentions the saying, أَعْطَيْتُهُ سُمَيْرِيَّةً مِنْ دَرَاهِمَ كَأَنَّ الدُّخَانَ يَخْرُجُ مِنْهَا, without explaining it: [ISd says,] I think he meant, [*I gave him*] دَرَاهِمُ سُمْرٌ, i. e. *dusky dirhems, as though smoke were issuing from them* by reason of their duskiness: or *dirhems of which the whiteness was fresh.* (M.)

سَمُّورٌ [The *sable; mustela zibellina,* or *viverra zibellina;*] *a certain beast,* (Mgh, Ḳ,) or *animal,* (Mṣb,) *well known,* (Mgh,) *found in Russia, beyond the country of the Turks, resembling the ichneumon; in some instances of a glossy black; and in some, of the* [*reddish*] *colour termed* شُقْرَة: (Mṣb, TA:) *costly furred garments are made of its skin:* (Ḳ, TA:) pl. سَمَامِيرُ. (Mṣb.) — Also *A* جُبَّة [or *any garment*] *made with its fur.* (TA.)

سَمِيرٌ *A companion of* [or *one who habitually indulges in*] *conversation,* or *discourse, by night.* (M, Ḳ.)

سَامِرٌ A man *holding,* or *who holds, a conversation,* or *discourse, by night:* (Ṣ:) pl. سُمَّارٌ (Ṣ, M, Ḳ) and سُمَّرٌ. (TA.) It is also a quasi-pl. n., (M, Ḳ,) [as such occurring in a verse cited voce مُزْمِرٌ, in art. زمر,] and is syn. [as such] with سُمَّارٌ, signifying persons *holding,* or *who hold, conversation,* or *discourse, by night:* (Ṣ, M:) or persons *waking, continuing awake, not sleeping;* as also ▼ سَامِرَةٌ [a fem. sing., and therefore applicable as an epithet to a broken pl. and to a quasi-pl. n. and to a coll. gen. n.]: (M, Ḳ:) سَامِرٌ is a pl. [or rather quasi-pl. n.] applicable to males and to females: (T, TA:) or it is a sing., and, like other sings., is used as a qualificative of a pl. only when the latter is determinate; as in the phrase تَرَكْتُهُمْ سَامِرًا [*I left them holding a conversation* &c.]. (Lḥ, M.) — Also *A camel pasturing by night.* (TA.) — See also سَمَرٌ.

سَامِرَةٌ: see سَامِرٌ. — السَّامِرَةُ (M, Mṣb, Ḳ) and ▼ السَّمَرَةُ (TA) [*The Samaritans; a people said to be*] *one of the tribes of the Children of Israel;* (M;) or *a sect,* (Mṣb,) or *people,* (Ḳ,) *of the Jews, differing from them* (Mṣb, Ḳ) *in most,* (Mṣb,) or *in some,* (Ḳ,) *of their institutes:* (Mṣb, Ḳ:) Zj says, *they remain to this time in Syria, and are known by the appellation of* ▼ السَّامِرِيُّونَ: (M:) most of them are in the mountain of En-Nábulus: (TA:) ▼ سَامِرِىٌّ is the rel. n. of السَّامِرَةُ. (M, Mṣb, Ḳ.)

سَامِرِىٌّ, and its pl.: see the next preceding paragraph.

أَسْمَرُ [*Tawny,* or *brownish; dusky; dark-complexioned* or *dark-coloured;*] *of the colour termed* سُمْرَة [q. v.]: (Ṣ, M, Ḳ, &c.:) fem سَمْرَاءُ: (Mṣb, &c.:) and pl. سُمْرٌ. (A.) You say بَعِيرٌ أَسْمَرُ *A camel of a white colour inclining to* شُهْبَة [which is *a hue wherein whiteness predominates over blackness*]. (M.) And قَنَاةٌ سَمْرَاءُ [*A tawny spear-shaft*]. (M.) And حِنْطَةٌ سَمْرَاءُ [*Tawny wheat*]. (M.) — [Hence,] السَّمْرَاءُ *Wheat:* (Ṣ, Mṣb, Ḳ:) because of its colour. (Mṣb.) And الأَسْمَرَانِ *Wheat and water:* (AO, Ṣ, Ḳ:) or *water and the spear.* (Ṣ, Ḳ.) — الأَسْمَرُ, also, signifies *Milk:* (M:) or *milk of the gazelle:* (IAạr, M, Ḳ:) app. because of its colour. (M.) — And [for the same reason] السَّمْرَاءُ signifies also *Coarse flour,* or *flour of the third quality, full of bran;* syn. خُشْكَار. (Ḳ.) You say خُبْزُ السَّمْرَاءِ *Bread made of such flour.* (L in art. خرج.) — And The [*kind of milking-vessel called*] عُلْبَة. (Ṣgh, Ḳ.) — And عَامٌ أَسْمَرُ † *A year of drought, in which is no rain.* (M.)

أُسَيْمِرُ dim. of أَسْمَرُ: see سَمَرٌ, in two places.

مِسْمَارٌ *A nail; a pin,* or *peg, of iron;* (Mgh;) *a certain thing of iron;* (Ṣ, Ḳ;) *a thing with which one makes fast, firm,* or *strong:* (M, Ḳ:) pl. مَسَامِيرُ. (Ṣ, Mṣb, Ḳ.) — Also, (Ḳ, TA,) or مِسْمَارُ إِبِلٍ, (A, O,) ‡ *A good manager of camels;* (A, O, Ḳ, TA;) *a skilful, good pastor thereof.* (A.)

مُسَمَّرٌ *Nailed; made fast, firm,* or *strong, with a nail* [or *nails*]. (Ṣ,* Mgh.) — † A man, (TA,) *having little flesh, strongly knit in the bones and sinews.* (Ḳ, TA.) — And, with ة, ‡ A woman, (M,) or girl, or young woman, (A, O, Ḳ,) *compact,* or *firm, in body,* (M, A, O, Ḳ,) *not flabby in flesh.* (M, O, Ḳ.) — عَيْشٌ مُسَمَّرٌ ‡ *A turbid life:* (M, O,* Ḳ,* TA:) from سَمَارٌ applied to milk. (M, TA.)

مُسَامِرٌ: see سَمِيرٌ, in two places.

سمرج

Q. 1. سَمْرَجَةٌ [inf. n. of سَمْرَجَ] The *collecting of the* [*tax called*] خَرَاج: (Ibn-'Abbád, O:) [and the *giving,* or *paying, thereof:* for] one says, سَمْرِجْ لَهُ, meaning *Give thou to him* [*the tax so called*]. (ISh, O, Ḳ. [It seems to be intentionally indicated in the O and Ḳ, by what immediately precedes the explanation of this phrase, which explanation is أَعْطِهِ, that الخَرَاجَ is to be understood after it.])

سمرج [written without any syll. signs, and therefore probably سَمْرَجٌ,] sing. of سَمَارِجُ, (TA,) which signifies *Even,* or *plain, places* [or *tracts*] *of land.* (T,* Ibn-'Abbád, O, TA.*)

سَمْرَجٌ and ▼ سَمْرَجَةٌ, (Ṣ, O, Ḳ,) each a Pers. word arabicized, (Ṣ, O,) [or rather a compound of the Pers. سه "three" and the Arabic مَرَّة for مَرَّةٌ "a time,"] The *levying of the* [*tax called*] خَرَاج *at three several times* [or *instalments*]: (Ṣ, O, Ḳ:) or the *name of the day on which payment of the* خَرَاج *is received;* (Ḳ;) thus the former word is expl. by ISh; (O;) the *day of the collecting of the* خراج; (Ibn-'Abbád, ISd, O, TA;) *a day when the foreigners,* or *Persians,* (العَجَم) *levy the* خراج *at three several times* [or *instalments*]: also mentioned as written with ش. (TA.)

سَمْرَجَةٌ: see the next preceding parapraph.

سمس

سَمَاسٌ: see art. سمو.

سمسر

Q. 1. سَمْسَرَ, inf. n. سَمْسَرَةٌ, *He acted as a* سِمْسَار [q. v.]. (Ḳ.)

سِمْسَارٌ *A broker;* or *one who acts as an intermediary between the seller and the buyer,* (Lth, Mgh, Ḳ,) *for effecting the sale; whom people call* دَلَّال, because he directs the purchaser to the merchandise, and the seller to the price: (TA:) pl. سَمَاسِرَةٌ: (Mgh, Ḳ:) a Pers. word, arabicized: (Lth, Mgh:) or *one who sells wheat to the people:* (M, TA:) or (TA, in the Ḳ "and") the *possessor of a thing:* (Ḳ:) or (TA, in the Ḳ "and") *one who has the care of a thing.* (Ḳ.) — ‡ *A messenger,* or *mediator,* (سَفِير,) *between two lovers* or *friends.* (Ḳ.) — سِمْسَارُ الأَرْضِ ‡ *He who is acquainted with the land,* or *country;* (Ḳ;) *an acute scrutinizer of its circumstances:* (TA:) fem. with ة. (Ḳ.) — هُوَ ابْنُ سِمْسَارِهَا [app. means † *He is the careful and skilful manager of it*]. (Fr, TA voce جلس.)

سمط

1. سَمَطَهُ, and ـِ; and ـُ, (Ṣ, M, Mṣb, Ḳ,) inf. n. سَمْطٌ, (Ṣ, M, Mṣb,) namely, a kid, (Ṣ, M, Mṣb, Ḳ,) and a lamb, (M,) *He removed its hair,* (Mṣb,) or *wool,* (Ḳ,) or *cleansed it of the hair,* [or *wool,*] (Ṣ,) *by means of hot water;* (Ṣ, Mṣb, Ḳ;) in order to roast it; (Ṣ;) or it is generally done for this purpose: (TA:) or *he plucked from it the* [*hair,* or] *wool, after putting it into hot water.* (A.) — [And *It scalded it:* for] you say, of boiling water, يَسْمُطُ الشَّىْءَ [*it scalds the thing*]. (TA.) — سَمَطَهُ, (M, Ḳ,) inf. n. as above, (M,) also signifies *He hung it; suspended it;* namely, a thing; (M, Ḳ;) as also ▼ سَمَّطَهُ, inf. n. تَسْمِيطٌ: (TA:) or the latter, *he hung it,* or *suspended it, upon,* (Ṣ, Ḳ,) or *by means of,* (so in some copies of the Ḳ and in the TA,) سُمُوط, (Ṣ, Ḳ,) meaning *thongs,* or *straps.* (TA.) And سَمَطَ ▼ الدِّرْعَ, (M,) inf. n. تَسْمِيطٌ, (TA,) *He hung the coat of mail upon the hinder part of his horse.* (M.)

2: see 1, in two places. — سَمَّطْتُ الشَّىْءَ, inf. n. تَسْمِيطٌ, also signifies *I kept,* or *clave, to the thing:* hence a verse cited voce دَرِينٌ. (TA in art. درن.)

5. تَسَمَّطَ *It* (a thing, TA) *was,* or *became, hung,* or *suspended.* (Ḳ.)

سِمْطٌ *A thread,* or *string, having upon it beads*

(Ṣ, Mgh) or *pearls*; (Mgh;) otherwise it is called سِلْكٌ: (Ṣ, Mgh:) *a string of beads or the like*; (M, Ḳ;) so called because it is hung, or suspended; (M;) *a single string thereof*; like يَكْ رَسَنْ [in Persian]; a necklace of two strings thereof being called ذَاتُ سِمْطَيْنِ: (IDrd:) or it signifies, (M,) or signifies also, (Ḳ,) *a necklace longer than the* مِخْنَقَة: (IDrd, M, Ḳ:) or [simply] *a necklace*: (Mṣb:) pl. سُمُوطٌ: (M, Ḳ:) which also signifies the *things that are suspended* (مَعَالِيقُ) *from necklaces*. (TA.) — *A thong, or strap, that is suspended from the horse's saddle*; (Ṣ, Ḳ;) sing. of سُمُوطٌ. (Ṣ.) — The *redundant part of the turban, which is left hanging down upon the breast and the shoulder-blades*: (Ḳ:) pl. as above. (TA.) — *A coat of mail which the horseman hangs upon the hinder part of his horse*. (M, Ḳ.) — ‡ *A trail, or long and elevated tract*, (حَبْل,) of sand, (Ḳ, TA,) *regularly disposed, as though it were a necklace*. (TA.) = See also سُمْطٌ, in two places.

نَعْلٌ سُمْطٌ, (M, Ḳ,) and ▼ سَمِيطٌ, (Ṣ, M, Ḳ,) and ▼ أَسْمَاطٌ, (M, Ḳ,) which last is pl. of سَمِيطٌ, (TA,) *A sandal, or sole, that is of a single piece* [*of leather, not of two or more pieces sewed together, one upon another*], (طَاقٌ وَاحِدٌ, Ṣ, TA,) *in which is no patch*: (Ṣ, M, Ḳ:) or the last, (Ṣ,) or all, (M,) *not having a second piece sewed on to it*; (AZ, Ṣ, M;) as also ▼ سِمْطٌ. (So in the Ḳ, voce فَرْدٌ.) — [ثَوْبٌ سُمُطٌ (the latter word occurring twice in art. لبغ in the TA, and there opposed to مُبَطَّنٌ, and said to be masc. and fem.), i. q.] ▼ ثَوْبٌ سِمْطٌ *A garment having no lining*; [either] *a* طَيْلَسَان, or *such as is of cotton*: (ISh, Ḳ:) but one does not say مِلْحَفَةٌ سِمْطٌ nor كِسَآءٌ سِمْطٌ, because such are not [ever] lined: (ISh:) or [accord. to some] سِمْطٌ signifies a garment *that is lined below*; expl. by saying, أَوِ السِّمْطُ مِنَ الثِّيَابِ مَا ظُهِرَ مِنْ تَحْتُ, (Ḳ, TA, [in the CḲ, and in a MS. copy of the Ḳ, for ظُهِرَ, we find ظَهَرَ,]) i. e. جُعِلَ لَهُ ظِهْرٌ: (TA:) [but I think that ظَهَرَ is undoubtedly the right reading; and that سِمْطٌ means *any portion that appears of a garment worn beneath a shorter garment*:] see سَنَدٌ, last sentence. — ▼ سَرَاوِيلُ أَسْمَاطٌ *Trousers, or drawers, not stuffed*: (M, Ḳ:) i. e., (Ḳ,) or, as Th says, (M,) *of single cloth*, طَاقٌ وَاحِدٌ. (M, Ḳ.) — نَاقَةٌ سُمُطٌ, (Kr, M, Ḳ,) and ▼ أَسْمَاطٌ, (Ḳ,) *A she-camel without any brand, or mark made by a hot iron*. (Kr, M, Ḳ.) = سُمُطٌ is also a pl. of سِمَاطٌ [q. v.]. (Ḳ.)

سِمَاطٌ *A rank* of people: (M, Ḳ:) or *a side*, or *lateral part* or *portion*: (Mṣb:) *each of the two sides, or lateral portions*, of men, and of palm-trees. (Ṣ, Mṣb.) You say, قَامَ بَيْنَ السِّمَاطَيْنِ *He stood between the two ranks*. (TA.) And قَامَ القَوْمُ حَوْلَهُ سِمَاطَيْنِ *The people stood around him in two ranks*. (TA.) And هُمْ عَلَى سِمَاطٍ وَاحِدٍ *They are according to one order*. (Ḳ.) And مَشَى بَيْنَ السِّمَاطَيْنِ *He walked between the two sides*. (Ṣ, Mṣb.) And خُذُوا سِمَاطَيِ الطَّرِيقِ *Take ye the two sides of the fresh, or moist*. (TA.) And اِجْعَلِ الأَمْرَ سِمَاطًا وَاحِدًا *Make thou the affair, or case*, [*uniform, or*] *one uniform thing*. (Fr, TA in art. بأج.) — The *part* of a valley *which is between the upper extremity and the lower*: (M, Ḳ:) pl. سُمُطٌ. (Ḳ) — سِمَاطُ الطَّعَامِ *The thing upon which food is spread*: (Ḳ:) pronounced by the vulgar سَمَاط: [and applied by them to *such as is long, prepared for a large company of people*:] pl. أَسْمِطَةٌ [a pl. of pauc.] and سِمَاطَاتٌ. (TA.)

سَمِيطٌ and ▼ مَسْمُوطٌ, applied to a kid, (Ṣ, M, Mṣb, Ḳ,) and to a lamb, (M,) *Of which the hair*, (Mṣb,) or *wool*, (Ḳ,) *has been removed*, (Mṣb, Ḳ,) or *cleansed of its hair* [or *wool*], (Ṣ,) *by means of hot water*; (Ṣ, Mṣb, Ḳ;) in order to its being roasted: (Ṣ:) or *of which the* [*hair* or] *wool has been plucked off from it, after its having been put into hot water*: (M:) or the former, *plucked of its* [*hair* or] *wool, and then roasted with its skin*: (Lth:) and a *roasted* sheep or goat: the former word of the measure فَعِيلٌ in the sense of the measure مَفْعُولٌ. (TA.) = See also سَمِيطٌ, and its pl. أَسْمَاطٌ, voce سُمْطٌ; the pl. in three places.

سَامِطٌ *Boiling* water, *that scalds* (يَسْمُطُ) *a thing*. (TA.) = *Hanging a thing by a rope behind him*; from السُّمُوطُ [pl. of السِّمْطُ]. (TA.)

مَسْمُوطٌ: see سَمِيطٌ.

سمع

1. سَمِعَهُ, (Ṣ, Mṣb, Ḳ,*) aor. ـَ, (Ḳ,) inf. n. سَمْعٌ (Ṣ, Mṣb, Ḳ) and سِمْعٌ, or this latter is a simple subst., (Lḥ, Ḳ,) and سَمَاعٌ, (Ṣ, Ḳ,) or this last [also] is a simple subst., (Mṣb,) and سَمَاعَةٌ and سَمَاعِيَةٌ (Ḳ) and مَسْمَعٌ, (TA,) [*He heard it*, (namely, a thing, as in the Ṣ,) or ‡ *him*;] and ▼ تَسَمَّعَ, (Mṣb, Ḳ,) also written and pronounced ▼ اِسَّمَّعَ; (Ḳ, TA;) and ▼ اِسْتَمَعَ; (Mṣb;) are syn. with سَمِعَ (Mṣb, Ḳ) as trans. by itself; (Mṣb;) and ▼ اِسْتَمَعَ [also] is syn. with سَمِعَ [as trans. by itself]: (Ḥam p. 694, where occurs a usage of its act. part. n. showing the verb to be trans. by itself:) or ▼ اِسْتَمَعَ denotes what is intentional, signifying only *he gave ear, hearkened*, or *listened*: but سَمِعَ, [as also ▼ تَسَمَّعَ and ▼ اِسْتَمَعَ,] what is unintentional, as well as what is intentional. (Mṣb.) You say, سَمِعَ الشَّىْءَ [*He heard or listened to, the thing*]. (Ṣ.) And تَسَمَّعَ ▼ الصَّوْتَ [*He listened to, or heard, the sound*]. (TA.) [And سَمِعْتُ لَهُ صَوْتًا *I heard him, or it, utter*, or *produce, a sound*; lit. *I heard a sound attributable to him, or it*. And سَمِعَهُ مِنْهُ *He heard it from him*. And سَمِعَهُ عَنْهُ *He heard it as related from him*; *he heard it on his authority*. And سَمِعَهُ يَقُولُ كَذَا *He heard him say such a thing*.] And سَمِعَ بِهِ [*He heard of it*; for سَمِعَ التَّكَلُّمَ بِهِ, or the like]. (Ḳur xii. 31 and xxviii. 36 and xxxviii. 6, Ṣ, Ḳ, TA.) [When trans. by means of لِ alone, or إِلَى, it denotes what is intentional.] You say, سَمِعْتُ لَهُ, (Ṣ, Mṣb, TA,) and إِلَيْهِ, (Ṣ, TA,) meaning *I gave ear, hearkened*, or *listened, to him, or it*; (Ṣ, Mṣb,* TA;) and ▼ تَسَمَّعتُ له, (Mṣb,) or اليه, and ▼ اِسَّمَّعْتُ, (Ṣ, TA,) signify the same; (Ṣ, Mṣb, TA;) and so ▼ اِستمعت له, (Ṣ, Mṣb, Ḳ,) and اليه. (Ḳ.) It is said in the Ḳur [xxxvii. 8], accord. to different readings, لَا يَسَّمَّعُونَ إِلَى المَلَإِ الأَعْلَى, and ▼ لَا يَسْمَعُونَ, *They shall not listen* [*to the archangels*]: (Ṣ:) or the former has this signification, *they shall not listen to the angels* (Bḍ, Jel) *in heaven*, (Jel,) or *the exalted angels*: (Bḍ:) and ▼ the latter, *they shall not seek*, or *endeavour, to listen* &c. (Bḍ.) And in the same [xvii. 50], ▼ نَحْنُ أَعْلَمُ بِمَا يَسْتَمِعُونَ بِهِ إِذْ يَسْتَمِعُونَ إِلَيْكَ [*We are cognizant of that on account of which they hearken when they hearken to thee*]; بِهِ meaning بِسَبَبِهِ, (Bḍ, Jel,) and لِأَجْلِهِ, (Bḍ,) alluding to scoffing, or derision. (Bḍ, Jel.) [For various usages of سَمْعٌ and other inf. ns., whether employed as inf. ns. or as simple substs., see those words below.] — It also signifies *He understood it*; (TA;) *he understood its meaning*; i. e., the meaning of a person's speech. (Mṣb.) You say, لَمْ تَسْمَعْ مَا قُلْتُ لَكَ *Thou didst not understand what I said to thee*. (TA.) And such is the most obvious meaning of the verb in the saying, إِنْ كَانَ يَسْمَعُ الخَطِيبَ [*If he understand the words of the preacher*]; for this is the proper meaning in this case: but it may be rendered tropically, ‡ *if he hear the voice of the preacher*. (Mṣb.) — Also *He knew it*: as in the saying, سَمِعَ اللّٰهُ قَوْلَكَ [*God knew thy saying*]. (Mṣb.) — Also † *He accepted it*; namely, evidence, and praise: or, said of the latter, † *he recompensed it by acceptance*: (Mṣb:) ‡ *he paid regard to it, and answered it*; namely, prayer: ‡ *he answered*, or *assented to*, or *complied with, it*; namely, a person's speech. (TA.) The saying سَمِعَ اللّٰهُ لِمَنْ حَمِدَهُ means *May God accept the praise of him who praiseth Him*: or, accord. to IAmb, *may God recompense by acceptance the praise of him who praiseth Him*: (Mṣb:) or *may God answer the prayer of him who praiseth Him*. (TA, as on the authority of IAmb.) — Also † *He obeyed him*: as in the saying in the Ḳur [xxxvi. 24], إِنِّى آمَنْتُ بِرَبِّكُمْ فَاسْمَعُونِ † [*Verily I believe in your Lord, and do ye obey me*]. (TA.) — Lth says that the phrase سَمِعَتْ أُذُنِى زَيْدًا يَفْعَلُ كَذَا وَكَذَا means † *My eye saw Zeyd doing such and such things*: but Az says, I know not whence Lth brought this; for it is not of the way of the Arabs to say سمعت اذنى as meaning *my eye saw*: it is in my judgment corrupt language, and I am not sure but that it may have been originated by those addicted to innovations and erroneous opinions. (TA.)

2. تَسْمِيعٌ [inf. n of سَمَّعَ, as also تَسْمِعَةٌ, q. v. infrà, voce سُمْعَةٌ,] is *syn. with* ▼ إِسْمَاعٌ [The *making* one *to hear*]. (Ḳ.) You say, سَمَّعَهُ الصَّوْتَ and ▼ اسمعهُ [*He made him to hear the sound*]. (Ṣ.) And سَمَّعَهُ الحَدِيثَ (TA) and ▼ اسمعهُ (Ṣ, TA) [*He made him to hear the narra-*

tive]; both signifying the same. (TA.) [And سمّع به *He made to hear of it,* or *him.*] It is said in a trad., مَنْ سَمَّعَ النَّاسَ بِعَمَلِهِ سَمَّعَ اللّٰهُ بِهِ أَسَامِعَ خَلْقِهِ وَحَقَّرَهُ وَصَغَّرَهُ (Ṣ,* Mgh, TA) [*Whoso maketh men to hear of his deed,*] *God will make the ears of his creatures to hear of him* on the day of resurrection; (TA;) or *whoso maketh his deed notorious, that men may see it and hear of it, God will make notorious his hypocrisy, and fill with it the ears of his creatures, and they shall be generally acquainted with it,* [*and He will render him contemptible, and small in estimation,*] *so that he will become disgraced;* (Mgh;) or the meaning may be, *God will manifest to men his internal state, and fill their ears with the evilness of his secret intentions,* in requital of his deed: or, as some relate it, [for أَسَامِعَ خَلْقِهِ] we should say, سَامِعُ خَلْقِهِ, which is an epithet applied to God; so that the meaning is, *God* [*the Hearer of his creatures*] *will disgrace him:* (TA:) [for] سَمَّعَ بِهِ, (Ṣ, Mgh, Mṣb,) inf. n. تَسْمِيعٌ, (Ṣ, Mgh, Ḳ,) signifies [also] *He rendered him,* or *it, notorious,* and *infamous:* (Ṣ, Mgh, Ḳ:*) or *he spread it abroad, for men to speak of it.* (Mṣb.) — Also *He raised him from obscurity to fame.* (Ṣ, Ḳ.*) — And *He made him to hear what was bad, evil, abominable,* or *foul,* and *he reviled him:* (AZ, T and L in art. ندد:) and ▼ اسمعهُ [also] has the latter of these two significations. (Ṣ, Ḳ.)

4. اسمعهُ, inf. n. إِسْمَاعٌ: see 2, in four places. — *He told him* [a thing]. (Mṣb) — *He made him to understand:* the verb being used in this sense in the Ḳur [viii. 23], لَوْ عَلِمَ اللّٰهُ فِيهِمْ خَيْرًا لَأَسْمَعَهُمْ [*Had God known any good in them, He had made them to understand*]. (TA.) — أَسْمَعَكَ اللّٰهُ *May God not make thee to be deaf.* (TA.) — أَسْمَعَتْ *She sang.* (TA.) One says to a female singer, أَسْمِعِينَا *Sing thou to us:* thus used in a verse of Ṭarafeh. (TA.) — أَسْمَعْتَ *Thou hast said a saying that ought to be heard and followed.* (Ḥar p. 398.) — اسمع الدَّلْوَ ‡ *He made, or put, a* مِسْمَع [q. v.] *to the bucket.* (Ṣ, Ḳ, TA.) And in like manner, اسمع الزَّبِيلَ (Ḳ) ‡ *He made, or put, what are termed* مِسْمَعَانِ *to the basket.* (TA.) — أَسْمِعْ بِهِمْ وَأَبْصِرْ; and أَبْصِرْ بِهِ وَأَسْمِعْ; see art. بصر.

5. تَسَمَّعَ, also written and pronounced اِسَّمَّعَ: see 1, in the former half of the paragraph, in six places.

6. تسامع بِهِ النَّاسُ (Ṣ, Ḳ) *The people heard of it,* [or *him,*] *one from another:* (PṢ, TḲ:) [or *the people heard one another talk of it,* or *him:*] or *it,* or *he, became notorious among the people.* (TA.) — تسامع also signifies *He feigned himself hearing.* (KL.)

8: see 1, in the former half of the paragraph, in four places.

10: see 1, in the first sentence, in two places.

سَمْعٌ inf. n. of سَمِعَ, (Ṣ, Mṣb, Ḳ,) like ▼ سَمَاعٌ, (Ṣ, Ḳ,) [&c.,] or the latter is a simple subst. [used in the abstract sense of the former]. (Mṣb.) You say, أَسْمَعُ سَمْعًا وَأُطِيعُ طَاعَةً, [for سَمْعًا وَطَاعَةً, an emphatic mode of expression, meaning *I hear and I obey,* or for سَمِعْتُ سَمْعًا وَأَطَعْتُ طَاعَةً, which means the same, but more emphatically; طَاعَةٌ being a quasi-inf. n. for إِطَاعَةٌ;] the verb [of each] being understood: and سَمْعٌ وَطَاعَةٌ, meaning أَمْرِى سَمْعٌ وَطَاعَةٌ [i. e. أَمْرِى ذٰلِكَ *My affair is hearing and obeying*]. (Ḳ.) You say also, [in like manner,] اَللّٰهُمَّ سَمْعًا لَا بَلْغًا, (Ḳ,) and سَمْعٌ لَا بَلْغٌ: (TA:) see سِمْعٌ. And سَمْعَ أُذُنِى فُلَانًا يَقُولُ ذٰلِكَ, (Ḳ,) [said to be] the only instance of the kind among inf. ns. of trans. verbs except رَأْىَ عَيْنِى, (TA in art. رأى,) [in a copy of the M, in art. رأى, written رَأْىَ عينى and سَمْعَ اذنى,] and ▼ سِمْعَةَ اذنى, and ▼ سَمْعَةَ اذنى, and ▼ سِمْعَ اذنى [*My ear heard* (lit. *my ear's hearing*) *such a one say that*]. (Ḳ.) — [As a simple subst., it signifies] The *sense of the ear;* (Ḳ;) [i. e., *of hearing;*] the *faculty in the ear whereby it perceives sounds.* (TA.) Thus in the Ḳur [l. 36], أَوْ أَلْقَى السَّمْعَ, (TA,) meaning, *Or who hearkeneth.* (Bḍ, Jel.) [And hence,] أُمُّ السَّمْعِ *The brain;* (Z, O, Ḳ;) as also ▼ أُمُّ السَّمِيعِ. (O, Ḳ.) One says, ضَرَبَهُ عَلَى أُمِّ السَّمْعِ [*He struck him upon the brain*]. (TA.) — [It is also used for the inf. n. of أَسْمَعَ. Hence] one says, قَالُوا ذٰلِكَ سَمْعَ أُذُنِى, and in like manner, ▼ سِمْعَ اذنى, and ▼ سَمَاعَ اذنى, and ▼ سَمَاعَةَ اذنى, i. e. إِسْمَاعًا [*They said that making my ear to hear*]: (Ḳ:) and one may say, سَمْعًا [*making to hear*]: this latter one says when he does not particularize himself. (Sb, Ḳ.) And ▼ كَلَّمَهُ سِمْعَهُمْ, with kesr, meaning, [*He spoke to him making them to hear,* or] *so that they heard.* (TA.) And a poet says,

* سَمَاعَ ▼ اللّٰهِ وَالعُلَمَاءِ أَنِّى *
* أَعُوذُ بِخَيْرِ خَالِكَ يَا ابْنَ عَمْرٍو *

[*Making God and the learned men to hear that I seek protection by the goodness of thy maternal uncle, O son of 'Amr;* or أَعُوذُ بِحَقْوِ خَالِكَ, i. e. *I have recourse for protection to thy maternal uncle;* thus in the TA in art. حقو;] using the subst. in the place of the inf. n., as though he said إِسْمَاعًا. (TA.) One says also, أَخَذْتُ ذٰلِكَ عَنْهُ سَمْعًا, and in like manner, ▼ سَمَاعًا, [i. e. *I received that from him by being made to hear,* which virtually means, *by hearsay,* or *hearing it from him,*] making the inf. n. [in each case] to be of a different form from that of the verb to which it belongs [in respect of signification; i. e., using an inf. n. of سَمِعَ for that of أَسْمَعَ]. (Ḳ,* TA.) [See also سُمْعَةٌ.] — It also signifies The *ear;* (Ṣ,* Mgh, Mṣb,* Ḳ;) as also ▼ مِسْمَعٌ, (Ṣ, Mṣb, Ḳ, TA,) because it is the instrument of hearing, (TA,) and ▼ مَسْمَعٌ, [because it is the place thereof,] (Aboo-Jebeleh, TA,) and ▼ سَامِعَةٌ; (Ṣ, Ḳ;) or ▼ مِسْمَعٌ signifies the *ear-hole;* (TA;) and so ▼ مَسْمَعٌ, and ▼ مُسْتَمَعٌ: (Er-Rághib, TA:) and سَمْعٌ is also used as a pl., (Ṣ, Ḳ,) being originally an inf. n.; but sometimes (Ṣ) it has for its pl. أَسْمَاعٌ (Ṣ, Mṣb, Ḳ) and أَسْمُعٌ, (Mgh, O, Ḳ,) a pl. of pauc., (TA,) [as is also the former,] and أَسَامِعُ is a pl. pl., (Ṣ, Mgh, O, Ḳ,) i. e. pl. of أَسْمَاعٌ, (Ṣ,) or of أَسْمُعٌ: (Mgh, O:) [for an ex. of the pl. pl., see 2:] the pl. of ▼ مِسْمَعٌ is مَسَامِعُ; (Mṣb, Ḳ;) or this may be an irreg. pl. of سَمْعٌ, like as مَشَابِهُ is of شِبْهٌ. (Ṣgh, TA.) You say, سَمْعَكَ إِلَىَّ i. e. [Incline *thine ear to me;* or] *hear thou from me.* (Ṣ, Ḳ.) And طَرَقَ الكَلَامُ السَّمْعَ [*The speech struck the ear*]. (Mṣb.) سَمْعٌ is used as a pl. in the Ḳur [ii. 6], where it is said, خَتَمَ اللّٰهُ عَلَى قُلُوبِهِمْ وَعَلَى سَمْعِهِمْ [*God hath set a seal upon their hearts and upon their ears*]. (Ṣ.) One also says, فُلَانٌ عَظِيمُ ▼ المِسْمَعَيْنِ *Such a one is great in the ears.* (Ṣ.) The phrase هُوَ بَيْنَ سَمْعِ الأَرْضِ وَبَصَرِهَا means † *It is not known whither he has repaired:* (AZ, Ḳ:) or *he is between the ears of the people of the land and their eyes,* [so that they neither hear him nor see him,] the prefixed noun أَهْل being suppressed: (AO, Ḳ,* TA:) or † *in a void land, wherein is no one;* (ISk, Ḳ;) i. e., none hears his speech, nor does any see him, except [the wild animals of] the desert land: (Ḳ:) or ‡ *between the length and breadth of the land.* (Ḳ, TA.) You say also, أَلْقَى نَفْسَهُ بَيْنَ سَمْعِ الأَرْضِ وَبَصَرِهَا † *He exposed himself to perdition,* or *imperilled himself, and cast himself no one knew where:* (IAạr, Th:) or † *he cast himself where no voice of man was heard, nor eye of man seen.* (Ḳ,* TA.) — Also *What rests in the ear, of a thing which one hears.* (L, Ḳ.) — See also سِمْعٌ, in three places, beside the two places before referred to.

سِمْعٌ *i. q.* سَمْعٌ, either as an inf. n. or as a a simple subst. (Lḥ, Ḳ.) You say, اَللّٰهُمَّ سِمْعًا لَا بِلْغًا, (Ṣ, Ḳ,) and ▼ سَمْعًا لَا بَلْغًا, (Ḳ,) and سِمْعٌ لَا بِلْغٌ, and ▼ سَمْعٌ لَا بَلْغٌ, (TA,) a form of prayer, (Ḳ,) meaning *O God, may it be heard of but not fulfilled:* (Ṣ, Ḳ:) or *may it be heard but not come to:* or *may it be heard but not need to be come to:* or it is said by him who hears tidings not pleasing to him: (Ḳ:) Ks says that it means *I hear of calamities but may they not come to me.* (TA.) You say also, سِمْعَ أُذُنِى فُلَانًا يَقُولُ ذٰلِكَ: see سَمْعٌ. — Also *i. q.* إِسْمَاعٌ: so in the phrase قَالُوا ذٰلِكَ سِمْعَ أُذُنِى: (Ḳ:) and in the phrase كَلَّمَهُ سِمْعَهُمْ: (TA:) both explained above: see سَمْعٌ. — Also *Mention, fame, report, that is heard;* as also ▼ سَمْعٌ, and ▼ سَمَاعٌ: (Ḳ:) *fame,* or *good report;* (Ṣ, Mṣb, Ḳ, TA;) and so ▼ سَمْعٌ and ▼ سَمَاعٌ. (TA.) You say, ذَهَبَ سِمْعُهُ فِى النَّاسِ *His fame,* or *good report, went among mankind.* (Ṣ.) And the Arabs say, لَا وَسِمْعِ ▼ اللّٰهِ, [or وَسِمْعُ الله,] meaning لَا وَذِكْرِ اللّٰهِ [*No, by the glory of God*]. (TA.) — [It is also used as an epithet: thus,] رَجُلٌ سِمْعٌ means يُسَمِّعُ [*A man who makes others to hear of him*]: or one says, هٰذَا ٱمْرُؤٌ ذُو سِمْعٍ, and ▼ ذُو سَمَاعٍ, [*This is a man of fame, or notoriety*], (Ḳ,) whether *good* or *bad*. (Lḥ, TA.) — Also *A certain mongrel beast of prey,* (Ṣ,) the *offspring of the wolf, begotten from the hyena:* (Ṣ, Mgh, Mṣb, Ḳ:) fem. with ة: they assert that it does not die a natural death, like the serpent, (Ḳ, TA,) but by some accident that befalls it, not knowing diseases and maladies; and that it is unequalled by any other animal in running, (TA,) its running being quicker than [the flight of] the bird; and its leap exceeding thirty cubits, (Ḳ, TA,) or twenty. (TA.) It is said in a prov., أَسْمَعُ ▼ مِنَ ٱلسِّمْعِ ٱلأَزَلِّ [*More quick of hearing than the* سمع *that is lean in the buttocks and thighs; or than the light,* or *active,* سمع]: and sometimes they said أَسْمَعُ مِنْ سِمْعٍ [*more quick of hearing than a* سمع]. (Ṣ.)

سَمْعَةٌ *A single hearing,* or *hearkening,* or *listening.* (Ḳ.) — سَمْعَةُ أُذُنِى فُلَانًا يَقُولُ ذٰلِكَ : see سَمْعٌ. — See also سُمْعَةٌ. — أُذُنٌ سَمْعَةٌ : see سَامِعٌ.

سُمْعَةٌ is *syn. with* تَسْمِيعٌ, like as سُخْرَةٌ is with تَسْخِيرٌ. (TA.) You say, فَعَلَهُ رِئَآءً وَسُمْعَةً *He did it* [*to make men to see it and hear of it,* or] *in order that men might see it and hear of it.* (Ṣ.) And مَا فَعَلَهُ رِئَآءً وَلَا سُمْعَةً, and ▼ سَمْعَةً, and ▼ سِمْعَةً, *He did it not making it notorious so as to make* [*men*] *to see and to hear* [*it*]. (Ḳ.) And فَعَلْتُهُ ▼ تَسْمِعَتَكَ, and تَسْمِعَةً لَكَ, *I did it in order that thou mightest hear it.* (AZ, Ḳ.) [See also سَمْعٌ, where similar phrases are mentioned and explained.] — السُّمْعَةُ, also, signifies *What is heard, of fame,* or *report, &c.:* (Ḥar p. 34:) and [particularly] *good report.* (Id. p. 196.)

سِمْعَةٌ *A mode,* or *manner, of hearing, hearkening,* or *listening.* (Ḳ.) You say, سَمِعْتُهُ سِمْعَةً حَسَنَةً [*I heard it with a good manner of hearing*]. (TA.) — سِمْعَةُ أُذُنِى فُلَانًا يَقُولُ ذٰلِكَ : see سَمْعٌ.

سَمَعَةٌ : see سُمْعَةٌ. — أُذُنٌ سَمَعَةٌ : see سَامِعٌ.

أُذُنٌ سَمِعَةٌ : see سَامِعٌ.

سِمْعَنَّةٌ نِظْرَنَّةٌ, and سُمْعُنَّةٌ نُظْرُنَّةٌ, (Ṣ, Ḳ,) the former accord. to AZ, the latter accord. to El-Aḥmar, (Ṣ,) and سِمْعَنَةٌ نِظْرَنَةٌ, (Ḳ,) or the second and third are without teshdeed, and mentioned by Yaạḳoob also, (TA in art. نظر, [but this, I think, is a mistake,]) applied to a woman, *Who listens,* or *hearkens, and endeavours to see, and, not seeing nor hearing anything, thinks it,* or *opines it:* (Ṣ,* Ḳ,* [the latter in art. نظر,] and TA:) and one also applies to her the epithet سِمْعَنَةٌ, meaning *who listens,* or *hearkens, and does so much,* or *habitually.* (Ḳ.)

سَمَعْمَعٌ (of the measure فَعَلْعَلٌ, Ṣ) *Small in the head,* (Ṣ, Ḳ,) and *in the body;* for او اللِّحْيَة in the Ḳ is a mistranscription for وَالجُثَّةِ : (TA:) *cunning,* or *very cunning:* (Ḳ, TA:) *light of flesh, quick in work, wicked,* and *clever:* (TA:) or [simply] *light and quick:* and applied as an epithet to a wolf. (Ḳ.) — Also A woman *that grins and frowns in thy face when thou enterest, and wails after thee when thou goest forth.* (Ḳ,* TA.) — And A *tall and slender* man: (Ḳ, TA:) fem. in this sense with ة. (TA.) — And A *wicked, deceitful,* or *crafty,* devil. (TA.)

سَمَاعِ [an imperative verbal n.] *Hear thou:* (Ṣ, Ḳ:) like دَرَاكِ and مَنَاعِ, meaning أَدْرِكْ and إِمْنَعْ. (Ṣ.)

سَمَاعٌ : see its syn. سَمْعٌ; first sentence. — Also syn. with إِسْمَاعٌ, as in three exs. expl. above; see سَمْعٌ, in the middle portion of the paragraph. — Also [an inf. n. used in the sense of a pass. part. n., meaning *What has been heard,* or *heard of:*] *a thing that one has heard of, and that has become current, and talked of.* (TA.) [Hence, used in lexicology and grammar as meaning *What has been received by hearsay;* i. e. *what is established by received usage:* as in the phrase, مَقْصُورٌ عَلَى السَّمَاعِ *restricted to what has been received by hearsay;* &c.: and in the phrase شَاذٌّ فِى السَّمَاعِ *deviating from the constant course of speech with respect to what has been received by hearsay;* &c.; which virtually means *deviating from what is established by received usage:* "what has been received by hearsay" always meaning "what has been heard, either immediately or mediately, from one or more of the Arabs of the classical times."] — [Also *What is heard,* or *being heard,* of discourse, or narration, and of matters of science. See an ex. voce مُورِدٌ, in art. ورد.] — And [hence,] *Singing,* or *song;* and *any* [*musical performance whether vocal or instrumental or both combined,* or *any other*] *pleasant sound in which the ears take delight:* as in the saying, بَاتَ فِى لَهْوٍ وَسَمَاعٍ [*He passed the night in* the enjoyment of *diversion and singing, &c.*]. (TA.) [See an ex. in a verse cited voce مِشْوَارٌ, in art. شور.] — See also سِمْعٌ, in three places.

سَمُوعٌ : see سَامِعٌ, in two places.

سَمِيعٌ : see سَامِعٌ, in six places. — It is also *syn. with* مُسْمِعٌ [*Making to hear; &c.*]. (Ṣ, Ḳ.) Az remarks its being wonderful that persons should explain it as having this meaning in order to avoid the assigning to God the attribute of hearing, since that attribute is assigned to Him in more than one place in the Ḳur-án, though his hearing is not like the hearing of his creatures: he, however, adds, I do not deny that, in the language of the Arabs, سميع may be syn. with سَامِعٌ or مُسْمِعٌ; but it is mostly syn. with سَامِعٌ, like as عَلِيمٌ is with عَالِمٌ, and قَدِيرٌ with قَادِرٌ. (TA.) — Also [*Made to hear;* or] *told;* applied to a man. (Mṣb.) — أُمُّ السَّمِيعِ : see سَمْعٌ. — السَّمِيعَانِ *Two long pieces of wood* [*fixed*] *in the yoke with which the bull is yoked for ploughing the land.* (Lth, TA.)

سَمَاعَةٌ an inf. n. of سَمِعَ. (Ḳ.) — And i. q. إِسْمَاعٌ, whence a phrase expl. above: see سَمْعٌ.

[سَمَاعِىٌّ, in lexicology and grammar, applied to a word &c., means *Relating,* or *belonging, to what has been received by hearsay;* i. e., *to what is established by received usage.* See سَمَاعٌ.]

سُمَّعٌ *Light, active,* or *agile:* and applied as an epithet to a غُولٌ. (Ḳ.)

سَمَّاعٌ One *who hearkens,* or *listens, much to what is said, and utters it.* (TA.) [Its primary signification is simply One *who hears, hearkens,* or *listens, much,* or *habitually:* and it signifies also *quick of hearing.*] See also سَامِعٌ. — *A spy, who searches for information, and brings it.* (TA.) — † *Obedient.* (TA.)

سَامِعٌ and ▼ سَمِيعٌ are syn.; [signifying *Hearing;* and *hearkening,* or *listening;*] (Az, Ṣ, Mṣb, Ḳ;) like عَالِمٌ and عَلِيمٌ, and قَادِرٌ and قَدِيرٌ. (Az, TA.) [▼ The latter has also an intensive signification; and hence,] ▼ السَّمِيعُ, applied to God, signifies *He whose hearing comprehends everything; who hears everything.* (TA.) And [hence, also,] ▼ this same epithet is applied to *The lion that hears the faint sound* (Ḳ, TA) *of man and of the prey* (TA) *from afar.* (Ḳ, TA.) You say also, أُذُنٌ سَامِعَةٌ, and ▼ سَمِيعَةٌ, and ▼ سَمِيعٌ, and ▼ سَمْعَةٌ, and ▼ سَمَعَةٌ, and ▼ سَمِعَةٌ, and ▼ سَمَّاعَةٌ, and ▼ سَمُوعٌ : [the first signifying *A hearing,* or *a hearkening* or *listening, ear:* and the last two, and app. all but the first, *an ear that hears,* or *hearkens* or *listens, much;* or *that is quick of hearing:*] the pl. of ▼ the last is سُمُعٌ. (Ḳ.)

سَامِعَةٌ fem. of سَامِعٌ [q. v.]. — [It is also used as an epithet in which the quality of a subst. is predominant]: see سَمْعٌ, in the latter half of the paragraph.

أَسْمَعُ [*More,* and *most, quick of hearing*]: see سِمْعٌ; last sentence.

تَسْمِعَةٌ [an inf. n. of 2]: see سُمْعَةٌ.

مَسْمَعٌ *A place whence* [and *where*] *one hears,* or *hearkens,* or *listens.* (IDrd, Ḳ.) You say, هُوَ مِنِّى بِمَرْأًى وَمَسْمَعٍ *He is where I see him and hear his speech;* (IDrd, Ḳ;) and in like manner, هُوَ مِنِّى مَرْأًى وَمَسْمَعٌ; (TA;) and مَرْأًى وَمَسْمَعًا, (M and Ḳ in art. رأى, q. v.,) and sometimes they said مَرًى. (TA.) And فُلَانٌ فِى مَنْظَرٍ وَمَسْمَعٍ *Such a one is in a state in which he likes to be looked at and listened to.* (T, A, TA, in art. نظر.) — See also سَمْعٌ, in the latter half of the paragraph, in two places. — It is also an inf. n. of سَمِعَ. (TA.)

مُسْمَعٌ [pass. part. n. of 4, q. v.]. — وَٱسْمَعْ غَيْرَ مُسْمَعٍ, in the Ḳur [iv. 48], means [*And hear thou without being made to hear;* i. e.] *mayest thou not be made to hear:* (Ibn-'Arafeh, Ḳ:) or *mayest thou not hear,* (Akh, Ṣ, Bḍ, Jel,) by reason of deafness, or of death; (Bd;) said by way of imprecation: (Az, Er-Rághib:) or *hear thou without being made to hear speech which thou wouldest approve*: or *not being made to hear what is disliked*; accord. to which explanation, it is said hypocritically: or *hear thou speech which thou wilt not be made* [*really*] *to hear*; because thine ear will be averse from it; accord. to which explanation, what follows the verb is an objective complement: or *hear thou without having thine invitation assented to*: (Bd:) or *without having what thou sayest accepted*. (Mujáhid, Ḳ.)

مُسْمِعٌ [act. part. n. of 4, q. v.] — [Hence,] مُسْمِعَةٌ *A female singer*. (Ṣ, Ḳ.) [See an ex. of the pl. in a verse cited voce شَارِبٌ.] — And hence, (TA in art. زمر,) the former is applied to ‡ *A shackle*. (Ḳ, and TA in art. زمر.)

مِسْمَعٌ *An instrument of hearing*. (TA.) — See سَمْعٌ, in the latter half of the paragraph, in four places. ═ † *A loop which is in the middle of the* [*large bucket called*] غَرْب, *and into which is put a rope in order that the bucket may be even*; (Ṣ, Ḳ;) so called as being likened to an ear: (El-Mufradát, TA:) or the *part of the* [*leathern water-bag called*] مَزَادَة *which is the place of the loop*: or *what goes beyond*, or *through, the hole of the loop*. (TA.) — Also, (Ḳ,) or مِسْمَعَانِ, (El-Aḥmar, TA,) ‡ *The two pieces of wood that are put into the two loops of the* [*basket called*] زَبِيل *when earth is taken forth with it from a well*. (El-Aḥmar, Ḳ, TA.) — And the latter, (i. e. the dual,) *A pair of socks*, or *stockings, worn by the sportsman when he is pursuing the gazelles during midday*, or *during midday in summer when the heat is vehement*. (TA.)

مُسَمَّعٌ ‡ *Shackled*: the explanation in the Ḳ, *shackled and collared*, applies to مُسَمَّعٌ مُسَوْجَرٌ together; not to the former of these two words alone. (TA.) [See مُسْمِعٌ.]

مَسْمُوعَاتٌ [*Things heard*]. See 4 in art. جوز.

مَسَامِعُ is pl. of مِسْمَعٌ (Mṣb, Ḳ) [and of مَسْمَعٌ]. — As a pl. without a sing., it is applied to *All the holes of a human being; such as are* [*the holes of*] *the eyes, and such as the nostrils, and the anus*. (TA.)

مُسْتَمَعٌ: see سَمْعٌ, in the latter half of the paragraph.

سمغ

السَّامِغَانِ *The two sides of the mouth, beneath the two extremities of the mustache, on the right and left*; a dial. var. of الصَّامِغَانِ [q. v.]. (IDrd, Ḳ.)

سمق

1. سَمَقَ, (Ṣ, O, L, Ḳ,) aor. ـُ, (O, L,) inf. n. سُمُوقٌ (Ṣ, O, L, Ḳ) and سَمْقٌ, (L,) *It was*, or *became, high*, or *tall*: (Ṣ, O, L, Ḳ:) or *tall in the highest degree*: (JK:) said of a plant, or herbage, (JK, L,) of a tree, and [particularly] of a palm-tree. (L.) — See also سُمَاقٌ.

سَمِقٌّ *Tall*; applied to a man. (Kr, TA.) [See also سَامِقٌ.]

سُمَاقٌ *Pure; sheer; unmixed*. (Ṣ, O, Ḳ.) You say كَذِبٌ سُمَاقٌ *A sheer, unmixed, lie*; (Ṣ, O;) and حُبٌّ سُمَاقٌ *pure, unmixed, love*; meaning *such as have overtopped* (سَمَقَا ↓) *every lie and love*. (O.)

سُمُوقٌ: see سُمَاقٌ.

سَمِيقٌ: see سَامِقٌ. ═ The dual, سَمِيقَانِ, signifies The [*yokes* or] *two pieces of wood that belong to the* نِير, *surrounding the necks of the two bulls*, (Ṣ, Z, O, Ḳ,) *like the neck-ring*, (Ṣ, O,) *the two extremities of each being made to meet together beneath the bull's dewlap, and bound with a cord*: (Z, TA:) pl. أَسْمِقَةٌ. (TA.) — And [its pl.,] أَسْمِقَةٌ, *Certain pieces of wood in the utensil upon which bricks*, or *crude bricks*, (لَبِن,) *are conveyed*. (Ibn-'Abbád, O, L, Ḳ.)

سُمَّاقٌ (Ṣ, O, Ḳ) and سُمُوقٌ ↓, (O, Ḳ,) in the Tekmileh with teshdeed, [i. e. سُمُّوقٌ ↓,] (TA,) [*Sumach*; the *rhus coriaria* of Linn.; or *its berry*:] *a certain fruit*, (Ḳ,) *well known*; (Ṣ, Ḳ;) *a certain acid thing, with which one cooks*; (O;) the *fruit of certain trees of the* [*high grounds termed*] قِفَاف *and of the mountains, acid, consisting of bunches of small berries, which are cooked*; (AḤn, TA;) *not known to AḤn as growing in any part of the land of the Arabs except in Syria*; and he says that it is *intensely red*: in the T, said to be the *acid berry called* عُبْرُب: n. un. with ة: (TA:) *it excites appetence; stops chronic diarrhœa; and the application of water in which it has been steeped*, or *macerated, as a collyrium, is beneficial for the* [*disorder termed*] سُلَاق *and for ophthalmia*. (Ḳ.)

سُمُّوقٌ: see the next preceding paragraph.

قِدْرٌ سُمَّاقِيَّةٌ: see عَرَبْرَبِيَّةٌ, in art عرب.

سَامِقٌ and سَمِيقٌ ↓ *High*, or *tall*; applied to a plant, or herbage, and to a tree, and [particularly] to a palm-tree. (L.) [See also سِمِقٌّ.]

سمقر

مُسْمَقِرٌّ: see art. سقر.

سمك

1. سَمَكَ, [aor. ـُ,] inf. n. سُمُوكٌ, *It* (a thing) *rose*, or *became high* or *elevated* or *lofty*. (Ṣ, Ḳ.) — And, aor. and inf. n. as above, *He ascended*. (TA.) One says, أُسْمُكْ فِى الرَّيْمِ *Ascend thou the stairs*. (Ṣ, TA. [See رَيْمٌ.]) ═ And سَمَكَهُ, (Ṣ, Ḳ,) aor. as above, (TA,) inf. n. سَمْكٌ, *He raised, elevated, upraised*, or *uplifted, it*. (Ṣ, Ḳ.) So in the phrase, سَمَكَ اللّٰهُ السَّمَآءَ [*God raised the heaven*]. (Ṣ.)

سَمْكٌ The *roof* of a house, or chamber: (Ṣ, Mgh,* Ḳ:*) or the *interior uppermost part* [i. e. the *ceiling*] of a house, or chamber; the exterior uppermost part thereof being called صَهْوَة: (Ḥam p. 725:) or [the *height*] *from the top to the bottom* of a house or chamber. (Ḳ.) [And hence, The *canopy* of the heaven or sky: or] the *measure of the height* of the heaven *from the earth*: or the *thickness* thereof, *upwards*. (Bd in lxxix. 28.) And The *stature*, or *height in a standing posture*, of anything: (Ḳ:) thus expl. by Lth: one says بَعِيرٌ طَوِيلُ السَّمْكِ [*A camel tall of stature*]. (TA.) [In the present day, it signifies The *extent* of anything *from top to bottom*; its *height, depth*, and *thickness*: and is vulgarly pronounced سُمْك.]

سَمَكٌ *Fish*; syn. حُوتٌ; (Ḳ;) *a kind of aquatic creatures*: [a coll. gen n.:] n. un. with ة: pl. of the former سِمَاكٌ and سُمُوكٌ. (Ṣ, TA.) شَوَى سَمَكَتَهُ فِى الحَرِيقِ [*He broiled his fish in the fire of a burning house*] is a post-classical prov. of the people of Baghdád, relating to the concealing, disguising, or cloaking, of a fault, for the purpose of seizing an opportunity; orginating from the fact that the thief used, when he saw the fire of a burning house in a place, to go thither for the purpose of theft; and if it were in his power, he did what he desired; and if he were lighted on, he said, I came to broil a fish. (Mṭr, in Ḥar pp. 481-2.) — السَّمَكَةُ [is a name of ‡ *The constellation Pisces*; also called السَّمَكَتَانِ;] *a certain sign of the Zodiac*; (Ḳ, TA;) thought by ISd to be so called because it is a watery sign; and also called الحُوتُ. (TA.)

سِمَاكٌ *A thing with which a thing is raised, elevated, upraised*, or *uplifted*; (Ḳ, TA;) *whether a wall or a roof*: (TA:) pl. سُمُكٌ. (Ḳ.) ═ السِّمَاكَانِ is the name of *Two bright stars*; السِّمَاكُ الأَعْزَلُ and السِّمَاكُ الرَّامِحُ: (Ṣ, O, Ḳ:) the former is *a star* [namely *a*] *in Virgo, called by astrologers* السُّنْبُلَة [or *Spica Virginis*]; (Ḳzw;) and is *one of the Mansions of the Moon*, (Ṣ, O, and Ḳzw in his descr. of the Mansions of the Moon,) *the Fourteenth thereof*; (Ḳzw ibid.;) it is *one of the* أَنْوَآء [pl. of نَوْءٌ, q. v.], *and rises aurorally in* تِشْرِينُ الأَوَّلُ [*October*, O. S.; its auroral rising, in Central Arabia, about the commencement of the era of the Flight, began *on the 4th of that month*]; it is called الاعزل because it has no star [near] before it, like the اعزل that has with him no spear; or, as some say, because, when it rises [aurorally], it is not accompanied by wind nor by cold: (TA:) the latter سِمَاك, i. e. الرَّامِح, [thus called for a reason expl. in art. رمح, q. v., is *the star Arcturus*, and] is *not of the Mansions of the Moon*, (Ṣ, O, TA,) *and has not any* نَوْء [here meaning *supposed influence in bringing rain &c.*]; *it is towards the north; the former being towards the south*; (TA;) *and is also called* السِّمَاكُ المِرْزَمُ: (AZ, TA in art. رمح:) [it is erroneously said that] *the* سماكان *are in the sign of Libra*: (TA:) and it is said that *they are the two hind legs of Leo* (رِجْلَا الأَسَدِ): (Ṣ, O, Ḳ:*) [for it appears, as I have before observed, (voce ذِرَاعٌ,) that the ancient Arabs, or many of them, extended the figure of Leo (as they did also that of Scorpio) far beyond the limits which we assign to it: and hence,] السماك الاعزل was also called سَاقُ الأَسَدِ [*the thigh*, or *the hind shank, of Leo*]. (Ḳzw in his descr. of Virgo.) The rhyming-proser says, إِذَا طَلَعَ السِّمَاكُ ذَهَبَ العِكَاكُ فَأَصْلِحْ فِنَاكَ وَأَجِدَّ حِذَاكَ فَإِنَّ الشِّتَآءَ قَدْ أَتَاكَ [*When* السماك الاعزل *rises* aurorally, (i. e. السماك الاعزل,) *the sultriness has gone, therefore do thou put thy court, or yard, in good condition, and renew thy sandal, for the winter has come to thee:* فِنَاكَ and حِذَاكَ being contractions of فِنَآءَكَ and حِذَآءَكَ, for the sake of the rhyme]. (O, TA.) The نَوْء [here app. meaning the rain consequent upon the auroral setting] of السماك الاعزل [about the 4th of April, O. S. in Central Arabia] is abundant, but disapproved, because it gives growth to the نَشْر [q. v.], which diseases the camels that pasture upon it. (Ḳzw in his descr. of the Mansions of the Moon.) [The epithet ▼ سِمَاكِيٌّ is applied to the rain above mentioned.] — السِّمَاكُ also signifies, (Ḳ,) or سِمَاكُ التَّرْقُوَةِ, (Ibn-'Abbád, O,) *The upper part of the chest, next to the collar-bone.* (Ibn-'Abbád, O, Ḳ.)

سِمَاكِيٌّ: see the next preceding paragraph.

سُمَيْكَآءُ *i. q.* حُسَاسٌ; (Ṣ, O, Ḳ;) i. e. *Certain small fish, which are dried; also called* حِفٌّ. (O, TA.)

سَمَّاكٌ *A fishmonger.* (MA.)

سَنَامٌ سَامِكٌ *A high*, (Ṣ, TA,) or *long and high, and plump*, (TA,) *camel's hump.* (Ṣ, TA.) — ‡ شَرَفُكَ تَامِكٌ وَإِقْبَالُكَ سَامِكٌ [*Thy nobility is lofty, and thy good fortune is high*]. (A and TA in art. تمك.)

المُسْمَكَاتُ *The heavens;* (Ḳ;) which are seven in number: (TA:) or so ▼ المَسْمُوكَاتُ: (Ṣ:) or this is wrong; or it is a dial. var.: (Ḳ:) the latter word is used by the vulgar, but is correct. (TA.)

مِسْمَاكٌ *A pole of a* [*tent such as is called*] خِبَآء, (Ṣ, Ḳ,) *which latter is raised thereby.* (Ṣ.)

مَسْمُوكٌ *Tall;* (IDrd, O, Ḳ;) applied to a man. (IDrd, O.) — And, applied to a horse, [مِنَ الحَبْلِ in the CḲ being a mistake for مِنَ الخَيْلِ,] ‡ *Firm* (Ibn-'Abbád, Z, O, Ḳ, TA) *in the* [*ribs called*] جَوَانِح. (Z, TA.) — المَسْمُوكَاتُ: see المُسْمَكَاتُ.

بَيْتٌ مُسْتَمِكٌ and ▼ مُنْسَمِكٌ *A tall house* or *tent.* (TA.)

مُنْسَمِكٌ: see what next precedes.

سمل

1. سَمَلَ عَيْنَهُ, (Ṣ,* M, Mgh,* Mṣb, Ḳ,) aor. ـُ, (M, Mṣb,) inf. n. سَمْلٌ, (Ṣ, M, Mṣb,) *He put out, or blinded,* (فَقَأَ,) *his eye* (Ṣ, M, Mgh, Mṣb, Ḳ, TA) *with an iron instrument* (Ṣ, Mṣb, TA) *made hot;* (Ṣ, Mṣb;) or *with some other thing;* sometimes *with a thorn;* (TA;) like سَمَرَهَا: (M and Ḳ in art. سمر:) and *he pulled it out:* (Mgh:) and ▼ استملها signifies the same. (Fr, Ḳ.) — سَمَلَ الحَوْضَ, (Ṣ, M, Ḳ,) inf. n. as above; (M;) and ▼ سَمَّلَهُ, (M, Ḳ,) inf. n. تَسْمِيلٌ; (TA;) *He cleansed*, or *cleared, the watering-trough*, or *tank*, (Ṣ, M, Ḳ,) *from the* سَمَلَة, (M, Ḳ,) [i. e.] *from the black mud*, or *black fetid mud*, [*that was in it*,] and *from the mud*, or *clay*. (Ṣ.) And سَمَلْتُ البِئْرَ *I cleansed*, or *cleared out, the well.* (Mṣb.) — سَمَلَ بَيْنَهُمْ, (Ṣ, M, Mṣb, Ḳ,) aor. and inf. n. as above, (Ṣ, M,) *He effected a rectification of affairs*, or *an adjustment*, or *a reconciliation, between them;* as also ▼ اسمل: (Ṣ, M, Ḳ:) or *he strove, laboured*, or *exerted himself, in effecting a rectification between them;* and so فِى المَعِيشَةِ [*in respect of the means of subsistence*]. (Mṣb.) — سَمَلَ, (Ṣ, M, Ḳ,) aor. ـُ, (M,) inf. n. سُمُولٌ (Ṣ, M, Ḳ) and سُمُولَةٌ, [or this is probably the inf. n. of the latter of the next two following syn. verbs,] (Ḳ,) *It* (a garment, or piece of cloth,) *was*, or *became, old, and worn out;* as also ▼ اسمل; (Ṣ, M, Ḳ;) and so سَمُلَ, like كَرُمَ; (Ḳ;) and ▼ اِسْمَألَّ, inf. n. اِسْمِئْلَالٌ. (TA.) — See also the next paragraph.

2. سَمَّلَ الحَوْضَ: see 1. — سَمَّلَ الحَوْضُ, (M, Ḳ,) inf. n. تَسْمِيلٌ, (Ḳ,) *The watering-trough*, or *tank, yielded but little water.* (Lḥ, M, Ḳ.) And in like manner, (Ḳ,) سَمَّلَتِ الدَّلْوُ, (M, Ḳ,) inf. n. as above, (Ḳ,) *The bucket yielded*, (M,) or *produced* [from the well], *only what is termed* السَّمَلَة, (Ḳ,) i. e., (TA,) *little water;* (M, TA;) as also ▼ سَمَلَتْ, (Ḳ,) inf. n. سَمْلٌ; but the former verb is said by Fr to be preferable. (TA.) — سَمَّلَ فُلَانًا بِالقَوْلِ *He was soft*, or *tender*, or *easy and sweet*, or *elegant, graceful*, or *ornate, to such a one*, (رَقَّقَ لَهُ, in the CḲ رقق له,) *in speech.* (Ḳ.) — And accord. to IDrd, تَسْمِيلٌ signifies *A laxness of the* ذَكَر *on the occasion of* جِمَاع. (TA.)

4: see 1, in two places.

5. تَسَمَّلَ, (Ḳ,) or تَسَمَّلَ سَمَلًا, (M,) *He drank*, or *took, remains in a vessel*, (M, Ḳ,) of wine, or beverage, &c. (M.) — And تَسَمَّلَ النَّبِيذَ *He persevered*, or *persisted, in the drinking of the* [*beverage called*] نبيذ. (Lḥ, M, Ḳ.)

8: see 1, first sentence.

Q. Q. 4. اِسْمَأَلَّ, (Ṣ, O, Ḳ,) inf. n. اِسْمِئْلَالٌ, (Ṣ,) *He* (a man, O) *was*, or *became, slender, lean*, or *lank*, (Ṣ, O, Ḳ,) *in the belly.* (Ṣ,* O,* Ḳ.) — Said of the shade, *It contracted;* or *went away;* syn. قَلَصَ, (O,) or اِرْتَفَعَ. (TA.) The phrase إِذَا اسْمَأَلَّ التُّبَّعُ, in a verse which is here cited in the Ṣ and O and TA, [and which I have cited in art. تبع,] means [accord. to J,] إِذَا رَجَعَ الظِّلُّ إِلَى أَصْلِ العُودِ [app. *When the shade* cast by the leaves of a tree *returns to the lower part of the branch;* i. e. when the sun becomes high: virtually the same as *when the shade contracts*]: (Ṣ, TA:) or, as some say, by التُّبَّع is meant [the star, or asterism, called] الدَّبَرَان, and the phrase means *when* الدبران *rises.* (TA. [See art. تبع.])

— Said of a person's face, *It became altered in consequence of emaciation.* (TA.) — See also 1, last sentence but one.

سَمَلٌ: see سَمَلَةٌ, in three places. — Applied to a garment, or piece of cloth, *Old, and worn out;* (Ṣ, M, Ḳ;) as also ▼ سَمَلَةٌ and ▼ سَمِيلٌ and ▼ سَمُولٌ (M, Ḳ) and ▼ سَمِلٌ and ▼ مُسْمَئِلٌّ: (Ḳ:) the pl. of سَمَلٌ is أَسْمَالٌ: (A'Obeyd, TA:) and one says also ثَوْبٌ أَسْمَالٌ, (Ṣ, M, Ḳ,) like رُمْحٌ أَقْصَادٌ and بُرْمَةٌ أَعْشَارٌ. (Ṣ.) The phrase سَمَلُ قَطِيفَةٍ occurs in a trad. [as meaning *An old and worn-out garment of the kind called* قطيفة]: and in another trad., أَسْمَالُ مُلَيَّتَيْنِ [meaning *two old and worn-out small garments of the kind called* مُلَآءَة]; مُلَيَّة being a dim. of مُلَآءَة. (TA.) And ▼ سَوْمَلٌ signifies [in like manner] *An old and worn-out* [*garment of the kind called*] كِسَآء, on the authority of Ez-Zejjájee. (M.) — Also, (i. e. سَمَلٌ,) applied to a ewe, *Having ragged wool:* — and سَمَلْ سَمَلْ is *A cry by which a ewe is called to be milked.* (O, TA.)

سَمِلٌ: see the next preceding paragraph.

سَمْلَةٌ *Tears poured forth* (AZ, Ḳ) *by the eyes affected with pain in consequence of hunger*, (AZ,) or *on an occasion of vehement hunger*, (Ḳ,) *as though putting out the eye.* (AZ, Ḳ.) — See also the next following paragraph.

سَمَلَةٌ *A small quantity of water* (Ṣ, M, Ḳ) *remaining in the bottom of a vessel &c.;* like ثَمِيلَةٌ: (Ṣ:) as also ▼ سَمْلَةٌ: (Ṣ, M,* Ḳ: [app., accord. to the M, the latter is syn. with the former absolutely:]) pl. ▼ سَمَلٌ, (Ṣ, M, Ḳ,) which is used of wine, or beverage, &c., (M,) [or rather this is a coll. gen. n.,] and [the pl. properly so termed is] سُمُولٌ (Aṣ, Ṣ) and أَسْمَالٌ [a pl. of pauc.]: (AA, Ṣ:) and ▼ سُمْلَانٌ [app. pl. of ▼ سَمَلٌ, agreeably with analogy,] signifies *remains* of [the beverage called] نَبِيذ, (M, Ḳ,) and of water also. (TA.) Also *A remaining portion of water in a watering-trough*, or *tank:* (M, Ḳ:) and, (Ḳ,) as some say, (M,) *black mud*, or *black fetid mud*, (M, Ḳ,) *therein:* (M:) pl. ▼ سَمَلٌ [or rather this is a coll. gen. n., as observed above,] and سِمَالٌ; (M, Ḳ;) and سَمَائِلُ is pl. of the latter of these pls. (TA.) — See also سَمَلٌ.

سُمْلَانٌ: see the next preceding paragraph.

سَمُولٌ: }
سَمِيلٌ: } see سَمَلٌ.

سَمَّالٌ [*One who puts out the eyes of others*]. A certain tribe were called بَنُو السَّمَّالِ, (M, Ḳ,*) or بَنُو سَمَّالٍ, (Ṣ, TA,) because their founder had put out the eye of a man. (Ṣ, M, Ḳ.)

سَامِلٌ One *who strives, labours*, or *exerts himself*, (Ṣ, M, Ḳ,) *in*, (Ṣ,) or *for*, (M, Ḳ,) *the right management of affairs for procuring the means of subsistence.* (Ṣ, M, Ḳ.)

سَوْمَلٌ: see سَمَلٌ.

سُوَمْلَةٌ *A small* [*cup of the kind called*] فِنْجَانَةٌ, (Ṣ, M, Ḳ, TA,) which latter is a post-classical word, originally فِلْجَانَةٌ: or the سومله, as some say, is *a small* فِيَالَجَة, an arabicized word from the Pers. پِيَالَهْ; which is also called طَرْجِهَارَةٌ; (TA;) and this is the same as the فِلْجَان. (TA voce طرجهارة.)

مُسْمَئِلٌّ *Slender, lean,* or *lank, in the belly;* (M, Ḳ;) applied to a man. (TA.) — See also سَمَل. ═ Also *A certain bird.* (Ḳ.)

سملق

سَمْلَقٌ *An even plain;* (Ḳ, TA;) like سَلَقٌ; mentioned by J in art. سلق; or *a desert in which is no herbage:* or *an even tract of land destitute of herbage:* and [the pl.] سَمَالِقُ signifies [*deserts such as are termed*] صَحَارَى: or, accord. to El-Wáhidee, *far-extending, long land.* (TA.) [See an ex. in a verse cited voce أَرْقَلَ: and another voce رِيَاغٌ, in art. ريغ.] — [Hence,] † A woman *that bears no offspring:* likened to land that does not give growth to anything. (TA.) — † *A* woman *bad in sexual intercourse;* as also with ة. (TA.) And the latter, † A woman *that has no* إِسْكَتَانِ [or *labia majora of the vulva*]: (TA:) [or] a woman *having no buttocks.* (ISk, TA in art. رقع.) — And † *A clamorous* old woman: or, accord. to AA, one *of evil disposition.* (TA.)

كَذِبٌ سَمْلَقٌ [like سُمَاقٌ] *A sheer, unmixed, lie.* (TA.)

سمن

1. سَمِنَ, (Ṣ, M, L, Mṣb, Ḳ,) aor. ـَ; (L, Mṣb, Ḳ;) and سَمُنَ, aor. ـُ; (Mṣb;) inf. n. of the former سِمَنٌ (Ṣ, M, L, Ḳ) and سَمَانَةٌ, (M, L, Ḳ,) or the former is a simple subst. (Mṣb) [and the latter by rule inf. n. of the latter verb]; *He was,* or *became, fat,* or *plump;* (Ṣ, M, L;) or *in the condition of having much flesh and fat:* (Mṣb:) and ▼ تسمّن has a like meaning [i. e. *he was,* or *became, fattened, rendered plump,* or *made to have much flesh and fat*]. (Ṣ, L.*) A poet says,

رَكِبْنَاهَا سَمَانَتَهَا فَلَمَّا
بَدَتْ مِنْهَا السَّنَاسِنُ وَالضُّلُوعُ

(IAar, M, L,) meaning *We rode her during her state of fatness,* or *plumpness,* [*but when the edges of her vertebræ, and the ribs, became apparent, . . .*] (M, L.) — [Hence,] سَمِنَ البُرُّ, inf. n. سِمَنٌ, † *The wheat became full in the grain.* (A in art. صفر.) ═ سَمَنَهُ, (Ṣ, M, L, Ḳ,) aor. ـُ, inf. n. سَمْنٌ, (Ṣ, M, L,) *He made it,* [or *prepared it,*] namely, food, *with* سَمْن [q. v. infrà]; (M, L, Ḳ;) as also ▼ سمّنه, and ▼ اسمنهُ: (Ḳ:) or the first signifies, (Ṣ,) or signifies also, and so ▼ the second and ▼ third, (M, L,) *he moistened it, and stirred it about,* (Ṣ, M, L,) namely, food, (Ṣ, L,) or bread, (M, L,) *with* سَمْن, (Ṣ, M, L,) لَهُمْ *for them.* (Ṣ.) — Also, and ▼ اسمنهُ, (L,) or سَمَنَ القَوْمَ, (M, Ḳ,) aor. and inf. n. as above, (M,) *He fed him,* or *the people,* or *party, with* سَمْن. (M, L, Ḳ.) — And سَمَنْتُ لَهُ *I seasoned his bread for him with* سَمْن. (L.)

2. سمّنهُ, (Ṣ, M, L, Mṣb, Ḳ,) inf. n. تَسْمِينٌ; (Ḳ;) *He,* or *it, rendered him fat,* or *plump;* (Ṣ, M, L, Ḳ;*) or *caused him to have much flesh and fat:* (Mṣb:) and ▼ اسمنهُ signifies the same. (M, L, Mṣb.) It is said in a prov., سَمِّنْ كَلْبَكَ يَأْكُلْكَ [*Fatten thy dog, and he will eat thee*]. (Ṣ, L, Mṣb. [See Freytag's Arab. Prov., i. 609.]) — سمّنهم, (Ṣ, M, L,) inf. n. as above, (Ṣ, L,) *He furnished them with* سَمْن *for travelling-provision, &c.* (Ṣ, M, L.) — See also 1, in two places. ═ تَسْمِينٌ also signifies The act of *cooling,* (Ṣ, M, L, Ḳ,) in the dial. of Eṭ-Ṭáïf (Ṣ, M, L) and El-Yemen. (Ṣ.) A fish was brought to El-Ḥajjáj, (Ṣ, M, L,) broiled, (L,) and he said to the cook, (Ṣ,) or to the man who brought it, (M, L,) سَمِّنْهَا, (Ṣ, M, L,) meaning *Cool it:* (Ṣ:) the man who brought it knew not what he meant; so 'Ambeseh Ibn-Sa'eed said to him, He says to thee *Cool it* (M, L) *a little.* (L.)

4. اسمن *He* (a man, M, L) *was fat,* or *plump, by nature.* (M, L, Ḳ.) — *He* (a man, Ṣ, M, L) *possessed a thing that was fat,* or *plump:* (Ṣ, M, L, Ḳ:) or *bought such:* (M, L, Ḳ:) or *gave such* (Ṣ, M, L, Ḳ) *to another.* (Ṣ.) And اسمن القَوْمُ *The people,* or *party, became in the state of those whose cattle had become fat,* or *plump.* (M, L, Ḳ.*) — Also *He bought* سَمْن. (L.) — And اسمنوا *They became in the condition of having much* سَمْن. (M, L, Ḳ.) ═ اسمنهُ: see 2: — and see also 1, in three places.

5: see 1. — [Hence,] تسمّن also signifies † *He prided himself in the abundance of his wealth, and collected it but did not expend it:* (TA in art. هنأ:) or *he made a boast of abundance of goodness,* or *goods, which he did not possess;* and *laid claim to nobility that was not in him:* or *collected wealth for the purpose of attaining to the condition of the noble:* or *loved to indulge himself largely in eatables and drinkables that are the causes of fatness,* or *plumpness.* (L.)

10. استسمنهُ *He deemed,* or *reckoned,* (Ṣ, L, Mṣb, Ḳ,) or *he found,* (M, L, Ḳ,) *it,* or *him,* (namely, a thing, M, L, and flesh-meat, L, or a man, Ḳ,) *to be fat,* or *plump,* (Ṣ, M, L, Ḳ,) or *to have much flesh and fat:* (Mṣb:) or *he sought it,* or *demanded it, fat,* or *plump.* (M, L.) ═ And جَاؤُوا يَسْتَسْمِنُونَ *They came seeking,* or *demanding, that* سَمْن [in the CḲ السِّمِين i. e. *that which was fat or plump*] *should be given to them.* (Ṣ, M, L, Ḳ.*)

سَمْنٌ *Clarified butter; ghee;* i. e. سِلَاءٌ *of fresh butter,* (M, L, Ḳ,) or *of milk;* (L;) it is *of the cow,* and sometimes *of the goat:* (Ṣ, L:) *what comes forth,* (Mgh,) or *is made,* (Mṣb,) [or *clarified, by cooking it, or boiling it, sometimes with an admixture of* سَوِيق (or *meal of parched barley or wheat*), or *dates,* or *globules of gazelles' dung,* (see خُلَاصَةٌ, and قِشْدَةٌ, and قِلْدَةٌ,)] *from the milk of cows,* and *of goats,* (Mgh, Mṣb,) or *sheep:* (Mṣb:) [n. un. with ة:] pl. [of mult.] سُمْنَانٌ (Ṣ, M, L, Mṣb, Ḳ, in the CḲ [erroneously] سِمْنَانٌ) and سُمُونٌ and [of pauc.] أَسْمُنٌ: (M, L, Ḳ:) *it counteracts all poisons, clears away the filth from foul ulcers, matures all tumours, and removes the* [*discoloration and spots termed*] كَلَف and نَمَش *from the face, applied as a liniment.* (Ḳ.) — سَمْنُ الهَبِيدِ [*Decocted juice of the colocynth,* or *of its pulp,* or *seed*]. (TA voce خَوْلَعٌ, q. v.)

سِمَنٌ *Fatness,* or *plumpness; contr. of* هُزَالٌ; (M, L;) or the *condition of having much flesh and fat.* (Mṣb.) [See 1, first sentence.]

سُمْنَةٌ, (M, L,) or ▼ سُمُنَةٌ, with ḍamm, (Ḳ,) *A certain herb,* (M, L, Ḳ,) *having leaves, and slender twigs, and a white flower:* said by AḤn to be *of the* [*kind called*] جَنْبَة, (M, L,) *which grows forth* بِنُجُومِ الصَّيْفِ [which may mean either *by the influence of the stars of the season called* الصيف, i. e., *of its rains,* or *with the herbs of that season,* in either case *in spring* or *summer,*] *and is evergreen.* (M, L, Ḳ.)

سُمْنَةٌ *A medicine for fattening,* or *rendering plump:* (M, L, Ḳ:) or *a medicine by which women are fattened,* or *rendered plump.* (T, Ṣ, L.) — See also سُمْنَةٌ.

السُّمَنِيَّةُ *A certain sect of idolaters, who assert the doctrine of metempsychosis, and deny that knowledge comes from informations;* (Ṣ, Mṣb;) *a certain people, of the Indians, who hold that the duration of the present world is from eternity,* or *that it is everlasting,* (M, L, Ḳ,) *and assert the doctrine of metempsychosis:* (Ḳ:) the word is said to be an irregular rel. n. from سُومَنَات, a town of India. (Mṣb.)

سَمِينٌ *Fat,* or *plump;* (Ṣ, M, L, Ḳ;*) *contr. of* مَهْزُولٌ; (Ṣ, L;) or *having much flesh and fat;* (Mṣb;) and ▼ سَامِنٌ signifies the same: (M, L, Ḳ:) fem. with ة: (M, L, Mṣb:) [see سَاحٌ:] pl. (of the first, and of its fem., Mṣb) سِمَانٌ, (Sb, M, L, Mṣb, Ḳ,) used instead of سُمَنَاءُ, which they did not say: (Sb, M, L:) accord. to Lḥ, (M, L,) ▼ مُسْمِنٌ signifies *fat,* or *plump, by nature;* (M, L, Ḳ;) applied to a man: and some say اِمْرَأَةٌ ▼ مُسْمَنَةٌ meaning *a woman fat,* or *plump,* syn. سَمِينَةٌ, (M, L,) or ▼ امرأة مُسَمَّنَةٌ, like مُكَرَّمَةٌ [in measure], meaning [*a woman rendered fat,* or *plump,*] *by nature;* (Ḳ;) and ▼ مُسَمَّنَةٌ بِالأَدْوِيَةِ [*rendered fat, or plump, by medicines*]; (M, L, Ḳ;) and woe, on the day of resurrection, by reason of languor in the bones, is denounced in a trad. against women who make use of medicine to render themselves thus. (L.) — [Hence,] أَرْضٌ سَمِينَةٌ † [*Fat land;* i. e.] *land of good soil, with few stones, strong to foster plants* or *herbage:* (M, L:) or *land consisting of soil in which is no stone.* (Ḳ.) — And كَلَامٌ سَمِينٌ † *Chaste, eloquent,* or *excellent, language.* (L in art. قصد.) — See also مَسْمُونٌ.

سُمَانَى [accord. to those who make the alif to be a sign of the fem. gender] or سُمَانًى [accord. to those who make that letter to be one of quasi-coordination] *A certain bird,* (Ṣ, M, L, Mṣb, Ḳ,) well known; (Mṣb;) [the *quail; tetrao coturnix:* so called in the present day: and also called سَلْوَى:] used as a pl. and as a sing.; (M, L, Ḳ;) sometimes as a sing.: (M, L:) [or] the n. un. is سُمَانَاةٌ: (Ṣ, M, L, Ḳ:) pl. سُمَانَيَاتٌ: (Ṣ:) one should not say سُمَّانَى, with teshdeed. (Ṣ, L.)

سَمَّانٌ *A seller of* سَمْن. (Ṣ, M, L.) ═ Also *Certain dyes* [or *pigments*] *with which one decorates,* or *embellishes.* (M, L, Ḳ.) [See also سِمَّانٌ, in art. سمر.] ═ سُمَّانٌ, the name of *A certain plant,* see in art. سمر.

سَامِنٌ: see سَمِينٌ. — Also *A possessor of* سَمْن: (M, L, Ḳ:) like لَابِنٌ and تَامِرٌ as meaning "a possessor of milk" and "of dates." (L.)

أُسْمَانٌ *Waist-wrappers;* syn. أُزُرٌ [pl. of إِزَارٌ]: and *old and worn-out garments* or *pieces of cloth:* (L:) or *old and worn-out* أُزُر. (Ḳ.)

مُسْمَنٌ: see its fem., with ة, voce سَمِينٌ.

مُسْمِنٌ; and its fem., with ة: see سَمِينٌ. — قَوْمٌ مُسْمِنُونَ *A people,* or *party, whose cattle have become fat,* or *plump.* (L.)

طَعَامٌ مَسْمَنَةٌ لِلْجِسْمِ [*Food that is a cause of fattening to the body*]. (M, L, Ḳ:* in the CḲ [erroneously] مُسْمِنَةٌ.) [See also an ex. voce كِظَّةٌ.]

مُسَمَّنٌ: see its fem., with ة, voce سَمِينٌ.

مَسْمُونٌ Food *made* [or *prepared*] *with* سَمْن: (L:) or *moistened, and stirred about, therewith:* (Ṣ:) [and ▾ سَمِينٌ signifies the same; for] a rájiz says,

* فَبَاكَرَتْنَا جَفْنَةٌ بَطِينَهْ * لَحْمُ جَزُورٍ غَثَّةٍ سَمِينَهْ *

[*And a capacious bowl came to us early in the morning, flesh of a slaughtered camel, lean, prepared with clarified butter*]: i. e. مَسْمُونَة, from السَّمْن, not from السِّمَن. (Ṣ, L.)

سمندل

سَمَنْدَلٌ [The *phenix;*] *a certain bird that is in India; that enters into the fire without having its plumage burned:* (Kr, M, Ḳ:* [mentioned in the M as a quadriliteral-radical word; the ن being regarded by ISd as augmentative:]) also called سَبَنْدَلٌ, with ب [in the place of م]: *it is said that when it becomes extremely aged, and is without offspring, it casts itself into burning coals, and returns to its youthful state.* (TA.) [See also سَنْدَلٌ, in art. سدل.]

سمهدر

سَمَهْدَرٌ *Fat,* as an epithet, (Ṣ, Ḳ,) applied to a boy, in praise of his fleshiness; (Fr, Ṣ;) a boy *fat and fleshy.* (TA.) — ‡ The *penis,* (Ḳ,) as likened to a fat, or fat and fleshy, boy. (TA.) — Applied to a country, or region, (بَلَد,) *Ample,* (Ṣ, Ḳ,) *wide,* or *far-extending, in its limits:* or *in which the sight is perplexed by its levelness.* (TA.) — A land *far-extending; that causes one to lose his way in it.* (Ḳ, TA.)

سمهر

Q. 1. سَمْهَرَ, said of seed-produce, *It did not multiply; as though every grain* [*of the seed*] *had its* [*single*] *head.* (T, Ḳ.)

Q. 4. اِسْمَهَرَّ *It* (a spear, TA) *was,* or *became, hard.* (Ṣ, Ḳ.) — *It* (a thorn) *was,* or *became, dry,* or *tough, and hard.* (Ṣ.) — *It was,* or *became, strong;* (said of a rope; TA;) or *pressing,* or *severe,* or *difficult;* (said of an affair; TA;) or *intense;* (Ṣ, Ḳ;) said of darkness: (Ṣ, TA:) and, said of darkness, *it became disagreeable, and intense.* (Ḳ.) — *He* (a man) *became vehement in fight.* (Ṣ.) — *It* (a penis) *became straight and erect.* (Ḳ, TA.)

رُمْحٌ سَمْهَرِىٌّ, (Ṣ, Ḳ,) and قَنَاةٌ سَمْهَرِيَّةٌ, (Ṣ,) *A hard spear,* (Ṣ, Ḳ,) and *a hard spear-shaft:* (Ṣ:) or so called in relation to a man named سَمْهَر, (Ṣ, Ḳ,) husband of رُدَيْنَة, (Ḳ,) who (as well as his wife, Ḳ) used to straighten spears: (Ṣ, Ḳ:) or in relation to a town or village of Abyssinia, (Ḳ,) called سَمْهَر: so says Ez-Zubeyr Ibn-Bekkár, but Ṣgh distrusts this; and the former opinion is the more common. (TA.) You say also رِمَاحٌ سَمْهَرِيَّةٌ [*Hard spears;* &c.]. (Ṣ.) — وَتَرٌ سَمْهَرِىٌّ *A strong bow-string.* (TA.) — قَدٌّ سَمْهَرِىٌّ *A straight stature.* (TA.)

مُسْمَهِرٌّ A tough thorn. (TA.) — A penis *hard and strong;* or *distended and erect and hard:* (L, TA: [but in both, عود, as an epithet applied to ذَكَر, is put by mistake for عَرْد]:) or the *penis* [itself]. (Ḳ.) — *Straight.* (AZ.)

سمو

1. سَمَا, (Ṣ, M, Mṣb, Ḳ,) first pers. سَمَوْتُ, like عَلَوْتُ, (Ṣ,) aor. يَسْمُو, (Mṣb, TA,) inf. n. سُمُوٌّ; (Ṣ, M, Ḳ;) and سَمِىَ, first pers. سَمِيتُ, (Th, Ṣ, TA,) like عَلِيتُ; (Ṣ;) *He,* (a man, Th, Ṣ,) or *it,* (a thing, M,) *was,* or *became, high, lofty, raised, upraised, uplifted, upreared, exalted,* or *elevated; it rose,* or *rose high:* (Ṣ, M, Mṣb, Ḳ:) and ▾ تَسَامَى signifies the same. (MA. [See also 6.]) — سَمَا لِىَ الشَّىْءُ *The thing became raised from afar so that I plainly distinguished it:* (Ḳ:) or, as in the Ṣ, سَمَا لِى الشَّخْصُ *the form,* or *figure, seen from a distance, rose,* or *became raised, to me* [i. e. *to my view*] *so that I plainly distinguished it.* (TA.) — سَمَا الهِلَالُ *The moon near the change rose* [app. meaning *upreared, not decumbent:* see أَدْلَقُ]. (TA.) — سَمَا لَهُ or نَحْوَهُ *He rose, and betook himself, to,* or *towards, him,* or *it.* Hence, [مَا سَمَوْتُ لَكُمْ *I will not* [or (unless the phrase be an apodosis) *I did not*] *rise and hasten to fight you.* (TA.) — سَمَا بَصَرُهُ *His sight,* or *eye, rose,* or *became raised.* (Ṣ, TA.) [And سَمَا طَرْفُهُ lit. signifies the same; but means † *His look was lofty;* or *he was proud:* see بَامٍ, below.] — سَمَا is also said of him who is termed حَسِيبٌ and شَرِيفٌ [i. e. it signifies *He was,* or *became, noble;* or *high,* or *exalted, in rank*]. (TA.) — سَمَتْ هِمَّتُهُ إِلَى مَعَالِى الأُمُورِ [*His ambition soared,* or *aspired, to high things,* or *the means of attaining eminence;*] *he sought glory,* or *might, and eminence.* (Mṣb, TA.) — سَمَا بِى شَوْقٌ بَعْدَ أَنْ كَانَ أَقْصَرَ [*A yearning,* or *longing, of the soul arose in me after it had ceased*]. (TA.) — هُمْ يَسْمُونَ عَلَى المِائَةِ *They exceed* [or *are above*] *the number of a hundred.* (TA.) — سَمَوْا, (Ṣ, Ḳ, TA,) and ▾ استموا, (Ṣ,) *They went forth to pursue the animals of the chase* (Ṣ, Ḳ, TA) *in their deserts:* (TA:) [or] one says of the hunter, or sportsman, يَسْمُو الوَحْشَ, and ▾ يَسْتَمِيهَا, meaning *he sees,* or *looks to see,* (يَتَعَيَّنُ,) *the coming forth of the wild animals, and pursues them.* (M. [See also 8 below.]) — سَمَا الفَحْلُ, inf. n. سَمَاوَةٌ, *The stallion sprang,* or *rushed, upon,* (Ṣ,) or *he overbore,* (Ṣ,* M, Ḳ,) *his she-camels that had passed seven or eight months since the period of their bringing forth.* (Ṣ, M, Ḳ.) ═ سَمَا بِهِ: see 4. ═ See also 2.

2. سَمَّاهُ فُلَانًا and بِفُلَانٍ, (Ṣ, M, Mṣb, Ḳ,) accord. to Sb originally with ب, but Lḥ says that the former is that which is usual, (M,) [inf. n. تَسْمِيَةٌ,] and in like manner ▾ اسماهُ, (Ṣ,) i. e. اسماهُ فُلَانًا and بِفُلَانٍ, (M, Ḳ,) and accord. to Th, ▾ سَمَاهُ فُلَانًا and بِفُلَانٍ, (Ḳ, [in the correct copies of which the form of the verb first mentioned is without teshdeed, while in the CḲ the first and last are both alike with teshdeed, or, as is said in the M, Th has mentioned سَمَوْتُهُ, but none other has mentioned it,]) *He named him,* or *called him, Such a one;* (Ṣ, M, Mṣb, Ḳ;) as Zeyd; i. e., he made Zeyd to be his name, his proper name. (Mṣb.) — [One says also, سَمَّى اللّٰهَ عَلَى شَىْءٍ, or simply سَمَّى عَلَيْهِ, which is the more common, meaning *He pronounced the name of God, saying* بِسْمِ اللّٰهِ (*In the name of God*), *upon,* or *over, a thing;* such as food, and an animal about to be slaughtered.] The Prophet said, سَمُّوا وَسَمِّتُوا وَدَنُّوا, [cited, with some variations, and expl., in arts. سمت and دنو,] meaning سَمُّوا اللّٰهَ [*Pronounce ye the name of God,* &c.]; i. e. whenever ye eat, [before ye begin to do so, accord. to the general custom, or] between two mouthfuls. (M.)

3. ساماهُ, (Ṣ, M, Ḳ, TA,) inf. n. مُسَامَاةٌ, (TA,) *He vied, competed,* or *contended for superiority, in highness, loftiness,* or *eminence,* or *in glory,* or *excellence,* [or in an absolute sense,] *with him;* syn. عَالَاهُ, (M,) or فَاخَرَهُ, and بَارَاهُ. (Ḳ.) It is said in the trad. respecting the lie [against 'Áïsheh], لَمْ تَكُنْ آمْرَأَةٌ تُسَامِيهَا غَيْرُ زَيْنَبَ, meaning *There was not any woman that vied with her in eminence* (تُعَالِيهَا and تُفَاخِرُهَا) *except Zeyneb;* المُسَامَاةُ meaning المُطَاوَلَةُ فِى الحُظْوَةِ. (TA.) And one says, فُلَانٌ لَا يُسَامَى وَقَدْ عَلَا مَنْ سَامَاهُ [*Such a one will not be vied with in highness,* &c.: *and he has overcome him who vied with him,* &c.]. (Ṣ.) And إِنَّ أَمَامِى مَا لَا أُسَامِى, said when one fears an affair, or event, before him; on the authority

of IAạr; meaning [*Verily before me is an affair, or event,*] *with which I cannot vie.* (M.) A poet cited by Th says,

* بَاتَ ٱبْنُ أَدْمَآءَ يُسَامِى ٱلْأَنْدَرَا *
* سَامَى طَعَامَ ٱلْحَيِّ حَتَّى نَوَّرَا *

and he says that سَامَى means ٱرْتَفَعَ, and صَعِدَ; but [it seems that the verse should be rendered, *Ibn-Admà passed the night aspiring to reach the heap of reaped wheat: he aspired to attain the wheat of the tribe until it attained to maturity:* for ISd says,] in my opinion he means, as the seed-produce rose by growth, he rose to it, until it attained to maturity, when he reaped it and stole it: and he cites also the saying,

* فَٱرْفَعْ يَدَيْكَ ثُمَّ سَامِ ٱلْحَنْجَرَا *

[*And raise thy hands, then endeavour to reach the windpipe*]; explaining سَامِ ٱلْحَنْجَرَ as meaning *raise thy hands to his* حَلْق [or *throat*, properly, *fauces*]. (M.)

4. اسماه *He raised, upraised, uplifted, upreared, exalted,* or *elevated, him,* or *it*; as also ▼ سَمَا بِهِ [lit. *he rose, &c., with him,* or *it*]. (M, Ḳ.) أَسْمَيْتُهُ مِنْ بَلَدٍ *I made him to go up,* or *away, from a town,* or *country.* (TA.) — اسمانا, (TA,) or ▼ اِسْتَمَانَا, (M,) *He,* or *it, incited us to hunt,* or *chase*: so says Th. (M, TA.) ═ Also *He looked at,* or *towards, his,* or *its* سَمَاوَة [expl. immediately before the mention of this phrase in the M as meaning the *form,* or *figure, seen from a distance,* and the *aspect,* of anything]. (M, TA.) ═ And اسمى *He* (a man) *took the direction of,* (Ṣ,) or *came to,* (M,) *Es-Semáweh* (ٱلسَّمَاوَةُ, Ṣ, M) *a certain water in the desert* (ٱلْبَادِيَة, M) or *a place between El-Koofeh and Syria,* (Ḳ,) *a well-known desert.* (TA.) ═ See also 2.

5. تسمّى [expl. by Golius, first, as meaning *Altus fuit, eminuit*; like سَمَا; but for this he names no authority, and I find none for it. ═] *He named himself.* (KL.) — تَسَمَّى بِزَيْدٍ *He was named Zeyd:* (Ṣ,* M,* Mṣb, Ḳ:*) تَسَمَّى بِكَذَا means *Such a thing became his name*: it is quasi-pass. of سَمَّاهُ and أَسْمَاهُ. (TA.) — And تَسَمَّى بِبَنِى فُلَانٍ, (M,) or بِٱلْقَوْمِ, (Ḳ,) and إِلَيْهِمْ, (M, Ḳ,) *He asserted his relationship to the sons of such a one* [*by the assumption of a name of relationship to them*], *or to the people.* (M, Ḳ.)

6: see 1, first sentence. — تَسَامَوْا عَلَى ٱلْخَيْلِ *They mounted upon the horses.* (TA.) — And تساموا *They vied, competed,* or *contended for superiority,* [*in highness, loftiness,* or *eminence,* or *in glory,* or *excellence,* or in an absolute sense, (see 3,)] *one with another.* (Ṣ, Ḳ.) ═ And تساموا signifies also *They called one another by their names.* (TA.)

8. استمى *He* (a hunter, or sportsman, [ٱلصَّاعِدُ in the CḲ being a mistranscription for ٱلصَّائِدُ,]) *attired himself with the socks,* or *stockings, called* مِسْمَاةٌ, (M, Ḳ, TA,) *to protect himself from the heat of the burning ground,* (TA,) *for the hunting of gazelles, in the time of heat.* (M.) And (M, in the Ḳ "or") استماهُ *He asked of him the loan of the socks,* or *stockings, above named, for that purpose,* (M, Ḳ,*) i. e. *for the hunting of gazelles at midday.* (TA.) And استمى, (M, CḲ,) or استمى ٱلظِّبَآءَ, (so in some copies of the Ḳ and in the TA,) *He sought,* or *pursued, the gazelles in their caves,* or *hiding-places,* (فِى غِيرَانِهَا, M, and so in copies of the Ḳ, by the غِيرَان being meant the كُنُس, M,) or *in what was not their time,* or *season,* (فِى غَيْرِ آنِهَا, thus in some copies of the Ḳ,) *at the auroral rising of Canopus* (سُهَيْل) [which rose aurorally, in Central Arabia, about the commencement of the era of the Flight, on the 4th of August, O. S.]): (M, Ḳ:) so says IAạr. (M.) [Freytag says, on the authority of scholia to the Deewán of Jereer, as follows: In the time of the greatest heat, they drive out a wild animal repeatedly from its hiding-place, permitting it to return thither at night, when, thus disturbed, it does not issue from its place; in order that they may be able to strike it.] — And *He hunted,* or *chased, wild animals.* (M.) — See also 1, latter part, in two places. — And see 4. ═ اِسْتَمَيْتُهُ also signifies *I made him the object of a visit*: or *I perceived in him good,* or *goodness, by a right opinion formed from its outward signs.* (Ḳ.) — And استماهُ *He chose it, took it in preference,* or *selected it.* (IAạr, L voce اِقْتَرَحَ.) — And IAạr mentions the saying, ٱلْبَكْرَةُ مِنَ ٱلْإِبِلِ تُسْتَمَى بَعْدَ أَرْبَعَ عَشْرَةَ لَيْلَةً أَوْ بَعْدَ إِحْدَى وَعِشْرِينَ, as meaning [*The youthful she-camel*] *is tested for the purpose of discovering whether or not she be pregnant* [*after fourteen nights or after one and twenty*]: but Th disallows this, and says that the word is تُسْتَمْنَى, from ٱلْمُنْيَةُ, which means "the period by the end of which one knows whether or not the she-camel is pregnant." (M.)

10. استمى [or اِسْتَمَى فُلَانًا, the word فلانا having app. been inadvertently omitted by a copyist,] *He asked,* or *demanded, his* [or *such a one's*] *name.* (TA.)

سِمٌ and سُمٌ and سَمٌ: see اِسْمٌ, in three places, near the beginning of the paragraph; and in four places near the end of the same.

سُمًا: see سَمَآءٌ: ═ and see also اِسْمٌ, near the beginning of the paragraph.

سِمًا and سُمًا: see اِسْمٌ, in two places, near the beginning of the paragraph; and in the last sentence but one of the same.

سَمَآءٌ *The higher,* or *upper,* or *highest,* or *uppermost, part of anything*: [in this sense] masc. (M.) — [In its predominant acceptation,] a word of well-known meaning; (Ḳ, TA;) i. e. (TA) [*The sky,* or *heaven*;] *the canopy of the earth*: (M, Mṣb, TA:) in this sense (M, Mṣb) masc. and fem.; (IAmb, Ṣ, M, Mṣb, Ḳ;*) sometimes fem.; (M;) rarely so, and thus as having the next but one of the significations here following: (Fr, Mṣb:) Az says that it is fem. because it is pl. [or coll. gen. n.] of سَمَآءَةٌ: (TA:) or it is as though it were pl. of ▼ سَمَاوَةٌ, [or rather its coll. gen. n.,] like as سَحَابٌ is of سَحَابَةٌ: (Mṣb, TA:) Er-Rághib says that the سَمَآء as opposed to the أَرْض is fem., and sometimes masc.; and is used as a sing. and as a pl.; as the latter in the Ḳur. ii. 27 [where it is shown to apply to seven heavens]; and that it is like نَخْلٌ and شَجَرٌ and other [coll.] gen. ns.: (TA:) in this sense (M) the pl. is أَسْمِيَةٌ [a pl. of pauc.] (Ṣ, M, Ḳ) and سُمِىٌّ, (M, Ḳ,) the latter [originally سُمُوىٌ] of the measure فُعُولٌ, and both [also] pls. of سَمَآءٌ in another sense, mentioned in what follows, (TA,) and سَمَوَاتٌ or سَمَاوَاتٌ, (Ṣ, M, Mṣb, Ḳ,) and accord. to the Ḳ, [in which all of these are mentioned as though pls. of سَمَآءٌ in all its senses,] ▼ سَمَا, [in the CḲ سُمًا,] but in the M سَمَآءٌ [like the sing., as mentioned above], where it is said that it must be a pl. in the Ḳur ii. 27 for the reason already stated, as though pl. of سَمَآءَةٌ or سَمَاوَةٌ; (TA;) and a poet assigns to سَمَآءٌ the anomalous pl. سَمَآءٍ, by his saying,

* سَمَآءُ ٱلْإِلٰهِ فَوْقَ سَبْعِ سَمَائِيَا *

[*The heaven of God, above seven heavens*]: (Ṣ, M:) the dim. is ▼ سُمَيَّةٌ. (Ḥam p. 452.) — And *Any canopy,* or *covering over-head, of a person.* (Ṣ, Mṣb,* TA.) — And hence, (Ṣ, TA,) *The ceiling,* or *roof,* (Ṣ, Mṣb, Ḳ, TA,) of a house, or chamber, or tent, (Ṣ, Ḳ, TA,) and of anything; (Ḳ, TA;) in this sense masc.; (Mṣb, TA;) and ▼ سَمَاوَةٌ also has this meaning. (Ṣ.) — And *The* رِوَاق, (M, Ḳ,) i. e. *the* شُقَّة [or *oblong piece of cloth*] *that is beneath the upper,* or *uppermost,* شُقَّة, (M,) *of a* بَيْت [or *tent*]; (M, Ḳ;) in which sense it is fem., and sometimes masc.; (M;) as also ▼ سَمَاوَةٌ; (M, Ḳ;) [and so, app., ▼ سِمَايَةٌ; for] one says, أَصْلَحَ سِمَايَتَهُ, with kesr, [*He repaired his* سماية,] meaning, his سَمَاوَة. (TA.) — And *The clouds*; (Zj, Ḳ;) because of their height: (Zj, TA:) or *a cloud.* (Mṣb.) — And *Rain*; (Ṣ, M, Mṣb, Ḳ;) because it comes forth from the سَمَآء [i. e. sky or clouds]: (TA:) or *a good rain* (مَطْرَةٌ جَيِّدَةٌ): (Ḳ, TA:) or *a new rain* (مَطْرَةٌ جَدِيدَةٌ): (T, TA:) or, as some say, *rain that has not fallen upon the earth*; so called in consideration of what has been said above [of its meaning the "clouds" &c.]: (Er-Rághib, TA:) [but] one says, مَا زِلْنَا نَطَأُ ٱلسَّمَآءَ حَتَّى أَتَيْنَاكُمْ [*We ceased not to tread upon the rain until we came to you*]: (Ṣ, TA:) applied to rain, it is masc., and fem. also because of its connexion with the سَمَآء that canopies the earth; (M;) or it is fem., as meaning سَحَابَة: (Mṣb:) the pl. [of mult.] is سُمِىٌّ (Ṣ, M, Mṣb, TA) and [of pauc.] أَسْمِيَةٌ. (Ṣ, TA.) بَنُو مَآءِ ٱلسَّمَآءِ is an appellation of *The Arabs*; [signifying *the sons of the water of the heaven*;] because of their keeping much to the deserts which are the places of the falling of rain [by means of which they subsist]: or by مَآءُ ٱلسَّمَآءِ is meant *Zemzem*, which God made to well forth for the Arabs, who are therefore like the sons thereof. (TA.) — [Hence, app., as being likened to rain by reason of the swiftness of his running,] a certain horse, (M, Ḳ,) belonging to Ṣakhr the brother of El-Khansà, (M,) was named السَّمَآءُ. (M, Ḳ.) — [Hence, likewise, as being likened to rain, † *Bounty.*] One says, أَصَابَنِى بِرَشْحَةٍ مِنْ سَمَائِهِ † [*He gave me a gift from his store of bounty*]. (A in art. رشح.) — Also † *Herbage;* because produced by the rain, which is thus called. (TA.) — And The *back* of a horse; (Ṣ, Mṣb, Ḳ;) because of its height: coupled with [its opposite] أَرْضٌ [q. v.]. (Ṣ, TA.) — And of a sandal, [in like manner opposed to أَرْض,] The *upper part* [*of the sole,* i. e. the *upper surface thereof*], *upon which the foot is placed.* (M.) — See also سَمَاوَةٌ.

سَمَاوٌ : see سَمَاوَةٌ.

سَمِىٌّ : see سَامٍ, in two places. — [Also] *A competitor,* or *contender for superiority, in highness, loftiness,* or *eminence,* or *in glory,* or *excellence;* i. q. ↓ مُسَامٍ, (Ṣ, TA,) and مُطَاوِلٌ: (TA:) thus the word, in the accus. case, is said to signify in the Ḳur xix. 66: (Ṣ, TA:) or it there has the meaning here next following. (Ṣ, M, TA.) — *A like,* or *an equal:* (Ṣ, M, Ḳ, TA:) and this meaning the word, in the accus. case, is said by some to have in the Ḳur xix. 8: or in this instance it has the meaning here following. (M, TA.) — *A namesake* of another. (Ṣ, M, Ḳ, TA.) — The fem. is سَمِيَّةٌ. (M, TA.)

سُمَىٌّ dim. of اِسْمٌ, q. v.

سُمَيَّةٌ dim. of سَمَآءٌ, q. v.

سِمَوِىٌّ and سُمَوِىٌّ : see اِسْمِىٌّ.

سَمَاوَةٌ : see سَمَآءٌ, in three places. — Also The *form,* or *figure, seen from a distance,* (Ṣ, M, Ḳ, TA,) [or] *such as is high,* or *elevated,* (TA,) of anything; (Ṣ, M, Ḳ, TA;) and the *aspect* thereof: pl. [or rather coll. gen. n.] ↓ سَمَآءٌ and ↓ سَمَاوٌ; the latter mentioned by Ks. (M, TA.) El-'Ajjáj says,

* سَمَاوَةَ الهِلَالِ حَتَّى ٱحْقَوْقَفَا *

[*The form,* &c., *of the moon when near the change, until it became curved*]. (Ṣ.)

سِمَايَةٌ : see سَمَآءٌ, in the middle of the paragraph.

سَمَائِىٌّ and سَمَاوِىٌّ [*Of,* or *relating to, the sky* or *heaven; heavenly; celestial;*] rel. ns. from سَمَآءٌ. (Mṣb, TA.)

سَامٍ [*High,* or *lofty;* as also ↓ سَمِىٌّ: pl. of the former سَوَامٍ; applied to women as pl. of سَامِيَةٌ, whence the phrase سَوَامِى الطَّرْفِ in a verse cited voce بَضْعٌ; and to irrational animals, as in an instance here following]. One says القُرُومُ السَّوَامِى *The stallions* [meaning *the stallion-camels high in their heads,* or] *raising their heads high.* (Ṣ, TA.) And سَامِيَاتٌ, [pl. of سَامِيَةٌ,] applied to camels, *That raise,* or *raise high, their eyes and their heads.* (Ḥam p. 791.) And رَدَدْتُ مِنْ سَامِى طَرْفِهِ [app. an elliptical phrase, نَخْوَتَهُ (which is expressed in the explanation) or a similar word being understood; i. e. † *I repelled the pride,* or *haughtiness, of him who was lofty in look;*] meaning *I contracted to him* [or *to the lofty in look*] *his soul, and annulled his pride,* or *haughtiness.* (Ṣ, TA.) And ↓ سَمِىُّ الأَنْفِ [lit. *High-nosed*] means † *disdainful,* or *scornful.* (T and Ḳ in art. انف.) — [Also act. part. n. of 1 in all its senses. — And hence,] سُمَاةٌ, (Ṣ, M, Ḳ,) of which it is the sing., (M,) signifies *Hunters* (Ṣ, M, Ḳ) *going forth to the chase:* (Ḳ:) an epithet in which the quality of a subst. predominates: or, as some say, *hunters in the day-time,* peculiarly: or *hunters wearing the socks,* or *stockings, called* مِسْمَاة. (M.)

اِسْمٌ, (Ṣ, M, Mṣb, Ḳ,) with the conjunctive ا, [i. e. written ٱسْمٌ,] but this is made disjunctive by poetic license [as well as when the word commences a sentence], (Ṣ,) usually with kesr [when the ا is disjunctive], (Lḥ, M, TA,) and أُسْمٌ, (Ṣ, M, Ḳ,) of the dial. of Benoo-'Amr-Ibn-Temeem and of Ḳuḍá'ah, (M, TA,) mentioned by IAar, (TA,) and ↓ سِمٌ and ↓ سُمٌ (Ṣ, M, Ḳ) and ↓ سَمٌ, (Ḳ,) and ↓ سُمًا (M, Ḳ) and ↓ سِمًا and ↓ سَمًا, (Ḳ,) [The *name* of a thing; i. e.] *a sign* [*such as may be uttered or written*] *conveying knowledge* of a thing; syn. عَلَامَةٌ: and *a word applied to denote a substance or an accident or attribute, for the purpose of distinction:* (M, Ḳ:) [or *a substantive in the proper sense of this term,* i. e. *a real substantive;* and *a substance in a tropical sense of this term,* i. e. *an ideal substantive:*] as expl. by El-Munáwee, in the "Towḳeef," the اسم is *that which denotes a meaning in itself unconnected with any of the three times* [*past and present and future*]: *if denoting what subsists by itself, it is termed* اِسْمُ عَيْنٍ; and *if denoting what does not subsist by itself,* [i. e. *an accident* or *attribute,*] *whether existent, as* العِلْمُ [i. e. *knowledge*], *or non-existent, as* الجَهْلُ [i. e. *ignorance*], *it is termed* اِسْمُ مَعْنًى: (TA:) the pl. is أَسْمَآءٌ [a pl. of pauc.] and أَسْمَاوَاتٌ, (Ṣ, M, Ḳ,) the latter said by Lḥ to be a pl. of اِسْمٌ, but it is rather a pl. of أَسْمَآءٌ, for otherwise there is no way of accounting for it, (M,) and أَسَامٍ (Ṣ, M, K) and أَسَامِىُّ (M, Ḳ) are [likewise] pls. of أَسْمَآءٌ: (Ḳ,* TA:) the word ٱسْمٌ [i. e. اِسْمٌ or أُسْمٌ] is derived from سَمَوْتُ, (Ṣ, TA,) or from السُّمُوُّ, (Mṣb, Er-Rághib, TA,) because the اسم is a means of raising into notice the thing denoted thereby, and making it known: (Ṣ,* Er-Rághib, TA:) it is of the measure اِفْعٌ [or أُفْعٌ, accord. to different dialects], the last radical, و, being wanting in it, (Ṣ, Mṣb, TA,) and the hemzeh [or rather ا] being prefixed by way of compensation for it, accord to a general rule; (Mṣb, TA;) for it is originally سِمْوٌ (Ṣ, Mṣb, Er-Rághib, TA) or سُمْوٌ, (Ṣ, Mṣb, TA,) its pl. being أَسْمَآءٌ, and its dim. being ↓ سُمَىٌّ [originally سُمَيْوٌ]: (Ṣ, Mṣb, Er-Rághib,* TA:) some of the Koofees hold that it is from الوَسْمُ, meaning العَلَامَةُ, the و, which is the primal radical, being rejected, and the hemzeh [or ا] being substituted for it, so that its measure is اِعْلٌ [or أُعْلٌ]; but this is a weak opinion, for, were it so, the dim. would be وُسَيْمٌ and the pl. would be أَوْسَامٌ. (Mṣb, TA.) One says, اِسْمُ هٰذَا كَذَا [*The name of this is thus,* or *such a word*]; and if you will you may say, أُسْمُ هٰذا كذا; and in like manner, ↓ سِمُهُ and ↓ سُمُهُ: Lḥ says that اِسْمُهُ فُلَانٌ [*His name is Such a one*] is the [common] phrase of the Arabs; and he mentions أُسْمُهُ فُلَانٌ as heard from [the tribe of] Benoo-'Amr-Ibn-Temeem: and Ks cites, as heard from some of [the tribe of] Benoo-Ḳuḍá'ah, the saying,

* بِٱسْمِ ٱلَّذِى فِى كُلِّ سُورَةٍ سُمُهْ ↓ *

[*In the name of Him whose name is in every chapter of the Ḳur-án*], and ↓ سِمُهْ as heard from others, not of Ḳuḍá'ah. (M.) سِرْ عَلَى ٱسْمِ ٱللّٰهِ is an elliptical phrase [for سِرْ مُعْتَمِدًا عَلَى ذِكْرِ ٱسْمِ ٱللّٰهِ *Journey thou relying upon the mention of the name of God*]. (IJ, M in art. دل: see دَلِيلٌ.) — [Hence,] اسم signifies also † *Fame, renown, report,* or *reputation,* of a person: (TA:) and so ↓ سُمًا, *in relation to good,* (Ḳ, TA,) not to evil; mentioned by Az. (TA.) One says, ذَهَبَ ٱسْمُهُ فِى النَّاسِ, i. e. *His fame* &c. [*went,* or *spread, among mankind,* or *the people*]. (TA.)

اِسْمِىٌّ [*Of,* or *relating to, a name* or *noun* or *substantive;*] rel. n. from اِسْمٌ; as also ↓ سِمَوِىٌّ and ↓ سُمَوِىٌّ. (Ṣ, TA.) [Hence, جُمْلَةٌ ٱسْمِيَّةٌ *A nominal proposition* or *phrase;* as distinguished from فِعْلِيَّةٌ, or verbal.]

[اِسْمِيَّةٌ The *quality of a name* or *noun* or *substantive.*]

مِسْمَاةٌ The *socks,* or *stockings, worn by a hunter,* (M, Ḳ, TA,) *to protect him from the heat of the burning ground.* (TA.)

مُسَمًّى [*Named*]. — [Hence,] one says, هُوَ مِنْ مُسَمَّى قَوْمِهِ and مُسَمَّاتِهِمْ, meaning † *He is of the best of his people* or *party.* (TA.)

مُسَامٍ : see سَمِىٌّ.

سن

1. سَنَّهُ, (M, L, Ḳ,) [aor. ـُ,] inf. n. سَنٌّ, (M,) *He* (a man, M, L) *bit him* (another man, M, L) *with his* أَسْنَان [or *teeth*]. (M, L, Ḳ: but in the Ḳ, *with the* أَسْنَان.) [Hence, app.,] سُنَّتِ الأَرْضُ *The herbage of the land was eaten.* (L, Ḳ.) — And, (M, L, in the Ḳ "or,") aor. and inf. n. as above, (M, L,) *He broke his* (a man's, M, L) أَسْنَان [or *teeth*]. (M, L, Ḳ.) — سُنَّتِ البَدَنَةُ: and سَنَّهَا ٱللّٰهُ: see 4. — Also, (accord. to the M and L, but accord. to the Ḳ "or,") aor. and inf. n. as above, (M, L,) *He pierced him,* or *thrust him, with the* سِنَان [or *spear-head*]. (M, L, Ḳ.) And سَنَّهُ بِالرُّمْحِ *He pierced him,* or *thrust him, with the spear.* (L.) — And *He fixed,* or *mounted, upon it* (i. e. the spear) *the* سِنَان [or *iron head*];

(M, L, K;) and ♦ أَسَنَّهُ *he put to it a* سِنَان. (L.) —— Also, (Ṣ, M, L, Mṣb, K,) aor. and inf. n. as above, (M, L, Mṣb,) *He sharpened it, whetted it,* or *made it sharp-pointed,* (Ṣ, M, L, Mṣb, K,) *and polished it,* (M, L, K,) namely, a thing, (M, L,) or a knife; (Ṣ, L, Mṣb, K;) and so ♦ سَنَّنَهُ: (M, L, K:) and سَنَّ *he sharpened, whetted,* or *made sharp-pointed,* a spear-head *upon the* مِسَنّ: (L:) and *he rubbed,* or *grated,* a stone upon a stone. (Fr, L.) —— [Hence,] سَنَّنِى هٰذَا الشَّىْءُ † *This thing* [*sharpened my appetite;*] *made me desirous of food.* (K.) The Arabs say [also] الحَمْضُ تَسُنُّ الإِبِلَ عَلَى الخُلَّةِ † *The* [*plants, or trees, called*] حمض *strengthen the camels* [or *sharpen their appetites*] *for the* [*plants, or trees, called*] خلّة, *like as the whetstone strengthens* [or *sharpens*] *the edge of the knife.* (L.) —— [Hence also,] سَنَّ أَضْرَاسَهُ, (M, L, K,*) [aor. and] inf. n. as above, (M, L,) *He rubbed and cleaned his teeth with the stick used for that purpose;* (M, L, K;) as though he polished them. (M, L.) —— And سَنَّ الإِبِلَ, (ISk, Ṣ, M, L,) or المَالَ, (K,) aor. and inf. n. as above, (M, L,) *He tended well,* (K,) or *pastured and tended well,* (ISk, Ṣ, L,) or *pastured, and rendered fat,* or *plump,* (M, L,) *the camels,* (ISk, Ṣ, M, L,) or *the cattle;* (K;) [*so that they became in good condition, free from mange* or *the like;*] as though he polished them. (ISk, Ṣ, M, L, K.) —— And سَنُّوا المَالَ *They sent the cattle into the pasturage.* (El-Muärrij, Ṣ, L, K.*) —— And سَنَّ الإِبِلَ, (M, L, K,) [aor. and] inf. n. as above, (M, L,) *He drove the camels quickly:* (M, L, K:) or, as some say, السَّنُّ signifies السَّيْرُ الشَّدِيدُ [i. e. *the making to go vehemently;* السَّيْر being here syn. with التَّسْيِير]: (M, L:) you say, سَنَنْتُ النَّاقَةَ *I made the she-camel to go* (سَيَّرْتُهَا, Ṣ, or سِرْتُهَا, L) *vehemently.* (Ṣ, L.) —— إِنَّمَا أُنَسَّى لِأَسُنَّ, occurring in a trad., meaning *I am made to forget only that I may drive* men *by directing to the right way, and show* them *what is needful* for them *to do when forgetfulness occurs* to them, may be from سَنَّ [expl. above as] meaning "he pastured and tended well" the camels. (L.) —— سَنَّ عَلَيْهِ المَآءَ, [aor. and inf. n. as above,] *He poured forth the water upon him,* or *it;* (M, L, K;) as also ♦ اسنّه: (Ḥam p. 611:) or *he discharged the water gently upon him,* or *it.* (M, L.) You say, سَنَنْتُ المَآءَ عَلَى وَجْهِى, (Ṣ, L,) or سَنَّ المَآءَ عَلَى وَجْهِهِ, (L,) or عَلَى الوَجْهِ, (Mṣb,) or فِى وَجْهِهِ, (Mgh,) aor. as above, (Mgh, L,) and so the inf. n., (L,) *I* [or *he*] *discharged the water without scattering upon his face:* if scattering it in pouring, you say, شَنَنْتُ: (Ṣ, L:) or *I,* or *he, poured the water gently* (Mgh, L, Mṣb) *upon the face,* (Mṣb,) or *upon his face.* (Mgh, L.) And سَنَّ التُّرَابَ *He poured the dust,* or *earth, gently* upon the ground: (Ṣ, L:) and *he put it gently* upon a corpse. (L.) And سَنَّتِ العَيْنُ الدَّمْعَ, aor. and inf. n. as above, *The eye poured forth tears.* (M, L.) And أَسْنِنْ قُرُونَ فَرَسِكَ *Make the* [*issues of*] *sweat to flow from thy horse by plying him hard,* in order that he may become lean, or light of flesh: and سُنَّ لَهُ قَرْنٌ, and قُرُونٌ, *An issue,* and *issues, of his sweat, was,* and *were, made to flow.* (L.) سَنَّ عَلَيْهِ الدِّرْعَ, (Ṣ, M, L, K,) aor. and inf. n. as above, (Ṣ, M, L,) *He put* (lit. *poured*) *upon him the coat of mail.* (Ṣ, M, L, K.) —— سَنَّ الفَحْلُ النَّاقَةَ *The stallion threw down the she-camel* (كَبَّهَا, in copies of the K [erroneously] رَكِبَهَا,) *upon her face.* (L, K.*) [See also 3.] —— سَنَّ الطِّينَ *He plastered pottery with the clay:* (M, L:) or *he made the clay into pottery.* (M, L, K.) —— سَنَّهُ, (Ṣ, L, K,) aor. as above, (Ṣ,) and so the inf. n., (Ṣ, L,) also signifies *He formed it, fashioned it,* or *shaped it;* (Ṣ, L, K;) namely, a thing: (K:) and some say, *he made it long.* (L.) —— And [from the former of these two meanings, app.,] *He instituted, established,* or *prescribed, it,* i. e. a custom, practice, usage, or the like, whether good or bad; *set the example of it; originated it as a custom* &c. *to be followed by others after him.* (L.) You say, سَنَنْتُ لَكُمْ سُنَّةً فَٱتَّبِعُوهَا [*I have instituted* &c., *for you an institute, a custom, a practice, a usage,* or *the like, to be followed, therefore follow ye it*]. (L.) And سَنَّ فُلَانٌ طَرِيقًا مِنَ الخَيْرِ, aor. and inf. n. as above, *Such a one originated* [or *instituted*] *an act of goodness,* or *piety,* [or *a good,* or *pious, way of acting,*] *which his people knew not, and which they afterwards followed,* or *pursued.* (L.) And سَنَّ ٱللّٰهُ سُنَّتَهُ لِلنَّاسِ *God manifested,* or *made known, his statutes,* or *ordinances,* and *commands and prohibitions,* [i. e. *his laws,*] *to men:* (M, L:) and سَنَّ ٱللّٰهُ سُنَّةً *God manifested,* or *made known, a right way* [*of acting* &c.]: (L:) [and in like manner one says of any one,] سَنَّ الأَمْرَ *He manifested,* or *made known, the thing, affair,* or *case.* (K.) —— And سَنَّ سُنَّةً, (M, L,) or طَرِيقَةً, (K,) [aor. and] inf. n. as above, (M, L,) *He pursued* [*a way, course, rule, mode,* or *manner, of acting* or *conduct* or *life* or *the like*]; as also ♦ اِسْتَنَّهَا; (M, L;) or ♦ اِسْتَسَنَّهَا; (so in the K;) and ♦ اِسْتَنَّ بِهَا: (K in art. سير:) and ♦ اِسْتَنُّوا بِطَرِيقٍ مِنَ الخَيْرِ [*They followed,* or *pursued, a good,* or *pious, way of acting*]. (L.) It is said in a trad. respecting the Magians, سُنُّوا بِهِمْ سُنَّةَ أَهْلِ الكِتَابِ, i. e. *Pursue ye with them the way of the People of the Scripture,* or *Bible; act with them as ye act with these;* granting them security on the condition of receiving [from them] the [tax called] جِزْيَة. (Mgh, L.*) ═ سَنَّ is also expl. as meaning *He,* or *it, became altered for the worse,* or *stinking:* so in a trad. of Barwaạ the daughter of Wáshik, where it is said, كَانَ زَوْجُهَا سُنَّ فِى بِئْرٍ [*Her husband had become altered for the worse,* or *stinking,* having died, *in a well* which he had descended]: from the saying in the Ḳur مِنْ حَمَإٍ مَسْنُونٍ: [see مَسْنُونٌ:] but some say that he [who used this phrase] meant [to say, or meant thereby,] أُسِنَ, i. e. *his head became affected with vertigo by reason of a foul odour that he smelt, and he swooned.* (L.)

2. سَنَّنَهُ: see 1, near the beginning. —— [Hence,] سَنَّنَ المَنْطِقَ † *He made the speech good,* or *beautiful;* (M, L, K;) as though he polished it. (M, L.) —— And سَنَّنَ إِلَيْهِ الرُّمْحَ, (M, L, K,) inf. n. تَسْنِينٌ, (M, L,) *He directed,* or *pointed, the spear towards him,* or *it.* (M, L, K.)

3. سَانَّ النَّاقَةَ, inf. n. مُسَانَّةٌ and سِنَانٌ, (Ṣ, M, L, K,) *He* (the stallion-camel) *bit the she-camel with the fore part of the mouth:* (L:) or *he opposed himself to her,* (M, L,) or *drove her,* (Ṣ, L,) or *bit her with the fore part of the mouth, and drove her,* (K,) *to make her lie down,* (Ṣ, M, L, K,) *in order that he might cover her:* (Ṣ, M,* L, K:) or *he covered her without her desiring it,* or *before she desired it, by force.* (IB, L.)

4. اسنّ, (Ṣ, M, L, Mṣb, K,) inf. n. إِسْنَانٌ, (Mgh, L, Mṣb,) said of a man, (Ṣ, M, L, Mṣb, K,) and of other than man, (Mṣb,) i. q. كَبِرَ [meaning *He became advanced in age,* or *full-grown*], (Ṣ, L, Mṣb,) or كَبِرَتْ سِنُّهُ [which means the same]; (M, L, K;) as also ♦ اِسْتَسَنَّ: (K:) but Az says that الإِسْنَانُ in the case of an animal of the ox-kind and of the sheep or goat, is not the same as in that of a man: for in such animals it means [*the attaining to the age of*] *the coming forth of the* [*permanent*] ثَنِيَّة [or *central incisor*]: (Mṣb:) or in such animals it means at least [*the attaining to the age of*] *the shedding of the* [*tooth called*] ثَنِيَّة [which is generally said to be *in the third year*]; and at the utmost in such animals, [*the attaining to the age of*] *what is termed* الصُّلُوغ or السُّلُوغ [which is *in the sixth year*]; and at the utmost in camels, [*the attaining to the age of*] *what is termed* البُزُول [which is generally *in the ninth year*]. (Mgh, L.) [It is also expl. in the K as meaning *His tooth grew forth:* but the right explanation is one given in the Mgh and L; i. e. *his tooth whereby he became* مُسِنّ *grew forth.*] لَمْ يُسْنِنْ, occurring in a trad. of Ibn-'Omar, as some relate it, is a mistake for لَمْ يُسْنِنْ. (Mgh, L.) And ♦ سَنَّتِ البَدَنَةُ, a phrase mentioned by Kt, as meaning *The teeth of the* بدنة *grew forth,* is also a mistake [for أَسَنَّتْ]. (L.) —— You say also, اسنّ سَدِيسُ النَّاقَةِ *The* [*tooth called*] سديس *of the she-camel grew forth,* i. e. *in the eighth year.* (Ṣ, L.) ═ Also, said of God, *He made a tooth to grow forth.* (Ṣ, L, K.) ♦ سَنَّهَا ٱللّٰهُ, [referring to the teeth of a بَدَنَة,] a phrase mentioned by Kt, is a mistake [for أَسَنَّهَا]. (L.) —— See also 1, in the former half of the paragraph, in two places.

5. تَسَنَّنَ بِهِ [*He took him,* or *it, as an exemplar, example,* or *object to be imitated*]. (K voce قُدْوَة.) —— تسنّن فِى عَدْوِهِ *He* (a man) *went at random, heedlessly,* or *in a headlong manner, in his running;* as also ♦ اِسْتَنَّ. (M, L.) ═ See also 5 in art. سنه, last signification.

6. تَسَانَّتِ الفُحُولُ i. q. تَكَادَمَتْ [meaning *The stallion-camels bit one another with the fore part of the mouth*]. (L, K.)

8. اِسْتَنَّ *He rubbed and cleaned his teeth with the* سِوَاك [or *piece of stick used for that purpose*];

(Ṣ, M, L, Ḳ;) *he made use of the* سِوَاك, *passing it over his teeth.* (L.) — And *He took,* or *seized, with the teeth.* (KL.) = استنّت العَيْنُ *The eye poured forth its tears.* (M, L.) — استنّ said of the blood of a wound made with a spear or the like, *It issued in a gush.* (AZ, L.) — Said of the سَرَاب [or mirage], *It was,* or *became, in a state of commotion, went to and fro,* or *quivered.* (M, L, Ḳ.) — Said of a horse, *i. q.* قَمَصَ [app. as meaning *He pranced, leaped, sprang,* or *bounded*]: (Ṣ, Ḳ:) *he frisked;* or *was brisk, lively,* or *sprightly: he ran, in his friskiness, briskness, liveliness,* or *sprightliness, in one direction: he ran, by reason of his friskiness, briskness, liveliness,* or *sprightliness, a heat,* or *two heats, without a rider upon him:* (L:) *he ran to and fro, by reason of briskness, liveliness,* or *sprightliness:* from سَنَّ as signifying "he poured forth" water, and as signifying "he sharpened" iron upon a whetstone. (Ḥar p. 47.) It is said in a prov., اِسْتَنَّتِ الفِصَالُ حَتَّى القَرْعَى, (Ṣ, Meyd, L,) or الفُصْلَانُ, (Meyd,) i. e. *The young weaned camels leaped, sprang,* or *bounded;* (Ṣ,* L;) *even those affected with the small pustules called* قَرَع; (Meyd, L;) which are small white pustules, the remedy for which is salt, and the butter (جُبَاب) of camels' milk: (Meyd:) when the healthy young weaned camels do thus, those affected with such pustules do the like in imitation, but become disabled from doing it by weakness: the prov. is applied to the man who introduces himself among a people, or party, to whom he does not belong: (L:) or to him who speaks with one before whom he should not speak by reason of the greatness of his rank: and some related it differently, saying, القُرَيْعَى [which is the dim. of القَرْعَى]; (Meyd;) and القُرْعُ [which is pl. of الأَقْرَع, q. v.]: and some say that استنّت الفِصَالُ signifies *the young weaned camels became fat,* or *plump, and their skins became* [*sleek*] *like* مَسَانّ [or *whetstones*]. (L.) And it is said in a trad. of 'Omar, رَأَيْتُ أَبَاهُ يَسْتَنُّ بِسَيْفِهِ كَمَا يَسْتَنُّ الجَمَلُ, meaning [*I saw his father*] *exulting with briskness, liveliness,* or *sprightliness, and brandishing his sword,* [*like as the camel exults with briskness, and lashes with his tail.*] (L.) See also 5. — [Also *He took, held,* or *followed, the* سَنَن, i. e., *road,* or *way,* or *main and middle part thereof:* and *he,* or *it, was,* or *lay, in the way.* Hence,] one says, خُذْ مَا آسْتَنَّ, meaning [*Take thou what lies in the way;*] *what is easily attainable; what offers itself without difficulty.* (AA, TA voce اِنْتَدَبَ.) — See also 1, near the end of the paragraph, in two places.

10: see 4: = and see also 1, near the end of the paragraph, in two places. — اِسْتَسَنَّتِ الطَّرِيقُ *The road was travelled.* (Ḳ.)

R. Q. 1. سَنْسَنَتِ الرِّيحُ *The wind blew coldly,* or *coolly;* as also نَسْنَسَت: so in the Nawádir. (L.)

سِنٌّ *i. q.* ضِرْسٌ [as meaning *A tooth;* in which sense this latter word is often used; though it is frequently restricted to a molar tooth, or to any of the teeth except the central incisors]: (M, L, Ḳ:) [or, accord. to some, *a single tooth;* i. e. *one that is not of the double,* or molar, *kind;* as shown by a description in what follows:] of the fem. gender: (Ṣ, M, L, Mṣb:) pl. أَسْنَانٌ (Ṣ, M, L, Mṣb, Ḳ) and أَسِنَّةٌ and أُسُنٌّ, (M, L, Ḳ,) the last of these mentioned by Lḥ, and this and the second anomalous; (M, L;) or the second is allowable as pl. of the first of these pls.; (Ṣ;) or it is pl. of the سِنَان of the spear; but may also be pl. of أَسْنَانٌ as pl. of سِنٌّ applied to herbage upon which camels pasture, in an instance to be cited in what follows: (A'Obeyd, T, L:) the vulgar say إِسْنَان and أُسْنَان, which are wrong: (Mṣb:) the أَسْنَان of a human being consist of four ثَنَايَا, and four رَبَاعِيَات, and four أَنْيَاب, and four نَوَاجِذ, and sixteen أَضْرَاس: or, as some say, four ثنايا, and four رباعيات, and four انياب, and four نواجذ, and four ضَوَاحِك, and twelve أَرْحَآء: (Mṣb:) or the أَسْنَان and أَضْرَاس together make up the number of thirty-two; the ثنايا are four, two above and two below [in the middle]; next are the رباعيات, which are four, two above and two below; next are the انياب, which are four [likewise, two above and two below]; and next are the اضراس, which are twenty, on each side five above and five below; and of these [last] the four that are next to the انياب are the ضواحك; next to each ناب, above and below, is a ضَاحِك; next to the ضواحك are the طَوَاحِن, also called the أَرْحَآء, which are twelve, on each side [above and below] three; and next to these are the نواجذ, which are the last of the teeth in growth, and the last of the اضراس, on each side of the mouth one above and one below: (Zj in his "Khalḳ el-Insán:") the dim. of سِنٌّ is ↓ سُنَيْنَةٌ, because it is fem. (Ṣ.) One says, لَا آتِيكَ سِنَّ الحِسْلِ, (Ṣ, M, L,) i. e. *I will not come to thee as long as remains the tooth of the young one of the* [*kind of lizard called*] ضَبّ; (M, L;) meaning, *ever;* (Ṣ, M,* L;) because the حسل never sheds a tooth: (Ṣ, L:) or, as Lḥ relates it, on the authority of El-Mufaḍḍal, سِنَّىْ حِسْلٍ; [using the dual form of سِنّ;] and [it may be rendered, accord. to the former reading, † *during the life of the young one of the* ضبّ, for] he says, they assert that the ضبّ lives three hundred years, and that it is the longest-lived creeping thing upon the earth. (M, L.) A poet (Aboo-Jarwal El-Jushamee, whose name was Hind, L) says, describing camels taken as a bloodwit,

* فَجَآءَتْ كَسِنِّ الظَّبْيِ لَمْ أَرَ مِثْلَهَا *
* بَوَآءَ قَتِيلٍ أَوْ حَلُوبَةَ جَائِعِ *

[*And they came;* † *like the age of the gazelle* was the age of every one of them: *I have not seen the like of them for an equivalent of a slain person, or a milch camel of one hungry:* (I have given a reading of this verse that I have found in the M and TA in art. ظبى, instead of that in the present art. in the Ṣ and L, in which سناء and سَنَاة are put in the place of بَوَآء, app. for سِنَاء, an inf. n. of سَانَاهُ, and as such here meaning *a soothing, or the like:*)] he means that they were ثُنْيَان, [pl. of ثَنِىّ], because the ثنىّ is one shedding [or that has shed] his ثَنِيَّة, and the gazelle has no ثَنِيَّة [in the upper jaw], so that he is always [one that may be termed] a ثَنِىّ. (Ṣ, L.) It is said in a trad., إِذَا سَافَرْتُمْ فِى الخِصْبِ فَأَعْطُوا الرُّكْبَ أَسِنَّتَهَا, [expl. as] meaning *When ye journey in the land abounding with herbage, enable ye the ridden beasts to take of the pasturage:* (Ṣ, L:) but Az states that A'Obeyd says, I know not أَسِنَّة except as pl. of the سِنَان of the spear; and if the trad. be [correctly] preserved in memory, it seems to be pl. of أَسْنَان; for سِنٌّ [sometimes] signifies the [*portion of*] *herbage upon which camels pasture;* and its pl. is أَسْنَانٌ; one says, أَسْنَانٌ مِنَ المَرْعَى; and the pl. of أَسْنَانٌ is أَسِنَّةٌ: Aboo-Sa'eed says that this last is pl. of سِنَانٌ, not of أَسْنَانٌ, and ↓ سِنَانٌ is applied to the [plants, or trees, called] حَمْض, as meaning † *a strengthener* [i. e. *a sharpener of the appetite*] of the camels for the [plants, or trees, called] خُلَّة: [see a phrase in the earlier part of the first paragraph:] in like manner, also, [he says,] when they light upon what is termed سِنٌّ مِنَ المَرْعَى [*a portion of pasturage*], this is termed ↓ سِنَانٌ عَلَى السَّيْرِ [*a strengthener,* or *sharpener, for journeying*]: this explanation is approved by Az, and likewise that of A'Obeyd: it is also related, on the authority of Fr, that السِّنُّ signifies *the eating vehemently:* [a signification mentioned in the K as well as in the L:] and Az says, I have heard more than one of the Arabs say, أَصَابَتِ الإِبِلُ اليَوْمَ سِنًّا مِنَ المَرْعَى [*The camels have obtained to-day a good portion of pasturage*] when they have eaten well of the best of the pasturage: Z says that ↓ أَعْطُوا الرُّكْبَ أَسِنَّتَهَا means † *Give ye to the ridden beasts what will prevent their being slaughtered;* for when their owner pastures them well, they become fat, and goodly in his eye, and therefore he withholds himself, with niggardliness, from slaughtering them, and this [condition of them] is likened to أَسِنَّة [as meaning "spear-heads"] pl. of سِنَان: [see also أَخَذَتْ رِمَاحَهَا, said of camels, voce رُمْح:] or if the pl. of سِنّ be intended by it, the meaning is, *enable ye them* [i. e. *the ridden beasts*] *to take of the pasturage;* and hence the trad., أَعْطُوا السِّنَّ حَظَّهَا مِنَ السِّنِّ, i. e. *Give ye the possessors of the* سِنّ [meaning *tooth*] *their share of the* سِنّ which is the *pasture.* (L.) السِّنُّ is also used for ذَوَاتُ السِّنِّ [*The possessors of the tooth*] as meaning *the slave and horses and the like and other animals,* [*collectively,* in like manner as خُفّ and حَافِر are used,] in a trad. of 'Omar. (L.) And it is said in a trad. of Ibn-Dhee-Yezen, لَأُوطِئَنَّ أَسْنَانَ العَرَبِ كَعْبَهُ, for ذَوِى أَسْنَانِ العَرَبِ, meaning [*I will assuredly make*] *the great men and the nobles* [*of the Arabs to tread upon his ankle*]. (L.) [But اسنان in this instance may be pl. of سِنّ in the sense here next following; so that ذوى اسنان

may be rendered *the advanced in age.*]) — Hence, (L,) ‡ *Life;* (Ṣ, M, L, Mṣb;) metaphorically used in this sense as indicative of its length and its shortness; (L;) [for the teeth vary with the length of life;] the *measure,* (Ḳ,) or *extent, of life;* (Mṣb, Ḳ;) [the *age attained;*] used in relation to human beings and others: (M, L, Ḳ:) of the fem. gender in this sense also, (M, L, Mṣb,) because meaning مُدَّةٌ: (Mṣb:) pl. أَسْنَانٌ, (M, L, Ḳ,) only. (M, L.) You say رَجُلٌ حَدِيثُ السِّنِّ, meaning † *A young man.* (Ṣ, Mṣb, Ḳ, all in art. حدث.) And جَاوَزْتُ أَسْنَانَ أَهْلِ بَيْتِى † [*I have exceeded*] *the lives of the people of my house.* (L.) And صَدَقَنِى سِنَّ بَكْرِهِ [and سِنُّ بَكْرِهِ, expl. in art. بكر]. (L.) — And † *A like, an equal,* or *a match, in age,* of another; (M, L, Ḳ;) like تِنٌّ; (M, L;) as also ▼ سَنِينٌ, (M, L, Ḳ,) and ▼ سِنِينٌ, (L,) or ▼ سَنِينَةٌ: (M, Ḳ:) in this sense also fem.; and [therefore] the dim. is ▼ سُنَيْنَةٌ; (L;) one says, ابْنِى سُنَيْنَةُ ابْنِكَ [*My son is the equal in age of thy son*]: (El-Ḳanánee, L:) and the pl. is أَسُنٌّ and أَسْنَانٌ. (L.) — Also † *A tooth* of a مِنْجَل [or *reaping-hook*]: (M, L, Ḳ:*) pl. أَسْنَانٌ, signifying its أُشُر. (L and Ḳ in art. اشر.) — [And † *A tooth* of a comb.] The Arabs say كَأَسْنَانِ المُشْطِ meaning † [*Like the teeth of the comb*] in equality, in respect of any state, or condition: but if they mean equality in respect of evil, they say

سَوَاسِيَةٌ كَأَسْنَانِ الحِمَارِ

[*Equals like the teeth of the ass*]; سواسية being an anomalous pl. of سَوَآءٌ. (Ḥar p. 39.) — And † The *nib,* i. e. the *place of paring,* of a writing-reed: (Ṣ, L, Ḳ:) [and *each lateral half of that part;* for] the writing-reed has a right سِنّ and a left سِنّ: (TA in art. حرف:) [and ▼ سِنَّةٌ occurs in the Ḳ voce جِلْفَةٌ as meaning the *point* of a writing-reed.] One says, أَطِلْ سِنَّ قَلَمِكَ وَسَمِّنْهَا وَحَرِّفْ قِطَّتَكَ وَأَيْمِنْهَا [*Make long the nib, or pared portion, of thy writing-reed, and make it thick* (lit. *fat*), *and make thy mode of cutting the extremity of the nib oblique, and make it to incline towards the right*]. (Ṣ, L.*) — *A tooth* [or *pin*] of a key [app. of the kind of wooden lock called ضَبَّة, q. v.]. (MA.) — See also سِنْسِنٌ. — Also, (M, Ḳ, and A and Ḳ in art. فص,) or ▼ سِنَّةٌ, (Ṣ, JM,) *A clove,* (فُصّ, Ṣ and A as syn. with سِنّ in art. فص, and JM in explanation of سِنَّة in the present art., or فُصَّة, Ṣ and L in explanation of سِنَّة,) or *a* حَبَّة [app. here meaning *small distinct portion*] *of the head* [app. here meaning bulb], (M and L and Ḳ in explanation of سِنّ,) of garlic. (Ṣ, M, A, L, Ḳ, JM.) ═ [Accord. to some,] one says, وَقَعَ فُلَانٌ فِى سِنِّ رَأْسِهِ, meaning *Such a one fell into* [*what equalled*] *the number of his hairs, of good,* (M,* L, Ḳ,*) and *of evil:* (L:) or, as some say, *into what he willed,* or *wished, and had authority to decide:* (L, Ḳ:) but this is a mistranscription: (Meyd:) the correct saying is فِى سِىِّ رَأْسِهِ, (Az, Meyd, L,) and سَوَآءِ رَأْسِهِ, meaning *he fell into a state of enjoyment,* or *welfare;* (Meyd;) the former sometimes expl. as meaning, [*he lighted upon,* or *came upon, what equalled*] *the number of the hairs of his head, of wealth,* or *good:* (A'Obeyd, Meyd:) or *what equalled* [*the hairs of*] *his head, of abundance of herbage,* or *of the goods, conveniences,* or *comforts, of life:* (Az, L, and Meyd* on the authority of IAạr:) the saying is a prov. (Meyd.) ═ السِّنُّ also signifies *The wild bull.* (L, Ḳ.)

سُنَّةٌ, (Ḳ,) or ▼ سِنَّةٌ, (so in the L,) *A she-bear;* syn. دُبَّةٌ. (Ḳ: in the L دِبَّة.) And *A she-lynx:* syn. فَهْدَةٌ. (L, Ḳ.)

سُنَّةٌ *A way, course, rule, mode,* or *manner, of acting* or *conduct* or *life* or *the like;* syn. طَرِيقَةٌ, (Mgh, L, Mṣb,) as also ▼ سَنَنٌ, (Ṣ, L,) and سِيرَةٌ; (Ṣ, M, L, Mṣb, Ḳ;) whence the saying, سُنُّوا بِهِمْ سُنَّةَ أَهْلِ الكِتَابِ, expl. in the first paragraph of this art., last sentence but one, (Mgh,) and the saying of the Hudhalee [Khálid Ibn-Zuheyr] cited in the first paragraph of art. سير; (Ṣ;) and this is [said to be] the primary signification; (L;) whether *good,* or *bad;* (M, L;) *approved* or *disapproved:* (Mṣb:) or, accord. to Sh, *a way* [*of acting* &c.] *that has been instituted,* or *pursued, by former people, and has become one pursued by those after them;* and this, he says, is the primary signification: (L:) it signifies also [particularly] *a way of acting* &c. *that is commended,* or *approved, and right;* wherefore one says, فُلَانٌ مِنْ أَهْلِ السُّنَّةِ [*Such a one is of the people of the commended and right way of acting* &c.; generally meaning, *of those who follow the institutes,* or *ways, of the Prophet*]; and is from ▼ سَنَنٌ signifying "a way," or "road;" (T, L;) and is also *syn. with* سَنَنٌ: (L:) and [the *laws,* i. e] the *statutes,* or *ordinances,* and *commands and prohibitions,* of God: (Lḥ, M, L, Ḳ:) [also *a practice or saying,* or the *practices and sayings collectively, of Moḥammad, or any other person who is an authority in matters of religion, namely, any prophet, or a Companion of Moḥammad,* (see Kull p. 203,) *as handed down by tradition:*] when used unrestrictedly in matters of the law, السُّنَّةُ means only *what the Prophet* [*Moḥammad*] *has commanded, and what has been handed down from him by tradition,* [or, as in the JM, *and what he forbade,*] *and what he has invited to do, by word or deed, of such things as are not mentioned in the Ḳur-án;* wherefore one says, in speaking of the directions, or evidences, of the law, الكِتَابُ وَالسُّنَّةُ meaning *the Ḳur-án and the Traditions:* (L:) [thus used, it may be rendered *the institutes of the Prophet;* or *his rule* or *usage:*] or in the law it signifies *the way of acting* &c. *that is pursued in religion without being made obligatory,* or *necessary;* it is *what the Prophet persevered in doing,* or *observing, with omitting,* or *neglecting,* [it] *sometimes; and if the said persevering is in the way of religious service, it constitutes* [*what are termed*] سُنَنُ الهُدَى; *if in the way of custom,* سُنَنُ الزَّوَائِدِ: *so that* سُنَّةُ الهُدَى [*the* سُنَّة *of right direction*] *is that of which the observance is a completion of religion, and it is that to the omission, or neglect, whereof attach blame and misdemeanour;* and سُنَّةُ الزَّوَائِدِ [*the* سُنَّة *of supererogatory acts*] *is that of which the observance is good, but to the omission, or neglect, whereof neither blame nor misdemeanour attaches, such as the ways of the Prophet in his standing and sitting and clothing and eating:* (KT:) سُنَنٌ is the pl. (Mṣb.) سُنَّةُ الأَوَّلِينَ, in the Ḳur xviii. 53, i. e. سُنَّتُنَا فِى الأَوَّلِينَ [*The way pursued by us in respect of the former,* or *preceding peoples*], means the destruction decreed to befall them; (Jel;) or extirpation; (Bd;) or, as Zj says, their beholding punishment; (أَنَّهُمْ عَايَنُوا العَذَابَ; [or, as expl. in the Ḳ, مُعَايَنَةُ العَذَابِ;]) for the believers in a plurality of gods said, [as is related in the Ḳur viii. 32,] O God, if this be the truth from Thee, then do Thou rain down upon us stones from heaven. (M, L.) — Also *Nature; natural,* or *native, disposition, temper,* or other *quality* or *property:* (M, L, Ḳ:) pl. سُنَنٌ. (M, L.) — And The *face;* (M, L, Ḳ;) because of its polish and smoothness: (M, L:) or the *ball of the cheek* (حُرُّ الوَجْهِ): or the *circuit* (دَائِرَة) *of the face:* or *the form:* (M, L, Ḳ:) or the *form* of the face: (Ṣ:) or the *forehead and two sides thereof:* (M, L, Ḳ:) all from the meaning of polish and smoothness and evenness: (M, L:) or the *principal part* of the face; the *part* thereof *in which beauty is generally known to lie:* (M in art. امر:) or the *side* of the cheek: pl. سُنَنٌ. (L.) You say, رَجُلٌ قَبِيحُ السُّنَّةِ *A man foul,* or *ugly, in respect of the form, and of what confronts one, of the face.* (L.) And هُوَ أَشْبَهُ شَىْءٍ سُنَّةً وَأُمَّةً *He is the most like thing in form,* and *face, and in stature.* (L.) — And The *black line,* or *streak, on the back of the ass.* (L.) ═ Also, (Ṣ, Ḳ,) or ▼ سِنَّةٌ, (so in the L,) *A sort of dates, of El-Medeeneh,* (Ṣ, L, Ḳ,) *well known.* (L.)

سِنَّةٌ: see سِنٌّ, in the last quarter of the paragraph, in two places. — Also *i. q.* سِكَّةٌ, meaning *A ploughshare;* i. e. the *iron thing with which the ground is ploughed up:* (AA, IAạr, Ṣ, L: [see also لُؤْمَةٌ:]) pl. سِنَنٌ. (L.) — [And] *A two-headed* فَأْس [i. e. *hoe* or *adz* or *axe*]: (Ḳ:) or [its pl.] سِنَنٌ signifies [simply] *i. q.* فُؤُوس [pl. of فَأْس]. (L.) ═ See also سُنَّةٌ: ═ and see سُنَّةٌ, last sentence.

سَنَنٌ *A way,* or *road:* (T, L:) the *main and middle part* thereof; (A'Obeyd, Mgh, L;) the *beaten track,* or *part along which one travels,* thereof; as also ▼ سُنَنٌ: (A'Obeyd, L:) the نَهْج [i. e. *plain,* or *open, track*] of the road; and so ▼ سُنُنٌ and ▼ سُنَنٌ (M, L, Ḳ) and ▼ سِنَنٌ: (Ḳ:) and, all of these, the *course,* or *direction,* of the road: (M, L, Ḳ:) but ISd says, [in the M,] I know not ▼ سِنَنٌ on any other authority than that of Lḥ. (L.) One says, تَنَحَّ عَنْ سَنَنِ الطَّرِيقِ (Ṣ, L, Mṣb) and ▼ سُنَنِهِ and ▼ سُنُنِهِ [*Go thou away,* or *aside, from the main and middle part of the road,* or *from the beaten track thereof;* &c.]

(Ṣ, L:) and عَنْ سَنَنِ الخَيْلِ (Ṣ, Mṣb) *from the way of the horses,* (Mṣb,) or *from the course,* or *direction, thereof.* (Ṣ.) And تَرَكَ فُلَانٌ لَكَ سَنَنَ الطَّرِيقِ and ▼ سُنَنَهُ (Lḥ, M, L) and ▼ سُنَنَهُ (L) and ▼ سِنَنَهُ (Lḥ, M, L) [respecting which last see what precedes] *Such a one left,* or *has left, to thee the course,* or *direction, of the road.* (Lḥ, M, L.) And امْضِ عَلَى سَنَنِكَ and ▼ سُنَنِكَ (L) or ▼ سُنُنِكَ (M) *Go along on thy course.* (M, L.) — سَنَنٌ also signifies *A way of acting* or *the like;* syn. طَرِيقَةٌ; (Ṣ, L;) as also سُنَّةٌ: (Mgh, L, Mṣb: see the latter word, in the former half of the paragraph, in two places:) you say, اسْتَقَامَ فُلَانٌ عَلَى سَنَنٍ وَاحِدٍ [*Such a one went on undeviatingly in one way*]: (Ṣ, L, Mṣb:*) and [in like manner] ▼ جَآءَتِ الرِّيحُ سَنَائِنَ *The wind came in one way,* (Ṣ, Ḳ,) *in one course,* or *direction,* and *one way,* (M, L,) *not varying:* (Ṣ, L:) and [similar to the former of these two phrases is the saying] بَنَى القَوْمُ بُيُوتَهُمْ عَلَى سَنَنٍ وَاحِدٍ i. e. [*The people,* or *party, built their houses,* or *constructed their tents,*] *in one mode,* or *manner.* (M, L.) Also The *aim,* or *intention,* of a man. (ISh, M,* L.) [Accord. to Fei,] السَّنَنُ also signifies الوَجْهُ مِنَ الأَرْضِ [by which may be meant *The place,* or *tract,* or *quarter, of the land, towards which one goes;* or it may mean *the face,* or *surface, of the ground*]: and so ▼ سُنَنٌ and ▼ سَنَنٌ. (Mṣb.) — السَّنَنُ also signifies الإِبِلُ تَسْتَنُّ فِى عَدْوِهَا [app. meaning *The camels that leap, spring,* or *bound, in their running;* (see 8;) or rather السَّنَنُ مِنَ الإِبِلِ has this meaning, as appears from what here follows]: (Ḳ:) or [a horse, or camel,] *that perseveres in his running and advancing and retiring:* and one says, جَآءَ سَنَنٌ مِنَ الخَيْلِ, i. e. شَوْطٌ [app. meaning *There came a number of horses running a heat;* for شوط in this explanation seems, from the phrase to which it relates and from what immediately precedes the mention of that phrase, to be an inf. n. used as an epithet in which the quality of a subst. predominates, and therefore, agreeably with a common rule, applied to a pl. number as well as to a single individual]: (M, L:) and جَآءَ مِنَ الخَيْلِ سَنَنٌ لَا يُرَدُّ وَجْهُهُ [app. meaning, in like manner, *There came, of the horses, a number running a heat, the course of which was not to be turned away*]; (Ṣ, L; not expl. in either;) and so, مِنَ الإِبِلِ [*of the camels*]. (L.) — And Sh explains سَنَنٌ as applied in a verse of El-Aạshà to People, or a party, *hastening to fight,* or *slay.* (L.) — Also, [as a quasi-inf. n.,] *The leaping, springing,* or *bounding,* [so I here render اسْتِنَان, inf. n. of 8, which see for other, similar, meanings,] of camels and of horses. (L. [It is there mentioned in another place, and in the M, as a subst., meaning a quasi-inf. n., from اسْتَنَّ.])

سُنَنٌ: see the next preceding paragraph, in six places. — It is also pl. of سُنَّةٌ [q. v.]. (Mṣb, &c.)

سُنُنٌ: see سَنَنٌ, in five places.

سِنَنٌ: see سَنَنٌ, in three places.

سَنَان, also pronounced سَنَّان: see سَنًا, in art. سنو and سنى, last sentence.

سِنَانٌ, (Ḳ,) or سِنَانُ رُمْحٍ, (Ṣ, M, Mgh, Mṣb,) *A spear-head;* (Ḳ;) *the iron* [*head*] *of a spear:* so called because of its polish: (M, L:) pl. أَسِنَّةٌ. (T, Ṣ, Mṣb, Ḳ.) One says, هُوَ أَطْوَعُ السِّنَانِ *He is one to whom the spear-head is subservient, howsoever he will.* (Ḳ.) — See also an ex. of its pl. voce سِنٌّ, in the middle of the paragraph. — And سِنَانٌ is *syn. with* مِسَنٌّ, q. v. (Ṣ, M, L.) — See also سِنٌّ, near the middle of the paragraph, in two places. — Also *Flies;* syn. ذِبَّانٌ [pl. of ذُبَابٌ]. (El-Muärrij, L.)

سَنُونٌ *A dentifrice;* (Ṣ, M, L, Ḳ;) *a medicament with which the teeth are rubbed and cleansed, compounded for the purpose of strengthening and freshening them:* (L:) pl. سُنُوفَاتٌ. (Ḳ in art. سوط [where, in the CḲ, سُفُوفَاتٌ is erroneously put in its place].) — See also سَنِينَةٌ.

سِنُونَ and سُنُونَ pls. of سَنَةٌ: see this last in art. سنه.

سَنِينٌ: see مَسْنُونٌ, in two places. — Also *What flows* [*upon,* or *from, the whetstone*] *on the occasion of sharpening iron* [*or a knife or the like*], and which is always stinking. (Fr, L.) And *What falls from a stone when one rubs,* or *grates, it* (Fr, Ṣ, L, Ḳ) *upon another stone.* (Fr, L.) — See also سِنٌّ, in the latter half of the paragraph.

سِنِينٌ: see سِنٌّ, in the latter half of the paragraph. — See also سَنَةٌ (of which it is a pl.) in art. سنه.

سَنِينَةٌ *Elevated sands extending lengthwise upon the ground:* or *sands having the form of* حِبَال [pl. of حَبْلٌ, q. v.]: and ▼ سَنُونٌ is syn. therewith in the former or latter of these senses: (M, L:) or سَنَائِنُ has the former of these meanings, and سَنِينَةٌ is its sing. (Ṣ, Ḳ.) — Also *Wind:* (M, L, Ḳ:) [or *a gentle wind:* (Freytag, from the Deewán of the Hudhalees:)] pl. سَنَائِنُ. (L.) — See also the pl., in relation to wind, voce سَنَنٌ, near the middle of the paragraph. — See also سِنٌّ, in the latter half of the paragraph.

سُنَيْنَةٌ: see سِنٌّ, of which it is the dim., in the former half of the paragraph: — and again, in the latter half of the same. — See also سَنَةٌ (of which it is an irreg. dim.) in art. سنه.

سِنْسِنٌ The *edge* (Ṣ, M, L, Ḳ) *of a vertebra* (Ṣ, M, L) or *of the vertebræ* (Ḳ) *of the back;* (Ṣ, M, L, Ḳ;) as also ▼ سِنْسِنَةٌ and ▼ سِنٌّ: (M, L, Ḳ:) pl. سَنَاسِنُ: (Ṣ, L:) and the *head* [*of any*] *of the bones of the breast:* and the *extremity of the rib in the breast:* (Ḳ:) or, as some say, سَنَاسِنُ signifies the *heads of the extremities of the bones of the breast, which are the soft heads of the bones of the* زَوْر: or the *extremities of the ribs in the breast:* or, of a horse, the *prominent* [*ribs,* or *anterior parts of the ribs, called*] جَوَانِح, *resembling the* ضُلُوع, *but stopping short of the* ضُلُوع: (M, L:) or the *upper part of the hump of a camel:* (Ḥam p. 689:) [or the *middle of the lower part of the hump;* for,] accord. to Az, لَحْمُ سَنَاسِنِ البَعِيرِ signifies *the flesh that is between the two sides,* or *halves, of the hump of the camel; which is the best of the sorts of flesh, and is marbled with fat:* (L:) or سَنَاسِنُ signifies *bones* [in general]; as also شَنَاشِنُ: (IAạr, L:) and (Ṣ) accord. to Ibn-'Amr [or Aboo-'Amr?] and others, (L,) it signifies the *heads of the* مَحَالَة [app. here meaning *vertebræ*]; (Ṣ, L;) and [it is also said that the sing.] سِنْسِنٌ signifies the *head of the* مَحَالَة [which signifies *a vertebra* as well as vertebræ, or is more correctly without ة when applied to the latter]. (Ḳ.) — Also *Thirst.* (Ḳ.)

سِنْسِنَةٌ: see the next preceding paragraph.

سَنْسَانٌ [app. *A blast* of smoke]. One says نَسْنَاسٌ مِنْ دُخَانٍ and سَنْسَانٌ, meaning [of] the smoke of fire. (L in the present art. and TA in art. نس.)

رِيحٌ سَنْسَانَةٌ *A cold,* or *cool, wind;* as also نَسْنَاسَةٌ. (L.)

أَسَنُّ *More* [and *most*] *advanced in age:* (M, L, Ḳ:) a correct Arabic word. (M, L.) You say, هٰذَا أَسَنُّ مِنْ هٰذَا *This is more advanced in age than this:* (M, L, Ḳ:*) and Th says, speaking of Moosà Ibn-'Eesà El-Leythee, أَدْرَكْتُهُ أَسَنَّ أَهْلِ البَلَدِ [meaning *I lived in his time,* he *being the most advanced in age of the people of the town,* or *country*]. (M, L.)

مُسِنٌّ *Advanced in age,* or *full-grown;* (L, Mṣb;) applied to a beast, *contr. of* فَتِىٌّ: (Ṣ and Mgh and Mṣb in art. فتو:) or, applied to an animal of the ox-kind and to the sheep or goat, [at the least,] *in the third year:* (L: [see the verb, 4:]) fem. with ة: (Mṣb:) pl. مَسَانٌّ, (L, Mṣb,) which, applied to camels, is [said to be] *syn. with* كِبَارٌ [as meaning *advanced in age,* or *full-grown*], (Ḳ,) *contr. of* أَفْتَآءٌ [pl. of فَتِىٌّ] so applied. (Ṣ, L.)

مِسَنٌّ *A whetstone;* i. e. *a stone,* (Ṣ, M, L, Mṣb,) or *anything,* (Ḳ,) *with which,* (Ṣ, Ḳ,) or *upon which,* (M, L, Mṣb, Ḳ,) *one sharpens,* or *whets,* or *makes sharp-pointed,* (Ṣ, M, L, Mṣb, Ḳ,) *and polishes,* (M, L, Ḳ,) *a knife and the like;* (Mṣb;) and ▼ سِنَانٌ signifies the same. (Ṣ, M, L.)

مَسْنُونٌ [*Bitten with the teeth:* whence, app., what next follows]. You say أَرْضٌ مَسْنُونَةٌ and ▼ سَنِينٌ meaning *Land of which the herbage has been eaten.* (L, Ḳ.) — *Sharpened,* or *whetted,* or *made sharp-pointed, and polished;* as also ▼ سَنِينٌ; (M, L, Ḳ;) applied to a knife (Ḳ) or thing [of any kind]. (M, L.) *Made smooth.* (Ṣ, L.) *Formed, fashioned,* or *shaped.* (Ṣ, M, L.) *Made long.* (L.) You say وَجْهٌ مَسْنُونٌ † *A face in which is length, without breadth;* (مَخْرُوطٌ;) *smooth and even;* or *smooth and long;* or *long, and not high in the ball;* or *soft, tender, thin, and even;* as though the flesh were ground (سُنَّ)

[like as a thing is ground in sharpening and polishing]) from it. (M, L.) And رَجُلٌ مَسْنُونُ الوَجْهِ † *A man beautiful and smooth in the face:* (Lḥ, M, L, Ḳ:) or *a man in whose nose and face is length:* (Ṣ, L, Ḳ:) or *beautiful and long in the face.* (L.) مِنْ حَمَإٍ مَسْنُونٍ, in the Ḳur [xv. 26 and 28 and 33], (L,) means † [*Of black mud*] *altered* [*for the worse in odour*]; (AA, Ṣ, L;) in which sense مَسْنُون is also applied to water; (AHeyth, L;) [or] *stinking:* (AA, Ṣ, M, L, Ḳ:) from سَنَنْتُ الحَجَرَ عَلَى الحَجَرِ "I rubbed, or grated, the stone upon the stone;" what flows between them, termed سَنِين, being always stinking: (Ksh and Bḍ in xv. 26: [and the like is said in the L, on the authority of Fr:]) or, accord. to I 'Ab, it means *moist:* accord to AO, *poured forth:* or, as some say, *poured forth in a form,* or *shape:* (L:) or *formed, fashioned,* or *shaped:* (Ksh, Bḍ:) or *poured forth in order to its drying* [or *hardening*], *and becoming formed, fashioned,* or *shaped, like as molten,* or *liquified, substances are poured forth into moulds.* (Ksh,* Bḍ.)

مُسْتَنُّ الحَرُورِ is said to mean *The place of the running of the* سَرَاب [or *mirage,* app. *in consequence of the hot wind*]: or *the place of the vehement heat of the hot wind;* as though it were running to and fro therein (كَأَنَّهَا تَسْتَنُّ فِيهِ عَدْوًا): or it may mean *the place whence issues the* [*hot*] *wind:* but the first is the explanation given by the preceding authorities. (M, L.) ═ المُسْتَنُّ [an epithet used as meaning] *The lion.* (Ḳ. [Thus applied, act. part. n. of اِسْتَنَّ.])

مُسْتَسَنٌّ and مُسْتَسِنٌّ: see what follows.

مُسَنْسَنٌ *A travelled road;* (T, M, L, and so in the CḲ; in some copies of the Ḳ ▼ مُسْتَسِنٌّ;) as also ▼ مُسْتَسَنٌّ. (Ḳ.)

سنبق

سُنْبُوقٌ *A small* زَوْرَق [or *skiff*], (Ṣgh, Ḳ, TA,) *made on the coasts of the sea:* a word of the dial. of the people of all the coasts of the Sea of El-Yemen: (Ṣgh, TA:) whether the ن be radical requires consideration: Ṣgh says, in the Tekmileh, that the word is of the measure فُنْعُول, from السَّبْق. (TA.)

سنبك

سُنْبُكٌ [mentioned in the Ṣ and Mṣb in art. سبك, and said in the latter to be of the measure فُنْعُل, The *toe of a horse or mule or ass;* i. e] the *extremity of the fore part of the solid hoof;* (Ṣ, Mṣb;) or the *extremity of the solid hoof* (Lth, O, Ḳ) *and its two sides anteriorly:* (Lth, O:) pl. سَنَابِكُ. (Ṣ, O, Mṣb.) — † The *extremity* (T, O, Ḳ, TA) *of the* نَعْل [or *iron shoe at the lower end of the scabbard*], (T, TA,) or *of the* حِلْيَة [or *gold or silver ornament*], (O, Ḳ,) of a sword. (T, O, Ḳ, TA.) — † The قَوْنَس [or *tapering top*] of an iron helmet. (O, Ḳ.) — Of a بُرْقُع, † The شِبَام [meaning *each,* or *either, of the two threads,* or *strings,* of the face-veil called برقع, *by which the woman draws and binds the two upper corners to the back of her head*]: (Ḳ, TA: [in the CḲ, شِيام is erroneously put for شِبَام:]) the سَنَابِك of the بَرقع are its شُبُم. (O.) — † *A rugged region* or *tract of the earth or land, in which is little,* or *no, good:* (Ṣ, O, Mṣb, Ḳ:) likened to the سنبك of the solid hoof. (Ṣ, O.) And سَنَابِكُ الأَرْضِ † *The extremities of the earth* or *land.* (TA.) — † The *first* of rain: (O, Ḳ:) and, (TA,) as some say, (Mṣb,) of anything. (Mṣb, TA.) One says, أَصَابَتْنَا سُنْبُكُ السَّمَآءِ † [*The first of the rain fell upon us*]. (TA.) And one says also, سُنْبُكٌ مِنْ كَذَا † *Preceding such a thing.* (O, Ḳ.) And كَانَ ذٰلِكَ عَلَى سُنْبُكِهِ † *That was in the time thereof,* (O, Ḳ, TA,) *and in the first thereof.* (TA.) ═ It is also said to signify The [*tax called*] خَرَاج: (O:) so says IAạr. (TA.) ═ And *A sort of run.* (Ḳ.)

سنبل

Q. 1. سَنْبَلَ الزَّرْعُ *The seed-produce put forth its* سُنْبُل [or *ears*]; (M, Ḳ;) as also أَسْبَلَ [q. v.]: the former of the dial. of Temeem, and the latter of that of El-Ḥijáz. (TA.) ═ سَنْبَلَ ثَوْبَهُ, (Ḳ,) inf. n. سَنْبَلَةٌ, (TA,) *He* (a man) *dragged a skirt of his garment behind him;* so says Khálid Ibn-Jembeh: (TA:) or *he dragged his garment behind him* or *before him.* (Ḳ.)

سُنْبُلٌ [*Ears of corn:* n. un. with ة: pl. سَنَابِلُ and سُنْبُلَات, the latter pl. occurring in the Ḳur xii. 43 and 46: it is said in the M, in art. سنبل, that سُنْبُلَةٌ signifies *one of the* سُنْبُل *of* زَرْع; in the Ḳ, in this art., that it signifies *one of the* سَنَابِل *of* زَرْع: see سَبَلٌ]. السُّنْبُلَةُ is also the name of *A certain sign of the Zodiac* [i. e. *Virgo*]; (Ḳ, TA;) *the sixth sign; the third of the summer signs:* (TA:) [or *Spica Virginis;*] *a certain star in Virgo.* (Ḳzw.) [See, again, سَبَلٌ.] — Also *A certain perfume;* (M;) *a certain plant of sweet odour, also called* سُنْبُلُ العَصَافِيرِ, (Ḳ,) *and* الرَّيْحَان الهِنْدِىُّ; (TA;) [*spikenard,* called in the present day السُّنْبُلُ الهِنْدِىُّ;] *the best whereof is the* سُورِىّ, (Ḳ,) *what is brought from* سُور [or سُورَى?], *a town,* or *district, of El-'Irák;* (TA;) *and the weakest is the* هِنْدِىّ: *it is an aperient; a discutient of flatulences;* (Ḳ,* TA;) *strengthening to the brain and the spleen and the kidneys and the bowels; and diuretic; and has the property of arresting the excessive flow of blood from the womb.* (Ḳ, TA. [Mentioned also voce سَبَلٌ, as called سُنْبُلُ الطِّيبِ.]) السُّنْبُلُ الرُّومِىُّ [also signifies *Spikenard,* or perhaps *a variety thereof;*] i. q. النَّارِدِينُ. (Ḳ.)

سُنْبُلَةٌ The [*kind of trees called*] عِضَاه [q. v.]. (Fr, Ḳ.) [It is said in the TA that the ن in this word is augmentative: but the same is held by some to be the case in other words mentioned in this art.]

قَمِيصٌ سُنْبُلَانِىٌّ *A shirt ample in length,* or *reaching to,* or *towards, the ground:* or so called in relation to a town, or district, in the Greek Empire. ('Abd-El-Wahháb El-Ghanawee, Ḳ, TA.)

سنت

2. سَنَّتَ القِدْرَ, inf. n. تَسْنِيتٌ, *He put* سَنُّوت, (Ṣ, Ḳ,) meaning كَمُّون [i. e. *cumin,* or *cumin-seed*], (Ṣ,) *into the cooking-pot.* (Ṣ, Ḳ.)

3. سَانَتُوا الأَرْضَ *They sought after the herbage of the land, doing so diligently,* or *with labour* or *perseverance,* or *time after time.* (M, Ḳ.)

4. اسنتوا *They experienced drought,* or *barrenness:* (Ṣ, M, A, Ḳ:) derived from سَنَةٌ; the و being changed into ت, [for سَنَةٌ is originally سَنَوَةٌ, or, accord. to one dial. سَنَهَةٌ,] to distinguish between this verb and أَسْنَى as signifying "he remained in a place a year:" or, as Fr says, they imagined the ه [meaning ة, in سَنَة,] to be a radical letter, finding it to be the third letter, and therefore changed it into ت: (Ṣ:) accord. to Sb, the ت [in أَسْنَتَ] is substituted for the ى [in أَسْنَى]; and there is no instance of the like except ثِنْتَانِ [in which the ت is substituted for the final radical, ى], (M in the present art.,) and in words of the measure اِفْتَعَلَ [as اِتَّسَرَ for اِيتَسَرَ]. (M in art. ثنى.)

5. تَسَنَّتَهَا [*He married her,* or *took her as his wife, he being an ignoble,* or *a low-born, but rich, man, and she being a noble,* or *high-born, but poor, woman;* or] *he,* an ignoble, or a low-born, man, *married her,* a noble, or high-born woman, *because of the paucity of her property and the abundance of his property.* (Ṣ) And تسنّت كَرِيمَةَ آلِ فُلَانٍ *He married the noble* or *high-born, woman of the family of such a one in the year of drought, dearth,* or *scarcity.* (TA.)

أَصَابَتْهُمْ سَنْتٌ, for سَنَةٌ, *Drought,* or *barrenness, afflicted them,* or *befell them.* (Ṣ, TA.)

رَجُلٌ سَنِتٌ, (Ṣ, A,* Ḳ,*) or سَنِتُ الخَيْرِ, (M,) *A man possessing little,* or *no, good; possessing few,* or *no, good things;* or *poor:* (Ṣ, M, A,* Ḳ:*) pl. سَنِتُونَ: (M, Ḳ:) it has no broken pl. (M.) And the former, *A man afflicted with drought,* or *barrenness;* (TA in art. بقع;) as also ▼ مُسْنِتٌ: (TA in the present art.:) and رَجُلٌ مُسْنِتٌ ▼ *a man indigent and desolate, possessing nothing:* probably from أَرْضٌ مُسْنِتَةٌ, or عَامٌ مُسْنِتٌ, [both expl. below,] or from أَسْنَتُوا meaning as expl. above. (MF.) — And أَرْضٌ سَنِتَةٌ and ▼ مُسْنِتَةٌ *Land that has not given growth to anything,* (AḤn, M, Ḳ,) *in consequence of its not having been rained upon:* but if containing any of the dry herbage of the preceding year, it is not termed مسنتة: it is not thus termed unless having in it nothing. (AḤn, M.) [See also سَنِيتٌ.]

رَجُلٌ سَنُوتٌ *A man evil in disposition.* (M, L.) [See also مَسْنُوتٌ.]

عَامٌ سَنِيتٌ and ▼ مُسْنِتٌ *A year of drought,* or *barrenness.* (AḤn, M, Ḳ.) [See also سَنِتٌ.]

سَنُّوتٌ, also pronounced سِنَّوْتٌ, (Ṣ, M, Ḳ,) the

latter a dial. var. mentioned by Kr, (M,) and سُنُّوتٌ, a form mentioned by IAth and others, but the first is that which is commonly known, and the most chaste; (TA;) a word of which the meaning is differently explained, as follows: (M, TA:) *Honey:* (Ṣ, M, A, Ḳ:) *i. q.* رُبٌّ [i. e. *rob*, or *inspissated juice*, &c.]: (M, Ḳ:) *a species of dates: fresh butter;* syn. زُبْدٌ: *cheese:* (Ḳ:) *i. q.* كَمُّونٌ [i. e. *cumin*, or *cumin-seed*]; (Yaạkoob, Ṣ, M, Ḳ;) so in the dial. of El-Yemen: (M:) or *a certain plant resembling the* كَمُّون: (IAạr, M:) *i. q.* شِبِتٌّ [i. e. *anethum graveolens*, or *dill, of the common garden-species*; in the CḲ شِبِتّ]: and *i. q.* رَازِيَانَجٌ; (M, Ḳ;) which last is what is called in the Egyptian dial. شَمَرٌ [a name given in Egypt to the *anethum graveolens*, above mentioned, and to *its seed*; and also to the *anethum fœniculum*, or *fennel*]. (TA.)

مُسَنَّتٌ; and its fem., with ة: see سَنِتٌ, in three places: and see also سَنِيتٌ.

مُسْنُوتٌ One *who associates with another and is angry without cause,* (Ḳ, TA,) *by reason of his evil disposition.* (TA.) [See also سَنُوتٌ.]

سنج

1. سَنَجَ *He smeared* anything *with a colour different from its own colour.* (O, Ḳ.)

سُنُجٌ The عُنَّاب [or *jujube*]. (IAạr, Ḳ.)

سَنْجَةٌ, as also صَنْجَةٌ, but the former is the more chaste, (T, O, Mṣb, Ḳ,) accord to Fr, (O,) because ص and ج do not both occur in any [genuine] Arabic word, (Mṣb,) or the former only is allowable accord. to Fr, (T, Mṣb,) or, accord. to ISk, (T, O, Mṣb, and Ṣ in art. صنج,) and IḲt, (T, Mṣb,) the latter only is allowable; (T, O, Mṣb, and Ṣ and O in art. صنج;) an arabicized word, (O, Mṣb, and Ṣ and A and Ḳ in art. صنج,) from [the Pers.] سنك [or سَنْگ, as meaning "a weight"]; (O;) [or rather from the Pers. سَنْجَه meaning "a balance" and "a weight;"] *i. q.* مِيزَانٌ [*A balance*]: (A in art. صنج:) [in the present day, applied to *a steelyard:* and also, more commonly, (agreeably with the explanation of صَنْجَة in the MA,) to *a weight of a balance;* which last seems to be intended in the Ṣ and O and Mṣb and Ḳ &c. by the expressions سَنْجَةُ المِيزَانِ and صَنْجَةُ, unless these expressions be instances of what is termed إِضَافَةُ الشَّىْءِ إِلَى نَفْسِهِ (i. e. the prefixing a noun, governing the gen. case, to another noun signifying the same thing), which I think unlikely:] pl. سَنَجٌ (A, Mṣb) and سَنَجَاتٌ. (Mṣb.) One says, اَلْوَزْنُ مِنِّى بِالسَّنْجَةِ الرَّاجِحَةِ [*He received by weight from me with the inclining balance, or with the preponderating weight*], and بِالسَّنَجِ الوَافِيَةِ [*with the full weights*]. (A.) And a rájiz says,

* كَأَنَّهَا سَنْجَةُ أَلْفٍ رَاجِحَهْ *

[*As though it, or she, were the weight of a thousand, preponderating*]: or, as some relate it, صَنْجَةُ. (O.)

سُنْجَةٌ *i. q.* رُقْطَةٌ [i. e. *Blackness mixed with speckles of white: or the reverse: or speckles of white,* and *of black,* and *of red,* and *of yellow,* in an animal]: (AA, O, Ḳ:) pl. سُنَجٌ, (O, Ḳ, TA, in the CḲ سُنْجٌ,) like حُجَرٌ (Ḳ, TA, in the CḲ like حُجْرٌ,) as pl. of حُجْرَةٌ. (TA.)

سِنَاجٌ The *mark,* or *effect, of the* سِرَاج [i. e. *lamp,* or *its lighted wick*], (A, O, Ḳ,) *upon the wall.* (O, Ḳ, TA.) One says, لَا بُدَّ لِلسِّرَاجِ مِنَ السِّنَاجِ [*The lamp, or its lighted wick, cannot but have the mark, or effect, thereof upon the wall*]. (A.) — Also The سِرَاج [*itself;* i. e. *a lamp,* or *its lighted wick*]: (ISd, Ḳ:) as also ▼ سَنِيجٌ. (Ḳ.)

سَنِيجٌ: see what next precedes.

بُرْدٌ مُسَنَّجٌ A [*garment of the kind called*] بُرْد *striped.* (O, Ḳ.) [SM thinks that it may be a mistranscription for مُسَبَّجٌ, meaning "wide," applied to a كِسَآء: but this I think improbable.]

سنجاب

سِنْجَابٌ [a Pers. word, arabicized; in the present day applied to The *squirrel;* and particularly the *gray squirrel:* and the *minever:*] *a certain animal, of the length of the jerboa, larger than the* فَأْر [or *rat*], *the fur of which is of the utmost softness: furred garments are made with its skin; and the best skins of this animal are the smooth and gray.* (Dmr, TA.)

[سِنْجَابِىٌّ *Gray; of the colour of the* سِنْجَاب.]

سنح

1. سَنَحَ is *syn. with* عَرَضَ [signifying *It showed, or presented, its side:* and hence, *it presented itself; it occurred*]. (A, O, L.) One says of a gazelle, (Ṣ, Ḳ,) or of a bird, (Ṣ,* A, Mṣb,) or some other thing, (IF, Ṣ, Mṣb, as implied by explanations of the part. n. سَانِحٌ,) سَنَحَ (Ṣ, A, Mṣb, Ḳ) لِى, (Ṣ,) or لَهُ, (A,) and عَلَيْهِ, (L,) and سَنَحَهُ, (A,) aor. ـَ, (Ṣ, L,) inf. n. سُنُوحٌ (Ṣ, L, Ḳ) and سَنْحٌ and سُنْحٌ; (L;) and ▼ سانح, inf. n. سِنَاحٌ; (Ṣ, TA;) [*It presented to me, or to him, its right side, or its left side, in its passage;*] *it passed along from the direction of my* [or *his*] *left hand to the direction of my* [or *his*] *right hand:* (Ṣ:) or *it passed along from the direction of* [*my* or] *his right hand* (A, L, Mṣb) *to the direction of* [*my* or] *his left hand:* (L, Mṣb:*) *contr. of* بَرَحَ. (Ḳ. [See سَانِحٌ, below.]) And سَنَحَ لِى فِى المَنَامِ *He presented himself to me in sleep;* syn. عَرَضَ: occurring in a saying of 'Alee, referring to the Prophet. (O.) And سَنَحَ لِى رَأْىٌ (Ṣ, A, Mṣb, Ḳ) فِى كَذَا, (Ṣ, Mṣb,) aor. ـَ, inf. n. سُنُوحٌ and سَنْحٌ and سُنْحٌ, (Ḳ, TA,) the second with ḍamm and sukoon and the third with two ḍammehs, (TA, [but written in the CḲ سُنْح and سُنُح,]) ‡ *An idea, or an opinion, presented itself,* or *occurred,* syn. عَرَضَ, (Ṣ, A, Ḳ,) or *appeared,* syn. ظَهَرَ, (Mṣb,) *to me,* (Ṣ, A,* Mṣb, Ḳ,) *respecting such a thing.* (Ṣ, Mṣb.) سَنَحَ is also said of poetry, (L, Ḳ,) meaning † *It presented itself,* or *occurred,* syn. عَرَضَ, to me (لِى): (L:) or *it became easy;* (L, Ḳ;) and in this last sense, said of a thing, aor. ـُ, inf. n. سُنُوحٌ (Mṣb.) And it is related in a trad. of 'Áïsheh, that she said, [referring to the Prophet,] أَكْرَهُ أَنْ أَسْنَحَهُ, meaning *I dislike that I should confront him* with my hands [engaged] in prayer; from سَنَحَ as signifying عَرَضَ. (L.) — سَنَحَ بِكَذَا † *He mentioned such a thing obliquely,* or *indirectly,* (Ṣ, Ḳ,) *in terms understood by the person addressed but unintelligible to others,* (Ṣ,) *not speaking explicitly.* (Ḳ.) — جَادَ سَنَحَ الخَاطِرُ بِهِ *i. q.* † [*The mind granted it liberally*]. (Mṣb.) — سَنَحَهُ *He turned him away,* or *back,* (O, Ḳ,) عَمَّا أَرَادَ [*from that which he desired,* or *meant*], (O,) or عَنْ رَأْيِهِ [*from his opinion*]. (Ḳ.) — And سَنَحَ بِهِ and عَلَيْهِ *He caused him to fall into straitness,* or *difficulty;* or *into sin,* or *crime;* syn. أَحْرَجَهُ; (Ḳ, TA; in the CḲ, [erroneously,] أَخْرَجَهُ;) [i. e. أَوْقَعَهُ فِى الحَرَجِ;] and *did evil to him.* (Ḳ.)

3: see 1, second sentence.

5: see 10. — تَسَنَّحْ مِنَ الرِّيحِ means اِسْتَدْبِرْ مِنْهَا [i. e. *Shelter thyself from the wind*]: so says Aboo-'Amr Esh-Sheybánee. (O [and so, probably, in correct copies of the Ḳ: in my MS. copy of the Ḳ, اِسْتَدْبِرْ منها: in the CḲ, اِسْتَدِرْ منها: in the TA, strangely, استدرّ منها, and expl. as meaning أُطْلُبْ منها الدَّرَّ: in the TḲ, استدبر منها, and expl. as meaning ولّها ظهرك: Freytag, app. having to choose only between the reading in the CḲ and that in the TḲ, has followed the latter, without mentioning their disagreement; though, if the meaning were "turn thy back towards the wind," the explanation should be اِسْتَدْبِرْهَا, not اِسْتَدْبِرْ مِنْهَا].)

10. اِسْتَسْنَحْتُهُ عَنْ كَذَا, and ▼ تَسَنَّحْتُهُ, *i. q.* اِسْتَفْصَحْتُهُ [meaning *I asked him, or desired him, to explain such a thing*]: (O, Ḳ:) and so اِسْتَسْنَحْتُهُ عن كذا, and تَسَنَّحْتُهُ. (TA.)

سُنْحٌ *Prosperity, good fortune, good luck,* or *auspiciousness; blessing, increase,* or *plenty:* syn. يُمْنٌ and بَرَكَةٌ. (O, Ḳ.) — Also, (Ḳ,) or ▼ سُنُحٌ, with two ḍammehs, (O,) The *middle of a road:* (O, Ḳ:) like [سُجْحٌ or] سُجُحٌ. (O.) [Both are also inf. ns. of 1, q. v.]

سِنْحٌ *i. q.* أَصْلٌ [i. e. *Origin,* &c.]; like سِنْخٌ [q. v.]. (O, TA.) — And *i. q.* هَيْئَةٌ and سَحْنَآءٌ [i. e. *Form, aspect, appearance,* &c.]. (O.)

سُنُحٌ: see سُنْحٌ.

غَارَةٌ سُنْخَاةٌ [app. as meaning *An incursion into the territory of an enemy taking by surprise*], accord. to one reading of a trad., is from سَنَخ الرَّأْى [expl. above]: but the reading commonly known is سَحَّاءُ [q. v.]. (IAth, TA.)

سَنِيخٌ: see سَانِحٌ. ═ Also *Pearls*; or *large pearls*; syn. دُرّ: (O, Ḳ:) or (Ḳ, but accord. to the O, "also") the *string upon which they are to be strung, before they are strung thereon*: (O, Ḳ:) when they have been strung, it is termed عِقْدٌ: (O:) pl. سُنُخٌ. (TA.) ── And [*Ornaments such as are termed*] حُلِىّ. (O, Ḳ.)

سِنَاحَةٌ i. q. سُتْرَةٌ [i. e. *Anything by which a person or thing is veiled, concealed, hidden, or covered*; &c.]. (O.)

سَنَحْنَحٌ A man *who sleeps not during night*: (Ḳ:) or سَنَحْنَحُ اللَّيْلِ a man who is *vigilant*; *who sleeps not*; *who journeys during the night*. (O.)

سَانِحٌ (Ṣ, A, Mṣb, Ḳ, &c.) and ▼ سَنِيحٌ (Ṣ, A, Ḳ) both signify the same, (Ṣ, A, Ḳ,) applied to a gazelle, (Ṣ, Ḳ,*) or to a bird, (Ṣ, A, Mṣb,) &c., (Ṣ, Mṣb,) *Turning its right side towards the spectator*; thus expl. by Ru-beh to Yoo, in the presence of AO; i. e. *passing from the direction of the left hand of the spectator towards the direction of his right hand*: (Ṣ:) or *coming from the direction of the right side of the spectator* (Aboo-'Amr Esh-Sheybánee, IF, A, L, Mṣb) *towards the direction of his left hand*; *turning towards him its left side*, which is that termed الإِنْسِىّ: *contr. of* بَارِحٌ [q. v.]: (Aboo-'Amr Esh-Sheybánee, L:) the pl. [of the former] is سَوَانِحُ and سَانِحَاتٌ and [of either] سُنُحٌ: and this last is also employed to signify *auspicious* and *inauspicious* gazelles [&c.], accord. to the different opinions of the Arabs. (L.) The Arabs [who apply the epithet in the latter of the two senses first explained] regard the سَانِح as a good omen, and the بَارِح as an evil omen; (Aboo-'Amr Esh-Sheybánee, Ṣ, L;) because one cannot shoot at the latter without turning himself: (Ṣ in art. برح:) but some of them hold the reverse of this: (Aboo-'Amr Esh-Sheybánee, L:) the people of Nejd hold the سانح to be a good omen; but sometimes a Nejdee adopts the [contr.] opinion of the Ḥijázee. (IB, TA.) It is said in a prov., مَنْ لِى بِالسَّانِحِ بَعْدَ البَارِحِ [expl. in art. برح]. (Ṣ, Ḳ.) ── [It is said in Ḥar p. 671 that السَّانِحُ also signifies المتطيّر المتفآل بالطيور, as though meaning *The person auguring*, or *who augurs, evil or good, from birds*: but I think that the right reading is المُتَطَيَّرُ بِهِ وَالمُتَفَآلُ بِهِ مِنَ الطُّيُورِ, i. e. *what is regarded as an evil omen and as a good omen, of birds*.]

سنخ

1. سَنِخَتْ أَسْنَانُهُ, (JḲ, A, TA,) [aor. ـَ,] inf. n. سَنَخٌ, (A,) *His teeth became eroded at the roots*. (JḲ, A, TA.) ── And سَنِخَ, said of a man, *He had his teeth eroded at the roots*. (A, TA.) ── And said of the mouth, *It lost the roots* (أَسْنَاخ) *of its teeth*. (Mṣb.) ── Also, (JḲ,) inf. n. as above, (Ḳ,) i. q. تغيّر [meaning † *It became altered for the worse in odour or otherwise, stinking, rancid, bad, or corrupt*]. (JḲ, Ḳ.) It is said [in this sense] of oil, (Ṣ, Ḳ,) or food, (A, L,) &c., (L,) as a dial. var. of زَنِخَ, (Ṣ, Ḳ,*) or from سَنِخَ الأَسْنَانِ, and therefore tropical; as also ▼ تسنّخ; (A;) *its odour became bad*. (Ṣ,* TA.) And سَنِخَ مِنَ الطَّعَامِ *He ate much food*; syn. أَكْثَرَ. (L, Ḳ.) ═ سَنَخَ, aor. ـُ, inf. n. سُنُوخٌ, (L, Ḳ,) *He*, or *it, was*, or *became, firm, steady, steadfast, stable, fixed, fast, settled*, or *established*; syn. رَسَخَ. (L, Ḳ.*) So in the phrase سَنَخَ فِى العِلْمِ, (Ṣ, L, Mṣb,) aor. ـُ, (L,) or ـَ, (Mṣb,) inf. n. سُنُوخٌ, (Ṣ, L, Mṣb,) [*He was*, or *became, firmly rooted* or *established, in knowledge*, or *science*;] and this means also *he attained to eminence therein*. (L.)

2. تَسْنِيخٌ The *seeking, desiring*, or *demanding*, a thing. (Ḳ.) You say, سَنَّخَ مِنْهُ الشَّىْءَ *He sought, desired*, or *demanded, from him the thing*. (TḲ.)

5: see 1.

سِنْخٌ The أَصْل [i. e. *origin, source, root, foundation*, &c.,] (JḲ, Ṣ, Mṣb, Ḳ) of anything: (JK, Mṣb, TA:) as also ▼ سِنْخ: (L:) pl. [of pauc.] أَسْنَاخٌ (L, Mṣb) and [of mult.] سُنُوخٌ. (L.) One says, رَجَعَ فُلَانٌ إِلَى سِنْخِ الكَرَمِ [app. meaning *Such a one traced back his lineage to* an ancestor who was *the origin*, or *source, of generosity* or *nobility*: or *such a one returned*, or *reverted, to the original state*, or *condition, of generosity*: the latter I think the more probable, as it is immediately added], and إِلَى سِنْخِهِ الخَبِيثِ [which seems to mean, *to his bad original state*]. (L.) And it is said in a trad., أَصْلُ الجِهَادِ وَسِنْخُهُ المُرَابَطَةُ عَلَيْهِ i. e. الرِّبَاطُ فِى سَبِيلِ اللّٰهِ [meaning *The very essence of fighting against unbelievers, and the first principle thereof, is constancy*, or *perseverance*, or *assiduity, in the way*, or *cause, of God*]. (L.) ── Also The *place of growth* (مَنْبِت) [i. e. the *socket*] of a tooth: (Ḳ:) or the *part of a tooth that enters into the flesh* [*of the gum*]; (Zj in his "Khalḳ el-Insán;") [i. e.] the أَسْنَاخ of the teeth, (Ṣ,) or of the central incisors, (Mṣb,) are the *roots* thereof (أُصُولُهَا). (Ṣ, Mṣb.) ── And [The *tongue*, or *tang*, of a blade;] the *part* of a knife, and of a sword, *that enters into*, or *is inserted in, the handle*: and the *part* of an arrow-head *that enters into*, or *is inserted in, the head of the shaft*. (L.) ── And The *paroxysm* of a fever. (Ḳ.) ── أَسْنَاخُ النُّجُومِ, accord. to IAạr, as is related by Th, means *The stars that do not make their* [*temporary*] *abode in the Mansions of the Moon, which* [*latter*] *are called* نُجُومُ الأَخْذِ: ISd says, I am not sure whether he mean the أُصُول [a term applied to *the seven*, or *five, planets*], or others: some say, [and so IAạr is stated in the TA in art. شيخ to have said,] that they are called only أَشْيَاخُ النُّجُومِ [q. v.]. (L, TA.*)

طَعَامٌ سَنِخٌ ‡ [*Food altered for the worse in odour* or *otherwise, stinking, rancid, bad*, or *corrupt*: see 1]. (A.) ── And بَلَدٌ سَنِخٌ † *A town*, or *country, in which is fever*, or *much fever*. (Ḳ.)

سَنْخَةٌ and ▼ سَنَاخَةٌ *A fetid odour*: and the latter, [and app. the former also,] *dirt*; and *remains of matter used for tanning*. (Ḳ, TA.) One says بَيْتٌ لَهُ سَنْخَةٌ (Ṣ, TA) and ▼ سَنَاخَةٌ (TA) or ▼ سِنَاخَةٌ (so in three copies of the Ṣ) [*A tent*, or *house*, or *chamber, that has a fetid odour*; as is indicated in the Ṣ and TA]. And Aboo-Kebeer says,

* فَأَتَيْتُ بَيْتًا غَيْرَ بَيْتِ سِنَاخَةٍ ▼ *

(so in three copies of the Ṣ,) or

* فَدَخَلْتُ بَيْتًا غَيْرَ بَيْتِ سَنَاخَةٍ ▼ *

(so in the TA,) i. e. [*And I came to*, or *and I entered*,] *a tent*, or *house*, or *chamber, not one of tanning-matter nor of clarified butter*. (Ṣ.)

سُنْخُتَانِ The *measure of two statures of a man*. (Ḳ.)

سِنَاخَةٌ or سَنَاخَةٌ: see سَنْخَةٌ, in five places.

بَيْتُ فُلَانٍ بَيْتُ سَنِيخَةٍ means [*The house of such a one is a house of unstableness*; or] *is not one of stableness*. (JḲ.)

[أَسْنَخُ, as stated by Freytag, is expl. by Reiske, in his additions to the Lex. of Golius, as meaning *Pulled out from the root* (سنخ): but no authority for this is named by him.]

سند

1. سَنَدَ إِلَيْهِ, (Ṣ, M, Mṣb, Ḳ,) aor. ـُ, (Ṣ, M, Mṣb,) inf. n. سُنُودٌ; (Ṣ, M, Mṣb, Ḳ;) and سَنِدَ, aor. ـَ; (Mṣb;) and ▼ استند, [which is the most common,] (Ṣ, M, Mṣb, Ḳ,) and ▼ تساند, (Ṣ, M, A, Ḳ,) and ▼ اسند; (M, TA;) signify the same; (Ṣ, M,* Mṣb, Ḳ*;) i. e. *He* (a man, Ṣ, Mṣb, [and in like manner it is said of a thing,]) *leaned, rested*, or *stayed himself, against it*, or *upon it*; syn. اِعْتَمَدَ; (TḲ;) [or اعتمد عَلَيْهِ;] namely, a thing, (Ṣ, M, Mṣb,) or a wall, (A, Mṣb,) &c. (Mṣb.) ── سَنَدَ فِى الجَبَلِ, (M, Ḳ,) aor. ـُ, inf. n. سُنُودٌ, (M,) *He ascended the mountain*; as also ▼ اسند. (M, Ḳ.) And [hence,] أَسْنَدْتُ ▼ إِلَى فُلَانٍ ‡ *I ascended to such a one*. (A.) ── And سَنَدَ فِى الخَمْسِينَ, (M, and so in some copies of the Ḳ,) or لِلْخَمْسِينَ, (so in other copies of the Ḳ,) ‡ *He approached*, or *drew near to*, [the age of] *fifty*: (Ḳ, TA:) [likewise] from سَنَدَ فِى الجَبَلِ. (M, TA.*) ── سَنَدَ ذَنَبُ النَّاقَةِ, (Ḳ,) or ▼ أَسْنَدَ, (so in the O,) *The tail of the she-camel tossed about, and lashed her croup*, or *rump, on the right and left*. (O, Ḳ.)

2. سنّد, inf. n. تَسْنِيدٌ, *He set up* [pieces of] wood [*as stays*, or *props*,] against a wall. (KL.

[See the pass. part. n., below. And see also 3 and 4.]) — Also, inf. n. as above, *He* (a man) *wore*, or *clad himself with, the kind of* برد *called* سَنَد. (IAạr, Ḳ.)

3. سَانَدْتُهُ إِلَى الشَّىْءِ: see 4. [Hence,] سُونِدَ المَرِيضُ [*The sick man was stayed*, or *propped up*, against a pillow or the like]: and قَالَ سَانِدُونِى [*He* (the sick man) *said, Stay ye me*, or *prop ye me up*]. (A, TA.) And يُسَانِدُ بَعْضُهُ بَعْضًا [*One part of it stays*, or *supports, and so renders firm* or *strong, another part*]. (Sh, O, Ḳ. [See مُسَانَدَةٌ.]) — [And hence,] سُونِدَ خَلْقُهَا, referring to a she-camel, † *Her frame*, or *make, was symmetrical*; or *conformable in its several parts*. (Ḥam p. 783.) — And سَانَدَهُ, (Ṣ, Ḳ,) inf. n. مُسَانَدَةٌ, (Ṣ,) *He aided*, or *assisted, him*; namely, another man. (Ṣ, Ḳ.) — And ‡ *He requited, compensated*, or *recompensed, him*, (A, Ḳ, TA,) عَلَى العَمَلِ [*for work*, or *for the work* or *deed*]. (Ḳ.)

4. أَسْنَدْتُهُ إِلَى الشَّىْءِ (AZ, Ṣ,* M,* Mṣb, Ḳ,* TA) *I made him*, or *it, to lean, rest*, or *stay himself* or *itself, against*, or *upon, the thing*; (TḲ;) and ▼ سَانَدْتُهُ إِلَيْهِ signifies the same. (AZ, TA.) You say, اسند ظَهْرَهُ إِلَى الحَائِطِ *He leaned his back against the wall*. (MA.) And اسندهُ *He stayed, propped*, or *supported, it*; namely, a thing leaning; syn. دَعَمَهُ. (TA in art. دعم.) — [Hence,] أَسْنَدْتُ إِلَيْهِ أَمْرِى ‡ [*I rested*, or *stayed, upon him my affair*]. (A.) — And اسند الحَدِيثَ إِلَى قَائِلِهِ, (T, M,* L, Mṣb,) inf. n. إِسْنَادٌ [q. v. infrà], (Ṣ, &c.,) ‡ *He traced up*, or *ascribed*, or *attributed, the tradition to the author thereof*, [*resting it upon his authority*,] (T, Ṣ, M, L, Mṣb, TA,) *by mentioning him*, (Mṣb,) or *by mentioning, uninterruptedly, in ascending order, the persons by whom it had been transmitted, up to the Prophet*; (T, L, KT;) [or *by mentioning the person who had related it to him from the Prophet if only one person intervened*;] *saying, "Such a one told me, from such a one," [and so on, if more than one intervened between him and the Prophet,] "from the Apostle of God;"* (KT;) [or it may be *with an interruption in the mention of the person by whom it had been transmitted*: see مُسْنَدٌ, below.] — إِسْنَادُ أَمْرٍ إِلَى آخَرَ إِيجَابًا أَوْ سَلْبًا [is a conventional phrase, used in logic, meaning † *The judging a thing to stand to another* thing *in the relation of an attribute to its subject, affirmatively or negatively*]. (Kull p. 157, in explanation of الحُكْمُ as a logical term [meaning "judgment"].) — إِسْنَادٌ مَجَازِىٌّ is another conventional term, used in lexicology and rhetoric, meaning † *A tropical attribution* of an act or a quality or a meaning; as in عِيشَةٌ رَاضِيَةٌ for مَرْضِيَّةٌ, and in زَبُونٌ (q. v.) in one of its senses: see Ḥar p. 432. — أُسْنِدَ الفِعْلُ إِلَى زَيْدٍ, another conventional phrase, is said of the verb in the phrases زَيْدٌ قَامَ and قَامَ زَيْدٌ and ضُرِبَ زَيْدٌ, meaning *The verb is made an attributive to Zeyd*: and, in an unusual manner, it is said (in the Mṣb in art. سلب) of the verb in the saying سَلَبْتُ زَيْدًا ثَوْبَهُ; so that it means in this instance *The verb is made to have Zeyd for its object*. And أُسْنِدَ إِلَيْهِ فَاعِلَانِ فَصَاعِدًا is said (in the TA in art. سوى) of the verb in the phrase اِسْتَوَى زَيْدٌ وَعَمْرٌو وَخَالِدٌ فِى هٰذَا; so that it means *Two and more agents are assigned to it*.] — اسندهُ فى الجَبَلِ *He made him to ascend the mountain*. (Ḳ.) — اسند as an intrans. verb: see 1, in four places. — You say also, اسند فِى العَدْوِ, (M, L,) inf. n. إِسْنَادٌ, (L,) *He was vehement in running; he strove, laboured, or exerted himself, therein*. (M, L.) — And *He* (a camel) *went a pace between that called* ذَمِيلٌ *and that called* هَمْلَجَةٌ. (L.)

6: see 1, first sentence. — تساند القَوْمُ means *The people went forth, every commander of them with a* [*separate*] *corps*. (Ḥam p. 783.) [See also the act. part. n., below.]

8: see 1, first sentence.

سِنْدٌ, (Ṣ, L,) or السِّنْدُ, (M, L, Ḳ,) *A certain country*, (Ṣ, L, Ḳ,) *well known*, (Ḳ,) said in the "Maráṣid" to be *a country between India* (الهِنْد) *and Karmán and Sijistán*: (TA:) or *a people*; (Ḳ;) [*the people of that country*;] *a well-known nation*; (M, L;) *a nation bordering upon India, whose colours incline to yellowness, and who are generally slender*: (Mgh:) or one of these meanings is the original of the other: (TA:) ▼ سِنْدِىٌّ signifies *a single person thereof*: (Ṣ, Ḳ:) and سِنْدٌ is the pl., (Ḳ,) or [rather] is applied to the people collectively; (Ṣ;) these two words being like زِنْجِىٌّ and زِنْجٌ: (TA:) the pl. of سِنْدٌ is سُنُودٌ and أَسْنَادٌ. (M, L.) السِّنْدُ is also the name of *A great river of* الهِنْد [or *India*; i. e. *the Indus*]: and of *a district in El-Andalus*: and of *a town in Western Africa* (المَغْرِب). (Ḳ.)

سَنَدٌ The *part that faces one*, of a mountain, *and rises from* (عَن) *the* سَفْح [i. e. *base*, or *foot*]; (Ṣ, Ḳ;) *the acclivity*, or *rising part, in the face*, or *front*, [or *side*,] of a mountain or a valley: (T, M, A:) or *a rising*, or *an elevated, portion* of ground: (Mgh:) pl. أَسْنَادٌ, (M, A,) [properly a pl. of pauc., but] the only pl. form. (M.) — *A thing, such as a wall &c., against*, or *upon, which one leans, rests*, or *stays himself*: (Mgh, Mṣb:) and ▼ مُسْنَدٌ and ▼ مُسْنِدٌ [the latter in the TA said to be with fet-ḥ, but this is evidently a mistake, occasioned by a copyist's writing ويفتح for ويضم,] signify [the same,] *a thing against*, or *upon, which one leans, rests*, or *stays himself*; [and the former of these two particularly signifies *a cushion*, or *pillow*, and more particularly *a large cushion* or *pillow, against which one leans*; as expl. by Golius on the authority of Meyd;] pl. مَسَانِدُ. (L, Mṣb.) — Applied to a man, *i. q.* مُعْتَمَدٌ [meaning ‡ *A person upon whom one leans, rests, stays himself*, or *relies*]; (Ṣ;) a man's مُعْتَمَد [i. e. ‡ *stay, support*, or *object of reliance*]; (Ḳ, TA;) as also ▼ مُسْتَنَدٌ. (TA.) You say سَيِّدٌ سَنَدٌ ‡ [*A lord*, or *chief, upon whom people lean*, &c.]. (A, TA.) And هُوَ سَنَدِى and ▼ مُسْتَنَدِى ‡ [*He is my stay, support*, or *object of reliance*]. (A.) And حَدِيثٌ قَوِىُّ السَّنَدِ ‡ [*A tradition valid in respect of the authority upon which it rests*, or *to which it is traced up* or *ascribed*]. (A, TA. [See also إِسْنَادٌ, below.]) — See also مُسْنَدٌ. — Also *A sort of garment of the kind called* بُرُود, (IAạr, Ḳ,) *of the fabric of El-Yemen*: (IAạr:) pl. أَسْنَادٌ: (Ḳ:) or the pl. is like the sing.: (IAạr, Ḳ:) one says أَثْوَابٌ سَنَدٌ [meaning *garments of the kind called* سَنَد]: (TA, from a trad.:) Ibn-Buzurj says that السَّنَدُ means الأَسْنَادُ مِنَ الثِّيَابِ, i. e. *garments of those called* بُرُود: and he cites, from a poet, the phrase جُبَّةُ أَسْنَادٍ, which, he says, means *a red jubbeh of those* [*made*] *of what are called* بُرُود. (TA.) Accord. to Lth, it signifies *A sort of clothing*, [*consisting of*] *a shirt with a shirt over it*: and in like manner, *short shirts made of pieces of cloth, one whereof is concealed beneath another*: whatever appears (كُلُّ مَا ظَهَرَ) thereof is termed سِمْطٌ [q. v.]: (O:) [this app. explains the meaning of what here follows:] السَّنَدُ is [a term used in the case of] thy wearing a long shirt beneath a shirt shorter than it. (M.)

سِنْدِىٌّ: see سِنْدٌ [of which it is the n. un.].

سَنْدَانٌ, with fet-ḥ, (Mgh, Mṣb, Ḳ,) or ▼ سِنْدَانٌ, (thus in a copy of the M, [and thus I have generally found it written, agreeably with the common modern pronunciation,]) The عَلَاة, (M,) or زُبْرَة, (Mṣb,) [both meaning *anvil*,] of the blacksmith. (Mṣb, Ḳ.)

سِنْدَانٌ *Great and strong*; applied to a man and to a wolf. (Ḳ.) — See also the next preceding paragraph.

سِنْدَانَةٌ *A she-ass* [either *domestic* or *wild*: probably the latter, because of her strength]. (Ḳ.)

سِنْدِيَانٌ [The *ilex*, or *evergreen oak*; so called in the present day;] *a kind of tree*. (TA.) [See إِسْنَادٌ.]

سِنَادٌ, applied to a she-camel, (Ṣ, M, &c.,) *Strong*: (Ḳ:) or *strong in make*: (AA, Ṣ:) or *tall in the hump*: (M:) or *long in the legs*, (A, L,) *and elevated* [so I render مسندة, conjecturally, as though meaning propped up,] *in the hump*: (L:) or *lean, and lank in the belly*; (AO, M, L;) but Sh disapproves of this last explanation. (L.)

سَنِيدٌ: see مُسْنَدٌ.

أَسْنَدُ [a comparative and superlative epithet from أُسْنِدَ الحَدِيثُ, q. v., though (like أَسْوَدُ and أَبْيَضُ when used as epithets of this kind) deviating from a general rule, which requires that such an epithet be formed from an unaugmented triliteral-radical verb]. You say أَسْنَدُ لِلْحَدِيثِ, meaning أَنَصُّ لَهُ, q. v. (TA in art. نص.)

إِسْنَادٌ inf. n. of 4 [q. v.]. (Ṣ, &c.) — [Used as a simple subst., signifying ‡ The *ascription* of a tradition *to an authority in the manner expl. voce* أَسْنَدَ it has a pl., namely, أَسَانِيدُ; as in the saying,] الأَسَانِيدُ قَوَائِمُ الأَحَادِيثِ ‡ [*The ascrip-*

tions to authorities, whereon they rest, &c., are the foundations of traditions]. (A, TA. [See also سَنَدٌ.]) — Also used in the sense of رِوَايَةٌ [q. v., as a simple subst.]: pl. as above. (Ḥar p. 32.) ═ Also *A certain kind of tree.* (M.) [In the TA, it is said that the name commonly known is سِنْدِيَان: but I think that this is a mistake: see the latter word.]

مُسْنَدٌ *A place in*, or *upon, which one leans, rests*, or *stays himself:* [and hence applied to *a couch*, and *a throne:*] pl. مَسَانِدُ. (KL. [See also مُسْنَدٌ, voce سَنَدٌ.])

مُسْنَدٌ [pass. part. n. of 4, *Made to lean, rest, &c., against, or upon, a thing:* and *stayed, propped*, or *supported;* or *set up.* — Hence used in the sense of مُسْنَدٌ, as being a thing set up]: see سَنَدٌ. — Also ‡ A tradition (حَدِيثٌ) *traced up*, or *ascribed*, or *attributed, to the author thereof*, (T, L, Ḳ, TA,) [*rested on his authority by the mention of him*, (see 4,) or] *by the mention, uninterruptedly, in ascending order, of the persons by whom it has been transmitted, up to the Prophet;* (T, L, KT;) [or *by the mention of him who has related it from the Prophet when only one has intervened;*] opposed to مُرْسَلٌ and مُنْقَطِعٌ; (T, L;) or *it may be* منقطع, i. e. *interrupted in the mention of the persons by whom it has been transmitted:* (KT:) pl. مَسَانِدُ, (Ḳ,) agreeably with analogy, (TA,) and مَسَانِيدُ, (Esh-Sháfi'ee, Ḳ,) which latter has ى added to render the sound of the kesreh more full; or, accord. to some, it is a dial. var.; and accord. to some, agreeable with analogy. (TA.) — And i. q. دَعِىٌّ [as meaning † One *who claims as his father a person who is not his father;* or *an adopted son;* or one *whose origin*, or *lineage*, or *parentage, is suspected*]; (Ṣ, M, L, Ḳ;) as also ↓ سَنِيدٌ; (M, L, Ḳ; [see an ex. in a verse cited voce أَسَرَ;]) opposed to صَرِيحٌ. (L.) — المُسْنَدُ, accord. to Sb, signifies † *The first portion* [i. e. *the subject*] *of a proposition;* and المُسْنَدُ إِلَيْهِ, † *the second portion* [i. e. *the attribute*, or *predicate*,] *thereof:* (M, L:) or, accord. to Kh, a proposition consists of a ↓ سَنَد and a مُسْنَد إِلَيْهِ; and in the phrase عَبْدُ ٱللّٰهِ رَجُلٌ صَالِحٌ, [for ex.,] عبد الله is a سند, and رجل صالح is a مسند اليه: (O, L:) [but accord. to other authors, and general modern usage, and agreeably with the proper meanings of the terms, المُسْنَدُ (meaning the attributed) signifies *the attribute*, or *predicate;* and المُسْنَدُ إِلَيْهِ, (meaning that to which a thing or an accident is attributed) signifies *the subject.*] — Also *The Ḥimyeree*, or *Ḥimyeritic, character of writing; the character of Ḥimyer;* (Ṣ, M, A, O, Ḳ;) *differing from the modern Arabic character:* (Ṣ, O:) they used to write it commonly in the days of their rule; and AḤát says that it continued in use among them in El-Yemen in his day [i. e. in the latter half of the second century of the Flight and the former half of the third century]: (M, TA:) Abu-l-'Abbás says, المُسْنَدُ was *the language of the sons of Seth;* (O, TA;) [i. e. the language written in the character so called;] and the like is said in the "Sirr eṣ-Ṣiná'ah" of IJ. (TA.) [See also De Sacy's Chrest. Ar., sec. ed., vol. ii., p. 122 of the Ar. text, and 311 of the transl.] — And i. q. الدَّهْرُ [i. e. *Time, from the beginning of the world to its end;* or *time absolutely;* or *a long time;* or *a long unlimited time;* or *time without end;* &c.]. (Ṣ, M, A, Ḳ.) So in the saying, لَا أَفْعَلُهُ آخِرَ المُسْنَدِ [*I will not do it to the end of time*]. (A, TA.) One says also, لَا آتِيهِ يَدَ المُسْنَدِ, meaning [*I will not do it*, or *I will not come to him or it*,] *ever.* (IAạr, TA.)

مُسْنَدٌ: see سَنَدٌ, second sentence.

مُسَنَّدٌ [pass. part. n. of 2, q. v.]. In the phrase خُشُبٌ مُسَنَّدَةٌ, [in the Ḳur lxiii. 4, meaning *Pieces of wood made to lean*, or *incline, against a wall*, (Jel,)] the latter word is with teshdeed because of its relation to many objects (لِلْكَثْرَةِ). (Ṣ.) ═ مُسَنَّدَةٌ also signifies *A certain sort of cloths*, or *garments;* and so ↓ مُسَنْدِيَّةٌ. (M, TA.)

مُسَنْدِيَّةٌ: see what next precedes.

مُسَانِدَةٌ (O, Ḳ, and Ḥam p. 783, in the CḲ and TḲ [erroneously] مُسَانَدَةٌ) † A she-camel *having the breast and fore part prominent:* (Aṣ, O, Ḳ:) or *whereof one part of her frame stays*, or *supports*, (يُسَانِدُ,) [*and so renders firm* or *strong*,] *another part:* (Sh, O, Ḳ:) or *having prominent withers:* (Ibn-Buzurj, L:) or *strong in the back:* or *whose frame*, or *make, is symmetrical*, or *conformable in its several parts:* or, as some say, *whose frame*, or *make, is dissimilar*, or *unconformable, in its several parts;* because the hump differs from the other parts; so that it is from the phrase تَسَانَدَ القَوْمُ meaning as expl. above [see 6]: (Ḥam p. 783:) and مُسَانِدَةُ القَرَا ‡ a she-camel *hard, firmly compacted, in the back.* (M, L, TA.)

مُتَسَانِدٌ: see سَنَدٌ, in two places.

خَرَجَا مُتَسَانِدَيْنِ ‡ *They two went forth aiding*, or *assisting, each other;* (A,* L, TA;) as though each of them leaned, or stayed himself, upon the other, and aided himself by him. (L, TA.) The latter word is used, in this sense, of two men going on a hostile, or hostile and plundering, expedition: and of two wolves attacking a person. (A.) And one says, خَرَجُوا مُتَسَانِدِينَ, meaning ‡ *They went forth under sundry*, or *different, banners*, or *standards*, (Ṣ, A, M, L, Ḳ,*) *every party by itself*, (A, L,) *the sons of one father under one* [*separate*] *banner*, (L,) *not all under the banner of one commander.* (Ṣ, L, Ḳ.)

سندر

Q. 1. سَنْدَرَةٌ (M, Ḳ) inf. n. of سَنْدَرَ, which signifies *He* (a man) *went quickly:* (TḲ:) [or *was quick* or *expeditious:*] syn. of the former سُرْعَةٌ: (M, Ḳ:) Sgh mentions it in art. سدر, regarding the ن as augmentative. (TA.) Hence, accord. to some, the saying of 'Alee,

أَنَا الَّذِى سَمَّتْنِى أُمِّى حَيْدَرَهْ
كَلَيْثِ غَابَاتٍ غَلِيظِ القَصَرَهْ
أَكِيلُكُمْ بِالسَّيْفِ كَيْلَ السَّنْدَرَهْ

[*I am he whom my mother named Ḥeydereh, like a lion of forests, thick in the neck: I will measure you with the sword with a quick measuring:*] meaning, I will slay you quickly, before flight. (TA. [But see what follows.]) — *A large*, or *an ample, sort of* كَيْل [or *measuring*]: (M, Ḳ:) so expl. by some in the saying of 'Alee above quoted: or in that saying it is from سَنْدَرَة as the name of a certain woman, who used to sell wheat and give full measure, or of a man who did so. (TA.) [See also سَنْدَرَةٌ as a subst., below.] — Also The *being bold*, or *daring:* or *boldness*, or *daringness.* (TA.) — And The *being sharp in affairs, and acting with penetrative energy:* or *sharpness in affairs, and penetrative energy.* (TA.)

سَنْدَرٌ: see the next paragraph but one.

سِنْدَرٌ A man *bold*, or *daring, in his affair, not frightened at anything.* (TA.)

سَنْدَرَةٌ, [said in the TḲ to be the inf. n. of Q. 1, q. v.,] (Ṣ in art. سدر,) or ↓ سَنْدَرٌ, (so in a copy of the M,) or ↓ سَنْدَرِىٌّ, (IAạr, Ḳ, TA,) *A* مِكْيَال [or *measure, for measuring corn, &c.*], (Ṣ, M, Ḳ,) *well known*, (M,) *of large size*, (Ṣ, Ḳ,) *like the* قَنْقَل *and the* جُرَاف: this is said in explanation of the first of these words as used in the saying of 'Alee quoted above: (Ṣ, TA:) i. e., the saying has hence been expl. as meaning, I will make a wide and quick slaughter of you: (TA:) or it may be *a measure* (مكيال) *made of the tree called* سَنْدَرَة: (Kt, TA:) [for] — it is also the name of *A certain tree*, (Ṣ, M, Ḳ,) *of which bows and arrows are made.* (M, Ḳ.)

سَنْدَرِىٌّ A man *quick*, or *expeditious*, (Ḳ, TA,) *in his affairs; who strives, exerts himself*, or *is diligent, therein.* (TA.) — And the pl. سَنَادِرَة signifies [*the contr.*, or] *Persons without occupation; people of sport and idleness;* as also سَبَادِرَة. (TA.) — Also, the sing., *Bold*, or *daring;* (O, Ḳ, TA;) *who makes a boast of more than he possesses.* (TA.) — The *lion;* (Ḳ;) because of his boldness, or daringness. (TA.) — *Strong*, or *vehement;* (O, Ḳ;) thus applied to anything. (TA.) — *Tall*, or *long;* (O, Ḳ;) thus in the dial. of Hudheyl. (O.) — *Large in the eyes.* (Ḳ.) — *Good:* and *the contr.*, i. e. *bad.* (M, Ḳ.) — *A certain sort of arrows*, and *of arrow-heads* or *the like:* (M:) or *the white of these*, (M, Ḳ,) i. e. of the latter: (Ḳ:) and a spear-head *very clear* or *bright*, (Ḳ, TA,) *and sharp:* (TA:) or, applied to an arrow, it means *made of the tree called* سَنْدَرَة: (Ṣ* in art. سدر, and M, and TA:) and قَوْسٌ سَنْدَرِيَّةٌ means *a bow made of that tree:* (TA:) or *a bow having its string braced, and strongly*, or *skilfully*, or *well, made.* (Ḳ, TA.) — Also *A species of bird.* (Ḳ.) — See also the next preceding paragraph.

سندس

سُنْدُسٌ *Thin*, or *fine*, دِيبَاج [or *silk brocade*]: (Th, M, Bḍ and Jel in xviii. 30, Jel in xliv. 53, Mṣb, Ḳ, TA:) or *thin*, or *fine*, حَرِير [q. v.]: (Bḍ in xliv.:) opposed to إِسْتَبْرَق: (TA:) or *i. q.*

بِزْيَوْن [expl. by IB as meaning *thin*, or *fine*, دِيبَاج : so in the TA in art. بزن] : (Ṣ :) or *a kind of* بِزْيَوْن ; (Lth, Ḳ, TA ;) *made of* [*the kind of down called*] مِرْعِزّى : (Lth, TA :) or *a kind of* بُرُود [pl. of بُرْد, q. v.] : (M, Ḳ :) [accord. to Golius, *præstans et subtile panni serici genus* ; as on the authority of Ibn-Maạroof : and *Attalicus pannus, aurum argentumve intextum habens* ; as on the authority of J, who, however, explains it only by the word بِزْيَوْن : it is mentioned in the Ṣ and Mṣb in art. سدس ; and in the latter, is said to be of the measure فُنْعُل ; but accord. to the Ḳ, the ن is a radical letter :] it is [said to be] an arabicized word, without contradiction, (Lth, Ḳ,) as well as إِسْتَبْرَق : (Lth :) but both these words occur in the Ḳur-án, and Esh-Sháfi'ee and others deny that any arabicized word occurs therein : [though they are opposed by Bḍ (xvii. 37) and others :] some say that they are instances of the agreement of different languages. (MF.)

سندق

سُنْدُوق a dial. var. of صُنْدُوق, q. v. ; (Fr, L, Ḳ ;) like زُنْدُوق : (TA :) pl. سَنَادِيق. (L.)

سندل

سَنْدَل : see art. سدل.

سنر

1. سَنِرَ, aor. ـَ , (TḲ,) inf. n. سَنَرٌ, (M, Ḳ,) *He* (a man, TḲ) *was*, or *became*, *illnatured*, or *very perverse* or *cross* : (Ḳ, TḲ :) or *narrow in disposition*. (M.) Hence is derived سِنَّوْر, in the first of the senses expl. below. (M.) [Or perhaps the reverse may be the case.]

سُنَّار, or سُنَّار : see the last paragraph.

سَنَوَّر *A coat made of thongs*, (Ṣ, M, Ḳ,) *worn in war*, (M,) *like a coat of mail* : (Ṣ, Ḳ :) [and] *any weapon of iron* : (A :) and *weapons*, or *arms*, *collectively* : (M, Ḳ :) or, accord. to some, *coats of mail* : (M :) so Aṣ means in explaining السَّنَوَّر as signifying *what consists of rings* : (TA :) or, as some say, *a coat of mail* : (Ḥam p. 352 :) or *all iron*. (AO.)

سِنَّوْر The *cat* ; of the masc. gender ; syn. هِرّ ; (M, A, Mṣb ;) as also ▼ سُنَّار, (Ḳ,) or ▼ سُنَّار : (as in a copy of the M :) fem. with ة : (Mṣb :) pl. سَنَانِير : (Ṣ, Mṣb, Ḳ :) but سنور is rare in the language of the Arabs : هِرّ and ضَيْوَن are more common. (IAmb, Mṣb.) And اِبْنُ السِّنَّوْر *The* دَرْص [or دِرْص, i. e. *kitten*, or *the like*]. (T in art. بنى.) —— *A lord, master*, or *chief* ; (M, Ḳ ;) in some copies of the Ḳ, سيد is erroneously put for سَيِّد ; (TA ;) *a chief of a tribe* : (Ṣgh :) pl. as above. (Ṣgh, Ḳ.) —— *A vertebra* (M, Ḳ) *of the upper part* (TA) *of the neck* (M, Ḳ) *of a camel* : (M, TA :) pl. as above. (TA.) —— The *root of the tail* : (Er-Riyáshee, Ḳ :) pl. as above. (Ḳ.)

سنط

1. سَنُطَ, aor. ـُ ; (M, Ḳ ;) or سَنِطَ, aor. ـَ , inf. n. سَنَطٌ ; (Mṣb ;) or both ; (TA ;) *He was*, or *became*, *such as is termed* سِنَاط [q. v.]. (M, Mṣb, Ḳ.)

سَنْط [The *mimosa Nilotica* ; also called *acacia Nilotica* ;] *a* قَرَظ, [or this is properly the name of its fruit,] (M, Ḳ,) *which grows in the* صَعِيد [or *Upper Egypt*], (M,) or [rather] *in Egypt* ; [for it grows in Lower, as well as Upper, Egypt ;] (Ḳ ;) *it is the best kind of firewood of the people of that country, who assert that it has most of fire, and least of ashes* ; so says AḤn, on the authority of a person well informed ; and he adds that *they tan with it* [or rather *with its pods*] : the word is foreign : (M :) and is also written صَنْط : Ṣgh says that is an arabicized word, from the Indian حبد. [So in the TA, doubtless a mistranscription. In the CḲ, السَّنْطُ is erroneously put for الشَّنْطُ.]

سِنَاطٌ (Ṣ, M, Mgh, Mṣb, Ḳ) and سُنَاطٌ (M, O, L, CḲ) and ▼ سَنُوطٌ (Ṣ, M, Ḳ) and ▼ سَنُوطِىّ (Ṣ, Ḳ) A man (Mṣb) *having no beard* : (M, Mgh, Mṣb :) or *having no hair at all upon his face* : (M :) or *having no hair upon the sides of his face* [so I render كَوْسَج], *and no beard at all* : (Ṣ, Ḳ :) or *having little hair upon the sides of the face*, (Mgh, Mṣb,) or *upon the side of the face*, *but not reaching to the state of the* كَوْسَج : (IAạr, Ḳ :) or *i. q.* كَوْسَج : (Mgh :) or *whose beard is on his chin* [*only*], *having nothing on the sides of the face* : (Aṣ, Ḳ :) or this last signification, accord. to Aṣ, applies to سَنُوط : (TA :) the pl. (of سَنُوط accord. to some copies of the Ḳ and the TA) is سُنُطٌ (IAạr, Ḳ) and أَسْنَاطٌ [which is a pl. of pauc.] : (Ḳ :) سناط is used as a sing. and pl. epithet : it is used as a pl. by Dhu-r-Rummeh. (IB, TA.)

سَنُوطٌ : see the next preceding paragraph. —— Also *A well-known medicine*. (Ḳ.)

سَنُوطِىّ : see سِنَاطٌ.

سنف

1. سَنَفَ البَعِيرَ, aor. ـُ and ـِ , (Ṣ, M, Ḳ,) inf. n. سَنْفٌ ; (M, Ḳ ;) and ▼ اسنفهُ ; (Ṣ,* M, Ḳ ;) or, accord. to Aṣ, the latter only ; (Ṣ ;) *He bound the* سِنَاف [q. v.] *upon the camel* : (Ṣ, M, Ḳ :) and the latter, *he put to him* (i. e. the camel), or *made for him*, *a* سِنَاف ; (Ḳ, TA ;) thus expl. by El-'Ozeyzee. (TA.) [Hence, accord. to some,] one says, in a prov., of a person confounded or perplexed, and unable to see his right course, in his affair, عَىَّ بِالإِسْنَافِ ▼, (Ṣ, Meyd,) meaning *He was confounded*, or *perplexed*, *and unable to see his right course*, *by reason of fright*, *like him who knows not where to bind the* سِنَاف : (Z, TA :) it originated from the fact of a man's being thus confounded, or perplexed : (Meyd :) a poet says, (namely, Ibn-Kulthoom, TA,)

* إِذَا مَا عَىَّ بِالإِسْنَافِ قَوْمٌ *
* مِنَ الأَمْرِ المُشَبَّهِ أَنْ يَكُونَا *

[as though meaning *When a people are unable to find the right way to bind the* سناف, *in consequence of the affair that is uncertain to be* : (thus related by Meyd ; but in the TA with حَىّ in the place of قوم, and عَلَى in the place of من :)] Az, however, says that this is not the meaning : that الاسناف here signifies *the advancing*, or *preceding* ; and that the meaning is, *are unable to find the right way of advancing*, or *preceding* ; (Meyd, TA ;) from أَسْنَفَ said of a horse, expl. below (TA.) —— See also the next paragraph.

4. اسنف, inf. n. إِسْنَافٌ : see above, in two places. —— Hence, i. e. from this verb in the sense expl. in the first sentence, (Ṣ, TA,) اسنف أَمْرَهُ ‡ *He performed his affair skilfully*, *soundly*, or *thoroughly*. (Ṣ, M, Ḳ, TA.) —— Also *He* (a horse) *preceded the other horses* : (Ṣ, TA :) and اسنفت *she* (a camel) *preceded the other camels* (Ḳ, TA) *in going*, or *journeying*, or *pace* ; (TA ;) as also ▼ سَنَفَتْ. (Ḳ, TA.) [See the verse cited in the preceding paragraph, and the explanation of it by Az.] Said of a camel, it means also *He put forward his neck*, *to go on* : (Ḳ, TA :) or *he advanced*, or *preceded*. (TA.) —— Said of lightning, *It appeared*, or *was seen*, *near* ; and so said of the clouds (السَّحَاب). (Ḳ.) —— And اسنفت الرِّيحُ *The wind blew violently*, *and raised the dust*. (Ibn-'Abbád, Ḳ.)

سَنْف : see the next paragraph.

سِنْف *A leaf* ; (M, and so in copies of the Ḳ, and in the TA ;) or *leaves* : (so in other copies of the Ḳ :) pl. سِنْف ; thus in the copies of the Ḳ, [like the sing.,] but this requires consideration ; and it seems that it is سُنُوف, a pl. assigned to سِنْف in a sense that will be mentioned in what follows : (TA :) [or the pl. is سِنَفَة, likewise mentioned, as a pl. of سِنْف, in what follows, in three places :] also (Ḳ) the *leaf of the* [*tree called*] مَرْخ : (AA, Ṣ, O, Ḳ :) or the *pericarp of the* مَرْخ : (Ṣ, M, O, Ḳ :) this, says IB, is the correct meaning, as those acquainted with the مرخ affirm ; for, as 'Alee Ibn-Ḥamzeh says, the مرخ has not leaves, nor thorns, but consists of slender twigs ; it grows in [water-courses such as are termed] شُعَب : (TA :) a poet likens thereto the ears of horses : (Ṣ :) the pl. is سِنَفَة : (M :) or the *pericarps of any tree having a produce consisting of grains in a long pod*, (AḤn, O, Ḳ,) *that become scattered*, *when they dry*, *from that pod*, *the shale thereof remaining* ; (AḤn, O ;) *one such pod is termed* ▼ سِنْفَة ; (AḤn, O, Ḳ ;) and the pl. [or coll. gen. n.] is سِنْف ; (Ḳ ;) and this last has for its pl. سِنَفَة : (AḤn, O, Ḳ :) Aboo-Ziyád says that it is *like* [*the pod of*] *the* بَاقِلّى [or *bean*], *except that it is wider*, *and pointed at the extremity* ; wherefore a poet likens thereto the ear of a horse : (O :) or, accord. to AḤn, ▼ سِنْفَة signifies *any pericarp*, *whether oblong or not oblong* ; and the pl. [or coll. gen. n.] is سِنْف ; and the pl. of سِنْف is سِنَفَة : (M :) [see also حُبْلَة :] and the *shale of the* [*bean called*]

بَاقِلَّآء, and of the [species of kidney-bean called] لُوبِيَآء, and of the lentil, and the like; (IAạr, TA;) or the shale of the first of these three when what was in it has been eaten; (Ḳ;) and the pl. is سُنُوف. (IAạr, TA.) — Also, (Ḳ,) or ▼ سَنَف, with fet-ḥ, (IAạr, O, L,) A branch, or twig, (عُود,) stripped of its leaves. (IAạr, O, L, Ḳ.) — And the former, The [grain called] دَوْسَر [i. e. زُؤَان, q. v.,] which is sometimes in wheat and barley, (O, Ḳ,) and which vitiates them, and lowers their prices. (O.) — Also i. q. صِنْف [A sort, or species]. (Ḳ.) One says, هٰذَا طَعَامٌ سِنْفَانِ [This is food, or wheat,] of two sorts, good and bad. (AA, O.) — And A company of men. (Ibn-'Abbád, O, Ḳ.) One says, جَآءَنِى سِنْفٌ مِنَ النَّاسِ A company of men came to me. (Ibn-'Abbád, O.)

سَنَفَةٌ: see the next preceding paragraph, in two places.

سُنْفَتَانِ and سِنْفَتَانِ Two pieces of wood set upright, between which is put the [pulley called] مَحَالَة [by means whereof water is drawn.] (Ḳ.)

سِنَافٌ The [breast-girth called] لَبَب: (Ḳ:) or the appertenance of the camel that is as the لَبَب to the horse or similar beast: (Kh, Ṣ:) or a cord which you tie to the تَصْدِير [or breast-girth of the camel], then you bring it forward so as to put it behind the callous protuberance upon the breast, [and there, app., make it fast in some manner,] and it keeps the تصدير in its place: (Aṣ, Ṣ, O, Ḳ:) this is done only when the belly of the camel has become lank, and his تصدير has [consequently] become unsteady: (Ṣ, O, Ḳ:*) or a cord that is tied from the hind girth of the camel to his breast-girth and is then tied to his neck, when he has become lank: (M:) pl. [of mult.] سُنُفٌ (M, Ḳ) and سُنْفٌ (Ḳ) and [of pauc.] أَسْنِفَةٌ: (TA:) and a leathern strap or thong, or some other thing, that is put behind the [breast-girth called] لَبَب, in order that it may not slip [from its place]. (M.)

سَنُوفٌ A horse that shifts the saddle forwards. (Ibn-'Abbád, O, Ḳ.) [See also مِسْنَافٌ.]

سَنِيفٌ A cloth that is put, (AA, O, Ḳ,) or tied, (M,) upon the shoulders of the camel: pl. سُنُفٌ (AA, M, O, Ḳ) and سُنْفٌ: (Ḳ:) the cloths that are similarly placed upon the hinder parts of camels are called أَشِلَّة [pl. of شَلِيل]. (AA, O.) — Also The حَاشِيَة [properly meaning selvage, or selvedge,] of a carpet; (Ibn-'Abbád, O, Ḳ;) i. e., its خَمْل [which generally means nap; but this addition I think doubtful]. (Ibn-'Abbád, O.)

مُسْنَفَةٌ A she-camel having the سِنَاف [q. v.] tied upon her. (Ṣ, TA.) — And خَيْلٌ مُسْنَفَاتٌ Horses having the [withers, or parts called] مَنَاسِج high, or elevated: denoting a quality approved in them; for it is only in the best, and the generous, thereof: and when they are thus, the saddles recede upon their backs; wherefore the سِنَاف is put to them, to keep the saddles in their places. (M.)

مُسْنِفَةٌ A mare, (Ṣ, M, Ḳ,) and a she-camel, (M,) preceding others in going, or journeying, or pace; (Ṣ, M, Ḳ;) as also ▼ مِسْنَافٌ: (M:) and مَسَانِيف [being pl. of the latter] signifies the same; and is applied to camels: (Th, TA:) or [so in the Ḳ, but more properly "and"] مُسْنَفَةٌ, with fet-ḥ to the ن, is specially applied to the she-camel, (Ḳ, TA,) in the sense first assigned to it above: (TA:) or مُسْنِفَةٌ, (Ḳ, TA,) with kesr to the ن, (TA,) signifies a [youthful she-camel such as is termed] بَكْرَة that has completed the tenth month of her pregnancy, and whose udder has become swollen. (Ibn-'Abbád, Ḳ, TA.) — Also, (El-'Ozeyzee, O, Ḳ,) or مُسْنِف and ▼ مِسْنَاف, (AA, M,) applied to a she-camel, Lean, or light of flesh, (AA, El-'Ozeyzee, M, O, Ḳ,) or lank in the belly. (AA, M.) — And مُسْنِفَةٌ signifies also Land affected with drought, barrenness, or dearth: (El-'Ozeyzee, O, Ḳ:) or a year of drought, barrenness, or dearth: [thus expl. as a subst., or an epithet in which the quality of a subst. is predominant:] pl. مَسَانِف. (AḤn, M.)

مِسْنَافٌ ‡ A camel that makes the saddle to shift backwards; (Ṣ, M, Ḳ, TA;) wherefore a سِنَاف is put to him: (Ṣ, TA:) and, (Ḳ,) or as some say, (Ṣ,) that makes it to shift forwards: (Ṣ, Ḳ, TA:) so says Lth: but ISh disallows his explanation, saying that it means a she-camel that makes the load to shift forwards; and that مِجْنَاة [a word which I have not found anywhere except in this instance] signifies the contrary: (TA:) or that makes her fore girth to slip forward; contr. of مُدْرِج and مِدْرَاج. (TA in art. درج.) — See also مُسْنِفَةٌ, in two places.

سنق

1. سَنِقَ, (Ṣ, Ḳ,) aor. ـَ, (Ḳ,) inf n. سَنَقٌ, (Ṣ,) He (a young camel) suffered indigestion (Ṣ, Ḳ) مِنَ اللَّبَنِ [from the milk]. (Ḳ.) One says, of a young camel, شَرِبَ حَتَّى سَنِقَ He drank until, or so that, he suffered indigestion. (Ṣ.) And one says, of an ass, and of any beast, سَنِقَ, inf. n. as above, meaning, He was affected with what resembled indigestion from eating fresh herbage. (TA.)

4. اسنقهُ النَّعِيمُ i. q. تَرَّفَهُ [i. e. Ease and plenty caused him to exult, or to exult greatly, or excessively, and to behave insolently and unthankfully, or ungratefully: or wealth made him to enjoy, or lead, a plentiful, and a pleasant or an easy, and a soft or delicate, life; or a life of ease and plenty]. (O, Ḳ.)

سَنِقٌ Satiated, or sated, like him who is suffering indigestion: (A'Obeyd, TA:) applied by Lebeed as an epithet to a horse. (TA.)

سُنَّوقٌ A house, or chamber, plastered with gypsum: (Ibn-'Abbád, O, Ḳ:) pl. سُنَّيقَاتٌ and سَنَانِيقُ: (Ḳ:) or, accord. to Sh, these are pls. of the word in the sense next following. (TA.) — Any [hill of the kind termed] أَكَمَة: pl. as above: so accord. to Sh: (T, O, TA:) or it is the name of a particular أَكَمَة, (T, O, Ḳ,* TA,) well known; occurring, without ال, in a poem of Imra-el-Ḳeys. (T, O, TA.) — And السُّنَّيْق, A certain white star. (Ibn-'Abbád, O, Ḳ.)

سنم

1. سَنِمَ, (M, Mṣb, Ḳ,) aor. ـَ, (Mṣb, Ḳ,) inf. n. سَنَمٌ; (M, Mṣb;) so some say; others saying سُنِمَ, in the pass. form; and ▼ أَسْنَمَ, as some say; others saying ▼ أُسْنِمَ; (Mṣb;) He (a camel) was, or became, large in the سَنَام [or hump]. (M, Mṣb, Ḳ.)

2. سَنَّمَهُ, (M, Ḳ,) inf. n. تَسْنِيمٌ, (Ḳ,) It (herbage, or pasture,) made him (a camel) large in the سَنَام [or hump]; as also ▼ اسنمهُ: (M, Ḳ:) or both signify it made him fat. (TA.) — And He made it gibbous, namely, a grave; i. e. he raised it from the ground like the سَنَام: (Mṣb:) تَسْنِيمٌ (Ṣ, Ḳ) of a grave (Ṣ) is the contr. of تَسْطِيح. (Ṣ, Ḳ.) He raised it, [app. so as to make it gibbous,] namely a thing. (M.) — And He filled it, namely, a vessel, (AZ, M, Mṣb, Ḳ,) and then put upon it what was like a سَنَام of wheat or some other thing, (AZ, Mṣb,) or so that there was above it what was like the سَنَام. (M.) — See also 5. — [And see تَسْنِيمٌ, below.]

4: see 1, in two places: — and 2, first sentence. — اسنم الدُّخَانُ, (Ṣ, Ḳ,) inf. n. إِسْنَامٌ, (Ṣ,) The smoke rose, or rose high. (Ṣ, Ḳ.) And اسنمت النَّارُ The fire became large in its flame: (M, Ḳ:) or the fire had a high flame. (TA.)

5. تسنّم النَّاقَةَ He mounted, or rode upon, the سَنَام [or hump] of the she-camel. (Ḥar pp. 332, and 300.) — He (the stallion) mounted the she-camel; (M, TA;) he leaped the she-camel. (TA.) — And تسنّمهُ He, or it, mounted, ascended, got, was, or became, upon it, (Ṣ, M, Mṣb, Ḳ,) namely, a thing; (M, Mṣb, Ḳ;) as also ▼ سَنَّمَهُ, (M, Ḳ,) inf. n. تَسْنِيمٌ. (TA. [Freytag adds اسنمهُ in this sense, as on the authority of J, whom I do not find to have mentioned it.]) And He mounted, or ascended, upon it from its side, namely, a wall. (TA.) And He rode upon it, namely, anything, [meaning any animal,] advancing, or retiring. (TA.) — Also It became abundant upon him, and spread; said of hoariness; as also تَشَيَّمَهُ; (IAạr, M, TA;) like أَوْشَمَ فِيهِ. (TA.) — And تسنّم السَّحَابُ الأَرْضَ The clouds rained copiously, or abundantly, upon the land. (TA.) — التَّسَنُّمُ also signifies The taking, or seizing, suddenly, unexpectedly, or by surprise. (M, Ḳ.)

سَنَمٌ [a coll. gen. n.]: see سَنَمَةٌ [its n. un.].

سَنِمٌ A camel having a large سَنَام [or hump]: (Lth, Ṣ, M, Ḳ:) fem. with ة. (Lth, TA.) — Also A tall plant, of which the سَنَمَة, (Ṣ, Ḳ,) i. e. the head, resembling the ear of corn, (Ṣ,) or the blossom, (Ḳ,) has come forth. (Ṣ, Ḳ.) [And] سَنِمَةٌ signifies Any tree (شَجَرَة) that does not *bear; its extremities having dried up, and become altered.* (M. [In the TA, the word in this sense is said to be سَنِمَةٌ: but the former is app. the right reading.]) —— Also, (TA,) or سَنِمٌ عَلَى وَجْهِ الأَرْضِ, (Ṣ, in which it is only mentioned as said of water,) Water *rising,* or *rising high, and appearing upon the surface of the earth.* (TA.)

سَنَمَةٌ The *blossom* (M, Ḳ) of a plant; (Ḳ;) i. e. (TA) the *head* thereof, *resembling the ear of corn,* (Ṣ, TA,) [or] it is of the طَرِيفَة [q. v.], not of the [herbs called] بَقْل: (M:) and signifies also the *extremities* [or *an extremity*] of the صِلِّيَان, *which are* [or *is*] *shed* thereby: (M, TA:) and the *head* of a tree [or plant] of the kind termed دِقّ [q. v.], *in form like what is upon the head of the reed,* or *cane, except that it is soft, and the camels eat it in the manner termed* خَضْم [inf. n. of خَضَمَ, q. v.]: (TA:) [it is the n. un. of ↓ سَنَم, the latter being a coll. gen. n., as is shown by what follows:] AḤn says, some assert that the سَنَمَة is *such of the produce of herbs as resembles the produce of the* إِذْخِر [q. v.] *and the like;* and *such as the produce of the reed,* or *cane;* and that *the most excellent of the* سَنَم *are the* سَنَم *of a herb called the* ↓ إِسْنَامَة [n. un. of إِسْنَام]; *and the camels eat it in the manner termed* خَضْم, *because of its softness;* or, as in some of the copies [of his work], *the camels do not eat it.* (M.)

سَنَامٌ of the camel, (Ṣ,) of the he-camel and of the she-camel, [The *hump;* i. e.] the *highest part of the back:* (M, TA:) [*in substance,*] *it is to the camel like the* أَلْيَة [here meaning the *fat of the tail*] *to the sheep:* (Mṣb:) pl. أَسْنِمَةٌ (Ṣ, M, Mṣb, Ḳ) [and app. أُسْنَام also, as seems to be indicated by an explanation of this latter pl. in what follows]. Hence, in a trad., نِسَآءٌ عَلَى رُؤُوسِهِنَّ كَأَسْنِمَةِ البُخْتِ [*Women upon whose heads are the like of the humps of the Bactrian camels*]; meaning such as wind the head-coverings as turbans upon their heads so as to enlarge them [in appearance] thereby. (TA.) [Hence, also, سَنَامُ النَّاقَةِ † *The name of a star in the constellation of Cassiopea:* mentioned by Freytag, with a reference to Ideler Untersuch. p. 84.] —— Also The *highest,* or *highest part,* of anything: (TA:) and the *best,* or *choice part,* (M, TA,) of anything; (TA;) because the سَنَام is the best, or the choice part, of what is in the camel. (M.) [Hence,] أَسْنِمَةُ الرِّمَالِ *The protuberant,* or *elevated, parts of the sands;* as being likened to the hump of the she-camel: (M, TA:) and أَسْنِمَةُ الرَّمْلِ *the backs of the sands, that rise from the main portions thereof.* (TA.) And سَنَامُ الأَرْضِ *The* نَحْر [q. v.] (Ṣ, TA [in some copies of the Ṣ نَحْر, perhaps correctly نَجْد, i. e. *high,* or *elevated, part*]) *of the land:* (Ṣ, TA:) and *the middle of the land.* (Ṣ, Ḳ.) And سَنَامُ النَّعْلِ *The rising part of the middle of the upper side of the sandal, which is in the place of the hollow of the foot.* (Ḥar p. 559.) And أُسْنَامُ نَارٍ *The highest parts of a fire:* (EM p. 156, and TA:) أُسْنَام being pl. of سَنَام, which signifies the *highest part* of a thing. (EM ubi suprà.) And سَنَامُ المَجْدِ † *The highest* [of a people] *in respect of glory.* (TA.)

السُّنُمُّ *The ox,* or *cow;* syn. البَقَرَةُ: (M, Ḳ:) or, as some say, *the wild* بَقَرَة. (TA.)

إِسْنَامٌ The *fruit,* or *produce, of the* حَلِيّ [q. v.]; (M, Ḳ, TA; [in the CḲ, of the حَلْيَا;]) mentioned by Seer on the authority of Aboo-Málik: (M:) n. un. with ة. (Ḳ.) And the latter signifies *A certain herb:* (see سَنَمَة:) or *a species of tree:* pl. [or rather coll. gen. n.] إِسْنَام. (M.)

تَسْنِيمٌ [originally inf. n. of 2, q. v.,] *A certain water in Paradise;* so called because running above the elevated chambers (Ṣ, Ḳ*) and the pavilions: mentioned in the Ḳur lxxxiii. 27: (Ṣ:) or *a certain fountain,* or *source,* (عَيْن,) *in Paradise:* so they assert; and this requires its being determinate, imperfectly decl.: or, accord. to Zj, *a water coming upon them from above,* from the elevated chambers: (M:) or *a certain fountain,* or *source, coming upon them from above.* (Ḳ [and in like manner Az explains it].)

أَرْضٌ مُسْنِمَةٌ *A land that gives growth to the* إِسْنَامَة, n. un. of إِسْنَام. (Ḳ, TA.)

مُسَنَّمٌ *A camel left unridden* [*so that he is made to have a large hump*]. (Ḳ,* TA.) —— And قَبْرٌ مُسَنَّمٌ *An elevated* [or *a gibbous*] *grave:* from السَّنَام. (Mgh.) —— And مَجْدٌ مُسَنَّمٌ † *Great glory.* (M, TA.)

سنه

1: see 5, in two places.

3. سَانَهَهُ, inf. n. مُسَانَهَةٌ and سِنَاهٌ; and سَانَاهُ, inf. n. مُسَانَاةٌ; (Ḳ;) or عَامَلَهُ مُسَانَهَةً, and مُسَانَاةً; (Mṣb;) *He made an engagement,* or *a contract, with him for work or the like, by the year:* (Ḳ:) and اِسْتَأْجَرْتُهُ مُسَانَهَةً, and مُسَانَاةً, [*I hired him by the year:*] (Ṣ:) مُسَانَهَة and مُسَانَاة from السَّنَة are like مُعَاوَمَة from العَام, and مُشَاهَرَة from الشَّهْر, and مُرَابَعَة from الرَّبِيع, &c. (TA in art. ربع.) —— سَانَهَتِ النَّخْلَةُ *The palm-tree bore one year and not another;* (Aṣ, Ḳ;) as also عَاوَمَت. (Aṣ, TA.)

4. In this form of the verb, the final radical letter is changed into ت, so that they say أَسْنَتُوا, meaning *They experienced drought,* or *barrenness.* (TA. [See also art. سنت.])

5. تَسَنَّهْتُ عِنْدَهُ, (Ṣ,) and تَسَنَّيْتُ عنده, (Ṣ, Mṣb,) *I remained, stayed, dwelt,* or *abode, with him,* or *at his abode, a year:* (Mṣb:) both signify the same. (TA.) [See also 5 in art. سنو and سنى.] —— تَسَنَّهَتِ النَّخْلَةُ † *The palm-tree underwent the lapse of years;* (Ṣ, Mṣb;) as also ↓ سَنِهَت: (Ṣ:) and in like manner one says of other things. (Mṣb.) —— تسنّه said of food and of beverage, (Fr, Ṣ, TA,) † *It became altered* [*for the worse*]; as also ↓ سَنِهَ, aor. ـَ, inf. n. سَنَهٌ: (TA:) or *it became altered* [*for the worse*] *by the lapse of years:* (Fr, Ṣ, TA:) and التَّسَنُّه in relation to bread and beverage &c. means *the becoming mouldy,* or *musty,* or *spoiled.* (Ṣ: and so in some copies of the Ḳ and in the TA: in other copies of the Ḳ, السَّنِهُ, like كَتِف, is put in the place of التَّسَنُّه; and المُتَكَرِّج in the place of the explanation التَّكَرُّج.) فَانْظُرْ إِلَى طَعَامِكَ وَشَرَابِكَ لَمْ يَتَسَنَّهْ, in the Ḳur [ii. 261], means † [*But look at thy food and thy beverage,*] *it has not become altered* [*for the worse*] *by the lapse of years:* (Fr, Ṣ, TA:) Az says that this is the right way of reading, by pronouncing the ه in يتسنه in pausing after it and in continuing without pausing: Ks used to suppress the ه in the latter case and to pronounce it in the former: and Aboo-'Amr Esh-Sheybánee says that the original form [of يَتَسَنَّ] is يَتَسَنَّنْ; the like change being made in it as is made in تَظَنَّيْتُ [for تَظَنَّنْتُ] and in قَصَّيْتُ أَظْفَارِى [for قَصَّصْتُ اظفارى]. (TA. [See also 5 in art. سنو and سنى, last sentence.])

سَنَةٌ a word of which the final radical letter is rejected, (Ṣ, Mṣb,) and of which there are two dial. vars., (Mṣb,) being, accord. to some, originally سَنْهَةٌ, (Ṣ, Mṣb,) like جَبْهَةٌ (Ṣ) or سَجْدَةٌ, (Mṣb,) and accord to others, سَنْوَةٌ, (Ṣ,* Mṣb,) like شَهْوَةٌ, and upon each of these originals are founded modifications of the word, (Mṣb,) therefore it is mentioned in the Ḳ [and Ṣ and other lexicons] in the present art. and again in art. سنو, (TA,) *A year;* syn. حَوْلٌ; (Mṣb;) or عَامٌ: (M, Ḳ:) or, as Suh says, in the R, the سَنَة is *longer than the* عَام; the latter word being applied to the [twelve] Arabian months [collectively], and thus differing from the former word: (TA:) with the Arabs *it consists of four seasons,* mentioned before [in art. زمن, voce زَمَن]: but sometimes it is tropically applied to ‡ *a single* فَصْل [or *quarter*]; as in the saying, دَامَ المَطَرُ السَّنَةَ كُلَّهَا, meaning [*The rain continued*] *during the* فَصْل [or *quarter, all of it*]: (Mṣb:) [see more in art. سنو and سنى:] the dim. is ↓ سُنَيْهَةٌ (Ṣ, Mṣb) accord. to those who make the original of سَنَة to be سَنْهَة, (Mṣb,) and ↓ سُنَيَّةٌ (Ṣ, Mṣb) accord. to those who make the original of سَنَة to be سَنْوَة; (Mṣb;) and some say سُنَيْنَة, but this is rare: (TA:) the pl. is سَنَهَاتٌ (Mṣb, Ḳ) accord. to those who make the original of سَنَة to be سَنْهَة, (Mṣb,) and سَنَوَاتٌ (Mṣb, Ḳ) accord. to those who make the original of سَنَة to be سَنْوَة; (Mṣb;) and سِنُونَ also, (Ṣ, Mṣb, Ḳ,) like the masc. perfect pl., (Mṣb,) [agreeably with a rule applying to other cases of this kind,] with kesr, to the س, (Ṣ, TA,) and سِنِينَ [in the accus. and gen. cases], (Mṣb, TA,) so that one says, هٰذِهِ سِنُونَ [*These are years*], and رَأَيْتُ سِنِينَ [*I saw years*], (TA,) and the ن is elided when it is prefixed to another noun, governing the latter in the gen. case, (Mṣb,) and some say سُنُونَ, with damm to the س; (Ṣ, TA;) and in one dial., the ى is retained in all the cases, and the ن is made a letter of declinability, with tenween when the word is indeterminate, [so that one says سِنِينٌ,] and is not elided when the word is prefixed to another noun, governing the latter in the gen. case, because it is [regarded as] one of the radical letters of the word; and of this dial. is the saying of the Prophet, اَللّٰهُمَّ اجْعَلْهَا عَلَيْهِمْ سِنِينًا كَسِنِينِ يُوسُفَ [*O God, make them to be to them years like the years of Joseph*]; (Mṣb; [but in my copy of the Mgh, I find كَسِنِى يُوسُفَ;]) or with respect to سِنِينٌ, like مِئِينٌ, with refa [and tenween], there are two opinions; one is, that it is of the measure فِعْلِينٌ, like غِسْلِينٌ, with a rejection [of one letter], though this is an anomalous pl., for there sometimes occurs among pls. that which has no parallel, as عِدًى, and this is the opinion of Akh; the other is, that it is of the measure فَعِيلٌ, changed to فِعِيلٌ because of the kesreh of the second letter; the pl. being in some instances of the measure فَعِيلٌ, like كَلِيبٌ and عَبِيدٌ; but he who holds this opinion makes its final ن to be a substitute for و, and that of مِائَةٌ a substitute for ى: (Ṣ:) you may also suppress the tenween in سِنِينٌ; [in which case it seems that one says سِنِينَ in the nom. case (assimilating it to سِنُونَ) as well as in the accus. and the gen.; like as one does in the instances of بُرِينَ and بِرِينَ, pls. of بُرَةٌ, accord. to the Ḳ, though, as I have shown in art. برو, there is some doubt on this point;] but the suppression of the tenween in سِنِينٌ is more rare than its pronunciation: (I'Aḳ p. 18:) and another pl. is سُنِىٌّ, [originally سُنُوٌّ,] of the measure فُعُولٌ. (Er-Rághib, TA in art. سنو.) The phrase ثَلٰثَ مِائَةٍ سِنِينَ, in the Ḳur [xviii. 24], is said by Akh to be for ثَلٰثَمِائَةٍ مِنَ السِّنِينَ [*Three hundred of years*]: and he says that if the سِنُون be an explicative of the مِائَة, it is in the gen. case [to agree with مِائَةٍ]; and if an explicative of the ثَلٰث, it is in the accus. case [to agree with ثَلٰثَ]. (Ṣ. [See also Bḍ on this phrase; and see De Sacy's Ar. Gr., 2nd ed., i. 423.]) [لِسَنَةٍ, relating to an animal or a plant or the like, means *To the completion of a year:* and لِسَنَتِهِ, *to the completion of his,* or *its, year;* i. e. *in his,* or *its, first year.*] And one says, لَقِيتُهُ مُنْذُ ▼ سُنَيَّاتٍ [*I met him some years ago; three or more, to ten, years ago*]: a phrase like لَقِيتُهُ ذَاتَ العُوَيْمِ. (Az, TA in art. عوم.) And ▼ سُنَيَّةٌ is a dim. of enhancement, of سَنَةٌ: one says سُنَيَّةٌ حَمْرَآءُ *A severe year of drought* or *barrenness* or *dearth:* (TA:) and وَقَعُوا فِى السُّنَيَّاتِ ▼ البِيضِ [*They lapsed into the severe years of scantiness of herbage*]: these were years that pressed hard upon the people of El-Medeeneh. (Ḳ, TA.) — سَنَةٌ [alone] also signifies ‡ *Drought,* or *barrenness:* (Mṣb, Ḳ, TA:) or *vehement,* or *intense, drought:* (TA in art. سنو:) an instance of a noun used especially in one of its senses, like دَابَّةٌ applied to "a horse," and مَالٌ applied to "camels:" pl., in this, as in the former, sense, سَنَهَاتٌ [and سَنَوَاتٌ] and سِنُونَ and سِنِينٌ. (TA.) One says of a land (أَرْض), أَصَابَتْهَا السَّنَةُ ‡ *Drought,* or *barrenness, befell it.* (Mṣb.) And in like manner one says of people, أَصَابَتْهُمُ السَّنَةُ ‡ [*Drought, &c., befell them*]. (TA.) A seeker of herbage and of a place in which to alight was sent to a tract, and found it dried up by want of rain, and when he returned, being asked respecting it, he said, السَّنَةُ, meaning ‡ *Drought,* &c. [has befallen it]. (TA.) And it is said in a trad., اَللّٰهُمَّ أَعِنِّى عَلَى مُضَرَ بِالسَّنَةِ, i. e. ‡ [*O God, aid me against Muḍar*] *by drought* &c. (TA.) ═ It is also [used as an epithet,] applied to land (أَرْض), as meaning ‡ *Affected with drought,* or *barrenness;* (Aṣ, Ṣ, Ḳ;) as also ▼ سَنْهَآءُ and سَنْوَآءُ. (Mṣb.) One says likewise, هٰذِهِ بِلَادٌ سِنِينٌ ‡ *These are countries,* or *tracts, affected with drought* &c.: and Eṭ-Ṭirimmáḥ says

بِمُنْخَرَقٍ تَحِنُّ الرِّيحُ فِيهِ
حَنِينَ الجُلْبِ فِى البَلَدِ السِّنِينِ

‡ [*In a gusty tract, the wind moaning therein like the moaning of the milch ewes* or *goats* (see حَلُوبٌ) *in the country affected with drought,* or *the countries,* &c., بَلَد being regarded as a coll. gen. n. and therefore qualified by a pl., like قَوْمٌ in the phrase قَوْمٌ كَافِرُونَ]. (TA.)

سَنَّهُ سَنَهٌ, also pronounced with teshdeed to the ن: see سَنًا, in art. سنو and سنى, last sentence.

طَعَامٌ سَنِهٌ † [*Food,* or *wheat,*] *that has undergone the lapse of years;* (AZ, Ḳ;) as also سَنٍ. (AZ, TA.) — See also مُتَسَنِّهٌ.

نَخْلَةٌ سَنْهَآءُ † *A palm-tree that bears one year and not another:* (Ṣ, Ḳ:) or *a palm-tree affected by a year of drought.* (Ṣ.) And سَنَةٌ سَنْهَآءُ *A year in which is no herbage nor rain.* (TA.) — See also سَنَةٌ, last sentence but one.

سُنَيْهَةٌ and سُنَيَّةٌ (dims. of سَنَةٌ), and the pl. سُنَيَّاتٌ: see سَنَةٌ, in five places: and see also سُنَيَّةٌ in art. سنو and سنى.

مُتَسَنِّهٌ, applied to bread, (Ṣ, Ḳ,) and so ▼ سَنِهٌ applied to bread and to beverage &c., (CḲ, but see 5, third sentence,) † *Mouldy,* or *musty,* or *spoiled.* (Ṣ, Ḳ.)

سنو and سنى

1. سَنَا, [aor. يَسْنُو,] inf. n. سُنُوٌّ and سِنَايَةٌ and سِنَاوَةٌ, i. q. سَقَى [as meaning *He watered,* or *irrigated,* land]. (M.) [Hence,] one says أَرْضٌ ▼ مَسْنُوَّةٌ and ▼ مَسْنِيَّةٌ, (Ṣ, M, Ḳ,) meaning *Watered,* or *irrigated, land:* (M:) the و in مَسْنِيَّةٌ being changed into ى, (Ṣ, M,) in the opinion of Sb, (M,) like as it is in قِنْيَةٌ; (Ṣ;) for he knew not سَنَيْتُهَا [as meaning *I watered it*], holding مَسْنِيَّةٌ to be from [سَنَاهَا having for its aor.] يَسْنُوهَا. (M.) One says [also], سَنَتِ النَّاقَةُ, aor. تَسْنُو, (Ṣ, Ḳ,) inf. n. [as above, or] سِنَاوَةٌ and سِنَايَةٌ, (TA,) *The she-camel watered,* or *irrigated, land.* (Ṣ, Ḳ, TA.) And السَّحَابَةُ تَسْنُو الأَرْضَ (Ṣ, Mṣb) *The cloud waters the land.* (Mṣb.) And سَنَاكَ الغَيْثُ † [*The rain gave thee water* for thy land, or *may the rain give thee water*], inf. n. سنو and سنى [app. سُنُوٌّ and سُنِىٌّ]. (TA.) And السَّحَابُ يَسْنُو المَطَرَ † [*The clouds send down rain*]. (TA.) And سَنَتِ السَّحَابَةُ بِالمَطَرِ † [*The cloud watered,* or *irrigated, with rain*], aor. تَسْنُو and تَسْنِى. (M, TA.) And سَنَتِ السَّمَآءُ, aor. تَسْنُو, inf. n. سُنُوٌّ, ‡ *The sky rained.* (TA.) — سَنَتِ الدَّابَّةُ, aor. تَسْنِى; (M in art. سنى;) or سَنِيَتْ, (Ḳ,* TA,) aor. تَسْنَى, like رَضِىَ; (Ḳ, TA;) *The beast* [by which is app. meant, in the M, *the horse,* for it is there added وَغَيْرُهَا, meaning that the verb is said in like manner of other animals, which is the case, for it is generally said of a camel,] *was used for the drawing of water upon it* [to irrigate land: see سَانِيَةٌ, below]. (M, Ḳ.) And سَنَا, aor. يَسْنُو, said of a beast [turning a water-wheel], *He turned round about the well.* (R, TA.) And القَوْمُ يَسْنُونَ لِأَنْفُسِهِمْ, (Ṣ, Ḳ,) inf. n. سِنَايَةٌ, and sometimes سَانِيَةٌ, (TA,) *The people,* or *party, draw water for themselves;* (Ṣ, Ḳ; [in some copies of the former of which, إِذَا أَسْتَقَوْا is erroneously put for إِذَا ٱسْتَقَوْا, the reading in both of my copies;]) and so ▼ اِسْتَنَوْا لأنفسهم. (M,* TA.) And سَنَا عَلَى البَعِيرِ, inf. n. سَنَايَةٌ [app. a mistranscription for سِنَايَةٌ], *He drew water upon the camel;* which camel is termed سَانِيَةٌ. (MA.) And بَعِيرٌ يُسْنَى عَلَيْهِ *A camel upon which water is drawn.* (Mgh and Mṣb in explanation of سَانِيَةٌ.) And بِئْرٌ يُسْنَى مِنْهَا [*A well from which water is drawn,* app. *by means of the camel called* سَانِيَةٌ]. (M.) And سَنَوْتُ الدَّلْوَ, inf. n. سِنَايَةٌ, *I drew the bucket from the well.* (TA.) ═ سَنَتِ النَّارُ, (M, Ḳ,) aor. تَسْنُو, inf. n. سَنَآءٌ, (M,) *The fire became high in its light.* (M, Ḳ.) And سَنَا البَرْقُ, (M, Ḳ,) aor. يَسْنُو, inf. n. سَنَآءٌ, (TA,) *The lightning shone, shone brightly,* or *gleamed:* (M, Ḳ, TA:) [or *gleamed upwards,* or *shot up:* for, in the Ḳur xxiv. 43,] some read, يَكَادُ سَنَآءُ بَرْقِهِ يَذْهَبُ بِالأَبْصَارِ, meaning *The rising and gleaming upwards of his lightning* [*nearly taketh away the sight,* lit. *sights*]; others reading سَنَا, of which سَنَآء is not a dial. var. (M.) And ▼ اسنى البَرْقُ signifies [in like manner] *The lightning shone,* or *gleamed;* or *diffused itself, and rose.* (M.) And سَنَا إِلَى مَعَالِى الأُمُورِ † *He rose* [or *aspired*] *to the means of attaining eminence.* (M.) And سَنَا فِى حَسَبِهِ, inf. n. سَنَآءٌ, † *He became high,* or *exalted, in his grounds of pretension to respect* or *honour.* (M.) And سَنِىَ, like رَضِىَ, *He* (a man, TA) *was,* or *became, high,* or *exalted, in rank.* (Ḳ,* TA.) ═ See also 2, in two places. ═ And see 5.

2. سَنَّاهُ, (M, TA,) inf. n. تَسْنِيَةٌ, (TA,) *He ascended, rose, mounted, got, was,* or *became, upon it,* namely, a thing; (M, TA;) as also ▼ تَسَنَّاهُ. (M.) And تَسَنَّى ▼ البَعِيرُ النَّاقَةَ *The he-camel mounted the she-camel to compress her.* (Ḳ.) ═ And سَنَّاهُ, (Ṣ, Ḳ,) inf. n. as above, (Ḳ,) *He opened it;* (Ṣ, Ḳ, TA;) namely, a knot, and a lock: (TA:) and *made it easy.* (Ṣ, Ḳ, TA. [In the last of these, said to be tropical.]) A poet says,

وَأَعْلَمُ عِلْمًا لَيْسَ بِالظَّنِّ أَنَّهُ
إِذَا اللّٰهُ سَنَّى عَقْدَ شَىْءٍ تَيَسَّرَا

[*And I know with a knowledge that is not mere opinion, that, when God opens, and makes easy, the tying*, or *knotting, of a thing, it becomes easy*]. (Ṣ.) And one says, سَنَّيْتُ الشَّىْءَ, and الأَمْرَ, † *I opened the way of doing the thing*, and *the affair*. (TA.) And سَنَّيْتُ ↑ البَابَ, (Ḳ,) inf. n. سنى [app. سَنْىٌ], (TA,) *I opened the door*; as also ↑ سَنَوْتُهُ; (Ḳ, TA;) the verb in this sense having ى and و for its last radical. (TA.) —— See also 5.

3. سَانَيْتُ الرَّجُلَ, (Ṣ, M,* Ḳ,*) inf. n. مُسَانَاةٌ (TA) [and سِنَآءٌ (see what I have said respecting a verse cited voce بين)], ‡ *I vied with the man in being pleased, well pleased*, or *content*; or *I agreed, consented, accorded*, or *was of one mind* or *opinion, with him*: (Ṣ, M,* Ḳ:*) and *I treated him with gentleness*, or *blandishment*; *soothed*, or *coaxed, him*: and *behaved well to him in my social intercourse with him*: (Ṣ, Ḳ:) or مُسَانَاةٌ signifies the *treating* one *with gentleness*, or *blandishment, in suing for a thing*: (Az, TA:) or the *endeavouring to conciliate* one. (TA.) —— And سَانَاهُ, inf. n. مُسَانَاةٌ and سِنَآءٌ, *He hired him for* [or *by*] *the year*; (M, Ḳ;) or *he made an engagement*, or *a contract, with him for work* or *the like, by the year*; like سَانَهَهُ: (Ḳ in art. سنه:) and اِسْتَأْجَرَهُ مُسَانَاةً and عَامَلَهُ مُسَانَاةً signify the same as مُسَانَهَةً [q. v.]. (M, TA.)

4. اسناه *He raised, exalted*, or *elevated, him*, or *it*. (Ṣ, Mṣb, Ḳ.) — اسنى النَّارَ *He raised the light of the fire*. (M.) — اسنى لَهُ الجَائِزَةَ *He raised* [*in value*], *to him, the* جائزة [i. e. *gift*, or *present*]. (TA.) And أَسْنَيْنَا لَهُ الجِعَالَةَ *We made much and high* [*in amount*], *to him, the pay*. (Ḥar p. 134.) — And اسنى جِوَارَهُ *i. q.* أَحْسَنَهُ [app. meaning *He made good his covenant of protection*]. (TA.) —— اسنى البَرْقُ *The lightning sent its light into the house*, or *tent*, or *chamber*: or *fell upon the ground*: or *flew along in the clouds*; (Ḳ, TA;) or, sometimes, *elsewhere, not in the clouds*: but it is only *in the night*. (TA.) See also another explanation near the end of the first paragraph. —— اسنى القَوْمُ, (Ṣ, M, Ḳ,) inf. n. إِسْنَآءٌ, (Ṣ,) *The people*, or *party, tarried a year* (Ṣ, Ḳ) in a place: (Ṣ:) or it signifies أَتَى عَلَيْهِمُ العَامُ [*the year passed over them*; meaning *they remained to the end of the year*]. (M.) But أَسْنَتُوا signifies *They were afflicted with drought*, or *barrenness*: (Ṣ, M,* Ḳ: [Freytag has erroneously assigned this signification to اِسْتَنْتُوا:]) the و, (Ṣ,) or the ى, which is originally وَ, (M,) being changed into ت, (Ṣ, M,) to distinguish between this verb and اسنى in the sense expl. above. (Ṣ. [See art. سنت.])

5. تسنّى: see 2, in two places. — Also *i. q.* رقى رقية [in the CḲ رَقَّى رُقْيَةً, and in my MS. copy of the Ḳ رَقَّى رُقْيَةً, but correctly رَقِىَ, meaning *He ascended*: agreeably with this rendering, the inf. n. is expl. in the TḲ as meaning يوقسكه چقمق:] said of a man. (Ḳ,* TA.) —— Also *It opened*, or *became opened* or *open*: said of a lock [&c.]. (TA.) — *It was*, or *became, facilitated*, or *easy*; and *ready*, or *prepared*. (Ḥar pp. 159 and 508.) —— And *i. q.* تَسَهَّلَ فِى أُمُورِهِ, said of a man, (Ḳ,) i. e. *He found*, or *experienced, ease*, or *facility, in his affairs*. (TḲ.) —— Also *i. q.* تَرَضَّى: so in the phrase تسنّى فُلَانًا [*He sought to please, content*, or *satisfy, such a one*; or *he pleased, contented*, or *satisfied, such a one, after striving, labouring*, or *toiling*]: (Ḳ:) but it is said in the M, [app. a mistake, perhaps for the T, for in the M I do not find it,] that سنيت فلانا [by which may be meant either ↑ سَنَيْتُ or ↑ سَنَّيْتُ] means ترضّيته. (TA.) —— تَسَنَّيْتُ عِنْدَهُ *I remained, stayed, dwelt*, or *abode, with him*, or *at his abode, a year*; like تَسَنَّهْتُ عِنْدَهُ: (Mṣb in art. سنه:) or it means ↑ أَقَمْتُ عِنْدَهُ سَنَيَاتٍ [*I remained*, &c., *with him*, or *at his abode, some years*; *three* or *more, to ten, years*]. (TA.) — Hence, (TA,) تسنّى signifies also *It became altered* [*for the worse*], (Ṣ, Ḳ, TA,) accord. to Er-Rághib, *so that it lost its freshness, by the lapse of years*: (TA: [see also تَسَنَّهَ:]) but accord. to AA, it is from the phrase in the Ḳur [xv. 26 and 28 and 33] مِنْ حَمَإٍ مَسْنُونٍ; one of the نs being changed into ى; and is similar to تَقَضَّى for تَقَضَّضَ. (Ṣ, TA.)

8. اِسْتَنَوْا لِأَنْفُسِهِمْ: see 1. —— استنى النَّارَ *He looked at the light of the fire*. (IAạr, M.)

سَنًا *Light*: (Mṣb, MF:) or the *light of lightning*, (Ṣ, M, Ḳ,) and *of fire*: (M:) or the *point*, or *extremity, of the light of lightning*: (T, TA:) or *light shining* or *gleaming*, or *diffusing itself and rising*: (Er-Rághib, TA:) or *a high light*: and applied also to the *shining*, or *gleaming, of weapons*: (Ḥam p. 271:) MF says that the apparent particularization in the Ḳ [&c.] seems to have been taken from the verse of the Ḳur [xxiv. 43], and that the word is correctly a general term, meaning as expl. in the Mṣb: (TA:) [it is originally سَنَوٌ, though mentioned in the Ḳ as belonging to art. سنى; for] the dual is سَنَوَانِ: Aṣ knew not a verb belonging to it. (TA.) —— Also [The *cassia senna* of Linn.; the *common senna of medicine*; so called in the present day; and also called سَنَا مَكَّة, and سَنَا حِجَازِىّ;] *a certain plant*, (Ṣ, M, Mṣb, Ḳ,) *used as a medicine*; (Ṣ, TA;) and recommended in a trad.; (TA;) *an attenuant of the yellow bile and the black bile and the phlegm*, (Ḳ, TA,) *howsoever used*; (TA;) [and] *used as a collyrium*; (M;) AḤn describes it as *a shrub*, or *small tree, of the* [*class called*] أَغْلَاث [pl. of غَلْثٌ], *which is mixed with* حِنَّآء, *and improves and strengthens its colour, and blackens it*; *and which has a fruit of such kind that, when it dries up, and is put in motion by the wind, it causes to be heard a sound such as is termed* زَجَل [q. v.]: (M in arts. سنو and سنى, and TA:) its name is as above and ↑ سَنَآءٌ: (M, Ḳ:) and the n. un. is سَنَاةٌ and سَنَآءَةٌ: (M in arts. سنو and سنى:) the dual of سَنًا is سَنَيَانِ, and some say سَنَوَانِ. (M in art. سنى.) [Accord. to a gloss. in a copy of the Ṣ, as stated by Golius, the dual سَنَوَانِ is applied to The *leaves of cyprus* (or حِنَّآء) *and senna mixed together*, with which the hair is dyed black.] In the phrase سَنَا المِسْكِ, in a verse of El-Jaadee, the plant [above mentioned] may be meant, as though it were mixed with musk: or it may be from سَنًا signifying "light;" because the diffusion of odour is like that of light. (M.) —— سَنَا, (JM,) or سَنَا سَنَا, (TA,) without teshdeed, and also with teshdeed, to the ن, is an Abyssinian expression, meaning حَسَنٌ [q. v.], (JM, TA,) occurring in a trad. of Umm-Khálid; but it is differently related; some saying سَنَهْ سَنَهْ; and some, سَنَاه; and pronouncing each with, as well as without, teshdeed: so in the Nh. (TA.)

طَعَامٌ سَنٍ [*Food*, or *wheat*,] *that has undergone the lapse of years*; as also سَنِهٌ. (AZ, TA in art. سنه.)

سَنَةٌ, applied to a portion of time, (M,) signifying *A year*, syn. حَوْلٌ, (Mgh,) or عَامٌ, (Ḳ,) but a distinction is made between عَامٌ and سَنَةٌ, [as has been stated in art. سنه,] (TA,) belongs to arts. سنو and سنه [in both of which it is mentioned in many of the lexicons: see what has been said respecting it in art. سنه in the present work]: (M:) accord. to Suh, in the R, it is from سَنَا, aor. يَسْنُو, said of a beast [turning a water-wheel], meaning "he turned round about the well;" so that it signifies *a single revolution of the sun*; and it is sometimes termed دَارٌ: he says also that it is *longer than the* عَام, which is applied to the [twelve] Arabian months [collectively]: but سَنَةٌ is also applied to *twelve revolutions of the moon*: the سَنَة شَمْسِيَّة [or *solar year*] is *three hundred and sixty-five days and a quarter of a day*: and the سَنَة قَمَرِيَّة [or *lunar year*] is *three hundred and fifty-four days and a third of a day*: it is also said, on the authority of Er-Rághib, that سَنَةٌ is used as denoting a year in which is difficulty, and drought, or barrenness, or dearth; and عَامٌ, as denoting that in which is ampleness of the means, or circumstances, of life, and abundance of herbage or the like; and by this is explained the nice point in the words of the Ḳur [xxix. 13], أَلْفَ سَنَةٍ إِلَّا خَمْسِينَ عَامًا [*a thousand years save fifty years*]; because the fifty years passed before the mission of the prophet [Noah], before which no harm happened to him from his people; but after his mission, the years were difficult to him. (TA.) [Respecting the dims., (which are سُنَيَّةٌ and سُنَيْهَةٌ, the former accord. to those who make the original of سَنَةٌ to be سَنْوَةٌ, and the latter accord. to those who make it to be سَنْهَةٌ,) and the pls., (which are سَنَوَاتٌ and سَنَهَاتٌ and سِنُونَ and سُنُونَ and سِنِينَ and سِنِينٌ, the last whereof is originally سِنِينٌ, and سُنِىٌّ also,) see سَنَةٌ in art. سنه. — Also respecting سَنَةٌ used alone as signifying ‡ *Drought*, or *barrenness*, or *vehement* or *intense drought*, see that word in art. سنه. —— Also respecting the same word used as an epithet, applied to land (أَرْضٌ), as meaning ‡ *Affected with drought* or *barrenness*, like سَنْوَآءُ and سَنْهَآءُ, see that same word in art. سنه.]

سَنَةٌ سَنْوَآءُ † *A hard, rigorous*, or *distressing, year*. (M, Ḳ.) And أَرْضٌ سَنْوَآءُ † *A land affected with drought* or *barrenness* [like أَرْضٌ سَنَةٌ]. (TA.) [See also سَنْبَآءُ, in art. سنه.]

سَنَآءٌ inf. n. of سَنَتْ said of fire, (M,) and of سَنَا said of lightning, (TA,) and of سَنُوَ. (M.) — [Used as a simple subst.,] *High*, or *exalted, rank* or *condition*. (Ṣ,* Mṣb, Ḳ, TA.) ═ See also سَنًا.

سَنِىٌّ *High*, or *exalted, in rank* or *condition*: (Ṣ, M:) as also ↓ سَنَايَا, applied to a man. (Ḳ,* TA.)

سُنَيَّةٌ dim. of سَنَةٌ, (Ṣ and Mṣb in art. سنه,) accord. to those who make the latter word to be originally سَنْوَةٌ: (Mṣb in that art.:) pl. سُنَيَّاتٌ. (Ḳ and TA in that art., and TA in the present art.) See 5, last sentence but one; and see also سَنَةٌ, in art. سنه, in four places.

أَخَذَهُ بِسَنَايَتِهِ (Ṣ, Ḳ) and بِصِنَايَتِهِ (Ṣ) *He took it wholly*. (Ṣ, Ḳ.)

سَنَايَا: see سَنِىٌّ.

سَانٍ *Watering*: [and *drawing water*:] applied [as an epithet] to a man and to a camel: pl. سُنَاةٌ; which is applied by Lebeed to men [as meaning] *drawing water by means of* سَوَانٍ [pl. of سَانِيَةٌ, q. v.]. (TA.)

سَانِيَةٌ [a subst. from سَانٍ, made so by the affix ة,] *A she-camel*, (Ṣ,* M, Ḳ,) or *a camel*, (Mgh, Mṣb,) *a he-camel* as well as *a she-camel*, (TA,) *upon which water is drawn* (Ṣ,* M, Mgh, Mṣb, Ḳ, TA) *from a* [*deep*] *well* (Mgh, Mṣb) [*by a man riding* or *leading it away from the well, it having the two extremities of a long rope tied to the saddle, and the upper end of the well-rope being tied to the middle of the former rope*, as expl. voce ثِنَايَةٌ]; i. q. نَاضِحَةٌ: (Ṣ, TA:) [it seems also to signify, sometimes, *a camel that carries water for irrigating seed-produce*; a meaning likewise assigned to نَاضِحَةٌ and نَاضِحٌ:] and *a beast* (دَابَّة) *that turns round about a well* [*raising water from it by means of the machine called* دُولَاب]: (R, TA:) pl. سَوَانٍ. (Ṣ, Mgh, TA.) Hence the prov.,

سَيْرُ السَّوَانِى سَفَرٌ لَا يَنْقَطِعُ

[*The course of the beasts that draw water* in either of the ways described above *is a journey that does not end*]. (Ṣ, Mgh, TA.) — Also the غَرْبٌ [or *large bucket with which water is drawn*] *together with its gear*, or *apparatus*. (M, Mgh, Ḳ.) — And † *A cloud watering the earth*. (Mṣb.)

أَرْضٌ مَسْنُوَّةٌ and مَسْنِيَّةٌ: see 1, second sentence.

مُسَنَّاةٌ i. q. عَرِمٌ [q. v.]: (Ṣ, Ḳ:) [or rather] *A dam*; i. e. *a thing constructed* [or *raised*] *to keep back the water of a torrent*; (Mgh;) *a* [*kind of*] *wall built in the face of water*: (Mṣb in art. سن:) so called because there are in it sluices, or openings for the water, according to what may be required; from سَنَّيْتُ الشَّىْءَ, and الأَمْرَ, expl. above: so in the T: (TA:) pl. مُسَنَّيَاتٌ. (MA.)

مَسْنُوَّةٌ, (M, TA,) or بِئْرٌ مَسْنُوَّةٌ (Az, TA,) *A well* (Az, M, TA) *of which the rope is long*, (Az, TA,) *from which one draws water only by means of the camel called* سَانِيَةٌ. (Az, M,* TA.)

سه

سَهْ and سَهْ سَهْ: see اِسْتٌ, in art. سته, in four places.

سهب

1. سَهْبٌ The act of *taking*. (JK, Ḳ.) You say, سَهَبَ الشَّىْءَ, aor. ـَ, inf. n. سَهْبٌ, *He took the thing*. (TḲ.)

2. تَسْهِيبٌ The *departure of reason*, or *intellect*: its verb [which was probably سُهِّبَ, like أُسْهِبَ, q. v.,] is obsolete. (TA.)

4. اسهب *He went far*, or *to a great* or *an extraordinary length*, in a thing; for instance, in journeying; as in a trad., in which it is said of horses, or horsemen, أَسْهَبَتْ شَهْرًا *They went far for a month*; and in eating and drinking; as in another trad.: (TA:) it is from سَهْبٌ, signifying "a plain and far-extending land;" as though meaning *He traversed a plain and far-extending tract of land*; like as one says أَسْهَلَ and أَحْزَنَ. (Ḥar p. 572.) *He* (a horse) *ran with wide steps, and preceded*, or *outstripped*. (Ṣ, TA. [See also سَهْبٌ, below.]) And [hence,] *He was*, or *became, loquacious*, or *profuse of speech*; (IAạr, Ṣ, Ḳ;) like اسهر; (Ḳ* and TA in art. سهر;) [and] so اسهب فِى المَنْطِقِ: (JK:) or *he doted*; or *was disordered in his intellect*; but when a man makes many mistakes in his speech, you say of him أَفْنَدَ: (Aṣ, TA:) or *he doted much*, or *often*; or *was much*, or *often, disordered in his intellect*: (AO, TA:) [and it seems from an explanation of the part. n. مُسْهِبٌ that it probably signifies also *he was eloquent*, or *profuse of correct speech*:] or *he was very greedy, and* (in some copies of the Ḳ "or") *covetous, so as to refrain from nothing*: (Ḳ, TA:) and you say also اسهب كَلَامَهُ *He prolonged*, or *was prolix in, his speech*: and فِى كَلَامِهِ إِسْهَابٌ *In his speech is prolixity*. (A, TA.) Also *He* (a man) *gave much*, or *largely*; and so ↓ استهب: (Lth, Ḳ:) [or, in this sense,] you say, اسهب فِى العَطَآءِ. (A.) — اسهبوا *They reached sand*, in digging [a well], *and water came not forth*: (Ṣ:) or *they dug, and came upon sand or a current of air*: (Ḳ:) or *they dug, and came upon a current of air, and the water disappointed them of its coming*: (Az, TA:) or *they dug without attaining any good*: (Ḳ:) or اسهب signifies *he dug until he reached sand*: and, accord. to Th, *he dug a well and reached water*. (TA.) — اسهبوا الدَّابَّةَ *They left the beast alone*, or *by itself*, (Ḳ, TA,) *to pasture* [*where it would*]. (TA.) ═ اسهب الشَّاةَ وَلَدُهَا *Her young one sucked*, (Ḳ,) or *licked*, (TA,) *the ewe*, or *she-goat*. (Ḳ.) ═ أُسْهِبَ *He* (a man, Ṣ) *lost his reason*, (Ṣ, Ḳ, TA,) as some say, (TA,) *from the bite of a serpent*, (Ṣ, Ḳ, TA,) or *the sting of a scorpion*: (TA:) or *his colour became altered in consequence of love* or *fright* or *disease*: (Ḳ:) or, accord. to AḤát, اسهب, [so in the TA, in which it seems to be implied that أَسْهَبَ, not أُسْهِبَ, is meant,] inf. n. إِسْهَابٌ, signifies *he* (a man bitten by a serpent, or stung by a scorpion,) *lost his reason and lived*. (TA. [See also the part. n., مُسْهَبٌ, below.]) إِسْهَابُ اللُّبِّ [in which the former word is probably the inf. n. of أُسْهِبَ, not of أَسْهَبَ,] means *The mind's being confounded*, or *perplexed, by* [*love of*] *a woman*. (JK.)

8: see 4, in the middle of the paragraph.

سَهْبٌ *A desert*, or *waterless desert*; syn. فَلَاةٌ: (Ṣ, Ḳ:) pl. سُهُبٌ. (TA.) [See also سُهْبٌ.] ═ *A horse wide of step in running*, (Ṣ, Ḳ, TA,) and (TA) *vehement therein*, (JK, Ḳ,* TA,) *slow to sweat*; (JK, TA;) and ↓ مُسْهَبٌ and ↓ مُسْهِبٌ, (Ḳ,) but the latter of these is said to be peculiarly the chaste form in this sense, (TA,) signify the same. (Ḳ.) — بِئْرٌ سَهْبَةٌ *A deep well*; (Ṣ, A, O, Ḳ;) as also ↓ بِئْرٌ مُسْهَبَةٌ: (Ṣ,* O:) or the former, *a deep well* (JK, TA) *from which sand comes forth* (JK) or *from which wind*, or *a current of air, comes forth*: (TA:) and ↓ the latter, *a well of which the coarse sand baffles one so that he cannot reach the water* [*in digging it*]; (Ḳ;) or *a well that people dig until they reach pouring earth, which baffles them by its pouring down, so that they leave it*; (Sh, TA;) or *a well of which the bottom and the water are not reached*; (Ks, TA;) or *a well that is dug until one reaches the water upon which is the earth*. (Az, TA. [See 4.]) ═ *A portion of time*; as in the saying, مَضَى سَهْبٌ مِنَ اللَّيْلِ [*A portion of the night passed*]. (TA.)

سُهْبٌ *A plain and smooth*, or *plain and smooth and soft, tract of land*: pl. سُهُوبٌ: (Ḳ:) or the pl. signifies *plain and far-extending tracts of land*: (JK, A, TA:) or *wide land* [or *lands* (for the sing. is expl. in the TA in one place as signifying *a wide land*)]: (AA, TA:) or سُهُوبُ الفَلَاةِ signifies, (Ḳ,) or signifies also, (JK,) *tracts*, or *regions, of the* فلاة [i. e. *desert*, or *waterless desert*,] *in which there is no way*. (JK, Ḳ.) [See an ex. in a verse cited in art. رقل, conj. 4: and see also سَهْبٌ, above, first sentence.]

مُسْهَبٌ, with fet-ḥ to the ه, [contr. to rule, being of the measure مُفْعَلٌ in the sense of the measure مُفْعِلٌ,] *Going far*, or *to a great* or *an extraordinary length*, in a thing: and *prolonging*. (TA.) — See also سَهْبٌ: and its fem., with ة, see in two places in the same paragraph. — Also *Long*, or *tall*: (JK:) applied [in the latter sense] as an epithet to a man: and طَوِيلٌ مُسْهَبٌ *excessively tall*. (A.) — Also, and ↓ مُسْهِبٌ, (Ḳ,) both said to have been mentioned by ISk, (TA,) or the former, but not ↓ the latter, (AZ, IAạr, IḲt, Zbd, Ṣ, TA,) though the former is extr. [with respect to rule], (Ṣ, TA,) *Loquacious*, or *profuse of speech*: (AZ, IAạr, ISk, IḲt, Zbd, Ṣ, Ḳ, TA:) or, accord. to Aboo-'Alee El-Baghdádee, as is stated by IB, the former signifies *profuse and erroneous in speech*: and the ↓ latter, *eloquent*, or *profuse and correct in speech*: and in like manner says El-Aạlam, adding that ↓ the latter is shown to have this meaning by its being applied to a horse that is *fleet*, or *swift, and excellent*; (TA:) or the former signifies *doting*; or *disordered in his intellect*: (Aṣ, TA:) or *doting much*, or *often*; or *much*, or *often, disordered in his intellect*: (AO, TA:) [and similar explanations of it will be found below:] other instances of verbs of the measure أَفْعَلَ having مُفْعَل as the measure of the part. n. used in the sense of the measure مُفْعِل are أَلْفَجَ and أَحْصَنَ and أَجْرَشَتِ الإِبِلُ and أَقْتَرَ: as used in the first of the senses expl. in this sentence, مُسْهَبٌ is from سَهْبٌ signifying "a wide land:" or, as some say, it is from أُسْهِبُوا الدَّابَّةَ, expl. above; as though the person to whom it is applied were left to speak what he would, or made to have ample scope to say what he would. (TA.) — Both مُسْهَبٌ and ▼ مُسْهِبٌ signify also *Very greedy, and covetous, so as to refrain from nothing*. (TA.) — And the former, One *who has lost his reason*; as some say, *from the bite of a serpent*, or *the sting of a scorpion*: or one *who talks irrationally*, or *foolishly*, or *deliriously, in consequence of doting*, or *disorder of his intellect*: or *whose colour has become altered in consequence of love* or *fright* or *disease*. (TA.) And مُسْهَبُ الجِسْمِ A man *whose body is wasting away in consequence of love*: so says Yaạkoob: and Lḥ mentions the phrases ▼ مُسْهِبُ العَقْلِ, with kesr, and مُسْهِبُ الجِسْمِ, and مُسْهِمٌ, which is formed by substitution [of م for ب], as meaning a man *whose reason is departing*, and *whose body is wasting away, in consequence of love*: and accord. to AḤát, مسهب, [app. ▼ مُسْهِبٌ, as the context seems to imply,] applied to one bitten by a serpent or stung by a scorpion, signifies *who has lost his reason, and lives*. (TA.) — Also Land *far-extending, and plain, with depression, consisting of low tracts, the depression whereof is little, extending for the space of a day and a night* [*of journeying*], *and thereabout: the* بُطُون [or *low tracts*] *of land of which it consists are in* [*deserts such as are termed*] صَحَارَى, *and in elevated and plain*, or *hard and elevated, tracts of ground, and sometimes they flow* [*with torrents*], *and sometimes they do not flow, for they comprise parts that are rugged, and parts that are plain*, or *soft, producing much herbage, and in them are places wherein are trees* [or *shrubs*], *and places wherein are none*. (L, TA.) — Also A place *that does not obstruct nor retain water*. (TA.)

مُسْهِبٌ: see سَهْبٌ, second signification: — and see مُسْهَبٌ, in seven places. — Also A man *who overcomes*, or *surpasses, and is bountiful, in his gifts*. (TA.)

سهج

1. سَهَجَتِ الرِّيحُ, (Ṣ, A, Ḳ,) aor. ـَ, (JK,) inf. n. سَهْجٌ, (TA,) *The wind blew violently*: (Ṣ, A, Ḳ, TA: [like سَهَكَتْ:]) or *continually and violently*. (TA.) — سَهَجَتِ الإِبِلُ *The camels journeyed*, or *went, quickly*, or *hastily*. (JK.) — سَهَجَ القَوْمُ لَيْلَتَهُمْ, (Ṣ, Ḳ,) inf. n. as above, (Ṣ,) *The people*, or *party, passed their night journeying* (Ṣ, Ḳ) *continually*. (TA.) — سَهَجَتِ الرِّيحُ الأَرْضَ [like سَحَجَتْ] *The wind pared the ground*: (Ṣ, Ḳ:) or *pared its surface*. (TA.) — And سَهَجَ الطِّيبَ, (Ṣ, Ḳ,) aor. and inf. n. as above, (TA,) *He bruised, brayed*, or *pounded*, or *he pounded small, powdered*, or *pulverized, the perfume*: (Ṣ, Ḳ:) or سَهْجٌ signifies any *bruising, braying*, or *pounding*. (TA.)

رِيحٌ سَهُوجٌ and سَهُوجٌ (O, Ḳ) and ▼ سَيْهَجٌ (Ṣ, O, Ḳ) and ▼ سَيْهُوجٌ, (Ṣ, A, O, Ḳ,) in the last two of which the ج is asserted by Yaạkoob to be a substitute for ك, (Az, TA,) and ▼ سَيْهَجَةٌ, (TA,) *A violent wind*. (Ṣ, A, O, Ḳ.) And you say also رِيَاحٌ سُهُجٌ (JK, Ṣ, O) and سَاهِجَاتٌ (JK) [both pls. of ▼ رِيحٌ سَاهِجَةٌ, and signifying, accord. to the context in the JK and O, *Violent winds*: or, accord. to the context in the Ṣ, *winds that pare the ground*: the sing. like رِيحٌ سَهُوكٌ and سَاهِكَةٌ &c.].

رِيحٌ سَاهِجَةٌ; pl. رِيَاحٌ سُهُجٌ and سَاهِجَاتٌ: see the next preceding paragraph. — غُبَارٌ سَاهِجٌ *Dust rising high*. (JK.)

سَيْهَجٌ, and with ة: } see سَهُوجٌ.
سَيْهُوجٌ:

أَسَاهِيجُ [like أَسَاهِيكُ and أَسَاهِىُّ] *Various sorts* (JK, O, Ḳ) *of running*, (JK,) or *of going*, or *pace*, (O, Ḳ,) or, as in one copy of the Ḳ, *of the going*, or *pace, of camels*. (TA.) — And *Varieties of false*, or *vain, things* or *sayings* or *deeds*. (JK, TA.)

مَسْهَجٌ [like مَسْهَكٌ] *A place where the wind passes along* [or *blows violently*]. (AA, Ṣ, O, Ḳ.) AA cites, as an ex., the saying,

* إِذَا هَبَطْنَ مُسْتَحَارًا مَسْهَجَا *

[*When they descend into*, or *enter, a place of confusion*, or *perplexity, where one is unable to see his right course, a place where the wind blows*, or *blows violently*]. (Ṣ, O.)

مِسْهَجٌ One *who runs on, in speech, like the wind*: (JK:) *eloquent*; or *fluent in speech*: (O, Ḳ, TA:) applied to an orator; (JK, T, TA;) as also مِسْهَكٌ. (T, TA.) — And One *who speaks on every true and false subject*. (O, Ḳ.)

سهد

1. سَهِدَ, aor. ـَ, (Ṣ, L, Ḳ,) inf. n. سُهَادٌ (Ṣ,* A,* L) and سُهُدٌ (A,* L, Ḳ*) and سَهَدٌ, (Ṣ, L,) [all these are mentioned as inf. ns. in the L and TA, and app. in the Ḳ, but the first seems to be mentioned in the Ṣ as a simple subst.,] *He was sleepless*: syn. أَرِقَ; (Ṣ, A,* L, Ḳ;) *he did not sleep* (لَمْ يَنَمْ); *contr. of* رَقَدَ. (L.) [See also سُهَادٌ below.]

2. سَهَّدَهُ, (Ṣ, A, L, Ḳ,) inf. n. تَسْهِيدٌ; (PṢ;) and ▼ اسهدهُ; (A, TA;) *He*, (a man, Ṣ, L, Ḳ,) and *it*, (anxiety, or grief, A, L, and pain, L,) *rendered him sleepless*. (Ṣ, A, L, Ḳ.) And فُلَانٌ يُسَهَّدُ *Such a one is not suffered to sleep*. (L.)

4: see 2. — اسهدت بِالوَلَدِ *She* [a woman] *brought forth the child with a single moan*, or *hard breathing*; (IAạr, Ḳ;) [or *with a single impulse*;] like زَكَبَتْ بِهِ, &c. (IAạr, L in art. حفد.)

[5. تسهّد is said by Freytag, as on the authority of the Ḳ, in which I do not find it, to signify *He was sleepless*; like سَهِدَ: if used, it more probably signifies *he was rendered sleepless*; as quasi-pass. of سَهَّدَهُ.]

شَىْءٌ سَهْدٌ مَهْدٌ *A good*, or *beautiful, thing*: (L, Ḳ:) مهد is here an imitative sequent to سهد. (L.)

سُهُدٌ: see سُهَادٌ, in two places.

سُهُدٌ One *who sleeps little*; (Ṣ, A, L, Ḳ;) as also ▼ مُسَهَّدٌ: (A:) and some say سُهَدٌ, like عُمَرُ; but this is [of a measure used] only in proper names: (Ḥam p. 39:) and an eye (عَيْنٌ) *that sleeps little*. (L.) — [Hence,] ‡ *Vigilant*; *cautious*; applied to a man; as also ▼ مُسَهَّدٌ. (A, TA.) — And *Little sleep*. (L.)

سُهْدَةٌ ‡ *Vigilance*: so in the saying, هُوَ ذُو سُهْدَةٍ فِى أَمْرِهِ ‡ [*He is possessed of vigilance*] (A, Ḳ) [*in his affair*]. (A.) — You say also, مَا رَأَيْتُ مِنْهُ سُهْدَةً, meaning ‡ *I experienced not*, or *I have not experienced, from him any mindfulness of what is good, nor any desire for it*: (A, TA:) or *anything upon which to place reliance, of words or of good actions*, (Ṣ, L, Ḳ,) or *of good actions or satisfactory words*. (L.)

سُهَادٌ (Ṣ, A, L) and ▼ سُهُدٌ (A, L, Ḳ) *Sleeplessness*. (Ṣ, A, L, Ḳ. [Both mentioned in the L and TA as inf. ns. of 1.]) One says فِى عَيْنِهِ ▼ سُهُدٌ and سُهَادٌ *In his eye is sleeplessness*. (A.)

سَهْوَدٌ, applied to a boy, or young man, *Tender*, or *flourishing, and fresh*: (Sh, Ḳ:) or *tall and strong*. (Ḳ.)

أَسْهَدُ [*More, and most, sleepless*.] — [Hence,] هُوَ أَسْهَدُ رَأْيًا مِنْكَ ‡ *He is more cautious and vigilant in judgment*, or *opinion, than thou*. (A, Ḳ,* TA.)

مُسَهَّدٌ *Rendered sleepless*. (Ṣ, L, Ḳ.) — See also سُهُدٌ, in two places.

سهر

1. سَهِرَ, aor. ـَ, inf. n. سَهَرٌ, *He waked, was sleepless* or *wakeful*, or *did not sleep, by night*; (Ṣ, Ḳ;) *he abstained from sleep by night*; (Lth;) *he remained awake* all the night or a part thereof: you say سَهِرَ اللَّيْلَ, or بَعْضَ اللَّيْلِ, *He remained awake during the night, or a part of the night*: (Mṣb:) [*he passed the night*, or *a part of the night, sleepless*, or *without sleeping*:] and سَهِرْتُ البَارِحَةَ *I remained awake last night*. (A.) — مَا لَهُ سَهِرَ وَعَبِرَ *What aileth him? May he be*

sleepless by night, and may he grieve, or *mourn,* is an imprecation of the Arabs. (AZ, TA in this art. and art. عبر.) — سَهِرَ البَرْقُ ‡ *The lightning gleamed,* or *glistened, during the night.* (A.)

3. مُسَاهَرَةٌ signifies The *being sleepless,* or *awake, with another:* (KL, and Ḥar p. 329:) [and the *vying with another in remaining sleepless* or *awake:*] and [like إِسْهَارٌ, but I think this doubtful,] the *making* [one] *sleepless* or *awake.* (KL.) سَاهِرِ النُّجُومَ means *He passed the night sleepless like as do the stars.* (Ḥar ubi suprà.)

4. اسهرهُ *He,* (Ṣ, Mṣb,) or *it,* (A,) as anxiety, or trouble of mind, and pain, (TA,) *caused him to wake, to be sleepless,* or *wakeful,* or *to remain awake.* (Ṣ, A, Mṣb, TA.)

سَهَرٌ : see سَاهُورٌ.

سُهَرَةٌ :
سَهْرَانُ : } see سَاهِرٌ.

سُهَارٌ *A state of waking; sleeplessness,* or *wakefulness;* (Ḳ;) *i. q.* سُهَادٌ; (T;) as also ↓ سَاهُورٌ. (Ḳ.)

سَهَّارٌ : see سَاهِرٌ, in two places.

سَاهِرٌ and ↓ سَهْرَانُ (Ṣ, Mṣb, Ḳ) and ↓ سَهَّارٌ (Ḳ) and ↓ سُهَرَةٌ, (Ṣ, Ḳ,) the last of which is an intensive epithet, (Ṣ,) [and so is the third, and sometimes the second,] *Waking, sitting up, sleepless, wakeful,* or *not sleeping, by night;* (Ṣ, Ḳ;) [*abstaining from sleep by night;*] *remaining awake* all the night or a part thereof: (Mṣb:) and the last, [and third, and sometimes the second,] *wakeful,* or *waking much, &c.* (Ṣ.) You say, رَجُلٌ سَهَّارُ العَيْنِ *A man whom sleep does not overcome.* (Lḥ.) — بَرْقٌ سَاهِرٌ ‡ *Lightning gleaming,* or *glistening, during the night.* (A.) — لَيْلٌ سَاهِرٌ ‡ *A night of waking* or *sleeplessness* or *wakefulness:* (Ḳ:) like as one says لَيْلٌ نَائِمٌ. (TA.) — سَاهِرَةُ العِرْقِ † A she-camel *that yields milk long and abundantly.* (TA.) — عَيْنٌ سَاهِرَةٌ ‡ *A running spring* or *fountain:* (Ḳ:) *a spring* or *fountain that runs night and day, unremittingly.* (A,* TA.) It is said in a trad., خَيْرُ المَالِ عَيْنٌ سَاهِرَةٌ لِعَيْنٍ نَائِمَةٍ ‡ *The best of property is a spring of water that runs night and day while its owner is sleeping;* (TA;) its owner having his mind unoccupied by it. (A.) — أَرْضٌ سَاهِرَةٌ ‡ *Land that produces plants quickly:* as though it passed the night doing so. (A.) — Also سَاهِرَةٌ [alone], ‡ *A wide,* or *an extensive, tract of land, the traverser of which remains awake during the night:* (A:) or the *earth,* or *land:* (Ḳ:) or the *surface of the earth:* (Fr, Lth, Ṣ, Ḳ:) because it produces plants or herbage alike by night and day: (Ibn-Es-Seed:) so in the Ḳur lxxix. 14: (Ṣ:) or (TA, but in the Ḳ "and") *a desert,* syn. فَلَاةٌ, (Ḳ,) *the traverser of which remains awake during the night:* (TA:) or (TA, but in the Ḳ "and") *an untrodden land:* (Ḳ:) or (TA) *a land which God will create anew on the day of resurrection:* (Ḳ:) or *a land on which none has disobeyed God:* (Ibn-Es Seed:) or (TA) *Hell:* (Ḳatádeh, Ḳ:) or (TA) [in the Ḳur ubi suprà] *a certain mountain of Jerusalem:* (Wahb Ibn-Munebbih, Ḳ:) or (TA) the *land of Syria.* (Muḳátil, Ḳ.)

سَاهِرَةٌ fem. of سَاهِرٌ [q. v.]. — See also سَاهُورٌ.

سَاهِرِيَّةٌ *A certain perfume:* [so called] because one is caused to be sleepless in preparing it, and making it good. (Ṣgh, Ḳ.)

سَاهُورٌ : see سُهَارٌ. ═ Also The *sheath of the moon,* (Ṣ, Ḳ,) *which it enters when it is eclipsed,* (TA,) accord. to the assertion of the Arabs; (Ṣ, TA;) as also ↓ سَاهِرَةٌ. (Ḳ.) One says, of the moon, when it is eclipsed, دَخَلَ فِى سَاهُورِهِ *It has entered into its sheath.* (Ḳt.) [Or] The *shade,* or *shadow, of the* سَاهِرَة, i. e., of the *surface of the earth.* (Ṣ, Ḳ.) — The *moon* (Ḳ, TA) itself; as also ↓ سَهَرٌ; of Syriac origin, accord to IDrd. (TA.) — The *halo* (دَارَة) *of the moon:* (Ḳ:) a Syriac word. (TA.) — And السَّاهُورُ, *The last nine nights of the lunar month:* (Ḳ:) or so لَيَالِى السَّاهُورِ: because the moon is absent in its first part. (ISk.) — Also سَاهُورٌ, The *source* of a spring of water. (Ḳ,* TA.) — And *Multitude; abundance.* (Ḳ.)

الأَسْهَرَانِ ‡ *Two ducts* (عِرْقَانِ) *in the two nostrils,* (Ṣ, Ḳ,*) *in the inside,* (TA,) *which, when an ass is excited by lust, flow with water,* (Ṣ, TA,) or *with blood:* (TA:) so in the verse of Esh-Shemmákh,

* تُوَائِلُ مِنْ مِصَكٍّ أَنْصَبَتْهُ *
* حَوَالِبُ أَسْهَرَيْهِ بِالذَّنِينِ *

[*She seeks to escape from a strong* (*he-ass*) *whom the ducts of his two nostrils flowing with mucus have fatigued*]: (Ṣ:) or *the nose and the penis:* (Sh, Ḳ:) or (TA, but in the Ḳ "and") *two ducts in the flesh and sinew next the back-bone, through which runs the seminal fluid into the penis:* (Ḳ:) or (TA) *two ducts rising from the two testicles, and meeting together in the interior of the penis,* (Ḳ,) or *of the* فَيْشَلَة [or *glans of the penis*]; *which are the ducts of the seminal fluid:* (TA:) or *the two veins or ducts of the penis which become prominent when it is in a state of erection:* (TA:) and *two veins or ducts in the eye:* (Ḳ:) but Aṣ disallows اسهريه, and says that the true reading, in the verse of Esh-Shemmákh, is أَسْهَرَتْهُ, meaning, [*that*] *have not suffered him to sleep.* (TA.) [See also حَالِبٌ.]

سهك

1. سَهِكَ, aor. ـَ, (Mṣb, Ḳ,) inf. n. سَهَكٌ, (Mṣb,) *He* (a man, Mṣb) *had a disagreeable smell proceeding from sweat.* (Mṣb, Ḳ.) [And app. *It* (a thing) *had a foul smell* from fish, and from the rust of iron, &c.: see سَهِكٌ below.] ═ سَهَكَتِ الرِّيحُ *The wind blew vehemently.* (Ṣ, O. [And so سَهَجَت.]) — And سَهَكَتِ الدَّابَّةُ, (Ṣ, O, Ḳ,) inf. n. سُهُوكٌ, (O, Ḳ,) *The beast ran lightly,* or *with agility:* (Ṣ, O, Ḳ:) or *frisked away to the right and left.* (O.) ═ سَهَكَهُ, (Ṣ, O, Ḳ,) aor. ـَ, inf. n. سَهْكٌ, (Ṣ, O,) *i. q.* سَحَقَهُ [*He bruised, brayed,* or *pounded, it;* &c.]; (Ḳ;) a dial. var. of the latter: (Ṣ, O:) or it is like the latter, except that سَهْكٌ appears to be coarser than سَحْقٌ; for you say of the perfumer, سَهَكَ العَطَّارُ الطِّيبَ عَلَى الصَّلَاءَةِ وَلَمَّا يَسْحَقْهُ [*The perfumer bruised, brayed, pounded,* or *crushed, coarsely, the perfume, upon the stone used for that purpose, and did not as yet powder it,* or *pulverize it*]. (IDrd, O.) — And سَهَكَتِ الرِّيحُ الأَرْضَ, (O,) or التُّرَابَ عَنْ وَجْهِ الأَرْضِ, (Ḳ,) or التراب عَنِ الأَرْضِ, (TA,) *The wind made the dust to fly* [*from the ground,* or *from the surface of the earth*]. (O, Ḳ, TA.) [And سَهَجَتِ الرِّيحُ الأَرْضَ, q. v., has a similar meaning.]

سَهَكٌ (Ṣ, O, Mṣb, Ḳ) and ↓ سُهْكَةٌ (Fr, O, Ḳ) and ↓ سَهَكَةٌ (O, Ḳ) *A disagreeable smell which one perceives from a human being when he sweats;* (Mṣb,* Ḳ;) and the *smell of fish;* (Ṣ, O, Ḳ;) and *of the rust of iron;* (Ṣ, Mṣb;) or they signify also the *rust of iron;* (O, Ḳ;) and the *foulness of the smell of stinking flesh-meat:* (Ḳ:) and Ḥar uses ↓ سُهُوكَةٌ in the first of these senses for the purpose of assimilation to سُهُومَةٌ, agreeably with a practice often observed. (Ḥar p. 449.) — The first is also inf. n. of سَهِكَ [q. v.]. (Mṣb.)

سَهِكٌ *Having a disagreeable smell proceeding from sweat.* (Ḳ.) You say, إِنَّهُ لَسَهِكُ الرِّيحِ *Verily he is one who has a disagreeable smell, &c.* (Moheeṭ, L.) And يَدِى مِنَ السَّمَكِ وَمِنْ صَدَإِ الحَدِيدِ سَهِكَةٌ [*My hand is disagreeable in smell from fish and from the rust of iron*]; like as you say وَضِرَةٌ when it is from milk and butter, and غَمِرَةٌ when it is from flesh-meat. (Ṣ.)

سَهَكَةٌ and سُهْكَةٌ : see سَهَكٌ.

رِيحٌ سَهُوكٌ and ↓ سَاهِكَةٌ (Ḳ) and ↓ سَيْهَكٌ and ↓ سَيْهُوكٌ (Ṣ, Ḳ) [like سَهُوجٌ and سَاهِجَةٌ &c.] *A vehement,* or *violent, wind,* (Ṣ, Ḳ, TA,) *paring* [*the ground*]; (TA;) as also ↓ مِسْهَكَةٌ: (O, Ḳ:) [pl. of ↓ the second سَوَاهِكُ:] El-Kumeyt says,

* رَمَادًا أَطَارَتْهُ السَّوَاهِكُ رِمْدِدَا *

[*Ashes which the violent winds made to fly away reduced to the most minute particles*]. (Ṣ.) — السَّهُوكُ *The eagle.* (Ḳ.)

سُهُوكَةٌ : see سَهَكٌ.

سَهَّاكٌ : see مِسْهَكٌ.

سَاهِكٌ *Ophthalmia;* syn. رَمَدٌ. (Ḳ.) So in the phrase, بِعَيْنِهِ سَاهِكٌ [*In his eye is ophthalmia*]. (TA.) — رِيحٌ سَاهِكَةٌ : see سَهُوكٌ, in two places.

سَيْهَكٌ :
سَيْهُوكٌ : } see سَهُوكٌ.

أَسَاهِكُ [like أَسَاهِيجُ] *Various sorts of running* (Ibn-'Abbád, O, Ḳ) of beasts; and their *frisking away* (Ḳ, TA) *to the right and left.* (TA.)

مَسْهَكٌ [like مَسْهَجٌ] *A place where the wind passes along* [or *blows violently*]; as also ↓ مَسْهَكَةٌ. (Ṣ, Ḳ.)

مِسْهَكٌ A horse *swift in running;* (Ṣ;) *that*

.runs much; (Ḳ;) *that runs like the wind.* (TA.) — And [like مِسْبَح, q. v.,] *Eloquent,* or *fluent, in speech; running therein like the wind;* (O, Ḳ;) as also ▼ سَحَّالٌ. (Kr, Ḳ.)

مَسْحَكَة : see سَحُوكٌ: — and see also مُسْحَك.

سهل

1. سَهُلَ, said of a place, (Ṣ,) or of a thing, and, accord. to IKṭṭ, they said also سَهَلَ and سَهِلَ, (Mṣb,) and سَهُلَتْ, said of land, (أَرْض,) aor. ـُ, (Ḳ,) inf. n. سُهُولَةٌ, (Ṣ, Mṣb, Ḳ, KL,) *It was,* or *became, smooth* or *soft, plain* or *level,* or *smooth and soft;* (Ṣ, Mṣb, Ḳ, KL, TA;) i. e. *contr. of* حَزُنَ and حَزُنَتْ, (Ṣ,* Ḳ,* TA,) inf. n. حُزُونَةٌ (TA.) — And سَهُلَ, (MA, Mṣb, Ḳ,) inf. n. سُهُولَةٌ, (MA, KL,) or سَهَالَةٌ, (Ḳ,) [but the former is the more common,] *It* (a thing, Mṣb) *was,* or *became, easy.* (MA, Mṣb,* Ḳ,* KL.) — One says كَلَامٌ فِيهِ سُهُولَةٌ ‡ [*Language,* or *speech, in which is smoothness,* or *easiness*]. (TA.)

2. سَهَّلَهُ, (Mṣb, Ḳ,) inf. n. تَسْهِيلٌ, (Ṣ, Ḳ,) i. q. صَيَّرَهُ سَهْلًا [which may mean *He rendered it smooth* or *soft, plain* or *level,* or *smooth and soft;* namely, a place &c.: or what next follows]. (TA.) — *He made it easy; he facilitated it;* (Ṣ, Ḳ;) namely, a thing; said of God (Mṣb) [and of a man]. — One says, سَهَّلَ سَبِيلَ المَآءِ [*He smoothed, made easy,* or *prepared, the way, course, passage,* or *channel, of the water*], (Ṣ and Ḳ in art. اتى,) in order that it might pass forth to a place. (Ṣ in that art.) And سَهَّلَ مَسِيلًا لِمَآءٍ [*He smoothed, made easy,* or *prepared, a channel for water*]. (M in that art.) — And سَهَّلَ ٱللّٰهُ عَلَيْكَ الأَمْرَ, and لَكَ, a form of prayer, meaning *May God* [*make easy,* or *facilitate, to thee the affair;* or] *take upon Himself, for thee, the burden of the affair;* and *lighten* [*it*] *to thee.* (TA.) [And in like manner سَهَّلَ ٱللّٰهُ عَلَيْكَ is often said with الأَمْرَ or أُمُورَكَ understood.] — [And أَهَّلَ بِهِ وَسَهَّلَ, or أَهَّلَهُ وَسَهَّلَهُ, inf. ns. تَأْهِيلٌ and تَسْهِيلٌ, *He said to him* ▼ أَهْلًا وَسَهْلًا, meaning (as expl. in the Mṣb in art. اهل) أَتَيْتَ قَوْمًا أَهْلًا وَمَوْضِعًا سَهْلًا, i. e. *Thou hast come to a people who are like kinsfolk, and to a place that is smooth, plain, or not rugged:* see أَهْلٌ and أَهَّلَ: and see also Ḥam p. 184.]

3. ساهلهُ, (MA, Ḳ,) inf. n. مُسَاهَلَةٌ, (TA,) *He was easy,* or *facile, with him;* (MA, Ḳ;*) or *gentle with him;* syn. يَاسَرَهُ: (Ḳ:) and ▼ تساهل عَلَيْهِ [has a similar meaning, i. e. *he acted,* or *affected to act, in an easy,* or *a facile, manner towards him;* or *gently*]. (Ṣ and Ḳ in art. غمض: see 4 in that art.) [See also the paragraph here following.]

4. اسهلوا *They descended to the* سَهْل [i. e. *smooth* or *soft,* or *plain* or *level,* or *smooth and soft, tract*]: (JK, Mṣb:) or *they betook themselves to the* سَهْل: (Ṣ:) or *they became in the* سَهْل: (Ḳ:) and *they alighted and abode in the* سَهْل, *after they had been alighting and abiding in the* حَزْن [i. e. *rugged,* or *rugged and hard,* or *rugged and high, ground*]. (TA.) Hence, in a trad. respecting the throwing of the pebbles [at Minè], يُسْهِلُ occurs as meaning *He betakes himself to the interior of the valley.* (TA.) — Also *They used smoothness,* or *easiness,* (سُهُولَة,) with men: opposed to أَحْزَنُوا. (TA.) [See also 3.] ══ اسهل is also trans., signifying *He found* [a thing, a place, &c.,] *to be smooth* or *soft, plain* or *level,* or *smooth and soft.* (Ḥam p. 675.) — اسهل الطَّبِيعَةَ (Ṣ) or البَطْنَ, (Mṣb, Ḳ,) said of medicine, (Ṣ, Mṣb, Ḳ,) *It relaxed,* or *loosened, the bowels;* syn. أَلَانَ, (Ḳ,) or أَطْلَقَ. (Mṣb.) And أُسْهِلَ الرَّجُلُ [*The man was relaxed* in his *bowels*]: and أُسْهِلَ بَطْنُهُ [*His bowels were relaxed*]. (Ḳ.) [Hence the inf. n. إِسْهَالٌ signifies *A diarrhœa.* And اسهل, likewise said of medicine, signifies also *It attenuated* a humour of the body.] — اسهلت بِهِ *She brought it forth* (i. e. her fœtus, or offspring,) *prematurely;* i. q. أَمْلَصَتْ بِهِ [q. v.] &c. (Abu-l-'Abbás [i. e. Th], TA in art. ملص.)

5. تَسَهَّلَ [*It was,* or *became, rendered easy,* or *facilitated;*] quasi-pass. of 2: (Mṣb:) or [like سَهُلَ] *it was,* or *became, easy.* (KL.) You say, تَسَهَّلَ لَهُ الأَمْرُ [*The affair was,* or *became, rendered easy to him*]. (Mṣb in art. اتى.) And تَسَهَّلَتْ طَرِيقُ الأَمْرِ [*The way of* accomplishing *the affair was,* or *became, rendered easy*]. (TA in that art.) — And تَسَهَّلَ فِى أُمُورِهِ, said of a man, (Ḳ in art. سنى,) *He found,* or *experienced, ease,* or *facility, in his affairs.* (TḲ in that art.)

6. تَسَاهَلَ is *syn. with* تَسَامَحَ. (Ṣ, Ḳ.) You say تساهلوا meaning *They acted in an easy,* or *a facile, manner, one with another;* (MA, TA in art. يسر;) or *gently;* syn. تَيَاسَرُوا. (TA in that art.) — See also 3. — [In the present day it is used as meaning The *being negligent,* or *careless,* فِى أَمْرٍ *in an affair.*] — [As a conventional term in lexicology, or in relation to language, it means *A careless mode of expression occasioning*] *a deficiency in the language of a* [*writer or*] *speaker without reliance upon the understanding of* [*the reader or*] *the person addressed:* (KT: [in one of my copies of that work, this explanation is omitted in the text, but written in the margin; and it is there added that it is what commonly obtains:]) or it means [sometimes *such a mode of expression*] *that a phrase is not correct if held to be used according to the proper meaning, but is correct if held to be used according to a tropical meaning:* or the *mention of the whole when meaning a part.* (Marginal notes in the copy of the KT above mentioned.) [See also تَسَامُحٌ, for which it is often used.]

8. استهل, of the measure افْتَعَلَ from السَّهْلُ, occurs in a trad., where it is said, مَنْ كَذَبَ عَلَىَّ فَقَدِ ٱسْتَهَلَ مَكَانَهُ فِى جَهَنَّمَ, meaning [*He who lies against me*] *takes for himself easily his place of abode in Hell.* (TA.)

10. استسهلهُ *He reckoned it* سَهْل, (Ṣ, Ḳ,) i. e. *easy,* or *facile.* (TḲ.) [See an ex. in a verse cited voce أَوْ, p. 123.]

سَهْلٌ *Smooth* or *soft, plain* or *level,* or *smooth and soft:* (Mṣb:) or anything *inclining to smoothness* or *softness, plainness* or *levelness,* or *smoothness and softness;* (JK, M, Ḳ;) *inclining to have little roughness,* or *ruggedness and hardness;* (JK, M, TA;) and ▼ سَهِلٌ signifies the same. (Ḳ.) You say أَرْضٌ سَهْلَةٌ, [meaning the same as سَهْلٌ used as a subst., expl. in what follows,] (Ṣ, Mṣb,) *contr. of* حَزْنَةٌ. (TA.) See also 2, last sentence. — Also *Easy,* or *facile;* (MA, Mgh, KL;) *contr. of* صَعْبٌ. (Mgh.) You say رَجُلٌ سَهْلُ الخُلُقِ [*A man easy of disposition*]: (Ṣ, Mṣb,* TA:) [and] سَهْلُ القِيَادَةِ [*easy to be led*]. (TA.) And كَلَامٌ سَهْلُ المَأْخَذِ ‡ [*Language easy in respect of the source of derivation*]. (TA.) رَجُلٌ سَهْلُ الوَجْهِ, (Ḳ, TA,) a phrase mentioned, but not explained, by Lḥ, (TA,) means *A man having little flesh in the face,* (Ḳ, TA,) in the opinion of ISd: and [it is said that] سَهْلُ الخَدَّيْنِ, in a description of the approved characteristics of the Prophet, means *having expanded cheeks, not elevated in the balls thereof.* (TA.) ══ [As a subst.,] *A smooth* or *soft, plain* or *level,* or *smooth and soft, tract of land;* [generally meaning *a soft tract,* or *a plain;*] (IF, Ṣ, MA, Mgh, Mṣb, Ḳ, TA;) i. e. *contr. of* جَبَلٌ, (Ṣ, Mṣb,) or *of* حَزْنٌ: (IF, Mgh, Mṣb, Ḳ, TA:) it is one of the nouns that are used as adv. ns. [of place]: (TA:) [for ex. you say, نَزَلُوا سَهْلًا, (a phrase occurring in the TA,) meaning *They alighted and abode in a* سهل:] pl. سُهُولٌ (MA, Mṣb, Ḳ) and سُهُولَةٌ [of which latter an ex. occurs in a verse cited voce رَأْسٌ]. (MA.) ══ Also The *crow;* i. e. *raven, carrion-crow, rook,* &c.; syn. غُرَابٌ. (Ḳ.)

سَهِلٌ: see سَهْلٌ, first sentence. — نَهْرٌ سَهِلٌ, (Ṣ, Ḳ,) and أَرْضٌ سَهِلَةٌ, (Ḳ,) [*A river, and a land,*] *having,* (Ṣ,) or *abounding with,* (Ḳ,) *what is termed* سِهْلَةٌ [q. v.]. (Ṣ, Ḳ.)

سِهْلَةٌ *Sea-sand:* (IAạr, TA:) or *sand such as is not fine:* (Ṣ:) or *coarse sand, such as is not fine and soft:* (IAth, TA:) or *a sort of earth like sand,* (JK, Ḳ,) *brought by water:* (Ḳ:) or *sand of a conduit in which water runs:* (Ṣ in art. رض:) سِهْلَةُ الزُّجَاجِ is *sea-sand that is made an ingredient in the substance of glass:* (Mgh:) Az says that he had not heard the word سِهْلَة except on the authority of Lth. (TA.) [And *Coarse sand that comes forth from the bladder;* (Golius on the authority of Meyd;) what we commonly term *gravel.*]

سُهْلِىٌّ, with ḍamm, [*Of,* or *relating to,* and *growing in,* and *pasturing in, the kind of tract termed* سَهْل;] a rel. n. from سَهْلٌ, (Ṣ, Mṣb, Ḳ,) or from أَرْضٌ سَهْلَةٌ, (Aboo-'Amr Ibn-El-'Alà, TA,) irregularly formed. (Ṣ, Mṣb.) You say نَبْتٌ سُهْلِىٌّ [*A plant growing in the* سَهْل]. (The Lexicons passim.) And بَعِيرٌ سُهْلِىٌّ *A camel that pastures in the* سَهْل. (Ḳ.)

سَهُولٌ *Laxative* to the bowels; syn. مَشُوٌّ; (O, Ḳ; in the CḲ [erroneously] مُشُوٌّ;) as also ▼ مُسْهِلٌ; applied to a medicine. (Mṣb, TA.)

سُهَيْلٌ *A certain star* [*well known*; namely, *Canopus*]; (T, Ṣ, Ḳ;) *not seen in Khurásán, but seen in El-'Irák;* (T, TA;) as Ibn-Kunáseh says, *seen in El-Ḥijáz and in all the land of the Arabs, but not seen in the land of Armenia; and between the sight thereof by the people of El-Ḥijáz and the sight thereof by the people of El-'Irák are twenty days:* (TA:) it is said that سهيل was a tyrannical collector of the tithes on the road to El-Yemen, and God transformed him into a star: (Lth, TA:) [*it rose aurorally, in Central Arabia, about the commencement of the era of the Flight, on the 4th of August, O. S.: the place where it rises, in that latitude, is S. 29° E.; and the place where it sets, in the same latitude, S. 29° W.:* (see 10 in art. حب: and see جَنُوبٌ:)] *at the time of its* [*auroral*] *rising, the fruits ripen, and the* قَيْظ [q. v., here meaning the *greatest heat*,] *ends.* (Ḳ.) [بَالَ سُهَيْلٌ, which is a prov., and the saying of a poet,

• بَالَ سُهَيْلٌ فِى الفَضِيخِ فَفَسَدْ •

have been expl. in art. بول.] 'Omar Ibn-'Abd-Allah Ibn-Abee-Rabeea says respecting Suheyl Ibn-'Abd-Er-Raḥmán Ibn-'Owf, and his taking in marriage Eth-Thureiyà El-'Ableeyeh of the Benoo-Umeiyeh, deeming their coming together to be a strange thing by likening them to the stars named Eth-Thureiyà and Suheyl,

• أَيُّهَا المُنْكِحُ الثُّرَيَّا سُهَيْلًا •
• عَمْرَكَ ٱللّٰهَ كَيْفَ يَلْتَقِيَانِ •
• هِىَ شَامِيَّةٌ إِذَا مَا ٱسْتَقَلَّتْ •
• وَسُهَيْلٌ إِذَا ٱسْتَقَلَّ يَمَانِى •

[*O thou marrier of Eth-Thureiyà to Suheyl, by thine acknowledgment of the everlasting existence of God,* (or, as it sometimes means, *I ask God to prolong thy life,*) tell me, *how can they meet together? She is of the northern region when she rises, and Suheyl, when he rises, is of the southern region*]. (Ḥar p. 276. [But I have substituted ٱللّٰهَ for ٱللّٰهُ, and يَمَانِى for يَمَانٍ. See also the notice of the poet above named in the work of Ibn-Khillikán: (I have the express authority of the TA for thus writing this name:) and De Sacy's Anthol. Gramm. Arabe, p. 139.]) [Freytag states that قَدَمَا سُهَيْلٍ is the name of *Two stars which are behind Canopus;* on the authority of Meyd: and also mentions the name of سهيل الشام, and سهيل الفرد, as given to *Certain stars in the constellation Anguis;* adding that Canopus is distinguished from سهيل الشام by the name of سهيل اليمن.] The name of أُخْتَا سُهَيْلٍ [*The two sisters of Canopus*] is applied to الشِّعْرَى العَبُورُ [or *Sirius*] *and* الشِّعْرَى الغُمَيْصَآءُ [or *Procyon*], *together.* (Ṣ and Ḳ in art. شعر.) [See also حَضَارِ and الوَزْنُ.]

أَكْذَبُ مِنْ سُهَيْلَةَ is a prov., (O, Ḳ,) said to mean [*More lying than*] *the wind:* (O:) or سهيلة was a certain liar. (Ḳ.)

مُسْهَلٌ *Relaxed,* or *loosened,* by medicine; applied to the belly: no credit is to be given to people's saying مَسْهُولٌ, unless an express authority be found for it. (Mṣb.)

مُسْهِلٌ: see سَهُولٌ. [Also an *attenuant* medicine.]

سهم

1. سَهَمَهُ, aor. ـَ, inf. n. سَهْمٌ: see 3. —— سَهَمَ, (Ṣ, MA, Ḳ,) aor. ـَ; (Ḳ;) and سَهُمَ, aor. ـُ; inf. n. سُهُومٌ, (Ṣ, MA, Ḳ,) of both verbs, (Ṣ, TA,) and of the latter سُهُومَةٌ also, agreeably with analogy; (Ḥar p. 449;) *He,* (a man, TA,) or *it,* (one's face, Ṣ, MA, and Ḥar ubi suprà,) *was,* or *became, altered in colour,* (MA,) or *he was,* or *became, lean* or *lank, in the belly, and altered* [*in colour*]; (Ṣ, Ḳ, and Ḥar ubi suprà;) [or, accord. to an explanation of سُهُومٌ in the Ḥam p. 360, *he,* or *it, was,* or *became, altered in colour, and emaciated, and dried up;*] and سُهِمَ, also, aor. يُسْهَمُ, inf. n. سُهُومٌ, has the first of these meanings: (MA:) [see also سُهُومٌ below:] or سُهِمَ signifies *he* (a man) *was,* or *became, lean,* or *lank, in the belly:* (TA:) or *he* (a man, Ṣ) *was,* or *became, smitten,* or *affected, by the heat of the* [*wind called*] سَمُوم, (Ṣ, Ḳ, [see سَهَام,]) or *by the burning,* or *vehement heat, of summer.* (Ḳ, TA.)

2. تَسْهِيمٌ The *making* a garment *to be marked with stripes* or *lines* [*like* سِهَام, i. e. *arrows:* see the pass. part. n. below]. (KL. [And the same meaning is indicated in the TA.]) Dhu-r-Rummeh says, describing a dwelling, [or rather the traces thereof,]

• كَأَنَّهَا بَعْدَ أَحْوَالٍ مَضَيْنَ لَهَا •
• بِالأَشْيَمَيْنِ يَمَانٍ فِيهِ تَسْهِيمُ •

[*As though it were, after years had passed with respect to it, in El-Ashyamán, a garment of El-Yemen in which was a marking with stripes* or *lines:* the epithet يَمَانٍ being often applied to a garment of this kind, and ثَوْبٌ being here understood]: (TA:) الأَشْيَمَانِ, or, as some call them, الأَشْأَمَانِ, are two places, or two mountains, mentioned by Dhu-r-Rummeh in several places in his poetry. (TA in art. شيم.)

3. سَاهَمَهُ, (Ṣ, MA, Mgh, Mṣb,) inf. n. مُسَاهَمَةٌ, (Mṣb,) *He shot arrows* [سِهَام] *with him* [*in competition*]. (MA.) —— [And hence,] *He cast,* or *drew, lots* [or more properly *arrows for sortilege,* as expl. in the PṢ,] *with him; practised sortilege* [or *sortilege with arrows*] *with him;* or *competed with him in doing so.* (Ṣ, MA, Mgh, Mṣb.) You say, سَاهَمْتُهُ فَسَهَمْتُهُ ♦; (Ṣ;) or سَاهَمْتُهُ فَسَهَمْتُهُ; (TA;) aor. of the latter verb ـَ, (Ṣ,) and inf. n. سَهْمٌ; (TA;) *I competed with him in casting,* or *drawing, lots* [or *arrows for sortilege*] or *in practising sortilege* [or *sortilege with arrows*] *with him, and overcame him therein;* or *He did so with them, and overcame them therein.* (Ṣ,* TA.) Hence, فَسَاهَمَ in the Ḳur xxxvii. 141, (TA,) where [the objective complement] أَهْلَ السَّفِينَةِ is understood. (Jel.) —— [And hence, *He shared with him,* فِى كَذَا *in such a thing.* See an ex. voce مُشَدٌّ, and another voce تَاوَبَ. —— And app. *He contended with him* for a thing: see 6.]

4. اسهم بَيْنَهُمْ i. q. أَقْرَعَ [i. e. *He ordered,* or *commanded, them to cast,* or *draw, lots,* or *to practise sortilege,* or *sortilege with arrows, among themselves,* for a thing; or *he prepared,* or *disposed, them for doing so;* or *he cast,* or *drew, lots,* or *practised sortilege,* or *sortilege with arrows, among them:* see أَقْرَعَ]. (Ṣ.) —— And أَسْهَمْتُ لَهُ *I gave him a lot, share,* or *portion.* (Mṣb.) —— And أَسْهَمَ is syn. with أَسْهَبَ, (Ḳ, TA,) meaning *He was,* or *became, loquacious,* or *profuse of speech:* its م is said by Yaḳoob to be a substitute for ب. (TA.) [See also مُسْهَمٌ, below.]

6. تساهموا: see 8. —— [Hence, *They shared together.*] El-Ḥakam El-Khudree says,

• تَسَاهَمَ ثَوْبَاهَا فَفِى الدِّرْعِ رَادَةٌ •
• وَفِى المِرْطِ لَفَّاوَانِ رِدْفُهُمَا عَبْلُ •

i. e. *Her two garments shared together; for in the shift was a soft,* or *tender, body, with a slender waist, and within the waist-wrapper were too thick thighs whereof the part above them, behind, was large.* (Ḥam p. 579.) —— Also *They contended* [for a thing], *one with another.* (JM.)

8. استهموا (Ṣ, Mṣb) and ♦ تساهموا (Ṣ) *They cast,* or *drew, lots,* or *practised sortilege,* [or *sortilege with arrows,*] *one with another;* syn. اقترعوا (Ṣ, Mṣb) and تقارعوا, (Ṣ,) both of which signify the same. (Ṣ &c. in art. قرع.)

سَهْمٌ *An arrow;* i. e. *one of what are called* نَبْل, (Mṣb, Ḳ, TA,) *having the iron head* [*and the feathers*] *affixed:* (TA:) the سهم before it has its feathers and its iron head affixed to it is [generally] called قِدْحٌ: (Ṣ and Ḳ in art. قدح:) accord. to some it signifies the *iron head* itself; i. q. نَصْلٌ; (Mṣb;) ISh says that this is its meaning; and he says, if one pick up a نصل, you say "What is this سَهْم with thee?" but if one pick up a قدح, you do not say thus; and the نَصْل is the broad and long سَهْم, and may be nearly of the length of the space between the extremity of the thumb and that of the fore finger when they are stretched out; and the مِشْقَص is of half the size of the نَصْل: (TA:) [but this meaning of سَهْمٌ seems to be very rare, and little known:] the pl. [of mult.] is سِهَامٌ (Ṣ, TA) and [of pauc.] أَسْهُمٌ. (TA.) [Hence,] سَهْمُ الرَّامِى † [*The arrow of the archer*], (Ḳ,) or [simply] السَّهْمُ [*the arrow*], (Ḳzw,) *a certain constellation,* (Ḳ,* Ḳzw,) [namely *Sagitta,*] *one of the northern constellations, composed of five stars, between the bill* [meaning *the star β*] *of* الدَّجَاجَةُ [which is *Cygnus*] *and* النَّسْرُ الطَّائِرُ [which consists of *the stars α and β and γ of Aquila*], *in the Great Milky Way, having its head towards the east and its notch towards the west; and its length, as it appears to the eye, when it is in the middle of the sky, is about two cubits* (نَحْوُ ذِرَاعَيْنِ: see ذِرَاعٌ). (Ḳzw.) —— Also The قِدْح [or *featherless and headless arrow*] *with which one casts,* or *draws, lots,* (IAth, Mgh, TA,) *in the game called* المَيْسِر; (IAth, TA;) and the قِدْح *with which one plays at a game of hazard* [*of any kind;* i. e. *an arrow for sortilege,* and *a* *gaming-arrow*]; the primary meaning of the word being the missile سَهْم; (Mgh;) or the primary meaning is the قِدْح with which one casts, or draws, lots in the game called المَيْسِر: (IAth, TA:) pl. سِهَام (Ḳ) [and أَسْهُم, as above]. See a verse cited voce رَقِيب. — Then applied to The *thing won by him whose arrow is successful* [in *the game above mentioned*]. (IAth, TA.) — And then (IAth, TA) applied also to *A lot, share,* or *portion,* (Ṣ, IAth, Mgh, Mṣb, Ḳ, TA,) *whatever it be;* (IAth, TA;) as also ▼ سُهْمَةٌ: (Ṣ, Mṣb, Ḳ:) pl. of the former سُهْمَانٌ (Ṣ, Mgh, Mṣb, Ḳ) and سِهَام [both pls. of mult.] and أَسْهُم [pl. of pauc.] (Mgh, Mṣb, TA) and [quasi-pl. n.] ▼ سُهْمَة, (M, Ḳ, TA,) this last like أُخْوَة. (TA.) It is said in a trad., كَانَ لَهُ سَهْمٌ مِنَ الغَنِيمَةِ شَهِدَ أَوْ غَابَ [*There was,* or *is, for him a share of the spoil whether he were,* or *be, present or absent*]. (TA.) And one says, ▼ سُهْمَةُ فُلَانٍ مِنْ هٰذَا كَذَا *The share of such a one, of this, is such a thing:* and it may be from السِّهَام meaning the arrows (قِدَاح) that are shuffled among the persons competing in sortilege, in order that each one may appropriate to himself what comes forth for him as his share. (Ḥam p. 579.) — سَهْمُ السَّفِينَةِ [*The mast of the ship:* so called as being likened to an arrow, because the curved yard of the sail, resembling a bow, is suspended from the top]: (Ṣ and Ḳ in art. دقل:) [in like manner] *called in Pers.* تير كشتى. (PṢ in that art.) — سَهْمُ البَيْتِ *The beam* (جَائِز) *of the house* or *chamber;* (Ṣ, Ḳ;) [similarly] *called in Pers.* تير. (Ṣ voce جَائِز, q. v.) — سَهْم also signifies The *measure of six cubits* [as used] in men's sales and purchases in their measurings of land. (Ḳ.) — And *A stone which is placed upon the entrance of a chamber constructed for the purpose of capturing therein the lion, so that, when he enters it, it falls upon the the entrance and closes it.* (Ḳ,* TA.) [The word in this sense is also mentioned in the Ḳ as written with ش.]

سُهُم, thus, with two ḍammehs, [The *fine filmy substance termed gossamer,*] with the article ال, i. q. غَزْلُ عَيْنِ الشَّمْسِ [lit. *the spun-thread of the rays of the sun*]: (IAạr, Ḳ:) and ▼ سَهَام [signifies the *same*], with the article ال i. q. مُخَاط الشَّيْطَانِ [q. v., lit. *the snivel of the devil*]. (Ḳ.) — And *Overpowering heat.* (IAạr, Ḳ.) — Also [a pl. of which the sing. is not mentioned, signifying] *Intelligent, knowing,* or *skilful* or *judicious, working* men; (Ḳ, TA;) and so with ش. (TA.)

سُهْمَةٌ: see سَهْم, in the latter half of the paragraph, in three places. — Also *Relationship.* (Ṣ, Ḳ.) Whence ذُو السُّهْمَةِ [*A relation*]. (Ṣ, TA.)

سَهَام The *heat of the* [*wind called*] سَمُوم; (Ṣ, Ḳ;) and the *burning,* or *vehement, heat of summer;* (Ḳ;) and the *clouds of dust thereof:* or *a hot wind;* and *hot winds;* used alike as sing. and pl. (TA.) — See also سُهُم. — And see what next follows.

سُهَام (Ṣ, Ḳ) and ▼ سَهَام, (Ḳ, and only thus in some copies of the Ḳ,) the former mentioned by several authors, (TA,) *Leanness,* or *lankness in the belly, and an altered state* (Ṣ, Ḳ, TA) *of the colour, and dryness of the lips.* (TA.) — And the former, [in some copies of the Ḳ the latter, but the former, as is said in the TA, is the right, agreeably with analogy as a word signifying a disease,] *A certain disease incident to camels.* (El-Umawee, Ṣ, Ḳ.)

سَهُوم, with fet-ḥ [to the س, by Freytag erroneously written سَهْوَم, in consequence of his having been misled by a double mistranscription immediately preceding in the CḲ], The *flying eagle:* (Ḳ:) the epithet "flying" being here used only as an explicative. (TA.)

سُهُوم an inf. n. of 1. (Ṣ, &c.) — Also *A frowning* (عُبُوس, Ḳ, TA) *of the face by reason of anxiety.* (TA. [In the CḲ, السَّهُوم and العَبُوس are erroneously put for السُّهُوم and العُبُوس: in the TA, السهوم is expressly said to be with ḍamm, in this case, and the meaning is shown by two verses there cited.])

سَهَّام *A maker of arrows.* (MA.)

سَاهِمُ الوَجْهِ, applied to a man, *Altered in face.* (TA.) The saying of 'Antarah,

وَالخَيْلُ سَاهِمَةُ الوُجُوهِ كَأَنَّمَا
تُسْقَى فَوَارِسُهَا نَقِيعَ الحَنْظَلِ

is expl. by Th as meaning *And the owners of the horses were altered in their complexions* in consequence of the state of difficulty wherein they were [*as though* they, i. e. *the riders thereof, were given to drink infusion of colocynth*]. (TA.) [But] سَاهِمُ الوَجْهِ, is applied as an epithet to a horse as meaning *Urged,* or *made, to perform a distressing act of running:* and in like manner to a man when he is *urged,* or *made, to perform a distressing part in war, or battle.* (TA.) — [The fem.] سَاهِمَةٌ, applied to a she-camel, means *Lean,* or *lank in the belly:* (Ṣ, Ḳ: [see also مَسْهُوم:]) and [its pl.] سَوَاهِم, applied to camels, *altered by journeying.* (Ṣ.)

مُسْهَم A horse *half-blooded, got by a stallion of generous race out of a mare not of such race;* syn. مُجَيَّن: (Ḳ:) to [the rider of] such is given less than the سَهْم [or share] of the spoil that is given to [the rider of] the horse of generous race. (TA.) [It is applied in this sense to a stallion-camel as well as to a horse.] A poet says,

بَنِي يَثْرِبِيٍّ حَصِّنُوا أَيْنُقَاتِكُمْ
وَأَفْرَاسَكُمْ مِنْ ضَرْبِ أَحْمَرَ مُسْهَمِ

[*Sons of Yethribee, keep ye your she-camels and your mares from the being covered by one that is red,* (i. e. of goodly appearance, for the red among camels are the most admired by the Arabs, and in like manner the bay among horses,) but *half-blooded*]: he means, keep ye your women from being taken as wives by such as are not their equals. (TA.) — You say also, رَجُلٌ مُسْهَمُ الجِسْمِ *A man whose body is wasting away in consequence of love:* (Ḳ:) and in like manner, مُسْهَمُ العَقْلِ [*whose reason is departing*]: mentioned by Lḥ: (TA:) and so ▼ مُسْهِم, in both cases: (TA voce مُسْهَب, q. v.:) the م being a substitute for ب. (TA in the present art.) — And مُسْهَم, (Ḳ, TA,) or ▼ مُسْهِم, (CḲ,) [both app. correct,] from أَسْهَمَ, is like مُسْهَب [q. v.], (Ḳ, TA,) or مُسْهِب, (CḲ,) from أَسْهَبَ, in measure and in meaning; (Ḳ, TA;) meaning *Loquacious,* or *profuse in speech:* the م, accord. to Yaḳoob, being [in this case also] a substitute for ب. (TA.)

مُسْهِم: see the next preceding paragraph, in two places.

مُسَهَّم A [garment of the kind called] بُرْد *marked with stripes,* or *lines,* (Ṣ, Ḳ, TA,) *like* سِهَام [i. e. *arrows*]. (TA.) — See also the following paragraph.

مَسْهُوم, applied to a man, *Lean,* or *lank in the belly:* [see also سَاهِم:] or *affected with what is termed* سهام [app. سُهَام, and meaning *the heat of the wind called* سَمُوم]. (TA.) — And, applied to a camel, *Smitten with the disease termed* سُهَام: and so ▼ مُسَهَّمَة applied to camels. (Ṣ, Ḳ.)

سهو

1. سَهَا عَنْهُ, (Ṣ, Mṣb,) or فِيهِ, (Ḳ,) aor. يَسْهُو, inf. n. سَهْو (Ṣ, Mṣb, Ḳ) and سُهُوّ, (M, Ḳ,) *He was,* or *became, unmindful, forgetful, neglectful,* or *heedless, of it,* or *inadvertent to it;* (Ṣ, Mṣb;) namely, a thing; syn. غَفَلَ عَنْهُ: (Ṣ,* Mṣb:) or *he forgot it,* or *neglected it,* (نَسِيَهُ,) and *was,* or *became, unmindful, forgetful,* &c., *of it,* or *inadvertent to it,* (غَفَلَ عَنْهُ,) *his mind adverting to another thing* or *affair* or *case;* (Ḳ, TA;) thus expl. in the M and T; so that السَّهْو and الغَفْلَة and النِّسْيَان are made to be one [in signification]; (TA;) but accord. to Esh-Shiháb, السَّهْو is *a slight* غَفْلَة [or *unmindfulness* &c.] *of that which is within the scope of the retentive faculty, such as when one's attention is roused by the least rousing thereof;* whereas النسيان denotes its passing away from the memory entirely; though all are used in one sense by a careless reliance upon the understanding of the reader or hearer: in the Mṣb it is said that a distinction is made between السَّاهِى and النَّاسِى by the latter's being applied to him who, when he is reminded, remembers, and the former's being applied to him who is in the contrary case: accord. to IAth, سَهَا فِى الشَّىْءِ means *he neglected,* or *omitted, the thing unknowingly;* and سَهَا عَنْهُ, *he neglected,* or *omitted, it knowingly:* or, as some say, السَّهْو is *the doing wrong from unmindfulness* (عَنْ غَفْلَة); as when an insane person reviles another, which is pardonable; and as when one drinks wine and then some unpleasing action proceeds from him unintentionally, which is punishable. (TA.) One says, سَهَا فِى الصَّلَاةِ, and عَنْهَا, i. q. غَفَلَ [*He was,* or *became, unmindful in prayer,* and *of it*]. (TA.) — [Hence, app., as implying an unexpected event,] حَمَلَتْ سَهْوًا *She* (a woman, Ṣ)

conceived in menstruis. (Az, Ṣ, Z, Ḳ.) And حَمَلَتْ بِهِ أُمُّهُ سَهْوًا *His mother conceived him in menstruis.* (JK.) —— السَّهْوُ also signifies السُّكُونُ (JK, Ṣ, Ḳ) and اللِّينُ (JK, Ṣ) [app. as an inf. n., i. e. as meaning *The being still,* or *quiet, and gentle;* though it is immediately added in the Ṣ that the pl. is سِهَآءٌ; for it seems that an early transcriber of the Ṣ has omitted to insert after اللِّين the words وَالسَّاكِنُ وَاللَّيِّنُ: see سَهْوٌ below]. One says, فَعَلَهُ سَهْوًا رَهْوًا *He did it voluntarily, without its being asked,* or *demanded;* (Ḳ, TA;) and *without constraint:* (TA:) or *quietly,* or *calmly, without being hard,* or *difficult.* (TA in art. رهو.) And سَهَا إِلَيْهِ *He looked at him,* or *it, with motionless eye.* (Mṣb, TA.) And العَيْنُ تَسْهُو فِيهِ *The eye expatiates in it;* syn. تَنْبَسِطُ. (JK.) —— سَهَاوَةٌ, as denoting a quality of a camel, *The being easy to ride;* (Ḳ;) an inf. n., of which the verb is سَهُوَ. (TA.) —— مَالٌ لَا يُسْهَى وَلَا يُنْهَى [*Cattle*] *of which the end is not to be reached.* (AA, JK, Ṣ, Ḳ.) You say, يُرَاحُ عَلَى بَنِى فُلَانٍ مِنَ المَالِ مَا لَا يُسْهَى وَلَا يُنْهَى [*There returns from the place of pasture in the evening,* or *afternoon, to the sons of such a one, of cattle,*] *what is not to be numbered for multitude:* (T, TA:) or *what is not to be computed,* or *computed by conjecture.* (IAạr, TA.) And ذَهَبَتْ تَمِيمٌ فَلَا تُسْهَى وَلَا تُنْهَى, meaning لَا تُذْكَرُ [i. e. *Temeem went away, and will not be remembered,* or *will not be mentioned*]: a saying of El-Aḥmar. (TA.)

3. ساهاهُ, inf. n. مُسَاهَاةٌ, *i. q.* غَافَلَهُ [app. meaning *He acted with him in the manner of him who is unmindful, forgetful, neglectful, heedless,* or *inadvertent*]. (TA.) [Or] the inf. n. signifies [The *acting with moderation with another;* or] the *abstaining from going to the utmost length* in social intercourse: (Ṣ, Ḳ:) or the *being easy,* or *facile,* with another: (A, TA:) or the *behaving in a good* [or *pleasing*] *manner in social intercourse:* (T, TA:) or the *comporting oneself with another,* or *others,* (مُخَالَقَةٌ,) *in a good manner,* in social intercourse. ('Eyn, M, TA.) And one says, هُوَ يُسَاهِي أَصْحَابَهُ *He comports himself with his companions,* or *does so with good nature;* syn. يُخَالِقُهُمْ. (TA.) And ساهاهُ means also *He mocked at him,* or *derided him.* (TA.)

4. اسهى *He* (a man, TA) *constructed what is termed a* سَهْوَة (Ḳ, TA) *in a* بَيْت [or *chamber* &c.]. (TA.)

السُّهَا [often written السُّهَى] *A certain dim star,* (Ṣ, Ḳ,) *in* [*the asterism called*] بَنَاتُ نَعْشٍ الكُبْرَى, (Ṣ, [in the Ḳ, erroneously, بنات نعش الصُّغْرَى,]) *by the middle star of those thus called;* (TA;) [i. e.] *a small star by that called* العَنَاقُ, (*which latter is the middle star* [ζ] *of the three in the tail of Ursa Major,* Ḳzw,) *by looking at which persons try their powers of sight;* (Ḳzw, TA;) mentioned in art. قود [voce قَائِدٌ, q. v.]; (Ḳ;) [it is *the star* 80, *by* ζ;] *also called* ▼ السُّهَيَّا, which is the diminutive. (TA.) It is said in a prov., أُرِيهَا السُّهَا وَتُرِينِى القَمَرَ [*I show her Es-Suhà and she shows me the moon*]. (Ṣ, TA. [See also Freytag's Arab. Prov. vol. i. pp. 527—9.]) And one says, أَنَّى يَلْتَقِى سُهَيْلٌ وَالسُّهَا *How can Suheyl* [or *Canopus*] *meet Es-Suhà?* for the former is southern and the latter is northern. (Ḥar p. 276.)

سَهْوٌ [an inf. n. used as an epithet,] *Easy;* applied to a man, and to an affair, (Ḳ, TA,) and to an object of want: (TA:) and so [the fem.] سَهْوَةٌ, applied to a mare; and applied to a she-mule as meaning *easy in pace, that does not fatigue her rider:* the epithet سَهْوٌ, however, is not applied to a he-mule: so in the T: (TA:) [but] it is applied to a he-camel, meaning *easy to ride;* and سَهْوَةٌ to a she-camel, (Ḳ, TA,) meaning *gentle, easy to ride:* and ▼ سَاهٍ, applied to a he-camel, means [likewise] *gentle* in pace; and so [the pls.] سَوَاهٍ and رَوَاهٍ applied to camels: (TA:) [and so ▼ سَهْوَآءُ applied to a mare; for] a certain mare was named السَّهْوَآءُ because of the gentleness of her pace. (TA.) Also, applied to water, *Cool, sweet,* or *limpid; easy of descent in the throat.* (Ḳ,* TA.) And قَوْسٌ سَهْوَةٌ *A bow that is compliant,* (Ḳ, TA,) and *easy.* (TA.) And رِيحٌ سَهْوٌ *A gentle wind:* [or *a quiet, gentle wind:*] pl. سِهَآءٌ: (TA:) a poet (said to be El-Ḥárith Ibn-'Owf, TA) says,

* تَنَاوَحَتِ الرِّيَاحُ لِفَقْدِ عَمْرٍو *
* وَكَانَتْ قَبْلَ مَهْلِكِهِ سِهَاءَا *

i. e. [*The winds blew violently for the loss of 'Amr; but they were before his death*] *quiet and gentle.* (Ṣ, TA.) One says also أَرْضٌ سَهْوَةٌ *Soft land, without barrenness.* (TA.) —— And السَّهْوُ means *The moon,* in the language of the Nabathæans. (JK.)

سِهْوٌ: see سِهْوَآءٌ.

سَهْوَةٌ *An instance,* or *a case, of unmindfulness, forgetfulness, neglectfulness, heedlessness,* or *inadvertence.* (Mṣb.) —— *A rock,* or *great mass of stone,* (Ḳ,) in the dial. of Ṭeiyi, who call nothing else by this name: so in the M: or, accord. to the T, in that dial., the *rock,* or *great mass of stone, upon which the waterer* [app. *of camels*] *stands:* (TA:) or *a rock,* or *great mass of stone, standing up, not having any foundation* [app. meaning *not partly imbedded*] *in the ground:* and in the dial. of Ṭeiyi, *a single stone, great* or *small.* (JK.) — *A* بَيْت [app. here meaning *booth, or the like,*] *which the Arabs of the desert set up at the water, and by the shade of which they shelter themselves.* (TA.) *A* صُفَّة [or *kind of roofed vestibule,* or *the like,* or *a covering for shade and shelter*], (Ḳ, TA,) *between two houses:* (TA:) or *a thing like the* صُفَّة, *which is before,* or *in the front of, houses:* (Aṣ, JK, Ṣ:) or [in some copies of the Ḳ "and"] *a kind of closet* (مُخْدَع) *between two chambers,* (Ḳ, TA,) *in which the waterers of the camels shelter themselves:* or, as some say, *a small wall which is built between the two* [*opposite main*] *walls of the chamber, the roof being placed over the whole; what is in the middle* [or *main part*] *of the chamber being* [*called*] *a* سَهْوَة; [see عَرْش;] *and what is within it,* [app. *behind,*] *a* مُخْدَع: (TA:) or the *like of a* رَفّ *and* طَاق, [app. meaning *a kind of arched construction with a flat top which forms a shelf, against a wall;* or simply *a shelf,* or *ledge projecting from a wall,* (see رَفّ and طَاق,)] *in which,* or *upon which, a thing is placed:* (ISd, Ḳ:) or *a small* بَيْت [or *chamber*], (Ṣ, Ḳ,) *descending into the earth, having its roof elevated above the ground,* (Ṣ,) *resembling a small* خِزَانَة [or *closet,* or *storeroom*], (Ṣ, Ḳ,) *in which are* [*deposited*] *the household-goods,* or *furniture and utensils;* thus as heard by A'Obeyd from more than one of the people of El-Yemen: (Ṣ:) or it signifies, (Ḳ,) or signifies also, (JK,) *four sticks,* or *pieces of wood,* (JK, Ḳ,) or *three,* (Ḳ,) *which are placed crosswise, one upon another, and upon which is then put anything of the household-goods,* or *furniture and utensils:* (JK, Ḳ:) so in the M: (TA:) and (accord. to the T, TA) *i. q.* كُنْدُوجٌ, (Ḳ,) which means *a small closet* or *store-room:* (TA:) and *i. q.* رَوْشَنٌ and كُوَّةٌ [i. e. *a window,* or *mural aperture*]: and *a* [*kind of curtained canopy,* or *the like, such as is called*] حَجَلَة: and *a curtain,* or *screen, before the court,* or *yard, of a house,* (Ḳ, TA,) and sometimes, *surrounding the house, like a wall:* (TA:) its pl. (in all of these senses, Ḳ, TA) is سِهَآءٌ (JK, Ḳ, TA) and سَهَوَاتٌ. (JK.)

سَهْوَآءُ: see سَهْوٌ: —— and see also what here follows.

سِهْوَآءٌ, (IAạr, JK, Ṣ, TA,) like سِعْوَآءٌ and تِهْوَآءٌ, all with kesr, on the authority of IAạr, but in the Ḳ ▼ سَهْوَآءٌ, (TA,) *A* [*portion,* or *short portion, such as is termed*] سَاعَة, of the night; (Ṣ, Ḳ, TA;) and (Ṣ, TA) the *first part* thereof: (JK, Ṣ, TA:) or it may be like ▼ سَهْوَانٌ, [which is app. in this case with tenween, and] which seems to mean *a period in which people are unmindful of the places,* or *ways, in which things are,* or *should be, sought by them;* or سهوان may be from سَاهِيَة, expl. below: and ▼ سِهْوٌ مِنَ اللَّيْلِ signifies the same as سِعْوٌ and سَعْو [and سِهْوَآءٌ] and سِعْوَآءٌ. (Ḥam p. 708.) One says, لَقِيتُهُ بَعْدَ سِهْوَآءٍ مِنَ اللَّيْلِ i. e. [*I met him after a portion,* or *short portion, of the night;* or] *after the first part of the night had passed.* (JK.)

سَهْوَانٌ: see سَاهٍ: —— and see also سِهْوَآءٌ.

السُّهَيَّا dim. of السُّهَا, q. v.

سَاهٍ *Unmindful, forgetful, neglectful, heedless,* or *inadvertent;* (JK, Ṣ, Mṣb, Ḳ;) as also ▼ سَهْوَانٌ; (Ṣ, Ḳ;) whence the prov.,

* إِنَّ المُوَصَّيْنَ بَنُو سَهْوَانٍ *

(Ṣ) i. e. *Only the unmindful* [lit. *the sons of the unmindful*] *are* such as require to be *enjoined:* (Ṣ, Meyd:) or, as some say, by بنو سهوان are meant *all mankind;* because all become unmindful: but the most correct explanation is, that *those who are enjoined* to do a thing *are subject to unmindfulness:* it is applied to him who is unmindful of pursuing that which he is commanded to do: and سهوان may be syn. with [the inf. n.] سَهْوٌ; or it may be an epithet, syn. with سَاهٍ, and is applied to Adam, because he forgot his covenant, so that بنو سهوان may mean the sons of Adam, and hence, the unmindful. (Meyd. [See also Freytag's Arab. Prov. i. 3-4.]) — See also سَهْو.

سَاهِيَةٌ *A tract of land long and wide, without any covert of trees, or the like,* [*to obstruct the view,* or] *to repel the eye.* (JK, and Ḥam p. 708.)

أُسْهَاةٌ and أُسْهِيَّةٌ: see what follows.

أَسَاهِىُّ, (JK, TA,) in the K, erroneously, أَسَاهِىّ ▼, (TA,) *i. q.* أَلْوَانٌ [generally signifying *Colours*; but also meaning *sorts,* or *species*; and here used in this latter sense, as is indicated in the TA]: a pl. having no sing.: (K, TA:) so in the M: (TA:) or it signifies, (JK,) or signifies also, (TA,) *various sorts* (ضُرُوبٌ مُخْتَلِفَةٌ, JK, TA) *of pace of camels*; like أَسَاهِيجُ: (TA:) and its sing. is ▼ أُسْهَاةٌ. (JK.)

سو

سَوْ *i. q.* سَوْفَ, q. v.

سوأ

1. سَآءَ, (Lth, M, Mṣb, K,) aor. يَسُوْءُ, (Lth, Mṣb,) inf. n. سُوْءٌ, (Lth, M,) or سَوَآءٌ, like سَحَابٌ, (K,) [but the former is that which is commonly known,] *It* (a thing, Lth, M) *was,* or *became, evil, bad, abominable, foul, unseemly, unsightly,* or *ugly.* (Lth, M, Mṣb, K.) It is used in this sense, (IKt, TA,) or [rather] is like بِئْسَ, (Bd, Jel,) in the Kur [xvii. 34], where it is said, سَآءَ سَبِيلًا [*Evil,* &c., *is it as a way of acting*]: (IKt, Bd, Jel, TA:) which is like the saying, سَآءَ هٰذَا مَذْهَبًا [*Evil,* &c., *is this as a way of acting* or *believing,* &c.]: the noun being in the accus. case as a specificative. (IKt, TA.) And so in the saying, سَآءَ مَا فَعَلَ فُلَانٌ صَنِيعًا [*Evil,* &c., *as an action, is that which such a one has done*]. (TA.) — One says also, أَسَأْتُ ▼ بِهِ الظَّنَّ, سُؤْتُ بِهِ ظَنًّا, and [lit. *I was evil in opinion respecting him,* or *it,* and *I made the opinion respecting him,* or *it, to be evil,* each virtually meaning *I held,* or *formed, an evil opinion respecting him,* or *it,*] the noun being determinate, with the article ال, in the latter case, (ISk, Ṣ, Mṣb, TA,) because it is an objective complement, for the verb is trans., (IB, TA,) and the noun being indeterminate in the former case, (IB, Mṣb, TA,) because it is in the accus. case as a specificative; (IB, TA;) but some allow it to be indeterminate after أَسَأْتُ ▼, which is here the *contr. of* أَحْسَنْتُ. (Mṣb.) — It is also trans.: (Lth, TA:) you say, سَآءَهُ, (Ṣ, M, K,) aor. يَسُوْؤُهُ, (Ṣ,) inf. n. سُوْءٌ (Ṣ, M, K) and سُوْءٌ, with ḍamm also, (TA, [and said to be an inf. n. in the Ksh and by Bd in ii. 46, but as it is not mentioned as an inf. n. in the Ṣ nor in the M nor in the K, but is expressly said in all these to be a subst., I think that it should be rejected, or regarded as a quasi-inf. n. like كَلَامٌ and ثَوَابٌ &c.,]) and سَوَآءٌ (K) and سَوَآءَةٌ (AZ, M, K) and سَوَائِيَةٌ, (Ṣ, M, K,) of the measure فَعَالِيَةٌ, like عَلَانِيَةٌ, (Kh, Ṣ, M,) and سَوَايَةٌ, (Ṣ, M, K,) which is a contraction of that next preceding, (Kh, Ṣ, M,) and مَسَآءٌ (M, K) and مَسَآءَةٌ, (Ṣ, M, K,) originally مَسْوَأَةٌ, (Ḥar p. 81,) and مَسَائِيَةٌ, which is originally مَسَاوِئَةٌ, (Kh, Ṣ, M, K,) and مَسَايَةٌ, (Ṣ, M, K,) which is a contraction of that next preceding, (Kh, Ṣ,) and مَسَائِئَةٌ, (M, K,) this last written in the L with two ى s, [i. e. مَسَايِيَةٌ,] (TA,) [*He did evil to him;*] *he did to him that which he disliked,* or *hated;* (M, K;) *he displeased, grieved,* or *vexed, him;* *contr. of* سَرَّهُ. (Ṣ.) One says, سُؤْتُ الرَّجُلَ, meaning *I displeased, grieved,* or *vexed, the man by what he saw* [or *experienced*] *from me.* (Ṣ.) And أَرَدْتُ مَسَآءَتَكَ and مَسَائِيَتَكَ [*I desired to displease, grieve,* or *vex, thee*]. (Lth, TA.) And إِنَّ اللَّيْلَ طَوِيلٌ وَلَا يَسُؤْ بَالُهُ [*Verily the night is long, and may the state thereof not displease, grieve,* or *vex,* me]: meaning لَا يَسُوْؤُنِى بَالُهُ; and expressing a prayer. (Lḥ, M. [In the TA, in the place of بَالُهُ is put مَا لَهُ; as though meaning مَا لَهُ مِنَ الحَوَادِثِ or the like, i. e. *its events,* or *accidents,* &c.]) And لَهُ عِنْدِى مَا سَآءَهُ وَنَآءَهُ [*I have, belonging to him,* or *I owe him, what grieved him, and oppressed him by its weight*], and مَا يَسُوْؤُهُ وَيَنُوْؤُهُ [*what does,* or *will, grieve him,* &c.]. (Ṣ.) تَرَكَ مَا يَسُوْؤُهُ وَيَنُوْؤُهُ [*He left,* or *has left, what will grieve him, and oppress him by its weight,* on the day of judgment, by the responsibility that it has imposed upon him,] is a prov., said of him who has left his property to his heirs. (Meyd, TA.) It is said that El-Maḥboobee was possessed of riches; and when death visited him, he desired to make a testament; so it was said to him, "What wilt thou write?" and he answered, "Write ye, 'Such a one,' meaning himself, 'has left what will grieve him, and oppress him by its weight:'" i. e., property which his heirs will devour, while the burden thereof will remain upon him. (Meyd, TA.) [See also 4.] — One says also, سُؤْتُ وَجْهَ فُلَانٍ, aor. أَسُوْؤُهُ, inf. n. مَسَآءَةٌ and مَسَائِيَةٌ, (Lth, TA,) *i. q.* قَبَّحْتُهُ [i. e. *I said, May God remove the person* (lit. *the face*) *of such a one far from good,* or *prosperity,* &c.]. (TA. [It is said in a copy of the M, that سُؤْتُ لَهُ وَجْهَهُ means قَبَّحْتُهُ: but I think that the right explanation is قَبَحْتُهُ, without teshdeed, meaning *I said to him,* قَبَحَ ٱللّٰهُ وَجْهَكَ: see art. قبح.])

2. سَوَّأَ [*He corrupted,* or *marred*]. You say, سَوِّ وَلَا تُسَوِّئْ *Rectify thou, and do not corrupt,* or *mar.* (A, TA.) [See also 4.] — سَوَّأَ عَلَيْهِ *He said to him* أَسَأْتَ [*Thou hast done ill*]. (M.) You say, سَوَّأْتُ عَلَيْهِ مَا صَنَعَ, (Ṣ,) or صَنِيعَهُ, (K,) i. e. فِعْلَهُ, (TA,) inf. n. تَسْوِئَةٌ and تَسْوِىءٌ, *I discommended to him what he had done,* or *his deed;* and *said to him* أَسَأْتَ [*Thou hast done ill*]. (Ṣ, K.) And إِنْ أَسَأْتُ فَسَوِّئْ عَلَىَّ [*If I do ill, say thou to me, Thou hast done ill*]. (Ṣ.)

4. أَسَآءَ, [inf. n. إِسَآءَةٌ,] *He did evil,* or *ill;* or *acted ill;* *contr. of* أَحْسَنَ: (Ṣ, M, K:) [and so] اسآء فى فعله. (Mṣb.) You say, اسآء إِلَيْهِ (Ṣ, K) and لَهُ and عَلَيْهِ and بِهِ (TA) *He did evil* or *ill,* or *acted ill, to him.* (Ṣ, K, TA.) — [See also أَسْوَى, in several senses, in art. سوى.] — اساءه *He corrupted it,* or *marred it;* (M, K;) [*did it ill;*] *did it not well;* namely, a thing. (M.) It is said in a prov., أَسَآءَ كَارِهٌ مَا عَمِلَ [*An unwilling person did ill what he did*]; relating to a man who was compelled against his will, by another, to do a thing, and marred it, or did it not well: it is applied to the man who seeks an object of want and does not take pains to accomplish it. (M, Meyd.*) See also 1, in two places, in the former half of the paragraph. [And see 2.]

8. استآء *He experienced evil,* or *that which he disliked* or *hated,* (Ṣ,* K, TA,) or *displeasure,* (TA,) or *grief,* or *anxiety.* (M, TA.) اِسْتَآءَ لَهَا occurs in a trad. as meaning *He* (the Prophet) *became displeased,* or *grieved,* or *anxious, on account of it;* i. e., on account of a dream that had been related to him: or, accord. to one relation, the right reading is اِسْتَأْلَهَا, meaning "he sought the interpretation of it, by consideration." (TA.)

سُوْءٌ is an inf. n. of سَآءَ, (Lth, Ṣ, M, K,) intrans., (Lth, M,) and trans.: (Ṣ, M, K:) and is also used as an epithet, applied to a man, (M, Mṣb, and Ḥam p. 712,) and to an action. (Mṣb.) You say رَجُلُ سَوْءٍ (Ṣ, M, Mṣb, K) [*A man of evil nature* or *doings;* or] *a man who does what is evil, displeasing, grievous,* or *vexatious:* (M, TA:) and رَجُلُ السَّوْءِ [*the man of evil nature* or *doings* &c.]: (Ṣ, K:) and ذِئْبُ السَّوْءِ [*the wolf of evil nature* &c.], as in a verse cited voce أَحَالَ, in art. حول: (Ṣ:) and عَمَلُ سَوْءٍ [*a deed of evil nature*]: (M, Mṣb:) and عَمَلُ السَّوْءِ [*the deed of evil nature*]: (Ḥam p. 498:) and نَعْتُ سَوْءٍ [*an epithet of evil nature*]: (O and K in art. سحق:) and سَعْفُ سَوْءٍ *a bad commodity:* (O and TA in art. سعف:) and if you make the former word determinate [by means of the article ال], you use the latter as an epithet [also], (M,* Mṣb, and Ḥam, p. 712,*) and you say الرَّجُلُ السَّوْءُ [*the evil man,* or *the man who does what is evil* &c.]: (Mṣb, and Ḥam p. 712:) and العَمَلُ السَّوْءُ [*the evil deed*]: (Mṣb:) [this last phrase I hold to be correct, regarding السَّوْءُ in this case as originally an inf. n. of the intrans. verb سَآءَ, and therefore capable of being used as an epithet applied to anything; though] IB says that السَّوْءُ used as an epithet is applied to a man but not to a deed: (TA:) [in what here follows from the Ṣ, denying the correctness of another phrase mentioned above on the authority of lexicologists of high repute, there is, in my opinion, an obvious mistranscription, twice occurring, السُّوْءُ for السَّوْءُ, which I suppose to have passed from an early copy of that work into most other copies thereof, for I find it alike in all to which I have had access:] Akh says, one should not say الرَّجُلُ السُّوْءُ, though one says حَقُّ اليَقِينِ as well as الحَقُّ اليَقِينُ; for السُّوْءُ is not the same as الرَّجُلُ, but اليَقِينُ is the same as الحَقُّ: he says, also, nor should one say, هٰذَا رَجُلُ السُّوْءِ, with ḍamm: (Ṣ:) [here the expression "with ḍamm" may perhaps be meant to refer to السوء in all of the three instances above; not in the last only:] IB says, [in remarking on this passage of the Ṣ, in which he appears to have read السُّوْء, with ḍamm, in all of the three instances,] Akh allows one's saying رَجُلُ السَّوْءِ and رَجُلُ سَوْءٍ, with fet-ḥ to the س in both; but not رَجُلُ السُّوْءِ, with ḍamm to the س, because السُّوْء is a subst., meaning "harm, injury, hurt, mischief, or damage," and "evilness of state or condition;" and رَجُل is prefixed, as governing a gen. case, only to the inf. n.: and he adds that one says, هٰذَا الرَّجُلُ السَّوْءُ, not prefixing [the former noun to the latter, but using the latter as an epithet]. (TA.) —— See also the next paragraph, in six places.

سُوْءٌ is the subst. from سَآءَهُ; (Ṣ, M,* Ḳ;) [so, app., accord. to the generality of the lexicologists;] or inf. n. (Ksh and Bḍ in ii. 46) of سِيْءَ, (Ksh ibid.,) or of سَآءَ, aor. يَسُوْءُ, (Bḍ ibid.,) or of سَآءَهُ [q. v.]; (TA;) signifying *Evilness, badness, abominableness, foulness,* or *unseemliness;* [and *displeasingness, grievousness,* or *vexatiousness;*] as, for instance, of natural disposition, and of doings: (Ksh ubi suprà:) *vitious, immoral, unrighteous, sinful,* or *wicked, conduct:* [hence, رَمَاهُ بِسُوْءٍ: see art. رمى:] *anything disapproved,* or *disallowed;* or *regarded as evil, bad, abominable, foul,* or *unseemly:* (Ṣ, TA:) [*an evil action* or *event:*] *evilness of state* or *condition: harm, injury, hurt, mischief,* or *damage:* (IB, TA:) *anything that is mentioned as being* سَيِّئ [i. e. *evil,* &c.]: (Lth, TA:) *any evil, evil affection, cause of mischief* or *harm* or *injury, noxious* or *destructive thing, calamity, disease,* or *malady:* (M, Ḳ, TA:) [pl. أَسْوَآءٌ, accord. to a general rule.] The saying مَا أُنْكِرُكَ مِنْ سُوْءٍ means *I do not disacknowledge thee in consequence of* سُوْء [i. e. *evilness,* &c.,] that I have seen in thee, but only in consequence of my little knowledge of thee. (Ṣ.) لِنَصْرِفَ عَنْهُ السُّوْءَ وَالْفَحْشَآءَ, in the Ḳur [xii. 24], is said by Zj to mean, [*In order that we might turn away from him*] *unfaithfulness to his master, and adultery.* (M, TA.) And سُوْءُ الحِسَابِ, in the Ḳur [xiii. 18, i. e. *The evilness of the reckoning*], is expl. by him as meaning a reckoning in which no good work will be accepted, and no evil work passed over; because infidelity will have made the former to be of no avail: or, as some say, it means a reckoning pursued to the utmost extent, in which no evil work will be passed over. (M, TA.) لَا خَيْرَ فِى قَوْلِ السُّوْءِ means *There is no good in* thy *saying* سُوْء [i. e. *a thing that is evil;* قول being here used in its original sense of an inf. n.]: but if you say ▼ السَّوْءِ, [you use قول in the sense of مَقُول, and] the meaning is, *in evil speech.* (TA as from the Ḳ, but not in the CḲ nor in my MS. copy of the Ḳ.) سُوْءٌ accord. to one reading, and ▼ سَوْءٌ accord. to another, (Ḳ, TA, [but all that is given in this sentence as from the Ḳ is so given only on the authority of the TA, not being in the CḲ nor in my MS. copy of the Ḳ,]) the latter of which readings is the more common, (TA,) in the phrase دَائِرَةُ السَّوْءِ, (Ḳ, TA,) in the Ḳur [ix. 99 and xlviii. 6], (TA,) mean *Defeat,* and *evil;* (Ḳ, TA;) and *trial,* or *affliction,* and *torment;* (TA;) and *perdition,* and *destruction,* or *corruption:* (Ḳ, TA:) and in like manner in the saying, أُمْطِرَتْ مَطَرَ السَّوْءِ, (Ḳ, TA,) in the Ḳur [xxv. 42]: (TA:) or السُّوْءُ means *harm, injury, hurt, mischief,* or *damage;* and *evilness of state* or *condition;* [as expl. before;] and ▼ السَّوْءُ, *corruption,* or *destruction,* or *perdition:* (Ḳ,* TA:) or السَّوْء in the phrase دَائِرَةُ السَّوْءِ means *defeat* and *evil;* and the reading ▼ السُّوْء is from [i. e. *syn. with*] المَسَآءَة [as inf. n.]. (Ṣ. [See also دَائِرَةٌ, in art. دور.]) Accord. to Zj, in the saying in the Ḳur [xlviii. 6], ▼ ٱلظَّآنِّينَ بِٱللّٰهِ ظَنَّ ٱلسَّوْءِ, (TA,) meaning ظَنَّ الأَمْرِ السَّوْءِ [i. e. *Who opine, of God, the opining of the evil thing*], (Bḍ,) it is allowable to read ظَنَّ السُّوْءِ; (T, TA;) and thus some read in this instance: (Jel:) but AM says, in the saying in the Ḳur [xlviii. 12], ▼ وَظَنَنْتُمْ ظَنَّ السَّوْءِ [*And ye opined the evil opining*], it is read only with fet-ḥ, and ḍamm to the س is not allowable in this instance, for there is in it no meaning of trial, or affliction, and torment: (TA:) [for this distinction, however, I see no reason; and it is not correct; for] السوء is with fet-ḥ and with ḍamm to the س in the three sentences [whereof this last is one] in which it occurs in this chapter. (Jel.) —— In the Ḳur vii. 188, it is said to mean † *Diabolical possession;* or *insanity,* or *madness.* (M, TA.) —— ‡ *Leprosy,* syn. بَرَصٌ, (Lth, Ṣ, M, Ḳ, TA,) is said to be its meaning in the Ḳur xx. 23 and xxvii. 12 and xxviii. 32. (Ṣ, TA.) —— † The *fire:* so in the Ḳur xxx. 9, accord. to the reading السُّوْءَى: (Ḳ, TA:) said to mean there *Hell:* but the reading commonly known is ▼ السُّوْأَى. (TA.) —— And † *Weakness in the eye.* (Ḳ. [Thus, i. e. with ḍamm to the س, in the CḲ and TḲ: in the TA said to be بِالفَتْحِ; but this is evidently a mistake for بالضمّ.])

سَيِّءٌ: see سَىْءٌ.

سَوْءَةٌ The عَوْرَة [or *pudendum*], (Ṣ, Mgh, Mṣb,) i. e. (Mṣb) the فَرْج [which means the same, or the *external portion of the organs of generation*], (Lth, M, IAth, Mṣb, Ḳ,) of a man, and of a woman: (Lth, Mṣb, TA:) and the *anus:* (Az and TA in art. سوى:) dual سَوْءَتَانِ: and pl. سَوْآتٌ: so called because its becoming exposed to men displeases [or shames] the owner thereof; (Mṣb;) or because of its unseemliness. (Ḥam p. 510.) In the Ḳur vii. 19, for سَوْآتِهِمَا, some read سَوَّاتِهِمَا; and some, سَوَاتِهِمَا. (Bḍ.) —— In the Ḳur v. 34, it means The *dead body,* or *corpse;* (Bḍ, Jel;) because it is deemed unseemly to be seen. (Bḍ.) —— Accord. to IAth, the former is the primary signification: and hence it is transferred to denote *Any saying,* or *action, of which one is ashamed when it appears:* (TA:) *any evil, bad, abominable, foul,* or *unseemly, saying* or *action;* (Ṣ, Ḳ, TA;) as also ▼ سَوْآءُ: (M:) *any disgracing action* or *thing:* (Lth, TA:) *an evil, abominable,* or *unseemly, property, quality, custom,* or *practice;* (Ḳ, TA;) as also ▼ سَوْآءُ, or ▼ سَوْءَى; (accord. to different copies of the Ḳ; [the latter perhaps fem. of ▼ أَسْوَأُ like the former, of the same class as دَنْيَا and دَنْيَا, or fem. of ▼ سَوْآنُ, like عَطْشَى fem. of عَطْشَانُ;]) or so both of these; (TA;) or so ▼ سَوْءَةٌ سَوْآءُ: (Ṣ:) [or this last means *a property,* &c., *that is very evil* &c.] One says, سَوْءَةً لِفُلَانٍ *May a disgracing action* or *thing befall such a one;* [or *disgrace,* or *shame, to such a one;*] using the accus. case because it is an expression of reviling and imprecation. (Lth, TA.) [See also سَيِّئَةٌ and سُوْءَى —— ▼ السَّوْءَةُ السَّوْءَى.] [or ▼ السَّوْءَةُ السَّوْآءُ] also means *The contrarious wife* or *woman.* (TA.)

سَايَةٌ as used in the saying ضَرَبَ فُلَانٌ عَلَى فُلَانٍ سَايَةً is held by some to be originally with ء, and of the measure فَعْلَةٌ, from السُّوْء; so that the saying means *Such a one did to such a one a thing that caused displeasure to him;* and *did evil to him:* others hold that the saying means *such a one made a way to do what he desired to such a one;* in which case, ساية is of the measure فَعْلَةٌ from سَوَّيْتُ; originally سَوْيَةٌ, which is changed into سَيَّةٌ, and then into سَايَةٌ, in like manner as دِوَّانٌ is changed into دِيوَانٌ. (Aboo-Bekr, TA.) [See the same word in art. سوى.]

سَوْءَى: see سَوْءَةٌ, in two places.

سُوْءَى is [fem. of ▼ أَسْوَأُ, q. v., as meaning *More,* and *most, evil, bad, abominable, foul, unseemly, unsightly,* or *ugly:* and is also] a subst. signifying *an evil, a bad, an abominable, a foul,* or *an unseemly, action;* (Mṣb, TA;) i. q. فَعْلَةٌ سَيِّئَةٌ [and سَيِّئَةٌ alone]: in this sense, [as well as in the former,] (TA,) *contr. of* حُسْنَى. (Ṣ, M, Ḳ, TA.) —— In the Ḳur xxx. 9, (Ṣ, TA,) accord. to the reading commonly known, (TA,) [as *contr. of* الحُسْنَى,] السُّوْءَى means † *The fire* (Ṣ, Ḳ, TA) *of Hell.* (TA.) See also سُوْءٌ, last explanation but one.

سَوْآءُ: see أَسْوَأُ (of which it is said by some to be fem.) in two places: —— and see also سَوْءَةٌ, in four places.

خَزْيَانُ سَوْآنُ is [app. an instance of the alteration of the latter of two epithets to assimilate it to the former, originally خَزْيَانُ أَسْوَأُ, meaning *Ashamed,* or *base,* or *vile,* or *ignominious,* and *evil, bad,* &c.,] from القُبْحُ. (M, TA.) —— See also سَوْءَةٌ.

سَيِّئٌ, [originally سَيْوِئٌ (as will be shown below, voce سَيِّئَةٌ), then سَيْيِئٌ, and then سَيِّئٌ,] applied to a thing [of any kind], (Lth, TA,) *Evil, bad, abominable, foul, unseemly, unsightly,* or *ugly;* (Lth, Mṣb, TA;) contr. of حَسَنٌ: (Mṣb:) sometimes contracted into ▼ سَيْءٌ, like as هَيْنٌ is contracted in هَيِّنٌ, and لَيْنٌ into لَيِّنٌ; as in the saying of Eṭ-Ṭuhawee,

• وَلَا يَجْزُونَ مِنْ حَسَنٍ بِسَيْءٍ •
• وَلَا يَجْزُونَ مِنْ غِلَظٍ بِلِينٍ •

[*And they will not requite good with evil, nor will they requite roughness with gentleness*]. (Ṣ.) You say قَوْلٌ سَيِّئٌ [*An evil saying*; or] *a saying that displeases*. (M, TA.) And فَعْلَةٌ سَيِّئَةٌ [*An evil action or deed*]. (TA.) And it is said in the Ḳur [xxxv. 41], وَمَكْرَ ٱلسَّيِّئِ وَلَا يَحِيقُ ٱلْمَكْرُ ٱلسَّيِّئُ إِلَّا بِأَهْلِهِ [*And in the plotting of that which is evil; but the evil plotting shall not beset* any save *the authors thereof*]. (M, TA.) One says also, فُلَانٌ سَيِّئُ الإِخْتِيَارِ [*Such a one is evil in respect of choice*, or *preference*]. (Ṣ.) [See also the next paragraph.]

سَيِّئَةٌ [fem. of سَيِّئٌ, q. v.: and also a subst., being transferred from the category of epithets to that of substs. by the affix ة], originally سَيْوِئَةٌ, (Ṣ,) *An evil act* or *action*; *contr. of* حَسَنَةٌ; (Mṣb;) *a fault, an offence*, or *an act of disobedience*; or *such as is intentional*; *a sin, a crime*, or *an act of disobedience for which one deserves punishment*; syn. خَطِيئَةٌ: (M, Ḳ:) pl. سَيِّئَاتٌ. (TA.) It is said in a trad., الحَسَنَةُ بَيْنَ السَّيِّئَتَيْنِ [*The good act is between the two evil acts*]; meaning that the exceeding of the just bounds is a سَيِّئَة, and the falling short thereof is a سَيِّئَة, and the pursuing a middle course between these two is a حَسَنَة. (TA.) [See also سَوْءَةٌ and سُوْءَى.] — Also, tropically, ‡ The *recompense of a* سَيِّئَة *properly so termed* [i. e. as expl. above]. (Mṣb in art. مكر.) — *An evil*, or *evil accident*; *a calamity*; *a misfortune*; (Kaṣh in iv. 81;) *a trial*, or *an affliction*; opposed to حَسَنَةٌ; (Kaṣh and Bḍ in iv. 80;) *scarcity of herbage*, or *of the goods, conveniences, and comforts, of life*; *straitness of circumstances*; and *unsuccessfulness*; thus [likewise] opposed to حَسَنَةٌ in the Ḳur iv. 80. (Er-Rághib, TA in art. حسن.)

أَسْوَأُ; fem. سُوْءَى: see the latter word. One says, هُوَ أَسْوَأُ القَوْمِ *He is the most evil*, &c., *of the people*, or *party*; syn. أَقْبَحُهُمْ: and هِىَ السُّوْءَى *She is the most evil*, &c. (Mṣb.) And the [common] people say أَسْوَأُ الأَحْوَالِ, meaning *The* [*worst*, or] *most scanty*, and *weakest, of states* or *conditions*. (Mṣb.) ═ [Also,] applied as an epithet to a man, (El-Umawee, M, TA,) *Evil, bad, abominable, foul, unseemly, unsightly*, or *ugly*: (El-Umawee, M, Ḳ, TA:) fem. ↓ سَوْآءُ, (El-Umawee, M, Ḳ,) which is thus applied to a woman; (El-Umawee, Ṣ, M;) or this is an instance of the measure فَعْلَآءُ having no [masc. of the measure] أَفْعَلُ. (M, TA.) See also سَوْءَةٌ, in four places. It is said in a trad. (M, TA) of the Prophet, or of 'Omar, (TA,) ↓ سَوْآءُ وَلُودٌ خَيْرٌ مِنْ حَسْنَآءَ عَقِيمٍ [*An ugly prolific woman is better than a beautiful barren one*]. (M, TA.)

مَسَآءَةٌ an inf. n. of سَآءَ: (Ṣ, M, Ḳ:) and [also a subst. signifying *An evil*, as being] *a cause of grief* or *vexation*; *contr. of* مَسَرَّةٌ: originally مَسْوَأَةٌ: and therefore the pl. is ↓ مَسَاوٍ, for مَسَاوِئُ; (Mṣb;) signifying also *vices, faults, defects*, or *imperfections*; (Ṣ, Mṣb, Ḳ, TA;) and *diseases*; (Ṣ, TA;) and *acts of disobedience*: (Mṣb:) so in the saying, بَدَتْ مَسَاوِيهِ *His acts of disobedience*, and *vices, faults*, &c., *appeared*: (Mṣb:) and الخَيْلُ تَجْرِى عَلَى مَسَاوِيهَا *Horses run, notwithstanding their vices*, or *faults*, &c., (Ṣ, Meyd, Ḳ,) and *diseases*; (Ṣ, Meyd;) for their generousness impels them to do so: (Ṣ, Meyd, Ḳ: but omitted in the CḲ:) and in like manner, the ingenuous generous man bears difficulties, and defends, or protects, what he is bound to defend or protect, or to regard as sacred, or inviolable, though he be weak, and practises generosity in all circumstances: (Meyd, TA:) or it is applied in relation to the protection and defence of what should be sacred, or inviolable, or of wives, or women under covert, and the members of one's household, notwithstanding harm, or injury, and fear: or it means that one may seek to defend himself by means of a man though there be in him qualities disapproved: (MF, TA:) but accord. to Lḥ, المَسَاوِى has no proper sing., like المَحَاسِنُ: (Meyd, TA:*) accord. to some of the writers on inflection, it is the contr. of المَحَاسِنُ, and an anomalous pl. of السُّوْءُ, being originally with ء. (TA.)

مَسَاوٍ: see the next preceding paragraph.

سوب

سُوبَةٌ *A long*, or *far, journey*; like سُبَاةٌ; (Ḳ, TA;) of which it is a dial. var.: a short journey is termed سُوَيْبَةٌ. (TA.)

سُوبِيَةٌ *A well-known* [*beverage of the kind called*] نَبِيذ, *prepared from wheat, and much drunk by the people of Egypt*, (L, TA,) *at their festivals*: (TA:) *and also prepared from rice*: (MF, TA:) [*also from the pips of a species of melon, called in Egypt* عَبْدَلَّاوِىّ; (see art. عبد; and see also White's "Abdollatiphi Hist. Aegypti Compendium," pp. 52-3; or De Sacy's transl., pp. 34-5;) *moistened and pounded, and steeped in water, which is then strained, and sweetened with sugar*:] it is mentioned in a trad. and by several writers. (TA.)

سوج

1. سَاجَ نَسِيجَهُ بِالمِسْوَجَةِ, said of a weaver, *He passed the* مِسْوَجَة, i. e. the *sprinkling instrument, to and fro over his web* [*to dress the warps with the preparation termed* سَوْج]. (A, TA.*) — [Hence, app., unless the reverse be the case, the inf. n.] سَوَجَانٌ signifies The act of *going and coming*: (AA, O, Ḳ, TA:) asserted by some to be سُوجَانٌ, [and thus it is in the CḲ,] but this is a mistake. (TA.) You say, سَاجَ, aor. يَسُوجُ, inf. n. سَوْجٌ [and سَوَجَانٌ], *He*, or *it, went and came*. (TA.) — And سَاجَ, (IAạr, O, Ḳ,) aor. as above, (IAạr, O,) inf. n. سَوْجٌ and سُوَاجٌ and سَوَجَانٌ, *He went along gently, softly*, or *in a leisurely manner*. (IAạr, O, Ḳ.) IAạr cites the following [as an ex. of an epithet hence derived]:

* غَرَّآءُ لَيْسَتْ بِالسَّؤُوجِ ↓ الجِلْبِجِ *

[A female *fair in face: she is not the ugly old woman that goes along gently*, or *softly*, by reason of decrepitude]. (O.)

2. سَوَّجَ عَلَى الكَرْمِ (A, Mṣb) وَنَحْوِهِ (Mṣb) *He made a* سِيَاج, i. e. *an enclosure* (A, Mṣb) *composed of thorns and the like*, (Mṣb,) *around the grape-vines* (A, Mṣb) *and the like*; as also سَيَّجَ, with ى, agreeably with the word سِيَاج [from which it is derived]: (Mṣb:) and سَيَّجَ حَائِطَهُ, inf. n. تَسْيِيجٌ, *he made an enclosure* (Ḳ and TA in art. سيج) *of thorns and the like* (TA in that art.) *around his garden* of palm-trees or vines. (Ḳ and TA in the same art.)

سَاجٌ [The *teak-tree*; *tectona grandis*; to which the name of سَاج is applied in Pers.; *remarkable for its huge size, and enormous leaves*: or the *Indian*, or *Oriental, plane-tree*: or the *Indian plantain-tree*: (see De Sacy's Chrest. Ar., sec. ed., iii. 473:)] *a certain species of tree*, (Ṣ, A, Mgh, O, Mṣb, Ḳ,) *of great size*, (Mṣb,) *growing to a very great size*, (Mgh,) *that grows only in India, and is conveyed thence to other countries*; (Mgh, Mṣb;) so they say: (Mgh:) Z says, (Mṣb,) it is *a black, heavy, wood, which is brought from India*, (A, Mṣb,) *in pieces made of an oblong form, and squared*, (A,) *and which the wood-fretter can hardly*, or *not at all, wear*, or *waste*; (A, Mṣb;) and he says that its pl. is سِيجَانٌ: (Mṣb: [but this is said in the A only to be pl. of سَاج meaning "a rounded, wide, طَيْلَسَان:"]) some say that *it resembles ebony, but is less black*: (Mṣb:) accord to the A, Noah's ark was made of it: but several authors say that it is related in the Book of the Law revealed to Moses that it was made of the صَنَوْبَر [or pine-tree]; and some say that the صنوبر is a species of the سَاج: (TA:) AḤn describes it, (O, TA,) on the authority of one who had seen it in its places of growth, (O,) as *a species of tree that grows to a great size, tall and wide, having leaves like the shields of the Deylem* (الدَّيْلَم, q. v.), *with one of which leaves a man may cover himself, and it will protect him from the rain, and it has a sweet odour, like the odour of the leaves of the walnut, and is fine and soft*, or *smooth*; (O, TA,) *the elephants* [he says] *are fond of it, and of the leaves of the banana, both of which they eat*: *it is not of the trees that grow in the land of the Arabs, nor does it grow in any country except those of India and the Zenj*; *nor does any tree grow so tall, nor any so big*: (O:) ↓ سَاجَةٌ is the n. un.; and its pl. is سَاجَاتٌ: (Mṣb:) and it signifies *a piece of wood of the tree called* سَاج, *made of an oblong form, and squared, as brought from India*; (A,* Mgh, TA;) *such as is cut and prepared for a foundation and the like*: (Mgh:) one says, فِى أَسَاسِ بِنَائِهِ سَاجَةٌ [*In the foundation of his building is a piece of wood of the* سَاج *cut in an oblong form, and squared*]: (A:) a سَاجَة from which a door is cloven, or divided off lengthwise, is called سَلِيجَةٌ: (TA:) and the term سَاجَةٌ is also applied to the *board*, or *tablet*, [*of wood of the* سَاج,] *upon which stand* [or *rest*] *the two scales of the balance when one weighs with it*. (Ḥam. p. 818.) ═ Also *A* [*garment of the kind* called] طَيْلَسَان of the colour termed خُضْرَة [here meaning a dark, or an ashy, dust-colour]: (Ṣ, A, O, Ḳ:) or a black طيلسان: (IAạr, O, Ḳ:) or a large, thick, or coarse, طيلسان: (TA:) or a طيلسان made of a round form, (A, TA,) and wide: (A:) or a طيلسان hollowed out in the middle (مُقَوَّر); so woven: (Az, O, Mṣb:) this last is said to be meant in a trad. in which it is said that the Prophet used to wear in war such قَلَانِس [pl. of قَلَنْسُوَةٌ, q. v.,] as were [made] of سِيجَان: (TA:) سِيجَانٌ is the pl.: (T, Ṣ, A, O, Mṣb:) the dim. is ▾ سُوَيْجٌ. (TA.) It is tropically applied to signify ‡ A [garment of the kind called] كِسَآء made of a square form, or four-sided; and is described as a sort of مِلْحَفَة, woven. (TA.) As meaning a طيلسان, it is said by some, that its ا is originally ى. (L, TA.) — It is also used, by a poet, in the manner of an epithet, as meaning Of the colour termed خُضْرَة [expl. above]. (TA.)

سَوْجٌ *A preparation of clay,* [app. *made into a sort of ooze, and*] *cooked; with which the weaver does over* [i. e. *dresses*] *the warps of the web.* (TA. [See 1, first sentence.])

سَاجَةٌ n. un. of سَاجٌ, q. v. (Mṣb.)

سَوُوجٌ [an epithet from سَاجَ in the last of the senses assigned to it above]: see 1, last sentence.

سُوَيْجٌ *A small* طَيْلَسَان *of the kind called* سَاج, q. v. (TA.)

سِيَاجٌ *An enclosure* (A, Mṣb) *made with thorns and the like* (Mṣb) *around grape-vines* (A, Mṣb) *and the like:* (Mṣb:) *an enclosure made with trees around grape-vines* or *a garden:* (L in art. سيج:) *an enclosure* (O and Ḳ in that art.) *of any kind* (O) *around a thing, such as palm-trees and grape-vines:* (O, Ḳ:) and *a wall* (O, Ḳ) *of any kind, whether roofed or not roofed:* (O:) pl. [of pauc.] أَسْوِجَةٌ and [of mult.] سُوجٌ; (A, Mṣb;) the latter originally سُوُجٌ, like كُتُبٌ pl. of كِتَابٌ. (Mṣb.) Fei makes the medial radical letter to be و, and so do [Z and] AHei and most of the grammarians: Az [and Ṣgh] and IM hold it to be ى. (TA.)

مِسْوَجَةٌ The *sprinkling instrument* (مِرَشَّة, A) *which the weaver passes to and fro over his web* [*to dress the warps with the preparation termed* سَوْج]. (A, TA.*)

كِسَآءٌ مُسَوَّجٌ *A* [*garment of the kind called*] كِسَآء *made into a* سَاج: (A:) or, *made round* (O, Ḳ, TA) *and wide,* or *ample:* (TA:) and also applied to signify *such as is made square,* or *four-sided.* (TA.)

سوح

سَاحٌ [originally سَوْحٌ]: see what follows.

سَاحَةٌ [originally سَوَحَةٌ] The *court,* or *open area,* of a house; i. e. *a spacious vacant part* or *portion* thereof, *in which is no building;* (Mṣb voce عَرْصَة;) *a part of a house in which is no building nor roof:* (Ḥar p. 33:) its بَاحَة: (Ṣ:) or its *yard;* i. e. *a spacious place in front* of a house: (Mṣb in the present art.:) or *a wide,* or *spacious, place, among the dwellings of a tribe:* and *a side, region, quarter,* or *tract;* or *a lateral,* or *an outward* or *adjacent, part* or *portion;* syn. نَاحِيَة: (Ḳ:) the pl. is ▾ سَاحٌ [or rather this is a coll. gen. n. of which ساحة is the n. un.] and [the pl. is] سَاحَاتٌ (Ṣ, Mṣb, Ḳ) and سُوحٌ; (Ṣ, Ḳ;) the last like بُدْنٌ pl. of بَدَنَةٌ, and خُشْبٌ pl. of خَشَبَةٌ: (Ṣ:) the dim. is ▾ سُوَيْحَةٌ. (TA.) [See also 7 in art. سبح.] One says, عَمَرَ اللّٰهُ سَاحَتَكَ [*May God people thy court,* or *yard;* or *make it to be well stocked with people and the like*]. (A.) And in a case of drought you say, احْمَرَّ اللُّوحُ وَاغْبَرَّتِ السُّوحُ [*The air,* or *atmosphere, has become red, and the courts,* or *yards, have become very dusty*]. (A.) You say also, إِنَّهُ لَبَرِىْءُ السَّاحَةِ, a phrase like إِنَّهُ لَبَرِىْءُ العَذِرَةِ [expl. in art. عذر]. (TA in art. عذر.)

سُوَيْحَةٌ dim. of سَاحَةٌ, q. v. (TA.)

سوخ

1. سَاخَتْ قَوَائِمُهُ, (Ṣ, Mṣb, Ḳ,) or قَوَائِمُ الدَّابَّةِ, (A,) فِى الأَرْضِ, (Ṣ, Mṣb,) or بِالأَرْضِ, (A,) aor. تَسُوخُ, (Ṣ, A, Mṣb,) inf. n. سَوْخٌ (L, Mṣb) and سُؤُوخٌ and سَوَخَانٌ, (L,) *His legs,* or *the legs of the beast, sank into the ground:* (Mṣb,* TA:) or *sank, and became concealed, in the ground* or *earth:* (Ṣ, Mṣb,* TA:) and so سَاخَتْ, aor. تَسِيخُ, (Ṣ, Mṣb, TA,) inf. n. سَيْخٌ (Mṣb) [and سَيَخَانٌ: see art. سيخ]: and in like manner one says of the feet: (A, TA:) like ثَاخَتْ. (Ṣ, Ḳ.) — And سَاخَ, (L, Ḳ,) aor. يَسُوخُ, (L,) *It* (a thing) *sank* [in water &c.], or *subsided;* syn. رَسَبَ. (L, Ḳ.) — And سَاخَتْ بِهِمُ الأَرْضُ, (A, L, Mṣb, Ḳ,) aor. تَسُوخُ, (L, Mṣb,) inf. n. سَوْخٌ (L, Mṣb, Ḳ) and سُؤُوخٌ and سَوَخَانٌ, (L, Ḳ,) *The ground,* or *earth, sank with them;* or *sank with them and swallowed them up* or *enclosed them;* syn. انْخَسَفَتْ, (L, Ḳ,) or خَسَفَتْ: and so سَاخَتْ, aor. تَسِيخُ, inf. n. سَيْخٌ. (Mṣb.)

4. اساخهُ *He* (God) *made him,* or *it, to sink into,* or *to sink and become concealed in, the ground* or *earth.* (Mṣb.)

5. تَسَوَّخَ *He fell into a place rendered very slimy by rain;* (L, Ḳ;) or *into mud rendered very watery by rain;* as also تروّخ. (L.)

صَارَتِ الأَرْضُ سُوَاخًا (L, Ḳ) and ▾ سُوَّاخًا (L) and ▾ سُوَّاخَى, (L, Ḳ,) or ▾ سَوَاخَى, of the measure فَعَالَى, (Ṣ,) said in the Ḳ to be a mistake, but the Ṣ is not the only lexicon in which it is thus written, (TA,) *The earth became very slimy by reason of rain.* (Ṣ, L, Ḳ.)

سَوَاخَى: see the next preceding paragraph.

فِيهِ سَوَاخِيَةٌ *In it is much mud.* (Ḳ.)

صَارَتِ الأَرْضُ سُوَّاخًا i. q. سُوَاخًا, q. v. (L.)

سُوَّاخَى *Mud rendered very watery by rain.* (L.) See صَارَتِ الأَرْضُ سُوَاخًا, above. — Also, and ▾ مَسْوَخَةٌ, *Tumid earth that breaks in pieces when trodden upon.* (L voce رَخَّاةٌ.) — بَطْحَآءُ سُوَّاخَى [*A wide water-course,* or *channel of a torrent, containing fine,* or *minute,* or *broken, pebbles, &c.,*] *into which the feet sink,* or *in which the feet sink and become concealed.* (L.)

سُوَيْوِخَةٌ dim. of سُوَّاخَى. (L, Ḳ.)

مَسْوَخَةٌ: see سُوَّاخَى.

سود

1. سَادَ, aor. يَسُودُ, inf. n. سِيَادَةٌ (Mṣb, TA) and سُودٌ and سُودَدٌ [and its vars. mentioned in the next sentence] and سَيْدُودَةٌ, (TA,) or سُودَدٌ is a simple subst. signifying as expl. below, (Mṣb,) *He was,* or *became,* [*a* سَيِّد, i. e. *chief, lord, master,* &c.; or] *possessed of glory, honour, dignity, eminence, exalted* or *elevated state,* or *nobility.* (Mṣb, TA.) — [It is also trans.:] you say, سَادَ قَوْمَهُ, (Ṣ, M,* A,) aor. يَسُودُهُمْ, (Ṣ, A,) inf. n. سِيَادَةٌ (Ṣ, M, Ḳ*) and سُودٌ (M, Ḳ*) and سُودَدٌ, (Ṣ, M, A, Ḳ,*) in which last the [final] د is added to render the word quasi-coordinate to words of the measure فُعْلَل, as جُنْدَبٌ and بُرْقُعٌ, (Ṣ,) and سُودُدٌ and سُؤْدَدٌ (M, TA*) and سُؤْدُدٌ (M, Ḳ,*) of the dial. of Ṭeiyi, (M,) and سَيْدُودَةٌ, (Ṣ, M,) *He was,* or *became, the* سَيِّد [or *chief, lord, master,* &c.,] *of his people;* (Ṣ;) [*he ruled his people,* or *held dominion over them;*] and ▾ اسْتَادَهُمْ signifies the same. (M, L.) And سَادَهُ, inf. n. سِيَادَةٌ and سِيَادٌ and سُودَدٌ [&c.], *He exercised rule,* or *dominion, over him.* (MA.) [See also سُودَدٌ below.] — [Hence,] سَادَتْ نَاقَتِى المَطَايَا ‡ *My she-camel left behind the* [other] *camels* or *beasts.* (A, TA.) — سَاوَدَنِى فَسُدْتُهُ: see 3. — سَوِدَ and سَادَ as syn. with اسْوَدَّ: see this last, in three places. — سَادَهُ as syn. with سَاوَدَهُ: see this latter. — سَادَ, aor. يَسُودُ, also signifies *He drank water such as is termed* مَسْوَدَة, *which occasions a disease termed* سُوَاد. (M, Ḳ.) — And سِيدَ, (M,) or سُئِدَ, like عُنِىَ, (Ḳ,) *He was,* or *became, affected with* السُّوَاد. (M, Ḳ. [In the former, the context indicates that this means here a disease that attacks the liver from eating dates: in the latter, that it here means a disease incident to sheep or goats.])

2. سَوَّدَهُ قَوْمُهُ, [inf. n. تَسْوِيدٌ,] *His people made him a* سَيِّد [i. e. *chief, lord,* &c.; generally meaning *over them*]. (Ṣ, M,* A.) It is said in a trad. of 'Omar, تَفَقَّهُوا قَبْلَ أَنْ تُسَوَّدُوا, (M,) or ▾ تَسُودُوا [for تَتَسَوَّدُوا], (O,) meaning *Learn ye knowledge,* or *science, before ye be* [*made*] *chiefs,* looked at; for if ye learn not before that, ye will be ashamed to learn after becoming advanced in age, or attaining to full growth, (بَعْدَ الكِبَرِ,) and so will remain ignorant, taking it [i. e. knowledge] from the younger ones, and that will lower your estima-

tion: (M:) or the meaning is, *before ye be married, and become masters of houses,* or *tents,* and be diverted by the marriage-state from [the acquisition of] knowledge, or science. (Sh, O.) [See also 5.] —— سَوَّدَ also signifies *He slew:* (Az, TA:) or [the inf. n.] تَسْوِيدٌ signifies the *slaying of* سَادَة [i. e. *chiefs, lords,* &c., pl. of سَيِّدٌ]. (Ḳ.) —— [And accord. to the Ḳ, تَسْوِيدٌ is also *syn. with* جُرْأَةٌ The *being bold, daring, brave,* or *courageous:* but accord. to the O, سَوَّدَ signifies خَرِئَ *He voided his excrement,* or *ordure;* as though from what next follows: which of these two explanations is right (for it seems improbable that both are right) I find no ex. to indicate.] —— سَوَّدْتُهُ, (Ṣ, M,* TA,) or سوّدته بِالسَّوَادِ, inf. n. تَسْوِيدٌ, (Mṣb,) *I blackened it; made it,* or *rendered it,* أَسْوَد [i. e. *black*]; (Ṣ,* M, Mṣb;*) *I changed its* بَيَاض [or *whiteness*] *to* سَوَاد [or *blackness*]. (TA.) —— [Hence, سوّد وَجْهَهُ lit. *He,* or *it, blackened his face:* meaning † *rendered his face expressive of sorrow,* or *displeasure;* or *grieved,* or *displeased, him:* and also, *disgraced him:* see the contr. بيّض: and see also 9. —— Hence also سوّد meaning *He wrote* anything *in a rough manner, as one writes the first draught,* or *original copy, of a book or the like; contr. of* بيّض in this sense also: probably post-classical.] —— And سَوَّدَ الإِبِلَ, (Ṣ, M, O,) inf. n. تَسْوِيدٌ, (Ṣ, Ḳ,) † *He beat,* or *pounded, old worn-out hair-cloth, and applied it as a remedy to the galls,* or *sores, on the backs of the camels.* (Fr, A'Obeyd, Ṣ, M, O, Ḳ.*) —— And سَوِّدُوا ضَيْفَكُمْ † *Feed ye your guest with something to allay the craving of his stomach before the morning-meal* (الغَدَآء). (El-Umawee, TA in art. لهج.)

3. ▼ سَاوَدَنِى فَسُدْتُهُ (Ṣ, A, Ḳ,* &c.) *He vied with me,* or *contended with me for superiority, in the rank,* or *quality,* or *qualities, of a* سَيِّد [or *chief, lord,* &c.], *and I overcame,* or *surpassed, him therein:* (Ṣ, A, L, Ḳ:*) —— and also *He vied with me in blackness, and I surpassed him therein.* (Ṣ, L, Ḳ.*) —— And سَاوَدَهُ, inf. n. سِوَادٌ, *He met him in the blackness of the night.* (M, L.) —— And سَاوَدْتُهُ, (Ṣ, A, O,) inf. n. سِوَادٌ (Ṣ, O, Ḳ*) and مُسَاوَدَةٌ, (Ṣ,) ‡ *I spoke secretly with him;* (Ṣ, A, O, Ḳ;*) because you bring near your سَوَاد [or person] to his [when you so speak with another]; or [because] originally meaning *I brought near my* سَوَاد, i. e. *person, to his:* (Ṣ:) or سَاوَدَهُ, inf. n. سِوَادٌ, signifies *he spoke secretly with him, and so brought near his* سَوَاد *to his* [the other's]; as also ▼ سَادَهُ, inf. n. سَوْدٌ. (M.) It was said to the daughter of El-Khuss, Wherefore didst thou commit fornication? (Ṣ, O, L,) or What caused thee to commit fornication? or Wherefore didst thou become pregnant? (M, L,) thou being the mistress of thy people? (Ṣ, O, L:) and she answered, قُرْبُ الوِسَادِ وَطُولُ السِّوَادِ, (Ṣ, M, O, L, [in my two copies of the Ṣ قُرْبَ and طُولَ, as though a verb were understood,]) i. e. [*The nearness of the pillow, and the long continuance of*] *secret speaking with another:* (Lḥ, M, L:) or, as some say, السواد here means *the enticing to* جِمَاع: or, as others say, الجماع *itself* [if the question put to her were the last mentioned above]. (M, L.) —— ساودهُ also signifies † *He acted deceitfully,* or *guilefully, with him:* (Ḳ:) or *he endeavoured to turn him* [*to a thing*] *by blandishment,* or *by deceitful arts;* or *to entice him;* as shown above. (TA.) —— And † *He drove him away;* namely, a lion. (O, Ḳ.) —— And سَاوَدَتِ الإِبِلُ النَّبَاتَ † *The camels laboured at the herbage with their lips, and could not master it, because of its shortness* (O, Ḳ) *and its scantiness.* (Ḳ.)

4. أَسَادَ and أَسْوَدَ *He begat a boy that was a* سَيِّد [or *chief, lord,* &c.]: (Ṣ, O, Ḳ:) or they signify, (O, Ḳ,) or signify also, (Ṣ,) *he begat a black boy:* (Ṣ, O, Ḳ:) or *he had a black child born to him:* (M:) and اسودت *she brought forth black children.* (A.)

5. تَسَوَّدَ *He became married:* (Ḳ:) or *he became married, and master of a house,* or *tent.* (Sh, O.) See 2, second sentence.

8: see 1. —— اِسْتَادُوا بَنِى فُلَانٍ *They slew the* سَيِّد [or *chief, lord,* &c.,] *of the sons of such a one:* (AZ, Ṣ, M, O, Ḳ:) or (so in the Ḳ, but in the Ṣ and O "and in like manner") *they took him captive:* (Ṣ, O, Ḳ:) or *they asked,* or *demanded, of him a woman in marriage.* (IAạr, Ṣ, M, O, Ḳ.) And اِسْتَادَ القَوْمَ, and فِى القَوْمِ, and مِنْهُمْ, *He asked,* or *demanded, in marriage, a* سَيِّدَة [or *woman of rank* or *quality*], *among the people:* (M:) or اِسْتَادَ فِى بَنِى فُلَانٍ, and مِنْهُمْ, *he married one of the chief,* or *noble, women of the sons of such a one.* (IAạr, O.) And استاد *He married among* سَادَة [or *chiefs, lords,* &c.]. (L.)

9. اِسْوَدَّ, (Ṣ, M, Mṣb, Ḳ,) inf. n. اِسْوِدَادٌ; (Ṣ, Ḳ;) and ▼ اِسْوَادَّ, (Ṣ, M, Ḳ,) inf. n. اِسْوِيدَادٌ; (Ṣ, Ḳ;) and in poetry it is allowable to say ▼ اِسْوَأَدَّ, to avoid the concurrence of two quiescent letters; imperative [of ▼ the second] اِسْوَادِدْ, and the last two letters in this may be incorporated together [so that you may say اِسْوَادَّ]; (Ṣ;) said of a thing; (Ṣ, Mṣb;) and ▼ سَوِدَ, (Ṣ, M, Mṣb,) said of a man, (Ṣ, TA,) and of a thing, (TA,) aor. يَسْوَدُ; (Mṣb;) and ▼ سَادَ, (M,) first pers. سُدْتُ, a form used by some; (Ṣ;) *It,* and *he, became* أَسْوَد [i. e. *black*]: (Ṣ, M, Mṣb, Ḳ:) and ▼ اسوادّ *it,* or *he, became intensely so.* (TA.) Nuṣeyb says,

سَوِدْتُ ▼ فَلَمْ أَمْلِكْ سَوَادِى وَتَحْتَهُ
قَمِيصٌ مِنَ القُوهِىِّ بِيضٌ بَنَائِقُهْ

[*I am black,* (for Nuṣeyb was a slave,) *and am not master of my person; but beneath it,* or *within it, is a shirt like the cloth of Ḳoohistán, the gores of which are white:* by this قميص he means his heart; قَمِيصُ القَلْبِ, or القَمِيصُ, tropically meaning "the pericardium;" and, by a synecdoche, "the heart itself, with its appertenances"]. (Ṣ, TA.) —— [Hence,] اسودّ وَجْهُهُ [lit. *His face became black:* meaning] ‡ *his face became expressive of grief,* or *sorrow,* or *displeasure, occasioned by fear* [&c.]: (Bḍ in iii. 102:) *he became grieved, sorrowful,* or *displeased;* and *confounded,* or *perplexed, and unable to see his right course, by reason of shame,* or *in consequence of a deed that he had done* (Bḍ in xvi. 60) [&c.: and often meaning *he became disgraced*]: opposed to اِبْيَضَّ. (Bḍ in iii. 102.)

11: see 9, in three places.

Q. Q. 4. اِسْوَأَدَّ: see 9, first sentence.

سُودٌ *A* سَفْح (M, Ḳ, TA) *of a mountain,* (M, TA,) [app. meaning, in this case, *a low tract at the base,* or *foot, of a mountain,*] *forming a narrow strip of ground,* (M, TA,) *rough and black,* (M,) or *level, abounding with black stones,* (Ḳ, TA,) *which are rough, and the predominant colour whereof is blackness; seldom found but at a mountain in which is a mine:* so says Lth: or *a piece of ground in which are black rough stones resembling dry human dung:* (TA:) or *land,* or *ground, in which blackness predominates, which is seldom anywhere but at a mountain in which is a mine:* (Mṣb:) pl. أَسْوَادٌ: (M, TA:) and ▼ سُودَةٌ signifies *a portion thereof;* (M, Mṣb, Ḳ, TA;) and the pl. of this is سُودَاتٌ, and the pl. of سُودَاتٌ is ▼ أَسْوِدَاتٌ, which occurs in a trad. (TA.)

سُودَدٌ: see سُودَدٌ.

سَيْدٌ a contraction of سَيِّدٌ, q. v.

سِيدٌ: see art. سيد.

سُودَةٌ: see سُودٌ. —— Also † *Land in which are palm-trees:* opposed to بَيْضَةٌ. (TA in art. بيض. [See also السَّوْدَآء, voce أَسْوَدُ, near the end.])

سُودَدٌ a subst. from سَادَ, inf. n. سِيَادَةٌ; signifying [The *rank, station,* or *condition,* or the *quality* or *qualities, of a* سَيِّد; i. e. *chiefdom, lordship, mastery,* &c.; or] *glory, honour, dignity,* (Mṣb,) or *eminence, exalted* or *elevated state,* or *nobility:* (M, Mṣb:) or this word, (Ṣ, M, Ḳ,) and its vars. سُودَدٌ and سُؤْدَدٌ (M, TA) and سُؤْدُدٌ, (M, Ḳ,) of the dial. of Ṭeiyi, (M,) and ▼ سُودٌ, (M, Ḳ,) are syn. with سِيَادَةٌ (Ṣ, M, Ḳ) and سَيْدُودَةٌ as inf. ns. of سَادَ [q. v.]. (Ṣ, M.)

سَوْدَآءُ fem. of أَسْوَدُ [q. v.]. (Mṣb.)

سُودَانِيَّةٌ or سُوَدَانَةٌ: see سُودَانِيَّةٌ.

سِيدَانَةٌ: see سِيدٌ, in art. سيد.

سُودَانِيَّةٌ, (M, A, TA,) or سُوَدَانِيَّةٌ, (Mgh, O,) and ▼ سُوَدَانَةٌ, (M, O,) or سُودَانَةٌ, with ḍamm, like the first, (TA,) and ▼ سُوَادِيَّةٌ (A, Ḳ) and ▼ أُسْوُدٌ (Ḳ) all signify the same; (TA;) *A certain bird, that eats grapes:* or i. q. عُصْفُور [i. e. the *sparrow;* or *a bird of the passerine kind*]: (Ḳ:) or *a certain small bird,* (A, Mgh, O, TA,) *having a long tail,* (Mgh,) *resembling the* عصفور, (TA,) *sometimes* (Mgh) *called also* ▼ العُصْفُورُ الأَسْوَدُ, (Mgh, O,) *of such a size that it may be grasped in the hand, that eats grapes* (A, Mgh, O, TA) *and dates* (A, TA) *and locusts.* (Mgh, O, TA.)

سَوَادٌ *Blackness; contr. of* بَيَاضٌ; (M, Mgh;) *a certain colour,* (Ṣ, Mṣb,) *well known.* (Mṣb.) One says, لَقِيَهُ فِى سَوَادِ اللَّيْلِ [*He met him in the blackness of night*]. (TA.) And الشَّاةُ تَمْشِى فِى سَوَادٍ وَتَأْكُلُ فِى سَوَادٍ وَتَنْظُرُ فِى سَوَادٍ [*The sheep,* or *goat, walks in blackness, and eats in blackness, and looks in blackness*]; meaning the blackness of its legs and of its mouth and of what is around its eyes. (Mgh,* Mṣb.) And إِذَا كَثُرَ البَيَاضُ قَلَّ السَّوَادُ [*When whiteness becomes much, blackness becomes little*]; by whiteness meaning *milk;* and by blackness, *dates.* (TA.) — *Black clothing.* (Mgh in art. بيض. [See its contr. بَيَاضٌ.]) — [Hence,] سَوَادُ القَلْبِ (Ṣ, M, A, Ḳ) and ↓سَوَادَتُهُ (M) and ↓أَسْوَدُهُ and ↓سُوَدَاؤُهُ (Ṣ, M, Ḳ) and ↓سُوَيْدَاؤُهُ, (Ṣ, M, A, Ḳ,) the last a dim., (TA,) *The heart's core; the black,* or *inner, part of the heart:* or *a black thing in the heart:* or *the black clot of blood that is within the heart* [*resembling a piece of liver* (Zj in his "Khalḳ el-Insán")]: or *the heart's blood:* i. q. حَبَّتُهُ: (Ṣ, M, Ḳ, TA:) or, as some say, دَمُهُ. (M, TA.) One says, اِجْعَلْهُمْ فِى سَوَادِ قَلْبِكَ (A, TA) and ↓سُوَيْدَائِهِ (A) ‡ [*Place them in the inmost part of thy heart;* i. e. *give them the best,* or *most intimate, place in thy affections*]. (A, TA.) — سَوَادُ البَطْنِ signifies *The liver.* (L, TA.) — سَوَادٌ is also *syn. with* شَخْصٌ ‡ [as meaning *A person;* and also, in a more general sense, *a bodily,* or *corporeal, form* or *figure* or *substance*]; (A'Obeyd, Ṣ, M, A, Mṣb, Ḳ;) of a man, and of other things; (Mṣb;) expressly said by A'Obeyd to be of any article of household goods or utensils and furniture and the like, and of other things: (M:) because appearing black when seen from a distance: (TA:) pl. أَسْوِدَةٌ and أَسَاوِدُ, (Ṣ, M, A,) the latter a pl. pl. (Ṣ, M.) El-Aạshà says,

تَنَاهَيْتُمُ عَنَّا وَقَدْ كَانَ فِيكُمُ
أَسَاوِدُ صَرْعَى لَمْ يُوَسَّدْ قَتِيلُهَا

[*Ye refrained from* retaliating upon *us when there were among you prostrate persons the slain whereof had not been pillowed* in graves]: by the اساود meaning the شُخُوص of the slain. (Ṣ.) And it is said in a trad., إِذَا رَأَى أَحَدُكُمْ سَوَادًا بِلَيْلٍ فَلَا يَكُنْ أَجْبَنَ السَّوَادَيْنِ فَإِنَّهُ يَخَافُكَ كَمَا تَخَافُهُ [*When any one of you sees a bodily form,* or *a person, by night, let him not be the more cowardly of the two bodily forms,* or *persons; for he feareth thee, like as thou fearest him*]: سوادا here meaning شَخْصًا. (L.) The saying لَا يُزَايِلُ سَوَادِى بَيَاضَكَ is expl. by Aṣ as meaning لَا يُزَايِلُ شَخْصِى شَخْصَكَ [i. e. *My person will not separate itself from thy person*]: سَوَادٌ, with the Arabs, meaning شَخْصٌ, and in like manner بَيَاضٌ. (IAạr, L.) [Hence, app.,] قَالَ لِى الشَّرُّ أَقِمْ سَوَادَكَ [as though lit. signifying *Evil said to me, Erect thy person*]; meaning † *be thou patient:* a prov. (TA.) — As its pl. أَسَاوِدُ means the شُخُوص of the vessels of a house, [accord. to the statement of A'Obeyd cited above,] such as the مِطْهَرَة and the إِجَّانَة and the جَفْنَة, these being called أَسَاوِدُ الدَّارِ, it is also used as meaning † *Household goods* or *utensils* or *furniture* and *the like,* absolutely. (Ḥar p. 495.) [And in like manner] the sing. is also used as meaning † The *travelling-apparatus and baggage and train* (ثَقَل) of a commander: (Ṣ:) and † the *tents and apparatus and beasts and other things, collectively,* of an army. (TA.) — Also, the sing., † *Property,* or *cattle, &c.;* syn. مَالٌ: (Aboo-Málik, TA:) or *much thereof;* (A'Obeyd, Ṣ, Ḳ;) as in the saying لِفُلَانٍ سَوَادٌ [*To such a one belongs much property, &c.*]. (A'Obeyd, Ṣ.) — Also ‡ *A collection, company,* or *collective body,* of men; (M, A, L;) as in the saying كَثَّرْتُ سَوَادَ القَوْمِ بِسَوَادِى ‡ [*I increased the number of the collective body of the people,* or *party, by my person*]: (A, TA:) and ↓أَسْوِدَاتٌ and أَسَاوِدُ are used in the same sense; (M;) or [rather] as pls. of this meaning: (L, TA:) or all these as meaning † *sundry, distinct* or *separate, sorts* of men, or people: (M:) [but] سَوَادُ المُسْلِمِينَ means † *the collective body of the Muslims:* (Mgh, Mṣb:) and so السَّوَادُ مِنَ المُسْلِمِينَ, a tropical phrase [in which الأَعْظَمُ is understood]: (A:) or this means ‡ *the great number of the Muslims agreed in obedience to the Imám.* (TA.) † The *commonalty,* or *generality,* of men or people: (Ṣ, Ḳ:) † the *bulk,* or *main part,* of a people: (M, TA:) or † the *greater number.* (Mṣb.) And † *A great number* (Ṣ, Mṣb, Ḳ) of any kind. (Ṣ.) — † *A collection of palm-trees and of trees in general;* on account of their greenness and blackness, because greenness nearly resembles blackness. (M, L.) — And ‡ The *rural district* of any province; i. e. the *district around the towns* or *villages,* and the رَسَاتِيق [i. e. *districts of sown fields with towns* or *villages*], of any province: (M, TA:) or the *environs, consisting of towns,* or *villages, and of cultivated land,* (A, TA,) [but more properly applied to the latter than to the former,] of a city, (A,) or *of the chief city* of a province: (TA:) or the *towns,* or *villages,* [but properly *with the cultivated lands pertaining to them,*] of a province or city: (Ḳ:) thus [particularly] of El-Koofeh and El-Baṣrah: (Ṣ, O:) hence, (A,) سَوَادُ العِرَاقِ, (A, Mgh, O, Mṣb,) or [simply] السَّوَادُ, (Ḳ,) *the district of towns* or *villages, and cultivated lands, of El-'Irák;* (O, Ḳ;*) or *the district between El-Baṣrah and El-Koofeh, with the towns,* or *villages, around them;* (A;) or *extending in length from Ḥadeethet El-Mowṣil to 'Abbádán, and in breadth from El-'Odheyb to Ḥolwán;* (Mgh;) so called because of the خُضْرَة [which means both greenness and a colour approaching to blackness] of its trees and its seed-produce; (Mgh, Mṣb;) for that which is أَخْضَر the Arabs term أَسْوَد because it appears to be thus at a distance. (Mṣb.)

سِوَادٌ *Secret speech with another;* as also سُوَادٌ: (M, Ḳ, TA:) each a subst. from سَاوَدَهُ, accord. to A'Obeyd: (M, TA:) but [ISd says,] in my opinion the latter is the inf. n. of سَاوَدَ, [and as such it has been mentioned above, (see 3,)] and the former is the simple subst., the two words being like مِزَاحٌ and مُزَاحٌ: (M:) Aṣ disallowed the former, but it is authorized by AO and others. (TA.) ═ Also *A certain disease incident to sheep* or *goats.* (Ḳ.) — And *A certain disease incident to man;* (Ḳ;) *a pain that attacks the liver, in consequence of eating dates, and that sometimes,* or *often, kills.* (M, TA.) — And *A yellowness in the complexion, and a greenness* (خُضْرَة [app. here meaning *a blackish hue inclining to greenness*]) *in the nail,* (Ḳ, TA,) *incident to people from* [*drinking*] *salt water.* (TA.)

سَيِّدٌ, (Ṣ, M, Ḳ, &c.,) of the measure فَيْعِلٌ; [originally سَيْوِدٌ, for a reason to be mentioned below; the kesreh upon the و, being deemed difficult of pronunciation, is suppressed, and the quiescent و and ى thus coming together, the latter receives the rejected kesreh, and the و is changed into ى and incorporated into the augmentative ى; as in the case of جَيِّدٌ with those who hold it to be originally جَيْوِدٌ;] or, accord. to the Baṣrees, it is of the measure فَيْعَلٌ; [originally سَيْوَدٌ;] (Ṣ;) and also ↓سَيْدٌ; (Mz, 40th نوع, section on the class of هَيِّنٌ and هَيْنٌ;) *A chief, lord,* or *master:* (M, L, Mgh, Mṣb: [accord. to the last of which, this is a secondary signification, as will be seen below:]) *a prince,* or *king:* (Fr, L:) *one who is set before,* or *over, others:* *a master of a household:* (L:) a woman's *husband:* (Fr, M, Mṣb:) *a possessor, an owner,* or *a proprietor:* (L, Mṣb:) a slave's *master,* or *owner:* (Fr, M, Mṣb:) *a superior in rank* or *station* or *condition; one possessing pre-eminence* or *excellence; a man of rank* or *quality; a personage; a man of distinction:* (L:) *one who surpasses others in intelligence and property, and in repelling injury, and in beneficence,* or *usefulness, who makes a just use of his property, and aids others by himself:* (ISh, L:) *one possessed of glory, honour, dignity, eminence, exalted* or *elevated state,* or *nobility;* (L, Mṣb; [accord. to the latter of which, this is the primary signification;]) *generous, noble,* or *high-born:* (L:) the *most generous, noble,* or *high-born,* of a people: (Mṣb:) *a liberal, bountiful,* or *munificent, person:* (Fr, L:) *clement; forbearing; one who endures injurious treatment from his people:* (L:) *devout, abstaining from unlawful things, and clement,* or *forbearing:* (Ḳatádeh, L:) *one who is not overcome by his anger:* ('Ikrimeh, L:) accord. to Aṣ, the Arabs say that it signifies *any one who is subdued,* or *repressed, by his principle of clemency,* or *forbearance:* (L:) and ↓سَائِدٌ signifies the same as سَيِّدٌ: or *one inferior to a* سَيِّد: (Ḳ:) or, accord. to Fr, one says, هٰذَا سَيِّدُ قَوْمِهِ اليَوْمَ [*this is the lord, &c., of his people today*]; but if you announce that he will be their سيّد after a little while, you say هُوَ سَائِدُ قَوْمِهِ عَنْ قَلِيلٍ, and سَيِّدٌ: (Ṣ:) the fem. of سَيِّدٌ [and of ↓سَائِدٌ] is with ة: (M, L, Mṣb:) pl. of سَيِّدٌ, (Ṣ, Mṣb,) or of ↓سَائِدٌ, (M, Ḳ,) سَادَةٌ (Ṣ, M, Mṣb, Ḳ) and سَيَائِدُ (Ṣ, Ḳ) and [pl. of سَادَةٌ,] سَادَاتٌ: (Mṣb:) [J says that] سَادَةٌ is of the measure فَعَلَةٌ, [originally سَوَدَةٌ,] because سَيِّدٌ is of the measure فَيْعِلٌ; [as has been before mentioned;] and it is like سَرَاةٌ as pl. of سَرِىٌّ, the only other instance of the kind; this being shown to be the case by the fact that سَيِّدٌ has also as a pl. سَيَائِدُ, with ء, [and with the و changed into ى because it is so changed in the sing.,] like as أَفِيلٌ has أَفَائِلُ, and like as تَبِيعٌ has تَبَائِعُ; but the Basrees, who hold سَيِّد to be of the measure فَيْعِل, say that it becomes of the measure فَعَلَةٌ in the pl. as though it were سَائِدٌ, like قَائِدٌ, which has قَادَةٌ as a pl., and like ذَائِدٌ, which has ذَادَةٌ as a pl.; and they also say that سَيَائِدُ, with ء, as pl. of سَيِّدٌ, is contr. to analogy; for by rule it should be without ء. (Ṣ.) — [In the present day it is also particularly applied to signify, like شَرِيفٌ, Any *descendant of the Prophet*.] — One of the poets has used it in relation to the jinn, or genii; saying,

* جِنٌّ هَتَفْنَ بِلَيْلٍ * يَنْدُبْنَ سَيِّدَهُنَّهْ *

[*Genii that were roused* from their sleep *by night, summoning*, or perhaps *bewailing and eulogizing, their chief*]: Akh says that this is a well-known verse of the poetry of the Arabs: but it is asserted by one, or more, likewise deserving of reliance, that it is of the poetry of El-Weleed [and therefore post-classical]. (M.) — And the wild ass is called † the سَيِّد of his female. (TA.) — Also, (Ks, Ṣ, M, Mgh, Mṣb, Ḳ,) and ▼ سَيْدٌ, (Ḳ,) the latter on the authority of Aboo-'Alee, (TA,) applied to a he-goat, † *Advanced in years*: (Ks, Ṣ, M, Mgh, Mṣb, Ḳ:) or *in its third year*: (Mgh:) or *great*, though not advanced in years: (TA:) or it is of general application, for it occurs in a trad. applied to the camel and the ox-kind. (M, TA.) — And the former also signifies † *What is most eminent, exalted*, or *noble*, of any things: and is applied by Zj to the Ḳur-án, because, he says, it is سَيِّدُ الكَلَامِ † [*The paragon of speech*]. (M.)

سَيْدٌ: see the last sentence but one above.

سُوَيْدٌ the abbreviated dim. of أَسْوَدُ: (Ṣ, Mgh, Mṣb:) see the latter. — Also [as a subst., or an epithet in which the quality of a subst. predominates,] *Water*; (M, Mgh, L;) as also ▼ أَسْوَدُ: (M: [but see الأَسْوَدَانِ, voce أَسْوَدُ:]) the former is [said to be] used in this sense in negative phrases only: (M, L:) one says, مَا سَقَاهُمْ مِنْ سُوَيْدٍ قَطْرَةً *He gave them not to drink a drop of water*. (M, Mgh,* L.) — أُمُّ سُوَيْدٍ means *The anus*; syn. الإِسْتُ; (Ḳ;) [and] so ▼ السُّوَيْدَاءُ. (M.)

سُوَادَةُ القَلْبِ: see سَوَادٌ, near the beginning of the paragraph.

سَوَادِىٌّ [or perhaps سُوَادِىٌّ, i. e. "belonging to the Sawád of El-'Irák,"] i. q. سِهْرِيزٌ (M) *A well-known sort of dates*, (Ḳ voce سهريز,) *found in abundance at El-Basrah*. (TA ibid.)

سُوَادِيَّةٌ: see سُودَانِيَّةٌ.

سُوَيْدَاءُ dim. of سَوْدَاءُ, fem. of أَسْوَدُ, q. v.: (Mgh:) — see also سَوَادٌ, in two places: — and سُوَيْدٌ: — and أَسْوَدُ, near the end of the paragraph. — Also *A certain bird*. (M.) — And *Salt tracts* (سِبَاخ) of [plants of the kind called] نُجِيل: Kr explains it by نَبْتَة [app. a mistranscription for نَبْتَةٌ *a plant*]; without describing it. (M.)

سَائِدٌ: see سَيِّدٌ, in the middle of the paragraph, in three places.

أَسْوَدُ *Greater*, and *greatest, in respect of estimation, rank*, or *dignity*; syn. أَجَلُّ: (Ṣ, Ḳ:) and, as some say, *more* [and *most*] *liberal* or *bountiful* or *munificent*: or *more* [and *most*] *clement* or *forbearing*. (TA.) One says, هُوَ أَسْوَدُ مِنْ فُلَانٍ *He is greater* &c. (أَجَلُّ) *than such a one*. (Ṣ.) And الأَسْوَدُ مِنَ القَوْمِ means *The greatest* &c. (الأَجَلُّ) *of the people*, or *party*. (Ḳ, TA.) — Also *Black*; i. e. *having* سَوَاد, (M,* Mgh,) which is *the contr. of* بَيَاض: (M, Mgh:) and ▼ أُسْوُدِىٌّ signifies the same as أَسْوَدُ: (Ḥam p. 379:) [or has an intensive signification, like أَحْمَرِىٌّ:] the fem. of أَسْوَدُ is سَوْدَاءُ: (Mgh, Mṣb:) the dim. of أَسْوَدُ is ▼ أُسَيِّدٌ, (Ṣ, Mṣb,) and it is allowable to say ▼ أُسَيْوِدٌ, [as is shown by an ex. voce أَسَدٌ,] meaning [*a little black thing*; or *blackish*, or] *approaching to black*; (Ṣ;) and the abbreviated dim. is ▼ سُوَيْدٌ: (Ṣ, Mgh, Mṣb:) the dim. of سَوْدَاءُ is ▼ سُوَيْدَاءُ: (Mgh:) the pl. of أَسْوَدُ (M, Mṣb) and of سَوْدَاءُ (Mṣb) is سُودٌ (M, Mṣb) and سُودَانٌ [which latter is especially applied to human beings]. (M.) السُّودَانُ is said in the R to denote [*The negroes*;] *that particular people*, or *race, who are the most stinking of mankind in the armpits and sweat*, and the more so those who are eunuchs. (TA.) [It (i. e. السودان) is also sometimes used for بِلَادُ السُّودَانِ, or أَرْضُ السُّودَانِ, (*The land*, or *the country, of the negroes*,) or the like: it is thus used in the TA voce سُمْغُرَةٌ.] And the epithet أَسْوَدُ is also applied by the Arabs to a thing that is أَخْضَرُ [i. e. *green*]; because it appears to be thus at a distance. (Mṣb. [See أَخْضَرُ: and see حَدِيقَةٌ دَهْمَآءُ and مُدْهَامَّةٌ, voce أَدْهَمُ.]) — [Hence,] أَسْوَدُ القَلْبِ and سُوَيْدَاؤُهُ: see سَوَادٌ. — [And السَّوْدَاءُ *The black bile; one of the four humours of the body*; of which the others are the yellow bile (الصَّفْرَآءُ), the blood (الدَّمُ), and the phlegm (البَلْغَمُ).] — أَسْوَدُ as opposed to أَحْمَرُ [and meaning The *Arab race*, and also, accord. to some, in this case also, the *black*]: see أَحْمَرُ, in two places. — As applied to a certain bird: see سُودَانِيَّةٌ, in two places. — Also, as a subst., (Ṣ,) or an epithet in which the quality of a subst. predominates, (Sh, M,) so that it is used as a subst., (Sh, TA,) but imperfectly decl., (TA,) ‡ *A great serpent*, (Ṣ, M, Ḳ,) *in which is blackness*: (Ṣ, M:) *the worst and greatest and most noxious of serpents, than which there is none more daring, for sometimes it opposes itself to a company of travellers, and follows the voice, and it is that which seeks retaliation, and he who is bitten by it will not escape death*: (Sh, TA:) it is pluralized as a subst., (Sh, Ṣ, M,) its pl. being أَسَاوِدُ (Ṣ, M) and أَسَاوِيدُ and ▼ أَسْوَدَاتٌ: (M:) were it an epithet [used as such], its pl. would be سُودٌ: it is also called أَسْوَدُ سَالِخٌ, because it casts off its slough every year: you do not say أَسْوَدُ سَالِخٌ: (Ṣ:) the female is called ▼ أَسْوَدَةٌ, (Ṣ, M,) which is extr.; (M;) and to this the epithet سَالِخَةٌ is not applied. (Ṣ.) — الأَسْوَدَانِ means † *The serpent and the scorpion*; (Sh, Mgh, Mṣb, Ḳ;) which are to be killed during prayer: (Sh, Mgh, Mṣb:) so called by the attribution of predominance [to the former]. (Sh, TA.) — And ‡ *Dates and water*; (El-Ahmar, Aṣ, Ṣ, M, A, Mgh, Mṣb, Ḳ;) both together being thus called by a term which properly applies to one only, [acord. to some,] for [they say that] الأَسْوَدُ alone signifies *dates*, not water, and especially, or mostly, *the dates of El-Medeeneh*; and in like manner, Aboo-Bekr and 'Omar together are called العُمَرَانِ; and the sun and the moon together, القَمَرَانِ: (TA:) or, as some say, it means *water and milk*; and is applied by a rájiz to *water and the herb called* الفَثّ, of [the grain of] which bread is made, and is eaten [in time of dearth or drought]. (M, L.) See also سُوَيْدٌ. — Also † *The* حَرَّة [or *tract strewn with black and crumbling stones*] *and night*: (Ṣ, M, L:) so called because of their blackness. (M, L.) A party came as guests to Muzebbid El-Medenee, and he said to them, "There is nothing for you with us but the أَسْوَدَانِ:" and they replied, "Verily therein is a sufficiency: dates and water:" but he said, "I meant not that: I only meant the حَرَّة and the night." (Ṣ, M.) And as to the saying of 'Áisheh, that she was with the Prophet when they had no food, but only the أَسْوَدَانِ, which is expl. by the lexicologists as meaning dates and water, [and thus by Mṭr in the Mgh, ISd says,] in my opinion she only meant the حَرَّة and night. (M.) — هُوَ أَسْوَدُ الكَبِدِ [lit. *He is black-livered*] means ‡ *he is an enemy*: (A, TA:) and سُودُ الأَكْبَادِ means ‡ *enemies*. (M, A.) — You say also, جَآءَ فُلَانٌ بِغَنَمِهِ سُودَ البُطُونِ, and, in like manner, حُمْرَ الكُلَى, both meaning ‡ *Such a one brought his sheep, or goats, in a lean*, or *an emaciated, state*. (Aṣ, Ṣ, and A in art. حمر.) — And رَمَى بِسَهْمِهِ الأَسْوَدِ ‡ *He shot with his lucky arrow*, (A, Ḳ,) *that was smeared with blood*, (A,) *by means of which he looked for good fortune*, (Ḳ, TA,) because he had shot with it and hit the object shot at, (TA,) or as though it were black (Ḳ, TA) with blood, (TA,) or by its having been much handled. (Ḳ, TA.) — And كَلَّمْتُهُ فَمَا رَدَّ عَلَىَّ سَوْدَاءَ وَلَا بَيْضَاءَ ‡ *I spoke to him, and he did not return to me a bad word nor a good one*: (Ṣ, L:) or *a single word*. (A.) — وَطْأَةٌ سَوْدَاءُ means † *A footstep*, or *footprint, that is becoming effaced*: a recent one is termed حَمْرَاءُ. (Ṣ.) — السَّوْدَاءُ † *Cultivated*, or *planted, land*; opposed to البَيْضَاءُ [q. v.]. (TA in art. بيض. [See also سَوْدَةٌ.]) — [But سَنَةٌ سَوْدَاءُ means † *A very severe year; more severe than such as is termed* حَمْرَاءُ; which is more severe than the بَيْضَاءُ, and still more so than the شَهْبَاءُ: see arts. شهب and حمر.] — الحَبَّةُ السَّوْدَاءُ, said in a trad. to be a remedy for every disease except death, (TA,) i. q. الشُّونِيزُ [q. v.], (Ḳ,) as also ▼ حَبَّةُ السُّوَيْدَآءِ, (TA,) [i. e.] this latter signifies الشُّونِيز, (M,) or properly الشِّينِيز, for thus the Arabs called it accord. to IAạr: or, as some say, i. q. الحَبَّةُ الخَضْرَآءُ [q. v. in art. حب], because the Arabs [often] call black أَخْضَر, and green أَسْوَد. (TA.) ═ It is also used as an epithet denoting excess; but as such is anomalous, being formed from a verb whence the simple epithet is of the measure أَفْعَلُ: so in the saying, أَسْوَدُ مِنْ حَلَكِ الغُرَابِ [*Blacker than the blackness*, or *intense blackness, of the crow*, or *raven*: see حَلَكٌ]. (I'Aḳ p. 237. [See also its contr. أَبْيَضُ, voce بَيَاضٌ; and see Ḥar p. 286.])

أَسْوَدَةٌ fem. of أَسْوَدُ, q. v., used as a subst. (Ṣ, M.)

أَسْوِدَاتٌ: see سَوَدٌ: — and سَوَادٌ: — and أَسْوَدُ.

أُسْوُدِيٌّ: see أَسْوَدُ, fourth sentence.

أُسَيْدِيٌّ, rel. n. of أُسَيْدٌ with the movent ى rejected, *Of*, or *relating to*, [*a blackish colour*, or] *a colour approaching to black.* (Ṣ.)

أُسَيْدٌ and أُسْوُدٌ: see أَسْوَدُ, fourth sentence.

مِسْآدٌ, *A skin for clarified butter*, or *for honey.* (TA in this art. [See also art. مسد; and see مِسْأَدٌ, in art. سأد.])

مَسُودٌ One *over whom rule*, or *dominion, is exercised*; or *of whom another is* سَيِّد [or *chief, lord, master*, &c.]. (TA.)

مُسْوِدٌ [act. part. n. of أَسْوَدَ, q. v.:] with ة, i. e. مُسْوِدَةٌ, A woman *who brings forth black children*: the contr. is termed مُبِيضَةٌ, (Fr, Ḳ in art. بيض,) or, more commonly, مُوضِحَةٌ. (O and TA in that art.)

مَآءٌ مَسْوَدَةٌ *Water that is a cause of* [*the disease called*] سُوَاد (M, Ḳ, TA) *to such as drink it.* (TA.)

ظَلَّ وَجْهُهُ مُسْوَدًّا, in the Ḳur [xvi. 60 and xliii. 16], means † [*His face becomes*, or *continues*, or *continues all the day*,] *expressive of sorrow*, or *displeasure.* (Mgh. [See the verb, 9.]) And أَيَّامٌ مُسْوَدَّةٌ means † [*Days of*] *evil state* or *condition*, and *hardness*, or *difficulty, of living.* (Ḥar p. 304.) — [مُسْوَدَّةٌ The *first draught*, or *original copy, of a book*, or *the like*: (not called مُسَوَّدَةٌ:) opposed to مُبَيَّضَةٌ, q. v.: probably post-classical.]

مُسَوَّدٌ *Guts* (مُصْرَان) *containing blood drawn by venesection from a she-camel, bound at the head, roasted and eaten.* (IAạr and Ḳ as expl. by MF.)

المُسَوِّدَةُ *The partisans of the dynasty of the 'Abbásees*; [*so called because they made their clothes black*;] opposed to the مُبَيِّضَة. (Ṣ and Ḳ in art. بيض.)

مُسْوُودٌ part. n. of سِيدَ. (Ḳ. [See 1, last signification.])

سور

1. سَارَ, aor. يَسُورُ, (Ṣ, M, Ḳ,) inf. n. سُؤُورٌ, (Ṣ,) or سَوْرٌ, (M,) or both, (Ḳ,) or سَوْرَةٌ, (Mgh,) [but this last is an inf. n. of un.,] *He leaped* or *sprang*, (Ṣ, M, A, Mgh, Ḳ,) إِلَيْهِ *to*, or *towards, him*, (Ṣ, M, Ḳ,) and عَلَيْهِ *upon him.* (A.) — *He leaped*, or *sprang*, [or *committed an assault*, upon another,] *like as he does who behaves in an annoying manner towards his cup-companion in his intoxication.* (TA. [See also 3.]) — [Hence,] سَارَ الشَّرَابُ فِى رَأْسِهِ, (Ṣ, M, A, Ḳ,) inf. n. سَوْرٌ and سُؤُورٌ (M, Ḳ) and سُؤُورٌ, agreeably with the root, (M,) and سُوَارٌ, (TA,) ‡ [*The wine assaulted*, or *rushed into, his head*]: (A:) [or] *the wine circulated in his head, and rose into it*: (M, Ḳ:) or سَارَ الشَّرَابُ, inf. n. سَوْرٌ and سَوْرَةٌ, *the wine had an overpowering influence upon the head*: (Mṣb:) and سَارَتْ فِيهِ حُمَيَّا الكَأْسِ *the force* or *overpowering influence*, (سَوْرَة,) [or *fumes*,] *of the cup of wine mounted*, or *rose, to his head*, or *into his head.* (TA in art. حمى.) — And سار, aor. as above, † *He was angry.* (Mṣb.) — سار, aor. as above, inf. n. سَوْرٌ, also signifies *He* (a man) *rose*, or *became elevated.* (M.)

• سُرْتُ إِلَيْهِ فِى أَعَالِى السُّورِ •

means *I rose to him* [*upon the upper*, or *uppermost, parts of the wall* of the city or town &c.]. (TA.) — And one says to a man, سُرْ سُرْ [*Rise thou, rise thou*, to eminence,] in enjoining aspiration to the means of acquiring eminence, or nobility: (IAạr, Ḳ,* TA:) from سُرْتُ الحَائِطَ, meaning *I ascended*, or *mounted, upon the wall.* (TA.) — See also 5, in two places. ═ سُوِّرَ بِهِ: see 2 in art. سير.

2. [سَوَّرَ,] inf. n. تَسْوِيرٌ, *He walled* a city or town &c. (See 2 in art. خفر.)] — See also 5. ═ And سَوَّرْتُهُ, [inf. n. as above, (see an ex. voce دَهْقَنَ,)] *I put upon him* [or *decked him with*] *the* سِوَار [or *bracelet*; or *I decked him with bracelets*]. (Ṣ.)

3. مُسَاوَرَةٌ signifies The *leaping*, or *springing*, of two antagonists, *each upon the other*, or their *assaulting*, or *assailing, each other, in mutual fight.* (Ḥar p. 329.) — And سَاوَرَهُ, (Ṣ, M, Ḳ,) inf. n. مُسَاوَرَةٌ and سِوَارٌ, (M, Ḳ,) *He leaped*, or *sprang, upon him*; *he assaulted*, or *assailed, him*; syn. وَاثَبَهُ. (Ṣ, M, Ḳ.) You say, الحَيَّةُ تُسَاوِرُ الرَّاكِبَ [*The serpent springs upon*, or *assaults, the rider*]. (A.) And it is said in a trad. of 'Omar, فَكِدْتُ أُسَاوِرُهُ فِى الصَّلَاةِ, meaning *And I was near to leaping upon him*, or *assaulting him, and fighting him, during prayer.* (TA.) [See also 1.] You say also, سَاوَرَتْنِى الهُمُومُ ‡ [*Anxieties assaulted*, or *assailed, me*]. (A.) — Also i. q. أَخَذَ بِرَأْسِهِ [which, as it is mentioned immediately after سِوَار in the last of the senses assigned to that word below, is app. said of speech, or language, meaning † *It had an overpowering influence upon his head*]. (M, Ḳ.)

5. تَسَوَّرَهُ *He ascended*, or *mounted, upon it*; (namely, a wall;) as also ▼ سَارَهُ, inf. n. سَوْرٌ: (TA:) *he climbed, ascended*, or *scaled, it*, (namely, a wall,) *like a thief*; (IAạr, Ṣ,* M, A,* Ḳ,* TA;) as also تَسَوَّرَ عَلَيْهِ; (M;) and ▼ سَاوَرَهُ, inf. n. as above: (Ḳ:) *and he climbed*, or *ascended, and took, it*; as also تسوّر عليه, and ▼ سَوَّرَهُ: (TA: [this last from a trad., in which, however, the verb is, in my opinion, probably mistranscribed:]) *he climbed*, or *ascended, its* سُور [or *wall*]. (Bḍ in xxxviii. 20.) ═ And تَسَوَّرَ *He put on himself* [or *decked himself with*] *the* سِوَار [or *bracelet*; or *he decked himself with bracelets*]. (Ṣ.)

6. تَسَاوُرٌ signifies The *leaping*, or *springing, one with* [or *upon*] *another.* (KL. [See also 3.]) — And رَفَعْتُ لَهَا شَخْصِى means تَسَاوَرْتُ لَهَا [*I raised*, or *elevated, my person to her*, or *it*, or *them*; or *stretched myself up* &c.; like تَطَاوَلْتُ]. (TA.)

8. اِسْتَارَ: see اِشْتَرَى in art. سرو, from which it is formed by transposition.

سُورٌ The *wall* of a city [or town &c.]: (Ṣ, M, A, Mṣb, Ḳ:) [properly] masc.; but Ibn-Jurmooz, in a verse, makes it fem., because it is a part of the مَدِينَة: (M:) pl. أَسْوَارٌ (Ṣ, M, Mṣb, Ḳ) and سِيرَانٌ. (Ṣ, Ḳ.) — And The *upper*, or *uppermost, part* of the head; occurring in a trad., as some relate it; or, accord. to others, it is ▼ سَوْرَة; or شُؤُون, which is said by some of the later authors to be the reading commonly known. (TA.) ═ See also سُورَةٌ, in three places. ═ And see سِوَار. ═ Also *An entertainment of a guest or guests*; (Ḳ;) *a repast to which people are invited*: (Abu-l-'Abbás, TA:) a Pers. word, honoured by the Prophet; (Ḳ;) i. e. by his saying to his companions, as is related in a trad., قُومُوا فَقَدْ صَنَعَ جَابِرٌ سُورًا [*Arise ye, for Jábir has made an entertainment*, or *a repast*]. Abu-l-'Abbás, TA.) ═ [It is also the name of *A species of fig*, called by Forskål (Flora Aegypt. Arab., pp. cxxiv. and 180,) *ficus sur*, (not "mimosa sur," as in Freytag's Lex.,) observed by him at Jubleh, in El-Yemen.]

سَوْرَةٌ *A leap*, or *spring.* (TA.) — † The *assault* of wine *upon the head*; or its *rush into the head*: and in like manner, the *assault*, or *rush*, of venom, such as that of the scorpion: (Ṣ:) or the *force*, or *strength*, of wine &c.; (M, Ḳ, Mṣb, and MF voce حَدٌّ;) as also ▼ سُوَارٌ; (M, Ḳ;) and in like manner, of hunger: (Mṣb:) the *overpowering influence* of wine *upon the head*: (Mṣb:) or ▼ سُوَار signifies the *creeping* of wine *in the head*: and سَوْرَة is said to signify the *assault*, or *force*, or *intoxicating operation*, or *overpowering influence upon the head*, (حُمَيَّا,) *produced by the creeping* of wine, *in*, or *through, the drinker*: and in like manner, سُوَارُ ▼ فَرَحٍ means † *a motion of joy like the creeping of wine in the head.* (TA.) — [† *A paroxysm of fever.* — † *An ebullition, a fierceness*, or *an impetuousness*, of anger; as when] one says إِنَّ لِغَضَبِهِ لَسَوْرَةً † [*Verily his anger has an ebullition, a fierceness*, or *an impetuousness*]: (Ṣ:) [‡ *an outburst*, or *outbreak*, of anger: and] † *anger itself*: [or † *a fit of anger*, or *irritation*:] pl. سَوْرَاتٌ. (Mṣb.) — [† The *flush*, or *impetuosity*, of youth: see حَمِيًّا.] — *Impetuousness* in war. (A.) [It is said in the TA that فُلَانٌ ذُو سَوْرَةٍ فِى الحَرْبِ means ذُو نَظَرٍ شَدِيدٍ, i. e. *Such a one has strong inspection in war*: but I think that نَظَر is here a mistranscription for سَطْو, i. e. *impetuousness*.] — *Violence, force*, or *oppression, and tyranny*, of a Sultán: (Ṣ, Ḳ:) and *might*, or *valour*, (Mṣb, TA,) of a Sultán. (TA.) — † *Vehemence*, or *intenseness*, of cold: (Ḳ:) or *vehement*, or *intense, cold*. (M.) You say, أَخَذَتْهُ السَّوْرَةُ † *Intense cold seized him*. (TA.) — See also سُورَةٌ.

سُورَةٌ ‡ *Eminence*, or *nobility*: (Ṣ, A, Ḳ:) *rank* or *station*: (Ṣ, M, A, Ḳ:) or *high*, or *exalted, rank* or *station*: (Ibn-Es-Seed:) *excellence*: (A:) pl. سُوَرٌ and ▼ سُوْرٌ: [the latter of which is an anomalous pl.; or a coll. gen. n. of which سُورَةٌ is the n. of un., as in another sense mentioned below:] (M:) and سُوْرَةٌ, (M,) or ▼ سَوْرَةٌ, (Ḳ,) *a mark*, or *sign*, of glory, honour, dignity, or nobility; and *height* thereof. (M, Ḳ.) You say, لَهُ سُورَةٌ فِى المَجْدِ ‡ *He has eminence in glory*. (A.) And لَهُ سُورَةٌ عَلَيْكَ ‡ *He has superiority, and rank* or *station, over*, or *above, thee; he is of higher rank* or *dignity than thou*. (A.) And سُوَرٌ مِنَ الإِبِلِ, (M,) [in the A سُوَرُ الإِبِلِ,] or ▼ سُورٌ الإِبِلِ, (Ḳ,) means † *The excellent ones of camels*: (M, Ḳ:) sing. سُورَةٌ, which, accord. to some, signifies *hardy and strong*. (M.) — سُورَةٌ also signifies *What is goodly and tall, of structures*. (M, Ḳ.) — And The *extremity* (حَدّ) of anything. (IAạr, TA.) — See also سُورٌ. — Also *A row of stones or bricks of a wall*: (L, Ḳ: in the L, عِرْقٌ من عُرُوقِ الحَائِطِ: in the Ḳ, عِرْقٌ مِنْ أَعْرَاقِ الحَائِطِ, or, as in the CḲ, عِرْقُ الحائطِ:) *any degree of a structure*: (Ṣ:) (مَنْزِلَةٌ) pl. ▼ سُوَرٌ, (Ṣ, Ḳ,) [or this is a coll. gen. n.,] like as بُسْرٌ is of بُسْرَةٌ, (Ṣ,) and سُوَرٌ. (Ḳ.) — Hence its application in relation to the Ḳur-án, [to signify *A chapter* thereof,] because each of what are thus called forms one degree, or step, (Ṣ, M,* Ḳ,) distinct from another, (Ṣ, Ḳ,) or [leading] to another: (M:) or from the same word signifying "eminence:" (IAạr:) or as being likened to the wall of a city: (B:) some pronounce it with hemz; (see art. سأر;) but it is more common without: (TA:) pl. سُوَرٌ, (Ṣ, Mṣb,) and سُورَاتٌ and سُوَرَاتٌ are also allowable. (Ṣ.) — *A sign*, or *token*. (IAạr, M, Ḳ.) You say, بَيْنَهُمَا سُورَةٌ *Between them two is a sign*, or *token*. (IAạr, M.)

سُوَارٌ: see سُورَةٌ, in three places: — and see what here follows.

سِوَارٌ (Ṣ, M, Mṣb, Ḳ) and ▼ سُوَارٌ (M, Mṣb, Ḳ) and ▼ أُسْوَارٌ (Ṣ, MF, and others) and ▼ إِسْوَارٌ (M, Ḳ) *A woman's bracelet*, (Ṣ,* M, Mṣb,* Ḳ,) syn. قُلْبٌ, (M, Ḳ, [in the CḲ, erroneously, قَلْب,]) *of silver* or *of gold*; (Zj;) [and *a man's bracelet* also: see 2 and 5, and see also مُسَوَّرٌ:] all arabicized, from the Pers. دستوار [دَسْتْوَار or دِسْتْوَار or دَسْتَوَار]: (B, TA:) pl. [of pauc.] of سِوَارٌ, (Ṣ, M, Mṣb,) and of سُوَارٌ, (M,) أَسْوِرَةٌ, (Ṣ, M, Mṣb, Ḳ,) and (pl. pl., M) أَسَاوِرُ, (Ṣ, M, Ḳ,) accord. to Aboo-'Amr Ibn-El-'Alà pl. of إِسْوَارٌ, (Ṣ,) and أَسَاوِرَةٌ, (Ṣ, Mṣb, Ḳ,) also pl. of إِسْوَارٌ or أُسْوَارٌ, (M, TA,) or of أَسْوِرَةٌ, or perhaps of أَسَاوِرُ; (Ṣ;) and (pl. of mult., M) ▼ سُوْرٌ, (M, Mṣb, Ḳ,) originally سُوُرٌ, like كُتْبٌ pl. of كِتَابٌ, (Mṣb,) and سُؤُورٌ, (Ḳ, [in a copy of the M سُوُورٌ,]) said by Sb to be used by poetic license. (M, TA.)

سَوَّارٌ is an epithet applied to a dog [as meaning *Wont to spring* or *leap* or *assault*]. (A.) — And it signifies The *lion*; (TṢ, Ḳ;) because of his leaping, or springing; (TA;) as also ▼ مُسَاوِرٌ. (TṢ, TA.) — Also One *who is wont to leap* or *spring upon another*, or *to assault him*; (Ṣ;) *who behaves in an annoying manner towards his cup-companion in his intoxication*; (Ṣ, A, Mgh;) *who assaults* [or *insults*] *his cup-companion when he drinks*. (TA.) — † One *into whose head wine quickly rises*: (M, Ḳ:) as though it were he himself that rose. (M.) — And † Speech, or language, *that has an overpowering influence upon the head* (الَّذِى يَأْخُذُ بِالرَّأْسِ). (M, Ḳ.)

سُوَارَى *Height*: so expl. by Th as used in the saying,

* أُحِبُّهُ حُبًّا لَهُ سُوَارَى * كَمَا تُحِبُّ فَرْخَهَا الحُبَارَى *

[*I love him with a love that has height* (i. e. *rising to a high degree*), *like as the bustard loves her young one*]: meaning that the bustard is stupid, and, when she loves her young one, is excessive in stupidity. (M.)

أُسْوَارٌ: see the next paragraph: — and see also سِوَارٌ.

إِسْوَارٌ (Ṣ, M, Mṣb, Ḳ) and ▼ أُسْوَارٌ (Ṣ, M, Ḳ) The *leader of the Persians*; (M, A, Mṣb, Ḳ;) *like the* أَمِير *among the Arabs*: (Mṣb:) or *their greatest king*: arabicized [from the Pers. سُوَار]: (TA: [but said in the A to be tropical:]) or *a horseman of the Persians*, (A'Obeyd, Ṣ, TA,) *who fights*: (A'Obeyd, TA:) or *one who is firm on the back of his horse*: (Ḳ:) or *one who excels in sitting firmly on the back of his horse*: (M:) or (so in the M, but in the A and Ḳ "and") *one who is skilful in shooting arrows*: (M, A, Ḳ:) pl. أَسَاوِرَةٌ (Ṣ, M, A, Mṣb, Ḳ) and أَسَاوِرُ; (M, Ḳ;) in the former of which the ة is to compensate for the ى of the original form, which is أَسَاوِيرُ. (Ṣ.) — See also الخَضَارِمَةُ. — And see سِوَارٌ.

مِسْوَرٌ *A leathern pillow, upon which one leans*, or *reclines*; as also ▼ مِسْوَرَةٌ: (M, Ḳ:) pl. مَسَاوِرُ. (TA.)

مِسْوَرَةٌ: see what next precedes.

مُسَوَّرٌ [*Decked with a bracelet* or *bracelets*. And hence,] ‡ *Made a king* [or *chief*]. (A, TA. [See دِهْقَانٌ.]) — And The *place of the bracelet*; (M, Ḳ;) like as مُخَدَّمٌ signifies the "place of the خَدَمَة." (M.)

مُسَاوِرٌ: see سَوَّارٌ.

سوس

1. سَاسَ الدَّوَابَّ, aor. يَسُوسُ, (A, Mgh,) inf. n. سِيَاسَةٌ, (TA,) *He managed*, or *tended, the beasts, and trained them*. (قَامَ عَلَيْهَا) (Mgh, TA.) [And سَاسَ المَالَ *He managed*, or *tended, the camels* or *other property*. See سَائِسٌ.] — Hence, (Mgh,) سَاسَ الرَّعِيَّةَ, aor. and inf. n. as above, (Ṣ, A,* Mgh, Ḳ, &c.,) ‡ *He ruled*, or *governed, the subjects; presided over their affairs as a commander*, or *governor*, or *the like*; (Ṣ,* Mgh;) *he commanded and forbade them*. (A, Ḳ.) And سَاسُوهُمْ, inf. n. سَوْسٌ, ‡ *They were*, or *became, heads, chiefs, commanders*, or *the like, over them*. (TA.) One says, فُلَانٌ مُجَرَّبٌ قَدْ سَاسَ وَسِيسَ عَلَيْهِ (Ṣ, Ḳ) ‡ [*Such a one is experienced: he has ruled and been ruled*: or] *he has commanded and been commanded*: (Ṣ:) or *he has taught and been taught*; or *has disciplined and been disciplined*. (Ḳ.) — سَاسَ الأَمْرَ, aor. as above, inf. n. سِيَاسَةٌ, ‡ *He managed, conducted, ordered*, or *regulated, the affair*; syn. دَبَّرَهُ, (Mṣb,) and قَامَ بِهِ: (M, Mṣb, TA:) سِيَاسَةٌ signifies the *managing* a thing (قِيَامٌ عَلَى شَىْءٍ) *in such a manner as to put it in a right*, or *proper, state*. (TA.) [Used as a simple subst., the inf. n. may be rendered *Management, rule, government*, or *governance*.] — سَاسَ, aor. يَسَاسُ, (Ṣ, M, Ḳ,) and يَسُوسُ, (Ṣ, M, A, Ḳ,) aor. يَسَاسُ, (Ṣ, M, Ḳ,) and يَسُوسُ, (Kr, M,) inf. n. سَوْسٌ, (M,) or سُوْسٌ; (Ibn-'Abbád, Ḳ;) and سَوِسَ, aor. يَسْوَسُ; (Ḳ, TA; but the aor. is omitted in the CḲ;) or سَاسَ, aor. يَسُوسُ, inf. n. سَوْسٌ and سَاسٌ; and سَاسَ, aor. يَسُوسُ, inf. n. سُوسٌ; (Mṣb;) and سِيسَ; (Yoo, Ḳ;) and ▼ أَسَاسَ; and ▼ سَوَّسَ; (Ṣ, M, A, Mṣb, Ḳ; but the last is omitted in the TA;) and ▼ اِسْتَاسَ; and ▼ تَسَوَّسَ; (M, TA;) *It* (wheat, or other food, [&c.,]) *had in it*, or *became attached by*, [*the grub called*] سُوس; [*the grub called*] سُوس *fell upon it*, or *into it*. (Ṣ, M,* A,* Mṣb, Ḳ,* TA.) One says also, سَاسَتِ الشَّجَرَةُ, aor. تَسَاسُ, inf. n. سِيَاسٌ; and ▼ اساست; [*The tree had in it*, or *became attached by, the grub called* سُوس.] (AHn, M, TA.*) And سَاسَتِ الشَّاةُ, aor. تَسَاسُ, (Ṣ, M, Ḳ,) inf. n. سَوْسٌ, (Ṣ, Ḳ,) or سُوسٌ; (M;) and ▼ اساست, (Ṣ, M, Ḳ,) inf. n. إِسَاسَةٌ; (TA;) *The sheep*, or *goat, abounded with* قَمْل. (AZ, Ṣ, M, Ḳ. [In a copy of the Ṣ and in one of the Ḳ, I find قُمَّل: in another of the Ṣ and another of the Ḳ, and in the CḲ, and in a copy of the M, قَمْل: the right reading apears to be قُمَّل; for this last word is said by some to be syn. with سُوس.]) You also say, when you are gradually perishing by reason of grief, (إِذَا تَهَالَكْتَ) سَوَّسَ ▼ عَظْمِى وَدَوَّدَ لَحْمِى (غَمًّا) ‡ [*My bone has bred grubs, and so my flesh*]. (A.) — سُوِّسَتِ الدَّابَّةُ, inf. n. سَوْسٌ, *The beast was attached by the disease termed* سُوس [q. v. infrà]. (TḲ.)

2. سَوَّسُوهُ ‡ *They made him*, or *appointed him, ruler*, or *governor, over them*; (M,* TA;) as also ▼ اساسوه. (TA.) — سُوِّسَ الرَّجُلُ أُمُورَ النَّاسِ, (Ṣ, Ḳ,) or أَمْرَ النَّاسِ, (as in the TA,) or أَمْرَ قَوْمِهِ, (A,)

‡ *The man was made ruler of the affairs of the people;* (Ṣ;) [*or of the affairs of his people,* accord. as the phrase is given in the A:] or *was made king.* (Ḳ.) Accord. to a relation of a verse of El-Ḥoṭei-ah, he uses the expression سُوِّسْتَ أَمْرَ بَنِيكَ [as though meaning *Thou hast ruled the affairs of thy sons*]; but Fr says that سُوِّسْتَ is a mistake. (Ṣ. [Thus I find it in one copy of the Ṣ: but in another copy of the Ṣ, I find سُوِّسْتَ, which is clearly wrong; and in the TA, سُوِّسْتَ, which Fr can hardly be supposed to have disallowed.]) — سَوَّسَ لَهُ أَمْرًا † *He made an affair easy to him;* syn. رَوَّضَهُ and ذَلَّلَهُ. (TA.) You say, سَوَّسَ فُلَانٌ لَهُ أَمْرًا فَرَكِبَهُ † [*Such a one made an affair easy to him,* or, perhaps, *commended it to him by making it seem easy, and so he embarked in it,* or *undertook it*]: like as you say, سَوَّلَ لَهُ, and زَيَّنَ لَهُ. (AZ, Ḳ.*) — سَوَّسَ الْمَرْأَةَ *He slit the vulva of the woman.* (TA.) ═ See also 1, in two places.

4: see 2: ═ and see 1, in three places.

5: } see 1.
8: }

سَاسٌ : see سُوسٌ. — Also *A canker,* or *corrosion,* (قَادِحٌ,) *in a tooth:* (AZ, Ḳ:) without ء and without teshdeed. (AZ.) ═ And A tooth *that has been eaten,* or *corroded:* (L, Ḳ,* TA:) originally سَائِسٌ; like هَارٌ and هَائِرٌ. (Ḳ.) — See also مَسُوسٌ, in two places.

سُوسٌ [The *grub,* or *larva of the phalæna tinea* and *of the curculio;* i. e. the *moth-worm* and the *weevil;*] the *kind of worm that attacks wool* (Ṣ, A, Ḳ) *and cloths* (TA) *and wheat* or *other food:* (Ṣ, TA:) and with ة, [a n. un.,] *i. q.* عُثَّةٌ; (Mgh, Mṣb;) as also ↓ سَاسٌ; (TA;) i. e., *a worm that attacks wool and cloths* (Mgh, Mṣb) *and wheat* or *other food:* (Mgh:) and سُوسٌ, the *kind of worm* (M, Mṣb) *called* عُثٌّ, (M,) *that eats grain* (M, Mṣb) *and wood:* (Mṣb:) n. un. with ة: (M, Mṣb:) and *any eater of a thing* is termed سُوسَةٌ, *whether worm or other thing.* (M.) One says, الْعِيَالُ سُوسُ الْمَالِ † [*The persons who compose a household are the grubs of property*]: i. e., they consume it by little and little like as سُوس consume grain, which can scarcely be cleared of them when they attack it. (Mṣb.) ═ [The *licorice-plant;* so called in the present day;] *a kind of tree,* (AḤn, M, Ḳ,) or *plant,* (Mgh,) *well known,* (Mgh, Ḳ,) *with which houses are covered above the roofs,* (AḤn, M, Mgh,) *the expressed juice of which is an ingredient in medicine,* (AḤn, M,) *the leaves of which are put into* [*the beverage called*] نَبِيذ, *and make it strong like* [*the strong drink called*] دَاذِىّ, (Mgh,) *in the roots of which is sweetness* (AḤn, M, Ḳ) *intense in degree,* (AḤn, M,) *and in its branches is bitterness,* (AḤn, M, Ḳ,) *and it abounds in the countries of the Arabs:* (AḤn, M:) or *a kind of tree that grows in leaves without twigs:* (M:) or *a certain herb resembling* [*the species of trefoil called*] قَتّ. (TA.) [The root is vulgarly called, in the present day, عِرْقُ سُوس: and so is a strong infusion prepared from it, which is a very pleasant drink: and its inspissated juice is called رُبُّ السُّوسِ.] ═ *Nature; natural disposition:* (Ṣ, M, A, Ḳ:) and *origin.* (Ṣ, A, Ḳ.) One says, الفَصَاحَةُ مِنْ سُوسِهِ (Ṣ, M) *Chasteness of speech,* or *eloquence, is* [a quality] *of his nature.* (Ṣ.) And الكَرَمُ مِنْ سُوسِهِ (Lḥ, M, A) *Generosity is* [a quality] *of his nature.* (A.) And فُلَانٌ مِنْ سُوسِ صِدْقٍ *Such a one is of good origin.* (Ṣ.)

سَوَسٌ *A certain disease in the rump of a horse or similar beast,* (M, Ḳ, TA,) *between the hip and the thigh, occasioning, as its result, weakness of the hind leg:* (TA:) or *a disease that attacks the beast in its legs.* (M.) [See 1, last sentence.]

سَوَاسٌ *A certain kind of tree:* n. un. with ة: (M, Ḳ:) AḤn says, (M, TA,) on the authority of Aboo-Ziyád, (TA,) *it is of the kind called* عِضَاه, *resembling the* مَرْخ, *having a pericarp like that of the* مرخ, (M, TA,) *without thorns and without leaves, growing high; and persons shade themselves beneath it;* one of the Arabs said that it is *the same that is called* ↓ سَوَاسٍ (written with the article السَّوَاسِى); and AḤn says, I asked him respecting it, and he said that *this and the* مَرْخ *and the* مَتْخ *all three resemble one another;* (M;) *and it is one of the best of materials used for producing fire,* (Lth,* M, Ḳ,*) *not giving a sound without emitting fire,* (M,) or *because it seldom gives a sound without emitting fire.* (Lth, TA.)

سُوَاسٌ *A certain disease in the necks of horses, rendering them rigid,* (ISh, Ḳ, TA,) *so that they die.* (ISh, TA.)

سَوَاسٍ (with the article السَّوَاسِى): see سَوَاسٌ. ═ And for the same word, and سَوَاسِوَةٌ and سَوَاسِيَةٌ: see art. سوى.

سَائِسٌ [*A groom, who has the care and management of a horse* or *horses* or *the like;*] *one who manages,* or *tends, beasts* or *horses* or *the like, and trains them:* (TA:) pl. سَاسَةٌ and سُوَّاسٌ. (A.) And سَائِسُ مَالٍ [*A manager,* or *tender, of camels* or *cattle* or other *property*]. (Ḳ in art. ازى, &c.) — [And hence,] ‡ *A manager, a conductor, an orderer,* or *a regulater,* of affairs: pl. as above. (M, TA.)

أَسْوَسُ A beast *having the disease termed* سَوَسٌ. (Ḳ.) [Freytag, misled by an ambiguity in the Ḳ, assigns to it a signification belonging to سُوسٌ.] ═ Also, [or أُسْوُسٌ, unless originally an epithet,] *A kind of stone upon which is generated the salt called* زَهْرَةُ أُسْوُس: the author of the "Minháj" says that this may be caused by the moisture and dew of the sea falling upon it. (TA in art. سوس.)

طَعَامٌ مَسُوسٌ and ↓ مُسَوَّسٌ, (TA,) or ↓ مُسَوِّسٌ, [which is app. the more correct,] (Ṣ,) and ↓ سَاسٌ, (M,) *Wheat,* or *other food, attacked by* [*the grub called*] سُوس: (M, TA:) and ↓ حِنْطَةٌ مُسَوِّسَةٌ *wheat so attached.* (Mgh.) And أَرْضٌ مَسُوسَةٌ and ↓ سَاسَةٌ [*Land attacked by such grubs*], (M, TA,) in like manner. (TA.) And ↓ شَجَرَةٌ مُسِيسٌ [or مُسِيسَةٌ *A tree containing,* or *attacked by, such grubs*]. (TA.) And ↓ شَاةٌ مُسِيسٌ, (M,) or مُسِيسَةٌ, (TA,) *A sheep,* or *goat, abounding with* قَمْل [i. e. قُمَّل: see 1, near the end of the paragraph]. (M, TA.)

مُسِيسٌ : see مَسُوسٌ, in two places.

مُسَوِّسٌ and مُسَوَّسٌ : see مَسُوسٌ, in three places.

سوسن

سَوْسَنٌ, (M, Mṣb, Ḳ,) like جَوْهَرٌ [in measure], (Mṣb, Ḳ,) by the vulgar pronounced سُوسَنٌ, with damm to the first letter, (Mṣb, [and thus written in one of my copies of the Ṣ, in the other of those copies, and app. in most others, omitted,]) a Pers., or foreign, word, (أَعْجَمِىٌّ,) current in the language of the Arabs, (M,) [i. e.] an arabicised word, [app. from the Pers. سُوسَنْ, in Hebr. שׁוֹשַׁן,] (Ṣ,) [applied in the present day to The *lily:* and also the *iris:* and the *pancratium:* and app. to *other similar flowers:*] *a certain plant,* (M, Mṣb, Ḳ,*) *of sweet odour,* (Ḳ,) *resembling what are called* رَيَاحِين, *with broad leaves, but not having an odour that diffuses itself like the* رياحين; (Mṣb;) *it is well known, and of many kinds, the sweetest of which is the white:* (Ṣ: [but only, as mentioned above, in one of my two copies thereof:]) *there is a wild kind; and the garden-kind is of two sorts, namely, the* آزَاد, *which is the white, and the* إِيرِسَا, [i. e. *the iris,* in the CḲ, erroneously, آبُرسا,] *which is the* آسْمَانْجُونِى, [i. e. *azure-coloured,* from the Pers. آسْمَانْ كُونْ,] *beneficial as a remedy against the dropsy, an attenuant of thick matters; and the* آزاد *is of a delicate,* or *subtile, nature,* [so I here render لَطِيف, but it has other meanings,] *beneficial as a remedy for cold disorders in the brain, a discutient of the thick kinds of flatus that collect therein; its* أَصْل [app. here meaning *root*] *is a detergent of the skin, discutient; and its leaves are beneficial as a remedy against the burning of hot water, and against the sting of venomous reptiles or the like, and particularly of the scorpion:* the n. un. is with ة. (Ḳ.)

سوط

1. سَاطَهُ, [aor. يَسُوطُ,] (M,) inf. n. سَوْطٌ, (Ṣ, M, Ḳ,) *He mixed it,* (Ṣ, M, Ḳ,) *one part with another,* (Ṣ,) *and stirred it about, and beat it;* (M;) as also ↓ سَوَّطَهُ, (M, Ḳ,*) inf. n. تَسْوِيطٌ: (Ḳ:) or سَوْطٌ signifies the *putting together two things in a vessel, then beating them with the hand until they become mixed:* (Jm, Ḳ:) or, accord. to some, it relates particularly to a cooking-pot, when its contents are mixed: (M:) you say, سَاطَ قِدْرَهُ بِالْمِسْوَطِ [*he mixed, and stirred about, and beat, the contents of his cooking-pot with the* مِسْوَط, q. v.]: (TA:) but you say also, سَاطَ الهَرِيسَةَ, and ↓ سَوَّطَهَا, *he stirred about the* [*food called*] هريسة *with a piece of wood, in order that it might become mixed:* (TA:) or ↓ سَوَّطَهُ signifies *he mixed it much.* (Ṣ.) — [Hence,] سِيطَ حُبُّكَ بِدَمِى and مِنْ دَمِى † [*The love of thee is*

mixed with my blood]. (TA.) And هُوَ يَسُوطُ الأَمْرَ † *He turns over the affair* [*in his mind*]. (TA.) And فُلَانٌ يَسُوطُ الحَرْبَ and ▼ يَسُوطُهَا † *Such a one superintends, manages,* or *conducts, in person, the war.* (A, TA.) And سَوَّطَ ▼ فُلَانٌ أُمُورَهُ, inf. n. as above, (Ṣ, TA,) ‡ *Such a one rendered his affairs confused,* or *disordered,* or *perplexed:* (TA:) and in like manner, رَأْيَهُ [*his opinion*]. (M.) And سَوَّطَ ▼ أَمْرَهُ ‡ *He created confusion,* or *disorder, in his affair,* or *case.* (Ḳ, TA.) ══ سَاطَهُ, (M,) aor. يَسُوطُ, (Ṣ,) inf. n. سَوْطٌ, (M, Ḳ,) *He whipped him; struck him with a* سَوْط; (Ṣ, M, Ḳ;) namely, a beast, and a man. (TA.) —— سَاوَطَنِى فَسُطْتُهُ: see 3.

2: see 1, in six places. ══ سَوَّطَ الكُرَّاثُ, (M, Ḳ,) inf. n. تَسْوِيطٌ, (Ḳ,) ‡ *The leeks put forth their* سِيَاط [or *seed-stalks:* see سَوْطٌ]. (M, Ḳ, TA.)

3. ▼ سَاوَطَنِى فَسُطْتُهُ, aor. of the latter أَسُوطُهُ: thus mentioned by Lḥ, without any addition: app. meaning *He acted roughly with me with his whip,* or *he contended with me therewith, and I overcame him* [*with my whip*]: a mode of expression which is rare in relation to substances; rather relating to accidents, or attributes. (M.)

8. اِسْتَوَطَ, which is extr., [for by rule it should be اِسْتَاطَ,] *It* (a thing) *was,* or *became, mixed.* (M.) —— [Hence,] اِسْتَوَطَ عَلَيْهِ أَمْرُهُ ‡ *His affair,* or *case, was,* or *became, confused,* or *disordered, to him.* (M, Ḳ,* TA.)

سَوْطٌ [*A whip;*] *a certain thing,* (Ṣ, M,) namely, *plaited skin,* (Bḍ in lxxxix. 12,) [or *a lash,*] *with which one beats,* or *strikes,* (Ṣ, M,) *well known;* (Mṣb;) *i. q.* مِقْرَعَةٌ: (Ḳ:) so called because it mixes the flesh with the blood (IDrd, M, Ḳ) when a man or a beast is struck with it; (IDrd, TA;) or because its several component parts are mixed together: (Bḍ, ubi suprà:) pl. [of pauc.] أَسْوَاطٌ and [of mult.] سِيَاطٌ: (Ṣ, M, Mṣb, Ḳ:) the latter originally سِوَاطٌ. (TA.) The saying ضَرَبْتُ زَيْدًا سَوْطًا means ضَرَبْتُ زَيْدًا بِسَوْطٍ [*I struck Zeyd with a whip*]: (M, Mṣb:*) or it is one of those rare instances in which a prefixed n. is suppressed; being originally ضَرَبْتُهُ ضَرْبَةَ سَوْطٍ [*I struck him a stroke,* or *lash, of a whip*], meaning ضَرْبَةً بِسَوْطٍ [*a stroke,* or *lash, with a whip*]: (M:) or ضَرْبَةً وَاحِدَةً بِسَوْطٍ [*one stroke,* or *lash, with a whip*]. (Mgh.) One says also, ضَرَبَهُ مِائَةَ سَوْطٍ [*He struck him a hundred strokes,* or *lashes, of the whip*]. (Ṣ and Ḳ in art. سحل.) —— In the Ḳur [lxxxix. 12], where it is said, فَصَبَّ عَلَيْهِمْ رَبُّكَ سَوْطَ عَذَابٍ, (Ṣ, Mṣb,) it signifies ‡ *A portion,* or *share:* (Ṣ, Ḳ:) or (Ṣ, Mṣb, but in the Ḳ, "and") ‡ *vehemence,* or *severity;* (Ṣ, Mṣb, Ḳ;) as being likened to the paining of a whip; (Mṣb;) because punishment is sometimes with the سَوْط; (Ṣ;) and this word is used by the Arabs to denote every kind of punishment when it is extreme, though there be in it no beating: (Fr:) [therefore,] the above-cited saying in the Ḳur means, ‡ [*And thy Lord poured upon them a portion,* or *a share,* or *vehemence,* or *severity, of punishment:* or it means,] *a mixture,* prepared for them, *of various punishments:* or it is designed to show that what befell them in the present world was, in comparison with what is prepared for them in the final state, like the whip in comparison with the sword: (Bḍ:) or the meaning is † *a kind of punishment.* (Jel.) [Agreeably with this last explanation, it is said that] the phrase هُمَا يَتَعَاطَيَانِ سَوْطًا وَاحِدًا means ‡ *They two are agreed upon one mode:* (A:) or the meaning is ‡ [*they two enter,* or *plunge, into;* or *venture boldly upon, and do;*] *one thing,* or *affair;* (Ṣ, and Ḳ; but wanting in one copy of the former; and in the latter, in the place of هما is put ما;) i. e., *one sort* [*of thing* or *affair*]. (Ṣ.) —— [قِيدُ سَوْطٍ *The measure of a whip,* i. e. *a whip's length,* is an astronomical measure, which seems, from several instances that I have noted, in the work of Ḳzw &c., to be the same as رُمْحٌ is in modern usage; i. e. *four degrees and a half,* by rule; but, like the latter, not precise nor uniform in every instance.] —— [The pl.] سِيَاطٌ also signifies ‡ The *seed-stalks of leeks;* (TḲ;) the *stalks, of leeks, upon which are the* زَمَالِيق *thereof:* (M, Ḳ:) so called as being likened to the سِيَاط with which one strikes. (M.) —— And سَوْطٌ signifies also ‡ *A remaining portion* (A, Ḳ) *of water,* (A,) or *of a pool of water left by a torrent,* (Ḳ, [in some copies of which الغَدِيل is erroneously put for الغَدِير,]) *extended like the* سَوْط [*with which one strikes*]: (A:) pl. سِيَاطٌ. (TA.) —— And † *A place where water collects and stagnates:* (Ḳ:) pl. أَسْوَاطٌ. (TA.) —— And ‡ *A road,* or *track, of little width, between two elevations:* pl. أَسْيَاطٌ [or سِيَاطٌ?] and أَسْوَاطٌ: so in the A: but some say شَوْطٌ, q. v. (TA.) —— Also † *A kind of tent, of* [*goats'*] *hair.* (Ibn-El-Kelbee, TA voce بَيْتٌ, q. v.) —— And سَوْطُ بَاطِلٍ ‡ *Light entering from an aperture in a wall, in sunshine;* (Ḳ, TA;) also termed خَيْطُ بَاطِلٍ: but as some say, with ش. (TA: and it is mentioned with ش in art. شوط in the Ṣ, and again in the Ḳ.)

سُوَيْطٌ; fem. with ة: see مَسُوطٌ.

سَوَّاطٌ The شُرْطِىّ [or *officer of the prefect of police*] *who has with him the* سَوْط [or *whip*]. (TA.)

مَسُوطٌ *Mixed.* (TA.) So in a trad. of 'Alee with Fáṭimeh, [in which the former expresses the intimacy of her union with him, as though they two were one person,] مَسُوطٌ لَحْمُهَا بِدَمِى وَلَحْمِى † *Her flesh is blended and mixed with my blood and my flesh.* (TA.) You say also, أَمْوَالُهُمْ ▼ سُوَيْطَةٌ بَيْنَهُمْ *Their possessions are mixed among them;* (AZ, Ṣ, Ḳ;) *i. q.* ▼ مُسْتَوِطَةٌ. (M.)

مِسْوَطٌ: see what next follows.

مِسْوَاطٌ *A thing with which one mixes a thing,* (Ṣ,* M, Ḳ,) *and stirs it about;* (M;) i. e., *a stick,* or *the like, used for that purpose;* as also ▼ مِسْوَطٌ. (Ḳ.) ══ A horse *that will not put forth his power of running unless by means of the whip;* (Ibn-'Abbád and Ḳ; and so in a copy of the Ṣ, on the authority of AO, but omitted in another copy;) *as though* (TA) *keeping it in store.* (Ṣ, TA.)

مُسْتَوِطٌ; fem. with ة: see مَسُوطٌ.

سوع

1. سَاعَتِ الإِبِلُ, aor. تَسُوعُ, (Ṣ, Ḳ,) inf. n. سَوْعٌ, (Ṣ,) *The camels were left to themselves,* (Ṣ, Ḳ,) *without a pastor;* (Ḳ;) as also سَاعَت with تَسِيعُ for its aor. and سَيْعٌ for its inf. n. (Sh.)

3. عَامَلَهُ مُسَاوَعَةً [*He bargained with him for work by,* or *for, the hour,*] is from السَّاعَةُ, like مُيَاوَمَةٌ from اليَوْمُ. (Ṣ, Ḳ. [See also the last sentence of the second paragraph of art. سعى.]) [It is added in the Ṣ, that neither of them is used otherwise than thus: but accord. to SM one says also,] سَاوَعَهُ, inf. n. سِوَاعٌ, *He hired him,* or *took him as a hireling, for the hour.* (TA.)

4. أَسَاعَهُ *He left to himself,* or *itself, left alone,* or *neglected,* and *lost,* or *destroyed, him,* or *it.* (Ḳ.) Er-Rághib says, [but why, I do not well see,] that the meaning of neglecting, or the like, is imagined as derived from السَّاعَةُ. (TA.) You say, أَسَعْتُ الإِبِلَ *I left the camels to themselves, left them alone,* or *neglected them.* (Ṣ.) And رُبَّ نَاقَةٍ تُسِيعُ وَلَدَهَا حَتَّى تَأْكُلَهُ السِّبَاعُ, meaning [*Scarce,* or *many, a she-camel*] *leaves to itself,* or *leaves alone,* or *neglects, her young one* [*so that the beasts of prey devour it*]. (TA.) [See also 4 in art. سيع.] ══ أَسْوَعَ *He* (a man, Zj) *passed from* سَاعَة *to* سَاعَة [i. e. *time to time,* or *hour to hour*]; (Zj, Ḳ;) as also اساع, inf. n. إِسَاعَةٌ: (Zj, TA:) or *he remained behind,* or *held back,* or *delayed, for a* سَاعَة [i. e. *a time,* or *an hour*]. (Ibn-'Abbád, Ḳ.)

سَاعٌ: see سَاعَةٌ, in two places.

سَوْعٌ and ▼ سُوَاعٌ *i. q.* هَدْءٌ, as used in the phrase, جَآءَنَا بَعْدَ سَوْعٍ مِنَ اللَّيْلِ [*He came to us after a period,* or *portion, of the night;* or *after about a third or fourth part of the night had elapsed, when men were asleep,* or *at rest, and the night, and the foot of the passenger, were still;* or *after a third part of the night*]: (Ṣ, Ḳ:*) or this phrase means *he came to us after a* سَاعَة [i. e. *a short period,* or *an hour,*] *of the night.* (TA.).

سَاعَةٌ [*An hour;*] *one of the divisions of the night and the day;* (Lth, Ḳ, TA;) *both of which together consist of four and twenty of those divisions; each of them, when they are of equal length, consisting of twelve such divisions;* (TA;) [also termed سَاعَةٌ فَلَكِيَّةٌ (*an astronomical hour; fifteen* دَرَجَات *of time; sixty minutes of time;*) because سَاعَة alone is often used in a vague sense, as meaning what is termed سَاعَةٌ زَمَانِيَّةٌ; i. e.] *a time of night* or *of day:* but used absolutely by the Arabs as meaning *a time; a while; a space,* or *period; an indefinite* [*short*] *time;* and *a little while;* (Mṣb;) *a* [*short* or] *little portion,* or *division,* [or *space,* or *period,*] *of the night* and *of the day:* (TA:) and السَّاعَةُ signifies the present time: (Ṣ, Ḳ:) pl. سَاعَاتٌ and ▼ سَاعٌ, (Ṣ, Mṣb, Ḳ,) [or the latter is rather a coll. gen. n. of which ساعة is the n. un.,] and سِوَاعٌ. (Mṣb.) It is used unrestricted in the Ḳur [vii. 32 and in other places], where it is said, لَا يَسْتَأْخِرُونَ سَاعَةً (Mṣb) *They will not remain behind* (Bḍ) *for a time,* or *any while,* (Mṣb,) or *the shortest time:* or *they shall not seek to remain behind,* by reason of intense terror. (Bḍ.) And so in a trad., where it is said, مَنْ رَاحَ فِى السَّاعَةِ الأُولَى *Whoso goeth in the first time;* not in the first astronomical ساعة, for then it would necessarily mean that he who should come in the latter part thereof would be on a par with the former person, which is not the case. (Mṣb.) [سَاعَةً signifies, as shown above, *For,* or *during, an hour:* and *awhile; for a little while; during a short time;* as in the phrase,] جَلَسْتُ عِنْدَكَ سَاعَةً *I sat with thee,* or *at thine abode, for a little while,* or *during a short time.* (TA.) [And فِى سَاعَةٍ, *In a short time: in a moment.* And السَّاعَةَ, *Now: just now: this moment.* And سَاعَتَئِذٍ, *Then; at that time:* or *in that hour.*] And مُذْ سَاعَةٍ [*A little while ago;*] *in the first time near to us:* (Ḳ in art. انف:) or this signifies السَّاعَةَ [expl. above]. (Zj, T and M in art. انف.) [And مِنْ سَاعَتِهِ *At the moment thereof; instantly.* Hence, سَمُّ سَاعَةٍ *An instantaneous poison.*] — السَّاعَةُ also signifies ‡ *The resurrection;* (Ṣ, Ḳ, TA;) *the raising of mankind for the reckoning;* also termed السَّاعَةُ الكُبْرَى: (Er-Rághib, B:) or *the time thereof:* (Ḳ:) because of the quickness with which its reckoning will be accomplished: (TA:) or because it will come suddenly upon mankind, in a moment, and all creatures will die at one cry. (Zj, Az, TA.) Hence, in the Ḳur [liv. 1], اِقْتَرَبَتِ السَّاعَةُ ‡ *The resurrection* [or *the time thereof*] *hath drawn nigh.* (Jel, TA.) And [in vii. 186 and lxxix. 42,] يَسْأَلُونَكَ عَنِ السَّاعَةِ ‡ *They ask thee concerning the resurrection* [or *the time thereof*]. (Bḍ, Jel, TA.) And [in xxxi. last verse and xliii. 85,] عِنْدَهُ عِلْمُ السَّاعَةِ ‡ *With Him is the knowledge of the resurrection,* (TA,) or *of the time thereof.* (Bḍ, Jel.) — Also † *The death of one generation;* termed, for distinction, السَّاعَةُ الوُسْطَى: as in the saying of Moḥammad, when he saw 'Abd-Allah Ibn-Uneys, إِنْ يَطُلْ عُمْرُ هٰذَا الغُلَامِ لَمْ يَمُتْ حَتَّى تَقُومَ السَّاعَةُ † [*If the life of this boy last long, he will not die until the death of the generation shall come to pass*]: accordingly it is said that he was the last that died of the Companions. (Er-Rághib, B.) — Also † *The death of any man;* termed, for distinction, السَّاعَةُ الصُّغْرَى: as in the Ḳur [vi. 31], قَدْ خَسِرَ الَّذِينَ كَذَّبُوا بِلِقَآءِ اللّٰهِ حَتَّى إِذَا جَآءَتْهُمُ السَّاعَةُ بَغْتَةً † [*They have suffered loss who disbelieved in, or denied as false, the meeting with God until, when death came to them suddenly*]. (Er-Rághib, B.) — Also † *Difficulty, distress,* or *affliction;* and so ▼ السَّاعُ. (TA.) — And † *Distance,* or *remoteness.* (TA.) = See also سَائِعٌ.

سَاعَةٌ سَوْعَآءُ *A severe, grievous,* or *distressing* [*hour* or *time*]; (Ṣ, Ḳ;) like the phrase لَيْلَةٌ لَيْلَآءُ. (Ṣ.)

سُوَاعٌ: see سَوْعٌ. = Also, (Ṣ, Ḳ, [in the CḲ erroneously without tenween,]) and سَوَاعٌ, (Kh, Ḳ,) *A certain idol* (Ṣ, Ḳ) *which belonged to the people of Noah,* (Ṣ,) *in whose time it was worshipped; then the deluge buried it, but Iblees exhumed it, and it was worshipped* [*again*]; (Ḳ;) so says Lth; (TA;) *then it became the property of* [*the tribe of*] *Hudheyl,* (Ṣ, Ḳ,) *and was at Ruhát,* (Ṣ,) *and pilgrimage was performed to it:* (Ṣ, Ḳ:) or *it belonged to* [*the tribe of*] *Hemdán:* (Bḍ, TA:) Abu-l-Mundhir says, I have not heard the mention of it in the poems of Hudheyl: but one of the Arabs, in verse, mentions Hudheyl as paying devotion to it: (TA:) it is said that *it had the form of a woman:* (Ḥar p. 362:) [if so, as a fem. proper name, it would be without tenween: but] it is mentioned in the Ḳur [lxxi. 22, and is there with tenween]. (TA.) [See also وَدٌّ.]

هُوَ ضَائِعٌ سَائِعٌ *He is left to himself, left alone,* or *neglected.* (Ṣ,* Ḳ,* TA.) ▼ سَاعَةٌ [is pl. of سَائِعٌ; and also signifies] *In a state of perdition* or *destruction; perishing;* or *dying; in a pl. sense;* like جَاعَةٌ as signifying جِيَاعٌ, (Ḳ,) and طَاعَةٌ as signifying مُطِيعُونَ. (TA.)

مُسِيعٌ: see the following paragraph.

مِسْيَاعٌ A she-camel *that leaves her young one so that the beasts of prey devour it:* (Sh, Ḳ:) or a she-camel *that goes away in the place of pasturing:* (Ṣ:) belonging to this art. and to art. سيع, q. v. (Ḳ.) You say also, رَجُلٌ مِضْيَاعٌ مِسْيَاعٌ لِلْمَالِ [*A man who is wont to neglect the camels* or *the like; or to leave them to themselves,* or *alone;* or *to lose them*]; and accord. to A'Obeyd, مُضِيعٌ ▼ مُسِيعٌ. (Ṣ.)

سوغ

1. سَاغَ, (Ṣ, Mgh, Mṣb, Ḳ,) or سَاغَ فِى الحَلْقِ, (JK,) aor. يَسُوغُ, (Ṣ, Mṣb,) inf. n. سَوْغٌ (JK, Ṣ, Mgh, Mṣb, Ḳ) and سُوَاغٌ, or سَوَاغٌ, accord. to different copies of the Ḳ, (TA,) or سَوَغَانٌ, (CḲ, [not in my MS. copy of the Ḳ nor in the TA,]) and مَسَاغٌ, (MA,) *It* (beverage, or wine, JK, Ṣ, Ḳ, or food, Mgh, or each of these, TA) [*was easy and agreeable to swallow;*] *was easy of entrance into the fauces;* (Ṣ, Mgh, Mṣb, Ḳ;*) or *passed the fauces easily and agreeably.* (Bḍ in xiv. 20.) [See an ex. in a verse cited voce خَمِيرٌ.] — [Hence,] one says, ▼ سُغْ فِى الأَرْضِ مَا وَجَدْتَ مَسَاغًا † *Enter thou into the land while thou findest a place of entrance.* (TA.) — And سَاغَ فِعْلُ الشَّىْءِ ‡ *The doing of the thing was allowable;* or *passed for lawful.* (Mṣb.) And سَاغَ لَهُ مَا فَعَلَ ‡ *What he did was allowable to him;* or *passed for lawful to him.* (Ṣ, Ḳ, TA.) — And سَاغَ النَّهَارُ ‡ *The day was,* or *became, easy.* (TA.) — سَاغَتْ بِهِ الأَرْضُ, (Ḳ,) inf. n. سَوْغٌ, (TA,) i. q. سَاخَتْ † [*The ground,* or *earth, sank with him;* or *sank with him and swallowed him up,* or *enclosed him*]. (AA, Ḳ, TA.) — And سَاغَتِ النَّاقَةُ † *The she-camel became apart,* or *alone,* syn. شَذَّتْ, (Ḳ, TA,) or *ran,* syn. شَدَّتْ, (JK, and so in the CḲ and in my MS. copy of the Ḳ,) *and went far away.* (JK, TA.) = See also 4, in two places.

2. [سَوَّغَهُ is app., in its primary sense, *syn.* with أَسَاغَهُ: and hence what here follows.] — You say, سَوَّغَهُ مَا أَصَابَ, (JK, TA,) inf. n. تَسْوِيغٌ, (JK,) † *He made pleasant,* or *agreeable, to him what he attained:* or, as some say, *he left clear to him what he had attained.* (TA.) — And سَوَّغَهُ, (inf. n. as above, Ḳ,) ‡ *He made it allowable, lawful,* or *free,* (Ṣ, Mṣb, Ḳ,) لَهُ *to him.* (Ṣ.) And سَوَّغَهُ مَالًا ‡ [*He made property allowable,* &c., *to him*]: so in the "Mufradát." (TA.) — And سَوَّغَ لَهُ كَذَا † *He gave him such a thing.* (IDrd, Ḳ.) — [See also تَسْوِيغَاتٌ, below.]

4. اساغهُ, (JK, Mṣb,) inf. n. إِسَاغَةٌ, (JK,) or إِسَاغٌ, (Mṣb,) said of God, (JK,) or of a man, (Mṣb,) [*He made it easy and agreeable to swallow;*] *he made it easy of entrance into the fauces;* (Mṣb;) [or *made it to pass the fauces easily and agreeably;*] namely, beverage [&c.: see 1, first sentence]; (JK;) as also ▼ سَاغَهُ. (Mṣb.) — [Hence,] أَسِغْ لِى غُصَّتِى [*Make thou easy to me to swallow the thing that is choking me;* or *let me swallow it;*] meaning † *grant thou to me some delay,* or *respite;* or *act gently,* or *in a leisurely manner, towards me,* or *with me;* (Ṣ, Ḳ;) and *do not hurry me.* (Ṣ.) — And أَسَغْتُهُ, (Ṣ, Mgh, Mṣb,) inf. n. as above, (Ṣ, Mṣb, TA,) *I swallowed it:* (Mṣb, and Jel in xiv. 20:) or *I received it into my fauces easily* (Ṣ, Mgh, and Bḍ in xiv. 20) *and agreeably;* (Bḍ ibid.;) namely, beverage, or wine, (Ṣ, Ḳ,) or food, (Mgh,) or each of these; (TA;) and ▼ سُغْتُهُ and سِغْتُهُ, aor. أَسُوغُهُ and أَسِيغُهُ, (Ṣ, Ḳ,) inf. n. سَوْغٌ and سَيْغٌ, (TA in art. سيغ,) signify the same. (Ṣ, Ḳ.) — اساغ فُلَانٌ بِفُلَانٍ means † *Such a one completed his affair by means of such a one,* (Ibn-Buzurj, Ḳ, TA, [in the CḲ, ثُمَّ أَمْرُهُ بِهِ is erroneously put for تَمَّ أَمْرُهُ بِهِ,]) *and accomplished the object of his want by means of him:* (Ibn-Buzurj, TA:) the case is that of one's desiring a certain number of men or of pieces of money of which one remains to complete the affair: when he obtains it, one says, اساغ بِهِ. (Ibn-Buzurj, Ḳ.) = أَسْوَغَ أَخَاهُ *He* (a man, Lḥ) *was born with his brother:* (Lḥ, Ḳ:) or *he was born* [*next,* or *immediately,*] *after his brother.* (Ibn-'Abbád, Ḳ.) [See what next follows.]

هٰذَا سَوْغُ هٰذَا and سَيْغُهُ (Ṣ, Ḳ) and ▼ سَوْغَتُهُ (Ḳ) mean ‡ *This is he who was born next after this,* (Ṣ, Ḳ, TA,) or, as in the "Mufradát," *immediately after this;* (TA;) and the like is also said of the female: (Ḳ:) one says, هِىَ أُخْتُهُ سَوْغُهُ and ▼ سَوْغَتُهُ [*She is his sister that was born* &c.], (Ṣ, TA,) as well as هُوَ أَخُوهُ سَوْغُهُ and ▼ سَوْغَتُهُ [*He is his brother that was born* &c.]: or سَوْغُ الرَّجُلِ means *he who was born after the man,* or *near after him,* though not his brother: and Fr heard a man of Benoo-Temeem say سُوغُهُ, and another of the same tribe say ▼ سَوْغَتُهُ, meaning *he who followed him*: (TA:) [the pl. of سَوْغ is أَسْوَاغ; and it is said that] أَسْوَاغُ الرَّجُلِ means *those who were born with the man in one case of childbirth, after him, no other childbirth having occurred between him and them*: (TA:) or *those born next after him*: (JḲ:) and أَصْوَاغ is a dial. var. thereof: but IF says that هٰذَا سَوْغُ هٰذَا means *This is of the cast, mould, form,* or *fashion, of this*; and that the س may be a substitute for ص; as though the one were cast, moulded, formed, or fashioned, like the other: (TA:) and [in like manner] one says, هٰذَا سَيْغُ هٰذَا *this is proportionate to this,* or *of the proportion of this.* (TA in art. سيغ.)

سَوْغَةٌ: see the next preceding paragraph in four places.

سَوَاغٌ *A thing whereby one makes to enter easily into his fauces [and to pass down his throat] that which is choking him.* (Ṣ, Mṣb, Ḳ.) One says, المَآءُ سِوَاغُ الغُصَصِ [*Water is that whereby one makes easy of entrance into the fauces and of passage down the throat the things that are choking him*]. (Ṣ.)

سَائِغٌ, applied to beverage, or wine, (JK, Ḳ, TA,) and food, (TA,) *Descending easily [and agreeably] down the throat*; (JK, Mṣb, Ḳ, TA, and Bḍ and Jel in xvi. 68 and Bḍ in xxxv. 13;) [or *easy and agreeable to swallow*;] *not choking*; (Jel in xvi. 68;) and ▼ أَسْوَغُ signifies the same; (IDrd, Ḳ, TA;) and so ▼ سَيِّغٌ, applied to food [&c.]; (TA;) [and ▼ مُسْتَسَاغٌ, accord. to Freytag, as from the Ḳ, in which I do not find it.]

سَيِّغٌ: see the next preceding paragraph.

أَسْوَغُ: see سَائِغٌ. [Freytag assigns to it also another signification, which belongs not to it, but to سَوْغٌ.]

تَسْوِيغَاتُ السَّلَاطِينِ is a post-classical term, (O, Ḳ,) from سَوَّغْتُهُ لَهُ, inf. n. تَسْوِيغٌ, meaning "I made it allowable, lawful, or free, to him:" (O:) and what is meant by [the sing. of تسويغات i. e.] تَسْوِيغٌ is The *permission* [of the Sulṭán] *for the taking of that which is one's right, or due, on a particular account, with facilitation thereof to the taker.* (MF.)

مَسَاغٌ [*A place of easy entrance* or *passage* for beverage, or food, into the fauces or throat. — And hence,] † *A place of entrance* into a land [&c.]; as in a saying cited in the first paragraph of this art., q. v. (TA.) — And [hence] one says, هٰذَا لَا أَجِدُ لَهُ مَسَاغًا ‡ *This, I do not find to it a passage,* or *an [easy] entrance*; or *a way,* or *place, of entrance.* (TA.)

مُسْتَسَاغٌ: see سَائِغٌ.

سوف

1. سَافَ الشَّىْءَ, aor. يَسُوفُ (Ṣ, M, Mṣb) and يَسَافُ, (M,) inf. n. سَوْفٌ; (Ṣ, M, Ḳ;) and so ▼ سَاوَفَهُ; (M, TA;) and ▼ اِسْتَافَهُ, (M, Mṣb, Ḳ,*) inf. n. اِسْتِيَافٌ; (Ṣ;) [and, accord. to Freytag, ▼ سَوَّفَهُ; but he has not named his authority; if correct, probably having an intensive signification;] *He smelled the thing.* (Ṣ, M, Mṣb.) A poet says, (Mṣb,) namely, Ru-beh, (Ṣ, M,)

إِذَا الدَّلِيلُ ٱسْتَافَ ▼ أَخْلَاقَ الطُّرُقْ

[*When the guide smells the natures of the roads to know whether he be pursuing the right course or deviating therefrom*]. (Ṣ, M, Mṣb.) — [And hence, *He hunted.* (Freytag, from the Deewán el-Hudhaleeyeen.)] == سَوْفٌ is also *Syn. with* صَبْرٌ. (IAạr, Ḳ.) You say, of a man, سَافَ عَلَيْهِ, inf. n. سَوْفٌ, *He endured it with patience.* (TḲ.) == سَافَ, (Ṣ, M, O, Ḳ) aor. يَسُوفُ (Ṣ, O, Ḳ) and يَسَافُ, (O, Ḳ,) inf. n. سَوْفٌ, (M,) said of a man, (M,) and of cattle, (مَال, M, O, Ḳ,) *He,* or *they, perished,* or *died*: (Ṣ, M, O, Ḳ:) or, said of cattle, *they had a murrain occurring among them.* (Ḳ.) == [سَافَ expl. by Freytag in this art., as though having for its aor. يَسُوفُ, and meaning *He smote a person with a sword*, is a mistake, caused by a mistranscription (of سُفْتُهُ for سِفْتُهُ) in art. سيف in some copies of the Ḳ.]

2. سَوَّفَهُ, (Ṣ, M, Ḳ,) or سَوَّفَ بِهِ, (Mṣb,) inf. n. تَسْوِيفٌ, (Ṣ, M, Mṣb, Ḳ,) *He said to him time after time* سَوْفَ أَفْعَلُ [*I will do* such a thing]; (Ṣ, Mṣb, TA;) derived from the particle سَوْفَ: (IJ, M:) and hence, (Mṣb,) *he delayed,* or *deferred, with him*; or *put him off with promises*; syn. مَطَلَهُ; (Ṣ,* Mṣb, Ḳ, TA;) *saying* سَوْفَ أَفْعَلُ; (TA;) or *promising to be faithful to his engagement*; (Mṣb;) mostly used in relation to a promise that is not to be fulfilled; as is said by Ibn-Abil-Ḥadeed: (MF, TA:) and ▼ سَاوَفَهُ signifies [the same, as is implied in the M, being *syn. with*] مَاطَلَهُ: see an ex. in a verse cited voce سَوْفَ, last sentence. (TA.) التَّسْوِيفُ is [also expl. as] *Syn. with* التَّأْخِيرُ [app. as meaning *the postponing, putting off, delaying,* or *deferring,* anything]. (TA.) [And it is implied in art. عطب of the TA that it is *Syn. with* التَّمْرِينُ and التَّصْبِيرُ: so that you say, سَوَّفَهُ عَلَيْهِ, meaning *He inured,* or *accustomed, him to it*; and *made him to endure it with patience*: see سَافَ عَلَيْهِ, above.] — You say also, سَوَّفْتُهُ أَمْرِى, meaning *I made him* (a man) *to have the ordering and deciding of my affair,* or *case,* (Ṣ, Ḳ,) *to do what he would*: (Ṣ:) and so سَوَّمْتُهُ. (TA.) == See also 1, first sentence.

3. سَاوَفَهُ: see 1: == and 2. == Also *i. q.* سَارَّهُ [*He spoke,* or *discoursed, secretly to him* or *with him*; or *acquainted him with a secret*]. (Ḳ.) — And سَاوَفَ المَرْأَةَ *i. q.* ضَاجَعَهَا [*He slept with the woman in,* or *on, one bed*]. (Ḳ.)

4. اساف, (Ṣ, M, Ḳ,) inf. n. إِسَافَةٌ, (TA,) said of a man, (Ṣ, M,) *His cattle perished,* or *died*: (Ṣ, Ḳ:) or *he had murrain occurring among his cattle*: so in a verse of Ṭufeyl, cited voce اِسْتَرْخَى, in art. رخو. (M.) [Hence,] one says, أَسَافَ حَتَّى مَا يَشْتَكِى السُّوَافَ, (AA, Ṣ, Meyd, Ḳ,) or السَّوَافَ, (Aṣ, Meyd,) [*He had murrain among his cattle until he did not complain of the murrain*:] a prov., (Meyd,) applied to him who has become accustomed to casualties; (Ṣ, Ḳ;) or to him who has become inured to calamities, (A'Obeyd, Meyd, A,) so that he is not impatient of the vicissitudes of fortune. (A'Obeyd, Meyd.) — اساف الوَالِدَانِ *The two parents lost their child by his death*: in which case, the child is said to be ▼ مُسَافٌ; and his father, ▼ مُسِيفٌ; and his mother, ▼ مُسِيفَةٌ. (Ibn-'Abbád, Ḳ.) == اساف اللّٰهُ *God destroyed him,* or *took away his life.* (M.) — اساف الخَرْزَ *i. q.* خَرَمَهُ [i. e. *He spoiled the sewing* of the skin, or hide; *as when one uses a thick instrument for sewing* or *perforating, and a thin thong*; or *as when one rends two stitch-holes into one*]. (M.) And اساف الخَارِزُ *The sewer* of a skin, or hide, *perforated,* or *sewed, in such a manner that the two stitch-holes became rent* [*into one*]. (A'Obeyd, Ḳ.)

8: see 1, first and second sentences.

سَافٌ *Any row,* or *course,* (Ṣ, M, L, Ḳ, TA,) [i. e.] *a single row,* or *course,* (Mgh,) *of bricks,* (Ṣ, M, Mgh, L, Ḳ, TA,) or (so in the Mgh, but in the TA "and") *of clay,* (Mgh, TA,) of a wall, (Ṣ, Mgh, Ḳ, TA,) or in a wall, (TA,) or in a building; (M, L, TA;) as also مِدْمَاكٌ: (TA:) pl. of pauc. آسُفٌ [formed by transposition, like آدُرٌ pl. of دَارٌ,] (L,) and سَافَاتٌ: (Mgh:) Lth explains السَّافُ as signifying *what is between the* سَافَات *of the building*: its ا is originally و. (TA.) [سَافَةٌ mentioned by Freytag as signifying "a single series of stones in a wall," on the authority of the Ḳ, I do not find there, nor in any other lexicon.] == Also *A certain bird, that preys.* (M.)

سَوْفَ, for which one also says سَفْ, (M, Mughnee, Ḳ,) rejecting the medial radical letter, (M, Mughnee,) and سَوْ, (M, Mughnee, Ḳ,) rejecting the final radical, (M, Mughnee,) and سَىْ, (M, Mughnee, Ḳ,) rejecting the final radical and changing the medial into ى for the purpose of alleviation [of the utterance], (M, Mughnee,) and accord. to the L سَا, (TA,) is a particle, (IJ, M, Ḳ,) denoting inception; (Ḳ;) or a word denoting تَنْفِيس, (Sb, Ṣ, M, Ḳ,) i. e. amplification, because it changes the aor. from the strait time, which is the present, to the ample time, which is the future; (Mughnee voce سَ [q. v.];) i. e., denoting تنفيس with respect to that which has not yet happened; (Sb, Ṣ, Ḳ;) and postponement; (M;) and it is used in terrifying and threatening and promising; (IDrd, Ḳ;) or it is a word denoting promising or threatening: (Mṣb:) it is *syn. with* سَ accord. to some, or *has a larger meaning than this latter* accord. to others. (Mughnee.) You say, سَوْفَ أَفْعَلُ [*I will do* such a thing]. (Sb, Ṣ.) And one may not introduce a separating word between it and its verb, [except in a case mentioned in what follows,] because it occupies the place of the س in سَيَفْعَلُ [&c.]. (Sb, Ṣ.) [But] it is distinct from س by its [sometimes] having ل prefixed to it; as in [the phrase in the Ḳur xciii. 5], وَلَسَوْفَ يُعْطِيكَ رَبُّكَ فَتَرْضَى [*And thy Lord will give thee, and thou wilt be well pleased*]: (Mughnee:) in this phrase, [however,] the ل is [considered as] prefixed to the verb, not to the particle: (M:) or the phrase is elliptical, for لَأَنْتَ سَوْفَ يُعْطِيكَ. (Bd.) And it is distinct from سَ in this, that it is sometimes separated [from its verb] by a verb divested of government both as to the letter and the meaning; as in the saying,

• وَمَا أَدْرِى وَسَوْفَ إِخَالُ أَدْرِى •
• أَقَوْمٌ آلُ حِصْنٍ أَمْ نِسَآءُ •

[*And I know not, but I shall, I think, know, whether the family of Hisn be a company of men or women*]. (Mughnee.) — When you desire to make it a subst., [i. e. to use it as a subst.,] you make it to have tenween [when it is indeterminate]. (IDrd, K.) IDrd cites as an ex.,

• إِنَّ سَوْفًا وَإِنَّ لَيْتًا عَنَآءُ •

[*Verily* سَوْف *and verily* لَيْت *are a weariness*]: but one reading is إِنَّ لَيْتًا; إِنَّ لَوًّا; and another, وَإِنَّ لَوًّا إِنَّ سَوْفًا; and there is no such reading as إِنَّ سَوْفًا. (O, TA.) One says also, فُلَانٌ يَقْتَاتُ السَّوْفَ [lit. *Such a one feeds upon the word* سَوْف]; meaning ‡ *Such a one lives by means of things hoped for*: (S, K, TA:) and in like manner, مَا قُوتُهُ إِلَّا السَّوْفُ [lit. *His food is not anything but*, or *other than, the word* سَوْف]. (A, TA.) — In the following verse of Ibn-Mukbil, cited by Sb,

• لَوْ سَاوَفَتْنَا ▼ بِسَوْفٍ مِنْ تَحِيَّتِهَا •
• سَوْفَ العَيُوفِ لَرَاحَ الرَّكْبُ قَدْ قَنِعَا •

[*Had she put us off with a* سَوْف *as part of her greeting, with the putting off even of such as is affected with dislike, the riders had gone contented*], سَوْف is put in the accus. case [for مُسَاوَفَةَ, i. e.] as an inf. n. with the augmentation [meaning the augmentative letters] rejected. (M.)

سِيفَةٌ: see مَسَافَةٌ, in two places.

سُوَافٌ The [*murumber commonly called*] قِثَّآء [q. v.]: (M, K, TA:) so says AHn, (M, TA,) on the authority of Et-Toosee. (TA.) ═ See also what next follows.

سُوَافٌ and ▼ سَوَافٌ; with damm accord. to As, and so, he says, all the names of diseases, as نُحَازٌ and زُكَامٌ and قُلَابٌ and خُمَالٌ [&c.]; accord. to AA, not so, but with fet-h, and in like manner said 'Omárah Ibn-'Akeel; (S;) or none relates it with fet-h except AA, and his relation is nought; (IB;) *Disease of cattle, and death thereof*: (S:) or each signifies *death among mankind and cattle*: (M:) or the latter, *a mortality*, or *murrain, among camels*; or so the former: or the latter, *a mortality among mankind and cattle*: (K:) and the former, *disease of camels*; (AHn, M, K;) and so the latter. (K.) One says, وَقَعَ فِى المَالِ سُوَافٌ [or سَوَافٌ] *Death* [or *a murrain*] *happened among the cattle*. (S.)

مِسَافٌ *The nose*: because one smells (يُسَافُ, K, i. e. يُشَمُّ, TA) with it: (K:) so in the Moheet. (TA.) — See also مَسَافَةٌ, in two places.

مُسَافٌ A child *taken from his parents by death*: see 4. (Ibn-'Abbád, K.)

مُسِيفٌ A man *whose cattle have died*. (TA.) — And A father *having lost his child by death*: see 4. (Ibn-'Abbád, K.)

مَسَافَةٌ [properly *A place of smelling*: — and hence,] ‡ *Distance*; (S, K, TA;) and ▼ مَسَافٌ and ▼ سِيفَةٌ signify the same in this sense [or in others here following]: (K:) [*a space*, or *tract*, or *an extent, over which one journeys*:] *a far-extending tract that one traverses*: originally *a place of smelling* of the guides, in order that they may know whether it be far or near, out of the way or in the right way: (A, TA:) or *a* [*desert*, or *such as is termed*] مَفَازَة: (M:) said to be from سَافَ الشَّىْءَ meaning "he smelled the thing;" for the guide smells the dust of the place wherein he is; and if he smell the odour of urine and dung of camels, he knows that he [or some other] has traversed it; but otherwise, not: (Msb:) or because the guide, when he is in a desert, (S, M, K,) and has lost his way therein, (M,) smells its dust, (S, M, K,) in order that he may know, (S, K,) or and thus knows, (M,) whether he be in the right way, (S, M, K,) or not: (S, K:) then, by reason of frequency of usage of this word [as meaning "a place of smelling of the guides"] it became a term for "distance:" (S, K:) pl. مَسَاوِفُ (A, TA) and مَسَافَاتٌ. (Msb.) One says, كَمْ ▼ سِيفَتُهَا and ▼ مَسَافُهَا and مَسَافَةُ هٰذِهِ الأَرْضِ ‡ [*How long is the distance*, or *how much is the extent, of this land?*]. (TA.) And بَيْنَهُمْ مَسَافَةٌ بَعِيدَةٌ ‡ [*Between them is a far-extending distance* or *space*]. (Msb.) And بَيْنَنَا مَسَافَةُ عِشْرِينَ يَوْمًا ‡ [*Between us is the distance*, or *space, of twenty days*]. (TA.) — In the following saying of Dhu-r-Rummeh, it is doubly tropical:

• وَأَبْعَدُهُمْ مَسَافَةَ غَوْرِ عَقْلٍ •
• إِذَا مَا الأَمْرُ ذُو الشُّبُهَاتِ عَالَا •

‡‡ [*And the furthest of them in the extent of the depth of intelligence when the affair*, or *case, in which are dubiousnesses overcomes and is onerous*]. (A, TA.)

مُسَوِّفٌ One *who does what he will*, [*as though he said time after time* سَوْفَ أَفْعَلُ,] *whom no one will make to turn back*. (K.) — And, with ة, A woman *who will not comply with the desire of her husband when he calls her to his bed, and strives with him to repel him in respect of that which he desires of her, and says* سَوْفَ أَفْعَلُ: such is said, in a trad., to be cursed. (TA.) — Also, with ة, A well (رَكِيَّةٌ) *of which one says, Water will be found* (سَوْفَ يُوجَدُ) *in it*: or *of which the water is smelt* (يُسَافُ), *and disliked, and loathed*. (Ibn-'Abbád, Z, K.) — And, without ة, *Very patient* or *enduring*. (TA.)

مُسْتَافٌ *A place of smelling*, or *that is smelt*. (O, K.)

مُسِيفٌ A mother *having lost her child by death*: see 4. (Ibn-'Abbád, K.)

إِنَّهَا لَمُسَاوِفَةٌ لِلسَّيْرِ [app. referring to a she-camel] *Verily she is one that has ability for journeying*. (M.)

سوق

1. سَاقَ المَاشِيَةَ, (S, K,) or النَّعَمَ, (Mgh,) or الدَّابَّةَ, (Msb,) aor. يَسُوقُ, (S, Mgh, Msb,) inf. n. سَوْقٌ (S, Mgh, Msb, K) and سِيَاقٌ, (S, [so in both of my copies, but it is said in the JK that this latter is used in relation to death, and such is generally the case,]) or سَيَاقٌ, like سَحَابٌ, (TA, [but this I have not found elsewhere, and I doubt its correctness,]) and سِيَاقَةٌ and مَسَاقٌ, (O, K, TA,) *He drove the cattle* [or *the beast*]; *he urged the cattle* [or *the beast*] *to go*; (Mgh;) and ▼ استاقها signifies the same, (S, K,) as also ▼ اساقها, and ▼ سَوَّقَهَا; (TA;) or تَسْوِيقٌ, the inf. n. [of this last], signifies the *driving well*: (KL:) [and accord. to Freytag, ▼ استساق, followed by an accus., signifies the same as سَاقَ as expl. above; but for this he names no authority.] Hence, in the Kur [lxxv. 30], إِلَى رَبِّكَ يَوْمَئِذٍ المَسَاقُ (TA) i. e. *To thy Lord*, and his judgment, *on that day shall be the driving*. (Bd, Jel.) And the saying, in a trad., لَا تَقُومُ السَّاعَةُ حَتَّى يَخْرُجَ رَجُلٌ مِنْ قَحْطَانَ يَسُوقُ النَّاسَ بِعَصَاهُ [properly rendered *The resurrection*, or *the hour thereof, shall not come to pass until a man come forth from* the tribe of *Kahtán driving the people with his staff*], allusive to his having the mastery over them, and their obeying him; the staff being mentioned only to indicate his tyrannical and rough treatment of them. (TA.) [And hence the saying, سَاقَ عَلَىَّ فُلَانًا † *He urged such a one to intercede for him with me*.] — [Hence also,] سَاقَهُ القَدَرُ إِلَى مَا قُدِّرَ لَهُ † [*Destiny drove him*, or *impelled him, to that which was destined for him*]. (TA.) [And in like manner one says of desire, &c.] — And سَاقَ إِلَى المَرْأَةِ مَهْرَهَا, (K,) or صَدَاقَهَا, (S, Msb,) inf. n. سِيَاقٌ; (TA;) and ▼ اساقه; (Msb, K;) ‡ *He sent to the woman her dowry*; (K, TA;) or *conveyed it*, or *caused it to be conveyed, to her*; (Msb;) though consisting of dirhems or deenárs; because the dowry, with the Arabs, originally consisted of camels, which are driven. (TA.) And hence, مَا سُقْتَ إِلَيْهَا, meaning ‡ *What didst thou give her as her dowry?* occurring in a trad.; or, as some related it, مَا سُقْتَ مِنْهَا, i. e. *What didst thou give for her*, or *in exchange for her?* (TA.) And سَاقَ إِلَيْهِ الشَّىْءَ ‡ [*He made*, or *caused, the thing to go, pass*, or *be conveyed* or *transmitted, to him*; *he sent to him the thing*]. (M and K in art. اتى.) And سَاقَ إِلَيْهِ خَيْرًا ‡ [*He caused good*, or *good fortune, to betide him*]. (TA.) And سَاقَ لِأَرْضِهِ أَتِيًّا † [*He made a rivulet*, or *a channel for water, to run to his land*]. (M in art. اتى.) — [Hence likewise,] سَاقَتِ الرِّيحُ السَّحَابَ ‡ [*The wind drove along the clouds*]. (S,* TA.) — [And سَوْقٌ, inf. n. سَاقَ الحَدِيثَ, and سِيَاقٌ and مَسَاقٌ, ‡ *He carried on the narrative*, or *discourse*.] You say, فُلَانٌ يَسُوقُ الحَدِيثَ أَحْسَنَ سِيَاقٍ ‡ [*Such a one carries on the narrative*, or *discourse, in the best manner of doing so*]. (Mgh, TA.) And إِلَيْكَ يُسَاقُ الحَدِيثُ ‡ [*To thee* as its object *the narrative*, or *discourse, is carried on*]. (TA.) And كَلَامٌ مَسَاقُهُ إِلَى كَذَا ‡ [*Speech whereof the*

carrying-on is pointed *to such a thing*]. (TA.) And جِئْتُكَ بِالحَدِيثِ عَلَى سَوْقِهِ ‡ [*I uttered to thee the narrative,* or *discourse, after the proper manner of the carrying-on thereof*]. (TA.) [In like manner also one says,] سَاقَ الأُمُورَ أَحْسَنَ مَسَاقٍ † [*He carried on,* or *prosecuted, affairs,* or *the affairs, in the best manner of doing so*]. (A in art. حود.) — سَوْقُ المَعْلُومِ مَسَاقَ غَيْرِهِ [from ساق الحديث expl. above] means † *The asking respecting that which one knows in the manner of one's asking respecting that which he knows not:* a mode of speech implying hyperbole: *as when one says,* أَوَجْهُكَ هٰذَا أَمْ بَدْرٌ [*Is this thy face or a full moon?*]. (Ḳull p. 211.) — ساق said of a sick man, (Ḳ,) and ساق نَفْسَهُ, [app. thus originally,] (Ks, Mṣb, TA,) and ساق بِنَفْسِهِ, (TA,) aor. يَسُوقُ, (Ks, Ṣ, O, Mṣb, TA,) inf. n. سِيَاقٌ, (Ṣ, O, Mṣb, Ḳ,) originally سِوَاقٌ, (TA,) and سَوْقٌ (O, Ḳ) and سُؤُوقٌ, (TA,) ‡ *He cast forth,* or *vomited, his soul;* (Ks, TA;) *he gave up his spirit;* or *was at the point of death, in the agony of death,* or *at the point of having his soul drawn forth;* (Ṣ, O, Mṣb, TA;) or *he began to give up his spirit,* or *to have his soul drawn forth.* (Ḳ.) You say, رَأَيْتُ فُلَانًا يَسُوقُ ‡ *I saw such a one giving up his spirit at death.* (Ṣ, O, TA.) And رَأَيْتُ فُلَانًا بِالسَّوْقِ [or فِى السِّيَاقِ, as in the Mṣb,] ‡ *I saw such a one in the act* [or *agony*] *of death;* and يُسَاقُ [*having his soul expelled*], inf. n. سَوْقٌ: and إِنَّ نَفْسَهُ لَتُسَاقُ ‡ [*Verily his soul is being expelled*]. (ISh, TA.) = سَاقَهُ, (Ḳ,) first pers. سُقْتُهُ, (Ṣ,) aor. as above, inf. n. سَوْقٌ, (TA,) also signifies *He hit,* or *hurt, his* (another man's, Ṣ) سَاق [or *shank*]. (Ṣ, Ḳ.)

2. سوّق, inf. n. تَسْوِيقٌ: see 1, first sentence. — سوّق فُلَانًا أَمْرَهُ † *He made such a one to have the ruling,* or *ordering, of his affair,* or *case.* (Ibn-'Abbád, Ḳ.) — See also 5. = Said of a plant, (TA,) or of a tree, (Ḳ,) more properly of the former, (TA,) † *It had a* ساق [i. e. *stem, stock,* or *trunk*]. (Ḳ, TA.)

3. ساوقهُ *He vied,* or *competed, with him, in driving:* (Ḳ: [in the CḲ, for فِى السَّوْقِ, is put فى السُّوقِ:]) or *he vied,* or *competed, with him to decide which of them twain was the stronger;* from the phrase قَامَتِ الحَرْبُ عَلَى سَاقٍ. (Ṣ.) [Hence,] one says بَعِيرٌ يُسَاوِقُ الصَّيْدَ ‡ [*A camel that vies with the animals of the chase in driving on,* or *in strength*]. (JK, Ibn-'Abbád, O, Ḳ, TA.) — مُسَاوَقَةٌ is also *syn. with* مُتَابَعَةٌ [app. as meaning † The *making to be consecutive,* or *successive,* for it is added], *as though driving on one another,* or *as though one portion were driving on another.* (TA. [See 6, its quasi-pass.].) — [Freytag also assigns to ساوق the meaning of *He,* or *it, followed* (*secutus fuit*), as on the authority of the Ḥamáseh; but without pointing out the page; and it is not in his index of words explained therein.]

4: see 1, in two places. — أَسَقْتُهُ إِبِلًا ‡ *I made him to drive camels:* (Ḳ:) or *I gave to him camels, to drive them:* (Ṣ, TA:) or ‡ *I made him to possess camels.* (TA.)

5. تسوّق القَوْمُ *The people,* or *party,* [*trafficked in the* سُوق, or *market;* or] *sold and bought:* (Ṣ, TA:) the vulgar say ▼ سَوَّقُوا. (TA.)

6. تَسَاوَقَتِ الإِبِلُ ‡ *The camels followed one another;* (Az, O, Mṣb, Ḳ, TA;) and in like manner one says تَقَاوَدَتْ; (O, Ḳ,* TA;) *as though, by reason of their weakness and leanness, some of them held back from others.* (TA.) And تَسَاوَقَتِ الغَنَمُ ‡ *The sheep,* or *goats, pressed, one upon another,* (Ḳ,) or *followed one another,* (O,) *in going along,* (O, Ḳ,) *as though driving on one another.* (O.) [See also 7.] — The lawyers say, تَسَاوَقَتِ الخِطْبَتَانِ, meaning † [*The two demandings of a woman in marriage*] *were simultaneous:* but [Fei says] I have not found it in the books of lexicology in this sense. (Mṣb.)

7. انساقت المَاشِيَةُ *The cattle went,* or *went along, being driven;* [or *as though driven;* or *drove along;*] quasi-pass. of سَاقَهَا. (Ṣ, TA.) And انساقت الإِبِلُ [has the like signification: or means] † *The camels became consecutive.* (TA. [See also 6.])

8: } see 1, first sentence.
10: }

سَاقٌ The *shank;* i. e. the *part between the knee and the foot* of a human being; (Mṣb;) or the *part between the ankle and the knee* (Ḳ, TA) of a human being; (TA;) the ساق of the human foot: (Ṣ, TA:) and [the *part properly corresponding thereto,* i. e. the *thigh commonly so called,* and also the *arm,* of a beast;] the *part above the* وَظِيف of the horse and mule and ass and camel, and the *part above the* كُرَاع of the ox-kind and sheep or goat and antelope: (TA:) [it is also sometimes applied to the *shank commonly so called, of the hind leg,* and, less properly, *of the fore leg,* of a beast: and to the *bone of any of the parts above mentioned:* and sometimes, by synecdoche, to the *hind leg,* and, less properly, to the *fore leg* also, of a beast: it generally corresponds to ذِرَاعٌ: of a bird, it is the *thigh commonly so called:* and sometimes the *shank commonly so called:* and, by synecdoche, the *leg:*] it is of the fem. gender: (Mṣb, TA:) and for this reason, (TA,) the dim. is ▼ سُوَيْقَةٌ: (Mṣb, TA:) the pl. [of mult.] is سُوقٌ (Ṣ, Mgh, O, Mṣb, Ḳ) and سِيقَانٌ and [of pauc.] أَسْؤُقٌ, (Ṣ, O, Ḳ,) the و in this last being with ء in order that it may bear the ḍammeh. (O, Ḳ.) A poet says,

لِلْفَتَى عَقْلٌ يَعِيشُ بِهِ *
حَيْثُ تَهْدِى سَاقَهُ قَدَمُهْ *

meaning *The young man has intelligence whereby he lives when his foot directs aright his shank.* (IAạr, TA.) And one says of a man when difficulty, or calamity, befalls him, كَشَفَ عَنْ سَاقِهِ [lit. *He uncovered his shank;* meaning † *he prepared himself for difficulty*]: so says IAmb: and hence, he says, (TA, [in which a similar explanation is cited from ISd also,]) they mention the ساق when they mean to express the difficulty of a case or an event, and to tell of the terror occasioned thereby. (Ḳ, TA.) Thus, the saying يَوْمَ يُكْشَفُ عَنْ سَاقٍ, (Ṣ, Ḳ, TA,) in the Ḳur [lxviii. 42], (Ṣ, TA,) [lit. *On a day when a shank shall be uncovered,*] means † *on a day when difficulty,* or *calamity, shall be disclosed.* (I'Ab, Mujáhid, Ṣ, Ḳ, TA.) It is like the saying, قَامَتِ الحَرْبُ عَلَى سَاقٍ, (Ṣ, TA,) which means † *The war,* or *battle, became vehement,* (Mṣb in this art. and in art. حرب,) *so that safety from destruction was difficult of attainment:* (Id. in art. حرب:) and كَشَفَتِ الحَرْبُ عَنْ سَاقٍ, [as also شَمَّرَتْ عَنْ سَاقِهَا,] i. e. † *The war,* or *battle, became vehement.* (Jel in lxviii. 42.) And in like manner, وَٱلْتَفَّتِ ٱلسَّاقُ بِٱلسَّاقِ, (Ḳ, TA,) in the Ḳur [lxxv. 29], (TA,) means † *And the affliction of the present state of existence shall be combined with that of the final state:* (Ḳ, TA:) or it means *when the* [one] *leg shall be inwrapped with the other leg by means of the grave-clothes.* (TA.) One says also, قَامَ القَوْمُ عَلَى سَاقٍ † *The people or party, became in a state of toil, and trouble,* or *distress.* (TA.) And قَرَعَ لِلْأَمْرِ سَاقَهُ, [originating from one's striking the shin of his camel in order to make him lie down to be mounted; lit. *He struck his shank for the affair;*] meaning † *he prepared himself for the thing,* or *affair;* syn. تَشَمَّرَ: (JK:) or *he was,* or *became, light,* or *active, and he rose,* or *hastened, to do the thing;* or † *he applied himself vigorously,* or *diligently,* or *with energy, to the thing,* or *affair;* i. q. شَمَّرَ لَهُ [q. v.]; (TA;) or تَشَمَّرَ لَهُ. (A and TA in art. قرع [q. v.: see also ظُنْبُوبٌ, in several places].) [It is also said that] كِدْتُ أَوْهَتْ بِسَاقٍ means أَفْعَلُ [i. e. *I nearly,* or *almost, did* what I purposed: but this explanation seems to have been derived only from what here, as in the TA, immediately follows]: Ḳurṭ says, describing the wolf,

وَلٰكِنِّى رَمَيْتُكَ مِنْ بَعِيدٍ *
فَلَمْ أَفْعَلْ وَقَدْ أَوْهَتْ بِسَاقِ *

[i. e., app., *But I shot at thee from afar, and I did not* what I purposed, *though it* (the shot, الرَّمْيَةُ, I suppose, being meant to be understood,) *maimed a shank:* which virtually means, *though I nearly did what I purposed:* the poet, I assume, says اوهت بساق for the sake of the measure and rhyme, for أَوْهَتْ سَاقًا: see what is said, in the explanations of the preposition بِ, respecting the phrase وَٱمْسَحُوا بِرُؤُوسِكُمْ]. (TA.) — By a secondary application, سَاقٌ signifies † [*A greave;* i. e.] *a thing that is worn on the* ساق [or *shank*] *of the leg, made of iron or other material.* (Mgh.) — Also ‡ [The *stem, stock,* or *trunk,* i. e.] the *part between the* أَصْل [here meaning *root,* or *foot,* (though it is also syn. with ساق in the sense in which the latter is here explained,)] *and the place where the branches shoot out;* (TA;) or the *support;* (Mṣb;) or the جِذْع; (Ṣ, Ḳ;) of a tree, or shrub: (Ṣ, Mṣb, Ḳ, TA:) pl. [of mult.] سُوقٌ (Mṣb, TA) and سُوُقٌ and سُؤُوقٌ and

and [of pauc.] أَسْوُقٌ and أُسْوُقٌ. (TA.) It is related in a trad. of Mo'áwiyeh, that a man said, I applied to him to decide in a litigation with the son of my brother, and began to overcome him therein; whereupon he said, Thou art like as Aboo-Duwád says,

أَنَّى أُتِيحَ لَهُ حِرْبَآءُ تَنْضُبَةٍ

لَا يُرْسِلُ السَّاقَ إِلَّا مُمْسِكًا سَاقَا

[*Whencesoever, or however, a preparation is made for him*, to catch him, he is like *a chameleon of a tree of the kind called* تَنْضُب, *he will not loose the stem* thereof *unless grasping a stem*]: he meant that no plea of his came to nought but he clung to another; likening him to the chameleon, which places itself facing the sun, and ascends half-way up the tree, or shrub, then climbs to the branches when the sun becomes hot, then climbs to a higher branch, and will not loose the former until it grasps the other. (O, TA.*) — [Hence, perhaps, as it seems to be indicated in the O,] one says, وَلَدَتْ فُلَانَةُ ثَلَاثَةَ بَنِينَ عَلَى سَاقٍ, (Ḳ, [in the copies of which, however, I find ثَلَاثٌ put for ثَلَاثَةَ,]) or عَلَى سَاقٍ وَاحِدٍ, (Ṣ,) or وَاحِدَةٍ, (O,) i. e. ‡ *Such a woman brought forth three sons, one after another, without any girl between them:* (Ṣ, O, Ḳ, TA:) so says ISk: and وُلِدَ لِفُلَانٍ ثَلَاثَةُ أَوْلَادٍ سَاقًا عَلَى سَاقٍ, i. e. ‡ *Three children were born to such a one, one after another.* (TA.) And بَنَى القَوْمُ بُيُوتَهُمْ عَلَى سَاقٍ وَاحِدٍ † [*The people, or party, built their houses, or constructed their tents, in one row or series*]. (TA.) — سَاقٌ also signifies † The *soul*, or *self*; syn. نَفْسٌ: hence the saying of 'Alee (in the war of the [schismatics called] شُرَاة), لَا بُدَّ لِى مِنْ قِتَالِهِمْ وَلَوْ تَلِفَتْ سَاقِى † [*There is not for me any way of avoiding combating them, though my soul, or self, should perish* by my doing so]. (Abu-l-'Abbás, O, TA.) So too in the saying, قَدَحَ فِى سَاقِهِ [as though meaning ‡ *He cankered his very soul*]: (IAạr, TA in art. قدح:) [or] *he deceived him, and did that which was displeasing to him:* (L in that art.:) or ‡ *he impugned his honour, or reputation;* from the action of canker-worms (قَوَادِح) cankering the stem, or trunk, of a shrub, or tree. (A in that art.) — سَاقُ حُرٍّ [is said to signify] The *male of the* قُمَارِىّ [or *species of collared turtle-doves of which the female is called* قُمْرِيَّة (see قُمْرِىّ)]; (Ṣ, Mṣb, Ḳ;) i. e. the وَرَشَان: (Ṣ, Mṣb:) the former appellation being given to it as imitative of its cry: (Aṣ, Ḳ:) it has neither fem. nor pl.: (AḤát, TA:) or السَّاقُ is *the pigeon;* and الحُرُّ, *its young one:* (Sh, Ḳ:) the poet Ibn-Harmeh uses the phrase كَسَاقِ ٱبْنِ حُرٍّ. (O, TA.) [See more in art. حر.]

سَوْقٌ: see سِيَاقٌ.

سُوقٌ [*A market, mart, or fair;*] *a place in which commerce is carried on;* (ISd, Mṣb, TA;) *a place of articles of merchandise:* (Mgh, TA:) so called because people drive their commodities thither: (TA:) [in the Ṣ unexplained, and in the Ḳ only said to be well-known:] of the fem. gender, and masc., (Ṣ, Mgh, Mṣb, Ḳ,*) the former in the dial. of the people of El-Ḥijáz, and the latter in that of Temeem, (Ṣ and Mṣb voce زُقَاقٌ, q. v.,) the former the more chaste, or the making it masc. is a mistake: (Mṣb:) pl. أَسْوَاقٌ: (TA:) the dim. is ▼ سُوَيْقَةٌ [with ة, confirming the opinion of those who hold سُوق to be only fem.]: also signifying *merchandise*, syn. تِجَارَةٌ; as in the phrase, جَآءَتْ سُوَيْقَةٌ [*Merchandise came*]. (TA.) — [Hence,] سُوقُ الحَرْبِ ‡ *The thickest*, or *most vehement part* (حَوْمَة,) *of the fight;* (Ṣ, Ḳ, TA;) and so ▼ سُوقَةُ الحَرْبِ; i. e. *the midst thereof.* (TA.)

سَوَقٌ *Length of the shanks:* (Ṣ, Ḳ:) or *beauty thereof:* (Ḳ:) or it signifies also *beauty of the shank.* (Ṣ.)

سَاقَةٌ ‡ The *rear*, or *hinder part*, of an army: (Ṣ, Mgh, Ḳ, TA:) pl. of ▼ سَائِقٌ; being those who drive on the army from behind them, and who guard them: (TA:) or as though pl. of سَائِقٌ, like as قَادَةٌ is of قَائِدٌ. (Mgh.) And hence, سَاقَةُ الحَاجِّ ‡ [*The rear of the company of pilgrims*]. (TA.)

سُوقَةٌ † *A subject*, and the *subjects*, of a king; (Ḳ, TA;) so called because driven by him; (TA;) *contr. of* مَلِك; (Ṣ, Mgh, Mṣb;) whether practising traffic or not: (Mgh:) not meaning of the people of the أَسْوَاق [or markets], as the vulgar think; (Mṣb;) for such are called سُوقِيُّونَ, sing. سُوقِىٌّ: (Ḥam p. 534:) it is used alike as sing. and pl. (Ṣ, Mgh, Mṣb, Ḳ) and dual (Mgh, Mṣb) and masc. and fem.: (Ṣ, Ḳ:) but sometimes it has سُوَقٌ for its pl. (Ṣ, Ḳ.) — سُوقَةُ الطُّرْثُوثِ [in the CḲ, erroneously, الثُّرْثُوث] *The part of the* [*plant called*] طرثوث *that is below the* نُكَعَة [or نُكْعَة or نُكَعَة, which is the *head from the top to the extent of a finger*, or the *flower at the head thereof*]; (O, Ḳ;) *sweet and pleasant:* so says Ibn-'Abbád: (O:) AḤn says [of the طرثوث], *it is like the penis of the ass, and there is no part of it more pleasant, nor sweeter, than its* سوقة; *which is in some instances long; and in some, short.* (TA.) — See also سُوقٌ, last sentence.

سُوقِىٌّ [*Of*, or *relating to, the* سُوق, or *market*]. Its pl., سُوقِيُّونَ, means The *people of the* سوق (Ḥam p. 534.) — [Hence,] أَدِيمٌ سُوقِىٌّ *A skin, or hide, prepared, or dressed; in a good state:* or *not prepared* or *dressed:* it is ascribed to the vulgar: and there is a difference of opinion respecting it: the second [explanation, or meaning,] is that which is commonly known. (TA.)

سَوِيقٌ *Meal of parched barley* (شَعِير), or *of* [*the species thereof, or similar grain, called*] سُلْت, *likewise parched;* and it is also *of wheat;* but is *mostly made of barley* (شعير); (MF, TA;) *what is made of wheat* or *of barley;* (Mṣb, TA;) *well known:* (Ṣ, Mṣb, Ḳ, TA:) [it is *generally made into a kind of gruel*, or *thick ptisan, being moistened with water*, or *clarified butter*, or *fat of a sheep's tail, &c.;* (see لَتَّ;) and is therefore said (in the Mṣb in art. حسو and in the KT voce أُكْل, &c.,) to be supped, or sipped, not eaten: but it is *likewise thus called when dry;* and in this state is taken in the palm of the hand and conveyed to the mouth, or licked up: (see سَفَّ, and قَمِحَ:) it is *also made of other grains beside those mentioned above;* and *of several mealy fruits; of the fruit of the Theban palm;* (see حَتِىّ;) and *of the carob;* (see خَرُّوبٌ;) &c.:] it is also, sometimes, with ص: so says IDrd in the Jm: and he adds, I think it to be of the dial. of Benoo-Temeem: it is peculiar to that of Benu-l-'Ambar: (O, TA:) the n. un. [meaning *a portion, or mess, thereof*] is with ة: (AAF, TA in art. جش:) and the pl. is أَسْوِقَةٌ. (TA.) — And *Wine:* (AA, Ḳ:) also called سَوِيقُ الكَرْمِ. (AA, TA.)

سِيَاقٌ [an inf. n. of 1 (q. v.) in several senses. — As a subst., properly so termed,] ‡ *A dowry*, or *nuptial gift;* (Ḳ, TA;) as also ▼ سَوْقٌ [which is likewise originally an inf. n.: see 1]. (TA.) — [Also, as a subst. properly so termed, † The *following part* of a discourse &c.; opposed to سِبَاق: you say سِبَاقُ الكَلَامِ وَسِيَاقُهُ † *the preceding and following parts of the discourse; the context, before and after:* see, again 1. And † The *drift, thread, tenour*, or *scope*, of a discourse &c.]

سُوَيْقَةٌ dim. of سَاقٌ, q. v.: (Mṣb, TA:) — and of سُوقٌ, also, q. v. (TA.)

سَوَّاقٌ: see سَائِقٌ. — Also *A seller*, and *a maker, of* سَوِيق. (Mgh.)

أَسْوَقُ *Long in the* سَاق [or *shank*]. (AA, Ḳ. [See also أَسْوُقٌ.]) — And † *Having a* سَاق [or *stem*]; applied to a plant. (Ibn-Abbád, Ḳ.) — And † The طَلْع [or *spadix*] *of a palm-tree, when it has come forth, and become a span in length.* (Ḳ.)

سَائِقٌ [*Driving*, or *a driver;*] the agent of the verb in the phrase سَاقَ المَاشِيَةَ: as also ▼ سَوَّاقٌ (Ṣ, Ḳ) in an intensive sense [as meaning *Driving much* or *vehemently*, or *a vehement driver*]: (Ṣ, TA:) pl. of the former سَاقَةٌ, q. v. (TA.) مَعَهَا سَائِقٌ وَشَهِيدٌ, in the Ḳur [l. 20], is said to mean *Having with it a driver to the place of congregation* [*for judgment*] *and a witness to testify against it of its works:* (TA:) i. e. *an angel driving it, and another angel testifying of its works:* or *an angel performing both of these offices:* or *a writer of evil deeds and a writer of good deeds:* or *its own person*, or *its consociate* [*devil*], *and its members*, or *its works.* (Bḍ.)

سَيِّقٌ, [originally سَيْوِقٌ,] † Clouds (سَحَابٌ, AZ, Aṣ, Ṣ, Ḳ) *driven by the wind*, (AZ, Aṣ, Ṣ,) *containing no water*, (AZ, Ṣ, Ḳ,) or *whether containing water or not.* (Aṣ.)

سَيِّقَةٌ, [a subst. formed from the epithet سَيِّق by the affix ة,] originally سَيْوِقَةٌ, (TA,) *Beasts* (دَوَابّ) *driven by the enemy;* (Ṣ, Ḳ;) like وَسِيقَةٌ: so in a verse cited voce جَبَأَ: (Ṣ:) or *a number of camels, of a tribe, driven away together*, or *attacked by a troop of horsemen and driven away.* (Z, TA.) — [Hence,] one says, المَرْأَةُ سَيِّقَةُ القَدَرِ

† [*Man, or the man, is the impelled of destiny*]; i. e. destiny drives him to that which is destined for him, and will not pass him by. (TA.) —— سَيِّقَةٌ signifies also *An animal by means of which* [in the O بِهَا, for which فِيهَا is erroneously put in the K,] *the sportsman conceals himself, and then shoots, or casts, at the wild animals*: (O, K:) like قَيِّدَةٌ: (A in art. قود:) said by Th to be *a she-camel* [*used for that purpose*]: (TA:) [so called because driven towards the objects of the chase: see دَرِيَّةٌ:] pl. سَيَائِقُ. (K.) [See also مِسْوَقٌ.]

أَسْوَقُ A man (S,* TA) *long in the shanks*: (S, K: [see also سُوَاقٌ:]) or *thick in the shanks*: (IDrd, TA:) or it signifies, (K,) or signifies also, (S,) *beautiful in the shank* or *shanks*, (S, K,) applied to a man: and so سَوْقَاءُ applied to a woman: (S:) Lth explains the latter as meaning a woman *having plump shanks, with hair*. (TA.)

إِسَاقَةٌ (Lth, O, K, in the CK أَسَاقَة,) *The strap of the horse's stirrup*. (Lth, O, K.)

بَعِيرٌ مِسْوَقٌ, (JK, O, and TA as from the Tekmileh,) or مُسْوِقٌ, like مُحْسِنٌ, (K, [but this I think to be a mistake,]) means الَّذِى يُسَاوِقُ الصَّيْدَ [i. e. ‡ *A camel that vies with the animals of the chase in driving on*, or *in strength*]; (JK, O, K;) so says Ibn-'Abbád: (O:) accord. to the L, *a camel by means of which one conceals himself from the animals of the chase, to circumvent them*. (TA. [See also سَيِّقَةٌ, last signification.])

[مِسْوَقَةٌ *A staff*, or *stick, with which cattle are driven*: pl. مَسَاوِقُ: perhaps post-classical.]

مُنْسَاقٌ *i. q.* تَابِعٌ [app. as meaning † *A follower*, or *servant*; as though driven]. (Ibn-'Abbád, O, K.) —— And † *A relation*; syn. قَرِيبٌ. (Ibn-'Abbád, O, K.) —— And عَلَمٌ مُنْسَاقٌ † *A mountain extending along the surface of the earth*. (Ibn-'Abbád, O, K.*)

سوك

1. سَاكَ الشَّىْءَ, (IDrd, O, Msb, K,) aor. يَسُوكُ, inf. n. سَوْكٌ, (IDrd, O, Msb,) *He rubbed the thing*, or *rubbed it well*. (IDrd, O, Msb, K.) —— See also 2. ═ And see 6.

2. سَوَّكَ فَاهُ, (S, O, Msb,) or سَوَّكَ فَمَهُ بِالعُودِ, (K,) inf. n. تَسْوِيكٌ; (S, O, Msb, K;) and † سَاكَهُ, (O, K,) aor. and inf. n. as in the first paragraph, (O,) or inf. n. سِوَاكٌ; (M..; [there said to be an inf. n., as well as a subst. syn. with مِسْوَاكٌ, but without the mention of its verb;]) and † اسْتَاكَ and † تَسَوَّكَ, these two used without the mention of the mouth (S, O, Msb, K) or the stick; (K;) [*He rubbed and cleaned his teeth with the* سِوَاك, or مِسْوَاك.]

5: see the next preceding paragraph.

6. تَسَاوُكٌ and سِوَاكٌ [each an inf. n., the verb of the latter, if it have one, being app. † سَاكَ,] *A weak manner of going*: or *a bad manner of going, resulting from slowness or emaciation*: (K, TA:) so says ISk. (TA.) One says, جَآءَتِ الإِبِلُ تَسَاوَكُ, [for تَتَسَاوَكُ,] i. e. *The camels came inclining from side to side, in consequence of weakness, in their going along*. (S, O.) [Or] تَسَاوَكَتِ الإِبِلُ means *The camels had an agitation of their necks in consequence of leanness*. (IF, Msb.) In the M it is said that جَآءَتِ الغَنَمُ مَا تَسَاوَكُ means *The sheep*, or *goats, came, not moving their heads, in consequence of weakness*. (TA.)

8: see 2.

سِوَاكٌ and † مِسْوَاكٌ signify the same; (S, Mgh, O, Msb, K;) i. e. *A tooth-stick*; *a piece of stick with which the teeth are rubbed* [*and cleaned, the end being made like a brush by beating or chewing it so as to separate the fibres*]; (K,* TA;) [commonly] *a piece of stick of the* [*kind of tree called*] أَرَاك: (Msb:) accord. to IDrd, derived from سُكْتُ الشَّىْءَ meaning "I rubbed, or rubbed well, the thing;" (O, Msb;) accord. to IF, from تَسَاوَكَتِ الإِبِلُ [expl. above]: (Msb:) accord. to Lth, (T, TA,) سِوَاكٌ is masc. and fem., (IDrd, T, M, O, K,) though it is the more approvable way to make it masc.; (O;) but Az holds this to be a mistake, and the word to be masc. [only]; and Hr says that this assertion of Lth is one of his foul mistakes: (TA:) its pl. is سُوُكٌ (S, O, Msb, K) and سُوْكٌ (Az, TA) and سُؤُكٌ, (AHn, TA,) and [of pauc.] أَسْوِكَةٌ; and the pl. of † مِسْوَاكٌ is مَسَاوِيكُ. (TA.) In the saying, in a trad., خَيْرُ خِلَالِ الصَّائِمِ السِّوَاكُ, a prefixed n. is [said to be] suppressed [so that the meaning is *The best of the habits*, or *customs, of the faster is* the use of *the tooth-stick*: but see 2, where سِوَاكٌ is said, on the authority of the Msb, to be also an inf. n.].

مِسْوَاكٌ: see سِوَاكٌ, in two places.

سول

1. سَالَ, aor. يَسَالُ, (Akh, and S, M, Msb, K, all in art. سأل,) like خَافَ, aor. يَخَافُ, (Msb and K ibid.,) first pers. pret. سِلْتُ, [like خِفْتُ,] (Sb, M in the present art., [in the K in this art., erroneously, سَلْتُ,]) and aor. أَسَالُ, (Sb, M and K in this art.,) imperative سَلْ, (S, Msb, K, TA, all in art. سأل,) dual سَلَا, and pl. سَلُوا, these two being irregular, (Msb in that art.,) inf. n. سُوَالٌ, (M and K in the present art.,) mentioned by Sb and by Th, (M ibid.,) and سِوَالٌ, (M and K ibid.,) mentioned by Th, (M ibid.,) *i. q.* سَأَلَ [*He asked*, &c.], (Akh, and S, M, Msb, K, all in art. سأل,) and سَالْتُ; a dial. var. of the verb with ا, (Sb, M and K in the present art.,) the medial radical being originally و, (M and K ibid.,) not a substitute for أ, (M ibid.) as is shown by the phrase هُمَا يَتَسَاوَلَانِ, (M and K ibid.,) mentioned by AZ: (M ibid.:) it is of the dial. of Hudheyl. (TA in art. سأل.) [For the pass. (سِيلَ &c.), see سَأَلَ.] A certain elegant scholar says,

• سَالَتْ هُذَيْلٌ رَسُولَ ٱللّٰهِ فَاحِشَةً •

i. e. [*Hudheyl*] *asked of the Apostle of God as a thing wished for* [*something beyond measure evil*]: it is not from سَأَلَ, [i. e. it is originally سَوِلَ, not formed from سَأَلَ by the substitution of ا for أ,] as many of the elegant scholars say. (Er-Rághib, TA.) ═ سَوِلَ, (M, K,) [aor. يَسْوَلُ] inf. n. سَوَلٌ, (M,) *He*, or *it, was*, or *became, lax, flaccid*, or *uncompact*; or *it hung down loosely*; *was*, or *became, pendent*, or *pendulous*: (M, K:) [or, said of a man, *he was*, or *became, flaccid*, or *pendulous, in the belly*, or *in the part of the belly below the navel*; as appears from an explanation of أَسْوَلُ and from what here follows:] سَوَلٌ, (S, TA,) in the K, erroneously, † سَوْلَةٌ, (TA,) signifies *flaccidity*, or *uncompactness*, or *pendulousness*, (S, K, TA,) of the belly, (K,) and so † تَسَوُّلٌ and تَسَوُّنٌ, (TA,) or of the part of the belly below the navel; (S, TA;) and of other things, (K, TA,) as, for instance, (TA,) of a cloud also. (S, TA.)

2. سَوَّلَتْ لَهُ نَفْسُهُ أَمْرًا, (S,) or كَذَا, (M, K,) or الشَّىْءَ, (Msb,) inf. n. تَسْوِيلٌ, (TA,) *His soul embellished* [or *commended*] *to him* (S, M, Msb,* K) *a thing*, or *an affair*, (S,) or *such a thing*, (M, K,) or *the thing*: (Msb:) or *made it* [*to appear*] *easy to him*, and *a light matter in his eyes*; from سَوَلٌ signifying "laxness" or the like: (Bd in xii. 18:) the inf. n. signifies the *embellishing*, a thing, and *making it to be loved* or *approved*, in order that one may do it or say it: (TA:) or the soul's *embellishing* a thing that is eagerly desired, and *picturing what is foul* thereof *as goodly*: (Er-Rághib, TA:) and it is said to be from سُوْلٌ signifying "an object of a man's desire, which embellishes to the seeker thereof that which is false, or vain, and other things of the deceptions of the present world." (TA.) —— You say also, يُسَوَّلُ إِلَىَّ كَذَا *Such a thing is imaged in the mind to me*; *is an object of fancy to me*; or *seems to me*. (L in art. هد.) —— And سَوَّلَ لَهُ said of the Devil, *He led him into error*; or *made him to err*: (M, K:) or *facilitated to him the commission of great sins*; from سَوَلٌ meaning as expl. above in this paragraph: or *incited him to indulgence in appetences*, or *lusts*; from السُّوْلُ meaning [by implication] التَّمَنِّى: (Bd in xlvii. 27:) or [as though meaning] *let down his rope* [*to him to aid in the accomplishment of his desire*]. (Ham p. 748.)

5: see 5 in art. سأل; ═ and 1, last sentence, in the present art.

6. هُمَا يَتَسَاوَلَانِ [*They two ask*, or *beg, each other*; *i. q.* يَتَسَاءَلَانِ, q. v.]: (M, K:) a phrase mentioned by AZ. (M.)

سُولٌ *i. q.* مَسْأَلَةٌ [as signifying *A petition*; or *a request*; meaning *a thing that is*, or *has been, asked*, or *begged*; see سُؤْلٌ]; (TA;) as also † سُولَةٌ; (K, TA;) each, (TA,) a dial. var. of the word with ء: (K, TA: [but it is also said in the latter that سُؤْلٌ is the original of سُولٌ because the readers of the Kur-án read the word with ء in chap. xx. verse 36:]) or *an object of desire* or *wish* (أُمْنِيَّةٌ), *which one asks*: (TA:) or *an object of want, which the soul eagerly desires:* (Er-Rághib, TA:) or *an object of* a man's *desire* (أُمْنِيَّة), *which embellishes to the seeker thereof that which is false,* or *vain, and other things of the deceptions of the present world:* but there is a difference between سُول and ▼ سُولَة on the one hand and أُمْنِيَّة on the other hand, in that the former relate to what is sought, or demanded, and امنية relates to what is meditated (قُدِّرَ); (TA;) [for] this last primarily signifies "a thing that a man meditates (يُقَدِّرُهُ) in his mind," from مَنَى signifying قَدَّرَ; (Bd in ii. 73;) so that the سُول ▼ seems to be after the أُمْنِيَّة: (TA:) سُولَة may be from سَوَّلَتْ لَهُ نَفْسُهُ كَذَا in the first of the senses assigned to it above, and [from] سَوَّلَ said of the Devil in the last of the senses assigned to it above. (Ham p. 748.) [See also سُؤَال, below.]

سُولَة: see 1, last sentence.

سُوَلَة: see سُول, in three places.

سُوَلَة, (M, Ḳ,) applied to a man, (M,) *One who asks,* or *begs, much;* (Ḳ;) i. q. [سُؤَلَة and] سَؤُول. (M.)

سُوَال an inf. n. of سَالَ as syn. with سَأَلَ: (Sb, Th, M, Ḳ:) [and used as a simple subst., like سُول and سُولَة, for] IJ mentions أَسْوِلَة as its pl. (M, TA.)

سَوِيل *An equal.* (M, Ḳ.) So in the saying, أَنَا سَوِيلُكَ فِى هٰذَا الأَمْرِ [*I am thy equal in this affair*]. (M.)

أَسْوَل *Lax, flaccid,* or *uncompact;* or *hanging down loosely;* or *pendent,* or *pendulous; in the lower part:* (M, Ḳ:) or a man *flaccid,* or *pendulous, in the part of the belly below the navel:* fem. سَوْلَآءُ: and pl. سُول. (Ṣ.) And سَحَابٌ أَسْوَلُ *Clouds that are uncompact,* (Ṣ, TA,) *their skirts,* or *fringes, hanging down;* and in like manner, سَحَابَةٌ سَوْلَآءُ; sing. سَحَائِبُ سُولٌ. (TA.) And دَلْوٌ سَوْلَآءُ *A large bucket.* (M, Ḳ.*)

سوم

1. سَوْمٌ, inf. n. of سَامَ, primarily signifies The *going,* or *going away, engaged,* or *occupied, in seeking,* or *in seeking for* or *after,* or *in seeking to find and take* or *to get,* a thing: and sometimes it is used as meaning the *going,* or *going away;* as when it is said of camels [or the like]: and sometimes, as meaning the *seeking,* or *seeking for* or *after,* or *seeking to find and take* or *to get;* as when it relates to selling or buying. (Er-Rághib, TA.) — You say, سَامَتِ المَاشِيَةُ, (Ṣ, Mgh, Mṣb, TA) or النَّعَمُ (M) or المَالُ, (Ḳ,) aor. تَسُومُ, (Ṣ, M, Mṣb,) inf. n. سَوْمٌ, (Ṣ, M, Mgh, Mṣb,) *The cattle pastured* (Ṣ, M, Mgh, Mṣb, Ḳ, TA) *by themselves* (Mṣb) *where they pleased;* and in like manner, الغَنَمُ [*the sheep* or *goats*]: or *went away at random,* or *roved, pasturing where they pleased.* (TA.) — [Hence, سَامَ, inf n. as above, *He did as he pleased.*] You say, خَلَّيْتُهُ وَسَوْمَهُ *I left him to do as he pleased.* (Ṣ, M, Ḳ.*) [In the CḲ, خَلَّاهُ وَسَوْمَهُ لِمَا يُرِيدُهُ is put for خَلَّاهُ وَسَوْمَهُ لِمَا يُرِيدُهُ; and the like is done in one of my copies of the Ṣ. See also 2.]) — And سَامَ, (Ṣ,) or سَامَتِ الإِبِلُ, and الرِّيحُ, (M, Ḳ,) or الرِّيَاحُ, (Ṣ,) inf. n. as above, (Ṣ, M,) *He,* or *it,* (Ṣ,) or *the camels,* and *the wind,* (M, Ḳ,) or *the winds,* (Ṣ,) *passed, went,* or *went on* or *along:* (Ṣ, M, Ḳ:) or سَوْمٌ signifies the *passing,* &c., *quickly;* one says of a she camel, سَامَتْ, aor. and inf. n. as above, *she passed,* &c., *quickly;* (Aṣ, TA;) and hence the saying of Dhu-l-Bijádeyn cited in art. عرض, voce تَعَرَّضِى: or the *passing,* &c., *quickly, with the desire of making a sound in going along.* (TA.) — And سَامَتِ الطَّيْرُ عَلَى الشَّىْءِ, (M, Ḳ,) aor. and inf. n. as above, (M,) *The birds went,* [or *hovered,*] or *circled, round about the thing:* (M, Ḳ:) or, as some say, سَوْمٌ signifies any *going,* [or *hovering,*] or *circling, round about.* (M.) = [As mentioned in the first sentence of this art.,] سَوْمٌ is also in selling and buying. (Ṣ.) You say, سَامَ السِّلْعَةَ, (Mgh, Mṣb,) aor. and inf. n. as above, (Mṣb,) *He* (the seller) *offered the commodity,* or *article of merchandise,* (Mgh, Mṣb,) *for sale,* (Mṣb,) *and mentioned the price:* (Mgh:) and it is also said of the purchaser, like ▼ اِسْتَامَهَا, (Mgh, Mṣb,) meaning *he sought to obtain the sale of the commodity,* or *article of merchandise:* and one says also of the seller, and of the purchaser, سَامَ بِالسِّلْعَةِ, meaning *he mentioned the price of the commodity* [*in offering it for sale,* and *in offering to purchase it*]: (Mṣb:) and in like manner, سُمْتُ فُلَانًا بِسِلْعَتِى, inf. n. as above, *I said to such a one, "Wilt thou take* [or *purchase*] *my commodity for such a price?"* (TA:) and سَامَنِى بِسِلْعَتِهِ *he* (the seller, Mṣb) *mentioned to me the price of his commodity* [*in offering it for sale*]: (Mṣb, TA:) [and, agreeably with these explanations,] Kr says that السَّوْمُ signifies العَرْضُ [i. e. *the act of offering,* &c.]: (M, TA:) or سُمْتُ بِالسِّلْعَةِ, inf. n. سَوْمٌ (M, Ḳ) and سُوَامٌ, with ḍamm; (Ḳ, TḲ; [in the former only said to be syn. with سَوْمٌ in selling and buying;]) and ▼ سَاوَمْتُ, (M, Ḳ,) inf. n. سِوَامٌ; (TA;) and ▼ اِسْتَمْتُ بِهَا and عَلَيْهَا; signify غَالَيْتُ [which means *I offered the commodity for sale, mentioning its price, and was exorbitant in my demand:* and also *I purchased the commodity for a dear,* or *an excessive, price:* and both these meanings are app. here intended]: (M, Ḳ, TA:) and in like manner, ▼ اِسْتَمْتُهُ السِّلْعَةَ [*I offered to him the commodity for sale,* &c.: and *I purchased of him the commodity,* &c.]: (TA:) or, as some say, (so in the TA, but in the M and Ḳ "and,") this last, as also ▼ اِسْتَمْتُهُ عَلَى السِّلْعَةِ, means ▼ سَأَلْتُهُ سَوْمَهَا [i. e. *I asked him the price at which the commodity was to be sold*]: (M, Ḳ, TA:) and سَامَنِيهَا, (M,) or ▼ سَاوَمَنِيهَا, (TA, [but the former is app. the right,]) means ▼ ذَكَرَ لِى سَوْمَهَا [i. e. *he mentioned to me the price at which it was to be sold*]: (M, TA:) you say also, ▼ اِسْتَمْتُ عَلَيْهِ بِسِلْعَتِى when you mention the price of the commodity [i. e. it means *I mentioned to him the price at which I would sell my commodity*]: and you say, ▼ اِسْتَامَ مِنِّى بِسِلْعَتِى when he is the person who offers to thee the price [i. e. it means *he offered to me a price for my commodity;* or *he sought to obtain from me the sale of my commodity by offering a price for it*]: (TA:) and ▼ اِسْتَامَ عَلَىَّ *he contended* [*by bidding*] *against me in a sale:* (Ṣ,* PṢ:) or ▼ اِسْتَامَ عَلَىَّ السِّلْعَةَ, which means اِسْتَامَ عَلَى سَوْمِى [i. e. *he sought to obtain the sale of the commodity in opposition to me,* or *to my seeking it*]. (Mṣb. [See also 3.]) Hence, [Mohammad is related to have said,] لَا يَسُومُ الرَّجُلُ عَلَى سَوْمِ أَخِيهِ, (Mgh,) or لا يسوم أَحَدُكُمْ على سوم اخيه, (Mṣb,) i. e. [*The man,* or *any one of you,*] *shall not purchase* [*in opposition to his brother*]: (Mgh, Mṣb:) and it may mean *shall not sell;* the case being that of a man's offering to the purchaser his commodity for a certain price, and another's then saying, "I have the like thereof for less than this price:" so that the prohibition relates in common to the seller and the buyer: (M:) and the saying is also related otherwise, i. e. ▼ لَا يَسْتَامُ, meaning *shall not purchase.* (Mgh.) And it is said in a trad., نَهَى عَنِ السَّوْمِ قَبْلَ طُلُوعِ الشَّمْسِ, meaning, accord. to Aboo-Is-ḥáḳ, أَنْ ▼ يُسَاوِمَ بِسِلْعَتِهِ [i. e. *He* (Mohammad) *forbade the offering a commodity for sale before the rising of the sun*]; because that is a time in which God is to be praised, and one should not be diverted by other occupation: or, he says, it may mean *the pasturing of camels;* because, before sunrise, when the pasturage is moist with dew, it occasions a fatal disease. (TA.) You say also, سُمْتُكَ بَعِيرَكَ ▼ سِيمَةً حَسَنَةً [*I have mentioned to thee a good price for thy camel*]. (Ṣ.) And ▼ اِسْتَامَ فِيهِ ▼ سِيمَةً غَالِيَةً [*He demanded for it a dear price*]. (TA in art. حشر.) And سَامَهُ بِعَمَلٍ [*He made to him an offer of working, mentioning the rate of payment;* or *bargained,* or *contracted, with him for work*]. (Ḳ in art. عمل. [See also 3.]) — The Arabs also say, عَرَضَ عَلَىَّ سَوْمَ عَالَّةٍ [*He offered to me in the manner of offering water to camels taking a second draught*]; meaning like the saying of the vulgar, عَرْضَ سَابِرِىٍّ: (Ks, TA: [see art. سبر:]) a prov. applied to him who offers to thee that of which thou hast no need. (Sh, TA. [See also art. عل; and see Freytag's Arab. Prov. ii. 84.]) — And you say, سَامَهُ الأَمْرَ, (M, Ḳ,) aor. as above, (TA,) inf. n. سَوْمٌ, (M, TA,) *He imposed upon him,* or *made him to undertake, the affair, as a task,* or *in spite of difficulty* or *trouble* or *inconvenience;* or *he ordered, required,* or *constrained, him to do the thing, it being difficult* or *troublesome* or *inconvenient:* (M, Ḳ, TA:) or *he brought upon him the affair,* or *event;* (Zj, M, Ḳ, TA;) as also ▼ سَوَّمَهُ, (Ḳ,) inf. n. تَسْوِيمٌ: (TA:) or *he endeavoured to induce him,* or *incited him,* or *made him, to do,* or *to incur, the affair,* or *event:* (Sh, TA:) it is mostly used in relation to punishment, and evil, (Zj, M, Ḳ, TA,) and wrong-doing: and hence the saying in the Ḳur [ii. 46 and vii. 137 and xiv. 6], يَسُومُونَكُمْ سُوْءَ العَذَابِ *They bringing upon you evil punish-*

ment or torment: (Zj, M, TA:) or seeking, or desiring, for you evil punishment: (Ksh and Bḍ in ii. 46:) or endeavouring to induce you to incur it: (Ksh ibid.:) from سَامَهُ خَسْفًا [expl. by what here follows]. (Ksh and Bḍ ibid.) You say, سُمْتُهُ خَسْفًا *I brought upon him* خَسْف [i. e. *wrong*, or *wrong treatment*, as expl. in the Ksh and by Bḍ ubi suprà]: or *I endeavoured to induce him to incur it* (أَرَدْتُهُ عَلَيْهِ): (Ṣ:) [see also خَسْف: and سُمْتُهُ خُطَّةَ خَسْفٍ; expl. in art. خط:] and سِيمَ الخَسْفَ *He was constrained to incur, or to do, what is termed* الخَسْف [meaning *abasement* or *ignominy*, or *that which was difficult*]: (TA:) and سُمْتُهُ ذُلًّا *I abased him.* (Mṣb.) ═ سَامَهُ, aor. as above, also signifies *He kept*, or *clave, to it, not quitting it.* (M,* TA.) ═ See also 4.

2. سَوَّمَ الخَيْلَ, (Ṣ, Ḳ,) or الإِبِلَ, (M,) [inf n. تَسْوِيمٌ,] *He sent forth* (Ṣ, M, Ḳ) *the horses*, (Ṣ, Ḳ,) or *the camels*, (M,) [sometimes meaning] *to the pasturage, to pasture where they would.* (TA. [See also 4.]) — [Hence,] سوّمهُ means خَلَّاهُ وَسَوْمَهُ, (AZ, Ṣ, M, Ḳ,) i. e. [*He left him*] *to do as he pleased*; namely, a man. (AZ, Ṣ, Ḳ. [In the CḲ is a mistranscription in this place, before mentioned: see 1, fourth sentence.]) Whence the prov., عَبْدٌ وَسُوِّمَ, *A slave, and he has been left to do as he pleases.* (TA.) — And سَوَّمْتُ فُلَانًا فِى مَالِى *I gave such a one authority to judge, give judgment, pass sentence, or decide judicially, respecting my property.* (AO, Ṣ: and in like manner سوّمهُ فى مَالِه is expl. in the M and Ḳ.) And سَوَّمْتُهُ أَمْرِى *I made him to have the ordering and deciding of my affair, or case, to do what he would*; like سَوَّفْتُهُ أَمْرِى. (TA in art. سوف.) — And سَوَّمَ عَلَى القَوْمِ *He urged his horses* [خَيْلَهُ being understood] *against the people, or party, and made havoc among them.* (Ṣ, Ḳ.) — And تَسْوِيمٌ signifies also The *making* a horse *to sweat well.* (KL.) — See also 1, in the last quarter of the paragraph. ═ And سَوَّمَ الفَرَسَ, (M, Ḳ,) inf. n. تَسْوِيمٌ, (Ḳ,) *He put a mark upon the horse*: (M, Ḳ:) *he marked the horse with a piece of silk* (بِحَرِيرَةٍ) [perhaps a mistranscription for بِحَدِيدَةٍ, i. e. *with an iron* such as is used for branding]), or *with something whereby he should be known.* (Lth, TA.) See also 5. [And see 4.]

3. سَاوَمْتُهُ (Ṣ, Mṣb) بِالسِّلْعَةِ (MA) [and فِى السِّلْعَةِ agreeably with what here follows and with an ex. in art. بكر], inf. n. سِوَامٌ (Ṣ, Mṣb) and مُسَاوَمَةٌ, (TA,) [*I bargained*, or *chaffered, with him*, or] *I contended with him in bargaining*, or *chaffering, for the commodity*, or *article of merchandise*, (MA, Mṣb,* TA,) *and in deciding the price*: (TA:) and ↓ تَسَاوَمْنَا (Ṣ, Mṣb, TA*) فِى السِّلْعَةِ (TA) [and بِالسِّلْعَةِ agreeably with what here precedes] *We bargained*, or *chaffered, for the commodity*, or *article of merchandise*, [or *contended in doing so*,] *one offering it for a certain price, and another demanding it for a lower price.* (Mṣb.) See also 1, in three places.

4. اسام المَاشِيَةَ, (Ṣ, Mgh, Mṣb,) or الإِبِلَ, (M, Ḳ,) inf. n. إِسَامَةٌ, (Mgh,) *He pastured the cattle*, or *the camels*: (M, Mgh, Ḳ, TA:) or *he sent forth*, or *took forth, the cattle*, or *the camels, to pasture*: (Ṣ, TA:) or *he made the cattle* [or *the camels*] *to pasture by themselves* [*where they pleased* (see 1)]: (Mṣb:) and [in like manner] سُمْتُ ↓ الإِبِلَ *I left the camels to pasture* [*by themselves where they pleased*]. (Th, TA. [See also 2.]) Hence, in the Ḳur [xvi. 10], فِيهِ تُسِيمُونَ (Ṣ) *Upon which ye pasture* your beasts. (Jel.) — [And accord. to Freytag, اسام occurs in the Deewán of Jereer as meaning *He urged* a horse *to run*: or, as some say, *he marked* a horse *with some sign.* See also 2.] — اسام إِلَيْهِ بِبَصَرِهِ *He cast his eye*, or *eyes, at him*, or *it.* (Ḳ.) ═ See also سَامَةٌ.

5. تسوّم *He set a mark, token, or badge, upon himself, whereby he might be known* [in war &c.]. (Ṣ.) In a trad. (Ṣ, TA) respecting [the battle of] Bedr, (TA,) occur the words, تَسَوَّمُوا فَإِنَّ المَلَائِكَةَ قَدْ تَسَوَّمَتْ, (Ṣ, TA,) or ↓ سَوِّمُوا فانّ الملائكة قد سَوَّمَتْ, accord. to different relations; i. e. *Make ye a mark, token, or badge, for yourselves, whereby ye may know one another* [in the fight, *for the angels* that are assisting you *have done so*]. (TA.)

6: see 3.

8. أَرْضٌ تُسْتَامُ فِيهَا الإِبِلُ, (M,) or ↓ مُسْتَامَةٌ تُسْتَامُ, (TA,) means *A land in which the camels pasture by themselves where they please* (تَسُومُ فِيهَا): (M:) or *a land into which they go away* [*to pasture*]. (TA.) [See also مَسَامٌ.] ═ اِسْتَامَ السِّلْعَةَ: &c.: see 1, in ten places.

سَامٌ *Death*: (IAạr, Ṣ, M, Mgh:) and سَامَةٌ [as its n. un.] *a death*: (IAạr, TA:) but the former [signifies the same in Pers., and] is said to be not Arabic. (TA.) It is related in a trad., respecting the salutation of the Jews, that they used to say, السَّامُ عَلَيْكُمْ [*Death come upon you*, instead of السَّلَامُ عَلَيْكُمْ]; and that he [i. e. Moḥammad] used to reply, عَلَيْكُمْ; accord. to the generality of the relaters, وَعَلَيْكُمْ, but correctly without the و, because the و implies participation: and it is related of 'Áisheh that she used to say to them, عَلَيْكُمُ السَّامُ وَالذَّامُ وَاللَّعْنَةُ, as mentioned in art. سأم: (TA:) the Jews are also related to have said [to the Muslims], عَلَيْكُمُ السَّامُ الدَّامُ meaning المَوْتُ الدَّائِمُ. (TA in art. دوم: see دَائِمٌ in that art.) ═ Also *A kind of tree, of which are made the masts* (دَقَاقِلُ [pl. of دَوْقَلٌ]) *of ships*: (Kr, M, TA:) accord. to Sh, (TA,) the [*tree called*] خَيْزُرَان. (Ḳ, TA. [And accord. to some copies of the Ḳ, سَامَةٌ also has this signification, and the signification expl. in the sentence here next following: but accord. to the text of the Ḳ as given in the TA, وَالسَّامَةُ has been erroneously substistituted in the copies above referred to for وَالسَّاقَةُ, which, by reason of what precedes it, means that سَامَةٌ also signifies the same as سَاقَةٌ; and if the former reading were right, the context in the Ḳ would imply that السامة is also the name of a son of Noah, which is incorrect; the name of that son being only سَامٌ.]) ═ Also *A* [*hollow*, or *cavity, in the ground, such as is called*] نُقْرَة, *in which water remains*, or *stagnates, and collects.* (Ḳ. [For the verb in this explanation, which is written يَنْقَعُ in the CḲ and in my MS. copy of the Ḳ, I read يَتَنَقَّعُ.]) ═ Also a pl. [or rather coll. gen. n.] of which the sing. [or n. un.] is سَامَةٌ: (M, Ḳ:) the former signifies *Veins of gold*: and the latter, *a single vein thereof*: (Ṣ:) or the latter, *a vein in a mountain, differing from its* [*general*] *nature*; (M, Ḳ;) *if running from east to west, not failing of its promise to yield silver*: (M:) or the former, (M,) or latter, (Ḳ, TA,) *gold*, and *silver*; (M, Ḳ, TA;) accord. to Aṣ and IAạr: (M, TA:) or, as some say, *an ingot of gold*, and *of silver*: (TA:) or *veins of gold*, and *of silver, in the stone* [or *rock*]: (M, Ḳ:) En-Nábighah El-Jaạdee, (M,) or Edh-Dhubyánee, (TA,) uses السام as meaning *silver*; for he likens thereto a woman's front teeth in respect of their whiteness: (M, TA:) and Aboo-Sa'eed says that silver is called in Pers. سِيمْ, and in Ar. سَامٌ: (TA:) but the meaning most commonly known is *gold.* (M, TA.) A poet says, (M,) namely, Ḳeys Ibn-El-Khaṭeem, (Ṣ,)

* لَوَ انَّكَ تُلْقِى حَنْظَلًا فَوْقَ بَيْضِنَا *
* تَدَحْرَجَ عَنْ ذِى سَامِهِ المُتَقَارِبِ *

(Ṣ, M,) [i. e. *If thou threwest colocynths upon our helmets, they would roll along from what is gilded thereof*, they being *near together*: لَوَ انَّكَ is for لَوْ أَنَّكَ: and] the ه in سامه relates to the بيض [which are described as] gilded therewith: (Ṣ:) the poet is describing the party as being close together in fight, so that colocynths, notwithstanding their smoothness and the evenness of their parts, if they fell upon their heads, would not reach the ground. (Th, Ṣ,* M.)

سَوْمٌ [is originally an inf. n.: see 1, passim: ═ and is also used as a subst. signifying The *price* of any commodity, or article of merchandise; like ↓ سِيمَةٌ and ↓ سُومَةٌ]. You say, سَأَلْتُهُ سَوْمَهَا, and ذَكَرَ لِى سَوْمَهَا, referring to a سِلْعَة [or commodity]: see 1, in the former half of the paragraph. And سُمْتُكَ بَعِيرَكَ ↓ سِيمَةً حَسَنَةً, and اِسْتَامَ فِيهِ ↓ سِيمَةً غَالِيَةً: see again 1, in the latter half of the paragraph. And إِنَّهُ لَغَالِى ↓ السِّيمَةِ, (Ṣ, M, Ḳ) and ↓ السُّومَةِ, meaning السَّوْمِ [i. e. *Verily it is dear in price*]. (M, Ḳ.) ↓ سِيمَةٌ and ↓ سُومَةٌ are both substs. from سَامَ as used in the phrase سَامَنِى الرَّجُلُ بِسِلْعَتِهِ [and the like]; (TA;) syn. with قِيمَةٌ. (Ḥar p. 435 in explanation of the former.)

سَامَةٌ [as n. un. of سَامٌ: see the latter, first sentence, and last but one. ═ Also] *A* حُفْرَة, (M, and so in copies of the Ḳ,) or حُفَيْرَة, (Ḳ accord. to the TA,) [i. e. *hollow dug in the ground*, app. to be filled with water for cattle,] *by a well* (عَلَى رَكِيَّةٍ): its pl. is سِيَمٌ [originally سِوَمٌ]: and you say, ↓ أَسَامَهَا, (M, Ḳ, TA,) inf. n. إِسَامَةٌ, meaning *He dug it* [i. e. the سامة]. (TA.) ═ Also i. q. سَاقَةٌ [q. v.], (Ḳ, accord. to the TA, [as mentioned above, see سَامٌ,]) on the authority of IAạr. (TA.)

سُومَةٌ: see سَوْمٌ, in three places. ═ Also, (Ṣ,

M, Ḳ,) and ▾ سِيمَةٌ (M, Ḳ) and ▾ سِيمَى, also written سِيمَا, (Ṣ, M, Ḳ, TA, but omitted in some copies of the Ḳ,) and ▾ سِيمَآءٌ and ▾ سِيمِيَآءٌ, (Ṣ, M, Ḳ,) the last mentioned by Aṣ, (TA,) [and it occurs with tenween by poetic license, being properly like كِبْرِيَآءُ, a rare form, q. v.,] *A mark, sign, token,* or *badge, by which a thing is known,* (Ṣ,* M, Ḳ,) or *by which the good is known from the bad:* (TA:) accord. to J, (TA,) the سُومَةٌ is *a mark,* &c., *that is put upon a sheep* or *goat,* and *such as is used in war* or *battle;* (Ṣ, TA;) whence the verb تَسَوَّمَ [q. v.]: (Ṣ:) and accord. to IAạr the ▾ سِيمَةٌ is *a mark upon the wool of sheep;* and its pl. is سِيَمٌ: [see also سِمَةٌ, in art. وسم:] accord. to IDrd, one says, ▾ عَلَيْهِ سِيمَى حَسَنَةٌ, meaning *Upon him,* or *it, is a good mark* &c.; and it is from وَسَمْتُ, aor. أَسِمُ; being originally وِسْمَى; the و being transposed, and changed into ى because of the kesreh before it: (TA:) this form occurs in the Ḳur [xlviii. 29], where it is said, سِيمَاهُمْ فِى وُجُوهِهِمْ [*Their mark is upon their faces;* and in several other places thereof]. (Ṣ.)

سِيمَةٌ: see سُومَةٌ, in five places: ═ and see also سُومَةٌ, in two places. [For the meanings "pactus" and "pastum missus," assigned to it by Golius, as from the Ṣ, and copied by Freytag, I find no foundation.]

سِيمَى, also written سِيمَا: see سُومَةٌ, in two places.

سِيمَآءٌ: see سُومَةٌ.

سِيمِيَآءٌ: see سُومَةٌ. — [In the present day it is applied to *Natural magic:* from the Pers. سِيمِيَا.]

سَوَامٌ: see سَائِمٌ. ═ Also *Two small hollows* (نُقْرَتَانِ) *beneath the eye of the horse.* (Ḳ.) ═ [And accord. to Freytag, it occurs in the Deewán el-Hudhaleeyeen in a sense which he explains by "*Malum*" (*an evil,* &c.).]

سُوَامٌ [The *offering* a commodity *for sale,* &c.: see 1. ═ Also] *A certain bird.* (Ḳ.)

لَا سِيَّمَا: see art. سوى.

سَائِمٌ [*Going,* or *going away, engaged,* or *occupied, in seeking,* or *in seeking for* or *after,* or *in seeking to find and take* or *to get,* a thing: (see 1, first sentence:)] *going away at random,* or *roving, wherever he will.* (TA.) And [particularly], (Ṣ,) as also ▾ سَوَامٌ (Aṣ, Ṣ, M, Ḳ) and سَائِمَةٌ, (Aṣ, Ṣ, M, Mgh, Mṣb, Ḳ,) Cattle, (مَالٌ, Ṣ, TA, or مَاشِيَةٌ, Mgh, Mṣb,) or camels, (Aṣ, M, Ḳ, TA,) and sheep or goats, (TA,) *pasturing* (Ṣ, M, Mgh, Mṣb, Ḳ, TA) *by themselves* (Mṣb) *where they please;* (TA;) or *sent forth to pasture, and not fed with fodder among the family* [*to whom they belong*]; (Aṣ, Mgh, TA;) or *pasturing in the deserts, left to go and pasture where they will:* (TA:) the pl. of سَائِمٌ and of سَائِمَةٌ is سَوَائِمُ: (Ṣ:) the pass. part. n. مَسُومٌ is not used. (Mṣb.) It is said in a trad., فِى سَائِمَةِ الغَنَمِ زَكَاةٌ [*In the case of pasturing sheep* or *goats, there is a poor-rate*]. (TA.) And in another trad., السَّائِمَةُ جُبَارٌ, i. e. *The beast* (دَابَّةٌ) *that is sent away into its place of pasture,* if it hurt a human being, *the injury committed by it is a thing for which no mulct is exacted.* (TA.) And it is related in a trad. respecting the emigration to Abyssinia, that the Nejáshee said to those who had emigrated to his country, اُمْكُثُوا فَأَنْتُمْ سُيُومٌ بِأَرْضِى, i. e. [*Tarry ye, and ye will be*] *secure* [*in my land*]: IAth says that thus it is explained: and سيوم is [said to be] an Abyssinian word: it is related also with fet-ḥ to the س: and some say that سُيُومٌ is pl. of سَائِمٌ [like as شُهُودٌ is said to be of شَاهِدٌ]; i. e., *ye shall rove* (تَسُومُونَ) *in my country like the sheep,* or *goats, pasturing where they please* (كَالغَنَمِ السَّائِمَةِ), no one opposing you: (TA:) or, as some relate the trad., it is شُيُومٌ. (TA in art. شيم.)

[مَسَامٌ *A place where cattle pasture by themselves where they please; a place where they rove about, pasturing:* like أَرْضٌ مُسْتَامَةٌ. — Freytag explains it as meaning *A place of passage:* — and *A quick passage:* from the Deewán el-Hudhaleeyeen.]

مَسَامَةٌ *A wide and thick piece of wood at the bottom of the* قَاعِدَتَانِ [or *two side-posts*] *of the door.* (Ḳ.) — And *A staff in the fore part of the* [*women's camel-vehicle called*] هَوْدَج. (Ḳ.)

الخَيْلُ المُسَوَّمَةُ means *The pastured horses:* (Ṣ, Mṣb, TA:) or *the horses sent forth with their riders upon them:* (AZ, Az, Mṣb, TA:) or it means, (TA,) or means also, (Ṣ, Mṣb,) *the marked horses;* (Ṣ, Mṣb, TA;) *marked by a colour differing from the rest of the colour;* or *by branding:* (TA:) or *the horses of goodly make.* (Ḥam p. 62, and TA. [See the Ḳur iii. 12.]) — مُسَوِّمِينَ, in the Ḳur [iii. 121], may mean, accord. to Akh, either *Marked* [*by the colours,* or *the like, of their horses, so as to be distinguished from others*], or *sent forth;* and is thus with ى and ن [because applied to rational beings, namely, angels, and] because the horses were marked, or sent forth, and upon them were their riders. (Ṣ.) — And حِجَارَةً مِنْ طِينٍ مُسَوَّمَةً عِنْدَ رَبِّكَ, (Ṣ,* M, Ḳ,*) in the Ḳur [li. 33 and 34], (Ṣ, M,) means [*Stones of* baked *clay*] *having upon them the semblance of seals* [*impressed in the presence of thy Lord*], (Ṣ, Ḳ, Er-Rághib,) in order that they may be known to be from God: (Er-Rághib:) or *marked* (Zj, M, Bḍ, Ḳ, Jel) *with whiteness and redness,* (Zj, M, Ḳ,) as is related on the authority of El-Ḥasan, (Zj, M,) or *with a mark whereby it shall be known that they are not of the stones of this world* (M, Ḳ) *but of the things wherewith God inflicts punishment,* (M,) or [*each*] *with the name of him upon whom it is to be cast:* (Jel:) or *sent forth:* (Bḍ, TA:) but Er-Rághib says that the first is the proper way of explaining it. (TA.)

مُسْتَامَةٌ, applied to a land (أَرْضٌ): see 8.

سون

5. تَسَوَّنَ: see 1 in art. سول, last sentence.

سوى

1. سَوِىَ, aor. يَسْوَى: see 3, in two places. ═ [Accord. to Golius, سَوَى, inf. n. سِوًى, signifies *He intended,* or *proposed to himself:* this he says as on the authority of the KL, in which only the inf. n. is mentioned with the explanation قصد وآهنگ كردن: and to this, Freytag adds the authority of Meyd; and also that the verb governs the thing which is its objective complement in the accus. case. In the Ṣ and other lexicons of good repute, I find the meaning of قَصَدَ assigned to اِسْتَوَى followed by إِلَى; but in none to سَوَى.]

2. سَوَّاهُ, (Ṣ, M, &c.,) inf. n. تَسْوِيَةٌ, (Ḳ,) *He made it equal, equable, uniform, even, level, flat, plane* or *plain;* (Ṣ,* M, MA, Mṣb, Ḳ;) or *equal in respect of elevation* or *of depression;* (Er-Rághib, TA;) [and *straight, right, direct,* or *rightly directed;* (see its quasi-pass. 8;)] and ▾ اسواه signifies the same; (M, Ḳ;) namely, a place, (Mṣb, Ḳ,) or a thing, (Ṣ, M, Er-Rághib, TA,) or an uneven, or a crooked, thing. (Mgh.) It is said in a trad., فَأَمَرَ بِالخَرِبِ فَسُوِّيَتْ [*And he gave orders respecting the ruins, and they were levelled*]. (TA in art. خرب.) And in another trad., سَوَّيْنَا عَلَى رُقَيَّةَ, meaning *We buried Rukeiyeh, and made the earth of the grave even,* or *level, over her.* (Mgh.) [Hence also,] سُوِّيَتْ عَلَيْهِ الأَرْضُ: see 8. And hence the saying in the Ḳur [iv. 45], لَوْ تُسَوَّى بِهِمُ الأَرْضُ, (TA,) i. e. *That they were buried, and that the ground were made level over them;* (Ṣ,* Bḍ;) ب being here syn. with عَلَى: (TA in art. ب:) or the meaning is, *that they became like the dust of the earth;* (M, Jel;) thus expl. by Th; (M;) or *that they had not been created, and that they and the earth were alike.* (Bḍ.) [Hence also,] بَلَى قَادِرِينَ عَلَى أَنْ نُسَوِّىَ بَنَانَهُ, in the same [lxxv. 4], is said to mean [*Yea: we are able*] *to make his hand like the foot of the camel, without fingers:* or *to make his fingers uniform, of one measure* or *size:* (TA:) or the meaning is, *we are able to put together the bones of his fingers* [*consistently*] *as they were.* (Bḍ, Jel.) And حَتَّى إِذَا سَاوَى ▾ بَيْنَ الصَّدَفَيْنِ, in the Ḳur [xviii. 95], means سَوَّى بَيْنَهُمَا [i. e. *Until, when he had made the space between the two sides of the mountains even,* or *level,* by filling it up]. (TA.) — [Also *He made it uniform, equal,* or *consimilar,* with another thing.] One says, سَوَّيْتُهُ بِهِ, (M, Ḳ,) inf. n. as above; (Ḳ;) and ▾ سَاوَيْتُهُ بِهِ, (M,* TA, TḲ,) and ▾ أَسْوَيْتُهُ بِهِ; *I made it uniform,* or *equal, with it;* or *like it:* (M, Ḳ, TA:) and ▾ سَاوَيْتُ هٰذَا بِذَاكَ *I raised this so as to make it equal in measure,* or *quantity,* or *amount, with that.* (TA.) And سَوَّيْتُ بَيْنَهُمَا, and ▾ سَاوَيْتُ, (Ṣ, M, Ḳ,) *I made them uniform,* or *equal, each with the other;* or *like each other.* (M, Ḳ, TA.) — [And *He made it symmetrical* or *symmetrically, by,* or *with, a just adaptation of its component parts; made it congruous* or *consistent in its several parts,* or *with congruity* or *consistency in its several parts:* he made it, formed it, or fashioned

it, in a suitable manner: he made it to be adapted, or *so as to be adapted, to the exigencies*, or *requirements, of its case*, or *of wisdom: he made it complete*, or *in a complete manner; completed it*, or *completed its make: he made it right* or *good*, or *in a right* or *good manner; rectified it; adjusted it;* or *put it into a right*, or *good, state.*] In the Ḳur xxxii. 8, it means *He made him symmetrical* [or *symmetrically*], *by the fit*, or *suitable, formation of his members.* (Bḍ.) And سَوَّيْتُهُ in the same, xv. 29 and xxxviii. 72, *I made his creation symmetrical:* (Bḍ:) or *I completed him*, or *made him complete.* (Jel.) And سَوَّى in the same, lxxxvii. 2, *He made* what He created *congruous* or *consistent in the several parts.* (Jel.) And اَلَّذِى خَلَقَكَ فَسَوَّاكَ, in the same [lxxxii. 7], means [*Who created thee,*] *and made thy creation to be adapted to the exigencies*, or *requirements, of wisdom.* (TA.) وَنَفْسٍ وَمَا سَوَّاهَا, in the same, [xci. 7, means *By a soul and what made it to be adapted to its exigencies*, i. e., to the performance of its functions, for it] is indicative of the faculties of the soul: this explanation is more proper than that which makes ما to mean [*Him who*, i. e.] God. (TA.) And رَفَعَ سَمْكَهَا فَسَوَّاهَا, in the same, lxxix. 28, means *He hath raised high* [*its canopy*, or] *the measure of its elevation from the earth*, or *its thickness upwards, and made it symmetrical*, or *even*, (Bḍ,) or *completed it by adorning it with the stars*, (Bḍ, TA,*) agreeably with what is said in the Ḳur xxxvii. 6, (TA,) *and by means of the revolvings* [*thereof*], *&c.*: from the saying next following. (Bḍ.) سَوَّى فُلَانٌ أَمْرَهُ *Such a one rectified*, or *adjusted, his affair;* or *put it into a right*, or *good, state.* (Bḍ in lxxix. 28.) [Hence,] one says, سَوِّ وَلَا تُسَوِّ *Rectify thou, and do not corrupt*, or *mar.* (A and TA in art. سوأ.) [One says also, سَوَّى الطَّعَامَ *He cooked the food thoroughly:* see 8 as its quasi-pass.] And سَوَّى فُلَانٌ مَنْصُوبَةً [*Such a one framed a stratagem*, or *plot*]. (TA in art. نصب.) ═ سَوَّى [as an intrans. verb, if not a mistranscription for سَوِىَ], inf. n. as above: see 8. ═ And سَوَى, [app. for سَوِىَ,] inf. n. as above, signifies *It was*, or *became, altered* [*for the worse*]; syn. تَغَيَّرَ. (TA.)

3. سَاوَاهُ, (Ṣ,* M,* Mṣb,) inf. n. مُسَاوَاةٌ (M, Er-Rághib, Mṣb, TA) and سِوَآءٌ, (M,) *It was*, or *became, equal to it*, (Ṣ, Er-Rághib, Mṣb, TA,) and *like it, in measure, extent, size, bulk, quantity*, or *amount*, and *in value*, (Mṣb, TA,) or *in linear measure*, and *in weight*, and *in the measure of capacity*, [*as well as in value:*] one says هٰذَا الثَّوْبُ مُسَاوٍ ▼ لِذٰلِكَ الثَّوْبِ [*This garment*, or *piece of cloth, is equal in length and breadth to that garment*, or *piece of cloth*]; and هٰذَا الثَّوْبُ مُسَاوٍ ▼ لِذٰلِكَ الدِّرْهَمِ [*This garment*, or *piece of cloth, is equivalent to that dirhem*]: and sometimes it means *in mode*, or *manner of being:* one says, هٰذَا السَّوَادُ مُسَاوٍ ▼ لِذٰلِكَ السَّوَادِ [*This blackness is equal in quality to this blackness*]. (Er-Rághib, TA.) It is said in a trad., سَاوَى الظِّلُّ التِّلَالَ *The shade*, or *shadow, was like, in its extent, to the mounds, in their height.* (TA.) [And سَاوَى الشَّىْءُ رَأْسَهُ means *The thing equalled in height his head:* see an ex. of the verb tropically used in this sense voce بَنِى.] One says also, هٰذَا يُسَاوِى دِرْهَمًا *This is worth*, or *equal in its value to, a dirhem:* and in a rare dial., one says, سَوِىَ ▼ دِرْهَمًا, aor. يَسْوَاهُ; (Mṣb, TA;) which AZ disallows, saying, one says سَاوَاهُ, but not يَسْوَاهُ. (Mṣb.) And هٰذَا الشَّىْءُ لَا يُسَاوِى كَذَا *This thing is not equivalent to* [or *is not worth*] *such a thing:* (Fr, Ṣ:) or لَا يُسَاوِى شَيْئًا [*It* (a garment, or some other thing, M) *is not worth anything*]: (M, Ḳ:) ▼ لا يَسْوَى is of a rare dial., (Ḳ,) unknown to Fr, (Ṣ,) disallowed by A'Obeyd, but mentioned by others: (M:) Az says that it is not of the language of the Arabs [of pure speech], (Mṣb, TA,) but is post-classical; and in like manner ▼ لا يُسْوِى is not correct Arabic: this last is with ḍamm to the [first] ى: MF says that the generality of authorities disallow it, and the Fṣ expressly disallows it, but the expositors thereof say that it is correct and chaste, of the dial. of the people of El-Ḥijáz, though an instance of a verb of which the aor. only is used. (TA.) One says likewise, سَاوَى الرَّجُلُ قِرْنَهُ *The man equalled his opponent*, or *competitor*, in knowledge, or in courage. (TA.) — See also 6. ═ And see 2, in four places, in the former half of the paragraph.

4. اسوى as a trans. verb: see 2, in two places, in the former half of the paragraph. — لَا يُسْوِى, in the sense of لَا يُسَاوِى, is not correct Arabic: see 3, in the latter part of the paragraph. ═ As an intrans. verb: see 8. — Also *He was like his son*, or *offspring*, [in some copies of the Ḳ *his father*, which, as is said in the TA, is a mistake,] *in make*, (M, Ḳ,) or *in symmetry*, or *justness of proportion;* (Fr, TA;) or simply *he was like his son*, or *offspring.* (M.) [In this instance, and in all the senses here following that are mentioned in the Ḳ, the verb is erroneously written in the CḲ استوى.] — اسوى فِى المَرْأَةِ i. q. أَوْعَبَ, (M, Ḳ, TA,) i. e. *He inserted the whole of his* ذَكَر *into the* فَرْج [*of the woman*]. (TA.) ═ Also, [as though originally أَسْوَأَ,] *He was*, or *became, base, abased, abject, vile, despicable*, or *ignominious;* syn. خَزِىَ; (M, Ḳ;) from السَّوْأَةُ. (TA.) — And *He voided his ordure;* syn. أَحْدَثَ; (Az, M, Ḳ;) [likewise] from السَّوْأَةُ, as meaning "the anus." (Az, TA.) — And hence, in the opinion of Az, and thought by J to be originally أَسْوَأَ [as he says in the Ṣ], (TA,) [though trans.,] *He dropped, left out, omitted*, or *neglected*, (Ṣ, M, Ḳ,) and *did so through inadvertence*, (Ṣ, Ḳ,) a thing, (Ṣ,) or a letter, or word, of the Ḳur-án, (M, Ḳ,) or a verse thereof: (M:) mentioned by A'Obeyd: (Ṣ:) and in like manner, accord. to IAth, in reckoning, and in shooting, or casting: and Hr says that أَشْوَى, with ش, is allowable, as meaning أَسْقَطَ. (TA.) — Also *He was*, or *became, affected with* بَرَص [or *leprosy*, which is sometimes termed السُّوْءُ; so that the verb in this sense also seems to be originally أَسْوَأَ]. (TA.) — And *He was*, or *became, restored to health*, [or *free from* سُوْء as meaning *an evil affection*, (as though the verb were in this sense likewise originally أَسْوَأَ, the incipient ا being privative, as it is in many other instances, like the Greek privative α,)] *after a disease*, or *malady.* (TA.) ═ أَسْوَيْتُهُ بِهِ: see Q. Q. 1 in art. اسو.

5: see 8.

6. تَسَاوَيَا *They two were*, or *became, equal, like each other*, or *alike;* as also ▼ اِسْتَوَيَا. (M, Ḳ.) ▼ استوى has two and more agents assigned to it: one says, استوى زَيْدٌ وَعَمْرٌو وَخَالِدٌ فِى هٰذَا [*Zeyd and 'Amr and Khálid were equal*, or *alike, in this*]; i. e. تَسَاوَوْا: whence the saying in the Ḳur [ix. 19], لَا يَسْتَوُونَ ▼ عِنْدَ اللّٰهِ [*They will not be equal*, or *alike, in the sight of God*]. (TA.) And one says, تَسَاوَوْا فِى المَالِ *They were*, or *became, equal in respect of the property, none of them exceeding another;* as also ▼ اِسْتَوَوْا فِيهِ. (Mṣb.) It is said in a trad., as some relate it, مَنْ ▼ سَاوَى يَوْمَاهُ فَهُوَ مَغْبُونٌ, in which the meaning is said to be تَسَاوَى [i. e. *He whose two days are alike*, neither being distinguished above the other by any good done by him, *is weak-minded*]. (TA.) And in another it is said, لَا يَزَالُ النَّاسُ بِخَيْرٍ مَا تَفَاضَلُوا فَإِذَا تَسَاوَوْا هَلَكُوا, (Ṣ,* TA,) i. e. [*Men will not cease to be in a good state while they vie in excellence,*] *but when they cease from vying in excellent qualities and are content with defect* [*and thus become alike, they perish*]: or *when they become equal in ignorance:* or *when they form themselves into parties and divisions, and every one is alone in his opinion, and they do not agree to acknowledge one exemplar* or *chief* or *leader* [*so that they are all alike*]: or, accord. to Az, *when they are alike in evil, there being none among them possessed of good.* (TA.)

8. استوى [seems, accord. to Bḍ, to signify primarily *He sought*, or *desired, what was equal, equable, uniform, even*, or the like: for he says (in ii. 27) that the primary meaning of الاِسْتِوَآءُ is طَلَبُ السَّوَآءِ; app. indicating the sense in which السواء is here used by what follows. — And hence, accord. to him, but I would rather say primarily, as being quasi-pass. of سَوَّاهُ,] *It was*, or *became, equal, equable, uniform, even, level, flat, plane* or *plain*, [or *equal in respect of elevation* or *of depression*, (see 2, first sentence,)] *straight, right, direct*, or *rightly directed;* syn. اِعْتَدَلَ (Ṣ, M, Mṣb, Ḳ, TA, and Ksh and Bḍ in ii. 27) فِى ذَاتِهِ, (TA,) said of a place, (Mṣb,) and اِسْتَقَامَ, said of a stick, or piece of wood, &c. (Ksh ubi suprà.) And ▼ سَوِىَ, [if not a mistranscription for سَوِىَ,] inf. n. تَسْوِيَةٌ, signifies the same as استوى [app. meaning as above], accord. to IAar; and so does ▼ أَسْوَى, as also أَوْسَى, formed from it by transposition. (TA.) One says, اِسْتَوَتْ بِهِ الأَرْضُ [lit. *The earth*, or *ground, became equable, uniform, even, &c., with him*, he having been buried in it], meaning *he perished in the earth;* as also ▼ تَسَوَّتْ, and ▼ سُوِّيَتْ عَلَيْهِ. (M, Ḳ.) And استوت أَرْضُهُمْ *Their land became* [*even in its surface, being*] *affected with drought*, or *barrenness.* (M,*

TA.) And اِسْتَوَى المَآءُ وَالخَشَبَةَ, meaning مَعَ الخَشَبَةِ [i. e. *The water became even*, or *level, with the piece of wood*]. (TA.) See also 6, in four places. One says also, اِسْتَوَى المُعْوَجُّ [or المُعْوَجُ (as in the MA) i. e. *The crooked*, or *uneven, became straight*, or *even*]: (Mgh:) and اِسْتَوَى مِنْ اعْوِجَاجٍ [*It became even from a state of unevenness*]. (Ṣ.) فَٱسْتَوَى عَلَى سُوقِهِ, in the Ḳur xlviii. last verse, means *And has stood straight*, or *erect*, (Bḍ,) or *become strong, and stood straight*, or *erect*, (Jel,) *upon its stems*. (Bḍ, Jel. [Golius erroneously assigns a similar meaning to اِسْتَوَى, a verb which I do not anywhere find.]) And فَٱسْتَوَى in the same, liii. 6, *And he stood straight*, or *erect, in his proper form in which God created him*: or *was endowed by his strength with power over the affair appointed to him*: (Bḍ:) or *became firm*, or *steady*. (Jel.) اِسْتَوَى said of a stick &c. means *It stood up* or *erect*: and *was*, or *became, even*, or *straight*: hence one says, اِسْتَوَى إِلَيْهِ كَالسَّهْمِ المُرْسَلِ *He*, or *it, went towards him*, or *it, with an undeviating, a direct*, or *a straight, course, like the arrow shot forth*: and hence, ثُمَّ ٱسْتَوَى إِلَى السَّمَآءِ is metaphorically said of God, in the Ḳur ii. 27 [and xli. 10]; (Ksh;) meaning ‡ *Then He directed himself by his will to the* [*heaven*, or] *elevated regions*, (Ksh, Bḍ,) or *upwards*, (Ksh,) or *to the heavenly bodies*; (Bḍ;) syn. عَمَدَ, (Zj, M, Ḳ,) and قَصَدَ (Zj, Ṣ, M, Ḳ, and Ksh and Bḍ) بِإِرَادَتِهِ; (Ksh, Bḍ;) for when الإِسْتِوَآءُ is trans. by means of إِلَى, it imports the meaning of *the directing of oneself*, or, as in this case, *of one's design*: (TA;) you say of any one who has finished a work and has directed himself to another, قَدِ ٱسْتَوَى لَهُ and إِلَيْهِ. (Ḥar p. 631:) or the meaning here is صَعِدَ, (Zj, M, Ḳ,) or صَعِدَ أَمْرُهُ [i. e. *his command ascended*]; (M;) and this is what is intended here by صَعِدَ: (TA:) or أَقْبَلَ عَلَيْهَا [i. e. *He advanced to it*, namely, the heaven]; (Fr, Th, M, Ḳ;) like as one says, كَانَ فُلَانٌ مُقْبِلًا عَلَى فُلَانٍ ثُمَّ ٱسْتَوَى عَلَيَّ and إِلَيَّ also, meaning أَقْبَلَ يُشَاتِمُنِي [i. e. *Such a one was advancing against such a one, then he advanced against me*, and *to me, reviling me*, or *contending with me in reviling*]: (TA:) or it means اِسْتَوْلَى, (M, Ḳ,) as some say: (M:) J says, [in the Ṣ,] but not explaining thereby the verse above cited, that it signifies also اِسْتَوْلَى and ظَهَرَ [as meaning *He had*, or *gained, the mastery*, or *victory*]: and hence the saying of El-Akhṭal, cited by him [in the Ṣ,]

• قَدِ ٱسْتَوَى بِشْرٌ عَلَى العِرَاقِ •
• مِنْ غَيْرِ سَيْفٍ وَدَمٍ مُهْرَاقِ •

[*Bishr has gained the mastery over El-'Irák without sword and without shed blood*]: Er-Rághib says that when this verb is trans. by means of عَلَى, it imports the meaning of الإِسْتِيلَآء; as in the saying in the Ḳur [xx. 4], الرَّحْمٰنُ عَلَى العَرْشِ ٱسْتَوَى [which may be rendered, *The Compassionate hath ascendancy over the empyrean so as to have everything in the universe equally within his grasp*; agreeably with what here follows]: he then adds, it is said to mean that everything is alike in relation to Him in such manner that no one thing is nearer to Him than another thing, since He is not like the bodies that abide in one place exclusively of another place. (TA.) The saying لَمَّا ٱسْتَوَتْ بِهِ رَاحِلَتُهُ عَلَى البَيْدَآءِ means [*When his riding-camel*] *ascended with him upon the desert*: or *stood up with him straight upon its legs*. (Mgh.) And one says, اِسْتَوَى عَلَى ظَهْرِ دَابَّتِهِ, (Ṣ, TA,) or عَلَى الفَرَسِ, (Mṣb,) *He was*, or *became, firm*, or *steady*, [or *he settled himself*, or *became firmly seated*, or *sat firmly*,] *upon the back of his beast*, or *upon the horse*: (Ṣ, Mṣb, TA:) and اِسْتَوَى جَالِسًا [*He became firm*, or *steady, sitting*; or *he settled himself in his sitting place*; or *sat firmly*]. (Mṣb.) [اِسْتَوَى as quasi-pass. of سَوَّاهُ also signifies *It was made*, or *became, symmetrical; congruous*, or *consistent in its several parts*: *was made, formed*, or *fashioned, in a suitable manner*: *was made*, or *became, adapted to the exigencies*, or *requirements, of its case*, or *of wisdom*: *was made*, or *became, complete*: *was made*, or *became, right*, or *good*; *became rectified, adjusted*, or *put into a right* or *good state*. And hence,] اِسْتَوَى الرَّجُلُ i. q. بَلَغَ أَشُدَّهُ [q. v.]; (M, Ḳ;) [generally meaning] *The man* [*became full-grown, of full vigour*, or *mature, in body*, or *in body and intellect*; i. e.] *attained the utmost limit of* [*the period termed*] *his* شَبَاب; (Ṣ;) or *attained the utmost limit of his* شَبَاب, *and the completion of his make and of his intellect, by the completion of from twenty-eight to thirty* [*years*]: (T, TA:) or *attained to forty* (T, M, Ḳ) *years*. (Ḳ.) And اِسْتَوَى الطَّعَامُ *The food became thoroughly cooked*. (Mṣb.) [خَطُّ الإِسْتِوَآءِ means *The equinoctial line*.]

سَيٌّ, [app. a dial. var. of سِيٌّ]: see لَا سِيَّمَا, in the next paragraph.

سِيٌّ, originally سِوْيٌ; and its dual: see سَوَآءٌ, in ten places, all except one in the latter half of the paragraph. — [Hence,] of him who is, or has become, in a state of wealth, or welfare, [or rather, of abundant wealth or welfare,] one says, وَقَعَ فِي سِيِّ رَأْسِهِ and ▼ هُوَ فِي سَوَآءِ رَأْسِهِ, (Fr, Ṣ,) or فِي سِيِّ رَأْسِهِ [in the CḲ (erroneously) سَيِّ] and وَقَعَ ▼ فِي سَوَآءِ رَأْسِهِ (M, Ḳ) and ▼ سُوَآءِ رَأْسِهِ, (Ḳ,) or مِنَ النِّعْمَةِ فِي سَوَآءِ ▼ رَأْسِهِ, (Ks, M,) i. e. † [*He is in*, or *has lighted upon*, or *come upon*,] *what is in the predicament of his head* (حُكْمِ رَأْسِهِ) [*in point of eminence, of wealth*, or *welfare*]: or *what covers his head* [*thereof*]: (M, Ḳ:) or *what equals his head* [*in eminence*] (يُسَاوِي رَأْسَهُ), *of wealth*, or *welfare*: (T, TA:) or *what has equalled his head* [*in eminence*], *of wealth*, or *welfare*; i. e. *what has accumulated upon him, and filled* [or *satisfied*] *him*: (M:) or [*what equals*] *the number of the hairs of his head, of wealth*, or *good*; (A'Obeyd, Ṣ, Ḳ;) as some explain it. (A'Obeyd, Ṣ.) See also سِيٌّ, last sentence but one. — [Hence likewise,] لَا سِيَّمَا, (Ṣ, M, Mṣb, Ḳ,) also pronounced لَا سِيَمَا, without teshdeed, (Mṣb, Mughnee, Ḳ,) and ▼ لَا سَيَّمَا is a dial. var. thereof, (Mṣb,) a compound of سِيّ and مَا, denoting exception: (Ṣ:) one says, لَا سِيَّمَا زَيْدٌ, i. e. لَا مِثْلَ زَيْدٍ [lit. *There is not the like of Zeyd*; virtually, and generally, meaning *above all Zeyd*, or *especially Zeyd*]; مَا being redundant: and لَا سِيَّمَا زَيْدٍ also; like as one says, دَعْ مَا زَيْدٌ: (M, Ḳ:) [J says,] with respect to the case of the noun following مَا, there are two ways: you may make مَا to be in the place of الَّذِي, and mean that an inchoative is to be understood, [namely, هُوَ or the like,] and put the noun that you mention in the nom. case as the enunciative; thus you may say, جَآءَنِي القَوْمُ لَا سِيَّمَا أَخُوكَ, meaning لَا سِيَّ الَّذِي هُوَ أَخُوكَ [i. e. *The people*, or *party, came to me, and there was not the like of him who is thy brother*; or *above all*, or *especially, he who is thy brother*]: (Ṣ, TA: [thus in a copy of the Ṣ: in other copies of the same, and in the TA, for سِيَّمَا, سِيَّ:]) but this rendering is invalidated in such a phrase as وَلَا سِيَّمَا زَيْدٌ by the suppression of the correlative of the noun in the nom. case where there is no lengthiness, and by the applying مَا to denote a rational being: (Mughnee:) or you may put the noun after it in the gen. case, making مَا redundant, and making سِيّ to govern the noun in that case because the meaning of سِيّ is مِثْل: [and this is the preferable way:] (Mughnee:) in both of these ways is recited the saying of Imra-el-Ḳeys,

• أَلَا رُبَّ يَوْمٍ لَكَ مِنْهُنَّ صَالِحٍ •
• وَلَا سِيَّمَا يَوْمٌ بِدَارَةِ جُلْجُلِ •

[*Verily many a good day was there to thee by reason of them; but there was not the like of a day*, or *above all a day*, or *especially a day, at Dárat Juljul*, a certain pool, where Imra-el-Ḳeys surprised his beloved, 'Oneyzeh, with others, her companions, bathing: see EM pp. 9 and 10]: you say also, أَضْرِبُ القَوْمَ وَلَا سِيَّمَا أَخِيكَ, meaning وَلَا مِثْلَ ضَرْبِ أَخِيكَ [i. e. *I will beat the people*, or *party, but there shall not be the like of the beating of thy brother*]: and if you say, وَلَا سِيَّمَا أَخُوكَ, the meaning is, وَلَا مِثْلَ الَّذِي هُوَ أَخُوكَ [*and there shall not be the like of him who is thy brother*]: in the saying إِنَّ فُلَانًا كَرِيمٌ وَلَا سِيَّمَا إِنْ أَتَيْتَهُ قَاعِدًا, accord. to Akh, مَا is a substitute for the affixed pronoun هُ, which is suppressed; the meaning being, وَلَا مِثْلَهُ إِنْ أَتَيْتَهُ قَاعِدًا [i. e. *Verily such a one is generous, and there is not the like of him if thou come to him sitting*]: (Ṣ, TA:) it is said in the Mṣb, [after explaining that مَا in سِيَّمَا may be redundant, and the noun after it governed in the gen. case as the complement of a prefixed noun; and that مَا may be used in the sense of الَّذِي, and the noun following put in the nom. case as the enunciative of the inchoative هُوَ which is suppressed;] that, accord. to some, the noun following may be in the accus. case, as being preceded by an exceptive; [or, as a specificative; (Mughnee;) in which case we must regard مَا as a substitute for the affixed pronoun هُ;]

but that this is not a good way; [and in this case, accord. to the generality of the authorities, it must be an indeterminate noun, not, like زَيْد, determinate: (Mughnee:)] also that سِيَّمَا should not be used without لَا preceding it: and that it denotes the predominance of what follows it over what precedes it: but it is added that لَا is sometimes suppressed [as is said in the Mughnee] because known to be meant, though this is rare. (TA.) One says also, لَا سِيَّ لِمَا فُلَانٌ (Lḥ, M, Ḳ) i. e. *There is not the like of such a one:* (TA:) and لَا سِيَّكَ مَا فُلَانٌ (Lḥ, M, Ḳ) i. e. *Such a one is not the like of thee.* (TA.) [In both of these instances, ما is obviously redundant. Other (similar) usages of سِيّ are mentioned voce سَوَآءٌ, to which reference has been made above.] —— سِىٌّ also signifies *A* [*desert such as is termed*] مَفَازَة; (Ṣ, M, Ḳ;) because of the evenness of its routes, and its uniformity. (TA.) [Hence السِّىُّ is the name of a particular tract, said in the M to be a certain smooth place in the بَادِيَة.] —— See also art. سيو.

سِيَّةٌ: see سَوَآءٌ, near the end of the paragraph.

سُوًى: see سَوَآءٌ, in seven places: —— and see also سِوًى, in two places.

سِوًى: see سَوَآءٌ, in seven places. —— Also, and likewise ↓ سُوًى, (Akh, Ṣ, Mṣb, Mughnee, Ḳ,) and ↓ سَوَآءٌ, (Akh, Ṣ, M, Mughnee, Ḳ,) and ↓ سِوَآءٌ, (Mughnee,) i. q. مَكَانٌ, (Mughnee,) or غَيْر, (Akh, Ṣ, M, Mṣb, Mughnee, Ḳ,) accord. to different authorities: each used as an epithet, and as denoting exception, like غَيْر; accord. to Ez-Zejjájee and Ibn-Málik, used in the same sense and manner as غَيْر: but accord. to Sb and the generality of authorities, an adv. n. of place, always in the accus. case, except in instances of necessity: (Mughnee:) one says, عِنْدِى رَجُلٌ سِوَى زَيْدٍ, meaning بَدَلَ زَيْدٍ and مَكَانَ زَيْدٍ [i. e. *I have with me a man instead of Zeyd* and *in the place of Zeyd*]: (Ḥam p. 570, and TA:*) [but] one says [also], مَرَرْتُ بِرَجُلٍ سِوَاكَ and ↓ سُوَاكَ and ↓ سَوَائِكَ, meaning غَيْرِكَ [i. e. *I passed by a man other than thee*]: (Ṣ:) and ↓ جَآءَنِى سَوَاؤُكَ [and سِوَاكَ &c. *Other than thou came to me*], using it as an agent; and ↓ رَأَيْتُ سَوَآءَكَ [and سِوَاكَ &c. *I saw other than thee*], using it as an objective complement: and ↓ مَا جَآءَنِى أَحَدٌ سَوَآءَكَ [and سِوَاكَ &c. *None except thou came to me*]: and مَا جَآءَنِى أَحَدٌ ↓ سَوَاؤُكَ [and سِوَاكَ &c. *None other than thou came to me*]: (Mughnee:) and قَصَدْتُ القَوْمَ سِوَى زَيْدٍ, meaning غَيْرَ زَيْدٍ [i. e. *I betook myself to,* or *towards, the people,* or *party, others than Zeyd,* which is virtually the same as *except Zeyd*]: (Mṣb:) and لَئِنْ فَعَلْتَ ذَاكَ وَأَنَا سِوَاكَ لَيَأْتِيَنَّكَ مِنِّى مَا تَكْرَهُ, meaning [*If thou do that*] *when I am in a land other than thy land,* [*what thou dislikest,* or *hatest, shall assuredly come to thee from me.*] (Ibn-Buzurj, TA.) —— The Arabs also said, عَقْلُكَ سِوَاكَ, meaning *Thine intellect has departed from thee.* (IAạr, M.) ═══ The strangest of the meanings of سِوَى, in this sense with the short alif and with kesr, is قَصْدٌ. (Mughnee.) سِوَى الشَّىْءِ means قَصْدُهُ [i. e. *The tendency,* or *direction, of the thing*]. (M.) And one says, قَصَدْتُ سِوَى فُلَانٍ, meaning قَصَدْتُ قَصْدَهُ [i. e. *I tended,* or *betook myself, in the direction of,* or *towards, such a one*]. (Ṣ, Ḳ.* [In the CḲ, and in my MS. copy of the Ḳ, سَوَاهُ is erroneously put for سِوَاهُ.]) And hence, (Mughnee,) a poet says, (namely, Ḳeys Ibn-El-Khaṭeem, TA,)

* وَلَأَصْرِفَنَّ سِوَى حُذَيْفَةَ مِدْحَتِى *

[*And I will surely turn towards Ḥodheyfeh my eulogy*]. (Ṣ, Mughnee.)

سَوَآءٌ [in some copies of the Ḳ erroneously written without ء] in its primary acceptation is an inf. n., [but without a proper verb, used as a simple subst.,] meaning *Equality, equability, uniformity,* or *evenness;* syn. اِسْتِوَآءٌ; (Mughnee;) as also ↓ سَوِيَّةٌ: (M, Ḳ:) or [rather] it is a subst., (Ṣ, and Ksh and Bḍ in ii. 5,) meaning اِسْتِوَآءٌ, (Ksh and Bḍ ibid.,) from اِسْتَوَى in the sense of اِعْتَدَلَ; (Ṣ;) and signifies [as above: and] *equity, justice,* or *rectitude;* syn. عَدْلٌ; (Ṣ, M, Ḳ;) as also ↓ سَوِيَّةٌ; (M;) and ↓ سِوًى and ↓ سُوًى, as well as سَوَآءٌ, accord. to Fr, are syn. with نَصَفٌ; and accord. to him, (TA,) and to Akh, (Ṣ, TA,) syn. with عَدْلٌ; (Ṣ, Ḳ, TA;) [but app., only syn. with عَدْلٌ and نَصَفٌ not as a subst. but as an epithet, like وَسَطٌ thus used, as will be shown by what follows, although] each said by Er-Rághib to be originally an inf. n. (TA.) One says, هُمَا عَلَى سَوِيَّةٍ ↓ مِنْ هٰذَا الأَمْرِ, meaning سَوَآءٌ [i. e. *They two are on an equality,* or *on a par, in respect of this affair,* or *case*]: (Ṣ, TA:) and ↓ هُمْ عَلَى سَوِيَّةٍ, meaning [likewise] اِسْتِوَآءٍ [i. e. *They are on an equality,* or *on a par*], (M, Ḳ,) فِى هٰذَا الأَمْرِ [*in this affair,* or *case*]. (M.) And ↓ قَسَمْتُ الشَّىْءَ بَيْنَهُمَا بِالسَّوِيَّةِ, (Ṣ,) meaning بِالعَدْلِ [i. e. *I divided the thing between them two with equity, justice,* or *rectitude*]. (TA.) And it is said in the Ḳur [viii. 60], فَانْبِذْ إِلَيْهِمْ عَلَى سَوَآءٍ, meaning عَدْلٍ [as expl. in art. نبذ, q. v.]. (Ṣ,* TA.) [Hence,] لَيْلَةُ السَّوَآءِ *The night of the thirteenth* [*of the lunar month;* the first being that on which the new moon is first seen]; (Aṣ, Ṣ, Ḳ, TA;) *in which the moon becomes equable* or *uniform* (يَسْتَوِى) [*in illumination*]: (TA:) or *the night of the fourteenth.* (M, Ḳ.) —— And i. q. وَسَطٌ [as meaning The *middle,* or *midst,* of a thing]; (Ṣ, M, Mughnee, Ḳ;) as also ↓ سُوًى and ↓ سِوًى. (Lh, M, Ḳ.) Hence, سَوَآءُ الشَّىْءِ *The middle,* or *midst, of the thing;* (Ṣ, M;) as also ↓ سُوَاهُ and ↓ سِوَاهُ. (Lh, M.) It is said in the Ḳur [xxxvii. 53,] فَرَآهُ فِى سَوَآءِ الجَحِيمِ [*And he shall see him*] *in the middle* or *midst* [*of the fire of Hell*]. (Ṣ,* Mughnee, TA.) In like manner also one says سَوَآءُ السَّبِيلِ [*The middle of the road*]: or, accord. to Fr, it means *the right direction of the road* or *way.* (TA.) And one says, اِنْقَطَعَ سَوَائِى, meaning *My waist* [*broke*], or *my middle.* (TA.) And سَوَآءُ النَّهَارِ means *The middle of the day.* (M, Ḳ. [In some copies of the Ḳ, مُنْشَعَهُ is erroneously put for مُنْتَصَفُهُ.]) —— [Hence, perhaps, as being generally the middle or nearly so,] The *summit* of a mountain. (M, Ḳ.) And *An* [*eminence,* or *a hill,* or *the like, such as is termed*] أَكَمَة: or *a* [*stony tract such as is termed*] حَرَّة: or the *head of a* حَرَّة. (M.) ═══ It is also used as an epithet; (Mughnee;) and signifies *Equal, equable, uniform,* or *even;* syn. ↓ مُسْتَوٍ; (M, Mughnee, Ḳ;) applied in this sense to a place; (Mughnee;) as also, thus applied, ↓ سِوًى, and ↓ سِىٌّ; (M, Ḳ;) or these two signify, thus applied, [like سَوَآءٌ as expl. hereafter,] *equidistant in respect of its two extremities.* (TA.) And as syn. with ↓ مُسْتَوٍ, it is applied [to a fem. noun as well as to a sing., and] to one and more than one, because it is originally an inf. n.; whence the phrase لَيْسُوا سَوَآءً [*They are not equal;* in the Ḳur iii. 109]. (Mughnee.) Using it in this sense, one says أَرْضٌ سَوَآءٌ [*An even land*]: and دَارٌ سَوَآءٌ *A house uniform* (↓ مُسْتَوِيَةٌ) *in respect of the* [*appertenances termed*] مَرَافِق: and ثَوْبٌ سَوَآءٌ *A garment,* or *piece of cloth, equal,* or *uniform,* (↓ مُسْتَوٍ,) *in its breadth and its length and its two lateral edges:* but one does not say جَمَلٌ سَوَآءٌ, nor حِمَارٌ سَوَآءٌ, nor رَجُلٌ سَوَآءٌ: (M, TA:) though one says رَجُلٌ سَوَآءُ البَطْنِ *A man whose belly is even with the breast:* and سَوَآءُ القَدَمِ *having no hollow to the sole of his foot.* (TA.) One says also رَجُلٌ سَوِىُّ ↓ الخَلْقِ, (Ṣ, M,) meaning ↓ مُسْتَوٍ [i. e. *A man uniform in make,* or *symmetrical;* or *full-grown, of full vigour,* or *mature in body,* or *in body and intellect:* see 8]: (Ṣ:) and رَجُلٌ ↓ سَوِىٌّ *A man equally free from excess and deficiency in his dispositions and his make:* (Er-Rághib, TA:) or *sound in limbs:* (TA voce مِرَّة, q. v.:) and ↓ غُلَامٌ سَوِىٌّ *A boy,* or *young man, uniform in make,* or *symmetrical,* (مُسْتَوِى ↓ الخَلْقِ,) *without disease, and without fault,* or *defect:* (Mgh:) and the fem. is سَوِيَّةٌ. (M.) Accord. to Er-Rághib, ↓ السَّوِىُّ signifies *That which is preserved from excess and deficiency:* and hence ↓ الصِّرَاطِ السَّوِىّ [in Ḳur xx. last verse, as though meaning *The road,* or *way that neither exceeds, nor falls short of, that which is right*]; (Er-Rághib, TA;) *the right,* or *direct, road:* (Bḍ, Jel:) and some read السَّوَآءِ, meaning *the middle, good, road:* and السُّوْء (Ksh, Bḍ) i. e. *the evil,* or *bad,* road: (Bḍ:) and السُّوأَى [i. e. *most evil,* or *worst;* fem. of أَسْوَأُ; for الصِّرَاط is fem. as well as masc.]: (Ksh, Bḍ:) [and] ↓ السُّوَى, of the measure فُعْلَى from السَّوَآءِ, [with which it is syn.,] or originally السُّوأَى [mentioned above]: (Ḳ:) and ↓ السُّوَىّ, (Ksh, Bḍ,) which is dim. of السَّوَآء, (Lth, TA,) [or] as dim. of السُّوْء [in which case it is for السُّوَىْء]. (Ksh, Bḍ.) —— [Hence,] it signifies also *Complete:* (Mughnee:) you say, هٰذَا

دِرْهَمٌ سَوَآءٌ (M, Mughnee) *This is a complete dirhem*; (Mughnee;) using the last word as an epithet: and سَوَآءً also, using it as an inf. n., as though you said ٱسْتِوَآءً: and in like manner in the Ḳur xli. 9, some read سَوَآءٌ; and others, سَوَآءٍ. (M.) — And *Equitable, just,* or *right*; syn. عَدْلٌ: used in this sense in the saying in the Ḳur [iii. 57], تَعَالَوْا إِلَى كَلِمَةٍ سَوَآءٍ بَيْنَنَا وَبَيْنَكُمْ [*Come ye to an equitable,* or *a just,* or *right, sentence,* or *proposition, between us and you*]. (Az, TA.) — And *Equidistant,* or *midway,* (عَدْلٌ, and وَسَطٌ, Ṣ, or نَصَفٌ, Mughnee,) *between two parties,* (Ṣ,) or *between two places*; (Mughnee;) applied as an epithet to a place; as also ▼ سِوًى and ▼ سُوًى; (Ṣ, Mughnee;) of which three words the second (سِوًى) is the most chaste; (Mughnee;) or the last two signify *equal* (مُسْتَوٍ) *in respect of its two extremities*; and are used as epithets and as adv. ns.; originally, inf. ns. (Er-Rághib, TA.) ▼ مَكَانًا سُوًى and ▼ سِوًى, (M, Ḳ,) in the Ḳur xx. 60, accord. to different readings, means *A place equidistant,* or *midway,* (Ksh, Bḍ, Jel,) between us and thee, (Ksh, Bḍ,) or to the comer from each of the two extremities: (Jel:) or مَكَانٌ سُوًى and سِوًى means مَعْلَمٌ [i. e. *a place marked*], (so in a copy of the M and in one of the Ḳ,) or مَعْلَمٌ, (so in other copies of the Ḳ and in the TA,) which is for ذُو مَعْلَمٍ, meaning *having a mark,* or *sign, by which one is guided,* or *directed, thereto.* (MF, TA.) — [Also *Equal,* or *alike,* in any respect.] One says, مَرَرْتُ بِرَجُلٍ سَوَآءٍ وَالعَدَمُ, (M, Mughnee, Ḳ,) and ▼ سُوًى وَالعَدَمُ, and ▼ سِوًى وَالعَدَمُ, (M, Ḳ,) meaning وُجُودُهُ وَعَدَمُهُ سَوَآءٌ [i. e. *I passed by a man whose existence and whose non-existence are equal,* or *alike,* to me, or in my opinion]: (M, Ḳ:*) and Sb mentions the phrase, سَوَآءٌ هُوَ وَالعَدَمُ [as meaning *His existence and his non-existence are equal,* or *alike,* to me]. (M.) And سَوَآءٌ عَلَىَّ قُمْتَ أَوْ قَعَدْتَ [*It is equal,* or *alike, to me, that thou stand or that thou sit,* or *whether thou stand or sit*; or *that thou stand or that thou sit is equal,* or *alike, to me*: see Ḳur ii. 5, and the expositions thereof]. (Ṣ.) [And ▼ سُوًى is used as an adv. n., or as an inf. n. adverbially, meaning *Alike*: see an ex. in a verse cited voce سَمْتٌ.] — Also *A like; a similar person* or *thing*; (Ṣ, M, Ḳ;) and so ▼ سِىٌّ: [each used as masc. and fem.; and the former as sing. and dual and pl., though having proper dual and pl. forms:] the pl. of the former is أَسْوَآءٌ, (Ṣ, M, Ḳ,) and also, (Ṣ,* Ḳ,) but anomalous, (Ṣ,) or [rather] quasi-pl. ns., all anomalous, (M,) ▼ سَوَاسِيَةٌ (Ṣ, M, Ḳ) and ▼ سَوَاسٍ and ▼ سَوَاسِوَةٌ: (M, Ḳ:) and أَسْوَآءٌ is also pl. of ▼ سِىٌّ: (TA:) as to ▼ سَوَاسِيَةٌ, Akh says, سَوَآءٌ is of the measure فَعَالٌ, and سِيَةٌ may be of the measure فِعَةٌ or فِلَةٌ, the former of which is the more agreeable with analogy, the و being changed into ى in سِيَةٌ because of the kesreh before it, for it is originally سِوْيَةٌ; and it is from أَسْوَيْتُ الشَّىْءَ meaning "I neglected the thing:" [see 4:] (Ṣ:) accord. to Aboo-'Alee, the ى in سَوَاسِيَةٌ is changed from the و in سَوَاسِوَةٌ, in which latter some preserve it to show that it is the final radical: (M:) accord. to Fr, سَوَاسِيَةٌ has no sing., and relates only to equality in evil: (T, TA:) so in the saying,

سَوَاسِيَةٌ كَأَسْنَانِ الحِمَارِ

[*Equals like the teeth of the ass*]. (TA.) It requires two [or more nouns for its subjects]: you say, سَوَآءٌ زَيْدٌ وَعَمْرٌو, meaning ذَوَا سَوَآءٍ [i. e., lit., *Two possessors of equality,* or *likeness, are Zeyd and 'Amr*], (M, Ḳ,) because it is [originally] an inf. n.: (M:) and هُمَا فِى هٰذَا الأَمْرِ سَوَآءٌ [*They two are in this affair,* or *case, likes*]: (Ṣ:) and هُمَا سَوَآءَانِ (Ṣ, M, Ḳ) and ▼ سِيَّانِ i. e. *They two are likes*: (Ṣ, M, Mgh, Mṣb, Ḳ:) and هُمْ سَوَآءٌ and أَسْوَآءٌ and ▼ سَوَاسِيَةٌ i. e. *They are likes*; (Ṣ; [the first and last of these three are mentioned in the Mgh as identical in meaning;]) or, accord. to Fr, the last means *they are equals in evil,* not in good: (T, TA:) and ▼ مَا هُوَ لَكَ بِسِىٍّ *He is not a person like to thee*: and مَا هُمْ لَكَ بِأَسْوَآءٍ [*They are not persons like to thee*]: (Lḥ, M:) and ▼ مَا هِىَ لَكَ بِسِىٍّ (Lḥ, M, Ḳ*) i. e. *She is not a person like to thee*: (TA:) and مَا هُنَّ لَكَ بِأَسْوَآءٍ [*They* (females) *are not persons like to thee*]: and لَا سِىَّ ▼ لِمَنْ فَعَلَ ذَالِكَ [*There is not a like to him who did that*]: and لَا سِيَّكَ ▼ إِذَا فَعَلْتَ ذَالِكَ [*There is not the like of thee when thou doest that*]: (Lḥ, M, Ḳ:) and لَا سِيَّةَ ▼ فُلَانٍ (Ḳ) [*There is not the like of such a one*: in the CḲ, لَا سِيَّكَ ▼ فُلَانٌ: perhaps the right reading is لَا سِيَّكَ فُلَانٌ, *Such a one is not the like of thee*]. سَوَآءٌ and ▼ سِيَّانِ should not be used with أَوْ in the place of وَ, except by poetic license: one of the exceptions to this rule is the saying of Aboo-Dhu-eyb,

وَكَانَ سِيَّانِ أَلَّا يَسْرَحُوا نَعَمًا
أَوْ يَسْرَحُوهُ بِهَا وَٱغْبَرَّتِ السُّوحُ

[*And they were two like cases that they should not send forth cattle to pasture or send him forth with them when the tracts were very dusty* by reason of drought]. (M.) For two other exs. of لَا سِيَّمَا, [as well as of its syn. سِىٌّ, and for سَوَآءٌ also,] see سِىٌّ. — See also سِوًى in six places.

سُوَآءٌ: see سِىٌّ, second sentence, in two places: and سَوَآءٌ also, in the latter half of the paragraph: — and see سِوًى. — بَعَثُوا بِالسَّوَآءِ وَاللَّوَآءِ means † *They sent seeking,* or *demanding, aid,* or *succour.* (Ḳ in art. لوى. [The proper signification of السَّوَآء in this instance I do not find explained.])

سِوًى: see سَوَآءٌ, in the former half of the paragraph, in six places.

سُوًى: see سَوَآءٌ, in the middle of the paragraph.

سَوِيَّةٌ: see سَوَآءٌ, in five places. — [Also fem. of سَوِىٌّ. — And hence, as a subst.,] *A kind of vehicle of female slaves and of necessitous persons*: (Ḳ:) or *a* [*garment of the kind called*] كِسَآء, *stuffed with panic grass* (ثُمَام), (Ṣ, M, Ḳ, and L in art. كوب,) or *palm-fibres* (لِيف), (M,) or *the like,* (Ṣ, M, and L ubi suprà,) *resembling the* بَرْذَعَة [q. v.], (Ṣ, and L ubi suprà,) *which is put on the back of the camel,* (M,) or *on the back of the ass &c.,* (L ubi suprà,) *and which is one of the vehicles of female slaves and of necessitous persons*: (M:) and likewise *such as is put upon the back of the camel, but in the form of a ring because of the hump, and* [*also*] *called* حَوِيَّة [q. v.]: pl. سَوَايَا. (Ṣ.)

سَوَاسٍ and سَوَاسِوَةٌ and سَوَاسِيَةٌ: see سَوَآءٌ, in the latter half of the paragraph; the last of them in three places.

سَوَآءِ لَوَآءِ, each of the measure فَعَالِ, irregularly derived from ٱسْتَوَى and ٱلْتَوَى; a prov., applied to women, meaning *Straight* and *bending,* and *collecting together* and *separating*; *not remaining in one state,* or *condition.* (Meyd.) — And أَرْضٌ سَوَآءٌ *Land of which the earth, or dust, is like sand.* (IAth, TA.)

سَايَةٌ is [held by some to be] of the measure فَعْلَةٌ from التَّسْوِيَةُ [inf. n. of سَوَّى]; (Ḳ;) mentioned by Az on the authority of Fr; but in copies of the T, فَعْلَةٌ from الشَّوِيَّة. (TA.) One says, ضَرَبَ لِى سَايَةً, meaning *He prepared for me a speech*: (Ḳ:) or *an evil speech, which he framed* (سَوَّاهَا) *against me to deceive me*: mentioned by Az on the authority of Fr. (TA.) [See the same word in art. سوأ.]

أَسْوَى [*More,* and *most, equal, equable, uniform,* or *even*: and *more,* or *most, equitable,* &c.]. One says, هٰذَا المَكَانُ أَسْوَى هٰذِهِ الأَمْكِنَةِ i. e. [*This place is*] *the most even* [*of these places*]. (M.)

تَسْوَآءٌ *An even place*; occurring in a trad.: the ت is augmentative. (TA.)

مُسْوٍ [act. part. n. of 4]. One says in answer to him who asks, "How have ye entered upon the morning?" (Ṣ,) or "How have ye entered upon the evening?" (M, TA,) مُسْوُونَ صَالِحُونَ [as enunciatives of نَحْنُ understood], (Ṣ, M,) or مُسْتَوِينَ ▼ صَالِحِينَ [as enunciatives of أَصْبَحْنَا or أَمْسَيْنَا understood, but I think that مُسْتَوِينَ is a mistranscription for مُسْوِينَ], meaning *In a good, right, state, with respect to our children and our cattle.* (Ṣ, M, TA.)

مُسَاوٍ: see 3, in three places.

مُسْتَوٍ: see سَوَآءٌ, in the former half of the paragraph, in six places: and see also مُسْوٍ. [هِلَالٌ مُسْتَوٍ: see أَدَقُّ.]

سى

سَىْ i. q. سَوْفَ, q. v.

سَىٌّ and سِىٌّ: see art. سوى; and see the latter in art. سو.

سيأ

2. سَيَّأَ النَّاقَةَ, (Ḳ,) or ▼ تَسَيَّأَهَا, (M,) or both,

(TA,) *He drew forth the she-camel's* سَىْءٌ, or *milk that descended before the full flow:* (M, Ḳ:) from El-Hejeree. (M.)

5: see above. ═ تَسَيَّأَتْ, (Ṣ, M, and so in copies of the Ḳ,) or اِسْيَأَتْ, [a variation of the former,] (TA, as from the Ḳ,) *She* (a camel) *emitted her milk,* (Fr, Ṣ, Ḳ,) i. e., *what is termed* سَىْءٌ, (M,) *without its being drawn forth.* (Fr, Ṣ, Ḳ.) — Hence, إِنَّ فُلَانًا لَيَتَسَيَّأُ لِى بِشَىْءٍ قَلِيلٍ † [*Verily such a one yields me,* or *gives me, little*]. (TA.) — تَسَيَّأَ بِحَقِّى † *He acknowledged my right,* or *due, after he had denied it.* (Ḳ.) — تَسَيَّأَتْ عَلَىَّ الأُمُورُ † *The affairs have become discordant,* or *diverse, to me,* (Ḳ,* TA,) *so that I know not which of them to pursue;* (TA;) as also تَسَأْسَأَتْ. (TA in art. سأ.)

7. انسيأ اللَّبَنُ *The milk, such as is termed* سَىْءٌ, *issued without being drawn forth.* (Fr, Ṣ.)

سَىْءٌ (Fr, Ṣ, M, Ḳ) and ↓ سِىْءٌ (M, Ḳ) The *milk that issues without being drawn forth;* (Fr, Ṣ;) the *milk* (Ṣ, M, Ḳ) *that is in the extremities of the camel's teats,* (Ṣ, Ḳ,) or *in the fore part of the udder,* (IAth, TA,) *descending* (Ḳ) *before,* (قَبْلَ, so in copies of the Ṣ and M and Ḳ,) or *at the first of,* (قُبُلَ, so in the TA as from the Ḳ,) *the full flow.* (Ṣ, M, Ḳ.) ═ See also the former word in art. سوأ.

سِىْءٌ: see the next preceding paragraph.

سَيْئٌ: and سَيِّئَةٌ: see art. سوأ.

سَيَّآءٌ, occurring in a trad., is expl. as meaning *One who sells grave-clothes, and* [*therefore*] *wishes for people's death:* it may be from السُّوْءُ and المَسَآءَةُ: or from السَّىْءُ meaning "the milk that is in the fore part of the udder:" or it may be from سَيَّأْتُهَا meaning "I milked her." (IAth, TA.)

سيب

1. سَابَ, (Ṣ, M, A, Mgh, Mṣb, Ḳ,) aor. يَسِيبُ, (Ṣ, A,) inf. n. سَيْبٌ, (Ṣ, M, A, Ḳ,) *It ran;* (Ṣ, M, A,* Mgh, Mṣb, Ḳ;) said of water: (Ṣ, M, A, Mṣb:) and ↓ انساب, likewise said of water, *it ran of itself.* (Mṣb.) — [Hence,] سَابَتِ الحَيَّةُ, (M,) aor. as above; (M, A;) and ↓ انسابت; (Ṣ, M, A, Mṣb;) ‡ *The serpent ran:* (Ṣ, A,* Mṣb:) or *went along* (M, TA) *in a uniform,* or *continuous, course,* (M,) or *quickly.* (TA.) ساب and ↓ انساب both signify † *He,* or *it, walked,* or *went along, quickly:* (Ḳ, TA:) [or] so the former verb. (M.) It is said in a trad., respecting a man who drank from the mouth of a skin, انْسَابَتْ ↓ فِى بَطْنِهِ حَيَّةٌ ‡ *A serpent entered and ran into his belly* with the running of the water: wherefore it was forbidden to drink from the mouth of a skin. (TA.) El-Ḥareeree, in [his first Maḳámeh, entitled] the Ṣan'áneeyeh, [p. 20,] uses the phrase, انساب ↓ فِيهَا عَلَى غَرَارَةٍ, meaning *He entered into it as the serpent enters into its lurking place.* (TA.) And you say of a viper, ساب and ↓ انساب, meaning ‡ *It came forth from its lurking-place.* (TA.) And ↓ انساب نَحْوَكُمْ † *He returned towards you.* (Ṣ.) — ساب, (Mgh, Mṣb,) aor. as above, inf. n. سَيَبَانٌ, said of a horse and the like, † *He went away at random:* (Mṣb:) or † *he* [app. a horse or the like] *went any,* or *every, way:* (Mgh:) or سَابَتِ الدَّابَّةُ ‡ *The beast was left alone,* or *by itself, to pasture, without a pastor.* (Ṣ,* A, TA.) — And سَابَ فِى مَنْطِقِهِ ‡ *He took every way* [or *roved at large*] *in his speech:* (TA:) or *he dilated,* or *was profuse, without consideration, in his speech.* (A, TA.) And سَابَ فِى الكَلَامِ ‡ *He entered into talk,* or *discourse, with loquacity,* or *irrationality.* (TA.) It is said in a trad., إِنَّ الحِيلَةَ بِالمَنْطِقِ أَبْلَغُ مِنَ السُّيُوبِ فِى الكَلِمِ, meaning ‡ [*Verily art,* or *skill, in speech is more eloquent,* or *effective,*] *than what is loose,* or *unrestrained,* [or *rambling,*] *in words;* i. e. *elegance of speech, with paucity,* [*is more eloquent,* or *effective,*] *than profusion.* (L, TA. [السُّيُوب is here an inf. n.])

2. سَيَّبَ † *He left, left alone,* or *neglected,* a thing. (M.) — ‡ *He left* a beast, (Ṣ, A,) or a she-camel, (Mgh,) *alone,* or *by itself, to pasture where it would, without a pastor.* (Ṣ, A, Mgh.) — † *He emancipated* a slave *so that he* (the emancipator) *had no claim to inherit from him, and no control over his property; he made* him *to be such as is termed* سَائِبَةٌ. (Mṣb.) — See also what next follows.

4. اساب, said of a horse, [and سَيَّبَ ↓ جُرْدَانَهُ has the same or a similar meaning,] *i. q.* رَفَضَ, q. v. (TA in art. رفض.)

7: see 1, in seven places.

سَيْبٌ [is an inf. n. of 1, used in the sense of سَائِبٌ (q. v.), as will be shown in what follows in this paragraph. — And hence,] ‡ *A gift:* (Ṣ, M, A, Mgh, Mṣb, Ḳ:) and *a voluntary gift, by way of alms,* or *as a good work:* (TA:) and *a benefaction, an act of beneficence* or *kindness, a favour,* or *a benefit:* (M, Ḳ:) pl. سُيُوبٌ. (L, TA.) It is said in a trad. respecting a prayer for rain, وَٱجْعَلْهُ سَيْبًا نَافِعًا ‡ *And make Thou it to be a beneficial gift:* or the meaning in this instance may be, *a flowing rain.* (TA.) And one says, فَاضَ سَيْبُهُ عَلَى النَّاسِ ‡ *His gifts flowed abundantly upon the people.* (A, TA.) [See also an ex. in a verse cited voce جَبَا.] — Also *i. q.* رِكَازٌ ‡ [i. e. *Metal,* or *mineral;* or *pieces of gold* or *silver, that are extracted from the earth;* or *any metals* or *other minerals;* or *buried treasure of the people of the Time of Ignorance*]: (A, Mṣb:) or so سُيُوبٌ; (A'Obeyd, Ṣ, M, Mgh, Ḳ;) which is the pl.: (A, Mṣb:) the latter signifies, accord. to Th, *metals,* or *minerals:* (M, TA:) accord. to Aboo-Sa'eed, *veins of gold* and *of silver, that come into existence, and appear, in the mines:* so called because of their running (لِٱنْسِيَابِهَا) in the earth: accord to Z, *treasure buried in the Time of Ignorance:* or *metal,* or *mineral:* (TA:) because of the gift of God, (M, Z, Mgh, TA,) to him who finds it. (Z, TA.) The Prophet said, (Mgh, TA,) فِى السُّيُوبِ الخُمُسُ, i. e. *In the case of* رِكَاز, *the fifth part* [is for the government-treasury]. (A, Mgh, TA.) ═ Also The *hair of the tail* of a horse. (M, Ḳ.) ═ And *A pole with which a ship or boat is propelled.* (M, Ḳ.)

سِيبٌ *A place,* or *channel, in which water runs:* (Ṣ, M, Ḳ:) or so سِيبُ مَآءٍ: (A:) pl. سُيُوبٌ. (M.) ═ And The *apple:* in this sense a Pers. word [arabicized]: and hence the name of [the celebrated grammarian] سِيبَوَيْهِ; as though meaning "the scent of apples;" (M, Ḳ,* TA;) accord. to Abu-l-'Alà, (M, TA,) and Seer: (TA:) by some, [app. such as mispronounce it,] this name is said to be from the Pers. سِى signifying "thirty" and بُويَهْ signifying "odour;" as though meaning "thirty odours:" (MF, TA:) and some say that وَيْهِ is an ejaculation; and that the relaters of traditions dislike pronouncing this name therewith, as also other similar names, and therefore say سِيبُوَيَهْ, changing the ه into ة, but pausing upon it [so as to pronounce it ه]. (TA.)

سَيَابٌ and ↓ سُيَّابٌ (Ṣ, M, Ḳ) and ↓ سَيَّابٌ (Ḳ) [*Unripe dates in the state in which they are called*] بَلَح: (Ṣ, M, Ḳ:) or [*in the state in which they are called*] بُسْر: (Ḳ:) or *green* بُسْر: (AḤn, M:) Aṣ says that the *flowers of the palm-tree when they have become* بَلَح are termed سَيَابٌ, without teshdeed: (TA:) [but see بُسْرٌ:] the n. un. is سَيَابَةٌ (Ṣ, M) and سُيَّابَةٌ (Ṣ) [and سَيَّابَةٌ]: Sh says that they are called سَدَآء in the dial. of El-Medeeneh, and one is called سَيَابَة in the dial. of Wádi-l-Ḳurà: and he adds, I have heard the Baḥránees say ↓ سُيَّاب and سُيَّابَة. (TA.)

سُيَّابَةٌ n. un. of سُيَّابٌ; (Ṣ, M;) like as سَيَابَةٌ is of سَيَابٌ. (Ṣ.) — Also *Wine.* (Ḳ.)

سُيَّابٌ and سَيَّابٌ: see سَيَابٌ, in three places.

سَائِبٌ *Running* water. (Mṣb.) [See also سَيْبٌ, first sentence.]

سَائِبَةٌ ‡ *Any beast that is left to pasture where it will, without a pastor:* (M, A, Ḳ:*) pl. سَوَائِبُ and سُيَّبٌ. (A.) † *A camel that has lived until his offspring have had offspring, and is therefore set at liberty, and not ridden,* (M, Ḳ,) *nor laden with a burden.* (M.) In the Ḳur v. 102, (TA,) † *A she-camel that was set at liberty to pasture where it would,* (Ṣ, Mgh, Mṣb, Ḳ,) *in the Time of Ignorance,* (Ṣ, Ḳ,) *on account of a vow* (Ṣ, Mgh, Mṣb, Ḳ) *and the like:* (Ṣ, Ḳ:) or the *mother of a* بَحِيرَة; (Ṣ, Mgh; [in the Mṣb, said to be *a* بَحِيرَة (itself); and in one place in the TA said to be *a she-camel of which the dam is a* بَحِيرَة; but both of these explanations require consideration, as will be seen from what follows;]) or (Ḳ) *a she-camel which, having brought forth females at ten successive births, was set at liberty to pasture where she would,* (Ṣ, Ḳ,) *and not ridden, nor was her milk drunk except by her young one or a guest, until she died, when the men and the women ate her together; and the ear of her last female young one was slit, and she was* [*therefore*] *called* بَحِيرَة, *and was a* سَائِبَة *like her mother:* (Ṣ:) or *a she-camel of which a man,* (M, IAth, Ḳ,) *in the Time of Ignorance,* (M,) *when he came from a far journey,* (M, IAth, Ḳ,) *or re-*

covered from a disease, (IAth, TA,) *or had been saved by his beast from difficulty* or *trouble,* (M, IAth,) or *when his beast had been saved therefrom,* (Ḳ,) *or from war, said,* هِىَ سَائِبَةٌ; (M, IAth, Ḳ;) i. e. *she was left to pasture where she would, without a pastor, and no use was made of her back, nor was she debarred from water, nor from herbage, nor ridden:* (IAth, TA:) thus it signifies in the Ḳur: (M:) or *a she-camel from whose back a vertebra or* [*some other*] *bone was taken forth,* (M, Ḳ,) *so that she became known thereby,* (M,) *and which was not debarred from water nor from herbage, nor ridden,* (M, Ḳ,) *nor milked:* (TA:) the pl. is سُيَّبٌ, like نُوَّمٌ pl. of نَائِمٌ, and نُوَّمٌ pl. of نَائِمَةٌ; (Ṣ;) and سَوَائِبُ. (TA.) It is said in a trad., "I saw 'Amr Ibn-Lohei dragging his intestines in the fire [of Hell]:" and he was the first who set at liberty سَوَائِب: the doing of which is forbidden in the Ḳur v. 102. (TA.) And it is related that a hostile attack was made upon a certain man of the Arabs, and he found not any [other] beast to ride, so he rode a سَائِبَة: whereupon it was said to him, "Dost thou ride what is forbidden?" and he replied, يَرْكَبُ الحَرَامَ مَنْ لَا حَلَالَ لَهُ [He rides what is forbidden who has not what is allowed]: and this saying became a proverb. (M.) السَّائِبَتَانِ means *The* بَدَنَتَانِ [i. e. *two camels,* or *cows* or *bulls, for sacrifice,*] *which the Prophet brought as offerings to the House* [*of God at Mekkeh*], *and which one of the believers in a plurality of gods took away:* they are thus called because he gave them up (سَيَّبَهُمَا) to God. (TA.) — Also † *A slave emancipated so that the emancipator has no claim to inherit from him,* (Ṣ, M, A, Mgh, Mṣb, Ḳ,) *except,* accord. to Esh-Sháfi'ee, *in the case of the slave's dying without appointing any heir, in which case his inheritance belongs to his emancipator,* (TA,) [*for*] *such an emancipated slave may bestow his property where* [or *on whom*] *he pleases,* (Ṣ, Mgh, Mṣb, TA,) agreeably with a trad.: (Mgh, TA:) [in the Ṣ, and in the Mṣb as on the authority of IF, it is added, that "this is what is related to have been forbidden:" but from what has been stated above, this appears to be a mistake; and I think that these words have been misplaced in the Ṣ and Mṣb, and that they relate only to the she-camel termed سَائِبَة:] a slave is thus emancipated by his owner's saying to him, أَنْتَ سَائِبَةٌ. (Ṣ.) 'Omar said, السَّائِبَةُ وَالصَّدَقَةُ لِيَوْمِهِمَا [*The sáïbeh and alms are for their day*]: i. e., for the day of resurrection; so that one may not return to the deriving of any advantage from them in the present world. (AO, Mgh, TA.)

سيج

2. سَيَّجَ : } see art. سوج.
سِيَاجٌ : }

سيح

1. سَاحَ, (Ṣ, Mgh, Ḳ,) or سَاحَ عَلَى وَجْهِ الأَرْضِ, (A,) aor. يَسِيحُ, (Ṣ, Ḳ,) inf. n. سَيْحٌ (Ṣ, A, Mgh, Ḳ) and سَيَحَانٌ, (Ḳ,) *It* (water) *ran upon the surface of the earth.* (Ṣ, A, Mgh, Ḳ.) — And hence, (TA,) سَاحَ فِى الأَرْضِ, (Ṣ, A, Mṣb,) aor. as above, (Ṣ, Mṣb,) inf. n. سِيَاحَةٌ, (A,) or سَيْحٌ, (Mṣb,) or both, and سُيُوحٌ and سَيَحَانٌ, (Ṣ, Ḳ,) said of a man, (A,) ‡ *He went,* or *journeyed, through the land,* or *earth,* (Ṣ, L, Ḳ, &c.,) *for the purpose of devoting himself to religious services* or *exercises:* (L, Ḳ:) or in this restricted sense, which MF asserts to be unmentioned in most of the older books, and thinks to be conventional, the verb has only the first of the inf. ns. above, and in the absolute sense it has the second and third and fourth. (TA.) It is said in a trad., لَا سِيَاحَةَ فِى الإِسْلَامِ (Ṣ, A, TA) i. e. ‡ [*There shall be no going about through the land,* or *earth, in the way of devotees, in El-Islám:* or] *no quitting of the cities,* or *towns, and going,* or *journeying, through the land,* or *earth:* (TA:) or *no quitting of the cities,* or *towns, and dwelling in the deserts, and forsaking the being present at the congregational prayers and at assemblies:* or *no going about through the land,* or *earth, doing evil,* or *mischief, and calumniating and corrupting.* (IAth, TA.) The سِيَاحَة of the Muslims [in a religious sense, and such as is approvable,] is † *Fasting.* (TA.) — [Hence also,] سَاحَ الظِّلُّ *The shade changed,* or *turned,* or *moved, from side to side,* or *from place to place.* (Ṣ, Ḳ.)

2. [سَيَّحَ is said by Golius, as on the authority of the Ḳ, to signify *He made* water *to flow:* and this is probably its primary and proper signification, whence other meanings, which are tropical: but it is not in the Ḳ.] — See 4. — سَيَّحَ فُلَانٌ, [app. for سَيَّحَ كَلَامَهُ,] inf. n. تَسْيِيحٌ, ‡ *Such a one talked much.* (A, TA.) — And سُيِّحَ, inf. n. as above, † *It* (a garment, or piece of cloth,) *had in it* [or *was diversified with*] *various stripes.* (L.) [And in like manner it is said of other things: see its part. n., مُسَيَّحٌ.]

4. اساح نَهْرًا *He made a river,* or *rivulet, to flow,* or *run.* (A, Ḳ.) [See also 2.] — اساح الفَرَسُ جُرْدَانَهُ (A) or ذَكَرَهُ (L) ‡ *The horse put forth his veretrum from its prepuce;* (L;) and ♦ سيّح signifies the same: (A, L:) or both of these verbs, said of a horse, are *syn. with* رَفَضَ [q. v.]. (TA in art. رفض.) — And اساح بِذَنَبِهِ, said of a horse, † *He let his tail hang down loosely:* (Ḳ:) accord. to the Ḳ, J is in error in writing this verb اشاح; and Az says that اساح is right, and that اشاح is a mistranscription: the like is also said in the TṢ: but اشاح is asserted by more than one to be the right word. (TA.)

7. انساح بَطْنُهُ † *His belly became large* (Ḳ, TA) *and wide,* (TA,) *and approached* [*the ground*] *by reason of fatness.* (Ḳ, TA.) One says of a she-ass, انساح بَطْنُهَا, meaning † *Her belly became big, and approached the ground.* (IAṣr, T.) — انساح بَالُهُ ‡ [*His,* or *its, state,* or *condition,*] *became free from straitness.* (Ṣ, O, Ḳ.) A poet says, (Ṣ,) namely, Dhu-r-Rummeh, (O,)

أَمْنِّى ضَمِيرَ النَّفْسِ إِيَّاكِ بَعْدَمَا
يُرَاجِعُنِى بَثِّى فَيَنْسَاحُ بَالُهَا

‡ [*I make the secret thoughts of the soul to wish for thee after my grief,* or *sorrow, returns to me; and then the state,* or *condition, thereof, becomes free from straitness*]. (Ṣ, O.) — انساح said of a garment, or piece of cloth, (Ḳ, TA,) &c., (TA,) † *It became much rent,* or *rent in several places.* (Ḳ, TA.) In like manner it is said of the dawn [as meaning † *It broke*]. (TA.) And it is said in the trad. relating to the cave (الغَار) [mentioned in the Ḳur ix. 40]) فَانْسَاحَتِ الصَّخْرَةُ, meaning † [*And the mass of rock*] *became impelled and riven:* and hence, [accord. to some,] the ♦ سَاحَة of a house [expl. in art. سوح]: but as some relate it, the verb in this instance is [انصاحت,] with ص and ح. (TA.)

سَيْحٌ *Running water;* (Ṣ, Mṣb;) an inf. n. used as a subst.: (Mṣb:) or *running external water:* (Ḳ:) or *external water running upon the surface of the earth:* (T, TA:) the *water of rivers and valleys:* (Mgh:) pl. سُيُوحٌ. (T, TA.) [And it is used as an epithet:] you say also (TA) مَآءٌ سَيْحٌ (A, TA) and ♦ سَائِحٌ (A) *Water running upon the surface of the earth:* (A, TA:) pl. of the former أَسْيَاحٌ. (TA.) — Also † *A striped* [*garment of the kind called*] كِسَآء, (Ḳ, TA,) *with which one covers himself, and which one spreads:* (TA:) or *a striped* [*garment such as is called*] عَبَآءَة: and *a sort of* [*the garments called*] بُرُود: (Ṣ:) pl. سُيُوحٌ. (TA.) See also مُسَيَّحٌ.

سَاحَةٌ: see 7; and see also art. سوح.

سَيَّاحٌ ‡ *An itinerant, a roamer,* or *frequent traveller:* (A,* MA:) from سَاحَ فِى الأَرْضِ. (A.)

سَائِحٌ: see سَيْحٌ. — [Hence,] ‡ A man *going,* or *journeying,* [*as a devotee, or otherwise,*] through the land or earth. (A.) — And, as being likened thereto, ‡ *Fasting,* or *a faster:* (A:) or *a faster who keeps to the mosques:* (Ḳ:) the faster is said to be thus called because he who journeys as a devotee does so without having any provision with him, and eats only when he finds provision: therefore the faster is likened to him. (TA.) السَّائِحُونَ in the Ḳur ix. 113 means ‡ *The fasters:* (Bḍ, Jel, TA:) so say Zj and I'Ab and Ibn-Mes'ood: (TA:) or *those who observe the obligatory fasts:* or *those who fast constantly:* (TA:) or *those who journey to war against unbelievers,* or *to seek knowledge.* (Bḍ.) And سَائِحَات in the Ḳur lxvi. 5 means † Women *who fast:* or *who forsake their country or homes* [*for the sake of God*]. (Bḍ, Jel.) — This last (سائحات [if not a mistranscription for سَابِحَات]) also means † *Swift horses:* — and † The *planets.* (KL.)

مَسَاحٌ or مَسَاحَةٌ, the latter of the measure مَفْعَلَةٌ, from السِّيَاحَة, [each app. meaning † *A place of* سِيَاحَة, or *journeying,*] is sing. of مَسَايِح, in which the ى is like that in مَعَايِش, as in other similar words of which the medial radical is an infirm letter, except مَصَائِبُ, by rule مَصَاوِبُ. (Ḥar p. 15.) —— [The pl. مَسَايِح is also expl. by Freytag as applied in the Deewán of Jereer to † The *part of the head between the temples as far as the forehead* (where the hairs are).]

مُسَيَّحٌ † *Striped*; applied in this sense to a [garment of the kind called] بُرْدٌ; (Ṣ, Ḳ;) and also, with ة, to a [garment such as is called] عَبَآءَة: (Ṣ:) or applied to [the garments called] عَبَآء as meaning *having alternate stripes of white and black, the latter not intensely black*: every عباءة also is termed ↑ مُسَيَّحٌ and مُسَيَّحَةٌ: but that which has not stripes is a كِسَآء, not an عباءة. (ISh, TA.) So too applied to locusts (جَرَاد); (Ḳ;) and with ة applied to a single locust [i. e. جَرَادَة]: (TA:) or, applied to locusts, it means *marked with black and yellow and white stripes* or *streaks*. (Aṣ, TA.) It is also applied as an epithet to the [bird called] حَيْقُطَان. (Ṣ.) —— ‡ The *wild ass*: so called because of his streak that makes a division between the belly and the side. (Ḳ, TA.) مُسَيَّحُ العَجِيزَةِ ‡ [*He that has the rump streaked*] is an epithet applied to the [wild] ass because of the whiteness on his rump. (A, TA.) —— ‡ A road *of which the tracks* (شَرَك or شُرُك in different copies of the Ḳ) *are rendered apparent*: (Ḳ, TA:) likened to the عَبَآء thus termed. (TA.)

مِسْيَاحٌ ‡ One *who goes about calumniating, and making mischief, in the land*: (Ṣ, A, Ḳ:) pl. مَسَايِيحُ: so in the trad., لَيْسُوا بِالمَسَايِيحِ وَلَا بِالمَذَايِيعِ البُذُرِ ‡ [*They are not of those who go about calumniating, &c., nor of the babblers who cannot keep secrets.*] (Ṣ, TA.) Sh derives it, not from السِّيَاحَةُ, but, from تَسْيِيحُ الثَّوْبِ. (L, TA.)

سيخ

1. سَاخَ, aor. يَسِيخُ, inf. n. سَيْخٌ and سَيَخَانٌ, i. q. رَسَخَ and ثَاخَ [both app. as signifying *It sank into the ground*: or by the former may here be meant *it was*, or *became, firm, steady, steadfast, stable, fixed, fast, settled*, or *established*]. (Ḳ.) See also 1 in art. سوخ, in two places.

سِيَاخٌ *A building of clay*, (JK, TḲ,) *of any kind*: (JK:) pl. سُيُوخٌ. (JK, TḲ.) In the copies of the Ḳ, بُنَاةُ الطِّينِ is erroneously put for بِنَآءُ الطِّينِ. (TḲ.)

سيد

سَيْدٌ a contraction of سَيِّدٌ, q. v. in art. سود.

سِيدٌ *A wolf*: (Ṣ, M, A, Ḳ: mentioned in the Ḳ in art. سود; and in the Ṣ, at the close of that art.:) accord. to Sb, its medial radical letter is ى; its dim. being ↑ سُيَيْدٌ: not like رِيحٌ [of which the dim. is رُوَيْحَةٌ], nor like دِيمَةٌ: (M:) and ↑ سِيدَانَةٌ signifies the same: (Ḳ:) or so ↑ سِيدَانٌ; (M;) which is the pl. (Ṣ, M, A) also: (M:) and ↑ سِيدَانَةٌ signifies *a she-wolf*; (M, A, and Ḥam p. 274;) [and] so ↑ سِيدَةٌ; (Ks, Ṣ;) or this is not allowable. (Ḥam ubi suprà.) One says سِيدُ رَمْلٍ [*A wolf of sands*; i. e., that frequents the sands; meaning *a savage wolf*]. (Ṣ.) Hence, ↑ اِمْرَأَةٌ سِيدَانَةٌ ‡ *A bold woman*, (M, A,) *like the she-wolf*. (A.) —— And *A lion* (Ṣ, M, K) is sometimes thus called, (Ṣ,) in the dial. of Hudheyl. (M.) The former is the primary signification accord. to J and others; though the contr. seems to be indicated in the Ḳ. (TA.)

سِيدَةٌ fem. of سِيدٌ, q. v., accord. to Ks: (Ṣ:) but said to be not allowable. (Ḥam p. 274.)

سِيدَانٌ: see سِيدٌ.

سِيدَانَةٌ: see سِيدٌ, in three places.

سُيَيْدٌ dim. of سِيدٌ, q. v. (Sb, M.)

سَيِّدٌ: and سَيْدٌ: see art. سود.

مَسْيِدٌ mentioned by Ez-Zarkeshee as a dial. var. of مَسْجِدٌ [q. v.]: thought by MF to be post-classical: and in the [classical] language of the Arabs *i. q.* مَكْتَبٌ [*A place where the art of writing is taught*]. (TA.)

سير

1. سَارَ, aor. يَسِيرُ, inf. n. سَيْرٌ and مَسِيرٌ, (Ṣ, M, A, Mgh, Mṣb, Ḳ,) which latter is extr., for by rule it should be of the measure مَفْعَلٌ, with fet-ḥ [to the ع], (Ṣ,) and مَسِيرَةٌ (M, Ḳ) and سَيْرُورَةٌ (M, Mgh, Ḳ) like قَيْلُولَةٌ, but [Mṭr says] we have not heard it, (Mgh,) and تَسْيَارٌ, (Ṣ, M, Ḳ,) which last denotes repetition or frequency of the action, (M,) *He*, or *it, went* [*in any manner*, or *any pace*]; *went*, or *passed, along*; *marched, journeyed*, or *proceeded*; *went away, passed away*, or *departed*; (M,* Ḳ,* TA;) *by night* and *by day*. (Mṣb, TA.) You say, سَارَتِ الدَّابَّةُ [*The beast went, went along, &c.*]. (Ṣ.) [And سار سَيْرًا شَدِيدًا *He* (a camel or other beast, and a man,) *went a vehement pace*, or *vehemently*. And سار العَنَقَ *He* (a camel, or a horse,) *went the pace*, or *in the manner, termed* العَنَق: and the like.] And سَارُوا مِنْ بَلَدٍ لِبَلَدٍ [*They went*, or *journeyed, from town to town*, or *from country to country*]: (A:) or سار مِنْ بَلَدٍ إِلَى بَلَدٍ [*he went, &c.*]. (Mgh.) And بَارَكَ ٱللّٰهُ فِى مَسِيرِكَ i. e. سَيْرِكَ [*May God bless thy journeying*]. (Ṣ.) And سِرْ عَنْكَ *Go thou from thy place; pass thou from it*: (L in art. نفذ:) or † *feign thou heedlessness, and bear*, or *endure*, or *be forbearing*; an elliptical phrase; as though it were originally سِرْ وَدَعْ عَنْكَ المِرَآءَ وَالشَّكَّ [*go thou, and leave wrangling and doubt*]. (Ṣ.) —— [Hence, سارت السَّفِينَةُ ‡ *The ship went*, or *sailed*: for] سَيْرُ السَّفِينَةِ is a tropical phrase. (Mgh.) —— And سار سِيرَةً حَسَنَةً ‡ [*He pursued a good way, course, mode*, or *manner, of acting*, or *conduct*, or *the like*], (Ṣ, A, Mṣb,) and سِيرَةً قَبِيحَةً [*a bad way, &c.*]. (Mṣb.) —— And سَارَ فِى النَّاسِ † *It became current*, or *commonly known, among the people*; [as also ↑ تَسَيَّرَ, alone; (see Ḥar p. 318;)] i. e. a proverb, and a saying. (M.) —— And سارت سُنَّةٌ † [*A way, course, mode*, or *manner, of acting*, or *conduct*, or *the like, obtained*, or *was usual, among people*]. (M.) —— سار is also trans., *syn. with* سَيَّرَ. (Ṣ, M, Mṣb, Ḳ.) See the latter, in five places. —— [Hence,] سار سُنَّةً † *He made*, or *caused, a way, course, mode*, or *manner, of acting*, or *conduct*, or *the like, to obtain*, or *became usual, among people*. (Ṣ, M,* TA.) The Hudhalee (Khálid Ibn-Zuheyr, M) says,

* فَلَا تَجْزَعَنْ مِنْ سُنَّةٍ أَنْتَ سِرْتَهَا *
* فَأَوَّلُ رَاضٍ سُنَّةً مَنْ يَسِيرُهَا *

[*Then by no means be thou impatient of a way of acting which thou hast made usual; for the first who should be content with a way of acting is he who makes it usual*]. (Ṣ, M, L, TA: but in the M and TA, in the place of تجزعن, we find تَغْضَبَنْ.)

2. سَيَّرَهُ, (M, A, Mṣb, Ḳ,) inf. n. تَسْيِيرٌ; (TA;) and ↑ اسارهُ; (M, A, Ḳ;) and ↑ سارهُ, (Ḳ,) inf. n. سَيْرٌ and سِيرَةٌ and مَسَارٌ and مَسِيرَةٌ [or مَسِيرٌ, as below]; (TA;) and سار ↑ بِهِ; (IJ, M, Ḳ;) *He made him* (a man, A, Mṣb) *to go* [*in any manner*, or *any pace*]; *to go*, or *pass, along*; *to march, journey*, or *proceed*; *to go away, pass away*, or *depart*: (M, A, Mṣb, K, TA:) and سُورَ ↑ بِهِ [for سِيرَ بِهِ, the reg. pass. form of سَارَ بِهِ,] is mentioned; like هُوبَ and طُولَ. (M.) And سَيَّرَ الدَّابَّةَ; (M, A, Mṣb;) and ↑ اسارها; (M;) and ↑ سارها, (Ṣ, M, Mṣb,) inf. n. سَيْرٌ and سِيرَةٌ and مَسَارٌ and مَسِيرٌ [or مَسِيرَةٌ, as above]; (M;) *He made the beast to go &c.*: (Ṣ, M, A, Mṣb:) or ↑ سِرْتُ الدَّابَّةَ signifies *I rode the beast* [*and thus made it to go &c.*]: (Ibn-Buzurj, TA:) but when you ride it to pasture, you say, ↑ أَسَرْتُهَا, (Mṣb,) or اسرتها إِلَى الكَلَإِ (Ibn-Buzurj, TA) or الى المَرْعَى. (A.) And سَيَّرَهُ مِنْ بَلَدِهِ *He made him to go*, or *depart, from his town*, or *country*; *expelled*, or *banished, him from it*. (Ṣ, A.) —— [Hence] سَيَّرَ ‡ *He removed*, or *put off*, or *took off*, the horse-cloth, or covering, (Ṣ, A, Ḳ,) from the horse, (Ḳ,) or beast, (A,) or from the back of the beast. (Ṣ.) —— And ‡ *He made* a proverb, (Ḳ,) and a saying, (TA,) *to become current*; (Ḳ;) *he published* it *among the people*. (TA.) —— And سَيَّرَ سِيرَةً † *He related stories of the ancients*. (M, Ḳ.) —— سَيَّرَهُ, [from سَيْرٌ meaning "a thong"] *He made stripes upon it*; namely, a garment, or piece of cloth, and an arrow. (M.) And سَيَّرَتْ خِضَابَهَا *She* (a woman) *made her dye to have the form of stripes, like thongs*. (Ḳ,* A,* TA.)

3. سَايَرَهُ, (Ṣ, M, A,) inf. n. مُسَايَرَةٌ, (A,) *He went, went along, &c.*, (سَارَ,) *with him*: (M:) *he went at an equal rate*, or *kept pace, with him*: (PṢ:) *he ran with him*; syn. جَارَاهُ. (Ṣ, A.) —— [And *He vied, contended*, or *competed, with him in going*, or *in running*: and hence, † *in any affair*; like جَارَاهُ.] See also 6.

4: see 2, in three places.

5: see 8: — and see also 1, in the latter half of the paragraph. ═ تسيّر [from سَيْرٌ meaning "a thong"] said of a man's skin, *It peeled off,* (A, Ḳ, TA,) *and became like thongs.* (TA.)

6. تسايرا *They two* [*went,* or *went along,* (see 3,) or] *went at an equal rate,* or *kept pace, each with the other:* (PṢ:) or *ran, each with the other.* (Ṣ, A.) — One says of a great, or frequent, liar, لَا تَسَايَرُ خَيْلَاهُ [lit. *His two troops of horses will not run together, each troop with the other:* meaning † *his assertions will not be found to agree together*]: (so in a copy of the M:) or ↓ لَا تُسَايِرُ خَيْلَاهُ. (So in the Ḳ and TA voce خَيْلٌ, q. v.; and so in the TA in the present art. [See also 6 in art. سلم.]) — [And *They two vied, contended,* or *competed, each with the other, in going,* or *in running:* and hence, † *in any affair.*] — One says also, تَسَايَرَ عَنْ وَجْهِهِ الغَضَبُ ‡ *Anger went* [or *disappeared by degrees*] *from his face.* (TA, from a trad.)

8. استار بسيرته, (O, Ḳ, TA,) or ↓ تسيّر بسيرته, (as in the CḲ,) † *He pursued his way, course, mode,* or *manner, of acting,* or *conduct,* or *the like.* (O, Ḳ,* TA.) ═ And استار [from سِيرَةٌ in the last of the senses assigned to this word below] *He procured for himself wheat, or other provision, from a place, to be laid up in store.* (Ṣ, O, Ḳ.)

سَارٌ: see سَائِرٌ.

سَيْرٌ an inf. n. of 1 [q. v.]. (Ṣ, M, A, &c.) [Used as a simple subst., *A going, in any manner,* or *any pace; passage, march, journey, progress,* or *course: a pace: pace as meaning degree of celerity,* or *rate of going: departure:* see also سِيرَةٌ.] ═ Also *A thong,* or *strap,* or *strip of skin* or *leather;* (Ṣ, Mṣb, Ḳ;) *i. q.* شِرَاكٌ: (M:) pl. [of mult.] سُيُورٌ (Ṣ, M, A, Mṣb) and سُيُورَةٌ and [pl. of pauc.] أَسْيَارٌ. (M.) It is said in a prov., قُدَّتْ سُيُورُهُ مِنْ أَدِيمِكَ [*His thongs have been cut from thy hide*]: applied to two things exactly resembling each other. (AHeyth, Meyd.) And لَيْسَ فِي العَصَا سَيْرٌ is a post-classical prov., (Meyd,) meaning *There is not in the staff,* or *stick, a thong:* the سير in this case being the thong that is inserted into the perforation of the head of the staff, or stick, and whereof a ring is tied, into which the hand is put: the prov. is applied to him who is unable to perform that which he desires to do. (Ḥar p. 232.)

سَيْرَةٌ: see the next paragraph, in two places.

سِيرَةٌ [*i. q.* سَيْرٌ as meaning *A going, in any manner,* or *any pace;* &c.: see above:] a subst. from 1 in the first of the senses assigned to it above. (M, Ḳ.) Lḥ mentions the saying, إِنَّهُ لَحَسَنُ السِّيرَةِ [*Verily he is good in going,* &c.]. (M: in the TA, ↓ السَّيْرَةِ, as having the meaning here next following.) — Also, (M,) or ↓ سَيْرَةٌ, (Ḳ,) [but the former seems to be the right, being agreeable with analogy, whereas the latter is anomalous,] *A mode,* or *manner, of going,* &c. (M, Ḳ.) — And the former, ‡ *A way, course, rule, mode,* or *manner, of acting* or *conduct* or *life* or *the like;* syn. طَرِيقَةٌ (Ṣ, M, Mgh, Mṣb, Ḳ) and سُنَّةٌ (M, Ḳ) and مَذْهَبٌ: (Mgh:) pl. سِيَرٌ. (Mgh, Mṣb.) You say, سَارَ بِهِمْ سِيرَةً حَسَنَةً ‡ [*He pursued with them a good way of acting*]. (Ṣ.) And سَارَ الوَالِى فِى الرَّعِيَّةِ سِيرَةً حَسَنَةً ‡ [*The prefect,* or *governor, pursued among the subjects a good way of acting*]; (A, Mṣb;*) and in like manner, سِيرَةً قَبِيحَةً [*a bad way of acting*]. (Mṣb.) — † The *record of* a man's *actions and pious works;* the prefixed noun صَحِيفَةُ being understood. (Mgh.) — ‡ *Stories of the ancients:* (M, Ḳ:) [or so سِيرَةُ أَوَّلِينَ:] you say, هٰذَا فِى سِيرَةِ الأَوَّلِينَ ‡ [*This is in the stories of the ancients*]. (A.) — [Hence it is used in the present day as meaning † The *mention* of a person or thing: and † *a matter,* or *subject, of discourse.*] — Also, as a law term, (Mgh,) or so [the pl.] سِيَرٌ, (Mgh, Mṣb,) † *Military expeditions;* or the *memorable actions thereof;* (Mṣb;) or the *affairs thereof.* (Mgh.) And they say السِّيَرُ الكَبِيرُ [meaning † *The great book of military expeditions;* for كِتَابُ السِّيَرِ الكَبِيرُ]; using a masc. epithet in lieu of the [suppressed] prefixed noun كِتَابُ. (Mgh.) — Also, the sing., † *Mode,* or *manner, of being; state,* or *condition;* syn. هَيْئَةٌ. (M, O, Mṣb, Ḳ,) and حَالَةٌ. (O, Mṣb.) So in the Ḳur xx. 22. (M, O, TA.) ═ Also *Wheat, or other provision, that is brought from a place to be laid up in store.* (Ṣ, O, Ḳ.)

سَيُّرٌ *That goes,* or *journeys, much:* or *a great goer:* (IJ, M, Ḳ:) and ↓ سَيُورٌ is applied as an epithet [in the same sense] to a hackney, and to an ass. (Az, TA in art. فره.)

سِيَرَاءُ (Ṣ, M, Ḳ, &c.) and سِيَرَاءٌ (TA) [which latter, according to analogy, should be with tenween, but perhaps it is without tenween as being a contraction of the former,] *A sort of garment,* or *cloth, of the kind called* بُرُود, (Fr, Ṣ, M, Mgh, Mṣb, Ḳ,) *having yellow stripes;* (Ṣ, Mgh, Mṣb, Ḳ;) or *mixed with silk;* (Ḳ;) or *mixed with* [*the silk termed*] قَزّ: (AZ, A'Obeyd, Mgh:) or *a sort of* بُرُود *of silk:* (A:) or *a sort of garment,* or *cloth, having stripes, made of* قَزّ: or *certain garments,* or *cloths, of El-Yemen;* (M;) *which are now commonly known by the name of* مُضَلَّعْ: (TA:) or *a sort of* برود *mixed with silk like thongs;* and hence its appellation, from سَيْرٌ, "a thong:" it is asserted by certain of the later writers that it is a subst., not an epithet; and he who says so cites Sb as asserting that a word of the measure فِعَلَاءُ is not an epithet, but is a subst.: hence, he says, it is used with a prefixed noun, as in the ex. حُلَّةُ سِيَرَاءَ; and is expl. as signifying *clear silk.* (IAth, TA.) — Also ‡ The *diaphragm,* or *midriff:* (M, Ḳ:*) metaphorically used in this sense by a poet. (M.) — And † The *peel* [or *pellicle*] *adhering to the stone of a date.* (M, Ḳ.) — And *A palm branch stripped of its leaves.* (M, Ḳ.) — And *Gold:* (M:) or *clear, pure, gold.* (Ḳ,* TA.) — And *A certain plant,* (M, Ḳ, TA,) *not described by Ed-Deenawaree* [i. e. AḤn]; *as some say,* (TA,) *resembling the* خُلَّة [q. v.]: (Ḳ, TA:) so in the Tekmileh. (TA.)

سَيُورٌ: see سَيُّرٌ.

سَيَّارٌ *A journeyer,* or *traveller:* (A:) and سَيَّارَةٌ, (Ṣ, M, Mgh, Mṣb, Ḳ,) for جَمَاعَةٌ سَيَّارَةٌ, (Mgh,) or قَوْمٌ سَيَّارَةٌ, (A,) *a company of persons journeying:* (Ṣ, M, A, Mgh, Mṣb, Ḳ:) [accord. to ISd,] سَيَّارَةٌ is made fem. because meaning رُفْقَةٌ, or جَمَاعَةٌ. (M.) — [السَّيَّارَةُ and السَّيَّارَاتُ] † *The five planets; Mercury, Venus, Mars, Jupiter, and Saturn.* (TA in art. كنس.)

سَائِرٌ [part. n. of 1, *Going,* &c. — Hence,] † A proverb [and a saying] *current,* or *commonly known.* (TA.) ═ Also, and ↓ سَارٌ, (Ṣ, M, Ḳ,) both are syn., (Ḳ,) signifying The *rest,* or *remainder,* of a thing: (M:) [and accord. to some,] the *whole,* or *all,* of a thing or of people. (Ṣ, TA.) [See the former word in art. سار.]

مُسَيَّرٌ: see the next paragraph.

مَسِيرٌ an inf. n. of سَارَ. (Ṣ, M, A, &c.) — [Also *A place,* and *a time, of going,* or *journeying.*] — And pass. part. n. of سَارَ; (Mṣb, MF;) [and so ↓ مَسْيُورٌ, for] you say طَرِيقٌ مَسِيرٌ, (Ḳ,) or مَسْيُورٌ فِيهِ, (IJ, M,) [*A travelled road,*] and رَجُلٌ مَسِيرٌ بِهِ [*A man made to go, or journey,* &c.]: (IJ, M, Ḳ:) accord. to Kh, in this case, and in others like it, the ى is changed into و [so that مَسْيُورٌ, the original form of مَسِيرٌ and of مَسْيُورٌ, becomes مَسْوُورٌ, and is then contracted into مَسُورٌ]: (M:) or, accord. to Kh, the ى is rejected: but accord. to Akh, it is the و that is rejected [so that مَسْيُورٌ becomes مَسْيُرٌ; and then, مَسِيرٌ; and then مَسُورٌ]. (TA.)

مَسِيرَةٌ *A space which one traverses in journeying; a journey as measured by the time that it occupies;* as in the phrase, مَسِيرَةُ شَهْرٍ *a month's journey;* (TA;) and بَيْنَهُمَا مَسِيرَةُ يَوْمٍ [*Between them two is the space of a day's journey*]. (Ṣ, TA.) مَسِيرَةُ يَوْمٍ [*A day's journey*] is *twenty-four miles.* (MF in art. قرطس.)

مُسَيَّرٌ A garment, or piece of cloth, *figured with stripes* (Ṣ, M, A, Ḳ) *like thongs,* (Ṣ, M, A,) *made of silk:* or *a* بُرْد *mixed with silk.* (TA.) [See also سِيَرَاءُ.] — And عُقَابٌ مُسَيَّرَةٌ *A striped eagle.* (M.) — And المُسَيَّرُ, (Ḳ,) or مُسَيَّرُ القرع, (TA, [but the orthography of the latter word I think doubtful,]) *A certain sweetmeat,* (Ḳ, TA,) *well-known.* (TA.)

مُسْتَارٌ [*A place whence one procures wheat, or other provision, for subsistence, to be laid up in store:* from اِسْتَارَ in the latter of the senses assigned to it above, agreeably with analogy, and as is indicated in the Ṣ]. A rájiz says, [namely, Aboo-Wejzeh, as in a copy of the Ṣ,]

• أَشْكُو إِلَى ٱللّٰهِ العَزِيزِ الغَفَّارْ •
• ثُمَّ إِلَيْكَ اليَوْمَ بُعْدَ المُسْتَارْ •

[*I complain unto God, the Mighty, the Very Forgiving, then unto thee, this day, the remoteness of the place whence I have to procure provision for subsistence*]: or, accord. to some, المُسْتَار, in this verse, is of the measure مُفْتَعَل from السَّيْر [and, like it, meaning *the journey*]. (Ṣ.)

سيع

1. سَاعَ, aor. يَسِيعُ, inf. n. سَيْعٌ and سُيُوعٌ, *It* (water, and the سَرَاب [or mirage],) *ran, and was in a state of commotion, upon the surface of the ground;* (Ṣ, O, Ḳ;) as also ▼ انساع: (Ṣ:) or the latter, said of water, *it ran upon the surface of the ground;* as also ▼ تسيّع: and ▼ انساع, said of a thing in a congealed or solid state, signifies also *it melted; became fluid,* or *liquid.* (TA.) — سَاعَتِ الإِبِلُ, (Sh, Ḳ,) aor. as above, inf. n. سَيْعٌ, (Sh,) *The camels were left to themselves, without a pastor;* (Sh, Ḳ;) as also ساعت having تَسُوعُ for its aor. and سَوْعٌ for its inf. n. (Sh, Ṣ* and Ḳ* in art. سوع.) — And ‡ سَاعَ الشَّىْءُ, aor. as above, *The thing became left,* or *neglected,* or *lost;* or *it perished.* (TA.)

2. تَسْيِيعٌ The act of *plastering with mud* [or *with* سِيَاع]. (Ḳ.) You say, سَيَّعْتُ الحَائِطَ *I plastered the wall with mud and chopped straw.* (Ṣ.) — And The act of *anointing with fat* and *the like.* (Ḳ.) You say, سَيَّعَتِ المَرْأَةُ مَزَادَتَهَا *The woman anointed* [*with fat,* or *the like, her leathern water-bag*]. (TA.)

4. اساعهُ *He left it, neglected it, lost it,* or *destroyed it.* (TA.) [See also art. سوع.]

5: see 1. — تسيّع البَقْلُ *The herbs,* or *leguminous plants, dried up;* or *became yellow.* (TA.)

7: see 1, in two places.

سَيْعٌ *Water running upon the surface of the ground.* (Lth, Ḳ.)

سَيَاعٌ, (Ḳ,) or سِيَاعٌ, (Ṣ,) or both, (MF, TA,) *Mud:* (TA:) or *mud* [*mixed*] *with chopped straw, with which one plasters.* (Kr, Ṣ, Ḳ.) The saying of the poet, (Ṣ, Ḳ,) namely El-Ḳuṭámee, (Ḳ,) describing his she-camel, (TA,)

* فَلَمَّا أَنْ جَرَى سِمَنٌ عَلَيْهَا *
* كَمَا طَيَّنْتَ بِالفَدَنِ السِّيَاعَا *

presents an inversion, the meaning being كما طَيَّنْتَ بِالسِّيَاعِ الفَدَنَ [i. e. *And when fatness extended upon her, as when thou plasterest with mud and chopped straw the pavilion*]; الفَدَن signifying القَصْر. (Ṣ, Ḳ: [but in the former, only the latter hemistich is cited; and in some copies of the former, and in the O, we find بَطَّنْتَ in the place of طَيَّنْتَ.]) — Also *Fat with which a* مَزَادَة [*or leathern water-bag*] *is anointed.* (Ḳ.) — And ‡ *Pitch,* or *tar;* syn. زِفْتٌ; as being likened to mud, because of its blackness. (TA.)

ضَائِعٌ سَائِعٌ, mentioned in this art. in the TA: see art. سوع.

سَرَابٌ أَسْيَعُ *A mirage* [*running upon the surface of the ground,* (see 1,) *and*] *in a state of commotion:* (Ṣ,* TA:) or, as some say, [*in a state of exceeding commotion;* for] the form of the epithet in this case denotes مُفَاضَلَة. (TA.)

مِسْيَعَةٌ *A plasterer's trowel;* syn. مَالَجَةٌ: (Ṣ:) *a piece of wood made smooth, used by skilful plasterers with mud.* (Lth, Ḳ.)

مِسْيَاعٌ A she-camel *that goes away in the place of pasturing:* (Ḳ:) mentioned by J in art. سوع, q. v.: (TA:) or *that bears, or suffers, neglect,* or *being left alone,* (الَّتِى تَحْمِلُ الضَّيْعَةَ,) [for the last of which words we find in some copies of the Ḳ الضِّيعَةَ, but it is said in the TA that the former is the right reading, as is shown by its being added,]) *and bad superintendence* or *management;* (Ḳ, TA;) thus expl. by Aṣ: (TA:) or *upon which one journeys and returns;* (Ḳ;) thus expl. by Ṣgh, but this is the explanation of مِرْيَاعٌ, with which it is coupled. (TA.)

سيغ

1. سِغْتُهُ, aor. أَسِيغُهُ, inf. n. سَيْغٌ: see 4, in art. سوغ.

هٰذا سَيْغُ هٰذَا: see هذا سَوْغُ هذا, in art. سوغ, in two places.

سَيِّغٌ: see سَائِغٌ, in art. سوغ.

سيف

1. سَافَهُ, (Ṣ, M, O, Ḳ,) first pers. سِفْتُهُ, (Ṣ, O, Mṣb, Ḳ, [in the CḲ, erroneously, سُفْتُهُ,]) aor. يَسِيفُ, (Ṣ, O, Mṣb, Ḳ,) inf. n. سَيْفٌ, (M,) *He struck him,* or *smote him, with the* سَيْف [or *sword*]; (Ṣ, M, O, Mṣb, Ḳ;) as also ▼ تسيّفهُ. (TA.) — See also 3. — سَيِفَ, inf. n. سَيَفٌ; and ▼ انساف; [app., as seems to be indicated by the context, said of palm-trees (نَخْل) or of palm-branches (سَعَف), as meaning *They had upon them what is termed* سَيَف, q. v.:] (M, TA:*) and سَيِفَت and ▼ انسافت are said of a palm-tree (نَخْلَة) [app. as meaning *it had* سيف *upon it*]. (TA.)

3. مُسَايَفَةٌ signifies The *contending with another in fight,* or *in smiting, with the sword.* (Ṣ, Mgh.) ▼ سَايَفَنِى فَسِفْتُهُ, a phrase mentioned, without his adding anything thereto, by Lḥ, app. means [*He contended with me in smiting with the sword, and*] *I was more skilled in the use of the sword* (كُنْتُ أَسْيَفَ) *than he.* (M.) — See also 6.

4. اساف القَوْمُ *The people,* or *party, came to the* سيف [or *sea-shore*]. (AAF, M.) — اساف الخَرَزُ (Ṣ, Ḳ) *i. q.* خَرَمَهُ (Ṣ, TA) [expl. in art. سوف] is said to belong to the present art., in which it is mentioned by IF as well as J. (TA.)

5: see 1. — [Accord. to Freytag, تَسَيَّفَ signifies *He was slain with the sword:* but he mentions no authority for this. Perhaps the pass. form of this verb may have this meaning.]

6. تسايفوا *They contended, one with another, in smiting with swords;* (Ṣ, M, Ḳ;) as also ▼ سايفوا; (Ḳ;) and so ▼ استافوا, (M, Ḳ,) as expl. by the lexicologists; but this last properly signifies *they took,* or *took hold of, the swords.* (IJ, M.)

7: see 1, in two places.

8. اِسْتِيَافٌ signifies The act of [*putting to the sword,*] *destroying,* or *killing.* (KL.) One says, أُسْتِيفَ القَوْمُ [app. meaning *The people,* or *party, were put to the sword*]: (Ḳ:) a phrase mentioned by Lth. (TA.) — See also 6.

سَيْفٌ *A sword;* (MA, PṢ, &c.;) *a certain thing with which one smites;* (M;) *well known:* its names exceed a thousand: (Ḳ: in which it is added that its author has mentioned these names in [his book entitled] الرَّوْضُ المَسْلُوفُ: [for the names of particular parts thereof, see ذُبَابٌ:] pl. [of pauc.] أَسْيَافٌ (Ṣ, M, O, Mṣb, Ḳ) and أَسْيُفٌ (Lḥ, M, O, Ḳ) and [of mult.] سُيُوفٌ (Ṣ, M, O, Mṣb, Ḳ) and [quasi-pl. n.] ▼ مَسْيَفَةٌ, like مَشْيَخَةٌ, (O, Ḳ, TA,) or مَسِيفَةٌ, like مَشِيخَةٌ. (CḲ.) [Hence,] سَيْفُ الجَبَّارِ † [*The sword of Orion;*] *the three stars* [η, θ, κ, *beneath the girdle*] *of* الجبّار, *in a sloping direction, near together, disposed in a row.* (Ḳzw.) — † *A certain fish,* (Ibn-'Abbád, O, Ḳ,) *resembling a* سَيْف [or *sword*]; (Ibn-'Abbád, O;) as also ▼ سَيِّفٌ. (Ḳ.) — † The سَبِيب, (M,) [i. e.] the *hair of the tail,* (Ḳ,) *of a horse.* (M, Ḳ.) — سَيْفُ الغُرَابِ † i. q. الدَّلْبُوثُ; (Ḳ;) *A certain plant, the stem* (أَصْل) *and leaves of which are exactly like those of the saffron, and the bulb of which is enclosed in a covering of* [*fibres of the kind called*] لِيف; (AḤn;) so called because its leaves are slender at the extremity like the سَيْف [or *sword*]. (AḤn, Ḳ.) — هُمْ أَسْيَافٌ [lit. *They are swords*] means أَحْزَابٌ [i. e. † *they are bodies, or parties, of men prepared,* or *ready, for fighting, &c.*]. (Ibn-'Abbád, O, Ḳ.) — And one says, بَيْنَ فَكَّيْهِ سَيْفٌ صَارِمٌ ‡ [*Between his two jaws is a sharp tongue;* lit., *a cleaving sword*]. (TA.)

سِيفٌ The *shore* (سَاحِل) *of the sea* or *of a great river:* (Ṣ, M, O, Mgh, Mṣb, Ḳ:) and the *side* (سَاحِل) of a valley: or [the *margin* of the shore of a sea or of a great river; for it is added,] every سَاحِل has a سيف: or السِّيفُ is applied only to the سيف [or sea-shore, or seaboard,] of 'Omán: (Ḳ:) [if otherwise applied,] its pl. is أَسْيَافٌ. (Ṣ, M.) One says, هُمْ أَهْلُ أَسْيَافٍ وَأَرْيَافٍ [*They are people of the shores of the sea* or *of a great river, and of the tracts of towns,* or *villages, and cultivated lands*]. (TA.) — Also *A thing that adheres to the lower parts,* or *roots, of palm-branches, like* [*the fibres called*] لِيف, *but not the same as* لِيف: (Ṣ: in which is added, "this I have taken from a book, without having heard it:") or the [*fibrous substance called*] لِيف, (Ḳ,) or the *thick,* or *coarse,* لِيف, (M,) *adhering to the lower parts, or roots, of palm-branches, which is the worst sort thereof,* [i. e. of لِيف,] (M, Ḳ,) *and the harshest, and coarsest.* (M.) [See شِيفٌ.] — See also سَيْفٌ.

سِيفَةٌ: see art. سوف.

سَيْفَانٌ, applied to a man, *Tall and slender,* (Ks, Ṣ, M, O, Ḳ,) *like the* سَيْف [or *sword*], (M,) *lank in the belly:* (Ks, Ṣ, O:) and with ة applied to a woman, (Ks, Ṣ, M, O, Ḳ,) meaning *tall; resembling a sword-blade:* (O:) or it is peculiar to women; (K;) [i. e.] accord. to Kh, one does not apply to a man the epithet سَيْفَانٌ. (O.)

سَيَّافٌ An owner, or a possessor, of a سَيْف [or sword]; (S, M, O, K;) as also ▼ مُسِيفٌ: (M:) pl. [or rather coll. gen. n.] of the former سَيَّافَةٌ: (S, M, O, K:) or this last signifies a people, or party, whose حُصُون [or fortresses] are their سُيُوف [or swords; i. e. whose only means of defence are their swords]. (Lth, O, K.*) — Also ‡ A man who is a frequent shedder of blood; or who sheds much blood. (TA.) [An executioner who slays with the sword.] — And A maker of سُيُوف [or swords]. (TA.) [And A seller of swords.]

سَائِفٌ Striking, or smiting, with the سَيْف [or sword]. (S.) — And A man having a سَيْف [or sword]: (S, O, K:) or having with him a سَيْف. (Msb.)

أَسْيَفُ [More, and most, skilled in the use of the sword]: see 3.

مُسِيفٌ One having upon him a سَيْف [or sword]; (S, O, K;) having hung upon himself a سَيْف: (Ks:) and (K) accord. to Ibn-'Abbád, a courageous man having with him a سَيْف. (O, K.) — See also سَيَّافٌ. ═ And see art. سوف.

مَسِيفَةٌ, or مَسْيَفَةٌ: see سَيْف.

مُسَيَّفٌ, applied to a [garment of the kind called] بُرْد, Having upon it what resemble the forms of سُيُوف [or swords]: (M, TA:) and, so applied, having broad stripes, like the سَيْف [or sword]. (TA.) — And, applied to a dirhem, of which the sides are plain, or clear of any impress or the like. (IAar, O, K.)

مِسْيَافٌ A wind (رِيحٌ) that cuts like the سَيْف [or sword]. (M.) ═ See also art. سوف.

سيل

1. سَالَ, (S, M, Msb, K,) said of water, (S, Msb, TA,) or of a thing, (M,) aor. يَسِيلُ, (Msb, K,) inf. n. سَيْلٌ and سَيَلَانٌ (S, M, Msb, K, TA) and مَسِيلٌ and مَسَالٌ, (TA,) It flowed, or ran: (M, K, TA:) or, said of water, it rose so as to become excessively copious, and flowed, or ran: and سال said of thing, it was, or became, fluid, or liquid; contr. of جَمَدَ. (Msb.) — The Arabs say, سَالَ بِهِمُ السَّيْلُ وَجَاشَ بِنَا البَحْرُ [The torrent flowed with them, and the sea estuated with us so as to be unnavigable;] meaning, † they fell into a hard case, and we fell into one that was harder than it: (M, Meyd:) a proverb. (Meyd.) — And سَالَتْ عَلَيْهِ الخَيْلُ ‡ [The horsemen poured upon him]. (TA. [See also 6.]) — And سالت الغُرَّةُ † [The blaze upon the face of a horse] extended, or spread, long and wide: (S:) [or, simply, extended down the face; as appears from an explanation of the word شِمْرَاخ in the S and K &c.: see also سَائِلَةٌ, below. And in like manner سال is often said of flowing, or defluent, hair.] ═ سِيلَ &c. for سُئِلَ, pass. of سَأَلَ: see this last word, in art. سأل.

2: see 4.

3. سَايَلْتُ: see 3 in art. سأل.

4. اسالهُ, (S, M, Msb, K,) inf. n. إِسَالَةٌ, (Msb,) He made it to flow, or run; (S,* M, Msb, K;) as also ▼ سَيَّلَهُ, (S, TA,) inf. n. تَسْيِيلٌ. (TA.) It is said in the Kur [xxxiv. 11], وَأَسَلْنَا لَهُ عَيْنَ القِطْرِ (M, TA) i. e. And we made [the source of copper, or of brass,] to flow, or run, for him. (TA.) — And † He made it long, (M, K,) and complete; (M;) namely, the point of the iron head or blade of an arrow or of a spear &c. (M, K.)

6. تَسَايَلَتِ الكَتَائِبُ ‡ [The troops of horse] poured [together] from every quarter. (S, TA. [See also 1.]) ═ هُمَا يَتَسَايَلَانِ: see 6 in art. سأل.

سَيْلٌ A torrent, or flow of water; (MA;) [i. e.] much water, (M, K,) or a collection of rainwater, (Msb,) flowing, or running, (M, Msb, K,) in a valley, or water-course, or torrent-bed: (Msb:) or water that comes to one [from rain, in any case, or] from rain that has not fallen upon one: (TA:) originally an inf. n.: (Msb, TA:) pl. سُيُولٌ: (S, M, Msb, K:) ▼ سَائِلَةٌ, also, signifies the same as سَيْلٌ; and its pl. is سَوَائِلُ [expl. in the M as meaning flowing, or running, waters]. (TA.) — And they said also, مَآءٌ سَيْلٌ, meaning ▼ سَائِلٌ [i. e. Flowing, or running, water]; (M, K;) putting the inf. n. in the place of the epithet. (M.) وَجَدْتُ بَقْلًا وَبُقَيْلًا وَمَآءً غَلَلًا سَيْلًا, meaning I found herbs full-grown and large and tall, and herbs not full-grown and therefore small, [and water among trees, flowing, or running,] is a saying of one sent to seek for herbage and water; mentioned by Th. (M.)

سِيلَةٌ A mode, or manner, of flowing or running of water. (K.)

سِيلَانٌ The سِنْخ [or tongue] of [meaning that enters into] the hilt, or handle, of a sword (M, K) and of a knife (M) and the like; (M, K;) the part, (S, TA,) in the A the tail, (TA,) that enters into the hilt, or handle, of a sword and of a knife: heard by A'Obeyd, though not from a learned man: (S, TA:) but AA cites the following ex. from Ez-Zibrikán Ibn-Bedr:

وَلَنْ أُصَالِحَكُمْ مَا دَامَ لِي فَرَسٌ
وَٱشْتَدَّ قَبْضًا عَلَى السِّيلَانِ إِبْهَامِي

[And I will not make peace with you while I have a horse and my thumb grasps firmly upon the tongue of the sword]. (El-Jawáleekee, IB, TA.)

سَيَالٌ pl. of سَيَالَةٌ, (K,) [or rather the former is a coll. gen. n. of which the latter is the n. un., applied in the present day to A species of mimosa, or acacia, mentioned by Forskål in his Flora Aegypt. Arab., pp. lvi. and cxxiv., and by Delile in his Floræ Aegypt. Illustr. (in the Descr. de l'Égypte), no. 965: and to a species of thistle; carduus lacteus; or wild artichoke:] a species of trees having thorns, of the kind called عِضَاه: (S:) certain trees having white thorns: (M:) or the [thorny plant called] شُبْرُم: (AA, M:) a certain plant; (K;) said to have white thorns, from which, when these are plucked, there issues what resembles milk: (AA, M, K:*) certain trees having lank branches and white thorns of which the bases resemble the middle pairs of the teeth of virgins: (TA:) or, (K,) accord. to Aboo-Ziyád, (AHn, M,) tall سَمُر [or gum-acacia-trees]: (AHn, M, K:) accord. to the A, the trees called خِلَاف [now applied to the salix Aegyptia of Linn.] in the dial. of El-Yemen. (TA.)

سَيَّالٌ [Flowing, or running, much]. One says, نَزَلْنَا بِوَادٍ نَبْتُهُ مَيَّالٌ وَمَاؤُهُ سَيَّالٌ [We alighted in a valley the herbage whereof was inclining much, by reason of its luxuriant growth, and the water whereof was flowing, or running, much, by reason of its copiousness]. (TA.) — [And Distilling much: see وَدَقٌ.] ═ Also A certain mode of calculation. (O, K, TA. [In the CK, الجِيتَانِ is erroneously put for الحِسَابِ.])

سَيَّالَةٌ: see سَائِلَةٌ. — Also A bending in a sea or great river. (TA.)

سَائِلٌ: see سَيْلٌ. — Also Fluid, or liquid. (Msb.) — سَائِلُ الأَطْرَافِ, in a description of the Prophet, means † Extended in the fingers: or, as some relate it, سَائِنُ, with ن, which has the same meaning. (O.) And غُرَّةٌ سَائِلَةٌ means † [A blaze upon the face of a horse] extending, or spreading, long and wide: (S:) or [extending so as to be] equable, or uniform, upon the bone of the nose: or that has extended upon the extremity of the nose so as to make it white: (M, K:) or that has spread widely upon the forehead and the bone of the nose: (TA:) if narrow, it is termed شِمْرَاخ. (S, TA.)

سَائِلَةٌ [as a subst. formed from the epithet سَائِلٌ by the affix ة]; pl. سَوَائِلُ: see سَيْلٌ. — [Hence the saying,] رَأَيْتُ سَائِلَةً مِنَ النَّاسِ † I saw a company of men that had poured from some quarter; and so ▼ سَيَّالَةٌ. (TA.) — The pl. سَوَائِلُ also signifies Valleys [app. flowing with water, or because they flow with water]. (T in art. ذنب.)

مَسِيلٌ: see مَسَلٌ.

مُسَالُ الخَدَّيْنِ [app. meaning ‡ Having expanded cheeks, not elevated in the balls thereof, like مَسِيلُ الخَدَّيْنِ,] is a tropical phrase. (TA.) — مُسَالَا الرَّجُلِ † The two sides of the beard of the man: (O, and so in one of my copies of the S:) or, of his jaws: (so in the TA and in my other copy of the S; i. e. لَحْيَيْهِ instead of لِحْيَتِهِ:) sing. مُسَالٌ: and pl. مُسَالَاتٌ. (S, O.) And also † The two sides of the man [himself]; syn. عِطْفَاهُ. (S, O.)

مَسِيلٌ A place [or channel] in which a torrent flows: (Msb:) or مَسِيلُ مَآءٍ and ▼ مَسَلُ مَآءٍ, (S, K,) the latter anomalous, so much so that a parallel to it is scarcely, or in no wise, known, (MF,) a water-course; i. e. a place [or channel] in which water flows, or runs: pl. [of pauc., of the former,] أَمْسِلَةٌ, (S, K,) and [of mult.] مَسَايِلُ and مُسُلٌ and مُسْلَانٌ; (S, Msb, K, TA;) the second pl. regular, without ء, (TA, [though written in the CK with ء,]) and the rest irregular, (Ṣ,* TA,) the sing. being likened to رغيف, (Ṣ, Mṣb, TA,) which has for its pl. أرْغِفَةٌ and رُغُفٌ (Ṣ, TA) and رُغْفَانٌ. (Ṣ, Mṣb, TA.) — It is also an inf. n. (TA. [See 1, first sentence.]) — Also Rain *causing much flowing;* opposed to مُوْزِغٌ [q. v.]. (Ḥam p. 632.) [See also what follows.]

مُسِيلٌ Rain *that causes the valleys and water-courses* (تِلَاع) *to flow;* opposed to مُوْزِغٌ [q. v.]. (Ṣ in art. وزغ, and Ḥam p. 632.) [See also what next precedes.]

Quasi سيم

سِيمَةٌ and سِيمَى and سِيمَآءٌ and سِيمِيَآءٌ: see art. سوم.

سُيُومٌ: see سَائِمٌ [of which it is said to be pl.], in art. سوم.

لا سِيَّمَا and لا سِيمَا and لَا سِيَمَا: see art. سوى.

سين

سِينٌ *One of the letters of the alphabet:* (Ṣ, M, L, Ḳ:) [i. e., the *name of that letter:* (see art. س:)] of the masc. gender as being supposed to be a حَرْف [or letter], and fem. as being supposed to be a كَلِمَة [or word]. (L.) The saying فُلَانٌ لَا يُحْسِنُ سِينَهُ means *Such a one will not form well* one of the three شُعَب [i. e. teeth, or cusps,] of *his* س. (Ṣ, L.)

سِينَآءُ *Certain stones,* (M, L, Ḳ,) so says Zj, (M, L,) *well-known:* (Ḳ:) whence the name of a certain mountain in Syria. (M, L.)

سِينِيَّةٌ *A certain tree;* (M, L, Ḳ;) mentioned by AḤn on the authority of Akh: (M, L:) pl. سِينِينٌ. (M, L, Ḳ.)

سيو

سِيَةٌ The *curved part of each of the two extremities* of a bow: pl. سِيَاتٌ: (Ṣ, Ḳ:) the ة in the sing. is a substitute for و: AO says that Ru-beh used to pronounce it [سِئَةٌ,] with ء; and the rest of the Arabs, [سِيَةٌ,] without ء. (Ṣ, TA.) [See also art. سأو.]

سَىٌّ: see art. سوى.

سِىٌّ, with the compound سِيَّمَا: see art. سوى. — [Hence, perhaps, because of its uniformity, and, if so, belonging to art. سوى,] كَلَأٌ سِىٌّ *Much,* or *abundant, herbage:* mentioned by Ṣgh. (TA.)

سِيَّةٌ: see art. سوى.

سِيَوِىٌّ *Of,* or *relating to, the* سِيَة *of a bow.* (Ṣ.)

ش

The thirteenth letter of the alphabet: called شِينٌ. It is one of the letters termed مَهْمُوسَة [or non-vocal, i. e. pronounced with the breath only, without the voice]; and of the letters termed شَجْرِيَّة, (TA,) from الشَّجْرُ, which means "the place of the opening of the mouth." (TA on the letter ج. See also شين in art. شين.) It is sometimes substituted for the affixed pronoun of the second pers. fem., كِ; as in رَأَيْتُشِ for رَأَيْتُكِ, and as in the following verse,

فَعَيْنَاشِ عَيْنَاهَا وَجِيدُشِ جِيدُهَا
وَلٰكِنَّ عَظْمَ السَّاقِ مِنْشِ رَقِيقُ

[*And thy two eyes are her two eyes, and thy neck is her neck; but the bone of thy shank is slender*]; i. e. عَيْنَاكِ and جِيدُكِ and مِنْكِ: this substitution for the affixed pronoun of the second pers. fem. is of dial. of Benoo-'Amr and Temeem; and is not restricted to cases of pausation, as is shown by the verse above cited, though some assert it to be so: it is also substituted for the ك of دِيك, when with kesr, so that they said دِيشٍ: also for ج, as in مُدْمَشٌ [or مُدَمَّشٌ], for مُدْمَجٌ [or مُدَمَّجٌ]: and for س, as in جَعْشُوشٌ, for جُعْسُوسٌ. (MF. [See also De Sacy's Chrest. Arabe, sec. ed., iii. 530-31.]) — [As a numeral, it denotes *Three hundred.*]

شاب

شُؤْبُوبٌ *A shower,* or *fall,* or *what pours forth at once* or *without intermission,* of rain (Ṣ, A, O, Ḳ) &c.: (Ṣ, O:) or of rain with hail; for otherwise this term is not applied to rain: (ISd, TA:) pl. شَآبِيبُ: (Ṣ, A, O, Ḳ:*) this is the pl. of شُؤْبُوبٌ (Ḳ, TA) in all its senses: (TA:) or *rain that falls upon one place and misses another;* like نَجْوٌ and نَجَآءٌ. (AZ, TA.) — [*A thin, not wide, cloud, of which the rain falls with vehemence.* (Freytag, from the Deewán of the Hudhalees.)] — *A heat,* or *an unintermitted act,* of running. (TA.) — *Sharpness, vehemence, force,* or *strength,* of anything: (Ḳ:) *violence,* or *vehemence, of impetus* or *pushing* or *driving,* (Ṣ, A, O, Ḳ,) of rain, (A,) or of anything. (Ḳ.) Kaab Ibn-Zuheyr says, speaking of a he-ass and she-asses,

إِذَا مَا ٱنْتَحَاهُنَّ شُؤْبُوبُهُ
رَأَيْتَ لِجَاعِرَتَيْهِ غُضُونَا

i. e. *When he runs vehemently* [*towards them,* or rather *when his vehemence of running is directed towards them*], *thou seest a wrinkling* [or *wrinkles*] *in his* جَاعِرَتَانِ [dual of جَاعِرَةٌ, q. v.]. (Ṣ, O.) — *The first appearance* [or *bloom*] *of beauty.* (Ḳ.) One says of a girl, or young woman, إِنَّهَا لَحَسَنَةُ شَآبِيبِ الوَجْهِ *Verily she is goodly in respect of the first appearances* [or *bloomings*] *of beauty of countenance in the eye of the beholder.* (O.) — *The vehemence of the heat of the sun.* (Ḳ.) — And The طَرِيقَة *of the sun:* (Ḳ:) شَآبِيبُ الشَّمْسِ signifies *the lines,* or *streaks,* (طَرَائِق,) *of the sun when it rises.* (O.) — شَآبِيبُ الصَّمْغِ *What flows, of the* [*manna,* or *gum, called*] مُغْفُر [q. v.], *and remains like strings,* or *threads, between the trees and the ground.* (T, L.) [See also سَعَابِيبُ.]

شأت

شَئِيتٌ A horse *that has a habit of stumbling;* or *that stumbles often:* (Ṣ, Ḳ:) it has no corresponding verb: and accord. to Aṣ, it signifies (Ṣ) a horse *whose hind hoofs fall short of reaching* [*the spots that have been trodden by*] *his fore hoofs:* (Ṣ, Ḳ:) [but see شَبُوبٌ:] pl. شُؤُوتٌ. (TA.) [See also أَحَقّ.]

شأف

1. شَئِفَتْ رِجْلُهُ, (Ṣ, O, Ḳ,) aor. ـَ, (Ḳ,) inf. n. شَأَفٌ; (Ṣ, O;) and شُئِفَتْ رجله; (O, Ḳ;) *His foot became affected with an ulcer,* or *imposthume, such as is termed* شَأْفَة, *breaking out in it.* (Ṣ, O, Ḳ.) — Accord. to some, (O,) شَأَفَ الجُرْحُ (O, Ḳ, [in my MS. copy of the Ḳ شَأْفَ, and so accord. to the TḲ, and in the CḲ without ء, but I think that the right reading is شَأِفَ, and that its verb is شَئِفَ, or it may be شَأَفَ, and inf. n. of شَئِفَ,]) signifies *The wound's becoming in a corrupt state, so that it will hardly,* or *not at all, be cured.* (O, Ḳ.) — شَئِفَ صَدْرُهُ عَلَىَّ *His bosom bore concealed enmity and violent hatred,* or *rancour, malevolence, malice,* or *spite, against me.* (TA.) — شَئِفَتْ أَصَابِعُهُ, (Az, O, Ḳ,) or يَدُهُ, (M, TA,) *His fingers,* or *his hand, became cracked,* or *disintegrated, in the parts around the nails;* (Az, M, O, Ḳ;) as also سَئِفَتْ, (O, TA,) and سَعِفَتْ: so say AZ and IAạr, and in like manner says Th. (TA.) — شَئِفْتُهُ, (Ṣ, O, Ḳ,) and شَنِفْتُ لَهُ, (AZ, O, Ḳ,) aor. ـَ, (Ḳ,) inf. n. شَأَفٌ, (Ṣ, O, Ḳ,) in the Bári' شَأْفٌ, with fet-ḥ to the ء, (TA,) and شَآفَةٌ; (O, Ḳ;) and شَئِفْتُ مِنْهُ, inf. n. شَأْفٌ, omitted in the Ḳ [and Ṣ, and O], but correct, as Ṣgh has indicated in the Tekmileh; (TA;) *I hated him;* (Ṣ, O, Ḳ;) like شَنِفْتُ لَهُ; (Ṣ and O in art. شنف;) namely, a man: (Ṣ, O:) or the first and second signify, (Ḳ,) or the first also signifies accord. to IAạr, (O,) *I feared, when I saw him,* namely, a man, *that I should smite him with an evil eye,* or *should guide against him one whom he disliked,* or *hated;* (O;) or *I feared that he would smite me with an evil eye,* or *I guided against him one whom he disliked,* or *hated.* (Ḳ.) — And شَئِفَ *He* (a man, A'Obeyd, O) *was frightened,* or *afraid.* (A'Obeyd, O, Ḳ.)

10. اِسْتَشْأَفَتْ, said of a قُرْصَة, [so in the TA, an evident mistranscription, app. for قَرْحَة, and so in the next paragraph, i. e. an ulcer, or imposthume,] means صَارَ لَهَا أَصْلٌ [*It had,* or *acquired, root,* or *rootedness,* or *permanence;* as though it became a شَأْفَة]. (TA.)

شَئِفٌ [part. n. of شَئِفَ, and properly meaning *Having an ulcer,* or *imposthume, such as is termed* شَأْفَة,] is applied as an epithet to a heart, in the following verse, cited by IḲṭṭ,

يَا أَيُّهَا الجَاهِلُ أَلَّا تَنْصَرِفْ
وَلَمْ تُدَاوِ قُرْصَةَ القَلْبِ الشَّئِفْ

[in which قُرْصَة is doubtless a mistranscription (like that in the next preceding paragraph) for قَرْحَة; the obvious meaning of the verse being, † *O thou ignorant one, wherefore wilt not thou revert, when thou hast not cured the sore of an ulcerated heart?*]. (TA.)

شَأْفَة *An ulcer,* or *imposthume,* (قَرْحَة,) *that breaks out in the bottom of the foot, and is cauterized,* (Ṣ, IAth, O, Ḳ,) or *is cut,* (Yaạḳoob, IAth, O,) *and goes away;* (Yaạḳoob, Ṣ, IAth, O, Ḳ;) and the word is also pronounced without ء [i. e. شَافَة]: (IAth, TA:) or *an ulcer,* or *imposthume, in the foot of a person, who dies if it is cut:* (O, Ḳ:) and it is also said to be *a tumour in the hand, and foot, from the entering of a piece of wood,* or *stick, into the flesh of the foot,* or *the palm of the hand, and its remaining therein,* so that the place swells, and becomes large. (TA.) اِسْتَأْصَلَ ٱللّٰهُ شَأْفَتَهُ (Ṣ, O, Ḳ) is a prov. (Ṣ, O) meaning † *May God cause him to go away like as the* شأفة *above mentioned goes away:* (Ṣ, O, Ḳ:) or this means *may God extirpate him:* for — شَأْفَةٌ is also syn. with أَصْلٌ [i. e. *Root,* &c.]: (O, Ḳ:) so says Sh. (O.) [See also 10 in art. اصل: and see what here follows.] — It is also said to signify The *family and household* of a man: and hence the form of imprecation, اِسْتَأْصَلَ ٱللّٰهُ شَأْفَتَهُمْ [*May God extirpate their family and household*]. (TA.) — And ‡ *Enmity.* (TA.)

شَأَفَةٌ, thus with fet-ḥ to the ء, is an epithet applied to a man, meaning *Mighty, potent, powerful,* or *strong; inaccessible,* or *difficult of access.* (TA.)

رِجْلٌ مَشْؤُوفَةٌ *A foot affected with an ulcer,* or *imposthume, such as is termed* شَأْفَةٌ, *breaking out in it:* (O, Ḳ:) from شُئِفَتْ رِجْلُهُ. (O,* Ḳ,* TA.) — And مَشْؤُوفٌ, from شُئِفَ, *Frightened,* or *afraid;* (A'Obeyd, O, Ḳ;) applied to a man. (A'Obeyd, O.)

شأم

1. شَؤُمَ عَلَيْهِمْ, (Ṣ, MA, Ḳ,) inf. n. شُؤْمٌ, (MA,) *He* (a man, Ṣ) *was,* or *became, unlucky,* or *inauspicious,* (صَارَ شُؤْمًا, Ṣ, Ḳ, in the MA شوم شد,) *to them:* (Ṣ, MA, Ḳ;) as also شَأَمَهُمْ, and شَأَمَ عليهم, and شُؤِمَ عليهم: (Ḳ:) or شَأَمَهُمْ, (AZ, Ḥam p. 224,) or شَأَمَ عَلَيْهِمْ, (Ṣ,) or both of these, (TA,) aor. ـَ, (Ṣ, TA,) inf. n. شَأْمٌ, (TA,) *he drew upon them ill luck,* or *evil fortune;* (Ṣ, TA;) or *caused ill luck,* or *evil fortune, to befall them from him:* (AZ, Ḥam ubi suprà, TA:) or شُؤْمٌ as an inf. n. signifies the *being unlucky:* and the *rendering unlucky:* and so شُومٌ [as it is commonly pronounced: see شُؤْمٌ below]. (KL.) — And شَأَمَهُمْ, inf. n. شَأْمٌ, so in the L; in the Ḳ, ↓ شَأَّمَهُمْ, inf. n. تَشْئِيمٌ; but the former is the right; (TA;) *He made them to go,* or *journey, to* ٱلشَّأْم [i. e. *Syria*]. (Ḳ, TA.)

2: see what next precedes.

3. شَائِمْ بِأَصْحَابِكَ *Take thou the direction of the left hand with thy companions:* (Ṣ, Ḳ, TA:) يَامِنْ signifies "take thou the direction of the right hand." (TA.) — And شَآمَ *He* (a man) *came to* ٱلشَّأْم [i. e. *Syria*]: like يَامَنَ signifying "he came to El-Yemen." (TA. [See also 4.])

4. اشأم *He desired the left:* like as أَيْمَنَ signifies "he desired the right." (TA in art. يمن.) — And *He* (a man, Ṣ) *came to* ٱلشَّأْم [i. e. *Syria*]: (Ṣ, Ḳ, TA: [see also 3:]) or *he went thither:* and أَيْمَنَ signifies "he came to El-Yemen." (TA.) — مَا أَشْأَمَهُ (Ṣ, Ḳ, TA) *How unlucky,* or *inauspicious, is he!* (TA:) the vulgar say, مَا أَيْشَمَهُ. (Ṣ, TA.)

5. تشأم به, (MA, TA,) from ٱلشُّؤْمُ, (TA,) *He found him,* or *it, unlucky,* or *inauspicious:* and *he became unlucky by means of him,* or *it:* (MA:) or تشأم signifies *he had ill luck,* or *evil fortune.* (KL.) See also 6. — And تشأم *He took the direction of his left hand:* (Ḳ, TA:) and in like manner تَيَامَنَ, [whence it seems that تشأم in the sense expl. above may be a mistake for ↓ تشآم,] "he took the direction of his right hand." (TA.) — And *He asserted his relationship to* [*the people of*] ٱلشَّأْم [i. e. *Syria*]: (Ṣ, Ḳ:) a verb similar to تكوّف and تقيّس. (Ṣ.)

6. تَشَاءَمُوا بِهِ, (Ṣ, Mṣb, Ḳ, TA, &c.,) in some of the copies of the Ḳ ↓ تشأموا, (TA,) [and in like manner تشأم به, which is often opposed to تَيَمَّنَ بِهِ, (see an instance in Bḍ xvii. 14,) is used in the Ḳ in art. عطس, and تشأم منه in the TA in the same art. as on the authority of IKh, whence it seems that both these verbs are correct in the sense here following, though the former is probably preferable, and ↓ استشأم به is used in the same manner in "Les Oiseaux et les Fleurs," p 83, as mentioned by Freytag, so that تشأم به and استشأم are the contr. of تيمّن به and استيمن,] *They augured evil from him,* or *it; regarded him,* or *it, as an evil omen;* (Mṣb, KL;*) like تَطَيَّرُوا بِهِ: (Mṣb:) *deemed him,* or *it, unlucky,* or *inauspicious.* (KL.) — تشآءم, thus, with medd, also signifies *He took the direction of* ٱلشَّأْم [i. e. *Syria*]. (TA.) — See also 5.

10: see the next preceding paragraph.

ٱلشَّأْمُ, the name of a certain country [i. e. *Syria*], is masc. and fem.; (Ṣ;) sometimes masc.: (Ḳ:) and may also be pronounced ٱلشَّامُ [as it commonly is in the present day]. (Mṣb.) — [And as this country lies on the north of Arabia, ٱلشَّأْمُ also signifies *The northern region;* opposed to ٱلْيَمَنُ.]

شُؤْمٌ, (Ṣ, Mṣb, Ḳ, &c.,) thus, with ء, but always pronounced شُومٌ, without ء, (TA,) is an inf. n.: (MA, KL: [see 1, first sentence, in two places:]) and signifies [as a simple subst.] *Unluckiness, inauspiciousness, unfortunateness, unprosperousness, evil fortune,* or *ill luck;* contr. of يُمْنٌ; (Ṣ, Ḳ;) [i. e.] i. q. نَحْسٌ: (Ḥar p. 158:) *evil* [*of any kind*]; syn. شَرٌّ: (Mṣb:) [and particularly] *an evil omen:* (PṢ:) and ↓ مَشْأَمَةٌ signifies the same as شُؤْمٌ: (TA:) [or, like مَنْحَسَةٌ, *a cause of unluckiness,* &c.:] مَشَائِمُ is a pl. of شُؤْمٌ, [or of ↓ مَشْأَمَةٌ: if of the former,] irreg., like as its syn. مَنَاحِسُ is [said to be] of نَحْسٌ. (TA in art. نحس.) It is said in a trad., إِنْ كَانَ ٱلشُّؤْمُ فَفِى ثَلَاثٍ ٱلْمَرْأَةِ وَٱلدَّارِ وَٱلْفَرَسِ, meaning *If there be that whereof the consequence is disliked,* or *hated, and feared,* [or *if there be unluckiness,*] *it is in three things, the wife, and the house, and the horse:* i. e., if any of you have a wife whose companionship he dislikes, or a house in which he dislikes dwelling, or a horse that he dislikes taking for the purpose of keeping post on the enemies' frontier, let him separate himself therefrom, by divorcing the wife, and removing from the house, and selling the horse: or, as some say, the شؤم of the wife is her not producing children; and that of the house, its straitness, and the badness of its neighbour; and that of the horse, one's not going to war upon it. (JM.) — See also مَشْؤُومٌ. — Also *Black* camels: and حِضَارٌ signifies "white" camels, (Ḳ, TA,) and is also written and pronounced حَضَارِ: (TA:) neither of these has a sing.: (Ḳ:) both occur in a verse of Aboo-Dhu-eyb: but accord. to one reading thereof it is شِيمٌ; pl. of أَشْيَمُ: so says AA: and IJ says that شُومٌ, [without ء,] being originally شُيْمٌ, of the measure فُعْلٌ, may also be pl. of أَشْيَمُ. (TA.)

شَأْمَةٌ and ↓ مَشْأَمَةٌ The *left,* meaning the *left side* or *direction* or *relative location* or *place;* (Ṣ, Ḳ;) i. q. [يَسْرَةٌ and] مَيْسَرَةٌ; (Ṣ;) *contr. of* يَمْنَةٌ and مَيْمَنَةٌ. (Ḳ.) One says of a man, قَعَدَ شَأْمَةً [*He sat on the left*]. (Ṣ.) And one says, خُذْ بِهِمْ شَأْمَةً i. e. [*Take thou with them*] *the direction of the left hand.* (Ṣ.) And نَظَرْتُ يَمْنَةً وَشَأْمَةً [*I looked in a right direction and in a left direction*]. (TA.) And hence ↓ أَصْحَابُ ٱلْمَشْأَمَةِ, in the Ḳur [lvi. 9 and xc. 19], (TA,) meaning [*The occupants of the left:* or] *those who shall have their records given to them in their left hands:* or *the occupants of the low,* or *ignoble, place,* or *station:* or *the havers of unfortunateness* (ٱلشُّؤْم): and أَصْحَابُ ٱلْمَيْمَنَةِ is expl. as having the contr. senses. (Ksh and Bḍ in lvi. 9.) — Also, the former, *A mole* (خَالٌ) *upon the person:* thus, with ء, as mentioned by IAth: also mentioned without ء in art. شيم. (TA.) — See also شَامَةٌ as meaning "a black she-camel," in art. شيم.

شِئْمَةٌ *Nature; natural, native,* or *innate, disposition, temper,* or other *quality* or *property:* (Ḳ, TA:) mentioned thus, as with ء, by AZ and Lḥ, and said by IJ to be sometimes thus pronounced; but the pronunciation thereof with ء is held by ISd to be extraordinary. (TA.) [See art. شيم.]

شَامِىٌّ, (Ṣ, Mṣb, Ḳ, TA,) without ء, (TA,) and ↓ شَآمٍ, (Ṣ, Mṣb, Ḳ,) of the measure فَعَالٍ, (Ṣ,) an allowable form, without ى, (Mṣb,) like تَهَامٍ and يَمَانٍ, (TA,) and ↓ شَآمِىٌّ, (Sb, Ṣ, Ḳ,) [*Syrian;*] *of,* or *relating to,* ٱلشَّأْم: (Ṣ, Mṣb, Ḳ:) one should not say شَأْمِىٌّ; any instance [of this] occurring by poetic license being accounted for as a case of the use of the name of the country for the rel. n.: (Ṣ:) the fem., applied to a woman, is شَامِيَّةٌ and ↓ شَآمِيَةٌ, the latter without teshdeed: (Ṣ, TA:) the pl. of شَامِىٌّ is شَوَامٌ, like غُرَابٌ [in measure]. (TA.) — [And hence, *Northern.*]

شَآمٍ, and شَآمِيَةٌ the fem. of the former; and شَآمِىٌّ: see the next preceding paragraph.

شَائِمٌ: see مَشْؤُومٌ.

أَشْأَمُ [*More,* and *most, unlucky, inauspicious, unfortunate,* or *unprosperous*]. The Arabs say,

أَشْأَمُ كُلِّ ٱمْرِئٍ بَيْنَ لَحْيَيْهِ, (Meyd, TA,) as some relate it, or, as others relate it, فَكَّيْهِ, which means the same, (Meyd,) [app. meaning accord. to the TA, *The most unlucky thing of every man is between his two jaws,* or *the two lateral portions of his lower jaw;* but it is said that] أَشْأَمُ is here used in the sense of شُؤْمٌ [i. e. *the unluckiness,* &c.]; and in a similar manner [the contr.] أَيْمَنُ is used [in the sense of يُمْنٌ]: so says AHeyth: (Meyd:) the prov. meaning the tongue. (AHeyth, TA.) The fem. is شُؤْمَى. (TA.) — Hence, (TA,) اليَدُ الشُّؤْمَى *The left hand* or *arm*; *contr. of* اليُمْنَى; (Ḳ, TA;) *i. q.* الشِّمَالُ. (TA.) It is said in a trad., respecting camels, لَا يَأْتِى خَيْرُهَا إِلَّا مِنْ جَانِبِهَا الأَشْأَمِ [*Their goodness comes not save from their left side*]: i. e. they are milked and mounted only from the left side. (TA.) — See also مَشْؤُومٌ, in three places. — Zuheyr, in the following saying,

* فَتُنْتَجْ لَكُمْ غِلْمَانَ أَشْأَمَ كُلُّهُمْ *
* كَأَحْمَرِ عَادٍ ثُمَّ تُرْضِعْ فَتَفْطِمِ *

uses it in the sense of the inf. n. شُؤْمٌ; (Ṣ;) meaning غِلْمَانَ شُؤْمٍ: (Ṣ, and EM p. 124:) he says, *And it,* i. e. war, *will bring forth for you boys of ill luck,* or *evil omen; all of them like Aḥmar of 'Ád: then it will suckle* these boys, *and wean* them: by Aḥmar of 'Ád, he means Aḥmar of Thamood, for Aḥmar was the surname of him who hamstrung the she-camel of Ṣáliḥ, and his name was Ḳudár: he says thus for the sake of the measure: or, as some say, Thamood were called 'Ád-el-Ákhireh. (EM.)

مَشْأَمَةٌ: see شُؤْمٌ, in two places: — and see also شَأْمَةٌ, likewise in two places.

مَشْؤُومٌ, (Ṣ, MA, Ḳ, KL,) and مَشُومٌ, (Ṣ, Ḳ,) the latter like مَقُولٌ, (TA,) [a contraction of the former,] *Unlucky,* or *inauspicious,* (Ṣ, MA, Ḳ, KL,) عَلَى قَوْمِهِ [*to his people,* or *party*], (Ṣ, MA, Ḳ,) and عَلَى نَفْسِهِ [*to himself*]: (Ksh and Bḍ in lvi. 9:) [and so ↓ شُؤْمٌ; (as in an ex. in the first sentence of this art.;) this being an epithet as well as a subst., like its syn. نَحْسٌ; syn. with مَشْؤُومٌ, like as نَحْسٌ is syn. with مَنْحُوسٌ; and app., like نَحْسٌ, used alike as sing. and pl., for it seems to be originally an inf. n.:] and so ↓ شَائِمٌ; (Ḳ;) or this signifies *drawing ill luck,* or *evil fortune,* upon his people [and upon himself]: (Ṣ, TA:) and أَشَائِمُ, a pl., likewise signifies *unlucky,* or *inauspicious;* (KL;) *contr. of* أَيَامِنُ; (Ṣ, Ḳ, TA;) these being pls. of ↓ أَشْأَمُ and أَيْمَنُ: (TA:) the pl. of مَشْؤُومٌ is مَشَائِيمُ, (Ṣ, KL, TA,) which is extr., for by rule it should be مَشْؤُومُونَ. (TA.) One says also طَائِرٌ ↓ أَشْأَمُ meaning [*An omen*] *happening,* or *occurring,* (جَارٍ,) *with unluckiness, or inauspiciousness;* [i. e. *an unlucky,* or *inauspicious, omen;*] (Ḳ, TA;) and [in like manner] طَيْرٌ ↓ أَشْأَمُ: and the pl. is أَشَائِمُ [as above]. (TA.)

شأن

1. شَأَنْتُ شَأْنَهُ *i. q.* قَصَدْتُ قَصْدَهُ [meaning *I pursued his* (another's) *way,* or *course, doing as he did*]; (Ṣ, L, Ḳ:* in the Ḳ, شَأَنَ شَأْنَهُ and قَصَدَ قَصْدَهُ;) and in like manner one says, ↓ اشْتَأَنَ شَأْنَهُ. (Ḳ.) — And اشْأَنْ شَأْنَكَ *Do thou what thou dost well.* (Ṣ, L, Ḳ.*) And *Keep thou to thy affair.* (IAạr, L.) — And مَا شَأَنَ شَأْنَهُ *He did not know,* or *had not knowledge of, him,* or *his affair* or *case* or *state:* (Lḥ, IAạr, L, Ḳ:) [from a passage in the L, imperfectly written, it seems, accord. to Lḥ, to be said of one who does what another likes or dislikes, app. without regard to his liking it or disliking it, agreeably with what here follows:] or (Ḳ) this means, (Ṣ, Ḳ,) or means also, (L,) *he did not care for, mind, heed,* or *regard, him.* (Ṣ, L, Ḳ. [In the Ṣ and L, the verb in the sense thus expl. is in the first pers.: and in one place in the L it is expl. by أَرَادَ, which often has this meaning.]) One says also, لَأَشْأَنَنَّ شَأْنَهُمْ, meaning *I will assuredly know,* or *try, prove,* or *test,* (لَأَخْبُرَنَّ,) *their affair* or *case* or *state:* (L:) or this means *I will assuredly corrupt,* or *pervert,* or *mar, their affair* or *case* or *state:* (Ṣ, L, Ḳ:*) and لَأَشْأَنَنَّ خَبْرَهُمْ, (L,) or خَبْرَهُ, (Ḳ,) means *I will assuredly know,* or *try, prove,* or *test,* [*his,* or *their, state,* or] *him,* or *them.* (L, Ḳ. [In the CḲ and in my MS. copy of the Ḳ, لَأُخْبِرَنَّهُمْ, is erroneously put for لَأَخْبُرَنَّهُمْ.]) — شَأَنَ بَعْدَكَ means صَارَ لَهُ شَأْنٌ [i. e., app., *He became a person to whom importance attached* (accord. to the general meaning of لَهُ شَأْنٌ) *after thou knewest,* or *sawest,* or *mettest, him;* بَعْدَكَ being for بَعْدَ عَهْدِكَ بِهِ, agreeably with common usage]. (Ḳ.)

[4. اشْأَنَ شَأْنَهُمْ is mentioned by Golius as meaning "*Corrupit ac pervertit rem eorum,*" as on the authority of the Ṣ, (the right reading in which has been given above,) and on that of the KL, in my copy of which I find nothing of the sort.]

8: see 1, first sentence.

شَأْنٌ *A thing, an affair,* or *a business;* syn. أَمْرٌ; (Ṣ, L, Ḳ;) and خَطْبٌ [in the same sense, or in that next following]: (L, Ḳ:) *a great thing* or *affair:* (Ḥar p. 274:) *state, condition, case, quality,* or *manner of being;* syn. حَالٌ: (Ṣ, L:) [also *property,* or *nature:* and *importance* attaching to a person or thing:] pl. شُؤُونٌ and شِئَانٌ, (L, Ḳ,) the latter mentioned by IJ on the authority of AAF, and شُونٌ occurs in poetry for the former of these, or as another pl. originally شُؤْنٌ, of the measure فُعْلٌ. (L.) It is said in the Ḳur [lv. 29], كُلَّ يَوْمٍ هُوَ فِى شَأْنٍ [*Every day He is* employing Himself *in an affair* of some kind]: expl. as meaning that, of his business (مِنْ شَأْنِهِ [which may also be rendered "of his property"]) it is to render mighty one who is brought low, and to bring low one who is mighty, and to enrich one who is poor, and to impoverish one who is rich; and no affair occupies him so as to divert him from an affair (لَا يَشْغَلُهُ شَأْنٌ عَنْ شَأْنٍ). (L.) [And one says, مَا شَأْنُكَ *What is thy affair?* or *what is thy case?* And شَأْنَكَ, for اشْأَنْ شَأْنَكَ i. e. *Pursue thy way* or *course,* or *thy affair;* or *do what thou dost well;* or *keep to thy affair:* or the like: and to this is often added, وَمَا تُرِيدُ i. e. *and what thou wilt,* or *wishest,* or *desirest.* And مِنْ شَأْنِهِ أَنْ يَفْعَلَ كَذَا *It is of his business,* or *of his property,* or *nature, to do,* or *that he should do, such a thing.* And رَجُلٌ سَهْلُ الشَّأْنِ (a phrase occurring in the Ṣ and Ḳ in art. هش) *A man of easy nature.* And لَهُ شَأْنٌ, sometimes meaning *There is for him,* or *he has, a great thing* or *affair* to perform or transact: but more commonly, *great importance attaches to him,* or *to it:* see 1, last sentence. And a grandee, or a prince, is said to be عَظِيمُ الشَّأْنِ i. e. *Of great importance* or *rank* or *dignity.*] = Also [*A suture of the skull;* i. e.] the *place of junction of the* قَبَائِل [or *principal bones,* namely, the *frontal, occipital,* and *two parietal, bones,*] *of the head:* (Ḳ:) sing. of شُؤُونٌ, (Mgh,) which signifies the *places of junction,* (Aṣ, Ṣ, Mgh, L,) and *of meeting,* (Ṣ, L,) *of the* قَبَائِل (Aṣ, Ṣ, Mgh, L) *of the head;* (Ṣ, L;) *between every two of which* قبائل *is a* شَأْن: (Aṣ, L:) [it is fancifully said that] from them come the tears: (Aṣ, Ṣ, L:) the pl. is also expl. as meaning the سَلَاسِل [i. e. *sutures* as being likened to the سلاسل (or lines) of writing] *that unite the* قبائل: by Lth, as the نَمَائِم [likewise meaning *sutures resembling lines of writing*] *of the skull; between the* قبائل: by AHát, as the شُعَب [meaning *serrated edges*] *that unite the* قبائل *of the head.* (L.) — And The *channel by which the tears flow,* or *run, to the eye:* pl. [of pauc.] أَشْؤُنٌ and [of mult.] شُؤُونٌ: (L, Ḳ:) [perhaps thus called because supposed to come from the sutures of the skull: but they may have been supposed to come thence because tears are called مَآءُ الشُّؤُونِ (as in a verse cited voce وَسَمَ); for this phrase may have been misunderstood as signifying "the water of the sutures of the skull," whereas it seems to be properly rendered "the water of the channels of the tears:"] it is said that the شُؤُون connect the قبائل of the head [expl. above] to the eye: Lth says that they are the *ducts* (عُرُوق) *of the tears from* [*the interior of*] *the head to the eye:* and Th, that they are *certain ducts* (عروق) *above the* قبائل, *which become strong by degrees as the man advances in age:* (L: [but it seems that Th has confounded explanations of شؤون in two different senses:]) accord. to ISk, (Ṣ,) or AA and others, (L,) the شَأْنَانِ are *two ducts* (عِرْقَانِ) *descending from* [*the upper part of*] *the head to the eyebrows and then to the eyes.* (Ṣ, L.) — [The pl. شُؤُون is also expl. as though meaning *Tears* themselves, in a phrase mentioned voce ذَرَّ (q. v.), on the authority of the Ḳ.] — And شُؤُونُ الخَمْرِ means † *The effluvia of wine that creep* (مَا دَبَّ مِنَ الخَمْرِ) *in the veins of the body.* (L.) — شَأْنٌ also signifies *A vein of earth in a mountain,* (L, Ḳ,) i. e. *a cleft therein,* (L,) *in which palm-trees are planted;* (L, Ḳ;) or *in which trees of the kind called* نَبْع *grow;* or *that produces plants,* or *herbage:* (L:) pl. شُؤُونٌ: (L, Ḳ:) which is said by ISd to mean *lines,* or *streaks, in a mountain:* or, as some say, *cracks,* or *clefts:* and to these cracks, or clefts, the poet Ḳeys Ibn-Kuráả likens [imaginary] clefts in the liver, occasioned by love. (L.)

إِنَّهُ لَيَشْأَنُ شَأْنٍ أَنْ نَفْسُدَكَ is a saying mentioned by Lḥ, expl. [only] by the words اى ان نعمل فى فسادك [i. e. أَنْ نَعْمَلَ فِى فَسَادِكَ], app. meaning *Verily he is busying himself in the doing of a thing in order that we may labour in causing thee to be in a bad, or corrupt, state*]. (L.)

شاهبلوط

شَاهْبَلُّوط [a Pers. word, and also used by the Arabs in the present day, applied to The *chestnut*]: also written شَاهْ بَلُّوط. (TA voce بَلُّوطٌ and voce جَمْلٌ.)

شاهين

شَاهِينٌ *A certain well-known bird,* (Ḳ, TA,) *of those that prey;* (Mṣb,* TA;) it is *of the birds called* صُقُور [pl. of صَقْر], as are also the يُؤْيُؤ and the بَاشَق and the بَازِى and the زُرَّق; (AHát in "the Book of Birds," TA in art. بشق;) [said by Golius, on the authority of Dmr, to be the *white falcon;* and to this bird it is perhaps applied by some of the Arabs; but some of them, I believe most of them, and I believe also that they do so most properly, apply this appellation in the present day to the *gerfalcon,* which is not wholly white; and some, to the *falcon gentle:*] the word is [of Pers. origin,] not genuine Arabic; (TA;) it is an arabicized word: the pl. is شَوَاهِين, and sometimes شَيَاهِينُ is used in its stead, formed by substituion [of ى for و] for facilitating the pronunciation. (Mṣb.) — Also † The عَمُود [meaning *beam*] *of the balance.* (Ḳ.) — And *i. q.* صَنْجَة [which signifies *A balance,* and *a steelyard,* and *a weight of a balance*]: so in the Expos. of the "Muwaṭṭa." (MF, TA.)

شأو

1. شَأَوْتُ القَوْمَ, (AZ, Ṣ,) aor. ُ, (JM, PṢ,) or َ, (Ḥam p. 786,) inf. n. شَأْوٌ, (AZ, Ṣ, Ḳ,) *I preceded,* or *outwent, the people,* or *party.* (AZ, Ṣ, Ḳ.*) Accord. to [several of] the copies of the Ḳ, شَأَهُ i. e. like شَاعَهُ in measure, which is incorrect, [in other copies ▼ شَاءَاهُ, agreeably with what is said in the Ṣ,] signifies *He strove,* or *contended, with him to precede him,* or *outgo him:* or *he preceded him,* or *outwent him:* but in the Ṣ it is said, شَاءَاهُ, of the measure فَاعَلَهُ, signifies *he strove,* or *contended, with him to precede him,* or *outgo him:* and شَآهُ like شَاعَهُ, [the former belonging to art. شوأ and] formed by transposition, signifies *he preceded him,* or *outwent him;* and both of these are used by the poet (El-Ḥárith Ibn-Khálid El-Makhzoomee, TA) in his saying,

مَرَّ الحُدُوجُ وَمَا شَأَوْنَكَ نَقْرَةً •
وَلَقَدْ أَرَاكَ تُشَآءُ بِالأَظْعَانِ •

this [passage in the Ṣ], however, is taken from what is said by A'Obeyd, in [his work] "El-Ghareeb el-Muṣannaf," which is as follows: شَآنِى الأَمْرُ, like شَاعَنِى [in measure], and شَأَنِى, like شَعَانِى, mean *the affair,* or *event, grieved me;* and thus in the verse of El-Ḥárith Ibn-Khálid, which he cites; and the same is said in the T on the authority of IAạr, who says that the poet has used two dial. vars.: [accordingly the verse may be rendered, *The camels with their saddles upon them passed along and they grieved thee not at all; but I see thee that thou art grieved by the women borne in the camel-vehicles:*] it is said in the M, شَآنِى الشَّىْءُ means *the thing preceded me,* or *outwent me:* and also *the thing grieved me:* formed by transposition from شَأَنِى, as is proved by its having no inf. n.: IAạr says that they are two dial. vars. because of his not being a grammarian. (TA.) [See also 8.] — And شَأَوْتُ البِئْرَ, (Lḥ, TA,) or شَأَوتُ مِنَ البِئْرِ, (Ṣ,) inf. n. شَأْوٌ, (Ḳ, TA,) *I drew forth the earth from the well:* (Ṣ, Ḳ:*) or *I drew forth a basketful of earth* (شَأْوًا) or *two basketfuls of earth* (شَأْوَيْنِ) *from the well.* (Lḥ, TA.)

3. شَاءَاهُ: see 1. يُشَاوِى occurs in a verse of Milḥah El-Jarmee, meaning يُسَابِقُ, from شَأْوٌ meaning طَلَقٌ: one says شَاءَاهُ, aor. يُشَائِيهِ, meaning سَبَقَهُ: but the verb of the measure regularly formed from الشَّأْوُ is شَاءَى; so that يشاوى is formed by transposition and by the change of the ء into ى. (Ḥam p. 786.)

6. تَشَاءَى مَا بَيْنَهُمَا, (Ṣ, Ḳ, TA, [in the CḲ, erroneously, تَشَاوَى,]) like تَشَاعَى [in measure], (Ṣ,) *The space between them two became far-extending.* (Ṣ, Ḳ.) — And تَشَاءَى القَوْمُ *The people,* or *party, became scattered,* or *dispersed.* (Ṣ, Ḳ.)

8. اِشْتَأَى *He preceded,* or *outwent:* (Ṣ, Ḳ:) so says El-Mufaḍḍal. (Ṣ.) — And *He gave ear, hearkened,* or *listened.* (Ṣ, Ḳ.)

شَأْوٌ The *utmost extent, term, limit, point, reach,* or *goal.* (Ṣ, Mṣb, Ḳ.) — And *A heat,* or *single run to a goal* or *limit:* so in the saying, عَدَا شَأْوًا (Ṣ) or جَرَى شَأْوًا (Mṣb) [*He* (a horse, TA) *ran a heat*]. — And *i. q.* هِمَّةٌ: thus in the saying, إِنَّهُ لَبَعِيدُ الشَّأْوِ † [*Verily he is far-aiming,* or *far-aspiring, in purpose, desire,* or *ambition*]: (Lḥ, TA:) and سَأْوٌ is a dial. var. thereof. (TA.) — Also *A* [*basket such as is termed*] زَبِيل; and so ▼ مِشْآةٌ: (Ḳ:) or ▼ the latter signifies *a* زَبِيل *in which the earth of a well is taken forth;* of the measure of مِشْعَاةٌ; and the pl. is مَشَآءٍ: (Ṣ:) and شَأْوٌ signifies, (Ṣ,) or signifies also, (Ḳ,) the *earth that is taken forth from a well* (Ṣ, Ḳ) *with the like of the* مِشْآة, (as in a copy of the Ṣ,) or *such as fills the* مِشْآة: (so in another copy of the Ṣ [agreeably with what next follows]:) *a* زَبِيل *of the earth of a well.* (Aṣ, T, TA.) — And hence, i. e. as being likened to a زبيل of the earth of a well, † The *dung that the he-ass and the she-ass casts forth:* (Aṣ, T, TA:) or the *dung* of the she-camel; (M, Ḳ;) but the more approved word is [سَأْوٌ,] with س. (M, TA.) — Also The *nose-rein* (زِمَام) *of a she-camel.* (Lth, Ḳ.)

مِشْآةٌ; see the next preceding paragraph, in two places.

مُشْتَأٍ [part. n. of 8, q. v.: — and] *i. q.* مُخْتَلِفٌ [app. as meaning *Disagreeing, differing,* or *discordant*]. (TA.)

شب

1. شَبَّ, aor. ِ, (Ṣ, Mgh, Mṣb, Ḳ,) inf. n. شَبَابٌ (Ṣ, Mgh, Mṣb, Ḳ*) and شَبِيبَةٌ (Ṣ, Mṣb, Ḳ*) and شُبُوبٌ and شَبِيبٌ, (TA,) *He became a youth,* or *young man;* i. e. *he attained to the state termed* شَبَابٌ *meaning as expl. below;* (Ṣ, Mgh, Mṣb, Ḳ;) said of a boy. (Ṣ, Mṣb.) [And in like manner شَبَّتْ is said of a girl, i. e. *She became a young woman.*] — شَبٌّ used as a noun: see below. — [Perhaps as an inf. n. of which the verb is شَبَّ, (as Freytag has assumed,) but more probably of شُبَّ, which will be found mentioned in this paragraph, for I do not find the former verb in the requisite sense,] شَبٌّ signifies Anything's *being,* or *becoming, raised,* or *elevated.* (Ḳ.) — شَبَّ said of a horse, (Ṣ, Mṣb, Ḳ,) aor. ِ, and ُ, (Ṣ, Ḳ,) inf. n. شِبَابٌ and شَبِيبٌ (Ṣ, Mṣb, Ḳ) and شُبُوبٌ, (Ḳ,) *He was brisk, lively,* or *sprightly,* (Ṣ, Mṣb, Ḳ,*) *and raised his fore legs* (Ṣ, Mṣb, Ḳ) *together,* (Ṣ, Mṣb,) *as though in leaping,* (TA,) *and played.* (Ṣ. [See also شَبَّتْ in art. شبو, said of a mare.]) And likewise *He was* or *became, restive,* or *refractory:* one says, بَرِئْتُ إِلَيْكَ مِنْ شِبَابِهِ and شَبِيبِهِ and عِضَاضِهِ and عَضِيضِهِ [*I am irresponsible to thee for his being restive,* or *refractory,* and for *his biting*]. (Ṣ.) — شَبَّتِ النَّارُ, [aor., accord. to rule, ِ,] (Mṣb, Ḳ,) and شُبَّتْ [pass. of the trans. verb شَبَّ, q. v. infrà], inf. n. شُبُوبٌ (which is of the intrans., TA) and شَبٌّ (which is of the trans. verb, TA), *The fire burned, burned up, burned brightly* or *fiercely, blazed,* or *flamed.* (Mṣb, Ḳ. [See also 5.]) [And hence,] شَبَّتِ الحَرْبُ بَيْنَهُمْ ‡ [*War,* or *the war, burned,* or *burned fiercely, between them*]. (A, TA.) — شُبَّ *It was raised,* or *elevated.* (O, TA.) — شَبَّ النَّارَ, aor. ُ, (Ṣ, O, Mṣb,) inf. n. شَبٌّ (Ṣ, O, Ḳ) and شُبُوبٌ, (Ṣ, Ḳ,) or the latter is the inf. n. of the intrans. verb mentioned above, (TA,) *He kindled the fire;* or *made it to burn, burn up, burn brightly* or *fiercely, blaze,* or *flame;* (Ṣ, O, Mṣb, Ḳ;*) as also ▼ شَبَّبَهَا, inf. n. تَشْبِيبٌ; (L;) and ▼ اِشْتَبَّهَا: (A and TA in art. حش:) and so شَبَاهَا. (TA in art. شبو.) And in like manner, شَبَّ الحَرْبَ ‡ *He kindled war,* or *the war;* or *made it to burn,* or *burn fiercely.* (Ṣ.) — [Hence,] شَبَّ, aor. ُ, said of the blackness of a garment, (Sh, A, TA,) ‡ *It heightened and increased,* (A,) or *made to appear bright and beautiful, and* [*as it were*] *burning,* or *glowing,* (Sh, TA,) the whiteness of the wearer. (Sh, A, TA.) And شَبَّ لَوْنَهَا (aor. as above, Ṣ) † *It*

(a woman's hair) *showed*, [or *set off*,] *and rendered beautiful, her colour*, or *complexion*: (Ṣ:) *it* (a woman's head-covering, and her hair,) *increased, and showed*, [or *heightened, and set off*,] *her beauty*: (Ḳ:) *it* (a woman's black head-covering) *increased her fairness, and rendered her beautiful.* (TA.) And يَشُبُّ الوَجْهَ, said of patience, † *It gives beauty and colour to the countenance.* (TA, from a trad.) —— See also 4, in two places.

2. شَبَّبَ النَّارَ, inf. n. تَشْبِيبٌ: see the preceding paragraph. —— Hence, تَشْبِيبُ الشِّعْرِ ‡ *The making the commencement of poetry elegant*, or *ornate, by the mention of women*: (L, TA:) or the primary meaning of التَّشْبِيبُ is *the mention of the days of youth and of play* or *sport, and amatory language*; and *it is in the commencing of odes*; and *the commencement thereof* is so called, absolutely, though there be not in it any mention of youth: (TA:) it means النَّسِيبُ, (Ṣ, O,) or النَّسِيبُ بِالنِّسَآءِ, (Ḳ, TA, [in the CḲ, erroneously, التَّشَبُّبُ بالنساء,]) i. e. بِذِكْرِهِنَّ: (TA:) one says, يُشَبِّبُ بِفُلَانَةَ, (Ṣ, O,) and ▼ يتشبّب بها [if this be not a mistranscription for يُشَبِّبُ], (TA,) meaning يَنْسُبُ بِهَا: (Ṣ, O, TA:) [see this fully expl. in art. نسب: i. e.] شَبَّبَ بِفُلَانَةَ, inf. n. تَشْبِيبٌ, means, ‡ *He spoke of such a female in amatory language* [*in the commencement of his ode*], (Mṣb, TA,) *and alluded to the love of her*: (Mṣb:) and شَبَّبَ قَصِيدَتَهُ † *He embellished* [*the commencement of*] *his ode by the mention of women*: (Mgh, Mṣb:) and شَبَّبَ قَصِيدَتَهُ بِفُلَانَةَ ‡ [*He embellished the commencement of his ode by mentioning, in amatory language, such a female*]: (A, TA:) and ▼ شَبَابٌ is used in the sense of تَشْبِيبٌ; thus a قَصِيدَةٌ is said to be حَسَنَةُ الشَّبَابِ ‡ [*Beautiful in the mention of women* &c.]; and Jereer is said to have been أَرَقُّ النَّاسِ شَبَابًا ‡ [*The most elegant of men in the mention of women* &c.]. (A, TA.) —— Hence, i. e. from تَشْبِيبُ القَصِيدَةِ, may be derived التَّشْبِيبُ as a conventional term in the science of the division of inheritances; meaning † *The mention of daughters according to the different degrees* [*of descent*]: (Mgh:) it is as when one says, "he died, and left three daughters of a son, subordinate one to another, and three daughters of a son's son, in like manner, and three daughters of a son's son's son, in like manner, and the sons died and the daughters remained." (O.) —— تَشْبِيبُ الكُتُبِ signifies † *The commencing of books*, or *writings*: and hence شَبَّبَ بِمُجَاوَبَتِهِ, occurring in a trad., meaning † *He commenced answering him*: not from the تَشْبِيب of women in poetry. (TA.)

4. أَشَبَّهُ ٱللّٰهُ *God made him*, or *may God make him, to become a youth*, or *young man*; i. e., *to attain to the state termed* شَبَابٌ *meaning as expl. below*: and أَشَبَّ ٱللّٰهُ قَرْنَهُ means the same: (Ṣ, A, TA:) the latter [lit. means *God made*, or *may God make, his equal in age to become a youth*, &c., (see Ḥar p. 572,) and therefore] is tropical. (A, TA.) —— أَشْبَبْتُ الفَرَسَ *I excited the horse to be brisk, lively*, or *sprightly, and to raise his fore legs together, as though in leaping, and to play.* (Ṣ,* Ḳ,* TA.) —— أَشَبَّ النَّارَ: see 1. —— أُشِبَّ لِىَ الرَّجُلُ, inf. n. إِشْبَابٌ; as also ▼ شُبَّ; ‡ *The man appeared before my upraised eyes when not hoped for.* (AZ, TA.) —— And أُشِبَّ لِى كَذَا, and ▼ شُبَّ, ‡ *Such a thing was prepared*, or *appointed*, or *ordained, for me.* (Ṣ, Ḳ,* TA.) ═ أَشَبَّ ‡ *He became one whose child, or children, had attained to the state of* شَبَاب [i. e. *youth*, or *young manhood*, &c.]: (Ḳ:) [or] أَشَبَّ الرَّجُلُ بَنِينَ ‡ *the man became one whose children had attained to that state*: (Ṣ, TA:) and in like manner, أَشَبَّتْ أَوْلَادًا is said of a woman. (TA.) —— And أَشَبَّ said of [the species of bovine antelope called] the wild bull, (Ṣ, Ḳ,) *He became such as is termed* شَبَبٌ [q. v.], i. e., (Ṣ,) *he became advanced in age*, or *full-grown*; (مُسِنّ, Ṣ, Ḳ;) *one whose state termed* إِسْنَان [q. v.] *had ended.* (Ṣ.)

5. [تَشَبَّبَتِ النَّارُ *The fire became kindled*; or *made to burn, burn up, burn brightly* or *fiercely, blaze*, or *flame*: see also 1.] One says on the occasion of kindling fire,

تَشَبَّبِى تَشَبُّبَ النَّمِيمَهْ •
جَآءَتْ بِهَا تَمْرٌ إِلَى تَمِيمَهْ •

[*Be thou kindled like the state of kindling of the calumny that Temr brought to Temeemeh*: but to what this alludes I know not]: it is like the saying, أَوْقَدَ بِالنَّمِيمَةِ نَارًا [*He kindled a fire with calumny*]. (A, TA.) —— See also 2.

10. It is said in a trad., يَجُوزُ شَهَادَةُ الصِّبْيَانِ عَلَى الكِبَارِ يُسْتَشَبُّونَ [*The boys' giving testimony against those that are full grown is allowable, when they* (the former) *are deemed to have attained to the state of youths*, or *young men*]: it is as though it were said that if they take upon themselves the bearing witness in boyhood, and give their testimony when full grown, it is allowable: (TA:) or يُسْتَشَبُّونَ means *they shall be sought youths, such as have attained to puberty*, or *maturity*, in the case of giving testimony: or *they shall be waited for*, in the case of giving testimony, *until the period of becoming youths*, or *young men.* (Mgh.) —— And it is said in another trad., اِسْتَشِبُّوا عَلَى أَسْوُقِكُمْ فِى البَوْلِ, i. e. *Sit upon your shanks as one does when preparing to rise, not stooping with the whole body near to the ground*; [*having your feet only upon the ground; in the voiding of urine*:] from شَبَّ الفَرَسُ meaning "the horse raised his fore-legs together from the ground." (TA.)

R. Q. 1. شَبْشَبَ *He completed* [a thing]; (AA, O, Ḳ;) said of a man. (AA, TA.)

شَبٌّ, and its fem. شَبَّةٌ: see شَابٌّ. ═ Also *The stones of* زَاج [or *vitriol*]: (Ḳ:) or the *stones from which* زاج *and the like thereof are obtained; the best whereof is that which is brought from El-Yemen, which is white* شَبّ, *and is very glistening*: (TA:) [but شَبٌّ يَمَانِىٌّ, as also شَبٌّ alone, is a name now commonly given to *alum*:] or it is *a certain thing resembling* زاج: (Ṣ, Mṣb:) or *a species thereof*: accord. to El-Fárábee, the *stones from which come* زاج *and the like*: Az says, it is *one of the minerals produced by God in the earth, with which one tans, and resembling* زاج, and the name [correctly] heard is thus, with ب, but is by some mistranscribed with the three-dotted ث, [i. e. شَثّ,] which is a kind of tree of bitter taste, and I know not whether one tans with it or not: accord. to Mṭr, in the saying that one tans with شبّ, this word is a mistranscription; for شبّ is a dye, and one does not tan with a dye; it is mistranscribed for شَثّ, which is a kind of tree like the dwarf apple-tree, whereof the leaves are like those of the عَلَاف [q. v.], and with them one tans: El-Fárábee also says, in the section of ث, that the شَثّ is a species of mountain-tree, with which one tans: from all which it appears that one tans with both of them; for an affirmation is to be preferred to a negation: (Mṣb:) and it is *a well-known medicine*; (Ḳ, TA;) as some say: so accord. to the correct copies of the Ḳ, in some of which, دَآءٌ is put for دَوَآءٌ. (TA.)

شُبَّ and دُبَّ, though originally verbs, are used as nouns, by the introduction of مِنْ before them: one says, أَعْيَيْتَنِى مِنْ شُبَّ إِلَى دُبَّ and مِنْ شُبٍّ إِلَى دُبٍّ [expl. in art. دب]: (Ṣ:) and in like manner they are used in another saying expl. in art. دب [q. v.]: (Ṣ in that art.:) or, without tenween, they may be regarded as verbs used in the way of حِكَايَة [or imitation]. (MF.)

شَبَّةٌ The *burning, burning up, burning brightly* or *fiercely, blazing*, or *flaming*, of fire. (TA.)

شَبَبٌ and ▼ شَبُوبٌ, applied to a [bovine antelope of the species called the] wild bull, (Aṣ, Ṣ, Ḳ,) and to a sheep or goat, (Ḳ,) and ▼ مُشِبٌّ, applied to the former, and ▼ مِشَبٌّ, (Aṣ, Ṣ, Ḳ,) sometimes, applied to the former, (Aṣ, Ṣ,) or to both, (Ḳ,) *Advanced in age*, or *full-grown*, (مُسِنٌّ, Ṣ, Ḳ,) *whose state termed* إِسْنَان [q. v.] *has ended*; (Aṣ, Ṣ;) and ▼ مُشِبَّةٌ is in like manner applied to a she-camel as meaning مُسِنَّةٌ: (TA:) or ▼ شَبُوبٌ, (AA, Ḳ,) applied to both, (Ḳ,) as also ▼ مُشِبٌّ, (TA,) or to a bull, (AA,) is syn. with ▼ شَابٌّ [meaning *youthful*, or *in the prime of life*]: (AA, Ḳ, TA:) and accord. to AO, شَبَبٌ, applied to a bull, means *that has attained to the end of* شَبَاب [i. e. *youthfulness*, or *the prime of life*]: (Ṣ, TA:) or, as some say, *that has attained to the end of his full growth and strength*; as also ▼ شَبُوبٌ, which is likewise applied to the female; or, accord. to AḤát and ISh, when he is a year old, and weaned, he is called دَبَبٌ; and then, شَبَبٌ [meaning *more than a year old*]; and the female, شَبَبَةٌ. (TA.)

شَبَابٌ and ▼ شَبِيبَةٌ [both mentioned above as inf. ns.] (Ṣ, Mṣb, Ḳ) [and ▼ شَبَابِيَّةٌ which is a simple subst.] *Youth, youthfulness*, the *prime of man-*

hood, or *young manhood*; syn. فَتَآءٌ; (Ḳ;) or حَدَاثَةٌ; *contr. of* شَيْبٌ: (Ṣ:) or *the state from puberty to the completion of thirty years*; or *from sixteen years to thirty-two*; after which a man is called كَهْلٌ; (TA;) the *age before* الكُهُولَة: (Mṣb:) or the *state between thirty and forty*: (Mgh:) or, accord. to Moḥammad Ibn-Ḥabeeb, the *state from the seventeenth year to the completion of fifty-one years* is termed ▼ شَبَابِيَّةٌ; the period before, from birth, being termed غُلُومِيَّةٌ; and in the period after, a man being called شَيْخٌ, until he dies. (TA.) One says, سَقَى ٱللّٰهُ عَصْرَ ▼ الشَّبِيبَةِ [*May God freshen as with rain the times*, or *mornings*, or *afternoons*, *of youth*, &c.], and عُصُورَ الشَّبَائِبِ [*the times*, &c., *of the states of youth*, &c.]. (A, TA.) — [شَبَابٌ often signifies † The *sap*, or *vigour*, *of youth* or *young manhood*.] One says, ٱسْتَحَارَ شَبَابُهَا, as in a verse of Aboo-Dhu-eyb, † *The sap* [or *vigour*] *of youth* (مَآءُ الشَّبَابِ) *flowed in her*. (IB, TA in art. حير.) And ٱمْتَلَأَ شَبَابًا † [*He became full of the sap*, or *vigour*, *of youth* or *young manhood*]. (The lexicons, &c., passim.) [But] مَآءُ الشَّبَابِ signifies [also] ‡ *The freshness*, or *brightness*, *and beauty*, *of youth*. (Ḥar p. 340.) [And ▼ شَبِيبَةٌ app. signifies also † *Youthful folly*, or *the like*; (see an ex. voce غَمْرَةٌ;) and so, probably, does شَبَابٌ.] — [Hence,] شَبَابٌ also signifies † The *first*, or *beginning*, or the *new*, or *recent*, *state*, of a thing; (Ḳ, TA;) and so ▼ شَبِيبَةٌ. (TA.) One says, قَدِمَ فِى شَبَابِ الشَّهْرِ (A, TA) ‡ *He came*, or *arrived*, *in the beginning of the month*. (TA.) And لَقِيتُهُ فِى شَبَابِ النَّهَارِ (A, TA) ‡ *I met him in the beginning of the day*: (TA:) and جِئْتُكَ فِى شَبَابِ النَّهَارِ and بِشَبَابِ النَّهَارِ † *I came to thee in the beginning of the day*: (Lḥ, TA:) or شَبَابُ النَّهَارِ means *the period when the sun has risen high*, *when one fifth of the day has passed*. (A in art. وراد.) And one says also ▼ فَعَلَ ذٰلِكَ فِى شَبِيبَتِهِ *He did that at the commencement thereof*. (TA.) — See also شَابٌّ — And see 2.

شِبَابٌ an inf. n. of شَبَّ said of a horse. (Ṣ, Mṣb, Ḳ.) — See also the next paragraph, in two places.

شَبُوبٌ: see شَبَبٌ, in three places. — Also A horse *whose hind feet pass beyond his fore feet*; (Ḳ;) which is a fault: accord. to Th, such is termed ▼ شَبِيبٌ: IM says that the correct word is شَئِيتٌ: [but] see this in its proper place. (TA.) — Also *A thing with which a fire is kindled*, or *made to burn*, *burn up*, *burn brightly* or *fiercely*, *blaze*, or *flame*; (Ṣ, Ḳ;) and so ▼ شِبَابٌ. (Ḳ.) — And [hence, as also ▼ شِبَابٌ,] ‡ *A thing that serves* [*as a foil*] *for beautifying*, or *setting off*, (Ḳ,) [or *making to appear bright and beautiful*,] or *for increasing*, or *enhancing*, and *strengthening*, [or *heightening*, *in beauty*,] (Ṣ, TA,) to another thing. (Ṣ, Ḳ, TA.) So in the saying, هٰذَا شَبُوبٌ لِهٰذَا ‡ *This is a thing that serves for increasing*, or *enhancing*, [or *heightening*, *in beauty*,] *to such a thing*. (Ṣ, TA.) One says of a woman's head-covering, هُوَ شَبُوبٌ لِوَجْهِهَا ‡ [*It is a thing that serves for giving an appearance of additional brightness and beauty to her face*]. (A.)

شَبِيبٌ: see the next preceding paragraph.

شَبِيبَةٌ: see شَبَابٌ, in five places.

عَسَلٌ شَبَابِىٌّ *Honey of Shebábeh* (شَبَابَة); (A, TA;) or, *of Benoo-Shebábeh*, (Mgh,) a people of Eṭ-Ṭáïf, (A, Mgh, TA,) of [the tribe of] Khath'am, who possessed bees, and hence it was thus called. (Mgh.)

شَبَابِيَّةٌ: see شَبَابٌ, in two places.

شَبَّذَا زَيْدٌ *i. q.* حَبَّذَا [q. v. in art. حب]. (Th, TA.)

شَابٌّ part. n. of شَبَّ said of a boy; (Mṣb;) [*Youthful*, or *in the prime of manhood*; *a youth*, or *a young man*;] *in the state from puberty to the completion of thirty years*; or *from sixteen years to thirty-two*; after which a man is called كَهْلٌ; (TA;) *in the age before* الكُهُولَة: (Mṣb:) or *in the state between thirty and forty*: (Mgh:) [or *in the state from the seventeenth year to the completion of fifty-one years*: (see شَبَابٌ:)] and IAạr mentions ▼ شَبٌّ as an epithet applied to a man [in the same sense as شَابٌّ]: (TA:) a female is termed شَابَّةٌ (Ṣ, Mṣb, Ḳ) and ▼ شَبَّةٌ; both signifying the same: (Ṣ, Ḳ:) the pl. of شَابٌّ is شُبَّانٌ (Ṣ, A, Mgh, Mṣb, Ḳ) and شَبَبَةٌ (Ṣ, A, Ḳ) and ▼ شَبَابٌ, (Ṣ, A,* Ḳ,) or the last is an inf. n. used as an epithet applied to a pl. number, (Mgh, and Ḥam p. 50,) or it is a quasi-pl. n.: (TA:) females, (Mṣb,) or women, (Ḳ,) are termed شَوَابُّ (Mṣb, Ḳ) and شَبَائِبُ, (Ḳ,) the latter said by AZ to be allowable in the sense of the former, (TA,) which is pl. of شَابَّةٌ, (Mṣb,) شَبَائِبُ, accord. to Az, being pl. (not of شَابَّةٌ but) of شَبَّةٌ, like as ضَرَائِرُ is of ضَرَّةٌ: (TA:) the dim. of شَابَّةٌ is ▼ شُوَيْبَّةٌ, and some of the Arabs say ▼ شُوَابَّةٌ, changing the ى into ا before a double letter [as in دُوَابَّةٌ for دُوَيْبَّةٌ]. (ISd, L in art. هد.) One says, مَرَرْتُ بِرِجَالٍ شَبَبَةٍ meaning شُبَّانٍ [i. e. *I passed by men that were youths*, or *persons in the prime of manhood*]. (Ṣ.) — See also شَبَبٌ.

شُوَابَّةٌ: } شُوَيْبَّةٌ: } dims. of شَابَّةٌ fem. of شَابٌّ, q. v.

شَوْشَبٌ The *scorpion*. (IAạr, Ḳ.) — And The *louse*; syn. قَمْلٌ: (Ḳ in this art.:) or the *ant*; syn. نَمْلٌ: (Ḳ in art. ششب:) fem. [or perhaps n. un.] with ة. (TA.)

مِشَبٌّ, and its fem., with ة: see شَبَبٌ, in three places. — Also the former, *A lion*: (Ḳ:) or *a full-grown lion*: syn. أَسَدٌ كَبِيرٌ. (TA.)

مُشِبٌّ: see شَبَبٌ.

مُشَبَّبُ الأَظَافِرِ [or rather الأَظَافِيرِ, pl. of the pl. أَظْفَارٌ or of أُظْفُورٌ,] ‡ *Having sharp-pointed nails* or *talons* or *claws*; as though they flamed, by reason of their sharpness. (A, TA.)

مَشْبُوبٌ [pass. part. n. of 1]. You say نَارٌ مَشْبُوبَةٌ *A fire kindled*, or *made to burn*, *burn up*, *burn brightly* or *fiercely*, *blaze*, or *flame*: شَابَّةٌ in this sense is not allowable. (Ḳ.) — [Hence,] applied to a man, (A, TA,) ‡ *Comely*, (Ṣ, TA,) *of goodly countenance*; (A, TA;) as though lighted up: *bright*, or *fair*, *in complexion*, *and of goodly countenance*; as though his countenance were lighted up with fire: pl. مَشَابِيبُ. (TA.) And ‡ A man *of acute mind*. (TA.) And طَلَعَتِ المَشْبُوبَتَانِ الزُّهَرَتَانِ [or الزُّهَرَاوَانِ?] ‡ *Venus and Jupiter*, so called on account of their beauty and splendour, *rose*. (A, TA.)

شبت

شِبِتٌّ [*Anethum graveolens*, or *dill*, *of the common garden-species*;] *a certain herb*, or *leguminous plant*, *well known*: (Ḳ:) it is said that سِبِتٌّ is an arabicized word from شِبِتٌّ; but it has been stated before [in art. سبت, q. v.,] that both these are arabicized words from شِوِدْ [or شُود]; and that سبط [i.e. سِبِطٌّ] is a dial. var. (TA.) [See also شِبِثٌّ.]

شبث

1: see the next paragraph, in two places.

5. تَشَبَّثَ بِهِ *He*, or *it*, *clung*, *caught*, *clave*, or *adhered*, *to it*, (Ṣ, A, L, Mṣb, Ḳ,* TA,) namely, a thing; (Ṣ, L, TA;) as also ▼ شَبِثَ بِهِ, aor. ـَ, inf. n. شَبَثٌ: (L, TA:) or, accord. to Esh-Shiháb, in the Expos. of the Shifà, to a thing in which was weakness: or, accord. to the 'Ináyeh, *he*, or *it*, *clung*, &c., *to it with weakness*; and therefore ▼ مُتَشَبِّثٌ is used as an epithet applied to a spider; and تَمَسَّكَ signifies a stronger action; and تَشَبَّثَ بِهِ is also expl. as meaning *he*, or *it*, *took fast*, or *firm*, *hold upon it*: (L, TA:) and *he stuck*, or *fixed*, or *struck*, *the claw*, or *talons*, or *nails*, *into it*: (MA, PṢ:) and ▼ شَبِثَ الشَّىْءَ *he laid hold upon the thing*, *and took it*: IAạr was asked respecting some verses, and he said, مَا أَدْرِى مِنْ أَيْنَ شَبِثْتُهَا *I know not whence I laid hold upon them* [*and took them*]. (L, TA.)

Q. Q. 1, accord. to the Ṣ and L, شَنْبَثَ: see art. شنبث.

شَبَثٌ The *spider*: (Ḳ:) or *a large spider*, *with many legs*. (TA.) — Also (Ḳ) *A certain small creeping thing*, (Ṣ, A, Mṣb, Ḳ,) *having many legs*, (Ṣ, A, Ḳ,) *of the* أَحْنَاش [or *creeping things* &c.] *of the earth*: (Ṣ, Mṣb:) it should not be called شِبِثٌ: (Ṣ:) or *a certain small creeping thing*, *having six long legs*, *yellow in the back*, *and in the outer sides of the legs*, *black in the head*, *and blue in the eye*: or *a certain small creeping thing*, *having many legs*, *large in the head*, *of the* احناش *of the earth*: or *a certain small creeping thing*, *wide in the mouth*, *high in the hinder part*, *that perforates the ground*, *is found where there is moisture*, *and eats scorpions*; and it is *what is called* شَحْمَةُ الأَرْضِ: (TA:) pl. شِبْثَانٌ. (Ṣ, A, Mṣb, Ḳ.) The [marks termed] أُثْر of the blade of a sword are likened by a poet, (Ṣ, TA,) namely, Sá'ideh Ibn-Ju-eiyeh, (TA,) to the tracks of شِبْثَان. (Ṣ, TA.)

رَجُلٌ شَبِثٌ *A man whose nature it is to cling, catch, cleave, or adhere, to a thing.* (Ṣ, Ḳ.) And ضِرْسٌ ضَبِثٌ شَبِثٌ [*A tooth, or molar tooth,*] *that catches, or fastens, to a thing.* (TA.)

شُبَثَةٌ, (Ḳ,) or شُبَثَةٌ ضُبَثَةٌ, (TA,) A man (TA) *who cleaves to his* قِرْن [i. e. *opponent*, or *adversary*], *not quitting him.* (Ḳ, TA.)

شِبِتٌّ [erroneously written in some copies of the Ḳ شِبِثٌّ, and in the L شِبِثٌ,] *A certain well-known plant;* (AḤn, L, Mṣb;) *a certain herb*, or *leguminous plant;* (Ḳ;) [*i. q.* شِبِتٌّ and سِبِتٌّ, q. v.; i. e. *anethum graveolens*, or *dill, of the common garden-species:*] Ṣgh says that شبث is a foreign word of which سِبِتٌّ is an arabicized form; and it is made of the measure فِعِلّ because this measure has many examples; whereas the measure فِعِل, of which إِبِل is an instance, is extraordinary. (Mṣb.)

شَبَاثٌ: see what next follows.

شُبُوثٌ and ▼ شَبَاثٌ [so in the CḲ and in my MS. copy of the Ḳ, but the latter is strangely said in the TA to be with kesr,] sings. of شَبَابِيثُ, which signifies The *flesh-hooks* (كَلَالِيب) of the fire. (Ḳ.)

الشَّنَبِثُ: } see art. شنبث.
الشَّنَابِثُ: }

مُتَشَبِّثٌ an epithet applied to a spider: see 5.

شبح

1. شَبُحَ, (Ṣ, Ḳ,) inf. n. شَبَاحَةٌ, (TḲ,) said of a man, (Ṣ,) *He was*, or *became, broad in the fore arms:* (Ṣ, Ḳ, TA:) or *long therein.* (TA.) — شَبَحَهُ, (A, O, Mgh, L, Mṣb, Ḳ,) aor. ـَ, (Ḳ,) inf. n. شَبْحٌ, (TḲ,) *He extended, stretched,* or *stretched out, it,* or *him;* (A, O, Mgh, L, Mṣb, Ḳ;) namely, a thing; (IF, L, Mṣb;) a hide, or skin, (A, L, Ḳ,) or some other thing, (L,) *between pegs,* or *stakes;* (Ḳ;) and a man, (Mgh, L, Mṣb,) *between two things, to be flogged,* (L,) [i. e.,] *between two stakes inserted and fixed in the ground,* (Mgh, Mṣb,) which are called عُقَابَانِ, (Mgh,) *when he was beaten,* or *crucified,* (Mgh, Mṣb,) or *like him who is crucified;* and ▼ شبّحهُ is used, accord. to some, in the same manner. (L.) And شَبَحَ يَدَيْهِ *He extended,* or *stretched forth, his arms,* or *hands:* (L:) or شَبَحَ [alone] *he extended his arm,* or *hand, to offer a prayer,* or *supplication;* (Ḳ;) or *he extended and raised his arms,* or *hands, in his prayer,* or *supplication.* (A.) And الحِرْبَآءُ يَشْبَحُ عَلَى العُودِ ‡ *The chameleon extends* (Ṣ, A, O) *itself* (Ṣ, O) or *its fore legs* (A) *upon the branch.* (Ṣ, A, O.) — Also, inf. n. as above, *He cut, hewed,* or *pared, it,* namely, a stick, or piece of wood, *so as to make it wide.* (O, L. [See also 2.]) — And *He clave it,* or *split it,* (Ḳ,* TA,) namely, another's head, or anything whatever. (TA.) — شَبَحَ لَنَا *He* (a man, Ḳ) *stood erect* [as though drawing himself up] *to us.* (O, Ḳ.) — And شَبَحَ لَكَ *It* (a thing) *appeared,* or *became apparent, to thee.* (L.) — شَبِحَ بِأَمْرٍ *He was,* or *became, attached,* or *addicted, to an affair;* or *fond of it.* (O.)

2. شبّحهُ: see 1. — Also, (Ḳ,) inf. n. تَشْبِيحٌ, (Ṣ,) *He made it* (a thing) *wide.* (Ṣ, Ḳ.) — And تَشْبِيحٌ signifies also The act of *paring,* or *peeling,* or *the like.* (O. [See also 1.]) — And The act of *pulling,* or *plucking, out,* or *up.* (O.) — And شبّح, (O, Ḳ,) inf. n. as above, (Ḳ,) *He* (a man, TA) *became aged, and saw a* [*thing such as is termed*] شَبَح *appearing as though it were two.* (O, Ḳ.)

شَبْحٌ: see شَبَحٌ, in two places: — and see also مَشْبُوحٌ.

شَبَحٌ (Ṣ, A, O, Mṣb, Ḳ) and ▼ شَبْحٌ (Ṣ, O, Ḳ) *i. q.* شَخْصٌ [i. e. The *body,* or *bodily* or *corporeal form* or *figure* or *substance, of a man* or *some other thing* or *object, which one sees from a distance*]: (Ṣ, A, O, Mṣb, Ḳ:) *a man,* or *some other creature, of which the* شَخْص [or *body,* &c.,] *appears to one:* (L:) and *a thing that is perceived by sense* (A, O, L) and *by sight:* (O, L:) pl. أَشْبَاحٌ, (A, O, Mṣb, Ḳ,) which is of the former, (A, Mṣb,) and [of the latter] شُبُوحٌ. (Ḳ.) One says, لَاحَ لِى شَبَحٌ, meaning شَخْصٌ [i. e. *A body,* or *bodily form, appeared, loomed,* or *gleamed, to me*]. (A.) And هُمْ أَشْبَاحٌ بِلَا أَرْوَاحٍ [*They are bodies without souls*]. (A.) And أَدَقُّ مِنْ شَبَحِ بَاطِلٍ, (A, O,) and مِنْ خَيْطِ بَاطِلٍ, a prov., (O,) meaning [*More minute,* or *inconsiderable, than*] *the atoms that are seen in the rays of the sun entering from a mural aperture in a chamber:* (A,* O:) or, as some say, *than the thread that comes forth from the mouth of the spider;* [meaning *gossamer;*] *called by the children* مُخَاط الشَّيْطَان. (O.) And الأَسْمَآءُ ضَرْبَانِ أَسْمَآءُ أَشْبَاحٍ وَأَسْمَآءُ أَعْمَالٍ, meaning [*Nouns are of two sorts,*] *the names of things perceived by sense, and the names* [*of actions,* or rather *of accidents* or *attributes,* i. e.] *of other things;* like as they say أَسْمَآءُ المَعَانِى and أَسْمَآءُ الأَعْيَانِ. (A.) And هَلَكَ أَشْبَاحُ مَالِهِ *The known ones of his camels, and sheep* or *goats, and other cattle, perished.* (O, Ḳ.*) — شَبَحٌ also signifies *A door* or *gate, of high structure;* (O, Ḳ;) and so ▼ شَبْحٌ: (Ḳ:) [but the latter may have originated from a mistranscription; for Ṣgh says,] and so شَبَحٌ. (O.) — See also شَبَحَةٌ.

شَبَحَةٌ *A rafter,* or *timber,* (عُود,) *of the ceiling,* or *roof, of a house:* so in a trad. where it is said, فَنَزَعَ سَقْفَ بَيْتِى شَبَحَةً شَبَحَةً [*And he pulled off the roof of my house, rafter by rafter,* or *timber by timber*]. (JM,* TA.)

شَبَحَةٌ of horses: what is thus called is well known [as being *A rope which is extended from a horse's fore leg to his hind leg:* so in the present day]. (TA.)

شَبَحَةٌ a word occurring in the Ḳ and TA voce مُشْط and in the TA voce مِحْوَر &c. [app. as meaning *A broad piece of wood*]. — الشَّبَحَتَانِ signifies *The two pieces of wood of the* مِنْقَلَة, (O, Ḳ,) *which is the thing upon which bricks are carried from place to place:* the pl. is الشَّبَحَاتُ and [the coll. gen. n., of which شَبَحَة is the n. un., is] ▼ الشَّبَحُ. (O.)

شَبْحَان [whether with or without tenween is not apparent, as the fem. is not mentioned,] *Tall;* (AA, Ṣ, O, Ḳ;) an epithet applied to a man. (TA.)

شَبِيحَةٌ sing. of شَبَائِحُ, (O,) which signifies *Pieces of wood,* (O, Ḳ,) *broad,* (O,) *placed transversely,* (O, Ḳ,) *contrariwise,* or *on contrary sides,* (O,) *in the* [*camel's saddle called*] قَتَب (O, Ḳ) *that is of wood:* so expl. by Shujáa. (O.)

مُشَبَّحٌ, applied to a [garment of the kind called] كِسَآء, *Strong,* or *stout:* (O, Ḳ:*) or, as some say, *wide.* (O.) — And [applied to a stick, or piece of wood,] *Pared,* (Ḳ, TA,) and *cut,* or *hewed* [app. *so as to be made wide:* see 1]. (TA.) — And *A species of fish..* (TA.)

مَشْبُوحٌ *Wide between the shoulders.* (L.) — مَشْبُوحُ الذِّرَاعَيْنِ and شَبْحُ ▼ الذِّرَاعَيْنِ *A man broad in the fore arms:* (Ṣ, Ḳ:) or *long therein:* but AAF and Ibn-El-Jowzee prefer the former explanation. (TA.) — مَشْبُوحٌ بِأَمْرٍ *Attached,* or *addicted, to an affair;* or *fond of it.* (O.)

شبر

1. شَبَرَ, aor. ـُ (Ṣ, A, Mṣb) and ـِ, (Ṣ,) inf. n. شَبْرٌ; (IAạr, Ṣ, Mṣb, Ḳ;) and ▼ شبّر, inf. n. تَشْبِيرٌ; (IAạr, Ḳ;) *He measured by the* شِبْر [or *span*] (IAạr, Ṣ, A, Mṣb, Ḳ) a garment, or piece of cloth, (Ṣ, Ḳ,) or a thing: (A, Mṣb:) from الشِّبْرُ; like as one says بَاعَهُ from البَاعُ. (Ṣ.) مَنْ لَكَ أَنْ تَشْبُرَ البَسِيطَةَ ‡ [*Who will be guarantee for thee that thou wilt measure the earth with thy span?*] is a prov. applied to him who imposes upon himself that which he is unable to accomplish. (A, TA.) — شَبَرَ المَرْأَةَ, inf. n. as above, † *He compressed the woman.* (TA.) — شَبَرَهُ, (ISk, Ṣ, A,) aor. ـُ and ـِ, (TA,) inf. n. as above; (Ṣ, Ḳ;) and ▼ اشبرهُ, (Ṣ, A,) inf. n. إِشْبَارٌ; (Ḳ;) and ▼ شبّرهُ, inf. n. تَشْبِيرٌ; (TṢ, TA;) *He gave him* (ISk, Ṣ, A, TṢ, Ḳ*) *wealth,* or *property,* (ISk, Ṣ, A,) or *a sword,* (ISk, Ṣ,) or *a coat of mail.* (Ṣ, IB.) — شَبِرَ, aor. ـَ, *He exulted;* or *exulted greatly,* or *excessively;* and *behaved insolently and unthankfully,* or *ungratefully.* (TṢ, Ḳ, TA.)

2: see 1, in two places. — Also شبّرهُ, (AHeyth, Ḳ,) inf. n. تَشْبِيرٌ, (AHeyth, TA,) *He magnified him,* or *honoured him;* namely, a man: (AHeyth, Ḳ, TA:) and *made him a near companion, a familiar,* or *a favourite.* (AHeyth, TA.)

4. اشبر *He* (a man) *begat children tall in the* أَشْبَار, i. e. *statures:* and *he begat children short therein.* (IAạr, TA.) — اشبرهُ: see 1.

5. تشبّر *He was, or became, magnified,* or *honoured:* and *made a near companion, a familiar,* or *a favourite.* (AHeyth, TA.)

6. تشابرا *They* (two bodies of men, Ṣ) *drew near, each to the other:* (Ṣ, Ḳ:) as though they became a span (شِبْر) distant, one from the other; or as though each extended the span to the other. (Ṣ.)

شَبْرٌ The *measure* [*of the width* (see ذِرَاعٌ)], *by the span,* of a garment, or piece of cloth: so in the saying, كَمْ شَبْرُ ثَوْبِكَ [*How much is the measure of the width, by the span, of thy garment,* or *piece of cloth?*]. (Mṣb.) — *Stature;* (Fr, Ḳ;) and so ▼ شِبْرَةٌ; whether short or tall: (TA:) pl. [app. of the latter] أَشْبَارٌ. (IAạr, TA.) You say, مَا أَطْوَلَ شَبْرَهُ *How tall is his stature!* (TA.) — *Life,* or *age;* as also ▼ شِبْرٌ. (TṢ, Ḳ.) Thus in the saying, قَصَّرَ ٱللّٰهُ شَبْرَهُ and ▼ شِبْرَهُ [*May God shorten,* or *God shortened, his life*]. (TṢ, TA.) — ‡ The *act of giving:* (A, IAth:) like as بَاعٌ and يَدٌ are said for "generosity." (A.) — See also شِبْرٌ, in two places. — † The *due for marriage,* and *for concubitus;* (Sh, Ṣ,* Ḳ;*) *such as what are termed* مَهْرٌ and عُقْرٌ. (Sh, TA.) You say, أَعْطَيْتُ المَرْأَةَ شَبْرَهَا *I gave the woman her due for marriage,* or *for concubitus.* (Ṣ.) — † The *hire that is given for the stallion-camel's covering of the female.* (IAạr, T, Ṣ, Mṣb, Ḳ.*) The taking of this is forbidden. (T, Ṣ, Mṣb.) — ‡ *Marriage:* (IAth, Ḳ:) because it is accompanied by a gift. (IAth, TA.) بَارَكَ ٱللّٰهُ فِى شَبْرِكُمَا *May God bless your marriage* is a saying mentioned in a trad. (IAth, TA.)

شِبْرٌ *A span;* the *space between the extremity of the thumb and that of the little finger* (Mṣb, Ḳ) *when extended apart in the usual manner:* (Mṣb:) of the masc. gender: (Ḳ:) pl. أَشْبَارٌ, (Ṣ, Mṣb, Ḳ,) the only pl. form. (Sb.) [See also بُصْرٌ, and ذِرَاعٌ.] [Hence,] قَصِيرُ الشِّبْرِ (applied to a man, Ṣ) ‡ *Contracted,* or *short, in make:* (Ṣ, A, Ḳ:) or, accord. to some of the lexicons, *in step.* (TA.) — [As a measure in astronomy, it is said in several of the law-books to be The *twelfth part of the* رُمْح; and therefore *twenty-two minutes and a half,* accord. to modern usage: but there is reason to believe that ancient usage differed from the modern with respect to both of these measures, and was not precise nor uniform. See رُمْحٌ.] — قِبَالُ الشِّبْرِ † *The serpent:* (IAạr, Ḳ:) and so قِبَالُ الشِّبْعِ. (IAạr, TA.) — See also شَبْرٌ, in two places.

شِبْرٌ ‡ *A gift;* (Ṣ, Mgh, Ḳ, TA;) as also ▼ شَبْرٌ (Mgh, TA) and ▼ شِبْرَةٌ: (IAạr, TA:) and *wealth,* or *the like;* syn. خَيْرٌ: (Ḳ:) the first is a word similar to خَبْطٌ and نَقْضٌ; and he who says that it is used by poetic license for شَبْرٌ [as it is said to be in the Ṣ] is in error: ▼ شَبْرٌ and شِبْرٌ are said to be two dial. vars., like قَدْرٌ and قَدَرٌ. (TA.) — Also *A certain thing which the Christians give, one to another,* (يَتَعَاطَاهُ النَّصَارَى, Ḳ, TA, بَعْضُهُمْ لِبَعْضٍ, TA,) *like the* قُرْبَان [or *Eucharist*], (Ḳ, TA,) *seeking to ingratiate themselves thereby:* (TA:) or the *Eucharist* (قُرْبَان) *itself:* (Ḳ:) or *a thing which the Christians give* (تُعْطِيه), *one to another, as though seeking to ingratiate themselves thereby:* (Kh, Ṣgh, TA:) or (TA, in the Ḳ "and") *bodies:* and *powers,* or *faculties:* (Ḳ, TA:) or (TA, in the Ḳ "and") the *Gospel.* (Ḳ, TA.)

شِبْرَةٌ: see شَبْرٌ: — and see also شِبْرٌ.

شَبُّورٌ *A trumpet;* syn. بُوقٌ; (Ṣ, Ḳ;) *a certain thing in which one blows:* (Mgh:) said to be an arabicized word; (Ṣ;) not genuine Arabic: (Mgh, TA:) accord. to IAth, it is Hebrew: (TA:) [app. from the Hebr. שׁוֹפָר, as observed by Golius.] — See also أُشْبُورٌ.

رَجُلٌ شَابِرُ المِيزَانِ † *A man that is a thief.* (Ṣgh, Ḳ.)

أَشْبَرُ *Wider in span;* syn. أَوْسَعُ شِبْرًا. (A, TA.) So in the saying, هُوَ أَشْبَرُ مِنْ صَاحِبِهِ [*He is wider in span than his companion*]. (A.)

أُشْبُورٌ *A certain fish;* (Ḳ;) called by the vulgar ▼ شَبُّور. (TA.)

مَشْبَرٌ sing. of مَشَابِرُ, (TA,) which signifies *Certain notches* (حُزُوزٌ [pl. of حَزٌّ, in the CḲ erroneously written خُوُوز,]) *in the cubit, by means of which buying and selling are transacted:* (Ḳ, TA:) *of them is the notch* (حَزّ) *of the span, and the notch of the half of the span, and of the quarter thereof: every notch of these, small or great, is termed* مَشْبَر: mentioned by Ṣgh, from Aboo-Sa'eed. (TA.) — مَشَابِرُ also signifies *Rivers,* or *rivulets,* (أَنْهَار,) *that are depressed, so that the water comes to them from several places,* (Ḳ, TA,) *of such as overflows from the lands:* (TA:) pl. of مَشْبَرٌ and ▼ مَشْبَرَةٌ. (Ḳ, TA.)

مَشْبَرَةٌ: see what next precedes.

مُشْبُورَةٌ *A liberal, bountiful,* or *generous,* woman. (IAạr, Ḳ.)

شبط

شُبَاطُ (AA, Ḳ) and شَبَاطُ, being perfectly and imperfectly decl., (AA, TA,) *The name of a month in Greek;* (AA, Ḳ;) i. q. سُبَاط, q. v. (AA, TA.)

شَبُّوطٌ (Ṣ, Ḳ) and شَبُوطٌ, (Ḳ,) the latter mentioned in the O on the authority of Lth, but in the L on the authority of Lḥ, and said by him to be a Greek word, (TA,) [a coll. gen. n.,] n. un. with ة, and sometimes that with fet-ḥ is without teshdeed, (Ḳ,) i. e. شَبُوطَةٌ, mentioned by ISd, but with the expression of a doubt as to its correctness, (TA,) [now applied to *A species of cyprinus,* or *carp:* or, accord. to Golius, *a fish resembling the alosa,* or *shad, but three times larger; wont to be brought from the Euphrates to Aleppo:*] *a species of fish,* (Lth, Ṣ, Ḳ,) *slender in the tail, wide in the middle part, soft to the feel, small in the head, resembling a* بَرْبَط [or *Persian lute*]: (Lth, Ḳ:) the بربط when long, not broad, is likened to this fish; and this fish, to the بربط: the pl. is شَبَابِيطُ. (TA.) [See شُبُّوحٌ.]

شبع

1. شَبِعَ, [aor. ـَ,] inf. n. شِبَعٌ (IDrd, Ṣ, Mṣb, Ḳ) and شِبْعٌ, (IDrd, Mṣb, TA,) which is a contraction of the former, or accord. to some it is a subst., having the signification assigned to it below, (Mṣb,) or it is both, (TA,) and شَبْعٌ, (Ibn-'Abbád, Ḳ,) *He was,* or *became, satiated, sated,* or *satisfied in stomach;* شِبَعٌ being the *contr. of* جُوعٌ, (Ṣ, Ḳ,) and one of those inf. ns. [which are of a measure often] denoting natural affections or qualities [such as رِوًى and سِمَنٌ &c.]. (Ṣ.) You say بَلَدٌ قَدْ شَبِعَتْ غَنَمُهُ *A country of which the sheep,* or *goats, have become completely satiated,* or *satisfied, by abundance of herbage.* (TA.) And شَبِعْتُ خُبْزًا, and لَحْمًا, (Ṣ, Mṣb, Ḳ,) and مِنْ خُبْزٍ, and مِنْ لَحْمٍ, (Ṣ, Ḳ,) *I was,* or *became, satiated, sated,* or *satisfied, with bread,* and *with flesh-meat.* (Ṣ, Ḳ.) — Hence, metaphorically, شَبِعْتُ مِنْ هٰذَا الأَمْرِ وَرَوِيتُ ‡ *I have become,* or *I became, disgusted* [or *satiated to loathing*] *with this thing,* or *affair.* (Ṣ,* TA.) — [See also another metaphorical usage of this verb voce خَزَانَةٌ.] — شَبِعَ عَقْلُهُ † *His intellect was,* or *became, full, perfect,* (Ḳ,) *strong,* or *solid.* (TA.)

2. شَبَّعَتْ غَنَمُهُ, (Ṣ, Ḳ, [in some copies of the former, erroneously, شَبِعَتْ,]) inf. n. تَشْبِيعٌ; (Ḳ;) and شُبِّعَتْ; (as in one place in the TA;) ‡ *His sheep,* or *goats, were,* or *became, nearly, but not quite, satiated,* or *satisfied.* (Ṣ, Ḳ, TA.)

4. اشبعهُ [signifying *It satiated him, sated him,* or *satisfied his stomach,*] is said of food and of abundance of drink. (TA.) — أَشْبَعْتُهُ [*I satiated him, sated him,* or *satisfied his stomach;* or] *I fed him so that he became satiated, sated,* or *satisfied.* (Mṣb.) And أَشْبَعْتُهُ مِنَ الجُوعِ [*I fed him so as fully to relieve him from hunger*]. (Ṣ, Ḳ.) [Hence,] أَشْبَعْتُ الثَّوْبَ مِنَ الصِّبْغِ (Ṣ, TA) (Ṣ) ‡ *I saturated the garment,* or *piece of cloth, with the dye.* (TA.) — [Hence also,] اشبعهُ ‡ *He made it* (namely anything, TA) *full, without lack* or *defect,* or *abundant,* or *copious.* (Ḳ,* TA.) It is said of other things beside substances; as, for instance, of blowing, and of reading or reciting, and of any expression. (TA.) You say also, سَاقَ فِى هٰذَا المَعْنَى فَصْلًا مُشْبَعًا [*He carried on, respecting this idea, a full section*]. (TA.) [And اشبع حَرَكَةً *He rendered a vowel full in sound, by inserting after it its analogous letter of prolongation.* And such a letter of prolongation is said to be inserted, or added, لِلْإِشْبَاعِ *to render the sound full;* as in نُكَاتٌ for نُكَتٌ, and أَنْظُورُ for أَنْظُرُ, and مَرَاضِيعُ for مَرَاضِعُ. And إِشْبَاعًا is also used as signifying *For the sake of,* or *by way of, pleonasm,* or *giving fulness of expression.*] — اشبع الرَّجُلُ *The man's beasts were,* or *became, completely satiated,* or *satisfied, by abundance of herbage.* (TA.)

5. تشبّع *He ate immediately after eating.* (Ḳ.) — *He feigned himself satiated, sated, or satisfied in stomach, not being so.* (Ḳ, TA.) — [And hence,] ‡ *He made a boast of abundance or riches,* (Mṣb, Ḳ,* TA,) or *of more than he possessed;* and *invested himself with that which did not belong to him.* (TA.) [See مُتَشَبِّعٌ.]

شِبْعٌ a subst., signifying *A thing that satiates one, sates one, or satisfies one's stomach;* (Ṣ, Mṣb, Ḳ;) *consisting of bread,* and *of flesh-meat, &c.;* (Mṣb;) as also ▼ شِبَعٌ: (Ḳ:) accord. to some, the former is an inf. n.: (Mṣb:) or it is an inf. n. and also a subst. signifying as above. (TA.) You say, الرَّغِيفُ شِبْعِى *The cake of bread* [*is that which*] *satiates me,* &c. (Mṣb.)

شِبَعٌ inf. n. of 1 [q. v.]. — Also ‡ *Thickness in the shanks.* (TA.) — See also شِبْعٌ. You say, أَرْضٌ ذَاتُ شِبَعٍ *A land having abundance of herbage, and plenty.* (Mgh.)

شَبْعَةٌ مِنْ طَعَامٍ The *quantity with which one is satiated, sated, or satisfied, once, of food.* (Ṣ, Ḳ.)

أَرْضٌ شَبِعَةٌ *i. q.* ذَاتُ شِبَعٍ [q. v.]. (Mgh.)

شَبْعَانُ *Satiated, sated, or satisfied in stomach;* (Ṣ, Mṣb,* Ḳ;) as also ▼ شَابِعٌ, but this is allowable only in poetry: (Ḳ:) fem. of the former شَبْعَى, (Ṣ, Mṣb, Ḳ,) and شَبْعَانَةٌ (Ṣgh, Ḳ) is sometimes used: (Ṣgh:) the pl. of شبعان and of شبعى is شِبَاعٌ and شَبَاعَى. (TA.) [Hence the saying,] قَوْمٌ إِذَا جَاعُوا كَاعُوا وَتَرَاهُمْ سِبَاعًا إِذَا كَانُوا شِبَاعًا [*A people who, when they are hungry, are fearful and cowardly, and thou seest them to be beasts of prey when they are satiated*]. (A, TA.) — [And hence,] شَبْعَى الخَلْخَالِ ‡ A woman *who fills up the anklet by reason of her fatness.* (Ṣ, Ḳ, TA.) And شَبْعَى السِّوَارِ ‡ *Who fills up the bracelet by reason of fatness.* (Ḳ, TA.) And شَبْعَى الوِشَاحِ ‡ A woman *large in the belly.* (TA.) And شَبْعَى الدِّرْعِ ‡ A woman *bulky in make:* (A, O, L, TA:) in the Ḳ erroneously written شَبْعَى الذِّرَاعِ, and expl. as meaning *bulky in the forearm.* (TA.)

شَبِيعٌ Food *that satiates, sates, or satisfies the stomach.* (Fr.) — † An arrow *that kills much* or *many or often.* (Ibn-'Abbád.) — ثَوْبٌ شَبِيعُ الغَزْلِ ‡ *A garment, or piece of cloth,* [*of full texture,* or] *of many threads:* (Ṣ, Ḳ, TA:) pl. ثِيَابٌ شُبْعٌ. (TA.) And حَبْلٌ شَبِيعٌ, (Ḳ,) or شَبِيعُ الثَّلَّةِ, (TA,) † *A rope abundant,* (Ḳ, TA,) *and firm,* or *strong, in the wool,* (TA,) or *in the hair,* or *fur,* [of which it is composed:] (Ḳ, TA:) pl. شُبْعٌ. (TA.) — رَجُلٌ شَبِيعُ العَقْلِ † *A man full,* or *perfect,* (Ḳ, TA,) *and strong,* or *solid,* (TA,) *in intellect;* (Ḳ, TA;) from IAạr; (TA;) as also ▼ مُشْبَعُهُ. (Ḳ.) And رَجُلٌ مُشْبَعُ ▼ القَلْبِ [or perhaps ▼ مُشْبِعُ القَلْبِ] † *A man strong,* or *firm, in heart.* (TA.)

شُبَاعَةٌ *A portion of food that remains,* or *is redundant, after one is satiated,* or *satisfied.* (Ibn-Abbád, Ḳ.*)

شَابِعٌ: see شَبْعَانُ. — بَهِيمَةٌ شَابِعٌ *A beast that has attained to eating;* an epithet applied to such a beast *until it is nearly weaned.* (TA.)

فُلَانٌ فِى رِىٍّ وَمَشْبَعٍ [*Such a one is in a state in which he is satiated, or satisfied, with drink and food*]. (T, A, TA, in art. نظر.) [See مَنْظَرٌ.]

مُشْبَعٌ pass. part. n. of 4 [q. v.]. See also شَبِيعٌ, in two places.

مُشْبِعٌ: see شَبِيعٌ. — البَآءُ المُشْبَعُ [or المُشْبَعَةُ] *The letter* پ. (TA in art. بلس.)

مُتَشَبِّعٌ ‡ One *who invests himself with, and makes a boast of, more than he possesses; who invests himself with that which he does not possess;* (Ṣ, TA;) *who affects goodly qualities more than he possesses; like him who feigns himself satiated, or satisfied in stomach, not being so:* (TA:) or he *who feigns himself satiated, or satisfied in stomach, not being so:* and hence, † a *lying* person, *who affects to be commended or praised for, or boasts of, or glories in, that which he does not possess.* (Mgh.) Thus in a trad., (Ṣ, Mgh,) in which it is said, المُتَشَبِّعُ بِمَا لَا يَمْلِكُ كَلَابِسِ ثَوْبَىْ زُورٍ, (Ṣ, TA,) or بِمَا لَيْسَ عِنْدَهُ, (Mgh,) ‡ [*He who invests himself with, and makes a boast of, more than he possesses, &c., is like the wearer of two garments of falsity:* or] accord. to A'Obeyd, it means [that such *is like*] *the hypocrite who wears the garments of the devotees in order that he may be thought to be a devotee, not being so:* or, as some say, *the person who wears a shirt to the sleeves of which he attaches two other sleeves in order to make it appear that he is wearing two shirts:* or [*the wearer of the garments of the false witness;* for] it is said that there used to be in the tribe the man of goodly exterior, and when false witness was needed, he bore [such] witness, and was not rejected, because of the goodliness of his apparel. (Mgh.) [See also art. زور, in which this trad. is cited with a small variation.]

شبق

1. شَبِقَ, (Ṣ, M, O, Mṣb, Ḳ,) aor. ـَ, (Mṣb, Ḳ,) inf. n. شَبَقٌ, (Ṣ, M, Mgh, O, Mṣb,) *He was,* or *became, affected with vehement lust, or carnal desire:* (Ṣ, M, Mgh, O, Mṣb, Ḳ:) said of a man; (M, Mṣb;) and in like manner one says of a woman; and also, sometimes, of other than human beings. (M, TA.) — And شَبِقَ مِنَ اللَّحْمِ *He suffered indigestion,* or *turned away with disgust, from flesh-meat.* (Ibn-'Abbád, O, Ḳ.)

شَبِقٌ *Affected with vehement lust or carnal desire;* (Mṣb, TA;) applied to a man; and sometimes to other than man: (Mṣb:) fem. with ة. (Mṣb, TA.)

شُوبَقٌ *A certain wooden implement of the baker, or maker of bread;* (Ḳ;) *a baker's rolling-pin;* (MA;) [thus called, and also شُوبَك, in the present day;] an arabicized word, (Ibn-'Abbád, O, Ḳ,) from [the Pers.] چُوبَه [or چُوبَك, or from the Pers. شُوبَنْج]. (TA.) [See also كُرِيب.]

شبك

1. شَبَكَهُ, aor. ـِ, (Ḳ, TA,) inf. n. شَبْكٌ; (TA;) and ▼ شَبَّكَهُ, inf. n. تَشْبِيكٌ; *He infixed,* (Ḳ, TA,) and *inserted,* (TA,) *one part thereof into another,* or *parts thereof into others:* (Ḳ, TA:) so in the M: (TA:) [but the latter more usually signifies *he infixed,* and *inserted, many parts thereof into others:* (see 8, first sentence, respecting its quasi-pass.:) and hence, *he made it reticulated, retiform, like a net;* and *like a lattice,* or *trellis,* or *grating,* or *cage:* and both signify also *he made it commingled in its several parts, intricate, complicated, perplexed,* or *confused;* either properly, as when the object is a fabric, or anything made by art, or created; or tropically, as when the object is ideal:] primarily, (TA,) الشَّبْكُ signifies الخَلْطُ [i. e. *the mixing together* a thing or things]; and [implies] التَّدَاخُلُ [i. e. *the entering of one part* of a thing *into another part,* or *of parts* of a thing or things *into other parts;* or *the being intermixed,* or *intermingled*]. (Ṣ, TA.) Hence, ▼ تَشْبِيكُ الأَصَابِعِ, (Ṣ, TA,) meaning *The inserting of some of the fingers* [i. e. *those of one hand*] *amid the other fingers;* (Mṣb, TA;) which it is forbidden to do in prayer: (TA:) one says, شَبَّكَ بَيْنَ أَصَابِعِهِ, or] شَبَّكَ أَصَابِعَهُ, *He inserted,* or *interserted, his fingers together* [*so as to conjoin his two hands*]: (MA:) or, as some interpret it, تَشْبِيكُ الأَصَابِعِ which is forbidden in prayer is † *the mixing,* and *entering, into contentions,* or *altercations.* (TA.) [Hence also,] ▼ كَانَتِ الرِّيحُ شَبَّكَتْهُمْ, a saying of Mohammad Ibn-Zekereeyà, meaning † *The wind had made them like the* شَبَكَة [or *net*], *in the interknitting and contraction of the limbs.* (Mgh.) — شَبَكَهُ عَنْهُ, inf. n. as above, means † *He,* or *it, diverted him,* or *occupied him so as to divert him, from him,* or *it.* (TA.)

2: see above, in three places: — and see also 8, in two places.

3. شَابَكَ بَيْنَهُمَا, inf. n. مُشَابَكَةٌ, [app. † *He caused an embroilment between them two,*] occurring in a tradition. (TA.)

4. اشبكوا *They dug wells* (O, Ḳ) *such as are called* شِبَاك (O) or *such as are called* شَبَكَةٌ. (Ḳ.) — And أَشْبَكَ *It* (a place) *had* [*such*] *wells dug in it by many persons.* (TA.)

5: see 8, in four places.

6: see 8, in three places. — تشابكت السِّبَاعُ *The beasts of prey leaped* [*the females*]; syn. نَزَتْ: (Ḳ:) or *desired to do so* (أَرَادَتِ النِّزَاءَ). (IAạr, TA.) — تَشَابَكَا [app. † *They became embroiled, each with the other;*] quasi-pass. of شَابَكَ بَيْنَهُمَا. (TA.)

8. اشتبك, quasi-pass. of شَبَكَهُ, *It had one part thereof infixed,* (Ḳ, TA,) and *inserted,* (TA,) *into another,* or *parts thereof into others;* as also ▼ تشبّك, quasi-pass. of شَبَّكَهُ: (Ḳ, TA:) so in the M: but ▼ the latter imports muchness, or multiplicity: (TA:) [i. e. it signifies *it had many parts thereof infixed,* and *inserted, into others;* and hence, *it was reticulated, retiform,*

like a net; and *like a lattice,* or *trellis,* or *grating,* or *cage:* and both signify also *it was,* or *became, commingled in its several parts, intricate, complicated, perplexed,* or *confused;* either properly, as when said of a fabric, or anything made by art, or created; or tropically, as when said of what is ideal.] One says, اشتبكت النُّجُومُ, and ▼ تشابكت, and ▼ شُبِّكَت, [or the last may be a mistranscription for ▼ تشبّكت,] *The stars were intermixed among themselves, and confused:* (TA:) [or *were clustered together:*] or اِشْتِبَاكُ النُّجُومِ signifies *the stars' being numerous, and being intermixed among themselves;* from شَبَكَةُ الصَّائِدِ ["the net of the fisherman" or "sportsman"]: (Mgh:) or *their being numerous, and* [as though] *gathered* [or *clustered*] *together:* (Mṣb:) or, as some say, *the appearing of all the stars* [which causes them to appear confused]. (TA.) And اشتبكت العُرُوقُ *The veins were knit together, commingled,* or *intricately intermixed* or *intermingled;* syn. اِشْتَجَرَتْ. (O, TA.) And اشتبك السَّرَابُ *The mirage became intermixed,* or *confused.* (TA.) And اشتبك الظَّلَامُ ‡ *The darkness became confused.* (Ṣ, O, TA.) And اشتبكت الأُمُورُ, and ▼ تشابكت, and ▼ شُبِّكت, (Ḳ, TA,) and ▼ تشبّكت, (TA,) † *The affairs became intricate, complicated, perplexed,* or *confused.* (Ḳ, TA.) And اشتبكت الحُرُوبُ بَيْنَهُمْ † *The war,* or *fight, became intricate, and entangled between them;* syn. نَشِبَت. (TA in art. نشب.) And اشتبكت أَنْيَابُهُ وَٱخْتَلَفَتْ [*His canine teeth locked together, and were dissimilar*]; referring to a lion. (O. [See also شَابِكٌ.]) اِشْتِبَاكُ الرَّحِمِ means ‡ *The close* [or *intimate*] *connexion of relationship by birth:* (TA:) [and in like manner, ▼ تَشَابُكُ الأَرْحَامِ *such connexion of relationships by birth:* see an ex. of its part. n., voce مُشْتَبِكٌ.]

شَبْكٌ: see شَبَكَةٌ. — Also The *teeth of a comb;* (O, Ḳ;) because of their nearness together. (TA.)

بَيْنَهُمَا شُبْكَةٌ, (Ḳ,) or شُبْكَةُ نَسَبٍ, (Ṣ, Mṣb,) ‡ *Between them two is* [*a close* or *an intimate connexion of*] *relationship by birth:* (Ṣ, Ḳ, TA:) and بَيْنَ القَوْمِ شُبْكَةُ نَسَبٍ ‡ *Between the people,* or *party, is an intermingling* [*of relationship*]. (O, TA.)

شَبَكَةٌ The شَرَكَة [meaning *net*] *of the* صَيَّاد [i. e. *fisherman,* and *fowler* or *sportsman*]; (Ḳ;) the مِصْيَدَة, (Lth, O, TA,) or *instrument of* الصَّيْد, (Ṣ,) *that is used in the water* [i. e. *for catching fish*] and *on the land* [i. e. *for catching fowls* or *wild animals*]; (Lth, O,* TA;) applied by some peculiarly to the مِصْيَدَة *of the water;* (TA;) and ▼ شُبَّاكٌ signifies the same: (Ḳ:) pl. of the former شِبَاكٌ (Ṣ, Mṣb, Ḳ) and شَبَكَاتٌ (Mṣb) and [coll. gen. n.] ▼ شَبَكٌ: (Mṣb, Ḳ:) and the pl. of ▼ شُبَّاكٌ is شَبَابِيكُ (Ḳ.) — And *A certain thing for the head;* (Lth, O;) [*a small net, for the head, a veil of net-work, in order that the face may not be known.* (Golius, on the authority of Meyd.)] ═ Also *Wells near together,* (Ḳ, TA,) *of which the water is near* [*to the mouths*], *communicating* [app. *by filtration*] *one with another:* so accord. to El-Ḳutabee: (TA:) or *wells separate, one from another:* (M and L in art. مأد:) and, (Ḳ,) or as some say, (TA,) *wells* (O, Ḳ, TA) *that are open to view,* (Ḳ, TA,) *dug in a rugged place, of the depth of the stature of a man,* and *twice* and *thrice that measure, in which the rain-water becomes retained:* so called because of their mutual proximity, and confusedness: a single one of them is not called شَبَكَةٌ; for this is only a name for a plural number; but the pl. شِبَاكٌ is applied to *aggregates thereof in sundry places:* (O, TA:) or شِبَاكٌ, (Ṣ,) or شَبَكَةٌ, (Mṣb,) signifies *wells that are numerous and near together in a* [*tract of*] *land;* (Ṣ, Mṣb;) from اِشْتِبَاكُ النُّجُومِ: (Mṣb:) or, accord. to Aṣ, شَبَكَةٌ signifies *wells,* or *other pits or hollows dug in the ground, that are numerous;* and the pl. is شِبَاكٌ. (IDrd, O.) — And *A* [*tract of*] *land in which are many wells,* (Ḳ, TA,) *not tracts that exude water and produce salt, nor such as give growth to plants,* or *herbage:* (TA:) or [the pl.] شِبَاكٌ signifies *places,* of the earth, *that are not such as exude water and produce salt, nor such as give growth to plants,* or *herbage; such as the* شِبَاك *of El-Baṣrah.* (Lth, O.) — And The *burrow* of the [field-rat called] جُرَذ: (Ḳ, TA:) or the *burrows* thereof, which are near together: pl. شِبَاكٌ. (TA.)

شِبَاكٌ, (thus in the 'Eyn and O and L and TA,) or ▼ شُبَّاكٌ, (thus in the Ḳ, there said to be like زُنَّارٌ,) but [SM says that] the latter is a manifest mistake, (TA,) *A thing,* (Ḳ, TA,) or *anything,* (Lth, O,) *composed of canes,* or *reeds,* (Ḳ, TA,) or *such as canes,* or *reeds,* (Lth, O,) *firmly bound together,* (Lth, O, TA,) *in the manner of the manufacture of mats:* (Lth, O, Ḳ, TA:) a single piece whereof is termed ▼ شِبَاكَةٌ, (Lth, O, TA,) or ▼ شُبَّاكَةٌ. (So in the Ḳ.) — And likewise, (i. e. شِبَاكٌ, as in the 'Eyn and O and L, but in the Ḳ ▼ شُبَّاكٌ, TA,) *What is between the curved pieces of wood of the* [*vehicles called*] مَحَامِل, [pl. of مَحْمِل, q. v., *composed*] *of net-work of thongs* (مِنْ تَشْبِيكِ القِدِّ [القدّ being here used as a coll. gen. n.: see art. قد]). (Ḳ, TA.)

شِبَاكَةٌ: see the next preceding paragraph.

شَبَائِكُ [a pl. of which the sing. is not mentioned,] *Contentions,* or *altercations.* (TA.)

شَبَّاكٌ means مَنْ يَعْمَلُ الشِّبَاكَ الوَطِيَّاتِ [app. *A maker of soft netted fabrics of thongs for* مَحَامِل; (see شِبَاكٌ, latter sentence;) supposing الوَطِيَّات to be for الوَطِيئَات, agreeably with a well-known license]. (TA.)

شُبَّاكٌ: see شَبَكَةٌ, in two places: — and شِبَاكٌ, likewise in two places: — and شُبَّاكَةٌ, also in two places. — Applied to a دِرْع *i. q.* مَحْبُوكَةٌ [app. as signifying *Woven well,* or *well and compactly;* in which sense this epithet seems to be more properly applicable to a woman's "shift" than to "a coat of mail;" but دِرْع in the former of these senses is seldom, if ever, fem.; and in the latter sense, seldom, if ever, masc.]. (TA.) ═ [It is also a pl., of which the sing., if used, is probably ▼ شَابِكٌ, accord. to analogy; as a possessive epithet, meaning ذُو شَبَكَةٍ, like لَابِنٌ meaning ذُو لَبَنٍ, &c.:] one says, رَأَيْتُ عَلَى المَآءِ الشُّبَّاكَ *I saw, upon the water, the fishermen with the nets.* (Az, Z, TA.)

شُبَّاكَةٌ, (Ṣ, O, KL,) or ▼ شُبَّاكٌ, (Mṣb, TA,) *A thing formed of grating,* or *lattice-work,* (▼ مُشَبَّكَة, Ṣ, O, or مُشَبَّك, KL, TA,) of iron, (Ṣ, O, Mṣb, Ḳ, TA,) and of other material [i. e. of wood &c.]: (TA:) and [particularly] *a window so formed:* (KL:) pl. شَبَابِيكُ. (Ṣ, O, TA.) One says, رَأَيْتُهُ يَنْظُرُ مِنَ الشُّبَّاكِ ▼ [*I saw him looking from the grated,* or *latticed, window*]. (TA.) — See also شِبَاكٌ.

شَابِكٌ [app. a possessive epithet, meaning ذُو شَبَكَةٍ]: see شُبَّاكٌ. — [Also meaning ذُو ٱشْتِبَاكٍ.] One says طَرِيقٌ شَابِكٌ *A road,* or *way, that is confused and intricate.* (O, Ḳ.) — [Hence,] أُمُّ النُّجُومِ الشَّوَابِكِ may mean *The sun;* as being the chief of the [confused] stars: or *the milky way;* [as being composed of confused stars;] الشَّوَابِك [pl. of الشَّابِكَة] meaning ▼ المُشْتَبِكَة. (Ḥam pp. 43 and 44.) — And لُحْمَةٌ شَابِكَةٌ: see مُشْتَبِكٌ. — And شَابِكٌ applied to a lion, *Having the canine teeth locking together,* (▼ مُشْتَبِكُ الأَنْيَابِ, Ḳ, TA, [see 8, near the end, in the CḲ مُتَشَبِّكُ الأَنْيَابِ,]) *dissimilar:* (TA:) and شَابِكُ الأَنْيَابِ is applied to a camel, (O, TA,) in like manner. (TA.) [Hence,] الشَّابِكُ is one of the names for *The lion.* (TA.) — And one says رَجُلٌ شَابِكُ الرُّمْحِ, meaning *A man whom one sees,* by reason of his skill, *thrusting with the spear* [*indiscriminately*] *in all the faces.* (O, TA.)

مُشَبَّكٌ: see شُبَّاكَةٌ. — المُشَبَّكُ is *A certain sort of food.* (TA.)

مُشْتَبِكٌ: see شَابِكٌ, in two places. — رَحِمٌ مُشْتَبِكَةٌ (A'Obeyd, Ṣ, TA) means ‡ [*Relationship by birth*] *closely,* or *intimately, connected.* (A'Obeyd, TA.) And one says also, بَيْنَهُمَا أَرْحَامٌ مُتَشَابِكَةٌ ▼ ‡ [*Between them two are relationships by birth closely,* or *intimately, connected*]: and ▼ لُحْمَةٌ شَابِكَةٌ [which means the like]. (TA.)

أَرْحَامٌ مُتَشَابِكَةٌ: see what next precedes.

شبل

1. شَبَلَ, (Ḳ,) aor. ُ, (TḲ,) inf. n. شُبُولٌ, *He* (a boy, TA) *became a youth,* or *young man,* (Ḳ,) or *grew up, and became a youth,* or *young man,* (TA,) *in a state of ease and plenty.* (Ḳ, TA. [In the CḲ, فى نِعْمَةٍ is erroneously put for فى نَعْمَةٍ.]) Accord. to Ks, one says, شَبَلْتُ فِى بَنِى فُلَانٍ, meaning *I grew up,* or *became a youth,* or *young man, among the sons of such a one:* (Ṣ, TA:) and قَدْ شَبَلَ الغُلَامُ أَحْسَنَ شُبُولٍ *The boy has grown up,* or *become a youth,* or *young man, in the best manner:* (Ṣ:) but accord. to others,

it is not said except in the case of being in a state of ease and plenty. (TA.)

4. أَشْبَلَتِ المَرْأَةُ بَعْدَ بَعْلِهَا † *The woman bore with her children, [tending them patiently, after* the loss of *her husband,] without marrying:* (Ṣ, O:) [and] اشبلت عَلَى وَلَدِهَا ‡ *She* (a woman) *applied herself constantly to the care of her children, after [the loss of] her husband,* (Ḳ, TA,) *and bore with them,* (TA,) *not marrying:* (Ḳ, TA:) and the epithet applied to her is ▼ مُشْبِلٌ [without ة]. (TA.) One says, هِىَ فِى إِشْبَالِهَا كَاللَّبُوَةِ عَلَى أَشْبَالِهَا ‡ [*She is, in her constant application of herself to the care of her children,* &c., *like the lioness over her whelps*]. (TA.) — And اشبل عَلَيْهِ ‡ *He inclined to him; affected him;* or *was,* or *became, favourably inclined towards him:* (Ṣ, O, Ḳ, TA:) and *he aided, helped,* or *assisted, him.* (Ḳ, TA.)

[7. انشبل is expl. by Golius as signifying "*Leviter e loco exivit, effluxit;*" as on the authority of the KL; but I do not find it in my copy of that work; and think that it is some other word to which this meaning is there assigned.]

شِبْلٌ The *whelp,* or *young one, of the lion:* (Ṣ, Mgh, O, Mṣb:) or the *young one of the lion when it has attained to the seeking,* or *taking, of prey:* (Ḳ, TA:) [and Freytag says, on the authority of Meyd, *of any wild beast:*] pl. أَشْبَالٌ (Ṣ, O, Mṣb, Ḳ) and أَشْبُلٌ (Ṣ, O, Ḳ) [both properly pls. of pauc.] and [pl. of mult.] شُبُولٌ and شِبَالٌ. (Ḳ.)

شَابِلٌ A lion *whose canine teeth have become such as lock together, dissimilar;* expl. by the words الَّذِى ٱشْتَبَكَتْ أَنْيَابُهُ. (Ḳ. [Perhaps, in this sense, a mistranscription for شَابِكٌ, q. v.]) — And (Ḳ) † A boy, or young man, *full* [or *plump*] *in body, by reason of ease and plenty and of youthfulness:* (IAạr, O, Ḳ:*) and so شَابِنٌ, and حِضْجْر. (IAạr, O.) — [شَابِلَةٌ, expl. by Golius as signifying "*Diminuta lacte camela, pulli septimestris mater,*" as on the authority of the KL, is a mistake for شَائِلَةٌ.]

[أُشْبُلٌ, expl. by Golius as signifying "*Magno veretri præputio* camelus," as on the authority of the KL, is a mistake for أَثْيَلُ.]

مُشْبِلٌ A lioness *whose whelps,* or *young ones, accompany her,* (Ṣ, O, Mṣb,) *going with her.* (Ṣ, O.) And A she-camel *whose young one has become strong, and goes with her.* (AZ, Ṣ, O.) — See also 4.

مَشْبُولٌ A place *in which are lions' whelps* or *young ones.* (Ḥam p. 416.)

شبم

1. شَبِمَ, (Ṣ, Ḳ,) aor. ـَ, (Ḳ,) inf. n. شَبَمٌ, (TA,) *It was,* or *became, cold;* (Ṣ, Ḳ;) said of water. (Ṣ.) ═ شَبَمَ الجَدْىَ, (Ḳ,) aor. ـُ, inf. n. شَبْمٌ, (TḲ,) *He put the* شِبَام [q. v.] *in the mouth of the kid;* as also ▼ شَبَّمهُ, (Ḳ,) inf. n. تَشْبِيمٌ. (TA.)

2: see what next precedes.

شَبَمٌ *Cold,* or *coldness;* (Ṣ, Mṣb, Ḳ;) accord. to the M, of water: (TA:) but one says غَدَاةٌ ذَاتُ شَبَمٍ [*A morning having coldness*]: (Ṣ:) and يَوْمٌ ذُو شَبَمٍ *A day having coldness.* (Mṣb.) — Jureybeh Ibn-El-Ashyam El-Faḳ'asee says,

وَقَدْ شَبَّهُوا العِيرَ أَفْرَاسَنَا ✱ فَقَدْ وَجَدُوا مِيرَهَا ذَا شَبَمْ

[*And they likened our horses to the camels carrying provision of corn; but they found their provision to be something having coldness*]; meaning, accord. to Aboo-Riyásh, that they found *death;* for death is cold; and poison also is cold: but there is another reading, accord. to which the last word is بَشَمْ, meaning "heaviness," such as results from food. (Ḥam p. 363.) See also the next paragraph.

شَبِمٌ *Cold,* as an epithet, (Ṣ, Mṣb, TA,) applied to water, (Ṣ, TA,) and to rain; and one says غَدَاةٌ شَبِمَةٌ, meaning *A cold morning.* (TA.) [And] *Feeling cold:* (Ḳ:) or *feeling cold together with hunger.* (AA, Ṣ, Ḳ.) — Also *A weapon,* or *weapons;* as being cold: and such has been said to be the meaning [of ▼ ذَا شَبَمْ] in the verse cited above. (TA.) — And *Death;* because of its coldness: — and *Poison;* for the same reason. (Ḳ. [But see the verse cited above, and the explanation of it.]) ═ And بَقَرَةٌ شَبِمَةٌ *A fat ox* or *cow,* or *beast of the bovine kind:* (Ḳ, TA:) but the epithet commonly known is سَنِمَةٌ, [meaning "having a large hump,"] with س and ن. (TA.)

شُبُمٌ: see شِبَامٌ.

شَبَامٌ *A certain plant,* (AḤn, Ḳ,) *resembling in colour the* حِنَّآء [q. v.]. (AḤn, TA.)

شِبَامٌ *A piece of wood which is put crosswise in the mouth of a kid,* (Ṣ, Ḳ, TA,) or, as in the M, *in the two sides of the mouth of a kid* or lamb, *and tied behind its head,* (TA,) *in order that it may not suck its mother;* (Ṣ, Ḳ;) as also ▼ شُبُمٌ: (Ḳ:) and so حِشَاكٌ. (IDrd and Ṣ in art. حشك.) — Also, (Ḳ,) or the dual, شِبَامَانِ, (Ṣ, TA,) *Two threads,* or *strings, attached to the* [*kind of face-veil called*] بُرْقُع, *by which the woman* [*draws and*] *binds* [*the two upper corners of*] *it to the back of her head:* (Ṣ, Ḳ:) [also called ثِبَاتٌ:] pl. شُبُمٌ. (O in art. سنبك.)

مُشَبَّمٌ: see the following paragraph. Applied to a lion, it means *Having his mouth tied,* or *bound;* from شِبَامٌ in the former of the senses expl. above: (Meyd, TA:) thus in the following prov.:

تَفْرَقُ مِنْ صَوْتِ الغُرَا ✱ بِ وَتَفْرِسُ الأَسَدَ المُشَبَّمْ

[*She is frightened at the cry of the crow,* or *raven, and breaks the neck of the lion whose mouth is tied*]: (Meyd, Ḳ, TA:) or, accord. to another relation, المُشَتَّمْ, [meaning "the grim-faced,"] from شَتَامَةُ الوَجْهِ: (Meyd:) a saying originating from the fact of a woman's breaking the neck of a lion, and then hearing the cry of a crow, or raven, and being frightened: applied to him who advances boldly to undertake that which is of high account, [or attended with peril,] and fears that which is contemptible. (Meyd, Ḳ.)

مَشْبُومٌ [and ▼ مُشَبَّمٌ] A kid, or lamb, *having the piece of wood called* شِبَام *put into its mouth and tied behind its head, in order that it may not suck its mother.* (TA.)

شبه

2. شَبَّهَهُ إِيَّاهُ and شَبَّهَهُ بِهِ, (MA, Ḳ,) inf. n. تَشْبِيهٌ, (Ṣ, Ḳ, KL,) *He made it to be like it,* or *to resemble it; he assimilated it to it;* (MA, KL;) i. q. مَثَّلَهُ [meaning thus: and also meaning *he likened it to it,* or *compared it with it;* agreeably with the explanation here next following]: (Ṣ,* Ḳ:) شَبَّهْتُ الشَّىْءَ بِالشَّىْءِ *I put the thing in the place,* or *predicament, of the* [other] *thing, by reason of an attribute connecting them* [or *common to them*]; which attribute may be real and ideal; real as when one says, "this dirhem is like this dirhem," and "this blackness is like this blackness;" and ideal as when one says, "Zeyd is like the lion" or "like the ass" i. e. in his strength or his stupidity, and "Zeyd is like 'Amr" i. e. in his power and his generosity and similar qualities; and sometimes it is tropical, as when one says, "the absent is like the non-existent," and "the garment is like the dirhem" i. e. the value of the garment is equivalent to the dirhem. (Mṣb.) شَبَّهَهُ, [app. for شَبَّهَ شَيْئًا بِشَىْءٍ,] accord. to IAạr, means *He made a thing equal to a thing,* or *like a thing.* (TA.) — [Hence,] شَبَّهَهُ عَلَيْهِ, inf. n. as above, *He rendered it confused to him* [*by making it to appear like some other thing*]; (JḲ,* TA;) *he rendered it ambiguous, dubious,* or *obscure, to him.* (MA.) See also 8, [with which it is, in its pass. form, and in its act. form likewise, nearly or exactly syn. in one of the senses,] in two places. — [And شَبَّهَتْهُ إِلَيْهِ النَّفْسُ, or الحَالُ, *The mind,* or *the case, imaged it to him;* like خَيَّلَتْهُ: see art. خيل.] See also 5, [with which, in its pass. form, this verb is nearly or exactly syn. in one sense.] — [تَشْبِيهٌ used as a simple subst. means *A comparison, simile, similitude,* or *parable:* and has for its pl. تَشْبِيهَاتٌ. Hence, عَلَى التَّشْبِيهِ *By way of comparison.*]

3: see the next paragraph, in four places.

4. اشبههُ, [inf. n. إِشْبَاهٌ;] and ▼ شَابَهَهُ, [inf. n. مُشَابَهَةٌ;] (Ṣ, Ḳ;) *He was,* or *became, like him; he resembled him;* syn. مَاثَلَهُ. (Ḳ.) One says أَشْبَهَ الوَلَدُ أَبَاهُ, and ▼ شَابَهَهُ, *The child* [*resembled his father,* or] *shared with his father in some one of his qualities,* or *attributes.* (Mṣb.) And مَنْ أَشْبَهَ أَبَاهُ فَمَا ظَلَمَ, (Meyd, TA,) or مَنْ يُشَابِهْ ▼ أَبَهُ فَمَا ظَلَمْ, as some relate it, (TA,) [*Whoso resembles his father, he has not done that which is wrong:*] a prov., meaning, he has not put the likeness in the wrong place; for there is not any one more fit, or proper, for him to resemble than he: or it may mean that the father has not done

that which is wrong. (Meyd. [See also Ḥar pp. 667-8.]) And اشبه الرَّجُلُ أُمَّهُ, (IAạr, Ḳ,) and ▾ شَابَهَهَا, (Ḳ,) [*The man resembled his mother,*] meaning †*the man became impotent, and weak.* (IAạr, Ḳ.) And it is said in a trad. of 'Omar, إِنَّ اللَّبَنَ يُشْبِهُ عَلَيْهِ [*Verily one becomes like by feeding upon milk*]: i. e. the infant that is suckled often becomes like the woman who suckles it, because of the milk: (JK:) or اللبن يشبه [app. for اللَّبَنُ يُشْبِهُ عَلَيْهِ]: i. e. one acquires a likeness to the natural dispositions of the woman who suckles [him]: or, as it is also related, ▾ يتشبّه [app. for يُتَشَبَّهُ عَلَيْهِ]. (TA.) ═ [اشبه is also a verb of wonder: hence the saying,

مَا أَشْبَهَ اللَّيْلَةَ بِالبَارِحَةْ

How like is this night to yesternight! expl. in art. برح.]

5. تشبّه به [*He became assimilated to him,* or *it: and he assumed,* or *affected, a likeness,* or *resemblance, to him,* or *it; he imitated him,* or *it;*] *he made himself to be like,* or *to resemble, him,* or *it;* (MA, KL;*) i. q. تمثّل: (Ṣ,* TA: [in the former, this meaning is indicated, but not expressed:]) said of a man. (Ṣ.) See also 4, last sentence but one. — [Hence,] تشبّه لَهُ أَنَّهُ كَذَا *It became imaged to him* [*in the mind,* i. e. *it seemed to him,*] *that it was so;* syn. تَخَيَّلَ, (Ṣ and Ḳ* in art. خيل,) and تَخَايَلَ: (Ṣ in that art.:) and شُبِّهَ ▾ إِلَيْهِ أَنَّهُ كَذَا [signifies the same; or] *it was imaged to him* [*in the mind*] *that it was so;* syn. خُيِّلَ. (PṢ in that art.)

6. تَشَابُهٌ signifies The *being equal,* or *uniform;* syn. اِسْتِوَآءٌ: (TA:) [or rather the *being consimilar.*] You say, تَشَابَهَا *They were like,* or *they resembled, each other.* (MA.) And الخُطُوطُ تَتَشَابَهُ *The lines are like one another; the lines resemble one another.* (Mgh.) — See also the next paragraph, in two places.

8. اشتبها and ▾ تشابها *They resembled each other so that they became confounded,* or *confused,* or *dubious.* (Ḳ.) And اشتبه (Ṣ, MA) and ▾ تشابه (MA) *It* (a thing, Ṣ, MA, or an affair, MA) *was,* or *became, ambiguous, dubious,* or *obscure,* (MA,) عَلَىَّ [*to me*], (Ṣ,) or عَلَيْهِ [*to him*]: (MA:) and شُبِّهَ ▾ عَلَيْهِ الأَمْرُ *the thing,* or *affair, was rendered confused,* or *dubious, to him:* (Ḳ,* TA:) and شُبِّهَ ▾ الشَّىْءُ, also, [see مُشْتَبِهٌ,] *the thing was,* or *became, confused,* or *dubious.* (IAạr, TA.)

شِبْهٌ and ▾ شَبَهٌ are syn., (Ṣ, Mṣb, Ḳ,) like مِثْلٌ and مَثَلٌ, and بِدْلٌ and بَدَلٌ, and نِكْلٌ and نَكَلٌ, the only other instances of the kind, i. e. of words of both these measures, that have been heard, having the same meaning, (Ṣ and TA in art. بدل,) i. q. ▾ شَبِيهٌ, (Ṣ, Mṣb, Ḳ,) syn. مِثْلٌ, (Ḳ,) [i. e.] *A like; a similar person* or *thing;* (MA, Mṣb;) [*an analogue; a match;*] *a fellow:* (MA:) pl. (of all, TA) أَشْبَاهٌ. (Ḳ, TA.) One says, هٰذَا شِبْهُهُ [and ▾ شَبَهُهُ], i. e. ▾ شَبِيهُهُ [meaning *This is the like, &c., of him, or it*]. (Ṣ.) And فُلَانٌ شِبْهُكَ and ▾ شَبَهُكَ and ▾ شَبِيهُكَ [*Such a one is the like, &c., of thee*]. (JK.) [And هٰذَا شَبِيهٌ ▾ بِهِ *This is like him,* or *it.* And hence, in lexicology, الأَشْبَاهُ وَالنَّظَائِرُ *The words that are alike in form:* generally applied to rare instances.] — See also the next paragraph, in two places.

شَبَهٌ: see the next preceding paragraph, in three places. — [Hence,] syn. with شَكْلٌ [signifying *A likeness, resemblance,* or *semblance,* as meaning *something resembling*]; (AA, Ḳ and TA in art. شكل;) and ▾ شُبْهَةٌ is syn. with مِثْلٌ [*in the same sense*]: (Ḳ in the present art.: [see exs. of the latter voce عُقْرٌ:]) pl. of the former [in this sense, as is indicated in the Ṣ,] ▾ مَشَابِهُ, contr. to rule, like مَحَاسِنُ and مَذَاكِيرُ; (Ṣ, TA;) or this is a pl. having no proper sing. (TA.) One says, بَيْنَهُمَا شَبَهٌ [*Between them two is a likeness, &c.*]. (Ṣ.) And نَزَعَ إِلَى أَبِيهِ فِى الشَّبَهِ [*He inclined to his father in likeness*]. (Ṣ, in art. نزع.) And a poet cited by IAạr says,

أَصْبَحَ فِيهِ شَبَهٌ مِنْ أُمِّهِ

مِنْ عِظَمِ الرَّأْسِ وَمِنْ خُرْطُمِهِ

[*He became so that there was in him a resemblance of his mother, in respect of bigness of the head, and of his nose*]. (TA.) And one says also, بِهِ شُبْهَةٌ ▾ لَهُ i. e. مِثْلٌ [*In him is a likeness,* or *something having a likeness, to him,* or *it*]. (TḲ.) — Also, (JK, Ṣ, Mṣb, Ḳ, &c.,) and ▾ شِبْهٌ, (JK, Ṣ, Ḳ,) and ▾ شَبَهَانٌ, (Ḳ, TA, but not in the CḲ,) [*A sort of fine brass;*] *a metal resembling gold in its colour,* the *highest in quality of* صُفْر [or *brass*]; (Mṣb;) *yellow* نُحَاس; (Ḳ;) *a sort of* نُحَاس (JK, T, Ṣ, M*) *rendered yellow by the addition of an alloy* (lit. *a medicament*): (T, M,* TA:) so called because resembling gold in its colour: (M, TA:) pl. أَشْبَاهٌ. (Ḳ.) One says كُوزُ شَبَهٍ and ▾ شِبْهٍ [*A mug of* شبه]. (Ṣ.) ═ See also شَبَهَانٌ.

شُبْهَةٌ: see شَبَهٌ, in two places. — [Hence,] *Confusedness,* or *dubiousness:* (Ṣ, Ḳ:) pl. شُبَهٌ (TA) [and شُبُهَاتٌ and شُبَهَاتٌ and شُبْهَاتٌ]: whence the phrase أَصْحَابُ الشُّبُهَاتِ *Those persons who are of dubious characters; those who are objects of suspicion*]. One says, لَيْسَ فِيهِ شُبْهَةٌ [*There is not any confusedness,* or *dubiousness, in respect of it*]: referring to property. (Mṣb voce شَائِبَةٌ, in art. شوب.)

شَبَهَانٌ and ▾ شَبَهٌ, (Ḳ accord. to the TA,) the latter on the authority of IB, (TA, [and mentioned also in the M voce سَيَالٌ on the authority of AA,]) *A certain thorny plant,* (Ḳ accord. to the TA,) *resembling the* سَمُر [or *gum-acacia-tree*], (TA,) *having an elegant red blossom, and grains like the* شَهْدَانَج [or *hemp-seed*], *an antidote for the bite,* or *sting, of venomous reptiles, beneficial for the cough, lithotriptic, and binding to the bowels.* (Ḳ accord. to the TA: but see what here follows.) And ▾ شُبْهَانٌ, (Ḳ accord. to the TA,) or شُبَهَانٌ, (so in a copy of the Ṣ,) or both, (so in copies of the Ḳ,) or ▾ شَبْهَانٌ, or ▾ شُبُهَانٌ, (so in different copies of the Ṣ, [the latter of these two I find in one copy only,]) *A kind of trees, of the* [*kind called*] عِضَاه: (Ṣ, Ḳ:) or the ثُمَام [i. e. *panic grass*]: (Ḳ, TA, but not in the CḲ:) or the نَمَّام [now commonly applied to *wild thyme, thymus serpyllum*], (Ṣ, Ḳ), *one of the sweet-smelling plants,* (Ṣ,) *having an elegant red flower,* &c., as in the next preceding sentence. (So in copies of the Ḳ. [See شُبْهَانٌ.]) ═ See also شَبَهٌ.

شَبْهَانٌ, or شُبْهَانٌ, or شُبُهَانٌ: see the next preceding paragraph.

شُبَاهٌ (Lth, JK, Ḳ) and شَبَاهٌ (CḲ [but not in my MS. copy of the Ḳ nor in the TA]) *A certain grain, like that called* حُرْف (Lth, JK, Ḳ) *in colour,* [see حُرْف and رَشَادٌ,] *which is taken,* i. e. *swallowed, as a medicine.* (Lth, JK.)

شَبِيهٌ: see شِبْهٌ, in four places.

أَشْبَهُ [*More, and most, like*]. أَشْبَهُ مِنَ التَّمْرَةِ بِالتَّمْرَةِ [*More like than the date to the date*] is a prov.: and so أَشْبَهُ مِنَ المَآءِ بِالمَآءِ [*More like than water to water*]. (Meyd.) — [And *More,* or *most, suitable.* One says, هٰذَا أَشْبَهُ بِكَ *This is more suitable to thee.* And هٰذَا الأَشْبَهُ *This is the most suitable.*]

مُشَبَّهٌ: [see its verb: — and] see مُشْتَبِهٌ. — Also, applied to the plant called نَصِىّ, *Becoming yellow.* (TA.)

مُشَبِّهٌ: [see its verb: — and] see مُشْتَبِهٌ.

مَشَابِهُ: see شَبَهٌ, of which it is said to be an anomalous pl.

مُشْتَبِهٌ [part. n. of 8, q. v.]. مُشْتَبِهَاتٌ, (Ṣ,) and ▾ مُشَبِّهَاتٌ, [thus agreeably with an explanation of its verb by IAạr, (see 8, last sentence,)] (JK,) or أُمُورٌ مُشْتَبِهَةٌ, and ▾ مُشَبَّهَةٌ like مُعَظَّمَةٌ, (Ḳ,) *Things,* or *affairs, that are confused* or *dubious* [*by reason of their resembling one another or from any other cause*]: (JK, Ṣ, Ḳ:) [and *uncertain:* (see an ex. of مُشَبَّه in this sense in a verse cited voce سَنَفٌ:)] ▾ مُشْتَبِهًا وَغَيْرَ مُتَشَابِهٍ, in the Ḳur [vi. 99], means *resembling one another so that they become confounded,* or *confused,* or *dubious, and not resembling one another* &c. (TA.)

مُتَشَابِهٌ *Consimilar,* or *conformable, in its several parts:* thus مُتَشَابِهًا means in the Ḳur xxxix. 24. (Jel.) And مُتَشَابِهَاتٌ Things *like,* or *resembling, one another.* (JK, Ṣ.) — See also مُشْتَبِهٌ. — مُتَشَابِهَاتٌ in the Ḳur iii. 5 means Verses that are *equivocal,* or *ambiguous;* i. e. *susceptible of different interpretations:* (Ksh:) or verses *unintelligible;* such as the commencements [of many] of the chapters: (Jel:) or the مُتَشَابِه in the Ḳur is that *of which the meaning is not to be learned from its words;* and this is of two sorts; one is that *of which the meaning is known by referring it to what is termed* مُحْكَم [q. v.]; and the other is that *of which the knowledge of its real meaning is not attainable in any way:* (TA:) or it means what is *not understood without repeated con-*

sideration: (TA in art. فسر:) Ed-Ḍaḥḥák is related to have explained المُحْكَمَاتُ as meaning "what have not been abrogated;" and المُتَشَابِهَاتُ as meaning *what have been abrogated*. (TA in the present art.)

شبو

1. شَبَا, (Ḳ,) [aor. ـُ ,] inf. n. شُبُوٌّ, (TA,) *It was* or *became, high, elevated,* or *lofty*. (Ḳ. [See also 4, first sentence.]) — شَبَتِ الفَرَسُ, (Ḳ,) inf. n. as above, (TA,) *The mare stood upon her hind legs*. (Ḳ.) [It is added in the TA that the vulgar say شَبَّت: but see art. شب, where a similar meaning is assigned to شَبَّ said of a horse.] — شَبَا وَجْهُهُ *His face shone after having become altered*. (Ḳ.) ═ شَبَا النَّارَ, (Ḳ,) inf. n. as above, (TA,) *He kindled the fire*; or *made it to burn, burn up, burn brightly* or *fiercely, blaze,* or *flame*; (Ḳ;) as also ↓ أَشْبَاهَا. (TA.)

4. أَشْبَتِ الشَّجَرَةُ, (Ṣ,) or اشبى الشَّجَرُ, (Ḳ,) inf. n. إِشْبَآءٌ, (TA,) *The tree,* (Ṣ,) or *the trees,* (Ḳ,) *became tall,* (Ṣ, Ḳ, TA,) *and tangled and dense, by reason of luxuriance* (Ḳ, TA) *and sappiness*. (TA.) — اشبى said of a man, *He begat a boy* [*sharp*] *like the point of iron* (كَشَبَا الحَدِيدِ): (Yz, TA:) or *he had a son born to him sharp in intellect*: (Ṣ, Ḳ, TA:) or *he begat generous,* or *noble, children, by whom he had sharp means of attack and defence, like the points of spear-heads*. (Ḥam p. 384.) ═ وَجَدْتُ لَهُ i. q. أَشْبَيْتُ الرَّجُلَ ↓ شَبَاةً [app. meaning *I found the man to have sharpness*]. (Ḥam p. 385.) — And اشباهُ *He exalted him,* syn. رَفَعَهُ, (Ṣ,) and *honoured him*; namely, a man. (Ṣ, Ḳ.) — And *He cast him into a well,* or *into an evil,* or *a hateful, plight*: thus having two contr. meanings. (Ḳ.) ═ اشبى is also *syn. with* دَفَعَ [*He impelled, pushed, thrust,* &c.]. (Ḳ. [But perhaps this is a mistake for رَفَعَ, a syn. of اشبى mentioned before: if not, it may be from شَبَاةٌ signifying the "point" of anything.]) ═ And i. q. أَعْطَى [*He gave*]. (Ḳ. [In this sense, accord. to the TḲ, trans. without a prep.; which I think doubtful.]) — And i. q. أَشْبَلَ, (Ḳ,) meaning أَشْفَقَ [i. e. *He was,* or *became, favourably inclined*; &c.]. (TA. [In this sense, also, both اشبى and اشبل, accord. to the TḲ, are trans. without a prep.; but this I think a mistake with respect to both of these verbs, the latter of which is well known to be trans. only by means of عَلَى.]) ═ [And i. q. أَشْبَهَ.] One says, اشبى زَيْدًا أَوْلَادُهُ, (Ṣ,) or اشبى فُلَانًا وَلَدُهُ, (Ḳ,) *His children resembled such a one,* or, *Zeyd*; syn. أَشْبَهُوهُ. (Ṣ, Ḳ.)

شَبًا: see شَبَاةٌ, in two places. ═ Also The *green substance that overspreads stagnant water*; syn. طُحْلُب. (Ḳ.)

شُبُوٌّ [written in my original شُبُو] i. q. اذى [i. e., app., أَذًى, *A state of annoyance* or *molestation*: or *annoyance, molestation, harm,* or *hurt*: or *a thing that annoys,* &c.]. (TA.)

شَبَاةٌ The *point* (Ṣ, Ḳ) *of the extremity* (Ṣ) of anything: (Ṣ, Ḳ:) pl. ↓ شَبًا [or rather this is a coll. gen. n.] and [the pl. properly so termed is] شَبَوَاتٌ. (Ṣ, Ḳ.*) — And The *sting* of the scorpion; (Ḳ;) [and] so ↓ شَبًا [mentioned above as having a pl. meaning]. (Sh, TA in art. شول; and Ḥam p. 385.) — And The *portion with which one cuts,* of a sword. (Ḥar p. 17.) — And The *two sides of the* أَسَلَة [i. e. *toe,* or *tapering head* or *foremost part,*] of a sandal: pl. as above [app. in all of the senses of the sing.]. (Ḳ.) — [And app. † *Sharpness,* as a quality of a man:] see 4. — Also The *scorpion*: (Fr, TA:) or the *scorpion when just born*: or *a yellow scorpion*: (Ḳ:) so in the M. (TA.) [See also the next paragraph.] — And *A mare raising her head* (عَاطِيَةٌ) *in the bridle*. (Ḳ.) And [*A mare*] *standing upon her hind legs*. (Ḳ.)

شَبْوَةُ *The scorpion*; (A'Obeyd, Ṣ, Ḳ, TA; [in the CḲ, شَبْوَةُ العَقْرَبِ is erroneously put for شَبْوَةُ العَقْرَبُ;]) a proper name thereof; it may be from الشَّبَا signifying its *sting*; (Ḥam p. 385;) determinate; (TA;) imperfectly decl.: (A'Obeyd, Ṣ, TA:) it is said in the Ḳ, "and [the article] ال is prefixed to it;" but this is a mistake: it should be, "and ال is not prefixed to it: (TA:) [but, although a proper name, it has a pl.;] the pl. is شَبَوَاتٌ. (Ṣ.) [See also شَبَاةٌ, which signifies "a scorpion," and of which شَبَوَاتٌ is a pl.] — جَارِيَةٌ شَبْوَةٌ *A girl,* or *young woman, that is bold, much in motion, foul in speech* or *actions*. (TA.)

مُشْبًى [pass. part. n. of 4,] *Honoured* [&c.]. (TA.) ═ See also what next follows.

مُشْبٍ [act. part. n. of 4,] A man *having a son born to him sharp in intellect*; (Th, Ḳ, TA;) and so ↓ مُشْبًى, (Ḳ, TA, [in the CḲ, erroneously, مُشْبِى,]) accord. to IAạr, but disallowed by Th. (TA.) And the former, accord. to IAạr, A man *who begets generous offspring*. (TA.) — And مُشْبِيَةٌ A woman *affectionate, kind,* or *favourably inclined, to her children*. (TA.)

شت

1. شَتَّ, (Ṣ, A, Mgh, Ḳ,) aor. ـِ , (Mṣb,) inf. n. شَتٌّ (Ṣ, Mṣb, Ḳ*) and شَتَاتٌ, (Ṣ, A, Ḳ,*) or the latter is a simple subst., (Mṣb,) and شَتِيتٌ (Ḳ, by implication,) and شُتُوتٌ; (MA;) and ↓ انشتّ, (Ḳ,) and ↓ استشتّ, and ↓ تشتّت; (Ṣ, Ḳ; [but the last, app., has an intensive signification;]) *It* (the state of affairs, Ṣ, or the state of union of a people or party, A, TA) *became dissolved, broken up, discomposed, deranged, disorganized, disordered,* or *unsettled*; syn. تَفَرَّقَ, (Ṣ, A, Mṣb, Ḳ, TA,) or إِنْفَرَقَ; (CḲ;) and of the third and fourth verbs, [or rather of all,] إِنْتَشَرَ. (TA.) And ↓ تشتّتوا *They became separated, disunited, dispersed,* or *scattered*. (A.) ═ See also 2, in two places.

2. شتّت, (Ṣ, Ḳ,) inf. n. تَشْتِيتٌ; (Ṣ;) and ↓ اشتّ; and ↓ شَتَّ, aor. ـُ , [which is anomalous in the case of a trans. verb of this class,] inf. n. شَتٌّ and شَتَاتٌ and شَتِيتٌ; (Ḳ;) [the first and second mentioned in the Ḳ only with reference to God as the agent;] *He dissolved, broke up, discomposed, deranged, disorganized, disordered,* or *unsettled,* syn. فَرَّقَ, (Ṣ, Ḳ,) the state of affairs [&c.], (Ṣ,) and the state of union of a people or party. (TA.) And one says also, اشتّ ↓ بِى قَوْمِى *My people,* or *party, dissolved, broke up,* &c., *my state of affairs*. (Ṣ, TA.) And شَتَّ ↓ بِقَلْبِى كَذَا وَكَذَا *Such and such things discomposed,* or *disorganized,* (فَرَّقَ, [which may also be rendered *frightened,*]) *my mind,* or *heart*. (Aṣ, TA.) And شَتَّتَهُمُ اللّٰهُ *God separated, disunited, dispersed,* or *scattered, them*. (A.)

4: see 2, in two places. ═ [أَشَتَّ عَلَيْكَ *It* (a thing) *was,* or *became, distinct,* or *clear, to thee*. (Freytag, from the Deewán of the Hudhalees.)]

5: see 1, in two places.

7 and 10: see 1.

شَتٌّ an inf. n. of 1 [q. v.] (Ṣ, Mṣb, Ḳ.) — And signifying *Separation, disunion,* or *dispersion*: so in the saying, الحَمْدُ لِلّٰهِ الَّذِى جَمَعَنَا مِنْ شَتٍّ [*Praise be to God who has brought us together from* a state of *separation, disunion,* or *dispersion*]: (TA:) a saying mentioned by AA, as heard by him from an Arab of the desert: (Ṣ, TA:) and ↓ شَتَاتٌ is [similar in meaning, being] likewise an inf. n. of 1; (Ṣ, A, Ḳ;) or it is a subst. from the intrans. verb شَتَّ, (Mṣb,) and signifies *a state of separation* or *disunion*; as in the saying, أَخَافُ عَلَيْكُمُ الشَّتَاتَ [*I fear for you separation,* or *disunion*]. (TA.) ═ Also i. q. مُتَفَرِّقٌ [meaning *Dissolved, broken up, discomposed, deranged, disorganized, disordered,* or *unsettled*; and *separated, disunited, dispersed,* or *scattered*]; as also ↓ شَتِيتٌ, (Ṣ, A, Mṣb,) [and ↓ شَتَاتٌ, as will be shown in what follows;] or ↓ شَتِيتٌ is syn. with مُفَرَّقٌ, [which is virtually the same as مُتَفَرِّقٌ,] and مُشَتَّتٌ: (Ḳ:) the pl. of شَتٌّ is أَشْتَاتٌ (Ṣ) [and شُتُوتٌ also, as will be shown by an ex. in what follows]: and ↓ شَتَّى is pl. of ↓ شَتِيتٌ, like as مَرْضَى is of مَرِيضٌ; (Jel in xx. 55, and MF;) or, accord. to some, it is a sing. noun. (MF.) One says أَمْرٌ شَتٌّ i. e. مُتَفَرِّقٌ [*A state of affairs dissolved, broken up,* &c.]; (Ṣ;) and [so] ↓ أَمْرٌ شَتَاتٌ, the latter word being an inf. n. used as an epithet. (Ḥam p. 176.) And ↓ صَارَ جَمْعُهُمْ شَتِيتًا i. e. مُتَفَرِّقًا [*Their company,* or *congregated body, became separated, disunited, dispersed,* or *scattered*]. (A.) And جَاؤُوا أَشْتَاتًا *They came separated, disunited, dispersed,* or *scattered*; syn. مُتَفَرِّقِينَ: (Ṣ, Mṣb, Ḳ:) and so ↓ جَاؤُوا شَتَاتَ شَتَاتَ, (Ḳ,) in one copy of the Ḳ شَتَاتَ وَشَتَاتَ; and MF allows ↓ شُتَاتَ, like ثُلَاثَ and رُبَاعَ; but there is no apparent reason for the repetition; and accord. to the L, the phrase as transmitted from the authorities worthy of confidence is جَآءَ القَوْمُ شَتَاتًا ↓ and شَتَاتَ i. e. *The people,* or *party, came separated,* &c. (TA.) And ↓ قَوْمٌ شَتَّى (Ṣ, Mṣb, Ḳ, TA) *A people,* or *party, separated,* &c.; syn. مُتَفَرِّقُونَ: (Mṣb, TA:) or *consisting of sundry,* or *distinct, bodies*; *not of one* tribe. (Ḳ.) And إِنَّ المَجْلِسَ لَيَجْمَعُ شُتُوتًا مِنَ النَّاسِ, (Ṣ, TA,) and شَتَّى ▼ مِنَ النَّاسِ, *Verily the assembly comprises sundry*, or *distinct, bodies of men*; (TA;) or *men not of one tribe.* (Ṣ, TA.) And أَشْيَآءُ شَتَّى ▼ [*Things of sundry*, or *different*, or *distinct, kinds* or *sorts*]. (Ṣ.) أَزْوَاجًا مِنْ نَبَاتٍ ▼ شَتَّى, in the Ḳur xx. 55, means *Sorts, of plants, various*, or *different*, in colours, tastes, &c. (Jel.) شَتَّى ▼ تَؤُوبُ: see expl. voce أَمَّ. And أُمَّهَاتُهُمْ شَتَّى ▼ الحَلَبَةُ حَالِبٌ, a prov., see expl. voce حَالِبٌ.

شَتَاتٌ and شَتَاتٌ and شَتَاتًا: see شَتٌّ, in five places.

شُتَاتٌ: see شَتٌّ.

شَتِيتٌ: see شَتٌّ, in four places. ثَغْرٌ شَتِيتٌ means [*Fore teeth*] *separate*, or *wide-apart, one from another.* (Ṣ, A, Ḳ.) Ṭarafeh says,

• مِنْ شَتِيتٍ كَأَقَاحِ الرَّمْلِ غُرّ •

[meaning *From separate* fore teeth *like white chamomiles of the sands*: ثَغْرٍ being understood, and غُرّ being for غُرٍّ]. (TA.)

شَتَّى: see شَتٌّ, in seven places:—and see also the last sentence of the following paragraph.

شَتَّانَ بَيْنُهُمَا, (Ḳ, TA, but omitted in the CḲ,) with ḍamm to the ن of بين, (TA,) [*Different*, or *distinct, are they two*: or *widely different* or *distinct are they two*: or *how very*, or *widely, different* or *distinct, are they two!* lit., *the union of them two is severed*: or *the interval between them two is far-extending*, or *wide*: or *how greatly is the union of them two severed!* as will be shown below.] AZ quotes, in his "Nawádir," with بين in the nom. case, the following verse:

• شَتَّانَ بَيْنُهُمَا فِي كُلِّ مَنْزِلَةٍ •
• هٰذَا يَخَافُ وَهٰذَا يَرْتَجِي أَبَدَا •

[*Different*, or *widely different*, &c., *are they two in every predicament: this fears, and this hopes, ever*]. (TA.) The manṣoob form, however, is also employed (Ḳ, TA, but omitted in the CḲ) by some of the Arabs in the above-mentioned phrase, so that one says, شَتَّانَ بَيْنَهُمَا, مَا being understood, as though one said, شَتَّ الَّذِي بَيْنَهُمَا [meaning, as above explained, *Different*, or *widely different*, &c., *are they two*: lit., *separated*, or *disunited*, or *severed, is that which is between them two*: or *far-extending*, or *wide, is the interval between them two*: or *how greatly separated*, or *severed, is the union between them two!*]: Ḥassán Ibn-Thábit says,

• وَشَتَّانَ بَيْنَكُمَا فِي النَّدَى •
• وَفِي البَأْسِ وَالخُبْرِ وَالمَنْظَرِ •

[*And different*, or *widely different*, &c., *are ye two in munificence and in valour and internal state and external appearance*]. (TA.) In like manner also, [but with ما,] one says, شَتَّانَ مَا بَيْنَهُمَا, (A, Mṣb, Ḳ,) accord. to Th. (TA.) This [as also, consequently, the same phrase without ما] is disallowed by Aṣ and IḲt: IB, however, says that this phrase occurs in the verses of chaste Arabs: for instance, Abu-l-Aswad Ed-Duälee says,

• وَشَتَّانَ مَا بَيْنِي وَبَيْنَكَ إِنَّنِي •
• عَلَى كُلِّ حَالٍ أَسْتَقِيمُ وَتَظْلَعُ •

[*And different*, or *widely different*, &c., *are I and thou: for I, in every case, go erect, and thou haltest*]: and similar is the saying of El-Ba'eeth,

• وَشَتَّانَ مَا بَيْنِي وَبَيْنَ ابْنِ خَالِدٍ •
• أُمَيَّةَ فِي الرِّزْقِ الَّذِي يَتَقَسَّمُ •

[*And different*, or *widely different*, &c., *are I and Ibn-Khálid Umeiyeh, with respect to the supplies for the wants of life that are divided among mankind*]. (TA.) One says also, شَتَّانَ هُمَا; (Ṣ, A, Ḳ;) and شَتَّانَ مَا عَمْرٌو وَأَخُوهُ; (Ṣ, Ḳ;) *Different*, or *distinct*, or *widely different*, &c., *are they two*; and *'Amr and his brother*: [lit., *separate*, or *distinct, are they two*; &c.: or *remote are they two, one from the other*; &c.:] or *how greatly*, or *widely, are they two separated*; &c.! (Ṣ, A, Ḳ:) here ما is redundant; and in the former phrase, هما is the agent of شتان; as is the former of the two nouns, to which the latter noun is conjoined, in the latter phrase. (TA.) El-Aạshà says,

• شَتَّانَ مَا يَوْمِي عَلَى كُورِهَا •
• وَيَوْمُ حَيَّانَ أَخِي جَابِرِ •

[*Different*, or *widely different*, &c., *are* (or *were*) *my day upon her* (the camel's) *saddle, and the day of Ḥeiyán the brother of Jábir*: in which, for يَوْمِي and يَوْمُ, some read نَوْمِي and نَوْمُ]. (Ṣ, TA.) And in like manner, [but without ما,] one says, شَتَّانَ أَخُوهُ وَأَبُوهُ [*Different*, or *widely different*, &c., *are his brother and his father*]. (TA.) [See also an ex. in a verse cited voce دَائِمٌ, in art. دوم.]— شَتَّانَ, is a preterite verbal noun, signifying افْتَرَقَ, [and so expl. above,] accord. to many authorities, [including most of the grammarians,] and therefore they have made it a condition that its agent must be what denotes more than one: [for اشترطوا فى فعله التردّد, I read اشترطوا فى فاعله التعدّد, which agrees with what is afterwards said in the TA and here; though the former phrase may be so rendered as to convey essentially the same meaning: but this condition is not necessary if we render شتان by بَعُدَ:] (TA:) or it signifies افْتَرَقَ and تَبَاعَدَ; (Ibn-Umm-Ḳásim;) or بَعُدَ; [and so expl. above;] (Ṣ, A, Mṣb, Ḳ;) and is inflected from شَتُتَ; (Ṣ, Ḳ;) [which is a verb not used; in the CḲ, incorrectly, شَتَتَ;] the fet-ḥah of the ن being the fet-ḥah originally pertaining to the [final] ت [of the verb]; and this fet-ḥah shows the word to be inflected from the preterite verb, like as سَرْعَانَ is from سَرُعَ, and وَشْكَانَ from وَشُكَ: (Ṣ:) or, accord. to Er-Raḍee, it implies wonder, [like several verbs of the measure فَعُلَ, as shown in remarks on هَيُؤَ &c.,] and means *how greatly separated, disunited*, or *severed*, &c.! (TA:) or, accord. to El-Marzooḳee and Hr and Zj and some others, it is an inf. n.: El-Marzooḳee says, in his Expos. of the Fṣ, that it is an inf. n. of a verb not used, [namely شَتُتَ,] and is indecl., with fet-ḥah for its termination, because it is put in the place of a pret. verb, being equivalent to شَتَّ, [for شَتُتَ,] i. e., تَشَتَّتَ أَوْ تَفَرَّقَ جِدًّا [as expl. above]: and Zj says that it is an inf. n. occupying the place of a verb, of the measure فَعْلَان, and therefore indecl., because differing thus from others of its class: Aboo-'Othmán El-Mázinee says that شَتَّان and سُبْحَان may receive tenween, whether they be substs, or occupying the place of substs.: upon which AAF observes that if شتان be in its proper place, it is a verbal noun, meaning شَتَّ: if with tenween, it is indeterminate; if without tenween, determinate; and if translated from its office of a verbal noun, and made a subst. answering to التَّشْتِيتُ, and determinate, it is similar to سبحان in the phrase سُبْحَانَ مِنْ عَلْقَمَةَ الفَاخِرِ, which is a subst. answering to التَّنْزِيهُ. (TA.) The ن in شَتَّان (sometimes, TA) receives kesreh; (Ḳ;) though this is contr. to what is said by AZ and by IDrst: its being sometimes with kesreh is mentioned by Th, on the authority of Fr: and Er-Raḍee seems to infer that its being so was an opinion of Aṣ; and gives two reasons for his disallowal of the expression شتان ما بين; first, because شتان occurs with kesr to the ن; and second, because its agent cannot be otherwise than what denotes more than one: [but see what has been observed above on this point:] IAmb says that one must not say شَتَّانِ مَا بَيْنَ أَخِيكَ وَأَبِيكَ, because, in this case, شتان [virtually] governs only one noun in the nom. case: but that one may say, شَتَّانِ مَا أَخُوكَ وَأَبُوكَ, and شَتَّانِ أَخُوكَ وَأَبُوكَ, using شَتَّانِ as the dual of شَتٌّ; though correctly شتان is a verbal noun: MF, however, observes that the Expositors of the Fṣ seem to say that Fr makes شَتَّانِ to be the dual of شَتٌّ; but that he only mentions it as a dial. var. of شَتَّانَ: the following is adduced as an ex.

• لَشَتَّانِ مَا أَنْوِي وَيَنْوِي بَنُو أَبِي •

[*Different*, or *widely different*, &c., *are that which I intend and that which the sons of my father intend*]: in which شتان is read with both fet-ḥah and kesreh: and it is said in the O that شَتَّانِ is a dial. var. of شَتَّانَ. (TA.)—IJ mentions شَتَّى ▼ as an accidental syn. of شَتَّان; and says that it is not the fem. of the latter: therefore the assertion of some, that it is used by poetical license in the following verse of Jemeel requires consideration:

• أُرِيدُ صِلَاحَهَا وَتُرِيدُ قَتْلِي •
• وَشَتَّى بَيْنَ قَتْلِي وَالصَّلَاحِ •

[*I desire to make peace with her, but she desires to slay me: and different*, or *widely different*, &c., *are slaying me and making peace*]. (TA.)

شتر

1. شَتَرَ, aor. ـِ, (Ṣ, Mṣb, Ḳ, &c.,) inf. n. شَتْرٌ; (T, Ṣ, A, Mṣb, Ḳ, &c.;) and شَتَرٌ; (Ṣ, Ḳ;) *He* (a

man) *had an inversion in the eyelid;* (T, Ṣ;) *seldom natural:* (T:) or *an inversion of,* (A,) or *in,* (Mṣb,) *the lower eyelid:* (A, Mgh, Mṣb:) or *an inversion of the eyelid above and below,* (M, Ḳ,) or *above or below,* (Mgh,) *and a contraction thereof:* (M:) or *a cracking thereof,* (Ḳ,) *so that the edge* [for العتار, in the TA, I read العِتار,] *became separate:* (Mgh, TA:) or *a flaccidity of its lower part.* (Ḳ.) — And شَتِرَتِ العَيْنُ, and شُتِرَت, (Ḳ,) and ▾ انشترت, (Ṣ, Ḳ,) *The eye had an inversion in the lid:* (Ṣ:) [or *in,* or *of, the lower lid:*] or *an inversion of the lid above and below,* (Ḳ,) *and a contraction thereof:* (TA:) or *a cracking thereof,* (Ḳ,) *so that the edge became separate:* (TA:) or *a flaccidity of its lower part.* (Ḳ.) — And شَتِرَ, (TḲ,) inf. n. شَتَرٌ, (Ḳ,) *He* (a man) *had his lower lip cracked.* (Ḳ,* TA.) = شَتَرَهُ, and ▾ اشترهُ, (Ṣ,) or the latter but not the former, (Sh, TA,) *He caused him to have an inversion in the eyelid.* (Ṣ.) — And شَتَرَ العَيْنَ, (Ḳ,) aor. ـِ, inf. n. شَتْرٌ; (TA;) and ▾ اشترها; and ▾ شتّرها; (Ḳ;) *He caused the eye to have an inversion of the lid above and below,* (Ḳ,) *and a contraction thereof:* (TA:) or *a cracking thereof,* (Ḳ,) *so that the edge became separate:* (TA:) or *a flaccidity of its lower part.* (Ḳ.) — شَتْرٌ also signifies The *cutting off of the lower eyelid:* for which a quarter of the whole price of blood must be paid. (TA.) = شَتَرَ بِهِ *He reviled him;* (Ḳ;) *found fault with him; blamed him;* or *censured him; in verse or in prose:* (TA:) and ▾ شتّر به, inf. n. تَشْتِيرٌ, *he detracted from his reputation; found fault with him; blamed him;* or *censured him;* (Ṣ, TA;) *made him to hear what was bad, evil, abominable,* or *foul:* (TA:) Sh says that it is شتر, and he disallows ▾ شتّر: but IAạr and AA say شتّر; and AM holds this to be correct. (TA.) [See also شذّر به.]

2: see 1, in three places.

4: see 1, in two places.

7: see 1, second sentence.

أَشْتَرُ A man *having the affection of the eyelid described above, voce* شَتَرَ: (Ṣ, A, Mgh, Mṣb:) or *having the eyelid slit:* (IAạr, TA in art. شرم:) fem. شَتْرَآءُ. (Mṣb.) — A man *having his lower lip cracked:* and شَفَةٌ شَتْرَآءُ *a cracked lip.* (TA.)

شتم

1. شَتَمَهُ, (MA, Mṣb, Ḳ,) aor. ـِ (Mṣb, Ḳ) and ـُ, (Ḳ,) inf. n. شَتْمٌ (Ṣ, MA, Mṣb, Ḳ) and مَشْتِمَةٌ and مَشْتَمَةٌ, (Ḳ, TA,) the last of these [written مَشْتُمَة in the CḲ] with ḍamm to the ت, or this and the next before it, though said to be inf. ns., may be simple substantives, as A'Obeyd inclines to think them, (TA,) *He reviled him, vilified him, upbraided him, reproached him, defamed him,* or *gave a bad name to him;* (Ṣ,* MA, Ḳ, TA;) syn. سَبَّهُ: (Ḳ, TA:) or, as some say, شَتْمٌ signifies [the *addressing with*] *foul speech, without* قَذْف [here meaning the *casting an accusation,* though commonly used and expl. as syn. with شَتْم]: (TA:) and ▾ شاتمهُ signifies the same as شَتَمَهُ, (MA, Mṣb,) being a rare instance of a verb of the measure فَاعَلَ denoting an act of a single agent when it has an unaugmented verb of the same radical letters [and the same signification], as صَادَمَهُ الحِمَارُ meaning صَدَمَهُ, and زَاحَمَهُ meaning زَحَمَهُ. (Mṣb.) Hence the saying, فَإِنْ شُتِمَ فَلْيَقُلْ إِنِّى صَائِمٌ [*And if he be reviled, let him say, Verily I am fasting*], which may mean that he should say this with his tongue, which is the more proper meaning, or mentally: or ▾ فَإِنْ شُوتِمَ, which is allowable, though the former is the more proper. (Mṣb.) — شاتمهُ فَشَتَمَهُ: see 3. = شَتُمَ, aor. ـُ, (Ṣ, Ḳ,) inf. n. شَتَامَةٌ (Ṣ, IB) and شُتْمٌ, (IB, TA,) † *He* (a man, Ṣ) *was,* or *became, displeasing,* or *hateful, in countenance.* (Ṣ, Ḳ.) = [شَتِمَ, trans. by means of بِ, expl. by Golius as meaning *He rejoiced at evils,* or *misfortunes,* of an enemy, is, I doubt not, a mistake for شَمِتَ; though it might be supposed to be formed by transposition, like جَبَذَ from جَذَبَ.]

[**2.** شتّم, accord. to Reiske, said of a camel when haltered, and of a lion, as mentioned by Freytag, signifies † *He was harsh, and surly, in countenance, and uttered a grumbling sound:* if used, it must be شَتُمَ, agreeably with the part. n., expl. below.]

3. مُشَاتَمَةٌ is *syn. with* مُسَابَّةٌ, (Ṣ,) signifying The *reviling, vilifying, upbraiding, reproaching, defaming,* or *giving a bad name to, each other:* (KL:) and [in like manner] ▾ تَشَاتُمٌ is *syn. with* تَسَابٌّ, (Ṣ,) signifying as above [but used in relation to two persons and more than two]: (KL:) you say, شَاتَمَا and ▾ تَشَاتَمَا meaning تَسَابَّا [*They reviled, vilified,* &c., *each other*]: (Ḳ:) and ▾ تشاتموا *They reviled,* &c., *one another;* like تَسَابُّوا. (MA.) [شاتمهُ may therefore be rendered *He reviled him,* &c., *being reviled,* &c., *by him:* but sometimes it is syn. with شَتَمَهُ:] see 1, in two places. — One says also, ▾ شَاتَمَهُ فَشَتَمَهُ, aor. ـُ, meaning [*He vied,* or *contended, with him in reviling, vilifying,* &c.,] *and he overcame him* [*therein,* i. e.] *in reviling,* &c. (TA.)

[**5.** تشتّم is said by Freytag to signify *He exposed himself to contumelies;* on the authority of the Ḥam p. 310: but I there find only the part. n., مُتَشَتِّمٌ, signifying as expl. below: so that the verb, if used, means *he became exasperated by reviling, vilifying,* &c., *and addressed,* or *applied, himself thereto.* — He also explains it as signifying † *He contracted the face very austerely;* on the authority of the Deewán of the Hudhalees.]

6: see 3, in three places.

شِتَامٌ: see the next paragraph.

شَتِيمٌ: see مَشْتُومٌ. — Also † *Displeasing,* or *hateful, in countenance;* (Ṣ, Ḳ;) applied to a man, and to a lion; (Ṣ;) and to an ass, as meaning thus, *and foul,* or *ugly:* (TA:) or to a lion as meaning ‡ *grim-faced;* or *stern, austere,* or *morose, in countenance;* as also ▾ مُشَتَّمٌ; and ▾ شُتَامَةٌ; (Ḳ, TA;) the last like جُبَانَةٌ [in measure, but in the CḲ written شَتَامَة]. (TA.) One says, فُلَانٌ شَتِيمُ المُحَيَّا † *Such a one is displeasing,* or *hateful, in countenance.* (Ṣ.) = Also, and ▾ شِتَامٌ, *An obstruction* (سُدَّة) *of the fauces, combined with foulness,* or *ugliness, of face.* (TA.)

شَتِيمَةٌ a subst., (Ṣ, Mṣb, Ḳ, and Ksh in lxxiv. 41, [by Bḍ, in explaining the same passage of the Ḳur, improperly said to be an inf. n.,]) from شَتَمَهُ, (Mṣb, Ḳ,) in the sense of شَتْمٌ [meaning The *act of reviling, vilifying,* or *upbraiding; reproach, obloquy,* or *contumely*]; (Ṣ,* and Ksh ubi suprà;) as also ▾ مَشْتِمَةٌ, and ▾ مَشْتَمَةٌ, or, as mentioned above, [see 1, first sentence,] these two are inf. ns. (TA.)

شَتَّامٌ [One *who reviles,* &c., *much*]. (Ḥam p. 310.)

شَتَّامَةٌ One *who reviles,* &c., [*very*] *much.* (TA.) — See also شَتِيمٌ.

[شَاتِمٌ act. part. n. of 1, *Reviling,* &c. — It is also said by Golius, on the authority of the Mirḳát el-Loghah, to signify *Rejoicing at another's evils,* or *misfortunes:* but this I believe to be a mistake for شَامِتٌ: see 1, last sentence.]

الاشتيام, with kesr, [which seems to indicate that it is الإِشْتِيَامُ,] is expl. by IB as meaning رئيس الركاب [app. رَئِيسُ الرُّكَّابِ *The headman,* or *master, of the riders:* but whence this is derived I know not, unless it be arabicized, from the Pers. أُشْتَا يَامْ (if there be such an appellation), meaning "the master of the post-horse"]. (TA.)

مَشْتِمَةٌ and مَشْتَمَةٌ: see شَتِيمَةٌ.

مُشَتَّمٌ: see شَتِيمٌ; and see also مُتَشَتِّمٌ.

مَشْتُومٌ *Reviled, vilified, upbraided, reproached, defamed,* or *called by a bad name:* and so with ة applied to a female, as also ▾ شَتِيمٌ; (Ḳ, TA;) this last, without ة, mentioned on the authority of Lḥ. (TA.)

مُتَشَتِّمٌ *Exasperated by reviling,* &c., *and addressing,* or *applying, himself thereto.* (Ḥam p. 310: there expl. by the words متحكك بالشتم ومعترض له [i. e. مُتَحَكِّكٌ بِالشَّتْمِ وَمُعْتَرِضٌ لَهُ: see 5].)

شتو

1. شَتَا الشِّتَآءُ, aor. يَشْتُو, inf. n. شتو [app. شُتُوٌّ], *The winter commenced:* like as one says, رَبَعَ الرَّبِيعُ, inf. n. رُبُوعٌ]. (TA.) — And شَتَا اليَوْمُ, aor. as above, *The day was,* or *became, intensely cold.* (Mṣb.) — And شَتَا بِهِ, (Ḳ,) and شَتَوْتُ بِهِ, (Ṣ,) and شَتَوْنَا بِهِ, aor. as above, inf. n. شَتْوٌ, (Mṣb,) *He,* and *I,* and *we, remained, stayed, dwelt,* or *abode,* (Ṣ, Mṣb, Ḳ,) *during the* شِتَآء [or *winter,* &c.], (Ṣ,) or *during a* شِتَآء, (Mṣb, Ḳ,) *in it,* (Ṣ, Mṣb, Ḳ,) namely, a place, (Ṣ, Mṣb,) or a country or town; (Ḳ;) as also ▾ شَتَّى, (Ḳ,) inf. n. تَشْتِيَةٌ; (TA;) and ▾ تَشَتَّى, (Ṣ, Ḳ,) said by AZ to be from الشِّتَآء, like تَصَيَّفَ from الصَّيْف: (TA:) [and all are also app. trans. in this sense without a prep.:] or, as some say, شَتَا الشِّتَآءَ means *he re-*

mained, stayed, dwelt, or abode, in the صَمَّان [q. v., meaning a particular place and also a particular sort of place,] in the شِتَآء; and ▾ تَشَتَّاهَا, *he pastured* [*his cattle*] *therein in the* شتآء. (TA.) — And شَتَا القَوْمُ, (Ḳ,) aor. as above, (TA,) *The people, or party, experienced drought, or barrenness, or dearth, in the* شتآء; as also ▾ أَشْتَوْا. (Ḳ.) — See also 4. = شَتِىَ, like رَضِىَ [in measure], *He was smitten by the* شتآء. (IḲṭṭ, TA.)

2. شَتَّى, inf. n. تَشْتِيَةٌ: see 1. — One says also, هٰذَا الشَّىْءُ يُشَتِّينِى *This thing will suffice me for my* شتآء [*or winter, &c.*]. (Ṣ.)

3. عَامَلَهُ مُشَاتَاةً (Ṣ, Ḳ) and شِتَآءً (Ḳ) [*He bargained with him for work by, or for, the season called* شتآء]; and in like manner, اسْتَأْجَرَهُ [*He hired him, or took him as a hireling*]: (TA:) from الشِّتَآء [i. e. the subst.]; (Ṣ;) like مُرَابَعَةٌ from الرَّبِيع, &c.: (TA in art. ربع:) شتآء being here in the accus. case as an inf. n., not as an adv. n. [of time]. (TA.)

4. أَشْتَوْا, (Ṣ, Ḳ,) and أَشْتَيْنَا, (Mṣb,) *They, and we, entered the* [*season called*] شتآء; (Ṣ, Mṣb, Ḳ;) and ▾ شَتَوْنَا signifies the same as اشتينا in this sense. (Ḥam p. 117.) — See also 1, near the end.

5: see the first paragraph, in two places.

شَتًا *A rough, or rugged, place.* (Ḳ.) — And *The* صَدْر [i. e. *higher, or upper, part, or front, or fore part,*] *of a valley.* (Az, Ḳ.)

شَتْوَةٌ: see شِتَآء, in three places.

شَتْوِىٌّ and شَتَوِىٌّ, (Ṣ, Mṣb, Ḳ,) like خَرْفِىٌّ and خَرَفِىٌّ, (Ṣ,) [signifying *Of, or relating to, the season called* شتآء,] are rel. ns. of شتآء (Ṣ, Mṣb, Ḳ) regarded as pl. of شَتْوَة: (Mṣb:) or it may be that they formed the rel. n. from شَتْوَة, and discarded that of شِتَآء; as is said in the M: (TA:) or those who regard شتآء as a sing. make its rel. n. to be ▾ شِتَائِىٌّ and ▾ شِتَاوِىٌّ. (Mṣb, TA.) — الشَّتَوِىُّ, (Ṣ, Ḳ,) thus with fet-ḥ to the ش and ت, (Ḳ,) signifies also *The rain of the* [*season called*] شتآء; and so ▾ الشَّتِىُّ; (Ṣ, Ḳ;) the latter occurring in a verse (Ṣ, TA) of En-Nemir Ibn-Towlab. (TA.) [See the latter of the tables inserted voce زَمَنٌ; and see also نَوْءٌ.] — Also *The increase, or offspring,* (نِتَاج,) *of sheep and goats in the* [*season called*] رَبِيع [by which is here meant *the season called* رَبِيعُ الكَلَإِ *and* الرَّبِيعُ الأَوَّلُ, *commencing in January and ending in March*: see the former of the two tables mentioned above]: (Aboo-Naṣr, TA voce صَفَرِىٌّ [q. v.]:) [and in like manner, *of camels*; for] شَتْوِىٌّ and شَتَوِىٌّ and ▾ شَتِىٌّ are applied to the young camel *brought forth by her that is termed* ▾ مُشْتٍ, meaning مُرْبِع [i. e. *that brings forth in the* (*season called*) رَبِيع]. (TA.)

شِتَآءٌ a word of well-known meaning [in the sense in which it is most commonly used, i. e. *Winter*]; (Ṣ;) *one of the quarters* [*of the circle*] *of the seasons*; (Ḳ;) and ▾ شَاتَاةٌ signifies the same; (Ṣgh, Ḳ;) [and so does ▾ شَتِيَّةٌ; (see an ex. voce رِبْعِىٌّ;)] and so does ▾ مَشْتَاةٌ: (Mṣb, TA:) [also *the half-year commencing at the autumnal equinox*:] ISk says, السَّنَةُ is with the Arabs a name for twelve months: then they divided it into two halves, and commenced the سَنَة [or year] at the commencement of the شتآء because this word is masc. and the word صَيْف [meaning in this case the "half-year commencing at the vernal equinox"] is fem.: then they divided the شتآء into two halves; the شتوى being the former; and the ربيع, the latter; [but this is a manifest mistake, probably attributable to a copyist; for, as is well known, the former half is called the ربيع; and the latter, the شتآء or ▾ شَتْوَة;] each consisting of three months; and in like manner the صَيْف and the قَيْظ consist, each, of three months: (TA:) also *one of the six seasons into which the year is divided, each whereof consists of two months*; namely, the *season* [*commencing in November and ending in January,*] *next after that called* الخَرِيف: (Ṣ and Ḳ voce رَبِيع: [see this word; and see, again, the former of the two tables mentioned above:]) accord. to Mbr, (Ṣ,) شتآء is pl. of ▾ شَتْوَةٌ; (Ṣ, Mṣb, Ḳ;) it is said to be so by IF on the authority of Kh, and by some on the authority of Fr or some other: or شتآء and ▾ شَتْوَةٌ signify the same, (Ḳ,) as is said in the M; (TA;) [i. e.] some say that الشِّتَآء is a proper name for the quarter [&c.]: (Mṣb:) the pl. is أَشْتِيَةٌ, (Ṣ, Mṣb, Ḳ,) i. e. pl. of شتآء, (Ṣ, Mṣb,) because أَفْعِلَة, as pl. of فِعَال, is peculiar to a masc. [noun]; (Mṣb;) and شُتِىٌّ also, (Ḳ, TA,) originally أُشْتُوىٌ [a mistake for شُتُوىٌ], written in the Tekmileh شُتِىٌّ, as on the authority of Fr.: (TA:) the pl. of its syn. ▾ مَشْتَاةٌ is مَشَاتٍ. (Mṣb.) — Also, i. e. شتآء, *Hail*, syn. بَرَدٌ, (Ḳ, TA, [in the CḲ بُرْدٌ,]) *that falls from the sky.* (TA.) — And *Drought, or dearth*: (Ḳ, and Ḥam pp. 117 and 150:) this meaning being assigned to the شتآء exclusively of the صَيْف because in it the people keep to the tents, not going forth to seek after herbage. (TA.)

شُتِىٌّ: see شَتْوِىٌّ, in two places.

شَتِيَّةٌ: see شتآء [with which it is syn.].

شِتَائِىٌّ and شِتَاوِىٌّ: see شَتْوِىٌّ.

شَاتٍ *Entering the* شتآء, which, with them, [i. e. the Arabs, and app. in this case,] means [*a season of*] *drought, or dearth.* (Ḥam pp. 149-50.) — يَوْمٌ شَاتٍ *A day intensely cold*: (Mṣb:) or *a day in which is* بَرَد [i. e. *hail* (accord. to the CḲ بُرْد)]; and in like manner غَدَاةٌ شَاتِيَةٌ [*a morning in which is hail*]. (Ḳ, TA.)

شَاتَاةٌ: see its syn. شِتَآء.

مَشْتًى *The place* [*in which one resides, stays, dwells, or abides, during the season*] *of the* شتآء [*or winter, &c.*]; as also ▾ مَشْتَاةٌ: (Ḳ:) pl. مَشَاتٍ. (TA.)

مُشْتٍ: see شَتَوِىٌّ, last sentence. — It is said in a trad., as some relate it, وَالنَّاسُ مُرْمِلُونَ مُشْتُونَ, meaning *The people being in a state of straitness, or dearth, and hunger, and paucity of milk*: but IAth says that the reading commonly known is مُسْنِتُونَ. (TA.)

مَشْتَاةٌ: see شِتَآء, in two places: — and مَشْتًى.

شث

شَثٌّ *A species of tree,* (Aṣ, IDrd, ISd, Mṣb,) *of those that grow upon the mountains,* (Aṣ,) or *a certain plant,* (Ṣ, Ḳ,) *of sweet odour,* (Ṣ, Mṣb, Ḳ,) *but bitter to the taste,* (Ṣ, Mṣb,) *with which one tans,* (Ṣ, Ḳ,) *growing in the mountains of El-Ghowr* (ADḲ, Mṣb) *and Tihámeh and Nejd*; (ADḲ;) *a kind of tree like the dwarf-apple-tree,* (AḤn, Mgh,) *in size,* (AḤn,) *the leaves of which are like those of the* خِلَاف [q. v.], (AḤn, Mgh,) *and are used for tanning therewith,* (Mgh,) *without thorns, and having a small rose-coloured* [*fruit of the kind called*] بَرَمَة, *in which are three or four black grains, resembling the* شُونِيز [q. v.], *which, when scattered, are eaten by the pigeons*: n. un. with ة. (AḤn:) the word occurs in a trad. as the name of a tan: Az says that it is a mistake for شَبّ, though he knew not whether the شَثّ were used for tanning, or not: (TA:) [Mṭr, however, says that] شبّ is a mistake in this case, for it is a species of زَاج, and is a dye, not a tan: (Mgh:) accord. to some, (TA,) the شَثّ is the *wild nut* (جَوْزُ البَرِّ). (Ḳ [in which this last is mentioned as a distinct signification] and TA.) [See also شَبٌّ.] = *The honey-bee.* (AA, Ḳ.) = *A broken portion of the head of a mountain, remaining in a form like the* [*kind of acroterial ornament of a wall called*] شُرْفَة: pl. شِثَاثٌ. (Ḳ.) = Also *Many, or much,* of anything. (TA.)

شج

1. شَجَّهُ, aor. ُ and ِ, (Ṣ, Mṣb, Ḳ,) the former reg., (Mṣb,) [the latter irreg.,] inf. n. شَجٌّ, (Ṣ, Mṣb,) *He broke it,* [*so as to cleave its skin or its flesh,*] namely, another's head: (Ṣ,* Ḳ, TA:) or *he clave his skin of the face or of the head*; or *he clave its skin*, i. e. the skin of the face or of the head: (Mṣb:) originally *he struck it*, namely, the head, *so as to wound it and cleave it* [*in the skin or flesh thereof*]; and then used in relation to other members: (TA:) or شَجَّهُ فِى رَأْسِهِ and فِى وَجْهِهِ [*he wounded him so as to cleave the skin or the flesh in his head and in his face*]. (A.) Accord. to some, [contr. to the authority of the A,] it is from شَجَّتِ السَّفِينَةُ البَحْرَ [expl. below]. (Mṣb.) — [Hence,] it is said in a prov., فُلَانٌ يَشُجُّ بِيَدٍ وَيَأْسُو بِأُخْرَى [*Such a one breaks a head with one hand and cures with another*]; meaning † *such a one corrupts, or mars, one time, and*

rectifies, or repairs, another time. (TA.) And زَيْدٌ يَشُجُّ مَرَّةً وَيَأْسُو مَرَّةً ‡ Zeyd does, or says, wrong one time, and right one time. (A, TA.) — And شَجَّتِ السَّفِينَةُ البَحْرَ ‡ The ship clave the sea: (Ṣ, A, L, Mṣb:) and [in like manner] شَجَّ البَحْرَ ‡ he clave the sea; (Ḳ, TA;) said of a swimmer. (TA.) And شَجَّ المَفَازَةَ ‡ He traversed the desert. (Ṣ, A, Ḳ.) And شَجَّ الأَرْضَ بِرَاحِلَتِهِ † He traversed the land, with his camel that he rode, at a vehement rate. (TA.) — And شَجَّ الشَّرَابَ, (Ḳ, TA,) or شَجَّ الخَمْرَ بِالمَآءِ, aor. ـُ and ـِ, inf. n. شَجٌّ, [as above,] (TA,) ‡ He mixed the beverage, or the wine, (Ḳ, TA,) with water. (TA.) Hence, فَكَأَنْ يَشُجُّ عَلَى مِسْكًا, occurring in a trad., means ‡ And it was as though it mixed with her odour of musk the breath of wind that reached my organ of smell. (TA.)

2. تَشْجِيجٌ [The breaking of another's head much, so as to cleave the skin or the flesh: or the breaking of heads so as to cleave the skin or the flesh. — And hence, perhaps,] † The acting with penetrative energy, vigour, or effectiveness; syn. تَصْمِيمٌ. (O, Ḳ.)

3. بَيْنَهُمْ شِجَاجٌ (A, O, Ḳ) and ▼ تَشَاجٌّ (A, TA) Between them is a mutual breaking of heads. (A, O, Ḳ, TA. [In the CḲ, شُجَاجٌ is erroneously put for شِجَاجٌ.])

6: see what next precedes.

شَجَّةٌ A single act of breaking of one's head [so as to cleave its skin or its flesh]. (TA.) — And A wound by which the head is broken (Ṣ,* A,* L, Mṣb) so as to cleave its skin or its flesh: (L:) and [such] a wound in the face: (A,* Mṣb:) pl. شِجَاجٌ (Ṣ, A, L, Mṣb) and شَجَّاتٌ. (Mṣb.) What are termed شِجَاج are of ten different kinds, (A, L,) distinguished by the following epithets: [1] حَارِصَةٌ, which peels off the [external] skin, but does not bring blood: [2] دَامِيَةٌ, which brings blood: [3] بَاضِعَةٌ, [which cleaves the flesh slightly, and brings blood, but does not make it to flow: (but in art. دمغ, voce دَامِغَةٌ, q. v., what are here mentioned as the second and third are transposed:) 4, مُتَلَاحِمَةٌ,] which cleaves the flesh much: [5] سِمْحَاقٌ, which leaves between it and the bone only a thin skin: these are five شجاج for which there is no retaliation nor any determinate mulct, but respecting which a judge must give his sentence: [6] مُوضِحَةٌ, which reaches to the bone, and for which the mulct is five camels: [7] هَاشِمَةٌ, which breaks the bone, and for which the mulct is ten camels: [8] مُنَقِّلَةٌ, from which bone is removed, from one place to another, and for which the mulct is fifteen camels: [9] مَأْمُومَةٌ, also called آمَّةٌ, which leaves between it and the brain only a thin skin, and for which the mulct is one third of the whole price of blood: [10] دَامِغَةٌ, which reaches the brain, and for which the mulct is also one third of the whole price of blood. (L.)

The شَجَّة of 'Abd-El-Ḥameed, [who was the goodliest man of his age,] the son of 'Abd-Allah the son of 'Omar the son of El-Khaṭṭáb, was the subject of a prov. on account of its beauty [and is said to have increased his goodliness]. (MF.)

شَجِيجٌ The mark, or scar, of a wound by which the forehead has been broken. (Ṣ,* A, Ḳ,* TA.)

شَجْجَى The عَقْعَق [or magpie]; (Ḳ, TA; omitted in the CḲ;) [and] so ▼ شَجَوْجَى. (Ḳ and TA in art. شجو.)

شَجِيجٌ and ▼ مَشْجُوجٌ A head broken [so that its skin or its flesh is cloven]: or a man having his head [so] broken: (Ṣ, TA:) pl. [of the former] شَجَّى: you say قَوْمٌ شَجَّى. (AZ, TA.) — Each is also applied as an epithet to a wooden peg or stake [as meaning † Having its head broken, or mangled, by blows]: and so is ▼ مُشَجَّجٌ, but in an intensive sense. (Ṣ, L.) — And both the first and ▼ last signify ‡ A wooden peg or stake; (A, TA;) each as an epithet in which the quality of a subst. predominates: because its head is separated, or uncompacted, in its component parts [or fibres by its being battered]. (TA.) One says, مَا بِالدَّارِ شَجِيجٌ and ▼ مُشَجَّجٌ ‡ There is not in the house [even] a wooden peg or stake. (A, TA.)

شَجَوْجَى: see شَجْجَى.

سَابِحٌ شَجَّاجٌ ‡ A swimmer that cleaves the water vehemently. (TA.)

أَشَجُّ A man having a mark, or scar, of a wound by which his forehead has been broken. (Ṣ, A, Ḳ.)

مُشَجَّجٌ: see شَجِيجٌ, in three places.

مَشْجُوجٌ: see شَجِيجٌ.

شجب

1. شَجِبَ, aor. ـَ, (Ṣ, A, O, Mṣb, Ḳ,) inf. n. شَجَبٌ; (Ṣ, O, Mṣb, Ḳ;) and شَجَبَ, aor. ـُ, (Ṣ, A, O, Ḳ,) inf. n. شُجُوبٌ; (Ṣ, O, Ḳ;) He perished: (Ṣ, A, O, Mṣb, Ḳ:) or, accord. to AO, he perished in relation to religion or the present worldly state: the former verb said by Ks to be the better: (TA:) or the former, (Ṣ,) or each, (O,) signifies he grieved, or mourned; or was sorrowful, sad, or unhappy. (Ṣ, O.) [See also شَجَبٌ, below.] — And شَجَبَ, aor. ـُ, inf. n. شَجْبٌ and شُجُوبٌ, It (a thing) went, went away, or passed away. (TA.) — And شَجَبَ, aor. ـِ, inf. n. شَجْبٌ, said of a raven (غُرَاب), It uttered the croak that is ominous of separation: (TA:) [or it croaked vehemently: or it (a raven of separation) bemoaned, by its croak, a misfortune: see شَاجِبٌ.] — See also 6. == شَجَبَهُ, (Ṣ, Ḳ,) aor. ـُ, inf. n. شَجْبٌ, (Ṣ,) He (God, Ṣ) destroyed him: (Ṣ, Ḳ:) one says مَا لَهُ شَجَبَهُ اللّٰهُ [What aileth him? May God destroy him!]: thus the verb is trans. as well as intrans. (Ṣ.) — And He grieved him; or caused him to mourn or lament, or to be sorrowful, sad, or unhappy: (Ṣ, Ḳ, TA:) [and so, app., ▼ أَشْجَبَهُ; for] one says, أَشْجَبَهُ الأَمْرُ فَشَجِبَ لَهُ, inf. n. شَجَبٌ, i. e. حَزَنٌ, [which seems to mean The affair grieved him and he grieved at it,] and [in like manner] أَشْجَبَكَ الأَمْرُ فَشَجِبْتَ. (TA,) — And He cast, or shot, at him, namely, a gazelle, (O, Ḳ, TA,) with a spear, (O,) or with an arrow, or some other thing, (TA,) and severed one of his legs, so that he could not move from his place. (O, Ḳ, TA.) — Also He drew, or pulled, him, or it. (O, Ḳ.) One says of a horseman, and of a horse, شَجَبَ اللِّجَامَ and يَشْجُبُهُ, He pulled the bit and bridle, and he pulls it. (O.) And إِنَّكَ لَتَشْجُبُنِي عَنْ حَاجَتِي Verily thou drawest me from the thing that I want. (Aṣ, O.) — And He occupied him, or busied him, or occupied him so as to divert his attention [from a thing]. (ISk, Ṣ, O, Ḳ.) — And شَجَبَهُ بِشِجَابٍ He stopped it with a stopper; syn. سَدَّهُ بِسِدَادٍ. (Ṣ, O, TA.)

4: see the preceding paragraph.

5. تشجّب i. q. تَحَزَّنَ [app. as meaning He expressed pain, grief, or sorrow, or he lamented, or moaned]. (O, Ḳ.)

6. تشاجب It (an affair, Nh, Mṣb, TA) became confused: (Nh, Mṣb, Ḳ, TA:) and (Mṣb, Ḳ, TA) it (a thing, IDrd, TA) became intermixed, or intermingled, one part of it entering into, or within, another; (IDrd, Mṣb, Ḳ, TA;) as also شجب [app. ▼ شَجَبَ], inf. n. شجب [app. شَجْبٌ]. (IDrd, TA.)

شَجْبٌ Want, or a want, syn. حَاجَةٌ: and anxiety: (A, O, Ḳ:) pl. شُجُوبٌ. (TA.) == Also, as an epithet, applied to a skin for water or milk, as though a contraction of شَجِبٌ meaning "perishing," Old, and worn out; (O, TA;*) as also ▼ شَاجِبٌ: (O:) or the latter, so applied, signifies dry. (TA.) — And [as a subst., or an epithet in which the quality of a subst. is predominant,] A skin for water or milk of which half is cut off and the lower part made into a bucket: (O, Ḳ:) pl. شُجُبٌ. (TA.) And A dry skin for water or milk into which pebbles are put and then shaken for the purpose of frightening camels. (L, Ḳ.*) Az says, on the authority of an Arab of the desert, that it signifies An old, worn-out, skin for water or milk, of which, sometimes, the mouth is cut off, and fresh ripe dates are put in it. (TA.) Suh says, in the R, that A water-skin was thus called [app. meaning absolutely]. (MF, TA.) And it is said in a trad. that a man of the Anṣár used to cool water for the Prophet فى اشجابة [app. a mistranscription for فِى أَشْجَابِهِ, meaning in his water-skins, or worn-out water-skins; and cited to show that أَشْجَابٌ is a pl. of شَجْبٌ, like as أَنْهَارٌ is pl. of نَهْرٌ]. (TA.) == Also One of the poles of a tent: (A, Ḳ:) pl. شُجُوبٌ [agreeably with an explanation in the Ṣ]. (TA.) == And [as an epithet,] Long, or tall. (Ḳ.)

شَجَبٌ Grief, or sorrow; and anxiety: (Ḳ, TA:) but the word more commonly known is with ن [i. e. شَجَنٌ]. (TA.) [The pl. is أَشْجَابٌ (like أَشْجَانٌ) occurring in the O. See also شَجِبَ, of which it is the inf. n.: and see شَجْبٌ, first sentence.] —— And *Distress that befalls a man by reason of disease* or *of fight.* (Ḳ,* TA.)

شَجِبٌ and ↓ شَاجِبٌ *Perishing:* (Ṣ, O, Ḳ:) [accord. to an explanation of their verbs by AO, *in relation to religion* or *to the present worldly state:*] or the former, (Ṣ,) or each, (O,) signifies, *grieving,* or *mourning;* or *sorrowful, sad,* or *unhappy.* (Ṣ, O.)

شُجُبٌ *Three pieces of wood* [*set up as a tripod*] *upon which the pastor hangs his bucket* (Ḳ, TA) *and his skin for water or milk.* (TA.) [See also شِجَابٌ (voce مِشْجَبٌ), of which it is said in the TA to be pl.]

شِجَابٌ: see مِشْجَبٌ. —— Also *A stopper;* syn. سِدَادٌ. (Ṣ, O, TA.)

شَجُوبٌ A woman *affected with anxiety, whose heart is given up thereto.* (O, Ḳ.)

شَاجِبٌ: see شَجِبٌ: —— and شَجْبٌ. —— Also A raven (غُرَابٌ) *croaking vehemently,* or *that croaks vehemently:* (Ṣ, O, Ḳ:) a raven *uttering the croak that is ominous of separation:* a raven of separation *that bemoans, by its croak, a misfortune.* (TA.) —— Also *Irrational in talk, and loquacious.* (Ḳ.) It is said in a trad., النَّاسُ ثَلَاثَةٌ شَاجِبٌ وَغَانِمٌ وَسَالِمٌ, i. e. *Men are* [*of*] *three* [*sorts;*] *a speaker of what is bad, or an utterer of foul, or obscene, language, aiding in wrongdoing; and a speaker of what is good, and an enjoiner thereof, and a forbidder of what is disapproved, so that he obtains good fortune; and one who is silent:* or, accord. to A'Obeyd, شَاجِبٌ signifies *perishing,* or *in a state of perdition, and sinning.* (TA.) [Or] the Prophet said, الْمَجَالِسُ ثَلَاثَةٌ فَسَالِمٌ وَغَانِمٌ وَشَاجِبٌ, meaning [*Assemblies are of three sorts;*] *secure from sin; and acquiring recompense; and perishing, or in a state of perdition, and sinning.* (O.)

مِشْجَبٌ *Pieces of wood,* (T, Mṣb, Ḳ,) *bound together* [*at the top*], *upon which clothes are spread,* (T, Mṣb,) or *upon which clothes are put;* as also ↓ شِجَابٌ; (Ḳ;) of which latter the pl. is شُجُبٌ: (TA: [see this last word above:]) *pieces of wood, or sticks, of which the heads are joined together, and the feet parted asunder, upon which clothes are put, and sometimes the water-skins are hung thereon for the purpose of cooling the water:* (Nh, TA:) or *a piece of wood upon which clothes are put:* (Ṣ:) Suh says, in the R, that they used to call the water-skin شَجْبٌ, and they used not to hold it otherwise than suspended, so that مِشْجَبٌ properly signifies the *piece of wood, or stick, to which the water-skin is suspended:* then they amplified the application of this word so as to call thereby the *thing upon which clothes are suspended:* (MF, TA:) the pl. is مَشَاجِبُ. (A.)

شجر

1. شَجْرٌ is an inf. n. of شَجَرَ, and signifies The *being,* or *becoming, intricate, complicated, perplexed, confused,* or *intricately intermixed;* as also ↓ اِشْتِجَارٌ. (TA.) You say, شَجَرَ الأَمْرُ بَيْنَهُمْ, (Mṣb, Ḳ,) aor. ـُ, inf. n. شَجْرٌ (Mṣb, TA) and شُجُورٌ, (Ḳ, TA,) *The affair, or case, was, or became, complicated, intricate, or confused, so as to be a subject of disagreement, or difference, between them;* syn. اِضْطَرَبَ; (Mṣb;) and so شَجَرَ بَيْنَهُمْ [in which الأَمْرُ is understood]; syn. اِخْتَلَفَ: (Ṣ:) *it was, or became, an occasion of contention,* or *dispute,* or *of disagreement,* or *difference, between them.* (Ḳ, TA.) فِيمَا شَجَرَ بَيْنَهُمْ, in the Ḳur iv. 68, means *Respecting that which hath become complicated,* or *intricate,* or *confused,* [*so as to be a subject of disagreement,* or *difference,*] *between them:* and hence the word شَجَرٌ, ["trees," and "shrubs,"] because of the intermixing, or confusion, of the branches: (Bḍ:) or *respecting the disagreement,* or *difference, that has happened between them.* (Zj, Mgh.) And it is said in a trad., إِيَّاكُمْ وَمَا شَجَرَ بَيْنَ أَصْحَابِى *Avoid ye the disagreement,* or *difference, that hath occurred among my companions.* (TA.) ═ شَجَرَهُ, (Ḳ,) aor. ـُ, (TA,) inf. n. شَجْرٌ, *He tied it;* namely, a thing. (Ḳ.) —— شَجَرَهُ بِالرُّمْحِ *He thrust,* or *pierced, him with the spear,* (Ṣ, A, Ḳ, TA,) *so that it stuck fast in him.* (TA.) —— شَجَرَهُ عَنْهُ, (Ṣ, A, Ḳ,) aor. ـُ, (TA,) inf. n. شَجْرٌ, (Ṣ,) *He,* or *it, averted,* or *diverted, him, from it;* (Ṣ, A, Ḳ;) namely, an affair: (Ḳ:) *he removed,* or *put away,* (TṢ, Ḳ,) *him,* (Ḳ,) or *it,* (TṢ,) *from it:* (TṢ, Ḳ:) *he withheld,* or *debarred,* and *repelled, him from it.* (Ḳ.) You say, مَا شَجَرَكَ عَنْهُ *What has averted thee,* or *diverted thee, from it?* (Ṣ, A.) —— شَجَرَ الْبَيْتَ, (Ṣ, Ḳ,) aor. and inf. n. as above, (TA,) *He propped up the* بيت [or *tent*] *with a pole.* (Ṣ, Ḳ, TA. [In some copies of the Ḳ, بِعُودٍ is erroneously put for بِعَمُودٍ.]) In like manner شَجَرْتُهُ is said of anything as meaning *I propped it up with a pole or the like.* (TA.) And شَجَرَ الشَّجَرَةَ, (T, Ḳ, TA,) and النَّبَاتَ, (T, TA,) inf. n. as above, (TA,) *He raised the hanging branches of the tree, or shrub,* (T, Ḳ, TA,) and *of the plant.* (T, TA.) And شَجَرَ الثَّوْبَ *He raised the garment, it having gone down.* (T, TA.) And شَجَرَ, inf. n. as above, is said of anything as meaning *It was raised, upraised, uplifted,* or *elevated.* (TA.) —— شَجَرَ فَاهُ *He opened his mouth* (A, Ḳ,* TA) *with a stick, or a piece of wood,* (A, TA,) *by inserting this into the part of the mouth called its* شَجْر, (TA,) فَأَوْجَرَهُ [*and then put, or poured, medicine, or water, &c., into his mouth*]. (A, TA.) And شَجَرَ الدَّابَّةَ, (TṢ, Ḳ, TA,) aor. and inf. n. as above; or, accord. to one relation of a trad. in which it occurs, ↓ اشْتَجَرَهَا بِلِجَامِهَا; (TA;) *He made the beast to open its mouth by jerking its bridle to curb it.* (TṢ, Ḳ, TA.) —— And شَجَرَ الشَّىْءَ *He threw the thing upon the* مِشْجَر [q. v.], (Ṣ, Ḳ,) i. e. the مِشْجَب. (Ṣ.) ═ شَجِرَ, aor. ـَ, i. q. كَثُرَ جَمْعُهُ [app. meaning *Its aggregate became large in quantity;* or *it became much in the aggregate*]: (TṢ, Ḳ, TA:) but accord. to Aṣ, [it seems to signify *it became collected together, and then scattered,* or *dispersed, by something:* for he says that] ↓ شَجِيرٌ [its reg. part. n.] is applied to anything *collected together, and then scattered,* or *dispersed, by something* (TA.)

2. تَشْجِيرُ النَّخْلِ i. q. تَشْخِيرُهُ, (Ḳ,) *The laying of the racemes of the palm-trees upon the branches, lest they should break:* (Ḳ in art. شخر:) this is done when the fruit is much in quantity, and the racemes are large, and one fears for the heart of the tree, and for the base, or lower part, of the raceme. (TA in the present art.)

3. شاجر المَالُ *The cattle pastured upon* شَجَر [i. e. *trees,* or *shrubs*], (ISk, Ṣ, A, Ḳ,) *having consumed the herbs and leguminous plants.* (ISk, Ṣ, A.*) —— شاجر فُلَانٌ فُلَانًا, (Ḳ,) inf. n. مُشَاجَرَةٌ, (Ṣ,) *Such a one contended, disputed,* or *litigated, with such a one.* (Ṣ,* Ḳ, TA.)

4. اشجرت الأَرْضُ *The land produced* شَجَر [i. e. *trees,* or *shrubs*]. (Ḳ.)

6: see 8, in three places.

7: see 8, in two places, and see 7 in art. سجر.

8. اشتجر *It was, or became, knit,* or *connected, together, one part with another;* as also اِشْتَبَكَ: *it was, or became, commingled, one part amid,* or *within, another;* (TA;) and so ↓ تشاجر: (Ḥam p. 161:) *it was,* or *became, intricate, complicated, perplexed, confused,* or *intricately intermixed.* (TA: see 1, first sentence.) It is said in a trad., relating to conflict and faction (فِتْنَة), يَشْتَجِرُونَ فِيهَا اشْتِجَارَ أَطْبَاقِ الرَّأْسِ *They become knit together therein, like the knitting together of the bones of the head that interjoin, one with another, one entering into another:* or the meaning is, *they disagree,* or *differ, one with another.* (TA.) You say, اشتجروا بِرِمَاحِهِمْ (TA) and ↓ تشاجروا بِهَا (Ṣ, A, Mṣb, TA) *They became knit together,* or *commingled, one with another,* [*in conflict,*] *with their spears:* (TA:) or *they thrust,* or *pierced, one another with their spears.* (Ṣ, A, Mgh, Mṣb, TA.) And اشتجروا (Zj, Ṣ, A, Mṣb, Ḳ) and ↓ تشاجروا (Zj, Ṣ, A, Mgh, Ḳ) *They became commingled,* or *confused,* or *embroiled, disagreeing,* or *differing:* (Zj, TA:) *they contended,* or *disputed, together;* (Ṣ, A, Mgh, Mṣb;) or *disagreed,* or *differed.* (Ṣ,* A,* Mgh, Mṣb,* Ḳ.) —— Also *He preceded, outwent,* or *outstripped;* (Ḳ,* TA;) and so ↓ انشجر. (Ḳ.) —— And, said of sleep, *It withdrew,* or *kept aloof,* from one; (Ḳ,* TA;) as also ↓ انشجر. (Ḳ.) ═ Also (Ṣ, Ḳ) said of a man, (Ṣ,) *He put his hand beneath his* شَجْر, *against the part beneath his chin:* (Ṣ:) or *he put his hand beneath his chin and leaned upon his elbow,* (Ḳ, TA,) *not laying his side upon the bed.* (TA.) —— [And, said of a horse, *He was bridled, reined,* or *curbed:* (Freytag, from the Deewán of the Hudhalees:) or perhaps the verb in this sense is in the passive form:] ═ see 1, last sentence but two.

شَجْرٌ *A discordant,* or *complicated,* or *confused, affair,* or *case.* (O, Ḳ.) ═ Also The *part,* of a رَحْل [or camel's saddle], *that is between the* كَرَّانِ, (Ḳ, TA, [this word erroneously written in the CḲ with ز,]) which are the قَادِمَة and the آخِرَة, (TA in art. شخر,) [i. e. the شَرْخَانِ,] the كَرّ

being what conjoins the ظَلِفَتَانِ [in the fore part of the saddle and in like manner in the hinder part]: the part between the ظَرَّانِ is also called the شَجْر. (TA in the present art. [It is there said that this part is also called the شَرْخ as well as the شَجْر: but this is a mistake.]) — And The *chin*: (Aṣ, O, Ḳ:) or (TA, in the Ḳ "and,") the *place of opening* (مَفْرَج, [as in the Ḳ voce شِين,] in the Ḳ here erroneously written مَخْرَج, the meaning being مَفْتَح,) *of the mouth*: (Ḳ,* TA:) or the *part between the two lower jaws*: (AA, Ṣ, Ḳ:) or the *hinder part of the mouth*: or the *side of the mouth, where the upper and lower lips unite*: or *what has opened of the part where the mouth closes* [when medicine or the like is put into it]; expl. by مَا ٱنْفَتَحَ مِنْ مُنْطَبَقِ الفَمِ: or the *place of meeting of the* لِهْزِمَتَانِ [q. v., a word variously explained]: (Ḳ:) or the *part where the two sides of the lower jaw unite, beneath the hair that grows between the lower lip and the chin*: and, in a horse, the *part between the upper, main, portions of the two sides of the lower jaw*: (TA:) pl. [of pauc.] أَشْجَارٌ and [of mult.] شُجُورٌ and شِجَارٌ. (Ḳ.)

شَجَرٌ (Ṣ, A, Mgh, Mṣb, Ḳ, &c.) and ↓ شِجَرٌ and شِيَرٌ, (Ḳ,) in which last the ج is changed into ى, like as the ى is changed into ج, as in فُقَيْمِجّ, originally فُقَيْمِىّ, or, accord. to IJ, the ى in شِيَرٌ is not changed from ج because it remains ى in the dim., in which, where it so changed, it should be changed back into ج, whereas the dim. of شِيَرَةٌ is said to be شُيَيْرَةٌ and شِيَيْرَةٌ, and because it has kesr instead of fet-ḥ to the ش, [whence it appears that IJ knew not شِجَرٌ,] (TA,) [as coll. gen. ns., *Trees*; and *shrubs*, or *bushes*; which latter are also called, for distinction, دِقُّ الشَّجَرِ; and sometimes applied to *plants* in general; and, as a gen. n., sometimes meaning the *tree*, &c.;] the *kind of plant that has a trunk*, or *stem*: (Ṣ, A, Ḳ:) or the *kind that has a hard trunk*, or *stem*, (Mgh, Mṣb,) *like the* نَخْل *&c.*: (Mṣb:) or *such as produces seed, and does not come to an end in its year*: (Mgh:) or *such as rises*, or *rises high, of itself, whether slender or large, and whether it withstand the winter or lack strength to do so*: (Ḳ:) called شَجَرٌ from شَجَرَ, because of the intermixing, or confusion, of the branches: (Bḍ in iv. 68, and TA:*) n. un. with ة, (Mṣb, Ḳ,) i. e. شَجَرَةٌ (Ṣ, Mgh, Mṣb, TA) and ↓ شِجَرَةٌ and شِيَرَةٌ: (TA:) the pl. [of شَجَرٌ] is أَشْجَارٌ (Ṣ, Mṣb) and [of شَجَرَةٌ] شَجَرَاتٌ (Mṣb, TA) and [of شِيَرَةٌ] شِيَرَاتٌ: (TA:) ↓ شَجْرَآءُ also signifies the same as شَجَرٌ: (Ḳ:) or it is a pl. [or rather a quasi-pl. n.] of شَجَرَةٌ; a pl. [or quasi-pl. n.] of which there are few other instances; قَصْبَآءُ of قَصَبَةٌ, and طَرْفَآءُ of طَرَفَةٌ, and حَلْفَآءُ of حَلَفَةٌ; or, accord. to Aṣ, the sing. [or n. un.] of حَلْفَآءُ is حَلِفَةٌ: and accord. to Sb, شَجْرَآءُ is sing. and pl., and so are قَصْبَآءُ and طَرْفَآءُ and حَلْفَآءُ: (Ṣ:) or شَجْرَآءُ signifies *tangled*, or *luxuriant*, or *abundant and dense*, شَجَر: (A:) or *a collection of* شَجَر. (TA.) — شَجَرَةُ البَقِّ &c.: see in arts. بق &c. — In the saying in a trad., that the شَجَرَة and the صَخْرَة are of, or from, Paradise, by the former is said to be meant *The grape-vine*: or *the tree beneath which allegiance was sworn to the Prophet*; and which, it is said, was a سَمُرَة [or gum-acacia-tree]: (TA:) and by the latter, the صخرة [or rock] of Jerusalem. (TA in art. صخر, q. v.) — By الشَّجَرَةُ الطَّيِّبَةُ, mentioned in the Ḳur in xiv. 29, is said to be meant *The palm-tree*: or *a certain tree in Paradise*: and by الشَّجَرَةُ الخَبِيثَةُ, in the next verse but one, *the colocynth*, and *the* كَشُوث: [see art. خبث:] or each may have a more general application. (Bḍ in xiv. 31.) And الشَّجَرَةُ المَلْعُونَةُ, mentioned in the Ḳur xvii. 62, means *The tree called* الزَّقُّوم: and some explain it as meaning *the Devil*: and *Aboo-Jahl*: and *El-Ḥakam Ibn-Abi-l-'Áṣ*. (Bḍ.) — شَجَرَةٌ also signifies ‡ The *stock*, or *origin*, of a man: (O, TA:) [hence,] one says, هُوَ مِنْ شَجَرَةٍ طَيِّبَةٍ ‡ [*He is of a good stock* or *origin*]; and مِنْ شَجَرَةِ النُّبُوَّةِ ‡ [*of the prophetic stock*, meaning *of the stock of the Prophet*]. (A.) [And † *A genealogical tree; a pedigree*.] — Also, (CḲ,) or ↓ شُجْرَةٌ, (O, and Ḳ accord. to the TA, [but probably thus in the TA only because found to be so in the O,]) † *A small speck*, or *speckle, on the chin of a boy*: (O, Ḳ:) on the authority of IAạr. (TA.) — And one says, مَا أَحْسَنَ شَجَرَةَ ضَرْعِهَا, (so in my copy of the A, and accord. to the CḲ,) or ↓ شُجْرَةَ ضرعها, (O, and so accord. to the text of the Ḳ as given in the TA, [but Z has, in the A, distinguished the phrase as tropical, and hence it seems that he held the former reading to be the right,]) ‡ *How goodly are the shape*, (A,) or *the size*, (O, Ḳ,) *and the appearance, of her udder!* (A, O, Ḳ:) or *the veins and skin and flesh thereof!* referring to a she-camel. (O, Ḳ.)

شَجِرٌ: see 1, last sentence: — and its fem., with ة, see voce شَجِيرٌ.

شِجَرٌ; and its n. un., with ة: see شَجَرٌ.

شُجْرَةٌ: see شَجَرٌ, last two sentences.

شَجْرَآءُ, as a quasi-pl. n.: see شَجَرٌ. — Also fem. of أَشْجَرُ as syn. with شَجِيرٌ.

الحُرُوفُ الشَّجْرِيَّةُ [*The letters of which the* شَجْر *is the place of utterance*; (in the CḲ, الشَّجَرِيَّةُ;)] *the letters* ج *and* ش *and* ض. (Ḳ.)

شِجَارٌ: see مِشْجَرٌ, in two places.

شِجَارٌ: see مِشْجَرٌ, in four places. — Also The *wood of a well*, (Ṣ, Ḳ, KL,) *by means of which the bucket is drawn out therefrom*: (KL:) pl. شُجُرٌ: (Ṣ:) this pl. occurs in a verse, accord. to J; but the right reading in that instance is سُجُل, as is shown by the rhyme of the poem. (Ṣgh, TA.) — Also [*A wooden bar of a door*;] *a piece of wood which is put behind a door*; *called in Pers.* مَتْرَس, (Ṣ, Ḳ, TA,) written by Az مِتْرَس. (TA.) — And *A piece of wood with which a couch-frame* (سَرِير) *is repaired, by its being affixed as a* ضَبَّة [q. v.], (Ṣ, Ḳ,) *beneath it*. (Ṣ.) — And *A piece of wood which is put in the mouth of a kid, to prevent its sucking*. (TṢ, Ḳ.) — And *A certain brand*, or *mark made with a hot iron, upon camels*. (Ṣ, Ḳ.)

وَادٍ شَجِيرٌ, and ↓ أَشْجَرُ, (Ḳ,) or the former, (Ṣ, A,) but not the latter, (Ṣ,) and ↓ مُشْجِرٌ; (Ḳ;) and أَرْضٌ شَجِيرَةٌ, (Ṣ, TA,) and ↓ شَجِرَةٌ, (A, Ḳ,) and ↓ شَجْرَآءُ, (Ṣ, Mṣb, Ḳ,) and ↓ مُشْجِرَةٌ; (AḤn, Ṣ,* Ḳ;) *A valley*, and *a land, abounding with* شَجَر or أَشْجَار [i. e. *trees*, or *shrubs*]. (Ṣ, A, Mṣb, Ḳ.) — شَجِيرٌ also signifies *Strange*, or *a stranger*; applied to a man, (Ṣ, A, Ḳ,) and to a camel. (Ṣ, Ḳ.) — And *An arrow that is used in the game called* المَيْسِر, *thrown among arrows not from its kind of tree*: (Ṣ, Ḳ:) or *one that is borrowed, and from the winning of which* [on former occasions] *one augurs good*. (TA.) — Also *Bad, corrupt*, or *disapproved*. (Kr, Ḳ.) — And *A companion*: (M, Ḳ:) or *a friend*: (A:) pl. شُجَرَآءُ. (M, TA.) — And *A sword*. (Ḳ.)

شِجَارَةٌ: see مِشْجَرٌ.

شَوَاجِرُ [pl. of شَاجِرَةٌ fem. of شَاجِرٌ]: see مُشْتَجِرٌ. — Also *Withholding*, or *debarring*, and *diverting, things*. (TA.) You say, شَجَرَتْنِى عَنْهُ شَوَاجِرُ [*Withholding*, or *debarring*, or *diverting, things withheld*, or *debarred*, or *diverted, me from it*]. (Ṣ.)

أَشْجَرُ; and its fem., شَجْرَآءُ: see شَجِيرٌ. — Also (Ḳ) *Containing more* شَجَر [i. e. *trees*, or *shrubs*]: (Ṣ, Ḳ:) so in the saying, هٰذِهِ الأَرْضُ أَشْجَرُ مِنْ هٰذِهِ [*This land is one containing more trees than this*]. (Ṣ, Ḳ.*) It has no known verb. (TA.)

مَشْجَرٌ (Ṣ, Ḳ, TA) [and] ↓ مَشْجَرَةٌ (Mgh, Mṣb) *A place* (Ṣ, Mgh, Mṣb, Ḳ) *of growth* (Mgh, Ḳ) *of* شَجَر or أَشْجَار [i. e. *trees*, or *shrubs*]: (Ṣ, Mgh, Mṣb, Ḳ:) or, as some say, the former signifies *many* شَجَر. (TA.) — The former also signifies *A place of* مُشَاجَرَة [i. e. *contending, disputing*, or *litigating*]: pl. مَشَاجِرُ: and, some say, it is an inf. n. (Ḥar p. 473.) — See also مِشْجَرٌ, in two places.

أَرْضٌ مُشْجِرَةٌ: see شَجِيرٌ. — You say also مُشْجِرٌ meaning *A land giving growth to* شَجَر [i. e. *trees*, or *shrubs*]. (TA. [See also مَشْجَرٌ.])

مِشْجَرٌ i. q. مِشْجَبٌ [i. e. *A thing composed of pieces of wood*, or *sticks, the heads of which are bound together, and the feet parted asunder, upon which clothes &c. are put*]: (Ṣ:) or *pieces of wood*, or *sticks, tied together, like the* مِشْجَب, *upon which articles of furniture*, or *utensils, are put*: (M, Mṣb:) pl. مَشَاجِرُ. (M, TA.) — And hence, (M,) The *wood*, (Ḳ,) or *pieces of wood*, (M,) *of the* [*kind of camel-vehicle for women called*] هَوْدَج; (M, Ḳ;) as also ↓ مَشْجَرٌ and ↓ شِجَارٌ: (L, Ḳ:) n. un. مَشْجَرَةٌ and ↓ شِجَارَةٌ: (TA:) or *a vehicle used by women, smaller than the* هَوْدَج, *having the head uncovered*; (AA, Ḳ,* TA;) as also ↓ مَشْجَرٌ and ↓ شِجَارٌ and ↓ شِجَارٌ: (Ḳ:) accord. to Lth, ↓ شِجَارٌ signifies the *wood* [or *frame-work*] *of the* هودج, *which when covered becomes a* هودج: (TA:) Aṣ says that مَشَاجِرُ signifies the *pieces of wood of a* هودج: AA, that it signifies *vehicles smaller than* هَوَادِج, *having the heads uncovered; also called* شُجُر, of which the sing. is ▼ شِجَارٌ. (Ṣ.)

مَشْجَرَةٌ: see شَجِيرٌ: — and see also مَشْجَرٌ.

مُشَجَّرٌ Figured work (TA) *having the form of* شَجَر [i. e. *trees,* or *shrubs*]: (Ḳ,* TA:) and silk brocade (دِيبَاج) *figured with the forms of* شَجَر. (Ṣ, Ḳ.)

مُشْتَجَرُ الرِّمَاحِ [*The place of the commingling of spears;* or *of the thrusting,* or *piercing, therewith*]. (Ḥam p. 161.)

مُشْتَجِرٌ and ▼ مُتَشَاجِرٌ *Commingled* [*and confused*]: you say رِمَاحٌ مُشْتَجِرَةٌ and ▼ مُتَشَاجِرَةٌ and ▼ شَوَاجِرُ *Spears commingled and confused.* (TA.)

مُتَشَاجِرٌ: see what next precedes, in two places.

شجع

1. شَجُعَ, aor. ـُ, (Ṣ, Mṣb, Ḳ,) inf. n. شَجَاعَةٌ, (Ṣ, Mṣb,) *He* (a man, Ṣ) *was,* or *became, courageous, brave, valiant, bold, daring,* or *strong-hearted* (Ṣ, Mṣb, Ḳ) *on the occasion of war,* or *fight,* (Ṣ, Ḳ,) *making light of wars, by reason of his boldness.* (Mṣb.) AZ says that شَجَاعَةٌ sometimes denotes a comparative quality in relation to him who is weaker than the person to whom it is ascribed. (Mṣb.) = شَجَعَهُ, aor. ـَ, [which in this case is contr. to the general rule, notwithstanding the guttural letter, for by rule it should be ـُ,] *He overcame him,* or *surpassed him, in* شَجَاعَة [or *courage,* &c.]. (Ḳ.) [See 3.] = شَجِعَ, aor. ـَ, (Mṣb,) inf. n. شَجَعٌ, (IDrd, Mṣb, Ḳ,) *He was,* or *became, tall.* (IDrd, Mṣb, Ḳ.)

2. شجّعهُ, (Ṣ, Ḳ,) inf. n. تَشْجِيعٌ, (Ḳ,) *He encouraged him;* or *strengthened his heart;* (Ṣ, Ḳ;) and *emboldened him:* (Ḳ:) or *he said to him, Thou art* شُجَاع [or *courageous,* &c.]. (Sb, Ṣ, Ḳ.)

3. شَاجَعْتُهُ فَشَجَعْتُهُ [*I strove to overcome* or *surpass him, or contended with him for superiority, in* شَجَاعَة (or *courage,* &c.), *and*] *I overcame him,* or *surpassed him, therein.* (TA.)

4. مَا أَشْجَعَهُ [*How courageous, brave, valiant, bold, daring,* or *strong-hearted, is he, on the occasion of war,* or *fight!*]. (TA in art بسل.)

5. تشجّع *He affected* (تَكَلَّفَ) *courage, bravery, valour, boldness, daringness,* or *strength of heart on the occasion of war,* or *fight;* (Ṣ, Ḳ;) [*he encouraged himself; made himself,* or *constrained himself to be, courageous:*] and *he feigned,* or *pretended to have, courage,* &c., *on the occasion of war,* or *fight, not having it in him.* (TA.)

شَجَعٌ *Penetrating energy; boldness.* (Aṣ.) — *Quickness of the shifting of the legs,* in camels, (Ṣ, Ḳ,) or, accord. to IB, in horses. (TA.)

شَجِعٌ; fem. with ة: see شُجَاعٌ, in three places. — شَجِعُ القَوَائِمِ *Quick in the shifting of the legs,* applied to a he-camel; and so شَجِعَةٌ and ▼ شَجْعَاءُ, applied to a she-camel. (Ṣ, Ḳ.) And قَوَائِمُ شَجِعَاتٌ *Quick, and light, active,* or *nimble, legs.* (TA.) — *Mad,* applied to a camel. (Ibn-'Abbád, Ḳ.)

شُجْعٌ: see شُجَاعٌ.

شُجْعَةٌ: see شُجَاعٌ: = see also شَجْعَةٌ: — also *Tall, and uncompact in frame:* — and *crippled by disease;* or *having a protracted disease:* [whence] it is said in a prov., أَعْمَى يَقُودُ شُجْعَةً [*A blind man leading one crippled by disease,* or *having a protracted disease:* but in Freytag's Arab. Prov. ii. 119, the last word is written شَجَعَةً, and said to be pl. of ▼ شَاجِعٌ, and to signify, app., *suffering paralysis*]. (TA.)

شَجْعَةٌ: see شُجَاعٌ. = Also *Cowardly, weak,* (Ibn-'Abbád,) *lacking strength* or *power* or *ability, lean,* or *emaciated, and small in body, having no heart;* (Ibn-'Abbád, Ḳ;) as also ▼ شُجْعَةٌ: (Lḥ, Ḳ:) the former seems to have the meaning of a pass. part. n., [i. e. of مَشْجُوعٌ, q. v.,] like سُخْرَةٌ and other words. (Ibn-'Abbád.)

شَجَعَةٌ: see شُجَاعٌ.

شَجْعَآءُ [or شَجِعَآءُ or شُجَعَآءُ]: see شُجَاعٌ.

شَجْعَمٌ *A bulky serpent:* or *a malignant and audacious serpent:* regarded by Sb as a quadriliteral-radical word. (TA.) [See also شُجَاعٌ.]

شَجَاعٌ: see what next follows.

شُجَاعٌ and ▼ شِجَاعٌ (Lḥ, ISk, Ṣ, Mṣb, Ḳ) and ▼ شَجَاعٌ, (Mṣb, Ḳ,) which is of the dial. of Benoo-'Okeyl, being made by them to accord with its contr., which is جَبَانٌ, (Mṣb,) and ▼ شَجِيعٌ (Lḥ, Ṣ, Mṣb, Ḳ) and ▼ أَشْجَعُ (Ṣ, Ḳ) and ▼ شَجِعٌ (Ḳ) and ▼ شِجِعٌ, (as in some copies of the Ḳ,) or ▼ شَجْعَةٌ, (as in other copies of the Ḳ and in the TA,) [of all which forms the first is the most common,] *Courageous, brave, valiant, bold, daring,* or *strong-hearted* (Ṣ, Mṣb, Ḳ) *on the occasion of war,* or *fight,* (Ṣ, Ḳ,) *making light of wars, by reason of boldness:* (Mṣb:) fem. [of the 1st and 2nd and 3rd respectively] شُجَاعَةٌ and شِجَاعَةٌ (Ṣ,* Mṣb,* Ḳ) and شَجَاعَةٌ (Mṣb,* Ḳ) and شجاع also [without ة] (Mṣb) and [of the 4th] ▼ شَجِيعَةٌ (Mṣb, Ḳ) and [of the 5th] ▼ شَجْعَآءُ and [of the 6th] ▼ شَجِعَةٌ: (Ḳ:) pl. masc. (of the 1st, Ṣ, Mṣb) شِجْعَةٌ [a pl. of pauc.] (AO, Ṣ, Mṣb, Ḳ) and [of the first three, and perhaps of the 4th also,] شَجَعَةٌ (Ṣ, Ḳ) and (of the 1st, Ṣ) شِجْعَانٌ (Lḥ, Ṣ, Ḳ) and (of the 4th, Ṣ) شُجْعَانٌ (Lḥ, ISk, Ṣ, Ḳ) [or, accord. to IDrd, شجعان is a mistake, as is said in the TA, but the word is there written without any syll. signs,] and (of the 4th, Ṣ, Mṣb) ▼ شُجَعَآءُ (Ṣ, Mṣb, Ḳ) and [of the 4th, and perhaps of others also,] شِجَاعٌ, (Ḳ,) and also, (but these are quasi-pl. ns., TA,) ▼ شَجْعَةٌ (AO, Ṣ, Ḳ) and ▼ شُجْعَةٌ (Ḳ) and ▼ شَجْعَآءُ [app. a mistake for شُجَعَآءُ or شِجْعَآءُ]: (TA:) pl. fem. [all of شَجِيعَةٌ, or the last of شَجْعَآءُ or of شَجِعَةٌ,] شَجَائِعُ and شُجُعٌ and شُجْعٌ: (Lḥ, Ḳ:) or شُجَاعٌ is [an epithet] peculiar to men: (Ḳ,* TA:) AZ says, "I have heard the Kilábees say, رَجُلٌ شُجَاعٌ, but they do not apply this epithet to a woman:" (Ṣ:) ▼ شَجِيعَةٌ and ▼ شَجْعَةٌ, however, are applied to a woman, and signify *bold,* (Ibn-'Abbád, Ḳ,) *long-tongued, and vehemently clamorous, towards men;* (Ibn-'Abbád, TA;) *audacious in her speech,* (Ibn-'Abbád, Ḳ, [but these two epithets as applied to a woman and signifying "bold" &c. are omitted in the CḲ,]) *and in her length of tongue, and vehement clamorousness.* (Ibn-'Abbád, TA.) — شُجَاعٌ (Ṣ, Mṣb, Ḳ) and ▼ شِجَاعٌ (Ḳ) also signify † *The serpent;* (Ḳ;) and so does ▼ أَشْجَعُ: (TA:) or ‡ *the male serpent:* (Mgh, Ḳ:) or *a certain species of serpent,* (Sh, Ṣ, Mṣb, Ḳ,) as also ▼ أَشْجَعُ, (Ṣ,) *small,* (Ḳ,) or *slender, and asserted to be the boldest of the serpent-kind:* (Sh:) pl. شِجْعَانٌ (Lḥ, IDrd, Ḳ) and شُجْعَانٌ, (IDrd, Ḳ,) the former of which is the more common: (IDrd:) the pl. of أَشْجَعُ is أَشَاجِعُ; or, as some say, this is pl. of أَشْجِعَةٌ, which is pl. [of pauc.] of شجاع, signifying the *serpent.* (TA.) [See also شَجْعَمٌ, above.] — Also ‡ *The serpent called* صَفَرٌ, *that presents itself in the belly* (Ṣ, Ḳ,* TA) *of a man,* as the Arabs assert, *when he has been long hungry:* (Ṣ, TA:) but Aṣ says that شُجَاعُ البَطْنِ signifies † *vehemence of hunger.* (Az, TA.)

شِجَاعٌ: see شُجَاعٌ, in two places.

شَجِيعٌ; fem. with ة: see شُجَاعٌ, in three places.

شَاجِعٌ: see شُجْعَةٌ.

أَشْجَعُ; fem. شَجْعَآءُ: see شُجَاعٌ, in four places. You say also, لَبُؤَةٌ شَجْعَآءُ *A bold lioness.* (TA.) — Applied to a man, accord. to some, it signifies, (Ṣ,) or it signifies also, (Ḳ,) *In whom is lightness,* or *unsteadiness, like what is termed* هَوَج, (Ṣ, Ḳ,) *by reason of his strength.* (Ṣ.) See also شَجِعٌ. — *Mad;* or *possessed by a devil:* (TA:) Lth says that, applied to a man, it signifies one *who is as though there were in him madness,* or *diabolical possession;* but Az says that this is a mistake; for, were this its meaning, the poets would not have used it in praise. (TA, in another part of the art.) — *Tall:* (IDrd, Mṣb, Ḳ:) and so the fem. applied to a woman. (IDrd, Mṣb.) — *Bulky; big-bodied;* or *stout:* or, as some say, *youthful;* or *in a state of youthful vigour.* (TA.) — The *lion.* (Lth, Ṣ, Ḳ.) — It is said in the Ḳ that الأَشْجَعُ also signifies الدَّهْرُ [i. e. *Time;* or *fortune;* &c.]; and J says that this is what the poet means by the expression, أَشْجَعُ أَخَّاذٌ: but this cannot be the correct meaning, for the poet, namely El-Aạshà, says,

• بِأَشْجَعَ أَخَّاذٍ عَلَى الدَّهْرِ حُكْمَهُ •

by الاشجع meaning himself, or some other thing. (TA.) = Also, (Ṣ, Ḳ,) and إِشْجَعٌ, (Ḳ,) or the latter accord. to some, but this was not known to Abu-l-Ghowth, (Ṣ,) sing. of أَشَاجِعُ, [in some copies of the Ṣ written أَشَاجِيعُ,] but the former, which, as is mentioned in the TA, is found in the handwriting of J, is that which is commonly known,] which signifies [The *knuckles nearest to the wrist;* this being what is meant by] the *bases* (أُصُول) *of the fingers, which are connected with the tendons of the outer side of the hand:* (Ṣ, Ḳ:) in the T, we find the *heads* (رُؤُوس) *of the fingers,* instead of اصول: (TA:) or اشجع in the hand and foot [but see what follows] signifies the *tendons extended above the* سُلَامَى [here meaning the *metacarpal and metatarsal bones*] *from the wrist to the bases* (أُصُول) *of the fingers* or *toes, which are called* أَطْنَابُ الأَصَابِعِ, *above the outer side of the hand:* or the *bone which connects the finger with the wrist;* [i. e. the *metacarpal bone;*] *every finger having to it a bone thus called:* he who says that the أَشَاجِع [so here instead of اشجع as above] are the tendons calls those bones the أَسْنَاع. (TA.) Aboo-Bekr is described as عَارِى الأَشَاجِعِ عَنْ مَفَاصِلِ الأَصَابِعِ, meaning *Having little flesh upon what are thus termed:* or *having their tendons apparent.* (TA.) [See also رَاجِبَةٌ and بُرْجُمَةٌ.] ═ أَشْجَعُ مِنْ دِيكٍ, [*More courageous than a cock*] is one of the proverbs of the Arabs. (Mgh.)

مُشْجَعٌ, like مُجْمَلٌ, (Ḳ, TA,) i. e. having the form of a pass. part. n., (TA,) [in the CḲ مَشْجَع, like مَجْمَل,] *In the utmost state of madness,* or *diabolical possession:* (Ḳ:) so says Ibn-Abbád; and hence, accord. to him, شُجَاعٌ [but in what sense he does not say]. (TA.)

مَشْجُوعٌ *Overcome,* or *surpassed, in* شَجَاعَة [or *courage,* &c.]. (Ḳ, TA.)

شجن

1. شَجِنَ, (Ṣ, L, Ḳ,) aor. ـَ; (Ḳ;) and شَجُنَ, aor. ـُ; inf. n. [of the former] شَجَنٌ [in some copies of the Ḳ شَجْنٌ] and [of the latter, or of both,] شُجُونٌ; (L, Ḳ;) *He grieved, mourned,* or *lamented;* or *was sorrowful, sad,* or *unhappy;* (Ṣ, L, Ḳ;) and *was anxious:* and ▼ تشجّن signifies the same: (L:) or this last signifies, (Ḳ,) or, as Lth says, it seems to signify, (L,) *he remembered;* syn. تَذَكَّرَ. (L, Ḳ.) And شجنت الحَمَامَةُ, [app. both شَجِنَت and شَجَنَت,] inf. n. شُجُونٌ, *The pigeon cooed in a wailing and plaintive manner.* (L.) [See also شَجْنٌ below.] ═ شَجَنَهُ, (Ṣ, L, Ḳ,) [aor. ـُ, accord. to the usual rule of the Ḳ,] inf. n. شَجْنٌ and شُجُونٌ, (L, Ḳ,) signifies the same as ▼ اشجنهُ, (Ṣ, L, Ḳ,) i. e. *He,* (another person, Ṣ,) or *it,* (an affair, or an event, or a case, L, Ḳ,) *caused him to grieve* or *mourn* or *lament,* or *to be sorrowful* or *sad* or *unhappy.* (Ṣ, L, Ḳ.) ═ شَجَنَتْنِى الحَاجَةُ, (Ṣ, L,) and شَجَنَتْهُ, (L, Ḳ,) aor. ـُ, inf. n. شَجْنٌ, (Ṣ, L,) *Want,* or *the want, detained,* or *withheld,* (Ṣ, L, Ḳ,) *me,* (Ṣ, L,) or *him.* (L, Ḳ.) And مَا شَجَنَكَ عَنَّا *What detained,* or *withheld, thee from us?* (L.)

4. اشجنهُ: see the preceding paragraph. ═ اشجن الكَرْمُ *The grape-vine had a branchlet of a bunch of which all the grapes came to maturity.* (L, Ḳ. [See شِجْنَةٌ.])

5: see 1, first sentence. ═ تَشَجَّنَ الشَّجَرُ *The trees were,* or *became, tangled,* or *luxuriant,* or *abundant and dense.* (L, Ḳ.)

شَجْنٌ (Ṣ, L, Ḳ [in the CḲ شَجَنٌ, but expressly said in the Ṣ to be بِالتَّسْكِينِ]) *A road* of a valley; (Ṣ, L;) or *a road in a valley:* or *in the upper,* or *uppermost, part thereof:* as also ▼ شَاجِنَةٌ: (Ḳ:) pl. of the former شُجُونٌ: (Ṣ, L, Ḳ:) and of ▼ the latter شَوَاجِنُ: (Ḳ:) or ▼ شَاجِنَةٌ signifies *a valley in which are many trees;* (Ṣ, L;) or *a place in which are* شُجُون, which means *tangled trees;* (Ḥam pp. 761-2;) and شَوَاجِنُ is its pl.: (Ṣ, L, and Ḥam p. 762:) or ▼ شَاجِنَةٌ signifies *a sort of valley producing good herbage:* or, as some say, شَوَاجِنُ signifies the *upper,* or *uppermost, parts of a valley;* and its sing. is ▼ شَجَنٌ [thus written in the L in this instance], as ISd mentions on the authority of A'Obeyd, but adding that, as such, it is irregular, and that it is more properly to be regarded as pl. of ▼ شَاجِنَةٌ. (L.) — [Hence,] one says, الحَدِيثُ ذُو شُجُونٍ, (Ṣ, Meyd, L, Ḳ,) شُجُون being pl. of شَجْنٌ, with the ج quiescent; (Meyd;) a prov., (Meyd, L,) meaning † *The story is involved,* or *intricate;* (Ṣ, Meyd, L;) or *has several ways* [*in which it may be understood*]; (Meyd;) or *has several modes,* or *manners; and objects of aim:* (L, Ḳ:) applied to a story by which one calls to mind another: (A'Obeyd, Meyd, L:) the first who said it was Ḍabbeh Ibn-Udd Ibn-Ṭábikhah: he had two sons, named Saad and So'eyd: and some camels belonging to him ran away by night, so he sent his two sons to seek them; and they separated; and Saad found them and restored them; but So'eyd went on seeking them; and El-Ḥárith Ibn-Kaab met him; and there were upon the young man two [garments such as are called] burds (بُرْدَانِ), which El-Ḥárith asked him to give to him, but he refused to comply with his desire; whereupon he slew him, and took his two burds: and Ḍabbeh, when he saw a dark object in the night, used to say, أَسَعْدٌ أَمْ سُعَيْدٌ [“Is it Saad or So'eyd?” (see سَعْدٌ)]; and this saying of his became current as a prov.: some time after this, having gone on pilgrimage, he met El-Ḥárith Ibn-Kaab at 'Okáḍh, and saw upon him the two burds of his son So'eyd, and asked him respecting them; and he answered that he had met a young man wearing them, and slain him, and taken them: Ḍabbeh said, “With this thy sword?” and he answered, “Yes:” and he said, “Give it me that I may look at it, for I think it to be sharp:” and El-Ḥárith gave it him: and he took it, and shook it, and said, إِنَّ الحَدِيثَ ذُو شُجُونٍ; and slew him with it: whereupon it was said to him, “O Ḍabbeh, in the sacred month?” and he said, سَبَقَ السَّيْفُ العَذَلَ [“The sword preceded the censure”]: these three provs. he originated. (Meyd.)

شُجْنَةٌ and شِجْنَةٌ: see the next paragraph.

شَجَنٌ *Grief, mourning, lamentation, sorrow, sadness,* or *unhappiness;* (Ṣ, L, Ḳ;) and *anxiety:* (L, Ḳ:) pl. أَشْجَانٌ (Ṣ, L, Ḳ) and شُجُونٌ; (L, Ḳ; [in the latter of which these pls. are mentioned after all the explanations of the sing.;]) the former a pl. of pauc., and the latter of mult. (Ḥam p. 404.) [See a verse cited voce عَرَضٌ, in which it means *A cause of anxiety.*] — And The *soul's love,* or *its inclination,* or *its blamable inclination:* (L:) [or] *love that is followed by anxiety and grief.* (Kull p. 165.) — And *A want,* (Ṣ, L, Mṣb, Ḳ,) as also ▼ شَجِينٌ, (L,) wherever it be: (Ṣ, L, Ḳ:) pl. شُجُونٌ (Ṣ, L, Mṣb, Ḳ) and أَشْجَانٌ; (L, Mṣb, Ḳ;) the latter being pl. of شَجِينٌ also. (L.) A rájiz says,

لِى شَجَنَانِ شَجَنٌ بِنَجْدِ
وَشَجَنٌ لِى بِبِلَادِ السِّنْدِ

[*I have two wants; a want in Nejd, and I have a want in the country of Es-Sind*]. (Ṣ.) ═ Also *An intricately-intermingling branch* of a tree; (L, Ḳ;) and a شُعْبَة [i. e. *branch,* or *branchlet,* or *the like,*] of anything; (Ḳ;) like ▼ شِجْنَةٌ and ▼ شُجْنَةٌ and ▼ شَجْنَةٌ (L, Ḳ) in the former sense: (L: [accord. to the Ḳ, app., in the latter sense:]) or, accord. to IAar, one says ▼ شُجْنَةٌ and ▼ شُجَنٌ meaning *a branch* of a tree, [or the latter app. means *branches,* for it seems to be a coll. gen. n.,] and ▼ شِجْنَةٌ and ▼ شِجَنٌ, and [the pl. of ▼ شُجْنَةٌ is] شُجُنَاتٌ and : (L:) or, accord. to J, (L,) ▼ شِجْنَةٌ and ▼ شُجْنَةٌ signify *roots of trees intricately intermingling:* (Ṣ, L:) [but] the primary signification of ▼ شِجْنَةٌ and ▼ شُجْنَةٌ is *a branchlet* (a شُعْبَة *of a* غُصْن) *of a tree:* (L:) or ▼ شُجْنَةٌ signifies *tangled,* or *luxuriant,* or *abundant and dense, trees.* (Mṣb.) — See also شُجْنَةٌ. — And see شَجْنٌ. — Also, (Ḳ,) or شجنة, (L, [thus written without any syll. signs, perhaps fem. of شَجَنٌ, i. e. شَجَنَةٌ, but it seems to be indicated by the context in the L that it is ▼ شُجْنَةٌ,]) A *she-camel compact in make, of which the several parts are interknit, one with another,* (L, Ḳ,*) *like the parts of a tree.* (L.)

شَجْنَةٌ: see the next preceding paragraph.

شُجْنَةٌ: see شَجَنٌ, in six places: and شِجْنَةٌ. ═ Also, as some say, *Leanness;* or *slenderness, and leanness;* or *leanness, and lankness in the belly.* (L.)

شِجْنَةٌ: see شَجَنٌ, in five places. — Also, i. e. with kesr, (Ḳ,) or ▼ شَجَنٌ and ▼ شِجِنَّةٌ, (L,) *A branchlet of a bunch of a grape-vine of which all the grapes come to maturity.* (L, Ḳ.) — شِجْنَةٌ signifies also † *Relationship closely,* or *intimately, connected.* (L.) One says, بَيْنِى وَبَيْنَهُ شِجْنَةُ رَحِمٍ, and ▼ شُجْنَةُ رَحِمٍ, † *Between me and him is a relationship closely,* or *intimately, connected.* (Ṣ.) And it is said in a trad., الرَّحِمُ شِجْنَةٌ مِنَ ٱللّٰهِ i. e. [الرَّحِمُ] *is derived from* الرَّحْمٰن: (Ṣ, L: [see رَحِمٌ:]) or, accord. to AO, (L,) the meaning is, [الرَّحِمُ *is*] *relationship, from God, closely,* or *intimately, connected, like the roots of trees.* (Ṣ, L.) — Also *A crack,* or *cleft, in a mountain.* (Lḥ, L, Ḳ.)

شَجَنَّةٌ: see the next preceding paragraph.

شَاجِنَتِى ↑ شُجُونٌ is a saying of the Arabs like their saying غَابِلَتِى غَبُولُ [i. e., app., *My withholder is death*, or *shall be death* alone; for شَجَنَتْهُ شُجُونٌ may be rendered *Death withheld him*, like as غَبَلَتْهُ غَبُولُ is rendered "death separated him"]. (L.)

شَجِنٌ : see شَجَنٌ.

شَاجِنٌ *Grieving, mourning*, or *lamenting; or sorrowful, sad*, or *unhappy;* (Ṣ, L;) and *anxious.* (L.) — See also an ex. of its fem., with ة, voce شُجُونٌ.

شَاجِنَةٌ [as a subst.]; pl. شَوَاجِنُ : see شُجْنٌ, in five places.

شجو

1. شَجِىَ, aor. ـَ, inf. n. شَجًا, *He was choked;* or *his throat*, or *fauces, became obstructed;* (Ṣ, Ḳ;) بِهِ *by it;* i. e. a bone or the like. (Ḳ.) One says, عَلَيْكَ بِالْكَظْمِ وَلَوْ شَجِيتَ بِالْعِظَامِ [*Keep thou to self-restraint though thou be choked by the bones*]. (TA.) — And, [hence, by a metaphor, (see Ḥar p. 33,)] aor. and inf. n. as above, † *He grieved, mourned*, or *lamented;* or *was sorrowful, sad*, or *unhappy:* (Ṣ, Mṣb:) and *he was*, or *became, anxious*, or *disquieted in mind.* (Ṣ.) — Also, aor. and inf. n. as above, said of a creditor (غَرِيم), *He went away,* عَنْهُ [*from him*]. (Ḳ. [See 4.]) — شَجَا بَيْنَهُمْ *It was*, or *became, an occasion of contention*, or *dispute*, or *of disagreement*, or *difference, between them.* (Ḳ.) — شَجَاهُ, (Ṣ, Mṣb, Ḳ,) aor. ـُ, inf. n. شَجْوٌ, (Ṣ, Mṣb,) [app. originally *syn. with* أَشْجَاهُ in the first of the senses assigned to the latter in the next paragraph: — and hence,] † *It* (anxiety, Mṣb) *grieved him;* or *caused him to mourn* or *lament*, or *to be sorrowful* or *sad* or *unhappy;* (Ṣ, Mṣb, Ḳ;) as also ↑ اشجاهُ. (Ḳ.) And, said of wealth (الغِنَى), inf. n. شَجْوٌ, *It excited his griefs, mournings*, &c., and *his desire.* (TA.) — Also, and ↑ اشجاهُ, † *It caused him to be mirthful,* (Ks, Ḳ, TA,) and *excited him.* (Ks, TA.) Thus each of these verbs has two contr. significations. (Ḳ.) But MF observes that طَرِبَهُ, the explanation here given in the Ḳ, is said by the author of the Ḳ [in art. طرب] to denote a lightness arising from joy or grief. (TA.) [Generally, however, it means as rendered above.]

4. اشجاهُ, inf. n. إِشْجَآءٌ, *It choked him;* or *caused his throat*, or *fauces, to be obstructed;* syn. أَغَصَّهُ; (Ṣ, TA;) said of a bone lying across in the throat, or fauces. (TA.) [This is clearly shown to be the meaning in the Ṣ, as well as in the TA, intended by أَغَصَّهُ; with which it is also syn. in another sense; for] — It signifies [also] † *It*, or *he, caused him to fall into grief, mourning, lamentation, sorrow, sadness*, or *unhappiness.* (Ḳ.) See also 1, in two places. — Also † *He subdued, overpowered*, or *overcame, him,* (Ḳ, TA,) *so that he grieved*, or *was sorrowful.* (TA.) — And † *He angered him.* (Ks, TA.) — And † *He made him to go away.* (Az, TA.) And أَشْجَيْتُهُ عَنِّى † *I gave him* (i. e. a creditor or petitioner) *what contented him, so that he went away.* (TA.)

6. تَشَاجَتْ عَلَيْهِ, (Aṣ, T, Ḳ,* TA,) said of a woman of the desert with reference to a young man who had been dallying, and holding amorous converse, with her, (Aṣ, T, TA,) † *She resisted him*, and *expressed grief*, or *unhappiness, to him*, or *on account of him*, [i. e. *on account of his advances*,] *saying, Alas, my grief*, or *my unhappiness!* (Aṣ, T, Ḳ,* TA.) And said of a woman with reference to her husband, meaning † *She expressed grief*, &c., as above. (A, TA.)

شَجًا *A bone*, or *some other thing* (Ṣ, Ḳ) *of the like sort,* (Ḳ,) *sticking fast,* (Ṣ,) or *lying across*, or *forming an obstruction,* (Ḳ,) *in the throat*, or *fauces,* (Ṣ, Ḳ,) of a human being, and of a beast; (TA;) *a thing in the throat*, or *fauces, that* [*chokes one*, or] *prevents from swallowing:* (Ḥar p. 69:) an inf. n. used as a subst. [properly thus termed]. (Ḥar p. 33.) — See also the next paragraph.

شَجْوٌ † *Anxiety*, or *disquietude of mind;* and *grief, mourning, lamentation, sorrow, sadness*, or *unhappiness;* (Ṣ;) [and] so ↑ شَجًا: thus termed because a man is choked thereby. (Ḥar p. 33.) — And † *A want; an object of want.* (Az, Ḳ, TA.) One says, بَكَى فُلَانٌ شَجْوَهُ [app. meaning † *Such a one wept for his object of want*]: and دَعَتِ الحَمَامَةُ شَجْوَهَا [app. † *The pigeon called for its object of want*]. (TA.)

شَجٍ † *Grieving, mourning*, or *lamenting;* or *sorrowing, sad*, or *unhappy;* applied to a man; (Ṣ, Mṣb;) and شَجِيَةٌ, of the measure فَعِلَةٌ, applied to a woman: one says, وَيْلٌ لِلشَّجِى مِنَ الخَلِىِّ [mentioned and expl. voce خَالٍ, in art. خلو, where each of these epithets is written with teshdeed to the ى; and likewise in another saying there mentioned]: (Ṣ:) or, in this saying, (TA,) it signifies *occupied* [*by anxiety* or *grief*]; (Ḳ, TA; [in the CḲ, الشَّجَا is erroneously put for الشَّجِى;]) and خَلِىّ means "free [therefrom]:" so says AZ: and in this instance الشَّجِى may mean *occupied by a bone choking*, or *obstructing, his throat*, or *fauces*, or *by anxiety, and not having found a way of escape therefrom;* or *by his opponent*, or *adversary, whom he has been unable to withstand:* (TA:) and sometimes one says ↑ شَجِىٌّ, like as one says حَزِنٌ and حَزِينٌ; though this is rare; (Mṣb;) it is mentioned in the 'Eyn; but شَجٍ is more known; and is said by Az to be the chaste form: (TA:) Mbr says, the ى of الخلى is with teshdeed, and the ى of الشَّجِى is without teshdeed, (Ṣ,) and sometimes this ى is with teshdeed in poetry; (Ṣ, Ḳ;) but if you make it to be from شَجَاهُ, it is ↑ شَجِىٌّ only, syn. with مَشْجُوٌّ [i. e. *grieved*, &c.]: (Ṣ;) and so it is said to be by Az and Z: and Az adds, the second way of accounting for it is, that they often lengthen فَعِل with a ى, saying, فُلَانٌ قَمِنٌ and قَمِينٌ لِكَذَا, and سَمِجٌ and سَمِيجٌ, and كَرٍ and كَرِىٌّ: and the third way is, that they assimilated one word in measure to another, as in الغَدَايَا وَالعَشَايَا, the [proper] pl. of غَدَاةٌ being only غَدَوَاتٌ. (TA.)

شَجِىٌّ: see the next preceding paragraph, in two places.

مَفَازَةٌ شَجْوَآءُ [*A desert*, or *waterless desert*,] *difficult to travel.* (Ṣ, Ḳ.*)

شَجَوِىٌّ, with fet-ḥ to the ج; rel. n. of شَجٍ. (Ṣ.)

شَجَوْجًى, (Ṣ, Ḳ,) of the measure فَعَوْعَلٌ [and therefore with tenween], (Mz 40th نوع, and MF and TA,) like حَجَوْجًى &c., (Ṣ,* and Mz ibid.,) and ↑ شَجَوْجَاةٌ, (Ḳ,) applied to a man, (Ṣ,) *Long in the legs:* (Ṣ, Ḳ:) or *very tall:* or *very tall, with bigness* (ضِخَم, in the CḲ ضَخْم,) *of the bones:* or *long in the back, short in the leg;* (Ḳ;) thus in the M; but Az says the reverse, i. e. *long in the legs, short in the back.* (TA.) — Also, (Ḳ,) or the former, (TA,) *A bulky horse.* (Ḳ.) — And The عَقْعَق [or *magpie*]; (Ḳ;) [and] so شَجَّجَى; (Ḳ and TA in art. شج;) fem. with ة [i. e. شَجَوْجَاةٌ]. (Ḳ.) — And *A wind continually blowing;* as also شَجَوْجَاةٌ. (Ḳ.) All this is in the M. (TA.)

شَجَوْجَاةٌ: see the next preceding paragraph.

أَمْرٌ شَاجٍ *An affair*, or *event, grieving;* or *causing to mourn* or *lament*, or *to be sorrowful* or *sad* or *unhappy.* (TA.)

شح

1. شَحَّ, (Mṣb,) sec. pers. شَحِحْتَ, aor. يَشِحُّ and يَشَحُّ, (Ṣ, O, Mṣb, Ḳ,) the latter of these aors. agreeable with analogy as the verb is intrans., and the former deviating therefrom; (MF;) and sec. pers. شَحَحْتَ, aor. يَشُحُّ; (Ṣ, O, Mṣb, Ḳ;) [the first of which, having for its aor. يَشِحُّ, is the most common;] inf. n. شُحٌّ (Ṣ, A, O, Mṣb, Ḳ) and شِحٌّ and شَحٌّ, (ISk, O, Ḳ,) of which three inf. ns. the first is the most approved; (TA;) *He was*, or *became, niggardly, tenacious, stingy, penurious*, or *avaricious;* syn. بَخِلَ: (Mṣb:) or بخل relates to single things, or particulars; and شح, to things in general: or بخل relates to wealth, or property; and شحّ, to wealth, or property, and to kindness, or beneficence: or شحّ, signifies *he was*, or *became, niggardly*, &c., as above, *in the utmost degree:* (TA:) or *he was*, or *became, niggardly*, &c., as above, (Ṣ, A, O, Ḳ,) *and covetous*, or *vehemently* or *greedily* or *excessively* or *culpably desirous,* (Ḳ,) or *with covetousness*, or *vehement* or *greedy* or *excessive* or *culpable desire.* (Ṣ, A, O.) You say, شَحَّ بِهِ and شَحَّ عَلَيْهِ; (T, M, Ḳ;) by the former meaning *He was*, or *became, niggardly*, &c., *of it*, i. e., of his property, or the like; and by the latter, *he was*, or *became, niggardly*, &c., *to him*, i. e., to an asker, or a beggar, or a seeker, or the like: (MF:) or [in some cases, as will be seen from phrases mentioned below, (see شَحِيحٌ,)] meaning by the latter the same as by the former. (L.) [Thus] one says, هُوَ يَشُحُّ بِمَالِهِ [*He is niggardly*, &c., *of his property*; and sometimes, in the same sense, يَشُحُّ عَلَى مَالِهِ]. (A.) And شَحَّ بَعْضُهُمْ

عَلَى بَعْضٍ [Some of them were niggardly, &c., to some; meaning they were niggardly, &c., one to another]. (Mṣb, Ḳ.)

3. هُوَ يُشَاحُّنِى بِكَذَا [He is niggardly, tenacious, &c., as above, with me, of such a thing]. (A.) [The inf. n.] مُشَاحَّةٌ [in the CḲ erroneously written مُشاحَةٌ] is syn. with ضِنَّةٌ: (Ḳ, TA:) hence the saying, لَا مُشَاحَّةَ فِى الاِصْطِلَاحِ [There shall be no acting in a niggardly manner, of one with another, in the making of peace, one with another]. (TA.) And one says, فُلَانٌ يُشَاحُّ عَلَى فُلَانٍ Such a one is tenacious of such a one; syn. يَضَنُّ بِهِ. (Ṣ, L.)

6. تَشَاحَّ القَوْمُ The people, or party, were niggardly, tenacious, &c., as above, [see 1,] one to another, (Mṣb, Ḳ, TA,) فِى الأَمْرِ [in the affair], (Ḳ, TA,) and عَلَيْهِ [for it], (TA,) and vied in hastening to it, (TA,) fearing lest it should become unattainable. (Ḳ, TA.) And تَشَاحَّا عَلَى الأَمْرِ لَا يُرِيدَانِ أَنْ يَفُوتَهُمَا (Ṣ, O, Ḳ, TA) They two (i. e. two men, Ṣ, O) contended together for the thing, or affair, each of them being unwilling that it should become beyond his reach, or attainment. (TA.) And تَشَاحَّا المَآءَ [or تَشَاحَّاهُ] i. q. تَجَاشَعَاهُ [i. e. They straitened each other in pressing to the water, and vied, each with the other, in endeavouring to satisfy their thirst]. (TA in art. جشع.)

R. Q. 1. شَحْشَحَةٌ [inf. n. of شَحْشَحَ] The being cautious, wary, or vigilant; or fearing. (O, Ḳ.) — The crying of the [bird called] صُرَد. (Ḳ.) You say, شَحْشَحَ الصُّرَدُ The صرد uttered its cry. (O, TA.) — The camel's reiterating of his voice, [or his being not clear, or his being sparing,] in his braying. (Ḳ.) You say of the camel, شَحْشَحَ فِى هَدِيرِهِ [He reiterated his voice, or] he was not clear, (Ṣ,) or he was sparing, (L,) in his braying. (Ṣ, L.) — And The flying swiftly. (Ṣ, Ḳ.)

نَفْسٌ شَحَّةٌ : see شَحِيحٌ.

أَوْصَى فِى صِحَّتِهِ وَشِحَّتِهِ means [He made his will during his state of soundness, or health, and] in his state of which he is tenacious [or the state which he is reluctant to quit] (فِى حَالِهِ الَّتِى يَشُحُّ عَلَيْهَا). (O, Ḳ.)

شَحَاحٌ : see the next paragraph in four places.

شَحِيحٌ (Ṣ, A, Mṣb, Ḳ) and ▼ شَحَاحٌ (Ṣ, A, Ḳ) and ▼ شَحْشَحٌ and ▼ شَحْشَاحٌ and ▼ شَحْشَحَانٌ, (Ḳ,) applied to a man, Niggardly, tenacious, stingy, penurious, or avaricious: (Mṣb:) or niggardly, &c., as above, in the utmost degree: (TA:) or niggardly, &c., as above, (Ṣ, A, Ḳ,) and covetous, or vehemently or greedily or excessively or culpably desirous, (Ḳ,) or with covetousness, or vehement or greedy or excessive or culpable desire: (Ṣ, A:) and ▼ نَفْسٌ شَحَّةٌ signifies the same as شَحِيحَةٌ [a soul that is niggardly, &c.]: (IAạr, TA:) the pl. (of شَحِيحٌ, Ṣ, Mṣb) is أَشِحَّةٌ [a pl. of pauc.] (Ṣ, A, Mṣb, Ḳ) and شِحَاحٌ (Ṣ, A, Ḳ) and أَشِحَّآءُ. (Mṣb, Ḳ.) You say, هُوَ شَحِيحٌ [and شَحِيحٌ عَلَى شَىْءٍ and بِشَىْءٍ] He is niggardly, &c., of a thing. (L in art. شد.) أَشِحَّةً عَلَى الخَيْرِ, in the Ḳur [xxxiii. 19], means [They being niggardly, or vehemently desirous. of the good things, i. e.] of the wealth and spoils: (TA:) and أَشِحَّةً عَلَيْكُمْ, in the same verse, means [They being niggardly] of aid [to you]. (Jel.) — [Hence,] إِبِلٌ شَحَائِحُ, [in which the latter word is pl. of شَحِيحَةٌ,] (O, Ḳ,) or شِحَاحٌ, (A,) ‡ Camels that yield little milk. (A, O, Ḳ, TA.) And ▼ زَنْدٌ شَحَاحٌ ‡ A piece of stick, or wood, for producing fire, that does not yield fire. (Ṣ, A, Ḳ.) And مَآءٌ ▼ شَحَاحٌ † Water little in quantity; not copious. (Ḳ.) And ▼ أَرْضٌ شَحَاحٌ † Land that will not flow with water unless in consequence of much rain; (Ṣ, O, Ḳ;) as also ▼ شَحْشَحٌ: (O, Ḳ:) and also, (ISk, L, TA,) or ▼ the latter word, (so accord. to the Ḳ,) † Land that flows in consequence of the least rain; (ISk, Ḳ, TA;) as though it were niggardly of itself to the water; (TA;) like حَشَادٌ [in this, or in the former, sense]: (ISk, L:) thus having two contr. meanings. (Ḳ.) And accord. to AḤn, شَحَاحٌ signifies † [Small water-courses such as are termed] شِعَاب any one of which is made to flow if a skinful of water is poured into it. (TA.)

شَحْشَحٌ : see شَحِيحٌ, in three places. — Also Evil in disposition; (O, Ḳ;) and so ▼ شَحْشَاحٌ. (TA.) — Very jealous; (Fr, Ṣ, O, Ḳ;) as also ▼ شَحْشَاحٌ and ▼ شَحْشَحَانٌ, (Fr, O, Ḳ.) — Courageous; (Ṣ, Ḳ;) and so ▼ شَحْشَاحٌ. (TA.) — Also, (Ṣ, O, Ḳ, TA,) applied alike to a male and to a female, (TA,) and ▼ شَحْشَاحٌ, (Ḳ, TA,) or ▼ شَحْشَحَانٌ, (Ṣ,* O,) One who keeps, attends, or applies himself, constantly, perseveringly, or assiduously, to a thing: (Ṣ, O, Ḳ, TA:) who strives, labours, or exerts himself, therein: (TA:) or, as some say, (Ṣ, O,) penetrating, sharp, vigorous, or effective, therein: (Ṣ, O, TA:) the first, (Ṣ, O, Ḳ, TA,) and ▼ second, (TA,) applied to an orator, or a preacher, (Ṣ, O, Ḳ, TA,) in this last sense, (Ṣ, O, TA,) or as meaning eloquent (Ḳ, TA) and powerful: (TA:) and both, as epithets of general application, penetrating, sharp, vigorous, or effective, in speech, or in going or journeying: the first is also applied to an orator, or a preacher, as meaning skilful: (TA:) and ▼ the last of these three epithets is applied by Dhu-r-Rummeh to a driver of camels, who urges them by singing to them. (Ṣ, O, TA.) — Also the first, applied to a raven, or crow, (غُرَاب,) That croaks much. (O, Ḳ.) — And Light, or agile; applied to an ass; as also ▼ شُحْشُحٌ, (O, Ḳ,) as some say. (O.) — And Swift in flight; applied to a قَطَاة. (Ṣ, O, Ḳ.) — Also, and ▼ شَحْشَحَانٌ, Tall, or long, (Fr, O, Ḳ, TA,) and strong. (TA.) — And the former, applied to a [desert such as is termed] فَلَاة, Wide; (O, Ḳ, TA;) in which the places of alighting are far apart, and in which is no herbage. (TA.)

شُحْشُحٌ : see the next preceding paragraph.

شَحْشَاحٌ : see شَحِيحٌ: — and see also شَحْشَحٌ, in five places. — Also, applied to a woman, Resembling a man in her strength, (O, Ḳ,) and her exertion, or energy. (O.)

شَحْشَحَانٌ : see شَحِيحٌ: — and see also شَحْشَحٌ, in four places.

مُشَحْشِحٌ Niggardly, tenacious, stingy, penurious, or avaricious; [like شَحِيحٌ;] (TA;) possessing little, or no, good. (O, Ḳ, TA.)

شحب

1. شَحَبَ, aor. ـَ (Ṣ, A, O, Ḳ, &c.) and ـُ, (A, O, Ḳ, &c.,) but the former more commonly obtains, (TA,) inf. n. شُحُوبٌ; (Ṣ, O, Ḳ;) and شَحُبَ, (Fr, Ṣ, A, O, Ḳ, &c.,) inf. n. شُحُوبَةٌ, (Fr, Ṣ, O, Ḳ,) but this form of the verb is disapproved by AZ and 'Iyáḍ; (TA; [in which, however, nine authorities for it are mentioned;]) said of one's body; (Fr, Ṣ, O;) or of one's colour, or complexion, (A, Ḳ,) and so شُحِبَ, (A, O, Ḳ,) inf. n. شُحُوبٌ; (A;) [It was, or became, altered [for the worse, wan, or haggard], (Fr, Ṣ, A, O, Ḳ, &c.,) in consequence of emaciation, (Ḳ,) or hunger, (A, Ḳ,) or sleeplessness, and the like, (A,) or travel, (Ḳ,) or work, or disease, or impatience, or distress or fatigue: or, accord. to the author of the "Wá'ee," شُحُوبٌ signifies emaciation itself: (TA:) in this sense, it is of the dial. of Benoo-Kiláb. (A, TA.) — شَحَبَ الأَرْضَ, (IDrd, O, Ḳ,) aor. ـَ, inf. n. شَحْبٌ, (IDrd, O,) He pared the ground, or scraped off its superficial part, with a shovel, (IDrd, O, Ḳ,) or some other thing: of the dial. of El-Yemen. (IDrd, O.)

شَحِبٌ : see what follows.

شَاحِبٌ A man having his colour, or complexion, altered [for the worse, wan, or haggard], (TA,) or so شَاحِبُ اللَّوْنِ, (A,) in consequence of disease, or travel, or the like: (TA: [see 1:]) and emaciated, or lean; (TA, KL;) as also ▼ شَحِبٌ. (KL.) It is said in a trad., لَا تَلْقَى المُؤْمِنَ إِلَّا شَاحِبًا [Thou wilt not find the believer otherwise than wan, or haggard; or emaciated, or lean]; because شُحُوب is one of the effects of fear, and of paucity of food, and of little enjoying of plentifulness and pleasantness or easiness, and softness or delicacy, of life. (TA.) — It is also applied as an epithet to a sword, meaning Altered in its colour by blood that has dried upon it: used in this sense by the poet Taäbbaṭa-sharrà. (TA.)

شحج

1. شَحَجَ, aor. ـِ and ـَ, inf. n. شَحِيجٌ (Ṣ, O, Ḳ) and شُحَاجٌ (Aṣ, Ṣ, O, Ḳ) and شَحَجَانٌ (O, Ḳ) and تَشْحَاجٌ; (O, L;) and ▼ تشحّج; and ▼ استشحج; (L, TA;) He uttered his voice or cry; [brayed;

croaked;] said of a mule, (Ṣ, O, Ḳ, &c.,) and of an ass, (ISd, O,) and of a raven, or crow; (Ṣ, O, Ḳ, &c.;) and sometimes, ‡ of a man: (L:) or شَحِيجٌ is used in relation to a mule; and شَحَجَانٌ, in relation to a raven, or crow: (T, TA:) or the former of these two signifies the *reiterating of the voice* or *cry* of the raven, or crow; and when it stretches forth its head [and croaks], you say نَعَبَ: and accord. to the L, the first and second inf. ns., used in relation to an ass, signify the *uttering certain of his voices* or *cries:* Th is thought by ISd to have mentioned also شَحِيجٌ; but the latter doubts its correctness: and شُحَاجٌ is also expl. as signifying the *raising of the voice;* but as used more especially in relation to the mule and the ass. (TA.) شَحَجَ is also said of a raven, or crow, meaning *He, being advanced in age, had a rough,* or *harsh, voice* or *cry:* (O, Ḳ:) [*he croaked roughly,* or *harshly, by reason of age:*] it is said in the M that شَحِيجٌ and شُحَاجٌ signify the *crying* of a raven, or crow, when advanced in age. (TA.)

5: see the preceding paragraph.

10. استشحج [*He desired* a raven, or crow, *to croak*]. One says of ravens, or crows, أُسْتُشْحِجْنَ فَشَحَجْنَ [*They were desired to croak, and they croaked*]. (O, Ḳ.) — See also 1.

شَحَّاجٌ, applied to a mule, an ass, and a raven or crow, *that brays,* or *croaks,* or *raises its voice, much:* and by Er-Rá'ee it is applied to ‡ a مُؤَذِّن. (TA.) — بَنَاتُ شَحَّاجٍ, (Ṣ, A, O, Ḳ,) and ▼شَاحِجٍ, (J,) *Mules:* (Ṣ, A, O, Ḳ:) and *asses.* (A, TA.) — And شَحَّاجٌ and ▼مِشْحَجٌ The *wild ass:* (Ṣ, O, Ḳ:) in the L said to be the *wild pigeon:* [but حمام is evidently there a mistranscription for حِمَار:] each an epithet in which the quality of a subst. predominates. (TA.)

شَوَاحِجُ [pl. of شَاحِجَةٌ] *Ravens, or crows:* which are also called ▼مُسْتَشْحِجَاتٌ and ▼مُسْتَشْحَجَاتٌ, meaning *desired to croak* and *croaking.* (O, Ḳ.) Dhu-r-Rummeh uses the phrase ▼مُسْتَشْحِجَاتٌ بِالفِرَاقِ [*Ravens croaking by reason of separation*]. (O, TA.)

شَاحِجٌ: see بَنَاتُ شَاحِجٍ — شَحَّاجٌ.

مِشْحَجٌ: see شَحَّاجٌ.

مُسْتَشْحِجَاتٌ: see the next but one of the preceding paragraphs, in three places.

شحذ

1. شَحَذَ, (Ṣ, A, Mṣb, Ḳ,) aor. ـَ, (Ṣ, Mṣb, Ḳ,) inf. n. شَحْذٌ, (Ṣ,) *He sharpened* (Ṣ, A, Mṣb, Ḳ) a knife, (Ṣ, A, L, Ḳ,) and a sword, and the like, (L,) or an iron implement, (Mṣb), with a whetstone or other similar thing; (TA;) as also ▼اشحذ; (Ḳ;) and ▼شَحَّذَ, inf. n. تَشْحِيذٌ. (KL.) — [Hence,] شَحَذْتَ عَلَيْنَا لِسَانَكَ ‡ [*Thou hast sharpened against us thy tongue*]. (A and TA in art. رهف.) And اشْحَذْ لَهُ غَرْبَ ذِهْنِكَ ‡ [*Sharpen thou for it the edge of thine intellect*]. (A.) And شَحَذَهُ بِعَيْنِهِ, (Ḳ,) or بِبَصَرِهِ, (A,) ‡ *He looked sharply at him.* (Ḳ,* TA.) And شَحَذَ الجُوعُ مَعِدَتَهُ † *Hunger made his stomach keen, and strengthened it,* (L,) *and inflamed it.* (L, Ḳ.) — Hence also, i. e. from شَحَذَ in the sense first expl. above, (Ḥar p. 377,) فُلَانٌ يَشْحَذُ النَّاسَ, (inf. n. شَحْذٌ, Ḳ,) ‡ *Such a one begs importunately of men:* (A, Ḳ,* and Ḥar ubi suprà:) and شَحَذْتُهُ *I begged importunately of him.* (Mṣb.) — And شَحَذَهُ † *He drove him away;* namely, a man; (Ḳ;) as also ▼تَشَحَّذَهُ, (CḲ, and so accord. to the O,) or ▼شَحَّذَهُ, (Ḳ accord. to the TA,) inf. n. تَشْحِيذٌ. (TA.) [See also 5 below.] And شَحَذْتُهُ, (O, TA,) inf. n. as above, (Ḳ,) † *I drove him vehemently.* (O, Ḳ,* TA.) — شَحْذٌ also signifies † The *being angry.* (Ḳ.) You say, شَحَذَ عَلَيْهِ † *He was angry with him.* (TḲ.) — And *i. q.* قَشْرٌ [The act of *paring,* or *peeling,* &c.]. (O, Ḳ.) You say, شَحَذَهُ, i. e. قَشَرَهُ [*He pared it, peeled it,* &c.]. (TḲ.)

2: see above, in two places.

3. شَاحَذَنِى, inf. n. شِحَاذٌ, *He assisted me, by alternating with me,* (رَاسَلَنِى,) *and did like as I did, in sharpening a sword* and *the like.* (Ḥam p. 533.) — شاحذت النَّاقَةُ *The she-camel raised her tail, and then twisted it vehemently,* when in labour, being near to bringing forth. (O, Ḳ.)

4: see 1, first sentence.

5. رَأَيْتُهُ يَتَشَحَّذُ ‡ [*I saw him applying himself to importunate begging*]. (A, TA. [In both this meaning is indicated by the context.]) — تَشَحَّذَنِى فُلَانٌ † *Such a one drove me away,* and *subjected me to trouble,* or *difficulty.* (TA.) See also 1.

شَحْذَانٌ † [*Having a keen appetite;*] *hungry.* (Ṣ, M, L, Ḳ.) — And † *A vehement driver.* (Ḳ, TA. [See also مِشْحَذٌ.]) — And † *Light,* or *active, in his work* (فِى عَمَلِهِ). (O, Ḳ.)

شُحْذُوذٌ, applied to a man, *i. q.* نَزِقٌ † [*Light, and unsteady,* or *lightwitted;* &c.]. (TA.)

شَحِيذٌ, applied to a knife [&c.], *Sharpened;* (Lth, A, TA;) as also ▼مَشْحُوذٌ. (Lth, TA.)

شَحَّاذٌ ‡ *An importunate beggar:* (A, Ḳ:*) one should not say شَحَّاثٌ: (Ḳ:) the latter is said by IB to be a vulgar corruption; but several authors assert it to be correct, because ذ is changed into ث without any error in speech, as is asserted by El-Khafájee and others; and accord. to the A, both these words signify as above: (TA in art. شحث, and partly repeated in the present art.:) [it is said, however, that] شَحَّاذٌ meaning *a beggar* does not occur in the language of the Arabs. (Ḥar p. 377.)

مِشْحَذٌ *A whetstone;* or *thing with which,* or *upon which, one sharpens.* (Ṣ, Ḳ.) — And [hence,] A *rough, severe,* or *violent,* driver: (O, Ḳ: [see also شَحْذَانٌ:] and applied also as an epithet to a driving. (O.)

مَشْحَذَةٌ [*A cause,* or *means, of sharpening:* a word of the class of مَجْبَنَةٌ &c.]. One says, هٰذَا كَلَامٌ مَشْحَذَةٌ لِلْفَهْمِ ‡ [*This is discourse that is a cause,* or *means, of sharpening of the understanding*]. (A.)

مِشْحَاذٌ An [*elevation such as is termed*] أَكَمَةٌ, *wide within,* (O, Ḳ, TA,) *not rough in the stones* [*thereof*], *but extending long upon the earth, not having in it trees nor soft ground:* (O, TA:) or, accord. to ISh, (O, TA,) *level ground,* (O, Ḳ, TA,) *in which are pebbles like those* [*that are strewn in the court*] *of the mosque, and in which is no mountain;* but he says that ADḳ disapproves the word: (O, TA:) accord. to Fr, (O,) the *head of a mountain,* (O, Ḳ, TA,) *when sharp,* or *pointed:* pl. مَشَاحِذُ. (O.)

مَشْحُوذٌ: see شَحِيذٌ. — فُلَانٌ مَشْحُوذٌ عَلَيْهِ ‡ *Such a one is an object of anger.* (O, TA.)

شحط

1. شَحَطَ, aor. ـَ, inf. n. شَحْطٌ (Ṣ, Ḳ) and شَحَطٌ (Ḳ) and شُحُوطٌ (Ṣ, Ḳ) and مَشْحَطٌ; (Ḳ;) and شَحِطَ, aor. ـَ, (Ḳ,) inf. n. شَحَطٌ; (TA;) *It was,* or *became, distant,* or *remote:* (Ṣ, Ḳ:) or شَحْطٌ and شَحَطٌ signify the *being distant,* or *remote, in all states* or *circumstances.* (TA.) You say, شَحَطَ المَزَارُ *The place of visiting was,* or *became, distant,* or *remote.* (Ṣ.) And لَا أَنْسَاكَ عَلَى شَحْطِ الدَّارِ *I will not forget thee notwithstanding the distance of the dwelling.* (TA.) And El-'Ajjáj says,

وَالشَّحْطُ قَطَّاعٌ رَجَآءَ مَنْ رَجَا *

[*And distance is the severer of the hope of him who hopeth*]. (TA.) — شَحَطَ فِى السَّوْمِ *He went far,* or *far from what was right,* and *exceeded the due limit, in the demanding of a price.* (TA.) — Hence, (TA,) شَحَطَ البَعِيرَ فِى السَّوْمِ, (Ḳ, TA, [in the CḲ, and in a MS. copy of the Ḳ, البَعِيرُ,]) aor. ـَ, inf. n. شَحْطٌ, (TA,) *He went to the utmost of the value of the camel in the demanding of a price:* (Ḳ, TA:) or *he went far from what was right,* and *exceeded the due limit:* (Ḳ:) and شَحِطَ signifies the same; (Ḳ;) or is thought to do so by ISd. (TA.) Hence, also, what is said in a trad., by Rabee'ah, respecting a man emancipating a portion of a slave: يَكُونُ عَلَى المُعْتِقِ قِيمَةُ أَنْصِبَآءِ شُرَكَائِهِ يُشْحَطُ الثَّمَنُ ثُمَّ يُعْتَقُ كُلُّهُ [*The value of the portions of his copartners shall be imposed upon the emancipater;*] *the price* of the slave *shall be carried to the utmost;* [*then he shall emancipate the whole of him:*] or the meaning is, *the price* of the slave *shall be collected;* from شَحَطَ الإِنَآءَ, which see below. (TA.) — شَحَطَ فُلَانًا *He preceded, outwent, got before,* or *passed beyond, such a one, and became far from him:* (Ḳ, TA:) and in like manner, الخَيْلَ [*the horses,* or *horsemen*]. (T, TA.) One says also, شَحَطَتْ بَنُو هَاشِمٍ العَرَبَ *The sons of Háshim surpassed,* and *outstripped, the Arabs* [in general] *in excellence.* (TA.) — شَحَطَ الإِنَآءَ *He filled the vessel.* (Fr, Ḳ.) — See also 5.

2. شَحَّطَهُ, inf. n. تَشْحِيطٌ, (Ṣ, Ḳ,) *He made him* (a slain man) *to struggle,* or *flounder,* بِدَمِهِ

in his blood: (Ṣ:) or *he besmeared, bedawbed, befouled*, or *defiled, him*, بِالدَّمِ *with blood*. (Ḳ.)

4. اشحطهُ *He made him*, or *caused him, to be*, or *become, distant*, or *remote; he put him, sent him*, or *removed him, far away*. (Ṣ, Ḳ.)

5. تشحّط *He* (a slain man) *struggled*, or *floundered*, بِدَمِهِ *in his blood*: (Ṣ:) and ↑ شَحْطٌ [inf. n. of شَحَطَ] also signifies the *struggling*, or *floundering*, in blood: (Lth, ISd, Ḳ:) or the former signifies *he struggled*, or *floundered, and rolled*, or *wallowed*, فِى دَمِهِ *in his blood*: (TA:) or *became besmeared, bedawbed, befouled*, or *defiled*, (Mgh, Ḳ,) *and he rolled*, or *wallowed*, (Mgh,) or *struggled*, or *floundered*, (Ḳ,) فِى دَمِهِ *in his blood*. (Mgh, Ḳ.*) And *It* (the fœtus) *struggled*, or *floundered*, فِى السَّلَى *in the membrane enclosing it*. (Ḳ.)

شَحَّاطٌ: see what next follows.

مَنْزِلٌ شَاحِطٌ *A distant*, or *remote, place of abode*; as also ↑ شَحَّاطٌ. (TA.) — شَوَاحِطُ الأَوْدِيَةِ, [the former word being pl. of شَاحِطَةٌ,] *The distant*, or *remote, parts of the valleys*. (TA.)

شَوْحَطٌ *Certain trees*, (Ḳ,) *a species of the trees of the mountains*, (Ṣ,) meaning *of the mountains of the* سَرَاة, [the mountain-range extending from near 'Arafát to Nejrán in El-Yemen,] *for there they grow*, (TA,) *of which bows are made*: (Ṣ, Ḳ:) AḤn says, One acquainted with [the kind of trees called] the شوحط has informed me that *it grows in the manner of the* أَرْز [or *pine-tree*], *many rods growing from one stem; its leaves are thin and long, and it has a fruit like the long grape*, [the word here rendered "grape" is عنبة, but it has been altered in the MS., and may therefore be incorrect,] *except that its extremity is more slender, and it is soft, and is eaten*: (TA:) or *i. q.* نَبْعٌ: (IB:) or *a species of the* نبع, (Ḳ,) *of which bows are made*: (TA:) or *the* شوحط *and* نبع *and* شِرْيَان *are one; the name varying according to the excellence of their places of growth; what is upon the summit of the mountain being called* نبع; *what is upon its base*, or *foot*, or *lowest* or *lower part*, شريان; *and what is in the depressed tract by its base*, شوحط: (Mbr, Az, Ḳ:) IB says the same with respect to the نبع, but that *the* شوحط *is that which is upon the lowest part of the mountain*; and this is confirmed by what is said by AZ and others: El-Ghanawee El-Aạrábee says, *the* نبع *and* شوحط *and* سَرَاء *are one*: as to the شريان, no one holds it to be of the نبع except Mbr: Aboo-Ziyád says that bows are made of the شريان, and they are good, but of a black colour tinged with redness: and AḤn says in one place, that *the* نبع *and* شوحط *are yellow in the wood, heavy in the hand; and when they become old, they become red*: (TA:) the n. un. is with ة. (Ḳ.)

شحم

1. شَحُمَ, (Ṣ, Mṣb, Ḳ,) aor. ـُ, (Ḳ,) inf. n. شَحَامَةٌ, (MA, Mṣb,) *He* (a man, Ṣ, Ḳ) *was*, or *became, fat*; (Ṣ, MA, Ḳ;) as also شَحِمَ, aor. ـَ: (TA:) or *he was*, or *became, abundant in the fat of his person*. (Mṣb.) And شَحُمَتْ إِبِلُهُ (Ḳ) *His camels were*, or *became, fat*. (TA.) And شَحِمَتِ النَّاقَةُ; and شَحُمَت, aor. ـُ; of the classes of غَنِىَ and نَصَرَ; inf. n. شَحْمٌ and شُحُومٌ; *The she-camel became fat after leanness*. (TA.) — شَحِمَ, (Ṣ, Ḳ,) aor. ـَ, (Ḳ,) inf. n. شَحَمٌ, (TA,) *He was*, or *became, eagerly desirous of fat*. (Ṣ, Ḳ, TA.) And *He ate much fat*. (TA.) ═ شَحَمَهُ, (Ḳ,) or شَحَمَ أَصْحَابَهُ, (Ṣ,) aor. ـَ, (Ḳ,) inf. n. شَحْمٌ, (TA,) *He fed him*, or *his companions, with fat*; or *gave him*, or *them, fat to eat*. (Ṣ, Ḳ.)

4. اشحم *He had much fat in his possession*: like as الحم signifies "he had much flesh in his possession." (TA.)

شَحْمٌ, (Ṣ, Mṣb, Ḳ,) of an animal, (Mṣb,) a word of well known meaning, (Ṣ, Mṣb, Ḳ,) *Fat*; (MA, KL;) the *substance of fatness*: (ISd, TA:) شَحْمَةٌ is a more special term, (Ṣ, Mṣb,) [i. e. a n. un.,] signifying *a piece thereof*: (Ḳ:) the pl. of the former is شُحُومٌ. (Mṣb, TA.) It is said of the Jews, in a trad., حُرِمَتْ عَلَيْهِمُ الشُّحُومُ فَبَاعُوهَا وَأَكَلُوا أَثْمَانَهَا [*Fats have been forbidden to them; but they have sold them, and have devoured the prices thereof*: see Lev. vii. 23]: the fat that is forbidden to them is that of the kidneys and of the stomach and of the intestines into which the food passes from the stomach; but not that of the أَلْيَة [meaning the "rump," and also the "tail of a sheep,"] nor of the back. (TA.) One says, لَقِيتُهُ بِشَحْمِ كُلَاهُ [lit. *I met him, or found him, with the fat of his kidneys*,] meaning, ‡ *in his state of briskness, liveliness*, or *sprightliness*. (Ḳ, TA.) And of him who is deemed weak, one says, فُلَانٌ شَحْمٌ لِلْمُبْتَلِعِ ‡ [lit. *Such a one is fat for the swallower*]. (Ḥam p. 771.) — Also The *hump of the camel*: (TA:) heard by Az from the Arabs in this sense. (TA in art. حجر.) — And The *whiteness* [app. meaning the *white part*] *of the belly*. (TA.) — شَحْمَةُ الأُذُنِ [*The lobe*, or *lobule, of the ear*;] *the part, of the ear, to which the* قُرْط [i. e. *ear-ring* or *ear-drop*] *is suspended*; (Ṣ, Mṣb, Ḳ;) i. e. *the soft portion of the lower part of the ear*: or *the place of the perforation for the* قُرْط. (TA.) — شَحْمَةُ العَيْنِ *The* مُقْلَة *of the eye*; (TA;) i. e., *what comprises the white and the black of the eye*: (Zj in his "Khalḳ el-Insán;" and Ṣ and Mṣb and Ḳ voce مُقْلَةٌ:) [this is what is generally meant by it; i. e. *the globe of the eye*:] in the T it is said to be *the* حَدَقَة [i. e. *black*, or *what is in the middle of the white*,] *of the eye*: and some say that it is *the* شَحْمَة [app. meaning the *whole substance*] *that is beneath* [or *behind*] *the* حَدَقَة. (TA.) — شَحْمَةُ الحَنْظَلِ [and شَحْمُهُ, as in the Ḳ in art. حنظل,] *The inner part* [i. e. the *pulp*] *of the colocynth, exclusive of its seeds*. (Ḳ.) — شَحْمَةُ الرُّمَّانِ *The thin yellow* [*pulp*] *that is amid the seeds of the pomegranate*; (Ḳ;) or, as in the M, *the substance that separates the seeds of the pomegranate*. (TA.) — شَحْمُ النَّخْلِ *The heart pith*, or *cerebrum*, (جُمَّار,) *of palm-trees*: (Ṣ in art. جذب:) and شَحْمَةُ النَّخْلَةِ *the heart* (جُمَّارَة) *of the palm-tree*. (M, TA.) — شَحْمَةُ المَرْجِ *The* خِطْمِىّ [or *marsh-mallow*]. (Ḳ.) — شَحْمُ الأَرْضِ *The truffle*; as a gen. n.; syn. الكَمْءُ: (TA in art. كمأ:) and شَحْمَةُ الأَرْضِ *the truffle*; as a n. un.; syn. الكَمْأَةُ: (Ḳ:) or *the white truffle*; syn. الكَمْأَةُ البَيْضَآءُ. (Ṣ.) [It should be observed that الكَمْءُ is generally held to be a n. un.; and الكَمْأَةُ, to be a coll. gen. n.; contr. to analogy: but they are here evidently used in the reverse manner.] — شَحْمَةُ الأَرْضِ also signifies *A certain white worm*: or is *of* (مِنْ [which is omitted in some of the copies of the Ḳ]) *the* [*long worms, found in moist earth, and in the mud of rivers, called*] خَرَاطِين: (Ḳ, TA:) or *a white* عَظَايَة [n. un. of عَظَآء, q. v.], *not big*: or, as some say, it is *not of the* [*species called*] عَظَآء; *it is more pleasant* [*to the taste*], *and better*: *and* [*because it dwells in the sand-hills*,] *they say* [i. e. *call it*] *also* شَحْمَةُ النَّقَا, *like as they say* بَنَاتُ النَّقَا: (TA:) it is *the* [*reptile called*] حُلَكَة, *which dives into the sand, and to which the fingers* (بَنَان) *of virgins are likened*. (TA in art. ارض. [See حُلَكَة: and see also شَبَثٌ.]) أَبُو شَحْمٍ is an appellation of *The small species of what is called* حِمَارٌ قَبَّانَ. (TA in art. قب, q. v.) — [See also شَحْمَةٌ below.]

شُحْمٌ, with ḍamm, [as though pl. of أَشْحَمُ, which I do not find mentioned,] *White*; applied to men. (IAạr, TA.)

شَحِمٌ *Eagerly desirous of fat*. (Ṣ, Ḳ.) One says, رَجُلٌ شَحِمٌ لَحِمٌ *A man eagerly desirous of fat and of flesh*. (TA.) — عِنَبٌ شَحِمٌ *Grapes having little juice* (Ḳ, TA) *and thick skin*. (TA.) — And رُمَّانَةٌ شَحِمَةٌ *A pomegranate having thick* شَحْمَة [or *pulp amid the seeds*]. (TA.)

شَحْمَةٌ [n. un. of شَحْمٌ, which see throughout. ═ Also] *A certain bird*. (Ḳ. [For طَائِرٌ, which I regard as the right reading, in the CḲ, I find in other copies of the Ḳ الطَّائِرُ as an explanation of الشَّحْمَة.]) ═ And *A certain game of the children of the Arabs of the desert*. (Ḳ,* TA.)

شَحِيمٌ *Fat*, as an epithet applied to a man: (ISk, Ṣ, Ḳ:) or *abundant in the fat of his person*. (Mṣb.)

شَحَّامٌ *A seller of fat*; (Ṣ, Ḳ;) as also ↑ شَاحِمٌ. (Ḳ.) — And One *who feeds men much with fat*. (TA.)

شَاحِمٌ One *who feeds men with fat*. (Ṣ, TA.) — And A man *having*, or *possessing, fat*; like لَاحِمٌ signifying "having, or possessing, flesh:" possessive epithets like لَابِنٌ and تَامِرٌ. (TA.) — See also شَحَّامٌ.

مُشْحِمٌ, (Ṣ, [so in my copies, see 4, of which it is the part. n.,]) or ↑ مُشَحِّمٌ, like مُحَدِّثٌ [in measure], (Ḳ,) [both perhaps correct,] A man *having much fat in his house or tent*. (Ṣ, Ḳ.) — And the former, A man *whose camels are fat*. (Ḳ.)

مَشْحُومٌ: see مُشَحِّمٌ.

مُشْحِمٌ: see مُشَحِّمٌ.

مَشْحُومٌ Food, and bread, *into which fat has been put;* (TA;) [and so ▼مُشَحَّمٌ, for] one says خُبْزَةٌ مُشَحَّمَةٌ [*a cake of bread, &c., into which fat has been put*]. (Ḳ in art. ودق.)

شحن

1. شَحَنَ, (Ṣ, L, Mṣb, Ḳ,) aor. ـَ, inf. n. شَحْنٌ, (L, Mṣb,) *He filled* (Ṣ, L, Mṣb, Ḳ) a ship, (Ṣ, L, Ḳ,) or a house, or chamber, &c.: (Mṣb:) *he filled,* [or *laded,*] *and completely equipped* or *furnished,* a ship. (L.) And in like manner, *It* (i. e. what was in it) *filled* a ship. (L.) And, (Ṣ, L, Ḳ,) as also ▼اشحن, (Ḳ,) *He filled* a town or city (Ṣ, L, Ḳ) بِالخَيْلِ [*with horsemen* or *the horsemen*]. (Ṣ, L.) ═ Also, (L, Mṣb, Ḳ,) aor. as above, (L,) and so the inf. n., (L, Mṣb,) *He drove away* (L, Mṣb, Ḳ) a people, or party, (L,) or him. (Mṣb.) And (L) one says, مَرَّ يَشْحَنُهُمْ, (Ṣ, L,) inf. n. as above, (Ṣ,) *He passed along driving them away, and pursuing them.* (Ṣ, L.) AZ heard an Arab of the desert say, اشْحَنْ عَنْكَ فُلَانًا, meaning *Remove thou, and put far away, from thee such a one.* (L.) And one says of a thing that is intensely acid, إِنَّهُ يَشْحَنُ الذُّبَابَ i. e. *Verily it drives away the flies.* (TA.) ═ شَحْنٌ also signifies The *running vehemently.* (L.) And شَحَنَ, *He went far,* or *far away.* (Ḳ.) And one says, شَحَنَتِ الكِلَابُ, (L,) [and شَحِنَت, as appears from what follows,] aor. تَشْحَنُ and تَشْحُنُ, (L, Ḳ,) like تَمْنَعُ and تَعْلَمُ and تَنْصُرُ, (Ḳ,) inf. n. شُحُونٌ, (L,) *The dogs went far in pursuit without catching any prey,* or *game.* (L, Ḳ.) ═ شَحِنَ عَلَيْهِ, aor. ـَ, (L, Mṣb, Ḳ,) inf. n. شَحْنٌ; (L, Mṣb;) and شَحَنَ, aor. ـَ, inf. n. شَحْنٌ; (Mṣb;) *He bore rancour, malevolence, malice,* or *spite, against him;* (Mṣb, Ḳ;) and (Mṣb) *bore,* (L,) or *showed,* (Mṣb,) *enmity towards him.* (L, Mṣb.)

[2. شحّنهُ *He made him,* or *appointed him to the office of, a* شِحْنَة, q. v.; occurring in post-classical works.]

3. شاحنهُ, (L, Mṣb, Ḳ,) inf. n. مُشَاحَنَةٌ, (L, Mṣb, KL,) *He regarded him,* or *treated him, with rancour, malevolence, malice,* or *spite;* (Mṣb;) or *with enmity; being so regarded,* or *treated, by him:* (L, Mṣb, Ḳ, KL:) or, as some say, مُشَاحَنَةٌ is *such reviling, and blaming, upbraiding,* or *reproaching, reciprocally, as does not amount to fighting one another;* from شَحْنَآءُ meaning "enmity." (L.)

4. اشحن: see 1. — Also, (Ḳ,) inf. n. إِشْحَانٌ, (L,) *He sheathed* the sword: (L,* Ḳ:) and *he drew* the sword: thus having two contr. significations. (Ḳ.) ═ Also, (Ṣ, L, Ḳ,) inf. n. as above, (Ṣ, L,) *He* (a boy, or child, Ṣ, L, and, as some say, a man, L) *was ready,* or *about, to weep:* (Ṣ, L, Ḳ:) or *his eyes watered at the approach of weeping.* (L.) — And اشحن لَهُ بِسَهْمٍ *He prepared himself to shoot him,* or *to shoot at him, with an arrow.* (Ḳ.)

6. تَشَاحُنٌ The *regarding,* or *treating, one another* [*with rancour, malevolence, malice,* or *spite;* (see 1, last sentence; and 3;) or] *with enmity.* (L.)

شَحْنَةٌ [thus written, with fet-ḥ to the ش, but I incline to think that it is correctly ▼شِحْنَةٌ,] The *contents of a ship, that fill it.* (L.)

شِحْنَةٌ: see what next precedes. — [Also] *A body of men sufficing for the guarding, controlling,* or *firm holding,* of a province, or city, *on the part of the Sultán.* (Az, L, Ḳ.*) And (Ḳ) *A troop of horsemen keeping post* (Ṣ, L, Ḳ) in a country or town. (Ṣ, L.) IB says that the vulgar usage of this word as syn. with أَمِيرٌ [i. e. *A commander* or *commandant,* &c., being used app. only in post-classical times, from the Pers. شحنه, meaning in Pers., and hence in Arabic also, *a viceroy, prefect, chief of the police,* or *the like,*] is a mistake. (L.) — And The *quantity of fodder appointed to beasts as sufficing them for a day and a night.* (Az, L, Ḳ.) ═ See also what next follows.

شَحْنَآءُ *Rancour, malevolence, malice,* or *spite:* (L:) or *vehement hatred:* (Mṣb:) and *enmity;* (Ṣ, L, Mṣb, Ḳ;) as also ▼شِحْنَةٌ. (Ṣ, L, Ḳ.) Hence the saying, كَانَ بَيْنَهُ وَبَيْنَ أَخِيهِ شَحْنَآءُ i. e. [*There was between him and his brother*] *enmity.* (L.)

شُحُونٌ in the following verse, cited by ISd,

تَأَطَّرْنَ فِى المِينَآءِ ثُمَّ تَرَكْنَهُ
وَقَدْ لَجَّ مِنْ أَحْمَالِهِنَّ شُحُونُ

may be, accord. to him, an inf. n. of شَحَنَ, or an extr. pl. of شِحْنَةٌ: (L:) [but I rather think that it is a pl. of ▼شَاحِنٌ, like as شُهُودٌ is of شَاهِدٌ; and accordingly I would render the verse (which evidently relates to ships) thus: *They kept close in the port, then they left it, and laders had persisted in contention by reason of their burdens,* i. e. the burdens of the ships, because of the labour that they occasioned.]

شَاحِنٌ [act. part. n. of شَحَنَ]: see the next preceding paragraph. — See also مَشْحُونٌ. ═ Also A dog *going far in pursuit without catching any prey,* or *game:* pl. شَوَاحِنُ. (L.) ═ And *Bearing enmity* [or *rancour* &c. (see 1, last sentence,)] towards another: one says, هُوَ شَاحِنٌ لَكَ [*He is bearing enmity* &c. *towards thee*]. (L.)

مَشْحُونٌ A ship (فُلْكٌ, so in the Ḳur [xxvi. 119 &c.], Ṣ, L, or مَرْكَبٌ, Ḳ [in the L, erroneously, رَكْبٌ],) *Filled* [or *laded, and completely equipped* or *furnished:* see 1, first sentence]; (Ṣ, L, Ḳ;) as also ▼شَاحِنٌ, like كَاتِمٌ in the sense of مَكْتُومٌ, (L, Ḳ,) mentioned by Kr. (L.)

مُشْحَنٌ *Becoming angered;* or *made angry.* (Ḳ.)

عَدُوٌّ مُشَاحِنٌ [*An enemy who regards,* or *treats, another with rancour,* &c., *being so regarded,* or *treated by him:* see 3]. (Ṣ, L.) المُشَاحِنُ as used in a trad. means *The schismatic innovator in religion:* (L, Ḳ:) so says El-Owzá'ee: or *the transgressor:* (L:) or it means *he who has in his heart rancour* &c. (شَحْنَآء) *towards the Companions of the Apostle of God:* or *he who forsakes the institutes,* or *rule and usage, of his prophet; who speaks against his people; who sheds their blood.* (TA.)

شحو

1. شَحَا, (Ḳ,) or شَحَا فَاهُ, (Ks, Ṣ,) aor. ـُ, (Ks, TA,) or ـَ, (Ṣ,) inf. n. شَحْوٌ, (Ks, Ṣ, TA,) said of a man, (TA,) *He opened his mouth;* (Ṣ, Ḳ, TA;) as also ▼اشحى [or app., اشحى فَاهُ], (Ḳ,) and ▼شحّى فَاهُ, inf. n. تَشْحِيَةٌ. (TA.) شَحَا فَاهُ [meaning as above] is also said of the ass when about to bray. (TA.) And one says of the bit, شَحَا فَمَ الدَّابَّةِ [*It opened the mouth of the beast*]. (TA.) [See also art. شحى.] ═ And شَحَا فُوهُ, (Ṣ, Ḳ,*) aor. ـَ, (Ṣ,) inf. n. as above, (TA,) *His mouth opened;* (Ṣ, Ḳ;) as also ▼شحّى فوه; (TA;) but one should not say اشحى فوه. (IAạr, TA.) — And شَحَا, inf. n. as above, *He stepped, paced,* or *walked.* (TA.) Hence it is related in a trad. of 'Alee, that, having mentioned sedition, or conflict and faction, or the like, he said to 'Ammár, لَتَشْحُوَنَّ فِيهَا شَحْوًا لَا يُدْرِكُكَ الرَّجُلُ السَّرِيعُ, meaning *Thou shalt assuredly go* [or *step* or *pace*] *quickly, and advance, therein* [so that *the swift man shall not overtake thee*]. (TA.) And it is said that شَحَا فِيهِ signifies *He went far;* and *took a wide,* or *an ample, range; in it.* (TA. [See also 5.])

2: see the preceding paragraph, in two places.

4: see 1, first sentence.

5. تشحّى, accord. to Aboo-Sa'eed, primarily signifies *He took a wide,* or *an ample, range* in anything. (TA. [See also 1, last explanation.]) — [Hence,] تشحّى عَلَيْهِ *He spread out,* or *stretched out, his tongue,* [or *he gave wide range to his tongue,*] *respecting him* [or *against him*]. (Ḳ.)

شَحًا, (Ḳ,) thus with the short ا, (TA,) *Wide;* applied to anything: and ▼شَحْوَآءُ, applied to a well, signifies the same: (Ḳ:) or the latter, thus applied, *wide in the head* [or *upper part*]. (TA.)

شَحْوَةٌ *A step, pace,* or *single act of stepping* or *pacing.* (Ṣ, Ḳ.) One says, فَرَسٌ بَعِيدُ الشَّحْوَةِ *A horse having a far extent of step:* (Ṣ, TA:) and رَغِيبُ الشَّحْوَةِ (Ṣ in art. رغب) a horse *wide of step; that takes a large space of ground with his legs.* (TA: but there, الشَّحْوِ [which is the inf. n.].) — [Hence,] رَجُلٌ بَعِيدُ الشَّحْوَةِ فِى مَقَاصِدِهِ ‡ [*A man who strides along in his pursuits*]. (TA.) — And إِنَآءٌ وَاسِعُ الشَّحْوَةِ i. e. ‡ [*A vessel wide*] *in the interior.* (TA.)

شَحَآءٌ: see the next paragraph.

شَحْوَآءُ: see شَحًا. — Also A she-camel *wide of step:* and it is said in a trad. that the Prophet had a horse named ▼الشَّحَآءُ, thus related, with medd, [app. الشَّحَّآءُ, like الوَسَّاعُ,] expl. as meaning *the wide of step:* so says IAth. (TA.)

شَاحٍ [act. part. n. of 1: fem. شَاحِيَةٌ; pl. of the latter شَوَاحٍ and شَاحِيَاتٌ]. One says, جَآءَتِ الخَيْلُ

شَوَاحِيَ *The horses came opening their mouths:* (Ṣ, A, Ḳ,* TA:) and so أَقْبَلَتِ الخَيْلُ شَاحِيَاتٍ. (M, TA.) — And جَآءَنَا شَاحِيًا *He came to us stepping along.* (TA.) — And † *He came to us without any want.* (TA.) — الشَّوَاحِى is applied by the vulgar to *The large pieces of wood resembling columns:* but [SM says,] I have not seen any mention thereof in the [classical] language. (TA.)

شحى

1. شَحَى, like رَضِىَ, inf. n. شَحْىٌ, is said by ISd and in the Ḳ to be a dial. var. of شَحَا, inf. n. شَحْوٌ, i. e., as ISd says, meaning *He opened* his mouth; but the latter, he says, is the better known: this, however, requires consideration: for it is said in the Tekmileh that شَحَى فُلَانٌ, aor. يَشْحَى, inf. n. شَحْىٌ, is a dial. var. of [شَحَا, aor.] يَشْحُو, inf. n. شَحْوٌ, on the authority of Lth. (TA.)

شخب

1. شَخَبَ, (Mgh, TA,) aor. ُ [and ِ], inf. n. شَخْبٌ, said of milk, (Mgh,) and of anything, *It flowed.* (Mgh, TA.) And شَخَبْتُهُ *I made it to flow.* (Mgh.) You say, شَخَبَ اللَّبَنُ, aor. ُ and ِ, (Ṣ, O, CḲ,) inf. n. شَخْبٌ, (Ṣ, O,) *The milk flowed in an extended stream from the udder when milked;* (Ṣ, O, CḲ;) and † in like manner one says of blood: (O:) or شَخَبَ اللَّبَنَ, aor. ُ and ِ, *he made the milk to flow in a continuous stream from the udder* (Ḳ accord. to the TA [and accord. to the context in the Ḳ, in which it is immediately added فَانْشَخَبَ, showing that ▼ انشخب has the former of these two significations as quasi-pass. of شَخَبَ, and the like is said in the A,]) *between the vessel and the teat.* (TA.) Hence, i. e. from شَخَبَ اللَّبَنَ, the saying of El-Kumeyt,

وَوَحْوَحَ فِى حِضْنِ الفَتَاةِ ضَجِيعُهَا
وَلَمْ يَكُ فِى النُّكْدِ المَقَالِيتِ مَشْخَبُ ▼

[*And he who lay upon his side with her, or her bedfellow, breathed audibly, by reason of the cold, in the bosom of the young woman, and there was not, among the she-camels that had no young ones living, and that should therefore abound with milk, because not suckling, any flowing of milk in a continuous,* or *an extended, stream,* or *any time,* or *place, thereof,* for مَشْخَب may be, agreeably with a general rule, an inf. n. or a n. of time or of place]. (Ṣ.) And some expl. شَخْب as signifying *The sounding,* or *sound, of milk when it is being drawn from the udder.* (TA.) One says also, شَخَبَتْ أَوْدَاجُ القَتِيلِ دَمًا i. e. ‡ [*The external jugular veins of the slain person*] *streamed,* or *flowed with blood:* (Mṣb, TA:* [and the like is said in the Mgh:]) and شَخَبْتُهُ أَنَا † [*I made it to stream,* or *flow*]: the verb being intrans. and trans. (Mṣb.) And هُوَ يَشْخُبُ دَمًا † *He,* or *it, flows* [or *streams*] *with blood;* the last word being in the accus. case as a specificative: and *he,* or *it, pours forth,* or *makes to flow* [or *stream*], *blood;* the last word, when this is the meaning, being in the accus. case as an objective complement: but the former is that which is commonly known. (Mgh.) And شَخَبَتْ يَدَاهُ حَتَّى مَاتَ † [*His hands flowed,* or *streamed, with blood, until he died:* or *poured forth blood,* &c.]: said, in a trad., of one whose knuckles, or finger-joints, were cut. (TA.) ▼ انشخب, also, is said of blood [as meaning † *It flowed,* or *streamed*]. (TA.) And انشخب ▼ دَمًا, said of a vein, means † *It flowed,* or *streamed, with blood.* (Ṣ, Ḳ, TA.) And it is said in a trad. respecting the حَوْض [or pool (of the Apostle)], يَشْخُبُ فِيهِ مِيزَابَانِ مِنَ الجَنَّةِ † [*Two spouts will pour forth into it from Paradise*]. (TA.) And one says, شَخَبْتُ اللِّقَاحَ *I milked the milch camels.* (A, TA.) — And مَرَّ يَشْخَبُ فِى الأَرْضِ † *He went,* or *passed by,* (O,) or *ran,* (El-Fáïḳ, TA,) *swiftly* [*in the land,* or *upon the ground*]. (El-Fáïḳ, O, TA.)

7: see the preceding paragraph, in three places.

شَخَبٌ: see the next paragraph. — Also † *Blood.* (Ḳ.)

شُخْبٌ *Milk coming forth,* (A,) or *milk that has come forth,* (Ḳ,) *from the udder,* (A, Ḳ,) *when drawn therefrom;* (TA;) and so ▼ شَخْبٌ; (A, Ḳ;) which is also an inf. n.; (TA;) or this latter is an inf. n., (Ṣ, O,) and the former [is a subst. properly so called, and] signifies *an extended stream of milk,* (Ṣ, A, O,) *like a thread,* or *string,* (A,) *when it is drawn from the udder;* (Ṣ, A, O;) of the measure فُعْل in the sense of the measure مَفْعُول: (A:) or the *milk that comes forth from beneath the hand of the milker at each squeeze of the udder of the ewe or she-goat.* (TA.) It is said in a prov., شُخْبٌ فِى الإِنَآءِ وَشُخْبٌ فِى الأَرْضِ, (Ṣ, Meyd, A, O,) i. e. *One extended stream of milk from the udder into the vessel, and one &c. upon the ground:* (Meyd:) applied to him who hits the mark one time and misses another time (Ṣ, Meyd, A, O) in what he says; or says right one time and wrong another time. (Meyd.) And in another prov., شُخْبٌ طَمَحَ *An extended stream of milk from the udder that has fallen upon the ground* so as to be unprofitable; for such is the meaning of طَمَحَ in this case: applied to a man who has made a slip, or mistake: or it means a good hap that has escaped one's opportunity to avail himself of it. (Meyd.) See also the next paragraph.

شُخْبَةٌ *A single stream of milk from the udder;* (A, Ḳ;) pl. شِخَابٌ [q. v.]: (Ḳ:) or it signifies, (Ḳ,) or so ▼ شُخْبٌ, (TA,) *an extended stream of milk* (Ḳ, TA) *when it is drawn* (TA) *from the udder, streaming continuously* (Ḳ, TA) *between the vessel and the teat.* (TA.)

شِخَابٌ *Milk when it is drawn from the udder:* (A, Ḳ: [in which latter it is also said to be pl. of شُخْبَةٌ:]) of the dial. of El-Yemen. (TA.)

وَدَجٌ شَخِيبٌ † [*An external jugular vein*] *cut so that its blood has flowed,* or *streamed, forth.* (TA.)

أُشْخُوبٌ The *sound of the streaming of milk.* (Ṣ, O, Ḳ.) — [And it seems to be used as an epithet; for it is added that] one says, إِنَّهَا لَأُشْخُوبُ الأَحَالِيلِ [app. meaning *Verily she is one whereof the orifices of the teats produce a sound by the streaming of the milk*]. (Ṣ, O.)

مَشْخَبٌ: see the verse in the first paragraph.

شخت

1. شَخُتَ, (Ṣ, Ḳ,) aor. ُ, inf. n. شُخُوتَةٌ, (Ḳ,) said of a man, (Ṣ,) [and app., in like manner, of anything,] *He* [or *it*] *was,* or *became, thin,* or *slender,* (Ṣ, L, Ḳ,) *lean, and lank in the belly, not in consequence of emaciation.* (L, Ḳ.)

2. تَشْخِيتٌ The *bringing, conveying,* or *causing to come;* syn. إِبْلَاغٌ. (Ḳ.) One says, شَخَّتَهُ إِلَيْهِ *He brought it,* &c., *to him.* (TḲ.)

شَخْتٌ and ▼ شَخِيتٌ, (Ṣ, A, Ḳ,) the former also pronounced ▼ شَخَتٌ, (Ḳ, TA,) by some, (TA,) applied to a man, (Ṣ,) *Thin,* or *slender,* (Ṣ, A, L, Ḳ,) *lean, and lank in the belly, not in consequence of emaciation:* (A, L, Ḳ:) *slender in the body:* fem. of the first with ة: (TA:) pl. شِخَاتٌ: (Ṣ, A, Ḳ:) or شَخْتٌ signifies *thin,* or *slender,* as applied to anything: thus it is applied to him who is thin, or slender, in the neck, and in the legs: one says, [of a beast,] إِنَّهُ لَشَخْتُ الجُزَارَةِ *Verily he is thin,* or *slender, in the legs:* (TA:) and قَوَائِمُهُ شِخَاتٌ *His legs are thin,* or *slender:* (A:) and حَطَبٌ شَخْتٌ *Slender firewood.* (TA.) — [Hence,] إِنَّهُ لَشَخْتُ العَطَآءِ † *Verily he is one who gives little.* (TA.) And زَيْدٌ شَخْتُ الخُلُقِ ‡ *Zeyd is low, ignoble,* or *mean, in natural disposition.* (A, TA.) — Some say that it is arabicized, from the Pers. سَخْت. (TA.)

شَخَتٌ: see the next preceding paragraph.

شَخِيتٌ: see شَخْتٌ: — and also what here follows.

شَخِيتٌ and ▼ شِخِّيتٌ and شِخْتِيتٌ Dust (غُبَارٌ) *rising,* or *spreading,* or *diffusing itself.* (Ḳ.)

شِخْتِيتٌ: see what next precedes.

شخر

1. شَخَرَ, aor. ِ, inf. n. شَخِيرٌ (Ṣ, Ḳ) and شَخْرٌ, (Ḳ,) *He raised his voice, with snorting;* said of an ass: (Ṣ:) *he uttered a sound from the fauces:* or *from the nose:* (Ḳ:) or *from the mouth, without the nose:* (TA:) *he* (a horse) *neighed:* (Ḳ:) or *uttered a sound after neighing:* (TA:) or *uttered a sound from his mouth,* (Ḳ, TA,) *without the nose:* (TA:) Aṣ says that among the sounds made by horses are those termed شَخِير and نَخِير and كَرِير; the first of which is from the mouth; the second, from the nostrils; and the third, from the chest: some say that شَخَرَ is like نَخَرَ [*he snorted*]. (TA.)

شَخْرٌ The *first period* or *stage of youth;* (Ḳ, TA;) and the *sharpness* thereof: like شَرْخٌ. (TA.)

— The *part*, of a رَحْل [or camel's saddle], *that is between the* قَادِمَة *and the* آخِرَة, (O, Ḳ, TA,) which are the حَقْوَانِ: (TA:) [said to be] also called the شَرْخ, [which is an evident mistake, perhaps originating from its having been said that شَخْر and شَرْخ are syn., meaning in another sense, mentioned above,] (O, TA,) and the شُخْر [q. v.]: (TA:) or the *space between the upper part of the two extremities* [*at the fore part and hind part*] of the [saddle called] قَتَب. (JK.) — And The *chink* of the buttocks. (JK, O. [In the Ḳ, for وَشَخْرُ الإِسْتِ شَقُّهَا, the reading in the JK and O, is put وَشَخْرَ الإِسْتَ شَقَّهَا.])

شَخِيرٌ *That utters much,* or *often, the sound* termed نَخِير: (Ḳ:) or, as in some copies of the Ḳ [and in the O], شَخِير: (TA:) [see نَخَرَ and شَخَرَ:] applied to an ass in this sense, (O,) or as signifying *vociferous*. (TA.)

شخس

1. شَخَسَ, aor. ـَ, (Ḳ,) inf. n. شَخْسٌ, (Ṣ, A, O, Ḳ,) *It was,* or *became, conflicting, incongruous,* or *dissimilar, in its several parts;* شَخْسٌ being *syn. with* اضْطِرَابٌ and اخْتِلَافٌ [here used in the same, or nearly the same, sense]. (Ṣ, A, O, Ḳ.) — Also, (Ḳ,) inf. n. as above; (Lth, O, Ḳ;) or ▼ شاخس; (so says Lth, TA; and so in a copy of the A;) and ▼ تشاخس; (O, Ḳ;) said of an ass, (Lth, A, O, Ḳ,) *He opened his mouth on the occasion of gaping* (Lth, O, Ḳ) *and smelling the urine of a she-ass:* (Lth, O:) or *he opened his mouth, raising his head, after smelling the dung.* (A.) It is said that the primary signification of الشَّخْسُ is *The opening of the mouth to gape.* (Ḥam p. 196.)

3. شاخس فَاهُ, said of time, *It caused his teeth to become incongruous;* (ISk, A, O;) *some of them being long and some of them being broken:* (ISk, O:) this is the case in extreme old age: (A, TA:) مُشَاخَسَةٌ and شِخَاسٌ, [as inf. ns. of the pass. verb,] in relation to the teeth, signify their *being in such a condition that some of them incline and some of them have fallen out:* (JK, TA:*) one says, [شُوخِسَ فَاهُ, or شُوخِسَتْ أَسْنَانُهُ, and] ▼ تشاخس فُوهُ, (A,) or تشاخست أَسْنَانُهُ, (Ṣ, O, Ḳ,) *His teeth became incongruous,* (Ṣ, A, O, Ḳ,) *and some of them inclined and some of them fell out,* (Ṣ, O, Ḳ,) *by reason of extreme old age.* (Ṣ, A,* O, Ḳ.) — شاخس الصَّدْعَ, said of the repairer of a wooden bowl, *He made the crack* of the bowl *to incline, so that it remained not closed up.* (O, Ḳ.) = See also 1.

4. اشخس † *He showed a sour, a crabbed,* or *an austere, face,* (Aboo-Sa'eed, O, Ḳ,) لَهُ *to him,* (Aboo-Sa'eed, TA,) فِى المَنْطِقِ *in speech;* as also اشخص. (Aboo-Sa'eed, O, TA.) — And اشخسهُ, (O, Ḳ,) and اشخس بِهِ, (TA,) † *He spoke evil of him behind his back,* or *in his absence,* or *otherwise, with truth,* or *though it might be with truth;* syn. اِغْتَابَهُ; (O, Ḳ, TA;) as also اشخص بِهِ. (TA.)

6. تشاخس: see 1: and 3. — *It* (a crack in a wooden bowl) *was made* by the repairer *to incline, so that it remained not closed up.* (TA.) — *It,* said of the upper part of a man's skull, (i. e. said of his قِحْف, IDrd, O,) or said of his head, (Ḳ,) *became severed in twain,* in consequence of a blow: (IDrd, O, Ḳ:) or said of the two [lateral] bones of his head (قِحْفَا رَأْسِهِ), meaning تدانيا واختلفا; [but the former of these two verbs is app. a mistranscription for تَبَايَنَا; and the meaning, *they became separated, each from the other, and not fitting together:*] and it is sometimes said of the thumb; and of a vessel. (TA.) — تشاخس القَوْمُ † *The people,* or *party, became distant,* or *remote, one from another.* (JK.) — تشاخس أَمْرُ القَوْمِ † *The state of affairs of the people,* or *party, became divided,* (O, Ḳ,* TA,*) *and conflicting,* or *inconsistent.* (TA.) And تشاخس مَا بَيْنَ القَوْمِ † *The state between the people,* or *party, became bad,* or *corrupt.* (ISk, Ṣ, O, Ḳ.*)

شَخِيسٌ † An affair, or a state of affairs, (أَمْرٌ,) *disorganized, disordered,* or *unsettled;* syn. مُتَفَرِّقٌ. (Ḳ.) — † Speech *in which is a sour, a crabbed,* or *an austere, look:* (JK: [like شَخِيصٌ:]) or ‡ *incongruous,* or *discordant, speech;* (O, Ḳ, TA;) as also ▼ مُتَشَاخِسٌ, (A'Obeyd, TA, in art. شخص,) and مُتَشَاخِصٌ. (Ḳ ibid.) — [A man] *adverse to that which he is commanded to do.* (TA.)

مُتَشَاخِسٌ: see the next preceding paragraph.

شخص

1. شَخَصَ, (Ṣ, A, Mṣb, Ḳ,) aor. ـَ, (A, Mṣb, Ḳ,) inf. n. شُخُوصٌ, (Ṣ, Mṣb, Ḳ,) *He,* or *it, rose;* or *became raised,* or *elevated.* (Ṣ, A, Mṣb, Ḳ.) — [Hence,] *It* (a star) *rose.* (Ḳ.) And شَخَصَ لَهُ شَخْصٌ [*A figure seen from a distance rose to his view*]. (TA in art. زول.) — شَخَصَ بَصَرُهُ, (Ṣ, Mgh, Mṣb, Ḳ, [in some copies of the Ḳ, بَصَرَهُ, but this occurs afterwards in that work,]) is said when a man opens his eyes and then does not move his eyelids; [and signifies ‡ *His eyes,* or lit., *his eye, became fixedly open:*] (Ṣ, Ḳ:*) or it signifies *his eye became raised:* (Mṣb:) or *his sight became stretched and raised.* (Mgh.) [See the Ḳur xiv. 43, and xxi. 97.] You say, شَخَصَ إِلَيْكَ بَصَرِى ‡ [*My eye,* or *eyes, became fixedly open,* or *raised,* or *my sight became stretched and raised, towards thee*]. (A.) And شَخَصَ بَصَرُ المَيِّتِ, (A,) inf. n. as above, (IAth,) ‡ [*The eye,* or *eyes, of the dying man became fixedly open:* or] *the eyelids of the dying man became raised upwards, and he looked intently, and became disquieted,* or *disturbed.* (IAth.) — شَخَصَتِ الكَلِمَةُ مِنَ الفَمِ † *The word,* or *sentence, rose* [*from the mouth*] *towards the palate:* this is sometimes natural: i. e., one's raising his voice, and not being able to lower it. (Ḳ.) — شَخَصَ السَّهْمُ (inf. n. as above, Mṣb,) ‡ *The arrow rose* [*so as to deviate*] *from the butt,* or *object of aim:* (Ḳ:) or *the arrow passed beyond the butt,* or *object of aim, going above it:* (A, Mṣb:) or *rose in the sky.* (ISh.) — شَخَصَ (aor. as above, Mṣb, and so the inf. n., Ṣ, Mṣb,) also signifies *He went,* or *went away,* from one town or country to another: (Ṣ, A, Ḳ:) or *he went forth* from one place to another, (Mṣb,) or from his place of alighting or abiding: (TA:) or [so accord. to the TA, but in the Ḳ "and"] *he journeyed upwards.* (Ḳ, TA.) You say also, شَخَصَ مِنْ قَوْمِهِ *He went forth from his people:* and شَخَصَ إِلَيْهِمْ *he returned to them.* (TA.) — Also, (M, Ḳ,) aor. and inf. n. as above, (M,) *It* (a thing) *rose;* or *swelled;* or *became swollen:* (M:) *it* (a wound) *rose, and became swollen:* (M, Ḳ:) [*it was,* or *became, protuberant,* or *prominent.*] = شَخَصَ بَصَرَهُ, (Mṣb, Ḳ, TA,) or شَخَصَ بِبَصَرِهِ, (Mgh,) or both, (TA, [in which it is said to be tropical,]) and شَخَصَ بِبَصَرِهِ إِلَى السَّمَآءِ, (Mṣb,) or شَخَصَ [alone], (so in a copy of the A, [in which it is mentioned among proper expressions,]) † *He raised his eye,* or *sight,* (Ḳ, TA,) *towards the sky, and did not move his eyelids;* said of a dying man: (TA:) or *he stretched and raised his sight:* (Mgh:) or *he opened his eyes,* (A, Mṣb,) *and did not move his eyelids,* (A,) or [*looking fixedly,*] *not moving his eyelids.* (Mṣb.) — يَشْخَصُ بِصَوْتِهِ فَلَا يَقْدِرُ عَلَى خَفْضِهِ ‡ [*He raises his voice, and is not able to lower it*]. (Ḳ.) — شُخِصَ بِهِ, (Ṣ, Ḳ,) coordinate to عُنِىَ, (Ḳ,) or شُخِصَ [alone], (so in a copy of the A,) or شُخِصَ بِهِ أَمْرٌ, coordinate to تَعِبَ, inf. n. شَخَصٌ, (Mṣb,) ‡ [*He was disquieted by a thing that happened to him:* or] *a thing that disquieted him happened to him:* (Ṣ, A, Ḳ:) or *a thing happened to him and disquieted him:* (Mṣb:) as though he were raised from the ground by reason of his disquietude. (TA.) [See also 4.] = شَخُصَ, aor. ـُ, (Ṣ, Ḳ,) inf. n. شَخَاصَةٌ, or this is a simple subst., [for] ISd says, I have not heard a verb of which it may be the inf. n., (TA,) [if used, signifying] *He* (a man, Ṣ) *was,* or *became, big, bulky,* or *corpulent.* (Ṣ, Ḳ.)

2. شخّص الشَّىْءَ, (A,) inf. n. تَشْخِيصٌ, (TA,) ‡ *He individuated the thing;* syn. عَيَّنَهُ. (A, TA.) [From شَخْصٌ, q. v.]

4. اشخصهُ [*He made him,* or *it, to rise,* or *become raised* or *elevated*]. You say, اشخص نَفْسَهُ [*He raised himself;* or *drew,* or *stretched, himself up*]. (Ṣ and Ḳ in art. علب.) — اشخص بِسَهْمِهِ ‡ *He made his arrow to pass beyond the butt,* or *object of aim, going above it.* (A.) — And اشخصهُ *He made him to go,* or *go away,* from one town or country to another: (Ṣ:) or *to go forth* from one place to another: (A,* Mṣb:) or *to go,* or *journey:* (A in art. سير:) or *to journey upwards.* (TA.) — ‡ *He disquieted him,* (Ḳ, TA,) *so that he went away* from a place. (TA.) [See also 1.] = اشخص ‡ *His* (an archer's) *arrow passed beyond the butt,* or *object of aim,* (Ṣ, A, Mṣb, Ḳ,) *going above it.* (Ṣ, A, Mṣb.) = *The time of his journeying, going away,* or *departing, came,* or *arrived.* (Ṣ, Ḳ, TA.) = اشخص إِلَيْهِ ‡ *He showed him a sour, a crabbed,* or *an austere, face,* or *countenance;* looked at him *in a sour, a crabbed,* or *an austere, manner;* (A, TA;) or so اشخص لَهُ, (TA in art. شخس,) فِى المَنْطِقِ *in speech;* as also اشخس. (Aboo

Sa'eed, O and TA in art. شخص.) — اشخص بِفُلَانٍ ‡ *He spoke evil of such a one behind his back*, or *in his absence*, or *otherwise, with truth*, or *though it might be with truth*; syn. اِغْتَابَهُ; (Yaḳkoob on the authority of AO, Ṣ, A, Ḳ;) as also اشخص. (AO, Yaḳkoob, Ṣ.)

5. تشخّص [quasi-pass. of 2; † *It was*, or *became, individuated; it*, or *he, had*, or *assumed, the quality of individuality* or *personality*; syn. تَعَيَّنَ].

شَخْصٌ The *body*, or *bodily* or *corporeal form* or *figure* or *substance*, (سَوَادٌ,) *of a man*, (Ṣ, A, Mṣb, Ḳ,) or *some other object* or *thing*, (Ṣ, A, Ḳ,) *which one sees from a distance*: (Ṣ, A, Mṣb, Ḳ:) applying in common to *what is termed* جُثَّةٌ and *what is termed* طَلَلٌ, *in relation to a man*; i. e., *in relation to a man sitting* or *sleeping* [or *lying down*], and *in relation to a man standing erect*: (Mṣb, voce جُثَّةٌ:) or it is applied only to *a body*, or *material substance, composed*, [*not simple*,] *and having height*: (El-Khaṭṭábee, Mṣb, TA:) or *any body*, or *material thing* or *substance*, [*that is somewhat high, and conspicuous*, or] *having height and appearance*: (IAth, TA:) pl. (of pauc., Ṣ) أَشْخُصٌ (Ṣ, Ḳ) and (of mult., Ṣ) أَشْخَاصٌ [which is properly another pl. of pauc.] and شُخُوصٌ (Ṣ, A, Ḳ) and شِخَاصٌ. (TA.) — Then used as signifying † *A man himself; a man's self*, or *person; his* ذَات; (Mṣb;) [i. e.,] *a person; a being; an individual*; syn. نَفْسٌ [also syn. with ذَاتٌ]; (L, TA;) as in the following verse of 'Amr Ibn-Rabee'ah, cited by Sb:

• فَكَانَ مِجَنِّى دُونَ مَنْ كُنْتُ أَتَّقِى •
• ثَلَاثُ شُخُوصٍ كَاعِبَانِ وَمُعْصِرُ •

† [*And three persons*, namely, *two girls whose breasts were beginning to swell and one who had attained the age of puberty, were my shield against such as I was fearing*]: meaning ثَلَاثَةُ أَنْفُسٍ: (L:) [the poet making the word in question fem. because it relates here to females: but] Rubeh is related to have said ثَلَاثَةُ أَشْخُصٍ, meaning, of women. (M, voce نَفْسٌ.) A شخص [meaning *a person*] ceases to be a شخص by its being divided; whereas, when a جسم is divided, no part of it ceases to be a جسم. (Er-Rághib, TA in art. جسم.) It is said in a trad., لَا شَخْصَ أَغْيَرُ مِنَ ٱللّٰهِ ‡ [*There is not any being more jealous than God*]; شخص being here metaphorically used for ذات: or the meaning is, *a person* (شخص) *should not be more jealous than God*: but accord. to one relation, the words are لَا شَىْءَ أَغْيَرُ مِنَ ٱللّٰهِ [which has the first of the two meanings mentioned above]. (IAth, TA.) [It is also used in a pl. sense: see a verse of Ziyád el-Aạjam in art. الى.]

شَخِيصٌ *Big, bulky*, or *corpulent*: (Ṣ, Ḳ, TA:) or *great in* شَخْص [or *person*] *and make*: (TA:) applied to a man: (Ṣ:) fem. with ة; (Ṣ, A, Ḳ;) applied to a woman. (Ṣ, A.) — *A lord, master, chief, man of rank* or *quality*, or *a personage*. (AZ, Ḳ.) — مَنْطِقٌ شَخِيصٌ ‡ *Sour, crabbed*, or *austere, speech*. (Ibn-'Abbád, A, Ḳ. [See also شَخِيسٌ.])

شَخَاصَةٌ *Bigness, bulkiness*, or *corpulence*: or *greatness of* شَخْص [or *person*] *and make*. (TA.) [Said to be a subst.: but see شُخُوص.]

شَاخِصٌ [part. n. of the intrans. verb شَخَصَ]. [Hence,] بَصَرٌ شَاخِصٌ ‡ [*An eye fixedly open*: or *raised*: or *sight stretched and raised*: see 1]: you say, سَمِعْتُ بِقُدُومِكَ فَقَلْبِى بَيْنَ جَنَاحَىَّ رَاقِصٌ وَبَصَرِى تَحْتَ حِجَاجِى شَاخِصٌ ‡ [*I have heard of thy coming, and my heart is throbbing between my two sides, and my eye beneath my bone of the eyebrow fixedly open*, &c.]. (A, TA.) With the pl., أَبْصَارٌ, you say شَاخِصَةٌ, (A, Mṣb, TA,) and شَوَاخِصُ, (A, TA,) or شُخُوصٌ [like شُهُودٌ as pl. of شَاهِدٌ; if not an inf. n., as which it may be applied, in the place of an epithet, to a pl. subst.]. (Mṣb.) — سَهْمٌ شَاخِصٌ ‡ *An arrow passing beyond the butt*, or *object of aim, going above it*. (Ṣ, A.) You say, رُمِىَ بِالشَّاخِصَاتِ ‡ [*He was shot at with arrows which passed beyond him, going above him*: perhaps doubly tropical, meaning *he was assailed with invectives which did not harm him*]. (A.) — شَاخِصٌ also signifies A man *prosecuting war* [*during three or more days together*,] *not on alternate days*: and of such it is said in a trad., that he may shorten prayer. (TA.) = شَاخِصٌ as the act. part. n. of the trans. verb, [for شَاخِصٌ بَصَرَهُ,] (Mṣb,) † [A man *raising his eye*, or *sight, and looking fixedly*; as does a dying man: or *stretching and raising his sight*: (see 1:) or] a man *opening his eyes and not moving his eyelids*. (Ṣ,* Mṣb.)

[مَشْخَصٌ, as though signifying The *place of a* شَخْص used in the sense of صُورَة: accord. to modern usage sing. of] مَشَاخِصُ *deenárs* [or *pieces of gold*] *figured* [or *stamped with effigies*]. (TA.)

مُشَخَّصٌ ‡ A thing *individuated*. (A, TA.)

مُتَشَاخِصٌ *Discordant*; (A'Obeyd, Ḳ;) applied to language, or speech; (A'Obeyd, TA;) and to a thing, or an affair; (TA;) and مُتَشَاخِسٌ signifies the same. (A'Obeyd, TA.)

شد

1. شَدَّ, as an intrans. verb, aor. ـِ, inf. n. شِدَّةٌ: see 8; and see also شَدَّ. — [Hence,] لَشَدَّ مَا is an expression used in the same sense as لَعَزَّ مَا (A and Ḳ in art. عز) and لَحَقَّ مَا: (A and TA in that art.:) [and in like manner without the ل: thus] one says, شَدَّ مَا أَنَّكَ ذَاهِبٌ, meaning حَقَّ أَنَّكَ ذَاهِبٌ [i. e. *It is distressing*, or *it distresses me, that thou art going away*]: and if you please, you may consider شَدَّ as similar to نِعْمَ; as when you say, نِعْمَ العَمَلُ أَنَّكَ تَقُولُ الحَقَّ [Excellent, or most excellent, is the deed, thy saying the truth]. (Sb, TA.) [And it is also used to render intensive a verb following it; as in the saying, لَشَدَّ مَا أَبْغَضَنِى *Much indeed*, or *greatly indeed, did he hate me*.] — شَدَّ عَلَيْهِ, aor. ـِ (Ṣ, L) and ـُ, (L,) inf. n. شَدٌّ (Ṣ, L) and شُدُودٌ, (L,) *He charged*, or *made an assault* or *attack, upon him*, in war, or battle. (Ṣ, L.) You say, شَدَّ عَلَى العَدُوِّ شَدَّةً وَاحِدَةً, and شَدَّاتٍ كَثِيرَةً, *He made one charge*, or *assault*, or *attack, upon the enemy*, and *many charges*, &c. (L.) And شَدَّ عَلَى قِرْنِهِ بِسِكِّينٍ, or بِعَصًا, *He made an assault*, or *attack, upon his adversary, with a knife*, or *with a staff*; as also اشتدّ ▼ عَلَيْهِ. (Mgh.) And شَدَّ الذِّئْبُ عَلَى الغَنَمِ *The wolf assaulted*, or *attacked, the sheep or goats*. (L.) In the phrase, شَدُّوا الإِغَارَةَ, the meaning is شَدُّوا لِلْإِغَارَةِ [*They made a charge for the purpose of a sudden attack* upon an enemy, or *a predatory incursion*]; and therefore الاغارة is put in the accus. case, not as an objective complement. (Ḥam p. 8.) — شَدَّ, (Ṣ,) aor. ـِ and ـُ, (TḲ,) inf. n. شَدٌّ, (Ṣ, L, Ḳ,) also signifies *He ran*; (Ṣ, L,* Ḳ;*) and so ▼ اشتدّ. (Ṣ, L, Ḳ.) رُبَّ شَدٍّ فِى الكُرْزِ [*Many a run is in the sack*] is a prov., originating from the fact that a man riding a pregnant mare was pursued by an enemy, and she cast her foal, which ran with its mother, whereupon the horseman alighted, and carried it off in a sack; and the enemy overtook him, and said to him, "Throw to me the foal;" and he replied in these words, meaning that the foal was of generous race: it is applied to him whose internal, or intrinsic, qualities are commended. (Meyd.) And one says, شَدَّ فِى العَدْوِ, (A, Mgh, L,) inf. n. شَدٌّ; (L;) and ▼ اشتدّ; (A, Mgh, L;) *He hastened*, or *was quick, in running*: (Mgh, L:) and شَدَّ الإِحْضَارَ [meaning the same]. (Ṣ in art. افر.) — شَدَّ النَّهَارُ, (Ṣ, L,) and الضُّحَى, (L,) inf. n. شَدٌّ; (L, Ḳ; but in the latter, النَّار is erroneously put for النَّهَار; TA;) and ▼ اشتدّ; (L;) *The day*, and *the morning, became advanced, the sun being high*. (Ṣ,* L, Ḳ.*) [See also شَدٌّ below.] = شَدَّهُ, aor. ـُ (Ṣ, A, L, Mṣb) and ـِ, the latter anomalous, for the aor. of a trans. verb of this class, of the measure فَعَلَ, should be ـُ only, and that of an intrans. verb of the same class and measure should be ـِ, and this is the only instance, or almost the only one, of its kind, with both of these forms of aor., except عَلَّ [and نَمَّ] and بَثَّ] and [الحَدِيثَ, but there is one trans. verb of the same class having the latter form of aor. only, namely, حَبَّ, (Fr, Ṣ, L,) inf. n. شَدٌّ, (L, Mṣb, Ḳ,) *He made it*, or *rendered it, hard*; used in relation to substances and attributes: (L:) *he made*, or *rendered, it*, or *him, firm, compact*, or *sound*; and *strong, powerful*, or *forcible*; *vigorous, robust*, or *sturdy*; syn. أَحْكَمَهُ, (L,) and قَوَّاهُ; (Ṣ, A, L, Ḳ;*) as also ▼ شَدَّدَهُ, [inf. n. تَشْدِيدٌ,] i. e. as syn. with احكمهُ (L) and قوّاهُ: (Ṣ, A, L:) *he bound*, or *tied, him*, or *it, firmly, fast*, or *strongly*; syn. أَوْثَقَهُ: [which may also be meant to convey the signification immediately preceding this last:] (Ṣ, L, Mṣb, Ḳ:) and [simply] *he tied, bound*, or *made fast, him*, or *it*; syn. رَبَطَهُ. (Ṣ and Mṣb and Ḳ &c. in art. ربط.) One says, شَدَّ عَضُدَهُ i. e. *He*

strengthened [*his fore arm*, or perhaps *his upper arm*, but the former is app. here meant]. (Ṣ, L.) And شَدَّ عَلَى يَدِهِ *He strengthened him*, [lit. *his arm*, or *hand*,] *and aided him*. (L.) And شَدَّ اللّٰهُ مُلْكَهُ, and ↓شَدَّدَهُ, *God strengthened*, or *may God strengthen, his dominion*. (Ṣ, L. [See also a similar ex. voce أَزْرٌ.]) And شَدَّ العُقْدَةَ [*He tied firmly* or *fast* or *strongly*, or *he pulled tight*, or *tightened, the knot*], (A, Mgh, Mṣb,) and الوَثَاقَ [*the bond*]. (Ḳur xlvii. 4.) [And شَدَّ الدَّابَّةَ *He bound the saddle on the beast*: see an ex. voce دَلِيلٌ.] شَدُّ الرِّحَالِ [lit. *The binding of the camels' saddles* upon their backs] is a metonymical phrase for ‡ *the going a journey*. (Mgh, Mṣb.) And شَدُّ المِئْزَرِ, occurring in a trad., [lit. *The binding of the waist-wrapper* upon the waist] is a metonymical phrase for ‡ *the avoiding of women*: or *the exerting oneself*, or *employing oneself vigorously* or *laboriously, in work*: or for both of these together. (L.) مَا أَمْلِكُ شَدًّا وَلَا إِرْخَآءً [lit. *I possess not power to tighten nor to slacken*] means *I am not able to do anything*. (TA.) [And شَدَّهُ also signifies *He pressed, compressed*, or *squeezed, it*: and *he pulled*, or *strained, it*.] وَاشْدُدْ عَلَى قُلُوبِهِمْ, in the Ḳur [x. 88], means *And put Thou a seal upon their hearts*, so that they may not heed admonition, nor be disposed, or directed, to that which is good. (L.) ═ أَشُدُّ لَقَدْ كَانَ كَذَا, as also أَشُدَ without teshdeed, means أَشْهَدُ [q. v.]: (Ḳ:) a strange saying. (TA.)

2: see the preceding paragraph, latter half, in two places. — شَدَّدَهُ, inf. n. تَشْدِيدٌ, also signifies *He made it*, or *rendered it*, namely, a beating, and anything, *hard to be borne, heavy, vehement, violent, intense, severe, strict, rigorous*, or *excessive*; *he intensified it*, or *aggravated it*: (L:) تشديد is the *contr. of* تَخْفِيفٌ [in this sense and in other senses here following]. (Ṣ.) [Hence, the objective complement being understood,] one says, شَدَّدَ عَلَيْهِ, (A, Mṣb,) which is the *contr. of* خَفَّفَ [i. e. of خَفَّفَ عَنْهُ; thus meaning *He rendered his burden, suffering, distress, uneasiness*, or *the like, hard to be borne, heavy, vehement, violent, intense, severe, strict, rigorous*, or *excessive*; *intensified it*, or *aggravated it*; or *he pressed hard upon him*; *treated him with hardness, strictness, severity*, or *rigour*]: (Mṣb:) and مَنْ شَدَّدَ شَدَّدَ اللّٰهُ عَلَيْهِ [*Whoso treateth* others *hardly, God will treat him hardly*]. (A. [See also 8.]) — [تَشْدِيدٌ, as opposed to تَخْفِيفٌ, also signifies The *characterizing of a letter by a lengthened pronunciation equivalent in grammatical analysis and in prosody to doubling, denoted in writing by the sign called* ↓شَدَّةٌ, i. e. *by the sign* ّ over that letter; as also تَثْقِيلٌ.] — See also شَدَّدَهُ.

3. شَادَّهُ, (A, L,) inf. n. مُشَادَّةٌ and شِدَادٌ, (L,) *He vied with him, contended with him for superiority*, or *strove to surpass him, in strength, power*, or *force*. (A, L.) [Hence,] مَنْ يُشَادِدِ الدِّينَ يَغْلِبْهُ, (A,) or مَنْ يُشَادَّ هٰذَا الدِّينَ يَغْلِبْهُ, i. e. *Whoso contendeth for superiority in strength with this religion, and withstandeth it*, or *opposeth it, and tasketh himself with religious service beyond his power, it* (the religion) *will overcome him*: a trad. (L.) And لَنْ يُشَادَّ الدِّينَ أَحَدٌ إِلَّا غَلَبَ *No one shall contend for superiority in strength with religion, &c. but he will be overcome* by the religion. (Ḳ,* TA.) — See also 5.

4. اشدّ, (Ṣ, A, L, Ḳ,) inf. n. إِشْدَادٌ, (Ḳ,) *He*, (a man, Ṣ, L, Ḳ,*) or *they*, (a company of men, A, L,) *had*, (A, L,) or *had with him*, (Ṣ, L, Ḳ,) [or *had with them*,] *a strong beast*, (Ṣ, L, Ḳ,) or *strong beasts*. (A, L.) ═ [مَا أَشَدَّ كَذَا *How hard, hard to be borne, vehement, violent, intense*, or *the like*, or *how great, is such a thing!*]

5. تشدّد *He acted*, or *behaved, with forced hardness, firmness, strength, vigour, hardiness, courage, vehemence, severity, strictness*, or *rigour*; *he exerted his strength, force*, or *energy*; *strained*, or *strained himself*, or *tasked himself severely*; syn. تَصَلَّبَ; (A and TA in art. صلب;) and جَهَدَ نَفْسَهُ; (L;) [فِى الشَّىْءِ *in the thing*; as also ↓شَادَّ فِيهِ;] for التَّشَدُّدُ فِيهِ and المُشَادَّةُ فِى الشَّىْءِ signify the same: (Ṣ, L, Ḳ:* [see an ex. of تشدّد in the first paragraph of art. جلد:]) [and] both of these phrases signify *the showing hardness*, &c., *in the thing*. (PṢ.) You say also تَشَدَّدَ لِلْأَمْرِ *He applied himself with hardness, firmness, vigour, hardiness, severity*, or *rigour, to the affair*. (MA.) And تَشَدَّدَتِ القَيْنَةُ *The slave-songstress strained herself*, or *tasked herself severely*, in raising her voice in singing. (L.) — Also *He* (a man) *was*, or *became, hard*, or *difficult*: you say, سَأَلْنَا فُلَانًا حَاجَةً فَتَشَدَّدَ عَلَيْنَا [*We asked of such a one a thing wanted, and he was hard*, or *difficult, to us*]. (TA in art. وعر.) — And *He was*, or *became, niggardly, tenacious*, or *avaricious*. (MA, KL.)

6. تَشَادُّوا [*They vied, contended for superiority*, or *strove to surpass one another, in strength, power*, or *force*: see 3]. (TA in art. حمس: there coupled with اِقْتَتَلُوا.) — See also the next paragraph.

8. اشتدّ; (Ṣ, A, L, Mṣb;) and ↓شَدَّ, aor. ـِ, (L, Mṣb,) the only form of its aor., (L,) inf. n. شِدَّةٌ, (Ṣ, Mṣb,) whence the former verb; (Ṣ;) and ↓تَشَادَّ; (L;) *It was*, or *became, hard*, (L, and MA and KL and PṢ in explanation of the first,) said of a substance and of an attribute: (L:) *it*, or *he, was*, or *became, firm, compact*, or *sound*; (L &c. as above;) *strong, powerful*, or *forcible*; *vigorous, robust*, or *sturdy*; (L, and A and MA and KL in explanation of the first, and Mṣb in explanation of the second:) [also *it was*, or *became, bound*, or *tied, firmly, fast*, or *strongly*:] and the first of these verbs, [and the second also,] *it was*, or *became, hard to be borne, heavy, vehement, violent, intense, pressing, severe, strict, rigorous, tight, strait* or *difficult, distressing* or *distressful, afflictive, calamitous*, or *adverse*. (MA, L, KL.) It is said in a trad., لَا تَبِيعُوا الحَبَّ حَتَّى يَشْتَدَّ i. e. [*Ye shall not sell grain*] *until it becomes hard*, or *firm*, or *strong*. (L.) And you say, اشتدّت العُقْدَةُ [*The knot became tied firmly, fast*, or *strongly*; or *became tight*]. (A, Mgh, Mṣb.) And اشتدّ الزَّمَنُ عَلَيْهِمْ *The time*, or *fortune, became hard upon them*; or *severe, rigorous, distressful, afflictive, calamitous*, or *adverse, to them*. (L. [See also 2.]) And اشتدّ بِهِ الأَمْرُ [*The affair*, or *event, distressed*, or *afflicted, him*; like اشتدّ عَلَيْهِ]. (L in art. جهد, &c.) — See also 1, former half, in four places.

شَدٌّ an inf. n. of 1 [q. v.]. (Ṣ, L, &c.) — [Hence,] شَدُّ النَّهَارِ, and شَدُّ الضُّحَى, *The time when the day*, and *the morning, is advanced, the sun being high*. (L.) One says, جِئْتُكَ شَدَّ النَّهَارِ, and شَدَّ الضُّحَى, (L, and the like is said in the A,) and فِى شَدِّ النَّهَارِ, and فِى شَدِّ الضُّحَى, (L,) *I came to thee in the time when the day*, and *the morning, was advanced, the sun being high*. (A,* L.)

شَدَّةٌ [inf. n. of un. of شَدَّهُ: as such signifying] *A single act* [*of making*, or *rendering, hard, firm, compact*, or *sound*; *strong, powerful*, or *forcible*: and] *of binding*, or *tying, firmly, fast*, or *strongly*. (Mṣb.) — See also 2, last sentence but one. ═ Also [inf. n. of un. of the intrans. verb شَدَّ: as such signifying] *A single charge* or *assault* or *attack* in war or battle. (Ṣ, A,* Mgh, L, Ḳ.*)

شِدَّةٌ inf. n. of ↓شَدَّ (L, Mṣb) as syn. with اشتدّ: (L:) [and] a subst. from [i. e. syn. with] اِشْتِدَادٌ: (Ḳ:) The *attribute denoted by the epithet* شَدِيدٌ: (Ṣ:) *hardness*, (A, MA, L,) in substances and in attributes; (L;) *firmness, compactness*, or *soundness*; *strength, power*, or *force*; *vigour, robustness, sturdiness*, or *hardiness*; (MA, L; see أَشُدٌّ, which, accord. to some, is a pl. of شِدَّةٌ;) *courage, bravery, firmness of heart*: (L:) *niggardliness, tenaciousness*, or *avarice*: (A: [see also 5, last sentence:]) *vehemence, violence, intenseness, stress, pressure, severity, strictness, rigour, tightness, straitness* or *difficulty*: (MA:) *hardship, rigour of fortune*: (MA, L:) *famine, dearth, want of victuals*; *hardness, straitness*, or *difficulty*, of subsistence [&c.]: (L:) *trouble, distress, affliction, calamity*, or *adversity*; (MA, L;) as also [↓شُدَّى, in these as well as in some of the preceding senses, and] ↓شَدِيدَةٌ, [rather meaning *a hard*, or *distressing, event, an affliction*, or *a calamity*, and rarely used,] of which, (L,) or of شِدَّةٌ, (MA, L,) the pl. is شَدَائِدُ, (MA, L,) agreeably with analogy if of شَدِيدَةٌ, but extr. if of شِدَّةٌ: and this pl. also signifies *seditions, discords*, or *dissensions, whereby men are put into a state of commotion*: (L:) and the *rigours*, or *pangs*, (غَمَرَات,) of death: (Ṣ and Mṣb in art. غمر:) accord. to Sb, the pl of شِدَّةٌ is شِدَدٌ, which, he says, preserves its original form [without idghám] because it does not resemble a verb. (L.) One says, قَاسَيْتُ مِنْهُ شِدَّةً [*I endured, from him, hardness*, &c.; or *from it, hardship*, &c.]. (A.) And خِفْتُ ↓شُدَّى فُلَانٍ meaning شِدَّتَهُ

[i. e. *I feared the hardness*, &c., *of such a one*]: so says AZ: and he cites this verse:

* فَإِنِّى لَا أَلِينُ لِقَوْلِ شُدَّى ✝ *
* وَلَوْ كَانَتْ أَشَدَّ ✝ مِنَ الحَدِيدِ *

[*And*, or *for*, *I will not become gentle for a hard saying*, (lit. *a saying of hardness*,) *though it should be harder than iron*]. (L.) And أَصَابَتْنِى ✝ شُدَّى meaning شِدَّةٌ [i. e. *Hardship*, &c., *befell me*]. (AZ, Ṣ.) [And شِدَّةٌ also signifies *A strong, an intense*, or *a great, degree* of any quality &c.]

شُدَّى: see the next preceding paragraph, in four places.

شَدِيدٌ *Possessing the quality of* شِدَّةٌ: (Ṣ, L:) i. e. *hard*; applied to a substance and to an attribute: *firm, compact*, or *sound*: (L:) *strong, powerful, forceful; vigorous, robust, sturdy*, or *hardy*; (A, Mgh, L, Mṣb;) applied to a thing, (Mṣb,) and to a man; (A, Mgh, L;) as also شَدِيدُ القُوَى: (Mgh:) pl., applied to men, أَشِدَّآءُ and [applied to things and men] شِدَادٌ (A, L) and شُدُدٌ, (Sb, L,) which last preserves its original form [without idghám] because not resembling a verb: (L:) also *courageous, brave, firm of heart*: (L, Ḳ:*) and *niggardly, tenacious*, or *avaricious*; (A, L, Mṣb, Ḳ;) as also ✝ مُتَشَدِّدٌ: (Ṣ, A, L, Ḳ:) and [as is implied by the first explanation above, and shown by frequent usage,] *vehement, violent, intense, pressing, severe, strict, rigorous, tight, strait* or *difficult, hard* as meaning *hard to be borne, troublesome, distressing* or *distressful, afflictive, calamitous*, or *adverse*. (L, KL, PṢ, &c.) You say, هُوَ شَدِيدٌ عَلَى قَوْمِهِ [*He is hard*, or *severe*, or *rigorous, to his people*]. (A.) [And شَدِيدٌ عَلَى كَذَا *Niggardly, tenacious*, or *avaricious, of such a thing.*] Aboo-Dhu-eyb says, using شَدِيدٌ in the sense of شَحِيحٌ,

* حَدَرْنَاهُ بِالأَثْوَابِ فِى قَعْرِ هُوَّةٍ *
* شَدِيدٍ عَلَى مَا ضُمَّ فِى اللَّحْدِ جُولُهَا *

[*We lowered him, with the grave-clothes, into the bottom of a cavity in the ground, the sides whereof were tenacious of what was comprised in the lateral hollow which was the place of the corpse*]. (L.) And the words of the Ḳur [c. 8], وَإِنَّهُ لِحُبِّ الخَيْرِ لَشَدِيدٌ, accord. to Zj, mean *And verily, on account of the love of wealth, he is niggardly*, or *tenacious*, or *avaricious*. (L.) شَدِيدُ العَيْنِ applied to a man, and شَدِيدَةُ جَفْنِ العَيْنِ metaphorically applied by a poet to a she-camel, mean *Whom sleep does not overcome.* (L.) And الشَّدِيدُ means *The lion*; (Ḳ;) because of his strength and hardiness. (TA.) [شَدِيدٌ with a subst. or an inf. n. following it in the gen. case, the latter having the article ال prefixed to it, or being prefixed to another noun in the gen. case, supplies the place of an intensive epithet; as in شَدِيدُ السَّوَادِ *Intensely*, or *very, black*; and شَدِيدُ الغَضَبِ *Vehemently*, or *exceedingly*, or *very, angry*; and] مِسْكٌ شَدِيدُ الرَّائِحَةِ *Strong-smelling musk*; (L;) [and رَجُلٌ شَدِيدُ بَيَاضِ العَيْنِ *A man intensely white in the eye.*] — الحُرُوفُ الشَّدِيدَةُ [*The strong letters*] are *those letters which, in a state of quiescence, prevent the current of the voice in their utterance*; namely ا, ب, ت, ج, د, ط, ق, and ك; (TA;) *the letters comprised in the words* أَجَدْتَ طَبَقَكَ. (Ḳ.)

شَدِيدَةٌ [as a subst. from شَدِيدٌ, rendered such by the affix ة]: see شِدَّةٌ.

أَشَدُّ [*Possessing the quality of* شِدَّةٌ, *in a greater*, and *in the greatest, degree*; i. e. *more*, and *most, hard*, &c.]. See an ex. in a verse cited voce شِدَّةٌ. حَلَبْتُهَا الخ, or حَلَبْتَ بِالسَّاعِدِ الأَشَدِّ, is a prov., expl. in art. حلب. And بَقِىَ أَشُدُّهُ. [*The hardest part of it has remained*] is another prov., applied to him who attains a part of that which he wants, and is unable to attain the completion thereof. (TA. [See also Freytag's "Arab. Prov.," i. 169.]) [With an indeterminate subst. or inf. n. following it in the accus. case, it supplies the place of a simple epithet denoting the comparative and superlative degrees; as in أَشَدُّ سَوَادًا *More*, and *most, black*; and أَشَدُّ غَضَبًا *More*, and *most, angry*.] — أَشَدُّ النَّهَارِ *The time when the day is most advanced, the sun being at the highest.* (L. [See شَدُّ النَّهَارِ.])

أَشُدٌّ, (Ṣ, A, Mgh, L, Ḳ, &c.,) also pronounced أُشُدٌّ, (Seer, Ḳ,) but the latter form is rare, (TA,) is both masc. and fem., (Zj, TA,) and as used in the Ḳur it has somewhat different meanings: (Az, TA:) in the phrase حَتَّى يَبْلُغَ أَشُدَّهُ, (Ṣ, Ḳ,) and other phrases in the Ḳur, (TA,) أَشُدٌّ is expl. as meaning *The state of strength*; (Ṣ, Mgh, L, Ḳ;) which is *from eighteen to thirty years*: (Ṣ, L, Ḳ:) or *from about seventeen to forty*: (Zj:) or *from thirty to forty*: (Zj in another place:) or *puberty*: (Az, Mgh, L:) or *firmness*, or *soundness, of judgment, produced by experience*: (L:) or *puberty together with such maturity as gives evidence of rectitude of conduct* or *course of life*; (Zj, Az, Mgh, L;) *which may be at*, or *before, the age of eighteen years*; accord. to most of the men of science, and among them Esh-Sháfi'ee; (Zj, Az, L;) *and the extreme term of which is three and thirty years*: (Mgh:) or the *age of forty years*; as in the Ḳur xlvi. 14: (L:) أَشُدٌّ [originally أَشْدُدٌ] is a sing. having a pl. form, like آنُكٌ; and these two words are [said to be] the only instances of the kind: (Ṣ, Ḳ: [but see آنُكٌ:]) or a pl. having no proper sing., (Ṣ, Mgh, Ḳ,) like آسَالٌ and أَبَابِيلُ and عَبَادِيدُ and مَذَاكِيرُ: (Ṣ:) or its sing. is ✝ شِدَّةٌ, (AHeyth, Ṣ, Mgh, Ḳ,) accord. to Sb; and this is good with respect to the meaning, because one says, بَلَغَ الغُلَامُ شِدَّتَهُ; (Ṣ;) but فِعْلَةٌ does not form a pl. of the measure أَفْعُلٌ; (Ṣ, Ḳ;) for as to أَنْعُمٌ, (Ṣ,) which is said by AHeyth to be pl. of نِعْمَةٌ, (TA,) [and respecting which Mṭr says that] أَشُدٌّ is said to be pl. of شِدَّةٌ like as أَنْعُمٌ is of نِعْمَةٌ, formed by regarding the ة as elided, (Mgh, [and AHeyth says the like,]) it is only pl. of نُعْمٌ in the phrase يَوْمُ نُعْمٍ: (Ṣ:) or its sing. is شَدٌّ, like as كَلْبٌ is of أَكْلُبٌ; or شِدٌّ, like as ذِئْبٌ is of أَذْؤُبٌ; (Ṣ, Ḳ;) accord. to some; (Ṣ;) but neither شَدٌّ nor شِدٌّ has been heard from the Arabs [as sing. of أَشُدٌّ]; and they are only deduced from analogy: (Ṣ, Ḳ:) or it is pl. of أَشَدٌّ; and the أ is not regarded in the formation of this pl. (IJ, from A'Obeyd.)

مَشَدُّ العِصَابَةِ [*The place*, or *part, where the fillet*, or *the like, is bound*, or *tied*]. (A.)

مُشِدٌّ A man *having*, (A, Mgh, L,) or *having with him*, (L,) *a strong beast*, (A, Mgh, L,) or *strong beasts*; (L;) *contr. of* مُضْعِفٌ. (Mgh, L.) It is said in a trad., يَرُدُّ مُشِدُّهُمْ عَلَى مُضْعِفِهِمْ [*He among them who has a strong beast*, or *strong beasts, shall give back* a portion of the spoil *to him of them who has a weak beast*, or *weak beasts*]; meaning that the strong warrior and plunderer shall share with (يُسَاهِمُ) the weak in the plunder that he gains. (L.)

مُتَشَدِّدٌ: see شَدِيدٌ.

شدخ

1. شَدَخَ, (Ṣ, A, Mṣb, &c.,) aor. ـَ, (Mṣb, Ḳ,*) inf. n. شَدْخٌ, (Ṣ, A, Mṣb, Ḳ, &c.,) *He broke*, or *crushed*, syn. كَسَرَ, (Ṣ, A, Mṣb, Ḳ,) and فَضَخَ, (TA, and Ḥam p. 363,) or هَشَمَ, (TA,) a hollow thing, (Ṣ, A, L, TA,) or a soft, or tender, or an easily-broken, thing, (A,) or a moist thing, (Ḳ,) or a moist and soft thing, such as the عَرْفَج and the like, (L, TA,) a person's head, (Ṣ, A, L, Mṣb, TA,) and a colocynth, and an unripe date, (A,) and any hollow bone, and a rod, (Mṣb,) or, as some say, a dry thing, (Ḳ,) with the hand, or with a stone &c.: (Ḥam ubi suprà:) or *he pressed*, or *squeezed*, syn. غَمَزَ, [app. *so as to crush*,] a hollow thing, or a soft, or tender, or an easily-broken, thing, as a head, and a colocynth, and an unripe date. (A.) — [Hence,] شَدَخَ دِمَآءَهُمْ تَحْتَ قَدَمِهِ ‡ *He made their blood* (lit. *bloods*) *to go for nothing*, or *to be of no account.* (A, Ḳ.*) And [simply] شَدَخَ الدِّمَآءَ † *He made the blood* [of men] (lit. *bloods*) *to go for nothing, unretaliated*, or *uncompensated by mulcts*; or *to be of no account.* (Ḥam p. 91.) And شَدَخْتُ الدِّيَاتِ تَحْتَ قَدَمَىَّ † *I made the bloodwits to be of no account* [*so that they should not be exacted*]. (Ḥam ibid.) — And شَدَخَهُ *He hit*, or *hurt, his* مُشَدَّخ, i. e. the part of the neck so called. (Ḳ.) — And شَدَخَ aor. ـَ, (TA,) inf. n. شَدْخٌ (Ḳ, TA) and شُدُوخٌ, (TA,) *He*, (a man, TḲ,) or *it*, (a thing, or an affair, TA,) *deviated*, or *declined*, (Ḳ, TA,) *from the right course, aim*, or *scope*, (TA,) or *from the* [*proper*] *way.* (AO, TA.) — شَدَخَتِ الغُرَّةُ, (Ṣ, TA,) aor. ـَ, (TA,) inf. n. شَدْخٌ (Ḳ, TA) and شُدُوخٌ, (TA,) *The blaze on the horse's forehead spread widely upon the face* (Ṣ) [*from the forelock to the nose, without reaching to the eyes*: see شَادِخَةٌ]: or *spread, and extended downwards*, (Ḳ, TA,) *filling the forehead, without reaching*

to the eyes: or *covered the face from the root of the forelock to the nose.* (TA.)

2. شَدَّخْتُ الرُّؤُوسَ *I broke,* or *crushed, the heads;* or *did so much:* the verb is with teshdeed to denote muchness, or frequency, or application to many objects. (Ṣ, TA.) — [And شدّخ البُسْرَ *He pressed,* or *squeezed, the unripe dates, so as to crush them:* see مُشَدَّخ.]

5: see what next follows.

7. انشدخ *It was,* or *became, broken,* or *crushed;* (Ṣ, A, Mṣb, Ḳ, TA;) said of a hollow thing, (Ṣ, A, TA,) or a soft, or tender, or an easily-broken thing, (A,) or a moist thing, (Ḳ,) or a moist and soft thing, (TA,) a person's head, (Ṣ, A, Mṣb, TA,) a colocynth, and an unripe date, (A,) and any hollow bone, and a rod, (Mṣb,) or, as some say, a dry thing; (Ḳ;) and so ↓ تشدّخ [but app. implying muchness, or frequency, or relation to many things, as quasi-pass. of 2, q. v., whereas the former verb is quasi-pass. of 1]: (Ḳ:) or *it was,* or *became, pressed* or *squeezed* [app. *so as to be crushed;* or *it was,* or *became, crushed by being pressed* or *squeezed:* see مُشَدَّخ]. (A.)

شَدَخ *An abortive fœtus,* (L, Ḳ, TA,) *in a soft,* or *tender, state, before it has become firm.* (L, TA.) — See also شَادِخ, in two places

شَدْخَة A *soft,* or *tender,* or *succulent,* plant: (Ḳ:) applied in the M as an epithet to the species of plant called عِجْلَة. (TA.)

شَادِخ A child that is *soft,* or *tender;* (Ḳ;) as also ↓ شَدَخ: (IAạr, L:) or غُلَامٌ شَادِخٌ signifies *a youth:* (A:) accord. to IAạr, a boy is called جَفْرٌ; then, يَافِعٌ; then, ↓ شَدَخٌ; then, مُطَبَّخٌ; and then, كَوْكَبٌ. (TA. [See also مُطَبَّخ.]) — Also A thing, or an affair, *deviating from the right course, aim,* or *scope,* (Ḳ, TA,) or *from its* [*proper*] *way.* (AO, TA.) — See also the next paragraph.

شَادِخَةٌ, [as a subst.,] (Ṣ, L, Ḳ, TA,) or غُرَّةٌ ↓ شَادِخَةٌ, (A,) *A blaze on a horse's forehead spreading* [*widely* (see 1)] *upon the face,* (Ṣ,) or *covering the face,* (A,) *from the forelock to the nose,* (Ṣ, A,) *without reaching to the eyes:* (Ṣ:) or *spreading, and extending downwards,* (Ḳ, TA,) *filling the forehead, without reaching to the eyes:* or *covering the face from the root of the forelock to the nose:* (TA:) or *such as is long;* such as is round being called وَتِيرَة. (AO, TA.) — [Hence,] † *A notorious,* and *a bad,* or *an evil, an abominable,* or *a foul, deed.* (Ṣ, TA.) A rájiz says,

لَاهُمَّ إِنَّ الحَارِثَ بْنَ جَبَلَهْ

زَنَى عَلَى أَبِيهِ ثُمَّ قَتَلَهْ

وَرَكِبَ الشَّادِخَةَ المُحَجَّلَهْ

i. e. [*O God,* (لَاهُمَّ being for اَللّٰهُمَّ,) *verily El-Ḥárith Ibn-Jebeleh straitened,* or *oppressed, his father,* (زَنَى being for زَنَّأَ,) *then slew him,*] and *committed a bad and notorious deed* in slaying him. (Ṣ.)

أَشْدَخُ A horse *having a blaze such as is termed* شَادِخَة: fem. شَدْخَآءُ. (Ḳ, L, TA.) — الأَشْدَخُ *The lion.* (Ḳ.)

مُشَدَّخٌ *Unripe dates pressed,* or *squeezed,* (بُغْمَرُ, in some copies of the Ṣ and Ḳ and in the L and TA يُغْمَزُ, [but the former I think to be evidently the right reading,]) *until they become broken* or *crushed* (يَنْشَدِخ), (Ṣ, A,* L, Ḳ,) *and dried for the winter,* (A,) or *then dried in the winter.* (L.) — المُشَدَّخُ i. q. مُقَطَّعُ العُنُقِ [app. meaning *The part of the neck where it is cut up* by the butcher]. (Ḳ.)

مِشْدَاخ [A post-classical term] *A surgical instrument with which the head of the fœtus is crushed* [*in the womb*]. (Albucasis de Chirurgia, p. 342.)

شدق

1. شَدِقَ, inf. n. شَدَقٌ, said of a man, *He was wide in the* شِدْق [q. v.]. (M, TA.*) — And *He was eloquent.* (TA.)

5. تشدّق *He twisted his* شِدْقَانِ, [i. e. *the two sides of his mouth,* or *the quivering flesh of his mouth, inside his cheeks,*] *in order to affect clearness, or distinctness, of speech,* or *to be more clear,* or *distinct, in speech.* (Ḳ.) And تشدّق فِى كَلَامِهِ *He opened his mouth and was diffuse in his speech.* (M, TA.)

شَدْق: see what next follows.

شِدْقٌ (Lth, Ṣ, M, Mgh, O, Mṣb, Ḳ) and ↓ شَدْقٌ (Lth, M, O, Mṣb, Ḳ) The *quivering flesh* (طَفْطَفَة) *of the mouth, inside the two cheeks;* (Lth, O, Ḳ;) or so the dual of each: (M:) or the *side of the mouth;* (Ṣ, Mgh, Mṣb;) so says Az: (Mṣb:) pl. (of the former, Ṣ, Mṣb) أَشْدَاقٌ (Lth, Ṣ, M, O, Mṣb, Ḳ) and (of the latter, Mṣb, TA) شُدُوقٌ. (M, Mṣb, TA.) One says, نَفَخَ فِى شِدْقَيْهِ [*He blew in the sides of his mouth* so as to distend them]. (Ṣ.) And إِنَّهُ لَوَاسِعُ الأَشْدَاقِ, meaning [*Verily he is wide*] *in the* شِدْق; using the pl. as a sing.; a phrase mentioned by Lḥ. (M, TA.) شِدْقَا الفَرَسِ means *The chink of the mouth of the horse, to the extremity thereof at* [*the place of*] *the bit* [*on each side*]. (M.) تَرْكَبُ شِدْقَيْهَا مِنَ النَّشَاطِ [app. meaning † *She goes at random,* (like تَرْكَبُ رَأْسَهَا,) *by reason of briskness, liveliness,* or *sprightliness,*] is said of a woman and of a she-camel and of a mare. (Ḳ voce مِضْرَار.) — And ‡ The *two sides* of a valley; as also ↓ شَدِيقٌ: (Ḳ:) or the duals, شِدْقَانِ and شَدْقَانِ, have this signification; the sings. signify the *side* of a valley; (O;) or so شِدْقٌ, with kesr; (Mṣb;) and so ↓ شَدِيقٌ. (O.)

شَدَقٌ [mentioned above as inf. n. of 1] *Wideness of the* شِدْق: (Ṣ, Ḳ:) or, as in the T, *wideness of the* شِدْقَانِ. (TA.) — And *Eloquence.* (Ṣ,* TA.) — And † *A bending,* or *winding, in a valley.* (TA.)

شِدَاقٌ *A certain brand with which a camel is marked upon the* شِدْق. (M, TA.)

شَدِيقٌ: see شِدْقٌ, in two places.

شَدْقَمٌ and شَدْقَمِىٌّ: see the next paragraph; the former in three places: and see also art. شدقم.

أَشْدَقُ A man *wide in the* شِدْق: (M:) or a man *wide in the* شِدْقَانِ: (Mgh, Mṣb:) or *wide in the* شِدْق, *and inclining therein in any manner:* (TA:) fem. شَدْقَآءُ: (M, Ḳ:) and pl. شُدْقٌ: (Ḳ:) and ↓ شَدْقَمٌ and ↓ شَدْقَمِىٌّ signify the same as أَشْدَقُ; the م being augmentative, as in فُسْحُمٌ and سُتْهُمٌ; or, accord. to IJ, it is radical: (M, TA:) whence, i. e. from شَدْقَمٌ in the sense expl. above, (I'Ab, TA,) one says also ↓ شِدْقٌ شَدْقَمٌ, meaning *a wide* شِدْق: (I'Ab, M, TA:) and شَفَةٌ شَدْقَآءُ means *a lip wide in the part where each* شِدْق *is cleft* [*by the extremity of the mouth*]. (M, TA.) — It is also applied as an epithet to an orator, (Ṣ, M, Ḳ, TA,) meaning *Eloquent;* (M, Ḳ, TA;) *good and eloquent in speech;* (M,* TA;) and so ↓ شَدْقَمٌ. (TA.)

مُتَشَدِّقٌ One *who twists his* شِدْقَانِ *in order to affect clearness, or distinctness, of speech,* or *to be more clear,* or *distinct, in speech.* (Ṣ. [See 5.]) — *Diffuse in speech, without preparation,* or *caution,* or *precaution:* or one *who ridicules men, twisting his* شِدْقَانِ *with them and against them.* (TA.) And مُتَشَدِّقٌ فِى مَنْطِقِهِ *Diffuse in his speech.* (TA.)

Quasi شدقم

شَدْقَمٌ *Wide in the* شِدْق [or *side of the mouth*]; (Ṣ, Ḳ;) applied to a man; as also ↓ شَدْقَمِىٌّ; (TA;) and ↓ شُدَاقِمٌ: (Ḳ, TA:) [mentioned under this head in the Ṣ and Ḳ, but] the م is augmentative. (Az, Ṣ.) It has been erroneously said that it is with the pointed ذ. (MF.) — See also أَشْدَقُ. — Also The *lion;* (Ḳ;) and so ↓ شُدَاقِمٌ. (IB, TA.) — And *A certain stallion-camel belonging to En-Noạmán Ibn-El-Mundhir:* whence ↓ شَدْقَمِيَّاتٌ *Certain camels, so called in relation to that stallion.* (Ṣ, Ḳ.)

شَدْقَمِىٌّ: and شَدْقَمِيَّاتٌ: see the preceding paragraph.

شُدَاقِمٌ: see the first paragraph, in two places.

شدن

1. شَدَنَ, (Ṣ, Ḳ,) aor. ـُ, (Ṣ,) inf. n. شُدُونٌ, (Ṣ, Ḳ,) said of a gazelle, and of the young of any cloven-hoofed animal, and camel, and solid-hoofed animal, *He became strong, and in no need of his mother:* (Ḳ:) or *he became strong, and in a good state of body, and active and grown up, and vied with his mother in his faculties* [so I render

مَالَكَ أُمَّهُ of which I do not find any explanation] *so that he went along with her*; and [in this sense] it is said of a colt also: (TA:) or, said of a young gazelle, *he became strong, and his horns came forth, and he became in no need of his mother*: and sometimes it is said of a colt [in a similar sense]. (Ṣ.) Hence, it is said of a boy, meaning *He became strong, and active and grown up*. (Ḥar p. 536.)

4. اشدنت *She* (a gazelle) *had a young one that had become such as is termed* شَادِن. (Ṣ, Ḳ.)

شَدَنٌ *A kind of tree*, (Ḳ, TA,) *having weak, or soft, and thick stems*, (TA,) *the flower of which is like the jasmine* (Ḳ, TA) *in form, but tinged with redness, and more pleasant* [*in odour*] *than the jasmine*; said by IB to be *of pleasant odour*. (TA.)

شَدَنِيَّاتٌ *Certain she-camels, so called in relation to a place in El-Yemen*, (Ṣ, Ḳ, and EM p. 229,) *named* شَدَن: (TA, EM:) or *in relation to a certain stallion*. (IAṭr, Ḳ, TA. [In the CḲ, فَحْلٍ is erroneously put for فَحْلٍ.])

شَادِنٌ A young gazelle *that has become strong, and whose horns have come forth, and that has become in no need of his mother*: (A'Obeyd, TA: [see شَصَرٌ:]) when used alone, [not as an epithet, in which quality it seems to be applied also to the young of any cloven-hoofed animal, and camel, and solid-hoofed animal, (see 1,)] it means [simply] *a young gazelle*. (Ṣ, TA.)

مُشْدِنٌ [without ة] A doe-gazelle *whose young one has become such as is termed* شَادِن: (Ṣ, Ḳ, TA:) or *who has a* شَادِن *following her*: and in like manner applied to other animals of the cloven-hoofed kind, and of the solid-hoofed, and to a camel: (TA:) pl. مَشَادِنُ and مَشَادِينُ, (Ṣ, Ḳ,) like مَطَافِلُ and مَطَافِيلُ, (Ṣ,) [pls. of مُطْفِل,] the latter pl. anomalous. (TA.)

مَشْدُونَةٌ, applied to a girl, i. q. عَاتِقٌ [i. e. *That has newly attained to puberty, and has not been married; or that is between the periods of puberty and middle age*; &c.]. (IAṭr, Ḳ.)

شده

1. شُدِهَ, (JK, Ṣ, Ḳ,) inf. n. شَدْهٌ, (Ṣ,) *He* (a man, JK, Ṣ) *became confounded*, or *perplexed, and unable to see his right course*; or *became bereft of his reason* or *intellect*; i. q. دُهِشَ: (JK, Ṣ, Ḳ:) and also, (Ḳ,) or, accord. to AZ, only, (Ṣ,) *he was*, or *became, busied, occupied*, or *employed*; or *busied, &c., so as to be diverted* from something; or *diverted* from a thing *by being busied*; syn. شُغِلَ: (Ṣ, Ḳ:) and *he was caused to become confounded*, or *perplexed, and unable to see his right course*; (Ḳ;) as also ↑ انشده, or ↑ اشتده, (Ḳ, accord. to different copies: the former accord. to the TA.) Accord. to Az, شَدْهٌ is not from الدَّهَش, as it is thought to be by some [and as is implied by what here follows]. (TA.) — شَدَهَهُ *He confounded*, or *perplexed, him, so that he was unable to see his right course*; or *bereft him of his reason* or *intellect*; syn. أَدْهَشَهُ; (Ḳ;) as also ↑ اشدهه: (A'Obeyd, Ḳ:) or the former verb, in the act. form, has not been heard: (Ḥar p. 64:) and [it is asserted that] one does not say ↑ اشدهه. (JK.) — شَدَهَ رَأْسَهُ i. q. شَدَخَهُ [i. e. *He broke his head*]. (Ḳ.)

4: see the preceding paragraph, in two places.

7 and 8: see 1, first sentence.

شَدْهٌ: see what next follows.

شُدْهٌ (Ṣ, Ḳ) and ↑ شَدَهٌ (Ṣ, and so in some copies of the Ḳ and in the TA) and ↑ شَدْهٌ (so in some copies of the Ḳ in the place of the second, and in others together with the second, and in the TA) [app. *A state of confusion*, or *perplexity, so that one is unable to see his right course*; or *a state of alienation of mind*;] substs. from شُدِهَ: (Ṣ: [but in the Ḳ they are mentioned after شَدَهَهُ and أَشْدَهَهُ meaning أَدْهَشَهُ, and مَشَادِهُ meaning مَشَاغِل, as being the substs.; so that they may signify as above, and also *business, occupation*, or *employment*, &c.; agreeably with renderings in the TḲ:]) and ↑ شُدَاهٌ is a subst. from شُدِهَ [app. in the former, or in both, of these senses]. (Ḳ.)

شَدَهٌ: } see the next preceding paragraph.
شُدَاهٌ: }

مَشْدُوهٌ A man *confounded*, or *perplexed, and unable to see his right course*; or *bereft of his reason* or *intellect*. (Ṣ, TA. [But accord. to AZ, it seems to signify only مَشْغُولٌ, i. e. *Busied, occupied*, or *employed*, &c.: see 1, first sentence.])

مَشَادِهُ [a pl. of which the sing. is app. مَشْدَهَةٌ] *Things that cause one to be busied, occupied*, or *employed*; or *busied, &c., so as to be diverted* from something; or *diverted* from a thing *by being busied*; syn. مَشَاغِل [pl. of مَشْغَلَةٌ]. (Z, Ḳ.)

شدو

1. شَدَا, (Mṣb, Ḳ,) first pers. شَدَوْتُ, (Ṣ,) aor. ـُ, (Mṣb,) inf. n. شَدْوٌ, (Ṣ, Mṣb,) *He drove* camels: (Ṣ, Ḳ:) or *he collected and drove* a detached number of a herd of camels. (Mṣb.) — Hence, (Mṣb,) شَدَا, (Mṣb, Ḳ,) inf. n. as above, (TA,) † *He acquired somewhat of polite literature*, (Ṣ, Mṣb, Ḳ, TA,) or *of science, and guided himself thereby to the knowledge of somewhat more*, (Mṣb,) and likewise *of song*; (TA;) as though he drove it and collected it: (Ṣ, TA:) or شَدَا مِنَ الْعِلْمِ, and مِنَ الغِنَآءِ, (MA, TA,) شَيْئًا, (TA,) inf. n. as above, (MA, TA,) *he acquired somewhat of science*, and *of song*: (MA:) or *he knew well some sort of science*, and *of song*; and so of other things. (TA.) شَدْوٌ signifies † A man's *doing well*, or *knowing well, somewhat* of a thing or an affair. (TA.) And شَدَوْتُ مِنْهُ بَعْضَ المَعْرِفَةِ means *I knew* [*somewhat of*] him, or it, [*but*] *not well*. (TA.) — Also † *He recited a verse*, or *two verses*, (Ṣ, Ḳ,) *singing*, (Ḳ,) or *prolonging*, or *straining, his voice, as in singing* [*and as is commonly done in the driving of camels*; whence, app., this meaning of the verb]. (Ṣ.) And شَدَا شِعْرًا, (Ṣ, Ḳ,) or غِنَآءً, (Ṣ,) † *He sang poetry*, (Ṣ, Ḳ,) or *a song*: (Ṣ:) or *he recited it with a trilling*, or *quavering*, or *prolonging and modulating of the voice*. (Ṣ.) — And شَدَا شَدْوَهُ i. q. نَحَا نَحْوَهُ † [*He tended, repaired, betook himself*, or *directed his course, towards him*, or *it*; agreeably with the explanation in the TḲ: or *he purposed his* (another's) *purpose*]. (Ḳ.) — And شَدَا فُلَانًا فُلَانًا † *He assimilated such a one to such a one*; or *he likened such a one to such a one*; syn. شَبَّهَهُ إِيَّاهُ. (ISd, Ḳ, TA. [In the CḲ, فُلَانًا is not repeated.])

4. اشدى † *He became a good*, or *an excellent, modulator of his voice*, or *maker of melody*. (Ḳ.)

شَدًا *A remnant of strength*; and *a portion*, or *somewhat, thereof*: (Ḳ:) a dial. var. of شَذًا. (TA. [See شَذَاةٌ, in art. شذو.]) *A remnant*, or *remainder*, of anything. (TA.) *A small quantity* or *number*: (TA:) and so ↑ شَدْوٌ, (M, Ḳ,) *whatever it be*, (M, TA,) *of much or many*, (M, Ḳ,) *whatever the latter be*. (Ḳ.) And The *extremity* of anything: (Ḳ:) a dial. var. of شَذًا. (TA.) — Also *Heat*. (Ḳ.) — And *Mange*, or *scab*: (Ḳ: [in the CḲ, الحَرْبُ is put for الجَرَبُ:]) a dial. var. of شَذًا. (TA.)

شَدْوٌ: see the next preceding paragraph.

شَادٍ act. part. n. of 1; signifying *Driving*, or *a driver of*, camels: &c.: (Ḳ,* TA:) pl. شُدَاةٌ. (TA.) — [And particularly] † *One who acquires somewhat of polite literature*, (Ṣ, Mṣb,) and *of science, and guides himself thereby to the knowledge of somewhat more*. (Mṣb.) — Also † *A reciter of verses, who sings in reciting*, or *prolongs*, or *strains, his voice, as in singing*: *a singer of poetry*: (TA:) [and simply] *a singer*. (Ṣ.)

شذ

1. شَذَّ, (Ṣ, M, A, &c.,) aor. ـِ and ـُ, (Ṣ, M, L, Mṣb, Ḳ,) the former agreeable with analogy, and that which is mentioned by the leading writers on inflection, and the latter anomalous, (TA,) and Esh-Shiháb mentions ـَ, but this is not known, and there is no reason for it unless فَعِلَ be established as a form of the pret., and this has not been mentioned, (MF,) inf. n. شُذُوذٌ (Ṣ, M, Mgh, L, Mṣb, Ḳ) and شَذٌّ, (M, L, Ḳ,) *It* (a thing, M, L) *was*, or *became, apart*, (Ṣ, A, L, Mṣb,) and *it fell*, or *went*, or *came, out*, or *forth*, (Ṣ, M, L, Ḳ,) *from the generality of things*, or *the general assemblage, main body, bulk*, or *common mass*, (Ṣ, M, A, L, Ḳ,) *to which it pertained*, (M, L,) or *from other things*: (Mṣb:) *it* (anything) *was*, or *became, apart*, or *alone*: and *he* (a man) *was*, or *became, apart from his companions*, or *alone*: (Lth, L:) and † *he* [app. a beast] *took fright, and ran away*. (Mṣb.) You say, شَذَّ عَنْهُ *It was*, or *became, apart*, &c., *from it*. (Ṣ, L.) And شَذَّ عَنِ الجَمَاعَةِ *He was*, or *became, apart from the collective body* [or *generality*] *of people*. (Mgh.) And مَا يَشِذُّ عَلَيْهِ شَىْءٌ † [*Nothing is out of his way*, or *sphere*, or *compass*]. (Ṣ and Ḳ in art. حوذ.) And شَذَّ الحَصَى *The pebbles became scat-*

tered, or dispersed. (L.) —— شَذَّ, aor. ـِ and ـُ, inf. n. شُذُوذٌ and شَذٌّ, also signifies ‡ *It* (a word, form or measure, construction, or government,) *deviated from the common,* or *constant, course of speech in respect of analogy,* or *rule; deviated from common,* or *constant, analogy,* or *rule; was extraordinary,* or *exceptional, as to rule;* or *was anomalous, abnormal,* or *irregular:* and *it* (the same) *deviated from the common,* or *constant, course of speech in respect of usage; deviated from common,* or *constant, usage; was extraordinary,* or *exceptional, as to usage;* or *was unusual:* [the verb is used absolutely to express each of these meanings; the context in general showing clearly which meaning is intended: the former is that which is most frequently intended: and] the former meaning is also expressed by the phrase شَذَّ عَنِ القِيَاسِ or شَذَّ فِى القِيَاسِ: and the latter, by the phrase شَذَّ فِى الاِسْتِعْمَالِ. (Mz, 12th نوع.) [See also the contr. اِطَّرَدَ: and see شَاذٌّ, below.] —— See also 4.

2: see what next follows.

4. اشذّهُ; (Ṣ, M, Ḳ;) and ▼شذّذهُ; (Ḳ;) and ▼شَذَّهُ, aor. ـُ, only; (M, Ḳ;) but Aṣ disallows this last form of the verb; (IJ, L;) *He,* or *it, caused it to be,* or *to become, apart,* (Ṣ, L,) *to fall,* or *go,* or *come, out,* or *forth, from the generality of things,* or *the general assemblage, main body, bulk,* or *common mass,* (Ṣ, M, L, Ḳ,) *to which it pertained:* (M, L:) and the first signifies *he removed it,* and *put it far away;* namely, a thing: (Ḳ:) and *he set him,* or *exposed him, apart from his companions,* or *alone:* (IJ, L:) and *he scattered,* or *dispersed, it.* (IKṭṭ.) A poet says,

* فَأَشْذَّنِى لِمُرُورِهِمْ فَكَأَنَّنِى *
* غُصْنٌ لِأَوَّلِ عَاضِدٍ أَوْ عَاصِفِ *

[*And he,* or *it,* (perhaps meaning fortune,) *exposed me apart from my companions, to their passing by,* or *by reason of their passing away, so that I was as though I were a branch* that should become a prey *for the first lopper or stormy wind*]. (IJ, L.) And one says of a she-camel, اشذّت الحَصَى *She scattered,* or *dispersed, the pebbles* [with her feet]. (TA.) —— اشذّ also signifies جَآءَ بِقَوْلٍ شَاذٍّ ▼ نَادٍّ † [*He said what deviated from the common course of speech*]. (Ḳ, TA.)

شَذَّانٌ: see شَاذٌّ, in four places.

شِذَّانٌ The [*species of lote-tree called*] سِدْر. (Ḳ.)

شَاذٌّ A thing *that is,* or *becomes, apart,* (Ṣ, L, Mṣb,) and *that falls,* or *goes,* or *comes, out,* or *forth, from the generality of things, general assemblage, main body, bulk,* or *common mass,* (Ṣ, L,) *to which it pertains:* (L:) anything *apart,* or *alone:* and a man *apart from his companions,* or *alone:* (Lth, L:) and [app. a beast] *taking fright, and running away:* (Mṣb:) شُذَّانٌ is a pl. thereof, like as شُبَّانٌ is of شَابٌّ; [and so is شُذَّاذٌ, agreeably with analogy;] and ▼ شَذَّانٌ is used in a similar sense, but is an epithet of the measure فَعْلَانٌ, not a pl. of شَاذٌّ. (L.) مَا يَدَعُ فُلَانٌ شَاذًّا وَلَا نَادًّا إِلَّا قَتَلَهُ [*Such a one does not leave any one apart from his companions, nor any one taking fright and running away, but he slays him,*] is said of a courageous man whom no one encounters without his slaying him. (IAạr, L.) And one says شُذَّانُ قَوْمٍ *Those, of a people, who have become apart,* or *separate, from their companions.* (L, from a trad.) And شُذَّاذُ النَّاسِ *Those who are among a people but do not belong to their tribes* (Ṣ, L) *nor to their places of abode:* (L:) and *those who are scattered,* or *dispersed, of people;* (A, L;) as also ▼ شَذَّانُ النَّاسِ, (Ṣ, L,) and شُذَّاذُهُمْ. (L.) And قَوْمٌ شُذَّاذٌ *A people not among their own tribe nor in their own places of abode:* (L, Ḳ:*) or *a people among another people, not among their own tribes nor in their own places of abode.* (M, TA.) And شُذَّاذُ الآفَاقِ *The strangers.* (Ḥar p. 352.) And جَآؤُوا شُذَّاذًا *They came few in number.* (L, Ḳ.*) And ▼ شَذَّانُ الإِبِلِ and شُذَّانُهَا *Those that are scattered,* or *dispersed, of the camels.* (L.) And شُذَّانُ الحَصَى (M, L) and ▼ شَذَّانُ الحَصَى (Ṣ, IJ, M, L, Ḳ) *What are scattered,* or *dispersed, of pebbles;* (Ṣ, L, Ḳ;) *what have flown about, and become scattered* or *dispersed, thereof:* (M, L:) and in like manner one says of other things, (L, Ḳ,) or of similar things. (M, L.) —— Applied to a word, form or measure, construction, or government, it signifies ‡ *Deviating from the common,* or *constant, course of speech in respect of analogy,* or *rule; deviating from common,* or *constant, analogy* or *rule; extraordinary,* or *exceptional, as to rule;* or *anomalous, abnormal,* or *irregular:* such a word, &c., though itself admitted if agreeable with common usage, is not taken as an example to be imitated: also, applied to the same, *deviating from the common,* or *constant, course of speech in respect of usage; deviating from common,* or *constant, usage; extraordinary,* or *exceptional, as to usage; unusual:* [used absolutely to express each of these significations; the context in general showing clearly which signification is meant: the former is that which is most frequently intended:] a word, &c., may be شاذّ in respect of usage but agreeable with common analogy or rule; as the pret. of يَذَرُ and يَدَعُ; and the regular phrase مَكَانٌ مُبْقِلٌ, the epithet more commonly heard being بَاقِلٌ: and شاذّ in respect of analogy, or rule, but agreeable with common usage; as أَغْوَصَ, اِسْتَصْوَبْتُ الأَمْرَ, and الرِّمْثُ: and شاذّ in respect of analogy, or rule, and of usage, together; as ثَوْبٌ مَصْوُونٌ, and مِسْكٌ مَدْوُوفٌ: (Mz, 12th نوع: [and the like is said, but less fully, in the Mṣb:]) the pl. masc. is شُذَّاذٌ; and pl. fem. شَوَاذُّ. (Mz, ib.) See 4, last sentence. [See also the contr. مُطَّرِدٌ: and see شَذَّ, latter part.] —— Applied to a tradition, † *Having a single ascription, attested by a* [*single*] *sheykh, whether he be trustworthy or not:* in the latter case, not accepted: in the former case, one hesitates respecting it, and does not adduce it as an argument, or evidence. (KT.)

شذب

1. شَذَبَ, aor. ـِ and ـُ, (Ḳ,) inf. n. شَذْبٌ, (TA,) *He stripped off,* or *removed,* the bark of a tree; as also ▼ شذّب, inf. n. تَشْذِيبٌ: (Ḳ:) *he cut off* portions of a tree, or the bark thereof. (TA.) *He cut,* or *cut off,* a thing; (O, Ḳ;) aor. ـِ, inf. n. شَذْبٌ. (O.) *He cut,* or *lopped,* a tree: or *he divested* it *of its bark.* (A.) *He pruned,* or *pared,* a tree *by cutting off its* شَذَب, i. e. its *straggling branches,* or its *thorns,* or *its bark;* aor. ـِ, inf. n. شَذْبٌ; and ▼ شذّب has the like meaning, but importing muchness, or relation to many objects: and شَذَبَ also signifies *he trimmed,* or *cleared,* anything *by removing another thing from it:* (Mṣb:) or *he pruned* a tree *by lopping off its branches so that it became apparent:* (Ḳ, TA:) and *he pruned* a palm-tree *by cutting off from it its* شَذَب, meaning its *branches:* (TA:) and [in like manner] ▼ شذّب, (Ṣ, TA,) inf. n. تَشْذِيبٌ, (Ṣ, Ḳ, TA,) *he pruned* a tree *by cutting off its* شَذَب, meaning its *straggling branches not in the choice,* or *best, part thereof:* (Ṣ:) or *he trimmed* a palm-trunk (Ḳ, TA) *by lopping off the stumps of the branches:* (TA:) ▼ تَشْذِيبُ الرَّيَاحِينِ [likewise] signifies *the pruning,* or *cutting off, the superfluous portions of the straggling extremities of the sprigs of sweet-smelling plants:* (Mgh:) and شُذِبَ عَنْهُ, said of anything, signifies *it was removed from it,* namely, another thing. (TA.) —— See also 2, in two places.

2. شذّب, inf. n. تَشْذِيبٌ: see above, in four places. —— [Hence,] تَشْذِيبٌ signifies also The *shaping* an arrow *by the first operation:* (AḤn, Ḳ:) the second operation is termed تَهْذِيبٌ. (AḤn.) —— And شذّبهُ, (Sh, TA,) inf. n. as above, (Sh, Ḳ,) *He drove away him,* or *it,* (Sh, Ḳ,* TA,) from a thing; (TA;) as also ▼ شَذَبَهُ, aor. ـِ, inf. n. شَذْبٌ: (Sh, TA:) and ▼ شَذَبَ عَنْهُ *he repelled from him,* or *defended him.* (Ṣ, Ḳ.) —— And شَذَّبْتُ المَالَ, (Kt, TA,) inf. n. as above, (Ḳ,) † *I dispersed,* or *scattered, the property.* (Kt, Ḳ,* TA.) —— [And accord. to Golius, on the authority of a gloss in a copy of the KL, شذّب also signifies *He made long.*]

5. تشذّبوا ‡ *They became dispersed,* or *scattered.* (A, Ḳ.)

شَذَبٌ *Pieces,* or *cuttings, of trees;* (Aṣ, A'Obeyd, Ḳ;) n. un. with ة: (Aṣ, A'Obeyd:) or *bark of trees:* (Ḳ:) *pieces of bark,* and *pieces of wood,* or *sticks,* or *twigs* or *branches, in a dispersed,* or *scattered, state;* (O, Ḳ;) pl. أَشْذَابٌ: (Ḳ:) *what fall from,* or *of, the branches of a tree,* [*when it is pruned,*] *in a dispersed,* or *scattered, state:* or, as some say, the *thorns:* and the *bark:* (Mṣb:) the *stumps of the cut branches upon the trunk of a palm-tree,* and *other portions, which are lopped off;* (O;) [i. e., also] the *branches thereof which are lopped off:* (TA:) and in like manner, (O,) as pl. of شَذَبَةٌ, (Ṣ,) [or rather as a coll. gen. n. of which the n. un. is with ة,] *what are cut off from,* or *of, the branches of trees,* (Ṣ, O,) *others than palm-trees,* (O,) i. e. *of the straggling branches,* (Ṣ,) *such as are not in the choice*, or *best, part thereof*: (Ṣ, O:) also the *superfluous portions of the straggling extremities of the sprigs* of sweet-smelling plants, *which are pruned*, or *cut off*. (Mgh.) — *Anything in a scattered*, or *dispersed, state*. (Ḳt, TA.) — ‡ *Somewhat remaining* of herbage [&c.]: (Ṣ, A, O, Ḳ: [in the first and third of which is added وَهُوَ المَأْكُولُ, app. referring to the herbage of which the remainder is thus called, meaning, "it being what has been eaten:"]) pl. as above, i. e. أَشْذَابٌ. (Ṣ, O, Ḳ.*) One says, فِى الأَرْضِ شَذَبٌ مِنْ كَلَإٍ ‡ *In the land is somewhat remaining of herbage*. (A, TA.) And one says also, بَقِىَ عِنْدَهُ شَذَبٌ مِنْ مَالٍ ‡ [*There remained in his possession a remnant of property*]. (A, TA.) And مَا بَقِىَ لَهُ إِلَّا شَذَبٌ مِنَ العَسْكَرِ ‡ [*There remained not to him save a relic of the army*]. (A, TA.) — Also † *Household goods*, or *furniture and utensils, consisting of what are termed* قُمَاش [q. v., perhaps here meaning the *meaner sorts thereof*,] *&c.*: (A'Obeyd, O, Ḳ:) pl. as above. (Ḳ,* TA.) — And *A dam*; or *thing constructed*, or *raised, to keep back the water of a torrent*. (Ṣ, O, Ḳ.)

رَجُلٌ شَذِبُ العُرُوقِ † *A man whose veins are apparent*. (Ṣ, Ḳ.) — And شذب [app. شَذِبٌ] is syn. with عَطِبٌ, meaning A man *alighting*, or *abiding, in places of dried-up herbage, and in a waterless desert*. (TA in art. عطب.)

شَاذِبٌ ‡ *Going*, or *being, away from his home*, or *place of settled abode*. (Ṣ, Ḳ, TA.) — ‡ *Solitary*, or *alone, and whose prosperity is despaired of*; (Ḳ, TA;) as though stripped of good. (TA.)

شَوْذَبٌ: see مُشَذَّبٌ, in three places.

مِشْذَبٌ *A pruning-hook*. (O,* Ḳ,* TA.)

مُشَذَّبٌ A palm-trunk *pared* (Ṣ, O, TA) *of its prickles* (TA) [or *of the stumps of its branches* or *of its lower branches*: see the verb of which it is the pass. part. n.]. — ‡ *Tall*; (Ṣ, A;) as also ▼ شَوْذَبٌ; (Ṣ;) the former as an epithet applied to a horse, (Ṣ, A,) from the same epithet as applied to a palm-trunk: (A:) and † *tall, and goodly in make*; (A, Ḳ;) and so ▼ شَوْذَبٌ; (Mgh, Ḳ;) as though pruned: (Mgh:) and ▼ the latter, applied to anything [meaning any animal], † *tall, and excellent* or *of high breed* or *strong and light and swift*: A'Obeyd says that the former signifies † *excessively tall*, and is applied in this sense to anything [i. e. a man and any animal]: Ḳt says, after explaining شَذَّبْتُ المَالَ as it has been expl. above, that he who is excessively tall is as though his frame were disconnected, and not compact; and therefore he is thus termed: but IAmb says that Ḳt has made a mistake in asserting that this epithet signifies † *tall, conspicuous for tallness*, and that it is from the palm-tree from which the branches have been lopped off, (in consequence of which, as is said in the Fáïḳ, it becomes taller, MF, TA,) and that he who is † *conspicuous for tallness* is not thus called unless *somewhat deficient in flesh*: it is applied to a horse as meaning ‡ *tall, and not very fleshy*. (TA.)

شذر

2. شَذَّرَ النَّظْمَ, inf. n. تَشْذِيرٌ, *He divided the strung beads with other beads*. (O. [See شَذْرٌ, below.]) — Hence, by way of comparison, (TA,) شَذَّرَ كَلَامَهُ بِشِعْرٍ ‡ [*He interspersed his language with poetry*]: but this is post-classical. (O, TA.) — شَذَّرَ بِهِ *He rendered him notorious*, or *infamous*: or *made him to hear what was bad, evil, abominable*, or *foul*: (O, TA:) and in like manner شَتَّرَ بِهِ. (TA.)

5. تشذّر *It* (a people, or party, TA, or a collected body, Ḳ, and a flock of sheep or a herd of goats, TA) *dispersed*, or *became dispersed*, (A, Ḳ, TA,) *and went in every direction*. (TA.) — تشذّر بِالثَّوْبِ *He turned back the extremity of the garment between his legs, and stuck it in the part where it was bound round his waist, behind*. (Ṣ, Ḳ.) And تشذّر بِالذَّنَبِ *He put the tail between his thighs, making it to cleave to his belly*. (Ṣ, TA.) — Hence, (TA,) تشذّر فَرَسَهُ *He mounted his horse from behind*. (Ṣ, Ḳ.) — Also, تشذّر, *He prepared himself for fight*, (Ṣ, Ḳ, TA,) and *for a charge*, or *an assault*; *he equipped*, or *accoutred, himself for it*. (TA.) — *He threatened*; (Ṣ, A, Ḳ;) and *became angered*: (Ḳ:) A'Obeyd says, I doubt not its being with ذ; but some, he adds, say تشزّر, with ز. (Ṣ.) [See a verse of Lebeed cited among the exs. of the preposition بِ.] — *He was*, or *became, brisk, lively*, or *sprightly*. (Ḳ.) — *He hastened to do a thing*; (TṢ, Ḳ, TA;) or *in a thing*, or *an affair*. (So in some copies of the Ḳ.) — تشذّروا فِى الحَرْبِ i. q. تَطَاوَلُوا [app. as meaning *They behaved overbearingly in war*]: (Ṣ, Ḳ:) or تَشَذُّرٌ signifies the *protracting of war*. (KL.) — تشذّرت النَّاقَةُ *The she-camel pastured upon herbage* (Ḳ, TA) *that rejoiced her*, (TA,) *and she shook her head by reason of joy thereat*. (Ḳ, TA.) And *The she-camel drew together her two sides, and raised her tail*. (TA.) — And تشذّر السَّوْطُ *The whip inclined, and became in motion*. (Ḳ.)

شَذْرٌ *Pieces of gold that are picked up from the mine* (Ṣ, A, Ḳ) *without the melting*, or *smelting*, (Ṣ, Ḳ,) *of the ore*: (Ṣ:) n. un. with ة: (Ṣ, Ḳ:) and pl. شُذُورٌ. (A.) And *Beads made of gold to form divisions between pearls and jewels*: (TA:) or *beads by means of which other beads of a string are divided*: (Ḳ:) or *small pearls*: (Ṣ, Ḳ:) or *small things of gold, like the heads of ants, which are affixed to a* [*ring of the kind called*] خَوْق: (Sh:) or, as some say, *green beads*: (Ḥar p. 600:) n. un. with ة. (Ḳ.) — شذر [app. شَذْرٌ] signifies [also, like تَشَذُّرٌ,] *Briskness, liveliness*, or *sprightliness*: and *quickness in an affair*. (Ḥam. p. 54.)

تَفَرَّقُوا شَذَرَ مَذَرَ, and شِذَرَ مِذَرَ, *They* [*dispersed*, or *became dispersed*, or] *went*, or *went away, in every direction*: (Ṣ, L, Ḳ:) it is not said of a people coming: (L:) the م in مذر is sometimes changed into ب; or, accord. to some, بذر is the original, being from التَّبْذِيرُ; but MF thinks that مذر is the original, as it is only an imitative sequent, in which no regard is had to the meaning of "dispersion." (TA.)

شَوْذَرٌ *A* [*garment of the kind called*] مِلْحَفَة: an arabicized word; (Ṣ, Ḳ;) from the Pers. چَادَرْ [or چَادُرْ or چَادِرْ]. (Ṣ.) And i. q. إِتْبٌ; (A, Ḳ, TA;) i. e. *A* [*garment of the kind called*] بُرْد, *which is slit* [*in the middle*], *and worn by a woman, who throws it upon her neck*, [*putting her head through the slit*;] *having neither sleeves nor an opening at the bosom*: (TA:) or [*a garment*] *like the* صِدَار, [*which is said by some to be the same as the* إِتْب,] *worn by a young woman*: (Ḥar p. 55:) *a garment which a woman wears beneath her* ثَوْب: (Fr:) *a certain garment which a woman and a girl wear, extending to the extremity of the upper half of the arm*. (Lth.) [The modern چادر of Persia and El-'Irák seems to be generally what is commonly called in Egypt a "miláyeh," correctly "mulááh" (مُلَآءَة), figured and described in my work on the Modern Egyptians: or, in some instances, a similar covering of plain white, or dark blue, cotton; the former of which is now called in Egypt an "izár." (See Dozy's "Dict. des Noms des Vêtements chez les Arabes," pp. 216-219.)]

شِيذَارَةٌ A *very jealous* man; (Ḳ;) as also شِنْذَارَةٌ and شِنْذِيرَةٌ. (TA.)

المُتَشَذِّرُ *The lion*: (Ḳ:) because of his briskness, or quickness to act, or readiness to leap. (TA.)

شذو

شَذَا, aor. ـُ: see 4. — Also *He perfumed himself* (تَطَيَّبَ) *with musk*, (Ḳ, TA,) which is termed شَذْوٌ, or, as in copies of the M, شِذْوٌ. (TA.) — And شَذَا بِالخَبَرِ, (Ḳ, TA,) inf. n. شَذْوٌ; or, accord. to the Tekmileh, ▼ شَذَّى بالخبر, there written with teshdeed; (TA;) ‡ *He knew the information*, or *story, and made it known*, or *understood*. (Ḳ, TA.)

2: see the preceding paragraph.

4. اشذى *He annoyed, molested, harmed*, or *hurt*: or *he did what annoyed, molested, harmed*, or *hurt*: syn. آذَى: (Ṣ, Mṣb, TA:) and (TA) so ▼ شَذَا, (Ḳ,) aor. ـُ, inf. n. شَذًا, (TA,) or شَذْوٌ. (TḲ [accord. to which the latter verb is trans.].) — And اشذاهُ عَنْهُ, (Ḳ,) inf. n. إِشْذَآءٌ, (TA,) *He put aside*, or *away*, and *removed far off, him*, or *it, from him*, or *it*. (Ḳ, TA.)

شَذًا *Annoyance, molestation, harm*, or *hurt*; or *a thing that annoys, molests, &c.*: (Ṣ, Mṣb, Ḳ:) and *evil*, or *mischief*; (Ṣ, Mṣb;) as also ▼ شَذَاةٌ; as in the saying إِنِّى لَأَخْشَى شَذَاةَ فُلَانٍ i. e. [*Verily I fear*, or *dread*,] *the evil*, or *mischief, of such a one*. (TA.) — *Dog-flies*; (Ṣ, Ḳ;) *which also sometimes light upon the camel*: (Ṣ:) or *flies in general*: (Ḳ:) or *large blue flies that light upon beasts, and annoy*, or *molest*, or *hurt, them*: (TA:) n. un. ▼ شَذَاةٌ. (Ṣ. [It is said in the Mṣb that شَذًا, of which the n. un. is شَذَاةٌ, is also with kesr (i. e. ▼ شِذًا); but in what sense is not specified.]) One says of him who is vehemently hungry, ضَرِمَ شَذَاهُ [lit. *His flies have become vehemently hungry*, or *burning with hunger*]. (Ṣ.) — And [app. because of the annoyance that it occasions,] *Mange*, or *scab*: (ISd, Ḳ:) and so شَذًا. (Ḳ in art. شدو.) — And [app.

because of its pungency,] *Salt:* (Ṣ, Ḳ:) said in the M to be pl. [but properly coll. gen. n.] of ▼شَذَاةٌ, which signifies *a piece of salt.* (TA.) — See also شَذْوٌ. — Also *Fragments of aloes-wood* (Ṣ,* Ḳ,* TA) *with which one perfumes himself.* (TA. [The same is also indicated in the Ṣ.]) — And *Sharpness,* (Ṣ,) or *strength,* (Fr, T, Ḳ,) *of pungency of odour;* (Fr, T, Ṣ, Ḳ;) accord. to the M, *of sweet odour.* (TA.) — See also شَذَاةٌ. — Also The *extremity* of anything: (TA:) and so شَذًا. (Ḳ and TA in art. شذو.) = And *A sort of trees,* (Ṣ, Ḳ,) *used for* مَسَاوِيك [i. e. *sticks with which the teeth are cleansed*], (Ḳ,) *growing in the Sarāh* (السَّرَاة) *and having gum.* (TA.) = And *A sort of ships* or *boats:* (Lth, Ṣ, Ḳ:) n. un. ▼شَذَاةٌ: (Lth, Ṣ:) [or] ▼شَذَاوَةٌ signifies *one of a sort of small ships,* or *boats, like those called* زَبَازِبُ [pl. of زَبْزَبٌ]: and its pl. is شَذَاوَاتٌ. (Mṣb.)

شِذًا: see the next preceding paragraph.

شَذْوٌ, so accord. to the Ḳ, but written in copies of the M with kesr [i. e. ▼شِذْوٌ], (TA,) *Musk;* (IAạr, Ḳ, TA;) as also ▼شَذًا: (IJ, TA:) or the *odour thereof:* (Aṣ, T, Ṣgh, Ḳ:) or the *colour thereof.* (Ḳ.)

شِذْوٌ: see the next preceding paragraph.

شَذَاةٌ: see شَذًا, in three places. — Also *Sharpness.* (TA.) — And *Strength,* and *boldness,* of a man. (Lth, TA.) — [Or] *A remnant of strength:* (Ṣ, Ḳ:) pl. شَذَوَاتٌ (TA) and [coll. gen. n.] ▼شَذًا. (Ṣ,* TA. [See also شَذًا, in art. شذو.]) = As an epithet applied to a man, (TA,) *Evil in disposition,* (Ḳ, TA,) *sharp in temperament, that annoys,* or *molests,* or *hurts, by his evil,* or *mischief:* in some of the copies of the Ḳ, الشَّىْءُ الخَلْقِ is erroneously put for السَّيِّئُ الخُلُقِ. (TA.) = See again شَذًا, last sentence.

شَذَاوَةٌ: see شَذًا, last sentence.

شر

1. شَرَّ, (L, Ḳ,) sec. pers. شَرِرْتَ, (Ṣ, Mṣb, Ḳ, MF,) aor. يَشَرُّ; (L, Mṣb, MF;) and sec. pers. شَرُرْتَ, (Ṣ accord. to some copies, L, Mṣb, Ḳ, MF,) aor. يَشُرُّ; (L, Mṣb, Ḳ,* MF;) and sec. pers. شَرَرْتَ, (Ṣ accord. to some copies, M, Ḳ, MF,) aor. يَشِرُّ; (M, Ḳ, MF;) of which three vars. the first is the best known; and the last is strange, and disallowed by most authorities; (MF;) inf. n. [of the first or third] شَرٌّ (Ṣ, Ḳ) and [of the first] شُرٌّ (Ṣ) and [of the second or third] شَرَارَةٌ, (Ṣ, Ḳ,) and شِرَّةٌ also is an inf. n. [syn. with شَرٌّ]; (Ṣ;) *He* (a man) *was,* or *became, evil, a wrongdoer, unjust, bad, corrupt, wicked, mischievous, vitious,* or *depraved.* (Ṣ,* L, Mṣb, Ḳ,* &c.) The manner in which the Ḳ mentions شَرَّ with the two aors. يَشُرُّ and يَشِرُّ [only, omitting the most common aor., i. e. يَشَرُّ,] obviously demands consideration. (MF.) One says, شَرِرْتَ يَا رَجُلُ [*Thou hast been evil,* or *a wrongdoer,* &c., *O man*], (Ṣ, Ḳ,) and so شَرُرْتَ and شَرَرْتَ. (Ṣ accord. to different copies, and Ḳ.) — شَرَّ, aor. يَشُرُّ, also signifies *He increased in evil, wrongdoing,* &c. (L.) It is said in a prov., كُلَّمَا تَكْبَرُ تَشُرُّ [*In proportion as thou growest old, thou increasest in evil,* &c.]. (AZ, L.) — مَا شَرَّهُ: see 4, last sentence. = شَرَّهُ, (O, Ḳ,) aor. يَشُرُّ, (O, TA,) inf. n. شَرٌّ, (O, Ḳ,) with ḍamm, (Ḳ, [which is said in the TA to indicate that the aor., not the inf. n., is with ḍamm, but this is inconsistent with the common practice of the author of the Ḳ, and is evidently wrong,]) *He blamed him; found fault with him; attributed* or *imputed to him, charged him with,* or *accused him of, a vice, fault, defect, blemish,* or *something amiss.* (O, Ḳ,* TA. [See also 4.]) One says, مَا قُلْتُ ذَالِكَ لِشَرِّكَ وَإِنَّمَا قُلْتُهُ لِغَيْرِ شَرِّكَ *I said not that to find fault with thee, but I only said it for a different purpose than that of finding fault with thee:* (Ṣ, TA:) or this has a different meaning, which see below, voce شَرٌّ. (TA.) One says also, قَدْ قَبِلْتُ عَطِيَّتَكَ ثُمَّ رَدَدْتُهَا عَلَيْكَ مِنْ غَيْرِ شَرِّكَ وَلَا ضَرِّكَ, meaning [*I have accepted thy gift; then I have given it back to thee*] *without rejecting it to thee or blaming thee* [*and without injuring thee*]. (IAạr, TA.) = Also شَرَّهُ, (Ṣ,) or شَرَّهُ فِي الشَّمْسِ, (A,) [aor. and inf. n. as in the next sentence;] and ▼شَرَّرَهُ, (A,) inf. n. تَشْرِيرٌ; (Ṣ;) and ▼اشرّهُ; and ▼شَرْشَرَهُ; (A;) *He spread it* (i. e. a garment, or piece of cloth, Ṣ, or some other thing, TA) *in the sun:* (Ṣ, A, TA:) this is the primary signification. (TA.) And [hence,] شَرَّهُ, (Ṣ, Ḳ,) aor. يَشُرُّ, (Ṣ,) inf. n. شَرٌّ; (Ṣ, Ḳ;) and ▼اشرّهُ, (Ḳ,) inf. n. إِشْرَارٌ; (TA;) and ▼شَرَّرَهُ, (Ḳ,) inf. n. as above; (TA;) and شَرَّاهُ [or شَرَاهُ without teshdeed?]; (Ḳ;) *He put it* (i. e. [the preparation of curd called] أَقِط, and flesh-meat, Ṣ, Ḳ, and the like, and salt, Ṣ, and a garment, or piece of cloth, and the like, Ḳ) *upon a* خَصَفَة, (Ṣ, Ḳ,) i. e. a *mat,* (TA,) or *some other thing,* (Ḳ,) *to dry.* (Ṣ, Ḳ.) And شَرَّهُ *He sprinkled it;* namely, salt. (R, MF.)

2. شرّرهُ inf. n. تَشْرِيرٌ, *He rendered him notorious,* or *infamous, among men.* (Yz, Ḳ.) = See also 1, latter part, in two places.

3. شارّهُ, (Ḳ,) inf. n. مُشَارَّةٌ, (Ṣ,) *He acted with him in an evil manner;* (Ḳ;) *he treated him with enmity,* or *hostility:* (L, TA:) *he contended,* or *disputed, with him:* (Ṣ, L, TA:) *he did evil to him, obliging him to do the like in return.* (L, TA.) [See also 3 in art. شرى: and see an ex. voce جَارٌّ.]

4. اشرّهُ *He attributed,* or *imputed, to him evil, wrongdoing, injustice,* or *the like:* (Ṣ, Ḳ:) but some disallow this. (Ṣ. [See also 1.]) — أَشَرُّوهُ *They banished him,* or *drove him away, and caused him to be alone.* (TA.) = See also 1, latter part, in two places. — [Hence, app.,] اشرّهُ signifies also ‡ *He manifested it, revealed it, published it,* or *made it known.* (Ṣ, A, Ḳ.) Thus in a verse of Imra-el-Ḳeys, where he says, لَوْ يُشِرُّونَ مَقْتَلِى ‡ [*that they might publish,* or *make known, my slaughter*]; as related by Aṣ; but it is better with س. (Ṣ.) = مَا أَشَرَّهُ, and ▼مَا شَرَّهُ, [the latter of which is extr. with respect to form, but more commonly used than the former, meaning *How evil, wrongdoing, unjust, bad, corrupt, wicked, mischievous, vitious,* or *depraved, is he!*] phrases similar to مَا خَيْرَهُ and مَا أَخْيَرَهُ [which have the contr. meaning]. (TA in art. خير.)

8. اشترّ, said of a camel, [and of any cloven-hoofed animal,] i. q. اجترّ, i. e. *He ruminated,* or *chewed the cud:* ج and ش being from one place of utterance. (IAth, TA.)

10. استشرّ *He became possessor of a great herd, such as is termed* إِشْرَارَة, *of camels.* (Ḳ.)

R. Q. 1. شَرْشَرَهُ, (A'Obeyd, Ḳ,) inf. n. شَرْشَرَةٌ, (Ṣ,) *He split it,* or *clave it:* (A'Obeyd, Ṣ:) and *cut it much,* or *in many pieces.* (A'Obeyd, Ṣ, Ḳ.) — *He bit it, and then shook it;* namely, a thing. (O, Ḳ, TA. [In the CḲ, نَقَضَهُ is erroneously put for نَفَضَهُ.]) — شَرْشَرَتْهُ الحَيَّةُ *The serpent bit him.* (L, Ḳ.*) — شرشرت المَاشِيَةُ النَّبَاتَ *The cattle ate the herbage.* (Ḳ.) — شرشر السِّكِّينَ *He sharpened,* (Ḳ,) or *rubbed,* (O,) *the knife upon a stone,* (O, Ḳ, TA,) *so that its edge became rough.* (O, TA.) — See also 1, latter part. = شَرْشَرَ, inf. n. as above, *It* (a bird) *expanded and flapped its wings, without alighting;* like رَفْرَفَ. (TA in art. فرش.)

R. Q. 2. تَشَرْشَرَ *It became separated,* or *scattered.* (A.)

شَرٌّ (Ṣ, A, Mṣb, Ḳ, &c.) and ▼شُرٌّ, (Kr, Ḳ,) the former of which is the more chaste, (TA,) and ▼شَرَّةٌ (Ḥam p. 629) *Evil,* [*moral and physical;*] (L, Mṣb;) *wrongdoing, injustice, badness, corruptness, wickedness, mischievousness, vitiousness,* or *depravity:* (Mṣb:) [and *evil fortune, misfortune, woe,* or *unhappiness:*] *contr.* of خَيْرٌ: (Ṣ, A, Ḳ:) pl. شُرُورٌ. (Mṣb, Ḳ.) It is said in a trad., in a form of prayer, (TA,) used by the Prophet, (Mṣb,) وَالخَيْرُ كُلُّهُ بِيَدَيْكَ وَالشَّرُّ لَيْسَ إِلَيْكَ, (Mṣb,* TA,) meaning [*And all good is in thy hands, and evil* i. e.] *wrongdoing,* or *injustice,* or *corruptness, is not imputable to Thee:* (Mṣb, TA:) or *evil is not a means of advancement in thy favour,* or *of obtaining thine approval:* or *evil speech does not ascend to Thee.* (Nh, L.) — شَرٌّ also signifies † *Poverty.* (Ḳ.) — And † *Fever.* (Ḳ.) — It is also an epithet, applied to a man, (Yoo, Ṣ,) and so is ▼شَرِيرٌ, (Akh, Ṣ, A, Mṣb, Ḳ,) meaning *Evil, wrongdoing, unjust, bad, corrupt, wicked, mischievous, vitious,* or *depraved:* (Yoo,* Akh,* Ṣ,* A,* Mṣb, Ḳ:*) [fem. of the former شَرَّةٌ, like as خَيْرَةٌ is fem. of its contr. خَيْرٌ; and شُرَّى, fem. of أَشَرُّ, is used in the same sense, as will be shown in what follows:] the pl. of شَرٌّ, (Yoo, Ṣ,) or of ▼شَرِيرٌ, (Akh, Ṣ, Mṣb, Ḳ,) is أَشْرَارٌ, (Yoo, Akh, Ṣ, Mṣb, Ḳ,) and of the former شِرَارٌ; (Ḥam p. 514;) and you say قَوْمٌ أَشْرَارٌ [pl. of شَرٌّ or of ▼شَرِيرٌ]. (Ṣ.) A woman of the Arabs, (Ṣ, L,) who, accord. to some, was of the Benoo-'Ámir, (L,) is related to have said, ▼أُعِيذُكَ بِاللّٰهِ مِنْ نَفْسٍ حَرَّى وَعَيْنٍ شُرَّى, meaning [*I charm thee by* invoking *God, against* a thirsty soul, and] an evil, or a malignant, eye: (Ṣ, L:) or an eye that looks at one with vehement hatred. (TA.) And الشَّرُّ [The evil one] is an appellation of Iblees. (Ḳ.) —— [It is also used to denote the comparative and superlative degrees; like the contr. خَيْرٌ.] You say, هُوَ شَرٌّ مِنْكَ [He is worse, or more evil or wrongdoing &c., than thou]. (Ḳ.) And هٰذَا شَرٌّ مِنْ ذَاكَ [This is worse, &c., than that]. (Mṣb.) And فُلَانٌ شَرُّ النَّاسِ [Such a one is the worst, &c., of mankind]; (Ṣ;) and ▼ أَشَرُّ; (Ṣ, Mṣb, Ḳ;) this latter being the original, (Mgh, Mṣb,) but rare, (Ḳ,) or bad, (Ṣ, Ḳ,) peculiar to the dial. of the Benoo-'Ámir, (Mṣb,) or unused. (Mgh.) The fem. [of شَرٌّ] is شَرَّةٌ, [like as the fem. of its contr., خَيْرٌ, is خَيْرَةٌ,] (Ḳ,) and (of أَشَرُّ, Ṣ,* or of شَرٌّ, which is used for أَشَرُّ, Kr) ▼ شُرَّى. (Ṣ, Kr, Ḳ.) And [using the dim. form of شَرٌّ,] you say, هُوَ ▼ شُرَيْرٌ مِنْكَ [He is a little worse, &c., than thou]. (Ibn-Buzurj, TA in art. خير. [See خَيْرٌ.]) ▬ مَا أَشَرَّهُ for مَا شَرَّهُ: see 4.

شُرٌّ A vice, fault, defect, blemish, or something amiss: (TA:) a thing disapproved, disliked, or hated. (Ḳ, TA.) You say, مَا رَدَدْتُ هٰذَا عَلَيْكَ مِنْ شُرٍّ بِهِ I did not give this back to thee on account of any fault &c., in it, but I preferred to give it to thee. (TA.) And مَا قُلْتُ ذَاكَ لِشُرِّكَ I said not that on account of a thing that thou disapprovest, &c.: (Ḳ, TA:) or this has a different meaning, expl. above in the first paragraph. (TA.) —— See also شَرٌّ, first sentence.

شِرَّةٌ: see شَرٌّ, first sentence. —— Also The inordinate desire, or eagerness, (Ṣ,) and sprightliness, of youth: (Ṣ, Ḳ:) and in an absolute sense, inordinate desire, or eagerness; and [simply] desire; and sprightliness: (TA:) [and] sharpness, and angriness. (Ḥar p. 35.) It is said in a trad., إِنَّ لِهٰذَا الْقُرْآنِ شِرَّةً ثُمَّ إِنَّ لِلنَّاسِ عَنْهُ فَتْرَةً [Verily there is an eagerness for this Ḳur-án: then men have a weariness of it]. (L.)

شَرَرٌ; n. un. with ة: see what next follows.

شَرَارٌ, (Ṣ, A, O, Mṣb, TA,) accord. to the Ḳ شِرَارٌ, but this is a mistake, (MF,) and ▼ شَرَرٌ, (Ṣ, A, O, Mṣb, Ḳ,) which is a contraction of شَرَارٌ, (Mṣb,) Sparks of fire: (Ṣ, O, Mṣb, Ḳ:) n. un. of each with ة. (Ṣ, A, O, Mṣb,* Ḳ.) See an ex. voce شَرَّارٌ.

شَرِيرٌ: see شَرٌّ, in three places. ▬ Also The side of the sea, or of a great river; (AḤn, Ḳ;) the shore thereof: (Kr, TA:) or the part that is near to a sea or great river: pl. أَشِرَّةٌ: (AA, TA:) which signifies also seas or great rivers [themselves]. (TA.) —— And (as some say, TA) A kind of tree that grows in the sea, or in a great river. (Ḳ, TA.)

شُرَيْرٌ dim. of شَرٌّ: see the latter, last sentence but one.

شُوَيْرَةٌ A [large needle such as is termed] مِسَلَّةٌ (Ḳ, TA) of iron. (TA.)

شَرَّارٌ [Emitting many sparks]. One says, أَبُوكَ نَارٌ شَرَّارَةٌ وَأَنْتَ مِنْهَا ▼ شَرَارَةٌ [Thy father is a fire that emits many sparks, and thou art a spark from it]. (A.)

شَرَّانٌ Certain insects (Ḳ) resembling بَعُوض [or gnats], (Ṣ, Ḳ,) which cover the face of a man, but do not bite; sometimes called الأَذَى: (Ṣ:) of the dial. of the people of Es-Sawád: (T, TA:) [it is with tenween; for] the n. un. is with ة. (Ḳ.)

شِرِّيرٌ (Ṣ, A, Ḳ) Abounding in شَرّ [or evil or wrongdoing &c.; very evil &c.]; applied to a man: (Ṣ, A:) pl. شِرِّيرُونَ (Ḳ) and أَشْرَارٌ, which latter is anomalous. (Ḥam. p. 690.)

شَرْشَرٌ, (IAạr, Ṣ, Ḳ,) or (so in the Ṣ, but in the Ḳ "and") ▼ شُرْشُرٌ, (Ibn-Ziyád, Ṣ, Ḳ,) A certain plant, (Ṣ, Ḳ,) which extends along the ground like ropes, (Ibn-Ziyád, AḤn, Ḳ,) in the same manner as the قُطْب, but having no thorns that hurt any one: (Ibn-Ziyád, AḤn:) Az says that it is a well-known plant, seen by him in the desert; that it fattens the camels, and makes their milk plentiful; and that it is mentioned by IAạr and others among the plants of the desert: ▼ شِرْشِرَةٌ is expl. in the Ḳ as though it were the name of another plant; but it is not so; for شِرْشِرٌ is the pl. [or rather coll. gen. n.] thereof: it is a herb smaller than the عَرْفَج, having a yellow flower, and twigs, or shoots, and large dust-coloured leaves: it grows in plain, or soft, ground; and spreads wide, as though it were ropes, by reason of length, of the measure of a man in a standing posture; and has berries (حَبّ), like those of the هَرَاس. (TA.) ▬ شِوَآءٌ شَرْشَرٌ Roasted flesh-meat, of which the grease, or gravy, drips; (Ṣ, Ḳ;) like شَلْشَلٌ and رَشْرَاشٌ. (TA.)

شُرْشُرٌ: see the next preceding paragraph.

شُرْشُرَةٌ, ('Ináyeh, and so in some copies of the Ḳ,) or ▼ شَرْشَرَةٌ, (so in other copies of the Ḳ, accord. to the TA,) sing. of شَرَاشِرُ, (Ḳ,) which signifies The fringe-like extremities of a tail; (Ṣ,* Ḳ,* A, TA;) and of wings. (TA.) —— Hence, metaphorically, [or synecdochically,] the pl. is used as signifying ‡ The whole: and hence the saying, أَلْقَى عَلَيْهِ شَرَاشِرَهُ ‡ He betook himself altogether to it; as though, says Aṣ, by reason of his eagerness, he threw himself altogether upon it: accord. to Esh-Shiháb, it means he betook himself [to it], openly or secretly: or شَرَاشِرُ signifies † the whole body; (Ḳ;) and أَلْقَى عليه شراشره and أَجْرَانَهُ and أَجْرَامَهُ, all signify the same, provs. mentioned by Meyd, [app. † he threw upon it the weight of his body: see Freytag's Arab. Prov., ii. 409 and 410: and see art. جرم]: or the first of these means † he loved it so that he courted death, or destruction, (اِسْتَهْلَكَ,) in his love of it: (TA:) or he loved it with a love that he would not give up, because of his necessity: (Lth, TA:) or ‡ he desired it inordinately, or eagerly, and loved it. (A.) [See also أَلْقَى عَلَيْهِ أَرْوَاقَهُ, voce رَوْقٌ. Accord. to different authorities,] شَرَاشِرُ also signifies † Burdens, or weights; (Ṣ, Ḳ;) sing. شُرْشُرَةٌ: (Ṣ:) and it is so expl. as used in the saying mentioned above: or it there signifies † weight, and whole person: or the reduplication implies intensiveness; as though this word originally signified weight of evil: but F, in his comments on the Preface of the Ksh, objects to this, as the word does not imply the contr. of خَيْرٌ, but dispersion. (TA.) Also ‡ Self: (Ḳ, TA:) and the saying mentioned above is expl. as meaning ‡ He threw himself upon it, through inordinate, or eager, desire, and love. (Ṣ, TA.) And † Love: (Ḳ:) or † love of self. (Kr, TA.)

شُرْشُورٌ: see the next preceding paragraph.

شِرْشِرَةٌ A piece of anything. (Ḳ.) ▬ See also شَرْشَرٌ.

شُرْشُورٌ A certain bird, (Ḳ, TA,) of small size; said by Aṣ to be thus called by the people of El-Ḥijáz; and by the Arabs of the desert, بَرْقَش [a mistranscription for بِرْقِش]: it is said to be dust-coloured; in elegance, like the حُمَّرَة; and to be a little larger than the عُصْفُور [or sparrow]. (L, TA.) [Freytag, on the authority of Dmr, says that it is the same as is called ابو براقش: (but see بِرْقِش:) and describes it as being of an ashy colour, with some mixture of redness; and of the passerine kind.]

أَشَرُّ; and its fem., شُرَّى: see شَرٌّ, latter half, in three places. —— شُرَّى is also applied to a woman as meaning A great imputer of vices, faults, or the like, to others. (AA, L.)

إِشْرَارَةٌ A خَصَفَة, (Ṣ, Ḳ,) i. e. mat, (TA,) upon which [the preparation of curd called] أَقِط (Ṣ, Ḳ) and other things (Ṣ) are spread (Ṣ, Ḳ*) to dry; (TA;) [as also ▼ مِشَرٌّ or ▼ مَشَرٌّ, as written in different copies of the Ṣ voce عَبْثَ:] or a piece of cloth, of those whereof a tent is composed, used for that purpose: (TA:) or a tablet of stone or wood, upon which flesh-meat is dried: (Lth, IAạr:) pl. أَشَارِيرُ: or this pl. signifies pieces of flesh-meat cut into strips and dried: (Ṣ:) or the sing. signifies also flesh-meat cut into strips and dried. (Ḳ, TA.) ▬ Also A great herd of camels: (Ḳ:) because scattered. (TA.)

مِشَرٌّ or مَشَرٌّ: see the next preceding paragraph.

المُشَرْشِرُ The lion: (Ṣgh, Ḳ:) from الشَّرْشَرَةُ "the biting" a thing "and then shaking" it. (Ṣgh, TA.)

شرب

1. شَرِبَ, (Ṣ, A, Ḳ, &c.,) aor. ـَ, (A, Ḳ,) inf. n. شُرْبٌ and شَرْبٌ (Ṣ, A, Mṣb, Ḳ, &c.) and شِرْبٌ, (Ṣ, A, Ḳ,) agreeably with three different readings of the Ḳur lvi. 55, (Ṣ, TA,) the first of which (with ḍamm) is that generally obtaining, (Fr, TA,) and is the only one admitted by Jaạfar Ibn-Moḥammad, notwithstanding which the second form (with fet-ḥ) is said by MF to be the most chaste as well as the most agreeable with analogy, (TA,) or the second (with fet-ḥ) is an inf. n., and the first is a simple subst., (AO, Ṣ, Mṣb, Ḳ,) and so is the third, (AO, Ṣ, Ḳ,) and مَشْرَبٌ, (Ṣ, Ḳ,) which is

also a n. of place [and of time], (Ṣ,) and تَشْرَابٌ, (Ṣ, Ḳ, TA,) a form used when muchness of the act is meant, (TA,) and تِشْرَابٌ, which is anomalous, (TA voce تَبْيَانٌ, q. v.,) *He drank,* (KL, PṢ, TḲ,) or *he swallowed,* syn. جَرِعَ, (A, Ḳ, [but the former meaning is evidently intended by this explanation, and such I shall assume to be the case in giving the explanations of the derivatives in the A and Ḳ &c.,]) water, &c., (Ṣ,) or a liquid, properly *by sucking in,* or *sipping;* and *otherwise* tropically; (Mṣb;) [generally, *gulping* it; for] you say, شَرِبَ المَآءَ فِى جَرْعَةٍ [*He drank the water at once,* or *at a single draught*]; and ▼ تَشْرَبَهُ فِى مُهْلَةٍ [*He drank it leisurely,* or *gently,* or *slowly*]: (Mgh:) شُرْبٌ signifies *the conveying to one's inside, by means of his mouth, that in the case of which chewing is not practicable:* (KT:) [but] Es-Saraḳusṭee says, one does not say of a bird شَرِبَ المَآءَ, but حَسَاهُ. (Mṣb.) In the saying of Aboo-Dhu-eyb, describing clouds,

• شَرِبْنَ بِمَآءِ البَحْرِ ثُمَّ تَرَفَّعَتْ •

[which is evidently best rendered *They drank of the water of the sea, then rose aloft,* agreeably with what has been stated respecting بِ in the sense of مِنْ in p. 143, it is said that] the ب is redundant, or, as رَوِينَ is rendered trans. by means of بِ, [though I do not think that this is the case unless ب be used as meaning "by means of," and I do not remember to have met with an instance of it,] شَرِبْنَ is thus rendered trans. (TA.) [See a similar ex. in the 28th verse of the Mo'allaḳah of 'Antarah, EM p. 232. One says also, شَرِبَ فِى إِنَآءٍ, meaning *He drank out of a vessel;* agreeably with an explanation of مِشْرَبَةٌ, in the Ṣ and Ḳ, as meaning إِنَآءٌ يُشْرَبُ فِيهِ.] And one says, إِنِّى لَأَمْكُثُ اليَوْمَيْنِ مَا أَشْرَبُهُمَا مَآءً, meaning [مَا أَشْرَبُ فِيهِمَا مَآءً i. e. *Verily I tarry the two days not drinking in them water*]. (O.) — [شَرِبَ الدَّوَآءَ, in the conventional language of the physicians, as is indicated in the Mgh, voce بَشِعَ (q. v.), on the phrase شَرِبَ البَشِعَ, and as is shown in many instances in the Ḳ &c., means *He took,* i. e. *swallowed, the medicine,* whether fluid or solid. — And in the present day, they say, شَرِبَ الدُّخَانَ, meaning *He inhaled,* properly *imbibed, smoke* of tobacco; or, *he smoked tobacco,* or *the tobacco.*] — One says of seed-produce, or corn, when its culms have come forth, قَدْ شَرِبَ الزَّرْعُ فِى القَصَبِ † [*The seed-produce,* or *corn, has imbibed into the culms*]: (O, TA:) and when the sap (المَآء) has come into it, شَرِبَ قَصَبُ الزَّرْعِ † [*The culms of the seed-produce,* or *corn, have imbibed*]. (TA.) And one says, شَرِبَ السُّنْبُلُ الدَّقِيقَ ‡ [*The ears of corn imbibed the farina;* or] *became pervaded by the farina;* (En-Naḍr, A, O;) or *had in them the alimentary substance;* as though the farina were water which they drank. (TA.) And وَقَدْ شَرِبَ الزَّرْعُ الدَّقِيقَ, occurring in the story of Oḥod, (O, TA,) as some relate it, or ▼ شُرِّبَ as others relate it, means ‡ [*And the seed-produce,* or *corn, had imbibed,* or *had been made to imbibe, the farina,* or] *had become hardened in its grain, and near to maturity.* (TA.) [And ▼ أُشْرِبَ means the same: for one says,] أُشْرِبَ الزَّرْعُ ‡ [*The seed-produce,* or *corn, was made to imbibe* the farina; or] *became pervaded by the farina:* and in like manner, أُشْرِبَ الزَّرْعُ الدَّقِيقَ, i. e. ‡ [*The seed-produce,* or *corn, was made to imbibe the farina,* or] *its alimentary substance.* (TA.) — One also says, أَكَلَ غَنَمِى وَشَرِبَهَا ‡ [*He ate* the flesh of *my sheep,* or *goats, and drank* the milk of *them*]. (TA in art. اكل.) And [in like manner] أَكَلَ فُلَانٌ مَالِى وَشَرِبَهُ ‡ [*Such a one fed upon, devoured,* or *consumed, my property*]. (A.) And أَكَلَ عَلَيْهِ الدَّهْرُ وَشَرِبَ ‡ [*Time wasted him,* or *wore him away;* as though it fed upon him]. (A.) — And أَشْرَبْتَنِى ▼ مَا لَمْ أَشْرَبْ [lit. *Thou hast made me to drink what I have not drunk,*] meaning ‡ *thou hast charged against me,* or *accused me of doing, what I have not done;* (Ṣ, A, Ḳ;) like أَكَلْتَنِى مَا لَمْ آكُلْ. (Ṣ in art. اكل.) = شَرِبَ also signifies *He was,* or *became, satisfied with drinking:* (TA:) and in like manner شَرِبَتْ is said of camels. (A'Obeyd, Ṣ, TA.) And *He was,* or *became, thirsty;* (Ḳ, TA;) thus having two contr. significations; (TA;) as also ▼ أَشْرَبَ. (Ḳ, TA.) — Also, and ▼ أَشْرَبَ, *His camels were,* or *became, satisfied with drinking:* and, i. e. both these verbs, *his camels were,* or *became, thirsty:* (Ḳ, TA:) or the former verb signifies, or signifies also, (accord. to different copies of the Ḳ,) *his camel was,* or *became, weak.* (Ḳ, TA.) = شَرِبَ بِهِ, and ▼ أَشْرَبَ بِهِ, *He lied against him.* (Ḳ.) = شَرُبَ, aor. ـُ, (O, Ḳ, TA,) inf. n. شَرْبٌ, (O, TA,) *He understood:* (O, Ḳ, TA:) on the authority of AA. (TA.) [In a copy of the A, the verb in this sense is written شَرِبَ; and app. not through the fault of the transcriber, for it is there mentioned as tropical: but in the O, it is said to be like كَتَبَ, aor. ـُ, inf. n. كَتْبٌ; and in the Ḳ, to be like نَصَرَ.] One says, شَرُبَ مَا أُلْقِىَ إِلَيْهِ, i. e. *He understood* [*what was told to him*]. (TA.) And one says to a stupid person, أَحْلُبْ ثُمَّ اشْرُبْ *Kneel thou; then understand.* (O, TA. See also 1 in art. حلب.)

2. شَرَّبَهُ, inf. n. تَشْرِيبٌ, *He made him to drink* water &c.; and so, as is indicated in the Ṣ and Ḳ &c., and as is well known, ▼ أَشْرَبَهُ: and] شَرَّبْتُهُ المَآءَ *I gave to drink the water;* as also ▼ أَشْرَبْتُهُ. (TA.) — [Hence,] one says, ظَلَّ مَالِى يُؤَكَّلُ وَيُشَرَّبُ [lit. *My cattle passed the day made to eat and made to drink,*] i. e. † *pasturing as they pleased.* (Ṣ, TA.) And شَرَّبَ مَالِى وَأَكَّلَهُ [lit. *He made people to drink my property, and made them to eat it;* or *to drink the milk of my cattle, and to eat the flesh thereof;*] i. e. † *he fed people,* (Ṣ,) or *gave people to drink and to eat,* (TA,) [of] *my property,* or *cattle.* (Ṣ, TA.) — And شَرَّبَ الأَرْضَ وَالنَّخْلَ † *He gave drink to the land and the palm-trees.* (TA.) — And شَرَّبَ لُقْمَةً بِالدَّسَمِ † [*He imbued,* or *soaked, a morsel,* or *mouthful, with grease,* or *gravy*]. (TA in art. ودع.) — And شَرَّبْتُ القِرْبَةَ, (A'Obeyd, Ṣ,) inf. n. تَشْرِيبٌ, (A'Obeyd, Ḳ,) † *I rendered the water-skin sweet;* (Ḳ;) *I put into the water-skin,* it being new, *clay and water, in order to render its savour sweet.* (A'Obeyd, Ṣ.) — And شَرَّبَ الزَّرْعُ الدَّقِيقَ: see 1, in the latter half of the paragraph.

3. شَارَبَهُ, (Ṣ, A, Ḳ, TA,) inf. n. مُشَارَبَةٌ and شِرَابٌ, *He drank with him;* namely, a man. (TA.) — [And *He watered his camels,* &c. *with his,* i. e. with another's: or *he drew water with him for the watering of camels* &c.:] see an ex. of the latter inf. n. in a verse cited voce شَرِيبٌ.

4: see 2, in two places. One says, أَشْرَبْتُ الإِبِلَ حَتَّى شَرِبَتْ [*I made the camels to drink until they were satisfied with drinking;* or *I watered the camels,* or *gave them to drink,* &c.]; (Ṣ, TA;) [for] أَشْرَبَ is *syn. with* سَقَى. (Ḳ.) — [Hence,] أُشْرِبَ الثَّوْبُ يُشْرَبُ الصِّبْغَ: see 5. And أُشْرِبَ الثَّوْبُ حُمْرَةً ‡ *The garment,* or *piece of cloth, was imbued,* or *saturated, with redness.* (A.) And أَشْرَبَ اللَّوْنَ ‡ *He saturated the colour* [*with dye*]. (Ḳ, TA.) And أُشْرِبَ لَوْنًا † *It was intermixed with a colour;* as also ▼ اِشْرَابَّ. (TA.) And أُشْرِبَ الأَبْيَضُ حُمْرَةً † *The white was suffused,* or *tinged over, with redness.* (Ṣ, TA.) — [Hence,] أُشْرِبَ is also said of a sound, as meaning † *It was mixed with another sound;* as appears from the words here following: [حِسُّ الصَّوْتِ فِى الفَمِ مِمَّا لَا إِشْرَابَ لَهُ مِنْ صَوْتِ الصَّدْرِ † *The faint,* or *gentle, sound of the voice in the mouth, of such kind as has no mixture of the voice of the chest*]. (Ḳ in art. همس.) — [Hence also,] أُشْرِبَ الزَّرْعُ: see 1, latter half. — And أُشْرِبَ فِى قَلْبِهِ حُبَّهُ, (Ṣ,) or أُشْرِبَ حُبَّ فُلَانٍ, (Ḳ,) or حُبَّ فُلَانَةَ, (A,) ‡ [*He was made to imbibe into his heart the love of him,* or *of such a man,* or *of such a female;*] meaning that the love of him, or of her, pervaded, or commingled with, his heart, (Ṣ, A, Ḳ, TA,) like beverage. (TA.) Whence, in the Ḳur [ii. 87], وَأُشْرِبُوا فِى قُلُوبِهِمُ العِجْلَ, for حُبَّ العِجْلِ, (Ṣ, TA,) i. e. † *And they were made to imbibe* [*into their hearts*] *the love of the calf.* (Zj, TA.) — And رَفَعَ يَدَهُ فَأَشْرَبَهَا الهَوَآءَ ثُمَّ قَالَ بِهَا عَلَى قَذَالِهِ ‡ [*He raised his hand, and made the air to swallow it up,* (i. e. raised it so high and so quickly that it became hardly seen,) *then gave a blow with it upon the back of his head*]. (A, TA.) — And أَشْرَبْتَنِى مَا لَمْ أَشْرَبْ: see 1, latter half. — And one says to his she-camel, لَأُشْرِبَنَّكِ الحِبَالَ ‡ [*I will assuredly put upon thee the ropes,* or *cords*], and العِقَالَ [*the cord,* or *rope, with which the fore shank and the arm are bound together*]. (A.) [Or] اشربهُ means ‡ *He put the rope,* or *cord, upon his neck;* namely, a man's, (Ḳ, TA,) and a camel's, and a horse's or the like: (TA:) and اشرب الخَيْلَ *he put the ropes,* or *cords, upon the necks of the horses.* (Ḳ.) And اشرب إِبِلَهُ ‡ *He tied his camels, every one to* *another*. (K, TA.) ═ اشرب as an intrans. verb: see 1, last quarter, in two places. — Also *He* (a man, TA) *attained to the time for the drinking of his camels*. (K,* TA.) ═ اشرب بِهِ: see 1, near the end of the paragraph.

5: see 1, first sentence. — Hence one says, (Mgh,) تَشَرَّبَ الثَّوْبُ العَرَقَ, (S, Mgh,* K,) and الصِّبْغَ, (A, Mgh, L,) ‡ *The garment*, or *piece of cloth, imbibed*, or *absorbed*, (S, A, Mgh,* L, K,) *the sweat*, (S, Mgh, K,) and *the dye*; (A, Mgh, L;) as though it drank it by little and little: (Mgh:) and [in like manner] one says, الثَّوْبُ يشرب الصِّبْغ [app. ▾ يُشْرَبُ, (like as one says يُشْرَبُ حُمْرَةً, as shown in the next preceding paragraph,) meaning † *The garment*, or *piece of cloth, is made to imbibe*, or *absorb, the dye*]. (TA.) [It is said that] the verb is not used intransitively in the [proper] language of the Arabs. (Mgh.) [But] one says, تَشَرَّبَ الصِّبْغُ فِى الثَّوْبِ, meaning ‡ *The dye pervaded the garment*, or *piece of cloth*: (K,* TA:) and الصِّبْغُ يَتَشَرَّبُ الثَّوْبَ ‡ [*The dye pervades the garment*, or *piece of cloth*]. (TA.) [See also the explanation of a verse cited voce تَسَقَّى.]

10. استشرب لَوْنُهُ † *His*, or *its, colour became intense*. (K.) And استشربت القَوْسُ حُمْرَةً † *The bow became intensely red*: such is the case when it is made of the [tree called] شَرْيَان. (AHn, TA.)

11. إِشْرَابَّ: see 4, near the beginning.

Q. Q. 4. إِشْرَأَبَّ, (S, A, O, K,) inf. n. إِشْرِئْبَابٌ, (S, O,) ‡ *He raised his head like the camel that has satisfied his thirst on the occasion of drinking*: (A:) or *he stretched forth his neck to look*: (S, A, O, K:) not improbably, from الشُّرْبُ in its well known sense, as though he did so when preparing to drink: (O:) or, as is said in the L, from مَشْرَبَةٌ as syn. with غُرْفَةٌ: (TA:) you say, اِشْرَأَبَّ لَهُ, (S, A,) or إِلَيْهِ, (K,) or both; (TA;) [the former of which may be rendered *He raised his head at it*, or *he stretched forth his neck at it to look*; or, as also the latter, *he stretched forth his neck to look at it*;] namely, a thing: (S:) or اشرأبّ originally means *he stretched forth his neck in preparing to drink water*: and then, in consequence of frequency of usage, *he raised his head, and stretched forth his neck, in looking*; and hence is trans. by means of إِلَى: (Har p. 152:) or *he raised*, or *exalted, himself*. (K,* TA.) يَشْرَئِبُّونَ لِصَوْتِهِ, occurring in a trad., means ‡ *They will raise their heads at his voice to look at him*. (TA.) And اِشْرَأَبَّ النِّفَاقُ وَارْتَدَّتِ العَرَبُ, in another trad., means ‡ *Hypocrisy exalted itself* [*and the Arabs apostatized*, or *revolted from their religion*]. (TA.)

شَرْبٌ an inf. n. of شَرِبَ [q. v.]. (S, A, Msb, K, &c.) ═ And a pl., (S, Msb,) or [rather] a quasi-pl. n., (ISd, TA,) of شَارِبٌ, q. v. (S, ISd, Msb, TA.) ═ [Golius assigns to it also the meaning of "*Linum tenue*," as on the authority of Meyd.]

شُرْبٌ an inf. n. of شَرِبَ [q. v.]; (S, A, Msb, K, &c.;) like ▾ شِرْبٌ: (S, A, K:) or a simple subst. [signifying The act of *drinking*]; (AO, S, Msb, K;) as also ▾ شِرْبٌ. (AO, S, K.) ═ In the phrase ذُو أُصُولٍ شُرْبٍ it is used as [an epithet,] meaning شُرْبٌ [which may be regarded as virtually syn. with شَارِبٌ or as similar to this latter but intensive in signification]. (Ham p. 194.)

شِرْبٌ: see the next preceding paragraph, in two places. — Also *Water*, (K, TA,) itself; so some say; (TA;) as also ▾ مِشْرَبٌ, (K, accord. to the TA,) with kesr, (TA,) or ▾ مَشْرَبٌ, (so in the CK and in my MS. copy of the K,) i. e. *water that one drinks*; so says AZ: pl. of the former أَشْرَابٌ. (TA.) [See also شَرَابٌ.] — [And *A draught* of milk: see an ex. in a verse cited in art. سلف, conj. 4.] — And *A share*, or *portion that falls to one's lot, of water*: (S, Mgh, Msb, K:) or so شِرْبٌ مِنْ مَآءٍ. (ISk, TA.) It is said in a prov., آخِرُهَا أَقَلُّهَا شِرْبًا [*The last of them is the one of them that has the least share of water*]: originating from the watering of camels; because the last of them sometimes comes to the water when the watering-trough has been exhausted. (S. [See also Freytag's Arab. Prov. i. 61.]) — As a law-term, it means The *use of water* [or the *right to use it*] *for the watering of sown-fields and of beasts*. (Mgh.) — Also *A watering-place*; syn. مَوْرِدٌ: (AZ, K:) pl. as above. (TA.) — And † *A time of drinking*: (K:) but they say that it denotes the time only by a sort of tropical application; and they differ respecting the connexion of this meaning with the proper meaning. (MF, TA.)

شُرَبٌ: see شَرَبَةٌ, in two places.

شَرْبَةٌ *A single act of drinking*. (S.) — And *A single draught*, or the *quantity that is drunk at once*, of water. (S.) It is said in a prov., نِعْمَ مُعَلَّقُ الشَّرْبَةِ هٰذَا [*Excellent*, or *most excellent, is the traveller's drinking-cup*, or *bowl, that will hold a single draught*, namely, *this!*]: the مُعَلَّق is said by As to be a drinking-cup or bowl which the rider upon a camel suspends [to his saddle]: (Meyd:) it is said in describing a camel: (TA:) and it means that, to the place of alighting to which he desires to go, he is content with a single draught, not wanting another: (Meyd, TA:) the prov. is applied to him who, in his affairs, is content with his own opinion, not wanting that of another person. (Meyd.) شَرْبَةُ أَبِى الجَهْمِ [*The draught of Abu-l-Jahm*] is said of a thing that is sweet, or pleasant, but in its result unwholesome: (MF, TA:) Abu-l-Jahm was a frequent visiter of the Khaleefeh El-Mansoor El-'Abbásee, who, finding him troublesome, ordered that a poisoned draught should be given to him, in his presence: which having been done, Abu-l-Jahm, pained by the draught, rose to depart; and being asked by the Khaleefeh whither he was going, he answered, Whither thou hast sent me, O Prince of the Faithful. (MF.) — In the Mo'allakah of Tarafeh, it is applied to *A draught of wine*. (EM p. 87.) — [In the conventional language of the physicians, it is a term applied to *A dose of medicine*, *such as is drunk* and also *such as is eaten*.] ═ Also *A palm-tree that grows from the date stone*: (K:) pl. شَرَبَاتٌ. (TA. [It seems to be there added that شَرَائِبُ and شَرَابِيبُ are also its pls.: the former may be like ضَرَائِرُ pl. of ضَرَّةٌ: the latter is app. a mistranscription, and should perhaps be شَرَائِيبُ, for شَرَائِبُ; like مَحَامِيرُ for مَحَامِرُ, &c.])

شُرْبَةٌ, (K,) or شُرْبَةٌ مِنْ مَآءٍ, (S,) The *quantity of water that satisfies thirst*. (S, K.) — شُرْبَةٌ is also *syn. with* ▾ إِشْرَابٌ [originally an inf. n.] meaning † *A colour tinged over with another colour*; as in the saying, فِيهِ شُرْبَةٌ مِنْ حُمْرَةٍ † [*In him is a colour tinged with redness*]: (S, TA:) [and] ‡ *somewhat of redness*; as in the phrase, فِيهِ شُرْبَةٌ ‡ [*In him is somewhat of redness*]: (A:) or † *a redness in the face*: (K:) or † *whiteness mixed with redness*. (IAar, TA voce خُشْبَةٌ.)

شَرَبَةٌ [The *act*, or *habit, of*] *much drinking*. (K.) One says, إِنَّهُ لَذُو شَرَبَةٍ, meaning *Verily he is one who drinks much*. (AA, AHn, TA.) ═ It is also allowable as a pl. of شَارِبٌ [q. v.]. (Msb.) ═ Also *A small trough*, (S, K, TA,) *made*, (S,) or *dug*, (TA,) *around a palm-tree*, (S, K, TA,) and *around any other kind of tree, and filled with water*, (TA,) *holding enough to irrigate it fully*, (K, TA,) *so that it is plentifully irrigated thereby*: (S, TA:) pl. ▾ شَرَبٌ [or rather this is a coll. gen. n., of which the former is the n. un.,] and [the pl. properly so termed is] شَرَبَاتٌ. (S.) — And *i. q.* كُرْدُ دَبْرَةٍ, (K, TA,) which is *syn. with* مَسْقَاةٌ: (TA:) [from a comparison of the explanations of all of these words, it seems to mean *A channel of water for the irrigation of a plot*, or *tract, of sown land*: or, if the explanation مسقاة, in the TA, be conjectural, the meaning may be *a portion of such land, having a raised border to retain the water admitted upon it*:] pl. شَرَبَاتٌ and [coll. gen. n.] ▾ شَرَبٌ [as above]. (TA.) ═ Also *Thirst*. (Lh, T, O, K.) One says, لَمْ تَزَلْ بِهِ شَرَبَةٌ اليَوْمَ *He has not ceased to have thirst to-day*. (Lh, TA.) And جَآءَتِ الإِبِلُ وَبِهَا شَرَبَةٌ *The camels came thirsty*. (T, O.) And طَعَامٌ ذُو شَرَبَةٍ *Food wherewith one has not sufficient water to satisfy thirst*. (O, TA.) Accord. to the L, شَرَبَةٌ signifies The *thirst of cattle after the being satisfied with fresh pasture*; because this invites to drink. (TA.) — And *Vehemence of heat*. (K.) One says, يَوْمٌ ذُو شَرَبَةٍ *A day of vehement heat, in which is drunk more water than at other times*. (TA.)

شِرِّيبٌ One *who drinks much*; (ISk, S, K;) as also ▾ شَرُوبٌ and ▾ شَرَّابٌ. (S.) One says رَجُلٌ أُكَلَةٌ شُرَبَةٌ *A man who eats and drinks much*. (ISk, S.)

شُرْبُبٌ, applied to herbage, *i. q.* غُمْلُولٌ; (O, K;) i. e. *Tangled and dense, one part above another*. (O.)

شُرُبَّةٌ, [said to be] the only word of this form except جُرُبَّةٌ, (K,) [but to this should be added بُغُتَّةٌ, inf. n. of بَغَتَهُ,] *A way, mode*, or *manner*, *of being*, or *acting* &c. (Ṣ, O, Ḳ.) One says, مَا زَالَ فُلَانٌ عَلَى شَرْبَةٍ وَاحِدَةٍ *Such a one ceased not to be* [*employed*] *upon one affair.* (Ṣ, O.) ═ And *A tract of land*, (Ḳ, TA,) *soft*, or *plain*, (TA,) *producing herbs, but having in it no trees.* (Ḳ, TA.) — [And] The *side of a valley.* (Mgh.)

شَرَابٌ *A beverage*, or *drink*, (Mgh, L, Mṣb, Ḳ,) *of any of the liquids*, (Mgh, Mṣb,) or *of anything that is not chewed*, (L,) or *of whatever kind and in whatever state it be*; thus in a copy of the Ḳ: (TA:) and syn. with شَرَابٌ are ▼ شَرِيبٌ and ▼ شَرُوبٌ, (Ḳ,) accord. to a saying attributed to AZ: (TA:) or these two have another meaning, expl. in the next paragraph: (Ḳ:) the pl. of شَرَابٌ is أَشْرِبَةٌ; (Mgh, TA;) or it has no pl., as is said in the Ḳ in art. نهر [accord. to one or more of the copies; but see نَهَارٌ, where it is shown that in copies of the Ḳ, as well as in the Ṣ, the word to which this statement relates is سَرَابٌ, with the unpointed س]. (TA.) The lawyers [and generally the post-classical writers, and sometimes others,] mean thereby [*Wine*, and] *such beverage as is forbidden.* (Mgh.) [Also *Sirup*: pl. شَرَابَاتٌ: so in the language of the present day.]

شَرُوبٌ and ▼ شَرِيبٌ are *syn. with* شَرَابٌ, q. v.: or both signify Water *inferior to the* عَذْب [or *sweet*]: (Ḳ:) or [*brackish* water; i. e.] water *between the salt and the sweet*: (AO, Ṣ:) or water *drinkable*, or *fit to be drunk*, *but in which is disagreeableness*: (Mṣb:) or the former signifies water *that has some degree of sweetness, and is sometimes drunk by men notwithstanding what is in it*; and ▼ the latter, water *inferior to what is sweet, and not drunk by men save in cases of necessity, but sometimes drunk by cattle*: (IḲṭṭ, TA:) or ▼ the latter, the *sweet*: and the former is said to signify water *that is drunk*: (TA:) or ▼ the latter, water *that has no sweetness in it, but is sometimes drunk by men notwithstanding what is in it*; and the former, water *inferior to this in sweetness, and not drunk by men save in cases of necessity*: (AZ, T, M, TA:) or, accord. to Lth, ▼ شَرِيبٌ and ▼ شَرِّيبٌ signify water *in which are bitterness and saltness, but not abstained from as drink*: and مَآءٌ شَرُوبٌ and طَعِيمٌ are *syn.*: and ▼ مَآءٌ مَشْرَبٌ is syn. with شَرُوبٌ: this last word is used alike as masc. and fem. and sing. and pl. (TA.) It is said in a prov., originally in a trad., جُرْعَةُ شَرُوبٍ أَنْفَعُ مِنْ عَذْبٍ مُوبٍ [expl. in art. وبأ]. (TA.) ═ Also, شَرُوبٌ, A man *who drinks vehemently.* (TA.) See also شُرْبَةٌ: and شِرِّيبٌ. — And † A she-camel *desiring the stallion.* (Ḳ.)

شَرِيبٌ: see شَرَابٌ: and شَرُوبٌ; the latter in five places. ═ Also *One who drinks with another*: (Ṣ, Ḳ:) and *one who waters his camels with those of another*: of the measure فَعِيلٌ in the sense of the measure مُفَاعِلٌ: (Ṣ:) and *one who draws water, or is given to drink, with another.* (IAạr, Ḳ.) You say, هُوَ شَرِيبِى [*He is my companion in drinking*; or *in watering his camels with mine*: &c.]. (TA.) And a rájiz says,

* رُبَّ شَرِيبٍ لَكَ ذِى حُسَاسِ *
* شِرَابُهُ ▼ كَالحَزِّ بِالمَوَاسِى *

[*Many a one who waters his camels with thine*, or *who draws water with thee* for the watering of camels, *having an evil disposition, his watering* &c. *is like the cutting with razors*]: i. e., thy waiting for him at the watering-trough is [a cause of] killing to thee and to thy camels. (TA.)

شَرِيبَةٌ is expl. in the Ṣ as meaning *A sheep*, or *goat, which one drives back*, or *brings back, from the water, when the sheep*, or *goats, are satisfied with drinking, and which they follow*: but in some of the copies is a marginal note stating that the correct word is سَرِيبَةٌ, with the unpointed س. (TA.)

شَرَابِىٌّ *A cup-bearer*: or *a butler*: and *a seller of wine* or *of sirup.* (MA.)

شُرَأْبِيبَةٌ a subst. (Ḳ) from اشْرَأَبَّ [q. v.; as such signifying ‡ *A raising of the head like the camel that has satisfied his thirst on the occasion of drinking*: &c.]: (Ṣ, Ḳ, TA:) like طُمَأْنِينَةٌ [from اِطْمَأَنَّ]. (Ḳ, TA.)

شُرَّابٌ: see شُرْبَةٌ: and what here next follows.

شِرِّيبٌ *Addicted to* شَرَاب [i. e. *drink*, or *wine*]; (Ṣ, Ḳ, TA;) like خِمِّيرٌ; (Ṣ;) as also ▼ شَرَّابٌ and ▼ شَرُوبٌ and ▼ شَارِبٌ. (TA.) ═ See also شَرُوبٌ.

[شُرَّابَةٌ *A tassel*: so in the language of the present day: probably post-classical: pl. شَرَارِيبُ.]

شَارِبٌ *Drinking*, or *a drinker*: pl. شَارِبُونَ (Mṣb) and ▼ شُرْبٌ, like as صَحْبٌ is of صَاحِبٌ, (Ṣ, Mṣb,) or, accord. to ISd, (TA,) شَرْبٌ, which signifies *people drinking*, (Ḳ, TA,) and *assembling for drinking*, is a quasi.-pl. n. of شَارِبٌ, being like رَكْبٌ and رَجْلٌ; and شُرُوبٌ, which is said by IAạr [and in the Ṣ] to be pl. of شَرْبٌ, is pl. of شَارِبٌ, like as شُهُودٌ is of شَاهِدٌ; (TA;) شَرَبَةٌ also is allowable as a pl. of شَارِبٌ, like as كَفَرَةٌ is pl. of كَافِرٌ; (Mṣb;) and أَشْرُبٌ is pl. of شَرْبٌ, or it may be an anomalous pl. of شَارِبٌ: (MF:) the pl. شُرُوب occurs in the saying of El-Aạshà,

* هُوَ الوَاهِبُ المُسْمِعَاتِ الشُّرُو *
* بَ بَيْنَ الحَرِيرِ وَبَيْنَ الكَتَنْ *

[*He is the giver of female singers to the drinkers, some clad in silk and some in linen*]. (Ṣ.) — See also شِرِّيبٌ. — [Hence, The *mustache*; i. e.] the *defluent hair over the mouth*; (Mṣb;) or so شَوَارِبُ, (Lḥ, A, Ḳ,) which is the pl., (Lḥ, Ṣ, Mṣb,) as though the sing. applied to every distinct part: (Lḥ:) the two [halves] are called شَارِبَانِ: (Ṣ, TA:) or, as some say, only the sing. is used, and the dual is a mistake: (TA:) accord. to AḤát (Mṣb, TA) and AAF, (TA,) the dual is is scarcely ever, or never, used; but accord. to AO, the Kilábees say شَارِبَانِ, with regard to the two extremities: (Mṣb, TA:) and the pl., (A, Ḳ,) or, accord. to the T &c., the dual, (TA,) signifies the *long portions* [*of the hair*] *on the two sides of the* سَبَلَة [q. v.]: (T, A, Ḳ, TA:) or (Ḳ, TA) شَارِبٌ signifies the سَبَلَة *altogether*, (A, Ḳ, TA,) as some say; but this is not correct. (TA.) One says, طَرَّ شَارِبُ الغُلَامِ [*The mustache of the boy*, or *young man, grew forth*]. (Ṣ.) — And hence, as being likened to the two long portions of hair on each side of the سَبَلَة, the شَارِبَانِ of the sword, (T, TA,) i. e. ‡ *Two long projections* (أَنْفَانِ طَوِيلَانِ) *at the lower part of the hilt*, (A,* Ḳ, TA,) [*extending from the guard*,] *one on one side and the other on the other side of the blade*, (T,* TA,) *the* غَاشِيَة [or *leathern covering of the scabbard*] *being beneath them*: so says ISh. (TA.) — الشَّوَارِبُ also signifies ‡ *The* عُرُوق [or *ducts*] *of the* حُلْقُوم [or *windpipe*]: (A:) or *certain ducts* (عُرُوق) *in the* حَلْق [i. e. *fauces* or *throat*], (Ḳ, TA,) *that imbibe the water* [or *saliva?*], *being the channels thereof*: (TA:) and, (Ḳ,) or, as some say, (TA,) *the channels of the water* [or *saliva?*] (Ṣ, Ḳ, TA) *in the* حَلْق [i. e. *fauces* or *throat*] (Ṣ) or *in the neck*: (Ḳ, TA:) or *certain ducts* (عُرُوق) *adhering to the windpipe, and the lower parts thereof to the lungs*: so says IDrd: or rather, some say, *the hinder part thereof* [*adhering*] *to the* وَتِين [or *aorta*], *having tubes from which the voice issues, and in which choking takes place, and whence the saliva issues*: and those of the horse are said to be [*certain ducts*] *by the side of the* أَوْدَاج [or *external jugular veins*], *where the veterinary surgeon draws blood by cutting the* اوداج: the sing. seems by implication to be شَارِبٌ. (TA.) Hence the phrase حِمَارٌ صَخِبُ الشَّوَارِبِ † *An ass that brays vehemently.* (Ṣ, TA.) And صَخِبُ الشَّوَارِبِ ‡ [*A man*] *having a disagreeable voice*: thus likened to an ass. (A, TA.) — Accord. to IAạr, الشَّوَارِبُ signifies [also] مَجَارِى المَآءِ فِى العَيْنِ, which AM supposes to mean *The channels of water in the spring*, or *source*; not in the eye. (L, TA.) — سُنْبُلٌ شَارِبٌ قَمْحًا means ‡ *Ears of corn becoming*, or *being, pervaded by the farina*: (A, TA:) or, *in which the grain has hardened, and nearly come to maturity.* (TA.) ═ Also † *Weakness*, or *feebleness*, in any animal: (Ḳ,* TA:) or *a strain* (عِرْق) thereof; as in the saying, نِعْمَ البَعِيرُ هٰذَا لَوْ لَا أَنَّ فِيهِ شَارِبَ خَوَرٍ † [*Excellent*, or *most excellent, were the camel, this one, were there not in him a strain of weakness* or *feebleness*]. (TA.)

شَارِبَةٌ [a subst. from شَارِبٌ, made such by the affix ة,] *A people*, or *party, dwelling upon the side* (ضَفَّة, in some copies of the Ḳ صُفَّة,) *of a river*, (Ṣ,* A, Ḳ,) *and to whom belongs the water thereof.* (Ṣ.)

إِشْرَابٌ as syn. with شُرْبَةٌ: see the latter.

مَشْرَبٌ is a noun of place, [and of time,] as well as an inf. n.: [i. e.] it signifies [*A place*, and *a time, of drinking*: or] the *quarter* (وَجْه) *whence one drinks*: (Ṣ, TA:) and *a place to which one comes to drink at a river* or *rivulet*: (TA:) and ▼ مَشْرَبَةٌ, (Ṣ, Mṣb, Ḳ, TA,) not, as is implied in the Ḳ, مَشْرُبَةٌ also, (TA,) signifies [the same, as is indicated in the A; or] *a place whence people drink;* (Mṣb, TA;*) *i. q.* مَشْرَعَةٌ; (Ḳ;) or *like a* مَشْرَعَة. (Ṣ, TA.) One says, هٰذَا مَشْرَبُ القَوْمِ and ▼ مَشْرَبَتُهُمْ [*This is the people's, or party's, drinking-place, or place whence they drink*]. (A.) And it is said in a trad., مَلْعُونٌ مَنْ أَحَاطَ عَلَى مَشْرَبَةٍ ▼, (Ṣ, TA,) i. e. [*Cursed is he*] *who takes entirely to himself, debarring others from it, a place whence people drink.* (TA.) — See also شُرْب.

مُشْرَبٌ حُمْرَةً ‡ A man *whose complexion is tinged over* [or *intermixed*] *with redness.* (TA.) [See 4: and see also مُشَرَّبٌ.]

رَجُلٌ مُشْرِبٌ *A man whose camels have drunk* [*until satisfied with drinking:* see أَشْرَبَ near the end of the first paragraph]. (TA.) And *A man whose camels are thirsty, or who is himself thirsty.* (TA.) اِسْقِنِى فَإِنَّنِى مُشْرِبٌ is a saying mentioned by IAạr, and expl. by him as meaning عَطْشَانُ: it means [*Give thou me to drink, for*] *I am thirsty* or *my camels are thirsty.* (TA.)

مَشْرُوبٌ: see شُرْبٌ: and see also شَرُوبٌ.

مَشْرُبَةٌ: see مَشْرَبٌ, in three places. — Hence, (A, TA,) *An upper chamber;* syn. غُرْفَةٌ; (Ṣ, A, Mṣb, Ḳ, TA;) and عِلِّيَّةٌ; (Ṣ,* Ḳ;) both of which signify the same; (MF, TA;) because people drink therein; (A, TA;) as also ▼ مَشْرَبَةٌ: (Ṣ, Mṣb, Ḳ, TA:) pl. مَشَارِبُ, (TA,) syn. with عَلَالِىُّ, (Ṣ,) and مَشْرُبَاتٌ. (TA.) — And the former, (Ḳ, TA,) not, as is implied in the Ḳ, the latter also, (TA,) *A* صُفَّة [i. e. *roofed vestibule* or *the like*]: (Ḳ, TA:) or the *like of a* صُفَّة *in the front of a* غُرْفَة [expl. above]. (TA.) — Also the former, (Ḳ, TA,) not, as is implied in the Ḳ, both words, (TA,) *Soft,* or *plain, land, in which is always herbage,* (Ḳ, TA,) i. e. *green and juicy herbage.* (TA.) — See also مَشْرَبَةٌ. ═ [Also *A cause of drinking:* a word of the class of مَبْخَلَةٌ &c.] One says طَعَامٌ مَشْرَبَةٌ *Food* [*that is a cause of drinking,* or] *upon which one drinks much water:* (T, TA:) or طَعَامٌ ذُو مَشْرَبَةٍ *food upon which the eater drinks.* (A.)

مَشْرَبَةٌ: see the next preceding paragraph.

مِشْرَبَةٌ, (Ṣ, A, Ḳ,) and MF says that ▼ مَشْرَبَةٌ is allowable in the same sense, mentioning it as on the authority of Fei, [in my copy of whose lexicon, the Mṣb, I do not find it,] (TA,) *A drinking-vessel.* (Ṣ, A, Ḳ.)

مُشَرَّبٌ حُمْرَةً ‡ A man *whose complexion is much tinged over* [or *much intermixed*] *with redness.* (TA.) [See also مُشْرَبٌ.] — مُشْرَبَةٌ is an epithet applied to Certain letters *the utterance of which, in pausing, is accompanied with a sort of blowing, but not with the same stress as the* [*generality of those that are termed*] مَجْهُورَة: they are زَاى and ظَآء and ذَال and ضَاد: [and Lumsden (in his Ar. Gr. p. 47) states that رَآء belongs to the same class, likewise: and, as some say, نُون when movent:] Sb says that some of the Arabs utter with more vehemence of voice than others. (TA.)

شرج

1. شَرَجَ: see 4. — Also, (Ṣ, A, O, TA,) [aor. ـُ,] inf. n. شَرْجٌ, (Ṣ, O, Ḳ, TA,) *He put,* or *set, together* bricks (لَبِن), *in order, side by side,* or *one upon another, compactly;* (Ṣ, A, O, Ḳ, TA;) and (O) so ▼ شرّج, (O, Mgh, Mṣb,) with teshdeed, (Mṣb,) inf. n. تَشْرِيجٌ. (O, Mgh.) — And *He collected together,* (O, Ḳ,) or *put together,* or *joined,* (L,) any thing or things, *one part to another,* or *one thing to another;* (O, L;) as also ▼ شَرَّجَ. (L.) — [And app. *He wove* palm-leaves: see شَرِيجَةٌ, below; and see also شَرِيطٌ.] — And *He mixed* (A, O, Ḳ) beverage, or wine: and in like manner ▼ شرّج *he mixed* honey &c. with water. (O.) — And شَرَجَهُ فِى الأَمْرِ, aor. ـُ, (TḲ,) inf. n. as above, (Ḳ, TḲ,) *He was,* or *became, a partner,* or *sharer,* (Ḳ, TḲ,) *with him in the affair.* (TḲ.) ═ Also, (O,) inf. n. as above, (Ḳ,) *He lied;* (O, Ḳ;) like سَرَجَ and سَدَجَ. (O.) ═ شَرِجَ, (O, TA,) with kesr to the ر, (O,) *He was,* or *became, beautifully fat.* (O, TA.)

2. شرّج, inf. n. تَشْرِيجٌ: see above, in three places. — Also, said of pasture, or herbage, *It caused* the flesh of an animal *to be intermixed with fat.* (L.) And شُرِّجَ, said of the flesh of an animal, *It was intermixed with fat:* (Ṣ, O:) or *was made to be of two colours by reason of the fat and the flesh:* (TA:) and ▼ تشرّج بِالشَّحْمِ *it* (the flesh) *became intermixed with fat.* (Ṣ, O, Ḳ.) ═ And تَشْرِيجٌ also signifies The *sewing with stitches far apart.* (Ṣ, O, Ḳ.) — See also 4.

3. مُشَارَجَةٌ The *being like, one to another.* (O, Ḳ.) One says, شارجهُ *He was like to him;* or it, *to it:* and تَشَارَجَا *They two were like, each to the other.* (TḲ.)

4. اشرج, (AZ, Ṣ, A, O, Mṣb,) inf. n. إِشْرَاجٌ; (Ḳ;) and ▼ شرّج, (AZ, O,) inf. n. تَشْرِيجٌ; (Ḳ;) and ▼ شَرَجَ, (AZ, O,) inf. n. شَرْجٌ; (Ḳ;) *He closed,* or *made fast,* the [leathern receptacle called] خَرِيطَة (AZ, O, Ḳ) or عَيْبَة, (Ṣ, A, O, Mṣb,) *by inserting its* أَشْرَاج [or *loops*] *one into another.* (Ṣ, A,* O, Mṣb.) — [Hence,] اشرج صَدْرَهُ عَلَيْهِ ‡ [*He closed his bosom upon it*]. (A, TA.)

5: see 2.

7. انشرج, (Ḳ,) or انشرجت, said of a bow, (ISk, Ṣ, O,) *It split.* (ISk, Ṣ, O, Ḳ.)

شَرْجٌ *A place in which water flows from a* [*stony tract such as is termed*] حَرَّة *to a soft,* or *plain, tract;* (Ṣ, Ḳ;) as also ▼ شَرْجَةٌ: (TA:) or the latter signifies [simply] *a place in which water flows;* and some elide the ة, saying شَرْجٌ: (Mṣb:) pl. شِرَاجٌ (Ṣ, Mgh, Mṣb, Ḳ, expl. in the Mgh agreeably with the former explanation above, and said in the Mṣb to be pl. of شَرْجَةٌ,) and شُرُوجٌ. (Ṣ, Ḳ.) ═ Also *A party,* or *distinct body* or *class* [of men]. (Ṣ, Ḳ.) One says, أَصْبَحُوا فِى هٰذَا الأَمْرِ شَرْجَيْنِ i. e. [*They became, in this affair,*] *two parties.* (Ṣ.) And it is said in a trad., أَصْبَحَ النَّاسُ شَرْجَيْنِ فِى السَّفَرِ [*The people,* or *men, became two parties in the journey*]; meaning, half of them fasting, and half of them breaking the fast. (TA.) — And The *like* of another; (Ṣ, Ḳ;) as also ▼ شَرِيجٌ: (O, Ḳ:) the latter from the same word as meaning "a piece of wood [or a branch] that is split into two halves;" each of which is the شريج of the other. (O.) One says, هٰذَا شَرْجُ هٰذَا *This is the like of this.* (Ṣ.) — And *A sort,* or *species.* (Ṣ, Ḳ.) One says, هُمَا شَرْجٌ وَاحِدٌ *They two are one sort,* or *species.* (Ṣ.) — And شَرْجَانِ Any *two different colours:* (Ṣ:) [and] ▼ شَرِيجَانِ signifies [the same, i. e.] *two different colours* (Ḳ, TA) of anything; or, accord. to IAạr, *two mixed colours, not black and white:* (TA:) and ▼ this latter, also, the *two lines of the* نِيرَانِ [or *two ornamental borders*] *of a* [*garment of the kind called*] بُرْد, (O, Ḳ,) *one of which is* أَخْضَر [here meaning *of a dark,* or *an ashy, dust-colour*], *and the other white* or *red.* (O.) — And الشَّرْجُ, like فَلْس [in measure, not to be confounded with الشَّرَجُ], signifies The [*perinæum,* or] *part between the anus and the testicles.* (IḲṭṭ, TA.)

شَرَجٌ The *loops* (Ṣ, Mgh, O, Mṣb, Ḳ) of the [leathern receptacle called] عَيْبَة, (Ṣ, Mgh, O, Mṣb,) and of the [tent called] خَيْمَة, (O, TA,) and the like, and of the مُصْحَف [or copy of the Ḳur-án, &c.]: (TA:) [the loops here meant being such as are inserted one into another, to close a bag &c.: see 4:] pl. أَشْرَاجٌ. (Ṣ, Mṣb.) [And it seems also, from what here follows, to signify *A single loop.*] — † The *anus:* (Mṣb, TA:) or hence شَرَجُ الدُّبُرِ signifies † *the anus.* (Mgh.) — And † The *vulva* of a woman: (O, Ḳ:) pl. as above. (TA.) — And شَرَجُ الدَّوَاهِرِ [*The purse for money*]. (M and Ḳ in art. صر: in the CḲ, شَرْج.) ═ Also *A place of expanding* of a valley: (Ṣ, O, Ḳ:) pl. as above. (Ṣ.) — And *The Milky Way in the sky:* (Ṣ:) or so الشَّرَجُ. (Ḳ.) ═ Also *A splitting,* or *cracking,* (انْشِقَاق, Ṣ, and so in some copies of the Ḳ, or شُقَاق, so in other copies of the Ḳ and in the O,) *in a bow.* (Ṣ, O, Ḳ.) — And in a beast, The *having one of the two testicles larger than the other.* (Ṣ, O, Ḳ.)

شَرْجَةٌ: see شَرْجٌ. — Also *A hollow dug in the ground, in which a piece of skin is spread, and from which camels are watered,* (O, Ḳ,) *water being poured upon the skin.* (O.)

شَرِيجٌ *A branch,* or *rod, that is split into two halves:* and ▼ شَرِيجَةٌ, *a bow that is made thereof:* (Ṣ, O, Ḳ:) or the former, *a branch,* or *rod, from which are split two bows:* and *either of the bows thus made:* or *a split bow:* pl. شَرَائِجُ: accord. to AA, *a bow that is split from a branch,* or *rod, in two halves;* also called فِلْق: accord. to Lḥ, a bow *in which is a splitting* (شَقّ, used as an inf. n.), and [*such as is*] *a* شِقّ, by which is meant the subst. [i. e. *half* of a branch or rod *divided lengthwise*]; شريج being used by him as an epithet: and some say that ▼ شَرِيجَةٌ signifies a bow *that is not* [*made*] *from a sound*, or *whole, branch;* like فِلْق. (TA.) — Also *An arrow used in the game called* المَيْسِر *belonging to the person who plays with it, not borrowed.* (TA in art. شجر.) — See also شَرْج, in three places. — المَرْءُ بَيْنَ شَرِيجَىْ غَمٍّ وَسُرُورٍ is a tropical saying [app. meaning ‡ *Man is between the two different conditions of grief and happiness*]. (A, TA.)

شَرِيجَةٌ *A thing* (Ṣ, Mgh, Mṣb, Ḳ) *that is woven* (Ṣ, Mgh, Mṣb) *of palm-leaves* (Ṣ, Mgh, Mṣb, Ḳ) and *the like,* (Mṣb,) *in which are carried melons and other things* (Ṣ, Mgh, Mṣb, Ḳ) *of the like kind:* (Ṣ, Mgh, Ḳ:) pl. شَرَائِجُ. (Mṣb.) — *A door,* (Mgh,) or *a thing like a door,* (Mṣb,) *made of reeds,* or *canes, for a shop.* (Mgh, Mṣb.) — *A cage,* or *coop,* (جَدِيلَة,) *of reeds,* or *canes,* (O, Ḳ, TA,) *made* (TA) *for pigeons.* (O, Ḳ, TA. [The explanation in the Ḳ is strangely misunderstood and rendered by Freytag as meaning "Zona ex arundine facta, qua utuntur in balneo."]) — And The *sinew with which the feathers of an arrow are attached:* (O, Ḳ:) if it is feathered by means of glue, the glue is called رُومَةٌ. (O.) — [Also, accord. to Golius, as on the authority of Meyd, The *tie*, or *band*, ("ligamentum") *of a book.*] — See also شَرِيجٌ, in two places.

شَيْرَجٌ, (Mṣb, TA,) or شِيرِجٌ, (so in my copy of the Mgh,) or the latter is not allowable, (Mṣb, TA,) vulgarly pronounced سِيرِج, [q. v.,] with س and kesr, (TA,) an arabicized word, (Mgh, Mṣb, TA,) from [the Pers.] شِيرَهْ, (Mgh, Mṣb,) *Oil of sesame,* or *sesamum:* (Mṣb, TA:) and *white oil* (Mgh, Mṣb, TA) is sometimes thus called: (Mṣb, TA:) and *expressed juice* (عَصِير), (Mgh, Mṣb, TA,) or [*beverage of the kind called*] نَبِيذ, (Mgh,) *before it alters;* (Mgh, Mṣb, TA;) as being likened to oil of sesame because of its clearness. (Mṣb, TA.)

أَشْرَجُ A beast *having one of his testicles larger than the other.* (Ṣ, Mgh, Ḳ.) — A man *having one testicle.* (A, TA.)

[سَهْمٌ مُشَرَّجٌ *An arrow having cracks.* (Freytag, from the Deewán of the Hudhalees.)]

فَتَيَاتٌ مُتَشَارِجَاتٌ [in the CḲ, erroneously, مُتَشارَجات,] *Young women equals in age.* (O, Ḳ.)

شرح

1. شَرَحَ, aor. ـَ, (Ḳ,) inf. n. شَرْحٌ, (Ṣ, O,) *He uncovered, laid open, displayed, exposed to view, discovered, revealed,* or *disclosed.* (Ṣ, O, Ḳ.) — [Hence,] one says, شَرَحَ أَمْرَهُ ‡ *He showed, discovered, disclosed,* or *made apparent, his affair,* or *case.* (A, TA.) And شَرَحَ مَسْأَلَةً (A, TA) ‡ *He explained a question;* (TA;) *he explained,* or *made manifest, the answer to a question.* (A.) And شَرَحَ الغَامِضَ † *He expounded, explained,* or *interpreted, what was obscure, recondite,* or *abstruse.* (Ṣ, O.) And شَرَحَ الحَدِيثَ, inf. n. as above, † *He expounded, explained,* or *interpreted, the tradition; showed,* or *made apparent, its meaning.* (Mṣb.) — And شَرَحَ, aor. as above, (Ḳ,) and so the inf. n., (O, TA,) *He opened* (O, Ḳ, TA) a thing of any kind, of any substance or material. (TA.) — ‡ *He deflowered* a virgin: (O, Ḳ, TA:) or ‡ *he compressed* a woman, (A, L,) or a virgin, (Ḳ,) *lying on her back;* (A, L, Ḳ;) or *he threw,* or *laid, upon her back, and then compressed,* his female slave, or young woman. (O, L.) — *He widened,* or *dilated,* a thing. (Ḳ.) — Hence, (TA,) شَرَحَ اللّٰهُ صَدْرَهُ, (Ṣ, A, Mgh, O, Mṣb, TA,) aor. as above, (TA,) and so the inf. n., (Mṣb, TA,) † *God dilated his bosom,* (Mgh, O, Mṣb, TA,) لِقَبُولِ الخَيْرِ [*for the acceptance,* or *favourable acceptance, of what was good*], (O, TA,) and لِلْإِسْلَامِ (Mgh, Mṣb, TA) *for the acceptance,* or *favourable acceptance,* [*of El-Islám,* or] *of the truth,* (Mṣb, TA,) as in the Ḳur [xxxix. 23]. (TA. [Said in the TA to be tropical; but not so in the A, being mentioned in the latter as proper.]) [And hence, an objective complement being app. understood,] فُلَانٌ يَشْرَحُ إِلَى الدُّنْيَا ‡ *Such a one manifests desire for the things of the present world:* (A:) or *such a one becomes dilated in the bosom at the prospect of the things of the present world, and desirous of acquiring them, with large desire.* (O,* L.) And مَا لِى أَرَاكَ تَشْرَحُ إِلَى كُلِّ رِيبَةٍ ‡ *What aileth me that I see thee manifesting desire for everything occasioning doubt,* or *suspicion,* or *evil opinion?* (A, TA.) — Also *He cut;* and so ▼ شرّح. (Ḳ.) You say, شَرَحَ اللَّحْمَ, (A, O, Mṣb, TA,) inf. n. as above; (O;) and ▼ شرّحه, (A, O, Mṣb, TA,) inf. n. تَشْرِيحٌ; (Ṣ, O, TA;) the former meaning *He cut the flesh-meat lengthwise* [or *into an oblong slice* or *into such slices*]: and the latter, *he so cut it much* or *into many* [*such*] *pieces* [or *slices*]: (Mṣb:) or the former, *he cut the flesh-meat from the joint or limb:* or both signify *he cut the flesh-meat upon the bone:* (L, TA:) or شَرْحُ اللَّحْمِ signifies تَصْفِيفُهُ; and so ▼ تَشْرِيحُهُ: (O:) or التَّصْفِيفُ is a kind of ▼ تَشْرِيح; i. e. *the cutting* a piece of flesh-meat *thin, so that it is translucent by reason of its thinness, and then throwing it upon the live coals.* (TA.) — Also, (Ḳ,) inf. n. as above, (O,) *He understood* (O, Ḳ) speech, or language. (TḲ.) — And شَرْحٌ also signifies The act of *keeping, preserving,* or *guarding.* (TA.) [And particularly The *guarding* of seed-produce *from the birds;* (see شَارِحٌ;) as also شِرَاحَةٌ; (see 1 in art. خفر, fourth sentence;) each an inf. n., of which the verb is شَرَحَ.]

2. The inf. n. تَشْرِيحٌ signifies The *expounding, explaining,* or *interpreting, well,* language, or discourse. (KL.) — See also 1, latter half, in four places. — [Also The *dissecting,* or *anatomizing,* a body.]

7. انشرح صَدْرُهُ (Ṣ, A, O) *His bosom became dilated,* (O,) [with joy or the like, or] لِلْإِسْلَامِ [*for the acceptance,* or *favourable acceptance, of El-Islám*]. (Ṣ.)

10. استشرح *He asked for language to be expounded, explained,* or *interpreted, to him:* or *for flesh-meat to be cut for him in the manner termed* شَرْح. (O.)

شَرْحٌ inf. n. of 1. (Ṣ, O, &c.) — [*An exposition, explanation,* or *interpretation, in the form of a running commentary, comprising the entire text of the work which it expounds;* distinguished from a حَاشِيَة, which is a commentary only on particular words and passages: pl. شُرُوحٌ.]

شُرْحَةٌ: see شَرِيحَةٌ. — شُرْحَةٌ مِنَ الظِّبَآءِ *Flesh-meat of gazelles cut in the manner termed* شرح [i. e. *into oblong slices*], (TA,) *such as is brought in a dry state, just as it was, not* مُقَدَّد [which means *cut into strips and then dried by exposure to the sun*]. (ISh, O, Ḳ, TA.)

شَرَاحٌ The *discovery, disclosure,* or *explanation,* of an affair or a case: so in the prov., النَّجَاحُ مَعَ الشَّرَاحِ [*The accomplishment of one's want is with the discovery,* or *disclosure,* or *explanation,* thereof]; meaning, discover thou, or disclose, or explain, to me my affair, or case, for the doing so is one of the means of accomplishing my want: thus expl. by Aṣ. (Meyd. [In the TA, من is put in the place of مع. See a similar prov. voce سَرَاحٌ.])

شَرِيحٌ, applied to flesh-meat, *i. q.* ▼ مَشْرُوحٌ [i. e. *Cut into oblong slices*]. (O.) — See also شَرِيحَةٌ, in two places.

شُرَيْحٌ The *vulva of a woman;* (O, Ḳ;) and (Ḳ) so ▼ مُشَرَّحٌ: (A, Mgh, Ḳ:) or a proper name for *the vulva of a woman;* like as رُمَيْحٌ is a proper name for "the penis." (TA in art. رمح. [Golius appears to have found in the Ḳ الحَرُ in the place of الحِرُ.])

شَرِيحَةٌ *A cut piece of flesh-meat,* (Ṣ, A, O, Ḳ,) as also ▼ شَرِيحٌ and ▼ شُرْحَةٌ, (Ḳ,) *such as is* مَشْرُوح [or *cut into oblong slices*]; (O;) [i. e. *an oblong slice of flesh-meat:*] or *a thin piece,* or *slice, of flesh-meat:* (L, TA:) and *any extended piece of fat flesh-meat;* (Ṣ, O;) as also ▼ شَرِيحٌ: (Ṣ:) pl. of the first شَرَائِحُ. (A.)

شَارِحٌ [*An expositor, explainer,* or *interpreter,* of a book or the like. — And] *A keeper,* or *guardian.* (TA.) In the dial. of El-Yemen, (O, TA,) *A guardian of seed-produce from the birds* (O, Ḳ, TA) &c. (O, TA.)

مُشَرَّحٌ: see شُرَيْحٌ. — [Also] The سَافِلَة [i. e. *podex,* or *anus,*] of a man. (O.)

مَشْرُوخٌ: see شَرِيخٌ. — Also The سَرَاب [or *mirage*]: (Ḳ: [In the CḲ, الشَّرَابُ is put in the place of السَّرَابُ:]) mentioned on the authority of Th: and مَسْرُوخ [q. v.] is a dial. var. thereof. (TA.)

شرخ

1. شَرَخَ, (Ṣ, A, L, Ḳ,) aor. ـَ, (L,) inf. n. شَرْخٌ (Ṣ, Ḳ) and شُرُوخٌ, (L, Ḳ,) said of the نَاب [or tush] of a camel, *It clave the flesh,* (Ṣ, A,* L, Ḳ,) *and came forth.* (L.) — And شَرَخَ, inf. n. شُرُوخٌ (Ṣ, L) and شَرْخٌ, (L,) said of a boy, *He became a youth,* or *young man, such as is termed* شَارِخٌ. (Ṣ, L.)

شَرْخٌ The *rising, protruding, prominent,* or *projecting, extremity* or *edge* of a thing. (L, Ḳ.) [Hence,] شَرْخَا الفُوقِ, (ISh, Ṣ, A, TA,) or شَرْخَا السَّهْمِ, (Mṣb, TA,) both alike in meaning, (TA,) *The* زَنَمَتَانِ, (ISh, A, Mṣb, TA,) or *two edges* or *extremities* [or *cusps*], (Ṣ, TA,) *of the arrow,* (ISh, TA,) [i. e.] *of the notch of the arrow,* (Ṣ, A, Mṣb, TA,) *between which is the place of the bow-string.* (ISh, Ṣ, A, Mṣb, TA.) And in like manner, (Ṣ,) شَرْخَا الرَّحْلِ signifies *The* آخِرَة *and* وَاسِطَة *of the camel's saddle;* (Ṣ, L, Mṣb;) *the two extremities of the camel's saddle;* or, as some say, [more precisely,] *its two* [*upright*] *pieces of wood,* [*corresponding to the* قَرَبُوسَانِ *of the horse's saddle, rising from it*] *behind and before* [or *at the fore and hind parts*]: (L, TA:) [whence] one says of him who journeys much, لَا يَزَالُ فُلَانٌ بَيْنَ شَرْخَىْ رَحْلِهِ [*Such a one ceases not to be between the two uprights of his camel's saddle:* for between them the rider sits: see آخِرَةُ الرَّحْلِ, voce آخِر]. (A, TA.) — The نَاب [or *tush*] of a camel. (L.) — *A sword-blade* (نَصْل) *that has not yet been tempered* (لَمْ يُسْقَ بَعْدُ), *nor had its hilt affixed to it:* (Ṣ, Ḳ:) pl. شُرُوخٌ. (Ṣ.) — The *origin, source,* or *root,* syn. أَصْل and عِرْق, (L, Ḳ,) of anything; like سِنْخ. (L.) — The *beginning, commencement,* or *first period* or *state,* (Ṣ, A, L, Mṣb, Ḳ,) of a thing, or an affair, and also, (Ṣ, A,) of youth; (Ṣ, A, L, Mṣb, Ḳ;) the *prime and best part* or *period* of youth, (A,) and its *beauty and brightness, and its strength.* (L. [See also شَغْر.]) — *A youth,* or *young man, such as is termed* شَابّ; and *youths,* or *young men;* originally an inf. n., and [therefore, when used as an epithet in which the quality of a subst. is predominant,] applied to one and to two and to a pl. number: (L:) or it is a pl. of ▼ شَارِخٌ in the sense of شَابّ, (Ṣ, L, Ḳ,) or [rather] a quasi-pl. n., (L,) like as صَحْب is of صَاحِب, (Ṣ,) [i. e.] a noun used as a pl. in the sense expl. above: (Sh:) or, accord. to some, it signifies *strong young men, profitable for service:* and accord. to others, *young children:* (A'Obeyd, L:) it has also for pls. شُرُوخٌ and شُرْخٌ: (L:) and شُرُوخٌ شُرَّخٌ is an expression used in an intensive sense. (L, Ḳ.) — The *offspring* of a man: (Ḳ, TA:) or the *sperma by which offspring is produced.* (TA.) — The *increase,* or *offspring,* or *brood,* syn. نِتَاج, (AO, Ṣ, L, Mṣb, Ḳ,) *of camels,* (Mṣb,) [i. e.] *consisting of the young ones of camels,* (Ṣ, Ḳ,) *in any year,* (Ṣ, Mṣb, Ḳ,) or *of camels &c., of one year, while they continue small.* (L.) One says, هٰذَا مِنْ شَرْخِ فُلَانٍ *This is of the increase* (نِتَاج) [*of the camels &c.*] *of such a one.* (AO, L.) — *An equal in age, a contemporary in birth;* (Ṣ, A, Ḳ;) *an equal, a match, fellow, peer,* or *compeer;* pl. شُرُوخٌ. (Ṣ, Ḳ.) You say, هُوَ شَرْخِى *He is my equal in age,* (A, TA,) or *my equal* or *match.* (TA.) And هُمَا شَرْخَانِ *They two are equals* [*in age,*] or *matches.* (Ṣ, Ḳ.) — [The pl.] شُرُوخٌ also signifies [*Trees of the kind called*] عِضَاه. (Ḳ.)

شَارِخٌ: see the next preceding paragraph. You say صَبِىٌّ شَارِخٌ, meaning *A young boy.* (A.)

شرد

1. شَرَدَ, aor. ـُ, inf. n. شُرُودٌ (Ṣ, L, Mṣb, Ḳ) and شِرَادٌ, (Ṣ, L, Ḳ,) or the latter is a simple subst., (Mṣb,) and شَرَادٌ (Ḳ) and شَرْدٌ, (L,) said of a camel, (Ṣ, A, L, Mṣb,) and of a horse or the like, (L,) *He took fright,* or *shied, and fled,* or *ran away at random;* or *became refractory, and went away at random,* or *ran away,* or *broke loose, and went hither and thither by reason of his sprightliness;* syn. نَفَرَ, (Ṣ, L, Mṣb, Ḳ,) and نَدَّ: (Mṣb:) and [simply] *he fled,* or *ran away;* said of a camel &c. (Aboo-Bekr, TA.) The saying of the Prophet, أَمَا يَشْرُدُ بِكَ بَعِيرُكَ ‡ [*Does not thy camel take fright and run away with thee?*], addressed by him to Khowwát, who answered, أَمَّا مُنْذُ قَيَّدَهُ الإِسْلَامُ فَلَا [*As to the period since El-Islám shackled him, no*], mentioned in the A, points to a story related of Khowwát Ibn-Jubeyr, (TA,) that, being found by the Prophet sitting by some strange women, he endeavoured to excuse himself by saying that he had a camel which took fright and ran away, and he was seeking for something wherewith to shackle him: the Prophet used afterwards to taunt him by inquiring of him respecting the running-away of his camel: what Kr says, and J in the Ṣ [in art. نحى], is incorrect. (IAth, L.) You say also, شَرَدَ عَنِّى فُلَانٌ *Such a one fled,* or *went away* or *aside* or *apart* or *to a distance, from me;* syn. نَفَرَ. (A.) [Or] شَرَدَ said of a man, inf. n. شُرُودٌ, means *He departed, driven away.* (L.) And you say, شَرَدَ عَلَى اللّٰهِ, meaning *He departed from obedience to God, and seceded,* or *separated himself from the community* [*of the faithful*]. (L.)

2. شَرَّدَهُ, (L, Mṣb,) inf. n. تَشْرِيدٌ, (Ṣ, L, Mṣb, Ḳ,) *He made him to take fright, and flee,* or *run away at random;* or *to become refractory, and to go away at random,* or *run away,* or *break loose, and go hither and thither by reason of his sprightliness;* namely, a camel [and a horse or the like: see 1]: (Mṣb:) or *he drove him away,* or *expelled him;* (Ṣ,* L, Ḳ;*) as also ▼ اشردهُ; (L;) [and so شَرَّدَ بِهِ: for] you say شَرَّدْتُ بِهِ and شَرَّدْتُهُ عَنِّى [*I drove him away from me*]. (A.) And تَشْرِيدٌ signifies also The act of *dispersing,* or *scattering.* (Ḳ.) [Hence,] شَرِّدْ بِهِمْ مَنْ خَلْفَهُمْ, in the Ḳur [viii. 59], means *Disperse thou,* or *scatter thou, by them, those* [who shall come] *after them:* (Ṣ, L:) or *terrify thou, by them, those* [who shall come] *after them:* or *make thou them notorious to those* [who shall come] *after them:* (L:) [for] — شَرَّدَ بِهِ (inf. n. as above, TA) signifies *He rendered him notorious by exposing his vices* or *faults.* (L, Ḳ.)

4. اشردهُ *He made him to be driven away,* or *expelled,* (L, Ḳ,) *and not received into a place of refuge, covert,* or *lodging.* (L.) See also 2.

5. تشرّد القَوْمُ *The people,* or *party, went away,* or *departed.* (L.)

شَرَدٌ: see شَارِدٌ.

شِرَادٌ an inf. n. of شَرَدَ [q. v.]: (Ṣ, L, Ḳ:) or a simple subst. from شَرَدَ [and as such signifying *A taking fright,* or *shying, and fleeing,* or *running away at random;* &c.: or *a disposition thereto*]. (Mṣb.) You say, of a camel, بِهِ شِرَادٌ [*He has a disposition to take fright,* or *shy, &c.*]. (A.)

شَرُودٌ: see شَارِدٌ, in five places.

شَرِيدٌ *Driven away,* or *expelled:* (Ṣ, L, Ḳ:) or, accord. to Aboo-Bekr, when following طَرِيد, it signifies *fleeing,* or *running away:* or, as Aṣ says, *alone,* or *solitary.* (TA.) — Also *A remainder* of anything; as of water in a vessel, and as of property, or camels and the like; pl. شَرَائِدُ, deviating from rule: or شَرِيدَةٌ is a syn. [or rather fem.] of شَرِيدٌ [and شَرَائِدُ is its reg. pl.]. (L.)

شَارِدٌ and ▼ شَرُودٌ, (Ṣ, A, L, Ḳ,) applied to a camel, (Ṣ, A, L,) and to a horse or the like, (L,) *Taking fright,* or *shying, and fleeing,* or *running away at random;* or *refractory, and going away at random,* or *running away,* or *breaking loose, and going hither and thither by reason of sprightliness:* or *that takes fright,* or *shies, &c.:* (Ṣ, L, Ḳ:) [or] the latter [signifies *wont to take fright,* or *shy, &c.:* and] is applied to a male animal and to a female: (L:) [the fem. of the former is with ة:] pl. of the former شُرَّدٌ (A,* L) and ▼ شَرَدٌ, (Ṣ, L, Ḳ,) [or rather this is a quasi-pl. n.,] like as خَدَمٌ is of خَادِمٌ; (Ṣ, Ḳ;) [and the pl. of شَارِدَةٌ is شَوَارِدُ and شُرَّدٌ;] and the pl. of ▼ شَرُودٌ is شُرُدٌ, like as زُبُرٌ is of زَبُورٌ. (Ṣ, L, Ḳ.*) You say ▼ فَرَسٌ شَرُودٌ *A horse,* or *mare, refractory towards the rider:* and ▼ نَاقَةٌ شَرُودٌ *A she-camel that runs away,* or *breaks loose and goes hither and thither by reason of her sprightliness.* (L.) — [Hence,] ▼ قَافِيَةٌ شَرُودٌ ‡ *A rhyme,* or *verse,* or *poem, current through the countries, lands,* or *regions,* or *through the cities,* or *towns.* (Ṣ, A, Ḳ.) — And قَوَافٍ شَوَارِدُ (Ṣ in art. ابد) and قَوَافٍ شُرَّدٌ (Ḳ ibid.) [pls. of قَافِيَةٌ شَارِدَةٌ] ‡ *Strange, unusual, unfamiliar,* or *extraordinary, rhymes* or *verses* or *poems;* syn. أَوَابِدُ. (Ṣ and Ḳ ibid.) And [in like manner] لَفْظَةٌ شَارِدَةٌ,

in lexicology, signifies † *A barbarism;* or *a strange,* or *an uncouth, unusual, unfamiliar,* or *extraordinary, word* or *expression* or *phrase;* as also لفظة غَرِيبَةٌ and وَحْشِيَّةٌ and حُوشِيَّةٌ; opposed to لفظة فَصِيحَةٌ. (Mz, 13th نوع.)

شردم

شِرْدِمَةٌ: see the art. here following.

شرذم

شِرْذِمَةٌ *A party,* or *company,* (طَائِفَةٌ,) of men, or people: (Ṣ:) or *a small company:* (TA:) or *a small number of men,* or *people:* (Ḳ:) and so شِرْدِمَةٌ, with the unpointed د, on the authority of AA: (IB, TA:) the former occurring in the Ḳur xxvi. 54. (TA.) —— *A piece,* or *portion,* (Ṣ, Ḳ,) of a thing, (Ṣ,) of a quince &c.: pl. شَرَاذِمُ and شَرَاذِيمُ. (Ḳ.) —— [Hence,] ثَوْبٌ شَرَاذِمُ, (Ṣ,) or ثِيَابٌ شَرَاذِمُ, (Ḳ,) *A garment,* or *garments, old and worn out,* (Ṣ, Ḳ,) *much rent.* (Ḳ.)

شرس

1. شَرِسَ, aor. ـَ, (Mṣb, TA,) inf. n. شَرَسٌ (Mṣb, TA, TḲ) and شَرَاسَةٌ and شِرِيسٌ, (TḲ, the first and second also mentioned and explained, but not said to be inf. ns., in the Ṣ and O and Ḳ, and the third in like manner in the Ḳ,) or the second is a simple subst., (Mṣb,) or an inf. n. of which the verb is with ḍamm [to the medial radical letter, as shown below], (TA,) *He was,* or *became, evil in disposition,* or *illnatured,* (Ṣ,* A,* Mṣb, Ḳ,* TA,) *and very perverse* or *cross* or *repugnant,* (Ṣ,* A,* Ḳ,* TA,) *and averse.* (TA.) And شَرِسَتْ نَفْسُهُ, (Mṣb, TA,) inf. n. شَرَسٌ; (TA;) and شَرُسَتْ, (Mṣb, TA,) inf. n. شَرَاسَةٌ; (TA;) [*His mind was,* or *became, evil in disposition,* &c.:] ISd and others make this distinction [in respect of the inf. ns.] in the usages of the two verbs. (TA.) —— And شَرِسَ *He showed,* or *manifested,* or *he made himself an object of, love,* or *affection, to men.* (IAạr, O, Ḳ.) [Thus it has two contr. meanings.] ═══ Also, شَرِسَ, *He kept continually,* or *constantly, to the pasturing upon the trees called* شِرْس. (IAạr, O, Ḳ.) ═══ And شَرِسَتِ المَاشِيَةُ, (AZ, AḤn, O, Ḳ,*) aor. ـَ, (AZ, O, Ḳ,) or, as written by El-Umawee and AḤn, ـِ, (TA,) inf. n. شَرَاسَةٌ, *The cattle ate vehemently:* (AZ, AḤn, O, Ḳ:) thus expl. without the particularizing of the شِرْس [as the pasture eaten]. (TA.) ═══ And شَرَسَهُ, (Ibn-'Abbád, O,) inf. n. شَرْسٌ, (Ḳ,) *He pained him,* or *distressed him,* (Ibn-'Abbád, O, Ḳ,*) namely, his companion, (Ḳ,) *with speech,* (Ibn-'Abbád, O,) [i. e.,] *with rough speech.* (Ḳ.)

3. شارسهُ, (A, TA,) inf. n. شِرَاسٌ (A, O, Ḳ) and مُشَارَسَةٌ, (O, Ḳ,) *He treated him,* or *behaved towards him,* or *dealt with him, with hardness,* (A, O,* Ḳ,* TA,) or *harshness,* or *illnature.* (A, TA.)

6. تشارسوا *They treated one another* [*with hardness,* or *harshness,* or *illnature,* (see 3,) or] *with enmity,* or *hostility,* (Ṣ, O, Ḳ,) *and contrariety,* or *perverseness.* (TA.)

مَكَانٌ شَرْسٌ, (Ṣ, O, TA,) and ▾ شَرِسٌ, (Ṣ, [both of these forms I find in my two copies of the Ṣ, the former in a poetical ex., and therefore it may perhaps be a contraction of the latter by poetic license,]) and ▾ شَرَاسٌ, (TA,) *A place that is rugged,* or *rough,* (Ṣ, O, TA,) *and hard:* or, as in the M, *rough to the feel.* (TA.) And أَرْضٌ ▾ شَرْسَآءُ, and ▾ شَرَاسِىٌّ, and ▾ شَرَاسٌ, (O, Ḳ, TA, [the last written by Freytag شُرَّاسٌ,]) *Land that is rugged,* or *rough,* (O,) or *hard,* (Ḳ,) or *hard and rugged* or *rough.* (TA.)

شِرْسٌ *Such as are small, of thorny trees;* (Mgh,* Ḳ;) as also ▾ شَرَسٌ; (Ḳ;) the latter word thus expl. by AḤn: (O:) or the عِضَاه *of the mountain,* which are the *small kind of thorny trees,* (Ṣ, O, TA,*) *having yellow thorns,* or, as some say, *such as have slender thorns, growing in depressed tracts, and in the deserts* (الصَّحَارِى), *but not in the plain,* or *soft, tracts of valleys;* (TA;) *such as the* شُبْرُم *and* حَاج (Ṣ, O) *and* قَتَاد *and* شُكَاعَى. (O. [See عِضٌ.]) See also أَشْرَسُ.

شَرَسٌ: see next preceding paragraph.

شَرِسٌ (Ṣ, A, O, Mṣb, Ḳ) and ▾ شَرِيسٌ (A, O, Ḳ) and ▾ أَشْرَسُ (Ṣ, O, Ḳ) A man (Ṣ, O) *evil in disposition,* or *illnatured,* (Ṣ, A, O, Mṣb, Ḳ,) *and very perverse* or *cross* or *repugnant,* (Ṣ, A, O, Ḳ,) *and averse:* (TA:) and شَرِسَةٌ and ▾ شَرِيسَةٌ [both fem.] *abounding in evilness of disposition* or *illnature, and in excessive perverseness* &c. (TA.) One says also ▾ نَفْسٌ شَرِيسَةٌ *A mind evil in disposition,* &c. (A, TA.) And ▾ نَاقَةٌ شَرِيسٌ, (TA,) or ذَاتُ شِرِيسٍ, (O,) or the latter also, (TA,) *i. q.* شَرِسَةٌ [*A she-camel evil in disposition,* &c.]. (O.) See also أَشْرَسُ. —— شَرِسُ الأَكْلِ, (O, Ḳ,) or, accord. to AḤn, ▾ شَرِيسُ الأَكْلِ, (TA,) *Vehement in respect of eating.* (AḤn, O, Ḳ.) —— See also شَرْسٌ. ═══ شَرِسَةٌ and ▾ شَرِيسَةٌ [A land (أَرْضٌ)] *abounding with* شَرَس [or شِرْس, i. e. the trees thus called]; (TA;) [and] ▾ أَرْضٌ مُشْرِسَةٌ *a land abounding with* شِرْس. (Yaạkoob, Ṣ.)

شَرَاسٌ: see شَرْسٌ, in two places.

شَرَاسِىٌّ: see شَرْسٌ.

شَرِيسٌ: see شَرِسٌ, in six places: and أَشْرَسُ.

أَشْرَسُ: see شَرِسٌ. Hence, (O,) الأَشْرَسُ *The lion;* (O, Ḳ;) as also ▾ الشِّرْسُ, (O,) or ▾ الشَّرِيسُ; (Ḳ;) because of his evil disposition. (O.) —— And *Bold,* or *daring, in fight:* (O, Ḳ:) or this is a mistranscription for أَشْوَسُ, mentioned in the T as having this meaning. (TA.) —— Also *i. q.* أَفْعَلُ [*More,* and *most, evil in disposition* or *illnatured* &c.]. (TA in art. فعل.) —— عَثَرَ بِأَشْرَسِ الدَّهْرِ, meaning † [*He stumbled upon,* or *chanced to meet with,*] *hardship, calamity,* or *adversity:* a prov. (O, Ḳ. [In Meyd (and so in Freytag's Arab. Prov., ii. 96,) عَثَرْنَا بِشِرْسِ ▾ الدَّهْرِ, and expl. as lit. meaning the trees called شِرْس.]) —— See also شِرْس.

مُشْرِسٌ *Whose camels pasture upon the* [*trees called*] شِرْس. (Ṣ.) —— أَرْضٌ مُشْرِسَةٌ: see شَرِسٌ.

شرسف

شُرْسُفَةٌ *Badness of natural disposition; illnature.* (Ibn-'Abbád, O, Ḳ.)

شُرْسُوفٌ The غُضْرُوف [or *cartilage*] *attached to each rib;* (Ṣ, O, Ḳ;) *like the* غُضْرُوف *of the scapula:* (Ṣ, O:) or the *extremity of the rib, projecting over the belly:* (Ṣ, O, Ḳ:) or the *head of the rib, next the belly:* (IAạr, O:) or *a rib having a* غُضْرُوف [or *cartilage*] *at its extremity:* (ISd, TA:) pl. شَرَاسِيفُ. (Ṣ, O.) ═══ A camel *shackled.* (IAạr, O, Ḳ.) —— And A camel *hocked,* or *hamstrung, in one of his legs.* (IAạr, O, Ḳ.) —— And A captive *having his arms bound behind his back.* (IAạr, O.) ═══ *Calamity,* or *misfortune:* and the *commencement of hardship.* (Ḳ.) One says, أَصَابَتِ النَّاسَ الشَّرَاسِيفُ *The commencements of hardships befell the people.* (IF, O.)

شَاةٌ مُشَرْسَفَةٌ *A sheep,* or *goat, having in its sides a whiteness covering the* شَرَاسِيف [pl. of شُرْسُوف, q. v.,] (Lth, O, Ḳ) *and the* شَوَاكِل [pl. of شَاكِلَةٌ, q. v.]. (Lth, O.)

شرط

1. شَرَطَ عَلَيْهِ كَذَا, (Ṣ, Mṣb, Ḳ,) aor. ـِ and ـُ, (Ṣ, Mṣb,) inf. n. شَرْطٌ; (Mṣb;) and ▾ اشترط عليه كذا; (Ṣ,* Mṣb,* Ḳ,* TA;) both signify the same; (Ṣ, Mṣb, Ḳ;) [*He imposed such a thing as a condition,* or *by stipulation, upon him;*] *he made such a thing a condition against him.* (TḲ.) And شَرَطَ عَلَيْهِ فِى البَيْعِ *He imposed a thing as obligatory upon him in the sale, and took it upon himself as such.* (TḲ.) ═══ شَرَطَ, aor. ـِ and ـُ, (Ṣ, Mṣb, Ḳ,) inf. n. شَرْطٌ, (Mṣb, Ḳ,) *He* (a cupper) *scarified;* syn. بَزَغَ; (Ṣ, Ḳ;) as also ▾ شرّط, inf. n. تَشْرِيطٌ. (JK in art. بزغ, and TA.*) [Hence, and from the verb in the sense first mentioned, the saying,] رُبَّ شَرْطِ شَارِطٍ أَوْجَعُ مِنْ شَرْطِ شَارِطٍ [*Many a condition of one making a condition is more painful than the scarifying of a scarifier*]. (TA.) —— *He slit* the ear of a camel. (TA.) —— *He slit, and then twisted,* [or *wove together,* (see شَرِيطٌ,)] palm-leaves. (TA.) ═══ شَرِطَ *He fell into a momentous,* or *formidable, case.* (O, Ḳ.)

2: see the next preceding paragraph.

3. شارطهُ, (Ḳ,) inf. n. مُشَارَطَةٌ, (TA,) *He made a condition,* or *conditions,* or *he stipulated, with him, mutually; each of them made a condition,* or *conditions,* or *each of them stipulated, with the other.* (O, L, Ḳ.) And ▾ تشارط عَلَيْهِ is like شَارَطَ [app. meaning *He made a condition,* or *conditions, with another,* or *others;* or *they* (a party of persons) *made a condition,* or *conditions, together; against him*]. (TA.)

4. اشرط نَفْسَهُ *He marked himself, and prepared himself,* (Ṣ, Ḳ,) لِأَمْرِ كَذَا (Ḳ) or لِكَذَا [*for such an affair*]. (Ṣ.) — *He* (a courageous man) *marked himself for death.* (TA.) — اشرط نَفْسَهُ وَمَالَهُ فِى هٰذَا الأَمْرِ *He put forward,* or *offered, himself and his property in this affair.* (TA.) — اشرط إِبِلَهُ *He made known that his camels were for sale.* (Ḳ.) And اشرط طَائِفَةً مِنْ إِبِلِهِ وَغَنَمِهِ *He set apart a portion of his camels, and of his sheep, or goats, and made known that they were for sale.* (TA.) And اشرط مِنْ إِبِلِهِ, (Ṣ, Ḳ,) and غَنَمِهِ, (Ṣ,) *He prepared for sale some of his camels,* (Ṣ, Ḳ,) and *of his sheep, or goats.* (Ṣ.) — أَشْرَطْتُ فُلَانًا لِعَمَلِ كَذَا *I prepared such a one for such a work, or such an agency or employment, and made him to have the charge,* or *management, thereof.* (AA.) — اشرط إِلَيْهِ الرَّسُولَ *He hastened to him the messenger,* (Ḳ,* TA,) *and sent him forward:* from أَشْرَاطٌ signifying the "beginnings" of things. (TA.) ═ اشرط بِهَا, and فِيهَا, *He held it to be, or made it, a thing of mean account, and perilled, hazarded, or risked, it.* (TA.) [It is not said to what the pronoun refers.]

5. تشرّط فِى عَمَلِهِ *He acted,* or *performed, well, soundly and skilfully,* or, *nicely and exactly, in his work,* (O, L, Ḳ,) *and constrained himself to observe whatever conditions were imposed upon him.* (L.)

6: see 3.

8: see 1, first signification. — [أُشْتُرِطَ *It was made conditional,* or *a condition.* And *He,* or *it, was made to be conditionally intended,* in, or by, a saying, دُونَ غَيْرِهِ *exclusively of any other.*]

10. استشرط المَالُ *The camels,* or *the like, became in a bad state after having been in a good state.* (Ṣgh, Ḳ.) [See شَرَطٌ.]

شَرْطٌ [*A condition; a term; a stipulation;* said to signify] the *imposition of a thing as obligatory* [*upon a person*], *and the taking it upon oneself as such, in a sale and the like;* (Ḳ;) [but this is a loose explanation, as is observed in the TḲ; the meaning being *a thing imposed upon a person as obligatory, and taken upon oneself as such:* in the Ṣ, it is merely said to be well known:] and ♦ شَرِيطَةٌ signifies the same: (Ṣ, Mṣb, Ḳ:) pl. of the former, شُرُوطٌ: (Ṣ, Mṣb, Ḳ:) and of the latter, شَرَائِطُ. (Mṣb, TA.) It is said in a trad., لَا يَجُوزُ شَرْطَانِ فِى بَيْعٍ [*Two conditions in a sale are not allowable*]; as when one says, "I sell to thee this garment, or piece of cloth, for ready money for a deenár, and on credit for two deenárs." (TA.) And it is said in a prov., الشَّرْطُ أَمْلَكُ عَلَيْكَ أَمْ لَكَ (TA) *The condition is most valid,* or *binding,* [whether it be *against thee or in thy favour:*] (Mgh in art. ملك:) relating to the keeping of conditions between brothers. (Ṣgh, TA.) [شَرْطٌ also relates to other things beside sales and the like: for instance, you say, شَرْطُ المَصْدَرِ كَذَا وَكَذَا, meaning *What is required to justify the application of the term* مصدر *is such a thing, and such a thing.*] ═ شَرْطَا نَهْرٍ *The two banks of a river.* (TA.) — [The pl.] شُرُوطٌ also signifies *Roads leading in different directions.* (TA.) ═ See also شَرَطٌ, in two places.

شَرَطٌ *A sign, token,* or *mark,* (Ṣ, Mṣb, Ḳ,) *which men appoint between them;* (TA;) as also ♦ شَرِيطٌ: (TA:) pl. of the former, أَشْرَاطٌ. (Mṣb, Ḳ.) And hence, (Mṣb,) أَشْرَاطُ السَّاعَةِ *The signs of the resurrection,* or *of the time thereof;* (Ṣ, Mṣb, TA;) mentioned in the Ḳur [xlvii. 20]: or *the small events prior thereto, which men deny:* (El-Khaṭṭábee:) or *the means thereof, exclusive of the main circumstances thereof, and of the event itself.* (TA.) — [Hence also,] الشَّرَطَانِ *The two stars* [α *and* β] *which are the two horns of Aries;* (Ṣ, Ḳ, Ḳzw;) *the brighter whereof is called* النَّاطِحُ; (Ḳzw;) [*and the other,* النَّطْحُ;] *the First Mansion of the Moon:* (Ḳzw:) *towards the north of them is a small star which some of the Arabs reckon with those two, saying that it* (*namely this mansion,* Ḳ) *consists of three stars, and calling them* الأَشْرَاطُ: (Ṣ, Ḳ:) IAạr mentions an instance of the use of the sing., الشَّرَطُ; but the dual is more approved, and more commonly known: (TA:) *the two stars above mentioned are the first asterism of the spring.* (ISd, Z.) [See مَنَازِلُ القَمَرِ, in art. نزل.] Ḥassán Ibn-Thábit says,

* فِى نَدَامَى بِيضِ الوُجُوهِ كِرَامٍ *
* نُبِّهُوا بَعْدَ هَجْعَةِ الأَشْرَاطِ *

meaning [*Among fair-faced, generous cup-companions, roused from sleep after*] *the setting of the* اشراط: though another meaning, which see below, has been assigned to the last word. (Ṣgh.) — And hence, (ISd, Z,) شَرَطٌ also signifies † The *beginning* of a thing; (ISd,* Z,* Ḳ;) as also ♦ مِشْرَاطٌ: (Ibn-'Abbád, Ḳ:) pl. of the former, أَشْرَاطٌ, which is applied to the *beginnings* of any event that happens because the شَرَطَانِ are the first asterism of the spring: (ISd, Z:) the pl. of ♦ مشراط in the sense here expl. is مَشَارِيطُ. (Ḳ.) Hence, accord. to some, أَشْرَاطُ السَّاعَةِ, expl. above. (TA.) ═ The *refuse,* (Ṣ, Mṣb, Ḳ, TA,) *such as the galled in the back, and the emaciated,* (TA,) and the *young,* (Ḳ,) and the *bad,* (A'Obeyd,) of camels or the like, (Ṣ, Ḳ,) or of goats, (Mṣb,) or of goats also: (Ṣ:) used alike as sing. and pl. and masc. and fem.: and applied particularly to the *young* of camels, as a pl. and as a sing.: also, to a she-camel and to a he-camel: and to *such,* of camels, *as is brought,* or *driven, from one place to another for sale; as the aged she-camel, and the camel that is galled in the back:* (TA:) also the same, not ♦ شَرْطٌ as in the Ḳ, [without restriction of its application,] *low, base, vile,* or *mean;* (Ḳ,* TA;) and so ♦ أَشْرَطُ: (TA:) pl. أَشْرَاطٌ, (Ṣ, Ḳ,) and pl. pl. أَشَارِيطُ. (Ṣ,* TA.) You say, الغَنَمُ أَشْرَاطُ المَالِ [*Sheep, or goats, are the refuse,* or *meanest sort, of beasts that people possess*]. (Ṣ.) And شَرَطٌ is also applied to men; (Ṣ, TA;) شَرَطُ النَّاسِ signifying *The refuse,* or *lowest* or *basest* or *meanest sort, of mankind* or *people.* (TA.) In the verse of Ḥassán Ibn-Thábit cited above, الأَشْرَاطُ is said to mean *The guards,* or *watchmen,* and *the lowest* or *basest* or *meanest sort of people;* (Ṣ, Ṣgh;) [so that هَجْعَة must be understood in the sense of "a light sleep in the first part of the night;"] but the correct meaning is that expl. before. (Ṣgh.) — Also أَشْرَاطٌ, The *noble, eminent,* or *honourable, sort* of men: thus the word has two contr. significations. (Yaạḳoob, Ṣ, Ḳ.) ═ And *A small water-course coming from a space of ten cubits:* (AḤn, O, Ḳ:) or *what flows from even tracts of ground into the* [*larger water-courses called*] شِعَاب. (TA.)

شَرْطَةٌ *A single act of scarifying; a scarification.* (Mṣb.)

شُرْطَةٌ *A thing which one has made a condition.* (Ṣgh, Ḳ.) You say, خُذْ شُرْطَتَكَ *Take thou that which thou hast made a condition.* (Ṣgh, Ḳ.) ═ Also, and ♦ شُرَطَةٌ, (Mgh,) or شُرَطٌ, (Ḳ,) which is the pl. (Mgh, Ḳ) of the former, (Ḳ,) The *choice men of the army:* (Mgh:) and *such as compose the first portion of the army that is present in the war* or *fight,* (Mgh, Ḳ,) *and prepare for death;* (Ḳ;) [the *braves of an army;*] they are *the Sultán's choice men of the army;* and the term شُرْطَةٌ is applied in a trad. to *a party making it a condition to die, and not return, unless victorious:* (TA:) or this appellation, and ♦ شُرَطَةٌ, which is a rare form, are applied to *a body of soldiers;* and the pl. is شُرَطٌ: and the pl. is applied to the *aids* (أَعْوَان [here app. meaning *guards*]) *of the Sultán:* (Mṣb:) شُرْطَةٌ, also, is applied to *a well-known body of the aids* (أَعْوَان [here meaning *armed attendants, officers,* or *soldiers,*]) *of the prefects* [*of the police*]; (Ḳ;) pl. شُرَطٌ: (TA:) the شُرَط, (Aṣ, Ṣ, Mṣb,) or the شُرْطَة, (Ḳ,) are so called because they assumed to themselves signs, or marks, whereby they might be known (Aṣ, Ṣ, Mṣb, Ḳ) to the enemies: (Mṣb:) or the شُرَط are so called because they were prepared: (AO, Ṣ:) or as being likened to the شَرَط, or "refuse," of goats; because they were low persons: (Mṣb:) [or, probably, because they were prepared, or exposed, to be slain:] *a single person of the* شُرَط is called شُرْطِىٌّ (Ṣ, Mṣb) and ♦ شُرَطِىٌّ: (Ṣ:) or ♦ شُرْطِىٌّ and ♦ شُرَطِىٌّ are applied to *a single person of the* شُرْطَة: (Ḳ:) ♦ شُرْطِىٌّ is a rel. n. from شُرْطَة; and such also is ♦ شُرَطِىٌّ from شُرَطَة; not from شُرَط, because this is a pl. (Mgh.) صَاحِبُ الشُّرْطَةِ signifies *The governor,* or *prefect,* (Mgh, Mṣb,) [*of the police,* or] *of a town,* or *city,* or *district,* or *province;* to whom formerly pertained both religious and civil affairs; but now it is not so. (Mgh. [See رِدْف.]) [In later times, this title has been commonly applied to *The chief,* or *prefect, of the police.*] — Also The *best, best part,* or *choice,* of anything; as also ♦ شَرِيطَة: the latter occurring in a trad., as related by Sh; but Az thinks it should be the former word. (TA.)

شُرَطَةٌ: see شُرْطَةٌ, in two places.

شَرَطِىٌّ *Of,* or *relating to,* [*the asterism called*]

the شَرَطَان and *the* أَشْرَاط; as also ▼ أَشْرَاطِىٌّ; the latter being formed from the pl., (IB, TA,) because the stars thus called are regarded as composing one thing. (TA.) You say, رَوْضَةٌ ▼ أَشْرَاطِيَّةٌ, meaning [*A garden, or meadow,* &c.,] *rained upon by the* نَوْء [q. v.] *of the* شَرَطَان. (Ṣ, TA.) In the A we find ▼ نَوْءٌ شِرَاطِىٌّ: but probably it should be شَرَطِىٌّ. (TA.)

شُرْطِىٌّ and شُرَطِىٌّ: see شُرْطَةٌ, in five places.

شَرِيطٌ *A rope, or cord, of twisted palm-leaves:* (Ṣ, Mṣb:) and *threads of wool* and *of fibres of the palm-tree* [*twisted together*]: (TA:) or *palm-leaves twisted together, with which is woven* (يُشْرَطُ, as in the Ḳ, or, as in the O, accord. to the TA, يُشْرَجُ, [app. a mistake for يُشْرَعُ,]) *a couch,* or *bier,* [app. meaning the part thereof upon which a man or corpse lies,] and *the like:* (O, Ḳ:) so called because its palm-leaves are split, and then twisted together: if of fibres of the palm-tree, it is called دِسَارٌ: (TA:) or *a wide rope* [or *flat plait*] *woven of fibres* or *leaves of the palm-tree:* (Mgh in art. قمط:) or *a rope of any kind:* pl. شَرَائِطُ and شُرُطٌ. (TA.) Also *Threads of silk,* or *of silk and of gold, twisted together* [or *woven, so as to form a kind of flat lace, like tape*]: so called as being likened to the threads of wool and of fibres of the palm-tree [twisted together]. (TA.) — Also The [*sort of basket,* or *small box, called*] عَتِيدَة *in which a woman puts her perfumes* (IAạr, O, Ḳ) *and her utensils* or *apparatus.* (IAạr, O.) And The [*sort of receptacle called*] عَيْبَة [q. v.]. (IAạr, O.)

شَرِيطَةٌ: see شَرْطٌ: — and see also شُرْطَةٌ, last sentence. — Also A she-camel *having her ear slit:* (Ḳ, TA:) of the measure فَعِيلَةٌ in the sense of the measure مَفْعُولَةٌ. (TA.) — And A sheep or goat *having a slight scar made upon its throat, like the scarification of the cupper, without the severing of the* [*veins called*] أَوْدَاج, *and without making the blood to flow copiously:* thus they used to do in the Time of Ignorance, cutting a little of the animal's throat, (Ḳ, TA,) and then leaving it to die; (TA;) and they considered it a lawful mode of slaughtering it; but the eating of such an animal is forbidden in a trad.: (Ḳ, TA:) or one *scarified on account of some disease;* and when such died, they said that they had slaughtered it. (TA.)

شَرَطِىٌّ: see شِرَاطِىٌّ.

شِرْوَاطٌ, applied to a man, *Tall:* (O, Ḳ:) and, applied to a camel, (Ibn-'Abbád, O,) or to a he-camel, (Ḳ,) *swift:* (Ibn-'Abbád, O, Ḳ:) or it is applied in the former sense to a man, and is also applied to a camel, male and female alike, ('Eyn, Ṣ,) as meaning *tall and slender:* ('Eyn:) or it means *tall, spare of flesh, slender;* applied to a man and to a camel, and to the female likewise, without ة. (L.)

الغَنَمُ أَشْرَطُ المَالِ *Sheep, or goats, are the vilest sort of beasts that one possesses:* an instance of a noun of superiority without a verb; which is extr.: (Ḳ, TA:) this is from the "Iṣláh el-Al-fádh" of ISk: but in some of the copies of that work, we find أَشْرَاط in the place of أَشْرَط. (ISd, TA.) See شَرَطٌ.

أَشْرَاطِىٌّ: fem. with ة: see شَرَطِىٌّ, in two places.

مِشْرَطٌ *A lancet* (Ṣ, Ḳ, TA) *with which the cupper scarifies;* (TA;) as also ▼ مِشْرَاطٌ. (Ṣ, Ḳ, TA.)

مِشْرَاطٌ: [pl. مَشَارِيطُ:] see مِشْرَطٌ: — and see شَرْطٌ, in two places. — أَخَذَ لِلْأَمْرِ مَشَارِيطَهُ *He took his apparatus,* [or *prepared himself,*] *for the thing,* or *affair.* (Ibn-'Abbád, Ḳ.)

شرع

1. شَرَعَتِ الدَّوَابُّ فِى المَآءِ, (Ṣ, Ḳ,) aor. َ, (Ṣ,) inf. n. شَرْعٌ and شُرُوعٌ, [the latter of which is the more common,] and ▼ مَشْرُوعٌ, (TA, [there said to be syn. with شُرُوعٌ, like as مَيْسُورٌ is with يُسْرٌ,]) *The beasts entered into the water,* (Ṣ, Ḳ, TA,) *and drank of it:* (TA:) and شَرَعَ, aor. as above, and so the inf. ns., *he* (one coming to water to drink) *took the water with his mouth:* (TA:) or شَرَعْتُ فِى المَآءِ, inf. ns. as above, *I drank the water with my hands:* or *I entered into the water:* and شَرَعَ المَالُ *the cattle came to the water to drink:* (Mṣb:) and ▼ شُرِّعَتِ الدَّابَّةُ [if not a mistranscription for شُرِعَتْ] *the beast was,* or *became, at the watering-place.* (TA.) — [Hence,] شَرَعَ فِى الأَمْرِ, (Ṣ, Mṣb, Ḳ,) aor. as above, (Mṣb,) inf. n. شُرُوعٌ, (Ṣ, Mṣb, Ḳ,) *He entered into the affair;* (Ṣ, Ḳ;) *he entered upon, began,* or *commenced, the affair.* (Mṣb.) — شَرَعَ البَابُ إِلَى الطَّرِيقِ, inf. n. شُرُوعٌ, *The door, or entrance, communicated with the road.* (Mṣb.) And شَرَعَ المَنْزِلُ *The dwelling was upon,* (Ṣ, Ḳ,) or *had its door* [*opening*] *upon,* (TA,) *a road that was a thoroughfare.* (Ṣ, Ḳ, TA.) — شَرَعَ said of a spear, *It pointed directly* [towards a person: see an explanation of the trans. verb in what follows]. (Ṣ, Ḳ: but in the latter, شَرَعَت, said of spears.) See also شَرَعٌ. — And, said of a road, (Mgh,) and of an affair, or a case, (TA,) *It was,* or *became, apparent, manifest,* or *plain.* (IAạr, Mgh, TA.) — شَرَعَ المَالَ, aor. as above, [inf. n., app., شَرْعٌ,] *He brought the cattle to the watering-place;* as also ▼ اشرعهُ: (Mṣb:) and the former is trans. in this sense by means of بِ: (Ḥar p. 21:) or شَرَعَ (TA) and ▼ شَرَّعَ, inf. n. of the latter تَشْرِيعٌ, (Ṣ, TA,) *he made the beasts,* (Ṣ,) or his camels, (TA,) *to enter into the water* [*to drink*]: (Ṣ, TA:) and ▼ اشرع نَاقَتَهُ *he made his she-camel to enter into the watering-place:* (TA:) or ▼ تَشْرِيعٌ signifies the *bringing camels to the watering-place to drink without requiring in doing so to draw with the pulley and its appertenances nor to give them to drink in a watering-trough* or *tank.* (O, Ḳ.) It is said in a prov, (Ṣ,) أَهْوَنُ ▼ السَّقْىِ التَّشْرِيعُ (Ṣ, Ḳ) *The easiest mode of watering is the making* of the camels *to enter into the water:* applied to him who takes an easy way of performing an affair, and does not exert himself therein. (Meyd. [See Freytag's Arab. Prov. ii. 889.]) — شَرَعَ البَابَ إِلَى الطَّرِيقِ *He made the door, or entrance, to communicate with the road:* (Mṣb:) and ▼ اشرعهُ الى الطريق (Ṣ, Mṣb, Ḳ, TA) signifies the same; (Mṣb, TA;) or *he opened it* (i. e. the door, or entrance,) *to the road.* (Ṣ, Mṣb, Ḳ, TA.) And ▼ اشرع الجَنَاحَ إِلَى الطَّرِيقِ *He put the* جناح [meaning *projecting roof*] *towards the road.* (Mṣb.) — And شَرَعَ (Ḳ) and ▼ اشرع (Ṣ, Ḳ, TA) and ▼ شَرَّعَ (TA) *He directed* (Ṣ, Ḳ, TA) a spear, (Ṣ, TA,) or spears, (Ḳ,) and a sword, (TA,) قِبَلَهُ (Ṣ) or نَحْوَهُ (TA) [i. e. *towards him*]: or ▼ اشرع signifies *he inclined* a spear. (Mṣb.) — And شَرَعَ, (Mgh, Mṣb, TA,) aor. as above, (Mṣb,) inf. n. شَرْعٌ, (TA,) *He made apparent, manifest,* or *plain,* (Mgh, Mṣb, TA,) a road; (Mgh, TA;) as also ▼ اشرع; and ▼ شَرَّعَ, inf. n. تَشْرِيعٌ: (Ḳ, TA:) and in like manner, an affair, or a case; and religion. (TA.) Accord. to Az, this meaning of شَرَعَ is from شَرَعَ الإِهَابَ [which see in what follows]. (TA.) One says, شَرَعَ اللّٰهُ لَنَا كَذَا *God made apparent, manifest,* or *plain, to us, such a thing.* (Mṣb.) And شَرَعَ فُلَانٌ *Such a one made apparent, manifest,* or *plain, the truth,* or *right.* (TA.) — And شَرَعَ لَهُمْ *i. q.* سَنَّ [i. e. *He instituted, established,* or *prescribed, for them,* or *to them,* a religious ordinance, a law, &c.]: (Ṣ, Ḳ:) whence [accord. to some,] شِرْعَةٌ and شَرِيعَةٌ. (TA.) — شَرَعَ الإِهَابَ, (Ṣ, Ḳ,) aor. as above, inf. n. شَرْعٌ, (Ṣ,) *He stripped off the hide:* (Ṣ, Ḳ:) or, accord. to Yaḳoob, as heard by him from Umm-El-Ḥomáris El-Bekreeyeh, *he slit the hide in the part between the two hind legs,* (Ṣ, TA,) and *then stripped it off:* or *he slit the hide,* [*and then stripped it off,*] *not making of it a* زِقّ [q. v.], *nor stripping it off* [*entire*] *by commencing from one hind leg.* (TA.) — شَرَعَ الحَبْلَ *He loosed,* or *undid, the rope,* or *cord,* or *the slip-knot thereof,* (أَنْشَطَهُ,) [*then, app., doubled it in the middle,* to put that part round something to be carried,] *and inserted its two halves* (قُطْرَيْهِ) *into the loop.* (O, Ḳ.) — And شَرَعَ الشَّىْءَ *He raised,* or *elevated, the thing much;* (Ḳ;) as also ▼ اشرعهُ. (TA.)

2: see 1, in six places. — شَرَّعَ السَّفِينَةَ, inf. n. تَشْرِيعٌ, *He made,* or *put, a sail* (شِرَاع) *to the ship,* or *boat.* (TA.)

4: see 1, former half, in two places. — [Hence,] one says, اشرع يَدَهُ إِلَى المِطْهَرَةِ † *He put his hand* [*to and*] *into the* مطهرة [or *vessel for purification*]. (TA.) And it is said in a trad. (respecting the [ablution termed] وُضُوء), حَتَّى أَشْرَعَ فِى العَضُدِ meaning *Until,* or *so that, he made the upper half of the arm to reach to* (lit. *to enter*) *the water.* (TA. [This ex. is elliptical and inverted; for حَتّى اشرع العَضُدَ فِى المَآءِ.]) — And أَشْرَعَنِى الرَّجُلُ † *The man sufficed me; or gave me what sufficed me:* and اشرعنى الشَّىْءُ † *The thing sufficed me.* (TA.) — And أَشْرَعَ said of a plant, or of herbage, [app. for أَشْرَعَ الإِبِلَ,] † *It became full-grown, and satiated the camels.* (TA.) — See, again, 1, latter half, in six places.

8. فُلَانٌ يَشْتَرِعُ شِرْعَتَهُ [meaning *Such a one originates,* or *embraces,* or *follows, his way of religion*] is similar to the phrases يَفْتَطِرُ فِطْرَتَهُ and يَمْتَلُّ مِلَّتَهُ; from شِرْعَةُ الدِّينِ and فِطْرَتُهُ and مِلَّتُهُ. (TA.)

شَرْعٌ, originally an inf. n.: — then applied as a name for *A manifest, a plain,* or *an open, track,* or *road,* or *way:* — and then, metaphorically, to The *divine way of religion;* so says Er-Rághib; (TA;) syn. with شَرِيعَةٌ, q. v. (Mṣb.) — In the saying مَرَرْتُ بِرَجُلٍ شَرْعِكَ, (so in the Ḳ,) or مررت بِرَجُلٍ شَرْعُكَ مِنْ رَجُلٍ, (so in the Ṣ and O, [for هُوَ شَرْعُكَ,]) with kesr and with ḍamm to the ع [of شرعك], (TA,) i. e. [*I passed by a man*] *sufficing thee* [*as a man*], (Ṣ, O, Ḳ,) the meaning is, *of the sort to which thou directest thyself and which thou seekest* (تَشْرَعُ ▼ فِيهِ وَتَطْلُبُهُ): (Ṣ, O:) and the word in this sense is used alike as sing. and pl. (Ṣ, O, Ḳ) and dual, because it is [originally] an inf. n. (Ṣ, O.) You say, شَرْعُكَ هٰذَا [and هٰذَانِ and هٰؤُلَآءِ] i. e. *Sufficient for thee* [*is this* and *are these two* and *are these*]. (Ṣ: and the like is said in the Mgh.) And it is said in a prov.,

• شَرْعُكَ مَا بَلَّغَكَ المَحَلَّا •

thus correctly, for it is a hemistich; not المَحَلَّ, as in the Ṣ and Ḳ; (TA;) i. e. *Sufficient* travelling-provision *for thee is that which will cause thee to reach the place* [*of alighting*] to which thou repairest: (Ḳ, TA:) applied to the case of being content with little. (Ṣ, Ḳ.) — See also شَرَعٌ, in two places. — And see شِرْعَةٌ.

شِرْعٌ [in the CḲ, erroneously, شَرْعٌ,] The *like* of a thing; as also ▼ شِرْعَةٌ: (Ḳ, TA:) [but the former is masc. and ▼ the latter is fem.; for] one says, هٰذَا شِرْعُ هٰذَا *This is the like of this;* and so هٰذِهِ شِرْعَةُ ▼ هٰذِهِ: and هٰذَانِ شِرْعَانِ *these two are likes.* (Ṣ, O, TA.) [The pls., or rather coll. gen. ns. and pls., following this meaning in the Ḳ belong to شِرْعَةٌ and شِرْعَةٌ in another sense; as is shown by exs. in the O and TA.] — Also The *chords of the* بَرْبَط, (O, Ḳ, TA,) which is the [*Persian*] عُود [or *lute*]. (TA.) [In this sense, a coll. gen. n.:] see its n. un. شِرْعَةٌ. — And hence, as being likened thereto, (TA,) ‡ The [*thong called*] شِرَاك *of a sandal.* (O, Ḳ, TA.) It is related in a trad. that a man said, إِنِّى أُحِبُّ الجَمَالَ حَتَّى فِى شِرْعِ نَعْلِى (O, TA) i. e. ‡ [*Verily I love elegance, even*] *in the* شراك *of my sandal.* (TA.)

شَرَعٌ: see شَرِيعَةٌ. — One says, النَّاسُ فِى هٰذَا الأَمْرِ شَرَعٌ and ▼ شَرْعٌ, (Ṣ, Mṣb, Ḳ,) the latter a contraction of the former, (Mṣb,) allowed by Kr and Ḳz, but disallowed by Yaạḳoob, (IDrst, TA,) *The people are in this affair equals:* (Ṣ, Mṣb, Ḳ:) in this sense, used alike as sing. and pl. and fem. (Ṣ, TA) and masc.: (TA:) [of شَرَعٌ] Az says that it seems to be pl. [or quasi-pl. n.] of ▼ شَارِعٌ, like as خَدَمٌ is of خَادِمٌ; i. e., [the phrase means] *the people enter into this affair* (يَشْرَعُونَ فِيهِ) *together.* (TA.) One says also, النَّاسُ شَرَعٌ وَاحِدٌ and ▼ شَرْعٌ وَاحِدٌ, meaning *The people are one sort.* (Ḳ.)

شُرْعَةٌ: see the next paragraph, in two places.

شِرْعَةٌ: see شَرِيعَةٌ, in two places. — Also *A custom.* (TA.) — See also شِرْعٌ, first sentence, in three places. — Also *A snare for the birds called* قَطًا, (Lth, O, Ḳ, TA,) *with which to capture them,* (O, TA,) *made of sinews:* (Lth, O, TA:) pl. شِرَعٌ. (O.) — Also, (Ṣ, O, Ḳ,) and ▼ شُرْعَةٌ, (Ḳ,) *A string,* or *chord:* (Ṣ, O, Ḳ, TA:) or *such as is slender:* or *while continuing stretched upon the bow;* (TA;) and so ▼ شِرَاعٌ; (Lth, O, Ḳ;) or *upon the lute;* and so ▼ شِرَاعٌ: (TA:) the pl. [or rather coll. gen. n.] (of ▼ شُرْعَةٌ, Ṣ, O, [i. e. of this n. un. meaning the "chord of a lute," as is shown by exs. in the O and TA,]) is ▼ شِرْعٌ (Ṣ, O, Ḳ) and (that of ▼ شُرْعَةٌ, TA) ▼ شُرَعٌ, (O, Ḳ, TA,) like as تُمَرٌ is of تُمْرَةٌ, (O, TA,) and [the pl. properly so termed] (of شِرْعَةٌ, Ṣ, O) شِرَعٌ, and pl. pl. شِرَاعٌ: (Ṣ, O, Ḳ:) and the pl. of ▼ شِرَاعٌ as a sing. syn. with شِرْعَةٌ is شُرُعٌ. (TA.)

شَرَعَةٌ i. q. سَقِيفَةٌ [i. e. *A roof,* or *covering, such as projects over the door of a house &c.;* or *a place roofed over*]: pl. أَشْرَاعٌ. (O, Ḳ.)

[شَرْعِىٌّ *Of,* or *relating to, the religion* or *law.* — And *Accordant to the religion* or *law; legal,* or *legitimate.*]

شَرَاعٌ A plant, or herbage, *full-grown,* (O, Ḳ, TA,) *that satiates the camels.* (TA.)

شِرَاعٌ: see شِرْعَةٌ. — The شِرَاع of a ship or boat (Ṣ, Mgh, O, Mṣb) is called in Pers. بَادْبَان [i. e. *A sail*]; (MA, Mgh, KL;) i. q. قِلْعٌ; (MA, TA;) *a thing like a wide* مُلَآءَة [q. v.], (O, Ḳ, TA,) *of cloth* or *of matting,* (TA,) [*raised,* or *attached,*] *upon a piece of wood* [i. e. *a mast* or *a yard*]; *which is beaten upon by the wind* (تُصَفِّقُهُ الرِّيحُ,) *and causes the ship,* or *boat, to go along:* (O, Ḳ, TA:) so called because it is raised (يُشْرَعُ) i. e. (يُرْفَعُ) above the ship, or boat: (TA:) pl. أَشْرِعَةٌ and شُرُعٌ; (O, Ḳ;) the former a pl. of pauc. (O.) — And hence, as being likened thereto, (TA, [and the same is implied in the Ṣ and O,]) ‡ The *neck* of a camel. (Ṣ, O, Ḳ, TA.) Sometimes they said of a camel, رَفَعَ شِرَاعَهُ, meaning ‡ *He raised his neck.* (Ṣ, O, TA.) — One says also رَجُلٌ شِرَاعُ الأَنْفِ, meaning † *A man having the nose extended,* and *long.* (TA. [See أَشْرَعُ.]) — See also شِرْعَةٌ, in three places.

شَرِيعٌ *Courageous;* (O, Ḳ, TA;) applied to a man. (O, TA.) — Also *Good,* or *excellent, flax.* (Ḳ.) — And The لِيف [or *fibres that grow at the base of the branches of the palm-tree*] *of which the prickles* (شَوْك) *are strong, and such as, by reason of their thickness, are fit for the sewing of leather therewith.* (TA.)

شَرَاعَةٌ *Courage;* (O, Ḳ;) as an attribute of a man. (O.)

شَرِيعَةٌ and ▼ شِرْعَةٌ (Ṣ, O, Mṣb, Ḳ) and ▼ مَشْرَعَةٌ (Mṣb, Ḳ) and ▼ مَشْرَعٌ (TA) and ▼ شَرَعٌ (O, TA*) and مَآءٌ ▼ شِرَاعٌ (TA) *A watering-place; a resort of drinkers* [*both men and beasts*]; (Ṣ, O, Ḳ, TA;) *a place to which men come to drink therefrom and to draw water,* (Mṣb,* TA,) *and into which they sometimes make their beasts to enter, to drink:* (TA:) but the term ▼ مشرعة, (Az, Mṣb,) or شريعة, (TA,) is not applied by the Arabs to any but [*a watering-place*] *such as is permanent, and apparent to the eye,* (Az, Mṣb, TA,) *like the water of rivers,* (Mṣb,) *not water from which one draws with the well-rope:* (Az, Mṣb, TA:) the pl. of شَرِيعَةٌ is شَرَائِعُ; and that of ▼ مَشْرَعَةٌ or ▼ مَشْرَعٌ [or of both] is مَشَارِعُ; which is also expl. as meaning *gaps,* or *breaches, in the banks of rivers or the like by which men or beasts come to water:* (TA:) and [in like manner it is said that] شَرِيعَةٌ signifies *a place of descent to water:* (Lth, TA:) or *a way to water.* (Bḍ in v. 52.) — And hence, (Lth, Kr, Mṣb, TA, and Bḍ ubi suprà,) الشَّرِيعَةُ, (Lth, Kr, Ṣ, Mṣb, Ḳ, &c.,) as also ▼ الشِّرْعَةُ, (Mṣb, Ḳ, &c.,) and ▼ الشَّرْعُ, (Mṣb,) signifies likewise الدِّينُ; (Mṣb, and Bḍ ubi suprà;) because it is a way to the means of eternal life; (Bḍ ibid.;) or because of its manifestness; (Mṣb;) [i. e.] *The religious law of God;* (Lth, Kr, Ṣ, O, Ḳ,* TA;) *consisting of such ordinances as those of fasting and prayer and pilgrimage* (Lth, Kr, TA) *and the giving of the poor-rate* (Kr, TA) *and marriage,* (Lth, TA,) *and other acts* (Lth, Kr, TA) *of piety,* or *of obedience to God,* or *of duty to Him and to men:* (Kr, TA:) pl. as above. (Mṣb.) شَرِيعَةٌ signifies also [*A law, an ordinance,* or *a statute:* and] *a religion,* or *way of belief and practice in respect of religion:* (Fr, TA:) and *a way of belief or conduct that is manifest* (Ibn-'Arafeh, Mgh, Ḳ) *and right* (Ibn-'Arafeh, Ḳ) *in religion;* (Mgh;) and so ▼ شِرْعَةٌ. (Ḳ.)

شُرَاعِىٌّ, as an epithet applied to A spear-head and a spear, *of Shurạạ,* (TA,) which was the name of a certain man who made spear-heads and spears, (Ḳ, TA,) as they assert: but IAạr says that it may be a reg. rel. n. from شُرَاعٌ, or an irreg. rel. n. from some other name of which the radical latters are شرع: and [SM says also that,] applied to a spear, it signifies *long:* (TA:) or ▼ شِرَاعِىٌّ, thus applied, has this meaning, a rel. n. [from شِرَاعٌ]. (Ṣ, O.) شُرَاعِيَّةٌ and ▼ شِرَاعِيَّةٌ [in the

CĶ without teshdeed], applied to a she-camel, signify ‡ *Long-necked*: (O, Ķ, TA:) thus expl. by ISh: but Az thinks the latter to be the more probably correct; the neck being likened to the شِرَاع of the ship or boat, because of the height thereof. (O.)

شِرَاعِىٌّ; and its fem., with ة: see the next preceding paragraph.

شَرَّاعٌ *A seller of the flax called* شَرِيع. (IAar, Ķ.)

شَارِعٌ *Entering into water* [*to drink*]: pl. شُرَّعٌ and شُرُوعٌ: (KL:) these pls. are applied in this sense to camels. (Ṣ, Ķ.) — [Hence,] *Entering* into an affair (فِى أَمْرٍ). (Az, TA.) See شَرَعٌ. — And sing. of شُرَّعٌ in the phrase حِيتَانٌ شُرَّعٌ, (TA,) which means *Fishes lowering their heads to drink*: (Aboo-Leylà, TA:) or *raising their heads*: (Ķ, TA:) or *directing themselves*, or *repairing*, (شَارِعَاتٌ,) *from the deep water to the bank*, or *side*: (Ṣ, TA:) and حِيتَانٌ شُرُوعٌ signifies the same: (TA:) or شُرَّعًا in the Ķur vii. 163, referring to fish, means *appearing upon the surface of the water*. (Bḍ, Jel.*) — Also, applied to a place of alighting, or an abode, (مَنْزِلٌ,) *Situate upon a road that is a thoroughfare*: and شَارِعَةٌ applied to a house (دَارٌ) signifies the same; (Ķ;) or *having its door* [*opening*] *upon such a road*; (TA;) or *near to the road and to the people* [or *passengers*]: (Mgh,* TA:) and دُورٌ شَارِعَةٌ *houses having their doors opening into the streets*: or دُورٌ شَوَارِعُ, as expl. by IDrd, *houses upon one open road*. (TA.) It is said in a trad., كَانَتِ الأَبْوَابُ شَارِعَةً إِلَى المَسْجِدِ *The doors were opening towards the mosque*. (TA.) — And Anything *near* (Ķ, TA) to a thing, or *overlooking* it: whence شَارِعَةٌ applied to a house (دَارٌ) near to the road and to the people, as expl. above. (TA.) [Hence,] نُجُومٌ شَوَارِعُ *Stars near to setting*. (Ķ.) — [Also *Pointing directly* towards a person; applied to a spear.] One says رِمَاحٌ شَارِعَةٌ and شَوَارِعُ (Ķ, TA) and شُرَّعٌ as in some of the copies of the Ṣ (TA) *Spears pointing directly*: and ▼ رِمَاحٌ مُشْرُوعَةٌ and ▼ مُشْرَعَةٌ *spears directed*. (Ķ, TA.) — Also [used as a subst.] *A main road*: (Ṣ, O:) or it signifies, (Mgh, TA,) or so طَرِيقٌ شَارِعٌ, (Mṣb,) ‡ *a road*, or *way, into which people enter* (يَسْلُكُهُ النَّاسُ, Mṣb, or يَشْرَعُ فِيهِ النَّاسُ, Mgh, TA) *in common*, or *in general*; (Mgh, Mṣb, TA;) by a tropical attribution; (Mgh;) [i. e.] شَارِعٌ in this case has the meaning of مَشْرُوعٌ [or مَشْرُوعٌ فِيهِ]; (Mṣb;) or as meaning ذُو شَرْعٍ مِنَ الخَلْقِ [*having an entering of people*]: (TA:) or it signifies *a manifest, plain*, or *conspicuous, road* or *way*: (Mgh, TA:) [in the present day, شَارِعٌ commonly signifies *any great street that is a thoroughfare*:] the pl. is شَوَارِعُ. (Mṣb.) ═ الشَّارِعُ also means *The learned man who practises what he knows and instructs others*: (Ķ, TA:) or so الشَّارِعُ الرَّبَّانِىُّ. (O.) And hence it is applied to designate the Prophet: [or as meaning *The legislator*: or *the announcer of the law*:] or because he made manifest and plain the religion, or religious law of God. (TA.)

أَشْرَعُ A nose *of which the end is extended* (Ķ, TA) *and elevated, and long*. (TA.)

مَشْرَعٌ: see شَرِيعَةٌ, in two places.

مُشْرَعٌ: see its fem., with ة, voce شَارِعٌ.

مَشْرَعَةٌ and مَشْرُعَةٌ: see شَرِيعَةٌ, in four places.

بَيْتٌ مُشْرَعٌ *A high*, or *lofty, house* or *tent*. (TA.)

مَشْرُوعٌ: see its fem., with ة, voce شَارِعٌ: ═ see also 1, first sentence.

شرف

1. شَرُفَ, (Ṣ, O, Mṣb, Ķ,) aor. ـُ, (Ķ,) inf. n. شَرَفٌ (Ṣ,* O,* Mṣb,* Ķ, TA) and شَرَافَةٌ, (TA,) said of a man, (Ṣ, O, TA,) *He was*, or *became, high, elevated, exalted*, or *eminent*, (Ṣ, O, Mṣb, Ķ, TA,) [*in rank, condition*, or *estimation*,] *in respect of religion* or *of worldly things*: (Ķ, TA:) [generally meaning *he was high-born*, or *noble*:] part. n. شَرِيفٌ [q. v.]. (Ṣ, O, Mṣb, Ķ, TA.) [See also شَرَفٌ, below.] — [Hence one says,] شَرُفَتْ نَفْسُهُ عَنِ الشَّىْءِ *His soul was above the thing; disdained*, or *scorned, it*. (L in art. انف.) — شَرُفَتِ النَّاقَةُ, and شَرَفَتْ, (O, Ķ,) aor. of each ـُ, inf. n. شُرُوفٌ, (Ķ,) reg. as of the former verb, and irreg. as of the latter, (TA,) *The she-camel was*, or *became, such as is termed* شَارِفٌ [q. v.]. (O, Ķ.) ═ شَرَفَهُ, aor. ـُ, (IJ, Ṣ, O, Ķ, TA,) inf. n. شَرْفٌ, (TA,) *He overcame him*, or *surpassed him, in* شَرَف [i. e. *highness, elevation*, or *eminence, of rank, condition*, or *estimation*; or *nobility*]; (IJ, Ṣ, O, Ķ, TA;) and so شَرُفَ عَلَيْهِ: (Z, TA:) or *he excelled him* (طَالَهُ, Ķ, TA, in the CĶ [erroneously] طاوَلَهُ) *in the grounds of pretension to respect or honour* (فِى الحَسَبِ). (Ķ, TA.) See 3. — شَرَفَ الحَائِطَ, (Ķ, TA,) aor. ـُ, inf. n. شَرْفٌ, (TA,) *He put to the wall a* شُرْفَة [q. v.]. (Ķ, TA.) [See also 2.] ═ شَرِفَتِ الأُذُنُ, and شَرِفَ المَنْكِبُ, aor. ـَ, (Ķ, TA,) inf. n. شَرَفٌ, (TA,) *The ear*, and in like manner *the shoulder, was*, or *became, high*, (Ķ, TA,) *and prominent*: or, as some say, *stood up*. (TA.) ═ And شَرِفَ, [from شَرَفٌ signifying the "hump" of a camel,] (O, Ķ,) said of a man, (O,) *He kept constantly*, or *continually, to the eating of the* [*camel's*] *hump*. (O, Ķ.)

2. شَرَّفَهُ, inf. n. تَشْرِيفٌ, *He* (God) *rendered him high, elevated, exalted*, or *eminent*, [*in rank, condition*, or *estimation*; or *ennobled him*:] (Ṣ, KL,* PṢ:*) and *he held him*, or *esteemed him, to be so*. (MA, PṢ.) ISd thinks that the verb may also mean *He regarded with more*, or *exceeding, honour*. (TA.) [And Golius explains it as meaning *He decked with a royal garment*; on the authority of the KL; in my copy of which I find no other meaning assigned to it than the first mentioned above.] One says, شَرَّفَ اللّٰهُ الكَعْبَةَ, (O, Ķ, TA,) inf. n. as above, (TA,) [*God rendered*, or *may God render, the Kaabeh an object of honour*, or *glorious*,] from الشَّرَفُ, (O, Ķ, TA,) i. e. المَجْدُ. (TA.) [تَشْرِيفٌ is also used as a subst. properly so called; and as such is expl. by itself in this art.] — Also *He put to it* شُرَف [pl. of شُرْفَةٌ, q. v.]; (O, Ķ;) namely, his house, (Ķ,) or a [palace, or pavilion, or other building such as is called] قَصْر, &c.; inf. n. as above. (O.) [See also شَرَفَ الحَائِطَ.] — شَرِّفِ المَرْبَأَ, expl. in the Ķ as syn. with شارفه and اشرفه, is a mistake for تَشَرَّفَهُ [q. v.]. (TA.) — شَرَّفَ النَّاقَةَ, inf. n. as above, means *He almost severed the teats of the she-camel by binding them* [*tightly*] with the صِرَار [q. v.]: (IAar, O, TA:) this being done for the preservation of her [stoutness of] body, and her fatness, so that burdens may be put upon her in the coming year. (TA.) — [شَرَّفَ, app. for شَرَّفَ العُنُقَ, is also said by Reiske, as mentioned by Freytag in his Lexicon, to signify *He* (a camel going along) *raised the neck*: but his authority for this is not stated.]

3. شارفهُ, (Ṣ, O, Ķ,) inf. n. مُشَارَفَةٌ, (TA,) *He vied with him*, or *contended with him for superiority, in* شَرَف [i. e. *highness, elevation*, or *eminence, of rank, condition*, or *estimation*; or *nobility*]; (Ṣ, O, Ķ, TA;) ▼ فَشَرَفَهُ *and he overcame*, or *surpassed, him therein*. (TA.) — See also 5. — Also *He was*, or *became, near to it*; *he drew near to it*, or *approached it*; namely, a thing: and *he was*, or *became, near to attaining it*, [and in like manner شارف عَلَيْهِ, as used in the Ṣ and Ķ in the beginning of art. بلغ, *he was*, or *became, at the point of reaching it*, or *attaining it*, namely, a place,] or *of obtaining it*, or *getting possession of it*: [and *he was*, or *became, at the point of experiencing it*, (See Bḍ in lxxviii. 14,) and *doing it*; followed by أَنْ and an aor.:] and, as some say, *he looked for it*, or *expected it*; *his mind told him of it*; *he looked for its coming to pass*. (TA.) See also 4, in two places.

4. اشرف *It rose*; or *it was*, or *became, high* or *elevated*; [*so as to overtop*, or *overlook, what was around it or adjacent to it*: *overtopped, surmounted, overpeered, overlooked, overhung*; *was*, or *became, protuberant, prominent*, or *projecting*: and *rose into view, came within sight* or *view*, or *became within a commanding*, or *near, view*:] said of a place [&c.]. (Mṣb.) One says of a piece of ground, أَشْرَفَ عَلَى مَا حَوْلَهُ [*It rose above*, or *overtopped, what was around it*]. (Sh, TA.) And أَشْرَفَ لِى شَرَفٌ فَمَا زِلْتُ أَرْكُضُ حَتَّى عَلَوْتُهُ [*An eminence rose into view to me, and I ceased not to urge on my beast until I ascended*, or *mounted, upon it*]. (TA.) — [Hence,] أَشْرَفْتُ عَلَيْهِ *I looked upon it*, or *viewed it*, (Ṣ, O, Mṣb, Ķ,*) *from above*; (Ṣ, O, Ķ;) [*I overlooked it*, or *looked down upon it*:] and *I came in sight of it*: *got a view of it*: and *got knowledge of it*; *became acquainted with it*; or *knew it*: all of which meanings may be intended to be conveyed by the explanation in the Mṣb, which is إِطَّلَعْتُ عَلَيْهِ:]

and أَشْرَفْتُ عَلَيْهِ signifies the same as شَارَفْتُ ▼ الشَّىْءَ [app. in the first of the senses expl. in this sentence, as well as in another sense expl. in what follows]: (Ṣ, O:) and شَارَفُوهُمْ ▼ signifies the same as أَشْرَفُوا عَلَيْهِمْ. (TA.) — And اشرف عَلَى المَوْتِ *He* (a sick man) *was, or became, on the brink, or verge, or at the point, of death.* (O, Ḳ.) And اشرف بِهِ عَلَى المَوْتِ [*He made him to be on the brink, or verge, or at the point, of death*]. (T and Ḳ in art. ذرف.) — And أَشْرَفَتْ نَفْسُهُ عَلَى شَىْءٍ *His soul was vehemently eager for a thing.* (Mgh. [See also 10.]) إِشْرَافٌ signifies The *being eager*, and the *being vehemently eager*: and hence the saying, in a trad., مَنْ أَخَذَ الدُّنْيَا بِإِشْرَافِ نَفْسٍ لَمْ يُبَارَكْ لَهُ فِيهَا [*Whoso takes the enjoyments of the present world with eagerness, or vehement eagerness, of soul, he will not be blessed therein*]. (TA.) — And اشرف عَلَيْهِ *He regarded him with solicitous affection* or *pity* or *compassion.* (O,* Ḳ.) — [And اشرف لِى *He, or it, came within sight, or view, to me; or came within a commanding, or near, view of me*: see an ex. voce أَجْهَدَ; and another voce رُبَّ.] — And [hence,] اشرف لَكَ الشَّىْءُ *The thing became, or has become, within thy power* or *reach*; or *possible, practicable,* or *easy, to thee.* (TA.) = See also 5, in two places.

5. تشرّف, said of a man, is from الشَّرَفُ, (O,) and signifies صَارَ مُشَرَّفًا [*He became elevated,* or *exalted, in rank, condition,* or *estimation*; or *ennobled*]. (Ḳ.) — تشرّف بِهِ *He became elevated,* or *exalted, in rank, condition,* or *estimation*; or *ennobled*; *by,* or *by means of, him,* or *it*: (MA:) [or *he gloried,* or *prided himself, by reason of it,* or *in it*; i. e.] *he reckoned it,* (Ṣ,) or *regarded it,* (O,) *as a glory* or *an honour* [*to himself*], (Ṣ, O,) *and a favour.* (O.) = تشرّف المَرْبَأَ, (Ṣ, O, TA,) in the Ḳ, erroneously, شَرَّفَهُ; (TA;) and اشرفهُ ▼; (Ṣ, O, Ḳ;) and شارفهُ ▼, (Ḳ,) inf. n. مُشَارَفَةٌ; (TA;) *He* (a man, Ṣ, O) *ascended,* or *mounted, upon the elevated place of observation.* (Ṣ, O, Ḳ.) And اشرف ▼ الشَّىْءَ and عَلَى الشَّىْءِ signify the same as [تشرّفهُ and] تشرّف عَلَيْهِ, i. e. *He ascended,* or *mounted, upon the thing.* (TA.) — It is said in a trad., with reference to certain future trials, or conflicts and factions, (فِتَن,) مَنْ تَشَرَّفَ لَهَا تَسْتَشْرِفْهُ ▼ i. e. *Whoso finds a place of refuge* [*for* escaping, or avoiding *them, let them invite him,* or *cause him, to seek,* or *take, refuge,* virtually meaning] *let him seek,* or *take, refuge* therein. (O, TA.*) = تُشُرِّفَ القَوْمُ *The people,* or *party, had their* أَشْرَاف [or *eminent,* or *noble, men,* pl. of شَرِيف,] *slain.* (O, Ḳ.)

8. اشترف *He,* or *it, stood up,* or *upright,* or *erect*; (Ṣ, O, TA;) and (TA) so استشرف ▼ [if this be not a mistranscription, which I incline to think it may be as the former verb (of which see the part. n. below) is not mentioned in the Ḳ]. (Ḳ, TA.)

10. استشرف الشَّىْءَ, (Ṣ, O, Mṣb, Ḳ,) and لِلشَّىْءِ, (Mṣb in art. طمح,) *He raised his eyes* (Ṣ, O, Mṣb, Ḳ) *towards the thing,* (O, Ḳ,) or *to look at the thing,* (Mṣb,) or *looking at the thing,* (Ṣ,) *and expanded his hand over his eyebrow like as does he who shades* [*his eyes*] *from the sun.* (Ṣ, O, Ḳ.) A poet says,

تَطَاوَلْتُ وَٱسْتَشْرَفْتُهُ فَرَأَيْتُهُ
فَقُلْتُ لَهُ آأَنْتَ زَيْدُ الأَرَامِلِ

[*I stretched up myself, and raised my eyes towards him, expanding my hand over my eyebrow like him who is shading his eyes from the sun; and I said to him, Art thou Zeyd-el-Arámil?*]. (O.) — Hence, (TA,) أُمِرْنَا أَنْ نَسْتَشْرِفَ العَيْنَ وَالأُذُنَ, (Mgh,* O, Ḳ, TA,) in a trad. (O, TA) relating to the sheep or goat to be slaughtered as a victim on the day of sacrifice, (TA,) means *We have been commanded to pay much attention to the eye and the ear,* and *to examine them carefully, in order that there may not be any such defect as blindness of one eye or mutilation* (Mgh,* O, Ḳ, TA) *of an ear*: (TA:) or, (Mgh, O,) as some say, (O,) [in the Ḳ "that is,"] *to seek that they be of high estimation, by being perfect* (Mgh,* O, Ḳ) *and sound*: (Mgh, O:) or, accord. to some, it is from الشُّرْفَةُ signifying "the choice ones," or "best," of cattle; and the meaning is, *we have been commanded to select them.* (TA.) — And يَسْتَشْرِفُ مَعَالِىَ الأُمُورِ ‡ *He desires,* or *seeks,* [or *raises his eye to,*] *the means of attaining eminence.* (Mṣb in art. شوف.) — استشرف إِبِلَهُمْ means *He* (a man) *smote their camels with the* [*evil*] *eye*; syn. تَعَيَّنَهَا: (Ṣ, TA:) or *he looked at them* (تعيّنها) *to smite them with the* [*evil*] *eye.* (TA.) — استشرفهُ حَقَّهُ *He defrauded him of his right,* or *due.* (O, Ḳ.) = See also 5: = and 8.

Q. Q. 1. شَرْيَفْتُ الزَّرْعَ *I cut off the* شِرْيَاف [q. v.] *of the seed-produce*; (Ṣ, O;) and so شَرْنَفْتُهُ: (O and Ḳ* in art. شرنف:) of the dial. of El-Yemen: but Az doubts whether the word be with ن; and the ى and ن are both held by him to be augmentative. (O.)

شَرْفٌ: see the next paragraph, near the end.

شَرَفٌ *Highness, elevation, exaltation,* or *eminence,* [*in rank, condition,* or *estimation, in respect of religion* or *of worldly things*: (see the first sentence of this art.:)] (Ṣ, O, Mṣb, Ḳ:) [generally meaning *high birth*:] *glory, honour, dignity,* or *nobility*; syn. مَجْدٌ: or not unless [*transmitted*] *by ancestors*: (Ḳ:) [for] accord. to ISk, شَرَفٌ and مَجْدٌ may not be unless [transmitted] by ancestors; but حَسَبٌ and كَرَمٌ may be in a man though he have not ancestors [endowed therewith]: (O:) or, (Ḳ,) accord. to IDrd, (O,) it signifies *highness of* حَسَب [which means *grounds of pretension to respect* or *honour, consisting in any qualities* (*either of oneself* or *of one's ancestors*) *which are enumerated,* or *recounted, as causes of glorying*]: (O, Ḳ:) and شُرْفَةٌ ▼ signifies the same as شَرَفٌ; (TA;) or the same as فَضْلٌ and شَرَفٌ [meaning *a favour* and *a glory* or *an honour*]; as in the saying, أَعُدُّ إِتْيَانَكُمْ شُرْفَةً [*I reckon your coming a favour, and a glory* or *an honour*]; (O, Ḳ;) and أَرَى ذٰلِكَ شُرْفَةً [*I regard that as a favour, and a glory* or *an honour*]: (O:) the pl. of شَرَفٌ is أَشْرَافٌ, like as that of سَبَبٌ is أَسْبَابٌ. (TA.) نُهْبَةٌ ذَاتُ شَرَفٍ means *Spoil,* or *booty, of high value, at which men raise their eyes, and look,* or *which they smite with the* [*evil*] *eye*: [see اِسْتَشْرَفَ إِبِلَهُمْ:] but the phrase is also related with س. (TA. See سَرَفٌ.) — See also شَرِيفٌ, with which, or with the pls. of which, it is said to be syn. — Also *An elevated place*; *an eminence*: (Ṣ, Mgh, O, Ḳ:) accord. to Sh, *any piece of ground that overtops what is around it, whether extended or not, only about ten cubits,* or *five, in length, of little or much breadth in its upper surface*: (TA:) pl. أَشْرَافٌ: (TA voce وَطْءٌ:) and مَشَارِفُ الأَرْضِ signifies *the high,* or *elevated, places,* or *parts, of the earth* or *ground*: (Ṣ, Mṣb, Ḳ:) sing. مُشْرَفٌ ▼, with fet-ḥ to the م and ر. (Mṣb. [See also مُشْرُفٌ.]) A poet says,

آتِى النَّدِىَّ فَلَا يُقَرَّبُ مَجْلِسِى
وَأَقُودُ لِلشَّرَفِ الرَّفِيعِ حِمَارِى

[*I come to the assembly, and my sitting-place is not made near* to the chief person or persons, *and I lead to the high elevated place my ass*]: he means, I have become unsound in my intellect in consequence of old age, so that no profit is gotten from my opinion, and I am not able to mount my ass from the ground, unless from a high place. (Ṣ.) — [Hence, ‡ The *brink, verge,* or *point,* of some event of great magnitude, or of any importance: not well expl. as meaning] the *being on the brink,* or *verge,* or *at the point,* of some event of great importance, good or evil: (O, Ḳ:) one says in the case of good, هُوَ عَلَى شَرَفٍ مِنْ قَضَآءِ حَاجَتِهِ ‡ [*He is at the point of accomplishing the object of his want*]: and in the case of evil, هُوَ عَلَى شَرَفٍ مِنَ الهَلَاكِ ‡ [*He is on the brink,* &c., *of destruction*]. (O, TA.) — And ‡ The *hump* of a camel. (O, Ḳ, TA.) — And app. sing. of أَشْرَاف in a sense expl. below: see the latter word. (TA.) = And *A heat*; *a single run,* or *a run at once, to a goal,* or *limit*: (O, Ḳ:) or, (Ḳ,) accord. to Fr, *about a mile*: (O, Ḳ:) or *about two miles.* (TA as from the Ḳ and on the authority of Fr.) One says, عَدَا شَرَفًا أَوْ شَرَفَيْنِ [*He ran a heat, or two heats*]: (O:) and [in like manner,] اِسْتَنَّتْ شَرَفًا أَوْ شَرَفَيْنِ, (O, Ḳ,) occurring in a trad., said of a mare, or of horses. (O.) = Also, (O, TA,) accord. to IAạr, (O,) *A red clay* or *earth*: and *i. q.* مَغْرَةٌ [i. e. *red ochre*]; as also شَرْفٌ ▼: accord. to Lth, *a kind of trees, having a red dye*: and said to be *the same as* [the Pers.] دار پرنیان [i. e. دَارْ بَرْنِيَان, meaning *Brazil-wood,* which is commonly called in Arabic بَقَّم]. (O, TA:* in the former of which, the Pers. word here mentioned is written without the points to the پ; and in the latter, الدابرنيان.)

شُرْفَةٌ: see the next preceding paragraph, first quarter. — Also The *choice ones,* or *best,* of مَال [meaning cattle]. (Ṣ, O, Ḳ.) — The شُرْفَةٌ of a [palace, or pavilion, or other building such as is called] قَصْر (Ṣ, O, Mṣb, Ḳ) [and of a mosque] is well-known; (Ḳ;) [*An acroterial ornament, forming a single member of a cresting of a wall or of the crown of a cornice, generally of a fanciful form, and pointed, or small, at the top:*] pl. شُرَفٌ, (Ṣ, Mgh, O, Mṣb, Ḳ, TA,) a pl. of mult., and شُرُفَاتٌ and شُرَفَاتٌ and شُرْفَاتٌ, which are pls. of pauc., or, as some say, شرفات [i. e. شُرُفَاتٌ] is pl. of ▼ شُرُفَةٌ, with two dammehs: Esh-Shiháb says that شُرُفَات is expl. as meaning the *highest portions* of a قَصْر; but what are thus termed are only *what are built on the top of a wall, distinct from one another, [side by side, like merlons of a parapet,] according to a well-known form:* (TA:) the شُرْفَة is what is called by the [common] people ▼ شُرَّافَة: (Ḥam p. 824:) the شُرَّافَة of a mosque is a word used by the lawyers, and is one of their mistakes, as IB has notified: so says MF: its pl. is شَرَارِيف. (TA.) — The شُرُفَات (thus with two ḍammehs, Ḳ) of a horse are The *neck and* قَطَاة [i. e. *croup*, or *rump*, or *part between the hips* or *haunches*,] thereof. (O, Ḳ.)

شُرُفَةٌ: see the next preceding paragraph.

شَرِيفٌ *High, elevated, exalted,* or *eminent,* (Ṣ, O,* Mṣb, Ḳ, TA,) [*in rank, condition,* or *estimation,*] *in respect of religion* or *of worldly things:* (TA:) [generally meaning *high-born,* or *noble:*] *possessing glory, honour, dignity,* or *nobility:* or *such, and having also* [*such*] *ancestry:* (TA:) [using it as not implying highness, or nobility, of ancestry,] you say, هُوَ شَرِيفُ اليَوْمَ [*He is high,* or *noble, to-day*], and شَارِفٌ ▼ عَنْ قَلِيلٍ as meaning *one who will be* شريف [*after a little while*]: (Fr, Ṣ, Ḳ:) the pl. [of pauc.] is أَشْرَافٌ and [of mult.] شُرَفَآءُ (Ṣ, O, Mṣb, Ḳ) and ▼ شَرَفٌ, so in the Ḳ, app. denoting that this last is one of the pls. of شريف, and it is said in the O that شَرَفٌ is syn. with شُرَفَآءُ; but in the L it is said that it is syn. with شَرِيف; and hence the saying هُوَ شَرَفُ قَوْمِهِ meaning *He is the* شريف *of his people,* and كَرَمُهُمْ meaning *the* كَرِيم *of them;* and thus it has been expl. as used in a trad.: (TA:) [but both these assertions are probably correct; for it seems to be, agreeably with analogy, an inf. n. used as an epithet, and therefore applicable to a single person and to a pl. number, and also to two persons, and likewise to a female as well as to a male.] — [By the modern Arabs, and the Turks and Persians, it is also applied, as a title of honour, to Any *descendant of the Prophet;* like سَيِّد. And, with the article ال, particularly to the descendant of the Prophet who is *The governor of Mekkeh;* now always a vassal of the Turkish Sulṭán.]

شُرَافِىٌّ, applied to a [lizard of the kind called] ضَبّ, and to a jerboa, *Large in the ears, and in the body:* (TA:) and so شُرَافِيَّةٌ applied to a she-camel; (O, Ḳ, TA;) as also ▼ شَرْفَآءُ. (TA.) And أُذُنٌ شُرَافِيَّةٌ *i. q.* شُفَارِيَّةٌ [q. v.], (Ḳ, TA,) or *An ear that is high, long, and having hair upon it.* (IDrd, O, TA.) See also أُذُنٌ شَرْفَآءُ, voce أَشْرَفُ. — Also *A kind of white garments* or *cloths:* (O, Ḳ:*) or *a garment,* or *piece of cloth, that is purchased from a country of the foreigners adjacent to the land of the Arabs.* (Aṣ, O, Ḳ.*)

شُرَّافَةٌ; pl. شَرَارِيفُ: see شُرْفَةٌ.

شِرْيَافٌ (Ṣ, O, Ḳ) and شِرْنَافٌ (O and Ḳ in art. شرنف) [but see Q. Q. 1] *The leaves of seed-produce that have become so long and abundant that one fears its becoming marred; wherefore they are cut off.* (Ṣ, O, Ḳ.)

شَارِفٌ: see شَرِيفٌ. — Applied to a she-camel, † *High* [app. meaning *much advanced*] *in age:* (A, TA:) or *advanced in age;* (Ṣ, O, Ḳ;) *decrepit;* (IAạr, Ḳ;) as also شَارِفَةٌ: (Ḳ:) [see عَوْزٌ, in three places:] pl. شُرُفٌ, like بُزْلٌ and دَلُوقٌ, pls. of بَازِلٌ and عَائِذٌ, (Ṣ, O,) or شُرْفٌ, like كُتْبٌ, (Ḳ,) or the latter is allowable in poetry, (O,) or the former is a contraction of the latter, (IAth, TA,) and شَوَارِفُ [also pl. of شَارِفَةٌ] (O, Ḳ) and شُرَّفٌ and شُرُوفٌ: (Ḳ:) it is said that شَارِفٌ is not applied to the he-camel; but it is so applied, as well as to the she-camel, accord. to the Towsheeḥ of El-Jelál. (TA.) Hence, as being likened to black decrepit she-camels, (Aboo-Bekr, TA,) الشُّرُفُ الجُونُ, with two ḍammehs, [which I think a mistake, unless it mean with a ḍammeh to each word,] (Ḳ,) or الشُّرْفُ الجُونُ, (O, IAth, TA,) occurring in a trad., meaning † [*Trials,* or *conflicts and factions,*] *like portions of the dark night:* (O,* Ḳ,* TA:) thus expl. by the Prophet: (O, TA:) but some relate it otherwise, with ق, (Ḳ,) saying الشُّرْقُ الجون, pl. of شَارِقٌ, (O,* TA,) meaning "[trials, &c.,] rising (O, Ḳ, TA) from the direction of the east." (O, TA.) — Also applied to an arrow, as meaning *Old:* (Ṣ, O, Ḳ:) and applied to a garment or a piece of cloth [app. in the same sense]: (A and TA voce طَرِيدٌ:) or an arrow *long since laid by* [expl. by بَعِيدُ العَهْدِ بِالصِّيَابَةِ; but I think that the right reading is بعيد العهد بِالصِّيَانَةِ, and have assumed this to be the case in my rendering]: or *of which the feathers and the sinews* [*wherewith they are bound*] *have become uncompact:* or *slender and long.* (TA.) — دَنٌّ شَارِفٌ [*A wine-jar*] *of which the wine is old.* (TA.) — And شَارِفٌ [alone] *A receptacle for wine, such as a* خَابِيَة *and the like thereof.* (O, Ḳ.)

الشَّارُوفُ *A kind of cord* or *rope;* syn. حَبْلٌ: [so in the O, and in one of my copies of the Ṣ: in my other copy of the Ṣ, and in the Ḳ, جَبَلٌ, i. e. the name of a certain mountain:] a post-classical word. (Ṣ, O.) — And شَارُوفٌ also signifies *A broom:* (Ṣ, O, Ḳ:) a Pers. word, (Ṣ,) arabicized, from جَارُوبْ, (O, Ḳ,) originally جَاىْ رُوبْ, which means "a place-sweeper." (O.)

أَشْرَفُ [*More,* and *most, high, elevated, exalted,* or *eminent, in rank, condition,* or *estimation;* &c.; generally meaning *more,* and *most, high-born* or *noble;* (see شَرِيفٌ;)] *surpassing in* شَرَف. (Ṣ, O.) — مَنْكِبٌ أَشْرَفُ *A high shoulder;* (Ṣ, O, Ḳ;) *such as has a goodly rising;* which implies what is termed إِهْدَآءٌ [inf. n. of أَهْدَأَ, and here app. meaning the "being curved in the back"]. (TA.) And أُذُنٌ شَرْفَآءُ *A long ear;* (Ṣ, O, Ḳ;) *standing up; rising above what is next to it:* and so اذن ▼ شُرَافِيَّةٌ. (TA.) — See also شُرَافِىٌّ. [أَشْرَفُ also signifies *Having a prominent,* or *an apparent, ear:* opposed to أَسَكُّ, q. v. — Hence,] الأَشْرَفُ is an appellation of *The bat;* (O, Ḳ, TA;) because its ears are prominent and apparent: it is bare of downy and other feathers, and is viviparous, not oviparous: so in the saying of Bishr Ibn-El-Moạtemir,

* وَطَائِرٌ أَشْرَفُ ذُو جُرْدَةٍ * وَطَائِرٌ لَيْسَ لَهُ وَكْرُ *

[*And a flying thing that has prominent and apparent ears and a denuded body, and a flying thing that has no nest*]: (O, TA:) in the Ḳ is added, and *another bird, that has no nest,* &c.: but this is taken from an explanation of the latter hemistich of the verse cited above; which explanation is as follows: (TA:) the bird that has no nest is one of which the Baḥránees [so in the TA, but accord. to the O "the sailors,"] tell that it does not alight save while it makes, of the dust, or earth, a place in which it lays its eggs, and which it covers over; then it flies into the air, and its eggs break open of themselves at the expiration of the term thereof; and when its young ones are able to fly, they do after the habit of their parents. (O, L, TA: and the same is said, less fully, in the Ḳ.) — مَدِينَةٌ شَرْفَآءُ *A city having* شُرَف, (Mgh, O, Ḳ,*) pl. of شُرْفَةٌ [q. v.]: (O:) the pl. of أَشْرَفُ, and of شَرْفَآءُ, accord. to rule, is شُرْفٌ. (Mgh. [In the copies of the Ḳ, الشُّرْفُ is erroneously said to be pl. of الشَّرْفَآءُ.]) It is said in a trad. of Ibn-'Abbás, أُمِرْنَا أَنْ نَبْنِىَ المَدَائِنَ شُرْفًا وَالمَسَاجِدَ جُمًّا i. e. *We have been commanded to build cities with* شُرَف *and mosques without* شُرَف. (Mgh, O.*)

أَشْرَافٌ *The ears and nose of a man:* (O, Ḳ, TA:) its sing. in this sense is not mentioned: it is app. ▼ شَرَفٌ; like سَبَبٌ, sing. of أَسْبَابٌ. (TA.)

تَشْرِيفٌ inf. n. of 2 [q. v.]. (Ṣ &c.) — [And also a post-classical term applied to *An honorary present, such as a garment &c.:* and *a letter,* i. e. *an epistle,* considered as conferring honour: pl. تَشْرِيفَاتٌ.]

مَشْرَفٌ: see شَرَفٌ, in the middle of the paragraph: and see also what here next follows.

مُشْرَفٌ, (O, Ḳ,) like مُكْرَمٌ, (Ḳ,) or ▼ مَشْرَفٌ [q. v. voce شَرَفٌ], (so in my two copies of the Ṣ,) *A place from which one overlooks,* i. e. *looks upon,* or *views,* [*a thing*] *from above.* (Ṣ, O, Ḳ.) — Hence the saying in a trad., مَا جَآءَكَ مِنْ هٰذَا المَالِ وَأَنْتَ غَيْرُ مُشْرِفٍ وَلَا سَائِلٍ فَخُذْهُ (O, TA) i. e. [*What comes to thee of this property*] *thou not coveting nor looking for it* [*nor asking it, take it*]. (O.)

مُشْرِفٌ [part. n. of 4;] *High;* (Ṣ, Mgh, Mṣb;)

[or *overtopping*; &c.;] applied to a mountain, (Ṣ,) or a place. (Mgh, Mṣb.)

سُيُوفٌ مَشْرَفِيَّةٌ *Certain swords*, (Ṣ, O, Ḳ,) so called in relation to مَشَارِفُ, (Ṣ,) or in relation to مَشَارِفُ الشَّامِ, (O, Mṣb, Ḳ,) i. e. certain towns, or villages, of the land of the Arabs, near to the رِيف [q. v.]: (Ṣ, O, Mṣb, Ḳ:) so says AO: (Ṣ, O:) or, as some say, this is a mistake, and they are so called in relation to a place of El-Yemen: (Mṣb:) [or, accord. to some, in relation to المَشَارِفُ, certain towns, or villages, near Ḥowrán: (see De Sacy's Chrest. Ar., sec. ed., iii. 53:)] and it is said that مَشْرَف was the name of a blacksmith who made swords: (TA:) one says سَيْفٌ مَشْرَفِىٌّ, (Ṣ, O, Mṣb,) not مَشَارِفِىٌّ, because a rel. n. is not formed from a pl. of the measure of مَشَارِفُ. (Ṣ, O.)

مُشَرَّفٌ [*Elevated*, or *exalted, in rank, condition*, or *estimation*; or *ennobled*]; (Ḳ, TA;) an epithet applied to a man; from الشَّرَفُ. (TA.) ═ Also A garment, or piece of cloth, *dyed with the red clay* or *earth* [&c.] *called* شَرَف. (IAạr, TA.)

مَشْرُوفٌ (Ṣ, TA) and مَشْرُوفٌ عَلَيْهِ (Z, TA) *Overcome*, or *surpassed, in* شَرَف [i. e. *highness, elevation*, or *eminence, of rank, condition*, or *estimation*; or *nobility*]. (Ṣ, Z, TA.)

مُشْتَرِفٌ A horse *high in make.* (Ṣ, O, Ḳ.)

شرق

1. شَرَقَتِ الشَّمْسُ, (Ṣ, M, Mgh, Mṣb, Ḳ,) aor. ُ, (Ṣ, M, Mṣb,) inf. n. شُرُوقٌ (Ṣ, M, Mgh, Mṣb, Ḳ) and شَرْقٌ, (Ṣ, Mṣb,) *The sun rose*; (Ṣ, M, Mgh, Mṣb, Ḳ;) as also ↓ أَشْرَقَتْ: (Ḳ:) *the sun rose from the east*; and in like manner one says of the moon, and of the stars: (M:) or *the sun rose so that its light began to fall upon the earth and trees*: (T and TA in art. ذر:) and ↓ اشرقت signifies, as distinguished from شَرَقَت, (Ṣ, M, Mgh, Mṣb,) or signifies also, (Ḳ, TA,) for both verbs are correctly expl. in the Ḳ as above, (TA,) *it shone*, or *gave its light*, (Ṣ, M, Mgh, Mṣb, Ḳ, TA,) *and spread* (M, TA) *upon the earth*, or *ground*: (TA:) or, as some say, شَرَقَت, and ↓ اشرقت are syn., (M, Mṣb,) as meaning *it* (the sun) *shone*: (M:) and شَرْقٌ [as inf. n. of the former verb] signifies the *shining* of the sun. (Ḳ.) — And شَرَقَ النَّخْلُ, and ↓ اشرق, *The palm-trees showed redness in their fruit*: (M, Ḳ:*) or *showed the colours of their dates.* (AḤn, M.) [See also شَرِقَ in what follows.] ═ شَرَقَ الشَّاةَ, (Ṣ, O, Mṣb, Ḳ,) aor. ُ, (Ṣ, O, Mṣb,) inf. n. شَرْقٌ, *He slit the ear of the sheep*, or *goat*, (Ṣ, O, Mṣb, Ḳ,) *in the manner expl. voce* شَرْقَآءُ. (Mṣb.) — And شَرَقَ الثَّمَرَةَ, (Az, Ḳ,) inf. n. شَرْقٌ, (IAmb, Az, TA,) *He plucked the fruit*: (Az, Ḳ, TA:) or *cut it.* (IAmb, Az, TA.) One says in crying بَاقِلَّآء [or beans], شَرْقُ الغَدَاةِ طَرِىٌّ *The cutting of the morning, fresh!* meaning *what has been cut*, and *picked, in the morning.* (IAmb, Az, TA.) ═ شَرِقَ, [aor. َ,] inf. n. شَرَقٌ, *It* (a place) *was*, or *became, bright by reason of the sun's shining upon it*; as also ↓ اشرق; (M, TA;) [whence,] وَأَشْرَقَتِ ↓ الأَرْضُ بِنُورِ رَبِّهَا occurs in the Ḳur [xxxix. 69 as meaning *And the earth shall shine with the light of its Lord*]: (M:) [in other instances,] أَشْرَقَتِ الأَرْضُ means *The earth was*, or *became, bright with the sunshine.* (TA.) — [Hence, perhaps, or, though not immediately, from what here next follows, some other applications of this verb, to denote redness.] — شَرِقَ بِرِيقِهِ, (Ṣ, M, Mṣb, Ḳ,) and بِالمَآءِ, and the like, (M,) aor. َ, (Mṣb,) inf. n. شَرَقٌ, (M, Mṣb,) *He* (a man, M, Mṣb) *was*, or *became, choked with his spittle*, (Ṣ, M, Mṣb, Ḳ,) and *with water*, &c. (M.) [And جَرِضَ and غَصَّ and شَجِىَ are sometimes used in the same sense in relation to spittle &c.] — [Hence,] شَرِقَ الجُرْحُ بِالدَّمِ † *The wound became* [*choked* or] *filled with blood.* (Mṣb.) — And شَرِقَ المَوْضِعُ بِأَهْلِهِ ‡ *The place became* [*choked* or] *filled and straitened by its occupants.* (TA.) — And شَرِقَ الجَسَدُ بِالطِّيبِ ‡ [*The body became choked in its pores with perfume*]. (TA.) — [And شَرِقَ الثَّوْبُ بِالجَادِىِّ † *The garment*, or *piece of cloth, became glutted*, or *saturated, with* the dye of *saffron*: see the part. n. شَرِقٌ.] — And شَرِقَتْ عَيْنُهُ ‡ *His eye became red* [*being surcharged with blood*]; as also ↓ اِشْرَوْرَقَتْ: (M, TA:) and so شَرِقَ الدَّمُ فِى عَيْنِهِ: (Ḳ, TA:) or this last signifies *the blood appeared in his eye*: (M:) and شَرِقَتْ بِالدَّمِ *it* (the eye) *had the blood apparent in it*, [*as though it were choked therewith*,] *without its running from it.* (TA.) — And شَرِقَ لَوْنُهُ, inf. n. شَرَقٌ, † *His colour*, or *complexion, became red, by reason of shame*, or *shame and confusion.* (TA.) — And [hence, app.,] شَرِقَ الشَّىْءُ, inf. n. as above, † *The thing became intensely red, with blood*, or *with a beautiful red colour.* (M, TA.) — And also † *The thing became mixed, commingled*, or *blended.* (M, TA.) — شَرِقَتِ الشَّمْسُ, inf. n. as above, means ‡ *The sun had a duskiness blended with it, and it* [app. the duskiness] *then became little*: (TA:) or *it was near to setting*: (M, Ḳ:) or *became feeble in its light*; (O, Ḳ;) app. from شَرِقٌ applied to flesh-meat as meaning "red, having no grease, or gravy," and applied to a garment, or piece of cloth, as meaning "red, that has become glutted, or saturated, (شَرِقٌ,) with dye;" because its colour, in the last part of the day, when it is setting, becomes red. (O.) — The phrase يُؤَخِّرُونَ الصَّلَاةَ إِلَى شَرَقِ المَوْتَى, (Ṣ, M, O, Ḳ, [in the CḲ, erroneously, شَرْقِ,]) occurring in a trad., (Ṣ, M, O,) in a saying of the Prophet, (O, Ḳ,) is expl. as meaning *Who postpone*, or *defer, the prayer until there remains not*, (Ṣ, M, O, Ḳ,) *of the sun*, (Ṣ,) or *of the day*, (M, O, Ḳ,) *save as much as remains* (Ṣ, M, O, Ḳ) *of the life*, (Ṣ,) or *of the breath*, (M, O, Ḳ, [but in the CḲ, نَفْسِ is put in the place of نَفَسِ,]) *of the dying who is choked with his spittle*: (Ṣ, M, O, Ḳ:) or the meaning is, *until the sun is* [*but just*] *above the walls, and* [*diffusing its feeble light*] *among the graves* (M, O, Ḳ*) *as though it were a great expanse of water.* (M, O.) AZ says, يُكْرَهُ الصَّلَاةُ بِشَرَقِ المَوْتَى means *Prayer is disapproved when the sun becomes yellow*: and فَعَلْتُ ذٰلِكَ بِشَرَقِ المَوْتَى *I did that when the sun was becoming yellow.* (TA.) ═ شَرِقَتِ الشَّاةُ, (Ṣ, Mṣb, Ḳ,) aor. َ, (Mṣb, Ḳ,) inf. n. شَرَقٌ, (Ṣ, Mṣb,) *The sheep*, or *goat, had its ear slit* (Ṣ, Mṣb, Ḳ) *in the manner expl. voce* شَرْقَآءُ. (Mṣb, Ḳ.)

2. شرّق, (TA,) inf. n. تَشْرِيقٌ, (Ṣ, O, Ḳ,) *He took to the direction of the east*, or *place of sunrise*: (Ṣ, O, Ḳ, TA:) *he went to the east*: *he came to the east*: (M, TA:) and *he directed himself to the east.* (TA.) — And *He prayed at sunrise*: and hence, app., *He performed the prayer of the festival of the sacrifice*: (TA:) or this meaning is from شَرَقَتِ الشَّمْسُ. (Mgh: it is also mentioned in the M.) — شرّقت الأَرْضُ, inf. n. as above, *The land became affected with drought, and dryness of the earth, being* [*parched by the sun and*] *not reached by water*: whence the term ↓ شَرَاقِىّ [q. v.] in the dial. of Egypt. (TA.) — تَشْرِيقٌ also signifies The *being beautiful, and* [*sunny* or] *shining in face.* (Sh, O, Ḳ.) ═ شرّق اللَّحْمَ, (M, Mgh, Mṣb,) inf. n. as above, (Ṣ, M, Mgh, O, Mṣb, Ḳ,) *He cut the flesh-meat into strips, and dried it in the sun*, or *spread it in the sun to dry*: (Ṣ, M, Mgh, O, Mṣb, Ḳ:) or [simply] *he cut it into pieces, and into strips.* (Mṣb.) [In like manner also] تَشْرِيقُ الشَّعِيرِ signifies *The throwing barley in a sunny place in order that it may dry.* (Mgh.) And one says of the [wild] bull, يُشَرِّقُ مَتْنَهُ, meaning *He exposes his back to the sun in order that what is upon it of the dew of night may dry*: in this sense the phrase is used by Aboo-Dhu-eyb. (M.) — أَيَّامُ التَّشْرِيقِ is an appellation of *The three days next after the day of sacrifice*: (Ṣ, M, O, Mṣb:) [i. e. the eleventh and twelfth and thirteenth days of Dhu-l-Ḥijjeh:] these days were so called because the flesh of the victims was therein cut into strips, and dried in the sun, or spread in the sun to dry: (Ṣ, M, Mgh, O, Mṣb, Ḳ:*) or because the victims were not sacrificed until the sun rose: (IAạr, Ṣ, O, Ḳ:) or from the prayer of the day of sacrifice, which they follow: (Mgh:) or because they used to say, [on that day,] (Ṣ, M, O,) in the Time of Ignorance, (M,) أَشْرِقْ ↓ ثَبِيرُ كَيْمَا نُغِيرُ, (Ṣ, M, O,) which means *Enter thou upon the time of sunrise, Thebeer*, (addressing one of the mountains of Mekkeh, M,* Mgh,) *that we may push*, or *press, on*, or *forward*, (M, Mgh, Mṣb,) *to return from Minà*: (M: [see also 4 in art. غور:]) Aboo-Ḥaneefeh used to hold that التَّشْرِيقُ means التَّكْبِيرُ [i. e. *the saying* أَللّٰهُ أَكْبَرُ]; but none beside him has held this opinion. (TA.) It is said in a trad. that the days thus called are days of eating and drinking, and of celebrating the praises of God. (O.) — شرّق الثَّوْبَ † *He made* [or *dyed*] *the garment*, or *piece of cloth, yellow*: (Ibn-'Abbád, O:) [or *he dyed it red*: (see the pass. part. n., below:)] or تَشْرِيقٌ signifies the *dyeing with saffron*, (M, L,) *so that the thing dyed is saturated*, (L,) or *not so that the thing is saturated*: (so in a copy of the M:) it is not with safflower. (M, L.

[See also 4, last signification.]) ═ شَرَقَ الحَوْضَ is sometimes said for صَرَّجَهُ, meaning *He plastered the watering-trough*, or *tank*, *with* شَارُوق [q. v.], or صَارُوج. (M in art. صرج.)

4. اشرق: see 1, in six places. One says also, اشرق وَجْهُهُ, (Ṣ,) and لَوْنُهُ, (M,) *His face*, (Ṣ,) and *his colour*, or *complexion*, (M,) *shone*, (Ṣ, M,) *and was bright, with beauty*. (Ṣ.) — Some allow its being made trans.; [meaning *It caused*, or *made, to shine*;] as in the saying,

• ثَلَاثَةٌ تُشْرِقُ الدُّنْيَا بِبَهْجَتِهَا •
• شَمْسُ الضُّحَى وَأَبُو إِسْحَاقَ وَالقَمَرُ •

[There are *three things, with the beauty of which the world is made to shine; the sun of the bright early morning, and Aboo-Is-ḥáḳ, and the moon*]: but there is no proof in this, because [the right reading may be تَشْرُقُ, and so] الدنيا may be an agent; therefore the making the verb trans. [in this sense] is said to be post-classical, though it is mentioned by the author of the Ksh. (MF, TA.) — It signifies also *He entered upon the time of sunrise*: (Ṣ, M, Mgh, Mṣb, Ḳ:) similarly to أَفْجَرَ, and أَصْبَحَ, and أَظْهَرَ. (TA.) See 2. ═ اشرق عَدُوَّهُ *He caused his enemy to become choked* [with his spittle, or with water, or the like: see 1]. (O, Ḳ.) And أَشْرَقْتُ فُلَانًا بِرِيقِهِ ‡ [*I choked the utterance*, or *impeded the action*, *of such a one*;] *I did not allow such a one to say, or to do, a thing*. (Z, TA.) — اشرق الثَّوْبَ بِالصِّبْغِ, (Moḥeeṭ, A, O,) or فِى الصِّبْغِ, (Ḳ,) ‡ *He exceeded the usual degree in dyeing the garment*, or *piece of cloth*; [*saturated it with dye*;] or *dyed it thoroughly*. (Ḳ, TA. [See also 2, last signification but one.])

5. تشرّق *He sat in a sunny place* (Ṣ, O, Ḳ) [*at any season*, (see مَشْرُقَةٌ,) or particularly] *in winter*. (O, Ḳ.) — And تشرّقوا *They looked through the* مِشْرِيق *of the door*, i. e. *the chink thereof into which the light of the rising sun falls*. (O.)

7. انشرقت القَوْسُ *The bow split*. (Ibn-'Abbád, O, Ḳ.)

12. اِشْرَوْرَقَتْ عَيْنُهُ: see 1, latter half. — اِشْرَوْرَقَ بِالدَّمْعِ ‡ *He became drowned in tears*. (Ibn-'Abbád, O, Ḳ, TA.)

شَرْقٌ [an inf. n.: see 1, first sentence. — Also] *The sun*; (Ṣ, O, Ḳ;) and so ▼ شَرْقٌ: (Ḳ, and thus in one of my copies of the Ṣ in the place of the former:) [or] ▼ شَرْقَةٌ has this signification: (M, Mṣb:) and شَرْقٌ signifies the *rising sun*; (M, TA;) as some say; (M;) thus accord. to AA and IAạr; (TA;) and so ▼ شَرِقٌ, (M, Mṣb,) and ▼ شَرْقَةٌ, and ▼ شَرَقَةٌ, (M, Ḳ,) and ▼ شَرِقَةٌ, (TA,) and ▼ شَارِقٌ, (Ṣ,* M, Ḳ,) and ▼ شَرِيقٌ: (M, Ḳ:) one says, طَلَعَتِ الشَّرْقُ *The sun rose*; (Ṣ, M, O; in one of my copies of the Ṣ ▼ الشَّرَقُ;) but not غَرَبَتِ الشَّرْقُ: (M:) and ▼ آتِيكَ كُلَّ شَارِقٍ *I will come to thee every day that the sun rises*: or, as some say, شَارِقٌ signifies the *upper limb* (قَرْن) *of the sun*: (M:) and one says, لَا آتِيكَ مَا ذَرَّ شَارِقٌ [*I will not come to thee as long as a sun*, or *the upper limb of a sun*, *rises*, or *begins to rise*]. (Ṣ, M.) — See also مَشْرُقٌ, in three places. — Also *A place where the sun shines* (حَيْثُ تُشْرِقُ الشَّمْسُ). (Ḳ.) See مَشْرُقَةٌ. — The *warmth* of the sun. (TA.) — The *light that enters from the chink of a door*; (IAạr, Th, Ḳ;) as also ▼ شَرَقٌ. (Ḳ.) In a trad. of I'Ab, (TA,) it is said of a gate in Heaven, called ▼ المَشْرِقُ [q. v.], قَدْ رُدَّ حَتَّى مَا بَقِىَ إِلَّا شَرْقُهُ (O, Ḳ, TA) i. e. *It had been closed so that there remained not save its light entering from the chink thereof*: so says I'Ab. (O, TA.) — And *A chink*, or *fissure*. (Ḳ, TA.) One says, مَا دَخَلَ شَرْقَ فِيَّ شَىْءٌ *Nothing entered the chink of my mouth*. (Z, TA.) ═ Also *A certain bird*, (Sh, M, Ḳ,) *one of the birds of prey*, (M,) *between the kite and the hawk*, or *falcon*, (Sh, Ḳ,) or *between the kite and the* [*species of falcon called*] شَاهِين [q. v.]: (O:) pl. شُرُوقٌ. (M.)

شَرْقٌ: see the next preceding paragraph.

شَرَقٌ [inf. n. of شَرِقَ, q. v. — And also a subst.]: see شَرْقٌ, in three places. — Also *A thing* [*such as spittle* and *the like* (see شَرِقَ)] *obstructing*, or *choking, the throat*, or *fauces*. (Ṣ, and Ḥar p. 477.)

شَرِقٌ A place *bright by reason of the sun's shining upon it*; as also ▼ مُشْرِقٌ. (M, TA.) — A man *choked* with his spittle, or with water, or the like. (M, TA.) — † A plant, or herbage, *having plentiful irrigation*; or *flourishing and fresh*, or *juicy*, *by reason of plentiful irrigation*; syn. رَيَّانُ. (TA.) — † A garment, or piece of cloth, *red*; *that is glutted*, or *saturated*, [so I render شَرِقٌ بِالجَادِىِّ,] *with dye*: (O:) and الَّذِى شَرِقَ applied to a garment, or piece of cloth, [app. signifies † *glutted*, or *saturated*, *with* the dye of *saffron*: see also مُشْرَقٌ, and see 4.] (TA.) One says also صَرِيعٌ شَرِقٌ بِدَمِهِ † [*Prostrated*,] *dyed with his blood*. (M, TA.) — ‡ Flesh-meat (Ṣ, M, O, TA) that is *red*, (M, O, TA,) *having no grease*, or *gravy*. (Ṣ, M, O, TA.) — † A thing *intensely red*, *with blood*, or *with a beautiful red colour*. (M.) — And † A thing *mixed*, *commingled*, or *blended*. (M.)

شَرْقَةٌ: see شَرْقٌ, in two places: — and see مَشْرُقَةٌ, in two places.

شَرْقَةٌ † *Anxiety, grief*, or *anguish*; syn. in Pers. أَنْدُوه. (KL.)

شَرَقَةٌ: see شَرْقٌ: — and see مَشْرُقَةٌ. ═ Also *A brand with which a sheep, or goat, such as is termed* شَرْقَآءُ, *is marked*. (O, Ḳ.)

شَرِقَةٌ: see شَرْقٌ.

شَاةٌ شَرْقَآءُ *A sheep, or goat, having its ear slit* (Ṣ, Mgh, O, Ḳ) *lengthwise*, (Ḳ,) *without its being separated*: (TA:) or *having the ear slit in two*, (Aṣ, Mṣb, TA,) *as though it were a* زَنَمَة [q. v.]: (Aṣ, TA:) or شَرْقَآءُ applied to an ear signifies *cut at its extremities, without having anything thereof separated*: and applied to a she-goat (مَعْزَة), *having its ear slit lengthwise, without its being separated*: and, as some say, applied to a شَاة, *having the inner part of its ear slit on one side with a separating slitting, the middle of its ear being left sound*: or, accord. to Aboo-'Alee in the "Tedhkireh," شَرْقَآءُ signifies *having its ears slit with two slits passing through, so as to become three distinct pieces*. (M.)

شَرْقِىٌّ [*Of*, or *relating to*, *the east*, or *place of sunrise*; *eastern*, or *oriental*]. — لَا شَرْقِيَّةٍ وَلَا غَرْبِيَّةٍ, (Ḳ, TA,) in the Ḳur [xxiv. 35], (TA,) means *Not such that the sun shines upon it at its rising only* (Fr, Ḳ, TA) *nor at its setting only*, (Fr, TA,) *but such that the sun lights upon it morning and evening*: (Fr, Ḳ, TA:) or, accord. to El-Ḥasan, it means *not of the trees of the people of the present world, but of the trees of the people of Paradise*: Az, however, says that the former explanation is more fit and more commonly received. (TA.) And مَكَانٌ شَرْقِىٌّ signifies *A place, of the earth*, or *ground*, *in*, or *upon*, *which the sun rises*, or *shines*. (TA.) See also شَارِقٌ [and شَرْقٌ and مَشْرُقَةٌ]. ═ Also *A certain red dye*. (TA.)

شَرِيقٌ: see شَرْقٌ. — Also A boy, or young man, *goodly*, or *beautiful*, (Ḳ, TA,) *in face*: (TA:) pl. شُرُقٌ, (Ḳ, TA, [in the CḲ شَرْقٌ, but correctly]) with two ḍammehs. (TA.) — And A woman *small in the vulva*: (Ibn-'Abbád, O, Ḳ:) or *having her vagina and rectum united by the rending of the separation between them*; syn. مُفْضَاةٌ. (M, Ḳ.) — And الشَّرِيقُ is the name of *A certain idol*. (M, TA.)

[شُرَيْقَةٌ The *first part of the rising sun*. (Freytag, from the Deewán of the Hudhalees.) See also شَارِقٌ, voce شَرْقٌ.]

شَرَاقِىٌّ [The *lands that are not reached by the water*, or *inundation*, *and that are consequently parched by the sun*]: a word of the dial. of Egypt. (TA.) See 2.

شَارِقٌ: see شَرْقٌ, in two places. — Also The *side that is next the east*; (O;) the *eastern side*; (Ḳ;) of a hill, and of a mountain: you say, هٰذَا شَارِقُ الجَبَلِ and ▼ شَرْقِيُّهُ [*This is the eastern side of the mountain*], and هٰذَا غَارِبُ الجَبَلِ and غَرْبِيُّهُ [in the opposite sense]: (TA:) pl. شُرُقٌ. (O, Ḳ.) Hence, in a trad., as some relate it, الشُّرُقُ الجُونُ [meaning † *Trials*, or *conflicts and factions*, *like portions of the dark night, rising from the direction of the east*]: but it is otherwise related, with ف [in the place of the ق: see شَارِفٌ]. (TA.) — And الشَّارِقُ is the name of *A certain idol*, *of the Time of Ignorance*; (IDrd, M, Ḳ;) whence عَبْدُ الشَّارِقِ, a proper name [of a man]. (IDrd, M.) ═ Also [if not a mistranscription for شَارُوقٌ, q. v., app. *Clay*, or *some other substance or mixture, with which a place is plastered,]* مَا يُطَيَّنُ بِهِ مَكَانٌ. (Ibn-'Abbád, O.)

شَارُوقٌ signifies [The *kind of plaster called*] جِلْسٌ, [q. v.,] (Kr, M,) *i. q.* صَارُوجٌ. (Ḳ. [See this last word: and see also the last sentence of the next preceding paragraph above.])

مَشْرَقٌ: see what next follows.

مَشْرِقٌ (Ṣ, M, O, Mṣb, Ḳ,) which by rule should be ▼ مَشْرَقٌ, (M, Mṣb,) but this latter is rarely used, (Mṣb,) The *place,* (M,) or *quarter,* or *direction,* (Mṣb,) *of sunrise;* (M, Mṣb;) [the *east,* or *orient;*] and ▼ شَرْقٌ signifies the same; (Ṣ, M, O, Mṣb, Ḳ;) as also ▼ مُشْرِيقٌ: (Seer, M:) the pl. of the first is مَشَارِقُ; and the pl. of ▼ شَرْقٌ is أَشْرَاقٌ. (M.) The dual, المَشْرِقَانِ, means *The place of sunrise of summer and that of winter* [E. 26° N. and E. 26° S. in Central Arabia]. (Ṣ, O, TA.) And also *The place of sunrise and the place of sunset;* [or *the east and the west;*] (M, O;) the former being thus made predominant because it denotes existence, whereas the latter denotes non-existence: (M:) thus in the saying, (M, O,) in the Ḳur [xliii. 37], (O,) يَا لَيْتَ بَيْنِى وَبَيْنَكَ بُعْدَ ٱلْمَشْرِقَيْنِ [*O, would that between me and thee were the distance of the east and the west*]. (M, O.) And [in like manner] one says ▼ مَا بَيْنَ الشَّرْقَيْنِ, meaning *What is between the place of sunrise and the place of sunset.* (M.) — See also مَشْرُقَةٌ. — The saying, cited by IAạr,

* قُلْتُ لِسَعْدٍ وَهُوَ بِالأَزَارِقِ *
* عَلَيْكَ بِالْمَحْضِ وَبِالْمَشَارِقِ *

he explains as meaning [*I said to Saad, he being at El-Azárik* (a certain water in the بَادِيَة, TA in art. زرق)], *Keep thou* [*to pure milk, and*] *to the sun* [or *the places of sunshine*] *in winter:* but [ISd says,] in my opinion, المَشَارِق is here pl. of ▼ مُشَرَّقٌ applied to flesh-meat that is "[cut into strips and] spread in the sun [to dry];" and this is confirmed by his saying بالمحض, each of them being food. (M.)

مُشْرِقٌ: see شَرْقٌ. — Also *Entering upon the time of sunrise:* the pl. occurs in this sense in the Ḳur xv. 73 and xxvi. 60. (TA.)

مَشْرُقَةٌ and مَشْرَقَةٌ (Ṣ, M, O, Ḳ) and مَشْرِقَةٌ, (M, O, Ḳ,) the last mentioned by Ks, (O,) *A place of sitting in the sun;* (Ṣ, O, Ḳ;) accord. to some, peculiarly, (TA,) *in the winter;* (O, Ḳ, TA;) and ▼ شَرْقَةٌ and ▼ مِشْرَاقٌ (Ṣ, O, Ḳ) and ▼ مُشْرِيقٌ (O, Ḳ) signify the same: (Ṣ, O, Ḳ:) or *a place upon which the sun shines;* accord. to some, peculiarly, *in the winter,* (M,) as also ▼ شَرْقَةٌ and ▼ شَرَقَةٌ (M, TA) and ▼ شَرْقٌ (M) and مشرق [app. ▼ مَشْرِقٌ, of the pl. of which, or of one of the first three words in this paragraph, see an ex. in a verse cited voce مَشْرِقٌ if the explanation of that verse by IAạr be correct]. (TA.)

مَشْرِقِيٌّ (Mṣb, TA) and مَشْرَقِيٌّ both [applied to a man] signify *Of the east;* or *eastern:* (Mṣb:) pl. مَشَارِقَةٌ. (TA.)

مُشَرَّقٌ *A place of prayer;* syn. مُصَلًّى; (Aṣ, Ṣ, M, Mgh, Ḳ;) i. e., in an absolute sense: (TA:) or the *place of prayer of the festival* (العِيد): (TA:) or the *place of prayer of the two festivals:* and المُشَرَّقُ is said to mean *the place of prayer of the festival at Mekkeh:* (M, TA:) and *the mosque of El-Kheyf.* (Ṣ, Ḳ.) — And The *festival* (العيد) [itself]: because the prayer thereon is after the شَرْقَة, i. e. the [rising] sun. (M.) — Also Flesh-meat [*cut into strips and*] *spread in the sun* [to dry: see its verb, 2]. (M.) See also مَشْرِقٌ, last sentence. — And A garment, or piece of cloth, [*dyed yellow:* or *with saffron:* see, again, its verb: or] *dyed with a red colour.* (O, Ḳ.) — And a fortress [or a watering-trough or tank (see 2, last sentence,)] *plastered with* شَارُوق. (O, Ḳ.)

مُشَرِّقٌ *Taking to the direction of the east,* or *place of sunrise:* one says, شَتَّانَ بَيْنَ مُشَرِّقٍ وَمُغَرِّبٍ [*Different,* or *widely different, are one going towards the east and one going towards the west*]. (Ṣ.)

مِشْرَاقٌ: see مَشْرُقَةٌ. — Also A man *accustomed to make his enemy to be choked with his spittle.* (Z, TA.)

مُشْرِيقٌ: see مَشْرِقٌ: — and مَشْرُقَةٌ. — Also, (M, O, Ḳ,) of a door, (M, Ḳ,) *A chink into which the light of the rising sun falls.* (M,* O, Ḳ.*) — And المُشْرِيقُ is the name of *A gate for repentance, in Heaven.* (I'Ab, O, Ḳ.) See شَرْقٌ.

شرقرق

شِرِقْرَاقٌ and its vars.: see art. شقرق.

شرك

1. شَرِكَهُ فِيهِ, aor. ـَ, inf. n. شِرْكَةٌ (Ṣ, Mgh,* Mṣb, Ḳ) and شَرِكَةٌ, the former a contraction of the latter, but the more usual, (Mṣb,) and شِرْكٌ (Mgh, Mṣb) and شَرِكٌ, the former of these two a contraction of the latter, but the more usual, (Mṣb,) or شِرْكٌ [q. v. infrà] is a simple subst., (Ṣ, Ḳ,) [*He shared, participated,* or *partook, with him in it;*] *he was,* or *became, a* شَرِيك [or *copartner* &c.] *to him in it;* (Mṣb;) namely, a sale or purchase, and an inheritance, (Ṣ, Ḳ,) or an affair; (Mṣb;) and ▼ شاركه فيه [signifies the same]. (Mgh, Mṣb,* Ḳ.* [It is said in the TA, after the mention of شَرِكَهُ with its inf. n. شِرْكَةٌ, that it is more chaste than ▼ اشركه; by which it is implied that this latter is sometimes used as syn. with the former; for which I do not find any express authority.] And *He entered with him into it;* [or *engaged with him in it;*] namely, an affair. (TA.) — شَرِكَتِ النَّعْلُ, aor. ـَ, *The sandal had its* شِرَاك *broken;* (Ibn-Buzurj, Ḳ;) inf. n. شَرَكٌ. (TḲ.)

2: see 4. — [The inf. n.] تَشْرِيكٌ also signifies The *selling a part* [or *share*] *of what one has purchased for that for which it was purchased.* (Mgh, Ḳ.) — شَرَّكَ النَّعْلَ, (Ṣ,* Mgh, Mṣb, Ḳ,) inf. n. تَشْرِيكٌ, (Ṣ, Ḳ,) *He put a* شِرَاك *to the sandal;* (Ṣ, Mgh, Mṣb, Ḳ;) as also ▼ أَشْرَكَهَا, (Ṣ, TA,) inf. n. إِشْرَاكٌ. (TA.)

3. شَارَكْتُ فُلَانًا, (Ṣ, TA,) inf. n. مُشَارَكَةٌ, (TḲ,) [*I shared, participated,* or *partook, with such a one;*] *I was,* or *became, the* شَرِيك [or *copartner* &c.] *of such a one.* (Ṣ, TA.) El-Jaadee says,

* وَشَارَكْنَا قُرَيْشًا فِى تُقَاهَا *
* وَفِى أَحْسَابِهَا شِرْكَ ▼ العِنَانِ *

[*And we shared with Kureysh in their piety and in their several grounds of pretension to respect, with a sharing exclusive of other properties*]. (Ṣ.) See also 1. [And see 8.]

4. أَشْرَكْتُهُ فِى الأَمْرِ *I made him a* شَرِيك [or *copartner* &c.] *to me in the affair:* and ▼ شَرَّكْتُ بَيْنَهُمْ فِى المَالِ [*I made them copartners in the property;* and شَرَّكَهُمْ, occurring in this art. in the TA, on the authority of Esh-Sháfi'ee, means, in like manner, *he made them copartners;* and أَشْرَكَ بَيْنَهُمْ is used in this sense in the present art. in the Ḳ]. (Mṣb.) وَأَشْرِكْهُ فِى أَمْرِى, in the Ḳur [xx. 33], means *And make Thou him my* شَرِيك [or *copartner,* or *associate,* or *colleague,*] *in my affair.* (Ṣ.) And one says also, اشركهُ مَعَهُ فِى الأَمْرِ *He made him to enter* [or *engage*] *with him in the affair:* and اشرك فُلَانًا فِى البَيْعِ *He made such a one to enter* [or *share*] *with him in the sale or purchase.* (TA.) — [Hence,] اشرك بِٱللّٰهِ *He attributed to God a* شَرِيك [or *copartner* &c.] (Mgh, TA) *in his dominion:* (TA:) [or *he attributed to God* شُرَكَآء i. e. *copartners* &c., such as the angels and the devils: (see Ḳur vi. 100, &c., and any of the expositions thereof:) i. e. *he believed in a duality,* or *a plurality, of gods:*] and [in a wider sense,] *he disbelieved* [or *misbelieved*] *in God:* syn. كَفَرَ: (Ṣ,* Mṣb, Ḳ, TA:) used in this latter sense because الكُفْرُ is not free from some kind of شِرْك. (Kull p. 49.) — See also 1: — and 2.

6: see the next paragraph, in three places.

8. اشتركوا and ▼ تشاركوا, (Mgh, Mṣb,) and اشتركا and ▼ تشاركا, (Ḳ,) and اشتركنا and ▼ تشاركنا, (Ṣ,) [*They,* and *they two,* and *we, shared, participated,* or *partook, one with another,* and *each with the other;* or *were,* or *became, copartners,* &c.;] فِى كَذَا [*in such a thing*]. (Ṣ.) — [Hence,] الاِشْتِرَاكُ in lexicology signifies *The being homonymous;* lit. *the being shared,* or *participated,* in by several meanings: [used as a subst., *homonymy:*] (Mz, 25th نوع; and Intr. to the TA:) one says of a noun [or word] that is termed مُشْتَرَكٌ [q. v.], تَشْتَرِكُ فِيهِ مَعَانٍ كَثِيرَةٌ [*Many meanings share, or participate, in it*]. (TA.) — And اشترك الأَمْرُ † *The affair,* or *case, was,* or *became, confused,* and *dubious.* (TA.)

شَرْكٌ: see what next follows.

شِرْكٌ is an inf. n. of شَرِكَهُ, as mentioned in the

first sentence of this art.: (Mgh, Msb:) or a subst. therefrom: (Ṣ:) and is *syn. with* ↑ شِرْكَةٌ, [signifying *A sharing, participating* or *participation, partaking,* or *copartnership,* and mentioned before as an inf. n.,] (Ḳ,) as also are ↑ شَرِكٌ and ↑ شِرْكَةٌ, [likewise mentioned before as inf. ns.,] and ↑ شَرْكٌ and ↑ شَرْكَةٌ, (MF, TA,) and so is ↑ شُرْكَةٌ, with damm, (Ḳ,) this last said by MF to be unknown, but it is common in Syria, almost to the exclusion of the other dial. vars. mentioned above. (TA.) An ex. of the first occurs in a trad. of Mo'ádh, أَجَازَ بَيْنَ أَهْلِ الْيَمَنِ الشِّرْكَ, meaning [*He allowed, among the people of El-Yemen,*] *the sharing, one with another,* (الإِشْتِرَاك,) *in land* [and app. *its produce*], *by its owner giving it to another for the half* [app. *of its produce*], or *the third,* or *the like thereof:* and a similar ex. of the same word occurs in another trad. (TA.) See also an ex. in a verse cited above, conj. 3. And one says, رَغِبْنَا فِى شِرْكِكُمْ, meaning *We are desirous of sharing with you in affinity,* or *relationship by marriage.* (Ḳ,* TA.) — And *A share:* (Mgh, O, Msb, TA:) as in the saying, بِيعَ شِرْكٌ مِنْ دَارِهِ [*A share of his house was sold*]: (Mgh:) and as in the saying, أَعْتَقَ شِرْكًا لَهُ فِى عَبْدٍ [*He emancipated a share belonging to him in a slave*]: (Msb:) pl. أَشْرَاكٌ. (O, Msb, TA.) [See a verse of Lebeed cited voce زَعَامَةٌ.] — It is also a subst. from أَشْرَكَ بِاللّٰهِ; (Mgh, Msb, Ḳ, TA;) thus in the Ḳur xxxi. 12; (Mgh, TA;) meaning The *attribution of a* شَرِيك [or *copartner* &c., or *of* شُرَكَآء i. e. *copartners* &c., (see 4,)] *to God:* (Mgh:) [so that it may be rendered *belief in a plurality of gods:*] and [in a wider sense,] *unbelief* [or *misbelief*]; syn. كُفْر. (Ṣ, Msb, Ḳ, TA.) And it is also expl. as meaning *Hypocrisy:* (Mgh, TA:) so in the saying of the Prophet, إِنَّ أَخْوَفَ مَا أَخَافُ عَلَى أُمَّتِى الشِّرْكُ [*Verily the most fearful of what I fear for my people is hypocrisy*]: (Mgh:) and so in the trad., الشِّرْكُ أَخْفَى فِى أُمَّتِى مِنْ دَبِيبِ النَّمْلِ [*Hypocrisy is more latent in my people than the creeping of ants*]. (IAth, TA.) — See also شَرِيكٌ, in two places.

شَرَكٌ The حِبَالَة [properly a sing., meaning *snare,* but here app. used as a gen. n., meaning *snares,* as will be seen from what follows,] *of the* صَائِد [i. e. *sportsman,* or *catcher of game,* or *wild animals,* or *birds*]; one of which is called ↑ شَرَكَةٌ: (Ṣ, O:) the meaning of the شَرَك of the صَائِد is well known; and the pl. is أَشْرَاكٌ; like سَبَبٌ and أَسْبَابٌ: or, as some say, شَرَكٌ is the pl. of ↑ شَرَكَةٌ, [or rather is a coll. gen. n. of which ↑ شَرَكَةٌ is the n. un.,] like قَصَبٌ and قَصَبَةٌ: (Msb:) [i. e.,] شَرَكٌ signifies the حَبَائِل [or *snares,* or by this may perhaps be meant the *cords composing a snare,* for حَبَائِل is an anomalous pl. of حِبَالَة,] *for catching wild animals or the like;* and *what is,* or *are, set up for* [catching] *birds:* (Ḳ, TA:) one whereof is said to be called ↑ شَرَكَةٌ [a term used in the Ḳ, in art. شبك, as the explanation of شَبَكَةٌ, which means *a net*]: (TA:) and the pl. of شَرَكٌ is شُرُكٌ, with two dammehs, which is extr. [with respect to analogy, like فُلُكٌ pl. of فَلَكٌ]. (Ḳ.) Hence the trad., أَعُوذُ بِكَ مِنْ شَرِّ الشَّيْطَانِ وَشَرَكِهِ, meaning حَبَائِلِهِ وَمَصَايِدِهِ [i. e. *I seek protection by Thee from the mischief of the Devil, and his snares*]. (TA.) — شَرَكُ الطَّرِيقِ means *The main and middle parts of the road;* (Ṣ, Ḳ;) syn. جَوَادُّهُ: or *the tracks that are* [*conspicuous and distinct,*] *not obscure to one nor blended together:* (Ḳ:) pl. [or rather coll. gen. n.] of ↑ شَرَكَةٌ: (Ṣ:) or *the* أَنْسَاع *of the road;* (Aṣ, TA;) i. e. *the furrows of the road, made by the beasts with their legs* [or *feet*] *in its surface, a* ↑ شَرَكَة *here and another by the side of it:* (TA:) or أَشْرَاكٌ [is its pl., and] signifies the *small tracks that branch off* from the main road *and then stop,* or *terminate.* (Sh, TA.) [See أُسٌّ.]

شَرْكٌ: }
شَرْكَةٌ: } see شِرْكٌ, first sentence.
شُرْكَةٌ: }

شِرْكَةٌ: see شِرْكٌ, first sentence. — Also *A piece of flesh-meat;* of the dial. of El-Yemen; originally, *of a slaughtered camel, in which people share, one with another.* (TA.)

شَرَكَةٌ: see شَرَكٌ, in six places.

شَرِكَةٌ: see شِرْكٌ, first sentence.

شُرَكِىٌّ and شُرُكِىٌّ A *quick,* or *swift,* pace: (Ḳ:) so says ISd. (TA.) And لَطْمٌ شُرَكِىٌّ *A quick and consecutive slapping,* (Ṣ, O, Ḳ,) like the camel's slapping when a thorn has entered his foot and he beats the ground with it with a consecutive beating. (Ṣ,* O.) Ows Ibn-Hajar says,

• وَمَا أَنَا إِلَّا مُسْتَعِدٌّ كَمَا تَرَى •
• أَخُو شُرَكِىِّ الوِرْدِ غَيْرُ مُعَتِّمِ •

[*And I am none other than one who is ready, as thou seest; one in the habit of quick and consecutive coming to water; not one who is dilatory*]: i. e., *one coming to water time after time, consecutively:* he means, I will do to thee what thou dislikest, not delaying to do that. (Ṣ.)

شِرَاكٌ The *thong,* or *strap, of the sandal,* (Mgh, Msb, Ḳ, TA,) *that is on the face thereof,* (TA,) *upon the back* [meaning *upper side*] *of the foot,* (Mgh, Msb,) [*extending from the thong,* or *strap, that passes between two of the toes, towards the ankle, and having two arms* (its عَضُدَانِ), *which are attached to the* أُذُنَانِ (q. v.), or *pass through these and unite behind the foot:* see also حِزَامَةٌ, and قُرْصَةٌ, whence it appears to mean also *each arm,* and the *two arms, of the* شِرَاك *properly so called:* and see سَيْرٌ, where it appears to be used as meaning *a thong* or *strap,* absolutely:] the شِرَاك of the sandal is well known: (O:) pl. شُرُكٌ, (O, Ḳ, TA,) and accord. to the Ḳ أَشْرُكٌ also, but this is a mistake. (TA.) To this is likened, in a trad., the shadow at the base of a wall, on the eastern side thereof, when very small [or narrow], showing that the sun has begun to decline from the meridian. (Mgh, Msb,) — [Hence,] † *A streak of herbage:* (Ṣ, O, Ḳ:) pl. شُرُكٌ, (Ṣ, O, TA,) expl. by AHn as meaning *herbage in streaks; not continuous.* (TA.) One says, الكَلَأُ فِى بَنِى فُلَانٍ شُرُكٌ † *The herbage among the sons of such a one is composed of streaks.* (Aboo-Nasr, Ṣ, O.) — [In the Ḳ voce بَتِّق it is used as meaning † *A row* of shoots, or offsets, cut from palm-trees and planted, such as are termed, when planted, مُبَتَّق and مُنَبَّق.] — [Hence,] one says, مَضَوْا عَلَى شِرَاكٍ وَاحِدٍ ‡ [*They went away in one uniform line or manner*]. (TA.) And اِجْعَلِ الأَمْرَ شِرَاكًا وَاحِدًا † *Make thou the affair,* or *case,* [*uniform,* or] *one uniform thing.* (Fr, TA in art. بأج.)

شَرِيكٌ act. part. n. of شَرِكَهُ; (Mgh;) *i. q.* ↑ مُشَارِكٌ [*A sharer, participator, partaker,* or *partner, with another; a copartner, an associate,* or *a colleague,* of another]; (Ḳ;) and ↑ شِرْكٌ signifies the same: (Az, Ḳ, TA:) *a sharer in what is not divided:* (Ḳ and TḲ in art. خلط:) or *a sharer in the rights of a thing that is sold:* (Mgh in that art.:) pl. شُرَكَآءُ and أَشْرَاكٌ, (Ṣ, O, Msb, Ḳ, TA,) like شُرَفَآءُ and أَشْرَافٌ pls. of شَرِيفٌ; (Ṣ, O, TA;) or the latter is pl. of ↑ شِرْكٌ: (Az, TA:) a woman is termed شَرِيكَةٌ; (Ṣ, O, Ḳ;) which is applied to a man's جَارَة [i. e. *wife,* or *object of love*]; (TA;) and the pl. of this is شَرَائِكُ. (Ṣ, O, Ḳ.) Az mentions his having heard one of the Arabs say, فُلَانٌ شَرِيكُ فُلَانٍ meaning *Such a one is married to the daughter,* or *to the sister, of such a one;* what people call *the* خَتَن [*of such a one*]. (TA.)

مُشْرِكٌ and ↑ مُشْرِكِىٌّ, (Ṣ, O, Ḳ,) like as one says دَوٌّ and دَوِّىٌّ, and قَعْسَرٌ and قَعْسَرِىٌّ, (Ṣ, O,) One *who attributes to God a* شَرِيك [or *copartner* &c., or شُرَكَآء i. e. *copartners* &c. (see 4)]: (O:) [i. e. *a believer in a duality,* or *a plurality, of gods:*] and [in a wider sense,] *a disbeliever* [or *misbeliever*] *in God.* (Ṣ, O, Ḳ.) Abu-l-'Abbás explains [the pl.] مُشْرِكُونَ in the Ḳur xvi. 102 as meaning Those *who are* مشركون *by their obeying the Devil; by their worshipping God and worshipping with Him the Devil.* (TA.) — [In one place, in the CḲ, the former word is erroneously put for مُشْتَرَك, q. v., last sentence.]

مُشْرِكِىٌّ: see the next preceding paragraph.

المَسْأَلَةُ المُشَرَّكَةُ, (O, Ḳ, TA,) or الفَرِيضَةُ المُشَرَّكَةُ, (Msb,) for المُشَرَّكُ فِيهَا, (Msb, TA,) is *That* [*assigned portion of inheritance,* or *the question relating thereto* (المَسْأَلَةُ المُشَرَّكَةُ being for مَسْأَلَةُ الفَرِيضَةِ المُشَرَّكَةِ),] *in which the brothers by the mother's side* [*only*] *and those by* [*both*] *the father's and the mother's sides are made to share together;* (O, Msb,* Ḳ, TA;) also called ↑ المُشَرِّكَةُ [*that makes to share*], tropically;

(Mṣb;) and called also ▼ المُشْتَرَكَةُ [for المُشْتَرَكُ فِيهَا i. e. *that is shared in*]: (Lth, Ḳ, TA:) this is the case of a husband and a mother and brothers by the mother's side and brothers by the father's and mother's sides: (O, Ḳ, TA:) for the wife is half; and for the mother, a sixth; and for the brothers by the mother's side, a third, and the brothers by the father's and mother's sides share with them: (O, TA:) 'Omar decided in a case of this kind by assigning the third to two brothers by the mother's side, and not assigning anything to the brothers by the father's and mother's sides; whereupon they said, يَا أَمِيرَ المُؤْمِنِينَ هَبْ أَنَّ أَبَانَا كَانَ حِمَارًا فَأَشْرِكْنَا بِقَرَابَةِ أُمِّنَا [*O Prince of the Believers, suppose that our father was an ass, and make us to share by reason of the relationship of our mother*]: *so he made them to share together* (فَأَشْرَكَ بَيْنَهُمْ [thus in the O and Ḳ, but correctly فَشَرَّكَ بينهم, or, as afterwards in the TA, فَشَرَّكَهُمْ]): (O, Ḳ, TA:) therefore it (i. e. the فَرِيضَة, TA) was called مُشَرَّكَة [and مُشْرِكَة] and مُشْتَرَكَة, [in the CḲ, erroneously, مُشْرَكَة,] and also حِمَارِيَّة: (Ḳ, TA:) and it is also called حَجَرِيَّة, because it is related that they said, هَبْ أَنَّ أَبَانَا كَانَ حَجَرًا مُلْقًى فِى اليَمِّ [*suppose that our father was a stone thrown into the sea*]; and [therefore] some called it يَمِّيَّة: and it was called also عُمَرِيَّة. (TA. [More is there added, explaining different decisions of this case.])

المُشْتَرَكَةُ: see the next preceding paragraph.

مُشَارِكٌ: see شَرِيكٌ. — رِيحٌ مُشَارِكٌ means *A wind to which the* نَكْبَآء [q. v.] *is nearer than the two winds between which this blows*. (Ḳ.)

مُشْتَرَكٌ, applied to a road (طَرِيقٌ, Mgh, Mṣb, TA), is for مُشْتَرَكٌ فِيهِ, (Mṣb,) meaning [*Shared in:* or] *in which the people are equal* [*sharers*]. (TA.) — Hence, الأَجِيرُ المُشْتَرَكُ [in my copy of the Mgh, erroneously, المُشْتَرِكُ,] *The hired man* [*that is shared in;* i. e.,] *whose work no one has for himself exclusively of others, but who works for every one who repairs to him for work, like the tailor in the sitting-places of the markets;* (Mṣb;) or *who works for whom he pleases:* as to أَجِيرُ المُشْتَرَكِ, it is not right, unless the word thus governed in the gen. case be expl. as an inf. n. (Mgh.) — See also الفَرِيضَةُ المُشْتَرَكَةُ, above. — اِسْمٌ مُشْتَرَكٌ [in like manner for مُشْتَرَكٌ فِيهِ] *A noun shared in* by several meanings; i. e. *a homonym;*] *a noun shared in by many meanings, such as* عَيْنٌ *and the like:* (Mz, 25th نوع; and TA in the present art. and in the Intr.:) or مُشْتَرَكٌ signifies a word *having two, or more, meanings;* and is applied to a noun, and to the pret. of a verb as denoting predication and prayer, and to the aor. as denoting the present and the future, and to a particle: (Mz ubi suprà:) [مُشْتَرَكٌ used as a subst., meaning *a homonym*, has for its pl. مُشْتَرَكَاتٌ.] — الحِسُّ المُشْتَرَكُ [for المُشْتَرَكُ فِيهِ,] signifies, in the conventional language of the philosophers, *The faculty of fancy;* so called because "participated in" by the five senses: but it is vulgarly used as meaning *common sense.*] — مُشْتَرِكٌ applied to a man, [for مُشْتَرَكٌ فِيهِ,] means † *Talking to himself, like him who is affected with anxiety;* (Aṣ, Ṣ, Ḳ, TA; [in the CḲ, erroneously, مُشْتَرَكٌ;]) *his judgment being shared in; not one.* (TA.)

شرم

1. شَرَمَهُ, (Ṣ, Ḳ,) aor. ـِ, (Ḳ,) inf. n. شَرْمٌ, *i. q.* شَقَّهُ [meaning *He slit it;* or *rent it;* and perhaps also *he clave it, split it,* &c.]. (Ṣ, Ḳ.) — It is also said in the Ḳ that الشَّرْمُ signifies قَطْعُ مَا بَيْنَ الأَرْنَبَةِ: but ما بين should be struck out: and the passage, moreover, is defective: it should be, as in the M, الشَّرْمُ and ▼ التَّشْرِيمُ signify The *cutting* (قَطْع [or rather شَقّ i. e. *slitting* or *rending*]) *of the end,* or *tip, of the nose,* and *of the* ثَفْر [here meaning the *vulva,* or the *orifice of the vagina,*] *of a she-camel:* specially said of these two things. (TA. [See also 2; and see شَرِيمٌ.]) — شَرَمَ الثَّرِيدَةَ, aor. and inf. n. as above, and the latter, by poetic license, شَرَمٌ, *He ate of the sides,* or *of the edge, of the* ثريدة [or mess of crumbled bread moistened with broth]. (TA.) — شَرَمَ لَهُ مِنْ مَالِهِ, (Ṣ, Ḳ,) aor. as above, (Ḳ,) and so the inf. n., (TA,) *He gave him little of his* مال (i. e. *property,* or *cattle*]. (Ṣ, Ḳ.) ═ شَرِمَ, aor. ـَ, is quasi-pass. of شَرَمَهُ; [i. e. it signifies *It was,* or *became, slit,* or *rent;*] (TA;) as also ▼ انشرم: (Ṣ, TA. [In the former it is implied that the meaning of the latter verb is اِنْشَقَّ.]) — Also, aor. as above, (Mṣb,) inf. n. شَرَمٌ, (Ṣ,* Mṣb, Ḳ,*) *He* (a man) *had his nose slit:* (Mṣb:) or *he had the end,* or *tip, of his nose cut.* (Ṣ,* Mṣb, Ḳ.*)

2. تَشْرِيمٌ *i. q.* تَشْقِيقٌ [meaning The *slitting,* or *rending,* and perhaps also *cleaving, splitting,* &c., *much,* or *in several places*]: (Ṣ, Ḳ, TA: [see 2 in art. خرم:]) one says, شرّمهُ [*he slit it* &c.], in relation to the ear &c.: (TA:) [it is used in relation to the end, or tip, of the nose; and to the orifice of the vagina of a she-camel; as shown above:] see 1, second sentence. تَشْرِيمُ الظِّئَارِ is [*The scarifying of the vulva,* or *of the orifice of the vagina, for the purpose of*] *the making a she-camel to affect and suckle a young one not her own* [*by causing her to imagine, from the pain thus occasioned, that she has recently brought forth that young one*]; (TA;) تشريم in this phrase signifying تَشْقِيق. (T in art. ظأر.) It is said in a trad. of Ibn-'Omar, that he purchased a she-camel, and, seeing in her what is thus termed, returned her: (Ṣ:) in this instance, تشريم الظئار means *The laceration of the two edges of the vulva on the occasion of* ظئار. (T and TA in art. ظأر: see 1 in that art.) — تَشْرِيمُ الصَّيْدِ is *The wounding of the skin of the animal of the chase without piercing into the belly,* or *inside,* (L in art. حق, [see 8 in that art.,]) *so that the animal escapes wounded.* (Ṣ, Ḳ.*)

5. تَشَرَّمَ, (Ṣ, Ḳ,) said of the skin, (TA,) or of a thing, (Ṣ,) *It was,* or *became, rent,* or *slit, in several places;* (Ṣ, Ḳ, TA;) quasi-pass. of شَرَّمَهُ. (TA.) It is said in a trad. of Kaạb, أَتَى عُمَرَ بِكِتَابٍ قَدْ تَشَرَّمَتْ نَوَاحِيهِ i. e. تَشَقَّقَتْ [meaning *He brought to 'Omar a book of which the sides were slit,* or *rent, in several places*]. (TA.)

7: see 1, near the end.

شَرْمٌ *A canal,* or *cut,* (خَلِيج,) from a بَحْر [i. e. sea, or large river]: (Ṣ, Ḳ:) [now applied to *a creek of a sea:*] or the لُجَّة [i. e. *main body,* or *fathomless deep,*] of the بَحْر [or sea]: (Ḳ:) or the *deepest part* thereof: (TA:) or *a* غَمْرَة [or *submerging deep*] thereof: pl. شُرُومٌ. (IB, TA.) — And *Any fissure in a mountain* or *rock, not passing through.* (TA.) ═ Also *A certain kind of tree.* (Ḳ.) — Also, (Ḳ,) or عُشْبٌ شَرْمٌ, (Ṣ, [in one of my copies of the Ṣ شَرِمٌ,]) *Abundant herbs* or *herbage, of which the upper parts are eaten, the middle parts not being required,* (Ṣ, Ḳ,) *nor the lower parts.* (Ṣ.)

شَرُومٌ: see what next follows.

شَرِيمٌ A woman *having her vagina and rectum united by the rending of the separation between them;* syn. مُفْضَاةٌ; (Ṣ, Mgh, Ḳ;) as also ▼ شَرُومٌ, (Ṣ, Ḳ,) and ▼ شَرْمَآءُ; (Ḳ;) or the last of these in this sense has not been heard, though mentioned in the sense here following. (Mgh.) — Also A she-camel *having her* ثَفْر [here meaning the *vulva,* or the *orifice of the vagina,*] *cut* [or rather *slit* or *rent*]; and so ▼ شَرْمَآءُ, and ▼ مَشْرُومَةٌ: (M, TA:) or ▼ شَرْمَآءُ applied to a she-camel and to a she-ass, accord. to the Tekmileh, means *having the vulva slit,* or *rent:* therefore the first-mentioned meaning of this epithet, applied to a woman, if correct, may be tropical. (Mgh.) — Also The فَرْج [or *vulva*]; (Ḳ;) because of its being cleft. (TA.)

شَارِمٌ An arrow *that slits,* or *rends,* (يَشْرِمُ,) *the side of the target.* (Ṣ, Ḳ, TA.)

أَشْرَمُ, applied to a man, (IAạr, Ṣ, Mṣb, Ḳ,) *i. q.* ▼ مَشْرُومُ الأَنْفِ; (Ṣ, Ḳ;) [i. e.] *Having the nose slit;* (IAạr, Mṣb, TA;) like أَخْرَمُ: (IAạr, TA:) or *having the end,* or *tip, of the nose cut:* (Mṣb:) and *having the lower lip slit;* like أَفْلَحُ: and *having the upper lip slit;* like أَعْلَمُ: and *having the ear slit;* like أَخْرَبُ: and *having the eyelid slit;* like أَشْتَرُ: it has all these meanings: (IAạr, TA:) fem. شَرْمَآءُ, applied to a woman. (Mṣb.) — For the fem., see also شَرِيمٌ, in three places. — The fem. is also applied to an ear (أُذُنٌ), meaning *Having a small portion cut from the upper part;* and so ▼ مُشَرَّمَةٌ. (TA.)

مُشَرَّمٌ *Slit,* or *rent, in several places:* so in a trad., where it is said, فَجَآءَهُ بِمُصْحَفٍ مُشَرَّمِ الأَطْرَافِ [*And he brought him a copy of the Ḳur-án having the extremities slit,* &c.]. (TA.) — See also أَشْرَمُ, last sentence.

مَشْرُومٌ: see أَشْرَمُ: — and see also شَرِيمٌ.

Quasi شرنف

شَرْنَفْتُ الزَّرْعَ, mentioned under this head in the O and Ḳ: see Q. Q. 4 in art. شرف. The ن is held by Az to be augmentative, if not a mistake for ى. (O.)

شِرْنَافٌ: see شِرْيَافٌ, art. in شرف.

شره

شَرِهَ (Ṣ, MA, Mgh, Mṣb, Ḳ) عَلَى الطَّعَامِ (MA, Mgh, Mṣb) وَغَيْرِهِ, (Mṣb,) or إِلَى الطَّعَامِ, (TA, [perhaps a mistranscription,]) aor. ـَ, (Mṣb, Ḳ,) inf. n. شَرَهٌ, (Ṣ, MA, Mgh, Mṣb,) said of a man, (Ṣ,) *He was vehemently desirous,* or *greedy;* (MA;) or *very vehemently desirous,* or *very greedy;* (Mgh, Mṣb;) or *overcome by vehement desire,* or *greediness;* (Ṣ, Ḳ;) *of the food* (MA, Mgh, Mṣb) *&c.:* (Mṣb:) or, as some say, *he was affected with the worst of vehement desire,* or *of greediness.* (TA.)

شَرِهٌ (Ṣ, Mṣb, Ḳ) and ▼ شَرْهَانُ (Lth, Ḳ) [*Vehemently desirous,* or *greedy;* (see 1;) or] *very vehemently desirous,* or *very greedy;* (Mṣb;) or *overcome by vehement desire,* or *greediness:* (Ḳ:) or, accord. to some, *affected with the worst of vehement desire,* or *of greediness.* (TA.)

شَرْهَانُ: see the next preceding paragraph.

إِهْيَا أَشْرَ إِهْيَا, with kesr to the ء in اهيا, and with fet-ḥ to the ء in اشر, and to the ش, (Ḳ, TA,) and with the ر quiescent, (TA,) [mentioned in this art. in consequence of the supposing اشر with اهيا after it to compose one word,] but this is not its proper place; (Ḳ, TA;) so says Ṣgh; (TA;) an ancient Greek expression, (Ḳ, TA,) or Syriac, or, more correctly, Hebrew; (TA;) [the truth is that it is a mode of writing the Hebrew words אֶהְיֶה אֲשֶׁר אֶהְיֶה "I shall be that I am," in Exod. iii. 14, rendered in our Authorized Version "I am that I am;"] said in prayer; (TA;) [virtually] meaning *The existing from eternity, that will not cease to be:* (Ḳ:) Ṣgh says, thus one of the learned men of the Jews pronounced it to me in 'Adan Abyan: and some say هيا شراهيا, as though abridging it, meaning يَا حَىُّ يَا قَيُّومُ [which may be rendered *O Ever-living, O Self-subsisting by Whom all things subsist;* but the latter epithet is variously explained]; so says Lth: (TA:) the people now say أَهْيَا شَرَاهِيَا, (so in some copies of the Ḳ,) with fet-ḥ to the ء in اهيا, and dropping the ء in what follows this word, [which, however, probably means that they say أَهْيَا شَرْ أَهْيَا,] or, as in the handwriting of Ṣgh, with medd to the ء in the former; (TA;) [in my MS. copy of the Ḳ آهيا شَراهيا; in the CḲ, آهْيًا شَراهِيًّا;] which is said in the Ḳ to be a mistake accord. to the assertion of the learned men of the Jews: but this, which is said to be a mistake, is what commonly obtains in the books of the people, [i. e. of the Jews,] and they seldom, or never, pronounce it otherwise than thus: Aẓ says that the vulgar say يَا هَيَا, which is post-classical; correctly [يَا هَيَا or] يَا هَيَاهُ, with fet-ḥ to the ء: AḤát says, I think it to be originally يا هَيَا شراهيا [which is inconsistent with the Hebrew]: and Ibn-Buzurj says, they said يَا هيا and يَا هَيَا in speaking to one from a near place. (TA.)

شرو

شَرْوٌ *Honey:* (Ḳ:) or *white honey:* mentioned by Ṣgh: formed by transposition from شَوْرٌ: (TA:) and also written ▼ شِرْوٌ. (Ḳ.)

شِرْوٌ: see what precedes.

شَرَوِىٌّ, originally شَرْيِىٌّ: } see art. شرى.
شِرَوِىٌّ, originally شِرْيِىٌّ: }

شرول

شِرْوَالٌ is [said to be] a dial. var. of سِرْوَالٌ: (Ḳ:) IAmb says that Es-Sijistánee mentions his having heard some of the Arabs of the desert say شروال for سِرْوَال; but that it seems he heard them use the Pers. word, [which, it appears, is شَرْوَال as well as شَلْوَار,] and knew it not: (O, TA:*) شروال is a vulgar word, [now commonly pronounced شَرْوَال,] and some of the vulgar say شَلْوَار, with fet-ḥ to the ش. (TA.)

شرى

1. شَرَاهُ, (Ṣ, Mgh, Mṣb, Ḳ, &c.,) aor. ـِ, (Ṣ, Mṣb, Ḳ,) inf. n. شِرًى (Ṣ, Mgh, Mṣb, TA) and شِرَآءٌ, (Ṣ,* Mgh, Mṣb,* TA,) the former inf. n. the more in repute, (Mṣb, TA,) and this is of the dial. of Nejd, the latter being of the dial. of El-Ḥijáz, or the latter may be said to be with medd for the purpose of assimilating it to a preceding word, accord. to El-Munádee, or it may be regarded as an inf. n. of شَارَاهُ, (TA,) *i. q.* بَاعَهُ [in the sense in which this is generally used, i. e. *He sold it*]; (Ṣ, Mgh, Ḳ;) *he gave it for a price:* (Mṣb:) and *i. q.* ▼ اِشْتَرَاهُ [in the sense in which this is generally used, i. e. *he bought it*]; (Ṣ, Mgh;) i. e. شَرَاهُ signifies also *he took it,* or *acquired it, for a price:* (Mṣb:) or this and ▼ اشتراه both signify بَاعَهُ [as meaning *he sold it*]; (T,* Ḳ, TA;) but the former is more used than the latter in this sense: (T, TA:) and both signify also [*he bought it;* i. e.] *he possessed it by sale;* (Ḳ;) which is the more usual meaning of the latter: (T, TA:) thus the former has two contr. meanings, (Ṣ, Mṣb, Ḳ,) and the latter also: (Ḳ:) for the two persons selling and buying sell and buy the price and the thing upon which the price is put; so that each of the things given in exchange is sold in one point of view and bought in another. (Mṣb, TA.) It is said in the Ḳur [ii. 203], وَمِنَ ٱلنَّاسِ مَنْ يَشْرِى نَفْسَهُ ٱبْتِغَآءَ مَرْضَاةِ ٱللّٰهِ i. e. [*And of men is he*] *who sells* [*himself in the endeavour to obtain the approval of God*]. (Ṣ,* TA.) And in the same, [xii. 20], وَشَرَوْهُ بِثَمَنٍ بَخْسٍ i. e. *And they sold him* [*for a deficient,* or *an insufficient, price*]. (Ṣ, TA.) And in the same [ii. 15], أُولٰئِكَ ٱلَّذِينَ ٱشْتَرَوُا ٱلضَّلَالَةَ بِٱلْهُدَى, originally ٱشْتَرَيُوا, (Ṣ,) [lit. *Those are they who have purchased error with right direction,*] meaning, ‡ *who have taken* الضلالة *in exchange for* الهدى: (Ksh, Bḍ, Jel:) or ‡ *who have preferred* الضلالة *to* الهدى: (Ksh, Bḍ:) [for] of any one who relinquishes a thing and lays hold upon another thing, one says اشتراه; (Ḳ, TA;) which is thus tropically used [as meaning ‡ *he took it in exchange* بِغَيْرِهِ *by* giving up *another thing*]; (TA;) and hence this saying in the Ḳur-án. (Ḳ, TA.) — [Hence,] شَرَى بِنَفْسِهِ عَنِ ٱلْقَوْمِ ‡ *He advanced before the people,* or *party,* (Ḳ, TA,) *to their enemy,* (TA,) *and fought in defence of them:* or ‡ *he advanced to the Sultán, and spoke for the people:* (Ḳ, TA:) [as though he sold himself for them; the ب in بنفسه being app. redundant:] or, as in the Tekmileh, شَرَى بِنَفْسِهِ إِلَى ٱلْقَوْمِ ‡ *he advanced to the people,* or *party, and fought them.* (TA.) — And شَرَى فُلَانًا, (Ḳ,) inf. n. شَرْىٌ, (TA,) † *He mocked at, scoffed at, laughed at, derided,* or *ridiculed, such a one:* (Ḳ:) [and] so ▼ شَرَّاهُ. (TA voce جَدَّعَهُ [q. v.: thus there written, perhaps for the purpose of assimilating it to جَدَّعَهُ].) — And *i. q.* أَرْغَمَهُ † [*He angered such a one;* or *did evil to him, and angered him*]: (Lḥ, Ḳ, TA:) and so أَوْرَمَهُ, and غَطَاهُ [or perhaps عَطَاهُ, for both are expl. alike]: all said of God. (Lḥ, TA.) And فَعَلَ بِهِ مَا شَرَاهُ † *He did to him that which occasioned evil to him;* or *that which displeased, grieved,* or *vexed, him;* syn. سَآءَهُ. (TA.) And لَحَاهُ ٱللّٰهُ وَشَرَاهُ † [*May God remove him far from good* or *prosperity,* or *curse him, and do evil to him,* or *displease* or *grieve* or *vex him*]. (TA.) = شَرَى ٱللّٰهُ فُلَانًا, (Ḳ,) inf. n. شَرْىٌ, (TA,) also signifies *God smote him,* or *may God smite him, with the eruption termed* شَرًى [q. v.]. (Ḳ, TA.) = And شَرَاهُ, (Ḳ,) aor. ـِ, inf. n. شَرْىٌ, (TA,) *i. q.* شَرَّاهُ, (Ḳ, TA,) i. e. *He spread it* [*to dry*]; (TA;) [in copies of the Ḳ, in art. شر, written, in this sense, ▼ شَرَّاهُ;] namely, flesh-meat, and a garment, or piece of cloth, and [the preparation of curd called] أَقِط. (Ḳ.) = شَرِىَ, aor. ـَ, inf. n. شَرًى, (Ṣ, Ḳ,) said of lightning, (Ṣ, Ḳ, &c.,) *It shone,* or *gleamed, much:* (Ṣ:) or *it shone,* or *gleamed,* (Ḳ, TA,) *and spread in the face of the clouds,* or, as in the T, *became dispersed in the face of the clouds:* (TA:) and ▼ اشرى signifies the same; (Ḳ;) or *it shone,* or *gleamed, consecutively:* the latter verb mentioned by Ṣgh. (TA.) — And hence, (Ṣ,) said of the nose-rein of a camel, (Ṣ, TA,) *It was,* or *became, in a state of commotion,* (TA,) or, *of much commotion.* (Ṣ, TA.) [See also 12.]) — Also, (Ḳ,) aor. and inf. n. as above, (TA,) *He* (a man) *was,* or *became, angry:* (Ḳ, TA:) or *he was,* or *became, flurried by reason of anger.* (Ṣ, TA.) — And, said of evil, or mischief, *It spread,* بَيْنَهُمْ *among them:* (Ḳ, TA:) or *became great,* or *formidable;* and in like manner said of an affair, or event. (Nh, TA. [See also 10.]) — Also, and ▼ استشرى, *He* (a man, Ṣ) *persisted,* or *persevered,* (Ṣ, Ḳ,) *in an affair,* (Ṣ,) or *in his error, and his corrupt conduct:* and the former, said of a man, is like غَرِىَ in measure and meaning [i. e. *he persisted,* or *persevered, in his anger*]. (TA.) One says of a horse, شَرِىَ فِى سَيْرِهِ, (Ṣ, Ḳ,) inf. n. as above, (TA,) *He per-*

sisted, or persevered, in his pace, or going; as also ▼ استشرى: (Ṣ:) or *he exceeded the usual bounds therein,* (Ḳ, TA,) *and went on without languor:* (TA:) and فِى عَدْوِهِ ▼ استشرى *he* (i. e. a horse) *persisted, or persevered, in his running:* (Mgh:) and شَرِىَ فِى لِجَامِهِ *he* (a horse) *strained his bridle.* (A, TA.) And شَرِيَتْ عَيْنُهُ بِالدَّمْعِ *His eye persisted, or persevered, in the shedding of tears, the tears pouring forth consecutively.* (TA.) ═ And شَرِىَ, (Ṣ, Ḳ, TA,) aor. ـَ, inf. n. شَرًى, (Ḳ,* TA,) *He,* (TA,) or *his skin, broke out with the eruption termed* شَرًى [q. v.]. (Ṣ, Ḳ, TA.)

2: see the preceding paragraph, in two places.

3. شَارَاهُ, inf. n. مُشَارَاةٌ and شِرَآءٌ, i. q. بَايَعَهُ [as signifying *He sold and bought with him:* and *he bartered, or exchanged commodities, with him:* that شاراه has both of these meanings (like بايعه) is shown by the fact that مُشَارَاةٌ is also expl. in the TA, on the authority of Er-Rághib, as signifying the same as قَبَاضٌ]. (Ḳ.) — Also, (Mgh,) inf. n. مُشَارَاةٌ, (TA,) *He persisted in contention, litigation, or wrangling:* (Mgh:) one says, هُوَ يُشَارِيهِ (T, M, Ḳ) *He persists in contention, litigation, or wrangling, with him:* (M, TA:) or *he contends in altercation, disputes, or litigates, with him; or does so vehemently, or obstinately;* syn. يُجَادِلُهُ: (Ḳ, TA:) and it is said of the Prophet, in a trad., كَانَ لَا يُشَارِى وَلَا يُمَارِى [*He used not to persist in contention,* &c.]: (Mgh, TA:) meaning accord. to Th, كَانَ لَا يَسْتَشْرِى ▼ بِالشَّرِّ [*he used not to persist, or persevere, with evil conduct*]: (TA:) from اِسْتَشْرَى فِى عَدْوِهِ [expl. above (see 1 near the end)] as said of a horse: (Mgh:) or, accord. to Az, (TA,) originally يُشَارِرُ; one of the ر s being changed into ى. (Ḳ,* TA. [See 3 in art. شر: and see also 3 in art. جرى.])

4. اشرى, said of lightning: see 1, latter half. — Said of a camel, *He sped, or went quickly.* (IḲṭṭ, TA.) — اشرى بَيْنَهُمْ *He excited discord, strife, or animosity, between them, or among them.* (Az, Ḳ.) — اشرى الحَمَلُ (Ḳ accord. to the CḲ, [which, I think, evidently gives the right reading,] in the TA and in my MS. copy of the Ḳ الجمل,) i. q. تَفَلَّقَتْ عَقِيقَتُهُ [i. e. *The lamb had its wool cleaving open, or becoming cleft*]: (Ḳ: [Freytag, following the TḲ, and reading الجَمَلُ, explains the verb as said of fruit, and meaning "diffissos habuit nucleos;" but I cannot find any authority for the signification that he thus assigns to عقيقة:]) mentioned by Ṣgh. (TA.) — اشرت الشَّجَرَةُ *The plant* [*crept upon the ground,* or] *was like the cucumber and the melon;* as also ▼ استشرت. (TA.) — See also 5. ═ اشراهُ *He filled it;* (Ṣ, Ḳ;) namely, a watering-trough: and in like manner اشرى جَفْنَةً *he filled a bowl,* (Ṣ,) or جِفَانَهُ *his bowls* for the guests. (TA.) — And *He made it to incline,* (Ḳ, TA,) فِى نَاحِيَةِ كَذَا [*in the direction of such a thing*]. (TA.) Hence the saying of a poet,

• وَإِنِّى حَيْثُمَا يُشْرِى الهَوَى بَصَرِى •
• مِنْ حَوْثُمَا سَلَكُوا أَدْنُو فَأَنْظُورُ •

[*And that I, wherever love makes my eye, or eyes, to incline, wherever they travel, approach and look:* فانظور being for فَأَنْظُرُ]: or, as some relate it, أُثْنِى فَأَنْظُورُ [i. e. *turn myself,* or *my eyes, and look*]. (TA.) — [Also *He put it in motion;* namely, a bridle. (Freytag, from the Deewán of the Hudhalees.)]

5. تشرّى *It became scattered, or dispersed:* (Ḳ:) accord. to the M, said in this sense of a company of men. (TA.) — Also, said of a man, (Ṣ,) or of a party, or company of men, (TA,) *He,* or *they, became like the* شُرَاة [pl. of شَارٍ q. v.] *in his,* or *their, actions;* (Ṣ,* TA;) and so ▼ اشرى. (IAth, TA.)

6. تَشَارَيَا *They sued each other; or cited each other before a judge;* syn. تَقَاضَيَا. (A, TA.)

8: see the first paragraph, in three places.

10. استشرى: see 1, latter part, in three places: and see 3. — Also *He persisted, or persevered, in consideration, or examination.* (TA.) — And استشرى فِى دِينِهِ *He strove, or exerted himself,* or *was diligent, or studious,* and *was careful,* or *mindful,* or *regardful, in his religion.* (TA.) — And استشرت الأُمُورُ بَيْنَهُمْ *The affairs, or events, were, or became, great, or formidable, between them, or among them.* (Ḳ,* TA. [See also شَرِىَ.]) — And see 4.

12. اِشْرَوْرَى *It was, or became, in a state of commotion.* (Ḳ. [See also شَرِىَ.])

شَرْىٌ *The colocynth:* (Ṣ, Ḳ:) or it signifies, (Ḳ,) or signifies also, (Ṣ,) *the plant thereof:* (Ṣ, Ḳ:) n. un. with ة: (Ṣ:) and ▼ شِرْيَانٌ also signifies the *colocynth;* as a dial. var. of شَرْىٌ: or the *leaves thereof.* (TA.) One says, هُوَ أَحْلَى مِنَ الأَرْىِ وَأَمَرُّ مِنَ الشَّرْىِ [*He, or it, is sweeter than honey and more bitter than colocynth*]. (TA.) And فُلَانٌ لَهُ طَعْمَانِ أَرْىٌ وَشَرْىٌ [*Such a one has two flavours,* that of *honey* and that of *colocynth*]. (Ṣ, TA.) — And *Any kind of plant that spreads upon the ground, running* [or *creeping*] *and extending; such as the melon and the cucumber.* (AḤn, O voce سُطَّاحٌ, q. v., and TA* in the present art.) — And *Palm-trees that grow from the date-stones:* (Ḳ:) and with ة [as the n. un.] *one of such palm-trees.* (Ṣ.) — And, accord. to IJ, *A kind of tree of which bows are made.* (L voce حَتٌّ, q. v. [See also شِرْيَانٌ.]) ═ See also شَرًى. ═ And see شَرْوَى.

شَرًى *A road,* (Ḳ, TA,) in a general sense. (TA.) And, (Ḳ,) with the article ال, [particularly] *A road of Selmà,* (Ṣ, Ḳ, TA,) *the mountain so called,* (TA,) *abounding with lions:* (Ṣ, Ḳ, TA:) whence they say of courageous men, مَا هُمْ إِلَّا أُسُودُ الشَّرَى [*They are no other than the lions of Esh-Sharà*]. (TA.) — And i. q. نَاحِيَةٌ [as meaning *An adjacent tract* or *region*]; (Ṣ, Ḳ;) as also ▼ شَرَاةٌ: (Ḳ:) accord. to some, *of the right hand:* (TA:) pl. أَشْرَآءٌ. (Ṣ, Ḳ.) Hence, شَرَى الفُرَاتِ *The adjacent tract* (نَاحِيَة) *of the Euphrates:* (TA:) and أَشْرَآءُ الحَرَمِ *the adjacent tracts of the Sacred Territory;* syn. نَوَاحِيهِ. (Ṣ.) — And *A mountain.* (Ḳ.) ═ Also The *bad,* or *worse,* or *worst, of cattle:* accord. to J, [in the Ṣ,] ▼ شَرِىٌّ, [said in the Ṣ to be like شَوَى المَالِ,] which is [said to be] a mistake: (Ḳ:) but El-Bedr El-Ḳaráfee questions it being so: (TA:) and the *good,* or *better,* or *best, thereof;* as also ▼ شَرَاةٌ: thus having two contr. significations: (Ḳ:) and so says ISk: but ISd says that إِبِلٌ ▼ شَرَاةٌ, like سَرَاةٌ, means *choice camels.* (TA.) ═ And *A certain eruption upon the body, resembling dirhems:* (TA:) or *small pimples or purulent pustules, having a burning property:* (Ṣ:) or *small pimples or purulent pustules, red, itching, and distressing, generally originating at once,* (Ḳ, TA,) *but sometimes gradually,* (TA,) *and becoming* [*more*] *severe by night in consequence of a hot vapour breaking forth at once upon the body:* (Ḳ, TA:) thus in the "Ḳánoon" of Ibn-Seenà [or Avicenna]. (TA.) ═ ذُو الشَّرَى *A certain idol of* [*the tribe of*] *Dows* (دَوْس), (Ḳ, TA,) *in the Saráh* (السَّرَاة): so says Naṣr. (TA.)

شَرٍ *Having the eruption termed* شَرًى, *described in the next preceding paragraph.* (Ṣ, Ḳ.)

شِرًى, (Ṣ, TA,) an inf. n. of شَرَى, aor. يَشْرِى, (TA,) [when used as a simple subst., signifying *A sale* and also *a purchase,*] has أَشْرِيَةٌ for its pl., which, as pl. of a sing. of the measure فِعَلٌ, is anomalous. (Ṣ, TA.)

شَرَاةٌ: see شَرًى, in two places.

شَرَآءٌ: see شِرًى.

شَرِىٌّ *Sold:* and also *bought:* applied in this sense to a male slave; and شَرِيَّةٌ to a female slave. (Mṣb.) — Also A horse *that persists, or perseveres, in his pace, or going:* (Ṣ:) or *that exceeds the usual bounds therein,* (Ḳ, TA,) *and goes on without languor:* (TA:) or a *choice* horse: (A, TA:) or an *excellent, choice* horse. (TA.)

شَرِيَّةٌ *A way, course, mode, or manner, of acting* or *conduct* or *the like:* and *a nature;* or *a natural, a native,* or *an innate, disposition* or *temper* or *the like.* (Ḳ.) ═ Also, of women, *Such as bring forth females.* (Ḳ.) One says, تَزَوَّجَ فِى شَرِيَّةِ نِسَآءٍ *He married among women such as bring forth females.* (TA.)

شَرْوَى, in which the و is a substitute for ى, as it is in تَقْوَى and the like, (TA,) The *like* (Ṣ, Ḳ) of a thing: (Ṣ:) because a thing is sometimes bought with the like thereof: (TA:) [used alike as sing. and pl.: and, accord. to the TA, it seems that ▼ شَرْىٌ signifies the same.] It is said of Shureyḥ, كَانَ يُضَمِّنُ القَصَّارَ شَرْوَى الثَّوْبِ الَّذِى أَهْلَكَهُ [*He used to make the washer responsible for the like of the garment, or piece of cloth, that he destroyed*]. (TA.) And it is said in a trad. of 'Omar, relating to the [collecting of the] poor-rate, فَلَا يَأْخُذُ إِلَّا تِلْكَ السِّنَّ مِنْ شَرْوَى إِبِلِهِ [i. e. *And he shall not take* any *save of that age, of the likes of his camels*]. (TA.)

شِرَوِىٌّ, in which the و is a substitute for ى, and ▼ شِرَائِىٌّ, [both signifying *Of,* or *relating to, selling,* and also *of,* or *relating to, buying,*] are rel. ns.; the former, of the inf. n. شِرًى; and the latter, of the inf. n. شِرَآءٌ. (Mṣb, TA.)

شِرْيَانٌ see شَرْىٌ: — and see what next follows.

شِرْيَانٌ and ▼ شَرْيَانٌ, (Ṣ, Ḳ,) the former of which is the more in repute, (TA,) the former said to be quasi-quadriliteral, like جِرْيَالٌ, [and therefore mentioned also in the TA in art. شرن,] but held by IB to be of the measure فِعْلَانٌ, (TA in art. شرن,) *A kind of tree,* (Ṣ, Ḳ, TA,) *of the* عِضَاه [q. v.] *of the mountains,* (TA,) *of which bows are made:* (Ṣ, Ḳ, TA:) n. un. with ة: *the tree thus called grows in the manner, and of the height and width, of the* [*species of lote-tree called*] سِدْر, *and has a yellow, sweet* نَبِقَة [or *drupe*]: so says AḤn: and he adds, Aboo-Ziyád says, *bows are made of the* شريان, *and the bow made thereof is good, but black tinged with redness; its wood being of those woods of which good bows are* [*commonly*] *made; and they assert that it seldom, or never, becomes crooked:* Mbr says that *the* نَبْع *and* شَوْحَط [q. v.] *and* شريان *are one kind of tree, but differing in name and estimation according to the places of growth; such thereof as is upon the summit of the mountain being the* نبع; *and such as is at the base,* or *foot,* or *lowest* or *lower part, thereof, the* شريان. (TA. [But see شَوْحَط.]) — Also sing. of شَرَايِين signifying *The arteries;* i. e. *the pulsing veins;* (Ṣ, Ḳ;) *which spring from the heart:* (Ṣ:) but the anatomists assert that they spring from the liver, and pass by the heart. (TA.) — شِرْيَانٌ, with kesr, signifies also *A crack,* or *fissure,* [in a rock,] *such as is termed* ثَتّ. (Az, TA.)

شِرَائِىٌّ: see شِرَوِىٌّ.

شَارٍ *Selling,* or *a seller:* (Mgh, TA:) and *buying,* or *a buyer:* as also ▼ مُشْتَرٍ [in both senses, but generally in the latter sense; whereas شَارٍ is generally used in the former sense]: (TA:) pl. of the former شُرَاةٌ. (Mgh.) — Also, (Ṣ, TA,) and ▼ شَارِىٌّ, in which latter the ى is not the ى of a rel. n. but is an affix corroborative of the epithet, as in the cases of أَعْوَرُ and أَعْوَرِىٌّ [or أَحْمَرُ and أَحْمَرِىٌّ] and صُلَّبٌ and صُلَّبِىٌّ, (TA,) *One of the people to whom is applied the appellation* الشُّرَاةُ, (Ṣ, TA,) which means *the* [*heretics,* or *schismatics, commonly known by the name of*] خَوَارِج [pl. of خَارِجِىٌّ, q. v.]: (Ṣ, M, Mgh, Ḳ, &c.:) so called because they said, We have sold ourselves in obedience to God, i. e., for Paradise, when we separated ourselves from the erring Imáms: (Ṣ:) or because they sold themselves for the sake of what they believed: or because they said, Verily God has purchased us and our possessions: (Mgh:) but ISk says, because of their vehement hatred of the Muslims: and the author of the Ḳ says that it is from شَرِىَ signifying "he was angry," and "he persisted, or persevered;" and he charges J with error in his explaining it as above, from their saying "we have sold ourselves" &c.; but this charge is senseless, for J has followed herein more than one of the leading authorities: the author of the Ḳ has followed ISd, who, however, adds, as to themselves, they say "We are the شُرَاة" because of the saying in the Ḳur ii. 203 [cited in the first paragraph of this art.], and the saying [in ix. 112] "Verily God hath purchased, of the believers, themselves" [&c.]; and the like is said in the Nh, with this addition, that شُرَاةٌ is the pl. of شَارٍ; i. e., it is from المُشَارَاةُ, شَرَى, aor. يَشْرِى; or it may be from شَرِىَ meaning المُلَاجَّةُ: moreover, the part. n. of شَرِىَ is شَرٍ; and this has not شُرَاةٌ for its pl. (TA.)

شَارِىٌّ: see the next preceding paragraph.

مُشْتَرٍ: see شَارٍ. — المُشْتَرِى *A certain star,* (Ṣ, Ḳ,) *well-known;* (Ḳ;) [*Jupiter;*] *one of the Seven Stars.* (TA.) — And *A certain bird.* (Ḳ.)

شزب

1. شَزَبَ, (Ṣ, A, O, Ḳ,) and شَزُبَ, (O, Ḳ,) aor. of each ـُ, (Ḳ,) inf. n. شُزُوبٌ (Ṣ, A, O, Ḳ) and شَزَبٌ, (Ḳ,) *He was, or became, such as is termed* شَازِب meaning as expl. below: (Ṣ, A, O, Ḳ:) [mostly] said of a horse. (Ṣ, A, O, TA.)

2. شَزَّبَهُ, (O, Ḳ,) inf. n. تَشْزِيبٌ, (Ḳ,) *He,* or *it, caused it* (a rod, O) *to wither:* (O, Ḳ, TA:) and *he,* or *it, made him to become lean,* or *light of flesh; slender, and lean;* or *lean, and lank in the belly.* (TA.)

شَزِبَةٌ: see what follows.

شَازِبٌ *Lean,* or *light of flesh; slender, and lean;* or *lean, and lank in the belly;* applied to a horse: (Ṣ, O:) [or] ▼ شَزِبَةٌ signifies thus, applied to a she-ass, (Ḳ, TA,) and a she-camel: (so accord. to the CḲ:) and شَازِبٌ, *lean,* &c., as above; *and tough;* (A, Ḳ;) applied to a horse, (A, TA,) and to a man, &c.: (TA:) or *lean,* or *light of flesh, though not emaciated:* (Aṣ, TA:) and, applied to a man, *very slender* or *slim* or *spare:* (A:) pl. شُزَّبٌ, (Ṣ, A, O, Ḳ,) applied to horses, (Ṣ, A, O,) and [as also of شَازِبَةٌ] شَوَازِبُ. (Ḳ.) And شَازِبَةٌ *A she-gazelle lean,* or *light of flesh;* or *slender, and lean;* or *lean, and lank in the belly; in consequence of her having come from afar:* pl. شَوَازِبُ. (TA.) — And *Rough;* (Ṣ, Ḳ, TA;) applied to a place. (Ṣ, TA.)

شزر

1. شَزَرَهُ, and شَزَرَ إِلَيْهِ, aor. ـِ, (Ḳ,) inf. n. شَزْرٌ, (TA,) *He looked askew,* or *sideways, at him,* (IAmb, Ḳ,) *not turning his face towards him,* (TA,) [or *with a slight turning of the face,* (see لَحْظَة,)] *by reason of hatred* or *of awe:* (IAmb:) or *he looked at him with a look of aversion:* or *he looked at him from the right and left:* (Ḳ:) or *from the outer angle of the eye:* generally, *in anger:* or *with hatred and anger:* (TA:) or, (Ḳ,) as also نَظَرَ إِلَيْهِ شَزْرًا, (Ṣ, A, Mgh, Mṣb,) *he looked at him from the outer angle of the eye,* (Ṣ, A, Mṣb, Ḳ,) *with anger,* (Ṣ, Ḳ,) or *with aversion, like as one looks who hates another,* (A, Mgh,) or *like one who is averse and angry:* (Mṣb:) or شَزَرَهُ signifies *he looked at him with the look of an enemy.* (TA.) The saying of 'Alee, الْحَظُوا الشَّزْرَ وَٱطْعُنُوا اليَسْرَ, is expl. as signifying *Look ye from the right and left* [*and thrust ye straight forward*]. (TA.) — Also شَزَرَهُ, (Fr, Ḳ,) aor. and inf. n. as above, (Fr,) *He smote him with the* [*evil*] *eye.* (Fr, Ḳ.) — Also شَزَرَهُ *He thrust him,* or *pierced him,* (Ḳ,) with a spear-head. (TA.) And طَعَنَهُ شَزْرًا *He thrust him,* or *pierced him, sideways.* (A.) — شَزَرَ الحَبْلَ, aor. ـِ and ـُ, (Ḳ,) inf. n. شَزْرٌ, (TA,) *He twisted the rope,* or *cord, from the left* [*by rolling it against his body from left to right*]: (ISd, Ḳ:) or *he twisted it upwards* [*by rolling it upwards against his thigh or body*]: (Aṣ, AM:) or *he twisted it from without* [*by rolling it against his thigh*], *and turned it towards his belly* [contrarily to the usual manner, which is termed يَسْر, and which is the twisting downwards, by rolling the rope or cord downwards either against the body or against the thigh]; (ISd, Ḳ;) as also ▼ استشزرهُ. (Ḳ.) [See also شَزْر, below.]

3. شازرهُ, inf. n. مُشَازَرَةٌ, *He treated him,* or *regarded him, with enmity,* or *hostility:* whence [the manner of looking termed] الشَّزْرُ. (AA.)

4. اشزرهُ ٱللّٰهُ *God cast him into an evil case from which he could not extricate himself.* (TA.)

5. تشزّر *He was angry.* (Ḳ.) [See also تشذّر.] — *He prepared himself,* لِلْقِتَالِ *for fight,* (Ḳ,) and لِلسُّجُودِ [*for prostration* in prayer]. (Mgh.)

6. تشازروا *They looked, one at another, in the manner termed* شَزْر, (Ṣ, Ḳ,) *from the outer angle of the eye.* (TA.) [See 1.]

10. استشزر: see 1, last sentence but one. — Also *It* (a rope or cord) *was twisted in the manner described above, in the explanation of* شَزَرَ الحَبْلَ. (Ḳ.)

طَعْنٌ شَزْرٌ *A thrusting,* or *piercing, from the right and from the left:* (Ṣ, M, TA:) or *with the right hand and the left.* (TA.) — فَتْلٌ شَزْرٌ *A twisting upwards, contrarily to the manner in which the spindle* [*usually*] *turns.* (Ṣ.) [See 1.] — غَزْلٌ شَزْرٌ *Spun thread* [*app. twisted in a manner the reverse of that which is usual:* (see 1; and see also رَدْنٌ:) or] *that is uneven.* (Ḳ.) — طَحَنَ بِالرَّحَى شَزْرًا, [in which شَزْرًا appears to be an inf. n., though its verb is not mentioned,] *He ground with the hand-mill turning it from his right:* [i. e., making it to revolve in the same course as do the hands of a watch:] (Ṣ, A, Ḳ:*) the contrary [which is the common way] is termed بَتًّا. (A, TA.) — And مَا زَالَ شَزْرًا *He ceased not to be taking the wrong way.* (IAạr, TA.) — شَزْرٌ also signifies *Difficulty* (Ḳ) in an affair. (TA.)

فِى لَحْظِهِ شَزْرٌ [*In his glance is a sidelong and*

angry look, from the outer angle of the eye: see 1]. (Ṣ, Ḳ.*) — شُزُرٌ signifies [also] *Disquietude.* (Mgh.)

أَتَاهُ الدَّهْرُ بِشَزْرَةٍ لَا يَنْحَلُّ مِنْهَا [*Time,* or *fortune, brought him a calamity from which he was not to be extricated;*] meaning, *destroyed him.* (TA.)

شُزْرَةٌ ‡ *Redness in the eye, and,* or *with,* (so in the Ḳ accord. to the TA, but in the CḲ "or,") *what is termed* شَزْرٌ *in the glance thereof.* (Ḳ.)

عَيْنٌ شَزْرَآءُ ‡ *Red milk.* (TṢ, Ḳ.) — لَبَنٌ أَشْزَرُ ‡ *An eye that is red, and* (so in the Ḳ accord. to the TA, but in the CḲ "or,") *with what is termed* شَزْرٌ *in the glance thereof.* (Ḳ.)

حَبْلٌ مَشْزُورٌ *A rope,* or *cord, twisted from the left;* (Lth, A, Mṣb, TA;) which is the stronger way: (Lth, A:) or *upwards:* (Aṣ, T, Ṣ:) [see 1:] and ▼ مُسْتَشْزَرٌ. — غَدَائِرُ مُسْتَشْزِرَاتٌ, (Ṣ, TA,) and ▼ مُسْتَشْزَرَاتٌ, (TA,) [*Pendent locks of hair*] *so twisted.* (Ṣ, TA.)

مُسْتَشْزَرٌ: see the next preceding paragraph.

شسع

1. شَسَعَ النَّعْلَ, (Ṣ, O, Mṣb, Ḳ,) aor. ـَ, (Mṣb, Ḳ,) inf. n. شَسْعٌ, (O, Ḳ,) *He put a* شِسْع [q. v.] *to the sandal;* (Ṣ,* Mṣb,* Ḳ;) as also ▼ شَسَّعَهَا, and ▼ أَشْسَعَهَا. (Ṣ, O, Ḳ.) — شَسِعَتِ النَّعْلُ, aor. ـَ, *The sandal had its* شِسْع *broken.* (Ibn-Buzurj, O, Ḳ.) — شَسِعَ الفَرَسُ, aor. as above, inf. n. شَسَعٌ, *The horse had a gap, or space, between his central incisor and the tooth next to it.* (Aboo-Málik, IDrd, O, Ḳ.*) — شَسَعَ, aor. as above, inf. n. شَسْعٌ and شُسُوعٌ, *It was,* or *became, distant,* or *remote;* said of a place of alighting, or abode. (Ḳ.) And, said of anything, *i. q.* تَنَاءَى [*It was* or *became, far from another thing*]: and شَخَصَ [*it rose,* &c.]. (TA.) — شَسَعَ بِهِ *He put,* or *sent,* or *removed, him,* or *it, away,* or *far away;* as also ▼ اشسعهُ. (TA.)

2: see the preceding paragraph.

4: see 1, first and last sentences.

شِسْعٌ (Ṣ, O, Mṣb, Ḳ, &c.) and شِسِعٌ (Ḳ) and ▼ شِسْعُنٌ, so in some of the copies of the Ḳ, (TA,) [thus in my MS. copy of the Ḳ, and also in the O,] with an augmentative ن, (O, TA,) The قِبَال *of the sandal;* (Ḳ;) [i. e.] the *appertenance of the sandal that is attached,* or *tied, to its* زِمَام; (Ṣ;) [meaning] *one of the thongs,* or *straps,* or *strips of leather, of the sandal, being that which passes between two toes, of which the* [*lower*] *end enters the hole,* or *perforation, that is in the fore part of the sandal, and which is attached* [*at its upper end*] *to the* زِمَام [or, as it is also called, the شِرَاك, *a thong,* or *strap,* or *strip of leather, extending towards the ankle, and having two arms,* (its عَضُدَانِ,) *which are attached to the* أُذُنَانِ (q. v.), or *pass through these and unite behind the foot*]: (IAth, TA:) a poet says, referring to camels,

أَحْدُو بِهَا مُنْقَطِعًا شِسْعَنِى ▼

[*I urge them on by singing to them, with the interdigital thong of my sandal broken*]: (Lth, O, TA:) the pl. of شِسْعٌ is شُسُوعٌ (Ṣ, O, Mṣb, Ḳ, TA) and أَشْسَاعٌ: (O, Ḳ, TA:) ISd and Z affirm that it has only the former pl.; but AḤei contradicts this: (TA:) the latter pl. [a pl. of pauc.] occurs in the saying of 'Obeyd Ibn-Eiyoob El-'Amberee,

يُدِيرُ نَعْلَيْهِ لِئَلَّا تُعْرَفَا

يَجْعَلُ أَشْسَاعَهُمَا نَحْوَ القَفَا

[*He turns round his sandals, in order that they may not be known* by their prints upon the ground; *putting the interdigital thongs thereof in the direction of the back of the neck*]. (O, TA.) — [Hence,] قِبَالُ الشِّسْعِ signifies † *The serpent;* mentioned by IAạr with قِبَالُ الشِّبْرِ. (TA.) — And شِسْعٌ also signifies † The *extremity* of a place. (O, Ḳ.) One says, حَلَلْنَا شِسْعَ الدَّهْنَآءِ † [*We alighted in the extremity of the sandy desert,* or *of* the desert called *Ed-Dahnà*]. (O.) — And † *A narrow tract* of land. (O, Ḳ.) — And ‡ *Somewhat remaining* of property or cattle. (IAạr, O, Ḳ, TA.) And (Ḳ) ‡ *A small quantity* or *number* of property or cattle. (Moḥárib, O, Ḳ, TA.) One says, لَهُ شِسْعُ مَالٍ ‡ *He has a small quantity of property, or a small number of cattle;* (Moḥárib, O, Ḳ, TA;) or *a small collection of camels and of sheep* or *goats:* (Ḳ, TA:) and Fr adds ▼ شَسِيعُ مَالٍ [app. in the same sense: but see another explanation of شِسْعُ مَالٍ in what follows]. (O.) — And ‡ The *greater portion* or *number* of property or cattle. (El-Mufaḍḍal, O, Ḳ, TA.) Thus it has two contr. [?] significations. (Ḳ.) One says, ذَهَبَ شِسْعُ مَالِهِ ‡ *The greater portion of his property, or the greater number of his cattle, went,* or *passed, away.* (El-Mufaḍḍal, O, TA.) — And فُلَانٌ شِسْعُ مَالٍ ‡ *Such a one is a good manager of cattle* or *camels &c.;* (Ṣ, O, Ḳ, TA;) *one who keeps assiduously to the tending,* or *pasturing, thereof:* (A, TA:) and Fr says, هُوَ شِسْعُ مَالٍ ▼ شَسِيعُ مَالٍ, as syn. with شِسْعُ مَالٍ. (TA: [but see above.])

شِسْعُنٌ: see شِسْعٌ, in two places.

شُسُوعٌ: see شَاسِعٌ.

شَسِيعُ مَالٍ: see شِسْعٌ, in two places.

شَاسِعٌ A man *having his* شِسْع *broken.* (O, Ḳ.) — Also *Distant,* or *remote;* and so ▼ شَسُوعٌ: (Ṣ, O, Ḳ:) both applied to a place of alighting, or abode: (O, Ḳ:) pl. [of either, irreg.,] شُسْعٌ. (Ḳ.) One says بِلَادٌ شَاسِعَةٌ [*Distant countries* or *towns*]. (Mṣb.) And رَجُلٌ شَاسِعُ الدَّارِ *A man whose house,* or *abode,* or *country, is distant.* (TA.) And سَفَرٌ شَاسِعٌ *A far journey.* (TA.)

شصب

شَوْشَبٌ, mentioned in the Ḳ under this head and in art. شب: see the latter art.

شصر

1. شَصَرَ, (A'Obeyd, O,) aor. ـِ, (O,) inf. n. شَصْرٌ, (A'Obeyd, Ṣ, O, Ḳ,) *He sewed* (a garment, or piece of cloth, A'Obeyd) *with wide stitches,* or *with stitches far apart,* (Ṣ, O, Ḳ,) *as in the manner termed* بَشْك. (A'Obeyd.) — شَصَرَ عَيْنَ البَازِى, (Ṣ, O,) aor. and inf. n. as above, (Ṣ,) *He sewed up the eye of the hawk.* (Ṣ, O.) — شَصَرَ النَّاقَةَ, (M, O, Ḳ,) aor. ـِ and ـُ, (O, Ḳ,) inf. n. as above, (Ṣ, M, O, Ḳ,) *He transfixed the sides of the she-camel's vulva with small sharp-pointed pieces of wood, or prickles,* (M, O,* Ḳ,*) *and twisted round behind them sinews,* (M,) or *a string made of hairs from her tail,* (M, O,* Ḳ,*) *on account of the protruding of her womb on the occasion of her bringing forth;* (M, O, Ḳ;) syn. of the inf. n. تَزْنِيدٌ. (Ṣ.) See also شِصَارٌ, below. — And شَصَرَ النَّاقَةَ, (Ḳ,) inf. n. as above, (TA,) signifies also *He inserted the piece of wood called* شِصَار *between the nostrils of the she-camel;* and so ▼ شَصَّرَهَا, (Ḳ,) inf. n. تَشْصِيرٌ. (TA.) — شَصَرَتْهُ شَوْكَةٌ, (O, Ḳ,) inf. n. as above, (Ḳ,) *A thorn pricked,* or *pierced, him.* (O, Ḳ.) — شَصَرَهُ بِالرُّمْحِ, (O,) inf. n. as above, *He pierced him* (O, Ḳ*) *with the spear.* (O.) — شَصْرٌ also signifies A *bull's,* (O, Ḳ,) and a *gazelle's,* (TA,) *smiting* (O, Ḳ, TA) a man (O, TA) *with his horn.* (O, Ḳ, TA.) = And شَصَرَ, (IAạr, O,) inf. n. as above, (Ḳ,) *He leaped,* or *leaped upwards;* syn. طَفَرَ. (IAạr O, Ḳ.*) — شَصَرَ بَصَرُهُ, aor. ـُ, (O, Ḳ, in the L ـِ,) inf. n. شُصُورٌ, *His eye,* or *eyes, became fixedly open,* or *raised,* or *stretched and raised,* or *his eyelids became raised and he looked intently and became disquieted* or *disturbed,* (syn. شَخَصَ,) *and the eye became inverted;* at the time of death: (O, Ḳ:) thus, nearly in the same words, expl. by Lth and IF and Ibn-'Abbád: (O:) or the correct word is شَصَا, or شَطَرَ; (so accord. to different copies of the Ḳ, the latter being the reading in the TA;) or both; for Az says that this explanation of شصر بصره is in his opinion a mistake, and that it is correctly شَصَا بَصَرُهُ and شَطَرَ, meaning that *he was as though he looked at thee and at another.* (O, TA.*)

2: see the preceding paragraph.

شِصْرٌ, and its dual: see شِصَارٌ.

شَصْرٌ (A'Obeyd, Ṣ, Ḳ) and ▼ شَاصِرٌ (Lth, Ṣ, Ḳ) and ▼ شَوْصَرٌ (Ḳ) The *young one of the gazelle, when he has become strong and active:* (A'Obeyd, Ṣ, L, &c.:) in the Ḳ, *when he has become strong, but not active;* but this is a mistake: (TA:) or *that has become old enough to smite with his horn:* or *that has become a month old:* or *that has not yet cropped the herbage* [*but only sucked his mother*]; expl. by الَّذِى لَمْ يَحْتَنِكْ: (Ḳ:) A'Obeyd states that it is said by more than one of the Arabs of the desert that the young one of the gazelle is called طَلًا; then, خِشْفٌ; and when his horns come forth, شَادِنٌ; and when he has become strong and active, شَصْرٌ, of which the fem. [as is also said in the Ḳ] is شَصْرَةٌ; then, جَذَعٌ; and then, ثَنِىّ, which name he continues to have until he dies: (Ṣ:) [perhaps correctly corresponding to our six terms which are as follows: a fawn (applied to a buck or doe of the first year), a pricket (to a buck of the second year), a sorel (to a buck of the third year), a sore (to a buck of the fourth year), a buck of the first head (to one of the fifth year), and a great buck (to one of the sixth year):] or ▼ شَاصِرٌ is applied to *a young gazelle when his horn has come forth:* (Lth:) pl. [of شَصَرٌ,] أَشْصَارٌ. (Ḳ.) — شَصَرٌ also signifies *A certain bird, smaller than the* عُصْفُور [or *sparrow*], (AA, O, Ḳ,) *of the colour thereof.* (AA, O.)

شِصَارٌ The *small sharp-pointed piece of wood,* or *prickle,* (Ḳ,) or the *small sharp-pointed pieces of wood,* or *prickles,* (IDrd, Ṣ,) *with which the operation termed* تَزْنِيدٌ [which is that described above in the explanation of شَصَرَ النَّاقَةَ] *is performed;* (IDrd, Ṣ, Ḳ;) as also ▼ شِصْرٌ: (Ḳ:) or ▼ شِصَارَانِ, or شِصَارَانِ, is a term applied to *two pieces of wood, which are thrust through the edge of the rectum of a she-camel, and then bound with a strong string of the fibres of the palm-tree, behind them:* this is done when they desire to make a she-camel affect the young one of another: they take a stuffed دُرْجَة [q. v.], and insert it into her rectum, and transfix the rectum with two sharp-pointed pieces of wood, which they bind as above described: this operation is termed ▼ شَصْرٌ and تَزْنِيدٌ. (ISh.) [See also 1.] — Accord. to the T, *A piece of wood, which is bound between the two edges of a she-camel's vulva.* (TA.) — And *A piece of wood, which is inserted between the nostrils of a she camel.* (Ḳ.)

شَصِيرٌ *A prick of a thorn.* (O, Ḳ.)

شَاصِرٌ: see شَصَرٌ, in two places.

شَوْصَرٌ: see شَصَرٌ.

شَاصِرَةٌ *One of the snares with which beasts of prey are caught.* (O, Ḳ, TA.)

شصو and شصى

1. شَصَا بَصَرُهُ, (Ṣ, Ḳ,) aor. ـُ, (Ṣ, TA,) inf. n. شُصُوٌّ, (Ṣ, TA, and so in copies of the Ḳ, accord. to the CḲ شَصْوٌ, [and this, though wrong, is agreeable with a rule generally observed in the Ḳ, as it is not there followed by any indication of the form,]) like عُلُوٌّ, (TA,) *His eye,* or *eyes, became fixedly open,* or *raised,* or *stretched and raised,* or *his eyelids became raised and he looked intently and became disquieted* or *disturbed,* syn. شَخَصَ, (Ṣ, Ḳ, TA,) [at the time of death, (see شَخَصَ,)] *as though he looked at thee and at another.* (TA.) — And شَصَا السَّحَابُ *The clouds rose,* or *rose high,* (T, Ṣ, Ḳ,) *in their first appearing.* (T, TA.) And شَصَا said of anything, *It rose,* or *rose high.* (T, TA.) — [Hence,] شَصَتِ القِرْبَةُ, (Ḳ,) inf. n. as above, (TA,) *The water-skin being filled with water,* (Ḳ, TA,) and in like manner, *being inflated,* (TA,) *its legs became raised,* or *raised high.* (Ḳ, TA.) And thus also, شَصَا الزِّقُّ, *The wine-skin being filled with wine, its legs became raised,* or *raised high.* (TA.) — And شَصِىَ, aor. ـَ; (Ks, Ṣ, TA;) or شَصَا, aor. ـُ; and and شَصِىَ aor. ـُ; (Ḳ;) but this last requires consideration, differing as it does from what is in the Ṣ [without any allusion to the latter's being wrong]; (TA; [see also شَظِىَ;]) said of a corpse; (Ks, Ṣ, Ḳ;) *Its arms and legs rose,* or *rose high;* (Ḳ;) or *it became inflated,* or *swollen, and its arms and legs rose,* or *rose high.* (Ks, Ṣ.) — And شَصَى بِرِجْلِهِ *He raised,* or *raised high, his leg.* (TA.)

4. اشصى بَصَرَهُ [*He made his eye,* or *eyes, to become fixedly open,* or *raised,* &c.: see 1, first sentence: or] *he raised,* or *he raised high, his eye,* or *eyes.* (Ṣ, Ḳ,* TA.)

شَصْوٌ i. q. شِدَّةٌ [app. as meaning *Hardship, distress,* or *adversity*]. (Az, Ḳ.) — And *A* سِوَاك [or *piece of stick with which the teeth are cleansed*]. (IAạr, Az, TA. [See also شَوْصٌ.])

شَاصٍ; fem. شَاصِيَةٌ, pl. of the latter شَاصِيَاتٌ and شَوَاصٍ; part. n. of 1 (Ṣ, TA) as said of the eyes [i. e. *Fixedly open,* or *being raised,* &c.]: (TA:) and of a water-skin, meaning *Filled,* or *inflated, so that its legs are raised;* and of a wine-skin, meaning *filled, so that its legs are raised:* and of a corpse, meaning *Inflated,* &c. (Ṣ, TA.) It is said in a prov.,

إِذَا ٱرْجَحَنَّ شَاصِيًا فَٱرْفَعْ يَدَا

[expl. in art. رجحن, q. v.]. (Ṣ, TA.)

شط

1. شَطَّ, aor. ـُ and ـِ, (Ṣ, Mṣb, Ḳ,) [the latter contr. to analogy,] the pret. like ضَرَبَ and قَتَلَ, (Mṣb, [and the like is said in the TA,]) inf. n. شَطٌّ and شُطُوطٌ, (Ṣ, Ḳ,) *It* (a house, or dwelling, Ṣ, Mṣb, TA, and a place of visitation, TA) *was,* or *became, distant, remote,* or *far off.* (Ṣ, Mṣb, Ḳ.) — شَطَّ فِى السَّوْمِ, (Mṣb, Ḳ,) aor. ـُ and ـِ, (Mṣb,) inf. n. شَطٌّ and شَطَطٌ; (TA;) or ▼ أَشَطَّ فيه; (Ṣ;) or both, (Mṣb, Ḳ,) but the latter is the more common; (Ḳ;) and ▼ اشتطّ; (Ṣ;) *He went far,* (Ṣ, Ḳ,) or *beyond the due bounds, in offering a thing for sale and demanding a price for it,* or *in bargaining for a thing:* (Ṣ, Mṣb, Ḳ:) the verb in this phrase is also followed by عَلَيْهِ [*against him*]. (TA.) IB says that شَطَّ signifies بَعُدَ [meaning *He,* or *it, was,* or *became, distant,* &c.]: and that ▼ أَشَطَّ signifies أَبْعَدَ [meaning *he went far,* &c.]. (TA.) You say also, أَشَطُّوا ▼ فِى طَلَبِى *They went far,* or *very far,* or *to a great* or *an extraordinary length, in seeking me.* (Ṣ, Ḳ.*) And ▼ أَشَطَّ القَوْمُ فِى طَلَبِنَا *The people,* or *company of men, sought us walking and riding.* (TA.) And ▼ أَشَطَّ فِى المَفَازَةِ *He went away in the desert:* (Ḳ:) as though he went far in it. (TA.) And شَطَّ فِى سِلْعَتِهِ, inf. n. شَطَطٌ, *He exceeded the due bounds, and went far from what was right, in respect of his commodity,* or *article of merchandise.* (Ḳ.) And شَطَّ فِى حُكْمِهِ, (Mṣb, Ḳ,) aor. ـُ, (Ḳ, TA,) only, (TA,) or ـُ and ـِ, (Mṣb,) the latter aor. is mentioned in the L, (TA,) inf. n. شَطَطٌ, (Mṣb, TA,) in the Ḳ, erroneously, شَطِيطٌ, (TA,) and شُطُوطٌ also; (Mṣb;) and ▼ اشطّ; (Mṣb, Ḳ;) and ▼ اشتطّ; (Ḳ;) or ▼ اشطّ فِى القَضِيَّةِ; (Ṣ;) *He acted unjustly, wrongfully, injuriously,* or *tyrannically,* (Ṣ, Mṣb, Ḳ,) *in his judging,* or *exercising jurisdiction* or *rule,* or *passing sentence,* (Mṣb, Ḳ,) or *in judging,* &c., (Ṣ,) عَلَيْهِ *against him.* (Ḳ.) And شَطَطْتَ عَلَيْهِ, (Ṣ, L,) aor. ـِ, (L,) and ▼ أَشْطَطْتَ; (Ṣ, L;) *I acted unjustly, wrongfully, injuriously,* or *tyrannically, against him:* mentioned by A'Obeyd. (Ṣ, L.) It is said in the Ḳur [xxxviii. 21], وَلَا تَشْطُطْ, or ▼ تُشْطِطْ, or ▼ تَشْطُطْ, or ▼ تُشَاطِطْ, accord. to different readings, *And go not thou far from what is right:* (Ḳ, TA:) all having this meaning: (TA:) or *exceed not the due bounds.* (Bḍ.) شَطَطٌ signifies The *exceeding the due bounds* (AA, Ṣ, Mgh) in selling, and in demanding or seeking, and in exercising jurisdiction, &c., (AA,) or in everything. (Ṣ.) It is said in a trad. لَهَا مَهْرُ مِثْلِهَا لَا وَكْسَ وَلَا شَطَطَ [*She shall have the dowry of her like:*] *there shall be no falling short nor exceeding.* (Ṣ.) And you say of a just sale, لَا بَخْسَ فِيهِ وَلَا شَطَطَ, (Ṣ in art. بخس,) or وَلَا شُطُوطَ, (T and TA in that art.,) [*There is no deficiency in it nor excess.*] You also say شَطَّ فِى القَوْلِ, aor. ـُ and ـِ, inf. n. شَطَطٌ and شُطُوطٌ, *He was rough, harsh,* or *coarse, in speech.* (Mṣb.) — شَطَّ used transitively, [aor. ـُ,] *He passed,* or *passed beyond,* [or, probably, *passed far away from,*] a place. (TA.) — شَطَّ فُلَانًا, (Ḳ,) aor. ـُ, (TA,) inf. n. شَطٌّ and شُطُوطٌ, (Ḳ,) *He distressed,* or *afflicted, such a one, and treated him,* or *used him, unjustly, wrongfully, injuriously,* or *tyrannically:* (Ḳ:) so say AZ and Aboo-Malik. (TA.) — شَاطَّهُ فَشَطَّهُ: see 3.

2. شطّط, inf. n. تَشْطِيطٌ, *He strove, laboured, exerted himself,* or *did his utmost, in acting unjustly, wrongfully, injuriously,* or *tyrannically, and exceeding the due bounds.* (Ḳ,* TA.) See also 1, in the latter half of the paragraph.

3. شَاطَّهُ, (Ḳ,) inf. n. مُشَاطَّةٌ, (TA,) *He vied with him in* اِشْتِطَاط [i. e. *going far,* or *beyond the due bounds,* in offering a thing for sale and demanding a price for it, or in bargaining for a thing; or *acting unjustly, wrongfully, injuriously,* or *tyrannically,* in judging, &c.]. (Ḳ.) You say, ▼ شَاطَّهُ فَشَطَّهُ [*He vied with him in so doing, and surpassed him,* or *overcame him, therein*]. (TA.) See also 1, in the latter half of the paragraph.

4: see 1, in nine places.

8: see 1, in two places.

شَطٌّ The *bank,* or *side,* of a river: (Ṣ, Mṣb, Ḳ:) and of a valley: (Ṣ, Mṣb:) or, of the latter, the *rising ground next the bottom:* (AḤn:) pl. شُطُوطٌ (Mṣb, Ḳ) and شُطَّانٌ; (Ḳ;) the latter occurring in a verse, accord. to one relation; but accord. to another relation, it is شُطَّانٌ, pl. of شَاطِئٌ, which is syn. with شَطٌّ. (TA.) — † The *side* of a camel's hump; (Ṣ, Ḳ;) *any side* thereof: (Ṣ:) or the *half* thereof: (Ḳ:) pl. شُطُوطٌ. (Ṣ, Ḳ.)

شَطَّةٌ: see شَاطٌّ.

شِطَّةٌ: see شَطَاطٌ, in two places.

شَطَطٌ, for أَمْرٌ ذُو شَطَطٍ, (Mgh,) and قَوْلٌ ذُو شَطَطٍ, (Bḍ in lxxii. 4,) *An action*, or *affair*, (Mgh,) and *a saying*, (Bḍ,) *that is extravagant*, or *exorbitant*, or *exceeding the due bounds.* (Mgh, Bḍ.) [See 1, of which it is an inf. n.]

شَطَاطٌ *Distance; remoteness;* (Ṣ, Ḳ, TA;) as also ▼ شِطَاطٌ and ▼ شِطَّةٌ, with kesr, (Ḳ,) and ▼ مَشَطَّةٌ. (TA.) It is said in a trad., اَللّٰهُمَّ إِنِّى أَعُوذُ بِكَ مِنْ وَعْثَآءِ السَّفَرِ وَكَآبَةِ ▼ الشِّطَّةِ وَسُوْءِ الْمُنْقَلَبِ i. e. [*O God, verily I seek protection by Thee from trouble of travel, and grievousness*] *of distance of the space to be journeyed over,* [*and evilness of return* to my home.] (TA.) — And *Distance,* or *farness, between the two extremities* of a man; as also ▼ شِطَاطٌ and ▼ شَطَاطَةٌ. (Ḳ.) And *Tallness, and beauty of stature:* (Ḳ:) or *justness of stature:* (IDrd, Ṣ, Ḳ:) as also ▼ شِطَاطٌ, (Ṣ, Ḳ,) in either sense. (Ḳ.) — Also, and ▼ شِطَاطٌ, *Fragments of baked bricks.* (Ḳ.) — [Freytag erroneously assigns the first and last meanings in this paragraph to شَطَّةٌ: and he adds, from Reiske, a meaning belonging to شِطَاطٌ.]

شِطَاطٌ: see شَطَاطٌ, in four places.

شَطُوطٌ A she-camel *having a large hump;* (Aṣ, Ṣ, Ḳ;) as also ▼ شَطُوطَى: (Ḳ:) or *large in the two sides of the hump:* (TA:) pl. شَطَائِطُ. (Ḳ.)

شَطَاطَةٌ: see شَطَاطٌ.

شَطُوطَى: see شَطُوطٌ.

شَطْشَاطٌ *A certain bird:* (Ḳ:) IDrd says that it is asserted to have this meaning; but is not of established authority. (O.)

شَاطٌّ Anything *Distant, remote,* or *far.* (TA.) — A man *whose two extremities are far from each other.* (Ḳ.) — جَارِيَةٌ شَاطَّةٌ, (Ṣ, Ḳ,) and ▼ شَطَّةٌ, (Ḳ,) *A girl tall, and of beautiful stature:* (Ḳ:) or *of just stature.* (Ṣ, Ḳ.) — إِنَّكَ لَشَاطِى *Verily thou art acting unjustly, wrongfully, injuriously,* or *tyrannically, towards me* in judging: occurring in a trad. (A'Obeyd, Az, Ṣ.)

مَشَطَّةٌ: see شَطَاطٌ. — Also *Difficulty, distress, affliction, trouble,* or *inconvenience.* (TA.)

شطأ

1. شَطَأَ: see 4. — Also *He walked on the* شَاطِئ, i. e. *bank,* or *side, of the river.* (Ḳ,* TA.) — And *He cut lengthwise* [*into slices,* or *strips,*] the hump of a camel, and a skin, or hide. (TA.) — *He subdued, overcame, overpowered,* or *mastered,* a man. (Ḳ.) — *He compressed* his wife. (Ḳ.) [And طَشَأَ and طَشَأَ signify the same.] — شَطَأَ النَّاقَةَ, (AA, Ṣ, Ḳ,) aor. َ [as in other senses], (TA,) inf. n. شَطْءٌ, (AA, Ṣ,) *He bound the saddle upon the she-camel.* (AA, Ṣ, Ḳ.) — And شَطَأَ بِالْحِمْلِ *He burdened heavily,* or *overburdened,* the camel *with the load;* (Ḳ;) inf. n. as above. (TA.) [But see what follows.] — Accord. to ISk, (TA,) this last phrase signifies also, (Ḳ,) or شَطَأَتْ بِالْحِمْلِ, as in the L, (TA,) *He,* (a man, Ḳ,) or *she,* (a camel, L, TA,) *had strength,* or *power, to bear the load.* (L, Ḳ, TA.) — شَطَأَتْ بِهِ *She* (his mother) *cast him forth* [*from her womb*]. (Ḳ.) One says, لَعَنَ ٱللّٰهُ أُمًّا شَطَأَتْ بِهِ, and so قَطَأَتْ بِهِ, *May God curse a mother who cast him forth* [*from her womb*]. (TA.)

2. شَطَّأَ, inf. n. تَشْطِئٌ, *It* (a valley) *had its two sides* (شَاطِئَاهُ, TA) *flowing* [*with water*]. (IAạr, Ḳ.)

3. شَاطَأْتُهُ *I walked upon one* شَاطِئ [i. e. *bank,* or *side, of a river* or *valley,*] *while he walked upon the other* شَاطِئ. (Ṣ, Ḳ.*)

4. اشطأ; (Ṣ, Mṣb;) or ▼ شَطَأَ, aor. َ, inf. n. شَطْءٌ and شُطُوءٌ; (Ḳ;) or both; (TA;) *It put forth its* شَطْء [or *sprouts,* &c.]; (Ṣ, Ḳ;) syn. فَرَّخَ; (Mṣb;) said of seed-produce; (Ṣ, Mṣb, Ḳ;) and in like manner said of palm-trees (نَخْل); and the former verb, said of trees (شَجَر), *they put forth sprouts around their bases,* or *stems.* (Ḳ.) And اشطأت الشَّجَرَةُ بِغُصُونِهَا *The tree put forth its branches.* (TA.) — And the former verb, † *He* (a man) *had a son who had attained to manhood and become like him;* (AḤn, Ḳ;) like أَصْحَبَ. (TA.)

Q. Q. 1. شَطْبَأَ, (Ḳ, TA,) said of a man, (TA,) i. q. رَهْيَأَ, (Ḳ, TA,) meaning *He was weak* (TA) in his opinion, or judgment, (Ḳ, TA,) and in his affair. (TA.)

شَطْءٌ (Ṣ, Mṣb, Ḳ, &c.) and ▼ شَطَأٌ (TA as from the Ḳ [but not in the CḲ nor in my MS. copy of the Ḳ, though a known dial. var. of the former as will be shown in what follows,]) The فِرَاخ [or *sprouts*] of seed-produce, (IAạr, Ṣ, Mṣb, Ḳ,) and of plants, or herbage, (Ṣ,) and of palm-trees: or the *leaves* thereof; (Ḳ, TA;) i. e. of seed-produce: (TA:) and the *shoots that come forth* (Mṣb, Ḳ) *from,* (Mṣb,) or *around,* (Ḳ,) *the bases,* or *stems,* (Mṣb, Ḳ,) of plants, or herbage, (Mṣb,) or of trees: (Ḳ:) pl. أَشْطَآءٌ, (Ṣ,) or شُطُوءٌ. (Ḳ.) أَخْرَجَ شَطْأَهُ, in the Ḳur xlviii. last verse, means *That has put forth its* فِرَاخ [or *sprouts*]: (Bḍ, Jel:) or, accord. to Akh, *its extremity:* (Ṣ:) or *its ears,* (Mṣb, TA,) accord. to Fr; each grain, he says, producing ten, or eight, or seven: or, accord. to Zj, *its plants:* (TA:) and some read ▼ شَطَأَهُ, (Bḍ, Jel,) which is a dial. var.; and شَطَاءَهُ, and شَطْأَهُ, and شَطَهُ, and شُطُوءَهُ. (Bḍ.) — [See also شَطْأَةٌ.] — And see شَاطِئٌ.

شَطَأٌ: see the next preceding paragraph, in two places.

شَطْأَةٌ [app. a n. un. of شَطْءٌ, q. v. — Also] *A green palm-branch:* one says, لَهَا قَدٌّ كَالشَّطْأَةِ *She has a figure like the green palm-branch.* (A, TA.) — And *A slice,* or *strip,* i. e. *a piece cut lengthwise,* of a camel's hump, and of a skin, or hide. (A, TA.)

شَاطِئٌ (Ṣ, Mṣb, Ḳ) and ▼ شَطْءٌ (Ḳ) The *bank,* or *side,* (شَطّ, Ṣ, Ḳ, and جَانِب, Ṣ, Mṣb,) of a valley (Ṣ, Mṣb, Ḳ) and of a river: (Ḳ:) and some say that the former signifies the *extremity,* or *edge,* or *side,* (طَرَف,) of a river; and the *shore* of the sea: the pl. of the latter is شُطُوءٌ; and of the former, شَوَاطِئُ and شُطْآنٌ; (Ḳ, TA;) or this last, as is said in the M, may be pl. of شَطْءٌ. (TA.) Accord. to the Ṣ, one says also شَاطِئُ الْأَوْدِيَةِ [meaning *The sides of the valleys*]; not assigning to شاطئ any pl.: but the truth is that the pl. is as stated above. (TA.)

شطب

1. شَطَبَ, (Ḳ, TA,) aor. ُ, (TA,) inf. n. شَطْبٌ, (AZ, TA,) *He cut* (Ḳ, TA) *into oblong pieces,* or *strips,* flesh-meat, and a camel's hump, and a hide, or leather: (TA:) or *he cut into strips, but without separating them,* a camel's hump. (AZ, TA.) — And شَطَبَتِ الْجَرِيدَ, [aor. ُ,] inf. n. شَطْبٌ, *She* (a woman) *split the palm-sticks,* or *palm-branches stripped of their leaves, to make of them mats:* which being done, says A'Obeyd, [or when they have been peeled,] the شَاطِبَة [q. v.] throws them to the مُنَقِّيَة. (Ṣ.) [Or] شَطَبَتْ, aor. ُ, inf. n. شُطُوبٌ, *She removed the upper peel of the* شَطْب, or [*fresh, green*] *palm-branches.* (ISk, TA.) — شَطَبَ also signifies *It inclined,* or *declined, turned aside* or *away, deflected,* or *deviated,* and *became distant,* or *remote;* (Aṣ, O, Ḳ;) and so شَطَفَ; and both signify *it went away.* (Aṣ, TA.) One says, شَطَبَ عَنْهُ *It turned aside* or *away,* and *became distant,* or *remote, from him,* or *it.* (Ḳ.) Thus, in a trad., شَطَبَ الرُّمْحُ عَنْ مَقْتَلِهِ *The spear deflected from,* and *failed to reach, his vital part.* (O, TA.*) And one says also, شَطَبَتِ الدَّارُ *The dwelling was,* or *became, distant,* or *remote.* (O.)

7. انشطب *It flowed;* (Ṣ, Ḳ;) said of water, &c. (Ḳ.)

شَطْبٌ pl. of ▼ شَطْبَةٌ, (Ṣ, Mṣb,) [or rather a coll. gen. n., of which the latter is the n. un.,] like تَمْرٌ as is of تَمْرَةٌ; (Mṣb;) *Fresh,* (A,) or *green,* (Mṣb,) or *green and fresh,* (Ṣ, Ḳ,) *palm-branches* (Ṣ, A, Mṣb, Ḳ) *stripped of their leaves:* (A:) or they are *less than what are termed* شَطَائِب, of which the sing. is ▼ شَطِيبَة; and the شطائب are less than the كَرَانِيف: [i. e. the كِرْنَاف is the thickest part of the palm-branch; next is the شَطِيبَة; and next to this, the شَطْبَة:] or ▼ شَطْبَةٌ signifies *a green palm-branch.* (Ḳ.) عَسِيلٌ

▼ شُطْبَةٌ, in a trad. of Umm-Zarạ, [as expl. in art. سل, q. v.,] means *Like a green palm-stick drawn forth* from its skin: or *like a sword drawn forth* [from its scabbard]: (TA in art. سل:) [for] — ▼ شُطْبَةٌ signifies also *A sword.* (Aboo-Saʼeed, Ḳ.) — [Hence, app.,] شَطْبٌ is used also as an epithet, meaning ‡ *Tall, and well made;* (A, Ḳ, TA;) applied to a man and to a horse. (TA.) And, applied to a boy, or young man, ‡ *Plump;* or *fat, soft, thin-skinned, and plump:* and so ▼ شَطْبَةٌ applied to a girl, or young woman: (A:) or the former, applied to a boy, or young man, *well made, and neither tall nor short:* (TA:) or, so applied, *light,* or *active, in body, and sharp-headed:* (IAạr, TA in art. عضب, voce عَضْبٌ:) or it means, so applied, *long and even* (سَبِطٌ) *in the bones, light of flesh;* likened to the palm-stick that is split: but this epithet is mostly used with ة, i. e. ▼ شَطْبَةٌ, which is applied to a mare: (Ḥam p. 208:) or this epithet, شَطْبَةٌ, applied to a mare, means *lank* (سَبِطَةٌ) *in flesh;* (Ḳ, TA;) or *tall;* (TA;) as also ▼ شَطْبَةٌ in the former sense, (Ḳ, TA,) or in the latter; and the masc. is not thus used, applied to a horse: (TA:) and ▼ شَطْبَةٌ, (Ṣ,) or ▼ شُطْبَةٌ, (Ḳ,) or both, but the former is the more approved, (TA,) *beautiful; plump;* or *fat, soft, thin-skinned, and plump;* (Ḳ, TA;) *and tall:* (Ḳ:) or simply *tall;* (Ṣ, TA;) as also ▼ مَشْطُوبٌ and ▼ مُشَطَّبٌ applied to a man. (TA.)

شَطْبَةٌ: see the next preceding paragraph, in seven places: — and see what next follows.

شُطْبَةٌ (Ṣ, Ḳ) and ▼ شِطْبَةٌ (Ḳ) and ▼ شَطْبَةٌ (TA) and ▼ شُطَبَةٌ, (Ḳ,) which last is said by some to be a n. un. of شُطَبٌ [mentioned in what follows as a pl.], (MF,) *A* [*raised*] *line* (طَرِيقَةٌ, Ṣ, O, or طَرِيقٌ, Ḳ, [meaning *a ridge,* and sometimes also *a depressed line,* as shown voce مُشَطَّبٌ, i. e. *a channel,*]) *in the* مَتْن [i. e. *broad side,* or *middle of the broad side, of the blade*] (Ṣ, O) *of a sword:* (Ṣ, O, Ḳ:) pl. شُطَبٌ and شُطُبٌ, (Ṣ, O,) or شُطُوبٌ and شُطْبٌ and شُطُبٌ: (Ḳ: [in which it is said that the pl. is شُطُوبٌ and شُطُبٌ like غُرَفٌ and كُتُبٌ: but I think that شُطُوبٌ is a mistranscription, and that the right reading is شُطَبٌ and شُطُبٌ like غُرَفٌ and كُتُبٌ:]) hence it would seem that شُطَبٌ and شُطُبٌ are pls. of one sing.; but Ibn-Hishám El-Lakhmee expressly states that the former is pl. of ▼ شُطْبَةٌ; and the latter, of ▼ شَطِيبَةٌ; (MF;) of which شَطَائِبُ also is a pl.; (L in art. عمد;) and which signifies [the same as شُطْبَةٌ, i. e.] the *rising* عَمُود [i. e. *the ridge*] *in the* مَتْن *of a sword.* (ISh, TA.) [See also مُشَطَّبٌ: and see عَمُودٌ and مَتْنٌ.]

شَطْبَةٌ: see شطب (near the end) in two places: — and see also شُطْبَةٌ: — and شَطِيبَةٌ, in three places.

شُطَبَةٌ: see شُطْبَةٌ.

شِطَابٌ The *instrument with which a* بَرْذَعَة [or *cloth put beneath a camel's saddle*] *is quilted.* (Ḳ.)

شَطِيبَةٌ *A slice,* or *strip,* of flesh-meat: (TA:) or *a piece cut lengthwise* of a camel's hump; (Ṣ, O, Ḳ, TA;) as also ▼ شِطْبَةٌ: (O, Ḳ:) or *a piece cut in the form of a strip, but not separated,* of a camel's hump; and so ▼ the latter word: pl. of the former شَطَائِبُ. (AZ, TA.) — And *A piece cut lengthwise* of a hide or of leather; (Ṣ, O;) as also ▼ شِطْبَةٌ. (O.) — And *A piece of* [the tree called] نَبْع *of which a bow is made.* (Ṣ, O.) — See also شَطْبٌ. — And see شُطْبَةٌ. — Also, applied to a she-camel, *Tough;* syn. يَابِسَةٌ. (Ḳ.) — And [the pl.] شَطَائِبُ *Different,* or *various, parties, sects,* or *classes,* (Ḳ, TA,) *and sorts,* of men &c. (TA.) — And *Difficulties,* or *distresses;* (Abu-l-Faraj, O, Ḳ;) as also شَصَائِبُ. (Abu-l-Faraj, O, TA.)

شَطِيبَةٌ, (as in the TA,) or ▼ مُشَطَّبَةٌ, (as implied in the Ḳ,) A *quilted* بَرْذَعَة [or cloth that is put beneath a camel's saddle]. (Ḳ, TA.)

شَطَّابٌ *A butcher.* (Fr, TA in art. سطر.)

شَاطِبٌ [act. part. n. of the trans. verb شَطَبَ]. — [Hence,] شَوَاطِبُ [the pl. of شَاطِبَةٌ] signifies Women *who cut skin,* or *leather, into strips, after having shaven it* or *measured it:* so accord. to different copies of the Ḳ; i. e. بَعْدَ مَا يَحْلِقْنَهُ or يَخْلُقْنَهُ. (TA.) — And Women *who split palm-leaves, and peel the* [*palm-branches stripped of their leaves,* or *the portions thereof termed*] عَسِيب, *to make of them mats, and then throw them to the* مُنَقِّيَات: (TA:) or the sing., شَاطِبَةٌ, signifies a woman *who peels the* عَسِيب, (Aṣ, TA,) or *who splits the palm-sticks, to make of them mats,* (Ṣ,) *and then throws them to the* مُنَقِّيَة, (Aṣ, Ṣ, TA,) *who removes all that is upon them with her knife until she has made them slender, when she throws them back to the* شَاطِبَة: (Aṣ, TA:) or a woman *who makes mats of* شَطْب, i. e. [*green, fresh*] *palm-branches* [*stripped of their leaves*]: (ISk, TA:) the pl. occurs in a verse cited voce تَذَرَّعَ. (Ṣ, TA.) — Also, [from the intrans. verb شَطَبَ,] طَرِيقٌ شَاطِبٌ *A road inclining, declining,* or *turning aside* or *away.* (Ṣ, Ḳ.) — And رَمْيَةٌ شَاطِبَةٌ *A shot,* or *throw, that deflects,* or *deviates, from a vital part;* as also شَاطِفَةٌ. (TA.) — And رَجُلٌ شَاطِبُ المَحَلِّ i. q. شَاطِنٌ [i. e. *A man remote,* or *distant, in respect of the place of alighting* or *abode*]. (TA.)

مُشَطَّبٌ A sword (Ṣ, A, Ḳ) *having* شُطَب [pl. of شُطْبَةٌ], (A, Ḳ,) i. e. (A, TA) *having* طَرَائِق [here meaning *ridges,* as expl. above, voce شُطْبَةٌ], (Ṣ, A, TA,) in its مَتْن; [or *ridges and channels,*] *these being in some cases elevated and depressed* [*lines*]; (TA;) as also ▼ مَشْطُوبٌ: (Ḳ, TA:) said by some, [but not so accord. to the A,] to be tropical, as being likened to pieces of a camel's hump cut in strips. (TA.) And in like manner, A garment, or piece of cloth, *having* طَرَائِق [as meaning *lines,* or *streaks,* or *stripes*]. (Ṣ, TA.) And أَرْضٌ مُشَطَّبَةٌ ‡ *Land that is furrowed* (A, Mṣb, Ḳ) *a little,* (Ḳ,) *not much,* (Mṣb,) *by a torrent.* (A, Mṣb, Ḳ.) — And † *Flowing* [water &c.; because of the streaks, or lines, with which its surface is diversified]. (TA.) — See also شَطِيبَةٌ. — And see شَطْبٌ, last sentence.

مَشْطُوبٌ: see the next preceding paragraph. — فَرَسٌ مَشْطُوبُ المَتْنِ وَالكَفَلِ means *A horse swollen with fat in the two portions of flesh and sinew next the back bone, on each side,* [*and in the rump,*] (O, Ḳ,) *and whose creases of the skin are far apart.* (O.) — See also شَطْبٌ, last sentence.

شطر

1. شَطَرَهُ, (A, MA, O, TA,) [aor. ـُ,] inf. n. شَطْرٌ; (MA;) and ▼ شَطَّرَهُ, (Ḳ,) inf. n. تَشْطِيرٌ; (TA;) *He halved it; divided it into halves.* (A, MA, O, Ḳ, TA.) — شَطَرَهَا, aor. ـُ, (Ṣ,) inf. n. شَطْرٌ, (Ṣ, Ḳ,) *He milked one* شَطْر *of her,* (namely, a camel, or a ewe or goat, Ṣ, [i. e., in the former case *one pair of teats,* and in the latter case *one teat,*]) *and left the other* شَطْر. (Ṣ, Ḳ.) — شَطَرَتْ and شَطُرَتْ, aor. ـُ, (Ḳ,) inf. n. شِطَارٌ, (TA,) *She* (a ewe or goat) *had one of her teats dried up:* or *had one teat longer than the other.* (Ḳ.) [شِطَار seems to be also *Syn. with* حِضَان as expl. in this Lex.: see also the latter word in Freytag's Lex.: Reiske, as cited by Freytag, explains the former word as meaning "*quando latus unum vulvæ præ altero propendet.*"] — شَطَرَ بَصَرُهُ, (Ṣ, Ḳ, TA, and so in the O voce شَفَر, q. v., [in some copies of the Ṣ and Ḳ and in a copy of the A, erroneously, بَصَرَهُ,]) aor. ـُ, (Ṣ,) inf. n. شُطُورٌ (Ṣ, Ḳ) and شَطْرٌ, (TA,) *He was as though he were looking at thee and at another:* (Ṣ, A, Ḳ:) on the authority of Fr. (TA.) — شَطَرَ شَطْرَهُ *He repaired,* or *betook himself, in the direction of him,* or *it:* or الشَّطْر in the sense of الجِهَة and النَّاحِيَة has no verb belonging to it. (Ḳ.) — شَطَرَتِ الدَّارُ *The house,* or *abode, was distant,* or *remote.* (Mgh, Mṣb.) — شَطَرَ, (Ṣ, Ḳ,) aor. ـُ; (Ḳ;) and شَطُرَ, aor. ـُ; inf. n. شَطَارَةٌ, of both verbs, (Ṣ, Ḳ,) or this is a simple subst., (Mṣb,) and شُطُورٌ; (L;) [and ▼ تشاطر; (A in art. عنر;)] *He was,* or *became,* or *acted, like a* شَاطِر [q. v.]. (Ṣ, Ḳ.) And شَطَرَ عَنْهُمْ, (A, Mṣb,) or شَطَرَ عَلَى أَهْلِهِ, (Ṣ,* Ḳ,) aor. ـُ, (Mṣb,) inf. n. شُطُورٌ and شُطُورَةٌ and شَطَارَةٌ, (Ḳ,) or this last is a simple subst., (Mṣb,) *He withdrew far away* (Ṣ,* A, Ḳ*) *from his family;* or *broke off from them,* or *quitted them, in anger:* (A, Ḳ:) or *he disagreed with his family, and wearied them by his wickedness* (Mṣb, TA) *and baseness.* (Mṣb.)

2: see 1, first sentence. — شَطَّرَ نَاقَتَهُ, (Ṣ,) or بِنَاقَتِهِ, (Ḳ,) inf. n. تَشْطِيرٌ, (Ṣ, Ḳ,) *He bound two of the teats of his she-camel with the* صِرَار [q. v.], (Ṣ, Ḳ,) *leaving* [*the other*] *two* [*unbound*]. (Ḳ.)

3. شَاطَرْتُهُ مَالِى *I halved with him my property;* (Ṣ, Ḳ;) *I retained half of my property and gave him the other half.* (M, TA.) — And شَاطَرَتْ

طَلِيِّى I left for my lamb, or kid, one teat [of the mother], having milked the other teat and bound it with the صِرَار [q. v.]. (Ṣ.)

6: see 1, last sentence but one.

شَطْرٌ The *half* of a thing; (Ṣ, A, Mgh, Mṣb, Ḳ;) as also ↑شَطِيرٌ: (TA:) pl. [of pauc.] أَشْطُرٌ (Ṣ, Ḳ) and [of mult.] شُطُورٌ. (Ḳ.) It is said in a prov., أَحْلُبْ حَلَبًا لَكَ شَطْرُهُ [*Milk thou a milking of which half shall be for thee*]. (Ṣ.) And one says شَعَرٌ شَطْرَانِ *Hair* [*half*] *black and* [*half*] *white*. (A.) Accord. to Ibráheem El-Ḥarbee, (O,) the saying of the Prophet, مَنْ مَنَعَ صَدَقَةً فَإِنَّا آخِذُوهَا وَشَطْرَ مَالِهِ [*Whoso refuses to render a poor-rate, verily we take it* from him, *and half of his property*], thus related by Bahz, is a mistake, and the right wording is, وَشُطِرَ مَالُهُ, meaning *and his property shall be divided into two halves*, and the collector of the poor-rate shall have the option given him and shall take that rate from out of the better of the two halves, as a punishment for the man's refusal of the rate; (O, Ḳ;) but it is said that this law was afterwards abrogated: (O:) Esh-Sháfi'ee, however, says that, in the old time, when one refused the poor-rate of his property, it was taken from him, and half of his property was taken as a punishment for his refusal; and he adduces this trad. as evidence thereof; but says that in recent times, only the poor-rate was taken from him, and this trad. was asserted to be abrogated. (TA. [More is there said on this subject, but I omit it as unprofitable.]) — It occurs in two trads. as meaning *Half a* مَكُّوك [q. v.], or *half a* وَسْق [q. v.], of barley. (TA.) — [In prosody, *Half a verse.*] — Also ‡ *A part*, or *portion*, or *somewhat*, of a thing; (Mgh, Ḳ;) and so ↑شَطِيرٌ. (TA.) In the trad. of the night-journey, فَوَضَعَ شَطْرَهَا means † [*And He remitted*] *part*, or *somewhat*, *thereof*; (Ḳ;) i. e., of the prayer. (TA.) And similar is the saying in another trad., الطُّهُورُ شَطْرُ الإِيمَانِ † [*Purification is part of faith*]. (TA.) — Either *the fore pair* or *the hind pair of the teats* of a she-camel: she has two pairs of teats, a fore pair and a hind pair, and each pair is thus called: (Ṣ, Ḳ:) and *either of the two teats* of a ewe or she-goat: (IAạr, TA:) pl. أَشْطُرٌ. (Ṣ, TA.) Hence the saying, (Ṣ,) فُلَانٌ حَلَبَ الدَّهْرَ أَشْطُرَهُ ‡ *Such a one has known*, or *tried*, *varieties of fortune*: (Ṣ,* TA:) *has experienced the good and evil of fortune*; (Ṣ, Ḳ, TA;) *its straitness and its ampleness*: being likened to one who has milked all the teats of a camel, that which yields plenty of milk and that which does not; the fore pair being the good; and the hind pair, the evil: or, as some say, أَشْطُر means *streams*, or *flows*, *of milk*: and [in like manner] one says, حَلَبَ الدَّهْرَ شَطْرَيْهِ. (TA.) And, as is said in the "Kámil" of Mbr, one says of a man experienced in affairs, فُلَانٌ قَدْ حَلَبَ أَشْطُرَهُ ‡ *Such a one has endured the difficulties and* [*enjoyed*] *the ampleness of fortune, and managed his affairs in poverty and in wealth*: lit., *has milked his pairs of teats*, one pair after another. (TA.) — Also *A direction* in which one looks or goes or the like. (Ṣ, A, Mṣb, Ḳ.) One says, قَصَدَ شَطْرَهُ *He went in his*, or *its*, *direction*; *towards him*, or *it*. (Ṣ, A.) And it is said in the Ḳur [ii. 139 and 144 and 145], فَوَلِّ وَجْهَكَ شَطْرَ ٱلْمَسْجِدِ ٱلْحَرَامِ *Then turn thou thy face in the direction of the Sacred Mosque*. (Fr, Ṣ.) The noun in this sense has no verb belonging to it: or one says, شَطَرَ شَطْرَهُ [expl. above: see 1]. (Ḳ.) — Also *Distance*, or *remoteness*. (TA.)

شُطُرٌ: see شَطِيرٌ [of which it is both a syn. and a pl.].

وَلَدُ فُلَانٍ شِطْرَةٌ *The offspring of such a one are half males and half females*. (Ṣ, A, Ḳ. [In the Ḥam p. 478, it is written شُطْرَة.])

شَطْرَانُ, (Ṣ, A, Ḳ,) fem. شَطْرَى, (Ḳ,) *A bowl*, (Ṣ, Ḳ,) or *vessel*, (A, Ḳ,) *half full*. (Ṣ, A, Ḳ.)

شَطُورٌ *A ewe*, or *she-goat*, *having one teat longer than the other*; (Ṣ, O, Ḳ;) like حَضُونٌ in this sense [and perhaps in others also, agreeably with what is said of شَطَّار in the first paragraph of this art.]: (Ṣ in art. حضن:) and (so in the Ṣ and O, but in the Ḳ "or") one *having one of her teats dried up*: (Ṣ, O, Ḳ:) and a she-camel *having two of her teats dried up*; for she has four teats. (Ṣ, O.) And *A garment*, or *piece of cloth*, *having one of the two extremities of its breadth longer than the other*. (O, Ḳ.) — See also the next paragraph.

شَطِيرٌ: see شَطْرٌ, in two places. — Also *Distant*, or *remote*; (Aṣ, Ṣ, A, Mgh, Mṣb, Ḳ;) applied to a town, or country, (Aṣ, Ṣ,) an abode, (A, Mgh, Mṣb,) and a tribe. (A.) And so ↑شُطُرٌ in the phrase نَوًى شُطُرٌ [*A distant tract*, or *region*, *towards which one journeys*]: (Ṣ, Ḳ:) so too ↑شَطُورٌ in the phrase نِيَّةٌ شَطُورٌ [which may mean as above, (like نِيَّةٌ شَطُونٌ,) or *a remote*, or *far-reaching*, *intention*, or *aim*, or *purpose*]. (TA.) — Also *A stranger*; (Ṣ, O, Mṣb, Ḳ;) because of his remoteness from his people; (TA;) as in a verse cited voce إِذًا: (Ṣ, O:) or *one who is alone*, or *solitary*: (A:) pl. شُطُرٌ. (TA.)

شَاطِرٌ [One *who withdraws far away from his family*; or *breaks off from them*, or *quits them*, *in anger*: (see 1, last sentence:) or] one *who disagrees with his family*, (Mṣb,) and *who wearies them by his wickedness* (Ṣ, Mṣb, Ḳ) *and baseness* (Mṣb) *and guile*: (TA:) *i. q.* خَلِيعٌ [meaning as above, and having other similar meanings; generally *vitious*, or *immoral*; *bad*, *evil*, *wicked*, or *mischievous*]: (A:) accord. to some, it is post-classical: Aboo-Is-ḥáḳ says that it signifies one *who takes a wrong course*: it is also expl. as signifying one *who outstrips*; like the [messenger called] بَرِيد, who takes a long journey in a short space of time: and hence, [as a conventional term of the mystics,] it is applied to one *who outstrips, and is quick, in attaining nearness to God*: or as meaning one *who has wearied his family, and withdrawn far from them* [*in spirit*], *though with them* [*bodily*], *because of their inviting him to carnal lusts, and accustomed ways* [*of the world*]: (TA:) [in the present day, it is applied to *a sharper*, or *clever thief*: and to *any clever*, or *cunning*, *person*:] pl. شُطَّارٌ. (TA.)

مَشْطُورٌ [*Halved*. — And hence,] A verse of the metre termed الرَّجَز, (O, Ḳ,) and of that termed السَّرِيع, (TA,) *having three of its six feet wanting*; (O, Ḳ;) properly, *having half thereof taken away*. (O.) — Also Bread *done over with* [*the seasoning*, or *condiment*, *called*] كَامَخ. (O, Ḳ.)

هُمْ مُشَاطِرُونَا *They are persons whose houses adjoin ours*. (O, Ḳ.)

شطرنج

شِطْرَنْجٌ (O, L, Mṣb, Ḳ) and شَطْرَنْجٌ; (L, Mṣb;) some say the former; and some, the latter; (Mṣb;) the latter said to be of established authority, as a dial. var., though disallowed in the Ḳ [and in the O]; but the former is the more approved on account of its being conformable with Arabic words, (Mṣb, TA,) such as جِرْدَحْل, (TA,) which the latter is not; (Mṣb, TA;) and sometimes it is pronounced with the unpointed س, (O,) this being a dial. var.; (Ḳ;) *A well-known game*; [namely, *chess*:] (O, L, Ḳ:) a Pers. word, (TA,) arabicized; (Mṣb, Ḳ, TA;) [said to be] from صَدْ رَنْگ "a hundred stratagems;" or from شُدْ رَنْج "trouble departed," meaning that trouble departs from him who plays at it; (TA;) [or from شَاهْ رَنْج "the royal care or sorrow;" or from شَشْ رَنْگ "six species or ranks," because the pieces are of so many species: (Richardson's Pers. Arab. and Engl. Dict., Johnson's ed.:)] or [accord. to some] it is from الشَّطَارَة, (O, Ḳ,) or المُشَاطَرَة, referring to the word شطرنج; (TA;) or from التَّسْطِير, (O, Ḳ,) referring to the word سطرنج; so says Ibn-Hishám El-Lakhmee: but, as IB and others have said, these derivations are only partial, making the ن and the ج to be augmentative letters, and are manifestly incorrect. (MF, TA.)

شطن

1. شَطَنَ, (Ṣ, TA,) [aor. ـُ,] inf. n. شُطُونٌ, (PṢ,) *He was*, or *became*, *distant*, or *remote*, (Ṣ, TA,) عَنْهُ [*from him*, or *it*]. (Ṣ.) And شَطَنَتِ الدَّارُ, (Mṣb, TA,) aor. as above, (Mṣb,) and so the inf. n., *The abode*, or *dwelling*, *was distant*, or *remote*. (Mṣb, TA.) — And † *He was*, or *became*, *remote*, or *far*, *from the truth, and from the mercy of God*. (Mṣb.) — And شَطَنَ فِى الأَرْضِ, (Ḳ,) inf. n. as above, (TA,) *It entered into the earth*, either رَاسِخًا [app. as meaning *becoming firmly fixed* therein], or وَاغِلًا [app. as meaning *penetrating, and becoming concealed*]. (Ḳ.) — شَطَنَهُ, (Ṣ, Ḳ,) aor. ـُ, inf. n. شَطْنٌ, (Ṣ,) *He turned away in opposition to him* (namely, his companion, Ḳ) *from his design*, or *aim*, or *his direction that he was pursuing, and his way*, or

course; expl. by the words خَالَفَهُ عَنْ نِيَّتِهِ وَوَجْهِهِ (ISk, Ṣ, Ḳ.) ― And شَطَنَهُ, (Ṣ, Ḳ,) aor. ـُ, (Ṣ,) inf. n. شَطْنٌ, (TA,) *He bound him with the* شَطَن [or *rope*, or *long rope*, &c.]. (Ṣ, Ḳ.)

4. اشطنهُ *He made him*, or *caused him, to be*, or *become, distant*, or *remote*. (Ṣ, Ḳ.)

Q. Q. 1. شَيْطَنَ *He acted as a* شيطان [i. e., as implied in the context, a *devil*; or *one excessively*, or *inordinately, proud* or *corrupt* or *unbelieving* or *rebellious*, or *one insolent and audacious in pride and in acts of rebellion*]; (Ḳ;) and ▾ تَشَيْطَنَ; (Ṣ, Ḳ;) both signify the same; (Ḳ, TA;) *he became, and acted, like the* شَيْطَان. (TA.)

Q. Q. 2. تَشَيْطَنَ: see what next precedes.

شَطَنٌ *A rope*, (Ṣ, Mṣb, Ḳ,) in a general sense: (Ḳ:) or *a long rope*: (Kh, Ṣ, Ḳ:) or *a long and strongly-twisted rope by means of which one draws water*: (TA:) pl. أَشْطَانٌ. (Ṣ, Mṣb, Ḳ.) Mention is made, in a trad., of a horse as being مَرْبُوطٌ بِشَطَنَيْنِ [i. e. *Tied with two ropes*, or *long ropes*, &c.,] because of his strength. (TA.) And one says of a strong-spirited horse, إِنَّهُ لَيَنْزُو بَيْنَ شَطَنَيْنِ [*Verily he leaps between two ropes*, or *long ropes*, &c.]: a saying applied as a prov. to him who exults, or exults greatly, or excessively, and behaves insolently and ungratefully, and is strong. (TA.) An Arab of the desert described a horse (Ṣ, Mṣb) that did not become abraded in the sole of his hoof (so in a copy of the Ṣ) by saying, كَأَنَّهُ شَيْطَانٌ فِى أَشْطَانٍ [*As though he were a devil in ropes*, or *long ropes*, &c.]. (Ṣ, Mṣb.)

نِيَّةٌ شَطُونٌ (Ṣ) or نَوًى شَطُونٌ (Ḳ) [*A place to which one purposes journeying*] *that is distant*, or *remote*. (Ṣ, Ḳ.) And غَزْوَةٌ شَطُونٌ [*A warring and plundering expedition*] *that is distant*. (Ḳ.) And حَرْبٌ شَطُونٌ [*Distant war*: or] † *war that is difficult* [*because distant*]. (TA. See an ex. in a verse cited voce جُنَّةٌ.) [See also شَطِينٌ, and شَاطِنٌ.] ― بِئْرٌ شَطُونٌ † *A deep well*, (Ṣ, Ḳ, TA,) *curving in its interior*: (TA:) or *a well from which the bucket is drawn out by means of two ropes, from its two sides, wide in the upper part and narrow in the lower part*; (Ḳ, TA;) *so that if one draws out the bucket from it by means of one rope, one draws it against the casing, and it becomes rent*. (TA.) And رُمْحٌ شَطُونٌ † *A long and crooked spear*. (TA.)

شَطِينٌ *Distant*, or *remote*. (TA. [See also شَطُونٌ, and شَاطِنٌ.])

شَاطِنٌ [*Distant*, or *remote*, in respect of the place of alighting or abode]; i. q. شَاطِبٌ [q. v.]. (TA in art. شطب. [See also شَطُونٌ, and شَطِينٌ.]) ― And † *Far from the truth* [*and from the mercy of God*: see 1]. (TA.) ― And i. q. خَبِيثٌ † [*Bad, corrupt*, &c.; like شَيْطَانٌ]. (Ḳ.) Umeiyeh (Ṣ, TA) Ibn-Abi-ṣ-Ṣalt, referring to Solomon, (TA,) says,

أَيُّمَا شَاطِنٍ عَصَاهُ عَكَاهُ
ثُمَّ يُلْقَى فِى السِّجْنِ وَالأَغْلَالِ

[*Whatever bad one disobeyed him, he bound him in irons; then he was cast into the prison and the shackles for the neck and hands*]. (Ṣ, TA.)

شَيْطَانٌ a word of well-known meaning [i. e. *A devil*; and with the article ال, *the devil, Satan*]: (Ṣ, Ḳ:) *any that is excessively*, or *inordinately, proud* or *corrupt* or *unbelieving* or *rebellious*, or *that is insolent and audacious in pride and in acts of rebellion, of mankind*, and *of the jinn*, or *genii*, and *of beasts*; (A'Obeyd, Ṣ, Mṣb, Ḳ;) as is shown in relation to the first and second of these by what is said in the Ḳur vi. 112, and ii. 13 and 96: (TA:) the ن is radical, (Ṣ, Mṣb, TA,) the word being of the measure فَيْعَال, from شَطَنَ, (Mṣb, TA,) signifying "he was, or became, distant, or remote," (TA,) or signifying "he was, or became, remote, or far, from the truth, and from the mercy of God;" (Mṣb;) as is indicated by the pl. شَيَاطِينُ; [for] the reading of El-Ḥasan in the Ḳur xxvi. 210, الشَّيَاطُونَ, is anomalous, [like بَسَاتُونَ for بَسَاتِينُ,] and is said by Th to be a mistake: (TA:) or, as some say, the ن is augmentative, (Ṣ, Mṣb, TA,*) and the ى is radical, so that the word is of the measure فَعْلَان, (Mṣb,) from شَاطَ, aor. يَشِيطُ, (Mṣb, TA,) signifying "it was, or became, null, void, of no account," and the like, and "it burned," or "became burnt," (Mṣb,) or signifying "he burned with anger:" but the former opinion is the more common: (TA:) [in the Ḳur, the word is always perfectly decl.; and so it is said to be by SM, in art. شيط of the TA; unless used as a proper name: but J says,] if you make it to be of the measure فَيْعَال from تَشَيْطَنَ said of a man, [or rather because they say of a man تشيطن,] you make it perfectly decl.; but if you make it to be from شَيَّطَ ["he burned" a thing], you make it imperfectly decl., because it is of the measure فَعْلَان. (S.) ― Also The *serpent*: (Ṣ, Ḳ:) or *a certain species of serpents*; (Fr, Ṣ, TA;) *having a mane, of foul aspect*: or, as some say, *a slender, light*, or *active, serpent*. (TA.) ― Respecting the saying in the Ḳur [xxxvii. 63], طَلْعُهَا كَأَنَّهُ رُؤُوسُ الشَّيَاطِينِ [*Its fruit is as though it were the heads of the* شياطين], Fr says that there are three ways in which it may be explained: one is, that the طلع is likened to the heads of the شياطين [meaning *devils*] in respect of foulness, or ugliness, because these are described as foul, or ugly: (Ṣ:) or it is likened to the *evil in disposition of the jinn*, because these are imagined as foul, or ugly: Zj says, in explaining it, that one says of a thing deemed foul, or ugly, كَأَنَّهُ وَجْهُ شَيْطَانٍ [*as though it were the face of a devil*], and كَأَنَّهُ رَأْسُ شَيْطَانٍ [*as though it were the head of a devil*]; for though the شيطان is not seen, he is conceived in the mind as the foulest, or ugliest, of things: (TA:) the second is, that [the meaning is *foul*, or *ugly, serpents*; for] the Arabs apply the name شيطان to *a sort of serpents, having a mane, foul*, or *ugly, in the head and face*: (Ṣ, TA:*) the third is, that *a certain foul*, or *ugly, plant* is named رُؤُوسُ الشَّيَاطِينِ; (Ṣ, TA;) which is expl. in the Ḳ only as meaning *a certain plant*. (TA.) ― شَيْطَانُ الفَلَا [lit. *The devil of the waterless deserts*] means † *thirst*. (Ḳ.) ― شَيْطَانٌ signifies also † *Any blamable faculty*, or *power*, [or *propensity*,] of a man. (Er-Rághib, TA.) One says, رَكِبَهُ شَيْطَانُهُ i. e. † [*His anger got the ascendency over him*; or] *he was*, or *became, angry*. (TA.) And نَزَعَ شَيْطَانَهُ † *He plucked out his pride*. (TA.) ― Also, [probably as being likened to a serpent,] † *A mark made with a hot iron in the upper part of the haunch of a camel, perpendicularly, upon the thigh, extending to the hock*; (Ḳ, TA;) from the "Tedhkireh" of Aboo-'Alee; (TA;) likewise called ▾ مُشَيْطَنَةٌ. (AZ, Ḳ, TA.)

الشَّيْطَانِيَّةُ *A certain sect of the extravagant zealots of* [*the schismatics called*] *the* شِيعَة; so named from [their founder] شَيْطَانُ الطَّاقِ, (TA,) an appellation of Mohammad Ibn-En-Noamán. (Ḳ and TA in art. طوق.)

مُشَاطِنٌ *One who draws out the bucket from the well* بِشَطَنَيْنِ, (Ḳ, TA,) i. e. *with two ropes*. (TA.)

مُشَيْطَنَةٌ: see شَيْطَانٌ, last sentence.

شظ

1. شَظَّ الجُوَالِقَ, (Ṣ,) or الوِعَآءَ, (Ḳ,) aor. ـُ, inf. n. شَظٌّ, (TA,) *He fastened its* شِظَاظ [q. v.] *upon the sack*: (Ṣ:) or *he put the* شِظَاظ *into the bag*; [meaning *into its loop*, or *handle*;] as also ▾ اشظّهُ: (Ḳ:) or the latter signifies *he put to it*, or *made for it*, (namely the sack,) *a* شِظَاظ. (Ṣ.)

4: see the preceding paragraph.

شِظَاظٌ The *stick*, or *piece of wood, which is inserted into the loop*, or *handle, of a sack*; (Ṣ;) *a curved piece of wood*, (Ḳ, TA,) *with a pointed extremity*, (TA,) *which is put into the two loops*, or *handles, of a pair of sacks*, (Ḳ, TA,) *when they are bound upon the camel*: (TA:) there are two such pieces of wood: (Ṣ,* TA:) pl. أَشِظَّةٌ. (Ḳ.) And *A piece of wood*, or *peg, with which they make fast the rope of a burden*. (Ibn-Maaroof, as cited by Golius.)

شَظِيظٌ A sack *made fast*, or *bound*. (Fr. Ḳ.) ― A stick, or piece of wood, *split in several places*. (Fr, Ḳ.)

شظف

1. شَظِفَ الشَّجَرُ, (Ṣ, O, Ḳ,) aor. ـَ; (Ḳ;) and شَظُفَ, (O, Ḳ,) aor. ـُ; (Ḳ;) inf. n. شَظَافَةٌ, (O, Ḳ,) of the former verb; (O;) *The trees, not being sufficiently watered, became hard, without losing their moisture*. (Ṣ, O, Ḳ.) ― And شَظِفَتْ يَدُهُ *His hand became rough*, or *coarse*. (Ḥar p. 70.) ― And شَظُفَ العَيْشُ *The means of subsistence became dry and hard*. (Ḳ,* TA.) ― شَظَفَ السَّهْمُ, (Ṣ, Mṣb, Ḳ,) aor. ـِ, (Ḳ,) *The arrow entered between the skin and the flesh*. (Ṣ, Mṣb, Ḳ. Omitted in the TA.) ― شَظَفْتُهُ عَنِ الشَّىْءِ,

(O, TA,) inf. n. شَظْفٌ, (O, Ḳ,) *I withheld, restrained,* or *debarred, him from the thing.* (O, Ḳ,* TA.) — And شَظْفٌ signifies also The *drawing forth the testicles of a ram:* (O, Ḳ:) or the *compressing them between two pieces of wood,* or *stick, and binding them with sinew* (بِعَقَبٍ, in the CḲ [erroneously] بِعَقِبٍ,) *so that they wither.* (Ḳ.)

5. تشظّف *He subjected himself to a hard,* or *difficult, life.* (L in art. معد.)

شَظْفٌ *A splinter,* or *piece split off, of a staff,* or *stick.* (IAạr, O, Ḳ.)

شِظْفٌ *Dry bread.* (O, Ḳ.) — And *A small piece of wood,* or *stick, like a peg:* pl. شِظَفَةٌ. (Ibn-'Abbád, O, Ḳ.)

شَظَفٌ and ▼ شِظَافٌ *Straitness;* and *hardness,* or *difficulty,* or *distress;* (AZ, Ṣ, O, Ḳ;) like ضَفَفٌ: (AZ, Ṣ, O:) ISd thinks that the second is a dial. var. of the first; and IB mentions that, in a verse of El-Kumeyt, as related by some, it is with kesr, i. e. شِظَاف [which see in what here follows]: (TA:) and (Ḳ) as some say, (TA,) *dryness,* and *hardness, of the means of subsistence:* (Ḳ:) or شَظَفٌ signifies *hardness,* and *straitness, of the means of subsistence:* (Mṣb:) or *hardness,* and *coarseness,* or *roughness, thereof;* from شَظِفَتْ يَدُهُ [expl. above]: (Ḥar p. 70:) pl. شِظَافٌ. (Ḳ.) — Also *A disintegration of the flesh, separating it from the border around the nail.* (TA.)

شَظِفٌ *Dry and hard* means of subsistence. (Ḳ,* TA. [See 1.]) — *Evil in disposition.* (O, Ḳ.) — *Vehement in fight.* (Ibn-'Abbád, O, Ḳ.) — A man *alighting,* or *taking up an abode, in places where the herbage is dried up, and in a desert where is no water* (فَلَاة). (TA in art. عظب.) — بَعِيرٌ شَظِفُ الخِلَاطِ [*A stallion-camel*] *vehement in leaping,* or *compressing, the she-camels.* (Ṣ, O, Ḳ.) — أَرْضٌ شَظِفَةٌ *Rough,* or *rugged, land* or *ground.* (Ibn-'Abbád, O, Ḳ.)

شِظْفَةٌ *Bread that has become burned.* (IAạr, O.)

شِظَافٌ : see شَظَفٌ.

شظاف *Distance,* or *remoteness.* (O, Ḳ.)

شَجَرٌ شَظِيفٌ *Trees that, not being sufficiently watered, have become hard, without losing their moisture.* (Ṣ, O, Ḳ.)

مُشَظِّفٌ *One who utters oblique, indirect,* or *ambiguous, speech* or *language, deviating from the right way* or *course.* (O, Ḳ. Omitted in the TA.)

شظى

1. شَظِىَ, [aor. and inf. n. as in the next sentence,] said of a stick, or branch, or piece of wood, [&c.,] *It was,* or *became, split.* (AḤn, TA.) — Said of a horse, (Aṣ, Ṣ, Mgh, Ḳ,) aor. ـَ , inf. n. شَظًى, (Ḳ,) *His* شظى, (Aṣ, Ṣ, Mgh, Ḳ,) i. e. the *small bone called* الشَّظَى, (Aṣ, Ṣ, Mgh,*) *moved from its place,* (Aṣ, Ṣ, Mgh,) or *became displaced,* syn. زَوِىَ, (A, TA,) or *became unsteady,* or *wabbling:* (Ḳ:) and so ▼ تشظّى, (Ḳ, TA,) this latter on the authority of ISd: (TA:) or [the inf. n.] شَظًى, accord. to some, signifies the sinews' *becoming split,* or *slit:* (Aṣ, Ṣ, Mgh:) or شَظًى has this meaning also; (Ḳ;) and so ▼ تَشَظٍّ. (ISd, Ḳ, TA.) = Accord. to the Ḳ, شَظِىَ, said of a corpse, is *syn. with* شَصِىَ: but correctly, the former verb is شَظَى, aor. ـِ , inf. n. شُظِىٌّ, and the latter verb is شَصَا [q. v.], as they are said to be by Az: and in like manner, شَظَى, aor. ـِ , is said of a سِقَآء [or skin for water or milk], meaning *It being filled, its legs became raised,* or *raised high.* (TA.)

2. شظّى, (TA,) inf. n. تَشْظِيَةٌ, (Ḳ, TA,) *He separated into several,* or *many, portions* or *divisions;* or *dispersed,* or *scattered;* (Ḳ,* TA;) [a thing; or] ‡ a company of men. (TA.) — And *He made* [a horse] *to be such that his* شظى (شَظَاهُ) *became unsteady,* or *wabbling.* (TA.)

4. اشظاهُ *He,* or *it, hit,* or *hurt, his* شظى (شَظَاهُ): (Ḳ:) Ṣgh says, by rule it should be شَظَاهُ [i. e. the verb should be thus, being derived from الشَّظَى, like قَفَاهُ from القَفَا]. (TA.)

5. تشظّى, said of a stick, or branch, or piece of wood, (A, Mṣb, Ḳ, TA,) or of a thing, (Ṣ, TA,) *It split,* or *became split, in pieces,* or *in several* or *many places:* (A, Mṣb, TA:) or *it became scattered,* or *dispersed, in splinters,* or *pieces split off:* (Ṣ, Ḳ:) and *it* [i. e. anything, nothing in particular being specified,] *became separated into several,* or *many, portions* or *divisions;* or *dispersed,* or *scattered.* (TA.) One says also, تَشَظَّى اللُّؤْلُؤُ عَنِ الصَّدَفِ ‡ [*The pearls became separated,* or *scattered, from the oyster-shells*]. (A, TA.) See also 1, in two places.

7. انشظى *It broke,* or *became broken.* (TA.) One says, انشظت الرَّبَاعِيَةُ *The* [*tooth called the*] رباعية *broke,* or *became broken.* (TA.)

شَظًى, of a staff, or stick, The *like of a* لِيطَة [i. e. *a piece,* or *sharp piece, of the exterior portion*], *that enters into the hand, and wounds it.* (Ḥam p. 474. [But شَظِيَّةٌ is more commonly used in this and similar senses.]) — *A small bone,* (عُظَيْمٌ, Ḳ, TA, [in the CḲ عَظْمٌ, i. e. *a bone,* and so in my copy of the Mgh,]) or *a slender small bone,* (Aṣ, Ṣ,) *adhering to the* ذِرَاع [here app. meaning the *arm-bone* of a horse], (Aṣ, Ṣ, Ḳ,) or *to the bone of the* ذِرَاع, (Mgh,) *which sometimes moves from its place;* (Aṣ, Ṣ, Mgh; [see شَظِيَّةٌ;]) or *to the knee;* (Ḳ;) thus in the M; (TA;) or to the وَظِيف [app. here meaning the *fore shank* of a horse]; (Ḳ;) thus in the A: (TA:) or *certain small sinews* (عَصَب) *therein;* (Ḳ;) i. e. *in the* وظيف; thus in the T. (TA.) AO says that تَحَرُّكُ الشَّظَى [i. e. *The motion of the* شظى from its place (see 1)] is like what is termed اِنْتِشَارُ العَصَبِ, except that the horse has more power of endurance of the latter than of the former. (T, TA.) — And *Portions* of a thing *that are separated,* or *dispersed,* or *scattered.* (Ḥar p. 160.) It is said by ISd to be a pl. [or rather it is a coll. gen. n.] of which the sing. [or n. un.] is شَظَاةٌ. (TA.) — Also *A portion of fur upon the mark left by a gall,* or *sore, on the back* [*of a camel*], *such as reaches the utmost extent thereof:* (Ḳ, accord. to the TA: [الشَّظَى being there expl. by the words الوبرة على اثر الدبرة حتى تبلغ اقصاها: in the CḲ, and in my MS. copy of the Ḳ, الدُّبْرَةُ على أَثَرِ الدَّبَرَةِ فى المَزْرَعَةِ حَتَّى تَبْلُغَ أَقْصَاهَا; which Freytag renders "sulcus ad latus alterius in arvo ductus, ut ejus extremum attingeret;" but which, I think, evidently presents a mistranscription and an interpolation:]) the pl. is أَشْظِيَةٌ: and sometimes there are ten [?] portions of fur [of this description, app. meaning, upon one camel: the word that I here render "ten" is more like عشه than عشر; but the final letter, as is often the case in the MS. of the TA, is written in a form differing little from a common form of ر]: mentioned by ISh, from Eṭ-Ṭáïfee; as is said in the T. (TA.) — Also † The *followers,* and *incorporated confederates,* of a people, or party; (Ṣ, Ḳ;) *contr. of* the صَمِيم thereof: (Ṣ:) or the *freedmen* and *followers.* (M, TA.)

شَظِىٌّ and شِظِىٌّ : see the next paragraph.

شَظِيَّةٌ *A splinter,* or *piece split off,* (T, Ṣ, M, Mgh, Mṣb, Ḳ,) of a staff, or stick, and the like, (Ṣ,) or of wood, (T, Mgh, Mṣb,) and the like, (Mṣb,) or of a reed, or cane, (T, Mgh,) or of silver, (T, TA,) or of bone, (T, Mgh,) or of anything: (M, Ḳ:) pl. شَظَايَا (Ṣ, Mṣb, Ḳ, &c.) and ▼ شَظِىٌّ, (Ḳ,) [or rather this is a coll. gen. n.,] like رَكِىٌّ as is of رَكِيَّةٌ, (TA,) or a quasi-pl. n., like عَبِيدٌ, improperly said by IAạr to be pl. of شَظًى, (ISd, TA,) and ▼ شِظِىٌّ, (Ḳ, TA, [in the latter as omitted in the Ḳ, with kesr to the ش on account of the same vowel-sound following,]) mentioned by Ṣgh, from Ks. (TA.) AO terms the إِبْرَة [q. v.] at the head of the elbow [of the horse] a شَظِيَّة adhering to the ذِرَاع, but not [forming a portion] of it. (TA. [See شَظًى.]) — Also *A bow:* (Ḳ:) because its wood is split: on the authority of AḤn. (TA.) — And The *shank-bone.* (Ḳ.) — And *A great mass of rock wrenched from the side of a mountain;* (Ḳ, TA;) *as though it were a piece split off, broken* [*off*] *but not parted so as to form an interstice, or a gap:* and also *a piece cut from a mountain, like a house or a tent:* and it is said in the copies of the Ḳ that شِظْيَة, with kesr, signifies the same; but the word is correctly ▼ شِنْظِيَةٌ, with an augmentative ن, as in the T, and mentioned also by Hr in the "Ghareebeyn:" pl. of the former شَظَايَا. (TA.) — See also شُنْظُوَةٌ.

شَاظٍ part. n. of شَظِىَ [q. v.] said of a horse. (TA.)

شُنْظُوَةٌ The *head,* or *top, of a mountain,* (Ḳ, TA,) [and so ▼ شِنْظِيَةٌ, (Freytag, from the Deewán of the Hudhalees,)] *resembling the* شُرْفَة [q. v.]

of a mosque: pl. شَنَاظٍ: and الجِبَالِ ▾ شَوَاظِى [likewise] signifies the heads, or tops, of the mountains. (TA.)

شِنْظِيَةٌ: see شَظِيَّةٌ, near the end.

شَوَاظِى الجِبَالِ: see شَنْظَاةٌ.

[مِشْظًى, pl. مَشَاظٍ, *A fragment of wood*: (Freytag, from the Deewán of Jereer:) but the pl., when indeterminate, is correctly مَشَاظٍ.]

شع

1. شَعَّ, (O, Ḳ, TA,) aor. ـَ, (O, TA,) inf. n. شَعَاعٌ (Ṣ,* O,* Ḳ,* TA) and شَعٌّ, (TA,) *It became scattered*, or *dispersed*; (Ṣ, O, Ḳ, TA;) said of a thing; like شَاعَ, aor. يَشِيعُ; (TA;) of the urine of a camel; (O, Ḳ;) and of a people, or party; (IAạr, O, Ḳ;) [like شَعَّ;] and [in like manner] شَعَاعٌ is used in relation to blood, &c., as meaning the *being scattered*. (Ṣ, O, Ḳ, TA. [See also شَعَاعٌ, below; and شُعَاعٌ.]) ═ شَعَّ بَوْلَهُ, (Ṣ, O, Ḳ,) aor. ـُ, (Ṣ, O,) inf. n. شَعٌّ (O, TA) and شَعَاعٌ, (Ḳ,* TA,) *He* (a camel) *scattered his urine*; as also ▾ اشعّهُ: (Ṣ, O, Ḳ:) or both signify *he scattered his urine, and stopped it.* (TA.) — And شَعَّ الغَارَةَ عَلَيْهِمْ, (Ḳ, TA,) inf. n. شَعٌّ; and ▾ شَعْشَعَهَا; (TA;) *He poured upon them the horsemen making a sudden attack and engaging in conflict*, or *urging on their horses*; (Ḳ, TA;) and in like manner, الخَيْلَ. (TA.)

4: see 1. ═ اشعّت الشَّمْسُ *The sun spread*, or *diffused, its* شُعَاع [or *beams*], (Ṣ, Ḳ,) or *its light*. (TA.) — اشعّ الزَّرْعُ *The corn put forth its* شَعَاع, (Ṣ, Ḳ, TA,) i. e., its *awn*. (TA.) — And اشعّ السُّنْبُلُ *The ears of corn became compact in their grain*, (Ḳ, TA,) *and dry therein.* (TA.)

7. انشعّ الذِّئْبُ فِى الغَنَمِ *The wolf made an incursion among the sheep or goats.* (O, Ḳ, TA.)

R. Q. 1. شَعْشَعَهُ, (Ṣ, O, Ḳ,) inf. n. شَعْشَعَةٌ, (TA,) *He mixed it*, namely, wine, (Ṣ, O, Ḳ,) with water. (O.) And *He mixed one part of it*, namely, a thing, *with another part*, (O,* Ḳ,) like as one mixes wine with water. (O.) And شَعْشَعَ الثَّرِيدَةَ *He mixed the* ثريدة [or *mess of crumbled bread*] with olive-oil: (O:) or *he put much clarified butter to it*, (ISh, O, Ḳ,) and *much grease*, or *gravy*: (Ḳ:) or *he raised its head*; (O, Ḳ;) as some say: (Sh, O:) or *he made its head high*; (O, Ḳ;) as some say; from شَعْشَاعٌ as an epithet applied to a man, meaning "tall." (O.) But the verb is used more in relation to wine than to ثريد. (TA.) — See also 1.

R. Q. 2. تَشَعْشَعَ, said of a man, is from ▾ شَعْشَاعٌ applied to a man as meaning حُلْوٌ خَفِيفٌ [i. e. "such as is excited to briskness, liveliness, or sprightliness, and esteemed pleasing in the eye, and is light, or active;" so that the verb may be rendered *He was*, or *became, such as is excited to briskness*, &c.: or *he was*, or *became, such as is* termed شَعْشَاعٌ, q. v.]. (Ḥam, p. 246.) — Said of the month *It nearly came to an end; little remained of it*: (Ḳ, TA:) occurring in a trad.: but accord. to one relation thereof, it is تَشَعْسَعَ; from الشَّسُوعُ "the being distant, or remote:" and accord. to another, تَسَعْسَعَ, with two س. (TA.)

شَعٌّ: see شَعَاعٌ, first and last sentences. ═ Also *Haste*: (IAạr, Ḳ, TA:) and so شَعِيعٌ accord. to the Ḳ; but this is wrong; the meaning of the latter word being only that given below, voce شَعَاعٌ. (TA.)

شُعٌّ *A spider's web.* (AA, Ḳ.) — See also شُعَاعٌ.

شَعَاعٌ [an inf. n. (see 1) used as an epithet, and therefore as masc. and fem. and sing. and pl.;] *Scattered*, or *dispersed*; and *disordered*, or *unsettled*; syn. مُتَفَرِّقٌ; (Ṣ, Ḳ;) as also ▾ شَعٌّ, [likewise an inf. n. used as an epithet,] applied [like the former] to anything, (Ḳ, TA,) such as blood, and an opinion, and a purpose, or an intention; (TA;) and ▾ شَعِيعٌ, which is wrongly expl. in the Ḳ as syn. with شَعٌّ in another sense, as stated above; (TA;) and ▾ شَعْشَاعٌ. (Ṣ, Ḳ.) One says, ذَهَبَ دَمُهُ شَعَاعًا *His blood went scattered*, or *dispersed*: (TA:) or شَعَاعٌ applied to blood signifies *spirtling* from a wound made with a spear or the like; as in a verse cited voce نَفَذَ. (Az, TA. [See also شُعَاعٌ.]) And ذَهَبُوا شَعَاعًا *They went away scattered*, or *dispersed*. (Ḳ.) And أُمَّةٌ شَعَاعٌ *A nation*, or *people, scattered*, or *dispersed*. (TA, from a trad.) And تَطَايَرَتِ العَصَا شَعَاعًا *The staff*, or *stick, broke into scattered pieces*; as when one has broken it by striking with it upon a wall: and in like manner, القَصَبَةُ *the reed*, or *cane*. (TA.) And رَأْىٌ شَعَاعٌ *A disordered*, or *an unsettled, opinion.* (Ṣ, Ḳ.) And نَفْسٌ شَعَاعٌ *A mind of which the purposes*, or *intentions*, (هَمُّهَا, as in the Ṣ [and O], for which, in the Ḳ, هُمُومُهَا is erroneously substituted, TA,) *and the opinions*, (Z, TA,) *are disordered*, or *unsettled*, (Ṣ, Ḳ, TA,) *so that it is not directed to a decided affair.* (Z, TA.) And طَارَ فُؤَادُهُ شَعَاعًا [*His mind fled in a disordered*, or *an unsettled, state, as though dissipated*; expl. as] meaning تَفَرَّقَتْ هُمُومُهُ [a mistranscription, as before: correctly تفرّقت هَمُّهُ i. e. *his purposes*, or *intentions, became disordered*, or *unsettled*: see also Ḥam p. 44, and Ḥar p. 366]. (Ḳ.) And a rájiz says,

• صَدْقُ اللِّقَآءِ غَيْرُ شَعْشَاعِ ▾ الغَدَرْ •

meaning [*Firm*, or *steady, in encounter*, or *conflict*,] *not disordered*, or *unsettled, in respect of purpose*, or *intention*. (Ṣ.) — Hence, app., (TA,) Milk *mixed with much water*; (ISh, O;) syn. ضَيَاحٌ. (ISh, O, Ḳ, TA.) ═ Also [as a subst.] The *awn*, or *beard*, of the ears of corn; (Ṣ, O, Ḳ;) and so ▾ شُعَاعٌ and ▾ شِعَاعٌ (Ḳ) and ▾ شَعٌّ: (TA:) or the *awn*, or *beard, when it has become dry, as long as it remains on the ears*; as also ▾ شُعَاعٌ. (Lth, O.)

شُعَاعٌ (Ṣ, O, Ḳ) and ▾ شُعٌّ (AA, Ḳ) [*The rays*, or *beams*, of the sun; or] *what one sees*, (Ṣ, O, Ḳ,) *of the light, like rods*, (Ṣ,) or *extending like spears*, (O, Ḳ,) *at the rising*, or *the beginning of the rising*, (Ṣ,) or *a little after the rising*, (O, Ḳ,) of the sun; (Ṣ, O, Ḳ;) or *what one sees, like cords coming towards him, when looking at the sun*; or the *dispersing light* of the sun: (Ḳ:) n. un. with ة: (Ṣ, O, Ḳ:) [and Freytag states that ▾ شَعْشَعَةٌ is said by Jac. Schultens to signify *rays*: but this I do not find in any lexicon:] the pl. (of شُعَاعٌ, O) is أَشِعَّةٌ, (O, Ḳ,) accord. to analogy, (O,) [a pl. of pauc.,] and شُعُعٌ (O, Ḳ) and ▾ شِعَاعٌ; (Ḳ;) the last anomalous. (TA.) Hence, in a trad. respecting [the night called] لَيْلَةُ القَدْرِ, it is said, إِنَّ الشَّمْسَ تَطْلُعُ مِنْ غَدِ يَوْمِهَا لَا شُعَاعَ لَهَا [*Verily the sun will rise on its morrow having no rays*]. (Ṣ: in the O, مِنْ غَدِهَا.) — In the verse cited voce نَفَذَ, Aṣ is related to have read الشُّعَاعُ instead of الشَّعَاعُ, as meaning *The light*, [or *brightness*] *and redness, and scattered state*, of the blood: ISd says, I know not whether he said it meaning by original application or by way of comparison. (TA.) — See also شَعَاعٌ, last sentence, in two places.

شِعَاعٌ: see شُعَاعٌ, last sentence: — and see also شَعَاعٌ.

شَعِيعٌ: see شَعَاعٌ, first sentence.

شَعْشَعٌ, (Ṣ, O,) or ▾ شَعْشَاعٌ, (Ḳ,) or both, (TA,) and ▾ مُشَعْشَعٌ, (Ṣ, TA,) Shade *that is not thick*, or *dense*; (Ṣ, O, Ḳ, TA;) or *which has not wholly shaded one, having in it interspaces*. (TA.) — See also شَعْشَاعٌ, in two places.

شُعْشُعٌ: see the next paragraph but one, in two places: and see شُلْشُلٌ.

شَعْشَعَةٌ: see شُعَاعٌ.

شَعْشَاعٌ: see شَعَاعٌ, in two places: and شَعْشَعٌ. — Also, (Ṣ, O, Ḳ,) and ▾ شَعْشَعٌ (O, Ḳ) and ▾ شَعْشَعَانٌ (IDrd, Ṣ, O, Ḳ) and ▾ شَعْشَعَانِىٌّ, (O, Ḳ,) in which last the relative ى is without cause, as in أَحْمَرِىٌّ and دَوَّارِىٌّ, (TA,) applied to a man, (Ṣ,) *Tall*: (O, Ḳ:) or *tall and goodly* (Ṣ, TA) *and light of flesh*; applied to a man as being likened to the thin [or much diluted] wine termed مُشَعْشَعَة: or the first signifies *long-necked*; and so ▾ the third, and ▾ the fourth; applied to anything, or the last, accord. to the R, applied to a man only: and the first, *long* applied to a neck: (TA:) and *light*, or *active*: (O, Ḳ:) or *so in journeying*; as also ▾ شُعْشُعٌ like هُدْهُدٌ, applied to a man, or, accord. to Th, to a boy, or young man: or *light in spirit*: (TA:) see also R. Q. 2: and (Ḳ) as some say, (O,) the first signifies *goodly*, or *beautiful*, (O, Ḳ, TA,) *in face*: (TA:) and ▾ شَعْشَعٌ, (so in the O,) or ▾ شُعْشُعٌ, with ḍamm to the ش, (TA,) a boy, or young man, *goodly*, or *beautiful*, *in face*, *light in spirit*; (O, TA;) on the authority of AA. (TA.) ═ Also *Certain trees*; or *a kind of tree*. (TA.)

شَعْشَعَانٌ : see شَعْشَاعٌ, in two places. With ة, applied to a she-camel, meaning *Tall*: (Ṣ,* O:) or *large in body*: (TA:) pl. شَعْشَعَانَاتٌ. (Ṣ, O. [In the TA, شَعْشَعَانَاتٌ is said to be mistranscribed in the Ṣ شَعْشَعَانَان: but it is not so in either of my copies.])

شَعْشَعَانِىٌّ : see شَعْشَاعٌ, in two places. Also *Long and thin*; applied to a camel's lip. (TA.)

مُشَعْشَعٌ : see شَعْشَعٌ. — With ة, applied to wine (خَمْرٌ), *Mixed with water*: (O,* EM p. 183:) accord. to some, [*much diluted*; i. e.] *mixed so as to be thin*. (TA.)

شعب

1. شَعَبَ, (Ṣ, Mṣb,) aor. ـَ, (Mṣb,) inf. n. شَعْبٌ, (A, Mṣb, Ḳ,) *He collected*; *brought*, *gathered*, or *drew*, *together*; or *united*; (Ṣ, A, Mṣb, Ḳ;) a thing, (Ṣ,) any thing or things, and a people or party: (Mṣb:) and *he separated*; *put apart*, or *asunder*; *divided*; *disunited*; or *dispersed* or *scattered*; (Ṣ, A, Mṣb, Ḳ;) a thing, (Ṣ,) any thing or things, and a people or party: (Mṣb:) thus having two contr. significations: (Ṣ:) so expressly state A'Obeyd and Aboo-Ziyád: (TA:) but accord. to IDrd, it has not two contr. significations [in one and the same dial.]: he says that the two meanings are peculiar to the dials. of two peoples, (Mṣb, TA,*) each meaning belonging to the dial. of one people exclusively. (TA.) [Hence, as it seems to be indicated in the Ṣ and A, or from شَعْبٌ meaning "a tribe," as it seems to be indicated in the Ḥam p. 538,] one says, تَفَرَّقَ شَعْبُهُمْ, (Ṣ,) or شَتَّ شَعْبُهُمْ, (A, Ḥam,) ‡ [*Their union became dissolved*, or *broken up*; or *their tribe became separated*;] meaning *they became separated after being congregated*: (Ṣ, Ḥam:) and ٱلْتَأَمَ شَعْبُهُمْ (Ṣ, A, Ḥam) ‡ [*Their separation became closed up*, or *their tribe drew together*;] meaning *they drew together after being separated*. (Ṣ, Ḥam.) And شَعَبَتْهُمُ ٱلْمَنِيَّةُ *Death separated them*: (Ṣ:) and شَعَبَتْهُ شَعُوبُ [*Death separated him* from his companions]; (TA;) said of a man when he has died. (O in art. عبل: in the Ḳ, in that art., ↓ اشْتَعَبَتْهُ [perhaps a mistranscription].) And it is said in a trad., مَا هٰذِهِ ٱلْفُتْيَا ٱلَّتِى شَعَبْتَ بِهَا ٱلنَّاسَ i. e. [*What is this judicial decision*] *with which thou hast divided the people?* (Ṣ. [In the TA, on the authority of IAth, ٱلتى شَغَبَتْ فِى ٱلنَّاسِ, which means, "which has excited evil among the people."]) One says also, شَعَبَ ٱلرَّجُلُ أَمْرَهُ † *The man broke up*, *discomposed*, *deranged*, or *disorganized*, [or *rendered unsound*, *impaired*, or *marred*, (agreeably with another explanation of the verb in what follows,)] *his state of affairs*: (Aṣ, A'Obeyd, TA:) whence the saying of 'Alee Ibn-El-'Adheer El-Ghanawee,

وَإِذَا رَأَيْتَ ٱلْمَرْءَ يَشْعَبُ أَمْرَهُ
شَعْبَ ٱلْعَصَا وَيَلِجُّ فِى ٱلْعِصْيَانِ

† [*And when thou seest the man break up his state of affairs as with the breaking up of the staff*, *and persevere in disobedience*, or *rebellion*]. (A'Obeyd, TA.) — Also, aor. as above, (Mṣb,) and so the inf. n., (Ṣ, A, Mṣb, Ḳ,) *He repaired* a cracked thing [such as a wooden bowl or some other vessel, *by closing up its crack* or *cracks*, or *by piecing it*: see 2, which has a similar signification, but implying muchness]: (Ṣ, Mṣb:) and [in a general sense,] *he repaired*, *mended*, *amended*, *adjusted*, or *put into a right*, or *proper*, *state*: (A, Ḳ, TA:) and it signifies the contr. also [of the former meaning and] of this, in the same, or in another, dial.: (TA:) [i. e.] *he cracked* a thing [such as a wooden bowl &c.]: (A, Mṣb:) and *he corrupted*, *rendered unsound*, *impaired*, or *marred*. (A, Ḳ, TA.) شَعْبٌ صَغِيرٌ مِنْ شَعْبٍ كَبِيرٍ, occurring in a trad. of 'Omar, means *A little repairing*, *of*, or *amid*, *much impairing*. (TA.) — [*He gave* a portion of property; as though he broke it off.] One says, ٱشْعَبْ لِى شُعْبَةً مِنَ ٱلْمَالِ *Give thou to me a portion of the property*. (TA.) — *He* (the commander, or prince, Ṣ) *sent* a messenger (Ṣ, Ḳ) إِلَيْهِ [*to him*], (Ḳ,) or إِلَى مَوْضِعِ كَذَا [*to such a place*]. (Ṣ.) — *He turned*, or *sent*, him, or it, *away*, or *back*: (Ḳ, TA:) aor. and inf. n. as above. (TA.) And شَعَبَ ٱللِّجَامُ ٱلْفَرَسَ *The bridle turned away* or *back*, or *withheld*, or *restrained*, *the horse from the direction towards which he was going*. (Ḳ.) — *He*, or *it*, *diverted* a man *by occupying him*, *busying him*, or *engaging his attention*. (Ḳ, TA.) One says, مَا شَعَبَكَ عَنِّى [*What diverted thee*, or *what has diverted thee*, &c., *from me?*]. (TA.) ═ It is also intrans.: see 4. — [Thus it signifies *He quitted his companions*, *desiring others*.] One says, شَعَبَ إِلَيْهِمْ (Ḳ, TA) فِى عَدَدِ كَذَا (TA) *He yearned towards them* [*with such a number of* men], *and quitted his companions*. (Ḳ, TA.) — And *He*, or *it*, *appeared* [distinct from others]: (Ḳ, TA:) whence the month [شَعْبَانُ, q. v.,] is [said to be] named. (TA.) ═ Also, (Ḳ, TA,) aor. and inf. n. as above, (TA,) said of a camel, *He cropped* (ٱهْتَصَرَ) *the upper*, or *uppermost*, *parts of trees* [or *shrubs*]. (Ḳ, TA.) ═ شَعِبَ, aor. ـَ, (Ḳ,) inf. n. شَعَبٌ, (Ṣ,* Ḳ,* TA,) *He* (a goat, Ṣ, TA, and a gazelle, TA) *was wide*, (Ḳ,) or *very wide*, (Ṣ,) *between the horns*, (Ṣ, Ḳ,) and *between the shoulders*. (Ḳ,* TA.) [See also شَعَبٌ, below.]

2. شعّب [app. signifies *He collected* several things; or *he collected much*: and] *he separated* several things; or *he separated much*. (O.) — Also *He repaired* a cracked wooden bowl [or some other vessel] *in several places* [*by closing up its cracks*, or *by piecing it*]: (Ṣ, O:) [and app., in a general sense, *he repaired*, *mended*, *amended*, *adjusted*, or *put into a right*, or *proper*, *state*, several things; or *he repaired*, &c., *much*: and it seems to signify also the contr. of these two meanings: i. e. *he cracked* several things; or *he cracked in several places*: and *he corrupted*, *rendered unsound*, *impaired*, or *marred*, several things; or *he corrupted*, &c., *much*.] ═ It is also intrans.: see 4. — Thus, said of seed-produce, *It branched forth*, or *forked*, *after being in leaf*, or *blade*; (TA;) like ↓ تشعّب. (Ḳ,* TA.) [Hence,] one says, إِنِّى أَرَى ٱلشَّرَّ شَعَّبَ † [*Verily I see the evil to have grown like seed-produce when it branches forth*]; like as one says, قَصَّبَ, and نَبَّبَ. (TA in art. نب.)

3. شَاعَبَهُ *He became distant*, or *remote*, *from him*; (Ḳ, TA;) namely, his companion. (TA.) [Hence,] شَاعَبَ ٱلْحَيَاةَ † [*He quitted life*]. (TA.) And شَاعَبَتْ نَفْسُهُ (Ḳ, TA) *His soul* [*departed*, or] *quitted life*; (TA;) meaning *he died*; (Ḳ, TA;) as also ↓ انشعب [i. e. انشعب هُوَ]. (Ḳ.) [See also what next follows.]

4. اشعب *He died*: (Ṣ, Ḳ: [see also 3:]) or (so in the Ṣ and TA, but in the Ḳ "and") *he separated himself* from another or others, *never to return*; (Ṣ, Ḳ;) as also ↓ شعّب or ↓ شَعَبَ, accord. to different copies of the Ḳ, the latter as in the L. (TA.) A poet says, (Ṣ,) namely, En-Nábighah El-Jaadee, (IB, TA,)

وَكَانُوا أُنَاسًا مِنْ شَعُوبٍ فَأَشْعَبُوا

(Ṣ, IB, TA,) or وَكَانُوا شُعُوبًا مِنْ أُنَاسٍ, accord. to different readings: [app. meaning, *And they were men of divided races* or *tribes*, or *were divided races* or *tribes of men*; *so they perished*; or *separated*, *never to return*:] IB says, after mentioning the former reading, i. e. they were of men who should perish; so they perished: having previously mentioned the latter reading, and added, i. e. they were of those whom شعوب should overtake. (TA. [IB's explanations seem at first sight to indicate that he read شُعُوبَ and شَعُوبًا; neither of which is admissible: each of his explanations app. relates to both readings; as though he understood the poet to mean, they were men separated from different tribes, to be overtaken by others; so they perished.])

5. تشعّب and ↓ انشعب are quasi-pass. verbs, the former of شَعَّبَ and the latter of شَعَبَ: (TA:) [the former, therefore, is most correctly to be regarded and used as intensive in its significations, or as relating to several things or persons: but it is said that] both signify alike: [app. *It became collected*; *it became brought*, *gathered*, or *drawn*, *together*; or *it became united*: and also] *it became separated*, *put apart* or *asunder*, *divided*, *disunited*, or *dispersed* or *scattered*: (Ṣ, Ḳ:) and *it*, or *he*, *became distant*, or *remote*. (Ḳ.) One says, تَشَعَّبُوا فِى طَلَبِ ٱلْمِيَاهِ [*They became separated*, &c., or *they separated themselves*, &c., *in search of the waters*], and فِى ٱلْغَارَاتِ [*in predatory excursions*]. (TA.) And ↓ انشعب عَنِّى فُلَانٌ *Such a one became distant*, or *remote*, *from me*; or *withdrew to a distance*, or *far away*, *from me*. (TA.) And ↓ انشعب ٱلطَّرِيقُ [and تشعّب] *The road separated*. (Ṣ, A, Mṣb.) And ↓ انشعب ٱلنَّهْرُ and تشعّب *The river separated* [or *branched forth*] *into other rivers*. (TA.) And ↓ انشعبت أَغْصَانُ ٱلشَّجَرَةِ (Ṣ, Mṣb, TA) and تشعّبت (TA) *The branches of the tree separated*, *divided*,

straggled, or *spread out dispersedly*; (Ṣ, TA;) or *branched forth from the stem, and separated, divided*, &c. (Mṣb.) See also 2. One says also, تَشَعَّبَ أَمْرُ الرَّجُلِ † [*The state of affairs of the man became broken up, discomposed, deranged, disorganized*, or (agreeably with another explanation of the verb in what follows) *rendered unsound, impaired*, or *marred*]. (A.) — Also ▼ the latter verb, [or each,] *It became closed up*; [or *repaired by having a crack* or *cracks closed up*, or *by being pieced*;] said of a cracked thing: (TA:) and ▼ both verbs, *i. q.* اِنْصَلَحَ [which means, in a general sense, *it became rectified, repaired, mended, amended, adjusted*, or *put into a right*, or *proper, state*; &c.; but I have not found this verb (انصلح) in its proper art. in any of the Lexicons]: (Ḳ, TA:) and ▼ the latter signifies also *it became cracked*; (A;) [and in like manner the former, said of a number of things; or *it became cracked in several places* when said of a single thing: and hence ▼ both signify, in a general sense, *it became corrupted, rendered unsound, impaired*, or *marred*; a meaning which may justly be assigned to the former verb in the phrase mentioned in the next preceding sentence.]

7: see 5, in nine places: and see also 3.

8: see 1, in the former half of the paragraph.

شَعْبٌ inf. n. of شَعَبَ [q. v.]. (Mṣb.) — [Used as a simple subst., it signifies *Collection*, or *union*: and also *separation, division*, or *disunion*; and] *a state of separation* or *division* or *disunion*; (Ḳ, TA;) as also ▼ شُعْبَةٌ: (Ṣ, TA:) pl. of the former شُعُوبٌ. (TA.) — And [hence, perhaps, as implying both union and division,] *Such as is divided* [*into sub-tribes*], *of the tribes of the Arabs and foreigners*: (Ṣ: [in my copy of the Mṣb, ما انقسمت فيه قبائل العرب, as though it meant the tribes of the Arabs collectively, agreeably with another explanation to be mentioned below; but I think that there may be a mistranscription in this case:]) pl. شُعُوبٌ: (Ṣ, Mṣb:) or it signifies, as some say, (Mṣb,) or signifies also, (Ṣ,) *a great tribe*; syn. قَبِيلَةٌ عَظِيمَةٌ, (Ṣ, A, Ḳ,) or حَىٌّ عَظِيمٌ; (Mṣb;) *the parent of the* [*tribes called*] قَبَائِل, *to which they refer their origin, and which comprises them*: (Ṣ:) or, as some say, *a great tribe* (حَىٌّ عَظِيمٌ) *forming a branch of a* قَبِيلَة: or *a* قَبِيلَة *itself*: (TA:) A'Obeyd says, on the authority of Ibn-El-Kelbee, on the authority of his father, that the شَعْب is *greater than the* قَبِيلَة; next to which is the فَصِيلَة; then, the عِمَارَة; then, the بَطْن; then, the فَخِذ: (Ṣ, TA:) but IB says that the true order is that which Ez-Zubeyr Ibn-Bekkár has stated, and is as follows: (TA:) [i. e.] the genealogies of the Arabs consist of six degrees; (Mṣb;) first, the شَعْب; then, the قَبِيلَة; then, the عِمَارَة, (Mṣb, TA,) with fet-ḥ and with kesr, to the ع; (Mṣb;) then, the بَطْن; then, the فَخِذ; and then, the فَصِيلَة: thus, Khuzeymeh is a شعب; and Kináneh, a قبيلة; and Ḳureysh, an عمارة; and Ḳuṣey, a بطن; and Háshim, a فخذ; and El-'Abbás, a فصيلة: (Mṣb, TA:) and Aboo-Usámeh says that these classes are agreeable with the order obtaining in the structure of man; the شعب is the greatest of them, derived from the شَعْب [or suture] of the head; next is the قبيلة, from the قبيلة [which is a term applied to any one of the four principal bones] of the head; then, the عمارة, which is the breast; then, the بطن [or belly]; then, the فخذ [or thigh]; and then, the فصيلة, which is the shank: to these some add the عَشِيرَة, which consists of few in comparison with what are before mentioned: (TA:) and some add after this the رَهْط: some also add the جِذْم before the شعب: (TA in art. بطن:) the pl. is as above. (TA.) It signifies also *A nation, people, race*, or *family of mankind*; syn. جِيلٌ; as expl. by IM and others: in the Ḳ, [and in a copy of the A,] erroneously, جَبَلٌ [a mountain]: (TA:) but it is [strangely] said by Aboo-'Obeyd El-Bekree that accord. to all except Bundár, the word in this sense is ▼ شِعْبٌ, with kesr. (MF.) And the pl., شُعُوبٌ, is [said to be] especially applied to denote the *foreigners* (العَجَم): (TA:) [thus it is said that] the phrase, in a trad., إِنَّ رَجُلًا مِنَ الشُّعُوبِ أَسْلَمَ means [*Verily a man*] *of the foreigners* (العَجَم) [*became a Muslim*: but see الشُّعُوبِيَّةُ]. (Ṣ.) — Also, [as implying separation,] *Distance*, or *remoteness*. (A, Ḳ.) So in the phrase شَعْبُ الدَّارِ [*The distance*, or *remoteness, of the abode*, or *dwelling*]. (TA.) — And *A crack* (Ṣ, A, Ḳ, TA) in a thing, (Ṣ,) which the شَعَّاب repairs. (Ṣ,* TA.) — And The *place of junction* [i. e. the *suture*] *of the* قَبَائِل [or *principal bones*] of the head; (Ḳ;) the شَأْن *which conjoins the* قبائل of the head: the قبائل in the head being [the frontal bone, the occipital bone, and the two parietal bones; in all,] four in number. (Ṣ.) — [Hence, perhaps,] هُمَا شَعْبَانِ † *They two are likes* [or *like each other*]. (Ṣ.) — See also شِعْبٌ. = Also *Distant*, or *remote*; (Ḳ;) as in the phrase مَآءٌ شَعْبٌ [*Distant*, or *remote, water*]: pl. شُعُوبٌ. (TA.)

شُعْبٌ: see the dual شُعْبَانِ voce شُعْبَةٌ.

شِعْبٌ *A road*: (Mṣb:) or *a road in a mountain*: (Ṣ, A, O, L, Mṣb, Ḳ:) primarily *a road in a mountain* (Ḥar p. 29) and *in valleys*: (Id. p. 72:) afterwards applied to *any road*: (Id. p. 29:) [see also مَشْعَبٌ:] pl. شِعَابٌ. (Ṣ, O, Mṣb.) And *A water-course*, or *place in which water flows, in* [*a low*, or *depressed, tract, such as is called*] *a* بَطْن *of land*, (ISh, A, O, Ḳ,) *having two elevated borders, and in width equal to the stature of a man lying down, and sometimes between the two faces*, or *acclivities, of two mountains*. (ISh, O.) Or it signifies, (Ḳ,) or signifies also, (A,) *A ravine*, or *gap*, [or *pass*,] *between two mountains*. (A, Ḳ.) — Also [*A reef of rocks in the sea*: so in the present day: or] *a* زِرْبَة or زَرْبَة (accord. to different copies of the Ḳ in art. جهن [but neither of these two words do I find in their proper art. in any Lex.]) *in the sea, such as is connected with the shore*: if not connected with the shore, a bow-shot distant, it is called جُهْنٌ. (Ḳ and TA in art. جهن.) — And *A brand*, or *mark made with a hot iron*, (Ṣ, Ḳ,) *upon camels*, (Ḳ,) *peculiar to the Benoo-Minḳar, in form resembling the* [*hooked stick called*] مِحْجَن: (Ṣ:) or *a brand upon the thigh, lengthwise*, [*consisting of*] *two lines meeting at the top and separated at the bottom*: (ISh, TA:) or *a brand united* [*at the upper part and*] *at the lower part separated*: (Aboo-'Alee in the "Tedhkireh," TA: [but there is an omission here, so that the reverse may perhaps be meant:]) or *a brand upon the neck, like the* مِحْجَن: (Suh in the R, TA:) in a marginal note in the copy of the L, it is said that شعب signifying *a brand* is with kesr to the ش and with fet-ḥ [i. e. شِعْبٌ and ▼ شَعْبٌ]. (TA.) — See also شُعْبَةٌ. — [And see the pl. شِعَابٌ below.]

شُعَبٌ *Width*, or *distance*, (A, Ḳ,) or *great width* or *distance*, (Ṣ,) *between the horns* (Ṣ, A, Ḳ) *of a goat* (Ṣ, TA) and *of a gazelle*, (TA,) and *between the shoulders*, (A, Ḳ,) and *between two branches*. (A.) [See also 1, last signification.]

شُعْبَةٌ: see شَعْبٌ, second sentence. — Also The *space*, or *interstice, between two horns*: and *between two branches*: (Ḳ:) pl. شُعَبٌ and شِعَابٌ, (Ḳ,* TA,) in this and all the following senses. (TA.) — And *A cleft in a mountain, to which birds* (الطَّيْر), for which المَطَر is erroneously substituted in [several of] the copies of the Ḳ, TA) *resort*: pl. as above. (Ḳ, TA.) — Also *A branch of a tree*, (Ṣ, A,* Mgh,* Mṣb, TA,) *growing out apart*, or *divaricating*, therefrom: (Mṣb,* TA:) or the *extremity of a branch*: (Ḳ, TA: [said in the latter to be tropical in this latter sense; but why, I see not:]) pl. شُعَبٌ (Ṣ, Mgh, Mṣb, TA) and شِعَابٌ, as above. (TA.) And شُعَبُ الغُصْنِ *The divaricating*, or *straggling*, [*branchlets*, or] *extremities* [or *shoots* or *stalks*] *of the branch*. (TA.) And [hence] عَصًا فِى رَأْسِهَا شُعْبَتَانِ [*A staff having at its head two forking portions* or *projections*]; (A, TA;) and Az mentions, as heard by him from the Arabs, ▼ شُعْبَانِ, without ت, instead of شُعْبَتَانِ in this phrase. (L, TA.) And شُعْبَةٌ مِنْ رَيْحَانٍ [*A sprig, spray, bunch*, or *branchlet, of sweet basil*, or *of sweet-smelling plants*]: and شُعْبَةٌ مِنْ شَعَرٍ [and مِنْ صُوفٍ *A lock*, or *flock, of hair* and *of wool*]. (JK in art. طوق.) And أَنَا شُعْبَةٌ مِنْ دَوْحَتِكَ ‡ [*I am a branch*, or *branchlet, of thy great tree*]. (A, TA.) And مَسْأَلَةٌ كَثِيرَةُ الشُّعَبِ † [*A question having many branches*, or *ramifications*]. (Mṣb.) And [the pl.] شُعَبٌ [as meaning] ‡ The *fingers*: (Ḳ, TA:) one says, قَبَضَ عَلَيْهِ بِشُعَبِ يَدِهِ ‡ *He laid hold upon it with his fingers*. (A, TA.) And قَعَدَ بَيْنَ شُعْبَتَيْهَا ‡ *He sat between her two legs*: (A:) and بَيْنَ شُعَبِهَا الأَرْبَعِ ‡ [He sat (in the Mgh قَعَدَ, as implied in the A, and in the Mṣb جَلَسَ,)] *between her arms and her legs*; (A, Mgh, Mṣb, Ḳ;) or *between her legs and the* شُفْرَانِ [dual of شُفْر, q. v.,] *of her* فَرْج; (A, Mgh, Ḳ;) occurring in a trad.; (Mgh, Mṣb;) an allusion to جِمَاع (A, Mgh, Mṣb, Ḳ.) And شُعْبَتَا الرَّحْلِ † *The* شَرْخَانِ [or *two upright pieces of wood*] *of the* *camel's saddle; its* قَادِمَة and its آخِرَة. (Mgh.) And اُغْرُزِ اللَّحْمَ فِى شُعَبِ السَّفُّودِ ‡ [*Infix thou the flesh-meat upon the prongs of the roasting-instrument*]. (A, TA.) And شُعْبَةُ مِنْجَلٍ † [*A tooth of a reaping-hook*]. (Ḳ in art. سن.) And شُعْبَةٌ مِنْ شُعَبِ السِّينِ † [*A tooth, or cusp, of the teeth, or cusps, of the* س]; the شُعَب of the س being three. (Ṣ and L in art. س.) And شُعَبُ الفَرَسِ ‡ *The outer parts, or regions, of the horse* (أَقْطَارُهُ, A, or نَوَاحِيهِ, Ḳ); *all of them:* (Ḳ:) or *the prominent parts* (Ṣ, Ḳ) *of them,* (Ḳ,) or *of him;* (Ṣ, and so in some copies of the Ḳ;) *as the neck, and the* مَنْسِج [or *withers,* &c.], (Ṣ, TA,) *and the crests of the hips,* (TA,) or *such as his head, and his* حَارِك [or *withers,* &c.], *and the crests of his hips.* (A.) — Also *A small water-course, or channel in which water flows;* as in the phrase شُعْبَةٌ حَافِلٌ *a small water-course filled with a torrent:* (Ṣ:) or *a water-course in sand;* (Ḳ;) or *in the elevated part of a depressed tract into which sand has poured and remained.* (TA.) And *A small portion of a* [*water-course such as is called*] تَلْعَة; or *what is smaller than a* تَلْعَة; accord. to different copies of the Ḳ; الشُّعْبَة being expl. as meaning مَا صَغُرَ مِنَ التَّلْعَةِ, and, in one copy, عَنِ التَّلْعَةِ. (TA.) And *Such as is large, of the channels for irrigation of valleys:* (Ḳ, TA:) or, as some say, *a branch from a* تَلْعَة, and *from a valley,* or *torrent-bed, taking a different course therefrom:* pl. as above. (TA.) — And *A portion, part,* or *piece, of a thing;* or *somewhat* thereof: (Ṣ, Mṣb, Ḳ, TA:) pl. as above. (TA.) One says, اشْعَبْ لِى شُعْبَةً مِنَ المَالِ *Give thou to me a portion of the property.* (TA.) And فِى يَدِهِ شُعْبَةُ خَيْرٍ † [*In his hand is somewhat of good,* or *of wealth*]. (TA.) And it is said in a trad., الحَيَآءُ شُعْبَةٌ مِنَ الإِيمَانِ † *Modesty is a part of faith:* and in another, الشَّبَابُ شُعْبَةٌ مِنَ الجُنُونِ † [*Youth is a part of insanity*]. (TA.) In explanation of the phrase, in the Ḳur [lxxvii. 30], إِلَى ظِلٍّ ذِى ثَلَاثِ شُعَبٍ [*Unto a shade,* or *shadow, having three parts,* or *divisions*], it is said that the fire [of Hell], on the day of resurrection, will divide into three parts; and whenever they shall attempt to go forth to a place, it will repel them: by ظِلّ being here meant that the fire will form a covering; for [literally] there will be no ظِلّ in this case. (Th, L.) — And *A piece such as is called* رُؤْبَة, *with which a wooden bowl* [or *the like*] *is repaired.* (Ṣ.) — Accord. to Lth, (T, TA,) شُعَبُ الدَّهْرِ means ‡ *The changes,* or *vicissitudes, of time* or *fortune;* (T, A, TA;) and he cites the saying of Dhu-r-Rummeh,

* وَلَا تَقْسِمُ شَعْبًا وَاحِدًا شُعَبُ *

which he explains by saying, i. e. I thought that one thing, or state of things, would not be divided into many things, or states: [i. e. *Nor* did I think that the *vicissitudes* of fortune would *divide one whole body of men* into many parties:] but Az disapproves of this explanation, and says that شُعَب here means *Intentions, designs,* or *purposes:* he says that the poet describes tribes assembled together in the [season called] رَبِيع, who, when they desired to return to the watering-places, differed in their intentions, or designs; wherefore he says, *Nor* did I think that various *intentions* would *divide* [*one whole body of men* who before had] a consentient intention. (L, TA.) — [See also the pl. شِعَابٌ below.]

شَعْبَانُ, imperfectly decl., (Mṣb,) *The name of a month* [i. e. *the eighth month of the Arabian year*]: pl. شَعْبَانَاتٌ (Ṣ, Mṣb, Ḳ) and شَعَابِينُ: (Mṣb, Ḳ:) so called from تَشَعَّبَ "it became separated;" (Ḳ, TA;) because therein they used to separate, or disperse themselves, in search of water [when the months were regulated by the solar year; this month then corresponding partly to June and partly to July, as shown voce زَمَنٌ, q. v.]; or, as some say, for predatory expeditions [after having been restrained therefrom during the sacred month of Rejeb]; or, accord. to some, as Th says, from شَعَبَ "it appeared;" because of its appearance between the months of Rejeb and Ramadán. (TA.) — غُزَالُ شَعْبَانَ *A certain insect,* (Ḳ,* TA,) *a species of the* جُنْدَب, or *of the* جُنْدُب. (TA.)

شِعَابٌ pl. of شِعْبٌ: (Ṣ, O, Mṣb:) and of شُعْبَةٌ. (Ḳ, TA.) — شَغَلَتْ شِعَابِى جَدْوَاىَ is a prov., [expl. as] meaning *The abundance of the food* [that I have to procure for my family] *has occupied me so as to divert me from giving* to people: (Ṣ, TA:) [Z considers شعاب, here, as pl. of شُعْبَة "a branch," and as meaning *duties, and relations:* (Freytag's Arab. Prov., i. 653:)] but El-Mundhiree says that شِعَابِى is a mistranscription: the other reading is سَعَاتِى, meaning "my expending upon my family." (Meyd. [See also سَعَاةٌ, in art. سعو and سعى.])

شَعُوبُ, (Ṣ, A, Mṣb, Ḳ,) without the article ال, and imperfectly decl., (Mṣb,) and الشَّعُوبُ, (A, Mṣb, Ḳ,) with the article, and perfectly decl., (Mṣb,) but several authors disallow this latter, accounting it wrong; (TA;) a name for *Death;* (Ṣ, A,* Mṣb, Ḳ;*) so called because it separates men: (Ṣ, Mṣb:) the former is a proper name: (Mṣb:) J says [in the Ṣ] that it is determinate, and does not admit the article ال: in the L, it is said that شَعُوبُ and الشَّعُوبُ both signify as above; and that in either case it may be originally an epithet, being like the epithets قَتُول and ضَرُوب; and if so, the article in this case is as in العَبَّاس and الحَسَن and الحَرِث: and this opinion is confirmed by what is said of its derivation: but he who says شَعُوب, without the article, makes the word a pure substantive, and deprives it literally of the character of an epithet; wherefore the article is not necessarily attached to it, as it is not to عَبَّاس and حَرِث; yet the essence of an epithet is in it still, as in the instance of جَابِرُ بْنُ حَبَّةَ, a name for "bread," so called because it reinvigorates the hungry; and as in وَاسِط, [a certain town] so called, accord. to Sb, because midway between El-'Irák ['Irák el-'Ajam] and El-Basrah: thus in the L. (TA.) One says of a person when he has been at the point of death and then escaped, أَقْصَتْهُ شَعُوبُ [*Death became near to him*]. (TA.) And it is said in a trad., فَمَا زِلْتُ وَاضِعًا رِجْلِى عَلَى خَدِّهِ حَتَّى أَزَرْتُهُ شَعُوبَ, i. e. [*And I ceased not putting my foot upon his cheek until*] *I made death to visit him.* (TA.)

شَعِيبٌ *A* [*leathern water-bag such as is called*] مَزَادَة [q. v.]; (A'Obeyd, Ṣ, Ḳ;) as also رَاوِيَةٌ and سَطِيحَة: (A'Obeyd, Ṣ:) or *one that has been repaired,* or *pieced:* (TA:) or *one that is made of two hides:* (Ḳ:) or *one that is made of two hides facing each other, without* فِئَام *at their corners;* فئام in [the making of] مَزَايِد being the taking of the hide and folding it, and then adding at the sides what will widen it: or *one that is pieced* (تُفْأَمُ) *with a third skin, between the two skins, that it may be rendered wider:* or *one that is made of two pieces joined together:* (TA:) or *one that is sewed* (مَخْرُوزَة, Ḳ and TA, in the CḲ مَحْزُوزَة,) *on both sides:* (Ḳ:) called thus because one part is joined to another: (L, TA:) pl. شُعُبٌ. (Ḳ,* TA.) — Also *An old, worn-out skin for water or milk:* (Ḳ:) because it is pieced, or repaired: (TA:) pl. as above. (Ḳ.) — And *A camel's saddle;* syn. رَحْلٌ: because it is joined, part to part: so in the saying of El-Marrár, describing a she-camel,

* إِذَا هِىَ خَرَّتْ خَرَّ مِنْ عَنْ يَمِينِهَا *
* شَعِيبٌ بِهِ إِجْمَامُهَا وَلُغُوبُهَا *

[*When she falls down,* or *fell down, there falls down,* or *fell down, from her right side a saddle by reason of which was her fevered and jaded state*]. (TA.) — And رَجُلٌ شَعِيبٌ i. q. غَرِيبٌ [*A man who is a stranger,* &c.]. (AA, TA voce غَرِيبٌ.)

شِعَابَةٌ The *art,* or *craft, of repairing cracks* [*in wooden bowls &c., by piecing them*]. (TA.)

شُعُوبِىٌّ: see what next follows.

الشُّعُوبِيَّةُ *A sect which does not prefer,* or *exalt, the Arabs above the 'Ajam* [or *foreigners* or *Persians*]: (Ṣ:) or *a sect which prefers,* or *exalts, the 'Ajam above the Arabs:* (Mṣb:) or *those who despise the circumstances,* or *condition, of the Arabs;* (A,* Ḳ;) one of whom is called شُعُوبِىٌّ; (A, Ḳ;) a rel. n. formed from the pl., (IM, Mṣb, TA,) شُعُوب being predominantly applied to the 'Ajam; (IM, TA;) like أَنْصَارِىٌّ [from الأَنْصَارُ]. (IM, Mṣb,* TA.) In the phrase إِنَّ رَجُلًا مِنَ الشُّعُوبِ أَسْلَمَ, occurring in a trad., [and mentioned before, voce شَعْبٌ,] الشعوب may mean العَجَمُ; or it may be [used as] a pl. of الشُّعُوبِىُّ, like as المَجُوسُ and اليَهُودُ are [used as] pls. of المَجُوسِىُّ and اليَهُودِىُّ. (IAth, TA.)

شَعَّابٌ *A repairer of cracks* [*in wooden bowls &c., by piecing them*]. (Ṣ, Mṣb, TA.)

الشَّعْبَانِ *The two shoulders:* (Ḳ:) because wide apart: of the dial. of El-Yemen. (TA.)

أَشْعَبُ A goat, (Ṣ, TA,) and a gazelle, (A, TA,) *wide,* (A,) or *very wide,* (Ṣ, TA,) *between the horns:* (Ṣ, A, TA:) [and app., *between the shoulders:* (see شَعْبٌ:)] fem. شَعْبَآءُ: (TA:) and pl. شُعْبٌ. (Ṣ, A, TA.) — It is also the name of a certain very covetous man [who became proverbial for his covetousness, and hence it is used as an epithet]: (Ṣ, Ḳ:) so in the saying, لَا تَكُنْ أَشْعَبَ فَتَتْعَبَ [*Be not thou an Ash'ab, for* in that case *thou wilt become fatigued,* or *wearied,* by thy endeavours]; (Ḳ;) a prov.: (TA:) and so in the prov., أَطْمَعُ مِنْ أَشْعَبَ [*More covetous than Ash'ab*]. (Ṣ.)

مَشْعَبٌ *A way, road,* or *path,* (Ṣ, Mṣb, Ḳ,) [in an absolute sense, or] *branching off from another.* (Mṣb.) مَشْعَبُ الحَقِّ means *The way* [*of truth,* or] *that distinguishes between truth and falsity.* (Ḳ.)

مِشْعَبٌ *An instrument by means of which a crack in a* [*wooden bowl or some other*] *thing is repaired* [*by piecing it*]; *an instrument used for perforating, a drill,* or *the like,* (Ḳ, TA,) *by means of which the* شَعَّاب *repairs a vessel.* (TA.)

قَصْعَةٌ مُشَعَّبَةٌ [*A wooden bowl*] *repaired in several places* [*by closing up its cracks,* or *by piecing it*]. (Ṣ.) — See also what follows.

مَشْعُوبٌ applied to a camel, (Ḳ,) and ▼ مُشَعَّبَةٌ applied to a number of camels, (TA,) *Marked with the brand called* شِعْب. (Ḳ, TA.)

شعبذ

Q. 1. شَعْبَذَ, and its inf. n. شَعْبَذَةٌ: see شَعْوَذَ and شَعْوَذَةٌ in art. شعذ.

مُشَعْبِذٌ: see مُشَعْوِذٌ in art. شعذ.

شعث

1. شَعِثَ, aor. ـَ, (Mṣb,) inf. n. شَعَثٌ, (A, Mgh, Mṣb,) *It* (hair) *was,* or *became, shaggy,* or *dishevelled,* (A, Mgh,) *and frouzy,* or *altered in odour,* (Mgh,) *in consequence of its being seldom dressed:* (A, Mgh:) or *it was,* or *became, defiled with dust, and matted,* or *compacted, in consequence of its being seldom anointed:* (Mṣb:) or, accord. to El-Ghooree, *it wanted oil,* or *ointment:* (Ḥar p. 50:) and ▼ تشعّث signifies [the same: or] *it was,* or *became, matted,* or *compacted,* (Ḳ, TA,) *and dusty.* (TA.) And the former verb, [and app. ▼ the latter also,] *It* (the head) *was,* or *became, dusty, not being renovated* [*by dressing* or *anointing*], *nor cleansed.* (Mṣb.) Also the former verb, aor. as above, (L, Ḳ, and Ḥam p. 469,) inf. n. شَعَثٌ (Ṣ, L, Ḳ, and Ḥam) and شُعُوثَةٌ, (L and Ḥam,) *He was,* or *became, shaggy,* or *dishevelled, in the hair,* (JM, PṢ,) *and frouzy,* or *altered in odour, in consequence of its being seldom dressed:* (JM:) or it signifies (or signifies also, JM) *he had a dusty head,* (Ṣ, L, Ḳ, JM,) *and plucked hair, unanointed;* (L;) or *he had matted,* or *compacted, and dusty, hair:* (L, and Ḥam p. 469:) and in like manner ▼ تشعّث. (L.) — شَعَثٌ, (Mṣb,) or ▼ تَشَعُّثٌ, (Ṣ, Ḳ, TA,) [or each,] also signifies ‡ *The being separated,* or *disunited,* (Ṣ, Mṣb, Ḳ, TA,) and *spread out,* (Mṣb,) and *uncompacted,* (TA,) *like as is the head of the* سِوَاك [or *tooth-stick, by its being bruised,* or *battered,* or *mangled by blows*]. (Mṣb, TA.) You say, تَشَعَّثَ ▼ رَأْسُ السِّوَاكِ, (Mṣb, TA,) and الوَتِدِ, (A, TA,) ‡ *The head of the tooth-stick,* and *of the wooden peg* or *stake, became disintegrated;* or *separated, disunited,* or *uncompacted, in its component parts* [or *its fibres;* or *rendered brushy; by its being bruised,* or *battered,* or *mangled by blows*]. (TA.) And ▼ تَشَعَّثُوا ‡ *They* [meaning men] *became separated, disunited, dispersed,* or *scattered.* (A.) — And شَعِثَ, aor. as above, (TḲ,) inf. n. شَعَثٌ, said of the state of affairs, † *It was,* or *became, dissolved, broken up, discomposed, deranged, disorganized, disordered,* or *unsettled.* (Ṣ,* A,* Ḳ,* TA, TḲ. [In the Ṣ and A and Ḳ, this is placed as the first of all the meanings in this art.; and in the A, it is mentioned among the meanings that are proper, not tropical; but in my opinion it is tropical. See also شَعَثٌ below.])

2. شَعَّثَهُ, inf. n. تَشْعِيثٌ, *He rendered it* (i. e. hair) [*shaggy,* or *dishevelled, and frouzy:* (see 1:) or] *matted,* or *compacted, and dusty:* or *he rendered him* [*shaggy,* or *dishevelled, and frouzy, in his hair:* or] *matted,* or *compacted, and dusty, in his hair.* (TA.) — تَشْعِيثٌ also signifies † The *separating, disuniting, dispersing,* or *scattering,* a thing. (Ṣ.) And † The *making to separate like as do rivers and branches.* (L.) [Hence,] شَعَّثَ رَأْسَ السِّوَاكِ ‡ [*He made the head of the tooth-stick to become disintegrated;* or *separated, disunited,* or *uncompacted, in its component parts* or *its fibres;* or *rendered it brushy; by bruising it, battering it,* or *mangling it by blows:* see 1]. (A.) — شَعَّثَ السَّنَا ‡ *He took of the straggling branches,* or *sprigs, of the senna,* without pulling it up by the roots. (TA, from a trad.) — See also 5, in two places. — شَعَّثَ النَّاسُ فِى الطَّعْنِ عَلَيْهِ † *The people took,* or *began, to impugn his character, censure him, reproach him,* or *speak against him, by befouling his reputation* (بِتَشْعِيثِ عِرْضِهِ). (TA, from a trad.) — And شَعَّثَ مِنْهُ † *He detracted from his reputation;* syn. غَضَّ مِنْهُ and تَنَقَّصَهُ: from التَّشْعِيثُ [as inf. n. of 1 in the last of the senses assigned to it above,] meaning انْتِشَارُ الأَمْرِ. (L.) — And also, inf. n. as above, † *He repelled from him,* or *defended him:* (Ḳ:) or *he defended his reputation.* (TA.) [Thus it has two contr. meanings.]

4. اشعث مِنِّى فُلَانٌ ‡ *Such a one was angry by reason of me;* syn. غَضِبَ. (A. [But this I have not found elsewhere; and I almost think that اشعث, in my copy of the A, may be a mistranscription for شَعَّثَ; and غَضِبَ, for غَضَّ.])

5: see 1, in six places. — تَشَعُّثٌ also signifies † The act of *taking;* syn. أَخْذٌ; (Ḳ, TA;) and so ▼ تَشْعِيثٌ. (TA.) One says, تَشَعَّثَهُ الدَّهْرُ † *Time,* or *fortune, took him.* (TA.) And تشعّث مَالَهُ *He took his property.* (TḲ.) — And † The *eating little of food;* (Ḳ, TA;) and so ▼ تَشْعِيثٌ: whence one says, شَعَّثْتُ مِنَ الطَّعَامِ *I ate little of the food.* (TA.)

شَعْثٌ: see the next paragraph.

شَعَثٌ inf. n. of 1 [q. v.]. (L, Mṣb, &c.) — [Hence,] لَمَّ ٱللّٰهُ شَعَثَكَ, (Ṣ,) and شَعَثَكُمْ, (A,) i. e. ‡ [*May God rectify,* or *repair, and consolidate, what is discomposed, deranged, disorganized, disordered,* or *unsettled, of thy,* and *your, affairs;* (see art. لم;) or] *consolidate thy,* and *your, disorganized, disordered,* or *unsettled, state of affairs:* (Ṣ, A:* [in the latter expressly distinguished as tropical:]) [and so ▼ شَعْثَكَ, and شَعْثَكُمْ; perhaps by poetic license; for] Kaab Ibn-Málik El-Anṣáree says,

لَمَّ الإِلٰهُ بِهِ شَعْثًا وَرَمَّ بِهِ
أُمُورَ أُمَّتِهِ وَالأَمْرُ مُنْتَشِرُ

† [*God rectified and consolidated, by him, a discomposed, deranged, disorganized, disordered,* or *unsettled, state of affairs, and repaired, by him, the affairs of his people, when the state of affairs was broken up*]. (TA.) It is said in a trad., as a form of prayer, أَسْأَلُكَ رَحْمَةً تَلُمُّ بِهَا شَعَثِى i. e. ‡ [*I ask of Thee mercy*] *whereby thou shalt consolidate what is discomposed, deranged, disorganized, disordered,* or *unsettled, of my state of affairs.* (TA.)

شَعِثٌ, applied to hair, *Shaggy,* or *dishevelled:* (MA:) [or *shaggy,* or *dishevelled, and frouzy,* or *altered in odour, in consequence of its being seldom dressed:* (see 1, first sentence:)] or *defiled with dust, and matted,* or *compacted, in consequence of its being seldom anointed.* (Mṣb.) And in a similar sense applied to the head of a مِسْوَاك [or tooth-stick, meaning † *Disintegrated;* or *separated, disunited,* or *uncompacted, in its fibres;* or *rendered brushy; by its being bruised,* &c.; and so as applied to the head of a wooden peg or stake; as indicated by an explanation of its verb]. (MA.) [And in the TA it is applied to a plant, as meaning † *Straggling.*] See also أَشْعَثُ. — And † A man *dirty in the body.* (Mṣb.)

شَعْثَةٌ *A place of* [or *in*] *the hair that is* شَعِث [or *shaggy,* or *dishevelled,* &c.]. (TA.)

شَعْثَانُ, and شَعْثَانُ الرَّأْسِ: see what next follows.

أَشْعَثُ, (Ṣ, Mgh, Mṣb, Ḳ,) and أَشْعَثُ الرَّأْسِ, (Ḳ,) and ▼ شَعِثٌ, (Mgh, TA,) [and شَعِثُ الرَّأْسِ,] and ▼ شَعْثَانُ, (TA,) and شَعْثَانُ الرَّأْسِ, (Ḳ,) applied to a man, (A, Mgh, Mṣb,) *Having the hair shaggy,* or *dishevelled, and frouzy,* or *altered in odour, in consequence of its being seldom dressed:* (Mgh:) or *having the hair defiled with dust, and matted,* or *compacted, in consequence of its being seldom anointed:* (Mṣb:) or *having the head dusty,* (Ṣ, A, Ḳ, TA,) *and the hair plucked, and unanointed:* (TA:) fem. of the first شَعْثَآءُ, applied to a woman: (A, Mṣb:) and شُعْثٌ [is its pl., and] is applied to horses, as meaning [*having shaggy coats,*] *not curried:* (Ṣ:) or *dusty by* *reason of long journeying.* (Ḥam p. 130. [See an ex. from a poet, voce أَلَا.]) The first [or each] is also applied to a head, as meaning *Dusty, not renovated* [*by dressing* or *anointing*], *nor cleansed.* (Mṣb.) — الأَشْعَثُ ‡ *The wooden peg* or *stake:* (A, Ḳ, TA:) so in a verse of El-Kumeyt cited in the first paragraph of art. حف: an epithet in which the quality of a subst. is predominant: (TA:) so called because its head is disintegrated; or separated, disunited, or uncompacted, in its component parts [or its fibres; by its being battered by blows]. (A,* TA.) — And † *What has dried up of the* [*barley-grass called*] بُهْمَى: (Ḳ, TA:) [or] it is so called *when its prickles have dried.* (TA.)

شعذ

Q. Q. 1. شَعْوَذَ, (A, Mṣb,) inf. n. شَعْوَذَةٌ, (A, L, Mṣb, Ḳ,) *He practised the art termed* شَعْوَذَة, expl. below: (A, L, Mṣb, Ḳ:) as also شَعْبَذَ, (Mṣb, Ḳ,) inf. n. شَعْبَذَةٌ: (A, Mṣb, Ḳ:) so some say. (Mṣb.) [See what here follows.]

شَعْوَذَةٌ *Legerdemain,* or *sleight-of-hand,* (A, L, Ḳ,) and *false miracles,* (TA,) and *fascinations,* (Ḳ,) or *fascination,* (A, L,) or *a kind of play,* (Mṣb,) *like* سِحْر, (A, L, Mṣb, Ḳ,) *making a thing to appear different from what it really is,* (L, Ḳ,) or *showing a man what has no real existence:* (Mṣb:) or *making what is false to assume the form of what is true:* (TA:) as also شَعْبَذَةٌ: (A, Mṣb:) vulgarly termed شَعْبَثَةٌ. (TA.) — Also *Quickness:* or *lightness,* or *agility, in any affair.* (L.) — It is not a word of the language of the people of the desert. (Lth, L, Mṣb.)

شَعْوَذِىٌّ *A messenger of princes or governors,* (L, Ḳ,) *who journeys on affairs of importance for them* (L) *upon post-horses* or *other beasts appointed for their conveyance:* (L, Ḳ:) so called because of his quickness. (L.) It is not a word of the language of the people of the desert. (Lth, L.) — See also what follows.

مُشَعْوِذٌ and مُشَعْوَذٌ A man *who practises the art termed* شَعْوَذَة; (L, Ḳ;) as also ▼ شَعْوَذِىٌّ: (TA in art. عجب:) improperly called مُشَعْبِذٌ, and surnamed أَبُو العَجَبِ. (Eth-Tha'álibee, TA.)

شعر

1. شَعَرَ بِهِ, (Ṣ, Mṣb, Ḳ, &c.,) and شَعُرَ بِهِ, (Ḳ,) which latter is disallowed by some, but both are correct, though the former is the [more] chaste, (TA,) aor. ـُ, (Ṣ, Mṣb, Ḳ,) inf. n. شِعْرٌ (Ṣ, Mṣb, Ḳ, &c.) and شَعْرٌ (Ḳ, TA) and شَعَرٌ, (TA, and so in the CḲ in the place of شِعْرٌ,) but the first is the most common, (TA,) and شِعْرَةٌ (Mṣb, Ḳ) and شَعْرَةٌ and شُعْرَةٌ, (Ḳ,) of which last three the first is the most common, (TA,) and شِعْرَى and شُعْرَى (Ḳ) and شَعْرَى (TA) and شُعُورٌ (Mṣb, Ḳ) and شُعُورَةٌ, (Ḳ,) which is said to be the inf. n. of شَعُرَ, (TA,) and مَشْعُورٌ and مَشْعُورَةٌ (Lḥ, Ḳ) and مَشْعُورَآءُ, (Ḳ,) which is of extr. form, (TA,) *He knew it; knew,* or *had knowledge, of it; was cognizant of it;* or *understood it;* (Ṣ,* A, Mṣb, Ḳ, TA;) as also شَعَرَ لَهُ: (Lḥ, TA:) or *he knew the minute particulars of it:* or *he perceived it by means of* [*any of*] *the senses.* (TA.) Lḥ mentions the phrase أَشْعُرُ فُلَانًا مَا عَمِلَهُ and أَشْعُرُ لِفُلَانٍ مَا عَمِلَهُ [*I know what such a one did* or *has done*], and مَا شَعَرْتُ فُلَانًا مَا عَمِلَهُ [*I knew not what such a one did*], as on the authority of Ks, and says that they are forms of speech used by the Arabs. (TA.) [See also شُعُور, below.] — شَعَرَ, (A, Mṣb, Ḳ,) aor. ـُ, (Mṣb, Ḳ,) inf. n. شِعْرٌ and شَعْرٌ, (Ḳ, TA,) or شَعُرَ, (so accord. to the CḲ instead of شِعْرٌ,) *He said,* or *spoke,* or *gave utterance to, poetry; spoke in verse; poetized;* or *versified;* syn. قَالَ شِعْرًا; [for poetry was always spoken by the Arabs in the classical times; and seldom written, if written at all, until after the life-time of the author;] (A, Mṣb, Ḳ;) as also شَعُرَ: (Ḳ:) or the latter signifies *he made good,* or *excellent, poetry* or *verses;* (Ḳ, MF;) and this is the signification more commonly approved, as being more agreeable with analogy: (MF:) or the latter signifies *he was,* or *became, a poet;* (Ṣ;) as also شَعِرَ, aor. ـَ. (TA.) One says, شَعَرْتُ لِفُلَانٍ *I said,* or *spoke, poetry,* &c., *to such a one.* (TṢ, O, TA.) And لَوْ شَعَرَ بِنَقْصِهِ لَمَا شَعَرَ [*Had he known his deficiency, he had not spoken poetry,* or *versified*]. (A.) = شَاعَرَهُ فَشَعَرَهُ: see 3. = شَعَرَ as a trans. verb syn. with اشعر: see 4. — As syn. with شاعر: see 3. = شَعِرَ, aor. ـَ, (Ḳ,) inf. n. شَعَرٌ, (TA,) *His* (a man's, TA) *hair became abundant* (Ḳ, TA) *and long:* (TA:) and said likewise of a goat, or other hairy animal, *his hair became abundant.* (TA.) — Also † *He possessed slaves.* (Lḥ, Ḳ.)

2. شعّر as an intrans. verb: see 4: — and as a trans. verb also: see 4.

3. شَاعَرَهُ ▼ فَشَعَرَهُ, (Ṣ, Ḳ,) aor. of the latter ـَ, that is with fet-ḥ, (Ṣ, MF,) accord. to Ks, who holds it to be thus even in this case, where superiority is signified, on account of the faucial letter; or, accord. to most, ـُ, agreeably with the general rule; (MF;) *He vied,* or *contended, with him in poetry, and he surpassed him therein.* (Ṣ, Ḳ, MF.) = And شَاعَرَهُ, (Ṣ,) and شاعرها, (A, Mṣb, Ḳ,) and ▼ شَعَرَهَا, (A, Ḳ,) *He slept with him,* and *with her,* (نَاوَمَهُ, Ṣ, and نَامَ مَعَهَا, Mṣb, Ḳ, or ضَاجَعَهَا, A,) *in one* شِعَار [or *innermost garment*]. (Ṣ, A, Mṣb, Ḳ.) = [Reiske, as mentioned by Freytag, explains شاعر as signifying also *Tractavit, prensavit, vellicavit:* but without naming any authority.]

4. اشعرهُ *He made him to know.* (Ṣ.) You say, اشعرهُ بِالأَمْرِ and الأَمْرَ, (Ḳ,) the latter of which is less usual than the former, because one says شَعَرَ بِهِ but not شَعَرَهُ, (MF,) *He aquainted him with the affair; made him to know it.* (Ḳ.) And أَشْعَرْتُ أَمْرَ فُلَانٍ *I made known the affair of such a one.* (A.) And أَشْعَرْتُ فُلَانًا *I made such a one notorious for an evil deed or quality.* (A.) — Also, (inf. n. إِشْعَارٌ, Mṣb,) *He marked it,* namely a beast destined for sacrifice at Mekkeh, (Ṣ,* Mgh, Mṣb,* Ḳ, TA,) *by stabbing it in the right side of its hump so that blood flowed from it,* (Ṣ,) or *by making a slit in its skin,* (Ḳ,) or *by stabbing it* (Ḳ, TA) *in one side of its hump with a* مِبْضَع *or the like,* (TA,) *so that the blood appeared,* (Ḳ, TA,) or *by making an incision in its hump so that the blood flowed,* (Mṣb,) *in order that it might be known to be destined for sacrifice.* (Ṣ, Mṣb.) — [Hence, app.,] † *He wounded him so as to cause blood to come.* (TA.) It is said in a trad. respecting the assassination of 'Othmán, أَشْعَرَهُ مِشْقَصًا † *He wounded him so as to cause blood to come with a* مشقص [q. v.]: (TA:) and in another trad., أُشْعِرَ أَمِيرُ المُؤْمِنِينَ † [*The Prince of the Faithful was wounded so that blood came from him*]. (Ṣ.) — And ‡ *He pierced him with a spear so as to make the spear-head enter his inside:* and اشعرهُ سِنَانًا ‡ *he made the spear-head to enter into the midst of him:* [but this is said to be] from اشعرهُ بِهِ "he made it to cleave to it." (TA.) أُشْعِرَ is said specially of a king, meaning *He was slain.* (A, TA.) — Also *He made it to be a distinguishing sign:* as when the performance of a religious service is made, or appointed, by God to be a sign [whereby his religion is distinguished]. (TA.) — And اشعروا *They called, uttering their* شِعَار [whereby they might know one another]: or *they appointed for themselves a* شِعَار *in their journey.* (Lḥ, Ḳ, TA. [See also 10.]) = مَا أَشْعَرَهُ [*How good,* or *excellent, a poet is he!*]. (TA in art. خزى: see مُخْزٍ in that art.) = اشعر [from شَعْرٌ or شَعَرٌ signifying "hair"] *It* (a fœtus, Ṣ, A, Ḳ, in the belly of its mother, TA) *had hair growing upon it;* (Ṣ, A, Ḳ;) as also ▼ تشعّر; (Ṣ, Ḳ;) and ▼ شعّر, inf. n. تَشْعِيرٌ; and ▼ استشعر. (Ḳ.) — And اشعرت *She* (a camel) *cast forth her fœtus with hair upon it.* (Ḳṭr, Ḳ.) — And اشعر *He lined* a boot, (A, Ḳ,) and a جُبَّة, (A,) and the مِيثَرَة of a horse's saddle, and a قَلَنْسُوَة, and the like, (TA,) *with hair;* (A, Ḳ;) as also ▼ شَعَرَ; (Lḥ, A, Ḳ;) and ▼ شعّر, (Ḳ,) inf. n. تَشْعِيرٌ: (TA:) or, said of a مِيثَرَة, *he covered it with hair.* (A.) — And اشعرهُ *He clad him with a* شِعَار [i. e. *an innermost garment*]. (Ṣ, A, Ḳ.) And *He put on him a garment as a* شِعَار, i. e., *next his body.* (TA.) [Hence,] اشعرهُ فُلَانٌ شَرًّا ‡ *Such a one involved him in evil.* (Ṣ, A.) And اشعرهُ الحُبُّ مَرَضًا † [*Love involved him in disease*]. (Ṣ.) And اشعرهُ بِهِ † *He made it* (i. e. anything) *to cleave,* or *stick, to it,* [*like the* شِعَار *to the body,*] i. e., to another thing. (Ḳ.) — [And † *It clave to him,* or *it, as the* شِعَار *cleaves to the body.* Hence,] اشعرهُ الهَمُّ ‡ [*Anxiety clave to him as the* شِعَار *cleaves to the body*]. (A.) And اشعر الهَمُّ قَلْبِى ‡ *Anxiety clave to my heart* (Ḳ, TA) *as the* شِعَار *cleaves to the body.* (TA.) And أَشْعَرَ الرَّجُلُ هَمًّا ‡ *The man clave to anxiety as the* شِعَار *cleaves to the body.* (Ṣ, TA. [In one of my copies of the Ṣ, أُشْعِرَ, accord. to which reading, the phrase

should be rendered *The man was made to have anxiety cleaving to him* &c.]) ═ اشعر السِّكِّينَ ‡ *He put a* شَعِيرَة [q. v.] *to the knife.* (Ṣ, A, Ḳ.*)

5: see 4, in the latter half of the paragraph.

[6. تشاعر *He affected*, or *pretended, to be a poet, not being such.* (See its part. n., below.)]

10. استشعرت البَقَرَةُ *The cow uttered a cry to her young one, desiring to know its state.* (A, TA.) — And استشعروا *They called, one to another, uttering the* شِعَار [*by which they were mutually known*], *in war*, or *fight.* (TA. [See also 4.]) ═ استشعر as syn. with اشعر and تشعّر: see 4, in the latter half of the paragraph. — Also, (A,) or استشعر شِعَارًا, (Ḳ,) *He put on*, or *clad himself with, a* شعار [i. e. *an innermost garment*]. (A, Ḳ.) [Hence,] اِسْتَشْعِرْ خَشْيَةَ ٱللّٰهِ ‡ *Make thou the fear of God to be* شِعَارَ قَلْبِكَ [i. e. *the thing next to thy heart*]. (TA.) And استشعر خَوْفًا ‡ *He conceived in his mind fear.* (Ṣ, A.*)

شَعْرٌ and ▼شَعَرٌ, (A, Mṣb, Ḳ, but only the latter in my copies of the Ṣ and in the O,) two well-known dial. vars., the like being common in cases of this kind, in which the medial radical letter is a faucial, (MF,) [but the latter I have found to be the more common,] *Hair*; i. e. *what grows upon the body, that is not* صُوف *nor* وَبَر; (Ḳ;) it is an appertenance *of human beings and of other animals*: (Ṣ, A, Mṣb:) [when spoken of as used in the fabrication of cloth for tents &c., the meaning intended is *goats' hair*: (see 4 in art. بنى:)] of the masc. gender: (Mṣb, TA:) pl. (of the former, Mṣb) شُعُورٌ and (of the latter, Mṣb) أَشْعَارٌ (Ṣ, Mṣb, Ḳ) and (of the latter also, TA) شِعَارٌ: (Ḳ, TA:) and ▼أُشْعَارٌ, properly dim. of أَشْعَارٌ, is used, accord. to Aboo-Ziyád, as dim. of شُعُور: (TA:) the n. un. is with ة: (Ṣ, A,* Mṣb, Ḳ:) and this, i. e. شَعْرَةٌ [or شَعَرَةٌ], is also used metonymically as a pl. (Ḳ, TA.) One says, شَقُّ الأُبْلُمَةِ بَيْنِي وَبَيْنَكَ المَالُ شَقَّ الشَّعَرَةِ and † [*The property is*, or *shall be, equally divided between me and thee*]. (TA.) And رَأَى فُلَانٌ الشَّعْرَةَ *Such a one saw*, or *has seen, hoariness*, or *white hairs*, (Yaạkoob, Ṣ, A, TA,) upon his head. (TA.) — [The n. un.] شَعْرَةٌ is also used, metonymically, as meaning ‡ *A daughter.* (TA.) — And ▼شَعْرٌ (Ḳ, and so accord. to the TA, but in the CḲ ▼شُعْرٌ,) signifies also ‡ *Plants and trees*; (Ḳ, TA;) as being likened to hair. (TA.) — And the same, (A, Ḳ, TA, but in the CḲ ▼شُعْرٌ,) ‡ *Saffron* (A, Ḳ) *before it is pulverized.* (A.)

شَعَرٌ: see the next two preceding sentences.

شِعْرٌ [an inf. n., (see 1, first sentence,) and used as a simple subst. signifying] *Knowledge*; *cognizance*: (Ḳ, TA:) or *knowledge of the minute particulars of things*: or *perception by means of* [*any of*] *the senses.* (TA.) One says, لَيْتَ شِعْرِى فُلَانًا مَا صَنَعَ, (Ks, Lḥ, Ṣ,* Mṣb,* Ḳ,*) and لَيْتَ شِعْرِى عَنْهُ مَا صَنَعَ, and لَيْتَ شِعْرِى لَهُ مَا صَنَعَ, (Ks, Lḥ, Ḳ,*) i. e. *Would that I knew what such a one did*, or *has done*; (Ṣ,* Ḳ,* Mṣb,* TA;) for *would that my knowledge were present at*, or *comprehending, what such a one did*, or *has done*; the phrase being elliptical: (TA:) accord. to Sb, لَيْتَ شِعْرِى is for ليت شِعْرَتِى, the ة being elided as in هُوَ أَبُو عُذْرِهَا [for هو ابو عُذْرَتِهَا], (Ṣ, TA,) the elision of the ة in this latter instance, as Sb says, being peculiar to the case of the words being preceded by ابو; [but see عُذْرَةٌ;] and as in إِقَامَة when used as a prefixed noun; though لَيْتَ شِعْرَتِى is not now known to have been heard. (TA.) One says also, لَيْتَ شِعْرِى مَا كَانَ *Would that I knew what happened*, or *has happened.* (A.) — The predominant signification of شِعْرٌ is *Poetry*, or *verse*; (Mṣb, Ḳ;) because of its preeminence by reason of the measure and the rhyme; though every kind of knowledge is شِعْر: (Ḳ:) or because it relates the minute affairs of the Arabs, and the occult particulars of their secret affairs, and their facetiæ: (Er-Rághib, TA:) it is properly defined as *language qualified by rhyme and measure intentionally*; which last restriction excludes the like of the saying in the Ḳur [xciv. 3 and 4], ٱلَّذِى أَنْقَضَ ظَهْرَكَ وَرَفَعْنَا لَكَ ذِكْرَكَ, because this is not intentionally qualified by rhyme and measure: (KT; and the like is said in the Mṣb:) and sometimes *a single verse* is thus termed: (Akh, TA:) pl. أَشْعَارٌ. (Ṣ, Ḳ.) — Also † *Falsehood*; because of the many lies in poetry. (B, TA.)

شُعْرٌ: see شَعْرٌ, in two places.

شَعِرٌ: see أَشْعَرُ. — [The fem.] شَعِرَةٌ signifies [particularly] A sheep or goat (شَاةٌ) *having hair growing between the two halves of its hoof, which in consequence bleed*: or *having an itching in its knees*, (Ḳ, TA,) *and therefore always scratching with them.* (TA.)

شَعْرَةٌ and شَعَرَةٌ ns. un. of شَعْرٌ [q. v.] and شَعَرٌ.

شِعْرَةٌ The *hair of the pubes*; (T, Mṣb, Ḳ;) as also ▼شِعْرَاءٌ, [accord. to general analogy with tenween,] or ▼شَعْرَاءُ, [and if so, without tenween,] accord. to different copies of the Ḳ; (TA;) *of a man* and *of a woman*; and *of the hinder part of a woman*: (T, Mṣb:) or the *hair of the pubes of a woman*, specially: (Ṣ, O, Mṣb:) and the *pubes* (عَانَة) [*itself*]: (Ḳ:) and the *place of growth of the hair beneath the navel.* (Ḳ,* TA.) — Also *A portion of hair.* (Ḳ,* TA.)

الشِّعْرَى [*The star Sirius*;] *a certain bright star, also called* المِرْزَمُ; (TA; [but see this latter appellation;]) *the star that rises* [*aurorally*] *after* الجَوْزَاء [by which is here meant *Gemini*], *in the time of intense heat*, (Ṣ, TA,) *and after* الهَقْعَة [app. a mistranscription for الهَنْعَة]: (TA:) [about the epoch of the Flight, it rose aurorally, in Central Arabia, on the 13th of July, O. S.: (see الثُّرَيَّا; and see also مَنَازِلُ القَمَرِ, in art. نزل:) on the periods of its rising at sunset, and setting aurorally, see دَبْرٌ and دبور:] the Arabs say, إِذَا طَلَعَتِ الشِّعْرَى جَعَلَ صَاحِبُ النَّخْلِ يَرَى [*When Sirius rises aurorally, the owner of the palm-trees begins to see* what their fruit will be]: (TA:) there are *two stars* of this name; الشِّعْرَى العَبُورُ and الشِّعْرَى الغُمَيْصَاءُ, (Ṣ, Ḳ,) together called الشِّعْرَيَانِ: the former is that [above mentioned] which is in [a mistake for "after"] الجَوْزَاء, and the latter is [*Procyon*,] *in the* ذِرَاع [by which is meant الذِّرَاعُ المَبْسُوطَةُ, not الذِّرَاعُ المَقْبُوضَةُ]; (Ṣ;) and both together are called *the two Sisters of Suheyl* (سُهَيْل [i. e. *Canopus*]): (Ṣ, Ḳ:) the former was worshipped by a portion of the Arabs; and hence God is said in the Ḳur-án to be Lord of الشِّعْرَى: (TA:) it is called العَبُور because of its having crossed the Milky Way; and the other is called الغُمَيْصَاء because said by the Arabs to have wept after the former until it had foul thick matter in the corner of the eye: (Ḳ in art. غمص:) the former is also called الشِّعْرَى اليَمَانِيَّةُ [*the Yemenian*, or *Southern*, شعرى]; and the latter, الشِّعْرَى الشَّامِيَّةُ [*the Syrian*, or *Northern*, شعرى]. (Ḳzw.)

شَعْرَاءُ fem. of أَشْعَرُ [q. v.: under which head it is also mentioned either as a subst. or as an epithet in which the quality of a subst. is predominant]. — See also شِعْرَةٌ.

شِعْرَاءٌ [app., if correct, with tenween]: see شِعْرَةٌ.

شِعْرِىٌّ [*Of*, or *relating to, poetry*; *poetical*. — And also † *False*, or *lying*]. One says أَدِلَّةٌ شِعْرِيَّةٌ † *False*, or *lying, evidences* or *arguments*: because of the many lies in poetry. (B, TA.) ═ [And *Of*, or *relating to*, الشِّعْرَى, i. e. *Sirius*.] You say, رَعَيْنَا شِعْرِىَّ المَرَاعِى *We pastured* our cattle *upon the herbage of which the growth was consequent upon the* نَوْء [i. e. the *auroral rising* or *setting*] *of* الشِّعْرَى [or *Sirius*]. (A.)

شُعَرِيَّاتٌ The *young ones of the* رَخَم [i. e. *vultur percnopterus*]. (Ḳ.)

شَعْرَانُ: see أَشْعَرُ. — شَعْرَان [app. without tenween, being probably originally an epithet, also] signifies † The [*shrub called*] رِمْث, (Ḳ,) or *a species thereof*, (Tekmileh, TA,) *green, inclining to dust-colour*: (Tekmileh, Ḳ, TA:) or *a species of* [*the kind of plants called*] حَمْض, *dust-coloured*: (TA:) or حَمْض *upon which hares feed, and in which they* [*make their forms*, i. e.] *lie, cleaving to the ground*; *it is like the large* أُشْنَانَة [here app. used as the n. un. of أُشْنَان, i. e. *kali*, or *glass-wort*], *has slender twigs, and appears from afar black.* (AḤn, TA.)

شُعْرُورٌ [*A poetaster*]: see شَاعِرٌ. ═ Also, accord. to analogy, sing. of شَعَارِيرُ, which is † *Syn. with* شُعْرٌ [as pl. of شَعْرَاءُ, q. v. voce أَشْعَرُ], meaning the *flies that collect upon the sore on the back of a camel, and, when roused, disperse themselves from it.* (TA.) [Hence the saying,] ذَهَبَ القَوْمُ شَعَارِيرَ † *The people dispersed themselves*, or *became dispersed*: (Ṣ:) and ذَهَبُوا شَعَارِيرَ بِقِذَّانَ, (Ḳ,) or بِقِذَّانَ, and (TA,) and بِقِنْذَحْرَةَ, (Ḳ,) and

بِقِنْذَحْرَةٍ, (TA,) † *They went away in a state of dispersion, like flies*: (Ḳ:) شعارير thus used being pl. of شُعْرُورٌ; (TA;) or having no sing. (Fr, Akh, Ṣ, TA.) And أَصْبَحَتْ شَعَارِيرَ بِقِرْذَحْمَةٍ, and بِقِنْذَحْرَةٍ, and بِقِذَّحْرَةٍ, and بِقِرْذَحْمَةٍ, † *They became beyond reach, or power.* (Lḥ, TA.) —— And the same pl. شَعَارِيرُ, having no sing., also signifies † *A certain game* (Ṣ, Ḳ, TA) *of children.* (TA.) You say, لَعِبْنَا الشَّعَارِيرَ [*We played at the game of* الشعارير]: and هٰذَا لَعِبُ الشَّعَارِيرِ [*This is the game of* الشعارير]. (Ṣ.) —— And † *A sort of women's ornaments, like barley* [-*corns*], *made of gold and of silver, and worn upon the neck.* (TA.) —— And شُعْرُورَةٌ [n. un. of شُعْرُورٌ] signifies *A small* قِثَّآء [or *cucumber*]: pl. شَعَارِيرُ [as above]. (Ṣ, Ḳ.)

شُعْرَانِىٌّ: see أَشْعَرُ. ═ أَرْنَبٌ شُعْرَانِيَّةٌ *A hare that feeds upon the* شُعْرَان [q. v.], *and that* [*makes its form therein, i. e.*] *lies therein, cleaving to the ground.* (AḤn, TA.)

شَعَارٌ ‡ *Trees*; (ISk, Er-Riyáshee, Ṣ, A, Ḳ;) as also ▼ شِعَارٌ: (As, ISh, Ḳ:) or *tangled*, or *luxuriant*, or *abundant and dense, trees*; (T, Ḳ;) as also ▼ شِعَارٌ: (Sh, T, Ḳ:) or (TA, but in the Ḳ "and") *trees in land that is soft* (Ḳ, TA) *and depressed, between eminences,* (TA,) *where people alight,* (Ḳ, TA,) *such as is termed* دَهْنَآء, and *the like,* (TA,) *warming themselves thereby in winter, and shading themselves thereby in summer,* as also ▼ مَشْعَرٌ: (Ḳ, TA:) or this last signifies *any place in which are a* خَمَر [or *covert of trees,* &c.,] *and* [*other*] *trees*; and its pl. is مَشَاعِرُ. (TA.) One says, أَرْضٌ كَثِيرَةُ الشَّعَارِ † *A land abounding in trees* [&c.]. (Ṣ.) —— See also the next paragraph, latter half.

شِعَارٌ *A sign of people in war,* (Ṣ, Mṣb, Ḳ,) and *in a journey* (Ḳ) &c., (TA,) i. e. (Mṣb) *a call or cry,* (A, Mgh, Mṣb,) *by means of which to know one another*: (Ṣ, A, Mgh, Mṣb:) and the شِعَار of soldiers is *a sign that is set up in order that a man may thereby know his companions*: (TA:) and شِعَار signifies also the *banners,* or *standards,* of tribes. (TA in art. برم.) It is said in a trad. that the شِعَار of the Prophet in war was يَا مَنْصُورُ أَمِتْ أَمِتْ [*O Manṣoor,* (a proper name of a man, meaning "aided" &c.,) *kill thou, kill thou*]. (TA.) And it is said that he appointed the شِعَار of the refugees on the day of Bedr to be يَا بَنِى عَبْدِ ٱلرَّحْمٰنِ: and the شعار of El-Khazraj, يَا بَنِى عَبْدِ ٱللّٰهِ: and that of El-Ows, يَا بَنِى عُبَيْدِ ٱللّٰهِ: and their شعار on the day of El-Aḥzáb, حٰمٓ لَا يُنْصَرُونَ. (Mgh.) —— And *Thunder*; (Tekmileh, Ḳ;) as being a sign of rain. (TḲ.) —— شِعَارُ الحَجِّ means *The religious rites and ceremonies of the pilgrimage*; and *the signs thereof*; (Ḳ;) and, (TA,) as also ▼ الشَّعَائِرُ, (Ṣ,) *the practices of the pilgrimage, and whatever is appointed as a sign of obedience to God*; (Ṣ, Mṣb,* TA;) *as the halting* [*at Mount 'Arafát*], *and the circuiting* [*around the Kaabeh*], *and the* سَعْى [*or tripping to and fro between Eṣ-Ṣafà and El-Marweh*], *and the throwing* [*of the pebbles at Minè*], *and the sacrifice,* &c.; (TA;) and ▼ شَعِيرَةٌ and ▼ شِعَارَةٌ and ▼ مَشْعَرٌ signify the same as شِعَارٌ: (L:) ▼ شَعِيرَةٌ is the sing. of شَعَائِرُ, meaning as expl. above; (Aṣ, Ṣ, Mṣb;) or, as some say, the sing. is ▼ شِعَارَةٌ: (Aṣ, Ṣ:) or ▼ شَعِيرَةٌ and ▼ شِعَارَةٌ, by some written ▼ شَعَارَةٌ, and ▼ مَشْعَرٌ, signify *a place* [*of the performance*] *of religious rites and ceremonies of the pilgrimage*; expl. in the Ḳ by مُعْظَمُهَا, which is a mistake for مَوْضِعُهَا; (TA;) and ▼ مَشَاعِرُ, *places thereof*: (Ṣ:) or ▼ شَعَائِرُ الحَجِّ signifies *the* مَعَالِم [or *characteristic practices*] *of the pilgrimage, to which God has invited, and the performance of which He has commanded*; (Ḳ;) as also ▼ المَشَاعِرُ: (TA:) and ▼ شَعَائِرُ ٱللّٰهِ, *all those religious services which God has appointed to us as signs; as the halting* [*at Mount 'Arafát*], *and the* سَعْى [*or tripping to and fro between Eṣ-Ṣafà and El-Marweh*], *and the sacrificing of victims*: (Zj, TA:) or *the rites and ceremonies of the pilgrimage, and the places where those rites and ceremonies are performed*; (Bḍ in v. 2 and xxii. 33;) among which places are Eṣ-Ṣafà and El-Marweh, they being thus expressly termed; (Ḳur ii. 153;) and so accord. to Fr in the Ḳur v. 2: (TA:) or *the obligatory statutes* or *ordinances of God*: (Bḍ in v. 2:) or *the religion of God*: (Bḍ in v. 2 and xxii. 33:) the camels or cows or bulls destined to be sacrificed at Mekkeh are also said in the Ḳur xxii. 37, to be مِنْ شَعَائِرِ ٱللّٰهِ, i. e. *of the signs of the religion of God*: (Bḍ and Jel:) and [hence the sing.] ▼ شَعِيرَةٌ signifies [sometimes] *a camel* or *cow* or *bull that is brought to Mekkeh for sacrifice*; (Ṣ, Ḳ;) *such as is marked in the manner expl. voce* أَشْعَرَ; (Mṣb;) and شَعَائِرُ is its pl.; (Ḳ;) and is also pl. of شِعَارٌ: and the [festival called the] عِيد is said to be a شعار of the شَعَائِر [i. e. *a sign of the signs of the religion*] of El-Islám. (Mṣb.) —— شِعَارُ الدَّمِ is said to mean ‡ *The piece of rag*: or ‡ *the vulva*: because each is a thing that indicates the existence of blood. (Mgh.) ═ Also The [*innermost garment*; or] *garment that is next the body*; (Ṣ, Mṣb;) the *garment that is next the hair of the body, under the* دِثَار; as also ▼ شَعَارٌ; (Ḳ;) but this is strange: (TA:) pl. [of pauc.] أَشْعِرَةٌ and [of mult.] شُعُرٌ. (Ḳ.) [Hence,] one says, لَبِسَ شِعَارَ الهَمِّ ‡ [*He involved himself in anxiety*]. (A.) And جَعَلَ الخَوْفَ شِعَارَهُ † [*He made fear to be* as though it were *his innermost garment*], by closely cleaving to it. (TA in art. درع.) [Hence, also,] it is said in a prov., هُمُ الشِّعَارُ دُونَ الدِّثَارِ, meaning † *They are near in respect of love*: and in a trad., relating to the Anṣár, أَنْتُمُ الشِّعَارُ وَالنَّاسُ الدِّثَارُ † *Ye are the special and close friends* [*and the people in general are the less near in friendship*]. (TA.) —— Also *A horse-cloth*; *a covering for a horse to protect him from the cold.* (Ḳ.) —— And † *A thing with which wine* [app. while in the vat] *is protected,* or *preserved from injury*: (L, Ḳ: [for الخَمْرُ, the reading in the CḲ, the author of the TḲ has read الخُمُرُ (and thus I find the word written in my MS. copy of the Ḳ) or الخُمْرُ, pls. of الخِمَارُ; and Freytag has followed his example: but الخَمْرُ is the right reading, as is shown by what here follows:]) so in the saying of El-Akhṭal,

فَكَفَّ الرِّيحَ وَالأَنْدَآءَ عَنْهَا
مِنَ الزَّرَجُونِ دُونَهُمَا الشِّعَارُ

[evidently describing wine, and app. meaning † *And the* شعار *of the wine,* (الشِّعَارُ مِنَ الزَّرَجُونِ, i. e. شِعَارُ الزَّرَجُونِ,) while yet in the vat, *intervening as an obstacle to them, kept off the wind and the rains, or dews, or day-dews, from it,* namely, the wine]. (L.) —— See also شَعَارٌ, in two places. ═ Also *Death.* (O, Ḳ.)

شَعِيرٌ, (Ṣ, Mṣb, Ḳ,) which may be also pronounced شِعِيرٌ, agreeably with the dial. of Temeem, as may any word of the measure فَعِيلٌ of which the medial radical letter is a faucial, and, accord. to Lth, certain of the Arabs pronounced in a similar manner any word of that measure of which the medial radical letter is not a faucial, like كِبِيرٌ and جِلِيلٌ and كِرِيمٌ, (MF,) [and thus do many in the present day, others pronouncing the fet-ḥ in this case, more correctly, in the manner termed إِمَالَة, i. e. as "e" in our word "bed:" *Barley*;] *a certain grain,* (Ṣ, Mṣb,) *well known*: (Mṣb, Ḳ:) of the masc. gender, except in the dial. of the people of Nejd, who make it fem.: (Zj, Mṣb:) n. un. with ة [signifying *a barley-corn*]. (Ṣ, Ḳ.) ═ Also *An accompanying associate*; syn. عَشِيرٌ مُصَاحِبٌ: on the authority of En-Nawawee: (Ḳ, TA:) said to be formed by transposition: but it may be from شَعَرَهَا meaning "he slept with her in one شِعَار;" [see 3; and so originally signifying *a person who sleeps with another in one innermost garment*;] then applied to any special companion. (TA.)

شَعَارَةٌ, and, as written by some, شِعَارَةٌ: see شِعَارٌ, in four places.

شَعِيرَةٌ *A sign,* or *mark.* (Mgh.) —— See this word, and the pl. شَعَائِرُ, voce شِعَارٌ, in seven places. ═ Also n. un. of شَعِيرٌ [q. v.]. (Ṣ, Ḳ.) —— And [hence,] ‡ The *iron* [*pin*] *that enters into the tang of a knife which is inserted into the handle, being a fastening to the handle*: (Ṣ:) or *a thing that is moulded of silver or of iron, in the form of a barley-corn,* (Ḳ, TA,) *entering into the tang of the blade which is inserted into the handle,* (TA,) *being a fastening to the handle of the blade.* (Ḳ, TA.) —— [And † *A measure of length,* defined in the law-books &c. as *equal to six mule's hairs placed side by side*;] the *sixth part of the* إِصْبَع [or *digit*]. (Mṣb voce مِيلٌ.) —— [And † The *weight of a barley-corn.*]

[شُعَيْرَةٌ dim. of شَعْرَةٌ and شَعَرَةٌ: pl. شُعَيْرَاتٌ.]

شُعَيْرَآءُ [dim. of شَعْرَآءُ fem. of أَشْعَرُ. ═ Also] *A kind of trees*; (Ṣgh, Ḳ;) in the dial. of Hudheyl. (Ṣgh, TA.) —— See also أَشْعَرُ, last signification but one.

شَعِيرِىٌّ *A seller of* شَعِير [or *barley*]: one does

not use in this sense either of the more analogical forms of شَاعِرٌ and شُعَّار. (Sb, TA.)

شَاعِرٌ *A poet:* (T, Ṣ, Mṣb, Ḳ:) so called because of his intelligence; (Ṣ, Mṣb;) or because he knows what others know not: (T, TA:) accord. to Akh, it is a possessive epithet, like لَابِنٌ and تَامِرٌ: (Ṣ:) pl. شُعَرَآءُ, (Ṣ, Mṣb, Ḳ,) deviating from analogy: (Ṣ, Mṣb:) Sb says that the measure فَاعِلٌ is likened in this case to فَعِيلٌ; and hence this pl.: (TA:) or, accord. to IKh, the pl. is of this form because the sing. is from شَعُرَ, and therefore should by rule be of the measure فَعِيلٌ, like شَرِيفٌ [from شَرُفَ]; but were it so, it might be confounded with شَعِير meaning the grain thus called, therefore they said شَاعِرٌ, and regarded in the pl. the original form of the sing. (Mṣb.) A wonderful poet is called خِنْذِيذٌ: one next below him, شَاعِرٌ: then, ▼شُوَيْعِرٌ [the dim.]: (Yoo, Ḳ:) then, ▼شُعْرُورٌ: and then, ▼مُتَشَاعِرٌ. (Ḳ.) — Also † *A liar:* because of the many lies in poetry: and so, accord. to some, in the Ḳur xxi. 5. (B, TA.) — شِعْرٌ شَاعِرٌ *Excellent poetry:* (Sb, T, Ḳ:) or *known poetry:* but the former explanation is the more correct. (TA.) One also says, sometimes, كَلِمَةٌ شَاعِرَةٌ, [by كلمة] meaning قَصِيدَةٌ: but generally in a phrase of this kind the two words are cognate, as in لَيْلٌ لَائِلٌ and وَيْلٌ وَائِلٌ. (TA.)

شُوَيْعِرٌ: see the next preceding paragraph.

أَشْعَرُ [*More,* and *most, knowing* or *cognizant* or *understanding:* see 1, first sentence. — And,] applied to a verse, (T,) or to a poem, (Ṣ,) *More* [and *most*] *poetical.* (T, Ṣ.*) — Also, (Ṣ, A, Ḳ,) and ▼شَعِرٌ, (A, Ḳ,) and ▼شَعْرَانِىٌّ, (Ḳ,) which last (SM says) I have seen written شُعْرَانِىٌّ, (TA,) A man *having much hair upon his body:* (Ṣ, A:) or *having hair upon the whole of the body:* (IAth, L voce أَجْرَدُ [q. v.], in explanation of the first:) or *having much and long hair* (Ḳ, TA) *upon the head and body:* (TA:) and the first and second, a goat *having much hair:* fem. of the first شَعْرَآءُ: (TA:) and pl. of the first شُعْرٌ. (Ṣ, Ḳ.) One says أَشْعَثُ أَشْعَرُ, meaning *Having his head unshaven and not combed nor anointed.* (TA.) And فُلَانٌ أَشْعَرُ الرَّقَبَةِ [lit. *Such a one is hairy in the neck*] is said of a man though he have not hair upon his neck, as meaning ‡ *such a one is strong, like a lion.* (A,* TA.) — [The fem.] شَعْرَآءُ also signifies *A testicle,* or *scrotum,* (خُصْيَةٌ,) *having much hair:* (TA:) and the سَوْءَة [or *pudendum*]: thus used as a subst. (IAṭr, TA in art. عمد.) See also شَعْرَةٌ. — And *A furred garment.* (Th, Ḳ.) — And as an epithet, ‡ *Evil, foul,* or *abominable:* [as being likened to that which is shaggy, and therefore unseemly:] (Ḳ,* TA:) in the Ḳ, الخَشِنَةُ is erroneously put for الخَبِيثَةُ. (TA.) One says, دَاهِيَةٌ شَعْرَآءُ, (Ṣ, A, Ḳ,) and وَبْرَآءُ, (Ṣ, A,) and زَبَّآءُ, (TA in art. زب,) ‡ *An evil, a foul,* or *an abominable,* (TA,) or *a severe,* or *great,* (Ḳ,) *calamity* or *misfortune:* pl. شُعْرٌ. (Ḳ, TA.) And one says to a man when he has said a thing that one blames or with which one finds fault, جِئْتَ بِهَا شَعْرَآءَ ذَاتَ وَبَرٍ ‡ [*Thou hast said it as a foul,* or *an abominable, thing*]. (Ṣ, A.*) — And أَشْعَرُ signifies also The *hair that surrounds the solid hoof:* (Ṣ:) or [the *extremity,* or *border, of the pastern, next the solid hoof;* i. e.] the *extremity of the skin surrounding the solid hoof,* (Ḳ, TA,) *where the small hairs grow around it:* (TA:) or the *part between the hoof* of a horse *and the place where the hair of the pastern terminates:* and the *part* of a camel's foot *where the hair terminates:* (TA:) pl. أَشَاعِرُ, (Ṣ, TA,) because it is [in this sense] a subst. (TA.) — Also The *side of the vulva,* or *external portion of the female organs of generation:* (Ḳ:) it is said that the أَشْعَرَانِ are the إِسْكَتَانِ, which are the *two sides* [or *labia majora*] *of the vulva of a woman:* or the *two parts next to the* شُفْرَانِ, which are the *two borders of the* إِسْكَتَانِ: or the *two parts between the* إِسْكَتَانِ *and the* شُفْرَانِ: (L, TA:) or the *two parts next to the* شُفْرَانِ, *in the hair, particularly:* (Zj, in his "Khalḳ el-Insán:") the أَشَاعِر of the حَيَآء [or vulva of a camel &c.] are the *parts where the hair terminates:* (TA:) and the أَشَاعِر of a she-camel are the *sides of the vulva.* (Ṣ, L, TA.) — And *A thing that comes forth from* [between] *the two halves of the hoof of a sheep* or *goat, resembling a* ثُؤْلُول [or *wart*]; (Lḥ, Ḳ;) for which it is cauterized. (Lḥ, TA.) — And *Flesh coming forth beneath the nail:* pl. شُعُرٌ, (Ḳ, TA,) with two ḍammehs, (TA,) or شُعْرٌ. (So in the CḲ.) — And [the fem.] شَعْرَآءُ also signifies ‡ Land (أَرْض) *containing,* or *having, trees:* or *abounding in trees:* (A, Ḳ:) [and so, app., ▼شَعْرَانُ; for] there is a mountain in [the province of] El-Mowṣil called شَعْرَانُ, said by AA to be thus called because of the abundance of its trees: (Ṣ:) or شَعْرَآءُ signifies *many trees:* (A'Obeyd, Ṣ:) or *i. q.* أَجَمَةٌ [i. e. *a thicket, wood,* or *forest;* &c.]: (TA:) and a meadow (رَوْضَةٌ, AḤn, A, Ḳ, TA) *having its upper part covered with trees,* (AḤn, Ḳ* TA,) or *abounding in trees,* (TA,) or *abounding in herbage:* (A:) and a tract of sand (رَمْلَةٌ) *producing* [*the plant called*] نَصِىّ (Ṣgh, L, Ḳ) *and the like.* (Ṣgh, Ḳ.) — And † *A certain tree of the kind called* حَمْض, (Ḳ, TA,) *not having leaves, but having* [*what are termed*] هَدَب [q. v.], *very eagerly desired by the camels, and that puts forth strong twigs* or *branches;* mentioned in the L on the authority of AḤn, and by Ṣgh on the authority of Aboo-Ziyád; and the latter adds that *it has firewood.* (TA.) — And † *A certain fruit:* (AḤn, TA:) *a species of peach:* (Ṣ, Ḳ:) sing. and pl. the same: (AḤn, Ṣ, Ḳ:) or *a single peach:* (IḲṭṭ, MF:) or الأَشْعَرُ is a name of the *peach,* and the pl. is شُعْرٌ. (Mṭr, TA.) — Also † *A kind of fly,* (Ṣ, Ḳ,) *said to be that which has a sting,* (Ṣ,) *blue,* or *red, that alights upon camels and asses and dogs;* (Ḳ;) as also ▼شُعَيْرَآءُ: (TA:) *a kind of fly that stings the ass, so that he goes round:* AḤn says that *it is of two species, that of the dog* and *that of the camel: that of the dog is well known, inclines to slenderness and redness, and touches nothing but the dog: that of the camel inclines to yellowness, is larger than that of the dog, has wings, and is downy under the wings: sometimes it is in such numbers that the owners of the camels cannot milk in the day-time nor ride any of them; so that they leave doing this until night: it stings the camel in the soft parts of the udder and around them, and beneath the tail and the belly and the armpits; and they do not protect the animal from it save by tar: it flies over the camels so that one hears it to make a humming,* or *buzzing, sound.* (TA. [See also شُعْرُورٌ, under which its pl. شُعْرٌ is mentioned.]) — And [hence, perhaps, as this kind of fly is seen in swarms,] † *A multitude of men.* (Ḳ.)

أَشْعَارٌ: see شَعْرٌ.

مَشْعَرٌ *i. q.* مَعْلَمٌ [meaning *A place where a thing is known to be*]. (TA.) — And hence, *A place of the performance of religious services.* (TA.) See this word, and its pl. مَشَاعِرُ, voce شِعَارٌ, in four places. — [The pl.] المَشَاعِرُ also signifies *The five senses;* (Ṣ,* A,* TA;) *the hearing, the sight, the smell, the taste, and the touch.* (Ṣ and Mṣb in art. حس.) — See also شِعَارٌ.

دِيَةُ المُشْعَرَةِ *The bloodwit that is exacted for killing kings: it is a thousand camels.* (A, TA. [See 4.])

مُتَشَاعِرٌ One *who affects,* or *pretends, to be a poet, but is not.* (Ṣ,* L,* Ḳ,* TA.) See شَاعِرٌ.

شعف

1. شَعَفَ, (Ṣ, O, Ḳ,) aor. ـَ, (Ḳ,) inf. n. شَعْفٌ, though it is implied in the Ḳ, by its being said that the verb is like مَنَعَ, that it is شَعَفٌ, (TA,) *He smeared, anointed,* or *overspread,* a camel [suffering from the mange, or scab], with tar, (Ṣ, O, Ḳ, and Bḍ in xii. 30,) *and burned him by so doing.* (Bḍ ibid.) Imra-el-Ḳeys says,

• لِيَقْتُلَنِى وَقَدْ شَعَفْتُ فُؤَادَهَا •

• كَمَا شَعَفَ المَهْنُوءَةَ الرَّجُلُ الطَّالِى •

[*That he should slay me, I having overspread her heart* with love of me, *like as the man anointing overspreads her* (meaning the camel) *that is smeared with tar*]: but it is also related otherwise, i. e. قَطَرْتُ فُؤَادَهَا كَمَا قَطَرَ: (O, TA:) Aboo-'Alee El-Ḳálee says that she [the camel] that is smeared with tar experiences, by reason of the tar, a pleasurable sensation with a burning. (TA.) — Hence, [as indicated above,] قَدْ شَعَفَهَا حُبًّا [*He has overspread and burned her* heart *with love*]; as some read in the Ḳur xii. 30; others reading شَغَفَهَا: (Bḍ:) [or *he has burned her heart with love;* for] شَعَفَهُ الحُبُّ means *love burned his heart:* (Ṣ:) there are two readings of the words of the Ḳur above; (O, Ḳ;) [as well as two other readings mentioned in art. شغف;] قَدْ شَعَفَهَا حُبًّا, (Ṣ, O, Ḳ,) one, a reading of El-Ḥasan (Ṣ, O) and others; meaning [as above: or], accord. to AZ, *he has diseased her heart with love,* (Ṣ,* O,) *and* *melted it:* (O:) or, accord. to El-Ḥasan, *he has penetrated into her with love:* (Ṣ:) the other reading is قَدْ شَعَفَهَا حُبًّا, (O, Ḳ,) meaning *he has become attached to her with love,* and *loved her excessively:* (O:) [but it is also said that] شَعَفَنِى حُبُّهُ means *The love of him overspread my heart from above;* (O, Ḳ;) from شَعَفَةٌ signifying the "head" of the heart, "at the place of suspension of [or from] the نِيَاط;" (O,* Ḳ;) and in like manner, شُعِفْتُ بِهِ and بِحُبِّهِ, (O, and so in the CḲ,) or شَعِفْتُ: (so in other copies of the Ḳ, in which, and in the CḲ, the verb in this case is said to be like فَرِحَ: [but this I regard as a mistake:]) and شَعَفَ القَلْبَ *He,* or *it, struck,* or *smote, the* شَعَفَة, or *uppermost part, of the heart:* (Ḥam p. 545:) Az, however, says, I know not any one that has assigned to the heart a شَعَفَة, except Lth; and vehement love takes possession of the core (سَوَاد) of the heart; not of its extremity: [but] accord. to Fr, شُعِفَ بِفُلَانٍ, like عُنِىَ, means *The love of such a one rose to the highest places of his heart:* others say that الشعف [app. الشَّعَفُ] signifies *the being frightened,* and *disquieted,* like the beast when it is frightened; and that the Arabs transferred its attribution from beasts to human beings: (TA:) Abu-l-'Alà says that الشَّعَفُ signifies a thing's *falling into the heart:* (IB, TA:) one says also, شَعَفَهُ المَرَضُ *Disease melted him:* (TA:) and accord. to AZ, شُعِفَ بِكَذَا means *He became diseased by such a thing.* (Ṣ.)

شَعَفٌ: see شَعَفَةٌ, in two places. — Also The *upper,* or *uppermost, part of the hump of the camel:* (O, Ḳ:) Lth says that it is *like the heads of truffles, and the three stones upon which the cooking-pot is placed, that are round in their upper,* or *uppermost, parts.* (O.) ═ Also *Vehemence of love:* (L:) [or simply *love:* for] one says, أَلْقَى عَلَيْهِ شَعَفَهُ, meaning [*He cast*] *his love* [*upon him,* or *it*]; as also شَغَفَهُ. (TA.)

شَعَفَةٌ The *head* [or *summit*] *of a mountain:* (Ṣ, O, Ḳ:) and the *upper,* or *uppermost, part of anything:* (Ḥam pp. 130 and 545:) pl. ↓ شَعَفٌ [or rather this is a coll. gen. n., and accord. to Freytag it is used as a sing., in the two senses above mentioned, in the Deewán of Jereer,] and [the pl. is] شُعُوفٌ and شِعَافٌ and شَعَفَاتٌ: (Ṣ, O, Ḳ:) and ↓ شَعَفٌ is also expl. as signifying *an elevated part of the earth* or *ground.* (TA.) — Also *A lock of hair* (خُصْلَة) *upon the head,* (Ḳ,) or *upon the upper,* or *uppermost, part of the head.* (O, TA.) And شِعَافٌ (its pl., TA) signifies The *hair of the head:* so in the phrase رَجُلٌ صُهْبُ الشِّعَافِ [*A man whose hair of the head is red,* or *red in the outer part and black beneath,* or *of a red colour tinged over with blackness,* &c.]. (Ṣ, O, Ḳ.) — And The [*pendent lock of hair termed*] ذُؤَابَة *of a boy,* or *young man.* (Ṣ.) — And شَعَفَةُ القَلْبِ signifies *The head of the heart, at the place of suspension of* [or *from*] *the* نِيَاط [q. v.]. (O, TA. [But see, in the first paragraph, what Az says respecting this meaning.])

شَعَافٌ, like سَحَابٌ, *Love's making away with the heart.* (TA.)

شُعَافٌ *Insanity,* or *madness.* (O, Ḳ.)

[شُعَيْفَةٌ dim. of شَعَفَةٌ: pl. شُعَيْفَاتٌ.] One says, مَا عَلَى رَأْسِهِ إِلَّا شُعَيْفَاتٌ *There is not upon his head* aught *save some small hairs of the* [*pendent lock of hair termed*] ذُؤَابَة. (Ṣ, O, Ḳ.)

مَشْعُوفٌ [*Burned* in the heart by love: (see 1:) or] *diseased* [therein]: (AZ, Ṣ:) or *struck,* or *smitten, in the* شَعَفَة *of his heart by love,* or *by fright,* or *by insanity,* or *madness.* (O, Ḳ.) *Insane,* or *mad.* (O, Ḳ.) *Bereft of his heart.* (TA.) [See also مَشْغُوفٌ.]

شعل

1. شَعَلَتِ النَّارُ: see 8. — [Hence,] شَعَلَتِ الخَيْلُ فِى الغَارَةِ † [*The horsemen became spread* or *dispersed,* or *spread* or *dispersed themselves, in the hostile,* or *predatory, incursion*]; quasi-pass. of أَشْعَلْتُهَا. (Ḥam p. 715.) — And شَعَلَ فِيهِ, aor. ـَ, (Ḳ,) inf. n. شَعْلٌ, (TA,) † *He went far in it;* (Ḳ;) namely, an affair. (TḲ.) ═ شَعَلَ النَّارَ: — and الحَرْبَ: see 4. ═ شَعِلَ, aor. ـَ, (Ḳ,) inf. n. شَعَلٌ, (TA,) *He* (a horse) *had the whiteness termed* شَعَل *and* شُعْلَة [expl. below]; (Ḳ;) as also ↓ اشعالّ, (Mgh, Ḳ, TA,) which occurs in poetry with the ا made movent, i. e. ↓ اِشْعَأَلَّ, inf. n. اِشْعِئْلَالٌ; (TA; [in my copy of the Mgh written اِشْعِلَال;]) or ↓ اشعلّ, (Ṣ,) or this last also, (TA,) inf. n. اِشْعِلَالٌ. (Ṣ, TA.) Among the faults in the "Khizánet el-Fiḳ-h" is ↓ الإِشْعَالُ, [expl. as meaning *The having*] *a whiteness of the* أَشْفَار [or *edges of the eyelids*]. (Mgh.)

2. شعّل النَّارَ: see what next follows.

4. اشعل النَّارَ; (AZ, Ṣ, O, Mṣb, Ḳ;) and ↓ شَعَلَهَا, (AZ, O, Mṣb, Ḳ,) aor. ـَ, inf. n. شَعْلٌ; (TA;) and [in an intensive sense] ↓ شعّلها, (Ḳ,) inf. n. تَشْعِيلٌ; (TA;) *He kindled the fire;* or *made it to burn up, burn brightly* or *fiercely, blaze,* or *flame;* syn. أَضْرَمَهَا, (Ṣ, O, TA,) or أَوْقَدَهَا, (Mṣb, by implication,) or أَلْهَبَهَا; (Ḳ, TA;) فِى الحَطَبِ [*in the firewood*]. (Ṣ, O, TA.) — [Hence,] one says also, أَشْعَلْتُ الحَرْبَ † [*I kindled war,* or *the war;* or *made it to burn fiercely,* or *to rage*]; and ↓ شَعَلْتُهَا; mentioned by Abu-l-'Alà. (Ḥam p. 715.) 'Amr Ibn-El-Iṭnábeh says,

لَيْسُوا بِأَنْكَاسٍ وَلَا مِيلٍ إِذَا
مَا الحَرْبُ شُبَّتْ أَشْعَلُوا بِالشَّاعِلِ ↓

(Ṣ, O, and Ḥam ubi suprà,) † *They are not persons in whom is no good, nor such as are not firm on their horses:* [*when war is kindled,*] *they make to burn fiercely,* and *excite, that which is slightly burning:* such may be the meaning; for it may be that the ب in بالشاعل is pleonastically inserted, and الشاعل may mean as above: or بالشاعل may mean *by him who makes it to burn fiercely,* [as is implied in the Ṣ and O,] or *by that which does so.* (Ḥam.) — And أَشْعَلْتُهُ غَضَبًا (O, TA, and Ḥam p. 194) ‡ *I excited him,* or *inflamed him, with anger.* (TA.) — And اشعل إِبِلَهُ بِالقَطِرَانِ † *He smeared his camels much with tar;* (Ṣ, O, Ḳ, TA;) [which has a burning effect;] *smearing them generally, and not merely the scattered scabs exclusively of the other parts of the body.* (TA.) — And اشعل الخَيْلَ فِى الغَارَةِ ‡ *He spread,* or *dispersed, the horsemen in the hostile,* or *predatory, incursion:* (O, Ḳ, TA:) and [in like manner] one says اشعلوا الغَارَةَ † [*They spread,* or *dispersed, themselves,* or *their horsemen, in the hostile,* or *predatory, incursion*]. (Ṣ and Ḳ in art. شعو.) And أَشْعَلْتُ جَمْعَهُمْ † *I dispersed* or *scattered, their congregation.* (O, TA.) And اشعل الإِبِلَ † *He dispersed the camels.* (Lḥ, Ḳ, (TA.) — And اشعل السَّقْىَ † *He made* [*the watering* or] *the water* [*of the irrigation*] *abundant.* (IAạr, Ḳ, TA.) ═ أَشْعَلَتِ الغَارَةُ † *The horsemen making a hostile,* or *predatory, incursion became dispersed,* or *dispersed themselves.* (Ṣ, Ḳ.) — اشعلت الطَّعْنَةُ † *The spear-wound,* or *the like, emitted its blood in a scattered state.* (Ibn-'Abbád, O, Ḳ.) And اشعلت القِرْبَةُ, and المَزَادَةُ, † *The water-skin,* and *the leathern water-bag, shed its water in a scattered state.* (Ṣ, Ḳ.) And اشعلت العَيْنُ † *The eye shed its tears copiously.* (O, Ḳ.) — See also 1, last sentence.

5: see what next follows.

8. اشتعلت النَّارُ; (Lḥ, Ṣ, O, Mṣb, Ḳ, TA;) and ↓ شَعَلَت, aor. ـَ; (Mṣb;) and [in an intensive sense] ↓ تشعّلت; (Ḳ, TA;) *The fire became kindled;* or *it burned up, burned brightly* or *fiercely, blazed,* or *flamed;* syn. تَأَجَّجَتْ, (Lḥ, TA,) or اِضْطَرَمَتْ, (Ṣ, O, TA,) or تَوَقَّدَتْ, (Mṣb,) and اِلْتَهَبَتْ; (Ḳ,* TA;) فِى الحَطَبِ [*in the firewood*]. (Lḥ, TA.) — Hence, اِشْتَعَلَ غَضَبًا ‡ *He became excited,* or *inflamed, with anger:* (TA:) or *he became filled with wrath.* (Mṣb.) — Hence also, اشتعل الشَّيْبُ فِى الرَّأْسِ ‡ *Whiteness of the hair became glistening in the head;* including the hair of the beard. (TA.) And اشتعل الرَّأْسُ شَيْبًا [in the Ḳur xix. 3, expl. in art. شيب]. (Ṣ, Mṣb.)

9: see 1.

11: see 1. — اشعالّ رَأْسُهُ, (O, Ḳ,) inf. n. اِشْعِيلَالٌ, (TA,) *His hair became separated,* or *loosened, and ruffled,* or *bristling up.* (O, Ḳ.)

Q. Q. 4. اِشْعَأَلَّ: see 1.

شَعْلٌ † A man *light, agile,* or *active,* and *clever, ingenious, acute,* or *sharp:* (O, Ḳ:) and so مِشْعَلٌ. (O, TA.)

شَعَلٌ [inf. n. of شَعِلَ (q. v.)] and ↓ شُعْلَةٌ [properly a subst. as distinguished from an inf. n.] † *A whiteness in the tail of a horse, and the forelock, and the* قَذَال [*or place where the* عِذَار, i. e. *each of the two cheek-straps of the headstall, is tied, behind the forelock*]: (Ḳ:) or *in some part of the forelock;* or, as some say, *in a side thereof:* and sometimes *in the* قذال: but mostly *in the tail*: (TA:) or the former signifies *a whiteness in the extremity of the tail of a horse*: or, accord. to Lth, *a whiteness in the forelock and the tail*: or, as some say, *in the head and the forelock*: [or the *quality of having such whiteness*: for it is added that] the subst. [app. signifying *such whiteness itself*] is ▼ شُعْلَةٌ: (Mgh:) or the former, *a whiteness in the side of the tail*: [or,] accord. to Aṣ, ▼ شُعْلَةٌ is a term applied to *a whiteness of the tail when it intermixes with any other colour*; and the horse is said to be بَيِّنُ الشَّعَلِ [i. e. *one that exhibits the quality of having such whiteness*]. (Ṣ.)

شُعْلَةٌ *A firebrand; a piece of wood in which fire is kindled*; (Az, Ḳ,* TA;) like جِذْوَةٌ and شِهَابٌ and قَبَسٌ: (Az, TA:) [this is what is meant by its being said that] what is termed شُعْلَةٌ مِنْ نَارٍ [the only indication of the meaning in the Ṣ and O] is well known: (Mṣb:) pl. شُعَلٌ; (Ṣ, O, TA;) erroneously said in the Ḳ to be like كُتُبٌ. (TA.) [Hence,] one says, فُلَانٌ شُعْلَةُ نَارٍ †[*Such a one is a firebrand*]. (Er-Rághib, TA voce ذُعْفَةٌ, q. v.) — And [*A lighted wick*: so in the present day: (see also شَعِيلَةٌ:) or] the *burnt* [or *lighted*] *extremity of a wick*. (Ṣ voce قُرَاطٌ. [And the same meaning is intended there in the Ḳ; and also in the TA voce جِذْوَةٌ.]) — And The *flame of fire*; as also ▼ شُعْلُولٌ. (Ḳ,* TA. [In the CḲ شُعُولٌ; as though it were a second pl. of شُعْلَةٌ.]) — And شُعْلَةُ, (O, Ḳ, TA,) without ال, (Ḳ, TA,) is the name of *A mare of Keys Ibn-Sebáa*; (O, Ḳ, TA;) likened to the kindling of fire, because of her swiftness. (TA.) — See also شَعَلٌ, in three places.

شُعْلُولٌ: see the next preceding paragraph. — Also *A party, division, sect*, or *distinct body* or *class*, of men &c. (TA.) [See شَعَالِيلُ, below.]

شَعِيلٌ The *like of stars, at the bottom of a cooking-pot*; and *in tinder*, or *burnt rag into which fire has fallen*. (Ibn-'Abbád, O, TA.) — See the next paragraph. — And see also أَشْعَلُ.

شَعِيلَةٌ [*A lighted wick*; i. e.] *a wick in which is fire*; (Ṣ, O, Ḳ;) *a wick soaked with oil* or *grease, in which is fire*, used for giving light, and not thus called unless *kindled with fire*: (TA: [see also شُعْلَةٌ:]) or the *fire that is kindled in a wick*: (Ḳ:) pl. شُعُلٌ, like as صُحُفٌ is pl. of صَحِيفَةٌ; (T, Ṣ, O, TA;) in the Ḳ erroneously said to be ▼ شَعِيلٌ [which, however, may be correct as a coll. gen. n.]. (TA.)

شَعَالِيلُ [a pl., of which the sing. is app. شُعْلُولٌ, q. v.; *Things*, and *persons, scattered*, or *dispersed*]. Aboo-Wejzeh says,

• حَتَّى إِذَا مَا دَنَتْ مِنْهُ سَوَابِقُهَا •
• وَلِلْغَامِ بِعِطْفَيْهِ شَعَالِيلُ •

[*Until*, or *until when, those of them that outstripped approached him, and there were scattered portions of foam upon his two sides*]. (TA.) And one says, ذَهَبُوا شَعَالِيلَ, (Ṣ, O, Ḳ,) like شَعَارِيرَ, i. e., (Ṣ, O,) [*They went away*] *in a state of dispersion*; (Ḳ;) [or] *they dispersed themselves*, or *became dispersed*. (Ṣ, O.)

شَاعِلٌ as used in a verse cited above (see 4) [may be the part. n. of the intrans. verb in the phrase شَعَلَتِ النَّارُ, and thus] may mean [*Burning* &c.; or] *slightly burning*: (Ḥam p. 715:) [or] it signifies ذُو إِشْعَالٍ [*having the quality of kindling*, &c.; being said to be a possessive epithet], (Ṣ, O, Ḳ,) like تَامِرٌ and لَابِنٌ, having no verb: (Ṣ, O: [but see 4, first sentence:]) or it may be for ذُو شُعْلٍ, meaning مُشْعِلٌ. (Ḥam ubi suprà. [See, again, 4.]) — See also the next paragraph.

أَشْعَلُ A horse *having the whiteness termed* شُعْلَةٌ (Aṣ, Ṣ, Mgh, O, Ḳ) or شَعَلٌ [q. v.]; (Mgh, Ḳ;) as also ▼ شَعِيلٌ and ▼ شَاعِلٌ: (O, Ḳ:) fem. of the first شَعْلَاءُ. (Ṣ, Ḳ.) — And غُرَّةٌ شَعْلَاءُ [*A blaze on a horse's forehead* or *face*] *taking in*, i. e. *including, one of the eyes*. (Mgh, TA.)

مُشْعَلٌ *A* [*lamp of the kind called*] قِنْدِيلٌ [q. v.]. (Ḳ.) — See also مَشْعَلَةٌ.

مُشْعَلٌ [pass. part. n. of 4, q. v.]. One says نَارٌ مُشْعَلَةٌ [*A fire kindled*, &c.; or] *burning up, burning brightly* or *fiercely, blazing*, or *flaming*. (Lḥ, TA.) And جَآءَ فُلَانٌ كَالْحَرِيقِ المُشْعَلِ i. e. [*Such a one came like the fire that is*] *kindled*, &c. (Ṣ, O.) See also the next paragraph.

جَرَادٌ مُشْعِلٌ ‡ *Locusts that are numerous*, (Ḳ, TA,) *spreading*, (Ṣ, O,) *in a state of dispersion*, (Ḳ,) *running in every direction*. (Ṣ, O.) One says, (Ṣ, O, TA,) of an army, (TA,) جَآؤُوا كَالْجَرَادِ المُشْعِلِ (Ṣ, O, TA) ‡ *They came* [*like locusts numerous and spreading*, &c.,] *coming forth from every direction*: thus the last word is written accord. to Az [and J] and Ṣgh; and thus, and also ▼ المُشْعَلِ, accord. to Z. (TA.) And كَتِيبَةٌ مُشْعِلَةٌ † [*A military force*] *spreading*, or *in a state of dispersion*. (Ṣ,O.)

مِشْعَلٌ *A certain thing*, (Ṣ, O, Ḳ,) *used by the Arabs of the desert*, (Ṣ, O,) *made of skins* (Ṣ, O, Ḳ) *sewed together*, like the نِطَع [q. v.], (Ṣ, O,) *having four legs* (Ṣ, O, Ḳ) *of wood, to which it is bound, so that it becomes like the watering-trough*; (Ṣ, O;) [*the beverage called*] نَبِيذ *is prepared in it*, (Ṣ, O, Ḳ,) *because* [*generally*] *they have not jars*: (Ṣ, O:) also called ▼ مِشْعَالٌ: (O, Ḳ:) pl. مَشَاعِلُ. (Ṣ, O.) شَرِبَ مِشْعَلًا occurs in a trad. [as meaning *He drank the quantity that filled a* مشعل *of* نَبِيذ]. (O.) — Also i. q. مِصْفَاةٌ [*A clarifier*, or *strainer*, for wine &c.]: (O, Ḳ:) pl. as above. (TA.)

مَشْعَلَةٌ *A particular sort of large support for a light*: (KL:) [i. e. *a sort of cresset, consisting of a staff with a cylindrical frame of iron at the top which is filled with flaming pine-wood or the like or tarred rags*, or, as is sometimes the case, *having two, three, four*, or *five, of these receptacles for fire*: it is borne before travellers and others at night; and is thus called in the present day, and also, more commonly, ▼ مَشْعَل: (two cressets of the sort thus called are figured in my "Modern Egyptians," ch. vi.: see also مَشَاعِلِيٌّ, below:)] *the place in which fire is kindled*: (TA: [a loose explanation, meaning a cresset:]) what is thus called is the *thing of which the pl. is* مَشَاعِلُ: (Ṣ, O:) [accord. to El-Wáḥidee, it is ▼ مِشْعَلَةٌ; for he says that] المشعلة with kesr to the م means *the instrument in which fire is carried*: and مَشْعلة [thus, with a fet-ḥah over the م,] means *fire kindled*; or *made to burn up, burn brightly* or *fiercely, blaze*, or *flame*; syn. نار موقدة. (W p. 51.)

مِشْعَلَةٌ: see the next preceding paragraph.

مِشْعَلٌ: see مِشْعَالٌ.

مَشَاعِلِيٌّ, a rel. n. formed from مَشَاعِلُ pl. of مَشْعَلَةٌ, is a n. un. of which the coll. gen. n. is مَشَاعِلِيَّةٌ, and signifies *A bearer of the cresset called* مَشْعَلَة: hence applied also to *a nightman*: and hence, to *a cleanser of wells*: *a scavenger*; or *remover of offal and the like*: and to *an executioner*. (See De Sacy's Chrest. Arabe, sec. ed., i. 201—203; and Quatremère's "Hist. des Sultans Mamlouks," sec. part, 4 and 5.)]

شعو

4. اشعى القَوْمُ الغَارَةَ, (Ṣ, Ḳ,) inf. n. إِشْعَآءٌ, (Ṣ,) *The people*, or *party, spread*, or *dispersed, themselves*, or *their horsemen, in the hostile*, or *predatory, incursion*; syn. أَشْعَلُوهَا. (Ṣ, Ḳ.) — And اشعى بِهِ, (Ḳ,) inf. n. as above, (TA,) *He was*, or *became, grieved*, or *disquieted, by it*; syn. اِهْتَمَّ. (Ibn-Ḥabeeb, Ṣgh, Ḳ.)

غَارَةٌ شَعْوَآءُ *A raid*, or *hostile* or *predatory incursion, spreading widely and dispersedly*. (Ṣ, Ḳ.*) [See an ex. in the last of the verses cited voce رَبٌّ.] — And شَجَرَةٌ شَعْوَآءُ *A tree having spreading branches*. (ISd, Ḳ.)

جَآءَتِ الخَيْلُ شَوَاعِيَ, (Ṣ, Ḳ,) and شَوَائِعَ, from which شواعى is [said to be] formed by transposition, (Ṣ,) *The horsemen came scattered*, or *dispersed*, or *in a state of dispersion*. (Ṣ, Ḳ.)

شغب

1. شَغَبَ عَلَيْهِمْ, (Ṣ, A, Mṣb, Ḳ,) and بِهِمْ, (Ṣ, Mṣb, Ḳ,) and فِيهِمْ, (TA,) and شَغَبَهُمْ, (Ṣ, Mṣb, Ḳ,) aor. ـَ, (A, Mṣb, Ḳ,) inf. n. شَغْبٌ, (Ṣ,* A,* Ḳ,* TA,) with which شَغَبٌ is syn., (A, Ḳ,) a syn. sometimes used, (A,) or this latter is not allowable, (Ṣ, Ḳ,) as some say, (Ḳ,) and is ascribed by IAth to the vulgar, and said by El-Ḥareeree in the "Durrat el-Ghowwáṣ" to be a mistake, but IB says in the commentaries on the "Durrah" that it is correct, mentioned by IDrd, and MF says that it is mentioned by IJ, as well as by Z in the A; (TA;) and one says also شَغِبَ عليهم, [and it seems to be implied that one says likewise شَغَبَ

شَغِبَ, and شَغْبُهُمْ, aor. as above, (Ṣ, Ḳ,) inf. n. شَغَبٌ; (Ṣ, TA;) but this latter form of the verb, with kesr, is of weak authority; (Ṣ,* TA;) [whence it seems that شَغَبٌ is correct as inf. n. of شَغِبَ, but disallowed by some who knew not this form of the verb;] *He excited*, or *stirred up*, (Ṣ, A, Mṣb, Ḳ, TA,) [*against them*, or] *among them*, (Mṣb,) *evil*, or *mischief*, (Ṣ, A, Mṣb, Ḳ, TA,) and *conflict, faction, sedition*, or *discord*, and *contention*, or *altercation*, and *opposition*: (TA:) and [it is said that] تَشْغِيبٌ is like شَغْبٌ signifying the *exciting*, or *stirring up, evil*, &c.; (Ḳ, TA;) [but] ↓ شغّب, inf. n. تَشْغِيبٌ, signifies *he excited*, or *stirred up, evil*, &c., *much*, or *often*. (O.) A trad. mentioned in [the first paragraph of] art. شعب is quoted by IAth thus: مَا هٰذِهِ الفُتْيَا الَّتِى شَغَبَتْ فِى النَّاسِ [*What is this judicial decision which has excited evil, &c., among the people?*]. (TA.) — [See also شَغْبٌ below.] — The saying of 'Amr Ibn-Ḳameeah,

فَإِنْ تَشْغَبِى فَالشَّغْبُ مِنِّى سَجِيَّةٌ

means ‡ *And if thou oppose*, or *contravene*, me, *and do that which is not agreeable* to me, [know that *opposition*, &c., *is a natural disposition of mine*; عَلَىَّ being understood after تشغبى, as appears from what here follows.] (TA. [See also 3, and 6.]) Accord. to El-Báhilee, ذَاتُ شَغْبٍ [applied to a she-ass] means ‡ *Having the quality of opposing* or *contravening* [the male]: so in the saying of El-'Ajjáj,

كَأَنَّ تَحْتِى ذَاتَ شَغْبٍ سَمْحَجَا

قَوْدَآءَ لَا تَحْمِلُ إِلَّا مُخْدَجَا

‡ [*As though beneath me were* a she-ass] *such as opposes* or *contravenes* [the male], *long-bodied, long-necked*, [*that would not bear in her womb* aught *save a fœtus imperfectly formed*;] meaning, لَا تُوَاتِيهِ وَتَشْغَبُ عَلَيْهِ [i. e. that *she* (the beast that he was riding) *would not comply with his desire*, and *was contravening him*]. (TA.) [Accord. to J,] ذَاتُ شَغْبٍ وَضِغْنٍ, [in the TA وصغب, and so in a copy of the A, an evident mistranscription,] applied to a she-ass that has not conceived during a year or two years or some years, means ‡ *Refractory*, or *incompliant, to the strong*, or *bulky, male*. (Ṣ: there expl. by the words إِذَا وَحِمَتْ وَٱسْتَصْعَبَتْ عَلَى الجَأْبِ [which have been misunderstood by Golius, and rendered by him, and by Freytag after him, as applied to a woman, and meaning *respuens maris congressum, aut picâ laborans*].) — And شَغَبَ signifies also † *He declined*, or *deviated, from the right way* or *course*: (Sh, TA:) or شَغَبَ عَنِ الطَّرِيقِ, aor. ـَ, (Ḳ,) inf. n. شَغْبٌ, (TA,) † *He declined*, or *deviated, from the road* or *way*. (Ḳ.)

2: see 1, end of the first sentence.

3. شاغبهُ, (Ṣ, A, Ḳ, TA,) inf. n. مُشَاغَبَةٌ and شِغَابٌ, (TA,) *He acted with him in an evil manner; treated him with enmity*, or *hostility; contended in altercation with him*; or *did evil to him, obliging him to do the like in return*: (A, Ḳ, TA:) *he opposed*, or *contravened, him*. (TA.)

6. طَلَبْتُ مِنْهُ كَذَا فَتَشَاغَبَ وَٱمْتَنَعَ ‡ *I sought*, or *demanded, of him such a thing, and he manifested incompliance* (تَعَاصَى), *and refused*. (A, TA.)

شَغْبٌ inf. n. of شَغَبَ [q. v. passim]. (Ṣ,* A,* Ḳ,* TA.) — Also *Clamour*, or *a confusion of cries* or *shouts* or *noises*: (Ḥam p. 505:) or *much clamour and confused* or *indistinct speech, leading*, or *conducing, to evil*, or *mischief*. (Ḥar p. 311.) One says شَغْبُ الجُنْدِ [*The clamour*, &c., *of the army*]. (Ṣ, and Ḥam ubi suprà.) — [Hence, app., this word, or the next, is used by some post-classical writers as signifying The *plaintive cry* of the بُلْبُل. (See De Sacy's Chrest. Ar., sec. ed., iii. 500—502.)]

شَغَبٌ inf. n. of شَغِبَ [q. v.]. (Ṣ, TA.)

شَغِبٌ, (Ṣ, O, Ḳ, TA, [in the CḲ, erroneously, شِغْبٌ,]) like كَتِفٌ, (O,) and ↓ شَغَّابٌ, (Ṣ, O, Ḳ,) the latter in an intensive sense, (TA,) and ↓ شِغَبٌّ, (O, Ḳ,) [also in an intensive sense,] and ↓ مِشْغَبٌ, (Ṣ, O, Ḳ,) [likewise] in an intensive sense, (O,) and ↓ مُشَغِّبٌ, [also in an intensive sense accord. to the explanation of its verb in the O,] (Ṣ,) and ↓ مُشَاغِبٌ, and ↓ ذُو مَشَاغِبَ, (Ḳ,) *One who excites*, or *stirs up, evil*, or *mischief*, (Ṣ,* Ḳ, TA,) and *conflict, faction, sedition*, or *discord*, and *contention*, or *altercation*, and *opposition*. (TA.)

شِغَبٌّ: see the next preceding paragraph.

شَغَّابٌ: see شَغِبٌ. — نَاقَةٌ شَغَّابَةٌ ‡ *A she-camel that does not pursue a direct course, but deviates* [*therefrom*]. (A, TA.)

مِشْغَبٌ: see شَغِبٌ. — فُلَانٌ مِشْغَبٌ † *Such a one is a person who deviates from what is right*, or *from the truth*. (O, TA.)

مُشَغِّبٌ: }
ذُو مَشَاغِبَ: } see شَغِبٌ.
مُشَاغِبٌ: }

شغر

1. The inf. n. شَغْرٌ, accord. to Ibn-Nubáteh, primarily signifies The *raising the leg* or *hind leg*, without restriction; and then by a metaphorical usage, the *doing so for the purpose of copulation*, and *for making water*: but the explanations of J [and of Z in the A] and of Fei and of F are at variance with his assertion. (MF.) [Accord. to these authorities,] شَغَرَ, (Ṣ, A, Mṣb, Ḳ,) aor. ـَ, (Ṣ, Mṣb, Ḳ,) inf. n. as above, (Mṣb, TA,) signifies *He* (a dog) *raised one of his hind legs* (Ṣ, A, Mṣb, Ḳ) *to make water*, (Ṣ, Mṣb,) or *and made water*, or *whether he made water or did not*: (A, Ḳ:) and شَغَرَ بِرِجْلِهِ *he* (a dog) *raised his hind leg, and made water*. (TA.) And شَغَرَتْ *She* (a camel) *raised her hind leg, and struck* [*with it*, or *kicked*,] *the young one*. (A.) And, said of a woman, (Mṣb, Ḳ,) *She raised her leg*, (Mṣb, and so in some copies of the Ḳ,) or *her legs*, (so in other copies of the Ḳ,) *for the purpose of copulation*. (Mṣb, Ḳ.) And the verb is also trans.: you say, شَغَرَ المَرْأَةَ, (Mṣb, Ḳ,) inf. n. شُغُورٌ, (Ḳ, [but this is a strange form in the case of a trans. verb,]) *He raised the woman's leg*, (Mṣb, and so in some copies of the Ḳ,) or *legs*, (IDrd, O, and so in some copies of the Ḳ,) *for the purpose of copulation*; and so ↓ اشغرها. (IDrd, O, Mṣb, Ḳ.) And شَغْرٌ as the act of a stallion [camel] signifies His *striking with his head beneath the she-camel, at the part next the udder, and so raising her, and throwing her down* [app. *for the purpose of copulation*]. (Ḳ.) — شَغَرْتُ بِرِجْلِى فِى الغَرِيبِ means † *I overcame the people in guarding*, or *protecting, the stranger*. (AA, O, Ḳ.) — And شُغُورٌ signifies also † The *being distant*, or *remote*. (Fr, Ḳ.) One says, شَغَرَ البَلَدُ, (Ṣ, Mṣb, Ḳ,) aor. ـُ, inf. n. شُغُورٌ, (Mṣb, [accord. to the Ḳ, app., شَغْرٌ,]) † *The country*, or *town, was*, or *became, remote from him who should aid it against the enemy, and him who should exercise sovereign sway*, (Ḳ, TA,) *and from him who should manage its affairs with prudence, precaution*, or *sound judgment*: (TA:) or *destitute of a guardian*, or *protector, to defend it*: (Mṣb:) or *destitute of people*: [and so, app., شَغَرَ البَلَدُ بِرِجْلِهِ; for it is immediately added,] one says بَلْدَةٌ شَاغِرَةٌ بِرِجْلِهَا meaning as expl. below: (Ṣ:) and شَغَرَتِ الأَرْضُ *the land had not remaining in it any one to defend it, and to manage its affairs with prudence, precaution*, or *sound judgment*. (Ḳ.) — Also, i. e. شَغْرٌ, The *making* [another, or others,] *to go forth* [from a place]. (Ḳ.) One says, شَغَرْتُهُ عَنِ الأَرْضِ *I made him to go forth from the land*: (AA, TA:) and شَغَرْتُ بَنِى فُلَانٍ مِنْ مَوْضِعِ كَذَا *I made the sons of such a one to go forth from such a place*: (Ṣ:) or شَغَرُوا فُلَانًا عَنْ بَلَدِهِ *They drove away, expelled*, or *banished, such a one from his country*, or *town*; and the inf. n. is شَغْرٌ and شِغَارٌ. (TA.) — And *i. q.* تَفْرِقَةٌ [The act of *scattering*, or *dispersing*]. (Ḳ.)

3. شاغرهُ, (Mgh, Mṣb, Ḳ,) inf. n. شِغَارٌ, (Ṣ, A, Mgh, Mṣb, Ḳ,) *He gave him in marriage a woman on the condition of his giving him in marriage another, without dowry* [*from either*]; *concubitus with each of the said women being* [*in lieu of*] *the dowry for the other*: or *it applies peculiarly to female relations* [*of the men so contracting*]; (Ḳ;) so that the meaning is only *he gave him in marriage his female relation on the condition of his doing the like to him*: (TA:) or *he gave him in marriage a female under his guardianship, the other man doing to him the like, on the condition that concubitus with each one of the said females should be* [*in lieu of*] *the dowry for the other*: (Mgh,* Mṣb:) or *he gave him in marriage his sister on the condition of receiving in marriage the other's sister, without any dowry beside this*: (A:) or *he said to him, Give me in marriage thy daughter*, or *thy sister, on the condition of my giving thee in marriage my daughter*, or *my sister, concubitus with each one of the said females being* [*in lieu of*] *the dowry of the other*. (Ṣ.) The practice of شِغَار was common in the Time of Ignorance, (Mṣb,) but is forbidden to the Muslims. (Ṣ, A.) — شِغَارٌ also signifies *Two men's going forth into the field from two armies, and, when one of them has almost overcome his fellow, two men's coming to aid one of them, whereupon the other cries out,* لَا شِغَارَ لَا شِغَارَ: (TA:) or *two men's acting wrongfully,* or *injuriously, towards another man:* (Ḳ, TA:) thus expl. by ISd. (TA.) And The *acting with enmity,* or *hostility.* (TA.)

4. اشغر المَرْأَةَ: see 1. — اشغرت الرُّفْقَةُ [and app. ▼ اشتغرت also (see the last sentence of this art.)] † *The party journeying together withdrew by themselves from the beaten road.* (Ḳ, TA.) — See also 8, first sentence. — اشغرت said of a she-camel, *She went with wide steps, and quickly.* (TA.) — See, again, 8.

5. تشغّر *He* (a camel) *exerted his utmost power,* (Ḳ,) or *spared no exertion,* (A'Obeyd, Ṣ,) *in his pace:* (A'Obeyd, Ṣ, Ḳ:) or *ran vehemently:* (Ḳ:) or *went a pace above that termed* اَلنَّبْطَةُ. (TA.) — تشغّر فِى أَمْرٍ قَبِيحٍ *He* (a man, O) *persevered in an evil,* or *a foul, affair, and went deep into it.* (O, Ḳ.*)

8. اشتغر, (JK, T,) or ▼ اشغر, (Ṣ, Ḳ,) *It* (a watering-place) *was on one side of the beaten track:* (JK, T, Ṣ, Ḳ:) [both verbs may be correct: that the former is so appears from the fact that] a poet, cited in the T, [describing a watering-place,] uses the phrase ▼ بَعِيدُ المُشْتَغِرِ [app. meaning *far off on one side of the road*]. (TA.) See also 4. — اشتغر العَدَدُ *The number was,* or *became, large.* (Ṣ, Ḳ.) — اشتغر الإِبِلُ *The camels were,* or *became, many and various.* (Ḳ.) — اشتغرت عَلَيْهِ ضَيْعَتُهُ *i. q.* فَشَتْ, (A,) i. e. *His affairs became disordered so that he knew not with which of them to begin.* (TA in art. فشو.) — اشتغر الأَمْرُ *The affair became confused:* (Ḳ:) or *became large,* or *wide, and great,* بِفُلَانٍ [*with such a one*]. (AZ, TA.) — اشتغرت الحَرْبُ *The war,* or *battle, became wide and great.* (TA.) — اشتغر عَلَيْهِ حِسَابُهُ, (T, Ṣ, A,) in the Ḳ ▼ أَشْغَرَ, but the former is the right, (TA,) ‡ *What he had to reckon was,* or *became, too diffuse and numerous to him;* (T, Ḳ;) *such that he could not find the way to sum it up.* (Ṣ, A.) — ذَهَبَ فُلَانٌ يَعُدُّ بَنِى فُلَانٍ فَاشْتَغَرُوا عَلَيْهِ *Such a one went to number the sons of such a one, and they were too numerous for him.* (TA.) — اشتغر فِى الفَلَاةِ *He went far into the desert.* (Ṣ, Ḳ.) — اشتغر عَلَيْنَا *He exalted himself above us, and boasted against us.* (Ḳ.)

تَفَرَّقُوا شَغَرَ بَغَرَ and شِغَرَ بِغَرَ *They dispersed themselves,* or *became dispersed, in every direction:* (Ṣ, Ḳ:) and in like manner one says of sheep or goats, تَفَرَّقَتِ الغَنَمُ شَغَرَ بَغَرَ: (TA:) شغر بغر is a compound of two nouns made into one, and indecl., with fet-ḥ for the termination. (Ṣ.) The like is not said in the case of [persons &c.] coming, or advancing. (TA.)

شَغْرَى *A stone at which dogs raise the hind leg and make water,* or *to make water:* (Ḳ:) so in the Tekmileh. (TA.)

شَغَّارٌ *Empty.* (Ṣgh, Mṣb, Ḳ.) — Also, used as sing. and pl., A well, and wells, *having much water:* (Ḳ:) or, as is said in the Nawádir, thus used, *having much water; wide,* or *spacious, in the adjacent part where the camels lie down.* (TA.) — Also, accord. to the Ḳ, *Two veins,* or *ducts,* (عِرْقَانِ,) *in the side of the camel:* but correctly, as in the Tekmileh, the شَغَّارَانِ are the حَالِبَانِ, i. e. *two veins or ducts,* (عِرْقَانِ,) *in the two sides of the camel.* (TA.)

شَغُورٌ A *tall* she-camel, *that raises her legs* (تَشْغَرُ بِقَوَائِمِهَا) *when she is taken to be ridden* (Ḳ, TA) or *to be milked.* (TA.)

شَغَّارَةٌ A she-camel *that raises her legs to strike* [*with them,* or *kick*]. (TA.)

شَاغِرٌ A dog *raising one of his hind legs, and making water,* or *whether making water or not.* (A.) — بَلْدَةٌ شَاغِرَةٌ بِرِجْلِهَا ‡ *A country,* or *town, that does not defend itself from a hostile attack* (Ṣ, A, Ḳ) *made by any one,* (Ṣ, Ḳ,) *by reason of its being destitute* (Ḳ, TA) *of any to protect it.* (TA.) And أَرْضٌ شَاغِرَةٌ † *A land having no one remaining in it, to defend it, and to manage its affairs with prudence, precaution,* or *sound judgment.* (Ḳ.) One says also, الأَرْضُ لَكُمْ شَاغِرَةٌ, meaning † *The land,* or *the earth, is wide,* or *ample, for you.* (TA.)

مُشْتَغَرٌ: see 8 [of which it is app. an inf. n.].

رُفْقَةٌ مُشْتَغِرَةٌ *A party journeying together far from the beaten road.* (TA.)

شغرب

Q. 1. شَغْرَبَهُ *i. q.* شَغْزَبَهُ, q. v. (AZ, TA.)

شَغْرَبِىٌّ (TA) and شَغْرَبِيَّةٌ (Ḳ) *i. q.* شَغْزَبِىٌّ and شَغْزَبِيَّةٌ. (Ḳ, TA.)

شغزب

Q. 1. شَغْزَبَهُ, inf. n. شَغْزَبَةٌ, *He threw him down by the trick called* شَغْزَبِيَّة, expl. below; (Ṣ, Ḳ;) and شَغْرَبَهُ signifies the same. (AZ, TA.) Accord. to IAth, the primary meaning of شَغْزَبَةٌ is *A twisting,* in a neuter sense; and *artifice.* (TA.) — Also *He took him,* or *seized him, violently.* (Ḳ.)

Q. 2. تَشَغْزَبَتِ الرِّيحُ *The wind whirled* (اِلْتَوَتْ) *in its blowing.* (Ḳ.)

شَغْزَبِىٌّ: see شَغْزَبِيَّةٌ.

شَغْزَبِىٌّ *Difficult;* (Ḳ;) anything *deemed difficult.* (IAth, TA.) — A [watering-place such as is termed] مَنْهَلٌ *lying out of the way.* (Ḳ, TA.) — الشُّغْزُبِىُّ *The jackal;* syn. اِبْنُ آوَى. (IAth, TA.)

شَغْزَبِيَّةٌ (Ṣ, Ḳ) and ▼ شَغْزَبِىٌّ, as also شَغْرَبِيَّةٌ (Ḳ) and شَغْرَبِىٌّ, but more chastely with ز, (TA,) *A sort of trick in throwing down* [or *wrestling*]; (Ṣ, TA;) the *twisting of one's leg with the leg of another,* (Ṣ, Ḳ, TA,) *and throwing him down* (Ḳ, TA) *in the manner termed* شَزْرًا [or *sideways*]: (TA:) and one says also, أَخَذَهُ بِالشُّغْزُبِيَّةِ, (Ṣ, TA, [in one of my copies of the Ṣ بِالشَّغْزَبَةِ,]) meaning the same: (TA:) and صَرَعَهُ صَرْعَةً شَغْزَبِيَّةً: (AZ, TA:) [the pl. is شَغَازِبُ:] Dhu-r-Rummeh says,

وَلَبَّسَ بَيْنَ أَقْوَامٍ فَكُلٌّ ⁂ أَعَدَّ لَهُ الشَّغَازِبَ وَالمِحَالَا

[*And he involved affairs in confusion between parties, so all prepared for him tricks by which to overthrow him, and artifice*]. (Ṣ, TA.)

حَتَّى يَكُونَ شُغْزُبًا occurs in the "Sunan" of Aboo-Dáwood, in the chapter on the عَقِيقَة and عَتِيرَة; but it is thought by El-Ḥarbee that the last word is for زُخْزُبًا, meaning *Firm in flesh, and thick, big,* or *bulky.* (L, TA.)

شغف

1. شَغَفَهُ, (Ṣ, O, Mṣb, Ḳ,) aor. ـَ, (Mṣb, Ḳ,) inf. n. شَغْفٌ, (Mṣb,) *He,* or *it, struck,* or *smote, his* شَغَاف; (O, Ḳ;) like كَبَدَهُ meaning "he, or it, struck, or smote, his كَبِد" [or "liver"]; (O, TA;) so says Yoo: (TA:) or *it* (i. e. love) *rent the* شَغَاف *of his heart:* (Fr, TA:) or *it* (love) *reached his* شَغَاف: (ISk, Ṣ, TA:) or شَغَفَ قَلْبَهُ *it* (love) *reached the* شَغَاف *of his heart,* i. e. *his pericardium.* (Mṣb.) I'Ab read, [in the Ḳur xii. 30,] قَدْ شَغَفَهَا حُبًّا, and expl. the meaning to be [*He has affected her so that*] *the love of him has entered beneath the* شَغَاف: (Ṣ, TA:) or the meaning is, *the love of him has struck,* or *smitten, her* شَغَاف: (Lth, O, TA:) or *he has rent the* شَغَاف *of her heart,* i. e. *its* حِجَاب, [app. meaning *her midriff,*] *so as to reach her heart, with love:* (Bḍ:) Abu-l-Ash-hab read قَدْ شَعَفَهَا حُبًّا, with kesr to the ع, [meaning *he has become attached to her,* or *has loved her,*] like the reading of Thábit El-Bunyánee, شَعِفَهَا, with kesr to the unpointed ع: (O, TA:) [for] شَغِفَهُ, aor. ـَ, [inf. n. app. شَغَفٌ,] signifies *he became attached to him,* or *loved him.* (Ḳ, TA.) One says also, شَغَفَهُ المَالُ, meaning *The property became embellished to him,* [or *pleasing to him,*] *so that he loved it.* (Mṣb.) And شُغِفَ بِالشَّىْءِ, like عُنِىَ, *He was,* or *became, vehemently desirous of the thing;* or *fond of it.* (TA.) And شَغِفَ بِالشَّىْءِ, like فَرِحَ, *He became disquieted,* or *disturbed, by the thing.* (TA.)

5. مَا هٰذِهِ الفُتْيَا الَّتِى تَشَغَّفَتِ النَّاسَ, a saying of I'Ab, means [*What is this judicial sentence*] *that has put vain suggestions into the minds of the people, and separated them?* as though it entered the شَغَاف of their hearts. (TA.) [See also 1 in arts. شعب and شغب.]

شَغْفٌ: see شَغَاف in two places.

شَغْفٌ [app. inf. n. of شَغَفَ: and accord. to Fei, app., *Love reaching to the pericardium*; or *heart-felt love*; see an ex. in a verse cited voce بَلْ; and see also حُبٌّ, and شَغَفَ;] a subst. from شَغَفَ قَلْبَهُ, said of love. (Mṣb.) ═ See also شَغَافٌ, in two places. ═ Also The *bark* (نَجَب, AḤn, O, or قِشْر, Ḳ) *of the kind of tree called* غاف. (AḤn, O, Ḳ.*)

شَغَافٌ The *pericardium*; i. e. the غِلَاف, (Ṣ, O, Ḳ,) or غِشَآء, (Mṣb,) *of the heart*: (Ṣ, O, Mṣb, Ḳ:) or [app. a mistake for "and," as will be shown by what follows,] *its* حِجَاب [generally meaning the *midriff*], (Ḳ,) [here said to be,] accord. to AHeyth, *a certain fat that clothes the heart*: (TA:) [J seems to confound the غلاف of the heart with its حِجَاب; for after "the غلاف of the heart," he adds, "and it is a skin beneath it (دُونَهُ), like the حِجَاب:"] or the حَبَّة (Ḳ) or the سُوَيْدَآء [both generally meaning the *core*] *thereof*: (O, Ḳ:) or the *place of entrance* (مَوْلِج) *of the phlegm*: (Lth, O, Ḳ:) and ▼ شَغْفٌ and ▼ شَغَفٌ signify the same in the two senses, (Ḳ,) or in the first and second senses: (TA:) or ▼ شَغْفُ القَلْبِ and ▼ شَغَفُهُ signify the same as شَغَافُهُ, accord. to AHeyth: (O:) the pl. of the شغاف of the heart is شُغُفٌ; which is metaphorically applied in a saying of 'Alee to the *place of the fœtus* [*in the belly*]. (TA.) ═ Also, (A'Obeyd, Ṣ, O, Ḳ,) and ▼ شُغَافٌ, (Ḳ,) the latter agreeable with analogy as the name of a disease, (TA,) *A certain disease that attaches one, beneath the* شَرَاسِيف [pl. of شُرْسُوف, q. v.], *in the right side*: (A'Obeyd, Ṣ, O, Ḳ:) and (some say, TA) *a pain of the belly*: (Ḳ, TA: [in the CḲ, البَطْر is erroneously put for البَطْن:]) and (some say, TA) *a pain of the* شغاف *of the heart*: (Ḳ, TA:) accord. to Aṣ, شَغَافٌ signifies *a certain disease in the heart, which, if it reaches to the spleen, kills the patient*. (TA.)

شُغَافٌ: see the next preceding paragraph.

مَشْغُوفٌ *Insane, or mad*; (O, Ḳ;) like مَشْعُوفٌ. (O.) And مَشْغُوفٌ بِمَالٍ One *to whom property is embellished* [or *rendered pleasing*,] *so that he loves it*. (Mṣb.)

شغل

1. شَغَلَهُ, (Ṣ, O, Mṣb, Ḳ,) aor. ـَ, (O, Ḳ, MṢ,) inf. n. شُغْلٌ (Mṣb, Ḳ) and شَغْلٌ, (Ḳ,) the latter on the authority of Sb, (TA,) *He, or it*, (a man, Ṣ, or an affair, Mṣb,) *busied him, occupied him*, or *employed him*; (Ḳ;) i. q. أَلْهَاهُ [signifying as above; and particularly *he, or it, busied him, &c., so as to divert him* from (عَنْ) something; or *diverted him* from a thing *by busying him, &c.*]: (Ṣ and Mṣb and Ḳ in art. لهو, and Bḍ and Jel in xv. 3, &c.:) [▼ شغّلهُ signifies *he, or it, busied him, &c., much*; i. e.] with teshdeed it denotes muchness: (Bḍ in xlviii. 11:) ▼ اشغلهُ is a good dial. var. of شَغَلَهُ; or is rare; or bad: (Ḳ:) accord. to IDrd [and J], (O,) one should not say أَشْغَلْتُهُ; (Ṣ, O;) for it is bad: (Ṣ:) accord. to IF, they scarcely ever say أَشْغَلْتُ, [thus in the O, but in the Mṣb ▼ اِشْتَغَلَ,] but it is allowable: (O:) none of the leading lexicologists is known to have pronounced it good. (TA.) [Hence the saying, شَغَلَتْ سَعَاتِى جَدْوَاىَ (see art. سعو and سعى), or, as some relate it, شغلت شِعَابِى جدواى (see art. شعب).] See another ex. voce شَاغِلٌ. One says also شُغِلَ بِهِ, (Mṣb, Ḳ,) meaning تَلَهَّى [i. e. *He was, or became, busied*, &c., *by it*], (Mṣb,) and ▼ اشتغل بِهِ [meaning the same]; (Az, Mṣb, Ḳ;) and شُغِلْتُ عَنْكَ بِكَذَا [*I was*, or *became, busied*, &c., *so as to be diverted from thee, by such a thing*], (Ṣ, O,) and ▼ اشْتَغَلْتُ [in the same sense]: (Ṣ:) and ▼ تشاغل عَنْهُ, (TA,) which likewise signifies تَلَهَّى [meaning as expl. above, or *he busied himself, &c., so as to divert himself from him, or it*]: (TA in art. لهو, and Bḍ and Jel in lxxx. 10:) some disallow ▼ اِشْتَغَلَ, in the form of an active verb, but say أُشْتُغِلَ, in the form of a pass. verb; but it is originally quasi-pass. of أَشْغَلْتُهُ, like as are اِحْتَرَقَ and اِكْتَحَلَ of أَحْرَقْتُهُ and أَكْحَلْتُهُ; [though why of أَشْغَلْتُهُ rather than of شَغَلْتُهُ, I do not see:] Az mentions the usage of its act. and pass. part. ns.: (Mṣb:) accord. to AḤát and IDrd, one should not say ▼ اِشْتَغَلَ; but IF mentions, as transmitted from the Arabs, أُشْتُغِلَ فُلَانٌ بِالشَّىْءِ, and the pass. part. n. (O.) — One says also, نَحْنُ نَشْغَلُ عَنْكَ المَرْتَعَ † [*We occupy the place of pasturage so as to keep it from thee*], and المَآءَ [*the water*]; meaning, it is sufficient for us without being more than sufficient. (Ṣ in art. شفه.) And شُغِلَ عَنْكَ مَا عِنْدَنَا † [*What we had was employed so as to be kept from thee*]. (JK in that art.)

2: see the preceding paragraph.

4. اشغلهُ: see 1. — مَا أَشْغَلَهُ [meaning *How much is he busied! &c.*], (Th, Ṣ, Ḳ,) denoting wonder, (Th, TA,) is anomalous, because one does not [regularly] form a verb of wonder from one in the form of a pass. verb. (Th, Ṣ, Ḳ.)

6. تشاغل عَنْهُ: see 1. [Accord. to Golius, تشاغلوا signifies *They occupied one another*, on the authority of the KL; in which, however, I find only تَشَاغُلٌ expl. as meaning خودرا بچيزى مشغول كردن i. e. *To make oneself busied, &c., with a thing.*]

8: see 1, in five places. — One says also, اِشْتَغَلَ فِيهِ السُّمُّ *The poison crept into him*, or *pervaded him*; syn. سَرَى: and اشتغل فِيهِ الدَّوَآءُ *The medicine entered into him, and produced an effect upon him*, or *showed its effect upon him*; syn. نَجَعَ. (TA.)

شَغْلٌ an inf. n. of 1. (Ḳ, Mṣb.) See the next paragraph. ═ And see also شَغْلَةٌ.

شُغْلٌ and ▼ شَغْلٌ and ▼ شُغُلٌ (Ṣ, O, Mṣb, Ḳ) and ▼ شَغَلٌ (Ṣ, O, Ḳ) *Business, occupation*, or *employment*; (PṢ;) *contr. of* فَرَاغٌ: (Ḳ:) [and particularly *business*, &c., *that diverts one* from a thing:] or *an occurrence that causes a man to forget, or neglect, or be unmindful*: (Er-Rághib, TA:) pl. [of pauc.] أَشْغَالٌ (Ṣ, O, Ḳ) and [of mult.] شُغُولٌ: (Ḳ:) شُغْلٌ is mentioned by Sb as an instance of an inf. n. having a pl., namely, أَشْغَالٌ; like عَقْلٌ and مَرَضٌ. (TA in art. مرض.) [See also أُشْغُولَةٌ.]

شُغُلٌ: see the next preceding paragraph.

شَغِلٌ *Busy*, or *busied, occupied*, or *employed*: (Ḳ:) [and particularly *busy*, &c., *so as to be diverted* from a thing:] thought by ISd to be a possessive epithet [meaning ذُو شُغْلٍ], because it has no verb to which it is conformable: (TA:) it is an epithet applied to a man, from الشُّغْلُ [or الشُّغُلُ]: (IAạr, in O:) and ▼ مَشْغُولٌ signifies the same; (Mṣb, TA;) and ▼ مُشْتَغِلٌ (Az, Mṣb, Ḳ) and ▼ مُشْتَغَلٌ, (Az, IF, O, Mṣb, Ḳ,) the latter [said to be] extr. [meaning anomalous, for أُشْتُغِلَ is not mentioned by F]. (Ḳ.)

شُغُلٌ: see شُغْلٌ.

شَغْلَةٌ *Reaped grain or wheat, collected together, in the place where it is trodden out*; syn. بَيْدَرٌ and كُدْسٌ (IAạr, O, Ḳ) and عَرَمَةٌ; (IAạr, O;) as also ▼ شَغَلَةٌ: (IAth, TA:) pl. [or coll. gen. n.] of the former ▼ شَغْلٌ, (O, Ḳ, TA, [in the CḲ, erroneously, شُغُلٌ,]) like as تَمْرٌ is of تَمْرَةٌ. (O, TA.)

شَغَلَةٌ: see the next preceding paragraph.

شَغَّالٌ signifies كَثِيرُ الشُّغْلِ [i. e. *Having much business* or *occupation* or *employment*; or *who busies* or *occupies* or *employs himself much*]. (TA.)

شَاغِلٌ act. part. n. of شَغَلَهُ; [*Busying, occupying, or employing*; &c.;] (Ṣ, Mṣb;) applied to a man, (Ṣ,) or to an affair. (Mṣb.) [Hence,] one says, شَغَلَتْنِى ▼ عَنْكَ الشَّوَاغِلُ [*Busying affairs busied me, or have busied me, so as to divert me from thee*]: the last word being pl. of شَاغِلٌ. (TA.) شُغْلٌ شَاغِلٌ [lit. *Busying business*, or *the like*,] has an intensive meaning: (Ḳ:) the latter word in this case is a corroborative, as in لَيْلٌ لَائِلٌ. (Ṣ.)

أَشْغَلُ مِنْ ذَاتِ النِّحْيَيْنِ [*More, and most, busy* &c.]. [*More busy than she who was the owner of the two skins of butter*] is a prov. [mentioned in the TA]: she was a woman of [the tribe of] Teym-Allah: she used to sell clarified butter, in the Time of Ignorance; and Khowwát Ibn-Jubeyr El-Anṣáree came to her, demanding to buy clarified butter of her, and saw no one with her, and he bargained with her: so she untied a skin, and he looked at it: then he said to her, "Hold thou it until I look at another:" and she said, "Untie thou another skin:" and he did so, and looked at it, and said, "I desire other than this; therefore hold thou it:" and she did so: and when her hands were [thus] occupied, he assaulted her, and she was unable to repel the him. (Meyd.)

أُشْغُولَةٌ an instance of the measure أُفْعُولَةٌ from الشُّغْل [similar to الْعُوبَةٌ and الْبِهَّةٌ and أُلْهُوَّةٌ, and to &c.; app. meaning *A thing with which one is busied*, &c.: and also *syn. with* شُغْل.] (O, Ḳ.)

مَشْغَلَةٌ *A thing that causes one to be busied*, &c.: (Ḳ,* TA:) pl. مَشَاغِلُ. (TA.)

مَشْغُولٌ: see شَغِلٌ.—[Hence,] فُلَانٌ فَارِغٌ مَشْغُولٌ *Such a one is devoted to that which is unprofitable.* (TA.)—And جَارِيَةٌ مَشْغُولَةٌ *A young woman having a husband.* (TA.)—And مَالٌ مَشْغُولٌ *Property devoted to commerce.* (TA.)—And دَارٌ مَشْغُولَةٌ *A house in which are inhabitants.* (TA.)

مُشْتَغَلٌ and مُشْتَغِلٌ: see شَغِلٌ.

شغى and شغو

1. شَغِىَ, aor. ـَ, inf. n. شَغًا, [signifies accord. to some] *He* (a man) *had a tooth*, or *teeth*, *exceeding the other teeth:* and [accord. to others, agreeably with what is said to be the right meaning of شَاغِيَةٌ below,] *he had a tooth*, or *teeth*, *differing in the manner of growth from the other teeth.* (Ṣ.) [And] شَغِيَتِ السِّنُّ, aor. ـَ; (Mṣb, Ḳ;) and شَغَتْ, aor. ـُ; (Ḳ;) inf. n. (of the former, Mṣb, TA) شَغًا (Mṣb, Ḳ, TA) and [of the latter] شُغُوٌّ, (Ḳ, TA, [in the CḲ شُغُو, but]) like عُلُوٌّ; (TA;) [accord. to some] *The tooth exceeded the other teeth:* (Mṣb:) and [accord. to others] (Mṣb) *the tooth differed from the other teeth* (Mṣb, Ḳ, TA) in an absolute sense, (TA,) or *in respect of its place of growth*, (Mṣb,) or *in its manner of growth, in length*, and *shortness*, and *receding*, and *projecting:* (Ḳ, TA:) or, accord. to the A, شَغًا signifies the *differing in respect of the manner of growth and of collocation:* or the *upper teeth's not falling upon the lower:* (TA:) or, as IF says, the *advancing of the upper teeth beyond the lower.* (Mṣb.) The epithet applied to a man is ↓ أَشْغَى; and to a woman, شَغْوَآءُ; and the pl. is شُغْوٌ: (Ṣ, Mṣb:) [and] the epithet applied to a tooth is شَغْوَآءُ and شَغْيَآءُ; (Ḳ;) or ↓ شَاغِيَةٌ; (Ṣ, Mṣb;) which last is said by Az to have two meanings; one whereof is *exceeding* [*the other teeth*]; and the other, *being longer and larger, and differing in respect of the place* [or more probably the *manner*] *of its growth from those next to it:* (Mṣb:) or, accord. to a marginal note in the Ṣ, in the handwriting of Aboo-Zekereeyà, this signifies *differing in the manner of its growth from the manner of growth of the others, whether exceeding or not exceeding:* or, accord. to a marginal note in the copy of Aboo-Sahl El-Harawee, *crooked;* not exceeding. (TA.)

2. تَشْغِيَةٌ signifies The *dribbling of the urine*, (Lth, Ḳ, TA,) *little by little.* (Lth, TA.) One says of a man, شَغَّى, (TḲ,) and ↓ اشغى بِبَوْلِهِ, (IAth, TA,) *He dribbled his urine*, (IAth, TA, TḲ,) *little by little.* (IAth, TA.)

4. أَشْغَوْا بِهِ † *They disagreed with, differed from*, or *opposed, the people, in respect of his affair*, or *case:* (Ḳ:) as though taken from شَغَا الأَسْنَانِ. (TA.)—See also 2.

شَغًا inf. n. of شَغِىَ said of a man, (Ṣ,) or of شَغِيَتْ said of a tooth. (Mṣb, Ḳ.)—Also a subst. signifying *A dribbling of the urine;* and so ↓ شُغْيَةٌ. (Ḳ.)

أُمُّ شَغْوَةَ: see شَغْوَآءُ, voce أَشْغَى.

شُغْيَةٌ: see شَغًا.

شَاغِيَةٌ: see 1, last sentence.

أَشْغَى; fem. شَغْوَآءُ and شَغْيَآءُ; and pl. شُغْوٌ: see 1, last sentence.—شَغْوَآءُ also signifies *An eagle;* (Ṣ, Mṣb, Ḳ;) because its upper mandible exceeds the lower: (Ṣ, Mṣb:) and so ↓ أُمُّ شَغْوَةَ. (T in art. ام.)

مُشْتَغٍ One *who separates himself from every yoke-fellow*, or *familiar:*—and *one whose age* (سِنُّهُ) *is deficient:*—in both of these senses expl. as an epithet applied by Ru-beh to a رُبَاعِىّ [or boy four spans in height]. (TA.)

شف

1. شَفَّ, aor. ـِ, inf. n. شُفُوفٌ (S, Mgh, O, Mṣb, Ḳ) and شَفِيفٌ (Ṣ, O, Ḳ) and شَفَفٌ, (CḲ, [but not in my MS. copy of the Ḳ nor in the TA,]) *It* (a garment, or piece of cloth,) *was thin, fine*, or *delicate*, (Ṣ, Mgh, O, Mṣb, Ḳ,) *so that what was behind it was visible*, (Ṣ,* IB, Mgh, [for خَلْفَهُ in some copies of the Ṣ, and خَلْقَهُ in others, I read مَا خَلْفَهُ, which is the right reading accord. to IB and the TA, agreeably with the reading in the Mgh, which is مَا وَرَآءَهُ,]) or *so as to tell what was beneath it:* (O, Ḳ:) [and *it*, (a gem, or the like,) *was translucent:* or *was transparent.* (See شَفَّاف.)] One says, شَفَّ عَلَيْهِ ثَوْبُهُ *His garment was thin*, &c., *upon him.* (Ṣ.)—And شَفَّ جِسْمُهُ, aor. ـِ, inf. n. شُفُوفٌ, *His body became lean*, or *emaciated.* (Ṣ, O, Ḳ.) ═ شَفَّ, aor. ـِ, inf. n. شَفٌّ, *It* (a thing, O, Mṣb) *exceeded;* or *was*, or *became, redundant.* (Ṣ, O, Mṣb, Ḳ.) Hence, in a trad., شَفَّ نَحْوًا مِنْ دَانِقٍ *It exceeded by about a* دانق. (Sh, O.) And one says, شَفَّ عَلَيْهِ, aor. يَشُفُّ, [so in the L and TA, contr. to rule, probably a mistranscription for يَشِفُّ,] inf. n. شُفُوفٌ; and ↓ شفّف, and ↓ استشفّ; [app. meaning, as seems to be indicated by the context, *It exceeded it:*] and شَفِفْتُ فِى السِّلْعَةِ [app. a mistranscription for شَفَفْتُ] *I gained in*, or *upon, the article of merchandise:* (TA: [and so, app., ↓ استشفّ فِى تِجَارَتِهِ and ↓ شَفَّفْتُ: see شِفٌّ:]) [*He obtained what is termed* شِفّ *in his traffic;* i. e.] *he made gain, or profit, in his traffic;* syn. رَبِحَ. (Ṣ and Ḳ in art. ربح.)—And sometimes (Mṣb) it signifies also the contr.; i. e. *It fell short;* or *was*, or *became, deficient.* (Mṣb, Ḳ.) One says, (O, Mṣb,) of a dirhem, (O,) هٰذَا يَشِفُّ قَلِيلًا *This falls short, or is deficient, a little.* (O, Mṣb.) And شَفَّ عَنْهُ الثَّوْبُ, aor. ـِ, *The garment was too short for him.* (TA.) ═ Also شَفَّ, (O, Ḳ,) aor. ـِ, (O,) *It* (a thing, O) *was*, or *became, in a state of motion, commotion*, or *agitation.* (O, Ḳ.) ═ And شَفَّ لَكَ الشَّىْءُ i. q. دَامَ and ثَبَتَ [app. meaning *The thing belonged*, or *pertained, to thee permanently*, or *constantly;* or *may the thing belong*, &c.]. (TA.) ═ شَفَّهُ, (Ṣ, M, O, Ḳ,) aor. ـُ, inf. n. شَفٌّ (Ṣ, M, TA) and شُفُوفٌ, (M, TA,) *It* (anxiety) *rendered him lean*, or *emaciated;* (Ṣ, O, Ḳ;) as also ↓ شَفْشَفَهُ; (Ṣ;) both are also expl. as meaning *it rendered him lean*, or *lank in the belly, so that he became slender:* (TA:) or, accord. to the M, *it* (grief, and love,) *pained his heart:* or *rendered him lean*, or *emaciated:* or *deprived him of his reason:* and it is said of grief as meaning *it manifested what he felt of impatience.* (TA.) And شَفَّ النُّفُوسَ, as used in a verse of Towbeh Ibn-El-Ḥomeiyir, *It hurt and melted the souls.* (Ḥam p. 594.) ═ See also 8, in two places.

2: see the preceding paragraph, in two places.

4. أَشْفَفْتُهُمْ *I preferred them*, or *judged them to excel.* (Ḳ.) You say, أَشْفَفْتُ بَعْضَ وَلَدِى عَلَى بَعْضٍ *I preferred some of my children above some.* (Ṣ. [And the like is said in the Mgh.]) And أَشْفَفْتُ هٰذَا عَلَى هٰذَا *I preferred this above this.* (Mṣb.)—And اشفّ فُلَانٌ الدِّرْهَمَ *Such a one made the dirhem to exceed:* or, *made it to fall short.* (TA.) ═ أَشَفَّ عَلَيْهِ [if not a mistranscription for أَشَفَّ, which I rather think it to be,] *He excelled him*, or *surpassed him.* (TA.) ═ أَشَفَّ الفَمُ *The mouth had in it a fetid odour.* (Ibn-Buzurj, TA.)

6. تَشَافَفْتُهُ *I took away his* or *its*, شِفّ, i. e. *excess*, or *redundance.* (O, Ḳ.)—See also the next paragraph, in three places.

8. اشتفّ مَا فِى الإِنَآءِ (Ṣ, O, Ḳ) كُلَّهُ (Ḳ) *He drank what was in the vessel, all of it*, (Ṣ, O, Ḳ,) *even the* شُفَافَة [or *last drop* or *remains*], (O,) *not leaving any of it remaining;* (Ṣ;) [and so ↓ اِجْتَفَّ;] as also ↓ تشافّ: (Ṣ, O, Ḳ:) and ↓ استشفّ المَآءَ *He drank the water to the uttermost, not leaving any of it remaining;* as also ↓ شَفَّهُ, aor. ـُ, inf. n. شَفٌّ: and ↓ شَفَفْتُ المَآءَ *I drank much of the water without having my thirst satisfied.* (TA.) [Hence,] in the trad. of Umm-Zarạ, وَإِنْ شَرِبَ اشْتَفَّ [*And if he drank, he drank up all that was in the vessel*]. (Ṣ, O.) And it is said in a prov., ↓ لَيْسَ الرِّىُّ عَنِ التَّشَافِّ (Ṣ, O, TA) i. e. *The satisfying of thirst is not from the drinking up all that is in the vessel;* for it is sometimes effected by less than this: (O, TA:) it is applied in forbidding one's going to the utmost in an affair, and persevering therein. (Ṣ,* O, TA.) Accord. to IAạr, one says also تَشَافَيْتُ المَآءَ *I exhausted the water;* which, ISd says, is originally ↓ تَشَافَفْتُ. (TA.)—'Abd-Allah Ibn-Sebreh El-Ḥarashee uses the first of these verbs metaphorically in relation to death; saying,

سَاقَيْتُهُ المَوْتَ حَتَّى ٱشْتَفَّ آخِرَهُ

meaning ‡ [*I vied with him in giving the draught of death*] *until he drank the last of it*, i. e., the last of death. (TA.) — And اشتفّ البَعِيرُ الحِزَامَ كُلَّهُ means *The camel filled, and took up wholly, the girth*, (O, Ḳ, TA,) *so that nothing remained of it redundant*, by reason of the largeness of the middle of his body. (TA.)

10. اِسْتَشَفَّهُ, (O, Ḳ,) or اِسْتَشَفَّ مَا وَرَآءَهُ, (Ṣ, Mṣb,) *He saw what was behind it.* (O, Mṣb, Ḳ.) [Thus the former signifies *He saw through it:* and it is used in this sense both properly and tropically.] — Hence the saying to the seller of cloths, اِسْتَشِفَّ هٰذَا الثَّوْبَ, [which may be rendered *Look thou through this garment*, or *piece of cloth*; but is expl. as] meaning *make thou this garment*, or *piece of cloth, single*, [*by unfolding it*,] *and raise it*, or *hold it up*, *in shade, in order that I may see whether it be close in texture or flimsy.* (TA.) — استشفّ also signifies [agreeably with the explanation of اِسْتَشَفَّ مَا وَرَآءَهُ mentioned above] † *He distinguished a thing plainly, like as one distinguishes plainly a thing behind glass.* (Ḥar p. 244.) — And one says, كَتَبْتُ كِتَابًا فَٱسْتَشَفَّهُ, meaning † [*I wrote a letter*, or *writing*, &c., *and*] *he examined attentively what was in it.* (TA.) — See also 8. — And see 1, in two places. — [Freytag mentions as a signification of استشفّ "*Desiderio* alicujus rei *impleri*;" with الى before the object: but he names no authority for this; and I doubt its correctness.]

R. Q. 1. شَفْشَفَهُ: see 1, latter part. — Also, accord. to IAạr, (O, TA,) inf. n. شَفْشَفَةٌ, (Ḳ, TA,) *It* (heat, and cold,) *dried it up*; namely, a thing, (O, Ḳ, TA,) such as herbage, (O, TA,) &c. (TA.) And accord. to AA, الشَّفْشَفَةُ signifies *The* hoar-frost's *burning* [meaning *blasting*] the herbage of the earth: or *the burning* of a medicament that is sprinkled upon a wound: (O:) or it has the former of these two meanings, and signifies also *the sprinkling* of a medicament upon a wound. (Ḳ. [But I think that, for وَذْرُ الدَّوَآءِ in the Ḳ, we should read وَذَرُّ الدَّوَآءِ, and thus reconcile the Ḳ in this case with the O: see, however, what next follows; which may be regarded either as confirming the reading in the Ḳ, or as having misled its author, in this instance.]) — الشَّفْشَفَةُ signifies also *The sprinkling* of urine and the like. (Ḳ.) You say, شَفْشَفَ بِبَوْلِهِ *He sprinkled his urine.* (O.) — Also *The trembling, and the being confused* (الاِخْتِلَاط), (O, Ḳ, TA,) *resulting from intense jealousy.* (TA. [See مُشَفْشَفٌ.]) — And شَفْشَفَ عَلَيْهِ *He was solicitously affectionate*, or *pitiful* or *compassionate, towards him.* (TA.) [See, again, مُشَفْشَفٌ.])

R. Q. 2. تَشَفْشَفَ, said of herbage, *It began to dry up.* (TA.)

شَفٌّ *A thin, fine*, or *delicate*, garment or piece of cloth; (AZ, Ṣ, Mgh, O,* Mṣb, Ḳ;*) as also ▼ شِفٌّ (AZ, Ṣ, O, Mṣb, Ḳ) and ▼ شَفِيفٌ: (Mṣb:) you say ثَوْبٌ شَفٌّ (Ṣ, Mgh, Mṣb) and ▼ شِفٌّ (Ṣ, Mṣb) and ▼ شَفِيفٌ. (Mṣb:) [see also شَفَّافٌ:] and the garment, or piece of cloth, itself, is termed شَفٌّ and ▼ شِفٌّ: (Ḥar p. 70:) [i. e. each of these words is also used as a subst.; and this is perhaps meant in the O and Ḳ: or] شَفٌّ signifies also *a certain thin, fine*, or *delicate, veil* or *covering*: or, accord. to Aboo-Naṣr, *a certain thin, fine*, or *delicate, veil or covering, of wool, through which one sees what is behind it*: (Ṣ:) pl. شُفُوفٌ. (O, Mṣb, Ḳ.) Among the verses of "the Book" [of Sb, cited as exs. therein], is the following:

لَلُبْسُ عَبَآءَةٍ وَتَقَرَّ عَيْنِى
أَحَبُّ إِلَىَّ مِنْ لُبْسِ الشُّفُوفِ

[*Verily the wearing of a woollen cloak, my eye being therewithal unheated by tears, is more pleasing to me than the wearing of thin, fine*, or *delicate, garments*]. (O.) — See also شِفٌّ. — شَفٌّ [app. شُفٌّ] also signifies *Pimples*, or *small pustules, that come forth and then go away.* (Ibn-Buzurj, TA.)

شِفٌّ: see شَفٌّ, in three places. — Also, (Ṣ, Mgh, O, Ḳ,) and ▼ شَفٌّ, (L, Ḳ,) but the former is that which is well known, (L, TA,) and ▼ شَفِيفٌ, (TA,) *Gain*, or *profit*; *increase obtained in traffic*: and *excess, surplus*, or *redundance*: syn. رِبْحٌ [q. v.]: and فَضْلٌ; (Ṣ, Mgh, O, Ḳ;) and زِيَادَةٌ. (Mgh, TA.) Hence (Mgh) نَهَى عَنْ شِفِّ مَا لَمْ يُضْمَنْ, meaning [*He* (the Prophet, TA) *forbade*] *the* رِبْح [i. e. *gain*, or *profit, of that for which one has not made himself responsible* to the purchaser]. (O, Mgh.) And one says, لِهٰذَا عَلَى هٰذَا شِفٌّ [*There is*, or *pertains, to this, an excess above this*]. (Kṣh in ii. 15.) And قَالَ قَوْلًا شِفًّا *He said a saying that was a redundance.* (TA.) — And *A deficiency*: thus having two contr. meanings. (ISk and Ṣ and O in explanation of the first word, Ḳ in explanation of the first and second words, and TA in explanation of all.) — Also, the first word, *i. q.* مَهْنَأً: one says to a person when regarding him with a wish for the like of a thing that he has attained, or that he possesses, without desiring that it should pass away from him, شِفٌّ لَكَ يَا فُلَانُ [*May it be an unalloyed gratification to thee, O such a one*]. (TA.) — And *A thing that is little*, or *small, in quantity*; *mean*, or *paltry*. (TA.) [See also شَفِيفٌ, last signification.]

شَفَفٌ: see شَفِيفٌ, last signification. — Also *i. q.* خِفَّةٌ [*Lightness*, &c.]. (TA.) — And sometimes it signifies *Evilness*, or *narrowness of the circumstances*, (رِقَّة,) *of one's state*, or *condition.* (TA.)

شُفَافٌ: see شُفَافَةٌ.

شَفِيفٌ: see شَفٌّ, in two places: — and see شِفٌّ. — Also *Cold*, as a subst.; (ISk, Ṣ, O, Mṣb;) thus in the saying, وَجَدَ فِى أَسْنَانِهِ شَفِيفًا [*He felt*, or *experienced, in his teeth, cold*]; (Ṣ, O;) and so ▼ شَفَّانٌ: (ISk, Mṣb:) or, as some say, (O,) the *hurting*, or *paining*, (لَذْع, [in the CḲ لَدْغ,]) *of cold*: (Ṣ, O, Ḳ:) and *intense cold, with rain and wind*; and شِفَافٌ is its pl.: (TA:) or *intense cold* [alone]: (Mṣb:) or *a cold wind in which is moisture*: (O:) and ▼ شَفَّانٌ signifies *the cold of a wind in which is moisture*: (Ṣ:) or شَفِيفٌ has this last signification; and ▼ شَفَّانٌ, the signification next preceding it: one says, أَلْجَأَهُ شَفَّانٌ ▼ لَهُ شَفِيفٌ *A cold and moist wind, having* [much] *cold and moisture, made him to betake himself to a covert*: (IDrd, IF, Mṣb:) or شَفِيفٌ signifies *rain and hail*: (O:) or so ▼ شَفَّانٌ; [or *rain and cold*: for برد is written in my original without any syll. sign;] wherefore some of the lawyers say that it is *rain and more*: (Mṣb:) or شَفِيفٌ signifies also *rain in which is hail*: (Ḳ, TA:) or *rain in which is cold*: (CḲ:) or *a cold wind*; (Ḳ;) as also ▼ شَفْشَافٌ: (O, Ḳ:) or this last signifies *a wind of mild cold*: (Ṣ, TA:) and ▼ شَفَّانٌ, *cold and wind*: (O, Ḳ:) one says, غَدَاةٌ ذَاتُ شَفَّانٍ *a morning having cold and wind* (Ṣ,* O, Ḳ) *with moisture.* (Ṣ.) — And *Intense heat* (IDrd, Es-Saraḳusṭee, O, Mṣb, Ḳ) *of the sun*: (IDrd, O, Ḳ:) thus having two contr. significations. (Ḳ.) — And *Pain* in the stomach. (Aboo-Sa'eed, O.) — [Also *Affected with pain*: or *with hurt*, or *grief.* (Freytag, from the Deewán of the Hudhalees.)] — Also *Small*, or *little, in number, quantity*, or *amount*; and so ▼ شَفَفٌ. (O, Ḳ.) [See also شِفٌّ, last signification.]

شُفَافَةٌ *A portion of water remaining in a vessel*; (Ṣ, O, Ḳ;) and likewise, *of milk*: (TA:) or the *last drop remaining in a vessel*: (Ḥam p. 239:) IAth says that some of the later writers mention it as being with س. (TA.) Dhu-r-Rummeh uses the phrase ▼ شُفَافُ الشَّفَا, in a verse, as meaning *In the remaining portion of the day.* (O.)

شَفَّافٌ *Extremely* [or *very*] *thin* or *fine* or *delicate, so that a thing behind it is visible*: (KL:) [*translucent*:] *transparent*; applied to a gem, or the like; and to a garment, or piece of cloth. (TA.) [See also شَفٌّ.]

شَفَّانٌ: see شَفِيفٌ, in six places.

شَفْشَافٌ A garment, or piece of cloth, *not well* or *strongly* or *compactly* [*woven* or] *made.* (O, Ḳ.) — See also شَفِيفٌ.

شُفَاشِفٌ *Vehement thirst.* (O, Ḳ.)

أَشَفُّ [a noun denoting excess]. It is said in a trad. of Ráfi', فَكَانَ الخَلْخَالُ أَشَفَّ مِنْهَا قَلِيلًا, meaning [*And the anklet*, or *pair of anklets, was*] *more than they* [*in value* or *weight*]; (syn. أَفْضَلُ and أَزْيَدُ;) i. e. more [in value or weight] than the dirhems. (Mgh.) And one says, فُلَانٌ أَشَفُّ مِنْ فُلَانٍ, meaning *Such a one is a little greater*, or *older*, (أَكْبَرُ قَلِيلًا,) *than such a one.* (TA.)

مُشَفْشَفٌ is said by Ibn-Buzurj to be like مُجَفْجَفٌ

[part. n. of جَفَّهُ; i. e. *Collected*; or *collected together and taken away*]. (TA.)

مُشَفْشَفٌ (O, Ḳ) and ▼ مُشَفْشِفٌ, (Ḳ,) the latter on the authority of IAạr, (TA,) *Slender, shallow,* or *weak, in intellect, and evil in disposition.* (O, Ḳ.) And [both words agreeably with different explanations of the verb] One *in whom is,* (Ḳ,) or, accord. to Saad, one *who is as though there were in him,* (O,) *a trembling, and confusion,* (O, Ḳ,) *resulting from jealousy,* (Ḳ,) or *from vehement jealousy,* (O,) *and solicitous affection,* or *pity* or *compassion, for his* حُرَم [or *wives,* or *women under covert, and household,* (in the CḲ his حَرَم,)] as though jealousy wasted his heart, and made him lank and lean: or *evil in disposition, and very jealous*: and ▼ the latter word, *solicitously affectionate*; or *pitying,* or *compassionating.* (TA.)

مُشَفْشِفٌ: see the next preceding paragraph, in two places.

شفر

1. The primary signification of [the inf. n.] شفر [i. e. شَفْرٌ, of which the verb is app. شَفَرَ,] is The act of *cutting,* or *cutting off*; syn. قَطْعٌ. (Ḥam p. 57.) ═ شَفَرَهَا, (Ḳ,) inf. n. شَفْرٌ, (TA,) *He struck her* (a woman's) شُفْر (Ḳ, TA) *in compressing her.* (TA.) — And شَفَرَ [or app. شَفَّرَ] إِنْسَانًا] *He annoyed, molested, harmed,* or *hurt, a man.* (IAạr, O, TA.) ═ شَفِرَتْ, aor. ـَ, inf. n. شَفَارَةٌ, *She* (a woman) *was one whose gratification of her venereal lust* (شَهْوَتُهَا) *soon took place*: (Ḳ:) or *she emitted*; [or, app., *emitted soon*;] syn. أَنْزَلَتْ. (TA.) ═ And شَفِرَ, aor. ـَ, *It decreased, diminished,* or *became defective* or *deficient.* (IAạr, Ḳ.)

2. شفّرها, (Ḳ,) inf. n. تَشْفِيرٌ, (Ibn-'Abbád, O, Ḳ,) *He compressed her* (i. e. a woman, Ibn-'Abbád, O) *on the* شُفْر *of her* فَرْج. (Ibn-'Abbád, O, Ḳ.) — And شَفَّرْتُ الشَّىْءَ, inf. n. as above, *I eradicated,* or *extirpated, the thing.* (TA.) ═ شفّر المَالُ, (O, Ḳ,) inf. n. as above, (Ḳ,) *The property became little*: (O, Ḳ:) and *went away*: (Ḳ:) from IAạr. (TA.) — And شفّر said of a man, *He gave little.* (Ḥam p. 242.) — And شفّرت الشَّمْسُ لِلْغُرُوبِ (O, Ḳ) (O) † *The sun became near to setting*; (O, Ḳ;) being likened to a man whose property has become little, and gone away. (TA.) — And in like manner, (TA,) شفّر عَلَى أَمْرٍ (Ibn-'Abbád, O, Ḳ) and لِأَمْرٍ, (Ibn-'Abbád, O,) said of a man, † *He was,* or *became, on the brink,* or *verge, of the affair,* or *event,* or *case.* (Ibn-'Abbád, O, Ḳ.)

4. اشفر is said in the Tekmileh to signify *He* (a camel) *strove,* or *exerted himself, in running*: but perhaps it should be اشغر, mentioned before [in art. شغر]. (TA.)

شَفْرٌ: see the next paragraph, in four places.

شُفْرٌ The *place of growth of the eyelash,* (Sh, T, Ṣ, A, Mṣb, Ḳ,) *which is the edge of the eyelid*; (Ṣ, Mṣb;) as also ▼ شَفْرٌ (Kr, A, Ḳ) and ▼ شَفِيرٌ: (Ḳ:) or, accord. to some, this last signifies the *upper side of the inner angle of the eye*: (TA:) and with the vulgar, the first signifies the *eyelash*; but this is [said to be] a mistake: (IḲt, Mṣb:) it occurs, however, in this sense, in a trad. of Esh-Shaạbee; (IAth, TA;) and in like manner the pl. occurs in another trad.; but the word شَعَر should be considered as understood before it; or what grows is thus called by the name of the places of growth, and the like of this is not rare: (Mgh:) it is of the masc. gender: (Lḥ, Ḳ:) and the pl. is أَشْفَارٌ, (Sb, Ṣ, Mgh, Mṣb,) the only pl. form. (Sb, TA.) [Hence,] one says, مَا بِالدَّارِ شُفْرٌ, (Ks, Fr, T, Ṣ, Mṣb, Ḳ,) and ▼ شَفْرٌ, (Lḥ, Mṣb, Ḳ,) but Sh disallows this latter, (TA,) and ▼ شُفْرَةٌ, (Fr, Ṣgh, Ḳ,) ‡ *There is not in the house any one*: (Ṣ, Mṣb, Ḳ, &c.:) and مَا رَأَيْتُ ▼ مِنْهُمْ شُفْرًا ‡ *I saw not of them any one*: from the شفر of the eye: meaning one having a شفر: (A:) and شفر is also used in this sense without a negation. (TA.) One says likewise, مَا تَرَكَتِ السَّنَةُ ظُفْرًا وَلَا شُفْرًا ‡ *The year of drought left not anything*: and sometimes they said ▼ شَفْرًا, with fet-ḥ, and in this case they said ظَفْرًا, for assimilation. (A.) — Also, (Ṣ, A, Mgh, Mṣb, Ḳ,) and ▼ شَفِيرٌ, (Ṣ, A, Mṣb, Ḳ,) The *edge, border, margin, brink, brow,* (Ṣ, Mgh, Mṣb,) or *side,* (A, Ḳ,) of anything; (Ṣ, A, Mgh, Mṣb, Ḳ;) as of a valley and the like, (Ṣ,) or as of a river &c.: (Mgh and Mṣb, in relation to the latter word:) one says, قَعَدُوا عَلَى شَفِيرِ النَّهْرِ, and البِئْرِ, and القَبْرِ, *They sat upon the side of the river,* and *of the well,* and *of the grave*: (A:) and both words signify the *side of the upper part* of a valley. (Ḳ.) — And الشُّفْرُ, (Ḳ,) or شُفْرُ الفَرْجِ, (Mṣb,) and شُفْرُ المَرْأَةِ, (TA,) *The edge,* (Mṣb, Ḳ,) or *border,* (TA,) *of the vulva,* or *external portion of the organs of generation,* [meaning, *of each of the labia majora,*] *of a woman*: (Mṣb, Ḳ, TA:) pl. أَشْفَارٌ: (Mṣb:) the إِسْكَتَانِ are the two sides [or labia majora] of the vulva of a woman; and the شُفْرَانِ are the *two borders of the said* اسكتان: (AḤeyth, Mgh, TA:) Lth says that the ▼ شَافِرَانِ are [*two parts*] *of the pudendum muliebre*: (TA:) and شُفْرُ الرَّحِمِ and ▼ شَافِرُهَا signify [in like manner] *the edges of the vulva*: (Ṣ:) and شُفْرَا المَرْأَةِ and ▼ شَافِرَاهَا, *the two edges of the* رَحِم [or *vulva* (for الرَّحِم is here used tropically, for الفَرْج, as it is in many other instances,)] *of a woman.* (TA.)

شِفْرٌ: see شَفْرَةٌ, first sentence.

شَفَرٌ: see سَفَنٌ, first sentence.

شَفِرٌ [an epithet of which the fem. only is mentioned]. شَفِرَةٌ and ▼ شَفِيرَةٌ signify A woman *who experiences the gratification of her venereal lust* (شَهْوَتَهَا) *in her* شُفْر; *so that she emits* (تُنْزِل) *speedily*: or [in the CḲ "and"] *who is content with the least of coïtus*: (Ḳ, TA:) contr. of قَعِيرَة and قَعِرَة. (TA.)

شَفْرَةٌ *A large knife*; (Ṣ, A, Ḳ;) as also ▼ شِفْرَةٌ, though this is mentioned only by the author of the Mgh; (MF; [but it is not in my copy of the Mgh; and Golius mentions ▼ شُفْرَةٌ as having this signification, on the authority of Meyd;]) or *a broad knife*: (Mgh, Mṣb:) pl. شِفَارٌ (Mṣb, Ḳ) and شَفَرَاتٌ (Mṣb) and [coll. gen. n., of which شَفْرَةٌ is the n. un., or it may be a quasi-pl. n. of شَفْرَةٌ,] ▼ شِفْرٌ. (TA.) — And hence, (Mgh, TA,) ‡ *A servant*; (Ṣ, Mgh, TA;) because of his utility. (TA.) It is said in a prov., أَصْغَرُ القَوْمِ شَفْرَتُهُمْ ‡ *The least of the party is their servant.* (Ṣ, Mgh.) — Also *A shoemaker's knife.* (Ṣ, Ḳ.) — And *A piece of iron made broad, and edged,* or *pointed.* (Ḳ.) — *A broad blade*: so says the author of the Mgh. (TA. [But not in my copy of the Mgh.]) — The *edge,* or *cutting part,* (حَدّ,) of a sword: (Ṣ, Mgh, Ḳ:) or the *edge of the cutting part* of a sword. (TA. [See ذُبَابٌ.]) The *side* of a blade: (Ḳ:) or *each of the two sides* thereof. (AḤn, TA.) [*Each of the two sharp sides* or *edges* of a spear-head and of an arrow-head.] — See also شُفْرٌ, second sentence.

شُفْرَةٌ: } see the next preceding paragraph.
شِفْرَةٌ: }

[شَفُورٌ i. q. زُنْبُورٌ The *hornet,* or *hornets.* (Golius, on the authority of Meyd.)]

شَفِيرٌ: see شُفْرٌ, in three places. — Also The *edge of the lip of a camel.* (Ḳ.) ═ شَفِيرَةٌ: see شَفِرَةٌ, voce شَفِرٌ.

يَرْبُوعٌ شُفَارِىٌّ *A jerboa having hair upon its ears*: (Ṣ:) or *having large ears*: or *having long ears, and bare toes,* [in the CḲ, for العَارِى البَرَاثِنِ, which is evidently the right reading, we find العالى البراثن,] *not quickly overtaken*: (Ḳ:) it is [*of*] *a species of jerboa called* ضَأْنُ اليَرَابِيعِ, *the fattest and the best, with ears somewhat long*: (TA:) or *having long legs, and soft and fat flesh*: (Ḳ:) it is said that *it has a nail in the middle of its shank.* (TA. [See تَدْمُرِىٌّ.]) — ضَبٌّ شُفَارِىٌّ *A long and bulky* [*lizard of the kind called*] ضَبّ. (Ḥam p. 242.) — أُذُنٌ شُفَارِيَّةٌ (as also شُرَافِيَّةٌ [q. v.], TA) *A large ear*: (Ḳ:) or *a bulky ear*: (A'Obeyd, TA:) or *a long ear*: (AZ, TA:) or *a broad ear, soft in the upper part*: (TA:) or *an ear having much hair and fur.* (Ḥam p. 242.)

شَفَّارٌ The *possessor of a* شَفْرَة [or *large knife*]. (A,* TA.)

شَافِرٌ, and its dual: see شُفْرٌ, last sentence, in three places. ═ Also One *who destroys,* or *makes away with, his property*: so in the Tekmileh. (TA.)

مَشْفَرٌ: see what next follows.

مِشْفَرٌ The *lip* of a camel; (Ṣ, Mgh, Mṣb, Ḳ;) as also ▼ مَشْفَرٌ: (Ḳ:) and ‡ of a horse: (Ṣ, TA:) and ‡ of a human being: (Ḳ, TA:) or ‡ of an Abyssinian, as being likened to that of a camel: (A'Obeyd, TA:) pl. مَشَافِرُ. (Ṣ, Ḳ.) It is said in a prov., أَرَاكَ بَشَرٌ مَا أَحَارَ مِشْفَرٌ [lit. *External skin hath shown thee what a lip hath transmitted to the stomach;*] meaning, *the external appearance hath rendered thee in no need of inquiring respecting the internal state:* (Ṣ, Ḳ:) originally said of a camel; (TA;) for when you see his external skin, whether he be fat or lean, you take it as an indication of the quality of his food. (Ḳ, TA.) — Also The *vulva*, or *external portion of the organs of generation*, of a woman: (R, MF:) but this is strange. (TA.) — And ‡ *A piece of land:* and *of sand:* (Ḳ, TA:) each by way of comparison [to the lip of a camel]. (TA.) ═ Also *A state of resistance; inaccessibleness*, or *unapproachableness:* (Ḳ:) *strength*, or *power;* (Ḳ,* TA;) *vehemence*, or *hardness*, or *firmness*. (Ḳ, TA.) — And *A state of perdition* or *destruction:* and thus it is expl. as used in the saying mentioned by Meyd [in his Proverbs, perhaps the origin of this explanation], تَرَكْتُهُ عَلَى مِثْلِ مِشْفَرِ الأَسَدِ [which may be rendered *I left him at the like of the lip of the lion*]; (TA;) applied to him who is exposed to destruction. (Meyd, TA.*)

عَيْشٌ مُشَفَّرٌ *Strait, scanty, subsistence.* (O, Ḳ.)

شفرج

شُفَارِجٌ *A tray* (طَبَقٌ) *on which are small saucers*, or *cups*, فَيْشَجَات and سُكُرُّجَات: (O, Ḳ:) a Pers. word, (Ṣ, O,) arabicized; (Ṣ, O, Ḳ;) from پِيشْبَارِجْ or پِيشْپَارِجْ (Ḳ, TA) or پِيشَارِجْ; (as in some copies of the Ḳ;) or what people call پِيشْبَارِجْ: (Yaḳoob, Ṣ:) [i. e. پِيشْ پَارَهْ or پِيشْ پَارْ, "pésh pár," and "pésh párah," meaning "sweetmeats presented to a guest:"] accord. to El-Jawáleeḳee, it signifies *different kinds of flesh-meat in* طبايع: [but what this means I know not: I suppose it to be a corruption of some word signifying saucers or the like:] in the "Kitáb el-Moheet," شَفَارِيجُ is said to be pl. of شُفَارِجٌ, signifying *a kind of food.* (TA.)

شفع

1. شَفَعَهُ, (Ṣ, Mgh, Mṣb, Ḳ,) aor. َ, (Mṣb, Ḳ,) inf. n. شَفْعٌ, (Ṣ, Mṣb,) *He made it to be a* شَفْع; (Ṣ, Ḳ, TA;) meaning (TA) *he made it* (a single thing) *to be a* زَوْج [i. e. *he made it to be one of a pair* or *couple;* and sometimes, *he made it to be a pair* or *couple together*]: (Mgh, TA:) or *he adjoined it to*, or *coupled it with, that which was a single thing:* (Mṣb:) accord. to Er-Rághib, الشَّفْعُ signifies *the adjoining* a thing *to its like.* (TA.) You say, كَانَ وِتْرًا فَشَفَعْتُهُ, (Ṣ,) or كَانَ وِتْرًا فَشَفَعْتُهُ بِآخَرَ i. e. [*It was a single thing, and*] *I made it to be one of a pair*, or *couple, with another.* (Mgh. [In Ḥar p. 194, I find the phrase كان وترا فشفّعه ↓ بآخر, expl. in like manner; but شفّعه thus used I do not find in any lexicon: it may, however, be correctly thus used; for تشفّع, which has the form, app. has also the signification, of its quasi-pass.]) [And شَفَعَ الْمِلْكُ بِمِلْكٍ آخَرَ *The possession* (here meaning *house*, or *piece of land*,) *was coupled by purchase with another possession:* and شُفِعَ بِهِ مِلْكٌ *It had a possession coupled with it by purchase:* see شُفْعَةٌ.] You say also, شَفَعْتُ الرَّكْعَةَ *I made the* رَكْعَة *to be two.* (Mṣb.) And a poet says,

* مَا كَانَ أَبْصَرَنِى بِغِرَّاتِ الصِّبَى *
* فَالْيَوْمَ قَدْ شُفِعَتْ لِىَ الأَشْبَاحُ *

[*How clear was my sight with the inadvertencies of youth! but to-day, objects have become doubled to me*]: i. e., I see the object [as] two objects, by reason of the weakness and dispersedness of my sight. (O, Ḳ.*) — [Hence,] one says of a she-camel, (Ṣ, O,) and of a ewe, or she-goat, (O,) شَفَعَتْ, (Ṣ, O,) inf. n. شَفْعٌ, (Ṣ,) meaning *She became such as is termed* شَافِع [q. v.]: (Ṣ, O:) she is thus termed لِأَنَّ وَلَدَهَا شَفَعَهَا أَوْ شَفَعَتْهُ [*because her young one has made her to be one of a pair*, or *couple, with itself, or because she has made it to be one of a pair or couple, with another that is in her belly*], (Ṣ, O, Ḳ,) inf. n. شَفْعٌ, or the inf. n. in this case is شِفْعٌ, with kesr. (O, Ḳ.) — One says also, إِنَّهُ لَيَشْفَعُ عَلَىَّ بِالعَدَاوَةِ, (Ḳ,) or لِى, (O,) i. e. ‡ *Verily he aids* [another, *becoming* to him *one of a pair, by enmity*] *against me, and acts injuriously to me* [*conjointly* with another]. (O, Ḳ, TA.) Accord. to Er-Rághib, يَشْفَعُ means *He joins himself to another, and aids him, becoming to him one of a pair*, or *a* شَفِيع [i. e. *an intercessor*], in doing good or evil, so that he aids him, or partakes with him, in [procuring] the benefit or the harm thereof; and thus it means in the saying in the Ḳur [iv. 87], مَنْ يَشْفَعْ شَفَاعَةً حَسَنَةً [and in what follows the same]: (TA:) or these words mean *Whoso adds a* [*good*] *deed to a* [*good*] *deed:* (O, Ḳ:) or, as some say, the شفاعة here is a man's *instituting, or prescribing, to another, a way of good or evil, so that he* [the latter] *imitates him, and thus becomes as though he were to him one of a pair.* (TA.) [But accord. to the expositors in general, and accord. to the general usage of the inf. n. شَفَاعَةٌ as distinguished from شَفْعٌ, what is here meant is *Intercession.*] — [Hence also,] شَفَعَ لَهُ إِلَى فُلَانٍ, (Ṣ,* Ḳ,* TA,) or الى الأَمِيرِ, (MA,) aor. َ, (Ḳ, TA,) inf. n. شَفَاعَةٌ; (MA, Ḳ, TA;) and ↓ تشفّع لَهُ, (MA,) or ↓ تشفّع فِيهِ; (Ṣ, TA;) *He made petition*, or *intercession, for him* [*to such a one*, or *to the prince* or *the like;* thus adjoining himself to him as an aider]; (MA, TA:) and شَفَعَ بَيْنَ النَّاسِ [*He interceded between the people*], inf. n. شَفَاعَةٌ: (Jel in iv. 87:) and شَفَعْتُ فِى الأَمْرِ, (Mṣb,) inf. n. شَفَاعَةٌ (IḲṭṭ, Mṣb, TA) and شَفْعٌ, (Mṣb, [but the latter is scarcely to be found elsewhere thus used,]) *I pleaded*, [or *interceded*,] *in the affair*, or *case*, [in favour of another,] *for some means of access* or *ingratiation*, or *some right* or *due:* (IḲṭṭ,* Mṣb, TA:*) شَفَاعَةٌ is mentioned, but not explained, in the Ḳ: (TA:) as distinguished from شَفْعٌ meaning as expl. above, it signifies the *joining oneself to another as an aider to him* or *a petitioner respecting him* [or *for him*]; and in most instances the former person is one of higher station than the latter: (Er-Rághib, TA:) or the *speaking of the* شَفِيع [or *intercessor*] *to the king* [or *some other person*] *respecting some object of want which the speaker asks for another person:* it is also expl. as signifying the *passing over without punishment*, or the *forgiving*, [or rather the *asking*, or *requesting*, *the passing over* &c., (for the word طَلَبُ, probably accidentally omitted by the transcriber at the commencement of the explanation, should doubtless be supplied,)] *of sins, crimes*, or *misdeeds.* (TA.) Hence, in a trad., اِشْفَعْ ↓ تُشَفَّعْ [*Intercede thou: thou shalt have thine intercession accepted*]. (TA.) The saying in the Ḳur [ii. 117], وَلَا تَنْفَعُهَا شَفَاعَةٌ [*Nor shall intercession profit it*] means that it shall have no شَافِع [or intercessor] for his شَفَاعَة [or intercession] to profit it; being a denial of the شافع; (Ibn-'Arafeh, O, Ḳ;) and the same is the case in the Ḳur lxxiv. 49, (Ibn-'Arafeh, O, TA,) and xx. 108. (TA.) شَفَعَ, inf. n. شَفْعٌ and شَفَاعَةٌ, also signifies *He prayed*, or *supplicated:* and thus Mbr and Th explain the words of the Ḳur [ii. 256], مَنْ ذَا الَّذِى يَشْفَعُ عِنْدَهُ إِلَّا بِإِذْنِهِ [*Who is he that shall pray, or supplicate, in his presence, except by his permission?*]. (TA.) — Accord. to El-Ḳutabee, (Mgh,) [i. e.] El-Ḳuteybee, (TA,) one says also, of a neighbour of one who desires to sell a dwelling [or land] شَفَعَ إِلَيْهِ فِى مَا بَاعَ, meaning *He made a demand to him*, i. e. to the latter, *respecting that which he sold* [*for the right of pre-emption*]: and of the latter person, ↓ شَفَّعَهُ [*and he admitted his right of pre-emption*, i. e.] *and he pronounced him to have a better right*, or *title*, or *claim*, [*as a purchaser*,] *to that which was sold, that he whose connexion was more remote.* (Mgh, TA.*) ═ شَفَعَ, inf. n. شَفْعٌ, signifies also *He*, or *it, was*, or *became, tall*, or *high.* (TA.) ═ And شُفِعَ, like عُنِىَ, *He* (a man) *was smitten by the* [*evil*] *eye.* (IḲṭṭ, TA. [But see شُفْعَةٌ, last sentence.])

2: see 1, near the beginning. — شَفَّعْتُهُ فِيهِ, inf. n. تَشْفِيعٌ, *I accepted his intercession* (شَفَاعَتَهُ) [*for him*]. (Ṣ,* O, Ḳ.) See, again, 1, in the last quarter of the paragraph. — And see another signification of the verb in a later part of the same paragraph.

5. تشفّع [signifies *It was made a pair* or *couple*, accord. to the Ḳ voce وِتْرٌ; this word being there expl. as meaning مَا لَمْ يَتَشَفَّعْ مِنَ العَدَدِ: but in the M and A, in the same place, instead of يَتَشَفَّعْ, we find يُشْفَعْ.] — تشفّع لَهُ, and فِيهِ: see 1, near the middle of the paragraph. — [It is said in the TA that تَشَفَّعَهُ also is quasi-pass. of اِسْتَشْفَعَ بِهِ: but تشفّعه is evidently, here, a mistranscription, app. for تَشَفَّعَ, meaning *He was granted intercession.*] ═ Also *He became a* شَافِعِىّ [i. e. *a follower of the Imám Esh-Sháfi'ee*] *in persuasion:* but this is post-classical. (TA.)

10. اِسْتَشْفَعْتُهُ إِلَى فُلَانٍ *I asked him to make intercession for me* (أَنْ يَشْفَعَ لِى) *to such a one.* (Ṣ, O, Ḳ.*) And اِسْتَشْفَعْتُ بِهِ *I sought,* or *demanded, intercession* (الشَّفَاعَة) [*by means of him*]. (Mṣb.) A poet, cited by Aboo-Leylà, says,

زَعَمَتْ مَعَاشِرُ أَنَّنِى مُسْتَشْفِعٌ
لَمَّا خَرَجْتُ أَزُورُهُ أَقْلَامَهَا

i. e. *Companies of men asserted me to be seeking intercession* (زَعَمُوا أَنِّى أَسْتَشْفِعُ) for the object of eulogy, [*when I went forth repairing to visit him,*] *by means of their writing-reeds* (بِأَقْلَامِهِمْ), meaning *by their letters* (بِكُتُبِهِمْ). (O, TA.)

شَفْعٌ *contr. of* وِتْرٌ; (Ṣ, Mgh, O, Ḳ;) *i. q.* زَوْجٌ [i. e., like زَوْجٌ, it signifies *One of a pair* or *couple;* and sometimes, but rarely, *a pair* or *couple together;* and sometimes, (see for instance زَكًا) *an even number, a number that may be divided into two equal numbers*]: (O, Ḳ:) also *one with which another is made to be a pair* or *couple:* (TA:) [and, as will be seen in what follows, *one with which an odd number is made to be an even number:*] pl. شِفَاعٌ, (TA,) and app. أَشْفَاعٌ, whence الصَّلَاةُ بَيْنَ الأَشْفَاعِ, meaning التَّرَاوِيح [q. v. voce تَرْوِيحَةٌ]. (Mgh.) — الشَّفْعُ also signifies *The day of the sacrifice;* (O, Ḳ;) thus in the words of the Ḳur [lxxxix. 2] وَالشَّفْعِ وَالْوَتْرِ; by الوتر being meant the day of 'Arafát: (O:) or in this instance it means *the creatures of God,* (O, Ḳ,) because of the saying in the Ḳur [li. 49], "and of everything we have created two of a pair;" (Ḳ;) الوتر meaning God: (O, Ḳ:) or *Adam's wife;* الوتر meaning Adam, who was made a pair with her: (I'Ab, O, TA:) or *Adam's children:* (TA:) or *the two days after the sacrifice;* الوتر meaning the third day: (O, TA:) or *God;* [and الوتر, those who compose an odd number;] because of the saying in the Ḳur [lviii. 8], "there can be no secret discourse of three, but He is the maker of them, with Himself, to be four:" (Ḳ:) or the meaning of الشَّفْعُ وَالْوَتْرُ is *the prayers;* of which some are شَفْع [i. e. an even number of rek'ahs], and some are وِتْر [i. e. an odd number of rek'ahs]: (O, TA:) [for] it is said that all the numbers consist of شَفْع [i. e. *even*] and وِتْر [i. e. *odd*]. (TA.)

شَفَعَةٌ: see the next paragraph, in two places, near the end.

شُفْعَةٌ is used in relation to a house and to land; (Ṣ, TA;) and ↓ شُفُعَةٌ, with two ḍammehs, is a dial. var. thereof thus used. (TA.) It signifies *A* مِلْك [here meaning *house,* or *piece of land,*] *that is coupled* (مَشْفُوع) [*by purchase*] *with one's* مِلْك [i. e. *house,* or *piece of land, previously possessed, and adjoining thereto*]; (Mgh, Mṣb;*) from the phrase كَانَ وِتْرًا فَشَفَعْتُهُ [expl. above, in the second sentence of this art.]; (Mgh; [and the like is said in the Mṣb;]) a noun of the same class as لُقْمَةٌ; being of the measure فُعْلَةٌ in the sense of the measure مَفْعُول: (Mgh, Mṣb:*) this is the primary signification: then it was applied to denote *a particular kind of obtaining possession;* (Mgh;) [i. e.] it is also used as meaning the *obtaining possession of that* مِلْك [or *house,* or *piece of land, by purchasing it, and coupling it with that previously possessed, and adjoining thereto*]; (Mṣb;) or one's *making a demand respecting that which he seeks* [*to possess, for the right of the pre-emption thereof*], *and adjoining it to that which he* [*already*] *has:* (O, Ḳ:) and with the lawyers it signifies the *right of obtaining possession of a piece of land,* [i. e. the *right of pre-emption thereof,* or *of a house,*] *against one's co-sharer whose possession is recent, by compulsion, for a compensation:* (Ḳ:) or the *right of obtaining possession of a piece of land, by compulsion, for* [*the payment of*] *what it cost the* [*former*] *purchaser, by reason of partnership* or *of* [*immediate*] *neighbourship:* (KT:) or the *right of* [*immediate*] *neighbourship with respect to* [*pre-emption of*] *a house* or *land.* (PṢ.) [See 1 in art. سقب.] El-Ḳutabee says, in explaining this word, in the Time of Ignorance, when a man desired to sell a house, his neighbour used to come to him and to make a demand to him (شَفَعَ إِلَيْهِ i. e. طَلَبَ) respecting that which he sold [for the right of pre-emption], and he pronounced him to have a better right, or title, or claim, [as a purchaser,] to that which was sold, than he whose connexion was more remote: as though he took it from الشَّفَاعَة: but the [right] derivation is that first mentioned. (Mgh.) We have not heard, (Mgh,) or there is not known, (Mṣb,) any verb belonging to it [in the classical language]. (Mgh, Mṣb.) Esh-Shaạbee uses it in the first and in the second of the senses expl. above, [or nearly so,] in his saying, مَنْ بِيعَتْ شُفْعَتُهُ وَهُوَ حَاضِرٌ فَلَمْ يَطْلُبْ ذٰلِكَ فَلَا شُفْعَةَ لَهُ [i. e. *He whose claimed possession to be coupled by purchase with one already belonging to him is sold when he is present without his demanding that* possession, *there shall be no obtaining possession for him by his purchasing it for that purpose*]. (Mgh. [And the like is said in the Mṣb.]) Esh-Shaạbee says [also], الشُّفْعَةُ عَلَى رُؤُوسِ الرِّجَالِ [*The possession that is coupled by purchase with another possession is* apportioned *according to the heads of the men* entitled thereto]: i. e., when the house is shared by a company of men whose shares are different, and one of them sells his portion, what is sold to his co-sharers is to be apportioned among them equally, according to their heads, not according to their [former] shares: (O, Ḳ, TA:) so in the Nh. (TA.) — شُفْعَةُ الضُّحَى *The two rek'ahs* (رَكْعَتَانِ) *of the* [*prayer that is performed in the period of the morning called the*] ضُحَى; as also ↓ شَفَعَةُ الضحى: (O, Ḳ:) occurring in a trad., thus accord. to two different relations. (O.) = Also *Diabolical,* or *demoniacal, possession;* or *madness,* or *insanity;* (AA, O, Ḳ;) and so ↓ شَفَعَةٌ; the latter expl. in this sense by IAạr; and as *syn. with* سَفْعَة and شُنْعَة and رَدَّة and نَظْرَة, [perceived] in the face: [see these words; the second and third of which generally mean *an unseemliness* or *ugliness;* and so, sometimes, does the last:] the pl. of شُفْعَة in the sense here expl. on the authority of AA is شُفَع. (TA.) — And IF states that it has been said to signify The [*evil*] *eye, by which one is smitten:* but he doubts its correctness; and thinks that it may be with the unpointed س. (O.) [See سَفْعَة, not سُفْعَة.]

شُفُعَةٌ: see شُفْعَةٌ, first sentence.

شَفُوعٌ A she-camel *that fills two milking-vessels in one milking.* (Ṣ, Ḳ.) — See also شَافِعٌ.

شَفِيعٌ *i. q.* صَاحِبُ شَفَاعَةٍ; (Ṣ, Ḳ, TA;) i. e. (TA) *An intercessor;* as also ↓ شَافِعٌ: pl. of the former شُفَعَآءُ. (Mṣb, TA.) [See الشُّفَعَآء, in art. سقف.] — Also *i. q.* صَاحِبُ شُفْعَةٍ; (Ṣ, Ḳ;) [meaning *A possessor of the right termed* شُفْعَة; or] *one who demands, and is granted, as a neighbour* [*or a partner*], *in preference to him whose connexion is more remote, the right of purchasing a house* [*or piece of land*] *that is to be sold.* (TA.)

شَفَائِعُ *Sorts of pasture,* or *herbage, that grow two and two:* (Ibn-Abbád, O, Ḳ:) or *twins* (تُؤَام [pl. of تَوْءَم]) *of plants.* (O, Ḳ.)

شَافِعٌ [act. part. n. of 1, q. v. — Hence], applied to a she-camel, ‡ *Having a young one in her belly and another following her:* (Fr, Sh, Ṣ, Mgh, Ḳ, TA:) or applied in this sense to a ewe or she-goat: (Ḳ:) or, thus applied, *having her young one with her:* (A'Obeyd, Ṣ, Mgh:) thus called because her young one has made her to be one of a pair [with it], or because she has made it to be one of a pair [with her]: (A'Obeyd, Ṣ, Ḳ:) and ↓ شَفُوعٌ, thus applied, signifies the same as شَافِعٌ: and one says also, هٰذِهِ شَاةُ الشَّافِعِ, like as one says صَلَاةُ الأُولَى and مَسْجِدُ الجَامِعِ. (TA.) — Also *A he-goat,* (O, Ḳ, TA,) himself: (O:) or *a ram:* or *such as, when he impregnates, impregnates with twins.* (O, Ḳ.) — عَيْنٌ شَافِعَةٌ *An eye* [*that makes a thing to appear a pair,* i. e.,] *that sees doubly.* (O, Ḳ.) — فُلَانٌ يُعَادِينِى وَلَهُ شَافِعٌ means ‡ *Such a one treats me with enmity, and has one who aids him to do so.* (A, TA.) — See also شَفِيعٌ and مُشَفَّعٌ.

أَشْفَعُ *Tall,* or *high.* (L, TA.)

مُشْفِعٌ *A ewe,* or *she-goat, that suckles any animal.* (IAạr, TA.)

مُشَفَّعٌ One *whose intercession is accepted:* hence the Ḳur-án is termed by Ibn-Mes'ood ↓ شَافِعٌ مُشَفَّعٌ, i. e. *An intercessor of which the intercession will be accepted,* for him who follows it and does according to what is in it, that his unpremeditated transgressions may be forgiven. (O, TA.)

مُشَفِّعٌ One *who accepts intercession.* (L, TA.)

مَشْفُوعٌ A possession (مِلْك [here meaning house, or piece of land,]) *coupled* [*by purchase*] with a man's possession [previously belonging to him, upon certain conditions expl. voce شُفْعَةٌ]. (Mgh, Mṣb.) —— Also *Affected with diabolical,* or *demoniacal, possession;* or *with madness,* or *insanity;* (O, Ḳ;) and مَسْفُوعٌ, with the unpointed س, is a dial. var. thereof. (TA.) — And مَشْفُوعَةٌ is said to signify A woman *smitten by the* [*evil*] *eye:* (IF, O, L: [but see شُفْعَةٌ, last sentence:]) the masc. is not used in this sense. (L, TA.)

شفق

1. شَفَقَ and شَفِقَ: see 4, in five places. — شَفِقَ عَلَيْهِ signifies *He was niggardly of it:* (TA:) [thus] the saying [of a poet]

كَمَا شَفِقَتْ عَلَى الزَّادِ العِيَالُ

means [*Like as the household*] *are niggardly of the provision:* (IDrd, M, O:) because he who is niggardly of a thing is ▼ مُشْفِقٌ عَلَيْهِ [i. e. *fearful,* or *cautious, on account of it*]. (M.)

2. تَشْفِيقٌ signifies ‡ The *making* [a gift or the like (see مُشَفَّقٌ)] *scanty,* or *little in amount* or *quantity;* as also ▼ إِشْفَاقٌ. (O, Ḳ, TA.) — And ‡ The *weaving badly.* (Ḳ, TA.) You say, شَفَّقَ المِلْحَفَةَ ‡ *He wove badly,* (M,) or *so as to make it scanty in the yarn,* or *unsubstantial,* (TA,) *the* [*kind of wrapper called*] ملحفة. (M, TA.) —— See also 4, last sentence.

4. اشفق signifies *He feared,* or *was cautious;* as also ▼ شَفَقَ [in the CḲ شَفَّقَ]; or only the former: (Ḳ, TA:) [accord. to ISd,] ▼ شَفِقَ, inf. n. شَفَقٌ, signifies *he feared:* (M:) IDrd says, ▼ شَفَقْتُ [in one of my copies of the Ṣ شَفِقْتُ] and أَشْفَقْتُ are syn., (Ṣ, O, TA,) as some assert, (O, TA,) but the lexicologists disallow this, (Ṣ, O,) saying that one should only say أَشْفَقْتُ: (O:) accord. to Er-Rághib, الإِشْفَاقُ signifies [*the being affected with*] *care,* or *solicitude, mixed with fear;* and when it is trans. by means of مِنْ, the meaning of fear is most apparent in it; but when trans. by means of عَلَى, the meaning of care, or solicitude, is most apparent in it: (TA: [and the like is said by Bḍ in xxi. 29:]) or it signifies [*the being affected with*] *fright* [or *fear*]; sometimes *mixed with faithful* or *sincere* or *honest advice;* and sometimes *divested thereof:* (Ḥam p. 179:) one says, أَشْفَقْتُ مِنْهُ, (Ṣ,) or مِنْ كَذَا, (Mṣb,) *I feared,* or *was cautious of,* (Ṣ, Mṣb,) *him,* or *it,* (Ṣ,) or *such a thing:* (Mṣb:) or اشفق منه *he feared him,* or *it:* (MA:) and أَشْفَقْتُ عَلَيْهِ, (Ṣ, [in which it is implied that this differs from أَشْفَقْتُ مِنْهُ,]) or عَلَى الصَّغِيرِ, *I was affectionate, kind,* or *compassionate,* and *favourably inclined,* [*towards him,* or] *towards the little one:* (Mṣb; [and a similar explanation is given in the MA:]) and ▼ شَفَقْتُ, aor. ـِ, is a dial. var. thereof [i. e. of أَشْفَقْتُ when trans. by means of عَلَى, and perhaps also when it is trans. by means of مِنْ]: (Mṣb:) or اشفق عليه signifies [*he was solicitously affectionate, &c., towards him;* agreeably with the explanation of Er-Rághib above, and with that here following;] *he was affected with pity,* or *compassion, and tenderness, and fear, for him, at the same time giving him faithful* or *sincere* or *honest advice,* أَنْ يَنَالَهُ مَكْرُوهٌ [*lest some disliked* or *evil event should betide him*]: (TA:) or *he feared,* or *was cautious, for him:* and اشفق منه *he was impatient of him,* or *it:* and ▼ شَفِقَ is a dial. var. [of اشفق when trans. by means of مِنْ, and app. also when trans. by means of عَلَى]. (M.) —— See also 2. —— Also *He entered upon* [*the time of*] *the* شَفَق [q. v.]. (M.) And *He came in a* [*time of*] شَفَق: and so ▼ شَفَّقَ. (M.)

شَفَقٌ *Fear:* (Ḳ:) [see also شَفِقَ, (of which it is the inf. n.) in the next preceding paragraph:] or *fear* [*arising*] *from strictness* (شِدَّة) *of faithful* or *sincere* or *honest advice;* (M, TA;) as also ▼ شَفَقَةٌ: (M:) or ▼ the latter signifies the *fear of him who gives faithful* or *sincere* or *honest advice, in consequence of his doing so, for him to whom such advice is given:* (O:) or the former, (Ḳ, TA,) and ▼ the latter also, (TA,) the *eagerness,* or *striving, of him who gives such advice, to rectify,* or *amend, the state of him to whom that advice is given:* (Ḳ, TA: [said in the latter to be a tropical application of the words; but why, I see not:]) ▼ شَفَقَةٌ is a subst. from الإِشْفَاقُ, (Ṣ, Mṣb, TA,) and شَفَقٌ is syn. therewith (Ṣ, O, Ḳ, TA) as being also a subst. from الإِشْفَاقُ: (Ṣ, TA:) [it is said that] the primary signification of ▼ شَفَقَةٌ is *weakness:* (Ḥam p. 179:) and it is conjoined with خَوْفٌ [fear]; therefore it is not applied as an attribute to God: (Idem p. 722:) [generally] it signifies *affection, kindness, benignity, compassion,* or *favourable inclination:* (MA:) [or *solicitous affection* &c.:] or *pity,* or *compassion, and tenderness, and fear of the betiding of some disliked* or *evil event, together with faithful* or *sincere* or *honest advice.* (TA.) —— شَفَقٌ also signifies The *redness* (Kh, Ṣ, Mṣb, Ḳ) *in the horizon* (Ḳ) *from sunset until the time of the last* عِشَآء [i. e. *nightfall*], (Kh, Ṣ, Mṣb, Ḳ,) when it disappears, (Kh, Ṣ, Mṣb,) and the white شَفَق remains until the middle [or rather until a late period varying at different seasons] of the night: (Mṣb:) or *until near that time:* or *until near the* عَتَمَة [q. v., generally meaning the same, or nearly so]: (Ḳ:) or the *redness that is seen in the sky at sunset:* (IDrd, O:) or the *remains of the light and redness of the sun in the first part of the night, until near the* عَتَمَة: (Ṣ:) or the *light and redness of the sun, seen at sunset, until the time of the prayer of nightfall:* (M:) or the *mixture of the light of day with the blackness of night at sunset:* (Er-Rághib, TA:) accord. to Zj, the *redness that is in the region of sunset after the setting of the sun:* this is the meaning given as of common repute in the books of lexicology; and Mṭr says [in the Mgh] that it means the *redness* accord. to a number of the Companions of the Prophet and of the people of the generation next succeeding them: but accord. to Aboo-Hureyreh, it means the *whiteness* [*after sunset,* which, to distinguish it from the شَفَق commonly so called, is often termed the white شَفَق, as in an instance above]: (Mṣb:) IAth says that this word has two contr. meanings; being applied to the *redness that is seen after sunset;* and to the *whiteness remaining in the western horizon after the said redness.* (TA.) Fr says, I heard one of the Arabs say, عَلَيْهِ ثَوْبٌ كَأَنَّهُ الشَّفَقُ [*Upon him is,* or *was, a garment as though it were the* شَفَق]: and it was red. (Ṣ.) —— [Hence,] ‡ A garment, or piece of cloth, *dyed red.* (AA, TA.) —— And *Day.* (Zj, M, Ḳ.) —— Also i. q. نَاحِيَةٌ † [*A side,* &c.; or *a remote side*]: pl. أَشْفَاقٌ. (O, Ḳ.) One says, أَنَا فِى أَشْفَاقٍ مِنْ هٰذَا الأَمْرِ i. e. نَوَاحٍ [meaning † *I am apart,* or *aloof, from this affair;* as though *in,* or *on, remote sides thereof*]: (O, TA:) and in like manner فِى عُرُوضٍ مِنْهُ [app. a mistranscription for عُرُوضٍ i. e. نَاحِيَةٍ] and فى أَعْرَاضٍ منه i. e. نَوَاحٍ. (TA.) —— And ‡ A bad thing; syn. رَدِىٌّ: (Lth, Ṣ, M, O, Ḳ, TA: [in the TA said to be written by J with kesr to the ف; but not so in either of my copies of the Ṣ:]) applied to a garment, or piece of cloth, (Mgh, TA, and Ḥam p. 179,) [in this sense, or] as meaning *bad and thin:* (Mgh in art. حوث:) [said to be] from شَفَقَةٌ signifying "weakness:" (Ḥam ubi suprà:) seldom pluralized: (O:) and used alike as masc. and fem., being applied as an epithet to a مِلْحَفَة, (M, O,) meaning رَدِيئَة. (M.)

شَفِقٌ: see شَفِيقٌ, in two places.

شَفَقَةٌ: see شَفَقٌ, in five places.

شَفُوقٌ: see the next paragraph.

شَفِيقٌ is *syn. with* ▼ مُشْفِقٌ as part. n. of 4 [signifying *Fearing,* or *fearful,* or *cautious;* and also *affectionate, kind,* or *compassionate,* &c.]; (Ṣ, O, Mṣb,* Ḳ;) as also ▼ شَفِقٌ (Mṣb) [and in an intensive sense ▼ شَفُوقٌ; and, from what follows, it appears that شَفِيقٌ also is used as an intensive epithet]: or ▼ شَفِقٌ signifies *fearing;* and its pl. is شَفِقُونَ: (M, TA:) and شَفِيقٌ, one *giving faithful* or *sincere* or *honest advice, eager,* or *striving, to rectify,* or *amend, the state of him to whom that advice is given.* (M.)

إِنَّ الشَّفِيقَ بِسُوْءِ ظَنٍّ مُولَعٌ

[*Verily the affectionate, &c., or the very affectionate &c., is addicted to evil opinion,*] is a prov., applied in the case of the man who fears, for his friend, the accidents of fortune, by reason of his excessive شَفَقَة [or affection, &c.]. (TA.) And it is said in the Ḳur [xxi. 50], وَهُمْ مِنَ السَّاعَةِ مُشْفِقُونَ ▼ [meaning *And who are fearful of the time of the resurrection*]; the signification of fear being most apparent when مُشْفِقٌ is thus trans. by means of مِنْ. (TA.) See also an instance of ▼ مُشْفِقٌ [in a similar sense] in the first paragraph of this art.

مُشْفَقٌ: see the last paragraph. —— [Accord. to Freytag, it signifies also *Fear:* but he names no authority for this.]

مُشْفِقٌ: see شَفِيقٌ, in three places.

عَطَآءٌ مُشَفَّقٌ ‡ *A gift made scanty,* or *little in*

amount or *quantity;* (Ṣ, TA;) as also ▼ مُشَفَّقٌ. (TA.)

شفه

1. شَفَهَهُ, aor. ـَ , (Ḳ,) inf. n. شَفْهٌ, (TḲ,) *He struck his* شَفَة [i. e. *lip*]. (Ḳ.)—— شُفِهَ, [said of a water, † *It had many lips of drinkers applied to it; i. e. it had many drinkers:* (see its part. n.:) and] said of food, ‡ *It had many eaters:* (Ḳ, TA:) or [as a consequence thereof] *it became little in quantity.* (TA.)—— And [hence], said of property, † *It had many seekers.* (Ḳ.)—— And, said of a man, † *He had many askers,* or *beggars,* (Ḳ, TA,) *so that they consumed what he had,* or *possessed.* (TA.) [Or † *He was importuned by begging, so that what he had,* or *possessed, was consumed:* as pass. of what next follows.]—— شَفَهَهُ † *He importuned him by begging, so that he consumed what he had,* or *possessed.* (Ṣ, Ḳ.) And one says, كَادَ العِيَالُ يَشْفَهُونَ مَالِى ‡ *The family,* or *household, almost consumed my property.* (Ḳ,* TA.)—— Also, (Ṣ, Ḳ,) inf. n. شَفْهٌ, (Ṣ,) i. q. شَغَلَ. (Ṣ, Ḳ.) You say, شَفَهَنِى عَنْ كَذَا † *He, or it, occupied me so as to divert me from such a thing;* syn. شَغَلَنِى. (Ṣ.) And نَحْنُ نَشْفَهُ عَلَيْكَ المَرْتَعَ, and المَآءَ, meaning † *We occupy the place of pasturage so as to keep it from thee,* and *the water,* (نَشْغَلُهُ عَنْكَ,) i. e. it is sufficient for us without being more than sufficient. (Ṣ, TA.) And شُفِهَ عَنْكَ مَا عِنْدَنَا † *What we had was employed so as to be kept from thee;* syn. شُغِلَ عَنْكَ. (JK.) ═ IAạr mentions the phrase شَفِهْتُ نَصِيبِى, with fet-ḥ, without explaining it; but Th says that it is سفهت, [i. e. سَفِهْتُ, with س, and with kesr to the ف,] meaning "I forgot [my share, or portion]." (TA.)

3. شافهه, (Ḳ,) inf. n. مُشَافَهَةٌ, (TA,) *He put his lip* (شَفَتَهُ) *near to his* [another's] *lip.* (Ḳ, TA.) And كَلَّمَهُ مُشَافَهَةً (Mṣb, TA) and شِفَاهًا (Mṣb) *He spoke to him putting his lip near to his lip:* (TA:) [or *mouth to mouth;* for,] accord. to J, (TA,) مُشَافَهَةٌ signifies the *talking with another mouth to mouth:* (Ṣ, TA:) but the usage of the inf. n. of a verb different from that which it is thus made to qualify is, as Sb says, restricted to instances that have been heard: the phrase كَلَّمَهُ مُفَاوَهَةً [has not been heard, and therefore] is not allowable. (TA.)—— [Hence,] شافه البَلَدَ, and الأَمْرَ, ‡ *He was,* or *became,* or *drew, near to the town,* or *country,* and *the affair.* (A, Ḳ, TA.)

شَفَةٌ, (T, Ṣ, Mṣb, Ḳ, &c.,) also pronounced ▼ شِفَةٌ, (Ḳ,) is a word of which the third, i. e. the final, radical letter is elided; (T, Mṣb;) and accord. to some, (Mṣb,) this letter is ه, (T, Mṣb, Ḳ, TA,) so accord. to all of the Baṣrees, (TA,) the word being originally ▼ شفهة, (T, Ṣ, Mṣb, TA,) i. e. شَفْهَةٌ, (so in copies of the Ṣ,) or شَفَهَةٌ, like طَلْحَةٌ and سَجْدَةٌ, (Mṣb,) because it has the former of the dims. mentioned below, and the first of the pls. mentioned below, with ه, (Ṣ, Mṣb,*) and it is sometimes pronounced شفهة; (T, TA;) or, as some assert, the deficient letter is و, (Ṣ, Mṣb,) the word being originally شَفْوَةٌ, like شَهْوَةٌ, (Mṣb,) because it has the last of the pls. mentioned below, (Ṣ, [but omitted in one of my copies,] and Mṣb,*) and the latter of the two dims. mentioned below; (Mṣb;) both of which assertions are stated on the authority of Kh; (IF, Mṣb;) [The *lip* of a human being;] شَفَتَا الإِنْسَانِ meaning *the two covers of the mouth of the human being:* (Ḳ:) it is [properly] only of a human being: (Mṣb:) but it is sometimes, metaphorically, of the horse: and in like manner, of the دَلْو [or leathern bucket] as used by A'Obeyd; but ISd has expressed a doubt whether he had heard this from the Arabs: (TA:) the pl. is شِفَاهٌ (Ṣ, Mṣb, Ḳ, &c.) and شَفَهَاتٌ (Lth, Mṣb, TA) and شَفَوَاتٌ, (Lth, Ṣ, Mṣb, Ḳ,) the second of which is said by Lth to be more agreeable with analogy than the third, though the third is more common, as being likened to سَنَوَاتٌ [pl. of سَنَةٌ]: (Az, (Mṣb, TA:) and Ks mentions the phrase, إِنَّهُ لَغَلِيظُ الشِّفَاهِ [as meaning *Verily he is thick in the lip*], as though the term شَفَة applied to every portion of the شَفَة: (TA:) the dim. is ▼ شُفَيْهَةٌ (Ṣ, Mṣb) and شُفَيَّةٌ. (Mṣb.)—— [Hence,] هُمْ أَهْلُ الشَّفَةِ † *They are those who have the right of drinking with their lips* (بِشِفَاهِهِمْ) *and of watering their beasts.* (Mgh.)—— And بِنْتُ شَفَةٍ ‡ *A word;* (Ṣ, Mṣb, Ḳ, TA;) as also ذَاتُ شَفَةٍ. (TA.) One says, مَا كَلَّمْتُهُ بِبِنْتِ شَفَةٍ † *I spoke not to him a word:* (Ṣ:) or مَا كَلَّمَنِى بِنْتَ شَفَةٍ † *He spoke not to me a word:* (TA:) and مَا سَمِعْتُ مِنْهُ بِنْتَ شَفَةٍ † *I heard not from him a word:* (Mṣb:) and مَا كَلَّمْتُ فُلَانًا ذَاتَ شَفَةٍ † *I spoke not to such a one a word.* (AZ, T voce ذُو.)—— And فُلَانٌ خَفِيفُ الشَّفَةِ ‡ *Such a one is a person who asks,* or *begs, little of people:* (ISk, Ṣ, Ḳ,* TA:) and also, ‡ *importunate,* (Ḳ, TA,) *one who asks,* or *begs, much of people:* (TA:) thus having two contr. meanings. (Ḳ.)—— And لَهُ فِى النَّاسِ شَفَةٌ † *He has praise,* or *commendation, among the people:* (Ṣ:) and لَهُ فِينَا شَفَةٌ حَسَنَةٌ ‡ *He has a good report,* or *reputation, among us.* (A, Ḳ, TA.) And إِنَّ شَفَةَ النَّاسِ عَلَيْكَ لَحَسَنَةٌ ‡ *Verily the people's speaking of thee is good.* (Lḥ, TA.) And مَا أَحْسَنَ شَفَةَ النَّاسِ عَلَيْكَ ‡ *How good is the people's speaking of thee!* (Ḳ, TA.)—— See also شَفًا, in art. شفو and شفى.

شِفَةٌ, and شُفَيْهَةٌ or شَفَهَةٌ: } see the next preceding paragraph.

شَفَهِىٌّ and شَفِىٌّ are both allowable as rel. ns. of شَفَة [i. e. as meaning *Labial:* and so, accord. to some, is شَفَوِىٌّ]. (Ṣ.) الحُرُوفُ الشَّفَهِيَّةُ (Kh, T, Ṣ, Mṣb, Ḳ) and الشَّفَوِيَّةُ, (Kh, T, Mṣb,) or the latter is not allowable, (Ṣ,) [i. e. *The labial letters,*] are ب *and* ف *and* م: (T, Ṣ, Ḳ:) [or, accord. to Lumsden (Ar. Gr. p. 28), ب, م *and* و: and, it seems, accord. to some, (see De Sacy's Gr. Ar. sec. ed. i. 27,) ع *and* ش *and* ض, which is strange:] so called because their place of utterance is from the شَفَة, without any action of the tongue. (T, TA.)

شُفَيْهَةٌ: dim. of شَفَةٌ, q. v.

شُفَاهِىٌّ A man (Ṣ, Mgh) *large* [in some copies of the Ṣ *thick*] *in the* شَفَتَانِ [or *lips*]; (Ṣ, Mgh, Ḳ;) as also ▼ أَشْفَهُ. (Mgh. [But see this latter below.])

شَافِهٌ *Thirsty,* (Ḳ, TA,) *not finding water enough to moisten his lip:* like سَافِهٌ, mentioned in art. سفه. (TA.)

أَشْفَهُ: see شُفَاهِىٌّ.—— [Accord. to some,] أَشْفَى signifies A man *whose lips do not close together:* (Ṣ, Ḳ:) but there is no proof of its correctness: (Ṣ:) the fem. in this sense is شَفْيَآءُ. (TA in art. شفى.)

مَشْفُوهٌ ‡ A water *at which there are many lips* (شِفَاه TA, and Ḥar p. 609,) *of those coming to drink,* (Ḥar,) *so that it has become little in quantity;* (TA;) or water *at which are many people:* (Ṣ, Ḳ:*) or water *that is sought:* or, as some say, *forbidden to those who come to drink of it because of its being little in quantity.* (TA.)—— And hence, (Ḥar ubi suprà,) ‡ Food *upon which are* [put] *many hands;* (Ḳ, TA, Ḥar;) *having many eaters:* or *that has become little in quantity.* (TA.)—— And † Property *sought by many:* (TA:) [or *little in quantity;* for] one says, أَتَانَا وَأَمْوَالُنَا مَشْفُوهَةٌ ‡ *He came to us when our possessions were little in quantity.* (Ḳ, TA.)—— And † A man *of whom people have asked,* or *begged, much,* (Ṣ,) or *importuned by begging,* (Ḳ,) *so that all that he had,* or *possessed, is consumed:* (Ṣ, Ḳ:) like مَثْمُودٌ, and مَضْفُوفٌ, and مَكْثُورٌ عَلَيْهِ: (so in one of my copies of the Ṣ:) and sometimes it means † one *whose household and guests have consumed his property.* (IB, TA.)

شفى and شفو

1. شَفَتِ الشَّمْسُ, aor. ـُ , [inf. n. app. شَفًا, but said in the TḲ to be شُفُوٌّ,] *The sun was,* or *became, near to setting:* (Ḳ in art. شفو:) and شَفَت, (Ḳ in art. شفى,) [aor. ـِ ,] inf. n. شَفًا, (TA,) *it* (the sun) *set;* as also شَفِيَت: (Ḳ:) or, accord. to IḲṭṭ, *set save a little;* and the like is said in the T. (TA.) قُبَيْلَ الشَّفَا means *A little before the setting of the sun.* (TA.) [See also شَفًا below.]—— And شَفَا said of the هِلَال [or moon a little after or before the change], *It rose.* (Ḳ.) And said of a شَخْص [or bodily form or figure seen from a distance, or a person], *It,* or *he, appeared,* or *became apparent.* (Ḳ.) ═ شَفَاهُ, (Ṣ, Mṣb, Ḳ,) aor. يَشْفِى, (Mṣb, Ḳ,) inf. n. شِفَآءٌ, (Ṣ, Mṣb,) *He* (God, Ṣ, Mṣb) *recovered him,* or *restored him to convalescence,* syn. أَبْرَأَهُ, so in the M, but in the Ḳ بَرَّأَهُ, (TA,) namely a sick person, (Mṣb,) مِنْ مَرَضِهِ [*from his disease,* or *sickness*]. (Ṣ, TA.)—— [Hence, شَفَيْتُهُ, in art. بضع in the Ṣ, said by a person respecting one who asked him concerning a

question, as meaning † *I relieved him from doubt:* and شَفَاهُ عَنِ المَسْأَلَةِ in the same art. in the Ḳ, as meaning † *He relieved him from doubt respecting the question.* See 8 as quasi-pass. of the verb thus used.] —— And يَشْفِيكَ إِنْ قَالَ † [*He will please thee if he speak;* i. e.] *his speech will please thee.* (Ḥar p. 433.) —— شَفَاهُ also signifies *He sought,* or *demanded,* or *desired, for him, recovery,* or *restoration to convalescence;* and so ↓ أَشْفَاهُ: (Ḳ, TA:) thus in the M. (TA.)

2. شَفَّاهُ بِكُلِّ شَىْءٍ, inf. n. تَشْفِيَةٌ, *He treated him medically,* or *curatively, with everything whereby he might attain recovery,* or *restoration to convalescence.* (TA.) ═ مَا شَفَّى فُلَانٌ أَفْضَلُ مِمَّا شَفَّيْتَ i. e. رَبِحَ and مَا ٱزْدَادَ [meaning *The gain of such a one* (ما being here what is termed مَصْدَرِيَّة, as اِزْدَادَ and رَبِحَ are intrans.,) *is more excellent than thy gain*] is said to be an instance of substitution, [originally شَفَّفَ and شَفَّفْتَ,] like [قَصَّى and تَقَضَّى and] [for قَصَّصَ and تَقَصَّصَ and تَقَضَّضَ]. (TA.)

3. مُشَافَاةٌ [an inf. n. of which the verb, if used, is شَافَى]: see 3 in art. شفه.

4. اشفى عَلَيْهِ *He was, or became, on the brink of it;* (Ṣ, Mṣb, Ḳ, TA;) namely, a thing; and death: (Ṣ, Mṣb:) mostly used in relation to evil, but also in relation to good: so says IḲṭṭ. (TA.) [See شَفًا.] —— And اشفى [alone] † *He was, or became, at the point of* [*giving* or *receiving*] *a charge* or *an injunction,* or *a trust* or *deposit.* (TA.) —— And † *He was, or became, in the last part of the night;* which is termed شَفَا اللَّيْلِ. (TA.) ═ أَشْفَى نَفْسَهُ عَلَى هُلْكٍ (Ḳ and TA in art. خطر) and اشفى بِهَا (TA in the same) i. e. عَلَى شَفَا هُلْكٍ [meaning † *He caused himself to be on the brink of destruction*]. (TA ibid.) ═ اشفاهُ *He gave him a remedial medicine.* (Az, TA.) And *He prescribed for him a remedy in which should be his recovery,* or *restoration to convalescence.* (TA.) And أَشْفَيْتُكَ الشَّىْءَ (Ṣ, Ḳ*) *I gave thee the thing in order that thou shouldst attain, or seek, recovery,* or *restoration to convalescence, thereby.* (Ṣ: in two copies thereof, تَشْتَفِى ↓ بِهِ: in two other copies thereof, and in like manner in the Ḳ, تَسْتَشْفِى ↓ بِهِ.) And اشفاهُ ٱللّٰهُ عَسَلًا *God made honey to be his remedy.* (AO, Ṣ: and the like is said by IḲṭṭ as cited in the TA.) —— See also 1, last sentence. —— اشفى also signifies † *He gave* [a person] *something.* (TA.)

5. تشفّى: see 8 [with which it is syn.]. —— [Hence,] تشفّى مِنْ غَيْظِهِ (Ṣ, MA, Ḳ) † *He recovered from his anger, wrath,* or *rage.* (MA.) And تشفّى مِنْ عَدُوِّهِ, (T, TA,) or بِالعَدُوِّ, and اشتفى ↓ بِهِ, (Mṣb,) † *He inflicted injury upon his enemy* [or *the enemy*] *in a manner that rejoiced him* [or *relieved him from his anger*]: (T, TA:) [or *he attained what he desired from his enemy* or *the enemy, and so appeased his anger:*] because latent anger is like a disease; and when it departs by reason of that which one seeks to obtain from his enemy, he is as though he became free, or recovered, from his disease. (Mṣb.)

6. تَشَافَيْتُ المَآءَ a phrase mentioned by IAạr as meaning *I exhausted the water:* said by ISd to be originally تَشَافَفْتُ. (TA in art. شف.)

8. اشتفى بِكَذَا (Ṣ, Ḳ, TA) *He attained recovery,* or *restoration to convalescence, by means of such a thing;* (TA;) and so ↓ تشفّى: (TḲ:) and استشفى ↓ مِنْ عِلَّتِهِ [if not a mistranscription for اشتفى] *he became free from his disease, sickness,* or *malady; recovered from it;* or *became convalescent.* (TA.) See 4, latter part. —— And see also 5. —— [Also † *He was,* or *became, content with such a thing;* or *relieved from doubt thereby:* and] † *he profited by such a thing.* (MA.) One says, اِشْتَفَيْتُ بِمَا أَخْبَرَنِى فُلَانٌ † *I was,* or *became, content with that which such a one told me,* [or *relieved from doubt thereby,*] *because it was true.* (IB in art. حلك, from Az.) And أَخْبَرَهُ فُلَانٌ فَٱشْتَفَى بِهِ † [*Such a one gave him information*] *and he profited by his veracity.* (TA.)

10. استشفى *He sought,* or *demanded, a remedy,* or *cure.* (TA.) See 4, latter part. —— And see also 8.

شَفًا The *point* or *extremity, verge, brink,* or *edge,* of anything; (Ṣ, Mṣb, Ḳ, &c.;) like ↓ شَفَةٌ; for شَفَا الحُفْرَةِ (Ksh in iii. 99) or شَفَا البِئْرِ (Bḍ ibid.) and شَفَتُهَا both signify the same, (Ksh, Bḍ,) i. e. حَرْفُهَا (Ksh) or طَرَفُهَا; (Bḍ;) but the final و in the former is changed into ا, and in the latter [accord. to those who hold شَفَةٌ to be originally شَفَوَةٌ] it is elided; (Ksh, Bḍ;) شَفًا being originally شَفَوٌ: (Bḍ:) [but شَفًا generally signifies as expl. above; and شَفَةٌ almost always signifies the "lip" of a human being:] the dual is شَفَوَانِ; this being known, as Akh says, by the fact that إِمَالَة in the word شَفًا is not allowable: (Ṣ:) and the pl. is أَشْفَآءٌ. (TA.) It is said in the Ḳur [iii. 99], وَكُنْتُمْ عَلَى شَفَا حُفْرَةٍ مِنَ ٱلنَّارِ فَأَنْقَذَكُمْ مِنْهَا [*And ye were on the verge,* or *brink, of a pit of the fire* of Hell, *and He saved,* or *rescued, you from it*]. (Ṣ.) And one says, هُوَ عَلَى شَفَا الهَلَاكِ ‡ [*He is on the brink of destruction*]. (TA.) —— Also ‡ *A little;* (Ṣ, A, Ḳ, TA;) *a small part,* or *portion; somewhat;* (A, TA;) *somewhat remaining* of the moon when near the change, (Ḳ, TA, [الهِلَاكِ in the CḲ is erroneously put for الهِلَالِ,]) and of the sight (البَصَرِ), and of the day, and the like, as in the T. (TA.) One says of a man on the occasion of his dying, and of the moon at [the last period of the month called] its مُحَاق, and of the sun at its setting, (Ṣ,) مَا بَقِىَ مِنْهُ إِلَّا شَفًا [and مِنْهَا when said of the sun] † *There has not remained of him,* or *it, save a little:* (Ṣ, Ḳ:*) and [in like manner] مِنَ العُمْرِ [*of life*]. (Ṣ.) And one says, أَتَيْتُهُ بِشَفًا مِنْ ضَوْءِ الشَّمْسِ † [*I came to him in a time when there was little remaining of the light of the sun*]. (TA.) El-'Ajjáj says,

* وَمَرْبَأٍ عَالٍ لِمَنْ تَشَرَّفَا * أَشْرَفْتُهُ بِلَا شَفًا أَوْ بِشَفَا *

meaning [*Many an elevated place of observation, high to him who ascends it, I have ascended*] *when the sun had set or when there was somewhat of it remaining.* (Ṣ.) One says also, صَارَ فِى شَفًا القَمَرِ meaning † *He was,* or *became, in the last part of the night.* (TA.) And it is said in a trad., (in relation to [the temporary marriage termed] المُتْعَة,) فَلَوْ لَا نَهْيُهُ عَنْهَا مَا ٱحْتَاجَ إِلَى الزِّنَا إِلَّا شَفًا, accord. to the T meaning [*Were it not for his* (i. e. God's) *forbidding it, none would need having recourse to fornication,*] *save a small number of men:* (T, TA:) or, accord. to 'Aṭà, it means, *but would be on the brink thereof, without falling into it;* شَفًا being thus used in the place of the inf. n. إِشْفَآء: so says IAth, as from Az. (TA.)

شَفَةٌ, in which the deficient letter is و, (Ḳ, TA,) for it has for pl. شَفَوَاتٌ, (TA,) or ه, (Ḳ, TA,) for it has [also] for pl. شِفَاهٌ, (TA,) has been mentioned before, (Ḳ, TA,) in art. شفه [q. v.]. (TA.) —— See also شَفًا above, first sentence.

شِفَآءٌ, (Ḳ, TA,) like كِسَآءٌ, (TA,) [in the CḲ erroneously written شَفاء,] primarily signifies The *becoming free from disease, sickness,* or *malady; recovering therefrom;* or *becoming convalescent:* —— and then, *Medical,* or *curative, treatment:* (TA:) the *giving of health:* (KL:) inf. n. of شَفَاهُ [q. v.]: (Ṣ, Mṣb, TA:) —— and [then], (TA,) *A medicine,* or *remedy:* pl. أَشْفِيَةٌ, and pl. pl. أَشَافٍ. (Ḳ, TA.) [Hence, دَارُ الشِّفَآءِ *The hospital.*] —— [And hence,] one says, شِفَآءُ العِىِّ السُّؤَالُ ‡ [*The remedy of inability is the asking information*]. (TA.)

شَفِىٌّ:
شُفَيَّةٌ: } see art. شفه.
شَفَوِىٌّ:

شَافٍ [*Recovering,* or *restoring to convalescence; remedial;*] *health-giving.* (KL.) —— [Hence, جَوَابٌ شَافٍ † *An answer that relieves from doubt.*]

أَشْفَى *More* [and *most remedial* or] *health-giving.* (KL.) ═ Also A man *whose lips do not close together:* fem. شَفْيَآءُ. (TA.) See أَشْفَهُ, in art. شفه.

إِشْفَى *An instrument for perforating;* (Ḳ;) *a thing pertaining to the makers or sewers of boots or shoes or sandals &c.;* (Ṣ;) [i. e.] *the awl used by them:* (MA, KL:) and the *instrument with which leather,* or *skin, is sewed:* (Mgh, Ḳ:) or, accord. to ISk, it is [*an instrument used*] *for water-skins and water-bags and the like;* and the مِخْصَف is for sandals: (Ṣ:) [see also art. اشف:] masc. and fem.: (Ḳ,* TA:) pl. أَشَافٍ. (Mgh, TA.) —— Th mentions the saying, إِنْ لَاطَمْتَهُ لَاطَمْتَ الإِشْفَى [*If thou contend with him in slapping, thou wilt do so with the* اشفى]; meaning that when one does so, it will be against himself. (TA.) —— And إِشْفَى المِرْفَقِ, a phrase used by a poet, means † *Sharp in the elbow.* (TA.)

شق

1. شَقَّهُ, (Ṣ, M, Mṣb, Ḳ,) aor. ـُ, (M, Mṣb,)

inf. n. شَقٌّ, (Ṣ, M, Mṣb,) *He cut it* [or *divided it*] *lengthwise;* (TA in art. قد;) [i. e.] *he clave it, split it, rived* or *rifted it,* or *slit it; so as to separate it;* [i. e. *he clave, split, rived* or *rifted, slit, rent, ripped, tore, broke,* or *burst, it asunder;*] or *without separating it;* [i. e. *he cracked, chapped, incided* or *incised, gashed, slashed, furrowed,* or *trenched, it;* or *clave, split, &c.,* or *cut, it open;*] syn. صَدَعَهُ; (Ḳ;) or [more explicitly] الشَّقُّ signifies الصَّدْعُ البَائِنُ [*the cleaving* &c. *that separates*]; or غَيْرُ البَائِنِ [*that which does not separate*]; or الصَّدْعُ [*the cleaving, &c.,*] *in a general sense:* (M:) and in like manner, [but with an intensive signification, or implying frequency or repetition of the action, or its application to several objects, generally meaning *he clave it, &c., much,* or *in pieces,* or *in several places,*] ↓ شقّقهُ: (M, Ḳ:) you say, شقّق الحَطَبَ (Ṣ, Ḳ) وَغَيْرَهُ (Ṣ) i. e. شَقَّهُ [but properly meaning *He clave in pieces the firewood* &c.]. (Ḳ. [In the CḲ, شَقَّ الحَطَبَ is erroneously put for شقّق الحطب.]) — شَقَّ رَأْسَهُ generally means *He clave his head,* or *his pericranium:* and sometimes, as in an instance in the Ḳ voce شَعَّأَ, *he divided the hair of his head.*] — شَقَّ العَصَا [lit. *He split the staff*] means ‡ *he separated himself from the community;* (Ṣ, Ḳ, TA;) and particularly, that of the Muslims: because the staff is not thus called but when it is whole, not when it is split: accord. to Lth, يَشُقُّ عَصَا المُسْلِمِينَ and ↓ يُشَاقُّهُمْ signify alike: but they differ in meaning, as will be shown hereafter. (TA.) شَقَّ عَصَا المُسْلِمِينَ, (Ḳ, TA,) said of a خَارِجِىّ [i. e. heretic or schismatic], also means † *He effected disunion and dissension in the body of the Muslims.* (TA.) And one says also, شَقَّ عَصَا الطَّاعَةِ † [*He broke the compact of allegiance,* or *obedience; became a rebel*]. (M.) لَا وَالَّذِى شَقَّ الرِّجَالَ لِلْخَيْلِ وَالجِبَالَ لِلسُّيُولِ — [app. meaning † *No, by Him who clave men for the riding upon horses, and the mountains for the flowing of the torrent,*] is a saying mentioned by IAạr, but not expl. by him. (M. [It is there added, وَعِنْدِى أَنَّهُ جَعَلَ الرِّجَالَ وَالجِبَالَ جُمْلَةً وَاحِدَةً ثُمَّ خَرَقَهَا فَجَعَلَ الرِّجَالَ لِلْخَيْلِ وَالجِبَالَ لِلسُّيُولِ: an expression of opinion which is, to me, by no means clear, though reconcilable with my rendering.]) — المَالُ بَيْنَنَا شَقَّ الأُبْلُمَةِ and الأَبْلُمَةِ [*The property is divided between us as in the dividing of the* ابلمة; or *the cattle are divided* &c.;] means we are equal in respect of the property, or cattle: for the ابلمة means the [kind of leaf called] خُوصَة, which, when it is split lengthwise, splits in halves: (M:) or, accord. to Aboo-Ziyád, the ابلمة is a herb, or leguminous plant, (بَقْلَةٌ,) to which there come forth pods, like [those of] the bean; and when you split them lengthwise, they split in halves, equally, from the first part to the last thereof: شَقَّ is in the accus. case as an inf. n., مَشْقُوقٌ being understood. (Ḥar p. 639.) [See also شِقٌّ.] — شَقَّ, (Ṣ, M, Ḳ,) aor. ـُ, inf. n. شُقُوقٌ, (M,) said of the canine tooth of a camel, ‡ *It* [*clave the gum and*] *came forth:* (Ṣ, M, Ḳ, TA:) [said to be] a dial. var. of شَقَأَ: (Ṣ:) and said of the canine tooth of a child, (M, TA,) in like manner, (TA,) meaning *it made its first appearance:* (M:) and said also of a plant, [as meaning *it came forth*] *on the ground's first cleaving open from it.* (M, TA.) — Also, aor. ـُ, inf. n. شَقٌّ, said of the dawn, ‡ *It rose;* as though it clave the place of its rising and came forth therefrom. (TA.) — Also, aor. ـُ, (TA,) inf. n. شَقٌّ, said of lightning, ‡ *It* [*clave the clouds, and*] *extended high, into the midst of the sky, without going to the right and left:* (Ḳ, TA:) so says A'Obeyd: (TA: [see شَقِيقٌ:]) and ↓ انشقّ and ↓ تشقّق, said of lightning, signify إِنْعَقَّ [probably meaning the same; (see عَقِيقَةٌ;) or, as expl. in the Ṣ and also in the O, in art. عق, *it was,* or *became, in a state of commotion,* (تَضَرَّبَ,) *in the clouds*]: (M, TA:) or ↓ تشقّق said of lightning means *it spread wide and long.* (JK.) — شَقَّ السَّبِيلَ (Ḳ in art. عبر) † *He passed along the way;* as though he cut it, or furrowed it. (TḲ in that art.) And شَقَّ النَّهْرَ † *He crossed the river by swimming.* (TA in art. قطع.) — شَقَّ المَآءَ † *He opened a way, passage, vent,* or *channel, for the water to flow forth;* syn. بَجَسَهُ. (A and Ḳ in art. بجس.) — شَقَّ أَمْرَهُ, aor. ـُ, inf. n. شَقٌّ, † *He,* or *it, discomposed, deranged,* or *disordered, so that it became incongruous,* or *inconsistent, his affair,* or *state of affairs.* (M, TA.) [A phrase similar to شَقَّ العَصَا, mentioned above. And so, app., what next follows.] — شَقَّ الكَلَامَ, i. q. قَدَّهُ [also expl. as *syn. with* قَطَعَهُ, which generally means † *He cut short,* or *broke off, the speech;* or *ceased from speaking;* but sometimes, and perhaps in this case, *he articulated speech,* or *the speech:* compare a signification of 2.]. (M and L in art. قد.) — See also 8. — شَقَّ بَصَرُ المَيِّتِ i. q. شَخَصَ [i. e. † *The eye,* or *eyes, of the dying man became fixedly open;* or *his eyelids became raised upwards, and he looked intently, and became disquieted,* or *disturbed*]: (M, TA:) and (TA) *the dying man looked at a thing, his sight not recoiling to him:* (Ṣ, Ḳ, TA:) said of him to whom death is present: (Ṣ, TA:) or [simply] *the eyes of the dying man became open:* (TA:) one should not say شَقَّ المَيِّتُ بَصَرَهُ: (Ṣ, M, Ḳ:) and شُقَّ, with ḍamm to the ش, is not approved. (IAth, TA.) — شَقَّ عَلَيْهِ, (M, Ḳ, in the Ṣ عَلَىَّ, and in the Mṣb عَلَيْنَا,) aor. ـُ, (Ṣ, M, Mṣb,) inf. n. شَقٌّ (Ṣ, M, Ḳ) and مَشَقَّةٌ, (Ṣ, Ḳ,) [or the latter is a simple subst., as seems to be indicated in the M and Mṣb,] † *It* (a thing, Ṣ, or an affair, or event, M, Mṣb, Ḳ) *affected him severely; had a severe effect upon him; distressed, afflicted, troubled, molested, inconvenienced, fatigued,* or *wearied, him:* (M:) *it was difficult, hard, distressing, grievous,* or *severe, to him;* (Ḳ, TA;) and *onerous, burdensome, oppressive,* or *troublesome, to him.* (TA.) And شَقَّ عَلَيْهِ, [inf. n., app., شَقٌّ only,] † *He caused him to fall into a difficult, hard, distressing, grievous,* or *severe, case:* (Ḳ, TA:) *imposed upon him that which was onerous, burdensome, oppressive,* or *troublesome.* (TA.) And شَقَّتِ الشُّقَّةُ † *The journey was* [*difficult, hard,* or] *far-extending.* (Mṣb.) — شَقَّ, said of the solid hoof, and of the pastern of a horse or the like, *It was,* or *became, affected with the disease termed* شُقَاق, *occasioning cracks.* (M, TA.)

2: see 1, first sentence. — شقّق الكَلَامَ, (Ṣ, Ḳ, TA,) inf. n. تَشْقِيقٌ, (TA,) ‡ *He uttered,* or *pronounced, speech,* or *the speech, in the best manner:* (Ṣ, Ḳ, TA:) and *he sought with repeated efforts, in speaking, to utter,* or *pronounce, the speech in the best manner.* (TA.)

3. شَاقَّهُ, (M, Mgh, Mṣb,) inf. n. مُشَاقَّةٌ (Ṣ, M, Mgh, Mṣb, Ḳ) and شِقَاقٌ, (Ṣ, M, Mṣb, Ḳ,) the latter inf. n. occurring in the Ḳur ii. 131 and iv. 39 [&c.], (TA,) † *He acted with him contrariously,* or *adversely,* (Ṣ,* M, Mgh, Mṣb, Ḳ,) *and inimically;* (Ḳ;) properly, *each of them doing to the other that which was distressing, grievous,* or *troublesome, so that each of them was in a* شِقّ [or *side*] *other than that of his fellow;* (Mṣb;) or *as though he became in a* شِقّ, i. e. *side, in respect of him:* (Mgh:) accord. to Er-Rághib, the inf. n. signifies the *being in a* شِقّ [or *side*] *other than that of one's fellow:* or it is from شَقُّ العَصَا بَيْنَكَ وَبَيْنَ صَاحِبِكَ [meaning "the effecting disunion and dissension between thee and thy fellow"], so that it is tropical: (TA:) or the primary meaning of الشِّقَاقُ is *the being* [*mutually*] *remote.* (Ḥam p. 326.) See also 1, in the first quarter of the paragraph.

4. اشقّ النَّخْلُ *The palm-trees put forth their* شَوَاقّ, pl. of شَاقَّةٌ [q. v.]: mentioned by Th, on the authority of some one or more of the Benoo-Suwáäh. (M.)

5. تشقّق quasi-pass. of 2: (Ṣ, M, Ḳ:) said of firewood (Ṣ, Ḳ) &c. (Ṣ) [as meaning *It became cloven in pieces*]. See 7, in two places. — Said of lightning: see 1, in two places, in the latter half of the paragraph. — Said of a horse, ‡ *He was,* or *became, lean,* or *light of flesh; slender and lean;* or *lean, and lank in the belly.* (A'Obeyd, TA.)

6. تَشَاقَّا, said of two adversaries, or litigants, as also ↓ اشْتَقَّا, *They wrangled, quarrelled,* or *contended, each with the other,* (M, TA,) *and took to the right and left in contention;* (TA;) فِى الشَّىْءِ [*in respect of the thing*]. (M.)

7. انشقّ quasi-pass. of شَقَّهُ as expl. in the first sentence of this art.: [i. e. it signifies *It became divided lengthwise, cloven, split, riven* or *rifted, slit, rent, ripped, torn, broken,* or *burst, asunder;* or *it became cracked, chapped, incided* or *incised, gashed, slashed, furrowed,* or *trenched;* or *cloven,* or *split, &c.,* or *cut, open:* or *it clave, split, &c.:*] (Ṣ, M:) and in like manner, ↓ تشقّق is quasi-pass. of شَقَّقَهُ: [i. e. it signifies *it became cloven* or *split* &c., or *it clave* or *split* &c., *much,* or *in pieces,* or *in several* or *many places:*] (M:) or the former signifies [sometimes] *it opened so as to have in it an interstice.* (Mṣb.) وَانْشَقَّ القَمَرُ, in the Ḳur liv. 1, means *And the moon hath been cloven* (Bḍ, Jel) *in twain,* (Jel,) as a sign to the

Prophet: (Bḍ, Jel:) or *shall be cloven* on the day of resurrection: but the former is confirmed by another reading, وَقَدِ ٱنْشَقَّ ٱلْقَمَرُ: (Bḍ:) or, accord. to Er-Rághib, the meaning is, † *the case hath become manifest.* (TA.) One says, انشقّ الشَّىْءُ بِنِصْفَيْنِ [*The thing became cloven*, &c., *in halves*]. (Ṣ.) [And انشقّ مِنْهُ *It became cloven*, &c., *from it:* and *it branched off from it;* as a river from another river, and the like. And انشقّ عَنْهُ *It clave asunder from over it, so as to disclose it:* see also 8.] — [Hence,] انشقّ فُلَانٌ مِنَ الغَضَبِ † *Such a one was as though his interior were filled with anger so that he split.* (TA.) — And انْشَقَّتِ العَصَا † *The affair,* or *state of affairs, became discomposed, deranged,* or *disordered:* (Ṣ, Ḳ, TA:) and انشقّت العَصَا بِالبَيْنِ, and ↓ تشقّقت, (Lth, M, TA,) † *the affair,* or *state of affairs, became discomposed, deranged,* or *disorganized, by separation:* (Lth, TA:) and انشقّ الأَمْرُ † *the affair,* or *state of affairs, became discomposed, deranged,* or *disorganized, being incongruous,* or *inconsistent.* (M, TA.) And انشقّت عَصَا الطَّاعَةِ † [*The compact of allegiance,* or *obedience, became broken*]. (M.) — انشقّ said of lightning: see 1, in the latter half of the paragraph.

8. اِشْتِقَاقٌ signifies The *taking the* شِقّ of a thing, (Ṣ, Ḳ,) i. e. the *half* thereof. (Ṣ.) One says, اشتقّ الشَّىْءَ *He took the* شِقّ [or *half*] *of the thing.* (TḲ.) — And † The *taking* [or *deriving*] *a word* from a word, (Ṣ, Ḳ,) *with the condition of reciprocal relation in meaning and* [*radical*] *composition, and of reciprocal difference in form:* [and it is of three kinds:] الاِشْتِقَاقُ الصَّغِيرُ is *that derivation in which there is a reciprocal relation between the two words in the letters and in the order* [*thereof*]; *as in* ضَرَبَ *from* الضَّرْبُ: الاشتقاق الكَبِيرُ is *that in which there is a reciprocal relation between the two words as to the letter and the meaning, exclusively of the order; as in* جَبَذَ *from* الجَذْبُ: الاشتقاق الأَكْبَرُ is *that in which there is a reciprocal relation between the two words in the place* [or *places*] *of utterance; as in* نَعَقَ *from* النَّهْقُ. (KT.) [You say, اشتقّ حَرْفًا or كَلِمَةً or لَفْظًا, and اِسْمًا, *He derived a word,* and *a name,* مِنْ آخَرَ *from another;* and ↓ شَقَّهُ sometimes signifies the same, as is shown by a citation voce زجر.] — [And, as *syn.* with اِخْتِرَاعٌ, (see 8 in art. خرع,)] The *constructing,* or *founding,* (بُنْيَانٌ,) of a thing *of,* or *from, what is originated without premeditation.* (M.) — And ‡ The *taking to the right and left,* (Ṣ, Ḳ, TA,) *not pursuing the right,* or *direct, course,* (Ṣ, TA,) in speech, and in contention, or disputation, or litigation: (Ṣ, Ḳ, TA:) or اِشْتِقَاقُ الكَلَامِ signifies *the taking to the right and left in speech:* (so in a copy of the M: [but I think that the right reading is الاِشْتِقَاقُ فِى الكَلَامِ, agreeably with what here follows:]) you say, اشتقّ فِى الكَلَامِ, and فِى الخُصُومَةِ. (TḲ.) See also 6. And [in like manner] one says of a horse, اشتقّ فِى عَدْوِهِ † *He went to the right and left in his running.* (M. [See also ↓ أَشَقّ.]) — اشتقّ الطَّرِيقُ فِى الفَلَاةِ ‡ *The road went* [or *branched off*] *into the desert.* (TA. [See also 7.])

10. استشقّ بِالجُوَالِقِ *He turned the sack upon one of his two sides* (عَلَى أَحَدِ شِقَّيْهِ), *in order to pass through a door.* (TA.) — [استشقّ, as stated by Freytag, is expl. by Jac. Schultens, but on what authority is not said, as signifying "*Prodiit, manifestus evasit.*"]

R. Q. 1. شَقْشَقَ, (JK, Ṣ, Ḳ,) inf. n. شَقْشَقَةٌ, (Ṣ,) said of a stallion [camel], *He brayed* [*in his* شِقْشِقَة, or *faucial bag*]. (JK, Ṣ, Ḳ.) [It is said that] the primary meaning of شَقْشَقَةٌ is *Loudness of voice;* or the *being loud in voice.* (JK.) — And said of a sparrow, *It uttered a cry:* (Ḳ, TA:) or one says of a sparrow, يُشَقْشِقُ فِى صَوْتِهِ [app. meaning *It makes a loud twittering in its cry*]. (Ṣ.)

شَقٌّ sing. of شُقُوقٌ; (Ṣ, Mgh, Mṣb, Ḳ;) originally an inf. n.; (Ṣ, Mṣb;) *An opening forming an interstice* in a thing: (Mṣb:) or *a fissure, cleft, chink, split, slit, rent, crack,* or *the like,* syn. صَدْعٌ, in wood or a stick, or in a wall, or in a glass vessel [&c.]: (T, TA:) [or] *a place that is* مَشْقُوق [i. e. *cloven* or *cleft, split,* &c.: (see 1, first sentence: and see also مَشَقّ:) and often signifying *an incision, a gash,* or *a furrow,* or *trench*]: (M, Ḳ:) as though an inf. n. used as a subst. in this sense: pl. as above, شُقُوقٌ: (M:) it differs from شُقَاقٌ, (Ṣ, Mgh,) by having a general signification: (Mgh:) accord. to Yaạḳoob, one says, بِيَدِ فُلَانٍ شُقُوقٌ (Ṣ, Mgh) and بِرِجْلِهِ (Ṣ) [i. e. *In the hand,* or *arm, of such a one are cracks,* or *the like,* and *in his foot,* or *leg*]: but [it is asserted that in this case] one should not say شُقَاقٌ: (Ṣ, Mgh: [see, however, this word:]) and hence, شَقُّ القَبْرِ *The trench,* or *oblong excavation, in the middle of the grave:* and accord. to Aṣ, شُقُوقٌ signifies صُدُوعٌ [i. e. *fissures,* &c.,] in mountains, and in the earth, or ground. (Mgh.) — The *rima vulvæ* of a woman; i. e. the *gap* [or *chink*] *between the two edges,* or *borders, of the labia majora of her vulva:* as also ↓ مَشَقٌّ. (M, Ḳ.) — And ‡ The *daybreak.* (Ṣ, Ḳ, TA.) = See also the next paragraph, first and fifth sentences. = And see the last two sentences of the same paragraph.

شِقٌّ The *half* (Ṣ, Mgh, Mṣb, Ḳ) of a thing (Ṣ, Mṣb, Ḳ) of any kind; as also ↓ شَقٌّ: (Ḳ:) or the *half* of a thing when it is cloven, or split, or divided lengthwise; (M;) as also ↓ شِقَّةٌ. (AḤn, Ṣ,* M, Ḳ.) One says, أَخَذْتُ شِقَّ الشَّاةِ and ↓ شِقَّةَ الشَّاةِ *I took the half of the sheep or goat:* (Ṣ, TA:) the vulgar pronounce the ش with fet-ḥ. (TA.) And خُذْ هٰذَا الشِّقَّ ↓ شِقَّةَ *Take thou this* [i. e. *half*] *of the sheep* or *goat.* (TA.) Hence the trad., تَصَدَّقُوا وَلَوْ بِشِقِّ تَمْرَةٍ i. e. [*Give ye alms though* it be but] *the half of a date;* meaning deem not anything little that is given as alms. (TA.) And المَالُ بَيْنِى وَبَيْنَكَ شِقَّ الشَّعَرَةِ and ↓ شَقَّ الشَّعَرَةِ, (O, Ḳ,* [in the CḲ and in my MS. copy of the Ḳ شِقّ, but the former reading appears to be the right, شَقّ being an inf. n. as in a similar saying in the former half of the first paragraph of this art., and شِقّ being a subst. used as an inf. n. or for كَشِقّ,]) meaning [*The property is between us*] *two halves, equal* [*in division*]. (Ḳ.) — [Hence,] *A certain kind of the jinn,* or *genii;* (Ibn-'Abbád, O, Ḳ;) *a species of diabolical beings having the form of the half of a human being.* (Ḳzw in his Descr. of the Jinn.) — The *lateral half,* or *half and side;* as when one says that a person paralyzed has a شِقّ inclining; and as when one speaks of the شِقّ of a مَحْمِل [meaning *either of the two dorsers,* or *panniers,* or *oblong chests, which are borne, one on either side, by a camel, and which, with a small tent over them, compose a* مَحْمِل: see this last word, and مَحَارَةٌ]. (Mgh.) — The *side* of the body; as when one says of a person that his left شِقّ was grazed, or abraded. (Mgh.) [Hence,] one says of a horse, يَمِيلُ عَلَى أَحَدِ شِقَّيْهِ [*He inclines,* or *leans, upon one of his two sides*]. (O.) [And مَشَى عَلَى شِقٍّ and فِى شِقٍّ *He went,* or *walked, inclining upon one side.*] — The *side,* or *lateral part,* (Lth, Mṣb, Ḳ, TA,) of a thing; the two sides of a thing being called شِقَّاهُ: (Lth, TA:) or, as some say, (TA,) the *side of a mountain.* (Ṣ, TA.) [Hence,] one says, فُلَانٌ مِنْ شِقِّ العَشِيرَةِ لَا مِنْ صَمِيمِهَا † [*Such a one is of the collateral class of the kinsfolk,* or *tribe, not of the main stock thereof*]. (Mgh in art. عرض.) — *I. q.* ↓ شَقِيقٌ; (Ṣ, Mṣb, Ḳ;) [which primarily signifies The *cloven-off half* of a thing; i. e.,] when a thing is cloven in halves, each of the halves is called the شَقِيق of the other. (Ṣ, Ḳ.) — [And hence, † The *counterpart* of a person or thing: and this appears to be meant by J, and accord. to SM in the Ḳ, where it is said that شِقّ is syn. with ↓ شَقِيق; for they add immediately after:] one says هُوَ أَخِى وَشِقُّ نَفْسِى ‡ [*He is my brother, and the counterpart of myself*]; (Ṣ, TA;) as though he were cloven from me, because of the resemblance of each of us to the other. (TA.) One says also, هٰذَا ↓ شَقِيقُهُ, meaning † *This is the like of him,* or *it.* (TA.) And [hence] it is said in a trad., النِّسَآءُ شَقَائِقُ الرِّجَالِ, [in which شَقَائِق is the pl. of ↓ شَقِيق as fem., or of شَقِيقَةٌ in the same sense,] meaning † *Women are the likes of men* in natural dispositions; as though they were cloven from them; or because Eve was created from Adam. (TA.) — And ‡ A man's *brother;* (M;) and so ↓ شَقِيقٌ; (Ṣ, M, O, Ḳ, TA;) meaning *a brother by the father and mother;* (TA;) from شَقِيق as meaning "either half of a thing that is cloven in halves;" (Ṣ, TA;) or as though the relationship of one were cloven from that of the other: (IDrd, O, Ḳ:) pl. of the latter أَشِقَّآءُ. (M, Mṣb.) — And a name for *A thing at which one looks:* (Lth, O, Ḳ:) [but this is app. taken from the following saying of Lth, in which I think الشَّقُّ is a mistranscription for الشِّقُّ, meaning "the crack," &c.:] الشَّقُّ is the inf. n. of شَقَقْتُ, and الشِّقُّ is a name for that at which one looks [i. e. for the visible effect of the act signified by the verb], and the pl. is الشُّقُوقُ [which is well known as the pl. of الشَّقُّ]. (JK.) ═ Also *i. q.* ↓ مَشَقَّةٌ (Ṣ, M, O, Mṣb, Ḳ) i. e. *Difficulty, hardship, distress, affliction, trouble, inconvenience, fatigue,* or *weariness;* (M, TA;) and *languor,* or *lack of power, that overtakes the mind and the body;* (Er-Rághib, TA;) and so ↓ شَقٌّ; (IJ, Ṣ, M, O, Ḳ;) thus it is sometimes pronounced with fet-ḥ; mentioned by A'Obeyd; (Ṣ;) and by AZ; (M;) or this is an inf. n., and شِقٌّ is the subst.; (O, Ḳ;) and ↓ شُقَّةٌ and ↓ شِقَّةٌ also signify the same as مَشَقَّةٌ, (Ḳ,) or *such as overtakes a man in consequence of travel;* (TA;) and the pls. of these two are شُقَقٌ, (Ḳ, TA,) mentioned by Fr, (TA,) and شِقَقٌ, (Ḳ, TA,) mentioned on the authority of some one or more of [the tribe of] Ḳeys: (TA:) the pl. of ↓ مَشَقَّةٌ is مَشَاقُّ and مَشَقَّاتٌ. (TA.) Hence, in the Ḳur [xvi. 7], لَمْ تَكُونُوا بَالِغِيهِ إِلَّا بِشِقِّ ٱلْأَنْفُسِ [*Which ye would not reach save with difficulty,* or *distress, &c., of the souls*]; where some read ↓ بِشَقِّ. (Ṣ,* TA.)

شُقَّةٌ primarily signifies The *half of a garment* [*consisting of two oblong pieces sewed together, side by side*]: then it was applied to [*such*] *a garment as it is* [*when complete:* in both of these senses it is used in the present day]: (Er-Rághib, TA:) or *a piece* (قِطْعَة) *of a garment:* (Mgh:) or the شُقَّة of ثِيَاب [thus, and thus only, in the Ṣ, meaning of garments and of cloths, for it is of both,] is *an oblong piece;* syn. سَبِيبَةٌ مُسْتَطِيلَةٌ: (M, Ḳ:) [it is often applied to *an oblong piece of cloth of those pieces of which a tent is composed:*] pl. شُقَقٌ and شِقَاقٌ. (M, Mgh, TA.) One says, فُلَانٌ يَبِيعُ شِقَاقَ الكَتَّانِ [*Such a one sells pieces,* or *oblong pieces, &c., of linen*]. (Mgh.) — Also *A piece of a* مَزَادَة [q. v.]. (B, TA in art. بصر.) — And *A piece,* or *portion,* [or *tract,*] of Hell; likewise pronounced ↓ شِقَّةٌ. (Ḥam p. 816.) — And *A far journey;* as also ↓ شِقَّةٌ, (Ṣ, M, Ḳ,) sometimes thus pronounced with kesr: (Ṣ:) *a far, long journey: a far-extending space:* (TA:) or *a road difficult to him who travels it:* (Mgh:) or [simply] *a journey:* and *i. q.* ثنيا [so in my copy of the Mṣb, app. a mistranscription for ثَنِيَّة, i. e. *a mountain-road,* &c.]: pl. شُقَقٌ. (Mṣb.) — And *A part, region, quarter,* or *tract,* (Ibn-'Arafeh, Er-Rághib, Ḳ, TA,) *towards which one draws near,* (Ibn-'Arafeh, TA,) or *towards which the traveller directs himself,* (Ḳ, TA,) [like شُقَّةٌ,] or *in the reaching of which one is overtaken by difficulty,* or *distress;* (Er-Rághib, TA;) And ↓ شِقَّةٌ signifies the same. (Ḳ.) — And *Distance;* and so ↓ شِقَّةٌ. (Ḳ.) — See also شِقٌّ, last sentence but one.

شِقَّةٌ *A splinter* (Ṣ, Ḳ) *that splits off,* (Ṣ,) or *a piece* (M, Mgh, TA) *split off,* (M, TA,) of a plank, (Ṣ, M, Ḳ, TA,) or of wood, (TA,) or of a piece of wood, (Ṣ, Mgh,) or other thing: (M, TA:) *a piece split,* or *divided, lengthwise,* of a staff, or stick, and of a garment, or piece of cloth, &c.: (IDrd, O, Ḳ:) and *a piece split* (Ḳ, TA) from anything; *such as the half:* (TA:) pl. شِقَقٌ. (O, TA.) One says of him who is angry, اِحْتَدَّ فَطَارَتْ مِنْهُ شِقَّةٌ فِى الأَرْضِ وَشِقَّةٌ فِى السَّمَآءِ † [*He became excited by sharpness of temper,* or *angriness, and* he was as though *a bit flew from him upon the ground, and a bit into the sky*]. (Ṣ,* M, TA: in the Ṣ, فى الارض &c. is omitted.) See also شِقٌّ, first three sentences. — See also شُقَّةٌ, in four places. — And see شِقٌّ, again, last sentence but one.

شَقَقٌ The *quality,* in a horse, (M, Ḳ,) and in a man, (M,) *denoted by the epithet* أَشَقُّ [q. v.]. (M, Ḳ.)

شُقَقَةٌ [a pl. of which the sing. is not mentioned] *Enemies.* (TA.)

شُقَاقٌ *A cracking in several places,* (تَشَقُّق, Ṣ, Ḳ,) or *cracks,* (Mgh,) or *a certain disease occasioning cracks,* (M,) *in the pasterns of horses* or *the like,* (Ṣ, M, Mgh, Ḳ,) *and in their hoofs,* (M, Mgh,) *and sometimes rising to their shanks:* so says Yaḳoob: (Ṣ:) and, accord. to Lth, (Mgh,) and Az, (TA,) *a cracking in several places* (تَشَقُّق) *of the skin, from cold or some other cause, in the hands* or *arms, and the face:* (Mgh, TA:) or it signifies also *any crack,* or *slit, in the skin, from disease:* (M, TA:) Aṣ says that it is *in the hand* or *arm, and the foot* or *leg, of a human being,* and *in the fore leg and hind leg of an animal:* (Mgh, TA:) but this is inconsistent with what is said by Yaḳoob [as stated voce شِقٌّ, first sentence]. (Mgh.) See also أَسْعَدُ: and شَرَجٌ.

شَقِيقٌ: see شِقٌّ, in five places. — شَقِيقُ البَرْقِ [so in a copy of the M, but the right reading may be شَقِيقَةُ البَرْقِ, which occurs in the next sentence of the M,] *i. q.* عَقِيقَتُهُ [expl. in the Ṣ, in art. خفو, as meaning *Lightning that cleaves the clouds, and extends high, into the midst of the sky, without going to the right and left:* but see شَقِيقَةٌ]. (M.) ═ Also *A calf that has become firm,* or *strong:* (O, Ḳ:) and applied likewise to † *a man* [*that has become so;* by way of comparison]: (O:) or *a bull such as is termed* جَذَعٌ [i. e. *in his second,* or *third, year*]. (JK.)

شَقْوَقَةٌ *A certain bird;* also called ↓ شُقَيْقَةٌ: (M, Ḳ:) and ↓ شُقَيْقَةٌ is the dim. thereof: (Ḳ:) AḤát says, the ↓ شَقْوَقَة is *a very little thing, grayish* (زُرَيْقَاء), *of the colour of ashes; ten and fifteen of what are thus called congregate; and I think it to be the* ↓ شُقَيْقَة, *which is a* دُخَّلَة *of the* دُخَّل [q. v.]; *it is somewhat dusky; and its form is the form of these, but it is smaller than they:* it is called ↓ شُقَيْقَة because of its smallness: IDrd, in the class of فُعَيْعِل, mentions ↓ الشُّقَيْق as signifying *a certain species of birds* [app. as a coll. gen. n., of which the n. un. is with ة]. (O, TA.)

شَقِيقَةٌ [accord. to Golius, *A fissure;* as from the KL; but not so expl. in my copy of that work. —] *An intervening space* or *tract between two elongated,* or *extended, tracts of sand,* (Ṣ, M,* O, Ḳ,* [in the last of which الجَبَلَيْنِ is erroneously put for الحَبْلَيْنِ,]) thus expl. to AḤn by an Arab of the desert, (TA,) *producing herbage:* (Ṣ, M, O, Ḳ:) or *a rugged tract between two elongated,* or *extended, tracts of sand, producing good herbage;* (M, TA;) so in the T, as expl. to its author by an Arab of the desert: (TA:) pl. شَقَائِقُ, (T, Ṣ, O, Ḳ, TA,) expl. by some as meaning *sands* themselves: (TA:) or *a great piece of sand:* or *a piece of sand between two pieces thereof.* (Ḥam p. 282.) — [In the A and TA voce قدّ, it is used as meaning *A slice cut off* of a melon &c.] ═ *A rain,* (M,) or *a violent rain, consisting of large drops,* (Ḳ, TA,) *wide in extent:* so called because the clouds cleave asunder from it: (M, Ḳ, TA:) pl. as above. (TA.) — The pl., شَقَائِقُ, is expl. by Az as signifying *Clouds that have cloven asunder with copious rains.* (O, TA.) — شَقِيقَةُ بَرْقٍ, (O, Ḳ,) and عَقِيقَتُهُ, both as expl. by Aboo-Sa'eed, (O,) *A flash of lightning that has spread* (O, Ḳ) *in the horizon,* (O,) or *from the horizon:* (Ḳ: [but see شَقِيقٌ:]) or شَقِيقَةُ البَرْقِ signifies *a flash of lightning that has spread in the breadth of the clouds, and filled the sky:* pl. as above. (Ḥam p. 557.) ═ *A headache,* (JK, T, TA,) or *a pain,* (Ṣ, O, Ḳ,) or *a certain disease,* (M,) *in the half of the head,* (JK, T, Ṣ, M, O, Ḳ,) [i. e. *hemicrania,*] and *of the face:* (JK, T, Ṣ, O, Ḳ:) or, accord. to IAth, *a sort of headache in the fore part of the head and towards the sides thereof.* (TA.) ═ شَقَائِقُ النُّعْمَانِ, used alike as sing. and pl., (Ṣ, O, Ḳ,) having no proper sing., (Mṣb,) or its sing. is شَقِيقَةٌ; (M, O, Mṣb;) [The *red,* or *blood-coloured, anemone;*] *a certain plant;* (M;) *a certain red flower;* (Lth, O;) *well known;* (Ṣ, Ḳ;) the شَقِرُ; (Mṣb;) or, as AḤn says, on the authority of AA and Aboo-Naṣr and others, it is the شَقِرَة [n. un. of شَقِر]; and the sing. of شقائق is شَقِيقَةٌ: (O, TA:) it is called شقائق النعمان because of its redness, as being likened to the شَقِيقَة of lightning: (M, Ḳ:) or from النُّعْمَان as meaning "blood," as resembling blood in colour; (Mṣb, TA;) so that it signifies "pieces of blood:" (TA:) or in relation to En-Noạmán Ibn-El-Mundhir, because he prohibited to the public a piece of land in which it abounded: (Ṣ, Ḳ, TA:) or because he alighted upon شَقَائِق of sand that had produced red شَقِر, and he deemed them beautiful, and commanded that they should be prohibited to the public; so the شَقِر were called the شقائق of En-Noạmán, by the name of the place of their growth. (TA.) ═ See also شَقْوَقَة.

شُقَيْقٌ, and with ة: see شَقْوَقَة, in four places.

شَقَّاقٌ, meaning One *who glories,* or *boasts, vainly, and praises himself for that which is not in him,* is not of the [classical] language of the Arabs. (L, TA.)

شَقِّىٌّ A horse *with which his rider ex-*

periences difficulty in striving to master him. (JK.)

شِقَّةٌ *A certain mode of* جِمَاع, (K, TA,) *in which the woman lies upon her* شِقّ [or *side*]. (TA.)

شِقْشِقَةٌ [The *bursa faucium*, or *faucial bag, which is placed behind the palate of the he-camel, and which, when excited, he inflates, and blows out from the side of his mouth;*] *a thing resembling the lungs, or lights, which the he-camel protrudes from his mouth when he is excited by lust;* (S, O, K;) *a skin in the fauces of the Arabian camel, which he inflates with wind, and in which he brays; whereupon it appears from the side of his mouth;* so says En-Nadr; and he adds that *it does not pertain to any but the Arabian camel,* [as is said in the M, and] as Hr says; but this requires consideration; (TA;) [also expl. as] the لَهَاة [q. v.] *of the he-camel,* (M, and Har p. 16,) *which he protrudes from his mouth when he brays:* (Har ubi suprà:) pl. شَقَاشِق. (TA.) — To this is likened the tongue of the chaste, or eloquent, and able speaker; himself being likened to the braying stallion-camel: (O:) and hence they say of an orator, or a preacher, that he is ذُو شِقْشِقَةٍ: (S:) one says likewise of an orator, or a preacher, that is loud in voice and skilful in speech, هُوَ أَهْرَتُ الشِّقْشِقَةِ [lit. *He is wide,* or *ample, in respect of the* شقشقة]: (TA:) and one says, هَدَرَتْ شِقْشِقَتُهُ † [meaning *His utterance was sonorous and fluent*]. (A and TA in art. هدر.) Orators, or preachers, are also termed شَقَاشِق [for ذَوُو شَقَاشِق]: and one says, فُلَانٌ شِقْشِقَةُ قَوْمِهِ, meaning † *Such a one is the noble, and the chaste in speech,* or *eloquent, of his people.* (M.) And in a trad. of 'Omar, (M, O, TA,) accord. to A'Obeyd and others, or of 'Alee accord. to Hr, (TA,) شَقَاشِق are assigned to the Devil, in his saying, إِنَّ كَثِيرًا مِنَ الخُطَبِ مِنْ شَقَاشِقِ الشَّيْطَانِ [lit. *Verily many of the orations,* or *harangues, are from the* شقاشق *of the Devil*]; because of the lying introduced into them. (M, O,* TA.*)

الخُطْبَةُ الشِّقْشِقِيَّةُ an appellation applied to a certain خُطْبَة [i. e. oration, or harangue, or sermon,] of 'Alee, because of his saying to Ibn-'Abbás, (O, K,) on his having cut short his speech, (O,) in reply to a remark of the latter person upon his not having continued his speech uninterruptedly, تِلْكَ شِقْشِقَةٌ هَدَرَتْ ثُمَّ قَرَّتْ [*That was a* شقشقة *that uttered a braying, then became still*]. (O, K.)

شَاقٌّ *Difficult, hard, distressing, grievous, afflicting, troubling, molesting, fatiguing,* or *wearying.* (KL.) One says أَمْرٌ شَاقٌّ [*An affair,* or *event, that is difficult,* &c.]; from شَقَّ عَلَيْنَا الأَمْرُ. (Msb.) And شُقَّةٌ شَاقَّةٌ (S, Msb) *A long journey* [*that is difficult,* &c.]. (Msb.)

شَاقَّةٌ The *spadix of a palm-tree, that has become a span in length;* so called because it cleaves the envelope: pl. شَوَاقّ. (M.)

أَشَقُّ, (S, M, O, K,) fem. شَقَّاء, and pl. شُقٌّ, (K,) applied to a horse, *Wide between the hind legs:* (IAar, Th, T, O,* K,* TA:) and the fem. signifies *wide in the* أَرْفَاغ [or *groins,* or *similar parts*]; (TA;) and is applied to a mare: (IDrd, O, TA:) and *wide in the vulva;* (IAar, O, K;) applied in this sense to a woman. (IAar, O, TA.) And أَشَقُّ المَنْخِرَيْنِ, applied to a horse, *Wide in the nostrils.* (Lth, O, TA.) — Also, (O, K,) *Tall,* or *long;* (T, S, M, O, K;) applied to a horse; (T, S, M, K;) thus expl. by As; (T, TA;) and so too applied to a man: (M, TA:) and the fem., as above, applied to a mare. (S.) — And, applied to a horse, *That goes to the right and left in his running,* (JK,* O, K, TA, [in the CK, يَسْبِقُ is erroneously put for يَشِقُّ, and in like manner in my MS. copy of the K, with the additional mistranscription of مِن عَدْوِهِ for فِى عَدْوِهِ,]) *as though* (O, TA) *leaning upon one of his sides:* (JK, O, TA:) so says Lth; and he cites as an ex.,

* وَتَبَازَيْتُ كَمَا يَمْشِى الأَشَقّ *

[as though meaning *And I moved my posteriors in walking, like as goes the horse that inclines to the right and left in his running:* but this may be rendered *and I stepped wide, like as does the tall,* or *long-bodied, horse*]. (O, TA.)

مَشَقٌّ [properly *A place of cleaving, splitting,* &c.: and hence *a fissure, cleft,* &c., like شَقٌّ: pl. مَشَاقّ]: see شَقٌّ. — مَشَقُّ العَيْنِ [*The slit of the eye*]. (TA in art. حوص.)

مَشَقَّةٌ [said in the S and K to be an inf. n. of شَقَّ trans. by means of عَلَى]: see شِقٌّ, in the last quarter of the paragraph, in two places.

شقأ

1. شَقَأَ, (S, K,) aor. ـَ, (K,) inf. n. شَقْءٌ and شُقُوءٌ, said of the نَاب [or tush] (S, K) of a camel, (S,) *It grew forth;* (S, K;) *it appeared;* (TA;) as also شَكَأَ. (K in art. شكأ.) [See also شَقَّ.] شَاقِى, with the ء softened [or changed into ى], occurs in a verse of Dhu-r-Rummeh [for the part. n. شَاقِئ]. (TA.) — شَقَأَ رَأْسَهُ *He divided his head;* syn. فَرَقَهُ: [meaning, *his hair:*] or *he separated it* (فَرَّقَهُ) [i. e. *his hair*] *with the* مِشْقَأ [or *comb*]: (K:) or شَقَأَ شَعَرَهُ بِالمُشْطِ, inf. n. شَقْءٌ, *he separated his hair with the comb.* (AZ, S.) — And شَقَأَهُ, (S, K,) inf. n. شَقْءٌ, (S,) *He hit his* مَشْقَأ, i. e. *the place of the parting of the hair of his head,* (S, K,) with a staff, or stick. (S.)

إِبِلٌ شُوَيْكِئَةٌ *Camels of the age when the* نَاب [or *tush*] *grows forth:* and so شُوَيْكِئَةٌ: (As, TA:) [or شُوَيْكِيَة, q. v. in art. شوك.]

مَشْقَأٌ (S, K) and ▼ مَشْقَئٌ, (Fr, O, TA,) like مَفْرَق and مَفْرِق, (O, TA,) The *place of the parting of the hair of the head.* (Fr, S, O, K.)

مِشْقَأٌ *A comb;* (IAar, S, K;) as also ▼ مِشْقَأَةٌ and ▼ مِشْقَاةٌ, and مِشْقًا [or مِشْقَى]. (K: the last also mentioned in the K in art. شقو.)

مَشْقِئٌ: see مَشْقَأٌ.

مِشْقَأَةٌ: see مِشْقَأٌ. — Also *i. q.* مِدْرَاةٌ; (K;) [i. e. *A thing,* or *an iron instrument, with which the head is scratched;* or *a thing like a large needle, with which the female hair-dresser adjusts,* or *puts in order, the locks of a woman's hair;*] or *a piece of wood,* or *stick,* [*like a skewer,*] *which a woman inserts in her hair;* or *a horn prepared for that purpose* (TA) [or *for adjusting the locks of a woman's hair:* see مِدْرَاةٌ].

مِشْقَاةٌ: see مِشْقَأٌ.

شقح

1. شَقَحَ النَّخْلُ, and ▼ شقّح, *The palm-trees were,* or *became, goodly with their fruit.* (TA.) [See also 4.] — شَقَحَ اللّٰهُ فُلَانًا, [inf. n. شَقْحٌ,] accord. to AZ, is *syn. with* قَبَحَهُ اللّٰهُ [i. e. *God removed such a one far from good,* or *prosperity,* &c.; or *may God remove* &c.]: (TA:) [or, as may be inferred from what follows, the former of these verbs is used by some as an imitative sequent to the latter of them:] and accord. to Sb, (TA,) شَقُحَ, (K, TA,) inf. n. [شُقْحٌ and] شَقَاحَةٌ, (TA,) is *syn. with* قَبُحَ [i. e. *He,* or *it, was,* or *became, bad* or *evil, foul* or *ugly,* &c.]: (K, TA:) [but in this case also it seems that the former of these verbs may be used by some as an imitative sequent to the latter of them: for] one says, قُبْحًا لَهُ وَشُقْحًا [*May removal far from good,* or *prosperity,* &c., *betide him*], (S, O, K,) in which شُقْحًا is an imitative sequent to قُبْحًا, or syn. therewith; (S, K;) and [in like manner] قَبْحًا لَهُ وَشَقْحًا; (O, K;) and, of a man, قَبُحَ وَشَقُحَ, inf. n. of the latter as above and in like manner of the former; (S;) and جَآءَ بِالقَبَاحَةِ وَالشَّقَاحَةِ [*He did,* or *said, what was bad* or *evil,* &c.]: (K:) and ▼ هُوَ قَبِيحٌ شَقِيحٌ [*He is bad* or *evil, foul* or *ugly,* &c.]: (S,* O, K:*) and ▼ قَعَدَ مَقْبُوحًا مَشْقُوحًا, [*He sat,* or *remained, far removed from good,* or *prosperity,* &c.]: in like manner: (K:) but Sb intimates that ▼ شَقِيحٌ is not an imitative sequent, by his stating that the Arabs say شَقِيحٌ وَدَمِيمٌ [*Bad,* or *evil,* &c., *and blamed,* &c.; or, more probably, شَقِيحٌ وَدَمِيمٌ, meaning *foul and ugly*]: (L, TA:) and [it is said that] ▼ شَقِيحٌ signifies *Recovering* (نَاقِهٌ [for which Freytag appears to have read نَاقَةٌ]) *from disease;* (O, K, TA;) and hence one says, فُلَانٌ قَبِيحٌ شَقِيحٌ [as though meaning *Such a one is unsightly,* being just *recovering from disease*]: (TA:) and accord. to AZ, ▼ مَشْقُوحٌ is [not an imitative sequent, but] *syn. with* مَقْبُوحٌ: (L, TA:) in the phrase above-mentioned, مَشْقُوحًا is said in the 'Ináyeh to mean *broken:* or *far removed:* (TA:) or it means *reviled.* (O.) — [As indicated above,] شَقَحَهُ, aor. ـَ, (Lh, O, K,) inf. n. شَقْحٌ, (Lh, O,) also

signifies *He broke it*. (Lḥ, O, Ḳ.) One says, لَأَشْقَعَنَّكَ شَقْعَ الجَوْزَةِ بِالجَنْدَلِ, i. e. *I will assuredly break* [or *crush*] *thee* [*as in the breaking of the walnut*] *with stones*: (O, TA:*) or *I will assuredly extract all that thou hast* [*as in the extracting of the contents of the walnut by means of stones*]: for شَقَعَ الجَوْزَةَ, inf. n. as above, means *He extracted what was in the walnut*. (TA.)

2: see 1, first sentence: and see also 4, in three places.

3. شاقعهُ *He reviled him*; or *contended with him in reviling*; (Ḳ, TA;) and *contended with him in annoyance*. (O, TA.)

4. اشقع النَّخْلُ; (Ṣ, A, Mgh, O, Ḳ;) as also ▾ شقّع, (Ṣ,* A, Mgh, O,) inf. n. تَشْقِيعٌ; (Ṣ;) *i. q.* أَزْهَى [meaning *The palm-trees showed redness*, or *yellowness, in their fruit*]: (Ṣ, A, O, Ḳ:) or *their dates became altered from greenness to yellowness*: (Mgh:) the former is said by Aṣ to be of the dial. of El-Ḥijáz: and ▾ the latter verb is also said of the [kind of tree called] أَرَاك, meaning *it became coloured in its fruit*. (TA.) And اشقع التَّمْرُ, (O,) or البُسْرُ, (Ḳ,) inf. n. إِشْقَاعٌ; (TA;) and ▾ شقّع, (O, Ḳ,) inf. n. as above; (TA;) *The dates, or the unripe dates, became coloured*, (O, Ḳ,) *red*, or *yellow*: (O, TA:) or, as some say, *became sweet*. (TA.) The Prophet forbade the selling of dates before their becoming in this state. (Ṣ,* A,* O, TA.) —— اشقعهُ *He removed him far away*. (O, Ḳ.*) —— أَقْبِحْ بِهِ وَأَشْقِعْ [app. *How foul*, or *ugly*, or the like, *is he!* as seems to be shown by what here follows]: IDrd cites,

* أَقْبِحْ بِهِ مِنْ وَلَدٍ وَأَشْقِعْ *
* مِثْلَ جُرَىِّ الكَلْبِ لَا بَلْ أَقْبَحْ *

[*How foul is he, as offspring, and how ugly! like the little whelp of the dog; nay, rather, more foul!*]. (O.)

شُقْعٌ [an inf. n. of شَقِعَ, q. v. —— And,] accord. to AZ, *i. q.* شُحٌّ [i. e. *Niggardliness*, &c.; or the *being niggardly*, &c.: see 1 in art. شح]. (TA.)

شُقْعَةٌ: see what next follows.

شُقْحَةٌ and ▾ شُقْعَةٌ *An unripe date altering in redness*, (Ḳ,) or *altered to redness*. (Aṣ, TA.) —— And the former signifies The [*ruddy*] *colour termed* شُقْرَة. (O, Ḳ.)

حُلَّةٌ شُقْحِيَّةٌ *A red* [*dress*, or *garment, such as is termed*] حُلَّة: (Ḳ:) the latter word being a rel. n. from شُقْحَة meaning "an unripe date altering to redness." (TA.)

تَشْقِيحٌ: see 1, in three places.

أَشْقَحُ *Red*; (TA;) or [*of a ruddy colour*;] *i. q.* أَشْقَرُ: (O, Ḳ, TA:) so says AḤát. (TA.) —— [Hence,] رَغْوَةٌ شَقْحَاءُ [*Froth*, app. of milk,] *that is not of a pure white hue*, (O, Ḳ, TA,) *but coloured*. (TA.)

مَشْقُوحٌ: see 1, in two places.

شقذ

1. شَقَذَ, aor. ـَ, (Ṣ, M, L, Ḳ,) inf. n. شَقَذٌ, (Ṣ, M, L,) *He scarcely ever, or never, slept, and had a malignant eye, affecting*, or *hurting, others, therewith*: (Ṣ, M, L, Ḳ:*) or *he had a strong*, or *powerful, eye, quickly affecting* or *hurting* [*others therewith*]. (M, L, Ḳ.) —— And شَقَذَ, (Ṣ, M, L, Ḳ,) aor. ـَ; (Ḳ;) and شَقِذَ, aor. ـَ; (L, Ḳ;) *He went away*, (Ṣ, M, L, Ḳ,) *and went far off*, (Ṣ, L,) *being driven away*. (Ṣ, L, Ḳ.)

3. شاقذهُ, (Ṣ, L,) inf. n. مُشَاقَذَةٌ, (Ḳ,) *He regarded him*, or *treated him, with enmity*, or *hostility*. (Ṣ, L, Ḳ.)

4. اشقذهُ, (inf. n. إِشْقَاذٌ, L,) *He drove him away*. (Ṣ, M, L, Ḳ.)

شَقَذٌ: see شَقَذَانٌ, in three places.

شُقُذٌ: see شَقَذَانٌ, in four places: —— and see also شَقَذٌ.

شِقِذٌ: see شَقَذَانٌ, in three places.

شَقَذٌ: see شَقَذَانٌ. —— مَا بِهِ شَقَذٌ وَلَا نَقَذٌ *There is not in him any motion*. (IAar, Ṣ, L.) —— And, (L, Ḳ, in the CḲ ما به شَقَذٌ ولا نَقَذٌ,) as also ما به شُقُذٌ ▾ ولا نُقُذٌ, (Ḳ,) *There is not in it* (namely, a commodity, or household furniture, L) *any fault, or defect*: and *there is not in it* (namely, language, or speech, L) *any defect, imperfection*, or *unsoundness*. (L, Ḳ.*) —— And مَا لَهُ شَقَذٌ وَلَا نَقَذٌ *He possesses not anything*. (L, Ḳ.) —— And مَا دُونَهُ شَقَذٌ وَلَا نَقَذٌ *There is not anything to be feared, nor anything to be disliked, in the way to the attainment thereof*. (Meyd, TA.)

شَقِذٌ: see شَقَذَانٌ, in six places.

شُقَذٌ: see شَقَذَانٌ, in two places.

شِقْذٌ: see شَقَذَانٌ, in the latter half.

شَقَذَةٌ and شِقْذَةٌ: see شَقَذَانٌ, near the end; the latter, in two places.

شَقَذَى: see what next follows.

عُقَابٌ شَقَذَانَةٌ *An eagle vehemently hungry*, (Ṣ, M, L, Ḳ,) *and eager in seeking food*; (M, L;) as also ▾ شَقَذَى. (Ḳ.) A poet likens a horse thereto. (M, L.)

شِقْذَانٌ, as a sing. n.: see شَقَذَانٌ (of which it is also a pl.), in two places, near the end.

شَقَذَانٌ One *who scarcely ever, or never, sleeps*; (Ṣ, M, L, Ḳ;) as also ▾ شَقِذٌ; (Ṣ, M, Ḳ;) *and who has a malignant eye*, (Ṣ, M,) *affecting*, or *hurting, others therewith*; as also ▾ شَقَذٌ (Ṣ, M, Ḳ, in the TA شَقْذٌ,) and ▾ شَقِيذٌ: (M:) or *who has a strong*, or *powerful, eye, quickly affecting* or *hurting* [*others therewith*]; (M, L, Ḳ;) as also ▾ شَقَذٌ and ▾ شَقِيذُ العَيْنِ: (M:) and شَقِذٌ one *who scarcely ever, or never, sleeps; whom drowsiness does not overcome*. (T, L.) —— Also *Driven away, and remote*; and so ▾ شَقِيذٌ. (L.) —— And شَقَذَانَةٌ A *light-spirited* woman: (Th, M, L:) *foul*, or *obscene, in her speech*; *clamorous, and foul-tongued*. (T, L.) —— Also The *male chameleon*; (M, L, Ḳ;) and so ▾ شَقَذٌ and ▾ شِقْذٌ and ▾ شُقُذٌ: or all these words signify *a slender and compact male chameleon, with a small head, that cleaves to the trunk of the kind of tree called* عِضَاه: (M, L:) pl. شِقْذَانٌ (M, L, Ḳ) and شَقَاذَى: (M:) the former pl. like كِرْوَانٌ, pl. of كَرَوَانٌ; (L;) and also used as a sing., meaning *a male chameleon*; (Th, M;) thus used by a poetess: (M:) also ▾ شِقْذٌ (Ṣ, M, L, Ḳ) and ▾ شُقَذٌ (M, L) and ▾ شُقُذٌ (M, L, Ḳ) and ▾ شَقِذٌ (Ḳ) the *young one of a chameleon*: (Lḥ, Ṣ, M, L, Ḳ:) pl. شِقْذَانٌ (Ṣ, M, L, Ḳ) and شَقَاذَى: (M, L, Ḳ:) the former pl. like صِنْوَانٌ, pl. of صِنْوٌ. (Ṣ.) A poet says, describing asses,

* فَرَعَتْ بِهَا حَتَّى إِذَا * رَأَتِ الشَّقَاذَى تَصْطَلِى *

And they pastured therein until the heat became vehement and *they saw the male chameleons* thirsty, desiring to go to water, and *repairing to the sun*: some say, that شقاذى here signifies *moths*, (فَرَاش), but this is a mistake. (M, L.) شِقْذَانٌ also signifies The *animals called* ضَبّ *and* وَرَل *and* طِحْن *and* سَامّ أَبْرَص *and* دَسَّاسَة: and the sing. is ▾ شِقْذَةٌ: (M, L:) or *any small animals that creep or walk upon the earth, and venomous* or *noxious reptiles and the like*: (M, L, Ḳ:) sing. ▾ شَقَذَةٌ (M, L) and ▾ شِقْذٌ, (M,) or ▾ شَقِذٌ, (L,) and ▾ شُقُذٌ, (M,) or ▾ شَقَذٌ; (L;) but it does not appear how ▾ شَقَذَةٌ can be a sing. of شِقْذَانٌ unless the augmentative letter be regarded as elided. (M, L.) —— Also The *wolf*; (M, L, Ḳ;) and so ▾ شِقْذَانٌ (Th, M, L, Ḳ) and ▾ شُقُذٌ, (M, L,) or ▾ شِقْذٌ, (Ḳ,) or ▾ شَقَذٌ. (TA.) —— Also The *hawk*; syn. صَقْرٌ; (M, L;) and so ▾ شِقْذَانٌ (Th, M, L) and ▾ شُقُذٌ, (M, L,) or ▾ شَقَذٌ. (TA.) —— And شِقْذَانٌ [the pl.] also signifies The *young ones of the kinds of birds called* حُبَارَى *and* قَطًا (M, L, Ḳ) and *the like*. (M, L.)

شَقِيذٌ: see شَقَذَانٌ, in two places.

طَرْدٌ مُشْقِذٌ *A driving far away*. (M, L.)

شقر

1. شَقِرَ, aor. ـَ, inf. n. شَقَرٌ (M, L, Mṣb, Ḳ [in the CḲ and TA شُقْر, which is evidently wrong,]) and شُقْرَةٌ, (Lth, Ḳ,) or the latter is a simple subst.; (M;) and شَقُرَ; and ▾ اِشْقَرَّ; (M, Ḳ;) *He was*, or *became, of the colour termed* شُقْرَة. (M, L, Mṣb, Ḳ.)

9: see 1.

شُقُورٌ: see شُقْرٌ.

شَقِرٌ [The *red*, or *blood-coloured, anemone*;] *i. q.* شَقَائِقُ النُّعْمَانِ: (Ṣ, M, A, Mṣb, Ḳ:) it is not a sweet-scented flower: (Mṣb:) n. un. with ة; (Ṣ, M, Mṣb, Ḳ;) pl. [of the n. un.] شَقِرَاتٌ: (Ḳ:) as also ▼ شُقَّار and ▼ شُقَرَان, (so in some copies of the Ḳ,) the latter so written by IDrd and Ṣgh, and thought by IDrd to be a place or a plant, (TA,) or ▼ شُقُرَان, (so in some copies of the Ḳ and in the TA,) and ▼ شَقَّارَى and ▼ شُقَّارَى: (Ḳ:) or شَقِرٌ is the name of *a certain other plant, not the* شقائق, *but red like it*: (M,* Ḳ,* TA:) or it signifies *cinnabar*: (A:) or شَقِرَةٌ has this signification, (T, Ḳ,) as well as that first assigned to it above: (Ḳ:) and accord. to AḤn, (M, TA,) ▼ شُقَّارَى is the name of *a certain plant* (Ṣ, M, TA) *that grows in sands, having a pungent odour, which is tasted in the flavour of milk*: and he adds that, accord. to some, it is the same as the شَقِر; but that this opinion is not well founded: (M, TA:) it is also said that it is *a certain plant having a flower of a dingy red colour, the seed, or grain, of which is called* خِمْخِم: (TA:) and that ▼ شُقَّارَى (M, TA) and ▼ شَقَّارَى, (M,) or ▼ شُقَّار, (TA,) are names of *a certain plant, having a flower of a colour somewhat of that termed* شُكْلَة, *with slender, or delicate, dust-coloured leaves, which grows in the manner of* قَضْب [a kind of trefoil], *is approved in pasturage, and grows only in fruitful years.* (M, TA.)

جَآءَ بِالشُّقَرِ وَالبُقَرِ: see جَآءَ بِالصُّقَرِ وَالبُقَرِ, in art. صقر.

شُقْرَةٌ The *colours described in the explanations of the epithet* أَشْقَر, *below.* (Ṣ, M, Mṣb, &c.)

شَقِرَانٌ, or شُقُرَانٌ: see شَقِرٌ.

شِقِرَّاقٌ and its vars.: see in art. شقرق.

شَقُورٌ: see the next paragraph, in four places.

شُقُورٌ (AHeyth, Fr, A'Obeyd, Ṣ, Ḳ) and ▼ شَقُورٌ (AHeyth, Aṣ, Abu-l-Jarráḥ, Ṣ, Ḳ) *A want*; or *a needful*, or *requisite, thing, affair*, or *business*: (Ṣ, Ḳ:) or the former signifies *wants*: (Ḥam p. 716:) A'Obeyd says that the former word is the more correct, because شُقُور signifies *things*, or *affairs, that cleave to the heart, disquieting it*; and is pl. of ▼ شَقْر; and that ▼ شَقُور, with fet-ḥ, has the signification of an epithet [meaning *cleaving to the heart and disquieting it*]: (Ṣ:) or, accord. to some, this latter signifies *grief, mourning, sorrow*, or *sadness*; *disquietude of mind*: or *disquietude of mind that causes one to be sleepless*: the former is also expl. as signifying a man's *case*, and his *secret*: and ▼ both are also said to signify *tidings*: and a man's *state*, or *condition*. (TA.) One says, أَخْبَرْتُهُ بِشُقُورِى *I acquainted him with my want*; like as one says أَفْضَيْتُ إِلَيْهِ بِعُجَرِى وَبُجَرِى: (Ṣ:) or *I acquainted him with my tidings.* (TA.) And أَفْضَيْتُ إِلَيْهِ بِشُقُورِى *I acquainted him with my case, and with what I kept secret from others*; (TA;) and so نَقَضْتُ لَهُ شُقُورِى: (Ḥam p. 716:) or *I revealed to him my secret, and acquainted him with all my affairs.* (Mgh.) And ▼ بَثَّهُ شَقُورَهُ, and شُقُورَهُ, *He complained to him of his state*, or *condition*. (M, TA.)

شُقَّارَى: see شَقِرٌ, in two places: ═ and see also جَآءَ بِالصُّقَرِ وَالبُقَرِ, in art. صقر.

شُقَّار: see شَقِرٌ, in two places.

شَقَّارَى: see شَقِرٌ, in three places.

أَشْقَرُ, applied to a man, [*Of a ruddy complexion combined with fairness*: or] *of a clear ruddy complexion, with the outer skin inclining to white*: (Ṣ:) or *having a red, or ruddy, tinge, over a white, or fair, complexion*: (M, Mṣb, Ḳ:) and applied to a horse, [*of a sorrel colour*;] *of a clear red colour*, (Ṣ, IF, Mṣb,) or *of a red colour inclining to* [*the dull red hue called*] مُغْرَة, (M, Ḳ,) *with a red mane and tail*: (Ṣ, M, Ḳ:) when the mane and tail are black, the epithet كُمَيْت [meaning bay, or dark bay, or brown,] is applied to the horse: (Ṣ:) the اشقر is said to be the best of horses: (IAạr, M: [but it is said in Ḥar p. 390 to be regarded by the Arabs as of evil omen:]) and applied to a camel, *intensely red*: (Ṣ:) or *of a colour resembling that of a horse thus termed*: (M:) fem. شَقْرَآءُ: and pl. شُقْرٌ. (Mṣb.) — Also, applied to blood, *That has become thick*, (مَا صَارَ عَلَقًا, M, Mṣb, TA,) *and not been overspread with dust.* (Mṣb, TA.) — And the fem., شَقْرَآءُ, is used as [a subst.] signifying *Fire*. (Ḥam p. 718.)

شقرق

شَقِرَّاقٌ and شِقِرَّاقٌ, (Ṣ, O, Mṣb, Ḳ,) the former accord. to IAạr, (Th, TA,) the latter accord. to Fr, (TA,) but disallowed by IḲt, and asserted by him to be a mispronunciation of the vulgar, (Mṣb,) and شُقَرَّاقٌ, (Mṣb, Ḳ,) and شَقَرَّاقٌ, (accord. to the CḲ,) and, (Ṣ, O, Ḳ,) as they sometimes said, (Ṣ, O,) شِرِقْرَاقٌ, (Ṣ, O, Ḳ,) and شَرَقْرَاقٌ, and شَرَقْرَقٌ, (Ḳ,) [the first and second now applied to The *green wood-pecker, picus viridis*: and to the *common roller, coracias garrula*:] *a certain bird*, (Ṣ, O, Mṣb, Ḳ,) *well known*, (Ḳ,) among the Arabs, (Fr, TA,) called أَخْيَل, (Fr, Ṣ, O, Mṣb, TA,) [a name likewise now applied to the *green wood-pecker*,] *and regarded by the Arabs as of evil omen*; (Ṣ;) *less than the pigeon, the colour of which is green, and the beak black, and having blackness in the extremities and exterior of its wings*: (Mṣb:) accord. to IAạr, the شِقِرَّاق is with the Arabs *the* أَخْطَب [q. v.]: (TA:) accord. to the Ḳ, or شقراق and شرقراق accord. to Lth, (TA,) *a certain bird speckled*, or *spotted, with green and red and white* (Ḳ, TA) *and black*, (TA,) *and found*, accord. to the copies of the Ḳ, *in the land of the Ḥaram*, but correctly, as in the words of Lth, بارض الجرم, thus, with ج, [perhaps rightly بِالأَرْضِ الجَرْمِ, *in the land that is hot*, or *very hot*,] *in the places in which palm-trees grow*; *of the size of the* هُدْهُد [or hoopoe]: accord. to Lth, شقراق is of the measure فعلال: شرقراق is mentioned by J and Ṣgh [as well as in the Ḳ] in the present art.; but should, properly, be mentioned under the head of شرقرق, as it is in the L. (TA.)

شقص

2. شَقَّصَهُ, (L, TA,) inf. n. تَشْقِيصٌ, (L, Mgh, Ḳ,) *He divided it into parts*, or *portions*: (Mgh:) or *he cut it up, and separated its members* (A, L, Ḳ*) *into just portions among the sharers*; (L, Ḳ;*) namely, a slaughtered animal, (Ḳ,) or particularly a slaughtered sheep or goat, and a pig: (L, A, TA:) or *he divided it* (namely, a pig,) *into parts or portions, and members*, for eating and selling. (Mgh.) Hence the trad. مَنْ بَاعَ الخَمْرَ فَلْيُشَقِّصِ الخَنَازِيرَ (L, A) *He who sells wine, let him cut up swine and divide their members*, as is done to a sheep or goat when its flesh is sold: meaning, he who holds the selling of wine to be lawful, let him hold the selling of swine to be so; for they are equally forbidden. (L, TA.)

شِقْصٌ *A piece*, or *part*, of a thing; (Ṣ, M, Mgh, Mṣb;) as also ▼ شَقِيصٌ: (M, Mgh:) or *a little*, of much; (M, TA;) as also ▼ the latter: (IDrd, M, Ḳ:) and ▼ the latter, *a little*, or *paltry, thing*: (TA:) and the former, *a piece of land*: (Ṣ:) or *a share*; syn. سَهْم, (A, Ḳ,) or حَظّ, (M,) and نَصِيب, (A, Mgh, Ḳ,) and شِرْك, (A, Ḳ,) which signifies the same as نَصِيب; (Sh, on the authority of Khálid;) as also ▼ شَقِيصٌ; (Sh, M, Mgh, Ḳ;) like نِصْف and نَصِيف: (M:) as, for instance, in property; (IDrd;) and of a slave: (TA:) or *a certain share not divided*: (Esh-Sháfi'ee, TA:) or if *divided* it may also be thus called: (Az, TA:) pl. [of pauc.] أَشْقَاصٌ (M, Mṣb) and [of mult.] شِقَاصٌ. (M, TA.)

شَقِيصٌ: see شِقْصٌ, throughout. ═ Also *A sharer*, or *partner*. (Ṣ, A, Ḳ.) You say, هُوَ شَقِيصِى *He is my sharer*, or *partner*, (Ṣ, A,) *in a piece of land.* (Ṣ.) ═ And *A fleet*, or *swift, and excellent* horse: (Ḳ:) but an epithet not known to Lth. (TA.)

مِشْقَصٌ *A broad* نَصْل [or *iron head*] (IDrd, Mṣb, Ḳ) *of an arrow*: (IDrd:) or *an arrow having such a* نصل, (Lth, IF, Ḳ,) *with which wild animals are shot*; (Lth;) but Az says that this explanation is at variance with what has been heard from the Arabs: (TA:) or it signifies, (M,) or signifies also, (Ḳ,) *a long* نصل; (M, Ḳ;) not a broad one: (M:) or *an arrow having such a* نصل; (M;) *with which wild animals are shot*: (Ḳ:) or *a long and broad* نصل: (Ṣ:) or it is *of half the size of a* نصل, *and is worthless; children play with it, and it is the worst kind of arrow* [-head], *and is used for shooting at objects of the chase and any other thing*: (TA:) pl. مَشَاقِصُ. (Ṣ.)

مُشَقِّصٌ *A butcher*. (A, Ḳ.)

شقو

1. شَقِىَ, (Ṣ, Mṣb, Ḳ,) originally شَقِوَ, (Ṣ, TA,) aor. َ, (Ṣ, Mṣb,) dual thereof يَشْقَيَانِ, (Ṣ,) inf. n. شَقَاوَةٌ and شِقَاوَةٌ, (Ṣ,* Ḳ,) the latter accord. to a reading of the Ḳur xxiii. 108, (Ṣ,) and شَقَآءٌ and شِقْوَةٌ and شُقْوَةٌ (Ṣ,* Ḳ) and شَقًا, (Ḳ,) or the last of these is the inf. n., and شَقَاوَةٌ and شِقْوَةٌ [and the rest, none of which is expressly specified as an inf. n. in the Ṣ,] are simple substs., (Mṣb,) *He*

was, or became, unprosperous, unfortunate, unhappy, or *miserable;* (Ṣ, Mṣb, TA;) شَقِىَ being *contr. of* سَعِدَ; (Mṣb;) and شَقَاوَةٌ &c. *contr. of* سَعَادَةٌ: (Ṣ, TA:) or *he was,* or *became, in a state of straitness, distress, adversity,* or *difficulty.* (Az, Ḳ, TA.) [See also شَقَاوَةٌ below.] — Also † *He suffered,* or *experienced, fatigue,* (TA, and Ksh and Bḍ and Jel in xx. 1,) فِى كَذَا [*in such a thing*]. (TA.) ═ شَقَاهُ: see 3: — and 4.

3. شَاقَاهُ, (Ḳ, TA,) inf. n. مُشَاقَاةٌ (Ṣ, TA) and شِقَآءٌ, (TA,) *He laboured, strove,* or *struggled, with him, to prevail,* or *overcome,* (Ṣ, Ḳ, TA,) in war, or battle, and the like; (Ḳ, TA;) so in the T; (TA;) *he struggled,* or *contended, with,* or *against, the difficulty,* or *trouble,* or *inconvenience, that he experienced from him;* (Ṣ,* TA;) syn. عَالَجَهُ; (Ḳ, TA;) or مَارَسَهُ; and عَانَاهُ. (Ṣ,* TA.) — And ↓ شَاقَاهُ فَشَقَاهُ, aor. of the latter verb ـُ, *He endeavoured to surpass him in mutual labouring,* or *striving,* or *struggling, to prevail,* or *overcome,* &c., غَالَبَهُ فِى الشِّقَآءِ, [in the CḲ, فى الشَّقاء, but the former seems to be the right reading, and may be best rendered *in the mutual striving against difficulty,*]) *and he surpassed him* [*therein*]. (Ḳ. [In the Ṣ, شَاقَانِى فُلَانٌ فَشَقَوْتُهُ, aor. أَشْقُوهُ; and only the latter verb as thus used is there explained.]) — مُشَاقَاةٌ signifies also † The *treating* [one] *with hardness, harshness,* or *illnature.* (TA.) — And ‡ The *vying, one with another, in patience,* or *endurance:* a rájiz says,

إِذَا يُشَاقِى الصَّابِرَانِ لَمْ يَرِثْ *
يَكَادُ مِنْ ضَعْفِ القُوَى لَا يَنْبَعِثْ *

[*When the two patient ones vie in endurance, he does not lag behind, almost, by reason of the weakness of powers, failing to hasten in pace*]: he means a camel vying with the attendant thereof in endurance of going. (TA.)

4. اشقاهُ اللّٰهُ *God caused him to be unprosperous, unfortunate, unhappy,* or *miserable;* *contr. of* أَسْعَدَهُ: (Ṣ,* Mṣb, TA:) or *God caused him to be in a state of straitness, distress, adversity,* or *difficulty:* and so ↓ شَقَاهُ. (Ḳ.) ═ And اشقى *He combed.* (AZ, Ḳ. [See مِشْقًى.])

شَقْوَةٌ an inf. n. of شَقِىَ, as also شِقْوَةٌ: (Ṣ,* Ḳ:) or a simple subst. (Mṣb.)

شَقِىٌّ *Unprosperous, unfortunate, unhappy,* or *miserable:* (Ṣ, Mṣb, TA:) [or *in a state of straitness, distress, adversity,* or *difficulty:* (see its verb:)] pl. أَشْقِيَآءُ. (TA.) وَلَمْ أَكُنْ بِدُعَائِكَ رَبِّ شَقِيًّا, in the Ḳur [xix. 4, *And I have not been, in supplicating Thee, my Lord, unprosperous*], means I have been one whose prayer has been answered. (TA.)

شَقَاوَةٌ an inf. n. of شَقِىَ; (Ṣ,* Ḳ;) or a simple subst.; (Mṣb;) signifying *Unprosperousness,* &c.; [see its verb;] *contr. of* سَعَادَةٌ: (Ṣ, Er-Rághib, TA:) it is of two kinds; أُخْرَاوِيَّةٌ [*relating to the world to come*] and دُنْيَاوِيَّةٌ [*relating to the present world*]: and the latter is of three kinds; نَفْسِيَّةٌ [*relating to the soul*] and بَدَنِيَّةٌ [*relating to the body*] and خَارِجِيَّةٌ [*relating to external circumstances*]. (Er-Rághib, TA.) — Also † *Fatigue;* syn. تَعَبٌ; but the latter has a more general signification; every شقاوة being تعب, but every تعب is not شقاوة. (TA.)

أَشْقَى [*More,* and *most, unprosperous,* &c. — And] ‡ *More* [and *most*] *fatigued.* (TA.)

مِشْقًى *A comb:* a dial. var. of مِشْقَأٌ. (AZ, Ḳ.)

شقى

1. شَقَى, inf. n. شُقِىٌّ, said of the نَاب [or tush] of a camel, *It grew forth:* a dial. var. of شَقَأَ. (Ḳ in art. شقو [but belonging to the present art.: mentioned in the TA, as not in the Ḳ, on the authority of ISd].) — [Freytag states, as on the authority of Abu-l-'Alà, that شَقَى is used for شَقَّ *He clave,* or *split,* &c.: — and that Reiske has explained it as signifying *He opened the mouth with a wide grinning* ("amplo rictu").]

شَاقٍ *A long prominence,* or *projecting portion,* or *ledge,* (حَيْدٌ طَالِعٌ طَوِيلٌ,) of a mountain, (Ḳ, TA,) *that cannot be ascended:* (TA:) by rule it should be with ء [i. e. شَاقِئٌ, as being derived from شَقَأَ]: (Sgh, TA:) pl. شَوَاقِى (Ḳ [correctly شَوَاقٍ]) and شُقْيَانٌ. (TA. [Mentioned in the Ḳ in art. شقو, but belonging to the present art.])

شك

1. شَكَّ is intrans. by itself, and trans. by means of the particle فِى: — one says, شَكَّ الأَمْرُ, aor. يَشُكُّ [contr. to analogy in the case of an intrans. verb of this class], inf. n. شَكٌّ, *The thing,* or *case,* or *affair, was,* or *became, dubious,* or *confused:* (Mṣb:) — and شَكَّ فِيهِ, (MA, Ḳ,) first pers. شَكَكْتُ فِيهِ, (Ṣ, Mṣb,) aor. as above, (JM, PṢ, &c.,) and so the inf. n., (MA, &c.,) *He doubted, wavered* or *vacillated in opinion,* or *was uncertain, respecting it;* (MA, Mṣb, and so accord. to explanations of شَكٌّ [q. v. infrà] in the Ṣ and Mṣb and Ḳ &c.;) syn. اِرْتَابَ; (Mṣb;) and ↓ تشكّك signifies the same. (Ṣ, Ḳ.) — شَكَّ عَلَىَّ الأَمْرُ means شَقَّ [i. e. *The case,* or *affair, was difficult, hard, distressing,* &c., *to me*]: (O, TA:) or, as some say, [*was such that*] *I doubted* (شَكَكْتُ) *respecting it.* (TA.) ═ شَكَّ said of a camel, (IAạr, Ṣ, Ḳ,) aor. and inf. n. as above, (Ṣ,) *He limped,* or *halted;* or *had a slight lameness,* (IAạr, Ṣ, TA,) *of his hind leg:* (IAạr, TA:) or *his arm stuck to his side,* (Ḳ, TA,) *and he had a slight lameness in consequence thereof:* (TA:) and ↓ اشتكّ, likewise said of a camel, *he had a slight lameness;* (Ibn-'Abbád, O, TA;) like شَكَّ. (Ibn-'Abbád, O.) — شَكٌّ also signifies The *cleaving* or *sticking* [of a thing to another thing]. (Ṣ, O, TA.) So in a verse of Aboo-Dahbal El-Jumahee cited voce يَلَبٌ. (Ṣ.) And one says, شَكَّتِ الرَّحِمُ *The relationship was,* or *became, closely united.* (O, TA. [See رَحِمٌ شَاكَّةٌ voce شَاكٌّ.]) — شَكَّ فِى السِّلَاحِ, (Ḳ, TA,) aor. and inf. n. as above, (TA,) *He put on* [or *around him,*] or *attired himself with, the arms,* or *weapons, completely, not leaving any of them;* (TA;) [*as though*] *he entered amid them.* (Ḳ, TA.) ═ شَكَكْتُهُ بِالرُّمْحِ, (Ṣ, O, Mṣb, in the Ḳ شَكَّهُ,) and بِالسَّهْمِ, and the like, aor. as above, (TA,) and so the inf. n., (Mṣb, TA,) *I pierced,* or *transpierced, him,* or *it,* (طَعَنْتُهُ, Mṣb, or خَزَقْتُهُ, O, and in like manner in the TA, but in my copies of the Ṣ خَرَقْتُهُ [meaning *I made a hole in him,* or *it*], and thus in one place in the TA, and اِنْتَظَمْتُهُ, Ṣ, O, and in like manner in the Ḳ,) *with the spear,* (Ṣ, O, Mṣb, Ḳ,) and *with the arrow,* &c.: (TA:) but IDrd says that, accord. to some, شَكٌّ is only *by the conjoining two things* with an arrow or a spear: (O, TA:) [thus,] فَشَكَّ رِجْلَهُ مَعَ رِكَابِهِ means *And he clave and transpierced his leg,* or *foot, together with his stirrup.* (Mgh.) — [Hence,] شَكَكْتُ إِلَيْهِ البِلَادَ *I traversed,* or *crossed,* or *cut through, the countries,* or *districts, to him.* (O, TA.) — And شُكَّ عَلَيْهِ الثَّوْبُ *The garment was put* [or *drawn*] *together upon him, and fastened with a thorn* or *a wooden pin:* or *was let down,* or *made to hang down, upon him.* (TA.) — شَكُّوا بُيُوتَهُمْ *They placed their tents in one row,* or *series,* (O, Mṣb, Ḳ,) *in one regular order,* (T, TA,) *near together.* (Mṣb.) — Hence, شَكُّوا الأَرْحَامَ *They made the relationships to be closely connected.* (Mṣb.) And شُكَّ *He was made,* or *asserted, to be connected with the lineage of another.* (IAạr, O.) — And شَكَكْتُهُ said of anything means *I drew and joined,* or *adjoined, it* [to another thing]. (Mṣb.) [And *I infixed it* in, or *thrust it* into, another thing.] — مَا شَكَّ كَفِّى خَلِيلَهَا, [or, more probably, مَا شَكَّ,] a phrase in a verse of El-Farezdaḳ,] in which it forms an apodosis,] means مَا قَارَنَ [i. e., app., *Its friend* (*the sword,* or *the spear,* both of which are meanings of الخَلِيل,) *would not be conjoined* (or *grasped*) *with my hand*]. (TA.) — شَكَّ الثَّوْبَ *He* (the sewer) *made the stitch-holes far apart* [*in sewing the garment,* or *piece of cloth*]. (O, TA.) [Thus the verb has two contr. meanings.] ═ شَكِكْتُ إِلَيْهِ, with kesr, and شَكَكْتُهُ, (Ibn-'Abbád, O, and so in the Ḳ accord. to the TA, as also in the TḲ, in the CḲ and in my MS. copy of the Ḳ شَكَكْتُهُ and اليه,) *I inclined to him,* or *it;* or *trusted to,* or *relied upon, him,* or *it, so as to be,* or *become, easy,* or *quiet, in mind;* or *leaned, rested,* or *relied, upon him,* or *it;* syn. رَكَنْتُ. (Ibn-'Abbád, O, Ḳ.)

2. شَكَّكَنِى فِيهِ, (Ṣ, O, Ḳ,*) inf. n. تَشْكِيكٌ, (O,) *He made me to doubt, to waver* or *vacillate in opinion,* or *to be uncertain, respecting it;* (Ṣ, Ḳ, TA;) *he threw me,* or *made me to fall, into doubt,* &c., *respecting it.* (O.)

5: } see the first paragraph.
8: }

شَكٌّ [used as a subst.] signifies *Doubt;* (Mṣb; [see 1;]) or the *contr. of* يَقِينٌ; (Ṣ, O, Mṣb, Ḳ;) by which explanation is meant *a wavering* or *vacillation in opinion between two things, whether they be equal* [*in probability*] *or such that one of them outweighs* [*therein*] *the other;* or, as the expositors explain its meaning in the Ḳur x. 94, *uncertainty:* (Mṣb:) or *a wavering* or *vacillation in opinion, between two inconsistent things, without making either of them to outweigh the other in the estimation of him who conceives the* شَكّ: or, as some say, *a pausing,* or *hesitation, between two extremes that are equal* [*in probability*], *without the mind's inclining to either of them:* when one of them is made to outweigh, without the other's being rejected, it is ظَنٌّ: (KT:) accord. to Er-Rághib, it is the *alternation,* or *confusedness, of two inconsistent things, in the judgment of a man, and their being equal:* this is sometimes because of there being two indications, equal in his judgment, of the two inconsistent things; or of there being no indication thereof: and sometimes it relates to the question whether a thing be, or be not; and sometimes, to the question of what kind it is; and sometimes, to some of its qualities; and sometimes, to the accident that is the cause of its being: it is a species of جَهْل; but is more special than this; for جهل is sometimes the utter nonexistence of knowledge of the two inconsistent things; so that every شك is جهل, but every جهل is not شك: (TA:) accord. to some, the primary meaning is *a state of commotion,* or *disturbance, of the heart and mind:* (Mṣb:) pl. شُكُوك. (Ḳ.) — [Hence, يَوْمُ الشَّكِّ *The day of which one doubts whether it be the last of one month or the first of the next month:* and generally, *whether it be the last of Shaabán or the first of Ramaḍán;* and to fast on this day is forbidden.] ═ Also *A small crack in a bone.* (Ḳ.) — And *A seam,* or *line of sewing, of a garment.* (L in art. صوح.) — [And accord. to Freytag, *A coat of mail composed of narrow rings:* but he names no authority for this.] ═ And [*Arsenic;*] *a certain medicament, that destroys rats; brought from Khurásán, from the mines of silver;* (Ḳ, TA;) *of two kinds,* (TA,) *white* and *yellow;* (Ḳ, TA;) *now known by the name of* سَمُّ الفَأْرِ [*ratsbane*]. (TA.)

شِكٌّ *A covering* (حُلَّة) *that is put upon the backs of the two curved extremities of the bow:* (Ḳ:) so says ISd. (TA.)

شَكَّةٌ [an inf. n. of un.] *A single piercing through two men on a horse.* (Ḥam p. 271.)

شُكَّةٌ i. q. شُقَّةٌ: (O, Ḳ:) so in the saying, إِنَّهُ لَبَعِيدُ الشُّكَّةِ [*Verily he is one whose region to which he directs himself is far distant*]. (O.)

شِكَّةٌ *Arms,* or *weapons,* (Ṣ, Ḳ, TA,) *that are worn.* (TA.) — And *A broad piece of wood,* (Ḳ,) or *small broad piece of wood,* (Ṣ, O,) *that is put into the hole* (خُرْت) [*in which is inserted the end of the handle*] *of the axe,* or *adz,* and *the like, in order to narrow it.* (IDrd, Ṣ, O, Ḳ.) ═ رَجُلٌ مُخْتَلِفُ الشِّكَّةِ means *A man discordant in natural dispositions.* (TA.)

شَكَكٌ A camel *having a slight lameness; that limps,* or *halts.* (TA.)

شُكُكٌ, with two dammehs, [a pl. of which the sing., in the sense here indicated, is not mentioned,] i. q. أَدْعِيَآءُ [*Persons who make a claim in respect of relationship; or who claim to be sons of persons not their fathers; or who are claimed as sons by persons not their fathers;* or *adopted sons:* pl. of دَعِىٌّ]. (IAạr, TA.) ═ [Also said to be pl. of شَكِيكَةٌ, q. v.]

شِكَاكٌ *Tents arranged in a row:* (O, Ḳ:) one says, ضَرَبُوا بُيُوتَهُمْ شِكَاكًا *They pitched their tents in one row:* but accord. to Th, it is سِكَاكًا, [q. v.,] from السِّكَّةُ. (TA.)

شَكُوكٌ ‡ A she-camel *of which one doubts whether she be fat or not* (Ṣ, Ḳ, TA) *in her hump,* (Ḳ, TA,) *by reason of the abundance of her fur, wherefore her hump is felt:* (Ṣ, TA:) pl. شُكُكٌ. (Ḳ.)

شُكُوكٌ *Sides;* syn. جَوَانِبُ. (Ibn-'Abbád, O, TA.) [Perhaps pl. of شَكَاكَةٌ (q. v.), next after which it is mentioned in the O; like as صُلِىٌّ (originally صُلُوىٌ) is pl. of صَلَايَةٌ.]

شَكَاكَةٌ *A region, quarter,* or *tract,* syn. نَاحِيَةٌ, of the earth. (Ibn-'Abbád, O, Ḳ.)

شَكِيكَةٌ *A party, sect,* or *distinct body* or *class,* (AA, Ṣ, O, Ḳ,) of men: (AA, Ṣ, O:) pl. شَكَائِكُ; (AA, Ṣ;) [and app. شُكُكٌ also, for,] accord. to IAạr, شُكُكٌ signifies *distinct bodies of soldiers.* (TA.) ═ *A way, course, mode,* or *manner, of acting* or *conduct* or *the like:* (IDrd, O, Ḳ:) thus in the saying, دَعْهُ عَلَى شَكِيكَتِهِ [*Leave thou him intent on pursuing his way,* &c.]: (IDrd, O:) pl. شَكَائِكُ (IDrd, O, Ḳ) and شُكُكٌ, (so in copies of the Ḳ,) or شُكُكٌ; if the latter of these two, extr. [with respect to analogy]. (TA.) — And *Natural disposition;* syn. خُلُق. (TḲ, as from the Ḳ. [The only reading that I find in copies of the Ḳ is with ح in the place of خ, i. e. حَلْق; and thus, but without any vowel-sign, in the TA: but I think that the right reading is evidently that in the TḲ.]) ═ Also The [*kind of basket called*] سَلَّة *in which are* [*put*] *fruits.* (Ibn-'Abbád, O, Ḳ,*) ═ And [the pl.] شَكَائِكُ signifies The *pieces of wood with which, they being joined together, are formed the tent-like tops* of the vehicles called هَوَادِج [pl. of هَوْدَج]. (AA, O, TA.)

شُكَّكَةٌ, applied to a woman, meaning *Just in proportion,* or *beautiful, and slender;* or *light,* or *active, in her work;* and *clever;* is vulgar. (TA.)

شَكِّىٌّ, (so in the O, occurring there in three instances,) or شُكِّىٌّ, (thus in the Ḳ, [but if this were the right reading, the rule of the author would require him to add "with ḍamm," therefore I suppose it to have been mistranscribed in an early copy of the Ḳ,]) applied to a لِجَام [i. e. bit, or bridle], *Difficult.* (O, Ḳ.) [See also شَكِىٌّ in art. شكو and شكى.]

شُكَّاكٌ: see شَاكٌّ.

شَكْشَكَةٌ *Sharp arms* or *weapons:* (IAạr, O, Ḳ:) or the *sharpness of arms* or *weapons:* (Ḳ:) or the latter should be the meaning accord. to analogy. (O.)

شَاكٌّ [act. part. n. of شَكَّ]. — رَجُلٌ شَاكُّ السِّلَاحِ and شَاكٌّ فِى السِّلَاحِ [*A man completely armed*]: the former expl. as meaning *a man wearing a complete set of arms,* or *weapons:* [pl. شُكَّاكٌ, agreeably with analogy:] you say قَوْمٌ شُكَّاكٌ فِى الحَدِيدِ [*a people,* or *party, completely clad in sets of iron arms or weapons*]. (Ṣ, O. [In one of my copies of the Ṣ, بِالحَدِيدِ.]) [Accord. to the TA, one says رَجُلٌ شُكَّاكٌ ▼ مِنْ قَوْمٍ شُكَّاكٍ: but شُكَّاكٌ seems evidently to be a mistranscription for شَاكٌّ. See also شَاكُّ السِّلَاحِ and شَاكِى السِّلَاحِ in arts. شوك and شكو.] — رَحِمٌ شَاكَّةٌ *Near relationship.* (O, TA. [See شَكَّتِ الرَّحِمُ.]) ═ See also what next follows.

شَاكَّةٌ *A tumour in the fauces;* (O, Ḳ;) *mostly in children:* (O:) pl. شَوَاكُّ: or, accord. to Abu-l-Jarráḥ, the sing. of شَوَاكُّ is ▼ شَاكٌّ, meaning the *tumour.* (TA.)

مِشَكٌّ The *thong with which the coat of mail is* [*in certain parts thereof*] *conjoined* (يُشَكُّ بِهِ): 'Antarah says,

• وَمِشَكِّ سَابِغَةٍ هَتَكْتُ فُرُوجَهَا •
• بِالسَّيْفِ عَنْ حَامِى الحَقِيقَةِ مُعْلِمِ •

(O, TA:) [but in the EM it is مَسَكِّ, thus with س, and with fet-ḥ to the م; a word which I do not find in any lexicon: it is said that] مسك signifies *a coat of mail narrow in the rings:* and the poet means, *And of many an ample coat of mail* [*narrow in the rings*] *have I rent open the middle parts with the sword, from over a man who was the defender of those who, or that which, it was his duty to defend, who was pointed to as being the cavalier of the army.* (EM p. 243.)

أَمْرٌ مَشْكُوكٌ [for مَشْكُوكٌ فِيهِ] *An affair,* or *a case, in which there is doubt.* (TA.) ═ مِنْبَرٌ مَشْكُوكٌ i. q. مَشْدُودٌ [i. e. *A pulpit made firm* or *strong* &c.]. (TA. [See also مَسْكُوك.])

شكد

1. شَكَدَهُ, aor. ـِ (Ṣ, L) and ـُ, (L,) inf. n. شَكْدٌ; (Ṣ, L, Ḳ;) and ▼ اشكدهُ, (M, L,) but this latter, which is erroneously said in the copies of the Ḳ to be syn. with شَكَدَ, instead of شَكَدَ, is, accord. to ISd, not of high authority; (TA;) *He gave him:* (Ṣ, L, Ḳ:) or *he gave him a thing as a free gift.* (L.)

4. اشكدهُ *He gave him of dates on their being cut,* and *of wheat on its being reaped.* (L.) *He gave him of a heap of reaped corn on the occasion of measuring,* and *of the bundles* (حُزَم) [*of corn*] *on the occasion of reaping:* of the dial. of El-Yemen. (L.) *He gave him food to eat, or milk to drink, after it had been deposited in the house* or *tent.* (L.) — See also 1.

10. استشكد *He sought*, or *demanded*, *what is termed* شُكْد [q. v.]. (L.) — And جَآءَ يَسْتَشْكِدُنِى *He came seeking*, or *demanding*, *of me* شُكْد; meaning *what is given of a heap of reaped corn on the occasion of measuring*, and *of the bundles* (حُزَم) [*of corn*] *on the occasion of reaping*: of the dial. of El-Yemen. (L.)

شُكْدٌ *A gift*: (Ṣ, L, Ḳ:) or *a free gift*: pl. أَشْكَادٌ. (L.) *A recompense*. (L.) [See شُكْر in two places.] *What is given of dates when they are cut*, and *of wheat when it is reaped*. (L.) *What is given of a heap of reaped corn on the occasion of the measuring*, and *of the bundles* (حُزَم) [*of corn*] *on the occasion of the reaping*: of the dial. of El-Yemen. (L.) *Travelling-provisions with which one is furnished, consisting of milk*, or [*the preparation of dried curd called*] أَقِط, or *clarified butter*, or *dates*, *and with which one goes forth from the abodes of a people*. (L.) And *Meat and drink deposited in a house* or *tent*. (L.)

شكر

1. شَكَرَ لَهُ, and شَكَرَهُ, (Ṣ, Mgh, Ḳ,) but the former is the more chaste, (Ṣ,) and the latter is for شَكَرَ نِعْمَتَهُ, (A,) aor. ـُ, (TA,) inf. n. شُكْر and شُكْرَانٌ (Ṣ, A,* Mṣb, Ḳ) and شُكُورٌ, (Ṣ, Ḳ,) which last, in the Ḳur lxxvi. 9, may be either an inf. n. or pl. of شُكْر [used as a simple subst.], (Ṣ,) *He thanked him*; or *praised*, *eulogized*, or *commended*, *him*, *for a benefit* or *benefits*: (Ṣ:) *he was grateful*, or *thankful*, *to him*; or *he acknowledged his beneficence*, and *spoke of it largely*: (Ṣ,* Ḳ: [but in the Ṣ, the verb in the former sense has شُكْر only for its inf. n., and it is implied that in the latter sense it has for its inf. n. only شُكْرَان, as will be seen below:]) and شَكَرَ اللّٰهَ, and شَكَرَ لِلّٰهِ, (Lḥ, Mṣb, Ḳ,) which latter is less common than the former, and even disallowed by Aṣ in prose, though allowed by him in verse, (Mṣb,) and شَكَرَ بِنِعْمَةِ اللّٰهِ, and شَكَرَ نِعْمَةَ اللّٰهِ and شَكَرَ بِاللّٰهِ (Lḥ, Ḳ,) and شَكَرَ لِلّٰهِ نِعْمَتَهُ, (A,) inf. n. شُكْر and شُكْرَانٌ (Mṣb) [and شُكُورٌ], *He thanked*, or *praised*, *God for his beneficence*: (A:) *he was grateful*, or *thankful*, *to God*; or *acknowledged his beneficence*, and *spoke of it largely*: (Ḳ:) *he acknowledged the beneficence of God*, *and acted in the manner incumbent on him in rendering Him obedience and abstaining from disobedience*; so that شُكْر is in word and in deed: (Mṣb:) and ↓ تَشَكَّرَ لَهُ signifies the same as شَكَرَ لَهُ: (Ṣ, A, Mṣb, Ḳ:) you say, تَشَكَّرْتُ ↓ لَهُ مَا صَنَعَ [*I thanked him*, &c., *for what he did*]: (A:) and تشكّر ↓ لَهُ بَلَآءَهُ [*He was grateful to Him*, &c., i. e. to God, *for his probation*]: (Ḳ:) and أَشْكُرُ إِلَيْكَ نِعَمَ اللّٰهِ [*I praise to thee*, or *mention to thee with thanks*, *the favours of God*]: (L in art. حمد:) [but there are many explanations of شَكَرَ beside those given above: its meanings will be more fully shown by what here follows:] شُكْر is the *thanking* a benefactor; or *praising*, *eulogizing*, or *commending*, him, (Ṣ, A,) *for a benefit* or *benefits*: (Ṣ:) or the *being grateful*, or *thankful*; or *acknowledging beneficence*; and *speaking of it largely*; and [in the copies of the Ḳ, "or," but this is evidently a mistake,] *it is only on account of favour received*; (Ḳ;) and شُكْرَان is [the same, being] *contr. of* كُفْرَانٌ: (Ṣ:) شُكْر [sometimes] differs from حَمْد; (Mṣb in art. حمد;) for شكر is only on account of favour received; whereas حمد is sometimes because of favour received, (Th, Az, TA in art. حمد, and Mṣb ubi suprà,) and sometimes from other causes; (Th ubi suprà;) [and thus] the latter is of more common application than the former; (Ṣ in art. حمد;) therefore you do not say شَكَرْتُهُ عَلَى شَجَاعَتِهِ, but you say حَمِدْتُهُ على شجاعته: (Mṣb ubi suprà:) or شُكْر is more common than حَمْد with respect to its kinds and means, and more particular with respect to the objects to which it relates; and the latter is more common with respect to the objects to which it relates, and more particular with respect to the means; for the former is, with the heart, the *being humble*, or *lowly*, *and submissive*; and with the tongue, the act of *praising*, *eulogizing*, or *commending*; and *acknowledging beneficence*; and with the members, the act of *obeying*, and *submitting one's self*; and the object to which it relates is the benefactor, exclusively of his essential qualities; therefore one does not say شَكَرْنَا اللّٰهَ عَلَى حَيَاتِهِ [*we thanked God for his existence*, or *praised Him*, &c.]; but He is مَحْمُود on that account, like as He is for his beneficence; and شُكْر is also for beneficence: thus حَمْد relates to every object to which, as an object, شُكْر relates; but the reverse is not the case: and everything whereby is حمد, thereby is شكر; but the reverse is not the case; for the latter is by means of the members, or limbs, and the former is by means of the tongue: شُكْر is of three kinds; with the heart, or mind, which is the *forming an* [*adequate*] *idea of the benefit*; and with the tongue, which is the *praising*, *eulogizing*, or *commending*, *the benefactor*; and with the members, or limbs, which is the *requiting the benefit according to its desert*: it rests upon five foundations; humility of him who renders it towards him to whom it is rendered; his love of him; his acknowledgment of his benefit; the eulogizing him for it; and his not making use of the benefit in a manner which he [who has conferred it] dislikes: it is also explained as *devotion of the heart to love of the benefactor*, and *of the members to obey him*, and *the employment of the tongue in mentioning him and eulogizing him*: [and there are several other explanations of it which it is unnecessary to add:] some say that it is formed by transposition from كَشْر, the "act of uncovering, or exposing to view:" others, that it is from عَيْنٌ شَكْرَى "a full fountain, or eye;" accord. to which etymology it would signify the *being full of the praise of the benefactor*. (B, TA.) — شُكْر on the part of God signifies ‡ The *requiting and commending* [a person]: (Ḳ:) or † the *forgiving* a man: or ‡ the *regarding* him *with content*, *satisfaction*, *good will*, or *favour*: and hence, necessarily, ‡ the *recompensing*, or *rewarding*, him: the saying شَكَرَ اللّٰهُ سَعْيَهُ signifies ‡ *May God recompense*, or *reward*, *his work*, or *labour*. (TA.) — شَكِرَتْ, aor. ـَ, (Ṣ, Ḳ,) inf. n. شَكَرٌ, (Ṣ,) ‡ *Her* (a camel's) *udder became full* (Ṣ, Ḳ, TA) *of milk*: (Ṣ, TA:) or *she* (a camel) *obtained a good share of leguminous herbage*, or [*other*] *pasturage*, *and in consequence abounded with milk after having had little milk*: (T, TA:) and *she* (a beast) *became fat*, (Ḳ, TA,) *and her udder became full of milk*. (TA.) — And شَكِرَ ‡ *He was*, or *became*, *liberal*, or *bountiful*, (A, Ḳ,) after having been niggardly: (A:) or *he gave largely after having been niggardly*. (Ḳ.) — شَكِرَتْ said of a tree (شَجَرَة), (Fr, Ṣ, A, Ḳ,) aor. ـَ, inf. n. شَكَرٌ, (Ṣ,) † *It produced*, or *put forth*, *what are termed* شَكِير, (Fr, Ṣ, Ḳ,) i. e. *what grow around it*, *from its* أَصْل [i. e. *root*, or *base*, or *stem*]; (Ṣ;) as also ↓ اشكرت, (Fr, TA,) and ↓ اشتكرت: (Ṣgh, TA:) or *its* شَكِير, i. e. *sappy twigs* or *shoots*, *from its stem*, or *small leaves beneath the large*, *became abundant*. (A.) — And شَكِرَ, aor. ـَ, (Ḳ,) inf. n. شَكَرٌ; (TA;) and شَكَرَ, aor. ـُ; and ↓ اشكر; (Ḳ;) said of palm-trees (نَخْل), † *They had many* شَكِير, i. e. *offsets*, or *suckers*. (AḤn, Ḳ,* TA.) — And شَكِرَ and ↓ اشكر and ↓ اشتكر are all verbs from شَكِير. (Ḳ.) [It is said in the Ḳ that these verbs are from شكير in all of certain significations there mentioned; app. meaning, all that are there mentioned after the next preceding verb: and hence they seem to have the significations here following: — said of palm-trees (نَخْل), † *They put forth leaves around their branches*: — and, said of trees in general (شَجَر), † *They put forth branches*: — and † *They produced bark*: — and, said of a grape-vine, † *It grew from a shoot planted*: — in the TA it seems to be implied that, said of a vine, they signify † *it put forth long shoots*, or *upper shoots*.]

3. شَاكَرْتُهُ *I showed him that I was thankful*, or *grateful*, (A, O, Ḳ,) *to him*. (A.) — And شَاكَرْتُهُ الحَدِيثَ *I commenced with him discourse*. (O, Ḳ.)

4. اشكر القَوْمُ † *The people's camels had their udders full of milk* (شَكِرَتْ إِبِلُهُمْ): (Ḳ:) or *the people's camels became fat*: (TA:) or *the people milked a camel* or *sheep* or *goat having her udder full of milk*, i. e., *such as is termed* شَكِرَة: (Ṣ:) or *the people milked camels* or *sheep* or *goats having their udders full of milk*, *one such after another*: (O, TA: [but for اِحْتَلَبُوا شَكِرَةً شَكِرَةً in the O, and شَكْرَةً شَكْرَةً in the TA, I read احتلبوا شَكِرَةً شَكِرَةً, agreeably with what here next precedes:]) or *the people*, *having alighted in a place where their camels found herbs*, or *leguminous plants*, *had abundance of milk from them*. (T, TA.) — اشكرت said of an udder: see 8. — اشكرت الأَرْضُ † *The land produced fresh herbage after other herbage that had become dried up and dusty*. (TA.) — See also 1, near the end of the paragraph, in three places.

5. تشكّر: see 1, in three places. — Also [*He affected*, or *made a show of*, *thankfulness*, or *gratitude*: (see تَحَمَّدَ:) or] *he seemed*, or *appeared*, *thankful*, or *grateful*. (KL.)

8. اشتكر ‡ *It* (an udder) *became full* (Ṣ, Ḳ, TA) *of milk*; (Ṣ, TA;) as also ↓ اشكر. (Ḳ.) — اشتكرت

السَّمَآءُ † The rain fell vehemently: (Ṣ:) or the sky rained much. (Ḳ.) — اشتكرت الرِّيَاحُ † The winds brought rain: (Ḳ:) or blew violently: or, as is said on the authority of A'Obeyd, were contrary; but ISd says that this is a mistake. (TA.) — Also اشتكر † It (heat, and cold,) became intense. (Ḳ.) — ‡ He (a man) strove, exerted himself, or did his utmost, in his running. (Ḳ, TA.) = Also † It became what is termed شَكِير [q. v.]. (TA.) — See also 1, near the end of the paragraph, in two places. — [Hence, app.,] ‡ It (a fœtus) put forth downy hair. (A.)

شَكْرٌ The vulva, or pudendum, of a woman: (Ṣ, M, Mṣb, Ḳ:) or the flesh thereof: (M, Ḳ,* MF:) as also ↓ شِكْرٌ, in either of these senses: (Ḳ:) pl. شُكَارٌ: (Mṣb, TA:) نَحْمُهَا, in the Ḳ, as the second explanation, is a mistake for لَحْمُهَا. (MF.) It is said in a trad., نَهَى عَنْ شَكْرِ البَغِيِّ, meaning He forbade the giving hire for prostitution; the word ثَمَن being understood as prefixed to شكر. (TA.) — Also i. q. نِكَاحٌ [i. e. The act of compressing, or of contracting marriage with, a woman]. (TṢ, Ḳ.)

شُكْرٌ an inf. n. of شَكَرَ: (Ṣ, A,* Mṣb, Ḳ:) and it may [be used as a simple subst., and, as such,] have for its pl. شُكُورٌ. (Ṣ. [See 1.])

شِكْرٌ: see شَكْرٌ.

شَكْرَةٌ † [Fulness of the udder of a camel; and so ↓ شَكْرِيَّةٌ is expl. in the TḲ;] a subst. from أَشْكَرَ الْقَوْمُ [q. v.]. (Ḳ.) One says, هٰذَا زَمَنُ الشَّكْرَةِ, so in the L and other lexicons, (TA,) or ↓ الشَّكَرَةِ, (so in my copies of the Ṣ,) or ↓ الشَّكْرِيَّةِ, (so in the O and Ḳ,) † [This is the time of the fulness of the udder,] when the camels abound with milk, or have their udders full, (إِذَا حَفَلَتْ, q. v.,) from the [herbage called] رَبِيع. (Ṣ, O, L, Ḳ.)

شَكَرَةٌ: see the next preceding paragraph.

شَكِرَةٌ ‡ A she-camel, (Aṣ, Ṣ, A, Ḳ,) and ewe or she-goat, (A,) having her udder full (Aṣ, Ṣ, A, Ḳ) of milk, (Ṣ,) whatever be the fodder, or herbage, she has eaten; (A;) as also ↓ مِشْكَارٌ: (Ḳ:) or the former, that has obtained a good share of leguminous herbage, or of [other] pasture, and in consequence abounds with milk after having had little milk: (T, TA:) and ↓ the latter, that abounds with milk though having had but a small share of pasture: (TA:) or that abounds with milk in summer and ceases in winter: (IAạr, TA:) pl. of the former شَكَارَى, (Ṣ, Ḳ,) applied to camels and to sheep or goats, (Ṣ,) and شَكْرَى (Ḳ) and شَكِرَاتٌ: (Ṣ, Ḳ:) and شَكَارَى is applied to camels, and sheep or goats, as meaning abounding with milk, or having their udders full, (إِذَا حَفَلَتْ) from the [herbage called] رَبِيع (Ṣ, TA.) [↓ شَكْرَى is also a sing. epithet, having a similar signification: as well as a pl.] One says ↓ ضَرَّةٌ شَكْرَى ‡ An udder abounding with milk: (A:) or having much milk. (Ṣ.) And ↓ عَيْنٌ شَكْرَى † A full source or eye. (B, TA.) And ↓ قِدْرَةٌ شَكْرَى † A fat piece of flesh-meat: (Ḳ:) or ‡ [a piece of flesh-meat] flowing with grease, or gravy: (A: [but in my copy, قُدْرَةٌ is erroneously put for قِدْرَةٌ:]) pl. شَكَارَى. (A.)

شَكْرَى: see the next four preceding sentences.

شَكْرِيَّةٌ: see شَكْرَةٌ, in two places.

شَكُورٌ an intensive epithet, (TA,) signifying كَثِيرُ الشُّكْرِ [i. e. One who thanks much; or who is very thankful or grateful: see 1]: (Ḳ, TA:) and one who is earnest, or does his utmost, in thanking his Lord, or in being thankful or grateful to Him, by obedience to Him, performing his appointed religious services: (TA:) or one who does his utmost in showing his thankfulness, or gratitude, with his heart and his tongue and his members, or limbs, with firm belief, and with acknowledgment [of benefits received]: or who sees his inability to be [sufficiently] thankful or grateful: or who renders thanks, or is thankful or grateful, for probation: or, for what is denied him: (ḲT:) pl. شُكُرٌ. (TA.) — ‡ A beast that is sufficed by little fodder or herbage, (Ṣ, A,) and that fattens upon it: (A:) or that fattens upon little fodder or herbage: (Ḳ:) as though thankful for that small benefit. (TA.) — الشَّكُورُ, applied to God, ‡ [He who approves, or rewards, or forgives, much, or largely:] He who gives large reward for small, or few, works: He in whose estimation small, or few, works performed by his servants increase, and who multiplies his rewards to them. (TA.)

شَكِيرٌ ‡ The shoots that grow around a tree, from its أَصْل [i. e. root, or base, or stem]: (Ṣ:) or sappy twigs or shoots, that grow from the stem of a tree: or small leaves beneath the large: (A:) or fresh and tender twigs or shoots, that grow among such as have become thick and tough: and what grow at, or upon, the أُصُول [i. e. roots, or bases, or stems,] of large trees: or small leaves that grow at, or upon, the root, or base, or stem, of a tree: (IAạr, TA:) and offsets, or suckers, or sprouts, of palm-trees: (Ḳ:) and the leaves that are around the branches of the palm-tree: (Yaạḳoob, Ḳ:) and plants, and hair, and feathers, and abundant ostrich-feathers (عِفَآء, Ḳ, TA, in the CḲ عَفاء), such as are small, growing among such as are large: or the first, of herbage, growing after other herbage that has become dried up and dusty: (Ḳ:) and downy hair, or down: and any soft, fine hair: (A:) or hair growing among the plaits: pl. شُكُرٌ: and weak hair: (TA:) and hair at the roots of a horse's mane, (Ḳ, TA,) like down, and in the forelock: (TA:) and the hair that is next to the face and the back of the neck: (A, Ḳ:) and branches: (AḤn, Ḳ: [in the CḲ, والقُصُون is erroneously put for والغُصُون:]) and the bark (لِحَآء) of trees: pl. شُكُرٌ: (Ḳ:) and the pl. also signifies the long shoots of a grape-vine: or its higher, or highest, shoots: (AḤn, TA:) and the sing., a grape-vine growing from a planted shoot. (AḤn, Ḳ, TA.) — Also ‡ Young men: (A:) or young offspring. (TA, from a trad.) — And ‡ The young ones of camels: (Ḳ, TA:) as being likened to the شَكِير of palm-trees. (TA.)

شَكَائِرُ † Forelocks: (Ḳ, TA:) as though pl. of شَكِيرَةٌ [which may be n. un. of شَكِير]. (TA.)

[شِكُورِيَةٌ a name applied in the present day to Cichorium, intybus and endivia; wild and garden-succory, and endive; as also هِنْدِبَى, correctly هِنْدِبَى.]

شَاكِرِيٌّ A hired man, or hireling; one taken as a servant: an arabicized word, from [the Pers.] چاكر. (O, Ḳ.)

شَوْكَرَانٌ: see the next paragraph.

شَيْكَرَانٌ (Ṣ, Ḳ) and شَيْكُرَانٌ, (Ḳ,) [in the CḲ, erroneously, شُكْرَان and with ḍamm to the ك,] or the correct form is شَيْكُرَانٌ, with ḍamm to the ك, as Ibn-Hishám El-Lakhmee and El-Fárábee have expressly affirmed; (TA;) or it is correctly with س, (Ḳ,) unpointed, and so it is mentioned by AḤn; (TA;) [but see سَيْكُرَانٌ;] or correctly ↓ شَوْكَرَانٌ, (Ḳ,) as Ṣgh holds to be the case, (TA,) [and thus it is written in several medical books, from the Pers. شَوْكَرَانْ; accord. to Golius, Cicuta herba, and applied in the present day to conium, i. e. hemlock, or a species thereof; and this is probably what is meant by Golius, as the conium maculatum, or common hemlock, is called by some cicuta;] a certain plant, (Ṣ, Ḳ,) of the kind called حَمْض, (so in a marginal note in a copy of the Ṣ,) the stem of which is like that of the رَازِيَانج [or fennel], and the leaves of which are like those of the [species of cucumber called] قِثَّآء, or, as some say, like those of the يَبْرُوح [q. v.], and smaller; having a white flower, and a slender stem, without any fruit; and its seed is like [that of] the نَانْخَوَاه [or ammi], or [of] the أَنِيسُون [or anise], without taste or odour, and mucilaginous. (TA.)

أَشْكَرُ [More, and most, thankful, or grateful, &c.: see an ex. voce بَرُوق].

عُشْبٌ مَشْكَرَةٌ (O, Ḳ, TA, in the CḲ مُشْكِرَةٌ,) † Herbage that causes milk to be copious. (O, Ḳ, TA. [In the CḲ, مُغْزَرَةٌ اللَّبَنِ is erroneously put for مَغْزَرَةٌ لِلَّبَنِ.])

مِشْكَارٌ: see شَكِرَةٌ, in two places.

رِيحٌ مُشْتَكِرَةٌ † A violent wind: (O, Ḳ:) or, as some say, a contrary wind; (O, TA;) but ISd says that this is a mistake. (TA.)

شكس

1. شَكِسَ, (T, Ṣ, Mṣb, TA,) aor. َ, inf. n. شَكَسٌ (T, Mṣb, TA) and شَكَاسَةٌ; (T, Ṣ, Mṣb, TA;) or شَكُسَ, aor. ُ, (O, Ḳ, TA,) inf. n. شَكَاسَةٌ; (O;) He was, or became, refractory, untractable, perverse, stubborn, or obstinate, in disposition: (Ṣ, O, Ḳ:) or hard in disposition, or illnatured, in behaviour or dealing: (TA:) or evil in disposition, or illnatured, and very perverse or cross or repugnant and averse; syn. شَرِسٌ. (Mṣb, TA.*)

3. شَاكَسَهُ *He treated him*, or *behaved towards him, with hardness, harshness*, or *illnature*. (O, Ḳ.)

6. تَشَاكَسُوا *They treated*, or *behaved towards, one another with hardness, harshness*, or *illnature*; or *disagreed, one with another*; in buying or selling: (IDrd, O, TA:) or *they treated*, or *behaved towards, one another with contrariety*, or *opposition*. (Ḳ,* TA.) [Hence,] اللَّيْلُ وَالنَّهَارُ يَتَشَاكَسَانِ ‡ *The night and the day are opposed to each other*: (TA:) or *alternate*. (Az, A, O, TA.)

شَكْسٌ: see شَكِسٌ. — مَحَلَّةٌ شَكْسٌ † *A strait place of alighting* or *abode*. (TA.) ═ الشَّكْسُ *A day*, or *two days, before the new moon*; i. q. المُحَاقُ. (AA, O, Ḳ.)

شِكْسٌ: } see the next following paragraph.
شُكُسٌ: }

شَكِسٌ, (Fr, Ṣ, Mṣb, Ḳ,) or ▼ شَكْسٌ, (Ṣ,) and ▼ شَكُسٌ, (Ḳ,) the first agreeable with analogy, (Ṣ,) A man (Ṣ) *refractory, untractable, perverse, stubborn*, or *obstinate, in disposition*: (Ṣ, Ḳ:) or *hard in disposition*, or *illnatured*: (TA:) or *evil in disposition*, or *illnatured, and very perverse* or *cross* or *repugnant and averse*; syn. شَرِسٌ: (Mṣb:) and ▼ شِكْسٌ and ▼ مِشْكَسٌ are likewise epithets applied [in the same sense, but the latter having an intensive signification,] to a man: (IAạr, TA:) pl. شُكُسٌ; (Ṣ, Ḳ;) a pl. of the first or third; (Ḳ;) or of the second, like as صُدُقٌ is pl. of صَدْقٌ. (Ṣ.) — Also the first, ‡ *Niggardly; tenacious; avaricious*. (Ḳ.)

مِشْكَسٌ: see the next preceding paragraph.

مُتَشَاكِسُونَ (Ḳur xxxix. 30) *Disagreeing, one with another*; (A,* Ḳ,* TA;) *and behaving with hardness, harshness*, or *illnature*: (A:) or *disputing*, or *contending, together*. (TA.) [See the verb, 6.]

شكل

1. شَكَلَ, as an intrans. verb: see 4, in three places. — And see 5. ═ شَكَلَ الفَرَسَ بِالشِّكَالِ, (Ṣ,) or شَكَلَ الدَّابَّةَ, (Mṣb, Ḳ,) aor. ـُ, inf. n. شَكْلٌ, (Mṣb,) *He bound* [*the horse* or] *the beast, with the* شِكَال; (Mṣb;) [i. e.] *he bound the legs of* [*the horse* or] *the beast with the rope called* شِكَال; as also ▼ شَكَّلَهَا, (Ḳ,) inf. n. تَشْكِيلٌ. (TA.) And شَكَلْتُ الطَّائِرَ [app. *I bound the legs of the bird in like manner*]. (Ṣ.) And شَكَلْتُ عَنِ البَعِيرِ *I bound the camel's* شِكَال *between the fore girth and the hind girth*; (Ṣ;) [i. e.] *I put* [or *extended*], *between the hind girth and the fore girth of the camel, a cord*, or *string, called* شِكَال, *and then bound it, in order that the hind girth might not become* [*too*] *near to the sheath of the penis*. (TA in art. حقب.) — And [hence, i. e.] from the شِكَال of the beast, (TA,) شَكَلَ الكِتَابَ, (AHát, Ṣ, Mṣb, Ḳ, TA,) inf. n. as above, (Mṣb, TA,) ‡ *He restricted* [*the meaning* or *pronunciation of*] *the writing*, (قَيَّدَهُ, AHát, Ṣ, TA,) or *he marked the writing*, (أَعْلَمَهُ, Mṣb,) *with the signs of the desinential syntax* (AHát,* Ṣ,* Mṣb, TA*) [*and the other syllabical signs and the diacritical points*]: or i. q. أَعْجَمَهُ: (Ḳ:) but AHát says that أَعْجَمَهُ has the former meaning; and شَكَلَ الكِتَابَ signifies *he dotted*, or *pointed, it* [*with the diacritical points*]: (TA:) and ▼ اشكل الكِتَابَ signifies the same as شَكَلَهُ; (Ṣ, Mṣb, Ḳ, TA;) as though [meaning] *he removed from it dubiousness and confusion*; (Ṣ, Ḳ,* TA;) so that the أ in this case is to denote privation: (TA:) this [J says (TA)] I have transcribed from a book, without having heard it. (Ṣ.) — And شَكَلَتْ شَعْرَهَا, (O, TA,) aor. ـُ; thus correctly, as pointed by IḲṭṭ; accord. to the Ḳ ▼ شكّلت; (TA;) † *She* (a woman) *plaited two locks of her hair, of the fore part of her head, on the right and left*, (O, Ḳ, TA,) *and then bound with them her other* ذَوَائِب [or *pendent locks* or *plaits*]. (TA.) — And شكل [thus in the TA, so that it may be either شَكَلَ or ▼ شَكَّلَ,] † *He* (the lion) *compressed* the lioness: on the authority of IḲṭṭ. (TA.) ═ شَكِلَتْ, aor. ـَ, (Ḳ, TA,) inf. n. شَكَلٌ, (TA,) *She* (a woman) *used amorous gesture* or *behaviour*; or *such gesture*, or *behaviour, with coquettish boldness, and feigned coyness* or *opposition*; *displayed what is termed* شِكْل, i. e. غُنْج *and* دَلّ *and* غَزَل; (Ḳ, TA;) and ▼ تشكّلت [signifies the same], i. e. تَدَلَّلَتْ [and in like manner تشكّل is said of a man]. (TA.) — See also شَكِلَ below, in two places. — And شَكِلْتُ إِلَى كَذَا, with kesr [to the ك], i. q. رَكَنْتُ [i. e. *I inclined to such a thing*; or *trusted to*, or *relied upon, it, so as to be*, or *become, easy*, or *quiet, in mind*]. (O.)

2. شَكَّلَ, as an intrans. verb: see 4: — and see also 5. ═ شَكَّلَهُ, inf. n. تَشْكِيلٌ, *He formed, fashioned, figured, shaped, sculptured*, or *pictured, it*; syn. صَوَّرَهُ; (Ḳ, TA;) namely, a thing. (TA.) — See also 1, in three places.

3. مُشَاكَلَةٌ signifies The *being conformable, suitable, agreeable, similar, homogeneous*, or *congenial*; syn. مُوَافَقَةٌ; (Ṣ, Ḳ;) as also ▼ تَشَاكُلٌ: (IDrd, Ṣ, Ḳ:) Er-Rághib [strangely] says that المُشَاكَلَةُ is from الشَّكْلُ signifying "the binding," or "shackling," a beast [with the شِكَال]. (TA.) You say, هُوَ يُشَاكِلُهُ [*He, or it, is conformable, &c., with him, or it*; or *resembles him, or it*]. (Mṣb.) And هٰذَا الأَمْرُ لَا يُشَاكِلُكَ i. e. لَا يُوَافِقُكَ [*This affair will not be suitable to thee*]. (TA.) And ▼ تَشَاكَلَا *They resembled each other*. (MA.)

4. اشكل [primarily] signifies صَارَ ذَا شَكْلٍ [meaning *It*, or *he, was*, or *became, such as had a likeness* or *resemblance*, or *a like*, or *match*, &c.]. (TA.) — [And hence, app.,] said of a thing, or case, or an affair; (Ṣ, Mgh, O, Mṣb, Ḳ;) as also ▼ شَكَلَ, (O, Ḳ, TA, [in the CḲ, erroneously, شَكِلَ, evidently not meant by the author of the Ḳ, as it is his rule, after mentioning a verb of this form, to add كَفَرِحَ or the like,]) inf. n. شَكْلٌ; (TA;) and ▼ شكّل, (Ḳ,) inf. n. تَشْكِيلٌ; (TA;) † *It was*, or *became, dubious*, or *confused*; syn. اِلْتَبَسَ, (Ṣ, O, Mṣb, Ḳ,) and اِخْتَلَطَ, (O, TA,) or اِشْتَبَهَ: (Mgh:) [and ▼ اشتكل is mentioned in this sense by Golius as on the authority of J (whom I do not find to have mentioned it either in this art. or elsewhere), and by Freytag as on the authority of Abu-l-'Alà: accord. to Sh, اشكل in this sense is from شُكْلَةٌ signifying "redness mixed with whiteness:" (see مُشْكَل:) but] accord. to Er-Rághib, إِشْكَالٌ in a thing, or case, or an affair, is metaphorical, [and] like اِشْتِبَاهٌ from الشِّبْهُ. (TA.) One says, اشكل الأَمْرُ عَلَى الرَّجُلِ † [*The thing*, or *case*, or *affair, was*, or *became, dubious*, or *confused, to the man*]; and ▼ شَكَلَ means the same. (Zj, O.) And أَشْكَلَتْ عَلَىَّ الأَخْبَارُ † [*The tidings were dubious*, or *confused, to me*], and أَحْكَلَتْ; both meaning the same. (TA.) And one says also, عَلَيْهِ إِشْكَالٌ and عليه إِشْكَالَاتٌ [meaning *There is doubt*, or *uncertainty*, and *there are doubts*, or *uncertainties, respecting it*: thus using the inf. n. as a simple subst., and therefore pluralizing it]. (Mz, 3rd نوع; &c.) — It is also said of a disease; [app. as meaning † *It became nearly cured*; because still in a somewhat doubtful state;] like as you say تَمَاثَلَ; and so ▼ شَكَّلَ. (TA.) — اشكل النَّخْلُ *The palm-trees became in that state in which their dates were sweet* (Ks, Ṣ, A, O, Ḳ) *and ripe*, (Ks, Ṣ, O, Mṣb,) or *nearly ripe*; (A, TA;) and ▼ تشكّل signifies the same. (O.) — And اشكلت العَيْنُ *The eye had in it what is termed* شُكْلَة [q. v.: see also شَكَل]. (Ḳ.) ═ اشكل الكِتَابَ: see 1.

5. تشكّل *It* (a thing, TA) *was*, or *became, formed, fashioned, figured, shaped, sculptured*, or *pictured*; syn. تَصَوَّرَ. (Ḳ, TA.) — And *He became goodly in shape, form*, or *aspect*. (TḲ in art. طوز.) — تَشَكَّلَ العِنَبُ, (Ṣ, Ḳ,) and ▼ شَكَّلَ, and ▼ شَكِلَ, (Ḳ,) *The grapes became in that state in which some of them were ripe*: (Ṣ, Ḳ:) or *became black, and beginning to be ripe*: (Ḳ:) thus in the M. (TA.) — See also 4, near the end. — And see 1, also near the end.

6: see 3, in two places.

8: see 4.

[10. استشكلهُ is often used by the learned in the present day as meaning *He deemed it* (i. e. a word or phrase or sentence) *dubious*, or *confused*.]

شَكْلٌ i. q. شِبْهٌ [as meaning *A likeness, resemblance*, or *semblance*; a well-known signification of the latter word, but one which I do not find unequivocally assigned to it in its proper art. in any of the lexicons]. (AA, Ḳ, TA. [In the CḲ, and in my MS. copy of the Ḳ, in the place of الشِّبْهُ as the first explanation of الشَّكْلُ in the Ḳ accord. to the TA, we find الشَّبَهُ; but that the explanation which I have given is correct, is shown by what here follows.]) One says, فِى فُلَانٍ شَكْلٌ مِنْ أَبِيهِ, meaning شَبَهٌ [i. e. *In such a one is a likeness*, or *resemblance, of his father*]: (AA, TA:) and ▼ شُكْلَةٌ and فيه أَشْكِلَةٌ ▼ مِنْ أَبِيهِ (AA, O, Ḳ, TA) and ▼ شَاكِلٌ, (O, Ḳ, TA,) [likewise] meaning شِبْهٌ, (AA, O, Ḳ, TA,) and مُشَابِهَةٌ: (TḲ:) and ▼ شَاكِلَةٌ also is *syn. with* شَكْلٌ [in the sense of شِبْهٌ]; (Ḳ, TA;) [for] one says, هٰذَا عَلَى شَاكِلَةِ أَبِيهِ as meaning شِبْهِ [i. e. *This is accordant to the likeness of his father*]. (TA.) — And *I. q.* مِثَالٌ: you say, هٰذَا عَلَى شَكْلِ هٰذَا, meaning على مِثَالِهِ [i. e. *This is according to the model*, or *pattern*, or *the mode*, or *manner*, *of this*]. (TA.) — And The *shape*, *form*, or *figure*, (صُورَة,) of a thing; *such as is perceived by the senses*; and *such as is imagined*: (Ḳ:) the *form* (هَيْئَة), of a body, *caused by the entire contents' being included by one boundary, as in the case of a sphere; or by several boundaries, as in those bodies that have several angles* or *sides, such as have four* and *such as have six* [&c.]: so says Ibn-El-Kemál: (TA:) pl. [of pauc., in this and in other senses,] أَشْكَالٌ and [of mult.] شُكُولٌ. (Ḳ.) — [It often means *A kind*, *sort*, or *variety*, of animals, plants, food, &c.] — [And The *likeness*, or the *way* or *manner*, *of the actions* of a person:] it is said in a trad. respecting the description of the Prophet, سَأَلْتُ أَبِى عَنْ شَكْلِهِ, meaning [*I asked my father respecting the likeness of his actions*, or] *respecting what was like his actions*; accord. to IAmb: or, accord. to Az, *respecting his particular way*, *course*, *mode*, or *manner*, *of acting*, or *conduct*: (O:) and ▼ شَاكِلَةٌ [likewise, and more commonly,] signifies *a particular way*, *course*, *mode*, or *manner*, *of acting*, or *conduct*; (Ṣ, O, Ḳ, TA;) as in the saying, كُلٌّ يَعْمَلُ عَلَى شَاكِلَتِهِ, (Ṣ, O, TA,) in the Ḳur [xvii. 86], (O, TA,) i. e. *Every one does according to his particular way*, &c., (Ibn-'Arafeh, Ṣ, O, Bḍ, Jel, TA,) *that is suitable to his state in respect of right direction* and *of error*, or *to the essential nature of his soul, and to his circumstances that are consequent to the constitution*, or *temperament*, *of his body*: (Bḍ:) and *according to his nature*, or *natural disposition*, (Ibn-'Arafeh, Er-Rághib, O, TA,) *by which he is restricted* [*as with a* شِكَال]: (Er-Rághib, TA:) and *his direction towards which he would go*: (Akh, Ṣ, O, Ḳ,* TA:) and *his side* [*that he takes*]: (Ḳatádeh, O, Ḳ,* TA:) and *his aim*, *intention*, or *purpose*: (Ḳatádeh, O, Ḳ, TA:) and شَكْلٌ [likewise] signifies *aim*, *intention*, or *purpose*; syn. قَصْدٌ. (TA.) — Also *A thing that is suitable* to one; or *fit*, or *proper*, for one: you say, هٰذَا مِنْ هَوَاىَ وَمِنْ شَكْلِى [*This is of what is loved by me and of what is suitable to me*]: (Ḳ, TA:) and لَيْسَ شَكْلُهُ مِنْ شَكْلِى [*What is suitable to him is not of what is suitable to me*]. (TA.) [And hence, app.,] one says, مَا شَكْلِى وَشَكْلُهُ, meaning *What is my case and* [what is] *his*, or *its*, *case?* because of his, or its, remoteness from me. (T and TA voce أَمْرٌ.) — And sing. of أَشْكَالٌ (L, K, TA) signifying *Discordant affairs* and *objects of want, concerning things on account of which one imposes upon himself difficulty and for which one is anxious*: (Lth, TA:) and *dubious*, or *confused*, *affairs*: (TA:) or *discordant*, and *dubious*, or *confused*, *affairs*. (Ḳ. [In the CḲ, الْمُشْكِلَةُ is erroneously put for الْمُشْكَلَة.]) — Also *A like*; syn. مِثْلٌ; (Ṣ, Mgh, O, Mṣb, Ḳ;) and so ▼ شِكْلٌ: (O, Ḳ:) or, as some say, the *like* of another *in nature* or *constitution*: (Mṣb: [and accord. to Er-Rághib, it seems that the attribute properly denoted by it is congruity between two persons in respect of the way or manner of acting or conduct: but in the passage in which this is expressed in the TA, I find erasures and alterations which render it doubtful:]) pl. أَشْكَالٌ (Ṣ, Mgh, O, Mṣb, Ḳ*) and شُكُولٌ [as above]. (Ṣ, O, Mṣb, Ḳ.*) One says, هٰذَا شَكْلُ هٰذَا *This is the like of this.* (Mṣb.) And فُلَانٌ شَكْلُ فُلَانٍ *Such a one is the like of such a one in his several states* or *conditions* [&c.]. (TA.) In the saying in the Ḳur [xxxviii. 58], وَآخَرُ مِنْ شَكْلِهِ, (O, TA,) meaning And other punishment *of the like thereof*, (Zj, TA,) Mujáhid read ▼ مِن شِكْلِهِ. (O, TA.) — Also sing. of أَشْكَالٌ signifying, (O, Ḳ,) accord. to IAạr, (O,) *Certain ornaments* (O, Ḳ) *consisting of pearls* or *of silver*, (Ḳ,) *resembling one another, worn as ear-drops by women*: (O, Ḳ:) or, as some say, the sing. signifies *a certain thing which girls*, or *young women*, *used to append to their hair, of pearls* or *of silver*. (O.) — And *A species of plant*, (IAạr, O, Ḳ,) *diversified in colour*, (Ḳ,) *yellow and red*. (IAạr, O, Ḳ.) — [And The *various syllabical signs*, or *vowel-points &c., by which the pronunciation of words is indicated and restricted*: originally an inf. n., and therefore thus used in a pl. sense.] — See also the next paragraph.

شِكْلٌ: see the next preceding paragraph, latter part, in two places. — Also, as an attribute of a woman, *Amorous gesture* or *behaviour*; or *such gesture*, or *behaviour*, *combined with coquettish boldness, and feigned coyness* or *opposition*; syn. دَلٌّ, (Ṣ, O, Mṣb, Ḳ,) and غُنْجٌ, and غَزَلٌ; (Ḳ; [in the CḲ, غَزْلٌ, which is a mistranscription;]) or her غُنْج, and *comely* or *pleasing* دَلّ, *whereby a woman renders herself comely* or *pleasing*; (TA;) and ▼ شُكْلٌ signifies the same. (Ḳ.) One says امْرَأَةٌ ذَاتُ شِكْلٍ [*A woman having amorous gesture* or *behaviour*; &c.]. (Ṣ, O, Mṣb.)

شَكَلٌ, in a sheep or goat, The *quality of being white in the* شَاكِلَة. (Ṣ, O. [See أَشْكَلُ.]) [In this sense, accord. to the TḲ, an inf. n., of which the verb is ▼ شَكِلَ, said of a ram &c.]. — And in an eye, The *quality of having what is termed* شُكْلَةٌ [q. v.]. (Ṣ, O.) [Accord. to the TḲ, in this sense also an inf. n., of which the verb is ▼ شَكِلَ, said of a thing, as meaning *It had a redness in its whiteness.*]

شُكْلَةٌ: see شَكْلٌ, first signification. — One says also, فِيهِ شُكْلَةٌ مِنْ سُمْرَةٍ [*In him*, or *it*, *is an admixture of a tawny*, or *brownish*, *colour*], and شُكْلَةٌ مِنْ سَوَادٍ [*an admixture of blackness*]: (TA:) [or] شُكْلَةٌ signifies *redness mixed with whiteness*: (Sh, Mṣb, TA:) in camels, (Ḳ, TA,) and in sheep or goats, (TA,) *blackness mixed with redness*, (Ḳ, TA,) or *with dust-colour*: in the hyena, accord. to IAạr, *a colour in which are blackness and an ugly yellowness*: (TA:) in the eye, *a redness in the white*: (Mgh:) or, in the eye, *i. q.* شُهْلَةٌ [q. v.]: (Ḳ:) or, accord. to AO, (TA,) the *like of a redness in the white* of the eye; (Ṣ, O, TA;) and such was in the eyes of the Prophet; (O;) but if in the black of the eye, it is termed شُهْلَةٌ: (Ṣ, O, TA:) and the like is in the eyes of the [hawks, or falcons, termed] صُقُور and بُزَاة: accord. to some, it is *yellowness mixing with the white* of the eye, *around the black*, as in the eye of the hawk (الصَّقْر); but he [i. e. AO] says, I have not heard it used except in relation to redness, not in relation to yellowness. (TA.) فِيهِ شُكْلَةٌ مِنْ دَمٍ means *In him*, or *it*, *is a little* [or *a small admixture*] *of blood*. (TA.)

شَكِلَةٌ A woman *using*, or *displaying*, *what is termed* شِكْل, i. e. غُنْج *and* دَلّ *and* غَزَل [meaning *amorous gesture* or *behaviour*, &c.], (Ḳ, TA,) *in a comely*, or *pleasing*, *manner*. (TA.)

شَكْلَآءُ fem. of أَشْكَلُ [q. v.]. (Ṣ, O.) — Also *A want*; syn. حَاجَةٌ; and so ▼ أَشْكَلَةٌ, (Ṣ, O, Ḳ, [both of these words twice mentioned in this sense in the Ḳ,]) and ▼ شَوْكَلَآءُ; this last and the second on the authority of IAạr; (O;) accord. to Er-Rághib, *such as binds*, or *shackles*, (تُقَيِّدُ,) *a man* [*as though with a* شِكَال]. (TA.) One says, ▼ لَنَا قِبَلَكَ أَشْكَلَةٌ [&c.] i. e. حَاجَةٌ [*We have a want to be supplied to us on thy part*; meaning *we want a thing of thee*]. (Ṣ, O.) — Also *i. q.* مُدَاهَنَةٌ. (So in the O and TA. [But whether by this explanation be meant the inf. n., or the fem. pass. part. n., of دَاهَنَ, is not indicated. Words of the measure فَعْلَآءُ having the meaning of an inf. n., like بَغْضَآءُ, are rare.])

شِكَالٌ, of which the pl. is شُكُلٌ, (Ṣ, O, Mṣb, Ḳ,) the latter also pronounced شُكْلٌ, (TA,) *i. q.* عِقَالٌ [*A cord*, or *rope*, *with which a camel's fore shank and arm are bound together*]: (Ṣ, O:) [or, accord. to the TA, by عقال is here meant what next follows:] *a rope with which the legs of a beast* (دَابَّة) *are bound*: (Ḳ:) *a bond that is attached upon the fore and hind foot* [or *feet*] *of a horse* [or *the like*] and *of a camel*: (KL:) [*hobbles for a horse* or *the like, having a rope extending from the shackles of the fore feet to those of the hind feet*: so accord. to present usage; and so accord. to the TḲ, in Turkish كوستك: Fei says only,] the شِكَال of the beast (دابّة) is well known; and the pl. is as above. (Mṣb.) In relation to the [camel's saddle called] رَحْل, (Ḳ, TA,) accord. to Aṣ, (Ṣ, O, TA,) *A string*, or *cord*, *that is put* [or *extended and tied*] *between the* تَصْدِير [or *fore girth*] *and the* حَقَب [or *hind girth*], (Ṣ, O, Ḳ, TA,) *in order that the latter may not become* [*too*] *near to the sheath of the penis*; also called the زِوَار, on the authority of AA: (Ṣ, O, TA:) and [in relation to the saddle called قَتَب,] *a bond* [*in like manner extended and tied, for the same purpose*,] *between the* حَقَب [or *hind girth*] *and the* بِطَان [by which is meant the *fore girth*, answering to the تَصْدِير of the رَحْل]: and *a bond* [probably meaning the rope mentioned in the explanation given from the Ḳ in the preceding sentence] *between the fore leg and the hind leg.* (Ḳ, TA.) —— Also, in a horse, ‡ *The quality of having three legs distinguished by* [*the whiteness of the lower parts which is termed*] تَحْجِيل, *and one leg free therefrom;* (Ṣ, O, Ḳ, TA;) [this whiteness] being likened to the عِقَال termed شِكَال: (Ṣ, O:) or *having three legs free from* تَحْجِيل, *and one hind leg distinguished thereby:* (Ṣ, O, Ḳ,* TA:*) accord. to A'Obeyd, it is *only in the hind leg;* not in the fore leg: (Ṣ, O:) or, accord. to AO, (TA,) *having the whiteness of the* تَحْجِيل *in one hind leg and fore leg, on the opposite sides,* (Mgh,* TA,) *whether the whiteness be little or much:* (TA:) [when this is the case, the horse is said to be ذُو شِكَالٍ مِنْ خِلَافٍ: see 3 (last sentence) in art. خلف:] the Prophet disliked what is thus termed in horses. (O.)

شَكِيلٌ ‡ *Foam mixed with blood, appearing upon the bit-mouth,* or *mouth-piece of the bit.* (Z, O, Ḳ, TA.)

شَاكِلٌ: see شَكْلٌ, first signification. —— Also *A whiteness between the* عِذَار [which see, for it has various meanings,] *and the ear.* (Ḳtr, Ṣ, O. [See also شَاكِلَةٌ.])

شَوْكَلٌ: see شَوْكَلَةٌ. —— One says, اِجْعَلِ الأَمْرَ شَوْكَلًا وَاحِدًا, meaning *Make thou the affair,* or *case,* [*uniform,* or] *one uniform thing.* (Fr, TA in art. باج.)

شَاكِلَةٌ: see شَكْلٌ, former half, in two places. ═ الشَّاكِلَةُ, also, signifies *The flank;* syn. الخَاصِرَةُ, i. e. الطِّفْطِفَةُ: (Ṣ, O:) [or,] in a horse, *the skin that is between the side* (عُرْض) *of the* خَاصِرَة *and the* ثَفِنَة, (Ḳ, TA,) which latter means [the *stifle-joint,* i. e.] the *joint of the* فَخِذ *and* سَاق: or as some say, the شَاكِلَتَانِ are *the two exterior parts of the* طِفْطِفَتَانِ [or *two flanks*] *from the place to which the last of the ribs reaches to the edge of* [*the hip-bone called*] *the* حَرْقَفَة *on each side of the belly.* (TA.) One says, أَصَابَ شَاكِلَةَ الرَّمِيَّةِ, meaning [*He hit*] *the* خَاصِرَة [or *flank*] *of the* رَمِيَّة [or *animal shot at*]. (TA.) [Hence,] one says, أَصَابَ شَاكِلَةَ الصَّوَابِ ‡ [*He hit the point that he aimed at, of the thing that was right*]: and هُوَ يَرْمِى بِرَأْيِهِ الشَّوَاكِلَ ‡ [*He hits, by his opinion,* or *judgment, the right points*]. (TA.) Ibn-'Abbád says that [the pl.] شَوَاكِل signifies [also] The *hind legs;* because they are shackled [with the شِكَال]. (O.) —— Also *The part between the ear and the temple.* (IAạr, Ḳ, TA.) —— And شَوَاكِل (which is the pl. of شَاكِلَة, TA) † *Roads branching off from a main road.* (Ḳ.) You say طَرِيقٌ ذُو شَوَاكِلَ † *A road having many roads branching off from it.* (O.) —— And شَاكِلَتَا الطَّرِيقِ means ‡ *The two sides of the road:* you say طَرِيقٌ ظَاهِرُ الشَّوَاكِلِ ‡ [*A road of which the sides are apparent,* or *conspicuous*]. (TA.)

شَوْكَلَةٌ, (so in the O, as on the authority of IAạr,) or ▼ شَوْكَلٌ, (so in the Ḳ,) thus says Ez-Zejjájee, but Fr says the former, [like IAạr,] (TA,) *i. q.* رَجَّالَةٌ [as meaning The *footmen* of an army or the like]: (Fr, IAạr, Ez-Zejjájee, O, Ḳ, TA:) or مَيْمَنَةٌ [meaning the *right wing* of an army]: or مَيْسَرَةٌ [meaning the *left wing* thereof]. (Ez-Zejjájee, Ḳ, TA.) —— And *i. q.* نَاحِيَةٌ [probably as meaning The *side, region, quarter,* or *direction, towards which one goes;* like شَاكِلَةٌ, as expl. by Akh and others, in a saying mentioned voce شَكْلٌ]. (IAạr, O, Ḳ.) ═ Also *i. q.* عَوْسَجَةٌ [i. e. *A tree of the species called* عَوْسَج, q. v.]. (IAạr, O, Ḳ.)

شَوْكَلَاةٌ: see شُكْلَاةٌ, above.

أَشْكَلُ *More,* and *most, like;* syn. أَشْبَهُ: so in the saying, هٰذَا أَشْكَلُ بِكَذَا [*This is more,* or *most, like to such a thing*]. (Ṣ, Ḳ.*) —— Also *Of a colour in which whiteness and redness are intermixed;* (Ṣ, Mṣb, Ḳ;) applied to blood; and, accord. to IDrd, a name for *blood,* because of the redness and whiteness intermixed therein; (Ṣ;) [and] applied to a man; (Mṣb;) or to anything: (TA:) or *in which is whiteness inclining to redness and duskiness:* (Ḳ:) or it signifies, with the Arabs, [*of*] *two colours intermixed.* (TA.) [Hence,] it is applied to water, (Ḳ, TA,) as meaning ‡ *Mixed with blood:* (TA: [see an ex. in a verse cited voce حَتَّى:]) pl. شُكْلٌ. (Ḳ.) And the fem., شَكْلَآءُ, is applied as an epithet to an eye, (Ṣ, Ḳ,) meaning *Having in it what is termed* شُكْلَةٌ, which is *the like of a redness in the white thereof;* like شُهْلَةٌ in the black: (Ṣ:) pl. as above. (Ḳ.) A man is said to be أَشْكَلُ العَيْنِ, meaning *Having a redness,* (Mgh,) or *the like of a redness,* (O,) *in the white of the eye:* (Mgh, O:) the Prophet is said to have been أَشْكَلُ العَيْنِ: and it has been expl. as meaning *long in the slit of the eye:* (Ḳ:) but ISd says that this is extraordinary; and MF, that the leading authorities on the trads. consentaneously assert it to be a pure mistake, and inapplicable to the Prophet, even if lexicologically correct. (TA.) —— Applied to a camel, (Ḳ, TA,) and to a sheep or goat, (TA,) *of which the blackness is mixed with redness,* (Ḳ, TA,) or *with dust-colour;* as though its colour were dubious to thee: (TA:) pl. as above, applied to rams &c., (Ḳ, TA,) in this sense. (TA.) —— Applied to a sheep or goat, *White in the* شَاكِلَة [or *flank*]: (Ṣ, O:) fem. شَكْلَآءُ; (Ṣ;) applied to a ewe, as meaning *white in the* شَاكِلَة, (Ḳ, TA,) *the rest of her being black.* (TA.) ═ Also The *mountain-species of* سِدْر [or *lote-tree*]; (Ṣ, O, Ḳ;) described to AḤn, by some one or more of the Arabs of the desert, as *a sort of trees like the* عُنَّاب [or *jujube*] *in its thorns and the crookedness of its branches, but smaller in leaf, and having more branches; very hard, and having a small drupe,* (نُبَيْقَة, [dim. of نَبِقَة, n. un. of نَبِق, which means the "drupes of the سِدْر,"]) *which is very acid: the places of its growth are lofty mountains; and bows are made of it* [as is shown by an ex. in the Ṣ and O]: (TA:) [app. with tenween, having a] n. un. with ة: (Ṣ, Ḳ:) AḤn says that *the growth of the* اشكل *is like* [*that of*] *the trees called* شِرْيَان [of which likewise bows are made]. (TA.)

أَشْكَلَةٌ: see شَكْلٌ, first signification. —— Also *i. q.* لَبْسٌ [meaning † *Dubiousness,* or *confusedness*]. (Ḳ.) ═ See also شُكْلَةٌ, in two places. ═ Also *A single tree of the species called* أَشْكَل [q. v.]. (Ṣ, Ḳ.)

مُشْكِلٌ, from أَشْكَلَ in the first of the senses assigned to it above, signifies *Entering among* [meaning *confused with*] *its likes.* (TA.) —— And [hence, app., or] accord. to Sh, from شُكْلَةٌ meaning "redness mixed with whiteness," it signifies † *Dubious,* or *confused.* (TA.) [Used as a subst.,] it has for its pl. مُشْكِلَاتٌ [and مَشَاكِلُ also: for] one says, هُوَ يَفُكُّ المَشَاكِلَ, meaning †[*He solves*] *the things,* or *affairs, that are dubious,* or *confused.* (TA.) —— مشكل [app. مُشَكَّلٌ], applied to a horse, means *Having a whiteness in his flanks.* (AA, TA in art. دعر.)

مُشَكَّلٌ *Endowed with a goodly aspect,* or *appearance,* and *form.* (TA.)

مَشْكُولٌ A horse *bound,* or *shackled, with the* شِكَال [q. v.]. (O, TA.) —— And ‡ A horse *distinguished by the whiteness in the lower parts of certain of the legs which is denoted by the term* شِكَال [q. v.]: (Ṣ, Mgh,* O, TA:) such was disliked by the Prophet. (Ṣ.) [See also مُحَجَّل.] —— And ‡ A writing *restricted* [*in its meaning* or *pronunciation*] *with the signs of the desinential syntax* [*and the other syllabical signs and the diacritical points*]. (AḤát, TA.)

شكم

1. شَكَمَهُ, aor. ُ, inf. n. شَكْمٌ, *He bitted him;* [namely, a horse or the like;] *he put the bit* (شَكِيمَة) *into his mouth.* (TA.) —— [Hence], شَكَمَ الوَالِىَ, (Ṣ, Ḳ,) aor. and inf. n. as above, (TA,) ‡ *He bribed the* والى [i. e. *prefect,* or *the like*]; as though he stopped his mouth with the شَكِيمَة, (Ṣ, Ḳ, TA,) i. e. the [bit, or] iron thing of the لِجَام. (TA.) And شَكَمَ فَاهُ بِالإِتَاوَةِ i. e. †[*He stopped* (lit. *bitted*) *his mouth*] *with the bribe.* (TA in art. اتو.) —— And فَعَلَ فُلَانٌ أَمْرًا فَشَكَمْتُهُ † *Such a one did a thing,* or *performed an affair, and I settled,* or *established, it.* (Lth, TA.) —— And شَكَمَهُ, (Ṣ, Ḳ,) aor. as above, (Ṣ,) and so the inf. n.; (Ḳ;) and ▼ اشكمهُ; (Th, Ḳ;) *He repaid, requited, compensated,* or *recompensed, him;* (Ṣ, Ḳ;*) or *gave him what is termed* شُكْم [q. v.]: (Ḳ:) *he gave him his hire,* or *pay.* (Ṣ, from a trad.) —— And, as some say, (Ṣ,) شَكَمَهُ, inf. n. شَكْمٌ and شَكِيمٌ, *He bit him.* (Ṣ, Ḳ.) ═ شَكِمَ, aor. َ, (Ḳ,) inf. n. شَكَمٌ, (TḲ,) *He was,* or *became, hungry.* (Ḳ.)

4: see the preceding paragraph.

شُكْمٌ (Ṣ, Ḳ, &c.) and ▼ شُكْمَى; (Ḳ;) of the latter, ISd says, "I think it to be a dial. var., but I am not certain of it;" (TA;) *A repayment, requital, compensation*, or *recompense*; (El-Umawee, A'Obeyd, Ṣ, Ḳ;) and شُكْبٌ is a dial. var. thereof: (TA:) when the gift is initial, it is termed شُكْدٌ: (Ṣ:) or *a substitute*; or *thing given, received, put, or done, by way of replacement* or *exchange*: (Ḳs, TA:) and (Ḳ) *a gift*; (Aṣ, Ḳ, TA;) as also شُكْدٌ; (Aṣ, TA;) or the latter signifies a gift without compensation: (TA:) or شُكْمٌ signifies *a benefaction, bounty*, or *gratuity*; syn. نُعْمَى. (Lth, TA.)

شَكْمٌ *A lion*: (Ḳ:) expl. in this sense as occurring in a verse of Aboo-Ṣakhr El-Hudhalee: or, accord. to Skr, as there used, *quickly*, or *soon, angry*; or *violently angry*. (TA.)

شُكْمَى: see شُكْمٌ.

شَكِيمٌ: see شَكِيمَةٌ, in three places. — Also The *loop-shaped handles* of the cooking-pot. (Ṣ, Ḳ.)

[شَكَامَةٌ expl. by Golius as meaning "*Malitia indolis, contumacia*," as on the authority of the KL, is app. a mistake for شَكَاسَةٌ, which I find expl. in the KL as signifying the "being evil in nature, or natural disposition," but not شكامة. — Freytag explains it as meaning also *Likeness*; a signification of شَكِيمَةٌ, also mentioned by him; but for this he names no authority, and I know of none.]

شَكِيمَةٌ, in the لِجَام, [The *bit-mouth*, or *mouth-piece of a bit*; i. e.] the *transverse piece of iron in the mouth of the horse, in which is the* فَأْس [q. v.]; (Ṣ, Ḳ;) as also ▼ شَكِيمٌ: (Ṣ:) [see also مِسْحَلٌ, and لِجَامٌ:] or ▼ شَكِيمٌ is pl. of شَكِيمَةٌ, as also شَكَائِمُ and شُكُمٌ, (Ḳ, TA,) this last with two ḍammehs, [but written in the CḲ شُكْمٌ,] or [rather ▼ شَكِيمٌ is a coll. gen. n., and] شُكُمٌ is said by some to be pl. of شَكِيمٌ, not of شَكِيمَةٌ. (TA.) — Hence, [as used in phrases mentioned below,] (TA,) ‡ *Resistance*, or *incompliance*: (Ṣ, TA:) *disdain, scorn*, or *disdainful and proud incompliance* or *refusal*: and *self-defence from wrong treatment*: (Ḳ:) and *self-magnification, pride*, or *haughtiness*; syn. شَمَمٌ; السُّمُّ in the copies of the Ḳ being a mistake for الشَّمَمُ: (TA:) *firmness, strength*, or *vehemence, of spirit*; (TA, and Ḥam p. 140;) and *evilness of nature* or *disposition*: (Ḥam ibid:) *strength of heart*: (IAạr, TA:) *hardiness*; *courage*, or *courage and energy*; or *determination*; syn. عَارِضَةٌ: *vigorousness, strenuousness*, or *energy*: (TA:) also [simply] *nature*, or *natural disposition*; syn. طَبْعٌ. (Ḳ, TḲ: in the CḲ الطَّبْعُ is [erroneously] put in the place of الطَّبْعُ.) One says, فُلَانٌ ذُو شَكِيمَةٍ ‡ *Such a one is resistant*, or *incompliant*: (Ṣ, TA:) or *disdainful*, or *scornful*; *resistant, unyielding*, or *incompliant*: *one who defends himself from wrong treatment*: *proud*: *hardy*; *courageous*: *one possessing prudence* or *discretion*, or *firmness* or *soundness of judgment*. (TA.) And فُلَانٌ شَدِيدُ الشَّكِيمَةِ, meaning [in like manner] ‡ *Such a one is firm, strong*, or *vehement, of spirit*; (Ṣ, TA, and Ḥam p. 140;) *disdainful*, or *scornful*; *resistant, unyielding*, or *incompliant*; (Ṣ, Ḳ, TA;) so says ISk: (TA:) or, as some say, *one possessing strength*, or *vehemence, of tongue*; and *perspicuity*, or *eloquence, of speech* or *language*; or *perspicuity of speech with quickness*, or *sharpness, of intellect*; and *much hardiness*, or *courage*, or *courage and energy*, or *determination*. (Ḥam p. 140.) — Also † *Likeness*, or *resemblance*. (Ḳ.) — And † *A compact*, or *covenant*; syn. عَهْدٌ: (Ḳ, TA:) in some copies of the Ḳ, الفَهْدُ is erroneously put for العَهْدُ. (TA.)

شكى and شكو

1. شَكَا, (Ḳ,) first pers. شَكَوْتُ, (Ṣ, Mṣb,) of which شَكَيْتُ is a dial. var., (Ḳ in art. شكى,) aor. ـُ, (Ṣ, Mṣb,) [and of the latter ـِ,] inf. n. شَكْوٌ, (Ṣ, Mṣb,) or شَكْوَى, (Ḳ,) or this is a simple subst., (Ṣ, Mṣb,) also pronounced شَكْوَى, (Ḳ,) and شِكَايَةٌ, (Ṣ, Ḳ,) with kesr, (Ḳ,) in which the ى is [said to be] substituted for و because most inf. ns. of the measure فِعَالَةٌ of verbs ending with an infirm radical letter are of verbs of which that letter is ى, (TA,) or this also is a simple subst., (Mṣb,) and شَكَاةٌ, (Ṣ, Ḳ,) or this too is a simple subst., (Mṣb,) and شَكَاوَةٌ, (Ḳ,) and شَكِيَّةٌ, (Ṣ, Ḳ,) is a trans. verb; (Ṣ, Mṣb, Ḳ;) and ▼ اشتكى signifies the same; (Ṣ, Ḳ;) as also ▼ تشكّى: (Ḳ:) one says, شَكَا أَمْرَهُ إِلَى ٱللّٰهِ and ▼ اشتكى [i. e. اشتكى أَمْرَهُ], and ▼ تشكّى [i. e. تشكّى أَمْرَهُ], (Ḳ, TA,) meaning [*He complained of his case to God*; or] *he told to God the weakness of his condition*: (TA:) and شَكَوْتُ فُلَانًا and ▼ اشْتَكَيْتُهُ [*I complained to such a one of his conduct to me*]; (Ṣ;) [or] شَكَا فُلَانًا means *he told such a one of his evil conduct to him*: (TA:) and شَكَا فُلَانًا إِلَى فُلَانٍ *He complained of such a one to such a one*: (MA:) [and شَكَوْتُ إِلَيْهِ كَذَا *I complained to him of such a thing*:] see 4: and [in like manner] اشتكى ▼ إِلَيْهِ كَذَا *He complained to him of such a thing*: (MA:) and ▼ اشْتَكَيْتُ مِنْهُ [*I complained of him, or it*; like شَكَوْتُهُ]: (Mṣb:) Er-Rághib says, الشِّكَايَةُ is *The showing*, or *revealing, of grief*, or *sorrow*; whence the saying in the Ḳur [xii. 86], إِنَّمَا أَشْكُو بَثِّي وَحُزْنِي إِلَى ٱللّٰهِ [*I only show my grief and my lamentation to God*]; and in the same [lviii. 1], وَتَشْتَكِي ▼ إِلَى ٱللّٰهِ [*And showeth her grief*, or *sorrow, to God*]; the primary signification of الشَّكْوُ being *the opening of the small skin for water or milk called* شَكْوَة, *and showing what is in it*; so that it is as though originally metaphorical [though what is termed حَقِيقَةٌ عُرْفِيَّةٌ (expl. in art. حق)]; like the phrases نَفَضْتُ لَهُ مَا فِي جِرَابِي and بَثَثْتُ لَهُ مَا فِي وِعَائِي, meaning "I showed him what was in my heart." (TA.) — شَكَا is also said of a camel as meaning *He stretched out his neck, and made much moaning*, or *prolonged utterance of a complaining voice, being fatigued by journeying*. (TA.) — And شَكَاهُ, (MA, Ḳ, TA,) inf. n. شَكْوٌ and شَكَاةٌ and شَكْوَى, (MA, TA,) is said in relation to a disease, or sickness; (MA, Ḳ, TA;) meaning *He* (a diseased, or sick, person) *complained of it*, namely, his disease, or sickness; (MA; [accord. to the TḲ, followed in this case, as in many others, by Freytag, it means *it* (i. e. disease, or sickness,) *afflicted him*; which I think to be indubitably a mistake;]) and ▼ تشكّى and ▼ اشتكى signify the same [as شَكَا مَرَضَهُ *he complained of his disease*, or *sickness*]: (TA:) [or] these two verbs (تشكّى and اشتكى) signify [or signify also] *he was*, or *became, diseased*, or *sick*. (TA in additions at the end of this art.) One says also, ▼ اشتكى عُضْوًا مِنْ أَعْضَائِهِ and ▼ تشكّى, both meaning the same [i. e., originally, *He complained of* a pain, or disease, in *some one of his members*; but generally meaning *he had a complaint of*, or *a pain* or *a disease in, some one of his members*; and شَكَا عُضْوًا not unfrequently occurs used in the same sense]: (Ṣ:) [thus one often says of a brute; for ex.,] Aṣ says, in explaining القُلَابُ as meaning "a certain disease that attacks the camel," يَشْتَكِي ▼ مِنْهُ قَلْبَهُ [*he has a pain in consequence thereof in his heart*; in which قَلْبَهُ, though determinate, may be considered as an explicative, like بَطْنَهُ in the phrase أَلِمَ بَطْنَهُ, q. v.]. (Ṣ in art. قلب.) — One says also, هُوَ يُشْكَى بِكَذَا, meaning *He is accused*, or *suspected, of such a thing*; syn. يُتَّهَمُ بِهِ: (Ḳ: [there mentioned as though it were from أَشْكَى, and held to be so by the author of the TḲ; but it is from شَكَى; as though meaning *he is complained of by reason of such a thing*:]) mentioned by Yaạḳoob, in the "Alfáḍh." (TA.) — شكى فُلَانٌ [thus in my original, app. شَكَا or شَكِىَ,] is mentioned by Az as meaning *The nails of such a one became split in several*, or *many, places*. (TA.)

2. شَكَّتِ النِّسَآءُ, inf. n. تَشْكِيَةٌ; and ▼ اشتكت; and ▼ تَشَكَّتْ; (Ḳ;) or, accord. to Th, only this last; (TA;) *The women took for themselves*, or *made, a* شَكْوَة [q. v.] *for the churning of milk*; (Ḳ, TA;) because it was little in quantity; the شكوة being small, so that only a small quantity can be churned in it: (TA:) or, as in the T, شكّى and ▼ تشكّى *he took for himself*, or *made, a* شَكْوَة: (TA:) [or] so ▼ اشتكى: (Ṣ:) and so ▼ اشكى. (IḲṭṭ, TA.) — شَكَّى شَاكِيَهُ, inf. n. تَشْكِيَةٌ, expl. in the Ḳ as meaning طَيَّبَ نَفْسَهُ and كَفَّ عَنْهُ, is a foul mistranscription: correctly, سَلَّى شَاكِيَهُ, meaning "He comforted his complainer, and consoled him for that which had befallen him;" as in the Tekmileh. (TA.)

3. شاكاهُ, inf. n. مُشَاكَاةٌ, *He complained of him, i. q.* شَكَاهُ: or *he told of his deceit, guile*, or *circumvention, and his vices*, or *faults*. (TA.)

4. اشكاهُ [*He made him*, or *caused him, to complain*;] *he did to him that which made him*, or *caused him, to have need to complain of him*. (Ṣ, Mṣb.) *He increased his annoyance and complaining*. (Az, Ḳ, TA.) — And *He removed*, or *did away with, his complaint*; or *made his complaint to cease*; (Ṣ,* Mgh, Mṣb, Ḳ;) *he caused him to be pleased* or *contented* [*and so relieved him from his complaint*]; syn. أَعْتَبَهُ مِنْ شَكْوَاهُ; (Ṣ, and Ḥar p. 337;) i. e. أَرْضَاهُ; (Ḥar ibid.;) and

he desisted from that of which he complained: (Ṣ,* Mṣb:) thus it has two contr. significations. (Ṣ, Ḳ.) Hence the saying, (Mgh, Mṣb, TA,) in a trad., (TA,) شَكَوْنَا ▼ إِلَى رَسُولِ ٱللّٰهِ حَرَّ ٱلرَّمْضَآءِ فِى صِيَامِنَا فَلَمْ يُشْكِنَا [*We complained, to the Apostle of God, of the heat of the burning ground, in our fasting,*] *and he did not remove,* or *cause to cease, our complaint.* (Mgh,* Mṣb, TA.) And [hence] one says, اشكى فُلَانًا مِنْ فُلَانٍ, meaning *He took for such a one, from such a one, what pleased* or *contented him* [*and so relieved him from complaining of him*]. (ISd, Ḳ, TA: omitted in the CḲ.) —— Also *He told him his complaint, and the desire,* or *longing of the soul, that he endured.* (TA.) —— And i. q. وَجَدَهُ شَاكِيًا [which may mean *He found him to be complaining,* or, as seems to be indicated by what immediately precedes it in the Ḳ, *he found him to be complaining of a disease of the slightest sort*]: (Ḳ:) or, as in the T, اشكى [app. meaning اشكى حَبِيبَهُ] signifies *he found the object of his love,* or *his friend, to be complaining;* expl. by صَادَفَ حَبِيبَهُ يَشْكُو. (TA.) ═ See also 2.

5. تشكّى *He expressed complaint* or *lamentation, pain, grief,* or *sorrow;* syn. تَوَجَّعَ; (Mṣb and Ḳ in art. وجع;) *he made complaint* or *lamentation.* (MA, KL.) See 1, in four places. —— [Hence] one says, تشكّى شَآئِى أَرْضَ كَذَا, meaning † [*My sheep* or *goats*] *forsook such a land,* [*as though they complained of it,*] *and did not go near it.* (TA. [But I have substituted شَآئِى for what is there written شاكى, an evident mistranscription.]) ═ See also 2, in two places.

6. تَشَاكَوْا *They complained, one to another.* (Ḳ.)

8: see 1, in nine places: ═ and see also 2, in two places.

شَكْوٌ inf. n. of شَكَا. (Ṣ, Mṣb.) —— It is also used in the sense of وَجْدٌ [meaning *Grief, mourning,* or *sorrow*]. (TA.) —— Also, and ▼ شَكْوَى, and ▼ شَكَاةٌ, and ▼ شَكَآءٌ, and ▼ شَكْوَآءُ, (Ḳ,) this last mentioned by Az, (TA,) [but it is omitted in some copies of the Ḳ,] *A complaint,* meaning *a disease, malady,* or *sickness.* (Ḳ.) ═ Also, the first, *A small,* or *young, lamb:* or *a small,* or *young, camel:* (Ḳ accord. to different copies: in some, الشَّكْوُ having for its explanation الحَمَلُ الصَّغِيرُ, and thus in the TA: in others, الجَمَلُ الصغير:) mentioned by ISd. (TA.)

شَكَاةٌ an inf. n. of شَكَا; (Ṣ, Ḳ;) or a simple subst., like شَكْوَى. (Mṣb.) —— See also شَكْوٌ. —— Also i. q. عَيْبٌ [*A vice, fault,* &c.]. (TA.) [See a verse cited voce رِفَاقٌ.]

شَكْوَةٌ *The skin of a sucking kid,* (T,* Ṣ, M,*) *for milk:* that of the جَذَع and of such as is above that [in age] is termed وَطْبٌ; (Ṣ;) or that of the جذع is termed سِقَآءٌ; and that of such as is weaned, بَدْرَةٌ: (T, TA:) or *a receptacle of skin* or *leather, for water* and *for milk,* (Ḳ, TA,) or, as some say, *in which water is cooled* and *in which milk is kept close:* (TA:) or *a small skin for water or milk:* or *a small receptacle in which water is put:* (Er-Rághib, TA:) the dim. is ▼ شُكَيَّةٌ: (TA:) and the pl. is شَكَوَاتٌ and شِكَآءٌ (Ḳ, TA) and شُكِىٌّ [like as بُدُورٌ is a pl. of بَدْرَةٌ], being originally شُكُوٌّ, like as دُلِىٌّ (pl. of دَلْوٌ) is originally دُلُوٌّ]. (TA.)

شَكْوَى an inf. n. of شَكَا, as also شُكْوَى; (Ḳ;) or a simple subst. [signifying *Complaint*]: (Ṣ, Mṣb:) pl. شَكَاوَى. (TA.) —— See also شَكْوٌ.

شَكْوَآءُ: } see شَكْوٌ.
شَكَآءٌ: }

شَكِىٌّ i. q. ▼ شَاكٍ [i. e. *Complaining*]; (Mṣb;) [or *a complainer;* i. e.] الشَّكِىُّ signifies الّذِى يَشْتَكِى, (Ṣ,) or الذى يَشْكُو. (JM.) —— And *Pained;* syn. مُوجَعٌ; (Ḳ, TA;) in this sense an instance of فَعِيلٌ in the sense of مَفْعُولٌ: (TA:) or *causing pain;* syn. مُوجِعٌ: [thus accord. to both of my copies of the Ṣ: and this appears to be correct; for it is there immediately added,] El-Ṭirimmáḥ says,

* وَسْمِى شَكِىٌّ وَلِسَانِى عَارِمُ *

[which is inconsiderately cited in the TA immediately after the former of these two explanations: I say "inconsiderately" because the meaning evidently is, not that thus indicated in the TA, but, *My branding,* or *stigmatizing,* by satire, (for one says وَسَمَهُ بِالهِجَآءِ,) *is such as causes pain, and my tongue is vehement:* or شَكِىٌّ may here have the last but one of the meanings expl. in this paragraph]: وَسْمِى is from السِّمَةُ. (Ṣ.) —— Also *Affected with a complaint,* meaning *disease, malady,* or *sickness,* [app. in an absolute sense, (see شَكْوٌ,) and also] *of the least,* or *lightest,* or *slightest, sort;* and so ▼ شَاكٍ. (M, Ḳ.) —— And i. q. ▼ مَشْكُوٌّ, (Ṣ, Mṣb, Ḳ,) which is a pass. part. n. of شَكَا; [and therefore signifies *Complained of;* and also *complained to;* but mostly seems to be used in the former of these senses;] as also ▼ مَشْكِىٌّ. (Ṣ, Mṣb.)

شِكَايَةٌ an inf. n. of شَكَا; (Ṣ, Ḳ;) or a simple subst., like شَكْوَى. (Mṣb.)

شَكِيَّةٌ an inf. n. of شَكَا. (Ṣ, Ḳ.) —— And also (TA) a subst. signifying *A thing complained of* (اِسْمٌ لِلْمَشْكُوِّ); like رَمِيَّةٌ a subst. signifying "a thing cast at or shot at" (اِسْمٌ لِلْمَرْمِىِّ): (Mṣb, TA:) pl. شَكَايَا. (TA.) ═ Also *A remainder,* or *remaining portion,* (Ḳ and TA in art. شكى,) of a thing: mentioned by Ṣgh. (TA.)

شُكَيَّةٌ dim. of شَكْوَةٌ, q. v. (TA.)

شَكِّىٌّ, (thus in copies of the Ḳ,) or شُكِّىٌّ, with ḍamm to the ش, (TA,) is mentioned in art. شك [q. v.], and J has committed a mistake (Ḳ, TA) in mentioning it here, as Ṣgh has observed: (TA:) [accord. to F, it seems to be a rel. n. applied to a bit, or bridle; for it is said to be so applied in the Ḳ, as well as in the O, in art. شك, in which both explain it as meaning *Difficult;* and also to a skin; for immediately after asserting that J has committed a mistake, F adds,] and شَكَّى, like حَتَّى, is a town in Armenia, whence [are brought] bits, or bridles, (لُجُم,) and skins, (Ḳ,) [and SM adds that they are termed شَكِّيَّة: but what I find J to have stated is as follows:] الشَّكِّىُّ, [thus in one of my copies of the Ṣ,] or الشُّكِّىُّ, [thus in the other of those copies,] in relation to weapons, is an arabicized word, and is in Turkish تُش or تَش. (Ṣ. [But in the JM, this last word is written, as from the Ṣ, تشن: it may therefore be correctly تُشْن, or تَشْن, which, though used in Turkish, is a Pers. word, meaning *smooth.*])

شَاكٍ: see شَكِىٌّ, in two places. ═ In the phrase رَجُلٌ شَاكِى السِّلَاحِ, (Ṣ,) which means *A man whose weapon is sharp,* or *whose weapons are sharp,* (Ṣ, Ḳ,*) Akh says that شاكى is formed by transposition from شَائِكٌ [q. v. in art. شوك]: (Ṣ:) and accord. to AZ, one says also شَاكٌ فِى السِّلَاحِ. (TA in art. شوك.) —— And الشَّاكِى [is app. formed in like manner from الشَّائِكُ, and] signifies *The lion.* (Ḳ.)

مِشْكَاةٌ *A niche in a wall;* i. e. *a hole,* or *hollow,* (كُوَّةٌ,) *in a wall, not extending through;* (Fr, Ṣ, M, Ḳ, &c.;) in which a lamp, placed therein, gives more light than it does elsewhere: thus expl. by the generality of the expositors [of the Ḳur-án]; and this is said by Ibn-'Aṭeeyeh to be the most correct explanation: (TA:) said by Aboo-Moosà to mean *the iron,* or *leaden, thing in which is the wick* [*of the lamp*]: thought by Az to mean *the tube which is the place of the wick in the glass lamp,* as being likened to the كُوَّة which is thus called: (TA:) some expl. it as having this meaning in the Ḳur xxiv. 35, and say that the مِصْبَاح there mentioned is the lighted wick: (Bḍ:) accord. to Mujáhid, *the pillar,* or *the like,* (العَمُود,) *upon the top,* or *head, of which the* مِصْبَاح [meaning *lamp*] *is put:* or the *iron things by means of which the* قِنْدِيل [or *lamp*] *is suspended:* IJ says that its ا is originally و, and hence it is [often] written مِشْكَوْةٌ: and Zj says that it is an Abyssinian word, and used in the language of the Arabs: (TA:) [the pl. is مَشَاكٍ, like مَسَاحٍ pl. of مِسْحَاةٌ:] Kaab says that, in the verse of the Ḳur [xxiv. 35], by the مشكاة is meant the breast of Moḥammad; and by the مصباح, his tongue; and by the زُجَاجَة, his mouth. (TA.)

مَشْكُوٌّ and مَشْكِىٌّ: see شَكِىٌّ, last sentence.

شل

1. شَلَّتْ يَمِينُهُ, (Ṣ, O,) or يَدُهُ, (Mgh, TA,) or اليَدُ, (Mṣb, Ḳ,) originally شَلِلَتْ, (Mgh, Mṣb, TA,) aor. تَشَلُّ, (Ṣ, O, &c.,) inf. n. شَلَلٌ (Ṣ,* O,* Mgh, Mṣb, Ḳ) and شَلٌّ, (Mṣb, Ḳ,) or the latter

is not allowable; (Ḥam p. 60;) this is the chaste form of the verb; (Th, TA;) and ▾ أُشِلَّتْ; (Th, Ḳ;) and شُلَّتْ, (Th, O, Ḳ,) but this last is bad, (Th, O, TA,) and is disallowed by Fr; (TA;) *His right hand or arm, or his hand or arm, or the hand or arm, was, or became, unsound,* or *vitiated:* (Ṣ, O, TA:) or *deprived of the power of motion by an unsound,* or *a vitiated, state of its* عُرُوق [meaning *veins* or *nerves*]: (Mṣb:) or *dried up;* or *stiff:* or *it went* [or *wasted*] *away.* (Ḳ, TA.) One says, in praying for a person, لَا تَشْلَلْ يَدُكَ [*May thy hand, or arm, not become unsound,* &c.]: (Ṣ, Mṣb,* Ḳ:*) and لَا شَلَلًا and ▾ لَا شَلَالِ, which mean the same; the last word like قَطَامِ. (Ḳ.) And شَلَّ عَشْرُهُ, and خَمْسُهُ, [*His ten fingers became unsound,* &c., and *his five fingers,*] and some say شَلَّتْ, but this is more rare; i. e., the suppression of the fem. ت is more usual in a case of this kind. (Lḥ, TA.) To one who has shot or thrown, or who has pierced or thrust, well, one says, لَا شَلَلًا وَلَا عَمًى [*Mayest thou not experience unsoundness,* &c., *nor blindness*]; and لَا شَلَّ عَشْرُكَ [*May thy ten fingers not become unsound,* &c.], meaning أَصَابِعُكَ. (Ṣ, O.)

He who says شَلَّتِ الأُذُنُ and شَلَّ البَائِنُ is a foreigner. (Mgh.) The lawyers [improperly] use الشَّلَل in relation to the ذَكَر. (Mṣb.) One says also, شَلِلْتَ يَا رَجُلُ [*Thou hast become unsound,* &c., in thy hand or thine arm, *O man*]. (Ṣ, O.) And لَا شَلَلَ, meaning لَا تَشْلَلْ, because it occupies the place of an imperative. (Lth, TA.) In the saying of the rájiz, (Ṣ,) namely, Abu-l-Khudree El-Yarboo'ee, (O, TA,)

• مُهْرَ أَبِى الحَبْحَابِ لَا تَشَلِّى •

[*Colt of Abu-l-Ḥabḥáb, mayest thou not become unsound,* &c., in the fore leg], (Ṣ, TA, [in the O, ابى الحُرِث, for ابى الحَبحاب,]) the last word is thus [for لا تشلل] on account of the rhyme: (Ṣ, O, TA:) [for] the next hemistich is

• بَارَكَ فِيكَ ٱللّٰهُ مِنْ ذِى أَلِّ •

[*God bless thee as one possessing fleetness,* or *swiftness*]; (O, TA;) ذى ألّ in this instance meaning ذِى سُرْعَةٍ. (Ṣ in art. ال.) ═ شَلَّهُ; (Ḳ;) and شَلَلْتُ الإِبِلَ, (Ṣ, O,) and الرَّجُلَ; (Mṣb;) aor. ـُ, (Ṣ, Mṣb,) inf. n. شَلٌّ (Ṣ, O, Mṣb, Ḳ*) and شَلَلٌ, (Ḳ,* and Ksh in xii. 3,) like as قَصَصٌ is inf. n. of قَصَّ, (Ksh ibid.,) or شَلَلٌ is a simple subst.; (Ṣ, O;) *He drove him away;* (Ḳ;) and *I drove away* (Ṣ, O, Mṣb) *the camels,* (Ṣ, O,) and *the man.* (Mṣb.) And مَرَّ فُلَانٌ يَشُلُّهُمْ بِالسَّيْفِ *Such a one passed along urging them on, and driving them, with the sword.* (Ṣ.) [See also 4. — Hence,] الصُّبْحُ يَشُلُّ الظَّلَامَ ‡ *The dawn drives away the darkness.* (TA.) — And شَلَّتِ العَيْنُ دَمْعَهَا † *The eye sent forth* [or *shed*] *its tears:* (Lḥ, Ḳ:) like شَنَّتْهُ: (Lḥ, TA:) asserted by Yaạkoob to be formed by substitution [of ل for ن]. (TA.) — And شَلَّ الدِّرْعَ, (O, TA,) and شَلَّهَا عَلَيْهِ, aor. ـُ, inf. n. شَلٌّ, (TA,) *He put on himself the coat of mail;* on the authority of ISh. (O, TA.) ═ شَلَلْتُ الثَّوْبَ, (Ṣ, O, Mṣb, TA,) inf. n. شَلٌّ, (O,) *I sewed the garment,* or *piece of cloth,* (Ṣ, O, Mṣb, TA,) *slightly;* (Ṣ, O, TA; [omitted, probably by inadvertence, in my copy of the Mṣb;]) [previously to the second sewing termed الكَفّ;] strangely omitted in the Ḳ: ▾ شِلَالَةٌ is [app. a subst., not an inf. n., signifying *The act,* or *art, of so sewing;*] the *contr.* of كِفَافَةٌ. (TA.)

4. اشلّ يَمِينَهُ, (Ṣ,) or يَدَهُ, (Fr, Ḳ,) *He* (i. e. God, Ṣ) *made his right hand or arm,* (Ṣ,) or *his hand, or arm,* (Ḳ,) *to become unsound,* or *vitiated:* (Ṣ:) or *to become dried up,* or *stiff:* or *to go* [or *waste*] *away:* (Ḳ:) or اشلّ اليَدَ *He* (i. e. God) *made the hand or arm to become deprived of the power of motion by an unsound,* or *a vitiated, state of its* عُرُوق [meaning *veins* or *nerves*]. (Mṣb.) And اشلّ ٱللّٰهُ يَدَهُ is said by way of imprecation [as meaning *May God render his hand or arm unsound,* &c.]. (O.) See also 1, first sentence. ═ [It is said that] إِشْلَالٌ signifies *The driving away* a camel, and a troop or company with the sword: [like شَلٌّ: see 1, latter half:] — and *The making war.* (KL.)

7. انشلّ *He became driven away.* (Ḳ, TA. [In some of the copies of the Ḳ, انشلّ بِهِ, meaning *He became driven away by,* or *with, him,* or *it.*]) And انشلّت الإِبِلُ *The camels became driven away.* (Ṣ.) And انشلّوا مَطْرُودِينَ [*They went driven away*]; referring to a company of people. (TA.) — [Hence,] انشلّ الذِّئْبُ فِى الغَنَمِ † *The wolf made an incursion among the sheep* or *goats;* as also انشنّ: mentioned by Az in art. نشغ. (TA.) — And انشلّ السَّيْلُ † *The torrent began to be impelled, before its becoming vehement:* (Sh, O, Ḳ:) and so انسلّ. (Sh, O.) — And انشلّ المَطَرُ † *The rain descended.* (Ḳ.)

R. Q. 1. شَلْشَلْتُ المَآءَ *I made the water to fall in drops;* (Ṣ;) *in consecutive drops.* (TA.) And شَلْشَلَ بَوْلَهُ, (Ḳ, TA, [in the CḲ, erroneously, تَشَلْشَلَ,]) and بِبَوْلِهِ, (Ṣ, O, Ḳ, TA,) inf. n. شَلْشَلَةٌ and شِلْشَالٌ, [both incorrectly written by Freytag,] (Ḳ, TA,) *He* (a boy, Ṣ, O, TA) *scattered his urine; emitted it dispersedly:* (Ḳ, TA:) the subst. [signifying the *act of doing so*] is ▾ شَلْشَالٌ with fet-ḥ. (Ḳ.) And شَلْشَلَ السَّيْفُ الدَّمَ, [in the CḲ, erroneously, بِالدَّمِ,] and ▾ تَشَلْشَلَ بِهِ, *The sword poured forth the blood.* (Ḳ, TA.)

R. Q. 2. تَشَلْشَلَ *It* (water) *fell in consecutive drops.* (TA.) And تَشَلْشَلَ دَمًا *It* (a wound) *dripped with blood in consecutive drops.* (TA.) See also R. Q. 1, last sentence.

شَلَّةٌ: see the next paragraph.

شُلَّةٌ *i. q.* نِيَّةٌ [app. as meaning The *thing,* or *place, that one proposes to himself as the object of his aim*]: (Ṣ, O, Ḳ:) the *place that a company of men have proposed to themselves as the object of their aim or journey:* so in the M: (TA:) or the نِيَّة [in the sense thus expl. in the M and TA] *in journeying:* (T, Ḳ:) and thus also ▾ شَلَّى, and likewise *in fasting,* and *in warring:* one says, ▾ أَيْنَ شَلَّاهُمْ [*Where is the place that they propose to themselves as the object of their aim in journeying,* &c.?]. (TA.) — And *A remote affair* (Ṣ, O, Ḳ) *that one seeks;* (Ḳ;) as also ▾ شَلَّةٌ. (O, Ḳ.) ═ See also شَلَلٌ. ═ And see شَلِيلٌ.

شَلَلٌ *An unsoundness in the hand or arm,* or *a vitiated state* thereof. (Ṣ, O.) [See also 1, first sentence, where it is mentioned as an inf. n.] — And ‡ *A stain,* (Ṣ, O,) or *a blackness,* (Ḳ,) or *a dust-colour,* (TA,) *in a garment,* or *piece of cloth, that does not become removed by washing.* (Ṣ, O, Ḳ, TA.) One says, مَا هٰذَا الشَّلَلُ فِى ثَوْبِكَ, (Ṣ, O,) or بِثَوْبِكَ, (TA,) ‡ [*What is this stain,* &c., *in thy garment?*] ═ Also The *act of driving away:* (Ṣ, O, Ḳ:) a subst.: (Ṣ, O:) or an inf. n., (Ksh in xii. 3,) [see 1, latter half,] *i. q.* طَرْدٌ, like [the inf. n.] شَلٌّ, (Ḳ,) as also ▾ شُلَّةٌ. (TA.)

شُلُلٌ and شَلَلٌ: see شُلْشُلٌ.

لَا شَلَالِ: see 1, second sentence.

جَآءُوا شِلَالًا *They came driving away the camels.* (Ṣ, O.) — And ذَهَبَ القَوْمُ شِلَالًا *The people went driven away* (انشلّوا مَطْرُودِينَ). (TA.) — And شِلَالٌ signifies *A company of men in a scattered,* or *dispersed, state.* (Ṣ, O.)

شَلُولٌ, of she-camels, and of women, (O, Ḳ, in the latter of which, in the place of وَالنِّسَآء, is found وَالشَّآء [i. e. and of sheep or goats], TA,) is like نَابٌ [meaning *Aged*]. (O, Ḳ.) — See also شُلْشُلٌ, in two places.

شَلِيلٌ, (Ṣ, O, Ḳ,) accord. to AO, (Ṣ,) or A'Obeyd, (O, TA,) *An innermost covering for the body, worn beneath the coat of mail,* (Ṣ, O, Ḳ,) *whether it be a* ثَوْب *or some other thing:* (Ṣ, O:) and, (Ṣ, O, Ḳ,) sometimes, (Ṣ, O,) *a short coat of mail,* (Ṣ, O, Ḳ,) *worn beneath the upper one,* (Ṣ, O,) or *worn beneath the large one:* or *in a general sense:* (Ḳ:) [i. e.] *a coat of mail* itself is called شَلِيل; (ISh, TA;) and also ▾ شُلَّةٌ: (TA:) pl. أَشِلَّةٌ; (Ṣ, O, TA;) in the Ḳ, erroneously, شِلَّةٌ. (TA.) — Also (Ṣ, O, Ḳ) *A* [*cloth such as is termed*] حِلْس, (Ṣ, O,) or مِسْح, *of wool* or *of* [*goats'*] *hair,* (Ḳ,) *that is put upon the rump,* or *croup, of the camel,* (Ṣ, O, Ḳ,) *behind the* [*saddle called*] رَحْل. (Ḳ.) [See also سَنِيف.] ═ And The *part,* of a valley, *in which the water flows:* (Ḳ:) or the *middle* of a valley, (Ṣ, O, Ḳ,) *where flows the main body of water:* (Ṣ, O:) so says A'Obeyd, on the authority of AO; but the word commonly known [in this sense] is سَلِيل, with the unpointed س. (O.) ═ And The نُخَاع [or *spinal cord*]; (Ḳ, TA;) [also called the سَلِيل;] i. e. the *white* عِرْق [or *nerve*] *that is in the vertebræ of the back:* mentioned by Kr. (TA.) — And *Long streaks,* or *strips, of flesh, extending with the back:* (Ḳ, TA:) n. un. with ة: also mentioned by Kr: but the more approved word is with [the unpointed] ص. (TA.) ═ And *Clouds in which is no water;* syn. جَهَامٌ. (AA, O.)

شَلَاثَةٌ: see 1, last sentence.

شُلَّى: see شَلَّةٌ, in two places.

شَلْشَلٌ Water, and blood, *falling in consecutive drops;* as also ♦ مُتَشَلْشِلٌ. (K, TA.) — A زِقٌّ [or skin for wine &c.] *flowing* [or *leaking*]. (TA.) And Roasted flesh-meat (شِوَآءٌ) *of which the grease, or gravy, drips;* like شَرْشَرٌ and رَشْرَاشٌ. (TA in art. شر.) — مَآءٌ ذُو شَلْشَلٍ (S, O) and ♦ شَلْشَالٌ (S, O*) *Water having a dripping.* (S, O.) ═ See also the next paragraph.

شُلْشُلٌ A man *light, active,* or *agile;* (S;) [and] so ♦ مِشَلٌّ, (O,) and ♦ شَلُولٌ: (O, TA:) or the first, a boy, or young man, *sharp-headed; light,* or *active, in spirit; brisk, lively,* or *sprightly, in his work;* and so شُغْشُغٌ, and جُلْجُلٌ: (IAar, TA:) or a man *clever, ingenious, acute,* or *sharp; light, active,* or *agile:* (O:) or *light, active,* or *agile, in accomplishing that which is wanted; quick; a good companion; cheerful in mind;* as also ♦ شَلْشَلٌ, and ♦ مِشَلٌّ [in the CK (erroneously) مُشِلٌّ], and ♦ شَلُولٌ, and ♦ شُلُلٌ, and ♦ شَلِلٌ, (K, TA,) of which last the pl. is شَلِلُونَ, it having no broken pl. because of the rareness of فَعِلٌ as the measure of an epithet: (Sb, TA:) and *having little flesh; light, active,* or *agile, in that which he commences,* (K, TA,) *of work &c.;* (TA;) as also ♦ مُتَشَلْشِلٌ: (K, TA:) or this latter [simply] *lean,* or *having little flesh.* (S, O.)

شَلْشَلَةٌ The *falling* of water *in drops,* (K, TA,) *consecutively.* (TA.) [If an inf. n. in this sense, its verb is most probably شَلْشَلَ.]

شَلْشَالٌ: see R. Q. 1: — and see also شَلْشَلٌ.

شُلَاشِلٌ, applied to a plant, or herbage, *Fresh, juicy,* or *sappy.* (TA.)

أَشَلُّ A man *whose hand,* or *arm, has become unsound, or vitiated:* (S, TA:) or *deprived of the power of motion by an unsound,* or *a vitiated, state of its* عُرُوق [meaning *veins* or *nerves*]: (Msb:) or *dried up,* or *stiff:* or *whose hand,* or *arm, has gone* [or *wasted*] *away:* (K, TA:) fem. شَلَّآءُ. (S, Msb.) — And يَدٌ شَلَّآءُ (Mgh, TA) A *hand,* or *an arm, that will not comply with that which its possessor desires of it, by reason of disease therein.* (TA.) — And عَيْنٌ شَلَّآءُ *An eye of which the sight has gone.* (O, Msb, K.)

مِشَلٌّ A [*spear of the kind called*] مِطْرَد [q. v.]. (TA.) — And A he-ass *that drives away* [his she-asses] *much.* (K. [In the CK, in this sense, erroneously written مُشِلٌّ. See مِشْلَلٌ.]) — See also شُلْشُلٌ, in two places. — One says also إِنَّهُ لَمِشَلٌّ عَوْنٌ [thus app., but written in my original without any syll. signs,] meaning *Verily he is a writer soundly,* or *thoroughly, learned;* or *skilled, intelligent, and experienced; and sufficing.* (TA.) ═ Also *A garment with which the neck is covered:* mentioned by the sheykh Zádeh in his Commentary on El-Beydáwee. (TA.)

مِشْلَلٌ A he-ass *much busied by the care of his she-asses.* (IAar, O, L, K. [See also مِشَلٌّ.])

مُتَشَلْشِلٌ: see شَلْشَلٌ: — and see also شُلْشُلٌ.

شلجم

شَلْجَمٌ *A well-known plant;* (S;) [*colza:* see سَلْجَمٌ:] mentioned by the author of the L, and other leading lexicologists, following J. (TA.)

شلم

شُلَمٌ *Sparks of anger:* so in the saying يَتَطَايَرُ شُلَمُهُ [*His sparks of anger fly about*]: (K:) and so شُتَمُهُ. (TA.)

شَالَمٌ:
شَوْلَمٌ: } see what follows.

شَيْلَمٌ The زُؤَان [now applied to *darnel-grass* (but see this latter word زؤان)] *that is* [*often found*] *in wheat;* also called ♦ شَالَمٌ (Msb, K) and ♦ شَوْلَمٌ; (K;) of Pers., or foreign, origin; (أَصْلُهُ أَعْجَمِيٌّ;) and *it is said that one of its two extremities is sharp and the other thick:* (Msb:) of the dial. of the Sawád: accord. to IAar, *i. q.* زِيوَان [sic.] and صَعِيع: AHn says that it is *a small, oblong, red, erect grain, resembling in form the* سُوس [or *grub*] *of wheat; and it does not intoxicate, but renders the wheat very bitter:* and in one place he says, *the plant of the* شيلم *spreads upon the ground, and its leaves are like those of the* خِلَاف [or *salix Aegyptia*] *that is termed* بَلْخِىّ, *very green, and juicy,* or *tender; people eat its leaves when they are fresh, and they are pleasant* [*to the taste*], *without bitterness; but its grain is more intensely,* or *nauseously, bitter* (أَعْقَى) *than aloes.* (TA.) [Forskål, in his Flora Aegypt. Arab. p. 199, after describing the زؤان, says, "شيلم etiam agri vitium; a priore tamen diversa species: decocto plantæ obtunduntur sensus hominis qui operationem chirurgicam subire debet; Avicenna sic referente." See also سَكْرَة.] ═ [Golius says, on the authority of a gloss in a copy of the KL, that it signifies also *A short,* or *little, avaricious, man;* "vir curtus, avarus:" a meaning, if correct, app. tropical.]

شلو

1. شَلَا, aor. ـُ, *He went,* or *journeyed.* (K.) ═ And *He raised, uplifted,* or *took up,* a thing; syn. رَفَعَ. (IAar, Az, K.)

4. اشلى, (S, Msb, K, &c.,) inf. n. إِشْلَآءٌ, (Msb,) *He called* a dog, (AZ, S, Msb,) &c.: (Msb:) and *he called* a she-camel, (ISk, S, K,) and a ewe or she-goat, *by her name,* (ISk, S,) *to milk her.* (ISk, S, K.) And اشلى دَابَّتَهُ *He showed the* مِشْلَاة [or *nose-bag* (in the CK erroneously المِخْلَاة)] *to his beast in order that it should come to him.* (K.) [See also 10.] Accord. to IAar and several others, one says, أَشْلَيْتُ الكَلْبَ عَلَى الصَّيْدِ, meaning *I incited,* or *urged, the dog* [*against the object,* or *objects, of the chase*]; like أَغْرَيْتُهُ in measure and in signification: (Mgh,* Msb, TA:) but this is disallowed by ISk, (S, Msb, TA,) and by Th; (S, Mgh, TA;) and in like manner, اشليته بالصَّيْدِ in the same sense; though they are allowed by others: one says, however, [by common consent,] أَشْلَيْتُ الكَلْبَ لِلصَّيْدِ, meaning *I called the dog to the chase.* (Mgh.)

8: see the next paragraph, in two places.

10. استشلاهُ, (S, K,) and ♦ اشتلاهُ, (S,* K, [accord. to my copies of the former, أَشْلَاهُ, but a verse immediately following as an ex. shows the right reading,]) *He called him in order to save him,* or *rescue him,* (S, K,) or *to make him come forth,* (S,) *from straitness,* or *perdition,* (K,) or *from a place:* (S:) this is the primary signification. (TA.) — And [hence] the former, (S, K, TA,) and ♦ the latter also, (S, TA, i. e. اشتلاهُ, [thus in this instance in the copies of the S,]) ‡ *He saved him,* or *rescued him.* (S, K, TA.) ═ And استشلى *He* (a man, TA) *was,* or *became, angry.* (K, TA.)

شَلًا: see the next paragraph.

شِلْوٌ *A limb,* or *member;* (Msb, K;) as also ♦ شِلْوَةٌ: (TA:) or *a limb,* or *member, of flesh-meat:* whence, in a trad., ايتِنِى بِشِلْوِهَا الأَيْمَنِ [*Bring thou to me its right limb*]: (S:) pl. أَشْلَآءٌ (S, Msb, TA) and أَشْلٍ, [originally أَشْلُوٌ,] like أَدْلٍ pl. of دَلْوٌ. (TA.) — And The *body* of anything [i. e. of any animal]; as also ♦ شَلًا; (K;) which latter is expl. by ISd as signifying the *skin* and *body* of anything; and is applied in a trad. to the inner side of a haunch as meaning *having no flesh upon it:* (TA:) [or,] accord. to IDrd, شِلْوُ الإِنْسَانِ signifies *the body of the man after its wasting,* or *decaying:* (Msb, TA:) [or] أَشْلَآءُ الإِنْسَانِ means *the members,* or *limbs, of the man after wasting,* or *decaying, and becoming dissundered:* (S, TA:) and (hence, Msb) one says, بَنُو فُلَانٍ أَشْلَآءٌ فِى بَنِى فُلَانٍ, meaning † *The sons of such a one are remains among the sons of such a one:* (S, Msb:) and هُوَ مِنْ أَشْلَآءِ القَوْمِ † *He is of the remains of the people:* [for] شِلْوٌ signifies † *a remain,* or *remaining portion:* and شلى [app. شُلِىٌّ, said to be like غِنىً, but this is, I doubt not, a mistranscription for عُنِىٌّ, i. e. originally of the measure فُعُولٌ, is another pl. of شِلْوٌ, and] signifies † *remains* of any thing. (TA.) [See also شَلِيَّةٌ.] — Also *Any skinned animal of which somewhat has been eaten and a portion remains:* (K:) or *a portion remaining, whether much or little, of a sheep or goat of which part has been eaten:* (L voce سَلِيخ:) pl. أَشْلَآءٌ. (K.) — And أَشْلَآءُ اللِّجَامِ † *The straps,* or *thongs, of the bit* or *bridle:* (A, K:) or *such as have become old, and of which the iron appertenance has become slender,* (K,

TA,) or, as in the M, [*of which*] *the iron appertenances* [*have become slender*], *without straps*, or *thongs*: app. likened to limbs, or members, of flesh-meat. (TA.)

شِلْوَةٌ : see the next preceding paragraph.

شَلِيَّةٌ *A piece*, or *portion*, of flesh-meat &c. (Ḳ,* TA.) — And † *A remnant*, or *remaining portion*; (Ḳ, TA;) only of property: (Ṣ, Ḳ,* TA:) pl. شَلَايَا. (Ṣ, TA.) One says, ذَهَبَتْ مَاشِيَةُ فُلَانٍ وَبَقِيَتْ لَهُ شَلِيَّةٌ † [*The cattle of such a one went away, but a remnant remained to him*]. (AZ, Ṣ.) [See also شِلْوٌ.]

مُشْلًى *Lean*, or *light of flesh*: (Ḳ, TA:) an epithet applied to a man. (TA.)

مَشَالٍ, in the dial. of El-Ḥijáz, The *things*, or *instruments*, *with which scarification is performed upon the cheeks*: app. pl. of مِشْلَاةٌ. (TA.)

شلياق

الشِّلْيَاقُ *A certain northern constellation*, [namely, *Lyra*,] *consisting of ten stars*, *the bright star* [*α*] *of which is called* النَّسْرُ الوَاقِعُ: *the Arabs liken it to a vulture* (نَسْر) *which has contracted its wings to itself*, *as though it had alighted upon a thing*: *the vulgar call* [*the three chief stars in*] *it* الأَثَافِى: *and before the bright star is a dim star which the Arabs call* الأَظْفَار [i. e. *the talons*]. (Ḳzw. [Not in any of my Lexicons.])

شم

1. شَمِمْتُ, aor. أَشَمُّ; and شَمَمْتُ, aor. أَشُمُّ; (Ṣ, Mgh, Mṣb, Ḳ;) the latter mentioned by AO; (Ṣ, TA;) third pers. of each شَمَّ; (Mgh;) inf. n. شَمٌّ (Ṣ, Mṣb, Ḳ) and شَمِيمٌ, (Ṣ, Ḳ,) which are of both verbs, (TA,) and شِمِّيمَى, mentioned by Z (Ḳ, TA) alone; (TA;) *I smelt*, i. e. *perceived by the nose*, (Ḳ,) a thing, (Ṣ, Mṣb, Ḳ,*) or an odour; (Mgh;) and ▼ اِشْتَمَمْتُ signifies the same; (Ṣ, Mṣb, Ḳ, TA; [أَشْمَمْتُهُ in the CḲ is a mistranscription for اِشْتَمَمْتُهُ;]) and ▼ تَشَمَّمْتُ also, (Ḳ,) and ▼ شَمَّيْتُ, thus in the copies of the Ḳ, but correctly ▼ شَمَّمْتُ: (TA: [both, however, are mentioned in the CḲ: the former like قَضَّيْتُ for قَضَّضْتُ:]) or تَشَمَّمْتُ ▼ الشَّىْءَ signifies شَمِمْتُهُ فِى مُهْلَةٍ [*I smelt the thing leisurely*, or *gently*]: (Ṣ, TA:) or تشمّم ▼ الشىءَ and ▼ اشتمّهُ both signify *he put the thing near to his nose in order that he might draw in its odour*. (AḤn, TA.) — See an ex. in a prov. mentioned voce حِمَارٌ. — [Hence,] † شُمَّ † *He was tried*, or *proved by trial* or *experiment* or *experience*; syn. أُخْتُبِرَ. (IAạr, Ḳ.) — شَمِمَ, sec. pers. شَمِمْتَ, aor. يَشْمَمُ, (Mṣb,) inf. n. شَمَمٌ, (Ṣ,* Mṣb, Ḳ,*) *He* (a man) *was high*, or *elevated*, *in the nose*. (Ṣ,* Mṣb, Ḳ.*) — [And hence,] شَمَّ, (Ḳ,) [sec. pers. شَمِمْتَ,] inf. n. شَمَمٌ, (TA,) ‡ *He* (a man, TA) *magnified himself*; or *behaved proudly*, or *haughtily*. (Ḳ, TA. [And اشمّ has a similar meaning.]) — [This verb is also probably used in other senses, said of a mountain, &c.: see شَمَمٌ below.] — See also 4, near the end.

2. شَمَّمْتُ and شَمَّيْتُ: see above, in two places.

3. شَامَّا, (Ḳ,) inf. n. مُشَامَّةٌ, (Ṣ, TA,) *They smelt each other*; (Ṣ,* Ḳ;) as also ▼ تَشَامَّا, (Ḳ,) inf. n. تَشَامٌّ. (Ṣ.) — [Hence,] شَامِمْهُ ‡ *Look thou to see what is with him*, or *in his mind*, (مَا عِنْدَهُ, Ṣ, Ḳ, TA,) and *draw near to him*, (Ḳ, TA,) and *seek after the knowledge of what is with him*, or *in his mind*, (ما عنده,) *by means of informations and disclosure*; as though each smelt what was with the other in order to act according thereto. (TA.) And hence the saying, شَامَمْنَاهُمْ ثُمَّ نَاوَشْنَاهُمْ ‡ [*We endeavoured*, or *looked*, *to ascertain their condition*; *then we engaged them in near*, *though not close*, *conflict*]. (TA.) You say also, شَامَمْتُ الرَّجُلَ meaning [simply] † *I drew near to the man*. (Ṣ.) مُشَامَّةٌ [used tropically] signifies † The *looking into* a thing. (KL.) And † The *approaching* the enemy *so that the two parties see each other*. (Ṣ.)

4. اشمّهُ إِيَّاهُ *He made him to smell it*, or *perceive it by the nose*. (Ḳ.) You say, أَشْمَمْتُهُ الطِّيبَ [*I made him to smell the perfume*]. (Ṣ, Mṣb.) — And [hence] one says to the prefect, or governor, or prince, or commander, أَشِمَّنِى يَدَكَ أُقَبِّلْهَا † [*Suffer me to approach thy hand that I may kiss it*]; (Ṣ,* TA;) a phrase like نَاوِلْنِى يَدَكَ, (TA,) but better than the latter phrase: so says Kh. (Ṣ.) — And اشمّ الخَتَّانُ, and اشمّت البَظْرَ, ‡ *He*, and *she*, i. e. the operator, *took*, (Ḳ, TA,) or *cut off*, (TA,) *a small portion of the prepuce*, and *of the* بَظْر [q. v.]: (Ḳ, TA:) or the latter signifies *she cut off a portion of the* نَوَاة [q. v.], *not extirpating it*. (TA.) — And اشمّ الحَرْفَ, (Ṣ,* Ḳ,) inf. n. إِشْمَامٌ, (Ṣ,) † *He made the consonant to have a smack of the ḍammeh or the kesreh*, (lit., *made it to smell*, Ṣ, or *to taste*, Ḳ, *the ḍammeh* or *the kesreh*,) *in such a manner* (Ṣ, Ḳ) *that the* إِشْمَام, (Ṣ,) or *that the ḍammeh* or *kesreh*, (Ḳ,) *was not heard*, (Ṣ, Ḳ,) *what is termed* إِشْمَام *being less than what is termed* رَوْمُ الحَرَكَةِ *the former being apparent only by the motion of the lip*, (Ṣ,) or *of the upper lip*, (so in one of my copies of the Ṣ,) *no account being taken of it*, (Ṣ, Ḳ,) i. e., *of the ḍammeh* or *kesreh*, (Ḳ,) *it not being reckoned as a* حَرَكَة *because of its feebleness*, *the consonant in this case being quiescent* or *like that which is quiescent*, (Ṣ,) *and the prosodical measure not being broken thereby*: (Ḳ:) for ex., in the following verse,

مَتَى أَنَامُ لَا يُؤَرِّقْنِى الكَرِى
لَيْلًا وَلَا أَسْمَعُ أَجْرَاسَ المَطِى

[meaning الكَرِىُّ and المَطِىّ, (as is said in one of my copies of the Ṣ,) i. e. *When I sleep, he who lets beasts on hire will not render me wakeful by night, nor do I hear the bells of the camels on which people ride*], the Arabs [or, as is said in the TA, some of the Arabs] make the ق [in يُؤَرِّقْنِى] to have a smack of the ḍammeh; but if you took account of the حَرَكَة of the إِشْمَام [in this case,] the measure of the verse would be broken, [the foot] رقنى الكرى becoming, in the scanning, مُتَفَاعِلُنْ, which may be only in the كَامِل; whereas this verse is of the رَجَز: (Sb, Ṣ:) another case of إِشْمَام is that of the ى in دُوَيْبَّة, [in which that letter is quiescent, but made to have a smack of kesreh,] as is the same letter in every similar case, in a dim. noun, when followed by a doubled letter. (Zj, T in art. دب.) Also *He pronounced the consonant with a* حَرَكَة [or vowel-sound] *between ḍamm and kesr*, *apparent only in utterance*, *not in writing*; as in قِيلَ and غِيضَ in the Ḳur xi. 46. (I'Aḳ pp. 130 and 131.) [See also رَامَ, voce رَوْمُ الحَرَكَةِ.] — [Golius explains اشمّ as signifying also "*Reduxit, fecit ut converteret se ab aliqua re*;" as on the authority of the KL; in my copy of which, however, I do not find this meaning.] — اشمّ, (Ṣ, Ḳ,) inf. n. إِشْمَامٌ, [as an intrans. verb,] said of a man, (Ṣ,) also signifies *He passed by*, or *along*, *raising his head*; (Ṣ, Ḳ, TA;) *and magnified*, or *exalted*, *himself*; *behaved proudly*, or *disdainfully*; or *elevated his nose*, *from pride*. (TA. [See also 1, near the end.]) — And *He turned away* from a thing. (Ḳ.) One says بَيْنَا هُمْ فِى وَجْهٍ إِذْ أَشَمُّوا, i. e. [*While they were in a certain direction*, *lo*,] *they turned away*; (Ṣ, TA, as from AA;) or ▼ شَمُّوا. (Thus in one of my copies of the Ṣ [but I think it to be a mistranscription].) And اشمّ القَوْمُ *The people*, or *party*, *deviated in their directions to the right and left*: a phrase heard in this sense by AA. (Ṣ.)

5: see 1, in three places.

6: see 3, first sentence.

8: see 1, in two places.

10. استشمّ *He desired to smell*. (KL.) — And *He perceived a smell*, or *an odour*, from a thing. (KL.) — دَخَلَ المُخَاطُ أَنْفَهُ فَاسْتَشَمَّهُ فَأَدْخَلَهُ فِى حَلْقِهِ, said of a man, means اِسْتَنْشَقَهُ [i. e. ‡ *The mucus entered his nose*, *and he snuffed it up*, *and made it to pass into his fauces*]; the verb being metaphorically thus used, like as الاِسْتِنْشَاقُ is metaphorically used for الشَّمُّ. (Mgh.)

شَمَمٌ inf. n. of the intrans. verb شَمَّ [q. v.]. (Mṣb, TA.) — [Used as a simple subst.,] *Highness of the nose*: (Mṣb:) or *highness of the bone of the nose*, (Ṣ, Ḳ,) *and beauty thereof*, (Ḳ,) *with evenness*, or *straightness*, *of its upper part*, (Ṣ, Ḳ, when there is in it a gibbousness it is termed قَنًا, Ṣ,) *and uprightness of the end*, or *lowest part*: (Ḳ:) or, as some say, *this last quality* [*alone*]: (TA:) or *length of the end*, or *lower part*, *of the nose*, *so that it extends over the middle of the mustache*, (وُرُودُ الأَرْنَبَةِ,) *with beautiful evenness*, or *straightness*, *of the bone*, *and highness thereof greater than the highness that is termed* ذَلَف: or *length and slenderness of the nose*, *and a downward extending of its* رَوْثَة [i. e. *end* or *tip*, or *part where the blood that flows from the nostrils drops* or *drips*]: (Ḳ:) or [*simply*] *length*.

in the nose. (Ham p. 789.) — And, in a man, The *quality of having what is termed* شَمَمٌ *of the nose.* (Ṣ.) — [And hence, ‡ *Self-magnification,* or *pride,* or *haughtiness:* see 1, near the end.] — And ‡ *Generosity.* (Ḥam p. 728.) — Also *Highness,* (Ḳ,) or *tallness of the head,* (Ṣ,) *of a mountain.* (Ṣ, Ḳ.) — And ‡ *Nearness:* and ‡ *remoteness:* thus having two contr. meanings. (Ḳ, TA.) It has both of such meanings in the phrase دَارُهُ شَمَمٌ ‡ [*His house, or abode, is near:* and, *remote*]: (Ḳ, TA:) and in the phrase رَأَيْتُهُ مِنْ شَمَمٍ ‡ [*I saw him, or it, from within a short distance:* and, *from afar*]. (TA.)

شَمُومٌ A thing [*odorous, fragrant,* or] *fit to be smelt.* (KL.)

شَمِيمٌ *High,* or *elevated:* (Ṣ, Ḳ:) applied in this sense to a [camel's saddle such as is called] قَتَب. (Ṣ.)

شَمَّامٌ *A sort of melon resembling a small colocynth,* [or rather *a small melon resembling a colocynth,*] *streaked with redness and greenness and yellowness:* called in Pers. دَسْتَنْبُويَه [i. e. "perfume"]; (Ḳ;) originally دَسْتْ بُوى [or دَسْتْ بُويَهْ]: (TA:) *its odour is cool, pleasant, lenitive, and narcotic; and the eating of it is laxative to the bowels:* (Ḳ:) [The *cucumis dudaïm* of Linn.; called by Forskål *cucumis schemmam:* the latter thus describes it (Flora Aegypt. Arab. p. 169): "*Caules* 5-sulcati, setis rigidis, scandentes, cirrhosi: *folia* cordato-oblonga, acuta, subsinuata, dentato-repanda, hispida: *calyces* villosi, molles: *flores* flavi, conferti in alis: *fructus* globoso-ovatus, glaberrimus, magnitudine citri, flavus, maculis inæqualibus, fulvo-ferrugineis, versus polos in lineas confluentibus; pulpa aquosa, seminibus tota plena: fructus juvenis villosus; maturus glaber: odor, fortis nec ingratus; eamque ob caussam cultus; non edulis:" in the present day, the same appellation is applied in Egypt to *several species of melon, of pleasant odour and taste;* but this application I believe to be of very late origin: see also لُفَّاحٌ: and see De Sacy's "Rel. de l' Égypte par Abd-allatif," pp. 126-7.]

شَمَّامَاتٌ *Sweet odours that one smells.* (Ḳ.)

شَمَاشِمُ *Ripe dates remaining upon the raceme.* (AZ, Ḳ.)

[شَامٌّ *Smelling,* or *perceiving by the nose.*] — يَا ٱبْنَ شَامَّةِ الوَذْرَةِ [*O son of her who smells the* وَذْرَة] is an expression of reproach. (Ṣ.)

أَشَمُّ, applied to a man, (Mṣb,) *Having that quality of the nose which is termed* شَمَمٌ; (Mṣb, Ḳ;) or so أَشَمُّ الأَنْفِ, thus applied: (Ṣ:) fem. شَمَّآءُ: (Mṣb, TA:) and pl. شُمٌّ. (TA.) — And [hence, ‡ *Self-magnifying,* or *proud,* or *haughty:* or] a chief *characterized by disdainfulness, scornfulness,* or *disdainful and proud incompliance,* (Ḳ, TA,) *and high-minded.* (TA.) — Also A mountain *tall,* (Ṣ, TA,) or *high,* (TA,) *in the head.* (Ṣ, TA.) [And *High,* as applied to a place of ascent in a mountain: see an ex. of the pl. in a verse cited voce تَصَدَّقَ.] — And A shoulder *high in the head of its bone.* (Ḳ.) — [Freytag mentions two other meanings: — "*Ventus ex alto veniens, qui penetrantioris est odoratus:* — [and] fem. شَمَّآءُ *Jugum extensum in monte:*" from the Deewán of the Hudhalees.]

مُشِمٌّ [*Turning away,* or *averse*]. One says, عَرَضْتُ عَلَيْهِ كَذَا فَإِذَا هُوَ مُشِمٌّ لَا يُرِيدُهُ [*I offered to him such a thing, and lo, he was averse, not desiring it*]. (Ṣ.)

[مِشَمٌّ *An instrument of smelling;* like as مِسْمَعٌ signifies "an instrument of hearing." — Hence, its pl.] مَشَامُّ signifies *Noses.* (KL.) — [This pl. is expl. by Jac. Schultens, as meaning *Perfumes* (*odoramenta*): so says Freytag.]

مَشْمُومٌ *A thing that is smelt;* such as *any sweet-smelling plant:* like as مَأْكُولٌ signifies "a thing that is eaten:" (Mṣb:) [and] *musk:* (Ṣ, Ḳ:) [pl. مَشْمُومَاتٌ.]

شمت

1. شَمِتَ, aor. ـَ, (Ṣ, A, Mṣb, Ḳ,) inf. n. شَمَاتَةٌ (Ṣ, Ḳ) and شَمَاتٌ, (Ḳ,) or the former is a simple subst., (Mṣb, [in which no inf. n. is mentioned,]) *He* (an enemy) *rejoiced:* (TA:) or *he* (a man, TA) *rejoiced at the affliction of the enemy:* (Ḳ, TA:) you say, شَمِتَ بِهِ *He rejoiced at his* [an enemy's] *affliction.* (Ṣ, A, Mṣb.)

2: see 4. — تَشْمِيتٌ is *syn. with* تَسْمِيتٌ: [i. e.] تَشْمِيتُ العَاطِسِ signifies *The uttering a prayer for the sneezer;* (Ṣ;) when he has, in obedience to an injunction of the Prophet, said الحَمْدُ لِلّٰهِ [Praise be to God]: (Ḥar p. 250:) you say, شَمَّتَ العَاطِسَ, (ISd, A, TA,) and شَمَّتَ عَلَيْهِ, meaning [as expl. in art. سمت: or] *He prayed for the sneezer that he might not be in a state in which his enemy might rejoice at his affliction:* (ISd, TA:) شمّت is better and more common than سمّت: (A'Obeyd, TA in art. سمت and in the present art.:) but the latter is said by Th to be the original word: or the meaning is, *he said to the sneezer, May God put away,* or *avert, from thee that on account of which one would rejoice at thy affliction:* or it is from الشَّوَامِتُ as signifying "the legs" of a quadruped, as though meaning *he prayed for the sneezer that he might be firm,* or *steadfast, in his obedience to God.* (L and TA from the Fáïḳ &c.) And شَمَّتَ لَهُ and عَلَيْهِ, inf. n. as above, *He prayed for what was good for him; prayed for a blessing upon him;* as also سَمَّتَ, but the former is the better and the more common. (L and TA from the T and Fáïḳ &c.) — Also *i. q.* تَخْيِيبٌ: (Ḳ:) you say, شَمَّتَهُ فُلَانٌ, meaning خَيَّبَهُ [*Such a one disappointed him;* or *caused him to be disappointed of attaining what he desired* or *sought:* or *denied him, refused him, prohibited him from attaining,* or *debarred him from, that which he desired* or *sought*]. (TA.) — And *i. q.* جَمْعٌ [The act of *collecting,* &c.]. (Ḳ. [But SM says that he had searched to the utmost for this meaning without finding it in any other lexicon.])

4. أَشْمَتَهُ ٱللّٰهُ بِهِ *God made him* (i. e. the enemy, A, Mṣb) *to rejoice at his affliction.* (A,* Mṣb, Ḳ, TA.) For فَلَا تُشْمِتْ بِىَ الأَعْدَآءَ [*Therefore make not thou the enemies to rejoice at my affliction*], in the Ḳur [vii. 149], Mujáhid is related to have read ▾ فَلَا تَشْمَتْ: but the correctness of this is doubted. (TA.)

5. تَشَمَّتَ sig...es A people's *returning disappointed of attaining their desire, without spoil.* (Ḳ.)

8. اِشْتِمَاتٌ [A camel's] *beginning to be fat.* (Ḳ. [See the part. n., below.])

شِمَاتٌ *Disappointment; frustration of one's endeavour or hope:* (IB, TA:) a subst. from تَشْمِيتٌ as signifying تَخْيِيبٌ. (TA.) — Also, thus written in copies of the Ḳ, [and in the Ṣ,] with kesr, (TA,) [but in the CḲ شَمَات,] and ▾ شَمَاتَى, (Ḳ,) Persons *suffering disappointment;* or *failing of attaining their desire;* (Ḳ, TA;) *without spoil:* (TA:) [pls.] without any sing.; (Ḳ:) or the latter has no sing. known to ISd: (TA:) [but] ▾ شَامِتٌ has this meaning as a sing. part. n., and شمات [app. شُمَّاتٌ] is its pl. (IB, TA.) One says, ▾ رَجَعُوا شَمَاتَى, (IAạr, TA,) or شِمَاتًا, (Ṣ,) *They returned suffering disappointment;* or *failing of attaining their desire;* (IAạr, Ṣ, TA;) *without spoil;* and so ▾ مُشَمَّتِينَ and ▾ مُتَشَمِّتِينَ. (TA.)

[شَمِيتٌ *Reproach* ("convicium"): so Golius, as from the KL; but I do not find it in my copy of that work.]

شَمَاتَى: see شِمَاتٌ, in two places.

شَامِتٌ One *rejoicing at the affliction of an enemy:* [fem. with ة: pl. masc. شُمَّاتٌ and fem. شَوَامِتُ; or the latter may be anomalously masc., like فَوَارِسُ &c.; and as such it is evidently used in the L, in one place; but in another place, where it cites an explanation by AO, as fem.: both are mentioned in the M and L and TA, and the latter in the Ṣ and A also.] One says, اَللّٰهُمَّ لَا تُطِيعَنَّ بِى شَامِتًا [*O God, comply not with the desire of one who is to me a rejoicer at my affliction*]; meaning, do not with me that which one who rejoices at my affliction likes, or approves; for in that case, Thou wouldst be as though Thou obeyedst him. (ISk, L, TA.) And بَاتَ فُلَانٌ بِلَيْلَةِ الشَّوَامِتِ *Such a one passed a night such as would make to rejoice those, or those females, that would rejoice at the affliction of an enemy;* (Ṣ, A, L, TA;) i. e., *a distressing night.* (A.) [And a verse cited in the next paragraph presents, as some read it, a similar ex. of الشَّوَامِت.] = See also شِمَاتٌ.

شَامِتَةٌ [fem. of شَامِتٌ, q. v. = Also], as a subst., sing. of شَوَامِتُ (Ṣ, TA) which signifies The *legs* of a beast. (Ṣ, A, Ḳ, TA.) One says, لَا تَرَكَ ٱللّٰهُ لَهُ شَامِتَةً, i. e. [*May God not leave to him*] *a leg* of a beast. (AA, Ṣ, A, TA.) And En-Nábighah [Edh-Dhubyánee] says,

* فَارْتَاعَ مِنْ صَوْتِ كَلَّابٍ فَبَاتَ لَهُ *
* طَوْعَ الشَّوَامِتِ مِنْ خَوْفٍ وَمِنْ صَرَدِ *

[*And that has been frightened at the voice of a huntsman with his dogs,*] *and passed the night in consequence thereof standing,* (lit. *obeying the legs,*) *by reason of fear and* [also] *of cold;* the poet describing a [wild] bull: (AO, L, TA:) but some read طَوْعُ (instead of طَوْعَ); and accord. to this reading, the meaning is, *and passed the night having, of fear and of cold, what was agreeable with the desire of such as would rejoice at his affliction;* the phrase being like the saying اَللّٰهُمَّ لَا تُطِيعَنَّ بِى شَامِتًا meaning as expl. in the next preceding paragraph: (ISk, L, TA:) or *he passed the night having* [*of fear and of cold*] *what would rejoice the* شَوَامِت *that heard thereof:* (AO, L, TA:) [and in like manner, Z says,] بَاتَ طَوْعَ الشَّوَامِتِ [without لَهُ, and with طوع in the accus. case, lit. *he passed the night obeying those, or those females, that rejoiced at his affliction,*] means, *as those that rejoiced at his affliction liked,* or *approved.* (A.)

مُشَمَّتٌ A king *prayed for* (Ḳ, TA) *with the prayers that are offered for kings.* (TA.) ═ See also شِمَاتٌ, last sentence.

مُشَمِّتٌ Any one *praying,* or *who prays, for what is good;* as also مُسَمِّتٌ. (Ṣ.)

إِبِلٌ مُشَمِّتَةٌ *Camels beginning to be fat.* (TA.)

مُتَشَمِّتٌ: see its pl. voce شِمَاتٌ, last sentence.

شمخ

1. شَمَخَ, (Ṣ, L, Ḳ,) aor. ـُ, inf. n. شُمُوخٌ, (L,) *It* (a mountain) *was high,* or *lofty.* (Ṣ, L, Ḳ.) — Hence, (Ḥar p. 442,) شَمَخَ بِأَنْفِهِ, (Ṣ, A, L, Ḳ,) and شَمَخَ أَنْفُهُ, aor. and inf. n. as above, (L,) *He* (a man) *magnified,* or *exalted, himself; was proud;* (Ṣ, A, L, Ḳ;) *behaved proudly,* or *disdainfully; elevated his nose, from pride.* (L.) [See also زَمَخَ.]

نِيَّةٌ شَمْخٌ (L, Ḳ) and ▼ شُمُوخٌ (L) *A distant, far-reaching,* or *far-aiming, intention, purpose,* or *design;* [in an action or a journey &c.;] (L, Ḳ;) as also نِيَّةٌ زَمْخٌ and زُمُوخٌ. (L.)

مَفَازَةٌ شَمُوخٌ *A desert,* or *waterless desert, far-extending;* (Ḳ;) as also زَمُوخٌ. (TA.) — See also شَمَخٌ.

شَمَّاخٌ: see what follows, in two places.

جَبَلٌ شَامِخٌ *A high,* or *lofty, mountain;* (Ṣ, A, L;) as also ▼ شَمَّاخٌ [but in an intensive sense, i. e. *a very high* or *lofty* mountain]: (L:) pl. جِبَالٌ شَوَامِخُ (Ṣ, A) and شُمَّخٌ. (A.) — Hence, شَامِخٌ signifies also *Proud;* (L, TA;) *elevating the nose, from pride,* or *disdain:* [like زَامِخٌ:] pl. شُمَّخٌ: (L, Ḳ:) and ▼ شَمَّاخٌ a man *who magnifies, or exalts, himself much;* or *elevates his nose much, from pride.* (L.) — And أُنُوفٌ شُمَّخٌ [*Noses elevated, from pride*]; like زُمَّخٌ. (Ṣ.) — And نَسَبٌ شَامِخٌ ‡ [*A proud,* or *high, lineage*]. (TA.)

شمر

1. شَمَرَ, aor. ـِ, inf. n. شَمْرٌ: see the next paragraph, in five places.

2. شمّر, (Ṣ, A, Mṣb, Ḳ,) inf. n. تَشْمِيرٌ, (Ṣ, Ḳ,) *He raised,* (Ṣ, Mṣb, Ḳ,) or *tucked up,* or *contracted,* (A,) *his garment,* (Mṣb, Ḳ,) or *his waist-wrapper,* (Ṣ,) [or *his sleeve,*] or *his skirts.* (A.) One says, شَمَّرَ عَنْ سَاقِهِ [*He raised,* or *tucked up, his garment, or waist-wrapper, or skirts, from his shank*]. (Ṣ.) [And in like manner, ▼ تشمّر signifies *He raised,* or *tucked up, his garment,* &c.: for] one says also, تَشَمَّرَ عَنْ سَاعِدَيْهِ [*He tucked up his sleeves from his fore arms*]. (TA.) It is said in a prov., شَمَّرَ ذَيْلًا وَادَّرَعَ لَيْلًا i. e. [lit.] *He contracted,* or *drew up, his* [or *a*] *skirt* [*and clad himself with night as with a tunic*]: (TA:) or شَمِّرْ ذَيْلًا وَادَّرِعْ لَيْلًا, meaning ‡ *Use thou prudence,* or *precaution,* or *good judgment, and journey all the night.* (Ṣ and Ḳ in art. درع.) — [Hence,] † *He strove,* or *laboured, exerted himself* or *his power* or *ability, employed himself vigorously* or *laboriously* or *with energy,* or *took extraordinary pains,* (AA, Mṣb, TA,) *and was quick,* (AA, TA,) فِى الْأَمْرِ [*in the affair*]; as also ▼ شَمَرَ, inf. n. شَمْرٌ: (TA:) and فِى العِبَادَةِ [*in religious service*]: (Mṣb:) and فِى سَيْرِهِ [*in his pace,* or *journeying*]; like تَجَرَّدَ and اِنْجَرَدَ. (L and TA in art. جرد.) Also, (Ḳ,) inf. n. as above; (TA;) and ▼ شَمَرَ, (Ḳ,) aor. ـِ, inf. n. شَمْرٌ; (TA;) and ▼ انشمر, and ▼ تشمّر; (Ḳ;) † *He passed along striving,* or *exerting himself,* or *vigorously:* or *he passed along with a proud and self-conceited gait;* (Ḳ;) [and] ▼ مَرَّ يَشْمُرُ, inf. n. as above, has the latter meaning. (Ṣ.) And شمّر فى الأمر † *He was,* or *became, light,* or *active,* (Ṣ, Mṣb, Ḳ,) *and quick,* (Mṣb,) *in,* or *for, the affair:* (Ṣ, Mṣb, Ḳ:) and شمّر للأمر, and شمّر للأمر أذياله, (A, TA,) and شمّر عن ساقه, (TA,) ‡ *He was,* or *became, light,* or *active, and he rose,* or *hastened, to do the thing,* or *affair.* (A, TA.) And شمّرت الحرب and شمّرت عن ساقها ‡ [*The war,* or *battle, became vehement;* like كَشَفَتْ عَنْ سَاقٍ]. (A.) — Also *He contracted* a thing; syn. قَلَّصَ; (TA;) [and so, perhaps, ▼ شَمَرَ; for] الشَّمْرُ signifies تَقْلِيصُ الشَّىْءِ, like التَّشْمِيرُ: (Ḳ:) [or the author of the TA may have misunderstood this explanation in the Ḳ, and the meaning may be *it* (a thing) *contracted,* or *became contracted;* for قلّص is trans. and also (like قَلَصَ) intrans.: that شمّر has this latter meaning, whether it have also, or have not, the former, is shown by the statement that] one says, شَمَّرَتِ الشَّفَةُ meaning قَلَصَتْ [i. e. *The lip became contracted,* or *became contracted upwards*]: (M in art. قلص:) and ▼ تشمّر [in like manner] signifies *it* (a thing) *contracted,* or *became contracted;* syn. تَقَلَّصَ. (TA.) — Also, (inf. n. as above, Aṣ, Ṣ,) ‡ *He launched forth* a ship, or boat; *let it go; let it take its course;* (Aṣ, IAṣr, Ṣ, A, Ḳ;) and in like manner, a hawk; (A;) and *he discharged,* or *shot,* an arrow: (Aṣ, IAṣr, Ṣ, A, Mṣb:) and hence, (Aṣ, Ṣ,) ‡ *he sent, sent forth,* or *sent away,* (Aṣ, Ṣ, M, A, Ḳ,) a thing. (M, A.) [See also سَمَّرَ.] And شمّر الإبل, inf. n. as above; (TA;) and ▼ اشمرها; (Ḳ;) † *He hastened the camels; made them to hasten;* syn. أَكْمَشَهَا, [which seems to be either syn. with, or a mistranscription for, كَمَّشَهَا, (see شَمَّرَ,)] and أَعْجَلَهَا. (O, Ḳ, TA.) — And شَمَّرْتُ النَّخْلَ *I cut off the fruit of the palm-trees;* syn. صَرَمْتُهُ; (A, TA;) or so ▼ شَمَرْتُهُ, (Ibn-'Abbád, O,) [for] الشَّمْرُ signifies صِرَامُ النَّخْلِ. (Ḳ.)

4. اشمر الإبل: see 2, last sentence but one. — اشمر الجَمَلُ طَرُوقَتَهُ *The he-camel impregnated the she-camel covered by him.* (O, Ḳ.) — اشمرهُ بِالسَّيْفِ *He destroyed him with the sword;* syn. أَدْرَجَهُ. (O, Ḳ.)

5. تشمّر: see 2, third sentence. — [Hence,] تشمّر للأمر, (Ṣ, Ḳ,) or لِلْعَمَلِ (A,) and ▼ انشمر للامر, (Ṣ,) † *He prepared himself* (Ṣ, A, Ḳ) *for the affair,* (Ṣ, Ḳ,) or *for the work.* (A.) [Freytag mentions اشمر للامر in a similar sense, "Paratus fuit ad rem peragendam," as on the authority of J; but I do not find it in the Ṣ.] — See also 2 as syn. with 1 and 7. ═ [Also, app., as quasi-pass. of 2, *It* (a garment, &c., *was,* or *became, raised,* or *tucked up,* or *contracted;* and so signifies ▼ انشمر.] — See 2 again, in the latter part of the paragraph.

7. انشمر: see 5, in two places. — See also 2 as syn. with 1 and 5. — Also *He* (a horse) *hastened,* or *went quickly.* (Ṣ, O. [Accord. to Freytag, the verb in this sense in the Ṣ is اشتمر; but this is a mistake.]) — And i. q. مَضَى and نَفَذَ [app. as meaning † *It,* or *he, acted with a penetrative force* or *energy* (see شِمْرٌ and شِمْرِىٌّ)]; and so ▼ اشتمر. (TA.) — And *It* (the water of a wall) *went away.* (A, TA.)

8: see the next preceding paragraph.

شِمْرٌ, applied to a man, † *Light, agile,* or *active; acute,* or *sharp,* or *quick, in intellect; clever, knowing,* or *intelligent;* syn. زَوْلٌ; and بَصِيرٌ; (El-Muärrij, O, Ḳ;) and نَاقِدٌ; (O, Ḳ;) thus accord. to the copies of the Ḳ [probably from the O]; but in the Tekmileh &c., نَافِذٌ, [which I regard as the right reading, meaning one *who acts with a penetrative energy,* or *who is sharp, vigorous,* or *effective,*] (TA,) *in everything.* (O, TA.) See also شِمْرِىٌّ. — Also † *Liberal, bountiful, munificent,* or *generous;* (O, Ḳ;) *and courageous.* (TA.)

شَمَّارٌ: see شِمْرٌ.

شِمْرَةٌ The *gait,* or *manner of walking, of a*

vitious, or *depraved*, *man*; (O, Ḳ;) or, accord. to IAạr, *of a man who goes to and fro, and round about.* (TA.) [See also شَنْزَةٌ.]

شَرٌّ شِمِّيرٌ *Severe evil.* (Ṣ, O, Ḳ.) It is said in a prov., أَلْجَأَهُ الخَوْفُ إِلَى شَرٍّ شِمِّيرٍ, (TA,) or أَجْأَهُ, (so in a copy of the A,) [*Fear compelled him to betake himself to* that which was *a severe evil:*] i. e. he feared an evil, and fear reduced him to a greater evil. (A.)

شَمَارٌ *i. q.* رَازِيَانِجٌ, in the dial. of Egypt, (O, Ḳ, TA,) also [and more commonly] called ▼ شَمَرٌ [applied to the *Anethum graveolens*, or *common garden-dill*, and to *its seed*; and also to the *anethum fœniculum*, or *fennel*: see also سَنُّوتٌ]. (TA.)

شَمَّرِىٌّ [in the CḲ شَمَرِىٌّ, without teshdeed to the م,] † A man, (Ṣ,) *penetrating*, or *acting with a penetrative energy*, or *sharp, vigorous, and effective, in the performing of affairs, and expert*, or *experienced*; (Ṣ,* Ḳ, TA;) mostly with respect to travel; (TA;) as though it were a rel. n. from شَمَّرَ; (Ṣ;) as also شِمَّرِىٌّ (Ṣ, Ḳ) and شِمِرِّىٌّ [in the CḲ شِمِرِىٌّ] and شُمُّرِىٌّ [in the CḲ شُمُرِىٌّ] and ▼ شِمْرٌ and ▼ شِمِّيرٌ, (Ḳ,) the last an intensive form, (TA,) and ▼ مُشَمِّرٌ: (Ḳ:) or *clever in the performing of affairs, and quick*: (Fr, TA:) or one *who strives, labours, or exerts himself, and is clever and skilful*: (Aboo-Bekr, TA:) or *quick in evil, and in what is vain, or false; who strives, labours, or exerts himself, therein*; from شَمَّرَ meaning "he strove, laboured, or exerted himself, and was quick:" (AA, Aboo-Bekr, TA:) or one *who goes his own way*, or *pursues a headlong*, or *rash, course, and will not refrain.* (Aboo-Bekr, TA.) —— نَاقَةٌ شَمَّرِيَّةٌ, (Ṣ, Ḳ,) and شِمَّرِيَّةٌ, and شِمِرِّيَّةٌ, and شُمُّرِيَّةٌ, (Ḳ, TA,) [all in the CḲ without teshdeed to the م,] and ▼ شِمِّيرٌ, (Ṣ, Ḳ,) † *A she-camel that is quick* (Ṣ, Ḳ) *in pace.* (TA.)

شَمُّورٌ, occurring in a trad. respecting 'Ooj Ibn-'Unuḳ, [or Ibn-'Oḳ,] as meaning something with which a mass of rock was hollowed out according to the size of his head, (TA,) *Diamond*: (Ḳ:) thought by El-Khaṭṭábee to have this meaning; but he says, "I have not heard respecting it anything upon which I place reliance." (IAth, TA.)

شِمِّيرٌ † One *who strives, labours*, or *exerts himself; who employs himself vigorously, laboriously*, or *with energy*; (Ḳ, TA;) *in the performance of affairs.* (TA.) See also شَمَّرِىٌّ, in two places.

شَاةٌ شَامِرٌ, and شَامِرَةٌ, *A ewe, or she-goat, having her udder drawn up to her belly*: (Ṣ, Ḳ:) an epithet having no verb. (TA.) —— شَفَةٌ شَامِرَةٌ, and ▼ مُتَشَمِّرَةٌ, *A contracted lip.* (TA.) —— لِثَةٌ شَامِرَةٌ, (A, Ḳ,) and ▼ مُتَشَمِّرَةٌ, (Ḳ,) or ▼ مُشَمِّرَةٌ, (so in a copy of the A,) *A gum cleaving to the roots of the teeth.* (A, Ḳ.)

مُشَمِّرٌ: see شَمَّرِىٌّ: —— and see also شَامِرٌ.

مُتَشَمِّرٌ: see its fem. voce شَامِرٌ, in two places.

شمرخ

Q. 1. شَمْرَخَ النَّخْلَةَ *He stripped off the unripe dates of the palm-tree.* (L.) And شَمْرِخِ العِذْقَ *Strip thou the* شَمَارِيخ [or *fruit-stalks*] *of the raceme of the palm-tree with the* مِخْلَب, *cutting off* [*the dates*]. (L,* Ḳ. [In the former, in the place of قَطْعًا, the last word in the explanation in the Ḳ, is put قَعْطًا, app. by a mistake of the copyist.])

شِمْرَاخٌ (Ṣ, Mgh, Mṣb, Ḳ) and ▼ شُمْرُوخٌ (Ṣ, Mṣb, Ḳ) *A* [*fruit-*] *stalk of the raceme of a palm-tree*; (Mgh;) the عِثْكَال, (Ṣ, L,) or *thing*, (Mṣb,) *upon which are the dates*; (L, Mṣb;) [i. e. *any one of the stalks that branch off from the main stem of the raceme, and on which hang the dates; each of these stalks comprising a number of dates, one below another*:] pl. of both شَمَارِيخُ: (Mṣb:) the عِذْق, or كِبَاسَة, [q. v.,] comprises the شَمَارِيخ: (Mṣb voce عِذْق:) or *an* عِثْكَال *upon which are unripe dates*, or *grapes*: (Ḳ:) originally relating to a raceme of dates; but sometimes, to grapes: (L:) and the former word [or each] signifies *a small bunch of grapes, growing apart, but attached to the lower portion of the stalk of a larger bunch.* (T, TA.) —— Also, شِمْرَاخٌ, The *head of a mountain*: (Ṣ, Ḳ:) or a *round, tall, slender head*, or *peak, of a mountain*: (L:) accord. to Aṣ, [the pl.] شَمَارِيخُ signifies the *heads of mountains*: (TA:) or it signifies the *upper*, or *uppermost, part* [or *parts*] of a mountain; and in like manner, of trees. (Ḥam p. 786.) And † The *upper*, or *uppermost, parts of clouds*: (Ḳ:) or [the pl.] شَمَارِيخُ is metaphorically applied to the *upper*, or *uppermost, parts* of clouds. (Ḥam ubi suprà.) —— And *A blaze upon the face of a horse, when it is narrow*, (Ṣ, Ḳ, TA,) *and long*, (TA,) *and extending so as to cover the* [*part of the nose called*] خَيْشُوم, *but not reaching to the lip*: (Ṣ, Ḳ, TA:) or *a blaze, upon the face of a horse, extending downwards on the nose.* (Lth, TA.) [See غُرَّةٌ سَائِلَةٌ, in art. سيل.] Accord. to J, The *horse itself* [*that has such a blaze*] is also thus called; but this is a mistake: (Ḳ:) it seems that he meant to have said ذُو شِمْرَاخٍ; but this, in a verse which he cites, is the name of a horse of Málik Ibn-'Owf En-Naḍree, as is said in the Ḳ. (MF.) —— [The pl.] الشَّمَارِيخُ is also a name applied by the Arabs to † *The stars of Centaurus* (قَنْطُورِس) *and Lepus* (الشَّبُعُ) *collectively.* (Kzw.)

شُمْرُوخٌ: see the next preceding paragraph, first sentence. —— Also *A slender, and soft* or *tender, branch, that has grown forth, within a year, upon the upper part of a thick branch.* (L.)

الشِّمْرَاخِيَّةُ *A sect of the heretics*, or *schismatics*, (الخَوَارِج,) *the companions* [or *followers*] *of 'Abd-Allah Ibn-Shimrákh.* (Ṣ, Ḳ.)

شمردل

شَمَرْدَلٌ *A youth, strong and hardy*; and in the like sense applied to a camel: (Lth, TA:) or *tall*; as also ▼ شَمَرْدَلِىٌّ: (Ḥam pp. 728 and 789:) or a *bulky* camel: (IAạr, TA:) or, of camels &c., (Ṣ, O, Ḳ,) the *swift*; (Ṣ, O;) or *youthful, swift, and goodly in make*: (Ḳ:) and with ة, a she-camel *goodly, beautiful in make.* (A'Obeyd, Ṣ, O, Ḳ.)

شَمَرْدَلِىٌّ: see the preceding paragraph.

شمرذل

شَمَرْذَلٌ a dial. var. of شَمَرْدَلٌ [q. v.]. (Lth, O, Ḳ.)

شمز

1. شَمَزَتْ نَفْسِى مِنْهُ, aor. ـُ, (TḲ,) inf. n. شَمْزٌ, (IAạr, Ḳ,) *My soul shrank from it in dislike* or *hatred.* (IAạr, Ḳ, TḲ.) [See also 5, and Q. Q. 4.]

5. تَشَمَّزَ وَجْهُهُ *His face became changed*, or *altered*, (T, Ṣ, Ḳ,) *by anger*, (Ḳ,) *and contracted.* (T, Ṣ, Ḳ.) See also what next follows.

Q. Q. 4. اِشْمَأَزَّ, (Ṣ, Ḳ,) inf. n. اِشْمِئْزَازٌ, (Ṣ,) *He* (a man, Ṣ) *shrank*, or *became contracted*; (Ṣ, Ḳ, TA;) as also ▼ تَشَمَّزَ: (TA:) *he quaked*, or *shuddered*: (IAạr, Ḳ:) or *he was frightened* (AZ, Ṣ, Ḳ) at a thing. (AZ, Ṣ.) It is said in the Ḳur xxxix. 46, وَإِذَا ذُكِرَ ٱللّٰهُ وَحْدَهُ ٱشْمَأَزَّتْ قُلُوبُ ٱلَّذِينَ لَا يُؤْمِنُونَ بِٱلْآخِرَةِ *And when God is mentioned alone, the hearts of those who will not believe in the world to come become contracted, and shrink with aversion*: (Bḍ, Jel:) or *quake*, or *shudder.* (Zj, TA.) And you say, قُلْتُ لَهُ كَذَا فَاشْمَأَزَّ مِنْهُ [*I said to him such a thing, and he shrank from it*; or *quaked*, or *shuddered, at it*; or *was frightened at it*]. (A.) And اِشْمَأَزَّ الشَّىْءَ, (Ḳ,) without a prep., accord. to Kr, (TA,) *He disliked*, or *hated, the thing.* (Ḳ.) [See also 1, and 5.]

شُمَأْزِيزَةٌ [a subst.] from Q. Q. 4, [*A shrinking*, or *contraction*: *a quaking*, or *shuddering*: or *fright*: and *dislike*, or *hatred*.] (Ṣ, Ḳ,* TA.) You say, رَجُلٌ فِيهِ شُمَأْزِيزَةٌ [*A man in whom is a shrinking*, &c.] (TA.)

مُشْمَئِزٌّ *Shrinking with aversion*; syn. نَافِرٌ: (Ḳ:) *disliking*, or *hating*, (Ḳ,) a thing: (TA:) *frightened*, or *afraid.* (Ḳ.)

شمس

1. شَمَسَ, aor. ـُ and ـِ, (Ṣ, Mṣb, Ḳ,) inf. n. شُمُوسٌ; (TA;) and شَمِسَ, aor ـَ (Ḳ) and ـُ also, like فَضِلَ, aor. يَفْضُلُ, accord. to the lexicologists, as ISd says, but he holds the aor. of شَمِسَ to be ـَ [only]; (TA;) and ▼ اشمس; (Ṣ, Ḳ;) *It* (a day) *was, or became, sunny*, or *sunshiny*; *it had sun*, or *sunshine*: (Ṣ, Mṣb, Ḳ:) or *it had sun*, or *sunshine, all the daytime*: or *it was*, or *became, clear*, or *unobscured*: (TA:) or *its sun was*, or *became, vehement.* (IF, Mṣb.) —— شَمَسَ, (Ṣ, Mṣb, Ḳ,) aor. ـُ (Mṣb, TA) and ـِ, (Mṣb,) inf. n. شُمُوسٌ

and شِمَاسٌ, (Ṣ, Mṣb, Ḳ,) *He* (a horse) *refused to be ridden* or *mounted:* (Ṣ, Ḳ:) or *took fright and broke loose and ran away, refusing to be ridden, by reason of the vehemence of his force of resistance,* [for لشدّة متعبه in the TA, I read لِشِدَّةِ مَنَعَتِهِ,] *and his sharpness of temper, so that he would not remain still:* (TA:) or *became rebellious against his rider.* (Mṣb.) — [Hence,] شَمَسَتِ المَرْأَةُ † *The woman abstained from looking at men, and from exciting their desire.* (TA.) — And شَمَسَ لِى فُلَانٌ ‡ *Such a one showed enmity to me:* (Ḳ:*) or *showed his enmity to me,* (T, Ṣ, A,) *and almost made it to take effect,* (A,) or *as though he purposed to act:* (T, TA:) or شَمَسَ فِى فُلَانٍ signifies, [unless فى be a mistake for لى, and فُلَانٍ for فُلَانٌ,] *he showed his enmity* [*towards such a one*], *and could not conceal it.* (M in TA.) [See also 3.] — And الخَمْرُ تَشْمُسُ بِصَاحِبِهَا † *Wine overcomes, and runs away with, its drinker.* (TA.)

2. شمّس, (TḲ,) inf. n. تَشْمِيسٌ, (Ḳ,) *He worshipped the sun.* (Ḳ, TḲ.) = And *He spread* a thing *in the sun,* or *sunshine,* (Ḳ, TḲ,) *in order that it might dry.* (TA.)

3. شامسهُ, inf. n. مُشَامَسَةٌ and شِمَاسٌ, *He opposed him, and treated him with enmity* or *hostility.* (Th, TA.) [See also 1.]

4: see 1, first signification. — [Also *He ascended a mountain towards the sun.* (Freytag, from the Deewán of the Hudhalees.)]

5. تشمّس *He* (a man) *sat in the sun,* or *sunshine:* (TA:) *he set himself up* [or *exposed himself standing*] *to the sun.* (Ṣ, TA.) = تشمّس عَلَيْهِ *He was niggardly, tenacious,* or *avaricious, to him.* (TA.) [See also the part. n., below.]

الشَّمْسُ [*The sun;*] *the body of the solar light, that runs its course in the firmament:* (Lth,* TA:) it is fem.: (Ṣ,* Mṣb, Ḳ:) and has neither dual nor pl.: (Mṣb:) or it has a pl., [though this is not used in a pl. sense,] namely, شُمُوسٌ, (Ṣ, Ḳ,) as though they called every part of it a شمس, like as they said مَفْرِقٌ for مَفَارِقُ. (Ṣ.) When it is made determinate without the article ال, [as] in the name عَبْدُ شَمْسَ, meaning *The Servant of the Sun,* (Mṣb, Ḳ,) i. e., of this luminous object, (Mṣb,) the شمس of heaven, because they used to worship it, (Ḳ,) it is imperfectly decl., (Aboo-'Alee, Mṣb, Ḳ,) because it is determinate and of the fem. gender, (Aboo-'Alee, Ḳ,) or because it is a proper name and of the fem. gender and altered from الشَّمْس: (Mṣb:) and a poet says,

* كَلَّا وَشَمْسَ لَنَخْضِبَنَّهُمْ دَمَا *

[*Nay verily, by the sun, we will assuredly dye them with blood*], making شمس imperfectly decl. because he means the art. ال to be understood: (IAṣr, TA:) but some say that in the former instance, (Mṣb, TA,) and in the latter, (TA,) the word in question has a different signification, which will be shown below: (Mṣb, TA:) and Sb says that none of the Arabs made شمس determinate without the art. ال, except in the proper name mentioned above, in which all of them made it so. (TA.) The dim. is ▼ شُمَيْسَةٌ. (Ṣ, TA.) — [Also *The sun,* or *sunshine.*] You say, قَعَدَ فِى الشَّمْسِ [*He sat in the sun,* or *sunshine*]. (TA.) — Also, (Ḳ, TA,) or شَمْسٌ, (Mṣb,) *A certain ancient idol.* (Mṣb, Ḳ.) Accord. to Ibn-El-Kelbee, it is this that is meant by the proper name mentioned above; and if so, it is perfectly decl.: (Mṣb:) and some say that it is this also that is meant in the words of the poet cited above, and that he makes the word imperfectly decl. because he uses it as a proper name of the image (الصُّورَة). (TA.) = شَمْسٌ also signifies *A kind of necklace* or *collar:* (Ṣ, Ḳ:) or *a pendant,* or *suspended ornament,* (مِعْلَاق,) *of the necklace* or *collar upon the neck:* or the *collar of a dog:* (TA:) or *a kind of women's ornament:* of the masc. gender: (Lḥ, TA:) pl. شُمُوسٌ. (TA.) — And *A kind of comb,* (Ḳ,) *with which women in the first age used to comb themselves;* (TA;) as also ▼ شُمَيْسَةٌ. (IDrd, TA.) = يَوْمٌ شَمْسٌ: see شَامِسٌ.

يَوْمٌ شَمِسٌ: see شَامِسٌ.

شُمَيْسَةٌ: see شَمْسٌ, last sentence but one.

شَمْسِىٌّ [*Of,* or *relating to, the sun; solar*]. السَّنَةُ الشَّمْسِيَّةُ *The solar year.* (Mgh.) — It is also a term applied by some of the Arabs to *The first* [*annual*] *increase* [*of sheep and goats*]. (Aboo-Naṣr, TA voce صَفَرِىٌّ, q. v.)

شِمَاسٌ The *disposition,* in a horse, *of refusing to be ridden,* or *mounted.* (Ṣ.) — [And hence,] † The *disposition,* in a woman, *of abstaining from looking at men, and from exciting their desire:* a subst. from شَمَسَتْ. (TA.)

شَمُوسٌ A horse *that refuses to be ridden* or *mounted;* (Ṣ, Ḳ;) as also ▼ شَامِسٌ: (Ḳ:) or *that takes fright and breaks loose and runs away, refusing to be ridden, by reason of the vehemence of his force of resistance and his sharpness of temper, so that he will not remain still:* (TA: [see 1:]) or *that will hardly remain still:* (A:) or *that rebels against his rider:* (Mṣb:) or *that refuses to be ridden or mounted, and will hardly remain still:* (Mgh:) also applied to a she-camel: (TA:) شَمُوصٌ, with ص, applied to a horse is not allowable: (Mṣb:) pl. شُمُسٌ (A, Mgh, Mṣb, Ḳ) and شُمْسٌ. (Ḳ.) — [Hence,] † A woman *who abstains from looking at men, and from exciting their desire;* as also ▼ شَامِسَةٌ: pl. of the former, شُمُسٌ; and of the latter, [شَوَامِسُ and] شُمُوسٌ. (TA.) — Hence also, (Mṣb,) ‡ A man *refractory, untractable, perverse, stubborn,* or *obstinate, in disposition:* (Ṣ, Mṣb, TA:) and a man *hard, harsh,* or *illnatured, in his enmity, vehement in contrariousness to him who opposes him:* (TA:) شَمُوصٌ [with ص] is not allowable. (Ṣ.) — [Hence too,] الشَّمُوسُ † *Wine:* (AḤn, Ḳ:) because it overcomes, and runs away with, its drinker, like the horse to which this epithet is applied. (AḤn.)

شُمَيْسَةٌ dim. of شَمْسٌ, q. v.

شَمَّاسٌ *One of the heads of the Christians, who shaves the middle of his head, and keeps to the church:* (Lth, A, Mgh, Ḳ:) [in the present day, *a deacon:* see جَاثَلِيقٌ:] not pure Arabic, (IDrd,) or not sound Arabic: (M:) [probably, as Golius says, from the Chaldee שַׁמָּשׁ:] pl. شَمَامِسَةٌ. (Mgh, Ḳ: [in the TA, شماسة; and in a copy of the A, شَمَّاسَةٌ; but the right reading is that in the Mgh.])

شَامِسٌ A *sunny,* or *sunshiny,* day; a day *having sun,* or *sunshine:* or *having sun,* or *sunshine, all the daytime:* or *clear; unobscured:* and in like manner, ▼ شَمْسٌ and ▼ شَمِسٌ, a *clear, cloudless,* day: and شَامِسٌ also signifies *intensely hot:* (TA:) and ▼ مُشْمِسٌ, applied to a day, signifies the *same as* شَامِسٌ; (A;) and so ▼ مَشْمُوسٌ. (Th, TA.) = A neck *having* [*ornaments of the kind called*] شُمُوس [pl. of شَمْسٌ, q. v.]: a possessive epithet. (TA.) = See also شَمُوسٌ, in two places.

أَشْمَسُ *More,* and *most, incompliant* or *resisting.* (Ḥam p. 324.)

مُشْمِسٌ: see شَامِسٌ.

مُشَمَّسٌ *Made* [or *spread to dry* (see 2)] *in the sun,* or *sunshine.* (Ṣ.)

مُشَمِّسٌ *A worshipper of the sun.* (O, TA.)

مَشْمُوسٌ: see شَامِسٌ.

مُتَشَمِّسٌ [*Sitting in* or] *setting himself up to* [or *exposing himself standing to*] *the sun.* (Ḳ.) = A man *who defends what is behind his back:* (ISh, TA:) a man *strong* (ISh, Ḳ, TA) *in that which sustains* or *supports him;* syn. قَوِىٌّ شَدِيدٌ القَوْمِيَّةِ: (ISh, TA:) Ṣgh says شَدِيدُ القُوَّةِ; but the former is the right reading: (TA:) and *niggardly, tenacious,* or *avaricious, to the utmost degree.* (Ḳ.)

شمط

1. شَمِطَ, aor. َ, inf. n. شَمَطٌ, *He* (a man, Ṣ, TA) *was,* or *became, grizzled in the hair of his head; he had whiteness in the hair of his head, mixed with its blackness:* (Ṣ, Mgh,* Ḳ:) as also ▼ أَشْمَطَ, (Ḳ, but wanting in one copy,) and ▼ اشْمَطَّ, and ▼ اشْمَاطَّ: (Ḳ:) [or *he had hair of two different colours, black and white:* or *he had whiteness of the hair,* or *hoariness, mixed with the blackness of youth:* or *he had whiteness,* or *hoariness, in his beard:* but شَمِطَتْ, said of a woman, *she had whiteness,* or *hoariness, in the head:* see شَمْطَآءُ, below.] = شَمَطَ, aor. ُ, (Ṣ, Ḳ,) inf. n. شَمْطٌ, (Ṣ,) *He mixed* a thing; (Ṣ, Ḳ;) *he mixed together* any two things: (Ṣ, Mgh:) and ▼ أَشْمَطَ signifies the same. (AZ, Ḳ.) You say, شَمَطَ بَيْنَ المَآءِ وَاللَّبَنِ *He mixed together the water and the milk.* (TA.) And أَشْمِطْ ▼ عَمَلَكَ بِصَدَقَةٍ † *Mix thou thy work with alms.* (AZ.) And Aboo-'Amr Ibn-El-'Alà used to say to his companions, اِشْمِطُوا, [i. e. either

اشمطوا or ▼ أشْمِطُوا,] meaning † *Betake yourselves at one time to reading, or reciting, somewhat of the Kur-án, and another time to some tradition, and another time to something strange* [*that is to be elucidated*], *and another time to poetry, and another time to lexicology*; i. e., *mix ye these* [*subjects of study*]: (TA:) or, accord. to one relation, ▼ شَمِّطُوا. (Ḥar p. 177; where it is expl. in a similar manner).

2: see above, last sentence.

4: see 1, in four places.

9:
11: } see 1, first sentence.
Q. Q. 4:

شَمَطٌ *Whiteness of the hair of the head mixed with its blackness*: (Ṣ, Mgh, Ḳ:) or *difference* in the hair *by being of two colours, black and white*: (M, TA:) or *mixture of whiteness of the hair*, or *hoariness, with the blackness of youth*: (Mgh:) or in a man, *whiteness*, or *hoariness, of the beard*: (Lth, Mgh, TA:) but in a woman, *whiteness*, or *hoariness, of the head*. (Lth, TA.) [See 1.] — Also شَمَطَاتٌ, which is its pl., *White hairs that are in the head*. (TA.)

شَمِيطٌ *Mixed*; as also ▼ مَشْمُوطٌ: (Ḳ:) *mixed together*; (Ṣ, TA;) applied to any two things; (Ṣ;) or any two colours. (TA.) — ذَنَبٌ شَمِيطٌ; in the Ḳ, ذِنْبٌ, which is a mistake; (TA;) *A tail* (TA) *in which are blackness and whiteness*. (Ḳ, TA.) And فَرَسٌ شَمِيطُ الذَّنَبِ *A horse in whose tail are two colours*. (TA.) And طَائِرٌ شَمِيطُ الذُّنَابَى *A bird having a whiteness* (Lth, Ḳ) *and blackness* (Lth) *in the tail*. (Lth, Ḳ.) — نَبْتٌ شَمِيطٌ *A plant of which part is dried up*, or *dried up and yellow*, (Lth, Ṣ, Ḳ,) *and part green*. (Lth, Ḳ.) — الشَّمِيطُ, [in a copy of the Mgh, ▼ شُمَيْطٌ, which is probably a mistranscription,] ‡ *The dawn*: (Ṣ, Ḳ:) because of the mixture of its whiteness with the remains of the darkness of night: (Ṣ, Mgh:) or because its colour is a mixture of darkness and whiteness. (TA.) — لَبَنٌ شَمِيطٌ ‡ *Milk which is such that one knows not whether it be sour or what has been collected in a skin, and had fresh milk poured upon it, by reason of its pleasantness*. (Ḳ, TA.) — وَلَدٌ شَمِيطٌ ‡ *Children of whom half are males and half are females*. (L, Ḳ.)

شُمَيْطٌ: see شَمِيطٌ. — See also صُرَدٌ.

أَشْمَطُ A man (Ṣ) *having the hair of his head grizzled; having whiteness in the hair of his head, mixed with its blackness*: (Ṣ, Ḳ:) [or *whose hair is of two different colours, black and white*: or *having whiteness of the hair*, or *hoariness, mixed with the blackness of youth*: or *having whiteness*, or *hoariness, in his beard*: see شَمَطٌ, above:] or *whose hair of his head is white in one place, the rest being black*: (Mgh:) fem. شَمْطَآءُ: (Lth, Ṣ, Mgh:) one should not apply to a woman the epithet شَيْبَآءُ: (Lth, Mgh:) pl. شُمْطَانٌ (Ṣ, Ḳ) and شُمْطٌ. (Ḳ.) — نَاقَةٌ شَمْطَآءُ *A she-camel having white lips*. (TA.) — لَحْمٌ أَشْمَطُ [*Flesh-meat marbled with fat*]. (Az, TA in art. هكرش.)

مَشْمُوطٌ: see شَمِيطٌ.

شمع

1. شَمَعَ, aor. ـَ, inf. n. شَمْعٌ and شُمُوعٌ and مَشْمَعَةٌ, *He played, sported, gamed, jested*, or *joked*: (Ṣ, O, Ḳ:) or *he was mirthful, and laughed*: and شَمَعَتْ, aor. as above, inf. n. شَمْعٌ and شُمُوعٌ, *She cheered by her discourse*. (TA.) It is said in a trad., مَنْ يَتَّبِعِ المَشْمَعَةَ يُشَمِّعِ ٱللّٰهُ بِهِ (Ṣ,* O) *He who follows the practice of play*, or *sport*, or *unprofitable play* or *sport, with men*, (Ṣ, O,) *and derision and laughter and enjoyment with them, God will requite him for that*, (O,) or *God will cause him to be in a state in which the like shall be done with him*. (Ṣ, O.) — And شَمَعَ, inf. n. شُمُوعٌ, *It was*, or *became, scattered*, or *dispersed*. (Ibn-'Abbád, O, Ḳ.)

2. شَمَّعَهُ, (Ḳ,) inf. n. تَشْمِيعٌ, (O, Ḳ,) *He*, or *it, made him to play, sport, game, jest*, or *joke*. (O,* Ḳ.) — شَمَّعَ الثَّوْبَ *He dipped the garment*, or *piece of cloth, in liquified* شَمَع [i. e. *wax*]. (O, Ḳ.)

4. اشمع السِّرَاجُ *The lamp*, or *lighted wick, diffused its light*. (Ṣ, Ḳ.)

شَمْعٌ and شَمَعٌ, both chaste accord. to ISd: (TA:) accord. to Fr, (Ṣ, O, Mṣb, TA,) the former is post-classical; (Ṣ, O, Mṣb, Ḳ, TA;) but ISd says that this is a mistake: (TA:) accord. to ISk one should say the latter, and not the former: (TA:) or accord. to him, the word is with fet-ḥ to the م, and some of the Arabs make the م quiescent: accord. to Th, it is with fet-ḥ to the م; and if you will, you may make it quiescent: accord. to IF, the م is sometimes with fet-ḥ; so that he gives one to understand that it is more frequently made quiescent: (Mṣb:) *A kind of thing with which one lights himself*: (Ṣ, O, Mṣb, Ḳ:) or i. q. مُومٌ [which, or rather مُوم, in Pers., signifies both *wax* and the *wax-candle*; both of which or rather the former and *wax-candles*, are meant by شَمْعٌ and شَمَعٌ]: (ISk, TA:) or the موم *of honey* [i. e. *bees' wax*]: (Lth, Ḳ:) the n. un., (CḲ,) or what denotes a piece, or portion, thereof, (so in copies of the Ḳ and in the TA,) is with ة, (Ḳ, TA,) شَمْعَةٌ and شَمَعَةٌ, (TA,) [i. e.] شمعة has a more particular signification. (Ṣ, O.)

شَمْعِىٌّ or شَمَعِىٌّ (Ḳ [as there mentioned app. meaning *A dealer in wax* or *wax-candles*, like ▼ شَمَّاعٌ in the present day,]) a rel. n. from شَمْعٌ or شَمَعٌ. (TA. [The latter said in the Ḳ to be the correct form.])

شِمَاعٌ *Mirth and laughter and jesting* or *joking*; as also ▼ شِمَاعَةٌ. (TA. [Not mentioned there as inf. ns.])

شَمُوعٌ, applied to a woman, (Ṣ, Ḳ,) *That jests*, or *jokes, much*; (Ḳ, TA;) *pleasant in discourse*; *that kisses one, and will not comply with one's desire otherwise than by doing thus*: (TA:) [or] *playful, sportful*, or *gamesome, and wont to laugh*; (Ṣ, Ḳ, TA;) and in this sense applied also to a man: or, applied to a woman, *that cheers by her discourse*. (TA.)

شِمَاعَةٌ: see شِمَاعٌ.

شَمَّاعٌ *A manufacturer of* شمع [meaning *wax-candles*]: (TA:) or a *melter of* شمع [meaning *wax*]. (KL.) See also شَمْعِىٌّ.

مِشْمَعَةٌ *A candlestick*: pl. مَشَامِعُ. (MA.)

مُشَمَّعٌ A garment, or cloth, *dipped in liquified* شَمَع [i. e. *wax*]. (TA.)

مِسْكٌ مَشْمُوعٌ *Musk mixed with ambergris*. (O, Ḳ.)

شمعل

Q. 1. شَمْعَلَ, (O, Ḳ, TA, [in the CḲ تَشَمْعَلَ,]) inf. n. شَمْعَلَةٌ, (TA,) *It became scattered* or *dispersed*. (O, Ḳ, TA.) — And شَمْعَلَةٌ signifies The *reading*, or *reciting*, of the Jews, (Ṣ, O, Ḳ, TA,) *when they assemble* فى مبرهم: (TA: [but I know not what this means:]) one says of them شَمْعَلَتْ [i. e. شَمْعَلَتِ اليَهُودُ]. (TA.)

Q. 4. اشْمَعَلَّ *He hastened, made haste*, or *went quickly*; syn. أَسْرَعَ: this is the primary signification. (Ḥam p. 282.) One says of a she-camel اشمعلّت meaning *She hastened*, &c. (Ṣ.) — And اشمعلّت الإِبِلُ *The camels went*, or *went away, and scattered* or *dispersed themselves, by reason of briskness, liveliness*, or *sprightliness*: (Kh, Ṣ, O, Ḳ:) or *spread themselves*, or *became scattered* or *dispersed*; as also اشمعطّت: (Aboo-Turáb, TA:) or *became scattered* or *dispersed, going* [*away*] *quickly*. (TA.) And in like manner, (Kh, Ṣ, O,) اشمعلّت الغَارَةُ فِى العَدُوِّ, (Kh, Ṣ, O, Ḳ,) meaning *The horsemen making a sudden attack upon the enemy scattered*, or *dispersed, themselves*; (Aboo-Turáb, Ḳ,* TA;) and so اشمعطّت. (Aboo-Turáb, TA.) And اشمعلّ القَوْمُ فِى الطَّلَبِ *The people*, or *company of men, hastened, and scattered* or *dispersed themselves, in seeking*; (Aboo-Turáb, Ṣ, O, Ḳ;) as also اشمعطّ. (Aboo-Turáb, TA.) — And i. q. أَشْرَفَ [q. v.]. (O, Ḳ.)

شَمْعَلٌ, and with ة: see the following paragraph.

مُشْمَعِلٌّ A *swift* she-camel; (Az, Ṣ;) or so مُشْمَعِلَّةٌ: (O:) and ▼ شَمْعَلٌ and ▼ شَمْعَلَةٌ (O, Ḳ) and مُشْمَعِلٌّ (Ḳ) a she-camel *brisk, lively*, or *sprightly*, (O, Ḳ,) *and swift*, (Ḳ,) *and light, active*, or *agile*. (TA.) مُشْمَعِلَّةٌ in the first of these senses is [said to be] from the phrase قِرْبَةٌ مُشْمَعِلَّةٌ *A water-skin of which the water flows out*. (Ḥar p. 111.) — Also A man *quick and penetrating* or *having a penetrative energy*: and with ة, *a very active woman*. (TA.) A man *light, active*, or *agile*; *excellent*, or *elegant, in mind, manners*, &c., or *clever, ingenious*, or *acute in mind*: or *tall*. (Ḳ.) A man *vigorous, strenuous*, or *energetic, and light, active*, or *agile.* (Ḥam p. 384.) —— Also applied to milk, meaning *Sour,* (Ḳ, TA,) *overcoming by its sourness.* (TA.)

شمل

1. شَمِلَهُمُ الأَمْرُ, aor. ـَ; and شَمَلَهُمْ, aor. ـُ; (Ṣ, Mṣb, Ḳ;) but the latter verb was unknown to Aṣ, (Ṣ, TA,) and is said by Lḥ to be rare; (TA;) inf. n. شَمْلٌ, (Mṣb, Ḳ,) which is of the former, (Mṣb,) and شُمُولٌ, (Mṣb, Ḳ,) and شَمَلٌ; (Ḳ;) i. q. عَمَّهُمْ [i. e. *The event,* or *case, included them in common, in general,* or *universally, within the compass of its effect* or *effects, its operation* or *operations, its influence,* or *the like*]: (Ṣ, Mṣb, Ḳ:) or شَمِلَهُمْ خَيْرًا or شَرًّا, or خَيْرًا and شَرًّا, (accord. to different copies of the Ḳ,) like فَرِحَ, (in the CḲ, or like فَرِحَ,) [app. means *he,* or *it, caused that*] *good* or *evil,* or *good* and *evil, betided them* [*in common, in general,* or *universally*]: and ▼ أَشْمَلَهُمْ شَرًّا [means] عَمَّهُمْ بِهِ [i. e. *he,* or *it, included them in common, in general,* or *universally, with,* or *by, evil*]: (Ḳ:) but one should not say, اشملهم خيرًا. (TA.) [Whether what precedes, or what next follows, should be regarded as giving the primary signification of شَمِلَ, is uncertain.] —— شَمِلَهُ, aor. ـَ, inf. n. شَمْلٌ and شُمُولٌ, *He covered* [or *enveloped*] *him with the* شَمْلَة, (Ḳ, TA,) or, *with the* مِشْمَلَة: such is thought by ISd to be meant by the explanation given by Lḥ, which is, غَطَّى عَلَيْهِ المِشْمَلَةَ. (TA.) —— هٰذِهِ شَمْلَةٌ تَشْمَلُكَ means تَسَعُكَ [i. e. *This is a* شملة *sufficient in its dimensions,* or *sufficiently large, for thee*]. (TA.) You say, اشْتَرَيْتُ شَمْلَةً تَشْمَلُنِى [*I bought a* شملة *sufficient in its dimensions, &c., for me*]. (ISk, Ṣ, O.) —— شَمَلَتْ لِقَاحًا, aor. ـُ, (Ṣ, O, Ḳ,) inf. n. شَمْلٌ, (Ṣ, O,) said of a she-camel, (Ṣ, O, Ḳ,) *She admitted impregnating seed,* (Ḳ,) or *she conceived,* مِنْ فَحْلِ فُلَانٍ, [*from the stallion of such a one*]. (Ṣ, O.) —— شَمَلَتْ إِبِلُكُمْ بَعِيرًا لَنَا *Your camels concealed among them a he-camel belonging to us, by his entering amid their dense multitude:* (Ḳ, TA:) so in the M and the Moḥeeṭ. (TA.) ═ شَمَلَ الشَّاةَ, aor. ـُ (Ṣ, Ḳ) and ـِ, (Ḳ,) inf. n. شَمْلٌ, (Ṣ,) *He suspended upon the ewe,* or *she-goat, the kind of bag called* شِمَال, *and bound it upon her udder:* (Ṣ,* Ḳ, TA:) and some say, شَمَلَ النَّاقَةَ, *he suspended a* شمال *upon the she-camel.* (T, TA.) Also, and ▼ اشملها, *He put to the ewe,* or *she-goat,* (Ḳ, TA,) or *he made for her,* (TA,) *a* شِمَال. (Ḳ, TA.) ═ شَمَلَ بِهِ, (Ḳ, TA,) inf. n. شَمْلٌ, (TA,) *He took* [*in it,* i. e. *in travelling it,* (see the pass. part. n.,)] *the direction of the left hand;* syn. أَخَذَ ذَاتَ الشِّمَالِ: (Ḳ, TA:) so expl. by IAạr. (TA.) —— شَمَلَتِ الرِّيحُ, aor. ـُ, inf. n. شُمُولٌ (Ṣ, O, TA) and شَمَالٌ, (O,) or شَمْلٌ, (TA,) *The wind shifted to a northerly direction* (شَمَالًا); (Ṣ, TA;) so expl. by Lḥ: (TA:) or *the wind blew northerly;* syn. هَبَّتْ شَمَالًا; as also ▼ أَشْمَلَتْ. (O. [In the TA, I find أَشْمَلَتِ الرِّيحُ: ذهبت شمائل مثل شَمَلت: but this, I doubt not, is a mistranscription of the passage in the O, which I have here followed; i. e. أَشْمَلَتِ الرِّيحُ: هَبَّتْ شَمَالًا مثل شَمَلَتْ; or of a similar passage in which إِذَا هَبَّتْ is put instead of هَبَّتْ alone.]) One says of two persons when they are separated, شَمَلَتْ رِيحُهُمَا † [*Their wind has become north,* or *northerly*]. (TA voce جَنُوبٌ, q. v. [See also مَشْمُولٌ.]) —— شَمَلَ الخَمْرَ, (Ḳ,) aor. ـُ, inf. n. شَمْلٌ, (TA,) *He exposed the wine to the* شَمَال [i. e. *north,* or *northerly, wind*], *so that it became cold,* or *cool.* (Ḳ.) —— And شُمِلُوا, (Ṣ, and in like manner in the Ḥam p. 595,) or شَمِلُوا, [expressly said to be] like فَرِحُوا, (Ḳ, [but this I think to be a mistake, the weight of authority, and the form of the part. n., which is مَشْمُولٌ, being against it,]) *They were smitten,* or *blown upon, by the wind called the* شَمَال. (Ṣ, Ḳ.) ═ شَمَلَ النَّخْلَةَ, (Ḳ,) aor. ـُ, inf. n. شَمْلٌ, (TA,) *He picked the ripe dates that were upon the palm-tree;* as also ▼ اشملها, and ▼ شَمْلَلَهَا: (Ḳ:) or this last (which is mentioned on the authority of Seer), accord. to some, signifies *he took of the* شَمَالِيل *of the palm-tree;* i. e., *of the few dates remaining upon it.* (TA.)

2. تَشْمِيلٌ [properly inf. n. of شَمَّلَ]: see 5, of which it is an anomalous inf. n. (TA.) —— And for its proper verb see 7. ═ Also The *taking by the* شِمَال [or *left hand*]. (TA.) ═ And شَمَّلَ النَّخْلَةَ *He bound pieces of* [*the garments called*] أَكْسِيَة [pl. of كِسَآء] *beneath the racemes of the palm-tree, because of its shaking off its fruit.* (TA.)

4. أَشْمَلَهُمْ شَرًّا: see 1, first sentence. —— اشمل الفَحْلُ شَوْلَهُ, (AZ, Ṣ, O,) inf. n. إِشْمَالٌ; (Ṣ;) or اشمل شَوْلَهُ لِقَاحًا; (Ḳ;) *The stallion-camel got with young from half to two thirds of the number of his* شَوْل [or *she-camels that had passed seven or eight months since the period of their bringing forth*]: (AZ, Ṣ, O, Ḳ:) when he has got them all with young, one says, أَقَمَّهَا; (AZ, Ṣ, O, TA;) and of the شول one says, قَمَّتْ, inf. n. قُمُومٌ. (TA.) —— اشمل فُلَانٌ خَرَائِفَهُ *Such a one picked the ripe dates that were upon his* خرائف [or *palm-trees of which he gathered the fruit for himself and his household*], *except a few.* (Ṣ, O.) —— See also 1, last sentence. ═ اشملهُ *He gave him a* شَمْلَة [q. v.]. (Ḳ, TA.) —— اشمل الشَّاةَ: see 1. ═ اشمل *He became possessor of a* مِشْمَلَة, (Lḥ, TA,) or, *of a* مِشْمَل. (Ḳ.) ═ اشملوا *They entered upon* [*a time in which blew*] *the* [*north,* or *northerly,*] *wind termed* الشَّمَال: (Ṣ, O, Ḳ:) like as they say, اجنبوا in the case of the جَنُوب. (TA.) —— أَشْمَلَتِ الرِّيحُ: see 1, latter half. —— See also 7.

5. تشمّل بِالشَّمْلَةِ, [and تشمّل الشَّمْلَةَ, (see 5 in art. درس,)] inf. n. تَشَمُّلٌ and ▼ تَشْمِيلٌ; (Ḳ;) the former reg.; the latter, which is mentioned by Lḥ, irreg., an instance like that in the saying [in the Ḳur lxxiii. 8], وَتَبَتَّلْ إِلَيْهِ تَبْتِيلًا; (TA;) *He covered himself with the* شَمْلَة [q. v.]. (Ḳ.) [See also 8.]

7. انشمل i. q. شَمَّرَ, (Ḳ, TA,) or انْشَمَرَ, (O, TA,) [both of which signify *He passed along striving,* or *exerting himself;* and the latter signifies also *he acted with a penetrative force* or *energy;* and *he hastened,* or *went quickly;*] فِى حَاجَتِهِ [*in his needful affair*]. (O, TA.) And i. q. أَسْرَعَ [*He hastened; went quickly;* or *was quick, swift,* or *fleet*]: (Ḳ:) or so ▼ أَشْمَلَ: (thus in the O, as on the authority of IDrd:) or so ▼ اشتمل, inf. n. اشتمال: (thus accord. to my copy of the Mṣb:) and likewise (O, Ḳ) ▼ شَمْلَلَ, (Ṣ, O, Ḳ,) inf. n. شَمْلَلَةٌ: (Ṣ:) and so ▼ شَمَّلَ, (Ḳ,) inf. n. تَشْمِيلٌ. (TA.) And i. q. انْشَمَرَ (O, TA) and انْضَمَّ, (TA,) [both meaning *It became contracted,*] as used by a poet in relation to a she-camel's udder. (O, TA.)

8. اشتمل بِثَوْبِهِ *He wrapped,* or *inwrapped, himself with his garment;* syn. تَلَفَّفَ: (Ṣ, O:) or اشتمل بِالثَّوْبِ signifies *he wrapped the garment around the whole of his body so that his arm,* or *hand, did not come forth from it:* (Ḳ:) or, as some say, *he wrapped himself with the garment, and threw* [*a part of*] *it upon his left side.* (TA.) [See also 5.] اِشْتِمَالُ الصَّمَّآءِ, which is forbidden by the Prophet, is, accord. to Aṣ, *The wrapping oneself with the garment so as to cover with it his body, not raising a side thereof in such a manner that there is in it an opening from which he may put forth his hand,* or *arm:* (O:) this is also termed التَّلَفُّعُ: and sometimes one reclines in the state thus described: (TA:) but A'Obeyd says, accord. to the explanation of the lawyers, it is *the wrapping oneself with one garment, not having upon him another, then raising it on one side and putting it upon his shoulders:* [so says Ṣgh; and he adds,] he who explains it thus has regard to the dislike of one's uncovering himself and exposing to view the pudenda; and he who explains it as do the lexicologists dislikes one's covering his whole body for fear of his becoming in a state in which his respiration would become obstructed so that he would perish: (O:) or it is *one's covering his whole body with the* كِسَآء or *with the* إِزَار; (Ṣ, Mṣb;) to which some add, *not raising aught of the sides thereof.* (Mṣb.) [See also art. صمّ.] One says also, يَشْتَمِلُ عَلَى السَّيْفِ [*He wraps his garment over the sword;* or] *he covers the sword with his garment.* (Ṣ, O.) —— [Hence,] اشتمل عَلَى كَذَا *It comprehended,* or *comprised, such a thing.*] One says, الرَّحِمُ تَشْتَمِلُ عَلَى الوَلَدِ † *The womb comprises* [or *encloses*] *the young.* (TA.) [And in like manner one says of a woman, اشتملت مِنْهُ عَلَى وَلَدٍ † *She became with child by him.* And الكِتَابُ يَشْتَمِلُ عَلَى كَذَا وَكَذَا † *The book,* or *writing, comprises such and such things.* And hence the phrase in grammar, بَدَلُ ٱشْتِمَالٍ † *A substitute for an antecedent to indicate an implication therein.*] —— One says also, اشتمل عَلَيْهِ الأَمْرُ, meaning ‡ *The event* [such as a misfortune or an evil of any kind *beset him,* or *beset him on every side,* or] *encompassed him;* (Ḳ, TA;) *like as the* كِسَآء *encompasses the body.*

(TA.) — One says of wine, تَشْتَمِلُ عَلَى العَقْلِ فَتَمْلِكُهُ وَتَذْهَبُ بِهِ † [*It compasses the intellect, and so takes possession of it, and makes away with it*]: (Ḥam p. 555:) or تَشْتَمِلُ عَلَى عَقْلِ الإِنْسَانِ فَتُغَيِّبُهُ † [*It compasses the intellect of the man, and conceals it*]; and thus one says of the present world or its enjoyments (الدُّنْيَا). (TA.) [اشتمل عَلَى شَىْءٍ often means † *He took,* or *got, possession of a thing; got it,* or *held it, within his grasp,* or *in his possession.*] — [Hence,] one says, اشتمل عَلَى نَاقَةٍ فَذَهَبَ بِهَا † *He mounted a she-camel and went away with her.* (AZ, O.) — And اشتمل عَلَيْهِ † *He shrouded, covered,* or *protected, him with himself,* or *his own person.* (TA.) — See also 7

R. Q. 1. شَمْلَلَ : see 1, last sentence: — and see also 7.

شَمْلٌ *A state of union* or *composedness:* and *a state of disunion* or *discomposedness:* thus having two contr. significations: (MF, TA:) or *a united,* or *composed, state of the affairs,* (Ṣ, Mṣb, TA,) and *of the number,* (TA,) of a people, or company of men: (Ṣ, Mṣb, TA:) and *a disunited,* or *discomposed, state of the affairs* [&c.] thereof. (Ṣ, Mgh, Mṣb.) In imprecating evil upon enemies, (O, TA,) [or upon an enemy,] one says, فَرَّقَ ٱللّٰهُ شَمْلَهُمْ, شَتَّتَ ٱللّٰهُ شَمْلَهُمْ, (O, TA,) or (Mṣb,) or فرّق الله شَمْلَهُ, (Ṣ,) i. e. [*May God dissolve, break up, discompose, derange, disorganize, disorder,* or *unsettle,*] *their,* (Mṣb,) or *his,* (Ṣ,) *united,* or *composed, state of affairs;* (Ṣ, Mṣb;) and شَتَّ شَمْلُهُمْ i. e. [*May their united,* or *composed, state of affairs* &c.] *become dissolved, broken up, discomposed,* &c.: (O, TA:) and [in the contr. case] one says, جَمَعَ ٱللّٰهُ شَمْلَهُمْ, (Ṣ, O, Mṣb, TA,) or شَمْلَهُ, (Mgh,) i. e. [*May God unite,* or *compose,*] *their,* (Ṣ, Mṣb,) or *his,* (Mgh,) *disunited,* or *discomposed, state of affairs* [&c.]. (Ṣ, Mgh, Mṣb.) And ▼ شَمَلٌ signifies the same: El-Ba'eeth says,

قَدْ يَنْعَشُ ٱللّٰهُ الفَتَى بَعْدَ عَثْرَةٍ •
وَقَدْ يَجْمَعُ ٱللّٰهُ الشَّتِيتَ مِنَ الشَّمَلِ •

[*Sometimes,* or *often, God raises the young man after a stumble: and sometimes,* or *often, God unites,* or *composes, what is dissolved,* or *broken up, of the state of affairs* previously *united,* or *composed*]: (Ṣ, O:) AZ cites this ex. in his "Nawádir:" (Ṣ:) but Aboo-'Omar El-Jarmee says that he had not heard the word thus except in this verse: (Ṣ, O:) Ibn-Buzurj, however, cites another verse as presenting an ex. of the same. (TA.) — دَخَلَ فِى شَمْلِهَا and ▼ شَمَلِهَا, said of a he-camel that has become concealed among a herd of [she-] camels, means *He entered amid their dense multitude:* (Ḳ, TA:) so in the M and the Moheeṭ. (TA.) — Also, (AḤn, O, Ḳ,) and so ▼ شَمَلٌ, and ▼ شِمْلٌ, (Ḳ,) *A raceme of a palm-tree:* (AḤn, O, Ḳ:) Eṭ-Ṭirimmáḥ likens thereto a camel's tail: (TA:) or *such as has little fruit:* (Ḳ:) or *of which some of the fruit has been plucked:* but AO used to say that it is the *produce* [or *spadix*] *of the male palm-tree, while not abundant and large.* (TA.) — See also شَمَالٌ. — And شَمْلٌ مِنْ جُنُونٍ signifies *Fear,* or *fright, like insanity:* and so ▼ شَمْلٌ [used alone, and thus written]. (TA.)

شِمْلٌ : see the next preceding paragraph, near the end.

شَمَلٌ : see شَمْلٌ, in two places. — Also *i. q.* كَنَفٌ [as meaning *Quarter,* or *shelter* or *protection*]: الكَنَفُ in the copies of the Ḳ being a mistake for الكَتَفُ: one says, نَحْنُ فِى شَمَلِكُمْ, i. e. فِى كَنَفِكُمْ [*We are in your quarter,* &c.]. (TA.) — And *A small quantity* (Ṣ, Ḳ) of dates upon a palm-tree (Ṣ) or of ripe dates: (Ḳ:) and of rain: (Ṣ, Ḳ:) and *a small number* (Ṣ, Ḳ) of men and of camels (Ṣ) or of men &c.: pl. أَشْمَالٌ: and in like manner ▼ شُمْلُولٌ [app. in all of these applications]; (Ḳ;) [or] as meaning *a light quantity* of fruit of the palm-tree; (TA;) and the pl. of the latter is شَمَالِيلُ: (Ḳ:) one says, مَا عَلَى النَّخْلَةِ إِلَّا شَمَلٌ and ▼ شَمَلَةٌ and ▼ شَمَالِيلُ *There is not upon the palm-tree save a small quantity remaining of its fruit:* (Ṣ, TA:) or مَا بَقِىَ فِى النَّخْلَةِ إِلَّا شَمَلَةٌ ▼ and ▼ شَمَالِيلُ *There remained not upon the palm-tree save somewhat in a sparse state* [of its fruit]: (TA:) and أَصَابَنَا شَمَلٌ مِنْ مَطَرٍ *A small quantity of rain fell upon us:* and رَأَيْتُ شَمَلًا مِنَ النَّاسِ وَالإِبِلِ *I saw a small number of men and of camels.* (Ṣ.) — See also شَمَالٌ, in two places: — And see شَمْلٌ, last sentence.

شَمِلٌ *Wrapping,* or *inwrapping, himself with a* شَمْلَة [q. v.]. (▼ مُشْتَمِلٌ) (TA.) — And *Thin;* syn. رَقِيقٌ: thus expl. by Sh, as applied in this sense by Ibn-Muḳbil to a she-camel's tail, which he terms لَيف. (TA.)

شَمْلَةٌ *A* [*garment of the kind called*] كِسَآء, *with which one wraps,* or *inwraps, himself* (يُشْتَمَلُ بِهِ), (Ṣ, Mgh, Ḳ,) *smaller than the* قَطِيفَة; as also ▼ مِشْمَلٌ (Ḳ) and ▼ مِشْمَلَةٌ; (Ṣ, Ḳ;) the last two expl. by Lth as *a* كِسَآء *having a sparse villous substance, with which one wraps himself, smaller than the* قَطِيفَة: (TA:) or the first signifies *a small* كِسَآء *which one wears in the manner of the* إِزَار [or *waist-wrapper*]: (Mṣb:) or with the Arabs it is *a* مِئْزَر [or *waist-wrapper*] *of wool* or *of* [*goats'*] *hair, which one wraps round him:* and ▼ مِشْمَلَةٌ, *such as is made of two pieces sewed together, with which a man wraps himself when he sleeps by night:* (Az, TA:) and this last, accord. to Meyd, signifies *a* كِسَآء *comprising the steel with which one strikes fire, with the apparatus of this latter:* (Ḥar p. 628:) the pl. of the first is شِمَالٌ (Mṣb, TA) and شَمَلَاتٌ. (Mṣb.) [See also مِشْمَالٌ.] — [Hence the saying,] ضَمَّ عَلَيْهِ اللَّيْلُ شَمْلَتَهُ ‡ [*The night contracted upon him its covering of darkness*]. (TA.) — And أُمُّ شَمْلَةَ ‡ *The present world,* or *its enjoyments;* syn. الدُّنْيَا: (IAạr, Ḳ, TA:) so called because compassing the intellect of a man (تَشْتَمِلُ عَلَى عَقْلِهِ), and concealing it. (TA.) — And † *Wine:* (AA, Ḳ, TA:) so called for the same reason. (TA.) — And *The sun.* (Z, TA; and T in art. امر.)

شِمْلَةٌ *A mode,* or *manner, of* اِشْتِمَال [or *wrapping oneself with a garment* as expl. above: see 8]. (Ḳ, TA.) الشِّمْلَةُ الصَّمَّآءُ is *That* [*mode of wrapping oneself*] *which is without a shirt and without drawers beneath;* in the case of which, prayer is disliked. (TA. [See 8, and see also art. صمّ.])

شَمَلَةٌ : see شَمَلٌ, in two places.

شَمَالٌ : see شِمَالٌ.

شِمِلٌّ : see شَمْلٌ, near the end of the paragraph. — Also, (TA,) and شِمِلَّةٌ; (Ṣ, O, Ḳ, TA;) the former applied to a he-camel; (TA;) and the latter to a she-camel, as also ▼ شِمْلَالٌ and ▼ شِمْلِيلٌ, (Ṣ, O, Mṣb, Ḳ, TA,) which are likewise applied to a he-camel, (TA,) and ▼ شِمَالٌ; (Ḳ;) *Light, active,* or *agile;* (Ṣ, O, Mṣb, Ḳ;) or *swift.* (Mṣb, Ḳ, TA.) Hence the phrase ▼ طَأْطَأْتُ شِمْلَالِى [*I hastened my light one,* or *my swift one*]: or, accord. to AA, he means his hand, or arm, called the شِمَال; [i. e. *I lowered my left hand* or *arm;*] شِمْلَالٌ and شِمَالٌ meaning the same. (Ṣ, O.)

شَمَالٌ, (Ṣ, O, Mṣb, Ḳ, &c.,) the most common form of the word, (Mṣb,) and ▼ شِمَالٌ, [a form which I think objectionable as likely to cause confusion, though it is probably the original form,] (Ḳ,) and ▼ شَمْأَلٌ, (Ṣ, O, Mṣb, Ḳ,) and ▼ شَأْمَلٌ, (Ṣ, O, Ḳ, [in one place in the O erroneously written شَآمَل,]) and ▼ شَأْمَلٌ, (Ṣ, O, Mṣb, Ḳ,) which last is formed by transposition, (Ṣ, O, Mṣb,) and ▼ شَامَلٌ, without ء, (MF, TA,) and ▼ شَوْمَلٌ, and ▼ شَيْمَلٌ and ▼ شَمُولٌ, (O, Ḳ,) and ▼ شَمِيلٌ, (Ḳ,) and ▼ شَمْلٌ, (Ṣ, O, Mṣb, Ḳ,) and ▼ شَمَلٌ, (Ṣ, Mṣb, Ḳ,) the last said by ISd not to have been heard except in the poetry of El-Ba'eeth, (TA,) and ▼ شَمِلٌ, (MF, TA,) [every one of these] used as a subst. and as an epithet, (Ḳ,) [so that one says رِيحُ الشَّمَالِ &c. as well as رِيحٌ شَمَالٌ &c. and شَمَالٌ &c. alone; The *north wind:* or *a northerly wind:*] the *wind that is the opposite to the* جَنُوب: (Mṣb:) the *wind that blows from the direction of the* قُطْب [or *pole-star*]: (Ṣ:) or the *wind that blows from the direction of the* جَدْي [which is on what is called the north, but what is rather to be called the north-west, side of the Kaabeh]: (M, Ḳ:) or the *wind that blows from the direction of the right hand of a person facing the Kibleh* [by which is meant the angle of the Black Stone; i. e., correctly speaking, *from the north*]: (Th, M, Ḳ:) or, correctly, the *wind that blows from between the place of sunrise and the constellation of the Bear* (بَنَات نَعْش): or *from between the place of sunrise and the place of setting of the constellation of the Eagle* (النَّسْر)

الطَّائِرِ): (IAạr, Ḳ:) [i. e. the *wind that blows from some point of the north-east quarter*, or *nearly so*: but it was probably thus named as being the *wind that blows from the direction of the* شِمَال (or *left side*) *of a person facing the rising sun*; and therefore the *north wind* or a *northerly wind*:] it seldom, or never, blows in the night: (Ḳ:) when it blows for seven days upon the people of Egypt, they prepare the grave-clothes, for its nature is deadly: it is cold and dry: (TA:) [see also نَكْبَآءُ:] the pl. of شَمَالٌ is شَمَالَاتٌ (Ṣ, O, Ḳ) and شَمَائِلُ, which is anomalous, as though pl. of شَمَالَةٌ: (Ṣ, O:) الأَشَامِلُ also occurs, coupled with الأَجَانِبُ, in a verse of Eṭ-Ṭirimmáh; and [as أَجَانِبُ is a reg. pl. of أَجْنُبٌ, which is a pl. of جَنُوبٌ,] ISd thinks that they formed from شَمْلٌ the pl. أَشْمُلٌ; and then from this last, the pl. أَشَامِلُ. (TA.) — [Hence,] one says, أَصَبْتُ مِنْ فُلَانٍ شَمَلًا ↑ رِيحًا i. e. [† *I perceived from such a one an odour*, app. meaning *a foul odour*]. (TA.)

شِمَالٌ, (Ṣ, O, Mṣb, Ḳ, &c.,) applied to one of the hands or arms, (Ṣ, Mṣb,) The *left*; *contr. of* يَمِينٌ; (Ṣ, O, Mṣb, Ḳ;) as also ↑ شِيمَالٌ, (Ḳ, TA, [in the CḲ, الشَّمال and الشِّمال are erroneously put for الشِّمَال and الشِّيمَال,]) the latter thought by ISd to be used only by poetic license, for شِمَال, (TA,) and ↑ شِمْلَالٌ, (AA, Ṣ, O, Ḳ,) this last not known to Ks nor to Aṣ: (TA:) of the fem. gender: (Ṣ, O, Mṣb:) pl. [of pauc.] أَشْمُلٌ, (Ṣ, O, Mṣb, Ḳ,) because it is fem., (Ṣ, O,) and [of mult.] شَمَائِلُ, (Ṣ, O, Mṣb, Ḳ,) which is anomalous, (Ṣ, O,) and شُمُلٌ, and شِمَالٌ like the sing. (Ḳ.) — And The *direction* [or *side*] *of the hand so called*: you say, اِلْتَفَتَ يَمِينًا وَشِمَالًا i. e. [*He looked*, or *turned his face*,] *in the direction of the* يمين *and in the direction of the* شمال: and the pl. in this sense also is أَشْمُلٌ and شَمَائِلُ: (Mṣb:) you say, ذَهَبَ إِلَى أَيْمُنِ الإِبِلِ وَأَشْمُلِهَا *He went to the right sides of the camels and the left sides thereof*. (TA in art. يمن.) — [Hence,] ‡ *Ill luck, unluckiness*, or *evil fortune*. (Ḳ, TA.) طَيْرُ الشِّمَالِ means ‡ *Birds of ill luck*: (A, TA:) *every bird from which one augurs evil*. (O, TA.) One says, جَرَى لَهُ غُرَابُ شِمَالٍ, meaning † *What was disliked*, or *hated, happened to him*: as though the bird [to which this is likened] came to him from the شِمَال [or direction of the left hand]. (TA.) And when the place that a person occupies is rendered evil, one says, فُلَانٌ عِنْدِى بِالشِّمَالِ † [*Such a one is with me*, or *in my estimation, in an evil plight*]. (TA.) — See also شَمَالٌ. — Also *Every handful of corn*, or *seed-produce, which the reaper grasps* [app. because grasped with his left hand]. (Ḳ.) ═ And *A sort of bag that is put upon the udder of the ewe* or *goat* (Ṣ, O, Ḳ) *when it* (i. e. *the udder*, TA) *is heavy* [*with milk*]: (Ḳ,* TA:) or it is *peculiar to the she-goat*: (Ḳ:) pl. شُمُلٌ. (Ḳ voce عَزَابَةٌ.) — And *A similar thing that is put to the raceme of a palm-tree, made with pieces of* [the *garments called*] أَكْسِيَة [pl. of كِسَآءٌ], *in order that the fruit may not be shaken off*. (Ṣ, O.) [In this sense it may perhaps be from the same word as pl. of شَمْلَةٌ.] ═ And *A mark made with a hot iron* (سِمَة) *upon the udder of a ewe or goat*. (Ḳ.) ═ Also *A nature*; or *a natural disposition* or *temper* or *the like*: (O, Mṣb, Ḳ:) accord. to Er-Rághib, so called because [it is as though it were a thing] inwrapping the man [and restricting his freedom of action], like as the [garments called] شِمَال [pl. of شَمْلَةٌ] inwrap the body: (TA:) the pl. is شَمَائِلُ, (O, Ḳ, TA,) and شِمَالٌ, also, [which seems to be rarely used as a sing. in this sense,] may be a pl., like دِلَاصٌ. (TA; and Ḥam p. 489, q. v.) 'Abd-Yaghooth El-Ḥárithee says,

* أَلَمْ تَعْلَمَا أَنَّ المَلَامَةَ نَفْعُهَا *
* قَلِيلٌ وَمَا لَوْمِى أَخِى مِنْ شِمَالِيَا *

[*Know not ye two that the utility of censure is little, and my censuring my brother is not of my nature*, or *of my natural dispositions*?]: (O, TA:) here it may be a pl., of the class of هِجَانٌ and دِلَاصٌ: or it may be [شِمَالِيَا,] an instance of transposition, for شَمَائِلِى. (TA.) ═ See also شِمْلٌ.

شَمْأَلٌ and شَمَأْلٌ: see شَمَالٌ.

شَمُولٌ: see شَمَالٌ. — Also *Wine*: (Ṣ, Ḳ:) or *wine that is cool* (Ḳ, TA) *to the taste*; but this is not of valid authority; (TA;) as also ↑ مَشْمُولَةٌ: [wine is said to be] thus called because it envelops (تَشْمَلُ) men with its odour: or because it has a strong puff (عَصْفَة), [when opened,] like that of the [wind called] شَمَال [in the CḲ شمال]. (Ḳ, TA.)

شَمِيلٌ: see شَمَالٌ.

شمالة [thus in my original, without any syll. signs, probably شَمَالَةٌ, like سِتَارَةٌ &c.,] The *lurking-place* (قُتْرَة) *of a hunter* or *sportsman*: pl. شَمَائِلُ. (TA.)

شَمَالِىٌّ *Of*, or *relating to, the quarter of the* شَمَال [or *north*, or *northerly, wind*]. (KL.) — And A *cold* day. (KL.)

شِمْلَالٌ: see شِمْلٌ, in two places: ═ and see شِمَالٌ.

شُمْلُولٌ; and its pl. شَمَالِيلُ: see شِمْلٌ, in three places. — شَمَالِيلُ also signifies The *shoots that divaricate at the heads of branches, like the fruit-stalks of the raceme of the palm-tree*. (Ṣ, O.) — [Hence,] ذَهَبُوا شَمَالِيلَ *They went away in distinct parties*: (Ḳ:) or *they dispersed themselves*. (Ṣ, O.) — And ثَوْبٌ شَمَالِيلُ *A garment*, or *piece of cloth, rent*, or *slit, in several places*; (O, TA;) like شَمَاطِيطُ. (Ṣ, O.) — شَمَالِيلُ النوى means بُقَايَاهُ [i. e. *The remains of* النوى: but I doubt whether this word be correctly transcribed]. (TA.)

شِمْلِيلٌ: see شِمْلٌ.

شَأْمَلٌ and شَأَمْلٌ: see شَمَالٌ.

أَمْرٌ شَامِلٌ i. q. عَامٌّ [i. e. *An event*, or *a case, that includes* persons or things *in common, in general*, or *universally, within the compass of its effect* or *effects, its operation* or *operations, its influence*, or *the like*; or *that is common, general*, or *universal, in its effect* &c.]. (Ṣ,* O,* Mṣb, TA.) — لَوْنٌ شَامِلٌ *A black colour overspread with another colour*. (O, TA.)

شَوْمَلٌ: } see شَمَالٌ.
شَيْمَلٌ: }

شِيمَالٌ: see شِمَالٌ.

مِشْمَلٌ: see شَمْلَةٌ. — Also *A short sword*, (Ṣ, O, Ḳ,) or *a short and slender sword, like the* مِغْوَل, (TA,) *over which a man covers himself with his garment*. (Ṣ, O, Ḳ.)

مَشْمَلَةٌ The *place* [or *quarter*] *whence blows the* [*north*, or *northerly, wind called*] شَمَال. (Ḥam p. 628.)

مِشْمَلَةٌ: see شَمْلَةٌ, in two places.

مِشْمَالٌ *A* [*garment of the kind called*] مِلْحَفَة, (Ḳ, TA,) *with which one wraps*, or *inwraps, himself* (يُشْتَمَلُ بِهِ). (TA.) [See also شَمْلَةٌ.]

مَشْمُولٌ A man *smitten*, or *blown upon, by the* [*north*, or *northerly*,] *wind called* شَمَال: (Ṣ, O:) and in like manner, a meadow, and a pool of water left by a torrent; (O;) or, applied to this last, *smitten by the wind thus called so as to become cool*: (Ṣ:) and hence, with ة, wine ‡ *cool to the taste*; (Ṣ, O, TA;*) or wine *exposed to the* شَمَال *and so rendered cool and pleasant*: (TA: see also شَمُولٌ:) and fire *upon which the wind called the* شَمَال *has blown*: (Ṣ, O:) and a night *cold, with* [*wind that is called*] شَمَال. (TA.) — [Hence,] ‡ One *whose natural dispositions are liked, approved*, or *found pleasant*: (Ḳ:) from [the same epithet applied to] water upon which the شَمَال has blown, and which it has cooled: or, as ISd thinks, from شَمُولٌ [q. v.]: (TA:) or مَشْمُولُ الخَلَائِقِ a man *whose natural dispositions are commended*; as being likened to wine that is commended: and also *whose natural dispositions are discommended*; as though from الشَّمَال, because they do not commend it when it disperses the clouds: (Ḥar p. 285:) [for] أَخْلَاقٌ مَشْمُولَةٌ [sometimes] means *discommended, evil, natural dispositions*. (IAạr, ISk, TA.) The saying of Aboo-Wejzeh,

* مَشْمُولَةُ الأُنْسِ مَجْنُوبٌ مَوَاعِدُهَا *

is expl. by IAạr as meaning † *Her familiarity passes away with the* شَمَال, *and her promises pass away with the* جَنُوب [which is the opposite of the شَمَال]: or, as some relate it,

* مَجْنُوبَةُ الأُنْسِ مَشْمُولٌ مَوَاعِدُهَا *

[meaning in like manner, as is said in the TA, on the authority of IAạr, in art. جنب: or,] accord. to ISk, meaning *her familiarity is commended*, because the جنوب, with rain, is desired for abundance of herbage; *and her promises are not commended.* (TA.) —— نَوًى مَشْمُولَةٌ, a phrase used by Zuheyr, is expl. as meaning † [*A tract, or place, towards which one journeys,*] *that separates friends;* because the [wind called] شَمَال disperses the clouds: (TA:) or it means *quickly* [or *soon*] *becoming exposed to view;* (ISk, O, TA;) from the fact that when the wind called the شَمَال blows the clouds, they delay not to become cleared away, and to depart: (O:) or, accord. to IAạr, it means مَأْخُوذٌ بِهَا ذَاتَ الشِّمَالِ [*in which the direction of the left hand is taken*]. (TA.) —— In the saying,

* حَمَلَتْ بِهِ فِى لَيْلَةٍ مَشْمُولَةٍ *

the meaning is, فَزِعَةٌ [i. e. *One in a state of fright became pregnant with him in a certain night*]. (TA, referring to the phrase شَمْلٌ مِنْ جُنُونٍ.)

مُشْتَمِلٌ: see شَمِلٌ. —— One says, جَآءَ مُشْتَمِلًا بِسَيْفِهِ like as one says مُرْتَدِيًا [i. e. *He came having his sword hung upon him*]. (TA.) —— And ‡ جَآءَ فُلَانٌ مُشْتَمِلًا عَلَى دَاهِيَةٍ [*Such a one came conceiving a calamity*]. (TA.)

شن

1. شَنَّ المَآءَ, (Ṣ, Mgh, Ḳ,) aor. ـُ, inf. n. شَنٌّ, (Mgh, TA,) *He scattered the water;* (Ṣ, Ḳ;) or *poured it scatteringly;* (Mgh;) or *poured it and scattered it;* or, as some say, *poured it in a manner like that which is termed* نَضْحٌ [i. e. *sprinkling*]; (TA;) عَلَى الشَّرَابِ [*upon the wine, or beverage*]: (Ṣ, Ḳ:) سَنَّهُ signifies "he poured it gently." (TA.) And شَنَّتِ العَيْنُ دَمْعَهَا *The eye poured forth its tears;* (TA;) or *sent forth* [or *shed*] *its tears;* like شَلَّتْ, (Lḥ, TA in art. شل,) which is asserted by Yaạḳoob to be formed by substitution [of ل for ن]. (TA in that art.) —— And, from the former, شَنَّ الغَارَةَ, (Ṣ, Mgh, Mṣb, Ḳ,) aor. and inf. n. as above, (Mṣb,) ‡ *He scattered,* (Ṣ, Mgh, Mṣb, TA,) or *poured,* (Ḳ, TA,) *the horsemen making a raid, or sudden attack, and engaging in conflict,* or *the horsemen urging their horses,* الغَارَةَ meaning الخَيْلَ المُغِيرَةَ, (Mgh, Mṣb,) *from every direction,* عَلَيْهِمْ [*upon them*]; (Ṣ, Ḳ;) as also ↓ أَشَنَّهَا; (Ṣ, Mṣb, Ḳ;) the latter mentioned in the Mj, (Mṣb,) by IF, but disapproved by the people of chaste speech. (TA.) —— And شَنَّ بِسَلْحِهِ (AA, Ṣ,* TA) *He cast forth his excrement, or dung, in a thin* [*and scattered*] *state:* and one says of the حُبَارَى [or bustard] تَشُنُّ بِذَرْقِهَا [*It casts forth its dung in a thin and scattered state*]. (AA, TA.) —— And شَنَّ عَلَيْهِ دِرْعَهُ *He put* (lit. *poured*) *on him his coat of mail.* (TA.) ═ شَنَّ الجَمَلُ مِنَ العَطَشِ, [aor. accord. to general rule ـِ,] *The camel became dried up* [*like a* شَنّ, q. v.,] *from thirst.* (TA.) And شَنَّتِ الخِرْقَةُ *The rag became dried up.* (TA.)

2. تَشْنِينٌ and تَشْنَانٌ [inf. ns. of شَنَّنَ] The *dripping, or dropping by degrees, of water from the* شَنَّة [or *old and worn-out water-skin* or *the like*]. (TA. [See also شَنِينٌ.])

4: see 1: —— and see also what next follows.

5. تَشَنَّنَتِ القِرْبَةُ, and ↓ تشانّت, (Ṣ, Ḳ,) and ↓ استشنّت and ↓ اشنّت, (Ḳ,) *The water-skin became old, and worn out:* (Ṣ, Ḳ:) or ↓ تشانّ, said of skin, or a skin, does not signify thus, but signifies, (AA, Ṣ,) or signifies also, (Ḳ,) and so تشنّن, (Ṣ, Ḳ, TA,) said of the skin of a man, in extreme old age, (Ṣ,) *it contracted, shrank, shrivelled,* or *wrinkled;* or *became contracted* or *shrunk* &c.; (Ṣ, Ḳ, TA;) *and dried up:* (Ṣ, TA:) and ↓ استشنّ is likewise said of the skin of a man, meaning *it became old, and worn out, like the old, and worn-out,* شَنّ. (Ḥar p. 675.) It is said in a trad., القُرْآنُ لَا يَتْفَهُ وَلَا يَتَشَانُّ ↓ [expl. in art. تفه]. (TA.) See also a tropical usage of ↓ استشنّ in a trad. cited in the first paragraph of art. بل. —— تشنّن is also said of the skin of a man as meaning *It became altered* [*for the worse*] *in odour,* in extreme old age. (TA.)

6. تَشَانَّ: see 5, in three places. —— Also *It was* or *became, mixed.* (Ḳ.)

7. [انشنّ *It became poured out,* or *forth; it flowed.* (Freytag, from the Deewán of the Hudhalees.) —— Hence,] انشنّ الذِّئْبُ فِى الغَنَمِ † *The wolf made an incursion among the sheep* or *goats;* as also انشلّ: mentioned by Az in art. نشغ. (TA.)

10. اِسْتَشَنَّ: see 5, in three places. —— Also, (Kh, Ṣ, Ḳ,) said of a man, (Kh, Ṣ, TA,) and of a camel, (TA,) ‡ *He became lean,* or *emaciated,* (Kh, Ṣ, Ḳ, TA,) *like the water-skin that has become old, and worn out:* so says Aboo-Kheyreh: (TA:) or, said of an animal, *he became dried up, and lean,* or *emaciated.* (Ḥar p. 530.) —— And استشنّ إِلَى اللَّبَنِ i. q. عَامَ, (Ḳ,) i. e. *He betook himself to milk,* or *the milk, and desired it eagerly,* or *longed for it.* (TA.)

R. Q. 1. شَنْشَنَةٌ [an inf. n., of which the verb, if it be used, is شَنْشَنَ,] The *motion* of paper, and of a new garment: [or rather the *making a kind of crackling sound by the motion* thereof:] mentioned by Az in art. قعقع: (TA:) and نَشْنَشَةٌ signifies the same: both thus expl. by IAạr. (TA in art. قع.)

شَنٌّ *A skin,* (Mṣb,) or *a water-skin,* (Ṣ, Mgh,) or *a small water skin,* (Ḳ,) or, as some say, *any vessel made of skin,* (TA,) applied by a poet to *a* دَلْو [or *leathern bucket*], (Ḥam p. 602,) *that is old, and worn out;* (Ṣ, Mgh, Mṣb, Ḳ, TA;) and so ↓ شَنَّةٌ; (Ṣ, Ḳ;) but app. *one that is small:* (Ṣ: [in which this addition to the explanation seems to relate peculiarly to the latter word: see an ex. of this latter word in some verses cited in the first paragraph of art. سقى:]) or both signify *an old water-skin;* as also ↓ مِشَنٌّ: (MA:) and ↓ شَنَنٌ, also, signifies *an old, worn-out, water-skin:* (TA:) pl. (of the first, Mgh, Mṣb) شِنَانٌ: (Ṣ, Mgh, Mṣb, Ḳ:) and Lḥ mentions the phrase قِرْبَةٌ أَشْنَانٌ, as though they applied the term شَنٌّ to every portion of the قربة and then pluralized it thus; but he says that he had not heard أَشْنَانٌ as a pl. of شَنٌّ except in this case: (TA:) the water in a شَنّ is cooler [than that in a skin not so old]. (Mgh.) It is said in a prov., لَا يُقَعْقَعُ لِى بِالشِّنَانِ [*A confused and clattering noise will not be made to me with the old and worn-out water-skins* to frighten me]: (Ṣ in the present art.: [in the Ṣ and Ḳ in art. قع, with مَا in the place of لا; and in the Ḳ in that art., with لَهُ in the place of لى:]) مَا يُقَعْقَعُ لَهُ بِالشِّنَانِ is applied to him who will not be abased by misfortunes, nor frightened by that which has no reality: (Ṣgh and Ḳ in art. قع:) or it means, he will not be deceived nor frightened: شِنَان being pl. of شَنٌّ, *a dried up skin,* which is shaken to a camel to frighten him. (L and TA in art. قع.) An old man is likened to the skin thus termed. (Ḥar p. 675.) And ↓ شَنَّةٌ signifies also ‡ *A worn-out old woman;* as being likened to the skin thus termed. (IAạr, TA.) And one says, رَفَعَ فُلَانٌ الشَّنَّ, meaning † *Such a man raised himself bearing upon the palm of his hand.* (IKh, TA.) —— Also i. q. غرض [app. غَرَضٌ, i. e. *A butt, at which one shoots or casts:* probably because an old water-skin was sometimes used as a butt]: pl. as above. (Mṣb.) —— [And, as Freytag states, on the authority of Meyd, † *Dry herbage.*] ═ Also *Weakness.* (TA.)

شَنَّةٌ: see شَنٌّ, in two places.

شَنَنٌ: see شَنٌّ, first sentence.

شَنَانٌ a dial. var. of شَنْآنٌ [inf. n. of شَنِئَ], (Ṣ, Ḳ,) signifying *Hatred;* [or the *hating* of another;] (Ṣ;) mentioned by AO. (Ṣ in art. شنأ.)

شُنَانٌ Water *in a scattered state,* or *being scattered.* (Ṣ, Ḳ.) —— And (Ḳ) *Cold* water: (Aṣ, Skr, ISd, Ḳ:) this explanation is preferred by Aboo-Naṣr. (TA.) —— And Clouds (سَحَابٌ) *pouring* (يَصُبُّ i. e. يَشُنُّ) *water.* (Skr, TA.)

شَنُونٌ A camel *in a state between that of the lean,* or *emaciated, and that of the fat;* (Ṣ;) so called because some of his fatness has gone: (Aboo-Kheyreh, TA:) one says مَهْزُولٌ; then شَنُونٌ, when he has become a little fat; then مُنْقٍ; then سَاحٌّ; and then مُتَرَطِّمٌ, when fat in the utmost degree: (Lḥ, TA:) so says Aboo-Ma'add El-Kilábee. (TA in art. سح.) [But it is said that] it signifies also *Lean,* or *emaciated;* (Ḳ;) applied to a beast: (TA:) and *fat:* thus having two contr. meanings. (Ḳ.) —— Also *Hungry:* (Ṣ, Ḳ:) applied in this sense by Eṭ-Ṭirimmáḥ to a wolf, because this animal is not described as fat or lean. (Ṣ.)

شَنِينٌ *Poured forth:* applied in this sense by the Hudhalee poet 'Abd-Menáf to thick blood (عَلَق). (TA.) —— And *Pure milk upon which cold water has been poured:* (IAạr, TA:) or any milk, whether fresh or collected in a skin at different times, *upon which water is poured.* (Ḳ, TA.) ═ And The *dropping* (Ṣ, Ḳ, TA) *by degrees,* (TA,) of water (Ṣ, Ḳ, TA) from a skin, (TA,) and of tears. (Ṣ, TA. [See also 2, and see شَنْشَنَةٌ.])

شَانَّةٌ *Water that drops* (Ṣ, Ḳ) *from a skin, or from a tree.* (Ṣ.)

شَانَّةٌ The [*channel called*] مَدْفَع [q. v.] *of a small valley: or a small* مَدْفَع *of a valley:* (TA: [the want of a vowel-sign in my original renders it doubtful which of these meanings is the right one:]) or شَوَانُّ, its pl., signifies the *channels of water*, of mountains, *that pour forth into valleys from a rugged place.* (AA, TA.)

شِنْشِنَةٌ *A nature; or a natural, a native, or an innate, disposition or temper or the like;* syn. طَبِيعَةٌ, (Ṣ, Mgh, Ḳ,) and خُلُقٌ, (Ṣ,) and سَجِيَّةٌ: (TA:) and *a custom, habit, or wont:* (Mgh, Ḳ:) [pl. شَنَاشِنُ.] One says فِيهِ مِنْ أَبِيهِ شَنَاشِنُ *In him are habits* [or *natural dispositions* inherited] *from his father.* (TA.) Hence,

* شِنْشِنَةٌ أَعْرِفُهَا مِنْ أَخْزَمِ *

[*A natural disposition, or a habit, which I know,* as inherited *from Akhzam*]: (Ṣ, Meyd, Mgh:) or, accord. to one relation, نِشْنِشَةٌ, which is app. formed by transposition from شِنْشِنَةٌ: (Meyd:) a prov.: (Meyd, Mgh:) [of its origin there are different explanations: see Freytag's Arab. Prov. i. 658, and Ḥar pp. 591 and 596:] أَخْزَم is the proper name of a man: (Meyd, Mgh, &c.:) or accord. to Lth, it is an epithet applied to a penis; one says كَمَرَةٌ خَزْمَآءُ "a glans of a penis having a short frænum," and ذَكَرٌ أَخْزَمُ; and شنشنة means the *dropping* of water [i. e., in this case, of the seminal fluid]: (Meyd:) the prov. is applied in relation to nearness of resemblance. (Meyd, Mgh.) — Also *A bit of flesh-meat, as much as is chewed at once;* syn. مُضْغَةٌ: or *a piece of flesh-meat;* (Ḳ, TA;) and so نِشْنِشَةٌ: on the authority of AA. (TA.) — And [the pl.] شَنَاشِنُ signifies *Bones;* like سَنَاسِنُ. (IAạr, L in art. سن.)

مِشَنٌّ: see شَنٌّ, first sentence.

مِشَنَّةٌ *A thing like the* مِكْتَل: [in the present day, *a round shallow basket* is thus called: pl. مَشَانُّ.] (TA.)

شنأ

1. شَنِئَهُ, (Th, Ṣ, Mgh, Mṣb, Ḳ, &c.,) and شَنَأَهُ, (Ḳ,) but this is said by AHeyth to be a bad dial. var. of the former, (TA,) aor. ـَ, (Mṣb, Ḳ,) inf. n. شَنْءٌ (AO, Ṣ, Mṣb, Ḳ) and شِنْءٌ and شُنْءٌ (Aboo-'Amr Esh-Sheybánee, Ṣ, Ḳ) and شَنْأَةٌ (Ḳ, TA, in the CḲ شناءة [i. e. شَنَآءَةٌ, which is afterwards added in the TA, not as in the Ḳ, and mentioned in the Ṣ but not there said to be an inf. n.,]) and شَنَأٌ (TA from Eṣ-Ṣafáḳusee) and شَنَآءٌ (TA [as from J, but perhaps from Az, for I do not find it in the Ṣ,]) and مَشْنَأٌ (Ṣ, CḲ, and TA as from Eṣ-Ṣafáḳusee, not as from the Ḳ,) and مَشْنَأَةٌ and مَشْنُؤَةٌ (Ḳ, TA, the last in the CḲ مَشْنُوءَةٌ [i. e. مَشْنُوءَةٌ],) and مَشْنِئَةٌ (TA from Eṣ-Ṣafáḳusee) and شَنَآنٌ, (Ṣ, Ḳ,) which is anomalous as being of a measure regularly employed [only] for the inf. n. of a verb signifying motion and agitation, as ضَرَبَانٌ and خَفَقَانٌ, (Ṣ, TA,) for though it has been said that [hatred (which it signifies) is attended by anger and] anger is accompanied by agitation of the heart, there is no necessary connexion between hatred and anger, and it is anomalous also as being of a measure not proper to [the inf. n. of] a trans. verb, (TA,) and شَنْآنٌ, (Ṣ, Mṣb, Ḳ,) which is also anomalous, and [said to be] the only instance of its kind (Ṣ, TA) except لَيَّانٌ, though some few others have been mentioned, as زَيْدَانٌ, but this is not well known, [and غَشْيَانٌ, of which the same may be said,] and وَشْكَانٌ [perhaps a simple subst.], and جَوْلَانٌ which is said to occur in a verse [perhaps contracted from جَوَلَان by poetic license], (TA,) and AO mentions شَنَانٌ, without ء, as being like شَنْآنٌ; (Ṣ;) these inf. ns. being fourteen, which is said by IḲṭṭ to be the greatest number of inf. ns. to any one verb, only seven other verbs, he says, having this number, namely, قَدَرَ, لَقِىَ, وَرَدَ, هَلَكَ, تَمَّ, مَكَثَ, and غَلَبَ; but Eṣ-Ṣafáḳusee makes the inf. ns. of شَنِئَ to be fifteen, [though the fifteenth form (which is perhaps مَشْنُؤَةٌ) I do not find mentioned,] and this is the greatest number known; (TA;) *He hated him:* (IḲooṭ, IF, Ṣ, ISd, IḲṭṭ, Mgh, Mṣb, Ḳ, &c.:) or, as some say, *he hated him vehemently.* (TA.) يشنى, [app. يَشْنَى, for يَشْنَأُ,] with the hemzeh changed into ى, occurs in a trad. (TA.) And شُنِئَ signifies *He* (a man, Ṣ) *was hated,* (Ṣ, and so accord. to some copies of the Ḳ,) or *was rendered hateful,* or *an object of hatred,* (so accord. to other copies of the Ḳ,) *even if beautiful* or *comely.* (Ṣ, Ḳ.) — شَنِئَ لَهُ حَقَّهُ, (Ḳ,) so says A'Obeyd, or, accord. to Th, شَنَأَ إِلَيْهِ, like مَنَعَ [in form], and this is the more correct, aor. of each ـَ, (TA,) *He gave him his right, or due.* (A'Obeyd, Th, Ḳ, TA.) And شَنِئَ بِهِ *He acknowledged it:* (Ṣ, Mṣb, Ḳ:) or *he gave him* (Ḳ) *his right,* or *due,* (TA,) [or the meaning in the Ḳ may be *he gave it,*] *and declared himself clear,* or *quit, of him* or *it;* as also شَنَأَ: (Ḳ:) [but accord. to SM, this is wrong, for he says that] the author of the Ḳ should have said, or شَنِئَ إِلَيْهِ, like شَنَأَ, aor. ـَ, *he gave him, and declared himself clear,* or *quit, of him* or *it.* (TA.) And شَنِئَ الشَّىْءَ *He produced the thing:* (Ḳ, TA:) or, as A'Obeyd says, شَنِئَ حَقَّهُ *he acknowledged his right,* or *due, and produced it from his possession.* (TA.)

6. تَشَانَؤُوا *They hated one another.* (Ṣ, O, Ḳ.)

شَنْءٌ and شِنْءٌ and شُنْءٌ [all mentioned above as inf. ns., when used as simple substs. signify *Hatred;* and thus ↓ شَنَآءَةٌ, likewise mentioned above as an inf. n., signifies accord. to the Ṣ; and so ↓ شَنِيئَةٌ accord. to Freytag, as on the authority of Meyd; and app. also شَنُوءَةٌ, q. v.; or all signify] *vehement hatred;* in which sense the first is expl. by AO: (TA:) or ↓ شَنَآءَةٌ signifies *hatred mixed with enmity and evilness of disposition.* (Ḥam p. 108.)

شَنُوْءَةٌ: see شَنُوءَةٌ, in three places.

شَنَآءَةٌ: see شَنْءٌ, in two places. — Also, and ↓ شَنَائِيَةٌ, epithets applied to a man, *Rendered hateful,* or *an object of hatred, evil in disposition.* (Lth, O, TA.) [See also the latter word voce شَنْآنٌ; and see مَشْنُوءٌ, and مِشْنَأٌ.]

شَنُوءَةٌ The *removing oneself far,* or *keeping aloof, from unclean things;* (Ṣ, Ḳ, TA;) and the *continual doing so,* or the *continual purification of oneself;* as also ↓ شَنُوْءَةٌ; and accord. to the Ḳ, شُنُوءَةٌ, but this is not found elsewhere. (TA.) — Hence, (Ṣ,) أَزْدُ شَنُوءَةَ, the appellation of a tribe of El-Yemen; (Ṣ, Ḳ;*) sometimes called أَزْدُ شَنُوَةَ: (ISk, Ṣ, Ḳ:) [or] this tribe was so called because of شَنَآن among them; (Ḳ, TA;) i. e. because of mutual hatred that occurred among them: (TA:) [whence it seems that شَنُوءَةٌ signifies also *Hatred:*] or because of their removing far from their [original] district: or, accord. to El-Khafájee, because of their high lineage, and good deeds; from the phrase رَجُلٌ شَنُوءَةٌ, meaning *A man of pure lineage and of manly virtue;* and AO says the like. (TA.) — [And accord. to Reiske, as stated by Freytag, (who has written it ↓ شُنُوءَةٌ in all its senses,) it is expl. by Meyd as meaning *What is esteemed sordid, of words* and *of actions.*] — Also *One who removes himself far,* or *keeps aloof, from unclean things;* (Ḳ, TA;) and so ↓ شَنُوْءَةٌ. (TA.) Thus both of these words are epithets, as well as substs. (TA.)

شَنِيئَةٌ: see شَنْءٌ.

شَنْآنٌ, of which the fem. is شَنْآنَةٌ and شَنْأَى, [so that one may say either شَنْآنُ or شَنْآنٌ,] is an epithet applied to a man; (Ḳ;) [signifying either *Hating* or (like مَشْنُوءٌ) *hated;* the former meaning seeming to be indicated by what immediately precedes it in the Ḳ; but the latter appears from what here follows to be the right meaning, and perhaps it may be that which is meant in the Ḳ;] as also ↓ شَنَآنَةٌ or ↓ شَنَائِيَةٌ [q. v. voce شَنَآءَةٌ]: so accord. to different copies of the Ḳ. (TA.) — In the Ḳur v. 3 and 11, it is accord. to some an inf. n., and some read there شَنْآن: [see 1, first sentence:] accord. to others, it is an epithet, signifying بَغِيضٌ or مُبْغَضٌ [i. e. *Hated* or *odious*]. (TA.) — شَنْآنُ الشِّتَآءِ, in a trad. of Kaab, is said to be a metaphorical expression for بَرْدُ الشِّتَآءِ ‡ [*The cold of winter*]; because it is hated: or, as some say, by the برد thereof is meant *ease and repose:* and the meaning intended is either *mutual hatred* or *ease and repose.* (TA.)

شَنَائِيَةٌ: see شَنَآءَةٌ, and شَنْآن.

شَنَآنَةٌ: see شَنْآن.

شَانِئٌ *Hating,* or *a hater,* (Fr, Ṣ, Mgh, Mṣb, TA,) and *an enemy:* (Fr, TA:) fem. with ة. (Mgh, Mṣb.) — لَا أَبَ لِشَانِئِكَ, as also لَا أَبَا لِشَانِئِكَ, (Ṣ, O, [but in my two copies of the Ṣ لِشَانِيكَ, which perhaps expresses the general pronunciation, and in the TA لا ابا لشانيك and لا اب لشانئك,]) means لِمُبْغِضِكَ [i. e., lit., *May there be no father* to thy hater]; and is said by ISk to be a metonymical expression for لَا أَبَا لَكَ [q. v., lit. an imprecation, but generally meant as an expression of praise]. (Ṣ, O, TA.)

شَوَانِئُ المَالِ means [*Camels, or the like,*] *not avariciously retained*; as though hated, and therefore liberally given away: (IAạr, Ḳ, TA:) شوانئ being app. an act. part. n. [in the pl.] used in the sense of a pass. part. n., like the instances in عِيشَةٌ رَاضِيَةٌ and مَآءٌ دَافِقٌ. (MF, TA.)

مَشْنَأٌ, applied to a man, (A'Obeyd, Ṣ, O,) like مَشْنَعٌ [in form, and perhaps in meaning], (A'Obeyd, TA,) *Foul*, or *ugly, in aspect*; as also ▾ مِشْنَآءٌ: (Ṣ, O:) or *foul*, or *ugly*, (Ḳ, TA,) *in face*, (TA,) *even if made an object of love* [*by good qualities*]: (Ḳ, TA:) [originally an inf. n., and therefore] used alike as sing. (Ṣ, O, Ḳ) and dual (Ṣ, O) and pl. (Ṣ, O, Ḳ) and masc. and fem.: (Ḳ:) so says Lth: (TA:) or one *who hates men*; (Ḳ;) and so ▾ مِشْنَآءٌ, accord. to 'Alee Ibn-Ḥamzeh El-Iṣbahánee: (TA:) or ▾ this last signifies one *whom men hate*: or it may be well rendered one *who does much for which he is to be hated*; for it is one of the measures of the act. part. n. [used in an intensive sense]. (A'Obeyd, Ḳ.)

مِشْنَآءٌ: see the next preceding paragraph, in three places.

مَشْنُوْءٌ, applied to a man, (Ṣ,) *Hated*, (Ṣ, and so in some copies of the Ḳ, [see also شَنْآن,]) or *rendered hateful*, or *an object of hatred*, (so accord. to other copies of the Ḳ,) *even if beautiful*, or *comely*; (Ṣ, Ḳ;) and مَشْنُوٌّ and مَشْنِىٌّ signify the same. (Ḳ in art. شنو.)

مَشْنِيئَةٌ, occurring in a trad. of 'Áïsheh, [*A kind of food that is supped*, or *sipped*;] i. q. حَسَآءٌ and تَلْبِينَةٌ: [see these two words:] said by IAth to be irregularly formed from مَشْنُوءَةٌ, by changing the ء into ى [so that the word becomes مَشْنُويَةٌ, and then, by rule, مَشْنِيَّةٌ, which is mentioned in the TA, in art. شنو, as occurring thus in a trad.,] and then by restoring the ء [in the place of the second ى], the meaning being *hated*. (TA.)

شنب

1. شَنِبَ, aor. ـَ, (Ḳ,) inf. n. شَنَبٌ, (TA,) *He had the quality termed* شَنَبٌ *meaning as expl. below*. (Ḳ.) — And *It* (a day) *was*, or *became, cool*, or *cold*. (A, Ḳ.)

شَنَبٌ *Lustre, and fineness*, or *delicacy*, or *thinness, and coolness, and sweetness, in the teeth*: (A, Ḳ:) or *lustre, and fineness*, or *delicacy*, or *thinness, in the fore teeth*: (TA:) or *these two qualities, together with coolness and sweetness, in the mouth*, accord. to Aṣ, or *in the teeth*: (TA:) or *coolness and sweetness in the teeth*: or *sharpness of the teeth*: (Ṣ:) or *sharpness of the canine teeth*, like غُرُوب, *so that they appear like a saw*: (Ḳ:) or *white specks in the teeth*: (A, Ḳ:) or the *state of the teeth when they appear somewhat tinged with blackness, like the appearance of blackness in hail*; غُرُوب signifying the "lustre" of the teeth; and ظَلْم, their "whiteness that is as though there were over it a blackness:" (ISh, TA:) Abu-l-'Abbás says, It is variously expl., as *a serrated state of the teeth*: and *their clearness and cleanness*: and *their being separate*, or *apart, one from another*: and the *sweetness of their odour*: (TA:) El-Jarmee says, I heard Aṣ say that this word signifies *coolness of the mouth and teeth*; and I said, Our companions say that it is *their sharpness when they come forth*; by which is meant *their new*, or *recent, and fresh state*; for when they have undergone the lapse of years, they become abraded, or worn: but he said, It is nothing but *their coolness*: and the saying of Dhu-r-Rummeh,

وَفِى اللِّثَاتِ وَفِى أَنْيَابِهَا شَنَبُ

[which should be rendered *And in the gums, and in her canine teeth, is coolness*], corroborates the assertion of Aṣ; for there is no sharpness in the gum: (Ṣ, L, TA:) it is also related of Aṣ that he said, I asked Ru-beh respecting the meaning of شَنَبٌ, and he took a grain of pomegranate, and pointed to its lustre: (Mz, TA:) [and ▾ شُنْبَةٌ signifies the same:] a poet says,

مُنَصَّبًا خَمْشُ أَحْمَرَ يَزِينُهُ

عَوَارِضُ فِيهَا شُنْبَةٌ وَغُرُوبُ

[*Her even set* of front teeth *are slender* and *white, side teeth in which are coolness and lustre adorning them*]. (O, TA.) — [In the present day, it signifies The *mustache*.]

شَنِبٌ and ▾ شَانِبٌ, (A, Ḳ,) the former regular, the latter on the authority of usage, (TA,) *A cool*, or *cold*, day. (A, Ḳ.)

شُنْبَةٌ *Coolness*, or *coldness*, of a day. (O, Ḳ.) — See also شَنَبٌ, near the end.

شَنِيبٌ: see أَشْنَبُ.

شَانِبٌ: see شَنِبٌ: — and what here follows.

أَشْنَبُ *Having the quality termed* شَنَبٌ *meaning as expl. above*; (A, O, Ḳ;) as also ▾ شَانِبٌ, (Ḳ,) which is irregular, (TA,) and ▾ شَنِيبٌ, (Ḳ,) [which is likewise irregular;] but the first of these three is the most common: (TA:) applied to a man, (O,) and to the ثَغْر [or front teeth], (A,) [and to the mouth, as in a verse cited voce زَرْنَبٌ:] fem. شَنْبَآءُ, (Ṣ, O, Ḳ,) applied to a woman, (Ṣ, O,) and also written شَمْبَآءُ, (Ḳ,) the ن being changed into م because of the following ب, and in like manner [the pl. شُنْبٌ is also written] شُمْبٌ. (TA.) — شَنْبَآءُ also signifies A pomegranate (رُمَّانَةٌ) *such as is termed* إِمْلِيسِيَّةٌ, *having no grains, but only juice within the rind*, (A, Ḳ, TA,) *in the form of grains without stones*. (TA.)

مُشَنِّبٌ *A young boy whose teeth are sharp and serrated by reason of his youthfulness*. (IAạr, O.)

مَشَانِبُ *Sweet mouths*. (O, Ḳ.)

شنبث

Q. 1. شَنْبَثَ الهَوَى قَلْبَهُ, (Ṣ and L in art. شبث, as Q. Q., and Ḳ in the present art.,) inf. n. شَنْبَثَةٌ, (Ṣ, L,) *Love clave to his heart*. (Ṣ, L, Ḳ.)

الشُّنْبُثُ *The lion*; as also ▾ الشُّنَابِثُ. (Ḳ.)

شُنَابِثٌ *Thick, gross, big, bulky, coarse*, or *rough*; syn. غَلِيظٌ. (Ḳ.) — See also الشُّنْبُثُ.

شنبر

خِيَارٌ شَنْبَرٍ: see the former word in art. خير.

شنج

1. شَنِجَ, aor. ـَ, inf. n. شَنَجٌ; and ▾ تشنّج, (Ṣ, A, Mgh, Ḳ,) and ▾ انشنج, (Ṣ, Ḳ,) and ▾ اشنج; (TA;) said of the skin (Ṣ, Mgh, Ḳ) in consequence of the touch [or proximity] of fire [&c.], (Mgh,) and of the face, and of a member or limb, (A,) of a finger, &c., (TA,) *It contracted, shrank, shrivelled*, or *wrinkled*; or *became contracted* or *shrunk* &c. (Ṣ, A, Mgh, Ḳ, TA.) [▾ تَشَنُّجٌ is often used as meaning *Spasmodic contraction* of a muscle &c.] And one says, ▾ فِى أَعْضَائِهِ تَشَنُّجٌ and ▾ تَشْنِيجٌ [*In his limbs*, or *members, is a contraction*]. (A.)

2. شَنَّجَهُ, inf. n. تَشْنِيجٌ, *He* [or *it*] *contracted, shrunk, shrivelled*, or *wrinkled, it*; namely, the skin [&c.]. (Ṣ, Ḳ.) See 1, last sentence. One says also, شَنَّجَ الخَيَّاطُ القَبَآءَ [*The tailor puckered the tunic*]. (A. [In the Mgh, the wrinkling around the anus is said to be like the تَشْنِيج of the قَبَآء.])

4: see 1.

5: see 1, in three places; and see مُتَشَنِّجٌ.

7: see 1.

شَنَجٌ inf. n. of 1. (Ṣ &c.) — Also *A camel*: (Lth, IDrd, Ḳ:) or *a heavy camel*. (L in art. غنج.)

غَنَجٌ عَلَى شَنَجٍ is a phrase of the tribe of Hudheyl, meaning *A man upon a camel*: (Lth, IDrd, O:) or *a man*, or *an old man, upon a heavy camel*. (L in art. غنج.) — It is also said, in the L, that it signifies *An old man*, in the dial. of Hudheyl. (TA.)

شَنِجٌ, applied to the skin &c., *Contracted, shrunk, shrivelled*, or *wrinkled*. (TA.) And, applied to a man, *Contracted*, &c., *in the skin*, and *in the arm*, or *hand*; as also ▾ أَشْنَجُ. (M, TA.) And ضَيِّقَةُ الكَفِّ يَدٌ شَنِجَةٌ means [i. e. *An arm contracted*, or *narrow, in the hand*; or *a hand contracted*, &c., *in the palm*, or *in the palm and fingers*]. (TA.) شَنِجُ النَّسَا means *Contracted in the* عِرْق *called* النسا [app., in this instance, *the sciatic nerve*]: (TA:) it is an epithet of commendation applied to a horse; because, when he is contracted therein, his hind legs are not relaxed: (Ṣ, Ḳ:) or it is an epithet of commendation applied to a horse of good breed; but not so when applied to a hackney: it is also applied to some other animals, that do not walk with freedom; to a gazelle, and to a wolf: (T, TA:) and sometimes to the raven, or crow, (T, Ṣ,) which hops as though it were shackled. (T, TA.)

أَشْنَجُ: see شَنِجٌ — شَنِجٌ أَشْنَجُ and شَنِجٌ مُشَنَّجٌ are expressions sometimes used; [أَشْنَجُ being syn. with شَنِجٌ, as shown above, and in this case a corroborative; and] مُشَنَّجٌ [when thus used] meaning *Intensely contracted* or *shrunk* &c. (Lth, TA.) ═ Also *Having one of his testicles smaller than the other*; like أَشْرَجُ, which is more approved. (TA.)

مُشَنَّجٌ: see أَشْنَجُ, in two places. — قَبَآءٌ مُشَنَّجٌ [*A puckered tunic*: see 2]. (A, Mgh.) سَرَاوِيلُ مُشَنَّجَةٌ, mentioned in a trad., in which they are forbidden, are said to be *Such* [*drawers*, or *trousers*,] *as are so ample that they fall down upon the boot so as to cover half of the foot*; as though meaning that, being ample and long, they cease not to rise, and become puckered (فَتَتَشَنَّجُ). (TA.)

شنر

2. شَنَّرَ عَلَيْهِ, inf. n. تَشْنِيرٌ, *He blamed him; found fault with him; attributed* or *imputed to him*, or *accused him of*, *a vice*, or *fault*: (Ḳ:) or the same, (Ḳ,) or شَنَّرَ بِهِ, (O,) or شَنَّرَهُ, (TA,) *he rendered him infamous; exposed his vices, faults*, or *evil qualities* or *actions*; *disgraced him*; or *put him to shame*. (O, Ḳ, TA.)

شِنْرَةٌ The *gait*, or *manner of walking, of a righteous man*. (O, Ḳ.) [See also شِمْرَةٌ.]

شَنَارٌ *A vice*, or *fault*: (Ṣ, O:) or the *foulest vice* or *fault*: (Ḳ:) and *a disgrace*, or *shame*, or *thing that occasions one's being reviled*: (Ṣ, O, Ḳ:) or *a disgraceful vice* or *fault*: seldom used unless conjointly with عَارٌ: (TA:) accord. to Sh, (O,) *a thing*, or *an affair, notorious for badness* or *foulness*: (O, Ḳ:) pl. شَنَائِرُ. (TA.)

شُنَارَى one of the names of *The cat*. (O, Ḳ.*)

شُنَّارٌ *A certain white bird, found in water*: of the dial. of Syria. (TA.)

شِنِّيرٌ and شِنِّيرَةٌ, (O, Ḳ,) [the latter having an intensive meaning,] applied to a man, (O,) *Abounding in evil* or *mischief, and in vices*, or *faults*; *bad in disposition*. (O, Ḳ.)

شِنِّيرَةٌ: see what next precedes.

مَشْنُورَةٌ A *liberal, bountiful*, or *generous, woman*: as also مَنْشُورَةٌ. (IAạr, T in art. نشر, TA.)

شنز

شُونِيزٌ, (Mgh, Ḳ,) so called by the Persians, (TA,) [and generally by the Arabs in the present day,] and شُونِيزٌ, as in the "Towsheeḥ" of El-Jelál Es-Suyootee, (TA,) and شِينِيزٌ, (AḤn, L, and so in some copies of the Ḳ,) without hemz, (AḤn, L,) the proper form, for so the Arabs called it, (IAạr, TA in art. سود,) or شِئْنِيزٌ, (as in some copies of the Ḳ, and in the TA,) with hemz, (TA,) and شُؤْنُوزٌ, or شُونُوزٌ, (as in different copies of the Ḳ,) and شِهْنِيزٌ, (ADḳ, Ḳ,) *A kind of seed*, (L,) or *grain*; (Mgh;) the *same as* اَلْحَبَّةُ السَّوْدَآءُ [*the black aromatic seed of a species of nigella*; *a sort of all-spice*]; (Ḳ;) or said to be so: (Mgh:) or it is of Persian origin: (Ḳ:) so it is accord. to Ed-Deenäwaree [AḤn]: (TA:) but some say that الحبّة السوداء is the same as الحَبَّةُ الخَضْرَآءُ. (TA in art. سود.)

شنع

1. شَنُعَ, aor. ـُ, inf. n. شَنَاعَةٌ (Ṣ, O, Mṣb, Ḳ) and شُنْعٌ and شَنَاعٌ, but this last, occurring in a verse, may be used by poetic license for شَنَاعَةٌ, (TA,) *It* (a thing, Ṣ) *was*, or *became, bad, evil, abominable, foul*, or *unseemly*; (Ṣ,* O,* Mṣb, Ḳ;) syn. قَبُحَ. (Mṣb. [In the Ṣ and O and Ḳ, it is said that شَنَاعَةٌ signifies the same as فَظَاعَةٌ; but the latter seems to import more than the former.]) ═ شَنَعَ فُلَانًا *He regarded such a one as bad, evil, abominable, foul*, or *unseemly*, (اِسْتَقْبَحَهُ, Ṣ, O, Ḳ, TA, in the CḲ اِسْتَخَفَّهُ,) *and reviled*, or *vilified, him*, (شَتَمَهُ, O, Ḳ, TA, and so accord. to one of my copies of the Ṣ,) or *loathed him*, (سَئِمَهُ,) thus in some of the lexicons, [and accord. to one of my copies of the Ṣ,] but [SM says that] شَتَمَهُ is shown to be the right reading by the saying of IAạr that شَنَعَهُ, inf. n. شَنْعٌ, means سَبَّهُ. (TA.) [See also 10.] — Also, (O, Ḳ,) inf. n. شَنْعٌ, (TA,) *He disgraced such a one; put him to shame*; or *exposed his vices, faults*, or *evil qualities* or *actions*. (O, Ḳ, TA.) — And شَنَعَ الخِرْقَةَ *He frayed the torn-off piece of cloth so that it became shaggy* (شَعَّثَهَا حَتَّى تَنْفَشَ): (O, Ḳ: [in the CḲ, in the place of the last word of the explanation, which is for تَتَنَفَّشَ, is put تَنْفَشُ:]) and in like manner one says of a thing similar to a خِرْقَة. (O.) ═ شُنِعَ بِهِ: see 10.

2. التَّشْنِيعُ signifies تَكْثِيرُ الشَّنَاعَةِ [app. meaning *The uttering*, or *saying, much*, or *often, what is bad, evil, abominable, foul*, or *unseemly*: and *the doing what is bad* &c. *much* or *often*]: (Ḳ:) or *the uttering*, or *saying, what is bad, evil, abominable, foul*, or *unseemly*, (KL, PṢ,) against any one: (PṢ:) and *the representing*, or *regarding, as bad*, &c.: (KL, PṢ:*) and *the committing* [*an action that is bad*, &c., or] *a fault*, or *vitious action*. (KL.) You say, شَنَّعْتُ عَلَيْهِ, inf. n. تَشْنِيعٌ, (Ṣ, O,) *I uttered*, or *said, what was bad, evil, abominable, foul*, or *unseemly, against him*: (PṢ:) from الشَّنَاعَةُ. (O.) And شَنَّعَ عَلَيْهِ الأَمْرَ, inf. n. as above, *He showed*, or *declared, to him that the affair was bad, evil*, &c.: (TA: [see also 5:]) or *characterized the affair to him as bad, evil*, &c. (Mṣb.) ═ And *The striving, labouring*, or *exerting oneself*, and *being quick*, and *vigorous*, or *energetic*, syn. التَّشْمِيرُ, (Ṣ, O, Ḳ, TA, [in the CḲ, erroneously, التَّشْهِيرُ,]) and الاِنْكِمَاشُ, and الجِدُّ, (O, Ḳ,) in pace, or going; (O,* Ḳ;) as also التَّشَنُّعُ (Ḳ) [and الإِشْنَاعُ]: thus شنّع is said of a man, meaning *He strove, laboured*, or *exerted himself, and was quick*: (TA:) and in like manner شَنَّعَتْ is said of a she-camel, (Aṣ, A'Obeyd, Ṣ, O,) and of camels, (O,) as also تشنّعت, (Ṣ,* O, expl. in the former by جَدَّتْ only,) and اشنعت; (O;) in pace, or going: (Ṣ, O:) or اشنعت said of a she-camel means *she was quick*, or *swift*. (Ḳ.)

4: see the next preceding sentence, in three places.

5. تشنّع القَوْمَ *He showed*, or *declared, the case of the people*, or *party, to be bad, evil, abominable, foul*, or *unseemly, by reason of their disagreement, and the unsound*, or *unsettled, state of their opinion*. (TA.) ═ And تشنّع *He* (a man) *purposed to do a bad, an evil, an abominable, a foul*, or *an unseemly, thing* or *affair*. (TA.) — See also 2, last sentence, in two places. — Hence, (IAạr, TA,) *He prepared himself for fight*: (IAạr, Ḳ, TA:) or, said of a party of men, *they prepared themselves for fight*: (O:) and accord. to AA, تشنّع للشَّرِّ *He prepared himself for evil*, or *mischief*. (O, TA.) — And *It* (a garment, or piece of cloth,) *became rent*, or *slit*. (O, Ḳ.) ═ تشنّع الغَارَةَ *He spread*, or *dispersed, the horsemen making a raid*, or *sudden attack, upon an enemy*. (AA, Ṣ, O, Ḳ, TA.) — And تشنّع الفَرَسَ *He mounted the horse*. (Ṣ, O, Ḳ.) — And تشنّع السِّلَاحَ *He put on the weapon*, or *weapons*. (Ṣ, O, Ḳ.)

10. استشنعهُ *He reckoned it bad, evil, abominable, foul*, or *unseemly*. (O, TA.) And accord. to Lth, (O, TA,) one says, رَأَى أَمْرًا شُنِعَ بِهِ, meaning استشنعهُ, (O, Ḳ, TA,) i. e. [*He saw a thing*] *which he regarded as bad, evil*, &c. (TA.) — And accord. to him, one says also, قَدِ اسْتَشْنَعَ بِفُلَانٍ جَهْلُهُ, (O, TA,) meaning *His ignorance has rendered such a one light, inconstant*, or *unsteady*. (TA.)

شَنْعٌ: see شَنِيعٌ.

شُنْعَةٌ the subst. from شَنُعَ; (Ṣ, O, Ḳ;) [i. e.] *Badness, evilness, abominableness, foulness*, or *unseemliness*; syn. قُبْحٌ; (Ḥar p. 196;) as also شُنُوعٌ: (O, Ḳ:) thus in the saying, فِى فُلَانٍ شُنُوعٌ [*In such a one is unseemliness*, or *ugliness*]; as also نَظْرَةٌ and رَدٌّ [or rather رَدَّةٌ]: (TA:) and one says also, فِى وَجْهِهِ شُنْعَةٌ and رَدَّةٌ and نَظْرَةٌ [app. meaning *In his face is unseemliness*, or *ugliness*]. (IAạr, TA voce شُقْعَةٌ.) — Also *Diabolical*, or *demoniacal possession*; or *madness*, or *insanity*. (IAạr, TA.)

شُنُوعٌ: see the next preceding paragraph, in two places.

شَنِيعٌ *Bad, evil, abominable, foul*, or *unseemly*;

(Ṣ, O, Mṣb, Ḳ;) as also ▼ شَنِعٌ (O, Ḳ) and ▼ أَشْنَعُ, (Ṣ, O, Ḳ,) the last like أَكْبَرُ in the phrase اللّٰهُ أَكْبَرُ, meaning كَبِيرٌ, accord. to one of the two interpretations of this phrase: (O, TA:) pl. of the first شُنُعٌ. (Mṣb, TA.*) It is applied to a day, in this sense: or as meaning *disliked*, or *hated:* (TA:) and so is ▼ أَشْنَعُ, (Ṣ, O, Ḳ, TA,) in the former sense, (TA,) or in the latter. (O, Ḳ, TA.) And you say مَنْظَرٌ شَنِيعٌ and ▼ مُشَنَّعٌ [*An aspect that is bad, evil,* &c.] and ▼ اِمْرَأَةٌ مُشَنَّعَةٌ, meaning قَبِيحَةٌ [i. e. *An unseemly,* or *ugly, woman*]. (TA.) And اِسْمٌ شَنِيعٌ [*An evil,* or *abominable, name*]: and قَوْمٌ شُنُعُ الأَسَامِى [*A people,* or *party, having evil,* or *abominable, names*]. (A, TA.) And ▼ قِصَّةٌ شَنْعَآءُ [*An evil,* or *abominable,* or *a foul, story*]. (TA.) And ▼ غَيْرَةٌ شَنْعَآءُ *Abominable, excessive jealousy:* (O, Ḳ, TA:) in [some of] the copies of the Ḳ, erroneously, غبرة. (TA.)

شَنْعَنَعٌ *Incongruous, unsound, weak,* or *faulty,* [and therefore *unseemly,*] *in make;* (IDrd, O, Ḳ, TA;) as also ▼ أَشْنَعُ ▼ الخَلْقِ; applied to a man: the former is from الشُّنُوعُ: and some say that it signifies *tall.* (TA.)

أَشْنَعُ; and its fem. شَنْعَآءُ: see شَنِيعٌ, in four places: and see also شَنْعَنَعٌ.

مَشْنَعٌ: see مَشْنَأٌ, in art. شنأ.

مُشَنَّعٌ; and its fem., with ة: see شَنِيعٌ, in two places.

مَشْنُوعٌ i. q. مَشْهُورٌ [*Well,* or *commonly, known; notorious;* &c.]. (O, L, Ḳ.)

شنف

1. شَنِفْتُ إِلَى الشَّىْءِ, (Ṣ,) aor. ـَ, (O, Mṣb,) inf. n. شَنَفٌ, (Ṣ, O, Ḳ,) *I looked in a state of opposition,* or *resistance,* (فِى ٱعْتِرَاضٍ,) *at the thing;* like شَفِنْتُ: (Ṣ, O:*) or الشَّنْفُ signifies *the looking* at a thing, (O,) or *the looking* at a thing *like him who is opposing it,* or *resisting it,* (كَالمُعْتَرِضِ عَلَيْهِ, Ḳ, TA,) and *the raising of the eyes in looking at a thing,* (TA,) *like him who wonders at it,* or *like him who dislikes it,* or *hates it;* (O, Ḳ, TA;) and so الشَّفْنُ, as AZ says. (TA.) [See also 2.] — شَنِفَ لَهُ, (Ṣ, O, Ḳ,) and also, or, correctly, accord. to ISd, this verb is trans. in the sense here next following without any particle, (TA,) [but two exs. are cited in the O from trads. in which it is trans. by means of ل,] aor. ـَ, (Ṣ, Ḳ,) inf. n. شَنَفٌ, (Ṣ, O,) *He hated him,* (أَبْغَضَهُ,) and *met him in a morose manner:* (Ṣ, O, Ḳ: [in the Ḳ, the latter meaning is expressed by تَنَكَّرَهُ, for تَنَكَّرَ لَهُ: in the Ṣ and O, the former meaning is expressed as above, on the authority of ISk; and it is also said that الشَّنَفُ is syn. with البُغْضُ and التَّنَكُّرُ:] in the former of these two senses it is like شَنِئَهُ, with ء: (Ṣ, O:) or الشنف [i. e. الشَّنْفُ] is a subst. signifying *vehemence of enmity.* (Ḥam p. 108.) — And شَنَفَ لَهُ, (IAạr, ISd, O,* Ḳ, TA,) and بِهِ, (ISd, TA,) i. q. فَطِنَ [i. e. *He knew it; knew, had knowledge,* or *was cognizant, of it;* or *knew it instinctively;* &c.]. (IAạr, ISd, O, Ḳ, TA.) — And شَنَفَ, (Ḳ, TA, [in the former of which it is erroneously implied that the verb is followed by لَهُ,]) *His upper lip turned upwards;* (Ḳ, TA;) inf. n. شَنْفٌ; (TA;) or this is a subst., signifying *a turning upwards of the upper lip:* so says AZ. (O.)

2. شَنَّفَهَا, inf. n. تَشْنِيفٌ, *He adorned her* (i. e. a woman, Ṣ, or a girl, or young woman, O, Ḳ) *with the* [*ornament called*] شَنْف; (Ṣ, O, Ḳ;) like as one says, قَرَّطَهَا; (Ṣ, TA;) as also ▼ أَشْنَفَهَا. (Zj, O, Ḳ.) — [Hence,] شَنَّفَ كَلَامَهُ وَقَرَّطَهُ ‡ [*He adorned and embellished his language*]. (TA.) — شَنَّفَ إِلَيْهِ, inf. n. as above, *He looked at him,* or *it, from the outer corner of the eye.* (Yaạḳoob, TA.) [See also 1.]

4: see the next preceding paragraph.

5. تشنّفت *She adorned herself with the* [*ornament called*] شَنْف; (Ṣ, O, Ḳ;) like as one says, تقرّطت. (Ṣ.)

شَنْفٌ (incorrectly pronounced with ḍamm, IDrd, O, Ḳ, i. e. شُنْفٌ, O, TA) *The upper* قُرْط [i. e. *ear-ring* or *ear-drop*]: (Ṣ, O, Ḳ:) or *a pendant* (مِعْلَاق) *in* [or *suspended from*] *the* قُوف [app. meaning the *upper part,* or perhaps, the *helix,* in the CḲ erroneously written فَوْق,] *of the ear;* (Lth, O, Ḳ;) and likewise *such as is attached to necklaces:* (Lth, O:) or *such as is suspended from the upper part of the ear;* what is suspended from the lower part [or lobe] thereof being termed قُرْط; (IDrd, O, Ḳ;) or this latter is termed رَعْثَةٌ: (IAạr, TA:) or, as some say, i. q. قُرْط: (TA:) pl. [of mult.] شُنُوفٌ (IDrd, Ṣ, O, Ḳ) and [of pauc.] أَشْنَافٌ. (TA.)

شَنِفٌ *Hating,* (Ṣ, O, Ḳ,) and *meeting in a morose manner.* (Ḳ.) IB cites, as an ex.,

* وَلَنْ تُدَاوِى عِلَّةَ القَلْبِ الشَّنِفْ *

[*And thou wilt not cure the hating heart*]. (TA.)

شَفَةٌ شَنْفَآءُ [*A lip,* meaning an upper lip] *turning upwards:* (O:) or شَاةٌ شَنْفَآءُ [*A sheep* or *goat*] *having the upper lip turning upwards.* (TA.)

شَانِفٌ *Turning away,* or *averse.* (O, Ḳ.) One says, مَا لِى أَرَاكَ شَانِفًا عَنِّى *What ails me that I see thee turning away, or averse, from me?* (O.) — And إِنَّهُ لَشَانِفٌ عَنَّا بِأَنْفِهِ ‡ *Verily he is raising his nose* [*in aversion*] *from us.* (O,* Ḳ.)

مَشْنُوفَةٌ † A she-camel *having a* زِمَام [or *nose-rein*] *attached to her.* (AA, O, Ḳ.)

شنق

1. شَنَقَ البَعِيرَ, aor. ـِ (Ṣ, M, Mṣb, Ḳ) and ـُ, (M, Ḳ,) inf. n. شَنْقٌ, (Ṣ, M, Mṣb,) *He curbed the camel by means of his* زِمَام [or *nose-rein*], (Ṣ, Ḳ,) or *pulled the* خِطَام [or *halter,* or *leading-rope,*] *of the camel,* (M,) *while riding him,* (Ṣ, M,) *in the direction of his* [*own*] *head,* (M,) *so as to make the prominences behind his* [*the camel's*] *ears cleave to the upright piece of wood rising from the fore part of the saddle:* (M, Ḳ:) or *he raised the camel's head* (M, Mṣb, Ḳ) *by pulling his* زِمَام, (M, Mṣb,) *while riding him,* (Mṣb, Ḳ,) *like as the rider of the horse does with his horse:* (Mṣb:) and ▼ اشنقهُ signifies the same: (Ṣ, M, Mṣb, Ḳ:) or ▼ اشنق is intrans.; you say, شَنَقَ البَعِيرَ and هُوَ ▼ اشنق, the reverse of the usual rule; (IJ, M;) or the latter is intrans. also; (Ṣ, Mṣb, Ḳ;) signifying *he* (the camel) *raised his head.* (Ṣ, M, Mṣb, Ḳ.*) — Hence, شَنَقْتُهَا, occurring in a trad., referring to a female hare, inf. n. as above, means, as implying restraint, *I cast,* or *shot, at her,* or *I struck her, so as to render her incapable of motion.* (O.) — And شَنَقَ البَعِيرَ, or النَّاقَةَ, (M, Ḳ,) inf. n. as above, (M,) *He bound the he-camel,* or *the she-camel, with the* شِنَاق [q. v.]. (M, Ḳ.) — And شَنَقَ رَأْسَ الدَّابَّةِ, (M,) or رَأْسَ الفَرَسِ, (Ḳ,) ‡ *He bound* (M, Ḳ) *the head of the beast,* (M,) or *the head of the horse,* (Ḳ,) *to the upper part of a tree,* (M,) or *to the head of a tree,* or *to a tree,* (accord. to different copies of the Ḳ,) or *to a peg,* (M,) or *to an elevated peg,* (Ḳ,) *so that his neck became extended and erect.* (M, TA.) — And شَنَقَ القِرْبَةَ, (IDrd, O, Ḳ,) aor. ـُ, (IDrd, O,) inf. n. as above, (TA,) † *He bound the mouth of the water-skin with the bond called* وِكَآء, *and then bound the extremity of its* وِكَآء *to its fore legs:* (IDrd, O, Ḳ, TA: [in the CḲ, أُوكَاهَا is erroneously put for أَوْكَاهَا, or, as in some copies of the Ḳ, وَكَاهَا:]) or *he suspended it:* and [in like manner] ▼ اشنق القِرْبَةَ, inf. n. as above, *he suspended the water-skin to a peg:* (TA:) or the latter signifies *he put a* شِنَاق *to the water-skin:* (M:) or he *bound the water-skin with a* شِنَاق, (Ṣ, Ḳ, TA,) i. e. *a cord with which its mouth is bound.* (Ṣ.) — [Hence شَنَقَهُ, as used in the present day, and in post-classical works, meaning † *He hanged him by the neck, till he died:* (see the pass. part. n., below:) whence ▼ مِشْنَقَةٌ, meaning *A gallows;* pl. مَشَانِقُ.] — شَنَقَ الخَلِيَّةَ, (M, Ḳ,) aor. ـُ, inf. n. شَنْقٌ; (M;) and ▼ شنّقها, (M, Ḳ,) inf. n. تَشْنِيقٌ; (TA;) *He put a piece of wood, which is called* ▼ شَنِيقٌ, (M, Ḳ,) *pared for the purpose,* (M,) *into the hive, and with it raised a portion of the honey-comb in the width of the hive,* (M, Ḳ,*) *having fixed the* شَنِيق *beneath it; and sometimes two portions of the honey-comb, and three:* (M: [accord. to which one says also, شَنَقَ فِى الخَلِيَّةِ القُرْصَيْنِ وَالثَّلَاثَةَ:]) *this is done only when the bees are rearing their young ones.* (M, Ḳ.*) — Accord. to Aboo-Sa'eed, شَنَقْتُهُ and ▼ أَشْنَقْتُ الشَّىْءَ signify the same: (TA: [in which the meaning is not expl.; but it is immediately added, app. to indicate the meaning here intended;]) El-Mutanakhkhil El-Hudhalee says, describing a bow and arrows,

* شَنَقْتُ بِهَا مَعَابِلَ مُرْهَفَاتٍ *

i. e. *I put its string into* [*the notches of*] *arrows* [*broad and long in the heads, made sharp or* *pointed*]. (O,* TA.) ▬ شَنِقَ, (M, Ḳ,) aor. ـَ; (Ḳ;) and شَنَقَ, (M, Ḳ,) aor. ـِ; (Ḳ;) *He loved a thing, and became attached to it*; (M, Ḳ, TA;) said of a man: (TA:) and شَنِقَ, inf. n. شَنَقٌ, is said of a man's heart, (O, TA,) meaning as above: (O:) or شَنَقٌ signifies the heart's *yearning towards*, or *longing for*, or *desiring, a thing*. (Mṣb.) ▬ شَنَقٌ also signifies The *being long*: (M:) or the *being long in the head*, (JK, Ṣ, TA,) *as though it were stretched upwards*: (TA:) one says of a horse, شَنِقَ inf. n. شَنَقٌ, meaning *He was long in the head*. (JK.) — شَنَقُ المَرْأَةِ, signifies اِسْتِنَانُهَا مِنَ الشَّحْمِ [app. meaning *The woman's becoming sleek, like* مِسَانّ (or *whetstones*) *by reason of fat*: see اِسْتَنَّتِ الفِصَالُ, in art. سن]: and the epithet applied to her is ▼ شَنِقَةٌ, pl. شَنِقَاتٌ. (JK, Ibn-'Abbád, O, TA.)

2. شَنَّقَ النَّخْلَةَ, inf. n. تَشْنِيقٌ: see 1, in the latter half of the paragraph. — تَشْنِيقٌ also signifies The *cutting* [a thing] *in pieces*. (O, Ḳ. [See the pass. part. n.]) — And The *adorning* [a person or thing]. (Ḳ. [See 5.]) — See also the next paragraph, near the end.

3. شانقه, inf. n. مُشَانَقَةٌ and شِنَاقٌ, *He mixed his cattle with his* [i. e. another's] *cattle*: (Ḳ, TA:) this is when [contributions to the poor-rate such as are termed] أَشْنَاقٌ [pl. of شَنَقٌ] are incumbent on a man, or two men, or three, when their cattle are separate, and one says to another, شَانِقْنِى, i. e. *Mix thou my cattle and thy cattle*; for if they are separate, a شَنَق will be obligatory, or incumbent, on each of us; and if they are mixed, the case will be light to us: so the شِنَاق signifies the *sharing in the* شَنَق or *in the* شَنَقَانِ. (L, TA.) [See also what follows in this paragraph: and see شَنَقٌ.] One says also ▼ لَا تَشَانَقُوا [for لَا تَتَشَانَقُوا] *Ye shall not put together what are separate* [of cattle]; التَّشَانُقُ being syn. with المُشَانَقَةُ. (TA.) — شِنَاقٌ signifies also The *taking somewhat from the* شَنَق: and hence the trad., لَا شِنَاقَ: (Ḳ, TA:) this means *There shall not be taken from the* شَنَق [any contribution to the poor-rate] *unless it is complete* [in number]: (A'Obeyd, Ṣ, TA:) the شَنَق being, of camels, such as exceed five, up to ten; and what exceed ten, up to fifteen: (A'Obeyd, TA:) Aboo-Sa'eed Eḍ-Ḍareer says, *up to nine*; and *up to fourteen*: but this is pronounced in the L to be wrong: (TA:) [Mṭr also says,] it means *there shall not be taken aught of what exceed five, up to nine*, for example: or, accord. to Aboo-Sa'eed Eḍ-Ḍareer, it is like the mixing; but this requires consideration: (Mgh:) Aboo-Sa'eed says that لَا شِنَاقَ means *a man shall not adjoin* (▼ لَا يُشْنِقُ [thus written here and thus expl. in the TA]) *his sheep* or *goats*, and *his camels, to the sheep* or *goats* [and *the camels*] *of another person*, in order to annul what is obligatory, or incumbent, on him, of the poor-rate: this is [for instance] in the case in which each of them has forty sheep or goats; so that it is incumbent on them to give two sheep or goats; but when one of them adjoins (فَإِذَا شَنَّقَ ▼ أَحَدُهُمَا [thus in this instance in the TA, perhaps a mistranscription for أَشْنَقَ,]) his sheep or goats to those of another, and the collector of the poor-rate finds them in his [the latter's] possession, he takes from them one sheep or goat. (TA.)

4. اشنق: see 1, in five places. — إِشْنَاقٌ [as inf. n. of أَشْنَقَ, from أَشْنَقَ القِرْبَةَ expl. in the first paragraph,] also signifies The *having the hand attached to the neck by means of a* غُلّ [q. v.]. (AA, TA.) — See also 3, in the latter half. ▬ Accord. to IAạr, (O, TA,) اشنق also signifies *He took* (O, Ḳ, TA) *the* شَنَق, i. e., (O, TA,) *the* [*fine termed*] أَرْش: (O, Ḳ, TA:) or *it was*, or *became, obligatory*, or *incumbent, on him to give the* أَرْش; thus having two contr. meanings [assigned to it]: (Ḳ:) or it signifies also, accord. to IAạr, *it was*, or *became, obligatory on him to give what is termed a* شَنَق; and this is the case until his camels amount to five and twenty, when what is due of them is [a she-camel such as is termed] اِبْنَةُ مَخَاضٍ. (O.) A man of the Arabs said, مِنَّا مَنْ يُشْنِقُ, which may mean *Of us is he who gives the* شُنُق, i. e. *cords*, pl. of شِنَاقٌ: or it may mean, *who gives the* شَنَق, i. e. أَرْش. (O.) — اشنق عَلَيْهِ *He exalted himself above him*; *domineered over him*; or *oppressed him*. (O, Ḳ.)

5. تشنّق *He adorned himself*; or *was*, or *became, adorned*: (JK, O:) and *he clad himself with garments*. (JḲ.)

6: see 3.

شَنَقٌ *What is between one* فَرِيضَة *and the next* فَرِيضَة, (A'Obeyd, Ṣ, M, Mgh, Mṣb, Ḳ, TA,) [meaning *a number that is between two other numbers whereof each imposes the obligation of giving a due termed* فَرِيضَة,] of camels, and of sheep or goats, (M, TA,) *in relation to the poor-rate*: (Ṣ, Mgh, Ḳ, TA:) so called because nothing is taken therefrom; so that it is adjoined (أُشْنِقَ i. e. أُضِيفَ) to that [number] which is next to it [of the numbers below it]: (JM:) accord. to some, it is syn. with وَقَصٌ; (Mgh, Mṣb;) but some say that it relates peculiarly to camels; (M, Mgh, Mṣb;) and وَقَصٌ, to bulls and cows: (Mgh, Mṣb:) used in relation to sheep or goats, it is *what is between forty and a hundred and twenty*; and in like manner as to other numbers [that impose the obligation of giving a فريضة]: (Ḳ, TA:) Aḥmad Ibn-Ḥambal is related to have said that the شَنَق is *what is above the* فريضة, absolutely; *as, for instance, what is above forty sheep* or *goats*: (TA: [I here render the word دُونَ "above," though it also means "below," because nothing is due from sheep or goats fewer than forty:]) as A'Obeyd says, it is, of camels, *such as exceed five, up to ten*; and *what exceed ten, up to fifteen*: (O,* TA: [see also 3:]) Ks states, on the authority of some one or more of the Arabs, that it is *up to twenty-five*; and says that it is *what does not impose the obligation of the* فريضة; meaning *what is between five and twenty-five*: (Fr, TA:) [but it is also expl. as applied to the *due itself that is to be contributed to the poor-rates for certain numbers of camels*: thus] Aboo-'Amr Esh-Sheybánee says, *the* شَنَق *for five camels is a sheep* or *goat*; *for ten, two sheep* or *goats*; *for fifteen, three sheep* or *goats*; and *for twenty, four sheep* or *goats*; the term شَنَق being applied alike to the sheep or goat, and to the two sheep or goats, and to the three sheep or goats, and to the four sheep or goats; what exceeds this last being termed فَرِيضَة: (TA:) or, *in the case of the poor-rate, the lowest* شَنَق (الشَّنَقُ الأَسْفَلُ) *is a sheep* or *goat for five camels*; and *the highest* شَنَق (الشَّنَقُ الأَعْلَى) *is a* بِنْت مَخَاضٍ *for five and twenty*: (O, Ḳ:) the pl. of شَنَقٌ is أَشْنَاقٌ (M, Mṣb, TA) and شِنَاقٌ. (M.) — Also *What is above the bloodwit* (مَا دُونَ الدِّيَةِ): (Aṣ, Ṣ, O, Mṣb, Ḳ:) the term أَشْنَاقٌ, (Ṣ, M, Mṣb,) pl. of شَنَقٌ, (M,) being applied to the *fines, for wounds, that are sent with the complete bloodwit* (Ṣ, M,* O, Mṣb) *by him upon whom rests the obligation to send such*; (Ṣ, O, Mṣb;) as though they were attached to the main, or greatest, fine: (Ṣ, M,* O:) and *an addition, in the bloodwit*, (M, Mṣb,) *of five*, (M,) or *of six*, (M, Mṣb,) or *of seven*, (Mṣb,) *to the hundred camels* [*which constitute the complete bloodwit*], (M, Mṣb,*) in order that it may be described as ample: (Mṣb:) [for,] as IAạr and Aṣ and El-Athram say, the man of rank or quality, when he gave [the bloodwit], used to add to it five [or more] camels, to show thereby his excellence and his generosity: (TA:) *a redundancy* [*in the case of the bloodwit*]; (O, Ḳ;) one of the explanations of the term given by Aṣ: (O:) or *in the case of bloodwits* (دِيَات), *the lowest* شَنَق (الشَّنَقُ الأَسْفَلُ) *is twenty camels whereof every one is a* بِنْت مَخَاضٍ; and *the highest* شَنَق (الشَّنَقُ الأَعْلَى) *is twenty camels whereof every one is a* جَذَعَة: (O, Ḳ:) and some say that أَشْنَاقُ الدِّيَاتِ means *the sorts of bloodwits*; *the bloodwit for purely-unintentional homicide being a hundred camels, which those who are responsible for it undertake to give in fifths, consisting of twenty whereof every one is an* اِبْنَة مَخَاضٍ, *and twenty whereof every one is an* اِبْنَة لَبُونٍ, *and twenty whereof every one is an* اِبْن لَبُونٍ, *and twenty whereof every one is a* حِقَّة, *and twenty whereof every one is a* جَذَعَة; *these also being termed* أَشْنَاق. (TA.) — It signifies also *A fine*, or *mulct, for a wound* or *the like*; (O, Mṣb, Ḳ;) *as, for instance, for a burn*, (O, TA,) or *such as a wound on the head that lays bare the bone*, (Mṣb, TA,) *and other wounds*, (Mṣb,) *and for a tooth* [*knocked out*], *and for an eye blinded*, *and for an arm* or *a hand vitiated*, or *rendered unsound and motionless*, or *stiff*; *and for anything short of what requires the complete bloodwit*: (TA:) or, as some say, *a fine for that which does not render obnoxious to retaliation*; *as a scratch*, or *laceration of the skin*, and *the like*: (M:) pl. أَشْنَاقٌ. (M, Mṣb.) ▬ Also *A burden borne on one side of a beast, equiponderant to another borne on the other side*; syn. عِدْلٌ: (Ḳ, TA: [in the CḲ and my MS. copy of the Ḳ, العَدْلُ is erroneously put for العِذْلُ :]) الشَّنَقَانِ signifies العِذْلَانِ. (JK, Ibn-'Abbád, O, TA.*) — And *A rope, or cord.* (Ibn-'Abbád, O, Ḳ.) — And *A bow-string;* (O, TA;) as also ▼ شِنَاقٌ; (O, Ḳ,* TA;) so called because it is bound to the head of the bow: (O, TA:) or, accord. to Sh, *a good bow-string,* i. e. *strong and long.* (TA.) [See what follows.] ═ الشَّنَقُ also signifies العَمَلُ [*The making a thing*]: (Ḳ:) thus accord. to some in the saying of Ru-beh, describing a sportsman [and his bow],

* سَوَّى لَهَا كَبْدَاءَ تَنْزُو فِي الشَّنَقْ *

[as though meaning *He prepared for it,* or *them,* a bow *such that the part whereby it was held filled the hand, springing in the making* by reason of its elasticity and strength: but the word which I have written تَنْزُو, and which is thus in one place in the TA, and in another place in the same, where the verse is repeated, تَنْزُوا, is illegible in the copy of the O, and may be a mistranscription]: accord. to others, however, the last word, الشَّنَق, here means *the bow-string.* (O, TA.)

شَنِقٌ, applied to a heart, *Loving intensely,* or *very passionately* or *fondly;* syn. هَيْمَانُ. (M, TA.) Accord. to Lth, ▼ قَلْبٌ شَنِقٌ مِشْنَاقٌ signifies طَامِحٌ إِلَى كُلِّ شَىْءٍ [app. meaning *A heart aspiring to everything*]: (O, L, TA:) in the Ḳ, قَلْبٌ شَنِقٌ كَكَتِفٍ مُشْتَاقٌ طَامِحٌ إِلَى كُلِّ شَىْءٍ; but the right reading is قَلْبٌ شَنِقٌ مِشْنَاقٌ كَكَتِفٍ وَمِحْرَابٍ, and the signification as above; primarily relating to the eye. (TA.) — Applied to a man, *Cautious;* or *fearful.* (TA.) — شَنِقَةٌ, applied to a woman: see 1, last sentence.

شِنَاقٌ *A rope,* or *cord, with which the head of a he-camel and of a she-camel is pulled:* [see 1, first sentence:] pl. [of pauc.] أَشْنِقَةٌ and [of mult.] شُنُقٌ. (M, TA.) — *A cord,* (A'Obeyd, Ṣ, Ḳ,) or *thong,* (A'Obeyd, Ḳ,) *with which the mouth of a water-skin is bound,* (A'Obeyd, Ṣ, Mgh, Ḳ,) and *that of a leathern water-bag, and which is untied in order that the water may pour forth:* (A'Obeyd, TA:) or the *suspensory cord of a water-skin:* and *any cord by which a thing is suspended.* (M.) — See also شَنَقٌ, in the last quarter of the paragraph. ═ As an epithet, *Tall:* (ISh, Ṣ, Ḳ:) used alike as masc. and fem. (ISh, Ḳ) and dual (ISh) and pl., (ISh, Ḳ,) not dualized nor pluralized: (ISh:) applied to a man, (Ṣ, TA,) and to a woman, and to a he-camel, and to a she-camel: applied to a she-camel as meaning *tall, and long-necked;* as also ▼ شَنْقَاءُ: and to a he-camel as meaning *tall and slender:* (ISh, TA:) also, and ▼ مَشْنُوقٌ, applied to a horse as meaning *tall.* (T, TA.) See also أَشْنَقُ.

شَنِيقٌ One *whose origin is suspected;* syn. دَعِىٌّ: a poet says,

* أَنَا الدَّاخِلُ البَابَ الَّذِى لَا يَرُومُهُ *

* دَنِىٌّ وَلَا يُدْعَى إِلَيْهِ شَنِيقُ *

[*I am he who enters the door that the ignoble seeks not, and to which one whose origin is suspected is not invited*]. (Ṣ.) ═ See also 1, latter half.

شِنِّيقٌ A man *evil in disposition:* (M, L:) or a *self-conceited* young man. (JK, Ibn-'Abbád, O, Ḳ.) And شِنِّيقَةٌ, like سِكِّينَةٌ, [in some copies of the Ḳ شَنِيقَةٌ, like سَكِينَةٌ,] A woman *talking, or conversing,* or *who talks,* or *converses, in an amorous and enticing manner.* (JK, Ibn-'Abbád, O, Ḳ.)

شَنْقَنَاقٌ a name for *A calamity* or *misfortune* (دَاهِيَةٌ): (Ibn-'Abbád, O, Ḳ:*) or, as some say, a name of *The chiefs of the Jinn,* or *Genii:* (Ibn-'Abbád, O:) or also *a certain chief of the Jinn.* (Ḳ.)

أَشْنَقُ *Long;* applied to a neck. (M.) And, as also ▼ مَشْنُوقٌ, *Long in the head;* applied to a horse and to a camel; and so شَنْقَاءُ [the fem. of the former] and ▼ شِنَاقٌ applied to the female. (M.) For the fem., see also شِنَاقٌ. ═ [The fem.] شَنْقَاءُ signifies [also] A female bird *that feeds her young ones with her bill, ejecting the food into their mouths.* (O, Ḳ.)

مَشْنَقَةٌ: see 1, in the latter half of the paragraph.

مُشَنَّقٌ Flesh-meat (Ks, Ṣ) *cut in pieces:* (Ks, Ṣ, Ḳ:) applied to flesh-meat, (M,) it is from the أَشْنَاق [pl. of شَنَقٌ] of the دِيَة [or bloodwit]. (Ks, Ṣ, M.) — And *Dough cut into pieces, and prepared with oil of olives:* (El-Umawee, Ṣ, M, Ḳ:) or *dough cut into lumps,* or *pieces, upon the table, before it is spread out;* also called فَرَزْدَقٌ and عَجَاجِيرُ. (IAạr, TA.)

مِشْنَاقٌ: see شَنِقٌ.

مَشْنُوقٌ [as pass. part. n. of شَنَقَ means *Curbed by means of his nose-rein,* &c. — And] † *Hanged:* one says, قُتِلَ مَشْنُوقًا † *He was put to death* [by being] *hanged.* (TA.) ═ See also شِنَاقٌ: and أَشْنَقُ.

شنو

مَشْنُوٌّ and مَشْنِىٌّ: see مَشْنُوءٌ, in art. شنأ.

مَشْنِيَّةٌ: see مَشْنِيئَةٌ, in art. شنأ.

شهب

1. شَهِبَ, (Ṣ, Mṣb, Ḳ,) aor. ـَ, (Mṣb, Ḳ,) inf. n. شَهَبٌ, (Ṣ, Mgh, Mṣb, Ḳ,*) *It* (a thing, Ṣ) *was,* or *became, of the colour termed* شُهْبَة, (Ṣ, Mṣb, Ḳ,) i. e. *of a* [*gray*] *colour in which whiteness predominated over blackness,* (Ṣ, Mgh, Mṣb,) or *in which whiteness was interrupted by blackness;* (Ḳ,* TA;) as also شَهُبَ, aor. ـُ; and ▼ اشهبّ; (Ḳ;) the last, inf. n. اِشْهِبَابٌ, said in the former sense of a horse; as also ▼ اشهابّ, inf. n. اِشْهِيبَابٌ; (Ṣ;) and this last verb, said of the head, *its whiteness predominated over its blackness;* (TA;) as also ▼ اشتهب. (Ṣ, TA.) ═ شَهَبَهُ, aor. ـَ, (Ḳ,) inf. n. شَهْبٌ, (TḲ,) said of heat and of cold, *It altered his colour;* as also ▼ شَهَّبَهُ: (Ḳ:) or, accord. to A'Obeyd, (TA,) شَهَّبَ ▼ الشَّجَرَ, (O, TA,) inf. n. تَشْهِيبٌ, (O,) said of cold, *It altered the colour of the trees:* and شَهَّبَ ▼ النَّاسَ is likewise said of cold [as meaning *It altered the colour of the men* or *people*]. (O, TA.) — And شَهَبَتِ السَّنَةُ القَوْمَ *The year of drought destroyed the cattle* (أَمْوَال) *of the people* or *party:* (so accord. to the CḲ and my MS. copy of the Ḳ:) or the verb in this sense is ▼ أَشْهَبَتْ. (So accord. to the text of the Ḳ as given in the TA.) — [Freytag erroneously assigns to this verb, as from the Ḳ, another meaning, belonging to 4.]

2: see the preceding paragraph, in three places.

4. اشهب, said of a stallion, *He had offspring of the colour termed* شُهْبَة *born to him:* so accord. to the Ḳ: but accord. to IM and the other lexicologists, it is said of a man, meaning *the offspring of his horses were of the colour termed* شُهْبَة: IAạr says that there are not, among horses, such as are termed شُهْب [pl. of أَشْهَبُ]: A'Obeyd, however, [as will be seen below,] explains شُهْبَة as meaning a colour of horses. (TA.) — See also 1, last sentence but one.

8 and 9: see 1, first sentence.

11: see 1, first sentence. — Also, said of seed-produce, ‡ *It dried up,* or *became yellow,* (Ṣ, A,) *but with somewhat green remaining in its interstices:* (Ṣ:) or *was near to yielding, and became white, and dried up, but with a little greenness remaining in its interstices.* (TA.) — Accord. to the L, one says also اشهابّت مَشَافِرُهُ [app. meaning *His lips became of an ashy hue*]. (TA.)

شَهْبٌ *A mountain overspread with snow.* (O, Ḳ.) ═ And a boy, or young man, *light,* or *active, in body, and sharp-headed.* (IAạr, TA voce عَضْبٌ. [See also شِهَابٌ.])

شَهَبٌ: see what next follows.

شُهْبَةٌ *A* [*gray*] *colour in which whiteness predominates over blackness,* (Ṣ, Mṣb,) or *in which whiteness is interrupted by blackness;* as also ▼ شَهَبٌ; (A, Ḳ;) which latter is [properly] an inf. n., of شَهِبَ: (Ṣ, Mṣb:) or *whiteness mixed with blackness:* (Ḥar p. 150:) not pure whiteness, as some have imagined it to be. (TA.) And in horses, *A colour in which the main hue is interrupted by a hoariness, or by some white hairs, whether the horse be* [*in his general colour*] أَدْهَم or أَشْقَر or كُمَيْت. (A'Obeyd, TA.)

شَهْبَانُ *A kind of plant* (شَجَرٌ), *resembling the* ثُمَام [or panic grass]; (Ḳ;) like شَبَهَانٌ. (TA. [But see this last word.])

شَهَابٌ (AḤát, Ṣ, Ḳ) and ▼ شَهَابَةٌ (AḤát, Kr, Ḳ) *Milk mixed with much water:* (AḤát, Ṣ:) or *a mixture of which one third is milk and the rest water:* (Ḳ, TA:) Az heard several of the Arabs apply the former term to *milk mixed with water:* so called on account of the alteration of its colour. (TA.)

شِهَابٌ, in its primary acceptation, *A* شُعْلَة [i. e. either *brand* or *flame* (app. the former, agreeably with what follows,)] *of fire*: (TA:) or *a* شُعْلَة *of fire gleaming* or *radiating*: (Ṣ, Ḳ:) accord. to ISk, *a firebrand*; i. e. *a stick in which is fire*: or, accord. to AHeyth, originally, *a piece of wood*, or *stick, in which is fire gleaming* or *radiating*: (Az, TA:) pl. شُهُبٌ, (Ṣ, Ḳ,) and some allow شُهْبٌ, (TA,) and شُهْبَانٌ (Akh, Ṣ, Ḳ) and شِهْبَانٌ, (Ḳ,) which is strange, (TA,) and أَشْهُبٌ, (Ḳ,) which last is [a pl. of pauc., but] thought by IM to be a quasi-pl. n. (TA.) The reading بِشِهَابِ قَبَسٍ, instead of بِشِهَابٍ قَبَسٍ, in the Ḳur [xxvii. 7], is an instance of a word prefixed to another identical therewith. (Fr. L.) — Hence, [*A shooting*, or *falling, star*;] *a star*, or *the like of a star, that darts down* [or *is hurled*] *by night*; and particularly *after a devil*; as occurring in the Ḳur [xv. 18 and] xxxvii. 10; and in a trad.; respecting the attempt of a devil to hear, by stealth, words uttered in heaven. (TA.) — [Hence also,] الشُّهُبُ signifies *The shining*, or *brightly-shining, stars*: (Ḳ:) or *the seven stars* [or *planets*; meaning, not the Pleiades (which are called النَّجْمُ), but *the Moon, Mercury, Venus, the Sun, Mars, Jupiter, and Saturn*: the first three of which are said by Freytag to be called صِغَارُ الشُّهُبِ]. (TA.) — For another meaning assigned in the K to الشُّهُبُ, see أَشْهَبُ. — شِهَابٌ also signifies ‡ *One who is penetrating, sharp*, or *energetic*, in an affair; (Ḳ, TA;) as being likened to the [shooting] star. (TA.) One says, إِنَّ فُلَانًا لَشِهَابُ حَرْبٍ ‡ *Verily such a man is one who is penetrating, sharp*, or *energetic, in war*. (Ṣ, A.*) And هٰؤُلَآءِ شُهْبَانُ الجَيْشِ ‡ [*These are the braves*, or *heroes, of the army*]. (A.) — Also the name of *A certain devil*: occurring in a trad.: hence the Prophet changed the name of a certain man [originally] thus named. (TA.)

شُهَابَةٌ: see شِهَابٌ.

كَتِيبَةٌ شُهَابَةٌ: see أَشْهَبُ.

شَاهِبٌ: see أَشْهَبُ, first sentence.

شَوْهَبٌ The *hedge-hog*; syn. قُنْفُذٌ. (Ṣ, Ḳ.)

أَشْهَبُ *Of the colour termed* شُهْبَة; (Ṣ, Mṣb, Ḳ;) as also ♦ شَاهِبٌ, (Ḳ,) occurring in the poetry of Hudheyl: (TA:) fem. of the former شَهْبَآءُ: (Ṣ, Mṣb, Ḳ:*) and pl. شُهْبٌ: (O:) the former epithet is applied to a horse, (Ṣ,) [contr. to an assertion of IAạr, (see 4,)] and to a he-mule, (Mṣb,) and شَهْبَآءُ to a she-mule. (Mgh, Mṣb.) [Golius, on the authority of Meyd, explains أَشْهَبُ أَدْهَمُ, applied to a horse, as meaning *Subniger, spadiceus*: and أَشْهَبُ أَخْضَرُ as meaning *lucide leviterve viridis*: the correct meaning of the former seems to be *of a blackish*, or *brownish, gray*: and that of the latter, *of a dark dust-coloured gray*: see أَدْهَمُ and أَخْضَرُ.] الشَّهْبَآءُ was the name of a mare belonging to El-Ḳattál El-Bejelee. (O, Ḳ; in the CḲ El-Bejlee.) Applied to a she-goat, شَهْبَآءُ signifies *Of a white colour intermixed with black*: thus applied, it is like مَلْحَآءُ applied to a ewe. (Ḳ.) Applied to a غُرَّة [or blaze on a horse's forehead], it means *In which are hairs differing from the whiteness* [*of the blaze*]. (Ṣ.) And الأَشَاهِبُ is [a pl. formed from الأَشْهَبُ as though this were a subst.] applied to the Benu-l-Mundhir, (Ḳ,) or one of the troops of En-Noamán Ibn-El-Mundhir, consisting of the sons of his paternal uncle and his maternal uncles, and their brethren; (TA;) so called because of their comeliness, (Ḳ,) or because of the whiteness of their faces. (TA.) — Applied to ambergris, (Ḳ, TA,) † *Of an excellent colour*, i. e., (TA,) *inclining to whiteness*. (Ḳ, TA.) And applied to an iron head or blade of an arrow or of a spear &c., ‡ *That has been filed so that its blackness has gone*: (Ṣ, A, TA:) or *that has been filed lightly, so that all its blackness has not gone*. (AḤn, TA.) [Hence,] كَتِيبَةٌ شَهْبَآءُ † *A great troop having numerous weapons*; (Ḳ;) so called because of the iron; (Ṣ;) or because of the whiteness of the weapons and iron, intermixed with blackness: or *a troop of which the iron* [*of the weapons and armour*] *is white and bright*: (TA:) or, as also ♦ كَتِيبَةٌ شُهَابَةٌ, *a troop upon which is* [*seen*] *the whiteness of the iron* [*weapons &c.*]. (T, TA. [See also كَتِيبَةٌ مَلْحَآءُ, voce أَمْلَحُ.]) And جَيْشٌ أَشْهَبُ *A strong army* [app. because of its numerous weapons]. (TA.) — أَرْضٌ شَهْبَآءُ † *A land in which is no verdure, by reason of the paucity of rain*. (TA.) And [hence,] سَنَةٌ شَهْبَآءُ ‡ *A year of drought*, or *sterility, white in consequence thereof*, (TA,) *in which is no verdure*, or *in which is no rain*: (Ḳ, TA:) next in degree is the بَيْضَآء; then, the حَمْرَآء, which is more severe than the بَيْضَآء; (TA;) and then, the سَوْدَآء: (TA in art. حمر:) or *a year that is white by reason of the abundance of snow and the want of herbage*: (IB, TA:) or *a year of drought*, or *sterility*; because the seed-produce dries up therein, and becomes yellow: and عَامٌ أَشْهَبُ signifies the same. (Ḥar p. 150.) And عَامَانِ أَشْهَبَانِ † *Two white years* (عَامَانِ أَبْيَضَانِ) *between which is no verdure* (Ḳ, TA) *of herbage*. (TA.) And يَوْمٌ أَشْهَبُ ‡ *A cold day*: (A, Ḳ:) or *a day of cold wind*; thought to be so called on account of the snow and hoar frost and hail therein: (L, TA:) or *a day of hoar-frost*: (Az, TA:) *a day of cold wind and hoar frost*; and [in like manner] the night (اللَّيْلَةُ) is termed شَهْبَآءُ. (Ṣ.) In the following verse, cited by Sb,

فِدًى لِبَنِي ذُهْلِ بْنِ شَيْبَانَ نَاقَتِي
إِذَا كَانَ يَوْمٌ ذُو كَوَاكِبَ أَشْهَبُ

[*May my she-camel be a ransom for the sons of Dhuhl Ibn-Sheybán when there is a day of difficulties, or distresses, . . .*] the meaning may be اشهب [or *whitish*] *by reason of the whiteness of the weapons, or by reason of the dust*. (TA.) And الشُّهْبُ [pl. of أَشْهَبُ], (O,) or ♦ الشُّهُبُ [pl. of شِهَابٌ], (Ḳ,) [but the former, I think, is evidently the right,] † *The white nights*; (اللَّيَالِي البِيضُ;) [i. e. *the thirteenth and fourteenth and fifteenth nights of the lunar month*; so called because lighted by the moon throughout; (see art. بيض;)] (O;) *three nights of the month*; (Ḳ, TA;) because of the alteration of their colour. (TA.) — أَشْهَبُ [or أَمْرٌ أَشْهَبُ] also signifies † *A hard*, or *difficult, affair* or *case*, (Ḳ, TA,) *such as is disliked*, or *hated*. (TA.) And أَشْهَبُ بَازِلٌ † *A hard*, or *difficult, affair* or *case, that is beyond one's power* [*of accomplishment* or *endurance*]: termed بازل because the camel thus termed is one that has attained its utmost strength. (O, TA. [See also art. بزل.]) — And الأَشْهَبُ signifies *The lion*. (O, K.) [And in the Deewán of Jereer, it is applied to *The swine*. (Freytag.)]

شهد

1. شَهِدَ, (Ṣ, A, Mgh, L, Mṣb, Ḳ,) aor. ـَ; (Ḳ;) and شَهُدَ, aor. ـُ; (Ḳ;) also pronounced and written شَهْدَ, (Akh, Ṣ, Ḳ,) and شِهِدَ, and شِهْدَ, accord. to a rule applying to all verbs of the measure فَعِلَ of which the medial radical letter is a faucial; (MF;) inf. n. شَهَادَةٌ (Ṣ, A, Mgh, L, Mṣb, Ḳ) and شهد; (TA; [there written without any syll. sign, and not found by me in any other Lex.;]) *He told*, or *gave information of, what he had witnessed*, or *seen or beheld with his eye*: (Mgh, L, Mṣb:) this is the primary signification: (L:) *he declared what he knew: he gave testimony, attestation*, or *evidence; he bore witness*: (L:) *he gave decisive information*. (Ṣ, A, L, Ḳ.) [See also شَهَادَةٌ below.] You say, شَهِدَ بِكَذَا, inf. n. as above, (Ṣ, A, Mgh, L, Mṣb, Ḳ,) *He told, or gave information of, such a thing, as having witnessed it*, or *seen or beheld it with his eye*; (Mgh, Mṣb;) or *declared such a thing as knowing it*; (L;) or *gave his testimony, attestation*, or *evidence, respecting it*; or *bore witness of it*, or *to it*; (Ṣ, A, L, Ḳ;) عِنْدَ الحَاكِمِ [*in the presence of the judge*]; لِفُلَانٍ [*for*, or *in favour of, such a one*], (Ṣ, Mgh, L, Ḳ,) and عَلَى فُلَانٍ [*against*, or *in opposition to, such a one*]. (Mgh.) And شَهِدَ عَلَى كَذَا *He gave decisive information* [*respecting such a thing* (as in the Ḳur xlvi. 9, and in many other instances); *he testified respecting it*]. (Ṣ, L. [See also another meaning of this phrase in what follows.]) [Hence,] شَهِدَ ٱللّٰهُ أَنَّهُ لَا إِلٰهَ إِلَّا هُوَ, in the Ḳur [iii. 16], means *God hath given evidence that there is no deity but He*: (Abu-l-'Abbás, IAmb, Jel:) or *God knoweth* &c.; (Aḥmad Ibn-Yaḥyà, Ḳ;) and so شَهِدَ ٱللّٰهُ throughout the Ḳur-án: (Aḥmad Ibn-Yaḥyà:) or *God saith* &c.: or *God hath written* &c. (Ḳ.) And أَشْهَدُ أَنْ لَا إِلٰهَ إِلَّا ٱللّٰهُ *I know*, (Mṣb, Ḳ,) [or *acknowledge*,] and *I declare*, [or *testify, that there is no deity but God*:] (Ḳ:) [Fei says,] the verb is trans. in this phrase by itself [i. e. without the intervention of a prep.] because it is used in the sense of أَعْلَمُ. (Mṣb.) [And hence, كَلِمَةُ الشَّهَادَةِ means *The sentence declaring that there is no deity but God and that Mohammad is God's apostle*.] — شَهِدَ بِٱللّٰهِ, (Mgh,* Mṣb,) aor. ـَ, inf. n. شَهَادَةٌ, (Mgh,) means *He swore by God*: (Mgh, Mṣb:) and أَشْهَدُ بِكَذَا *I swear by such a thing*. أَشْهَدُ بِٱللّٰهِ لَقَدْ كَانَ كَذَا (Ṣ, Ḳ.) *I swear by God that such a thing happened*, or *took place*, combines the meaning of witnessing with that of swearing and that of informing at the time of

uttering these words; as though the speaker said, *I swear by God that I witnessed such a thing, and now I inform of it.* (Mṣb.) Accord. to some, when one says only أَشْهَدُ, not adding بِاللّٰهِ, it is an oath. (TA.) — شَهِدَ عَلَى كَذَا, a phrase of which one meaning has been expl. above, means also *He became a witness* (شَاهِد) *of*, or *to, such a thing*; (Ṣ, Ḳ;) *he had knowledge of such a thing, and witnessed it*, or *saw it* or *beheld it with his eye*: (Mṣb:) and شَهِدَهُ, (Mgh, L,) inf. n. شَهَادَةٌ, (L,) [likewise] signifies *he witnessed it*; or *saw*, or *beheld, it*, or *him, with his eye*; (Mgh, L;) and (Mgh, L, Mṣb) so ↓ شَاهَدَهُ, (A, Mgh, L, Mṣb, Ḳ,) inf. n. مُشَاهَدَةٌ. (Ṣ, A, L, Mṣb.) [Hence,] one says, شُوهِدَتْ ↓ مِنْهُ حَالٌ جَمِيلَةٌ [*A comely*, or *pleasing, state*, or *condition, of him was witnessed*]. (A.) — And شَهِدَهُ, (aor. ـَ, Ḳ,) inf. n. شُهُودٌ, *He was*, or *became, present at it*, or *in it*; (Ṣ, A, Mgh, L, Mṣb,* Ḳ;) namely, a place, (Mgh,) or an assembly. (Mṣb.) Hence the saying, (Mṣb,) فَمَنْ شَهِدَ مِنْكُمُ الشَّهْرَ فَلْيَصُمْهُ, in the Ḳur [ii. 181], *Therefore whoever of you shall be present in the month, and stationary, not journeying, he shall fast therein* (Mgh, Mṣb) as long as he shall remain present and stationary: (Mṣb:) الشهر being here in the accus. case as an adv. n. of time. (Mgh, Mṣb.) [And hence,] شَهِدَ الجُمُعَةَ *He attained to* [*the being present at*] *the* جُمُعَة [here meaning, as in many other instances, the *prayer of Friday*]: (Mgh:) and شَهِدَ العِيدَ *he attained to* [*the being present at*] *the* عِيد [or *festival*, or *the prayer thereof*]. (Mṣb.) [Hence also,] it is said in a trad., يَشْهَدُ بَيْعَكُمُ الحَلِفُ وَاللَّغْوُ [*Swearing, and unprofitable speech, attend your selling*]. (TA in art. شوب: see 1 in that art.)

2: see 4.

3: see 1, latter half, in two places.

4. أَشْهَدْتُهُ عَلَى كَذَا *I made him to be a witness* (شَاهِد) *of*, or *to, such a thing*: (Ṣ, Mgh, L:) [and in like manner,] أَشْهَدْتُهُ الشَّىْءَ *I made him to have knowledge of the thing, and to witness it*, or *see it* or *behold it with his eye*. (Mṣb.) See also 10. إِشْهَادٌ in relation to criminal matters means [The *causing* one *to take notice of a thing that threatens to occasion some injury, with a view to the prevention of such injury; as, for instance*,] the *saying to the owner of a house, "This thy wall is leaning, therefore demolish it,"* or *"feared, therefore repair it."* (Mgh.) — اشهدهُ also signifies *He caused him to be present*. (Ḳ.) You say, أَشْهَدَنِى إِمْلَاكَهُ *He caused me to be present* [*at*, or *on the occasion of, his being put in possession*]. (Ṣ.) — أُشْهِدَ: see 10. — اشهد [as intrans.] † *Humorem tenuem e pene emisit* vir *propter lusum amatorium* vel *osculum*; (Ṣ, Ḳ;) as also ↓ شَهَّدَ, (Ḳ,) inf. n. تَشْهِيدٌ: (TA:) [from شَهْد signifying "honey;" for] عُسَيْلَة is a term for مَذْى. (Ṣ.) † *He rendered his* مِئْزَر [or *waist-wrapper*] *of a reddish hue and of a dark dust-colour* (أَغْبَر) [*by the act above-mentioned*]. (L.) † *He* (a boy) *attained to puberty*. (Th, TA.) And اشهدت *She* (a girl) *menstruated*: and *attained to puberty*. (Ḳ.)

5. التَّشَهُّدُ in prayer is well known; (Ṣ, Ḳ;) *The reciting of the form of words commencing with* التَّحِيَّاتُ لِلّٰهِ: [see art. حى:] from the occurrence therein of the words أَشْهَدُ أَنْ لَا إِلٰهَ إِلَّا اللّٰهُ وَأَشْهَدُ أَنَّ مُحَمَّدًا عَبْدُهُ وَرَسُولُهُ. (Mgh,* TA. [See also Ḥar p. 611.]) — And تَشَهَّدَ also signifies *He sought, or desired to obtain, martyrdom*. (L.)

10. استشهدهُ *He asked him*, or *required him, to tell what he had witnessed*, or *seen* or *beheld with his eye*; *to declare what he knew*; *to give testimony*, or *evidence*; *to bear witness*; or *to give decisive information*. (Ṣ, Mgh, L, Mṣb, Ḳ.) You say, اِسْتَشْهَدْتُ فُلَانًا عَلَى فُلَانٍ *I asked*, or *required*, [or *cited*, or *summoned*,] *such a one to give his testimony*, or *evidence*, or *to bear witness, against such a one*. (L.) And اِسْتَشْهَدْتُ الرَّجُلَ عَلَى إِقْرَارِ الغَرِيمِ and ↓ أَشْهَدْتُهُ *I asked*, or *required*, [&c., and *made*,] *the man to bear witness to*, or *to be witness of* or *to*, *the confession*, or *acknowledgment, of the debtor*. (L.) — [Hence,] استشهد بِبَيْتٍ عَلَى مَعْنَى كَلِمَةٍ [*He adduced*, or *urged*, or *cited, a verse as an evidential example of the meaning of a word*]. (A phrase of frequent occurrence in the larger lexicons.) — اُسْتُشْهِدَ (Ṣ, Ḳ) and ↓ أُشْهِدَ (Ḳ) *He was slain a martyr in the cause of God's religion*. (Ṣ, Ḳ. [See شَهِيدٌ.])

شَهْدٌ: see شَاهِدٌ, first sentence. = Also, and ↓ شُهْدٌ, (Ṣ, Mṣb, Ḳ,) the former of the dial. of Temeem, and the latter of the people of El-'Áliyeh, (Mṣb, TA,) *Honey*: (Ḳ:) or *honey in its wax* [i. e. *its comb*]; (Ṣ, Mṣb;) *honey not expressed from its wax* [or *comb*]: (TA:) pl. شِهَادٌ: (Ṣ, Mṣb, Ḳ:) شَهْدَةٌ is a more particular term, (Ṣ, Ḳ,) the n. un., [signifying *a portion thereof*; and *a honey-comb*, or *a portion of a honey-comb*;] as also شُهْدَةٌ. (TA.)

شُهْدٌ: see the next preceding paragraph.

شُهُودٌ: see شَاهِدٌ, in two places.

شَهِيدٌ is also written and pronounced شِهِيدٌ, with kesr to the ش: (Ḳ, TA:) and in like manner is every word of the measure فَعِيل having a faucial letter for its medial radical, whether an epithet, like this, or a subst., like رَغِيف and بَعِير: El-Hemdánee says, in the "Iạráb el-Ḳur-án," that the people of El-Ḥijáz, and Benoo-Asad, say رَحِيم and رَغِيف and بَعِير, with fet-ḥ to the first letter; and Ḳeys and Rabee'ah and Temeem say رِحِيم and رِغِيف and بِعِير, with kesr to the first letter: Suh says, in the R, that Temeem pronounce every فَعِيل of which the medial radical letter is hemzeh or any other faucial with kesr to the first letter: and En-Nawawee states, on the authority of Lth, that some of the Arabs do the same when the medial radical letter is not a faucial; as in كِبِير and كِرِيم and جِلِيل and the like thereof. (TA.) [This last pronunciation obtains extensively in the present day: and so, in similar cases, does the intermediate pronunciation termed إِمَالَةُ الفَتْحِ, (i. e. the pronouncing fet-ḥ like "e" in the English word "bed,") which may be justly regarded as the best to be followed because intermediate and because sanctioned by the usage of the classical times, except in cases that are pointed out by the grammarians as presenting obstacles to the pronunciation thus termed.] — شَهِيدٌ is syn. with شَاهِدٌ [in several senses, as shown below]: and its pl. is شُهَدَآءُ. (Ṣ, Ḳ.) See شَاهِدٌ, in six places. — Also *Possessing much knowledge with respect to external things*: خَبِيرٌ is used in the like sense with respect to internal things; and عَلِيمٌ, in the like sense absolutely. (L.) [Hence, perhaps,] وَادْعُوا شُهَدَآءَكُمْ, in the Ḳur ii. 21, [as though meaning *And call ye to your aid those of you who possess much knowledge*: or] the meaning here is, *your helpers*: (Bḍ:) or *your gods whom ye worship*. (Jel.) الشَّهِيدُ as a name of God means *The Faithful*, or *Trusty, in his testimony*, (Zj, L,) or *in testimony*: (Ḳ:) and (Zj, Ḳ) as some say, (Zj,) *He from whose knowledge nothing is hidden*; *the Omniscient*. (Zj, L, Ḳ.) — Also, derived from الشَّهَادَةُ, or from المُشَاهَدَةُ, or from الشُّهُودُ, [all inf. ns.,] accord. to different opinions; (TA;) and of the measure فَعِيل in the sense of the measure مَفْعُول; (Mṣb, TA;) or in the sense of the measure فَاعِل; (TA;) *A martyr who is slain in the cause of God's religion*; (Ṣ, Ḳ;) [i. e.] *one who is slain by unbelievers on a field of battle*; (Mṣb;) *one who is slain fighting in the cause of God's religion*: (IAth:) so called because the angels of mercy are present with him; (Ḳ;) because the angels are present at the washing of his corpse, or at the removal of his soul to Paradise: (Mṣb:) or because God and his angels are witnesses for him of his title to a place in Paradise: (IAmb, Mgh,* Ḳ:) or because he is one of those who shall be required to bear witness on the day of resurrection, (Ḳ, TA,) with the Prophet, (TA,) against the people of past times, (Ḳ, TA,) who charged their prophets with falsehood: (TA:) or because of his falling upon the ↓ شَاهِدَة, or ground: (Ḳ:) or because he is still living, and present with his Lord: (ISh, Mgh, Ḳ:) or because he witnesses, or beholds, God's world of spirits and his world of corporeal beings: (Ḳ,* TA:) [and several other reasons are assigned for this appellation:] the primary application is that expl. above: but it is also applied by the Prophet to *one who dies of colic*: *one who is drowned*: *one who is burned to death*: *one who is killed by a building falling to ruin upon him*: *one who dies of pleurisy*: (IAth, L:) *one who dies of plague*, or *pestilence*: *a woman who dies in a state of pregnancy*: (L:) and to some others: (IAth:) the pl. is شُهَدَآءُ. (A, Mṣb, Ḳ, &c.)

شَهَادَةٌ [see 1:] *Information of what one has witnessed*, or *seen* or *beheld with his eye*: (IF, Mgh, L, Mṣb:) this is the primary signification: (L:) said to be a subst. from المُشَاهَدَةُ: (Mṣb:) *declaration of what one knows*: *testimony, attestation, evidence*, or *witness*: (L:) *decisive information*. (Ṣ, A, L, Ḳ.) — *An oath*: pl. شَهَادَاتٌ: so in the Ḳur xxiv. 6 [and 8]. (TA.) — *Martyrdom in the cause of God's religion*.

(Ṣ, Ḳ. [See شُهْدٌ.]) — Also i. q. مَشْهَدٌ as expl. below: see the latter word. — [And it is used in the sense of مُشَاهَدٌ: thus,] عَالِمُ الغَيْبِ وَالشَّهَادَةِ, in the Ḳur vi. 73 &c., means *The Knower of what is unseen and of what is seen.* (Jel.)

شَهِيدَةٌ *A roasted lamb:* or [the *kind of food called*] هَرِيسَة [q. v.]: pl. شُهَادٌ. (Har. p. 609.)

[شُهَّادٌ *Always present.* (Freytag from the Deewán of the Hudhalees.)]

شَاهِدٌ (Ṣ, Mgh, L, Ḳ) and ✝ شَهِيدٌ (Ṣ,* Mgh, L) *One who tells,* or *gives information of, what he has witnessed,* or *seen* or *beheld with his eye:* (Mgh, L:) *one who declares what he knows:* (L:) one *who knows, and declares what he knows:* (ISd, TA:) *a witness,* as meaning *one who gives testimony,* or *evidence; who bears witness:* (Ṣ,* L, Ḳ:*) [*one who gives decisive information:* (see 1, first sentence:)] pl. of the former ✝ شَهْدٌ, (Akh, Ṣ, Ḳ,) or [rather] this is a quasi-pl. n., (Sb, TA,) like as صَحْبٌ is of صَاحِبٌ, and سَفْرٌ of سَافِرٌ, (Ṣ,) but some disallow this; (TA;) and ✝ شُهُودٌ [but see what is said of this in the latter half of the paragraph] and أَشْهَادٌ are also pls. of شَاهِدٌ, (Mgh, L,) or of شَهْدٌ: (Ṣ, Ḳ:) the pl. of ✝ شَهِيدٌ is شُهَدَآءُ. (Ṣ, Mgh.) [Hence,] ✝ مَعَهَا سَائِقٌ وَشَهِيدٌ, in the Ḳur l. 20: see art. سوق. — [Hence also] الشَّاهِدُ a name of the Prophet; (Ḳ;) meaning *The witness* against those to whom he has been sent. (Jel in xxxiii. 44.) — And شَاهِدٌ *An angel:* (Ṣ, L, Ḳ:) or *a guardian angel:* (Mujáhid:) pl. أَشْهَادٌ: or this means the *prophets.* (TA.) — And The *tongue:* (Ṣ, L, Ḳ:) from the saying, لِفُلَانٍ شَاهِدٌ حَسَنٌ *Such a one has an elegant diction.* (L.) One says also, مَا لِفُلَانٍ رُوَآءٌ وَلَا شَاهِدٌ *Such a one has neither goodliness of aspect nor tongue.* (Aboo-Bekr, L.) — [As a conventional term used in lexicology &c.,] *An evidential example,* generally poetical, of the form or meaning of a word or phrase: pl. شَوَاهِدُ: the sciences that require شواهد being those of اللُّغَة and الصَّرْف and النَّحْو and المَعَانِى and البَيَان and البَدِيع and العَرُوض and القَوَافِى. (MF on the خُطْبَة of the Ḳ.) [One says, هٰذَا شَاهِدٌ لِكَذَا and عَلَى كَذَا *This is an evidential example of such a thing.*] With respect to the classical language, absolutely, شواهد are taken, by universal consent, from the Ḳur-án, and from the language [both verse and prose (Kull p. 348)] of those Arabs who lived before the period of the corruption [in any considerable degree] of the Arabic tongue: [see مُوَلَّدٌ:] also, accord. to the general decision of the learned, from the Traditions of Moḥammad; [which last source is excluded by some because traditions may be corrupted in language by their transmitters, and interpolated, and even forged;] and electively from the language of those Arabs who lived after the first corruption of the Arabic tongue, but before the corruption had become extensive. (Mz, 1st نوع; and MF ubi suprà. [See, again, مُوَلَّدٌ.]) The classes of the poets from whose poetry شواهد are taken are the Pagan Arabs, the Mukhaḍrams, the Islámees, and the Muwelleds: [see جَاهِلِىٌّ and مُخَضْرَمٌ and إِسْلَامِىٌّ and مُوَلَّدٌ:] with respect to all the sciences above mentioned, they are taken from the poetry of the first, second, and third, classes; from that of the first and second by universal consent, and from that of the third electively: (MF ubi suprà:) but they are taken from the poetry of the fourth class with respect only to the sciences of المَعَانِى and البَيَان and البَدِيع. (Idem, and Kull p. 348.) [The age of the earliest existing classical poems (though some older fragments and couplets and single verses have been preserved) is only about a century before the birth of Moḥammad: that of the latest, about a century after his death. (See the Preface to this work.)] — Also *Knowing,* (Mṣb,) *and witnessing,* or *seeing* or *beholding with his eye; a witness,* as meaning *an eyewitness;* (L, Mṣb;) as also ✝ شَهِيدٌ: pl. of the former [or, as is said in the L in art. مجد, of the former or of the latter,] شُهُودٌ and أَشْهَادٌ; [but see what is said of these pls. in the first sentence of this paragraph;] and of the latter شُهَدَآءُ. (Mṣb.) [See an ex. of ✝ شَهِيدٌ in this sense in a verse cited voce رُبَّ.] — [Hence, in the present day, applied to *A notary, who hears and writes and attests cases to be submitted for judgment in the court of a ḳádee.*] — *Present; a witness* as meaning *one personally present;* (Ṣ, L, Mṣb, Ḳ;) as also ✝ شَهِيدٌ: (Mṣb:) pl. of the former شُهَّدٌ (Ṣ, L, Ḳ) [and أَشْهَادٌ, as above,] and ✝ شُهُودٌ, (Ḳ,) or this last is used as a pl. but is originally an inf. n. (Ṣ, L.) One says, الشَّاهِدُ يَرَى مَا لَا يَرَى الغَائِبُ, meaning *The present knows what the absent knows not.* (Mṣb.) And قَوْمٌ شُهُودٌ *People,* or *persons, present.* (Ṣ, A.) And كَلَّمْتُهُ عَلَى رُؤُوسِ الأَشْهَادِ [*I spoke to him before witnesses,* or *persons present*]. (A.) — [Hence, app., being opposed to غَائِبٌ,] *A running in which a horse exerts his force unsparingly;* (A, L;) as in the saying, لِلْفَرَسِ غَائِبٌ وَشَاهِدٌ *The horse has a run which he reserves* [*for the time of need*], *and a run which he performs unsparingly;* like the saying, لَهُ صَوْنٌ وَبَذْلٌ: (A: [see 1 in art. بذل:]) or شَاهِدٌ means *a running that testifies the excellence of a horse,* (IAạr, Ḳ,) *and his quality of outstripping others.* (IAạr, TA.) — *A star* [app. *when visible*]; (Aboo-Eiyoob, Ḳ;) as being present and apparent in the night. (TA.) — [Hence, accord. to some,] صَلَاةُ الشَّاهِدِ *The prayer of sunset;* (A, L, Mṣb, Ḳ;) because it is *the prayer that is performed when the star becomes visible;* (Sh, L;) also called صَلَاةُ البَصَرِ, because the stars are seen at the time thereof: or, accord. to some, *the prayer of daybreak;* (L;) [and so, accord. to some, صَلَاةُ البَصَرِ; (see art. بصر;)] as also ✝ المَشْهُودُ; (TA;) and it is said to be so called because he who is travelling must perform it without abridging it, like him who is present at his home: Aboo-Sa'eed Eḍ-Ḍareer says that the former prayer is so called for this reason [as is also said in the A and Mṣb]: AM asserts that the first reason assigned above is the right one, because the prayer of daybreak, in like manner, may not be abridged, and is not thus called; but it is thus called by a poet. (L.) — And الشَّاهِدُ is a name of *Friday;* (Fr, Ḳ;) as also ✝ المَشْهُودُ: or the latter is *the day of resurrection:* (Ḳ:) or *the day of 'Arafeh:* (Fr, Ḳ: [see عَرَفَةُ:]) because of the presence and congregation of people on each of those days. (TA.) — شَاهِدٌ also signifies *Matter resembling mucus, that comes forth with the fœtus:* (Ṣ, Ḳ:) pl. شُهُودٌ: which latter, accord. to ISd, means the أَفْرَاس [pl. of فَرْس, q. v.,] *upon the head of a young camel at the time of its birth.* (TA.) And شُهُودُ النَّاقَةِ means *The marks left by the blood,* or *by the membrane that enclosed the fœtus, of the she-camel, in the place where she has brought forth.* (Ṣ, Ḳ.) — Also *A quick,* or an *expeditious,* thing or affair. (Ḳ.)

الشَّاهِدَةُ *The earth,* or *ground.* (Ḳ.) See شَهِيدٌ, last sentence.

مَشْهَدٌ *A place where people are present* or *assembled; a place of assembling; an assembly;* (Ṣ, L, Ḳ;) as also ✝ مَشْهُدَةٌ and ✝ مَشْهَدَةٌ (Ḳ) and ✝ شَهَادَةٌ: (L:) pl. مَشَاهِدُ. (A.) [Hence,] مَشَاهِدُ مَكَّةَ *The places of religious visitation, where the ceremonies of the pilgrimage &c. are performed, at Mekkeh.* (L.) — [*A funeral assembly* or *procession.* — *A place where a martyr has died* or *is buried.* — And The *aspect,* or *outward appearance,* of a person; like مَرْأًى: see an instance voce عُودٌ.]

مُشْهَدٌ *Slain a martyr in the cause of God's religion.* (Ḳ. [See also شَهِيدٌ.])

اِمْرَأَةٌ مُشْهِدٌ, (Ṣ, A, Ḳ,) without ة, (Ṣ,) and مُشْهِدَةٌ, (A,) *A woman whose husband is present with her:* (Ṣ, A, Ḳ:) opposed to اِمْرَأَةٌ مُغِيبَةٌ; (Ṣ, A;) this last with ة. (Ṣ.)

مَشْهَدَةٌ and مَشْهُدَةٌ: see مَشْهَدٌ.

مَجْلِسٌ مَشْهُودٌ [*A place of assembling at which numerous persons are present*]. (A.) And يَوْمٌ مَشْهُودٌ [*A day on which numerous persons are present:* and particularly] *a day on which the inhabitants of heaven and earth will be present.* (TA.) And صَلَاةٌ مَشْهُودَةٌ مَكْتُوبَةٌ *A prayer at the performance of which the angels are present, and the recompense of which, for the performer, is written,* or *registered.* (L.) See also شَاهِدٌ, in two places, in the last quarter of the paragraph. — مَعْهُودٌ وَمَشْهُودٌ وَمَوْعُودٌ *Past and present and future;* the tenses of a verb. (Kh, L in art. عهد.)

شهدانج

شَهْدَانِجٌ, (Ḳ accord. to the TA,) with fet-ḥ to the ش and kesr to the ن, (TA,) and شَاهْدَانِجٌ, (Ḳ accord. to the TA,) or شَهْدَانَجٌ, (Mgh, Mṣb, and so in the CḲ, except that it is there written as though imperfectly decl.,) with fet-ḥ to the ن, (Mṣb,) and شَاهْدَانَجٌ, (CḲ,) arabicized from [the Pers.] شَاهْ دَانَهْ, which means "king of grains,"

(Ibn-El-Kutbee, TA,) The *seed of the* قِنَّب [or *hemp*]: (Mgh, Mṣb, Ḳ:) it is useful as a remedy for the quartan fever, (Ḳ,) prepared as a beverage, (TA,) and for the [kinds of leprosy called] بَهَق and بَرَص, (Ḳ,) applied as a liniment, (TA,) and it kills what are called حَبُّ القَرْعِ, (Ḳ,) which are worms in the belly, [tape-worms,] (TA,) when eaten, and also when applied to the belly externally. (Ḳ.)

شهر

1. شَهَرَهُ, (Ṣ, A, Ḳ,) aor. ـَ, (Ṣ, Ḳ,) inf. n. شَهْرٌ and شُهْرَةٌ; (Ṣ;) and ↓شَهَّرَهُ, (Ṣ, A, O, Ḳ,) inf. n. تَشْهِيرٌ; (Ṣ;) and ↓اشتهره; (Ṣ, Ḳ;) *He made it apparent, conspicuous, manifest, notorious, notable, commonly known,* or *public*: (Ṣ, O, MF:) or [it generally means] *he made it apparent, &c., as bad, evil, abominable, foul,* or *unseemly; he exposed it as such; or rendered it notorious in a bad sense,* or *infamous.* (A, Ḳ.) You say, شَهَرْتُ الحَدِيثَ, inf. n. as above, *I divulged the story,* or *discourse.* (Mṣb.) And لِفُلَانٍ فَضِيلَةٌ اشْتَهَرَهَا النَّاسُ [*Such a one has an excellent quality which the people have made commonly known*]. (Ṣ.) And شَهَرْتُهُ بَيْنَ النَّاسِ *I rendered him conspicuous* [or *notorious* or *celebrated* or *renowned*] *among the people.* (Mṣb.) And شَهَرْتُ زَيْدًا بِكَذَا and ↓شهّرته [*I rendered Zeyd conspicuous, notorious, celebrated,* or *renowned, for such a thing*]; (Mgh,* Mṣb;) [but] the latter has an intensive signification: ↓أَشْهَرْتُهُ, with ا, in the sense of شَهَرْتُهُ, has not been transmitted: (Mṣb:) or is not of established authority. (Mgh.) One says also, شُهِرَ بِكَذَا, and ↓اِشْتَهَرَ, [generally, but not always, in a bad sense, meaning] *He was rendered,* or *became, notorious,* or *infamous, for such a thing*: (A:) the latter verb being intrans. as well as trans. (TA.) And [hence one says,] ↓اِشْتَهَرْتُ فُلَانًا meaning ‡ *I held such a one in light,* or *little, estimation,* or *in contempt, and exposed his vices, faults,* or *evil qualities* or *actions.* (A.) — And شَهَرَ سَيْفَهُ, (Ṣ, A, Mṣb, Ḳ,) aor. ـَ, (Ṣ, Mṣb, Ḳ,) inf. n. شَهْرٌ, (Ṣ, Mṣb,) *He drew his sword* (Ṣ, Mṣb, TA) *from its scabbard*: (TA:) or *he drew his sword and raised it over the people*; (A, Ḳ;) as also ↓شهّره. (Ḳ.)

2: see above, in three places. [In modern Arabic, شهّر often signifies *He paraded* an offender *as a public example*; and it occurs in this sense in the Ṣ and TA in art. بلس, &c.: the offender, in this case, is generally mounted upon an ass or a camel, and often with his face towards the animal's tail.]

3. شاهره, (Ḳ,) inf. n. مُشَاهَرَةٌ (Ṣ, Ḳ) and شِهَارٌ, (Ḳ,) *He hired him, or took him as a hired man* or *hireling, for* [or *by*] *the month*: (Lḥ, Ḳ:) or *he made an engagement, or a contract, with him for work* or *the like, by the month,* or *month by month*: (TA:) المُشَاهَرَةُ from الشَّهْرُ is like المُعَاوَمَةُ from العَامُ. (Ṣ, TA.)

4: see 1. — أَشْهَرْنَا, (Ṣ, Mṣb,* Ḳ,) inf. n. إِشْهَارٌ, (Mṣb,) *A month passed* (lit. *came*) *over us.* (Ṣ, Mṣb,* Ḳ.) And اشهر الصَّبِىُّ [*The child became a month old;* or] *a month passed* (lit. *came*) *over the child*: similar to أَحْوَلَ, (A,) or to أَحَالَ. (Mṣb.) And اشهرت الدَّارُ *The house became altered, or changed, and months passed over it.* (TA in art. حول.) — Also *We remained, stayed, dwelt,* or *abode, a month in a place.* (ISk, Ṣ.) — And *We entered upon the month,* i. e., *the lunar month.* (Th, Ṣ.) — And اشهرت *She* (a woman) *entered upon the month of her bringing forth.* (Mṣb, Ḳ.)

8. اشتهر *It was,* or *became, apparent, conspicuous, manifest, notorious, notable, commonly known,* or *public*: (Ṣ:) or [it generally means] *it was, or became, apparent, &c., as bad, evil, abominable, foul,* or *unseemly; it was, or became, exposed as such, or rendered notorious in a bad sense* or *infamous.* (A, Ḳ.) *It* (a story, or discourse,) *became divulged,* or *public.* (Mṣb.) — اشتهر بكذا: see 1. — As a trans. verb: see 1 in three places.

شَهْرٌ The *new moon, when it appears*: (IF, A, Mgh, O, Mṣb, Ḳ:) so called because of its conspicuousness. (Mgh, Mṣb.) This is the original signification. (Mgh.) [See the last sentence of this paragraph.] You say, رَأَيْتُ الشَّهْرَ, meaning *I saw the new moon of the month.* (Mgh.) Hence it is said in a trad., صُومُوا الشَّهْرَ, meaning *Fast ye the first day of the lunar month.* (Lḥ, TA.) And hence the trad., إِنَّمَا الشَّهْرُ تِسْعٌ وَعِشْرُونَ, meaning The utility of watching for *the new moon is on the nine and twentieth* night. (L, TA.) [Or the meaning is, that the lunar month is a period of nine and twenty nights.] — Also The *moon*: or the *moon when conspicuous, and near to being full.* (Ḳ.) — And [A *lunar month*;] *a certain well-known number of days*: so called because made manifest by the moon: (ISd, Ḳ:) an arabicized word; or, as some say, Arabic; (Mṣb;) and so called because of its being manifest: (Mṣb, TA:) pl. [of pauc.] أَشْهُرٌ (Mṣb, Ḳ) and [of mult.] شُهُورٌ. (Ṣ, Mṣb, Ḳ.) The following are the modern names of the months: 1. المُحَرَّمُ [to which the epithet الحَرَامُ is often added]: 2. صَفَرٌ [to which the epithet الخَيْرُ is often added]: 3. رَبِيعٌ الأَوَّلُ: 4. رَبِيعٌ الآخِرُ [or الثَّانِى]: 5. جُمَادَى الأُولَى: 6. جُمَادَى الآخِرَةُ [or الثَّانِيَةُ]: 7. رَجَبٌ [to which is often added the epithet الأَصَمُّ, and that of الفَرْدُ]: 8. شَعْبَانُ [to which we often find the epithet المُعَظَّمُ added, and sometimes that of الشَّرِيفُ]: 9. رَمَضَانُ [to which the epithet المُبَارَكُ is appropriated]: 10. شَوَّالٌ [to which the epithet المُكَرَّمُ is frequently added]: 11. ذُو القَعْدَةِ: and 12. ذُو الحِجَّةِ: [see the second of the two tables in p. 1254:] and the following are the names by which they were called by the tribe of 'Ád, agreeably with the foregoing numeration: 1. مُؤْتَمِرٌ: 2. نَاجِرٌ: 3. خَوَّانٌ: 4. بُصَانٌ [q. v.]: 5. رُبَّى: 6. حَنِينٌ: 7. الأَصَمُّ: 8. عَاذِلٌ: 9. نَاتِقٌ: 10. وَعْلٌ: 11. وَرْنَةُ: and 12. بُرَكٌ [or بَرَكٌ?]. (Ibn-El-Kelbee, in TA, voce مُؤْتَمِرٌ. [But authors differ respecting some of these names, as will be seen in other articles.]) أَشْهُرٌ مَعْلُومَاتٌ, said, in the Ḳur [ii. 193], to be the period of the pilgrimage, for by الحَجُّ, which immediately precedes, is meant وَقْتُ الحَجِّ, (Mgh, Mṣb,) or زَمَانُ الحَجِّ, (Mṣb,) applies to *Showwál and Dhu-l-Ḳaadeh and ten days of Dhu-l-Ḥijjeh,* (Mgh, Mṣb,) accord. to Aboo-Ḥaneefeh (Mgh) and most of the learned, part of Dhu-l-Ḥijjeh being called a month tropically, as is often done by the Arabs in similar cases, relating to time; for ex. when they say, مَا رَأَيْتُهُ مُذْ يَوْمَانِ, the period of separation having been a day and a part of a day: (Mṣb:) or [and] *nine days of Dhu-l-Ḥijjeh with the night preceding the day of the sacrifice,* accord. to Esh-Sháfi'ee: (Mgh:) or [and] *all Dhu-l-Ḥijjeh,* accord. to Málik: (Mgh, Mṣb:) [in these two explanations the two months next preceding being meant to be included:] or *Showwál and Dhu-l-Ḳaadeh and Dhu-l-Ḥijjeh and Moharram,* accord. to Aboo-'Amr Esh-Shaabee. (Mṣb.) — Also † *A learned man*: (O, Ḳ:) [because of his celebrity:] pl. شُهُورٌ. (O, TA.) — [And accord. to the Ḳ, it signifies also The *like of a nail-paring*: but this is app. a mistake, perhaps originating from a mutilated transcript of what here follows:] a poet says, describing camels,

* أَبْدَأْنَ مِنْ نَجْدٍ عَلَى ثِقَةٍ *
* وَالشَّهْرُ مِثْلُ قُلَامَةِ الظُّفُرِ *

[*They went forth from Nejd in a state of confidence, the new moon being like the nail-paring*]. (O.)

شُهْرَةٌ a subst. from الاِشْتِهَارُ, (Mgh,) signifying The *appearance, conspicuousness, manifestness, notoriousness, notableness,* or *publicity,* of a thing: (Ṣ, O, Mṣb:) or [generally] its *appearance, &c., as bad, evil, abominable, foul,* or *unseemly*; its *notoriousness in a bad sense,* or *infamousness.* (A, Ḳ.) — *Any evil thing that exposes its author to disgrace; any disgraceful,* or *shameful, thing; a vice,* or *fault,* or *the like.* (IAar, O, TA.) — *A dress of the most excellent or superb kind*; and *one of the vilest or meanest kind*: both of which are forbidden. (Mgh.) — [It is also used in the sense of مَشْهُورٌ.] One says, جَعَلَهُ شُهْرَةً ‡ [*He rendered him notorious, either in a bad or in a good sense*]. (A.) And صَارَ شُهْرَةً, (Ḳ in art. دول,) i. e. مَشْهُورًا † [*He became notorious, &c.*]; said of a man. (TḲ in that art.)

بِرْذَوْنٌ شِهْرِىٌّ A برذون [or *hackney*] *between the* رَمَكَة [or *mare of mean breed*] *and the horse of generous breed*: one says, لَمْ يَرْكَبِ الشِّهْرِيَّةَ and الشَّهَارِىَ [*He did not ride hackneys of the sort above mentioned*]: (A:) or شِهْرِيَّةٌ signifies بَرَاذِين [or *hackneys*]; and its pl. is شَهَارٍ: (Mgh:) or *a sort of* بَرَاذِين [or *hackneys*]; (Lth, O, Ḳ;) *a horse of which the dam is Arabian but not the sire.* (Lth, O.)

شَهِيرٌ: see مَشْهُورٌ. — شَهِيرَةٌ *A woman, and a she-ass, broad* (O, Ḳ) *and bulky.* (O.)

[أَشْهَرُ *More, and most, apparent, conspicuous, manifest, notorious,* &c.; *better,* and *best, known.* —— Hence, الأَشْهَرَانِ *The drum and the banner.* (Gol., from Meyd.)]

أَشَاهِرُ [in the CK أَشَاهِيرُ] The *whiteness of the narcissus.* (K, TA.)

مُشْهِرٌ A child *a month old.* (O, TA.)

مُشَهَّرٌ: see the following paragraph.

مَشْهُورٌ *Of known place or station;* (K;) *well known; well spoken of; celebrated; held in repute; reputable; notable; eminent;* (O, K, TA;) applied to a man; (O, TA;) as also ↓ شَهِيرٌ, (O, K, TA,) and [in an intensive sense] ↓ مُشَهَّرٌ. (TA.) [And Anything *apparent, conspicuous, manifest, notorious, notable, commonly known,* or *public:* lit. *rendered apparent* &c. Applied to a word or phrase or meaning, *Commonly known* or *obtaining* or *received; well known;* or *held in repute.* Hence عَلَى المَشْهُورِ *According to common,* or *well-known, usage;* or *according to common repute.*]

شهق

1. شَهَقَ, aor. ـِ, (S, Msb,) inf. n. شُهُوقٌ, (Msb,) [said of a mountain, and of a building, &c., (see شَاهِقٌ,)] *It rose high;* or *became high,* or *elevated,* or *lofty.* (S, Msb.) —— شَهَقَ, aor. ـِ and ـُ, inf. n. شَهِيقٌ [and تَشْهَاقٌ], said of an ass, [*He uttered the ending of his braying,* or *the final sounds thereof;*] (S;) [for] شَهِيقٌ signifies the *ending,* or *final part, of the crying,* or *braying,* of the ass; (S, O;) and to this the cries of the punished in Hell are likened in the Kur xi. 108; (O;) and زَفِيرٌ signifies the "beginning, or commencing part, thereof:" (S:) or شهيق signifies the *drawing back of the breath;* and زفير the "emitting thereof:" (Lth, S: [but the reverse is said by Lth and in the S in art. زفر:]) and تَشْهَاقٌ signifies the same as شَهِيقٌ: (S:) or both of these words signify [absolutely] the *crying,* or *braying,* of the ass: (O, K:) Zj says that شَهِيقٌ as denoting one of the cries of the afflicted [in Hell] means *a very high-sounding moaning:* and that, accord. to some, زَفِيرٌ [as used in the Kur ubi suprà] is similar to the beginning of the cry of the ass, termed شَهِيقٌ; and that شَهِيقٌ is *in the chest.* (TA.) [Said of a man,] شَهَقَ, aor. ـِ and ـُ; and شَهِقَ, aor. ـَ; inf. n. شَهِيقٌ and شُهَاقٌ (O, K) and شُهُوقٌ (O) and تَشْهَاقٌ; signify *The* [*sound of*] *weeping became reiterated in his chest:* (O, K:) or, as in the L, *he reiterated the* [*sound of*] *weeping in his chest.* (TA.) [Or] شَهَقَ, aor. ـِ and ـُ, inf. n. شَهِيقٌ, signifies [or signifies also] *He reiterated his breath, making his voice audible, naturally.* (Msb.) One says also, شَهَقَ فُلَانٌ شَهْقَةً فَمَاتَ *Such a one uttered a single cry and died.* (S, TA.) —— And شَهَقَتْ عَيْنُ النَّاظِرِ عَلَيْهِ ‡ *The eye of the looker smote him with evil influence:* (O, K, TA:) or, *was pleased with him, and therefore continued looking at him.* (A, TA.)

شَهْقَةٌ *A single cry.* (S, TA.) [See 1, last sentence but one.]

شَهْقَةٌ *Height, elevation,* or *loftiness.* (TA.)

شَاهِقٌ *High,* or *lofty;* applied to a mountain, (S, O, Msb, K,) and to a building, &c.: (O, K:) or, applied to a mountain, *high and inaccessible:* (JK, TA:) pl. شَوَاهِقُ: (JK, Msb, TA:) you say جِبَالٌ شَاهِقَةٌ and شَاهِقَاتٌ and شَوَاهِقُ. (Msb.) —— Applied to a vein [or an artery], ‡ *Pulsing upwards:* (O, K, TA:) a term of the physicians. (O, TA.) —— ذُو شَاهِقٍ ‡ A man *whose anger is vehement:* (JK, S, A, O, L, TA:) wrongly expl. in the K by the words لَا يَشْتَدُّ غَضَبُهُ: (TA:) and so ذُو صَاهِلٍ. (A, TA.) And ‡ A stallion [camel] *Excited by lust, assaulting* [*the she-camels*], *and causing a sound to be heard from his inside;* as also ذُو صَاهِلٍ. (TA.)

تَشْهَاقٌ an inf. n. (S,* O, K. [See 1.]) —— [And also an epithet.] One says ضَحِكٌ تَشْهَاقٌ [app. meaning † *A loud laughing,* likened to the تَشْهَاق of the ass]. (S, O.)

شهل

1. شَهِلَ, aor. ـَ, (K,) inf. n. شَهَلٌ, (S,* O,* TA,) *He* (a man, S, O) *had that quality of the eye which is termed* شُهْلَةٌ [expl. below]; (S, O, K;) as also ↓ اِشْهَلَّ, inf. n. اِشْهِلَالٌ. (K.) [And in like manner each of these verbs is probably used as said of the eye.]

2. تَشْهِيلٌ is a vulgar dial. var. of تَسْهِيلٌ [inf. n. of سَهَّلَ, q. v.]. (TA.)

3. شَاهَلَهُ, (K,) inf. n. مُشَاهَلَةٌ, (S, O, TA,) *He acted with him in an evil manner;* or *contended,* or *disputed, with him;* syn. شَارَّهُ: (S,* O,* K, TA;) and لَاحَاهُ [which has the latter of these significations]: and *opposed him, being opposed by him;* syn. عَارَضَهُ: (TA:) *he reviled him;* or *reviled him, being reviled by him:* (K:) *he exchanged bad names with him;* syn. قَارَصَهُ: (S,* TA: [in the O, المُقَارَضَة is put for المُقَارَصَة:]) *he bandied words with him.* (S, O, TA.)

5. تَشَهَّلَ, said of the freshness, or brightness, and beauty, of the face, (مَآءُ الوَجْهِ,) *It went away,* or *departed,* (O, K, TA,) by reason of emaciation. (TA.)

9: see 1.

شَهْلٌ *A mixture of two colours.* (ISk, TA.) —— Hence, (ISk, TA,) one says, فِى فُلَانٍ وَلَعٌ and شَهْلٌ, (ISk, O, K,*) or فِى فُلَانٍ شَهْلٌ, (JK,) † *In such a one is lying.* (ISk, JK, O, K.) ═ See also شُهْلَةٌ.

شَهَلٌ [properly inf. n. of شَهِلَ]: see شُهْلَةٌ.

شَهْلَةٌ A *middle-aged, intelligent* woman: an epithet peculiarly applied to a woman: (S, O, K:) one says اِمْرَأَةٌ شَهْلَةٌ كَهْلَةٌ, but not رَجُلٌ شَهْلٌ ↓ كَهْلٌ; though IDrd mentions شَهْلٌ كَهْلٌ. (TA.) —— And An *old* woman. (K.)

شُهْلَةٌ *A tinge,* or *mixture, of* زُرْقَة [i. e. *blueness,* or *grayness,* or *a greenish hue,*] *in the black* of the eye: (S, O:) or, as also ↓ شَهَلٌ, [this latter mentioned above as inf. n. of شَهِلَ, *a tint*] *less than* زُرْقٌ, [in the CK الزُّرْقُ is erroneously put for الزُّرْقَة,] which is here used in the sense of الزُّرْقَة,] *and more beautiful than this, in the black of the eye:* (K, TA:) thus in the M: (TA:) or *a tinge of redness in the black of the eye, not in lines, like* شُكْلَةٌ, *but* [*consisting in*] *a paucity of blackness of the black of the eye, so that it is as though it inclined to redness:* (K:) or *a hue of the black of the eye between redness and blackness:* or *a lack of purity of the blackness thereof:* or *a redness in the black of the eye;* شُكْلَةٌ being the like of a redness in the white thereof; thus expl. by A'Obeyd; and in like manner by Es-Semmák. (TA.)

شَهْلَآءُ fem. of أَشْهَلُ [q. v.]. (S, O, K.) ═ Also *A want;* syn. حَاجَةٌ: (S, O, K:) said by IF to be originally شَكْلَآءُ. (O.)

دِرْهَمٌ شِهْلِيلِىٌّ A [app. meaning a silver coin] *of the measure of the breadth of the hand.* (Mgh.)

أَشْهَلُ, applied to a man, (S, O,) *Having that quality of the eye which is termed* شُهْلَةٌ: (S, O, K:) accord. to AZ, *syn. with* أَشْكَلُ: (TA: [but see this latter epithet:]) fem. شَهْلَآءُ; (K;) which is applied as an epithet to an eye. (S, O.) —— Also A mountain, and a wolf, *dust-coloured inclining to whiteness.* (En-Nadr, TA.) —— And الأَشْهَلُ is the name of *A certain idol.* (Ibn-El-Kelbee, O, K.)

شهم

1. شَهُمَ, aor. ـُ, (S, K,) inf. n. شَهَامَةٌ (S, TA) and شُهُومَةٌ, (TA,) *He* (a man) *was,* or *became, hardy, strong, sturdy, enduring,* or *patient;* (S;) [or] *acute of mind* or *intellect;* (S, K;) *clever, ingenious, sharp,* or *penetrating.* (K.) —— And ‡ *He* (a horse) *was,* or *became, swift; brisk, lively, sprightly,* or *agile; and strong.* (K, TA.) —— [And app. *It was,* or *became, rough, harsh,* or *coarse:* for] شَهَامَةٌ signifies خُشُونَةٌ. (Ham p. 609.) ═ شَهَمَهُ, (S, K,) aor. ـَ and ـُ, inf. n. شَهْمٌ and شُهُومٌ, (K,) *He frightened him,* or *made him afraid;* (S, K;) namely, a man. (K.) —— And شَهَمَ الفَرَسَ, aor. ـَ, (K,) inf. n. شَهْمٌ, (TA,) *He chid the horse;* (K;) or *incited him to quickness.* (JK, K, and Ham p. 609.)

شَهْمٌ, applied to a man, *Hardy, strong, sturdy, enduring,* or *patient;* (S;) *acute of mind* or *intellect;* (S, K;) *clever, ingenious, sharp,* or *penetrating;* and ↓ مَشْهُومٌ signifies the same: pl. of the former شِهَامٌ (K) [and app. شُهُمٌ also: see شَهُمٌ, and see what here follows]. —— *A chief whose judgment,* or *judicial decision,* or *exercise of authority, is effectual in affairs;* (K,* TA;) *courageous;* or *sharp,* or *vigorous and effective, in affairs which others are unable to accomplish:* or, accord. to Fr, *forbearing,* or *clement; who performs well that which is imposed upon him; whom one finds not otherwise than forbearing,* or *clement, and pleased,* or *content, with that which* *is imposed upon him*: and in like manner applied to other than a man: (TA:) pl. شُهُومٌ (Ḳ) [and app. شُهُمٌ]: see مُسْهُورٌ, with which شُهُمٌ is syn. (TA in art. سهم.) — And, applied to a horse, ‡ *Swift; brisk, lively, sprightly,* or *agile; and strong.* (Ḳ, TA.) ═ Also *A stone which is placed at the entrance of a trap* (مَصْيَدَة or مِصْيَدَة in different copies of the Ḳ) *for a lion, and which falls upon it when he enters*: as also ▼ شَيْهَمٌ: (Ḳ,* TA:) the latter is the word [better] known to the leading lexicologists. (TA.)

شَاهِمٌ *i. q.* سِعْلَاةٌ [app. meaning The *kind of goblin,* or *demon, thus called*]. (Aṣ, Ṣ, Ḳ.)

شَيْهَمٌ The دُلْدُل [q. v., i. e. *hedge-hog;* or *a certain species of hedge-hog;* &c.]: (Ḳ:) [see also the last sentence of this paragraph:] and, (Ḳ,) or accord. to AZ, (TA,) the *male hedge-hog*: (Ṣ, Ḳ, TA:) or *such as has large prickles* or *spines, of male hedge-hogs,* (Ḳ, TA,) and *the like.* (TA.) عَلَى ظَهْرِ شَيْهَمٍ, occurring in a verse of El-Aạshà, is said by AO to mean † *In a state of fright,* or *fear.* (TA.) — شَيْهَمَةٌ *An old woman*: (Ḳ:) or, accord. to IAạr, *a hedge-hog.* (TA.)

مَشْهُومٌ: see شَهْمٌ. ═ Also *Frightened,* or *made afraid.* (Ṣ, TA.) — And, applied to a horse, *Chidden;* or *incited to quickness.* (TA.)

شهنز

شِهْنِيزٌ *i. q.* شِينِيزٌ, (ADḳ, Ḳ,) and شُونِيزٌ, i. e. الحَبَّةُ السَّوْدَآءُ. (ADḳ, TA.)

شهو

1. شَهِيَهُ and شَهَاهُ: see 8. ═ شَهَا, aor. ـُ; and شَهِىَ, aor. ـَ; inf. n. شَهْوَةٌ; *It* [food &c.] *was good, sweet, pleasant,* or *the like.* (MA. [But this, the only meaning there assigned to these two verbs, I do not find elsewhere.])

2. شَهَّيْتُهُ [*I made him,* or *caused him, to desire, to long,* or *to desire eagerly*]. (Mṣb.) — [And شَهَّى *It excited desire, longing, eager desire,* or *appetence.* For ex., in art. سمق in the Ḳ, يُشَهِّى is said of the سُمَّاق, or berry of the sumach, meaning *It excites appetence.*] — And شَهَّى الشَّىْءَ *He,* or *it, caused the thing to be desired, longed for,* or *desired eagerly*: *made it to be good, sweet, pleasant,* or *the like.* (MA.) One says, هٰذَا شَىْءٌ يُشَهِّى الطَّعَامَ i. e. [*This is a thing that causes the food to be desired,* &c.; *that makes it sweet,* &c.; or] *that incites to desire,* or *eager desire, of the food.* (Ṣ, TA.) — [And accord. to an explanation of the inf. n., تَشْهِيَةٌ, in the KL, شَهَّاهُ seems to signify also *He said to him, I will give to thee what thou desirest, longest for,* or *eagerly desirest;* agreeably with a rendering of the verb alone, as on the authority of that work, by Golius.]

3. شَاهَاهُ, (Ḳ, TA,) inf. n. مُشَاهَاةٌ, (TA,) *He was,* or *became, like him; he resembled him.* (Ḳ, TA.) ═ Also *He jested,* or *joked, with him*: (IAạr, TA:) [and] so حَاشَاهُ. (Ḳ in art. حشو.) — And accord. to IAạr, it is also used in relation to the smiting action of the [evil] eye [perhaps meaning *He vied with him in smiting with the evil eye*: see also 4]. (TA.)

4. اشهاهُ *He gave him what he desired* or *eagerly desired.* (Ḳ.) — And *He smote him with an* [*evil*] *eye*: (Ḳ:) in this sense [said to be] formed by transposition from أَشَاهَهُ. (TA.) ═ مَا أَشْهَاهَا إِلَىَّ means that she is desired, or eagerly desired, [i. e. *How great an object of desire is she to me!*] as though it were from شُهِىَ, though this was not said: and مَا أَشْهَانِى لَهَا means that thou art desiring, or eagerly desiring, [i. e. *How desirous,* or *eagerly desirous, am I of her!*] so says Sb. (TA.)

5. تشهّى *He demanded with repeated desire.* (Ḳ, TA.) So in the saying, (TA,) تشهّى عَلَى فُلَانٍ كَذَا (Ṣ, TA) [*He demanded with repeated desire, of such a one, such a thing*]. — See also what next follows.

8. اشتهاهُ (Ṣ, &c.) *He desired it,* or *longed for it*: (Mṣb:) *he loved it;* and *desired it,* or *wished for it*: (Ḳ:) or *he desired it eagerly,* or *intensely*: (M in art. فرس: [see an ex. in a poetical citation voce فَرْسٌ:]) and ▼ شَهِيَهُ, (Ṣ, Mṣb, Ḳ,) aor. ـَ; (Mṣb, Ḳ;) as also ▼ شَهَاهُ, aor. ـُ; (AZ, Mṣb, Ḳ;) inf. n. شَهْوَةٌ (Ṣ, TA) and شَاهِيَةٌ, which last is an inf. n. [of a rare class] like عَاقِبَةٌ; (TA;) signifies the same: (Ṣ, Mṣb, Ḳ:) and so does ▼ تَشَهَّاهُ. (Ḳ.) [See what next follows.]

شَهْوَةٌ [mentioned above as an inf. n.] is a word of well-known meaning; (Ṣ;) *Desire,* or *longing,* or *yearning, of the soul for a thing;* (Er-Rághib, Mṣb, TA;) [meaning *for a thing gratifying to sense*: or *eager,* or *intense, desire;* particularly *for such a thing;* for] *it has a more intensive signification than* إِرَادَةٌ; *and* the intelligent agree in opinion that *it is not commendable*: (M in art. فرس:) [being either *lawful* or *unlawful,* it may be rendered as above: or *appetite*: or *appetence*: or *lust*: or *carnal lust*:] *in the present state of existence, it is of two sorts,* صَادِقَةٌ [i. e. *true*], and كَاذِبَةٌ [i. e. *false*]; the former being *that without which the body becomes in an unsound state, as the* شَهْوَة [or *desire* &c.] *for food on the occasion of hunger;* and the latter being *that without which the body does not become in an unsound state*: and sometimes it is applied to the *object of desire* &c., or *thing desired* &c.: (Er-Rághib, TA:) and agreeably with this last explanation the first of the following pls. is used in the Ḳur iii. 12: (Ksh, Bḍ, Jel:) sometimes also it is applied to the *faculty to which a thing is made an object of desire* &c.: (Er-Rághib, TA:) [also, to the *gratification of venereal lust;* thus in the Ḳ in art. شفر; see شَفْرَتْ and شَفْرَةٌ:] the pl. is شَهَوَاتٌ (Mṣb, TA) and أَشْهِيَةٌ and شُهًى; the last mentioned by AHei, and a rare instance of a pl. of the measure فُعَلٌ from a sing. of the measure فَعْلَةٌ having an infirm letter for its last radical, like جُهًى pl. of جَهْوَةٌ [and like قُرًى pl. of قَرْيَةٌ]. (TA.) [الشَّهْوَتَانِ means The *two appetites, that of the stomach and that of the generative organ.*] الشَّهْوَةُ الخَفِيَّةُ [*The latent desire* &c.] mentioned in a trad. is said to be *any act of disobedience which one conceives in his mind, and upon which he resolves*: or *one's seeing a beautiful young woman, and lowering his eyes, then looking with his heart, and imaging her to his mind, and so tempting himself.* (JM.) [شَهْوَةُ الطِّينِ, lit. *The longing for clay,* is app. used as a general term for *malacia*: see خُمَاضٌ.]

شَهْوَانُ (Ṣ, Mṣb, Ḳ, TA) and ▼ شَهْوَانِىٌّ and ▼ شَهِىٌّ, (Ḳ, TA,) applied to a man, *Desirous,* or *longing;* (Ṣ,* Mṣb,* Ḳ,* TA;) or *very desirous* or *longing; greedy;* or *voracious*: (TA:) fem. (of the first, Mṣb) شَهْوَى: (Mṣb, Ḳ, TA:) pl. [of the first] شَهَاوَى, (Ḳ, TA,) like سَكَارَى [pl. of سَكْرَانُ]. (TA.) [See an ex. of the pl. in a verse cited voce جَوْذَبَانٌ.] One says, رَجُلٌ شَهْوَانُ لِلشَّىْءِ [*A man desirous* &c. *of the thing*]. (Ṣ.)

شَهْوَانِىٌّ: see the next preceding paragraph.

شَهِىٌّ *i. q.* ▼ مُشْتَهًى (Ṣ, Mṣb) [i. e. *Desired, longed for,* or *eagerly desired*:] or *pleasant, delicious,* or *sweet*: (Mṣb, TA:) applied to food, (Ṣ,) and to water. (TA.) — [Hence,] أَبُو الشَّهِىِّ † *The* بَرْبَط [or *Persian lute*]. (KL.) — [And Golius adds, as on the authority of a gloss in a copy of the KL, † *The water-melon* (*anguria*).] ═ See also شَهْوَانُ.

شَهَّآءٌ A man *having much,* or *frequent, desire* or *longing* or *eager desire.* (TA.) [See also شَهْوَانُ.]

شَاهٍ [act. part. n. of 1; *Desiring,* or *longing;* &c.]. (Sb, TA.) ═ شَاهِى البَصَرِ A man *sharp of sight*: (Ṣ, Ḳ:) formed by transposition from شَائِهُ البَصَرِ. (Ṣ.)

أَشْهَى [*More,* and *most, desirable,* or *pleasant* or *delicious* or *sweet*]. One says, هُوَ أَشْهَى إِلَىَّ مِنْ كَذَا [*It is more desirable,* or *pleasant* &c., *to me,* or *in my estimation, than such a thing*]. (Mṣb voce إِلَى.) See also another ex. in a verse cited voce إِلَى, in art. الو.

مُشْتَهًى: see شَهِىٌّ. — [Used as a subst., its pl. is مُشْتَهَيَاتٌ.]

شوأ

1. شَآءَنِى, formed by transposition from شَأَنِى, aor. يَشُوءُ and يَشِىءُ, [but the latter form of the aor. is disallowed by MF,] *He preceded me,* or *outwent me.* (Ḳ.) ═ And *He grieved me.* (Ḳ.) — And *He pleased me.* (Ḳ.) Thus it bears two contr. significations. (TA.) And شُؤْتُهُ, aor. أَشُوؤُهُ, *I pleased him.* (Lth, O.) — And شُؤْتُ بِهِ *I was pleased with, and rejoiced in, him,* or *it.* (Lth, O, Ḳ.) [See also art. شأو.]

شَآءٌ, n. un. شَآءَةٌ: see art. شوه.

شَيَّآنٌ, (Ḳ, TA, and L in art. تمع,) in form like the dual of سَيِّدٌ [except as to the final vowel], (TA,) [erroneously written in the CḲ شَيْئَانٌ,]

and شَيْآنٌ, like تَيْحَانٌ and تَيَّحَانٌ [q. v.], (L in art. تيح,) [applied to a man,] *Far-sighted*; (K;) either in the proper sense, or metonymically applied to a man *characterized by deliberation, and reflection, and looking to the results of affairs.* (TA.) Each is also applied as an epithet to a horse. (L in art. تيح.) [The radical letters of this epithet are either شوأ or شيأ; therefore it is mentioned again in art. شيأ; and another form thereof, without ء, (شَيَّان,) is mentioned in art. شوى.]

شوب

1. شَابَهُ, aor. يَشُوبُهُ, (Ṣ, A, Mṣb,) inf. n. شَوْبٌ (Ṣ, A, Mṣb, K) and شِيَابٌ, (K,) *He mixed it*; (Ṣ, A, Mṣb, K;) such as milk with water; (Mṣb;) or honey with water. (A.) [And *It mingled with it*: for] one says also, كَأَنَّ رِيقَتَهَا خَمْرٌ يَشُوبُهَا عَسَلٌ [*As though her saliva were wine with which honey mingled*]. (A.) — [It is sometimes used in a good sense, but more frequently in a bad sense; and often means *He adulterated, vitiated,* or *sophisticated, it.*] It is said in a trad., يَشْهَدُ بَيْعَكُمُ الحَلِفُ وَاللَّغْوُ فَشُوبُوهُ بِالصَّدَقَةِ † [*Swearing, and unprofitable speech, attend your selling; therefore mix ye it with alms*]. (TA.) And it is said in a prov., هُوَ يَشُوبُ وَيَرُوبُ † *He mixes,* or *confounds,* or *makes a confusion* or *disorder, in speech* and *in actions*: (Ṣ, TA:) or *he says right one time and wrong another time*: (Aṣ, TA:) or *he defends without energy*: (TA:) or *he is sometimes incited to motion, or action, and defends himself, but without energy, and sometimes he is motionless, and does not become excited to motion,* or *action*; and it is not from [the words شَوْبٌ and رَوْبٌ applied to] milk: so says Aboo-Sa'eed [i. e. Aṣ]: and he says also that شَابَ عَنْهُ وَرَابَ means *he defended him at one time, and was sluggish,* or *indolent, at another time*: and that ▼ شوّب عنه, inf. n. تَشْوِيبٌ, means *he defended him without energy*: and thus this latter is expl. in the K, as is likewise شاب عنه: also that the Arabs say, لَقِيتُ فُلَانًا اليَوْمَ يَشُوبُ عَنْ أَصْحَابِهِ, meaning *I found such a one to-day defending his companions in some measure.* (TA.) [See also art. روب.] — شاب also signifies *He acted treacherously, perfidiously,* or *unfaithfully*: (Fr, TA:) *he lied*: *he deceived in selling* or *buying*: and *he acted dishonestly, insincerely,* or *with dissimulation.* (IAạr, TA.) — [See also Ḥar p. 448; where it is implied that it signifies also *He spoke truth,* or *was veracious.*]

2: see the preceding paragraph.

7: see what next follows.

8: اشتاب *It was,* or *became, mixed*; (O, K;) as also ▼ انشاب. (K.)

شَوْبٌ inf. n. of 1 [q. v.]. (Ṣ, A, &c.) — [Hence,] لَا شَوْبَ وَلَا رَوْبَ, occurring in a trad., means *There is,* or *shall be, no dishonesty, insincerity,* or *dissimulation, nor mixing, in the selling,* or *buying*: so says IAạr: or *I am irresponsible with respect to this commodity*: or, as he is related to have said, *thou art irresponsible for its being faulty,* or *defective.* (TA. [See also شَوْبَةٌ.]) — And شَوْبٌ (TA) and ▼ شِيَابٌ, (Ṣ, TA,) [each an inf. n. used as a subst. properly so termed,] or ▼ شِيَابَةٌ, (so in one copy of the Ṣ,) signify *A mixture; an admixture;* or *a thing mixed with another thing.* (Ṣ, TA.) Thus شَوْبًا signifies in the Kur xxxvii. 65: (TA:) or, accord. to one reading, the word there is ▼ شُوبًا, meaning *a thing with which another thing is mixed.* (Bḍ.) الشَّوْبُ also signifies [particularly] *What is mixed* [*with something else*], *of water* or *of milk*: (K:) one says, سَقَاهُ الذَّوْبَ بِالشَّوْبِ *He gave him to drink honey with water,* or *milk, mixed* [*therewith*]: (TA:) or سَقَاهُ الشَّوْبَ بِالذَّوْبِ *He gave him to drink milk* [*mixed*] *with honey.* (IDrd, TA.) And *Mixed honey*; as in the saying, مَا عِنْدِى شَوْبٌ وَلَا رَوْبٌ *I have not mixed honey nor milk such as is termed* رَائِب [q. v.]: (IAạr, TA:) or [simply] *honey* &c.; (A, Mṣb, TA;) so called because they mix it with beverages; (Mṣb;) as in the saying, سَقَاهُ الشَّوْبَ بِالرَّوْبِ *He gave him to drink honey with clarified butter,* or *with milk.* (A.) And *Broth*; as in the saying, مَا عِنْدَهُ شَوْبٌ وَلَا رَوْبٌ *He has not broth nor milk.* (Ṣ, K: but in the latter, مَا لَهُ.) And شَوْبٌ signifies also *A piece of dough.* (K.) — And [the pl.] أَشْوَابٌ signifies † *A medley,* or *mixed multitude, of sundry sorts*: a less particular term than أَوْبَاشٌ, which signifies a medley, or mixed multitude, of the low, or lower, or lowest, sort: (TA, from a trad.:) accord. to El-Jawáleekee, it is an arabicized word, from the Pers. آشُوبْ. (TA in art. وشب.)

شُوبٌ: see شَوْبًا in the next preceding paragraph.

شَوْبَةٌ *Deceit, delusion, guile,* or *circumvention*: (K: [see also شَوْبٌ:]) [or, app., *somewhat thereof*:] one says, فِى فُلَانٍ شَوْبَةٌ [*In such a one is deceit,* &c.]. (TA.)

شَيْبَآءُ *A virgin in the night of her devirgination*: (Ibn-Abi-l-Ḥadeed, MF:) [either from شَابَ having for its aor. يَشُوبُ, signifying "he mixed," or from شَابَ having for its aor. يَشِيبُ, signifying "he became white-headed, or hoary;" as shown by what follows:] one says, بَاتَتْ بِلَيْلَةِ شَيْبَآءَ, (Ṣ and A in art. شيب, and K in the present art.,) and بِلَيْلَةِ الشَّيْبَآءِ, (K,) *She passed the night of a virgin then devirginated,* (Ṣ, A, K,) and *of the virgin then devirginated*: (K, TA:) said of a virgin-bride when she is devirginated by the bridegroom in the night in which she has been first brought to him: (A, K, TA:) in the contr. case, when she is not devirginated, one says, بَاتَتْ بِلَيْلَةِ حُرَّةٍ: (Ṣ, TA:) and one says also, بِلَيْلَةٍ حُرَّةٍ and بِلَيْلَةٍ شَيْبَآءَ: (TA in art. حر:) Z, in the A, mentions the first phrase in art. شيب, and makes it to be tropical, as though the bride were in that night afflicted by an event so severe as to cause the locks of her hair to become white: in the L it is said that the ى in شيباء is substituted for و, because of [the allusion of the phrase to] the mixing of the sperma genitale of the man with that of the woman; but that شَوْبَآءَ has not been heard instead of شيباء: ISd, in the M, mentions it in arts. شوب and شيب; observing that the ى is said to take the place of و: J, as well as Z and others, mentions it in art. شيب [q. v.]. (TA.)

شِيَابٌ and شِيَابَةٌ: see شَوْبٌ.

شَائِبَةٌ sing. of شَوَائِبُ meaning *The whiteness* [*mixing*] *with the darkness of night.* (Ḥar p. 58.) — The saying لَيْسَ فِيهِ شَائِبَةُ مُلْكٍ may be from شَابَهُ "he mixed it;" meaning *There is not in it anything* [*of ownership,* or *right of possession,*] *mixed therewith, though small,* or *however small*; like as one says, لَيْسَ فِيهِ عُلْقَةٌ وَلَا شُبْهَةٌ; it being an instance of the measure فَاعِلَةٌ in the sense of the measure مَفْعُولَةٌ, as in عِيشَةٌ رَاضِيَةٌ: thus the lawyers use it. (Mṣb.) — شَائِبَةٌ is also sing. of شَوَائِبُ meaning *Uncleannesses, filths,* or *pollutions*; or *unclean, filthy,* or *foul, things.* (Ṣ, Mṣb, K.*)

مَشُوبٌ (Ṣ, Mṣb) and مَشِيبٌ, the latter from شِيبَ ["it was mixed"], *Mixed.* (Ṣ, Mṣb.) A poet says, (namely, Suleyk Ibn-Es-Sulakeh Es-Saadee, TA,)

وَمَآءِ قُدُورٍ فِى القِصَاعِ مَشِيبِ

i. e. [*And the water of cooking-pots, in the wooden bowls,*] *mixed* with seeds for seasoning and with sauces. (Ṣ.) — الفَتْحَةُ المَشُوبَةُ بِالكَسْرَةِ means [*The fet-ḥah that is mingled with kesreh*; which is] *the fet-ḥah that precedes the* ا *of* إِمَالَة; as in عَابِدٌ and عَارِفٌ [when they are pronounced "'ébidun" and "'érifun"]; for امالة consists in inclining [the sound of] fet-ḥah towards [that of] kesreh; whereby [the sound of] the ا that follows it is inclined, and is not a pure ا; for like as [the sound of] the fet-ḥah is mingled [with that of kesreh], so is [the sound of] the ا [mingled with that of ى]. (L, TA.)

مُشَاوَبٌ, with ḍamm [to the م], and fet-ḥ to the و, [not with both of these vowels to the و as supposed by Freytag,] *The case* (غِلَاف) *of a flask* or *bottle*; (K;) because it is mixed with redness and yellowness and greenness; mentioned by AHát on the authority of Aṣ: (TA:) pl. مَشَاوِبُ: (AHát, K:) or the pl. signifies [*receptacles of the sorts called*] أَسْفَاط [pl. of سَفَط] *and* حُقَق [pl. of حُقَّة] *made of palm-leaves.* (A.)

شوذ

2. شَوَّذَ السَّحَابُ الشَّمْسَ *The clouds covered the sun,* (K,) *as though it were turbaned with a dust-coloured haze inclining to yellow*; as is the case in a year of drought; i. e. (T, L) *thin clouds containing no water surrounding it,* (T, L, K,) *having the hue above described.* (T, L.) — شُوِّذَتِ الشَّمْسُ [thus in the L and K, not شَوَّذَتْ nor تَشَوَّذَتْ,] *The sun inclined to setting,* (T, L, K,) *and became covered with such clouds* [*as those above described*]: (T, L:) *became turbaned with clouds.* (AHn, L.) — شَوَّذَهُ, (inf. n. تَشْوِيذٌ, L,) † *He turbaned him*; *attired him with a turban*: (AZ, T, L, K:) app.

from شوّدت الشمس. (T, L.) And شوّد رَأْسَهُ † *He turbaned his head.* (Mṣb.)

5. تشوّد and ♦ اشتاد † *He turbaned himself; attired himself with a turban.* (AZ, T, Ṣ, L, Ḳ.) [See above.]

8: see what next precedes.

فُلَانٌ حَسَنُ الشِّيدَةِ † *Such a one is goodly in his manner of turbaning.* (Ḳ.)

خَيْرُ الأَشَاوِدِ † *The best of the creation,* or *of mankind,* or *people;* syn. خَيْرُ الخَلْقِ. (Ḳ.)

مِشْوَدٌ † *A turban;* (IAạr, Ṣ, Mgh, L, Mṣb, Ḳ;) as also ♦ مِشْوَادٌ: (Ḳ:) pl. of the former مَشَاوِدُ; (Ṣ, Mgh, L, Mṣb, Ḳ;) and of the latter مَشَاوِيدُ. (Ḳ.) — † *A king:* (Ḳ:) *a crowned king.* (TA.) — † *A lord,* or *chief,* (Ḳ,) *to whom obedience is paid.* (TA.)

مِشْوَادٌ: see the next preceding paragraph.

شور

1. شَارَ, (Ṣ, A, Mṣb, Ḳ,) aor. يَشُورُ, (Mṣb,) inf. n. شَوْرٌ (Mṣb, Ḳ) and شِيَارٌ and شِيَارَةٌ and مَشَارٌ and مَشَارَةٌ; (Ḳ;) and ♦ اشتار, and ♦ اشار, (Ṣ, Ḳ,) and ♦ استشار; (A, Ḳ;) *He gathered* honey; (Ṣ, Mṣb;) *extracted it from the small hollow* [*in the rock in which it had been deposited by the wild bees*]; (A, Ḳ;) *gathered it from its hives* and *from other places.* (TA.) ═ شار, inf. n. شَوْرٌ, *He exhibited, showed,* or *displayed,* a thing. (IAth, TA.) — شار الدَّابَّةَ, (Ṣ, A, Mgh, Mṣb, Ḳ,) inf. n. شَوْرٌ (Ṣ, Mgh, Mṣb, Ḳ) and شِوَارٌ, (Ḳ, TA,) or شَوَارٌ; (CḲ;) and ♦ شوّرها, (A, Ḳ,) inf. n. تَشْوِيرٌ; (TA;) and ♦ اشارها, (Th, Ḳ,) but this last is rare; (Th, TA;) *He exhibited,* or *displayed, the beast, for sale,* (Ṣ, A, Mgh, Mṣb,) *going to and fro with it,* (Ṣ, Mgh,) or *making it to run, and the like:* (Mṣb:) *he tried the beast, to know its pace,* or *manner of going:* (A, Mgh:) *he made the beast to run, that he might know its power:* (TA:) *he broke,* or *trained, the beast:* or *he rode it on the occasion of exhibiting,* or *displaying, it to its purchaser:* or *tried it, to see its powers:* or *he examined it, as though he turned it over;* and in like manner, الأَمَةَ *the female slave.* (Ḳ, TA.) [Hence] شار نَفْسَهُ *He displayed his agility, to show his power.* (TA, from a trad.) — And شُرْتُهُ *I ornamented,* or *decorated, it.* (TA.) ═ شار *He* (a man) *became goodly in countenance.* (Fr, TA.) — *He* (a horse) *became fat and goodly:* (Ṣ:) and so ♦ تشوّرت said of a she-camel: (TA:) [and شارت said of a woman: (Freytag, from the Deewán of the Hudhalees:)] or شارت said of a she-camel, *she became fat;* (Ḳ;) and in like manner ♦ اشتار, and ♦ استشار said of a he-camel: (Ṣ:) and ♦ اشتارت الإبل *the camels became somewhat fat:* (Ṣ:) and ♦ استشارت *they became fat and goodly:* (Ḳ:) or this last signifies ‡ *they became fat;* because their owner points to such with his fingers; as though they desired to be pointed to. (A.)

2. شوّر الدَّابَّةَ, inf. n. تَشْوِيرٌ: see 1. — شوّر بهِ *He did to him a deed of which one should be ashamed:* (Yaḳoob, Th, A, Ḳ:) or *he made bare his pudenda:* (O:) or *as though he made bare his pudenda.* (Ṣ.) — And شوّرهُ, (Lh, Ṣ,) and شوّر بهِ, (Lḥ, TA,) *He made him to be confounded,* or *perplexed, and unable to see his right course, by reason of shame;* or *ashamed, and confounded,* or *perplexed, and unable to see his right course, in consequence of a deed that he had done.* (Lḥ, Ṣ.) — شوّر القُطْنَ *He turned over* [or *separated and loosened*] *the cotton* by means of the مِشْوَار [q. v.]. (TA.) — See also 4, in two places.

3. شاورهُ, (inf. n. مُشَاوَرَةٌ and شِوَارٌ, TA,) and ♦ استشارهُ, both signify the same, (Ṣ, Mṣb,) *He consulted him,* or *consulted with him; he debated with him in order that he might see his opinion;* (Mṣb;) فِى الأَمْرِ *respecting the thing* or *affair:* (Ṣ, Mgh,* Mṣb:*) or ♦ the latter, (A, Ḳ,) or both, (TA,) *he sought, desired,* or *asked, of him counsel,* or *advice.* (A, Ḳ.) See also 6.

4: see 1, first sentence. — أَشِرْنِى عَسَلًا, (Ḳ,) or عَلَى العَسَلِ, (Sh, Ṣgh, L,) *Help thou me to collect honey,* or *the honey.* (Sh, Ṣgh, L, Ḳ.) ═ اشار الدَّابَّةَ: see 1. ═ اشار النَّارَ, and اشار بِهَا, (Ḳ,) or اَشْوَرَ بِهَا, or اَشْوَرَهَا, (accord. to different copies of the Ḳ, the former accord. to the text of the Ḳ in the TA,) and ♦ شوّر بِهَا, (Ḳ, TA,) *He stirred up the fire,* or *made it to burn up;* syn. رَفَعَهَا. (Ḳ.) ═ اشار إِلَيْهِ, (Ṣ, Mṣb, Ḳ,) inf. n. إِشَارَةٌ, (Mṣb,) *He made a sign to him,* with the hand, (Ṣ, Mṣb, Ḳ,) or with the head, (Mṣb,) or with the eye, or with the eyebrow, (Ḳ,) or with a thing serving to convey intelligence of what he would say; *as when one asks another's permission to do a thing, and the latter makes a sign with his hand* or *with his head, meaning that he should do it or not do it;* (Mṣb;) as also ♦ شوّر اليه, (ISk, Ṣ, Mṣb, Ḳ,) inf. n. تَشْوِيرٌ. (Mṣb.) — [And *He,* or *it, pointed to it* or *at it, pointed it out,* or *indicated it.* Hence, in grammar, اِسْمُ إِشَارَةٍ *A noun of indication;* as ذَا &c. And اشار إِلَى الحَرَكَةِ بِصَوْتٍ خَفِيٍّ [*He indicated the vowel by a somewhat obscure sound;*] meaning *he pronounced the vowel in the manner termed* الرَّوْمُ. (I'Aḳ p. 351.) And اشار إِلَى الإِعْرَابِ فِى الوَقْفِ [*He indicated the case-ending by the pronunciation termed* الرَّوْمُ *in pausing;* as when you say أَىٌّ with a slurring of the final vowel-sound to one who says to you مَرَّبِى رَجُلٌ]. (Ṣ voce أَىٌّ.) — اشار بهِ *He made it known.* (Ḥar p. 357.) — اشار عَلَيْهِ *He made known,* or *notified, to him the manner of accomplishing the affair that was conducive to good, and guided him to that which was right.* (Ḥar ibid.) — اشار عَلَيْهِ بِكَذَا [in the CḲ اليه] *He counselled him,* or *advised him, to do such a thing;* (Ṣ,* Mṣb;) *showed him that he held it right for him to do such a thing:* (Mṣb:) or *he commanded, ordered,* or *enjoined, him to do such a thing.* (Ḳ.)

5. تشوّر *He had a deed done to him of which one should be ashamed.* (Yaḳoob, Th, A, Ḳ.) [It occurs in a saying of Yaḳoob, respecting an indecent action of an Arab of the desert, app. as meaning *His pudenda became exposed;* (see 2;) but some disapprove it, and say that it is not genuine Arabic; as is stated in the TA.] — *He was,* or *became, confounded,* or *perplexed, and unable to see his right course, by reason of shame;* or *ashamed, and confounded,* or *perplexed, and unable to see his right course, in consequence of a deed that he had done.* (Lḥ, Ṣ.) ═ See also 1, last sentence.

6. تشاوروا and ♦ اِشْتَوَرُوا (A, Mgh, Mṣb) *They consulted one another,* or *consulted together; they debated together in order that they might see one another's opinion:* (Mṣb:) تَشَاوُرٌ signifies the *extracting,* or *drawing forth, opinion;* as also ♦ مُشَاوَرَةٌ and ♦ مَشُورَةٌ and ♦ مَشْوَرَةٌ, from شَارَ "he extracted honey;" (Bḍ in iii. 233;) and ♦ شُورَى signifies the same as تَشَاوُرٌ. (Bḍ in xlii. 36, and Mgh.) ═ تَشَايَرَهُ النَّاسُ occurs in a trad. as meaning اِشْتَهَرُوهُ بِأَبْصَارِهِمْ [app. *The people rendered him conspicuous,* or *notorious, by their looking at him*]. (TA. [There mentioned in the present art.; as though the ى were a substitute for و.])

8. اشتار: see 1, first sentence. — And see 10. ═ See also 1, last sentence, in two places. ═ اشتار ذَنَبَهُ i. q. اكْتَارَ [*He* (a horse) *raised his tail* in running]. (Ṣgh, TA.) ═ اِشْتَوَرُوا: see 6.

10. استشار: see 1, first sentence. — See also 3, in two places. — استشار النَّاقَةَ *He* (a stallion-camel) *smelt the she-camel and examined her, to know if she had conceived or not;* (Ḳ;) as also ♦ اشتارها. (A'Obeyd, TA.) ═ *It* (a man's case or affair) *became manifest.* (AZ, Ḳ.) — *He put on,* or *clad himself with, goodly apparel.* (Ḳ.) — See also 1, last sentence, in two places.

شَارٌ: see شَيِّرٌ, in two places.

شَوْرٌ *Honey gathered,* or *extracted, from its place:* (Ḳ, TA:) originally an inf. n. (TA.) — See also شُورَةٌ, with which it is syn. in several senses accord. to the O and some copies of the Ḳ.

شُورٌ: see شُورَةٌ, with which it is syn. in several senses accord. to the L and some copies of the Ḳ.

شَارَةٌ: see شُورَةٌ, in three places.

شَوْرَةٌ: see شُورَةٌ, in three places: ═ and see مَشُورَةٌ. ═ Also i. q. خَجْلَةٌ [i. e. *Confusion,* or *perplexity, and inability to see one's right course, by reason of shame:* &c.]. (Ḳ.)

شُورَةٌ, (Ṣ, IAth, O, L, Ḳ,) with ḍamm, (IAth, L,) and ♦ شَوْرَةٌ, (TA, and so in some copies of the Ḳ,) and ♦ شَارَةٌ, (Ṣ, O, L, Ḳ,) in which the ا is changed from و, (TA,) and ♦ شُورٌ, (so in the L and in some copies of the Ḳ,) or ♦ شَوْرٌ, (so in other copies of the Ḳ and in the O,) and ♦ شِوَارٌ, (Ṣ, O, Ḳ,) and ♦ شِيَارٌ, (O, Ḳ,) *Form,* or *appearance; figure, person, mien, feature,* or *lineament; external state* or *condition; state with respect to apparel and the like,* or *garb.* (Ṣ, IAth, O, L, Ḳ.) One says, فُلَانٌ حَسَنُ الشَّارَةِ ♦ and الشُّورَةِ *Such a one is goodly in form* or *appearance,* &c. (TA.) And هُوَ رَجُلٌ حَسَنُ الصُّورَةِ وَالشُّورَةِ *He is a man goodly in respect of form and of appear-*

ance, &c. (Fr. Ṣ. [See also below.]) — *Goodliness,* or *beauty:* (IAth, L, Ḳ:) so شُورَةٌ is expl. by IAạr: (O:) and ▼ شَوْرَةٌ, with fet-ḥ, is expl. as signifying *pleasing beauty:* (TA:) app. from شَوْرٌ, the "act of exhibiting, or showing," a thing. (IAth, TA.) — *Clothing,* or *apparel:* (Ṣ, O, L, Ḳ:) ▼ شَوْرَةٌ, with fet-ḥ, is said to have this signification by Th: and ▼ شَارَةٌ is also expl. as signifying *goodly,* or *beautiful, apparel.* (TA.) — *Ornament,* or*nature,* or *finery.* (Ḳ.) — *Fatness.* (Ḳ.) — And شُورَةٌ, with ḍamm, and ▼ مَشْوَارٌ, *Aspect,* or *pleasing aspect;* syn. مَنْظَرٌ: and *Internal,* or *intrinsic, state* or *quality;* syn. مَخْبَرٌ. (Ḳ,* TA.) One says, ▼ لَيْسَ لِفُلَانٍ مَشْوَارٌ i. e. مَنْظَرٌ [*Such a one has not a pleasing aspect*]. (TA.) And فُلَانٌ حَسَنُ الصُّورَةِ وَالشُّورَةِ *Such a one is good in respect of form, and of internal state* or *qualities, when tried.* (TA.) And ▼ فُلَانٌ حَسَنُ المَشْوَارِ *Such a one is good when one tries him.* (Aṣ, TA.) — For the first word (شُورَةٌ), see also مِشْوَارَةٌ. — And see مُسْتَشِيرٌ.

شُورَى *A certain marine plant;* (Ḳ;) a *sort of trees, of the trees of the shores of the sea:* (Ṣgh, TA:) [it is, as supposed by Freytag, the plant called by Forskål (Flora Aegypt. Arab, p. 37,) *sceura marina; of the class tetrandria, order monogynia; foliis lanceolatis, integris; floribus fulvis:* &c.: said by him to be called in Arabic "schura" شوره; and by the people of Maskaṭ, "germ" قرم:] *a sort of trees growing in inlets of the sea, in the midst of the water of the sea, resembling the* دُلْب *in the thickness of its stem and the whiteness of its bark, and also called* قُرْم. (O.)

شُورَى: see مَشُورَةٌ, in four places; and 6.

شُوَرَانٌ [whether with or without tenween is not shown] i. q. عُصْفُرٌ [i. e. *Safflower,* or *bastard saffron*]. (Ḳ.)

شَوَارٌ: see شُورَةٌ. — Also, (ISk, Ṣ, Mṣb, Ḳ,) and ▼ شِوَارٌ, and ▼ شُوَارٌ, (Mṣb, Ḳ,) The *furniture and utensils of a house* or *tent;* (ISk, Ṣ, Mṣb, Ḳ;) *such as are deemed goodly:* (Ḥam p. 305, in explanation of the first:) and *of a camel's saddle.* (Ṣ, Mṣb.) — And the first, (Ṣ, Mṣb, Ḳ,) and ▼ second, (Mṣb, Ḳ,) and ▼ third, (Ḳ,) The *pudendum,* or *pudenda,* (فَرْج, Ṣ, Mṣb,) of a woman and of a man: (Ṣ:) or a man's *penis,* [see also مِشْوَارٌ,] and his *testicles,* and his *posteriors* or *anus* (اِسْت). (Ḳ.) أَبْدَى ٱللّٰهُ شَوَارَهُ is a form of imprecation, (TA,) meaning *May God make bare his pudenda.* (Ṣ, A, TA.) — رِيحٌ شَوَارٌ *A soft,* or *gentle, wind:* (Ṣgh, Ḳ:) of the dial. of El-Yemen. (Ṣgh, TA.)

شُوَارٌ: } شِوَارٌ: } see شَوَارٌ; each in two places.

شِيَارٌ: see شُورَةٌ. — Also a name given by the Arabs to *Saturday,* (Ṣ in this art., and Ḳ in art. شير,) in the Time of Ignorance: (TA in art. شير:) pl. [of pauc.] أَشْيُرٌ and [of mult.] شُيُرٌ and شِيَرٌ: (Zj, Ḳ:) accord. to Zj, you may say ثَلَاثَةُ شِيَرٍ [*Three Saturdays,* using شير as a pl. of pauc.]: so in the Tekmileh. (TA.)

شَيِّرٌ One's *consulter,* or *counseller with whom he consults:* and one's وَزِير [q. v.]: (Ḳ:) one *qualified for consultation:* (Ṣ, TA:) pl. شُورَآءُ. (Ḳ.) One says, فُلَانٌ خَيِّرٌ شَيِّرٌ *Such a one is* [*good,*] *qualified for consultation.* (Ṣ, TA.) — A man *goodly in respect of* شَارَة [i. e. *appearance,* or *apparel,* &c.]: (Fr, Ṣ, A:) or *beautiful,* or *good:* in this or in the former sense, the fem., with ة, is applied to a woman. (TA.) One says, إِنَّهُ لَصَيِّرٌ شَيِّرٌ *Verily he is goodly in form and in appearance* or *apparel* &c. (Fr, Ṣ, A.) — A man *goodly in his internal,* or *intrinsic, states* or *qualities, when tried;* as also ▼ شَارٌ: one says رَجُلٌ شَيِّرٌ صَيِّرٌ and ▼ شَارٌ صَارٌ *A man goodly in his internal,* or *intrinsic, states* or *qualities, and equally so in his outward appearance.* (TA.) — *Fat:* (TA:) or *fat and goodly:* (Ṣ, Ḳ, TA:) pl. شِيَارٌ, applied to horses, (Ṣ, Ḳ,) and to camels. (Ṣ.) — قَصِيدَةٌ شَيِّرَةٌ *A beautiful ode;* (Ḳ;) *an excellent ode.* (TA.)

أَشْوَرُ [*More,* and *most, distinguished by* شُورَة or شَارَة, i. e., *form,* or *appearance;* &c.]. أَشْوَرُ عَرُوسٍ تُرَى [*The comeliest bride that was to be seen*] is a phrase occurring in a trad. relating to Ez-Zebbà [a queen of El-Ḥeereh, celebrated for her beauty]. (A, TA.)

مَشَارٌ A خَلِيَّة [or *habitation of bees,* generally *a hollow in a rock,*] (Ṣ, Ḳ,) *from which one gathers,* or *extracts, honey;* (Ṣ;) *a bee-hive;* as also ▼ مُشْتَارٌ. (KL.) See the next paragraph. [And see also مِشْوَارَةٌ.]

مَاذِىُّ مُشَارٍ *White honey* (TA) *gathered,* (Ṣ, TA,) or *which one has been assisted to gather.* (Ḳ, TA.) AA cites the following verse, (Ṣ,) of El-Ḳuṭámee, (accord. to a copy of the Ṣ,) or of 'Adee Ibn-Zeyd, (O, TA.)

* وَسَمَاعٍ يَأْذَنُ الشَّيْخُ لَهُ *
* وَحَدِيثٍ مِثْلِ مَاذِىِّ مُشَارْ *

[*And a singing,* or *a musical performance,* (or, instead of *And,* the meaning may be *Many,*) *to which the old man would lend ear, and a discourse like gathered white honey*]: but Aṣ disapproves of this, and says that the right reading is مَاذِىِّ ▼ مَشَارْ [*white honey of a habitation of bees from which it has been extracted*], the former of these words being prefixed to the latter, governing it in the gen. case, and the latter being with fet-ḥ to the م. (Ṣ, TA.)

مُشَوَّرٌ A thing *ornamented,* or *decorated.* (Ḳ.)

مِشْوَرٌ, (Ṣ,) or ▼ مِشْوَارٌ, (Ḳ,) or both, (TA,) The *wooden implement with which honey is gathered:* (Ṣ, Ḳ,* TA:) pl. of the former مَشَاوِرُ. (Ṣ.)

مَشَارَةٌ: see مِشْوَارٌ. — Also *A rivulet,* or *streamlet, for irrigation;* syn. سَاقِيَةٌ: (TA voce رَكِيب:) or *a channel of water:* (TA voce دَبْر:) or a دَبْرَة [i. e. either a *small channel of water for irrigation* or a *portion of ground*] *in land sown* or *for sowing:* (Ṣ, Ḳ:) or *a* دَبْرَة [app. here meaning a *portion of ground*] *cut off,* or *separated, from the adjacent parts,* (مُقْطَعَة,) *for sowing and for planting:* it may be of this art., or from ٱلْمَشْرَة: (ISd, TA:) or *what is surrounded by dams* [or *by ridges of earth*] *which confine,* or *retain, the water* [*for irrigation*]; as also دَبْرَةٌ and حِبْسٌ: (R, TA:) pl. مَشَاوِرُ and مَشَائِرُ. (Ḳ.)

مَشْوَرَةٌ: see the next paragraph, in four places.

مَشُورَةٌ and ▼ مَشْوَرَةٌ and ▼ شُورَى signify the same: (Ṣ:) the first and second are substs. from شَاوَرَهُ, and the third is a subst. from تَشَاوَرُوا: (Mṣb:) or the first (Lth) and second [which is written in the CḲ مَشُورَة] (Lth, Ḳ) and third (Ḳ) are from ٱلْإِشَارَة (Lth) or أَشَارَ عَلَيْهِ: (Ḳ:) [they signify *Consultation;* or *mutual debate in order that one may see another's opinion;* or *counsel,* or *advice:* or *a command, an order,* or *an injunction:* or] the *extracting,* or *drawing forth, opinion:* (Bḍ, as mentioned above: see 6:) ▼ مَشُورَةٌ [in the CḲ مَشْوَرَة] is of the measure مَفْعُلَةٌ, [originally مَشْوُرَةٌ, in the CḲ مَفْعَلَة,] not مَفْعُولَةٌ, (Ḳ, TA,) because it is an inf. n., [or rather a quasi-inf. n.,] and such a noun has not this last measure: (TA:) it is like مَعُونَةٌ; (Mṣb;) and is a contraction of مَشْوُرَةٌ: (Fr, TA:) and it is said also to be from شَارَ الدَّابَّةَ; or, accord. to some, from شَارَ العَسَلَ; good counsel or advice being likened to honey. (Mṣb.) One says, عَلَيْكَ بِٱلْمَشُورَةِ فِى أُمُورِكَ and ▼ بِٱلْمَشْوَرَةِ [*Keep thou to consultation,* or *take counsel, in thine affairs*]. (A.) And ▼ فُلَانٌ جَيِّدُ المَشْوَرَةِ and المَشُورَةِ [*Such a one is good,* or *excellent, in consultation,* or *counsel*]. (TA.) And ▼ أَمْرُهُمْ شُورَى بينهم, like امرهم فوضى بينهم, [*Their affair,* or *case, is a thing to be determined by consultation among themselves,*] i. e., none of them is to appropriate a thing to himself exclusively of others. (Mṣb.) It is said of 'Omar, ▼ تَرَكَ الخِلَافَةَ شُورَى (A, Mgh) *He left the office of Khaleefeh as a thing to be determined by consultation:* for he assigned it to one of six; not particularizing for it any one of them; namely, 'Othmán and 'Alee and Ṭalḥah and Ez-Zubeyr and 'Abd-Er-Raḥmán Ibn-'Owf and Saạd Ibn-Abee-Waḳḳáṣ. (Mgh.) And one says also, ▼ النَّاسُ فِيهِ شُورَى [*The people are to determine by consultation respecting it*]. (A.)

المُشِيرَةُ *The forefinger,* or *pointing finger.* (A, Ḳ.)

ثَوْبٌ مُشَوَّرٌ *A garment,* or *piece of cloth, dyed with* شُوَرَان, meaning عُصْفُر [i. e. *safflower*]. (Ḳ, TA.)

مِشْوَارٌ: see مِشْوَرٌ. — Also The *string of the* مِنْدَف [q. v.]: (Ḳ, TA:) because the cotton is turned over [or separated and loosened] (يُشَوَّرُ i. e. يُقَلَّبُ) by means of it. (TA.) — Also *A place in which beasts are exhibited,* or *displayed,*

(Ṣ, A, Mgh, Mṣb, Ḳ,) *for sale, and in which they run.* (Mgh, Mṣb.) Hence the saying, إِيَّاكَ وَالخُطَبَ فَإِنَّهَا مِشْوَارٌ كَثِيرُ العِثَارِ ‡ [*Avoid thou orations, for they are means of display in which one often stumbles*]. (Ṣ, A, Ḳ.) — And The *pace*, or *manner of going*, of a horse: one says فَرَسٌ حَسَنُ المِشْوَارِ [*A horse good in respect of pace*, or *manner of going*]. (A.) ═ See also شُورَةٌ, latter part, in three places. — One says of camels, (Ḳ,) or of a beast, (دَابَّة, TA,) أَخَذَتْ مِشْوَارَهَا and ▼ مَشَارَتَهَا *They*, or *it, became fat and goodly* (Ḳ, TA) *in appearance.* (TA.) ═ [It occurs in the O and Ḳ, in art. خوق, as signifying The *penis* of a horse: perhaps a mistranscription for شِوَار, q. v.: I find it expl. in this sense in Johnson's Pers., Arab., and Engl. Dict.; but he may have taken it from the Ḳ.] ═ [It is said to signify] also *A portion that a beast has left remaining of its fodder:* (O, Ḳ, TA:) but Kh says, "I asked ADḳ, Is it مِشْوَار or نِشْوَار? and he said نِشْوَار, and asserted it to be Pers.:" (O, TA:) it is an arabicized word, (Ḳ,) originally نُشْخُوار: (O, Ḳ: or, as in the CḲ, نُشْخوار: [correctly نُشْخُوار or نِشْخُوار:]) one says, نَشْوَرَتِ الدَّابَّةُ نِشْوَارًا. (TA.)

مَشْوَارَةٌ *A place in which bees deposit their honey;* as also ▼ شُورَةٌ; (Ḳ;) or, as written by Ṣgh, the latter word is [▼ شَوْرَةٌ,] with fet-ḥ. (TA.) [See also مَشَار.]

مُشْتَارٌ *A gatherer of honey.* (Ṣ, TA.) — See also مَشَار.

مُسْتَشِيرٌ *Fat;* (AA, Ṣ;) as also ▼ شُورَةٌ, with ḍamm, applied to a she-camel: (Ḳ:) or the latter signifies *of generous race;* or *excellent.* (TA.) [See also شَيِّر.] — And A stallion-camel (El-Umawee, T, Ṣ) *that knows the female which has not conceived, and distinguishes her from others.* (El-Umawee, T, Ṣ, Ḳ.)

شوس

1. شَوِسَ, (Ḳ,) aor. يَشْوَسُ, (TA,) inf. n. شَوَسٌ; (Ṣ, A, Ḳ, TA;) and شَاسَ, aor. يَشَاسُ, (Lth, Ḳ, TA,) or يَشُوسُ; (Ḥam p. 68;) *He looked from the outer angle of his eye, by reason of pride*, or *of anger*, or *rage:* (Ṣ, A, Ḳ:) or, as in the M, *he looked with one of his eyes, inclining his face towards the side of that eye; doing so naturally, or by reason of pride and self-conceit and anger:* or *he raised his head in pride:* (TA:) or *he made the eye small, contracting the lids, to look:* and ▼ تشاوس has the first of the meanings above mentioned; (A, Ḳ;) or the last: (A:) or one says, تشاوس فِى نَظَرِهِ, meaning *he looked with the look of the haughty*, or *proud:* (TA:) or تشاوس إِلَيْهِ *he looked at him from the outer angle of his eye, inclining his face towards the side of the eye with which he looked:* (AA, Ṣ, TA: [see also 3:]) or تشاوس signifies *he looked towards the sky with one of his eyes:* or it means *he showed*, or *manifested, pride and self-conceit, and haughtiness;* agreeably with the general analogy of verbs of this measure: and شَوَسٌ is in the natural disposition. (TA.) — Also *He was such as is termed* أَشْوَس meaning *bold*, or *daring, to engage in fight, and strong.* (TA.) ═ شَوْسٌ [inf. n. of شَاسَ] in relation to the سِوَاك [or tooth-stick] is a dial. var. of شَوْصٌ: (IAạr, Ḳ, TA:) one says, شَاسَ فَاهُ بِالسِّوَاكِ, like شَاصَهُ [q. v.]. (Fr, TA.)

3. شَاوَسَهُ [*He looked at him in the manner of him who is termed* أَشْوَس; like تشاوس إِلَيْهِ: see مُشَاوِس].

6: see the first paragraph.

أَشْوَسُ, applied to a man, (Ṣ, A,) *Who looks in the manner expl. above, in the first sentence of this art.:* (Ṣ, A, Ḳ:) or *in whose look is known anger;* or *rancour, malevolence, malice*, or *spite;* and *pride:* (TA:) or *raising his head by reason of pride:* (AA, TA:) fem. شَوْسَآءُ: (A, TA:) and pl. شُوسٌ. (Ṣ, A, Ḳ.) [Hence the saying,] بُلِىَ فُلَانٌ بِشُوسِ الخُطُوبِ ‡ [*Such a one was tried with terrifying*, or *severe, calamities* or *afflictions*]. (A, TA.) — Also *Bold*, or *daring, to engage in fight, and strong.* (TA. [See also شُوش: and see أَشْوَش.])

مُشَاوِسٌ ‡ Water *hardly to be seen, by reason of its paucity, and the depth to which it has sunk;* (A,* Ḳ;) as though it looked at him who came to it in the manner of him who is termed أَشْوَس (كَأَنَّهُ يُشَاوِسُ الوَارِدَ). (A, TA.)

شوش

2. شَوَّشَ عَلَيْهِ الأَمْرَ, inf. n. تَشْوِيشٌ, *He rendered the affair*, or *state*, or *case, confused, disordered*, or *perplexed, to him:* (El-Fárábee, Ṣ,* Mṣb: the inf. n., and that only, mentioned in the Ṣ in art. شيش:) or, accord. to certain of those skilled in the abstrusities and niceties of science, شوّش is a post-classical word, and the chaste word is هَوَّشَ: accord. to IAmb, the leading lexicologists hold that one should only say هوّش; and Az and others say the same: (Mṣb:) [F also says,] تَشْوِيش is a mistake for تَهْوِيش. (Ḳ.) See also شَوَاشِ.

5. تشوّش عَلَيْهِ الأَمْرُ *The affair*, or *state*, or *case, became confused*, or *perplexed, to him:* (El-Fárábee, Ṣ, Mṣb: mentioned in the Ṣ in art. شيش:) or this is post-classical: (Mṣb:) or تَشَوُّش is a mistake for تَهَوُّش. (Ḳ.)

6. تشاوش القَوْمُ *The people*, or *company of men, became mixed*, or *confounded, together;* syn. تَهَاوَشَ. (Ṣgh, Ḳ.*)

شُوش in the phrase أَبْطَالٌ شُوشٌ *i. q.* شُوسٌ [pl. of أَشْوَس, q. v.]. (O, Ḳ.)

شَوْشَآةٌ and شَوْشَاةٌ, (Lth, O, Ḳ,) or the former is a mistake, (TA,) the latter said by Az to be that which he heard from the Arabs, (O, TA,) applied to a she-camel, *Light*, or *agile:* (Lth, O, Ḳ:) or, so applied, *swift:* (A'Obeyd, O:) and applied to a woman as an epithet of discommendation. (O.) A poet, cited by AA, applies the epithet ▼ شَوَاشِئ, with hemz, by poetic license, to a نَاضِح [properly meaning a camel upon which water is drawn from a well]; originally from شَوْشَآة, (O,) or شَوْشَاة, (TA,) meaning "Light," or "agile," applied to a she-camel: so says AA. (O, TA.)

بَيْنَهُمْ شَوَاشِ, (O, and so in the TA as from the Ḳ,) or شَوَاشٌ, (so in the CḲ and in my MS. copy of the Ḳ,) *Between them is disagreement, dissension, discord*, or *difference:* (O, Ḳ:) the vulgar say ▼ تَشْوِيش. (O, TA.)

شَوَاشِئ: see شَوْشَآة.

مِشْوَش, (so accord. to my copy of the KL,) or مُشْوَش, (so accord. to Golius from the KL,) *A small turban* (دَسْتَارْچَهْ). (KL. [Comp. مِشْوَذ.])

مُشَاوِش Water *not to be seen*, (Ḳ,) or *hardly to be seen*, (TA,) *by reason of its remoteness* [*from the surface of the ground*] *or its paucity:* (Ḳ:) a dial. var. of مُشَاوِس [q. v.]. (TA.)

شوص

1. شَاصَ, aor. يَشُوصُ (Ṣ, A, Mgh, Mṣb, Ḳ) and يَشَاصُ, in all its senses, (O, Ḳ,) inf. n. شَوْصٌ, (Ṣ, Mgh, Mṣb, Ḳ,) *He set up* a thing *with his hand:* (Mṣb, Ḳ:) or *he put it into a state of commotion:* (Mṣb:) or it signifies also *he moved it violently from its place.* (IDrd, Ḳ.) — *He rubbed* a thing *with his hand.* (IAạr, Ḳ.) — *He washed* (A'Obeyd, Ṣ, Mgh, Mṣb, Ḳ) a thing, (Mṣb,) or anything: (A'Obeyd:) *he cleansed* (AO, Ṣ, Ḳ) a thing: (AO:) as, for instance, his mouth, with the سِوَاك [or tooth-stick]: (Ṣ:) *he rubbed and cleansed* the teeth and the side of the mouth. (IAạr.) You say شَاصَ فَاهُ *He cleansed and washed his teeth*, (Mgh,) بِالسِّوَاكِ [*with the tooth-stick*]. (Mṣb.) And شَاصَ أَسْنَانَهُ, (A,) or فَاهُ, (TA,) [or app., شَاصَ alone, accord. to the Ḳ,] *He cleansed his teeth with the* سِوَاك: (AA, Ḳ, TA:) or *he did so by passing it across his teeth:* (A, TA:) or *from below upwards:* (Ḳ, TA:) or *by thrusting it into them*, or *between them:* (TA:) and in like manner you say, ▼ اشاص فَاهُ, (TA,) inf. n. إِشَاصَةٌ; (Fr, Ḳ, TA;) and ▼ شوّص فاه, (TA,) inf. n. تَشْوِيصٌ. (Ḳ, TA.) — Also *He chewed* a سِوَاك [app. to separate the fibres at the end and so make it like a brush, to prepare it for cleaning his teeth with it]. (Ḳ,* TA.)

2: } see 1, near the end of the paragraph.
4: }

شَوْصُ السِّوَاكِ *The washings* (غُسَالَة) *of the tooth-stick:* or *what remains from the tooth-stick when one cleans his teeth with it:* each of these meanings is assigned to it in explanations of a trad.: اِسْتَغْنُوا عَنِ النَّاسِ وَلَوْ بِشَوْصِ السِّوَاكِ [*Be ye independent of other men, if it be only by means of possessing the washings*, &c., *of the tooth-stick:* i. e., as long ye possess anything]. (TA.)

شوط

1. شَاطَ, aor. يَشُوطُ, inf. n. شَوْطٌ, *He ran a heat*,

or *single run*, or *a run at once, to a goal*, or *limit*. (TA.)

2. شَوَّطَ, inf. n. تَشْوِيطٌ, *He* (a man, IAạr) *made a long journey; his journey was*, or *became, long.* (IAạr, Ḳ.) ═ شَوَّطَ الفَرَسَ: see 5. — شَوَّطَ سَفِينَتَهُ *He voyaged with his ship.* (TA.) ═ Also شَوَّطَ *He made* a cooking-pot *to boil.* (El-Kilábee.) — *He cooked thoroughly* flesh-meat; (Ibn-'Abbád, Ṣgh, Ḳ;) as also شَيَّطَ: (Ibn-'Abbád, Ṣgh:) or both signify *he smoked* it, or *made it smoky, and did not thoroughly cook* it. (TA.) — † *It* (hoar-frost, or rime,) *burned* (أَحْرَقَ, q. v.) a plant, or herbage: (Ḳ:) and in like manner one says of medicine which is sprinkled upon a wound. (TA.) See also 4 in art. شيط, in two places.

5. تَشَوَّطَ الفَرَسَ, [in the CḲ, ▼ شَوَّطَ, but as this, in the manner in which it is there mentioned, is a needless repetition, being implied, if correct, it is doubtless a mistranscription,] *He continued to drive*, or *urge on, the horse, until he was tired*, or *fatigued.* (Ḳ,* TA.)

شَوْطٌ *A heat; a single run*, or *a run at once, to a goal*, or *limit;* (Mgh, Mṣb, Ḳ;) syn. طَلَقٌ: (Ṣ, Mṣb:) pl. أَشْوَاطٌ. (Ṣ, Mgh, Mṣb, Ḳ.) You say, عَدَا شَوْطًا *He ran a heat.* (Ṣ.) And طَافَ بِالبَيْتِ سَبْعَةَ أَشْوَاطٍ *He performed seven circuits round the House* [of God, i. e. the Kaạbeh]: (Ṣ, TA:) from the [Black] Stone to the [Black] Stone [again] is one شَوْط: (Ṣ, Mṣb, TA:) but some of the lawyers disapprove of this application of the term اشواط. (IF, Ḳ, TA.) — [It is also, app., an inf. n. used as an epithet: for one says, جَآءَ شَوْطٌ مِنَ الخَيْلِ: see سَنَنٌ, in the latter part of the paragraph.] It is sometimes used in relation to the wind: so says Lth: and he cites the following as an instance in which the wind is meant:

* وَنَازِحٍ مُعْتَكِرِ الأَشْوَاطِ *

[app. meaning *And a wind*, or *many a wind, exhausting*, or *drying up, the waters, the blasts thereof bringing dust*]. (TA.) — And it is also [used as meaning *A bout*] of shooting arrows. (T and M in art. رشق.) — Also The *space of ground over which a horse runs; such as a* مَيْدَان, and *the like;* which is [said by some to be] the primary signification; [but the primary signification is said by others to be the first given above; (see Ḥar p. 574;)] and so ▼ تَشْوِيطَةٌ. (TA.) — Also † *A scope; an object to be reached*, or *accomplished;* syn. غَايَةٌ: whence the saying, الشَّوْطُ بَطِينٌ † *The scope is remote:* (Ḥar p. 574:) a prov., relating to the long extent of hope. (TA.) — And † *A place between two elevated tracts of ground, through which water and men pass, as though it were a road, extending as far as the voice of a caller can be heard, then ending*, (ISh, O, Ḳ,) *of such depth that it will conceal the camel and his rider, found only in plain*, or *soft, ground, and producing good herbage:* (ISh, O:) pl. شِيَاطٌ; (ISh, O, Ḳ;) originally شِوَاطٌ. (ISh, O.) Z writes it with س. (TA. See سَوْطٌ.) ═ شَوْطُ بَرَاحٍ *i. q.* اِبْنُ آوَى [*The jackal*]: (IDrd, Ṣ, Z, O, L, Ḳ:) or *some other beast.* (L.) ═ شَوْطٌ بَاطِلٍ: see سَوْطُ بَاطِلٍ, in art. سوط: accord. to IDrd, it is not of established authority. (O.)

تَشْوِيطَةٌ: see شَوْطٌ. — It is also, metonymically, applied to ‡ The *plague*, or *pestilence;* and *other destructive diseases.* (TA.)

شوظ

شُوَاظٌ and شِوَاظٌ, (Ṣ, Ḳ, &c., [but in one copy of the Ṣ, I find only the former, which is the more common,]) occurring in the Ḳur [lv. 35], where Ibn-Ketheer read شِوَاظٌ, (TA,) *Flame* (Ṣ, Bḍ, Jel, Ḳ) *without smoke:* (Ṣ, Jel, Ḳ:) or *smoke* of fire: and *heat* of fire: (ISh, Ḳ:) and *heat* of the sun: (Ḳ, TA:) or *a piece of fire in which is no smoke:* or *flame of fire:* or only *of fire and something mixed therewith.* (L.) — [And hence,] ‡ *Vehemence of thirst:* (Ḳ, TA:) or simply, *thirst.* (A, TA.) You say, جَمَلٌ بِهِ شواظ ‡ *A thirsting camel.* (A, TA.) — And ‡ *Clamour.* (Ḳ, TA.)

شوف

1. شُفْتُهُ, (Ṣ, O, Ḳ,) aor. أَشُوفُهُ, (O,) inf. n. شَوْفٌ, (O, Ḳ,) *I polished it;* (Ṣ, O, Ḳ;) namely, a thing, (Ṣ, O,) or an ornament of gold or silver. (Mgh.) — [Hence,] شِيفَتِ الجَارِيَةُ, (Ṣ, O, Ḳ,) also written شُيِّفَتْ, (thus in one of my copies of the Ṣ, in the other written شُيِّفَتْ, and thus only,) aor. تُشَافُ, (Ṣ, O, Ḳ,) inf. n. as above, (Ṣ,) *The girl*, or *young woman, was adorned.* (Ṣ, O, Ḳ.) — And [hence likewise,] شَوْفٌ also signifies The *smearing* of a camel *with tar.* (Ḳ.) One says, شُفْ بَعِيرَكَ *Smear thy camel with tar.* (O.) ═ [The inf. n.] شَوَفَانٌ as *syn. with* تَشَوُّفٌ [but in what sense is not said] is vulgar. (TA.) — So too is [the inf. n.] شَوْفٌ as meaning The act of *seeing* [and *of looking*]. (TA.) [شاف is much used in the present day as meaning *He saw*, and *he looked at*, a thing.]

2. شَوَّفَ الجَارِيَةَ, inf. n. تَشْوِيفٌ, *He adorned the girl*, or *young woman.* (TA.) ═ شَيَّفَ الدَّوَآءَ *He made the medicament to be what is termed* شِيَاف [q. v.]. (Ibn-'Abbád, O, Ḳ.) [The ى in this verb is substituted for و.]

4. اشاف عَلَيْهِ *i. q.* أَشْرَفَ [meaning *He was*, or *became, on the brink*, or *verge*, or *at the point, of it*], (Ṣ, O, Ḳ,) namely, a thing; like أَشْفَى; (Ṣ, O;) from which it is formed by transposition. (Ṣ.) — And اشاف *He feared.* (Ibn-'Abbád, O, Ḳ.) You say, اشاف مِنْهُ *He feared him*, or *it.* (Ḳ.) ═ See also 5, last sentence.

5. تشوّف *He adorned himself:* (Ḳ:) or تشوّفت *she* (a woman, IDrd, O, or a girl, or young woman, Ṣ) *adorned herself.* (IDrd, Ṣ, O.) One says of a woman divorced by a sentence that admits of her returning, تَتَشَوَّفُ لِزَوْجِهَا i. e. *She adorns herself for her husband, by making her face clear, and polishing her cheeks;* from 1 in the first of the senses assigned to it above. (Mgh.) ═ تشوّفت الأَوْعَالُ *The mountain-goats ascended upon the tops of the mountains*, (Lth, O, Mṣb,) *and looked down*, (Lth, O,) *to see the plain country and its freedom from those whom they feared, in order that they might repair to the water and the pasturage.* (Mṣb.) — Hence, تشوّف لِكَذَا *He* (a man) *raised*, or *stretched and raised, his eyes*, or *sight, towards such a thing:* and hence the verb became used to denote hope, or expectation, and desire, or seeking. (Mṣb.) And تشوّف مِنَ السَّطْحِ *He stretched himself up, and looked*, and *overlooked*, or *looked down, from the house-top.* (Ḳ.) One says, النِّسَآءُ يَتَشَوَّفْنَ مِنَ السُّطُوحِ *The women look*, [or *look down*,] *stretching themselves up, from the house-tops.* (Ṣ, O.) [See also 8.] And one says also, تشوّف إِلَى الشَّىْءِ, (Ṣ,) or إِلَى الخَبَرِ, (O, Ḳ,) or إِلى الخَيْرِ, (CḲ,) *He looked for* [*the thing*, or *good*, or *the news* or *tidings*], (Ṣ, O, Ḳ,) &c. (TA.) — And تشوّف الشَّىْءُ *The thing rose*, or *became high* or *elevated;* as also ▼ اشاف. (TA.)

8. اشتاف *He* (a man, Ṣ, O) *stretched himself up, and looked:* (Ṣ, O, Ḳ:) and in like manner one says of horses. (TA.) [See also 5.] — And اشتاف البَرْقَ *He looked at the lightning*, or *at the cloud thereof, to see whither it was tending, and where it would rain;* syn. شَامَهُ. (Ṣ, O, Ḳ.) ═ Also, said of a wound, *It became rough*, or *thick;* (AZ, O, Ḳ;) and so ▼ استشاف, thus without hemz. (TA.)

10: see what next precedes.

شَوْفٌ The مِجَرّ, (O, Ḳ,) i. e. *a wooden implement*, (O,) [meaning *a harrow*,] *by means of which the ploughed land is made even.* (O.)

شَائِفَةٌ: see شَائِفَةٌ, in art. شأف. (TA.)

شِيَافٌ *Medicaments for the eye and the like:* (O, Ḳ:) from 1 in the first of the senses assigned to it above: originally شِوَافٌ. (O.)

شَوَّافٌ A *sharp-sighted* man. (TA.)

شَيِّفَةٌ *A scout*, or *scouts*, (طَلِيعَةٌ,) *employed to look out for a party;* (IAạr, Ṣ, O, Ḳ;) as also ▼ شَيِّفَانٌ. (IAạr, O, Ḳ.)

شَيِّفَانٌ: see what next precedes.

مَشُوفٌ *Polished:* applied to a دِينَار [&c.]. (Ṣ, O, Ḳ.) 'Antarah says,

* وَلَقَدْ شَرِبْتُ مِنَ المُدَامَةِ بَعْدَ مَا *
* رَكَدَ الهَوَاجِرُ بِالمَشُوفِ المُعْلَمِ *

[*And verily I have drunk wine, after that the vehement noon-day-heats of summer had remitted*, purchased *with the polished, charactered* deenár]: (Ṣ, O, and EM p. 237:) he means the deenár polished by the minter thereof: (TA:) or, as some say, he means *the bright, charactered*, or *figured*, bowl. (O, TA.*) — Also A camel *smeared with tar;* (O, Ḳ;) because it polishes him. (TA.) — And (Ḳ) accord. to AA (O, TA) and A'Obeyd, (TA,) as used by Lebeed, (O, TA,) A camel *in a state of excitement by lust:* (O, Ḳ:*) but as some relate the verse in which it occurs, the word is with س, and means "smelt" by the [other] camels because smeared with tar. (O, TA.) — And, (Ḳ,) as some say, (O, TA,) it means [A camel] *decorated with wools of various colours, and with other things.* (O, Ḳ. [In the CḲ, المُزَيَّنُ is erroneously put for المُزَيَّنُ.])

مُشَوِّفَةٌ, like مُعَظِّمَةٌ [in measure], *A woman who exposes herself to view in order that men may see her.* (Aboo-'Alee, TA.)

شوق

1. شَاقَنِى, (Ṣ, Mṣb, Ḳ,) aor. يَشُوقُنِى, (Ṣ, Mṣb,) inf. n. شَوْقٌ; (Mṣb, TA;) and ♦ شَوَّقَنِى, (Ṣ, Mṣb,* Ḳ,) inf. n. تَشْوِيقٌ; (TA;) *It* (a thing, Ṣ and Mṣb in relation to the former verb, or the love of a female, Ḳ, and the mention of her, and her beauty, TA, or the latter verb is said of a man, Mṣb,) *excited my desire,* or *the yearning* or *longing of my soul.* (Ṣ, Mṣb,* Ḳ,* TA.) [Hence,] one says, شُقْ شُقْ فُلَانًا, meaning *Render thou desirous, render thou desirous, such a one* (♦ شَوِّقْهُ) for the ultimate abode or ultimate state of existence in the world to come (إِلَى الآخِرَةِ). (IAạr, Ḳ, TA. [See also 2.]) — And شَاقَ الطُّنُبَ إِلَى الوَتِدِ, (Ḳ,) aor. يَشُوقُهُ, inf. n. شَوْقٌ, (TA,) ‡ *He tied, and made fast, the tent-rope to the tent-peg;* (Ḳ, TA;) as also شاقه having for its inf. n. شَيْقٌ; (TA in art. شيق;) like نَاطَهُ بِهِ, inf. n. نَوْطٌ: mentioned also by Z. (TA.) — And شَاقَ القِرْبَةَ, (Ḳ,) inf. n. as above, (TA,) ‡ *He set up the water-skin, leaning it against the wall:* (Ḳ, TA:) mentioned by Ibn-Buzurj. (TA.)

2: see above, in two places. A poet says, (O,) a man of the tribe of Kelb, (Ḥam pp. 145 et seq.,)

• وَحَنَّتْ نَاقَتِى طَرَبًا وَشَوْقًا •
• إِلَى مَنْ بِالحَنِينِ تُشَوِّقِينِى •

[*And my she-camel uttered a yearning cry, by reason of lively emotion, and desire; whereupon I said, For whom, by the yearning cry, dost thou render me desirous?*]: تُشَوِّقِينِى being for تُشَوِّقِينَنِى. (O, and Ḥam p. 146, q. v.) Lth says that التَّشْوِيقُ in relation to reading or recitation [of the Ḳur-án], and [sacred] narratives, is as when one says, شَوِّقْنَا يَا فُلَانُ [lit. *Do thou render us desirous, O such a one*], meaning do thou mention [to us] Paradise and what is therein, by narratives, or reading or recitation; may-be we shall become desirous of it, and therefore work for it. (O, TA.)

4. وَجَدَهُ شَائِقًا signifies اشاقهُ [app. meaning, عَاشِقًا, i. e. *He found him to be an excessive,* or *attached,* or *admiring, lover*]. (IAạr,* TA.) — One says also, مَا أَشْوَقَنِى إِلَيْكَ [*How great is my desire,* or *the yearning* or *longing of my soul, for thee!*]. (TA.)

5. تشوّق *He was, or became, excited by desire,* or *yearning* or *longing of the soul;* quasi-pass. of شَوَّقَهُ (Ṣ, TA) and شَاقَهُ. (TA.) See also 8. — And (TA) *He showed,* or *made a show of,* (O, Ḳ, TA,) and *affected,* (O,) or *affecting,* (Ḳ, TA,) *desire,* or *a yearning* or *longing of the soul.* (O, Ḳ, TA.)

8. اشتاق إِلَيْهِ, (MA, O, Mṣb, Ḳ,) and اشتاقهُ, both signifying the same, (MA, O, Ḳ,) as also ♦ تشوّق إليه, i. e. *He was,* or *became, desirous of it;* or *affected with desire for it;* (MA;) [or *he yearned* or *longed for it in his soul;* for] اِشْتِيَاقٌ is *syn. with* شَوْقٌ, (q. v.) as expl. below. (Ṣ.)

شَوْقٌ *Desire,* or *yearning* or *longing of the soul,* (Ṣ, O, Mṣb, Ḳ,) *for a thing;* إِلَى شَىْءٍ (Ṣ, Mṣb;) as also ♦ اِشْتِيَاقٌ: (Ṣ:) [or] the *motion of love:* (IAạr, O, Ḳ:) pl. أَشْوَاقٌ. (Ḳ.) One says, بَرَّحَ بِى الشَّوْقُ [*Desire, &c., distressed me*]: and بَلَغَتْ مِنِّى الأَشْوَاقُ [meaning in like manner *Desires, &c., distressed me*]. (TA.) بَنَاتُ الشَّوْقِ means † *The effects of* الشوق [or *desire, &c.*]. (Ḥam p. 539.) — Also inf. n. of 1 [q. v.]. (Mṣb, TA.)

شَيْقٌ: see what next follows.

شِيَاقٌ † The *thing with which a thing is extended in order to its being tied to a thing;* (O, Ḳ;) like نِيَاطٌ; (Ṣ in art. شيق, O, TA;) originally شِوَاقٌ. and ♦ شَيْقٌ, originally شَوْقٌ, signifies the same. (TA.)

شَائِقٌ *Exciting* one's *desire,* or *the yearning* or *longing of the soul* of a person. (Ṣ, TA.) — Also [a possessive epithet, meaning ذُو شَوْقٍ. And hence,] *An excessive,* or *attached,* or *admiring, lover;* syn. عَاشِقٌ; and so ♦ مَشُوقٌ: (Ḥar, p. 142:) or ♦ the latter signifies one *whose desire,* or *yearning* or *longing of the soul, is excited:* (Ṣ, TA:) the former is sing. of شُوقٌ, (TA,) which is *syn. with* عُشَّاقٌ [pl. of عَاشِقٌ] (IAạr, O, Ḳ, TA) as well as pl. of أَشْوَقُ. (Ḳ.)

شَيِّقٌ *i. q.* ♦ مُشْتَاقٌ [i. e. *Desirous,* or *yearning* or *longing in the soul*]: (O, Mṣb, Ḳ:) or *i. q.* مَشُوقٌ [q. v. voce شَائِقٌ, in two places]: (JK:) originally شَيْوِقٌ, of the measure فَيْعِلٌ. (O, TA.)

شَوَّاقٌ [*Very desirous;* or *desiring,* or *yearning* or *longing, in the soul, much*]. (JK and Mṣb voce تَوَّاقٌ.)

أَشْوَقُ *Tall;* (IDrd, O, Ḳ;) applied to a man; but not of established authority: (IDrd, O:) pl. شُوقٌ. (Ḳ.)

مَشُوقٌ: see شَائِقٌ, in two places. — قِرْبَةٌ مَشُوقَةٌ ‡ *A water-skin set up, leaned against a wall.* (Ibn-Buzurj, O, Ḳ, TA.)

مُشْتَاقٌ: see شَيِّقٌ. المُشْتَاقُ, (so in the Ṣ,) or المُشْتَئِقُ, because مُشْتَاقٌ is originally مُشْتَوِقٌ, of the measure مُفْتَعِلٌ, (O,) is used by poetic license for مُشْتَاقٌ, (Ṣ, O,) as Sb says; (Ṣ;) for the poet, requiring to make the last letter but one movent, makes it so by the original vowel. (O.)

شوك

1. شَاكَتْنِى الشَّوْكَةُ, (Aṣ, Ṣ, O, Ḳ,*) aor. تَشُوكُنِى, (Aṣ, Ṣ, O,) inf. n. شَوْكٌ, (TA,) *The thorn entered into* [or *pierced me,* or] *my body* or *person.* (Aṣ, Ṣ, O, Ḳ.*) And شاكت إِصْبَعَهُ *It* (a thorn) *entered into* [or *pierced*] *his finger.* (TA.) And شَاكَتْنِى الشَّوْكَةُ, (Ḳ,) aor. as above, (TA,) *The thorn hurt me,* or *wounded me;* syn. أَصَابَتْنِى. (Ḳ, TA.) And شَاكَنِى الشَّوْكُ, aor. يَشُوكُنِى, *The thorns hurt,* or *wounded,* (أَصَابَ,) *my skin.* (Mṣb.) [Hence,] لَا يَشُوكُكَ مِنِّى ♦ شَوْكَةٌ ‡ *No harm,* or *hurt, shall ensue to thee from me.* (TA.) — شُكْتُهُ, aor. أَشُوكُهُ, [*I pierced him with a thorn;*] *I made a thorn to enter into his body* or *person;* (Ṣ, O, Ḳ;) as also ♦ أَشَكْتُهُ, (Ḳ,) inf. n. إِشَاكَةٌ: (TA:) the former verb from Ks; (T, Ṣ, O;) as though he made it to be doubly trans. [meaning that شَوْكَةً is to be understood]. (Az, TA.) And مَا شَاكَهُ بِشَوْكَةٍ and مَا أَشَاكَهُ ♦ شَوْكَةً [as is meant by its being added] وَلَا شَاكَهُ بِهَا *He did not hurt him with a thorn;* (Ḳ,* TA;) as expl. by IF: (TA:) and ♦ أَشَكْتُهُ *I hurt him with thorns:* (TA:) or شَوَّكْتُهُ ♦ بِهِ and ♦ بِالشَّوْكِ أَشَكْتُهُ *I hurt him,* or *wounded him, with thorns,* or *the thorns.* (Mṣb.) — Accord. to IAạr, (TA,) شاك الشَّوْكَةَ, (Ḳ, TA, [in the CḲ, erroneously, الشَّوْكَةِ,]) aor. يَشَاكُهَا, (TA,) signifies خَالَطَهَا [app. meaning *He pierced* (lit. *mixed* or *blended*) *himself with the thorn:* unless شَوْكَة be improperly used in this instance, by poetic license, as a coll. gen. n., as seems to be implied in the Ṣ and O by an explanation of a verse cited voce نَقَشَ, q. v., in which case the meaning is, *he entered among the thorns*]. (Ḳ, TA.) — [It is also said that] شاك الشَّوْكَةَ, aor. يَشَاكُهَا, inf. n. شَوْكٌ, signifies *He* (a man) *extracted the thorn from his foot.* (MA.) — شِيكَ, aor. يُشَاكُ, inf. n. شَوْكٌ, *He* (a man) *was,* or *became, pierced by a thorn.* (Ṣ, O.) — شَاكَ, (Ḳ,) or [first pers.] شِكْتُ, (Ṣ, O,) aor. يَشَاكُ, (Ḳ, and the like in the Ṣ and O,) inf. n. شَاكَةٌ and شِيكَةٌ, (Ṣ, O, Ḳ,) *He,* (Ḳ,) or *I,* (Ṣ, O,) *fell,* or *lighted, among thorns:* (Ṣ, O, Ḳ: [whence, accord. to the Ṣ and O, the verse above referred to, voce نَقَشَ:]) and شِكْتُ الشَّوْكَ, aor. أَشَاكُهُ, *I fell,* or *lighted, among the thorns:* (Ḳ:) accord. to IB, شِكْتُ, aor. أَشَاكُ, is originally شَوِكْتُ. (TA.) — شاكت الشَّجَرَةُ, aor. تَشَاكُ, inf. n. شَوْكٌ; and ♦ اشاكت; (Mṣb;) or ♦ شَوَّكَتْ, (Ḳ, TA,) inf. n. تَشْوِيكٌ; in some of the copies of the Ḳ شَوِكَتْ; (TA; [in the CḲ, شَوَكَت;]) and ♦ أَشْوَكَتْ; (Ḳ;) *The tree was thorny,* or *prickly; abounded with thorns,* or *prickles:* (Mṣb, Ḳ, TA:) [and] ♦ أَشْوَكَتْ said of a palm-tree has the like signification. (Ṣ, O.) — [Hence,] شاك لَحْيَا البَعِيرِ † *The two jaws of the camel put forth his canine teeth;* (Ṣ, O;) as also ♦ شوّك, (Ṣ, O,) inf. n. تَشْوِيكٌ: (Ṣ:) or the phrase with the latter verb means *The camel's canine teeth became long.* (Ḳ.) — And شاك ثَدْىُ الجَارِيَةِ † *The breast of the girl was ready to swell,* or *become protuberant* or *prominent;* as also ♦ شوّك, inf. n. تَشْوِيكٌ; (Ṣ;) and, accord. to Z, شَوَّكَ, like

قَرِحَ: (TA:) or شَوَّكَ ▾ ثَدْيُهَا signifies ‡ *her breast became pointed in its extremity,* (IDrd, O, Ḳ, TA,) *and its protrusion appeared.* (IDrd, O, TA.) — شَاكَ الرَّجُلُ, aor. يَشَاكُ, inf. n. شَوْكٌ, ‡ *The man exhibited his* شَوْكَة [i. e. *vehemence of might* or *strength,* or *of valour* or *prowess,* &c.], *and his sharpness.* (Ṣ, O, Mṣb, Ḳ, TA.) [And *The man was completely armed;* (as though meaning *he bristled with arms;*) for] the inf. n. شَوْكٌ signifies a man's *being completely armed.* (KL.) — And شِيكَ ‡ *He was,* or *became, affected with the disease termed* شَوْكَة [q. v.]. (Ḳ, TA.)

2. شَوَّكْتُهُ بِالشَّوْكِ: see 1, former half. — شَوَّكَ الحَائِطَ, (Ṣ, Ḳ,) inf. n. تَشْوِيكٌ, (TA,) *He put thorns upon the wall.* (Ṣ, Ḳ.) — See also 1, latter half, in four places. — شَوَّكَ الزَّرْعُ ‡ *The seed-produce,* or *corn, became white, before its spreading:* (Ḳ:) or *came forth* [*pointed,*] *without forking,* or *shooting forth into separate stalks,* (حَدَّدَ,) *and became white, before its spreading;* as also ▾ أَشْوَكَ: (TA:) [or *began to come forth:* see مُشَوِّكٌ.] — شَوَّكَ نَابُ البَعِيرِ † [*The canine tooth of the camel grew forth*]. (TA.) — شَوَّكَ رِيشُ الفَرْخِ, (IDrd, O,) and شَارِبُ الغُلَامِ, (IDrd, O, Ḳ,) ‡ *The feathers of the young bird,* (IDrd, O,) and *the mustache of the young man, became rough to the feel.* (IDrd, O, Ḳ, TA.) And شَوَّكَ الفَرْخُ † *The young bird put forth the heads of its feathers:* (Ṣ,* Ḳ, TA:) in [some of the copies of] the Ṣ and A, شَوَّكَ الفَرْخُ, thus with خ, expl. by أَنْبَتَ. (TA.) And شَوَّكَ الرَّأْسُ بَعْدَ الحَلْقِ ‡ *The head put forth its hair after the shaving.* (Ṣ, Ḳ, TA.)

4, as a trans. verb: see 1, former half, in four places: — as intrans.: see 1, latter half, in three places: and see also 2.

5. تَشَوُّكٌ The *having thorns;* expl. by بَا خَارْ شُدَنْ. (KL.)

شَاكٌ; and its fem., with ة: see شَائِكٌ, in four places.

شَوْكٌ, (Ṣ, Mṣb, Ḳ, &c.,) of a tree, (Mṣb,) or of a plant, (TA,) *Thorns, prickles,* or *spines;* (PṢ, TḲ;) the *kind of thing that is slender* [or *pointed*] *and hard in the head;* (TA;) well known: (Mṣb, Ḳ:) n. un. with ة. (Ṣ, O, Mṣb, Ḳ, TA.) [Hence the saying,] لَا يَشُوكُكَ مِنِّى شَوْكَةٌ: see 1, near the beginning. [The شَوْك of the palm-tree are commonly called سُلَّاء.] [شَوْكُ السُّنْبُلِ *The sharp prickles that compose the awn,* or *beard, of the ear of corn*]. (AḤn, TA in art. سهر.) — [For other significations of شَوْكَةٌ, see this word below.]

شَوِكٌ; and its fem., with ة: see شَائِكٌ, in three places.

شَوْكَةٌ n. un. of شَوْكٌ [q. v.]. (Ṣ &c.) [Hence various meanings here following; all of which seem to be tropical.] — أَصَابَتْهُمْ شَوْكَةُ القَنَا [app. † *The point of the spear hit, hurt,* or *wounded, them*]. (TA. [There expl. only by the words وَهِىَ شِبْهُ الأَسِنَّةِ, i. e. وهى شبه الاسنة; as though relating to a pl. number.]) — جَاؤُوا بِالشَّوْكَةِ وَالشَّجَرَةِ ‡ *They came with multitude* [app. meaning *of armed men*]. (TA.) — شَوْكَةُ العَقْرَبِ † *The sting of the scorpion.* (Ṣ, O, Ḳ.) — شَوْكَةُ الحَائِكِ ‡ *The weaver's implement with which he makes the warp and the woof even:* (Ṣ, O, TA:) i. e., (TA,) الشَّوْكَةُ signifies الصِّيصِيَةُ, (O, Ḳ, in the CḲ الصَّيصَةُ,) as having this meaning: — and also as meaning ‡ *The spur* of the cock. (O, TA.) — And الشَّوْكَةُ, (Lth, O,) or شَوْكَةُ الكَتَّانِ, (Ḳ, TA,) † *A piece of clay,* (Lth, O, Ḳ, TA,) *in a moist state,* (Ḳ, TA,) *made into a round form, and having its upper part pressed so that it becomes expanded, then* (Lth, O, TA) *prickles of the palm-tree are stuck into it,* (Lth, O, Ḳ, TA,) *and it dries;* (Ḳ, TA;) *used for clearing* [or *combing*] *flax therewith:* (Lth, O, Ḳ, TA:) mentioned by Az: and also called ▾ شُوَاكَةُ الكَتَّانِ. (TA.) — شَوْكَةٌ also signifies ‡ *A weapon,* or *weapons;* syn. سِلَاحٌ; (Ḳ, TA, and Ḥam p. 526;) as in the phrase فُلَانٌ ذُو شَوْكَةٍ ‡ [*Such a one is a possessor of a weapon* or *weapons;* though this admits of another rendering, as will be shown by what follows]: (TA:) or ‡ *sharpness* thereof: (Ḳ, TA:) or † the *point,* or *edge,* in a weapon. (Ṣ, O.) — And † *Vehemence of might* or *strength,* or *of valour* or *prowess,* (Ṣ, O, Mṣb, Ḳ, TA,) in respect of fighting: (Ḳ, TA:) and † *vehemence of encounter:* and † *sharpness:* (TA:) and † the *infliction of havock,* or *vehement slaughter* or *wounding,* syn. نِكَايَةٌ, [app. meaning *effectiveness therein,*] among the enemy: (Ḳ, TA:) and † *strength in weapons* [app. meaning *in the use thereof*]: (Mṣb:) and [simply] † *strength,* or *might.* (Ḥam p. 526.) One says, لَهُمْ شَوْكَةٌ فِى الحَرْبِ † [*They have vehemence of might* or *strength,* or *of valour* or *prowess, in war*]: and هُوَ ذُو شَوْكَةٍ فِى العَدُوِّ † [*He has effectiveness in the infliction of havock among the enemy*]. (TA.) And it is said in a trad., هَلُمَّ إِلَى جِهَادٍ لَا شَوْكَةَ فِيهِ † [*Come to a war in the cause of religion wherein is no vehemence of might* or *strength,* &c.]; meaning *the pilgrimage.* (TA.) — Also ‡ *A certain disease,* (IDrd, O, Ḳ, TA,) *well known;* (Ḳ;) namely, *plague,* or *pestilence;* syn. طَاعُون. (IDrd, O.) And † *A redness that arises* (A,* O, Ḳ) *upon the body* (Ḳ) or *upon the face, and part of the body, and is* [*said to be*] *allayed by means of charms,* or *spells:* (O:) because the sting of the scorpion, which is thus called, when it strikes a man, mostly produces redness. (A, TA.) — [In one instance, in the CḲ, شَوْكَةٌ is erroneously put for شَوِكَةٌ, as an epithet applied to a tree.]

شَوْكَاءُ, applied to a [garment such as is called] بُرْدَةٌ, (Ṣ, O,) or to a [garment or dress such as is called] حُلَّةٌ, (A, O, Ḳ,) ‡ *Rough to the feel, because new:* (AO, Ṣ, O, Ḳ, TA:) but Aṣ said, "I know not what it is." (O, L, TA.)

شَائِكٌ: see شَائِكٌ فِى السلاح and شَاكِى السِّلَاحِ, in three places.

شُوَاكَةُ الكَتَّانِ: see شَوْكَةٌ.

شُوَيْكَةٌ, like جُهَيْنَةٌ [in measure], accord. to the Ḳ, *A certain species of camels;* and thus in the Moḥeeṭ and the Moḥkam: but the correct word is that which here follows. (TA.)

إِبِلٌ شُوَيْكِيَّةٌ, (Ṣ, O, TA,) thus [says Ṣgh] I have seen the latter word in a verse in the Deewán of Dhu-r-Rummeh in the handwriting of Skr, with a distinct sheddeh to the [latter] ى, but in the handwriting of El-Bujeyrimee without a sheddeh; (O, TA;) † *Camels whose canine teeth have grown forth:* (Ṣ,* O, TA:) some say that it is شُوَيْكَة, with ة, and is for شُوَيْقَة [q. v.], the ق being changed into ك. (O, TA.)

شَجَرٌ شَائِكٌ (Ṣ, O) and ▾ شَوِكٌ and ▾ شَاكٌ (O) *Trees having thorns;* (Ṣ, O;*) and ▾ شَجَرَةٌ مُشِيكَةٌ *a tree having thorns:* (TA:) [or *thorny; having many thorns;* for] ▾ شَجَرَةٌ شَاكَةٌ signifies *a thorny tree,* or *a tree having many thorns,* (Ṣ, O, Ḳ,) accord. to ISk; (Ṣ, O;) as also ▾ شَجِرَةٌ شَوِكَةٌ [in the CḲ (erroneously) شَوْكَةٌ] and شَائِكَةٌ (Ḳ, TA) and ▾ مُشْوِكَةٌ. (Ṣ, O, Ḳ,* TA.) And ▾ أَرْضٌ شَاكَةٌ *A thorny land,* or *a land in which are many thorns:* (Ḳ, TA:) and [in like manner] ▾ أَرْضٌ مُشْوِكَةٌ (Ṣ, O, Ḳ) *a thorny land,* or *a land abounding with thorns;* (O;) *a land in which are the* [*thorny trees called*] سَعْدَان *and* قَتَاد *and* هَرَاس. (Ṣ, O, Ḳ.) — شَائِكُ السِّلَاحِ (Ṣ, O, Mṣb, Ḳ) and ▾ شَاكُ السلاح, (Fr, Ḳ, TA,) with refs to the ك, (TA,) [in the CḲ, erroneously, شَاكِ,] and ▾ شَوِكُ السلاح, (Ḳ,) which is of the dial. of El-Yemen, (TA,) and ▾ شَاكِى السلاح, (Fr, Ṣ, O, Mṣb, Ḳ,) this last formed by transposition from the first, (Ṣ, O, Mṣb, TA,) or, as Fr says, شَاكِى السلاح and شَاكُ السلاح are like جُرُفٌ هَارٍ and هَارٌ, (TA,) ‡ A man *who exhibits his* شَوْكَة [i. e. *vehemence of might* or *strength,* or *of valour* or *prowess,* &c.], *and his sharpness:* (Ṣ, O, Mṣb:) or a man *whose weapon is sharp,* or *whose weapons are sharp:* (Ḳ, TA:) or ▾ شَاكِى السلاح, as some explain it, a man *whose spear-head and arrow-head and the like are sharp:* (TA:) [or all may be rendered *bristling with arms:*] and accord. to AZ, one says شَائِكٌ and ▾ شَاكٍ فِى السِّلَاحِ. (TA.)

مَشُوكٌ *Affected with the disease,* (Ḳ,* TA,) or *redness,* (O, Ḳ,*) *termed* شَوْكَة; (O, Ḳ, TA;) applied to a man. (O.)

مُشْوِكٌ: see its fem. voce شَائِكٌ, in two places.

مُشِيكٌ: see its fem. voce شَائِكٌ.

زَرْعٌ مُشَوِّكٌ *Seed-produce of which the first portion has come forth.* (A, TA. [See also 2.])

شول

1. شَالَ, [aor. يَشُولُ,] (Ṣ, O, Mṣb, Ḳ,) inf. n. شَوْلٌ, (TḲ,) *It rose;* or *became raised,* or *elevated;* (Ṣ, O, Mṣb, Ḳ;) said, in this sense, of a she-camel's tail; (Ṣ, O, Ḳ;) [and in like manner of a star; (see Ḥam p. 230;)] and ▾ انشال signifies the

same, (O, Ḳ,) said of a stone, (Ḳ,) and so انشالت said of a jar (جَرَّة); (Ṣ, O;) and likewise ▼ اشتال. (TA.) — [Hence,] شال المِيزَانُ *The balance had one of its two scales higher than the other,* (Ṣ, O, Mṣb, TA,) *by reason of its lightness.* (Mṣb.) Whence the saying, شال مِيزَانُ فُلَانٍ, aor. يَشُولُ, inf. n. شَوَلَانٌ, meaning ‡ *Such a one was overcome in contending with another for superiority in glory* or *the like.* (TA.) — And شالت القِرْبَةُ, and شال الزِّقُّ, *The legs of the water-skin,* and *of the skin for wine &c., became raised,* or *elevated, on the occasion of its being filled,* or *inflated.* (TA.) — And شَالَ لَبَنُهَا [meaning *Her milk became drawn up,* or *withdrawn,*] is said of a camel. (TA.) — One says also, شالت نَعَامَتُهُ, meaning † *He was,* or *became, flurried, agitated,* or *excited,* (خَفَّ,) *and angry, and then became calm.* (Ḳ.) And شالت نَعَامَتُهُمْ † *Their might* (عِزُّهُمْ) *departed:* (O, Ḳ:) or *their abodes became clear of them, as though lightened of them,* (خَفَّتْ مَنَازِلُهُمْ مِنْهُمْ, Ḳ, TA,) *and they went away:* (TA:) or *their expression of opinion was,* or *became, discordant:* (تَفَرَّقَتْ كَلِمَتُهُمْ: Ḳ:) or *they died:* and *they became scattered,* or *dispersed;* as *though there remained not of them save a remnant;* [see شَوْلٌ;] النَّعَامَةُ signifying الجَمَاعَةُ: (TA:) or *they became irresolute, by reason of fear, and fled:* (Mṣb:) or *they were frightened, and fled.* (M in art. زال.) [See also نَعَامَةٌ: and see a verse cited voce إِمَّا.] = شُلْتُ بِهِ, and شُلْتُهُ, (Mṣb;) and ▼ أَشَلْتُهُ; (O, Mṣb;) or شُلْتُ بِالجَرَّةِ, for which one should not say شِلْتُ [which the vulgar say in the present day, making it trans. by itself]; (Ṣ, O;) and ▼ أَشَلْتُهَا; (Ṣ;) or شال بالحَجَرِ, and ▼ شاوله; (TA;) and ▼ اشاله, (Ḳ,) inf. n. إِشَالَةٌ; (Ḳ;) aor. of the first as above, inf. n. شَوْلٌ; (Ṣ, O, Mṣb;) *I raised,* (Ṣ, O, Mṣb,) or *he raised,* (Ḳ,) *it,* (O, Mṣb,) namely, a thing, (O,) or *the jar,* (Ṣ, O,) or *the stone.* (Ḳ.) And شالت بِذَنَبِهَا, (Ṣ, O, Mṣb, Ḳ,) aor. as above, (Ṣ, O, Ḳ,) inf. n. شَوْلٌ (O, Mṣb, Ḳ) and شَوَلَانٌ; (O, Ḳ;) and ▼ اشالته, (Ṣ, Mṣb, Ḳ,) inf. n. إِشَالَةٌ; and ▼ استشالته; (TA;) *She* (a camel) *raised her tail,* (Ṣ, O, Mṣb, Ḳ, TA,) *having become pregnant.* (Mṣb. [See شَائِلٌ: and see also 2.]) And شالت بِذَنَبِهَا *It* (a scorpion) *raised its tail.* (TA.) And شال يَدَهُ *He raised his arm* or *hand;* like شال بِهَا. (Mṣb.) And ▼ اشال بِضَبْعِهِ *He raised his* ضَبْع [generally expl. as meaning the *upper half of the arm, from the elbow to the shoulder-blade*]. (TA.)

2. شوّلت, said of a she-camel, (Ṣ, O, Ḳ,) *She became such as is termed* شَائِلَة: (Ṣ, O, TA: [in one of my copies of the Ṣ, صَارَ شَوْلًا is erroneously put for صَارَتْ شَائِلَةً:]) or *her supplies of milk dried up;* (جَفَّتْ أَلْبَانُهَا; Ḳ, TA; [but perhaps the right reading is خَفَّتْ, meaning *became scanty;* for SM adds,]) and *became little in quantity.* (TA.) And شوّلت الإِبِلُ *The camels became in such a state that their bellies* [*were drawn up as though they*] *reached their backs:* (Ḳ, TA:) or *became such as to have* [*only*] *a* شَوْل [or *small quantity remaining*] *of milk:* like as one says, شوّلت المَزَادَةُ (O, TA,) *The* مزادة [or *leathern water-bag*] *had little water remaining in it:* (O, Ḳ, TA:) one should not say شَالَت. (TA.) — [Hence, app.,] تَشْوِيلٌ of the ذَكَر signifies *Its being in a relaxed state on the occasion of* مُجَامَعَة. (O, Ḳ.) And شوّل said of a horse means, like رَفَّضَ, *He put forth his veretrum without being vigorously lustful.* (TA in art. رفض.) — شوّل said of a غَرْب [or large bucket], *Its water became little in quantity.* (O, Ḳ.) Said of a she-camel's milk, *It became deficient:* (Ḳ, TA:) and *it became withdrawn.* (TA.) And said of water, *It became little in quantity.* (Ḳ.) — In the following saying, (Ṣ, TA,) of Abu-n-Nejm, (TA,)

حَتَّى إِذَا مَا العِشْرُ عَنْهَا شَوَّلَا

the poet means, ذَهَبَ and تَصَرَّمَ [i. e. *Until, when the coming to water on the tenth day after the next preceding period of abstinence ceased from her* or *them* . . . referring to a camel or to camels]. (Ṣ, TA.) — شوّل فِى المَزَادَةِ *He left somewhat remaining* (أَبْقَى شَوْلًا) *of water in the* مزادة [or *leathern water-bag*]. (Ḳ,* TA.)

3. شاوله: see 1, latter half. — Also, and شاول بِهِ, [inf. n. مُشَاوَلَة,] and شاول بِهِ فِى الطِّعَانِ *He contended with him in thrusting* [with the spear]. (TA.) See also 6. — And شاول الفَحْلُ الفَحْلَ *The stallion* [*camel*] *fought with,* or *combated, the stallion* [*camel*]. (Ḥam p. 660.)

4: see 1, latter half, in five places.

6. تشاولوا *They reached,* or *smote, one another,* (تَنَاوَلَ بَعْضُهُمْ بَعْضًا,) *in fight, with the spears:* and ▼ مُشَاوَلَةٌ has a similar signification [to تَشَاوُلٌ, as shown above by an explanation of its verb, 3]. (AZ, Ṣ, O.)

7: see 1, first sentence.

8: see 1, first sentence. — اشتال لَهُ ‡ *He opposed himself to him, and reviled him.* (O, Ḳ, TA.)

10: see 1, near the end of the paragraph.

شَالٌ *A certain fish of the sea,* or *of great rivers* (سَمَكَةٌ بَحْرِيَّةٌ): (TA:) [in Egypt this name is applied to *a fish of the genus silurus, found in the Nile:* it is well described by Sonnini, in p. 407 of the 4to Engl. ed. of his Travels in Upper and Lower Egypt.] = Also *A certain kind of* رِدَآء [here meaning *shawl*], *made in Cashmere and Lahore, and brought for sale to other countries;* [erroneously] said to be made of camels' fur; and so called because raised to the shoulders, if it be an Arabic word [which is not the case, for it is from the Pers. شَالْ, whence our word "shawl"]: pl. شَالَاتٌ and شِيلَانٌ. (TA.)

شَوْلٌ: see شَائِلَةٌ, voce شَائِلٌ: = and شَوْلَةٌ: = Also *Somewhat remaining* of water in the skin and in the bucket, (Ḳ,) and of milk in the udder: (TA:) and *a small quantity of water* (Ṣ, O, Ḳ, TA) in the bottom of the water-skin (Ṣ, O, TA) and of the leathern water-bag: (TA:) [in the CḲ, المالُ القَلِيلُ is erroneously put for المَآءُ القَلِيلُ:] pl. أَشْوَالٌ. (Ṣ, O, Ḳ.) It is said in a prov.,

مَا ضَرَّ نَابًا شَوْلُهَا المُعَلَّقُ

(Meyd, TA,) i. e. *Her small quantity of water* [*that is hung* upon her *does not harm an aged she-camel*]: or نَابِى [*my aged she-camel*]: applied to the case of carrying that which will not harm thee if it be with thee, and will be useful to thee if thou be in want of it: (Meyd:) or applied to him who is enjoined to take the prudent course and to supply himself with travelling-provision though he be going to such provision. (TA.) = And *Light, active,* or *agile;* syn. خَفِيفٌ: (Ḳ:) so in the M. (TA.) [See also the next paragraph.]

شَوِلٌ One *that raises a thing.* (TA. [See also شَائِلٌ.]) — And A man *light, active,* or *agile,* (خَفِيفٌ,) *in work, and in service,* (Ṣ, O, Ḳ,) *and in respect of what is wanted; and quick:* (Ḳ:) thus in a verse of El-Aạshà: (O, TA:) [but accord. to the reading of AO of that verse, it is ▼ شُوَّلٌ, which has a similar, but intensive, meaning. (De Sacy's Chrest. Ar., 2nd ed., ii. 484-5.) See also what next follows.]

شُوَّلٌ, like صُرَدٌ [in measure], One *who aids,* or *assists, much* or *well;* syn. نَصُورٌ. (O, TA.) [See also what next precedes.]

شُوَّلٌ: see شَوِلٌ.

شَوْلَةٌ The *part that it raises of the tail* of the scorpion; (Ṣ, O, Ḳ;) and so ▼ شَوْلٌ: (Ḥam p. 649:) or, accord. to Sh, its *sting, with which it strikes.* (TA.) — [Hence,] الشَّوْلَةُ † *Two bright stars, near together,* [λ *and* υ,] (Ṣ, O,) *in the end of the tail of Scorpio,* (Ḳzw,) *which are one of the Mansions of the Moon,* (Ṣ, O, Ḳzw,) namely, *the Nineteenth Mansion;* (Ḳzw;) also called حُمَةُ العَقْرَبِ. (Ṣ, O.) [See مَنَازِلُ القَمَرِ, in art. نزل.] — And شَوْلَةُ is a proper name for *The scorpion;* (O, TA;) [and] so ▼ شَوَّالَةُ. (Ḳ, TA.) = Also *A foolish,* or *stupid,* woman. (IAạr, O, Ḳ.) شَوْلَةُ was the name of *A certain foolish female slave,* belonging to [the tribe of] 'Adwán, and she used to give advice to her masters, and it resulted in evil to them; whence the saying, أَنْتَ شَوْلَةُ النَّاصِحَةُ [*Thou art Showleh the giver of advice*]. (Ṣ, O, Ḳ.) — Also the name of *The mare of Zeyd-el-Fawáris Ed-Dabbee.* (O, Ḳ.)

شُوَيْلَآءُ *A certain plant,* (AḤn, O, Ḳ,) mentioned, but not described, by Aṣ; *of the kind termed* عُشْب, *growing in plain,* or *soft, land,* (AḤn, O,) *used as a medicament,* (AḤn, O, Ḳ,) and well known: (AḤn, O:) [Sgh says,] I have seen it: *it is dust-coloured, spreads upon the ground, has no thorns, and the cattle eagerly desire it:* (O:) *it is called* (O, Ḳ) *sometimes,* (Ḳ,) *by some of the people of El-'Irák,* (O,) ▼ شُوَيْلٌ, like قُبَيْطٌ [in measure]. (O, Ḳ.)

شَوَّالٌ The *tail of the scorpion.* (TA. [So called

because often raised.]) —— Also, (Ṣ, O, Mṣb, Ḳ,) and sometimes it is called الشَّوَّالُ, (Mṣb,) *The month of the festival of the breaking of the fast;* (Mṣb, Ḳ;*) *the month next after* رَمَضَان; (TA;) *the first of the months of the pilgrimage;* (Ṣ, O;) [*the tenth month of the lunar year:*] as some assert, (IDrd, O,) so called because [when first thus named] it coincided with the season when the she-camels [being seven or eight months gone with young] raised their tails: (IDrd, O, Mṣb, TA:) [for the camels generally couple in winter:] or because of their milk becoming then withdrawn; such being the case with the camels in the time of vehement heat and of the coming to an end of the juicy fresh herbage: [see a table of the months voce زَمَنٌ:] the Arabs used to regard the making of marriage-contracts in this month as of evil omen; and to say that the woman [then] married would resist him who married her, like as the she-camel resists the stallion and raises her tail; but the Prophet abolished their thus auguring, and he married 'Áisheh in this month: (TA:) the pl. is شَوَّالَاتٌ and شَوَاوِيلُ (Ṣ, Mṣb, Ḳ) and شَوَاوِلُ, this last formed by rejecting the augmentative letter [in the second]. (TA.)

شُوَيْلَ: see شُوَيْلَاءُ.

شَوَّالَةٌ [not (as is implied in the Ḳ) شُوَالَةٌ] *A certain bird,* (AḤát, O, Ḳ,) *a* دُخَّلَة [n. un. of دُخَّل q. v.], *of a dusky colour, which, when it alights upon a stone or a tree, moves up and down its tail like as does the camel;* so called because it raises its tail; *and in its belly and its hinder part is somewhat of redness.* (AḤát, O, TA.) —— See also شَوْلَةٌ. —— [Hence, as being likened to the scorpion, whence also the phrase إِنَّهُ تَدِبُّ عَقَارِبُهُ,] امْرَأَةٌ شَوَّالَةٌ † *A woman wont to calumniate.* (Ḳ.)

شَائِلٌ A she-camel *raising her tail,* (Ṣ, O, Mṣb, Ḳ,) *having conceived,* (Mṣb,) or *by reason of having conceived, and having no milk whatever:* (Ṣ, O, Ḳ:) or a she-camel *that has conceived, and raises her tail to the stallion as a sign of her having conceived, raising her head therewith, and elevating her nose:* (Az, TA:) the word is without ة because it is an epithet of peculiar application [to a female]: (Mṣb:) or it is without ة anomalously; for the male also raises his tail: (ISd, TA:) the pl. is شُوَّلٌ (Az, Ṣ, O, Mṣb, Ḳ) and شُيَّلٌ and شِيَّلٌ and شُوَّالٌ. (Ḳ.) Also, with ة, applied to a mare, as meaning *Raising the tail.* (TA.) —— And شَائِلَةٌ, which is anomalously with ة because it is an epithet denoting an attribute not shared with the female by the male, (ISd, TA,) A she-camel *that has passed seven months,* (Ṣ, O, Ḳ,) or *eight,* (Ṣ, O,) *since the period of her bringing forth,* (Ṣ, O, Ḳ,) or *of her becoming pregnant,* (Ḳ,) *and whose milk has dried up,* (جَفَّ لَبَنُهَا, Ḳ, and so in a copy of the Ṣ,) or *whose milk has become scanty,* (خَفَّ لَبَنُهَا, O, and so in another copy of the Ṣ,) *and her udder drawn up,* (Ṣ, O,) *there remaining in her udder no more than a* شَوْل, *a third of the quantity of the contents thereof when her bringing forth was recent:* (TA:) she-camels in this case are termed ▼شَوْلٌ, (Ṣ, O, Ḳ,) an anomalous pl., (Ḳ,) [or rather a quasi-pl. n.,] expl. by some as applied to she-camels *whose milk has become deficient,* which is the case when their young are weaned at the period of the [auroral] rising of سُهَيْل [or Canopus, a period which commenced, in Central Arabia, about the beginning of the era of the Flight, on the 4th of August, O. S.], and they cease not to be thus termed until the stallion is sent among them; (TA;) the pl. pl. [or pl. of شَوْلٌ] is أَشْوَالٌ; (Ḳ;) and شَوَائِلُ is a pl. of شَائِلَةٌ meaning [as expl. above, or] a she-camel *whose milk has become withdrawn.* (TA.) —— شَائِلٌ is also applied to Anything *that is raised,* or *drawn up,* or *withdrawn.* (TA.)

شُوشَلَاةٌ *Initus;* syn. نَيْكٌ: said to be an Abyssinian word. (Ibn-'Abbád, O, Ḳ.)

مِشْوَلٌ *A small* مِنْجَل [or *reaping-hook:* in the CḲ, erroneously, مُنْخُل]. (Ṣ, O, Ḳ, TA.)

مُشِيلٌ act. part. n. of 4. See an ex. in a verse cited voce خَافِضٌ; cited also in the present art. in the Ṣ and O.

مِشْوَلَةٌ is said by Yz to signify *A certain thing with which one plays.* (O, TA.)

مِشْوَالٌ *A stone that is raised.* (Lḥ, Ḳ.)

شوه

1. شَاهَ وَجْهُهُ, aor. يَشُوهُ; (Ḳ;) and شَاهَتِ الوُجُوهُ, aor. تَشُوهُ; (Ṣ, Mṣb;) inf. n. شَوْهٌ (Ṣ, Ḳ) and شَوْهَةٌ, (Ḳ,) or the latter is a simple subst.; (TA;) and شَوِهَ وَجْهُهُ, (Ḳ,) inf. n. شَوَهٌ; (TA;) *His face was,* (Ḳ,) and *the faces were,* (Ṣ, Mṣb,) *foul, unseemly,* or *ugly.* (Ṣ, Mṣb, Ḳ.) And شَوِهَ, (Mṣb,) and شَوُهَتْ, (Mgh,) inf. n. شَوَهٌ, (Mgh, Mṣb,) *He,* (a man, Mṣb,) and *she,* (a woman, Mgh,) *was,* or *became, foul, unseemly,* or *ugly,* (Mgh, Mṣb,) *in face,* (Mgh,) or *in make.* (Mṣb.) —— شَوَهٌ is also syn. with حُسْنٌ [app. as an inf. n., of which the verb is شَوِهَ signifying *He was,* or *became, beautiful:* thus having two contr. meanings]. (TA.) —— Also, (Ḳ,) as an inf. n., (TḲ,) The neck's *being long,* (Ḳ, TA,) *and high,* and the head's *overtopping;* whence ▼أَشْوَهُ applied to a horse: (TA:) and the neck's *being short:* thus [again] having two contr. meanings: (Ḳ:) one says, [app. of a horse,] شَوِهَتْ عُنُقُهُ *His neck was long* [&c.]: and *his neck was short:* (TḲ:) or شَوَهٌ said of the neck [of a horse] signifies the *being extended:* and said of the شِدْق [or side of the mouth], the *being wide,* (JK. [It probably signifies any of the attributes denoted by the epithet أَشْوَهُ, q. v.]) —— Also, [and app. in this sense likewise an inf. n. of which the verb is شَوِهَ,] The *being quick to smite with the* [*evil*] *eye.* (Ṣ.) —— And one says, شَاهَ فُلَانًا, (Ḳ,) inf. n. شَوْهٌ, (TA,) *He smote such a one with the* [*evil*] *eye;* (Ḳ, TA;) as also ▼اشاهه: (TA in art. شهو:) and in like manner, مَالَهُ [*his cattle,* or *property*]: (Lḥ, TA:) or شَوْهٌ signifies the *smiting vehemently therewith.* (TA.) And لَا تَشُوهْ ▼ عَلَىَّ *Smite not thou me with an* [*evil*] *eye:* (Ḳ:) or, accord. to Abu-l-Mekárim this means *say not, How eloquent art thou!* (Az, TA,) or *say not, How beautiful art thou!* (ISk, Ṣ,) *and so doing smite me with the* [*evil*] *eye,* or *with an* [*evil*] *eye.* (ISk, Az, Ṣ, TA.) ▼ تشوّه signifies *He practised artifice* to smite people with the evil eye. (JK.) And one says, هُوَ يَتَشَوَّهُ ▼ أَمْوَالَ النَّاسِ لِيُصِيبَهَا بِالْعَيْنِ i. e. *He raises his look towards the cattle,* or *possessions, of the people to smite them with the* [*evil*] *eye.* (TA.) [See also 1 in art. شيه.] —— Also, *He frightened,* or *terrified, such a one.* (Lḥ, Ḳ.) —— And *He envied such a one.* (Ḳ.) —— And شَاهَتْ نَفْسُهُ إِلَى كَذَا *His desire became raised towards such a thing.* (AA, Ḳ.)

2. شَوَّهَهُ, (Ṣ, Ḳ,) inf. n. تَشْوِيهٌ, (TA,) *He* (God) *rendered foul, unseemly,* or *ugly, his face:* (Ṣ, Ḳ, TA:) and *it,* i. e. the conformation of the face. (TA, from a verse of El-Ḥoṭei-ah.) And شَوَّهْتُ الوُجُوهَ *I rendered foul, unseemly,* or *ugly, the faces.* (Mṣb.) —— And شَوَّهَ اللّٰهُ حُلُوقَكُمْ *God rendered,* or *may God render, wide your throats,* or *fauces.* (TA.) —— لَا تُشَوِّهْ عَلَىَّ: see 1, latter half. —— شوّه بِيَدِهِ *He* (a man) *made a sign with his arm,* or *hand.* (JK.)

4. اشاهه: see 1.

5. تشوّه لَهُ *He became altered in countenance to him, so as to be not known by him,* (syn. تَنَكَّرَ, Ṣ, Ḳ,) *and assumed various appearances.* (Ṣ.) —— See also 1, in two places, near the end. —— تشوّه شَاةً *He hunted a* شاة [app. here meaning a *wild bull,* as seems to be indicated by the context in the Ṣ]. (Ṣ, Ḳ.)

شَاةٌ: see the next paragraph.

شَاةٌ, (Ṣ, Mṣb, Ḳ, &c.,) originally شَاهَةٌ, (Ṣ, Mṣb, TA,) *A sheep,* or *goat;* [*each* and *either,* but more commonly the *former;* see an instance voce صُوفٌ;] i. e. *one of what are termed* غَنَم; (Ṣ,* Mṣb,* Ḳ;) applied to the *male* and to the *female;* (Ṣ, Mṣb, Ḳ;) so that one says of the male, هٰذَا شَاةٌ, (Mṣb,) which is said by Kh to be like the phrase هٰذَا رَحْمَةٌ مِنْ رَبِّى; (Ṣb, TA;) and of the female, هٰذِهِ شَاةٌ; and شَاةٌ ذَكَرٌ and شَاةٌ أُنْثَى: (Mṣb:) or it may be [*one*] *of sheep,* and *of goats,* and *of gazelles* or *antelopes,* and *of the bovine kind* [app. *of the wild bovine kind* i. e. *of bovine antelopes*], and *of ostriches,* and *of wild asses;* (Ḳ;) it is applied to *a wild bull* by Ṭarafeh, in his saying,

* كَسَامِعَتَىْ شَاةٍ بِحَوْمَلَ مُفْرَدِ *

(Ṣ) i. e. *Like the two ears of a wild bull, in Ḥowmal, solitary;* the poet likening thereto the ears of a she-camel in respect of sharpness and erectness; (EM p. 76;) and likewise by Lebeed, and by El-Farezdaḳ: (IB, TA:) and it is also applied to [*a wild cow;* (though said in the Ḳ in art. شوى to signify the *wild bull,* specially the *male;*) and hence, as being likened thereto,] ‡ *a woman;* (Ḳ, TA;) thus by El-Aạshà; and thus also by Antarah, in his saying,

* يَا شَاةَ مَا قَنَصٍ لِمَنْ حَلَّتْ لَهُ *
* حَرُمَتْ عَلَىَّ وَلَيْتَهَا لَمْ تَحْرُمِ *

(TA) *O* شاة [i. e. *wild cow*] *of the chase* (ما being redundant) *for him to whom she is lawful: she has become forbidden to me, and would that she were not forbidden:* (EM p. 246:) pl. ↓ شَآءٌ, (Ṣ, Mṣb, Ḳ,) originally شَاهٌ, (Ḳ,) used when they are many in number, (Ṣ,) [but this is properly termed a coll. gen. n.,] and شِيَاهٌ, (Ṣ, Mgh, Mṣb, Ḳ,) with ه, which is used of a number from three to ten [inclusive], for more than which it is with ت [meaning ة, i. e. شَاةٌ, agreeably with a general rule], (Ṣ,) and شِوَاهٌ, [the original of شِيَاهٌ,] (Ḳ,) and ↓ شَوِىٌّ, (Ṣ, Ḳ, TA, [in the CḲ, erroneously, شَوِىٌ,]) which is pl. of شَاةٌ, (Ṣ, TA,) or rather a quasi-pl. n., originally شَوِيهٌ, the ه being changed into ى like as it is in ذِى for ذِهْ, (TA,) and أَشَاوِهُ, (Ḳ,) and ↓ شَيْهٌ, (so in copies of the Ḳ, [in the TA said to be like عَنْبٌ, which is a mistake, (perhaps for عَيْنٌ,) for it is there said to be a quasi-pl. n., which could not be said if it were شِيهٌ,]) and ↓ شِيهٌ, (CḲ, [but this, which is another quasi-pl. n., is not in my MS. copy of the Ḳ nor in the TA,]) and ↓ شَيِّهٌ, (Ḳ,) originally شَيْوِهٌ, but this, also, is a quasi-pl. n., (TA,) and ↓ شِيَةٌ also is syn. with شَاةٌ: (IAạr, Ḳ in art. شوى:) it has not a pl. formed with ا and ت, [i. e. it has not for a pl. شَاآتٌ,] whether it be used as a gen. n. or as a proper name: (TA:) the dim. is ↓ شُوَيْهَةٌ. (Ṣ, Mṣb.) The sing. is also used in the sense of the pl., in the saying فُلَانٌ كَثِيرُ الشَّاةِ وَالبَعِيرِ [*Such a one is possessor of a large number of sheep or goats, and of camels*], because the article ال denotes the genus. (Ṣ.) And it is said in a trad. فَأَمَرَ لَهَا بِشِيَاهِ غَنَمٍ [*And he ordered that sheep or goats should be given to her*]: شياه being prefixed to غنم, governing it in the gen. case, for the sake of distinction; because the Arabs [sometimes] call an animal of the wild bovine kind شاة. (IAth, TA.) —— الشَّاةُ is also the name of † *Certain small stars* (Ḳ in art. شوى) *between* الفرهد [or الفرجة, thus in the work of Ḳzw, in his descr. of Cepheus, and there said to be *the star in the breast of Cepheus*,] *and* الجَدْىُ [i. e. *the pole-star*]; (TA in that art.;) [the same that are described by Ḳzw as *certain small stars, called by the Arabs* الأَغْنَام, *between the legs of Cepheus and the star* الجَدْى.]

شَائِهُ البَصَرِ and شَاهِى البَصَرِ, شَاهُ البَصَرِ: see شَائِهٌ.

شَوَهٌ an inf. n., of شَوِهَ. (Mgh, Mṣb, TA. [See 1, in several places.]) ═ Also a subst. meaning *Unluckiness*, or *inauspiciousness*, of a woman. (TA.)

شَيْهٌ and شِيهٌ and شَيِّهٌ: see شَاةٌ.

شَوْهَةٌ *Remoteness:* (Ḳ, TA:) and so بَوْهَةٌ: one says, in dispraise, شَوْهَةً لَهُ وَبَوْهَةً [i. e. بُعْدًا لَهُ, lit. *Remoteness to him!* meaning *may God alienate him* or *estrange him, from good,* or *prosperity!* or, *curse him!*]. (TA.)

شَوِىٌّ, originally شَوِيهٌ: see شَاةٌ.

شُوَيْهَةٌ dim. of شَاةٌ, q. v. (Ṣ, Mṣb.)

شَائِهٌ *Envying:* pl. شُوَّهٌ: (Aṣ, Lḥ, TA:) or the latter signifies persons *practising artifice to smite men with the* [*evil*] *eye.* (JK.) —— And شَائِهُ البَصَرِ, (JK, Ṣ, Ḳ,) and ↓ شَاهُ البَصَرِ, (JK, Ḳ,) and شَاهِى البَصَرِ, (JK, TA, and Ṣ and Ḳ in art. شهو,) the last formed by transposition from the first, (Ṣ in art. شهو,) A man *sharp of sight.* (JK, Ṣ, Ḳ.)

شَائِىٌّ : } see the next paragraph.
شَاهِىٌّ :

شَاوِىٌّ and ↓ شَاهِىٌّ A man *possessing* شَاء [meaning *sheep* or *goats* or *both*]: (Ḳ:) the former is the rel. n. of شَآءٌ; and the latter, that of شَاةٌ: but used as a proper name of a man, it is ↓ شَائِىٌّ, and, if you will, شَاوِىٌّ. (Ṣ, TA.*)

شَيِّهٌ: see the next paragraph: ═ and see شَاةٌ.

أَشْوَهُ, applied to a man, (Mṣb,) *Foul, unseemly*, or *ugly,* (JK, Mṣb, Ḳ,) *in face,* (JK, Ḳ,) or *in aspect,* (Mṣb,) and, as also ↓ شَيِّهٌ, of which the pl. is شَيِّهُونَ, *in make:* (JK:) fem. شَوْهَآءُ: (JK, Mgh, Mṣb:) and pl. شُوهٌ. (Mṣb.) Any created thing *incongruous in its several parts;* as also ↓ مُشَوَّهٌ. (TA.) And the fem., A woman *frowning*, or *morose, in face;* (Ḳ,* TA;) *foul, unseemly,* or *ugly, in make:* (TA:) and also *beautiful, goodly,* or *comely;* (Ḳ,* TA;) *that excites admiration and approval by her beauty:* (TA:) thus having two contr. meanings. (Ḳ, TA.) Also, the fem., *Unlucky,* or *inauspicious.* (Ḳ.) —— And the masc. applied to a man, (Lth, Ṣ, TA,) and the fem. applied to a woman, (Lth, TA,) *That smites quickly with the* [*evil*] *eye:* (Lth, Ṣ, TA:) or *that smites people effectually with his,* and *her,* [*evil*] *eye.* (TA.) And أَشْوَهُ العَيْنِ *Having an evil eye.* (Fr, TA in art. شزر.) —— The fem. is also applied to a mare, (JK, T, Ṣ, Ḳ,) as an epithet of commendation, but not the masc. to a horse, meaning, it is said, *Wide in the* شِدْقَانِ [or *two sides of the mouth*]: (Ṣ:) or *long in the head, and wide in the nostrils:* (JK:) or *tall, and such as excites admiration and approval by her beauty* or *excellence:* (Ḳ,* TA:) or *exceedingly wide in the* شِدْقَانِ [or *two sides of the mouth*] *and the nostrils:* (Ḳ, TA:) or, as some say, *wide in the mouth:* (TA:) and *small in the mouth:* thus having two contr. meanings: (Ḳ, TA:) or *sharp-sighted:* (T, TA:) or *sharp in spirit:* (TA:) see also 1. —— Also, the masc., *Proud, and self-conceited.* (Ḳ.) —— And خُطْبَةٌ شَوْهَآءُ [*An oration from the pulpit*] *in which a blessing is not invoked on the Prophet.* (TA.)

أَرْضٌ مَشَاهَةٌ *A land in which are* شَآء; (A'Obeyd, Ṣ, Ḳ;) like as one says أَرْضٌ مَأْبَلَةٌ: (A'Obeyd, Ṣ:) or *in which are many thereof.* (Ḳ.)

مُشَوَّهٌ *Rendered foul, unseemly,* or *ugly, in face,* by God: (TA:) or *foul,* &c., *in shape.* (Ḳ.) See also أَشْوَهُ, second sentence. —— And *Bad in intellect.* (TA.)

شوى

1. شَوَى اللَّحْمَ, (aor. ـِ, TA,) inf. n. شَىٌّ, (Ṣ, MA, Mṣb, Ḳ,) *He roasted, broiled,* or *fried, the flesh-meat;* (MA, KL,* PṢ;) and ↓ اشواه signifies the same; as also ↓ اشتواه; (Mṣb, TA;) or this last, (TA,) or اشتوى [alone], (Ṣ, MA,) signifies *he prepared,* or *prepared for himself,* (Ṣ, MA,* TA,) شِوَآء, (Ṣ, TA,*) or *roasted, broiled,* or *fried, flesh-meat.* (MA.) —— And شَوَى المَآءَ, (IAạr, Ḳ,) aor. as above, (TA,) *He heated the water.* (IAạr, Ḳ.) —— [And accord. to Freytag, شَوَى signifies also *He cut off* from (من) roasted flesh-meat: but for this he has named no authority.] ═ See also 4.

2: see 4. —— Also شَوَّاهُ لَحْمًا *He gave him flesh-meat* [app. in an unrestricted sense]. (TA.)

3. يُشَاوِى, for يُشَائِى: see 3 in art. شأو.

4. اشوى اللَّحْمَ: see 1. —— أَشْوَاهُمْ; (Ṣ, Mṣb, Ḳ;) and ↓ شَوَّاهُمْ, inf. n. تَشْوِيَةٌ; (Ḳ;) *He fed them with* شِوَآء [i. e. *roasted,* or *broiled,* or *fried, flesh-meat*]. (Ṣ, Mṣb, Ḳ.) And (both verbs with their complements) *He gave them flesh-meat that they might roast,* or *broil,* or *fry, thereof.* (AZ, Ḳ.) ═ And اشوى ‡ *He left a portion remaining of his supper:* (Ṣ, Ḳ, TA:) or *he left some roasted,* or *broiled,* or *fried, flesh-meat of his supper.* (A, TA.) —— And اشوى القَمْحُ *The wheat became fit to be rubbed with the hands and to be roasted.* (ISd, Ḳ.) —— And اشوى السَّعَفُ † *The palm-branches became yellow on the occasion of their drying up;* (Ḳ, TA;) as though a roasting affected them. (TA.) ═ Also *He got,* or *acquired, the worse,* or *viler, sort of cattle.* (Ḳ.) ═ اشواه said of a shooter or caster, *He hit* (Ṣ,* Mṣb,* Ḳ) *his* شَوَى, (Ḳ,) i. e. [*one or more of his*] *extremities,* (TA,) *not a* [*vital*] *place where a wound would occasion death;* (Ṣ, Mṣb, Ḳ;) and so ↓ شَوَّاهُ, as in the Tekmileh: in the Ḳ, erroneously, شَوَاهُ. (TA.) —— [Hence, *He missed it,* i. e. the object of his aim. See مُشْوًى: and see also Ḥam p. 91.] —— [Hence, also, app.,] Hr says that اشوى is allowable in the sense of أَسْقَطَ † [*He dropped, left out, omitted,* &c., anything]; like أَسْوَى [q. v.]. (TA in art. سوى.) ═ In the saying مَا أَعْيَاهُ وَأَشْوَاهُ, (Ṣ, Ḳ, [in some copies of the Ḳ وَمَا أَشْوَاهُ,]) and so in ما اعياه واشواه, (Ṣ,* Ḳ,* TA,) the latter verb is an imitative sequent to the former [added only for the purpose of corroboration]. (Ṣ, Ḳ, TA.)

7. انشوى اللَّحْمُ *The flesh-meat became roasted, broiled,* or *fried;* (MA;) quasi-pass. of شَوَى اللَّحْمَ; (Ṣ,* M, Mṣb, Ḳ;) as also ↓ اشتوى; (M, Ḳ;) [or] the latter in this sense is not allowable. (Ṣ, Mṣb.)

8: see 1. —— [Hence,] اِشْتَوَيْتُهَا, referring to a she-camel, † *I journeyed upon her until the heat of the middays of summer emaciated her and she became as though she were burnt.* (Ḥam p. 783.) ═ See also 7.

شَاةٌ: see what next follows: and see more in art. شوه.

شِيَةٌ i. q. شَآءٌ [q. v. in art. شوه]; as also ↑ شَوِىٌّ; (IAar, Ḳ;) the latter is like غَنِىٌّ, [الشُّوَى in the CḲ as syn. with الشَّآء being a mistranscription,] and is said by IAth to be a quasi-pl. n., or [what lexicographers term] a pl., of ↑ شَاةٌ [n. un. of شَآءٌ]. (TA.)

شِىٌّ is originally شِوْىٌ. (ISd, TA.) One says, جَآءَ بِالعِىِّ وَالشِّىِّ, (Ṣ, Ḳ,) using the latter noun as an imitative sequent to the former [for the purpose of corroboration: see art. عى]. (TA.)

شَوًى is pl. of شَوَاةٌ: [or rather the former is a coll. gen. n. of which the latter is the n. un.:] the latter signifies The *skin of the head:* (Ṣ, TA:) so [accord. to some] in the Ḳur lxx. 16: (TA:) or the *exterior of the skin of the head, in which grows the hair:* (Aboo-Ṣafwán, TA in art. بشر:) and some say, the *exterior of all,* or *of any part, of the skin:* (TA in the present art.:) and the former signifies the *arms* or *hands* and the *legs* or *feet,* or the *fore* and *hind legs,* (Ṣ, Ḳ,) and (Ḳ) the *extremities* (Mṣb, Ḳ) *collectively,* (Ḳ,) and the *head* of a human being, (Ṣ,) or the قِحْف *of the head* [i. e. the *bone above the brain,* or *a separate portion of the skull,* or *a distinct bone of the skull*], (Ḳ,) but of a horse the *legs,* not the head, because one says عَبْلُ الشَّوَى [i. e. *thick in the legs*], for this cannot relate to the head of the horse, (Ṣ,) and *any part that is not a* [*vital*] *place* [i. e.] *where a wound causes death* (Ṣ, Mṣb, Ḳ) *such* [*for instance*] *as the legs.* (Mṣb.) ثَالِبَةُ الشَّوَى means A woman *having cracked,* or *chapped, feet.* (Ṣ and Ḳ in art. ثلب.) — It is also a subst. [app. meaning a quasi-inf. n.] from أَشْوَاهُ [q. v.] as said of a shooter or caster: (TA:) [and hence] the saying (Ṣ, TA) of the Hudhalee, (Ṣ, [accord. to the TA, Khálid Ibn-Zuheyr,])

* فَإِنَّ مِنَ القَوْلِ الَّتِى لَا شَوَى لَهَا *
* إِذَا زَلَّ عَنْ ظَهْرِ اللِّسَانِ ٱنْفِلَاتُهَا *

means † [*And,* or *for*] *verily of speech is that sentence* (كَلِمَة, a word understood,) *which does not hit a place where a wound will not occasion death,* [i. e. which does not miss its object, *when its escaping from the upper surface of the tongue is quick,*] but which kills. (Ṣ, TA.) And شَوًى is used [app. in like manner, as a quasi-inf. n.,] in the case of anything that has missed an object of aim, though there be to it [really] no place where a wound would occasion death nor anything that is [properly] termed شَوًى [as meaning a place where a wound will not occasion death]. (TA.) And [hence] it signifies † *A mistake;* syn. خَطَأٌ. (TA.) — Also ‡ *A thing,* (Ṣ,) or *an affair,* (Ḳ,) *that is paltry, mean, despicable,* or *of no account* or *weight* or *worth:* (Ṣ, Ḳ,* TA:) in this sense, from the same word as signifying the "extremities" [of an animal]. (IAth, TA.) Hence, in a trad. of Mujáhid, كُلُّ مَا أَصَابَ الصَّائِمَ شَوًى إِلَّا الغِيبَةَ ‡ [*Everything that befalls the faster is a matter of no account, except absence of mind*]; i. e. nothing that befalls the faster annuls his fast except الغيبة, for this does annul it. (TA.) — And † The *worse,* or *viler, sort of cattle,* (Ṣ, Ḳ, TA,) *of camels,* and *of sheep* or *goats;* and the *small,* or *young, thereof.* (TA.) [See also شُوَايَةٌ.] — And † *A remainder,* or *remaining portion.* (TA.) [See, again, شُوَايَةٌ.] — Also i. q. إِبْقَآءٌ † [The *making,* or *causing,* or *suffering, to remain;* or, perhaps, *to continue in life,* and if it mean thus, it may be from the same word in a sense expl. above, for the animal that one hits in a part that is not vital is suffered to continue in life]. (TA.)

شُوَآءٌ: see what next follows.

شِوَآءٌ *Roasted, broiled,* or *fried, flesh-meat;* (Ṣ,* MA, Mṣb, Ḳ,* KL;) as also ↑ شُوَآءٌ; (Ks, Ṣgh, Ḳ;) but the former is more usual and more chaste: (TA:) a subst. from شَوَى اللَّحْمَ: and ↑ شِوَآءَةٌ [as its n. un.] signifies *a piece thereof.* (Ṣ.)

شَوِىٌّ (Ḳ) and ↑ مَشْوِىٌّ (Mṣb) [*Roasted, broiled,* or *fried*], the latter originally مَشْوُوىٌ. (Mṣb.) [In the K the former is said to be like شِوَآءٌ; but it has the signification of the latter, i. e., of a pass. part. n.] — See also شِيَةٌ. — Ks says, (Ṣ,) in the phrase عَيِىٌّ شَوِىٌّ, and so in عَيِىٌّ شَيِىٌّ, (Ṣ, Ḳ,) some say (Ṣ) the latter word is an imitative sequent to the former [i. e. a corroborative: see art. عى]. (Ṣ, Ḳ.)

شِوَآءَةٌ: see شِوَآءٌ.

شَوِيَّةٌ:
شُوَايَةٌ: } see the next paragraph.

شُوَايَةٌ *What is cut off from,* or *of, flesh-meat:* (Ḳ, TA:) or *what the slaughterer cuts off from,* or *of, the extremities of a sheep* or goat. (TA.) — *A small thing* [or *portion*] *of that which is large; as a piece,* or *detached portion, of a sheep,* or *goat:* one says, مَا بَقِىَ مِنَ الشَّاةِ إِلَّا شُوَايَةٌ [*There remained not of the sheep,* or *goat, save a piece*]. (Ṣ.) — Also, (Ṣ, Ḳ,) and ↑ شِوَايَةٌ and ↑ شَوَايَةٌ, (Ḳ,) *A* قُرْص [or *round cake,* or *small round cake,*] of bread. (Ṣ, Ḳ.) — And, all the three, *A remaining portion of people,* or *of cattle, that have perished;* as also ↑ شَوِيَّةٌ; (Ḳ;) or this last, *a remaining portion of people that have perished:* (Ṣ:) pl. (of the last, Ṣ) شَوَايَا. (Ṣ, Ḳ.) [See also شَوًى.] — And ‡ The *bad,* or *vile, sort,* (Ḳ, TA,) or *worse,* or *viler, sort,* (TA,) of camels, and of sheep, or goats: (Ḳ, TA:) in this sense written by ISd with kesr and with fet-ḥ. (TA.) [See, again, شَوًى.] — [And accord. to Freytag, (شواية الرَّضْف (i. e. شُوَايَةُ الرَّضْفِ is expl. by Meyd as meaning *Cooked milk cast upon a hot stone, so that only a small portion remains.*]

شِوَايَةٌ: see the next preceding paragraph.

شَوَّآءٌ *A seller of roasted, broiled,* or *fried, flesh-meat.* (KL.)

شِيَانٌ [mentioned in this art. as though originally [شِوْيَانٌ] i. q. دَمُ الأَخَوَيْنِ [The *red, resinous, inspissated juice called dragon's blood:* see art. دمو]. (Ṣ, Ḳ.) — And *Far-seeing.* (Ṣ, Ḳ.)

شَاوِىٌّ *A possessor of* شَآء [meaning *sheep* or *goats* or *both*]. (Ṣ, Ḳ. [In the CḲ without teshdeed. Mentioned also in art. شوه, q. v.]) — سَعَفَةٌ شَاوِيَةٌ (with teshdeed to the ى, TA, [but in the CḲ without teshdeed,]) † *A palm-branch that has become yellow in drying up.* (Ḳ. [See 4.])

شَوْشَاةٌ, (Ṣ, Ḳ, [in some copies of the Ḳ شَوْشَآةٌ, but]) like مَوْمَاةٌ, (Ṣ,) A *swift* she-camel. (Ṣ, Ḳ.)

أَشَاوَى a pl. pl. of شَىْءٌ, q. v.

مُشْوِىٌّ, like مُهْدِىٌّ, (Ḳ, TA, [in the CḲ, مُشْوًى, like مُهْدًى,]) erroneously, as is proved by a verse cited as an ex. in the TA, pass. part. n. of 4,]) applied to a portion of a living serpent, (TA,) *That has been missed by the stone* [*cast at it*]. (Ḳ, TA.)

مِشْوًى (Ḳ in art. صول) *A frying-pan.* (TḲ in that art.)

مَشْوِىٌّ: see شَوِىٌّ.

مُشْتَوًى [*A place of roasting, broiling,* or *frying, flesh-meat*]. (Ṣ in art. طبخ.)

شى

4. أَشْيَاهُ an imitative sequent to أَعْيَاهُ in the phrase مَا أَعْيَاهُ وَأَشْيَاهُ: see 4 in art. شوى.

شِيَةٌ, syn. with شَاةٌ: see art. شوى.

شَىٌّ: and يَا شَىَّ مَا لِى: see شَىْءٌ, in art. شيأ.

شِىٌّ an imitative sequent to عِىٌّ: see art. شوى.

شَيِىٌّ an imitative sequent to عَيِىٌّ: see شَوِىٌّ.

شِيَانٌ: see art. شوى.

شيأ

1. شَآءَهُ, (Mṣb,) [originally شَيِئَهُ,] like خَافَهُ, [which is originally خَوِفَهُ,] (MF,) first. pers. شِئْتُهُ, (Ṣ, Ḳ,) aor. يَشَآؤُهُ, (Mṣb,) [and by poetic license يَشَاهُ, without ء,] first pers. أَشَآؤُهُ, (Ṣ, Ḳ,) inf. n. شَىْءٌ (Mṣb, Ḳ) and مَشِيئَةٌ, (Ṣ,* Ḳ,) or this is a simple subst., (Mṣb,) and مَشَآءَةٌ and مَشَائِيَةٌ, (Ḳ,) [or these two also are simple substs.,] *He, and I, willed, wished,* or *desired, it;* syn. أَرَادَهُ (Mṣb) and أَرَدْتُهُ: (Ṣ,* Ḳ:) most of the scholastic theologians make no difference between المَشِيئَةُ and الإِرَادَةُ, though they are [said to be] originally different; for the former, in the proper language, signifies *the causing to be* or *exist,* syn. الإِيجَادُ; and the latter, *the willing, wishing,* or *desiring;* syn. الطَّلَبُ. (TA.) A Jew objected, to the Prophet, his people's saying مَا شَآءَ ٱللّٰهُ وَشِئْتُ [*What God hath willed and I have willed*], as implying the association of another being with God: therefore the Prophet ordered them to say مَا شَآءَ ٱللّٰهُ ثُمَّ شِئْتُ [*What God hath willed, then I have willed*]. (TA.) [مَا شَآءَ ٱللّٰهُ as signifying *What hath God willed!* is used to express admiration. And as signifying *What God willed* it is a phrase often used to denote a vague, generally a great or considerable, but sometimes

a small, number or quantity or time: See De Sacy's Relation de l'Égypte par Abdallatif, pp. 246 and 394 &c.] ▬ See also 1 in art. شوأ.

2. شَيَّأْتُهُ عَلَى الأَمْرِ [in some copies of the Ḳ (erroneously) شَيَّتُّهُ] *I incited him*, or *made him, to do the thing*, or *affair*. (Aṣ, Ṣ, L, Ḳ, TA.) ▬ And شَيَّأَ ٱللّٰهُ وَجْهَهُ, (Ḳ, TA,) and خَلْقَهُ, (TA,) *God rendered*, or *may God render, foul, unseemly*, or *ugly, his face*, (Ḳ, TA,) and *his make*. (TA.)

4. أَشَآءَهُ إِلَيْهِ *He*, or *it, compelled him, constrained him*, or *necessitated him, to have recourse*, or *betake himself, to it*; syn. أَلْجَأَهُ; (Ṣ, Ḳ;) a dial. var. of أَجَآءَهُ; (Ṣ;) of the dial. of Temeem. (TA.) Temeem say, شَرٌّ مَا يُشِيْؤُكَ إِلَى مُخَّةِ عُرْقُوبٍ, meaning يُجِيْؤُكَ [q. v., i. e. *It is an evil thing that compels thee to have recourse to the marrow of a hock*]. (Ṣ.)

5. تَشَيَّأَ *His anger became appeased*: (Ḳ:) said of a man. (TA.)

شَيْءٌ [*A thing; anything; something; somewhat*;] a word of well-known meaning: (Ḳ:) [sometimes, in poetry, written and pronounced شَيّ: see an ex. in a verse cited voce صُوَّابَةٌ: see also the last sentence but one of this paragraph:] الشَّيْءُ properly signifies *what may be known, and that whereof a thing may be predicated*: (Mgh, KT:) accord. to Sb, it denotes existence, and is a name for *anything that has been made to have being, whether an accident*, or *attribute*, or *a substance, and such that it may be known, and that a thing may be predicated thereof*: (KT:) MF says that it is app. an inf. n. used in the sense of a pass. part. n., meaning *what is willed, and meant*, or *intended*, [in which sense ↓ مَشِيْئَةٌ (pl. مَشِيْئَاتٌ) is often used,] *without restriction to its actuality or possibility of being*, so that it applies to *that which necessarily is*, and *that which may be*, and *that which cannot be*; accord. to the opinion adopted by the author of the Ksh: [or, as an inf. n. in the sense of a pass. part. n., it may be expl., agreeably with what is said to be the proper meaning of the verb, as signifying *what is caused to be* or *exist*; accordingly,] Er-Rághib says that it denotes *whatever is caused to be* or *exist, whether sensibly, as material substances*, or *ideally, as sayings*; and Bḍ and others expressly assert that it signifies peculiarly *what is caused to be* or *exist*; but Sb says that it is the most general of general terms; and some of the scholastic theologians apply it to *what is non-existent*; such, however, are overcome in their argument by its not being found to have been thus used by the Arabs, and by such passages as كُلُّ شَيْءٍ هَالِكٌ إِلَّا وَجْهَهُ [*Everything is subject to perish except Himself* (Ḳur xxviii. last verse)] and وَإِنْ مِنْ شَيْءٍ إِلَّا يُسَبِّحُ بِحَمْدِهِ [*And there is not anything but it glorifies Him with praising* (Ḳur xvii. 46)], for what is non-existent cannot be described as perishing nor imagined to glorify God: (TA:) the pl. is أَشْيَآءُ, (Ṣ, Mṣb, Ḳ, &c.,) imperfectly decl., (Mṣb, TA,) or rather this is a quasi-pl. n., (Sb, TA,) respecting the formation of which there is much difference of opinion [as will be shown hereafter], (Mṣb, TA,) and أَشْيَاوَاتٌ, (Ṣ, Ḳ,) a pl. pl. [i. e. pl. of أَشْيَآءُ], (MF, TA,) and أَشَاوَاتٌ, [a contraction of that next preceding,] (Ḳ,) and أَشَاوَى, (Ṣ, Ḳ,) with fet-ḥ to the و, (MF, TA,) and it is also mentioned as with kesr, (TA,) [and is written in both of my copies of the Ṣ أَشَاوِى, though if with kesr it should be either أَشَاوٍ or أَشَاوِىُّ, but أَشَاوَى only is meant by J, as is shown by what here follows,] originally أَشَايِىُّ, with three ىs, not أَشَاوِىُّ as J says, [or rather as the word is written in copies of the Ṣ, for J may have held it to be أَشَاوِىُّ or أَشَايِىُّ, as he says that the ء was changed into ى, thus occasioning the combination of three ىs, so that he held its secondary form to be أَشَايِىُّ, as will presently be shown,] because the first ى is radical, not augmentative, (IB, Ḳ,) the medial ى of the three being suppressed, and the final one changed into ا [though written ى], and the initial one changed into و, (Ṣ,) and another form of pl. is أَشَايَا, (Ṣ, Mṣb, Ḳ,) with the ى preserved, not changed into و [as it is in أَشَاوَى], (TA,) [likewise] a pl. of أَشْيَآءُ, (Mṣb,) and أَشَايَا also is mentioned, (Ḳ,) as formed [from أَشْيَآءُ] by the change of ء into ى and adding ا, (TA,) and أَشَاوَهُ, which is strange, (Lḥ, Ḳ,) as there is no ء in أَشْيَآءُ, (Lḥ,) or in شَيْءٌ: (Ḳ:) with respect to the first of these forms, [the quasi-pl. n.] أَشْيَآءُ, the most probable opinion is that of Kh: (Mṣb, TA:) accord. to him, (Ṣ, Mṣb, Ḳ,) it is originally of the measure فَعْلَآءُ, (Ṣ, Ḳ,*) in lieu of أَفْعَالٌ, (Ḳ,) and therefore imperfectly decl., (Ṣ,) [i. e.] it is originally شَيْئَآءُ, (Mṣb,) and the two hemzehs combined in the latter portion being found difficult of pronunciation, the former of them is transposed to the beginning of the word, so that it becomes of the measure لَفْعَآءُ, (Ṣ, Mṣb,) as is shown by its having for its pls. أَشَاوَى and أَشَايَا and أَشْيَاوَاتٌ: (Ṣ:) accord. to Akh, it is [originally] of the measure أَفْعِلَآءُ; (Ṣ, Ḳ;) but if it were thus a broken pl., [not a quasi-pl. n.,] its dim. would not be ↓ أُشَيَّآءُ, as it is, but شُيَيْئَاتٌ: (Ṣ:) accord. to Ks, it is of the measure أَفْعَالٌ, and made imperfectly decl. because of frequency of usage, being likened to فَعْلَآءُ; but were it so, أَبْنَآءُ and أَسْمَآءُ would be imperfectly decl.: (Ṣ, Ḳ:) accord. to Fr, شَيْءٌ is originally شَيِّئٌ, and therefore has a pl. of the measure أَفْعِلَآءُ, afterwards contracted to أَفْعَآءُ; but were it so, it would not have for its pl. أَشَاوَى. (Ṣ. [Much more respecting this pl. is added in the TA, but it is comparatively unprofitable.]) The dim. of شَيْءٌ is ↓ شُيَيْءٌ and ↓ شِيَيْءٌ; (Ṣ, Ḳ, TA, but only the former in some copies of the Ḳ, the word being written in other copies شُيَىْءٌ;) not ↓ شُوَىٌّ, or ↓ شُوَىْءٌ; (the former accord. to my two copies of the Ṣ and accord. to the copies of the Ḳ followed in the TA, in which it is said to be with teshdeed to the ى, and the latter accord. to the CḲ and my MS. copy of the Ḳ;) or this is a dial. var. of weak authority, (Ḳ,) used by post-classical poets in their verses. (MF, TA.) — When a man says to thee, "What dost thou desire?" thou answerest, لَا شَيْئًا [*Nothing*]: and when he says, "Why didst thou that?" thou answerest, لِلَا شَيْءٍ [*For nothing*]: and when he says, "What is thine affair?" thou answerest, لَا شَيْءٌ [*Nothing*]: it is with tenween in every one of these cases. (Aṣ, AHát, TA.) [When one says لَا شَيْءَ, he means thereby *There is nothing*.] — لَيْسَ بِشَيْءٍ means [*It is nought, of no account* or *weight*; *it is not worthy of notice*, or *not worth anything*;] *it is not a good thing*; or *it is not a thing to be regarded*. (W p. 27.) — [لَيْسَ مِنَ الأَمْرِ فِى شَيْءٍ is a phrase of frequent occurrence, meaning *He has no concern with the affair*; see two exs. in the first paragraph of art. حوص. — حُسْبَانَةٌ فِيهِ شَيْءٌ مِنَ الطُّولِ occurs in the TA voce حُسْبَانَةٌ, meaning *In it is somewhat*, or *some degree, of length*; i. e. *it is somewhat long*; and is used in the present day in this sense.] — In the phrase هُوَ أَحْسَنُ مِنْكَ شَيْئًا, the last word is for بِشَيْءٍ [i. e. *He is better than thou in something*; meaning *he is somewhat better than thou*]. (IJ, L.) — مَا أَغْفَلَهُ عَنْكَ شَيْئًا is a phrase of the Arabs [app. lit. signifying *How unmindful of thee is he as to anything!*] mentioned by Sb as meaning دَعِ الشَّكَّ عَنْكَ [*Dismiss doubt from thee* (*respecting him as to anything*)]: IJ says that شيئا is here put in the accus. case as an inf. n., as though the saying were مَا أَغْفَلَهُ عَنْكَ غُفُولًا, because the verb of wonder does not require to be corroborated by the inf. n. [proper to it]: (L, TA:) [or it is a specificative:] IF says that it is a phrase of dubious meaning; and that the most probable explanation of it is this; that ما is here lit. interrogative, but in meaning denotative of wonder; and that شيئا is governed in the accus. case by some other word, or phrase, as though the saying were *dismiss a thing by which he is not occupied in mind, and dismiss doubt as to his being occupied in mind by it*. (TA in art. ما.) — [شَيْئًا فَشَيْئًا means *Thing by thing, part by part, bit by bit, piecemeal, inch by inch, drop by drop, little and little in succession, by little and little, by degrees*, or *gradually*.] — أَىُّ شَيْءٍ [meaning *What thing?*] is, by the alleviation of the ى [in أَىّ] and the suppression of the ء [in شىء], made into one word, أَيْشٍ: so says El-Fárábee: (Mṣb:) or, [as is commonly the case in the present day,] by reason of frequency of usage, it is contracted into أَيْش. (TA in art. جرم, as on the authority of Ks.) — شَيْءٌ in the Ḳur lx. 11 may mean *Any one* (Bḍ, Jel) or *more*. (Jel.) — [It is also applied to † The *penis* of a man; as in the explanation of a phrase mentioned voce ذَنَبٌ; like as its syn. هَنٌ is to the same and (more commonly) to the "vulva" of a woman.] — In algebra, it signifies [*A square root*;] *a number that is multiplied into itself*; which in arithmetic [and in algebra also] is called جذر [i. e. جَذْرٌ]; and in geometry, ضلع [i. e. ضِلْعٌ or ضِلَعٌ]; ("Dict. of the Techn. Terms used in the Sciences of the Musalmans," p. 202;) *an unknown number that is multiplied into itself.*

(Idem, p. 730.) ═ It is also said, on the authority of Lth, to signify *Water:* and he cites as an ex.,

تَرَى رَكْبَهُ بِالشَّىْءِ فِى وَسْطِ قَفْرَةٍ

[*Thou seest, or wilt see, his company of riders at the water in the midst of a desert*]: but AM says, I know not الشىء in the sense of "water," nor know I what it is. (TA.) ═ يَا شَىْءَ is an expression of regret, (El-Aḥmar, Ks, TA,) or of wonder, (Ḳ, TA,) [or of both,] meaning [*Oh!* or] *O my wonder!* (Ks, Lḥ, TA.) One says, يَا شَىْءَ مَا لِى, (El-Aḥmar, Ks, Lḥ, Ḳ,) and يَا هَىْءَ مَا لِى i. e. with and without ء, (Ks, TA,) and يَا فَىَّ مَا لِى, (Lḥ, Ḳ,) or يا هَىَّ ما لى, and يا فَىَّ ما لى, (El-Aḥmar, Ks, TA,) neither of these two with ء, (Ks, TA,) [meaning *Oh!* or *O my wonder! What has happened to me?*] in all of these, (Ks, TA,) ما being in the place of a noun in the nom. case. (Ks, Lḥ, TA.) — Some also say, يَا شَىْءَ and يَا فَىَّ and يَا هَىَّ, and some add مَا, saying, يَا فَىَّ مَا and يَا هَىَّ مَا and يَا شَىْءَ مَا, meaning *How good, or beautiful, is this!* (Ks, TA.)

شِيْئَةٌ [*Will, wish, or desire,*] a subst. from شَآءَهُ, (Lḥ, Ḳ,) [and] so is ↓ مَشِيْئَةٌ [which is mentioned in the Ḳ as an inf. n.]. (Mṣb.) One says, كُلُّ شَىْءٍ بِشِيْئَةِ ٱللّٰهِ, (Ṣ, Ḳ,) i. e. ↓ بِمَشِيْئَتِهِ [*Everything is by the will of God*]. (Ṣ.)

شُيَىْءٌ and شِيَىْءٌ and شُوَىٌّ or شُوَىْءٌ: see شَىْءٌ in the middle of the paragraph.

شِيَّانٌ and شَيَّآنٌ: see art. شوأ.

أُشَيَّآءُ dim. of أَشْيَآءُ: see شَىْءٌ, in the latter part of the former half of the paragraph.

مَشِيْئَةٌ: see شِيْئَةٌ, in two places: — and see also شَىْءٌ, near the beginning of the paragraph.

مُشَيَّأٌ *Incongruous, unsound,* (Ḳ, TA,) *foul,* or *ugly,* (TA,) *in make,* or *formation.* (Ḳ, TA. [See Ḥam p. 192.]) — And accord. to Aboo-Sa'eed, *A child born preposterously, the legs coming forth before the arms.* (TA.)

شيب

1. شَابَ, aor. يَشِيبُ, inf. n. شَيْبٌ and شَيْبَةٌ (Mṣb, TA) and مَشِيبٌ, (TA,) *He became white-haired,* or *hoary.* (Mṣb, TA.) And شاب رَأْسُهُ, (Ṣ,) and رَأْسُهَا, (Mṣb, TA,) inf. n. شَيْبٌ and شَيْبَةٌ, (Ṣ,) *His head,* and *her head, became white,* or *hoary.* (Ṣ, Mṣb, TA.) — [Hence,] ‡ شَابَتْ رُؤُوسُ ٱلْآكَامِ [*The heads, or summits, of the hills became white,* or *hoary*]. (A.) ═ And شاب الرَّأْسَ *It whitened the head:* so expl. by ISk as used in the following saying, (Ṣ,) ascribed by J to 'Adee, but it is of 'Abeed Ibn-El-Abraṣ: (IB, TA:)

تَصْبُو وَأَنَّى لَكَ ٱلتَّصَابِى
وَٱلرَّأْسُ قَدْ شَابَهُ ٱلْمَشِيبُ ↓

[*Thou inclinest to silly and youthful conduct: but whence cometh to thee the inclining to such conduct when hoariness,* or *the entering upon the period of hoariness, hath whitened the head?*]. (Ṣ,* IB, TA.) [See also 2.]

2. شَيَّبَهُ ٱلْحُزْنُ, (Ks, Ṣ, A,) and شَيَّبَ ٱلْحُزْنُ رَأْسَهُ, and بِرَأْسِهِ, (Ks, Ṣ, Mṣb, Ḳ,) which last is a strange phrase, as it exhibits together two means by which a verb is rendered trans., [namely, the doubling of the medial radical letter of the verb and the introduction of the prep. بِ,] (TA,) *Grief rendered him white-headed,* or *hoary-headed;* (Ks, Ṣ, A, Mṣb, Ḳ;) as also ↓ اشابهُ, (A,) and ↓ اشاب رَأْسَهُ and بِرَأْسِهِ. (Ks, Ṣ, Mṣb, Ḳ.*)

4. اشاب, said of a man, *He had children that had become white-headed,* or *hoary.* (Ṣ, TA.) ═ See also the next preceding paragraph, in two places.

شَيْبٌ The *hair* (Ḳ, TA) itself: sometimes it is thus called: (TA:) [but app. only *when white,* or *hoary;* in which sense it is often used; as in the TA in arts. خضب and صبغ &c.:] or (Ḳ, TA, in the CḲ "and") *whiteness of the hair,* or *hoariness;* (A, Ḳ, TA;) as also ↓ مَشِيبٌ: (Ḳ, TA:) both signify the same [and are thus used as simple substs. and are also inf. ns.]: (Ṣ:) or the former has the latter of the two significations given above; (Aṣ, Ṣ, Mgh, Mṣb;) and is *little and much* [*whiteness of the hair*]: one says, عَلَاهُ ٱلشَّيْبُ [*Whiteness of the hair,* or *hoariness, came upon him*]: (TA:) but ↓ مَشِيبٌ signifies a man's *entering upon the period of whiteness of the hair,* or *hoariness:* (Aṣ, Ṣ, Mṣb:) see an ex. of this latter in the first paragraph. In the phrase in the Ḳur [xix. 3], وَٱشْتَعَلَ ٱلرَّأْسُ شَيْبًا, (Ṣ,) meaning *And whiteness of the hair of the head hath spread therein like as the radiance of fire spreads in firewood,* (Jel,) [or *the head has become glistening with whiteness of the hair,* or *hoariness,*] شيبا is in the accus. case as a specificative: or, accord. to Akh, as an inf. n., as though it were said وَشَابَ ٱلرَّأْسُ شَيْبًا. (Ṣ, TA.*)

شِيبٌ, of a whip, a genuine Arabic word of well-known meaning; (Ṣ;) The *thong* (Ḳ, TA) *at the upper extremity* (TA) of a whip: (Ḳ, TA:) there are two of such thongs, called شِيبَانِ. (TA.) ═ Also *A word imitative of the sounds made by the lips of camels* (Ṣ, Ḳ) *in drinking.* (Ṣ.) ═ And pl. of أَشْيَبُ [q. v.]. (Ṣ, Ḳ, &c.)

شُيُبٌ a pl. of which the sing. is doubted: see أَشْيَبُ.

شَيْبَةٌ an inf. n. of 1 [q. v.]. (Ṣ, Mṣb.) — And accord. to El-Khafájee, *A white,* or *hoary, beard:* but MF says that this is a conventional post-classical meaning. (TA.) ═ [Also, in the present day, applied to *A species of artemisia;* (Forskål's Flor. Aegypt. Arab., p. lxxiii., no. 439;) the *artemisia arborescens* of Linn.: (Delile's Flor. Aegypt. Illustr., no. 790:) — and *Lichen;* (Forskål ubi suprà;) the *lichen prunastri* of Linn. (Delile, ib., no. 976†.) And شَيْبَةُ ٱلْجَبَلِ *Lichen scyphifer.* (Forskål, p. lxxviii., no. 559.)]

شَيْبَانُ: see أَشْيَبُ; near the end of the paragraph: — and see also the paragraph here following.

شِيبَانُ and مِلْحَانُ, (Ṣ, A,) thus in a verse of El-Kumeyt, as related by Ibn-Selemeh, with kesr to the ش and م, (Ṣ,) or the former word is written ↓ شَيْبَانُ, and sometimes شِيبَانُ, and the latter is as above, (Ḳ,) and sometimes مَلْحَانُ, (TA,) ‡ *The two months of winter;* (A, TA;) [as though meaning *the second of the Six Seasons,* commencing two months after the autumnal equinox; (see the former of the two tables in p. 1254;)] i. q. شَهْرَا قِمَاحٍ, (Ṣ, A, Ḳ, TA,) which are *the two coldest months;* (Ṣ, Ḳ, TA;) so called because of the earth's being then white with snow and hoar frost; (Ṣ, TA;) *falling at the period of the* [*auroral*] *rising of the Scorpion and the Vulture,* (العَقْرَب and النَّسْر, [by which latter is meant ٱلنَّسْرُ ٱلْوَاقِعُ, i. e. the star α of Lyra,]) *said by him who knows not to be the two Kánoons* [i. e. كَانُونُ ٱلْأَوَّلُ and كَانُونُ ٱلثَّانِى, corresponding to December and January O.S.]: (TA:) [it appears that they nearly agree with the two Kánoons; for El-Ḳazweenee and others say that ٱلْقَلْبُ (i. e. the heart of the Scorpion, which is the 18th of the Mansions of the Moon,) and ٱلنَّسْرُ ٱلْوَاقِعُ rise together, and their auroral rising in Central Arabia, about the commencement of the era of the Flight, accord. to my calculation, (see مَنَازِلُ ٱلْقَمَرِ in art. نزل,) was on the 25th of November O. S.: see also مِلْحَانُ, and قِمَاحٌ: it is also said that] شِيبَانُ [used alone] is a name of [*the month*] كانون الأوّل, because of the whiteness of the earth by reason of the hoar-frost and snow. (Mgh.)

شِيَابٌ and شِيَابَةٌ [the former erroneously written by Golius شَيَّابٌ]: see شَوْبٌ, in art. شوب.

شَيُوبٌ: see أَشْيَبُ.

شَائِبٌ [*Being,* or *becoming, white-haired,* or *hoary*]: see أَشْيَبُ. — شَيْبٌ شَائِبٌ is a phrase like لَيْلٌ لَائِلٌ, (Ṣ,) or like شِعْرٌ شَاعِرٌ: it means *Intense whiteness of the hair.* (TA.)

أَشْيَبُ *White-haired, white-headed,* or *hoary:* (Ṣ, A, Mgh, Mṣb, Ḳ:) [it is said to be] anomalous in form; (Ṣ, Mgh, Mṣb;) for an epithet of this measure is only formed [by rule] from a verb of the measure فَعِلَ, aor. يَفْعَلُ; (Ṣ, TA;) and it is a condition of the formation of such an epithet that it must denote a defect or the like, or a colour: but أَشْيَبُ signifies *white-headed,* or *hoary-headed;* [so that it does denote a colour;] and El-Khafájee says that it is reckoned among epithets denoting defects, or blemishes, like أَعْمَى and أَعْرَجُ: (MF, TA:) it is said in the Ḳ that it has no فَعْلَآءُ, i. e., (TA,) the epithet شَيْبَآءُ is not applied to a woman; (Mṣb, TA;) شَمْطَآءُ being used in its stead; (TA;) though one says شَابَ رَأْسُهَا: (Mṣb, TA:) [but see Ḥar p. 418, where شَيْبَآءُ is mentioned, applied to a woman, as meaning *aged,* and *white,* or *hoary, in the head:* and see شَيْبَآءُ in art. شوب:] the pl. is شِيبٌ; (Ṣ, A, Mgh, Mṣb, Ḳ;) with which is syn. شُيُبٌ; (TA, as from the Ḳ; [but not found by me in the copies of the Ḳ to which I have had access;]) and ▼ شُيْبٌ: (Ḳ, TA:) this last is said by IM to be allowable in poetry, عَلَى التَّمَامِ [here meaning as though it were a word composed of sound letters]; and this is the assertion of the lexicologists [in general]: ISd thinks it to be pl. of ▼ شَائِبٌ [q. v.], like as بُزْلٌ is of بَازِلٌ; or pl. of ▼ شُيُوبٌ [which app. means *very white* or *hoary in the head*], accord. to the dial. of the people of El-Ḥijáz, who say دَجَاجَةٌ دَجَاجٌ بُيُوضٌ and بُيُوضٌ. (TA.) — [Hence,] one says, رَأَيْتُ الجِبَالَ شِيبًا † *I saw the mountains white with snow and hoar frost.* (A, TA.) And شِيبٌ [used alone] signifies † *Mountains upon which snow falls, and which are white, or hoary, therewith*: (Ṣ, L:) or *mountains white with snow* or *with dust*: and, some say, *white clouds*: sing. أَشْيَبُ. (L, TA.) And, applied to truffles (كَمْأَة), † *White and large*: (TA:) or simply *white*. (Id. voce تَعَاشِيبُ.) — يَوْمٌ أَشْيَبُ † *A day in which are cold and clouds and* صُرَاد [correctly صُرَّاد, meaning *thin clouds*, or *cold and humid clouds, in which is no water*]; as also ▼ يَوْمٌ شَيْبَانُ. (Ḳ.) — لَيْلَةٌ شَيْبَاءُ, (Ḳ,) or لَيْلَةٌ شَيْبَاءُ, (TA,) and الشَّيْبَاءُ, (TA voce حُرٌّ,) † *The last night of the* [lunar] *month*: (Ḳ, TA:) its first night is called لَيْلَةٌ حُرَّةٌ and حُرَّةٌ. (Ḳ voce حُرٌّ.) بَاتَتْ بِلَيْلَةٍ شَيْبَاءَ, and بِلَيْلَةِ الشَّيْبَاءِ: see in art. شوب.

مَشِيبٌ: see شَيْبٌ, in two places.

شيح

1. شَاحَ: see 4. — [Also, accord. to Freytag, on the authority of the "Kitáb el-Aḍdád," *He was brave*, or *bold*: thus having two contr. significations. — Another meaning assigned to it by him, in common with شَايَحَ and أَشَاحَ, as on the authority of the Ḳ, i. e. "Diligens fuit," is a mistake.]

2. شَيَّحَهُ, (O,) inf. n. تَشْيِيحٌ, (Ḳ,) *He cautioned him*; or *made him to fear*, or *be in fear*. (O, Ḳ.*) — And *He removed him*, or *it, far away*. (O.) — And شَيَّحَ, (O, TA,) inf. n. as above, (Ḳ,) *He looked at his adversary*, or *antagonist, and straitened him*, or *treated him with hardness* or *harshness*: (O, Ḳ,* TA:) from IAạr. (TA.)

3: see the next paragraph, in two places. — Also *He fought*. (T, Ḳ.)

4. اشاح, (Ṣ, A, Ḳ,) inf. n. إِشَاحَةٌ, (IAạr, TA,) *He was cautious*, or *in fear*, (Ṣ, A, Ḳ,) مِنْهُ [*of it*], (A, TA,) i. e. a thing, or an affair, (TA,) and عَلَى حَاجَتِهِ [*for the thing that he wanted*]; (Ḳ;) as also ▼ شايح, (Ṣ, A, Ḳ,) inf. n. مُشَايَحَةٌ and شِيَاحٌ; and ▼ شَاحَ: (Ḳ:) or *he was cautious and in fear, endeavouring to repel death*. (L.) — But in the dial. of Hudheyl, (Ṣ,) *He strove, laboured, toiled*, or *exerted himself*, فِى أَمْرٍ [*in an affair*]; and so ▼ شايح. (Ṣ, A.) — And *He continued journeying*, or *going on*. (O.) — اشاح بِوَجْهِهِ *He turned away his face*, (Ṣ, A, TA,) from a [person or] thing, or from the heat of fire, or a hot odour, and from something hurtful: (TA:) or *he exerted himself in aversion or turning away*. (IAạr, TA.) One says, كَلَّمْتُهُ فَأَشَاحَ بِوَجْهِهِ *I spoke to him, and he turned away his face*. (A.) — اشاح also signifies *He advanced*, or *came forward*; syn. أَقْبَلَ. (Fr, O, TA.) [Thus it has two contr. meanings. See also the part. n., مُشِيحٌ.] — And *He defended what was behind his back*. (IAth, TA.) [See, again, the part. n.] — اشاح بِذَنَبِهِ, said of a horse, *He let his tail hang down loosely*. (Lth, Ṣ.) F, in the Ḳ, following Az and Ṣgh, says that this is a mistranscription of the verb, for اساح; but his assertion requires proof. (MF.) [See the latter verb, in art. سيح.] — اشاحت الأَرْضُ *The land produced the plant called* شِيح. (AḤn, O, Ḳ.)

شِيحٌ *Cautious*, or *fearing*; (A, Ḳ;) as also ▼ شَائِحٌ, (A, TA,) and ▼ مُشِيحٌ: (Aṣ, O:) or this last, *cautious*, or *fearing, and at the same time striving, labouring, toiling*, or *exerting himself*: (Az, TA:) or all signify *prudent*; *discreet*; or *having*, or *using, precaution*, or *good judgment*; (Ḥam p. 281;) and so ▼ شَيْحَانُ. (Id. p. 43.) — In the dial. of Hudheyl, (Ṣ, O,) *Striving, labouring, toiling*, or *exerting himself*, (Ṣ, A, O, Ḳ,) in affairs; (Ṣ, O, Ḳ;) and so ▼ شَائِحٌ, (A, Ḳ,) and ▼ مُشِيحٌ: (Aṣ, O, Ḳ:) pl. of the first [and app. of the second also] شِيَاحٌ: (Ṣ, O.) — Also [The *artemisia Judaïca*; and *absinthium Ponticum*; *species of wormwood*;] *a certain plant*, (AḤn, Ṣ, A, O, Ḳ,) *well known*, (AḤn, O, Ḳ,) *of several species*, (AḤn, O,) *of some* [*species*] *whereof brooms are made*, (L,) [*and which is also used for fumigation*,] *the leaves of which are* [*of the kind called*] هَدَب; (AḤn, O, L;) *it has a sweet odour, but its taste is bitter; is pasture for horses and camels; and the places of its growth are the plains and the meadows*: (AḤn, O, L:) pl. شِيحَانٌ. (Fr, O, L.) — Accord. to the Ḳ, [probably on the authority of Lth,] it signifies also *A* [*garment of the kind called*] بُرْد, *of El-Yemen*: but Az says that there is no kind of garment so called: the correct word is سَيْحٌ, with [the unpointed] س [and with fet-ḥ]. (TA.)

شَيْحَانُ [and probably with tenween also]: see شِيحٌ. — Also *Very jealous*; (Ṣ, O, Ḳ;) because such is cautious for his wives, or women under covert, or household or family; (Ṣ, O;) and so ▼ شَائِحٌ. (Ḳ.) — Also, (O, Ḳ,) and ▼ شِيحَانٌ, (Aṣ, O, Ḳ,) *Tall*: (O, Ḳ:) or *goodly in tallness*. (L.) — And the former, *That makes*, or *utters, a low sound in running*; [so I render يَتَهَمَّسُ عَدْوًا in the Ḳ and TA; in the O and in my MS. copy of the Ḳ, يَتَهَمَّشُ; but the former I think the right reading; app. *by reason of quickness*, or *swiftness*; for it is added,] quickness, or swiftness, is meant thereby: (O, TA:*) mentioned by Az, on the authority of Khálid Ibn-Jembeh. (TA.) [In this sense it seems to be with tenween: for] شَيْحَانَةٌ [is its fem. and] means *A quick*, or *swift*, she-camel. (Ṣ, O.) — Also A horse *strong in spirit*; syn. شَدِيدُ النَّفْسِ; (O, Ḳ, TA; in the CḲ, النَّفَسِ [i. e. *in breath*];) and so ▼ شِيحَانٌ: thus expl. by Skr. (O.)

شِيحَانٌ: see the next preceding paragraph, in two places.

شِيَاحٌ *Mutual caution* or *fear*. (And The *act of striving, labouring, toiling*, or *exerting oneself, in anything*. (Ḳ.) [But in both of these senses it seems to be an inf. n. of 3, q. v.] — Also (Ḳ) *Drought, dearth, scarcity*. (O, Ḳ.)

شَائِحٌ: see شِيحٌ, in two places: — and see also شَيْحَانُ.

مُشِيحٌ: see شِيحٌ, in two places. It is also expl. as meaning *Striving, labouring, toiling*, or *exerting himself, and persevering in his work*: (A:) and *striving* &c., *and hastening*, or *going quickly*. (TA.) — Also *Advancing*, or *coming forward*, to one. (Fr, O, Ḳ.) — And *Defending what is behind one's back*. (Fr, O, Ḳ.)

مُشَيَّحٌ is expl. as meaning *Striped*; applied to a garment: but Az says that there is no such word, so applied: the correct word is مُسَيَّحٌ, with [the unpointed] س. (TA.)

مَشِيحَى:
مَشِيحَاءُ: } see the following paragraph.
مَشْيُوحَى:

مَشْيُوحَاءُ (Ṣ, O, Ḳ) and ▼ مَشِيحَى (O, Ḳ) *A state of haste*: (Ṣ, O, Ḳ:) or *a state of confusion*: (Ḳ:) the latter meaning mentioned in the L: (TA:) you say, هُمْ فِى مَشْيُوحَاءَ مِنْ أَمْرِهِمْ (Ṣ, O, Ḳ) and فى مَشِيحَى من امرهم (O, Ḳ) *They are in a state of haste in respect of their affair*: (Ṣ, O, Ḳ:) or *in a state of confusion in their affair*: (L, Ḳ:) as having the latter meaning, Ibn-Málik says that it is مَشِيحَاءُ, with ح and medd, of the measure فَعِيلَاءُ, not مَفْعِلَاءُ; but this requires consideration: Ibn-Umm-Málik and others, following AḤei, say that ▼ القَوْمُ فِى مَشِيحَاءَ مِنْ أَمْرِهِمْ means *the people*, or *party, are in a state of striving, labour, toil*, or *exertion, and determination*, or *resolution, in respect of their affair*. (TA.) — مَشْيُوحَاءُ also signifies *A land that produces the plant called* شِيح; (Ṣ, O, Ḳ;) and so ▼ مَشْيُوحَى: (O, Ḳ:) or it signifies *many plants of the kind so called*: thus in the T, on the authority of Aṣ and A'Obeyd, and so says AḤn, as is stated [in the O and] in the R; (TA;) AḤn saying further that it is like مَشْيُوخَاءُ meaning a company of شُيُوخ [or elderly men], and مَعْيُورَاءُ meaning a herd of عُيُور [or asses], &c.; (O;) [so that it is a quasi-pl. n.;] but this is disallowed by El-Mufaḍḍal Ibn-Selemeh. (TA.)

شيخ

1. شَاخَ, (Ṣ, A, Mṣb, Ḳ,) aor. يَشِيخُ, (Ṣ, Mṣb, Ḳ,) inf. n. شَيَخٌ, with fet-ḥ to the ى, (Ṣ, Ḳ,) and

شُيُوخَةٌ (Ḳ) and شِيُوخَةٌ (TA) and شُيُوخِيَّةٌ (Ḳ) and شِيُوخِيَّةٌ (Zbd, TA) and شَيْخُوخَةٌ [the most common form, respecting which see what follows,] (Ṣ, A, Mṣb, Ḳ) and شَيْخُوخِيَّةٌ; (Ḳ;) and ▼ شَيَّخَ, inf. n. تَشْيِيخٌ; (Ṣ, A, Ḳ;) and ▼ تشيّخ; (Ḳ;) *He became a* شَيْخ [i. e. *an old*, or *elderly, man*; &c.]: (Ṣ, A, Mṣb, Ḳ:) in شَيْخُوخَةٌ, the ى is originally movent [with fet-ḥ], and afterwards made quiescent, for there is not in the language a word of the measure فَعْلُول [except صَعْفُوق, as is said in the Ṣ in art. حيد]: as to the similar words whose medial radical letter is و, as كَيْنُونَةٌ and قَيْدُودَةٌ and دَيْمُومَةٌ and هَيْعُوعَةٌ, these are originally كَيَّنُونَةٌ [for كَيْوَنُونَةٌ, of the measure فَيْعَلُولَةٌ,] and the like, and are contracted; for were it not so, they would be كَوْنُونَةٌ and the like. (Ṣ, L.)

2. شيّخ: see the preceding paragraph. ═ شَيَّخَهُ, (Ṣ, Ḳ,) inf. n. تَشْيِيخٌ, (TA,) *He called him by the appellation of* شَيْخ, *to pay him honour*, or *respect*. (Ṣ, Ḳ, TA.) ═ And شَيَّخَ عَلَيْهِ *He attributed* or *imputed to him*, or *charged him with, a vice*, or *fault; blamed*, or *reproached, him*; (Ḳ, TA;) *cast a bad, an evil, a foul*, or *an excessively bad* or *evil* or *foul, imputation upon him*. (TA.) And شيّخ بِهِ [and so شيّخهُ accord. to an explanation of شَيَّخْتُ الرجل, as on the authority of AZ, in the TA, but this may be a mistranscription for شَيَّخت بِالرَّجُلِ,] *He exposed his vices, faults*, or *evil actions; disgraced him*; or *put him to shame*. (Ḳ, TA.)

5. تشيّخ: see 1. — [It signifies also] *He feigned*, or *made a show of, old age*. (KL.)

شَيْخٌ (Ṣ, A, Mgh, L, Mṣb, Ḳ, &c.) and ▼ شَيْخُونٌ, (Ḳ,) but the latter is a strange word, mentioned by some of the expositors of the Fṣ, as expressing more than the former word, (MF,) [*An old*, or *elderly, man; an elder*, as meaning *a man whose age gives him a claim to reverence* or *respect*; *a senior*;] *one advanced in age*, (Mgh,) *such as is beyond him who is termed* كَهْل, (Mgh, Mṣb,) *which means him whose* شَبَاب [i. e. *youthfulness*, or *prime of manhood*,] *is ended*: (Mgh:) *one in whom age has become apparent*, (L, Ḳ,) *and hoariness*: (L:) or *a man from the age of fifty*, or *fifty-one, to the end of his life*, or *to the age of eighty*: (L, Ḳ:) also expl. as meaning *a man advanced in age but having strength*, or *vigour, to fight*: and *an old and weak*, or *a decrepit, man, who is of no service*: (Mgh:) [in the present day, شَيْخ is used in the senses above mentioned; and is also especially applied, as an appellation of honour, to *a doctor of religion and law; a head*, or *chief, of a religious confraternity; a chief of a tribe* or *the like*, and *of a village*; and to *a reputed saint*:] fem. ▼ شَيْخَةٌ, (Ṣ, A, Mṣb, Ḳ,) *an old*, or *aged, woman*; syn. عَجُوز: (A:) [and applied in the present day particularly to *a learned woman; an instructress*; and *the like*:] the pl. [of pauc.] of شيخ is أَشْيَاخٌ (Ṣ, A, Mgh, Mṣb, Ḳ) and شِيخَةٌ (Kr, ISd, A, Mgh, Mṣb, Ḳ) and [of mult.] شُيُوخٌ (Ṣ, A, Mgh, Mṣb, Ḳ) and شِيُوخٌ (Ḳ, with kesr, to agree with the ى, TA) and شِيخَانٌ (Ṣ, A, Mṣb, Ḳ) and شِيَخَةٌ (Ṣ, Mgh, Ḳ) and شَيَخَةٌ (A [there said to be like عَبَدَةٌ]) and ▼ مَشْيَخَةٌ, (Ḳ, and so in one of my copies of the Ṣ,) or this last is a quasi-pl. n., (Mgh, Mṣb,) and [so are] ▼ مَشْيُخَةٌ and ▼ مَشِيخَةٌ and ▼ مِشْيَخَةٌ (TA) and ▼ مَشِيَخَةٌ (Ḳ, and so in one of my copies of the Ṣ,) and ▼ مَشْيُوخَاءُ, (Ṣ, Ḳ,) the last like مَعْيُورَاءُ and مَعْلُوجَاءُ and مَسْلُومَاءُ and مَعْبُودَاءُ, which are said to be the only other instances of this form, (TA,) [but to these should be added مَتْيُوسَاءُ and مَكْبُورَاءُ and مَحْمُورَاءُ and perhaps some other instances,] and ▼ مَشْيَخَاءُ, (Ḳ,) and another pl. is ▼ مَشَايِخُ, (Ṣ, A, Ḳ,) or this last is pl. of مَشْيَخَةٌ, (Mgh, Mṣb,) and is disallowed by IDrd and Ḳz (TA) [though very commonly used in the present day, especially as applied to doctors of religion and law]; and the pl. of أَشْيَاخٌ is أَشَايِيخُ, like أَنَايِيبُ pl. of أَنْيَابٌ: (Z, TA:) the dim. of شَيْخٌ is ▼ شُيَيْخٌ (Ṣ, A, Ḳ) and ▼ شِيَيْخٌ, (Ṣ, Ḳ,) with kesr to the ش: (Ṣ:) ▼ شُوَيْخٌ is not allowable, (Ṣ, A,) or is rare. (Ḳ.) — [الشَّيْخَانِ, *The two Sheykhs*, is a title peculiarly applied to *the first two Khaleefehs, Aboo-Bekr and 'Omar*.] — شَيْخٌ also signifies † *A woman's husband*, (Ḳ,) though young: and in like manner, a man's wife, whether old or young, is called his عَجُوز. (Az, TA in art. عجز.) — [And ‡ *An ancestor*. Accord. to a copy of the A that seems to have been used by the author of the TA, one says, وَرِثَ مِنْ مَشْيَخَةِ الكَرَمِ and مِنْ أَشْيَاخِهِ, which is tropical, meaning مِنْ آبَائِهِ: but the right reading is evidently ▼ مِنْ مَشْيَخَتِهِ, and الكَرَمَ; and the meaning, ‡ *He inherited, from his ancestors, generosity*.] — شَيْخُ النَّارِ means ‡ *Iblees*: because he was created of fire, or because his ultimate place will be the fire of Hell. (Ḥar p. 130.) — And الشَّيْخُ † *The mountain-goat that is advanced in age*, or *full-grown*. (TA.) — And † *The milk-skin*. (TA.) — أَشْيَاخُ النُّجُومِ i. q. أُصُولُهَا, (Ḳ,) i. e. † *The seven* [or *five*] *planets*; (TḲ;) or *the* دَرَارِىّ [also applied by some to the five planets, *Mercury, Venus, Mars, Jupiter, and Saturn*]; accord. to IAạr, اشياخ النجوم, (TA in this art.,) or أَسْنَاخُ النُّجُومِ as is related by Th, (TA in art. سنخ,) means *the stars that do not make their* [*temporary*] *abode in the Mansions of the Moon, which* [*latter*] *are called* نُجُومُ الأَخْذِ: ISd says, I think that he means, by the نجوم, the fixed stars: Th says that they are called only أَسْنَاخُ النُّجُومِ, i. e. the أُصُول thereof, around which the [other] stars revolve, and pursue their courses. (TA. [See also سِنْخ, last sentence.]) ═ شَيْخٌ signifies also *A certain tree*; (AZ, Ḳ, TA;) *also called* شَجَرَةُ الشُّيُوخِ, *the fruit of which is a* جِرْو [q. v.] *like that of the* خِرْوَع, which is the *bastard saffron* (شَجَرَةُ العُصْفُرِ); *it grows in the meadows, and the* قِرْبَان [or *places where water runs to*, or *in*, or *into, meadows*, &c.]. (AZ, TA.)

شَيْخَةٌ fem. of شَيْخٌ, q. v. (Ṣ, A, Mṣb, Ḳ.)

شَيْخُونٌ: see شَيْخٌ.

شُيَيْخٌ and شِيَيْخٌ and شُوَيْخٌ: dims. of شَيْخٌ, q. v.

مَشْيَخَةٌ and مَشِيخَةٌ &c.; and the pl. مَشَايِخُ: see شَيْخٌ, in seven places.

مَشْيَخَاءُ: } see شَيْخٌ.
مَشْيُوخَاءُ: }

شيد

1. شَادَهُ, aor. يَشِيدُ, (Ṣ, Mṣb, Ḳ,) inf. n. شَيْدٌ, (Ṣ,) *He plastered it* (a wall) *with* شِيد, (Ṣ, Ḳ,) i. e. *gypsum*, or *the like*: (Ḳ:) *he built it* (a structure) *with* شِيد, meaning *gypsum*. (Mṣb.) — See also 2. — شَادُوا الدِّينَ † *They strengthened and exalted the religion*: from شَادَ in the first of the senses expl. above: (Ḥar p. 5:) [or rather from this verb as syn. with شَيَّدَ and أَشَادَ.] — See also 4. — As inf. n. of شَادَ in the phrase شَادَ بِالإِبِلِ, aor. as above, (TḲ,) شِيَادٌ signifies † The *calling* camels, (Ibn-'Abbád, O, Ḳ, TA,) as also ▼ إِشَادَةٌ, (Ibn-'Abbád, O,) *raising the voice in doing so*. (TA.) — Also, (Ḳ,) as inf. n. of the same verb, (TḲ,) † The *rubbing* perfume with the skin; (Ḳ;) as also ▼ تَشَيُّدٌ; in some copies of the Ḳ, ▼ تَشْيِيدٌ: (TA:) [the former of these two seems to be the right; and the meaning seems to be, the *rubbing the skin* with perfume; for,] accord. to AA, one says تَشَيَّدْ بِهٰذَا الطِّيبِ, meaning *Rub thy skin with this perfume*. (O.) ═ شَادَ, (said of a man, TA,) aor. as above, (Ḳ,) inf. n. شَيْدٌ, (TA,) also signifies *He perished*, or *died*. (Ḳ.)

2. شَيَّدَهُ, (A, L, Mṣb, TA,) inf. n. تَشْيِيدٌ, (L, Mṣb, TA,) *He raised it high*; (A, Mṣb, TA;) namely, a palace, (A,) or a building; (Mṣb, TA;) as also ▼ اشادهُ, (A, L, TA,) and ▼ شَادَهُ: (A: [this last is app. included with the two other verbs, in the A, as having this meaning, which is confirmed, as pertaining to it, by an explanation of its pass. part. n., مَشِيدٌ, q. v.:]) or شَيَّدَهُ [implies a repetition of the act of building: (see مُشَيَّدٌ:) or] signifies *he built it firmly*, or *strongly, and raised it high*. (L.) — See also 1.

4. اشادهُ: see 2. — Hence, (L,) إِشَادَةٌ signifies ‡ The *raising the voice* in saying a thing (Lth, Ṣ, L, Ḳ) [of any kind, or] such as one's companion dislikes; like تَنْدِيدٌ. (Lth, L.) See also 1. You say, اشاد صَوْتَهُ and بِصَوْتِهِ ‡ *He raised his voice*. (A.) And اشاد بِهِ ‡ *He proclaimed it*, or *cried it, raising his voice*; namely, a stray, or any other thing: (Aṣ, L:) ‡ *he made it known*; (AA, Ṣ, A,

Ḳ;*) namely, a stray. (Ṣ, Ḳ.) And اشاد بذكره ‡ *He raised his good fame, by praising him; raised a good report of him:* (Ṣ,* A, L:) and *he raised his ill fame, by dispraising him; raised an evil report of him:* and اشاده and ▼ شاده *he raised his notoriety* or *fame.* (L.) And اشاد عليه ‡ *He published against him* something disliked, disapproved, or odious: one says, اشاد عليه قبيحا and بقبيح ‡ [*He published against him something bad, evil, abominable,* or *foul*]. (A.) — And إِشَادَةٌ also signifies ‡ The act of *destroying:* (Ḳ, TA:) from the same word as syn. with تَنْدِيدٌ. (TA.)

5: see 1, in two places.

شَيْدٌ, a Pers. word, [or rather of Pers. origin, from شَيْدَا,] *Possessed;* or *mad,* or *insane:* or *intoxicated.* (TA.)

شِيدٌ *Anything with which a wall is plastered,* (Ṣ, A, Ḳ,) consisting of *gypsum* and *the like;* (A, Ḳ;) J says, of *gypsum* or بَلَاط; but this last word is a mistake, [probably originated by an early transcriber of the Ṣ,] for مِلَاط, i. e. *mud,* or *clay:* (Ḳ:) or [peculiarly] *gypsum.* (Mṣb.) — Az says that some of the Arabs sometimes call thus *A* حِصْن [i. e. *fortress, fort,* or *fortified place*]. (TA.)

مَشِيدٌ *Plastered with* شيد; and so, as some say, ▼ مُشَيَّدٌ: (T:) or *built with gypsum:* (Mṣb:) or *made with* شيد, (Ṣ, A, Ḳ,) i. e. *gypsum;* and so, some say, ▼ مُشَيَّدٌ: (A:) or the latter signifies *raised high,* or *made lofty;* (A'Obeyd, Ṣ, A, Ḳ;) and so the former, applied to a palace, (A,) or building: (TA:) the former has this meaning in the Ḳur xxii. 44: (Jel:) J says in the Ṣ, Ks says, مَشِيدٌ is applied to a sing., from the saying in the Ḳur, [ubi suprà,] وَقَصْرٍ مَشِيدٍ; and ▼ مُشَيَّدٌ, to a pl., from the saying in the same, [iv. 80,] فِى بُرُوجٍ مُشَيَّدَةٍ: but this is a mistake: what Ks says is that مُشَيَّدَةٌ, with ة and teshdeed, is a pl. [i. e. a lexicological, not a grammatical, pl.] of مُشَيَّدٌ: (IB, Ḳ:*) or the saying of Ks [if as quoted in the Ṣ] may be expl. accord. to the opinion of those who hold that مَشِيدٌ and مُشَيَّدٌ both signify *plastered with* شيد, on the supposition that the Arabs did not use مُشَيَّدَةٌ as applied to a pl., but only to a sing.: (Az, L:) [for] Fr says that the pass. part. n. of the unaugmented verb only is used when applied to a sing. and not denoting repetition, or muchness; but either this or the pass. part. n. of the verb of the measure فَعَّلَ may be used when applied to a sing. and denoting repetition, or muchness, and when applied to a pl.: thus you say كَبْشٌ مَذْبُوحٌ ["a slaughtered ram"]; but not مُذَبَّحٌ; but you may say ثَوْبٌ مُخَرَّقٌ [as meaning "a garment in which holes have been repeatedly made," or "in which many holes have been made," or "much pierced with holes," as well as ثَوْبٌ مَخْرُوقٌ meaning "a garment in which a hole has been made," or "in which holes have been made,"] and كِبَاشٌ مُذَبَّحَةٌ ["slaughtered rams"]: and hence you may say ▼ قَصْرٌ مُشَيَّدٌ; because تَشْيِيدٌ denotes building, and the act of building is repeated, and a building becomes high by degrees. (L.)

مُشَيَّدٌ: see the next preceding paragraph, in four places.

شير

6. تشاير: see 6 in art. شور.

شِيرٌ: n. un. with ة: pl. of the latter شِيرَاتٌ: and dim. شُيَيْرَةٌ and شِيَيْرَةٌ: see شَجَرٌ.

شِيَارٌ: } see art. شور.
شِيَرٌ: }

شيز

شِيزٌ and ▼ شِيزَى *A kind of black wood, of which bowls* (قِصَاع) *are made:* (Ṣ, Ḳ:) or the latter is *a certain black wood of which combs and bowls* (جِفَان) *are made:* (Mgh:) or *ebony:* or سَاسَم [*a certain wood of which bows or arrows are made*]: (AA, Ḳ:) or *walnut-wood:* (Aṣ, Ed-Deenáwaree [AḤn], Mgh, Ḳ:) Aṣ says of the شِيزَى, by the name of which the Arabs call *bowls* (جفان and قصاع) and the *sheaves of pulleys,* that it is *walnut-wood,* but it becomes blackened by grease, and therefore is thus called, and it is not شيز: so says AḤn: and he adds, the case is as he has described it; for the شيز does not become thick so as that bowls may be carved from it: (Ṣgh, TA:) of this latter, only combs and the like are made; and it is black: it is also said, in the T, that *bowls made from the walnut-tree* are called شِيزَى. (TA.)

شِيزَى: see the preceding paragraph.

شيش

4. اشاشت النَّخْلَةُ *The palm-tree produced dates such as are termed* شِيش. (O, Ḳ.)

شِيشٌ and ▼ شِيشَآءُ *A sort of dates which do not organize and compact stones;* (Fr, O, Ḳ;) *or, if they do so, they do not become hard; and when they dry, they become such as are termed* حَشَف, *not sweet:* (O, Ḳ:) dial. vars. of شيص and شِيصَآءُ: (Ṣ:) accord. to AḤn, (TA,) of Persian origin. (O, TA.)

شِيشَآءُ: see the next preceding paragraph.

شيص

2: see the next paragraph.

4. اشاصت النَّخْلَةُ *The palm-tree was not fecundated by the flowers,* or *pollen, of the male tree:* (A, Ḳ:) or *its dates dried up:* and *it bore dates such as are termed* شِيص: (Mṣb:) or *it became bad, and its dates became such as are termed* شيص; (TA;) as also ▼ شَيَّصت. (Ḳr, TA.)

5. تشيّص التَّمْرُ *The dates became such as are termed* شِيص. (Ṣ.)

شِيصٌ *Dates of which the stones do not become hard;* as also ▼ شِيصَآءُ; (Ṣ, A, Ḳ;) which is only the case when the palm-tree has not been fecundated by the flowers, or pollen, of the male tree: (Ṣ:) and sometimes, *having no stones:* (Fr, TA:) or *bad dates:* (A:) or the *worst of dates;* (IF, Mṣb, Ḳ;) as also ▼ the latter word: (Mṣb:) or the *worst of dates when full-grown but unripe:* (Lth, TA:) called in the dial. of Belhárith Ibn-Kaab, صِيص; and by the people of El-Medeeneh, سُخَّل: (El-Umawee, TA:) and said by some to be a Persian word, arabicized: (TA:) n. un. with ة; (A, Mṣb, Ḳ;) i. e., شِيصَةٌ and شِيصَآءَةٌ. (A, Mṣb.)

شِيصَآءُ: n. un. with ة: see شِيص, in two places.

شيط

1. شَاطَ, (Ṣ, Mṣb, Ḳ,) aor. يَشِيطُ, (Mṣb, Ḳ,) inf. n. شَيْطٌ and شِيَاطَةٌ (Ḳ) and شَيْطُوطَةٌ, (Lth, Ḳ,) *It* (a thing, Mṣb, TA, or, as some say, particularly, olive-oil, and rob, TA) *burned,* or *became burnt;* (Mṣb, Ḳ, TA;) as also ▼ تشيّط, (Ḳ,) said of flesh-meat: (TA:) or both, said of flesh-meat, signify *its upper part became burnt by the contact of fire:* (Lth, TA:) the latter is also said of wool; and the former likewise, of wool, and of hair: (TA:) the former also signifies *it was near to becoming burnt:* (TA:) and, said of clarified butter, and of olive-oil, (Ṣ, Ḳ,) *it became cooked so much that it burned;* (Ṣ;) because, in that case, it perishes; (O;) [which implies that a signification hereafter to be mentioned is held to be the primary one;] or *became thick;* or *became cooked so much that it almost perished.* (Ḳ.) You say also, شَاطَتِ القِدْرُ *The cooking-pot burned, and had something sticking in it:* (Ṣ:) or *had something burnt sticking in the bottom of it.* (O, Ḳ.) — شَاطَ, (Ṣ, Ḳ,) aor. as above, (Ṣ,) also signifies *He* (a man) *perished,* or *died.* (Ṣ, Ḳ.) [The art. in the Ṣ commences with this signification, which, as remarked above, seems to be regarded by some as the primary one.] — Also *He burned with anger.* (TA in art. شطن.) — And *It was,* or *became, null, void, of no account,* or *of no force.* (Mṣb, TA.) — *His* (a man's) *blood,* (Ṣ,) or *it,* (his blood,) (Mgh, Mṣb, Ḳ,) *went* (Ṣ, Mgh, Mṣb, Ḳ) *for nothing, unretaliated, and uncompensated by a mulct; it was,* or *became, of no account.* (Ṣ, Mgh,* Mṣb.) — And *It* (anything) *went away; passed away.* (TA.) — شَاطَتِ الجَزُورُ ‡ *The slaughtered camel became dispensed;* syn. تَنَقَّقَت; (Ṣ, Ḳ, TA;) *there remained not of it any portion that was not divided and given:* (Aṣ, Ṣ:) and شَاطَ لَحْمُ الجَزُورِ *The flesh of the slaughtered camel went away divided and distributed, nothing thereof remaining.* (A, TA.) — شاط also signifies ‡ *He hastened* (Ṣ, Ḳ, TA) in an affair. (Ḳ, TA.) — [شَاطَهُ seems to be a dial. var. of سَاطَهُ, as signifying *He mixed it.* — And hence,] شَاطَ الدِّمَآءَ ‡ *He mixed the bloods; as though he shed,* or *poured forth, the blood of the slayer upon that of the slain.* (Ṣ, Ḳ, TA.) A poet, (Ṣ,) namely, El-Mutalemmis, (TA,) uses the expression لَوْ تُشَاطُ دِمَاؤُنَا [*If our bloods were*

mixed]; (Ṣ, TA;) accord. to one relation; but accord. to another, the verb is with س. (TA.) — شَاطَ بِدَمِهِ: see 4.

2: see the next paragraph, in five places.

4. اشاطهُ, (Mṣb, Ḳ,) inf. n. إِشَاطَةٌ, (Mṣb,) *He burned it*, or *made it to burn*; (Mṣb, Ḳ;) namely, a thing, (Mṣb,) as, for instance, olive-oil; (TA;) as also ↓ شَيَّطَهُ, (Ḳ,) inf. n. تَشْيِيطٌ. (TA.) ↓ The latter also signifies *He burned its wool*, namely, that of a sheep, *in order to cleanse it*; and so شَوَّطَهُ: (Ṣ, TA:) and each of these, *he* (a cook) *set it on fire*, namely the foot of a bull or cow, or of a sheep or goat, and the head, *so that what was upon it, of hair, or wool, became burnt.* (TA.) You say also, شاط القِدْرَ *He made the cooking-pot to burn, and to have something sticking in it.* (Ṣ.) And ↓ شيّط القِدْرَ *He made the cooking-pot to boil*; as also شوّطها. (El-Kilábee.) And ↓ شيّط اللَّحْمَ *He cooked thoroughly the flesh-meat*; as also شوّطهُ: (Ibn-'Abbád:) or *he smoked it*, or *made it smoky, and did not thoroughly cook it*; (Ṣ;) and so the latter. (TA in art. شوط.) And ↓ شيّط الضَّبُعُ النَّبْتَ; and الدَّوَآءُ الجُرْحَ; ‡ *The year of drought burned the herbage*; and *the medicine, the wound.* (A, TA.) [See also شَوَّطَ.] — Also, (Ḳ,) inf. n. as above, (Ṣ,) *He destroyed him*, or *it.* (Ṣ, Ḳ.) — اشاط دَمَهُ, (Ṣ, Mgh, Mṣb, Ḳ,) and بِدَمِهِ, (Ṣ, Ḳ,) *He* (the Sultán, Mgh, Mṣb) *made his blood to go for nothing, unretaliated, and uncompensated by a mulct; made it to be of no account:* (Mgh, Mṣb, Ḳ,* TA:) or the latter, (TA,) or both, (Ḳ,) *he laboured to destroy him*, or *to kill him*: (Ḳ, TA:) or both, *he exposed him to slaughter*: (Ṣ, Ḳ:) or, accord. to IAmb, you say, ↓ شَاطَ بِدَمِهِ, meaning *he exposed him to destruction.* (TA.) You say also, اشاط دَمَ الجَزُورِ *He shed the blood of the camel that was to be slaughtered.* (Aṣ, Ḳ.) — اشاط اللَّحْمَ ‡ *He distributed the flesh*, (Ḳ, TA,) i. e. the flesh of a slaughtered camel: (TA:) or اشاط الجَزُورَ *he dispensed the last remaining portion of the slaughtered camel, after all beside had been distributed.* (Ṣ, TA.) Also † *He cut up*, or *cut in pieces, the flesh* of the slaughtered camel *before the distribution.* (ISh.)

5: see 1, first sentence.

10. استشاط ‡ *He became inflamed by anger*; عَلَيْهِ *against him*: (Ḳ, TA:) or *he became as though he were inflamed in his anger*; accord. to Aṣ, from مِشْيَاطٌ as applied to a she-camel: (Ṣ, TA:) [or] *he burned, and became inflamed, by vehement anger.* (TA.) — ‡ *He* (a man, TA) *became brisk*, or *sharp*; (Ḳ,* TA;) *he burned*; (TA;) مِنَ الأَمْرِ *by reason of the thing*, or *affair.* (Ḳ, TA.) — ‡ *It* (a pigeon) *flew briskly.* (Ḳ, TA.) — ‡ *He sought to be slain* in war or fight. (TA.) — ‡ *He became at the point of destruction.* (TA.) — ‡ *He* (a camel) *became fat*: (Ṣ, TA:) [as though he desired, or demanded, that he should be slaughtered, and that his flesh should be distributed:] or *fatness spread in him.* (TA.)

شَيْطَان [i. e. شَيْطَانٌ or شَيْطَانُ, accord. to different authorities, as shown below, *A devil*; and with the article ال, *the devil, Satan*;] is, accord. to some, from شَاطَ, (Mṣb, Ḳ, TA,) as signifying "it was, or became, null, void, of no account;" and the like: (Mṣb, TA:) or "he perished:" (Ḳ, TA:) or "he went away:" or "it burned," or "became burnt:" two reasons given for this derivation are, that among the names of the devil are المُذْهَبُ and البَاطِلُ: and another is this; that several read, in the Ḳur xxvi. 210, الشَّيَاطُونَ [instead of الشَّيَاطِينُ]: but some say that it is from شَطَنَ, signifying "he became distant," or "remote:" Sb gives both of these derivations: respecting the former of which, it should be observed that if from شاط as signifying "it burned," or "became burnt," it is proper; but if from the same in any of the other senses mentioned above, it is tropical: and if belonging to this art., it is imperfectly decl., being of the measure فَعْلَانُ: (Ṣ in art. شطن, in which see it:) [but in the Ḳur-án it is always perfectly decl.: and SM says that] it is perfectly decl., unless used as a proper name; in the latter case being imperfectly decl. (TA.)

شِيَاطٌ The *smell of a piece of cotton burning*, or *burnt.* (Ṣ, Ḳ.) — See also مِشْيَاطٌ.

شَائِطٌ and شَاطٍ, like هَائِرٌ and هَارٍ, [the latter being formed by transposition from the former, شَاطٍ and هَارٍ being for شَاطِئٌ and هَارِئٌ,] Flesh-meat [&c.] *burning*, or *being burnt.* (TA.)

تَشْيِيطٌ *Flesh-meat roasted*, (Ḳ,) or *made good, and roasted*, (TA,) *for a company of men*: (Ḳ:) a subst., like تَمْتِينٌ. (Ḳ, TA.) [In the CḲ, for وَاسْمٌ كَالتَّمْتِينِ, we find اِسْمٌ كَالتَّمْتِينِ.]

مِشْيَاطٌ ‡ A she-camel *that quickly becomes fat*: (Aṣ, Ṣ, A, Ḳ:) applied also to a he-camel: (TA:) pl. مَشَايِيطُ; (Ṣ, Ḳ;) in some of the copies of the Ṣ, مَشَايِطُ: and you say also ↓ إِبِلٌ شياط [app. a mistake for مِشْيَاطٌ, which is fem., like إِبِلٌ, as well as masc.]: AA says that مشايط, [or مَشَايِيطُ,] applied to camels, signifies *assigned for slaughter*; from شَاطَ said of a person's blood. (TA.)

مُسْتَشِيطٌ ‡ A *fat* camel. (Ḳ.) [See 10.] — ‡ *Laughing exceedingly*; (Ḳ;) *laughing vehemently, like one exerting himself in his laughing.* (ISh.)

شيع

1. شَاعَ, aor. يَشِيعُ, (Ṣ, O, Mṣb, Ḳ,) inf. n. شُيُوعٌ (O, Mṣb, Ḳ) and شَيْعُوعَةٌ (Ṣ, O, Ḳ) and شَيْعٌ (Ḳ) and شَيَعَانٌ and مَشَاعٌ, (O, Ḳ, the last, in the CḲ, مَشَاعَةٌ,) said of information, an announcement, a piece of news, or a narrative, or story, (TA,) or of a thing, (O, Mṣb,) *It became spread, published, divulged, revealed, made known*, or *disclosed*; (Ṣ, O, Ḳ, TA;) or *it became apparent*, or *manifest*; (Mṣb, TA;) فِى النَّاسِ [*among the people*]; *so as to reach every one, becoming equally known by the people, not known by some exclusively of others.* (TA.) — [Hence, app.,] شاع, aor. as above, said of a thing, signifies also † *It became scattered*, or *dispersed*; like شَعَّ. (TA in art. شع.) You say, شاع اللَّبَنُ فِى المَآءِ, (Mṣb,) or شاعت قَطْرَةٌ مِنَ اللَّبَنِ فِى المَآءِ, and ↓ تشيّعت, (TA,) † *The milk*, (Mṣb,) or *the drop of milk*, (TA,) *became dispersed in the water*, (Mṣb, TA,) *and mixed*: (Mṣb:) and ↓ شَيَّعَ فِيهِ likewise signifies *it became dispersed in it.* (TA.) And شاع الشَّيْبُ, inf. n. شَيْعٌ and شِيَاعٌ and شَيَعَانٌ and شُيُوعٌ and شَيْعُوعَةٌ and مَشِيعٌ, ‡ *Whiteness of the hair*, or *hoariness, appeared, and became scattered*: and شاع فِيهِ الشَّيْبُ, inf. n. as above, ‡ *Whiteness of the hair*, or *hoariness, spread upon him*; as also ↓ تشيّعهُ [or تَشَيَّعَ فِيهِ, agreeably with what has been said above]. (TA.) And شاع الصَّدْعُ فِى الزُّجَاجَةِ † *The crack spread, and became dispersed, in the glass*, or *glass vessel.* (Th, TA.) And ↓ تشايعت الإِبِلُ † *The camels became scattered*, or *dispersed*; or *they scattered*, or *dispersed, themselves.* (TA.) — As trans. by means of بِ: see 4, in two places. — [It is also trans. by itself.] شَاعَكُمُ السَّلَامُ is like the saying عَلَيْكُمُ السَّلَامُ [*Safety*, or *peace*, &c., *be*, or *light and abide, on you*]; (Ṣ, O, Ḳ;) but is only said by a man to his companions when he desires to quit them: (Ṣ, O:) or it means [*may safety*, &c.,] *follow you*: (O, Ḳ:) or, *not quit you*: (Ḳ:) whence, (TA,) one says also شَاعَكَ الخَيْرُ *may prosperity not quit thee*; and in like manner Lebeed says of praise (حَمْدٌ): (O, TA:) [and J says that] شاعهُ, inf. n. شِيَاعٌ, signifies *he*, or *it, followed him*: (Ṣ:) or شاعكم السلام, (Yoo, O, Ḳ,) aor. يَشَاعُكُمْ, inf. n. شَيْعٌ, (Yoo, O,) means [*may safety*, &c.,] *fill you*: (Yoo, O, Ḳ:) [app. from what next follows.] — One says also شِعْتُ الإِنَآءَ, (Ḳ, TA,) aor. أَشِيعُهُ, inf. n. شَيْعٌ, (TA,) *I filled the vessel.* (Ḳ, TA.)

2. شيّع فِيهِ: see 1. — شيّع said of a pastor, *He blew in the reed-pipe* [*called* شِيَاع, *by means of which the camels are called together*]. (Lth, Ḳ, TA.) — شيّع بِالإِبِلِ *He* (a pastor) *called to the camels, whereupon they followed one another*; (Mṣb;) in [some of] the copies of the Ḳ, *i. q.* ↓ أَشَاعَ بِهَا, [in the CḲ أَشَاهَا,] but correctly اشاء بها, (TA,) which means *he called to the camels*, (Ḳ in another part of the art., and TA,) *when some of them remained*, or *lagged, behind*: (TA:) and [in like manner] ↓ شايع بِإِبِلِهِ, (Ṣ, Ḳ,) inf. n. مُشَايَعَةٌ and شِيَاعٌ, (Ṣ,) *he* (a pastor, Ṣ) *shouted and called to his camels*, (Ṣ, Ḳ,) *when some of them remained*, or *lagged, behind*: (Ṣ:) or شيّع إِبِلَهُ *he* (a pastor) *called out among his camels, whereupon they went along, following one another*: (Mgh:) and شيّع الغَنَمَ *he urged on the sheep*, or *goats*, (Ḳ,* TA,) *because of their lagging behind*, (TA,) *in order that they might follow the others.* (Ḳ, TA.) [The last two phrases are app. from the second of the explanations here following.] — شيّعهُ, inf. n. تَشْيِيعٌ,

also signifies *He sent*, or *sent on, him*, or *it*. (TA.) — And *He made him*, or *it, to follow*. (TA.) — [And *He made it to be followed* by another thing.] One says, شَيَّعْتُ رَمَضَانَ بِسِتٍّ مِنْ شَوَّالٍ [or rather بِسِتَّةٍ] † *I made* [the fasting of] *Ramadán to be followed by* [the fasting of] *six* [days] *of Show-wál*; expl. by أَتْبَعْتُهُ بِهَا [a well-known phrase, of frequent occurrence, but one which I have not found in any of the lexicons, except in explanations; the approved phrase used in its stead being أَتْبَعْتُهُ إِيَّاهَا, lit. meaning "I made them to follow it;" this being virtually the same as "I made it to be followed by them"]: (Msb:) [and in like manner, the elliptical phrase] شَيَّعَ رَمَضَانَ, (K,) or شَيَّعَ شَهْرَ رَمَضَانَ, (O, TA,) means *He fasted after Ramadán*, or *the month of Ramadán, six days*; (O, K, TA;) i. e. أَتْبَعَهُ بِهَا. (TA.) — شَيَّعْتُهُ عِنْدَ رَحِيلِهِ (Lth,* S, O, Msb, K*) *I went forth with him* (Lth, O, Msb, K) *on the occasion of his departure*, (O, Msb,) namely, a guest, (Msb,) *in order to bid him farewell, and to conduct him to his place of alighting*, [app. meaning, *to his first place of alighting*,] (Lth, O, K,) or *to show honour*, or *courtesy, to him*; and *I bade him farewell*: (Msb:) or شَيَّعَ الضَّيْفَ signifies *he followed the guest* [app. on the occasion of his departure, *in order to bid him farewell*, &c.]: (Mgh:) or شَيَّعَهُ عِنْدَ رَحِيلِهِ *he went forth with him on the occasion of his departure, desiring to cheer him by his company to some place*: and ▼ شَايَعَهُ signifies the same. (TA.) — [شَيَّعَهُ sometimes signifies *He followed him, not coming up with him, but always going behind him*]. See المُشَيَّعَةُ, voce مُشَيَّعٌ. — [And *He followed*, or *imitated, him; conformed, agreed*, or *complied, with him*; like شَايَعَهُ]. See 3, in three places. — شَيَّعَ فُلَانًا ‡ *He encouraged such a one*, and *emboldened him*, (O, K, TA,) and *strengthened him*. (TA.) One says, فُلَانٌ يُشَيِّعُهُ عَلَى ذٰلِكَ ‡ *Such a one strengthens him to do that*. (TA.) And شَيَّعَ هٰذَا بِهٰذَا † *He strengthened this with this*. (TA.) — شَيَّعَ النَّارَ ‡ *He threw*, or *put, firewood upon the fire to make it blaze* or *flame, burn up*, or *burn brightly* or *fiercely*. (ISk, S, K, TA.) — And شَيَّعَهُ بِالنَّارِ † *He burned him*, or *it, with fire*. (S, K, TA.) Of anything that has been burned, one says, شُيِّعَ. (TA.)

3. مُشَايَعَةٌ primarily signifies The *following* another, or *conforming with* him, in, or as to, an affair, and an opinion; as also شِيَاعٌ; [an inf. n. of شَايَعَهُ, like the former;] and so too signifies ▼ تَشَيُّعٌ [if not a mistranscription for ▼ تَشْيِيعٌ, which I rather think it to be, agreeably with what follows]: and the *agreeing*, or *complying, with* him, or *obeying* him. (TA.) You say, شَايَعَهُ عَلَى أَمْرٍ, (Lth, O, Msb, K,) inf. n. مُشَايَعَةٌ (Msb) [and شِيَاعٌ], *He followed him*, or *conformed with him*, [&c.,] *in*, or *as to, an affair*: (Lth, O, Msb:) or *he did so, and strengthened him*; and likewise على رَأْيٍ *in*, or *as to, an opinion*; as also ▼ شَيَّعَهُ عَلَيْهِ, referring to an opinion [and an affair]. (TA.) And مَا تُشَايِعُنِي رِجْلِي وَلَا سَاقِي *My leg does not conform with* [my wish] *nor aid me to walk, nor does my shank*. (TA.) And شَايَعَتْهُ نَفْسُهُ عَلَى ذٰلِكَ *His soul conformed* [or *complied*] *with him*, [i. e. *with his wish*,] *and encouraged him, to do that*; as also ▼ شَيَّعَتْهُ. (L, TA.) — Also (O, K) *He befriended him*, or *was friendly to him*; syn. وَالَاهُ, (S, O, K,) from الوَلِيُّ. (S.) — شَايَعَهُ عِنْدَ رَحِيلِهِ: see 2, in the latter part of the paragraph. — شَايَعَ بِإِبِلِهِ: see 2, near the beginning. [Hence, app.,] one says also, شَايَعَ بِهِمِ الدَّلِيلُ فَأَبْصَرُوا الهُدَى *The guide called to them* [*and they saw the right direction*]. (TA.) ═ الشِّيَاعُ occurs in a trad., as some relate it, and is expl. as there meaning المُفَاخَرَةُ بِكَثْرَةِ الجِمَاعِ: but AA says that it is a mistranscription for البِيَاعُ, with س and ب; or that it may be from شَاعَةٌ signifying "a wife." (IAth, TA.)

4. اشاع الخَبَرَ, (S, O,) or الشَّىْءَ, (Msb, K,) or rather السِّرَّ, as in the L; (TA;) and اشاع بِهِ; (O,* K;) as also ▼ شَاعَ بِهِ, first pers. شِعْتُ بِهِ; (Msb, K;) *He spread, published, divulged, revealed, made known*, or *disclosed*, (S, O, K,) and (K) *made apparent* or *manifest*, (Msb, K,) *the information, announcement, news, narrative*, or *story*, (S, O,) or *the thing*, (Msb, K,) or *the secret*. (L, TA.) And اشاع ذِكْرَ الشَّىْءِ *He made the mention*, or *fame, of the thing to fly* [*abroad*, or *to spread*]. (TA.) — أَشَعْتُ المَالَ بَيْنَ القَوْمِ † *I dispersed*, or *distributed, the property among the people*, or *party*; and القِدْرَ فِى الحَىِّ *the* [*contents of*] *the cooking-pot among the tribe*. (A'Obeyd, TA.) [See also its pass. part. n.] — اشاعت بِبَوْلِهَا † *She* (a camel) *ejected her urine*, (S, K,) *scattering it*, (K,) *and stopped it*; (S, K; expl. in the K in two places;) but this is only when the stallion has leaped her, and is only said in relation to camels; and ▼ اشتاعت ببولها signifies the same: and in like manner اشاع is said of a he-camel. (TA.) — أَشَاعَكُمُ ٱللّٰهُ السَّلَامَ, (S, O,) or بِالسَّلَامِ, (K,) or both, (TA,) as also ▼ شَاعَكُمُ ٱللّٰهُ بِالسَّلَامِ, (K,) *May God make safety*, or *peace*, &c., [*to light and abide upon you*, or] *to accompany and follow you*. (S, O, K. [See also 1, latter half.]) — اشاع بِالإِبِلِ: see 2. — [اشاعت is also expl. in the TA as meaning خرجت: but I suspect a mistranscription or an omission in this case.]

5: see 1, in two places. — تشيّع said of a man, (S, O,) *He asserted himself to hold the tenets of the* شِيعَة [q. v.]: (S, O, K, KL, TA:) or *he became a* شِيعِىّ: a verb similar to تَحَنَّفَ and تَشَفَّعَ. (TA.) ═ [Accord. to Golius, it is expl. in the KL as meaning *He left a portion of a thing undistributed*: but this explanation is not in my copy of that work.] — تشيّع فِى الشَّىْءِ *He strove*, or *laboured*, or *he distressed himself*, or *he courted death*, (اِسْتَهْلَكَ,) *in his love of the thing*. (TA.) ═ تشيّعهُ الغَضَبُ *Anger excited him to lightness, levity*, or *unsteadiness*; or *flurried*, or *disquieted, him*. (TA.) — See also 3, first sentence.

6. تشايعت الإِبِلُ: see 1. — تشايعوا is from الشِّيعَة, (S, O,) and signifies *They became* شِيَع [i. e. *separate parties*, &c., pl. of شِيعَة, q. v.]. (TA.) — And *They went*, or *went along, together*. (KL.) — [See also the part. n., voce شَيِّع.]

8. اشتاعت بِبَوْلِهَا, said of a she-camel: see 4. — [See also the part. n., voce شَيِّع.]

شَاعٌ, originally شَائِعٌ: see the latter word. — Also The *urine of the she-camel, that becomes scattered when the stallion leaps her*. (As, O, K.) And, (As, O, [accord. to the K "or,"] The *urine of the he-camel when he is excited by lust*. (As, O, K.)

شَيْعٌ *A space* [of time]. (S, O, K.) One says, أَقَامَ فُلَانٌ شَهْرًا أَوْ شَيْعَهُ (S, O) i. e. *Such a one remained*, or *stayed, a month or the space thereof*: or *nearly the space thereof*. (TA.) — One says also, آتِيكَ غَدًا أَوْ شَيْعَهُ *I will come to thee to-morrow or after it*: (S, O, K:) or *to-morrow or the day after it*. (L, TA.) — And هٰذَا شَيْعُ هٰذَا *This is he that was born next after this*; like شَوْعُهُ: (S, O, K, all in art. شوع:) or *this is the like of this*. (A'Obeyd, O and K in the present art.) — شَيْعٌ signifies also *A follower*: and *a friend*, or *a comrade*, or *an assistant*. (KL.) — And *A lion's whelp*: (Lth, IDrd, S, O, K:) or *when he has attained to taking prey*; so in the L: and some say the *lion* [himself]. (TA.) ═ See also شَائِعٌ.

شَيْعُ نِسَآءٍ *One who follows after women, and mixes, associates*, or *converses, with them*. (K,* TA.)

شَاعَةٌ *A wife*: because she follows, or conforms with, [the wishes of] her husband. (Sh, O, K, TA.) ═ See also شَائِعٌ.

شِيعَةٌ *A certain tree*, (O, K,) *below the stature of a man, having knotted*, or *jointed, rods, and small, dark-red blossoms, smaller than the jasmine*: (O:) *the bees feed upon it*; (O, K;) *and men eat its tender extremities, being rendered healthy*, or *sound, thereby*; (يَتَصَحَّحُونَ بِهِ;) *and it has a hot quality in the mouth*; *and is sweet in odour*: (O:) *clothes become sweet-scented by adhering to it*, (O, K,* TA,) i. e. *to its blossom*, agreeably with what is said in the "Book of Plants," not to the tree, to which the pronoun refers in the O and K; (TA;) *and its honey is clear*, (O, K,) *very clear, and is well known*: *it is a pasture*; *and grows in the plains, and near to seed-produce*. (O.)

شِيعَةٌ *A separate*, or *distinct, party*, or *sect*, (O, K, TA,) *of men*: this is the primary signification: so called from their agreeing together, and following one another: or, accord. to some, the ى is originally و, and it is from شَوَّعَ قَوْمَهُ, which means "he collected his people or party:"

(TA:) the *followers and assistants* (Ṣ, O, Mṣb, Ḳ) of a man: (Ṣ, O, Ḳ:) *any people that have combined in*, or *for, an affair*: (Mṣb, TA:) accord. to Az, *persons who follow*, or *conform with, one another*, [*though*] *not all of them agreeing together*: (TA:) and *any assistant and partisan* of a man: (O, TA:) [for] the word is applied to *one* and to *two* and to *a pl. number* and to the *male* and to the *female*, (Ḳ, TA,) without variation: (TA:) the pl. is شِيَعٌ and أَشْيَاعٌ, (Ṣ,* O, Mṣb, Ḳ,) the latter a pl. pl.; (Mṣb;) and the former is applied to *any people*, or *party, whose affair*, or *case, is one, who follow one another's opinion*. (Ṣ.) The saying, in the Ḳur [xxxiv. last verse], كَمَا فُعِلَ بِأَشْيَاعِهِمْ مِنْ قَبْلُ means *As was done with the likes of them, of the same persuasion as they, of the peoples that have gone before*: (Ṣ,* TA:) and similar to this is the saying in the Ḳur liv. 51. (TA.) — Afterwards, الشِّيعَةُ became a name of *A particular party* [or *sect*]; (Mṣb, Ḳ;) being predominantly applied to *all who took as their friends*, or *lords, 'Alee and the people of his house*: (Ḳ:) *those who followed 'Alee, saying that he was the* [*rightful*] *Imám after the Apostle of God, and believing that the office of Imám should not depart from him and his descendants*: (KT:) they are *an innumerable people, who are innovators; the extravagant zealots among them are the Imámeeyeh, who revile the Two Sheykhs* [*Aboo-Bekr and 'Omar*]; *and the most extravagant of them call the Two Sheykhs disbelievers: some of them rise to the pitch of* [*that misbelief which is termed*] الزَّنْدَقَة [q. v.]. (TA.) [It is also applied to *A single person of this party*, or *sect*; agreeably with what has been said above; and such a person is likewise called ▼ شِيعِىٌّ: see 5.]

شِيعِىٌّ: see the next preceding sentence.

[شِيعِيَّةٌ and شِيعِيَّةٌ The *way of doctrine and practice*, or the *system of tenets, of the sect called* الشِّيعَة.]

شَيَاعٌ: see the next paragraph.

شِيَاعٌ The *reed-pipe of the pastor*; (IAạr, O, Ḳ;) the *instrument with which the pastor blows*; so named because he calls together the camels with it: (A, TA:) or the *sound of the pastor's reed-pipe*. (Ṣ, O, Ḳ.) — And *Callers*, or *summoners*; syn. دُعَاةٌ, (O, Ḳ,) pl. of دَاعٍ: (Ḳ:) in the Tekmileh, دُعَآءٌ [*a call, or calling*, &c.]. (TA.) ═ Also, (Ṣ, O, Ḳ,) and ▼ شَيَاعٌ, (O, Ḳ,) but the former is the more chaste, (O, [and the same is implied in the Ḳ,]) ‡ *Slender firewood, with which a fire is made to blaze* or *flame, burn up*, or *burn brightly* or *fiercely*: (Ṣ, O, Ḳ, TA:) and ▼ شُيُوعٌ signifies [the same, i. e.] *slender firewood* (AḤn, O, Ḳ) *that is quickly kindled by a weak fire, so that it prevails over the thick*, or *large, firewood*. (AḤn, O.)

شُيُوعٌ: see next preceding sentence.

شَيِّعٌ *A sharer*, or *partner*: (TA:) pl. شُيَعَآءُ. (O, Ḳ, TA.) One says, هُمْ شُيَعَآءُ فِيهَا [*They are sharers, or partners, in it*, i. e. a house (دَار) or land;] i. e. *every one of them is a* شَيِّع *to his fellow* [or *fellows*]. (O, Ḳ.) And ▼ هُمَا مُتَشَايِعَانِ فِى دَارٍ, (O, Ḳ,) or أَرْضٍ; (O;) and ▼ مُشْتَاعَانِ, (O, TA,) in the copies of the Ḳ, erroneously, مُتَشَاعَانِ; (TA;) *They two are sharers*, or *partners, in a house*, (O, Ḳ,) or *land*. (O.) — And الدَّارُ شَيِّعَةٌ بَيْنَهُمْ *The house is undivided* [i. e. *shared*] *among them*; syn. ▼ مُشَاعَةٌ. (O, Ḳ. [See also شَائِعٌ.])

شَائِعٌ Information, an announcement, a piece of news, a narrative, or a story, *spreading*; or *becoming spread, published, divulged, revealed, made known, disclosed, apparent*, or *manifest*; فِى النَّاسِ [*among the people*]; *so as to reach every one, becoming equally known by the people, not known by some exclusively of others*: (TA:) and ▼ شَاعَةٌ [is app. a pl. thereof, like as بَاعَةٌ is of بَائِعٌ, signifying, or so أَخْبَارٌ شَاعَةٌ,] *news*, or *tidings*, &c., *spreading*, or *becoming spread*. (IAạr, O, Ḳ.) — [† A thing *scattered*, or *dispersed*, or *in a state of dispersion*: fem. with ة: pl. of the latter شَوَائِعُ; which may also be pl. of the former applied to a rational being, like فَوَارِسُ pl. of فَارِسٌ.] One says, جَآءَتِ الخَيْلُ شَوَائِعَ † *The horsemen came scattered*, or *dispersed*, or *in a state of dispersion*; as also شَوَاعِىَ, formed by transposition. (TA. [But the latter is also mentioned as belonging to art. شعو.]) — Also A lot, share, or portion, (سَهْمٌ, Ṣ, O, Mṣb, Ḳ, and نَصِيبٌ, TA,) *undivided*; and so ▼ شَاعٌ, (Ṣ, O, Ḳ, TA,) like as one says سَائِرُ الشَّىْءِ and سَارُهُ; (Ṣ, O;) and ▼ مُشَاعٌ; (Ṣ, Ḳ;) [i. e. *shared in common*; as though] *spread*; (TA;) so called because *mixed, not being separated*: (Mṣb:) [and it seems, from the usage of a phrase in art. خلط of the Ḳ, (المُشَارِكُ فِى الشُّيُوعِ,) that ▼ شِيعٌ, as sing. of شُيُوعٌ, signifies *an undivided portion*.] — Also *Anything that is a supplement* to a thing: or *an addition*, or *augment*, thereto. (TA.)

مُشَاعٌ; and its fem., with ة: see شَائِعٌ and شَيِّعٌ.

مَشِيعٌ *Filled*; (O, Ḳ;) applied to a vessel. (Ḳ.) — [Hence,] † *Very rancorous, malevolent, malicious*, or *spiteful*; *filled with baseness, meanness*, or *sordidness*. (Ḳ, TA. [In the CḲ, erroneously said to be, in this sense, مُشِيع, like مُكِيل; instead of مَشِيع, like مَكِيل.]) Hence also, هُوَ ضَبٌّ مَشِيعٌ † *He is* [like *a lizard of the kind called* ضَبّ *that is*] *very rancorous*, &c. (TA.) IAạr says, I heard Abu-l-Mekárim revile a man, saying, هُوَ خَبٌّ مَشِيعٌ, [perhaps correctly ضَبٌّ, but see this word, which is used as a syn. sequent to خَبّ,] meaning *He is like a* ضَبّ *that is very rancorous*, &c., *and unprofitable*; (O, TA;) مَشِيع, here, being with fet-ḥ to the م; (O;) from شِعْتُهُ "I filled it." (O, TA.)

مِشْيَعَةٌ *A* قُفَّة [or *kind of basket*, of *palm-leaves*,] *in which a woman puts her cotton and other things*: (IDrd, O, L, Ḳ:) so called because it accompanies and follows her. (TA.)

مِشْيَاعٌ *One who will not keep*, or *conceal, a secret*; or *one who is unable to conceal his information, news*, or *tidings*; [*a babbler of secrets* &c.;] syn. مِذْيَاعٌ. (Ṣ, O, Ḳ.)

مُشَيَّعٌ ‡ *Courageous*: (Ṣ, O, Ḳ, TA:) as though he were encouraged and emboldened and strengthened by another, or encouraged and emboldened by the strength of his heart: (O, Ḳ:) or *whose heart is encouraged and emboldened by every formidable affair in which he has embarked*. (A, TA.) — And ‡ *Very quick* or *speedy* or *hasty*. (Ibn-'Abbád, Z, O, Ḳ.) — المُشَيَّعَةُ, in a trad. relating to sheep or goats to be slaughtered as victims on the day of sacrifice, in which trad. such are forbidden, (O, Mṣb, Ḳ,) means the sheep or goat (Mgh) *that requires one to urge it on after the* [*other*] *sheep or goats*, (Mgh, O, Mṣb, Ḳ,) *because of its weakness* (Mgh, Ḳ) *and leanness*, (Mgh,) or *because of its lack of strength to follow them*: (O:) or, as some relate it, the word is ▼ المُشَيِّعَةُ, (Mgh, O, Mṣb, Ḳ,) meaning *that ceases not to follow the* [*other*] *sheep* or *goats*, (لَا تَزَالُ تُشَيِّعُ ▼ الغَنَمَ, O, Ḳ,* i. e. تَتْبَعُهَا, Mgh, O, Ḳ,) or *that ceases not to lag behind the* [*other*] *sheep or goats*, (Mṣb,) *not coming up with them*, (Mgh, TA) *but always going behind them*, (TA,) *because of its leanness*; (Mgh, Mṣb, Ḳ;) from شَيَّعَ الضَّيْفَ [expl. above (see 2)]; (Mgh;) or as though urging on the [other] sheep or goats. (Mṣb.)

المُشَيِّعَةُ: see what next precedes.

مُشَايِعٌ *Overtaking*, or *coming up with another* or *others*; or *one that overtakes*, &c.: (Ṣ, Ḳ, TA:) as in the saying of Lebeed,

* كَمَا ضَمَّ أُخْرَى التَّالِيَاتِ المُشَايِعُ *

[*Like as he that overtakes collects together the last of those* cattle *that go behind* the others]. (TA.)

مُشْتَاعٌ:
مُتَشَايِعٌ: } see the dual of each, voce شَيِّعٌ.

شيف

2. شَيَّفَ الدَّوَآءَ [from شِيَافٌ]: see 2 in art. شوف.

شِيفٌ The *prickles* (شَوْك) *that are at the back of the* عَسِيب [or *leafless portion, next above the lowest and thickest part, of the branch*] *of the palm-tree*: (O, Ḳ:) so says AḤát: (O:) but Lth says that the word is [سِيفٌ, q. v.,] with the unpointed س. (TA.)

شِيَافٌ, originally شِوَافٌ:
شَيِّقَةٌ and شَيِّقَانٌ: } see art. شوف.

شيق

1. شِقْتُ الطُّنُبَ إِلَى الوَتِدِ, (Ṣ,) inf. n. شَيْقٌ, (TA,) is like نُطْتُهُ. (Ṣ.) [See 1 (last sentence but one) in art. شوق.]

شِيقٌ *A mountain:* (IAạr, Ṣ:) or the *highest part of a mountain:* (Skr, O, Ḳ:) or *a part that is even,* (Lth, O, Ḳ,) *and small in breadth, in the face of a mountain, resembling a wall,* (فِى لِهْبِ جَبَلٍ,) (Lth, O,) *that cannot be ascended:* (Lth, O, Ḳ:*) or the *most difficult place in a mountain.* (Ṣ, O, Ḳ.) A poet says, cited as using it in the last sense,

• شَغْوَآءُ تُوطِنُ بَيْنَ الشِّيقِ وَالنِّيقِ •

[*An eagle dwelling between the most difficult place in a mountain and the highest part thereof*]. (Ṣ, O.) See also a verse of Aboo-Dhu-eyb cited voce خَافَةٌ, in art. خوف. —— *A long,* or *tall, mountain;* (جَبَلٌ طَوِيلٌ;) (Ḳ;) thus accord. to some in the verse of Aboo-Dhu-eyb. (TA.) —— And accord. to some, it signifies in that verse (TA) *A narrow cleft in a mountain:* or *in the head thereof:* or *a cleft between two rocks.* (Ḳ, TA.) —— *A side;* syn. جَانِبٌ. (Skr, O, Ḳ.) One says, اِمْتَلَأَ مِنَ الشِّيقِ إِلَى الشِّيقِ *It became filled from side to side.* (TA.) ═ The *head* [or *glans*] *of the penis.* (IAạr, O, Ḳ.) ═ The *hair of a horse's tail:* n. un. with ة. (IAạr, O, Ḳ.) ═ *A species of fish.* (IAạr, O, Ḳ.) —— The *aquatic bird* [or rather *birds*] *called* بُرْك [pl. of بُرْكَةٌ, q. v.]: (Ḳ:) n. un. with ة. (TA. [In the Ḳ, شِيقَةٌ is mentioned in another place as meaning *a certain aquatic bird:* and in the O as meaning *a species of aquatic birds.*]) ═ And accord. to Ibn-'Abbád, *i. q.* كِتَابٌ [*A writing,* or *book,* &c.]. (O.) ═ See also art. شوق.

شِيَاقٌ: } see art. شوق.
شَيِّقٌ: }

شيل

1. شَيْلٌ is a bad [or vulgar] dial. var. of شَوْلٌ: one says, شِلْتُ بِهِ, [and now, more commonly, شِلْتُهُ,] like شُلْتُهُ, meaning *I raised it;* and, as now used, *I lifted it;* and hence, *I removed it,* or *took it away;* and *I carried it;* and *I loaded it,* namely, luggage upon a beast &c.;] aor. أَشِيلُ, inf. n. شَيْلٌ and مَشِيلٌ, the latter [in measure] like مَقْعَدٌ. (TA.)

شِيَالَةٌ The *occupation of the* شَيَّال, i. e. *porter,* or *carrier of burdens.* (TA.)

شُيَّلٌ and شُيُلٌ pls. of شَائِلٌ. (Ḳ in art. شول, in which see the singular.)

شَيَّالٌ, from شِلْتُ بِهِ [expl. above], *A porter,* or *carrier of burdens.* (TA.)

فَرَسٌ مِشْيَالُ الخَلْقِ *A horse incongruous, unsound, faulty,* or *weak, in make:* (AO, O and TA in the present art.:) mentioned in the L in art. شول. (TA.)

شيم

1. شَامَ الشَّىْءَ فِى الشَّىْءِ, (Ḳ,) [aor. يَشِيمُ,] inf. n. شَيْمٌ, (TA,) *He hid,* or *concealed, the thing in the thing:* (Ḳ, TA:) and *he inserted the thing in the thing.* (TA.) [Hence,] شَامَ سَيْفَهُ, (Ḳ,) first pers. شِمْتُهُ, (Ṣ,) aor. as above, (Ḳ,) inf. n. شَيْمٌ, (TA,) *He sheathed his sword;* (Ṣ, Ḳ;) and [in like manner] شَامَ نَبْلَهُ [*He put his arrows into the quiver*]: (TA:) and the former signifies also *He drew his sword:* thus having two contr. meanings: (Ṣ, Ḳ:) A'Obeyd doubted of the latter meaning; and Sh knew it not; but the verb is said to have this meaning in a verse of El-Farezdaḳ. (TA.) It is said in a trad. of Aboo-Bekr that a complaint was made to him against Khálid Ibn-El-Weleed, and he said, لَا أَشِيمُ سَيْفًا سَلَّهُ اللّٰهُ عَلَى المُشْرِكِينَ i. e. *I will not sheath a sword* [*which God has drawn against the believers in a plurality of gods*]. (TA.) [Hence also,] one says, شَامَ أَبَا عُمَيْرٍ (Ḳ, TA) i. e. [*He sheathed*] *the* ذَكَر; (TA;) meaning † *he attained his desire of the virgin.* (Ḳ, TA.) —— And شَامَ فِى الفَرَسِ سَاقَهُ *He struck the mare with his shank to make her run:* (Ḳ:) or *he impressed* (lit. *inserted*) *his leg* [or *shank*] *in the belly of the mare, striking her* [*with it*]. (Aboo-Málik, TA.) ═ شِمْتُ مَخَايِلَ الشَّىْءِ *I directed my look towards the indications,* or *symptoms, of the thing, waiting,* or *watching, for it.* (Ṣ.) —— And [hence, or the reverse may be the case,] شِمْتُ البَرْقَ, (Ṣ, Mṣb, Ḳ,*) aor. and inf. n. as above, (Mṣb, TA,) *I looked at,* (Ṣ, Ḳ,*) or *watched,* or *observed,* (Mṣb,) *the lightning,* (Mṣb, Ḳ,) or *the cloud thereof, to see where it would rain,* (Ṣ,) or *to see where it would pour,* or *bring rain,* (Mṣb,) or *to see whither it tended and where it would rain:* (Ḳ:) this is done only when it flickers and disappears without delay: and [it is said, but, in my opinion, fancifully, and with little reason, that] the drawing and sheathing of a sword are likened to lightning flickering and disappearing. (TA.) [Hence the phrase, شِمْتُ بَرْقَ فُلَانٍ † *I looked hoping for the benefits of such a one:* mentioned by Freytag on the authority of Meyd: and the like is said in Ḥar p. 319.] And شَامَ السَّحَابَ *He looked at the clouds from afar:* and [in like manner,] النَّارَ *the fire.* (TA.) It is said in a prov.,

• لَا تَشِمِ الغَيْثَ فَقَدْ أَوْدَى النَّقَدْ •

i. e. [*Look not thou hoping for rain, for*] *the lambs have perished:* addressed to him who mourns for that which has past. (Meyd.) And one says, فُلَانٌ مُوسِرٌ وَلَا أَشِيمُهُ مِنْ فَقْرٍ † [*Such a one is wealthy, and I do not look at him in hope by reason of poverty*]; meaning that he is independent of him. (Z, TA.) —— [Hence also,] شِمْ مَا بَيْنَهُمَا ‡ *Compute thou,* or *estimate,* or *consider,* (Ḳ, TA,) and *look,* or *see,* (TA,) *what* [*relation,* or *difference,*] *is between them two.* (Ḳ, TA. [In the CḲ, شُمْ is erroneously put for شِمْ; and قَدْرُهُ, in the explanation, for قَدِّرْهُ.]) ═ شَامَ also signifies *It* (a thing, TA) *entered,* فِى شَىْءٍ *into a thing;* (Ḳ, TA;) quasi-pass. of the same verb in the latter of the two senses expl. in the first sentence of this art.; (TA;) and so ▼اِنْشَامَ, (Ṣ, Ḳ, TA,) and ▼اشام, and ▼اشتام, and ▼تَشَيَّمَ, and ▼شَيَّمَ. (Ḳ, TA.) —— Also, (Ḳ,) aor. as above, (TA,) inf. n. شَيْمٌ and شُيُومٌ, *He made a valid charge,* or *assault,* or *attack, in war,* or *battle.* (Ḳ.) ═ Also, (Ḳ,) aor. as above, (TA,) *He* (a man) *had a black* رُقْعَة [app. meaning *spot,* or *mole,* i. e. شَامَة,] *apparent in his skin.* (Ḳ.) And شِيمَ, inf. n. شَيْمٌ, [perhaps a mistranscription for شَيَمٌ,] *He was marked with a* شَامَة [or *mole*]: or, as some say, [the pass. part. n.] مَشْيُومٌ [signifying "marked with a شامة"] has no verb: and AZ says that ▼شَيَمٌ, signifying the *having upon him a* شامة, has no known verb: (TA:) or شَيْمٌ is an inf. n. signifying the *having upon him* شام [i. e. *moles*]. (Ḥam p. 361.) ═ شَامَ فُلَانًا, (Ḳ,) aor. as above, (TA,) *He soiled the legs,* or *feet, of such a one with dust,* or *earth:* (Ḳ, TA:) in [some of] the copies of the Ḳ, غَيَّرَ رِجْلَيْهِ بِالشَّيَامِ; but correctly, [as in the CḲ and in my MS copy of the Ḳ,] غَبَّرَ; and accord. to the M, from الشَّيَام, [meaning that the verb is derived from this word,] i. e. التُّرَاب. (TA.)

2: see 1, in the latter half. ═ شَيَّمَ يَدَيْهِ فِى رَأْسِهِ, or ثَوْبِهِ, *He seized his head,* or *his garment, fighting him.* (Ḳ.)

4: see 1, in the latter half.

5: see 1, in the latter half. —— تَشَيَّمَهُ الضِّرَامُ *The kindling of fire entered it;* namely, a wood; as used in a verse of Sá'ideh: or, as some relate it, تَسَنَّمَهُ [q. v.]. (Ṣ, TA.) And تَشَيَّمَ الحَرِيقُ القَصَبَ *The fire entered, and mixed with, the reeds,* or *canes.* (TA.) —— And تَشَيَّمَهُ الشَّيْبُ ‡ *Hoariness came upon him,* (Ḳ, TA,) and *became intermixed upon him:* or, accord. to IAạr, *became abundant upon him, and spread;* (TA;) as also تَسَنَّمَهُ. (IAạr, M and TA in art. سنم.) ═ تَشَيَّمَ أَبَاهُ *He resembled his father in* شِيمَة i. e. *nature,* or *natural disposition.* (IAạr, Ḳ, TA.)

7. انشام: see 1, in the latter half. ═ Also *He* (a man) *became one who was looked at.* (Ṣ, Ḳ.)

8: see 1, in the latter half.

شَامٌ: see شَامَةٌ, in three places. ═ The country of الشَّام [i. e. *Syria*] has been mentioned in art. شأم [as originally الشَّأْم].

شِيمٌ *A certain species of fish.* (Ṣ, Ḳ.*) ═ Also pl. of أَشْيَمُ [q. v.]. (Ṣ, TA.) ═ And pl., in one sense, of شِيَام [q. v.]. (Ḳ.)

شَيَمٌ: see 1, near the end. ═ Also *Any land,* or *ground, in which one has not yet dug, remaining in its* [*original*] *hard state,* (Aboo-Sa'eed, Ḳ, TA,) *so that the digging therein is more difficult* [*than elsewhere*] *to the digger.* (Aboo-Sa'eed, TA.)

شَامَةٌ *A mole,* syn. خَالٌ, (Ṣ, Mṣb, TA,) upon the person; (Mṣb;) [i. e.] *a pimple inclining to blackness, upon the person;* (Mgh;) or *a* [*natural*] *mark differing from the colour of the person upon which it is:* (Ḳ,* TA:) its medial radical letter is originally ى: (Ṣ, TA:) and it is also with ة, i. e. شَامَةٌ: (IAth, TA:) pl. ↓شَامٌ, (Ṣ, Mṣb, Ḳ,) [or rather this is a coll. gen. n.,] and [the pl. properly so termed is] شَامَاتٌ. (Mṣb, Ḳ.) حَتَّى تَكُونُوا كَأَنَّكُمْ شَامَةٌ فِى النَّاسِ [*So that ye may be as though ye were a mole amid the people*], occurring in a trad., means [that ye may] be in the goodliest garb or guise, appearing like the شامة, at which one looks exclusively of the rest of the person. (IAth, TA.) And one says, صَارُوا ↓شَامًا فِى البِلَادِ, meaning † *They became scattered* [*in the countries*] *like the* شام [or moles] *upon the person.* (TA.) — Also *A black mark upon the person,* [an explanation which seems to apply, like the former in the Ḳ, to a mole, though given as differing therefrom,] and *upon the ground:* pl. [or coll. gen. n.] ↓شَامٌ. (Ḳ.) — It is also [*A mark,* or *spot,*] *upon a mare, upon a place that is disapproved, and sometimes upon her* دَوَائِر [which means what are termed *feathers,* pl. of دَائِرَةٌ, q. v.]. (ISh, TA.) — And *A spot* (نُكْتَة) [*upon the face*] *of the moon.* (Ḳ.) — And ‡ *A black she-camel:* (IAạr, Ṣ, Ḳ, TA:) accord. to Niftaweyh, شَآمَةٌ, with ء; but ISd says, I know not the reason of this, unless it be extr., like الخَأْتَمُ and العَأْلَمُ. (TA.) One says, مَا لَهُ شَامَةٌ وَلَا زَهْرَآءُ, meaning, ‡ *He has not a black she-camel nor a white one.* (Ṣ, Ḳ, TA.)

شِيمَةٌ *Nature; natural, native,* or *innate, disposition, temper,* or other *quality* or *property;* (Ṣ, Mṣb, Ḳ;) as also شِئْمَةٌ, (Ḳ,) which is an extr. dial. var.: (TA:) pl. شِيَمٌ. (Mṣb.) ═ Also *Dust,* or *earth, dug from the ground;* (Aṣ, Ṣ, Ḳ;) and so ↓شِيَامٌ. (Ṣ, as on the authority of Aṣ; but only in one of my two copies of the Ṣ.)

شَيَامٌ *Soft,* or *plain, land;* (AA, Ḳ, TA;) *of which the earth is soft,* or *uncompact.* (TA.) — See also the paragraph here following, in two places.

شِيَامٌ *Dust,* or *earth,* (Ḳ, TA,) *in a general sense;* (TA;) as also ↓شَيَامٌ: (Ḳ:) see also شِيمَةٌ: [or,] accord. to Kh, *a hollow dug in the ground:* or, as some say, *land of which the earth is soft,* or *uncompact.* (Ṣ, TA.) — And *A* [*covert such as is termed*] كِنَاس: so called because of the wild animal's entering (دُخُولِه i. e. لِانْشِيَامِ الوَحْشِ) into it. (Aṣ, Ṣ, TA.) ═ Also *The rat,* or *mouse;* syn. فَأْر: (IAạr, Ḳ, TA:) but written by Aboo-'Amr Ez-Záhid ↓شَيَامٌ, and said by him to be the جُرَذ [generally meaning *a large field-rat*]: (TA:) pl. شِيمٌ. (Ḳ.)

قَوْمٌ شُيُومٌ *A people,* or *party, in a state of security:* occurring in a trad.: and it is said that شيوم is an Abyssinian word: but, as some relate the trad., it is سُيُومٌ [q. v., voce سَائِمٌ, of which it is said to be pl.]. (TA.)

أَشْيَمُ A man (Ṣ, Mṣb) *having a* شَامَة [or *mole*] *upon his person;* (AZ, Ṣ, Mgh, Mṣb, Ḳ;*) and ↓مَشِيمٌ (Ṣ, Ḳ) and ↓مَشُومٌ (Ḳ) and ↓مَشْيُومٌ (Ṣ, Ḳ) signify the same [or rather *marked with a mole*]: (Ṣ,* Ḳ:) or أَشْيَمُ signifies *having upon him* شَام [or *moles*]: (Ḥam p. 361:) fem. شَيْمَآءُ: (TA:) and pl. شِيمٌ. (Ṣ, TA.) — And A beast, (Lth, AO, TA,) and anything, (Lth, TA,) *having upon him,* or *it, a* [*mark such as is termed*] شَامَة, (Lth, AO, TA,) or [*marks such as are termed*] شَام. (AO, TA.) — And شِيمُ الإِبِلِ † *Such as are black, of camels:* sing., masc. and fem., as above: (TA:) occurring in this sense in a verse of Aboo-Dhu-eyb, as related by AA: but as heard by Aṣ, in this verse, شُومُهَا, and thought by him to be a pl. [originally شُيْمٌ] of أَشْيَمُ. (Ṣ.) See also أَشْأَمُ (in art. شأم), last sentence.

مَشُومٌ: see the next preceding paragraph. ═ And see مَشْؤُومٌ, in art. شأم.

مَشِيمٌ: see أَشْيَمُ: ═ and see also the paragraph here next following.

مَشِيمَةٌ The غِرْس; (Ṣ, TA;) i. e. (TA) the *place of,* (Ḳ, TA,) or [*membrane that encloses,* or *forms the*] *covering of,* (Mṣb,) *the fœtus* (Mṣb, Ḳ, TA) *of a human being:* (Mṣb: [see غِرْسٌ:]) originally مَشْيِمَةٌ: (Ṣ, Mṣb:) pl. مَشَايِمُ (Ṣ, Ḳ) and [coll. gen. n.] ↓مَشِيمٌ. (IB, Ḳ.) [See also سَلًى.]

مَشْيُومٌ: see أَشْيَمُ.

شين

1. شَانَهُ, aor. يَشِينُهُ, (Ṣ, Mṣb, Ḳ, &c.,) inf. n. شَيْنٌ, (Ṣ,* Mṣb, TA,) *He,* or *it, disgraced him,* or *dishonoured him; rendered him ugly* or *unseemly, disfigured him,* or *blemished him;* (MA, PṢ;) *i. q.* عَابَهُ; (Mṣb, TA;) *contr. of* زَانَهُ; (Ṣ,* Ḳ;) [and ↓شَيَّنَهُ, inf. n. تَشْيِينٌ, signifies the same, (the verb alone rendered by Freytag, on the authority of Meyd, "dehonestavit,") like as the contr. زَيَّنَهُ signifies the same as زَانَهُ.] — The saying of Lebeed,

* يَشِينُ صَحَاحَ البِيدِ كُلَّ عَشِيَّةٍ *
* بِعُوجِ السَّرَآءِ عِنْدَ بَابٍ مُحَجَّبِ *

[*They deface what is unmarred of the deserts, every evening, with the crooked things* (i. e. the bows) *of the wood of the tree called* سَرَآء, *at a veiled door,* (referring to a company of men, and therefore the verb is sing.,)] means that they vie, one with another, in glorying, or boasting, and make marks, or lines, with their bows, upon the ground, as though they disfigured it (شَانُوهَا) with those marks, or lines. (Ṣ.)

2: see 1. ═ شَيَّنَ شِينًا حَسَنًا (T, TA) or حَسَنَةً (Ḳ) *He made,* (Th, TA,) or *wrote,* (Ḳ,) *a beautiful* ش. (Th, Ḳ, TA.)

شَيْنٌ is the *contr. of* زَيْنٌ: (Ṣ, Mṣb;) and ↓مَشَايِنُ [in the CḲ مَشَائِن] is an anomalous pl. thereof: (TA:) the latter signifies *Disgraces* or *dishonours,* i. e. *things,* or *qualities, that cause to be disgraced* or *dishonoured; things that render ugly* or *unseemly, that disfigure,* or *that blemish;* syn. مَعَايِبُ, (Ṣ, Ḳ, TA,) and مَقَابِحُ; (Ṣ, TA;) on the authority of Fr.: (TA:) [↓شَائِنَةٌ, also, signifies the same; and its pl. is شَوَائِنُ;] one says هٰذِهِ شَائِنَةٌ مِنَ الشَّوَائِنِ [*This is one of the things that disgrace or dishonour,* &c.]. (TA.) — [It is also used as epithet, like as is its contr. زَيْنٌ:] one says, وَجْهُهُ شَيْنٌ, i. e. *His face is ugly,* or *unseemly;* for ذُو شَيْنٍ; mentioned by Az. (TA.)

شِينٌ *One of the letters of the alphabet,* (Ṣ, Ḳ,) [i. e. the *name of that letter;* (see art. ش,)] *of the letters termed* مَهْمُوسَة [expl. in art. ش], *with somewhat of* التَّفَشِّيَة and التَّشْعِير [app. meaning *that kind of utterance which is undertoned, and muffled,* exactly like our "sh"], *its place of utterance being the* شَجْر, i. e. *the place of the opening of the mouth,* (Ḳ, TA,) *near the place of utterance of* ج: masc. [as meaning a حَرْف, or letter], and fem. [as meaning a كَلِمَة, or word]: pl. أَشْيَانٌ and شيانات [a mistranscription for شِينَاتٌ]. (TA.) ═ Also, thus with kesr, A man *having many* رِقَاع [i. e. *patches in his garment,* pl. of رُقْعَةٌ]. (Kh, TA.) ═ And *A long* مَرْكَب [app. meaning *ship or boat*]. (TA.)

فِعْلٌ شَائِنٌ [*An action that disgraces* or *dishonours,* &c.]. (TA.)

شَائِنَةٌ [a subst. from شَائِنٌ]: see شَيْنٌ.

مَشِينٌ *Disgraced,* or *dishonoured; rendered ugly* or *unseemly, disfigured,* or *blemished;* pass. part. n. of 1. (Mṣb.)

مَشَايِنُ an anomalous pl. of شَيْنٌ, q. v. (TA.)

شيه

1. شَاهَهُ, aor. يَشِيهُهُ, (Ḳ,) inf. n. شَيْهٌ, (TA,) *i. q.* عَانَهُ, (Ibn-Buzurj, Ḳ, TA, [in the CḲ, erroneously عَابَهُ,]) i. e. *He smote him with the* [*evil*] *eye.* (TA.) [See also 1 in art. شوه.]

شِيهٌ and شَيْهٌ: see شَاةٌ (of which they are quasi-pl. ns.) in art. شوه.

شِيَاهٌ: see شَاةٌ (of which it is a pl.) in art. شوه.

شَيُوهٌ *That smites vehemently with the* [*evil*] *eye.* (Ibn-Buzurj, Ḳ, TA. [In the CḲ, عَيُوبٌ is erroneously put for عَيُونٌ.])

شِيَهٌ: see شَاةٌ (of which it is a quasi-pl. n.) in art. شوه.

أَشْيَهُ [*More,* and *most, wont to smite with the evil eye*]. One says, هُوَ مِنْ أَشْيَهِ النَّاسِ [*He is of the most wont, of men, to smite with the evil eye:* this meaning being indicated by the context]. (Ibn-Buzurj, Ḳ, TA.)

ص

The fourteenth letter of the alphabet; called صَادٌ. It is one of the letters termed مَهْمُوسَة [or non-vocal, i. e. pronounced with the breath only, without the voice]; and of the letters termed أَسَلِيَّة, as also ز and س, because proceeding from the tip of the tongue; (TA;) and is one of the letters termed مُسْتَعْلِيَة, which are obstacles to إِمَالَة: (M in art. صود:) it is not conjoined with س, nor with ز, [nor, as some say, with ج,] (see إِجَّاص,)] in any Arabic word. (TA. [See also art. صود.]) It is a radical, and a substitute; not an augmentative. (M in art. صود.) It is sometimes substituted for س; and, as MF observes, what Ibn-Umm-Kásim says appears to mean that this substitution is allowable unrestrictedly; but Ibn-Málik, in the Tes-heel, makes it subject to conditions, saying that it is allowable accord. to a certain dial. when the س is followed by غ or خ or ق or ط, even when separated therefrom by a letter or by two letters: MF says that the dial. above mentioned is that of Benu-l-'Ambar, accord. to Sb and others; who give as exs. صَقَبٌ for سَقَبٌ, and صَخِرَ for سَخِرَ, and صَقْبٌ for سَقْبٌ, and صَلَغ for سَلَغ. (TA.) — [As a numeral, ص denotes *Ninety*.]

صأب

1. صَئِبَ رَأْسُهُ *His head abounded with* صُؤَاب [or *nits*]; (Ṣ, M, Ḳ;) as also ↓ اصأب. (Ṣ, Ḳ.) — صَئِبَ مِنَ الشَّرَابِ, (M, Ḳ,) aor. ـَ, (Ḳ,) inf. n. صَأَبٌ, (M,) *He was*, or *became, satisfied, and filled, with drink*: (M, Ḳ:) or صَئِبَ [alone] *he drank much water*. (Ṣ.)

4: see the preceding paragraph.

صُؤْبَةٌ *A granary*, or *granaries*, (أَنْبَار,) *of wheat* (طَعَام). (Ḳ.) — And *A place where dates are dried*: so in the dial. of the people of El-Felj. (TA in art. حضر.)

صُؤَابٌ: see the next paragraph, in three places.

صُؤَابَةٌ, (Ṣ, Ḳ,) vulgarly pronounced صُوَابَة, without ء, (MF, TA,) *A nit*; i. e. *an egg of a louse*; (Ṣ, Ḳ;) and *an egg of a flea*; (Ḳ;) but accord. to some, not applied to the latter unless tropically: (MF, TA:) accord. to IDrst, *a young louse*: (TA:) or the *eggs of the flea* and *of the louse*; as also ↓ صُؤَابٌ: (M:) [or,] accord. to the Ṣ and Ḳ, ↓ صُؤَابٌ and صِئْبَانٌ, (TA,) the latter of which is vulgarly pronounced صِيبَان, without ء, (MF, TA,) are pls. of صُؤَابَةٌ; but the former of them is a coll. gen. n., of which صُؤَابَةٌ is the n. un.: (TA:) Yaạkoob has erroneously asserted that one should not say صِئْبَانٌ. (M, TA.) — ↓ صُؤَابٌ is also sometimes applied to † *The small pieces of gold that are taken forth from the dust*, or *earth, of the mine*. (IDrst, TA.) In the following verse, cited by IAạr,

* يَا رَبِّ أَوْجِدْنِى صُؤَابًا ↓ حَيَّا *
* فَمَا أَرَى الطَّيَّارَ يُغْنِينِى شَيَّا *

the poet means, [*O my Lord*,] *cause me to find gold like* صُؤَاب [or *nits*], *whole*, or *sound, not broken into minute parts*; [*for I see not the* طَيَّار *to stand in any stead*; شَيَّا being for شَيْئًا;] by the طَيَّار meaning the *minutest pieces of gold that the wind blows away*. (M, L, TA.) — And [the pl.] صِئْبَانٌ signifies [also] † *Hoar-frost formed into grains like small pearls*. (A'Obeyd, L, TA.) [And drops of fine rain are said to be likened to صِئْبَان: see Ḥam p. 796. See also صَبِىٌّ (in art. صبو), last sentence.]

مِصْأَبٌ *A man who drinks much water*: (Ṣ:) or *who satisfies and fills himself with drink*. (Ḳ.)

صأك

1. صَئِكَ, aor. ـَ, (AZ, Ṣ, O, Ḳ,) inf. n. صَأَكٌ, (AZ, Ṣ, O,) *He* (a man, AZ, Ṣ, O) *sweated so that there arose from him a fetid odour*, (AZ, Ṣ, O, Ḳ,) *from* ذَفَر [app. as meaning *stench of the arm-pit*], or *otherwise*. (AZ, Ṣ, O.) — And, said of blood, *It congealed*. (O, Ḳ.) — And صَئِكَ بِهِ *It* (a thing, TA) *stuck*, or *clave, to him*. (Ḳ, TA.) Hence, accord. to the 'Eyn, صَاكَ, used in this sense in a verse of El-Aạshà: (TA:) or this belongs to art. صيك, (Ṣ and O in that art.,) agreeably with the opinion of ISd. (TA in that art.)

3. ظَلَّ يُصَائِكُنِى مُنْذُ الْيَوْمِ *He has continued vying with me*, or *contending with me for superiority*, or *striving to surpass me, in strength*, or *power*, or *force*, (يُشَادُّنِى,) *all this day*. (O, Ḳ,* TA.) [And so يُصَايِكُنِى, mentioned in the TA in art. صوك; but app. belonging to art. صيك.]

صَئِكٌ *A strong man*. (O, Ḳ.)

صَأْكَةٌ *The odour*, (Ḳ, TA,) i. e. *altered odour*, (TA,) *of a piece of wood when it has become moist*. (Ḳ, TA.) [And probably *The altered colour and odour* of rain-water trickling from trees: see what follows.]

صَائِكٌ, applied to rain trickling from trees, [app. a possessive epithet, meaning ذُو صَأْكَةٍ,] *Altered in colour and odour*. (TA in art. حلب.)

صأى

1. صَأَى, (Ṣ, M, Ḳ,) aor. يَصْئِى, (M,) like صَعَى aor. يَصْعِى, (Ṣ, [in one of my copies of the Ṣ يَصْعَى, which is wrong, or, accord. to the TA, both are correct, and in the Ḳ the pret. is said to be like سَعَى, which implies that the aor. is like يَسْعَى,]) inf. n. صَئِىٌّ (Ṣ, M, Ḳ) and صِئِىٌّ (Ks, M, Ḳ, TA) and صُئِىٌّ, (Ks, Ḳ, TA,) said of a young bird and the like, (Ṣ, Ḳ,) of a bird and of a young bird (M) and of a rat or mouse (Ṣ, M) and of a jerboa (Ṣ) and of a cat and of a dog (M) and of a pig and of an elephant, (Ṣ, M,) *It uttered a cry*, or *sound*; (Ṣ, M, Ḳ;) as also ↓ تَصَأَّى: (M, Ḳ:) and accord. to Fr, one says also of the scorpion, تَصِئُ and تَصْئِى. (Ṣ.) It is said in a prov., تَلْدَغُ الْعَقْرَبُ وَتَصْئِى or وَتَصِئُ, (Aṣ, Ṣ, Meyd,) this latter verb being formed by transposition, (Meyd,) i. e. *The scorpion stings while uttering a cry*; (Ṣ, Meyd;) the و being a denotative of state: (Aṣ, Ṣ:) applied to him who does wrong in the guise of him who complains of wrongdoing. (Meyd.) And one says also, جَآءَ بِمَا صَأَى وَصَمَتَ, (Ṣ, Ḳ,) and بِمَا صَآءَ وَصَمَتَ, (IAạr, Ṣ, TA,) صَآءَ being formed by tranposition from صَأَى, (Ṣ,) *He brought what was vocal and what was mute*; (Ṣ, Ḳ;) *such as slaves and beasts, and clothes and silver*; (Aṣ, TA;) or *sheep* or *goats, and camels, and gold and silver*; (IAạr, TA;) meaning *he brought much property*: and this is likewise a prov. (Ṣ.)

4. أَصْأَيْتُهُ *I made it* (i. e. a young bird &c.) *to utter a cry*, or *sound*. (M, Ḳ. [See 1.])

6: see the first paragraph above.

صَئِىٌّ, of the measure فَعِيلٌ, (TA, [originally an inf. n., written in a copy of the M صِئِىٌّ, but the former is evidently the right,]) The *bitch*: so called because of her cry. (TA.)

صب

1. صَبَّ, (Ṣ, M, Mṣb, Ḳ, &c.,) aor. ـُ, inf. n. صَبٌّ, (M, Mṣb,) *He poured out*, or *forth* (Ṣ, M, Mṣb, Ḳ) water (Ṣ, M, Mṣb) and the like. (M.) One says, صَبَبْتُ لِفُلَانٍ مَآءً فِى القَدَحِ لِيَشْرَبَهُ [*I poured out for such a one water into the drinking-cup that he might drink it*]. (TA. [See also 8.]) — Hence [† *He paid down* a price, or sum of money:] it is said in a trad., إِنْ أَحَبَّ أَهْلُكَ أَنْ أَصُبَّ لَهُمْ ثَمَنَكَ صَبَّةً ▼ وَاحِدَةً, meaning [† *If thy family like that I should pay down to them thy price*] *at once*, or *at one time*. (L, TA.) — And صَبَّ الحَبْلَ فِى البِئْرِ [† *He lowered*, or *let down, the rope into the well*] on the occasion of drawing water. (M in art. دلو.) — And لَمْ يَصُبَّ رَأْسَهُ † *He did not bend down his head*: occurring in a trad. relating to prayer. (T, TA.) — And صُبَّ رِجْلَا فُلَانٍ فِى القَيْدِ ‡ *The legs of such a one were* [*put into the shackles*, or] *shackled*. (Z, L, TA.) — And صَبَّ دِرْعَهُ ‡ *He put on*, or *clad himself with, his coat of mail*: (A, TA:) and صَبَبْتُهَا عَلَيْهِ ‡ [*I put it on him*]. (A.) — And صَبَّ عَلَيْهِ نَفْسَهُ ‡ [*He threw himself upon him*]. (A.) — And هُوَ يَصُبُّ إِلَىَّ الخَيْرَ ‡ [*He pours forth to me wealth*]. (A, TA.) — And صَبَّ ٱللّٰهُ عَلَيْهِمْ سَوْطَ عَذَابٍ ‡ [*God poured upon them a portion*, or *a share*, or *vehemence*, or *severity, of punishment*; or] *God punished them*. (A,* TA. [See also سَوْطٌ.]) And صَبَّ ٱللّٰهُ عَلَيْهِ صَاعِقَةً ‡ [*God poured upon him a thunderbolt*, or *a destructive punishment*, &c.]. (A, TA.) See also another ex. voce صَبٌّ. — And صُبَّ, (Ḳ, TA,) in the pass. form, said of a man, and of a thing, (TA,) † *He*, or *it, was annihilated, caused to pass away*, or *done away with*. (Ḳ, TA. [See also R. Q. 2.]) ═ See also 7, with which it is syn. in the first of the senses assigned to the latter below. — [Hence, app.,] صَبَّ فِى الوَادِى † *He descended into the valley*. (M, Ḳ.) And ٱنْصَبَّتْ ▼ قَدَمَاهُ فِى بَطْنِ الوَادِى, occurring in a trad., means † *His feet descended* [*into the interior*, or *bottom, of the valley*]: (TA:) or ٱنْصَبَّتْ قَدَمَاهُ فِى الوَادِى means † *his feet rested in the valley*; from ٱنْصَبَّ said of water. (Mgh.) — And صَبَّتِ الحَيَّةُ عَلَى المَلْدُوغِ, (Ṣ,* TA,) or ▼ انصبّت, (A,) ‡ [*The serpent darted down upon the* person *bitten* by it], said of the serpent when it has raised itself desiring to bite. (Ez-Zuhree, Ṣ, TA.*) And انصبّ ▼ البَازِى عَلَى الصَّيْدِ ‡ [*The hawk*, or *falcon, stooped upon the prey*, or *quarry*]. (A, TA.) And صَبَّ ذُؤَالَةُ عَلَى غَنَمِ فُلَانٍ (A,* TA) ‡ *The wolf* [*rushed upon* or] *made havock among the sheep*, or *goats, of such a one*. (TA.) ═ صَبَّ, (IAạr, A, TA,) sec. pers. صَبِبْتَ, (Ṣ, M,* Ḳ,) aor. يَصَبُّ, (IAạr, TA,) inf. n. صَبَابَةٌ, (IAạr, Ṣ,* M, A, Ḳ,* TA,) *He* (a man) *was*, or *became, affected with excessive love*, or *with attachment*, or *admiring love*, (IAạr, Ṣ, TA,) and *desire*: (Ṣ:) or *with desire*: (M, A, Ḳ:) or *with tenderness of desire*, (Ṣ, M, A, Ḳ,) and *ardour thereof*: (Ṣ:) or *with tenderness of love*. (M, Ḳ.) One says, صَبِبْتُ إِلَيْهِ [*I was*, or *became, affected with excessive love*, &c., *for him*]. (M, A,* TA.*) And صَبَّ بِهَا and إِلَيْهَا *He was*, or *became, affected with desire*, or *vehement desire*, [&c.,] *of*, or *for, her*. (MA.) — Lḥ mentions, among what is said by the women of the Arabs of the desert on the occasion of fascinating by means of charms, أَرِقَ فَأَرِقَ إِلَيْهِ صَبَّ ▼ فَأَصْبَبْ إِلَيْهِ, i. e. [as though meaning May he be *sleepless* by reason of love, *and I will be sleepless for him*: but I incline to think that the explanation has been corrupted by a copyist from رَقَّ فَأَرِقَّ إِلَيْهِ, or لَهُ, meaning *may he be tender-hearted* to me, *and I will be tender-hearted to him*]. (M, L, TA.)

4. أَصَبُّوا *They* (a company of men, TA) *took their way down a declivity*, or *declivous place*. (M, Ḳ, TA.)

5: see 7, in four places. — And see also what here follows.

6. تَصَابَبْتُ المَآءَ *I drank what remained of the water* (Ṣ, A, Ḳ) *in a vessel*: (Ṣ, A:) [or] you say, تصابّ الصُّبَابَةَ and ▼ اصطبّها and ▼ تصبّبها [*he drank what remained* of the water, or of the milk, *in a vessel*]; (M, L;) all signifying the same. (L, TA.) — And [hence,] تَصَابَّ فُلَانٌ المَعِيشَةَ بَعْدَ فُلَانٍ [lit. *Such a one drank the remains of life after such a one*], meaning ‡ *such a one outlived such a one*: (A,* TA:) and تَصَابَبْتُهُمْ أَجْمَعِينَ إِلَّا وَاحِدًا ‡ [*I outlived them all except one*]. (TA.) Esh-Shemmákh says, (M,) or El-Akhṭal, (TA,)

لَفَقْدُ قَوْمٍ تَصَابَبْتُ المَعِيشَةَ بَعْدَهُمْ •

أَعَزُّ عَلَىَّ مِنْ عِفَآءِ تَغَيَّرَا •

‡ [*Verily the loss of a people whom I have outlived is more severe to me than abundant and long hair that has become altered* in colour]: he means, the loss of those with whom I was in a state of ease and plenty is more severe to me than my hair's becoming white: (M:) Az says, he likens what remained of his life to the remains of beverage that he was sipping up. (TA.)

7. انصبّ *It* (water, Ṣ, M, and the like, M) *poured out* or *forth*, or *became poured out* or *forth*; (Ṣ, M, A, Ḳ;) as also ▼ صَبَّ, (M, Mṣb, Ḳ,) aor. ـِ, (Mṣb, TA,) inf. n. صَبِيبٌ; (Mṣb;) and ▼ تصبّب, (M, Ḳ,) which is of a form rarely occurring as that of a quasi-pass. of an unaugmented triliteral verb, being generally that of the quasi-pass. of a verb of the form فَعَّلَ; (MF, TA;) [but this app. denotes its doing so *repeatedly*; and *abundantly*, like تَدَفَّقَ, q. v.;] and ▼ اصطبّ. (Ḳ.) One says, المَآءُ يَنْصَبُّ مِنَ الجَبَلِ, (TA,) and ▼ يَتَصَبَّبُ من الجبل, (Ṣ, TA,) *The water descends, little by little, from the mountain*. (Ṣ, TA.) And ▼ تصبّب العَرَقُ [*The sweat flowed*], and الدَّمُ [*the blood*]. (A.) And ▼ تَصَبَّبْتُ عَرَقًا [which may be rendered *I flowed with sweat*] is a phrase of the Arabs, meaning تصبّب عَرَقِى [*my sweat flowed*]: thus the act is literally ascribed to the speaker, and what is essentially the agent becomes a specificative: it is not allowable to say عَرَقًا تَصَبَّبْتُ; for, as it is not allowable to put the agent before the verb, so it is not allowable to put the specificative, when it is virtually the agent, before the verb. (IJ, M.) — One says also, انصبّ الكُوزُ [*The mug had its contents poured out* or *forth*]. (TA in art. دفق.) — See also 1, in three places. — انصبّ النَّاسُ عَلَى المَآءِ [generally implies descent, but] means † *The people collected together*, or *assembled, at the water*. (Mṣb.) — [And انصبّ is often said of a place, or the ground, &c., meaning † *It sloped downwards*. — Ḥar (p. 125) uses the phrase تَنْصَبُّ إِلَى اللَّهْوِ, meaning (as there expl.) † *Thou inclinest to diversion*, or *sport*.]

8. اصطبّ المَآءَ is expl. by Sb as signifying *He took for himself the water*; agreeably with general analogy: (M:) [but it is more properly rendered *he poured out for himself the water*:] one says, اِصْطَبَبْتُ لِنَفْسِى مَآءً مِنَ القِرْبَةِ لِأَشْرَبَهُ [*I poured out for myself water from the skin that I might drink it*]: and اِصْطَبَبْتُ لِنَفْسِى قَدَحًا [*I poured out for myself a cup*]. (TA.) — See also 6. — And see 7.

R. Q. 1. صَبْصَبَهُ † *He annihilated it, caused it to pass away*, or *did away with it*; (M, Ḳ;*) namely, a thing. (M.) — And † *He dispersed it*, or *scattered it*: (Ḳ:) *he* (a man) *dispersed*, or *scattered, it*, namely, an army, or property or wealth. (AA, Ḳ.)

R. Q. 2. تَصَبْصَبَ † *It was*, or *became, annihilated, caused to pass away*, or *done away with*; (Ṣ, M, Ḳ;) *it passed*, or *went, away*; said of a thing. (Ṣ, M. [See also صُبَّ.]) — † *It* (the night, M, A, Ḳ, and the day, AZ, TA, and the heat, A) *passed*, or *went, away*, (AZ, M, A, Ḳ,) *except a small portion*, (AZ, M, TA,) or *for the most part*. (A, Ḳ.) — † *It* (what was in a water-skin, or milk-skin,) *became little in quantity*. (Fr, TA.) — † *It* (a company of men) *became dispersed*, or *scattered*. (M, TA.) ═ *He* (a man) *was*, or *became, very bold*, or *daring, and very adverse*, or *repugnant*, (M,* Ḳ,* TA,) عَلَيْنَا [*against us*]. (TA.) — And, said of a day, *It was*, or *became, intensely hot*. (M, Ḳ,* TA.)

صَبٌّ is an inf. n. [and is] used [as an epithet] in the sense of the measure فَاعِلٌ, or of the measure مَفْعُولٌ: (TA:) [thus it is used as an epithet] applied to water, [meaning *Pouring out* or *forth*, or *poured out* or *forth*,] like as are صَابٌّ and غَوْرٌ سَكْبٌ: (Ṣ, TA: [see also صَبِيبٌ:]) and hence, in 'Alee's description of Aboo-Bekr, when he died, كُنْتَ عَلَى الكَافِرِينَ عَذَابًا صَبًّا † [*Thou wast, against*, or *upon, the unbelievers, a punishment pouring forth*, or *poured forth*]. (TA.) — And [hence, app.,] one says, ضَرَبَهُ ضَرْبًا صَبًّا, meaning † *He smote him with the edge of the sword* [as though *with a smiting pouring down*, or *poured down*]; as also

حَذِرٌ. (IAar, L, TA.) — One says also, ضَرَبَهُ مِائَةً قَصَبًا, (TA,) or أَخَذَ مِائَةً قَصَبًا, (A,) meaning, ‡ [*He smote him* with *a hundred* blows, or *he took a hundred*,] *and less* than that, i. e. فَدُونَ ذٰلِكَ, (TA,) *contr. of* فَصَاعِدًا; (A;) or *and more* [than that], or *above* [that], i. e. *like* فَصَاعِدًا, (A, TA,) i. e. مَا فَوْقَ ذٰلِكَ. (TA.) — And صُبَّ ▼ عَلَيْهِ البَلَآءُ مِنْ صَبٍّ, meaning ‡[*Trial*, or *affliction, was poured upon him*] *from above*. (A, TA.) = Also, applied to a man, *Affected with excessive love*, or *with attachment*, or *admiring love*, (IAar, Ṣ, A,* TA,) and *desire*: (Ṣ:) or *with desire*: (M, A,* Ḳ:) or *with tenderness of desire*, (Ṣ,* M, A,* Ḳ,) and *ardour thereof*: (Ṣ:* [see صَبٌّ:]) or *with tenderness of love*. (M, Ḳ.) One says, هُوَ صَبٌّ بِهَا (and إِلَيْهَا) (see صَبَّ) *He is affected with excessive love of her*; &c.: (A:) fem. صَبَّةٌ: (M, Ḳ:) dual masc. صَبَّانِ, pl. masc. صَبُّونَ; dual. fem. صَبَّتَانِ, pl. fem. صَبَّاتٌ: thus accord. to those who hold رَجُلٌ صَبٌّ to be similar to رَجُلٌ فَهِمٌ and حَذِرٌ, originally صَبِبٌ: (TA:) [hence it appears that some hold صَبٌّ to be originally an inf. n., and therefore use it as an epithet in its original form, without regard to gender or number: but] accord. to Sb, صَبٌّ is [originally] of the measure فَعِلٌ, because you say صَبِبْتُ صَبَابَةً, like as you say قَنِعْتُ قَنَاعَةً. (M.) See also 1, last sentence.

صُبٌّ: see صُبَّةٌ. — Accord. to AO, it may also be pl. of ▼ صَبُوبٌ or of ▼ صَابٌّ: but As says that, accord. to others, it is not pl. of either of these two words; their pl. being صُبُبٌ: (L, TA:) it is said in a trad., (Ṣ, L, TA,) respecting conflicts and factions, or seditions, (L, TA,) لَتَعُودُنَّ فِيهَا أَسَاوِدَ صُبًّا يَضْرِبُ بَعْضُكُمْ رِقَابَ بَعْضٍ: (Ṣ, L, TA:) here by أَسَاوِد are meant "[great and noxious] serpents:" (L, TA:) and صُبًّا, accord. to Ez-Zuhree, is from الصَّبُّ ["the act of pouring out or forth"]; for the serpent, he says, when it desires to bite, raises itself, and then darts down (lit. pours down) upon him that is bitten: (Ṣ, L, TA:) [as though the meaning were, *Ye will be, therein*, like *great and noxious serpents, one portion of you smiting the necks of another portion*:] Ez-Zuhree says that صُبًّا is pl. of ▼ صَبُوبٌ, and originally صُبُبًا; like as رَجُلٌ صَبٌّ is originally صَبِبٌ; and so says IAmb: but IAar is related to have said that أَسَاوِد means *companies*, pl. of سَوَادٌ; and صُبًّا, *pouring*, one upon another, with slaughter: and some say that it is صُبَّى, in measure like حُبْلَى; and it is said to be from صَبَا, [for صَبَا إِلَى الدُّنْيَا,] aor. يَصْبُو, meaning "he inclined to the things of the present world;" and thus to be like غُزًّى, pl. of غَازٍ: [see صَابٍ, in art. صبو:] IAar used also to say that it is originally صُبَّأً, with ء, [pl. of صَابِئٌ,] from صَبَأَ عَلَيْهِ "he came, or came forth, upon him unexpectedly." (L, TA.)

صُبَّةٌ *A quantity* of wheat or food, &c., *that is poured out* or *forth* (M, Ḳ) *together*, or *collectedly*; (M;) also (M, Ḳ) sometimes (M) termed ▼ صُبٌّ. (M, Ḳ.) See also 1, near the beginning. — And *A* سُفْرَة [or *piece of skin in which the traveller puts his food*; or the *thing upon which one eats*]; (M, Ḳ;) so called because the food is poured into it, or upon it: (M:) or *a thing like the* سُفْرَة: (M, Ḳ:) and صِنَّة, with ن, signifies the same. (M.) — See also صُبَابَةٌ, with which it is syn. — Also *A company of men*: (M, Mṣb, Ḳ:) [app. tropical; but it is said that] this is the primary meaning, and it is used in relation to camels, and sheep or goats, and the like, tropically. (TA.) — ‡ *A detached number* of horses, (Ṣ, M, A, Mṣb, Ḳ,) and of camels, (A, Ḳ,) and of sheep or goats, (A, Mṣb, Ḳ,) and of dirhems, or pieces of money: (A:) or *from ten to forty*: (A, Ḳ:) or *from twenty to thirty and forty* of camels and of sheep or goats: or *less than a hundred* (M, A, Ḳ) of camels: (M, Ḳ:) or of camels *i. q.* صِرْمَة: (Ṣ:) and *from ten to forty* of goats: (AZ, Ṣ:) or *a flock* of sheep or *a herd* of goats, as being likened to a company of men: (TA:) or *from twenty to forty* of sheep and of goats; or peculiarly of goats: or *about fifty*: or *from sixty to seventy*: and of camels *about five or six*: (IAth, TA:) and *a collection* of dirhems, or pieces of money, and of wheat, or food, &c.: and *a piece* of a thing: (Mṣb:) [or] *a small quantity* or *portion* of wealth or property. (M, Ḳ.) — And † *A part*, or *portion*, of the night: so in the saying, مَضَتْ صُبَّةٌ مِنَ اللَّيْلِ † [*A part, or portion, of the night passed*]. (Ṣ.)

صَبَبٌ The *descent*, (تَصَوُّبٌ, M, L, TA, in the Ḳ erroneously written تَصَبُّبٌ, TA,) of a river, or rivulet, or channel of water, or of a road, *down a declivity*. (M, L, Ḳ, TA.) — And *A declivity, declivous place*, or *ground sloping down*; (M, A, Ḳ, TA;) and (TA) so ▼ صَبِيبٌ, of which the pl. is أَصِبَّةٌ; (Ṣ, TA;) so too ▼ صَبُوبٌ and ▼ صُبُوبٌ, with fet-ḥ and with ḍamm; (TA;) [i. e.] ▼ الصَّبُوبُ signifies *that down which you descend*, or *have descended*, (مَا ٱنْصَبَبْتَ فِيهِ,) and its pl. is صُبُبٌ [like عُمُدٌ pl. of عَمُودٌ]; (M, TA;) [and so ▼ الصُّبُوبُ;] or, as some say, ▼ الصَّبُوبُ, with fet-ḥ, is a name for *the water, &c.*, that is poured out upon a man, like طَهُورٌ and غَسُولٌ; and صُبُوبٌ, with ḍamm, is pl. of صَبَبٌ: but AZ mentions his having heard the Arabs apply ▼ صَبُوبٌ to *a declivity*, or *declivous place*; and says that its pl. is صُبُبٌ: (TA:) and الصَّبَبُ مِنَ الرَّمْلِ signifies *what has poured out* or *forth* or *down*, *of sand*: (M, Ḳ:*) and the pl. of صَبَبٌ is أَصْبَابٌ. (M, Ḳ.)

صُبَابٌ: see صُبَابَةٌ.

صَبُوبٌ [app. syn. with ▼ صَابٌّ as part. n. of the intrans. verb صَبَّ, signifying *Pouring out* or *forth* or *down*; or like the latter but having an intensive meaning]: see صُبٌّ, in two places. — See also صَبَبٌ, in four places.

صُبُوبٌ: see صَبَبٌ, in three places.

صَبِيبٌ [*Poured out* or *forth*: (see also صَبٌّ, first sentence:) or, as an epithet in which the quality of a subst. predominates,] *water poured out* or *forth*; syn. ▼ مَآءٌ مَصْبُوبٌ. (M, Ḳ.) — And (M, Ḳ) some say (M) *Blood*: (Ṣ, M, Ḳ:) and *sweat*; (Ḳ;) as in the saying,

• هَوَاجِرُ تَخْتَلِبُ الصَّبِيبَا

[*Vehement midday-heats that draw forth the sweat*]: (TA:) [or *what is poured forth* of sweat and of blood; for] one says, جَرَى صَبِيبُ العَرَقِ and الدَّمِ [*What was poured forth, of the sweat* and *of the blood, ran*, or *flowed*]. (A.) — And (M, Ḳ) some say (M) The *expressed juice of* عَنْدَم [or *dragon's blood*]. (M, Ḳ.) — And (M, Ḳ) some say (M) *A certain red dye*. (M, Ḳ.) — And (Ḳ) The *juice of the leaves of sesame*: (Ṣ, M,* Ḳ:*) A'Obeyd (so in a copy of the Ṣ, or Aboo-'Obeydeh accord. to the TA,) says, it is the *juice of the leaves of sesame*, or *of some other plant*, which was described to me in Egypt, *the colour of which juice is red tinged with blackness*: and some say, it is the *expressed juice of the leaves of the* حِنَّآء [q. v.]. (Ṣ, TA.) — And عُصْفُر [i. e. *Safflower*]: (Ḳ:) or *purified* عُصْفُر. (Ṣ.) — And *A kind of tree* [or *plant*] *resembling* سَذَاب [or *rue*], (M, Ḳ,) *with which the hair is dyed*. (M.) — And *Senna*, (M, Ḳ,) *with which beards are dyed, as with* حِنَّآء. (M.) — And *A certain thing* [or *plant*] *resembling the* وَسْمَة [or وَسِمَة, q. v.], (M, Ḳ, TA,) *with which beards are dyed*. (TA.) — Also *Hoar-frost*. (AA, Ḳ.) AA cites, as descriptive of the sky,

• وَلَيْسَ بِهَا إِلَّا صَبًا وَصَبِيبُهَا

[*And there is not in it aught save east wind and its hoar-frost*]. (TA.) — And *Good*, or *excellent, honey*. (Ḳ.) — Also, (Ḳ,) or صَبِيبُ سَيْفٍ, (TA,) The *extremity of a sword*: (Ḳ, TA:) or the *extremity next the* سِيلَان [q. v.] *thereof*: or, as some say, *its* سيلان absolutely. (TA.) — See also صَبَبٌ.

صَبَابَةٌ [is an inf. n., mentioned as such in the latter part of the first paragraph, and, when used as a simple subst.,] signifies [*Excessive love*, or *attachment*, or *admiring love*: (see its verb:) or] *desire*: (M, A, Ḳ:) or *tenderness of desire*, (Ṣ, M, A, Ḳ,) and *ardour thereof*: (Ṣ:) or *tenderness of love*. (M, Ḳ.)

صُبَابَةٌ and ▼ صُبَّةٌ *A portion*, (Ṣ, M, Mṣb, Ḳ,) or *a small quantity*, (Fr, A, and A'Obeyd in explanation of the former,) of water, (Fr, Ṣ, M, Mṣb, Ḳ,) and of milk, (M, Ḳ,) or of wine, or beverage, (A'Obeyd,) *remaining* (A'Obeyd, Ṣ, M, Mṣb, Ḳ) *in a vessel*. (A'Obeyd, Ṣ, M, Mṣb.)

• صُبَابَتِي تُرْوِي وَلَيْسَتْ غَيْلَا

My remaining portion of water in the vessel &c. *satisfies thirst, though it is not water running* [*copiously*] *upon the surface of the earth*, is a prov., applied to him who makes use of that which is bestowed though it be not much. (Meyd, TA.*) In the following verse, cited by IAar,

• وَلَيْلٍ هَدَيْتُ بِهِ فِتْيَةً

• سُقُوا بِصُبَابِ ▼ الكَرَى الأَغْيَدِ

‡ [*During many a night have I guided in the right way young men infused with the remains of drowsiness that made them to bend their necks from side to side*], صُبَاب may be put for صُبَابَة; or it may be pl. of the latter, [or rather a coll. gen. n. of which صُبَابَة is the n. un.,] like as شَعِيرٌ is of شَعِيرَةٌ: the poet uses this word metaphorically, in relation to drowsiness, like as he has used the word سُؤْرٌ. (M, L, TA.) One says also لَمْ أُدْرِكْ مِنَ العَيْشِ إِلَّا صُبَابَةً and إِلَّا صُبَابَاتٍ ‡ [*I did not attain*, or *obtain, of life, save a small remainder* and *small remains*]. (A, TA.)

صُبّ صَابٌ: see صَبُوبٌ: and see also صُبٌّ.

صَبْصَبٌ, (M, Ḳ,) applied to a camel, (M,) *Thick*, or *big, and strong*; as also ▼ صُبَاصِبٌ, (M, Ḳ, TA, in the CḲ صَبَاصِب,) so applied; (M;) and ▼ صَبْصَابٌ, (Ḳ,) likewise so applied. (TA.)

صَبْصَابٌ: see what next precedes. — Also, applied to a [journey such as is termed] قَرَبٌ, *Hard*, or *severe*: (M, TA:) and, applied to a [journey such as is termed] خِمْسٌ, i. q. بَصْبَاصٌ, (Aṣ, Ṣ, Ḳ) and حَصْحَاصٌ, i. e., *in which is no delay*, or *intermission, nor any flagging*. (Aṣ, TA.) ═ And الصَّبْصَابُ also signifies *What remains of the thing*: or *what is poured out from it*; (Ḳ, TA;) i. e., from the thing; by which is here said to be meant the water-skin or milk-skin. (TA.)

صُبَاصِبٌ: see صَبْصَبٌ.

الأَصَبُّ [app. a dial. var. of الأَصَمُّ], an epithet applied to the month رَجَبٌ: (TA in art. حرم:) see مُحَرَّمٌ.

[مَصَبٌّ *A place where water*, or *the like, pours out* or *forth*, *from a river into another river* or *into the sea* &c., *or from a tank* or *a gutter* &c., *and from high ground into a valley* (see ضَاجِعَةٌ); and *a sink*, or *sink-hole*: pl. مَصَابُّ (occurring in the Ṣ and Ḳ in art. رفق, &c.).]

[مِصَبَابٌ, accord. to Reiske, signifies *A ship*: so says Freytag: but for this I find no authority.]

مَصْبُوبٌ: see صَبِيبٌ, first sentence.

صبأ

1. صَبَأَ, (Ṣ, M, Ḳ,) aor. ـَ, (M, Ḳ,) inf. n. صُبُوءٌ, (Ṣ, M, Ḳ, [in the last of which it is implied that this verb in all its senses except the last has صَبْءٌ also for an inf. n., and likewise صَبُوٌّ as a syn. form, but this I do not find authorized by any other lexicon,]) said of the tush (Ṣ, M, Ḳ) of a camel (Ṣ, M) and of a cloven-hoofed animal and of a solid-hoofed animal, (M,) and said of a cloven hoof, (Ḳ, [but this, I doubt not, is a mistake, for in the place of صَبَأَ الظِّلْفُ وَالنَّابُ, the reading in the Ḳ, I find in the M صَبَأَ نَابُ الظِّلْفِ وَالخُفِّ وَالحَافِرِ, and the like in the L,]) *It grew forth*; (M, Ḳ;) or *its point*, or *extremity, grew forth*: (Ṣ:) and accord. to the Ḳ, it appears that ▼ اصبأ signifies the same; but this is not the case. (TA.) And صَبَأَتْ said of the ثَنِيَّة [i. e. a central incisor] of a boy, *It grew forth*. (Ṣ.) — Also, said of a star, (M, Ḳ,) and of the moon, (M,) *It rose*; and so ▼ اصبأ: (M, Ḳ:) or تَصْبَأُ النُّجُومُ *the stars come forth from their places of rising*: (AO, Ṣ:) or صَبَأَتِ النُّجُومُ *the stars appeared*: (TA:) and ▼ اصبأ النَّجْمُ *the Pleiades* [antonomastically called النجم] *rose*. (Ṣ.) — [Hence,] صَبَأَ, (Ṣ, M, Ḳ,) or صَبَأَ مِنْ دِينِهِ إِلَى دِينٍ آخَرَ, (AO, Ṣ, Mṣb,*) aor. ـَ, (M, Mṣb, Ḳ,) inf. n. صُبُوءٌ (Ṣ, M, Ḳ) and صَبْءٌ; and صَبُوٌّ, (M, Ḳ,) aor. ـُ, (TA,) inf. n. صُبُوءَةٌ; (CḲ [but not in the TA nor in my MS. copy of the Ḳ];) † *He departed from his religion to another religion*; (Ṣ, M, Mṣb, Ḳ;) like as the stars come forth from their place of rising. (AO, Ṣ.) And صَبَأَ, (Ṣ,) or صَبَأَ فِي دِينِهِ, aor. ـَ, inf. n. صُبُوءٌ, (T, TA,) *He was*, or *became, a* صَابِئ [or *Sabian*]. (T, Ṣ, TA. [See صَابِئٌ, below.]) — And صَبَأَ عَلَيْهِمْ, (Ṣ, M,) aor. ـَ, (Ṣ,) inf. n. صَبْءٌ and صُبُوءٌ, *He came forth upon them*; (Ṣ, M;) as also ▼ اصبأ: (M:) and accord. to IAạr, صَبَأَ عَلَيْهِ *he came forth*, or *went forth, upon him*, or *against him*: and *he inclined against him with enmity*: (TA:) or *he came*, or *came forth, upon him unexpectedly*: whence, he says, the word صُبًّا in the saying of the Prophet, لَتَعُودُنَّ فِيهَا أَسَاوِدَ صُبًّا, [which see in art. صب,] the said word being of the measure فُعْلًا, [originally صُبَأً,] and the ء being suppressed: (L in art. صب:) and ▼ أَصْبَأَهُمْ signifies *he came upon them suddenly, not having knowledge of their place*. (Ḳ.) ═ One says also, صَبَأَ عَلَيْهِمُ العَدُوَّ, (M,* Ḳ,) aor. ـَ, inf. n. صَبْءٌ; (M;) as also صَبَغَ; (TA;) *He guided to them* (M, Ḳ) *the enemy*: (Ḳ:) mentioned by IAạr, from AZ. (TA.) — And قُدِّمَ إِلَيْهِ طَعَامٌ فَمَا صَبَأَ وَلَا ▼ أَصْبَأَ *Food was presented to him, and he did not put* (M, Ḳ*) *his hand* (M) or *his finger* (إِصْبَعَهُ Ḳ) *into it*, or *upon it*: (M, Ḳ: [see also صَبَغَ:]) mentioned by IAạr. (M.) And صَبَأَ فِي الطَّعَامِ, aor. ـَ, *He* [app. a camel] *put his head into the food*: as also صَبَغَ. (O in art. صبغ.) And صَبَأَتْ فِيهَا رَأْسَهَا [or فِيهِ, *She put her head into it*]; like صَبَغَتْ. (TA in that art.)

4: see the preceding paragraph, in six places.

صَابِئٌ [part. n. of صَبَأَ: and as such signifying] *One who departs from his religion to another religion*. (Mṣb.) The Arabs used to call the Prophet الصَّابِى [for الصَّابِئ], because he departed from the religion of Ḳureysh to El-Islám; and him who entered the religion of El-Islám, مَصْبُوٌّ, changing the ء to و; and the Muslims [collectively], الصُّبَاةُ, as though pl. of الصَّابِى, without ء, like قُضَاةٌ and غُزَاةٌ pls. of قَاضٍ and غَازٍ. (TA.) And [the pl.] الصَّابِئُونَ in the Ḳur [v. 73, &c.,] is said by Zj to mean *Those who depart from one religion to another*. (TA.) — Then this appellation, صَابِئٌ, was applied to [*Any individual of*] *a certain sect of the unbelievers*, [*the Sabians*,] *said to worship the stars secretly, and openly to profess themselves to belong to the Christians*: they are called الصَّابِئَةُ and الصَّابِئُونَ: *and they assert that they are of the religion of Ṣábi the son of Sheyth* [or *Seth*] *the son of Adam*: their appellation may also be pronounced الصَّابُونَ, and thus Náfi' read it [in the Ḳur]: (Mṣb:) or the صَابِئُونَ are *a certain class of the people who possess revealed scripture*: (Ṣ:) or *a people whose religion resembles that of the Christians, except that their ḳibleh is towards the place whence blows the* [*south*, or *southerly, wind called*] جَنُوب: (Lth, T, TA:) [or] *whose ḳibleh is from* (مِنْ [or this may mean *some point of*]) *the place whence blows the* [*north*, or *northerly, wind called*] شَمَال *at midday*: (M, Ḳ:) or, accord. to some, *their ḳibleh is the Kaabeh*: (MF:) *and they assert that they are of the religion of Noah*, (Lth, T, M, Ḳ,) *lyingly*: (Lth, T, M:) in the R it is said that they are thus called in relation to Ṣábi the son of Lámak [or Lamech], the brother of Noah: Bḍ says, it is said that they are *worshippers of the angels*: and it is said that they are *worshippers of the stars*: and that their appellation is Arabic; from صَبَأَ "he departed from a religion;" or from صَبَا "he inclined," because of their inclining from truth to falsehood. (MF, TA.)

صبح

1. صَبَحَهُ, (Ṣ, Mgh, TA,) aor. ـَ, (Mgh, TA,) inf. n. صَبْحٌ; (Ṣ, TA;) and ▼ صبّحهُ, (Ḳ, TA,) inf. n. تَصْبِيحٌ; (TA;) *He gave him to drink a morning-draught*, or *what is termed a* صَبُوحٌ; (Ṣ, Mgh, Ḳ, TA;) [and] so صَبَحَهُ صَبُوحًا: (MA:) and the first [and second also] *he handed to him a morning-draught of milk* or *of wine*. (TA.) And صَبَحَ الإِبِلَ, aor. and inf. n. as above, *He watered the camels in the morning, between daybreak and sunrise*. (TA.) — And both are said respecting a غَارَة [meaning † *He made a hostile*, or *predatory, incursion upon him in the morning*; as though he made the غارة to be to him a morning-draught: see صَابِحٌ]. (Ḥam p. 66.) — [And accord. to Reiske, as stated by Freytag, صَبَحَ signifies *He drank in the early morning*: but I think that Reiske may have assigned to it this meaning from his having found the pass. form of the verb, not distinguished as such, used in a case in which it might be supposed to signify thus.]. — See also 2, in five places. ═ صَبْحٌ as an inf. n. [of which the verb is صَبِحَ accord. to a general rule] signifies The *being satiated*, or *having the thirst quenched, by a morning-draught*, or *what is termed a* صَبُوح. (L.) ═ And صَبِحَ, aor. ـَ, inf. n. صَبَحٌ [in the CḲ (erroneously) صَبْح] and صُبْحَةٌ, [*He*, or *it, was of the colour termed* صُبْحَة meaning as expl. below: or] *it* (hair) *had whiteness naturally intermixed in it with redness*; as also ▼ اصباحّ, (Ḳ, TA,) inf. n.

اِصْبِيحَاح. (TA.) = صَبُحَ, aor. ُ, inf. n. صَبَاحَةٌ, [q. v.,] *He was*, or *became, beautiful, comely, pretty*, or *elegant*; (Ṣ, A, Ḳ, TA;) as some say, peculiarly in the face: (TA:) or *he was*, or *became, bright* (Mṣb, TA) in the face. (Mṣb.)

2. صبّحهُ, (Ṣ,) or صَبَّحَهُمْ, (Ḳ,) inf. n. تَصْبِيحٌ, (TA,) *He came to him*, or *to them, in the morning, in the time termed the* صَبَاح; (Ṣ, Ḳ;) as also [صَبَحَهُ ▼, or] صَبَحَهُمْ, aor. َ: (Ḳ:) the teshdeed in the former does not imply muchness, or frequency: (Ṣ:) and صَبَّحَهُمُ الخَيْلُ and صَبَحَهُمْ ▼ *The horsemen came to them at daybreak, at the time termed the* صُبْح: (TA:) but Aboo-'Adnán says that there is a difference between صَبَّحْنَا and صَبَحْنَا ▼; which is this: you say, صَبَّحْنَا بَلَدَ كَذَا [*We came in the morning to such a town*, or *country*], and صَبَّحْنَا فُلَانًا [*We came in the morning to such a one*], with teshdeed; and صَبَحْنَا ▼ أَهْلَهَا خَيْرًا or شَرًّا [*We came in the morning to its people*, or *inhabitants, with good* or *with evil*, without teshdeed; as though we made the good or the evil to be a morning-draught, or putting the second of the nouns following the verb in the accus. case because of ب suppressed]: you say also, صَبَّحَهُ بِكَذَا; and you may also say, صَبَحَهُ ▼ بِكَذَا, as well as صَبَّحَهُ كَذَا; *He came to him in the morning with such a thing.* (L.) — And صَبَّحَكَ ٱللّٰهُ بِخَيْرٍ (Ṣ,* A, Mṣb) or بِالخَيْرِ (TA) † [*May God visit thee in the morning with good*, or *good fortune*, or *happiness*; or *make thee to be in*, or *during, the morning* attended *with good*, &c.; i. e. *make thy morning good*, or *happy*; or *grant thee a good*, or *happy, morning*]: a prayer for the person thus addressed, (Mṣb.) — And صَبَّحْتُهُ *I said to him* عِمْ صَبَاحًا [expl. below, see صَبَاحٌ]; (Ṣ;) and صَبَّحَهُمْ *he said to them* عِمُوا صَبَاحًا: (Ḳ:) or صَبَّحْتُهُ means *I said to him* صَبَّحَكَ ٱللّٰهُ بِخَيْرٍ [expl. above]. (Mṣb.) — See also 1, first sentence. — [Hence,] صَبَّحْتُ القَوْمَ المَآءَ, inf. n. as above, *I journeyed with the people*, or *party, by night until I brought them in the morning to the water.* (Ḳ.) — صَبَّحَنِى فُلَانٌ الحَقَّ ‡ *Such a one declared*, or *told clearly, to me the truth*; syn. مَحَّضَنِيهِ. (A, TA. [See صُبْحٌ.]) = تَصْبِيحٌ as a subst., see below.

4. اصبح *He entered upon the time of morning termed* صَبَاح [which means both *dawn* and *forenoon*]: (Ṣ,* Mṣb: [in the former this meaning is indicated, but not expressed:]) or *he entered upon the time of daybreak*, or *dawn, the time termed* صُبْح. (L, Ḳ.) By the following words of Esh-Shemmákh,

* وَقِيلُ المُنَادِى أَصْبَحَ القَوْمُ أَدْلِجِى *

is meant, [*And the saying of the crier is*,] *The people*, or *party, have nearly entered upon the time of dawn: prosecute the night-journey*: for the Arabs, when they have nearly arrived at a place which they desire to reach, say, قَدْ بَلَغْنَاهُ; and when travellers are near the time of day-break, they say, أَصْبَحْنَا. (T, L.) — [Hence,] ‡ *He awoke from sleep in the* جَوْف [i. e. *last third*, or *last sixth*,] *of the night.* (A, TA.) [And simply ‡ *He awoke*: for] one says to the sleeper, أَصْبِحْ, meaning ‡ *Awake thou from sleep.* (A, TA.) And one says also, أَصْبِحْ يَا رَجُلُ, meaning ‡ *Become roused, O man*, (A, Ḳ,* TA,) *from thy heedlessness* or *inadvertence*, (A, TA,) *and see thy right course*, (Ḳ, TA,) and *what will rectify thy state.* (TA.) And أَصْبِحْ لَيْلُ ‡ [*Become morning, O night*]: a prov.: (Meyd, A, TA:) said in a distressing night, that is long by reason of evil. (Meyd. [See Freytag's Arab. Prov., i. 727.]) — [Also *He*, or *it, became in the morning* in any particular state or condition: in this sense, and in that next following, an incomplete, i. e. a non-attributive, verb.] — And [hence, simply,] *He*, or *it, became*; syn. صَارَ. (Ṣ, Ḳ.) One says, اصبح عَالِمًا *He became knowing*, or *learned.* (Ṣ, TA.) Thus, فَأَصْبَحُوا ظَاهِرِينَ, in the Ḳur lxi. last verse, means *And they became victorious.* (Bḍ.) And فَأَصْبَحَ يُقَلِّبُ كَفَّيْهِ, in the Ḳur xviii. 40, [*And he became in a state*, or *condition, in which he turned over his hands*; i. e.] *and he became repentant*, or *grieved for what he had done.* (A in art. قلب, and Bḍ.) And فَأَصْبَحُوا لَا تَرَى إِلَّا مَسَاكِنَهُمْ, in the Ḳur xlvi. 24, i. e. [*And they became*] *in a condition such that*, if thou wert present in their country, *thou wouldst not see aught save their dwelling-places*; or, as Ḥamzeh and Ks read, لَا يُرَى إِلَّا مَسَاكِنُهُمْ [*there was not to be seen aught save their dwelling-places*]. (Bḍ.) [أَصْبَحَ يَفْعَلُ كَذَا is of frequent occurrence, meaning *He became occupied*, or *engaged, in doing such a thing*; *he betook, set*, or *applied, himself to doing such a thing*; *set about*, or *commenced, doing such a thing*; or *began to do such a thing.*] — [Also *He performed the prayer of daybreak.*] It is said in a trad., أَصْبِحُوا بِالصُّبْحِ, meaning *Perform ye the prayer of daybreak in the time of daybreak.* (L.) — See also 8. — Also *He acted gently.* (TA in art. ارش: see an ex. in a verse cited voce مَأْرُوشٌ.) = اصبح مِصْبَاحًا *He trimmed a lamp*, or *wick*; or *prepared it properly for use.* (TA.) — See, again, 8. = إِصْبَاحٌ as a subst., see صُبْحٌ, in two places.

5. تصبّح *He slept in the morning*; or *first part of day, before sunrise.* (Ṣ, Mṣb, Ḳ.) — And *He ate such food as is termed a* صُبْحَة. (Ḳ, TA.) It is said in a trad., مَنْ تَصَبَّحَ بِسَبْعِ تَمَرَاتٍ عَجْوَةٍ [*He who eats as a* صُبْحَة *seven dates of the sort called* عَجْوَة]. (TA.) = See also 8, in two places.

6. فُلَانٌ يَتَصَابَحُ and يَتَحَاسَنُ [*Such a one affects to be beautiful, comely, pretty*, or *elegant*: the latter verb is here added as an explicative of the former: see صَبُحَ]. (A, TA.)

8. اصطبح *He drank a morning-draught*, or *what is termed a* صَبُوح; (Ṣ, Ḳ, TA;) [and] so اصبح ▼. (Mṣb. [Thus in my copy of the Mṣb, but probably a mistranscription, for the former is the verb well known in this sense, and is not in that copy.]) It is said in a trad., مَا لَنَا صَبِىٌّ يَصْطَبِحُ [*We have not a child that drinks a morning-draught*]; meaning we have not as much milk as a child may drink in the early morning, in consequence of the drought. (TA.) = And i. q. أَسْرَجَ [as meaning *He lighted* a lamp or wick, or himself or another with a lamp &c.]; (Ḳ, TA;) and so اصبح ▼ (A, TA) [in the former sense], as in the phrase اصبح مِصْبَاحًا [*he lighted a lamp* or *wick*]; (A;) and اصبح alone has this meaning, i. e. أَسْرَجَ سِرَاجًا. (TA, from a trad.) [But it is used often in the latter sense:] one says, الشَّمْعُ مِمَّا يُصْطَبَحُ بِهِ *Candles are of the things with which one lights* [*himself*, or *others*]; syn. يُسْرَجُ: (Ṣ:) [and in like manner تصبّح ▼; for] one says, هُوَ يَتَصَبَّحُ بِالشُّمُوعِ [*He lights himself*, or *others, with candles*]: (A:) [and in like manner also استصبح ▼; for] one says, استصبح بِالمِصْبَاحِ (Ṣ, MA, Mgh, Mṣb, Ḳ*) *He lighted* [*himself*, or *another*,] *with the lamp*, or *wick*; (MA;) syn. أَسْرَجَ; (Ṣ;) or اِسْتَسْرَجَ: (Ḳ:) [hence it appears that اصطبح به and استصبح ▼ به and تصبّح ▼ به may be aptly rendered *he employed it as a means of light*; and thus the second of these three verbs, is expl. in treatises on practical law:] one says also, استصبح ▼ بِالدُّهْنِ [*He employed oil as a means of light*; or] *he made the lamp*, or *wick, to give light by means of oil*: (Mgh, Mṣb:) and it is said in a trad. respecting the several sorts of fat (شُحُوم) of carrion, يَسْتَصْبِحُ ▼ بِهَا النَّاسُ *The people* [*employ them as means of light*; or] *make their lamps*, or *wicks, to give light by means of them.* (TA.)

10: see the next preceding paragraph, in four places.

11: see 1, last sentence but one.

صُبْحٌ (Ṣ, A, Mṣb, Ḳ, &c.) and صَبَاحٌ ▼ (Mṣb, Ḳ) and صَبِيحَةٌ ▼ (Mṣb,* Ḳ) and إِصْبَاحٌ ▼ and مُصْبَحٌ ▼ (Ḳ [or perhaps the last should be مُصْبَح, q. v.]) *Daybreak*, or *dawn*; syn. فَجْرٌ; (Ṣ, A, Mṣb, Ḳ;) i. e. (so in the Mṣb, but in the Ḳ "or") the *beginning*, or *first part, of day*: (Mṣb, Ḳ:) إِصْبَاحٌ ▼ is an inf. n. [inf. n. of أَصْبَحَ] used in the sense of صُبْح, in the Ḳur vi. 96, (Jel,) and is similar to إِبْكَار; (TA;) [and مُصْبَحٌ ▼ is the n. of place and time from أَصْبَحَ:] the pl. of صُبْحٌ is أَصْبَاحٌ; (Ḳ;) and thus some read in the Ḳur vi. 96. (Bḍ.) See also أُصْبُح. One says, أَتَيْتُهُ لِصُبْحِ خَامِسَةٍ and لِصِبْحِ ▼ خامسة, (Ṣ, Ḳ,) meaning [*I came to him*] *in the morning* (صَبَاح) [*of the last*] *of five days*; (Ḳ;) i. e., *of a fifth day*; (TḲ;) [or rather, *of a fifth night*, as the last word is fem.;] like as one says, لِمُسْىِ خامسة. (Ṣ.) —

الصُّبْحُ is also used as meaning † *The truth;* and *the clear,* or *plain, thing* or *case.* (Ḥam p. 449.) —— And أُمُّ صُبْحٍ is one of the names of *Mekkeh.* (Ḳ,* TA.)

صُبْحٌ : see the next preceding paragraph.

صُبْحٌ : see صُبْحَةٌ. —— Also The *glistening* of iron (Ḳ, TA) and of other things. (TA.)

صَبْحَةٌ : see the next paragraph, in three places. —— Also *A watering of camels in the morning,* or *first part of day, before sunrise:* which is not esteemed by the Arabs wholesome: the time approved by them for watering is when the sun is near the meridian. (TA.)

صُبْحَةٌ The *early part of the forenoon, after sunrise;* syn. ضُحًى; as also ▾ صَبْحَةٌ: (Mṣb:) or the *period of* one's *entering upon the* صَبَاح [which means both *dawn* and *forenoon*]: so in the saying, لَقِيتُهُ ذَاتَ صُبْحَةٍ [*I met him when he was entering upon the dawn* or *forenoon*]. (TA.) —— And *A sleep in the morning,* or *first part of day, before sunrise;* as also ▾ صَبْحَةٌ; (Ṣ,* Ḳ;) or both signify *a sleep in the* ضُحًى [expl. above]; (A;) but the latter is by some disapproved: such sleep is forbidden in a trad., because it is in a time for the commemoration of the praises of God and then for seeking gain. (TA.) One says, فُلَانٌ يَنَامُ الصُّبْحَةَ and ▾ الصَّبْحَةَ [*Such a one sleeps in the first part of day, before sunrise*]. (Ṣ.) —— And *Food with which one contents,* or *diverts, himself* [*so as to allay the craving of his stomach*], *in the morning* or *first part of day, before sunrise.* (Ḳ.) —— See also صَبُوحٌ. ═ Also (Suh, Ḳ, TA,) and ▾ صَبَحٌ, (Lth, Ṣ, TA,) [each said in one place in the Ḳ to be an inf. n. of which the verb is صَبِحَ,] *Blackness inclining to redness:* (Ḳ:) or *intense redness in the hair:* (Lth, TA:) or *a colour inclining to that which is termed* صُهْبَةٌ: (Ḳ, TA:) or *nearly the same as* صُهْبَةٌ: (Lth,* Ṣ,* TA:) or *a colour inclining to that termed* شُهْبَةٌ: (Ḳ, TA:) or *whiteness that is not clear, or pure;* so the former is expl. by Suh. (TA. [See also أَصْبَحُ.])

صَبْحَانُ A man *who has drunk a morning-draught,* or *what is termed a* صَبُوح; (TA;) or *who has done so, and satisfied his thirst thereby:* (Aboo-'Adnán, TA:) [in the Ṣ and Ḳ it is implied that it is syn. with مُصْطَبِحٌ, q. v.:] fem. صَبْحَى. (Ṣ, TA.) Hence the prov., أَكْذَبُ مِنَ الأَخِيذِ الصَّبْحَانِ (Aboo-'Adnán, Ṣ, TA) *More lying than the captive who had satisfied his thirst with a morning-draught:* (Aboo-'Adnán, TA:) the person thus alluded to was a man who was among a people that gave him a morning-draught, after which he arose and quitted them, and was taken by another people, who said to him, "Guide us to the place where thou wast;" to which he replied, "I have passed the night in the bare desert:" but presently he sat down to make water, so they knew that he had passed the night with a people near by; and by his means they found their way to them, and exterminated them: (IAạr, TA:) or the prov. is أَكْذَبُ مِنَ الأَخِيذِ الصَّبْحَانِ *More lying than the young unweaned camel that has satisfied its thirst with drinking* [*its mother's milk in the morning*]; which [seems to be thirsty but] will not drink of its mother's milk when one desires it to do so: (IAạr, Sh, TA:) or, accord. to Fr, *than the young unweaned camel that is affected with indigestion,* or *heaviness of the stomach, from drinking much milk,* and therefore craves for milk again. (Meyd. [See also Freytag's Arab. Prov.: he seems to have followed a faulty text.]) —— Also the fem., صَبْحَى, A she-camel *that has been milked* [app. *in the morning*]. (Meyd, in his Proverbs, under the letter ص; and TA.) ═ See also صَبِيحٌ.

صَبْحَانُ A man *who hastens to take the morning-draught,* or *what is termed the* صَبُوح. (Ḳ.)

صَبَاحٌ : see صُبْحٌ. —— Also (Mṣb) *Contr. of* مَسَآءٌ, (Ṣ, A, Mṣb,) and so ▾ صَبِيحَةٌ, (Ṣ,) [and ▾ أُصْبُوحَةٌ (as in a phrase following in this paragraph), and ▾ مُصْبَحٌ, (see this last word,)] i. e. *Morning,* or *forenoon, counted from sunrise to noon:* (Mṣb and TA in art. مسو:) or, accord. to some, *from midnight to noon:* (TA in art. مسو:) or, accord. to the Arabs, *from the beginning of the latter half of the night to the time when the sun declines from the meridian;* then commences the مَسَآء, extending to the end of the former half of the night; thus expl. by Th; so says El-Jawáleekee. (Mṣb.) The Arabs say, when they regard a man, &c., as ominous of evil, صَبَاحُ ٱللّٰهِ لَا صَبَاحُكَ [*God's morning: not thy morning*]: and if you will, you may say, صَبَاحَ ٱللّٰهِ لَا صَبَاحَكَ. (Lḥ, TA.) And عِمْ صَبَاحًا, (Ṣ,) or عِمُوا صَبَاحًا, (Ḳ,) lit. imperative, but meaning a prayer, i. e. *May thy life,* or *your life, be pleasant during the morning,* (Ḥar p. 32, and TA* in arts. نعم and وعم,) is a salutation of the people of the Time of Ignorance. (TA.) One says also, لَقِيتُهُ صَبَاحًا, and ذَا صَبَاحٍ, (Ṣ,) or أَتَيْتُهُ ذَا صَبَاحٍ, (Ḳ,) which [i. e. ذا صباح] is only used adverbially, (Sb, Ṣ, Ḳ,) except in the dial. of Khath'am, (Sb, Ṣ,) meaning [*I met him,* or *I came to him,*] *in a morning,* [or] *between daybreak and sunrise:* (Ḳ:) the following verse (Ṣ, TA) by Anas Ibn-Nuheyk, of Khath'am, (TA,) or, as some say, by Iyás Ibn-Mudrikeh El-Ḥanafee, (so in a marg. note in a copy of the Ṣ,) presents an exception to the adverbial usage:

عَزَمْتُ عَلَى إِقَامَةِ ذِى صَبَاحٍ
لِأَمْرٍ مَا يُسَوَّدُ مَنْ يَسُودُ

(Ṣ, TA:) the poet means, *I determined to stay until the time of the* صباح [i. e. either *dawn* or *forenoon*]: for *it is on account of some particular thing,* i. e. some good quality, or some praiseworthy thing, *that he is made a chief who becomes a chief:* thus Ibn-Es-Seeráfee explains this verse. (TA.) And one says, ▾ أَتَيْتُهُ ذَا صَبُوحٍ, not used otherwise than adverbially, meaning the same as ذَا صَبَاحٍ, expl. above; (Ḳ;) and ▾ ذَاتَ الصَّبُوحِ *in the morning,* or *first part of day, before sunrise:* (IAạr, TA:) or ▾ ذَا صَبُوحٍ [properly means] *in a time of drinking the* [*morning-draught called*] صَبُوح. (TA.) And أَتَيْتُهُ صَبِيحَةَ ▾ يَوْمِ كَذَا [*I came to him in the dawn,* or *in the morning,* or *forenoon, of such a day*]: (A:) and ▾ أُصْبُوحَةَ كُلِّ يَوْمٍ [*in the morning of every day*]; and in like manner, أَتَيْتُهُ أُمْسِيَّةَ كُلِّ يَوْمٍ. (Ṣ.) And أَتَيْتُهُ صَبَاحَ مَسَآءَ, (Sb, A, TA,) for صَبَاحًا وَمَسَآءً, [*I came to him morning* and *evening,*] meaning *every morning and evening:* (Sharḥ esh-Shudhoor, p. 31:) the two nouns are thus constructed by some of the Arabs, after the manner of خَمْسَةَ عَشَرَ: but some prefix the former noun to the other, putting the latter in the gen. case, except when the expression is used as a denotative of state, or adverbially: (TA:) [or, accord. to IHsh,] صَبَاحَ مَسَآءٍ is allowable as [an adverbial expression] meaning صَبَاحًا ذَا مَسَآءٍ [lit. *in a morning having an evening,* or *in a forenoon having an afternoon*]; and a similar instance occurs in the Ḳur, ch. lxxix. last verse. (Sharḥ esh-Shudhoor, ubi suprà.) —— يَوْمُ الصَّبَاحِ means ‡ *The day of the hostile,* or *predatory, incursion.* (Ṣ, A, Ḳ.) The Arabs, when suddenly attacked in the morning by a troop of horsemen, cry aloud, يَا صَبَاحَاهْ † [*O! a hostile,* or *predatory, incursion!*]; warning the whole tribe: (TA:) this is said by him who calls for aid: (JM:) for they generally made a hostile, or predatory, incursion in the morning: (TA, JM:) or, as some say, the two conflicting parties used, when night came, to abstain; and when day returned, they recommenced; so that the case is as though he who said thus meant, The time of the صَبَاح [or morning] has come, therefore prepare yourselves for fighting. (JM.)

صُبَاحٌ The شُعْلَة [or *lighted wick*] *of a* قِنْدِيل [or *lamp*]. (Ḳ.) [See also مِصْبَاحٌ.] ═ And *I. q.* صَبِيحٌ, q. v. (Ks, Ṣ, Ḳ.)

صَبُوحٌ *A morning draught;* i. e. *a draught, drink,* or *potation, that is drunk in the morning,* or *first part of day, before sunrise,* (Ṣ, A, Mṣb, TA,) and *afterwards, before noon;* (TA;) *contr. of* غَبُوقٌ: (Ṣ, A:) and *whatever is eaten,* or *drunk, in the morning,* or *first part of day, before sunrise; contr. of* غَبُوقٌ: (TA:) [and particularly] *milk that is drunk at that time:* (AHeyth, L:) *milk,* or *wine, that is drunk at that time:* or *what is drunk at that time hot:* (L:) *milk that is milked at that time:* (Ḳ:) and شَرَاب [i. e. *beverage,* or *wine,*] *that people have,* (Ḳ, TA,) *and drink,* (TA,) *in the morning:* (Ḳ, TA:) pl. صَبَائِحُ. (TA.) أَعَنْ صَبُوحٍ تُرَقِّقُ [*Dost thou make a delicate allusion to a morning-draught?*] is a prov., [the origin of which is expl. in art. رق, q. v.,] applied to him who speaks obscurely, not plainly; and to him who alludes ambiguously to some great thing or affair; and to him who by blandishing expressions makes a thing incumbent on thee which is not really so. (TA.) — See also صَبَاحٌ, in three places. — Accord. to Lth, it signifies [absolutely] *Wine.* (T, TA.) — And The *quantity of milk* of a camel *that is drawn at dawn,* or *in the first part of day;* and so ▼ صُبْحَةٌ. (TA.) = Also A she-camel *that is milked at dawn,* or *in the forenoon,* (Lḥ, AHeyth, Ḳ,) or *in the morning,* or *first part of day, before sunrise;* and so with ة. (Ḳ.)

صَبِيحٌ (Ṣ, A, Mgh, Mṣb, Ḳ) and ▼ صُبَاحٌ (Ḳs, Ṣ, Ḳ) and ▼ صُبَّاحٌ and ▼ صَبْحَانُ (Ḳ) *Beautiful, comely,* (Ṣ, A, Mgh, Ḳ,) *pretty,* or *elegant;* (Ṣ, A, Ḳ;) as some say, peculiarly in the face; (TA;) or applied to the face: (A:) or *bright* (Mṣb, TA) in the face: (Mṣb:) the first is expl. by Lth as signifying *fair of face:* fem. صَبِيحَةٌ and صُبَاحَةٌ: and the pl. of صَبِيحٌ and صُبَاحٌ, and of their fems. here mentioned, is صِبَاحٌ. (L, TA.)

صَبَاحَةٌ *Beauty, comeliness, prettiness,* or *elegance;* (Ṣ, A, Ḳ;) as some say, peculiarly in the face: (TA:) or *brightness* in the face: (Mṣb:) it is said that صَبَاحَة is in the face; وَضَاءَة, in the skin; جَمَال, in the nose; حَلَاوَة, in the eye; مَلَاحَة, in the mouth; ظَرْف, in the tongue; رَشَاقَة, in the stature; لَبَاقَة, in the qualities of the mind; and that the completion of beauty is in the hair. (L, TA.) [See 1, last sentence.]

صَبِيحَةٌ: see صُبْحٌ: and صَبَاحٌ, in two places.

صُبَاحِىٌّ *Intensely red* blood: (Ḳ, TA:) from أَصْبَحُ signifying one "whose hair is overspread with redness." (TA.) = أَسِنَّةٌ صُبَاحِيَّةٌ *Wide spear-heads.* (Ḳ, TA. [In the CḲ the latter word is without teshdeed.]) ISd says, I know not the person or thing in relation whereto they are thus called. (TA.) [See also مِصْبَاحٌ.]

صُبَاحٌ: see صَبِيحٌ.

صَابِحٌ [*Giving to drink a morning-draught,* or *what is termed a* صَبُوح: act. part. n. of 1, q. v.: see also Ḥam p. 66. And] One *who waters his camels in the morning, between day-break and sunrise.* (TA. [See صُبْحَةٌ.]) — And † One *who makes a hostile,* or *predatory, incursion upon a people in the morning;* as though he made it to be to them a صَبُوح. (Ḥam p. 66.) — الحَقُّ الصَّابِحُ ‡ *The plain, manifest, clear, truth.* (Ḳ,* TA.)

أَصْبَحُ *Of a black colour inclining to redness:* (Ḳ:) or *having redness intermixed in his black hair:* (Sh, TA:) or *whose hair,* or *beard, has a red hue overspreading it:* (Aboo-Naṣr, Sh, TA:) or *having hair intensely red:* (TA:) it is *nearly the same as* أَصْهَبُ: (Lth, Ṣ:) and is an epithet applied to a man and to a lion: (Ṣ:) and to hair as meaning *having whiteness naturally intermixed in it with redness;* (Ḳ, TA;) of whatever kind it be: (TA:) fem. صَبْحَآءُ: (Ḳ:) and pl. صُبْحٌ: (TA:) and hence [accord. to some] ▼ الصُّبْحُ meaning "the dawn;" for, as Az says, the colour of the true dawn inclines a little to redness. (TA.) [Hence, because of his colour,] الأَصْبَحُ signifies *The lion.* (Ḳ.) In the phrase أَسْوَدُ أَصْبَحُ, the epithet is added as a corroborative. (Z, TA.) — And the fem., صَبْحَآءُ, signifies A female *conspicuous,* or *clear,* or *fair, in the* جَبِين [or *side of the forehead*]. (TA.)

أَصْبَحِىٌّ *A whip:* (Ṣ, Ḳ:) and سِيَاطٌ أَصْبَحِيَّةٌ *certain whips:* (AO, Ṣ, TA:) so called in relation to ذُو أَصْبَحَ, one of the Kings of El-Yemen, (AO, Ṣ, Ḳ, TA,) of Ḥimyer. (TA.)

إِصْبَاحٌ: see صُبْحٌ, in two places. — It is said to signify also *Darkness; contr. of* صُبْحٌ, which is its primary signification: and accord. to Esh-Shereeshee, *redness of the hair.* (Ḥar p. 284.)

أُصْبُوحَةٌ: see صَبَاحٌ, in two places.

تَصْبِيحٌ The *morning meal, that is eaten between daybreak and sunrise;* syn. غَدَآءٌ: (A, Ḳ:) a subst. of the measure تَفْعِيل, (Ḳ, TA,) similar to تَرْعِيب &c.: pl. تَصَابِيحُ. (A, TA.) One says, قَرَّبَ إِلَى الضُّيُوفِ تَصَابِيحَهُمْ [*He brought near to the guests,* or *put before them, their early morning-meals*]. (A, TA.)

مُصْبَحٌ, (Ṣ, Mṣb, and some copies of the Ḳ,) formed from the unaugmented verb, (Ṣ, Mṣb,) and ▼ مُصْبَحٌ, (Ṣ, Mṣb, Ḳ,) formed from the augmented verb أَصْبَحَ, (Ṣ, Mṣb,) The *place of entering upon the time of morning called* صَبَاح: and the *time of entering upon the same:* (Ṣ, Mṣb, Ḳ:) or the former signifies *i. q.* صَبَاحٌ, and the *time thereof,* and the *place thereof.* (Marg. note in a copy of the Ṣ.) See also صَبَاحٌ.

مُصْبَحٌ: see the next preceding paragraph: and see also صُبْحٌ, in two places.

مِصْبَحٌ: see the paragraph here following, in four places.

مِصْبَاحٌ *A lamp:* or its *lighted wick:* syn. سِرَاجٌ: (Ṣ, Ḳ:) the latter is the proper meaning (L) [though not the more usual], and is the meaning intended in the Ḳur xxiv. 35, (Bḍ, L, Jel,) or *a large, bright,* or *brilliant,* سِرَاج: (Bḍ:) and ▼ مِصْبَحٌ signifies *a lamp:* (L:) [the pl. of this is مَصَابِحُ: and] the pl. of مِصْبَاحٌ is مَصَابِيحُ. (Mṣb.) — مَصَابِيحُ النُّجُومِ means أَعْلَامُ الكَوَاكِبِ [i. e. † *The stars,* or *asterisms, that are signs of the way to travellers*]. (L, TA.) = Also *A large* [*drinking-vessel of the kind called*] قَدَح; (AḤn, Ḳ;) and so ▼ مِصْبَحٌ: (Ḳ:) or مَصَابِيحُ [the pl. of the former] signifies the [*vessels called*] أَقْدَاح [pl. of قَدَح] *with which one drinks the morning-draught called* صَبُوح. (Ṣ.) — And A she-camel *that remains in the morning in the place where she has lain down,* (Ṣ, Ḳ, TA,) *not going forth to pasture,* (Ṣ, TA,) *until the sun has risen high,* (Ṣ, Ḳ, TA,) *by reason of her strength* (Ḳ, TA) *and her fatness:* (TA:) the quality thus described is approved: (Aṣ, Ṣ, TA:) and such a she-camel is also termed ▼ مِصْبَحٌ: pl. of the former as above. (TA.) — And *A wide spear-head;* (Ḳ, TA;) [app. *of such as are termed* أَسِنَّةٌ صُبَاحِيَّةٌ;] as also ▼ مِصْبَحٌ. (TA.)

مُصْطَبِحٌ *Drinking a morning-draught,* or *what is termed a* صَبُوح. (Ṣ, Ḳ. [See also صَبْحَانُ, first sentence.])

صبر

1. صَبَرَهُ, aor. ـِ, (Ṣ, M, A, Ḳ,) inf. n. صَبْرٌ, (M, Ḳ,) *He confined him; held him in custody; detained, retained, restrained,* or *withheld, him,* or *it;* (Ṣ, M, A, Ḳ;) عَنْهُ *from it.* (M, A, Ḳ.) [Accord. to a copy of the A, ▼ صَبَّرَهُ signifies the same; but this may be a mistranscription. Hence,] صَبَرْتُ نَفْسِى *I restrained,* or *withheld, myself,* or *my soul;* (Ṣ, Mgh;) عَلَى كَذَا [*to endure such a thing*]. (Mgh.) 'Antarah says, mentioning a battle in which he was engaged,

• فَصَبَرْتُ عَارِفَةً بِذٰلِكَ حُرَّةً •
• تَرْسُو إِذَا نَفْسُ الجَبَانِ تَطَلَّعُ •

meaning حَبَسْتُ نَفْسًا صَابِرَةً [i. e. *And I restrained thereat a soul patient* and *ingenuous, that is firm when the soul of the coward yearns:* the last word (for تَتَطَلَّعُ) I have here rendered on the supposition that the poet describes the soul of the coward as one that is yearning for home]. (Ṣ.) [And hence,] صَبَرَ is also used intransitively: (Mṣb:) [or as a trans. verb of which the objective complement, namely, نَفْسَهُ, is understood:] you say, صَبَرَ, aor. and inf. n. as above, (Ṣ, M, Mṣb, Ḳ,) *He was,* or *became patient,* or *enduring; contr. of* جَزِعَ: (M, Ḳ:) or *he restrained,* or *withheld, himself,* or *his soul, from impatience:* (Ṣ, Mṣb:) or *he restrained,* or *withheld, himself,* or *his soul, from impatience, and his tongue from complaint, and his members from broil:* or, accord. to Dhu-n-Noon, *he shunned acts of opposition, and was calm in suffering the pangs of afflictions, and made a show of competence in a state of protracted poverty in places where the means of subsistence were found:* or, as some say, *he endured trial,* or *affliction, with good manners:* or *he was contented in trial,* or *affliction, without show of complaint:* or *he constrained himself to attempt things that he disliked:* or, accord. to 'Amr Ibn-'Othmán, *he maintained constancy with God, and received his trials with an unstraitened mind:* or, accord. to El-Khowwáṣ, *he steadily adhered to the statutes of the Ḳur-án and the Sunneh:* or, as some say, *he was content to perish for gaining the approval of him whom he loved:* or, accord. to El-Ḥareeree, *he made no difference between a state of ease, comfort, and affluence, and a state of affliction; preserving calmness of mind in both states:* (B:) and you also say ▼ اِصْطَبَرَ, (Ṣ, M, Mṣb, Ḳ,) and ▼ اِصَّبَرَ, (Ṣ, M, Ḳ, TA, [in the CḲ, erroneously, اِصْبَرَ,])

changing the ط into ص, but not اِطَّبَرَ, for ص is not to be incorporated into ط; (Ṣ;) and likewise ▾ تَصَبَّرَ; (M, Ḳ;) both syn. with صَبَرَ; (M;) or ▾ تصبّر signifies he constrained himself to be patient; (Ṣ, TA;) [or he took patience: and ▾ اصطبر, he acquired patience; and he was tried with patience: see صَابَرَ.] One says, صَبَرَ فُلَانٌ عِنْدَ المُصِيبَةِ Such a one was patient on the occasion of affliction. (Ṣ.) And صَبَرْتُ عَلَى مَا أَكْرَهُهُ [I was patient of, or I endured with patience, or bore with, what I dislike]. (A.) And صَبَرْتُ عَمَّا أُحِبُّ [I endured with patience the withholding of myself, or the being debarred, from what I love, or like; or I was patient of the loss, or want, of what I love, or like]: (A:) and ▾ تَصَبَّرْتُ عَنْهُ [I constrained myself to endure with patience the withholding myself, or the being debarred, from it, or him; or I constrained myself to be patient of the loss, or want, of it, or him]. (L, voce تَجَلَّدَ.) And ▾ أَفْضَلُ الصَّبْرِ التَّصَبُّرُ [The most excellent kind of patience is the constraint of oneself to be patient]: a saying of 'Omar. (IAạr.) And بَدَنِى لَا يَصْبِرُ عَلَى البَرْدِ ‡ [My body will not be patient of cold, or will not endure patiently cold]. (A.) And صَبْرٌ signifies also The being bold or daring [in enduring, or attempting, a thing]. (TA.) — Also He made him, or it, firm, or fast; or bound, or tied, him, or it, firmly, or fast. (TA.) [Hence,] صَبَرَهُ عَلَى القَتْلِ, inf. n. as above, He confined him, namely, a man, and other than man, [with bonds or otherwise,] (Ḳ, TA,) alive, (TA,) and shot, or cast, at him until he died: (Ḳ, TA:) or he set him up for slaughter: (M:) and you say also, قَتَلَهُ صَبْرًا; (Ṣ, M, Mṣb, Ḳ;) and صَبَرَهُ; meaning he confined him (i. e. a man) to die, until he died; and in like manner you say ▾ اصبرهُ; (Ṣ;) which latter signifies also he slew him in retaliation. (T in art. بوأ.) And قُتِلَ صَبْرًا He (i. e. any living thing) was confined alive, and then shot at, or cast at, until he was put to death: (Ṣ:) or he (any living thing) was bound until he was put to death: (Mṣb:) or he (a man) was bound hand and foot, or held by another man, until he was beheaded: (Mgh:) or he was slain [deliberately,] not on the field of battle, nor in war or fight, nor by mistake: (A'Obeyd:) and صُبِرَ he was confined, (A,) or held and confined, (B,) to be put to death. (A, B.) صَبْرُ الرُّوحِ [signifies The confining the living, and shooting, or casting, at him until he dies; as is shown in the TA: but it] occurs in a trad., in which it is forbidden, as meaning the act of gelding, or castrating. (A, TA.) — Also, (Ṣ, Mṣb,) aor. and inf. n. as above, (Mṣb,) He confined him to make him swear, until he swore, or took an oath; as also ▾ اصبرهُ: (Ṣ:) or he made him to swear a most energetic oath; (Mṣb;) as also صَبَرَ يَمِينَهُ, (A, Mgh,) which is a tropical phrase: (A:) and ▾ اصبره عَلَى يَمِينٍ, (TA in art. بلت,) or ▾ اصبرهُ, (TA in the present art.,) he (the judge, or governor,) constrained him to swear, or take an oath. (TA.) And صُبِرَ He was confined, or held in custody, in order that he might be made to swear, or take an oath. (A.) And حَلَفَ صَبْرًا He swore, or took an oath, being confined, or held in custody, (Ṣ, M,) by the judge, or governor, (M,) in order that he might be made to do so. (Ṣ, M.) And صَبَرَ يَمِينًا He swore, or took an oath: (TA in art. بلت:) and he compelled one to take an oath. (Mgh.) — See also 2. — Also He clave to him; namely, a man; syn. لَزِمَهُ. (M, Ḳ.) — صَبَرَ مِنْهُ: see 8. — صَبَرْتُ, (Ṣ, [thus in my copies, without any complement,]) or صَبَرْتُ بِهِ, (M, Mṣb, Ḳ,) aor. ـِ, inf. n. صَبْرٌ (Ṣ, M, Mṣb, Ḳ) and صَبَارَةٌ, (Ṣ, Mṣb, Ḳ,) I became responsible, or surety, for him, or it. (Ṣ, M, Mṣb, Ḳ.) — And اِصْبِرْنِى Give thou to me a surety. (Ṣ, Ḳ.) — صَبَرُوا طَعَامَهُمْ, (so in the CḲ, [agreeably with an explanation of the pass. part. n. مَصْبُور, q. v.,]) or ▾ صَبَّرُوهُ, (so in the M, and in my MS. copy of the Ḳ, [both probably correct,]) They collected their wheat together without measuring or weighing it; made it a صُبْرَة [q. v.]. (M, Ḳ.)

2. صبّرهُ, (M, Mṣb, Ḳ,) inf. n. تَصْبِيرٌ, (TA,) He urged him, or made him, to be patient, by a promise of reward: or he said to him, Be thou patient: and ▾ صَبَرَهُ he made him to be patient: (Mṣb:) or the former, he commanded him, or enjoined him, to be patient; as also ▾ اصبرهُ: (M, Ḳ:) and the first, he required of him that he should be patient: (Ṣgh, TA:) and ▾ اصبرهُ, he attributed to him (جَعَلَ لَهُ) patience; (M, Ḳ;) as also ▾ اصطبرهُ. (TA.) — See also 1, second sentence. — صَبَّرُوا طَعَامَهُمْ: see 1, last sentence. — صَبَّرَ الشَّىْءَ, inf. n. as above, He heaped up the thing. (O.) — [صبّر also signifies He embalmed a dead body with صَبِر, meaning accord. to Freytag myrrh; but for this I know not any authority: he mentions the verb as occurring in this sense in "Hamak. Waked." p. 94, last line. — Also He ballasted a ship: used in this sense in the present day. See صَابُورَة.]

3. صابرهُ, (A, MA,) inf. n. مُصَابَرَةٌ (A, Ḳ) and صِبَارٌ, (Ḳ,) [He vied with him in patience, or endurance; as shown in what follows: or] he acted patiently with him: (MA:) صَابِرُوا in the Ḳur iii. last verse means Vie ye in patience, or endurance: (Ksh, Bḍ, Jel:*) or in this instance, in the saying اِصْبِرُوا وَصَابِرُوا وَرَابِطُوا, the three verbs are progressive in meaning; the first meaning less than the second; and the second, less than the third: or the meaning is, [be ye patient] with yourselves, and [vie ye in patience] with your hearts in enduring trial with respect to God, and [remain ye steadfast] with your minds in desire for God: or [be ye patient] with respect to God, and [vie ye in patience] with God, and [remain ye steadfast] with God. (B, TA.) [See also 3 in art. ربط.]

4. اصبرهُ: see 1, latter half, in four places: — and see 2, in two places. — [مَا أَصْبَرَهُ How patient, or enduring, is he!] — مَا أَصْبَرَهُمْ عَلَى النَّارِ [in the Ḳur ii. 170] means How bold are they [to encounter the fire of Hell]! (Ḳ:) or how bold are they to do the deeds of the people of the fire [of Hell]! (TA:) or how much do they occupy themselves in doing the deeds of the people of the fire [of Hell]! (Ḳ:) this last explanation is in the Tekmileh. (TA.) — اصبرهُ also signifies He (the judge, A, TA, or the Sultán, El-Aḥmar, TA) retaliated for him. (El-Aḥmar, A, TA. [See 8.]) — اصبر [intrans.] It (a thing) was, or became, hard; syn. اِشْتَدَّ. (A. [See صَبِرٌ.]) — He fell into what is termed أُمُّ صَبُّورٍ, (Ḳ, TA,) i. e. a calamity: and he became in what is termed أُمُّ صَبَّارٍ, i. e. a حَرَّة. (TA.) — He sat upon the صَبِير, (Ḳ, TA,) i. e. the mountain. (TA.) — It (milk) was, or became, very sour, inclining to [the flavour of صَبِر, i. e.] bitterness. (Ḳ.) — He ate the صَبِيرَة, (IAạr, Ḳ,) i. e. the thin, round cake of bread so called. (TA.) — And He stopped the head of a flask, or bottle, with a صِبَار, (Ḳ, TA,) i. e. a stopper. (TA.)

5: see 1, near the middle of the paragraph, in four places.

6. تَصَابَرَ [relating to a number of persons] signifies The being patient, or enduring, one with another. (KL.) [You say, تصابروا They were patient, or enduring, one with another.] — And تصابروا عَلَى فُلَانٍ They leagued together, and aided one another, against such a one. (Ibn-Buzurj, TA in art. ضفر.)

8. اِصْطَبَرَ, and its var. اِصَّبَرَ: see 1, former half in three places. — اصطبر مِنْهُ He retaliated by slaying him, or wounding him, or the like; (A, Ḳ;) and so صَبَرَ مِنْهُ. (TA.) — [And accord. to Reiske, It was collected: (mentioned by Freytag:) app. as quasi-pass. of 1 in the last of the senses assigned to it above.] — اصطبرهُ: see 2.

10. استصبر It (a vapour, TA) became dense. (Ḳ, TA. [See صَبِير.])

R. Q. 1, accord. to the Ṣ, صَنْبَرَ: see art. صنبر.

صَبْرٌ [inf. n. of 1, q. v. — Used as a simple subst.;] Patience, or endurance; contr. of جَزَعٌ: (M, Ḳ:) or restraint of oneself, or of one's soul, from impatience. (Ṣ. [Several other explanations of this word are shown by explanations of the verb.]) — شَهْرُ الصَّبْرِ The month of fasting: (Ḳ:) fasting being called صَبْر because it is self-restraint from food and beverage and sexual intercourse. (TA, from a trad.) — [قَتَلَهُ صَبْرًا, and قُتِلَ صَبْرًا: see 1.] — يَمِينُ الصَّبْرِ The oath for which the judge, or governor, [in the CḲ الحُكْم is erroneously put for الحَكَم,] holds one in custody until he swears it: (M, Ḳ:) or the oath that is obligatory (Ḳ, TA) upon the swearer, (TA,) and which the swearer is compelled to take, (Mgh, Ḳ,) he being confined by the Sultán until he do so: (Mgh,* TA:) such an oath is also termed ▾ يَمِينٌ مَصْبُورَةٌ: (Mgh:) [i. e.] the term مَصْبُورَة is applied to an oath, (Ṣ, Ḳ, TA,) meaning one on account of which a man is confined, in order to make him swear it; (TA; [and this seems to be indicated by the context in the Ṣ and Ḳ;]) but the man being مَصْبُور, and not the oath, the latter is thus termed tropically. (TA.) — حَلَفَ صَبْرًا : see 1.] — See also صَبِيرٌ.

صُبْرٌ (Ṣ, M, Mṣb, Ḳ) and ↑ صُبُرٌ (M, Mṣb, Ḳ) The *side* of a thing: (Ṣ, M, Ḳ:) or *a side rising above the rest* of a thing: (Mṣb:) or its *upper part*, or *top:* (TA:) and the *edge* of a thing: (Ṣ, M, Ḳ:) and its *thickness:* formed by transposition from بُصْرٌ: (Ṣ:) pl. أَصْبَارٌ, (Ṣ, M, Mṣb, Ḳ,) and pl. pl. أَصَابِرُ. (Mṣb.) أَصْبَارٌ signifies The *sides* of a vessel, (Ṣ,) and of a grave. (TA.) And you say, He filled the drinking-cup, (Ṣ, M, A, Ḳ,) and the measure, (A, TA,) إِلَى أَصْبَارِهِ, (Ṣ, M, A, Ḳ,) *to its top*, (Ṣ, M, Ḳ,) as also الى أَصْبَارِهِ; (Ṣ;) or *to its uppermost parts;* (TA;) or *to its edges.* (A.) And أَخَذَهُ بِأَصْبَارِهِ *He took it altogether.* (Ṣ, M, A, Mṣb,* Ḳ.) And لَقِىَ الشِّدَّةَ بِأَصْبَارِهَا † *He met with complete distress*, or *adversity.* (Aṣ, Ṣ.) And in a trad., the tree called سِدْرَةُ المُنْتَهَى is said to be صُبْرُ الجَنَّةِ *in the highest part of Paradise.* (A, TA.) — Also the former, (Ṣ, M, Ḳ,) and ↑ صُبُرٌ, (M, Ḳ,) *Land in which are pebbles*, (Ṣ, M, Ḳ,) *not rugged.* (Ṣ, M.) Hence, ↑ أُمُّ صَبَّارٍ, q. v. (Ṣ, M.) — See also صَبِيرٌ, in two places.

صَبْرٌ : see صُبْرٌ: — and صَبِيرٌ in two places: — and see also صَبِرٌ.

صَبَرٌ *Ice;* syn. جَمَدٌ: (A, Ṣgh, Ḳ:) and [its n. un.] with ة, *a piece thereof:* (A, Ṣgh:) from أَصْبَرَ meaning اِشْتَدَّ. (A.)

صَبِرٌ (Ṣ, M, Mṣb, Ḳ) and ↑ صَبْرٌ, which latter is allowable only in cases of necessity in poetry, (Ṣ, Mṣb, Ḳ,) or it is allowable in other cases, as also ↑ صِبْرٌ, agreeably with analogy, (Ibn-Es-Seed, Mṣb,) [*Aloes;*] *a certain bitter medicine;* (Ṣ, Mgh, Mṣb;) the *expressed juice of a certain bitter tree;* (M, Ḳ;) the *expressed juice of a certain tree of which the leaves are like the sheaths of knives, long and thick, with a dusty and dull hue in their greenness, of rough appearance, from the midst of which there comes forth a stalk whereon is a yellow flower,* ثَمِدٌ [but what this means I know not] *in odour;* (Lth, TA;) *it grows like the green* سُوسَن [or *lily*], *save that the leaves of the* صبر *are longer and broader and much thicker, and it contains very much juice;* (AḤn, M, O, TA;) *it is crushed and thrown into the presses, then bruised with pieces of wood, and trodden with the feet until its expressed juice flows, when it is left until it thickens, then it is put into leathern bags, and exposed to the sun until it dries:* (AḤn, O:) *the best sort is the* سُقُطْرِى [i. e. *of the Island of Sukutrà*]: *and it is also known by the name of* ↑ صَبَارَة [a name now applied to the plant]: (TA:) the n. un. is صَبِرَةٌ [and صَبْرَةٌ and صِبْرَةٌ]: and the pl. is صُبُورٌ. (M, TA.) — [Accord. to Freytag, it signifies also *Myrrh:* but for this I know not any authority.]

صُبُرٌ : see صُبْرٌ.

صَبْرَةٌ : see صَبَارَةٌ: — and see صُبَارَةٌ, in two places. — Also *Urine, and dung of camels and other beasts, compacted together in a watering-trough.* (Ḳ.) — أَبُو صَبْرَةَ, (so in a copy of the M,) or ↑ أَبُو صُبَيْرَةَ, (so in the Ḳ and TA,) *A certain bird;* (M, Ḳ;) *red in the belly, black in the head and wings and tail, the rest of it being red;* (M;) thus in the L; (TA;) or *red in the belly, black in the back and head and tail;* (Ḳ;) thus in the Tekmileh: (TA:) [but] AḤát says, in "the Book of Birds," أَبُو صُبَيْرَةَ, which is [the same as] ↑ أَبُو صَبِرَةَ, is [*a bird*] *red in the belly, black in the head and wings and tail, the rest of it being red, of the colour of* صَبِر: and the pl. is صَبِرَاتٌ and صُبَيْرَاتٌ. (O.)

صُبْرَةٌ *A quantity collected together,* of wheat [&c.], *without being measured or weighed,* (Ṣ,* M, Mṣb,* Ḳ,) *heaped up:* (TA:) pl. صُبَرٌ. (Ṣ, Mṣb.) You say, اِشْتَرَيْتُ الشَّىْءَ صُبْرَةً *I bought the thing without its being measured or weighed.* (Ṣ, Mṣb.) — And *Reaped grain collected together;* or *wheat collected together in the place where it is trodden out:* (M, TA:) or *when trodden out and thrashed.* (Mṣb in art. كدس.) — And *Wheat sifted* (M, Ḳ) *with a thing resembling a* سَرَنْد [or سِرَنْد, which is a Pers. word, here app. meaning a kind of net]. (M.) — And *Rough,* or *rugged, stones, collected together:* pl. صِبَارٌ. (M, Ḳ.) [See also صُبَارَةٌ.]

أَبُو صُبَيْرَةَ : see صَبْرَةٌ.

صُبَارٌ : see صُبَارَةٌ, in two places.

صُبَّارٌ (M, Ḳ) and ↑ صُبَّارٌ (Ḳ) The *fruit of a kind of tree, intensely acid, having a broad, red stone, brought from India, said to be* (M) the *tamarind,* (M, Ḳ,) *used as a medicine.* (M.)

صِبَارٌ *A stopper* [of a bottle]; syn. سِدَادٌ. (Ḳ. [See 4, last sentence.]) — And The *fruit of a certain acid tree.* (Ḳ. [But in this sense it is probably a mistake for صُبَّارٌ, q. v.])

صَبُورٌ : see صَابِرٌ, in four places.

صَبِيرٌ : see صَابِرٌ, in two places. — Also *A surety.* (Ṣ, M, Mṣb, Ḳ.) You say, هُوَ بِهِ صَبِيرٌ *He is a surety for him, or it.* (TA.) — And صَبِيرُ قَوْمٍ *The chief, head, director, conductor,* or *manager, of the affairs of a people,* or *party:* (M, Ḳ:) *he who is patient for, and with, a people,* or *party, in* [*the managing of*] *their affairs:* (A:) pl. صُبَرَآءُ. (M.) — [And accord. to Golius, *A solitary man, having neither offspring nor brother:* but app. a mistake for صُنْبُورٌ, which is thus expl. in the Ṣ in this art.] — Also, (Ṣ, M, Ḳ,) and ↑ صَبَارَةٌ, (M,) *A white cloud;* (M, Ḳ;) and so ↑ صَبْرٌ and ↑ صُبْرٌ, of which the pl. is أَصْبَارٌ: (Ḳ:) or *white clouds;* (M, Ḳ;) as also أَصْبَانٌ, pl. of ↑ صَبْرٌ and ↑ صُبْرٌ: (Fr, Yaạkoob, Ṣ:) or *white clouds that scarcely ever, or never, give rain:* (Ṣ:) or *clouds,* (M, Ḳ,) or *white clouds,* (Aṣ, Ṣ,) *that become disposed one above another* (Aṣ, Ṣ, M, Ḳ) *in the manner of steps:* (Aṣ, Ṣ, M:) or *a dense cloud that is above another cloud:* (M, Ḳ:) or *a stationary portion of cloud:* (Ḳ:) or *a portion of cloud which one sees as though it were* مَصْبُورَة, i. e. *detained;* but this explanation is of weak authority: or, accord. to AḤn, *clouds remaining stationary a day and a night;* as though detained: (M:) or *clouds in which are blackness and whiteness:* or, as some say, *clouds slow in motion, by reason of their heaviness and the abundance of their water:* (Ḥam p. 786:) the pl. of صَبِير is the same as the sing., (M,) or it is صُبُرٌ. (Ṣ, M, Ḳ.) — And صَبِيرٌ, *A mountain:* (O, Ḳ:) or الصَّبِيرُ is the name of a particular mountain. (TA.) — [And accord. to Freytag, as from the Ḳ, in which I do not find this meaning, *A hill consisting of stones.*] — Also صَبِيرٌ, (Ḳ,) i. e. (TA) the صَبِير of a خِوَان [or table, or thing upon which one eats], (M, A, TA,) *A thin, round cake of bread, which is spread beneath the food that one eats:* (M, A, Ḳ:) or (Ḳ, TA, but in the CḲ "and") *upon which the food to be eaten at a wedding-feast is ladled* (Ḳ, TA) *by the maker of the bread:* (TA:) also called ↑ صَبِيرَةٌ. (Ḳ.)

صَبَارَةٌ : see the next paragraph: — and see صُبْرَةٌ.

صُبَارَةٌ (Ṣ, M, Ḳ) and ↑ صِبَارَةٌ and ↑ صَبَارَةٌ (Ḳ) *Stones:* (Ṣ, M, Ḳ:) or *smooth stones:* (TA:) or صُبَارَةٌ signifies, (M,) or صُبَارَةٌ signifies also, (Ḳ,) *a piece of stone,* or *portion of stones:* or *of iron.* (M, Ḳ.) A poet says, (Ṣ,) namely, El-Aạshà, (M,) or 'Amr Ibn-Milḳaț Eț-Țá-ee, addressing 'Amr Ibn-Hind, who had a brother slain, (IB,)

مَنْ مُبْلِغٌ عَمْرًا بِأَنَّ الْمَرْءَ لَمْ يُخْلَقْ صُبَارَهْ

(so in the Ṣ; but in the M and TA this verse is given differently, with شَيْبَانَ and أَنَّ in the places of عَمْرًا and بِأَنَّ; and it is said in the M that accord. to one relation the last word is صِيَارَهْ, [with ى,] which, it is added, is like صُبَارَهْ in meaning;) [i. e. *Who will tell 'Amr,* or *Sheybán, that man was not created stones?*] but IB says that the last word is correctly صِبَارَهْ, with kesr to the ص; and the poet means, man is not stone, that he should patiently endure the like of this: (TA:) [J says,] accord. to one relation, the last word is صَبَارَهْ, with fet-ḥ, which is pl. of ↑ صَبَارٌ, the ة being affixed to denote its being a pl. pl., for صَبَارٌ is pl. of ↑ صَبْرَةٌ, signifying *strong,* or *hard, stones:* [and he adds,] El-Aạshà says,

قُبَيْلَ الصُّبْحِ أَصْوَاتُ الصَّبَارِ ↑

(Ṣ:) but IB says that صَبَارٌ and صَبَارَةٌ are not pls. of صَبْرَةٌ; for فَعَالٌ is not a pl. form, but فِعَالٌ, with kesr, like حِجَارٌ and جِبَالٌ: (TA:) [and it is said that] the verse from which this is cited is not by El-Aạshà, and is correctly and completely as follows:

كَأَنَّ تَرَنُّمَ الْهَاجَاتِ فِيهَا
قُبَيْلَ الصُّبْحِ أَصْوَاتُ الصِّيَارِ

by الصيار being meant the صَنْج, (TṢ, Ḳ, TA,) the stringed instrument thus called: (TṢ, TA:)

accord. to the reading given in the Ṣ, the verse means, *As though the croaking of the frogs in it, a little before daybreak, were the sounds of falling stones:* and this is correct. (TA.) ═ See also صَبِرٌ.

صِبَارَةٌ: see the next preceding paragraph.

رَجُلٌ صَبُورَةٌ: see مَصْبُورٌ.

صَبِيرَةٌ: see صَبِيرٌ, last sentence.

أَبُو صُبَيْرَةَ: see صُبْرَةٌ.

صَبَارَّةٌ, [respecting the form of which see حَمَارَّةٌ,] (Ṣ, M, Ḳ,) and ▼ صَبَارَةٌ, without teshdeed, (Lḥ, M, Ḳ,) and ▼ صَبْرَةٌ, (Ḳ,) The *intenseness of the cold* (Ṣ, M, Ḳ) of winter: (Ṣ, M:) and [in an absolute sense] *intenseness* of cold: (TA:) and ▼ صَبْرَةٌ signifies also the *middle* of winter; (Ḳ;) and so ▼ صَوْبَرَةٌ. (TA.)

صَبَّارٌ: see صَابِرٌ, in two places. — أُمُّ صَبَّارٍ (Ṣ, M, A, Ḳ) and ▼ أُمُّ صَبُورٍ, (Ḳ,) or the former only is meant in the Ḳ as having the first of the significations here following, (TA,) *A stony tract, of which the stones are black and worn and crumbling, as though burned with fire;* syn. حَرَّةٌ; (T, Ṣ, M, A, &c.;) for which حَرٌّ is erroneously put in copies of the Ḳ: (TA:) from ▼ صُبْرٌ, q. v.; (Ṣ, M;) or from صُبَارَةٌ: or, accord. to some, *such as is level, abounding with stones, and difficult to walk upon:* (M:) or the former is [*the tract called*] حَرَّةُ لَيْلَى, and [that called] حَرَّةُ النَّارِ: (El-Fezáree:) or it has the first of the above-mentioned significations, and signifies also *a* [*mountain, or hill, such as is termed*] هَضْبَة: (ISk:) or *smooth rock upon which nothing makes an impression:* but the latter, accord. to Aboo-'Amr Esh-Sheybánee, signifies *a* هَضْبَة *without a pass.* (ISh.) — Also أُمُّ صَبَّارٍ (M, Ḳ) and ▼ أُمُّ صَبُورٍ (Ṣ, M, Ḳ) *A calamity,* or *misfortune:* and *a severe war:* (M, Ḳ:) or the latter, *a distressing case.* (Ṣ.) One says, وَقَعُوا فِى أُمِّ صَبَّارٍ (M) and ▼ أُمِّ صَبُورٍ, (Ṣ, M) *They fell into a calamity,* &c.: (M:) or the latter, *they fell into a distressing case:* (Ṣ:) or *into a perplexing and distressing case, from which they could not escape, like the* هَضْبَة, *above mentioned, without a pass:* (Aboo-'Amr Esh-Sheybánee:) but in some of the copies of the "Alfádh" [of ISk], أُمُّ صَبُورٍ, as though derived from صَبَارَةٌ, signifying "stones." (TA.)

صُبَّارٌ: see صَبَّارٌ.

أُمُّ صَبُورٍ: see صَبَّارٌ, in three places.

صَبَّارَةٌ *Rugged ground, rising above the adjacent part or parts, and hard,* (Ḳ, TA,) *in which is no herbage, and which produces none:* or i. q. أُمُّ صَبَّارٍ. (TA.) ═ See also صَبِرٌ.

صَابِرٌ and ▼ صَبُورٌ, (M, Ḳ,) the latter of which is also applied to a female, without ة, (M,) and ▼ صَبِيرٌ (M, Ḳ) and ▼ صَبَّارٌ, (M,) are epithets from صَبَرَ "he was patient, or enduring:" (M, Ḳ:) the five following epithets are said to denote different degrees of patience: صَابِرٌ is the most general of them [in signification, meaning simply *Patient,* or *enduring*]: ▼ مُصْطَبِرٌ signifies *acquiring patience;* and *tried with patience:* ▼ مُتَصَبِّرٌ, *constraining himself to be patient:* ▼ صَبُورٌ, *having great patience;* [or *very patient;*] *whose patience is greater than that of others;* [as also ▼ صَبِيرٌ; or this signifies *rendered patient,* from صَبَرَهُ;] denoting quality, or manner: and ▼ صَبَّارٌ, *having an intense degree of patience;* [or *having very great patience;*] denoting measure, and quantity: the pl. of ▼ صَبُورٌ is صُبُرٌ. (TA.) As an epithet applied to God, (Aboo-Is-ḥáḳ [i. e. Zj],) ▼ الصَّبُورُ signifies *The Clement,* or *Forbearing, who does not hastily avenge Himself upon the disobedient, but forgives,* or *defers:* (Aboo-Is-ḥáḳ, Ḳ:) [it may be well rendered *The Long-suffering:*] it is an intensive epithet. (TA.) One says also, هُوَ صَابِرٌ عَلَى البَرْدِ ‡ [*He is a patient endurer of cold*]. (A.)

صَنَبِرٌ; &c.: see art. صنبر.

صَوْبَرَةٌ: see صَبَارَّةٌ.

صَابُورَةٌ *Ballast of a ship;* the *weight that is put in the bottom of a ship.* (TA.)

أَصْبَرُ [*More,* and *most, patient* or *enduring*]. أَصْبَرُ مِنْ حِمَارٍ [*More patient than an ass*] is a prov. (Meyd.) And one says, هُوَ أَصْبَرُ عَلَى الضَّرْبِ مِنَ الأَرْضِ ‡ [*He is more patient of beating than the ground*]. (A.) [The fem.] صُبْرَى is applied to a she-camel by Ḥoneyf El-Ḥanátim [as meaning *Surpassingly patient* or *enduring*]. (IAạr, TA in art. بهى.)

أَصْبِرَةٌ Sheep or goats, and camels, *that return in the evening and morning to their owners, not remaining away from them:* (M, Ḳ:*) [a pl.] having no sing.: (Ḳ:) [ISd says,] I have not heard any sing. of it. (M.)

مَصْبُورٌ [pass. part. n. of 1, q. v. *Confined,* &c. —] *Confined* [*with bonds* or *otherwise*], (Ḳ,) or *set up,* (M,) *to be put to death:* (M, Ḳ:) and ▼ رَجُلٌ صَبُورَةٌ *a man confined,* (Ḳ,) or *set up,* (M,) *to be put to death;* (M, Ḳ;) i. q. مَصْبُورٌ لِلْقَتْلِ: (Th, M, Ḳ:) and مَصْبُورَةٌ, applied to a beast (بَهِيمَة, A), *confined* [or *bound*] *to be put to death* [*and in that state killed by arrows or the like*]; i. q. مَحْبُوسَةٌ عَلَى المَوْتِ: such is forbidden to be eaten. (Ṣ, A.) — مَصْبُورَةٌ applied to an oath: see صَبْرٌ. ═ Also *Made into a* صُبْرَة, *like a* صُبْرَة *of wheat; so gathered or collected together.* (TA.)

مُصْطَبِرٌ: see صَابِرٌ. [مصطبر is expl. by Reiske as signifying *Collecta caro* (ὄγκος τῆς σαρκός): mentioned by Freytag: if so, it is app. مُصْطَبَرٌ: see its verb.]

مُتَصَبِّرٌ: see صَابِرٌ.

صبع

1\. صَبَعَ بِهِ, aor. ـَ, (AZ, Ṣ, Ḳ,) inf. n. صَبْعٌ, (AZ, Ṣ,) *He pointed at him,* or *towards him, with his finger,* (بِإِصْبَعِهِ,) *disparagingly:* (AZ, Ṣ, Ḳ:) or, as some say, *he meant some evil thing to him when he* (the latter) *was inadvertent, not knowing.* (TA.) — And صَبَعَ فُلَانًا عَلَى فُلَانٍ *He directed such a one to such a one by pointing,* or *indication:* (Ṣ, Ḳ:) because, when one directs a man to a way, or road, or to a thing that is latent, or obscure, he points towards it with the finger. (TA.) One says, مَا صَبَعَكَ عَلَيْنَا *What directed thee to us?* (TA.) And صَبَعَ بَيْنَ القَوْمِ *He directed others to the people,* or *party.* (TA.) Of one who magnifies himself, or acts proudly, in his government, or administration, one says, ▼ صَبَعَهُ الشَّيْطَانُ † [app. meaning *The Devil has directed him*]: and أَدْرَكَتْهُ أَصَابِعُ الشَّيْطَانِ [*The fingers of the Devil have reached him*]. (TA. [See the pass. part. n. below.]) — And one says, قُرِّبَ إِلَيْهِ طَعَامٌ فَمَا صَبَعَ فِيهِ i. e. [*Food was presented,* or *offered, to him,* or *was placed,* or *put, before him, and*] *he did not put his finger into it.* (TA.) [See also صَبَأَ, near the end.] — And صَبَعَ الدَّجَاجَةَ, (O, Ḳ,) inf. n. as above, (TA,) *He inserted his finger into the hen in order that he might know if she were* [*near*] *laying an egg or not:* (O, Ḳ:) mentioned by Z. (TA.) — And صَبَعَ الإِنَآءَ *He put his finger upon the vessel so that what was in another vessel flowed upon it* [*into the former vessel*]: (A'Obeyd, Ṣ, O, Ḳ:) or, as some say, *he put together his two fingers,* [*or two of his fingers,*] *then discharged,* or *let flow, what was in the vessel,* of wine, or beverage, *into a thing with a narrow head* [or *mouth*]: or, accord. to Az, *he discharged,* or *let flow, what was in the vessel,* of wine, or beverage, *between the extremities of* [*either of*] *his two thumbs and fore fingers, in order that it might not become scattered, and pour forth copiously.* (TA.) — And صَبَعَهُ, inf. n. as above, *He hit,* or *hurt, his finger.* (TA.) ═ صَبَعَ عَلَى القَوْمِ, inf. n. as above, meaning *He came forth upon the people,* or *party,* is said to be originally صَبَأَ, with ء. (TA.)

[4. اصبع, followed by عَلَى, is said by Freytag, as on the authority of Meyd, to signify *He* (a pastor) *fed and managed well* his cattle: but this is perhaps taken from a mistranscription of the saying, mentioned by Meyd, لِلرَّاعِى عَلَى مَاشِيَتِهِ إِصْبَعٌ, q. v. infrà.]

صَبْعٌ ‡ *Self-magnification,* or *pride;* (O, Ḳ, TA;) *such as is consummate;* (TA;) and *haughtiness,* or *insolence,* or *vain glory;* (O, TA;) and ▼ مَصْبَعَةٌ signifies the same. (O, Ḳ, TA.)

صَبْعٌ i. q. صَبْحٌ [q. v.]: the ع being substituted for the ح. (MF on the letter ع.)

إِصْبَعٌ and أُصْبَعٌ and إِصْبِعٌ and أَصْبُعٌ and أُصْبِعٌ (Ṣ, O, Mṣb, Ḳ) and إِصْبُعٌ and أَصْبَعٌ (O, Mṣb, Ḳ) and أَصْبِعٌ and أُصْبُعٌ, the ء being thus trebly vowelled, and the ب likewise (Mṣb, Ḳ) with every one of the vowellings of the ء, (Ḳ,) and ▼ أُصْبُوعٌ also, (Mṣb, Ḳ,) of all which forms the first is the [only] one commonly known and the one approved by persons of chaste speech, (Mṣb,) all mentioned by Kr, (Ḳ,) and by Lḥ also on the authority of Yoo, (TA,) *A finger:* and *a toe:* (MA, KL, &c.:) of the fem. gender, (Mṣb,) or fem. and masc., (Ṣ, O, Mṣb, Ḳ,*) but generally fem.: (O, Mṣb, Ḳ:*) pl. (of اصبع, MA) أَصَابِعُ and (of اصبوع, MA) أَصَابِيعُ. (MA, Ḳ.) — One says, بِهِمْ تُثْنَى الأَصَابِعُ [*With the mention of them the fingers are bent*]; meaning that they are reckoned as the best, [or among the best,] for the best are not many. (M, on a verse cited in the first paragraph of art. ثنى.) [See also two similar exs. in the first paragraph of art. حنو and حنى.] — And لِلرَّاعِى عَلَى مَاشِيَتِهِ إِصْبَعٌ ‡ [*The pastor has a finger pointing at his cattle,* or camels or sheep or goats]; meaning, [has upon his cattle] *an impress of a good state* or *condition;* (Ṣ, Ḳ,* TA;) i. e. they are pointed at with the fingers because of their goodliness and fatness and good tending. (TA.) [See also a verse cited voce صُلْبٌ.] And similar to this saying is the prov., عَلَيْهِ مِنَ ٱللّٰهِ تَعَالَى إِصْبَعٌ حَسَنٌ, meaning † [*Upon him is, from God,* (*acknowledged be his absolute supremacy,*)] *an impress of a good state* or *condition.* (Meyd.) And one says also, إِنَّهُ لَحَسَنُ الإِصْبَعِ فِى مَالِهِ, meaning † *Verily he is good in respect of the impress upon his cattle* [*indicative of their state* or *condition*]. (IAạr, TA.) — And فُلَانٌ مُغِلُّ الإِصْبَعِ ‡ *Such a one is unfaithful, treacherous,* or *perfidious.* (O, Ḳ,* TA.*) — And لَهُ إِصْبَعٌ فِى هٰذَا الأَمْرِ ‡ [*He has a finger in this affair*]. (TA.) — The Prophet said قَلْبُ المُؤْمِنِ بَيْنَ إِصْبَعَيْنِ مِنْ أَصَابِعِ ٱللّٰهِ يُقَلِّبُهُ كَيْفَ شَآءَ ‡ [*The heart of the believer is between two of the fingers of God: He turneth it about as He pleaseth*]. (O.) — And a man says, in respect of a difficult affair, when he has been made to have recourse to a strong man, able to bear his burden, إِنَّهُ يَأْتِى عَلَيْهِ بِإِصْبَعٍ وَاحِدَةٍ † [*Verily he will make an end of it with one finger*]: and إِنَّهُ يَكْفِيهِ بِصُغْرَى أَصَابِعِهِ † [*Verily the smallest of his fingers will suffice him* for its accomplishment; the ب thus prefixed to the agent being redundant, as in كَفَى بِٱللّٰهِ شَهِيدًا and many other instances]. (O.) — أَبُو الإِصْبَعِ is one of the surnames of *The Devil.* (TA. [See صَبْغَةُ الشَّيْطَانِ, above.]) — [إِصْبَعٌ signifies also † *A prong,* as resembling a finger: so in the Ṣ and Ḳ in art. حفر, and in other instances.] — أَصَابِعُ الفَتَيَاتِ, (O, TṢ, Ḳ,) in the "Minháj" of Ibn-Jezleh اصابع الفتيان, [app. a mistranscription,] and in the L اصابع البُنَيَّاتِ, (TA,) † [*Common clinopodium,* or *wild basil,*] *the sweet-smelling plant called in Pers.* الفَرَنْجَمُشْك, (AḤn, O, Ḳ,) which grows abundantly in the southern parts of Arabia, and is not depastured by any animal. (AḤn, O.) — أَصَابِعُ العَذَارَى † *A species of grapes,* (AḤn, O, Ḳ,) *black,* (AḤn, O,) *long, like the acorn, likened to the dyed fingers of virgins;* (AḤn, O, Ḳ;*) *the bunch thereof is about a cubit* [*in length*], *compact* [so I render مُتَدَاخِس, supposing it to be similar to دخيس applied to herbage &c.,] *in the grapes; its raisins are good; and it grows in the Saráh* (السَّرَاة). (AḤn, O.) — أَصَابِعُ هُرْمُسَ † *The flowers* (فُقَّاح) *of the* سُورَنْجَان [or *Hermodactylus* (the *Iris* of Linn.?) now applied to *meadow-saffron, a species of colchicum*]; (O, Ḳ;) *the potency of which is like that of the* سورنجان [*itself*]. (TA.) — أَصَابِعُ فِرْعَوْنَ † [*Certain things*] *resembling the* مَرَاوِيد [or مَرَاوِد *with which* كُحْل *is applied*], *of the length of the finger,* (Ḳ, TA,) *red;* (TA;) *brought from the Sea of El-Ḥijáz; of proved efficacy for the speedy consolidation of wounds.* (Ḳ.) — أَصَابِعُ صُفْرٍ † *The root* (أَصْل) *of a certain plant of which the form is like the hand,* (O, Ḳ,) *variegated with yellowness and whiteness, hard, and having a little sweetness; and there is a species thereof yellow, with a dust-colour, but without whiteness:* (O, TA:) so says Ibn-Jezleh: (TA:) *it is beneficial as a remedy for madness,* or *diabolical possession, and for poisons,* (Ḳ, TA,) *and the sting,* or *bite, of venomous,* or *noxious, reptiles,* or *the like, and it acts as a dissolvent of thick excrescences.* (TA.) — As a measure, إِصْبَعٌ signifies [*A digit;* i. e. *a finger's breadth;*] the *width of six moderate-sized barley-corns;* (Mṣb voce جَرِيبٌ;) the *fourth part of the* قَبْضَة. (Mgh and Mṣb ibid.)

أُصْبُوعٌ: see إِصْبَعٌ, first sentence.

مَصْبَعَةٌ: see صُبْعٌ.

مَصْبُوعٌ ‡ *Self-magnifying,* or *proud.* (IAạr, O, Ḳ, TA.)

صبغ

1. صَبَغَهُ, aor. ـُ and ـَ (Ṣ, O, Mṣb, Ḳ, the former not in the copy of the Ḳ used by SM) and ـِ, (Fr, O, Mṣb, Ḳ,) inf. n. صَبْغٌ (Ṣ, O, Mṣb, Ḳ) and صِبَغٌ (Aṣ, O, Ḳ) and صِبْغَةٌ, (AḤn, TA,) [of which last, صِبْغَة (q. v.), also said to be an inf. n., is perhaps a contraction, or, as is said in the Ksh ii. 132, it means a mode, or manner, of صَبْغ,] *He dyed it,* or *coloured it;* (Ḳ, TA;) namely, a garment, or piece of cloth; (Ṣ, O, Mṣb, TA;) and white, or hoary, hair, and the like. (TA.) [It is said that] the primary meaning of الصَّبْغُ in the language of the Arabs is *The altering* [a thing]: and hence صَبِغَ الثَّوْبُ, meaning *The garment,* or *piece of cloth, was altered in colour* to blackness or redness or yellowness [&c.]. (TA.) — [Hence,] صَبَغَ اللُّقْمَةَ, aor. ـُ, inf. n. صَبْغٌ, † *He moistened the mouthful with oil* or *grease* [or *any kind of* صِبْغ i. e. *sauce* &c.]; and *he dipped it,* or *immersed it;* and in like manner any other thing. (TA.) [Thus] one says, صَبَغَ يَدَهُ بِالمَآءِ (Aṣ, O, Ḳ) and فِى المَآءِ (TA) ‡ *He dipped,* or *immersed, his hand,* or *arm, in the water.* (Aṣ, O, Ḳ, TA.) And صَبَغَتِ النَّاقَةُ مَشَافِرَهَا فِى المَآءِ (Aṣ, O) or بِالمَآءِ (TA) † *The she-camel dipped her lips in the water.* (Aṣ, O, TA.) — [Hence also,] the term صَبْغٌ is used by the Christians as meaning † The *dipping,* or *immersing,* of their children, [i. e. *baptizing* them,] *in water.* (Az, Ṣ,* TA.) One says, صَبَغَ وَلَدَهُ فِى النَّصْرَانِيَّةِ, inf. n. [صَبْغٌ (as shown in the next preceding sentence) and] صِبْغَةٌ, † *He introduced his child into the Christian communion,* it is said, *by dipping,* or *immersing, him in the water of baptism.* (TA.) And صَبَغَ وَلَدَهُ فِى اليَهُودِيَّةِ † *He introduced his child into the Jewish communion* [probably *by baptism combined with circumcision:* but see صِبْغَةٌ, an explanation of which seems to indicate that circumcision alone is meant in this case]. (TA.) — And يَصْبُغُونَ الحَدِيثَ † *They colour and alter information,* or *discourse.* (O.) — And صَبَغُوهُ فِى عَيْنِهِ † *They altered him in his estimation;* and *informed him that he had become altered from the state in which he was.* (TA.) And it is said that صَبَغُونِى فِى عَيْنِكَ and صَبَغُونِى عِنْدَكَ mean *They pointed me out to thee as one who would accomplish what thou desiredst of me;* from the saying of the Arabs, صَبَغْتُ الرَّجُلَ بِعَيْنِى and بِيَدِى *I pointed at the man with my eye* and *with my hand:* (O, Ḳ:*) but Az says that this is a mistake; that the Arabs when they mean thus say صَبَعْتُ, with the unpointed ع. (O.) — One says also, صَبَغَ يَدَهُ بِالعِلْمِ, (Mṣb,) or بِفَنٍّ مِنَ العِلْمِ, and بِالعَمَلِ, (TA,) ‡ *He laboured in science,* [or *in a species of science* or *knowledge,* and *in work,*] *and became notable therein* [or *thereby*]. (Mṣb.) = صَبَغَ ضَرْعُهَا, inf. n. صُبُوغٌ, ‡ *Her udder became full, and goodly in colour:* (O, Ḳ, TA:) said of a camel. (O, TA.) — And صَبَغَتْ عَضَلَتُهُ, (O, Ḳ,) aor. ـَ, (O, TA,) inf. n. صُبُوغٌ, (TA,) said of a man, (O,) *His* عضلة [or *muscle*] *became long:* (O, Ḳ:) like سَبَغَتْ. (O, TA.) And صَبَغَ الثَّوْبُ, inf. n. صُبُوغٌ, *The garment,* or *piece of cloth, was long and ample:* a dial. var. of سَبَغَ. (TA.) = And صَبَغَ فِى الطَّعَامِ, aor. ـَ, *He* [app. a camel] *put his head into the food:* as also صَبَأَ. (O.) And صَبَغَتِ الإِبِلُ فِى الرَّعْىِ [*The camels put their heads into the pasture,* or *herbage*]. (O, TA.) And صَبَغَتْ فِيهَا رَأْسَهَا [or فِيهِ, *She put her head into it*]; like صَبَأَتْ. (TA.)

2. صبّغت ثِيَابَهَا *She* (a woman) *dyed her garments much.* (O.) = صَبَّغَتِ الرُّطَبَةُ, (Ṣ, A, TA,) or البُسْرَةُ, (O, L, TA,) inf. n. تَصْبِيغٌ, (L, TA,) i. q. ذَنَّبَتْ ‡ [i. e. *The ripening date,* or *the full-grown unripe date, began to ripen,* or *showed ripening,* or *became speckled by reason of ripening,* or *ripened, at the part next the base and stalk*]: (Ṣ, O, L, TA:) or *became coloured.* (A, TA.) And ▼ اصبغت النَّخْلَةُ ‡ *The palm-tree showed ripening in its dates;* (O, Ḳ, TA;) as also صَبَّغَتْ, inf. n. as above: (Ḳ:) or, accord. to Az, تصبيغ in relation to the palm-tree [itself] is not known. (TA.) — And صَبَّغَتِ النَّاقَةُ, (Az, O, Ḳ,) inf. n. as above, † *The she-camel cast her young one when its hair had grown;* as also ▼ اصبغت: (O, Ḳ:) but سَبَّغَتْ, with س, which means the same, is more commonly used. (Az, O, TA.)

4: see 2, in two places. — أَصْبَغَ ٱللّٰهُ عَلَيْهِ النِّعَمَ

is a dial. var. of أَسْبَغَهَا, (O, Ḳ,*) meaning *God rendered benefits*, or *boons, complete, full*, or *ample, to him.* (O.)

5. تَصَبَّغَ فِى الدِّينِ is from الصِّبْغَةُ, (Lḥ, O, Ḳ,) and means † *He became settled*, or *established, in religion:* (TḲ:) and so تَصَبَّغَ صِبْغَةً حَسَنَةً; expl. by Z as meaning † *He was*, or *became, in a good state* [*in respect of religion*]. (TA.)

8. اصطبغ بِكَذَا *It was*, or *became, dyed*, or *coloured, with such a thing.* (TA. [There said to be tropical; but this I doubt.]) — And اصطبغ بِالصِّبْغِ, (Ṣ,* O, Ḳ,) or بِالخَلِّ, (El-Fárábee, Mgh, Mṣb,) and the like, and, as some say, مِنَ الخَلِّ, (Mṣb,) or فِى الخَلِّ, (Mgh, [so in my copy, but app. a mistranscription,]) ‡ *He made use of what is termed* صِبْغ [or *sauce*, &c.], (O, Ḳ, TA,) or *vinegar*, (TA,) *to render his bread savoury;* (O, Ḳ, TA;) الصِّبْغ including olive-oil, as well as vinegar, and similar seasonings. (TA.) One may not say, اصطبغ الخُبْزَ بِخَلٍّ. (Mgh, Mṣb.) — اصطبغ also signifies † *He made*, or *prepared, what is termed* صِبْغ [i. e. *sauce*, &c.]. (TA.)

صِبْغٌ (AZ, Aṣ, Ṣ, Mgh, O, Mṣb, Ḳ) and ▼ صِبْغَةٌ (Ṣ, O, Mṣb, Ḳ) and ▼ صِبَغٌ, (O, Ḳ,) or this is an inf. n., differing from صِبْغ, (AZ, Aṣ, L,) and ▼ صِبَاغٌ, (Mgh, O, Mṣb, Ḳ,) as some say, (O,) or this last is a pl. of the first, (O,* Mṣb,) [or] the pl. of صِبْغ is أَصْبَاغٌ, (Ṣ,) *A dye;* (AZ, Aṣ, Ṣ, Mgh, O, Mṣb, Ḳ;) *used for colouring clothes* [&c.]: (TA:) the pl. of ▼ صِبَاغ is أَصْبِغَةٌ; and أَصَابِيغُ is a pl. pl. [i. e. pl. of أَصْبَاغ]. (TA.) — [Hence, app.,] one says of a girl, or young woman, when one first takes her as a concubine, or when he first has her conducted to him as a bride, (AZ, O,) or when one first marries her, (Ḳ,) إِنَّهَا لَحَدِيثَةُ الصِّبْغِ † [*Verily she is one newly taken as a concubine*, or *a bride:* app. alluding to the recent application of the dye of the ḥinnà]. (AZ, O, Ḳ.) And one says also, مَا أَخَذْتُهُ بِصِبْغِ الثَّمَنِ, (AZ, O,) or مَا أَخَذَهُ بِصِبْغِ ثَمَنِهِ, (Ḳ,) i. e. [*I did not*, or *he did not, take it*, or *acquire it,*] *for its proper price*, [app. meaning *its cost-price*, or *primo-cost*,] but for a high [or raised] price. (AZ, O, Ḳ.*) — صِبْغ also signifies, (Ṣ, Mgh, O, Mṣb, TA,) and so does ▼ صِبَاغ, (Mgh, TA,) or the latter is pl. of the former, (Ṣ, O, TA,) ‡ *A seasoning*, or *condiment, for bread, to render it savoury;* (Ṣ, Mgh, O, Mṣb, TA;) particularly (Mṣb) *such as is fluid*, (Mgh in art. ادم, and Mṣb,) *as vinegar*, (Mgh, Mṣb, TA,) *and olive-oil*, (Mgh, TA,) *and the like*, (Mṣb, TA,) [i. e. any *sauce*,] *in which the bread is dipped:* (Mṣb:) so called because the bread is dipped in it, (Mgh, TA,) and coloured thereby: (Mgh:) the pl. of ▼ صِبَاغ is أَصْبِغَةٌ: one says, كَثُرَتِ الأَصْبِغَةُ عَلَى المَائِدَةِ ‡ [*The sauces*, or *fluid seasonings, were abundant upon the table*]. (TA.) صِبْغ is used in this sense, but not explained, in the Ḳ. (TA.) Hence, in the Ḳur [xxiii. 20], وَصِبْغٍ لِلْآكِلِينَ † [*And a sauce for those that eat*]; (Ṣ, O, Mṣb, TA;) where it means, accord. to Fr, *olive-oil;* but accord. to Zj, *the olive* [itself]; and Az prefers the latter explanation: (TA:) some read ▼ وَصِبَاغٍ. (Bd.)

صَبَغٌ, in a horse, The *having the whole of the fetlock white, without its whiteness conjoining with that of what is termed* التَّحْجِيل [q. v.]. (TA.)

صِبَغٌ: see صِبْغ, first sentence.

صُبْغَةٌ, in a sheep or goat, or in a ewe, † *Whiteness of the extremity of the tail;* the quality denoted by the epithet صَبْغَآءُ. (TA.) — Also † *A date that has become partly ripe*, i. e. *ripe in a part thereof.* (O, Ḳ.)

صِبْغَةٌ: see صِبْغ, first sentence. — It also means † *Religion*, syn. دِينٌ, (AA, O, Ḳ,) and مِلَّةٌ; (Ḳ;) and the *religious law*, syn. شَرِيعَةٌ; (TA;) and *anything whereby one advances himself in the favour of God:* (AA, TA:) [thus,] in the Ḳur [ii. 132], (O, TA,) صِبْغَةَ ٱللّٰهِ means *the religion of God*, syn. دِينَ ٱللّٰهِ, (O, Mṣb, Ḳ,) or فِطْرَةَ ٱللّٰهِ, (Ṣ, Mṣb,) which is the meaning of فِطْرَةَ ٱللّٰهِ; (Mṣb;) *the religion of God, with an adaptation to which mankind are created;* because its effect appears in him who has it like the dye in the garment; (Bḍ, Jel;) or because it intermingles in the heart like the dye in the garment; (Bḍ;) and it is said to be from the Christians' صَبْغ [or صِبْغَة i. e. *baptism*] of their children in a sort of water that they have; (Ṣ; [and the like is said in the O, and Ksh, &c.;]) صبغة being in this instance in the accus. case as an objective complement; (Mṣb;) for the meaning is "follow ye the religion of God;" (O, Mṣb;) or "we will follow the religion of God:" (O:) or it means *that which God has prescribed* to Moḥammad; i. e. *circumcision:* (O, Ḳ:) or صبغة is in this instance an inf. n., (Ksh, Bḍ, Jel,) signifying *a mode*, or *manner of*, صَبْغ [i. e. of *baptism*], (Ksh,) relating to the baptism of the Christians, (Ksh, Bḍ,) a corroborative of the saying آمَنَّا [in verse 130], as such put in the accusative case, (Ksh, Bḍ, Jel,) by reason of a verb understood, (Jel,) the meaning being صَبَغَنَا ٱللّٰهُ صِبْغَتَهُ [*God hath baptized us with his baptism*]; (Ksh, Bḍ, Jel;*) [so that صِبْغَةُ ٱللّٰهِ signifies *the baptism of God*, and may here be rendered We have received *the baptism of God;*] the Muslims being hereby commanded to say to the Christians, "Say ye, God hath baptized us (صَبَغَنَا) with the faith, with a baptism (صِبْغَة) not like ours [i. e. not like our Christian baptism], and purified us with a purifying not like ours;" or the Muslims being hereby commanded to say [of themselves], "God hath baptized us (صَبَغَنَا) with the faith, as a baptism (صِبْغَة), and we have not been baptized with your baptism (لَمْ نُصْبَغْ صِبْغَتَكُمْ)." (Ksh.)

صِبْغِىٌّ a rel. n. from صِبْغ. (Mṣb.) — [*A seller of dyes.* (Golius, on the authority of Meyd.)]

صِبَاغٌ: see صِبْغ, in five places.

صَبِيغٌ i. q. ▼ مَصْبُوغٌ [i. e. *Dyed*]; applied to a garment, or piece of cloth: and also used as a pl., applied to garments, or pieces of cloth. (L, TA.) [See also مُصَبَّغ.]

صِبَاغَةٌ The *craft*, or *art, of the dyer.* (O.)

صَبَّاغٌ *A dyer* (O, L, Ḳ) *of garments.* (O, Ḳ.) — And [hence,] † *A liar:* (Ḳ:) *one who colours and alters information*, or *discourse.* (O, Ḳ.*) The Prophet is related to have said, أَكْذَبُ النَّاسِ الصَّبَّاغُونَ وَالصَّوَّاغُونَ or مِنْ أَكْذَبِ النَّاسِ الخ [Which may mean *The most lying of men*, or *of the most lying of men, are the dyers and the goldsmiths;* or † *those who colour, and those who transform, information*, or *discourse*]: El-Khaṭṭábee says, the meaning is, that the persons who practise the two crafts to which these words relate make many promises as to returning the goods, and often break their promises; wherefore they are said to be of the most lying of men; not that every one of them is one who lies: but he adds that it has been said to mean the moulding and colouring of speech with falsehood. (O.)

نَاقَةٌ صَابِغٌ, (O, Ḳ,) without ة, (O,) *A she-camel having her udder full, and goodly in colour.* (O, Ḳ.) — And إِبِلٌ صَابِغَةٌ فِى الرَّعْىِ [meaning *Camels putting their heads into the pasture*], with ة. (O. [See 1, last sentence but one.])

أَصْبَغُ † A horse *white in the forelock*, (AO, Ṣ, Mgh, O, Ḳ,) *all of it:* (AO, Mgh: [see also أَسْعَفُ:]) or *white in the extremities of his tail:* (Ṣ, O:) or *white in the extremities of the ear:* (Ḳ:) when the whiteness is in his tail, he is termed أَشْعَلُ: or, accord. to AO, it signifies also *white in the whole of the tail, including its extremities.* (TA.) And ‡ A bird *white in the tail:* (Ṣ, O, Ḳ, TA:) or, accord. to the book entitled "Ghareeb el-Ḥamám" by El-Ḥasan Ibn-'Abd-Allah El-Iṣbahánee El-Kátib, *white in the whole of the head;* but used in the former sense by the keepers of pigeons. (TA.) And [the fem.] صَبْغَآءُ † A sheep or goat (شَاةٌ, Ṣ, O, Ḳ) or a ewe (AZ, TA) *white in the extremity of its tail*, (AZ, Ṣ, O, Ḳ, TA,) *the rest of it* (i. e. of the animal) *being black.* (TA.) — Also † *A species of weak birds.* (TA.) — Also, (applied to a man, O,) ‡ One *who voids his excrement* (O, Ḳ, TA) *in his clothes* (Ḳ, TA) *when he is beaten* (O, Ḳ, TA) and *when he is frightened:* mentioned by Z. (TA.) — And صَبْغَآءُ, † *A certain tree*, or *plant*, (شَجَرَةٌ,) *like the* ثُمَام [which is applied to several species of panic grass], *having a white fruit, growing in sands:* (Ḳ:) [but this seems to have been taken from three different explanations, here following:] accord. to Aboo-Ziyád, *a certain tree*, or *plant, that grows in the sands, resembling the* ضَعَة [which is applied to a species of the ثُمَام], *which is one of the abodes of the gazelles in the hot season, lurking-places being excavated by them at its roots:* accord. to another, of the Arabs of the desert, *it is like the* ثُمَام, but the ضَعَة *is larger in the leaves, and of a brighter green:* accord. to

Aboo-Naṣr, *a certain tree*, or *plant, having a white fruit.* (O.) And, (O, Ḳ,) as some say, (O,) † *A bunch of herbage, of which, when it comes up, the upper portions are green on the side next the sun, and white on the side next the shade.* (O, Ḳ.) —— Also (i. e. أَصْبَغ) The *greatest of torrents.* (Ibn-'Abbád, O, Ḳ.) [In this sense, though used as a subst., it seems to be, as in other senses, imperfectly decl., being originally an epithet: if not originally an epithet, it might, accord. to some authorities, be perfectly decl.]

مُصْبِغٌ [without ة] ‡ A palm-tree (نَخْلَةٌ) *showing ripening in its dates.* (O, TA.)

[مَصْبَغَةٌ *A dye-house:* so in the language of the present day.]

مُصَبَّغٌ *Dyed much.* (O.) In the phrase ثِيَابٌ مُصَبَّغَةٌ, [it is said that] the epithet is with teshdeed لِلْكَثْرَةِ [which means to denote muchness, and also to denote application to many objects, so that it may be rendered either *Garments much dyed,* or simply *dyed garments*]. (Ṣ.)

مُصْبِغٌ, like مُسْبِغٌ, which is the more commonly used, [each without ة,] applied to a she-camel, † *Casting her young one when its hair has grown.* (Az, TA.)

مَصْبُوغٌ : see صَبِيغٌ.

صبن

1. صَبَنَ, (Ṣ, M, Mṣb, Ḳ,) aor. ـِ, (Ṣ, Mṣb, Ḳ,) inf. n. صَبْنٌ, (Ṣ,) *He turned away* a gift, (Aṣ, Ṣ, Ḳ, TA,) or an act of kindness or beneficence, (Aṣ, Ṣ, TA,) from his neighbours, and his acquaintances, to others; and in like manner, كَبَنَ and خَضَنَ; (Aṣ, TA;) or *he withheld* it; عَنَّا [*from us*]: (Aṣ, Ṣ, Ḳ:) and صَبَنَ الكَأْسَ, (M, Mṣb,) aor. as above, (Mṣb,) *he* (the cupbearer) *turned away the cup of wine,* (M, Mṣb,) عَمَّنْ هُوَ أَحَقُّ بِهَا [*from him who was more,* or *most, entitled to it*], (M,) or عَنْهُ [*from him*]. (Mṣb.) 'Amr Ibn-Kulthoom says,

صَبَنْتِ الكَأْسَ عَنَّا أُمَّ عَمْرٍو
وَكَانَ الكَأْسُ مَجْرَاهَا اليَمِينَا

[*Thou hast turned away the cup of wine from us, O Umm-'Amr; when the proper course of the cup of wine was towards the right*]. (Ṣ. [See EM p. 184.]) —— And *He* (a man) *hid* a thing *in his hand,* (M, TA,) such as a dirhem &c., *without its being known.* (TA.) —— And صَبَنَ الكَعْبَيْنِ, (Ṣ, Ḳ,) or القَدَحَيْنِ, aor. and inf. n. as above, (M,) *He placed evenly,* or *suitably, in his hand,* (Ṣ, M, Ḳ,) *the pair of play-bones,* or *dice,* (Ṣ, Ḳ,) or *the pair of gaming-arrows,* (M,) *and then cast them:* (Ṣ, M, Ḳ:) said of a player at a game of hazard. (Ṣ, Ḳ.) To him who does so one says, أَجِلْ وَلَا تَصْبِنْ [*Shuffle thou, and do not pack*]. (Ṣ.)

[2. صَبَّنَ, from صَابُونٌ, *He soaped* a thing; or *washed* it *with soap:* so in the language of the present day.]

7: see what next follows.

8. اصطبن and ▼ انصبن (Ḳ, TA) and ▼ صَبْيَنَ (so in my MS. copy of the Ḳ) or ▼ صَيْبَنَ (so in the CḲ, but neither of these is in the TA,) *He,* or *it, turned away* or *back,* or *became turned away* or *back.* (Ḳ.)

Q. Q. 1. صَبْيَنَ or صَيْبَنَ : see what next precedes.

صَبِنَّاةٌ The hand of a player at a game of hazard *inclined for acting treacherously to a companion.* (IAạr, Ḳ.)

صَابُونٌ a word of well-known meaning, (Ṣ, M, Ḳ,) [*Soap;*] *a compound with which clothes* [*&c.*] *are washed: the best of which is made of pure olive-oil and clear potash and good* جير [meaning *lime*], *well cooked* [i. e. *boiled*], *and dried, and cut into particular shapes: the* مَغْرِبِيّ *sort is not cut, nor well cooked* [or *boiled*], *but is like cooked starch:* (TA:) *it is hot and dry; and produces a pleasurable sensation in the body;* (Ḳ;) *but the washing the head with it hastens hoariness:* (TA: [in which many other supposed properties of it are mentioned:]) IDrd says the word is not of the language of the Arabs: (TA:) [Fei, in the Mṣb, fancifully derives it from صَبَنَ الكَأْسَ, because it removes filths and impurities:] MF says that it is one of the words common to all languages, Arabic and Persian and Turkish and others [as Greek &c.]. (TA.) —— [Hence,] صَابُونُ الهُمُومِ is a term for † *Wine.* (TA voce تِرْيَاقٌ, q. v.)

[صَابُونِيٌّ *Of,* or *relating to, soap; saponaceous.* —— And *A maker,* or *seller, of soap:* mentioned in the Ḳ and TA only as a surname.]

صبو

1. صَبَا, (Ṣ, M, Ḳ,) aor. يَصْبُو, inf. n. صَبْوَةٌ, (Ṣ,) or صُبُوٌّ, (M, Ḳ,) and صُبُوٌّ (Ṣ, M, Ḳ) and صِبًا [also written صِبًى, in the CḲ (erroneously) صَبًى,] and صَبَآءٌ, (M, Ḳ,) [app., in its primary acceptation, *He was a youth,* or *boy,* or *child;* agreeably with an explanation of a phrase in what follows, and with explanations of صِبًا and صَبَآءٌ which will be found below: —— and hence,] *He was,* or *became, youthfully ignorant,* or *foolish,* or *silly:* (M, Ḳ:) [and, as seems to be indicated in the TA, *he indulged in amorous dalliance;* a sense in which the verb, more especially with صِبًا (q. v. infra) for its inf. n., is very frequently used:] or *he inclined to ignorant,* or *foolish,* or *silly, and youthful, conduct;* and in like manner ▼ تصابى; from الصَّبَا, which is from الشَّوْقُ [i. e. "desire"]: (Ṣ: [see an ex. of the inf. n. of the latter verb in a verse cited voce شَابَ, in art. شيب:]) or صِبًا and صَبَآءٌ, as inf. ns., signify the *inclining the heart* to any one; and have other significations expl. in what follows: and ▼ تَصَابٍ signifies the *manifesting passionate love,* and *desire:* (KL:) [but صِبًا and صَبَآءٌ are often used in different senses: thus Et-Tebreezee says that] in the following hemistich of a poem by Dureyd Ibn-Eṣ-Ṣimmeh,

صَبَا مَا صَبَا حَتَّى عَلَا الشَّيْبُ رَأْسَهُ

the first صبا may be from الصِّبَى [or الصِّبَا], and the second صبا from الصَّبَآءُ signifying الفَتَآءُ; so that the meaning may be, *He engaged in play,* or *sport, and* الصِّبَى [or *amorous dalliance,* &c.], *as long as he was a youth,* [*until hoariness came upon his head;*] or the meaning may be, *he engaged in* الصِّبَى *as long as he engaged therein,* &c. (Ḥam p. 380.) And صَبِىَ, (Ṣ, M, Ḳ,) [aor. يَصْبَى,] inf. n. صَبَآءٌ, (Ṣ,) or صِبًا, (M,) [or both, as will appear from what follows,] signifies *He played,* or *sported, with the* صِبْيَان [i. e. *youths,* or *boys,* or *children*]: (Ṣ:) or *he acted in the manner of the* صِبْيَان: (M, Ḳ:*) or both صِبًا and صَبَآءٌ, as inf. ns., signify the *acting as a youth,* or *boy,* or *child;* and the *playing,* or *sporting, with youths,* or *boys,* or *children:* (KL:) and ▼ تصبّى and ▼ تصابى, said of an old man, signify *he acted in a youthful, boyish,* or *childish, manner.* (TA.) —— صَبَا, inf. n. صُبُوٌّ and صَبْوَةٌ, also signifies *He inclined.* (Mṣb.) You say, صَبَا إِلَيْهَا *He inclined to her,* namely, a woman; as also صَبِىَ: and in like manner, صَبَتْ إِلَيْهِ and صَبِيَتْ [*She inclined to him*]. (M. [See also صَبَّ, in art. صب.]) And صَبَا إِلَيْهِ, (M,) or إِلَيْهَا, (Ḳ,) inf. n. صَبْوَةٌ (M, Ḳ) and صُبْوَةٌ (Ḳ) and صُبُوٌّ; (M, Ḳ;) and صَبِىَ; (Ḳ;) *He yearned towards, longed for,* or *desired,* (M, Ḳ,) *him,* (M,) or *her.* (Ḳ.) —— [Hence, app.,] صَبَتِ النَّخْلَةُ, (M, Ḳ,) aor. تَصْبُو, (M,) *The* [*female*] *palm-tree inclined,* or *leaned, towards the male palm-tree that was distant from it.* (M.) —— And صَبَتِ الرَّاعِيَةُ, (M, Ḳ,) aor. تَصْبُو, (M,) inf. n. صُبُوٌّ, *The pasturing beast inclined its head and put it upon the pasturage.* (M, Ḳ.) [See also 2.] —— صَبَتْ, (Ṣ, M, Ḳ,) aor. تَصْبُو, (Ṣ, M,) inf. n. صُبُوٌّ (Ṣ, M, Ḳ) and صَبًا, (M, Ḳ,) in [some of] the copies of the Ḳ صَبَآء, (TA,) said of the wind called الصَّبَا, (Ṣ, M, Ḳ,) *It blew.* (Ḳ.) —— And صُبِىَ القَوْمُ, (M, Ḳ,) like عُنِىَ, (Ḳ,) *The people,* or *party, were blown upon by the wind called* الصَّبَا. (M, Ḳ.)

2. صبّى رَأْسَهُ, inf. n. تَصْبِيَةٌ, *He inclined his head towards the ground.* (TA.) [See also 1, near the end.]

3. صابى رُمْحَهُ, (T, Ṣ,* M, Ḳ, TA,) inf. n. مُصَابَاةٌ, (TA,) *He inclined his spear,* (M, Ḳ,) or *he lowered the head of his spear towards the ground,* (T, TA,) [or, as the context in the Ṣ seems to indicate, *he inverted his spear,*] *to pierce,* or *thrust,* (T, M, Ḳ,) *with it.* (M, TA.) —— صابى السَّيْفَ *He put the sword into its* غِمْد [which generally means its *scabbard*] (Ṣ, M, Ḳ,) or *into its* قِرَاب [which generally means its *case for enclosing it together with its scabbard,*] (TA,) *reversed,* or *inverted:* (Ṣ, M, Ḳ, TA:) or, accord. to the A, صابى سَيْفَهُ, and سِكِّينَهُ, means *he put his sword,* and *his knife, into its* قِرَاب *not in the right manner:* and one says to one who hands a knife, صَابِ بِسِكِّينِكَ i. e. *Reverse thy*

knife, putting the handle towards me. (TA.) — صابى بِنَآءَهُ *He made his building to incline,* or *lean.* (Ḳ.) — صابى مَشَافِرَهُ *He* (a camel) *inverted his lips* on the occasion of drinking. (Ḳ.) — صابى الشَّيْخَ *He,* or *it, overturned the old man;* and *made him to incline.* (TA.) — صابى البَيْتَ, (M, Ḳ,) i. e. البَيْتَ مِنَ الشِّعْرِ, (TA,) *He recited the verse not rightly,* or *not regularly.* (M, Ḳ, TA. [In the CḲ, صاباهُ البَيْتَ.]) And صابى الكَلَامَ *He made the speech,* or *language, to deviate from its proper course,* or *tenour.* (M, Ḳ.) — صَابَيْنَا عَنِ الحَمْضِ is a phrase mentioned by AZ as meaning *We turned away from the* [*plants called*] حمض. (TA.) — And one says, الجَوَارِى يُصَابِينَ فِى السِّتْرِ, meaning يطلعن [i. e. يَطَّلِعْنَ, but I think that فِى is a mistranscription for مِن, and that the meaning is, *The girls,* or *young women, look from* within *the curtain*]. (TA:)

4. أَصْبَتْ *She* (a woman) *had a child such as is termed* صَبِىّ [i. e. *a boy,* or *a young male child*]; (Ṣ, M;) and *a child, male* or *female.* (Ṣ.) ═ أَصْبَتْهُ *She* (a woman, M, Ḳ, or a girl, or young woman, Ṣ) *excited his desire, and invited him,* (M, Ḳ,) or *made him to incline,* (Ṣ,) *to ignorant,* or *foolish,* or *silly, and youthful, conduct,* (Ṣ, M, Ḳ,) *so that he yearned towards her;* as also ↓ تَصَبَّتْهُ. (M, Ḳ.) And ↓ تَصَبَّاهَا *He invited her to the like thereof.* (M.) And ↓ تصبّاها also signifies *He deceived,* or *beguiled, her, and captivated her heart;* (M, Ḳ; [see also another rendering in an explanation of a verse cited voce إِصَارٌ;]) as also ↓ تصاباها. (Ḳ.) And اصبى عِرْسَ فُلَانٍ *He endeavoured to cause the wife of such a one to incline* [*to him*]. (TA.) ═ أَصْبَوْا *They entered upon* [*a time in which blew*] *the wind called* الصَّبَا. (M, Ḳ.)

5: see 1, latter half: ═ and see also 4, in three places.

6: see 1, in three places: ═ and see also 4.

[10. استصبى, as stated by Freytag, is expl. by Reiske as signifying *Pueriliter se et proterve gessit:* ═ and by Jac. Schultens as signifying *Pro puero habuit.* But the usage of this verb in any sense is app. post-classical.]

صَبًا [is of the fem. gender, and] is a subst. and an epithet, [so that one says رِيحٌ صَبًا, as well as صَبًا alone and رِيحُ الصَّبَا,] (M, TA,) [and signifies The *east wind:* or *an easterly wind:*] the *wind that blows from the place of sunrise:* (Mṣb:) or the *wind of which the mean place whence it blows is the place where the sun rises when the night and day are equal;* the opposite wind of which is the دَبُور: (Ṣ:) or the *wind that faces the House* [*of God,* i. e. *the Kaabeh;* app. meaning *that blows from the point opposite to the corner, of the Kaabeh, that is between the Black Stone and the door*]; as though yearning towards the House: (M, TA:) or, accord. to IAạr, (M,) the *wind of which the place whence it blows extends from the place of rising of* الثُّرَيَّا [or *the Pleiades*] *to* [*the place of*] بَنَات نَعْش [meaning *the tail of Ursa Major*]: (M, Ḳ:) [it is often commended by poets as a gentle and pleasant gale, like the Zephyr with us:] the dual is صَبَوَانِ and صَبَيَانِ: (IJ, M, Ḳ:) and pl. صَبَوَاتٌ and أَصْبَآءٌ. (M, Ḳ.)

صِبًا [also written صِبَى] and ↓ صَبَآءٌ, the former with kesr and the short alif, and the latter with fet-ḥ and the long alif, (Ṣ, Mṣb,) [both mentioned before as inf. ns.,] *Youth,* or *boyhood;* the *state of the* صَبِىّ [q. v.]: (Ṣ:) or *childhood.* (Mṣb.) One says, كَانَ ذٰلِكَ فِى صِبَاهُ and صَبَائِهِ [*That was in his youth* or *boyhood:* or *in his childhood*]. (Mṣb.) [See also an ex. in a verse cited in the first paragraph of art. شفع.] — And the former [or each, as is shown in the first sentence of this art.,] has also a signification derived from الشَّوْق [or "desire;" i. e., each signifies also *An inclining to ignorant,* or *foolish,* or *silly, and youthful, conduct; and amorous dalliance*]: (Ṣ:) and ↓ صَبْوَةٌ signifies [the same, as is also shown in the first sentence of this art., or, like صِبًا and صَبَآءٌ,] the *ignorance,* or *foolishness,* or *silliness, of youth;* (Lth, M, Ḳ;) *and amorous dalliance.* (Lth, TA.) [See an ex. of the first in a verse cited in the first paragraph of art. ادى; and another in a verse cited voce عَارِضٌ.]

صَبْوَةٌ: see the next preceding paragraph.

صَبَآءٌ: see صِبًا.

صَبِىٌّ *A youth, boy,* or *male child;* syn. غُلَامٌ: (Ṣ:) or *a young male child;* (Mgh, Mṣb;) *before he is called* غُلَام: (Mgh:) or *one that has not yet been weaned,* (M, Ḳ,) so called *from the time of his birth:* (M:) and ↓ صَابٍ signifies the same as صَبِىّ; these two words being like قَادِرٌ and قَدِيرٌ: (TA:) the pl. of the former is صِبْيَةٌ [a pl. of pauc., in which the و is changed into ى because of the kesreh before it, like as is said in the M respecting another of the pls.,] (Ṣ, M, Mṣb, Ḳ, but not in the CḲ,) and صِبْوَةٌ (M, Ḳ, TA, in the CḲ صَبْوَة,) and صَبْيَةٌ (M, Ḳ) and صُبْيَةٌ, (Ḳ, TA, but not in the CḲ,) [or rather the last two are quasi-pl. ns.,] and أَصْبٍ [another pl. of pauc.] (Ḳ) and أَصْبِيَةٌ [also a pl. of pauc.], (M, Ḳ,) but this last is said by J to have been unused, because the usage of صِبْيَة rendered it needless, (TA,) and صِبْيَانٌ, (Ṣ, M, Mṣb, Ḳ, but not in the CḲ,) in which the و is changed into ى because of the kesreh before it, (M,) and صُبْيَانٌ, (M, Ḳ,) as some say, preserving the ى notwithstanding the ḍammeh, (M,) and صِبْوَانٌ (M, Ḳ, but not in the CḲ,) and صُبْوَانٌ: (M, Ḳ:) and [ISd says,] accord. to Sb, the dim. of صِبْيَةٌ is ↓ أُصَيْبِيَةٌ, and that of أَصْبِيَةٌ is ↓ صُبَيَّةٌ, each irreg.; but in my opinion, صُبَيَّةٌ is the dim. of صِبْيَةٌ, and أُصَيْبِيَةٌ is that of أَصْبِيَةٌ: (M:) [J says,] أُصَيْبِيَةٌ occurs in poetry as being the dim. of أَصْبِيَةٌ. (Ṣ.) ↓ صَبِيَّةٌ signifies *A young woman, girl,* or *female child;* (Ṣ, TA;) and so too, [sometimes,] صَبِىّ: (TA:) and the pl. is صَبَايَا. (Ṣ, TA.) — أُمُّ الصِّبْيَانِ is a term applied to *The flatus,* or *flatulence,* (الرِّيحُ,) *that is incident to children.* (TA in art. ام.) [Golius, in that art., explains it as meaning *Larva, terriculamentum puerorum;* on the authority of Meyd.: and also as meaning *Epilepsy;* on the authority of Ibn-Beyṭár.] — صَبِىّ also signifies † The *pupil of the eye:* (M, Ḳ:) but Kr ascribes this meaning to the vulgar. (M.) — And ‡ The *extremity of each of the jaw-bones:* (Ḳ, TA:) i. e. (TA) الصَّبِيَّانِ signifies *the two extremities of the two jaw-bones* (Ṣ, M, TA) of the camel and of other animals: or, as some say, *the two edges curving outwards from the middle of the two jaw-bones:* (M, TA:) or, accord. to the A, *the thin portions of the two extremities thereof:* and it is [said to be] tropical. (TA.) And † *A bone below the lobe,* or *lobule, of each of the two ears:* (Ḳ:) or, as some say, the *head of the bone that is below the lobe,* or *lobule, of each of the two ears by the space of about three fingers put together.* (M.) — And ‡ The *edge* (حَدّ) of the sword: (M, Ḳ, TA:) or the *ridge* thereof, (M, TA, in the copies of the Ḳ أَوْ غَيْرُهُ is erroneously put for أَوْ عَيْرُهُ, TA,) *which rises in* [i. e. *along*] *its middle;* (M, Ḳ, TA;) and likewise of a spear-head: (M, TA:) or, accord. to the A, that *part* of a sword *below,* or *exclusive of,* (دُونَ,) *its* ظُبَة [q. v.]. (TA.) — And † The *head* of the human foot; (M, A, TA; in the copies of the Ḳ رَأْسُ القَوْمِ is erroneously put for رَأْسُ القَدَمِ; TA;) i. e. the *part* [thereof] *between its* حِمَارَة [q. v.] *and the toes.* (A, TA.) And الصَّبِيَّانِ signifies also † *The two sides of the* [*camel's saddle called*] رَحْل. (M.) — It is also said that صِبْيَانُ الجَلِيدِ signifies ‡ *The grains of hoar-frost that resemble pearls:* and صِبْيَانُ المَطَرِ ‡ *the small drops of rain:* but accord. to the author of the "Khaṣáïl," it is صُبَّان [pl. of صُؤَابَة, q. v.], with ء and then ب. (TA.)

صَبِيَّةٌ fem. of صَبِىّ, q. v.

صُبَيَّةٌ: see صَبِىّ, former half.

صَابٍ: see صَبِىّ, first sentence. — Also i. q. صَاحِبُ صَبْوَةٍ [i. e. One *who indulges in youthful folly, and amorous dalliance*]. (TA.) — Kureysh, (M,) or the Jews, (TA,) used to call the Companions of the Prophet صُبَاة. (M, TA. [See صَابِئٌ, in art. صبأ.]) And Náfi' read [in the Ḳur ii. 59 and xxii. 17] الصَّابِينَ instead of الصَّابِئِينَ; (TA;) and [in v. 73] الصَّابُونَ instead of الصَّابِئُونَ. (TA voce صَابِئٌ.) — صُبًّى, a pl. of صَابٍ, is expl. as meaning Those *who incline to conflicts and factions, seditions,* or *the like, and love to be foremost therein.* (TA. [See صَبٌّ, in art. صب.])

الصَّابِيَةُ *The oblique wind* (النُّكَيْبَآءُ, dim. of النَّكْبَآءُ,) *that blows in a direction between that of the east* or *easterly wind* (الصَّبَا) *and that of the* north or northerly wind (الشَّمَال): (Ṣ, Ḳ:) it is very cold, (Ṣ and TA voce نَكْبَآءُ,) and very boisterous, and unattended by rain or by any good. (TA ibid.)

أُصَيْبِيَةٌ: see صَبِىٌّ.

مُصْبٍ, (Ks, Az, M,) or مُصْبِيَةٌ, (Ṣ, A,) or both, (Ḳ,) applied to a woman, (Ḳs, Az, Ṣ, M, A, Ḳ,) and the former also applied to a man, (Er-Rághib, TA,) *Having* صِبْيَة [i. e. *children*, or *young children*, or *young unweaned children*], (Ṣ, Er-Rághib, A,*) or *having a child such as is termed* صَبِىّ. (M, Ḳ.) — Hence the latter is metaphorically applied by El-Ḥareeree to ‡ *Wine of which the sealed cover has been broken.* (Ḥar p. 450.) — [See also the verb, 4.]

مَصْبُوٌّ: see صَابِئٌ, in art. صبأ.

مُصَابِيَةٌ *A calamity*, or *misfortune*. (Ḳ.)

صح

1. صَحَّ, (Ṣ, A, MA, Mṣb, Ḳ,) aor. ـُ (MA, Mṣb, Ḳ) and ـِ, (MA,) inf. n. صِحَّةٌ (Ṣ,* A,* MA, Mṣb,* MF, TA) and صُحٌّ, (Ṣ,* Ḳ,* MF, TA,) two forms of the inf. n. of which there are some other exs., as قِلَّةٌ and قُلٌّ, and ذِلَّةٌ and ذُلٌّ, (MF, TA,) and صَحَاحٌ also, (Ḳ,* TA,* TḲ,) [like سَلَامٌ &c.,] *He was*, or *became*, *healthy*, or *sound*; (MA;) or *restored to health*, or *soundness*, مِنْ عِلَّتِهِ [*from his disease*]; (Ṣ, A;) as also ↓ اِسْتَصَحَّ: (Ṣ:) or *his disease departed*. (Ḳ, TḲ.) And † *It was*, or *became*, [or *proved*,] *sound*, *valid*, (MA,) [*substantial*, *real*, *sure*, *certain*,] *true*, *right*, (MA, Mṣb,) *correct*, *just* or *proper*, *whole* or *entire*, (MA,) or [*unmarred*, or *unimpaired*,] *free from every imperfection* or *defect* or *fault* or *blemish*, (L, Ḳ, TA,) *and from everything that would occasion doubt* or *suspicion* or *evil opinion*: (L, TA:) and ‡ *it was*, or *became*, *suitable to the case*, or *event*. (Mṣb.) You say, صَحَّتْ شَهَادَتُهُ ‡ [*His testimony was sound*, *valid*, &c.]. (A, TA.) And صَحَّ قَوْلُهُ ‡ [*His saying was*, or *proved*, *true*]. (A, TA.) And صَحَّ عِنْدَ القَاضِى حَقُّهُ ‡ [*His right*, or *due*, or *just claim*, *was*, or *became*, *established*, *substantiated*, *made good*, or *verified*, *in the estimation of the judge*; like ثَبَتَ]. (A, TA.) And صَحَّ لَهُ عَلَيْهِ كَذَا ‡ [*Such a thing became established*, or *verified*, *as due to him from him*; like ثَبَتَ]. (A, TA.) And صَحَّ العَقْدُ ‡ *The contract became established by its execution*. (Mṣb.) And صَحَّتِ الصَّلَاةُ, as used by the lawyers, ‡ *The prayer* [*was suitable to the ordinance thereof*, *so that it*] *annulled the obligation of performing it after the appointed time*. (Mṣb,* and Dict. of Techn. Terms of the Mussalmans pp. 815-816. [This meaning is expressed in the former by the phrase أَسْقَطَتِ القَضَآءَ; which is fully expl. in the latter work, with other conventional meanings of صِحَّةٌ, all reducible to explanations given above.] — صَحَّحَ الشَّىْءَ [if not a mistranscription for أَصَحَّ or صَحَّحَ] signifies † *He made the thing* صَحِيح [i. e. *sound*, *valid*, &c.]. (L, TA. [In the latter app. taken from the former.])

2. صَحَّحَهُ, [inf. n. تَصْحِيحٌ,] *He rendered him healthy*, *sound*, or *free from disease*; (Ṣ, A, MA, TA;) said of God; (Ṣ, TA;) and (A, TA) so ↓ اصحّهُ. (A, Ḳ, TA.) One says, أَصَحَّ ↓ اللّٰهُ بَدَنَكَ, and صَحَّحَ جِسْمَكَ, *May God render thy body healthy*, *sound*, or *free from disease*. (A.) — And † *He rendered it sound*, *valid*, (MA,) [*substantial*, *real*, *sure*, *certain*,] *true*, *right*, (MA, Mṣb,) *just* or *proper*, *whole* or *entire*, (MA,) [or *free from every imperfection* or *defect* or *fault* or *blemish*, *and from everything that would occasion doubt* or *suspicion* or *evil opinion*: see 1.] You say, صَحَّحْتُ الكِتَابَ, and الحِسَابَ, † *I corrected the book*, or *writing*, and *the reckoning*; *rectified what was wrong thereof*. (L, TA.) And صَحَّحَ بَرَآءَتَهُ [*He verified his being free* from a thing; *clear*, *quit*, or *guiltless*, of it; or *irresponsible* for it]. (Mgh in art. برأ.)

4. اصحّهُ: see 2, in two places. — Also *He found him to be* صَحِيح [or *healthy*, *sound*, or *free from disease*]; namely, a man. (L, TA.) — And اصحّ *He had his family and his cattle in a healthy*, or *sound*, *state*; (L, Ḳ;) whether he himself were in health or sick: (L:) or, said of a people, or party, *they had their cattle in a healthy*, or *sound*, *state*, *after they had been affected by a plague*, or *murrain*, or *distemper*. (Ṣ, L.)

5. تصحّح بِهِ [*He was rendered healthy*, or *sound*, *by it*]. (O and TA voce شُنْعَةٌ, q. v.)

10: see 1, first sentence. — One says also, أَنَا أَسْتَصِحُّ مَا تَقُولُ ‡ [*I hold to be true*, *right*, or *just*, *what thou sayest*]. (TA.)

R. Q. 1. صَحْصَحَ *It* (a thing, or an affair,) *was*, or *became*, *distinct*, *apparent*, or *manifest*; (Ḳ;) like حَصْحَصَ. (TA.)

صُحٌّ: see the next paragraph, in two places.

صِحَّةٌ (Ṣ, A, MA, O, Ḳ) and ↓ صُحٌّ (Ṣ,* O, Ḳ) and ↓ صَحَاحٌ (O, Ḳ) [all app. inf. ns., of صَحَّ, q. v.; and used as simple substs. meaning] *Health*, or *soundness of body*; (Ṣ, A, MA, O;) *contr. of* سُقْمٌ or سَقَمٌ: (Ṣ, A, O:) or *departure of disease*: (Ḳ:) صِحَّةٌ is said to be in the body and in religion; like as are [its contrs.] مَرَضٌ and سُقْمٌ: (Aboo-Is-ḥáḳ, TA in art. مرض:) in the body, it is *a natural state* or *condition*, *wherewith the actions* [*and functions*] *of the body have the natural course*: and it is metaphorically used in relation to [other things, including] attributes, or ideal things: (Mṣb:) and signifies [*a sound*, *valid*, *substantial*, *real*, *sure*, *certain*, *true*, *right*, *correct*, *just* or *proper*, *whole* or *entire*, *state* or *condition*; as is indicated in the first paragraph of this art.; or] *freedom from every imperfection* or *defect* or *fault* or *blemish*, (L, Ḳ, TA,) *and from everything that would occasion doubt* or *suspicion* or *evil opinion*. (L, TA.) One says, أَوْصَى فِى صِحَّتِهِ وَشِحَّتِهِ. (Ḳ in art. شح, q. v.) And كَانَ ذٰلِكَ فِى صُحِّهِ ↓ وَسُقْمِهِ [*That was in his state of health*, or *soundness*, *and his illness*, or *sickness*]. (AO, Ṣ.) And مَا أَقْرَبَ الصَّحَاحَ ↓ مِنَ السُّقَامِ [*How little removed is health*, or *soundness*, *from illness*, or *sickness*!]. (O.)

صَحَاحٌ: see صِحَّةٌ, in two places: — and see صَحِيحٌ, in four places. — صَحَاحُ الطَّرِيقِ means † *The hard part of the road*, *that has not been rendered soft*, or *plain*, (Ḳ, TA,) *nor smooth*, or *easy to walk or ride upon*. (TA.)

صُحَاحٌ: see the next paragraph.

صَحِيحٌ (Ṣ, A, MA, Mṣb, Ḳ, KL) and ↓ صَحَاحٌ (Ṣ, A, Mṣb, Ḳ) *Healthy*, *sound*, or *free from disease*; (Ṣ, A, MA, Ḳ, KL;) and so صَحِيحُ الجَسَدِ, applied to a man: (Mṣb:) and † *sound*, *valid*, (MA, KL,) [*substantial*, *real*, *sure*, *certain*,] *true*, *right*, (MA, KL, and Mṣb in explanation of the former word,) *correct*, *just* or *proper*, *whole* or *entire*, (MA, KL,) or [*unmarred*, or *unimpaired*,] *free from every imperfection* or *defect* or *fault* or *blemish*, (L, Ḳ, TA,) *and from everything that would occasion doubt* or *suspicion* or *evil opinion*: (L, TA:) [and † *suitable to the case*, or *event*: (see 1:)] fem. صَحِيحَةٌ, applied to a woman [and to other things]: (TA:) pl. صِحَاحٌ, (A, Mṣb, Ḳ,) a pl. of صَحِيحٌ, (Mṣb,) and applied to men [and other things], (A, Ḳ, TA,) and of صَحِيحَةٌ, and applied to women, (TA,) and أَصِحَّآءُ, (A, Mṣb, Ḳ,) a pl. of صَحِيحٌ, (Mṣb,) and applied to men, (A, Ḳ,) and أَصِحَّةٌ, likewise applied to men, (A,) and صَحَائِحُ, (Ḳ,) a pl. of صَحِيحَةٌ, and applied to women. (TA.) صَحِيحُ الأَدِيمِ means [lit. *Sound of skin*; or] *not* [*having the skin*] *cut*; as also ↓ صَحَاحُ الأَدِيمِ: (Ṣ:) [but each has a tropical signification; for] one says, فُلَانٌ صَحِيحُ الأَدِيمِ (Ḥam p. 628) meaning ‡ [*Such a one is sound*] *in respect of origin*, and *of honour*, or *reputation*. (Ḥar p. 135.) And دِرْهَمٌ صَحِيحٌ means *A dirhem free from defect*; as also ↓ صَحَاحٌ; and ↓ صُحَاحٌ, [which I find as syn. with صَحِيحٌ in my copy of the Ḳ,] with ḍamm, is allowable, like طُوَالٌ as syn. with طَوِيلٌ. (L, TA.) And it is said in a trad., يُقَاسِمُ ٱبْنُ آدَمَ أَهْلَ النَّارِ قِسْمَةً صَحَاحًا ↓ i. e. *The son of Adam*, meaning Ḳábeel [or Cain], who slew his brother Ḥábeel [or Abel], *will make a right division with the people of Hell*, so that half of it shall be for him, and half for them. (L, TA.)

صَحْصَحٌ (Ṣ, L, Mṣb, Ḳ) and ↓ صَحْصَاحٌ and ↓ صَحْصَحَانٌ (Ṣ, L, Ḳ) *A place*, (Ṣ, Mṣb,) or *ground*, or *land*, (L, Ḳ,) *that is plain*, or *even*,

(Ṣ, L, Mṣb, Ḳ,) *destitute of herbage*: pl. of the first صَحَاصِح: (L:) and the first signifies *a tract of land destitute of herbage, plain, or even, and containing small pebbles*: (L:) or *a smooth tract of land*: (R, MF:) and أَرْضٌ صَحَاصِحُ and ▼ صَحْصَحَانٌ *a land destitute of everything, containing no trees, nor any depressed resting-place for water*, said by AM to be *seldom found except in the rising ground of a valley, or in a mountain near to such rising ground, and not so plain as what is termed* صَحْرَآءُ. (L.) — [Hence, app., (see art. تره,)] تُرَّهَاتُ صَحَاصِحَ, and تُرَّهَاتُ صَحَاصِحٍ, [the latter preferred by J, as he says in the Ṣ,] ‡ *What is vain, or false*; (Ṣ, Ḳ, TA;) like تُرَّهَاتُ بَسَابِسَ: (Ṣ:) or [rather] *vain, false, untrue things, that have no foundation.* (TA.)

صَحْصَحٌ and ▼ صَحْصُوحٌ One *who pursues, or investigates, minute things, and retains them in his memory* (يُحْصِيهَا), *and knows them.* (Ḳ.)

صَحْصَاحٌ: see صَحْصَحٌ.

صُحْصُوحٌ: see صَحْصَحٌ.

صَحْصَحَانٌ: see صَحْصَحٌ, in two places.

مُصِحٌّ A man *having his family and his cattle in a healthy*, or *sound, state*; whether he himself be in health or sick: (L:) or *having his cattle in a healthy*, or *sound, state, after their having been affected by a plague*, or *murrain*, or *distemper*: pl. مُصِحُّونَ. (Ṣ, L.) It is said in a trad., لَا يُورِدَنَّ ذُو عَاهَةٍ عَلَى مُصِحٍّ (Ṣ, L) i. e. *One whose camels are affected by a murrain*, or *distemper, shall by no means bring them to water immediately after one whose camels are in a healthy*, or *sound, state*, so as to water the former beasts with the latter: a prohibition apparently given for fear that the latter beasts should become diseased like the former, and it should be supposed that the disease had passed by contagion, which ought not to be imagined. (L. [See also مُمْرِض.])

مَصَحَّةٌ *A cause of one's being rendered healthy*, or *sound in body.* (L, Ḳ.) So in the saying, الصَّوْمُ مَصَحَّةٌ [*Fasting is a cause of one's being rendered healthy*]. (L, Ḳ.) One says also, السَّفَرُ مَصَحَّةٌ [*Travel is a cause of one's becoming healthy*]. (Ṣ, A.) And أَرْضٌ مَصَحَّةٌ *A land free from plagues*, or *any common*, or *epidemic, diseases*; *in which maladies are not common* or *frequent.* (TA.)

مُصَحْصِحٌ *True, sincere*, or *honest, in love*, or *affection.* (Ḳ.) And it is also said to signify *Counselling*, or *admonishing*, or one *who counsels* or *admonishes, faithfully*, or *sincerely*: so in a verse of Melech El-Hudhalee; as though used by poetic license for مُصَحِّحٌ. (L.) ═ And ‡ One *who does, or says, vain*, or *false, things.* (A, Ḳ.)

صحب

1. صَحِبَهُ, aor. ـَ, inf. n. صُحْبَةٌ (Ṣ, A, Mṣb, Ḳ, &c.) and صَحَابَةٌ (Ṣ, A, Ḳ) and صِحَابَةٌ, (Ḳ,) *He associated, kept company*, or *consorted, with him*; (A, Ḳ;) [*he accompanied him*;] *he was*, or *became, his companion, associate, comrade, fellow, friend*, or *fellow-traveller*: (MA:) and ▼ صاحبهُ signifies the same. (TA. [See this latter verb below.]) — [Hence] one says, صَحِبَكَ ٱللّٰهُ and ▼ صَاحَبَكَ, (A, TA,) [inf. n. of the former (in the TA inadvertently said to be of the latter) صِحَابَةٌ, (said in the TA to be with kesr,) or صَحَابَةٌ, and, as will be shown by what follows, صُحْبَةٌ also,] ‡ *May God guard, keep, protect*, or *defend, thee*; *may God be thy guardian, keeper*, &c.: (TA in explanation of the former:) and أَحْسَنَ ٱللّٰهُ صَحَابَتَكَ (A, and Ḥam p. 443) or صِحَابَتَكَ (TA) ‡ [*May God make the guarding*, &c., *of thee to be good*]. And (TA) [in like manner,] ▼ اصحب فُلَانًا signifies † *He guarded, kept*, or *protected, such a one*; as also ▼ اصطحبهُ: and *he defended such a one*; syn. مَنَعَهُ: (Ḳ, TA:) one says, اَللّٰهُمَّ ٱصْحَبْنَا ▼ بِصُحْبَةٍ وَٱقْلِبْنَا بِذِمَّةٍ † *O God, guard us with* thy *guarding* in our journey, *and make us to return with* thy *safeguard* to our country, or land, &c.; occurring in a trad.: (TA:) and ▼ وَلَا هُمْ مِنَّا يُصْحَبُونَ, (A, TA,) in the Ḳur [xxi. 44], (TA,) means ‡ *Nor shall they* (i. e. the unbelievers, TA) *be defended from us*, (A, TA,) as expl. by Zj; (TA;) and *preserved in safety*: (A:) or, accord. to Ḳatádeh, *nor shall they be attended by good from us*: or, as some say, it is from the phrase صَحِبَكَ ٱللّٰهُ meaning as expl. above. (TA.) — See also 4, last sentence but one. ═ صَحَبَ, aor. ـَ, (Ḳ,) inf. n. صَحْبٌ, (TḲ,) *He skinned* a slaughtered animal. (Ḳ.)

3. صاحبهُ, (MA,) inf. n. مُصَاحَبَةٌ, (KL,) i. q. صَحِبَهُ; (TA;) *He associated, kept company*, or *consorted, with him.* (MA, KL.) See 1, first and second sentences. — And see the next paragraph, last sentence but one.

4. أَصْحَبْتُهُ فُلَانًا [*I made such a one to be a companion*, or *an associate, to him*]. (A.) And أَصْحَبْتُهُ ٱلشَّىْءَ ‡ *I made the thing to be* [*as it were*] *a companion to him*; (Ṣ, Ḳ, TA;) and so ▼ استصحبتهُ; as in the saying, استصحبته ٱلْكِتَابَ وَغَيْرَهُ ‡ *I made the book*, or *writing*, &c., *to be* [*as it were*] *his companion.* (Ṣ,* TA.) — And اصحبهُ ‡ *He did to him that which caused him to be a companion*, or *an associate, to him.* (A, TA.) — And ‡ *He left upon it*, namely, a skin, *its hair*, (Ṣ, A,) or *its wool*; *not subjecting it to the process termed* عَطْنٌ. (Ṣ.) — See also 1, in three places. ═ اصحب, intrans., *He* (a man) *became one having a companion*, or *an associate*: (Ḳ, TA: [in the latter said to be tropical; but, I think, without reason:]) and *he was*, or *became, one having companions*, or *associates.* (TA.) — And [hence,] ‡ *He* (a man) *had a son who had attained to manhood* (Ṣ, A, TA) *and so become like him*; (TA;) i. e. *he was alone, and became one having a companion*; (A;) or as though his son became his companion. (TA.) — And ‡ *He* (a camel, and a horse or similar beast, Ṣ, TA, or an animal, and a man to a man, A, TA*) *became tractable, submissive*, or *obsequious, after being refractory*, or *incompliant*; (Ṣ, A, TA;) [and so ▼ صَاحَبَ, as is implied by an explanation of its part. n. مُصَاحِبٌ; and ▼ استصحب, for] hence, (A,) one says also, ٱسْتَصْعَبَ ثُمَّ ٱسْتَصْحَبَ ‡ [*He was refractory*, or *incompliant*: *then he became tractable, submissive*, or *obsequious*]: (A, TA:) and accord. to A'Obeyd, one says, ▼ صَحِبْتُ ٱلرَّجُلَ, from الصُّحْبَةِ, and أَصْحَبْتُ [app. اصحبت لَهُ], meaning † *I became tractable, submissive*, or *obsequious, to the man.* (TA.) — And, said of water, ‡ *It became overspread with* [*the green substance termed*] طُحْلُب. (Ṣ, A.*)

5. يَتَصَحَّبُ مِنَّا † *He is ashamed*, or *bashful, with respect to us*; or *shy of us*; (Ḳ, TA;) i. e. *he is ashamed to sit with us*, or *shy of sitting with us.* (Ibn-Buzurj, TA.) And فُلَانٌ مَا يَتَصَحَّبُ مِنْ شَىْءٍ ‡ *Such a one does not guard himself against anything, and is not ashamed to do it*, or *shy of doing it, does not shun it*, or *avoid it.* (A.)

6: see the next paragraph, in two places.

8. اصطحبوا, (Ṣ, A, Ḳ,) originally اصتحبوا, (Ṣ,) *They associated, kept company*, or *consorted, one with another*; (Ṣ, A, Ḳ;) as also ▼ تصاحبوا: (A:) and in like manner اصطحبا and ▼ تصاحبا said of two men. (TA.) ═ اصطحبهُ: see 1.

10. استصحبهُ *He desired him*, or *demanded him, as a companion, an associate, a comrade*, or *a friend*: (MA:) or *he invited him to associate, keep company*, or *consort, with him*: and *he clave to him*: (A, Ḳ:) [*he chose him*, or *took him, as a companion*, &c.: and] *he had him with him.* (MA.) — [Hence,] one says, ٱسْتَصْحَبْتُ كِتَابًا لِى ‡ [*I made a book a companion to me*; or *I made a book belonging to me my companion*]. (A, L, TA.) And ٱسْتَصْحَبْتُ ٱلْكِتَابَ وَغَيْرَهُ † *I carried the book &c. with me.* (Mṣb.) And one says of anything, استصحبهُ as meaning † *It clave, adhered*, or *held fast, to it*; namely, another thing; (IF, Ṣ, Mṣb, TA;) or *coalesced*, or *united, with it.* (Ṣ, TA.) [See an ex. in a verse cited voce رَامِكٌ.] — See also 4, second sentence: ═ and see the last sentence but one of the same paragraph.

صَحْبٌ: see صَاحِبٌ.

صُحْبَةٌ an inf. n. of صَحِبَهُ [q. v.]. (Ṣ, A, Mṣb, Ḳ, &c.) — [As a simple subst., *Companionship.* Hence, لَهُ صُحْبَةٌ, often occurring in biographies as meaning *He had companionship* with the Prophet; i. e. he was one of the Companions of the Prophet. And خَرَجْتُ صُحْبَةَ ٱلرَّسُولِ, frequently occurring in trads., meaning *I went forth in the companionship of the Apostle*, or *in company with the Apostle.* Hence also] one says, حَمَلْتُ ٱلْكِتَابَ صُحْبَتِى † [*I carried the book with me*]. (Mṣb.) صُحْبَةُ ٱلسَّفِينَةِ [*The companionship of the ship*] is a post-classical phrase, denoting, by way of comparison, that which has no permanence. (Ḥar p. 258.) — See also صَاحِبٌ, of which it is a quasi-pl. n.

صَحَابَةٌ an inf. n. of صَحِبَهُ [q. v.]. (Ṣ, A, Ḳ.)

— See also صَاحِبٌ, of which it is a quasi-pl. n. [الصَّحَابَةُ is commonly applied to *The Companions of the Prophet*:] ▾ صَحَابِيٌّ [is the n. un., meaning *a Companion of the Prophet*; and] is conventionally applied to *one who saw Mohammad, and whose companionship with him was long, even if he have not related anything from him*; or, as some say, *even if his companionship with him was not long*. (KT.)

صَحَابِيٌّ: see the next preceding paragraph.

صَاحِبٌ *A companion, an associate, a comrade, a fellow, or a friend*; (A, MA, KL, TA;) *a fellow-traveller*: (MA:) [*an accomplice*: † *an accompanier*, or *attendant*, as applied to a thing:] and ‡ *a lord*, or *master*; *a possessor, an owner, an occupant, a haver*, or *a proprietor*; of anything: (A, TA:) it is not trans. like the verb, therefore you may not say, زَيْدٌ صَاحِبٌ عَمْرًا; (TA;) [i. e.] it is not used as an act. part. n., but as a subst., like وَالِدٌ; (Ham p. 32:) the pl., (Ṣ, Mṣb,) or term applied to a pl. number, (A, Ḳ, TA,) is ▾ صَحْبٌ, (Ṣ, A, Mṣb, Ḳ,) a pl. like رَكْبٌ of رَاكِبٌ, (Ṣ,) or [rather] a quasi-pl. n., (TA,) and أَصْحَابٌ, [the most common of all,] (A, Mṣb,) a pl. like أَشْهَادٌ of شَاهِدٌ, (TA,) or pl. of صَحْبٌ, like أَفْرَاخٌ of فَرْخٌ, (Ṣ,) and أَصَاحِيبُ, (Ṣ, Ḳ,) pl. of أَصْحَابٌ, (Ṣ,) and صُحْبَانٌ, (Ṣ, Ḳ,) a pl. like شُبَّانٌ of شَابٌّ, (Ṣ,) and صِحَابٌ, (Ṣ, A, Ḳ,) a pl. like جِيَاعٌ of جَائِعٌ, (Ṣ,) and صِحَابَةٌ, (A, Ḳ,) in which the ة may be regarded, agreeably with analogy, as an affix to the pl. صِحَابٌ characteristic of the fem. gender, (TA,) and ▾ صَحَابَةٌ, (Ṣ, A, Mṣb, Ḳ,) which is more common than صِحَابَةٌ, (TA,) but the only instance of فَعَالَةٌ as the pl. measure of a word of the measure فَاعِلٌ, (L, TA,) or originally an inf. n., (Ṣ,) or not so, but a quasi-pl. n., though written like the inf. n. [that is said to be its original], (from a marginal note in a copy of the Ṣ,) and ▾ صُحْبَةٌ, (Ṣ, A,) a pl. like فُرْهَةٌ of فَارِهٌ, (Ṣ, TA,) or [rather] a quasi-pl. n.: (TA:) the fem. is صَاحِبَةٌ, and its pl. is صَوَاحِبُ and صَاحِبَاتٌ, (Mgh, Mṣb,) the latter mentioned by AAF on the authority of Abu-l-Ḥasan: (TA:) hence, in a trad. of 'Áisheh, أَنْتُنَّ صَوَاحِبُ يُوسُفَ [*Ye are the female companions*, or *the mistresses, of Joseph*; meaning, enticers to lewdness]; or, as some relate it, صَوَاحِبَاتُ يُوسُفَ: (Mgh:) the dim. of صَاحِبٌ is ▾ صُوَيْحِبٌ (A) [and that of صَاحِبَةٌ is ▾ صُوَيْحِبَةٌ]. يَا صَاحِ for يَا صَاحِبِي [*O my companion*, &c.,] is the only allowable instance of such curtailing of a prefixed noun, related as heard from the Arabs. (Ṣ, TA.) One says, فُلَانٌ صَاحِبُ صِدْقٍ [*Such a one is a good companion*, &c.]. (A,* TA.) [And صَاحِبُ جَيْشٍ *The commander of an army*. And صَاحِبُ الشُّرْطَةِ and صَاحِبُ البَرِيدِ &c.: see arts. شرط and برد &c. And الصَّاحِبُ, alone, in post-classical times applied to *The Wezeer, when an officer of the pen*: see De Sacy's Chrest. Ar., sec. ed., ii. 59.] And صَاحِبُ اليَمِينِ [*The companion of the right hand*] and صَاحِبُ الشِّمَالِ [*The companion of the left hand*]; appellations of each man's recording angels, who write down his good and evil actions. (A trad. thus commencing in the Jámi' eṣ-Ṣagheer.) And صَاحِبُ الصُّورِ † The angel who is *the possessor of the horn*. (Idem.) [And صَاحِبُ بَيْتٍ † *The owner*, or *master, of a house* or *tent*.] And أَصْحَابُ الجَنَّةِ † [*The inmates*, or *occupants, of Paradise*]: (Ḳur ii. 76, &c.:) and أَصْحَابُ النَّارِ † [*The inmates*, &c., *of the fire* of Hell]. (Ḳur ii. 37, &c.) And صَاحِبُ سِجْنٍ † *An inmate of a prison*. (Bḍ and Jel in xii. 39.) And صَاحِبُ الصَّفِّ وَالجُمُعَةِ † *He who keeps to praying in the first rank and to the prayer of Friday*. (El-Munáwee on a trad. thus commencing in the Jámi' eṣ-Ṣagheer.) And أَصْحَابُ الشَّافِعِيِّ ‡ *The followers of the persuasion of Esh-Sháfi'ee*: and in like manner one says of the followers of other persuasions. (Mṣb.) [And صَاحِبُ كِتَابٍ † *The author of a book*.] And صَاحِبُ عِلْمٍ وَمَالٍ ‡ *A possessor of science and of wealth*. (A, TA.) And صَاحِبُ وِتْرٍ † [*One who has a claim for blood-revenge*: see an ex. in a verse cited voce دَرَّاكٌ]. (Keys Ibn-Rifá'ah, TA in art. درك.) [And صَاحِبُ أَمْرٍ وَنَهْيٍ † *One who possesses authority to command and to forbid*. And صَاحِبُ أَمْرٍ also signifies † *The author of an affair* or *event* or *action*; *the doer of a thing*; *the manager*, or *disposer, thereof*: and *one who keeps*, or *adheres, to a thing*. And صَاحِبُ دَيْنٍ † *A debtor*.] And one says, خَرَجَ وَصَاحِبَاهُ السَّيْفُ وَالرُّمْحُ ‡ [*He went forth, the sword and the spear being his companions*]. (A, TA.)

صُوَيْحِبٌ and صُوَيْحِبَةٌ dims. of صَاحِبٌ and صَاحِبَةٌ: see the next preceding paragraph.

أَصْحَبُ i. q. أَصْحَرُ, (Ṣ, Ḳ,) *Of a colour inclining to redness*: applied to an ass [app. to a wild ass]. (Ṣ, TA.)

مُصْحَبٌ [properly *Made to have a companion*. — And hence,] † A man *possessed by a jinnee* or *demon*; *a demoniac*; or *insane*. (Ḳ,* TA.) — See also مُصْحِبٌ. — And ‡ A skin, or hide, (A, Ḳ,) or a [skin such as is termed] زِقٌّ, (Ṣ,) *having its hair remaining upon it*, (Ṣ, A, Ḳ,) or *its wool*, or *its fur*; (Ḳ;) and ▾ مَصْحُوبٌ signifies the same. (A.) Hence, قِرْبَةٌ مُصْحَبَةٌ (Ḳ, TA) ‡ *A water-skin that has somewhat of its wool* [or *hair*] *remaining upon it, and that has not been subjected to the process termed* عَطْنٌ. (TA.) — And ‡ A branch, or stick, *that has not been stripped of its bark*, or *peel*. (TA.)

مُصْحِبٌ [properly *Having a companion*. — And hence,] A man *having a son that has attained to manhood, and become like him*. (Ḳ,* TA.) — And ‡ One *who talks to himself*; and so, sometimes, ▾ مُصْحَبٌ. (Ḳ, TA.) — And ‡ *Tractable, submissive*, or *obsequious, after being refractory*, or *incompliant*; (Ḳ;) as also ▾ مُصَاحِبٌ, (A, Ḳ,) and ▾ مُسْتَصْحِبٌ. (TA. [See also the next paragraph.]) — And † *Going straight on*, or *right on, without delay*. (Ḳ.)

هُوَ مُصْحَابٌ لَنَا بِمَا نُحِبُّ † *He is* [*very*] *submissive*, or *compliant, to us in that which we like*. (Ḳ.) [See also مُصْحِبٌ.]

مَصْحُوبٌ [*Associated with*, or *accompanied*]. — [Hence,] one says [to a person departing], اِمْضِ مَصْحُوبًا ‡ *Go thou, kept in safety, preserved from harm*; and [so] ▾ مُصَاحَبًا: (A, TA:) and [in like manner,] in bidding farewell, مُعَافًا ▾ مُصَاحَبًا ‡ [Be thou *kept in safety* or *health, preserved from harm*]: and a poet says,

• وَصَاحِبِي مِنْ دَوَاعِي السُّوءِ مُصْطَحَبُ ▾ •

† [*And my companion is preserved*, or *defended, from the causes of evil*]. (TA.) — See also مُصْحَبٌ.

مُصَاحَبٌ: see مَصْحُوبٌ, in two places.

مُصَاحِبٌ: see مُصْحِبٌ.

مُصْطَحَبٌ: see مَصْحُوبٌ.

مُسْتَصْحِبٌ: see مُصْحِبٌ.

صحر

1. صَحَرَهُ, aor. ـَ, (Ṣ, Ḳ,) inf. n. صَحْرٌ, (Ṣ, TA,) namely, milk, *He made it to become what is termed* صَحِيرَة: (Ṣ, TA:) or *he cooked it*, (Ḳ, TA,) *and then gave it to a sick person to drink*. (TA.) — صَحَرَتْهُ الشَّمْسُ *The sun pained his brain*: (Ḳ:) it is like صَهَرَتْهُ; (A;) or, as some say, *melted him*. (TA.) = صَحَرَ, aor. ـَ, inf. n. صَحِيرٌ and صُحَارٌ, *He* (an ass) *uttered a sound* [or *braying*] *more vehement than the neighing of horses*. (TA.) = [Golius explains صَحَرَ as meaning *It spread out wide*, said of a place, on the authority of J: but the verb is اصحر, q. v.; and the authority is not J.]

3. [صِحَارٌ is an inf. n. of صَاحَرَ, a verb not mentioned: hence,] أَبْرَزَ لَهُ مَا فِي نَفْسِهِ مِنَ الأَمْرِ صِحَارًا † [*He showed to him what was in his mind, of the thing*, or *affair, openly*]: a saying like جَاهَرَهُ بِهِ جِهَارًا. (Ḳ,* TA. [See also 4.])

4. اصحر, (Ṣ, A, Mgh, Ḳ,) or اصحر الصَّحْرَآءَ, (Mṣb, [but I think that this is a mistake for اصحر إِلَى الصَّحْرَآءِ,]) inf. n. إِصْحَارٌ, (Mṣb,) *He went forth to the* صحراء [or *desert*, &c.], (Ṣ, A, Mgh,) or *into the* صحراء: (Mṣb, Ḳ:) تصحّر [in this sense] has not been heard. (Mgh.) — Hence, in a trad., the saying of Umm-Selemeh to 'Áisheh, سَكَّنَ اللّٰهُ عُقَيْرَاكِ فَلَا تُصْحِرِيهَا [app. meaning, accord. to explanations of it in the TA in art. عقر, *God hath made thy dwelling and estate*, or, as Z explains it, *thy person* (نَفْسَكِ), *to be quietly settled, therefore do not thou remove it forth to the desert*]; i. e. لَا تُبْرِزِيهَا إِلَى الصَّحْرَآءِ; the verb, accord. to IAth, being made trans. by

the suppression of the prep.; [i. e. تُصْحِرِيهَا being for تُصْحِرِى بِهَا;] for it is [properly] intrans. (TA. [See also the next sentence but one, in which the verb is tropically made trans.]) — أَصْحِرْ لِعَدُوِّكَ means † *Be thou in a state of clearness* [or *certainty*] *with respect to the case of thy enemy*: (JM, TA:) occurring in a trad. of 'Alee. (TA.) — One says also, أَصْحَرَ بِالأَمْرِ and أَصْحَرَهُ ‡ *He revealed*, or *made manifest, the affair*, or *case*: and لَا تُصْحِرْ أَمْرَكَ ‡ [*Reveal not thy affair*, or *case*]: and أَصْحِرْهُ بِمَا فِى قَلْبِكَ ‡ [*Reveal to him what is in thy mind*]. (A, TA.) — اصحر said of a place, *It was*, or *became, wide*, or *spacious*; (O, K, TA;) i. e. *it became like the* صَحْرَآء. (TA.) = Said of a man, *He was*, or *became, blind of one eye*. (K.)

11. اصحارّ *It* (a plant) *dried up*; or *became yellow*; or *dried up and became yellow*: (S:) or *became of a dingy red colour, and then dried up and became yellow*: (TA:) and (TA) *it* (a plant, K, or an ear of corn, TA) *became red*: or *its first parts became white*. (K, TA.)

صَحْرٌ an imitative sequent to صَقْرٌ [q. v.]. (Kh, Ham p. 354.)

صَحَرٌ: see صُحْرَةٌ.

لَقِيتُهُ صَحْرَةَ بَحْرَةَ, in which the two nouns are imperfectly decl., (S, L,) being regarded as one, (L,) and صَحْرَةً بَحْرَةً, (K in art. بحر,) and صُحْرَةَ بُحْرَةَ, with damm, (O,) and ▼ صُحْرَةً بُحْرَةً, (MF in art. بحر,) and صَحْرَةَ بَحْرَةَ نَحْرَةَ, (O, K,) and صَحْرَةً بَحْرَةً نَحْرَةً, (K, [but this last is implicitly disallowed in the O, and expressly by MF in art. بحر,]) and with damm also in all these words, [i. e. صُحْرَةَ &c.,] (K,) *I met him openly*, or *in open view, nothing intervening to conceal him*. (S, L, K. [See also بَحْرَةٌ; and see صَرْحَةٌ.]) And one says likewise, أَخْبَرَهُ بِالأَمْرِ صحرة بحرة [*He acquainted him with the affair*, or *case, openly*]. (TA.)

صُحْرَةٌ (S, K, in the CK, صَحْرَةٌ [which is a mistake,]) and ▼ صَحَرٌ (K [in some copies of the K, صَحْرٌ, which, as observed in the TA, is wrong,]) *A colour in which is* [*the kind of red termed*] شُقْرَة: (S:) or *a colour nearly the same as* [*the kind of red termed*] صُهْبَة: (K:) or the latter, (TA, [and app. the former also,]) *a dust-colour with a slight redness*, (in the K, in حُمْرَةٌ خَفِيَّةٌ, the latter of these two words is a mistake for خَفِيفَةٌ, TA,) *inclining to a little whiteness*: (K, TA:) or the former, *redness inclining to dust-colour*: (TA:) or *dust-colour with redness*: (A:) and [*redness of the kind termed*] شُقْرَة *in the head*: (As, TA:) and both words, *a colour in which is whiteness and redness*: (TA:) and *whiteness overspreading blackness*; like سُحْرَة and سَحَر: (TA in art. سحر:) and the latter, accord. to Sgh, *whiteness*. (TA.) = Also, both words, The *quality of a* صَحْرَآء [q. v.]. (ISh.) — And the former, *A clear space in a* [*stony tract such as is called*] حَرَّة, (S, K,) *consisting of soft and clean soil with stones in it*: (TA:) pl. صُحَرٌ; (S, K;) the only pl. (TA.) — See also صَحْرَةٌ.

صَحْرَآءُ, imperfectly decl., (S, K,) though not an epithet; (S;) or it is an epithet in which the quality of a subst. predominates; (TA;) and is imperfectly decl. because it is of the fem. gender, (S,) and because the letter characteristic of the fem. gender [namely the long ا] is inseparable from it, (S, K,) *A desert; a waste*; syn. بَرِّيَّة: (S, Msb:) or *a tract of land like the back of a beast, bare*, or *destitute of herbage, without trees and without hills and without mountains; smooth* [*throughout*]: (ISh:) or *a plain*, or *level tract of land, with smoothness and ruggedness*, (A, K,) *less* [*rugged*] *than what is termed* قُفّ: (K:) or *a spacious tract of ground in which is no herbage*: (M, A, K:) or the *most plain and even of land, whether it have produced herbage or not, not having any mountain or hill near it*; as also جَهَادٌ: (ISh, TA in art. جهد:) you say صَحْرَآءُ وَاسِعَةٌ [*a wide desert* &c.]; (S;) but you do not say صَحْرَآءَةٌ, adding one fem. sign after another: (S, Msb:) the pls. are صَحَارِىُّ (S, Msb, K) and صَحَارٍ (S, M, Msb) [in the K, صَحَارِى, which, without the art. ال, and except when it is prefixed to another noun, and in a case of pausing, is a manifest mistake, as is shown in every complete treatise on inflection,] and صَحَارَى (S, Msb, K) and صَحْرَاوَاتٌ: (S, K:) the first of which four pls. occurs in poetry, and is the original form of the second: for when you form the pl. of صَحْرَآء, [which is originally صحرا‍ا,] you introduce an ا between the ح and the ر, and give kesr to the ر, as in all similar cases: then the first ا which is after the ر [in صحراا] is changed into ى, because of the kesreh preceding it; and the second ا, which is the characteristic of the fem. gender, is also changed into ى, and incorporated into the former: then they reject the first ى, and change the second into ا, [though still writing it ى,] and say صَحَارَى, with fet-h to the ر, that the ا may not be elided in the case of tenween, [which the word would have if the ر were with kesr]; and this they do to distinguish between the ى that is changed from the ا which is a characteristic of the fem. gender and the ى that is changed from the ا which is not a characteristic of the fem. gender as the ا of مَرْمًى when they say مَرَامٍ: some of the Arabs, however, do not reject the first ى [in صَحَارِىّ], but reject the second ى, and say الصَّحَارِى, with kesr to the ر, and هٰذِهِ صَحَارٍ, like as you say جَوَارٍ. (S. [In the Ham, p. 54, صُحْرٌ is mentioned as a pl. of صَحْرَآء; but I think it doubtful.])

صُحَارٌ The *sweat of horses*: (O, K:) or the *fever of horses*. (K.) [— See also 1.]

صُحُورٌ: see أَصْحَرُ.

صَحِيرٌ *A certain uttering of the voice of the ass*, (A, K,) *of a vehement kind*, (A,) *more vehement than the neighing of horses*: an inf. n. (TA. [See 1.])

صَحِيرَةٌ *Milk into which heated stones are thrown, so that it boils, after which some clarified butter is poured upon it, and it is drunk; and sometimes some flour is sprinkled upon it, and then it is supped*: or, accord. to Abu-l-Gheyth, it is called صَحِيرَةٌ, from الصَّخْرُ; like فَهِيرَةٌ, from الفِهْرُ: (S:) or *fresh milk into which heated stones are thrown*, or *which is put in the cooking-pot and made to boil in it once, until it burns; and sometimes flour is put into it, and sometimes clarified butter*: (TA:) or *fresh milk which is made to boil, after which some clarified butter is poured upon it*, (K,) *and it is drunk*: (TA:) or *fresh milk which is heated until it burns*: (A:) or *pure milk of camels*, or *of sheep*, or *of goats, which, when they want soup, and have not flour, it not being found in their land, they cook, and then give to drink to a sick person, hot*. (TA.)

ثَوْبٌ صُحَارِىٌّ *A kind of garment, so called in relation to* صُحَار, *a town of El-Yemen*: or, as some say, *of the colour termed* صُحْرَة, like ▼ أَصْحَرُ. (TA, from a trad.)

صُحَيْرَآءُ *A certain sort of milk*: (K:) so says Kr, without particularizing it. (TA.)

أَصْحَرُ *Of the colour termed* صُحْرَة: (S, K:) or *similar to* أَصْبَحُ: (As:) a man *of a red colour inclining to dust-colour*: (TA:) or *having a colour such as is termed* شُقْرَة *upon his head*: (As:) and an ass *in which is a red colour*: (S:) or *of a dust-colour with redness*: (A:) or *in which is whiteness and redness*; (TA;) and so ▼ صَحُورٌ applied to a she-ass; or this signifies *wont to kick with her hind leg*: (K, TA:) fem. صَحْرَآءُ: (S, TA:) and pl. صُحْرٌ. (TA.) See also صُحَارِىّ. — الأَصْحَرُ and ▼ المُصْحِرُ *The lion*. (Sgh, K.)

المُصْحِرُ: see what next precedes.

مُصَاحِرٌ One *who fights with his adversary in the desert* (الصَّحْرَآء), *and does not act deceitfully with him*. (S.)

صحف

2. تَصْحِيفٌ signifies (primarily, Msb) The *making a mistake* (S, O, Msb, K, TA) *in a* صَحِيفَة, (S, O, K, TA,) *by reason of the ambiguity*, or *dubiousness, of the letters*: a post-classical term: (TA:) or the *reading* a thing *in a manner at variance with what the writer intended*, or *at variance with the conventional usage* thereof: (Mgh:) a secondary signification is the *altering* a word, or an expression, *in such a manner that the meaning intended by the application* [thereof] *becomes altered*: (Msb:) or it consists in the *altering of a diacritical point* [or *points*]; *as in* النفى *for* النقى, or *vice versâ*: (KT, after التَّحْرِيف:) one says, صَحَّفَ اللَّفْظَ *He altered the word*, or *expression*, [*in such a manner that the meaning intended by the application thereof became altered*, or] *so that it became dubious* [*to the reader*]. (Msb.) [See also تَحْرِيف, in the first paragraph of art. حرف.]

4. أَصْحَفَ *It had* صُحُف [i. e. *written pieces of*

paper or of skin] (Ṣ, O, Ḳ, TA) collected in it, (Ṣ, O,) or put in it (Ḳ, TA) between two boards. (TA.)

5. تصحّف, said of a word, or an expression, *It became altered* [*so as to have a meaning different from that intended by the application thereof,* (see 2,) or] *so as to be dubious.* (Mṣb.) One says, تصحّف عَلَيْهِ لَفْظُ كَذَا [*Such a word, or such an expression, became altered so as to be dubious to him*]. (O, Ḳ.*)

صَحْفَةٌ [*A sort of bowl;*] *a vessel like the* قَصْعَة, (Ṣ, ISd, O, Mṣb, Ḳ,* TA,) *expanded, wide,* (ISd, TA,) or *a large, expanded* قَصْعَة, (Mgh,) or, accord. to Z, *an oblong* قَصْعَة, (Mṣb,) *that satisfies the hunger of five* [*men*] (Ks, Ṣ, ISd, Mgh, O, TA) *and the like of them:* (ISd, TA:) Ks says, (Ṣ, O,) the largest sort of قَصْعَة is the جَفْنَة; next to which is the قَصْعَة [properly so called], (Ṣ, O, Ḳ,) which satisfies the hunger of ten [men]; (Ṣ, O;) then, the صَحْفَة, (Ṣ, O, Ḳ,) which satisfies the hunger of five; (Ṣ, O;) then, the مِئْكَلَة, (Ṣ, O, Ḳ,) which satisfies two men, and three; (Ṣ, O;) and then, the ▼ صُحَيْفَة, (Ṣ, O, Ḳ,) which satisfies one man: (Ṣ, O:) the pl. of صَحْفَة is صِحَافٌ. (Ṣ, O, Mgh, Mṣb.) It is said in a prov., اِسْتَفْرَغَ فُلَانٌ مَا فِى صَحْفَتِهِ *Such a one chose for himself, as his share,* [or *exhausted, all of*] *what was in his* صحفة. (TA.)

صَحَفِىٌّ One *who makes mistakes in reading the* صَحِيفَة [or *writing,* or *written piece of paper* or *of skin*]; incorrectly termed by the vulgar صُحُفِىٌّ, with two ḍammehs; (O, Ḳ;) [for the formation of a rel. n. from a pl. of this kind (i. e. from صُحُف) is not allowable,] though the pl. is not restored to the sing. in forming the rel. n. in the case of proper names, such as أَنْمَارِىٌّ &c., nor in the case of words that are used in a manner like that of proper names, such as أَنْصَارِىٌّ &c.: (O:) or *a learner,* or one *who acquires knowledge,* (Mgh, Mṣb,) *from the* صَحِيفَة, (Mgh,) *inferior* [*in rank*] *to the* مَشَايِخ [pl. of شَيْخ]: (Mṣb:) a rel. n. from صَحِيفَة; (Mgh, Mṣb;) like حَنَفِىٌّ and بَجَلِىٌّ from حَنِيفَةُ and بَجِيلَةُ: (Mṣb:) and ▼ مُصَحِّفٌ signifies the same as صَحَفِىٌّ [in the former of these senses]. (TA.)

صِحَافٌ *Small places that are made for water to collect and remain therein* (مَنَاقِعُ صِغَارٌ تُتَّخَذُ لِلْمَآءِ): pl. صُحُفٌ. (Esh-Sheybánee, O, Ḳ.)

صَحِيفٌ [appears from what here follows, to be syn. with ▼ صَحِيفَة, or rather it is a coll. gen. n. of which the latter is the n. un.:] ‡ *The surface of the ground* or *earth;* (O, Ḳ, TA;) as being likened to the thing [i. e. paper or skin] that is written upon. (TA.) — See also the next paragraph.

صَحِيفَةٌ *A written piece of paper* (MA, Mgh, Mṣb) or *of skin;* (Mṣb;) *a writing,* or *thing written; a book,* or *volume; a letter,* i. e. *an epistle;* syn. كِتَابٌ; (Ṣ, O, Ḳ;) [syn. with كِتَاب in all of these senses; in the last of them in an anecdote related in Freytag's Arab. Prov. i. 721-2, and in Ḥar p. 119, q. v.;] and *a* [*portion of a book, such as is termed*] كُرَّاسَة; and *a register;* [for] in the إِنْقَاع [a title of several books, it is said that] the كُرَّاسَة and ▼ مُصْحَف and صَحِيفَة and كِتَاب and دَفْتَر are one: (MA:) pl. صُحُفٌ (Ṣ, Mgh, O, Mṣb, Ḳ) and صُحْفٌ, a contraction of the former, (TA,) and صَحَائِفُ, (Ṣ, O, Mṣb, Ḳ,) like سَفَائِنُ pl. of سَفِينَةٌ; (Lth, O;) the first of these pls. anomalous, (Lth, Sb, O, Ḳ,) the sing. being likened to قَضِيبٌ (Sb, O, TA) and رَغِيفٌ (Sb, TA) and قَلِيبٌ, (O,) of which the pls. are قُضُبٌ (Sb, O, TA) and قُلُبٌ (Sb, TA) and رُغُفٌ: (O:) [or صَحِيفٌ may be its original, as well as regular, sing.:] see the next preceding paragraph. صُحُفِ إِبْرٰهِيمَ وَمُوسَى, in the Ḳur [lxxxvii. last verse], means [In *the books of Abraham and Moses;* i. e.] *the books revealed to Abraham and Moses.* (O.) [صَحِيفَةٌ also means The *record of the actions* of anyone, that is kept in heaven: (see رَقّ:) one says, صَحِيفَتُهُ سَوْدَآءُ, meaning † *The record of his actions is black;* a phrase often used in the present day, in speaking of a bad man.] Moḥammad [the Ḥanafee Imám] speaks of صُحُف not written upon; saying, فَإِنْ كَانَتِ السَّرِقَةُ صُحُفًا لَيْسَ فِيهَا كِتَابٌ [*And if the stolen property be papers,* or *books, not having any writing upon them*]. (Mgh. [See, again, رَقّ.]) — صَحِيفَة signifies also *A plank, board,* or *leaf, of a door;* like صَفِيحَة [from which it is perhaps formed by transposition, or it may be tropical in this sense]: pl. صَحَائِفُ. (MA.) — Also ‡ *The external skin,* or *scarf-skin,* of the face: (O, TA:) or as some say, the *part* thereof *that fronts one:* pl. [or rather coll. gen. n.] ▼ صَحِيفٌ; or this may be used, in a verse in which it occurs, for صَحِيفَة. (TA.) — One says also صَحَائِفُ مِنْ شَحْمٍ [meaning † *Layers of fat*]. (A in art. نير.)

صُحَيْفَةٌ: see صَحْفَةٌ.

صَحَّافٌ [*A bookseller;*] *a seller of* صُحُف: or [*a bookbinder;*] *a maker* [meaning *binder*] *of* صُحُف. (TA.)

مَصْحَفٌ: see what next follows.

مُصْحَفٌ (Th, Ṣ, Mgh, O, Mṣb, Ḳ) and ▼ مِصْحَفٌ (Th, Ṣ, O, Mṣb, Ḳ) and ▼ مَصْحَفٌ; (Th, O, Ḳ;) the first of which is the original, (Fr, Ṣ, O, Mṣb,) being from أُصْحِفَ meaning as expl. above, and one of certain words that are pronounced by [some of] the Arabs with kesr to the م instead of ḍamm because the latter is deemed by them difficult of utterance, of which words are also مِخْدَعٌ and مِطْرَفٌ and مِغْزَلٌ and مِجْسَدٌ, (Fr, Ṣ, O,) or, accord. to AZ, Temeem pronounce the م with kesr, and Keys pronounce it with ḍamm, [as do most persons in the instance of مصحف in the present day,] and Th says that مَصْحَف, with fet-ḥ, is correct and chaste; (O;) [*A book,* or *volume, consisting of*] *a collection of* صُحُف, (Ṣ, Mgh, O, Ḳ, TA,) *written upon, and put between two boards:* (TA:) [generally applied in the present day to *a copy of the Ḳur-án:*] and also signifying *a* [*portion of a book, such as is termed*] كُرَّاسَة: but the former is the primary [and more common] signification: (Mgh:) pl. مَصَاحِفُ. (KL.) See also صَحِيفَة.

مِصْحَفٌ: see the next preceding paragraph.

مُصَحِّفٌ: see صَحَفِىٌّ.

صحل

1. صَحِلَ, aor. ـَ, inf. n. صَحَلٌ, *He was,* or *became, hoarse, rough, harsh,* or *gruff, in voice;* said of a man: (Ṣ, O:) [and] صَحِلَ صَوْتُهُ, aor. as above, (Ḳ,) and so the inf. n., (TA,) *His voice was,* or *became, hoarse, rough, harsh,* or *gruff:* or *sharp, together with hoarseness, roughness,* &c.: or صَحَل signifies *a roughness,* (خُشُونَة, Ḳ,) or *a rattling,* (حَشْرَجَة, Lḥ, TA,) *in the chest:* and *a cracking in the voice, without a right tenour thereof:* (Lḥ, Ḳ, TA:) one says, فِى صَوْتِهِ صَحَلٌ *In his voice is a hoarseness* [&c.]: (Ṣ, O:) and صَحِلَ حَلْقُهُ *His fauces became hoarse* [&c.]: (IB, TA:) but accord. to IAth and others, it is not Arabic [in origin]. (TA.) See also صَهَلَ.

صُحْل [app. a mistake for صَحَل]: see صَهَل.

صَحِلٌ, (Ḳ,) or صَحِلُ الصَّوْتِ, (Ṣ, O,) *Hoarse, rough, harsh,* or *gruff,* [&c.,] *in voice;* as also ▼ أَصْحَلُ. (Ṣ, O, Ḳ.) And صَوْتٌ صَحِلٌ [*A voice that is hoarse,* &c.]. (TA, from a trad.)

أَصْحَلُ: see the next preceding paragraph.

صحم

8. اصطحم i. q. اصطخم, q. v.

11. اِصْحَامَّ, (Ḳ,) inf. n. اِصْحِيمَامٌ, (TA,) said of a plant, or herbage, *It became intensely green:* and *it became yellow,* (Ḳ, TA,) *and altered in colour;* or, as J says, [in the Ṣ,] اصحامّت البَقْلَةُ *the herb,* or *leguminous plant, became yellow:* (TA:) thus it has two contr. meanings: or it (i. e. a plant, or herbage,) *became intermixed with yellowness in its dark greenness.* (AḤn, Ḳ.) And اصحامّت الأَرْضُ *The land became altered* [*for the worse*] *in its herbage, and its rain departed:* (Ḳ:) or, as some say, *the land became altered in the colour of its seed-produce, for the reaping:* and in like manner, اصحامّ الحَبُّ *the grain became thus altered.* (TA.) And اصحامّ الزَّرْعُ *The seed-produce was smitten by cold:* or *began to dry up.* (Ḳ.)

صُحْمَةٌ *Blackness inclining to yellowness:* or *a dust-colour inclining a little to blackness:* or *redness in whiteness:* (Ḳ:) or, as some say, *yellowness in whiteness.* (TA.)

أَصْحَمُ *Of the colour termed* صُحْمَة: (Ḳ:) i. e. *black inclining to yellowness:* (Ṣ, Ḳ:) &c.: (Ḳ:) or, accord. to AA, *intensely black:* (TA:) fem.

صَحْمَآءُ. (Ḳ.) — The latter, applied to a فَيْفَآء [or smooth, or waterless, desert], (Sh, Ḳ,) or to a بَلْدَة [or district, &c.], (Ṣ,) signifies *Dusty.* (Sh, Ṣ, Ḳ.) — And الصَّحْمَآءُ is the name of *A certain herb, or leguminous plant,* (Ṣ, Ḳ, TA,) *not intensely green.* (TA.)

مُصْحَامٌّ, applied to a plant, or herbage, [&c.,] part. n. of 11 [q. v.]. (TA.)

صحن

1. صَحَنَهُ, (Ṣ, Ḳ,) [aor. َ ,] inf. n. صَحْنٌ, (TA,) *He gave him something in a* صَحْن, (Ṣ, Ḳ,) i. e. the *bowl so called:* (Ṣ:) from Fr. (TA. [See 5.]) And صَحَنَهُ دِينَارًا *He gave him a deenár.* (TA.) — Also, (AA, Ṣ, Ḳ,) aor. as above, (Ḳ,) *He struck him.* (AA, Ṣ, Ḳ.) You say, صَحَنْتُهُ صَحَنَاتٍ i. e. *I struck him* [*strokes:* the latter word being pl. of ↓ صَحْنَةٌ, the inf. n. of un.]. (Ṣ.) And صَحَنَهُ عِشْرِينَ سَوْطًا *He struck him twenty strokes of the whip.* (TA.) — صَحَنَتِ الحَالِبَ بِرِجْلِهَا *She* (a camel) *kicked the milker with her hind leg.* (TA.) ═ صَحَنَ بَيْنَهُمْ, (Ṣ, Ḳ,) inf. n. as above, (TA,) *He made peace,* or *he effected a rectification of affairs, an agreement, a harmony,* or *a reconciliation, between them.* (Ṣ, Ḳ.)

5. تصحّن *He asked,* or *begged:* (Ḳ, TA:) one says, خَرَجَ فُلَانٌ يَتَصَحَّنُ النَّاسَ *Such a one went forth begging of the people;* (AZ, TA;) or, [as is a custom of many Arab and other Eastern mendicants,] *begging of them in a bowl,* [see 1, first sentence,] or *some other thing.* (TA.)

صَحْنٌ *A great* عُسّ [i. e. *bowl,* or *drinking-cup*]; (Ṣ, Ḳ;) *nearly as large as the* تِبْن [q. v.]: (Ks, Ṣ in art. تبن:) or *a shallow* عُسّ: (so accord. to a copy of the Ṣ:) or *a bowl,* or *drinking-cup,* (قَدَح) *that is neither large nor small:* (TA:) [now applied to *a plate,* and *a dish:*] pl. [of pauc.] أَصْحُنٌ (Mṣb,* TA) and [of mult.] صِحَانٌ (TA) [and app., agreeably with modern usage, صُحُونٌ]. — And [hence,] *A* [*kind of*] *cymbal;* (PṢ;) *a small brazen basin,* (طُسَيْت, [dim. of طَسْت,]) *one of what are termed* صَحْنَانِ, (Ṣ,) this meaning *two little brazen basins,* (طُسَيْتَانِ صَغِيرَتَانِ, Ḳ,) *which are struck together.* (Ṣ, Ḳ.) — And ‡ The *interior of the solid hoof;* (Ḳ, TA;) also called سكرجة [i. e. سُكُرُّجَة or سُكُرُّجَة]. (TA.) — And † The *interior* of the ear: or the مَحَارَة [i. e. *concha*] thereof. (TA.) And صَحْنَا الأُذُنَيْنِ [thus accord. to the TA and my MS. copy of the Ḳ, in the CḲ صَحْنَاه,] † *The resting-place* (مُسْتَقَرّ) *of the interior of each of the ears;* (Ḳ;) meaning *the place of hearing* [or *meatus auditorius*] *of the resting-place of the interior of each of the two ears* of the horse: pl. أَصْحَانٌ. (TA.) — Also The *middle* of a house; (Ṣ, Ḳ;) meaning the سَاحَة [i. e. *court*] *of the middle* of a house [and of a mosque &c.]: (TA:) [and also *a hall:* for] it is thus called *whether without,* or *with, a roof.* (Kull, voce بَيْت.) And The سَاحَة [or *spacious vacant part*] *of the middle* of a desert; and of an elevated and plain, or hard and elevated, tract; and of a wide space of low, or depressed, ground: pl. صُحُونٌ, the only pl. form. (TA.) *A wide part* of a desert: so in the saying, سِرْنَا فِى صَحْنِ الفَلَاةِ [*We journeyed in the wide part of the desert*]. (Mṣb.) And *A level,* or *plain, tract* of ground. (TA.) And *An acclivity* (سَنَد) of a valley, *in which is some elevation above* [*other*] *elevated ground, as though supported* [*by the latter*]; and in like manner, of a mountain, and of a hill such as is termed أَكَمَة; the صُحُون of the ground being the دُفُوف [i. e. *banks,* or *acclivities,*] thereof: it is *bare, and such as flows* [*with rain*]; and is not thus called unless *bare of everything, and even:* and it means also *an even tract of ground like the area of the place in which dates are put to dry.* (TA.) — [Hence,] one says, جَرَى الدَّمْعُ عَلَى صَحْنَىْ وَجْنَتِهِ ‡ [*The tears ran upon the middle of each of his cheek-balls*]. (TA.) ═ Also *A gift.* (TA. [See 1, first sentence.])

صَحْنَةٌ; pl. صَحَنَاتٌ: see 1. ═ Also *A bead* (خَرَزَة) *with which women fascinate men, and restrain them,* or *withhold them from other women.* (Lḥ, TA.)

صُحْنَةٌ *A clear space of a* [*stony tract such as is called*] حَرَّة. (Ḳ.)

صِحْنَاةٌ, (Ṣ, and so accord. to some copies of the Ḳ,) and صِحْنَآءُ, (thus also accord. to some copies of the Ḳ,) and with the short alif, [app. صِحْنَى and صَحْنَى,] (Ṣ, and so accord. to some copies of the Ḳ,) or صَحْنَاةٌ and صِحْنَاةٌ, (Mgh, Mṣb,) or thus also, (accord. to some copies of the Ḳ,) or thus, and also صِحْنَآءَةٌ and صَحْنَآءَةٌ, (accord. to other copies of the Ḳ,) or when with ة having a more special signification, [being a n. of un., and, if so, accord. to a general rule, with tenween when without ة, as is said to be the case in the TA, on the authority of Az, accord. to whom, as is also there stated, the word is pluralized by the elision of the ة,] (Ṣ,) *A certain condiment,* or *seasoning, made of fish,* (Ṣ, Ḳ,) *of small fish, which has the properties of exciting appetence, and rectifying the state of the stomach:* (Ḳ:) or *i. q.* صِير, (Mgh, Mṣb,) i. e. what is called in Pers. مَاهِى آوَه [*jelly of salted fish*]: (Mgh:) AZ is related to have said that صحناة is Pers., meaning what the Arabs call صير: IAth says that صير and صحناة are both of them Pers. words. (TA.)

صَحُونٌ A she-camel *that has a habit of kicking:* (AA, Ṣ, Ḳ:) and a *kicking* mare or horse: and a she-ass *that kicks the he-ass with her hind leg whenever he comes near to her:* or, as some say, a she-ass *in which are whiteness and redness* [app. meaning a wild she-ass]. (TA.)

مِصْحَنَةٌ *A vessel like the* [*bowls called*] صِحَاف, (Ḳ, TA) *and* قَصْعَة. (TA.)

صحو

1. صَحَا, said of a day, [aor. يَصْحُو,] inf. n. صَحْوٌ, *It was,* or *became, cloudless:* (TA:) and so ↓ أَصْحَى: (Mṣb, Ḳ, TA, but not in the CḲ:) [it is said that] صَحْو signifies the *departing of the clouds:* (Ṣ, Mgh, Ḳ:) [but] Es-Sijistánee says that the vulgar think it to have this meaning, whereas it only means the dispersing of the clouds with the departing of the cold. (Mṣb, TA.) And أَصْحَتْ ↓ السَّمَآءُ *The sky became cloudless.* (Ks, Ṣ, Mgh, Mṣb, Ḳ, TA, but not in the CḲ.) — And صَحَا مِنْ سُكْرِهِ, (Ṣ, Mṣb,) aor. يَصْحُو, (Mṣb,) inf. n. صَحْوٌ (Ṣ, Mṣb, Ḳ) and صُحُوٌّ, (Mṣb,) [*He recovered,* or *became free, from his intoxication;* or] *his intoxication ceased;* as also ↓ اصحى: (Mṣb:) and صَحِىَ, (Ḳ, TA,) inf. n. صَحًا; (TA;) as also ↓ اصحى; (IḲṭṭ, Ḳ, TA;) is [likewise] said of one intoxicated; (Ḳ, TA;) both meaning *he recovered from his state of insensibility;* (TA;) and in like manner both are said of one affected with desire, or yearning or longing in the soul; (Ḳ, TA;) [and also of one sleeping, meaning *he awoke:* see an ex. of the former of these two verbs in this last sense in the latter part of the second paragraph of art. فرط.] — صَحْوٌ signifies also ‡ The *relinquishing of youthful folly, and amorous dalliance, and of what is vain,* or *futile.* (Ḳ, TA.) Hence the saying of a poet,

* صَحَا القَلْبُ عَنْ سَلْمَى وَأَقْصَرَ بَاطِلُهْ *

‡ [*The heart relinquished,* or *has relinquished, youthful folly and amorousness by becoming rid of Selmà, and its vain,* or *futile, occupation ceased,* or *has ceased*]. (TA.) — And one says, صَحَتِ العَاذِلَةُ † *The censuring female relinquished censuring.* (TA.)

4. اصحى: see 1, in four places. — أَصْحَيْنَا *We became in a case of cloudlessness* [*of the sky or day*]; (Mṣb, TA;) *the sky became cloudless to us.* (Ṣ.) ═ أَصْحَيْتُهُ مِنْ سُكْرِهِ [*I recovered him,* or *roused him, from his intoxication*], and مِنْ نَوْمِهِ [*from his sleep*]. (TA.) — And sometimes إِصْحَآءٌ is used as meaning The act of *rousing,* and *recalling to mindfulness, from a state of heedlessness,* or *inadvertence.* (TA.)

صَحْوٌ [an inf. n. used as an epithet, and therefore applicable to a fem. as well as a masc. noun, and to a dual and a pl. as well as a sing.], applied to a day, *Cloudless;* (Ḳ, TA;) as also ↓ صَاحٍ; (Ṣ, TA;) and ↓ مُصْحٍ: (Mgh, Mṣb:) and (Ḳ) in the same sense applied to a sky; (Ks, Ṣ, Mgh, Mṣb, Ḳ;) as also ↓ مُصْحِيَةٌ, or, accord. to Ks, this is not allowable, but only صَحْوٌ, (Ṣ, Mgh, Mṣb,) though one says of the sky أَصْحَتْ. (Mṣb.)

صَحْوَةٌ *A state* [*of freedom from intoxication,* or] *of sensibility,* or *mental perception.* (TA voce سَكْرَة.) يُرِيدُ أَنْ يَأْخُذَهَا بَيْنَ الصَّحْوَةِ وَالسَّكْرَةِ [*He desires to take it being in a state between that of sensibility and that of insensibility,* or *mental perception and inability thereof,*] is a prov., applied to him who seeks a thing feigning ignorance while possessing knowledge. (TA.) [See also another ex. voce سَكْرَة.]

صَاحٍ: see صَحْوٌ. — It is also said of one intoxicated [as meaning *Recovering,* or *becoming free, from his intoxication*; or *ceasing to be intoxicated*: see 1]. (Ṣ, TA.)

مُصْحٍ; and its fem. مُصْحِيَةٌ: see صَحْوٌ.

مَصْحَاةٌ is like مَسْلَاةٌ in meaning as well as in measure, [signifying *A cause of freedom*,] except that the former is from the intoxication of grief and the latter is from distress of mind and anxiety. (TA.)

مِصْحَاةٌ *A sort of vessel*, (Ṣ, Ḳ,) *well known*, (Ḳ,) *used for drinking*; (TA;) *a* طَاس [q. v.], or *a* جَام [q. v.]: (Ḳ:) Aṣ says, "I know not of what it is:" (Ṣ, TA:) it is said to be *of silver*. (TA.) El-Aạshà speaks of wine being poured into it. (Ṣ, TA.) And one says وَجْهٌ كَمِصْحَاةِ اللُّجَيْنِ [*A face like the* مصحاة *of silver*.] (TA.)

صخ

1. صَخَّ الأُذُنَ, aor. ـُ, (Ṣ, A,* TA,) inf. n. صَخٌّ; (Ṣ, TA;) in a copy of the T, ▾ اصخّ, inf. n. إِصْخَاخٌ; (TA;) *It* (a sound) *deafened the ear by its vehemence*. (Ṣ, A, TA.) — And صَخَّهُ, aor. as above, *He struck him on the ear and rendered it deaf*. (A.) — And صَخَّنِى فُلَانٌ بِعَظِيمَةٍ ‡ *Such a one accused me of a great crime, and calumniated me*. (A, TA.) — And رَمَاهُ فَصَخَّهُ, inf. n. as above, *He shot*, or *cast*, *at him, and caused him extreme pain*: or, as some say, *killed him*. (JK.) — And صَخَّ الغُرَابُ *The crow pierced with his beak into the gall on the back of a camel*: (Ḳ,* TA:) or الغُرَابُ يَصُخُّ بِمِنْقَارِهِ فِى دَبَرَةِ البَعِيرِ *the crow pierces with his beak into the gall on the back of the camel*. (JK.) — صَخٌّ also signifies The *striking* with something hard, (L, Ḳ,) as a staff, (L,) upon something solid, (L, Ḳ,) and with iron upon iron. (L.) [Accord. to the TḲ, one says, صَخَّ الحَدِيدَ عَلَى الصَّخْرَةِ, meaning ضَرَبَهَا بِهَا: but I think that the right reading is بِالحَدِيدِ; and the meaning, *He struck with the iron upon the mass of rock*.] ═ صَخَّ الحَجَرُ, (A,) and صَخَّتِ الصَّخْرَةُ and the like, (L,) inf. n. صَخِيخٌ (A, L, Ḳ) and صَخٌّ, (L, Ḳ,) *The stone*, (A,) and *the mass of rock*, (L, Ḳ,) *caused a sound to be heard* (A, L, Ḳ) on its being struck (A, L) with a stone. (L.) — And صَخَّ لِحَدِيثِهِ *He listened to his narration*, or *discourse*. (A, TA.)

4: see above, first sentence.

صَخَّةٌ *A sound produced by the striking of a mass of rock with a stone*. (Ṣ, A,* Ḳ.)

صَاخَّةٌ *A cry that deafens by its vehemence*. (Ṣ, Ḳ.) — And hence, (Ṣ,) The *resurrection*: (AO, Ṣ, Ḳ:) so in the Ḳur lxxx. 33; accord. to AO: being either an act. part. n. from صَخَّ, aor. ـُ, or an inf. n.: (L:) or it there signifies the *cry on the occasion of which the resurrection shall take place, which will deafen the ears so that they shall hear nothing but the call to life*: (Zj, L:) or it there means the *second blast of the horn*. (Jel.) — Also *A calamity*, or *misfortune*: (Ḳ:) or *a severe calamity* or *misfortune*: and hence the resurrection is called الصَّاخَّةُ. (A, TA.)

صخب

1. صَخِبَ, (Ṣ, A, Mṣb, Ḳ,) aor. ـَ, (A, Mṣb, Ḳ,) inf. n. صَخَبٌ, (Ṣ,* A,* Mṣb, Ḳ,* TA,) of which سَخَبٌ is a syn., of the dial. of Rabee'ah, but [said to be] a bad word, (TA,) *He clamoured*; or *raised a loud*, or *vehement*, *cry*, (Ṣ, Ḳ, TA,) or *a confusion*, or *mixture*, *of cries* or *shouts* or *noises*; (Ṣ, A, TA;) accord. to some, in altercation, or contention: (TA:) or *he raised much clamour, and confusion of cries* or *shouts* or *noises*. (Mṣb.)

3. صاخبهُ, (A, MA,) inf. n. مُصَاخَبَةٌ, (A,) [*He raised a clamour*, or *confused noise, with him*;] *he spoke with him with a loud voice* or *noise* or *clamour*: *he clamoured with*, or *at*, or *against*, *him, with anger*. (MA.)

6: see the next paragraph.

8. اصطخبوا (Ṣ,* A, TA) and ▾ تصاخبوا (A, Ḳ, TA) *They clamoured*; or *raised loud*, or *vehement*, *cries*, or *clamours*, [or *confused noises*,] *and beat one another*, or *contended together in beating* or *in fight*. (Ḳ, TA.) A poet says,

إِنَّ الضَّفَادِعَ فِى الغُدْرَانِ تَصْطَخِبُ

[*Verily the frogs make a loud and confused croaking in the pools of water left by the torrents*]. (Ṣ.) And one says, سَمِعْتُ ٱصْطِخَابَ الطَّيْرِ (A, Ḳ*) i. e. [*I heard*] *the confused cries*, or *voices*, *of the birds*. (Ḳ. [See also صَخَبٌ.]) — And [hence,] ٱصْطَخَبَتْ أَمْوَاجُ الوَادِى ‡ [*The waves of the valley*, or *torrent-bed*, *flowing with water, dashed together, making a loud and confused sound*]. (A.)

صَخَبٌ inf. n. of 1: (Mṣb, TA:) [used as a simple subst., its pl. is أَصْخَابٌ:] one says, سَمِعْتُ أَصْخَابَ الطَّيْرِ *I heard the* [*confused*] *cries*, or *voices*, *of the birds*. (Mṣb. [See also 8.])

صَخِبٌ (A, Mṣb, Ḳ) and ▾ صَخَّابٌ (Ṣ, A, Mṣb, Ḳ) and ▾ صَخْبَانُ (Ṣ, Mṣb, Ḳ) and ▾ صَخُوبٌ (Ḳ) and ▾ صَاخِبٌ (A, Mṣb) are epithets from صَخَبٌ; (Ṣ, A, Mṣb, Ḳ;) all except the last signifying One *who clamours*, or *raises confused cries* or *shouts* or *noises*, *vehemently*, or *much*; (TA;) [the last having a similar, but not intensive, signification, i. e. *clamouring*, &c.:] and the first, though masc., is applied by the poet Usámeh El-Hudhalee to a female singer considered as a person (شَخْص [and meaning in this instance *loud of voice*]); for an epithet of the measure فَعِلٌ applied to a woman (ٱمْرَأَةٌ) is not known in the language: (L, TA:) the [proper] fem. epithet is صَخِبَةٌ and ▾ صَخَّابَةٌ (Ḳ) and ▾ صَخْبَى (Mṣb) and ▾ صَخُوبٌ (Ḳ, TA, in the CḲ [erroneously] صَخُوبَةٌ) and ▾ صُخْبَةٌ: (Ḳ:) the pl. of صَخْبَانُ is ▾ صُخْبَانٌ; (Kr, Ḳ;) [and the pl. of صَخُوبٌ is ▾ صُخُبٌ, like صُبُرٌ pl. of صَبُورٌ:] the hypocrites are described in a trad. as صُخُبٌ بِالنَّهَارِ خُشُبٌ بِاللَّيْلِ [expl. voce خُشُبٌ], meaning *clamorous and contentious*. (TA.) — [Hence,] حِمَارٌ صَخِبُ الشَّوَارِبِ *An ass that makes his braying to reciprocate* [*loudly*] *in the ducts of his throat*; (Ḳ;) *that brays vehemently*. (Ṣ in art. شرب, q. v.) — And عُودٌ صَخِبُ الأَوْتَارِ ‡ [*A lute of which the chords send forth loud sounds*]. (A, TA.) — And مَآءٌ ▾ مُصْطَخِبٌ الآذِىِّ (Ṣ, A,* Ḳ) and صَخِبُ الآذِىِّ (Ḳ) ‡ *Water of which the waves send forth a* [*loud*] *sound*, (Ṣ, TA,) or *are agitated*, (Ḳ,) or *dash together*. (TA.) See also what next follows.

عَيْنٌ صَخْبَةٌ, (Ḳ, TA,) with the خ quiescent, (TA,) or ▾ صَخِبَةٌ, (so in a copy of the A,) ‡ *A spring*, or *fountain*, *that is agitated* [app. *so as to make a confused sound*] *in estuating*. (A, Ḳ, TA.) ═ And صَخْبَةٌ signifies also The [*kind of bead* (خَرَزَة), *used for captivating*, or *fascinating*, *called*] عَطْفَة: (TA:) or *a bead* (خَرَزَة) *used* [*as a charm*] *in* [*cases of*] *love and hatred*. (Ḳ, TA.)

صَخْبَانُ; and its fem. صَخْبَى; and pl. صُخْبَانٌ: see صَخِبٌ.

صُخْبَةٌ: see صَخِبٌ.

صَخُوبٌ; and its pl. صُخُبٌ: see صَخِبٌ, in three places.

صَخَّابٌ, and its fem., with ة: see صَخِبٌ.

صَاخِبٌ: } see صَخِبٌ.
مُصْطَخِبٌ: }

صخد

1. صَخَدَ النَّهَارُ, aor. ـَ, (Ṣ, L, Ḳ,) inf. n. صَخْدٌ (Ṣ, L) and صَخَدَانٌ, (L,) *The day was*, or *became*, *intensely hot*. (Ṣ, L, Ḳ.) And صَخَدَ الحَرُّ, inf. n. صَخَدَانٌ, *The heat was*, or *became*, *intense*; as also ▾ اصخد, inf. n. إِصْخَادٌ. (L.) ═ صَخَدَتْهُ الشَّمْسُ, aor. ـَ, (Ṣ, L, Ḳ,) inf. n. صَخْدٌ, (Ṣ, L,) *The sun smote him*, (Ṣ, L,) and *burned him*: (Ṣ, L, Ḳ:) or *was*, or *became*, *hot upon him*. (L.) And صَخَدَهُ الحَرُّ *The heat pained his brain*. (A.) ═ صَخَدَ said of the [bird called] صُرَد, (Ṣ, L, Ḳ,) aor. ـِ, inf. n. صَخْدٌ and صَخِيدٌ, (L,) *It cried*: (Ṣ, L, Ḳ:) and so صَخَدَتْ said of the هَامَة [or owl]. (A, L.) ═ صَخَدَ إِلَيْهِ, (L, Ḳ,) aor. ـَ, (L,) inf. n. صُخُودٌ, *He listened to him*, (L, Ḳ,) and *inclined to him*. (L.)

4. اصخد *He* (a man, TA) *entered upon* [*a time of*] *heat*. (Ḳ.) — Also, (Ṣ, L, Ḳ,) and ▾ اصطخد, (A,) *It* (a chameleon) *warmed itself with the heat of the sun*; *basked in the sun*. (Ṣ, A, L, Ḳ.) — See also 1.

8: see 4. [And see also مُصْطَخِدٌ, below.]

صُخْدٌ a dial. var. of سُخْدٌ: meaning *Blood and water in the* سَابِيَآء [or *membrane enclosing the fœtus in the womb*]: — and i. q. رَهَلٌ: [see سُخْدٌ:] — and *Yellowness in the face*. (L.)

صَخَدَانٌ: see what next follows.

يَوْمٌ صَخْدَانٌ (Ṣ, L, Ḳ) and ▼ صَخَدَانٌ (Th, L, Ḳ) and ▼ صَيْخُودٌ (Ṣ, L, Ḳ [written by Freytag, as from the Ṣ, صَخُودٌ]) and ▼ صَاخِدٌ and ▼ صَيْخَدٌ (L) *A day intensely hot.* (Ṣ, L, Ḳ.) And لَيْلَةٌ صَخْدَانَةٌ *A night intensely hot.* (L.) And هَاجِرَةٌ ▼ صَيْخُودٌ *A midday intensely hot.* (A.) — [صَخَدَانٌ is originally an inf. n. Hence] one says, أَتَيْتُهُ فِى صَخَدَانِ الحَرِّ *I came to him during the intenseness of the heat:* (L:) and one says also, اتيته فى مَصَاخِدِ ▼ الحَرِّ *I came to him in the midday-intensities of the heat;* (TA;) for مَصَاخِدُ is pl. of ▼ مَصْخَدَةٌ signifying the *midday-intensity of heat;* (Ḳ, TA;) as also ▼ صَاخِدَةٌ: (L, TA:) and اتيته فى صَيَاخِيدِ ▼ الحَرِّ [meaning the same; or *I came to him during the intensities of the heat*]: (TA:) and رَمَانِى الحَرُّ بِصَيَاخِيدِهِ ▼ وَالبَرْدُ بِصَنَادِيدِهِ [*The heat smote me with its intensities, and the cold with its vehemencies*]. (A.)

صَاخِدٌ *Intense* heat. (L.) — See also صَخْدَانٌ. ═ [Also *Crying,* as a صُرَد and as an owl.] One says هَامٌ صَوَاخِدُ [in which the latter word is pl. of the fem. صَاخِدَةٌ] *Owls hooting.* (A.) ═ And *Listening,* and *inclining,* to one. (L.) ═ وَاحِدٌ قَاخِدٌ صَاخِدٌ [the second word here written in the TA and in my MS. copy of the Ḳ, فَاخِدٌ, but it is said in the TA in art. قحد, on the authority of the Ḳ, to be correctly with ق,] means صُنْبُورٌ, (Ḳ, TA,) i. e. *Single,* or *solitary, and weak:* or *i. q.* دَاهِيَةٌ [i. e. *very cunning,* or *very intelligent* or *sagacious, and crafty:* but this meaning I think improbable]. (TA. [See also art. قحد.])

صَيْخَدٌ: see صَخْدَانٌ. — Also الصَّيْخَدُ, (L, Ḳ,) or صَيْخَدُ الشَّمْسِ, (A,) *The rays* (عَيْن) *of the sun:* (A, L, Ḳ:) so called because of the heat thereof. (L.) One says, ذَابَ صَيْخَدُ الشَّمْسِ [*The rays of the sun became intensely hot*], (A,) and اِسْتَذَابَ الصَّيْخَدُ [which means the same]. (L.)

صَاخِدَةٌ: see صَخْدَانٌ.

صَيْخَادٌ: see the next paragraph, in two places.

صَيْخُودٌ; and its pl. صَيَاخِيدُ: see صَخْدَانٌ, in four places. — صَخْرَةٌ صَيْخُودٌ *A hard rock which becomes intensely hot when the sun shines fiercely upon it:* (L:) or [simply] *a hard rock;* (Ṣ, Ḳ;) as also ▼ صَيْخَادٌ: (Ḳ:) or *a solid, firm, and strong, rock;* and so ▼ صَيْخَادٌ: (TA:) or *a smooth and hard rock, that cannot be moved from its place, and upon which iron has not effect:* and *a great rock, which nothing can raise, and upon which neither a pickaxe nor any other thing has effect:* (L:) or *a rock upon which the pickaxe has no effect:* (A:) pl. as above. (L.)

صَيْخَدُونٌ *Hardness* (Ḳ, TA) and *strength.* (TA.)

مَصْخَدَةٌ; and its pl.: see صَخْدَانٌ.

مُصْطَخِدٌ A chameleon *standing erect, towards the sun;* [app. on a branch;] as also مُصْطَخِمٌ. (L. [See also 4.])

صخر

2. تَصْخِيرٌ [inf. n. of صَخَّرَ] *i. q.* تَسْخِيرٌ. (Ḳ.)

صَخْرٌ (Ṣ, A, Mṣb, Ḳ, &c.) and ▼ صَخَرٌ, (Ṣ, Mṣb, Ḳ,) the latter on the authority of Yaạḳoob, (Ṣ,) thus sometimes pronounced, (Mṣb,) *Rocks;* or *great masses of stone:* (Ṣ:) or *great masses of hard stone:* (A, Ḳ:) and صَخْرَةٌ (Ṣ, A, Mṣb, Ḳ, &c.) and صَخَرَةٌ (Ṣ, Mṣb, Ḳ) [are the ns. un., signifying] *one thereof,* (Ṣ, A, Ḳ,) or these have a more special signification [as meaning *a rock* and *a mass of rock*]: (Mṣb:) pl. صُخُورٌ (Ṣ, A, Mṣb, Ḳ) and صُخُورَةٌ (A, Ṣgh, L) and [of صَخْرَةٌ and صَخَرَةٌ] صَخَرَاتٌ. (Mṣb, Ḳ. [In the latter, صَخْرٌ and صَخَرٌ, as well as صُخُورٌ and صَخَرَاتٌ, are improperly termed pls. of صخرة.]) By صَخْرَةٌ in the Ḳur xxxi. 15 is meant a صخرة that is beneath the ground. (Zj, TA.) And by the صَخْرَة mentioned in a trad. as being of, or from, Paradise is meant the صخرة [or rock] of Jerusalem [in the centre of the building now called "the Dome of the Rock"]. (TA.)

صَخَرٌ; n. un. صَخَرَةٌ: see صَخْرٌ.

صَخِرٌ A place *abounding in rocks,* or *great masses of hard stone;* as also ▼ مَصْخَرٌ. (Ḳ.)

صَخِيرٌ *A certain plant.* (Ḳ.) [Golius explains this as meaning *Great,* applied to a rock, or mass of stone; and so مَصْخَرٌ; on the authority of J: but neither of these do I find in the Ṣ.]

صَخِيرَةٌ: see صَحِيرَةٌ.

صَاخِرٌ The *sound of iron* [*striking*] *upon iron.* (Ḳ.)

صَاخِرَةٌ *A kind of earthen vessel,* (Ṣ, A, Ḳ,) *out of which one drinks.* (A.)

أَصْخَرُ الوَجْهِ ‡ A *hard-faced* man; one *having little shame.* (A.)

مَصْخَرٌ; see صَخِرٌ.

صخم

1. صَخَمَتْهُ الشَّمْسُ *The sun smote,* or *hurt,* or *burned, him,* or *his face.* (Ḳ.)

8. اصطخم, (Ṣ, Ḳ,) and اصطخم, (Ḳ,) *He stood erect,* (Ṣ, Ḳ, TA,) and El-'Abbás adds, *silent, as though he were angry.* (TA.) [See also the part. n., below.]

صَخْمَآءُ A [stony tract such as is termed] حَرَّةٌ *in which the plain is intermixed with the rugged.* (Ḳ.)

مُصْطَخِمٌ part. n. of 8. (Ṣ.) Applied to a chameleon, *Standing erect, towards the sun;* [app. on a branch;] as also مُصْطَخِدٌ. (L in art. صخد.)

صد

1. صَدَّ عَنْهُ, (Ṣ, M, Ḳ, &c.,) aor. ـِ (Ṣ, M, A) and ـُ, (M,) the latter only agreeable with analogy, (MF,) [but the former, which is the more common, explainable on the ground that وَجْهَهُ or the like is understood,] inf. n. صُدُودٌ (Ṣ, M, A, Ḳ) and صَدٌّ, (M,) *He turned away from, avoided, shunned,* and *left, him, or it; he was averse from him, or it;* (Ṣ, M, A, Mṣb, Ḳ;) *he turned away his face from him* [or it]: (Ḥam p. 89:) and صَدَّهُ also, aor. ـُ, inf. n. صَدٌّ, *he forsook him, and turned away his face from him.* (L.) One says, أَرَى فِيكَ صُدُودًا [*I see in thee aversion*]. (A.) And لَا صَدَّ عَنْ ذَاكَ [lit. *There is no evading that*], meaning *truly thou didst that.* (Lḥ, M.) صَدَّ السَّبِيلُ ‡ [*The road,* or *way, turned aside*] is said when a difficult road up a mountain, (A, L,) or some other obstacle, (A,) presents itself before thee, and thou leavest it, and takest another way. (A, L.) — And صَدَّهُ عَنْهُ, (Ṣ, M, Ḳ, &c.,) aor. ـُ, (Mṣb,) inf. n. صَدٌّ; (Ṣ, Mṣb, Ḳ;) and ▼ أَصَدَّهُ, (Ṣ, M, Ḳ,) inf. n. إِصْدَادٌ; (TA;) and ▼ صَدَّدَهُ; (M;) *He averted him; turned him,* or *sent him, away,* or *back;* or *caused him to return,* or *go back,* or *revert; from it:* (Ṣ, M, Mṣb, Ḳ:) *prevented,* or *hindered, him from doing it:* (Ṣ, A, Mṣb, Ḳ:) or *did so by gentle means:* and so صَدَّدَهُ. (L in art. ضد.) ═ صَدَّ, aor. ـِ, (T, Ṣ, M, A, Ḳ,) agreeably with analogy, (MF,) and this is the more approved form, (T,) and ـُ, (T, Ṣ, Ḳ,) inf. n. صَدِيدٌ (Ṣ, A, Ḳ) and صَدٌّ, (M,) *He cried out, vociferated,* or *raised a clamour,* (T, Ṣ, M, A, Ḳ,) مِنْ كَذَا [*at,* or *by reason of, such a thing*]. (A.) — And صَدَّ, aor. ـِ, (Lth, M, Mṣb,) inf. n. صَدٌّ, (M,) *He laughed,* مِنْ كَذَا [*at such a thing*]: (Lth, Mṣb:) or *he laughed violently,* or *immoderately.* (M.)

2. صَدَّدَهُ عَنْهُ: see 1. ═ And صَدَّدَ, (T, TA,) inf. n. تَصْدِيدٌ; for which one says, صَدَّى, inf. n. تَصْدِيَةٌ, (T, M,* Ḳ,* TA,) changing one of the دد into ى, (T, Ḳ, TA,) like as one says قَصَّيْتُ أَظْفَارِى, which is originally قَصَّصْتُ; (T, TA;) and صَدَّى بِيَدَيْهِ; (TA in art. صدى;) *He clapped with his hands;* (T, M, Ḳ;) because, in the action of clapping the hands together, the صَدّ, i. e. "face," of one hand fronts that of the other; or, accord. to Aboo-Jaạfar Er-Rustamee, التَّصْدِيَةُ is from صَدًى meaning "a sound" [or "an echo"]; but the former derivation is the more probable: (TA:) [see art. صدى:] also *he raised his voice,* or *called out,* or *cried out.* (M, TA.) It is said in the Ḳur [viii. 35], وَمَا كَانَ صَلَاتُهُمْ عِنْدَ ٱلْبَيْتِ إِلَّا مُكَآءً وَتَصْدِيَةً *And their prayer at the House* [of God] *is nought but whistling, and clapping with the hands:* (M,* TA:) meaning, they do thus instead of praying as they have been commanded to do. (Jel.) ═ See also 4.

3. صَادَّهُ وَضَادَّهُ [*He treated him with aversion and opposition*]. (A.)

4. أَصَدَّهُ عَنْهُ: see 1. ═ اصدّ said of a wound, (Ṣ, M, Mṣb, Ḳ,) inf. n. إِصْدَادٌ; (TA;) as also

↑ صَدَّد ; (M, TA ;) *It contained*, or *generated*, *matter*, (Ṣ, M, Mṣb, Ḳ,) *such as is termed* صَدِيد : (M, Mṣb :) or *ran with such matter*. (A.)

5. تَصَدَّدَ لَهُ, for which one says تَصَدَّى لَهُ, [changing the last د into ى, as in the case of صَدَّدَ, q. v.,] from الصَّدَدُ, meaning "the place, or part, that is before, in front, facing, or opposite;" (Az, L ;) *He addressed*, or *applied*, or *directed*, *himself*, or *his regard*, or *attention*, or *mind*, *to him*, or *it* ; [as though he set himself over against the object to which the verb relates :] and *he asked him*, or *petitioned him*, *for a thing that he wanted :* syn. تَعَرَّضَ لَهُ ; (L and Ḳ* in the present art., and Ṣ and M and Ḳ in art. صدى ;) and أَقْبَلَ عَلَيْهِ ; (L ;) and تَضَوَّعَ لَهُ : (M in art. صدى :) *he inclined to him*, or *it :* (L :) *he raised his head towards it :* (M in art. صدى, in explanation of تصدّى :) *he raised his head and breast towards it*, *looking towards it*, or *regarding it :* (TA in art. صدى, in explanation of تصدّى :) the object is one at which you raise your eyes, looking at it : (Ṣ in art. صدى, in explanation of تصدّى :) *he applied*, or *gave*, *his whole attention to it*, (meaning an affair,) *having his mind unoccupied by other things* ; syn. تَفَرَّغَ لَهُ وَتَبَتَّلَ. (Mṣb.) One says also, تصدّى لِلرَّدِّ عَلَى المُصَنِّفِ [*He addressed*, or *applied*, *himself to reply against the author*]. (TA in art. حزب, &c.) And تصدّى لِلْمَعْرُوفِ وَطَلَبَهُ *He addressed himself*, or *applied himself*, *to obtain favour*, or *bounty* ; *and sought it* ; syn. تَعَرَّضَ لَهُ [and تَبَرَّى لَهُ]. (Mṣb in art. عرض.) And أَنْتَ لَهُ تَصَدَّى, [in the Ḳur, lxxx., 6,] originally تَتَصَدَّدُ, (L,) and accord. to one reading تَصَّدَّى, (Jel,) means *To him thou addressest thyself*, or *directest thine attention*, and *inclinest* ; syn. تَتَعَرَّضُ لَهُ, (L,) and تُقْبِلُ عَلَيْهِ, (Zj,) and تَمِيلُ إِلَيْهِ ; (L ;) or تَتَعَرَّضُ لَهُ بِالْإِقْبَالِ عَلَيْهِ : (Bḍ :) or *addressest thyself*, &c., and *humblest thyself :* (M in art. صدى : [in which, however, this explanation is not given with express reference to the above-cited phrase in the Ḳur :]) or it may signify *thou seekest to bring thyself near to him*, or *to advance thyself in his favour* ; from الصَّدَدُ as signifying القُرْبُ. (T.) [See also art. صدى.]

8. اصطدّت *She* (a woman) *covered herself with a* صِدَاد [q. v.], i. e. سِتْر. (Nawádir el-Aạráb, O, Ḳ.)

R. Q. 1. صَدْصَدَةٌ The *beating of the sieve with one's hand*. (TA.)

صَدٌّ a Pers. word [app. used by the Arabs] signifying *A hundred*. (TA.)

صَدٌّ : see صُدٌّ, in four places. — Also The *face*, or *front*, of the hand. (TA.)

صُدٌّ (M, A, L, Mṣb, Ḳ) and ↑ صَدٌّ (Ḳ) The *side* of a valley, (M, A, Mṣb, Ḳ,) or of a شِعْب [i. e. the kind of water-course so called, or a ravine], and of a mountain where it forms a ravine, (M, L,) and ‡ of a road : (A :) pl. [of pauc.] أَصْدَادٌ and [of mult.] صُدُودٌ. (TA.) And ↑ صَدٌّ (L) and ↑ صَدَدٌ (M, L) signify [in like manner] *A side* ; *a lateral*, or *an adjacent*, *part*, *quarter*, *tract*, or *the like* ; syn. of the former جَانِبٌ, (L,) and of the latter نَاحِيَةٌ. (M, L.) انْضَمَّ عَلَيْهِمُ الصُّدَّانِ [lit. *The two sides* of the road *confined them*] means ‡ *they occupied the middle of the road*. (A.) And الصُّدَّانِ signifies also ‡ *The two edges*, or *extremities*, or *cusps*, *of the notch of an arrow*, *between which is the place of the bow-string* ; syn. شَرْخَا الفُوقِ. (O. [In the Ḳ, erroneously, شَرْخَا الفَرْقِ.]) — Also صُدٌّ and ↑ صَدٌّ *A mountain :* (AA, Ṣ, M, L, Mṣb, Ḳ :) and so سُدٌّ and سَدٌّ : (AA, Ṣ, M :) pl. أَصْدَادٌ and صُدُودٌ. (M, L.) — And ↑ صُدٌّ [or صَدٌّ] *A cloud*, or *collection of clouds*, *rising high*, *and appearing like a mountain :* and so سُدٌّ [or سَدٌّ (q. v.)], which is the more approved word. (M, L.)

صَدَدٌ : see صُدٌّ. — Also i. q. قُرْبٌ [used as a n. of place, meaning *Vicinity*, or *a near place* or *spot* ; as in phrases here following] : (ISk, Ṣ, M, A, Mṣb, Ḳ :) and the *place*, or *part*, *that is before*, *in front*, *facing*, or *opposite*. (ISk,* T, Ṣ,* M, A,* L, Ḳ.*) One says, دَارُهُ بِصَدَدِ المَسْجِدِ [*His house is in the vicinity of*, i. e. *near to*, *the mosque* ; or *his house is opposite to the mosque*]. (Mṣb. [The former meaning is there indicated ; but no meaning is expressed.]) And أَخَذْتُهُ مِنْ صَدَدٍ i. e. مِنْ قُرْبٍ [*I took it from a near place* or *spot*]. (A.) And دَارِى صَدَدَ دَارِهِ, (ISk, Ṣ, A, Ḳ,) in which صدد is in the accus. case as an adv. n. of place, (Ṣ, Ḳ,) and بِصَدَدِهِ, (ISk, A,) and عَلَى صَدَدِهِ, (Lth, ISk,) *My house is opposite to*, i. e. *in the place*, or *part*, *that is in front of*, *his house :* (ISk, Ṣ, A, Ḳ :) and *in the vicinity of*, or *near to*, *his house*. (Ḳ.) And هٰذَا صَدَدَ هٰذَا, and بِصَدَدِهِ, *This is in front of*, or *opposite to*, *this*. (M.) — [Hence, app.,] لَاحَدَدَ لِى دُونَهُ وَلَا صَدَدَ *There is no impediment to me in the way of it*, *nor any obstacle*. (A.) — And هُوَ صَدَدَكَ i. q. قَصْدَكَ [i. e. *He*, or *it*, *is tending*, or *looking*, *in the direction of thee* ; or *is before thee*, or *before thy face :* see art. قصد]. (Sb, M.) — And أَنَا بِصَدَدِ مِنْ هٰذَا الأَمْرِ [*I am directing myself*, or *my attention*, *to this affair*]. (A.) [نَرْجِعُ إِلَى مَا نَحْنُ بِصَدَدِهِ, meaning *We will return to that* subject *to which our attention is directed*, is a phrase of frequent occurrence after a digression.]

صِدَادٌ *A woman's* سِتْر [app. meaning *veil*, or *covering*]. (Nawádir el-Aạráb, O, Ḳ.) — See also what next follows.

صُدُودٌ i. q. مِجْوَلٌ [app. meaning *A kind of garment for women* or *for young girls*, which is thus called] ; (O, Ḳ ; in the CḲ مِحْوَل ;) as also ↑ صِدَادٌ ; so says Th. (O.)

صَدِيدٌ an inf. n. of صَدَّ [q. v.] in one of its senses. (Ṣ, A, Ḳ.) — Also The *ichor*, i. e. *thin water*, [or *watery humour*,] of a wound, (Ṣ, A, Mgh, Ḳ,) *mixed* [or *tinged*] *with blood*, (Ṣ, A, Mgh,) *before the matter becomes thick :* (Ṣ, A :) or *matter*, or *pus*, *like water*, *in which is a mixture of red and white :* (M :) or *matter*, or *pus*, *like water in thinness and like blood in its having a mixture of red and white :* (AZ, Mṣb :) and some add that when it has thickened, it is مِدَّة : (Mṣb :) or *matter*, or *pus*, *mixed with blood*, (Lth, Mgh, Mṣb,) in a wound. (Lth.) In the Ḳur xiv. 19, it means *What flows from the skins of the inmates of Hell :* (M :) or *what flows from their insides*, *and is mixed with matter and blood :* (Jel :) or *hot water* (حَمِيم) *boiled until it thickens*. (M, Ḳ.) — And hence, as being likened thereto, ذُوَابَتُهَا i. e. صَدِيدُ الفِضَّةِ [app. meaning *What is melted of silver*]. (M.)

صُدَّى *A species of fig*, *white without*, *black within*, *and very sweet*. (AḤn, M, TA.)

صُدَّادٌ *A road to water*. (Ṣ, Ḳ.) = And الصُّدَّادُ *The serpent :* (Ḳ :) and (Ḳ, TA, in the CḲ "or") *a certain small animal* (دُوَيْبَّة, Ṣ, Ḳ) *of the kind of the* [*field-rats called*] جِرْذَان : (Ṣ :) or [*a species of lizard* ;] *what is called* سَامٌ أَبْرَصَ [q. v.] ; (AZ, Ṣ, M, Ḳ ;) used in this sense by Keys : (AZ, Ṣ :) or, accord. to Yaạkoob, *the* [*lizard called*] وَزَغ : or, as some say, *a species of the* [*field rats called*] جِرْذَان : (M :) pl. صَدَائِدُ, (Ṣ, M, Ḳ,) which is anomalous. (Ṣ, M.)

صَادٌّ *Turning away*, *avoiding*, *shunning*, and *leaving* ; or *averse :* fem. صَادَّةٌ : pl. of both صُدَّادٌ ; and of the fem. صَوَادُّ also. (M.)

مَصْدُودٌ [pass. part. n. of صَدَّهُ, q. v.]. One says, فُلَانٌ مَصْدُودٌ عَنِ الخَيْرِ [*Such a one is turned away from*, or *prevented from attaining*, *what is good*, or *prosperity*]. (A.)

صدأ

1. صَدِئَ, (Ṣ, M, L, Ḳ,) aor. ـَ, (L,) inf. n. صَدَأٌ, (Ṣ, M,) said of a horse, (Ḳ, TA,) and of a kid, (Ṣ, TA,) [or a goat,] *He was of the colour termed* صُدْأَة [i. e. *sorrel inclining to blackness* ; or *blackness intermixed*, or *tinged over*, *with redness* ; or *a colour like that of the rust of iron* ; probably from the same verb in the sense next following] ; (Ṣ, M, L, Ḳ, TA ;) as also صَدُؤَ, (Ḳ,) aor. ـُ ; (TA ; [and it is implied in the Ḳ that the latter verb is syn. with the former in all its senses ;]) but the former verb is that which is commonly known, and that alone which is required by analogy as a verb denoting a colour, and the latter is not known to have been heard ; (MF, TA ;) and in the L it is said that the verb in this sense is صَدِئَ and ↑ اِصْدَأَّ, this latter [formed from اِصْطَدَأَ, originally اِصْتَدَأَ,] of the measure اِفْتَعَلَ. (TA.) — Also, (M, Ḳ,) صَدِئَ, (Ṣ, M, Mṣb, Ḳ,) aor. as above, (Ṣ, Mṣb, TA,) and so the inf. n., (Ṣ, TA,) said of iron, *It was*, or *became*, *rusty*, or *rusted ;* (Ṣ, M, Mṣb, Ḳ ;) in which sense it is said also of the like of iron. (M.) = And صَدِئَ said of a man, *He stood erect*, *and looked*. (Ḳ.) = صَدَأَ المِرْآةَ, aor. ـَ, (Ḳ,) inf. n. صَدْءٌ, (TḲ,) *He polished the mirror*, (Ḳ, TA,) i. e., *removed from it the rust*, (TA,) *in order to use it as a collyrium ;* (Ḳ, TA ;) as also ↑ صَدَّأَهَا, (Ḳ,) inf. n. تَصْدِئَةٌ. (TA.) [Whether the mirrors

of the Arabs were made of bronze, or of what other metal they were made, is not said. See also 1 in art. حلأ.] ═ And, aor. as above, said of an owl, *He uttered a cry* or *cries*. (Sh, TA. [See also art. صدو.])

2: see the preceding paragraph.

5. تَصَدَّأَ لَهُ, (Ḳ,) as also تصدّع له, (TA,) i. q. تَصَدَّى له, (Ḳ, TA,) which is the original, meaning تعرّض له [i. e. *He addressed*, or *applied*, or *directed, himself*, or *his regard*, or *attention*, or *mind, to him*, or *it*; &c.]. (TA.)

8. اِصْدَأَ: see 1, first sentence.

صَدَأٌ inf. n. of صَدِئَ [q. v.]. (Ṣ, M.) — Also [a subst.] signifying The *rust* of iron, (Ṣ, M,* TA,) and of copper and the like. (Ḥar p. 481. [But there erroneously written صداء.]) ═ Also A man *slender in body*; (Ḳ, TA;) *light*, or *active, therein*: its ء is said to be substituted for ع. (TA. [See صَدَع; and see also صَدًى.])

صَدِئٌ [part. n. of صَدِئَ, q. v.]. — One says, يَدِى مِنَ الحَدِيدِ صَدِئَةٌ *My hand is disagreeable in smell* [*from the rust of iron*]. (Ṣ.) — And هُوَ صَاغِرٌ صَدِئٌ † *He is one to whom disgrace*, or *shame, and baseness*, or *meanness, attach*. (Ṣ, Ḳ.) — See also أَصْدَأُ.

صُدْأَةٌ, (Ṣ, M, Ḳ,) in a horse, (Ṣ, Ḳ,) and in a goat, or kid, (Ṣ,) *A sorrel colour* (شُقْرَة) *inclining to blackness*, (M, Ḳ, TA,) *the latter predominating*: (TA:) or *blackness intermixed*, or *tinged over, with redness* [app. *like the rust of iron*]. (Ṣ.)

أَصْدَأُ, (Ṣ, M, Ḳ,) applied to a horse, (Ḳ, TA,) or to a kid, (TA,) *Of a sorrel colour* (i. e. *of the colour termed* شُقْرَة) *inclining to blackness*, (M, Ḳ, TA,) *the latter predominating*: (TA:) or, applied to a horse, and to a goat, or kid, (Ṣ,) or applied to a kid, (Ḳ,) *of a black colour intermixed*, or *tinged over, with redness* [app. *like the rust of iron*]: (Ṣ, Ḳ:) fem. صَدْآءُ (Ṣ, M, Ḳ,) and ↑ صَدِئَةٌ. (M, L, TA.) And كُمَيْتٌ أَصْدَأُ [*A bay*, or *dark bay*, or *brown, horse*,] *tinged over with dinginess*. (Ṣ.) — Also *Rusty*, or *rusted*; applied to iron and the like. (M.) — And [hence] كَتِيبَةٌ صَدْآءُ, (M, and so in copies of the Ḳ,) or صَدْأَى, (Ḳ accord. to the TA,) and the former also, (TA,) [*A body of troops having their arms* or *armour*] *overspread with the rust of iron*. (M, Ḳ.) — And صَدْآءُ A land (أَرْض) *of which the stones are of a red colour inclining to blackness, and rugged, not even with the ground, these stones having beneath them* [*other*] *rough stones, or, sometimes, soil and stones*. (Sh, L.)

صدح

1. صَدَحَ, (Ṣ, A, Ḳ, &c.,) aor. ـَ, (Ḳ,) inf. n. صَدْحٌ (Ṣ, Ḳ, &c.) and صُدَاحٌ, (Ḳ,) in a verse of Wejeehah Bint-Ows Ed-Dabbeeyeh صُدَّاح, (Ḥam p. 617,) *He cried, or raised a loud cry*; (Ṣ, A;) or *raised his voice vehemently*; (Lth, T;) said of a cock [i. e. *he crowed*, or *crowed loudly* or *vehemently*]; (Lth, T, Ṣ, A;) and of a crow [i. e. *he croaked*, or *croaked loudly* or *vehemently*]: (Lth, T, Ṣ:) said of an ass, *he brayed loudly*: (L:) said of a bird, and † of a man, *he raised his voice in singing* (L, Ḳ) or *otherwise*; *cried out vehemently and sharply*; or *uttered a vehement and sharp voice*. (L.)

صَدْحَةٌ (Ṣ, L, Ḳ) and ↑ صُدْحَةٌ and ↑ صَدَحَةٌ (L, Ḳ) *A kind of bead* (خَرَزَة, Lḥ, Ṣ, L, Ḳ) *used for the purpose of captivating*, or *fascinating*: (Ḳ:) or *with which men are captivated*, or *fascinated*: (Ṣ:) or *with which women captivate*, or *fascinate, men*: (Lḥ:) or *with which men are conciliated*. (L.)

صُدْحَةٌ: } see the next preceding paragraph.
صَدَحَةٌ: }

صَدُوحٌ *Having a loud cry* or *voice*; as also ↑ صَدَّاحٌ; both applied to a cock [meaning *loud-crowing*]; (A;) [and to a crow as meaning *loud-croaking*]; and so the former applied to an ass [meaning *loud-braying*]; and so ↑ صَيْدَحٌ applied to a horse [meaning *loud-neighing*]; (Ṣ, Ḳ;) [and app. also applied to a camel as meaning *loud-braying*, for] صَيْدَحُ was the name of the she-camel of Dhu-r-Rummeh: (Ṣ, Ḳ:) or صَدُوحٌ (L, Ḳ) and ↑ صَدَّاحٌ (L) and ↑ صَيْدَحٌ and ↑ صَيْدَاحٌ and ↑ مِصْدَحٌ (L, Ḳ) signify *that raises his voice much in singing* or *otherwise*; (L;) [app. thus applied to a bird, and † to a man; (see 1;)] or *that cries out vehemently*, or *much*; or *has a loud*, or *strong, voice*; (L, Ḳ;) and so ↑ صَيْدَحِىٌّ. (Ḥam p. 558.) [Hence,] ↑ قَيْنَةٌ صَادِحَةٌ ‡ [*A loud-voiced female singer*]. (A, TA.) And ↑ حَادٍ صَيْدَحٌ ‡ [*A loud-voiced man urging camels by his singing*]. (A, TA.) And ↑ مِزْهَرٌ صَدَّاحٌ ‡ [*A loud-sounding lute*]. (Ṣ, A.)

صَدَّاحٌ: see the next preceding paragraph, in three places.

صَادِحَةٌ: see صَدُوحٌ.

صَيْدَحٌ: see صَدُوحٌ, in three places.

صَيْدَحِىٌّ: } see صَدُوحٌ.
صَيْدَاحٌ: }

الأَصْدَحُ *The lion*: (Ḳ:) so called because of his roaring. (TA.)

مِصْدَحٌ: see صَدُوحٌ.

صدر

1. صَدَرَ, (Ṣ, M, A, Mṣb, Ḳ,) aor. ـُ (Ṣ, M, Mṣb, Ḳ) and ـِ, (Ḳ,) inf. n. صَدْرٌ (Ṣ, M, A, Mṣb, Ḳ) and صُدُورٌ (A, TA) and مَصْدَرٌ (M, Ḳ) and مَزْدَرٌ because of the similarity [of the letters ص and ز], (M,) *He returned, went back*; (Ṣ, M, A, Mṣb, Ḳ;) and *went*, or *turned, away*; (Mṣb;) from (عَنْ) water, (Ṣ, M, A,) and a country, (Ṣ, M,) or a place, (Mṣb,) and † any affair. (Lth.) — Hence, صَدَرَ القَوْلُ, aor. ـُ, inf. n. صُدُورٌ, † [*The saying issued, proceeded*, or *emanated*, عَنْهُ *from him*.] (Mṣb.) [And صَدَرَ عَنْهُ الفِعْلُ, with the same aor. and inf. n., † *The action proceeded from him*.] — And صَدَرَ إِلَيْهِ *He went to it*; namely, a place: (TA:) *he came to it*. (Kull. p. 228.) ═ صَدَرَهُ: see 4. ═ Also, (M, Ḳ,) aor. ـُ, inf. n. صَدْرٌ, (M,) *He hit, struck*, or *hurt, his* صَدْر [i. e. *breast*]. (M, Ḳ.) You say, ضَرَبْتُهُ فَصَدَرْتُهُ *I struck him and hit his breast*. (A.) — And صُدِرَ *He had a complaint of the* صَدْر [or *chest*]. (M, Ḳ.) [See its part. n., below.]

2. صَدَّرَهُ: see 4. ═ صَدَّرَ بَعِيرَهُ, (Ḳ,) inf. n. تَصْدِيرٌ, (TA,) *He tied a cord from the girth of his camel to the part behind* [or *beyond*] *the callous lump on his breast*: (Ḳ, TA:) or, accord. to Lth, (L,) one says, صَدَّرَ عَنْ بَعِيرِهِ, (M, L,) and the meaning is, *he tied a cord from the* تَصْدِير [or *breast-girth*] *to the part behind* [or *beyond*] *the callous lump on the breast of his camel, to keep the* تصدير *in its place, when it had become loose in consequence of the animal's having become lank in the belly*: the cord above mentioned is called سِنَاف [q. v.]. (Lth, L.) — And صَدَّرَ عَلَى البَعِيرِ [app. *He put the breast-girth upon the camel*]: from التَّصْدِيرُ, i. e. "the girth" [thus called]. (MA.) — صُدِّرَ *His* (a horse's) *breast became wetted with sweat*. (Ṣ.) See 5. — صَدَّرَهُ, (TA,) or صَدَّرَهُ فِى المَجْلِسِ, (Ṣ,) † *He placed him*, or *seated him, in the upper*, or *highest, part in the sitting-room*, or *sitting-place*. (TA.) And صُدِّرَ *He was advanced*, or *promoted*. (A.) — صَدَّرَ كِتَابَهُ, (Ṣ, Ḳ,) inf. n. as above, (Ḳ,) ‡ *He put to his book*, or *writing, a* صَدْر, (Ṣ, Ḳ, TA,) i. e. a *title*, or a *commencement*. (TA.) And صَدَّرَ كِتَابَهُ بِكَذَا ‡ [*He commenced his book*, or *writing, with such a thing*]. (A.) ═ See also 5, where it is expl. as intrans., in two places.

3. مُصَادَرَةٌ signifies The *returning*, or *going back*, [app. *with another*, from water, &c.] (KL.) [The verb is probably trans., agreeably with general analogy, in all its senses; صَادَرَهُ app. signifying primarily *He returned*, or *went back, with him* from water &c. — Ibr D thinks that it signifies also † *He vied*, or *contended, with him for precedence*, or *priority*.] ═ Also † The *exacting a fine* or *the like* [app. *from another*: or the *suing*, or *prosecuting*, another, *for a debt &c*.]. (KL.) You say, صَادَرَهُ عَلَى كَذَا مِنَ المَالِ (Ṣ,* Ḳ,* TA) † *He desired*, or *sought, to obtain from him*; or *he demanded of him*; or *he sued*, or *prosecuted, him for*; *such a sum*, or *such an amount, of property*. (Ḳ,* TA.) — And صَادَرْتُهُ عَلَى كَذَا وَكَذَا † *I released him from my reckoning with him on such and such terms agreed upon by both*. (TA in art. فرق.) And صُودِرَ عَلَى مَالٍ يُؤَدِّيهِ † *He* (an agent) *was released from being reckoned with* (فُورِقَ) *on the condition of his paying certain property for which he became responsible*: a phrase of the registrars of accounts. (TA in the present art.)

4. اصدرهُ, (Ṣ, M, A, Mṣb, Ḳ,) and ♦ صَدَّرَهُ, (M, Ḳ,) and ♦ صدّرهُ, (Ḳ,) *He caused him to return; sent him,* or *brought him, back,* (Ṣ, M, A, Mṣb, Ḳ,) or *away;* (Mṣb;) from (عَنْ) water, and a country [or place], (Ṣ,) and † any affair. (Lth.) You say, أَصْدَرْنَا رِكَابَنَا *We sent,* or *brought, back our riding-camels satisfied with drink so that it was not necessary for us to remain with them for the sake of the water.* (TA.) And أَوْرَدَهُ وَأَصْدَرَهُ *He brought it and he took it away.* (Ḥar p. 361.) — [Hence,] أَوْرَدَ وَأَصْدَرَ ‡ *He began and completed.* (TA.) You say, إِذَا أَوْرَدَ أَمْرًا أَصْدَرَهُ ‡ *When he begins a thing,* or *an affair, he completes it.* (A.) And فُلَانٌ يُورِدُ وَلَا يُصْدِرُ ‡ *Such a one begins and does not complete.* (A.) — And اصدر القَوْلَ † [*He issued forth the saying; made it to issue, proceed,* or *emanate,* عَنْهُ *from him*]. (Mṣb. [See 1.]) [And اصدر عَنْهُ الفِعْلَ † *He,* or *it, made the action to proceed from him.*]

5. تصدّر *He* (a man, TA) *erected his chest in sitting.* (M, Ḳ.) — ‡ *He* (a horse) *outreached the other horses with his chest;* (M, Ḳ,* TA;) as also ♦ صدّر, (Ṣ,* M, MA, Ḳ,) inf. n. تَصْدِيرٌ: the latter verb is afterwards expl. in the Ḳ as meaning بَرَزَ بِرَأْسِهِ; but this is a mistake. (TA.) Ṭufeyl says, describing a horse,

كَأَنَّهُ بَعْدَ مَا صَدَّرْنَ ♦ مِنْ عَرَقٍ
سِيدٌ تَمَطَّرَ جُنْحَ اللَّيْلِ مَبْلُولُ

As though he were, after they had outreached with their chests, from a row of [other] *horses,* [*a wolf that had exposed himself to rain during a portion of the night,* and had become *wetted:*] but accord. to one relation, it is ♦ صُدِّرْنَ, meaning *their breasts were wetted* [مِنْ عَرَقٍ *by reason of sweat:* the former reading, however is the better. (Ṣ.) — Also † *He sat,* or *became placed* or *seated, in the upper,* or *highest, part in the sitting-room,* or *sitting-place.* (Ṣ,* Ḳ,* TA.) And *He became advanced,* or *promoted.* (A.) تصدّر لِأُمُورِ النَّاسِ † [*He became advanced to the foremost place for the conducting of the affairs of the people*]. (Ḥar p. 104.)

6. تصادروا [app. *They returned together* from water, &c.]. (A. [This meaning seems to be there indicated by the context.]) — And one says, تصادروا عَلَى مَا شَاؤُوا ‡ [app. meaning *They released one another from being reckoned with, by mutual agreement, on such terms as they would:* see 3]. (A.)

صَدْرٌ *Anything that fronts,* or *faces, one.* (M, Ḳ.) — And hence, (M,) The صدر [i. e. *breast,* or *chest,* or *bosom,*] of a man, [often meaning his *mind,*] (M, Mṣb, Ḳ,) and of other than man: (Mṣb:) of the masc. gender: (Lḥ, Ṣ, M, Ḳ:) pl. صُدُورٌ, (Ṣ, M, Mṣb,) the only pl. form. (M.) [See also صُدْرَةٌ.] As to the saying of the poet, (Ṣ, M,) El-Aạshà, (Ṣ,)

وَتَشْرَقُ بِالقَوْلِ الَّذِى قَدْ أَذَعْتَهُ
كَمَا شَرِقَتْ صَدْرُ القَنَاةِ مِنَ الدَّمِ

[*And thou becomest, or wilt become, red by reason of the saying that I have published, like as the fore part of the spear becomes red from blood*], (Ṣ,* M,) he has made صدر fem. because the صدر of the قناة is a part of the قناة; for they [sometimes] make a noun fem. when it is prefixed to a fem. noun: (Ṣ:) or if you will, you may say that he has made صدر fem. because he meant [thereby] the قناة; and if you will, you may say that the صدر of a قناة is a قناة. (M.) [Hence,] بَنَاتُ الصَّدْرِ ‡ *The spaces between the bones of the breast.* (M, TA.) [And also] † *Anxieties.* (T in art. بنى.) And ذَاتُ الصُّدُورِ † *What is in the minds.* (Ksh and Bḍ and Jel in iii. 115, &c.) And ضَاقَ صَدْرُهُ † *His bosom,* or *mind, became strait,* or *contracted.* (Mṣb in art. ضيق. [See the Ḳur xv. 97 and xxvi. 12.]) And شَرَحَ بِالكُفْرِ صَدْرًا † *He opened and dilated his bosom,* meaning, *was pleased, with infidelity.* (Jel in xvi. 108. [See also the similar phrases شَرَحَ اللّٰهُ صَدْرَهُ لِلْإِسْلَامِ and انْشَرَحَ لِقَبُولِ الخَيْرِ expl. in art. شرح.]) And انْشَرَحَ صَدْرُهُ † *His bosom became dilated* or *enlarged* [*with joy*]. (Ṣ in art. شرح.) And وَاسِعُ الصَّدْرِ and رَحِيبُ الصَّدْرِ † *Ample,* or *dilated, in the breast,* or *bosom;* [meaning *free-minded; free from distress of mind; without care:* and *free from narrowness of mind; liberal, munificent,* or *generous.*] (Ṣ and TA in art. رحب.) [And ضَيِّقُ الصَّدْرِ † *Having the bosom,* or *mind, strait,* or *contracted.*] And رَجُلٌ بَعِيدُ الصَّدْرِ ‡ *A man who is not to be turned,* or *bent,* or *inclined.* (M.) In the saying هَلْ يَسْتَطِيعُ مَنْ بِهِ صَدْرٌ إِلَّا أَنْ يَنْفُثَ [meaning *Is he who has the disease of the chest* (دَآءُ الصَّدْرِ) *able to do without spitting?*], if it be correct, the prefixed noun [دآء] is suppressed. (Mgh.) [صَدْرُ الدَّجَاجَةِ, as said by Freytag, is the name of † *The star γ of Cygnus.*] — Also † The *upper,* or *uppermost, part of the front* of anything. (M, Ḳ.) [Hence,] صُدُورُ الوَادِى † *The higher,* or *upper, parts,* and *fronts,* or *fore parts, of the valley;* (M, Ḳ;) as also صَدَائِرُهُ, which is pl. of ♦ صَدَارَةٌ, (Ḳ,) or ♦ صِدَارَةٌ, (as in a copy of the M,) or ♦ صَادِرَةٌ, (as in the L,) or of ♦ صَدِيرَةٌ. (M, L, Ḳ.) And صَدْرُ المَجْلِسِ † *The upper,* or *highest, part* [or *end*] *of the sitting-room,* or *sitting-place:* (TA:) *the elevated part thereof.* (Mṣb.) — [† The *fore part* of anything. † The *prow,* or *fore part,* of a ship.] † The *fore part* of the foot, *between the toes and the* [*protuberant part called the*] حِمَارَة. (M.) † The *fore part* of the sandal, *before the* [*hole through which is put the thong called the* شِرَاك, i. e. *the hole called the*] خُرْت. (M.) ‡ The *part* of the arrow *that is above the middle, as far as the* مراش: (so in a copy of the A: [an evident mistranscription for رأْس, i. e. *head:*]) or the *part* of the arrow *that is beyond the middle, as far as the slender part,* (Ṣ, M, Mṣb, Ḳ,) *which is next the head;* (M;) so called because it is the fore part when it is shot: (Ṣ, Mṣb, Ḳ:) and likewise of the spear [as in the verse cited above in this paragraph]. (M.) يَوْمٌ كَصَدْرِ الرُّمْحِ [lit. † *A day like the fore part of the spear*] means † *a day of straitness and distress:* accord. to Th, it is a day by which war, or battle, is peculiarly distinguished. (M, L.) — † The *first, first part,* or *commencement,* of anything; (Ṣ, M, Ḳ;) even † of the day, (M, Mṣb,) and † of the night, and † of the winter, and † of the summer, and † the like, (M,) and ‡ of an affair. (A. [See an ex. voce عَجُزٌ.]) ‡ The *title* of a book or writing: and the *first part,* or *commencement,* thereof. (TA.) [† The *first foot of the first hemistich* of a verse.] And The *first hemistich* (altogether) of a verse. (O voce عَجُزٌ.) [And † The *first verse* of a قَصِيدَة.] — صَدْرُ الطَّرِيقِ † *The wide,* or *widening, part of the road.* (Mṣb.) — صَدْرُ القَوْمِ † *The head,* or *chief, of the people,* or *party;* as also ♦ المَصْدَرُ. (TA.) And hence, صَدْرُ الصُّدُورِ † [*The chief of the chiefs;* a title applied to *the prime minister of the king;* and also to *the chief judge;* app., in the earlier times, to the former;] *he who performs the onerous duties of the king,* or *of the state.* (TA.) — And † *A part,* or *portion,* of a thing. (Ṣ, Ḳ.)

صَدَرٌ a subst. signifying *Return,* (Ṣ, M, Mṣb, Ḳ,) from (عَنْ) water, (Ṣ, M,) and a country, (Ṣ,) or a place, (Mṣb,) and † any affair: (Lth:) as some say, from anything. (M.) Hence, طَوَافُ الصَّدَرِ, (Ḳ, TA, in the CḲ الصَّدْرِ,) i. e. *The compassing* of the Kaạbeh *on the occasion of the return* of the pilgrims *from 'Arafát.* (TA.) [Hence also,] الصَّدَرُ *The fourth day of the days of the sacrifice* [*performed by the pilgrims*]: (M, Ḳ:) so called because the people then return from Mekkeh to their abodes. (M.) [And hence the saying,] تَرَكْتُهُ عَلَى مِثْلِ لَيْلَةِ الصَّدَرِ *I left him as in the night preceding the fourth day of the days of the sacrifice:* (A:) or [*as in the night preceding the day*] *when the people return from their pilgrimage;* (Ṣ;) meaning, † *possessing nothing.* (M.) — Also quasi-pl. n. of صَادِرٌ, q. v. (M, Ḳ.)

صُدْرَةٌ The صَدْر [or *breast*] (M, Ḳ) of a man [or beast]: (TA:) or the *prominent part of the upper portion thereof.* (T, Ṣ, M, Ḳ.) — Hence, (Ṣ,) *A certain garment* [*which covers the breast*], (Ṣ, M,) *well known:* (Ḳ:) *a short shirt:* a *short* دِرْع: and the dim., ♦ صُدَيْرَةٌ, is applied to *a short shirt which is worn next the body.* (TA.) [In the present day, صُدَيْرِى, which is a corruption of the dim., is applied to *A kind of waistcoat;* a *short vest without sleeves:* and its pl. is صُدَيْرِيَات.] See also the next paragraph.

صِدَارٌ *A certain garment, of which the head,* or *upper part, is like the* مِقْنَعَة, [*covering the head,*] *and the lower part of which covers the breast* (M, Ḳ) *and the shoulders:* (M:) *a woman in mourning for the death of her husband or relation used to wear a* صدار *of wool:* (Az:) or i. q. ♦ صُدْرَةٌ [q. v.] and مِجْوَلٌ and أُصْدَةٌ: (IAạr:) or *a certain garment with which the head and breast are covered, worn by a woman in mourning for her husband:* (A:) or *a small shirt worn next the body:* (Ṣ:) or *a* دِرْع *worn next the breast:* (Aṣ:) or i. q. إِتْبٌ [q. v.]. (T in art.

(.اتب) It is said in a prov., كُلُّ ذَاتِ صِدَارٍ خَالَةٌ [*Every female having a* صدار *is as a maternal aunt*]: i. e., it is incumbent on a man to be jealous for every woman like as he is jealous for his women under covert, or the females of his family whom he is under an obligation to respect and protect. (Ṣ. [See also Freytag's Arab. Prov. ii. 310.]) — Also *A certain mark made with a hot iron upon the breast of a camel.* (Ṣ.)

صَدَارَةٌ † *Precedence,* or *priority.* (TA.) — See also صَدْرٌ, near the middle of the paragraph.

صِدَارَةٌ : } see صَدْرٌ, near the middle of the paragraph.
صَدِيرَةٌ : }

صُدَيْرَةٌ dim. of صُدْرَةٌ, q. v. (TA.)

صَادِرٌ *Returning* [from water, &c.]; *going,* or *turning, back,* or *away:* (TA:) quasi-pl. n. صَدَرٌ ▼. (M, Ḳ.) — [Hence the saying,] مَا لَهُ صَادِرٌ وَلَا وَارِدٌ ‡ *He has not anything:* (M, Ḳ:) or *he has not a thing nor a people.* (Lḥ, M.) — And طَرِيقٌ صَادِرٌ ‡ *A road,* or *way, by which people return from water:* (Ṣ, M, A, Ḳ:) opposed to طَرِيقٌ وَارِدٌ. (M, A.)

صَادِرَةٌ : see صَدْرٌ, near the middle of the paragraph.

أَصْدَرُ A man (M) *having a large breast,* or *chest;* (M, Ḳ, TA;) i. e. *having the breast,* or *chest,* or *the upper part thereof, prominent;* as also مُصَدَّرٌ ▼. (TA.) — الأَصْدَرَانِ *Two veins* (M, Ḳ) *that beat,* or *pulse,* (M,) *beneath the temples:* (M, Ḳ:) or *the two sides* of a man: or *the two shoulder-joints:* (TA:) the word has no singular. (M.) [Hence the saying,] جَآءَ يَضْرِبُ أَصْدَرَيْهِ; (M, Meyd, Ḳ, TA;) and some say أَسْدَرَيْهِ [q. v.], (Meyd, TA,) and this is the original; (Meyd;) and some, أَزْدَرَيْهِ; (Meyd, TA;) a prov.; (M, Meyd, TA;) meaning *He came beating* [with his hand] *his two sides,* (TA,) or *his two shoulder-joints:* (Meyd, TA:) i. e. *he came empty* [-*handed*]; (M, Meyd, Ḳ,* TA;) *not having accomplished the object of his desire:* (Meyd:) or *he came exulting,* or *behaving insolently,* (Meyd, and Ḥar p. 603,) *not knowing where were his* أَصْدَرَانِ: so accord. to Yoo: and some say, جَآءَ يَضْرِبُ بِأَصْدَرَيْهِ. (Ḥar.)

تَصْدِيرٌ [a subst. like تَذْرِيعٌ and تَنْبِيتٌ] The [*fore-girth,* i. e. *breast-girth,* or] *girth that is upon the breast of the camel:* (Ṣ, A:*) [the hind girth, or belly-girth,] that which is next the ثِيل, is called the حَقَب: (Ṣ:) or the *girth of the camel's saddle* (الرَّحْل), and *of the* [*camel-vehicle called*] هَوْدَج. (M.)

مَصْدَرٌ *A place of returning* or *going back,* (Ṣ, TA,) or *of going,* or *turning, away* [from water, and from a country or place, and † from an affair or thing]. (TA. [See 1, first sentence.]) — [Hence, مَصْدَرُ أَمْرٍ ‡ *The way of return from,* or *of completing, a thing* or *an affair:* opposed to مَوْرِدُهُ.] One says, هُوَ يَعْرِفُ مَوَارِدَ الأُمُورِ وَمَصَادِرَهَا ‡ [*He knows the ways of betaking himself to things* or *affairs, and the ways of withdrawing himself from them;* or *of commencing them and of completing them*]. (A.) [See also another ex. in art. رحب, conj. 6.] — And hence [also], the مَصْدَرٌ [pl. of مَصَادِرُ] of verbs: (Ṣ, TA:) مَصْدَرٌ signifies † The *root* of a word, *from which proceed the derivatives of verbs:* (Lth, TA:) [in this sense it is a conventional term of grammar and lexicology, not belonging to the classical language; but on account of the importance of understanding its true application in lexicology, it is necessary to give here a full explanation of it: it is, agreeably with its etymology, the *source* (lit. place) *of derivation,* accord. to the grammarians of El-Baṣrah; and is what I term *an infinitive noun:* it is defined as] *a noun signifying, by its original application, an accident as subsisting in,* or *proceeding from, an agent* (as الفَرَحُ ["the being joyful"], الضَّرْبُ ["the act of beating"], and القُعُودُ ["the act of sitting"]), or *affecting an object of action,* (as الجُنُونُ ["the being possessed by a jinnee"]), *conformable to its verb, so as to comprise all the letters in that verb, either literally* (as in the instances above) *or virtually* (as in القِتَالُ ["the act of fighting"], which wants the ا that is before the ت in the verb, yet wants it as to the letter only, and not virtually, wherefore it is sometimes pronounced as if with the said letter, as in قَاتَلَ قِيتَالًا, but the ا is changed into ى on account of the kesr of the letter before it), or *substituting another letter for any of those letters that it wants* (as in العِدَةُ ["the act of promising"], which wants the و that is in its verb as to the letter and virtually, but has ة substituted for it [by way of compensation]): (from a comparison of definitions &c. in the Expos. of the "Kitab Ḥodood en-Naḥw" by the author of the work thus entitled, arts. مصدر and اسم مصدر; the Expos. of the "Shudhoor edh-Dhahab" by the author of the work thus entitled, section on the nouns that govern as verbs; I'Aḳ; &c.:) but the grammarians of El-Koofeh hold that the verb is the root, and that the مصدر is derived from it: (I'Aḳ p. 148:) some مصادر, moreover, are derived from real (as opposed to ideal) substantives, as التَّحَجُّرُ ["the becoming stone"] from الحَجَرُ ["stone"]. (Kull p. 327.) The مصدر has the same government as its own verb: it is often, and may be at pleasure, used as an ideal subst. or abstract noun: and it is often employed in the place of an act. or a pass. part. n.: (Kull, &c.:) [when thus used as an epithet, it is employed alike as sing. and pl. and masc. and fem.:] accord. to Zj, every مصدر used as an epithet is for ذُو [or ذَاتُ &c.] followed by the مصدر, and therefore it has no dual nor pl. [nor fem.] form. (TA voce حَرَضٌ.) [It has also other uses, which are expl. in the grammars. Used as a مَصْدَر, it is sometimes made fem.; as it is also when used in the sense of a noun that is properly fem.: see صَرْفٌ, third sentence.] — اِسْمُ مَصْدَرٍ, called by some اِسْمٌ لِلْمَصْدَرِ, is a term applied to [† *A quasi-infinitive noun;* i. e.] *a noun which is not a* مصدر, *but which is occasionally used in the place of a* مصدر; like as a مصدر is used in the place of an act. part. n., and in that of a pass. part. n.: such as الوُضُوْءُ for التَّوَضُّؤُ ["the performing of the ablution preparatory to prayer"], and الغُسْلُ for الاِغْتِسَالُ ["the washing of oneself"]; each of which wants somewhat that is in its verb without substituting anything for that which is wanting. (Expos. of the "Kitáb el-Ḥodood," cited above.) This kind of noun the grammarians of El-Koofeh and Baghdád allow to govern as a مصدر; but the grammarians of El-Baṣrah hold that the noun governed in the accus. case in each of the exs. adduced by the former as confirmatory of their opinion is so governed by a verb understood. (Expos. of the "Shudhoor," ubi suprà.) It is also applied to *A proper name signifying an accident* [or *attribute*]; as فَجَارِ and حَمَادِ, proper names, by original application, for الفَجْرَةُ and المَحْمَدَةُ ["vice" and "praise"]; and the like: and this kind does not govern as a مصدر. (Expos. of the "Kitáb Ḥodood en-Naḥw," ubi suprà; and Expos. of the "Shudhoor," ubi suprà.) It is also applied to [what is more properly termed اِسْمٌ لِلْمَعْنَى الحَاصِلِ بِالمَصْدَرِ, by some termed simply حَاصِلٌ بِالمَصْدَرِ, i. e. *An ideal substantive,* or *abstract noun;*] *a noun applied to signify an accident* [or *attribute*] *considered abstractedly* [such as صَدْرٌ signifying "return;" and this kind is commonly termed in the lexicons simply an اسم as distinguished from a مصدر]. (Kull p. 327.) Some apply it also to what is [properly] termed مَصْدَرٌ مِيمِىٌّ [i. e. *A* مصدر *commencing with an augmentative* م], if not of the measure مُفَاعَلَةٌ: but such is really a مَصْدَر. (Expos. of the "Shudhoor," ubi suprà.) And some of the grammarians [and of the lexicographers likewise] apply it to *A noun that signifies the instrument* [or *means*] *with* [or *by*] *which the action signified by a* مصدر *is performed:* as الأُكُلُ ["food," as being "that by means of which the act of eating (الأَكْلُ) is performed"]. (Kull, ubi suprà.) — See also صَدْرٌ, last sentence but two.

مُصْدِرٌ [act. part. n. of 4, q. v. —] ‡ A man *who completes things* or *affairs.* (A.) — And *One of the names of the month* جُمَادَى الأُولَى: (M, Ḳ:) [ISd says,] I think it to be of the dial. of [the tribe of] 'Ád. (M.)

مُصْدِرَةُ القَوْمِ ‡ *Those who are made to have the precedence,* or *priority, of the people,* or *party.* (A, TA.)

[مَصْدَرِىٌّ, as a grammatical term, *Of,* or *relating to, the* مَصْدَر. See the particles أَنْ and كَىْ &c.]

مُصَدَّرٌ A man (M) *strong in the chest;* (Ṣ, M, Ḳ;) and in like manner a lion, (M, A,) and a wolf: (M:) and the *lion;* (Ṣ, Ḳ;) and the *wolf;* (Ḳ;) because they are strong in the chest. (TA.) — See also أَصْدَرُ. — A horse *to whose breast the sweat has reached.* (M, Ḳ.) — A horse, and a sheep or goat, *white in the upper part* (لَبَّة) *of the breast:* (M, Ḳ:) or (with ة, A) a ewe *having a black breast,* (M, A, Ḳ,) *the rest of her being white.* (M.) —— ‡ A horse *that outreaches others* (IAạr, M, A, Ḳ) *with his breast:* (TA:) IAạr does not mention the breast. (M, TA.) [Accord. to rule, this should be مُصَدَّرٌ, as is shown by a verse cited above: see 5.] —— ‡ An arrow *thick in the part called the* صَدْر. (M, A, Ḳ.) —— And المُصَدَّرُ is a name applied to † *The first of the arrows termed* غُفْل, (M, Ḳ,) *which have no notches, and to which is assigned no portion* [*and no fine, in the game called* المَيْسِر]; these being added only to give additional weight to the collection of arrows from a dislike of suspicion [of foul play]. (Lḥ, M. [See السَّفِيح and المَنِيح.])

مَصْدُورٌ A man (A &c.) *having a complaint of the chest.* (Ṣ, A, Mgh, Mṣb.) 'Obeyd-Allah Ibn-'Abd-Allah Ibn-'Otbeh, on its being said to him, How long wilt thou utter this poetry? replied,

• لَا بُدَّ لِلْمَصْدُورِ مِنْ أَنْ يَسْعُلَا •

To him who has a complaint of the chest, there is no avoiding coughing. (TA. [See also نَفَثَ.]) —— It is also often used as meaning † *Grieved, afflicted,* or *vexed.* (TA in art. نفث.)

صدع

1. صَدَعَهُ, (Ṣ, Mṣb, Ḳ,) aor. َ , (Mṣb, Ḳ,) inf. n. صَدْعٌ, (Ṣ,* Mṣb, Ḳ,*) *He clave, split, slit,* or *cracked, it* [i. e. a hard thing, such as a glass vessel, and a wall, and the like of these; (see صَدْع below;) or so generally]; syn. شَقَّهُ; (Ṣ, Mṣb, Ḳ;) as also ↓ صَدَّعَهُ, [but app. in an intensive sense, or relating to a number of objects,] inf. n. تَصْدِيعٌ: (TA:) or *so as to divide it in halves:* or *so that it did not separate.* (Ḳ.) —— [Hence,] one says, صَدَعَهُ صَدْعَ الرِّدَآءِ [*He slit it,* or *rent it, as with the slitting,* or *rending, of the* garment called رِدَاء]. (TA.) —— And صَدَعَ الفَلَاةَ ‡ *He traversed,* or *crossed, the desert;* [*as though he clave it;*] (Ṣ, Mṣb, Ḳ, TA;) and in like manner, النَّهْرَ *the river.* (TA.) And هٰذَا الطَّرِيقُ يَصْدَعُ فِى أَرْضِ كَذَا وَكَذَا † [*This road extends through such and such a land*]. (TA.) And صَدَعَ اللَّيْلَ, inf. n. as above, ‡ *He journeyed during* [or *through*] *the night.* (IKṭṭ, TA.) —— صَدْعٌ also signifies The act of *separating,* or *dispersing,* or *scattering;* (Mṣb;) and so ↓ تَصْدِيعٌ; (Ṣ, O;) syn. تَفْرِيقٌ [with which each is probably syn. in other, but similar, senses]. (Ṣ, O, Mṣb.) One says, صَدَعَ الشَّىْءَ *He,* or *it, separated,* or *dispersed,* or *scattered, the thing.* (TA.) And صَدَعْتُ القَوْمَ, inf. n. صَدْعٌ, † *I separated,* or *dispersed,* or *scattered, the people,* or *party.* (Mṣb.) And صَدَعَتْهُمُ النَّوَى means [in like manner] فَرَّقَتْهُمْ [i. e. ‡ *The place that was the object of the journey separated them* from their homes &c.]; and so ↓ صَدَّعَتْهُمْ; whence التَّصْدَاعُ [as an inf. n., like التَّصْدِيعُ]. (TA.) And صَدَعْتُ الغَنَمَ صِدْعَتَيْنِ † *I separated,* or *divided, the sheep,* or *the goats, into two flocks* or *herds.* (Ṣ, TA.) —— [And hence,] صَدَعْتُ الشَّىْءَ † *I made the thing distinct* [*as though separate from others*], *apparent, manifest, evident, clear,* or *plain:* whence the saying of Aboo-Dhu-eyb in a verse cited in art. فيض, conj. 4. (Ṣ.) —— And صَدَعَ بِالحَقِّ ‡ *He spoke the truth openly,* or *aloud,* (Ṣ, Mṣb, Ḳ, TA,) *distinguishing,* or *discriminating, between it and falsehood:* and thus Kh has expl. the verb as used in the verse of Aboo-Dhu-eyb above referred to. (TA.) And صَدَعَ بِالأَمْرِ, (Ḳ, TA,) aor. and inf. n. as above, (TA,) † *He made known the affair,* or *case, by speaking of it.* (Ḳ, TA.) —— فَاصْدَعْ بِمَا تُؤْمَرُ, in the Ḳur [xv. 94], means † *Therefore cleave thou,* or *divide thou,* their congregation, [app. by separating the believers from the unbelievers, *with that wherewith thou art charged,* (بِهِ being understood after تؤمر,) i. e.,] with the declaration of the unity [of God]: (IAạr, O, Mṣb, Ḳ:) or † *distinguish thou* therewith between the truth and falsehood: (AO, O, Mṣb, Ḳ:) or † *dispense thou* among them in their collective state [*that wherewith thou art charged,* i. e.] the announcement [of the unity &c.]: (TA:) or † *reveal thou,* or *make manifest,* (Fr, Zj, Ṣ, Mṣb, Ḳ, TA,) *that with which thou art charged,* (Zj, Mṣb, TA,) and fear not any one, (Zj, TA,) or *the ordinance,* i. e., (Fr, TA,) thy religion; (Fr, Ṣ, TA;) ما [with what follows it] being held by Fr, who thus explains the phrase, to occupy the place of an inf. n., namely, الأَمْر: (TA:) or † *utter thou openly,* or *aloud,* (O, Ḳ, TA,) *that with which thou art charged,* meaning, accord. to Ibn-Mujáhid, (TA,) the Ḳur-án: (O, Ḳ, TA:) in the R it is said to be from الصَّدِيع meaning "the daybreak;" ignorance being likened to the darkness of night, and the Ḳur-án to light that cleaves that darkness: (TA:) or † *order thou,* or *ordain,* or *decree,* [*that with which thou art charged,* i. e.,] the truth: and † *decide thou according to the ordinance* [*prescribed to thee*]: (O, Ḳ, TA:) or ‡ *direct thy course by that* [revelation] *with* [the preaching of] *which thou art charged:* (O, Ḳ, TA:) so says Th, on the authority of an Arab of the desert; accord. to whom, (O, TA,) —— صَدَعَ فُلَانًا signifies ‡ *He directed his course to such a one because of his generosity.* (Th, O, Ḳ, TA.) —— صَدَعَ بِالأَمْرِ, (Ḳ, TA,) aor. and inf. n. as above, (TA,) also signifies † *He hit,* or *attained, with the affair, its proper place* [or *object*]. (Ḳ, TA.) —— And صَدَعْتُ إِلَى الشَّىْءِ, (AZ, Ṣ, Ḳ,) aor. as above, (AZ, Ṣ,) inf. n. صُدُوعٌ, † *I inclined to the thing.* (AZ, Ṣ, Ḳ.*) —— And صَدَعَهُ عَنْهُ † *He,* or *it, turned him away from him,* or *it.* (Ḳ.) One says, مَا صَدَعَكَ عَنْ هٰذَا الأَمْرِ † *What turned thee away from this affair?* (Ṣ, O, TA:) and some say, ما صَدَغَكَ, with the pointed غ, which is better. (O, TA.) ═ See also the next paragraph. ═ And see صَادِعٌ, last sentence.

2: see 1, in three places. ═ [Freytag adds two other explanations of صدّع: namely, "Immisit," followed by an accus. and فى; taken by inference from the Ḥam p. 196, l. 12 from the bottom: and "Rupit, perdidit;" from Reiske's additions to Golius: but both of these require consideration.] —— [صدّعهُ also signifies † *It affected him with headache; as though it made his head to split.*] One says, صَدَّعَنِى أَزِيزُ الرَّحَى † [*The sounding of the mill-stone affected me with headache*]. (A and TA in art. أز.) And صُدِّعَ, inf. n. تَصْدِيعٌ, † *He* (a man, Ṣ) *was,* or *became, affected with* صُدَاع [or *headache*]; (Ṣ, O, Ḳ; [see the Ḳur lvi. 19;]) and ↓ صُدِعَ [without teshdeed], pass. part. n. ↓ مَصْدُوعٌ, is allowable in poetry. (O, Ḳ.)

5. تصدّع, of which اِصَّدَّعَ is a var.: (O, Ḳ:) see 7, in four places. —— Also *It became separated,* or *dispersed,* or *scattered.* (Ḳ.) One says, تصدّع القَوْمُ ‡ *The people,* or *party, became separated,* or *dispersed,* or *scattered.* (Ṣ, Mṣb, TA.) And تصدّعوا عَنِّى † *They became separated,* &c., *from me.* (TA.) يَوْمَئِذٍ يَصَّدَّعُونَ, in the Ḳur [xxx. 42], means *On that day they shall become separated into two parties,* a party in Paradise and a party in Hell. (Zj, O, TA.) And one says, تصدّع السَّحَابُ † *The clouds became* [*scattered,* or] *dissundered.* (TA.) And تَصَدَّعَتِ الأَرْضُ بِفُلَانٍ † *Such a one, fleeing, became concealed in the earth* or *land* [*as though it became cloven with him*]. (O, Ḳ, and Ḥam pp. 136 and 418.) ═ تصدّع لهُ: see تَصَدَّى, in art. صدا.

7. انصدع [generally said of a hard thing, such as a glass vessel, and a wall, and the like of these, (see 1, first sentence,)] *It became cloven, split, slit,* or *cracked;* or, in an intrans. sense, *it clave, split, slit,* or *cracked;* syn. اِنْشَقَّ: (Ṣ, Mṣb, Ḳ:) [*or so as to become divided in halves:* or *so that it did not separate:* (see again 1, first sentence:)] as also ↓ تصدّع [but app. in an intensive sense, meaning *it became cloven* &c., or *it clave* &c., *much,* or *in several places*]. (O, Ḳ.) One says, تَصَدَّعَتِ ↓ البَيْضَةُ وَلَمْ تَتَفَلَّقْ [*The egg cracked,* or rather *cracked in several places, but did not split apart*]. (AZ, Ṣ in art. قيض.) And ↓ تصدّع الثَّوْبُ *The garment,* or *piece of cloth, became slit* or *rent,* or *much slit* or *rent;* i. q. اِنْصَاحَ. (Mṣb in art. صيح.) And انصدعت الأَرْضُ بِالنَّبَاتِ *The earth clave with,* or *became cloven by, the plants,* or *herbage;* as also ↓ تصدّعت. (TA.) And انصدع الصُّبْحُ † *The dawn broke;* like انفجر, and انفلق, and انفطر. (TA.)

صَدْعٌ [originally an inf. n.] *A cleft, split, slit,* or *crack,* (Lth, Ṣ, O, Ḳ, TA,) [generally] in a hard thing, (Lth, O, Ḳ, TA,) such as a glass vessel, and a wall, and the like of these: pl. صُدُوعٌ. (TA.) Ḥassán says, satirizing El-Ḥárith Ibn-'Owf El-Murree,

• وَأَمَانَةُ المُرِّيِّ حَيْثُ لَقِيتَهُ •
• مِثْلُ الزُّجَاجَةِ صَدْعُهَا لَمْ يُجْبَرِ •

[*And the fidelity of the Murree, where* (meaning *wherever*) *thou meetest him, is like the glass vessel, of which the crack is not repaired*]. (O, TA.) —— And *A part,* or *portion, separated,* of a thing, (O, Ḳ, TA,) of sheep or goats, and the like: (TA:) an inf. n. used as a subst. [properly thus termed]: (O, Ḳ, TA:) like خَلْقٌ in the sense of مَخْلُوقٌ, &c. (O, TA.) — And The *plants of the earth*; (Ḳ;) because they cleave it: (TA:) [i. e.] the *plants from over which the earth cleaves*: so in the phrase وَٱلْأَرْضِ ذَاتِ ٱلصَّدْعِ, in the Ḳur lxxxvi. 12: (Bḍ:) or this phrase means *And the earth which is cloven* by the plants (Th, Bḍ, TA) and by the springs. (Bḍ.) ═ And *i. q.* إِلْبٌ: (TA:) you say, النَّاسُ عَلَيْهِمْ أَلْبٌ وَاحِدٌ [or إِلْبٌ وَاحِدٌ, (Ḳ, TA,) and صَدْعٌ وَاحِدٌ], (TA,) *The people are one company combined in hostility against them*: (Ḳ, TA:) and in like manner ضِلَعٌ واحد and وَعْلٌ واحد: so says AZ. (TA.) ═ And A man *light of flesh*; and so ▼ صَدَعٌ, (Ṣ, Ḳ,) sometimes: (Ṣ:) or *of middling stature, light of flesh*: (Ks, TA:) *like the mountain-goat thus termed*. (TA.) — See also صَدَعٌ.

صِدْعٌ The *half* of a thing that is cloven, or split, or slit, in halves. (Ḳ,* TA. [See also صِدْعَةٌ.]) You say, صَدَعَ الشَّىْءَ صِدْعَيْنِ *He clave, or split, or slit, the thing in halves*. (TA.) — And † *A company of men*. (Ibn-'Abbád, O, Ḳ.) — And † *A woman who makes a division in the state of a people and does not repair it*. (Ibn-'Abbád, O, TA.)

صَدَعٌ and ▼ صَدْعٌ, (Ḳ,) or the former only, (Ṣ,) applied to a mountain-goat, and a gazelle, and an ass, [app. a wild ass,] (Ṣ, Ḳ,) and a camel, (Ḳ,) *Of a middling size, neither great nor small, but between the two*: (Ṣ:) or *youthful and strong*: [see also صَدِيعٌ:] or [in the CḲ "and"] the former word signifies a thing of any sort *between two things; between tall and short*, and *youthful and advanced in age*, and *fat and lean*, and *great and small*. (Ḳ.) — For the former word as applied to a man: see صَدْعٌ. — Also, thus applied *Penetrating, sharp*, or *effective, in his affair*. (TA.) ═ [It is said that] صَدَعٌ signifies also The صَدَأ [i. e. *rust*] of iron. (Ḳ.) [But this seems to be a mistake, which has arisen from what here follows.] It is said that [a certain person called] El-Uskuff [which generally means "the bishop"], being asked by 'Omar respecting the Khaleefehs, designated [him who was afterwards] the fourth of them ['Alee] as صَدَعٌ مِنْ حَدِيدٍ, meaning [lit.] thereby *A mountain-goat of iron*; using it as a hyperbolical appellation to denote his might and courage and endurance and hardness: or the phrase, as some relate it, is صَدَأٌ حَدِيدٌ [which may be rendered, "light or active in body" (a meaning assigned to صَدَأٌ and صَدَعٌ, the latter of which is said to be in this sense the original), and "sharp"]; or صَدَأُ حَدِيدٍ [i. e. "rust of iron," app. alluding to his frequent and long-continued wearing of mail and bearing of weapons]; which last is thought by Aṣ to be most probably correct. (O,* TA.)

صِدْعَةٌ The *half* of a thing that is cloven, split, or slit, in halves; as also ▼ صَدِيعٌ. (Ḳ. [See also صِدْعٌ.]) — And *A* [*herd such as is termed*] صِرْمَة of camels; (Ṣ, O, Ḳ;) and so ▼ صَدِيعٌ: (Ṣ, O, Ḳ:*) or, accord. to AZ, *a herd* of camels *amounting to sixty*. (O, TA.) And *A separate flock*, or *herd*, of sheep or goats; as also ▼ صَدِيعٌ: (Ṣ, O, Ḳ:) or, as some say, of these also, *amounting to sixty*: and it is said to signify also *a herd* of gazelles: (TA:) and ▼ صَدِيعٌ signifies also *a herd* of oxen [probably meaning wild oxen]. (O, TA.) — One says also, عَلَيْهِ صِدْعَةٌ مِنْ مَالٍ i. e. [*On him lies a debt of*] *a small amount of property*. (TA.)

صُدَعَاتٌ ‡ [*Divisions* in opinion &c.]. One says, بَيْنَهُمْ صُدَعَاتٌ فِى الرَّأْىِ وَالْهَوَى ‡ *Between them is division* [*in opinion and affection*; or rather *between them are divisions* &c.]. (O, Ḳ, TA.) And أَصْلِحُوا مَا فِيكُمْ مِنَ الصُّدَعَاتِ ‡ [*Repair ye the divisions that are among you*;] i. e. *become ye in a state of unity*. (O, TA.) And إِنَّهُمْ عَلَى مَا فِيهِمْ مِنَ الصُّدَعَاتِ أَلِبَّآءُ كِرَامٌ ‡ [*Verily they, notwithstanding the divisions that are among them, are intelligent* and *generous*]. (TA.) [It is stated in the TA, among the additions to the Ḳ in this art., that one says also, إِنَّهُمْ عَلَى مَا تَرَى مِنْ صَدَاعَتِهِمْ ▼ لَكِرَامٌ app. as meaning † *Verily they, notwithstanding what thou seest of their disunion, are generous*: but I think it most probable that صَدَاعَتِهِمْ is a mistranscription for صُدَعَاتِهِمْ.] ═ [Reiske, as stated by Freytag, explains it as signifying also *Camels going swiftly*.]

صُدَاعٌ † *Headache*: (Ṣ, O, Mṣb, Ḳ:) Er-Rághib says that it is *like a splitting in the head by reason of pain*; and is a metaphorical term. (TA.)

صَدِيعٌ *Either half* of a garment, or piece of cloth, (O, Ḳ,) that is slit in halves: (O:) and *a thing* [شَىْءٌ] accord. to the copies of the Ḳ, but I think that the right reading is شَىْءٍ i. e. "of a thing,"] that is cloven, or split, or slit, in halves: pl. صُدُعٌ. (Ḳ.) See also صِدْعَةٌ, first sentence. It is also said to signify *A* [*garment of the kind called*] رِدَآء, *that is slit in halves*. (TA.) And *A new patch in an old and worn-out garment*. (O, Ḳ.) And *A garment much rent*. (TA.) And *A black garment which a wailing woman wears with a white garment beneath it, and which she rends at her bosom so that the white one appears*: so says Ḳásim Ibn-Thábit. (TA.) And *A garment that is worn beneath the coat of mail*. (O, Ḳ.) And *A shirt* [*of a middling size*] *between two shirts, neither large nor small*. (TA.) — See also صِدْعَةٌ, second and third sentences, in three places. — Accord. to Ibn-'Abbád, (O,) applied to a mountain-goat, it signifies *Youthful*: and (some say, O) *of middling size*; syn. مَرْبُوعُ الْخَلْقِ; (O, Ḳ, TA;) i. e. *between two* [*in size*]; like صَدَعٌ [q. v.]. (TA.) ═ Also † *Daybreak*: (Ṣ, O, Ḳ:) because it cleaves the night. (O.) ═ And *Fresh milk which is put in a place, and becomes cool, and overspread by a thin skin*: (O, Ḳ:) so called because you skim off (تَصْدَعُ, lit. "cleave,") that thin skin from the clear milk. (O.)

صَدَاعَةٌ: see a saying mentioned above, voce صُدَعَاتٌ.

صَادِعٌ [act. part. n. of صَدَعَ; *Cleaving, splitting*, &c.] — [Hence,] applied to a valley, (O, Ḳ,) and a road, or way, (سَبِيلٌ, O, TA, in the Ḳ erroneously written سَيْلٌ [a torrent], TA, [or both may be correct,]) and a mountain, (Ḳ, TA, [in the O, حَبْلٌ is put for جَبَلٌ,]) † *Extending far along the earth*. (O, Ḳ, TA.) — And, applied to the daybreak, † *Shining*, or *bright*; syn. مُشْرِقٌ. (IDrd, O, Ḳ.) — Also † One *who decides*, or *judges, between*, or *among, a people*, or *party*. (TA.) — A poet (قيس بن ذريح) says,

• فَلَمَّا بَدَا مِنْهَا الْفِرَاقُ كَمَا بَدَا •
• بِظَهْرِ الصَّفَا الصَّلْدِ الشُّقُوقُ الصَّوَادِعُ •

[i. e. *And when separation from her appeared, like as appear the cleaving cracks in the surface of the hard and smooth rock*]: it may be that ▼ صَدَعَ is syn. with تَصَدَّعَ in some dial. [and that صَوَادِعُ is pl. of its part. n.]: or this may be an instance of a possessive epithet, meaning *having a cleaving*. (TA.)

هُوَ أَصْدَعُهُمْ بِالصَّوَابِ فِى أَسْرَعِ جَوَابٍ † [app. *He is the most effective of them in deciding rightly in a most quick answer*]. (TA.)

مَصْدَعٌ ‡ *A smooth*, or *plain, road, in a rugged tract of ground*: pl. مَصَادِعُ. (IDrd, O, Ḳ, TA.)

مِصْدَعٌ *A* [*sort of arrow-head, or arrow, such as is termed*] مِشْقَص [q. v.]: pl. مَصَادِعُ. (IDrd, O, Ḳ.) Hence the quiver is called خَابِئَةُ الْمَصَادِعِ [*The concealer*, or *guarder, of the* مصادع]. (TA.) — دَلِيلٌ مِصْدَعٌ † *A guide going his way* [app. *with energy*]. (TA.) — And خَطِيبٌ مِصْدَعٌ † *An orator*, or *a preacher, perspicuous*, (O, Ḳ, TA,) *eloquent*, (Ḳ, TA,) *and bold in speech*. (TA.)

مَصْدُوعٌ: see 2, last sentence.

صدغ

1. صَدَغَهُ, (A'Obeyd, Ṣ, O, Ḳ,*) aor. ـَ, (Ḳ,) inf. n. صَدْغٌ, (TḲ,) [may be rendered *I walked*, or *went along, cheek by jole with him*; lit.] *I had my* صُدْغ [or *temple*] *over against his* (another man's) *in walking*, or *going along*. (A'Obeyd, Ṣ, O, Ḳ.*) [See also 3. Accord. to Golius, it means also *I overtook him, and joined myself to him by his side*: but for this explanation he names no authority.] — And صَدَغَهُ, aor. as above [and probably ـُ also, like that of دَمَغَهُ], and inf. n. as above, *He struck his* صُدْغ [or *temple*]. (TA.) — And صَدِغَ, like عَنِىَ, inf. n. as above, *He had a complaint of his* صُدْغ [or *temple*]. (TA.) ═ صَدَغَهُ عَنِ الْأَمْرِ *He turned him away*, or *back, from the affair*. (Ḳ. [And so, accord. to Freytag, as from the Ṣ, on the authority of Aṣ, اصدغه: but he has app. taken this from a mistranscription in a copy of the Ṣ.]) One says, مَا صَدَغَكَ عَنْ هٰذَا الْأَمْرِ *What turned thee away*, or *back, from* *this affair?* (Aṣ, Ṣ, O:) and صَدَغَكَ also: (Ṣ and O in art. صدع:) but the former is the better. (O in that art.) And اِتَّبَعَ فُلَانٌ بَعِيرَهُ فَمَا صَدَغَهُ i. e. [*Such a one followed his camel, and*] *he did not turn him aside:* this is said when he has taken fright, or become refractory, and run away. (Aṣ, Ṣ, O.) And Selemeh is related to have said, اِشْتَرَيْتُ سِنَّوْرًا فَلَمْ يَصْدَغْهُنَّ [*I bought a cat, and he did not drive them away*]; meaning the rats, or mice. (O.) — One says also, فُلَانٌ مَا يَصْدَغُ نَمْلَةً *Such a one does not kill an ant;* (Ṣ, Ḳ;*) by reason of his weakness. (Ṣ.) — And صَدَغَهُ, inf. n. as above, *He straightened his,* or *its,* صَدَغ, i. e. *crookedness,* and *bending,* or *inclining.* (TA.) — صَدَغَ إِلَى الشَّىْءِ, inf. n. صُدُوغٌ, *He inclined to the thing.* (TA.) And صَدَغَ عَنْ طَرِيقِهِ *He declined from his way,* or *road.* (TA.) — صَدُغَ, aor. ?, (Ṣ, O, Ḳ,) inf. n. صَدَاغَةٌ, (Ṣ, O,) *He* (a man, Ṣ, O) *was,* or *became, weak.* (Ṣ, O, Ḳ.) [See its part. n. صَدِيغٌ.]

3. صادغه *i. q.* دَارَاهُ [*He treated him with gentleness,* or *blandishment; soothed, coaxed, wheedled,* or *cajoled, him;* &c.]: or عَارَضَهُ فِى المَشْىِ [*he went along over against him*]: (Ḳ:) Ibn-'Abbád says that صَادَغْتُ الرَّجُلَ means دَارَيْتُهُ: and he adds, وَهِىَ المُعَارَضَةُ فِى المَشْىِ: (O: [but the right reading seems to be أَوْ هِىَ:]) accord. to the A, one says, صَادَغْتُهُ فِى المَشْىِ صُدْغِى لِصُدْغِهِ [*I walked, or went along, with him, my temple towards his temple*]. (TA.) [See also 1, first sentence.]

صُدْغٌ [The *temple;* i. e.] the *part between the eye and the ear;* (Ṣ, O, Ḳ;) the *part between the outer angle of the eye and the root* (أَصْل) *of the ear;* (A, Mṣb;) the *part of the head that slopes down to the place of attachment of the jaws;* as expl. by AZ, it is [*from*] *the place of juncture between the* لحية [app. a mistranscription for لَحْى i. e. *jaw,* agreeably with the explanation next preceding,] *and* [*the main portion of*] *the head, to the part beneath the* قَرْن [which is the *temporal ridge*]; (TA;) *each of what are termed the* صُدْغَانِ: (AZ, A, TA:) ISd mentions also ▼ صُدُغٌ, as occurring in poetry, and expresses a doubt whether it be, or be not, peculiar to poetry: (TA:) and sometimes they said سُدْغٌ, with س: Ḳṭr says that certain persons of the Benoo-Temeem, called Bel'ambar [a contraction of Benu-l-'Ambar], change س into ص [or use these two letters indiscriminately] when followed by any of the letters ط and ق and غ and خ, whether the latter be second or third or fourth; saying سِرَاطٌ and صِرَاطٌ, and صَيْقَلٌ and سَيْقَلٌ, and بَسْطَةٌ and بَصْطَةٌ, &c.: (Ṣ, O:) the pl. is أَصْدَاغٌ (Ṣ, O, Mṣb, TA, [in all except the Mṣb mentioned after the signification expl. in the next sentence, and properly a pl. of pauc.,]) and also أَصْدُغٌ [which is probably used only as a pl. of pauc.]. (TA.) — And ‡ The *hair that hangs down upon the place above-mentioned.* (Ṣ, O, Mṣb, Ḳ.) One says صُدْغٌ مُعَقْرَبٌ ‡ [*A curled lock of hair hanging down upon the temple*]. (Ṣ, O, TA.)

صَدَغٌ *Crookedness,* and *bending,* or *inclining.* (TA. [See 1, near the end.])

صُدُغٌ: see صُدْغٌ.

صِدَاغٌ *A mark made with a hot iron upon the* صُدْغ [or *temple,* of a camel], (Ṣ, O, Ḳ, TA,) or, as in the A, *upon the even part of the* صُدْغ, *lengthwise.* (TA.)

صَدِيغٌ an epithet applied to a child (Ṣ, Ḳ) *In the stage extending to his completion of seven days:* (Ṣ:) or *that is seven days old:* (Mgh, O, Ḳ:) because his temple becomes firm (يَشْتَدُّ صُدْغُهُ) only to this period, (so in the O, [and the like is said in the Mgh,]) or because his temples are not bound (لَا يُشَدُّ صُدْغَاهُ) save for seven days: (so in the TA:) or it may be an instance of فَعِيلٌ in the sense of مَفْعُولٌ from صَدَغَهُ عَنِ الشَّىْءِ meaning "he turned him away, or back, from the thing." (O.) — And [hence, perhaps,] *Weak.* (Ṣ, O, Ḳ.)

الأَصْدَغَانِ [*The two temporal arteries;*] *two veins beneath the* صُدْغَانِ [or *two temples*], (O, Ḳ,) *which,* as is said by Aṣ, *are always pulsing, in everyone in the world:* a word having no sing., like as they say of المِذْرَوَانِ. (O.)

مِصْدَغٌ: see what next follows.

مِصْدَغَةٌ *A pillow,* or *cushion;* (Ṣ, O, Ḳ;) because placed beneath the صُدْغ [or temple]; also pronounced مِسْدَغَةٌ; and sometimes they said مِزْدَغَةٌ; (Ṣ, O;) and [▼ مِصْدَغٌ and] مِسْدَغٌ and مِزْدَغٌ signify the same. (TA in art. سدغ.)

مُصَدَّغٌ, and its fem.: see what follows.

مَصْدُوغٌ, A camel *marked with the mark termed* صِدَاغ; as also ▼ مُصَدَّغٌ: (Ḳ,* TA:) or the former is applied in this sense to a camel, and ▼ مُصَدَّغَةٌ in like manner to camels. (ISh, O, TA.)

صدف

1. صَدَفَ عَنِّى, (Ṣ, O,) or عَنْهُ, (Mṣb, Ḳ,) aor. ?, (O, Ḳ,) *He turned away from, avoided, shunned, and left,* (Ṣ, O, Mṣb, Ḳ,) *me,* (Ṣ, O,) or *him,* or *it;* (Mṣb, Ḳ;) so the verb signifies in the Ḳur vi. 158 [and a similar instance occurs in verse 46 of the same chap.]; (O;) and so ▼ تصدّف عنه: (O,* Ḳ:) and (so in the Ḳ [but more properly "or"]) صَدَفَ, (A'Obeyd, M, O, Ḳ,) aor. ?, (M, Ḳ) and ?, (Ḳ,) inf. n. صَدْفٌ and صُدُوفٌ, (M, O, Ḳ, TA, [صَدَفًا in the CḲ is a mistake,]) *he turned away,* (A'Obeyd, M, O, Ḳ, TA,) or *became turned away,* or *back,* (O, Ḳ, TA,) and *declined,* (Ḳ, TA,) عَنْهُ *from it,* (M, O,) namely, a thing; (O;) said of a man. (Ḳ.) And صَدَفَتْ, said of a woman, *She turned away her face.* (Mṣb.) — See also 4. — صَدَفٌ is an inf. n. (Ṣ, M, O, Mṣb) of which the verb is صَدِفَ, (M, Mṣb,) and from which is derived the epithet ▼ أَصْدَفُ, applied to a horse, or to a camel: (Ṣ, M, O:) it signifies, in relation to a horse, The *having the thighs near together, and the hoofs far apart, with a twisting of the pasterns:* (Ṣ, O, Ḳ:) or *a crookedness in the fore legs:* (M:) or *an inclining in the hoof towards the off side:* (ISk, Ṣ, M, Mgh, O, Ḳ:) or *an inclining of the foot* (Aṣ, Ṣ, M, Mgh, O, Mṣb, Ḳ) *of the fore leg* or *of the hind leg* (Aṣ, Ṣ, M, O, Mṣb) of the camel, *towards the off side;* (Aṣ, Ṣ, M, Mgh, O, Mṣb, Ḳ;) if towards the near side, the epithet applied to him is أَقْفَدُ, (Aṣ, Ṣ, O, Ḳ,) and the verb is قَفِدَ, inf. n. قَفَدٌ: (TA:) or *an inclining in the* قَدَم [or *human foot*]; Aṣ says, I know not whether *from the right* or *from the left:* or *an approaching of one of the knees towards the other;* thus, peculiarly, in the horse: or *a nearness together of* [*the two tendons called*] *the* عُجَايَتَانِ, *and a wideness apart of the hoofs, with a twisting of the pasterns; one of the natural faults of horses:* (M:) (Mṭr says,] as meaning *a twisting in the neck,* I have not found it. (Mgh.)

3. صادفهُ, (Ṣ, O, Ḳ, TA,) inf. n. مُصَادَفَةٌ, (M, TA,) *He found him;* or *lighted on him;* syn. وَجَدَهُ; (Ṣ, O, Ḳ, TA;) namely, another man; (Ṣ, O;) and لَقِيَهُ [which may also be rendered *he met with him;* or *encountered him*]; (O, Ḳ, TA;) and وَافَقَهُ [which signifies the same]. (M,* TA, and Ṣ and Ḳ in art. وفق.) One says, صَادَفْتُ فُلَانًا بِمَوْضِعِ كَذَا *I found,* or *met with, such a one in such a place;* syn. وَافَقْتُهُ. (TA in art. وفق.) And صَادَفْتَ أَمْرَكَ مُوَافِقًا لِإِرَادَتِكَ [*Thou foundest thine affair,* or *thy case, suitable to thy wish;* i. e., *foundest it to be so:* thus, in this instance, and in many others, like its syns. وَجَدْتَ and لَقِيتَ, the verb has two objective complements]. (Ṣ* and Ḳ* and TA in art. وفق.) — And مُصَادَفَةٌ signifies also The *being opposite, one to another;* or the *facing one another;* or the *matching one another;* syn. مُحَاذَاةٌ. (TA.)

4. اصدفهُ *He,* or *it, turned him away,* (Ṣ, M, O, Ḳ,) or *back;* or *caused him to return, go back,* or *revert;* (Ḳ, TA;) عَنْهُ *from it;* (M;) and ▼ صَدَفَهُ, (O, Ḳ,) inf. n. صَدْفٌ, (O,) signifies the same; (O, Ḳ;) the latter verb being trans. as well as intrans., but when trans. having only one inf. n., that mentioned above. (O.) One says, أَصْدَفَنِى عَنْهُ كَذَا وَكَذَا *Such and such things turned me away from it.* (Ṣ, O.)

5. تصدّف: see 1, first sentence. — Also *I. q.* تَعَرَّضَ: (TA:) in the saying of Muleyḥ El-Hudhalee,

• فَلَمَّا ٱسْتَوَتْ أَحْمَالُهَا وَتَصَدَّفَتْ •
• بِشُمِّ المَرَاقِى بَارِدَاتِ المَدَاخِلِ •

[app. describing a she-camel, or a number of camels, meaning *And when her,* or *their, burdens were,* or *became, adjusted,* or *firm* or *steady, and she,* or *they, went alternately to the right and left,* (see the phrase تَعَرَّضَتِ الإِبِلُ المَدَارِجَ, in art. عرض,) *in the high places of ascent, cold in the entrances thereof*, because of their height], Skr says, تَصَدَّفَتْ means تَعَرَّضَتْ. (M, TA.)

6. تَصَادَفَا, said of two sides of a mountain, *They met together*, and *faced each other*. (TA.)

صَدَفٌ inf. n. of صَدِفَ [q. v.]. (M, Mṣb.) = Also *Anything high*, or *lofty*, (Aṣ, Ṣ, M, O, Ḳ,) *such as a wall* and *a mountain*, (M,) or *such as a wall* and *the like*; (Ḳ;) *like what is termed* هَدَفٌ: (Aṣ, Ṣ, O:) and the *side of a mountain*: (M:) or صَدَفٌ and هَدَفٌ both signify *any building* or *structure, that is high*, or *lofty, and great*; (A'Obeyd, TA;) accord. to Az, likened to the صَدَف of a mountain, which is the *side that faces one*, thereof: (TA:) and صَدَفٌ and ↓ صُدُفٌ (Ṣ, M, O, Ḳ) and ↓ صُدْفٌ and ↓ صَدُفٌ, (O, Ḳ,) accord. to different readings of a passage in the Ḳur, (Ṣ, M, O, Ḳ,) [xviii. 95,] in which the dual occurs, (Ṣ, M, O,) signify the *place of ending*, or *breaking off*, (Ṣ, O, Ḳ,) *of a mountain*, (Ḳ,) or *of a lofty mountain*: (Ṣ, O:) or the *side of a mountain*: (Ḳ:) or the *part between two mountains*: (M:) or, as used in this instance, (Ḳ, TA,) in the verse of the Ḳur, (TA,) الصَّدَفَانِ, (M, Ḳ,) as also ↓ الصُّدُفَانِ, (M,) means *two mountains* (M, L, Ḳ) *meeting together*, (M, L, TA,) in the copies of the Ḳ, مُتَلَازِقَانِ [i. e. *cleaving together*], but the correct reading is مُتَلَاقِيَانِ, as in the L [and M], (TA,) *between Ya-jooj and Ma-jooj*: (M, L, Ḳ, TA:) and ↓ الصُّدُفَانِ, (M, Ḳ,) with ḍamm to the د, (M,) i. e. with two ḍammehs, especially, (Ḳ,) or this as well as الصَّدَفَانِ, (TA,) means *the two sides of the* شِعْب [app. here meaning *ravine*, or *gap*, *between two mountains*], or *of the valley*: (M, Ḳ, TA:) so says IDrd: (M, TA:) both signify *the two sides of the mountain when they* [*meet together, and*] *face each other*, so called لِتَصَادُفِهِمَا, i. e. because of their meeting together, and facing each other, *having between them a* [*road such as is termed*] فَجّ, or a شِعْب [expl. above], or *a valley*. (TA.) = Also [The *mother-of-pearl shell*; or *oyster-shell*; and *any shell of a mollusk*: and, by an extension of its primary application, the *oyster* itself; and *any shell-fish*, or *testaceous mollusk of the water*, and likewise *of the land*:] the *cover of the pearl*; (Ḳ;) or this is called صَدَفُ الدُّرَّةِ, (Ṣ, O,) or صَدَفُ الدُّرِّ; (Mṣb;) *a kind of cover created in the sea, composed of* [*what are termed*] صَدَفَتَانِ [i. e. *a pair of shell-valves*], *which are opened from* [i. e. *so as to disclose*] *a kind of flesh in which is life, called the* مَحَارَة [i. e. *oyster*], *and in the like thereof are found pearls*; (Lth, TA;) *i. q.* مَحَارٌ [which means *oyster-shells*, and also *oysters* themselves, and both of these may be here meant, as both are correct meanings of صَدَفٌ]: (M:) n. un. with ة: (Ṣ, M, O, Mṣb, Ḳ:) [in the Mṣb it is also said that الصَّدَفَةُ signifies *the* مَحَارَة, which is *the* مَحْمِل *of the pilgrims*; but I think that this is a mistake, caused by understanding مَحَارَة here in a wrong sense; for I find no other authority for assigning this meaning to الصَّدَفَةُ:] pl. أَصْدَافٌ. (O, Ḳ.) [See an ex. of the pl. voce حَلَزُونٌ.] — [Hence,] الصَّدَفَةُ signifies also, (M, TA,) or صَدَفَةُ الأُذُنِ, (O,) *The* مَحَارَة [or *concha*, i. e. *the external, deep, and wide, cavity, around the hole*,] *of the ear*. (M, O, TA.) — [And hence, also,] الصَّدَفَتَانِ signifies *The two small hollows*, or *sockets, in each of which is set the head of one of the two thigh-bones, and in each of which is a ligament* (عَصَبَة [app. *that called ligamentum teres, forming a tie*]) *to that head*. (M, TA.) [And in like manner, *The two sockets in the scapula, in each of which turns the head of one of the two upper arm-bones*: (see حَارِقَة:) or these, it seems, are called by some الصَّدَفَانِ; for it is said that] الصَّدَفُ signifies *the part of the scapula which is the place of the* وَابِلَة. (O, Ḳ.) — And صَدَفٌ also signifies ‡ *Flesh*, (O,) or *a piece of flesh*, (Ḳ, TA,) *growing in a wound of the head, next the skull, resembling the cartilages*. (O, Ḳ.) = And in the Tekmileh it is said that [the pl.] أَصْدَافٌ signifies *Waves of the sea*. (TA.) = See also صَدَفٌ.

صَدُفٌ: see صَدَفٌ, second sentence.

صُدُفٌ: see صَدَفٌ, second sentence. = Also, i. e. like صُرَدٌ, (O, Ḳ,) or ↓ صَدَفٌ, (so in a copy of the M,) *A species of animal of prey*: (M, O, Ḳ:*) or, as some say, *a bird*. (M, O, Ḳ.)

صُدْفٌ: see صَدَفٌ, in three places.

صَدَفِيٌّ *A camel of a certain sort*, (M, Ḳ,*) *of excellent quality*, (Ḳ,) [ISd says,] *so called*, (M, Ḳ,) I think, *in relation to a tribe of Arabs of El-Yemen*, (M,) or *in relation to a sub-tribe* (بَطْن) *of Kindeh*, (Ḳ,) *called* الصَّدِفُ. (M, Ḳ.) [See also صَرَفِيٌّ.] = [Also a rel. n. from صَدَفٌ; *Testaceous*.]

صَدُوفٌ A woman *who turns away her face* (Lḥ, M, Mṣb) *from her husband*: (Lḥ, M:) or a woman *who turns her face towards one and then turns away*: (Ṣ, O, Ḳ:) or *a woman who desires not kisses*: (M:) or *having a stinking mouth*, (Lḥ, Ibn-'Abbád, M, O, Ḳ,) as an epithet applied to a female, (Lḥ, M,) or to a male: (Ibn-'Abbád, O, Ḳ:) applied in this last sense to a man because he turns away his face whenever any one speaks to him. (TA.) — And A she-camel *that will not come to the watering-trough until it is left to her unoccupied*: like صَرُومٌ. (TA in art. صرم. [See also what next follows.])

صَوَادِفُ [pl. of صَادِفَةٌ] Camels *that come to others at the drinking-trough, and wait at their rumps until the drinkers have gone away, that they may go in*. (Ṣ, O. [See also what next precedes.])

أَصْدَفُ: see صَدَفٌ, in the first paragraph.

مُصَدَّفٌ meaning One *often attacked by diseases* is a word used by the vulgar. (TA.)

مَصْدُوفٌ *Veiled*, or *concealed*; *covered*; or *protected*; syn. مَسْتُورٌ. (TA.)

صدق

1. صَدَقَ, (Ṣ, M, O, Mṣb, Ḳ,) aor. ـُ, (M, TA,) inf. n. صِدْقٌ (Ṣ,* M, O,* Mṣb, Ḳ, TA) and صَدْقٌ, (M, Ḳ,) the former of which is the more chaste, (TA,) or the latter is an inf. n. and the former is a simple subst., (Ḳ,) and تَصْدَاقٌ (M) and مَصْدُوقَةٌ, (O, Ḳ, TA,) which is one of the [few] inf. ns. of the measure مَفْعُولَةٌ, (O, TA,) [or a fem. pass. part. n. used as an inf. n. like as is said of its contr. مَكْذُوبَةٌ,] *He spoke, said, uttered*, or *told, truth*, or *truly*, or *veraciously*; *contr. of* كَذَبَ: (Mṣb: [and in like manner it is said in the Ṣ and M and O and Ḳ that صِدْقٌ is the *contr. of* كِذْبٌ:]) Er-Rághib says that صِدْقٌ and كِذْبٌ are primarily in what is said, whether relating to the past or to the future, and [in the latter case] whether it be a promise or other than a promise; and only in what is said in the way of information: but sometimes they are in other modes of speech, such as asking a question, and commanding, and supplicating; as when one says, "Is Zeyd in the house?" for this implies information of his being ignorant of the state of Zeyd; and when one says, "Make me to share with thee, or to be equal with thee," for this implies his requiring to be made to share with the other, or to be made equal with him; and when one says, "Do not thou hurt me," for this implies that the other is hurting him: صِدْقٌ, he says, is [by implication] the agreeing of what is said with what is conceived in the mind and with the thing told of, together; otherwise it is not complete صِدْق, but may be described either as صِدْق or sometimes as صِدْق and sometimes as كِذْب according to two different points of view; as when one says without believing it, "Moḥammad is the Apostle of God," for this may be termed صِدْق because what is told is such, and it may be termed كِذْب because it is at variance with what the speaker conceives in his mind. (TA.) One says, صَدَقَ فِي الحَدِيثِ [*He spoke truth in the information*, or *narration*]. (Ṣ, O, Ḳ.) And صَدَقَهُ i. e. *He told him*, or *informed him, with truth*, or *veracity*, (AHeyth,* M, Mṣb,*) فِي القَوْلِ [*in the saying*]; for it is trans. as well as intrans. (Mṣb.) And صَدَقَهُ الحَدِيثَ (Ṣ, O, Ḳ, in the CḲ [erroneously] صَدَقَ فُلَانًا الحَدِيثَ) *He told him with truth*, or *veracity, the information*, or *narration*; for it is sometimes doubly trans. (TA.) And صَدَقَنِى سِنَّ بَكْرِهِ [*He hath told me truly the age*, or *as to the age, of his youthful camel*; or صَدَقَنِى سِنُّ بَكْرِهِ *the age of his youthful camel has spoken truly to me*]: (Ṣ, O, Ḳ:) a prov., (Ṣ, O,) expl. in art. بكر [q. v.]. (Ḳ.) And فُلَانٌ لَا يَصْدُقُ أَثَرَهُ and أَثَرَهُ, meaning *Such a one*, when asked, *will not tell truly whence he comes*. (M.) And صَدَقَتْ يَمِينُهُ *His oath was*, or *proved, true*. (Mṣb in art. بت.) صَدَقْتُ اللّٰهَ حَدِيثًا إِنْ لَمْ أَفْعَلْ كَذَا is an oath of the Arabs, meaning لَا صَدَقْتُ اللّٰهَ [*May I not utter truly to God a saying*, i. e. *may I not speak truth to God, if I do not such a thing*]. (AHeyth, O, Ḳ.) One says also, صَدَقَهُ النَّصِيحَةَ, and الإِخَآءَ, *He rendered to him truly*, or *sincerely, good advice*, and *brotherly affection*. (M.) And صَدَقُوهُمُ القِتَالَ (Ṣ, M, Ḳ,* TA) [*They gave them battle earnestly*,

not with a false show of bravery; as is implied in the Ṣ, and M, and Ḳ; i. e.] *they advanced against them boldly in fight*: (M, TA:) and in like manner, صَدَقُوا فِى القِتَالِ *they advanced boldly in fight*: or, accord. to Er-Rághib, the former means *they gave them battle so as to fulfil their duty*: and hence, in the Ḳur [xxxiii. 23], رِجَالٌ صَدَقُوا مَا عَاهَدُوا ٱللّٰهَ عَلَيْهِ *Men who fulfilled the covenant that they had made with God.* (TA.) And صَدَقَ اللِّقَآءَ, inf. n. صِدْقٌ, *He was firm*, or *steady, in encounter*, or *conflict.* (M, TA.) And صَدَقَ ظَنِّى *My opinion was*, or *proved, true*, or *correct*, like as one says [in the contrary case], كَذَبَ: (Er-Rághib, TA:) whence, in the Ḳur [xxxiv. 19], وَلَقَدْ صَدَقَ عَلَيْهِمْ إِبْلِيسُ ظَنَّهُ, meaning فِى ظَنِّهِ [i. e. *And assuredly Iblees was*, or *proved to be, correct in his opinion* that he had formed *against them*]: but some read ♦ صَدَّقَ, meaning, as Fr says, حَقَّقَ [i. e. Iblees *proved*, or *found, to be true*, his opinion &c.]. (TA.) And صَدَقَتْهُ نَفْسُهُ *His soul* [*told him truth*; meaning,] *diverted him*, or *hindered him*, or *held him back, from an undertaking, causing him to imagine himself unable to prosecute it.* (TA in art. كذب.) And صَدَقَ الصُّبْحُ [*The dawn shone clearly*]. (Ṣ in art. سفر.) [And one says of a word or the like, يَصْدُقُ عَلَى كَذَا, meaning *It applies correctly to such a thing.*] —— صَدَقَ الوَحْشِىُّ: see 2, near the end.

2. صَدَّقَهُ, (Ṣ, M, O, &c.,) inf. n. تَصْدِيقٌ, *contr. of* كَذَّبَهُ. (O,* Ḳ.) [This explanation implies several meanings here following.] *He attributed*, or *ascribed, to him truth, veracity*, or *the speaking truth.* (Mṣb.) And *He said to him, "Thou hast spoken truth."* (Mṣb.) *He accepted*, or *admitted*, [or *assented to*, or *believed*,] *what he said*: (M:) you say, صَدَّقَهُ فِى حَدِيثِهِ [*He accepted*, &c., *what he said in his information*, or *narration*]: (Ṣ:) and you say صدّق بلِسَانِهِ [*He assented to the truth of what was said with his tongue*]; as well as بِقَلْبِهِ [*with his heart*, or *mind*]. (T in art. أمن.) *He held him to be a speaker of truth.* (MA.) [*He found him to be a speaker of truth. He*, or *it, proved him to be a speaker of truth*; *verified him*; or *confirmed the truth of what he said*: see an ex. in a verse cited voce بَيْنَ.] *He found it* (an opinion) *to be true*, or *veritable.* (Ksh and Bḍ and Jel, in xxxiv. 19.) *He verified it*; *confirmed its truth*; or *proved it to be true*, or *veritable*; i. e. an opinion [&c.]; syn. حَقَّقَهُ: (Ksh and Bḍ, ibid.:) one says, صَدَّقَ الخَبَرَ الخُبْرُ [*The trial, proof*, or *test, verified the information*]. (Ṣ in art. خبر.) See 1, near the end. In the saying in the Ḳur [xxxix. 34], وَالَّذِى جَآءَ بِالصِّدْقِ وَصَدَّقَ بِهِ, [which seems to be best rendered *But he who hath brought the truth and* he who *hath accepted it as the truth*, (see كَذَّبَ بِالأَمْرِ,)] 'Alee the son of Aboo-Ṭálib is related to have said that by الذى جآء بالصدق is meant Moḥammad; and by الذى صدّق به, Aboo-Bekr: or, as some say, Gabriel and Moḥammad [are meant by the former and the latter respectively]: or by the former, Moḥammad; and by the latter, [every one of] the believers: (M:) accord. to Er-Rághib, by وصدّق به is meant *and hath found*, or *proved, to be true* (حَقَّقَ) *that which he hath brought by word*, by that which he hath aimed at (بِمَا تَحَرَّاهُ) by deed. (TA.) —— صدّق is also said to signify *He said, "This thing is the truth;"* like حَقَّقَ. (TA in art. حق.) —— And this verb also denotes المُبَالَغَةُ فِى الصِّدْقِ: thus in the saying,

صَدَّقَتْ فِيهِمْ ظُنُونِى

[*My opinions respecting them were*, or *proved to be, very true* or *correct*]. (Ksh, in xxxiv. 19.) —— صدّق الوَحْشِىُّ, (O, Ḳ, TA,) or ♦ صَدَقَ, (so in a copy of the M,) ‡ *The wild animal ran without looking aside, when charged upon*, or *attacked*: (M, O, Ḳ, TA:) mentioned by IDrd. (O, TA.) —— صَدَّقَهُمْ *He exacted from them the poor-rate.* (TA. [See صَدَقَةٌ.]) —— See also 5.

3. صَادَقَهُ, (M,) inf. n. مُصَادَقَةٌ (Ṣ, M, O, Ḳ) and صِدَاقٌ, (M, O, Ḳ,) the latter like كِتَابٌ, (TA, [in the CḲ erroneously written صَداق,]) *I acted*, or *associated, with him as a friend*, or *as a true*, or *sincere, friend.* (Ṣ,* M, O,* Ḳ.*) [See also 6.]

4. اصدق المَرْأَةَ *He named for the woman a* صَدَاق [or *dowry*]: (Ṣ, M,* O, Ḳ:) or *he gave her her* صَدَاق: (M,* Mṣb:) or *he appointed her*, or *assigned her, a* صَدَاق, *on taking her as his wife*: (TA:) and *he married her*, or *took her as his wife, on the condition of his giving her a* صَدَاق. (Mṣb.) And sometimes this verb is doubly trans.; whence, in a trad., مَا ذَا تُصْدِقُهَا فَقَالَ إِزَارِى [It was said, "*What is it that thou meanest for her, or givest her, as her dowry?*" *and he said, "My waist-wrapper"*]. (Mgh.)

5. تصدّق عَلَيْهِ *He gave him* (i. e. the poor, Mgh, Mṣb) *what is termed* صَدَقَة, (M, Mgh, Mṣb,) meaning [*an alms*, or] *what is given for the sake of God*, (M,) or *what is given with the desire of obtaining a recompense from God*: (M,* Mgh:) and عليه ♦ صَدَّقَ signifies the same; (M, TA;) and in this sense صَدَّقَ is [said by some to be] used in the Ḳur lxxv. 31. (TA.) Hence, in the Ḳur [xii. 88], وَتَصَدَّقْ عَلَيْنَا: (TA:) or this means † *And do thou confer a favour upon us* by giving that which is [not like the mean merchandise that we have brought, but of middling quality,] between good and bad. (M.) One says, تَصَدَّقْتُ بِكَذَا, meaning *I gave such a thing as a* صَدَقَة. (Mṣb.) See an ex. voce شَقَّ. The saying, in a trad., إِنَّ ٱللّٰهَ تَصَدَّقَ عَلَيْكُمْ بِثُلُثِ أَمْوَالِكُمْ, meaning ‡ [*Verily God*] *hath conferred a favour* [*upon you by giving you a third of your possessions* to bequeath to whom ye will], if correct, is tropical. (Mgh.) —— It is said by Ibn-Es-Seed, on the authority of AZ and IJ, and mentioned by IAmb, that تصدّق signifies also *He asked*, or *begged, for what is termed* صَدَقَة [or *alms*]: but Fr and Aṣ and others disallow the beggar's being called مُتَصَدِّق: (Az, TA:) IḲt says that the verb is improperly used in this sense by the vulgar: (Mṣb:) [and accord. to J and Ṣgh,] one says, مَرَرْتُ بِرَجُلٍ يَسْأَلُ, and one should not say يَتَصَدَّقُ. (Ṣ, O.)

6. تَصَادُقٌ signifies The *acting*, or *associating, as friends*, or *as true*, or *sincere, friends, one with another.* (Ḳ. [See also 3.]) And *I. q.* صِدْقٌ: (TA:) [or rather *mutual* صِدْق; *contr. of* تَكَاذُبٌ:] one says, تَصَادَقَا فِى الحَدِيثِ and فِى المَوَدَّةِ (Ṣ, O, TA) *They were true*, or *sincere, each to the other, in information*, or *narration*, and *in love*, or *affection*; *contr. of* تَكَاذَبَا. (O, TA.)

صَدْقٌ is an inf. n. of صَدَقَ [q. v.]: (M, Ḳ:) —— and is used as an epithet, applied to a man &c.: (Ṣ, M, O, Ḳ, TA:) [and] ♦ صِدْقٌ [also, if not a mistranscription for صَدْقٌ,] is an inf. n. used as an epithet, applied to a man and to a woman: (so in a copy of the M and in the TA:) [it is said that] the former signifies *Hard*, (Ṣ, M, O, Mṣb,) applied to a spear, (Ṣ, M, O,) and to other things: (M:) or *even*, or *straight*; (Ṣ, O;) or it signifies thus also, applied to a spear, and to a sword: (M:) or *hard and even* or *straight*, applied to a spear, (Ḳ, TA,) and to a man, (Ḳ,) or to the latter as meaning *hard*: or, as IB says, on the authority of IDrst, it is not from hardness, but means *combining those qualities that are commended*; and it is applied to a spear as meaning *long and pliant and hard*, and *the like*; and to a man, and to a woman likewise [without ة, but see what follows], as meaning *true in hardness and strength and goodness*; for, IDrst says, if it meant *hard*, one would say حَدِيدٌ صَدْقٌ and حَجَرٌ صَدْقٌ, which one does not: (TA:) and, applied to anything, (O, Ḳ, TA,) it means *complete*, or *perfect*, (Kh, O, Ḳ, TA,) thus applied to a man, (TA,) *such as is commended*; (O;) fem. with ة, (O, Ḳ, TA,) applied to a woman: (O:) the pl. is صُدْقٌ, applied to a company of men, (Ṣ, O, Ḳ,) and صَدْقُونَ (Ḳ) and صُدْقٌ, so applied, and صَدْقَاتٌ applied to women: (O, Ḳ:) and Ru-beh says, describing asses,

مَقْذُوذَةُ الآذَانِ صَدْقَاتُ الحَدَقْ

meaning [*Rounded, as though pared, in the ears*,] *penetrating in the eyes*; (O, TA;) which is [said to be] tropical. (TA.) صَدْقٌ signifies also *Firm*, or *steady, in encounter*, or *conflict*: (M:) or one says صَدْقُ اللِّقَآءِ, applying this epithet to a man, (Ṣ, O, Ḳ, TA,) meaning thus: (TA:) and صَدْقُ النَّظَرِ [*firm, or steady, in look*]. (Ṣ, O, Ḳ, TA. [Said in the TA to be tropical.])

صِدْقٌ is an inf. n. of صَدَقَ [q. v.]: (M, Ḳ, &c.:) or a simple subst., (Ḳ,) signifying [*Truth*; *veracity*; or] *agreement of what is said with what is conceived in the mind and with the thing told of, together*; otherwise it is not complete صِدْق, as expl. above in the first paragraph of this art. (Er-Rághib, TA.) —— It is also *syn.* with شِدَّةٌ [meaning *Hardness*; *firmness, compactness*, or *soundness*; *strength, power*, or *force*; *vigour, robustness, sturdiness*, or *hardiness*; and *courage, bravery*, or *firmness of heart*]: (Ḳ, TA: [in the latter of which it is said to be tropical; but this is evidently not the case accord. to the O, in which it is said that it radically denotes قُوَّةٌ (i. e. *strength, force,* &c.,) in a saying &c.: in the Ḳ it is implied by the context that it is syn. with شِدَّةٌ when used as the complement of a prefixed n. in instances mentioned in what here follows: but Ṣgh says, more correctly,]) a noun signifying anything to which goodness is attributed is prefixed to صِدْقٌ, governing it in the gen. case; so that one says (O) رَجُلُ صِدْقٍ (Sb, M, O, Ḳ) [*A man of good nature* or *disposition* or *character* &c.], *contr. of* رَجُلُ سَوْءٍ; (Sb, M;) and صَدِيقُ صِدْقٍ [*a friend of good nature* &c.]; (O, Ḳ;) and likewise اِمْرَأَةُ صِدْقٍ [*a woman of good nature* &c.]; (Ḳ;) and in like manner also حِمَارُ صِدْقٍ [*an ass of a good kind*]; (Sb, M, Ḳ;) and ثَوْبُ صِدْقٍ [*a garment,* or *piece of cloth, of good quality*]. (Sb, M.) The saying in the Ḳur [x. 93], (O,) وَلَقَدْ بَوَّأْنَا بَنِى إِسْرَائِيلَ مُبَوَّأَ صِدْقٍ means *And verily we assigned to the Children of Israel a good place of abode.* (O, Ḳ.) — See also صَدْقٌ.

صَدْقَةٌ: } see صَدَاقٌ; each in two places.
صُدْقَةٌ: }

صَدَقَةٌ [*An alms;* i. e.] *a gift* (Ṣ, M, Mgh, O, Mṣb, Ḳ) *to the poor* (Ṣ, O, Mṣb) *for the sake of God,* (M, Ḳ,) or *to obtain a recompense from God;* (M,* Mgh, Ḳ;*) *a portion which a man gives forth from his property by way of propitiation,* [*to obtain the favour of God,*] like زَكَاةٌ, except that the former is primarily applied to *such as is supererogatory,* and the latter to such as is obligatory: but it is said to be applied to *such as is obligatory* [i. e. to the زَكَاة, q. v., meaning the *poor-rate,* which is the *portion,* or *amount, of property, that is given therefrom, as the due of God, by its possessor, to the poor, according to a fixed rate,*] when the person who does so aims at conformity with the truth in his deed: (Er-Rághib, TA:) [in this latter sense, which is indicated in the Ṣ and O &c., and more plainly in the M, it is very frequently used:] and thus it is used in the Ḳur ix. 104, and in like manner its pl. in ix. 60: (Er-Rághib, TA:) the pl. is صَدَقَاتٌ. (Ṣ, M, O, Mṣb.) It is said in a trad., لَا صَدَقَةَ فِى الإِبِلِ الجَارَّةِ [*There is no poor-rate in the case of working camels*], because they are the riding-camels of the people; for the poor-rate is in the case of pasturing camels, exclusively of the working. (Ṣ in art. جر.) — See also صَدَاقٌ.

صَدُقَةٌ: see صَدَاقٌ, in two places.

صُدُقَةٌ: see the next paragraph.

صَدَاقٌ and ↓صِدَاقٌ, (Ṣ, M, Mgh, O, Mṣb, Ḳ,) the former of which is the most common of the dial. vars. here mentioned, (Mṣb,) [but] the latter is [said to be] more chaste than the former, (Mgh,) and ↓صَدُقَةٌ, (Ṣ, M, O, Mṣb, Ḳ,) of the dial. of El-Ḥijáz, (Mṣb,) and ↓صُدْقَةٌ, (Ṣ, M, O, Mṣb, Ḳ,) of the dial. of Temeem, (Mṣb,) and ↓صَدْقَةٌ (M, O, Mṣb, Ḳ) and ↓صُدُقَةٌ (M, O, Ḳ) and ↓صُدَقَةٌ, (M, Ḳ,) The مَهْر (Ṣ, M, Mgh, O, Ḳ) of a woman; (Ṣ, Mgh, O, Mṣb, Ḳ;) [i. e. *a dowry; nuptial gift;* or *gift that is given to,* or *for, a bride:*] the pl. of صداق is صُدُقٌ, (M, Mgh, Mṣb,) a pl. of mult., (M,) or صُدْقٌ, (O,) or both, (Ḳ,) and أَصْدِقَةٌ, a pl. of pauc., (M,) or this is accordant to analogy, but has not been heard; (Mgh;) the pl. of ↓صَدُقَةٌ is صَدُقَاتٌ; (Ṣ, Mṣb, Ḳ;) the pl. of ↓صُدْقَةٌ is صُدْقَاتٌ and صُدُقَاتٌ and صُدَقَاتٌ, (O,* Mṣb, Ḳ,) which last is the worst; (Ḳ;) and the pl. of ↓صُدْقَةٌ is صُدَقٌ, (Mṣb,) or صُدْقَاتٌ [by rule صَدَقَاتٌ]. (O.)

صِدَاقٌ: see the next preceding paragraph.

صَدُوقٌ *Having the quality of speaking, saying, uttering,* or *telling, truth,* or *truly,* or *veraciously, in a high,* or *an eminent, degree; very,* or *eminently, true* or *veracious:* (Mṣb:) pl. صُدُقٌ and صُدْقٌ. (Ḳ.) See also أَصْدَقُ.

صَدِيقٌ *A friend:* (O, Ḳ:) or *a true,* or *sincere, friend:* (Ṣ, M, Mṣb, TA:) applied likewise to a female, (Ṣ, M, O, Mṣb, Ḳ,) as also صَدِيقَةٌ, (Ṣ, M, Mṣb, Ḳ,) the former anomalous, the latter regular; (MF;) and to a pl. number, (Ṣ, M, O, Ḳ,) as in the Ḳur xxvi. 101 (M) [and in several other instances, of which see one in a verse cited voce رَوِىٌّ]: its proper pl. is أَصْدِقَآءُ (Ṣ, M, O, Ḳ) and صُدَقَآءُ and صُدْقَانٌ, (M, Ḳ,) the last on the authority of Fr, (TA,) and أَصَادِقُ, (M, O, Ḳ,) which is a pl. pl., (Ḳ,) said by IDrd to be anomalous, unless it be a pl. pl.: (O:) and the dim. is ↓صُدَيِّقٌ; one says, هُوَ صُدَيِّقِى, meaning *He is the most special,* or *most distinguished, of my friends,* or *of my true,* or *sincere, friends.* (Ṣ, O, Ḳ.)

صَدَاقَةٌ *Love,* or *affection:* (Ḳ:) or *truth,* or *sincerity, of love* or *affection:* (TA:) or *friendship,* or *friendliness;* (Ṣ, M;) or *true,* or *sincere, friendship* or *friendliness:* (Ṣ, M, Mṣb:) or *true firmness of heart in love* or *affection;* an attribute of a human being only. (Er-Rághib, TA.)

صُدَيِّقٌ dim. of صَدِيقٌ, q. v. (Ṣ, O, Ḳ.)

صِدِّيقٌ One *who speaks, says, utters,* or *tells, truth,* or *truly,* or *veraciously, much,* or *often:* (Mgh, O, Ḳ:) [or rather *having the quality of speaking, saying, uttering,* or *telling, truth,* or *truly,* or *veraciously, in a very high,* or *very eminent, degree;* for] it has a more intensive signification than صَدُوقٌ [q. v.]: (TA:) or *i. q.* مُصَدِّقٌ [which may have the latter of the two meanings expl. above, or may mean one *who accepts,* or *admits, the truth of what is said,* or *who verifies,* &c.: or مُصَدِّقٌ *in a high,* or *an eminent, degree;* for it is added that] the fem. as used in the Ḳur v. 79 means *superlative in* التَّصْدِيق *and* الصِّدْق; as a possessive epithet, i. e. ذَاتُ تَصْدِيقٍ: (M:) or it signifies دَائِمُ التَّصْدِيقِ [i. e. *always* مُصَدِّق in one or another or all of the senses assigned to this word above: it may be correctly rendered *eminently,* or *always, veracious:* and *eminently,* or *always, accepting,* or *confirming, the truth*]: and it may mean one *who verifies his saying by deed,* or *act:* (Ṣ:) it is said in the "Mufradát" [of Er-Rághib] that it has the first of the meanings expl. in this paragraph: or rather means, one *who never lies:* or rather, one *by whom lying cannot be practised because of his habitual veracity:* or rather, one *who is true in his saying and his belief, and who confirms his truth by his deed,* or *acting.* (TA.)

صَادِقٌ *Speaking, saying, uttering,* or *telling, truth,* or *truly,* or *veraciously; true* in respect of speech &c., or *veracious.* (Mṣb, TA.) — صِدْقٌ صَادِقٌ is a phrase like شِعْرٌ شَاعِرٌ, meaning *Eminent, and exalted, veracity.* (M, TA.*) — And حَمْلَةٌ صَادِقَةٌ [*A charge,* or *an assault, made with earnestness, not with a false show of bravery,*] is like the saying [in the contr. case] حَمْلَةٌ كَاذِبَةٌ. (M, TA:* said in the latter to be tropical.) See also مُصْدَقٌ, in two places. — One says also تَمْرٌ صَادِقُ الحَلَاوَةِ, meaning *Very sweet dates.* (IDrd, O.) — And بَرْدٌ صَادِقٌ *Vehement,* or *intense, cold.* (TA voce بَحْتٌ &c.)

الصَّيْدَقُ *The small star cleaving to the middle one of* [*those called*] بَنَاتُ نَعْشٍ الكُبْرَى [*which compose the tail of Ursa Major*]; (Kr, M, TA;) [i. e. *the star called* السُّهَا, q. v.; for] it is said that the first of بنات نعش الكبرى, that is at the extremity thereof, is named القَائِدُ; and the second is العَنَاقُ, and by the side of it is a small star named السُّهَا and الصَّيْدَقُ; and the third is الحَوَرُ: (O:) or, accord. to AA, (O, TA,) *the pole-star* (القُطْبُ). (O, Ḳ, TA. [But this is strange; and the more so as it is added in the Ḳ that it is expl. in art. قود; for the explanation in that art. (though not free from obvious mistakes) identifies الصَّيْدَقُ with السُّهَا.]) — And, (Ḳ,) accord. to Sh, (O, TA,) it signifies الأَمِينُ [*The trusted, trusted in,* or *confided in,* &c.]. (O, Ḳ. [But it is added in the O that Sh cites a verse of Umeiyeh Ibn-Abi-ṣ-Ṣalt in which الأَمِينُ is applied as an epithet to the star called الصيدق.]) — And, (Ḳ,) accord. to some, as AA says, (O,) it signifies *The king.* (O, Ḳ.)

فَعَلَهُ فِى غِبِّ صَادِقَةٍ [in the CḲ غِبُّ صادقةٍ] means *He did it after the affair,* or *case, had become manifest to him.* (IDrd, O, Ḳ, TA.)

صُنْدُوقٌ, mentioned in this art. in the Ṣ and Mṣb: see art. صندق.

أَصْدَقُ [*More,* and *most, true* or *veracious*]. One says أَصْدَقُ مِنْ قَطَاةٍ [*More veracious than a ḳaṭáh*]; because the bird thus called cries قَطَا قَطَا; [thus telling where it is to be found;] its name being imitative of its cry: (Meyd, and TA in art. قطو:) hence it is called by the Arabs ↓الصَّدُوقُ: the saying is a prov. (Meyd.)

ذُو مَصْدَقٍ, (JḲ, Ṣ, M, O,) with fet-ḥ, (Ṣ,) or ↓ذُو مِصْدَقٍ like مِنْبَرٌ, (Ḳ,) applied to a man, (JḲ, M,) [i. e.] applied to a courageous man, (Ṣ, O, Ḳ,) means ↓صَادِقُ الحَمْلَةِ [*Earnest, not making a false show of bravery, in the charge,* or *assault*]; (JK, Ṣ, M, O, Ḳ;) or *courageous* [*in the charge,* or *assault*]: (JK:) مُصَادِقٌ, occurring in a verse of Aboo-Dhu-eyb, may be for ذُو صِدْقٍ; or it may be an anomalous pl. of مُصَادِقٌ [used as an epithet], like مَلَامِحُ and مَشَابِهُ [pls. of لَمْحَةٌ and شَبَهٌ]. (M.) Also, (Ṣ, M, O, Ḳ,) applied to a horse, (M,) [i. e.] applied to a fleet and excellent horse, (Ṣ, O,) in like manner, (M,) meaning صَادِقُ ▼ الجَرْيِ [*Earnest in running*]; (Ṣ, O, Ḳ;) as though fulfilling his promise of running: (Ṣ, O: [said in the TA to be tropical:]) Khufáf Ibn-Nudbeh says,

إِذَا مَا ٱسْتَحَمَّتْ أَرْضُهُ مِنْ سَمَائِهِ
جَرَى وَهْوَ مَوْدُوعٌ وَوَاعِدُ مَصْدَقِ

meaning *When his hoofs are wetted with the sweat of his upper parts, he runs, being left to himself,* not beaten nor chidden, *and a fulfiller of his promise* to do his utmost. (Ṣ, O.) And sometimes it is applied to an opinion, in like manner [as meaning *True,* or *sincere*]. (M.) — مَصْدَقٌ also signifies *Hardness.* (Th, M.) — Also *i. q.* حَدٌّ [as meaning The *edge* of a sword]: (TA:) [in a copy of the M written جِدٌّ, which I think an evident mistake; for it is added,] and it is said to have this meaning in a verse of Dureyd Ibn-Eṣ-Ṣimmeh [relating to a sword]. (M, TA.)

مِصْدَقٌ: see the next preceding paragraph.

مُصْدِقٌ A man *from whom the poor-rate* (صَدَقَة) *of his cattle is exacted.* (TA.)

مُصَدِّقٌ One *who accepts, admits, assents to,* or *believes, another in his information,* or *narration.* (Ṣ, TA.) = Also The *exactor,* or *collector,* (Ṣ, M, O, Mṣb, Ḳ, TA,) *of the* صَدَقَات, (Ṣ, O, Mṣb, Ḳ, TA,) i. e. (TA) *of the* حُقُوق [or *dues,* meaning *poor-rates*], (M, TA,) *of the cattle,* (Mṣb,) or *of the sheep* or *goats,* (Ṣ, M, O, TA,) *and of the camels,* (M, O, TA,) *for the persons to whom pertain the shares* [*thereof*]. (TA.)

مُصَّدِّقٌ: see مُتَصَدِّقٌ.

مِصْدَاقٌ *A thing that confirms,* or *proves, the truth* of a thing: (Ṣ, Ḳ:) [and] *a verbal evidence of the truth,* or *veracity,* of a man. (Ḥar p. 106.) One says, هٰذَا مِصْدَاقُ هٰذَا *This is what confirms,* or *proves, the truth of this.* (Ṣ.) And شَىْءٌ لَيْسَ لَهُ مِصْدَاقٌ [*A thing having nothing to verify it*]. (IAạr, TA in art. برق.)

مَصْدُوقَةٌ [see 1, near the beginning]. One says لَيْسَ لِحَمْلَتِهِ مَصْدُوقَةٌ [meaning *There is no earnestness attributable to his charge,* or *assault*]; like as one says [in the contr. case], لَيْسَ لَهَا مَكْذُوبَةٌ. (M.)

مُتَصَدِّقٌ One *who gives what is termed* صَدَقَة [meaning *alms*]: (Ṣ, O, Mṣb, Ḳ:) accord. to Kh, it means thus, and also one *who asks* [*alms*]; (O, TA;) and IAmb says the like; but Az says that the skilful of the grammarians disallow this; and thus say Fr and Aṣ and others: (TA:) [J, also, and Ṣgh and Fei, say that] it has only the former meaning: (Ṣ, O, Mṣb:) it is also pronounced مُصَّدِّقٌ ▼, by substitution [of ص for ت] and incorporation [of one ص into the other]; (Ṣ,* O,* Mṣb, Ḳ;*) and this pronunciation of the pl. both masc. and fem. occurs in the Ḳur lvii. 17, (Ṣ, O, Ḳ,) where Ibn-Ketheer and Aboo-Bekr, differing from others, read without teshdeed to the ص. (O.)

صدل

صَيْدَلٌ *Stones* [i. e. *pieces of ore*] *of silver:* mentioned by IB on the authority of IDrst: and he says that حِجَارَةُ العَقَاقِيرِ [meaning drugs resembling pieces of stone, such as pieces of gum &c.,] are likened thereto. (TA.)

صَيْدَلَةٌ [The *trade of the* صَيْدَلَانِىّ; the *sale of* عِطَارَة [i. e. *drugs and perfumes*]. (Ḳ,* TA.)

صَيْدَلَانِىٌّ (Ṣ, M, Mgh, Mṣb, Ḳ) a word of well-known meaning: (M:) *A seller of medicines* (Mgh, Mṣb, TA) *and of drugs* (TA) *and of perfumes:* (Ḳ, TA:) a rel. n. from صَيْدَلَانُ, the name of a town or place, (Ḳ,) or from صَيْدَلٌ meaning as expl. above; (IB, TA;) or a Pers. word arabicized: (M:) and صَيْدَنَانِىٌّ signifies the same, (Ṣ, Mṣb, Ḳ, [in the CḲ, erroneously, صَنْدَنَانِىٌّ,]) and so صَنْدَلَانِىٌّ: (Ḳ in this art., and O and Ḳ in art. صندل:) the pl. of the first is صَيَادِلَةٌ. (M, Mgh, Mṣb, Ḳ.) — Also *A king:* and so صَيْدَنَانِىٌّ. (M in art. صدن.)

صدم

1. صَدَمَهُ, (Ṣ, M, Ḳ,) aor. ـِ, (M, Ḳ,) inf. n. صَدْمٌ, (Ṣ, M, Mgh, Ḳ,) *He dashed himself,* i. e. *his body,* (Ṣ, Mgh, TA,) *against him,* (Ṣ, TA,) or *against it,* (Ṣ, Mgh, TA,) i. e., a thing: (Mgh:) or *he struck it,* or *knocked it,* [or *struck* or *knocked against it,*] namely, a hard thing with the like thereof. (M, Ḳ.) Hence the saying, الكَلْبُ إِذَا قَتَلَ الصَّيْدَ صَدْمًا لَا يُؤْكَلُ [i. e. *When the dog kills the game by dashing himself against it, it shall not be eaten*]. (Mgh.) [See also 3.] — And صَدَمَهُ, aor. as above, (Mṣb,) and so the inf. n., (Mgh, Mṣb, Ḳ,) *He pushed, thrust,* or *repelled, him,* or *it.* (Mgh, Mṣb, Ḳ, TA.) One says, صَدَمْتُ الشَّرَّ بِالشَّرِّ [*I repelled evil with evil*]. (TA.) — And صَدَمَتْهُ حُمَيَّا الكَأْسِ i. e. ‡ [*The intoxicating influence of the cup of wine*] *smote him* [or *attacked him*] *in his head.* (TA.) — And صَدَمَهُمْ أَمْرٌ, (M, TA,) inf. n. as above, (Ḳ,) ‡ *An event befell them.* (M, Ḳ,* TA.) — And صَدَمَهُ بِالقَوْلِ † *He silenced him by speech.* (Mṣb.)

3. صادمهُ, (Ṣ, Ḳ, TA,) inf. n. مُصَادَمَةٌ, (TA,) *He,* or *it, dashed against him,* or *it, being dashed against by him,* or *it;* (Ṣ,* PṢ:) or *struck,* or *knocked, him,* or *it, being struck,* or *knocked, by him,* or *it:* (Ḳ,* PṢ:) or *pushed, thrust,* or *repelled, him,* or *it, being pushed,* &c., *by him,* or *it;* (Ḳ,* TA;) syn. دَافَعَهُ: (TA, and Ḥam p. 313:) and *i. q.* صَاكَّهُ [i. e. *he struck him,* or *it;* or *struck him,* or *it, vehemently, with a broad thing,* or *with anything;* or *slapped him with his hand; being struck,* &c., *by him*]: (Ḥam ibid.:) [but, like as دَافَعَهُ often signifies the same as دَفَعَهُ, so accord. to Fei,] صَادَمَهُ الحِمَارُ means صَدَمَهُ [i. e. *The ass dashed against him;* &c.]. (Mṣb in art. شتر.)

6. تَصَادَمَا, (Ṣ, Mgh,) said of two men running, (Mgh,) and اِصْطَدَمَا ▼, (Ṣ, Mgh, Ḳ,) said of two horsemen, (Mgh,) and of two stallion [camels], (TA,) *They dashed themselves together, each against the other:* (Ṣ,* TA, PṢ:) or *they struck,* or *knocked,* [*against*] *each other; they collided;* (Ḳ,* TA;) *each of them struck with himself the other:* (Mgh:) or both verbs, said of two horsemen, *they smote each other, each of them with his weight and his sharpness* or *vigorousness* or *valiantness:* (Mṣb:) [or *they pushed, thrust,* or *repelled, each other:* (see 1:)] and تصادموا *they pushed, pressed, crowded,* or *thronged, together;* or *dashed, one against another;* (M, Ḳ, TA; but in the M, only the inf. n. is mentioned;) *like two ships in the sea.* (TA.)

8: see the next preceding paragraph.

صِدْمٌ The *rugged portion* of a [stony tract such as is termed] حَرَّة; as also صِدْمَةٌ ▼. (ISh, TA.)

صَدْمَةٌ *A single shock,* or *collision:* (KL:) *a single impulsion, push,* or *thrust:* (TA:) and † *a vehement befalling of an event.* (KL.) It is said in a trad., الصَّبْرُ عِنْدَ الصَّدْمَةِ الأُولَى (Ṣ, Mṣb, TA) i. e. † [*Patience is* to be exercised] *at the first* [*shock,* or] *assault,* or *attack,* of the calamity: (TA:) meaning that patience is the last thing in the case of every misfortune, (Ṣ, Mṣb,) but it is [most] commended, (Ṣ,) or is most rewarded, (Mṣb,) on the occasion of the sharpness, or vehemence, thereof. (Ṣ, Mṣb.) And one says, أَتَيْتُ عَلَى الأَمْرَيْنِ صَدْمَةً وَاحِدَةً [*I made an end of the two affairs at one dash,* or *at one stroke*]. (TA.) = And *A baldness in the side of the forehead;* syn. نَزَعَةٌ. (Ḳ.) — See also الصَّدِمَتَانِ, in two places.

صِدْمَةٌ: see صِدْمٌ.

الصَّدِمَتَانِ (AZ, Ṣ, M, Ḳ) and الصَّدْمَتَانِ ▼ (Ḳ) *The* جَبِينَانِ [or *two parts whereof each is termed* جَبِين, *above the temple, on either side of the forehead*]: (Ḳ:) or *the two sides* (AZ, Ṣ, M, Ḳ) *of the* جَبِين (AZ, Ṣ, Ḳ) or *of the* جَبِينَانِ: (M:) or, accord. to AA, as is stated in a marginal note in a copy of the Ṣ, the correct meaning is *the two sides of the forehead.* (TA.) — And الصدمتان [i. e. الصَّدِمَتَانِ or ▼ الصَّدْمَتَانِ] signifies also *The two sides of the valley:* as though, by reason of their confronting, they struck each other. (TA.)

صُدَامٌ: see what next follows.

صِدَامٌ, (Ṣ, Ḳ,) or صُدَامٌ ▼, (M,) asserted by Az to be with ḍamm, (TA,) or the latter is vulgar, (Ṣ,) not allowable, (Ḳ,) though agreeable with analogy, (Ṣ, Ḳ,) being like صُدَاعٌ and زُكَامٌ and دُوَارٌ and other terms for diseases, (TA,) *A certain disease in the heads of horses* or similar *beasts*: (Ṣ, M, Ḳ:) or, accord. to ISh, *a certain disease that attacks camels, in consequence of which their bellies become affected with acidity, and they relinquish the water, though thirsty, for some days, until they recover or die.* (TA.)

أَصْدَمُ *Bald in the sides of the forehead.* (Ḳ.)

مِصْدَمٌ A man *vehement in war, and courageous*; or *a warrior*; or *known, experienced warrior*; syn. مِحْرَبٌ. (M.)

إِبِلٌ مُصَدَّمَةٌ : see what follows.

جَمَلٌ مَصْدُومٌ *A camel affected with* [*the disease termed*] صِدَام: and ▼ إِبِلٌ مُصَدَّمَةٌ [*camels affected therewith*]. (TA.)

صدن

صَيْدَنٌ *A firm, strong,* or *compact, building.* (M.) — And *A firm, strong,* or *compact, garment,* or *piece of cloth*: (M:) or *a* [*garment of the kind called*] كِسَآء *that is stout,* or *strong,* or *that is thick,* or *compact, in texture.* (Ḳ.) — And *A king*; (Ṣ, M, Ḳ;) because of the firmness of his rule, or his state, or condition; as also ▼ صَيْدَنَانِىٌّ and ▼ صَيْدَلَانِىٌّ. (M.) — And *A fox*; (Ṣ, M, Ḳ;) as also ▼ صَيْدَنَانِىٌّ: (Ḳ:) or الصَّيْدَنُ is one of the names thereof. (TA.) — And The *hyena.* (Ḳ.) — See also صَيْدَنَانِىٌّ. — Also *A species of fly, that makes a buzzing sound over the herbage.* (IKh, TA.) — And, as also صَيْدَلٌ, *Stones* [i. e. *pieces of ore*] *of silver*: to which are likened what are termed حِجَارَةُ العَقَاقِيرِ. (IDrst, TA. [See صَيْدَلٌ; and see also صَيْدَانٌ, below.])

صَيْدَانٌ *Pieces of silver,* (M, TA,) *when struck from the stone* [or *ore*] *thereof*: (TA:) n. un. with ة. (M, TA.) [See also صَيْدَنٌ, above, last signification. And see صَيْدَانٌ in art. صيد.] — And *Stone cooking-pots*: (M, TA:) in this sense [likewise] a coll. gen. n.: n. un. with ة. (IB and L in art. صيد, in which it is mentioned in the Ṣ and L and Ḳ.) [See, again, صَيْدَانٌ, and also صَيْدَانَةٌ, in art. صيد.] — And *Small pebbles*: (IAạr, M, TA:) or so صَيْدَانُ الحَصَى. (L in art. صيد.)

صَيْدَانَةٌ [as a n. un.: see صَيْدَانٌ, above. — Also] *Rugged, hard ground, in which is fine stone.* (M, TA.) — See also two other significations (mentioned here in the TA) in art. صيد.

صَيْدَنَانِىٌّ *A certain creeping thing,* (دَابَّةٌ, M,) or *a small creeping thing,* (دُوَيْبَّةٌ, Ṣ, Ḳ,) *that makes for itself a habitation in the ground,* (Ṣ, M, Ḳ,) *within the ground,* (M,) *and conceals it*; (Ṣ, M, Ḳ;) i. e. *covers it over*; (M;) so says A'Obeyd; (Ṣ;) also called ▼ صَيْدَنٌ: (Ṣ, Ḳ:) accord. to IKh, *a certain small creeping thing* (دويبّة) *that collects pieces of stick,* or *wood, from the plants*: accord. to IAạr, *a certain creeping thing* (دَابَّة) *having many legs, so many that they cannot be counted, which are short and long.* (TA.) — See also صَيْدَنٌ, in two places. — Also *i. q.* صَيْدَلَانِىٌّ (Ṣ, Mgh, Ḳ, TA) as meaning *A seller of medicines,* (Mgh,) or *of perfumes*: so called as being likened to the small creeping thing mentioned above: or from صَيْدَنٌ in a sense expl. above as syn. with صَيْدَلٌ. (TA.)

صدو

1. صَدْوٌ as an inf. n. of which the verb is صَدَا: see 2 in art. صدى, in two places.

صَدْوٌ as a subst. *A certain liquid poison which is applied upon arrow-heads,* or *spear-heads,* or *the like, resembling the blood of the* [*serpent called*] أَسْوَد. (M, TA.)

صدى

1. صَدِىَ, (Ṣ, M, Mgh, Mṣb, Ḳ,) aor. يَصْدَى, (Ṣ, Mgh, Mṣb,) inf. n. صَدًى, *He thirsted*: (Ṣ, M, Mgh, Mṣb, Ḳ:) or *he thirsted vehemently.* (M.) = صَدَا, inf. n. صَدْوٌ: see 2, in two places.

2. تَصْدِيَةٌ signifies The *clapping with the hands*; syn. تَصْفِيقٌ; (Ṣ, Ḳ;) accord. to Er-Rághib, as being like the echo (الصَّدَى), inasmuch as there is no profit in it; (TA;) or it is from الصَّدُّ, because they [who practised it in their worship] used to turn away (كَانُوا يَصُدُّونَ) from El-Islám; (Ḳ;) [see more in the second paragraph of art. صد;] and صَدْوٌ [an inf. n. of which the verb is ▼ صَدَا] signifies the same; (Ḳ;) and so ▼ تَصَدٍّ, of which AHeyth cites as an ex. the saying of Ḥassán

• صَلَاتُهُمُ التَّصَدِّى وَالْمُكَآءُ •

[*Their prayer is the clapping with the hands, and whistling*: like the saying in the Ḳur viii. 35]: (TA:) one says of a man, صَدَّى, (M,) or صَدَّى بِيَدَيْهِ, (TA,) meaning *He clapped with his hands*; (M, TA;) [said to be] originally صَدَّدَ; (M;) and ▼ صَدَا بِيَدَيْهِ, inf. n. صَدْوٌ [mentioned above], meaning the same. (TḲ.) = See also مُصَدِّيَةٌ.

3. صاداهُ, (Ḳ,) inf. n. مُصَادَاةٌ, (Ṣ,) *He imitated him,* or *it*; syn. عَارَضَهُ: (Ṣ,* Ḳ:) and *he,* or *it, corresponded,* and *was equal, to him,* or *it.* (TA.) In the Ḳur xxxviii. 1, some read صَادِ, with kesr, as an imperative from الْمُصَادَاةُ (Bḍ, TA) as meaning الْمُعَارَضَةُ; and hence الصَّدَى [i. e. the echo], because it imitates (يُعَارِضُ) the first sound: so that the meaning is, *Imitate thou* (عَارِضْ) the Ḳur-án by thy works. (Bḍ.) — [And] *i. q.* دَبَّرَهُ [i. e. *He considered,* or *forecast, its issues,* or *results*; *did, performed,* or *executed, it with thought,* or *consideration*; or *managed, conducted, ordered,* or *regulated, it*]; relating to an affair: (M:) [or] الْمُصَادَاةُ signifies *the turning about,* or *revolving, the opinion,* or *idea,* [*that one forms*] *respecting the management* (تَدْبِير) of a thing, *and the doing of it*: (Ḥam p. 35:) [or,] accord. to Aṣ, *the minding* a thing *attentively, carefully,* or *solicitously*: a man who had assisted his she-camel in her bringing forth said, بِتُّ أُصَادِيهَا طُولَ لَيْلِى [*I passed all my night minding her attentively, carefully,* or *solicitously*]; because he disliked binding her fore shank to her arm, as it would distress her; or leaving her, as she might go away at random and the wolf might devour her young one: and in like manner one says of the pastor, يُصَادِى إِبِلَهُ [*He minds attentively,* &c., *his camels*]; when they thirst before the completion of their usual period of being kept from drinking, he restricts them to journeying by night so as to arrive at water on the morrow. (TA.) — And *He soothed, coaxed, wheedled,* or *cajoled, him*; or *deceived, deluded, beguiled, circumvented,* or *outwitted, him*; or *strove, endeavoured,* or *desired, to do so*: syn. دَارَاهُ, (Ṣ, M, Ḳ, TA,) and دَاجَاهُ, and سَاتَرَهُ, (Ṣ, Ḳ, TA,) all of which have one meaning, (TA,) [though the last implies *concealing enmity*,] and لَايَنَهُ. (M.) مَنْ صَادَاكَ فَقَدْ صَادَكَ [*He who soothes thee,* or *coaxes thee, surely ensnares thee*] is a saying mentioned in the A. (TA.)

4. اصدى *It* (a mountain) *returned an echo.* (Ṣ,* Ḳ.) — And *He* (a man, TA) *died*; (Ḳ, TA;) as though [meaning] *his echo ceased*; the ا having a privative effect. (TA.)

5. التَّصَدِّى, accord. to Er-Rághib, signifies *The corresponding* to a thing *like as does the echo returning from the mountain.* (TA.) [But accord. to others,] تصدّى لهُ is originally تَصَدَّدَ; (Az and L in art. صد;) and signifies تَعَرَّضَ, (Ṣ, M, Ḳ,) and تَضَرَّعَ. (M.) [See 5 in art. صد; where the usages of this verb, except in the senses mentioned and indicated here below, are fully explained.] — It signifies also *The feigning oneself unmindful, negligent, inattentive, inadvertent, inconsiderate,* or *heedless, not being really so.* (TA.) — And *The diverting oneself.* (TA.) — See also 2.

صَدًى [sometimes written صَدًا] *An echo*; i. e. الصَّدَى signifies *what the mountain returns to him who utters a sound,* or *voice,* or *cry, therein*; (Ḳ;) or *the sound of the mountain and the like that responds to one*; (M;) or *what responds to one with the like of his voice,* or *cry, in the mountains* &c. (Ṣ.) One says, صَمَّ صَدَاهُ ‡ [*His echo became dumb,* or *may his echo become dumb*]; (Ṣ, TA;) meaning *he perished,* or *may he perish*: (Ṣ and Ḳ and TA in art. صم:) and أَصَمَّ اللّٰهُ صَدَاهُ ‡ [*May God make his echo to return no sound*]; (Ṣ, Ḳ, TA;) meaning *may God destroy him*: (Ṣ, Ḳ, and TA in art. صم:) for when a man dies, the صَدَى hears not from him anything, that it should respond to him. (Ṣ. [See also another explanation of this saying in what follows.]) — And *A sound, voice,* or *cry,* (M, TA,) in an absolute sense. (TA.) — Also The *part of the head,* (M,) or the *part of the brain,* (TA,) *which is the place* [or *seat*] *of hearing.* (M, TA.) And therefore one says, أَصَمَّ اللّٰهُ صَدَاهُ [*May God render deaf the part of his brain which is the seat of hearing*]. (TA.) — And The *brain,* (M, Ḳ, TA,) itself. (TA.) And The [*entire*] *contents* (lit. the *stuffing,* حَشْو,) *of the head*; (M, Ḳ, TA;) also called the هَامَة. (TA.) One says, صَدَعَ اللّٰهُ صَدَاهُ [*May God crack his brain,* or *the contents of his head*]. (M.) — And *A bird that cries in the*

هَامَة [or *head*] *of the slain when his blood has not been avenged by retaliation:* (M:) or *a bird that comes forth* (M, Ḳ) *from his head,* (مِنْ رَأْسِهِ, M,) or *from the head of the slain,* (Ḳ,) *when he,* or *it, has become consumed,* or *decayed,* (M, Ḳ,) also called the هَامَة; (M;) accord. to the assertion of the people of the Time of Ignorance; (M, Ḳ;) mentioned by A'Obeyd; and some of them used to say that the bones of the dead became a هَامَة, which flew: pl. أَصْدَآءٌ: (TA:) and [this may be meant by the saying that it signifies] the *male of the* بُومِ (Ṣ, M, Ḳ, TA) and هَام: pl. أَصْدَآءٌ: (M:) they used to say that when a man was slain and his blood was not avenged by retaliation, there came forth from his head a bird like the بُومَة, i. e. the هَامَة, the male being called the صدى; and it cried upon his grave, اِسْقُونِى اِسْقُونِى [*Give ye me to drink, give ye me to drink,* meaning, of the blood of the slayer]; and if the slayer was slain, it abstained from its crying: (TA:) and [it is said that] it signifies also the *body* [itself] *of a human being after his death;* (M, Ḳ;) or the *remains of the dead in his grave,* i. e. *his* جُثَّة [or *corpse*]. (Jm, TA.) — And, (Ḳ,) accord. to El-'Adebbes, (Ṣ,) [*A cricket;*] *a certain flying thing, that creaks by night, and hops,* (Ṣ, Ḳ,) *and flies, thought by the* [*common*] *people to be the* جُنْدَب, *but it is only the* صدى, *the* جندب *being smaller than the* صدى. (Ṣ. [See also الصَّرَّار.]) — And *A certain fish, black, long,* (Ḳ, TA,) *and bulky:* n. un. صَدَاةٌ. (TA.) — And [A man] *small,* or *slender, in person;* (AA, M, Ḳ, TA;) and so صَدًا, with ء, as mentioned by Az. (TA. [See also صَدْعٌ and صَدَغٌ.]) — And *Knowing in respect of what is conducive to the good of cattle:* (Ḳ:) or صَدَى مَالٍ means thus: (M:) or *gentle in the management of cattle;* like إِزَآءُ مَالٍ: so in the Jm: (TA:) or, as some particularly say, of camels: (M, TA:) [i. e.] you say, إِنَّهُ لَصَدَى إِبِلٍ, meaning *Verily he is knowing in respect of camels, and of what is conducive to their good.* (Ṣ.) = Also *Thirst:* (Ṣ, M, Ḳ:) or *vehement thirst:* (M:) [see the first paragraph, in which it is mentioned as an inf. n.:] it is said that thirst does not become vehement but the brain dries, and therefore the skin of the forehead of him who dies of thirst cracks. (TA.) — See also the next paragraph. = And The *act of the* مُتَصَدِّى, (M, Ḳ, TA,) i. e., [as is indicated in the M,] *of him who raises his head and breast, looking towards,* or *regarding, a thing;* and so ♦ صَدَاةٌ. (TA.)

صَدٍ and ♦ صَادٍ and ♦ صَدْيَانُ (Ṣ, M, Mṣb, Ḳ) and ♦ صَدًى [which last is an inf. n. used as an epithet] (M) *Thirsting:* (Ṣ, M, Mṣb, Ḳ:) or *thirsting vehemently:* (M:) fem. [of the first] صَدِيَةٌ (Mṣb) and [of the second] صَادِيَةٌ (Mṣb, Ḳ) and [of the third] ♦ صَدْيَا: (Ṣ, M, Mṣb, Ḳ:) and the pl. of صَادِيَةٌ is صَوَادٍ. (Ḥam p. 329.)

صَدَاةٌ: see صَدًى, last sentence.

صَدْيَانُ; and its fem., صَدْيَا: see صَدٍ.

صَادٍ (fem. with ة, and pl. of the latter صَوَادٍ): see صَدٍ. — As pl. of صَادِيَةٌ, (M,) صَوَادٍ signifies [also] *Tall* palm-trees: (Ṣ, Ḳ:) and sometimes, *such as drink not water:* (Ṣ:) or palm-trees *that drink water:* [thus in a copy of the M:] and some say, *such as are tall* thereof, and of other trees. (M.)

كَأْسٌ مُصْدَاةٌ [*A cup of wine*] *having much water: contr. of* مُعْرَقَةٌ, this meaning "having little water." (M.)

مِصْدَاةٌ A man *who thirsts much.* (M.)

مُصَدِّيَةٌ The woman *who faces,* or *decorates,* (♦ تُصَدِّى,) [which I thus render conjecturally, finding nothing to indicate its meaning except what here follows,]) *the* وِسَادَة [i. e. *pillow,* or *cushion,*] *with* الأَرَنْدَج, meaning *black lines, upon the leather* [*that forms its covering*]. (TA.)

صر

1\. صَرَّ, (Ṣ, A, TA,) aor. ِ, (Ṣ, TA,) inf. n. صَرِيرٌ, said of the جُنْدَب [which is app. a species of locust], and of a writing-reed, and of a door, (Ṣ, A, TA,) or of a dog-tooth, (نَاب, so in a copy of the Ṣ in the place of بَاب in other copies as in the A and TA,) *It made a sound,* or *noise;* (Ṣ, A, TA;) or *a prolonged sound* or *noise;* [meaning *it creaked;* or *made a creaking,* or *grating, sound;*] and so anything that makes a similar prolonged sound: and [in like manner] ♦ اِصْطَرَّتْ said of a mast (سَارِيَة), *it creaked,* or *made a creaking sound:* (TA:) but when there is a lightness, or slightness, and reiteration, of the sound, they use the reduplicative form, ♦ صَرْصَرَ, inf. n. صَرْصَرَةٌ, (Ṣ,* TA,) signifying *he* (the bird called أَخْطَب, Ṣ, A, TA, and the hawk, or falcon, Ṣ, M, TA, or other bird, or flying thing, M) *uttered his* [*reiterated quavering*] *cry;* (Ṣ, M, A, TA;) as though they imitated prolongation in the cry of the جُنْدَب [and the like], and reiteration in the cry of the أَخْطَب [and the like thereof]. (Ṣ, TA.) صَرَّ الجُنْدَبُ is a prov., expl. in art. جدب [q. v.]. (TA in that art.) — Also *He* (a sparrow) [*chirped,* or] *uttered a cry,* or *cries.* (TA.) — صَرَّ, aor. ِ, inf. n. صَرٌّ and صَرِيرٌ; and ♦ صَرْصَرَ; *He cried, called out,* or *raised a cry* or *clamour,* (M, Ḳ,) *with vehemence,* (Ḳ,) or *with the utmost vehemence:* (M:) and [in like manner] one says, جَآءَ يَصْطَرُّ♦ *He came* [*making a clamour,* or] *in clamour.* (TA.) — And صَرَّ صِمَاخُهُ, inf. n. صَرِيرٌ, *His ear-hole sounded,* (M, Ḳ,) or *tingled,* or *rang,* (A,) by reason of thirst. (M, A, Ḳ.) And صَرَّتِ الأُذُنُ *The ear tingled,* or *rang.* (ISk, A.) — And صَرَّ, aor. as above, *He thirsted* [app. *so as to hear a ringing in his ears*]. (IAạr.) = صَرٌّ [as inf. n. of صَرَّ] also signifies The act of *binding* [a captive, &c.: see the pass. part. n., مَصْرُورٌ]. (Mgh.) — You say, صَرَّ, [aor. ُ,] (Ṣ, M, A,) inf. n. صَرٌّ, (M, TA,) *He tied up* a purse, (Ṣ, M,* TA,) and money in a purse. (A.) — And صَرَّ النَّاقَةَ (Ṣ, M, Ḳ) and بِالنَّاقَةِ, (M, Ḳ,) or صَرَّ النَّاقَةَ بِالصِّرَارِ, (Mṣb,) aor. ُ, (M, Mṣb, Ḳ,) inf. n. صَرٌّ; (M, Ḳ;) [and app. ♦ صَرَّرَهَا; (see the pass. part. n., voce مَصْرُورٌ;)] *He bound the* صِرَار [q. v.] *upon the she-camel;* (Ṣ;) [i. e.] *he bound the she-camel's udder with the* صِرَار: (M, Mṣb, Ḳ,* TA:) and صَرَّ الأَطْبَآءَ بِالصِّرَارِ [*He bound the teats with the* صرار]. (A.) [See a verse of El-Kumeyt cited voce رِجْل: and see also what there follows it.] — [Hence,] صَرَّهَا means also † *He left off milking her* [i. e. the camel]. (Mṣb.) — And تُصَرُّ, [aor. of صُرَّتْ,] said of a leathern bucket (دَلْو) that has become flaccid, *It is tied, and has a loop-shaped handle affixed within it, having another such opposite to it.* (Ḳ,* TA.) — And one says, صُرَّ عَلَىَّ الطَّرِيقُ فَلَا أَجِدُ مَسْلَكًا ‡ [*He closed,* or *has closed, against me the road,* or *way, so that I find not any passage*]. (A.) And صُرَّتْ عَلَىَّ هٰذِهِ البَلْدَةُ فَلَا أَجِدُ مِنْهَا مَخْلَصًا ‡ [*This town has become closed against me so that I find not any way of escape from it*]. (A.) — And صَرَّ أُذُنَيْهِ, [aor. ُ, inf. n. صَرٌّ,] *He* (a horse) *contracted his ears to his head:* (ISk, Ṣ:) or *pointed and raised his ears;* which a horse does only when he exerts himself and hastens in his pace: (TA:) or *he* (an ass) *straightened and erected his ears to listen;* as also ♦ أَصَرَّهُمَا: (A:) and ♦ أَصَرَّ used intransitively, (ISk, Ṣ,) without the mention of the ears, (A,) signifies the same as صَرَّ أُذُنَيْهِ: (ISk, Ṣ, A:) and صَرَّ أُذُنَهُ and صَرَّ بِأُذُنِهِ, aor. and inf. n. as above; and ♦ أَصَرَّ بِهَا; *he* (a horse, and an ass,) *straightened and erected his ear to listen;* (M, Ḳ;) as also ♦ صَرَّرَهَا. (TA.) — [The inf. n.] صَرٌّ signifies also The act of *confining, withholding, hindering,* or *preventing.* (TA.) — And صُرَّ ‡ *He had an iron collar put upon his neck,* or *round his neck and hands together.* (A.) — And صَرَّ, aor. ُ, *He collected together* a thing, or things, (IAạr,) or anything. (TA.) And ♦ صَرَّرَ كَلَامًا † *He collected something to be said in his bosom,* or *mind.* (L and TA, from a trad.) And صَرْصَرَ المَالَ, inf. n. صَرْصَرَةٌ, *He collected together the property,* or *the camels* or *the like, and put back what had become scattered of the extreme portions thereof.* (T, TA.) = And صُرَّ *It* (a plant, or herbage,) *became smitten by cold, or by intense cold.* (M, Ḳ.)

2: see 1, in three places. = صَرَّرَتْ said of a she-camel, *She preceded.* (Aboo-Leylà, M, Ḳ.)

3\. صَارَّهُ عَلَى الشَّىْءِ *He compelled him against his will to do the thing.* (Ṣ, Ḳ.)

4: see 1, latter part, in three places. = أَصَرَّ عَلَيْهِ, (Ṣ, TA,) inf. n. إِصْرَارٌ, (TA,) † *He persevered,* or *persisted, in it;* or *kept to it perseveringly.* (Ṣ, TA.) You say, أَصَرَّ عَلَى فِعْلِهِ † *He persevered,* or *persisted, in doing it.* (Mṣb.) And أَصَرَّ عَلَى الذَّنْبِ ‡ *He persevered,* or *persisted, in the crime, sin,* or *act of disobedience.* (M, TA.) The verb is used in this sense when its object is evil, or crime, or the like. (TA.) — And † *He determined, resolved,* or *decided, upon it.* (M, Mgh, Ḳ.) You say, اصرّ عَلَى فِعْلِهِ † *He determined, resolved,* or *decided, upon going on in doing it, and not turning back.* (TA.) — اصرّ يَعْدُو † *He hastened* (M, Ḳ) *somewhat* (M) *in running:* (M, Ḳ: [in the CḲ, for أَصَرَّ يَعْدُو أَسْرَعَ, is put أَصَرَّ يَعْدُ وَأَسْرَعَ:]) accord. to A'Obeyd, the verb in this sense is أَضَرَّ; but Eṭ-Ṭooseè asserts that this is a mistranscription. (M.) ═ اصرّ السُّنْبُلُ *The ears of corn became such as are termed* صَرَر [q. v.]: (M, Ḳ:) [or] accord. to ISh, one says, اصرّ الزَّرْعُ, inf. n. إِصْرَارٌ, meaning *The seed-produce* [i. e. *corn*] *put forth the extremities of its awn, before its ears had become developed.* (TA.)

8: see 1, former half, in two places. ═ اصطرّ said of a solid hoof, *It was,* or *became, narrow,* or *contracted,* (Ṣ, TA,) *in an unseemly manner,* or *immoderately.* (TA.)

R. Q. 1. صَرْصَرَ, inf. n. صَرْصَرَةٌ: see 1, former half, in two places: ═ and the same paragraph, last sentence but one.

صَرٌّ *A leathern bucket* (دَلْو) *that, in consequence of its having become flaccid, is tied, and has a loop-shaped handle affixed within it, having another such opposite to it.* (Ḳ,* TA.) ═ See also صَرِيرَةٌ.

صِرٌّ (Ṣ, M, A, Mṣb, Ḳ) and ↓ صِرَّةٌ (M, A, Ḳ) *Cold:* (Th, M, A, Mṣb, Ḳ:) or *intense cold;* (Zj, M, A, Ḳ;) as also ↓ صَرْصَرٌ: (Ḥam p. 719:) or *cold that smites the herbage and the seed-produce of the field:* (Ṣ:) in the Ḳur iii. 113, the first of these words has the first of the meanings expl. above: (IAmb:) or the second meaning: (Zj:) or signifies *noise and commotion:* or, accord. to I'Ab, *fire.* (IAmb.) — And رِيحٌ صِرٌّ (M, A, Ḳ) and ↓ صَرْصَرٌ (Ṣ, M, A, Ḳ) *A wind intensely cold:* (Ṣ, M, A, Ḳ:) or *very intensely cold:* (T in explanation of the latter:) or *vehemently loud:* (M, A, Ḳ:) of ↓ صَرْصَرٌ some say that it is originally صَرَّرٌ, from صِرٌّ meaning "cold;" the incipient letter being repeated, and put in the place of the medial ر: others, that it is from صَرِيرُ البَابِ ["the creaking of the door"], and from صَرَّةٌ meaning "vociferation, or clamour." (ISk.) — And صِرٌّ is the name of *A certain bird, like the sparrow* (Ḳ, ṬA) *in size,* (TA,) *of a yellow colour:* (Ḳ, TA:) so called because of its cry: or, as some say, the *sparrow* (عُصْفُور) *itself.* (TA.)

صَرَّةٌ *Vociferation,* or *clamour:* (Ṣ, M, A, TA:) so in the Ḳur li. 29: (TA:) or the *most vehement vociferation* or *clamour* or *crying* (Zj, M, Ḳ*) of a man and of a bird &c. (Zj, M.) [In the Ḳ, this meaning is erroneously assigned to صِرَّةٌ.] — And *Vehemence* of grief or anxiety (Ṣ, M, Ḳ) and of war (M, Ḳ) and of heat, (Ḳ,) or of the hot season, (M,) &c.: (Ṣ, M:) and *vehemence of the heat* of summer. (Ṣ, A.) — And *A contraction,* or *much contraction, and sternness,* or *moroseness, of the face,* (Ḳ, TA,) *by reason of dislike,* or *hatred.* (TA.) ═ Also *A company, a collection,* or *an assemblage.* (Ṣ, M, Ḳ.) So in the following words of Imra-el-Ḳeys:

* جَوَاحِرُهَا فِى صَرَّةٍ لَمْ تَزَيَّلِ *

(Ṣ, M) i. e. *Those of them that remained behind, in a herd, not dispersed:* (EM p. 48: [see the entire verse voce دُونَ:]) or فِى صَرَّةٍ here means *in* [the midst of] *clamour:* (Ṣ:) or *in vehemence of grief* or *anxiety.* (Ṣ, M.) ═ Also *i. q.* عَطْفَةٌ (M, Ḳ) [i. e.] *A certain bead* (خَرَزَةٌ) *by which women fascinate men so as to withhold them from other women.* (Lḥ, M, Ḳ, TA. [This is evidently what is meant by عَطْفَةٌ, but is given in the M and Ḳ as a signification distinct therefrom.]) ═ See also مُصَرَّاةٌ.

صُرَّةٌ *A purse* (شَرَجٌ, M, Ḳ, in the CḲ شَرْجٌ,) *for money;* (Ṣ, M, A, Mṣb, Ḳ;) as also ↓ مَصَرٌّ, with fet-ḥ, (TA,) or ↓ مُصَرٌّ: (so in a copy of the A:) pl. of the first, صُرَرٌ. (Mṣb.) Hence the prov., اِفْتَحْ صُرَرَكَ تَعْلَمْ عُجَرَكَ, meaning † *Return to thyself,* [or *lay open the recesses of thy mind,*] and *thou wilt know* [*thy vices,* or *faults,* or] *thy good from thy evil.* (Meyd. [See also عُجَرٌ, last explanation.])

صِرَّةٌ: see صِرٌّ.

صَرَرٌ *Ears of corn* (سُنْبُل) *after the culm is produced,* (M, Ḳ, [in the CḲ, يُقَصِّبُ is put in the place of يُقَصِّبُ,]) *before they become apparent:* (M:) or *ears of corn while the farina has not come forth into them:* n. un. with ة: (AḤn, M, Ḳ:) or, accord. to ISh, *corn when the leaves become twisted, and the extremity of the ears becomes dry,* or *tough, though the farina have not come forth into them.* (TA.) [See 4, last sentence.]

صَرَارٌ: see صَرُورَةٌ, in two places.

صِرَارٌ The *thing with which a she-camel's udder is bound:* (M, Ḳ:) the *string which is tied over the she-camel's udder and over the* [*piece of wood called*] تَوْدِيَة, *in order that her young one may not suck her;* (Ṣ;) and in order that it may not make any impression upon her, they smear her teats with fresh [dung of the kind called] بَعَر: (TA:) or *a piece of rag which is bound upon the she-camel's teats, in order that her young one may not suck her:* (Mṣb:) pl. أَصِرَّةٌ. (M, A, Ḳ.) It is a custom of the Arabs to bind the صرار upon the udders of their milch camels when they send them to pasture by themselves; and when they return in the evening, they loose the اصرّة, and milk. (IAth.) — [Hence,] جَعَلْتُ دُونَ فُلَانٍ صِرَارًا ‡ *I put an obstruction,* or *obstacle, in the way of such a one.* (A.) ═ Also *Elevated places over which the water does not come.* (Ṣ.)

صَرُورٌ: see صَرُورَةٌ.

صَرَارَةٌ: see the next paragraph, in three places.

صَرُورَةٌ (Ṣ, M, A, Mṣb, Ḳ) and ↓ صَارُورَةٌ (Ṣ, M, Mṣb, Ḳ) and ↓ صَرُورٌ and ↓ صَارُورٌ (M, Ḳ) and ↓ صَرَارَةٌ (Ṣ, M, Ḳ) and ↓ صَرُورِىٌّ (Ṣ, M, Mṣb, Ḳ) and ↓ صَارُورِىٌّ (M) or ↓ صَارُورَاءُ, (Ṣgh, Ḳ,) the last like عَاشُورَاءُ, mentioned on the authority of Ks, (TA,) A man *who has not performed the pilgrimage to Mekkeh:* (Ṣ, M, A, Mṣb, Ḳ:) so called from صَرٌّ, signifying the "act of confining, withholding, hindering, or preventing;" (TA;) or because the person so called refrains from expending of his property in pilgrimage: (Mṣb:) you say also, اِمْرَأَةٌ صَرُورَةٌ *a woman who has not performed the pilgrimage to Mekkeh:* (Ṣ, Mṣb:) pl. ↓ صَرَارٌ and ↓ صَرَارَةٌ: (Ḳ:) [or, rather, the former is a coll. gen. n., of which صَرَارَةٌ is the n. of un.; and the latter is a quasi-pl. n., like صَحَابَةٌ, as well as n. un. of صَرَارٌ:] Fr cites, from certain of the Arabs, ↓ صَرَارٌ as used collectively; and one of the number is termed ↓ صَرَارَةٌ: (Ṣ:) each of the forms ending with the relative ى receives the dual and pl. and fem. inflections: and accord. to IAạr, the forms preceding those receive also the dual and pl. inflections: (M,* TA:) and some say that صَوَارِيرُ is pl. of ↓ صَارُورَةٌ: (TA:) or ↓ صَارُورَةٌ and ↓ صَارُورٌ, (M,) or صَرُورَةٌ, (Lḥ, Ṣ, M, A, Mṣb,) as occurring in the poetry of En-Nábighah, (Yaạḳoob, Ṣ,) not used without ة, (Lḥ, M,) or all the sing. forms above mentioned, (Ḳ,) signify one *who has not married:* (M, A, Ḳ:) or *who has not had intercourse with women:* as though he had determined (أَصَرَّ) upon relinquishing them: (Yaạḳoob, Ṣ, Mṣb:*) applied in like manner to a woman, and to a plurality of persons: (M, Ḳ:) the ة in صَرُورَةٌ applied to a man and to a woman is not to denote the fem. gender, but to give the utmost intensiveness to the signification. (IJ, M.) — It is said in a trad., لَاصَرُورَةَ فِى الإِسْلَامِ, (Ṣ, M,) meaning, accord. to A'Obeyd, *There is no abstinence from intercourse with women in El-Islám:* (M, TA:) i. e., no one should say, I will not marry: (TA:) thus he makes صرورة a noun signifying an accident: but it is better known as an epithet: (M:) and IAth says that the meaning is, he who slays another in the حَرَم [or sacred territory of Mekkeh] shall be slain: his saying, "I am a صرورة; I have not performed the pilgrimage, and I know not the sacredness of the حَرَم;" shall not be accepted of him: for in the Time of Ignorance, the Kaạbeh was a place of refuge. (TA.)

صَرِيرَةٌ دَرَاهِمُ *i. q.* مَصْرُورَةٌ [i. e. *Dirhems,* or *pieces of money, tied up in a purse*]: (Ḳ:) termed in the present day ↓ صَرٌّ. (TA.) ═ See also صَارَّةٌ.

صَرَارِىٌّ *A sailor:* (Ṣ, M, Ḳ:) like صَارٍ: (Ṣ:) pl. صَرَارِيُّونَ: (Ṣ, M, Ḳ:) it has no broken pl.: (M:) or صَرَارِىّ should be [without tenween, imperfectly decl., and] mentioned in art. صرى; for it is pl. of صُرَّاءٌ, which is pl. of صَارٍ, which J has mentioned in art. صرى: AḤát used to say that صُرَّاءٌ is a sing., like حُسَّانٌ; but without sufficient authority: and J has regarded صَرَارِىّ as a sing. in consequence of his finding it to have the same construction as a sing. in verses of Arabs;

whence he imagined the ى in it to be the relative ى, as is shown by his mentioning the word in this place. (IB.)

صَرُورِىٌّ : see صَرُورَةٌ.

صُرًّى : see صِرًّى : — and see also art. صرى.

صُرِّىَ : see the next paragraph.

هِىَ مِنِّى صِرِّى, said of an oath, (Ṣ,) or هُوَ مِنِّى صِرِّى, (M, Ḳ,) and ▼ أَصِرِّى, and ▼ صِرِّى, and ▼ أَصِرِّى, (Yaạḳoob, Ṣ, M, Ḳ,) and ▼ صُرِّى and ▼ صُرَّى, (Ḳ, TA,) or ▼ صُرًّى and ▼ صِرًّى, (as in a copy of the M,) *It is a determination,* or *resolution, from me;* (Ṣ, M, Ḳ;) *a serious assertion; not a jest.* (Ṣ, Ḳ.) Aboo-Semmál El-Asadee, his she-camel having strayed, said, "I swear to Thee, [O God,] that, if Thou restore her not to me, I will not serve Thee:" (Ṣ:) or, "O God, if Thou restore her not to me, I will not say a prayer to Thee:" (TA:) and he found her, her nose-rein having caught to a thorn-tree (عَوْسَجَة); and he took her, and said, عَلِمَ رَبِّى أَنَّهَا مِنِّى صِرِّى *My Lord knew that it was a determination,* or *resolution,* or *serious assertion, from me:* (Ṣ:) or *a confirmed determination:* (ISk:) it is derived from أَصْرَرْتُ عَلَى الشَّىْءِ "I persevered, or persisted, in the thing:" (Ṣ:) [or "I determined, or resolved, upon the thing:"] AHeyth says, ▼ صِرِّى, i. e., *Determine thou,* or *resolve thou;* as though he addressed himself; from أَصَرَّ عَلَى فِعْلِهِ "he determined, or resolved, upon going on in doing it, and not turning back:" it is also said that ▼ أَصِرِّى is changed into ▼ أَصِرَّى, like as they say بِأَبَا أَنْتَ and بِأَبِى أَنْتَ : and in like manner, ▼ صِرِّى is changed into صِرَّى ; the ا in أَصِرِّى being elided: not that they are two dial. vars., صَرَرْتُ عَلَى الشَّىْءِ and أَصْرَرْتُ : and Fr. says that صِرِّى and ▼ أَصِرِّى are originally imperatives; and that, when they desired to change them [i. e. the imperatives] into nouns, they changed the ى into ا [written ى after fet-ḥ]: and in like manner, [changing verbs into nouns,] they say, نُهِىَ عَنْ قِيلٍ وَقَالٍ ; &c. (TA.) Accord. to AZ, one says, ▼ إِنَّهَا مِنِّى لَأَصِرَّى meaning *Verily, it is a truth, or reality, from me;* and Aboo-Málik says the same of ▼ أَصِرَّى. (TA.)

صِرِّى : see the next preceding paragraph, in three places.

صَرًّى and ▼ صِرًّى A dirhem, (Ṣ, M, A, Ḳ,) and a deenár, (A,) *that sounds,* (Ṣ, M, Ḳ,) or *rings,* (A,) *when struck:* (Ṣ, M, A, Ḳ; in some copies of the last of which, in the place of إِذَا نُقِرَ, is put اذا نُقِدَ : TA:) accord. to some, used only in negative phrases: (IAạr, M:) thus used in the phrase, مَا لِفُلَانٍ صَرًّى, [expl. as] meaning *Such a one has not a dirhem nor a deenár:* (IAạr, A:*) and so used, as meaning *a dirhem,* by Khálid Ibn-Jembeh; who does not assign to it a dual nor a pl. (TA.)

صِرًّى : see صَرًّى.

صُرًّى : see صَرًّى : — and see also صِرِّى.

الصَّرَّارُ, (Mṣb,) or صَرَّارُ اللَّيْلِ, (Ṣ, Ḳ,) or both, (Mgh in art. خطب,) and ▼ الصُّرْصُرُ, (M and L in art. جد,) *The* جُدْجُد ; [*a cricket,* which is called the صرّار in the present day]; (Ṣ, M, Mgh, L;) *a certain thing that creaks* (يَصِرُّ); (Mṣb;) *a small flying thing;* (Ḳ;) it is *larger than the* جُنْدَب, and is *called by some of the Arabs* الصَّدَى : (Ṣ, Mgh:) A'Obeyd says that this last term signifies a certain flying thing that creaks (يَصِرُّ) by night, and hops, and flies, thought by the [common] people to be the جُنْدَب, and found in the deserts. (Mṣb.)

صُرَّانٌ *Such as grow in hard ground* (جَلَد [in the CḲ, erroneously, جِلْد]) *of the trees termed* شَجَرُ العِلْكِ, (Ḳ, TA,) *and of other trees.* (TA.)

صُرْصُرٌ : see صِرٌّ, in three places. — and see الصَّرَّارُ. — Also *A certain insect* (دُوَيْبَّة), (M, Ḳ, TA,) *beneath the ground, that creaks* (تَصِرُّ) *in the days of the* [*season called*] رَبِيع ; (TA;) and so ▼ صُرْصُورٌ and ▼ صُرْصُرٌ. (M, Ḳ, TA.) [Accord. to Forskål, (Descr. Animal., p. xxii.,) صرصر, pronounced "sursur," is applied to an insect which he terms *Blatta Aegyptiaca.*] — And *The cock:* (Ḳ, TA: [written by Golius and Freytag صِرْصِرٌ :]) so called because of his cry. (TA.) — See also صُرْصُورٌ.

صُرْصُرٌ : see صَرْصَرٌ : — and see also صُرْصُورٌ.

صَرْصَرَانٌ : see the next paragraph, in two places.

صَرْصَرَانِىٌّ sing. of صَرْصَرَانِيَّاتٌ, (Ṣ, Mṣb,) which signifies Camels *between the* بَخَاتِىّ [or *Bactrian* (in the CḲ, erroneously, نَجاتِى)] *and the Arabian:* (Ṣ, M, Mṣb, Ḳ:) or *such as are called* فَوَالِج : (Ṣ, M, Ḳ:) and ▼ صَرْصَرَانٌ [if not a mistranscription] signifies the same. (TA.) [See also صُرْصُورٌ.] — And صَرْصَرَانِىٌّ (Ṣ, M, Ḳ) and ▼ صَرْصَرَانٌ (M, Ḳ) *A species of fish,* (Ṣ,) *a certain smooth fish,* (M, Ḳ,) *of the sea.* (Ṣ, M.)

صُرْصُورٌ *Large* camels; (Ṣ, M, Ḳ;) as also ▼ صُرْصُرٌ and ▼ صَرْصَرٌ. (TA.) — And A camel *of the species called* بُخْتِىّ [i. e. *Bactrian*]: (M, Ḳ:) [see also صَرْصَرَانِىٌّ :] or *its offspring;* as also سُرْسُورٌ : (M:) or *an excellent stallion-camel.* (IAạr.) — See also صُرْصُرٌ. — Also *A ship,* or *boat:* [or *a long,* or *great, ship* or *boat:*] and so قُرْقُورٌ. (TA.)

الصَّرَاصِرَةُ *The Nabathæans of Syria.* (Ṣ, Ḳ.)

رَجُلٌ صَارٌّ بَيْنَ عَيْنَيْهِ *A man contracted in the part between the eyes, like him who is grieving,* or *mourning.* (TA.) — And صَارٌّ signifies Trees (شَجَر) *tangled,* or *luxuriant,* or *abundant and dense, not without shade* (Ḳ, TA) *in their lower parts, by reason of their perplexedness.* (TA.)

صَارَّةٌ *A want; a thing wanted; an object of want;* or *a needful,* or *requisite, thing:* (Ṣ, M, Ḳ:) pl. صَوَارُّ. (TA.) One says, لِى قِبَلَ فُلَانٍ صَارَّةٌ [*I have a want to be supplied to me on the part of such a one*]. (A'Obeyd, Ṣ.) — Also *Thirst:* (Ṣ, Ḳ:) pl. صَرَائِرُ, (Ḳ,) which is extr., (TA,) and صَوَارُّ : (Ḳ:) or the latter is pl. of صارّة in the sense first expl. above; as A'Obeyd says; and this is meant in the Ḳ: (TA:) AA says that its pl. in the latter sense is صَرَائِرُ ; and he cites the following words of Dhu-r-Rummeh:

• فَانْصَاعَتِ الحُقْبُ لَمْ تَقْصَعْ صَرَائِرَهَا •

[*And the wild asses turned back, retreating quickly, not having quenched their thirst*]: but fault has been found with AA for this; and it is said that صَرَائِرُ is pl. of ▼ صَرِيرَةٌ, [which is not expl.,] and that the pl. of صارّة is صَوَارُّ. (Ṣ.) One says, قَصَعَ الحِمَارُ صَارَّتَهُ, meaning *The ass* drank water until he *quenched his thirst.* (Ṣ.)

صَارُورٌ : see صَرُورَةٌ, in two places.

صَارُورَةٌ : see صَرُورَةٌ, in three places.

صَارُورَاءُ : } see صَرُورَةٌ.
صَارُورِىٌّ : }

صُوَيْرَةٌ *Narrow in disposition and in mind* or *judgment* or *opinion.* (Ṣgh, Ḳ.)

حَجَرٌ أَصَرُّ *A hard stone:* (Tekmileh, TA:) and صَخْرَةٌ صَرَّاءُ *a hard rock:* (M, Ḳ:) or *a smooth rock.* (L.)

أَصِرِّى : see صِرِّى, in four places.

أَصِرَّى : see صِرِّى, in three places.

مَصَرٌّ or مِصَرٌّ : see صُرَّةٌ.

مَصَرَّتَا البَوْلِ وَالغَائِطِ [*The two sphincters that serve as repressers of the urine and dung*]. (Ḳ in art. اسر.)

مُصِرَّةٌ A she-camel *that does not yield her milk copiously.* (M, Ḳ.)

مُصَرَّاةٌ *That has been left unmilked for some days, in order that the milk may collect in her udder, or until it has collected in her udder;* (M, Ḳ;) as also ▼ مُصَرَّةٌ ; applied to a ewe, or she-goat: or the former is from صَرَّى, aor. يُصَرِّى, (Ḳ,) inf. n. تَصْرِيَةٌ, and therefore should be mentioned in art. صرى [q. v.]. (TA.)

مُصَرَّرَةٌ : see the next paragraph.

مَصْرُورٌ *Bound, as a captive.* (Mgh.) — And مَصْرُورَةٌ and ▼ مُصَرَّرَةٌ A she-camel *having her udder bound with the* صِرَار. (IAth, TA.) — And مَصْرُورٌ applied to a solid hoof, *Contracted:* or *narrow:* (M, Ḳ:) or *narrow and contracted:* (Ṣ:) and ▼ مُصْطَرٌّ signifies the same; (M, Ḳ;) or *narrow in an unseemly manner, or immoderately.* (TA.) — Also ‡ A man *having an iron collar put upon his neck, or round his neck and hands together.* (A.)

مَصَارٌ [app. an irregular pl. of مَصِيرٌ, and therefore without tenween,] The أَمْعَآء [or *guts, bowels,* or *intestines, into which the food passes from the stomach*]. (M, Ḳ.) One says, شَرِبَ حَتَّى مَلَأَ مَصَارَهُ, meaning [*He drank until he filled*] *his* أَمْعَآء: mentioned by AḤn on the authority of IAạr, with no more explanation than this. (M.)

مُصْطَرٌ: see مَصْرُورٌ. — One says also اِمْرَأَةٌ مُصْطَرَةُ الحَقْوَيْنِ [meaning ‡ *A woman narrow in the flanks*]. (A.) — See also مُصْطَرٌ, in art. صرد.

صرب

1. صَرَبَ *He made the sour milk termed* صَرْب: (Ḳ,* TA:) [or] صَرَبَ اللَّبَنَ, (M, TA,) aor. ـِ, (M,) or ـُ, (TA,) inf. n. صَرْبٌ, *he made the milk to become what is termed* صَرْب: and *he milked some of the milk upon other milk, and left it to become sour:* (M, TA:) or صَرَبَ اللَّبَنَ فِى الوَطْبِ *he collected the milk in the skin, portion after portion, and left it to become sour;* as also ▼ اِصْطَرَبَهُ: (Ṣ:) or you say, صَرَبَ اللَّبَنَ فِى السِّقَآءِ and السَّمْنَ فِى النِّحْىِ [*he collected, portion after portion, and left, the milk in the* skin called سِقَآء, and *the clarified butter in the* skin called نِحْى]. (M, TA.) — [Hence,] صَرَبْتُ اللَّبَنَ فِى الضَّرْعِ † *I caused the milk to collect in the udder, not drawing it forth.* (Ḳt, TA.) — And صَرَبَ † *He kept in,* or *retained, and collected,* [*his*] *urine:* (Ḳ, TA:) or *withheld it long:* and accord. to some, particularly said of a stallion-camel: (TA:) [or] صَرَبَ بَوْلَهُ, (Ṣ, M,) aor. ـُ and ـِ, inf. n. صَرْبٌ, (M,) † *he kept in,* or *retained, and collected, his urine:* (Ṣ, M:) accord. to some, particularly said of a stallion-camel. (M.) — And صَرَبَ الصَّبِىُّ [ذَا بَطْنِهِ being app. understood] † *The boy remained some days without discharging his excrement,* or *ordure:* (M, TA:) and صَرَبَ بَطْنُ الصَّبِىِّ, inf. n. صَرْبٌ, † *the boy's belly became constipated* (عَقَدَ), *that he might become fat:* (M:) [or] صَرَبَ الصَّبِىُّ لِيَسْمَنَ † *the boy's excrement,* or *ordure,* (ذُو بَطْنِهِ,) *became confined, so that he remained a day without discharging it, when he was about to become fat.* (S.) [In the copies of the Ḳ, صَرَبَ is expl. as signifying عَقَدَ بَطْنَ الصَّبِىِّ لِيَسْمَنَ, to which, written without the syll. signs, the TA assigns the last of the meanings above; therefore, I doubt not, the right reading is بَطْنُ, agreeably with the explanation of صَرَبَ بَطْنُ الصَّبِىِّ in the M, given above: otherwise, the meaning must be † *He,* or *it, caused the boy's belly to become bound,* or *constipated, that he might become fat.*] — صَرِبَ, aor. ـَ, (Ḳ, TA,) inf. n. صَرَبٌ, (TḲ,) said of milk, (TA,) *It became collected* (Ḳ, TA) *in the udder.* (TA.) — صَرِبَتِ الأَرْضُ *The land produced herbs,* or *trees, such as are termed* صَرَب [a coll. gen. n. of which the n. un. is صَرَبَةٌ, q. v.]. (M, Ḳ.* [The meaning is indicated in both by the context.]) — صَرَبَ also signifies *He cut,* or *cut off;* (Ḳ, TA;) i. q. صَرَمَ; like as one says ضَرْبَةُ لَازِبٍ and لَازِمٍ. (TA.) — And i. q. كَسَبَ [*He gained, acquired,* or *earned;* &c.]. (Ḳ.)

2. تَصْرِيبٌ The *drinking of sour milk,* (O, Ḳ, TA,) *such as is called* صَرْب. (TA.) — And The *eating of gum,* (O, Ḳ, TA,) i. e., *what is called* صَرْب. (TA.)

4. اصرب *He* (a man, TA) *gave.* (O, Ḳ.) One says, اصرب إِلَيْهِ مَالًا *He* (a man) *gave to him property.* (TḲ.)

8: see 1, first sentence. — اصطرب صَرْبَةً *He provided,* or *took, for himself some milk, either fresh* or *sour, in a skin, for a journey.* (M, TA.)

11. اِصْرَابَّ [said by MF to be written by ISd ▼ اِصْرَأَبَّ] *It was,* or *became, smooth,* (M, O, Ḳ, TA,) *and clear;* (TA;) said of a thing, (M, Ḳ, TA,) or of milk. (O.)

Q. Q. 4. اِصْرَأَبَّ: see what next precedes.

صَرْبٌ and ▼ صَرَبٌ (Ṣ, M, &c.) *Sour milk* (M, Mgh, Ḳ) *that has been collected in a skin:* (M, Ḳ:) or *very sour milk:* (Ṣ, Mṣb:) or *milk that has been collected in a skin for some days so that it has become very sour:* (Aṣ, M:) n. un. ▼ صَرْبَةٌ and ▼ صَرَبَةٌ: (M, TA:) صِرَابٌ, occurring in some of the Expositions of the Jámi' eṣ-Ṣagheer, is a mistranscription; or it may be a pl. of صَرْبٌ accord. to the analogy of حَبْلٌ and حِبَالٌ, and رَمْلٌ and رِمَالٌ. (Mgh.) One says, جَآءَنَا بِصَرْبَةٍ تَزْوِى الوَجْهَ [*He brought us some sour milk,* or *very sour milk, that had been collected in a skin, making the face to contract in wrinkles*]. (Ṣ.) [SM here adds,] Az says that الصَّرْمُ is like الصَّرْبُ, and is better known. (TA. [But this evidently relates to the signification of "the act of cutting," or "cutting off;" not to الصَّرْبُ as applied to milk.]) — Also, (Ḳ,) or the former word, (M,) *Milk that is provided in a skin for a journey,* (M, Ḳ,) *whether fresh or sour.* (M.) — And both words, (M, Ḳ, TA,) or ▼ صَرْبٌ [only], (Ṣ, Mṣb,) *Gum:* (Mṣb:) or *red gum:* (T, Ṣ, M, L, TA: in the Ḳ, الصَّمْغ is erroneously put for الصَّمْغ الأَحْمَر: TA:) some say (M) it is the *gum of the* طَلْح (Ṣ, M) and *of the* عُرْفُط, peculiarly; *the pieces of which are red, as though they were ingots* [*of gold*], *and they are broken with stones:* (M:) the n. un. is ▼ صَرْبَةٌ: (Ṣ, M: [صَرْبَةٌ as a n. un. in this sense I do not find mentioned:]) and sometimes it [i. e. صَرْبٌ or صَرَبٌ] has صِرَابٌ for pl.: (M:) sometimes, (Ṣ,) what is called ▼ صَرَبَةٌ is *a thing like the head of the cat* [*in size*], *within which is a thing* [or *substance*] *like* دِبْس [or *honey of dates*], (Ṣ, Ḳ,) *and like glue,* (Ṣ,) *which is sucked and eaten.* (Ṣ, Ḳ.)

صِرْبٌ *A few tents* (بُيُوت) [in the O, erroneously, (بُيُوت)] *of the weak sort of the Arabs of the desert:* (IAạr, O,* Ḳ, TA:) and so صِرْمٌ. (O.)

صَرَبٌ: see صَرْبٌ, in two places. — Also *Red honey.* (TA in art. ضرب.) — See also صَرَبَةٌ.

صَرْبَةٌ: see صَرْبٌ, in two places. — Hence, ‡ The *water* [by which is meant the *seminal fluid*] *that collects in the back* [*of a man*]; as being likened to the [sour] milk that is collected in a skin. (M, TA.)

صَرَبَةٌ: see صَرْبٌ, in three places. — Also *A herb,* (M, Ḳ,) and *tree,* (M,) *that becomes green, and puts forth leaves, when dry,* or *that has grown,* or *become somewhat restored to a good state, after having been eaten* [or *depastured*], (يَتَجَبَّرُ, so in the M, [in the Ḳ يَتَغَيَّرُ, which, as is remarked in the TḲ, is a mistake,]) *after men* [*have fed their cattle therefrom*]: pl. [or rather coll. gen. n.] ▼ صَرَبٌ. (M.)

صَرِيبِىٌّ, (Ṣ, Ḳ,) accord. to Sa'eed Ibn-El-Museiyib, (TA,) The [*she-camel called*] بَحِيرَة, (Ṣ, Ḳ,) *whose milk was forbidden* [by *the pagan Arabs*] *for the sake of the idols* (الطَّوَاغِيت), *no man milking her* [*for himself*]: (TA:) thus called, (Ṣ, Ḳ, TA,) it is said, (TA,) because they used not to milk her save for the guest, so that her milk became collected [and retained] (Ṣ, Ḳ, TA) in her udder: (Ṣ, TA:) Ḳt says, it is from صَرَبْتُ اللَّبَنَ فِى الضَّرْعِ [expl. above]; or, as some say, from [الصَّرْبُ as signifying] "the act of cutting," or "cutting off;" and this seems to be the more correct of the two explanations: accord. to IAạr, it signifies *a she-camel having the ear slit,* like the بَحِيرَة, or *cut off:* and its pl., he says, is صُرُبٌ. (TA.)

صِرَابٌ *Seed-produce,* or *corn, which has been sown after that which has been carried off to the place where it is trodden in the autumn.* (O, Ḳ.)

صَرِيبٌ Milk *that has been made what is termed* صَرْب; as also ▼ مَصْرُوبٌ: (M, TA:) or *sour* milk: (A, Ḳ, TA:) pl. صُرُبٌ. (Ḳ.) So in the saying الصَّرِيبَ لَا الصَّرِيبَ, i. e. [Give me] *the thick* [milk], *from a number of milch camels, that has been mixed together; not the sour.* (A, TA.)

صَرَابَةٌ *Clearness,* and *smoothness:* thus in the phrase صَرَابَةُ حَنْظَلٍ in a verse of Imra-el-Ḳeys; as some relate it: (M, TA:) as others relate it, صَرَايَةٌ, (M,) or صَلَايَةٌ. (TA.)

مِصْرَبٌ *A vessel in which milk is collected, portion after portion, and left to become sour:* (Ṣ, Ḳ:*) and so مِكْرَصٌ and مِقْرَعٌ: pl. مَصَارِبُ. (TA.)

مَصْرُوبٌ: see صَرِيبٌ.

مُصَرَّبَةٌ † A she-camel *that is kept from being milked, in order that she may become fat.* (L in art. صفح, from the T.)

صرج

2. صَرَّجَ, inf. n. تَصْرِيجٌ, *He plastered with*

صَارُوج a watering-trough or tank (Ḳ,* TA) &c.: and sometimes they said شُرُق. (TA.)

صَارُوجٌ *Quick lime* (نُورَة), and the *mixtures thereof;* (T, Ṣ, M, Mgh, Mṣb, Ḳ;) *with which are plastered watering-troughs,* or *tanks, and baths, &c.:* (M, TA:) a Pers. word, (Ṣ, TA,) originally چَارُو, (TA,) arabicized, (Ṣ, M, Mṣb, Ḳ,) as is every word in which occur both ص and ج, (Ṣ, Mṣb,) or صَمْجَ is an exception to this rule: (TA in art. صوبج:) sometimes it is called شَارُوق. (TA.)

صرح

1. صَرُحَ, (Ṣ, O, Mṣb, Ḳ,) aor. ـُ, (Ḳ,) inf. n. صَرَاحَةٌ and صُرُوحَةٌ, (Ṣ, O, Mṣb,) [both strangely said in the Ḳ to be substs.,] *It was,* or *became, pure, sheer, free from admixture, unmingled, unmixed, genuine,* or *clear;* (Ṣ, O, Mṣb, Ḳ;) said of a thing (Ṣ, O, Mṣb) of any kind of which the meaning is predicable, (Ṣ, O,) [and particularly] said of one's race, or genealogy. (Ḳ.) —— صَرَحَ: see 2, in two places.

2. صَرَّحَتْ *She* (a camel) *yielded pure,* or *clear, milk.* (TA in art. حلب.) — [Hence, probably,] تَصْرِيحٌ signifies The *speaking clearly, plainly, explicitly, directly,* or *without ambiguity* or *equivocation; contr. of* تَعْرِيضٌ. (Ṣ, A, Ḳ.) You say, صَرَّحَ بِمَا فِى نَفْسِهِ, (Ṣ, A, L, Mṣb, Ḳ,) and بِمَا عِنْدَهُ, (A,) *He made apparent, manifest,* or *plain,* or *he manifested, exposed,* or *revealed,* (Ṣ, A, L, Ḳ,) *what was in his mind,* (Ṣ, L, Ḳ,) and *what he had;* (A;) as also ▼ صارح بِهِ; (L, Ḳ;) and ▼ صَرَحَ بِهِ: (TA:) or *he declared,* or *made clear, what was in his mind, so as to express the intended meaning according to the first* [or *most obvious*] *interpretation;* or *he made it free from expressions susceptible of tropical meanings and a secondary* [or *remote*] *interpretation.* (Mṣb.) And صَرَّحَ الشَّىْءَ, (TA,) inf. n. تَصْرِيحٌ; (Ḳ, TA;) and ▼ صَرَحَهُ, (TA,) inf. n. صَرْحٌ; (Ḳ, TA;) and ▼ اصرحهُ, (TA,) inf. n. إِصْرَاحٌ; (Ḳ, TA;) *He made the thing apparent, manifest, clear,* or *plain.* (Ḳ, TA.) —— This verb is also intrans. (Ḳ.) One says, صَرَّحَتِ الخَمْرُ, (Ṣ, A, Mṣb,) inf. n. تَصْرِيحٌ, (Ṣ, Ḳ,) *The wine became free from froth;* (Ṣ, A, Mṣb, Ḳ;) [*it became clear*] after fermenting and frothing. (Ṣ.) And صَرَّحَ النَّهَارُ *The day became free from clouds, and sunny:* (A:) or صَرَّحَ اليَوْمُ *the day became free from mists and clouds.* (Mṣb.) And صَرَّحَتْ كَحَلُ *The year of drought,* or *sterility, became one of unmixed severity;* (Ṣ, Meyd, L, Ḳ;) and in like manner, صَرَّحَتِ السَّنَةُ: (L:) or the former means *the sky became clear of clouds.* (Ṣ in art. كحل, and Meyd.) And صَرَّحَ, (Ṣ, Mṣb, TA,) inf. n. as above, (Ḳ, TA,) said of an affair, (Ḳ, TA,) or, as in a copy of the Ḳ, [and in the Ṣ and Mṣb,] said of the truth, (TA,) *It became apparent, manifest, exposed,* or *revealed;* (Ṣ, Mṣb, Ḳ, TA;) and so ▼ انصرح, (Ṣ, Ḳ, TA,) said of the truth. (Ṣ, TA.) Hence the prov. عِنْدَ التَّصْرِيحِ تُرِيحُ, meaning *On the appearing of the truth thou findest rest;* (Meyd, TA;) no doubt remaining in thy mind. (Meyd.) And صَرَّحَ الحَقُّ عَنْ مَحْضِهِ, (Ṣ, Meyd, A, Mṣb,) another prov., meaning ‡ *The truth,* or *affair, became revealed,* or *manifest,* (Ṣ, Meyd, Mṣb,) *after its being concealed:* (Meyd, Mṣb:) or, as AA says, *falsity became detected,* or *exposed, and the truth became apparent and known.* (Meyd. [See also زُبْدٌ.]) And صَرَّحَتْ بِجِلْذَانَ, another prov., (Meyd, L,) meaning *It* (the affair, or case,) *became apparent,* or *manifest,* to thee, *in Jildhán;* which last word is variously written, [see Freytag's Arab. Prov. i. 730, and Ḥar p. 106,] a place in Eṭ-Ṭáïf, soft and even, like the palm of the hand, containing no covert in which one may conceal himself; the ت in صرّحت denoting the قِصَّة or خُطَّة: (Meyd:) i. e. the man made apparent, or revealed, the utmost of what he desired, or meant. (L.) — See also a trad. cited in art. صوح, conj. 2. — صَرَّحَ said of an archer or the like means [*He made his arrow,* or *missile, to go clear of the butt* or *mark;* or] *he shot,* or *cast, and missed* (Ḳ, TA) *the butt* [or *mark*]. (TA.)

3. صارح بِهِ: see 2. —— [صارحهُ, inf. n. مُصَارَحَةٌ and صِرَاحٌ, *He confronted him,* or *faced him.*] One says, شَتَمَهُ مُصَارَحَةً, and صِرَاحًا, (Ṣ, Ḳ,) and ▼ صُرَاحًا, (Ḳ,) which last is a subst. [used as an inf. n., i. e. a quasi-inf. n.], (Ṣ, Ḳ,) *He reviled him confronting him,* or *face to face,* or *to his face.* (Ṣ, Ḳ.) And لَقِيتُهُ مُصَارَحَةً, (A, TA,) and صِرَاحًا, and ▼ صُرَاحًا, (TA,) *I met him face to face.* (A, TA.)

4: see 2.

5. تصرّح الزَّبَدُ عَنِ الخَمْرِ *The froth became cleared away from the wine.* (TA.)

7: see 2.

صَرْحٌ *A* قَصْر [i. e. *palace,* or *pavilion,* &c.]: (Zj, Ṣ, A, Ḳ:) and (as some say, TA) *any lofty building:* (Ṣ, A, Ḳ, TA:) or *a single house* or *chamber, built apart,* or *detached, large, and lofty:* (Mṣb, TA:) pl. صُرُوحٌ. (Ṣ, A.)

صَرَحٌ: see صَرِيحٌ.

صَرْحَةٌ The *court,* or *open area,* of a house; i. e. *a spacious vacant part* or *portion thereof, in which is no building;* its عَرْصَة, (Ṣ, TA,) or its بَاحَة [which means the same]: (A, Mṣb, TA:) pl. صَرَحَاتٌ. (Mṣb.) — And *A tract* of ground *that is hard and elevated* (Ṣ, L) *and even:* or *a tract that is even, and open to view,* of ground, and of a place where camels or other animals are confined, or where dates are dried, and of a house or dwelling: or *a tract that is even, and of goodly appearance, though not open to view:* Aboo-Aslam asserts it to mean *a* [*desert tract such as is called*] صَحْرَاء. (L.) — [Hence, app.,] one says, خَرَجَ لَهُمْ صَرْحَةً بَرْحَةً, (so accord. to the TA as from the Ḳ,) or صَرْحَةً بَرْحَةً, (O, and so in my MS. copy of the Ḳ,) or صَرْحَةَ بَرْحَةَ, (so in the CḲ,) *He went forth openly,* or *into the field* [*of battle*], *to them:* (O, Ḳ:) and إِنَّ خُرُوجَ صَرْحَةَ بَرْحَةَ لَكَثِيرٌ, (so accord. to the TA as from the Ḳ,) or صَرْحَةً بَرْحَةً, (O, and so in the CḲ,) or صَرْحَةَ بَرْحَةٌ, (so in my MS. copy of the Ḳ,) [accord. to SM,] with fet-ḥ in the end of each [app. in the former phrase], and with tenween in each [app. in the latter phrase], (TA,) [i. e. *Verily the going forth openly,* or *into the field of battle, is frequent.* See also صَحْرَة, and بَحْرَة.]

صُرْحَانٌ: } see صَرِيحٌ.
صُرَاحٌ: }

صُرَاحٌ: see صَرِيحٌ, in six places. — Also *Thin milk, containing much water, so that in some parts of it one sees a tawniness and* خُضْرَة [here app. meaning *a blackish hue*]. (L.) —— See also 3, in two places.

صِرَاحٌ: see the next paragraph, in two places.

صَرِيحٌ Anything *pure, sheer, free from admixture, unmingled, unmixed, genuine,* or *clear;* (Ṣ, A, Mṣb, Ḳ, TA;) as also ▼ صَرَحٌ, (Ṣ, Ḳ,) which is by some restricted by the [additional] epithet *white,* (TA,) and ▼ صُرَاحٌ, (L, Ḳ,) and ▼ صِرَاحٌ, which is [said to be] more chaste [though much less usual] than صُرَاحٌ, (L,) and ▼ صَرَاحٌ, (Ḳ,) and ▼ صُمَارِحٌ, (Ṣ, Ḳ,) in which last the م is augmentative, or, as is related on the authority of AA, it is صُمَادِحٌ, with د, but [J says] I do not think this to have been retained in the memory [as transmitted from the Arabs of classical times]. (Ṣ.) You say لَبَنٌ صَرِيحٌ *Milk of which the froth has gone,* (Ṣ, A, L,) or *free from froth,* (T, L,) *and clear:* (T, A, L:) or *just drawn.* (TA in art. زهر.) And بَوْلٌ صَرِيحٌ *Urine free from froth.* (T, L.) And ▼ خَمْرٌ صُرَاحٌ, (L,) and ▼ صُرَاحِيَةٌ, (L, Ḳ,) without teshdeed, (Ḳ,) *Pure wine,* (L, Ḳ,) *without admixture.* (TA.) And ▼ كَأْسٌ صُرَاحٌ *A cup of wine without admixture.* (Ṣ, A, Mṣb, Ḳ.) And جَآءَ بَنُو تَمِيمٍ صَرِيحَةً *The sons of Temeem came unmixed with any others.* (Ṣ.) And رَجُلٌ صَرِيحٌ, (T, Ṣ, L, Ḳ,*) and عَرَبِىٌّ صَرِيحٌ, (A, Mṣb,) *A man,* (T, Ṣ, L,) and *an Arab,* (A, Mṣb,) *of pure,* or *unmixed, race* or *genealogy;* pl. صُرَحَآءُ: (T, Ṣ, A, L, Mṣb, Ḳ:) and فَرَسٌ صَرِيحٌ *a horse of pure race;* (T, TA;) pl. صَرَائِحُ, (T, Ḳ, TA,) in this case as distinguished from the former. (T, TA.) And نَسَبٌ صَرِيحٌ *Pure,* or *unmixed, race* or *genealogy.* (A.) And كَلِمَةٌ ▼ صُرَاحٌ and ▼ صُرَاحِيَةٌ [*A word, an expression,* or *a sentence,*] *that is pure, genuine,* or *clear.* (Ḳ.) And ▼ كَذِبٌ صُرَاحٌ and ▼ صِرَاحٌ, the latter with kesr, and ▼ صُرَاحِيَةٌ and ▼ صُرَاحِىٌّ (TA) and ▼ صُرْحَانٌ with ḍamm, (Lḥ, TA,) † *A pure, sheer,* or *unmixed, lie,* (Lḥ, TA,) *manifest, and known* to men. (TA.) And قَوْلٌ صَرِيحٌ † *A saying* [*that is explicit, plain, or clear,*] *not requiring anything to be conceived in the mind, nor any interpretation.* (Mṣb.) And ▼ شَرٌّ صُرَاحٌ ‡ [*Pure unmixed, evil, or mischief*]. (A, TA.) And صَرِيحُ النُّصْحِ † *Pure,* or *sincere, in admonition,* or *counsel.* (L, TA.)

صَرَاحَةٌ : } inf. ns. of صَرُحَ [q. v.]. (Ṣ, O,
صُرُوحَةٌ : } Mṣb.)

صُرَاحِيَةٌ : see صَرِيحٌ, in three places. — [Hence the saying,] أَتَاهُ بِالأَمْرِ صُرَاحِيَةً [app. *He stated to him the affair,* or *case,*] *clearly,* or *without admixture.* (L, TA.)

صَرِيحٌ : see صُرَاحِيٌّ.

صَرِيحِيٌّ an epithet applied to a horse, in relation to a certain stallion named صَرِيحٌ, (Ṣ, TA,) or الصَّرِيحُ, (TA,) that begat a generous breed. (Ṣ, TA.)

صُرَاحِيَّةٌ *A vessel for wine:* (Ḳ:) [in Pers. صُرَاحِى :] but IDrd doubts its correctness. (TA.)

صُرَّاحٌ *A certain flying thing, resembling the* [*species of locust called*] جُنْدَب, *which is eaten.* (Ḳ.)

صَارِحٌ : see صَرِيحٌ.

يَوْمٌ مُصَرَّحٌ, (Ṣ, Ḳ,) like مُحَدَّثٌ [in measure], (Ḳ,) [in one of my two copies of the Ṣ مُصَرَّحٌ also, and in the other copy the latter only,] *A day free from clouds:* (Ṣ, Ḳ:) occurring in the poetry of Eṭ-Ṭirimmáḥ. (Ṣ.)

مِصْرَاحٌ A she-camel *that does not yield frothy milk;* (T, Ḳ; [in the CḲ, لا تَرْغَى is put for لا تُرْغِى ;]) *that yields pure milk, with little froth.* (M, TA.)

صرخ

1. صَرْخَةٌ, (L, Ḳ,) an inf. n. of صَرَخَ, (Ṣ,) signifies The *calling* or *calling out,* or *crying* or *crying out, vehemently;* [or *screaming;*] (L, Ḳ;) *on an occasion of fright,* or *alarm,* or *of some affliction,* or *evil accident:* (L:) one says, صَرَخَ, inf. n. صَرْخَةٌ ; and ▼ اصطرخ ; [*He called* or *called out,* &c.;] both meaning the same. (Ṣ.) And صُرَاخٌ is also an inf. n. of صَرَخَ, (A, Mgh, Mṣb,) and signifies The *raising the voice, calling* or *calling out, crying* or *crying out:* (Ṣ, A, L, Ḳ:) or *doing so vehemently:* (L, Ḳ:) and the *calling,* or *crying, for aid,* or *succour;* (A;) which last meaning is said to be tropical, but conventionally regarded as proper; (MF;) as also صَرِيخٌ, (Ṣ, TA,) which is likewise an inf. n. of صَرَخَ: (A, Mgh:) one says, صَرَخَ, aor. ـُ (A, MA, Mgh, L, Mṣb) and ـِ, (MA,) inf. n. صُرَاخٌ (A, MA, Mgh, L, Mṣb) and صَرِيخٌ, (A, Mgh,) *He raised his voice, called* or *called out, cried* or *cried out:* (A, MA, L, Mṣb:) or *did so vehemently:* (Mgh, L, Mṣb:*) and *he called,* or *cried, for aid,* or *succour,* (A, Mgh, L, Mṣb,) *saying,* وَا غَوْثَاهُ [*Alas, a crying for aid!*] and وَا صَرْخَتَاهُ [*Alas, a crying of alarm!*]; (L;) and ▼ استصرخ signifies the same: (AHát, L:) and ▼ اصطرخوا is syn. with صَرَخُوا ; (Ṣ, TA;) meaning ▼ تصارخوا ; as also ▼ استصرخوا ; (TA;) or [rather] meaning *They called* or *called out,* &c., (صَرَخُوا,) *one to another.* (TḲ.) كَانَتْ كَصَرْخَةِ الحُبْلَى [*It was like the vehement crying-out,* or *the screaming, of the pregnant woman*] is a prov., said of a thing that comes upon one suddenly, when he is not aware. (T.)

4. اصرخ *He aided,* or *succoured,* another; in answer to a call, or cry; (Ṣ, A, Mgh, Mṣb;) as also ▼ استصرخ : (AHát, L:) the أ in the former verb is said to have a privative effect, so that أَصْرَخْتُهُ signifies *I made his crying,* or *vehement crying,* &c., *to cease:* (TA:) and ▼ صَارِخَةٌ has the signification of the inf. n. of this verb, as an inf. n. [or rather quasi-inf. n.] of the measure فَاعِلَةٌ ; (Ḳ;) and ▼ صَرِيخٌ also may have this signification in the Ḳur xxxvi. 43, as is said in the Ksh [and by Bḍ]. (TA.)

5. تصرّخ *He made an effort to call* or *call out, to cry* or *cry out,* or *to do so vehemently;* [or, *to scream;*] (Ṣ, A, Ḳ;) or *he made an effort in calling* or *calling out,* &c., (PṢ,) *in calling* or *calling out,* &c., *vehemently,* and *in crying for aid* or *succour.* (KL.) One says, التَّصَرُّخُ بِهِ حُمْقٌ, (Ṣ,) meaning التَّصَرُّخُ بِالعُطَاسِ [i. e. *The making an effort to call* or *call out,* &c., or *in calling* or *calling out,* &c., *in sneezing, is stupidity*]. (Ṣ, TA.)

6. تصارخوا *They called* or *called out, cried* or *cried out,* or *did so vehemently, one to another;* (A;) [and so, accord. to a copy of the A, ▼ استصرخوا ; and app. ▼ اصطرخوا, as seems to be indicated in the L and Ḳ;] see 1.

8: see 1, in two places: and see also 6.

10. استصرخهُ *He called,* or *cried, to him for aid,* or *succour.* (Ṣ, A, Mgh, L, Mṣb.) — And *He incited him, urged him,* or *induced him, to call* or *call out, to cry* or *cry out,* [app. *for aid,* or *succour,*] or *to do so vehemently.* (L, TA.) — [Hence,] اُسْتُصْرِخَ الإِنْسَانُ *There came to the man a voice,* or *cry, informing him of an event on account of which his aid was invoked,* or *announcing to him a death.* (IAth, TA.) اِسْتِصْرَاخُ الحَيِّ means *The tribe's being invoked for aid to perform what is requisite for the dead:* and hence the trad. of Ibn-'Omar, فَاسْتُصْرِخَ عَلَى امْرَأَتِهِ, not بِامْرَأَتِهِ, meaning, *And he was called to aid in furnishing for the grave, and burying, the corpse of his wife:* or it may mean, *was informed that his wife was at the point of death.* (Mgh.) — See also 1, in two places; and 6: — and see 4.

صَرْخَةٌ an inf. n. of 1 [q. v.]. (Ṣ.) — Hence, (TA,) The *call to prayer.* (Ḳ, TA.)

صُرَاخٌ an inf. n. of صَرَخَ [q. v.]. (A, &c.)

صَرِيخٌ an inf. n. of صَرَخَ [q. v.]: (A, Mgh:) see also 4. — See also صَارِخٌ, in four places.

الصَّرَّاخُ [*He who calls* or *calls out,* or *cries* or *cries out,* or *does so vehemently,* or *screams,* &c., *much,* or *often.* — And hence,] *The peacock.* (IAạr, Ḳ.)

صَارِخٌ *Calling* or *calling out,* or *crying* or *crying out,* or *doing so vehemently;* [or *screaming;*] as also ▼ صَرِيخٌ. (A, Mṣb.) And *Calling,* or *crying, for aid,* or *succour;* (Ṣ, Mṣb, Ḳ;) and so ▼ صَرِيخٌ ; (Ṣ, Ḳ;) and ▼ مُسْتَصْرِخٌ. (Ṣ.) — Also, and ▼ صَرِيخٌ, (AHeyth, Ṣ, A, Ḳ,) or the latter [only] of these, (T, Mṣb,) and ▼ مُصْرِخٌ, (Ṣ, A, Mṣb, Ḳ,) and ▼ صَارِخَةٌ, (Lth, TA,) *Aiding,* or *succouring;* or *an aider,* or *a succourer:* (Lth, T, Ṣ, A, Mṣb, Ḳ:) Az says that he had not heard صَارِخٌ in this sense on the authority of any except Aṣ; but that all men agree that it has the second of the senses given above, and that ▼ مُصْرِخٌ has the last of those senses. (TA.) عَبْدٌ صَرِيخُهُ ▼ أَمَةٌ, meaning [*A male slave*] *whose aider* [*is a female slave*], is a prov. applied in the case of a mean man who is aided by one meaner than he. (Meyd.) And it is said in the Ḳur [xiv. 27], ▼ مَا أَنَا بِمُصْرِخِكُمْ وَمَا أَنْتُمْ بِمُصْرِخِىَّ *I am not your aiders, nor are ye my aiders.* (TA.) — الصَّارِخُ is an appellation of *The cock;* (Ḳ, TA;) because he cries much in the night: and it is said by some to be tropical. (TA.) — And صَارِخٌ signifies also *A voice,* or *cry, informing a man of an event on account of which his aid is invoked,* or *announcing to him a death.* (IAth, TA.)

صَارِخَةٌ The *voice,* or *cry, of the calling for aid,* or *succour.* (Ḳ.) Hence the saying, سَمِعْتُ صَارِخَةَ القَوْمِ [*I heard the cry of the people,* or *party, calling for aid,* or *succour*]. (TA.) — See also 4. — And see صَارِخٌ.

مُصْرِخٌ : see صَارِخٌ, in three places.

مُسْتَصْرِخٌ : see صَارِخٌ.

صرد

1. صَرِدَ, aor. ـَ, inf. n. صَرَدٌ, *He,* or *it, was,* or *became, cold:* or *intensely cold.* (M, L. [See صَرْدٌ.]) One says, صَرِدْتُ اليَوْمَ صَرَدًا شَدِيدًا [*I was,* or *became, to day, very cold;* or *very intensely cold*]. (A.) And صَرِدَ يَوْمُنَا [*Our day was,* or *became, very cold;* or *very intensely cold*]. (A.) — And صَرِدَ, aor. as above, (Ṣ, Ḳ,) and so the inf. n., (Ṣ,) *He* (a man) *was quickly sensible of cold.* (Ṣ, Ḳ.) — And صَرِدَ said of milk, *It became in a state of decomposition, by reason of cold.* (TA.) — And, said of a skin, (O, Ḳ,) inf. n. as above, (O, TA,) *It emitted its butter in clots:* (O, Ḳ:) of the doing of which it is cured with hot water. (O, TA.) — صَرِدَ عَنِ الشَّىْءِ,

inf. n. as above, means † *He abstained, refrained,* or *desisted, from the thing;* [as though he became cold with respect to it;] *he left, relinquished,* or *forsook, it:* (M:) and صَرِدَ قَلْبِى عَنِ الشَّىْءِ † *My heart refrained from the thing; left, relinquished,* or *forsook, it:* (Ṣ, A, O, Ḳ:) like as one says, أَصْبَحَ قَلْبِى صَرِدًا: (TA:) the [lizard called] ضَبّ is spoken of as saying,

أَصْبَحَ قَلْبِى صَرِدَا • لَا يَشْتَهِى أَنْ يَرِدَا

[† *My heart has become cold,* or *indifferent,* (meaning *disposed to abstinence,*) *not desirous of coming to drink*]. (O.) —— صَرِدَ, (M, L, Ḳ,) or صَرِدَ عَنِ الرَّمِيَّةِ, (Ṣ,) or مِنَ الرَّمِيَّةِ, (A,) said of an arrow, (Ṣ, M, A, Ḳ,) and of a spear, (M, L,) aor. as above, (L,) and so the inf. n., (M, A, L,) *It passed through,* or *transpierced,* or *a part of it passed through,* (Ṣ, M,) *the animal at which it was shot* [or *thrown*], *by reason of its sharpness;* expl. by نَفَذَ حَدُّهُ: (Ṣ:) or *it penetrated so that its extremity passed through;* expl. by نَفَذَ حَدُّهُ; (L, Ḳ;) or خَرَجَتْ شَبَاةُ حَدِّهِ; and so صَرَدَ, aor. ـُ. (A. [See صَارِدٌ: and see an ex. in a verse cited voce بُقْيَا.]) — And صَرِدَ, (Ḳ,) inf. n. صَرَدٌ and صُرُودٌ, (M, L,) [the latter inf. n. suggesting that one says also صَرَدَ,] said of an arrow, (M, Ḳ,) and of a spear and the like, (M,) *It missed* the object of aim: thus having two contr. significations: (M, L, Ḳ:) and ↓ اصرد also has the latter of these two significations. (L.) —— صَرِدَ said of a horse, aor. ـَ, [inf. n. صَرَدٌ,] ‡ *He became galled in the place of the saddle:* (Ḳ, TA:) [or *he had a white place,* or *white places, on his back, produced by galls,* or *by hair growing in the places of galls:* (see صُرَدٌ and صَرِدٌ:)] and, said of a camel, *he had white fur growing in the place of a gall produced by the saddle, after its healing.* (AO.) —— See also 4.

2. تَصْرِيدٌ, (Ṣ, M, Ḳ,) in the giving to drink, (Ṣ, Ḳ,) is The *giving to drink less than satisfies thirst.* (Ṣ,* M, Ḳ.*) One says, صرّدهُ *He gave him to drink less than satisfied his thirst.* (M.) And صَرَّدْتُ الشَّارِبَ عَنِ المَآءِ *I stopped short the drinker from drinking the water.* (A.) And سَقَى سَقْيًا غَيْرَ تَصْرِيدٍ [*He gave to drink a quantity not less than satisfied thirst*]. (A.) And صرّد السَّقْىَ *He stopped short the giving to drink before satisfying thirst.* (A.) And صرّد شُرْبَهُ *He cut short, or put a stop to, his drinking.* (TA.) And صرّد شَرَابَهُ *He made his beverage to be little in quantity.* (A.) And accord. to the T, تَصْرِيدٌ signifies The *drinking less than satisfies thirst.* (TA.) — Also, (Ṣ, Ḳ,) in giving, (Ṣ,) ‡ The *making to be little, or small, in quantity* or *number.* (Ṣ, Ḳ, TA.) One says, صرّد العَطَآءَ ‡ *He made the gift to be little, or small,* (M, A, TA,) لَهُ *to him.* (A, TA.) And it is said in a trad., [app. relating to a particular class of persons,] لَنْ يَدْخُلَ الجَنَّةَ إِلَّا تَصْرِيدًا, meaning قَلِيلًا [i. e. † *They will not enter Paradise save in small number*]. (TA.) —— [Also, app., An *arrow's hitting the object of aim:* see its part. n. مُصَرِّدٌ.]

—— And The act of *scattering,* or *dispersing.* (El-Ḳálee, TA.) —— And صرّد said of barley and of wheat, *It put forth its awn, but not its ears, though almost doing the latter.* (El-Hejeree, M.)

4. اصرد السَّهْمَ, (Ṣ, M, L, Ḳ,) and الرُّمْحَ; (M;) and ↓ صَرَّدهُ; (M, L, Ḳ;) *He made the arrow,* and *the spear,* or *a part thereof, to pass through* (Ṣ, M) the animal at which it was shot [or thrown]: (Ṣ:) or *to penetrate so that its extremity passed through.* (M, L, Ḳ.) [See صَرِدَ and صَارِدٌ.] —— See also 1, latter part.

7. اِنْصِرَادٌ is said to mean The *experiencing of cold.* (Meyd. [Mentioned by him, with the expression of a doubt as to the true meaning, and as only occurring, to his knowledge, in a prov., which see in Freytag's "Arab. Prov." i. 357: but أَكَّامِ, there, should be إِكَّامِ.])

صَرْدٌ (Ṣ, M, L, Ḳ) and ↓ صَرَدٌ, (M, L,) the former a simple subst. and the latter an inf. n., (Lth,) and ↓ صَرِيدٌ, (TA,) *Cold,* or *coldness:* (Ṣ, M, L, Ḳ:) or *intense cold:* (M, L:) صَرْدٌ is a Pers. word, [originally سَرْد,] arabicized: (Ṣ, Ḳ:) or, accord. to a number of authors, it is an Arabic word adopted by the Persians. (MF.) One says يَوْمُ صَرْدٍ and ↓ صَرَدٍ [*A day of cold:* or *of intense cold*]. (A.) — For the former, see also صَرِدٌ, in two places. — Also, the former, *A high place in mountains;* (AA, L, Ḳ;) being the coldest part. (AA, L.) —— صَرْدٌ signifies also *Pure, unmixed, unadulterated,* or *genuine;* (Ṣ, M, L, Ḳ;) applied to beverage, (L,) such as is termed نَبِيذ, (Ṣ, L,) and to wine, (L,) and to anything. (M, Ḳ.) One says كَذِبٌ صَرْدٌ † *An unmixed lie.* (Ṣ, L.) And أُحِبُّهُ حُبًّا صَرْدًا *I love him with a pure, genuine,* or *sincere, love.* (AZ, Ṣ, L.) — [Hence,] جَيْشٌ صَرْدٌ † *An army composed only of the sons of one father or ancestor:* (L:) or *an army altogether consisting of sons of one's paternal uncle* [meaning *of one's relations*]: (AO:) or, (M, A, L, Ḳ,) and ↓ جَيْشٌ صَرِدٌ (M, A, L) and ↓ صَرَدٌ, (Ḳ,) † *A great army;* (Ḳ;) ‡ *an army that appears, from the slowness of its motion, by reason of its great number, to be inanimate.* (M, A, L.) —— See also صُرَدٌ, near the end.

صَرَدٌ: see صَرْدٌ, in three places: —— and see صَرِدٌ, near the end.

يَوْمٌ صَرِدٌ *An intensely-cold day;* and لَيْلَةٌ صَرِدَةٌ *an intensely-cold night:* (M, L:) [or] ↓ يَوْمٌ صَرْدٌ *a cold day:* (Ṣ:) and رِيَاحٌ صَوَارِدُ [pl. of ↓ رِيحٌ صَارِدَةٌ] *cold winds.* (Ḥam p. 506.) And أَرْضٌ ↓ صَرْدٌ *A cold land:* pl. صُرُودٌ: (M:) the latter (i. e. the pl.) *contr. of* جُرُومٌ. (Ṣ.) And رَجُلٌ صَرِدٌ *A cold,* or *an intensely-cold, man:* and قَوْمٌ ↓ صَرْدَى *a cold,* or *an intensely-cold, company of men.* (M, L.) See also مِصْرَادٌ. — صَرِدٌ applied to milk, *In a state of decomposition,* (O, Ḳ, TA,) *by reason of cold.* (TA.) — صَرِدٌ عَنْ شَىْءٍ † *Abstaining, refraining,* or *desisting, from a thing;* [as though cold with respect to it;]

leaving, relinquishing, or *forsaking, it.* (M.) See 1. —— See also صَرْدٌ. —— And see صَارِدٌ. —— صَرِدٌ applied to a horse, ‡ *Galled in the place of the saddle:* (Ḳ, TA:) or, (L,) as also ↓ مُصْرَدٌ, (A, TA,) *having a white place,* or *white places, on his back, produced by galls,* (L, TA,) or *having on his back white places, termed* صِرْدَان, [pl. of صُرَدٌ,] *produced by hair growing in the places of galls.* (A.) [And app. applied in a similar sense to a camel: see صُرَدٌ.]

صُرَدٌ *A certain bird,* (Ṣ, M, Ḳ,) *above the size of the sparrow,* (M,) *having a large head,* (Ḳ,) *which preys upon sparrows:* (T, Ḳ:) *a certain bird, black and white,* or *party-coloured,* (أَبْقَع,) *with a white belly:* (A:) *a certain bird of the crow-kind, also called* الوَاقِى: (Mṣb:) the Arabs used to regard its cry, (L, Mṣb,) and the bird itself, (L,) as of evil omen, (L, Mṣb,) and used to kill it; and they are forbidden to kill it, in order to dispel the idea of a thing's being of evil omen: (Mṣb:) *there are two species thereof; one species is called by the people of El-'Irák* العَقْعَق [a name now applied to the *magpie, corvus pica*]; *the other species, called* الصُّرَدُ الهُمْهُم, [so in the L, but in my copy of the Mṣb الهمام,] *is the wild sort, which is found in Nejd, upon the trees called* عِضَاه; *it is never seen but upon the ground,* [so in the L, but in my copy of the Mṣb, *it is never seen upon the ground,*] *springing from tree to tree:* (Sukeyn En-Numeyree, L, Mṣb:) *when chased, and hard pressed, it is overtaken, and utters a cry like that of the hawk: it preys upon sparrows:* (Mṣb:) it is described by AḤát as *a bird black and white,* or *party-coloured,* (أَبْقَع,) *with a white belly, and a back of a dark,* or *an ashy, dust-colour* (أَخْضَر), [or, as is said in the L, *half white and half black, found in trees,*] *large in the head and beak, having a talon with which it preys upon sparrows and other small birds, as large as the point of a spear:* (Mgh, Mṣb:) some add to this that *it is called* المُجَوَّف, because of the whiteness of its belly; and الأَخْطَب, because of the dark, or ashy, dust-colour of its back; and الأَخْيَل [a name now applied to the *green woodpecker, picus viridis*], because of its diversity of colour; that *it is never seen but upon a branch* (فِى شُعْبَة, and so in the L,) *or a tree,* (Mgh, Mṣb,) *and can scarcely ever, or never, be taken,* (Mṣb,) or *can never be taken:* (Mgh, L:) *it is regarded as of evil omen:* (Mgh:) Ṣgh says that *it is called* سُمَيْط, [perhaps a mistranscription for شُمَيْط, because black and white,] in the dim. form: (Mṣb:) [it is said that] it was the first bird that fasted for the sake of God: (Ḳ:) the pl. is صِرْدَان: (Ṣ, M, Mṣb, Ḳ:) and the female is called صُرَدَة. (Mṣb.) — Also ‡ *A white place,* (Ṣ, M, L, Ḳ,) *produced by galls,* (Ṣ, L, Ḳ,) or *by the saddle;* (M;) or صُرَدَةٌ signifies *a white place produced by hair growing in the place of a gall;* likened to the colour of the bird thus called: (A:) pl. صِرْدَان. (M, A.) And † *A white place on the hump of a camel:* (M:) or *white fur growing in the place of a gall produced by the saddle, after its healing:* (AO:) pl. as above.

(AO, M.) — And † *A certain vein* (Aṣ, M) *beneath the tongue,* (Aṣ,) or *in the lower part of the tongue,* (M,) of the horse. (Aṣ, M.) And الصُّرَدَانِ † *Two veins,* (Lth, Ks, Ṣ, M, L, Ḳ,) *of a dark,* or *an ashy, dust-colour,* (أَخْضَرَانِ, Lth, Ks, M, L,) *in the lower part of the tongue, by means of which the tongue moves about,* (Lth, Ks, L,) or *penetrating within* (يَسْتَبْطِنَانِ) *the tongue:* (Ṣ, M, Ḳ:) or *two veins, on the right and left of the tongue:* (L:) or, as some say, *two bones, which erect* (يُقِيمَانِ) *the tongue.* (M.) Yezeed Ibn-Eṣ-Ṣa'iḳ in his saying

لَهُ صُرَدَانِ مُنْطَلِقَا اللِّسَانِ

means ذَرِبَانِ [i. e. ذَرِبَا اللِّسَانِ, for ذَرِبٌ لِسَانُهُمَا, as though he said لَهُ لِسَانٌ ذَرِبٌ *He has a long,* or *an unbridled, tongue;* the phrase that he uses being pleonastic]. (Ṣ.) — Also, (M, L,) or ▼ صُرَدٌ, (so in the Ḳ,) and ▼ صَرَدٌ, which is the more known, (TA,) *A nail in a spear-head,* (M, L, Ḳ,) *by means of which the shaft is fastened to it.* (L, Ḳ.*) — Accord. to Sh, فَتَحَ صُرَدَهُ means *He opened his mind, so as to reveal his secrets.* (TA. [But this is perhaps a mistranscription, for فتح صُرَّهُ: see صُرَّةٌ.])

صَرْدَى [pl. of صَرِدٌ; and, agreeably with analogy, of صَرِيدٌ]: see صَرِدٌ, and صُرَّادٌ.

صَرِيدٌ: see صَرِدٌ. — Also *Hoar-frost,* or *rime;* syn. جَلِيدٌ. (TA.) — See also صُرَّادٌ.

صَرِيدَةٌ [app. a subst.; for if it were an epithet, having the meaning of a pass. part. n. of the fem. gender, it should by rule be without ة;] *A female animal,* (M,) or *a ewe,* (Ḳ,) *injured,* (M, Ḳ,) *and emaciated,* (M,) *by cold:* pl. صَرَائِدُ: (M, Ḳ:) on the authority of IAạr. (Ḳ.)

صُرَّادٌ *Cold and humid clouds in which is no water:* (Aṣ:) or *cold and humid clouds which the wind carries away;* as also ▼ صُرَيْدٌ and ▼ صَرِيدٌ: (M:) or *thin clouds in which is no water;* (Ṣ, Ḳ;) as also ▼ صُرَيْدٌ (Ḳ) and ▼ صَرْدَى. (L, TA.)

صُرَيْدٌ: see what next precedes, in two places.

صَارِدٌ: see its fem., with ة, voce صَرِدٌ. — Also, (Ṣ, A, L, Ḳ,) and ▼ مِصْرَادٌ, (Ṣ, L, Ḳ,) and ▼ صَرِدٌ, (A,) *An arrow that has passed,* or *of which a part has passed, through the animal at which it has been shot;* syn. نَافِذٌ: (Ṣ, L, Ḳ:) or *of which the extremity only has passed through:* when part of the arrow has passed through, it is termed نَافِذٌ; and when the whole has passed through, مَارِقٌ. (A.) And نَبْلٌ صَوَارِدُ *Arrows of which the extremities have passed through the animals at which they have been shot.* (A.)

أَصْرَدُ *More* [and *most*] *cold;* or *more* [and *most*] *affected by cold:* — and *More* [and *most*] *transpiercing.* (Meyd, in explanations of provs. commencing with this word. [See Freytag's "Arab. Prov." pp. 743-4.])

مُصْرَدٌ: see what next follows.

مُصْرِدٌ, (Ḳtr, L,) or ▼ مُصْرَدٌ, (so accord. to the Ḳ, [the former agreeable with its verb, the latter app. a mistake,]) *An arrow missing the object of aim.* (Ḳtr, L, Ḳ.) [See also مُصْرِدٌ.]

مُصَرَّدٌ *Beverage,* (Ṣ,) or *drink,* (A,) *made little in quantity.* (Ṣ, A.) — And *Given little to drink:* or †*given a small gift.* (Ṣ.) — See also صَرِدٌ.

مُصْرِدٌ *An arrow hitting the object of aim.* (Ḳtr, L.) [See also مُصْرَدٌ.]

مِصْرَادٌ *A wind* (رِيحٌ) *cold;* or *intensely cold:* or *accompanied by cold and humid clouds.* (IAạr, M.) — Also, and ▼ صَرِدٌ, (T, Ṣ, M, Ḳ,) *A man quickly sensible of cold;* (Ṣ;) *weak in enduring cold;* (Ḳ;) *impatient of cold.* (T, M.) — And the former, *Strong in enduring cold.* (Ḳ.) — And *A land without trees, and without anything* (Ḳ, TA) *of herbage.* (TA.) — See also صَارِدٌ.

مُصْطَرِدٌ *A man vehemently angered* or *enraged:* (Ḳ:) and so مُصْطَرٌ, without د. (TA.)

صرط

صُرَاطٌ *A long sword:* a dial. var. of سُرَاطٌ [q. v.]. (Ḳ.)

صِرَاطٌ *A road,* or *way;* as also سِرَاطٌ, (Ṣ, Ḳ,) which is the original; (TA;) and زِرَاطٌ: (Ṣ:) [see the second of these three words:] Akh says that the people of El-Ḥijáz make it fem., and Temeem make it masc. (Ṣ and Mṣb voce زُقَاقٌ, q. v.) — الصِّرَاطُ, also written with س, is likewise [*The name of*] *a bridge extended over the midst of Hell,* (Ḳ, TA,) *sharper than a sword, and thinner than a hair, over which the creatures will pass, the people of Paradise passing over it with their works, some like the blinding lightning, and some like the wind sent forth, and some like coursers, and some running, and some walking, and some dragging themselves along; and a crier will cry, from the lower parts of the empyrean, "Lower your eyes until Fáṭimeh, the daughter of Moḥammad, (may God bless and save him, and may God be well pleased with her and her two sons,) pass over;" and the fire will say to the believer, "Pass thou over, O believer, for thy light hath extinguished my flame;" and thereupon, the feet of the people of the fire will slip.* (TA.)

مِصْرَطٌ and مَصْرَطٌ: see مَسْرَطٌ.

صرع

1. صَرَعَهُ, aor. َ, inf. n. صَرْعٌ (Ṣ, O,* Mṣb, Ḳ) and صِرْعٌ, (Ṣ, O,* Ḳ,) the former inf. n. of the dial. of Temeem and the latter of Ḳeys, (Ṣ, O,) and مَصْرَعٌ, which is also a n. of place, [and, accord. to rule, of time also,] (Ṣ, O, Ḳ,) said of a man, (Ṣ, Mṣb,) *He threw him down, or prostrated him, on the ground;* (O, L, Ḳ, TA;) namely, a man. (T, TA.) And صَرَعَتْهُ is also said of a beast, [the pronoun referring to the rider,] meaning *It threw him down.* (TA in art. قمص.) Hence the saying, المَنِيَّةُ تَصْرَعُ الحَيَوَانَ ‡ [*Death prostrates the animal*]. (TA.) And مَثَلُ المُؤْمِنِ كَالخَامَةِ مِنَ الزَّرْعِ تَصْرَعُهَا الرِّيحُ مَرَّةً فَتَعْدِلُهَا أُخْرَى i. e. [*The similitude of the believer is as the fresh,* or *juicy, plant of seed-produce,*] *which the wind bends at one time, throwing it from side to side,* [*and straightens at another.*] (TA, from a trad.) And صُرِعَ الشَّجَرُ *The trees were cut and thrown down.* (TA.) — See also 3. — [Hence also,] صُرِعَ *He was affected with the disease termed* صَرْعٌ [expl. below]. (Mṣb.) And *He* (a man) *was affected with diabolical possession,* or *madness;* inf. n. صَرْعٌ. (TA.) — See also 2, in two places.

2. صَرَّعَهُ, [inf. n. تَصْرِيعٌ,] *He threw him down or prostrated him, on the ground, vehemently;* namely, a man. (Ḳ.) — صَرَّعَ البَابَ, (Ḳ,) inf. n. as above, (TA,) *He made the door-way to have what are termed* مِصْرَاعَانِ [i. e. *a pair of folding doors*]; as also ▼ صَرَعَهُ. (Ḳ, TA.) — And [hence,] صَرَّعَ الشِّعْرَ ‡ *He made the poetry to have what are termed* مِصْرَاعَانِ; as also ▼ صَرَعَهُ: (Ḳ, TA:) تَصْرِيعُ البَيْتِ مِنَ الشِّعْرِ, or التَّصْرِيعُ فِى الشِّعْرِ, (Ṣ,) or مِصْرَاعُ الشِّعْرِ, (TA,) is *the making the first* [meaning *hemistich*] *to rhyme* [*like the second*]; (Ṣ;) [i. e.] *the making the last foot of the first hemistich like the last of the second* [*in rhyme*]: (TA:) derived from the مِصْرَاع of the door-way. (Ṣ, TA.)

3. صَارَعْتُهُ فَصَرَعْتُهُ ▼, (Ṣ, Mṣb, TA,) inf. n. of the former مُصَارَعَةٌ and صِرَاعٌ, (Mṣb, TA,) *I wrestled with him, each of us endeavouring to throw down the other,* [*and I overcame him in doing so,* or *and I threw him down.*] (TA.)

5. تصرّع لَهُ ‡ *He became lowly, humble,* or *abased, and abashed, to him;* as also تضرّع: (Az, TṢ, TA:) or ‡ *he lowered, humbled,* or *abased, himself to him:* one says, إِلَيْهِ مَا زِلْتُ أَتَصَرَّعُ لَهُ and ‡ [*I ceased not to lower, humble,* or *abase, myself to him*] حَتَّى أَجَابَنِى [*until he answered me,* or *gave me his assent*]. (Z, TA.)

6. تصارعوا *They wrestled, one with another, endeavouring to throw down one another;* and [▼ اصطرعوا signifies the same; or] ▼ اصطرعا *they two wrestled, each endeavouring to throw down the other.* (TA.)

7. انصرع [*He,* or *it, became thrown down,* or *prostrated, on the ground*]. (Occurring in the Ḳ in art. جاث.)

8: see 6, in two places.

صَرْعٌ an inf. n. of 1. (Ṣ, Mṣb, Ḳ.) — Also, [as a subst., *Epilepsy,* or *falling sickness:* and sometimes, app., *ecstatic catalepsy; a sort of trance into which a person falls:*] *a certain disease,* (Ṣ, O, Mṣb, Ḳ,) *well known,* (Ṣ, O,) *resembling madness,* or *diabolical possession,* (Mṣb,) accord.

to the Ra-ees [Ibn-Seenà, whom we call "Avicenna"], (TA,) *preventing, but not completely, the vital organs from performing their actions* [or *functions*]; *the cause of which is an obstruction that occurs in one or more of the venters* (بُطُون) *of the brain and in the ducts of the* أَعْصَاب [here meaning *nerves*] *by which the members are moved,* [*arising*] *from an abundant thick or viscous* خِلْط [or *humour*], *whereby the* رُوح [by which is here meant, as in many other instances, the *vital spirit,* or *nervous fluid,*] *is prevented from pervading them in the natural manner, and consequently the members become* [*spasmodically*] *contracted.* (K, TA.) ═ Also *A sort,* or *species:* and *a state, condition,* or *manner of being:* syn. ضَرْبٌ and فَنٌّ: (S, K:) of a thing: (K:) and so ▼ صِرْعٌ: and likewise ضَرْعٌ and ضِرْعٌ: (TA:) [see also صِرْعَةٌ:] pl. [of mult.] صُرُوعٌ (S, K) and [of pauc.] أَصْرُعٌ. (K.) One says, هُوَ ذُو صَرْعَيْنِ, meaning ذُو لَوْنَيْنِ [i. e. *He,* or *it, has two sorts,* or *species:* or *two distinctive qualities* or *properties*]. (Ibn-'Abbád, Z, O, K.) And تَرَكْتُهُمْ صَرْعَيْنِ *I left them changing from state to state.* (Ibn-'Abbád, O, K.) And لِلْأَمْرِ صَرْعَانِ, meaning طَرَفَانِ [i. e. *There are two ways of performing the affair, either of which may be chosen*]. (TA.) — See also صِرْعٌ, in three places. — صَرْعَانِ *Two camels of which one comes to the water when the other returns from it,* by reason of their [the camels'] multitude. (S, O, K.) — And [hence, perhaps,] الصَّرْعَانِ signifies *The night and the day;* (K;) [and] so ▼ الصِّرْعَانِ, with kesr, like الصِّرْفَانِ: (TA in art. صرف:) or *the forenoon and the afternoon; from the first part of day to midday and from midday to sunset;* each of these being termed صَرْعٌ: (S, O, K:) or *the morning, between daybreak and sunrise, and the evening, between sunset and nightfall;* as also العَصْرَانِ; (S and K in explanation of الأَبْرَدَانِ;) and some assert that it is formed by transposition from العَصْرَانِ: (TA:) or *the two extremities of the day.* (A, TA.) And one says, أَتَيْتُهُ صَرْعَىِ النَّهَارِ *I came to him in the morning and evening;* or *between daybreak and sunrise and between sunset and nightfall.* (S, O, K.) And لَقِيتُهُ صَرْعَىِ النَّهَارِ *I met him at the two extremities of the day.* (A, TA.) Dhu-r-Rummeh says,

كَأَنَّنِى نَازِعٌ يَثْنِيهِ عَنْ وَطَنٍ
صَرْعَانِ رَائِحَةٌ عَقْلٌ وَتَقْيِيدُ

meaning *As though I were one,* i. e. a camel, *yearning towards his place of abode, which an evening and a morning, in evening a binding of the fore shank to the arm and* in the morning *a shackling of the legs, turn* [or *keep*] *away from a settled abiding-place:* or, as Aboo-'Alee relates it, رَائِحَةً, [as a partial substitute for صَرْعَانِ,] meaning, *an evening,* when there is *a binding of the fore shank to the arm, and* a morning, when there is *a shackling of the legs;* for they bind the camel's fore shank to his arm in the evening when he is lying down, and they shackle his legs in the morning so that he may pasture [but not stray]: another reading is صَرْعَاهُ [*his morning and evening*]. (TA.) — One says also, هُوَ صَرْعُ كَذَا i. e. حِذَآءَهُ [app. meaning *It is over against,* or *corresponding to, such a thing*]. (O, K.)

صِرْعٌ an inf. n. of 1. (S, K.) ═ And *i. q.* مُصَارِعٌ. (K.) See the latter in two places. ═ See also صَرْعٌ, former half. — [Also *Either of two opposite conditions* in which one is or stands &c. in respect of an affair or case.] One says, طَلَبْتُ مِنْ فُلَانٍ حَاجَةً فَٱنْصَرَفْتُ وَمَا أَدْرِى عَلَى أَىِّ صِرْعَىْ أَمْرِهِ هُوَ [*I sought,* or *demanded, of such a one, an object of want, and then turned away, and I know not in which of the two opposite conditions he was in respect of his affair,* or *case*]; i. e., his affair, or case, did not become apparent, or clear, or known, to me. (S, O, K.*) And a poet says,

فَرُحْتُ وَمَا وَدَّعْتُ لَيْلَى وَمَا دَرَتْ
عَلَى أَىِّ صِرْعَىْ أَمْرِهَا أَتَرَوَّحُ

[*And I went, and bade not farewell to Leylà, and she knew not in which of the two opposite conditions in respect of her affair,* or *case, I was going*]; i. e., whether I went from her presence retaining attachment, or forsaking; (S, TA;) or, as Z says, in a condition of success or of disappointment. (TA.) — See also صَرْعٌ, in the middle of the paragraph. — Also *A like; a similar person* or *thing;* and so ▼ صَرْعٌ. (O, K.) One says, هُمَا صِرْعَانِ, (S, O) and ▼ صَرْعَانِ (O) *They two are likes:* (S, O:) and so شِرْعَانِ, &c. (S.) And هٰذَا صِرْعُهُ and ▼ صَرْعُهُ *This is the like of him,* or *it:* and so ضِرْعُهُ and ضَرْعُهُ, &c. (IAar, TA.) — And *A strand of a rope:* (O, K:) and so ضِرْعٌ: (O:) pl. صُرُوعٌ (O, K) and ضُرُوعٌ. (O.)

صَرْعَةٌ *A single act of throwing down,* or *prostrating, on the ground;* or *a single suffering of prostration.* (K, TA.) See also صِرْعَةٌ. — And *A state,* or *condition:* (O, K:) so in the saying, هُوَ يَفْعَلُهُ فِى كُلِّ صَرْعَةٍ [*He does it in every state,* or *condition*]: (O:) [see also صَرْعٌ:] or, accord. to the "Mufradát" [of Er-Rághib], the *state,* or *condition, of him who is thrown down,* or *prostrated.* (TA.)

صُرْعَةٌ One who is *often thrown down,* or *prostrated, by men.* (K.)

صِرْعَةٌ *A mode,* or *manner, of throwing down,* or *prostrating;* or *of being thrown down,* or *prostrated:* (S,* K, TA:) a word similar to رِكْبَةٌ and جِلْسَةٌ. (S.) Hence, (K,) one says, سُوْءُ الِاسْتِمْسَاكِ خَيْرٌ مِنْ حُسْنِ الصِّرْعَةِ [*The bad manner of holding fast* upon one's beast *is better than the good manner of being thrown down,* or *prostrated*]: (S, K:) i. e., when one holds fast, though he ride not well, it is better than one's being thrown down, or prostrated, in a manner that does not hurt him; because he who holds fast sometimes overtakes, but he who is thrown down will not attain: (TA:) a prov.: or, as some relate it, ▼ حُسْنِ الصَّرْعَةِ, which means *the good manner of the single suffering of prostration.* (K,* TA. [See also Freytag's Arab. Prov. i. 623.])

صُرَعَةٌ One *who throws down,* or *prostrates, others;* (S, O, K;) as also ▼ صِرِّيعٌ and ▼ صُرَّاعَةٌ: (K:) or one *who throws down,* or *prostrates, his antagonists much,* or *often;* (TA;) and so ▼ صِرِّيعٌ, (S, O,) and ▼ صُرَّاعَةٌ, with damm and teshdeed, mentioned by Ks: (O:) or ▼ صِرِّيعٌ signifies one *who throws down,* or *prostrates, vehemently, though he be not well known for doing so;* as also ▼ صَرَّاعٌ and ▼ صَرِيعٌ, the latter like أَمِيرٌ [in measure, but this I think doubtful, probably added from finding صِرِّيعٌ mistranscribed]: or ▼ صِرِّيعٌ, accord. to the T, one *whose occupation, whereby he is known, is the throwing down,* or *prostrating, others* [*as a wrestler*]. (TA.) It is said in a trad. that the Prophet asked, Whom do ye reckon the صُرَعَة among you? they said, Him *whom men will not throw down:* and he said, He is not such, but is † he *who governs himself on the occasion of anger:* or, as some relate it, † the *forbearing on the occasion of anger,* (O, TA.*)

صَرُوعٌ One *who wrestles much with others, endeavouring to throw them down:* (T, K, TA:) pl. صُرُعٌ. (K.)

صَرِيعٌ *i. q.* ▼ مَصْرُوعٌ [meaning *Thrown down,* or *prostrated, on the ground*]: pl. صَرْعَى. (O, K.) — [And *i. q.* ▼ مَصْرُوعٌ meaning (as the latter is expl. in the Msb) *Affected with the disease termed* صَرْعٌ, q. v.] — And [*i. q.* ▼ مَصْرُوعٌ meaning] *Affected with diabolical possession,* or *madness.* (TA.) — One says also, بَاتَ صَرِيعَ الكَأْسِ ‡ [*He passed the night prostrated by the influence of the wine-cup*]. (TA.) — And رَأَيْتُ شَجَرَهُمْ صَرْعَى and ▼ مُصَرَّعَاتٍ ‡ *I saw their trees cut down* [*and laid prostrate*]. (TA.) And نَبَاتٌ صَرِيعٌ ‡ *A plant,* or *plants,* or *herbage, growing upon the surface of the earth, not erect.* (TA.) And غُصْنٌ صَرِيعٌ ‡ *A branch falling down to the ground:* (TA:) or *a branch broken down and fallen to the ground:* (Msb:) and [in like manner] one says ▼ غُصْنٌ مَصْرُوعٌ; and مَصَارِعُ is said to occur in a verse of Lebeed as pl. of the latter word, the reg. pl. of which is مَصَارِيعُ: but in that verse some read ▼ مُصَرَّعٌ [which has a similar meaning. (TA. [See EM p. 157.])] — صَرِيعٌ also signifies † *Slain:* from the same word as applied to a branch and expl. above: pl. صَرْعَى. (Msb.) — And ‡ *A twig,* or *rod, drooping,* or *hanging down, to the ground, falling upon it, but with its base upon the tree, so that it remains falling in the shade, the sun not reaching it, and therefore becomes more soft,* or *supple, than the branch* [*from which it depends*], *and more sweet in odour; and it is used for rubbing and cleaning the teeth* [i. e. مَسَاوِيكُ *are made of it*]: pl. صُرُعٌ: (K, TA: [the pl. is thus in the L; but in some copies of the K صُرُوعٌ:]) or, accord. to the T, the sing. signifies *a twig*, or *rod, that falls from the tree called* بَشَام [q. v.]; and the pl. is صُرْعَانٌ: the former pl. occurs in a trad., in which it is said that the Prophet was pleased to rub and clean his teeth with صُرُع. (TA.) —— Also ‡ *A bow from which nothing has been pared off*: or *of which the wood has dried upon the tree*; (Ṣ, O, Ḳ, TA:) or this [latter] is only called صَرِيف. (TA.) —— And ‡ *A whip, in like manner*, (Ṣ, O, Ḳ, TA,) *from which nothing has been pared off*. (TA.) ═ See also صُرَعَةٌ.

صَرَّاعَةٌ The *quality of throwing down*, or *prostrating, vehemently*. (TA.)

صَرَّاعٌ : see صُرَعَةٌ.

صِرِّيعٌ : see صُرَعَةٌ, in four places.

صُرَّاعَةٌ : see صُرَعَةٌ, in two places.

صَارِعٌ act. part. n. of 1: pl. صَارِعُونَ and صُرَعَةٌ. [Hence,] قَوْمٌ صُرَعَةٌ *A people*, or *party, who throw down*, or *prostrate, those with whom they wrestle*. (TA.)

مَصْرَعٌ *A place* [and accord. to rule *a time* also] *of throwing down*, or *prostrating, on the ground*: (Ṣ, O, Ḳ:) [pl. مَصَارِعُ.] —— [And † *A place of slaughter*: for] مَصَارِعُ القَوْمِ signifies *the places of slaughter of the people*, or *party*. (TA.) ═ Also an inf. n. of 1 [q. v.]. (Ṣ, O, Ḳ.)

مِصْرَاعٌ : see مِصْرَعٌ.

مُصَرَّعٌ [pass. part. n. of 2, q. v.]. One says, مَرَرْتُ بِقَتْلَى مُصَرَّعِينَ [*I passed by slain persons thrown down*, or *prostrated, on the ground*]: with teshdeed because relating to many objects. (Ṣ.) —— See also صَرِيعٌ, in two places.

مِصْرَاعٌ *Either half* [i. e. *leaf*] *of a door* [meaning of a folding door]: (MA,* Mṣb, KL:*) *either one of what are termed the* مِصْرَاعَانِ *of a door or door-way*: (Ṣ, Mṣb:) مِصْرَاعَا بَابٍ means *two doors that are set up, meeting together, the place of entrance thereof being in the middle of them* [i. e. *between them*]: (T, O, Ḳ, TA:) [and in like manner, مِصْرَاعَا سِتْرٍ (occurring in the Ṣ in art. سجف) means *the two separate halves, that hang side by side, so as to meet together, of a curtain; like the two leaves of a folding-door*:] and the مِصْرَاع of a door [or curtain] is also called its ▼ مِصْرَع: (TA:) the pl. of مِصْرَاع is مَصَارِيعُ. (MA.) —— Hence, the مِصْرَاع in poetry; (Ṣ;) † *A hemistich*: (MA, KL:) [this is the general meaning: in a more restricted sense,] مِصْرَاعَانِ in poetry means *a single verse* [i. e. *a pair of hemistichs*] *having two rhymes*: (T, O,* Ḳ,* TA:) [using it in the latter sense, i. e. as meaning *a verse of which the former hemistich rhymes with the latter*, which is app. the primary signification,] Aboo-Is-ḥáḳ says, the مِصْرَاعَانِ are the two doors of the ode, like the مصراعان of the house, or chamber, or tent: and he says that the derivation of the word is from الصَّرْعَانِ meaning "the two extremities of the day." (TA.)

مَصْرُوعٌ : see صَرِيعٌ, in four places; where it is stated that مَصَارِعُ is said to occur as a pl. thereof; the reg. pl. being مَصَارِيعُ.

مُصَارِعٌ One *who wrestles with another, endeavouring to throw him down*; as also ▼ صِرْعٌ: you say, هُمَا ▼ صِرْعَانِ i. e. *They are two persons wrestling together, each endeavouring to throw down the other*. (Ḳ,* TA.)

صرف

الصَّرْفُ signifies *The turning*, or *sending*, or *putting*, a thing *away*, or *back, from its way*, or *course*; *the causing* it *to turn away*, or *back; therefrom; the averting* it, or *repelling* it *therefrom*: (M:) or *the shifting* a thing *from one state*, or *condition, to another*; (Bḍ in vi. 105;) and so ▼ التَّصْرِيفُ. (TA.) You say, صَرَفَهُ, (M, Ḳ,) or صَرَفَهُ عَنْ وَجْهِهِ, (Mṣb, TA,) i. e. عَنْ سَنَنِهِ, (TA in art. وجه,) aor. ـِ, (M, Mṣb, Ḳ,) inf. n. صَرْفٌ, (M, Mṣb,) *He turned, sent*, or *put, him*, or *it, away*, or *back*, &c., (M, Ḳ,) *from his*, or *its, way*, or *course*. (M.) And ▼ صارف نَفْسَهُ عَنِ الشَّىْءِ, meaning صَرَفَهَا عَنْهُ [*He turned himself away*, or *back, from the thing*]. (M.) And صَرَفْتُ الرَّجُلَ عَنِّى [*I turned the man away*, or *back*, or *I averted him*, or *repelled him, from me*]. (Ṣ.) And صَرَفَ الصِّبْيَانَ *He dismissed the boys*, or *sent them away*, syn. قَلَبَهُمْ, (Ṣ, Ḳ,) from the school: (Ḳ:) or صَرَفْتُ الصَّبِىَّ *I let the boy go his way*; and in like manner, الأَجِيرَ *the hired man*. (Mṣb.) And صَرَفَ اللّٰهُ عَنْكَ الأَذَى [*May God avert from thee harm*]. (Ṣ.) And ▼ اصطرف وَجْهَهُ (Ḳ in art. سفو and سفى) [meaning صَرَفَهُ i. e.] *He turned away his face*. (TḲ in that art.) صَرَفَ اللّٰهُ قُلُوبَهُمْ, in the Ḳur [ix. 128], means *God hath made them to err* in requital of that which they have done: (M, TA:) or *God hath turned them away*, or *may God turn them away, from belief*. (Bḍ.) And سَأَصْرِفُ عَنْ آيَاتِى, in the Ḳur [vii. 143], means [in like manner] *I will requite by causing to err from the direction of my signs*. (O, TA.) [And one says also, صَرَفَهُ إِلَى كَذَا *He turned him* (i. e. another man, or the like, as in the Ḳur xlvi. 28), or *it* (for ex. his mind or intention), *to such a thing*.] —— [Hence,] صَرَفَ الكَلِمَةَ, (TA,) inf. n. صَرْفٌ, (O,) *He declined*, or *inflected, the word* [i. e. *the noun*] *with tenween*. (O, TA.) See also 2. —— [Hence, also,] الصَّرْفُ means *The exchanging*, or *giving in exchange, gold for silver* [and *the reverse*]: because it is turned (يُصْرَفُ) thereby from one metal to another. (M.) You say صَرَفَ الدَّرَاهِمَ *He exchanged*, or *gave in exchange, the dirhems for* [other] *dirhems* or *for deenárs*. (Mgh.) And صَرَفْتُ الذَّهَبَ بِالدَّرَاهِمِ *I exchanged*, or *gave in exchange, the gold for dirhems*: (Mṣb:) and الدَّرَاهِمَ بِالدَّنَانِيرِ [*the dirhems for deenárs*]. (Ṣ.) —— It is said in a trad. respecting الشُّفْعَة [or the right of pre-emption], إِذَا صُرِفَتِ الطُّرُقُ فَلَا شُفْعَةَ i. e. *When the roads thereof are made distinct* [app. *by their being turned in different directions*, from the house, or piece of land, in question, to the possessions of different proprietors, *there is no right of pre-emption*]: (TA:) the inf. n. of the verb in this case is صَرْفٌ. (TA.) —— You say also, صَرَفْتُ المَالَ *I expended the property*; (Mṣb;) [and so ▼ صَرَّفْتُهُ; for] التَّصْرِيفُ, (M,) or تَصْرِيفُ الدَّرَاهِمِ, (O,) فِى البِيَاعَاتِ, (M, O, Ḳ,*) means *the expending of money* [*in the purchase of articles of merchandise*]. (M, O, Ḳ.*) —— And صَرَفْتُ الكَلَامَ *I embellished the speech* [app. *by distorting it*, or otherwise *altering it*]; and ▼ صَرَّفْتُهُ has a similar, but intensive, meaning: (Mṣb:) or صَرْفُ الحَدِيثِ means *the embellishing of discourse*, or *speech*, (A'Obeyd, Ṣ, M, O, Ḳ,) *by adding in it*, (A'Obeyd, Ṣ,) or *and adding in it*; (M, O, Ḳ;) and in like manner صَرْفُ الكَلَامِ: (Ḳ: [of which see another explanation voce صَرْفٌ:]) and is [said to be] from الصَّرْفُ in pieces of money, meaning "the superiority of one over another in value." (O, Ḳ.) —— صَرَفَ لِأَهْلِهِ [as though meaning صَرَفَ نَفْسَهُ لِأَهْلِهِ]: see 8. —— [See also صَرْفٌ, below.] ═ صَرَفَ الشَّرَابَ, (M, O, Ḳ,) inf. n. صُرُوفٌ, (M, TA,) *He did not mix the beverage*, or *wine*; (M, O, Ḳ, TA;) as also ▼ صرّفهُ, and ▼ اصرفهُ; the last mentioned by Th. (M, TA.) And صَرَفَ الخَمْرَ, (Ḳ, TA,) aor. ـِ, inf. n. صَرْفٌ, (TA,) [or perhaps this should be صُرُوفٌ, as in the next preceding sentence,] *He drank the wine unmixed*; (Ḳ, TA;) [and so ▼ صَرَّفَهَا; for] تَصْرِيفُ الخَمْرِ, (Ṣ, O,) or التَّصْرِيفُ فِى الخَمْرِ, (Ḳ,) signifies *the drinking of wine unmixed*. (Ṣ, O, Ḳ. [Freytag has erroneously expl. صَرَفَ as meaning simply *He drank wine*.]) ═ صَرَفَتِ البَكَرَةُ, (Ṣ, O, Ḳ,) aor. ـِ, (Ṣ, O,) inf. n. صَرِيفٌ, (Ṣ, M, O, Ḳ,) *The sheave of the pulley caused a sound to be heard on the occasion of the drawing of water*: (Ṣ, M,* O, Ḳ:) and the صَرِيف of the door, and of the tush of the camel, is like that of the sheave of the pulley; (Ṣ, O;) [i. e.] the صَرِيف of the door, (M, Ḳ,) and of the writing-reed (M, Mṣb) and the like, (M,) is *a creaking*, or *grating*; (M, Mṣb,* Ḳ;) and so that of the tush of the camel: (Ḳ: [وباب البعير in the CḲ is a mistake for وناب البعير:]) one says of a man, and of a camel, صَرَفَ بِنَابِهِ, (M, TA,) and صَرَفَ نَابَهُ, (TA,) aor. ـِ, inf. n. صَرِيفٌ, *He grated his canine tooth* [*against its opposite*] *so as to cause a sound to be heard*: (M, TA:) the صَرِيف of the stallion-camel is [indicative of] his threatening: (M:) or that of the canine tooth of the she-camel denotes her weariness; and that of the canine tooth of the he-camel, his lust: (IKh, TA:) or the صَرِيف of the stallion is from briskness, liveliness, or sprightliness; and that of the female, from fatigue. (Aṣ, TA.) [But] —— صَرَفَتْ, (IAạr, Ṣ, M, O, Ḳ,) aor. ـِ, (Ṣ, M, O,) inf. n. صُرُوفٌ (Ṣ, M, O, Ḳ) and صِرَافٌ, (Lth, Lḥ, IAạr, Ṣ, M, O, Ḳ,) said of a bitch, (Ṣ, O, Ḳ,) or of any female having a cloven hoof and of any having a claw, (Lḥ, M,) or of a ewe or she-goat and of bitch and of a cow, (Lth, TA,) or of any female animal of prey, but mostly of a bitch, (IAar, TA,) signifies *She lusted for the male:* (Lth, Lh, IAar, Ṣ, M, O, Ḳ:) and the epithet applied to such an animal is ▼ صَارِفٌ. (Lh, IAar, Ṣ, M, O, Ḳ.)

2. التَّصْرِيفُ [in its primary acceptation is like الصَّرْفُ in the primary acceptation of the latter, but generally relates to several objects, or is used in an intensive sense]: see 1, first sentence: it signifies *The turning* of the winds (Lth, O, Ḳ, TA) *from one state or condition, to another;* (O, TA;) or *from one direction, or course, or way, to another;* (Lth, O, Ḳ, TA;) and so of the torrents, and of the horse, and of affairs, and of the verses of the Ḳur-án; (Lth, TA;) *the making* of the winds *to vary,* or *differ;* and so of the clouds; (M;) *the changing* of the winds to south and north [&c.] and hot and cold [&c.]; (Jel in ii. 159, and xlv. 4;) or *the making* of the winds *to be south and north, and east and west, and to be of various sorts in their kinds:* (TA:) or تَصْرِيفُ الآيَاتِ signifies [*the varying,* or *diversifying, of the verses of the Ḳur-án, by repeating them in different forms;* or] *the making of the verses of the Ḳur-án distinct* [*in their meanings by repeating and varying them,* as expl. by many of the expositors in the instances occurring in vi. 46 and 65 and 105, and xlvi. 26]. (O, Ḳ.) — It signifies also *The deriving* one word from another [*by modification of the form for the purpose of modifying the meaning;* including what we term *the declining* of nouns (like الصَّرْفُ) and *the conjugating* of verbs]. (O, Ḳ.) [The science of التَّصْرِيف in language is commonly termed عِلْمُ الصَّرْفِ ▼.] — In relation to property, or money, see 1, near the middle of the paragraph. — And in relation to speech, see 1, near the middle of the paragraph. — One says also, صرّف الشَّىْءَ, (M,) inf. n. as above, (TA,) meaning *He employed the thing in other* [i. e. *more*] *than one way;* as though he turned it from one way to another way. (M, TA.) — And [hence,] صَرَّفْتُهُ فِى الأَمْرِ, (Ḳ,) or فِى أَمْرِى, speaking of a man, (Ṣ, O,) *i. q.* قَلَّبْتُهُ [meaning *I employed him to act in whatsoever way he pleased, according to his own judgment* or *discretion* or *free will,* or *I made him a free agent, in the disposal,* or *management, of the affair,* or *my affair:* or † *I made him,* or *employed him, to practise versatility,* or *to use art* or *artifice* or *cunning, in the affair,* or *in my affair;* for the quasi-pass., تصرّف, is said to be from الصَّرْفُ as signifying الحِيلَةُ, and is expl. as syn. with اِحْتَالَ: but the former meaning is the more common: and it is also used as meaning simply *I employed him in the managing of the affair,* or *my affair*]. (Ḳ.) — [Hence also, صرّف الفَرَسَ *He exercised the horse.*] — صرّف الشَّرَابَ: and صرّف الخَمْرَ: see 1, latter half.

3: see 1, third sentence. — The inf. n. مُصَارَفَةٌ signifies also † The *dealing,* or *buying and selling, with any one* يُصَرِّفُ [app. meaning *with art* or *artifice* or *cunning,* or it may perhaps mean *in the exchanging of money:* see صَيْرَفِىٌّ]. (KL.)

4. اصرف الشَّرَابَ: see 1, latter half.

5. تصرّف [quasi-pass. of 2: thus,] said of a man's face, *It turned about;* or *was,* or *became, turned about;* syn. تقلّب. (Jel in ii. 139.) — And *It* (a thing) *was,* or *became, employed in other* [i. e. *more*] *than one way;* as though it were turned from one way to another way. (M.) — [Hence,] تصرّف فِى الأَمْرِ, (Ḳ,) or فِى أَمْرِى, (Ṣ,) quasi-pass. of صَرَّفْتُهُ فيه, (Ṣ,* O, Ḳ,) thus syn. with تقلّب [meaning *He acted in whatsoever way he pleased, according to his own judgment* or *discretion* or *free will,* or *as a free agent, in the disposal,* or *management, of the affair,* or *my affair;* or *he was,* or *became, employed to do so*]: (Ḳ:) or it is from الصَّرْفُ as signifying الحِيلَةُ; (Ṣ, M, TA;) i. e. it means ‡ [*he practised versatility,* or] *he used art* or *artifice* or *cunning, in the affair,* or *in my affair;* syn. اِحْتَالَ. (TA [and in like manner Bd in xxv. 20: but the former meaning is the more common: see also 8].) [It is also used as meaning simply *He employed himself,* or *was employed, in the managing of the affair,* or *my affair;* because the management of affairs generally requires the practice of versatility, or the use of art or artifice or cunning.] — [Hence also, said of a horse, *He was exercised.*]

7. انصرف, (Ṣ, M, O, Ḳ,) inf. n. اِنْصِرَافٌ, (O,) and مُنْصَرَفٌ is also sometimes an inf. n. thereof as well as a n. of place, (Ṣ,) quasi-pass. of صَرَفَهُ, (Ṣ, M,) said of a thing, (M,) or of a man; (Ṣ;) as such signifying *It* [or *he*] *turned,* or *went, away,* or *back, from its* [or *his*] *way,* or *course;* or *was,* or *became, turned,* or *sent,* or *put, away,* or *back, therefrom;* or *averted,* or *repelled, therefrom:* (M:) [or *shifted from one state,* or *condition, to another:* (see 1, first sentence:)] or *i. q.* اِنْكَفَّ; so in the copies of the Ḳ; but [this is an inadequate explanation;] the right [or better] explanation is اِنْكَفَأَ [i. e. *he,* or *it, reverted,* or *returned;* or *was,* or *became, turned away* or *back*]; agreeably with what is said in the O. (TA.) ثُمَّ انْصَرَفُوا in the Ḳur [ix. 128] means *Then they return,* or *go back,* from the place in which they have listened: or *then they turn away* from doing aught of that which they have heard. (M.) — [Accord. to Golius, it signifies also *It ran in a small stream;* or *the like;* for he explains it as meaning "manavit:" but for this he names no authority. — Said of a noun, it means *It was inflected,* or *declined, with tenween.*]

8. اصطرف ‡ *He sought, sought after,* or *sought to gain, sustenance* or *the like,* (M, TA,) *and used art* or *artifice* or *cunning* [*in so doing*]; (M;) for his family, or household; (M, TA;) as also ▼ صَرَفَ, aor. ـِ; you say, صَرَفَ لِأَهْلِهِ [as though meaning صَرَّفَ نَفْسَهُ لِأَهْلِهِ] and اصطرف: (M:) or *he used art* or *artifice* or *cunning* (تصرّف) *in the seeking of gain:* (O, Ḳ, TA:) or [meaning thus] you say, اصطرف فِى طَلَبِ الكَسْبِ. (Ṣ.) — It is also trans.: you say, اصطرف وَجْهَهُ: see 1, first quarter. — And اصطرف الدَّرَاهِمَ *He procured the dirhems in exchange for* [other] *dirhems* or *for deenars.* (Mgh.)

10. اِسْتَصْرَفْتُ ٱللّٰهَ المَكَارِهَ, (Ṣ, O, Ḳ) *I begged God to avert from me the things,* or *events, that are objects of dislike* or *hatred.* (O, Ḳ.)

صَرْفٌ [as an inf. n.: see 1]. — Used as a subst., The *evil accidents, mishaps,* or *calamities,* of time, or fortune; [thus expl. as having a pl. signification;] صَرْفُ الدَّهْرِ meaning حَدَثَانُهُ, (Ṣ, M, O, Ḳ,) and نَوَائِبُهُ, (Ṣ, O, Ḳ,) or حَوَادِثُهُ; (Mṣb;) because it [i. e. time, or fortune,] turns things from their way, or course: (M:) [but it seems to be more properly rendered the *shifting* of fortune, or its *shifting about;* and to be an inf. n. sometimes used as a simple subst., and therefore having a pl., for] its pl. is صُرُوفٌ. (M, Mṣb.) In the phrase قَدْ شَسَعَتْ صَرْفُ نَوَاهَا, in a verse of Ṣakhr-el-Ghei, [ISd says,] he has made it fem. because of its dependance upon النَّوَى [which is fem.; as though the meaning were *The afflictions that are the consequence of the course taken by her in her journey have exceeded the bounds of moderation*]: (M:) [or it is here made fem. because having the signification of a broken pl., which is fem.:] or the meaning is, قَدْ بَعُدَتْ تَصَرُّفُ وَجْهِهَا الَّذِى أَخَذَتْ فِيهِ [i. e. *the shifting-about of her course that she has taken has become far-extending;* صَرْف being thus used as an inf. n.; for the Arabs sometimes make the inf. n. fem., saying أَوْجَعَتْنِى ضَرْبُكَ as well as أَوْجَعَنِى ضَرْبُكَ; (see EM p. 157;) and this I think the most preferable explanation]. (Skr in his Expos. of the Poems of the Hudhalees, p. 14 of the vol. edited by Kosegarten.) — Also *Repentance.* (Ṣ, M, O, Mṣb, Ḳ.) [See a phrase below, in which this and other meanings are assigned to it.] — And ‡ *Art, artifice,* or *cunning.* (Yoo, Ṣ, M, O, Ḳ, TA.) Hence, in the Ḳur [xxv. 20], فَمَا يَسْتَطِيعُونَ صَرْفًا وَلَا نَصْرًا ‡ [*And they are not able to put in practice art* or *artifice* or *cunning, nor aid*]: (Ṣ, TA:) or this means *and they are not able to avert,* or *repel,* from themselves punishment, (O, Ḳ, TA,) *nor to aid* themselves. (O, TA.) — And *Excellence,* or *superiority,* of a dirhem, (Ṣ, M, Mgh, O, Mṣb, Ḳ,) and of a deenár, (M,) over another, (Ṣ, M, &c.,) *in goodness,* (Ṣ, Mgh, Mṣb,) or *in value;* (M, Mgh, O, Ḳ;) as in the saying, بَيْنَ الدِّرْهَمَيْنِ صَرْفٌ [*Between the two dirhems is a difference of excellence*], because of the [superior] goodness of the silver of one of them: (Ṣ:) and in like manner, of speech; (O, Ḳ;) as in the saying فُلَانٌ لَا يَعْرِفُ صَرْفَ الكَلَامِ *Such a one knows not the excellence of speech* over other speech: (O:) and [in like manner] one says, لِهٰذَا عَلَى هٰذَا صَرْفٌ *There is,* or *pertains, to this, an excess,* and *an excellence, over this;* for when one is judged to excel, it, or he, is turned aside from its, or his, likes, or fellows. (O, Ḳ.*) — And The *night;* and the *day:* (Ḳ:) [because of their interchanging:] الصَّرْفَانِ signifies *the night and the day;* (Ṣ, O, Ḳ;) as also ▼ الصَّرَفَانِ; (Ḳ;) the latter accord. to Ibn-'Abbád; (O;) like الصِّرْفَانِ, with kesr also [as well as with fet-ḥ]. (TA.) — In the saying (Ṣ, M, O, Mṣb) of the Arabs, (M,) or of the Prophet, (O, Mṣb,) in a certain trad., (Ḳ,) لَا يُقْبَلُ مِنْهُ صَرْفٌ وَلَا عَدْلٌ

[*Neither* صَرْفٌ *nor* عَدْلٌ *shall be accepted from him*], (Ṣ, M,* O, Mṣb,*) by صَرْف is meant *repentance*; (Ṣ, M, O, Mṣb, Ḳ;) and by عَدْل, *ransom*: (M, Mṣb, Ḳ:) or by the former, *art*, or *artifice*, or *cunning*; (Yoo, Ṣ, M, O, Ḳ;) and by the latter, *ransom*: (M:) or by the former, *acquisition of gain*; and by the latter, *ransom*: (Ḳ:) or by the former, *a supererogatory act*; (A'Obeyd, M, O, Ḳ;) and by the latter, *an obligatory act*: (A'Obeyd, M, Ḳ:) or vice versâ: (Ḳ:) or by the former, *weight*; and by the latter, *measure*: (M, O, Ḳ:) or by the former, *deviation*; and by the latter, *a right*, or *direct*, *course*: (IAạr, M:) or by the former, مَا يُتَصَرَّفُ فِيهِ [app. meaning *an evasive artifice*]; and by the latter, *a like*: (Th, M:) or by the former, *value*, or *price*; and by the latter, *a like*; the saying originally relating to the bloodwit (الدِّيَة): one says, لَمْ يَقْبَلُوا مِنْهُمْ صَرْفًا وَلَا عَدْلًا, i. e. *They did not accept from them a bloodwit, nor did they slay one man for him, of their people, who had been slain*; but they required from them more than that; for the Arabs used [often] to slay two men, and three, for one man; when they slew a man for a man, that was العَدْل with them; and when they took a bloodwit, having turned from the blood to another thing, that was صَرْف, i. e. the value, or price, was صَرْف: then the saying was applied in relation to anything, so as to be proverbially used in the case of him who was to render more than was incumbent on him: it has also been said that by صَرْف is meant [in the saying cited above] *something additional*, or *in excess*; but this is nought. (M.)

صِرْفٌ: see its dual in the next preceding paragraph, near the middle. ═ Also *Pure*, *unmixed*, or *free from admixture*; (Ṣ, M, Mgh, O, Mṣb, Ḳ;) applied to wine, (Ṣ, M, O, Mṣb, Ḳ,) or beverage, as meaning *unmixed*, (Ṣ, M, O, Mṣb,) and so ▼ مَصْرُوفٌ, (O, Ḳ,) and to other things, (Ḳ,) to blood, and to phlegm, (TA,) and to anything (M, Mṣb) as meaning *free from turbid foulnesses*: (Mgh,* Mṣb:) and ▼ صَرِيفٌ likewise signifies anything *having in it no admixture*. (TA.) ═ And *A certain dye*, (Mṣb,) *a red dye*, (Ṣ, O, Ḳ,) *with which the thongs*, or *straps*, *of sandals are dyed*, (Ṣ, O,) or *with which the hide is dyed*: (Mṣb:) or *a certain red thing with which the hide is tanned* (يُدْبَغُ [perhaps a mistranscription for يُصْبَغُ]). (So in a copy of the M.)

الصَّرْفَةُ *One of the Mansions of the Moon*; [*the Twelfth Mansion*;] *a single very bright star*, [*β of Leo*,] (Ṣ, O, Ḳ, and Ḳzw in his Descr. of the Mansions of the Moon,) *by which are some small evanescent stars*; (Ḳzw;) *over against*, (يتلقّا, so in my copies of the Ṣ,) or *following*, (O, Ḳ and Ḳzw ubi suprà,) الزُّبْرَة; (Ṣ, O, Ḳ, Ḳzw;) [i. e.] it is *a single star behind the* خَرَاتَانِ *of the Lion*; (M;) it is *on the hinder part of the tail* (ذَنَب) *of the Lion*; [wherefore it is called by our astronomers *Deneb*;] *and is also called the* قُنْب, *which means the sheath of the penis, of the Lion*: (Ḳzw in his Descr. of Leo: [in the Ṣ and O, erroneously, "*the* قَلْب *of the Lion*:"]) [*it rose aurorally, in Central Arabia, about the commencement of the era of the Flight, on the 8th of Sept., O. S.; and set aurorally on the 9th of March*:] Ibn-Kunáseh says, (M,) it is called الصَّرْفَةُ because of the turning away of the cold (Ṣ, M, O, Ḳ) from the heat, (M,) and the coming of the heat, (Ṣ, O,) accord. to the [O and] Ḳ at its rising, but [as] IB says, correctly because of the turning away of the heat [at its rising], and the coming of the cold: (TA:) [i. e., correctly,] it is thus called because of the turning away of the cold at its setting in the early mornings, and the turning away of the heat at its rising from beneath the rays of the sun in the early mornings: (Ḳzw in his Descr. of Leo:) when it rises before the dawn, that is the beginning of autumn; and when it sets with the rising of the dawn, that is the beginning of spring. (M.) [Hence,] الصَّرْفَةُ is [called] نَابُ الدَّهْرِ الَّذِى يَفْتَرُّ, (Ibn-'Abbád, O, Ḳ,) or نَابُ الدَّهْرِ الَّذِى يَفْتَرُّ عَنْهُ [*The dog-tooth of time*, or *fortune*, *which it shows smiling*]: for when الصرفة rises, [a mistake for "sets, aurorally,"] the blossoms come forth and the herbage attains its full height: (M and Ḳ in art. فر:) in the T it is said that الصَّرْفَة is called by the Arabs نَابُ الدَّهْرِ [*the dog-tooth of time*, or *fortune*,] لِأَنَّهُ يَفْتَرُّ عَنِ البَرْدِ وَعَنِ الحَرِّ فِى الحَالَتَيْنِ [i. e. because it smiles revealing (the advent of) the cold and (that of) the heat, in its two states (of auroral rising and setting)]. (TA.) ═ صَرْفَةٌ also signifies *A certain kind of bead* (خَرَزَة); (Lḥ, Ṣ, M, O, Ḳ;) *mentioned among those by means of which men are captivated*, or *fascinated*, or *restrained by women from other women*; (Ṣ, O, Ḳ;*) or *by means of which men are conciliated*, *so as to be turned thereby from their ways of acting* or *conduct* or *the like*. (Lḥ, M.) ═ And A bow *having upon it a black mark* or *spot* (شَامَةٌ سَوْدَآءُ), *the arrows of which*, *when they are shot*, *will not hit the object of aim*. (O, Ḳ.) ═ And one says, حَلَبْتُ النَّاقَةَ صَرْفَةً, meaning *I milked the she-camel in the early morning*, *between dawn and sunrise*, *and then left her until the like time of the morrow*. (O, Ḳ.*)

الصَّرَفَانُ *Death*; (M, Ḳ;) *a name of death*. (IAạr, O.) ═ And صَرَفَانٌ signifies *Lead*; syn. رَصَاصٌ: (Ṣ, Mṣb, Ḳ:) or رَصَاصٌ قَلْعِىٌّ [q. v.]: (M:) and (Ḳ) accord. to Ibn-'Abbád, (O,) *copper*; syn. نُحَاس. (O, Ḳ.) ═ And *A sort of dates*; (Ṣ, M, O, Mṣb;) *a heavy sort of dates*: (Ḳ:) n. un. with ة: (M:) AḤn says, (M, O,) on the authority of certain of the Arabs, (O,) that the صَرَفَانَة is *a red date*, *like the* بَرْنِيَّة, (M, O, Mṣb,) *but* (M, O) *hard to be chewed*, (M, O, Ḳ,) *tough*, (M, O,) *and the heaviest of all dates*: (M, O, Mṣb:) *persons having households and slaves and hired men provide it*, *because of its satisfying quality*, (O, Ḳ, [but for لجزاتها in the O, referring to the n. un., and لِجَزَائِهَا in copies of the Ḳ, and لجزائها in the CḲ, I read لِجَزَائِهَا, which is evidently the right reading, and agrees with what here follows,]) *and its standing in great stead*: (O, Ḳ:) or it is the [*sort of dates called*] صَيْحَانِىّ [q. v.]: (Ḳ:) AḤn says, En-Nowshajánee told me that the صَرَفَانَة is [called] الصَّيْحَانِيَّة in El-Hijáz, and in like manner its palm-tree. (O.) صَرَفَانَةٌ رِبْعِيَّةٌ تُصْرَمُ بِالصَّيْفِ وَتُؤْكَلُ بِالشَّتِيَّة is one of their proverbs [expl. in art. ربع]. (AḤn, O, Ḳ.)

صَرَفِىٌّ *A camel of a certain excellent sort*; (M, O, Ḳ;) a rel. n.: (O, Ḳ:) or it is correctly with د; (O,* Ḳ;) i. e. صَدَفِىٌّ [q. v.]: (O:) some say that it is with د; and this is the right. (M.)

صَرُوفٌ A she-camel *that makes a grating*, or *creaking*, *sound with her tushes*, or *canine teeth*. (Ṣ, O, Ḳ.)

صَرِيفٌ inf. n. of 1 in the senses expl. in the last sentence but one of the first paragraph [q. v.]. (Ṣ, M, &c.) ═ See also صِرْفٌ. — Applied to milk, (Ṣ, M, O, Ḳ,) *Just milked*; (Ḳ;) *brought away from the udder while hot*, (Ṣ, M, O,) *when milked*. (Ṣ, O.) — Also *Dry* سَعَف [or *palm-branches*]: n. un. with ة: (AḤn, M:) [i. e.] ▼ صَرِيفَةٌ signifies a *dry* سَعَفَة. (Ḳ.) And AḤn says, (M, O,) in one place, (M,) الصَّرِيفُ signifies, (M, O, Ḳ,) as some assert, (O,) *What has become dry*, *of trees*; (M, O, Ḳ;) like الضَّرِيعُ; (M;) called in Pers. خُذْخُوش, (so in copies of the Ḳ, in the CḲ خُذْخُوش, and in the O الخذخوش, [all app. mistranscriptions, for I find nothing like them in Pers. except partially, i. e. خُوش meaning "dry," like خُشْك,]) and also called [in Arabic] القَفْلَةُ [*the tree that has become dry*]. (O.) [See also صَرِيعٌ, with the unpointed ص.] ═ Also *Silver*: so in a verse cited voce إِنْ (page 107, third col.): (ISk, Ṣ, O:) or *pure silver*. (Ḳ.) ═ See also the next paragraph.

صَرِيفَةٌ: see the next preceding paragraph. ═ Also *A thin*, *round cake of bread*; syn. رُقَاقَةٌ: pl. صُرُفٌ and صِرَافٌ and [coll. gen. n.] ▼ صَرِيفٌ. (Ḳ.)

خَمْرٌ صَرِيفِيَّةٌ *Wine of* صَرِيفُونُ, (Ṣ, O, Ḳ,) a place, (Ṣ, O,) i. e. a town, (O,) in El-'Iráḳ, (Ṣ, O,) in the Sawád of El-'Iráḳ near 'Okbarà; (O, TA;) not, as it is implied in the Ḳ, from another of the same name in Wásiṭ: (TA:) or, as some say, *wine just taken from the* دَنّ [or *jar*]; like [as one says] لَبَنٌ صَرِيفٌ. (O, Ḳ.)

صَارِفٌ: see صَيْرَفِىٌّ: ═ and see also صَرَّافٌ.

صِرِّيفٌ: see the next paragraph.

صَارِفٌ [act. part. n. of 1: as such having, among other meanings, the meaning of *Grating*, or *creaking*; or *making a grating*, or *creaking*, *sound*: and so ▼ صَرَّافٌ, but properly in an intensive sense; for] the dual of صَرَّاف is used by the poet Aboo-Khirásh as meaning *two thongs of a sandal that make a creaking sound*: (M:) [and ▼ صِرِّيفٌ likewise means *making a creaking sound with the teeth*: so accord. to Freytag, from Jereer.] One says, مَا فِى فِيهِ صَارِفَةٌ, meaning *He has not in his mouth a canine tooth* [lit. *a* grater or creaker; for سِنٌّ صَارِفَةٌ a tooth that makes a grating, or creaking, sound]. (M.) ═ See also 1, last sentence.

صَارِفَةٌ : pl. صَوَارِفُ : see تَصَارِيفُ, below.

صَيْرَفٌ One who practices art or artifice or cunning, in the disposal, or management, of affairs; (Ṣ, M, O, Ḳ;) as also ▼ صَيْرَفِىٌّ ; (Ṣ, O, Ḳ;) which latter is applied by the poet Suweyd Ibn-Abee-Káhil El-Yeshkuree [in the like sense] as an epithet to a tongue, in his saying,

* وَلِسَانًا صَيْرَفِيًّا صَارِمًا *
* كَحُسَامِ السَّيْفِ مَا مَسَّ قَطَعْ *

[And a cunning, sharp tongue, like the edge of the sword, what it touches it cuts]. (Ṣ, O.) — See also what next follows.

صَيْرَفِىٌّ i. q. ▼ صَرَّافٌ, (Ṣ, M, O, Mṣb,) or صَرَّافُ دَرَاهِمَ, (Ḳ,) and so ▼ صَيْرَفٌ, (M, Mṣb, Ḳ,) i. e. A money-changer; (M, Mṣb, TA;) except that صَرَّافٌ has an intensive signification [app. as meaning a skilful money-changer, and hence it is often used in the present day as meaning a banker]: (Mṣb:) all are applied to him who knows and distinguishes the relative excellence, or superiority, of pieces of money: (Mgh:) these appellations are from المُصَارَفَةُ, (Ṣ, O,) or from التَّصَرُّفُ, (M,) or from صَرْفٌ meaning "excellence," or "superiority," of one dirhem [or deenár] over another, (Mgh, and Mṣb on the authority of IF in relation to the first,) because such as excels, or is superior, is turned aside from the deficient: (Mgh:) the pl. is صَيَارِفَةٌ (Ṣ, M, O, Ḳ) and صَيَارِفُ (M) and صَيَارِيفُ, this last occurring in poetry, (Ṣ, M, O, Ḳ,) by poetic license, for the sake of the measure. (Ṣ, O.) — See also صَيْرَفٌ.

تَصَارِيفُ الأُمُورِ [and صَوَارِفُهَا pl. of ▼ صَارِفَةٌ] The varieties, or vicissitudes, of affairs or events. (M, TA.)

مَصْرِفٌ A place of turning away or back: [see also مُنْصَرَفٌ:] hence, in the Ḳur [xviii. 51], وَلَمْ يَجِدُوا عَنْهَا مَصْرِفًا, (TA,) meaning [And they shall not find] a place to which to turn away, or back, from it: (Bḍ, Jel:) or, a turning away, or back, from it: (Bḍ:) pl. مَصَارِفُ. (TA.)

مَصْرُوفٌ [pass. part. n. of 1: see its verb: — and] see مُنْصَرِفٌ: ═ see also صِرْفٌ.

مُتَصَرَّفٌ i. q. مُتَقَلَّبٌ [as meaning Place, or scope, or room, for free action]. (A, voce سُوبٌ [q. v.]; and so in the Fáïḳ.)

مُتَصَرِّفٌ is an epithet applied to a verb [as meaning That is perfectly inflected], opposed to جَامِدٌ [q. v.]. (TA, voce قَدْ.) — ظَرْفٌ مُتَصَرِّفٌ and ظَرْفٌ غَيْرُ مُتَصَرِّفٍ signify the same, respectively, as ظَرْفٌ مُتَمَكِّنٌ and ظَرْفٌ غَيْرُ مُتَمَكِّنٍ : see art. مكن. — وَكِيلٌ مُتَصَرِّفٌ means A factor, an agent, or a deputy, who acts according to his own free will in the disposal, or management, of an affair.]

مُنْصَرَفٌ is a n. of place, [meaning A place of turning away or back, like مَصْرِفٌ,] as well as an inf. n. [of 7]. (Ṣ.)

مُنْصَرِفٌ and غَيْرُ مُنْصَرِفٍ denote the two different sorts of nouns, (O, Ḳ,) meaning, respectively, [like ▼ مَصْرُوفٌ and غَيْرُ مَصْرُوفٍ,] Inflected, or declined, with tenween, and not so inflected or declined. (O, TA.)

صرم

1. صَرَمَهُ, (Ṣ, M, Mgh, Mṣb, Ḳ,) aor. ـِ, (M, Mṣb, Ḳ,) inf. n. صَرْمٌ (Ṣ, M, Mṣb, Ḳ) and صُرْمٌ, (M, Ḳ,) or the latter is a simple subst., (M, Mṣb,) He cut it, syn. قَطَعَهُ, (Ṣ, M, Mgh, Mṣb,) in any manner: [i. e. it signifies also he cut it through; or he cut it off, or severed it; for thus the meaning of قَطَعَهُ is generally explained:] (M:) or it signifies [only] he cut it (قَطَعَهُ) so as to separate it: (M, Ḳ:) namely, a thing, (Ṣ,) such as a rope, and a raceme of dates. (TA.) One says, صُرِمَتْ أُذُنُهُ i. q. صُلِمَتْ [i. e. His ear was cut off, entirely]. (TA.) And صَرَمَ النَّخْلَ, (Ṣ, M, Mṣb, Ḳ,) and الشَّجَرَ, (M, Ḳ,) and الزَّرْعَ, aor. as above, inf. n. صَرْمٌ, (M,) He cut off the fruit, or produce, of the palm-trees, (Ṣ, M, Mṣb,* Ḳ,) and the trees, (M, Ḳ,) and the corn, or the like; (M;) as also ▼ اصطرمه. (Ṣ, M, Ḳ.) — [Hence,] صَرَمَهُ, (Ṣ, M, MA, Ḳ,) [aor. as above,] inf. n. صَرْمٌ (Ṣ, MA,) or صُرْمٌ, (M, MA,) or the latter is a simple subst., (Ṣ,) † He cut him (i. e. another man); meaning he ceased to speak to him, or to associate with him; he cut him off from friendly, or loving, communion or intercourse; forsook him, or abandoned him; syn. قَطَعَ كَلَامَهُ ; (Ṣ, M, Ḳ;) and هَجَرَهُ : (A and Mgh and Ḳ in art. هجر:) or he cut himself off, or separated himself, from him, namely, his friend; he cut off [or withdrew] his friendship from him. (MA.) [See an ex. in a verse cited voce أَبٌّ.] And صَرَمَ وَصْلَهُ, aor. as above, inf. n. صَرْمٌ and صُرْمٌ, † [He cut, or severed, his bond of union,] as indicative of resemblance [to the act of cutting, or severing, properly thus termed]. (M.) — And صَرَمَ أَمْرَهُ † [He decided his affair]. (O voce ضَبًّا, q. v. [See also صَارِمٌ, and صَرِيمَةٌ.]) ═ صَرَمَ is also intrans., as syn. with انصرم, q. v. (M, Ḳ.) And [hence] one says, أَدْبَرَتِ الدُّنْيَا بِصَرْمٍ i. e. † [Worldly good departed] by becoming cut off, or by ceasing, and coming to an end. (TA.) — One says also, صَرَمَ عِنْدَنَا شَهْرًا, meaning † He stopped, stayed, or tarried, with us a month: (Ḳ, TA:) mentioned by El-Mufaḍḍal, on the authority of his father. (TA.) ═ صَرُمَ, (Mṣb,) [aor. ـُ,] inf. n. صَرَامَةٌ and صُرُومَةٌ, (M,) It (a sword) was, or became, sharp, (M, Mṣb,) and did not bend. (M.) — And [hence,] صَرُمَ inf. n. صَرَامَةٌ, said of a man, (Ṣ, M, Mṣb, Ḳ, TA,) as being likened to a sword, (TA,) ‡ He was, or became, courageous; (Mṣb;) or hardy, strong, or sturdy, (Ṣ, TA,) or sharp, penetrating, or vigorous and effective, (M, Ḳ, TA,) and courageous. (Ṣ, M, Ḳ, TA.)

2. صرّمهُ [He cut it; cut it through; or cut it off, or severed it; namely, a number of things considered collectively; or a single thing much, or in several places]: (M:) تَصْرِيمُ الحِبَالِ signifies تَقْطِيعُهَا [i. e. the severing of the ropes]: the verb being with teshdeed to denote muchness [of the action], or multiplicity [of the objects]. (Ṣ, TA.) [Hence, تَصْرِيمُ الأَطْبَآءِ The cutting off of the teats of camels: a phrase mentioned in the TA.]

3. صارمهُ, (MA,) inf. n. مُصَارَمَةٌ, (KL, TA,) † He effected a disunion with him: (MA:) or he cut him off from himself, being in like manner cut off by him: (KL:) or he cut him off from friendly, or loving, communion or intercourse, being so cut off by him: forsook him, or abandoned him, being forsaken, or abandoned, by him: cut him, i. e. ceased to speak to him, being in like manner cut by him: for المُصَارَمَةُ signifies المُهَاجَرَةُ and قَطْعُ الكَلَامِ. (TA.)

4. اصرم النَّخْلُ The palm-trees attained, or were near, to the time, or season, for the cutting off of their fruit. (Ṣ, M, Mṣb, Ḳ, TA.) — And [hence perhaps,] اصرم said of a man, (Ṣ, Ḳ, TA,) inf. n. إِصْرَامٌ, (TA,) † He was, or became, poor, (Ṣ, Ḳ,) having a numerous family, or household: (Ḳ:) or in a evil condition, though having in him intelligence (تَمَاسُك): [it is said that] the original meaning is he had a صِرْمَة, i. e. portion, of property remaining to him. (TA.)

5. تصرّم quasi-pass. of صَرَّمَهُ ; (M;) i. q. تقطّع [i. e. It became cut; cut through; or cut off, or severed; said of number of things considered collectively; or of a single thing as meaning it became cut, &c., much, or in many places, or into many pieces]. (Ṣ, Ḳ.) — See also 7, in three places. ═ Also † He affected hardiness, strength, sturdiness, and endurance, or patience; or constrained himself to behave with hardiness, &c. (Ṣ, Ḳ.)

6. تصارموا † They cut, forsook, or abandoned, one another; (MA;) they separated themselves, one from another; (KL, in which only the inf. n. is mentioned;) they severed the bond of union, or communion, that was between them; disunited, or dissociated, themselves, one from another; syn. تَقَاطَعُوا. (Ṣ,* MA, in the former of which only the inf. n. is mentioned.)

7. انصرم It became cut; cut through; or cut off, or severed; (Ṣ, M, Ḳ, TA;) quasi-pass. of صَرَمَهُ ; (M, TA;) said of a rope [&c.]; and so ▼ صَرَمَ. (M, Ḳ, TA.) — [Hence,] انصرم مِنَ النَّاسِ [or عَنِ النَّاسِ] † He separated himself from mankind; said of the wolf and of the crow [&c.]. (ISk, Ṣ, M.*) And انصرم اللَّيْلُ † The night went away, or departed; as also ▼ تصرّم: (Mṣb:) and انصرم الشِّتَآءُ † The winter ended; and ▼ تصرّمت السَّنَةُ † The year ended: (TA:) and ▼ تصرّم القِتَالُ † The fighting ended, or ceased. (Mgh.)

8. اصطرمهُ : see 1, third sentence.

صَرْمٌ *Skin:* [or *leather:*] (Ṣ, Mgh, Mṣb, Ḳ:) a Pers. word (Ṣ, Mṣb) arabicized, (Ṣ, Mgh, Mṣb, Ḳ,) originally جَرْم [correctly چَرْم]. (Mgh, Mṣb, TA.)

صُرْمٌ is an inf. n. like صَرْمٌ, (M, Ḳ,) or a simple subst.: (M, Mṣb:) [see the first paragraph, in three places: in one of its senses, there expl.,] it is syn. with هِجْرَانٌ and قَطِيعَةٌ: (TA:) and ↓ صَرِيمَةٌ [likewise] signifies † *Separation from a friend:* pl. صُرُومٌ. (MA. [This pl. is app. there mentioned as of صَرِيمَةٌ; but it is more probably of صُرْمٌ.]) ═ صُرْمُ الدِّيكِ : see دِيكٌ.

صِرْمٌ *Tents* (أَبْيَاتٌ), (Ṣ, M,) *of men,* (Ṣ,) *collected together,* (Ṣ, M,) *separate from* [*those of other*] *men:* (M:) or *i. q.* صِرْبٌ, (O in art. صرب,) which means *a few tents* (بُيُوت [in the O, erroneously, أَبْيُوت]) *of the weak sort of the Arabs of the desert:* (IAạr, O,* Ḳ, TA; all in art. صرب:) and hence, (M,) *a company* (M, Mṣb, Ḳ, TA) *of men,* (Mṣb, TA,) *not many;* or simply *a company* (TA) *alighting and abiding with their camels by the side of the water:* (Mṣb, TA:) pl. أَصْرَامٌ [a pl. of pauc.] (Ṣ, M, Mṣb, Ḳ) and أَصَارِمُ, (Ṣ,) or أَصَارِيمُ, (M,) or both, (Ḳ,) but accord. to IB the latter of these two is the right, [being a pl. pl., i. e. pl. of أَصْرَامٌ,] (TA,) and صُرْمَانٌ, (Sb, M, Ḳ,) with damm. (Ḳ.) — And *i. q.* ضَرْبٌ. (Ḳ. [So, app., in all the copies; accord. to the TḲ as meaning *A sort,* or *species:* but I think it most probable that this is a mistranscription for صِرْبٌ, with which, as has been stated above, صِرْمٌ is syn. accord. to the O.]) ═ Also *i. q.* خُفٌّ مُنْعَلٌ (M) or خُفٌّ مُنَعَّلٌ (Ḳ) [i. e. *A soled boot:* that خُفّ here means a boot, not a camel's foot, is indicated by its being immediately added by SM that] ↓ صَرَّامٌ signifies *A seller thereof.* (TA.)

صُرْمَةٌ [an epithet applied to a man, but used as a subst., and therefore having for its pl. صُرَمَاتٌ]. One says, هُوَ صُرْمَةٌ مِنَ الصُّرُمَاتِ, [the last word said to be thus (مُحَرَّكَة) in the TA, but in the CḲ (in which as well as in my MS. copy of the Ḳ من is omitted) written الصُّرْمَاتِ,] meaning ‡ *He is* [*a person*] *slow to revert from his anger.* (Ḳ, TA.) ═ Also, [if not a mistranscription for ↓ صَرِيمَة,] *A portion of silver, melted, and cleared of its dross, and poured forth into a mould.* (TA.)

صِرْمَةٌ *A herd, or detached number, of camels,* (Ṣ, M, Mgh, Mṣb, Ḳ,) *consisting of about thirty:* (Ṣ:) or *from twenty to thirty:* (M, Ḳ:) or *from thirty to five and forty:* (M:) or *to fifty,* and *forty;* (Ḳ;) if amounting to sixty, termed صِدْعَة: (TA: [but see this latter word:]) or *from ten to forty:* (M, Mṣb, Ḳ:) or *from ten to some number between that and twenty:* (M, Ḳ:) or *more than a* ذَوْد [which is at least two or three] *up to thirty:* (T voce إِبِلٌ:) or *about forty:* (Ḥam p. 753:) or *less than a* هَجْمَة, which is a hundred or nearly a hundred: (Id. p. 637:) pl. صِرَمٌ. (Ṣ,* M,* Mṣb.) — *A portion of property.* (TA.) — And *A detached portion of clouds:* (Ṣ, M, Mṣb, Ḳ:) pl. as above. (Ṣ, M.) — See also صَرِيمَةٌ. — And see صُرْمَةٌ.

صَرَامٌ and ↓ صِرَامٌ The *cutting off of the fruit of palm-trees:* (Ṣ,* Mṣb, and L voce جَدَادٌ:) and (L voce جَدَادٌ) the *time,* or *season, thereof:* (Ṣ, L:) or the *time,* or *season, of the ripening of the fruit* of palm-trees. (M, Ḳ.) ═ صَرَامِ : see the next paragraph, in two places.

صَرَامِ : see صَارِمٌ. ═ Also The *last milk* [*remaining in the udder*] *after what is termed* التَّغْرِيز [which is variously explained (see 2 in art. غرز), in the CḲ and in one of my copies of the Ṣ erroneously written التَّغْزِير,] *which a man draws when in need of it.* (Ṣ, Ḳ.*) Bishr says,

أَلَا أَبْلِغْ بَنِى سَعْدٍ رَسُولًا ✱ وَمَوْلَاهُمْ فَقَدْ حُلِبَتْ صَرَامِ

[*Now deliver thou to Benoo-Saad a message, and to their chief,* that *the last milk in the udder has been drawn*]: (Ṣ:) the last two words [the latter of which is written in the CḲ ↓ صِرَامِ] are a prov., meaning † *the excuse has reached its uttermost:* (Ṣ, Ḳ:) thus says AO: (Ṣ:) IB says that صَرَامِ in the saying of Bishr means *the she-camel that is termed* ↓ الصَّرْمَآءُ, *that has no milk;* [i. e. that the phrase means *the she-camel that has now no milk has been milked;*] and that he makes it a proper name; and that he [also] means thereby the latter of the two senses here following. (TA.) — الصَّرَامِ is also one of the names for *War,* or *battle;* (Aṣ, Ṣ, Ḳ;*) and so ↓ صَرَامِ, [indecl.,] like قَطَامِ: (Ḳ:) and one of the names for *calamity,* or *misfortune.* (Aṣ, Ṣ, Ḳ.* [See also صَيْرُومٌ.])

صِرَامٌ : see صَرَامٌ. — Sometimes it is applied to signify *Palm-trees* themselves; because the fruit is cut off: so in a trad. (TA.)

صَرُومٌ : see صَارِمٌ, in two places. — Also a she-camel *that will not come to the watering-trough to drink until it is left to her unoccupied;* (Ḳ, TA;) *cutting herself off from the other camels.* (TA.)

صَرِيمٌ *i. q.* ↓ مَصْرُومٌ, (M, Mṣb,) *Cut; cut through;* or *cut off,* or *severed:* (Ṣ, Mṣb, Ḳ:) and *having the fruit cut off;* syn. مَجْدُود; (Ṣ, Ḳ;) applied to palm-trees (نَخْل). (M.) And the former, A *heap* (كُدْس) of corn or the like *that has been cut,* or *of which the produce has been cut off;* syn. ↓ مَصْرُومٌ. (M, TA.) And *Whose ear has been cut off entirely* (الَّذِى صُرِمَتْ أُذُنُهُ): pl. صُرُمٌ. (TA. [See also the fem., with ة, voce بَحِيرَة, where the pl. is said to be صُرُمٌ.]) — [Applied to the lungs, it means properly *Burst asunder.* Hence the saying,] جَآءَ صَرِيمَ سَحْرٍ [so in copies of the Ḳ, accord. the TA سُحْرٍ, but correctly either سَحْرٍ or سُحْرٍ q. v., in the CḲ بادٍ and صَرِيمٌ, which last word is obviously wrong,] meaning ‡ *He came disappointed of attaining what he desired,* or *sought, and in a state of despair.* (Ḳ, TA.) And هُوَ صَرِيمُ سَحْرٍ عَلَى هٰذَا الأَمْرِ [i. e. صَرِيمُ سَحْرٍ or سَحَرٍ] ‡ *He is wearied and eager for this thing,* or *affair.* (TA.) — Also † An affair *decided, determined,* or *resolved, upon.* (M, TA.) — Used as a subst., see صَرِيمَةٌ, in two places. — Also † The *daybreak,* or *dawn;* (Ṣ, M, Ḳ;) because cut off from the night; (M;) as also ↓ صَرِيمَةٌ: (Ṣ:) and the *night;* (ISk, M, Ḳ;) because cut off from the day; (M;) or the *dark night:* (Ṣ:) thus having two contr. meanings: (Ṣ, Ḳ:) and *a portion thereof;* (Th, M, Ḳ;) i. e., *of the night;* (TA;) as also ↓ صَرِيمَةٌ: (M, Ḳ:) and صَرِيمَا اللَّيْلِ *the first and last parts,* or *beginning and end, of the night.* (TA.) The phrase in the Ḳur [lxviii. 20] فَأَصْبَحَتْ كَالصَّرِيمِ means [*And it became in the morning*] *burnt up and black like the night:* (Ṣ, M, Bḍ, TA:) or *like the dark night,* being burnt up: (Er-Rághib, TA:) or *like the black night:* (Ḳatádeh, TA:) or *like the day,* by its whiteness from excessive dryness: (Bḍ:) or *like that garden of which the fruits have been cut off:* (Bḍ, TA:*) or *like the sands* [that are termed صَرِيم (see صَرِيمَةٌ)]: (Bḍ:) or the meaning of صَرِيم in this instance is that which here next follows. (TA.) — *Black land, that does not give growth to anything.* (Ḳ.) — And *A piece of wood,* or *stick, which is placed across upon the mouth of a kid,* (M, Ḳ,) or *of a young weaned camel, and then tied to his head,* (M,) *in order that he may not suck.* (M, Ḳ.) ═ See also صَارِمٌ.

صَرَامَةٌ ‡ A man (TA) *who follows his own opinion, cutting himself off from consultation with others:* (M, TA:) or *who acts with penetrative energy,* or *vigorousness and effectiveness, in the performing of his affairs:* an inf. n. used as an epithet. (TA.)

صُرَامَةٌ *What is cut off* [*of the fruit*] *of palm-trees.* (Lḥ, M.)

صَرِيمَةٌ Land (أَرْض) *of which the seed-produce has been reaped:* (Ṣ, Ḳ:) of the measure فَعِيلَةٌ in the sense of the measure مَفْعُولَةٌ. (TA.) — And *A portion,* (Ṣ, M, Ḳ,) or *large portion,* (TA,) *detached from the main aggregate, of sand;* (Ṣ, M, Ḳ;) as also ↓ صَرِيمٌ: (M, Ḳ:) [or the latter is a coll. gen. n., being used in a pl. sense:] one says أَفْعَى صَرِيمَةٍ (Ṣ) or ↓ صَرِيمٍ (Ḳ) [*A viper of a detached sand-heap* or *of detached sand-heaps*]; like as one says حَيَّةُ خَلٍّ. (Ṣ in art. خل.) — And *A group,* or *an assemblage,* (Ṣ,) or *a detached number,* (M,) of the trees called غَضًا, and سَلَم, (Ṣ, M,) and أَرْطًى, and of palm-trees; and likewise ↓ صِرْمَةٌ, of أَرْطًى, and of سَمُر. (M.) — See also صَرِيمٌ, in two places. ═ Also † *Decision,* or *determination,* (Ṣ, M, Ḳ, TA,) عَلَى شَىْءٍ [*to do a thing*]: (Ṣ, TA:) and the *deciding of an affair,* (M, Ḳ, TA,) and the *firm,* or *sound, execution thereof:* (TA:) or *an object of want upon accomplishment of which one has decided,* or *determined;* as also عَزِيمَةٌ: (AHeyth, TA:) pl. صَرَائِمُ. (TA.) One says, هُوَ مَاضِى الصَّرِيمَةِ and الصَّرَائِمِ [*He is effective of decision* &c. and *of decisions* &c.]. (TA.) — See also صُرْمٌ.

صُرَيْمَةٌ *A detached number* [or *a small detached number,* for it is app. dim. of صِرْمَةٌ,] *of camels.* (TA.)

صَرَّامٌ: see صَارِمٌ. — Also *A preparer,* or *seller, of* صَرْم, (MA,) whence it is derived, (Mgh,) i. e. *skin,* or *leather:* (MA:) or it signifies as expl. voce صَرْم, last sentence. (TA.)

صَارِمٌ *Cutting; cutting through;* or *cutting off,* or *severing;* and Sb says that ↓ صَرِيمٌ is used in the same sense, like as ضَرِيبٌ in the phrase ضَرِيبُ قِدَاحٍ is used in the sense of ضَارِبٌ. (M.) إِنْ كُنْتُمْ صَارِمِينَ, in the Ḳur [lxviii. 22], means *If ye be deciding,* or *determining, upon the cutting off of the fruit of the palm-trees.* (TA.) — And † A man *cutting,* or *severing, his bond of union;* or one *who cuts,* or *severs, that bond;* and so [but in an intensive sense] ↓ صَرَّامٌ and ↓ صَرُومٌ; (M;) or this last signifies, (M, Ḳ,) as also ↓ صُرَامٌ, (Ḳ,) *having strength to cut,* or *sever,* (M, Ḳ,) *the bond of his union.* (M.) — Also, applied to a sword, (Ṣ, M, Mṣb, Ḳ,) and [in an intensive sense] ↓ صَرُومٌ, (M, Ḳ,) *Sharp,* (Ṣ, M, Mṣb, Ḳ,) *and not bending:* (M:) pl. of the former صَوَارِمُ. (TA.) — And the former, (Ṣ, M, Ḳ, TA,) applied to a man, (Ṣ, M, TA,) as being likened to a sword, (TA,) ‡ *Hardy, strong,* or *sturdy,* (Ṣ, TA,) or *sharp, penetrating,* or *vigorous and effective,* (M, Ḳ, TA,) *and courageous.* (Ṣ, M, Ḳ, TA.) — And الصَّارِمُ ‡ *The lion.* (Ḳ, TA.)

صَيْرَمٌ *A calamity* (Ḳ, TA) *that extirpates everything.* (TA. [See also صُرَامٌ, last sentence.]) — Also *Firm,* or *sound, of judgment.* (Ḳ.) — And i. q. وَجْبَةٌ, (Ṣ, M, Ḳ,) like صَيْلَمٌ, (TA,) i. e. *An eating once in the day:* (M, Ḳ,* TA:*) or, accord. to Yaạḳoob, *an eating at the time* [*of morning*] *called* الضُّحَى (M, TA) [*and not again*] *to the like time of the morrow:* (TA:) one says, فُلَانٌ يَأْكُلُ الصَّيْرَمَ (Ṣ, M,* Ḳ*) i. e. [*Such a one eats*] *once* (Ḳ, TA) *in the day:* but AḤát says, I asked El-Aṣma'ee respecting the بَزْمَة and the صَيْرَم, and he said, I know it not: this is the language of the devil. (TA.)

أَصْرَمُ A man *having the extremity of his ear cut off.* (Mgh.) — See also مُصْرِمٌ. — Also [the fem.] صَرْمَآءُ A she-camel *having little milk;* (M, Ḳ;) because her abundance of milk has become cut off: (M:) pl. صُرْمٌ. (Ḳ.) See also صُرَامٌ. [In the Ḥam, p. 230, it is implied that it signifies A she-camel such as is termed ↓ مُصَرَّمَةٌ as meaning *whose* أَخْلَاف (or *teats*) *have been cut off:* for it is there said that the poet 'Orweh has applied the term صَرْمَآء to † *a cooking-pot,* likening it to the she-camel termed مُصَرَّمَةٌ meaning as expl. above.] — Also, (Ṣ, Ḳ,) or فَلَاةٌ صَرْمَآءُ, (M,) *A desert in which is no water.* (Ṣ, M, Ḳ. [See also one of the explanations of the dual, here following.]) — الأَصْرَمَانِ signifies *The wolf and the crow;* (ISk, Ṣ, M, Ḳ;) because of their separating themselves (ISk, Ṣ, M) from mankind: (ISk, Ṣ:) and *the* [*bird called*] صُرَد *and the crow:* and *the night and the day;* (Ḳ, TA;) because each is cut off from the other. (TA.) El-Marrár says,

عَلَى صَرْمَآءَ فِيهَا أَصْرَمَاهَا •
وَخِرِّيتُ الفَلَاةِ بِهَا مَلِيلُ •

[*Upon a waterless desert, in which are its wolf and crow, and in which the skilful guide of the desert is burned by the sun*]. (ISk, Ṣ, M.) And تَرَكْتُهُ بِوَحْشِ الأَصْرَمَيْنِ is a saying mentioned by Lḥ, but not expl. by him: (M, TA:) ISd says, (TA,) in my opinion it means, [*I left him in*] *the desert,* or *waterless desert:* (M, TA:) or, accord. to Z, *in a desert,* or *waterless desert, in which was nothing but the wolf and the crow.* (TA.)

مَصْرِمٌ *A narrow place, that quickly flows with water:* (Ḳ, TA:) so called because the flow of water is quickly cut off from it. (TA.)

مُصْرِمٌ *A possessor of a* صِرْمَة *of camels.* (TA.) — And [hence], as also ↓ أَصْرَمُ, (M, Ḳ,) *Having little property:* (M:) or *poor,* [*and*] *having a numerous household,* or *family.* (Ḳ.) One says, كَلَأٌ تَيْجَعُ مِنْهُ كَبِدُ المُصْرِمِ [*Herbage by reason of which the liver of him who has little property is pained*]; i. e., abundant, so that when he who has little property sees it, he grieves that he has not many camels which he may pasture upon it. (M.)

مِصْرَمٌ The *curved knife of the parer of spindles.* (Ṣ, MA, Ḳ.)

مُصَرَّمَةٌ A she-camel *whose* [*fore* or *hind*] *pair of teats have been cut off,* (Ṣ, M, Ḳ,) *in order that the* إِحْلِيل [or *orifice through which the milk passes forth from the udder* of each teat] *may dry up and the milk not issue, for the purpose of giving greater strength to her:* and (AA used to say, Ṣ) *this is sometimes in consequence of the stoppage of the milk, something having happened to the udder, for which it is cauterized, and her milk stops,* (Ṣ, Ḳ,) *no milk ever issuing from the udder:* (Ṣ:) see also صَرْمَآءُ, voce أَصْرَمُ: or مُصَرَّمَةُ الأَطْبَآءِ means a she-camel *treated* (عُولِجَتْ) *so that her milk has stopped.* (Mgh.)

مَصْرُومٌ: see صَرِيمٌ, first and second sentences.

صرى

1. صَرِىَ, (Ṣ, M, Mṣb,) aor. ـَ, (Mṣb,) inf. n. صَرًى, (M, Mṣb,) said of water, *It remained,* or *stagnated, long:* or *it remained long, and became altered* [*for the worse*]: (Ṣ, Mṣb:) or, said of water and of milk, *it remained so that its flavour became altered* [*for the worse*]: (M:) or, said of milk, *it remained undrawn from the udder, so that its flavour became bad,* or *corrupt.* (TA.) And صَرِىَ الدَّمْعُ *The tears collected* [*in the eye*] *and did not run.* (TA.) — [Hence,] صَرِيَتِ النَّاقَةُ, (Fr, M, Mṣb, TA,) aor. as above, (Mṣb,) and so the inf. n.; (M, Mṣb, TA;) but Ibn-Buzurj says صَرَتْ, aor. ـِ; (TA;) *The she-camel's milk became collected in her udder;* (M, Mṣb, TA;) as also ↓ أَصْرَتْ. (M, TA.) — And صَرِىَ فِى يَدِهِ, (Ṣ, M, IḲṭṭ, TA,) with kesr; (Ṣ, TA;) or صَرَى فِى يَدِهِ; (thus accord. to the Ḳ;) *He* (a man) *remained in his hand, as a pledge,* (Ṣ, M, Ḳ, TA,) *held in custody.* (Ṣ, Ḳ, TA.) — And صرى [thus written without any syll. sign, app. صَرِىَ,] i. q. اِنْقَطَعَ [*It,* or *he, became cut off, cut short,* or *stopped;* &c.: quasi-pass. of صَرَاهُ in one of the senses of the latter]: from IAạr. (TA.) — صَرَاهُ, (IḲṭṭ, Mṣb, TA,) aor. ـِ, (Mṣb,) inf. n. صَرْىٌ, (IḲṭṭ, Mṣb, TA,) *He confined it,* namely, water, *in a resting-place* or *a vessel;* and in like manner, milk, and tears: (IḲṭṭ, TA:) or *he collected it,* namely, water, *and it remained long and became altered* [*for the worse*], or *remained* or *stagnated long;* and in like manner, but in an intensive sense, ↓ صَرَّاهُ. (Mṣb.) One says also of cows [and the like], تَصْرِى اللَّبَنَ فِى ضُرُوعِهِنَّ *They confine and collect the milk in their udders.* (TA.) And [of a man] one says, صَرَى المَآءَ فِى ظَهْرِهِ زَمَانًا *He retained the* ماء [i. e. *sperma*] *in his back a long time,* (Ṣ, M, Ḳ,*) *by abstaining from sexual intercourse.* (M, Ḳ.) — [Hence,] صَرَيْتُهَا, (M, Mṣb,) aor. ـِ, inf. n. صَرْىٌ; (Mṣb;) and ↓ صَرَّيْتُهَا, (Ṣ, M, Mṣb,) inf. n. تَصْرِيَةٌ, (Ṣ, Mṣb,) but the latter verb has an intensive meaning; (Mṣb;) and ↓ أَصْرَيْتُهَا; (M;) namely, a ewe or she-goat, (Ṣ,) or a she-camel, (M, Mṣb,) and any other milch animal, (M,) *I caused the milk to collect in her udder,* (Ṣ, M, Mṣb,) *by abstaining from milking her for some days.* (Ṣ, M.) — Also, i. e. صَرَاهُ, (M, Ḳ,) aor. ـِ, (Ḳ,) inf. n. صَرْىٌ, (M,) i. q. قَطَعَهُ [*He cut it off, cut it short,* or *stopped it;* &c.]; (M, Ḳ;) namely, a thing. (M.) You say, صَرَى بَوْلَهُ, inf. n. as above, meaning قَطَعَهُ [*He,* or *it, cut short,* or *stopped, his urine*]. (Ṣ.) And صَرَيْتُ المَآءَ [app. *I cut short,* or *stopped, the drawing of the water;* for it is expl. as said] إِذَا ٱسْتَقَيْتَ ثُمَّ قَطَعْتَ. (Ṣ.) And مَا يَصْرِيكَ مِنِّى أَىْ عَبْدِى, occurring in a trad., means *What cuts short* (يَقْطَعُ) *thine asking of Me* [*O my servant*]? (TA.) — And i. q. دَفَعَهُ [*He repelled it*]. (M, Ḳ.) One says, صَرَى ٱللّٰهُ عَنْهُ شَرَّهُ i. e. دَفَعَ [*God repelled,* or *may God repel, from him his,* or *its, evil,* or *mischief*]. (Ṣ.) — And i. q. مَنَعَهُ [*He prevented it,* &c.]. (Ṣ, M, Ḳ.) Dhu-r-Rummeh says,

وَوَدَّعْنَ مُشْتَاقًا أَصَبْنَ فُؤَادَهُ •
هَوَاهُنَّ إِنْ لَمْ يَصْرِهِ ٱللّٰهُ قَاتِلُهُ •

[*And they bade farewell to one affected with desire, whose heart they had smitten; the love of them, if God had not prevented it, had been his slayer*]. (Ṣ. [But this verse may be well rendered as an ex. of صَرَاهُ in the sense next following, which is also a meaning of مَنَعَهُ: in the M, it is cited as an ex. of صَرَاهُ in the sense of دَفَعَهُ.]) — Said of God, (M,) *He protected, defended, guarded,* or *preserved, him:* (M, Ḳ:) or (M) *He saved him* (M, Ḳ) *from destruction,* or *perdition:* (Ḳ:) or (M) *He sufficed him:* (M, Ḳ:) or *He aided him.* (TA.) — صَرَى بَيْنَهُمْ, (Ḳ,) or صَرَى مَا بَيْنَهُمْ, (Ṣ, M,) *He decided* [*between them,* or *the case between them*]; (Ṣ, Ḳ;) namely, persons who had applied to him as a judge: (Ṣ:) or *he rectified,* or *adjusted, the case between them.* (M.) ═ صَرَى also signifies عَطَفَ [*He bent,* or *inclined*]: (Ḳ, TA:) [app. intrans., or trans. by means of بِ, for] a poet uses the phrase صَرَيْنَ بِالأَعْنَاقِ [*They bent,* or *inclined, with the necks*]. (TA.) [But it is said in the TḲ that صَرَاهُ means عَطَفَهُ *He bent,* or *inclined, it.*] Accord. to Ibn-Buzurj, صَرَتِ النَّاقَةُ عُنُقَهَا means *The she-camel raised her neck by reason of the heaviness of the burden.* (TA.) ═ Also *He preceded,* or *went before;* syn. تَقَدَّمَ. (IAạr, Ḳ.) [Accord. to the TḲ, one says صَرَى القَوْمَ تَقَدَّمَهُمْ, meaning *He preceded,* or *went before, the people,* or *party.*] — And [*the contr.,* i. e.] *He receded,* or *retreated;* or *became,* or *remained,* or *lagged, behind;* syn. تَأَخَّرَ. (IAạr, Ḳ.) [Accord. to the TḲ, one says صَرَى عَنْهُمْ, meaning *He receded,* or *retreated, from them;* &c.]. — Also *He,* or *it, was,* or *became, high;* syn. عَلَا. (IAạr, Ḳ.) — And *the contr.,* i. e. *He,* or *it, was,* or *became, low;* syn. سَفُلَ. (IAạr, Ḳ.)

2: see 1, former half, in two places.

4: see 1, former half, in two places. — اصرى also signifies *He sold a ewe* or *she-goat,* (Ḳ, TA,) or *a she-camel,* (TA,) *whose milk had been caused to collect in her udder in consequence of her not having been milked for some days; such as is termed* مُصَرَّاةٌ. (Ḳ, TA.)

8. اِصْدَرَاهُ *i. q.* اِزْدَرَاهُ [the د in each being substituted for ت]: see the latter, in art. زرى.

صَرًى, (Ṣ, M, Mṣb, Ḳ,) an inf. n. used as an epithet, (Mṣb,) and ▼ صِرًى, (Ṣ, M, Ḳ,) [and Freytag adds ▼ صُرًى, as from the Ḳ, in which I do not find it,] Water *remaining,* or *stagnating, long,* accord. to Fr; (Ṣ;) or *that has remained,* or *stagnated, long:* (Mṣb:) or water *remaining long,* (Ḳ,) or *that has remained long, and become altered* [*for the worse*], (Ṣ, M, Mṣb,) accord. to AA. (Ṣ.) And the first, (M, Ḳ,) an inf. n. used as an epithet, (TA,) Milk *that has remained* (M, Ḳ) *long* (Ḳ) *so that its flavour has become altered* [*for the worse*]; (M, Ḳ;) as also ▼ صَرٍ, which is in like manner applied to water: (M:) or milk *left* [*long*] *in the udder of the camel, not drawn, so that it becomes salt and windy:* (IAạr, TA:) or milk *drawn in the night from a camel abounding therewith, having a bad and burning flavour.* (Az, TA.) And, (M, Ḳ,) some say, (M,) [used as a subst.,] *A portion remaining* (M, Ḳ) *of milk* (M) *in the udder,* (Ḥam p. 661,) and *of water.* (TA.) And Tears (دَمْعٌ) *that have become collected:* and the sing. [or epithet applied to a single tear (دَمْعَةٌ)] is صَرَاةٌ. (M.) And نُطْفَةٌ صَرَاةٌ [*Sperma of a man*] *altered* [*for the worse*]: and *long retained by him in his back.* (M. [This is also mentioned in the Ṣ, app. in the latter of these senses; the meaning being there only indicated by the context.]) — For the fem., صَرَاةٌ, see also مُصَرَّاةٌ.

صُرًى: see صَرًى, first sentence: — and see also مُصَرَّاةٌ.

صِرًى: see صَرًى, first sentence. — In relation to a she-camel it is Her *being pregnant twelve months, and bringing forth, and then yielding her biestings,* or *having her biestings milked:* mentioned by Az. (TA. [But what is meant by this is, to me, doubtful; for sometimes an inf. n., and sometimes an epithet, and sometimes a subst., is expl. in this manner.])

صَرٍ [part. n. of صَرِىَ]: see صَرًى. — Also A she-camel *whose milk has collected in her udder.* (Mṣb.) [See also مُصَرَّاةٌ.]

صَرْيَةٌ *Milk collected* [*in the udder*]: a poet says,

* وَكُلُّ ذِى صَرْيَةٍ لَا بُدَّ مَحْلُوبُ *

[*And whatever* udder *has milk must be milked*]. (TA.)

صَرْيَآءُ: see مُصَرَّاةٌ.

صَرْيَانُ, applied to a man and to a beast, *Whose* مَآء [i. e. *sperma*] *has collected in his back.* (TA.) ═ Also The [*bird called*] يَمَامَة [n. un. of يَمَام, q. v.]: and the [*bird called*] سَمَامَة [n. un. of سَمَام, q. v.]. (TA.)

صَرَآءٌ *Colocynths* (Ṣ, M, Ḳ, in the CḲ [erroneously] صِرَآءٌ [expressly said in the TA to be with fet-ḥ and medd,]) *when they become yellow;* (Ṣ, M;) as also صَرَايَاتٌ: (so in one of my copies of the Ṣ [in which it is shown to be correct by an ex. in a verse of Suleyk there cited: in the M and TA صَرَايَا, which I think a mistranscription]: in the other of my copies of the Ṣ omitted:) one thereof is termed ▼ صَرَايَةٌ. (Ṣ, M, Ḳ.*) [In the M and Ḳ, صَرَآءٌ is termed pl. of صَرَايَةٌ; but it is properly speaking a coll. gen. n., originally صَرَاىٌ.] — ▼ صَرَايَةٌ also signifies The *water in which colocynths have been steeped.* (M, Ḳ.)

صُرِّىٌّ One *who acts with boldness towards the wife of his father:* (Ḳ, TA:) such was Ibn-Muḳbil. (TA.)

صَرَايَةٌ: see صَرَآءٌ, in two places.

صُرًى: see مُصَرَّاةٌ, below.

صَارٍ [act. part. n. of صَرَى: as such signifying] *Guarding* or *preserving* [&c.], or *a guarder* or *preserver* [&c.]. (TA.) — [Hence,] *A sailor:* (Ṣ, M, Ḳ:) because he guards, or preserves, the ship: (TA:) pl. صُرَّآءٌ (Ṣ, M, Ḳ) and (M, Ḳ) pl. pl. (M) صَرَارِىُّ and صَرَارِيُّونَ. (M, Ḳ. [But see صَرَارِىُّ in art. صر.]) — Also [said to signify] The *transverse piece of wood in the middle of the ship:* (M, Ḳ:) [but] IAth says that it is the دَقَل [i. e. *mast*] *of the ship, which is set up in the middle thereof, and upon which is the* شِرَاع [or *sail:* it is now commonly called ▼ صَارِيَةٌ and سَارِيَةٌ: both of which are also sometimes applied to *a column*]: pl. صَوَارٍ. (TA.)

صَارِيَةٌ A well (رَكِيَّةٌ) *of which the water is old, altered for the worse, and overspread with* [*the green substance termed*] عَرْمَض: (Ḳ,* TA:) mentioned by Az. (TA.) ═ See also صَارٍ, last sentence.

مُصَرَّاةٌ A ewe, or she-goat, *whose milk has been caused to collect in her udder by her not having been milked for some days;* (Ṣ, Ḳ;) as also ▼ صُرًى, like رُبًى; (so in copies of the Ḳ; [but this, if correct, should be mentioned in art. صر, in which the former is also mentioned; accord. to the TA, however, it seems to be ▼ صُرًى, without teshdeed, for it is there said to be like رُبًى;]) both likewise applied to a she-camel, and to a cow; (TA;) and ▼ صَرَاةٌ signifies the same, (Ḳ,) applied to a she-camel and to a ewe or she-goat; (TA;) and so, applied to a she-camel, ▼ صَرْيَآءُ, of which the pl. is صَرَايَا, (M, Ḳ,) an irreg. pl. (M.) [See also صَرٍ.] — Aboo-'Alee, in the Bári', makes it *syn. with* مَصْرُورَةٌ; and so says the Imám Esh-Sháfi'ee; as though originally مُصَرَّرَةٌ: but Suh, in the R, disallows this. (TA.)

صطب

أَصَاطِبُ is the pl., and أُصَيْطِبٌ is the dim., of إِصْطَبْلٌ, q. v. (TA in art. اصطبل.)

أُصْطُبَّةٌ [*i. q.* أُسْطُبَّةٌ, q. v.;] *Tow;* i. e. *what falls from flax in the process of combing.* (M, Ḳ.)

مصطب [app. a mistranscription for ▼ مِصْطَبَةٌ or مُصْطَبَةٌ, like مِسْطَبَةٌ, q. v.,] *A blacksmith's anvil:* so in the T, on the authority of IAar. (TA.)

مِصْطَبَةٌ (so in copies of the Ḳ) [and مَصْطَبَةٌ, like مَسْطَبَةٌ], or مِصْطَبَّةٌ, (so accord. to the TA, with teshdeed to the ب, [but the word is of frequent occurrence and commonly written without teshdeed,]) *A place where people assemble,* (AHeyth, TA,) *like a* دُكَّان, [i. e. *a kind of wide bench, of stone or brick &c., generally built against a wall,*] *for the purpose of sitting upon it:* (AHeyth, Ḳ, TA:) Az heard an Arab of the desert, of the tribe of Fezárah, apply this word to *a square, flat-topped pile of earth, raised for the purpose of passing the night upon it:* (TA:) also, [sometimes, app. in late ages,] *a hospice for strangers;* or *a place in which the poor and the beggars assemble:* (MA, and Ḥar p. 375:) not [originally, or properly,] an Arabic word: (Ḥar ubi suprà:) [see more in art. سطب, for it is a dial. var. of مَسْطَبَةٌ,] of the dial. of Baghdád: (MA:) [the pl. is مَصَاطِبُ.] — See also the next preceding paragraph.

صعب

1. صَعُبَ, (Ṣ, A, MA, Mṣb, Ḳ,) aor. ـُ, (A, Ḳ,) inf. n. صُعُوبَةٌ; (Ṣ, MA, Mṣb, Ḳ;) and ▼ استصعب;

(Ṣ, A, MA, Mṣb, Ḳ;) and ▼ اصعب, (IAạr, Ḳ,) inf. n. إِصْعَابٌ; (IAạr, TA;) *It* (a thing, Mṣb, or an affair, or event, Ṣ, MA, Mṣb, Ḳ) *was*, or *became*, صَعْبٌ, (Ṣ, A, &c.,) i. e. *difficult, hard, hard to be done* or *accomplished, hard to be borne* or *endured*, or *distressing*. (A, MA, Ḳ.) One says, اِسْتَصْعَبَ ▼ عَلَيْهِ الأَمْرُ, (Ṣ, MA, Mṣb,) like صَعُبَ, (Ṣ, Mṣb,) *The affair*, or *event, was*, or *became, difficult*, &c., *to him*. (MA.)

2. صَعَّبَهُ, (Ḳ,) inf. n. تَصْعِيبٌ; (TA;) [and] ▼ اصعبهُ, (A,) inf. n. إِصْعَابٌ; (KL;) and ▼ تَصَعَّبَهُ (Ḳ;) *He made*, or *rendered, it* صَعْب, (A, Ḳ,) i. e. *difficult, hard*, &c. (A, Ḳ, KL.)

4. اصعب: see 1. — Said of a camel, *He was*, or *became*, صَعْب [meaning *refractory*, or *untractable*]: (Ḳ, TA:) [and in like manner one says ▼ استصعب: (see its contr. استصحب:) and ▼ تَصَعَّبَ, which is also said of a man:] and اصعب said of a camel, *he was unridden*, (A, TA,) *and untouched by a rope*. (A.) — Also, said of a man, *His camel was*, or *became, refractory*, or *untractable*. (L, TA.) ═ اصعبهُ: see 2. — Also *He left him* (i. e. a camel) *unridden*, (Ṣ, Ḳ, TA,) *and untouched by a rope, so that he became refractory*, or *untractable*. (Ṣ, Ḳ.) [See مُصْعَبٌ]. — And *He found it* (i. e. an affair, or event, Ṣ, Mṣb, or a thing, Ḳ) *to be* صَعْب [i. e. *difficult, hard*, &c.]; (Ṣ, Mṣb, Ḳ;) as also ▼ استصعبهُ: (Mṣb, Ḳ:) or both signify *he saw it*, or *held it, to be so*. (TA.) [See an ex. of the former in a verse cited voce رَيْثٌ.]

5. تَصَعَّبَ, intrans.: see 4. ═ تصعّبهُ: see 2.

10. استصعب, intrans.: see 1, in two places: — and see also 4. ═ استصعبهُ: see 4.

صَعْبٌ *Difficult, hard, hard to be done* or *accomplished, hard to be borne* or *endured*, or *distressing*; (A, MA, Ḳ;) *contr. of* سَهْلٌ; (Mgh, TA;) as also ▼ صُعْبُوبٌ: (T, O, Ḳ, TA:) pl. of the former صِعَابٌ; (Mṣb;) and of ▼ the latter, صَعَابِيبُ. (T, TA.) One says أَمْرٌ صَعْبٌ *A difficult, hard*, or *distressing, affair* or *event*. (A.) And عَقَبَةٌ صَعْبَةٌ (thus in the A, but in the Mṣb and TA without any syll. signs,) [*A mountain-road*] *difficult, hard*, or *distressing*: (TA:) pl. عِقَابٌ صِعَابٌ (A, Mṣb*) and صَعْبَاتٌ with sukoon [to the ع because the word is an epithet; for if it were a subst., it would be صَعَبَات]. (Mṣb.) [Or عُقْبَةٌ صَعْبَةٌ may perhaps be meant in the TA, i. e. *A difficult, hard*, or *distressing, stage of a journey*.] — Also *Refractory, untractable, incompliant, obstinate*, or *stubborn*; (Ḳ,* TA;) *contr. of* ذَلُولٌ; (Ṣ, A, TA;) applied to a camel, (Ṣ, A,) or to a beast; (TA;) [and to a man;] fem. صَعْبَةٌ, (Ṣ, TA,) which is applied to a woman: (Ṣ:) and the pl. of this is صِعَابٌ, [as of the masc.,] (TA,) and صَعْبَاتٌ, applied to women, with sukoon [to the ع because the word is an epithet]. (Ṣ, TA.) رَكِبَ النَّاسُ الصَّعْبَةَ وَالذَّلُولَ, occurring in a trad. of I'Ab, [lit. *The people rode the refractory and the tractable* she-camel,] means † *the people entered upon difficult and easy affairs*; i. e. they cared not for things, nor were cautious respecting what they said and did. (L, TA.) — [Hence,] الصَّعْبُ *The lion*; (O, Ḳ;) because of his untractableness. (TA.)

صُعْبُوبٌ: see the next preceding paragraph, first sentence, in two places.

صَاعِبٌ Land *containing stones such as fill the hand, and other stones, which is tilled*, or *cultivated*. (Ḳ, TA.)

مُصْعَبٌ *A stallion* [of camels]: (Ṣ, Ḳ:) and a camel, (Ṣ, A,) or a stallion [of camels], (ISk, TA,) *left unridden, and untouched by a rope*, (ISk, Ṣ, A, TA,) *so as to become refractory*, or *untractable*: (Ṣ:) or an *unbroken* camel, *upon whose back nothing is allowed to be put*: (L, TA:) pl. مَصَاعِبُ and مَصَاعِيبُ. (ISk, TA.) — It is also applied as an epithet to a man, (A, Mṣb, TA,) meaning مُسَوَّدٌ [i. e. † *Made a chief* or *lord* &c.]: (TA:) pl. مَصَاعِبُ. (A, Mṣb.) One says, فُلَانٌ مُصْعَبٌ مِنَ المَصَاعِبِ ‡ [*Such a man is one of those who have been made chiefs* or *lords* &c.]; like as one says, قَرْمٌ مِنَ القُرُومِ. (A.)

مُصْعِبٌ A man *whose camel is refractory*, or *untractable*: occurring in a trad. (L, TA.)

صعتر

صَعْتَرٌ *I. q.* سَعْتَرٌ [q. v.]: (Ḳ, and Ṣ and Mṣb in art. سعتر:) *it grows in the country of the Arabs, and is of two kinds*, سُهْلِيٌّ [i. e. *of the plain*] *and* جَبَلِيٌّ [i. e. *of the mountain*]: (AḤn, TA:) *when strewn in a place, it drives away venomous* or *noxious reptiles and the like*, (Ḳ,) *such as serpents and scorpions*. (TA.)

صعد

1. صَعِدَ فِى السُّلَّمِ, (Ṣ, A, Mṣb, Ḳ,) aor. ـَ, (Mṣb, Ḳ,) inf. n. صُعُودٌ (Ṣ, Mṣb, Ḳ) and صَعَدٌ and صُعُدٌ; (Ḥam p. 407;) and ▼ تصعّد, (A,) or اِصَّعَدَ, (L,) inf. n. اِصِّعَادٌ; (Ḳ;) and ▼ تصاعد, (A,) or اِصَّاعَدَ, (L,) inf. n. اِصَّاعُدٌ; (Ḳ;) and ▼ اصطعد; (Ḳ;) *He ascended*, or *went up, the ladder*, or *stair*: (L, Mṣb, Ḳ:) and so the verb is used of ascending a thing similar to a ladder, or stair: but in a case of this kind one should not say اصعد. إِلَى السَّطْحِ (L.) And صَعِدَ السَّطْحَ and (A, Mṣb) *He ascended*, or *ascended to, the flat house-top*. (Mṣb.) And صَعِدَ المَكَانَ, and فِى, and ▼ اصعد, and ▼ صعّد, المَكَانِ, *He ascended the place*, or *upon the place*. (L.) And صَعِدَ ▼ فِى الجَبَلِ, (Ṣ, A, Mṣb, Ḳ,) and عَلَى الجَبَلِ, inf. n. تَصْعِيدٌ; (Ṣ, Ḳ;) and صَعِدَ فِيهِ, a form rarely used, (Mṣb,) disallowed by AZ, (Ṣ, TA,) and said by him to have been unknown, (Ṣ,) or unheard, (Ḳ,) but he afterwards authorized it, and it is also authorized by IAạr and ISk, (TA,) and صَعِدَ الجَبَلَ; (Ṣ in art. دخل; [for صَعِدَ فِى الجَبَلِ, see دَخَلْتُ البَيْتَ;]) and ▼ تصعّد فيه, (MF, from a trad.,) and اِصَّعَّدَ فِيهِ, (AZ,) inf. n. اِصِّعَادٌ; (TA; [app. a mistranscription for اِصَّعُّدٌ; or اِصَّعَّدَ may be a mistranscription for ▼ اِصَّعَدَ, a var. of اِصْطَعَدَ, and its inf. n. is اِصِّعَادٌ;]) *He ascended the mountain*. (Mṣb, Ḳ.) And صعّد ▼ فِى الأَرْضِ *He ascended the land*. (AZ, TA.) One says, طَالَ فِى الأَرْضِ تَصْوِيبِى وَتَصْعِيدِى ▼ [*Long have continued my descending*, or *going down, and my ascending*, or *going up, in the land*]. (A. [There immediately following صَعَّدَ فِى الجَبَلِ, expl. above: see also رَكِبَ مُصَعِّدًا.]) ═ See also 4, last sentence.

2. صعّد, inf. n. تَصْعِيدٌ, as intrans.: see above, in four places. — And see also 4, in four places. ═ صعّدهُ *He made him*, or *caused him, to ascend*, or *mount*; syn. عَلَّاهُ; (Ḳ and TA in art. علو;) and رَقَّاهُ; (TA in art. رقى;) [and so ▼ اصعدهُ; and ▼ استصعدهُ; like as one says in the contr. sense نَزَّلَهُ and أَنْزَلَهُ and اِسْتَنْزَلَهُ.] You say, صعّدهُ جَبَلًا and دَابَّةً [*He made him to ascend*, or *mount, a mountain and a beast*]. (TA in art. علو.) And يُصَعِّدُونَهَا ▼ فِى الجَبَلِ is said with reference to wild bulls or cows [as meaning *They make them to ascend upon the mountain*]. (Ṣ and TA in art. سلع.) — [Hence,] one says also, صَعَّدَ فِىَّ النَّظَرَ وَصَوَّبَهُ, meaning † *He looked at me from head to foot, contemplating me*. (L, from a trad. [And a similar phrase occurs in Ḥar p. 640.]) — [صعّدهُ, inf. n. تَصْعِيدٌ, (the latter as used in the Ḳ voce كَافُورٌ,) also signifies † *He sublimated it*: often occurring in medical books, and used in this sense in the present day.] — And تَصْعِيدٌ signifies also The act of *liquifying, melting*, or *dissolving*. (Ḳ.) ═ See also 4, last sentence.

4. اصعد فِى المَكَانِ: see 1. — [Hence,] اصعد فِى الأَرْضِ *He went through the land towards a land higher than the other* [*from which he came*]: (A, TA:) taken from the saying of Lth, that اصعد, inf. n. إِصْعَادٌ, signifies *He went towards a declivity*, or *a river*, or *a valley, higher than the other* [*from which he came*]. (TA.) And اصعد فِى البِلَادِ *He went up*, or *upwards, through the countries*, or *lands*. (AA, Mṣb.) And اصعد مِنْ بَلَدِ كَذَا إِلَى بَلَدِ كَذَا *He journeyed* [*upwards*] *from such a region*, or *town, to such another region*, or *town*; *from one that was lower to one that was higher*. (Mṣb.) [And hence,] اصعد, inf. n. إِصْعَادٌ, *He journeyed*, or *went, towards Nejd*, and *El-Ḥijáz*, and *El-Yemen*: [or *towards a higher region*:] and انْحَدَرَ signifies "he journeyed, or went, towards El-'Irák, and Syria, and 'Omán:" (ISk, on the authority of 'Omárah:) or the former, *he journeyed*, or *went, towards the Ḳibleh*: and the latter, "he journeyed, or went, towards El-'Irák:" (Aboo-Ṣakhr, T:) or the former, *he came to Mekkeh*; (Ḳ;) but this is a defective explanation: (TA:) and مُصْعَدٌ, also, is used as an inf. n. of this verb; and مُنْحَدَرٌ, as an inf. n. of انحدر: (T, TA:) or اصعد, inf. n. إِصْعَادٌ, *he commenced a journey*, or *went forth*; as from Mekkeh, and from El-Koofeh to Khurásán, and the like: (Fr:) or *he* *commenced a journey, or the like, in any direction:* and انحدر signifies "he returned, from any town or country." (Ibn-'Arafeh.) And اصعد فى البِلَادِ, (Akh, Ṣ, Ḳ,) or فى الأَرْضِ, (Akh accord. to the T,) *He went away,* and *journeyed, through the land,* (Akh, Ṣ, Ḳ,) or *through the countries,* (Akh, T,) *in any direction.* (L.) And اصعدت السَّفِينَةُ, inf. n. إِصْعَادٌ; (L;) or ▼ صَعَّدَت; (A;) *The ship spread her sail, and was borne along by the wind,* (A, L,) *upwards* [app. meaning *up a river or the like*]. (L.) — اصعد فى الوَادِى; (Akh, Ṣ, L, Ḳ;) and ▼ صَعَّدَ فيه, inf. n. تَصْعِيدٌ; (Akh, Ṣ, Mṣb, Ḳ;) and ▼ اِصَّعَّدَ, (Lth,) but this last is disapproved by Az; (TA;) *He descended,* or *went down, into the valley,* (Akh, Ṣ, L, Mṣb, Ḳ,) *from the part whence the torrent comes; not going to the bottom of the valley:* and in like manner, اصعد فى الأَرْضِ *He descended,* or *went down, into the land:* (L:) and ▼ صَعَّدَ فى الجَبَلِ *He descended the mountain;* as well as he ascended it. (IB, L.) Akh cites the following words of 'Abd-Allah Ibn-Hemmám Es-Saloolee,

أُصَعِّدُ ▼ طَوْرًا فِى البِلَادِ وَأُفْرِعُ

(Ṣ, L,) as meaning *I descending,* or *going down, at one time, through the countries, and* [another time] *ascending,* or *going up:* this, says IB, is what induced Akh to explain صعّد as he has done; but it presents no proof, because إِفْرَاعٌ has two contr. significations, that of إِصْعَادٌ and that of اِنْحِدَارٌ: and accord. to AZ, by أُصَعِّدُ the poet means *I ascending,* or *going up,* to high places; and by أُفْرِعُ, the contrary. (L.) — اصعد also signifies *He advanced* towards another. (L.) — And *He went far;* syn. أَبْعَدَ. (Ḥam p. 22.) — And اصعد فى العَدْوِ *He exerted himself vehemently in running.* (L.) — اصعد as trans.: see 2, in two places. — اصعدت *She* (a camel) *became such as is termed* صَعُود [q. v.]. (Ṣ, L, Ḳ.) — And أَصْعَدْتُ النَّاقَةَ, (Ṣ, L, Ḳ,) and ▼ صَعَّدْتُهَا, [probably imperfectly transcribed for ▼ صَعْدَتُهَا,] (L,) *I made the she-camel to be,* or *become, such as is termed* صَعُود. (IAạr, Ṣ, L, Ḳ.)

5. تصعّد, and its var. اِصَّعَّدَ: see 1, in two places: — and see also 4. — تصعّد النَّفَسُ *The breath passed forth with difficulty.* (L.) — تصعّدهُ (Ṣ, A, Ḳ) and ▼ تصاعدهُ (A, Ḳ) *It* (a thing, Ṣ, Ḳ, or an affair, A) *was,* or *became, difficult,* or *distressing, to him; it distressed,* or *afflicted, him:* (A'Obeyd, Ṣ, A, Ḳ:) from صَعُودٌ as signifying "a mountain-road difficult of ascent:" (A'Obeyd:) or from الصَّعُودُ as the name of "a certain mountain in Hell." (TA.)

6. تصاعد, and its var. اِصَّاعَدَ: see 1: — and see also 5.

8. اصطعد, and its var. اِصَّعَدَ: see 1, in two places.

10. استصعدهُ: see 2. — استصعد البَرِيرَ *He plucked* or *gathered, the fruit of the* أَرَاك *to eat.* (TA in art. بر.)

صُعُدٌ; see صُعُدٌ.

صُعُدٌ: see صَعُودٌ, in two places. — عَذَابٌ صَعَدٌ *A vehement, severe, rigorous,* or *grievous, punishment;* (Ṣ, A, Ḳ;) i. e. ذُو صَعَدٍ: (TA:) or *a distressing,* or *an afflicting, punishment,* (Bd and Jel in lxxii. 17,) *that shall overcome the sufferer thereof,* the latter word being an inf. n. used as an epithet. (TA.)

صُعُدٌ an inf. n. of صَعِدَ [q. v.]. (Ḥam p. 407.) [Hence,] ذَهَبَ السَّهْمُ صُعُدًا [*The arrow went upwards*]. (A.) And هٰذَا النَّبَاتُ يَنْمِى صُعُدًا *This plant increases in height.* (Ṣ.) And تَنَفَّسَ صُعُدًا: see صُعَدَآءُ. And ▼ مِنْ صُعُدٍ [used by poetic license for مِنْ صُعُدٍ], said of a thing falling, i. e. *From above; from a higher place.* (Ḥam p. 349.) — Also a pl. of صَعُودٌ: and of صَعِيدٌ. (Ṣ, L, Ḳ.) — صُعُدٌ, thus, with two ḍammehs, is also the name of *A certain tree from which pitch is melted forth.* (L.)

صَعْدَةٌ *A high,* or *an elevated, piece of land* or *ground; contr. of* هَبْطَةٌ. (Mgh in art. هبط.) And صَعْدَةُ is said to be a proper name for *The earth.* (Ḥam p. 22.) — And *A she-ass:* (L, Ḳ:) or *a long-backed she-ass:* (L:) or *long* [*in the back*], applied to a she-ass as an epithet, and therefore the pl. is صَعْدَاتٌ, with the ع quiescent. (Ḥam p. 385.) And بَنَاتُ صَعْدَةَ *Wild asses:* (Ṣ, Ḳ:) said to be so called from صَعْدَةٌ meaning as expl. above; and if this be correct, it is like the appellation بَنَاتُ البَرِّ: (Ḥam p. 22:) or as being likened to the women [or rather woman (as will be shown in what follows)] termed صعدة; and in like manner, أَوْلَادُ صَعْدَةَ: (Ḥar p. 471:) the rel. n. [applied to *a single wild ass*] is ▼ صَاعِدِىٌّ, (Ṣ, L, Ḳ,) irregularly formed: thus in the saying of Aboo-Dhu-eyb,

فَرَمَى فَأَلْحَقَ صَاعِدِيًّا مِطْحَرًا
بِالكَشْحِ فَاشْتَمَلَتْ عَلَيْهِ الأَضْلُعُ

[*And he shot, and made a far-flying arrow to reach a wild ass in the flank, and the ribs enclosed it*]. (Ṣ, L.) — And *A spear,* or *spear-shaft;* syn. قَنَاةٌ: (L:) *a spear-shaft* (قَنَاة) *straight by its growth,* (Ṣ, L, Ḳ,) *not requiring to be straightened:* (Ṣ, L:) and *a kind of* أَلَّة [or *broad-headed dart*], which is *smaller than a* حَرْبَة: (L:) or [simply] *an* أَلَّة: (Ḳ, TA:) [in the CḲ أَلَة: and] in some copies of the Ḳ أَكَمَة, which is a mistranscription: (TA:) pl. صِعَادٌ and صَعَدَاتٌ; (L;) the latter with fet-ḥ to the ع because it is a subst. (Ḥam p. 385.) One says, تَطَاعَنُوا بِالصِّعَادِ, i. e. [*They thrust,* or *pierced, one another*] *with the spears.* (A.) — [Hence,] ‡ جَارِيَةٌ صَعْدَةٌ *A girl,* or *young woman, straight in figure,* (A, L,) *like a spear, or spear-shaft:* (L:) pl. جَوَارٍ صَعْدَاتٌ, the latter word with the ع quiescent, (A, L,) because it is an epithet. (L.)

صُعْدَةٌ: see صَعِيدٌ, last sentence but one.

صُعَدَآءُ: see صَعُودٌ, in two places.

صُعَدَآءُ *A sigh,* or *sighing; a breathing with an expression of pain, grief,* or *sorrow:* or *with difficulty:* (L:) *a long breathing:* (Ḳ:) or *a prolonged breathing:* (Ṣ:) or *a loud breathing:* (A:) accord. to some, *a breathing emitted upwards.* (L.) You say, تَنَفَّسَ الصُّعَدَآءَ, (L,) or تنفّس صُعَدَآءَ, (A,) and ▼ تنفّس صُعُدًا, (L,) *He sighed; uttered a sigh* or *sighing;* or *breathed with an expression of pain, grief,* or *sorrow:* (L:) [or *uttered a prolonged breathing:*] or *breathed loudly.* (A.) — [Hence,] فُلَانٌ يَتْبَعُ صُعَدَآءَهُ, (A,) or يَتَتَبَّعُ صُعَدَآءَهُ, (L, [in which the noun is evidently mistranscribed,]) ‡ *Such a one raises his head, and does not stoop it, by reason of pride:* (A:) or *does not raise his head nor stoop it.* (L. [The former explanation seems to be the right.]) — See also صَعُودٌ, in four places.

صُعْدُدٌ: see the next paragraph.

صَعُودٌ *An acclivity; contr. of* هَبُوطٌ, (Ṣ, L, Ḳ,) or *of* حَدُورٌ; (Mṣb;) and ▼ صَعَدٌ is [syn. therewith, being] *contr. of* صَبَبٌ: (L:) pl. صَعَائِدُ and صُعُدٌ. (Ṣ, Ḳ.) *An ascending road:* of the fem. gender: pl. [of pauc.] أَصْعِدَةٌ and [of mult.] صُعُدٌ. (L.) *A mountain-road difficult of ascent;* (Ṣ, A, L, Ḳ;) as also ▼ صَعُودَآءُ, (L, Ḳ,) and ▼ صُعَدَآءُ: (L in art. كأد:) *a difficult place of ascent.* (L in that art.) [Hence,] الصَّعُودُ *A certain mountain in Hell,* (L, Ḳ, MF,) *consisting of fire, which the unbeliever will ascend during a period of seventy years, after which he will fall down it, and thus he will do for ever:* (MF:) *it is of one live coal; the unbeliever will be compelled to ascend it, and will be beaten with* مَقَامِع [pl. of مِقْمَعَةٌ, q. v.]; *and whenever he puts his leg upon it, it will dissolve as high as the lower part of his hip, and will then become replaced whole and sound.* (L.) — [Hence also,] ‡ *Difficulty, grievousness, distress, affliction,* or *trouble;* (A, L, Mṣb;) as also ▼ صَعَدٌ (L) and ▼ صُعَدَآءُ, (Ḳ,) or ▼ صُعَدَآءُ, (L,) and ▼ صُعْدُدٌ. (Ḳ.) You say, أَرْهَقْتُهُ صَعُودًا, ‡ *I made him,* or *constrained him, to do a difficult, grievous, distressing, afflicting,* or *troublesome, thing:* (A:) or *I imposed upon him such a punishment.* (L.) And ▼ لِلسِّيَادَةِ صُعَدَآءُ [or ▼ صُعَدَآءُ? (see above)] ‡ *There is a difficult,* or *distressing, ascent to lordship,* or *mastery.* (A.) And أَكَمَةٌ ▼ ذَاتُ صُعَدَآءَ † *A hill difficult to ascend.* (L.) — Also A she-camel *that brings forth a young one imperfectly formed,* (Aṣ, Ṣ, Ḳ,) *after six or seven months,* (Aṣ,) *and is made to take an affection to the young one of the preceding year,* (Aṣ, Ṣ,) or *and takes an affection to the young one of the preceding year:* (Ḳ:) or *a she-camel whose young one dies, and which returns to her former young one, and yields it milk:* when she does this, her milk is the sweeter: (Lth:) or *a she-camel that brings forth her young one after its hair has grown, and then takes an affection to her former young one, or to the young one of another:* pl. صَعَائِدُ and صُعُدٌ; but this latter pl. is disapproved by Sb. (L.)

صَعِيدٌ *High,* or *elevated, land* or *ground:* or *high,* or *elevated, land* or *ground, above such as is low,* or *depressed:* or *even land* or *ground:*

(L:) or *even land* or *ground, without any trees:* (Lth, L:) or a [*desert such as is termed*] صَحْرَآء: (A:) or the *surface of the earth;* (Th, Zj, Ṣ, A, Mṣb, Ḳ;) *whether it be dust* or *earth,* or *otherwise:* Zj says, I know not any difference of opinion among the lexicologists on this point: (Mṣb:) [such is said to be its meaning in the Ḳur iv. 46 and v. 9; and therefore in performing the act termed التَّيَمُّم,] a man should strike his hands upon the surface of the earth, and not care whether there be in that place dust or not: (Zj:) [hence] one says, طَارَ صِيتُكَ فِى القَرِيبِ وَالبَعِيدِ وَبَلَغَ مُنْتَهَى الصَّعِيدِ [*Thy fame has flown through the near and the distant* regions, *and reached the extremity of the surface of the earth*]: (A:) or صَعِيدٌ signifies the *earth,* or *ground,* itself; (IAar, A, L;) as in the saying عَلَيْكَ بِالصَّعِيدِ, meaning *Sit thou upon the earth,* or *ground:* (A:) or *good earth* or *land:* or *earth,* or *land, not mixed with sand nor with salt soil:* (L:) or *dust,* or *earth,* (Fr, Ṣ, L, Mṣb, Ḳ,) *such as is pure, upon the surface of the ground* or *that has come forth from within it;* thus accord. to Az in the Ḳur iv. 46 and v. 9, in the opinion of most of the learned: (Mṣb:) or only *earth containing dust;* not applied to a coarse, nor to a fine, بَطْحَآء; nor to a coarse كَثِيب; although it be mixed with dust: (Esh-Sháfi'ee, L:) pl. صُعُدٌ and صُعُدَاتٌ, (Ṣ, L, Ḳ,) the latter a pl. pl. (Mṣb, TA.) — And *A wide,* or *an ample, place.* (L.) — And *A road,* (L, Mṣb, Ḳ,) whether wide or narrow: (L:) pls. as above (L, Mṣb) and صُعْدَانٌ. (L.) It is said in a trad., إِيَّاكُمْ وَالقُعُودَ بِالصُّعُدَاتِ إِلَّا مَنْ أَدَّى حَقَّهَا, i. e. *Beware ye of sitting in,* or *by, the roads, save he who performs the duty relating thereto:* [respecting which duty see طَرِيقٌ:] صُعُدَات is here the pl. of صُعُدٌ, which is pl. of صَعِيدٌ: or, as some say, it is pl. of ♦ صُعْدَةٌ, which signifies *A court,* or *an open space, before the door of a house,* and the *place through which men pass in front of it.* (L.) — Also *A grave.* (AA, Mṭr, L, Ḳ.)

إِنَّهَا لَفِى صَعِيدَةِ بَازِلَيْهَا ‡ *Verily she* (a camel) *is near to cutting her two teeth called the* بَازِلَانِ. (L, TA.)

صَعُودَآءُ: see صَعُودٌ.

صُعَادِيَّةٌ, applied to a she-camel, *Tall,* or *long;* syn. طَوِيلَةٌ. (Ḳ.)

صَعَّادٌ عَلَى الجِبَالِ One *who climbs the mountains much* or *often.* (TA in art. رقى.)

صَاعِدٌ [*Ascending,* &c.]. — [Hence,] عُنُقٌ صَاعِدٌ ‡ *A tall neck.* (A, L.) — And شَرَفٌ صَاعِدٌ ‡ [*High nobility*]. (A.) — [Hence also,] one says, بَلَغَ كَذَا فَصَاعِدًا ‡ *It reached such an amount and upwards:* (Ḳ, TA:) and أَخَذْتُهُ بِدِرْهَمٍ فَصَاعِدًا ‡ *I got it for a dirhem and upwards;* an elliptical phrase, for أَخَذْتُهُ بِدِرْهَمٍ فَزَادَ الثَّمَنُ صَاعِدًا *I got it for a dirhem and the price increased upwards,* or ذَهَبَ صَاعِدًا *went upwards:* you may not say وَصَاعِدًا, because you do not mean to tell that the dirhem with something more made the price, as when you say بِدِرْهَمٍ وَزِيَادَةٍ; but you mention the lowest price that you offered, and mean that you then offered more and more. (Ṣb, L.) And قَرَأَ فَاتِحَةَ الكِتَابِ فَصَاعِدًا † *He read the opening chapter of the Book* [i. e. of the Ḳur-án] *and more* is a phrase of the same kind. (L.)

صَاعِدِىٌّ rel. n. of صَعْدَةٌ, q. v.

مَصْعَدٌ [*A place of ascent:* pl. مَصَاعِدُ]. One says رُتْبَةٌ بَعِيدَةُ المَصْعَدِ and المَصَاعِدِ ‡ [meaning *A station,* or *post of honour, to which the ascent* and *ascents* (lit. *the place* and *places of ascent*) *is,* and *are, distant*]. (A.)

مُصْعَنْدٌ *A high* mountain. (L.) And رَكَبٌ مُصْعَنْدٌ, or ♦ مُصْعَنْفِدٌ, *A high,* or *prominent, pubes.* (L.) — Also *Beverage,* or *wine,* (Ḳ,) and *vinegar,* (TA,) *prepared with pains by means of fire,* or *well boiled,* (عُولِجَ بِالنَّارِ, Ḳ, TA,) *until it becomes altered in flavour and colour.* (TA.)

مُصْعَنْفِدٌ: see the next preceding paragraph.

مِصْعَادٌ The [*rope called*] حَابُول, [*made in the form of a hoop,*] *by means of which a man ascends palm-trees.* (Ḳ,* TA.) — [And *A scaling-ladder.* — And, accord. to Freytag, *A chain with which the feet of captives are shackled, to prevent their taking wide steps:* — and *A chain upon the feet of women, serving as an ornament:* in relation to which he refers to Schröder de vestitu mulierum Hebr. p. 123.]

صعر

1. صَعِرَ, aor. ـَ, (Mṣb, Ḳ,) inf. n. صَعَرٌ; (Ṣ, A, Mgh, Mṣb, Ḳ;) and ♦ تصعّر; (A, Ḳ;) *He had a wryness, or distortion, in the cheek,* (Ṣ,) or *in the face,* (A, Ḳ,) or *in either side* [*thereof*], (Ḳ,) or *in the neck,* (Lth, A, Mgh, Mṣb,) *by reason of pride,* (A,) *with a turning of the face on one side:* (Lth, Mgh, Mṣb:) [see also 5:] or *he* (a camel) *had a disorder by reason of which he twisted his neck,* (Ḳ,) *and distorted it.* (TA.) You say, فِى عُنُقِهِ وَخَدِّهِ صَعَرٌ *In his neck, and in his cheek, is a wryness,* or *distortion, arising from pride.* (A.) And لَأُقِيمَنَّ صَعَرَكَ [*I will assuredly straighten thy wryness,* or *distortion, of the neck,* or *cheek*]. (A.) And أَصَابَ البَعِيرَ صَعَرٌ *A disease which made him to twist his neck befell the camel.* (Mgh, TA.) — [See also صَعَرٌ below.] — Also صَعَرَ, (TḲ,) inf. n. صَعْرٌ, (Ḳ, TḲ,) *He* (a man, TḲ) *ate* صَعَارِير [pl. of صُعْرُورٌ, q. v.], (Ḳ,* TḲ,) i. e., *gum.* (TA.)

2. صعّره *He caused him to have a wryness,* or *distortion, in the neck, and a turning of the face on one side, by something smiting* or *befalling him.* (Mṣb.) — صعّر خَدَّهُ, (inf. n. تَصْعِيرٌ, Ḳ,) and ♦ صاعره, (Ṣ, A, Mṣb, Ḳ,) and ♦ اصعره, (Ḳ,) *He turned away his cheek* (Ṣ, A, Mṣb) *from the people,* (Mṣb,) *by reason of pride* (Ṣ, A, Mṣb) *and dislike;* (Ṣ, Mṣb;) *he turned away his cheek from looking towards the people, by reason of contempt arising from pride.* (Ḳ.) It is said in the Ḳur [xxxi. 17], وَلَا تُصَعِّرْ خَدَّكَ لِلنَّاسِ, (Mgh, TA,) and accord. to one reading, ♦ لَا تُصَاعِرْ, (TA,) meaning, *And turn thou not away from people through pride.* (Fr, Aboo-Is-ḥáḳ, Mgh.) [See also 5.]

3 and 4: see 2; the former in two places.

5. تصعّر and ♦ تصاعر *He distorted his cheek by reason of pride.* (Ṣgh, TA.) See also 1.

6: see what next precedes.

9. اصعرّت الإِبِلُ *The camels went a vehement pace:* or *became dispersed.* (TA.)

R. Q. 1. صَعْرَرَهُ, (Ṣ, Ḳ,) inf. n. صَعْرَرَةٌ, (TA,) *He made it round:* (Ṣ, Ḳ:) *he rolled it.* (TA.) [See مُصَعْرَرٌ.]

R. Q. 2. تَصَعْرَرَ *It became round:* (Ṣ, Ḳ:) *it rolled.* (TA.)

R. Q. 3. اِصْعَنْرَرَ, and اِصْعَرَّرَ, (Ḳ,) in which latter the ن is incorporated into the ر, (TA,) *He* (being beaten or struck) *writhed,* (TA,) *and turned round by reason of pain, in his place, and became contracted.* (Ḳ, TA.)

صَعَرٌ inf. n. of 1 [q. v.]. — The saying فِى الصَّعَرِ الدِّيَةُ is expl. as meaning *In* [the case of] *the distorting of the face* [*the whole bloodwit* shall be exacted: as though the verb of which صَعَرٌ is the inf. n. were trans.; but this is obviously a loose rendering]. (Mgh.) — صَعَرٌ also signifies *Pride:* (Mgh:) or the *being proud.* (TA.) — And *Smallness of the head:* (Ḳ:) or the *being small,* said of a man's head: (Ḳ,* TA:) one says, صَعِرَ رَأْسُهُ, inf. n. صَعَرٌ, meaning *his head was small.* (TḲ.)

صُعْرُورٌ (Ṣ, Ḳ, &c.) and ♦ صُعْرُرٌ (Ṣgh, Ḳ) *Long, slender, twisted gum:* (Ḳ:) or *a piece of gum having a long and twisted form:* (AZ, Ṣ:) and [*gum of the kind called*] لُثَى *that has become concrete:* (Ḳ:) or this is the signification of صَعَارِيرُ, (Ṣ, Ḳ,) which is the pl. [of صعرور], (TA,) accord. to AA: (Ṣ:) or the pl. signifies *concrete gum resembling fingers:* and صعرور is said to signify *a piece of gum:* accord. to Aboo-Naṣr, it is *like a reed-pen, and twisting like a horn:* and AḤn says that صُعْرُورَةٌ, with ة, signifies *a small round piece of gum:* (TA:) and the *fruit,* (Ḳ,) or *any fruit,* (TA,) *of a tree that is like* (*that of,* TA) *the* أَبْهَل, *and like pepper, and what resembles this, of such as are hard:* (Ḳ, TA:) or such they term صَعَارِير: (TA:) or *gum in general:* pl. صَعَارِيرُ. (Ḳ.) — Also, (Ḳ,) or صُعْرُورٌ [only], (TA,) † *A certain substance, yellow,* [in the CḲ اصعر is put for اصفر,] *thick, tough with* [*somewhat of*] *softness and moisture, that comes forth from the teat:* (Ḳ:) so called by way of comparison: (TA:) or *what is first milked, of biestings:* (Ḳ:) or *milk that is gummy* (مُصْمِغ), *in biestings, before it becomes clear.* (TA.) — صُعْرُورَةٌ The *little ball which is rolled along by the* [*kind of beetle called*] جُعَل. (Ḳ, TA.) — صَعَارِيرُ † *Long fingers.* (TA.)

صُعْرُور : see the next preceding paragraph.

صُقَّار *Proud*, or *haughty*: because he declines with his cheek, and turns away his face from people: occurring in a trad.: or the word as there used is صَقَّار, or صُقَّار, accord. to different relaters. (TA.)

صَيْعَرِىّ applied to a camel's hump, *Great*, or *large*, (Ḳ, TA,) *and round*. (TA.) — And أَحْمَرُ صَيْعَرِىّ *Intensely red*. (Ḳ.)

صَيْعَرِيَّةٌ *Obliquity in going* or *march* or *course*: (Ṣ, Ḳ:) from صَعَرٌ [inf. n. of صَعِرَ]. (Ṣ.) — Also *A mark made with a hot iron upon the neck of a camel*: (Ṣ:) or *of a she-camel* (Ḳ) *only*: (TA:) *a mark of the people of El-Yemen, only made upon she-camels*: (Tedhkireh of Aboo-'Alee:) *not upon a camel whether male or female*, (Ḳ,) as it is said to be by A'Obeyd [and J]. (TA.) J was led into error by a verse of El-Museiyab (Ḳ) Ibn 'Alas; wherein he uses the phrase بِنَاجٍ عَلَيْهِ الصَّيْعَرِيَّةُ [*With a swift he-camel marked with the* صيعرية]; (TA;) on hearing which, Tarafeh (Ḳ) Ibn-El-'Abd (TA) said, قَدِ اسْتَنْوَقَ الجَمَلُ [The male camel has assumed the characteristic of the female camel]. (Ḳ, TA.) El-Bedr El-Ḳaráfee urges that the term بعير, used by J, includes the female; and that the masc. epithet [نَاجٍ] is used [by the poet] because the male is the more honourable, being more hardy, and stronger than the female: but this demands consideration. (TA.)

أَصْعَرُ *Having a wryness*, or *distortion, in the cheek*, (Ṣ,) or *in the face*, (A, Ḳ,) or *in either side* [*thereof*], (Ḳ,) or *in the neck*, (A, Mṣb,) *by reason of pride*, (A,) *with a turning of the face on one side*: (Mṣb:) or a camel *having a disorder by reason of which he twists his neck*, (Ḳ,) *and distorts it*: (TA:) sometimes the being so is natural (Ṣ, A, Mṣb, Ḳ) in a man (Ṣ, Mṣb) and in an ostrich; (Ṣ, A, Mgh;) and sometimes it is accidental: (Mṣb:) pl. صُعْرٌ. (TA.) — It occurs in a trad. as signifying *Such as withdraws himself* [*from others, through pride*]; syn. ذَاهِبٌ بِنَفْسِهِ: (Ṣ, TA: [thought by Ibr D to be a mistake for زَاهٍ بِنَفْسِهِ: but this seems to me improbable:]) or *such as turns away his face, by reason of pride*: (IAth:) and in another trad. as signifying *such as turns away from the truth, and is faulty*. (TA.)

مُصْعَرٌ, (Ṣ,) in the Ḳ مُصْعَرٌ, said to be like مُكْرَمٌ, but the former is the right, as is shown by the ex. below, (TA,) applied to a night-journey to water, *Hard*, or *severe*. (Ṣ, Ḳ.) A poet says,

وَقَدْ قَرَبْنَ قَرَبًا مُصْعَرَا

[*And they had performed a hard night-journey to water*]. (Ṣ, TA.)

مُصَعْرَرٌ [*Made round*: and simply, *round*]. A rájiz says,

سُودٌ كَحَبِّ الفُلْفُلِ المُصَعْرَرِ

[*Black, like the round grains of pepper*]. (S.)

صعط

1. صَعَطَهُ, aor. ـِ and ـُ, (Ḳ,) inf. n. صَعْطٌ and صُعُوطٌ, (TA,) a dial. var. of سَعَطَهُ; and so is ▼ اصعطهُ of اسعطهُ. (Ḳ,* TA.) See art. سعط.

4: see what here precedes.

صَعُوطٌ i. q. سَعُوطٌ, q. v. (Lḥ, Ḳ.)

صعق

1. صَعَقَتْهُمُ السَّمَآءُ, (Ṣ, O, Ḳ,) aor. ـَ, (Ḳ,) inf. n. صَاعِقَةٌ, (O, Ḳ,) *The sky smote them with what is termed* صَاعِقَة [i. e. *a thunderbolt*]. (Ṣ, O, Ḳ.) [And صَقَعَتْهُمْ signifies the same.] — صُعِقَ is quasi-pass. of the verb in the phrase above; (Z, TA in art. سوف;) signifying *He was smitten by a* صَاعِقَة; (TA in art. صقع;) as also صُقِعَ; (Ḳ and TA in that art.;) and so صَعِقَ and صَقِعَ. (O in that art.) — And صَعِقَ, (Ṣ, O, Mṣb, Ḳ,) aor. ـَ, (Mṣb, Ḳ,) inf. n. صَعْقٌ, (Mṣb,) or صَعْقَةٌ, (Ṣ, O,) or both, and صَعَقٌ, (Ḳ,) and تَصْعَاقٌ, (Ṣ, O, Ḳ,) *He* (a man, Ṣ, O) *swooned*, or *became insensible*, (Ṣ, O, Mṣb, Ḳ, TA,) and *lost his reason*, (TA,) *in consequence of a sound that he heard*, (Mṣb, TA,) *such as the vehement sound of the fall of a wall or the like or of a part of a mountain*; (TA;) as also صُعِقَ. (Mṣb, TA.*) — And صَعِقَ, aor. ـَ, inf. n. صَعْقٌ and تَصْعَاقٌ, *He* (a man) *died*. (TA.) فَصَعِقَ مَنْ فِى السَّمٰوَاتِ وَمَنْ فِى الأَرْضِ, in the Ḳur [xxxix. 68], means *And those in the heavens and those upon the earth shall die*: (Ṣ, TA:) or *shall fall down dead*, or *in a swoon*: (Bḍ:) or *shall lose their reason*. (TA.) — And صَعِقَتِ الرَّكِيَّةُ, inf. n. صَعْقٌ, *The well fell in ruins*, or *to pieces*; or *collapsed*. (TA.) — صُعَاقٌ [as an inf. n.] signifies The *sounding* of thunder: and صَعَقَ, aor. ـَ, inf. n. صُعَاقٌ, is said of a bull, meaning *He bellowed*, or *lowed*: (TA:) and likewise of a man [app. as meaning *he bellowed*, or *roared*]. (ISk, TA in art. امر.)

4. أَصْعَقَتْهُ الصَّاعِقَةُ *The* صاعقة [or *thunderbolt*] *smote him*. (TA.) — And اصعقهُ *He, or it, caused him to swoon, or become insensible*. (Ṣ.) — And *He, or it, killed*, or *slew, him*. (TA.)

صَعْقٌ : see the next paragraph.

صَعَقٌ is an inf. n. of صَعِقَ [q. v.]: (Mṣb, Ḳ:) and primarily signifies *A swooning*, or *becoming insensible, in consequence of a vehement sound that one hears*; and sometimes, *such that one dies in consequence thereof*: — afterwards often used as meaning *Death*. (TA.) — [Also] *Vehemence of sound or voice*: (O, Ḳ:) and *vehemence of braying* of an ass; used in this sense by Rubeh; (O,* TA;) and said by Az to be originally ▼ صَعْقٌ. (TA.)

صَعِقٌ *Expecting*, or *looking for, a* صَاعِقَة [or *thunderbolt*]. (Ibn-'Abbád, O, Ḳ.) — Also *Swooning*, or *becoming insensible*; (Ḳ, TA;) and so ▼ مَصْعُوقٌ; or the latter signifies *dying suddenly*: and the former, *swooning*, or *becoming insensible*, and *losing his reason, in consequence of a sound that he has heard, such as the vehement sound of the fall of a wall or the like or of a part of a mountain*. (TA.) — And *Dying*, or *dead*. (TA.) — Also, (Ḳ, TA,) or صَعِقُ الصَّوْتِ, (Ṣ, O,) *Vehement in voice*, (Ṣ, O, Ḳ, TA,) and *in braying*; (TA;) applied to an ass. (Ṣ, O, TA.)

صَعْقَةٌ : see صَاعِقَةٌ. — Also The *sound proceeding from a* صَاعِقَة [or *thunderbolt*]. (TA.) — الصَّعْقَةُ الأُولَى means *The first blast* [*of the horn on the day of resurrection*]. (Mṣb.) — And صَعْقَةٌ also signifies *A death*. (TA.)

صَاعِقٌ A camel *meagre in his marrow*. (Ibn-'Abbád, O.)

صَاعِقَةٌ [*A thunderbolt*; i. e.] *a thing descending from the thunder, that smites not anything but it alters it and burns it*: (Mṣb:) or *fire that falls from the sky*, (AZ, Ṣ, O, Ḳ,) *in vehement thunder*: (AZ, Ṣ, O:) or *fire that God sends with vehement thunder*: (TA:) or the *scourge* (مِخْرَاق) *that is in the hand of* [*the angel who is*] *the driver of the clouds, and that comes not upon anything but it burns it*: (O, Ḳ:) or *a vehement sound from a thundering with which falls a piece of fire*: or the *sound of thunder*: (TA:) Wahb Ibn-Munebbih, being asked respecting it, whether it were a tangible thing or fire or what else, answered that he thought no one knew it except God: (O, TA:) accord. to some, (TA,) it signifies also the *cry*, or *vehement cry*, or *shout*, [*that is an efficient*] *of punishment*: (Ṣ, O, Ḳ:) and *death*; (O, Ḳ;) so accord. to Ḳatádeh (O, TA) and Muḳátil: (TA:) or *a cause of death*: (Zj, TA:) and *any destructive punishment*: (O, Ḳ:) and ▼ صَعْقَةٌ and صَاقِعَةٌ are dial. vars. thereof: (TA:) the pl. is صَوَاعِقُ. (O, Mṣb, TA.)

مَصْعُوقٌ : see صَعِقٌ.

صعل

1. صَعِلَ, aor. ـَ, (Ḳ,) inf. n. صَعَلٌ, (TA,) *He*, or *it, was*, or *became, such as is termed* صَعْلٌ *and* أَصْعَلُ meaning as expl. below; as also ▼ اصعالّ. (Ḳ, TA.) One says, ▼ اصعالّت النَّخْلَةُ meaning *The palm-tree was*, or *became, slender in the head*. (IDrd, O, TA.)

11: see the preceding paragraph, in two places.

صَعْلٌ *Small in the head*; applied to a man, (Aṣ, Ṣ, O,) and to an ostrich; (Ṣ, O;) as also ▼ أَصْعَلُ; (O;) and ▼ صَعْلَآءُ applied to a woman: (Ṣ:) or *small in the head and long and slender in the neck*; applied to a man: (Sh, TA:) or صَعْلٌ and its fem. صَعْلَةٌ, and ▼ أَصْعَلُ and its fem. ▼ صَعْلَآءُ, *such as is slender in the head and neck*, of mankind, and of ostriches, and [in like manner] of palm-trees: (Ḳ,* TA:) or, accord. to Aṣ, only the first is applied to a man, and its fem. (with ة) to a woman: but IB says that others mention ▼ صَعْلَآءُ as applied to a woman; and accord. to this, one applies ▼ أَصْعَلُ to a man. (TA.) And نَخْلَةٌ صَعْلَةٌ *A palm-tree that is crooked, and bare in the lower parts of its branches*: (Ṣ, O,

Ḳ:) or *a tall palm-tree*; which is disapproved, because often when it is tall it becomes crooked. (IB, TA.) And حِمَارٌ صَعْلٌ *An ass that has lost his soft hair*, (Ṣ, Ḳ,) or *his abundant and long hair*, (O,) or *both*. (TA.) And صَعْلٌ signifies also *Tall*, or *long*: (Ḳ:) applied by El-'Ajjáj to a mast of a ship as meaning *tall, and having its upper part even*, or *uniform, with its middle*; not as meaning slender in the head. (TA.) — Also, [used as a subst.,] *A male ostrich*; because small in the head: and with ة, *a female ostrich*. (TA.)

صَعَلٌ *Slenderness*. (Ṣ, O.)

صَعْلَةٌ, (O, TA,) or ▼ صَعَلَةٌ, which is preferred by Sh, (O,) *Smallness of the head*: (O, TA:) or *slenderness, and lightness of the body*. (TA.)

صَعَلَةٌ: see what next precedes.

أَصْعَلُ, and its fem. صَعْلَآءُ: see صَعْلٌ, in six places.

صعلك

Q. 1. صَعْلَكَهُ, (O, Ḳ,) inf. n. صَعْلَكَةٌ, (TA,) *He rendered him poor, or needy*. (O, Ḳ.) = صعلك الثَّرِيدَةَ *He made the* ثريدة [or *mess of crumbled bread moistened with broth*] *to have a head*: or *he raised its head*. (Ḳ.) And صعلك أَسْفَلَ السَّنَامِ *He stretched up the lower part of the camel's hump so as to make its upper part of a rounded form*. (Sh, O.) — And صعلك البَقْلُ الإِبِلَ *The herbs, or leguminous plants, fattened the camels*. (Sh, O, Ḳ.)

Q. 2. تَصَعْلَكَ *He was, or became, poor, or needy*. (Ṣ,* O,* Ḳ.) And *He made a show of poverty*. (KL.) [*He affected to be such as is termed* صُعْلُوك.] — تصعلكت الإِبِلُ *The camels cast, or shed, their fur*, (Ṣ, Ḳ, TA,) *and*, some add, *became bare*. (TA.) Accord. to Sh, *The camels became slender in their legs in consequence of fatness* [*of the body*; app. meaning that their legs became slender in comparison with their bodies]. (TA.) And accord. to Aṣ, تصعلك said of a horse, *He became slender, and shed his abundant and long hair*. (TA.)

صُعْلُوكٌ *Poor, or needy*; (Ṣ, O, Ḳ, TA;) [*a poor man*;] and ISd adds, *having no property*; and Az adds, *and having no reliance* [*upon any person or thing*]: (TA:) and *a thief*, or *robber*: (KL:) pl. صَعَالِيكُ. (Ṣ, O.) صَعَالِيكُ العَرَبِ means ذُؤْبَانُهَا [i. e., as expl. voce ذِئْبٌ, *The thieves*, or *sharpers, and paupers, of the Arabs*; or *the paupers of the Arabs who practise thieving*: because they act like wolves]. (Ṣ, O.) 'Orweh Ibn-El-Ward was called عُرْوَةُ الصَّعَالِيكِ because he used to collect the poor in a حَظِيرَة [i. e. an enclosure for cattle] and sustain them by means of the plunder that he took. (Ṣ, O, Ḳ.)

مُصَعْلَكُ الرَّأْسِ A man *round in the head*: (O, Ḳ, TA:) or, as some say, *small in the head*. (TA.) And مُصَعْلَكٌ applied to a camel's hump, *Such as is as though one rounded its upper part, and stretched up its lower part with the hand so as to make it assume that rounded form*. (Sh, O.)

صعو

1. صَعَا, aor. ـُ, *He*, or *it*, *was slender*; and *was small*: (IAạr, Ḳ:) from صَعْوٌ, here following. (TA.)

صَعْوٌ *A small* عُصْفُور [or *bird of the sparrow-kind*], (Ḳ, TA,) *red in the head*; (TA;) fem. with ة: (Ḳ:) or *small* عَصَافِير [or *birds of the sparrow-kind*], *the heads of which are red*; n. un. with ة: (Mṣb:) or صَعْوَةٌ signifies *a certain bird*; and its pl. is صَعْوٌ and صِعَآءٌ: (Ṣ:) or the pl. (of صَعْوَة, Mṣb) is صِعَآءٌ (Mṣb, Ḳ) and صَعَوَاتٌ, (Ḳ, in the CḲ صِعْوات,) and the pl. of صَعْوٌ is أَصْعَآءٌ: some say that صَعْوٌ is originally وَصْعٌ. (TA.) — Hence, (TA,) نَاقَةٌ صَعْوَةٌ *A she-camel small in the head*. (Ḳ.) = And the pl. أَصْعَآءٌ signifies أُصُولٌ [pl. of أَصْلٌ, q. v.]. (TA.)

صغر

1. صَغُرَ, aor. ـُ; (Ṣ, Mṣb, Ḳ;) and صَغِرَ, aor. ـَ; (Ḳ;) inf. n. صِغَرٌ, (Ṣ, Mṣb, Ḳ,) of the former, (Ṣ, Mṣb, TA,) and صَغَارَةٌ, (Ḳ,) also of the former, (TA,) and صَغَرٌ and صُغْرَانٌ, (IAạr, Ḳ,) which are both of the latter; (TA; [but Ibr D thinks that there is no reason for this assertion with respect to صغران;]) [*He* or] *it* (Ṣ, Mṣb) *was*, or *became*, *small*, or *little*; صِغَرٌ being the contr. of كِبَرٌ, (Ṣ,) or of عِظَمٌ, as also صَغَارَةٌ [&c.]: (M, Ḳ:) or صِغَرٌ is *in body*, or *corporeal substance*, (فِى الجِرْمِ,) [and *in years*, or *age*; and صَغُرَ, with this inf. n., said of a human being, signifies *he was a child*, or *in the state of childhood, not having attained to puberty*;] and صَغَارَةٌ is *in estimation* or *rank* or *dignity* (فِى القَدْرِ). (M, Ḳ.) — Also صَغُرَ, inf. n. صِغَرٌ and صَغَارٌ and صَغَارَةٌ and صُغْرَانٌ and صُغْرٌ (Ḳ) and صَغَرٌ, (TA,) *He was content with vileness, baseness, abasement*, or *ignominy*, (Ḳ,) and *tyranny*, or *injury*: (TA:) or صَغَرٌ is inf. n. of صَغِرَ, aor. ـَ, signifying *he was*, or *became*, *vile, base*, or *ignominious*; (Ṣ,* Mṣb;) and so صُغْرٌ and صَغَارٌ: (Mgh:) or صَغَارٌ signifies the *being small*, or *little, in estimation* or *rank* or *dignity*: (TA:) and you say, صَغُرَ فِى عُيُونِ النَّاسِ, with ḍamm, meaning, [*he became small*, or *little, in the eyes of men*; i. e.,] *he lost his reverence*, or *reverend dignity*. (Mṣb.) [See also 6.] One says also, هُوَ يَصْغُرُ عَنْ كَذَا *He*, or *it*, *is smaller than*, or *too small for*, *such a thing*; syn. يَقِلُّ. (TA in art. قل.) And صَغُرَتْ عَنِ الوَلَدِ [*She was too young to bear offspring*]. (Ṣ in art. جل, &c.) — مَا صَغُرَنِى إِلَّا بِسَنَةٍ, aor. ـُ, means مَا صَغُرَ عَنِّى [i. e. *He was not younger than I, save by a year*]. (IAạr, Ḳ.) — And صَغُرَتِ الشَّمْسُ *The sun inclined to setting*. (Th, Ḳ.)

2. صَغَّرَهُ, (inf. n. تَصْغِيرٌ, TA,) *He made him, or it, small, or little*; as also ▼ اصغرهُ. (Ṣ, Ḳ.) You say, ▼ اصغر القِرْبَةَ *He sewed the water-skin* [*so as to make it*] *small*. (Ṣ, Ḳ.) — صَغَّرَهُ فِى عُيُونِ النَّاسِ *He*, or *it*, *rendered him* [*small*, or *little*, i. e.,] *contemptible, vile, base*, or *ignominious*, [*in the eyes of men*:] (A:) and [in like manner] *he*, or *it*, *rendered him vile, base*, or *ignominious*, (TA,) or *content with vileness, baseness, abasement*, or *ignominy*. (Ḳ.) — صَغَّرْتُ شَأْنَهُ (TA in art. غمز) and مِنْ شَأْنِهِ (Ṣ and TA in the same art.) [*I lessened his rank*, or *dignity*]. — صغّر الاِسْمَ, inf. n. تَصْغِيرٌ, *He changed the noun into the diminutive form*. (Mṣb.) This is done for several purposes: to denote the smallness of the thing signified, in itself; as in the instance of دُوَيْرَةٌ ["a small, or little, house"]: to denote its smallness in the eye of the speaker, when it is not small in itself; as in the saying ذَهَبَتِ الدُّرَيْهِمُ إِلَّا دُوَيْهِمًا ["the dirhems went, except a small dirhem"]: to denote nearness; as in the instance of قُبَيْلَ الصُّبْحِ ["a little before daybreak"]: to denote affection and benevolence; as in the expression يَا بُنَىَّ ["O my little (meaning dear) son"]: to denote the greatness of the thing signified; as in the phrase سُنَيَّةٌ حَمْرَآءُ ["a very severe year"]: to denote praise; as when a man is described as كُنَيْفٌ مُلِئَ عِلْمًا ["a little pastor's-bag filled with knowledge"]: to denote blame; as in the expression يَا فُوَيْسِقُ ["O thou little transgressor"]. (L, TA.) [The inf. n., تَصْغِيرٌ, is also applied to *A diminutive noun* itself; as also اِسْمٌ مُصَغَّرٌ.] — See also 10.

4: see 2, in two places. = اصغرت الأَرْضُ *The land produced small plants or herbage*, (Ḳ,) *not tall*. (TA.) — اِرْتَبَعُوا لِيُصْغِرُوا [*They remained in the spring-pasture*] *in order that they might rear the younger ones*: (O, Ḳ: expl. in the former by لِيُوَلِّدُوا الأَصَاغِرَ [correctly لِيُوَلِّدُوا]: in the CḲ and my MS. copy of the Ḳ, by لِيُوَلِّدُوا الأَصَاغِرَ [which is a manifest mistake].) — أَصْغَرَتِ النَّاقَةُ وَأَكْبَرَتْ ‡ *The she-camel uttered her yearning cry to*, or *for*, *her young one, in a low tone, and loudly*. (A.)

6. تصاغر *He became small; he shrank*, or *became contracted*; (O* and TA in art. ضأل;) by reason of abasement, (TA ibid.,) or from fear. (Ḥam p. 658.) — *He became vile, base, ignominious, abject*, or *contemptible*; (Ḳ,* TA;) *came to nought*. (TA.) And تصاغرت إِلَيْهِ نَفْسُهُ *He* (lit. *his soul* or *his own self*) *became of little importance, by being vile, base*, or *ignominious, to himself*, or *in his own estimation*; (A, Mṣb;) *he became vile, base, ignominious, abject*, or *contemptible, to himself*, or *in his own estimation*. (Ṣ,* Ḳ,* TA.) — And [*He affected*, or *feigned*, *abjectness*; contr. of تَكَابَرَ: or] *he exhibited abjectness*. (KL.)

10. استصغرهُ *He counted, accounted, reckoned*, or *esteemed, him*, or *it*, *small*, or *little*: or *vile, base*, or *ignominious*: syn. عَدَّهُ صَغِيرًا: (Ṣ, Ḳ:) or *young*: as also ▼ صَغَّرَهُ. (TA.)

صُغْرٌ (Ṣ, Mṣb) and ▼ صَغَارٌ, with fet-ḥ, (Ṣ, [and

so in the Ḳur vi. 124,]) or ▼ صُغَار, with ḍamm, (Mṣb, [but perhaps there is an omission in my copy of the Mṣb after this word,]) and ▼ صُغْر, (Ṣ,) *Vileness, baseness, abasement,* or *ignominiousness:* (Ṣ, Mṣb:) so the second word signifies in the Ḳur vi. 124: (TA:) and *tyranny,* or *oppression,* or *injury.* (Ṣ.) One says, قُمْ عَلَى صُغْرِكَ, and ▼ صَغَرِكَ, [*Rise thou, notwithstanding thy vileness,* or *ignominiousness*]. (Ṣ.) [See also 1, of which it is an inf. n.]

صَغَرٌ : see صُغْرٌ, in two places. [And see 1, of which it is an inf. n.]

فُلَانٌ صِغْرَتُهُمْ *Such a one is the least,* or *youngest, of them:* (Ḳ,* TA:) and فُلَانٌ صِغْرَةُ أَبَوَيْهِ, and صِغْرَةُ وَلَدِ أَبَوَيْهِ, *Such a one is the least,* or *youngest, of the children of his parents:* opposed to كِبْرَةٌ. (TA.) And أَنَا مِنَ الصِّغْرَةِ *I am of the little-ones,* or *of the young:* (Ḳ:) said by an Arab child when he is forbidden to play. (TA.)

صُغْرَانٌ : see صَغِيرٌ.

صُغَارٌ : see صُغْرٌ.

صُغَارٌ : see صَغِيرٌ :— and صُغْرٌ.

صَغِيرٌ *Small,* or *little;* (Ṣ, Ḳ;) [*in body,* or *corporeal substance:* and *in estimation* or *rank* or *dignity;* as is implied in the K: and *in years,* or *age; a youngling; a young one* of any female; and of a tree and the like: applied to a human being, *a child;* i. e., *one who has not attained to puberty:* opposed to كَبِيرٌ:] as also ▼ صُغَارٌ (Ṣ, Ḳ) and ▼ صُغْرَانٌ (Ḳ) and ▼ أَصْغَرُ: (Mṣb in art. كبر:) fem. with ة: (Mṣb:) pl. masc. صِغَارٌ and صُغَرَآءُ, (a form used in poetry, Ṣ,) and ▼ مَصْغُورَآءُ, (Ṣ, Ḳ,) or the last is [correctly speaking] a quasi-pl. n.: (TA:) and pl. fem. صِغَارٌ, but not صَغَائِرُ when used as an epithet: (Mṣb:) the dim. of صَغِيرٌ is ▼ صُغَيِّرٌ and ▼ صُغَيْئِرٌ, (Sb, Ḳ,) the latter anomalous. (TA.) You say, هُوَ صَغِيرٌ فِى القَدْرِ; and فِى العِلْمِ; [*He is small,* or *little, in rank,* or *dignity;* as also صَغِيرُ الشَّأْنِ; and *in knowledge.*] (A.) And جَآءَ النَّاسُ صَغِيرُهُمْ وَكَبِيرُهُمْ *The people came:* [*the small in rank* or *dignity, of them, and the great therein, of them:* or] *those of no rank* or *dignity, and those of rank* or *dignity.* (Mṣb.) [See also صَاغِرٌ.]

صَغِيرَةٌ, [a subst. from صَغِيرٌ, made such by the affix ة,] applied to a sin, [signifying *A small* or *little, sin,*] has for its pl. صَغِيرَاتٌ and [more commonly] صَغَائِرُ; being, when thus applied, a subst. (Mṣb.) [See مُحَقَّرَاتٌ.]

صُغَيِّرٌ and صُغَيْئِرٌ dims. of صَغِيرٌ, q. v.

صَاغِرٌ *In a state of vileness, abasement, ignominiousness, abjectness,* or *contempt:* (Mṣb:) or *content with vileness, abasement,* or *ignominy,* (Ḳ,) *and tyranny,* or *injury.* (Ṣ, A, TA.) [See also صَغِيرٌ.]

أَصْغَرُ [*Smaller,* or *less;* and *smallest,* or *least; in body,* or *corporeal substance;* and *in estimation* or *rank* or *dignity;* and *in years,* or *age*]: (Ṣ, Mṣb, Ḳ:) fem. صُغْرَى: (Ṣ, Mṣb:) pl. masc. أَصَاغِرُ (Sb, Ṣ, Ḳ) and أَصَاغِرَةٌ, (M, Ḳ,) though the sing. is not of the nouns which regularly add ة to the pl., and it is added in this case because the sing. resembles in form قَشْعَمٌ, of which قَشَاعِمَةٌ is a pl., (ISd,) and أَصْغَرُونَ: (Sb, Ṣ:) and pl. fem. صُغَرٌ (Sb, Ṣ, Mṣb) and صُغْرَيَاتٌ: (Mṣb:) but Sb says, you do not say نِسْوَةٌ صُغَرٌ, nor قَوْمٌ أَصَاغِرُ, except with the article ال: and he adds, we have heard the Arabs says, الأَصَاغِرُ [perhaps miswritten for الأَصَاغِرَةُ;] and if you please, you may say الأَصْغَرُونَ. (Ṣ.) — الأَصْغَرَانِ [lit. *The two less,* or *least, things,*] means † *the heart and the tongue.* (Ḳ.) It is said in a prov., المَرْءُ بِأَصْغَرَيْهِ, meaning, † *The man* obtains power over things, and manages them thoroughly, *by means of his heart and his tongue.* (ISk, TA. [See Ḥar p. 446.]) — See also صَغِيرٌ.

أَرْضٌ مُصْغِرَةٌ *Land having small plants* or *herbage, not grown tall.* (ISk, Ṣ, Ḳ.*)

مُصْغَرَةٌ : }
مُصْغُورَةٌ : } see مَصْفُورٌ, in art. صفر.

مَصْغُورَآءُ : see صَغِيرٌ.

صغو and صغى.

1. صَغَا, aor. يَصْغُو; (Ṣ, Mṣb, Ḳ;) and [صَغَى, aor.] يَصْغِى, (Ṣ, TA, and so in some copies of the Ḳ,) or يَصْغَى; (Mṣb, and so in some copies of the Ḳ, and in the M, but it is said in the TA that it is correctly يَصْغِى, with kesr, as in the Ṣ;) inf. n. صُغُوٌّ; (Ṣ, Mṣb, Ḳ;) and صَغِىَ, aor. يَصْغَى, inf. n. صَغًا and صُغِىٌّ; (Ṣ, Mṣb, Ḳ;) *He,* or *it, inclined,* (Ṣ, Mṣb, Ḳ, TA,) إِلَى الشَّىْءِ [*to the thing*], (TA,) or إِلَى كَذَا [*to such a thing*]: (Mṣb:) or they signify [sometimes, for the meaning expl. above is unquestionably correct, and is that which is predominant,] *he* (a man, TA) *had an inclining of his* حَنَك [here app. meaning the *mouth* or the *part below the mouth*]; (Ḳ, TA;) or *of one of his lips;* thus correctly, as in the M and A; شِدْقَيْه in [some of] the copies of the Ḳ [and شِقَّيْه in others] being a mistake for شَفَتَيْه. (TA.) You say, صَغَتْ إِلَيْهِ أُذُنُهُ *His ear inclined to him, or it.* (TA.) And hence, in the Ḳur [lxvi. 4], فَقَدْ صَغَتْ قُلُوبُكُمَا [*For the hearts of you two have inclined* to that which is not right]. (Mṣb.) And صَغَتِ النُّجُومُ, (Ṣ, Mṣb,) and الشَّمْسُ, (Ḳ,) *The stars,* and *the sun, inclined to setting.* (Ṣ, Mṣb, Ḳ.) And صَغَا الرَّجُلُ *The man inclined,* or *leaned, on one side:* or *bent,* or *bowed, himself upon his bow.* (TA.) And صَغَى, عَلَى القَوْمِ inf. n. صَغًا, [as though meaning *He inclined to set himself against the people* or *party,*] is said of one when his love, or affection, is with such as are not of the said people, or party. (TA.) — And صَغَى, aor. يَصْغَى, (Ḳ, TA,) inf. n. صَغًا agreeably with the Ṣ and M, accord. to the copies of the Ḳ, erroneously, صَغْىٌ, (TA,) and صُغِىٌّ, (Ḳ, TA,) *He inclined and gave ear,* or *hearkened,* or *listened.* (Ḳ. [See also the next paragraph.])

4. اصغى الإِنَآءَ *He inclined the vessel:* (Ṣ, Mṣb, Ḳ:) or *he turned the vessel upon its side, in order that what was in it might collect together.* (M, TA.) — [Hence,] أُصْغِىَ إِنَآءُ فُلَانٍ † *Such a one perished,* or *died.* (Er-Rághib, TA.) And أَصْغَى إِنَآءَهُ † [*I. q.* اصغى حَقَّهُ expl. in what follows: (see also مُصْغًى:) or] *he detracted from his reputation; spoke evil of him;* or *slandered him.* (Z, TA.) اصغى حَقَّهُ, (A, TA,) or الشَّىْءَ, (Ḳ,) means ‡ *He diminished to him, impaired to him,* or *defrauded him of a portion of,* (Z, Ḳ, TA,) *his right* or *due,* (Z, TA,) or *the thing.* (Ḳ.) — You say also, أَصْغَيْتُ رَأْسِى, and سَمْعِى, *I inclined my head,* and *my ear.* (Mṣb.) And اصغى إِلَيْهِ, (Ṣ, Ḳ,) or اصغى إِلَيْهِ سَمْعَهُ, (M, TA,) *He inclined his ear to him.* (Ṣ, M, Ḳ.) And اصغى, alone, *He gave ear, hearkened,* or *listened.* (Ḳ. [See also 1, last explanation.]) And أَصْغَتِ النَّاقَةُ *The she-camel inclined her head towards the* رَحْل [or *saddle*], (Ṣ, Ḳ, TA;*) in some copies of the Ṣ إِلَى الرَّجُلِ [*towards the man*], (TA,) *as though she were listening to a thing:* (Ṣ, Ḳ:) this she does when the saddle is bound upon her. (Ṣ.)

صَغًا an inf. n. of صَغِىَ [q. v.]: and also [used as] a simple subst. [meaning *Inclination*]. (TA.) One says, أَقَامَ صَغَاهُ [*He rectified*] *his inclination.* (TA.) And صَغَاهُ, and ▼ صَغْوُهُ and ▼ صِغْوُهُ مَعَكَ, i. e. *His inclination* [*is with thee,* meaning, *is agreeable with thine*]. (AZ, Ṣ, Ḳ.) In [some of] the copies of the Ḳ صَغْوُهُ and صِغْوُهُ are written صَغْوَةً and صِغْوَةً, which would lead the inadvertent to imagine these two words to be syn. with the word there next preceding, namely, صَغْوَآءُ as an epithet applied to the sun. (TA.)

صِغْوٌ : see the next preceding paragraph. [هٰذَا ابْنُ صَغْوِكَ, or ▼ صِغْوِكَ, is a phrase similar to هذا ابن إِنْسِكَ, meaning *This is thy chosen,* or *special, friend* or *companion:* but perhaps post-classical.]

صَغْوٌ : see صَغًا and صِغْوٌ. ═ Also The *interior* of a ladle: — and the *side* of a well: — and the *part that is folded,* or *turned over, of the sides* of a دَلْو [or leathern bucket]: (Ḳ, TA:) so in the M: and its pl. in these senses is أَصْغَآءٌ. (TA.)

صَغْوَةٌ : see صَغْوَآءُ, voce أَصْغَى.

صَاغٍ [part. n. of صَغَا]: fem. صَاغِيَةٌ: and pl. صَوَاغٍ. — صَاغِيَتُكَ means *Those who incline to thee,* (Ḳ, TA,) *and come to thee,* (TA,) *in their cases of need:* (Ḳ, TA:) or *whoever, of thy family, come to thee as guests:* (TA:) or *those who incline to thee, of thy companions and relations:* (Ḥar p. 207:) ISd thinks it to be made fem. because meaning a جَمَاعَة. (TA.) أَكْرِمُوا فُلَانًا فِى صَاغِيَتِهِ means [*Honour ye such a one in respect of*] *those who incline to him, and who come to him seeking to obtain what he has.* (Ṣ.) — And الصَّوَاغِى means *The stars that have inclined to setting.* (TA.)

أَصْغَى, applied to a man, (TA,) *Having an inclining of the* حَنَك; (Ḳ, TA;) or *of one of the lips:* (Ḳ,* TA: [see 1:]) fem. صَغْوَآءُ. (TA.) — And the fem., applied to a قَطَاة [or bird of the species termed قَطًا], *Having an inclining of its beak, and of one of its mandibles:* and one says صَغْوَآءُ صَغُوَّةٌ ♦ to give intensiveness to the meaning; like as one says لَيْلٌ لَائِلٌ. (TA.) — Also, i. e. the fem., applied to the sun, *Inclining to setting.* (Ḳ.)

مَصْغًى [*A place of inclining, or to which to incline*]. It is said in a prov., الصَّبِىُّ أَعْلَمُ بِمَصْغَى خَدِّهِ [*The child best knows the place of inclining of his cheek*]: i. e. he best knows to whom he should betake himself, or whither it will profit him [to go]. (TA. [See also Freytag's Arab. Prov., i. 715.])

مُصْغًى *Inclined.* (Ḥam p. 260.) — One says, فُلَانٌ مُصْغًى إِنَاؤُهُ, meaning † *Such a one is abridged,* or *defrauded, of a portion of his right,* or *due:* (Ṣ, and Ḥam pp. 259-60:) because when the vessel is inclined, what it will hold becomes deficient. (Ḥam.)

صف

1. صَفَّ, (Ṣ, M, Mgh, O, Mṣb, Ḳ,) aor. ـُ, (Mṣb, TA,) inf. n. صَفٌّ, (O, Mṣb, Ḳ, TA,) *He set,* or *placed,* or *stationed,* (Ṣ, M, Mgh, O, Ḳ,) a company of men, (Ṣ, M, Mgh, O, Mṣb, Ḳ,) in war (Ṣ, O, Ḳ) &c., (O, Ḳ,) and a military force, (TA,) and also [in a similar sense] a thing, (Mṣb,) *in a rank,* or *row,* or *line:* (Ṣ, M, Mgh, O, Ḳ:) and likewise ♦ صفّف, (TA,) inf. n. تَصْفِيفٌ; (IDrd, O, Ḳ, TA;) but this has an intensive signification. (IDrd, O, TA.) — One says also of a she-camel, تَصُفُّ يَدَيْهَا عِنْدَ الحَلَبِ [*She sets her fore legs evenly, side by side,* not putting one of them in advance of the other, as if about to go onward, *on the occasion of being milked*]. (Ṣ, M, O, Ḳ. [See also صَفَنَ, said of a man: and see صَانَ in art. صون.]) And [in like manner] one says, صَفَّتِ الإِبِلُ قَوَائِمَهَا [*The camels set their legs in an even row*]. (Ṣ, O.) — And of a she-camel one says also, تَصُفُّ أَقْدَاحًا مِنْ لَبَنِهَا إِذَا حُلِبَتْ [as though meaning *She yields a row of bowls of her milk when she is milked*], because of the abundance of her milk. (Ṣ, O, Ḳ*.) And تَصُفُّ بَيْنَ مِحْلَبَيْنِ أَوْ ثَلَاثَةٍ, (Ṣ, O,) or simply تَصُفُّ, (M,) *She combines two milking-vessels, or three, at one milking;* (Ṣ,* M, O;*) الصَّفُّ meaning her *being milked into two milking-vessels,* or *three,* (Ṣ, O, Ḳ,) *so as to combine them.* (Ṣ, O. [In the CḲ, أَنْ تُحْلَبَ is a mistake for أَنْ تَحْلُبَ.]) And a rájiz, cited by AZ, says, referring to a she-camel,

• تَصُفُّ فِى ثَلَاثَةِ المَحَالِبِ •

[*She is milked into three milking-vessels at one milking*]. (Ṣ, O.) One says also صَفَّهَا, i. e. حَلَبَهَا صَفًّا [app. meaning *He milked her into two bowls, or three, at one milking; or into two bowls;* the pronoun referring to a she-camel]. (M. [One or the other of these two meanings appears to be indicated by what there precedes this.]) — صُفَّ عَلَى الجَمْرِ لِيَنْشَوِىَ (Ṣ, Ḳ) is said of flesh-meat (Ṣ) [app. meaning *It was laid, cut into a strip,* or *into strips, upon the live coals to broil*]; and فِى الشَّمْسِ لِيَجِفَّ [in like manner, *in the sun to dry*]: (Ḳ:) for one says of him who has prepared flesh-meat cut into strips, or oblong pieces, and dried in the sun, صَفَّ اللَّحْمَ; and [in like manner] one says also, صَفَّهُ عَلَى النَّارِ لِيَنْشَوِىَ: (Mṣb:) or صَفَّ اللَّحْمَ, aor. ـُ, inf. n. صَفٌّ, means *he cut the flesh-meat into broad slices:* (M:) and accord. to ISh, ♦ التَّصْفِيفُ is like التَّشْرِيحُ, i. e. *the cutting* a piece of flesh-meat *thin, so that it is translucent:* (TA in the present art.:) or التصفيف is a kind of تَشْرِيح; i. e. *the cutting* a piece of flesh-meat *thin, so that it is translucent by reason of its thinness, and then throwing it upon the live coals.* (TA in art. شرح.) [See صَفِيفٌ.] ═ See also 8, in three places. — صَفَّ said of a bird, (M, O, Mṣb, Ḳ,) aor. ـُ, (M, Mṣb,) inf. n. صَفٌّ, (Mṣb, Ḳ,) *It extended its wings in a line,* (M,) or *it expanded its wings,* (O, Mṣb, Ḳ,) in the sky, *and did not move them,* (M,) or *and struck* [an evident mistake for *and did not strike*] *with them its sides like the pigeon:* (Mṣb:) such as do so are not to be eaten; (Mṣb, Ḳ;) as the vulture and the hawk: (Mṣb:) it is said in a trad., يُؤْكَلُ مَا دَفَّ وَلَا يُؤْكَلُ مَا صَفَّ. (O, Ḳ, TA. See art. دف.) ═ صَفَفْتُ لِلسَّرْجِ, (Ṣ,) or صَفَفْتُ لِلسَّرْجِ صُفَّةً, (O,) or صَفَفْتُ السَّرْجَ, (Ḳ, and so in one place in the O,) and ♦ أَصْفَفْتُهُ, (O, Ḳ,) but this latter verb is of weak authority, (O,) ‡ *I put to the horse's saddle a* صُفَّة [q. v.]: (Ṣ, O, Ḳ, TA:) [and] صَفَّ لَهَا, and صَفَّ الدَّابَّةَ, *He made for the beast a* صُفَّة. (M.)

2: see above, first sentence: — and also in the latter half of the paragraph.

3. صَافُّوهُمْ (Ṣ, MA, O, Ḳ) فِى القِتَالِ (Ṣ, O, Ḳ) *They fought them in rank; they drew themselves out in a rank against them* [*in fight*]. (MA.) ═ [And app. one says also صَافَّهُ meaning *He had the* صُفَّة *of his house over against,* or *facing, his* (another's) صُفَّة. See هُوَ مُصَافِّى, below.]

4: see 1, last sentence.

6: see 8. — One says also تصافّوا عَلَيْهِ *They collected themselves together in a rank, or row, or line, against him.* (M, TA.) And تصافّوا عَلَى المَآءِ *They collected themselves together at the water;* as also تضافّوا عَلَيْهِ: like as one says تَصَوَّكَ فِى خُرْئِهِ and تَضَوَّكَ, and صَلَاصِلُ المَآءِ and ضَلَاضِلُهُ. (Lḥ, TA.)

8. اصطفّوا *They stood in,* (Ṣ, Mgh, O, Ḳ,) or *became,* (M,) [or *set, placed,* or *stationed, themselves in,*] *a rank,* or *row,* or *line;* (Ṣ, M, Mgh, Mṣb;*) or *ranks,* or *rows,* or *lines;* (O, Ḳ;) as also ♦ تصافّوا; (M, O,* Ḳ;* [التَّصَافُّ being expl. in the O and Ḳ by التَّسَاطُرُ; in the CḲ, erroneously, التَّشَاطُرُ;]) and so ♦ صَفُّوا, (M, Mgh, Mṣb,) aor. ـُ, (M, Mgh,) inf. n. صَفٌّ and صَفَفٌ, but [ISd says] this latter inf. n. I have not heard except in a phrase mentioned in what follows. (M.) Hence the saying, تَصُفُّ ♦ النِّسَآءُ خَلْفَ الرِّجَالِ وَلَا تَصُفُّ مَعَهُمْ [*The women shall stand in a rank behind the men* in the mosque, *and shall not stand in a rank with them*]. (Mgh.) And hence the saying of a woman of the desert to her sons, إِذَا لَقِيتُمُ العَدُوَّ فَدَغَوَى وَلَا صَفَفَ ♦ i. e. [*When ye meet the enemy, rush upon them without consideration, and*] *do not set yourselves in a rank.* (M. [See also 1, in art. دغو.])

R. Q. 1. صَفْصَفَ *He journeyed,* (سَارَ, O, and so in copies of the Ḳ,) or *became,* (صَارَ, so in the CḲ,) *alone in a* صَفْصَف, or *level tract of land.* (O, Ḳ.) ═ And *He pastured upon the trees called* صَفْصَاف. (O, Ḳ.) ═ And صَفْصَفَةٌ [as an inf. n., or as a simple subst.,] signifies *The crying* or *cry,* (صَوْت,) *of the sparrow,* which is called صُفْصُف (O, Ḳ) in some one or more of the dialects. (O.)

صَفٌّ *A rank, row,* or *line* [of things]; (KL, PṢ;) or *an even* صَدْر [i. e. *front,* or *fore part,*] of any things: (M:) and *a company of men standing in a rank,* or *row,* or *line:* (O, Ḳ:) pl. صُفُوفٌ; (Ṣ, M, O, Mṣb, Ḳ;) and the sing. may also be used in the sense of the pl.; it may be used either thus in the sense of the pl. or as a sing. in the Ḳur xviii. 46. (O.) Hence, in a trad., سَوُّوا صُفُوفَكُمْ [*Make even your ranks*] in prayer. (O, TA.) — Also *A station of* صُفُوف [or *ranks of men*]. (M. [See also مَصَفّ.]) And hence, (M,) as used in the Ḳur xx. 67, *i. q.* مُصَلًّى [i. e. *A place of prayer,* or *a place of prayer on the occasion of the* عِيد, or *festival*]; (Az, M, O;) because the people stand there in ranks: (M:) i. e. *a place where people assemble for their* عِيد: (Az, O:) or, in that instance, صَفًّا may mean مُصْطَفِّينَ [i. e. *standing in ranks*], (Az, M, O,) as a denotative of state. (M.) — And *A pair of bowls* (قَدَحَانِ) [app., as seems to be indicated, *that are filled at one milking of a camel*]; because they are put together. (M.) ═ Also *A certain medicament with which the teeth are whitened.* (O.)

صُفَّةٌ *An appertenance of a house,* (Ṣ, Mgh, O, Mṣb, Ḳ, [in none of which is it explained,]) or *of a building, like a wide* بَهْو [here used in a post-classical sense, as meaning a *kind of vestibule,* or *portico, for shade and shelter, open in front*], *with a long roof* or *ceiling;* (Lth, TA;) the طُرَّة of a building [app. meaning what is above described]; (M;) *i. q.* سَقِيفَةٌ: (Ṣ and Mṣb and Ḳ in art. سقف:) [see سَقِيفَةٌ; and see also سُدَّةٌ:] and *i. q.* ظُلَّةٌ [i. e. *a roof,* or *covering, for shade and shelter, over the door of a house;* or *extending from a house to another house opposite;* like سَقِيفَةٌ and سُدَّةٌ]: (M:) [for the meaning assigned to it by Golius as from the Ṣ, and by Freytag as from the Ḳ and Ṣ, ("*scamnum discubitorium, fere ex lapidibus structum,*") I find no authority in any Arabic work: in Egypt, it is applied to a *shelf of marble* or *of common stone, about four* feet high, supported by two or more arches, or by a single arch, figured and described in the Introduction to my work on the Modern Egyptians; this being app. so called because resembling in form, though not in size, a porch:] the pl. is صُفَفٌ (Ṣ, O, Mṣb, Ḳ) and صِفَافٌ and صُفَّاتٌ. (Mgh.) أَهْلُ الصُّفَّةِ [The people of the صُفَّة] was an appellation applied to certain persons who were the guests of El-Islám, [i. e. supported by the charity of the Muslims,] (O, Ḳ, TA,) consisting of poor refugees, and houseless men, (TA,) who passed the night in the صُفَّة of the mosque of the Prophet [in El-Medeeneh], which was a covered place, an appertenance of the mosque, (O, Ḳ, TA,) roofed over with palm-sticks; (Ḥar p. 379; [where see more;]) thither they resorted for lodging; and sometimes they were few, and sometimes they were many: [SM says,] I have drawn up a list of their names, in a tract, to the number of ninety-two, (TA in the present art.,) or ninety-three. (TA voce أَوْفَاضٌ.) [ISd says,] عَذَابُ يَوْمِ الصُّفَّةِ [The punishment of the day of the صُفَّة] is the same as عَذَابُ يَوْمِ الظُّلَّةِ [mentioned in the Ḳur xxvi. 189]: (M, TA:) Lth says that the former was a day on which a certain people disobeyed their apostle, wherefore God sent upon them heat and clouds which overspread them, so that they perished: and Az says that it is not the same as that mentioned in the Ḳur, and that he knew not what is meant by عذاب يوم الصفّة: (O, (TA:) it seems, however, that both mean the same, as الصُّفَّة and الظُّلَّة are one in meaning. (TA.) — Also † An appertenance of the سَرْج [or horse's saddle]; (Ṣ, M, IAth, Mgh, O, Ḳ, TA;) like the مِيثَرَة [q. v. in art. وثر] of the رَحْل [or camel's saddle]; (IAth, L, TA;*) the thing with which it is covered, between the قَرَبُوسَانِ, which are its fore part and its hinder part: (Mgh:) or, (M, TA,) as also of the رَحْل, (M,) the thing that comprises within it (تَضُمُّ) the [two pieces of wood called the] عَرْقُوَتَانِ and the [two pads, or stuffed things, called the] بِدَادَانِ, above them and beneath them: (M, TA:) pl. صُفَفٌ (Ṣ, M, O, Ḳ) and صِفَافٌ, the latter mentioned by Sb. (M.) — Also † A long period (زَمَانٌ) of time. (O, Ḳ, TA.) So in the saying, عِشْنَا صُفَّةً مِنَ الدَّهْرِ † [We lived, or have lived, a long period of time]. (O, TA.) — And † The quantity of grain that is put upon the palm of the hand: occurring in a trad. of Abu-d-Dardà, in the saying, أَصْبَحْتُ لَا أَمْلِكُ صُفَّةً وَلَا لُقَّةً [I became so that I possessed not the quantity of grain that might be put on the palm of the hand, nor a morsel of food]; اللُّقَّة meaning اللُّقْمَة. (TA.)

صَفَفٌ A thing that a man wears beneath the coat of mail (Ibn-'Abbád, O, Ḳ) in the day of battle. (Ibn-'Abbád, O.)

صَفُوفٌ A she-camel that yields a row of bowls of her milk (تَصُفُّ أَقْدَاحًا مِنْ لَبَنِهَا Ṣ, O, Ḳ) when she is milked, (Ṣ, O,) because of the abundance of her milk: (Ṣ, O, Ḳ:) or for which two vessels are set side by side (يُصَفُّ), and which fills them: (Ḥam p. 535:) or that sets her fore legs evenly, side by side, (تَصُفُّ يَدَيْهَا, [see 1,]) on the occasion of being milked. (Ṣ, M, O, Ḳ.) [See an ex. in a verse cited voce صُوفٌ. And see also صُفُوفٌ.]

صَفِيفٌ Flesh-meat (Ṣ, M) such as has been laid, cut into a strip, or into strips, (صُفَّ, Ṣ, Ḳ, and the like in the M and O, or شُرِّحَ وَصُفَّ, Mgh,) upon the live coals (Ṣ, Mgh, O, Ḳ) to broil (Ṣ, Mgh, Ḳ) or to become thoroughly cooked, (O,) or upon the pebbles, and then roasted, or broiled, (M,) or in the sun, to dry: (O, Ḳ:) or flesh-meat cut into strips, or oblong pieces, and dried in the sun, (M,* Mgh, Mṣb,) or, as Lth says, and in like manner Ks, spread in the sun [to dry]: (Mgh:) or flesh-meat cut into broad slices: (M:) or, accord. to Khálid Ibn-Jembeh, flesh-meat cut into slices, not in the manner of قَدِيد, but made broad, like cakes of bread [which are generally about a span, or somewhat less, in width, round and flat]: (TA:) [or cut thin so as to be translucent: (see 1, latter half:)] or flesh-meat made to boil once, and then taken up [from the fire]. (M.)

الصُّفِّيَّةُ The صُوفِيَّة: so called in relation to those called أَهْلُ الصُّفَّةِ. (TA. (See art. صوف.])

صَافٌّ [originally صَافِفٌ, act. part. n. of صَفَّ, q. v.]. صَافَّةٌ and [its pl.] صَوَافُّ are epithets applied to camels [as meaning Setting their legs in an even row], from صَفَّتْ قَوَائِمَهَا: (Ṣ, O:) [or] صَوَافَّ (in the Ḳur xxii. 37, O, Ḳ) means مَصْفُوفَةً [i. e. set in a row], (M, O, Ḳ, TA,) to be slaughtered; (M, TA;) of the measure فَوَاعِل in the sense of the measure مَفَاعِل [thus in the O, and also (probably copied therefrom) in the copies of the Ḳ; but correctly مَفَاعِيل]: or it means مُصْطَفَّةً [i. e. standing in a row]: (O, Ḳ:) or, as related by I'Ab, it is صَوَافِنَ. (TA.) In the phrase وَالصَّافَّاتِ صَفًّا in the Ḳur [xxxvii. 1], by الصَّافَّات are meant The angels standing in ranks in Heaven, glorifying God. (M, O, Ḳ.) — Applied to a bird, it means Expanding its wings and not moving [or flapping] them [in its flight]: opposed to دَافٌّ. (M and TA in art. دف.)

صَفْصَفٌ A level, or an even, tract of land or ground: (Ṣ, O, Mṣb, Ḳ:) thus expl. by AA, and by Mujáhid, as used in the Ḳur xx. 106: by others as meaning smooth: accord. to Fr, having in it no herbage: and accord. to IAạr, bald: pl. صَفَاصِفُ: (TA:) or أَرْضٌ صَفْصَفٌ signifies a smooth, and level, or even, land; and so, accord. to IJ, [the fem.] صَفْصَفَةٌ. (M.) Also, (M,) or صَفْصَفَةٌ [app. as an epithet in which the quality of a subst. is predominant], (TA,) A desert, or waterless desert; syn. فَلَاةٌ; (M, TA;) from IDrd. (TA.) — And The حَرْف [i. e. ridge, or brow, or ledge,] of a mountain. (Ibn-'Abbád, O, Ḳ.)

صُفْصُفٌ The sparrow, (IDrd, O, Ḳ,) in some one or more of the dialects. (IDrd, O.)

صَفْصَفَةٌ [fem. of صَفْصَفٌ, q. v. — Also] i. q. سُكْبَاجَةٌ [n. un. of سِكْبَاج, q. v., i. e., A mess of the kind of food thus called]; (AA, O, Ḳ;) as also ▼صَفْصَافَةٌ, (O, Ḳ,) which is of the dial. of Thaḳeef. (O.) — And A certain insect (دُوَيْبَّة, Lth, M, O), by the Persians (العَجَم) called the سِيسَك [i. e. weevil]: (Lth, O:) a word adventitious to the Arabic language. (Lth, M, O.)

صَفْصَافٌ The tree called خِلَاف: (Ṣ, M, O, Ḳ:) [accord. to modern usage, the latter is the salix Aegyptia of Linn.: (Forskål's Flora Aegypt. Arab., p. lxxvi., and Delile's Floræ Aegypt. Illustr., no 934:) and the صفصاف accord. to Forskål, ibid., is the salix Babylonica; or this is called صَفْصَاف رُومِىّ: (Delile, no. 932:) and another species of salix is called in Egypt صَفْصَاف بَلَدِىّ: (Forskål, ibid; and Delile, no. 933:)] or so in the dial. of Syria: (M, Mṣb:) or a kind of tree of which the خِلَاف is a species: (Ḳ in art. خلف:) n. un. with ة. (M, O, Ḳ.)

صَفْصَافَةٌ: see صَفْصَفَةٌ. — Also n. un. of صَفْصَاف [q. v.]. (M, O, Ḳ.)

مَصَفٌّ A station, (Ṣ, Mṣb,) or place where ranks are drawn up, (O, Ḳ,) in war, or battle: (Ṣ, O, Mṣb:) pl. مَصَافُّ. (Ṣ, O, Mṣb, Ḳ.)

هُوَ مُصَافِّى He is the person whose صُفَّة [of his house] is over against, or facing, my صُفَّة. (IDrd, O, Ḳ.)

صفح

1. صَفَحَ عَنْهُ, (Mgh, Mṣb, Ḳ,*) aor. َ, (Ḳ,) inf. n. صَفْحٌ, (TA,) properly signifying He turned towards [or from] him, or it, the صَفْحَة [i. e. side] of his face, (Mgh,) means he turned away from, (Mgh, Mṣb, Ḳ,*) and left, (Mṣb, Ḳ,) him, or it, (Mgh, Mṣb,) i. e. [a man, or] an affair. (Mṣb.) And ضَرَبْتُ عَنْهُ صَفْحًا I turned away from him and left him; (Ṣ, TA;) i. e. a man: (TA:) صَفْحًا being here an inf. n., and therefore in the accus. case, as in the phrase قَعَدْتُ جُلُوسًا; or it is in the accus. case as an adv. n., and the meaning is I turned away from him aside. (Ḥar p. 434. [See also, in art. ضرب, a similar phrase in the Ḳur xliii. 4, cited here in the TA, and in Ḥar ubi suprà.]) — And صَفَحَ عَنْهُ, (Ṣ, A, Ḳ, TA,) aor. and inf. n. as above, (TA,) means [also] He turned away from his crime, sin, fault, or offence: (Ṣ, A, TA:) or he forgave him. (Ḳ, TA.) And صَفَحْتُ عَنْ ذَنْبِ فُلَانٍ I turned away from the crime, sin, &c., of such a one, and did not punish him for it: (TA:) or صَفَحْتُ عَنِ الذَّنْبِ, aor. and inf. n. as above, I forgave the crime, sin, &c. (Mṣb.) — And صَفَحَتْ, (Ḳ, TA,) aor. as above, (TA,) inf. n. صُفُوحٌ, said of a she-camel, (Ḳ, TA,) and of a ewe, or she-goat, (TA,) [She ceased to yield her milk;] her milk went away. (Ḳ, TA.) — صَفَحَ as a trans. verb: see 5, in five places. — And see 2. — Also, aor. َ, inf. n. صَفْحٌ, He (a dog) spread forth, or stretched out, his fore legs: a rájiz says,

• صَفْحَ ذِرَاعَيْهِ لِعَظْمٍ كَلْبًا •

[*As the spreading forth of his fore legs, to,* or *for, a bone;* I mean *a dog*]; كلبا being put in the accus. case as an explicative: or he here uses an inversion; meaning صَفْحَ كَلْبٍ ذِرَاعَيْهِ. (L.) — And صَفَحَهُ, (Ṣ,) or صَفَحَهُ بِالسَّيْفِ; (Ḳ;) and ▼ اصفحهُ, (Ṣ,) or اصفحهُ بالسيف; (TA;) *He struck him with the side,* or *flat, of the sword,* (بِعُرْضِهِ, TA, or بِعَرْضِه, Ṣ, Ḳ,) [i. e. *with its* صَفْح, or صُفْح, or صَفْحَة,] *not with its edge.* (TA.) — And صَفَحَهُ, (Ṣ, IAth, Ḳ, TA,) aor. ـَ, inf. n. صَفْحٌ; (TA;) and ▼ اصفحهُ, (Ṣ, Ḳ, TA,) inf. n. إِصْفَاحٌ; (TA;) *He turned him back,* or *sent him away;* namely, a person asking, or begging; (Ṣ, Ḳ, TA;) *he refused his request:* (IAth, TA:) and صَفَحَهُ عَنْ حَاجَتِهِ and ▼ اصفحهُ عَنْهَا *He refused him the thing that he wanted.* (TA.) — And صَفَحَهُ also signifies *He gave to him.* (IAth, TA.) [Thus it has two contr. meanings.] — Also *He gave him to drink* any kind of beverage (Ḳ, TA) and at any time. (TA.) — And صَفَحَ الإِبِلَ عَلَى الحَوْضِ *He made the camels to pass by the watering-trough;* [app. *watering them;*] syn. أَمَرَّهَا عَلَيْهِ. (Ṣ, Ḳ.)

2. صفّح, (Ḳ,) inf. n. تَصْفِيحٌ, (Ṣ,) *He made a* thing *wide,* or *broad;* (Ṣ, Ḳ;) as also ▼ صَفَحَ; (Ḳ;) [and ▼ اصفح;] see مُصَفَّحٌ. One says of a sword, صُفِّحَ, inf. n. as above, *It was made broad,* or *wide, and lengthened out,* in the forging. (IAạr, Ṣ, TA.) = تَصْفِيحٌ is also *syn. with* تَصْفِيقٌ, (Ṣ, Mṣb, Ḳ,) meaning The *clapping with the hands.* (Ṣ, IAth, TA.) One says, صَفَّحَ بِيَدَيْهِ and صَفَّقَ [*He clapped with his hands*]; (A, TA;) *he struck one of his hands upon the other:* (Mgh:) or *he struck with the outer side of the right hand upon the inner side of the left hand.* (O in art. صفق.) [Golius gives صَفَحَ in this sense, erroneously, as from the Ṣ; and Freytag, this form as well as صفّح.] And it is said in a trad., التَّسْبِيحُ لِلرِّجَالِ وَالتَّصْفِيحُ لِلنِّسَآءِ, or, as some relate it, التَّصْفِيقُ instead of التصفيح, [*The saying* سُبْحَانَ ٱللّٰهِ *is for men, and the clapping with the hands is for women;*] (Ṣ, Mgh,* TA;) i. e., when the Imám is inadvertent, the person whom he leads should, if a man, rouse him by saying سبحان الله; and if a woman, should clap with her hands, instead of speaking. (IAth, TA.)

3. مُصَافَحَةٌ signifies The *taking by the hand;* (Ṣ, A, Ḳ;) as also ▼ تَصَافُحٌ; (A;) or the latter has a like meaning: (Ṣ, Ḳ:*) or the former signifies [the *joining hands;* i. e.] the *putting the hand* [*of one*] *in the hand* [*of another*] in meeting and saluting: (Ḥam p. 802:) or the *making the palm of the hand to cleave to* [*that of*] *the hand* [*of another*], *and turning face to face.* (L.) You say, صَافَحَهُ بِيَدِهِ *He took him by his hand.* (A.) And صَافَحْتُهُ, inf. n. as above [and صِفَاحٌ], *I applied my hand to his hand;* (Mṣb;) or *I put the palm of my hand upon the palm of his hand.* (TA.) — And لَقِيَهُ صِفَاحًا *He met him turning towards him the* صَفْح [or *side*] *of his face:* (TA:) or *he met him face to face; i. q.* صِقَابًا: (TA in art. صقب:) [and] *he met him suddenly,* or *unexpectedly.* (Ḥam p. 802.)

4. اصفحهُ: see 1, latter part, in three places: — and see also 2. — Also *He inverted it,* or *reversed it,* (Ibn-Buzurj, Ḳ,) namely, a sword; like صَابَاهُ [q. v.]. (Ibn-Buzurj.)

5. تصفّحهُ *He examined its* صَفَحَات [or *sides*]; i. e. a thing's: (Ṣ:) or *he considered it carefully,* or *attentively, and examined its* صَفَحَات. (A, Mgh.) And تَصَفَّحْتُ الكِتَابَ *I turned over,* or *examined, the* صَفَحَات, meaning *pages, of the book;* as also ▼ صَفَحْتُهُ, inf. n. صَفْحٌ: (Mṣb:) and ▼ صَفَحْتُ وَرَقَ المُصْحَفِ *I examined the leaves of the* مُصْحَف [i. e. *volume,* or *book,* or *copy of the Ḳur-án,*] *one by one.* (O, Ḳ.) And تصفّح القَوْمَ, (Lth, A,) and ▼ صَفَحَهُمْ, (Lth, O, Mṣb, Ḳ,) *He looked at the people, seeking for a particular man:* (Lth:) or *he examined the states,* or *conditions, of the people, and looked among them, to ascertain whether such a one was to be seen:* (A; in explanation of the former:) or *he made the people to pass before him, and examined them, one by one:* (O, Ḳ; in explanation of the latter:) or *he beheld* [or *looked at*] *the* صَفَحَات [or *sides*] *of the faces of the people.* (Mṣb.) And تصفّح وُجُوهَ القَوْمِ *He examined carefully,* or *attentively, the faces of the people, looking at their* (the people's) *external appearances and forms, and seeking to make himself acquainted with their cases:* and *he looked at the faces of the people, seeking to know them;* as also ▼ صَفَحَهَا. (Lth, TA.) And تصفّح الأَمْرَ, (A, TA,) and تصفّح فِى الأَمْرِ, (Ḳ, TA,) and ▼ صَفَحَ الأَمْرَ, (TA,) and صَفَحَ فِى الأَمْرِ, (Ḳ, TA,) *He looked into the affair,* or *case.* (Ḳ, TA.)

6. تَصَافَحَا *They took each the other's hand.* (TḲ.) See also 3. — Hence, تَصَافُحُ الأَجْفَانِ † *The closing together of the eyelids.* (Ḥar p. 364.)

10. استصفحهُ ذَنْبَهُ *He asked him,* or *begged him, to forgive his crime, sin, fault,* or *offence.* (L, TA.)

صَفْحٌ, (Ṣ, A, Mgh, Mṣb, Ḳ,) of a thing, (Ṣ, A, Mgh,) or of anything; (Mṣb;) and ▼ صَفْحَةٌ, (Ṣ, A, Mgh, Mṣb,) of a thing, (Mgh,) or of anything; (Ṣ, A, Mṣb;) The *side;* or *lateral,* or *outward, part* or *portion;* syn. of the former نَاحِيَةٌ; (Ṣ, A;) or of the same, (Ḳ,) or of the latter, (Ṣ, A,) or of each, (Mgh, Mṣb,) جَانِبٌ: (Ṣ, A, Mgh, Mṣb, Ḳ:) and both signify also the *face,* or *surface,* or *front,* of a thing: (Mgh:) pl. [of the former صِفَاحٌ, as below, and] of the latter صَفَحَاتٌ. (Mṣb.) صَفْحَا الشَّىْءِ signifies *The two sides of the thing;* syn. جَانِبَاهُ. (TA.) And صَفْحُ الإِنْسَانِ *The side of the human being;* (Ṣ, O, Ḳ;*) as also ▼ صَفْحَتُهُ. (O.) And hence, صَلَّى إِلَى صَفْحَةِ ▼ بَعِيرِهِ [*He prayed towards the side of his camel*]. (Mgh.) And صَفْحٌ and ▼ صُفْحٌ signify The عُرْض [i. e. *side*] (Ṣ, O, and Ḳ accord. to the TA, but in the CḲ and in my MS. copy of the Ḳ عَرْض, [which in this instance I think a mistake,]) of the face: (Ṣ, O, Ḳ:) and so of a sword; (Ḳ, TA; [in the former of which, in art. عرض, the عُرْض of a sword is said to be its صَفْح;]) or the عَرْض [i. e. *breadth,* or *width,*] (Ṣ, O, Mṣb, and so accord. to the CḲ and my MS. copy of the Ḳ,) of a sword; (Ṣ, O, Mṣb, Ḳ;) i. e. *contr. of* طُول; (Mṣb;) [but it may be well rendered its *side,* or its *flat,* and so ▼ صَفْحَة, for SM says that] صَفْحَتَا السَّيْفِ signifies *the two faces,* or *surfaces, of the sword:* (TA:) one says, نَظَرَ إِلَيْهِ بِصَفْحِ وَجْهِهِ (Ṣ, A) and ▼ بِصُفْحِ وجهه (Ṣ) [*He looked towards him with the side of his face* turned towards him] and ▼ بِصَفْحَتِهِ [which means the same]: (A:) but accord. to AO, one says, ضَرَبَهُ بِصُفْحِ ▼ السَّيْفِ [*He struck him with the side,* or *flat, of the sword*], and the vulgar say بِصَفْحِ السيف, with fet-ḥ: (Ṣ:) the pl. [of صَفْح] is صِفَاحٌ (Ḳ, TA) and [that of ▼ صُفْح is] أَصْفَاحٌ. (TA.) صَفْحَةُ ▼ الرَّجُلِ signifies *The side* (عُرْض) *of the breast of the man.* (L.) And one says, ضَرَبَهُ عَلَى صَفْحَةِ ▼ جَنْبِهِ [*He struck him on the surface,* or *flat part, of his side;* and so على صَفْحِ جنبه; but the former is the more common]. (A.) And جَلَا صَفْحَتَىِ ▼ السَّيْفِ [*He polished the two sides,* or *surfaces, of the sword*]. (A.) And كَتَبَ فِى صَفْحَتَىِ ▼ الوَرَقَةِ [*He wrote upon the two sides,* or *faces, of the piece of paper*]. (A.) صَفَحَاتُ ▼ الكِتَابِ signifies *The pages,* or *faces of the leaves, of the book.* (Mṣb.) And صَفْحُ الكَفِّ *The face* [i. e. *palm*] *of the hand.* (L.) And صَفْحَا الكَتِفِ *The two parts of the scapula that slope down from the* عَيْر [or *spine thereof*]: pl. صِفَاحٌ. (L.) And صَفْحُ الجَبَلِ *The part of the mountain where the side thereof rests upon the ground;* (Ṣ, Ḳ;) *its* سَفْح [q. v.]: (JM:) pl. صِفَاحٌ. (Ṣ.)

صُفْحٌ: see the next preceding paragraph, in four places.

صَفَحٌ *Excessive width* in the forehead. (IAạr, Ḳ.)

صَفْحَةٌ: see صَفْحٌ, in ten places. — [Hence,] أَبْدَى لَهُ صَفْحَتَهُ ‡ *i. q.* كَاشَفَهُ [which is used alone as meaning كَاشَفَهُ بِالعَدَاوَةِ *He showed open enmity,* or *hostility, with him*]: (A, TA:) or *he showed,* or *revealed, to him his deed* [or *crime*] *which he was concealing.* (TA in art. بدو, from a trad. [which shows it to be used in an evil sense].)

صِفَاحٌ, which is disapproved in horses, is [*A quality*] *like what is termed* مَسْحَة [app. meaning *a flatness,* or *an evenness,*] *in the side* (عُرْض) *of the cheek, by reason of which its width is excessive.* (O, Ḳ.) ▬ [It is also an inf. n. of 3, q. v.]

صَفُوحٌ One *who has the quality of turning away from the crimes, sins, faults,* or *offences, of others,* and *of forgiving*; [or rather *wont to turn away* &c.;] as also ▾ صَفَّاحٌ: (TA:) الصَّفُوحُ, (Ḳ, TA,) as an epithet applied to God, (TA,) means *the Very Forgiving*; or *He who forgives much.* (Ḳ, TA.) — And *Generous*; (Ḳ;) because the generous man forgives those who act injuriously towards him. (TA.) — And A woman *who turns away from one; who forsakes one's society*: as though not giving aught but her side. (Ḳ.)

صَفِيحٌ: see صَفِيحَةٌ, in four places. [It is properly a coll. gen. n.: as such signifying *Any kind of thing made flat and broad* or *wide*: as, for instance, *plate,* or *expanded metal*: n. un. with ة, meaning *a piece thereof.*] — [Hence, as it is supposed to be an expanded solid substance,] الصَّفِيحُ, (Ḳ,) or الصَّفِيحُ الأَعْلَى, (TA,) is one of the names of *Heaven.* (Ḳ, TA.)

صَفِيحَةٌ *A wide,* or *broad, stone*; (T, Ṣ;) as also ▾ صَفِيحٌ (T) and ▾ صُفَّاحٌ: (Ṣ:) or [صَفِيحٌ and] صُفَّاحٌ and صَفَائِحُ [which last is pl. of صَفِيحَةٌ] signify *wide,* or *broad, stones, which are put over graves*: (A:) or صَفَائِحُ and ▾ صُفَّاحٌ signify *wide,* or *broad, and thin, stones*; (Ḳ, TA;) one of which is called صَفِيحَةٌ and ▾ صُفَّاحَةٌ: (TA:) and *anything wide,* or *broad,* (Mgh, Mṣb, TA,) *such as a stone,* (TA,) and *a plank,* or *board,* (Mgh, TA,) and *the like,* (TA,) is termed صَفِيحَةٌ (Mgh, Mṣb, TA) and ▾ صُفَّاحَةٌ: (TA:) whence one says, اِشْتَرَى دَارًا فِيهَا صَفَائِحُ مِنْ ذَهَبٍ وَفِضَّةٍ [*He purchased a house in which were plates of gold and of silver*]. (Mgh.) The pl. صَفَائِحُ signifies also [particularly] The *planks, boards,* or *leaves,* (أَلْوَاح,) of a door. (Ṣ, Ḳ.) And *Wide,* or *broad, swords*; (A, Ḳ;) one such sword being termed صَفِيحَةٌ: (Ṣ:) or this latter signifies [simply] *a sword*; and ▾ صَفِيحٌ, *swords.* (Ḥam p. 323.) And The قَبَائِل [or *principal bones,* namely, the *frontal, occipital,* and *two parietal, bones,*] *of the head*; (Ḳ;) a single one of these being termed صَفِيحَةٌ. (TA.) And صَفِيحَةٌ, (Ṣ,) or ▾ صَفِيحٌ, (Ḳ,) or each of these, (TA,) signifies The *face,* or *surface,* of anything wide, or broad. (Ṣ, Ḳ, TA.) And صَفِيحَةُ الوَجْهِ *The exterior skin, cuticle,* or *scarf-skin, of the face.* (Ṣ.)

صَفَّاحٌ: see صَفُوحٌ.

صُفَّاحٌ; and its n. un., with ة: see صَفِيحَةٌ, in five places. — Also ‡ *Camels whose humps have become large,* (Ḳ, TA,) *so that the hump of the she-camel occupies the whole of her back*: n. un. with ة: (TA:) pl. صُفَّاحَاتٌ and صَفَافِيحُ: (Ḳ:) likened to wide, or broad, stones or similar things, because of their hardness. (TA.)

صَافِحٌ A she-camel, (Ḳ,) and a ewe, or she-goat, (TA,) [*ceasing to yield her milk*;] *whose milk is going away*: (Ḳ, TA:) or a she-camel *that has lost her young one, and whose milk has gone.* (IAạr, TA.) — غَيْرَ مُقْنِعٍ رَأْسَهُ وَلَا صَافِحٍ بِخَدِّهِ, occurring in a trad., means [*Not lifting up,* or *elevating, his head,*] *nor putting forth his cheek, nor inclining on one side.* (L.)

أَصْفَحُ A man *excessively wide in the forehead*: from صَفْحٌ. (Ḳ.)

مُصْفَحٌ *Wide,* or *broad*; (Ṣ, Ḳ;) as also ▾ مُصَفَّحٌ, (Ḳ,) which latter is the more common; both applied in this sense to a sword, and to anything; and ▾ مَصْفُوحٌ signifies the same. (TA.) One says, وَجْهُ هٰذَا السَّيْفِ مُصْفَحٌ *The face of this sword is wide,* or *broad*; from ▾ أَصْفَحْتُهُ. (Ṣ.) And ضَرَبَهُ بِالسَّيْفِ مُصْفَحًا, (Ṣ, A, Ḳ,) and ▾ مَصْفُوحًا, (IAạr, TA,) and ▾ مُصْفِحًا, (A, [this last relating to the agent,]) *He struck him with the breadth,* or *width,* [or *flat,*] *of the sword*; (Ṣ, A, Ḳ;) *not with its edge*: (A:) and ضربه بالسيف غَيْرَ مُصْفَحٍ *He struck him with the sword not with its breadth, but with its edge.* (TA.) And رَجُلٌ مُصْفَحُ ▾ الرَّأْسِ *A man wide,* or *broad, in respect of the head*; (Ṣ, TA;) and so مُصَفَّحُ الرَّأْسِ. (TA.) — Also *Having the two sides of his head depressed, and the side of the forehead prominent,* (Ḳ, TA,) *and the occiput also prominent and conspicuous*: (TA:) or *having the fore and hind parts of the head projecting.* (AZ, Mgh.) — And A head *compressed in the parts next the temples, so as to be long between the forehead and the back of the neck.* (Ḳ.) — A nose *straight in the bone*; (Ḳ, TA;) *having the bone even with the forehead.* (TA.) — And A *smooth,* or *soft,* or *smooth and soft, and beautiful,* face. (Lḥ, Ḳ.) — Applied to a sword, (TA,) *Inclined,* or *bent*: (Ṣ, Ḳ, TA:) and *inverted,* or *reversed*: (Ibn-Buzurj, Ḳ, TA:) *that is turned upon its edge when one strikes with it*: and *that is inclined,* or *bent, when one desires to sheath it.* (TA.) — It is said in a trad., قَلْبُ المُؤْمِنِ مُصْفَحٌ عَلَى الحَقِّ, meaning † *The heart of the believer is inclined to the truth*; (Ṣ, L;) as though its side (صَفْحُهُ i. e. جَانِبُهُ) were placed upon it. (L.) And مُصْفَحٌ applied to a heart signifies also † *Turned away from the truth*: (TA:) [or] so applied, *in which are combined faith and hypocrisy*: (Ḳ, TA:) or, accord. to Khálid, *that falls short of its duty*; *in which is latent rancour, malevolence, malice,* or *spite*; *and which is not sincere in its religion*: (Sh, TA:) or it means *double-faced*; *one who meets the unbelievers with one face, and the believers with another face*; صَفْحٌ signifying the "face," of anything. (IAth, TA.) ▬ And المُصْفَحُ is a name of *The sixth of the arrows used in the game called* المَيْسِر; (Ṣ, Ḳ;) as also المُسْبِلُ. (Ṣ.)

مُصْفِحٌ بِالسَّيْفِ *Striking with the side of the sword, not with the edge*; (TA;) *striking with the face of the sword.* (O.) See also مُصْفَحٌ.

مُصَفَّحٌ: see مُصْفَحٌ, in two places. — [Hence,] مُصَفَّحَةٌ signifies *A sword*; as also ▾ مُصْفَحَةٌ: (Ḳ: [but see what follows:]) accord. to IAạr, مُصَفَّحَاتٌ [its pl. (Ḳ)] signifies *swords*; because they are made broad, or wide, and lengthened out, in the forging: (Ṣ:) or, as some say, it signifies *broad,* or *wide, swords.* (TA. [See also صَفِيحَةٌ.]) Lebeed says, describing clouds,

كَأَنَّ مُصَفَّحَاتٍ فِى ذُرَاهَا
وَأَنْوَاحًا عَلَيْهِنَّ المَآلِى

[*As though there were swords,* or *broad swords, upon their summits, and wailing women having upon them the pieces of rag which such women hold in wailing and with which they make signs*]: (Ṣ, TA:) Az says that he likens the lightning, in the darkness of the clouds, to *broad swords*: (TA:) and IAạr says that مصفحات here means *swords*: but as some relate the verse, the word is ▾ مُصَفِّحَاتٌ [meaning *women clapping their hands*]; as though he likened the clouds' discovering themselves when the lightning shone from them, and they opened, and then met together after the lightning's becoming extinct, to the clapping of women's hands: (Ṣ: in some copies of which, الغَيْث is put for الغَمْر:) or, accord. to this reading, he likens the sound of the thunder to women's clapping of their hands. (TA.) — Also A she-camel (T, L) *that is kept from being milked, in order that she may become fat.* (T, L, Ḳ.)

مُصْفَحَةٌ, and its pl.: see مُصَفَّحٌ.

مَصْفُوحٌ: see مُصْفَحٌ, in two places.

مُصَافِحٌ One *who commits adultery,* or *fornication, with any woman, whether she be free or a slave.* (Ḳ.)

صفد

1. صَفَدَهُ, (Ṣ, M, A, Mgh, Ḳ,) aor. ـِ, (Ṣ, M, Mgh, Ḳ,) inf. n. صَفْدٌ (Ṣ, M, Mgh) and صُفُودٌ; (M;) *He bound him, bound him fast* or *made him fast,* (Ṣ, M, A, Mgh, Ḳ,) *shackled him,* or *fettered him, in iron* &c., (M,) or *with iron,* (A,) or *with a* [*collar of iron put upon the neck* or *around the neck and hands together, such as is called*] غُلّ; (L;) and ▾ صَفَّدَهُ, (M, Ḳ,) inf. n. تَصْفِيدٌ, (Ṣ,) signifies the same; (Ṣ, M, Ḳ;) and so ▾ اصفده, (Ḳ,) or this last has a different signification from the two other verbs mentioned above, as expl. below. (L.)

2: see above. — [Hence,] one says, صَفَّدْتُهُ بِكَلَامِى, inf. n. تَصْفِيدٌ *I overcame him by my speech.* (A, TA.)

4. اصفدهُ, (Ṣ, M, A, L,) inf. n. إِصْفَادٌ, (Ṣ,) *He gave him*; (Ṣ, M, A, L;) *gave him freely,* or *gratuitously*; (L;) property, or a slave: (Ṣ:) it is doubly trans. (M.) One says, إِنْ أَفَدْتَنِى حَرْفًا فَقَدْ أَصْفَدْتَنِى أَلْفًا [*If thou teach me a word, verily thou givest me* what is worth *a thousand* dirhems]. (A, TA.) ▬ See also 1.

صَفَدٌ: see the next paragraph, in three places.

صَفَدٌ *A bond;* (Ṣ, Ḳ, TA;) as also ▼ صَفْدٌ (TA:) or, (M, A,) as also ▼ صَفْدٌ, (M,) *i. q.* ▼ صِفَادٌ, (M, A,) which signifies *a rope,* (M,) or *a thong,* (Ṣ, Ḳ,) or *a shackle,* or *fetter,* (Ṣ, A, Ḳ,) or *a [collar of iron which is put upon the neck or around the neck and hands together, such as is called]* غُلّ, (Ṣ, M, A,) *with which one is made fast,* (M,) or *with which a captive is made fast:* (Ṣ, A, Ḳ:) pl. أَصْفَادٌ, [expl. in the Ṣ and A and Ḳ as signifying *shackles,* or *fetters,*] the only known pl., though of the form of a pl. of pauc. (M.) — Also *A gift;* (Ṣ, M, A, Ḳ;) [said to be] so called because he upon whom it is conferred is bound thereby; (Ksh and Bḍ in xxxviii. 37;) and so ▼ صَفْدٌ: (M:) pl. as above. (L.) One says, الصَّفَدُ صَفَدٌ *The gift is a shackle,* or *fetter.* (A.) — And *i. q.* ثَنَآءٌ [which generally means *Praise, eulogy,* or *commendation;* but is said by some to mean also *the contr.*]. (M.)

صِفَادٌ: see the next preceding paragraph.

نُهِىَ عَنْ صَلَاةِ الصَّافِدِ *The praying of him who puts his feet together as though they were fettered is forbidden.* (L, from a trad.)

إِصْفِدٌ is used by a poet for إِصْفِنْطٌ [q. v.]. (M.)

صفر

1. صَفِرَ, aor. ـَ, inf. n. صَفِيرٌ, (Ṣ, M, Ḳ,) with which ▼ صُفَارٌ is syn. in a phrase mentioned below; (Ṣ;) and ▼ صفّر, (M, Ḳ,) inf. n. تَصْفِيرٌ; (TA;) *He,* or *it,* (a bird, a vulture, Ṣ, and a serpent, or the أَسْوَد, or أَعْرَج, or ابْن قِتْرَة, or أَصَلَة, M,) *whistled;* syn. مَكَا; (Ṣ;) *made,* or *uttered, a certain sound,* (M, Mṣb,* Ḳ,) *without the utterance of letters.* (Mṣb.) [It is mostly said of a bird: see an ex. voce جُوّ.] One says [also], صَفَرَ فِى الصَّفَّارَةِ [*He whistled in the whistle*]. (M, Ḳ.) And صَفَرَ بِالْحِمَارِ, and ▼ صفّر, *He called the ass to water* [*by whistling;* for to do thus is the common custom of the Arabs]. (M, Ḳ.) And Fr mentions the phrase, ▼ كَانَ فِى كَلَامِهِ صُفَارٌ, meaning صَفِيرٌ [i. e. *There was in his speech a whistling*]. (Ṣ.) — صَفِرَ, aor. ـَ, inf. n. صَفَرٌ (Ṣ, M, A, Ḳ, &c.) and صُفُورٌ; (M, Ḳ;) and accord. to the T, صَفَرَ, aor. ـُ, inf. n. صُفُورَةٌ; (TA;) *It,* or *he, was,* or *became, empty, void,* or *vacant;* (Ṣ, M, A, Mṣb, Ḳ;) namely, a house or tent; (Ṣ;) or a vessel, (Ṣ, M, &c.,) مِنَ الطَّعَامِ وَالشَّرَابِ [*of food and beverage*]; and a skin, مِنَ اللَّبَنِ [*of milk*]; (TA;) and a hand; (A;) and a thing; (Ṣ, M;) and accord. to ISk, صَفِرَ, aor ـَ, inf. n. صَفِيرٌ, is said of a man. (TA.) [See also 4, last sentence but one.] One says, نَعُوذُ بِاللّٰهِ مِنْ قَرَعِ الفِنَآءِ وَصَفَرِ الإِنَآءِ (Ṣ, M, A) [*We seek preservation by God from the yard's becoming void of cattle, and the vessel's becoming empty;*] meaning, *from the perishing of the cattle.* (Ṣ.) And صَفِرَتْ وِطَابُهُ, (M, A, Ḳ, [in the CḲ, erroneously, وَطَابُهُ,]) and صَفِرَ إِنَاؤُهُ, (A,) [lit. *His milk-skins,* and *his vessel, became empty;*] meaning ‡ *he died;* (M, Ḳ;) *he perished.* (A. [See also other explanations in art. وطب.]) — صُفِرَ, (M, Ḳ,) inf. n. صَفْرٌ, (Ḳ,) *He had what is termed* صَفَار, i. e. *yellow water in his belly.* (M, Ḳ.)

2: see above, in two places. — and see 4. — Also صفّرهُ, (Ṣ, M, Ḳ,) inf. n. تَصْفِيرٌ, (Ḳ,) *He made it yellow:* (Ṣ:) *he dyed it yellow;* (M, Ḳ;) namely, a garment, or piece of cloth. (M.)

4. اصفرهُ *He emptied it;* or *made it void,* or *vacant;* namely, a house or tent [&c.]; (M, Ḳ;) as also ▼ صفّرهُ, (Ḳ,) inf. n. تَصْفِيرٌ. (TA.) The Arabs say, مَا أَصْفَيْتُ لَكَ إِنَآءً وَلَا أَصْفَرْتُ لَكَ فِنَآءً [*I have not overturned a vessel belonging to thee, nor have I emptied a yard belonging to thee*]; meaning I have not taken thy camels nor thy property, so that thy vessel should be overturned and thou shouldst find no milk to milk into it, and so that thy yard should be empty, plundered, no camel or sheep or goat lying in it: it is said in excusing oneself. (M.) — [Accord. to Freytag, اصفر signifies also *It* (a house) *was,* or *became, empty,* or *void,* of (مِنْ) household-goods: so that it is syn. with صَفِرَ: and this is probably correct: for —] أَصْفَرَ, (Ṣ, Ḳ,) also, (Ḳ,) signifies *He was,* or *became, poor;* (Ṣ, Ḳ;) said of a man. (Ṣ.)

5. تصفّر المَالُ *The cattle became in good condition, the vehement heat of summer having departed from them:* [or,] accord. to Ṣgh, تصفّرت الإِبِلُ signifies *The camels became fat in the* [*season called the*] صَفَرِيَّة. (TA.)

9. اصفرّ *It became* أَصْفَر [i. e. *yellow:* and also *black*]: (Ṣ, M, Ḳ:) and so ▼ اصفارّ: (Ṣ, Ḳ:) or the former signifies *it was so constantly:* and the latter, *it was so transiently.* (Az, TA. [See 9 in art. حمر.])

11: see the next preceding paragraph.

صِفْرٌ: see صَفْرٌ.

صُفْرٌ: see صِفْرٌ. — Also, (Ṣ, M, A, Mṣb, Ḳ,) and ▼ صِفْرٌ accord. to AO, (Ṣ, M, Mṣb,*) who allowed no other form, but the former is the better, (M,) [*Brass;*] the *metal of which vessels are made;* (Ṣ;) *i. q.* نُحَاس [which means both *copper* and *brass*]; (A, Mṣb;) or *a sort of* نُحَاس; or نُحَاس *made yellow;* (M;) or the *best sort of* نُحَاس; (Mṣb;) or *an excellent sort thereof:* (TA:) n. un. ▼ صُفْرَةٌ. (M.) — And *Gold:* (M, A, Ḳ: [see also الصَّفْرَآءُ, voce أَصْفَرُ:]) or *deenars;* either because they are yellow (صُفْر [pl. of أَصْفَرُ]), or thus called because resembling the صُفْر of which vessels are made. (M.) — And *Women's ornaments.* (A.) — إِنَّهُ لَفِى صُفْرِهِ, (Ṣ, O, TA, [thus in an old and very excellent copy of the Ṣ, in another copy of which I find, as in Freytag's Lex., ▼ صُفْرَةٍ,]) and ▼ صِفْرِهِ, (TA,) [app. means *He is in that state in which he requires to be rubbed with saffron;* for it] is said of him who is affected by madness, when he is in the days in which his reason fails; because they used to rub him with somewhat of saffron. (Ṣ, O, L.)

صِفْرٌ (Ṣ, M, A, Mṣb, Ḳ) and ▼ صُفْرٌ and ▼ صِفِرٌ (M, Ḳ) and ▼ صَفْرٌ (M) and ▼ أَصْفَرُ (Mṣb) *Empty, void,* or *vacant;* (Ṣ, M, A, Mṣb, Ḳ;) applied to a house or tent, (Ṣ, Mṣb,) and to a vessel, (M, A,) and to a hand: (A:) each of the first three is used alike as masc. and fem. and sing. [and dual] and pl.: (M:) [and so, app., is the last but one:] and each has also for its pl. أَصْفَارٌ. (M, Ḳ.) One says بَيْتٌ صِفْرٌ مِنَ المَتَاعِ *A house,* or *tent,* or *chamber, empty,* or *void, of furniture and utensils.* (Ṣ.) And [applying the pl. form of the epithet to a sing. subst.,] إِنَآءٌ أَصْفَارٌ *An empty vessel;* (M, Ḳ;) like as one says بُرْمَةٌ أَعْشَارٌ; on the authority of IAạr: (M:) and [applying the sing. form of the epithet to a pl. subst.,] آنِيَةٌ صِفْرٌ *empty vessels.* (M, Ḳ.) And رَجُلٌ صِفْرُ اليَدَيْنِ *A man empty-handed.* (Ṣ, Mṣb.) And صِفْرٌ مِنَ الخَيْرِ † *Void of good.* (TA.) And it is said, in a trad., of Umm-Zarạ, that she was صِفْرُ رِدَائِهَا meaning † *Lank in her belly;* as though her رِدَاء, which is a garment that falls upon the belly and there ends, were empty. (TA.) And هُوَ صِفْرٌ صِحْرٌ *It is* [*utterly*] *empty;* صحر being an imitative sequent. (Kh, Ḥam p. 354.) — صِفْرٌ in arithmetical notation, in the Indian method, is *A circle* [or the character ٥, denoting *nought,* or *zero;* whence our term "cipher:" when nought is thus denoted, five is denoted by a character resembling our B: but more commonly, in the present day, nought is denoted by a round dot; and five, by ٥]. (L, TA.) — See also صُفْرٌ, in two places.

صَفَرٌ [an inf. n. of صَفِرَ, q. v.: — and hence,] *Hunger:* and ▼ صَفْرَةٌ [the inf. n. un.] *a hungering once.* (M, Ḳ.) — Also *A certain disease in the belly, which renders the face yellow:* (M, Ḳ:) or *a collecting of water in the belly.* (Ḳt.) [See also صُفَار.] — Also *A kind of serpent,* (Ṣ, M, Ḳ,) *in the belly,* (Ṣ, Ḳ,) *which sticks to the ribs, and bites them,* (M, Ḳ,) or, as the Arabs assert, *which bites a man when he is hungry, its bite occasioning the stinging which a man feels when he is hungry:* (Ṣ:) used alike as sing. and pl.; or one is termed صَفَرَةٌ: (M:) and it is said to be what is meant by the word in a trad., in which it is disacknowledged: (Ṣ, TA:) or *a certain reptile* (دَابَّة) *which bites the ribs and their cartilages:* (M, Ḳ:) or *a certain serpent in the belly, which attacks beasts and men, and which, accord. to the Arabs* [*of the time of Ignorance*], *passes from one to another more than the mange or scab:* (Ru-beh:) the Prophet, however, denied its doing so: it is said also that *it oppresses and hurts a man when he is hungry:* (A'Obeyd:) this is the explanation approved by Az: (TA:) or, as also ▼ صُفَارٌ, *worms in the belly,* (M, Ḳ, TA,) *and in the cartilages of the ribs, which cause a man to become very yellow, and sometimes kill him.* (TA.) You say, عَضَّ عَلَى شُرْسُوفِهِ الصَّفَرُ, meaning, ‡ *He was hungry.* (A.) — Accord. to some, (M,) in the trad. above referred to, صَفَرٌ signifies *The postponing of* [*the month*] *El-Moharram, transferring it to Ṣafar:* (A'Obeyd, M, Ḳ:) [see نَسِىٌّ:] or it there means the disease called by this name, because they asserted it to be transitive. (Ḳ.) —

Also The *intellect*, or *understanding*; or the *heart*, or *mind*; syn. رُوعٌ: (M, Ḳ: [in the CḲ رَوْع:]) the *inmost part* (لُبّ) *of the heart*. (M, Ḳ.) Hence the saying, (TA,) لَا يَلْتَاطُ هٰذَا بِصَفَرِى *This will not adhere to me*, [or *to my mind*,] *nor will my soul accept it*: (Ṣ, TA:) said of that which one does not love. (A.) ═ Also *A contract*, *compact*, or *covenant*: or *suretiship*, or *responsibility*: syn. عَقْدٌ. (M, L, Ḳ. [In some copies of the Ḳ, فقد.]) ═ Also (Ṣ, M, Mṣb, Ḳ) and sometimes [صَفَرُ,] imperfectly decl., (Ḳ,) but all make it perfectly decl. except AO, who makes it imperfectly decl. because it is determinate [or a proper name] and similar in meaning to سَاعَةٌ, which is fem., meaning that all nouns signifying times are سَاعَات, (Th, M,) and, accord. to some, الصَّفَرُ, (Mṣb,) [*The second month of the Arabian calendar*;] *the month that is* [*the next*] *after El-Moharram* (المُحَرَّمُ): (Ṣ, M, Ḳ:) so called because in it they used to procure their provision of corn from the places [in which it was collected, their granaries having then become empty (صِفْر); agreeably with the opinion of my learned friend Mons. Fulgence Fresnel, that it was so called from the scarcity of provisions in the season in which it fell when it was first named; for it then fell in winter: see the latter of the two tables in p. 1254; and see also نَسِىْءٌ]: or because Mekkeh was then empty, its people having gone forth to travel: or, accord. to Ru-beh, because the Arabs in it made predatory expeditions, and left those whom they met empty: (M:) or because they then made predatory expeditions, and left the houses of the people empty: (Mṣb in art. جمد:) pl. أَصْفَارٌ, (Ṣ, M, Mṣb, Ḳ,) and, as some say, صَفَرَاتٌ. (Mṣb.) — الصَّفَرَانِ *The two months of El-Moharram and Ṣafar*; (M;) *two months of the year, whereof one was called by the Muslims El-Moharram*. (IDrd, M, Mṣb, Ḳ.)

صُفْرٌ: } see صِفْرٌ, first sentence.
صُفُرٌ: }

صَفْرَةٌ: see صَفْرٌ, [of which it is the n. un.,] first sentence.

صُفْرَةٌ [*Yellowness*;] *a certain colour*, (Ṣ, M, Mṣb,) *well known*, (M, Ḳ,) *less intense than red*, (Mṣb,) *found in animals and in some other things*, *and*, accord. to IAạr, *in water*. (M.) — Also *Blackness*. (M, Ḳ.) — See also صُفْرٌ, in two places. ═ صُفْرَةُ, imperfectly decl., is a proper name for *The she-goat*. (Ṣgh, Ḳ.)

صَفَرِىٌّ (Ṣ, M, Ḳ) and ♦ صَفَرِيَّةٌ (Ḳ) The *increase*, or *offspring*, (نِتَاج,) *of sheep or goats* (Ṣ, M, Ḳ [in the CḲ, او is erroneously put for و before this explanation]) *after that called* قَيْظِىٌّ: (Ṣ, TA:) or *at the period of the* [*auroral*] *rising of Suheyl* [or *Canopus*, which, in Central Arabia, at the commencement of the era of the Flight, was about the 4th of August, O. S.; here erroneously said in the M to be in the beginning of winter]: (M, Ḳ:) or ♦ the latter word signifies [as above, and also the *period itself above mentioned*: or] the *period from the rising of Suheyl to the setting of* الذِّرَاع [*the Seventh Mansion of the Moon*, which, in the part and age above mentioned, was about the 3rd of January, O. S.], *when the cold is intense*; and then breeding is approved: (M:) or the *period from the rising of Suheyl to the rising of* السِّمَاك [*the Fourteenth Mansion of the Moon*, which, in the part and age above mentioned, was about the 4th of October, O. S.], *commencing with forty nights of varying*, or *alternating*, *heat and cold*, *called* المُعْتَدِلَاتُ: (AZ:) the first increase [of sheep and goats] is the صَقَعِىّ, which is when the sun smites (تَصْقَعُ) the heads of the young ones; and some of the Arabs call it the شَمْسِىّ, and the قَيْظِىّ: then is the صَفَرِىّ, after the صَقَعِىّ; and that is when the fruit of the palm-tree is cut off: then, the شَتَوِىّ, which is in the [season called] رَبِيع: then, the دَفَئِىّ, which is when the sun becomes warm: then, the صَيْفِىّ: then, the قَيْظِىّ: then, the خَرَفِىّ, in the end of the [season called] قَيْظ: (Aboo-Naṣr:) or صَفَرِيَّةٌ signifies, (M, Ḳ,) and so صَفَرِىٌّ, (Ḳ,) the [*period of the*] *departure of the heat and the coming of the cold*: (AḤn, M, Ḳ:) or the *period between the departure of the summer and the coming of the winter*: (Aboo-Sa'eed:) or the *first of the seasons*; [app. meaning the *autumnal season*, *called* الخَرِيف, *which was the first of the four*, *and of the six*, *seasons*; or perhaps the *first of the seasons of rain*, *commonly called* الوَسْمِىّ;] and it may be *a month*: (AḤn, M, Ḳ:) or the latter, (M,) or both, (TA,) the *beginning of the year*. (M, TA.) [Hence,] أَيَّامُ ♦ الصَّفَرِيَّةِ *Twenty days of*, or *from*, (مِنْ,) *the latter part of the summer*, or *hot season*. (TA voce حُلْبٌ.) — Also the former, (Ṣ,) or ♦ both, (TA,) The *rain that comes in the beginning of autumn*: (Ṣ:) or *from the period of the rising of Suheyl to that of the setting of* الذِّرَاع [expl. above]. (TA.) — Also the latter, (Ṣ, M,) or ♦ both, (Ḳ,) *A plant that grows in the beginning of the autumn*: (Ṣ, M, Ḳ:) so called, accord. to AḤn, because the beasts become yellow when they pasture upon that which is green; their arm-pits and similar parts, and their lips and fur, becoming yellow; but [ISd says,] I have not found this to be known. (M.)

صُفْرِيَّةٌ *A sort of dates of El-Yemen*, *which are dried in the state in which they are termed* بُسْر, (AḤn, M, Ḳ,) *being then yellow*; *and when they become dry*, *and are rubbed with the hand*, *they crumble*, *and* سَوِيق *is sweetened with them*, *and they surpass sugar*; (AḤn, M;) [or] *they supply the place of sugar in* سَوِيق. (Ḳ.) ═ الصُّفْرِيَّةُ, (Ṣ, M, Ḳ,) and, (Ḳ,) or as some say, (Ṣ, M,) ♦ الصِّفْرِيَّةُ, (M, Ḳ,) *A sect of the* خَوَارِج, (Ṣ,) *a party of the* حَرُورِيَّة; (M, Ḳ;) so called in relation to Ṣufrah (صُفْرَة) [which is the name of a place in El-Yemámeh]): (M:) or in relation to Ziyád Ibn-El-Aṣfar, (Ṣ, Ḳ,) their head, or chief; (Ṣ;) or to 'Abd-Allah (Ṣ, M, Ḳ) Ibn-Eṣ-Ṣaffár, (Ṣ,) or Ibn-Ṣaffár, (Ḳ,) or Ibn-Ṣafár, (so in a copy of the M,) in which case it is extr. in form; (M;) or on account of the yellowness of their complexions; or because of their being void of religion; (Ḳ;) accord. to which last derivation, it is ♦ الصِّفْرِيَّةُ, with kesr; and Aṣ holds this to be the right opinion. (TA.) — And the former (الصُّفْرِيَّةُ) *The* مَهَالِبَة, (M, Ḳ,) who were celebrated for bounty and generosity; (TA;) so called in relation to Aboo-Ṣufrah, (M, Ḳ,) who was [surnamed] Abu-l-Mohelleb. (M.)

الصِّفْرِيَّةُ: see the next preceding paragraph in two places.

صَفَرِيَّةٌ: see صَفَرِىٌّ, in five places.

صِفْرِيتٌ is the sing. of صَفَارِيتُ, (Ṣ,) which signifies *Poor men*: (Ṣ, Ḳ:) the ت is augmentative. (Ṣ.)

صَفَارٌ, (Ṣ, M,) with fet-ḥ, (Ṣ,) or ♦ صُفَارٌ, like غُرَابٌ, (Ḳ,) *What is dry*, *of* [*the species of barley-grass called*] بُهْمَى: (Ṣ, M, Ḳ:) app. because of its yellowness: (M:) *it has prickles that cling to the lips of the horses*. (TA in art. شفه.) — And the former, accord. to ISk, *A certain plant*. (TA.)

صُفَارٌ: see 1, in two places. ═ Also *A certain disease*, *in consequence of which one becomes yellow*: (A:) the *yellow water that collects in the belly*; (M, Ḳ;) *i. q.* سِقْىٌ: (M:) or *a collecting of yellow water in the belly*, *which is cured by cutting the* نَائِط, *a vein in the* صُلْب [i. e. *backbone*, or *back*]. (Ṣ.) — See also صَفَرٌ. — And see صَفَارٌ. — Also *A yellowness that takes place in wheat before the grain has become full*. (A, TA.) — And *Remains of straw and of other fodder*, *at the roots of the teeth of beasts*; as also ♦ صِفَارٌ. (M, Ḳ.) — And The *tick*, or *ticks*: (M, Ḳ:) and, (Ḳ,) or as some say, (M,) *an insect*, or *animalcule*, (دُوَيْبَّة,) *that is found in the solid hoofs*, *and in the toes*, *or soles*, *of camels*, (M, Ḳ,) *in the hinder parts thereof*. (M.)

صِفَارٌ: see the next preceding paragraph.

صَفِيرٌ inf. n. of صَفَرَ [q. v.]. (Ṣ, M, Ḳ.) ═ [In the present day it signifies also The *sapphire*.]

صُفَارَةٌ *What has withered*, (M, Ḳ,) *and become altered to yellow*, (M,) *of plants*, or *herbage*. (M, Ḳ.)

صَفِيرَةٌ *A dam* (ضَفِيرَة) *between two tracts of land*. (Ṣgh, Ḳ.)

صُفَارَى *A species of bird*, *that whistles* (يَصْفِرُ). (M. [See also what next follows.])

صُفَارِيَّةٌ *A certain bird*; (IAạr, Ṣ;) as also صُفَارِيَةٌ, without teshdeed; (Ṣ;) the *bird called* تُبَشِّرُ, (Ṣ in art. بشر,) or تُبَشِّرٌ: (Ḳ in that art.:) [Golius (who writes the word صَفَارِيَّة) adds, "ut puto, quæ in Syria صُفَيْرَا dicitur, *flava*, *duplo major passere*, nam et *passer luteus*, ut reddit Meid.":] *i. q.* صَعْوَةٌ. (IAạr.) [See also الأَصْقَعُ.]

صُفُورِيَّةٌ, accord. to the Ḳ, *A kind of* نَبَات [i. e. *plant*]: but in the Tekmileh, *a kind of* ثِيَاب [i. e. *garments*, or *cloths*]; pl. of ثَوْب; and it bears the mark of correctness. (TA.)

صَفَّارٌ: see صَافِرٌ. — Also *A fabricator of* صُفْر [or *brass*]. (M, Ḳ.)

صُفَّارٌ, with ḍamm, The *entire quill of a feather.* (AA, O.)

صَفَّارَةٌ [*A whistle:* so in the present day: and also *a fife:*] *a hollow thing* (M, Ḳ) *of copper,* (Ḳ,) *in which a boy whistles* (M, Ḳ) *to pigeons,* (Ḳ,) or *to an ass, that he may drink.* (TṢ, L, Ḳ.) — [Hence,] الصَّفَّارَةُ *The anus;* syn. الإِسْتُ; (M, Ḳ;) in the dial. of the Sawád. (TA.)

صَافِرٌ *Whistling;* or *a whistler.* (TA.) — And hence, (TA,) *A thief;* (Ḳ;) as also ▼ صَفَّارٌ: [or this signifies *a frequent*, or *habitual, whistler:*] the thief being so called because he whistles in fear of his being suspected: whence, as some explain it, the saying أَجْبَنُ مِنْ صَافِرٍ [*More cowardly than a thief*]: (TA:) a prov.: accord. to AO, it means in this instance *one who whistles to a woman for the purpose of fornication* or *adultery;* because he fears lest he should be seen: or — accord. to A'Obeyd, *Any bird that whistles;* for birds of prey do not whistle, but only ignoble birds, that are preyed upon: (Meyd:) [or] *any bird that does not prey:* (M, Ḳ:) and *any bird having a cry:* and *a certain cowardly bird:* (Ḳ:) [accord. to Dmr, as stated by Freytag, it is *a bird of the passerine kind;* also called ▼ صَافِرِيَّةٌ:] accord. to Moḥammad Ibn-Ḥabeeb, (Meyd,) *a certain bird that suspends itself from trees, hanging down its head, whistling all the night in fear lest it should sleep and be taken;* and so in the prov. above mentioned: (Meyd, A:*) or, accord. to IAạr, it means ▼ مَصْفُورٌ بِهِ [*whistled to*]: i. e., when he is whistled to, he flees: and by ▼ المَصْفُورُ بِهِ is meant the *bird called* التنوط [i. e. التَّنَوُّط or التُّنَوِّط &c.], *the cowardice of which induces it to weave for itself a nest like a purse, suspended from a tree, narrow in the mouth and wide in the lower part, in which it protects itself, fearing lest a bird of prey should light upon it:* (Meyd: [see also art. نوط:]) or *any coward.* (TA.) — مَا بِهَا صَافِرٌ *There is not in it* (i. e. the house, الدَّار, TA) *any one:* (Ṣ, Ḳ:) [lit.] *any one who whistles:* (M:) or *any one to be called by whistling;* صافر being here an instance of the measure فَاعِلٌ in the sense of the measure مَفْعُولٌ followed by بِهِ. (T, TA.)

صَافِرِيَّةٌ: see the next preceding paragraph.

أَصْفَرُ [a comparative and superlative epithet from صَفَرَ]. One says أَصْفَرُ مِنْ بُلْبُلٍ [*A greater whistler*, or *warbler, than the* بلبل]. (Ṣ.) — See also صِفْرٌ. — [Also *More*, and *most, empty, void*, or *vacant.*] It is said in a trad., أَصْفَرُ البُيُوتِ مِنَ الخَيْرِ البَيْتُ الصِّفْرُ مِنْ كِتَابِ اللّٰهِ [*That one of houses which is the most void of good is the house that is destitute of the Book of God*]. (Ṣ.) — Also [*Yellow;*] *of the colour termed* صُفْرَةٌ: (Ṣ, M, Ḳ:) fem. صَفْرَآءُ: (Mṣb, &c.:) pl. صُفْرٌ. (TA.) And *Black* (A'Obeyd, Ṣ, Ḳ) is sometimes thus termed: (Ṣ:) applied to a camel, as in the Ḳur lxxvii. 33, because a black camel always has an intermixture of yellow: (TA:) or, applied to a camel, *of a colour whereof the ground is black, with some yellow hairs coming through.* (M.) Applied to a horse, *Of the colour termed in Pers.* زَرْدَهْ [*a kind of sorrel*], (Ṣ,) but not unless *having a yellow* [or *sorrel*] *tail and mane.* (Aṣ, Ṣ.) — بَنُو الأَصْفَرِ *The Greeks* (الرُّوم): (Ṣ, A:) or *their kings:* because the sons of El-Aṣfar the son of Room the son of 'Eesoo (or 'Eyṣoon, TA, [i. e. Esau,]) the son of Is-ḥáḳ [or Isaac] (Ḳ) the son of Ibráheem [or Abraham]: (TA:) or El-Aṣfar was a surname of Room: (TA:) or they were so called because their first ancestor, (A, IAth,) Room the son of 'Eyṣoon, (IAth,) was of a yellow complexion: (A, IAth:) or because they were conquered by an army of Abyssinians by whom their women had yellow children: (Ḳ:) [or] they are *the modern Muscovites.* (TA.) — الأَصْفَرَانِ *Gold and saffron;* (Ṣ, M, Ḳ;) which are said to destroy women: (TA:) or *the plant called* وَرْس *and saffron:* (Ṣ, Ḳ:) or *the plant called* وَرْس *and gold:* (M:) or *saffron and raisins.* (ISk, Ṣgh, Ḳ.) — And الصَّفْرَآءُ *Gold.* (M, Ḳ. [See also صُفْر.]) Hence the saying of 'Alee, يَا صَفْرَآءُ اصْفَرِّى وَيَا بَيْضَآءُ ابْيَضِّى وَغُرِّى غَيْرِى *O gold,* [*be yellow,*] *and O silver,* [*be white, and beguile other than me:*] and one says also, مَا لِفُلَانٍ صَفْرَآءُ وَلَا بَيْضَآءُ [*There is not belonging to such a one gold nor silver*]. (TA.) — Also *A kind of bile,* (M, Ḳ,) *well-known;* (Ḳ;) [*the yellow bile; one of the four humours of the body;* of which the others are the black bile (السَّوْدَآءُ), the blood (الدَّمُ), and the phlegm (البَلْغَمُ):] so called because of its colour. (M.) — And *The bow that is made of* [*the tree called*] نَبْع. (Ṣ,* Ḳ,* TA.) — And *The female locust that is devoid of eggs.* (M, Ḳ.) — And *A certain plant,* (Ṣ, M, Ḳ,) *of the plain or soft tracts, and of the sands,* (M, Ḳ,) *and sometimes growing in hard level ground:* (M:) or *a certain herb, that spreads upon the ground,* (AḤn, M,) *the leaves of which are like those of the* خَسّ [or *lettuce*], (AḤn, M, Ḳ,) *and which the camels eat vehemently:* (AḤn, M:) it is *of the kind called* ذُكُور. (Aboo-Naṣr, M.)

مُصْفَرٌ: see its fem., with ة, voce مَصْفُورٌ.

مُصْفِرٌ *A poor man.* (Ṣ.)

مُصَفَّرٌ; and its fem., with ة: see مَصْفُورٌ.

هُوَ مُصَفِّرٌ اسْتَهُ is from الصَّفِيرُ, [see صَفَرَ,] not from الصُّفْرَةُ, (Ṣ,) and means *He is a* ضَرَّاط; (Ṣ, Ḳ;) as though denoting cowardice: (TA:) or it is from صَفَّرَ "he dyed yellow;" (M;) and was applied to Aboo-Jahl; (M, TA;) meaning that he dyed his اِسْت with saffron, and was addicted to [the enormity termed] أُبْنَة: this, accord. to Ṣgh, is the correct explanation; and he adds that it is said of a luxurious man, whom experience and afflictions have not rendered firm, or sound, in judgment. (TA.) — المُصَفِّرَةُ is an appellation applied to *Those whose sign* [meaning *the colour of their ensign*] *is* صُفْرَة; (M, Ḳ;) [i. e. *whose ensign is yellow;*] and is similar to المُحَمِّرَةُ and المُبَيِّضَةُ. (M.)

مَصْفُورٌ: see صَافِرٌ, in two places. — Also *Hungry;* and so ▼ مُصْفَرٌ. (Ḳ.) — Of the fem., مَصْفُورَةٌ, (TA,) and ▼ مُصْفَرَةٌ, (Mgh, TA,) or ▼ مُصَفَّرَةٌ, (Mgh,) which one is forbidden to offer in sacrifice, (Mgh, TA,) it is said that the first is *Such as has the ear entirely cut off;* because its ear-hole is destitute of the ear: and the second, *the lean*, or *emaciated;* because devoid of fatness; or, accord. to Ḳt, the first and second have the latter meaning, as though destitute of fat and flesh: (TA:) or the second and third have the latter meaning; or the former meaning: (Mgh:) but accord. to the relation of Sh, what is thus forbidden is termed المَصْغُورَةُ, with غ, having the former of the meanings expl. above; which IAth disapproves: (TA in art. صغر:) or المُصْغَرَةُ. (Mgh in that art.) — Also *Having the disease termed* صُفَار: (A, TA:) or one *from whose belly comes forth yellow water.* (TA.)

صفرد

صِفْرِدٌ *A certain bird,* (Ṣ, M, Ḳ,) *of a cowardly nature,* (Ḳ,) *larger than the sparrow,* (M,) *that frequents houses, and is the most cowardly of birds;* (Lth;) *it is afraid of the* [*little bird called*] صَعْوَة; (IAạr;) *and is by the vulgar* (Ṣ) *called* أَبُو المَلِيح. (Ṣ, Ḳ. [Accord. to Golius, the *nightingale:* but this I think a mistake.]) أَجْبَنُ مِنْ صِفْرِدٍ [*More cowardly than a ṣifrid*] is a prov., (Ṣ, Meyd,) asserted by AO to be post-classical. (Meyd. [See Freytag's Arab. Prov. i. 372.])

صفط

إِصْفَنْطٌ a dial. var. of إِسْفَنْطٌ, q. v. (Aṣ, Ḳ.)

صفع

1. صَفَعَهُ, aor. َ, (O, Mṣb, Ḳ,) inf. n. صَفْعٌ, (Ṣ,* O, Mṣb, TA,) accord. to Lth, (O, TA,) *He struck him with his fist, not vehemently, on the back of his neck:* (O, Ḳ, TA:) or, (O, Ḳ,) accord. to Az (O, Mṣb, TA) and others, (Mṣb,) *he struck him* [i. e. *slapped him*] *with his expanded hand* (O, Mṣb, Ḳ, TA) *on the back of his neck, or on his body; not with the fist:* (O, Mṣb, TA:) or it is post-classical: (Ṣ, Ḳ:) [but Fei says,] the assertion that it is post-classical is not to be regarded: (Mṣb:) Az adds, IDrd says that it is from ▼ صَوْفَعَة, (O, TA,) which signifies the *top*, or *uppermost part, of the* [*cap called*] كُمَّة, *and of the turban:* (O, Ḳ, TA:) or this is a mistranscription, and is correctly with ق: (Ḳ, TA:) [Ṣgh says,] this which Az mentions, [as] on the authority of IDrd, I have not found in the Jm; and it is correctly with ق. (O.)

صَفْعَةٌ *A single act of striking* [or *slapping*] *with the expanded hand upon the back of the neck, or upon the body.* (Mṣb.)

صَفْعَانٌ or صَفْعَانٌ (accord. to different copies of the Ṣ and Ḳ) A man *who is struck* [or *slapped*] *in the manner expl. above in the first paragraph*; (Ṣ, Mṣb, Ḳ;) as also ▼ مُصْفَعَانِىٌّ. (O, Ḳ.)

صَوْفَعَةٌ: see the first paragraph of this art.

صَفْعَانٌ: see مُصْفَعَانِىٌّ.

صفق

1. صَفْقٌ [inf. n. of صَفَقَ] signifies The *striking* [a thing] *so as to cause a sound to be heard in consequence thereof*; (Ṣ, O, Ḳ;) as also تَصْفِيقٌ [inf. n. of ▼ صفّق, but this has an intensive signification]: (Ṣ:) and تَصْفَاقٌ is [also] an inf. n. of صَفَقَ, like صَفْقٌ in the phrase صَفْقُ الكَفِّ عَلَى الأُخْرَى [*the striking of the hand upon the other* hand], but denoting muchness of the action. (Sb, M, TA.) [Hence several meanings of both of these verbs, here following.] — صَفَقَ رَأْسَهُ, and عَيْنَهُ, (M,) and صَفَقَهُ عَلَى رَأْسِهِ, (Mṣb,) aor. ـُ, inf. n. صَفْقٌ, (M, Mṣb,) *He struck his head*, and *his eye*, (M,) and *he struck him on his head with the hand*. (Mṣb.) And صَفَقَهُ بِالسَّيْفِ, (O, Ḳ,) inf. n. صَفْقٌ, (O,) *He struck him with the sword*. (O, Ḳ.) And صَفَقَ بِهِ الأَرْضَ [lit. *He smote the ground with him*; meaning *he flung him upon the ground*]. (L, TA.) — صَفَقَ بِجَنَاحَيْهِ, (M, Ḳ,) aor. as above, (M,) [inf. n. صَفْقٌ,] said of a bird, *He beat* [his sides, or the air,] *with his wings*; (M, L, Ḳ;*) as also ▼ صفّق, (M, Ḳ,) inf. n. تَصْفِيقٌ. (TA.) — صَفَقَتْهُ الرِّيحُ, and ▼ صفّقته, *The wind smote it so as to cause a sound to be heard*: (Ṣ:) or the latter signifies [simply] *the wind smote it*, or *beat it*: (Ḥam p. 719:) [or *the wind beat upon it*; namely, a sail &c.: (see شِرَاعٌ:)] [and] both signify *the wind shifted it to the right and left, and turned it back*: (TA: [in the CḲ, التَّثْلِيبُ is erroneously put for التَّقْلِيبُ as an explanation of التَّصْفِيقُ:]) and ▼ صفّقت الرِّيحُ المَآءَ *The wind beat the water so that it made it clear*: (M:) and صَفَقَتِ الرِّيحُ الأَشْجَارَ, (Ḳ,) aor. as above, inf. n. صَفْقٌ, (O,) *The wind put the trees in motion*, or *into a state of commotion*, (O, Ḳ,) *and shook them*: (O, TA:) and ▼ صفّقت الرِّيحُ السَّحَابَ *The wind smote the clouds*, [for صَرَمَتْهُ in my original, an obvious mistranscription, I read ضَرَبَتْهُ,] *and blew in different directions upon them*. (TA.) — صَفَقَ العُودَ, (inf. n. صَفْقٌ, TA,) *He put in motion* [by striking them] *the chords of the lute*. (Ṣ, O, Ḳ.) — صَفَقَ يَدَهُ بِالبَيْعَةِ and صَفَقَ عَلَى يَدِهِ, inf. n. صَفْقٌ (M, Ḳ) and صَفْقَةٌ, (Ḳ,) [or the latter, which see below, is a simple subst.,] *He struck his hand upon his* [another's] *hand by way of ratifying the sale, or the covenant*; (M, Ḳ;) and so صَفَقَ لَهُ البَيْعَ, aor. ـِ, (Ḳ,) inf. n. صَفْقٌ: (TA:) or صَفَقْتُ لَهُ بِالبَيْعِ and بِالبَيْعَةِ, inf. n. صَفْقٌ, *I struck my hand upon his hand* [by way of ratifying the sale and the covenant]. (Ṣ, O, Mṣb.) [See also سَفَقَ. And see an ex. in a verse cited voce رَدَادٌ.] — صَفْقٌ (Ṣ, O, Ḳ) as inf. n. of صَفَقْتُهُ, (Ṣ, O,) also signifies The *shutting*, or *closing* [a thing]; and the *turning*, or *sending*, or *putting*, [a thing] *back*, or *away*; (Ṣ, O, Ḳ;) as also ▼ إِصْفَاقٌ. (Ḳ.) You say, صَفَقَ عَيْنَهُ *He shut*, or *closed, his eye*. (Ṣ, O, Ḳ.) And صَفَقَ البَابَ, (Ṣ, M, O, Mṣb, Ḳ,) aor. ـِ, (M,) inf. n. صَفْقٌ, (M, Mṣb,) *He shut or closed, the door*; (Ṣ, O, Mṣb, Ḳ;) as also ▼ اصفقهُ: (Ṣ, O:) or both signify *he locked the door*: (M, Ḳ:) and in like manner سَفَقَهُ [and اسفقهُ]. (TA.) And *He opened the door*: (ADk, O, Mṣb, Ḳ:) thus having two contr. significations. (Mṣb.) And صَفَقَ مَاشِيَتَهُ, inf. n. صَفْقٌ, *He turned, or sent, his cattle back, or away*. (M, TA.) And صَفَقَهُمْ عَنْ كَذَا *He turned them* [i. e. men] *back, or away, from such a thing*. (TA.) And one says, مَا زَالُوا يَصْفِقُونَنِى *They ceased not to turn me about in an affair*: [meaning that] they endeavoured to induce him to do it. (Ibn-'Abbád, O.) — صَفَقَهُمْ مِنْ بَلَدٍ إِلَى بَلَدٍ *They expelled them from town to town, or from country to country, forcibly and ignominiously*. (TA.) — صَفَقَ الشَّرَابَ: see 2. — صَفَقَ القَدَحَ, (O, Ḳ,) inf. n. صَفْقٌ, (O, TA,) *He filled the drinking-vessel*; as also ▼ اصفقهُ; (O, Ḳ;) and ▼ صفّقهُ: (O:) or صفّق ▼ الكَأْسَ, and ▼ اصفقها, *he filled the drinking-cup, or wine-cup*: (Lḥ, M:) and ▼ اصفقنا الحَوْضَ *We collected the water in the watering-trough*. (TA.) — And صَفَقَهَا, inf. n. صَفْقٌ, *He compressed her*; syn. جَامَعَهَا. (TA.) — And صَفْقٌ signifies also The *collecting together* [a thing or things]. (TA.) = صَفَقَ الرَّجُلُ, (M, Ḳ,) inf. n. صَفْقٌ, (M,) *The man went away*. (M, Ḳ.) — صَفَقَتْ عَلَيْنَا صَافِقَةٌ مِنَ النَّاسِ *A company of men alighted at our abode*. (IDrd, M,* O, Ḳ.*) — صَفَقَتْ, (IDrd, O, Ḳ,) inf. n. صَفْقٌ, (TA,) said of a she-camel, *Her womb closed against the passage of her fœtus*, [or أُرْتِجَتْ,] أُرْتِجَتْ رَحِمُهَا عَنْ وَلَدِهَا, i. e. *became closed*, the syll. signs of this word in the O being doubtful, in the CḲ erroneously written ارتَجَت,]) *so that the fœtus died*. (IDrd, O, Ḳ, TA.) = صَفُقَ, aor. ـُ, (M, O, Mṣb, Ḳ,) inf. n. صَفَاقَةٌ, said of a garment, or piece of cloth, (Ṣ, M, O, Mṣb, Ḳ,) *It was strong, stout, or firm*; (M;) *thick, substantial, close, or compact, in texture*: (O, Mṣb, Ḳ:) and so سَفُقَ. (T, Ṣ, &c., in art. سفق.) — And, said of a face, (Ṣ, O, Ḳ, TA,) ‡ *It was impudent*; or *had little shame*. (O, Ḳ, TA.)

2: see 1, former half, in five places. — التَّصْفِيقُ بِاليَدِ means *The making a sound with the hand* [by clapping]: (Ṣ:) one says, صفّق بِيَدَيْهِ [*He clapped with his hands*; or *clapped his hands*]: (O, Mṣb:) and النِّسَآءُ يُصَفِّقْنَ عَلَى المَيِّتِ [*The women clap their hands* in lamenting *over the dead*: thus they often do in the present day, over the corpse and over the grave]: (TA:) التَّصْفِيقُ is *syn. with* التَّصْفِيحُ: (Aṣ, O:) or (O) the former signifies *the striking with the palm of one hand upon that of the other*; (O, Ḳ;) but the latter is better expl. as the striking with the outer side of the right hand upon the inner side of the left hand. (O.) [See also 2 in art. صفح.] — صفّق القِرْبَةَ, (M, TA,) inf. n. تَصْفِيقٌ, (TA,) *He poured water into the skin*, (M, TA,) *and shook it about*, (TA,) *the skin being new, so that the water came forth yellow*. (M.) — See also 1, latter half, in two places. — صفّق الشَّرَابَ *He mixed the wine, or beverage*. (M.) — And, (M,) inf. n. as above; (Ṣ, O, Ḳ;) and ▼ صَفَقَهُ, (M,) inf. n. صَفْقٌ; (Ḳ;) and ▼ اصفقه, (M,) inf. n. إِصْفَاقٌ; (Ḳ;) *He transferred the wine, or beverage, from one vessel to another*, (Ṣ, M, O, Ḳ,) or *from one jar to another*, (Aṣ, TA,) *it being mixed*, (Ḳ,) *in order that it might become clear*. (M, Ḳ.) — تَصْفِيقُ الإِبِلِ means *The removing of camels from a place which they have depastured to a place in which is pasture*: (Ṣ, O, Ḳ:*) thus in the saying of the rájiz (Aboo-Mohammad El-Fak'asee, O) cited in the first paragraph of art. زل: (Ṣ, O:) or التَّصْفِيق in that instance, accord. to IAạr, is from صفّق القَوْمُ فِى البِلَادِ *The people, or party, went far in the country in search of pasture*: (M:) [or] صفّق, said of a man, (Ibn-'Abbád, O,) inf. n. as above, (Ḳ,) means *He went away*; and *he went round about*. (Ibn-'Abbád, O, Ḳ.) — And التَّصْفِيقُ signifies also *The forming a determined intention or purpose, and then reversing it*. (TA.)

3. صافق عِنْدَ صَفْقَةِ البَيْعِ [*He struck his hand upon that of another in token of the ratification of the sale*]. (T in art. دو. [See also 6.]) — صافقت said of a she-camel, *She lay, or slept, upon one side one time and upon the other side another time*: from صَفْقٌ meaning جَانِبٌ. (M. [And the same is indicated in the O.]) And فُلَانٌ يُصَافِقُ بَيْنَ جَنْبَيْهِ *Such a one turns over upon this* صَفْق [or *side*] *one time and upon the other another*. (O.) And بَاتَ فُلَانٌ يُصَافِقُ [*Such a one passed the night turning over from side to side*]. (Z, TA.) — [Accord. to the Ḳ, said of a she-camel, *She was taken with the pains of parturition*; *i. q.* مَخَضَتْ: but this is app. a mistake; for it seems to have been taken from the saying in the O, (one of the principal sources of the Ḳ,) إِذَا مَخِضَتِ النَّاقَةُ صَافَقَتْ, which evidently means *When the she-camel is taken with the pains of parturition, she turns over from side to side*; as is there indicated by the context both before and after.] — صافق بَيْنَ قَمِيصَيْنِ, (M,) or بين ثَوْبَيْنِ, (Ḳ,) *He wore two shirts*, (M,) or *two garments*, (Ḳ,) *one of them over the other*. (M, Ḳ.)

4: see 1, latter half, in five places: — and see also 2. = أَصْفَقُوا عَلَيْهِ *i. q.* تَبَايَعُوا عَلَيْهِ [i. e. *They made a covenant, or compact, respecting it, or to do it*, as though by striking their hands together], namely, the thing, or affair: (TA in art. بيع: [see صَفَقَ يَدَهُ بِالبَيْعَةِ; and see also 3, and 6, and صَفْقَةٌ:]) *they combined consentaneously, or agreed together, respecting it, or to do it*, namely, the thing, or affair; syn. أَطْبَقُوا عَلَيْهِ, (Ṣ, O, Ḳ,) or اِجْتَمَعُوا عَلَيْهِ. (M.) And أَصْفَقُوا عَلَيْنَا [*They combined, or collected themselves together, against us*]. (M, from a verse of Zuheyr.) أَصْفَقَتْ لَهُ

نِسْوَانُ مَكَّةَ occurs in a trad. as meaning *The women of Mekkeh collected themselves together to him*: or, as some relate it, ↓ انْصَفَقَتْ. (TA.) And one says, أَصْفَقُوا لَهُ meaning حَشَدُوا [i. e. *They collected themselves together to him; or they combined to treat him with courtesy and honour*]. (M.) — اصفق لَهُمْ *He brought them as much food as would satisfy their hunger*: (O, Ḳ:) said in relation to the entertainment of guests. (O.) — أَصْفَقَتْ يَدُهُ بِكَذَا, (Ṣ, O,) or يَدِى, (Ḳ,) *His hand, or my hand, lighted on, met with, or encountered, such a thing*; syn. صَادَفَتْهُ and وَافَقَتْهُ. (Ṣ, O, Ḳ.) En-Nemir Ibn-Towlab says, (Ṣ, O, TA,) describing a جَزَّار [or slaughterer of camels], (TA,)

* حَتَّى إِذَا قُسِمَ النَّصِيبُ وَأَصْفَقَتْ *
* يَدُهُ بِجِلْدَةِ ضَرْعِهَا وَحُوَارِهَا *

[*Until, or until when, the share was divided, and his hand lighted on the skin of her udder and her young one*]. (Ṣ, O, TA: but in the Ṣ, طُرِحَ is put in the place of قُسِمَ.) — أَصْفَقَ القَوْمُ *The people, or party, were, or became, in a state of commotion, or tumult*; syn. اِضْطَرَبُوا. (M, TA. [See also 8.]) — أُصْفِقَ لِى *It was appointed, or ordained, for me; or prepared for me.* (TA.) — اصفق الغَنَمَ *He milked the sheep, or goats, but once in the day*; (Ṣ, M, O, TA;) and so with س: (TA in art. سفق:) or الإِصْفَاقُ signifies *the milking once in the day and night.* (TA.) — اصفق الثَّوْبَ *He wove the garment* (M, TA) *strongly, stoutly, firmly*, (M,) *thickly, substantially, closely, or compactly.* (TA.)

5. تصفّق *He* (a man) *turned over and over*; (M;) *he moved repeatedly to and fro*, syn. تَرَدَّدَ, (M, O, Ḳ,) *from side to side.* (M.) And تصفّقت *She* (a camel) *turned herself over, upside down* (lit. *back for belly*), (O, Ḳ, TA,) *when taken with the pains of parturition.* (TA.) — تصفّق لِلْأَمْرِ *He addressed, or applied, or directed, himself, or his regard, or attention, or mind, to the affair*; syn. تَعَرَّضَ لَهُ. (Sh, O, Ḳ.)

6. تصافقوا (Ṣ, M, O) *They struck their hands upon the hands of others* (O) عِنْدَ البَيْعَةِ [*on the occasion of the ratifying of a sale, or covenant*]: (Ṣ, O:) or *they* [*struck a bargain*;] *bought and sold; or made a covenant, or compact; one with another.* (M, TA.)

7. انصفق *It* (a garment, or piece of cloth,) *was beaten by the wind, so that it moved to and fro.* (M, TA.) [See also 8.] — *It* (a door) *became shut, or closed*: and so with س: (TA in art. سفق:) [or *it shut again of itself*:] said of a door which, when opened, will not remain open. (TA in art. دلق.) — *He* (a man, TA) *turned, or became turned or sent or put, back, or away*: (Ṣ, O, Ḳ, TA:) *he* [or *it*] *returned.* (TA.) — And انصفقوا *They collected themselves together*: the contr. of the next preceding signification. (TA.) See also 4. — And one says, انصفقوا عَلَيْنَا يَمِينًا وَشِمَالًا *They came upon us on the right and left.* (M, TA.)

8. اصطفقت الأَشْجَارُ *The trees became shaken, or agitated*, by the wind. (Ṣ, O, Ḳ, TA.) And اصطفق العُودُ *The lute had its chords put in motion*, (Ṣ, O, Ḳ, TA,) *so that they responded, one to another.* (TA.) — اصطفق الآفَاقُ بِالبَيَاضِ *The tracts of the horizon flickered with whiteness, and the light thereof spread.* (TA.) — And اصطفق المَجْلِسُ بِالقَوْمِ *The sitting-place became a scene of commotion, or tumult, with the people, or party.* (TA. [See also 4, latter part.])

صَفْقٌ: see صَفْقَةٌ. — Also *A side; a lateral part or portion*; (Ṣ, M, O, Ḳ;) and so ↓ صُفْقٌ, (Ṣ, O, Ḳ,) and ↓ صَفْقٌ; (M, O, Ḳ;) syn. نَاحِيَةٌ, (Ṣ, M, O, Ḳ,) and جَانِبٌ. (M, TA.) Of a mountain, (Ṣ, O, Ḳ,) it signifies in like manner, (O,) its صَفْح, (Ṣ, O, Ḳ,) and its نَاحِيَة: (Ṣ:) [both of which signify as above: or by the former may be meant what here follows:] or its *face*, (M, Ḳ,) *in the upper part* thereof, *above the* حَضِيض [or *low ground at, or by, the base, or foot*]: (M:) pl. صُفُوقٌ. (Ṣ, O.) [In like manner also,] صَفْقَا العُنُقِ signifies *The two sides of the neck.* (M, Ḳ.) And صَفْقَا الفَرَسِ *The two cheeks of the horse.* (M, Ḳ.) — Also *A place.* (Ḳ.) — See also صِفْقٌ. — And see صَفَقٌ, in two places.

صُفْقٌ: see the next preceding paragraph.

صِفْقٌ, with kesr, The مِصْرَاع [i. e. *either half, or leaf*,] of a door [meaning of a folding door]: (Ḳ:) [or, accord. to the O, it is ↓ صَفْقٌ, for it is there said that صَفْقَا البَابِ means مِصْرَاعَاهُ; but SM follows the reading in the Ḳ without remarking upon the difference in the O; and adds,] and one says, بَابُ دَارِهِ صِفْقٌ وَاحِدٌ [meaning *The door of his house is one leaf*; i. e.] when it does not consist of what are termed مِصْرَاعَانِ. (TA.)

صَفَقٌ: see صِفْقٌ. — Also *Water that is poured into a new skin, and shaken in it, and in consequence becomes yellow*; (Ṣ, O, Ḳ;) or *yellow water that comes forth from a new skin upon which water has been poured*; (M;) and so ↓ صَفْقٌ. (M, Ḳ.) Hence, (TA,) one says, وَرَدْنَا مَآءً كَأَنَّهُ صَفَقٌ [*We came for the purpose of drinking to water as though it were the yellow water that comes forth from a new skin*]. (Ṣ, O.) — And *A new skin upon* [or *into*] *which water is poured, in consequence whereof yellow water comes forth from it.* (M.) — Also, accord. to AHn, (M,) or so ↓ صَفْقٌ, (Ḳ,) The *odour*, and *savour, of* دِبَاغ [or *tan*]. (M, Ḳ.) — And The former, accord. to Ibn-'Abbád, The *last of* دِبَاغ [or *tan*]: (O, TA:) in the Ḳ, آخِرُ الدِّمَاغِ is erroneously put for آخِرُ الدِّبَاغِ. (TA.)

صَفْقَةٌ *A striking of the hand* [*of one person*] *upon the hand* [*of another*] *in* [*ratifying*] *a sale or purchase and a covenant*: (Mgh:) and ↓ صَفْقٌ is [used in the same sense, being an inf. n. and also] a subst. from the verb in the phrase صَفَقَ يَدَهُ بِالبَيْعَةِ [expl. in the first paragraph of this art.]; (M, Ḳ;) as also ↓ صِفِقَّى, like زِمِجَّى, (Ḳ,) or ↓ صِفْقَى, (so in a copy of the M,) which is mentioned by Sb, (M, TA,) and of which Seer says that it may be from صَفْقُ الكَفِّ عَلَى الأُخْرَى (TA. [See 1, first sentence.]) — Hence it is used to signify The *contract itself that is made in the case of a sale*, (Mgh, Mṣb,) and the *covenant that one makes*: (Mgh:) or *an agreement respecting a thing*: (M, TA:) Az says that it relates to the seller and the buyer. (Mṣb.) [And it is sometimes with س in the place of ص.] One says, رَبِحَتْ صَفْقَتُكَ i. e. [*May*] *thy purchase* [*bring profit*]. (Ṣ, O.) And بَارَكَ ٱللّٰهُ لَكَ فِى صَفْقَةِ يَمِينِكَ i. e. [*May God bless thee in*] *the contract* [(lit. *the striking*) *of thy right hand*]. (Mṣb.) And صَفْقَةٌ رَابِحَةٌ, and صَفْقَةٌ خَاسِرَةٌ, (Ṣ, O, Ḳ,) *A sale or bargain* [*bringing gain, and a sale or bargain occasioning loss*]. (Ḳ.) And إِنَّهُ لَمُبَارَكُ الصَّفْقَةِ [*Verily he is blessed in respect of bargaining*]; meaning that he buys not anything without gaining in it. (TA.) And قَدِ ٱشْتَرَيْتُ اليَوْمَ صَفْقَةً صَالِحَةً [*I have purchased to-day a good purchase*]. (TA.) And البَيْعُ صَفْقَةٌ أَوْ خِيَارٌ *Selling is decisive or with the option of returning.* (Mgh.) And it is said in a trad. (of Ibn-Mes'ood, TA), صَفْقَتَانِ فِى صَفْقَةٍ رِبًا i. e. *Two bargains in a* [single] *bargain* [*are an unlawful gain*]: this is of two kinds: one is the seller's saying to the buyer, "I sell to thee such a thing for a hundred dirhems on the condition of thy buying of me this garment, or piece of cloth, for such a sum:" the other kind is his saying, "I sell to thee this garment, or piece of cloth, for twenty dirhems on the condition of thy selling to me thy commodity for ten dirhems." (O.) And it is said in another trad., إِنَّ أَكْبَرَ الكَبَائِرِ أَنْ تُقَاتِلَ أَهْلَ صَفْقَتِكَ i. e. [*Verily the greatest of great sins is*] *thy fighting those with whom thou hast made a covenant*: because each of the two persons making a covenant puts his hand in the hand of the other, like as is done by each of two persons selling and buying. (TA.)

صِفِقَّى or صِفْقَى: see the next preceding paragraph.

صِفَاقٌ The *inferior* [or *inner*] *skin, that is beneath the skin upon which is the hair*: (Ṣ, O, Ḳ:) *a thin skin beneath the upper skin and above the flesh*: (IAth, TA:) or the صِفَاق of the belly is the *skin*, (M,) the *inner skin*, (TA,) *that is next to the* سَوَاد, (M, TA,) *the* سَوَاد *of the belly*, (TA,) [i. e. *the liver*,] *and which is the part where the farrier perforates the beast* (يَثْقُبُ مِنَ الدَّابَّةِ) [at the navel, in order that a yellow fluid may issue forth]: (M, TA:) or the صِفَاق is the *part around the navel, where the farrier performs the operation above mentioned*: (AA, TA:) or the *skin which, when the* مَسْك [or *hide*] *is stripped off, remains cleaving to the belly, and the rending of which occasions a* [*rupture termed*] فَتْق; so says Aṣ, in the "Book of the Horse:" (TA:) or *what is between the* جِلْد [or *outer skin*] *and the* مُصْرَان [or *intestines into which the food passes from the stomach*]; (ISh, O, Ḳ;) *com-*

prising all of what are termed the مَرَاقّ *of the belly, beneath the* جِلْد *thereof, to the* سَوَاد *of the belly* [i. e. *the liver*]; the مَرَاقّ of the belly being all that has not a bone curving over it: (ISh, O:) or the *skin of the whole of the belly:* (O, Ḳ:) the pl. is صُفُقٌ, only. (M, TA.)

صَفُوقٌ *An abominable acclivity* or *ascending road* or *mountain-road difficult of ascent:* pl. صَفَائِقُ and صُفُقٌ. (M, Ḳ.) And *A mountain,* (Ḳ,) or *an obstacle,* or *elevated portion, of mountains,* (O,) *such as is inaccessible.* (O, Ḳ.) And *A smooth, high rock:* pl. صُفُقٌ. (Ibn-'Abbád, O, Ḳ.) — Also, applied to a bow, *Pliant.* (Fr, O, Ḳ.) — [In the TA, in a verse of Aboo-Dhu-eyb describing a bow, to which it seems to be there applied as an epithet, it is expl. as signifying راجعة; but I think that this is a mistranscription for وَاجِفَةٌ, meaning *Quivering.* — Freytag has assigned to it three explanations which belong to صِفَاقٌ.]

صَفِيقٌ, applied to a garment, or piece of cloth, (Ṣ, M, Mgh, O, Mṣb, Ḳ,) *strong, stout,* or *firm;* (M;) *thick, substantial, close,* or *compact, in texture:* (Mgh, O, Mṣb, Ḳ:) and سَفِيقٌ is a dial. var. thereof. (TA.) — Also † *Hardy, strong, sturdy, enduring,* or *patient.* (M.) — And applied to a face (Ṣ, O, Ḳ, TA) as meaning ‡ *Impudent;* or *having little shame.* (O, Ḳ, TA.) And رَجُلٌ صَفِيقُ الوَجْهِ † *A man having no shame.* (Ḥar p. 368.)

صَفِيقَةٌ: see صَافِقَةٌ.

صَفَائِقُ *Travelling-camels* (رِكَابٌ) *coming and going.* (Ibn-'Abbád, O.) — See also صَافِقَةٌ.

صَفَّاقٌ A cock *that beats with his wings when crowing.* (TA.) — It occurs in a trad., followed by أَفَّاقٌ in apposition, and is said by Aṣ to mean ٱلَّذِى يَصْفِقُ عَلَى أَمْرٍ عَظِيمٍ [app. One *who goes away on some great affair*]: but in the opinion of Az, it means one *who makes many journeys, and who employs himself,* or *uses art* or *artifice* or *cunning, in affairs of traffic;* thus nearly agreeing in meaning with أَفَّاقٌ. (O: the latter meaning only is assigned to it in the Ḳ.)

صَافِقَةٌ *A company* (IDrd, M, O, Ḳ) of men [*alighting* at one's abode]. (IDrd, M, O.) See 1, near the end. — Also *A calamity,* or *misfortune:* (M, TA:) pl. صَوَافِقُ: (M:) this pl. and ▼ صَفَائِقُ, (O, Ḳ, TA,) which latter may be pl. of ▼ صَفِيقَةٌ, (TA,) signify *accidents,* or *evil accidents,* (O, Ḳ, TA,) and *varieties,* or *vicissitudes, of events.* (O, TA.)

أَصْفَقُ A garment, or piece of cloth, *more* [*strong, stout, firm,*] *thick, substantial, close,* or *compact, in texture,* than another. (Mgh.)

أُصْفُقَانِيَّةٌ [written in one place with fet-ḥ, and in another with kesr, to the ف,] *i. q.* خَوَلٌ [A man's *slaves,* or *servants, and other dependents;* or *slaves, and cattle,* or *camels &c.;*] in the dial. of El-Yemen. (TA.)

مَصْفَقٌ *A place of passage; a way, road,* or *path;* syn. مَسْلَكٌ. (O, TA.)

مُصَفَّقٌ [pass. part. n. of 2, q. v.]. One says, لَكَ عِنْدِى وُدٌّ مُصَفَّقٌ وَنُصْحٌ مَرُوقٌ ‡ [*I have, for thee, an affection defecated like wine that has been transferred from one vessel to another and left to settle, and a benevolence purified like clarified wine*]. (TA.) — Also A *full* [or *filled*] drinking-vessel. (Fr, TA.)

مُصَافِقٌ A camel *lying,* or *sleeping, upon one side one time and upon the other side another time.* (O, Ḳ.) — And مُصَافِقٌ بَيْنَ ثَوْبَيْنِ *Wearing two garments, one of them over the other.* (Ibn-'Abbád, O.)

صفن

1. صَفَنَ, aor. ـِ, inf. n. صُفُونٌ, said of a horse, *He stood upon three legs and the extremity of the hoof of the fourth leg;* (AZ,* Ṣ, Ḳ, TA;) [thus expl.] without restriction to a fore leg or a hind leg: (TA:) or *he stood upon three legs, and turned back the extremity of the fore part of the fourth hoof, that of his fore leg:* (M, TA:) [or *he stood upon three legs,* and *otherwise:* (see صَافِنٌ:)] accord. to Fr, the poems of the Arabs indicate that صُفُونٌ signifies peculiarly, or specially, [or simply,] the act of *standing,* or *standing still.* (TA.) — Also, (M, Mṣb, Ḳ,) aor. and inf. n. as above, (M, Mṣb,) said of a man, (Ḳ,) or صَفَنَ صَفَّ قَدَمَيْهِ, (TA, from a trad.,) meaning قَدَمَيْهِ [*He set his feet evenly, side by side*], (M, Mṣb, Ḳ, TA,) standing, (Mṣb,) and praying. (TA.) [Or, said of a man standing in prayer, it signifies, or in this case it signifies also, *He put his feet close together:* or *he turned one of his feet backward, like as the horse turns one hoof when standing upon three legs:* see, again, صَافِنٌ.] — صَفَنَ الحَشِيشَ وَالوَرَقَ (M, TA), aor. ـِ, (M,) inf. n. صَفْنٌ, said of a bird, or flying thing, *It compacted the dry herbage* (M, TA) *and the leaves,* [*to make a habitation,*] *for its young ones,* (M,) or *around its place of entrance* [*into its habitation*]; (TA;) and ▼ صفّنهُ signifies the same: (M:) ▼ تَصْفِينٌ as the act of the hornet and the like is the *compacting for itself,* or *for its young ones, a habitation* (Ḳ, TA) *of dry herbage and of leaves:* so says Lth. (TA.) — And صَفَنَ ثِيَابَهُ *He collected together his clothes* (JM, TA) فِى السَّرْجِ [*upon his saddle*], (TA,) or فِى سَرْجِهِ وَنَحْوِهِ [*upon the saddle and the like thereof*]. (JM.) — صَفَنَ بِهِ الأَرْضَ, (Ḳ, TA,) aor. ـِ, inf. n. صَفْنٌ, (TA,) *He flung him,* or *it, upon the ground.* (Ḳ, TA.) — And صَفَنَهُ, aor. ـِ, inf. n. صَفْنٌ, *He rent,* or *slit, his* صَفَن, i. e. *scrotum.* (M.)

2. صفّن, and its inf. n.: see 1, in two places.

3. مُصَافَنَةٌ The *standing confronting a people,* or *party.* (TA.) — [Also The *dividing* of water among a people, or party, *in the manner described in the next paragraph:*] one says, صَافَنَ المَآءَ بَيْنَ القَوْمِ فَأَعْطَانِى صَفْنَةً ▼ i. e. مَقْلَةً [for جُرْعَةً مَقْلَةٍ, the meaning being *He divided the water in that manner among the people,* or *party, and gave me a gulp as much as would cover a pebble in the bottom of a vessel*]. (TA.)

6. تصافنوا المَآءَ, (AA, Ṣ, M, Ḳ,) said of people in a journey and having little water, (M,) *They divided the water among themselves* (AA, Ṣ, M, Ḳ) *by shares,* (Ṣ, Ḳ,) *by means of the pebble,* (AA, Ṣ, M,) *which they threw into the vessel to pour the water into it,* (AA,) *giving to each of them as much as would cover the pebble.* (AA, Ṣ.) See also 6 in art. حذى.

صَفْنٌ [if not a mistake for صُفْنٌ, q. v.,] signifies The [*round piece of skin,* or *leather, in which food is put, and upon which people eat; commonly called*] سُفْرَة; as also ▼ صَفْنَةٌ: (Ḳ:) the latter is expl. by AA and IAạr as a سُفْرَة *that is gathered together by a* [*running*] *string* [*near the edge, by means of which it is converted into a bag,* agreeably with a modern custom]. (TA.) — And The [*bursa faucium,* or *faucial bag, of the camel; commonly called*] شِقْشِقَة; as also ▼ صَفْنَةٌ: (Ḳ:) so expl. by AA. (TA.) — See also صُفْنٌ.

صُفْنٌ *A thing like the* سُفْرَة [described in the next preceding paragraph], *and between the* عَيْبَة *and the* قِرْبَة, *in which are* [*put*] goods or *utensils* or *the like:* or it is *of skin,* or *leather,* (M,) [i. e.] *a receptacle of skin,* or *leather,* (Ṣ, in which it is expressly said to be with ḍamm,) *like the* سُفْرَة, (Ṣ, M,) *pertaining to the people of the desert, in which they put their travelling-provisions, and* (M) *with which* (Ṣ, M) *sometimes* (M) *water is drawn,* (Ṣ, M,) *like* [*as is done with*] *the* دَلْو: (M:) occurring in a verse of Ṣakhr El-Hudhalee [cited in art. عضل]: (Ṣ:) or *a thing like the* [*small bucket,* or *small drinking-vessel, of skin* or *leather, called*] رَكْوَة, (Fr, Mgh, Ḳ,) *in which the ablution termed* وُضُوء *is performed:* (Fr, Ḳ:) or it signifies, (Mgh,) or signifies also, (Ḳ,) accord. to AA, (Ṣ,) a [*pouch such as is called*] خَرِيطَة, *pertaining to the pastor, in which are* [*put*] *his food, and his* زِنَاد [*for producing fire*], (Ṣ, Mgh, Ḳ,) *and his other utensils* or *apparatus,* (Ḳ,) or *what other things he requires;* (Ṣ, Mgh;) *and sometimes water is drawn with it, like* [*as is done with*] *the* دَلْو; (TA;) as also ▼ صُفْنَةٌ: (Ḳ:) or, accord. to A'Obeyd, ▼ صُفْنَةٌ signifies *a thing like the* عَيْبَة, *in which are* [*put*] *a man's goods* or *utensils, and his* [*other*] *apparatus;* and when the ة is elided, it is pronounced with ḍamm [i. e. صُفْنٌ]: (TA:) or ▼ صَفْنَةٌ, (TA,) or ▼ صَفْنٌ, (so in a copy of the M,) signifies *a small* دَلْو [or *leathern bucket*], *having a single* حَلْقَة [or *ring*]; and when it is large, it is called صُفْنٌ: and the pl. is أَصْفُنٌ. (M, TA.) — And † *Water* [app. considered as contained in the vessel thus called]: so expl. as used in the saying of Aboo-Du-ád,

هَرَقْتُ فِى حَوْضِهِ صُفْنًا لِيَشْرَبَهُ

[*I poured into his drinking-trough water that he might drink it*]. (TA.) — See also what next follows.

صَفَنٌ The *scrotum* (Ṣ, M, Mṣb, Ḳ) of a man; (Ṣ, Mṣb;) as also ▼ صُفْنٌ, (M,) or ▼ صَفْنٌ, (Ḳ,) and ▼ صُفْنَة and ▼ صُفْنَة: (M:) pl. أَصْفَانٌ (Ṣ, M, Mṣb) and صُفْنَانٌ. (Mṣb.) — And ‡ The *envelope of the ear of corn:* (Ḳ, TA:) so called by way of comparison [to the scrotum]. (TA.) — And The *habitation that is compacted* (M,* Ḳ, TA) *by a bird*, or *flying thing*, (M,) or *by the hornet and the like*, (Ḳ, TA,) *of dry herbage and of leaves*, (M, TA,) *for its young ones*, (M, Ḳ, TA,) or *for itself*. (Ḳ, TA.)

صَفْنَة: see صَفْنٌ, in two places: — and صُفْنٌ, in three places: — and صَفَنٌ: — and see also 3.

صُفْنَة: see صُفْنٌ, latter part: — and صَفَنٌ.

صَافِنٌ A horse *standing upon three legs and the extremity of the hoof of the fourth leg:* (A'Obeyd,* Ṣ, TA:) or *standing upon three legs, and turning back the extremity of the fore part of the fourth hoof, that of his fore leg:* (M, TA:) or *standing upon three legs*, and *otherwise:* thus, says Fr, I have found the Arabs use the word: (TA: [see 1, first sentence:]) pl. صُفُونٌ (M, TA) and صَوَافِنُ and [the pl. of صَافِنَة is] صَافِنَاتٌ. (TA.) صَافِنَاتٌ occurs in the Ḳur xxxviii. 30. (M, TA.) And in the same, xxii. 37, I'Ab and Ibn-Mes-'ood used to read صَوَافِنَ [instead of صَوَافَّ]: the former explaining it as meaning *Having the shank of one fore leg tied up to the arm;* for thus is done with the camel when he is slaughtered: the latter, as meaning *standing*, or *standing still*. (TA.) — And applied to a man, it means صَافٌّ قَدَمَيْهِ [*Setting his feet evenly, side by side*], (A'Obeyd, M, TA, and the like is said in the Ṣ and Mṣb,) *standing*. (A'Obeyd, Mṣb, TA.) It is said in a trad., (Ṣ, M, Mṣb, TA,) referring to the Prophet mentioned as praying, (Ṣ, M,) قُمْنَا خَلْفَهُ صُفُونًا [app. meaning *We stood behind him setting our feet evenly, side by side;* for so the context seems to indicate]. (Ṣ, M, Mṣb, Ḳ.) [But] in another trad., صَلٰوةُ الصَّافِنِ is said to be forbidden; meaning [*The praying*] *of him who puts his feet close together:* or, as some say, *of him who turns back his foot* [i. e. *one of his feet*] *like as the horse turns his hoof* [i. e. *one of his hoofs, when standing upon three legs*]. (TA.) ═ الصَّافِنُ signifies [*The saphena*, or *crural vein;* so in the present day; i. e.] *the vein of the* سَاق: (Ṣ: [see أَبْهَرُ, and see also النَّسَا:]) or *a vein lying deep in the arm* (الذِّرَاع) [and] *amid the sinews of the* [*fore*] *shank of a beast:* or the صَافِنَانِ are *two veins penetrating into the interior of the two shanks:* or *two veins in the legs:* or *two branches* [*of veins*] *in the two thighs:* and the صافن is [strangely said to be] *a vein in the interior of the back bone, extending lengthwise, uniting with the* نِيَاط [q. v.] *of the heart, also called the* أَكْحَل. (M.)

صفو

1. صَفَا, (Ṣ, M, Mṣb,) aor. يَصْفُو, (Ṣ, Mṣb,) inf. n. صَفَآءٌ (Ṣ, M, Mṣb, Ḳ*) and صُفُوٌّ (M, Mṣb, Ḳ*) and صَفْوٌ (Ḳ,* TḲ) and صَفْوَةٌ and صِفْوَةٌ, (MA,) said of wine, or beverage, (Ṣ,) or of water, (TḲ,) or of a thing, (M,) *It was*, or *became, clear, limpid*, or *pure; contr. of* كَدِرَ; (Ṣ, M, Ḳ;*) or *free from* الكَدَر [i. e. *turbidness, thickness*, or *muddiness*]; (Mṣb;) or *free from admixture*. (Er-Rághib, TA.) And, said of the air, or atmosphere, *It was*, or *became, cloudless; free from any particle of cloud*. (M, Ḳ.) [And it is also said, tropically, of life; and of the mind, or heart; and of love, or affection; &c.] — صَفَتْ, (AA, Ṣ, M, Ḳ,) aor. تَصْفُو; (AA, Ṣ;) and صَفُوَتْ; (M, Ḳ;) said of a she-camel, (AA, Ṣ, M, Ḳ,) and of a ewe, or she-goat, (AA, Ṣ,) *She abounded with milk*. (AA, Ṣ, M, Ḳ.) ═ صَفَا الشَّىْءَ *He took the clear*, or *pure, part*, or *portion, of the thing;* (M, TA;) as also ▼ استصفى صَفْوَهُ; (M;) and ▼ استصفاهُ [alone] signifies the same; (Ḳ, TA;) as also ▼ اصطفاهُ; (Er-Rághib, TA;) or *he took the best*, or *choice, part*, or *portion, of it*. (TA.) You say, صَفَوْتُ القِدْرَ *I took the clear*, or *pure, part*, or *portion*, [of the contents] *of the cooking-pot*. (Ṣ.)

2. صفّاهُ, inf. n. تَصْفِيَةٌ, *He cleared*, or *clarified, it*, namely, wine, or beverage, (Ṣ, TA,) *by means of the* رَاوُوق [or مِصْفَاة]. (TA.) And *He removed from it the floating particles*, or *motes*, or *the like, that had fallen into it;* (TA;) or so صفّاهُ مِنَ القَذَى. (Mṣb.) — And صفّى عَرَمَتَهُ, inf. n. as above, *He winnowed his heap of trodden-out corn*, or *grain*. (TA.)

3. صافاهُ, (Ṣ, M, Ḳ, TA,) inf. n. مُصَافَاةٌ, (TA,) ‡ *He regarded him*, or *acted towards him, with reciprocal purity of mind*, or *sincerity;* or *with reciprocal purity*, or *sincerity, of love*, or *affection;* syn. خَالَصَهُ; (Ṣ in art. خلص;) *he rendered him true*, or *sincere, brotherly affection;* (M, Ḳ, TA;) as also ▼ اصفاهُ; (Ḳ;) or اصفاهُ الوُدَّ, (Ṣ, Mṣb,) or المَوَدَّةَ, (TA,) *he rendered him pure*, or *sincere, love* or *affection;* (Ṣ, Mṣb, TA;) and [in like manner] one says also صافاهُ الإِخَآءَ. (TA.)

4. اصفاهُ الشَّىْءَ *He made the thing to be his*, or *he assigned*, or *appropriated, to him the thing, purely, absolutely*, or *exclusively*. (TA.) — See also 3 in two places. — And اصفاهُ (Ṣ, Mṣb, Ḳ, TA) بِالشَّىْءِ (Ṣ) or بِكَذَا (Ḳ, TA) ‡ *He chose him in preference to others* (Ṣ, Mṣb, Ḳ, TA) *for*, or *to give him, the thing* or *such a thing;* (Ṣ, Ḳ, TA;) and *he distinguished him particularly, peculiarly*, or *specially*, i. e. *above*, or *from*, or *exclusively of, others, by the thing* or *by such a thing*. (TA.) — And اصفى عِيَالَهُ بِشَىْءٍ قَلِيلٍ † *He contented*, or *satisfied, his family*, or *household, with something little*, or *scanty*. (TA.) — اصفى الأَمِيرُ دَارَ فُلَانٍ means † *The prince*, or *governor, took what was in the house of such a one:* (Ṣ,* TA:) and ▼ استصفى مَالَهُ ‡ *He took all his property*. (Ṣ, Ḳ, TA.) ═ اصفى, intrans., ‡ *He was*, or *became, destitute*, or *devoid*, مِنَ المَالِ [*of property*], and مِنَ الأَدَبِ [*of good education, good breeding*, or *polite accomplishments, &c.*]: (Ṣ, Ḳ, TA:) as though clear thereof. (TA.) — And ‡ *He* (a man, TA) *became exhausted of his sperma by women:* (Az, Ḳ, TA:) or *he ceased from sexual intercourse*. (IḲṭṭ, TA.) — And اصفت said of a hen, † *She ceased to lay eggs:* (Ṣ, M, Ḳ, TA:) as though she became clear. (TA.) — Hence, (TA,) اصفى said of a poet, ‡ *He ceased to utter poetry*, or *to poetize*. (Ṣ, M, A, Ḳ,* TA.) ═ اصفى القَوْمُ *The people had abundance of milk in their camels*, and *in their sheep* or *goats*. (TA.) ═ اصفى said of a digger, *He reached stone* (صَفًا, M, TA, i. e. حَجَرًا, TA), *so that he was repelled* [*thereby*], (M, TA,) or *prevented from digging* [*further*]. (TA.)

5. تصفّى [*It became cleared*, or *clarified*]. (Ḳ in art. نطب.)

6. تَصَافَيْنَا *We regarded one another*, or *acted reciprocally, with purity*, or *sincerity*, [*of mind*, or] *of love*, or *affection;* syn. تَخَالَصْنَا. (Ṣ. [See also 3.])

8. اصطفاهُ: see 1, last sentence but one. — Also *He took it clear, limpid*, or *pure;* (M, TA;) and so [accord. to SM, which, however, I think doubtful,] ▼ استصفاهُ, which is expl. in the Ḳ as signifying *he reckoned it clear, limpid*, or *pure;* though the former meaning is assigned in the M to اصطفاهُ only. (TA.) — And *He chose, made choice of, selected, elected*, or *preferred, it*, (Ṣ, M, Ḳ,) namely, a thing; (M;) as also ▼ استصفاهُ. (M, Ḳ.) And اِصْطَفَيْتُ كَذَا عَلَى كَذَا *I chose such a thing in preference to such a thing*. (TA.) But اِصْطِفَآءُ ٱللّٰهِ عِبَادَهُ [sometimes means *God's creating his servants pure;* for it] is sometimes by his bringing them into existence clear from the admixture that is found in others: and sometimes it is by his choice and judgment. (TA.)

10: see 1, last sentence but one, in two places: — see also 8, in two places: — and see 4.

صَفًا *Stones:* or *smooth stones:* and one thereof is termed صَفَاةٌ: [i. e. the former word is a coll. gen. n., and the latter is its n. un.:] the two words being like حَصًى and حَصَاةٌ: (Mṣb:) or صَفَاةٌ signifies *a smooth rock:* (Ṣ:) or *a hard and smooth stone, large, and such as does not give growth to anything:* (M, Ḳ:) and the pl. of this is صَفًا [improperly thus termed a pl.] (Ṣ, M, Ḳ) and صَفَوَاتٌ, (M, Ḳ,) and (Ṣ, M, Ḳ) that of صَفًا, (M, Ḳ,*) not of صَفَاةٌ, (M,) أَصْفَآءٌ and صُفِىٌّ (Ṣ, M, Ḳ) and صِفِىٌّ: (M, Ḳ:) or صَفًا signifies *stones that are broad and smooth:* (ISk, TA:) and [accord. to F,] ▼ صَفْوَآءُ signifies the same as صَفَاةٌ, as also صَفْوَانَةٌ [in the CḲ erroneously written صَفَوَاةٌ], of which the pl. is ▼ صَفْوَانٌ and ▼ صُفْوَانٌ, (Ḳ,) which last is said by El-Ḥáfidh to be a mistaken pronunciation of صَفْوَانٌ; (TA;) [but correctly,] ▼ صَفْوَآءُ [which is a quasi-pl. n.] and ▼ صَفْوَانٌ [a coll. gen. n.] (Aṣ, T, Ṣ, M, TA) of which the sing. or n. un. is صَفْوَانَةٌ (Ṣ, M, TA) signify the same as صَفًا, (Aṣ, T, M, TA,) or *stones*, (Ṣ,) or *soft, smooth stones;* (TA;) or ▼ صَفْوَانٌ is used as a pl. and as a sing.; as a pl. meaning *smooth stones*, one of which is termed صَفْوَانَةٌ; and as a sing., *stone*, or *a stone:* (Mṣb:) the dual of صَفًا is صَفَوَانِ. (ISk, TA.) مَا تَنْدَى صَفَاتُهُ is a prov., (Ṣ,) applied to the niggardly, like مَا يَبِضُّ حَجَرُهُ, (Ṣ, in art. بض,) meaning † *No good is obtained from him*. (TA in that art.) And one says also, قُرِعَ صَفَاتُهُ, meaning † *He im-*

pugned his character; blamed, or *censured, him;* or *spoke against him.* (Mgh in art. غمز.) — الصَّفَا *A certain place in Mekkeh* (Ṣ, Mṣb) may be masc. or fem., as meaning either the مَكَان or the بُقْعَة. (Mṣb.) — [بِنْتُ صَفَا, accord. to Reiske, as stated by Freytag, signifies *The echo.*]

صَفْوٌ *Clearness, limpidness,* or *purity; contr. of* كَدَرٌ; (M, Ḳ;) like [the inf. ns.] صُفُوٌّ and صَفَآءٌ [&c. when used as simple substs.: see 1, first sentence]. (Ḳ.) See also صَفَآءٌ, below. — Also, and ▼صَفْوَةٌ and ▼صِفْوَةٌ and ▼صُفْوَةٌ, (Ṣ, M, Mṣb, Ḳ,) but only with fet-ḥ when without ة, (AO, Ṣ,) The *clear,* or *pure, part,* or *portion,* of a thing; (Ṣ, M, Mṣb, Ḳ;) the *best,* or *choice, part,* or *portion;* (TA;) and so ▼صَفِىٌّ, (Ḳ,* TA,) of a thing. (Ḳ, TA.) One says ▼صَفْوَةُ المَآءِ, (T, TA,) and المَالِ, (AO, T, Ṣ, TA,) and الإِخَآءِ, (T, TA,) and ▼صُفْوَتُهُ, (AO, T, Ṣ, TA,) and ▼صِفْوَتُهُ, (AO, Ṣ,) [i. e. *The clear,* or *pure, part,* or *portion,* or *the best,* or *choice, of water,* and *of property,* and *of brothers,*] but only صَفْوُ الإِهَالَةِ [*the clear,* or *pure, part,* or *portion,* or *the best,* or *choice, of the grease,* or *melted fat,* &c.]. (T, TA.) And Mohammad is said to be ▼صَفْوَةُ ٱللّٰهِ مِنْ خَلْقِهِ and ▼مُصْطَفَاهُ [i. e. *God's choice one,* or *elect,* or *favourite, of his creatures*]: (Ṣ:) and [in like manner] Adam is said to be ▼صَفِىُّ ٱللّٰهِ i. e. *the chosen one,* or *elect, of God.* (TA.)

صَفَاةٌ as meaning صَافِيَةٌ: see صَافٍ. — Also n. un. of صَفًا [q. v.].

صَفْوَةٌ: see صَفْوٌ, in three places.

صُفْوَةٌ: see صَفْوٌ, in two places.

صِفْوَةٌ: see صَفْوٌ, in two places. — One says also, فِى الإِنَآءِ صِفْوَةٌ مِنْ مَآءٍ, or خَمْرٍ, i. e. [*In the vessel is*] *a small quantity* [*of water,* or *of wine*]. (M.)

صَفْوَآءُ: see صَفًا, in two places.

يَوْمٌ صَفْوَانٌ, (Ṣ, M, Ḳ,) and ▼صَافٍ, (M, Ḳ,) *A day in which the sun is clear, and which is very cold:* (Ṣ:) or *a cold day,* (Ḳ,) or *a very cold day,* (M,) *without clouds and without thickness* [*of the air*]. (M, Ḳ.) — صَفْوَانُ is also a name of *The second of the days of cold:* (Ḳ, TA:) so called because the sky therein is clear of clouds: [as a proper name,] it is determinate, and imperfectly decl. (TA. [See also صُفَيَّةُ.]) ═ صَفْوَانٌ [as a coll. gen. n., of which the n. un. is with ة; and said to be used as a sing. and as a pl.]: see صَفًا, in three places.

صَفْوَانٌ: see صَفًا.

صَفَآءٌ an inf. n. of صَفَا. (Ṣ, M, &c. [See 1, first sentence.]) — [It is often used by moderns as meaning † *Serenity of life,* and *of the mind; freedom from trouble; comfort; content; complacency; happiness, joy,* or *pleasure:* and so, sometimes, ▼صَفْوٌ.] — Also ‡ [*Reciprocal purity* or *sincerity of mind,* or *of love* or *affection,* or *of brotherly affection;* or *pure,* or *sincere, reciprocal love* &c.;] a subst. from صَافَاهُ. (TA.)

صَفِىٌّ: see صَافٍ. — Also ‡ *A friend who regards one,* or *behaves towards one, with reciprocal purity* or *sincerity of love* or *affection,* or *of brotherly affection:* (Ṣ,* M,* Ḳ, TA:) pl. أَصْفِيَآءُ. (TA.) One says, فُلَانٌ صَفِىُّ فُلَانٍ † [*Such a man is the friend* &c. *of such a man*]: and صَفِيَّةٌ and فُلَانَةُ صَفِىُّ فُلَانٍ † [*Such a woman is the friend,* &c. *of such a man*]. (Ḥam p. 430.) — See also صَفْوٌ, in two places. — Also ‡ *The portion, of the spoil, which the chief,* or *commander, chooses for himself before the division;* (Ṣ, Mṣb, Ḳ, TA;) and so ▼صَفِيَّةٌ, of which the pl. is صَفَايَا: (Ṣ, Mṣb:) or, accord. to Aṣ, صَفَايَا is pl. of صَفِىٌّ, which signifies the *portion which the chief chooses for himself, exclusively of his companions, such as the horse, and that which cannot be divided among the army:* or, as AO says, the *portion which the chief chose for himself, after* [*taking*] *the fourth part, such as the she-camel, and the horse, and the sword, and the girl* or *young woman;* and thus it continued to be in the case of El-Islám, but the fourth became reduced to the fifth. (Mṣb.) — Also, applied to a she-camel, (Ṣ, M, Ḳ,) and to a ewe, or she-goat, (Ṣ,) *Abounding with milk;* (Ṣ, M, Ḳ;) or so ▼صَفِيَّةٌ: (Z, TA:) or the former, a she-camel *whose milk lasts throughout the year:* (IAạr, TA in art. شكر:) pl. of the former, (Sb, Ṣ, M, Ḳ,) or of the latter, (Z, TA,) as above: (Sb, Ṣ, M, Z, Ḳ:) Sb says that it is not pluralized with ا and ت because the sing. is without ة. (M.) — And A palm-tree (نَخْلَةٌ) *abounding with fruit;* (M, Ḳ;) or so ▼صَفِيَّةٌ: (Z, TA:) pl. of the former, (TA,) or of the latter, as above. (Z, TA.)

صَفِيَّةٌ: see the next preceding paragraph, in three places.

صُفَيَّةُ a name of *The first of the days of cold:* (Ḳ, TA:) so called because the sky therein is clear of clouds. (TA. [See also صَفْوَانُ.])

صَافٍ *Clear, limpid,* or *pure; free from* كَدَر [or *turbidness,* &c.]; (Mṣb;) and so ▼صَفِىٌّ, applied to anything. (M.) Applied to pasturage, the former word may mean *Clear of dried-up leaves* or *similar rubbish:* or it may be formed by transposition from صَائِفٌ, meaning "of the [season called] صَيْف," and so belonging to art. صيف. (M. [See also صَافٍ in another sense as formed by transposition from صَائِفٌ, voce صَافٍ, in art. صوف.]) In the phrase ▼صَفَاةُ اللَّوْنِ, applied by the poet Kutheiyir-'Azzeh to honey (جَنَاةُ النَّحْلِ), and expl. as meaning *Clear in respect of colour,* [ISd says,] I think that صفاة is originally صَفِيَةٌ, as a possessive epithet. (M.) [صَافٍ is also applied to a sword, and the like, as meaning *Bright,* or *free from rust.*] And in the Ḳur xxii. 37, [instead of the common reading صَوَآفَّ, pl. of صَافٌّ and صَافَّةٌ,] some read صَوَافِىَ, [pl. of صَافِيَةٌ, as well as of صَافٍ applied to irrational animals,] as meaning that the animals there mentioned are [to be regarded *as*] *things purely* [or *exclusively*] *belonging to God.* (TA.) — See also صَفْوَانٌ. ═ Also *A certain fish, which* [*it is said*] *chews the cud;* pl. صَوَافٍ. (TA.)

صَافِيَةٌ [fem. of صَافٍ, q. v. — And also, as a subst.,] ‡ *One of what are termed* صَوَافِى الإِمَامِ, which means *the towns,* or *villages, of those who have rebelled against him, which the Imám* [or *Khaleefeh*] *chooses for himself* [*as his peculiar property*]: (A, TA:) or, as in the T, الصَّوَافِى signifies *what the Sulṭán appropriates exclusively to those persons whom he specially favours:* or, as some say, it means *the possessions and lands which their owners have abandoned,* or *of which the owners have died leaving no heirs thereof.* (TA.)

مِصْفَاةٌ i. q. رَاوُوقٌ; (Ṣ, MA, Ḳ, TA;) i. e. *A strainer;* (MA; [thus accord. to modern usage;]) *a clarifier;* i. e. *a thing from which clearing,* or *clarifying, is effected;* called by the vulgar مصفية [i. e. مِصْفِيَة, and also مِصْفَايَة]: pl. مَصَافٍ. (TA.)

عَسَلٌ مُصَفًّى [*Clarified honey;* or] *honey cleared of the floating particles,* or *motes,* or *the like, that had fallen into it.* (TA.)

مُصْطَفًى: see صَفْوٌ, last sentence.

صقب

1. صَقِبَ, (Ṣ, Ḳ,) aor. ـَ, (Ḳ,) inf. n. صَقَبٌ, (M, A, Ḳ,) [like سَقِبَ,] *He,* or *it, was,* or *became, near.* (Ṣ, M,* A,* Ḳ.) You say, صَقِبَتْ دَارُهُ, (Ṣ, A,) with kesr [to the ق], (Ṣ,) inf. n. as above, (Ṣ,* A,) *His house was near;* (Ṣ, A;) and (A) so ▼أَصْقَبَتْ دَارُهُ, (M, A, Ḳ, TA,) and أَسْقَبَتْ. (TA.) And it is said in a trad., (Ṣ, A,) الجَارُ أَحَقُّ بِصَقَبِهِ, (Ṣ, A, Ḳ,) i. e. [*The neighbour has a better,* or *the best, claim* to pre-emption *by reason of his being near:* see, with respect to this explanation, and other explanations also, what is said of another reading, بِسَقَبِهِ, voce سَقَبٌ: or *has a better,* or *the best, claim*] *to close connection,* and *nearness;* meaning *pre-emption:* (IAmb, O, TA:) or, *to what is next to him,* and *near to him:* (A, Ḳ, TA:) accord. to some, the meaning is *the partner:* (O, TA:) or *the partner who has not divided with his copartner;* this, says Az, being shown to be the meaning by another trad.: (Mṣb in art. جور:) or *the neighbour whose dwelling is adjoining.* (O, TA.) — Also *He,* or *it, was,* or *became, distant,* or *remote:* thus it has two contr. significations. (Ḳ.) ═ صَقَبَهُ, (Ḳ,) inf. n. صَقْبٌ, (M,) *He collected it,* or *gathered it together.* (M, Ḳ.) — And صَقَبَهُ *He raised it;* namely, a building, &c. (M, O, Ḳ.) — And صَقَبَهُ, (Ḳ,) or صَقَبَ قَفَاهُ, (M, TA,) *He struck* (M, Ḳ, TA) *him,* or *it,* (Ḳ,) or *the back of his neck, with his* صَقْب, (M, TA,) i. e. (TA) *with his fist.* (Ḳ, TA.) [The inf. n.] صَقْبٌ signifies The *striking* anything solid and dry or tough. (Ṣ, TA.) ═ صَقَبَ, (Ḳ, TA,) or ▼صقّب, (so in a copy of the M,) said of a bird, *It uttered a cry* or *cries:* (M, Ḳ:) from Kr. (M, TA.)

2: see what immediately precedes.

3. صاقبهُ *He drew near to him:* and *he faced*

him, or met him face to face: (A:) or صَاقَبَهُمْ, inf. n. مُصَاقَبَةٌ and صِقَابٌ, *he faced them, or met them face to face:* (Ḳ:) or صَاقَبْنَاهُمْ, inf. ns. as above, *we drew near to them:* and لَقِيتُهُ مُصَاقَبَةً and صِقَابًا *I met him face to face.* (M.)

4. أَصْقَبَتْ دَارُهُ: see 1, second sentence. ═ اصقبهُ *He made him,* or *it, to be near.* (Ṣ, Ḳ.) And اصقب ٱللّٰهُ دَارَهُ *May God make his house to be near.* (A.) [And so with س.] — And one says, أَصْقَبَكَ الصَّيْدُ *The game,* or *object of the chase, has become near to thee, so that thou art able to shoot, or cast, at it.* (Ḳ.)

صَقْبٌ The *young one of a camel:* (M, L, Ḳ:) and so سَقْبٌ [q. v.]: (M:) but the latter is the more chaste, and some have rejected the former word: (MF:) pl. صِقَابٌ and صُقْبَانٌ (M, Ḳ) [and app. صُقُوبٌ also, like سُقُوبٌ,] and [pl. of pauc.] أَصْقُبٌ. (TA.) — And Anything [i. e. any animal] *tall, together with plumpness,* or *with fatness, softness, thinness of the skin, and plumpness;* (Ṣ, M, Ḳ;) and so with س; (M;) as also ↓ صَقَبٌ. (TA.) Applied to a branch, *Juicy, thick, and long.* (TA.) — And *A tent-pole:* (M, Ḳ:) or the *middle tent-pole, which is the longest:* (Ṣ, M, Ḳ:) and so with س: (M:) pl. صُقُوبٌ. (Ṣ, M, Ḳ.) [See also this pl. below.] — And The *fist:* so in the phrase ضَرَبَهُ بِصَقْبِهِ [expl. above]. (TA.)

صَقَبٌ [is an inf. n., of صَقِبَ, as mentioned above: and, used as a simple subst.,] signifies *Vicinity,* or *nearness.* (M, A, &c.) Thus in the phrase هُوَ صَقَبَكَ [lit. *He is in thy vicinity;* meaning *he is near thee*]; mentioned by Sb among instances of adv. nouns which he classes apart because of their strangeness. (M.) And one says also, دَارِى مِنْ دَارِهِ بِصَقَبٍ [lit. *My house is in a situation of nearness with respect to his house:*] meaning, near [*his house*]. (TA.) — It [is also used as an epithet, and as such] signifies *Near:* (M, Ḳ:) you say مَكَانٌ صَقَبٌ, and سَقَبٌ, [q. v. voce سَاقِبٌ], *A near place;* (M;) and مَكَانٌ صَاقِبٌ ↓ and سَاقِبٌ: (A in art. سقب:) and دَارُهُ صَقَبٌ مِنِّى [*His house is near me*]. (A in the present art.) — See also صَقْبٌ.

صُقُوبٌ a pl. of صَقْبٌ [q. v.]. (Ṣ, M, Ḳ.) — Also The *hind legs* of camels; a dial. var. of سُقُوبٌ: (IAạr, M:) the س is changed into ص app. because the latter is more agreeable with ق. (M.)

صَاقِبٌ: see صَقَبٌ.

صَيْقَبَانِىٌّ *A seller of perfumes* [&c.: for the Arab dealer in perfumes sells a great variety of things, such as drugs, many articles of grocery, and the like]: (O, Ḳ:) so called because he collects [somewhat] of everything. (TA.)

أَصْقَبُ [*More, and most, near*]. One says, هٰذَا أَصْقَبُ مِنْ هٰذَا *This is nearer than this:* (M: [and the like is said in the A and TA:]) and so أَسْقَبُ. (M, TA.*)

هُوَ مُصَاقِبِى *He is my neighbour:* (TA in the present art.:) *he is one whose house, or tent, adjoins mine.* (TA in art. جور.)

صقر

1. صَقَرَ, (Ṣ, M, Ḳ,) aor. ـُ, (M,) inf. n. صَقْرٌ, (Ṣ, M,) *He broke,* (Ṣ, Ḳ,) or *struck,* (M,) stones, (Ṣ,) or a stone, (M, Ḳ,) *with a* صَاقُور [q. v.]. (Ṣ, M, Ḳ.) — صَقَرَهُ بِالعَصَا, (M, Ḳ,) inf. n. as above, (M,) *He struck him,* or *beat him,* (M, Ḳ,) *on his head,* (M,) *with the staff,* or *stick.* (M, Ḳ.) — صُقِرَ بِهِ الأَرْضُ *He was thrown,* or *cast, upon the ground;* lit. *the ground was struck with him.* (O, Ḳ. [In some copies of the Ḳ, صقر in this instance and the verb explaining it (ضرب) are in the act. form, and الارض is therefore in the accus. case.]) — صَقَرَ النَّارَ, (M, Ḳ,) inf. n. as above; (M;) and ↓ صَقَّرَهَا, (M, Ḳ,) inf. n. تَصْقِيرٌ; (TA;) *He lighted,* or *kindled, the fire;* or *made it to burn, burn up, burn brightly* or *fiercely, blaze,* or *flame.* (M, Ḳ.) — صَقَرَتْهُ الشَّمْسُ, (Ṣ, M, A,) aor. and inf. n. as above, (M,) ‡ *The sun hurt him by its heat:* (A:) or *pained his brain:* (Ṣ:) or *fell vehemently, with fierce heat, upon him,* or *upon his head:* or *was hot upon him.* (M, TA.) [See also 1 in art. سقر.] — صَقَرَنِى بِكَلَامِهِ ‡ [app. *He cursed me,* and *calumniated me*]. (A. [These meanings seem to be there indicated by the context.]) ═ صَقِرَ اللَّبَنُ *The milk was,* or *became, intensely sour;* as also ↓ اصقرّ, inf. n. اِصْقِرَارٌ; (Ḳ;) and ↓ صَمْقَرَ, (Ḳ in art. صمقر,) and ↓ اِصْمَقَرَّ. (Ḳ in that art and in the present art. also.) — [See also صَقْرٌ, below, last explanation but one.]

2. صقّر النَّارَ: see 1. ═ صقّر التَّمْرَ, (M,) or صَقَّرَ الرُّطَبَ, inf. n. تَصْقِيرٌ, (Aṣ, TA,) *He poured* صَقْر [q. v.], (M,) or دِبْس, [which is the same,] (Aṣ,) *upon the dates,* (M,) or *upon the fresh ripe dates.* (Aṣ.)

4. اصقرت الشَّمْسُ † *The sun was,* or *became, burning,* or *fiercely burning;* syn. اِتَّقَدَتْ; (M, Ḳ;) as also ↓ اِصْمَقَرَّتْ, (L and Ḳ in art. صمقر,) in which the م is augmentative: (L in that art.:) the former is from اصقرت said of fire. (M.)

5. تصقّرت النَّارُ: see 8. ═ تصقّر [*He hawked;*] *he hunted with the* صَقْر. (A, Ḳ.) ═ And *He tarried, stayed,* or *waited,* (Ḳ, TA,) in a place. (TA.)

8. اصطقرت and اصتقرت النَّارُ *The fire became lighted* or *kindled; burned, burned up, burned brightly* or *fiercely, blazed,* or *flamed;* (M, Ḳ;) as also ↓ تصقّرت. (Ḳ.)

9. اصقرّ: } see 1, last explanation.
Q. Q. 1. صَمْقَرَ: }

Q. Q. 1. صَوْقَرَ *He* (a bird) *uttered the cry termed* صَوْقَرِير [q. v.]: (Ḳ:) *reiterated his cry.* (TA.)

Q. Q. 4. اِصْمَقَرَّ: see 1, last explanation: — and see also 4.

صَقْرٌ [The *hawk;*] the *bird with which one hunts,* or *catches, game;* (Ṣ;) *whatever preys,* or *hunts* or *catches game, of the birds called* بُزَاة [pl. of بَازٍ] *and* شَوَاهِين [pl. of شَاهِين]; (M, A, Ḳ;) *a kind of bird including the* بَازِى *and the* شَاهِين *and the* زُرَّق *and the* يُؤْيُؤ *and the* بَاشَق: (AHát, TA in art. بشق:) [like our term "saker," and the French "sacre," &c.:] pl. [of pauc.] أَصْقُرٌ (M, Ḳ) and [of mult.] صُقُورٌ and صُقُورَةٌ (M, A, Ḳ) and صِقَارٌ and صِقَارَةٌ and صُقُرٌ; (M, Ḳ;) the last of which is said by Th to be pl. of صُقُور, which is pl. of صَقْر, but [ISd says] I hold it to be pl. of صَقْر: the fem. is ↓ صَقْرَةٌ. (M.) — [And accord. to Reiske, as mentioned by Freytag, *A liberal man:* perhaps *a noble man,* as likened to a hawk.] ═ Also, (Ṣ, Ḳ,) and ↓ صَقْرَةٌ, (Ṣ, M, Ḳ,) *Vehemence of the stroke of the sun,* (Ṣ, M, Ḳ,) and *fierceness of its heat:* (M:) or the *vehemence of its stroke upon the head:* (M:) pl. [of the latter] صَقَرَاتٌ. (Ṣ, A.) ═ Also the former, *Sour milk;* (Ḳ;) [and] so ↓ صَقْرَةٌ: (A:) or *milk rendered sour by a stroke of the sun:* (Sh:) or *milk sour in the utmost degree:* (Aṣ:) or *very sour milk;* as also ↓ صَقْرَةٌ: (Ṣ:) or this latter is *milk that has curdled, and of which the thick part has become separate, and the whey become clear, and that has become sour, so as to be a good kind of sauce.* (L.) One says, جَاءَنَا بِصَقْرَةٍ ↓ تَزْوِى الوَجْهَ [*He brought us some sour milk,* or *very sour milk,* &c., *such as contracts the face,* or *makes it to wrinkle:* like as one says بِصَرَبَةٍ]. (Ṣ, A, L.) — Also, (T, Ṣ, M, Mṣb, Ḳ,) and ↓ صَقْرَةٌ, (M,) [The *exuded,* or *expressed, juice called*] دِبْس; (Ṣ, Ḳ;) in the dial. of the people of El-Medeeneh: (Ṣ:) or the دِبْس *of dates;* (M;) or *of fresh ripe dates,* (Mgh, Mṣb,) *before it is cooked;* i. e. *what flows from them, like honey, and what, when it is cooked, is called* رُبّ: (Mṣb:) or the *honey of fresh ripe dates* and *of raisins;* as also ↓ صَقَرٌ: (Ḳ:) or the *honey of fresh ripe dates when it has become dry,* or *tough:* or *what exudes from grapes,* and *from raisins,* and *from dates, without their being pressed;* (M;) as also ↓ صَقَرٌ: (TA:) or, in the dial. of the Bahránees, [or people of El-Bahreyn,] the *crude* دِبْس, *resembling honey, which flows from baskets of dates when they* [i. e. the dates] *are deposited and congested, in an uncovered chamber,* [so I render بَيْت مُصَرَّح, but the meaning of the epithet is not clear,] *with green earthen pots beneath them.* (AM, TA.) — And the former, (صَقْر,) † *Water that has become altered for the worse in taste and colour.* (Ḳ, O, TA. [See also مُصْقَر and صَقْرَةٌ.]) ═ صَقْرٌ also signifies *A* دَائِرَة [or *feather,* i. e. *portion of the hair naturally curled* or *frizzled in a spiral manner* or *otherwise,*] *behind the place of the liver* (AO, Ḳ, TA) *of a horse* or *similar beast,* (Ḳ, TA,) *on the right* and *on the left,* (TA,) or *in the back of a horse:* (AO, TA:) there are two such feathers, (AO, Ḳ, TA,) which are the limit of the back. (AO, TA.) ═ Also, [probably as an inf. n., of which the verb is صَقَرَ,] The *acting the part,* or *performing the office, of a pimp to* [*men's*] *wives*, or *women under covert.* (IAạr, M, O, Ḳ. [In the CḲ, الحُرَم is erroneously put for الحُرَم.]) Hence the epithet صَقَّار, [as some explain it,] occurring in a trad. [which see below]. (TA.) — And *A cursing of such as is not deserving* [*thereof*]: pl. صُقُور and صِقَار. (Ḳ.)

صَقَر a name of *Hell*; a dial. var. of سَقَر [q. v.]. (Ḳ.) — صَقَر *Fallen leaves of the* [*kind of trees called*] عِضَاه, and [particularly] *of the* عُرْفُط, (M, Ḳ,) and *of the* سَلَم, and *of the* طَلْح, and *of the* سَمُر: not so called until they fall. (M.) — See also صَقْر, in two places.

رُطَبٌ صَقِرٌ, (Ṣ,) or صَقِرٌ مَقِرٌ, (M, Ḳ,) in which the latter word is an imitative sequent, (Ḳ,) *Fresh ripe dates containing* صَقْر: (M, Ḳ:) [*melliferous:*] or *proper for* دِبْس [or صَقْر]. (Ṣ.) — اِمْرَأَةٌ صَقِرَةٌ *A woman sharp*, or *acute, of mind*, (ذَكِيَّة, [in the CḲ, erroneously, زَكِيَّة,]) *strong-sighted.* (Ṣgh, Ḳ.)

جَآءَ بِالصُّقَرِ وَالبُقَرِ, (A, Ḳ, TA,) and ▼بِالصُّقَارَى وَالبُقَارَى, (Ḳ, TA,) ‡ *He came with lies, and excitements of dissension:* (A, TA:) or *with sheer lying:* (Ḳ:) or *with sheer, and excessive*, or *abominable, lying:* (TA:) each being a name for *that which is unknown:* (Ḳ, TA:) and in like manner one says جَآءَ بِالشُّقَرِ وَالبُقَرِ, and بِالشُّقَارَى وَالبُقَارَى; mentioned by IDrd, in the Jm; and by Meyd, in the Collection of Proverbs. (TA in art. بقر.) [See also Ḥar p. 399.]

صَقْرَةٌ: see صَقْر, in six places.

صَقَرَةٌ † *Water remaining in a watering-trough in which dogs and foxes void their urine*, (O, Ḳ, TA,) *altered for the worse in taste and colour.* (TA. [See also صَقْر and مُصَقَّر.])

صُقْرَةٌ † *A colour*, of a bird, *in which the* خُضْرَة [or *dark*, or *ashy, dust-colour*] thereof, or the *blackness* thereof, *is mixed with redness* or *yellowness*; as being likened to [the colour of] صَقْرَة [or صَقْر], i. e. دِبْس: a bird of that colour is termed ▼مُصَقَّر: so in the book entitled "Ghareeb el-Ḥamám," by Ḥoseyn Ibn-'Abd-Allah el-Kátib El-Iṣbahánee. (TA.)

صَقُور, (so in a copy of the M in two instances, and so in the O in one instance,) or ▼صُقُور, (so in the O in another instance, and so accord. to the Ḳ, in which latter it is expressly likened to تَنُّور,) *A wittol*, or *tame cuckold*; syn. دَيُّوث: (M, Ḳ:) or *one who acts the part of a pimp to his own wives*, or *women under covert*; as also ▼صَقَّار: (O:) the former epithet occurring in a trad. (M, O.)

صُقَارَى: see جَآءَ بِالصُّقَرِ وَالبُقَرِ, above.

صَقَّار [*A falconer*, or *rearer of hawks.* (Golius, from Meyd: and so in the present day.) — And] i. q. دَبَّاس [*A seller of* دِبْس, or صَقْر]. (O, Ḳ.) — Also † One who is *in the habit of cursing* (M, O, Ḳ) *those who are not deserving* [*of being cursed*]: (M, O, Ḳ:) and † *a calumniator:* and † *an unbeliever.* (M, O, Ḳ.) The Prophet, being asked the meaning of صَقَّار, (M, TA,) or of سَقَّارَة, (T, TA,) or of صَقَّارُونَ, (O,) occurring in a trad., said † *Young people who shall be in the end of time, whose mutual greeting will be mutual cursing.* (T, M, O, TA.) See also صَقُور.

صُقُور: see صَقُور.

صَاقِر, applied to a صَقْر [or hawk] *Sharp-sighted.* (Ḳ.)

صَاقُور: see صَاقُور.

صَاقِرَةٌ *A calamity*, (M, Ḳ,) or *a vehement calamity*, (O,) *befalling.* (M, Ḳ.)

صَاقُور [*A pickaxe;*] *a large* فَأْس (AA, Ṣ, M, Ḳ) *with one slender head, with which stones are broken;* (AA, Ṣ, M;) i. q. مِعْوَل; (AA, Ṣ, A;) and ▼صَوْقَر signifies the same; (M, Ḳ;) [but] this latter is expl. by IDrd as meaning *a thick* فَأْس *with which stones are broken.* (TA.) — And † The *tongue.* (M, Ḳ.) — See also what next follows.

صَاقُورَةٌ The *inner side of the cranium, over the brain*, (M, Ḳ, TA,) *as though it were the bottom of a bowl:* in the T said to be termed ▼صَاقُور. (TA.) — And صَاقُورَةٌ, (M,) and الصَّاقُورَةُ, (M, Ḳ,) a name of † *The Third Heaven.* (M, Ḳ.)

صَوْقَرِيرٌ *A cry of a bird*, (M, Ḳ,) *with a reiteration*, (M,) *resembling the sound of this word.* (M, Ḳ.)

أَصْقَرُ in the following saying, (M,) هٰذَا التَّمْرُ أَصْقَرُ مِنْ هٰذَا *These dates have more* صَقْر *than these*, (AḤn, M, Ḳ,) has no verb. (M.)

مُصْقَر Milk *that is sour and disagreeable:* (Ibn-Buzurj, TA:) and ▼مُصْمَقِر signifies milk *intensely sour.* (TA in art. صمقر.)

رُطَبٌ مُصَقَّرٌ *Fresh ripe dates*, (A,) or *fresh ripe dates that have become dry*, (Ṣ,) *upon which is poured* دِبْس (Ṣ, A) *of ripe dates*, (A,) *in order that they may become soft:* and sometimes it occurs with س; for they often change ص into س when there is in the word ق or ط or غ or خ, as in بُصَاق and صِرَاط and صُدْغ and صِمَاخ: (Ṣ:) or *excellent fresh ripe dates, picked from the raceme, which are put into* [*earthen vessels of the kind called*] بَسَاتِيق [pl. of بُسْتُوقَة] (in the TA erroneously written بَسَاتِين), *and upon which* صَقْر *is poured:* they remain moist and good all the year. (AḤn, L.) — And مَآءٌ مُصَقَّرٌ † *Water altered for the worse* [*in colour, as though* صَقْر, i. e. دِبْس, *had been mixed with it*]. (M. [See also صَقْر and صَقَرَة.]) — And طَائِرٌ مُصَقَّرٌ † *A bird of the colour termed*, صُقْرَة, q. v. (TA.)

مُصَقِّر One *who hunts with hawks.* (A,* TA.)

مُصْمَقِرّ A day *intensely hot:* the two م s in this word are augmentative. (TA.) — See also مُصْقَر.

صقع

1\. صَقَعَهُ, (Ṣ, Mgh, O, Ḳ,) aor. ـَ, (O, Mgh, Ḳ,) inf. n. صَقْعٌ, (O,) *He struck him*, or *beat him:* (Ḳ:) or *he struck* [or *slapped*] *him with his expanded hand:* (TA:) [like صَفَعَهُ:] or, (Ṣ, Mgh, O, Ḳ,) as also ▼صَوْقَعَهُ, (O, Ḳ,) *he struck him* (Ṣ, Mgh, O, Ḳ) *upon his head*, (O, Ḳ,) or *upon his* صَوْقَعَة, (Ṣ, O,) [i. e.] *upon the top of his head:* (Mgh:) this last is the primary signification: and hence, metaphorically, *he struck him*, or *beat him*, in an unrestricted sense: (Mgh,* O, TA:) and *he struck it*, namely, a dry, or tough, and solid thing, with a similar thing; as, for instance, a stone with a stone, and the like: or, as some say, *he struck it*, namely, anything dry, or tough. (TA.) It is said in a trad., respecting Munḳidh, صُقِعَ آمَّةً i. e. *He was struck on the top of his head:* (O:) or *he had his head broken so that the wound reached the membrane over his brain.* (TA.) — One says also, صَقَعَ بِهِ الأَرْضَ, (O, Ḳ) *He threw him down*, or *prostrated him, on the ground;* (Ḳ;) [lit.] *he smote the ground with him.* (Ibn-'Abbád, O.) — And صَقَعَتْهُ i. q. صَعَقَتْهُ الصَّاعِقَةُ الصَّاقِعَةُ, (Ṣ, O, Ḳ,) *The thunderbolt smote him.* (TA.) And صُقِعَ *He was smitten by a thunderbolt;* i. q. صُعِقَ; of the dial. of Temeem: (O:) and so صَقِعَ; (Ḳ, TA;) like صَعِقَ. (TA.) — And صَقَعَهُ بِكَيٍّ *He branded him*, or *marked him by cauterizing, upon his head*, [or *his* صَوْقَعَة,] or *his face.* (O, Ḳ.) — And صَقَعَ الثَّرِيدَةَ, aor. and inf. n. as above, *He ate the* ثَرِيدَة [or *mess of crumbled bread with broth*] *from its* صَوْقَعَة [or *top*, or *upper part*, or *hollow made therein*]. (TA. [See also Q. Q. 1.]) — صَقَعَ also signifies The *raising of the voice:* (O, TA:) and the *uttering it by consecutive emissions.* (TA.) You say, صَقَعَ بِصَوْتِهِ *He raised his voice.* (TA.) And hence, (TA,) صَقَعَ said of a cock, (Ṣ, O, Ḳ,) aor. ـَ, (O,) inf. n. صَقْعٌ and صُقَاعٌ (IDrd, O, Ḳ) and صَقِيعٌ, (Ḳ,) *He* [*crowed*, or] *uttered a cry:* (IDrd, Ṣ, O, Ḳ:) and so سَقَعَ. (Ṣ.) — And, accord. to IAạr, The *being eloquent in speech, and lighting upon the* [*proper*] *meanings.* (TA.) — صَقَعَ بِضَرْطَةٍ, said of an ass, *He emitted a sounding wind from the anus, in a moist and dispersed state.* (Ibn-'Abbád, O, Ḳ.) — صَقَعَ البَيْتَ *He attached to the tent the rope called* صِقَاع [q. v.]. (Az, O, TA.) — And صَقَعَ, (Ṣ, O, Ḳ,) said of a man, (Ḳ,) *He went away*, (Ṣ, O, Ḳ, TA,) فِى كُلِّ النَّوَاحِى [*in all directions*]: (TA:) one says, مَا أَدْرِى أَيْنَ صَقَعَ, (Ṣ, O, TA, [but in the second, لَا is put in the place of مَا,]) and بَقَعَ, (TA,) meaning *I know not whither he went away:* (O, TA:) and the verb is seldom used in this sense without the particle of negation. (TA.) Or it signifies, (Ḳ,) or signifies also, (O,) or so صَقِعَ, (Ṣ, TA,) like فَرِحَ, not صَقَعَ, (TA,) *He deviated from the way*, (Ṣ, O, Ḳ, TA,) *and alighted*, or *descended and abode, alone, by himself:* (TA:) or *he deviated from the way of goodness and generosity.* (IF, O, Ḳ, TA.) And صَقْع signifies The *going astray; losing one's way;* or *becoming lost;* and *perishing;*

or *dying*. (TA. [But I think that this is probably a mistranscription for صَقْع, inf. n. of صَقِعَ.]) You say also, صَقَعَ فُلَانٌ نَحْوَ كَذَا *Such a one repaired towards such a thing.* (TA.) — And صَقَعَتِ البِئْرُ, aor. ـَ, (A'Obeyd, Ṣ,) inf. n. صَقْعٌ, *The well collapsed; or broke down.* (A'Obeyd, Ṣ, Ḳ.*) = صَقِعَتْ, (TA,) inf. n. صَقَعٌ, (O, Ḳ, TA,) said of horses, and of birds, &c., *They became white* (O, Ḳ, TA) *in the* [صَوْقَعَة, or] *uppermost part of the head,* (TA,) or *in the middle of the head.* (O, Ḳ.) — And [the inf. n.] صَقَعٌ, in relation to the head, signifies The *being bald*: or, as some say, the *going away of the hair.* (TA.) = صُقِعَتِ الأَرْضُ *The earth, or ground, became overspread with the* صَقِيع [i. e. *hoar-frost, or rime*]; (Ṣ, O, Mṣb, Ḳ;) as also ↓ أُصْقِعَت; each with ḍamm. (IDrd, Ḳ.)

2. صقّع لهُ, inf. n. تَصْقِيعٌ, *He swore to him respecting a thing:* (Ibn-'Abbád, O, Ḳ:) and so بقّع له, inf. n. تَبْقِيعٌ. (Ibn-'Abbád, O.)

4. اصقع *He* (a man, O, TA) *entered upon* [*a time, or a tract, of*] صَقِيع [i. e. *hoar-frost, or rime*]. (IDrd, O, Ḳ, TA.) = And اصقع الصَّقِيعُ الأَرْضَ, (Ḳ, TA,) and الشَّجَرَ, (O, TA,) *The* صقيع [or *hoar-frost*] *fell, or lighted, upon the earth,* or *ground,* (Ḳ,* TA,) and *the trees.* (O, TA.) And أُصْقِعَتِ الأَرْضُ: see 1, last sentence. And أُصْقِعَ النَّاسُ *The men, or people, became overspread with the* صَقِيع. (TA.)

Q. Q. 1. صَوْقَعَهُ: see 1, first sentence. — صَوْقَعَ الثَّرِيدَةَ *He spread evenly the* ثريدة [or *mess of crumbled bread moistened with broth*]. (TA.)

صُقْعٌ *A district, quarter, or tract,* syn. نَاحِيَةٌ, (Ṣ, O, Mṣb, Ḳ,) *of a country:* (Mṣb:) and *a place, region, quarter, tract, or point, towards which a person, or thing, goes, tends, or is directed;* syn. جِهَةٌ: and *a place of alighting, or of descending and stopping or sojourning or abiding or lodging or settling; or a place of abode or settlement;* syn. مَحَلَّةٌ: (Mṣb:) pl. [of pauc.] أَصْقَاعٌ, (O, TA,) and pl. pl. أَصَاقِعُ: (TA:) and سُقْعٌ is a dial. var. thereof. (IJ, TA; and Ḳ in art. سقع.) One says, فُلَانٌ مِنْ أَهْلِ هٰذَا الصُّقْعِ i. e. مِنْ هٰذِهِ النَّاحِيَةِ [*Such a one is of the people of this district, &c.*]. (Ṣ, O.) And هُوَ فِى صُقْعِ بَنِى فُلَانٍ *He is in the* نَاحِيَة [or *district, &c.*], and *the* مَحَلَّة [or *place of alighting, &c.*], *of the sons of such a one.* (Mṣb.) See also مَصْقَع. — Also *A part, or portion, of the surrounding and inferior sides* of a well: pl. أَصْقَاعٌ: but the more approved word is with س. (TA.)

صَقْعٌ inf. n. of صَقِعَ. (Ṣ, &c.) — Also *An affection like* غَمّ, [i. e.] *that takes away the breath,* (يَأْخُذُ بِالنَّفَسِ, Ṣ, O, Ḳ, [in the CḲ, بالنَّفْسِ,]) *by reason of the vehemence of the heat.* (Ṣ, O, Ḳ.)

صَقِعٌ [*Smitten by a thunderbolt:* (see its verb, صَقِعَ:) or] *smitten as by a thunderbolt* from the enemy: so accord. to some: (O, TA:) 'Ows Ibn-Hajar says,

أَبَا دُلَيْجَةَ مَنْ لِحَيٍّ مُفْرَدٍ ٭ صَقِعٍ مِنَ الأَعْدَآءِ فِى شَوَّالِ

(Ṣ,* O, TA, but in the TA أَبَا [which may be rendered *O Aboo-Duleyjeh, who is for a solitary tribe, smitten as though by a thunderbolt from the enemies, in Showwál* (which was, in the time of the poet, a cold month) ?]: or, accord. to IAạr, the meaning here is, *in a state of retirement, remote from the enemies;* (Ṣ,* O;) for when the winter pressed severely upon the man, he used to retire to a distance, lest a guest should alight at his abode; the enemies being the strange guests; and by saying فِى شَوَّالِ, he means that the cold was in Showwál: (O, TA:) or صَقِعٌ means *absent and remote, so that one knows not where he is:* or *that has gone away, and alighted alone,* or *by himself:* (TA:) [pl. صَقْعَى:] see an ex. voce دَقِعَ. = أَرْضٌ صَقِعَةٌ, (TA,) and ↓ مَصْقُوعَةٌ, *Earth, or ground, overspread with the* صَقِيع [i. e. *hoar-frost, or rime*]: (Ṣ, Mṣb, TA:) and in like manner, شَجَرٌ صَقِعٌ, and ↓ مُصْقَعٌ, *trees overspread with the* صَقِيع. (TA.)

صَقْعَةٌ *Intenseness of cold;* from الصَّقِيعُ [meaning "hoar-frost," or "rime"]. (TA.)

صُقْعَةٌ *A whiteness in the middle of the head* of a horse and of a bird &c.; (Ṣ, O, Ḳ;) or *in the middle of the head* of a black sheep or goat, accord. to Abu-l-Wázi'. (TA.)

صَقْعَانُ *Stupid, dull, or wanting in intelligence:* but this is a vulgar word. (TA.)

صَقْعِىٌّ The *first increase, or offspring,* (نِتَاج,) [*of sheep, or goats,*] *when the sun smites* (تَصْقَعُ) *the heads of the lambs or kids:* (Aboo-Naṣr, O, Ḳ: [in the CḲ, البَهْم is erroneously put for البُهْم:]) and some of the Arabs call it the شَمْسِىّ, and the قَيْظِىّ: then is the صَفَرِىّ, after the صَقْعِىّ: (Aboo-Naṣr, TA:) it is also expl. as signifying *such as is brought forth in the* [*period called*] صَفَرِيَّة: (TA: [but see صَفَرِىٌّ:]) and, (O, Ḳ,) accord. to AZ, (O,) the *young camel that is brought forth in* [*the time of*] *the* صَقِيع [i. e. *hoar-frost, or rime*]; which is of the best of the increase [of camels]. (O, Ḳ.)

صِقَاعٌ *A piece of rag with which a woman protects her* خِمَار [or *muffler*] *from the oil* [*in her hair*], (Ṣ, O, Ḳ, TA,) *putting it on her head;* (TA;) as also ↓ صَوْقَعَةٌ: (Ḳ:) or this latter signifies *a thing by which the head is protected,* such as *a turban* and *a* خِمَار and *a* رِدَآء. (TA.) — And The [*woman's face-veil termed*] بُرْقُع (Ṣ, O, Ḳ) is sometimes thus called. (Ṣ, O.) — And *A thing with which a she-camel's nose is bound,* (Ṣ, O, Ḳ, TA,) as expl. in art. درج [voce دُرْجَةٌ], (Ṣ,) *when they desire her to affect her young one* or *the young one of another:* or, accord. to A'Obeyd, *a piece of rag with which her eyes are bound;* that with which her nose is bound, [or stopped, (see 1 in art. ظار,)] when she is made to affect a young one not her own, being termed غِمَامَةٌ. (TA. [But see دُرْجَةٌ.]) — And *A mark made with a hot iron upon the* قَذَال [or *back of the head*] *of a camel.* (Ibn-'Abbád, O, Ḳ.) — And *An iron thing that is in the place of* [*the kind of curb called*] *the* حَكَمَة *of the bit.* (O, Ḳ.) — And *A thing that is next to the head of the horse, beneath* (دُونَ) *the larger* بُرْقُع. (TA.) — The صِقَاع of a tent (خِبَآء) is *A rope that is extended from its top, and pulled tight, the two ends of which are tied to two pegs, or stakes, stuck into the ground, when the wind is violent and it is feared that the tent may be thrown down.* (O, TA.)

صَقِيعٌ The جَلِيد [i. e. *hoar-frost, or rime,*] *that nips, or blasts,* (lit. *burns,* [see أَحْرَقَ,]) *the plants, or herbage;* (Mṣb;) *what falls from the sky in the night, resembling snow.* (Ṣ, O, Ḳ.) = Also *A species of* زُنْبُور [or *hornet*]: (O, Ḳ:) so says AHát, as having been heard by him from a man of Eṭ-Ṭáïf. (O.)

صَاقِعٌ [*Deviating from the truth;* as is indicated in the TA: and hence,] *a liar:* (TA:) one says, صَهْ صَاقِعُ i. e. *Be silent, O liar.* (Yoo, O, Ḳ.)

صَاقِعَةٌ i. q. صَاعِقَةٌ [i. e. *A thunderbolt*]: (Fr, Ṣ, O, Ḳ:) of the dial. of Temeem: pl. صَوَاقِعُ. (TA.) [See also صَاعِقَةٌ.]

صَوْقَعَةٌ The *place of the whiteness termed* صُقْعَة *in the head* of a horse and of a bird &c.: (Ṣ:) or the *middle of the head* [in an absolute sense]: (O, Ḳ:) or the *top,* or *uppermost part,* [*of the head,* or] *of the* [*cap called*] كُمَّة, and *of the turban.* (O, Ḳ, TA: all in art. صقع. [See 1 in that art., where this last meaning is assigned to صَوْقَعَةٌ.]) — And *A turban* [itself]: (O, Ḳ:) and *any other thing that protects the head:* (TA:) accord. to IDrd, *a piece of rag which a woman puts upon her head as a protection.* (O. See صِقَاع, first sentence.) — *A piece of rag which is tied upon the top of the* [*kind of women's camel-vehicle called*] هَوْدَج, *and which the wind blows about.* (TA.) — The *head* [or *top*] of the [*woman's face-veil called*] بُرْقُع. (IAạr, TA in this art. and voce شِبَام [q. v.].) — The *hollow* (وَقْبَة) [*that is made in the upper part* of a dish] of ثَرِيد [or crumbled bread moistened with broth]: (Ṣ, O, Ḳ, TA:) or the *top,* or *upper part,* of ثَرِيد. (TA.) — Also The *place of a battle in which is much smiting.* (IDrd, O, Ḳ.)

أَصْقَعُ, applied to a horse, and a bird, &c., *Having a whiteness in the middle of the head:* (Ṣ, O, Ḳ:) or a horse *white in the top of his head:* (Mgh:) fem. صَقْعَآءُ, (Ṣ, O, Ḳ,) applied to an eagle (عُقَاب), (Ṣ, O, TA,) and to a female ostrich [&c.]. (TA.) — الأَصْقَعُ *A certain bird, resembling the* عُصْفُور [or *sparrow*], *in the feathers and head of which is a whiteness, found near water;* mentioned [in the Ḳ] in art. سقع [as with س in the place of ص]: (TA:) accord. to Ḳṭr, (O, TA,) the bird called الصُّفَارِيَّةُ [q. v.]: (O, Ḳ, TA:) you may form its pl. after the manner of substs. [i. e. saying أَصَاقِعُ], because it is an epithet in which the quality of a subst. predominates; or after the manner of the epithet [i. e. saying صُقْعٌ]. (TA.) — Accord. to AḤát, الصَّقْعَآءُ signifies *A* [*bird such as is termed*] دُخَّلَةٌ [q. v.], *of a dingy colour, small, with a yellow head, short in the* زِمِكَّى [or *tail*] *and the legs and the neck:* (TA:) or, accord. to him, the صَقْعَآء with a yellowness is *a* دُخَّلَة *of a dingy yellow colour, small, short in the* زِمِكَّى *and the legs and the neck:* and all دُخَّل are with the Arabs of the [birds termed] عَصَافِير and حُمَّر: but the صَقْعَآء with a blackness is *a* دُخَّلَة *of a dingy reddish colour, black in the head, and short in the* زِمِكَّى *and the neck.* (O.) — الأَصْقَعُ also signifies *The forelock* of a horse: or *the white forelock* thereof. (TA.) — And الصَّقْعَآءُ, *The sun.* (Ṣ, O, Ḳ.)

مَصْقَعٌ *A place towards which one tends, repairs,* or *betakes himself.* (TA.)

مُصْقَعٌ: see صَقِعٌ, last sentence.

خَطِيبٌ مِصْقَعٌ *An eloquent speaker* or *orator* or *preacher:* (Ṣ, O, Ḳ:) or one *loud in voice:* (Ḳ:) or one *who is not impeded in his speech, and who does not reiterate in speech by reason of inability to say what he would,* or *is not unable to find words to express what he would say:* (Katádeh, O, Ḳ:) or one *who is skilful, and penetrating,* or *effective, in his speech:* (O:) or one *who goes into every* ▼ صُقْع, i. e. نَاحِيَة, [meaning *province,*] *of speech:* (TA in this art. and in art. رقع:) [said to be] from الصَّقْعُ meaning "the raising of the voice;" (O, TA;*) or from الصُّقْعُ [expl. above]; or, as some say, from صَقَعَهُ meaning "he struck him upon his صَوْقَعَة;" but this last derivation is far-fetched: (TA:) pl. مَصَاقِعُ. (O, TA.)

أَرْضٌ مَصْقُوعَةٌ: see صَقِعٌ, last sentence.

صقل

1. صَقَلَهُ, (Ṣ, M, O, Mṣb, Ḳ,) aor. ـُ, (M, Mṣb,) inf. n. صَقْلٌ (Ṣ, M, O, Mṣb) and صِقَالٌ, (Ṣ, O, Mṣb,) or the latter is a simple subst., (M, Ḳ,) *He polished it;* (Ṣ, M, O, Mṣb, Ḳ;) i. e. a thing, (M,) or a sword, (Ṣ, O, Mṣb,) and the like: (Mṣb:) and so سَقَلَهُ. (Ṣ.) — صَقَلَ النَّاقَةَ † *He* (a man, AA, O) *made the she-camel lean,* or *light of flesh:* (AA, O, Ḳ:) and in like manner it is said of journeying: (AA, O:) and in like manner also, الفَرَسَ *the horse:* (Sh, TA:) or this means *he tended the horse well, with the coverings for protection from cold, and with fodder, and took good care of him.* (TA. [See صِقَال, below.]) — صَقَلَهُ بِالعَصَا ‡ *He struck him,* or *beat him, with the staff,* or *stick,* (Z, O, Ḳ, TA,) *and disciplined him.* (Z, TA.) — And صَقَلَ بِهِ الأَرْضَ † *He flung him upon the ground* (lit. *smote the ground with him*). (Aboo-Turáb, O, Ḳ.) — صَقِلَ, aor. ـَ, inf. n. صَقَلٌ, *It* (a thing, such as iron, and copper,) *was smooth, solid, and impenetrable to water.* (Mṣb.) — And صَقِلَ, inf. n. صَقَلٌ, *He* (a man) *differed,* or *varied, in his gait,* or *manner of walking.* (Ibn-'Abbád, O.)

صَقُلٌ, (so in a copy of the M,) or ▼ صُقُلٌ (Ḳ,) [the former, if correct, perhaps a contraction, by poetic license, of صَقِلٌ, for which it is not a mistranscription, as is shown by a verse cited as an ex. of it in the M,] *Light,* or *active;* applied to a beast (دَابَّة). (M, Ḳ.)

صُقْلٌ The خَاصِرَة [or *flank*]; as also ▼ صُقْلَةٌ: (Ṣ, M, O, Ḳ: [in the CḲ, erroneously, صَقْلَة:]) the former, in this sense, said by AA to be from صَقَلَ النَّاقَةَ: (TA:) seldom is the صُقْلَة of a horse long except his sides be short, which is a fault: (Ṣ, O:) and the صُقْلَانِ are the قُرْبَانِ [by which may be meant either the *two flanks* or the *two portions between the groin and the armpit on each side*] of a دَابَّة [i. e. horse or similar beast] &c. (M.) And The جَنْب [or *side*]. (M, Ḳ.) حُمُرٌ زَحَالِفُ الصُّقْلِ means *Asses having smooth and fat bellies.* (Ibn-'Abbád, TA in art. زحلف.) — And *i. q.* نَاحِيَة [meaning *A district, quarter, tract,* &c.]: (O, TA:) so in the saying, أَنْتَ فِي صُقْلٍ خَالٍ [*Thou art in a vacant district* &c.]; like صُقْعٍ خَالٍ. (TA.) — See also صَقَلٌ.

صَقَلٌ *Length of the flanks;* in a horse: (Ṣ, O:) or *depression* (اِنْهِضَام) *of the flank.* (M.)

صَقِلٌ A horse *long in the flanks:* (Ṣ, O:) or *long in the flanks and short in the sides:* (AO, TA: [see صُقُلٌ:]) and (O) *having little flesh,* (O, Ḳ, TA,) *whether long or short,* (O, Ḳ,) or *whether long in the flank* or *short.* (TA.) — Also, applied to a man, (Ibn-'Abbád, O,) *Differing,* or *varying, in his gait;* or *manner of walking.* (Ibn-'Abbád, O, Ḳ.)

صُقْلَةٌ: see صُقْلٌ. — Also *Leanness,* or *lankness in the belly,* and *slenderness.* (TA.)

صِقَالٌ an inf. n. of صَقَلَهُ, (Ṣ, O, Mṣb,) or a simple subst. (M, Ḳ.) [See 1, first sentence.] — صِقَالُ الفَرَسِ † *The tending of the horse well, taking good care of him, supplying him with fodder and fattening him.* (Ṣ,* M, O,* Ḳ.) One says, الفَرَسُ فِى صِقَالِهِ [*The horse is in his state of good tending and feeding*]. (Ṣ, O.) [See also 1, second sentence]. — Also The *belly.* (Ḳ.)

صَقِيلٌ A thing, (M,) or a sword, (Mṣb,) [and the like,] *Polished;* as also ▼ مَصْقُولٌ. (M, Mṣb, Ḳ.) — And A thing, such as iron, and copper, *smooth, solid, and impenetrable to water.* (Mṣb.) — [Also, as a subst., implying the meaning of an epithet,] *A sword.* (Ṣ, TA.)

صَيْقَلٌ: see صَقَّالٌ.

صَاقِلٌ *Polishing:* pl. صَقَلَةٌ. (Ṣ, M, Mṣb, Ḳ.)

صَيْقَلٌ One *who practises the art of polishing* (Ṣ, M, O, Mṣb, Ḳ) *and sharpening* (M, Ḳ) *swords* (Ṣ, M, O, Mṣb, Ḳ) *and the like:* (Mṣb:) [commonly called in the present day ▼ صَقَّال:] pl. صَيَاقِلَةٌ (Ṣ, M, O, Mṣb, Ḳ) and صَيَاقِيلُ: (so in a copy of the M:) the ة in the former pl. is affixed irregularly, as in مَلَائِكَة and قَشَاعِمَة. (M.)

مِصْقَلٌ: see the next paragraph. — Also, applied to a speaker, an orator, or a preacher, *i. q.* مِصْلَق, (M, Ḳ,) used by a poet in the sense of the latter word, i. e. as meaning *Eloquent.* (Th, M.)

مِصْقَلَةٌ (Ṣ, M, O, Ḳ, KL) and ▼ مِصْقَلٌ (KL) *An instrument,* (Ṣ, M, O, KL,) or *a* خَرَزَة [which may here mean either a *bead-shaped stone* or a *shell*], (Ḳ,) *with which one polishes* (Ṣ, M, O, Ḳ, KL) *a sword* (Ṣ, O, KL, TA) *and the like,* (Ṣ, TA,) *a knife,* (KL,) *a mirror, a garment,* or *piece of cloth,* and *paper.* (TA.)

مَصْقُولٌ: see صَقِيلٌ. — مَصْقُولُ الكِسَآءِ means † *Milk overspread with a pellicle:* (O,* TA:) a rájiz says,

• فَهُوَ إِذَا مَا اهْتَافَ أَوْ تَهَيَّفَا •
• يُبْقِى الدُّوَايَاتِ إِذَا تَرَشَّفَا •
• عَنْ كُلِّ مَصْقُولِ الكِسَآءِ قَدْ صَفَا •

[*And he, when he thirsts,* or *experiences the hot south-west wind* (الهَيْف), *leaves* only *the pellicles when he sucks in with his lips from every quantity of milk overspread with a pellicle, that has become clear*]: accord. to Aṣ, it means the *froth of milk:* (TA:) IAar explained it accord. to its apparent signification, as used in a verse of 'Amr Ibn-El-Ahtam El-Minḳaree, (O, TA,) i. e. as meaning a [glossy] red كِسَآء; [a sense not indicated by that verse, and clearly inconsistent with the ex. cited above;] and when told how Aṣ had explained it, replied that, when he had said it, he was ashamed to retract it. (TA.)

صك

1. صَكَّهُ, (Ṣ, O, Mṣb, Ḳ,) aor. ـُ, (TA,) inf. n. صَكٌّ, (Mgh,* Mṣb, TA,) *He struck him,* or *it:* (Ṣ, Mgh, O:) or *he struck him,* or *it, vehemently, with a broad thing;* or *in a general sense,* (Ḳ, TA,) *with anything whatever:* (TA:) or *he slapped him with his hand,* i. e. *struck him with his expanded hand,* (Mṣb,) like لَطَمَهُ, (TA in art. لطش, &c.,) *upon the back of his neck, and upon his face.* (Mṣb.) Hence, in the Ḳur [li. 29], فَصَكَّتْ وَجْهَهَا (Ṣ, TA) *And she slapped her face with her hand;* syn. لَطَمَتْهُ. (Jel.) And صَكَّ البَازِى صَيْدَهُ *The hawk,* or *falcon, struck his prey with his foot, and so cast it down.* (Ḥam p. 799.) And [hence, app.,] one says, خُذْ هٰذَا أَوَّلَ صَكٍّ, meaning أَوَّلَ مَا أَصُكُّ بِهِ [*Take thou this on my first striking with it*]: and so أَوَّلَ صَوْكٍ. (O, TA.) — Also *He pushed him,* or *thrust him;* (Aṣ, TA;) like دَكَّهُ and لَكَّهُ. (TA in art. دك.) — And صَكَّ البَابَ *He shut,* or *closed the door:* (Ṣ, O, Mṣb, Ḳ:) or *he locked the door.* (Lth, O, Ḳ.) — And صَكَّ, aor. and inf. n. as above, *He wrote what is termed a* صَكّ [expl. below]. (Mṣb.) — صَكِكْتَ, (Ṣ, O, Ḳ,) like مَلِلْتَ, (Ḳ,) third pers. صَكِكَ, (MA, in which it is mentioned

as said of an ass,) [and it is also implied in the TA that the third pers. is صَكِكَ, like لَحِحَتْ said of the eye, and some other instances, which are extr.,] a verb of the class of تَعِبَ, (Mṣb,) inf. n. صَكَكٌ, (Ṣ, Mgh,* O, Mṣb, Ḳ, TA,) [in the CḲ صَكِيكًا is erroneously put for صَكَكًا, and it seems from what follows that صَكٌّ is also an inf. n. like صَكَكٌ,] *Thou wast knock-kneed:* (Ṣ, O, Mṣb:) or *thou hadst a colliding* (اِضْطِرَاب) *of the knees,* and [when used in relation to an ostrich or a horse or the like] *of the* عُرْقُوبَانِ [which evidently means here, as in many other instances, the *hocks*]: (Ḳ:) [for] the verb is used in relation to a man, (Ṣ, O, Ḳ, TA,) and to other than man: (TA: [and the same is implied in the Ṣ and O, as is shown voce أَصَكُّ:]) صَكَكٌ [sometimes particularly] signifies the *colliding of the knees* [or *of the hocks*] *in running, so that it makes a mark,* or *scar, upon each of them:* (TA:) [and it is said that] this word, (Mgh,) or صَكٌّ, (TA, [perhaps a mistranscription for صَكَكٌ,]) signifies the *colliding of the* عُرْقُوبَانِ. (Mgh, TA.)

3. صَاكَّهُ [*He struck him,* or *it;* or *struck him,* or *it, vehemently, with a broad thing,* or *with anything;* or *slapped him with his hand; being struck, &c., by him*]. (Ḥam p. 313.)

8. اِصْطَكَّا *They* (two men, O, TA, and two bodies, TA) *struck each other.* (O, TA.) One says, تَصْطَكُّ رُكْبَتَاهُ [*His two knees collide,* or *knock together*]. (Ṣ, O, Mṣb.*) And اِصْطَكُّوا بِالسُّيُوفِ *They struck one another with the swords.* (TA.)

صَكٌّ inf. n. of صَكَّ. (Mgh,* Mṣb, TA.) —— Also a Pers. word (Ṣ, O) arabicized, (Ṣ, Mgh, O, TA,) *A certain writing,* (Ṣ, O, Ḳ,*) *called in Pers.* چَك, (O,) or چَكْ; (TA;) *a debenture,* or *written acknowledgement of a debt* (Mgh, Mṣb) *of money* or *property,* or *of some other thing:* (Mgh:) and *a written statement of a commercial transaction, purchase* or *sale, transfer, bargain, contract,* or *the like:* (Mṣb, TA:) i. q. سِجِلٌّ [in this last sense or in the senses next following]: (Ṣ and TA in art. سجل:) *a* سِجِلّ *of a* قَاضِى [i. e. *a sealed,* or *signed and sealed, statement of a judicial decision; a judicial record;* or the *record of a judge, in which his sentence is written*]: (KL:) and *a written order for the payment of subsistence-money,* or *of a stipend, salary, pension,* or *allowance;* which some persons used to sell, but the selling of which is forbidden: (Mṣb, TA:) pl. [of pauc.] أَصُكٌّ and [of mult.] صِكَاكٌ and صُكُوكٌ. (Ṣ, O, Mṣb, Ḳ.) [Hence,] لَيْلَةُ الصَّكِّ *The night of the middle* [*of the month*] *of Shaabán;* because in it are written the صِكَاك of the allowances of subsistence [of individuals]: also called لَيْلَةُ البَرَآءَةِ. (O, TA.) [Hence also] صَكُّ المُسَافِرِ *The traveller's pass, given him to prevent any one's offering opposition to him.* (A and Mgh in art. جوز.)

صَكَّةٌ The *vehemence of the midday-heat in summer:* (Ḳ:) or the *most vehement heat of midday in summer:* (Ṣ:) and it is prefixed to عُمَىٍّ: (Ḳ:) one says, لَقِيتُهُ صَكَّةَ عُمَىٍّ, (Ṣ, O,) a prov., meaning *I met him in the most vehement heat of midday in summer when the heat almost blinded by its vehemence:* (Lḥ, O, TA:) for عُمَىٍّ is said to be an abbreviated dim. of أَعْمَى: (Ṣ, O, TA:) and by it is said to be meant the gazelle, because he is dazzled and confounded in the midday-heats of summer, and knocks against the thing that is before him: some say, صَكَّةَ حُمَىٍّ, from حَمِيَتِ الشَّمْسُ: and some assert that عُمَىٍّ means the *heat, itself:* (O, TA:) or it is the name of a certain man [as will be found expl. in art. عمى, with variations of this saying]. (Ṣ, O, Ḳ, TA.)

صَكَاكٌ The *air* [or *atmosphere, between heaven and earth*]; like سُكَاكٌ; (Ibn-'Abbád, O, Ḳ;) a dial. var. of the latter word. (Ibn-'Abbád, O.)

صَكِيكٌ *Weak:* (IAmb, Hr, Ḳ, TA:) of the measure فَعِيلٌ in the sense of the measure مَفْعُولٌ; [lit.] meaning one *who is struck* much, or often, because deemed weak. (TA.)

صَكَّاكٌ [*A writer of the statements termed* صِكَاك, pl. of صَكٌّ: or, accord. to Golius, as on the authority of Meyd, *an actuary, who commits to writing the sentences of the judge*].

أَصَكُّ *Knock-kneed:* (Ṣ, O, Mṣb:) or *having a colliding* (اِضْطِرَاب) *of the knees,* and [when used in relation to an ostrich or a horse or the like] *of the* عُرْقُوبَانِ [which evidently means here, as in many other instances, the *hocks*]; as also ↓ مِصَكٌّ; (Ḳ;) which latter [in this sense is rare, and is written in the CḲ مَصَكٌّ, but] is with kesr to the م: (TA:) thus applied to a man; (Ṣ, O, Ḳ, TA;) and to other than man; (TA;) [i. e.] applied also to a horse; (O;) and to an ostrich, because he is long in step, long-legged, and sometimes, or often, his رُكْبَتَانِ [here improperly used as meaning "hocks"] being near together, his legs strike each other: (Ṣ, O:) and a man is also said to be أَصَكُّ الرِّجْلَيْنِ: (TA:) the fem. is صَكَّآءُ: (Mgh, Mṣb:) and the pl. is صُكٌّ. (TA.) —— Also One *whose teeth, both the* أَسْنَان *and the* أَضْرَاس, *cleave close together:* like أَلَصُّ. (Az, TA.) —— See also the next paragraph.

مِصَكٌّ *Strong;* (Ṣ, O, Ḳ;) applied to a man; and to other than man; (Ḳ;) [i. e.] applied to a camel, and to an ass, (Ṣ, O,) as in a verse cited in the last paragraph of art. سهر; (O;) and ↓ أَصَكُّ signifies the same: (Ḳ:) the fem. of the former is with ة; (Ṣ, O, TA;) which is held by Sb to be rare; for epithets of the measures مِفْعَلٌ and مِفْعَالٌ seldom have ة affixed to denote the fem. (TA.) —— One says also رَأْسٌ مِصَكٌّ لِلرُّؤُوسِ [app. meaning *A head strong to butt,* or *knock, against other heads*]. (Ḳ in art. رأس.) —— See also أَصَكُّ. —— Also *A lock;* syn. مِغْلَاقٌ. (Ḳ.)

مُصَكَّكٌ: see what follows.

مَصْكُوكٌ and ↓ مُصَكَّكٌ are epithets applied to a camel, [app. as meaning *Fleshy;*] as though flesh were thrust (صُكَّ, i. e. شُكَّ,) into him. (O.)

صكم

1. صَكَمَهُ, (Ṣ, Ḳ,) [aor. ـُ,] inf. n. صَكْمٌ, (TA,) *He* (a man, Fr, Ṣ) *struck him,* or *it.* (Fr, Ṣ, Ḳ.) See also صَوَاكِمُ. —— And *He* (a man, Fr, Aṣ, Ṣ) *pushed, thrust,* or *repelled, him,* or *it.* (Fr, Aṣ, Ṣ, Ḳ.) —— And one says of a horse, يَصْكُمُ, (Ṣ,) or صَكَمَ عَلَى لِجَامِهِ, (Ḳ,) or عَلَى فَأْسِ اللِّجَامِ, (TA,) *The horse champs,* (Ṣ,) or *champed,* (Ḳ,) *his bit,* (Ṣ, Ḳ,) or *the* فاس *of the bit,* (TA,) *and stretches forth his head,* (Ṣ,) or *then stretched forth his head, as though desiring to contend for superiority* [*with his rider*]. (Ḳ.)

صَكْمَةٌ *A vehement shock, collision, impetus, push,* or *thrust,* (Lth, Ṣ, Ḳ, TA,) *with a stone* or *some other thing.* (Lth, TA.)

صُكُمٌ i. q. أَخْفَافٌ [which means Camels' *feet,* and *boots;* probably, here, the former: in the TḲ it is expl. as meaning the *hoofs* of camels: and it is there said that the sing. is صَاكِمٌ]. (Ḳ.)

صَوَاكِمُ *Calamities, misfortunes,* or *evil accidents.* (Ḳ.) The Arabs say, صَكَمَتْهُ ↓ صَوَاكِمُ الدَّهْرِ [*The calamities of fortune smote him;* or *may the calamities of fortune smite him*]. (Ṣ.)

صل

1. صَلَّ, aor. يَصِلُّ, inf. n. صَلِيلٌ, *It sounded;* or *made, produced, emitted,* or *sent forth, a sound;* (Ṣ, M, O, Ḳ;) as also ↓ صَلْصَلَ, inf. n. صَلْصَلَةٌ and صِلْصَالٌ, (M, Ḳ, [in the CḲ صَلْصَلًا is erroneously put for صِلْصَالًا,]) or مُصَلْصَلٌ may be a n. of place; (M;) and صَلْصَلَةٌ [sometimes, or always, implies repetition, as will be shown by what follows, or], accord. to Lth, is more intensive, or more vehement, than صَلِيلٌ: (TA:) the former verb is said of iron [when struck with iron or the like, (see Ḥam p. 353, and what here follows,) meaning *it made a clashing,* or *a ringing, sound*], as also ↓ صَلْصَلَ; (TA;) of a nail &c., (Ṣ, O,) of a nail when struck so that it is forced to enter into a thing, (M, Ḳ,) as in a verse of Lebeed cited in art. حكم, conj. 4; (Ṣ, M, O;) of helmets of iron (بَيْض) when struck with swords, meaning *they made a ringing sound;* (M, Ḳ;*) [see an ex. of the inf. n. voce زَغْدٌ;] also of an empty jar when it is struck; (TA;) and of any dry clay, or baked pottery: (M:) also of a لِجَام [i. e. bit], meaning *it made a prolonged sound;* (M, Ḳ;) and ↓ صَلْصَلَ, (M, Ḳ,) inf. n. صَلْصَلَةٌ, (Ṣ,) said of the same, (Ṣ, M,* Ḳ,*) *it made repeated sounds,* (Ṣ, M, Ḳ,) and so ↓ تَصَلْصَلَ; (M, Ḳ;) which last is also said of a woman's, or other, ornament, meaning *it made a* [*tinkling,* or *ringing,*] *sound;* (Ṣ, Ḳ;) and of clay mixed with sand when it has become dry [app. as meaning *it made a crackling sound* when trodden upon]; (Ṣ;) mention is also made, in a trad., of the ↓ صَلْصَلَة [i. e. *ringing,* or *tinkling,*] of a bell; (Ḳ;) and

[its verb] صَلْصَلَ is said of anything dry [as meaning *it made a sound*, or *noise*, when struck, or put in motion]; (Lth, TA;) and also of thunder, meaning *it made a clear sound*. (M, Ḳ.) — [Hence,] صَلَّتِ الإِبِلُ, (M, Ḳ,) aor. تَصِلُّ, (M,) inf. n. صَلِيلٌ, *The camels made a* [*rumbling*] *sound to be heard on the occasion of drinking in consequence of their intestines' having become dry:* (M, Ḳ:) [and in like manner الخَيْلُ *the horses:*] one says, جَآءَتِ الخَيْلُ تَصِلُّ عَطَشًا *The horses came making a* [*rumbling*] *sound to be heard from their bellies in consequence of thirst:* (Ṣ, O:) and سَمِعْتُ لِجَوْفِهِ صَلِيلًا مِنَ العَطَشِ [*I heard a rumbling sound of his belly in consequence of thirst*]. (T, TA.) And صَلَّ السِّقَآءُ, inf. n. صَلِيلٌ, ‡ *The water-skin became dry,* (M, TA,) *not having any water in it, so that it was such as would make a kind of clattering* or *crackling noise* (يَتَقَعْقَعُ) [when struck or shaken or beat]. (TA.) And صَلِيلٌ also signifies The *sounding of the entering of water into the earth,* or *ground.* (M in art. صر.) — صَلَّ, (Ṣ, M, O, Ḳ,) aor. يَصِلُّ, (Ṣ, M, O,) inf. n. صُلُولٌ; (Ṣ, M, O, Ḳ;) and also, sec. pers. صَلِلْتَ, aor. تَصَلُّ; (O, TA;) and ↓ اصلّ; (Ṣ, M, O, Ḳ;) or only the latter; (Zj, TA;) or it may be الصُّلُول is said, as it occurs in a verse of El-Ḥoteí-ah, and not صَلَّ; like العَطَآءُ from أَعْطَى, and القُلُوعُ from أَقْلَعَتِ الحُمَّى; (IB, TA;) *It was,* or *became, stinking;* said of flesh-meat, (Ṣ, M, O, Ḳ,) whether cooked or raw; (Ṣ, O;) said by some to be used only in relation to that which is raw; but ↓ أَصَلَّتْ occurs, in a verse of Zuheyr, said of a مُضْغَة [or bit of flesh-meat that is chewed], which indicates that it is used in relation to that which is cooked and roasted; or, accord. to some, the verb here means أَثْقَلَتْ [*which has rendered heavy* the eater]: (M:) and one says also ↓ صَلَّلَتِ اللِّحَامُ [*the flesh-meats were,* or *became stinking* (in both of my copies of the Ṣ اللِّجَامُ is erroneously put for اللِّحَامُ, the reading in other copies of the Ṣ and in the O)]; the verb in this instance being with teshdeed لِلْكَثْرَةِ [i. e. because of its relation to many subjects, or to a pl.]. (Ṣ, O.) In the Ḳur [xxxii. 9], some read أَإِذَا صَلَلْنَا فِى الأَرْضِ, (M, O, TA,) [instead of the common reading, which is ضَلَلْنَا, with ض,] and some read صَلِلْنَا, (O, TA,) which has two meanings: i. e. *When we shall have become stinking, in the earth, and altered in ourselves and in our forms? and when we shall have become dried up?* from صَلَّة meaning "dry ground." (TA.) — And صَلَّ, (M, Ḳ,) inf. n. صُلُولٌ, (TA,) is also said of water, meaning *It became altered for the worse in taste and colour.* (M, Ḳ.) — صَلَّتْهُمُ الصَّالَّةُ, (Ṣ, M, O, Ḳ,) aor. تَصُلُّهُمْ, (Ṣ, O,) ‡ *Calamity,* or *the calamity, befell them.* (Ṣ, M, O, Ḳ, TA.) — صَلَّ الشَّرَابَ, (M, Ḳ,) aor. يَصُلُّهُ, (TA,) inf. n. صَلٌّ, *He cleared the wine,* or *beverage.* (M, Ḳ.) — And صَلَلْنَا الحَبَّ, (O,) or صَلَلْنَا الحَبَّ المُخْتَلِطَ بِالتُّرَابِ, (Ḳ,) [*We cleared the grain that was mixed with dust,* or *earth, from the dust,* or *earth, by pouring water upon it;* or] *we poured water upon the grain that was mixed with earth,* or *dust, so that each became separated from the other:* (O, Ḳ:) one says, ↓ هٰذِهِ صُلَالَتُهُ [app. meaning *This is its water with which it has been washed;* like as one says referring to anything that has been washed, هٰذِهِ غُسَالَتُهُ, and مُوَاصَتُهُ, meaning as above]. (Ḳ.) — صَلَلْتُ الخُفَّ: see the next paragraph.

2. صَلَّلَتِ اللِّحَامُ: see 1, latter half. — صَلَّلْتُ الخُفَّ; (so in my copies of the Ṣ;) or ↓ صَلَلْتُ الخُفَّ, (so accord. to the O and TA,) inf. n. صَلٌّ; (TA;) [meaning, as is indicated by what immediately precedes in the Ṣ and O, *He put a piece of skin such as is termed* صَلَّة *to the boot,* app., *to its sole* (see صَلَّة): or, as is indicated by what immediately precedes in the TA, *he put a lining* (termed صَلَالَة) *to the boot:* the verb without teshdeed (written in the O صَلَلْتُ) I think to be a mistranscription, notwithstanding the inf. n. assigned to it in the TA: general analogy is in favour of its being with teshdeed; and it is said that] تَصْلِيل signifies The *putting skin upon a thing.* (KL.)

4: see 1, latter half, in two places. — اصلّ المَآءَ *It* (oldness) *altered the water for the worse in taste and colour.* (M, Ḳ.)

R. Q. 1. صَلْصَلَ: see 1, former half, in four places. — Also *He threatened,* or *menaced;* and *frightened,* or *terrified.* (IDrd, O, Ḳ.) — And *He slew the chief man of the army.* (IDrd, O, Ḳ.) — And صلصل الكَلِمَةَ ‡ *He uttered the* كلمة [or *sentence*] *with a feigning,* or *making a show, of skilfulness.* (Z, O, TA.)

R. Q. 2. تَصَلْصَلَ: see 1, former half. — It is also said of a pool of water left by a torrent, as meaning *Its black mud became dry* [app. because such dry mud makes a crackling sound when trodden upon]. (IDrd, O, Ḳ.)

صَلٌّ: see صَلَّة, latter part.

صُلٌّ Flesh-meat, &c., *altered* [*for the worse*]. (Ḳ.)

صِلٌّ *A serpent:* (Ḳ:) or *a serpent against which charming is of no avail:* (Ṣ, O:) or *a serpent that kills at once when it bites:* (M:) or *a yellow serpent* (Ḳ) *in the case of which charming is of no avail:* (TA:) or *a yellow serpent that is found in the sand; when a man sees it, he ceases not to tremble until he dies:* (Ḥar p. 102:) pl. أَصْلَالٌ. (Ṣ, M,* O, Ḳ.*) One says, إِنَّهَا لَصِلُّ صَفًا [lit. *Verily it is a deadly serpent of smooth stones;* i. e., such as is found among smooth stones;] meaning, *an abominable serpent like the viper.* (Ṣ, O.) And إِنَّهُ لَصِلُّ أَصْلَالٍ [lit.] † *Verily he is a serpent of serpents;* thus one says of a man, likening him to a serpent; (Ṣ, O;) meaning *cunning,* or *crafty, and abominable,* (Ṣ, M, O, Ḳ,) *in contention,* (M,) or *in contention and in other cases:* (M, Ḳ:) like as one says ضِلُّ أَضْلَالٍ, and ضِرُّ أَضْرَارٍ. (TA in art. ضر.) — And ‡ *A calamity,* or *misfortune;* as also ↓ صَالَّة. (M, Ḳ, TA.) So the former in the saying, مُنِىَ فُلَانٌ بِصِلٍّ ‡ [*Such a one was tried with a calamity*]. (TA.) — And ‡ *A sharp sword:* pl. as above. (A, O, Ḳ, TA.) — And ‡ *An equal,* or *a match.* (Z, Ḳ, TA.) One says, هٰذَا صِلُّ هٰذَا ‡ *This is the equal,* or *match, of this.* (Z, TA.) And هُمَا صِلَّانِ † *They two are likes.* (Kr, M.) — See also صَلَّة, latter part. — Also *A certain plant:* (Ṣ, O:) or *a species of trees.* (M, Ḳ.)

صَلَّة [as an inf. n. of un.] The *sound of a nail and the like, when it is struck with force;* as also ↓ صِلَّة. (Ḳ.) And The *sound of the* لِجَام [or *bit*]. (Ḳ.) — Also *Dry ground:* (Ṣ, M, O, Ḳ:) or *ground,* or *land, not rained upon, between two tracts of ground,* or *land, that are rained upon;* (M, Ḳ;) because, being dry, it makes a sound [when trodden upon]: (M:) or accord. to IDrd, *ground,* or *land, rained upon, between two tracts not rained upon:* (O:) or simply *ground,* or *land,* (M, Ḳ,) *whatever it be;* like سَاهِرَة: (M:) pl. صِلَالٌ. (M, O, Ḳ.) — And *A sole:* (Ḳ:) [ISd says,] خُفٌّ جَيِّدُ الصَّلَّةِ means [*A boot good*] *in respect of the sole;* which is thus called by the name of the ground, not otherwise; in my opinion because of its dryness, and its making a sound on the occasion of treading. (M. [See also another explanation of this phrase in what follows.]) — Also *Skin:* one says خُفٌّ جَيِّدُ الصَّلَّةِ [*A boot good in respect of the skin;* somewhat differently expl. above]: (Ṣ, O:) or *dry skin, before the tanning.* (M, Ḳ.) And *Stinking skin in the tan.* (Ḳ.) — Also *An extensive rain:* (Ḳ:) and *a scattered, scanty rain:* (M, Ḳ:) and so ↓ صَلٌّ and ↓ صِلٌّ: thus having two contr. meanings: (Ḳ:) pl. as above: (M:) or صِلَالٌ, its pl., signifies *portions of scattered rains, falling by little and little.* (Ṣ, O.) — And † *A portion,* (Ḳ,) or *a scattered portion,* (M,) *of herbage:* (M, Ḳ:) pl. as above: (M:) or [the pl.] صِلَالٌ signifies † *herbage;* which is thus called by the name of the rain. (Ṣ, O.) — And *Moist earth.* (O, Ḳ.) — See also صُلَّة. — Also The اِسْت [i. e. *podex,* or *anus*]. (TA.)

صُلَّة, with ḍamm, (Ḳ,) or ↓ صَلَّة, (so in the O,) *Remains of water* (O, Ḳ) *in a watering-trough;* thus expl. by Fr; (O;) and *of other things,* (Ḳ,) *such as* [*the oils called*] دُهْن *and* زَيْت. (TA.) [See also صُلْصُلَة.] — And *A fetid odour.* (Ḳ.) — And The *flabbiness of moist flesh-meat.* (Ḳ.)

صِلَّة: see صَلَّة, first sentence. — هُوَ تِبْغُ صِلَّةٍ, or with ض, [i. e. ضِلَّةٍ,] accord. to different relaters, means *He is a very cunning man* (دَاهِيَة), *one in whom is no good.* (TA.)

صِلَال pl. of صَلَّة [q. v.]. (Ṣ, M, O, Ḳ.) — Also The *leg of a boot;* (Ibn-'Abbád, O, Ḳ;) and so ↓ صَلَالَة: (Ḳ:) or ↓ the latter signifies the *lining of a boot:* (M, Ḳ:) the pl. of the former is أَصِلَّة. (Ibn-'Abbád, O.)

صَلَالَة: see 1, last sentence but one.

صَلَالَةٌ : see صِلَالٌ, in two places.

صَلَالٌ Clay *that makes a sound like as does new pottery;* as also ▼ مِصْلَالٌ. (Ṣ, O.) — And رَجُلٌ صَلَالٌ مِنَ الظَّمَإِ [*A man making a rumbling sound to be heard from his belly in consequence of being thirsty:* see 1]. (TA.) ═ Also, (Ḳ,) i. e. like شَدَّادٌ, (TA,) or ▼ صُلَالٌ, (so in a copy of the M,) Water *altered for the worse in taste and colour.* (M, Ḳ.)

صُلَالٌ : see what next precedes.

صِلِّيَانٌ, of the measure فِعْلِيَانٌ, (Ṣ, O,) or, accord. to some, of the measure فِعِّلَانٌ, (TA in art. صلى,) *A certain plant;* (Ḳ;) *a certain herb,* or *leguminous plant;* (بَقْلَةٌ;) (Ṣ, O;) *a sort of plants* (شَجَرٌ [which means thus as well as "trees" &c.]), *said by AHn to be of the* [*kind called*] طَرِيقَة, *that grows upwards, the thickest portions whereof are the stems* (أَعْجَاز) *and the lower parts, of the size of the* حَلِىّ, *and the places of its growth are the plain,* or *soft, tracts, and the meadows* (رِيَاض): AA, he adds, says that *it is of the* [*kind called*] جَنْبَة, *because of its thickness and lastingness:* (M:) Az says that *it is of the best kind of herbage,* or *pasture, and has a* [*root such as is termed*] جِعْثِنَة, *and thin leaves:* (TA:) it is called خُبْزَةُ الإِبِلِ [*the bread of the camels*]: (TA in art. صلى:) the n. un. is with ة. (Ṣ, M, O, Ḳ.) It is said in a prov., (Ṣ, M, O,) of a man who hastens to swear an oath, (Ṣ, O,) or of one who boldly ventures to swear a false oath, (TA,) and has no impediment in his speech (Ṣ, O, TA) in doing so, (TA,) جَذَّهَا جَذَّ العَيْرِ الصِّلِّيَانَةَ (Ṣ, M, O, TA) *He hastened to it as the ass hastens to the* صِلِّيَانَة: (L in art. جذ:) because the ass often plucks out the صليانة by the root when he takes it for pasture. (Ṣ, O.)

صَالٌّ : see صَلْصَالٌ, in two places. — Also, [app. a part. n. used as a subst.,] *Water that falls upon the ground, which then cracks,* (O, Ḳ,) or, as in the L, *which then dries* (فَيَيْبَسُ فَتَجِفُّ [correctly فَتَيْبَسُ فَتَجِفُّ, as referring to الأَرْض, or rather فَتَيْبَسُ وَتَجِفُّ]), *causing a sound to be heard.* (TA.)

صَالَّةٌ : see صِلٌّ.

صُلْصُلٌ : see the next paragraph. ═ It is [also] said to signify *Stinking;* from صَلَّ said of flesh-meat. (O.)

صُلْصُلٌ : see صَلْصَالٌ. ═ Also *A certain bird:* (Ḳ:) *a certain small bird:* (M:) or (Ḳ) the [*collared turtle-dove called*] فَاخِتَة; (IAạr, Ṣ, O, Ḳ;) the *bird which the Persians* (العَجَم) *call by this latter name:* (Lth, TA:) or *a bird resembling the* فاختة: Az says, *it is what is called* موشجة [evidently a mistranscription for مُوشَّحَة, q. v.]: (TA:) pl. صَلَاصِلُ: (IAạr, TA:) and ▼ صُلْصُلَةٌ signifies *a pigeon,* (IAạr, O, Ḳ, TA,) or *a female pigeon.* (IAạr, TA.) ═ Also The *forelock of a horse;* (Ṣ, M, O, Ḳ;) and so ▼ صُلْصُلٌ: (Ḳ:) or *a whiteness in a horse's mane.* (M, Ḳ.) — And *Hair of the back of a horse, and of* [*the part of the breast called*] *the* لَبَّة, *that has become white in consequence of the falling-off of the hair.* (Ḳ.) ═ And *A* [*drinking-cup,* or *bowl, such as is called*] قَدَح (Ḳ:) or *a small* قَدَح; (Aṣ, O, Ḳ;) [i. e.] *a* قَدَح *such as is called* غُمَر. (AHn, M.) ═ And *A skilful pastor.* (IAạr, O, Ḳ.) ═ See also صُلْصُلَةٌ.

صَلْصَلَةٌ : see the next paragraph.

صُلْصُلَةٌ : see صُلْصُلٌ. ═ Also *A portion remaining of water* (Ṣ, M, O, Ḳ) *in a pool left by a torrent,* (M, Ḳ,) and *in a vessel,* or *in the* [*kind of small skin called*] إِدَاوَة, and *in the lower part of a pool left by a torrent,* (Ṣ, O,) and likewise *of* [*the kinds of oil called*] زَيْت (Ṣ,* M, O,* Ḳ) *and* دُهْن; (M, Ḳ;) as also ▼ صَلْصَلَةٌ, (Ibn-'Abbád, M, O, Ḳ,) and ▼ صُلْصُلٌ: (M, Ḳ:) pl. صَلَاصِلُ. (Ṣ, M, O.) [See also صُلَّةٌ.] — And i. q. وَفْرَة (IAạr, O, Ḳ) and جُمَّة (AA, TA) [i. e. *Hair collected together upon the head,* or *hanging down upon the ears,* or *extending beyond the lobe of the ear,* &c.].

صَلْصَالٌ *A noisy ass;* as also ▼ صُلْصُلٌ and ▼ صَلَاصِلٌ and ▼ مُصَلْصِلٌ: (M, Ḳ:) *an ass strong in voice* [or *bray*], *vehement therein.* (Aboo-Ahmad El-'Askeree, TA.) And A horse *sharp and slender* [or *shrill*] *in voice* [or *neigh*]. (M, TA.) And A wild ass *sharp in voice;* as also ▼ صَالٌّ: so says Aboo-Ahmad El-Askeree: and thus is expl. the saying in a trad., أَتُحِبُّونَ أَنْ تَكُونُوا مِثْلَ الحَمِيرِ الصَّالَّةِ ▼, app. meaning [*Would ye love to be like the asses*] *sound in bodies, vehement in voices, by reason of their strength and their briskness?* (TA.) — Also *Clay not made into pottery;* (M, Ḳ;) so called because of its making a sound (لِتَصَلْصُلِهِ): (M:) or *clay mixed with sand;* (Ṣ, O, Ḳ;) *which, when it becomes dry, makes a sound; and which, when baked, is* فَخَّار: (Ṣ, O:) or *dry clay, that makes a sound by reason of its dryness:* (Z, O, TA:) thus in the Ḳur lv. 13 [and xv. 26 and 28 and 33]: or, accord. to Mujáhid, *i. q.* حَمَأٌ مَسْنُونٌ [which means *black mud altered for the worse in odour*]. (TA.) ═ And صَلْصَالَةٌ *A land in which is no one.* (O, TA.)

صَلَاصِلٌ : see the next preceding paragraph.

مَصَلَّةٌ *A vessel in which wine, or beverage, is cleared:* (M, Ḳ:) of the dial. of El-Yemen. (M.)

مُصَلِّلٌ *Copious,* or *abundant, rain.* (IAạr, O, Ḳ.) ═ Also *A generous,* or *noble, and honourable, chief, pure in respect of parentage;* as also ▼ مُصَلْصَلٌ, with fet-ḥ: (Ḳ:) or one who is *pure in respect of generosity,* or *nobility, and of parentage:* (IAạr, O:) and ▼ رَجُلٌ مُصَلْصَلٌ [thus in the O] *a man who is a generous,* or *noble, chief, pure in respect of parentage, and honourable.* (Ibn-'Abbád, O.) — And The أَسْكَف [or *maker of boots*]; who is also called by the vulgar [or the people of the towns and villages] إِسْكَاف. (IAạr, O, Ḳ.)

مِصْلَالٌ : see صَلَالٌ.

مُصَلْصَلٌ may be either an inf. n. of صَلْصَلَ or a n. of place. (M. [See 1, first sentence.]) — [Also an epithet, if not a mistake for مُصَلْصِلٌ:] see مُصَلِّلٌ.

مُصَلْصِلٌ : see صَلْصَالٌ: — and see also مُصَلِّلٌ.

صلب

1. صَلُبَ, [aor. ـُ,] inf. n. صَلَابَةٌ; (Ṣ, M, A, Mṣb, Ḳ, &c.;) and صَلِبَ, aor. ـَ; (IḲṭṭ, A, Ḳ;) and ▼ صَلَّبَ, inf. n. تَصْلِيبٌ; (Ḳ; [but this last, accord. to the TA, is trans. only;]) said of a thing, (Ṣ, Mṣb,) [and of a man,] *It* [and *he*] *was,* or *became, hard, firm, rigid, stiff, tough, strong, robust, sturdy,* or *hardy;* syn. اِشْتَدَّ; (Ṣ,* A,* Mṣb, Ḳ;*) *contr. of* لَانَ. (M, TA.) — [Hence,] صَلُبَتِ الأَرْضُ مُنْذُ أَعْوَامٍ ‡ [*The land has been hard by lying waste for years*]; said of land that has not been sown for a long time. (A, TA.) — And صَلُبَ عَلَى المَالِ, inf. n. as above, † *He was,* or *became, tenacious,* or *avaricious, of property,* or *the property.* (M, L.) — [And صَلُبَ الشَّرَابُ, inf. n. as above, † *The wine became strong.* حَدُّ الشَّرَابِ is expl. in the Ṣ and L, in art. حد, as meaning صَلَابَتُهُ.] ═ صَلَبَ العِظَامَ, (M, Ḳ,) aor. ـِ, inf. n. صَلْبٌ; (M;) and ▼ اصطلبها; (M, Ḳ;) *He cooked,* (M,) or *collected and cooked,* (TA,) *the bones,* (M, TA,) *and extracted their grease,* or *oily matter,* (M, Ḳ, TA,) *to make use of it as a seasoning:* (TA:) or ▼ اصطلب [alone] *he extracted the grease,* or *oily matter, of bones,* (Ṣ,) or *he collected bones, and extracted their grease,* or *oily matter,* (Mṣb,) *to make use of it as a seasoning.* (Ṣ, Mṣb.) — And in like manner one says of one who roasts, or broils, or fries, flesh-meat and makes its grease to flow: (M:) i. e. one says, صَلَبَ اللَّحْمَ, (M,* Ḳ, TA,) and ▼ اصطلب [alone], (M,) *He roasted,* or *broiled,* or *fried, the flesh-meat,* (M, Ḳ, TA,) *and made its grease to flow.* (M, TA.) — And, (Ḳ,) as Sh says, (TA,) صَلَبَهُ, aor. ـُ and ـِ, (Ḳ, TA,) inf. n. صَلْبٌ, (TA,) *He,* or *it, burned him:* (Ḳ, TA:) and صَلَبَتْهُ الشَّمْسُ *The sun burned him* [app. *causing his sweat to flow*]. (TA.) — And صَلَبَهُ, (Ṣ, M, A, Mṣb, Ḳ,) aor. ـِ, (M, Mṣb, Ḳ,) inf. n. صَلْبٌ; (Ṣ, M, Mṣb;) and ▼ صَلَّبَهُ, (M, Ḳ,) inf. n. تَصْلِيبٌ, (Ḳ,) or the verb with teshdeed is said of a pl. number; (Ṣ, A;) [*He crucified him;*] *he put him to death in a certain well-known manner;* (M, L;) *he made him to be* مَصْلُوب; (Ḳ;) namely, one who had slain another; (Mṣb;) or a thief: (A:) from صَلَبَ العِظَامَ; because the oily matter, and the ichor mixed with blood, of the person so put to death flows. (M.) — [Hence] الصَّلْبُ in prayer means *The placing the hands upon the flanks, in standing, and separating the arms from the body:* a posture forbidden by the Prophet because resembling that of a man when he is crucified (إِذَا صُلِبَ), the arms of the man in this case being extended upon the timber. (TA.) — [Hence also,] صَلَبَ الدَّلْوَ, (M, Ḳ,) and ▼ صَلَّبَهَا, (M,) *He put upon the* دلو [or *leathern*

bucket] *what are called* ▼ صَلِيبَانِ, (M, L, Ḳ,) which are *two pieces of wood placed cross-wise* [*to keep it from collapsing*], *like what are called the* عَرْقُوَتَانِ. (M, L.) ═ صَلَبَتْ عَلَيْهِ حُمَّاهُ, (Ṣ, M, A, Mṣb,* Ḳ,) aor. ـِ, (Ṣ,) *His fever was continual,* (Ṣ, A, Mṣb, Ḳ,) *and vehement:* (Ṣ, A, Ḳ:) or *was of the kind termed* صَالِب [q. v.]. (M, TA.)

2. صَلَّبَهُ, (inf. n. تَصْلِيبٌ, TA,) *He, or it, rendered it, or him, hard, firm, rigid, stiff, tough, strong, robust, sturdy,* or *hardy.* (Ṣ, M, Ḳ, TA.) El-Aạshà says,

• مِنْ سَرَاةِ الهِجَانِ صَلَّبَهَا العُ •

• ضُّ وَرَعْىُ الحِمَى وَطُولُ الحِيَالِ •

(Ṣ, TA) i. e. [*Than the back of the excellent she-camel*] *which the provender of cities,* such as [the trefoil called] قَتّ, and date-stones, *and the pasture of El-Ḥimè,* meaning Ḥimè Ḍareeyeh, the place of pasture of the camels of the kings, *and the being long without conceiving,* (TA,) *have rendered hard,* or *firm,* or *strong.* (Ṣ, TA.) — [Hence] one says, صَلَّبَ النَّبِيذَ بِحَبِّ الدَّاذِىِّ † [*He made the* beverage termed نبيذ *to become strong by means of* the grain called حَبّ الداذى]. (Mgh in art. دوذ.) ═ صَلَّبَ الرُّطَبُ, (AA, Ṣ, Ḳ,) inf. n. تَصْلِيبٌ, (AA, TA,) *The ripe dates became dry:* (AA, Ṣ, Ḳ:) and صَلَّبَتِ التَّمْرَةُ *the date became dry.* (M, L.) — [Hence, perhaps, صَلَّبَ is said in the Ḳ to be syn. with صَلُبَ:] see 1, first sentence. ═ See also 1, latter half, in two places. — صلّب said of a monk, (M,) or صلّبوا (Ḳ, TA) said of monks, (TA,) *He,* (M,) or *they,* (Ḳ, TA,) *made,* or *took,* (M, Ḳ, TA,) *for himself,* (M,) or *for themselves,* (Ḳ, TA,) *a* صَلِيب [or *cross*], (M, Ḳ, TA,) in his church, (M,) or in their churches. (TA.) — التَّصْلِيبُ also signifies [*The making the sign of the cross.* And] *The figuring of a cross* [or *crosses*] upon a garment; (T, Mgh, TA;) and hence, *the figure thereof;* the inf. n. being thus used as a subst. properly so termed; (Mgh;) as in a trad. where it is said of the Prophet, قَضَبَ التَّصْلِيبَ; meaning قَطَعَ مَوْضِعَ التَّصْلِيبِ مِنْهُ [*He cut off the place of the figuring of the cross,* or *crosses, from it*]. (T, Mgh, TA.) And صَلَّبَ بَيْنَ عَيْنَيْهِ occurs in a trad., meaning *He made a mark like the cross between his eyes* by a blow. (TA.) — Also *A particular mode of wearing,* or *disposing, the* [*muffler called*] خِمَار, (M, Ḳ,) *for a woman.* (Ḳ.) One says of a woman, صَلَّبَتْ خِمَارَهَا [*She disposed her muffler cross-wise*]. (TA.) And a man's praying فِى تَصْلِيبِ العِمَامَةِ [*with the turban disposed cross-wise*] is disapproved: he should wind it so that one part [or fold] thereof is above [not across] another. (TA.)

4. اصلبت, (AA, Ḳ,) inf. n. إِصْلَابٌ, (AA, TA,) *She* (a camel) *stood stretching forth her neck towards the sky, in order to yield her utmost flow of milk to her young one.* (AA, Ḳ, TA.)

5. تصلّب ‡ *He acted,* or *behaved, with forced hardness, firmness, strength, vigour, hardiness, courage, vehemence, severity, strictness,* or *rigour;* *he exerted his strength, force,* or *energy; strained,* or *strained himself,* or *tasked himself severely;* syn. تَشَدَّدَ; (A, TA;) which means جَهَدَ نَفْسَهُ; (L in art. شد;) لِذٰلِكَ [*for that*]: (A:) said of a man. (TA.)

8: see 1, former half, in three places.

صُلْبٌ *Hard, firm, rigid, stiff, tough, strong, robust, sturdy,* or *hardy;* syn. شَدِيدٌ; (Ṣ, A, Mṣb,* Ḳ;) *contr. of* لَيِّنٌ; (M, TA;) as also ▼ صَلِيبٌ and ▼ صُلُبٌ (Ṣ, M, A, Ḳ) and ▼ صَلَبٌ: (M:) pl. of the first or second, [accord. to analogy of the latter, and also of the last,] صِلَابٌ. (M, A.) — [Hence,] مَكَانٌ صُلْبٌ and ▼ صَلَبٌ, (Ḳ,) or صُلْبٌ and ▼ صَلَبٌ, (M,) *A rugged, stony place:* (M, Ḳ:*) or صُلْبٌ signifies *a rugged, extending place,* of the earth or ground; and ▼ صَلَبٌ, *a hard part* of the earth or ground: (Ṣ:) or this last, *a tract of rugged depressed land stretching along between two hills:* (Sh, TA:) or the *acclivities of hills;* and its pl. is أَصْلَابٌ: (TA:) or أَصْلَابٌ signifies *hard, extending,* [*tracts of*] ground: (Aṣ, TA:) or *hard and elevated* [*tracts of*] ground: (IAạr, TA:) and مَكَانٌ صُلْبٌ, *a rugged, hard place:* (Mṣb:) the pl. (of صُلْبٌ, Ṣ) is صِلَبَةٌ. (Ṣ, M, Ḳ.) One says of land that has not been sown for a long time, إِنَّهَا أَصْلَابٌ ▼ مُنْذُ أَعْوَامٍ ‡ [*Verily it has been hard* by lying waste *for years*]. (A, TA.) — [Hence also,] هُوَ صُلْبُ المَعَاجِمِ ‡ [lit. *He is hard,* &c., *in respect of the places of biting;* meaning *he is strong,* or *resisting,* or *indomitable, of spirit;* عَزِيزُ النَّفْسِ;] thus صُلْبُ المَعْجَمِ is expl. in the Ṣ and Ḳ in art. عجم: and صُلْبُ العُودِ ‡ [which means the same]. (A, TA.) And صُلْبُ العَصَا and ▼ صَلِيبُ العَصَا, applied to a tender of camels; [lit. *Hard,* &c., *in respect of the staff;*] meaning † *hard, severe,* or *rigorous, in his treatment of the camels:* Er-Rá'ee says,

• صَلِيبُ ▼ العَصَا بَادِى العُرُوقِ تَرَى لَهُ •

• عَلَيْهَا إِذَا مَا أَجْدَبَ النَّاسُ إِصْبَعَا •

[*Hard,* &c., *having the veins* of his limbs *appearing: thou wilt see him to have a finger pointing at them,* i. e. his camels, because of their good condition, *when the people are afflicted with drought*]. (M, TA. But in the Ṣ, in art. صبع, we find ضَعِيف in this verse instead of صَلِيب.) — And [in like manner] هُوَ صُلْبٌ فِى دِينِهِ and ▼ صُلُبٌ ‡ [*He is hard, firm,* or *strong, in his religion*]. (A, TA.) — And جَرْىٌ صُلْبٌ (Lth, TA) or ▼ صَلِيبٌ (M, L, TA) ‡ *A hard,* or *vehement, running.* (Lth, M, L, TA.) — And صَهِيلٌ صُلْبٌ † *A vehement neighing.* (Lth, TA.) And صَوْتٌ ▼ صَلِيبٌ ‡ *A vehement sound* or *cry* or *voice.* (M, L, TA.) ═ Also, (Ṣ, M, A, Mṣb, Ḳ,) and ▼ صُلُبٌ (Mṣb, TA) and ▼ صَلَبٌ (Ṣ, M, A, Ḳ) and ▼ صَالِبٌ, (IAth, L, Ḳ,) which last is rarely used, (IAth, TA,) and is said to occur only in one instance, in poetry, but another instance of it in poetry is cited, (TA,) The *back-bone;* i. e. the *bone extending from the* كَاهِل [or *base of the neck*] *to the* عَجْب [or *rump bone*]; (M, A, Ḳ;) the *bones upon which the neck is set, extending to the root of the tail* [*in a beast*], and *in a man to the* عُصْعُص [or *os coccygis*]: (Zj in his "Khalḳ el-Insán:") or *a portion of the back:* (Ṣ:) and *any portion of the back containing vertebræ:* (Ṣ, Mṣb, TA:) [and particularly the *lumbar portion;* the *loins:*] and the *back* [absolutely]; as is said in an explanation of a verse of 'Adee Ibn-Zeyd cited in what follows: (M, TA:) pl. [of mult.] صِلَبَةٌ and [of pauc.] أَصْلُبٌ and أَصْلَابٌ, (M, Ḳ,) each of which two is used in poetry in a sing. sense, as though every part of the صُلْب were regarded as a صُلْب in itself, and صِلَبَةٌ, (M, TA,) of which last ISd says, [but this I do not find in the M,] I do not think it to be of established authority, unless it be a contraction of صِلَبَةٌ. (TA.) Lḥ mentions, as a phrase of the Arabs, هٰؤُلَآءِ أَبْنَآءُ صِلَبَتِهِمْ [*These are the sons of their loins:* because the sperma of the man is held to proceed from the صُلْب of the man, as is said in the Ksh &c. in lxxxvi. 7]. (M. [See also a similar phrase in the Ḳur iv. 27.]) — [Hence صُلْبٌ is used as signifying The *middle* of a page, as distinguished from the هَامِش (or margin): and in like manner, of other things.] — [Hence, likewise,] حَسَبٌ صُلْبٌ signifies also [meaning † *Rank* or *quality,* &c.]: (AA, Ṣ, M, Ḳ:) and *power,* or *strength.* (M, Ḳ.) A poet says, (M,) namely, 'Adee Ibn-Zeyd, (Ṣ, TA,)

• إِجْلِ أَنَّ ٱللّٰهَ قَدْ فَضَّلَكُمْ •

• فَوْقَ مَا أَحْكِى بِصُلْبٍ وَإِزَارْ •

† [*Because God hath made you to have excellence above what I can relate, in rank or quality,* or *in power, and abstinence from unlawful things*]: (Ṣ, M, TA:) AA says that صُلْب here signifies حَسَب; (Ṣ;) and إِزَار here signifies عَفَاف: (Ṣ, M, TA:) but some expl. صُلْب here by both حَسَب and قُوَّة: and some relate the latter hemistich otherwise, i. e.

• فَوْقَ مَنْ أَحْكَأَ صُلْبًا بِإِزَارْ •

meaning *above such as binds the back with an izár.* (M, TA.) And it is said in a trad., إِنَّ المُغَالِبَ صُلْبَ ٱللّٰهِ مَغْلُوبٌ, meaning † [*Verily he who strives to overcome*] *the power of God* [*is overcome*]. (TA.) — Also *Coïtus* (جِمَاع): because the sperma [of the man] issues from the part so called. (TA.)

صَلَبٌ, and its pl. أَصْلَابٌ: see صُلْبٌ, former half, in six places: ═ and see also صَلِيبٌ, in two places.

صُلَبٌ *A certain bird,* (O, Ḳ,) *resembling the* صَقْر [or *hawk*], *but which does not prey, and which is vehement,* or *loud, in its cry.* (O.)

صُلُبٌ: see صُلْبٌ, near the middle.

صَلِيبٌ: see صُلْبٌ, former half, in five places. — [Hence,] مَآءٌ صَلِيبٌ ‡ *Water upon which cattle grow fat and strong and hard.* (A, TA.) — And عَرَبِىٌّ صَلِيبٌ ‡ *An Arabian of pure race:* (A, Mgh, TA:) and اِمْرَأَةٌ صَلِيبَةٌ ‡ *A woman of noble,* or *generous, origin.* (A, TA.) ═ Also *Grease,* or *oily matter,* (Ṣ, M, A, Mṣb, Ḳ,) of bones; (Ṣ,

M,* Mṣb;) and so ▼ صَلَبٌ; (M, Ḳ;) which latter signifies also *ichor, or watery humour, mixed with blood, that flows from the dead:* (M:) pl. [of the former accord. to analogy, and perhaps of the latter also,] صُلْبٌ. (Ḳ.) Hence, in a trad., the phrase أَصْحَابُ الصُّلْبِ [in the CḲ ▼ الصَّلَبِ] *Those who collect bones,* (Ḳ, TA,) *when the flesh has been stripped off from them, and cook them with water,* (TA,) *and extract their grease, or oily matter, and use it as a seasoning.* (Ḳ, TA.) ══ Also [*A cross;*] *a certain thing pertaining to the Christians,* (Lth, Ṣ, M, Mṣb, Ḳ,) *which they take as an object to which to direct the face in prayer:* (Lth, TA:) pl. [of mult.] صُلْبَانٌ (Ṣ, M, A, Mṣb) and صُلُبٌ (Lth, Ṣ, M) and [of pauc.] أَصْلُبٌ. (Mṣb.) — [And *The figure of a cross* upon a garment &c.: see مُصَلَّبٌ.] — And *A certain brand,* or *mark made with a hot iron, upon camels;* (M, Ḳ;) *which,* as Aboo-'Alee says in the "Tedhkireh," *is sometimes large and sometimes small, and may be upon the cheeks, and the neck, and the thighs:* (M, TA:) or, as some say, it is *upon the temple;* and as some say, *upon the neck; being two lines, one upon* [or *across*] *the other.* (TA.) — And i. q. عَلَمٌ [as meaning *A banner,* or *standard;* properly, *in the form of a cross*]: (O, Ḳ:) En-Nábighah Edh-Dhubyánee is said to have thus called the عَلَم because there was upon it a صَلِيب [i. e. a cross]; for he was a Christian. (O.) — [And hence, as Freytag says, (referring to the "Historia Halebi" and "Locman. Fabul." p. ٢٢ l. 5. 8,) † *An army of ten thousand soldiers.*] — And الصَّلِيبُ is the name of *The four stars behind* النَّسْرُ الطَّائِرُ [which is *the asterism consisting of the three principal stars of Aquila;* whence it seems to be *the four principal stars of Delphinus*]: inconsiderately said by J to be behind النَّسْرُ الوَاقِعُ [which is α Lyræ]. (L, Ḳ, and so in the margin of some copies of the Ṣ.) [And Freytag says, (referring to Ideler Unters. p. 35,) that الصليب الواقع is the name of † *Stars in the head of Draco.*] — صَلِيبَانِ of a leathern bucket: see 1, last sentence but one. ══ See also مَصْلُوبٌ.

صَلَابَةٌ inf. n. of صَلُبَ. (Ṣ, M, A, &c.) — [Using it as a subst. properly so called,] one says, مَشَى فِى صَلَابَةٍ مِنَ الأَرْضِ ‡ [*He walked,* or *went along, upon hard ground*]. (A, TA.)

صَلِيبَةُ الرَّجُلِ *He who was,* or *those who were, in the loins* (صُلْب) *of the father* [or *ancestor*] *of the man:* hence the family of the Prophet, who are forbidden to receive of the poor-rate, are termed صَلِيبَةُ بَنِى هَاشِمٍ وَبَنِى عَبْدِ المُطَّلِبِ. (Mgh.)

صُلَّبٌ: see صُلْبٌ, former half, in two places. — Also *A hard stone, the hardest of stones.* (TA.) — And *Whetstones;* (Ṣ, M, Ḳ, TA;) as also ▼ صُلَّبَةٌ (TA) and ▼ صُلَّبِىٌّ (M, Ḳ, TA) and ▼ صُلَّبِيَّةٌ: (Ṣ, M, Ḳ, TA:) [or *a whetstone:*] or [*a thing*] *like a whetstone.* (A.) — See also صُلَّبِىٌّ.

صُلَّبَةٌ: see the next preceding paragraph.

صُلَّبِىٌّ: see صُلَّبٌ. — Also *A spear-head sharpened;* (Ṣ, TA;) and so ▼ مُصَلَّبٌ, (Ṣ,) or ▼ صُلَّبٌ: (TA: [but this last is perhaps a mistranscription for مُصَلَّبٌ:]) or a thing *polished and sharpened with whetstones:* (Ḳ:) and ▼ مُصَلَّبٌ signifies a spear *sharpened with the* صُلَّبِىّ, (M, TA,) or a spear-head *sharpened upon the* صُلَّب, which is like the whetstone. (A.)

صُلَّبِيَّةٌ: see صُلَّبٌ.

صُلْبُوبٌ The مِزْمَار [or *musical reed,* or *pipe*]: (O, Ḳ:) or, as some say, the قَصَبَة [or *tube*] *that is in the head of the* مزمار [app. meaning *its mouth-piece*]. (O.)

صَالِبٌ A *hot fever; contr. of* نَافِضٌ [which means "attended with shivering, or trembling"]: (Ṣ:) or a fever *not such as is termed* نَافِض: (M:) or a fever *attended with vehement heat, and not attended with cold:* (TA:) or a fever *attended with tremour* (A, Ḳ, TA) *and quivering of the skin:* (TA:) or a *continual* fever: (Mṣb:) or a fever *attended with* صُدَاع [or *headache*]: (Ḥam p. 345:) it is said by Ibn-Buzurj to be from the صُدَاع: (L, TA:) it is masc. and fem.: one says, أَخَذَتْهُ الحُمَّى بِصَالِبٍ [which may be rendered *Fever with burning heat, &c., seized him*] and أَخَذَتْهُ حُمَّى صَالِبٌ [virtually meaning the same]; the former of which is the more chaste: and one seldom or never makes one of the two nouns to govern the other in the gen. case: (M, TA:) or, accord. to Fr, they said حُمَّى صَالِبٌ and حُمَّى صَالِبٍ and صَالِبُ حُمَّى. (MF, TA.) صَالِبِى أَشَدُّ مِنْ نَافِضِكَ [*My burning fever,* or *continual fever, &c., is more severe than thy fever attended with shivering*] is a prov., (Meyd, TA,) applied to two things, or events, of which one is more severe than the other. (Meyd.) ══ See also صُلْبٌ, in the middle of the paragraph.

صَوْلَبٌ and ▼ صَوْلِيبٌ, (Lth, O, Ḳ, TA,) in some of the lexicons ▼ صَيْلِيبٌ, (TA,) *Seed that is scattered* (Lth, O, Ḳ, TA) *upon the earth,* (Lth, O, TA,) *and upon which the earth is then turned with the plough:* (Lth, O, Ḳ, TA:) Az thinks it to be not Arabic. (TA.)

صَوْلِيبٌ }
صَيْلِيبٌ } see the next preceding paragraph.

مُصَلَّبٌ A garment, or piece of cloth, *figured with the resemblance of the* صَلِيب [or *cross*]: (Ṣ, M, TA:) or *figured with a* صَلِيب: (A, Mṣb:) or *figured with the resemblances of* صُلْبَان [or *crosses*]. (TA.) [See 2.] — And A camel *marked with the brand called the* صَلِيب; (M, A, TA;) as also ▼ مَصْلُوبٌ: fem. of the latter with ة, applied to a she-camel; (M, TA;) as of the former also, applied to camels. (TA.) — And An Abyssinian (حَبَشِىّ) *marked with the figure of the* صَلِيب [or *cross*] *upon his face.* (A, TA.) ══ See also صُلَّبِىٌّ, in two places.

رُطَبٌ مُصَلِّبٌ, (Ṣ, Ḳ,) and تَمْرَةٌ مُصَلِّبَةٌ, (M,) [*Ripe dates, and a date,*] *becoming,* or *having become, dry.* (Ṣ, M, Ḳ.) When date-honey (دِبْس) has been poured on such dates, that they may become soft, they are termed مُصَقَّر. (Ṣ.) ══ مَطَرٌ مُصَلِّبٌ *Vehement, injurious rain.* (L, TA.)

مَصْلُوبٌ (M, A, Mṣb, Ḳ) and ▼ صَلِيبٌ (M, A, Ḳ) [*Crucified;*] *put to death in a certain well-known manner:* (M:) applied to a slayer of another, (Mṣb,) or to a thief. (A.) [See 1, latter half.] — See also مُصَلَّبٌ. ══ مَصْلُوبٌ عَلَيْهِ *Affected by a continual and vehement fever;* (Ṣ, TA;) or *by a fever such as is termed* صَالِبٌ. (TA.)

صلت

1. صَلُتَ, aor. ـُ, inf. n. صُلُوتَةٌ, said of the جَبِين [or side of the forehead], *It was such as is termed* صَلْت [i. e. *conspicuous,* or *clear,* or *fair;* &c.]: (Ṣ, Ḳ:) or *he* (a man) *was such as is termed* صَلْت *in respect of the* جَبِين, (Ṣ,* Ḳ,* TA,) or *of the face,* or *of the cheek.* (TA. [Accord. to the Ṣ and Ḳ, the verb is app. said of the جَبِين: accord. to the TA, of a man.]) ══ صَلَتَهُ, (Ṣ,) aor. ـُ, (TK,) inf. n. صَلْتٌ, (Ḳ,) *He urged him to run, by striking him with his foot,* or *leg;* or *struck him with his feet* or *legs, to urge him;* namely, a horse; syn. رَكَضَهُ. (Ṣ, Ḳ.*) — And *He poured it forth;* namely, what was in the cup, or bowl. (Ṣ.) ══ جَآءَ بِلَبَنٍ يَصْلِتُ, and بِمَرَقٍ يَصْلِتُ, *He brought milk,* and *broth, having much water,* (T, Ṣ, M,) *with little oily,* or *greasy matter.* (T, Ṣ.)

3. مُصَالَتَةٌ signifies The *taking to oneself a verse of another poet without altering anything in it.* (Ḥar p. 267. [But this I believe to be post-classical.])

4. اصلت سَيْفَهُ *He drew his sword from the scabbard.* (Ṣ, M, A.)

7. انصلت *He advanced with a penetrative energy,* and *outstripped;* syn. مَضَى, and سَبَقَ; (Ḳ;) or so انصلت فِى سَيْرِهِ [i. e., *in his pace*]: (Ṣ:) *he outstripped;* syn. تَجَرَّدَ: and *he was quick,* or *he hastened, in his pace,* or *going.* (TA.) One says of the eagle (العُقَاب), انْصَلَتَتْ مُنْقَضَّةً [*It was swift in making a stoop*]. (A. [This meaning is there indicated by the context.]) — انصلت يَعْدُو *He hastened in some measure, running:* and so انْكَدَرَ يَعْدُو. (A'Obeyd, TA.) — انصلتت السَّحَابَةُ † *The cloud was going to rain.* (TA, from a trad.)

صَلْتٌ, applied to the جَبِين [or side of the forehead], *Conspicuous,* or *clear,* or *fair;* syn. وَاضِحٌ: (Ṣ, A, Ḳ:) *open,* or *uncovered, and even:* (M, Ḳ:) or *smooth:* (TA:) anything *bare;* and *open,* or *uncovered:* (IAar, TA:) *wide, even, and beautiful,* or *comely.* (ISh, TA.) One says رَجُلٌ صَلْتُ الجَبِينِ *A man conspicuous,* or *clear,* or *fair*, *in respect of the* جبين: (M, TA:) or *smooth and shining*: (A:) or *wide, white, conspicuous*, or *clear*, or *fair*: (Khálid Ibn-Jembeh, TA:) or *even*: (A'Obeyd, TA:) or *hard*. (IAạr, TA.) And رَجُلٌ صَلْتُ الوَجْهِ وَالخَدِّ *A man conspicuous*, or *clear*, or *fair, in respect of the face and of the cheek*. (TA.) And فُلَانٌ يُكَوِّنُ الأَسْوَدَ صَلْتًا [*Such a one makes the black to be white*, or *fair*]. (TA.) — Also, and ▼ مُنْصَلِتٌ, (M, Ḳ,) and ▼ إِصْلِيتٌ, applied to a sword, (Ṣ, M, A, Ḳ,) *Sharp*: (Ṣ:) or *polished, and sharp*, or *penetrating*: (Ḳ:) or *unsheathed, and sharp*, or *penetrating*: (M:) or *such as penetrates into that which is smitten with it*: (A:) but some say that a sword is not termed صَلْتٌ unless *long*: (TA:) or ▼ إِصْلِيتٌ may have the same meaning as ▼ مُصْلَتٌ, i. e. *unsheathed*: (Ṣ:) accord. to AA, صَلْتٌ applied to a sword and to a knife and to a needle means *having no sheath*. (TA.) And one says, ضَرَبَهُ بِالسَّيْفِ صَلْتًا (Ṣ, M, A) and ▼ صُلْتًا (Ṣ, M) *He smote him with sword unsheathed*. (Ṣ, M, A.) — صَلْتٌ applied to a man, as also ▼ مِصْلَتٌ and ▼ أُصْلَتِيٌّ and ▼ مُنْصَلِتٌ (Ṣ, M, Ḳ) and ▼ مِصْلَاتٌ, (Ṣ, Ḳ,) pl. [of the last] مَصَالِيتُ, (Ṣ,) *Hard, firm, strong*, or *hardy*, (M,) *sharp*, or *penetrating*, (Ṣ, M, Ḳ,) *in affairs*, (Ṣ,) or *in needful affairs*, (M, Ḳ,) *light in clothing*: (M:) and [in like manner] ▼ صَلَتَانٌ signifies *sharp*, or *penetrating, and quick* (مُنْصَلِتٌ), *in his affair*. (Ḥam p. 536.) — See also صَلَتَانٌ below. — And see صُلْتٌ. — أَبُو الصَّلْتِ is a surname of *The* حِدَأَة [or *kite*]. (TA in art. حدأ.)

صُلْتٌ (Ṣ, M, Ḳ) and ▼ صَلْتٌ (M, Ḳ) *A large knife*: (Ṣ, M, Ḳ:) or *an unsheathed knife*: (M:) pl. أَصْلَاتٌ. (Ṣ, M.) — For the former, see also صَلْتٌ.

صِلْتٌ *A thief*, or *robber*: (Ḳ:) formed by transposition from لِصْتٌ. (TA.)

صَلَتَانٌ, applied to a man, and to an ass, *Strong, and hard, firm*, or *hardy*: pl. صِلْتَانٌ: (M:) or, applied to a man, as expl. above voce صَلْتٌ, q. v.: (Ḥam p. 536:) and, applied to an ass, *strong*: (Ṣ: [in some copies of which, for مِنَ الحِمَارِ, meaning مِنَ الحُمُرِ, we find الحِمَارِ, whence an error in the Lexicon of Golius:]) and, applied to a horse, *brisk, lively*, or *sprightly, and sharp of spirit*; (Ṣ, Ḳ;) and so applied to a man; like فَلَتَانٌ: (T and TA in art. فلت:) and, accord. to Aṣ, applied to an ass, *smooth, having short hair*: (TA:) or sometimes it means *having no hair upon him*; and so ▼ صَلْتٌ. (Ḥam p. 536.) — [And accord. to ISd, it seems to be an inf. n., of which the verb is not mentioned; for he says that] it signifies also The act of *leaping, springing*, or *bounding*. (M.)

أُصْلَتِيٌّ: see صَلْتٌ.

إِصْلِيتٌ: see صَلْتٌ, in two places.

مُصْلَتٌ / مِصْلَتٌ } see صَلْتٌ.

مِصْلَاتٌ: see صَلْتٌ. — مُصْلَاتُ العُنُقِ [app. applied to an ass] *Having the neck stretching out, and smooth*, or *with short*, or *little, hair upon it*. (Aṣ, TA.)

مُنْصَلِتٌ: see صَلْتٌ, in two places. — Also, applied to anything, *Quick*, or *swift*. (M, TA.) — Applied to a river, or rivulet, ‡ *Vehement in its manner of running*. (A, TA.)

صلح

1. صَلَحَ, (Ṣ, Mgh, Mṣb, &c.,) aor. ـُ, (Ṣ, MA, Mgh, Mṣb,) the well-known form, though omitted in the Ḳ, (TA,) and ـَ, (MA, Ḳ, Mṣb,) [said by some to be] the more chaste, because agreeable with analogy, (TA,) [but the former is the more common,] inf. n. صُلُوحٌ (Ṣ, MA, Mgh, Mṣb, Ḳ*) [in the CḲ الصَّلُوح is erroneously put for الصُّلُوح] and صَلَاحٌ (Ṣ,* MA, Mgh, Mṣb, Ḳ*) and مَصْلَحَةٌ; (MA;) and صَلُحَ, aor. ـُ, (Ṣ, MA, Mgh, Mṣb, Ḳ,) mentioned by Fr, on the authority of his companions, (Ṣ, TA,) but said by IDrd to be not well established, (TA,) inf. n. صَلَاحٌ and صَلَاحَةٌ, (MA,) or صَلَاحِيَةٌ; (TA;) said of a thing, (Ṣ, Mgh, Mṣb,) and of a man, (TA,) *It, and he, was*, or *became, good, incorrupt, right, just, righteous, virtuous*, or *honest*; *it was*, or *became, in a good, incorrupt, sound, right*, or *proper, state*, or *in a state of order*; *he*, or *it, throve*; *contr. of* فسد [i. e. فَسَدَ and فَسُدَ]; (MA; [and Ṣ and A and Mgh and Ḳ by implication; see صَلَاحٌ below;]) in Pers. نيك شد; (MA;) [and صَلَاحٌ signifies the same, for] ▼ استصلح and ▼ اِسْتِصْلَاحٌ both signify in Pers. نيك شدن. (KL.) One says, صَلَحَتْ حَالُ فُلَانٍ [*The state*, or *condition, of such a one became good, right*, or *proper*]. (A, TA.) — [Hence,] هٰذَا أَدِيمٌ يَصْلُحُ لِلنَّعْلِ ‡ [*This is leather that is suitable for the sandal*]. (A.) And هٰذَا الشَّىْءُ يَصْلُحُ لَكَ ‡ *This thing is suitable to thee*; or *fit*, or *meet, for thee*. (Ṣ, Ḳ,* TA.) And فُلَانٌ لَا يَصْلُحُ لِصُحْبَتِكَ ‡ [*Such a one is not fit for being thy companion*]. (A.)

3. صالحهُ, (A, Mṣb, Ḳ,) inf. n. صِلَاحٌ (Ṣ, Mṣb, Ḳ) and مُصَالَحَةٌ, (Ṣ, Ḳ,) the former of which is made fem. in a verse of Bishr Ibn-Abee-Ḥázim, (TA,) [*He made peace*, or *became at peace* or *reconciled, with him*; or *he reconciled himself with him*: for] مُصَالَحَةٌ is the *contr. of* مُخَاصَمَةٌ. (Mgh.) And صالحهُ عَلَى كَذَا *He made peace*, or *reconciliation*, [or *a compromise*,] *with him on the condition of such a thing*. (MA.) And صالحهُ عَلَى بَعْضِ مَا لَهُ [*He compounded with him for part of what was owed to him; he made a compromise with him on the condition of receiving part of what was due to him*]; said of a creditor and debtor. (Mgh in art. ضغط.) And صَالَحْتُ بَيْنَ القَوْمِ, inf. n. مُصَالَحَةٌ, *I made peace*, or *a reconciliation, between the people*, or *party*; syn. لَاءَمْتُ. (Mṣb in art. لأم.) [See also 4.])

4. اصلحهُ, (A, Mgh, Mṣb, Ḳ,) inf. n. إِصْلَاحٌ, (Ṣ, A,) and quasi-inf. n. صَلَاحٌ, (L in art. لقح,) said of a man, (A, Mṣb,) and of God, (TA,) [and of a thing,] *He, and it, made*, or *rendered, it*, or *him, good, incorrupt, right, just, righteous, virtuous*, or *honest*; *constituted it, disposed it, arranged it*, or *qualified it, well, rightly*, or *properly*; *rectified, corrected, redressed*, or *reformed, it*; *put it into a good, incorrupt, sound, right*, or *proper, state*; or *restored it to such a state*; *put it to rights*, or *in a state of order*; *set it right, set it in order, ordered it, managed it well, cultured it*; *adjusted, dressed*, or *trimmed, it*; *prepared it properly for use*; *repaired, mended, amended*, or *improved, it*; *made it*, or *him, to thrive*; *contr. of* أَفْسَدَهُ. (Ṣ,* Ḳ. [And so by implication in the Mgh &c.]) One says, أَصْلَحْتُ القِدْرَ بِالتَّابَلِ [*I made good, qualified properly*, or *seasoned*, (*the contents of*) *the cooking-pot with the seeds that are used in cooking*]. (Mṣb in art. تبل.) And أَصْلَحْتُ السِّقَآءَ بِالرُّبِّ [*I seasoned the skin with rob*, or *inspissated juice*]. (Ṣ in art. رب.) And أَصْلَحْتُ بَيْنَ القَوْمِ [in which الأَمْرَ is understood, so that the meaning is *I rectified*, or *reformed*, or *amended, the circumstances subsisting between the people*, or *party*; or] *I made peace*, or *I effected a rectification of affairs, an agreement, a harmony, a reconciliation, an accomodation*, or *an adjustment*; [or *I adjusted the affair*;] *between the people*, or *party*. (Mṣb.) And سَعَى فِى إِصْلَاحِ ذَاتِ البَيْنِ [*He laboured in rectifying*, or *improving, the bad*, or *the good, state of circumstances*, or *the disunion* or *union, subsisting between people*]. (A.) One says also, اصلح إِلَى الدَّابَّةِ, (TA,) and اصلح الدَّابَّةَ, (T, A, Mgh, TA,) the latter because اصلح implies the meaning of أَحْسَنَ, (Mgh,) ‡ *He acted well to the beast*, (T, A, TA,) *and put it into a good*, or *right*, or *proper, state*, or *took care of it*, or *paid frequent attention to it*. (A, TA.) And اصلح إِلَيْهِ ‡ *He acted well to him, did good to him*, or *benefited him*. (Ḳ, TA.) And اصلح [alone] † *He did that which was good, right*, or *just*. (Mṣb.)

6. تصالحا and اِصَّالَحَا &c.: see 8, in four places.

7. انصلح [quasi-pass. of أَصْلَحَهُ; thus signifying *It became rectified*, &c.: see تَشَعَّبَ]. (Ḳ in art. شعب.)

8. اصطلحا (Ṣ, A, Ḳ) and اصتلحا, (Ḳ,) and ▼ تصالحا (Ṣ, A, Ḳ) and ▼ اِصَّالَحَا, (Ṣ, Ḳ,) [the last a var. of تصالحا,] all signify the same, (TA,) and اصطلحوا, and ▼ تصالح القَوْمُ, (Mgh,) [*They two*, (i. e. two persons or two parties,) and] *the people*, or *party, made peace*, or *became at peace* or *reconciled*, [*each with the other*, and] *one with another*: (Mṣb:) [اِصْطِلَاحٌ is the *contr. of* اِخْتِصَامٌ, and] ▼ تَصَالُحٌ is the *contr. of* تَخَاصُمٌ. (Mgh.) — And اصطلحوا عَلَى أَمْرٍ *They* (a particular class of persons) *agreed together*, or *among themselves, respecting a particular thing*. (El-Khafájee, MF.) — [Hence,] اِصْطِلَاحٌ signifies also The *agreement* of a people *to name a thing by any name turned from the primary application*. (KT.) — And [as an inf. n. used in the sense of

a pass. part. n., for مُصْطَلَحٌ عَلَيْهِ,] *Conventional* [or *technical*] *language:* and *a conventional* [or *technical*] *term:* opposed to [لُغَةٌ and] تَوْقِيفٌ. (Mz 1st نوع.)

10. استصلح is the *contr. of* استفسد: (Ṣ, L, Ḳ:) [i. e. it signifies *He regarded,* or *esteemed,* a thing *good, incorrupt, right, just,* or *the like;* as expl. in the TḲ; and in like manner, a man. — *He wished,* or *desired,* a thing *to be good, incorrupt, right, just,* &c.; as in the TḲ; and in like manner, a man. — And *He sought to render good, incorrupt,* &c. — And hence, *He treated in such a manner as to render well affected,* or *obedient.*] — Also *He sought to do good* or *to act well* [إِلَى فُلَانٍ *to such a one*]. (KL.) — And *He sought peace,* or *concord.* (KL.) — And *It happened well.* (KL.) — See also 1.

صُلْحٌ a subst. from مُصَالَحَةٌ, (Ṣ, Mṣb, KT,) *syn. with the latter;* (Mgh;) masc. and fem.; (Ṣ, Ḳ;) *Peace, reconciliation,* or *agreement,* (Mgh, Mṣb, Ḳ, KT, TA,) *after contention:* and in the law it means *a compact to give over,* or *relinquish, contention.* (KT.) One says, وَقَعَ بَيْنَهُمَا صُلْحٌ (A, TA) *Peace,* or *reconciliation, took place between them two.* (TA.) [And أُخِذَ صُلْحًا *It* (a fortress or the like) *was taken peacefully,* or *by surrender.*] — Also *That in respect of which there has been made a peaceful compact:* or *which has been taken in the way of peace.* (Mgh.) — And *A party at peace with others.* (TA.) You say, هُمْ لَنَا صُلْحٌ *They are* [*a party*] *at peace with us.* (A, TA.) And you say also قَوْمٌ صُلُوحٌ ▼ *A people,* or *party, who are at peace:* the latter word in this case being app. an inf. n. used as an epithet. (TA. [See also صَالِحٌ.])

صِلْحٌ: see صَالِحٌ.

صَلَاحٌ an inf. n. of صَلَحَ (MA, Mgh, Mṣb) and of صَلُحَ: (MA:) [used as a simple subst., it signifies *Goodness, incorruptness, rightness* or *rectitude, justness, righteousness, virtue, honesty;* &c.: see 1:] *contr. of* فَسَادٌ; (Ṣ, A, Mgh, Ḳ;) as also صُلُوحٌ ▼: (Ḳ, TA: [الصَّلُوح in the CḲ being a mistake for الصُّلُوح:]) accord. to some, it is not used as an attribute of a prophet nor of an apostle, but only of a person inferior to these: accord. to others, however, this restriction is wrong. (MF.) — Also quasi-inf. n. of 4. (L in art. لقح.) — And [hence,] *A thing that is good,* and *right.* (Mṣb.) See also مَصْلَحَةٌ. — صَلَاحِ, like قَطَامِ, is a name of *Mekkeh;* (Ṣ, A, Ḳ;) either from الصُّلْحُ or from الصَّلَاحُ; (TA;) and sometimes it is perfectly decl. [pronounced صَلَاحٌ]. (Ṣ, Ḳ.)

صُلُوحٌ: see صُلْحٌ, and صَلَاحٌ: — and see also صَالِحٌ.

صَلِيحٌ: see what next follows.

صَالِحٌ, (MA, L, Mṣb, Ḳ,) from صَلَحَ; (MA;) and صَلِيحٌ ▼, (IAạr, L, Ḳ,) from صَلُحَ; (MA;) and صِلْحٌ ▼; (Ḳ;) applied to a thing, (Mṣb,) and to a man, (MA,) *Good, incorrupt, right, just, righteous, virtuous,* or *honest;* &c.; [see 1; *contr. of* فَاسِدٌ:] (MA, L, Ḳ:) pl. صُلَحَآءُ [accord. to general analogy of صَلِيحٌ, and app. applied only to rational beings, like صَالِحُونَ,] and صُلُوحٌ ▼ [q. v.; this being said by some to be a pl. of صَالِحٌ; and by others, to be originally an inf. n.; like as is said of شُهُودٌ]. (L.) One says رَجُلٌ صَالِحٌ فِى نَفْسِهِ [*A man good, incorrupt,* &c., *in himself*], مِنْ قَوْمٍ صُلَحَآءَ [*of a people good, incorrupt,* &c.]. (L.) And هُوَ عَلَى حَالَةٍ صَالِحَةٍ [*He is in a good, right,* or *proper, state* or *condition*]. (TA.) — [Hence,] صَالِحٌ signifies also † *Suitable, fit,* or *meet:* so in the saying, هُوَ صَالِحٌ لِلْوِلَايَةِ † [*He is fit for the office of prefect,* or *the like*]. (Mṣb.) — And ‡ *Much, copious,* or *frequent:* one says مَطَرَةٌ صَالِحَةٌ ‡ *A copious rain.* (Yaạḳoob, L, TA.) And hence the saying of IJ, أُبْدِلَتِ التَّآءُ مِنَ الوَاوِ إِبْدَالًا صَالِحًا, meaning ‡ [ت *is substituted for* و] *frequently.* (TA.) — The ا in صَالِحٌ is [often] omitted in writing [though not in pronunciation] when it is used as a proper name [so that the name is written صلح, or more properly صٰلِحٌ]. (Durrat el-Ghowwâṣ in De Sacy's Anthol. Gram. Ar. p. 66 of the Arabic text.)

صَالِحَةٌ [a subst. from صَالِحٌ, made so by the affix ة; *A good deed* or *action; an act of beneficence; a benefit*]. One says, لَا تُعَدُّ صَالِحَاتُهُ [*His good deeds,* or *beneficent actions, are not to be numbered*]. (A, TA.) And أَتَتْنِى صَالِحَةٌ مِنْ فُلَانٍ [*A benefit came to me from such a one*]. (TA.)

اِصْطِلَاحٌ [for مُصْطَلَحٌ عَلَيْهِ: see 8, last sentence].

اِصْطِلَاحِىٌّ *Conventional* [or *technical*] language: opposed to [لُغَوِىٌّ and] تَوْقِيفِىٌّ. (Mz 1st نوع.)

مُصْلِحٌ [act. part. n. of 4, q. v.]. One says, رَجُلٌ مُصْلِحٌ فِى أُمُورِهِ وَأَعْمَالِهِ [*A man who does well, rightly, justly,* or *properly, in his affairs and his actions*]. (L.)

مَصْلَحَةٌ *A cause, a means,* or *an occasion, of good; a thing, an affair,* or *a business, conducive to good,* or *that is for good;* [and hence it may often be rendered simply *an affair,* when the context shows it to mean what is conducive to good or done for a good purpose;] contr. of مَفْسَدَةٌ; (Ṣ and Mṣb and Ḳ in art. فسد;) *a good, right,* or *virtuous, affair;* (KL;) *a thing that is good and right;* syn. صَلَاحٌ ▼ [q. v.]: pl. مَصَالِحُ. (Ṣ, A, Mṣb, Ḳ.) One says, نَظَرَ فِى مَصَالِحِ النَّاسِ [*He considered the things that were for the good of the people*]. (A, TA.) And هُمْ مِنْ أَهْلِ المَفَاسِدِ لَا المَصَالِحِ [*They are of the people who occupy themselves in the things conducive to evil, not the things conducive to good*]. (A, TA.*) And فِى الأَمْرِ مَصْلَحَةٌ *In the affair is that which is good:* (Mṣb:) [or *a cause of good.*] And رَأَى الإِمَامُ المَصْلَحَةَ فِى كَذَا *The Imám saw what was good and right* [or *what was conducive to good*] *in such a thing.* (TA.) — It is also an inf. n. of صَلَحَ. (MA.)

مُتَصَلَّحٌ *A place,* of a garment [&c.], *that is to be repaired,* or *mended;* syn. مُتَرَدَّمٌ. (T in art. ردم.)

صلخ

1. صَلِخَ سَمْعُهُ, [and app. صَلِخَ alone,] aor. ـَ, (L,) inf. n. صَلَخٌ; (Ṣ, A, L;) as also صَلِحَ; (IAạr, L;) [the former of the dial. of El-Koofeh, and the latter of that of El-Baṣrah; (see أَصْلَخُ;)] *He was,* or *became, deaf, so as not to hear at all.* (Ṣ, A,* L.) صَلِخْتَ صَلَخًا كَصَلَخِ النَّعَامِ [Mayest thou, or may he, suffer *a deafness like the deafness of the ostrich*] is a form of imprecation uttered against a man; for all ostriches are [said to be] totally deaf. (L, TA.) — صَلَخَتْ جِلْدَهَا is said of a serpent (حَيَّة) [meaning *It cast off its slough:* like سَلَخَتْ]. (TA.) — And صَلَخَهُ, namely, a camel, is said of the mange, or scab, meaning [*It excoriated him;* like سَلَخَهُ; or] *it extended over the whole of his body.* (TA.)

6. تصالخ عَلَيْنَا *He feigned himself totally deaf to us;* (Ḳ,* TA;) as also تصالج, with ج. (TA.)

9. اصلخّ, inf. n. اِصْلِخَاخٌ, *He* (a man, TA) *lay upon his side.* (Ḳ, TA.)

دَاهِيَةٌ صَلُوخٌ *A destructive calamity.* (Ḳ.)

أَسْوَدُ صَالِخٌ i. q. أَسْوَدُ سَالِخٌ [q. v.], *A certain species of serpents, that casts off its slough.* (AHát, L.) — And جَرَبٌ صَالِخٌ i. q. سَالِخٌ [i. e. *Excoriating mange* or *scab*]: (Ḳ, TA:) it is *such as occurs in the hinder part of the camel, and one doubts not its extending over the whole of his body.* (TA.)

أَصْلَخُ, (Ṣ, Ḳ, &c.,) so accord. to all the people of El-Koofeh, but the people of El-Baṣrah and the Arabs of that region say أَصْلَحُ, (IAạr, TA,) *Deaf:* (Fr, A'Obeyd, TA:) or *deaf so as not to hear at all:* (Ṣ, Ḳ, TA:) or *very deaf:* (Mgh:) or أَصَمُّ أَصْلَخُ has this last meaning. (IAạr, TA.) Fr said, (Ṣ,) كَانَ الكُمَيْتُ أَصَمَّ أَصْلَخَ, meaning *El-Kumeyt was deaf so as not to hear at all.* (Ṣ, A.*) — Also A camel *affected with mange,* or *scab:* [or *having mange,* or *scab, by which he is excoriated: like* أَسْلَخُ:] fem. صَلْخَآءُ: and pl. صُلْخٌ. (Ḳ.) — And *Affected with* [*the malignant species of leprosy termed*] بَرَص. (TA.)

صلد

1. صَلَادَةٌ and صُلُودَةٌ, [inf. ns. of which the verb is صَلُدَ,] used in relation to a stone [&c.], signify The *being hard and smooth.* (M.) [And صَلَدَ has a similar meaning.] You say, صَلُدَتِ الأَرْضُ, and أَصْلَدَتْ ▼, *The land was,* or *became, hard:*

(Ḳ:) or ‡ *so that it produced no plants, or herbage:* (TA:) and صَلَدَ المَكَانُ, and ▼ أَصْلَدَ, (M, TA,) *the place was, or became, hard:* (TA:) or † *produced no plants, or herbage.* (M.) And صَلَدَ عَلَيْهِ الجَبَلُ, aor. ـِ, inf. n. صَلْدٌ; and صَلُدَ, [aor. ـُ,] inf. n. صَلَادَةٌ and صُلُودَةٌ and صُلُودٌ; *The mountain, or rock, baffled him,* namely, a well-digger, [*by its hardness,*] *and resisted his efforts.* (M.) — [Hence,] صَلَدَ الزَّنْدُ, (M, Ḳ, and so in some copies of the Ṣ,) aor. ـِ, inf. n. صَلْدٌ; (M;) or صَلِدَ, with kesr to the ل, aor. ـَ, inf. n. صُلُودٌ; (AZ, Ṣ;) *The* زند [*or piece of stick, or wood, for producing fire*] *gave a sound without emitting fire;* (Ṣ, M, Ḳ;) and ▼ اصلد signifies [the same, or] *it emitted no fire.* (Ḥam p. 407.) — And [hence,] صَلَدَتْ زِنَادُهُ [lit. "His pieces of stick, or wood, for producing fire, gave a sound without emitting fire"] means ‡ *He was, or became, niggardly, tenacious, penurious,* or *avaricious:* (AA, L, TA:) and صَلَدَ, alone, aor. ـِ, (M, A, Ḳ,) inf. n. صَلَادَةٌ; (M, A;) and صَلَدَ, (M, A,) aor. ـِ, (M,) or ـُ, (A,) inf. n. صَلْدٌ, (M,) or صُلُودٌ; (A;) and ▼ صلّد, inf. n. تَصْلِيدٌ; (Ḳ;) signify the same: (M, Ḳ:) or *he was, or became, very niggardly* &c. (A.) — And صَلَدَتْ صَلْعَتُهُ, or صَلِعَتُهُ, (accord. to different copies of the Ḳ, in the TA the former,) *The bald place on the front of his head shone,* or *glistened.* (Ḳ, TA.) صَلَدَ is also used in the same sense, in a trad., in relation to milk flowing forth. (TA.) — And one says, جَآءَ بِمَرَقٍ يَصْلِدُ, and بِلَبَنٍ يَصْلِدُ, meaning *He brought broth, and milk, containing little oily, or greasy, matter, and much water:* for يَصْلِتُ. (T in art. صلت.) — صَلَدَتْ أَنْيَابُهُ *His canine teeth caused a grating sound to be heard.* (Ḳ,* TA.) — صَلَدَ بِيَدَيْهِ *He clapped with his hands.* (M.) — صَلَدَتِ الدَّابَّةُ, aor. ـِ, (Ḳ,) inf. n. صَلْدٌ, (TA,) *The beast beat the ground with its fore feet in its running.* (Ḳ.) — صَلَدَ, (M,) or صَلَدَ فِى الجَبَلِ, (Ḳ,) aor. ـِ, inf. n. صَلْدٌ, said of a mountain-goat, (M,) *He ascended the mountain.* (M, Ḳ.) — تَصَلَّدُ, [or probably تَصْلِدُ,] said of a wild cow or wild ox (بَقَرَةٌ وَحْشِيَّةٌ), in a verse ascribed to a Hudhalee, [but not found by SM in the Deewán of the Hudhalees,] is expl. as meaning *She,* or *he, stands erect.* (TA.) — صَلَدَ السَّائِلَ † *He gave nothing to the asker,* or *beggar.* (L.)

2: see the preceding paragraph.

4. اصلد: see 1, in three places. — Also ‡ *He* (a man) *failed to produce fire with his* زند [*or piece of stick, or wood, used for that purpose*]. (Ṣ, A.) — And اصلد زَنْدَهُ ‡ *He made his* زند *to give a sound without emitting fire.* (M, TA.) And ‡ *He* (God) *caused his* زند *to emit no fire.* (A.) And سَأَلَهُ فَأَصْلَدَ † *He asked,* or *begged, of him, and found him niggardly:* thus related on the authority of IAạr; but by rule it should be فَأَصْلَدَهُ. (M.)

صَلْدٌ *Hard and smooth;* (Ṣ, M, A, Ḳ;) as also ▼ صَلِدٌ (Ḳ) and ▼ صَلُودٌ (M) and ▼ صَلِيدٌ (A) and ▼ أَصْلَدُ; (M;) applied to a stone; (Ṣ, M, A;) and so the first applied to land or ground (أَرْض); (Ṣ;) and to a solid hoof, as also ▼ صِلْدِمٌ and ▼ صُلَادِمٌ, which last is of the measure فُعَالِمٌ accord. to Kh, but فُعَالِلٌ accord. to others; (M;) and to a side of the forehead, (Ṣ, M,) or thus applied meaning *smooth and tough;* (L;) and to a head, as also ▼ صُلَادِمٌ, (M,) or thus applied meaning ‡ *upon which no hair grows:* (A:) and ▼ صَلَوْدَدٌ, (M, Ḳ,) which is of an extr. form, (M,) has the first of the significations above, (Ḳ,) or signifies [simply] *hard:* (M:) the pl. of صَلْدٌ (M, L) and of ▼ صَلُودٌ (M) is أَصْلَادٌ. (M, L.) — Also applied to a place, (مَكَان, M,) and صَلْدَةٌ applied to land, (أَرْض, A,) ‡ *That produces no plants, or herbage.* (M, A.) And أَصْلَادُ الجَبِينِ ‡ *The part of the side of the forehead upon which is no hair:* likened to smooth stone. (A Heyth.) — [Hence,] حَجَرٌ صَلْدٌ and ▼ صَلُودٌ ‡ *A stone that will not emit fire:* (L, TA:) and ▼ زَنْدٌ صَلُودٌ (M, A) and ▼ مُصْلِدٌ (M) [and ▼ مِصْلَادٌ] and ▼ صَلَّادٌ and ▼ صَالِدٌ ‡ [*A piece of stick, or wood, for producing fire*] *that gives a sound,* (M,) *not emitting fire:* (M, A:) and ▼ عُودٌ صَلَّادٌ ‡ *Wood, or a stick, from which fire cannot be produced.* (T, L, Ḳ.*) — And فَرَسٌ صَلْدٌ (Ḳ) and ▼ صَلُودٌ (Ṣ, M, A, Ḳ) ‡ *A horse that does not sweat:* (Ṣ, A, Ḳ:) such a horse is discommended: (Ḳ:) or *slow to sweat:* or *having little seminal fluid:* and *slow in impregnating.* (M.) — And رَجُلٌ صَلْدٌ (M) and ▼ صَلُودٌ (M, A) and ▼ أَصْلَدُ (Ṣ, M, A, Ḳ) ‡ *A niggardly, tenacious, penurious,* or *avaricious, man:* (Ṣ, M, Ḳ:) or *a man very niggardly* &c. (A.) — And نَاقَةٌ صَلْدَةٌ ‡ *A hardy, strong, enduring she-camel.* (Ḳ.) And خَيْلٌ صِلَادٌ ‡ *Hard, hardy,* or *strong, horses.* (A.) [And ▼ صِلْدَامٌ, also, signifies *Robust,* or *strong.* (Freytag, from Jereer.)]

صَلِدٌ: see صَلْدٌ, first sentence.

صَلْدَآءُ and صَلْدَاةٌ *Rugged and hard ground,* (ISk, Ḳ,) † *that produces no plants, or herbage.* (ISk.)

صِلْدِمٌ: see صَلْدٌ, first sentence.

صِلْدَامٌ: see صَلْدٌ, last sentence.

صَلُودٌ: see صَلْدٌ, in six places. — Also, applied to a well, *Such that its mountain, or rock, baffles the digger* [*by its hardness*], *and resists his efforts.* (M.) — ‡ A she-camel *having little, or no, milk;* as also ▼ مِصْلَادٌ: (Ṣ, A, Ḳ:) and the latter, [which in the former case is written in some copies of the Ḳ with ة,] *that has brought forth and has no milk.* (Ḳ. [But this is said in the TA to be a repetition.]) — † A woman *in whom is little,* or *no, good:* or *hard, having no compassion in her heart.* (M.) — ‡ A cooking-pot (قِدْر) *slow to boil.* (Ṣ, M, A, Ḳ.) — A beast (دَابَّة) *that beats the ground with its fore feet in its running.* (TA.) — One *who ascends a mountain by reason of fear;* (Ḳ, TA;) as also ▼ مِصْلَادٌ: (TA:) [or] a mountain-goat *that ascends the mountain.* (M.) — And *Alone, apart from others,* or *separate;* (Aṣ, L, Ḳ;) as also ▼ صَلِيدٌ. (Ḳ.)

صَلِيدٌ: see صَلْدٌ, first sentence: — and صَلُودٌ, last sentence. — Also *A shining, gleaming,* or *glistening.* (Ḳ.)

صَلَّادٌ: see صَلْدٌ, in two places; and مُصْلِدٌ.

صُلَادِمٌ: see صَلْدٌ, first sentence, in two places.

صَلَوْدَدٌ: see صَلْدٌ, first sentence.

صَالِدٌ: see صَلْدٌ. — أَنْيَابٌ صَالِدَةٌ *Canine teeth causing a grating sound to be heard;* (Ḳ,* TA;) as also صَوَالِدُ, (Ḳ, TA,) which is the pl. (TA.)

أَصْلَدُ: see صَلْدٌ, first sentence: — and see the same also near the end of the paragraph.

مُصْلِدٌ: see صَلْدٌ. — [Hence,] one says, لَيْسَ بِمُصْلِدِ القَدْحِ [lit. *He is not one whose wood gives only a sound when one endeavours to produce fire from it;* meaning † *he is not one who ungenerously refuses when asked*]; an expression of praise; (TA in art. كسر;) and [in like manner] لَيْسَ بِصَلَّادِ القَدْحِ. (TA in art. هش.) — Also Milk *milked into a greasy vessel, and therefore without froth.* (Ḳ.)

مِصْلَادٌ: see صَلْدٌ: — and صَلُودٌ, in two places.

صلط

2. صَلَّطَهُ اللّٰهُ عَلَيْهِ, inf. n. تَصْلِيطٌ, a dial. var. of سَلَّطَهُ, q. v. (Ibn-'Abbád, Ḳ.)

صلع

1. صَلِعَ, aor. ـَ, (Mṣb, Ḳ,) inf. n. صَلَعٌ, (Ṣ,* O,* Mṣb, Ḳ,* TA,) *He* (a man, Ṣ, O, Ḳ*) *was, or became, bald in the fore part of the head:* (Ṣ,* O,* Mṣb, Ḳ:* but in the Mṣb it is said in this sense of the head:) or *in the fore part of the head to the hinder part thereof:* and likewise *in the middle of the head.* (TA.) [See also جَلِحَ and جَلَحٌ.] Accord. to Ibn-Seenà, the baldness termed صَلَعٌ does not happen to women, because of the abundance of their moisture; nor to eunuchs, because their constitutions are nearly like those of women. (Mṣb.) — [Hence,] صَلِعَتِ العُرْفُطَةُ, inf. n. as above, ‡ *The* عرفطة [a species of mimosa] *dropped the heads of its branches:* and *had them eaten by the camels.* (TA.) — See also 7. — صَلَعَ رَأْسَهُ [perhaps a mistranscription for ▼ صَلَّعَ, and primarily signifying *He made his head bald in the fore part:*] ‡ *he shaved his head.* (Z, TA.) — صَلَعَ said of such as is termed عِذْيَوط, [but the verb in this sense is probably ▼ صَلَّعَ, (see this latter,)] *He voided his ordure* (أَحْدَثَ) *on the occasion of* جِمَاع. (TA.)

2. صلّع: see above, last sentence but one. — صلّعت الحَيَّةُ ‡ *The serpent came forth from concealment* (بَرَزَتْ) *without any earth, or dust, upon it.* (Ibn-'Abbád, O, Ḳ, TA. [But in the O, the verb in this and the following senses is carelessly written without the sheddeh.]) — صلّع, inf. n. تَصْلِيعٌ, (said of a man, IAạr, TA,) i. q. أَعْذَرَ

[meaning *He voided his ordure*: see تَصْلِيعٌ as a subst., below; and what here follows]. (IAạr, Ḳ, TA.) And صلّع فُلَانٌ, (inf. n. as above, TA,) *Such a one put his hand evenly expanded* (Ḳ, TA) *on the ground* (TA) *and voided his ordure* or *his ordure in a thin state* (سَلَحَ): (Ḳ, TA:) thus expl. by Lth. (TA.) See also 1, last sentence.

5. تصلّعت السَّمَآءُ † *The sky became bared by the disruption of its clouds.* (TA.) — See also what next follows.

7. انصلعت الشَّمْسُ ‡ *The sun rose,* or *began to rise*: syn. بَزَغَتْ: or *culminated*: or *came forth from the clouds,* (O, Ḳ, TA,) *appearing in the time of intense heat, with nothing intervening and concealing it;* (TA;) and so ▼ تصلّعت, (O, Ḳ, TA,) and ▼ صَلَعَت [or more probably صَلِعَت]. (TA.)

[8. اصطلع, accord. to Reiske, as stated by Freytag, signifies *He,* or *it, was defiled,* or *polluted;* "conspurcatus fuit:" but he names no authority.]

صَلَعٌ *Baldness in the fore part of the head:* (Ṣ, O, Mṣb, Ḳ:) or *in the fore part of the head to the hinder part thereof:* and likewise *in the middle of the head.* (TA. [See صَلِعَ, of which it is the inf. n.: and see also جَلَحٌ.]) — Also a dial. var. of صُلَّعٌ, q. v. (TA.) — One says also, لَأُقِيمَنَّ صَلَعَكَ meaning [*I will assuredly straighten*] *thy* [*natural*] *crookedness;* like ضَلَعَكَ. (TA in art. ضلع, from the T and M.)

صُلْعَةٌ: }
صُلَعَةٌ: } see what next follows.

صَلَعَةٌ *A place of baldness such as is termed* صَلَعٌ; (Ṣ, O, Mṣb, Ḳ;) as also ▼ صُلْعَةٌ; (Ṣ, O, Ḳ;) and ▼ صُلَعَةٌ is said to be a contraction of the first, (O, Mṣb,) by Lth, (O,) but it is disallowed by the thoroughly learned. (Mṣb.)

صِلَاعٌ, (O, Ḳ,) accord. to Ibn-'Abbád, with kesr, (O,) like كِتَابٌ, (Ḳ,) in the L [written] with ḍamm, (TA,) The *heat* of the sun. (O, Ḳ.)

صَلِيعٌ: see أَصْلَعُ. — [Hence,] ‡ A mountain *having upon it no plants,* or *herbage.* (O, Ḳ, TA.)

صُلَيْعَآءُ: see أَصْلَعُ, in six places.

صُلَّعٌ: see صُلَاعٌ. — Accord. to Aṣ, (Ṣ, O, TA,) ‡ *A place that produces no plants,* or *herbage;* (Ṣ, O, Ḳ, TA;) whether it be a mountain or land; (TA;) from صَلَعٌ in relation to the head; (Ṣ, O, TA;) and ▼ صَلَعٌ is also syn. with صُلَّعٌ in the sense expl. above. (TA.) And [the n. un.] صُلَّعَةٌ signifies *A smooth rock.* (TA.)

صُلَاعٌ, (Ṣ, O, Ḳ,) or ▼ صُلَّعٌ, (Ḳ,) or the latter also, which is app. a contraction of the former, (Ṣ, O,) † *Broad,* (Ṣ, O, Ḳ, TA,) *hard,* (Ḳ, TA,) *smooth,* (TA,) *rock:* (Ṣ, O, Ḳ, TA:) n. un. (of the former, Ṣ, O, [and of the latter also,]) with ة. (Ṣ, O, Ḳ.)

صَوْلَعٌ: see the next paragraph.

أَصْلَعُ, applied to a man, (Ṣ, O, Mṣb,) *Bald in the fore part of the head;* (Ṣ, Mgh, O, Mṣb, Ḳ;) denoting more than أَجْلَحُ: (Mgh:) or *bald in the fore part of the head to the hinder part thereof:* (TA:) and likewise, (TA,) or accord. to Aṣ, (O,) *bald in the middle of the head:* (O, TA:) and applied also to a head, (Mṣb, TA,) meaning *bald in the fore part:* (Mṣb:) and ▼ صَلِيعٌ signifies the same, applied to a head, (Mṣb, TA,) and to a man: (Mṣb:) fem. صَلْعَآءُ; (Ḳ;) but some disapprove this, and say that the fem. epithet is قَرْعَآءُ, and زَعْرَآءُ: (TA:) the pl. is صُلْعٌ (O, Mṣb, Ḳ) and صُلْعَانٌ: (O, Ḳ:) ▼ أُصَيْلِعُ is the dim. of the masc., [and ▼ صُلَيْعَآءُ is that of the fem.,] meaning as expl. above. (TA.) — [Hence,] the fem., applied to a tree such as is termed عُرْفُطَة, [a species of mimosa,] ‡ *That has dropped the heads of its branches:* (Ṣ, TA:) and *that has had its branches eaten by the camels.* (TA.) — And, applied to a tract of sand, (رَمْلَةٌ, Ṣ, O, Ḳ,) and to a land, (أَرْضٌ, Ḳ,) ‡ *In which are no trees:* (Ṣ, O, TA:) and (TA) *in which is no herbage.* (O, Ḳ, TA.) It also occurs, alone, as meaning † *A desert* (صَحْرَآء) *that produces nothing;* like the head termed أَصْلَعُ. (TA.) And ▼ صُلَيْعَآءُ, applied to a land, † *That produces no plants,* or *herbage.* (TA.) — And the masc., applied to a mountain, † *Open to view, smooth, and glistening.* (TA.) — And, applied to a spear-head, ‡ *Glistening and smooth:* (O, TA:) or *polished;* (Ḳ;) and so ▼ صَوْلَعٌ. (O, Ḳ.) — [Hence also,] ▼ الأُصَيْلِعُ signifies ‡ *The penis.* (O, Ḳ, TA.) And الأَصْلَعُ is said to signify ‡ *The head of the penis.* (TA.) — And ▼ الأُصَيْلِعُ, (Ṣ, O, Ḳ, TA,) or الأَصْلَعُ, (TA,) † *A certain serpent, slender in the neck,* (Ṣ, O, Ḳ, TA,) or, accord. to Az, *wide in the neck, round in the head,* (TA,) *its head being like a hazel-nut:* (Ṣ, O, Ḳ, TA:) thought by Az to be so called as being likened to the penis. (TA.) — أَصْلَعُ applied to an affair, or event, (أَمْرٌ,) means † *Hard, distressing,* or *calamitous;* (TA;) and so applied to a day; as also أَجْلَحُ: (A and TA in art. جلح:) or, applied to a day, ‡ *intensely hot.* (Ibn-'Abbád, Z, O, TA.) — Also, the fem., [used as a subst.,] ‡ *Any notorious affair* or *event;* or *any such affair that is dubious, of great magnitude* or *moment, to accomplish which,* or *to perform which, one finds not the way:* (O, Ḳ, TA:) and ‡ *a calamity,* or *misfortune,* (Ṣ, O, Ḳ, TA,) [or] *such as is hard to be borne;* [as though it were smooth and slippery;] because there is no escape from it: (TA:) and [in like manner] ▼ صُلَيْعَآءُ, (O, Ḳ, TA) and سَوْءَةُ صَلْعَآءُ, and ▼ صُلَيْعَآءُ, (TA,) *an evil, abominable,* or *unseemly, action* or *saying, such as is apparent, manifest,* or *unconcealed:* (O, Ḳ, TA:) or *a calamity,* or *misfortune, hard to be borne:* (Ḳ, TA:) and hence the saying of 'Áisheh to Mo'áwiyeh, (O, Ḳ, TA,) when she reproached him for his having asserted the relationship to him of Ziyád, and he replied that the witnesses gave testimony, (O, Ḳ,* TA, [see Abulfedæ Annales, i. 360,]) مَا شَهِدَتِ الشُّهُودُ وَلٰكِنْ رَكِبْتَ ▼ الصُّلَيْعَآءَ [*The witnesses did not bear witness* (in the CḲ, erroneously, ما شَهِدَتْ الشُّهُودُ,) *but thou committedst that which was an evil, abominable,* or *unseemly, action,* &c.]. (O, Ḳ, TA.) — ▼ صُلَيْعَآءُ is also said to signify † The *act of glorying,* or *boasting;* syn. فَخْرٌ. (TA.)

أُصَيْلِعُ, dim. of أَصْلَعُ: (TA:) see the latter, in three places.

تَصْلِيعٌ inf. n. of 2 [q. v.]. (Ḳ, TA.) — And a subst., like تَمْتِينٌ and تَنْبِيتٌ, signifying *Ordure,* or *dung;* or *such as is thin;* syn. سُلَاحٌ: (TA:) thus expl. by Lth. (O.)

صلغ

1. صَلَغَتِ البَقَرَةُ, and الشَّاةُ, (Ṣ, O, Ḳ,) aor. ـَ, (O,) inf. n. صُلُوغٌ, (Ṣ, O,) *i. q.* سَلَغَت, (Ṣ, O, Ḳ,) i. e. *The bovine animal,* and *the sheep* or *goat, shed the tooth* [*next*] *behind that called the* سَدِيس: (Ṣ and Ḳ in art. سلغ;) or *bred its* [*tooth called the*] نَاب: (Ḳ in that art. [in which see more]:) or صَلَغَ said of any cloven-hoofed animal, aor. and inf. n. as above, signifies *he entered the sixth year:* or, as some say, *the fifth:* this is the utmost of the ages thereof [that have verbs and epithets to denote them]: (Mṣb:) صُلُوغٌ (Mgh, Mṣb) in these animals (Mṣb) or in sheep or goats and animals of the bovine kind (Mgh) is like بُزُولٌ in camels. (Mgh, Mṣb.)

صَلَغٌ: see صَلَغَةٌ. — Also *A red* [*hill* or *mountain, such as is termed*] هَضْبَة [q. v.]. (O, Ḳ.)

صَلَغَةٌ *A large ship* or *boat.* (Lth, O, Ḳ.)

صَلَغَةٌ [a n. un. of which ▼ صَلَغٌ is the coll. gen. n., as is indicated in the O and TA,] applied to a she-camel *i. q.* رَبَاعِيَة [i. e. *In her seventh year*], *and fat:* or *i. q.* سَدِيس [i. e. *in the eighth year*]. (AA, O, Ḳ.)

صَالِغٌ part. n. of 1 [q. v.], (Ṣ, O, Mṣb, Ḳ,) an epithet applied to the male and the female of all cloven-hoofed animals, (Mṣb,) or to an animal of the bovine kind and to the sheep or goat, (Ṣ, O, Ḳ,) *I. q.* سَالِغ, (IDrd, O, TA,) which latter is said by Sb to be the original, the ص being substituted for the س because of the غ: (TA:) or, applied to a sheep or goat (Ibn-'Abbád, O, Ḳ) and to a bovine animal, (Ḳ,) it is *like* قَارِح [q. v.] *applied to a horse:* (Ibn-'Abbád, O, Ḳ:) or *in the fifth year,* (Aṣ, IF, O, Ḳ,) as applied to a sheep: (Aṣ, IF, O:) or *in the sixth year,* (AZ, O, Ḳ,) as applied to a sheep or goat: (AZ, O:) or a sheep or goat *advanced in age:* (IDrd, O:) [see more in art. سلغ:] the pl. is صُلَّغٌ (IAạr, Ṣ, O, Ḳ) and صَوَالِغُ, (IAạr, O, Ḳ,) both of which are applied to كِبَاش, (Ḳ,) [or rather] the former pl. is thus applied by Ru-beh, who by كِبَاش in this instance means "heroes," or "brave men." (Ṣ, O.)

صلف

1. صَلِفَ السَّحَابُ, [aor. ـَ,] inf. n. صَلَفٌ, *The*

clouds had in them no water: (M:) or صَلَفَتِ السَّحَابَةُ *the cloud had little water.* (A, TA. [It is implied in the TA that this is tropical; but I doubt its being so.]) See also its part. n., صَلِفٌ. — صَلَفَ said of a man's حَرْث [or seed-produce], *It did not increase,* or *multiply,* or *become plentiful* or *abundant.* (TA.) — صَلَفٌ as a quality of طَعَام [or wheat] signifies Its *having little increase* (نُزْل, Ṣ, or نَزَل, L, or نَمَآء and بَرَكَة, Ḳ) *and little goodness.* (L, TA: said in the latter to be tropical.) — [Hence, app., or from the verb as used in the sense expl. in the next sentence below,] مَنْ يَبْغِ فِى الدِّينِ يَصْلَفْ, (Ṣ, M, Meyd, &c.,) a prov., (Ṣ, Meyd, O, Ḳ,) relating to the holding fast to religion, (Ṣ,) or used in urging to the mixing in social intercourse with the holding fast to religion, (O, Ḳ,) or, accord. to IAth, a trad., (TA,) i. e., accord. to Aṣ, *He who exceeds the right bounds in religion* (Meyd) *will not be in favour with men,* or *beloved by them;* (Ṣ, Meyd;) or *will have little increase therein:* (M:) or *he who finds fault with men in respect of religion,* (O, Ḳ,) *and regards it as an excellence* [*that he possesses*] *above them, will have little goodness in their estimation, and* (O) *will not be in favour with them,* or *beloved by them:* (O, Ḳ:) or the meaning is, *he who seeks worldly good by means of religion, his share* of the former *will be little:* (Meyd:) or *he who seeks, in respect of religion, more than he has had revealed to him, his share will be little.* (IAth.) — صَلِفَتْ, (Ṣ, M, O,) aor. ـَ, (Ṣ, O,) inf. n. صَلَفٌ, said of a woman, means *She was not in favour with,* or *was not beloved by,* (Ṣ, M, O, Ḳ,*) *her husband,* (Ṣ, O, Ḳ,) or *him by whom she was supported;* (M;) and *was hated by him.* (Ṣ, O.) — صَلَفٌ, (O, Ḳ,) in a man and in a woman, (O,) signifies also The *saying that which one's companion dislikes,* or *hates.* (O, Ḳ.) — And, (O, Ḳ,) likewise in a man and in a woman, (O,) † The *commending,* or *praising, oneself for,* or the *boasting of,* or *glorying in, that which one does not possess:* (O, Ḳ:) or, (Ḳ,) as Kh asserts, (Ṣ, O,) the *overpassing the due limits in* الظَّرْف [here meaning *elegance of mind, manners, address, speech, person, attire, and the like*], (Ṣ, M, O, Ḳ,) and *in excellence in knowledge* or *courage* or *other qualities,* (TA,) and *arrogating to oneself more than is due, through pride:* (Ṣ, O, Ḳ:) but some say that this is post-classical: (M, TA:) [see an ex. voce آوَّهْ, in art. اوف; mentioned here in the TA as occurring in a trad.:] one says, of a man, صَلِفَ, (M, MA,) inf. n. صَلَفٌ, (M,) meaning † *He commended,* or *praised, himself* [&c.]; (MA;) and ▾ تصلّف, (Ṣ, MA, O,) meaning the same; (MA;) or this latter means تَكَلَّفَ الصَّلَفَ, (Ḳ, TA,) i. e. [*he affected the overpassing of the due limits in* الظَّرْف (meaning as expl. above); or *he took upon himself as a task*] *the arrogating to himself more than was due, through pride:* (TA:) [you say, تصلّف بِمَا لَيْسَ عِنْدَهُ † *He commended,* or *praised, himself for,* or *he boasted of,* or *gloried in, that which he did not possess:*] the epithet from the former verb is ▾ صَلِفٌ, (AZ, Ṣ, M, O, Ḳ,) applied to a man, (AZ, Ṣ, M, O,) and صَلِفَةٌ applied to a woman; (M;) and the pl. of صَلِفٌ is صَلَافَى (AZ, M, Ḳ) and صُلَفَآءُ and صَلِفُونَ: (AZ, O, Ḳ:) it is said to be from صَلِفٌ applied to a vessel, accord. to IAạr as meaning "that takes little water;" but rather, as others say, as meaning "thick and heavy:" the vulgar misapply it [app. by using it in the sense assigned to it by IAạr]. (TA.) — See also the next paragraph.

4. اصلف i. q. قَلَّ خَيْرُهُ [*His good things became few;* or *his wealth,* or *his goodness* or *beneficence, became little*]: (IAạr, O, Ḳ:) and (TA) so ▾ تصلّف. (M, TA.) — And *His soul,* or *spirit,* (رُوحُهُ,) *became heavy;* (IAạr, O, Ḳ;) and *he became oppressed as though by the nightmare.* (TḲ.) — And *He became one whose wife was not in favour with him,* or *not beloved by him.* (M.) — اصلفها *He hated her,* namely, his wife; (M;) as also ▾ صَلِفَهَا, (so in a copy of the M,) or صَلَفَهَا, aor. ـِ; (so in the L and TA;) the latter mentioned by IAmb: (L, TA:) or اصلفهُ *he hated him,* namely, another man. (Ibn-'Abbád, O, Ḳ.) — And اصلف نِسَآءَهُ *He divorced his wives:* and *he made their share of his favours to be small.* (A, TA.) — And one says to a woman, أَصْلَفَ اللّٰهُ رُفْغَكِ, meaning *May God make thee* [or *thy* فَرْج or *the like*] *to be hated by thy husband.* (Esh-Sheybánee, Ṣ, O, Ḳ.) — اصلف القَوْمُ, (thus in the O, on the authority of Ibn-'Abbád, [like أَحْزَنَ, and its contr. أَسْهَلَ, &c.,]) or ▾ تصلّف, (thus in the Ḳ, [but the former is preferable on the ground of analogy, and the latter I think a mistake,]) *The people,* or *party, became in the* [*kind of tract termed*] صَلْفَآء. (O, Ḳ.)

5. تصلّف: see 4, first sentence. — And see 1, latter part. — Also *He behaved in a loving,* or *an affectionate, and a blandishing,* or *coaxing, manner.* (O, Ḳ.) — And, said of a camel, *He loathed,* or *turned away with disgust from, the* [*pasturage termed*] خُلَّة, *and inclined to the* حَمْض. (O, Ḳ.) — See also 4, last sentence.

الصَّلَفُ *The branches of the heart of the palmtree that are next below the* قِلَبَة: [in the CḲ, حَوالَا فى قَلْبِ النَّخْلَةِ is erroneously put for حَوَالِى; قلب النخلة; and the same mistake was originally made in my MS. copy of the Ḳ:] n. un. with ة. (IAạr, O, Ḳ,* TA. [See خَافِيَة, last sentence.]

صَلِفٌ, applied to clouds (سَحَاب, Ṣ, M, O, Ḳ), *Containing no water:* (M:) or *having little water and much thunder.* (Ṣ, O, Ḳ. [Said in the TA to be tropical; but I doubt its being so.]) It is said in a prov., رُبَّ صَلِفٍ تَحْتَ الرَّاعِدَةِ, (Ṣ, and so in some copies of the Ḳ,) or ▾ رُبَّ صَلَفٍ, (M, O, and so in some copies of the Ḳ, [with an inf. n. in the place of an epithet,]) i. e. *Many a cloud is there,* [or *many clouds are there, lacking rain,* or] *having much thunder with little rain,* [*beneath that which thunders:*] (A'Obeyd, O:) applied to the wealthy niggard: (A'Obeyd, O, Ḳ:) or to him who threatens, and does not perform what he threatens: (Ṣ, O, Ḳ:) or to him who commends himself much, (M, O, Ḳ,) and is loquacious, (M, O,) but is destitute of good. (M, O, Ḳ.) — And A vessel *that takes little water:* (IAạr, Ṣ, M, O, Ḳ:) a *small vessel:* one *that leaks; that will not hold water.* (IAạr, TA. [This, also, is said in the TA to be tropical.]) And A *heavy* (Ḳ, TA) *and thick* (TA) vessel. (Ḳ, TA.) — Also High ground (قُفّ), or a hard plain, *that produces no plants* or *herbage:* (TA:) and so the fem., with ة, applied to land (أَرْض). (M, TA.) — Wheat (طَعَام) *having little increase* (قَلِيلُ النُّزْلِ and الرَّيْعِ): (M:) or *tasteless:* (M, O, Ḳ:) and ▾ صَلِيفٌ signifies the same, in the former sense or in the latter. (M.) — And [A man] *heavy in soul,* or *spirit;* syn. ثَقِيلُ الرُّوحِ. (TA. [See 4, second sentence, which shows that مُصْلِفٌ has this meaning: but the epithet thus expl. in the TA is there said to be like كَتِفٌ.]) — And صَلِفَةٌ signifies A woman *not in favour with,* or *not beloved by,* (Ṣ, M, O, Ḳ,) *her husband,* (Ṣ, O, Ḳ,) or *him by whom she is supported;* (M;) and *hated by him:* (Ṣ, O:) pl. صَلَائِفُ, (Ṣ, M, O, Ḳ,) which is extr. [in respect of analogy], (M,) and صَلِفَاتٌ. (O, Ḳ.) — See also 1, near the end.

صَلْفَآء and صَلْفَآء, and each with ة: see أَصْلَفُ, in five places.

صَلِيفٌ The *side* (عُرْض) [in one of my copies of the Ṣ عَرْض, and in the other copy عِرْق,]) *of the neck;* the two being called صَلِيفَانِ; (Ṣ, O, Ḳ;) [i. e.] الصَّلِيفَانِ signifies *the two sides of the neck* (جَانِبَا العُنُقِ): or this signifies *what are between the* لِيت [or *part beneath the earring*] *and the* قَصَرَة [or *base of the neck, on the two sides*]: (M:) or *the two heads of the vertebra that is next to the head, in the two sides of the neck.* (AZ, O,* Ḳ,* TA.) In this last explanation, in the copies of the Ḳ, رَأْس is put for رأسا. (TA. [And in some copies of the Ḳ, شِقَّيْهَا is there erroneously put for شِقَّيْهَا, which, as is said in the TA, refers to the neck.]) أَخَذَ بِصَلِيفِهِ and ▾ بِصَلِيفَتِهِ mean, accord. to Aṣ, *He took hold of the back of his neck:* (O, TA:) and one says also, ▾ أَخَذَهُ بِصَلِيفَتِهِ; meaning *He took him,* or *it, altogether.* (TA. [But I think it not improbable that ▾ بِصَلِيفَتِهِ in these two instances may be a mistranscription for بِصَلِيفَيْهِ.]) — الصَّلِيفَانِ signifies also *Two staves,* or *pieces of wood, which are placed across* [*horizontally*] *upon the* [*camel's saddle called*] غَبِيط, *by means of which the* مَحَامِل [pl. of مَحْمِل, q. v.,] *are bound.* (Ṣ, O, Ḳ.) And (TA) صَلِيفَا الإِكَافِ signifies *The two* [*similar*] *pieces of wood that are bound upon the upper part of the* [*saddle called*] إِكَاف. (M, TA.) — See also صَلِفٌ, latter half.

صَلِيفَةٌ: see صَلِيفٌ, in three places.

صَلَنْقَى and صَلَنْقَآءُ A *loquacious* man. (M, TA.)

أَصْلَفُ *Hard,* applied to a place; and so [the fem.] ▾ صَلْفَآءُ applied to land (أَرْض): (Ṣ, O:) or both signify *hard ground* (M, Ḳ) *containing* stones; (M;) or *hard and rugged ground;* (Aṣ, O;) and the pl. is صَلَافِ, (M, O, Ḳ,*) [in the last, erroneously, صَلَافِى, and in the O, correctly, الصَّلَافِى, being made determinate,]) thus pluralized in the same manner as صَحْرَآءُ because the quality of a subst. is predominant therein, (M,) and [for the same reason] أَصَالِفُ also; (O, Ḳ;) [the former pl. of صلفاء, and the latter of اصلف:] or ↓ صَلْفَآءُ (Ibn-'Abbád, O, Ḳ) and ↓ صِلْفَآءُ, [each, app., with tenween, the latter because of the measure فِعْلَآءٌ, and each because receiving the affix ة, for it is added,] and likewise ↓ صَلْفَاءَةٌ (Ḳ) and ↓ صِلْفَاءَةٌ, (Ibn-'Abbád, O, Ḳ,) *rugged, hard ground:* (Ḳ:) or *a smooth rock,* or *a hard, smooth, bare rock, even with the ground.* (Ibn-'Abbád, O, Ḳ.)

مُصَلَّفٌ A man *whose wife is not in favour with him* or *not beloved by him.* (IAạr, M, O, Ḳ.)

صلق

1. صَلَقَ, (Ṣ, M, O, Mṣb, Ḳ,) aor. ـِ , (Mṣb,) inf. n. صَلْقٌ, (Aṣ,* Ṣ,* M,* TA,) *He called out, cried out,* or *shouted, vehemently;* or *made a vehement sound;* (Aṣ, Ṣ, M, O, Mṣb, Ḳ;) as also ↓ اصلق: (Ṣ, M, O, Ḳ:) *he raised his voice on the occasion of a calamity,* and *of a death:* (TA:) and *he wailed;* (M, TA;) and so ↓ the latter verb: (M:) A'Obeyd mentions it as with س [in the place of ص]. (TA.) — Also, (Ṣ, O, TA,) inf. n. as above, (TA,) said of the tush of a camel; (Ṣ, O, TA;) and so ↓ اصلق; (Ṣ,* M, O;*) *It made a sound by its being grated against another.* (Ṣ,* M, O,* TA.) — And صَلَقَتِ الخَيْلُ, (M,* O, TA,) aor. ـِ, or, accord. to Lth, ـُ, inf. n. as above, (O,) *The horsemen dashed* amid others (فِيهِمْ) in making a sudden attack or incursion. (M,* O, TA.*) = صَلَقَ نَابَهُ, inf. n. صَلْقٌ, *He* (a camel) *grated his tush against another so as to make them produce a sound:* and ↓ اصلق, said of a stallion [camel], *he made his tushes to produce a grating sound:* (M, TA:) and ↓ اصطلق بِنَابِهِ, likewise said of a stallion [camel], *he made a grating sound with his tush.* (Ṣ, Mṣb, TA.) — صَلَقَهُ بِالعَصَا, (AZ, Ṣ, M, O, Ḳ,) aor. ـُ, inf. n. صَلْقٌ, (M,) *He struck him with the staff,* or *stick,* (AZ, Ṣ, M, O, Ḳ,) namely, another man, (Ḳ,) upon any part of his body. (M.) And صَلْقٌ is also said to signify The *striking* with stone-cutter's picks, or pickaxes. (O.) See also صَلَاقَةٌ. — صَلَقَتْهُ الشَّمْسُ *The sun smote him with its heat.* (O, Ḳ.) — صَلَقَ بَنِى فُلَانٍ (aor. ـِ, TA) *He attacked the sons of such a one with an abominable onslaught.* (IDrd, O, Ḳ.) — صَلَقَهُ بِلِسَانِهِ, aor. ـُ, inf. n. صَلْقٌ, † *He reviled him;* syn. شَتَمَهُ. (M.) Fr says that صَلَقُوكُمْ is allowable in the sense of سَلَقُوكُمْ in the Ḳur xxxiii. 19: (Ṣ* and TA in this art.:) but it is not allowable in the reading [of the Ḳur]. (TA in art. سلق, q. v.) — صَلَقَ جَارِيَتَهُ *He spread his girl,* or *young woman,* (Ḳ, TA,) *upon her back,* (TA,) *and compressed her.* (Ḳ, TA.) — صَلَقْتُ الشَّاةَ *I roasted the sheep,* or *goat, upon its sides.* (TA.) — صُلِقَ بِسَهْمِهِ *He was rendered unfortunate by his arrow* [in the game called المَيْسِر]. (Ibn-'Abbád, O.)

4: see 1, former half, in four places.

5. تَصَلَّقَتِ المَرْأَةُ *The woman, being taken with the pains of parturition, screamed,* or *cried out vehemently:* (Ṣ, O, Ḳ:) or *threw herself upon her sides, one time thus and another time thus.* (Lth, O.) And تَصَلَّقَتِ النَّاقَةُ, (Lth, O,) or الدَّابَّةُ, (Ḳ,) *The she-camel,* (Lth, O,) or *the beast,* (Ḳ,) *rolled over, back for belly, by reason of distress:* and in like manner the verb is used of any one suffering pain. (Lth, O, Ḳ.) And تصلّق عَلَى فِرَاشِهِ, occurring in a trad., means *He writhed about upon his sides on his bed,* (O, TA,) *and rolled over.* (TA.) And تصلّق الحُوتُ فِى المَآءِ *The fish went and came in the water.* (O.)

8: see 1, in the middle of the paragraph.

صَلْقٌ, (Aṣ, Ṣ, M,) an inf. n., (TA, [see 1, first sentence,]) and ↓ صَلَقٌ and ↓ صَلْقَةٌ, (M, TA,) *A vehement crying* or *shouting* (Aṣ, Ṣ, M, TA) or *sounding:* (Aṣ, Ṣ:) and *a wailing.* (M, TA.) = And the first, [thus written in a copy of the JK and in a copy of the M, but perhaps correctly ↓ صَلَقٌ, q. v.,] *A round plain:* (JK:) or *a depressed, soft, round plain:* (M:) pl. أَصْلَاقٌ (JK, M) and صُلْقَانٌ. (M.)

صَلَقٌ: see صَلْقٌ, first sentence. = Also *An even plain;* (Ṣ, O, Ḳ;) like سَلَقٌ [q. v.]: (Ṣ, O:) pl. أَصْلَاقٌ, and pl. pl. أَصَالِقُ, (O, Ḳ, TA,) in one copy of the Ḳ اصاليق. (TA.) See also صَلْقٌ, latter sentence.

صَلْقَةٌ: see صَلْقٌ. — Also *An onslaught,* or *a shock in battle.* (M, TA.) — صَلَقَاتُ الإِبِلِ *The tushes of camels, that make a sound by their being grated, one against another.* (Ṣ,* O,* TA.)

صَلِقٌ *Smooth.* (O, Ḳ.)

صَلَاقَةٌ *Water that has long preserved a still,* or *motionless, state,* (أَطَالَ صِيَامًا, JK, Ibn-'Abbád, O, Ḳ,* in which last صياما is omitted,) *in the place,* (JK, Ibn-'Abbád, O,) or *in a place,* (Ḳ,) i. e. *in one place,* (TA,) *and which the beasts have beaten* [*with their feet*], (صَلَقَهَا ↓ الدَّوَابُّ, [which, accord. to MF, should be صَلَقَهُ الدَّوَابُّ, referring to the word مَآء, but accord. to the TA it may refer to صَلَاقَة,]) wherefore it is [said to be] ↓ مَصْلُوقَةٌ. (JK, Ibn-'Abbád, O, Ḳ, TA.) In such water the ablution termed الوُضُوء should not be performed. (TḲ.)

صَلِيقَةٌ *Flesh-meat* (Jm, O, Ḳ) *thoroughly cooked,* (Jm, TA,) or *spread to dry,* (مُشَرَّرٌ, O,) or *roasted,* (مَشْوِىٌّ, Ḳ,) *and thoroughly cooked:* (O, Ḳ:) or *a piece of roasted flesh-meat:* (M:) pl. صَلَائِقُ: (Jm, M, O, Ḳ:) accord. to AA, سَلَائِقُ, with س, signifies "roasted lambs," from سَلَقْتُ الشَّاةَ "I roasted the sheep or goat." (TA. See also سَلِيقَةٌ.) — And *A thin cake of bread:* (M, TA:) accord. to some, (O,) [the pl.] صَلَائِقُ signifies *thin bread:* (JK, Ṣ, O:) but some say that it is صَرَائِقُ, with ر, that has this meaning. (TA.)

صَلَنْقَى [said in the copies of the Ḳ to be like عَلَنْدَى, but correctly عَلَنْدًى,] and صَلَنْقَاةٌ *Loquacious:* (O, Ḳ:) the ن is augmentative. (O.)

صُلَيْقَاءُ *A species of bird.* (M, TA.)

صَلَّاقٌ, applied to a speaker, an orator, or a preacher, (JK, IDrd, O, Ḳ,) is like سَلَّاقٌ, (JK,) [i. e.] *Eloquent;* as also ↓ مِصْلَقٌ [like مِسْلَقٌ], (IDrd, O, Ḳ) and ↓ مِصْلَاقٌ [like مِسْلَاقٌ]. (O, Ḳ.) — And ضَرْبٌ صَلَّاقٌ and ↓ مِصْلَاقٌ *A vehement striking* or *beating.* (M, TA.)

مِصْلَقٌ: see the next preceding paragraph.

مِصْلَاقٌ: see صَلَّاقٌ, in two places.

مَصَالِيقُ [a pl. of which the sing., if it have one, is not specified,] *Large,* or *bulky, stones.* (Ibn-'Abbád, O, Ḳ.) — And *Light,* or *active,* camels. (Ibn-'Abbád, O, Ḳ.)

مَصْلُوقٌ: see its fem., with ة, voce صَلَاقَةٌ.

صلم

1. صَلَمَ, aor. ـِ, [in one of my copies of the Ṣ ـُ,] inf. n. صَلْمٌ, (Ṣ, M, Mṣb, Ḳ,) *He cut off,* (Ḳ,) or *he cut off so as to extirpate,* (Ṣ, M, Mṣb,) a thing, (M, Ḳ,*) or an ear, (Ṣ, M, Mṣb, Ḳ,) and a nose; (M, Ḳ;) as also ↓ صلّم, (M, Ḳ,*) inf. n. تَصْلِيمٌ; (Ḳ;) [but] the latter verb is with teshdeed to denote muchness [of the action], or multiplicity [of the objects]: (TA:) and ↓ اِصْطَلَمَ [likewise] signifies *he cut off so as to extirpate* (Ṣ,* Mṣb,* Ḳ) a nose. (Mṣb.) = And صُلِمَ, aor. ـُ, inf. n. صَلْمٌ, *He had his ear extirpated* [*by amputation*]. (Mṣb.)

2: see the preceding paragraph.

8: see 1. — [Hence,] اُصْطُلِمَ القَوْمُ *The people,* or *party, were destroyed* [or *cut off*] (M, TA) *utterly.* (TA.)

صُلْمَةٌ i. q. مِغْفَرٌ. (Ḳ. [See the latter word, which is variously explained.])

صَلَمَةٌ [written by Golius and Freytag صُلَمٌ] *Strong* men: (Ḳ, TA:) as though pl. of صَالِمٌ. (TA.) = See also صُلَّمٌ.

صِلَامَةٌ (Ṣ, Ḳ) and صُلَامَةٌ and صَلَامَةٌ, (Ḳ,) the last on the authority of IAạr, (TA,) [all three written in a copy of the M with teshdeed to the ل,] *A party,* or *distinct body,* of men: (Ṣ, M, Ḳ:) pl. صلامات, signifying *companies,* and *parties,* or *distinct bodies:* (Ṣ:) or, as some say, صُلَامَةٌ, with ḍamm, means *a party,* or *company, equals in age and courage and liberality* or *bounty.* (TA.)

صُلَّمٌ and صُلَامٌ The *kernel of the stone of the* نَبِق [or *fruit of the lote-tree*]; (M, Ḳ;) *which is also called* أُنْبُوبٌ; *and is eaten:* mentioned by Az. (TA.)

صَيْلَمٌ A *difficult, severe,* or *distressing,* event; (M, Ḳ;) *such as extirpates:* you say أَمْرٌ صَيْلَمٌ: and such is termed ▼ صَيْلَمِيَّةٌ. (M.) And you say also وَقْعَةٌ صَيْلَمَةٌ i. e. [*An onslaught*] *that extirpates.* (Ḳ.) —— And *A calamity;* (Ṣ, M, Ḳ;) because it [often] extirpates; and so ▼ صَلْمَةٌ. (TA.) —— And *An abominable severing from friendly,* or *loving, communion* or *intercourse.* (TA.) —— And *A sword.* (Ṣ, Ḳ.) ═ Also *i. q.* وَجْبَةٌ: like صَيْرَمٌ [q. v.]: (M, Ḳ:) both mentioned by Yaạḳoob. (M.)

صَيْلَمِيَّةٌ: see the next preceding paragraph.

أَصْلَمُ A man (Ṣ) *having his ears* (Ṣ, Mgh) or *ear* (Mṣb) *extirpated* [*by amputation*]: (Ṣ, Mgh, Mṣb:) or a slave *whose ear has been cut off;* as also ▼ مُصَلَّمٌ: (M:) or a man *who is by nature as though his ears had been cut off;* and so ▼ مُصَلَّمُ الأُذُنَيْنِ: (Ḳ:) or this last is applied to a man as meaning *whose ears have been extirpated by amputation;* and to an ostrich as meaning *that is naturally as though his ears had been extirpated;* (Ṣ;) or [*small and short in the ears;* i. e.] because of the smallness and shortness of his ears; (M;) and it is said that when it is applied to a man, [or rather when a man is likened to an ostrich thus termed,] it means his being contemptible, or despised. (TA.) أُذُنٌ صَلْمَآءُ means *An ear that cleaves to its lobe,* or *lobule.* (M.) And الأَصْلَمُ is an appellation applied to *The flea.* (Ḳ.)

مُصَلَّمٌ: see the next preceding paragraph, in two places.

صلهب

Q. 4. اِصْلَهَبَّتِ الأَشْيَآءُ *i. q.* اِمْتَدَّتْ عَلَى جِهَتِهَا [*The things extended in their proper direction*]. (Ḳ. [In the O, اِشْتَدَّتْ is put in the place of اِمتدّت. Compare اِسْلَهَبَّ.])

صَلْهَبٌ A *tall* man; (Aṣ, IJ, O, Ḳ;) and so سَلْهَبٌ [q. v.]; (IJ, TA;) as also ▼ مُصْلَهِبٌّ or ▼ مُصْلَهَبٌ. (Ḳ accord. to different copies.) —— And A *strong* camel; (Ḳ;) and so ▼ صَلْهَبِىٌّ, (El-Umawee, Ṣ, Ḳ,) in which the final letter is [not a sign of the fem. gender but] to render the word quasi-coordinate to the quadriliteral-radical class; (Ṣ;) fem. صَلْهَبَةٌ (TA) and ▼ صَلْهَبَآةٌ: (Ṣ, Ḳ:) pl. صَلَاهِبُ. (AA, O, TA.) —— And A *large,* or *great,* house or tent. (Lth, O, Ḳ.) —— And A *hard* stone; as also ▼ صُلَاهِبٌ. (AA, TA.)

صَلْهَبِىٌّ, and its fem.: }
صُلَاهِبٌ: } see the next preceding paragraph.
مُصْلَهِبٌّ or مُصْلَهَبٌ: }

صلو

1. صَلَوْتُهُ, (Ḳ,) or صَلَوْتُ الظَّهْرَ, (M,) *I struck,* or *beat, that part,* [*of him,* or] *of the back, which is called* صَلًا: (M:) or *I hit that part* (M, Ḳ) with a thing, or with an arrow or some other thing: on the authority of Lḥ, who says that it is of the dial. of Hudheyl: and one says also صَلَيْتُهُ; which is extr. [with respect to derivation], unless it be an instance of interchangeableness [of و and ى]. (M.) ═ صَلِيَتْ and صَلَتْ, said of a mare, or she-camel: see 4.

2. صَلَّى, (Ṣ, M, Ḳ,) quasi-inf. n. صَلَاةٌ or صَلٰوةٌ, for which one should not say تَصْلِيَةٌ, (Ṣ, Ḳ,) or the latter is allowable as agreeable with rule and as occurring in old poetry, (MF, TA,) *He prayed, supplicated,* or *petitioned:* (Ṣ, M, Ḳ:) and [particularly] *he performed the divinely-appointed act* [*of prayer commonly*] *termed* صَلٰوةٌ or صَلَاةٌ. (Ṣ.) Hence, in the Ḳur [ix. 104], (TA,) وَصَلِّ عَلَيْهِمْ *And pray thou for them.* (Mṣb, TA.) صَلَّى عَلَى فُلَانٍ means *He prayed for such a one, and praised him.* (TA.) And hence the verse of El-Aạshà cited in art. رسم, conj. 8. (Ṣ, Mgh,* TA.) It is said in a trad., مَنْ دُعِىَ إِلَى وَلِيمَةٍ فَلْيُجِبْ وَإِلَّا فَلْيُصَلِّ [i. e. *Whoso is invited to a banquet,* or *a marriage-feast, let him comply,* or, *if not, let him pray* for the inviter]. (M.) And the saying, in a verse of El-Aạshà, عَلَيْكِ مِثْلَ الَّذِى صَلَّيْتِ means *Keep thou to the like of thy prayer;* i. e. he enjoined her to repeat the prayer for him: or, as some relate it, عَلَيْكِ مِثْلُ الَّذِى صَلَّيْتِ, meaning *upon thee be the like of that for which thou hast prayed:* (M:) these words he addressed to his daughter, on the occasion of her saying, "O my Lord, ward off from my father diseases and pain." (Mgh.) The saying عَبِيدُ فُلَانٍ يُصَلُّونَ [*The slaves of such a one perform the divinely-appointed act of prayer*] means that they have attained to the age of virility. (Mgh.) —— صَلَّى عَلَيْهِ, said of an angel, means *He prayed for,* or *begged, forgiveness,* or *pardon, for him:* and thus the verb sometimes means when said of other than an angel; as in the trad. of Sowdeh, in which it is said, إِذَا مِتْنَا صَلَّى لَنَا عُثْمَانُ بْنُ مَظْعُونٍ [*When we die, 'Othmán Ibn-Madh'oon will pray for forgiveness for us*]; he having then died. (TA.) —— [And, said of a man, *He blessed him,* meaning *he invoked* God's *blessing upon him;* namely, the Prophet; or he said, اَللّٰهُمَّ صَلِّ عَلَيْهِ (expl. by what here follows) accord. to the rendering of صَلُّوا عَلَيْهِ, i. e. عَلَى النَّبِىِّ, by Bḍ and others in the Ḳur xxxiii. 56.] One says, صَلَّيْتُ عَلَى النَّبِىِّ [*I blessed the Prophet;* &c.]. (Ṣ.) —— And, said of God, *He blessed him,* meaning *He conferred blessing upon him:* and *He had mercy on him:* and *He magnified him,* or *conferred honour upon him:* hence the saying, اَللّٰهُمَّ صَلِّ عَلَى آلِ أَبِى أَوْفَى, meaning *O God, bless the family of Aboo-Orfa:* or *have mercy on* &c.: but in the saying [in the Ḳur xxxiii. 56], إِنَّ ٱللّٰهَ وَمَلَائِكَتَهُ يُصَلُّونَ عَلَى النَّبِىِّ, the verb does not import two meanings; for it has there only one meaning, which is "magnification" [i. e. these words mean *Verily God and his angels magnify the Prophet;* or rather I would render them, *bless the Prophet,* as this rendering implies magnification and also a meaning of the quasi-inf. n. given in the M and Ḳ, which is "eulogy," or "commendation," bestowed by God upon his apostle, while it imports God's "conferring of blessing" and the angels' "invoking thereof"]: (Mṣb, TA:) [it is said that] اَللّٰهُمَّ صَلِّ عَلَى مُحَمَّدٍ means *O God, magnify Moḥammad in the present world by exalting his renown and manifesting his invitation* [*to El-Islám*] *and rendering permanent his law, and in the world to come by accepting his intercession for his people and multiplying his reward:* and it is disputed whether or not this form of prayer may be used for any but the Prophet [Moḥammad]: El-Khaṭṭábee says that it may not, though he himself used it for others. (TA.) [صَلَّى ٱللّٰهُ عَلَيْهِ وَسَلَّمَ is a phrase commonly used by the Muslims after the mention of their prophet: see art. سلم. See also صَلَاةٌ below.] ═ صَلَّى said of a horse, (Ṣ, Ḳ,) inf. n. تَصْلِيَةٌ, (TA,) *He followed next after the foremost* [*in a race, at the goal*]. (Ṣ, Ḳ.) Hence the saying [in a trad. of 'Alee], سَبَقَ رَسُولُ ٱللّٰهِ وَصَلَّى أَبُو بَكْرٍ وَثَلَّثَ عُمَرُ [expl. in art. سبق]. (Mgh.) —— And صَلَّى الحِمَارُ أُتُنَهُ, (Ṣgh, Ḳ,) inf. n. تَصْلِيَةٌ, (Ṣgh, TA,) *The* [*wild*] *ass drove together his she-asses, and made them to take the way* [*that he would follow*]. (Ṣgh, Ḳ, TA.)

4. أَصْلَتْ, (T, Ṣ, Ḳ, TA,) and ▼ صَلِيَتْ, (Fr, Ḳ, TA,) and ▼ صَلَتْ, (Zj, TA,) said of a mare, *The parts on the right and left of her tail,* (صَلَوَاهَا, Ṣ,) or *the part on either side of her tail,* (صَلَاهَا, Ḳ, [see صَلًا, below,]) *became relaxed, she being near to bringing forth:* (Ṣ, Ḳ:) or, said of a she-camel, *her young one fell into the part of her called* صَلًا, *and she was near to bringing forth.* (T, TA.)

صَلًا The *middle of the back* of a human being and of any quadruped: (M, Ḳ:) and, (Ḳ,) or as some say, (M,) [app. in a beast,] the *part that slopes down from the hips,* or *haunches:* or the *space intervening between the* جَاعِرَة [app. meaning the *hinder projection of the haunch* or *rump* of a beast] *and the tail:* (M, Ḳ:) or the *part on the right and left of the tail;* (Ṣ, M, Ḳ;) the two together being called [the] صَلَوَانِ, (Ṣ, Ḳ,) which is similarly expl. by Zj in relation to a she-camel; app. properly meaning the *two parts bordering upon the tail-bone:* (TA:) or the *place in which is set the tail* of the horse; dual as above: (Mṣb:) or the *bone upon which are the two buttocks:* (Mgh: [there thus expl. in relation to a man:]) or the *bone in which is the place of setting of the tail-bone;* thus expl. by IDrd: or the صَلَوَانِ are the *two bones projecting from the two sides of the rump:* or, accord. to some of the lexicologists, *two veins* (عِرْقَانِ) *in the place of the* رِدْف [i. e. *in the rump*]: (Ḥam p. 46:) the pl. is صَلَوَاتٌ, (M, Ḳ,) an instance of a pl. formed by the addition of ا and ت from a masc. sing., (M,) and أَصْلَآءٌ. (M, Ḳ.) —— [Hence,] one says, جِئْتُ فِى أَصْلَائِهِمْ, meaning *I came at their rears.* (TA.)

صَلٰوةٌ, or صَلَاةٌ, [accord. to El-Ḥareeree, to be written with ا when prefixed to a pronoun, and also in the dual number, (see De Sacy's Anthol. Gram. Arabe, p. 67 of the Arabic text,) but this rule I have not found to be generally observed, even in the best MSS., nor have I in the similar case of حَيٰوة, (to which it is also applied,) in the best copies of the Ḳur-án,] is said to be [originally صَلَوَةٌ,] of the measure فَعَلَةٌ, (Mgh, MF, TA,) or, accord. to some, [صَلْوَةٌ,] of the measure فَعْلَةٌ: (MF, TA:) it is a quasi-inf. n. of صَلَّى [q. v.]: (Ṣ, Ḳ:) and [used as a simple subst.] it signifies *Prayer, supplication,* or *petition:* (Ṣ, M, Mṣb, Ḳ:) this is said to be its primary signification: and ↑ مُصَلًّى is said to have the same meaning. (Mṣb, TA.) — Then applied to signify *A certain well-known mode,* or *manner,* [*of religious service,*] because comprising prayer; (Mṣb;) [the *divinely-appointed act of prayer;*] *one of the divinely-appointed* صَلَوَات; (Ṣ;) *a certain religious service in which are* رُكُوع [or *lowering of the head so that the palms of the hands reach the knees*] *and* سُجُود [or *prostration of oneself in a particular manner* expl. voce سَجَدَ]: (M,* Ḳ:) and ↑ مُصَلًّى is said to have the same meaning. (TA.) [The performance of this act is fully described in my work on the Modern Egyptians.] It is said to be, in this sense, a proper term of the law, not indicated by the language of the Arabs [before El-Islám] except as importing prayer, which is its primary signification: what Esh-Shiháb says respecting it necessarily implies its being a proper term of the law known to the Arabs [before El-Islám]: in the Mz it is said to be one of the words of El-Islám: but all of these sayings require consideration. (MF, TA, [Much more, which I omit as being unprofitable, is added on this point in the TA, partly from the Mṣb; as well as several different opinions respecting the derivation of the word as used in this sense, which are fanciful or absurd.]) The saying of the Prophet, لَا صَلٰوةَ لِجَارِ المَسْجِدِ إِلَّا فِى المَسْجِدِ means *There is no* صلوة [or *divinely-appointed act of prayer*] *that is excellent* or *complete* [*to the neighbour of the mosque unless in the mosque*]. (M.) And his saying, to Usámeh, الصَّلٰوةُ أَمَامَكَ means *The time of the* صلوة [or *divinely-appointed prayer*], or *the place thereof,* [*is before thee,*] alluding to that of sunset. (Mgh.) And he used the term الصَّلٰوةُ as meaning سُورَةُ الصَّلٰوةِ, i. e. *The* فَاتِحَة [or *Opening Chapter of the Ḳur-án,* because it is a form of prayer, or] because the recital thereof is excellent, or satisfactory. (Mgh.) In the Ḳur xxii. 41, (I'Ab, Ṣ, M, Ksh, Bḍ,) [the pl.] صَلَوَاتٌ means *Places of worship of the Jews:* (I'Ab, Ṣ, M, Ksh, Bḍ, Ḳ:) said to be (Ksh, Bḍ) originally صَلُوتَا, a Hebrew word, (Ksh, Bḍ, Ḳ,) arabicized: (Ksh, Bḍ:) this is the common reading of the word, and the most valid: other readings are صُلُوَاتٌ and صَلَوَاتٌ and صِلَوَاتٌ; and beside these, some others which are perverted forms. (TA.) — Also *Prayer for forgiveness* or *pardon.* (M, Mgh, Ḳ.) — [And *A blessing,* as meaning *an invocation of* God's *blessing* upon any one. See 2.] — And *i. q.* بَرَكَةٌ [as meaning *A blessing, such as is bestowed by God*]: (Mṣb:) and *mercy* (Ṣ, M, Mgh, Mṣb, Ḳ) of God (Ṣ, M) on his apostle: (M:) and *magnification;* and this is [said to be] specially denoted by its verb when the Prophet is the object: (Mṣb:) and God's *eulogy,* or *commendation,* bestowed upon his apostle. (M, Ḳ.)

= [from صَلًا] also means إِتْيَانُ المَرْأَةِ فِى دُبُرِهَا. (TA in art. صوم.)

مُصْلِيَةٌ part. n. of أَصْلَتْ [q. v.] said of a she-camel [or of a mare]. (T, TA.)

مُصَلًّى *A place of* الصَّلَاة [as meaning *the performance of the divinely-appointed act of prayer*]; (Mgh, Mṣb, Ḳ;) or *of any prayer* or *supplication:* (Mgh:) [and particularly] *a place of the performance of the divinely-appointed prayer on the occasion of the* [*festival termed*] عيد: (MA:) [and also *such a place at a burial-ground:* the place for this purpose is particularly termed مُصَلَّى الأَمْوَاتِ: see De Sacy's Chrest. Arabe, sec. ed., i. 192.] — And *A carpet upon which one performs the divinely-appointed act of prayer.* (MA.) — See also صَلَاةٌ, former half, in two places.

مُصَلٍّ Any one *praying* [in any manner: and particularly *performing the divinely-appointed act of prayer*]. (TA.) = And المُصَلِّى signifies, as applied to a horse, *The one that follows next after the foremost* [*at the goal*] (Ṣ, M, Mgh, Mṣb) *in a race:* (Mgh, Mṣb:) because his head is next to the part called صَلًا, (Lḥ, Ṣ, M, Mṣb,) or next to the صَلَوَانِ, (Mgh,) of the foremost. (Lḥ, Ṣ, M, Mgh, Mṣb.)

صلى

1. صَلَاهُ, (Ṣ, M, Mṣb, Ḳ,) aor. يَصْلِيهِ, (Ṣ, Mṣb, Ḳ,) inf. n. صَلْىٌ, (Ṣ, M, Ḳ,) *He roasted, broiled,* or *fried, it,* namely, flesh-meat, (Ṣ, M, Mṣb, Ḳ,) &c.; (Ṣ;) and صَلَاهُ فِى النَّارِ and صَلَّى عَلَى النَّارِ signify the same; and also *he burned it.* (TA.) And (so in the M, but in the Ḳ "or") صَلَاهُ (M, Ḳ) فِى النَّارِ (M) *He threw it into the fire to be burned;* as also ↑ اصلاهُ; and ↑ صلّاهُ, (M, Ḳ,) inf. n. تَصْلِيَةٌ; (TA;) namely, flesh-meat. (M, Ḳ. [But see the next sentence.]) And صَلَاهُ النَّارَ and فِى النَّارِ and عَلَى النَّارِ, (M, Ḳ,) inf. n. صَلْىٌ and صُلِىٌّ; (M;) and ↑ اصلاهُ النَّارَ, and ↑ صلّاهُ النَّارَ; *He made him to enter into the fire, and to remain, stay, dwell,* or *abide, therein:* (M, Ḳ:) and ↑ صُلِّىَ فُلَانٌ النَّارَ [*Such a one was made to enter into the fire,* &c.]: (M:) [or] you say, صَلَيْتُ الرَّجُلَ نَارًا, meaning *I made the man to enter fire and to be burned:* and ↑ أَصْلَيْتُهُ, with ا, when you mean *I threw him,* or *cast him, into the fire, as though intending burning* [*him*]; as also ↑ صَلَّيْتُهُ, inf. n. تَصْلِيَةٌ. (Ṣ.) — And صَلَيْتُ فُلَانًا, (T, TA,) or لِفُلَانٍ, (Ṣ, TA,) ‡ *I laboured in a case,* or *an affair, desiring to calumniate,* or *slander, such a one therein, and to cause him to fall into destruction:* (T, Ṣ, TA:) or صَلَيْتُ لَهُ and صَلَيْتُهُ both signify *I calumniated,* or *slandered, him, and caused him to fall into destruction,* (M, TA,) *in consequence thereof:* (M:) or, accord. to the Ḳ, صَلَى فُلَانًا, of which the inf. n. is صَلْىٌ, signifies *he soothed, coaxed, wheedled,* or *cajoled, such a one:* or *deceived, deluded, beguiled, circumvented,* or *outwitted, him:* which meanings are not in any of the three lexicons above mentioned: accord. to the A, صَلَيْتُ بِفُلَانٍ [probably a mistranscription for لِفُلَانٍ] means ‡ *I framed a stratagem,* or *plot, to cause such a one to fall;* there said to be tropical. (TA.) — صَلَى يَدَهُ بِالنَّارِ [said in the TA to be a mistake]: see 2. = صَلِىَ النَّارَ, (Ṣ, M, Mṣb, Ḳ,) and بِالنَّارِ, (M, Mṣb, Ḳ,) aor. يَصْلَى, (Ṣ, Mṣb,* Ḳ,*) inf. n. صَلًى, (Mṣb,) or صُلِىٌّ, (Ṣ, Ḳ, [صُلْيًا in the CḲ being a mistranscription for صُلِيًّا,]) or both, (M,) and صِلِىٌّ and صِلَآءٌ, (M, Ḳ,) and accord. to the Ḳ صَلَآءٌ, but this is a mistake for صَلًى, (TA,) *He was,* or *became, burned* [*by the fire*]: (Ṣ:) or *he endured,* or *suffered, the heat of the fire;* as also ↑ تصلّى النَّارَ: (M, Ḳ:) or *he felt the heat of the fire:* (Mṣb:) and one says ↑ تصلّى حَرَّ النَّارِ and ↑ اصطلاهُ [in this last sense or in the sense next preceding]: (Ḥam p. 792:) and صَلِىَ النَّارَ *he entered into the fire:* (TA in art. بله: see an ex. voce بَلْهَ:) or, accord. to Er-Rághib, صَلِىَ بِالنَّارِ means *he was tried* (بُلِىَ) *by fire,* or *by the fire;* and so بِكَذَا † [*by such a thing, as though by fire*]. (TA.) [In the Ḳur, in which are many exs. of it, (iv. 11, xiv. 34, xvii. 19, &c.,) it is always trans. by itself, without ب.] And صَلِىَ بِالأَمْرِ, (Ṣ, M,*) and بِالحَرْبِ; (Ṣ;) and ↑ تصلّى الأَمْرَ, and الحَرْبَ; (M;) *He endured,* or *suffered, the heat, and severity,* or *vehemence, of the affair,* or *case, and of the war,* or *fight:* (Ṣ, M:) Aboo-Zubeyd says,

• فَقَدْ تَصَلَّيْتُ ↑ حَرَّ حَرْبِهِمْ •
• كَمَا تَصَلَّى ↑ المَقْرُورُ مِنْ قَرَسِ •

[*And I have suffered the heat and vehemence of their war, like as he who is affected with cold suffers in consequence of coldest and most abundant hoar-frost*]. (M.) = [It is said that] صَلِىَ الرَّجُلُ signifies also لَزِمَ [i. e. *The man kept to,* or *clave to,* a thing]; and so ↑ اصطلى: whence Zj holds صَلَاةٌ [expl. in art. صلو] to be derived; because it is a keeping, or cleaving, to that which God has appointed: and hence also, [it is said,] مَنْ يَصْلَى ↑ فِى النَّارِ, i. e. يلزم [app. يُلْزَمُ], meaning مَنْ يُلْزَمُ النَّارَ *He who is made to keep,* or *cleave, to the fire;* nearly agreeing with صَلَاهُ النَّارَ as expl. above from the M and Ḳ]. (TA.) = And صَلَيْتُ الظَّهْرَ means *I struck,* or *beat, that part of the back which is called* صَلًا: or *I hit that part:* but this is extr.; for by rule it should be صَلَوْتُهُ, like as Hudheyl say. (M. [See 1 in art. صلو.])

2: see 1, second sentence; and third sentence in three places; and last sentence but one. — One says also, صلّى يَدَهُ بِالنَّارِ, (M, TA,) accord. to the Ḳ ↑ صَلَى, [without teshdeed,] but this is wrong, as is shown by a verse cited in the M, (TA,) *He warmed his hand with the fire.* (M, Ḳ, TA.) [And it is said in the TA that صلا أَوْقَاهُ ظَهْرَهُ بالنهر means: but I think that the right reading is صلّى ظَهْرَهُ بِالنَّمِرَةِ, i. e. *He warmed his* back with the woollen garment called نُمْرَة.] — And صَلَّيْتُ العَصَا بِالنَّارِ *I made the staff supple, and straightened it, by means of fire:* (Ṣ:) or صَلَّى العَصَا عَلَى النَّارِ, (M, Ḳ,) inf. n. تَصْلِيَةٌ; (Ḳ;) and ↓ تصلّاها; *he parched and darkened the staff upon the fire;* syn. لَوَّحَهَا: (M, Ḳ:) or صلّى العَصَا *he straightened the staff by turning it round over the fire:* (T in art. دوم: see an ex. in a verse cited in that art., conj. 10:) and صَلَّيْتُ القَنَاةَ *I straightened the spear-shaft by means of fire:* (A, TA:) and صَلَّيْتُ العُودَ بِالنَّارِ *I rendered supple the stick,* or *branch, by means of fire.* (Mṣb.)

4: see 1, second sentence; and third sentence in two places.

5: see the next paragraph, in two places: — see also 1, latter half, in five places: — and see 2, last sentence.

8. اصطلى *He warmed himself* (M, Ḳ) بِالنَّارِ [*by means of the fire*]: (M:) one says, اِصْطَلَيْتُ بِالنَّارِ and ↓ تَصَلَّيْتُ بِهَا [app. meaning *I warmed myself by means of the fire*]: (Ṣ:) or اصطلى النّارَ and بالنّارِ mean *he became warm by means of the fire:* and ↓ تصلّى بالنّار, *he became burnt by the fire.* (MA.) Hence, in the Ḳur [xxvii. 7 and xxviii. 29], لَعَلَّكُمْ تَصْطَلُونَ [*May-be ye will warm yourselves*]: (TA:) in relation to which it is said that the time was winter, and therefore الاِصْطِلَآء was needed. (M, TA.) — It is also said of the chameleon, as meaning *He repaired to the sun.* (M and L in art. شقذ: see an ex. in a verse cited voce شُقَذَانٌ.) — And one says of a courageous man, with whom one cannot cope, لَا يُصْطَلَى بِنَارِهِ [lit. *One cannot warm himself by means of his fire;* meaning † *one cannot approach him when he is inflamed with rage,* especially *in fight,* or *battle*]. (Ṣ.) The phrase may be also used satirically, as meaning † *One will not seek his hospitality.* (Meyd. [See Freytag's Arab. Prov. ii. 588.]) — See also 1, latter half, in two places.

صَلًى: see صِلَآءٌ.

صَلَآءٌ: see صَلَايَةٌ.

صِلَآءٌ *Roasted, broiled,* or *fried, flesh-meat.* (Ṣ, M, Ḳ.) — And, as also ↓ صَلًى, (Ṣ, M, Ḳ,) the former with kesr and the latter with fet-ḥ, (Ṣ,) *Fuel;* (Ṣ,* M, Ḳ;) syn. وَقُودٌ; (M, Ḳ, TA; [in the CḲ, erroneously, وقود;]) i. e. مَا تُوقَدُ بِهِ النَّارُ: (TA;) you say صَلَى النَّارِ and صِلَآءُ النَّارِ: (Ṣ:) or both signify *fire:* (M, Mgh, Ḳ:) or صِلَآءٌ signifies the *heat of fire.* (Mṣb.) One says, هُوَ أَحْسَنُ مِنَ الصِّلَآءِ فِى الشِّتَآءِ [*It,* or *he, is better than fire in winter*]. (TA.)

صَلِىٌّ: see مَصْلِىٌّ.

صَلَآءَةٌ: see what next follows.

صَلَايَةٌ and ↓ صَلَآءَةٌ, (Ṣ, M, Mgh, Ḳ,) the latter with ء because ↓ صَلَآءٌ is used as the pl., [or rather coll. gen. n.,] but not by those who say صَلَايَةٌ, (Sb, M,) [for] the pl. [of this] is صُلِىٌّ and صِلِىٌّ (Ḳ) and صَلَايَاتٌ, (MA,) i. q. فِهْرٌ [i. e. *A stone such as fills the hand; or of the size of that with which one bruises and breaks walnuts and the like*]: (Ṣ:) or *a thing with which perfume is bruised, brayed,* or *pounded:* (M, Ḳ:) or *a stone upon which one bruises,* or *powders,* (MA, Mgh,) *perfume* or *some other thing;* (Mgh;) that with which [not upon which] one does so being called مُدْوَكٌ. (MA.) Imra-el-Ḳeys [in a verse of his Mo'allaḳah, (see EM p. 45,) as some relate it,] uses the phrase صَلَايَةُ حَنْظَلٍ, because colocynths, when they have become dry, are split therewith. (Ṣ. [But there are two other readings, صَرَايَةٌ and صَرَابَةٌ.]) — Also, (Ḳ,) as being likened thereto, (TA,) † The *forehead.* (Ḳ.) — And the former word, *A rough, rugged,* سَرِيحَة [or *long strip*] *of* [*high ground such as is termed*] قُفّ. (ISh, Az, TA.)

صِلِّيَانٌ: see art. صل.

[صَالٍ is expl. by Freytag as meaning *Heated* or *warmed* ("calefactus"), and *burnt:* and the pl. is said by him to be صُلِىٌّ: but he names no authority: if this be correct, it must be a possessive epithet from صَلًى.]

صَالِيَةٌ *A support for the cooking-pot, such as is termed* أُثْفِيَّةٌ. (MA.)

مَصْلِىٌّ *Roasted, broiled,* or *fried;* as also ↓ صَلِىٌّ. (Ḥam pp. 13-14. [Both of these words are there without any syll. signs.]) It is said in a trad., أُتِىَ بِشَاةٍ مَصْلِيَّةٍ i. e. *A roasted sheep,* or *goat, was brought.* (Ṣ, TA.) — And صَيْحَانِيَّةٌ مَصْلِيَّةٌ means [*A date of the sort called* صَيْحَانِىّ] *dried in the sun.* (A, TA.)

أَرْضٌ مَصْلَاةٌ *A land abounding with the plant called* صِلِّيَان. (Ḳ.)

مِصْلَاةٌ *A snare that is set up for birds &c.:* (Ṣ, M:*) pl. مَصَالٍ. (Ṣ, M.) It is said in a trad., إِنَّ لِلشَّيْطَانِ فُخُوخًا وَمَصَالِىَ (Ṣ) or مَصَالِىَ وَفُخُوخًا i. e. [*Verily to the Devil belong snares and traps*] with which he catches men. (M.)

مُصْطَلًى The *limbs* of a man, or his *arms and legs and face and every prominent part,* which become cold at the time of death, and which are warmed at the fire: (AHeyth, L in art. برد:) or the *face and extremities.* (Z, TA.) One says, بَرَدَ المَوْتُ عَلَى مُصْطَلَاهُ. (AHeyth, L in art. برد: see 1 in that art.)

صم

1. صَمَّ, (Ṣ, M, Mṣb, Ḳ,) and صَمِمَ, which is extr., (M, Ḳ,) [first pers. of each صَمِمْتُ,] aor. يَصَمُّ, (M, Mṣb, Ḳ,) inf. n. صَمَمٌ (Ṣ,* M, Mṣb, Ḳ) and صَمٌّ; (M, Ḳ;) and ↓ أُصِمَّ; (Ṣ, M, Mṣb, Ḳ;) *He was,* or *became, deaf;* (M,* Mṣb, Ḳ;*) [or] *he had a stoppage of the ear, and a heaviness of hearing.* (M, Ḳ.) And صَمَّتِ الأُذُنُ, aor. as above, inf. n. صَمَمٌ, *The ear was,* or *became, deaf.* (Mṣb.) — [And *He was,* or *became, as though he heard not.*] One says, صَمَّ عَنْهُ † [*He was as though he heard not him,* or *it; he was deaf to him,* or *it*]; (M;) and ↓ أَصَمَّ عَنْهُ [meaning the same]. (Ṣ, M.) — [Hence صَمَّ signifies also † *He* or *it, uttered,* or *made, no sound* or *noise;* like him who, not hearing, returns no reply to a call or question; † *was dumb,* or *mute.*] One says, صَمَّتْ حَصَاةٌ بِدَمٍ ‡ [*A pebble made no sound in falling upon the ground by reason of blood*]; i. e. the blood was so copious that if one threw a pebble into it no sound would be heard in consequence thereof, (Aṣ, Ṣ, M, Meyd, Ḳ, TA,) because it would not fall upon the ground: (Aṣ, Ṣ, Meyd:) the saying is a prov. (Meyd.) And hence the saying of Imra-el-Ḳeys, صَمِّى ٱبْنَةَ الجَبَلِ, (Ṣ, Ḳ,) in the following verse:

بُدِّلْتُ مِنْ وَائِلٍ وَكِنْدَةَ عَدْ
وَانَ وَفَهْمًا صَمِّى ٱبْنَةَ الجَبَلِ

† [*I have been given in exchange, for Wáïl and Kindeh, 'Adwán and Fahm: make no sound, O pebble:* app. meaning that he would shed much blood]: (Ṣ, TA: but this verse is omitted in one of my two copies of the Ṣ:) or the meaning is, *O echo;* (Ṣ, M, Meyd, Ḳ;) so they assert: (AHeyth, TA:) or *O calamity;* the saying being a prov.; (Meyd, TA;) applied to the case of a severe calamity; as though meaning *be dumb, O calamity;* said by Aṣ to be applied in relation to an event deemed excessively foul or evil: (TA:) or *O serpent;* (Meyd, TA;) which is said to be the primary meaning: (Meyd:) or *O rock.* (AHeyth, Ḳ, TA. [See also the second of the sentences here following.]) One says also, صَمَّ صَدَاهُ ‡ [*His echo became dumb,* or *may his echo become dumb;*] meaning *he perished,* or *may he perish.* (Ṣ, Ḳ, TA.) And ↓ صَمِّى صَمَامِ [in the CḲ erroneously written صُمِّى] meaning ‡ *Increase, O calamity:* (Ṣ, Ḳ, TA:) or it is applied to a man who brings to pass a calamity, and means *be dumb, O calamity:* (TA:) or صَمَامِ means *calamity,* and *war;* but primarily, *the serpent;* and this saying, like صَمِّى ٱبْنَةَ الجَبَلِ, is a prov. said when two parties refuse to make peace, and persist in opposition; meaning *answer not the charmer, O serpent, but continue as thou art wont to be.* (Meyd.) — صَمَمٌ in relation to stones, (Lth, TA,) or stone, (M,) [app. as an inf. n.,] signifies The *being hard* [*and solid* (see أَصَمُّ)]; or [as a simple subst.] *hardness* [*and solidity*]: (Lth, M, TA:) and in relation to a spear-shaft, the *being compact;* or *compactness.* (M.) One says, صَمَّ الحَجَرُ, inf. n. صَمَمٌ, *The stone was hard* [*and solid*]. (MA.) And صَمَّتِ الفِتْنَةُ, meaning [*The trial,* or *civil war,* &c.,] *was,* or *became, hard, vehement,* or *severe.* (Mṣb.) — صَمَّ القَارُورَةَ, (Ṣ, Ḳ,) or صَمَّ رَأْسَ القَارُورَةِ, (M,) aor. ـُ, (PṢ, [in a copy of the M ـَ, contr. to a general rule in the case of a trans. verb of this class, and app. a mistranscription,]) inf. n. صَمٌّ, (M,) *He stopped the flask* or *bottle* [app. *with a* صِمَام]: (Ṣ, Ḳ:)

or *he stopped the head of the flask* or *bottle*, and *bound it*; as also ↓ اصمّه: (Ḳ:) or اصمّ القَارُورَةَ signifies *he put a* صِمَام *to the flask* or *bottle*. (Ṣ, Ḳ.) — And صَمَّ الجُرْحَ, aor. ـُ, inf. n. صَمٌّ, *He bound the wound, and put upon it a bandage with medicament.* (M.) — And صَمَّهُ, (Ṣ, M, Ḳ,) inf. n. صَمٌّ, (M,) *He struck him,* (Ṣ, Ḳ,) or *it*, i. e. his head, (M,) with a staff, or stick, (Ṣ, M,) and with a stone, (Ṣ, M, Ḳ,) and with the like thereof. (M.) And صُمَّ, with ḍamm, *He was struck vehemently.* (IAạr, TA.)

2. صمّم, said of a sword, (Ṣ, M, Ḳ, TA,) accord. to the Ḳ, signifies *It struck the joint, and cut,* or *severed, it*: or i. q. طَبَّقَ: but this is at variance with what is said by J and other leading authorities; which is as follows: (TA:) *it penetrated into the bone, and cut,* or *severed, it*; but when it strikes the joint, and cuts, or severs, it, one says طَبَّقَ; a poet says, describing a sword,

* يُصَمِّمُ أَحْيَانًا وَحِينًا يُطَبِّقُ *

[*It penetrates into the bone, &c., sometimes, and at one time it strikes the joint, &c.*]: (Ṣ, TA:) or *it passed into the bones*: (M:) and ↓ صَمْصَمَ, said of a sword, signifies the same: (M, TA:) or تَصْمِيم signifies a sword's *penetrating into that which is struck with it without its causing any sound to be heard*; from الصَّمَمُ in the ear. (Ḥam p. 326.) — And hence تَصْمِيم signifies also ‡ A man's *keeping constantly,* or *perseveringly, to the thing that he purposes, until he attains* [it]. (Ḥam ubi suprà.) One says, صَمَّمَ عَلَى كَذَا † *He kept constantly,* or *perseveringly, to his opinion in respect of such a thing, after his desiring to do it.* (IDrd, TA.) — And صمّم, (Ṣ, Mṣb, Ḳ, TA,) inf. n. تَصْمِيم, (M, Ḳ,) ‡ *He acted,* or *went on, with penetrative energy,* or *with sharpness, vigorousness, and effectiveness,* (Ṣ, M, Mṣb, Ḳ, TA,) in an affair, (M, Mṣb, Ḳ, TA,) and in journeying, (Ṣ, Ḳ, TA,) in this case said of a horse, (Z, TA,) and in other things; (Ṣ;) as also ↓ صَمْصَمَ. (Ḳ.) — And ‡ *He bit, and infixed his canine teeth,* (Ṣ, Ḳ, TA,) *and did not let go what he bit*: (Ṣ, TA:) or صمّم فِى عَضَّتِهِ *he infixed his teeth* [or *canine teeth*] *in his bite.* (A, TA.) — And صمّم الفَرَسَ العَلَفَ ‡ *He* (a man) *enabled the horse to take of the fodder to such a degree that fat and repletion stuffed him.* (Ḳ,* TA.) — And صمّم صَاحِبَهُ الحَدِيثَ ‡ *He made his companion to retain the narrative,* or *story, in his memory.* (Ḳ,* TA.) — See also the next paragraph.

4. اصمّ, intrans.: see 1, first and fourth sentences. ═ اصمّه *He,* (God, Ṣ, Mṣb, Ḳ,) or *it,* (a disease, M,) *rendered him deaf*; (Ṣ,* M,* Mṣb, Ḳ;*) [or] *caused him to have a stoppage of the ear, and a heaviness of hearing.* (M, Ḳ.) — [Hence,] أَصَمَّنِى الكَلَامُ † *He,* or *it, diverted me from hearing the speech*; as though he, or it, rendered me deaf. (TA.) — [Hence, اصمّه signifies also † *He,* or *it, caused him to be as though he heard not.* — And hence, † *He,* or *it, caused him, or it, to utter,* or *make, no sound* or *noise*; like him who, not hearing, returns no reply to a call, or question; *to be dumb,* or *mute.*] One says, أَصَمَّ اللّٰهُ صَدَاهُ ‡ [*May God make his echo to return no sound*;] meaning *may God destroy him*: (TA:) a prov., said in imprecating death upon a man; the صَدَى being that which returns the like of his voice, or cry, from the mountains &c.; and when a man dies, the صدى hears not from him anything that it should answer him, so that it is as though it were deaf. (Meyd.) [In the vulgar language, ↓ صَمَّمَ likewise signifies † *He silenced him, reduced him to silence,* or *closed his mouth*: so says De Sacy, in his Chrest. Arabe, sec. ed., iii. 379.] — And اصمّه [in the CḲ أَصْمَمَهُ] also signifies *He found him to be* أَصَمّ [i. e. *deaf*]. (Ṣ, M, Ḳ.) One says, نَادَاهُ فَأَصَمَّهُ [*He called him,* or *called to him, and found him to be deaf*]. (TA.) And أَصَمَّ دُعَاؤُهُ *His call found persons deaf to it,* (Th, M, Ḳ,) *who would not hear his censure.* (Ḳ.) — See also 1, near the end.

6. تصامّ *He feigned himself to be* أَصَمّ [i. e. *deaf*]. (Ṣ.) [It is intrans. and trans.] You say, تصامّ عَنْهُ ahd تصامّهُ *He feigned to him that he was deaf.* (M.) And تصامّ عَنِ الحَدِيثِ (M, Ḳ) and تصامّهُ (M) *He feigned* (M, Ḳ) to his companion (M) *that he was deaf to the narrative,* or *story.* (M, Ḳ.*) تَصَامَمْتُهُ means تَصَامَمْتُ مِنْهُ [or عَنْهُ], i. e. *I made a show of being deaf* [*to it*], *and feigned myself inattentive* [*to it*]. (Ḥam p. 169.)

R. Q. 1. صَمْصَمَ: see 2, in two places. ═ صَمْصَمَتِ الصِّمَّةُ, (TḲ,) inf. n. صَمْصَمَةٌ, (Ḳ, TḲ,) *The female hedge-hog uttered its cry.* (Ḳ,* TḲ.)

الصِّمّ a name for † *Calamity,* or *misfortune*; (Ṣ, TA;) as also ↓ الصِّمَّةُ, (TA,) and so ↓ صَمَامِ, like قَطَامِ, in a phrase mentioned in the first paragraph, q. v. (Ṣ, Ḳ. [See also this last word below.]) — And † *The lion*; (Ṣ, M, Ḳ;) as also ↓ الصِّمَّةُ, (M, Mṣb, Ḳ,) thus called because of his courage, [i. e. from the latter word as signifying "courageous," but accord. to the Mṣb the reverse is the case,] (M,) and so ↓ الصُّمْصُمُ and ↓ الصُّمَاصِمُ: (Ḳ:) the pl. of ↓ صِمَّة is صِمَمٌ. (TA.)

صِمَّةٌ *Courageous*; (Ṣ, M, Mṣb, Ḳ;) applied to a man; (Ṣ, M;) one *who renders deaf him whom he smites.* (Er-Rághib, TA.) — See also the next preceding paragraph, in three places. — Also *A male serpent*: (Ṣ, Ḳ:) pl. صِمَمٌ. (Ṣ.) — And *A female hedge-hog.* (Ḳ.) — See also صِمَام.

صَمَمٌ inf. n. of the intrans. verb صَمَّ [q. v.]. (Ṣ,* M, Mṣb, Ḳ.) ═ See also صَمِيم, in four places.

صَمَامِ [an imperative verbal noun, like نَزَالِ &c.]. One says, صَمَامِ صَمَامِ, meaning *Feign ye deafness, in silence.* (Ṣ, Ḳ.) Also meaning *Charge ye upon the enemy.* (AHeyth, TA.) ═ Also ‡ *Hard,* or *severe, calamity* or *misfortune*; and so ↓ الصَّمَّآءُ; (Ḳ, TA;) [*as though*] *closed up* [or *obdurate,* or *deaf to deprecation*]: (TA:) or الصَّمَّآءُ signifies [simply] *calamity,* or *misfortune*: (Ṣ:) and ↓ دَاهِيَةٌ صَمَّآءُ signifies *a calamity,* or *misfortune,* [*as though*] *closed up, and hard.* (M.) See also الصِّمّ, above.

صِمَام The سِدَاد [or *stopper*], (Ṣ, M, Ḳ,) [i. e.] the *thing that is put into the mouth,* (Mṣb,) of a flask, or bottle: (Ṣ, M, Mṣb, Ḳ:) and its شِدَاد [app. meaning the *piece of skin that is tied over the head*]: (M:) or accord. to some it signifies the عِفَاص [which has the latter meaning]: (Mṣb:) or it signifies the *thing that is put into the head* of the flask, or bottle; and عِفَاص signifies the "thing [or piece of skin] that is tied upon it:" (M:) and ↓ صِمَامَةٌ signifies the same as صِمَام, (IAạr, Ḳ,) as also ↓ صِمَّةٌ. (Ḳ.) — Also The فَرْج; perhaps for مَوْضِعُ صِمَامٍ: (Mgh, TA:) so in a trad., in which it is said that الوَطْء should be in one صِمَام: but, as some relate it, the word is there with س [i. e. سِمَام]. (TA.)

صَمِيم The *bone that is the* [*main*] *stay,* or *support,* of the limb or member or the like; (M, Ḳ, and Ḥam p. 302;) as the صميم [or principal bone] of the shank (M and Ḥam) of a beast, (M,) and that of the head; (M and Ḥam;) opposed to وَشِيظٌ, because the latter is smaller than the former: (M:) and the *thing that is the* [*main*] *stay,* or *support,* of another thing. (Ḥam p. 350.) — [Hence,] The *heart*: so in a saying of a poet cited voce دَلَفَ. (Ḥam p. 678.) — And hence, also, (TA,) ‡ The *prime, principal,* or *most essential, part*; (M, Ḳ, TA;) the *choice, best,* or *most excellent, part*; of a thing (Ṣ, M, Mṣb, Ḳ, TA) of any kind. (M.) One says, هُوَ فِى صَمِيمِ قَوْمِهِ ‡ [*He is of the choice, best,* or *most excellent, of his people* or *party*; *of the main stock thereof*; or *of those that constitute the members, exclusive of such as are followers,* or *incorporated confederates, thereof*]: (Ṣ, TA:) *contr. of* شَظًى (Ṣ in art. شظى) [and of شِقّ, q. v.]. — And ‡ The *greatest intenseness* or *vehemence* or *violence,* or the *most intense* or *vehement* or *violent degree,* of heat, and of cold: (Ṣ, Ḳ, TA:) or simply the *intenseness* or *vehemence* or *violence* thereof. (M.) — And † The *middle* [or *core*] of the heart. (Mṣb.) — And The *shell* (lit. the *dry,* or *hard, exterior covering*) of the egg. (Ḳ.) ═ Also an epithet, applied to a man, (M, Ḳ,) and to a woman, and to two persons, (M,) and to a pl. number, (M, Ḳ,) ‡ *Pure, unmixed,* or *genuine, in respect of race, lineage,* or *parentage.* (M, Ḳ, TA.)

صِمَامَةٌ: see صِمَام.

صَمَّانٌ *Hard ground,* (M,) [i. e.] *any such ground,* (Ḳ,) *containing stones, by the side of sands*; as also ↓ صَمَّانَةٌ: (M, Ḳ:) or the latter is a n. un.; and the former signifies *hard ground*: (Ḥam p. 285:) or *rugged ground,* (Ṣ, M,) *falling short of what is called* جَبَل: (M:) it is so called because of its hardness. (TA.)

صَمَّانَةٌ: see the next preceding paragraph.

صَمْصَمٌ *Very niggardly* or *tenacious*: (Ḳ:) or *niggardly,* or *tenacious, in the utmost degree.*

(IAạr, TA.) —— See also the next paragraph. —— [And see ضَمْضَمٌ.]

صَمْصَمٌ, (Ṣ, M, Ḳ,) applied to a man, (Ṣ, M,) *Thick:* (A'Obeyd, Ṣ:) or *short and thick:* (M, Ḳ:) or it signifies, (Ṣ,) or signifies also, (Ḳ,) *bold,* or *daring; that acts,* or *proceeds, with penetrative energy,* or *with sharpness, vigorousness, and effectiveness:* (Ṣ, Ḳ:) and applied to a man and to a horse, (M, Ḳ,) and to a mare, (M,) [in like manner,] i. q. ▼ مُصَمِّمٌ [and مُصَمِّمَةٌ (in the CḲ مُصَمَّمٌ is erroneously put for مُصَمِّمٌ) i. e. *that acts, or proceeds, with penetrative energy,* or *with sharpness, vigourousness, and effectiveness*], (M, Ḳ,) as also ▼ صِمٌّ, (Ḳ, TA,) or ▼ صِمْصِمٌ, (so in a copy of the M,) and ▼ صَمْصَامٌ, and ▼ صَمْصَامَةٌ, and ▼ صُمَصِمٌ, and ▼ صُمَاصِمٌ, (M, Ḳ, the last omitted in the TA,) and ▼ صُمَاصِمَةٌ: (Ḳ:) or *strong, robust,* or *hardy:* or *compact in make:* (M, in relation to all of these epithets:) or ▼ صِمٌّ, applied to a man, has the former of these two meanings: or the latter of them; as also صِمْصِمٌ, and ▼ صُمَصِمٌ: and, accord. to AO, ▼ صِمٌّ applied to a horse, and ▼ صِمَّةٌ to a mare, signify *strong, firm, compact in make.* (TA.) —— See also صِمْصِمَةٌ.

صُمَصِمٌ: see the next preceding paragraph, in two places: —— and see also الصِّمُّ.

صَمْصَمَةٌ inf. n. of R. Q. 1 [q. v.] —— See also the paragraph here following.

صِمْصِمَةٌ *A company,* or *collection,* (M, Ḳ,) *of men;* like زِمْزِمَةٌ; neither of which words is formed by substitution from the other: (M, TA: [in the TA in art. زم, this is said of زِمْزِمَةٌ and صِمْصِمَةٌ:]) pl. [or rather coll. gen. n.] ▼ صِمْصِمٌ. (M, Ḳ.) —— Also *The middle of a people* or *party;* and so ▼ صَمْصَمَةٌ. (Ḳ.) —— And *A rugged* [*hill such as is termed*] أَكَمَةٌ, *of which the stones are almost erect.* (En-Naḍr, TA.)

صَمْصَامٌ, (Ṣ, Ḳ,) or سَيْفٌ صَمْصَامٌ, (M,) and ▼ صَمْصَامَةٌ, (Ṣ, M, Ḳ, [in the CḲ, erroneously, صِمْصامَة,]) *A sword,* (Ḳ,) or *a sharp sword,* (Ṣ, M,) *that will not bend.* (Ṣ, M, Ḳ.) الصَّمْصَامُ, (Ṣ, Ḳ,) or ▼ الصَّمْصَامَةُ, (M,) was the name of *The sword of 'Amr Ibn-Maadee-Kerib.* (Ṣ, M, Ḳ.) And some of the Arabs make ▼ صَمْصَامَةُ, thus without tenween, imperfectly decl., to be the name of *A particular sword.* (IB, TA.) —— See also صِمْصِمٌ.

صَمْصَامَةٌ: see the next preceding paragraph, in three places: —— and see also صِمْصِمٌ.

الصِّمُّ: see صِمْصِمٌ: —— and see also صُمَاصِمٌ.

صُمَاصِمَةٌ: see صِمْصِمٌ.

أَصَمٌّ applied to any animal, (Mgh,) *Deaf;* (Ṣ,* M,* Mgh, Mṣb, Ḳ;*) [or] *having a stoppage of the ear, and a heaviness of hearing;* (M, Ḳ:) fem. صَمَّآءُ: (Mgh, Mṣb:) pl. صُمٌّ (M, Mṣb, Ḳ) and صُمَّانٌ. (M, Ḳ.) A poet says,

• أَصَمُّ عَمَّا سَاءَهُ سَمِيعُ •

(TA,) a prov., (Meyd,) meaning Feigning himself *deaf to that which displeases him,* (Meyd, TA,) i. e. to what is foul, (Meyd,) as though he heard it not, (TA,) but *hearing* (Meyd, TA) that which pleases him, i. e. what is good; as does the generous man. (Meyd.) And similar is the saying,

• وَلِى أُذُنٌ عَنِ الفَحْشَآءِ صَمَّا •

[*And I have an ear deaf to that which is foul*]. (TA.) [See also Ḥam p. 636, for another similar ex.] One says likewise, دَعَاهُ دَعْوَةَ الأَصَمِّ † *He called him* [*with the call of the deaf,* meaning,] *with extraordinary force.* (TA.) And ضَرَبَهُ ضَرْبَ الأَصَمِّ ‡ *He beat him* [*with the beating of the deaf,* meaning,] *uninterruptedly and excessively;* because the deaf, when he does thus, [not hearing any cry,] imagines that he is falling short of what he should do, and therefore will not leave off. (TA.) And لَمَعَ بِثَوْبِهِ لَمْعَ الأَصَمِّ † *He* (one warning a people from afar) *made a sign by waving his garment continually, as does the deaf;* as though he heard not the reply. (TA.) And حَيَّةٌ أَصَمُّ (M, Ḳ, TA) and صَمَّآءُ (TA) ‡ *A serpent that will not accept charming;* (M, Ḳ, TA;) as though it heard it not; (M;) *that will not obey the charmer:* (TA:) and [in like manner] the epithet صُمٌّ is applied to scorpions. (M.) And رَجُلٌ أَصَمُّ ‡ *A man whom one does not hope to win over, and who will not be turned back from the object of his desire;* (M, Ḳ, TA;) as though he were called and would not hear. (M, TA.) And دَهْرٌ أَصَمُّ † [*Inexorable fortune;*] as though one complained to it and it would not hear. (M.) And الصَّمَّآءُ and دَاهِيَةٌ صَمَّآءُ as expl. voce صَمَامِ, q. v. And فِتْنَةٌ صَمَّآءُ † *A sedition,* or the like, *that is severe,* or *hard to be borne;* (Ṣ, Mṣb;) *to the allaying of which there is no way;* because of its having gone to the utmost extent. (TA. [See also أَبْكَمُ.]) And أَمْرٌ أَصَمُّ † *An affair,* or *event, that is severe,* or *hard to be borne.* (TA.) And صَمَّ is tropically attributed to الحِلْمُ: (M:) a poet, cited by Th, says,

• قُلْ مَا بَدَا لَكَ مِنْ زُورٍ وَمِنْ كَذِبٍ •
• حِلْمِى أَصَمُّ وَأُذْنِى غَيْرُ صَمَّآءِ •

‡ [the last word I find written thus, app. for the sake of the rhyme: i. e. *Say what occurs to thee, of falsehood and of lying: my forbearance is deaf,* i. e. *insensible,* to it, *though my ear is not deaf*]. (M, TA.) صَمَّآءُ is applied to a قَطَاة [or bird of the species termed قَطًا, and may in this case be rendered † *Small-eared,* or *dull-eared,* being applied thereto] because of the سَكَك [i. e. smallness &c.] of its ear or because it is deaf when thirsting. (M.) And الأَصَمُّ [as though meaning ‡ *The deaf-mute*] is an epithet applied to رَجَب, (Ṣ, M, Mṣb, Ḳ,) the month thus named, (Mṣb,) which the people of the Time of Ignorance called شَهْرُ اللّٰهِ الأَصَمُّ, (Kh, Ṣ,) because the cry of the caller for aid was not heard in it, (Kh, Ṣ, M, Mṣb, Ḳ,*) and the shouting يَا صَبَاحَاهْ and يَا لَفُلَانٍ, (M, Ḳ,) nor the commotion of fight, (Kh, Ṣ, Mṣb,) nor the clash of arms, it being one of the sacred months: (Kh, Ṣ:) thus applied it is tropical, like نَائِمٌ in the phrase لَيْلٌ نَائِمٌ; as though, in it, the man were deaf to the sound of arms: (TA:) and in like manner it is also called مُنْصِلُ الأَلِّ. (M. [See also الأَصَبُّ, and مُحَرَّمٌ, and شَهْرٌ.]) —— And [as that which is without a cavity is generally non-sonorous,] one says حَجَرٌ أَصَمُّ meaning ‡ *Hard* (Ṣ, M, Mṣb, Ḳ) *and solid* (Ṣ, Mṣb, Ḳ) *stone:* (Ṣ, &c.:) and صَخْرَةٌ صَمَّآءُ ‡ *a hard and solid rock:* (Ḳ, TA:) or this latter signifies † *a rock in which is no crack nor hole:* pl. صُمٌّ. (TA.) And قَنَاةٌ صَمَّآءُ † *A compact spear-shaft.* (M.) —— الصَّمَّآءُ also signifies † *The earth,* or *ground.* (M:) And أَرْضٌ صَمَّآءُ † *Rugged ground:* pl. صُمٌّ. (Ḳ.) —— Also [app. † *The vermiform appendage of the cœcum;*] *the thin,* or *slender, extremity of the* عفجة: (Ḳ: [the last word in this explanation is thus, without any syll. signs, in my MS. copy of the Ḳ and in the TA: in the CḲ, عَفَجَة: but the right reading is evidently عِفَجَة, which is said in the TA, in art. عفج, to be, like أَعْفَاج, a pl. of عَفْج and its dial. vars.: see this last word:] thus called [in my opinion because resembling a meatus auditorius that is closed, and therefore deaf; though said to be so called] because of its hardness. (TA.) —— And نَاقَةٌ صَمَّآءُ ‡ *A fat she-camel:* (Ḳ, TA:) and, (Ḳ,) or as some say, (TA,) *one that has just conceived,* or *become pregnant.* (Ḳ, TA.) —— اِشْتِمَالُ الصَّمَّآءِ, (Ṣ, Mṣb, Ḳ, TA,) which is forbidden in a trad., (TA,) is † *The covering oneself with his garment, like* [*as is done in the case of*] *the* شَمْلَة *of the Arabs of the desert with their* [*garments called*] أَكْسِيَة [pl. of كِسَآء]; (A'Obeyd, Ṣ;) i. e. *the turning the* كِسَآء, *from the direction of one's right, upon his left arm and the part between his left shoulder-joint and neck, and then turning it a second time, from behind him, upon his right arm and the part between his right shoulder-joint and neck, so as to cover them both:* (A'Obeyd, Ṣ, Ḳ:) or *the wrapping oneself with the garment without making to it a place from which to put forth the hand:* (Mṣb:) or, (Ḳ,) as the lawyers explain it, (A'Obeyd, Ṣ,) it is *the wrapping one's body and arms with one garment, not having upon him another, and then raising it* [in the Ḳ, as is said in the TA, بَضْعَة is erroneously put for بِرُقْعَة] *on one of its sides, and putting it upon his shoulder, so that his pudendum appears from it:* (A'Obeyd, Ṣ, Ḳ:) [but] with the Arabs, لِبْسَةُ الصَّمَّآءِ means *the covering one's whole body with his garment, and not raising a side from which to put forth his hand:* (Mgh:) when you say, of a man, اِشْتَمَلَ الصَّمَّآءَ, it is as though you said, اِشْتَمَلَ الشِّمْلَةَ الصَّمَّآءَ; for الصَّمَّآءُ is a sort of اِشْتِمَال. (Ṣ. [See also اِشْتَمَلَ, and الشِّمْلَةُ الصَّمَّآءُ, in art. شمل.]) —— جَذْرٌ أَصَمُّ † *A surd,* or *an irrational, root, in arithmetic;* which is known only to God, accord. to a saying of 'Áïsheh: opposed to جَذْرٌ نَاطِقٌ. (Mgh in art. جذر.) —— فِعْلٌ أَصَمُّ *A surd verb*

is a term sometimes used in grammar, as meaning *a triliteral-radical verb of the class commonly called* مُضَاعَفٌ *of which the second and third radicals are the same letter.*]

صَوْتٌ مُصْمِرٌ *A sound, or noise, or voice, that deafens the ear-hole.* (TA.)

أَلْفٌ مُصَمِّرٌ † *A thousand completed;* like مُصَمَّتٌ and مُصْمَتٌ. (TA in art. صمت.)

مُصَمِّرٌ A sword *that passes into the bones:* (M:) or *that penetrates into that which is struck with it.* (TA.) — See also صِمْصِمٌ. — And † *A strong* camel: so says Aboo-'Amr Esh-Sheybánee: and he cites the saying,

* حَمَّلْتُ أَثْقَالِي مُصَمِّرَاتِهَا *

[as meaning *I loaded their strong camels with my burdens*]: (TA:) or the مُصَمِّرَات, here mentioned, are the camels *that do not utter a grumbling cry; patient of travel.* (Ḥam p. 791.)

صمت

1. صَمَتَ, (Ṣ, M, A, Mgh, Mṣb,) aor. ـُ, (Ṣ, M, Mṣb,) inf. n. صَمْتٌ (Ṣ, M, A, Mgh, Mṣb, Ḳ) and صُمْتٌ (M, L, TA) and صُمُوتٌ and صُمَاتٌ, (Ṣ, M, Mgh, Mṣb, Ḳ,) or the first of these is the inf. n. and the rest are simple substs.; (M;) and ▼اصمت, (Ṣ, M, Mṣb,) inf. n. إِصْمَاتٌ; (Ḳ;) and ▼صمّت, inf. n. تَصْمِيتٌ; (Ṣ, Ḳ; but only the inf. n. is mentioned;) *He was, or became, silent, mute, or speechless;* syn. سَكَتَ: (Ṣ, A, Mṣb, Ḳ:) or *he was,* or *became, long silent* or *mute* or *speechless:* (M, Mgh:) but there is a difference between سَكَتَ and صَمَتَ; for the former is said of him who has the power, or faculty, of speech, but abstains from making use of it; whereas the latter is sometimes said of that which has not the power, or faculty, of speech. (Er-Rághib, MF and TA in art. سكت.) The Arabs say, (Ks, TA,) and it is said in a trad., (TA,) لَا صَمْتَ يَوْمًا إِلَى ٱللَّيْلِ, or يَوْمٍ, or يَوْمٌ, i. e. *There shall be no keeping silence a whole day* [*until night*]. (Ks, Ḳ, TA. [In the "Jámi' eṣ-Ṣagheer," we find لا صُمَاتَ instead of لا صَمْتَ: and El-Munáwee, in his Commentary on that work, says that the keeping silence for a whole day is forbidden by the words of this trad. because it is an imitation of a Christian custom.]) And إِذْنُهَا صُمَاتُهَا [in another trad., relating to the asking a virgin if she consent to be married, lit. *Her permission is her silence,*] means *her silence* is like *her permission,* i. e. it suffices. (Mṣb.) One says also, جَآءَ بِمَا صَآءَ وَصَمَتَ † [*He brought what was vocal and what was mute*]; مَا صَآءَ meaning *sheep, or goats, and camels;* and مَا صَمَتَ, *gold and silver:* (IAạr, TA:) صَآءَ in this saying is formed by transposition from صَأَى [q. v.]. (Ṣ in art. صأى.)

2. صمّتهُ, (M, A, Ḳ,) inf. n. تَصْمِيتٌ; (Ṣ;) and ▼اصمتهُ; (M, A, Mṣb, Ḳ;) *He made him,* or *rendered him, silent, mute, or speechless:* (Ṣ, A, Mṣb, Ḳ:) or *he made him,* or *rendered him, long silent* or *mute* or *speechless.* (M.) — [Hence,] صَمِّتِي صَبِيَّكِ *Feed thy child with that which will silence it* [or *quiet it*]. (A, TA.) — And صمّت ٱلرَّجُلَ *He inclined to the man* who complained to him *by reason of his complaint* [and so *quieted him;* or *he cared for the complaint of the man and so quieted him:* see مُصَمِّتٌ]. (M, TA.) ═ See also 1, first sentence.

4. اصمتهُ: see 2. — [Hence,] لَمْ يُصْمِتْهُ ذٰلِكَ *That did not suffice him* [*so as to quiet him*]: said only of what is eaten and drunk. (TA.) — And اصمتهُ *He made it to be solid, not hollow; without a cavity.* (A'Obeyd, Ṣ, Ḳ.) [For that which is without a cavity is generally non-sonorous.] — And أُصْمِتَتِ ٱلْأَرْضُ, or أَصْمَتَت, (accord. to different copies of the Ḳ, the latter accord. to the O,) *The land became altered* (أَحَالَتْ) [*so as to be rugged, or hard,* app. *in consequence of its having been left untilled and unsown,*] *at the end of two years,* (O, Ḳ,) *and had rugged patches of urine and dung.* (O.) ═ See also 1, first sentence. — أَصْمَتَ also signifies *He was, or became, tongue-tied,* (O, TA,) *and spoke not;* (TA;) said of a sick man. (O, TA.)

صُمْتَةٌ a subst. from صَمَتَ [as such signifying *Silence, muteness,* or *speechlessness;* like صَمْتٌ used as a subst., and صُمْتٌ &c.; and like سُكْتَةٌ and سُكْتَةٌ]. (M, TA.) — And (M, TA) *A thing,* (M, A, Ḳ, TA,) i. e. *food,* (A, Ḳ, TA,) or *the like,* (Ḳ, TA,) *such as a date,* or *something pretty,* (TA,) *with which one silences* [or *quiets*] (M, A, Ḳ, TA) *a child;* (A, Ḳ, TA;) as also ▼صِمْتَةٌ; (Lḥ, M, TA;) like سُكْتَةٌ [in this sense as well as in the former sense]. (Ṣ.) A date is called صُمْتَةُ ٱلصَّبِيِّ [*The quieter of the child*], (M, TA,) and صُمْتَةُ ٱلصَّغِيرِ [*The quieter of the little one*], so in a trad., because when the little one cries, or weeps, he is silenced with it. (TA.) One says, مَا عِنْدَهَا صُمْتَةُ لَيْلَةٍ *She has not as much as would silence* [or *quiet*] *her child during one night.* (A.) And مَا لَهُ صُمْتَةٌ لِعِيَالِهِ and ▼صِمْتَةٌ *He has not what would feed and silence* [or *quiet*] *his household,* or *family.* (Lḥ, M.)

صِمْتَةٌ: see the next preceding paragraph, in two places.

مَا ذُقْتُ صَمَاتًا [*I did not taste,* or *have not tasted,*] *anything.* (Ḳ.)

رَمَاهُ بِصُمَاتِهِ, (AZ, Ṣ, A, Ḳ, [in a copy of the M بصماته, but this I think a mistranscription,]) or ▼بِصُمَاتَةٍ, (Ḳ accord. to the TA, and so in the M in art. سكت,) [both probably correct, for] one says also بِسُكَاتِهِ (AZ, Ṣ) and بِسُكَاتَةٍ, (Ṣ, M, A, Ḳ, in art. سكت,) *He* (a man, AZ, Ṣ, or God, A) *smote him, or afflicted him, with a thing that silenced him.* (AZ, Ṣ, M, A, Ḳ.) [See رَمَاهُ بِسُكَاتٍ, in art. سكت.] — صُمَاتٌ signifies also *Thirst:* (Aṣ, TA:) or *quickness of thirsting,* (M, Ḳ, TA,) in men and in beasts. (M, TA.)

فُلَانٌ عَلَى صُمَاتِ ٱلْأَمْرِ *Such a one is,* or *was, at the point of accomplishing the affair.* (Ṣ.) And أَنَا عَلَى صُمَاتِ حَاجَتِي *I am at the point of accomplishing my want.* (M.) And بَاتَ عَلَى صُمَاتِ أَمْرِهِ *He passed the night resolved upon his affair.* (TA.) And هُوَ بِصُمَاتِهِ *He is at the point of* [*attaining*] *his purpose:* (M, TA:) Aboo-Málik says that صُمَاتٌ signifies قَصْدٌ [i. e. *purpose, intention,* &c.]. (TA.) And one says, بَاتَ مِنَ ٱلْقَوْمِ عَلَى صُمَاتٍ *He passed the night in a place where he was seen and heard by the people, near to them.* (Ṣ, TA.)

دِرْعٌ صَمُوتٌ ‡ *A coat of mail from which no sound is heard to proceed when it is put on,* (Ṣ, A, L, TA,) *it being soft to the feel, not rough nor rusty:* (L, TA:) or *a heavy coat of mail.* (Ḳ.) And جَارِيَةٌ صَمُوتُ ٱلْخَلْخَالَيْنِ ‡ *A girl,* or *young woman, having thick legs, from whose pair of anklets no sound is heard to proceed,* (Ḳ, TA,) *by reason of their being depressed in her legs.* (TA. [لَبًا in the CḲ is erroneously put for لِغَمْهَا.]) And سَيْفٌ صَمُوتٌ † *A sword that penetrates deeply into the thing struck with it* [*so as not to make a sound by its being repelled by a bone*]. (Ḳ, TA.) And ضَرْبَةٌ صَمُوتٌ † *A blow* [*with a sword* or *the like*] *passing among the bones, not recoiling from a bone* (M, Ḳ, TA) *so as to make a sound.* (TA.) — And شُهْدَةٌ صَمُوتٌ ‡ *A honey-comb that is full: not having a cell empty.* (A, Ḳ.)

صُمَاتَةٌ: see رَمَاهُ بِصُمَاتِهِ, above.

صِمِّيتٌ, applied to a man, (Ṣ,) i. q. سِكِّيتٌ, (Ṣ, Ḳ, TA,) [i. e. *Much,* or *often, silent* or *mute* or *speechless;* or] *long silent* &c. (TA.)

صَامِتٌ *Silent, mute,* or *speechless:* (Mṣb:) pl. صَامِتُونَ (Ḳur vii. 192) [and صُمُوتٌ, occurring in the Ḳ in art. زم]. [Hence,] one says, مَا لَهُ صَامِتٌ وَلَا نَاطِقٌ ‡ [*He has not mute nor vocal property;* or *he has not dead nor live stock*]: (Ṣ, M, A:) by the former are meant *gold* and *silver;* (Ṣ, M, Mṣb, Ḳ;) and by the latter, *camels,* (Ṣ, Ḳ,) and *sheep* or *goats,* (Ṣ,) or *animals:* (M:) i. e. *he has not aught.* (Ṣ.) — Also, of camels, † *Twenty,* (O, Ḳ,) and *the like.* (O.) — And of milk, † *Such as is thick.* (Ṣ, O, Ḳ.)

أُصْمُتٌ: see مُصْمِتٌ.

بِبَلْدَةِ إِصْمِتَ and لَقِيتُهُ بِوَحْشِ إِصْمِتَ AZ explains as meaning [*I met him,* or *met with him,* or *found him,*] *in a desert place, in which was no one to cheer by his company:* (Ṣ: [and in like manner the latter phrase is expl. in the M:]) accord. to Kr, بِبَلْدَةِ إِصْمِتَ; but the phrase commonly known is بِبَلْدَةِ إِصْمِتَ: (M:) or تَرَكْتُهُ بِبَلْدَةِ إِصْمِتَ [*I left him*] *in the desert,* or *waterless desert:* or *in such a place that it was not known where he was:* (Ḳ:) and بِصَحْرَآءِ إِصْمِتَ (M, Ḳ) meaning as above, (Ḳ,) or having the latter of these two meanings: (M:) and بِوَحْشِ إِصْمِتَ and ▼إِصْمِتَةَ, (M, Ḳ,) mentioned, but not expl., by Lḥ, (M,) meaning as above, (Ḳ,) or app. meaning *in the desert,* or *waterless desert:* (M:) and some say, بِوَحْشِ ٱلْإِصْمِتَيْنِ: (TA:)

اصمت is as above, with the disjunctive alif; and also with the conjunctive [i. e. ٱصْمِتْ]: (O, Ḳ:) it is imperfectly decl., (Ṣ, MF, TA,) because combining the quality of a proper name with the fem. gender or with the measure of a verb: (MF, TA:) it is said that the desert, or waterless desert, is thus called because in it one fears much; as though everyone [therein] said to his companion, اصمت [i. e. أَصْمُتْ or أَصْمِتْ, "Be thou silent"]; like as they say of a مَهْمَه that it is so called because a man [therein] says to his companion, مَهْ مَهْ: (MA:) [for] accord. to some the word إِصْمِت is an imperative changed into a subst., and hence the ء is disjunctive, and it may be with kesr accord. to a dial. var. [of the imperative] that has not reached us: accord. to Yákoot, it is the name of a particular desert; but others say that the proper name [of that desert] is وَحْشُ إِصْمِتَ. (TA in art. وحش.)

إِصْمِتَة: see the next preceding paragraph.

مُصْمَتٌ [primarily signifies *Made, or rendered, silent, mute, or speechless.* — And hence,] *Solid; not hollow; having no cavity.* (A'Obeyd, Ṣ, M, Mgh, Mṣb, Ḳ.) [For that which is without a cavity is generally non-sonorous.] — And *A door,* (Ṣ, M, Mgh, Mṣb, Ḳ,) and *a lock,* (M, Ḳ,) *closed,* or *locked,* (Ṣ, M, Mgh, Mṣb, Ḳ,) *so that one cannot find the way to open it.* (Ṣ, M,* Ḳ.*) A poet says,

* وَمِنْ دُونِ لَيْلَى مُصْمَتَاتُ المَقَاصِرِ *

[*And in the way to Leylà are what are closed,* &c., *of chambers to which the owner alone has access:* مَقَاصِر being used by poetic license for مَقَاصِير, pl. of مَقْصُورَةٌ]. (TA.) — Also *A garment, or piece of cloth, of one, unmixed, colour.* (M, Mgh, Ḳ.) The garment thus termed that is disliked is That *of which the warp and woof are both of silk: or such as is woven of undressed silk, and then dressed, and dyed of one colour:* (Mgh:) [or] such as is termed مُصْمَتٌ مِنْ خَزٍّ, i. e. *consisting entirely of silk, not mixed with cotton nor with other material,* was forbidden by the Prophet. (TA.) — [Hence,] فَرَسٌ مُصْمَتٌ *A horse of one, unmixed, colour; in which is no colour differing from the rest:* (Ṣ, A, TA:) pl. خَيْلٌ مُصْمَتَاتٌ. (TA.) And أَدْهَمُ مُصْمَتٌ [applied to a horse] † *Black unmixed with any other colour.* (TA.) — [Hence also,] إِنَآءٌ مُصْمَتٌ † *A vessel not silvered, or not ornamented with silver.* (Mgh.) And بَيْضَةٌ مُصْمَتَةٌ † *A helmet made of one piece.* (AO, TA in art. بيض.) And حَلْىٌ مُصْمَتٌ † *A woman's ornament that is not intermixed with another:* or, accord. to Ahmad Ibn-'Obeyd, *that has stuck fast upon its wearer, so that it does not move about; such as the armlet, and the anklet, and the like.* (TA.) — The فَهْد [or lynx, an animal proverbial for much sleeping,] is said to be مُصْمَتُ النَّوْمِ ‡ [app. meaning *A heavy sleeper*]. (A, TA.) — الحُرُوفُ المُصْمَتَةُ are *All the letters* [*of the Arabic alphabet*] *except those called* حُرُوفُ الذَّلْقِ [or الحُرُوفُ الذُّلْقُ]; (M, TA;) i. e. (TA) *all the letters except those comprised in the phrase* مُرَّ بِنَفْلٍ. (Ḳ, TA.) [What is here rendered "except" (i. e. مَا عَدَا) is said by MF to be omitted in most of the copies of the Ḳ.] — See also مُصَمَّتٌ.

مُصْمِتٌ *Tongue-tied;* (O, TA;) *not speaking:* (TA:) applied to a sick man [when he is unable to speak]: (O, TA:) and ↓ أَصْمَتُ [signifies the same,] i. q. أَبْهَمُ and مُبْهَمٌ. (So in copies of the Ḳ in art. بهم. [In one of the explanations which I have given of مُبْهَمٌ, in consequence of an omission (to be supplied in Book II.), أَصْمَتُ is made syn. with مُصْمَتٌ.])

أَلْفٌ مُصَمَّتٌ † *A thousand completed;* (M, Ḳ;) like مُصَمَّمٌ; (M;) as also ↓ مُصْمَتٌ. (Ḳ.)

مُصَمِّتٌ [*A silencer,* or *quieter:* and hence, —] *One who cares for* another's *complaint.* (M,* Meyd, TA.) One says, (M, Meyd, TA,) i. e. a rájiz says, addressing a camel belonging to him, (Har p. 642,)

* إِنَّكَ لَا تَشْكُو إِلَى مُصَمِّتِ *

* فَٱصْبِرْ عَلَى الحِمْلِ الثَّقِيلِ أَوْ مُتِ *

[*Verily thou complainest not to one who cares for thy complaint; therefore endure with patience the bearing of the heavy burden, or die*]. (M, Meyd, TA.) تَشْكُو إِلَى غَيْرِ مُصَمِّتٍ, i. e. [*Thou complainest*] *to one who cares not for thy case,* is a proverb. (Meyd.)

صمج

صُمُجٌ [*Lamps of the kind called*] قَنَادِيلُ [pl. of قِنْدِيلٌ]: one of which is called صَمَجَةٌ: (Ṣ, Ḳ: [in the Ḳ, the former word is called pl. of the latter; but it is a coll. gen. n:]) an Arabic word, an exception to the rule that ص and ج cannot both occur in a genuine Arabic word: (TA:) or of Greek origin (رُومِىٌّ), arabicized: (Ṣ:) Esh-Shemmákh says,

* وَالنَّجْمُ مِثْلُ الصُّمُجِ الرُّومِيَّاتْ *

[*And the asterism,* meaning *the Pleiades, like the Greek lamps*]: (Ṣ, MF:) but this does not show the word to be Greek, as the epithet may be added for the purpose of restriction. (MF.)

صمخ

1. صَمَخَهُ, (Ṣ, A, L, Ḳ,) aor. ـَ, inf. n. صَمْخٌ, (L,) *He hit, or hurt, his* صِمَاخ [i. e. his *ear-hole,* or his *ear*]: (Ṣ, A, L, Ḳ:) and, accord. to Sh, صَمَخَتْهُ الشَّمْسُ *The sun smote,* or *hurt, his* صِمَاخ. (TA.) — صَمَخَتِ الشَّمْسُ وَجْهَهُ *The sun smote,* or *hurt, his face:* or [in the CḲ "and"] *fell vehemently upon it.* (A'Obeyd, Ḳ.) — صَمَخَ عَيْنَهُ, (ISk, Ḳ,) aor. and inf. n. as above, (ISk,) *He struck his eye with his fist:* (ISk, Ḳ:) in some of the lexicons, *with his hand.* (TA.) — And صَمَخَ أَنْفَهُ *He crushed,* or *bruised, his nose.* (Lḥ, TA.) [See also what next follows.]

صَمْخٌ inf. n. of 1 [q. v.]. (L.) — Also *Any blow that leaves a mark;* accord. to AZ, *upon the face.* (TA.)

صِمَاخٌ *The ear-hole:* (Ṣ, A, Mgh, Ḳ:) the *hole,* (Mṣb,) or *inner hole,* (L,) *of the ear, that penetrates to* [*the interior of*] *the head:* (L, Mṣb:) and ↓ أُصْمُوخٌ signifies the same: (L, Ḳ:) of the dial. of Temeem: (L:) and سِمَاخٌ is a dial. var., (Ṣ, L,) as also أُسْمُوخٌ: (L:) and, (Ṣ, L, Mṣb, Ḳ,) as some say, (Ṣ, L, Mṣb,) the *ear itself:* (Ṣ, L, Mṣb, Ḳ:) pl. أَصْمِخَةٌ, (L, Mṣb,) a pl. of pauc., (L,) and أَصْمَاخٌ, (A,) [also a pl. of pauc.,] and صُمُخٌ and صَمَائِخُ. (L.) One says, ضَرَبَ ٱللّٰهُ عَلَى صِمَاخِهِ, and عَلَى أَصْمِخَتِهِمْ, meaning *God made him,* and *them, to sleep:* phrases similar to ضَرَبْنَا عَلَى آذَانِهِمْ, in the Ḳur [xviii. 10: see art. ضرب]. (L.) And هٰذَا كَلَامٌ يُؤْلِمُ أَصْمَاخِى [*This is speech that pains my ears*]. (A.)

صَمُوخٌ [*Having merely an ear-hole;* as distinguished from أَذُونٌ, meaning "having an ear," i. e. "having an external ear"]. (Mṣb in art. بيض.)

أُصْمُوخٌ: see صِمَاخٌ.

صمد

1. صَمَدَهُ, (Ṣ, M, A, Mgh,) aor. ـُ, (Ṣ, Mgh,) inf. n. صَمْدٌ; (Ṣ, M, Mgh, Ḳ;) and صَمَدَ إِلَيْهِ; (M, A;*) *He tended, repaired, betook himself,* or *directed himself* or *his course* or *aim, to,* or *towards, him,* or *it;* or *endeavoured to reach,* or *attain,* or *obtain, him,* or *it;* or *had recourse to him,* or *it;* syn. قَصَدَهُ: (Ṣ, M, A, Mgh, Ḳ:*) and so سَمَدَهُ. (M in art. سمد.) One says, صَمَدَ إِلَيْهِ فِى الحَوَائِجِ *He repaired, betook himself,* or *had recourse, to him in exigencies;* syn. قَصَدَ. (M.) And صَمَدَ صَمْدَ الأَمْرِ, (A,) or صَمَدَ الأَمْرَ, (M,) *He betook himself to the thing,* or *affair; aimed at it; sought it,* or *endeavoured after it;* or *intended,* or *purposed, it;* syn. قَصَدَ قَصْدَهُ; (A;) or إِعْتَمَدَهُ. (M.) And ↓ تَصَمَّدَ لَهُ بِالعَصَا *He betook himself to him* or *towards him,* or *aimed at him, with the staff,* or *stick;* syn. قَصَدَ. (M.) And ↓ تَصَمَّدَ رَأْسَهُ بِالعَصَا *He aimed* (عَمَدَ) *at the main part of his head with the staff,* or *stick.* (M.) — Hence, صَمَدَ لَهُ *He faced it directly; directed his face exactly towards it.* (Mgh.) — And *He pointed towards it.* (Mgh.) — And صَمَدْتُ لَهُ حَتَّى أَمْكَنَتْنِى مِنْهُ غِرَّةٌ *I sprang and betook myself towards him, watching until heedlessness on his part made me to have him within my power.* (L, from a trad. respecting the slaying of Aboo-Jahl.) — And صَمَدَهُ بِالعَصَا, (A,) inf. n. صَمْدٌ, (Ḳ,) *He struck him,* or *beat him, with the staff,* or *stick.* (A, Ḳ.*) — الصَّمْدُ also signifies النَّصْبُ [*The setting up,* or *erecting,* a thing]: (Ḳ:) one says صَمَدَهُ *He set it up,* or *erected, it.* (TḲ.) — And صَمَدَتِ الشَّمْسُ وَجْهَهُ, (TḲ,) inf. n. صَمْدٌ, (Ḳ,) *The sun scorched his face.* (Ḳ,* TḲ.) — صَمَدَ القَارُورَةَ, (M, Ḳ,) aor. ـُ, (M,) or ـِ, (Ḳ,) but this is

strange, for there is no faucial letter, nor any other reason for it, (MF,) *He put a* صِمَاد [q. v.] *over*, or *into, the mouth of the flask*, or *bottle*. (M, Ḳ.)

2. [صَمَّدهُ, said of a number of persons, signifies the same as صَمَدَهُ as first expl. above; or, said of a single person, *He tended, repaired, &c., repeatedly*, or *frequently, to him*, or *it*; see its pass. part. n., below.] ═ صَمَّدَ رَأْسَهُ, inf. n. تَصْمِيدٌ, *He wound a piece of cloth*, or *a kerchief, called* صِمَاد, *round his head*. (TA.)

3. صَامَدَهُ, (TA,) inf. n. صِمَادٌ, (Ḳ, TA,) *He contended with him in fight*; syn. of the inf. n. جِلَادٌ. (Ḳ,* TA. [For جِلَاد, Golius appears to have found in his copy of the Ḳ جَلَّاد.])

4. اصمد إِلَيْهِ الأَمْرَ *He rested*, or *stayed, upon him the affair*; syn. أَسْنَدَهُ. (M.)

5: see 1, in two places.

صَمْدٌ inf. n. of 1. (Ṣ, M, &c.) [Hence صَمَدْتُ صَمْدَهُ, like قَصَدْتُ قَصْدَهُ, q. v.] ═ Also, (Ṣ, L, Ḳ,) or ▼ صَمَدٌ, (as in a copy of the Ṣ and in one of the M,) *Elevated ground*: (L:) or *elevated and rugged ground*, (Ṣ, M, L, Ḳ,) *not so high as to be a mountain*: (M, L:) or *hard, firm*, or *tough, ground*: (AA:) pl. أَصْمَادٌ and ▼ صِمَادٌ: (M:) or *a narrow, rugged, and low part of a mountain, producing trees*; as also ▼ صِمَادٌ. (Aboo-Kheyreh.)

صَمَدٌ (with the article ال an epithet applied to God, M) *A lord*; because one repairs, betakes himself, or has recourse, to him in exigencies; (Ṣ, A, Ḳ;*) or, when applied to God, because affairs are stayed, or rested, upon Him, (أُصْمِدَتْ إِلَيْهِ,) and none but He accomplishes them: (M, A, L:) or *a person to whom one repairs, betakes himself*, or *has recourse, in exigencies*: (M, A:*) you say, سَيِّدٌ صَمَدٌ, meaning *a lord*, or *chief, to whom recourse is had*: (A:) or صَمَدٌ signifies *a lord to whom obedience is rendered, without whom no affair is accomplished*: or *one to whom lordship ultimately pertains*: (M, L:) or *a lord whose lordship has attained its utmost point or degree*; in which sense it is not applicable to God: (T, L:) or the *Being that continues*, or *continues for ever* or *is everlasting*: (M, Ḳ:) or the *Being that continues*, or *continues for ever, after his creatures have perished*: (M:) or the *Creator of everything, of whom nothing is independent, and whose unity everything indicates*: or *one who takes no nourishment*, or *food*: (M, L:) also *high*, or *elevated*; (L, Ḳ;) applied to anything: (L:) a *man above whom is no one*: (L:) a *man who neither thirsts nor hungers in war*. (AA, Ḳ.) — Also *Solid*; *not hollow*; (M, Ḳ;) in which sense it may not be applied to God: (M:) and so ▼ مُصْمَدٌ, a dial. var. of مُصْمَتٌ. (Ṣ.) — And *A people having no trade*, or *occupation, nor anything by means of which they may live*. (Ḳ.) ═ See also صَمْدٌ.

صَمْدَةٌ *A rock firmly imbedded in the earth, even with the surface thereof*, or, in some instances, *somewhat elevated*; (M, Ḳ;*) as also ▼ صُمْدَةٌ. (M.) ═ And *A she-camel that has been covered and has not conceived*; (M, Ḳ;*) as also ▼ صُمُدَةٌ. (Kr, M.)

صُمْدَةٌ: }
صُمُدَةٌ: } see the next preceding paragraph.

صِمَادٌ The سِدَاد [or *stopper*, like صِمَام], (IAạr, Ḳ,) or the عِفَاص [or *piece of skin that is put as a cover over the mouth*], (Lth, Ṣ, M,) *of a flask* or *bottle*. (Lth, IAạr, Ṣ, M, Ḳ.) — And *A piece of cloth*, or *a kerchief, which a man winds round his head*, دُونَ العِمَامَةِ [which may mean either *exclusively of the turban* or *beneath the turban*]. (Ḳ.) ═ See also صَمْدٌ, in two places.

صَمُودٌ *A certain idol, which belonged to the tribe of 'Ád, who worshipped it*. (TA.)

مُصْمَدٌ: see صَمَدٌ, near the end of the paragraph.

مُصَمَّدٌ applied to a house, or tent, (بَيْتٌ, Ṣ) *repaired to* [*repeatedly*, or *frequently*, or *by many persons*, as is indicated by the teshdeed, though only expl. as] syn. *with* مَقْصُودٌ. (Ṣ, Ḳ.) ═ Also *A hard thing*; *in which is no softness*, or *fragility*. (Ḳ, TA.)

مِصْمَادٌ A she-camel *that endures cold, and drought*, or *barrenness of the earth, continuing to yield her milk*: pl. مَصَامِدُ and مَصَامِيدُ. (Ḳ.)

مُصْمَوْمِدٌ *Thick*, or *rough*, (Ḳ, TA,) and *high, overtopping*, or *prominent*. (TA.)

صمر

1. صَمَرَ, (M, Ḳ,) aor. ـِ, (M,) inf. n. صَمْرٌ and صُمُورٌ, *He was niggardly*, or *tenacious, and refused*; (M, Ḳ;) as also ▼ اصمر, and ▼ صمّر: (Ḳ:) [or] صَمَرَ, inf. n. صَمْرٌ, signifies *he collected, and refused*; and so ▼ اصمر, and ▼ صمّر: one says, صَمَرَ مَتَاعَهُ [*he collected, and refused, his goods*]: (O:) [but ISd says that] the phrase ▼ الصَّامِرِينَ مَتَاعَهُمْ, used by a poet, means الصَّامِرِينَ بِمَتَاعِهِمْ [i. e., accord. to the context, *those who are niggardly with their goods*]. (M.) ═ صَمَرَ المَآءُ, (M, O, Ḳ,) aor. ـُ, inf. n. صُمُورٌ, (M, O,) *The water ran from a declivity into a level place, and then became calm*, or *tranquil, while* [*continuing*] *running*. (M, O, Ḳ.) And ▼ صُمْرٌ signifies *The resting-place of such water*: (M, Ḳ:) and ▼ صُمْرُ الوَادِى *the resting-place of such water of the valley*. (TA.) ═ صَمُرَ, (O, Ḳ,) aor. ـُ; (Ḳ;) and صَمِرَ, (O, Ḳ,) aor. ـَ; (Ḳ;) said of milk, (O, Ḳ,) *It was*, or *became, sour*; (O;) or *very sour*; as also ▼ اصمر. (O, Ḳ.)

2: see above, first sentence, in two places: ═ and see the paragraph here following.

4: see 1, first sentence, in two places: ═ and see also the last sentence. ═ Also اصمروا, (O,* Ḳ,) inf. n. إِصْمَارٌ; (O;) and ▼ صمّروا, (Ḳ,) inf. n. تَصْمِيرٌ; (O;) *They entered upon the time of sunset*, which is called الصُّمَيْرُ. (O, Ḳ.)

5. تصمّر *He confined, restricted*, or *restrained, himself*. (O.) [See also its part. n., below.]

صَمْرٌ, (M, O, TṢ, Ḳ,) or ▼ صَمَرٌ, (Ṣ, A, L,) [the latter probably the correct, or the original, word, and, if so, app. an inf. n. of an unmentioned, and perhaps unused, verb, namely, صَمِرَ, whence the part. n. صَمِرٌ, q. v.,] *Stink, foul odour*, or *offensive smell*: (Ṣ, M, Ḳ:) and, (Ḳ,) accord. to IAạr, (O, TA,) the *odour of fresh musk*, (O, and so in copies of the Ḳ,) or *of fresh fish*: (TA, as from the Ḳ:) and, accord. to IAạr, (O, TA,) but in this sense more commonly ▼ صَمَرٌ, (O,) the *sultry heat*, (O,) or *foul smell, and sultry heat, and dew*, or *moisture, accompanying such heat*, (TA,) of the sea when it is agitated. (O, TA.)

صُمْرٌ i. q. صُبْرٌ [i. e. The *side* of a thing: or a *side rising above the rest* of a thing: or its *upper part*, or *top*: or its *edge*]: (Ṣ, M, Ḳ:) the م is said to be substituted for ب: (M:) pl. أَصْمَارٌ. (Ṣ, M, Ḳ.) You say, أَدْهَقْتُ الكَأْسَ إِلَى أَصْمَارِهَا, meaning الى أَصْبَارِهَا [i. e. *I filled the cup to its uppermost parts*; or *to its edges*]. (ISk, Ṣ, M,* Ḳ: in the M and TA is added, i. e. إِلَى أَعَالِيهَا.) And أَخَذَ الشَّىْءَ بِأَصْمَارِهِ, meaning بِأَصْبَارِهِ [i. e. *He took the thing altogether*: see art. صبر]. (M, TA.)

صُمْرٌ, and صُمْرُ الوَادِى: see the first paragraph.

صَمَرٌ: see صَمْرٌ, in two places.

صَمِرٌ: [*Stinking*; *having a foul*, or *an offensive, odour*, or *smell*]. One says, يَدِى مِنَ السَّمَكِ صَمِرَةٌ [*My hand is stinking from the fish*], (Ṣ, O, [in the former of which the meaning is indicated by the context,]) and مِنَ اللَّحْمِ [*from the flesh-meat*]. (TA.)

صَمْرَةٌ *Milk devoid of sweetness*. (O, Ḳ.)

صَمِيرٌ A man *whose flesh is dry*, or *tough, upon his bones*, (Ṣ, M, A, O, Ḳ,) *from whom the odour of sweat diffuses itself*. (IDrd, Ṣ, A, O, Ḳ.)

صُمَيْرٌ The *time of sunset*. (Ḳ, TA.)

صُمَارَى, (M, O, Ḳ,) and صَمَارَى, (O, Ḳ,) and ▼ صُمَارِىٌّ, (Ṣ, O, Ḳ,) and صِمَارَى, with kesr, [but whether otherwise like the first and second or the last, is not shown,] (TA, from Az,) The *podex*, or the *anus*; syn. دُبُرٌ, (Ṣ,) or اِسْتٌ, (M, A,) or سَافِلَةٌ: (O:) because of its foul smell. (O,* TA.)

صُمَارِىٌّ: see the next preceding paragraph.

صَامِرٌ A day *in which the wind is still*. (O, TA.) ═ See also 1, first sentence.

صَوْمَرٌ, a word of the dial. of El-Yemen, (IDrd, O,) The بَاذَرُوج; (M;) [i. e.] the *trees*, or *plants*, (شَجَر,) *called by the latter name*; (Ḳ;) or *a species of* بَقْل [or *herb*] *called in Pers. by the latter name* [which, commonly pronounced with د, is one of the names now applied to *basil*]: (IDrd, O:) accord. to AḤn, *a sort of tree*, or *plant, that does not grow by itself, but twines upon the* غَاف, *consisting of twigs with leaves like those of the* أَرَاك, (M, O,) *its twigs being more slender than thorns,* (O,) *and having a fruit resembling the acorn,* (M, O,) *in form, but thicker at the base and more slender at the extremity,* (O,) *which is eaten, and is soft, and very sweet:* (M, O:) *the stem of the* صَوْمَرَة [which is the n. un.] *is thicker than the upper half of the arm; and it increases in height with the* غَاقَة *while the latter does so:* (O:) 'Alee Ibn-'Abbás, author of the book entitled the "Kámil," says that the بَاذَرُوج has in it nothing beneficial when a man takes it internally; but when applied externally, it matures, or causes suppuration, [for انشج in the TA, an evident mistranscription, I read أَنْضَجَ,] and acts as a dissolvent. (TA.)

صَامُورَةٌ *Very sour milk.* (O, Ḳ.)

مُتَصَمِّرٌ *i. q.* مُتَشَمِّسٌ [app. as meaning *Niggardly, tenacious,* or *avaricious;* agreeably with the first explanation of 1]: (O, Ḳ:) and, (Ḳ,) or as some say, (TA,) *confining, restricting,* or *restraining, himself.* (Ḳ, TA.)

صمع

1. صَمِعَتِ الأُذُنُ, aor. ـَ, inf. n. صَمَعٌ, (Mṣb, TA,) *The ear was* [*small:* (see أَصْمَعُ:) or] *cleaving* [*to the head*], *and small:* (Mṣb:) or *was small, and not pointed,* or *tapering,* or *slender at the extremity, and had a contraction in the middle, and a cleaving to the head:* or *clave to the side of the face, from its base, and was short, not pointed,* or *tapering,* or *slender at the extremity:* or *was narrow,* or *contracted, in its hole, and pointed.* (TA.)

2: see the next paragraph.

Q. Q. 1. صَوْمَعَ الثَّرِيدَةَ *He made the* ثريدة [or *mess of crumbled bread with broth*] *slender in the head,* (Ibn-'Abbád, O, Ḳ,) *and pointed therein;* (Ibn-'Abbád, O;) as also ↓ صَمَّعَهَا. (TA.) — And صومع بِنَاءَهُ *He made his building high.* (Seer, TA.) — And صومع الشَّىْءَ *He collected together the thing.* (Ibn-'Abbád, O, Ḳ.)

صَمَعٌ inf. n. of 1 [q. v.]. (Mṣb, TA.) — Also *Courage:* because the courageous is described as compact in heart. (TA.)

صَمِعٌ *Courageous.* (TA.) — And *Sharp in intellect.* (TA. [See also أَصْمَعُ.])

صَوْمَعٌ: see what next follows.

صَوْمَعَةٌ *A Christian's cell,* or *chamber,* (Ḳ, KL,) *for retirement,* or *seclusion, having a high and slender head;* (KL;) [the *cell of a recluse;*] *a monk's* مَنَار [which, as here used, means likewise a *cell,* or *chamber, of the kind described above*]: (TA:) the صَوْمَعَة of the Christians is thus called because it is slender in the head; (Ṣ, O, Ḳ;) or because contracted; (Mṣb;) or, as Aṣ says, from the epithet أَصْمَعُ, meaning [that it is] pointed at the extremity, [or top,] and contracted: (TA:) and it is also called ↓ صَوْمَعٌ: (Ibn-'Abbád, O, Ḳ:) the pl. is صَوَامِعُ. (Mṣb.) — And *i. q.* مِئْذَنَةٌ [q. v.]. (Lḥ, M and Ḳ and TA in art. اذن.) — And ‡ The *upper,* or *uppermost, part of* [a *mess of*] ثَرِيد [or *crumbled bread moistened with broth*]: (Ḳ, TA:) and the *body thereof:* a ثريدة [or *mess of crumbled bread with broth*] is said to be thus called, when it is *made pointed in its head, and made even.* (TA.) — And ‡ *A* بُرْنُس [or *garment with a pointed hood*]: (Ḳ, TA:) Aboo-'Alee says, (TA,) صَوَامِعُ signifies بَرَانِس; (O, TA;) without mentioning a sing. thereof. (TA.) — And † The *eagle* is thus termed, because always upon the highest place to which it can ascend. (O,* Ḳ,* TA.)

أَصْمَعُ The *small in the ear;* (Ṣ, Mgh, O, Ḳ, TA;) of men and of others: (TA:) [see also 1:] fem. صَمْعَآءُ; (Ṣ, Mgh, O, Ḳ, TA;) applied in this sense to a woman, and to other than woman; (TA;) thus to a she-goat; and such I'Ab held to be allowable as a victim for sacrifice; (O, TA;) or, applied to a she-goat, *whose ear is like that of the gazelle, between such as is termed* سَكَّآء *and such as is termed* أَذْنَآء; or, accord. to Az, applied to a ewe or she-goat, *whose ear is little, and cleaving to the head:* (TA:) [pl. صُمْعٌ.] — Hence, The *ostrich;* because of the smallness of his ear, and its cleaving to his head. (TA.) — And the fem., applied to an ear, *Small,* or *little, and contracted towards the head.* (O, Ḳ.) — Also, the masc., applied to a كَعْب [as meaning a joint of the bones, and particularly an ankle-joint, and an ankle-bone, and also a joint, or knot, of a cane or reed], *Small,* or *slender, and even.* (O, Ḳ.) A woman is said to be صَمْعَآءُ الكَعْبَيْنِ *Small,* or *slender, in the* كَعْبَان [i. e. *ankle-joints* or *ankle-bones*]. (TA.) And dogs are said to be صُمْعُ الكُعُوبِ i. e. *Small in the* كعوب [app. meaning *joints of the legs,* i. e. *tarsal and other joints*]: (Ṣ, Ḳ:) so too the legs of a wild bull, meaning *slender, not swollen,* in the كُعُوب; *even and smooth therein;* thus in the saying of En-Nábighah Edh-Dhubyánee, describing dogs and a [wild] bull:

فَبَثَّهُنَّ عَلَيْهِ وَٱسْتَمَرَّ بِهِ
صُمْعُ الكُعُوبِ بَرِيْآتٌ مِنَ الحَرَدِ

[*And he* (the owner of the dogs) *has dispersed them* (the dogs) *against him; and legs* (قَوَائِمُ being understood) *slender and even and smooth in the joints, free from the disease that would render them unsteady,* (such being here meant by الحَرَد, which is properly in camels,) *have been strong to bear him.*] (L, TA. [See also De Sacy's Chrest. Arabe, sec. ed., ii. 438-9.]) You say also قَنَاةٌ صَمْعَآءُ الكُعُوبِ i. e. [*A spear-shaft*] *even and smooth* [*in the knots,* or *joints*]: or, as some say, *compact in the interior, hard, and slender in the knots.* (TA.) And رُمْحٌ أَصْمَعُ الكَعْبِ i. e. *A spear pointed in the* كعب [app. meaning the *knot that forms its lower extremity*]. (TA.) — أَصْمَعُ applied to a feather means *Slender in the* عَسِيب [or *shaft*]: (O, TA:) العَسِيبُ اللَّطِيفُ in the Ḳ is a mistake for اللَّطِيفُ العَسِيبِ: (TA:) or the *best of feathers;* (Ḳ, TA;) *such as is used for feathering an arrow, of the kind called* ظُهَار [q. v.]: (TA:) pl. صُمْعَانٌ, (O, Ḳ,) which is said to mean the *best* of the feathers of a bird. (O.) — Applied to a plant, it means *Having fruit come forth that has not yet broken open:* (O, Ḳ:) or, as some say, *saturated with moisture, and compact:* and صَمْعَآءُ is said to have this latter meaning applied to a plant such as is termed بَقْلَة: (TA:) and the same, (i. e. the fem.,) applied to the plant called بُهْمَى, *that has risen high,* (Az, Ṣ, O, Ḳ,) *and attained its complete growth,* (Az, O, TA,) *before the bursting open of its pericarps:* (Ṣ, O, Ḳ:) [and so as applied to any plant: (see بُسْرٌ:)] or, applied to a plant, *smooth and round and slender:* (O, Ḳ:) or any calyx (بُرْعُومَة) *that has not yet opened:* (AḤn, O, Ḳ:) and, applied to the plant called بهمى, *of which the calyxes have not opened, and the awn has not yet appeared:* (O:) or, thus applied, *fresh,* or *juicy, and not yet burst open:* or *having its fruit,* or *produce, coming forth upon its upper part:* accord. to IAar, thus applied, it is an intensive epithet, [app. meaning *full-grown and flourishing,*] like جَعْدٌ applied to the صِلِّيَان, and أَسْحَمُ applied to the نَصِىّ: (TA:) the pl. is صُمْعٌ. (O, Ḳ.) — أَصْمَعُ القَلْبِ means *Vigilant, and sharp,* or *acute, in mind:* (Ṣ, O, Ḳ:) and قَلْبٌ أَصْمَعُ *an intelligent and acute mind:* (TA:) and الأَصْمَعَانِ *the sharp,* or *acute,* (Ṣ, O, Ḳ,) *and vigilant* (Ḳ) *mind,* (Ṣ, O, Ḳ,) *and the resolute,* (عَازِم, Ṣ, and so in the L,) or *prudent,* or *discreet,* or *intelligent,* or *firm and sound,* (حَازِم, O, Ḳ,) *judgment,* or *opinion:* (Ṣ, O, Ḳ:) accord. to Aṣ, أَصْمَعُ applied to the mind (فُؤَاد), and to judgment, or opinion, means عَازِمٌ [expl. above]: and رَجُلٌ أَصْمَعُ القَلْبِ means *a man of acute intelligence.* (TA.) [See also صَمِعٌ.] And one says also عَزْمَةٌ صَمْعَآءُ i. e. *An effective resolution,* or *determination.* (TA.) — [It is said that] أَصْمَعُ signifies also A *sharp* sword: (O, Ḳ:) this and the next two significations are related as on the authority of El-Muarrij; but Az says that all that has been related as from him is of the things that are not to be regarded unless the transmission from him prove to be correct. (TA.) — And One *that ascends,* or *rises by degrees, to the most elevated of places.* (O, Ḳ.) — And *i. q.* سَادِرٌ [which means *In a state of confusion* or *perplexity, and unable to see his right course:* &c.: see this latter word]. (O, Ḳ.) — And الصَّمْعَآءُ also signifies *The* سَالِفَة [meaning the *side of the upper part of the neck*], (O, Ḳ,) *and the place of the ear:* (O:) this is said to be its meaning as used in a verse of Abu-n-Nejm, (O, TA,) describing a male ostrich. (TA.)

ثَرِيدَةٌ مُصَمَّعَةٌ: see what here follows.

ثَرِيدَةٌ مُصَوْمَعَةٌ (Ḳ) and ↓ مُصَمَّعَةٌ (Ṣ, O, Ḳ) [*A mess of crumbled bread with broth*] *made slender in the head,* (Ṣ, O, Ḳ,) *and pointed therein.* (Ṣ, O.)

صمغ

2. صَمَّغَهُ, inf. n. تَصْمِيغٌ, *He put* صَمْغ [i. e.

gum] into it; (O, Ḳ;) meaning, into ink. (O.) — And صَمَّغَ بِالصَّمْغِ, inf. n. as above, *He compacted the hair of his head* [with gum]. (Mṣb.)

4. اصمغت الشَّجَرَةُ *The tree produced* صَمْغ [i. e. *gum*]. (Ibn-'Abbád, O, Mṣb, Ḳ.) — Hence one says, يُصْمِغُ فُوهُ *His mouth is discharging like a tree producing gum,* and in like manner أُذُنَاهُ *his two ears,* and عَيْنَاهُ *his two eyes,* and أَنْفُهُ *his nose.* (Ibn-'Abbád, O, Ḳ.) And اصمغ شِدْقُهُ *The side of his mouth produced much spittle.* (O, Ḳ.) And اصمغ الرَّجُلُ *The man had foam coming forth upon the sides of his mouth.* (Ḥar p. 618.) And اصمغت الشَّاةُ is said of the sheep or goat when her biestings are fresh (كَانَ لِبَؤُهَا طَرِيًّا, Ibn-'Abbád, O, TA, in the Ḳ لَبَنُهَا, but the former is the right, TA) [i. e. *The sheep,* or *goat, yielded fresh biestings*] on the first occasion of her being milked. (Ibn-'Abbád, O, TA.)

10. استصمغ الصَّابَ *He scarified the species of tree that produces* صاب [q. v.] (Ṣ, O, Ḳ) *in order that its* غِرَآء [meaning *mucilage*] *might issue,* (Ḳ, TA,) i. e. (TA) *in order that a certain bitter substance might issue from it, and concrete like* صَبِر [i. e. *aloes*]: (Ṣ, O, TA:) thus expl. by Abu-l-Ghowth. (Ṣ.) — And استصمغ *He had a* صُمْغَة, i. e. *a small swelling,* or *pustule.* (Ibn-'Abbád, O, Ḳ.)

صَمْغٌ (Ṣ, O, Mṣb, Ḳ) and ▼ صَمَغٌ, (Ḳ,) the latter mentioned by ISd on the authority of AḤn, (TA,) [*Gum;* i. e.] the *fluid that exudes from the trees called* عِضَاه *and the like of these:* (Mṣb:) it is *of many sorts:* (Ṣ, O:) *that which is called* الصَّمْغُ العَرَبِىُّ *is the* صَمْغ *of the* طَلْح, (Ṣ, O, Mṣb,) which is said to be the same [tree] that is called أُمّ غَيْلَانَ: (Mṣb:) or the *mucilage* (غِرَآء) *of the* [*tree called*] قَرَظ [and more commonly سَنْط, i. e. the *mimosa Nilotica,* also called *acacia Nilotica*]; and *this is what is called* الصَّمْغُ العَرَبِىُّ; *not the* صَمْغ *of the* طَلْح; J [and others] having erred [in asserting it to be this]: [but] *every tree also has* صَمْغ: (Ḳ: [this last assertion, however, is questionable; for صمغ seems to signify properly *gum,* or *juice that exudes from certain trees and concretes*:]) the n. un., (Mṣb, TA,) or term applied to *a portion thereof,* (Ṣ, O,) is صَمْغَةٌ (Ṣ, O, Mṣb, TA) and صَمَغَةٌ: (TA:) and the pl. is صُمُوغٌ: (Ṣ, O, Mṣb, Ḳ:) among صُمُوغ [i. e. *sorts of* صَمْغ], the مُقْل [q. v.] is said to be included; but this is not known. (AḤn, TA.) It is said in a prov., تَرَكْتُهُ عَلَى مِثْلِ مَقْرِفِ الصَّمْغَةِ [*I left him in a condition like that of the place where the piece of gum has been pared off*]: this is when one has left a person nothing; for the صمغة is plucked off from its tree until there remains not upon it what would retain one's life: (Ṣ, O:) or, as some relate it, عَلَى مِثْلِ مَقْلَعِ الصَّمْغَةِ [*in a condition like that of the place where the piece of gum has been plucked off*]; (O, and so Meyd;) meaning, without anything remaining to him; because, when the gum is plucked off, there remains not any trace of it. (Meyd.) And in a trad. of El-Ḥajjáj occurs the saying, لَأَقْلَعَنَّكَ قَلْعَ الصَّمْغَةِ [*I will assuredly pluck thee away with the plucking away of the piece of gum*]; meaning I will assuredly extirpate thee. (TA.) [— Also *Resin;* see عِلْك.]

صَمَغٌ: see صَمْغٌ: — and see also الصَّامِغَانِ.

صَمْغٌ: see صَمْغٌ.

صَمْغٌ (AZ, O, Ḳ) and ▼ صِمَغَةٌ, (Ḳ,) or the latter is the n. un. of the former, and in like manner صَمَخ and صَمَخَة, the latter being the n. un., (AZ, O,) or ▼ صَمْغ and صَمْخ, of which ▼ صَمْغَة and صَمْخَة are the ns. un., (Az, on the authority of A'Obeyd, TA,) *A dry substance which is found upon the teats* (AZ, Az, O, Ḳ) *of a she-camel* (AZ, O, Ḳ) or *of a ewe or she-goat,* (Az, TA,) *when she is milked on the occasion of her bringing forth:* (AZ, Az, O:) when that is rent asunder (إِذَا فُطِرَ ذٰلِكَ [in the CḲ قُطِرَ]), the milk is clear and sweet. (AZ, O, Ḳ.)

صُمْغَةٌ *A small swelling,* or *pustule;* syn. قُرْحَةٌ. (Ibn-'Abbád, O, Ḳ.)

صَمْغَةٌ: see صَمْغٌ: — and see also صَمْغَانِ.

صَمَغَةٌ: see صَمْغٌ.

أَبَا صَمْغَانِ لَقِيتُ, (Ibn-'Abbád, O, Ḳ,) and ▼ صِمْغَةَ, (Ḳ,) *I met him whose mouth and ears and eyes and nose were discharging like the tree producing gum.* (Ibn-'Abbád, O, Ḳ.)

الصَّمَاغَانِ: see what next follows, in two places.

الصَّامِغَانِ, (IDrd, Ṣ, O, Ḳ,) like السَّامِغَانِ, [q. v.,] (IDrd, O,) but the former is said by Mṭr to be better known, (Ḥar p. 618,) and ▼ الصِّمَاغَانِ, (AO, O, Ḳ,) and ▼ الصَّمْغَانِ, (Lth, O, Ḳ,) *The two sides of the mouth,* (Ṣ, O, Ḳ,) *where the lips meet* [*and conjoin*], *next the* شِدْقَانِ: (O, Ḳ:) or *the two places where the spittle collects in the two sides of the lip;* (IAạr, O, Ḳ;) called by the vulgar الصَّوَارِين, (O in this art.,) or الصَّوَارِينِ, for الصَّوَارَانِ: (O and TA in art. صور:) or, as some say, [strangely,] *the hinder part of the mouth.* (TA.) It is said in a trad. that the ▼ صِمَاغَانِ are the two places where sit the two angels [that note and record the actions of a man]: a saying enjoining the use of the سِوَاك. (TA.)

لَبَنٌ مُصْمِغٌ [app. *Milk that is gummy;* describing biestings not yet clear]. (TA voce صُغْرُور, q. v.) — And شَاةٌ مُصْمِغَةٌ بِلَبَنِهَا, (O, TA,) in the copies of the Ḳ, erroneously, بِلَبَنِهَا, (TA,) *A ewe, or she-goat, yielding fresh biestings* on the first occasion of her being milked. (O, Ḳ,* TA.)

حِبْرٌ مُصَمَّغٌ *Ink made with* [*the addition of*] صَمْغ [or *gum*]: but [J says] I know not from whom I heard this. (Ṣ.)

صمقر

For words mentioned under this head in the Ḳ, see art. صقر.

صملخ

صُمْلَاخٌ The *interior of the ear-hole.* (Ḳ.) — And The *dirt* (Ṣ, A, Ḳ) *of the ear* (Ṣ) [i. e.] *of the ear-hole;* (A, Ḳ;) and the *scales that come forth therefrom;* (TA;) as also ▼ صُمْلُوخٌ; (Ṣ, Ḳ;) and so سِمْلَاخٌ and سُمْلُوخٌ: (Ḳ and TA in art. سملخ:) pl. صَمَالِيخُ. (TA.)

صُمْلُوخٌ: see above. — Also sing. of صَمَالِيخُ (TA) which signifies The *thin,* or *slender, shoots of the* أُصُول [i. e. *stems,* or *lower parts,*] *of the* نَصِىّ (Ḳ, TA) and *of the* صِلِّيَان: (TA:) or the sing. signifies the أُمْصُوخ *of the* نَصِىّ; which is *a kind of thing that is plucked therefrom, resembling a rod.* (AḤn, TA.)

صُمَالِخٌ *Thick* milk, (Ṣ, Ḳ,) *of a consistency resembling liver, so that it quivers.* (Ṣ.)

صُمَالِخِىٌّ and سُمَالِخِىٌّ signify the same; (ISh, Ḳ;) i. e. Milk *collected in a skin, and buried in a hole dug in the earth, and left until it becomes thick,* or *coagulates:* (ISh, TA:) or food, and milk, *having no taste.* (IAạr, TA.)

صمى

1. صَمَى, (Ḳ,) aor. يَصْمِى, (TḲ,) inf. n. صَمَيَانٌ, *He* (a man, TḲ) *hastened, made haste, sped,* or *went quickly;* (Ḳ, TA;) and *was light, active,* or *agile;* this is said by Aboo-Is-ḥáḳ [i. e. Zj] to be the primary signification; (TA;) as also ▼ اصمى. (Ḳ.) — And صَمَيَانٌ, (Ṣ, M, Ḳ,) likewise an inf. n. of which the verb is صَمَى, aor. as above, said of a man, (TḲ,) signifies [also] The act of *escaping,* or *getting loose* or *at liberty,* syn. تَفَلُّتٌ, (M, and so in some copies of the Ṣ, in other copies of the Ṣ and in the Ḳ تَقَلُّبٌ, [but the latter I regard as a mistake, and so it is said to be in the TḲ,]) and *leaping.* (Ṣ, M, Ḳ.) — صَمَى, aor. as above, (Ṣ, Mṣb, Ḳ,) inf. n. صَمْىٌ, (Mṣb,) said of an animal that is an object of the chase, means *He died* (Ṣ, Mṣb, Ḳ) *in one's sight,* (Ṣ, Mṣb,) or *on the spot.* (Ḳ.) — صَمَاهُ الأَمْرُ, (Lth, Ḳ,) aor. as above, (TA,) *The thing,* or *event, betided him,* or *befell him.* (Lth, Ḳ.) — And مَا صَمَاكَ عَلَيْهِ *What incited, urged, induced,* or *made, thee to do it?* (Ḳ, TA.)

3. صامى مَنِيَّتَهُ *He tasted,* or *experienced, his destiny,* or *death;* as also ▼ اصماها. (M.)

4: see 1, first sentence. — اصمى عَلَى لِجَامِهِ, said of a horse, *He champed his bit,* (Ṣ, M, Ḳ,) *and went away,* or *along.* (Ṣ, M.) — اصمى الصَّيْدَ *He shot the chase,* or *game, in such a manner that it died* (Ṣ, Mgh, Mṣb, Ḳ) *in his sight,* (Ṣ, Mṣb,) *before him,* (Mgh, Mṣb,) *quickly,* (Mgh,) or *on the spot:* (Ḳ:) accord. to Az, *he killed it by means of his dog, in his sight;* but it applies also to the case of killing with an arrow: (Mṣb, TA:) أَنْمَى is said when the chase, or game, goes out of one's sight (Mgh, Mṣb) after having been [seized by the dog or] hit [by the arrow], (Mgh,) and then dies, (Mgh, Mṣb,) so that one knows not whether it died by his dog or his arrow or by some accident. (Mṣb.) It is said in a trad., كُلْ مَا أَصْمَيْتَ وَدَعْ مَا أَنْمَيْتَ [*Eat thou what thou hast pursued*, or *shot, so that it has died in thy sight, and leave what thou hast pursued*, or *shot, in the case of its dying out of thy sight*]. (Ṣ, Mgh, Mṣb.) — And اصمى الرَّمِيَّةَ *He transpierced the animal that he shot at*, or *shot*. (M.) And اصمت القَوْسُ الرَّمِيَّةَ *The bow sent its arrow through the animal shot.* (TA.) — See also 3.

7. انصمى عَلَيْهِ *He darted down*, or *rushed*, (انْصَبَّ, Ṣ, Ḳ, or انْقَضَّ, M, [both meaning the same,]) *upon him*, (Ṣ, M, Ḳ,) and *advanced towards him*, (M,) to which Az adds, *like as the hawk*, or *falcon, darts down* (يَنْصَمِى, i. e. يَنْقَضّ). (TA.)

صَمَيَانٌ [an inf. n. used as] an epithet applied to a man, (Ṣ, M, A, &c.,) *Quick*, or *swift*: (Ḥar p. 93: [see 1, first sentence:]) *courageous*; (Ṣ, M, Ḳ;) *earnest, not making a false show of bravery, in the charge*, or *assault*: (M, Ḳ:) and *strong, and mature in age*: (M, TA:) or the same word, (accord. to the TA,) or ▼ صِمِّيَانٌ, (so in this sense accord. to a copy of the M,) one *who rushes* (يَنْصَمِى) *upon men injuriously*: (M, TA:) accord. to the T, one *who seizes upon men unjustly*: accord. to IAạr, *daring in acts of disobedience*: accord. to Z, applied to a man, it signifies تَمْضَآءٌ عَلَى الأُمُورِ [i. e. one *who executes, performs*, or *accomplishes, affairs with energy*; or *who keeps*, or *applies himself, thereto with much constancy* or *perseverance*: تَمْضَآءٌ being an intensive epithet, like تَلْقَامٌ and تِكْلَامٌ &c.]: (TA:) the pl. of صَمَيَانٌ is صِمْيَانٌ. (Kr, M, TA.)

صِمِّيَانٌ: see the next preceding paragraph.

صن

1. صَنَّ, [aor., accord. to rule, ـِ,] said of flesh-meat, *i. q.* صَلَّ [i. e. *It was*, or *became, stinking*]: either a dial. var. or formed by substitution. (M, TA. [See also the next paragraph.])

4. اصنّ *He, or it*, (a man, Ṣ, or a thing, Mṣb,) *had a foul*, or *fetid, odour, such as is termed* صُنَان: (Ṣ, Mṣb, Ḳ:) so too said of a he-goat, when excited by lust. (TA.) And said of flesh-meat, [like صَنَّ,] *It stank.* (TA.) And اصنّت البَقْلَةُ *The herb*, or *leguminous plant*, when held in the hand, *stank.* (TA.) And اصنّ said of water, *It became altered* [*for the worse*]. (Ḳ.) — Also *He elevated his nose*, (Ṣ, Ḳ,) or *his head*, (ISk, TA,) *from pride.* (ISk, Ṣ, Ḳ.) And hence, (Ṣ,) اصنّت said of a she-camel, *She, having conceived, behaved disdainfully to the stallion.* (Ṣ, Ḳ.) — And *He was*, or *became, angry.* (Ḳ.) — اصنّت said of a she-camel, (ISh, M,) or of a mare, (A'Obeyd, Ḳ,) when near to bringing forth, (A'Obeyd,) *Her young one struggled*, or *was in a state of commotion*, (A'Obeyd, M,) *in the part bordering upon her tail* [so I render فِى صَلَاهَا], (A'Obeyd,) or *its hind leg fell* [or *happened to come*] *into that part*; (M;) or *her young one stuck fast in her belly, and it pushed with its head*, (ISh, Ḳ,) or *with its shank and its nose*, (ISh,) *in the region of her anus.* (ISh, Ḳ.) The epithet applied to her in this case is ▼ مُصِنٌّ: (ISh:) and the pl. is مُصِنَّاتٌ and مَصَانٌّ. (Az, TA.) — اصنّت said of a woman, *She became old, but having in her some remains* [*of vigour*]: and such is termed ▼ مُصِنٌّ and مُصِنَّةٌ. (M.) — اصنّ also signifies *He spoke in a low, faint, gentle, or soft, manner.* (TA.) — And اصنّ عَلَى الأَمْرِ *He persevered*, or *persisted, in the affair.* (Ḳ.)

صَنٌّ, (Ṣ, M, TA,) with fet-ḥ, (Ṣ, TA,) accord. to the Ḳ صِنٌّ, which is wrong, (TA,) [*A kind of basket;*] *a thing like a covered* سَلَّة, *in which bread is put*, (Ṣ, Ḳ, TA,) *and* [*other*] *food*: (TA:) *a large* زَبِيل, *like the* سَلَّة. (M.)

صِنّ The *urine of the* وَبْر [or *hyrax Syriacus*], (Ṣ, M, TA,) in the copies of the Ḳ erroneously said to be of camels: (TA:) it is inspissated for medicines; (M, TA;) and is very fetid. (TA.) صِنُّ الوَبْرِ is also a term applied to *Small, round, flattened cakes*, (أَقْرَاص,) *which are brought from El-Yemen to El-Ḥijáz, found there in caves; having the property of dissolving tumours, applied as a plaster with honey*: mentioned by the ḥakeem Dáwood. (TA.) — Also, (M, TA,) thus, without the art., but written by Az and J with it, i. e. الصِّنُّ, as in the Ḳ, (TA,) *One of the days called* أَيَّامُ العَجُوزِ; (Ṣ, M, Ḳ;) said to be *the first of those days.* (M. [See art. عجز.])

صُنَّةٌ *i. q.* صُنَّةٌ [q. v.] as signifying *A* سُفْرَة, or *a thing like the* سُفْرَة. (M in art. صب.)

صِنَّةٌ: see the next paragraph.

صُنَانٌ *A stink*, or *stench*; (M, Mṣb;) whether of the armpit or otherwise: (Mṣb:) or, (Ṣ, Ḳ,) as also ▼ صِنَّةٌ, (Ḳ,) the *stink*, or *stench, of the armpit*, (Ṣ, Ḳ,) and *of the creases of the body when they are in a corrupt state*: and the former is likewise applied to the *odour* of the he-goat when excited by lust: (TA:) and it signifies also, (TA,) or as some say, (M,) *a sweet odour.* (M, TA.)

صَنَّانٌ *A courageous* man. (Ḳ.)

أَصَنُّ A man *feigning himself unmindful, inadvertent*, or *heedless.* (Ḳ.)

مُصِنٌّ A man *having a foul*, or *fetid, odour, such as is termed* صُنَان; fem. with ة: and likewise applied to a he-goat when excited by lust. (TA.) — And *Elevating the nose*, (Ṣ, M, TA,) or *the head*, (AA, TA,) *from pride*, (AA, Ṣ, M, TA,) or *from anger.* (M.) So in a verse cited in art. حفض. (Ṣ.) — And مُصِنٌّ غَضَبًا *Full of anger.* (Aṣ, Ṣ.) — See also 4, latter part, in two places. — Also *Silent.* (TA.) — And المُصِنُّ signifies *The serpent that, when it bites, kills on the spot*: one says, رَمَاهُ ٱللّٰهُ بِالمُصِنِّ المُسْكِتِ [*May God smite him with the silencing serpent that kills on the spot whomsoever it bites*]. (IKh, TA.)

صنب

صِنَابٌ *A sauce made of mustard* (Ṣ, M, A, Ḳ) *and raisins.* (Ṣ, A, Ḳ.) — And *Long in the back and belly*; as also ▼ صِنَابَةٌ: (IAạr, O, Ḳ:) and so each with س. (IAạr, O.)

صِنَابَةٌ: see what immediately precedes.

صِنَابِىٌّ, applied to a horse (M, A, TA) or similar beast, (M, TA,) or to a hackney, (TA,) and to a camel, (M, TA,) *Of a colour between redness and yellowness*, (M, A, Ḳ, TA,) *with abundance of hair, and of fur*: (TA:) or *of a bay, or dark bay, or brown, colour*; syn. كُمَيْتٌ: (Ṣ, O, Ḳ:) or *of a sorrel colour*; syn. أَشْقَرُ: (Ḳ:) or *of this last colour having some white hairs intermixed therewith*: (Ṣ, O, TA:) so called because his colour resembles the sauce termed صِنَاب: (TA:) صِنَابِىٌّ being a rel. noun from صِنَابٌ. (Ṣ, O, TA.)

مِصْنَبٌ *Addicted to*, or *fond of, eating the sauce termed* صِنَاب. (IAạr, O, Ḳ.)

صنبر

Q. 1. صَنْبَرَتِ النَّخْلَةُ *The palm-tree became solitary, or apart from others*: (M:) or *became slender in its lower part, and bared of the stumps of its branches, and scanty in its fruit.* (M, Ḳ.) And صَنْبَرَ أَسْفَلُ النَّخْلَةِ *The lower part of the palm-tree became slender, and stripped of the external parts* [or *of the stumps of the branches*]. (AO, and Ṣ in art. صبر, and TA.)

صُنْبُرٌ, (Ḳ, TA,) or ▼ صُنْبُورٌ, (O,) [both probably correct,] Anything *slender and weak*, (O, Ḳ, TA,) of animals and of trees [&c.]: (O, TA:) [the reg. pl. of the former is صَنَابِرُ: and hence, app.,] — ▼ صَنَابِرُ signifies *Slender arrows*; (T, M;) accord. to IAạr: [ISd says,] I have not found it save on his authority; and he has not mentioned a sing. thereof: (M:) [but] accord. to the T, they are so called as being likened to the صَنَابِر [a pl. of صُنْبُور] of the palm-tree: (TA:) occurring in this sense in a verse cited voce ذِلَّة. (IAạr, T, M.)

صِنَّبْرٌ, and صِنْبِرٌ, and الصِّنَّبْرُ: see صِنْبِرٌ.

صَنْبَرَةٌ *Ground that has become rough by reason of urine and of dung*, or *compacted dung, of oxen or sheep &c.*, (Ḳ, TA,) *and the like.* (TA.) — بِصَنُوبَرِهِ and أَخَذْتُ الشَّىْءَ بِصَنْبَرَتِهِ and بِصِنْبِرَتِهِ [which last is evidently, I think, a mistranscription for ▼ بِصَنُوبَرِهِ] is a saying mentioned by Ibn-'Abbád as meaning *I took the thing altogether.* (O.)

صِنَّبْرٌ, (Ṣ, in art. صبر, M, O, Ḳ,) originally ▼ صِنْبِرٌ, (O,) *Cold*, as a subst.; (M, O;) as also صِنَّبْرٌ: (O:) or *cold clouds*: (IDrd, O:) or *a cold wind* (M, Ḳ) *with mist* or *clouds*: (M:) occurring in a verse of Ṭarafeh with kesr to the ب: (M:) [see also صُنْبُورٌ:] or صِنَّبِرٌ, occurring in that verse, signifies the *intense cold* of winter; (Ṣ in art. صبر;) as also ▼ صَنَابِرٌ, (Ṣ, Ḳ,) of which the sing. is ▾صُنْبُورٌ. (TA.) On the expression of Ṭarafeh, حِينَ هَاجَ الصِّنَبِرْ, [when the cold wind, with mist, rises,] ending a verse, IJ says that the poet means الصِّنْبْرُ; but requiring to make the ب movent, he transfers to it the final vowel, as in the phrases هٰذَا بَكُرْ and مَرَرْتُ بِبَكِرْ: he should therefore have said الصِّنْبُرُ; but regarding the expression as meaning حِينَ هَيْجِ الصِّنَبْرِ, he makes the ب to be with kesr, as though he transferred to it the kesreh of the ر: this, he adds, is more probable than the opinion that the change is merely one of poetic necessity. (M.) For this last reason, another poet uses the word with teshdeed to the ن and ر, and with kesr to the ب; saying,

* نُطْعِمُ الشَّحْمَ وَالسَّدِيفَ وَنَسْقِى آلْ *

* مَحْضَ فِى الصِّنَّبِرِّ وَالصُّرَّادِ *

[We give to eat fat and the hump of the camel, and we give to drink pure milk, in the time of cold wind and chill mist]. (K.) — Also الصِّنَّبْرُ, (M, K,) or ▾الصِّنَّبِرُ, (as in two copies of the Ṣ in art. صبر,) and صِنَّبْرٌ, [without the article ال, occurring in a verse of which the metre requires it to be thus written, with teshdeed to the ن,] (TA,) One, (Ṣ,) namely, the second, (M, K,) of the days called أَيَّامُ العَجُوزِ: (Ṣ, M, K: [see عَجُوزٌ:]) [or الصِّنَّبْرُ] and الصِّنَّبِرُ may have the same meaning, [or meanings, or may both be applied to the day above mentioned, for the application of صِنَّبْرٌ to that day is certain;] poetic necessity requiring the ب to be movent. (Ṣ.) — صِنَّبْرٌ has also two contr. significations, namely, Hot: and cold: accord. to Th, on the authority of IAạr. (M.) You say غَدَاةٌ صِنَّبْرٌ, (M,) or صِنَّبْرٌ, (K,) and ▾صِنْبِرٌ, (as in a copy of the M,) or صِنَّبِرٌ, (K,) A cold morning: (M, K:) and a hot morning. (K.)

صُنْبُورٌ A solitary palm-tree, apart from others, (AO, Ṣ in art. صبر, and M, A in art. صبر, and K,) the lower part of which becomes slender, (Ṣ and A in art. صبر,) and stripped of the external parts [or the stumps of the branches]: (Ṣ ubi suprà:) and a palm-tree slender in its lower part, and bared of the stumps of its branches, and scanty in its fruit; (M, K;) as also ▾صُنْبُورَةٌ: (M:) and a palm-tree that comes forth from the root, or lower part, of another palm-tree, without being planted: (M:) or a little palm-tree that does not grow from its mother-tree: (Ibn-Sim'án:) and the lowest part of a palm-tree, (AHn, Ibn-Sim'án, M, K,) from which the roots branch off: (AHn, M:) and branches that come forth from the lowest part of a palm-tree: (M, K:) or a branch that comes forth from the trunk of a palm-tree, not from the ground: this is [said to be] the original signification: (T, TA:) or branches that come forth from the trunk of a palm-tree, not having their roots in the ground: such branches weaken the mother-tree, which is cured by pulling them off: the pl. is صَنَابِيرُ (IAạr) and ▾صَنَابِرُ: (T, TA:) and the صَنَابِير are also called رَوَاكِيبُ and عِقَّانٌ. (Ibn-Sim'án.) — Hence, (A,) applied to a man, Solitary; lonely: (IAạr:) or solitary, or lonely, without offspring and without brother: (Ṣ, A:) or solitary, weak, vile, or ignominious, having no family nor offspring nor assistant: (M, K:) or having no offspring, nor kinsfolk or near relations, nor assistant, whether of strangers or relations: and weak: (IAạr:) and mean, or ignoble. (M, K.) See also صِنَّبْرٌ. And A young, or little, (K,) or weak, (TA,) boy, or child. (K, TA.) It was applied as an epithet to Mohammad, by the unbelievers, as also [its dim.] ▾صُنَيْبِيرٌ, (M, TA,) or they called him صُنْبُورٌ, (O,) meaning that he had no offspring nor brother, so that, when he should die, his name would be lost; (M, TA;) likening him to a [solitary] palm-tree, of which the lower part had become slender, and the branches few, and which had become dry; (AO;) or to a branch growing from the trunk of a palm-tree. (TA.) ═ The tube, or pipe, that is in the [kind of leathern vessel, or bag, for water, called] إِدَاوَةٌ, of iron, (Ṣ, M, A, K,) or of lead, (Ṣ, M, K,) or brass, (A,) or of other material, (K,) from which one drinks. (Ṣ, M, A, K.) — The [aperture called] مَثْعَب of a watering-trough or tank [from which the water runs out]: (Ṣ, M, K:) or the hole, or perforation, thereof, from which the water issues when it is washed. (M, K.) — The pipe of copper or brass by which the water runs from one tank to another in a bath. (Mgh.) — And The mouth of a قَنَاة [or water-pipe]. (M, K.) ═ Also A cold wind: and a hot wind. (O, K.) See also صِنَّبْرٌ. — And A calamity, or misfortune. (O, K.)

صُنْبُورَةٌ: see صُنْبُورٌ, first sentence.

صَنَابِرُ: see صُنْبُورٌ: — and صُنْبُورٌ: ═ and صِنَّبْرٌ.

صَنَوْبَرٌ [The pine tree;] a certain kind of tree, (Ṣ in art. صبر, M, Mgh, Mṣb, K,) well known, from which, (Mṣb,) or from the roots of which, (Mgh,) زِفْت [i. e. pitch] is obtained, (Mgh, Mṣb,) green in winter and summer, (M,) the fruit of which is like small لَوْز [i. e. almonds, but this is app. a mistranscription], and the leaves whereof are [of the kind called] هَدَب [q. v.]: (Mgh:) or the fruit [i. e. the cone] (Ṣ, M, K) of that tree, (Ṣ,) [i. e.] of the أَرْز; (M, K;) the trees being called أَرْز: (M:) A'Obeyd says that it signifies the fruit of the أَرْزَة, and that the tree is called صَنَوْبَرَةٌ [which is the n. un.] on account of its fruit. (TA.) ═ See also صِنَّبْرٌ.

صَنَوْبَرَةٌ [n. un. of صَنَوْبَرٌ, q. v. ═ And] The middle of anything. (O.)

[الظِّلُّ الصَّنَوْبَرِىُّ The cone-shaped shade of the earth, on entering which the moon becomes eclipsed.]

صُنَيْبِيرٌ dim. of صُنْبُورٌ, q. v. (M, TA.)

نَخْلَةٌ مُصَنْبِرَةٌ A palm-tree that produces branches from its trunk: such branches spoil it; for they take the nourishment from the mother-tree, and weaken it. (Aboo-Sa'eed, TA.)

صنج

صَنْجٌ [A cymbal;] a thing made of brass, [having its fellow of the same kind,] one of which was struck with the other; (Ṣ, Mgh, Mṣb, K;) of a round form: (Mgh, Mṣb:) such was the instrument of this name known to the Arabs: (Ṣ, Mgh:) its use was disapproved: (Mgh:) pl. صُنُوجٌ: which was also applied by the Arabs to the small round things inserted in the hoop of the tambourine (Mgh, L,* Mṣb) and the like, (L,) of brass, or copper: (Mṣb:) an arabicized word (Ṣ, Mgh, Mṣb) [app. from the Pers. سَنْج or سِنْج]. — Also A certain stringed instrument [of music]; (Ṣ, Mgh, Mṣb, K;) [app. the kind of harp called by the Persians چَنْگ, and by the modern Arabs جُنْك, figured in Note 26 to Ch. iii. of my Translation of the Thousand and One Nights;] an instrument peculiar to the 'Ajam; (Ṣ, Mgh, Mṣb;) but the Arabs sometimes applied the name of صَنْج to this latter instrument: (L:) also an arabicized word when thus applied. (Ṣ, Mgh, Mṣb, K.) — صَنْجُ الجِنِّ signifies صَوْتُهَا [app. meaning The clamour of the Jinn, or Genii; or their raising of their voices in singing]: a phrase used [in this sense] in a verse of El-Kuṭámee. (TA.)

صَنَجَاتٌ: see سَنْجَةُ المِيزَانِ: its pl. is صَنَجٌ (Mgh) [and app. also صِنَجٌ, like سِنَجٌ].

صَنَّاجٌ A player with [or upon] the صَنْج, meaning [the cymbal, and also] the stringed instrument so called: and in like manner ▾صَنَّاجَةٌ: (L:) but this latter has an intensive signification [meaning an excellent player with, or upon, the صنج]: (Ḥar p. 617:) and signifies also a woman having [or playing with] a صَنْج, as in a verse cited voce جَذَا in art. جذو [where it evidently means a female player with cymbals]. (L.)

صَنَّاجَةٌ: see the next preceding paragraph. — صَنَّاجَةُ الجَيْشِ means † The singer of the army: — and also † The well-known بَطَل [or man of courage or valour] (Ḥar p. 617.) — Aạshà-Benee-Keys, (L, K,) also called Aạshà-Bekr, (L,) used to be called صَنَّاجَةُ العَرَبِ because of the excellence of his poetry, (L, K,) or because his poetry was much sung. (Ḥar ubi suprà.)

صند

صِنْدِدٌ: see what follows, in three places.

صِنْدِيدٌ A courageous lord or chief; (Ṣ, L, K;) as also ▾صِنْدِدٌ: (K:) or a great, or big, and courageous, lord or chief: (A:) or a great, or big, and courageous, king: (M:) or the former, (Aṣ, IAạr, L,) or ▾ the latter, (K,) a noble lord or chief: (Aṣ, L, K:) or a liberal, bountiful, munificent, or generous, lord or chief: or a clement, or forbearing, lord or chief: (IAạr, L, K:) a defender of an army: (IAạr, L:) جَمَاعَةُ العَسْكَرِ, by which the pl. الصَّنَادِيدُ is expl. in the K, is a mistake for حُمَاةُ العَسْكَرِ, the words used by IAạr: (TA:) a nobleman: a great man: (L:) or a great chief: (Kf:) one who presides over a people and their affairs of importance and things in general: or a lord, or chief, eminent among his people, possessing the qualities of courage and liberality or *munificence* or *generosity, who overcomes those that act with hostility and opposition towards him:* (MF:) pl. صَنَادِيدُ. (IAạr, A, L.) Accord. to some, the ن is augmentative; and the word is derived from الصَّدُّ, "the act of turning away;" and seems to have been formed to denote an intensive signification. (MF.) Also *Overcoming,* (Ḳ, TA,) and *great.* (TA.) دَآءُ الصَّنَادِيدِ is *The disease called* ذَاتُ الجَنْبِ. (T in art. جنب.) —— Also *A calamity; a misfortune;* or *a great,* or *formidable, event:* (TA:) pl. as above. (Ṣ, M, A, Ḳ.) Hence the saying of El-Ḥasan, نَعُوذُ بِٱللّٰهِ مِنْ صَنَادِيدِ القَدَرِ *We seek protection by God from the calamities,* &c., *of destiny:* (Ṣ, M:*) or *from its great and overpowering afflictions.* (L.) —— Also, (accord. to the TA,) or ↓ صِنْدِدٌ, (accord. to the Ḳ,) *An isolated ledge of a mountain.* (Ḳ, TA.) —— رِيحٌ صِنْدِيدٌ ‡ *Violent wind.* (A, Ḳ.) —— بَرْدٌ صِنْدِيدٌ ‡ *Vehement,* or *intense, cold.* (A, Ḳ.) —— One says, مَرَّتْ عَلَيْنَا صَنَادِيدُ مِنْ بَرْدٍ ‡ *Times of intense cold befell us.* (A.) [See also another ex. voce صَمَّدَانٌ.] —— And حَرٌّ صِنْدِيدٌ ‡ *Vehement,* or *intense, heat.* (A.) One says الصَّنَادِيدِ, يَوْمٌ حَامِي الصِّنْدِيدِ (Th, M, L,) or (A, Ḳ,) *A day of vehement,* or *intense, heat.* (Th, M, A, L, Ḳ.) —— غَيْثٌ صِنْدِيدٌ ‡ *Rain consisting of large drops:* (Ṣ, Ḳ:) or *that falls in large quantity:* pl. غُيُوثٌ صَنَادِيدُ. (A.) And one says, رَمَتِ السَّمَآءُ بِصَنَادِيدِ البَرَدِ ‡ *The sky cast down large hail-stones.* (A.) —— الصَّنَادِيدُ مِنَ السَّحَابِ † *Great clouds:* (M:) or *clouds that pour forth much rain, in large drops.* (L.)

صندق

صُنْدُوقٌ, (Ṣ and Mṣb in art. صدق, and Ḳ in a separate art.,) thus, with ص, accord. to ISk, (Ṣ,) and صَنْدُوقٌ, (Ḳ,) or the latter is vulgar, (Mṣb,) [*A chest, coffer,* or *trunk:* strangely expl. in the TA as meaning *a* جُوَالِق:] and زُنْدُوقٌ and سُنْدُوقٌ are dial. vars. thereof: (Ḳ:) pl. صَنَادِيقُ. (Ṣ, Mṣb, Ḳ.)

صَنَادِيقِيٌّ *A maker of* صَنَادِيق [or *chests, coffers,* or *trunks*]. (TA.)

صندل

Q. 1. صَنْدَلَ, said of a camel, (IAạr, M, O, Ḳ,) and of an ass, (Ḳ,) *He was big in the head,* (IAạr, M, O, Ḳ,) *and hard,* or *strong,* or *hardy, and large.* (Ḳ.)

Q. 2. تَصَنْدَلَ *He exerted himself in amatory conversation* or *dalliance with women.* (Ibn-'Abbád, O, Ḳ.) ═ And *He wore what is termed the* صَنْدَل, *a thing resembling the boot, with nails in the sole.* (Mṣb.)

صَنْدَلٌ, applied to an ass, (T, TA,) or to a camel, (Ṣ, O,) or to both, as also ↓ صُنَادِلٌ, (M, Ḳ,) *Big in the head:* (Ṣ, O:) or *strong in make, big in the head:* (T, TA:) or *large, strong, big in the head:* (M:) or *big in the head, and hard,* or *strong,* or *hardy, and large:* (Ḳ:) or accord. to IDrd, ↓ صُنَادِلٌ, applied to a camel, signifies *hard,* or *strong,* or *hardy:* (O:) the pl. of the former [or of each] is صَنَادِلُ. (Ṣ, O.) ═ Also, i. e. صَنْدَلٌ, *A species of trees,* (Ṣ, O, Mṣb,) or *a kind of wood,* (M, Ḳ,) *well known,* (Mṣb,) *of sweet odour,* (Ṣ, M, O,) *and of several sorts;* (TA;) [i. e. *sandal-wood;*] *the best of which is the red,* or *the white,* (Ḳ, TA,) or *the yellow;* (TA;) *a discutient of tumours, beneficial as a remedy for palpitation and for the headache and for weakness of the hot stomach and for fevers:* (Ḳ, TA:) *the infusion of its sawdust and the continual smelling of it weaken the venereal faculty.* (TA.) ═ It is also a Pers. word (كَلِمَةٌ أَعْجَمِيَّةٌ) [or rather an arabicized word from the Pers. سَنْدَل]) signifying *A thing resembling the boot* (الخُفّ), *in the sole of which are nails:* pl. صَنَادِلُ. (Mṣb.)

صَنْدَلَانِيٌّ i. q. صَيْدَلَانِيٌّ. (O, Ḳ.) See the latter, in art. صدل.

صُنَادِلٌ: see صَنْدَلٌ, above, in two places.

صنر

صِنَارٌ, as some say, or ↓ صِنَّارٌ, (M,) or both, but the former is the more common, (Ḳ,) The *kind of tree called* دُلْب [i. e. the *plane-tree*]: (AḤn, M, Ḳ:) n. un. with ة: (AḤn, M:) a Pers. word, introduced into the Arabic language; (Lth, AḤn, M;) or arabicized, from [the Pers.] چِنَار. (Ḳ.)

صِنَّارٌ, (Ḳ,) or ↓ صِنَّارَةٌ, (Ṣ, O, M,) or the latter is not allowable, (TA,) The *head of a spindle;* (Ṣ, O, Ḳ;) i. e. (Ṣ) the *crooked,* (Ṣ,) or *slender,* (M,) or *slender and crooked,* (TA,) *piece of iron* (Ṣ, M, TA) *that is in the head of the spindle:* (M, TA:) or, accord. to Lth, the latter signifies *a woman's spindle;* and is a foreign word introduced into the Arabic language. (TA.) ═ See also صِنَارٌ.

صَنُّورٌ A *niggardly* man, *of evil disposition:* (T, O, Ḳ:) mentioned by IAạr. (T, O.) [See also صِنَّارَةٌ.]

صَنَارَةٌ: see the next paragraph.

صِنَّارَةٌ: see صِنَّارٌ. —— Also The *handle* of the [kind of shield called] حَجَفَة: (Ṣ, Ḳ:) pl. صَنَانِيرُ. (Ḳ.) —— And The *ear:* (Ṣ, M, Ḳ:) of the dial. of El-Yemen. (Ṣ, M.) ═ Also A man *evil in disposition;* (M, Ḳ;) on the authority of IAạr; (M;) as also ↓ صَنَارَةٌ; (M, Ḳ;) on the authority of Kr: Aboo-'Alee says that the former has this meaning; but it is not of the form of words mentioned in the Book [of Sb], because [it is said that] this form does not occur as an epithet. (M.) And the former, (Ḳ, TA,) accord. to IAạr, (TA,) *Bad in respect of* أَدَب [or *discipline of the mind and manners,* &c.], *even though eminent,* or *celebrated,* or *well known:* (Ḳ, TA:) pl. as above. (TA.)

صنط

صَنَطٌ, thus pronounced by the people of Egypt, (TA,) a dial. var. of سَنَطٌ, q. v. (Ḳ.)

صنع

1. صَنَعَ الشَّىْءَ, aor. ـَ, inf. n. صُنْعٌ and صَنْعٌ, *He made, wrought, manufactured, fabricated,* or *constructed, the thing;* syn. عَمِلَهُ: (Ḳ:) [or *he made it,* &c., *skilfully,* or *well;* for] الصُّنْعُ signifies إِجَادَةُ الفِعْلِ; and every صُنْع is a فِعْل, but every فِعْل is not a صُنْع; and it is not predicated of [irrational] animals [unless tropically, (see أَصْنَعُ,)] nor of inanimate things, like as الفِعْل is. (Er-Rághib, TA.) —— [Hence,] صَنَعَ signifies also † [*He fabricated* speech or a saying or sentence or the like:] *he forged* a word; and poetry, عَلَى فُلَانٍ *in the name of such a one.* (Mz, 8th نوع.) —— And صَنَعَ, inf. n. صُنْعٌ [and صَنْعٌ] and صَنِيعٌ, [with the objective complement understood,] *He worked,* or *wrought; he practised,* or *exercised, an art, a craft,* or *a manufacture.* (MA.) —— And صَنَعَ إِلَيْهِ مَعْرُوفًا, (Ṣ, O, Ḳ,) aor. as above, (Ḳ,) inf. n. صُنْعٌ, with ḍamm, *He did to him a benefit, favour,* or *kind act:* and صَنَعَ بِهِ صَنِيعًا قَبِيحًا *he did to him an evil,* or *a foul, deed:* syn. فَعَلَهُ: (Ṣ, O, Ḳ:) and one says also [in the former of these two senses], اِصْطَنَعَ ↓ عِنْدَهُ صَنِيعَةً; (Ṣ, Mgh, Ḳ;) syn. اِتَّخَذَهَا; (Ḳ;) or أَحْسَنَ إِلَيْهِ. (Mgh.) The saying مَا صَنَعْتَ وَأَبَاكَ means مَعَ أَبِيكَ [i. e. *What didst thou together with thy father?*]. (Ṣ.) The saying of the Prophet, إِذَا لَمْ تَسْتَحْيِ فَٱصْنَعْ مَا شِئْتَ [*If thou be not ashamed, do what thou wilt,*] is said to be an instance of an imperative phrase of which the meaning is predicative; i. e. it is as though he said, he who is not ashamed does what he will: (O, L, TA:*) and other explanations of it are mentioned in the O and L: (TA:) [but] this is held by A'Obeyd to be the right meaning. (L.) In the phrase صُنْعَ ٱللّٰهِ, in the Ḳur [xxvii. 90, which may be rendered *By the doing of God*], صنع is in the accus. case as an inf. n.: but one may read it in the nom. case, meaning ذٰلِكَ to be understood before it. (Zj, O, TA.) One says also, صَنِيعَ ٱللّٰهِ and مَا أَحْسَنَ صُنْعَ ٱللّٰهِ عِنْدَكَ [*How good is the doing of God with thee,* or *at thine abode!*]. (Ḳ.) —— And صَنَعْتُ فَرَسِي, inf. n. صُنْعٌ and صَنْعَةٌ, ‡ *I tended well my horse;* or *took good care of him;* (Ṣ, O, Ḳ, TA;) *supplied him with fodder, and fattened him:* and صَنَعَ جَارِيَتَهُ ‡ *he reared,* or *nourished, his girl,* or *young woman:* (TA:) and صُنِعَتِ الجَارِيَةُ ‡ *the girl,* or *young woman, was treated* [or *nourished*] *well, so that she became fat;* as also ↓ صُنِّعَتْ, inf. n. تَصْنِيعٌ: (Ḳ, TA:) or you say اِصْنَعِ الفَرَسَ, (so accord. to my MS. copy of the Ḳ,) or ↓ أَصْنَعَ الفَرَسَ, (so accord. to other copies of the Ḳ, and in the O, [in the CḲ أَصْنَعَ الفَرَسَ,]) without teshdeed; [which seems to indicate that the right reading is صَنَعَ, agreeably with the reading in my MS. copy of the Ḳ which gives the imperative form; though it is stated in the TA that أَصْنَعَ الفَرَسَ is said by IḲṭṭ to be a dial. var. of صَنَعَهُ;] (O, Ḳ;) and ↓ صَنَّعَ الجَارِيَةَ,

with teshdeed, meaning *he treated* [or *nourished*] *well the girl*, or *young woman, and fattened her*; (O, Ḳ; [in my MS. copy of the Ḳ صَنَّعَ الجَارِيَةَ;]) because the تصنيع of the girl, or young woman, is by means of many things, and by careful tending: (O, Ḳ:) so says Lth: (O:) but Az says that by other, or others, than Lth, it is allowed to say صَنَعَ جَارِيَتَهُ, without teshdeed: and hence the phrase in the Ḳur [xx. 40.], وَلِتُصْنَعَ عَلَى عَيْنِى, (TA,) meaning † [*And this I did*] *that thou mightest be reared and nourished in my sight*; (O, TA;) for which some read وَلْتُصْنَعْ, as an imperative; and some, وَلِتَصْنَعَ, meaning *and that thou mightest work in my sight*, (Ksh, Bḍ,) lest thou shouldst do so contrary to my command. (Bḍ.) You say likewise, of a woman, صَنَعَتْ نَفْسَهَا: see 5. And you say also ↓ اِصْطَنَعْتُهُ, meaning ‡ *I reared him*; and *educated, disciplined*, or *trained, him well*. (Ṣ,* O, Ḳ, TA.) ═ Accord. to IDrst, صَنُعَ, inf. n. صَنَاعَةٌ, signifies *He was*, or *became, skilled*, or *skilful*: but IB says that صَنُعَ has not been heard. (TA.)

2: see 1, latter half, in two places.

3. مُصَانَعَةٌ primarily signifies The *doing to one a thing in order that he may do another thing to the doer of the former thing*. (TA.) — Hence, (TA,) † The *treating with gentleness*, or *blandishment; soothing, coaxing, wheedling*, or *cajoling*; and *endeavouring to conciliate*. (O, Ḳ, TA.) Or this is from the last of the following significations. (TA.) You say صانعهُ † *He treated him with gentleness*, or *blandishment*; &c. (O, TA.) And † *He acted hypocritically with him*. (TA.) And صانعهُ عَنِ الشَّىْءِ † *He strove*, or *endeavoured, to turn him from the thing by deceit*, or *guile*. (TA.) — And hence, (A, TA,) or from the last signification in this paragraph, (TA,) ‡ The act of *bribing*. (Ṣ, O, Mṣb,* Ḳ,* TA.) One says, صانع الوَالِىَ ‡ *He bribed* [*the prefect, ruler, judge*, or *the like*]. (TA.) And صانعهُ بِالمَالِ ‡ *He bribed him with property, wealth*, or *money*. (Mgh, TA.*) And it is said in a prov., مَنْ صَانَعَ بِالمَالِ لَمْ يَحْتَشِمْ مِنْ طَلَبِ الحَاجَةِ ‡ [*He who bribes with property is not ashamed of demanding the thing wanted*]. (Ṣ, O, TA.) — Also ‡ A horse's *not putting forth*, or *giving, the whole of his strength in going; reserving somewhat thereof*: one says, يُصَانِعُكَ بِبَذْلِهِ سَيْرَهُ ‡ [*He keeps back from thee somewhat by the manner in which he exerts his power of going*]. (O, Ḳ, TA.)

4. اصنع *He* (a man, O) *aided*, or *assisted, another*. (O, Ḳ.) And accord. to Ibn-'Abbád, followed in the O and TṢ and Ḳ, one says also, اصنع الأَخْرَقُ, meaning *The unskilful learned, and did soundly, thoroughly, skilfully*, or *well*: but this is a mistake, occasioned by his deeming dubious, or obscure, a passage in the Nawádir of IAạr, where the latter says that اصنع الرَّجُلُ means أَعَانَ الأَخْرَقَ [i. e. *The man aided*, or *assisted, the unskilful*]. (TA.) ═ اصنع الفَرَسُ: see 1, latter half. [Freytag states, as on the authority of the Ḳ, that أَصْنَعَ, said of a horse, signifies "Non omnibus viribus usus cucurrit, sed ita tamen ut eques eo contentus esset" (which is nearly the same as a signification of صَانَعَ likewise mentioned by him): but this is a mistake.]

5. تَصَنُّعٌ signifies The *affecting a goodly way, mode*, or *manner, of acting*, or *conduct*, or *the like*; (Ṣ, O, Ḳ, TA; [السَّمْتُ in the CḲ is a mistranscription for السَّمْت;]) and the *making a show thereof*; (TA;) and the *adorning oneself* (Ḳ, TA) *thereby, while internally unsound in the grounds of pretension to respect*. (TA.) And تصنّعت, said of a woman, means صَنَعَتْ ↓ نَفْسَهَا [*She cultivated and improved her person, so as to render herself comely, by art, and good nurture*]: (Ṣ, O:) or *she adorned*, or *embellished, herself*. (PṢ.)

8: see 1, former half. — Accord. to Er-Rághib, اِصْطِنَاعٌ signifies The *exceeding the usual*, or *ordinary, bounds*, or *degree, in putting* a thing *into a good, sound, right*, or *proper, state*. (TA.) — And hence, he says, the phrase in the Ḳur [xx. 43], وَٱصْطَنَعْتُكَ لِنَفْسِى, which means † *And I have chosen thee* [*for myself*] to establish my evidence and to serve as my spokesman between me and my creatures so that thy doing thus shall be as though I did it: (TA:) or it means *I have reared thee*, (Az, TA,) or *I have chosen thee*, (O, Ḳ, TA,) [*for myself*,] for a special affair which I require thee to accomplish in a sufficient manner, (Az, O, Ḳ, TA,) concerning Pharaoh and his forces. (Az, TA.) See also 1, last sentence but one. — One says also, اصطنع خَاتَمًا *He ordered that a signet-ring should be made for him*. (O, Ḳ.) [See also 10.] — And اصطنعهُ [in which the pronoun seems to refer to رِزْق i. e. sustenance, &c.,] also signifies قَدَّمَهُ [app. meaning *He offered it*]. (TA.) — And اصطنع [alone, for اصطنع مَصْنَعَةً,] ‡ *He made*, or *prepared, a repast, feast*, or *banquet, to which to invite friends*. (O, Ḳ, TA.) And ‡ *He prepared food to be dispensed in the way*, or *cause, of God*. (O and TA, from a trad.; mentioned also in the CḲ, but not in other copies of the Ḳ.)

10. استصنعهُ, accord. to the O, signifies *He asked for it to be made for him*: accord. to the L, استصنع الشَّىْءَ signifies *he invited*, or *he induced*, or *caused* (دَعَا,) [another] *to make the thing*. (TA.) In the saying of Es-Sarakhsee, اِسْتَصْنَعَ عِنْدَ الرَّجُلِ قَلَنْسُوَةً [app. meaning *He asked*, or *desired, the man to make for him a* قلنسوة (q. v.)], عند is redundant. (Mgh.) [See also 8.]

صَنْعٌ: see صَنَعٌ, in two places. ═ Also, and ↓ صُوَنَعٌ, *A certain small creeping thing*, or *insect*, (دُوَيْبَّةٌ,) or *a flying thing* (طَائِرٌ): (Ḳ, TA:) mentioned by Ṣgh: (TA:) also written in the Ḳ (in art. ضتع) ضَتْعٌ and ضُوَتَعٌ: in one case or the other mistranscribed. (TA in art. ضتع.)

صُنْعٌ an inf. n. of صَنَعَ [q. v.] (Ṣ, Ḳ, &c.) — And i. q. رِزْقٌ [*Sustenance*, &c.]. (TA.) ═ See also صَنَعٌ, in two places.

صَنَعٌ *A tailor*: (O, Ḳ:) or one who is *gentle, delicate*, or *skilful*, (رَفِيق, O,) or *thin, fine*, or *delicate*, (رَقِيق, so in the copies of the Ḳ,) or *slender*, or *small*, (دَقِيق, so in the TA,) [of which readings that in the O is app. the right,] *in respect of the hands*. (O, Ḳ.) See also صَنَعٌ, in five places. ═ Also *A* ↓ مَصْنَعَةٌ *of water*; (O, Ḳ, TA;) i. e. *a piece of wood* [app. *a plank or board*] *by means of which water is confined, and retained for a while*: (TA:) pl. أَصْنَاعٌ: (O, Ḳ:) [but this explanation in the TA seems to have been founded upon a statement there made, that Az heard the Arabs call أَحْبَاس of water أَصْنَاع; (see حِبْسٌ, of which احباس is the pl.;) for I do not find ↓ مَصْنَعَةٌ thus expl. in any lexicon except the TA:] and ↓ صَنَّاعَةٌ, with teshdeed, and ↓ صَنَاعٌ, (O, Ḳ,) like سَحَابٌ, (Ḳ,) accord. to Lth, (O,) signify *pieces of wood* [or *planks* or *boards*] *put together in water, to confine the water, and retain it for a while*; (O, Ḳ;) *like the* حِبَاسَة [q. v.]. (O.) — See also مَصْنَعَةٌ, in two senses. — Also *A manufactured thing* (Ḳ, TA) *of any kind*, (TA,) *such as a* سُفْرَة [q. v.], (Ḳ, TA,) &c. (TA.) — And ‡ *A garment*. (Ibn-'Abbád, O, Ḳ, TA.) You say, رَأَيْتُ عَلَيْهِ صِنْعًا جَيِّدًا ‡ [*I saw upon him a goodly garment*]. (Ibn-'Abbád, O, TA.) — And ‡ *A turban*. (IAạr, O, Ḳ, TA.) — And The [*iron instrument with which flesh-meat is roasted, called*] سُفُّود. (O, TṢ, Ḳ.) El-Marrár El-Faḳ'asee says, describing camels,

• وَجَآءَتْ وَرُكْبَانُهَا كَالشُّرُوبِ •
• وَسَائِقُهَا مِثْلُ صِنْعِ الشِّوَآءِ •

[*And they came, their riders being like drinkers*, or *drunkards, and their driver like the* سُفُّود *of roasted flesh-meat*]. (O.) In the L, السود is put in the place of السفود; and after citing the verse above, [and app. reading مِثْلَ, regarding it as relating to the camels,] the author says that the poet means, سُودَ الأَلْوَانِ. (TA.) — And *Roasted flesh-meat* [itself]; syn. شِوَآءٌ. (So in copies of the Ḳ. [SM says that the right reading, as the explanation of الصِّنْع in this instance, is الشَّوَا; and cites IAạr as saying الصِّنْعُ الشَّوَا نَفْسُهُ: but I think that the right reading is indicated by the addition نَفْسُهُ to be الشِّوَآء; and that IAạr gives this signification after mentioning that which here next precedes it.])

رَجُلٌ صَنَعٌ, (Mgh, L, Mṣb,) and رَجُلٌ صَنَعُ اليَدَيْنِ, (Ṣ, Mgh, O, Mṣb, Ḳ,) and صَنَعُ اليَدِ, (Th, TA,) and صِنْعُ ↓ اليَدَيْنِ, (Ṣ, O, Ḳ,) and صِنْعُ ↓ اليَدِ, (TA,) and صُنْعُ ↓ اليَدِ, (IB, TA,) and Sh is related to have said, رَجُلٌ ↓ صُنْعٌ, (TA,) and صَنِيعُ ↓ اليَدَيْنِ, (Ṣ, O, Ḳ,) and صَنِيعُ ↓ اليَدِ, (TA,) and صَنَاعُ ↓ اليَدَيْنِ, (Ḳ,) and صَنَاعُ ↓ اليَدِ, but not صَنَاع alone when applied to a male, (TA,) *A man skilful in the work of the hands* or *hand*: (Ṣ, Mgh, O, Mṣb, Ḳ, TA:) and a company of men you term قَوْمٌ صُنْعَى ↓ الأَيْدِى and ↓ صُنْعَى

صِنْعَى ▼ الأَيْدِى, and صَنَعَى ▼ الأَيْدِى, and الأَيْدِى, (Ḳ,) [all of which are instances of quasi-pl. ns., except, perhaps, the last, which is said in the TA to be a pl. of ▼ صِنع,] and أَصْنَاعُ الأَيْدِى, (Ḳ, [in the CḲ, erroneously, أَصْنَاعِى,]) which is pl. of ▼ صِنْعُ اليَدِ or of ▼ صَنِيعُ اليَدِ, or, accord. to Sb, as IB says, the only pl. of ▼ صِنْعٌ is صِنْعُونَ, and in like manner in the case of ▼ صَنَعٌ you say صَنَعُو اليَدِ, (TA,) and رِجَالٌ صُنُعٌ is mentioned as on the authority of Sb, (Ḳ,) and Sh is related to have said قَوْمٌ صَنْعُونَ, [using the latter word as pl. of ▼ صَنْعٌ,] with the ن quiescent. (TA.) And you say ▼ اِمْرَأَةٌ صَنَاعٌ, (ISk, Mgh, Mṣb, TA,) and ▼ صَنَاعُ اليَدِ, (Ṣ, O, Ḳ,) and ▼ صَنَاعُ اليَدَيْنِ, (IJ, TA,) an instance of an epithet applied to a woman like رَدَاحٌ and حَصَانٌ and ثَقَابٌ, (TA,) the ا of prolongation before the final letter resembling, and rendering needless, the ة in صَنَعَةٌ, (IJ, TA,) which is not allowable, (IJ,* Mgh, Mṣb, TA,*) though an instance of it occurs used on the ground of analogy: (Mgh:) *A woman skilful in the work of the hands* or *hand*; (ISk, Ṣ, O, Ḳ, TA;) *who makes things in a suitable manner; who sews, and cuts out or makes, leathern buckets*; (ISk, TA;) contr. of خَرْقَاءُ; (Mgh, Mṣb;) and ▼ اِمْرَأَةٌ صَنِيعَةٌ signifies the same: (TA:) and اِمْرَأَتَانِ صَنَاعَانِ: and نِسْوَةٌ صُنُعٌ. (Ṣ, O, Ḳ.) Th preferred صَنَعُ اليَدِ as applied to a man; and ▼ صَنَاعُ اليَدِ as applied to a woman. (IB, TA.) Accord. to IDrst, صَنَعٌ is an inf. n. used as an epithet. (TA. [But see 1, last sentence.]) It is said in a prov., لَا تَعْدَمُ صَنَاعٌ ▼ ثَلَّةً [expl. in art. ثل]. (TA.) — [Hence,] one says of a poet, and of any one who is eloquent, رَجُلٌ صَنَعُ اللِّسَانِ ‡ [*A man skilful in the use of the tongue*]: and in like manner, لِسَانٌ صَنَعٌ ‡ [*a skilful tongue*]. (Ḳ, TA.) And اِمْرَأَةٌ صَنَاعُ ▼ اللِّسَانِ † *A woman sharp-tongued*: or *long-tongued*: syn. سَلِيطَةٌ. (TA.)

صُنْعٌ: see صَنِيعٌ, last sentence.

صَنْعَةٌ *Work* or *handiwork, an art, a craft* or *handicraft*, or *a trade*; (KL;) as also ▼ صِنَاعَةٌ: (KL, PṢ:) *any habitual work* or *occupation* of a man; as also حِرْفَةٌ; (Ḳ in art. حرف;) [and so ▼ صِنَاعَةٌ, as is indicated in the Ḳ voce حِرْفَةٌ; whence] one says, صِنَاعَتُهُ رِعَايَةُ الإِبِلِ [*His habitual work* or *occupation*, or *his business*, *is the tending*, or *pasturing*, *of camels*]: (M, and Ḳ in art. رعى:) or صَنْعَةٌ [more particularly] signifies the *work of the* صَانِع; (Ṣ, O, Ḳ;) [*a manufacture*, or *work of art*; and *workmanship*, or the *skill of a worker*, which last meaning is plainly indicated in the O, and by common usage:] and ▼ صِنَاعَةٌ, the حِرْفَة [i. e. *craft*, or *habitual work* or *occupation*,] *of the* صَانِع, (Ṣ, Mgh, O, Mṣb,* Ḳ,) meaning *of him who works with his hand*: (Mgh:) the pl. of ▼ صِنَاعَة is [صَنَائِعُ and] صِنَاعَاتٌ. (KL.) — It is also an inf. n. of 1 as used in the phrase, صَنَعْتُ فَرَسِى [q. v.]. (Ṣ, O, Ḳ, TA.)

أَسْهُمٌ صُنْعَةٌ, with ḍamm, *Arrows that are equal, equable, uniform*, or *even, the work of one man*. (TA.) [Perhaps صُنْعَةٌ is a quasi-pl. n. of صَنِيعٌ applied to an arrow.]

صُنْعَى and صِنْعَى and صَنَعَى and صُنُعَى: see صِنْعٌ.

صَنَاعٌ: see صِنْعٌ: — and see also صَنَعٌ, in eight places.

صُنُوعٌ in a sense in which it is used in a verse of Aboo-Dhu-eyb is a pl. of which ISd says, "I know not any sing. thereof:" accord. to Skr, it means The خُرَز [app. either the *seams* or the *stitch-holes*] of a مَزَادَة or of an إِدَاوَة: or, as some say, *the thongs used in the sewing* thereof: and some say the *making* thereof, so that in this case it is an inf. n. (TA.)

صَنِيعٌ an inf. n. of 1 [q. v.]. (MA.) — And *i. q.* ▼ مَصْنُوعٌ [meaning *Made, wrought, manufactured, fabricated*, or *constructed*: or *made*, &c., *skilfully*, or *well*: see 1, first sentence]. (TA.) — [Hence,] ‡ *Food* (O, Ḳ, TA) *that is made*, or *prepared, and to which people are invited*; (TA;) and ▼ مَصْنَعَةٌ signifies [the same, i. e.] ‡ *a repast, feast*, or *banquet, to which friends are invited*: (O, Ḳ, TA:) one says, كُنْتُ فِى صَنِيعِ فُلَانٍ ‡ *I was at the repast of such a one, made*, or *prepared, by him, to which people were invited*: and ▼ المَصْنَعَة ‡ *the repast to which friends were invited*. (TA.) And (i. e. the former word) ‡ *Food prepared to be dispensed in the way*, or *cause, of God*. (TA.) — Also, applied to a sword, *Polished*, (Ṣ, O, Ḳ, TA,) *and proved by experience*; and so applied to an arrow: (Ḳ, TA:) or, applied to a sword, *frequently renovated by polishing*: (A, TA:) pl. صُنُعٌ. (TA.) — And, applied to a horse, ‡ *Well tended*; (Ṣ, O, Ḳ, TA;) *supplied with fodder, and fattened*. (TA.) And [in like manner it is applied to a human being:] one says, هُوَ صَنِيعِى ‡ *He is the person whom I have reared*; and *whom I have educated, disciplined*, or *trained, well*; (O, Ḳ, TA;) and so ▼ صَنِيعَتِى; (Ṣ,* O, Ḳ, TA;) and هُوَ مُصْطَنَعَةُ ▼ فُلَانٍ ‡ *he is the person whom such a one has reared*; &c. (Z, TA.) — And ‡ *A goodly and clean garment*. (A, L, TA.) — And *A deed*, or *an action*; (Ṣ, O, Ḳ, KL;) and so ▼ صَنِيعَةٌ: (Ḥam p. 198:) one says, صَنَعَ بِهِ صَنِيعًا قَبِيحًا *He did to him an evil*, or *a foul, deed*: (Ṣ, O, Ḳ:) and ▼ سُوْءُ صَنِيعَةٍ means *The evil* [*consequence*] *of a deed*. (Ḥam ubi suprà.) And [particularly] *A good deed, a benefit, favour*, or *kind act*; (O, Ḳ, TA;) and so ▼ صَنِيعَةٌ: (Ṣ,* O, Mṣb, Ḳ:) [see a verse cited voce مَصْنَعٌ:] pl. [of either, of the latter agreeably with rule,] صَنَائِعُ. (O, Ḳ.) — Also *Skilful in work* of the hands or hand: (Ṣ, O, Ḳ, TA:) fem. [in this sense] with ة. (TA.) See صَنَعٌ, in four places. Accord. to IDrst, ▼ صَنِعٌ [likewise] signifies *Skilled*, or *skilful*, as part. n. of صَنَعَ; but IB says that صَنِعَ has not been heard. (TA.)

صِنَاعَةٌ: see صَنْعَةٌ, in four places. The saying of 'Alee, يُؤْخَذُ مِنْ كُلِّ صِنَاعَةٍ صِنَاعَتُهُ, if correctly related, means يُؤْخَذُ مِنْ كُلِّ ذِى صِنَاعَةٍ مَصْنُوعُهُ [*From every one possessing skill in manufacture should be taken*, or *procured, that which he has manufactured*: or perhaps مِنْ is a mistake for عَنْ, and the meaning is, *from every craftsman is to be acquired his craft*]. (Mgh.)

صَنِيعَةٌ: see صَنِيعٌ, latter half, in four places.

صَنَاعِيَةٌ Persons *who tend their camels well, and fatten the young ones thereof, and give not their camels' milk to guests*: occurring in a verse of 'Ámir Ibn-Eṭ-Ṭufeyl. (TA, in this art. and in art. صلمع.)

صَنَائِعِىٌّ: see صَانِعٌ.

صَنَّاعٌ [*An expert* صَانِع i. e. *manufacturer* &c.] (TA. [There mentioned only as a proper name, or surname.])

صَنَّاعَةٌ: see صِنْعٌ, former half.

صَانِعٌ *A handicraftsman; manufacturer*; or *worker*, or *maker, with his hand*; (Ṣ,* Mgh, O,* Mṣb,* Ḳ;) or *one having a* صَنْعَة [i. e. *craft* &c.] *which he exercises*; (TA;) [*an artificer*, or *artisan*;] and ▼ صَنَائِعِىٌّ is [used in the same sense, and particularly as meaning *one who works for hire under a master*; being] a rel. n. from صَنَائِعُ [pl. of صِنَاعَةٌ], like أَنْصَارِىٌّ and أَنْمَاطِىٌّ: (TA:) the pl. of صَانِعٌ is صُنَّاعٌ. (Mṣb, TA.)

صَوْنَعٌ: see صَنَعٌ.

أَصْنَعُ [*More*, or *most, skilled in working with the hands, manufacturing, fabricating*, or *constructing*]. See an ex. voce سَرَقَةٌ, and another voce تَنَوُّطٌ.

مَصْنَعٌ [may be used, agreeably with analogy, as an inf. n.: and as a n. of place, and of time]. A poet says,

• إِنَّ الصَّنِيعَةَ لَا تَكُونُ صَنِيعَةً •
• حَتَّى يُصَابَ بِهَا طَرِيقُ المَصْنَعِ •

[which may be rendered *Verily that which is a good deed* considered abstractedly, or without relation to the manner or object &c., *will not be a good deed* in effect *except*, or *unless, the way of the doing*, or *the way that leads to the place* (here meaning *the object*) *of the doing, be rightly hit upon therewith*]. (O, TA.) — In the following verse of Náfi' Ibn-Laḳeeṭ, (TA in this art. and in art. ويش,) wrongly ascribed by J [in arts. ويش and موط] to Lebeed, (TA in art. ويش,) and ascribed by others to other poets, (TA in art. موط,) it is expl. by IAạr as signifying *A place that is deemed goodly* [in workmanship]; syn. مُسْتَمْلَحٌ [a n. of place, accord. to a general rule, as well as pass. part. n.: or مَصْنَعٌ may be here more literally rendered *a place of skilful workmanship*]: the poet says,

• مُرُطُ القِذَاذِ فَلَيْسَ فِيهِ مَصْنَعٌ •
• لَا الرِّيشُ يَنْفَعُهُ وَلَا التَّعْقِيبُ •

(TA in the present art.) meaning *Having no feathers upon it,* [*and having in it no place exhibiting skilful workmanship, neither the feathers being of use to it*] *nor the binding around with sinews.* (TA in art. ريش.) — See also what here follows.

مَصْنَعَةٌ (Ṣ, Mgh, O, Mṣb, Ḳ) and مَصْنُعَةٌ (Ṣ, O, Ḳ) and ▼ مَصْنَعٌ (O, Mṣb, Ḳ) [*A kind of tank, or reservoir, for rain-water;* i. e.] *a thing like a* حَوْض, (Ṣ, Mgh, O, Ḳ, TA,) or *like a* صِهْرِيج (Mṣb, TA) *and a* بِرْكَة, (Mṣb,) *that is made,* or *constructed,* (Mgh, Mṣb,) *for collecting the water of the rain:* (Ṣ, Mgh, O, Mṣb, Ḳ, TA:) pl. مَصَانِعُ, (O, Mṣb, Ḳ, TA,) a pl. of all the three words above, expl. by Aṣ as meaning *excavations which people make for the rain-water, which they fill therewith, and from which they drink;* and مَصَانِيعُ is another pl. of مَصْنَعَةٌ, the ى being inserted by poetic license; or it may be pl. of ▼ مَصْنُوعٌ or مَصْنُوعَةٌ: and ▼ صِنْعٌ [in like manner] signifies *a* حَوْض or *a thing like a* صِهْرِيج: and صُنُوعٌ is said to be a pl. thereof: (TA:) or صِنْعٌ signifies *a watering-trough, or tank, made for the rain-water, and not cased with baked bricks;* and its pl. is أَصْنَاعٌ. (TA voce بِرْكَةٌ.) See also صِنْعٌ, in two places. — [The pl.] مَصَانِعُ signifies also *Constructions such as* قُصُور [or *pavilions,* &c.], (O, Ḳ,) and *fortresses;* (Ṣ, O, Ḳ;) and ▼ صِنْعٌ also signifies *a fortress:* and the former, *wells* also. (TA.) And *Towns,* or *villages,* are thus called, (O, Ḳ,) by the Arabs, accord. to Aṣ: sing. مَصْنَعَةٌ: (O, TA:) one says, هُوَ مِنْ أَهْلِ المَصَانِعِ, meaning *He is of the people of the towns,* or *villages, and of the cultivated land.* (A, TA.) Also *Places set apart for horses, away from the tents* or *houses:* sing. مَصْنَعَةٌ. (AḤn, TA.) [In Abul. Ann. ii. 42, where it seems to mean "reservoirs for rain-water," Reiske renders it "Hospitia publica."] — See also صَنِيعٌ, in two places.

مَصْنُوعٌ: see صَنِيعٌ, and مَصْنَعَةٌ. — Also † [*Fabricated,* as applied to speech or a saying or sentence: a phrase, or word,] *innovated,* [or *coined,*] *and given by its author as chaste* (فَصِيح) *Arabic;* differing from مُوَلَّدٌ, which is applied to what is not so given: (Mz, 21st نوع:) *forged,* as applied to a word, and poetry. (Id. 8th نوع.)

صَنِيعٌ: see هُوَ مُصْطَنَعَةُ فُلَانٍ.

صنف

2. صَنَّفَهُ, (M, Ḳ,) inf. n. تَصْنِيفٌ, (Ṣ, M, O, Ḳ,) *He assorted it;* i. e. *made it into,* or *disposed it in, sorts,* or *species;* (Ṣ, O, Ḳ;) and *separated,* or *distinguished, its several parts* or *portions* or *constituents, one from another:* (Ṣ, M, O, Ḳ:) التَّصْنِيفُ is *the separating,* or *distinguishing,* of things, *one from another.* (Mṣb.) — And hence, (Z, Mṣb,* TA,) تَصْنِيفُ الكُتُبِ (Z, TA) or الكِتَابِ: (Mṣb:) you say, صَنَّفَ الكِتَابَ, inf. n. as above, *He composed the book.* (MA.) — صَنَّفَتِ العِضَاهُ *The* [*trees called*] عضاه *became green:* (M:) and صَنَّفَ الشَّجَرُ *the trees put forth their leaves:* (O, Ḳ: [and the like is said in the Mṣb:]) AḤn says that this signifies *the trees began to leaf, so that they were of two sorts, one sort that had leaved and one sort that had not leaved;* but this is not a valid saying; and in like manner ▼ تصنّف: (M:) accord. to the A, both signify *the trees became of different sorts;* and in like manner صنّف النَّبَاتُ [*the plants,* or *herbage*]: (TA:) and صنّف الثَّمَرُ, inf. n. as above, signifies *the fruits became so that some of them were ripe exclusively of others, and some of them coloured exclusively of others:* (Mṣb:) and ▼ تصنّف الأَرْطَى, and النَّبْتُ, *the* [*trees called*] ارطى, and *the plants,* or *herbage, broke forth to leaf.* (Ibn-'Abbád, O, Ḳ.) 'Obeyd-Alláh Ibn-Ḳeys-er-Ruḳeiyát says,

سَقْيًا لِحُلْوَانَ ذِى الكُرُومِ وَمَا
صَنَّفَ مِنْ تِينِهِ وَمِنْ عِنَبِهْ

[*May there be a sending down of rain to Ḥulwán, the possessor of vines, and of such as have put forth their leaves, of the fig-trees and the grape-vines thereof*]: (O, Ḳ:) it is said in the Ḳ that the verb in this verse is thus, from صنّف الشَّجَرُ, not from صَنَّفَهُ; and that J has erred in the reading that he has given; for the reading given by J, who ascribes this verse to Ibn-Aḥmar, is صُنِّفَ; but this is the reading of Fr, [as is said in the O,] and both readings are correct; and of the latter, [accord. to which the meaning is, *and of such as have been made to consist of various sorts or species, of the fig-trees and the grape-vines thereof,*] MF says, it is that which the case requires, the commendation being for the abundance and variety of the fruits of the trees, rather than for the trees putting forth their leaves. (TA.)

5: see above, in two places. — One says also, تصنّفت شَفَتُهُ *His lip became chapped.* (Ibn-'Abbád, O, Ḳ.) And تصنّف سَاقُ النَّعَامَةِ *The shank of the ostrich became chapped.* (TA.)

صَنْفٌ: see what next follows.

صِنْفٌ and ▼ صَنْفٌ *A sort,* or *species,* (Lth, Ṣ, M, O, Mṣb, Ḳ,) of a thing, (M, TA,) or of things, (Lth, TA,) as, for instance, of household-goods, or furniture and utensils: (TA:) [a term subordinate to جِنْس:] and *a part,* or *portion,* or *constituent,* of anything: (Lth, Mṣb, TA:) pl. (of the former, Mṣb) أَصْنَافٌ and (of the latter, Mṣb) صُنُوفٌ. (M, O, Mṣb, Ḳ.) — Also the former, *i. q.* صِفَةٌ [meaning *A quality, an attribute, a property;* or *a description,* as meaning the *aggregate of the qualities* or *attributes* or *properties,* of a thing, or the *state, condition,* or *case,* of a thing]. (M, Ḳ.) — See also صَنِفَةٌ.

صَنِفٌ: } see the next paragraph.
صِنْفَةٌ: }

صَنِفَةٌ (Ṣ, M, O, Ḳ) and ▼ صِنْفَةٌ and ▼ صِنْفٌ, (Sh, O, Ḳ,) the first of which is the most chaste, (O, TA,) of a waist-wrapper (إِزَار), (Ṣ, M,) or of a garment, (O, Ḳ,) The طُرَّة thereof, i. e. (Ṣ, O) the *side* thereof *that has no fringe of unwoven threads:* (Ṣ, O, Ḳ:) or (M, Ḳ) its طُرَّة [or *border*] (M) *upon which is the fringe consisting of unwoven threads:* (M, Ḳ:) or *any border,* or *side, thereof:* (Ṣ, M, O, Ḳ:) accord. to IDrd, it is, with the lexicologists, the *side* (حَاشِيَة) of a garment; and with others, the *part in which is the fringe of unwoven threads:* (O:) and the *corner* of a garment: the pl. of صَنِفَةٌ is صَنِفَاتٌ and [coll. gen. n.] ▼ صَنِفٌ. (M.) — صَنِفَاتٌ, as used by a poet describing the سَرَاب [or mirage], means, accord. to Th, ‡ *The sides,* or *borders,* of the سراب; the سراب being likened by him to a [garment such as is called] مُلَاءَة. (M.) — And صَنِفَةٌ signifies also † *A portion of a* قَبِيلَة [or *tribe*]. (Sh, TA.)

عُودٌ صَنْفِىٌّ *A species,* or *sort, of* عُودُ الطِّيبِ [i. e. *aloes-wood*] *not of good quality:* (M:) or *one of the worst kinds of* عُود, (O, Ḳ,) *little differing from* خَشَب [i. e. *wood used in carpentry and the like*]: (O:) or *inferior to the* قَمَارِىّ *and superior to the* قَاقُلِىّ: (Ḳ:) *used for fumigating therewith:* (TA:) so called in relation to a place [the situation of which I am unable to determine with certainty: see, respecting it, note 12 to ch. xx. of my Translation of the Thousand and One Nights]. (Ṣ, O.)

أَصْنَفُ, (O, Ḳ,) or أَصْنَفُ السَّاقَيْنِ, (M,) A male ostrich *having his shanks excoriated:* (M, O, Ḳ:) pl. صُنْفٌ. (Ḳ.)

تَصْنِيفٌ inf. n. of 2 [q. v.]. — [As a subst., *A literary composition;* as also ▼ مُصَنَّفٌ: pl. of the former تَصَانِيفُ; and of the latter مُصَنَّفَاتٌ.]

أَصْنَافٌ مُصَنَّفَةٌ [*Sorts,* or *species, separated,* or *distinguished, one from another; distributed,* or *classified;*] is a phrase similar to أَبْوَابٌ مُبَوَّبَةٌ. (Ṣ in art. بوب.) — See also تَصْنِيفٌ.

مُصَنِّفٌ [*A literary composer; an author* of a book or books]. — شَجَرٌ مُصَنِّفٌ, (Z, O, Ḳ, TA,) [in the CḲ مُصَنَّف, which is wrong, for it is] like مُحَدِّثٌ, (TA,) *Trees among which are two sorts, dry and fresh:* (O, Ḳ:) or, accord. to Z, *trees varying in colours and fruits.* (TA.)

صنم

2. صَنَّمَ, inf. n. تَصْنِيمٌ, *i. q.* صَوَّرَ [*He formed, fashioned, figured, shaped, sculptured,* or *pictured:* app. from the noun here following]. (Ḳ.)

صَنَمٌ [*An idol:* or *an idol of a particular kind:*] *a* وَثَن: (Ṣ:) or *a* وَثَن *that is worshipped:* (Ḳ:) or *a* وَثَن *that is made of stones,* and *of wood;* as is said on the authority of I'Ab: (Mṣb:) or *a thing well known, that is carved of wood,* and *that is made of molten and cast silver* and *copper* or *brass:* (M; and the like is said in the Mṣb on the authority of IF:) or the صنم is *made of metals that melt;* and the وثن is made of stone or of wood: (Mṣb:) or, accord. to Hishám El-Kelbee, the former is *made of wood* or *of gold* or *of silver* or *of other metal;* and the latter, of stones: or, accord. to Ibn-'Arafeh and El-Fihree, the former is *an image;* and the latter is a shapeless thing: or, as some say, the former is *a thing having corporeal form, carved of wood* or *of stone* or *of silver, and worshipped;* and [the latter (in the TA the صنم, but this I suppose to be a mistake for the وثن,)] is a incorporeal form: or the former is *a thing having the form of a human being;* and the latter, a thing having some other form: or the former is *a thing having material substance* or *shape;* and the latter, a thing not having material substance or shape: or the former is *of stones* or *other material;* and the latter, an embodied form: (TA:) or, accord. to IAth, the latter [?] is anything having corporeal form, made of metal or of wood and stones, like the form of a human being, made, and set up, and worshipped; and the former [?] *an incorporeal form:* (TA in art. وثن: [from explanations given above, it seems that the reverse of this is the case:]) and Abu-l-'Abbás states, on the authority of IAar, that ♦ صَنَمَةٌ and نَصَمَةٌ signify *an image* (صُورَةٌ) *that is worshipped;* (TA in the present art.;) each of these two words is thus (بالتَّحْرِيكِ), though it would seem that accord. to the K the latter is نُصْمَةٌ: (TA in art. نصم:) صَنَمٌ (S, K) it is said (S) is an arabicized word, from شَمَن (S, K) [which is Pers., though SM says,] I know not in what language, for in Pers. it is بت [i. e. بُتْ]: (TA:) the pl. is أَصْنَامٌ; (S, M, Msb;) which, as used in the Kur xiv. 38, is said by Er-Rághib to mean *things that divert one from God.* (TA.)

صَنَمَةٌ: see the next preceding paragraph. ═ Also *A calamity;* a dial. var. of صَلَمَةٌ; (K, TA;) which is mentioned by Az, but omitted in the K in art. صلم. (TA.) ═ And The قَصَبَة [or *quill*] of any feather. (K.)

صنو

4. اصنى النَّخْلُ *The palm-trees had pairs,* or *triplets,* or *more, growing together from single roots.* (IKtt, TA.)

صِنْوٌ: } see the next paragraph.
صُنْوٌ:

صِنْوٌ *One of a pair,* (AHn, S, M, K,) or *of three,* (S, M,) or *of more than two,* (K,) or *of more than three,* (M,) or *of five,* or *of six,* (TA,) of palm-trees, (S, M, K,) or of any trees, (AHn, M, K,) or of trees resembling one another, (M,) *growing from one root;* (AHn, S, M, K;) each [or every one] of such being called the صنو of the other [or others growing with it]; (AHn, M;) as also ♦ صُنْوٌ, (M, K,) mentioned by Zj: (M:) two of such are termed صِنْوَانِ (S, K) and صُنْوَانِ and صَنْوَانِ, [which last implies that ♦ صَنْوٌ as well as صُنْوٌ is a dial. var. of صِنْوٌ,] and also صِنْيَانِ and صُنْيَانِ and صَنْيَانِ, [which imply that صِنْىٌ and صُنْىٌ and صَنْىٌ are also dial. vars. of صِنْوٌ and صُنْوٌ and صَنْوٌ;] (K;) and the pl. is صِنْوَانٌ (AZ, S, M) and [of pauc.] أَصْنَآءٌ, (M,) the former pl. differing from the first of the duals mentioned above by being perfectly decl. (AZ, S,* TA.) Hence, in the Kur [xiii. 4], صِنْوَانٌ وَغَيْرُ صِنْوَانٍ, (TA,) i. e. Palm-trees *having one root and* [others] *having distinct roots:* Hafs read صُنْوَان, like قُنْوَان pl. of قِنْوٌ; of the dial. of Temeem. (Bd.) — And hence, (TA,) † *A brother;* but not so called unless coupled with another: (Sh, TA:) or *a brother by the same father:* (Az, TA:) [or *a brother by the same mother;* as is indicated by an explanation of one of the pls in what follows:] or *a brother such as is termed* شَقِيق, (M, K,) which means *by the father and mother:* (TA in art. شق:) and *a son;* (M, K;) because he has branched forth from one stock [with his father]: (TA:) and *a paternal uncle;* (M, K;) but this last meaning is taken from a trad. cited in what follows: (TA:) the fem. is with ة: and the pl. is أَصْنَآءٌ [a pl. of pauc.] and صِنْوَانٌ [as above]. (M, K.) It is said in a trad., عَمُّ الرَّجُلِ صِنْوُ أَبِيهِ ‡ [*The paternal uncle of the man is the* صنو *of his father*]; (T, S;) meaning that the stock of both is one. (T, TA.) [And it is said that] صِنْوَانٌ وَغَيْرُ صِنْوَانٍ, relating to a man's children, means † *Sons of one mother by different fathers, and children of different mothers by one father.* (Har p. 608.) — [Hence the pl.] أَصْنَآءٌ signifies also † *Likes,* or *fellows.* (IAar, TA.) — And رَكِيَّتَانِ صِنْوَانِ ‡ *Two wells near together,* (AZ, S, M, K, TA,) or (so in the TA and in some copies of the K) *that yield water from one spring.* (AZ, S, K, TA.) — صِنْوٌ also signifies *A widened well* (حَفْر) *from which water is not drawn and of the water of which no use is made:* (Ibn-Buzurj, K:) pl. صِنْوَانٌ. (Ibn-Buzurj, TA.) — See also what follows.

صُنَىٌّ *A small* حِسْى [q. v.] *to which no one comes for water,* (S, K,) *and for which no one cares:* dim. of ♦ صِنْوٌ: (S:) or, as some say, (S,) *a cleft in a mountain:* (S, TA:) or *a ravine,* or *gap,* (شِعْبٌ,) *in which water flows, between two mountains.* (TA.)

صنى

صِنْىٌ and صُنْىٌ and صَنْىٌ: see صِنْوٌ, in art. صنو.

صُنَىٌّ: dim. of صِنْوٌ: see art. صنو.

أَخَذَهُ بِصِنَايَتِهِ *He took it* (a thing, S) *wholly:* (Fr, S, M, K:) and so بِسِنَايَتِهِ. (M.)

صه

1. صَهَّ القَوْمَ *He chid the people* or *party* [app. *saying to them* صَهْ: see what next follows]. (TA.)

R. Q. 1. صَهْصَهَ بِهِمْ *He silenced them, saying to them* صَهْ صَهْ: (K, TA:) and they said also صَهْصَيْتُ [for صَهْصَهْتُ], like as they said دَهْدَيْتُ for دَهْدَهْتُ. (TA.)

صَهْ, as also صَهٍ, (S, IAth, K,) and صَهْ, and صَهًا, (TA,) a word used in chiding the person [or persons] to whom it is said, (K, TA,) thus in the M, or rather (TA) it is a verbal noun, (S, IAth, TA,) used in commanding silence, (S, TA,) meaning *Be silent,* (S, IAth, K, TA,) addressed to a single person, and to two persons, and to a pl. number, and to a male, and to a female: (IAth, TA:) and one says also صَهٍ صَهٍ: Mbr says, if you say, صَهٍ يَا رَجُلُ [*Be silent, O man*], it is to distinguish between that which is determinate and that which is indeterminate; صَهٍ being indeterminate: (S, TA:) [i. e.,] as IJ says, the saying صَهٍ, with tenween, is as though you said سُكُوتًا; and when you pronounce it without tenween, it is as though you said السُّكُوتَ: or, as IAth says, when with tenween, it is as though you said, أُسْكُتْ سُكُوتًا; and when without tenween, as though you said, أُسْكُتِ السُّكُوتَ المَعْرُوفَ مِنْكَ. (TA.)

صهب

1. صَهِبَ, (Mgh, L, Msb, TA,) aor. َ, (Msb,) inf. n. صَهَبٌ (Mgh,* L, Msb, TA) [and app. صُهُوبَةٌ also, and perhaps صُهْبَةٌ, q. v.], said of hair, [and of a camel's fur or hair,] *It was,* or *became, such as is termed* أَصْهَبُ, i. e., *of the colour termed* صُهْبَة; (Mgh, L, Msb, TA;) as also ♦ اصهبّ and ♦ اصهابّ. (L, TA.) ═ See also صَاهِبٌ.

4. اصهب *He* (a stallion [meaning a stallion camel]) *had young ones such as are termed* صُهْب [pl. of أَصْهَبُ] *born to him:* (K:) or, accord. to the M and L, *he* (a man) *had children such as are so termed born to him.* (TA.) ═ See also صَاهِبٌ.

9 and 11: see the first paragraph.

صَهَبٌ: see what next follows.

صُهْبَةٌ (S, A, Mgh, Msb, K) and ♦ صُهُوبَةٌ (S, Mgh, Msb, K) and ♦ صَهَبٌ, (A, Mgh, K,) [the last said in the L and Msb and TA to be an inf. n., (see 1,) and so may be each of the others, used as simple substs.,] *Redness,* (T, Mgh, Msb, K,) or [*a redness such as is termed*] شُقْرَة, (S, K,) *in the hair* (T, S, Mgh, Msb, K) *of the head* (T, S, Mgh) and *of the beard, when the exterior is red, with blackness in the interior:* (T, Mgh:) or *a tinge of redness over the hair, the roots being black, so that the hair when anointed appears as though it were black:* (As, TA:) or *redness in blackness:* (A:) or *redness, of the hair, tinged over with blackness:* or, as some say, *redness of the whole of the hair.* (TA.)

صُهُوبَةٌ: see the next preceding paragraph.

صُهَابِىٌّ, applied to a camel, *i. q.* أَصْهَبُ [q. v.]; (S, K;) and its fem., with ة, is syn. with صَهْبَآءُ [fem. of أَصْهَبُ]: or a camel *of which the origin is referred to a certain stallion,* or *a place, named* صُهَاب: (S, K:) or, if not used as a prefixed noun, it means sprung from a stallion named صُهَاب: Tarafeh uses the fem. as a prefixed noun in the phrase صُهَابِيَّةُ العُثْنُونِ [A she-camel *of the colour termed* صُهْبَة *in the long hairs beneath the lower jaw*]: (T, TA:) but Himyán [without using it as a prefixed noun] says,

• يُطِيرُ عَنْهَا الوَبَرَ الصُّهَابِجَا •

[*Making to fly from her,* or *it makes to fly from*

her, the fur of the colour termed [صُهْبَة]; meaning الصُّهَابِىّ; contracting it, and changing the ى into ج: and El-'Ajjáj applies صُهَابِىّ in a similar manner, as an epithet, to a camel's lip. (TA.) — Also *Full*, or *complete, without lack* or *defect.* (Ḳ.) — And applied to camels (نَعَم) as meaning *From which the poor-rate has not been taken;* (Ḳ, TA;) *they being left complete, without lack* or *deficiency.* (TA.) — And, applied to a man, (Ḳ, TA,) *Low, ignoble,* or *mean;* (TA;) *for whom,* or *to whom, there is no* دِيوَان [or *register of the names of pensioners* or *the like*]. (Ḳ, TA.) — And *Hard, strong, vehement,* or *violent.* (A, Ḳ.) Hence, مَوْتٌ صُهَابِىٌّ ‡ *A hard,* or *violent, death;* like مَوْتٌ أَحْمَرُ. (A, TA.)

صَاهِبْ ▼ أَصْهِبْ, (O,) or صَاهِبْ ▼ أَصْهِبْ, (so in a copy of the Ḳ, in the CḲ أَصْهِبْ صاهِبْ,) a call to ewes to be milked: (O, Ḳ:) it [i. e. صاهب] is a name for *Ewes:* (O:) in one copy of the Ḳ, a call to the stallion [meaning the stallion camel] on the occasion of covering. (TA.)

صَيْهَبٌ *A hard place:* (Sh, Ḳ:) pl. صَيَاهِبُ. (Sh, TA.) *Level ground:* (Ḳ:) so some say: (Sh, TA:) pl. as above: (TA:) or صَيَاهِبُ has this meaning. (O.) *Any place,* (Ḳ,) or *any high,* or *rugged,* or *high and rugged, ground,* or *place of a mountain,* (Θ,) *upon which the sun is vehemently hot so that flesh-meat is broiled upon it:* (O, Ḳ:) Lth assigns this meaning to صَيْهَبٌ; but AM says that the right word is صَيْهَدٌ. (TA in art. صهد.) And *A hard rock:* and *stones:* (Ḳ:) [or] by stones are here meant *hard rocks:* (O:) [but] this is a meaning of the pl. صَيَاهِبُ: (O:) (JK.) — *A hard,* or *strong,* camel; fem. with ة: likened to the stones so called. (T, O, TA.) — — And A *tall* man. (Ḳ.) — And A *hot* day: (Ḳ:) or a day *intensely hot:* (O, TA:) and so صَيْهَدٌ. (TA.) — And *Intenseness of heat:* (Ḳ:) so on the authority of IAạr alone; others explaining it as an epithet. (TA.)

أَصْهَبُ, applied to hair, (A, TA,) [and to camel's fur or hair,] and to a man, (Ṣ,) and to a camel, (A,) or to a male [of mankind and of camels], (Mgh, Mṣb,) fem. صَهْبَآءُ: (A, Mgh, Mṣb:) pl. صُهْبٌ: (Ṣ, A, Mṣb, Ḳ:) *Of the colour termed* صُهْبَة [expl. above]: (Ṣ, A, Mgh, Mṣb:) as some say, (TA,) applied to hair, it means *having redness intermixed with its whiteness:* (Ḳ, TA:) accord. to Aṣ, it is *nearly the same as* أَصْبَحُ: (TA:) applied to a camel, *having redness intermixed with his whiteness, the upper part of the fur being red, and the inner parts white:* (Ṣ:) or *not having the inner parts* [*of the fur*] *intensely white, the flanks and sides having somewhat of whiteness;* the اصهب being *less white than what is termed* آدَمُ, *having a dusky hue in the upper parts and a whiteness in the lower parts:* (T, TA:) or *not intensely white:* (Ḳ:) or, accord. to IAạr, *white:* and he says that the صُهْب and أُدْم were called by the Arabs "the Ḳureysh of camels," i. e. the most noble, and the best, as Ḳureysh were considered by them the best of them; also, that صُهْبَة was said to be the most famous and the best of colours, and that a she-camel of that colour was said to be the most swift of all: [see also أَحْمَرُ as applied to a camel:] but accord. to Aṣ, آدَمُ applied to a camel signifies white; and أَصْهَبُ, *white intermixed with redness:* (TA:) [see also صُهَابِىّ:] the dim. is ▼ أُصَيْهِبٌ. (Mṣb.) — صُهْبُ السِّبَالِ [lit. Persons *red,* or *reddish,* &c., *in respect of the mustaches,* &c.,] is a designation of ‡ *enemies;* and is applied to them even if not really صُهْبُ السِّبَالِ: (Aṣ, Ṣ, A,* L, Ḳ:) originally applied to the Greeks (الرُّوم), because redness of the hair was [common] among them, and they were enemies of the Arabs: (Ṣ, L, TA:) applied to others, it designates them as being as great enemies as the Greeks. (TA.) — الأَصْهَبُ is an appellation of *The lion:* (Ḳ:) because of his colour. (TA.) — And [for the same reason] أَصْهَبُ is a designation of The *male ostrich.* (L, TA.) — Hence also (Ṣ, TA) الصَّهْبَآءُ signifies *Wine:* (Ṣ, Ḳ:) or *wine expressed from white grapes:* (Ḳ:) used in this sense as a proper name: (AḤn, Ḳ:) but also used without the article ال; being originally an epithet. (TA.) — يَوْمٌ أَصْهَبُ ‡ *A cold day:* (Ḳ:) or *a day intensely cold.* (A, TA.)

أُصَيْهِبٌ dim. of أَصْهَبُ, q. v. (Mṣb.)

مُصَهَّبٌ ‡ Flesh-meat *mixed with fat.* (A, TA.) — † *What is termed* صَفِيفٌ [here app. meaning *cut into strips* or *slices, and laid upon live coals,* or *upon rocky ground vehemently heated by the sun* (see صَيْهَبٌ)], (O, Ḳ, and so in a copy of the Ṣ, in some copies of the Ḳ غَلِيظٌ, and in one copy ضَعِيفٌ,) of roast flesh-meat. (Ṣ, O, Ḳ.) — And Wild animals (وَحْش) [of various kinds or species] *mixed together.* (O, Ḳ, and in one of my copies of the Ṣ.)

صهر

1. صَهَرَ, (Ṣ, A, Ḳ,) aor. ـَ, inf. n. صَهْرٌ, (Ḳ,) *He melted,* or *liquefied,* a thing, (Ṣ, A, Ḳ,) such as fat, (A, TA,) and the like; (TA;) as also ▼ اصطهر. (Ḳ.) The saying لَأَصْهَرَنَّكَ بِيَمِينٍ مُرَّةٍ app. means † *I will assuredly melt thee* [in the fire of Hell *by* making thee to swear *a bitter oath*]: (Ṣ:) or ‡ *I will assuredly make thee to swear a hard oath.* (A.) One says also, صَهَرْتُ فُلَانًا بِيَمِينٍ كَاذِبَةٍ تُوجِبُ لَهُ النَّارَ † [*I caused such a one to melt, by* making him to swear *a false oath that would procure for him, as a consequence thereof, the fire* of Hell]. (AO.) — Also, inf. n. as above, *He,* or *it, burned: he thoroughly cooked* with fire. (TA.) — ‡ *It* (heat) *affected him severely.* (A.) And صَهَرَتْهُ الشَّمْسُ ‡ *The sun affected him severely by its heat,* (Ṣ,* A, Ḳ,* TA,) *so that it pained his brain.* (TA.) Ibn-Aḥmar says, describing the young one of a قَطَاة, (Ṣ, O,) which was bearing water to it, (O,)

تَرْوِى لَقًى أُلْقِىَ فِى صَفْصَفٍ
تَصْهَرُهُ الشَّمْسُ فَمَا يَنْصَهِرْ ▼

i. e. [*She bearing water to a castaway, cast upon a plain,*] *which the sun was melting,* [or *severely affecting,*] *and* [*which did not melt,* meaning] *which endured the sun's melting it.* (Ṣ,* O. [In both of my copies of the Ṣ, and in the O and TA, the first word is تَرْوِى, as above; not تُرْوِى.]) And you say, صَهَرَ الحَرُّ الحِرْبَآءَ ‡ *The heat made the chameleon's back to glisten.* (TA.) — And صَهَرَ خُبْزَهُ *He seasoned his bread with* صُهَارَة, (AZ, A, TA,) i. e. *melted fat.* (A, TA.) And صَهَرَ رَأْسَهُ *He anointed his head with* صُهَارَة. (A, Ḳ.) And صَهَرَ بَدَنَهُ *He anointed his body with* صُهَارَة [which is like صَهُور]. (L, TA.) — صَهَرَهُ also signifies † *He brought,* or *drew, it* (i. e. a thing, O) *near,* إِلَيْهِ [*to him* or *it*]; and so ▼ اصهره. (O, TA.)

3. صَاهَرَهُمْ, (Ḳ,) inf. n. مُصَاهَرَةٌ; (TA;) and ▼ اصهر بهم, and ▼ إِلَيْهِمْ; and صاهر فيهم; *He became that kind of relation to them termed* صِهْر; (Ḳ;) and so أَصْهَرَ إِلَيْهِمْ: (Mgh in art. ختن:) or صاهر إِلَيْهِمْ *he took to himself a wife from among them;* (Ṣ, A, Mṣb;) and so ▼ اصهر إِلَيْهِمْ: (A:) and ▼ اصهر بهم *he connected himself with them, and became,* or *made himself, an object of inviolable respect, by a covenant of mutual protection,* or *by relationship,* or *consanguinity,* or *by marriage:* (IAạr, Ṣ:) or اصهر بهم *he sought to bring himself near to them by the relationship termed* صِهْر. (T, TA.)

4: see 3, in three places. — One says also, اصهر الجَيْشُ لِلْجَيْشِ ‡ *The army drew near to the* [*other*] *army.* (A, O, Ḳ.) — See also 1, last sentence.

7. انصهر *It* (a thing, Ṣ, Ḳ, such as fat, and the like, TA) *became melted,* or *liquefied.* (Ṣ, Ḳ.) — See also 1.

8. اصطهر: see 1. — Also ‡ *His* (a chameleon's) *back glistened by reason of the heat of the sun;* (A,* Ḳ;) and so ▼ اصهارّ. (Ṣ, Ḳ.) — And *He ate* صُهَارَة. (O, Ḳ.)

11: see the next preceding paragraph.

صَهِيرٌ *Roasted, broiled,* or *fried;* syn. مَشْوِىٌّ. (TA.) — And *Hot;* syn. حَارٌّ. (Kr, Ḳ.)

صِهْرٌ *Relationship; nearness with respect to kindred;* syn. قَرَابَة: (A, Ḳ:) and [*affinity;* or] the *sacred,* or *inviolable, tie* (حُرْمَة) *of relationship consisting in being a father* or *brother* or *other kinsman of a man's wife:* (Mgh, Ḳ:) and ▼ صُهُورَة *the sacred,* or *inviolable, tie* (حُرْمَة) *of relationship by marriage:* (A:) Fr makes the former word of the fem. gender. (Ṣgh, TA.) — And *A relation,* or *kinsman,* or *kinswoman, of a* man's *wife:* (Kh, Ṣ, A, Mṣb:) and *of a* woman's *husband:* (A:) or the *father* or *brother* or *other kinsman of a* woman's *husband;* syn. حَمْوٌ [and حَمٌ &c. (see art. حمو)]: (Kh, Aṣ, ISk, Mṣb:) and the *father* or *brother* or *other kinsman of a* man's *wife:* (Kh, Aṣ, ISk, Ṣ, Mṣb, Ḳ:) so accord. to some of the Arabs: (Kh, Aṣ, Ṣ, Mṣb:) or none says otherwise, accord. to Aṣ, and IAạr says the like: (Mgh:) or *any relation of a man's wife* or *of a woman's husband whom it is unlawful to marry; as the father,* and *brother,* and *son,* and *paternal uncle*, and *maternal uncle*: (Az, Mṣb:) or a man's *relation by marriage*: and *a kinsman of a man's relation by marriage*: (A:) or *a man who has married among a people*: (Lth, Mgh:) and the *husband of a man's daughter*: and the *husband of a man's sister*: (IAạr, Ḳ:) Fr says that, in the Ḳur. xxv. 56, it signifies, *a relation whom it is lawful to marry; as the daughter of a paternal uncle*, and *of a maternal uncle*, and *the like*: and نَسَب in the same, a relation whom it is unlawful to marry: Zj, that the former signifies *a relation whom it is unlawful to marry*: and the latter, such as is not a صِهْر, of those mentioned in the Ḳur [iv. 27], from the words "your mothers are forbidden unto you" to the words "and your combining [as your wives] two sisters:" I'Ab explains نسب and صهر in the former passage of the Ḳur differently from Fr [altogether], and differently in part from Zj; saying that the former applies to the seven relations first mentioned in iv. 27 in the Ḳur, and صهر to the remaining six there mentioned and that mentioned in the next preceding verse; [so that it includes *a man's foster-mother, who has suckled him*; his *foster-sister, who has been suckled with him*; his *wife's mother*; his *step-daughter under his guardianship, born of his wife unto whom he has gone in*; his *son's wife*; his *wife's sister combined with that wife*; and his *father's wife*;] and this, says Az, is correct: (Mgh:) in the Ḳur xxv. 56, it means ذَوَاتُ صِهْرٍ, whether male or female: (Jel:) or ذُو صِهْرٍ: (Bḍ:) pl. أَصْهَارٌ (Ṣ, A, Mṣb, Ḳ, &c.) and صُهَرَآءُ; (Ḳ;) which latter is extr. (TA.) [صِهْرَةٌ, applied to a female, pl. صِهْرَاتٌ, is app. post-classical.] — And ‡ *A grave*, or *sepulchre*: (ISd, Ḳ:) for they used to bury their daughters alive, and say, "We have married them to the grave:" then, in the time of El-Islám, this expression was used, and it was said, نِعْمَ الصِّهْرُ القَبْرُ [*An excellent son-in-law is the grave*]: or it means, correctly, that which supplies the place of the صهر. (ISd.)

صِهْرِىٌّ *i. q.* صِهْرِيجٌ [q. v.]; (Ḳ;) a dial. var. of the latter word; signifying *A thing like a* حَوْض [or *watering-trough*, or *tank*]: (Ṣ:) accord. to Az, *a construction of clay and stones, built between* [and across] *two narrow branches* (مَأْزِمَانِ) *of a small water-course* (شُعْبَة) *of a valley, so that the water is kept back thereby, and they drink from it a long time.* (TA.)

صَهُورٌ *A melter of fat*: and *a roaster, broiler*, or *frier*: pl. صُهُرٌ. (Ḳ.)

صَهِيرٌ [*i. q.* ▼ مَصْهُورٌ as meaning] *Melted*, or *liquefied*. (Ṣ, Ḳ.) [And used also as a subst., in the sense of صُهَارَةٌ.] — Also Bread *seasoned with* صُهَارَة; and so ▼ مَصْهُورٌ. (A, O, TA.)

صُهَارَةٌ *What is melted* (Aṣ, Ḳ, TA) *of fat*, (Aṣ, TA,) and *the like*: (TA:) or (TA, in the Ḳ "and") *any piece of fat*, (Ḳ, TA,) whether *small* or *large*: (TA:) and ‡ *marrow*; syn. نِقْىٌ and مُخٌّ; (Ḳ, TA;) which mean the same. (TA.) One says, مَا بِالْبَعِيرِ صُهَارَةٌ ‡ *There is not in the camel any fatness* (طِرْقٌ); (ISk, Ṣ;) or *any marrow*. (TA.)

صُهُورَةٌ: see صِهْرٌ, first sentence.

صَاهُورٌ *The sheath of the moon.* (Ḳ. [See what is meant thereby voce سَاهُورٌ; of which it is a dial. var. in this sense, and app. in other senses also.])

مِصْهَرٌ *A thing* (A, O, Ḳ, TA) *like a* مِنْبَر [or *pulpit*], *of clay*, (Ḳ, TA,) or *of wood*, (TA,) *for the household utensils of brass* (A, O, Ḳ, TA) *and the like*, (O, Ḳ,) *which are put thereon*: (A, O:) but ISd says that it is not of established authority. (TA.)

مَصْهُورٌ: see صَهِيرٌ, in two places.

صهرج

Q. 1. صَهْرَجُوا صِهْرِيجًا *They plastered a* صِهْرِيج *with* صَارُوج [or *plaster of quick lime*]. (L.)

Q. 2. تَصَهْرَجُوا صِهْرِيًّا [*They made for themselves a* صِهْرِىّ, i. e. *a* صِهْرِيج]. (T and TA in art. صهر.)

صِهْرِيجٌ (Ṣ, A, Mṣb, Ḳ) and صُهْرِيجٌ, but this latter is of weak authority, (Mṣb,) and ▼ صُهَارِجٌ, (Ṣ, Ḳ,) as also صِهْرِىٌّ, by a change of the last letter, (ISd, TA,) *A* حَوْض [i. e. *watering-trough*, or *tank*], (Ḳ,) or *a thing like a* حَوْض, (Ṣ, A,) *in which water collects*; (Ṣ, A, Ḳ;) *a tank*, or *cistern, for rain-water*: (ISd, TA:) arabicized: (Mṣb:) originally Pers.: pl. صَهَارِيجُ. (Ṣ.) [See also صِهْرِىّ, in art. صهر.]

صُهَارِجٌ: see the next preceding paragraph: — and also that here following.

مُصَهْرَجٌ *Made with* صَارُوج, (Ḳ,) i. e. نُورَة [or *plaster of quick lime*]. (TA.) One says بِرْكَةٌ مُصَهْرَجَةٌ [*A tank*, or *the like*,] *made with* صَارُوج. (Ṣ.) And in like manner, حَوْضٌ ▼ صُهَارِجٌ [*A watering-trough*, or *tank*,] *plastered with* صاروج. (L.)

صهصلق

صَهْصَلِقٌ *A vehement* voice. (Ṣ, O, Ḳ.) A rájiz says,

• قَدْ شَيَّبَتْ رَأْسِى بِصَوْتٍ صَهْصَلِقْ •

[*She has rendered my head hoary by a vehement voice*]. (TA.) — And *A clamorous* old woman; (Ṣ, O, Ḳ, TA;) *vehement of voice*; (TA;) and so صَهْصَلَقٌ; (TA;) so too ▼ صَهْصَلِيقٌ. (Aṣ, Ṣ, O, Ḳ.) صَهْصَلِقُ الصَّوْتِ is applied to a man, as meaning *Vehement of voice*: and in like manner to a hawk. (TA.)

صَهْصَلِيقٌ: see the next preceding paragraph.

صهصى

Q. 1. صَهْصَيْتُ for صَهْصَهْتُ: see R. Q. 1 in art. صه.

صهل

1. صَهَلَ, said of a horse, aor. ـِ (Ṣ, O, Mṣb, Ḳ) and ـَ, (Mṣb, Ḳ,) inf. n. صَهِيلٌ, (Ṣ, O, Mṣb, Ḳ,) [and تَصْهَالٌ is an intensive inf. n., (see صَهِيل below,)] *He neighed*; lit. *uttered his voice*; or *voiced*. (Ṣ, O, Ḳ.)

[6. تَصَاهَلَتِ الخَيْلُ *The horses neighed, one to another.* See an ex. in a verse cited voce زُوْدٌ, where تَصَاهَلَ occurs for تَتَصَاهَلُ.]

صَهْلٌ: see the next paragraph, in two places.

صَحَلٌ *A voice with hoarseness, roughness, harshness*, or *gruffness*; [this is app. correct, or nearly so; but what follows I think evidently wrong; and probably taken from a copy of the O, in this instance incorrect;] like ▼ صَهْلٌ: and صَهَلٌ is *syn. with* صَحَلٌ: (Ḳ accord. to the CḲ and TA: [to which is added in the TA, i. e. *hoarseness, roughness, harshness*, or *gruffness, in the voice*:]) or *syn. with* صَحَلٌ: (so in my MS. copy of the Ḳ:) [the explanation given by Ṣgh appears to be correctly as follows:] one says, فِى صَوْتِهِ صَهَلٌ and صَحَلٌ, i. e. [*In his voice is*] *sharpness and hardness*: it is said in a trad. of Umm-Maạbad, فِى صَوْتِهِ صَهَلٌ or صَحَلٌ, accord. to different relations: and A'Obeyd says that الصَّهَلُ is *like* البَحَحُ [i. e. *hoarseness*, &c.], *not intense, but pleasing.* (Thus I find in the O.) [It is said in Ḥar p. 646 that الصحل and ▼ الصهل signify البَلَّهُ القليل: but I think that this has been taken from some commentator who had found الصحل and الصهل erroneously written for الصَّحَلُ and الصَّهَلُ, with ض.]

صُهَالٌ: see the next paragraph.

صَهِيلٌ [an inf. n., see 1,] and ▼ صُهَالٌ (Ṣ, O, Ḳ) and ▼ صَاهِلَةٌ, of which the pl. is صَوَاهِلُ, (O, Ḳ,) and ▼ تَصْهَالٌ, [which last is an intensive inf. n.,] (O,) The *neighing* or *neigh*, lit. the *voicing* or *voice, of the horse*: (Ṣ, O, Ḳ:) similar to نَهِيقٌ and نُهَاقٌ (Ṣ, TA) in relation to the ass. (TA.) أَهْلُ صَهِيلٍ وَأَطِيطٍ means *Possessors of horses and of camels*: (TA in art. اط:) it is said in a trad. of Umm-Zarạ, فَجَعَلَنِى فِى أَهْلِ صَهِيلٍ وَأَطِيطٍ [*And he set me among possessors of horses and of camels*]: (O, TA:) she meant that she was among people of little property, and he transferred her to people of much wealth; for the possessors of horses and of camels are more [rich] than the possessors of sheep or goats. (TA in the present art.)

صَهَّالٌ *Neighing*, lit. *uttering his voice*; [or rather *that neighs much* or *often*;] an epithet applied to a horse; (JḲ, * Ṣ, Mṣb, * Ḳ;) and so ▼ صَاهِلٌ and ▼ ذُو صَاهِلٍ. (JḲ. [But these two I find not elsewhere in this sense.]) — [Hence,] بَنَاتُ صَهَّالٍ *Horses.* (TA in art. بنى. [It should be observed that بَنَات applied to irrational beings is pl. of اِبْنٌ as well as of اِبْنَةٌ.])

صَاهِلٌ and ذُو صَاهِلٍ: see صَهَّالٌ. — صَاهِلٌ applied to a he-camel signifies *That strikes*, or *beats*, (O, Ḳ,) *with his fore leg and his hind leg*, (Ḳ,) *and bites, and does not ever utter a grumbling cry, in consequence of his disdainfulness*, (O, Ḳ,) *but whose inside makes a confused and continued*, or *rumbling, sound*, (Ḳ, TA,) *by reason of his disdainfulness*: (TA:) so expl. by Lth: one says جَمَلٌ صَاهِلٌ and نَاقَةٌ ذَاتُ صَاهِلٍ: (O, TA:) and ذُو صَاهِلٍ (O, Ḳ) and بِهَا صَاهِلٌ: (O, TA:) or ذُو صَاهِلٍ signifies a stallion camel *excited by lust, assaulting* [*the she-camels*], *and causing a sound to be heard from his inside*; as also ذُو شَاهِقٍ. (TA in art. شهق.) And ذُو صَاهِلٍ applied to a man, † *Vehement in springing* or *rushing*, or *in assaulting* or *attacking, and in excitement* or *provocation*: (M, Ḳ, TA:) or a man *whose anger is vehement*; as also ذُو شَاهِقٍ. (TA in art. شهق.)

[صَيْهَلٌ is expl. by Reiske as signifying *Firma ac tenax durities*: so says Freytag: but I find not any authority for this.]

صَاهِلَةٌ: see صَهِيلٌ: and see also ثُغَاءٌ, in art. ثغو. — Its pl., صَوَاهِلُ, is also applied (by the poet Aboo-Zubeyd Eṭ-Ṭá-ee, O, TA) to The *sounds of* مَسَاحٍ [i. e. *iron shovels* or *spades*]. (O, Ḳ.) Also (by the poet Temeem Ibn-Abee-Muḳbil, O, TA) to The *sounds of flies among herbage*; (O, Ḳ;) app. meaning the *humming* or *buzzing*, [*sounds*] *of their flying*. (O, TA.)

تَصْهَالٌ: see صَهِيلٌ.

صهو and صهى

1. صَهَا [or صَهِىَ], aor. يَصْهَى, inf. n. صَهًى, accord. to A'Obeyd; or صَهِىَ accord. to Kh; *It* (a wound) *was*, or *became, moist*: (Ṣ:) or صَهَا or صَهِىَ [as written in different copies of the Ḳ], aor. ـَ; and صَهِىَ; *he had a wound and it became moist*. (Ḳ.) — And the former, *He had much property*. (Az, Ḳ.) — And i. q. أَسَنَّ [*He became advanced in age*, or *full-grown*; &c.]. (TA.)

3. صَاهَاهُ, (Ḳ,) inf. n. مُصَاهَاةٌ, (TA,) as expl. by IAạr, (TA,) *He mounted upon its*, or *his*, صَهْوَة [q. v.]; (Ḳ, TA;) said with reference to a mountain and to an animal. (TA.)

4. اصهى *He had a complaint of the* صَهْوَة [q. v.]; (Ḳ, TA;) said of a horse. (TA.) — اصهى الصَّبِىَّ *He anointed the boy*, or *young male child, with clarified butter, and put him in the sun, in consequence of a disease* (M, Ḳ) *that had befallen him*: (Ḳ:) or *he so anointed him, and put him to sleep in the sun, in consequence of a disease*. (JK.)

صَهًا: see صَهْ, in art. صه.

صَهَاةٌ: see the next following paragraph, last sentence but one.

صَهْوَةٌ The *part of the back*, of a horse, *which is the place of the saddle-cloth*: (Ṣ:) or the *smooth*, or *soft, part* (ما أَسْهَلَ [so in copies of the Ḳ, but the right reading is app. ما أُسْهِلَ, lit. the *part that is found to be smooth*, or *soft*, to sit upon, see an ex. of this verb in the Ḥam p. 675,]) *of the two sides of the* سَرَاة [or *back*] of the horse: (Ḳ:) or the *part, of the back*, of the horse, *whereon the rider sits*: (Ḳ, and EM p. 43: [see an ex. of one of its pls. voce خَفِيفٌ:]) and (Ḳ) the *hinder part of the hump* of the camel; (JK, Ḳ;) also called the رَادِفَة; (JK;) or, as some say, the [*part called*] رَادِفَة, *which one sees above the rump*: (TA:) pl. صَهَوَاتٌ and صِهَآءٌ. (Ḳ.) [Hence, app.,] one says, تَيْسٌ ذُو صَهَوَاتٍ meaning ‡ *A fat he-goat*. (TA.) And صَهَوَاتٌ signifies also The *middle portions of the flesh extending along the two sides of the backbone* of a bird of the species termed قَطًا. (TA.) — Also The *uppermost part* of any mountain, (Ṣ,) and of anything. (Ḥar p. 374.) — And The *exterior uppermost part* of a house, or chamber; the interior uppermost part thereof being called سَمْكٌ. (Ḥam p. 725.) — And *A tower* (JK, Ṣ, Ḳ) *made* (JK, Ṣ) *upon a hill*, (JK, Ṣ, Ḳ,) *on the highest part thereof*: (JK, Ḳ:) pl. صَهَوَاتٌ, (JḲ,) or صُهًى, (Ḳ,) which is extr. [in respect of rule], like شُهًى pl. of شَهْوَةٌ: mentioned by AHei. (TA.) — And The *like of a cave*, or *cavern, in a mountain, in which is water* (Ḳ, TA) *of the rain*: (TA:) pl. صِهَآءٌ, (Ḳ, TA,) with kesr and the long ا: (TA:) or صِهَآءٌ signifies *places in which water falls, upon the heads of mountains, like the* قَلْب [a mistranscription for قَلْت, q. v.]: (JK:) [or,] accord. to AA, *places in which water wells forth*; pl. of صَهْوَةٌ: but in the handwriting of Az, الصُّهَا is expl. as meaning *the places in which water wells forth*; and as pl. of صُهْوَة: in the Mj, صِهَآءٌ is said to be pl. of ▼ صَهَاةٌ and of صَهْوَةٌ also. (TA.) — And *A depressed tract of land to which stray camels betake themselves*: (Ḳ:) or *a depressed place surrounded by mountains*; (JK;) [or] so ▼ صُهَاوِيَةٌ, accord. to Az. (TA.)

صُهَاوِيَةٌ: see what next precedes.

صو

2. صَوَّى صُوًى *He made* صُوًى [i. e. *signs set up for the guidance of travellers*] in the way. (TA. [The verb is originally صَوَّوَ: and صُوًى is pl. of صُوَّةٌ.]) = [See also art. صوى.]

4. اصوى القَوْمُ *The people*, or *party, alighted in what are termed* صُوًى, meaning *elevated* [or *rugged and elevated*] *tracts of land*. (IḲṭṭ, TA.) = [See also art. صوى.]

صَوٌ i. q. فَارِغٌ, (Ḳ,) so in the Tekmileh, (TA,) applied to a thing, meaning *Empty, void*, or *vacant*. (TḲ.)

صَوَّةٌ: see what follows, near the end.

صُوَّةٌ *A sign for the guidance of travellers, consisting of stones*, (AA, Ṣ, IAth, Mṣb,) *set up* (IAth, Mṣb) *in the way* (Mṣb) *in an unknown desert*: (IAth:) or *a stone that is a sign* [*for guidance*] *in the way*: (M, Ḳ:) or *an elevated sign of the way, set up in rugged ground*: (M:) pl. صُوًى (AA, Ṣ, M, IAth, Mṣb) and pl. pl. أَصْوَآءٌ, (M, Mṣb, Ḳ,) the latter like أَرْطَابٌ pl. of رُطَبٌ, (Mṣb, TA,) or, as some say, this is a pl., not a pl. pl. (TA.) It is said in a trad., إِنَّ لِلْإِسْلَامِ صُوًى وَمَنَارًا كَمَنَارِ الطَّرِيقِ † [*Verily El-Islám has signs and marks of guidance like those of the way*]. (Ṣ.) — Hence [the pl.] أَصْوَآءٌ is applied to signify *Graves*: (Ṣ:) occurring in a trad. in this sense. (TA.) — And the sing., (Ṣ, Ḳ,) accord. to Aṣ, (Ṣ,) signifies *Rugged and elevated ground*, (Ṣ, Ḳ,) *but inferior to a mountain*: (Ṣ:) or *an elevated and a rugged spot, upon which, sometimes, stones are set up in order that one may be directed thereby to the right way*; like تُوَّةٌ. (M in art. تو.) — And *A place of varying*, or *of coming and going*, (مُخْتَلَف) *of the wind*: (Ṣ, Ḳ:) a poet says, (namely, Imra-el-Ḳeys, TA,)

* وَهَبَّتْ لَهُ رِيحٌ بِمُخْتَلَفِ الصُّوَى *

[meaning, if the explanation be correct, and the citation appropriate, *And a wind blew them* (referring to the word جَمْر, i. e. live coals, in a verse immediately preceding) *in the place of varying of the places of varying of the wind*]: (Ṣ:) but Aboo-Zekereeyà, in the margin of his book [or his copy of the Ṣ], throws doubt upon the word meaning "wind" [in this explanation]. (TA. [See De Slane's "Diwan d' Amro'lkais," p. 20 of the Arabic text and p. 34 of his translation.]) = Also *An assemblage of beasts*, or *birds, of prey*: (M, Ḳ:) on the authority of Kr. (M.) = And The *sound of the echo*: (Ḳ:) mentioned by Az; but written by him with fet-ḥ [i. e. ▼ صَوَّةٌ]. (TA.) = أَخَذَهُ بِصُوَائِهِ, expl. in the Ḳ as meaning *He took it in its fresh state* (بِطَرَاءَتِهِ [in the CḲ erroneously بِأَطْرَافِهِ]), is a mistranscription; correctly, بِصَرَاهُ, with fet-ḥ to the ص, and with ر, as written by Az. (TA. [صَرًا and صَرَاوَةٌ, both omitted in the Ḳ, are expl. in their proper place in the TA as syn. with جِدَّةٌ and غَضَاضَةٌ.])

صوب

1. صَابَ, (Ṣ, M, A,) [aor. يَصُوبُ,] inf. n. صَوْبٌ (Ṣ, M, A, Ḳ) and مَصَابٌ, (Ḥar p. 240,) said of rain, (Ṣ, M, A,*) *It poured forth*; (M, A, Ḳ;) as also ▼ انصاب: (M, Ḳ:) or *it descended*; and ▼ تصوّب signifies the like. (Ṣ.) A poet says,

* فَسَقَى دِيَارَكَ غَيْرَ مُفْسِدِهَا *
* صَوْبُ الرَّبِيعِ وَدِيمَةٌ تَهْمِى *

which may mean, [*And may*] *the descending of* the rain called *the* ربيع [*and continuous rain*, or *continuous and still rain, pouring forth, water thy districts, not injuring them*]: or it may mean, [*may*] *the rain of* the season called *the* ربيع [&c.]: so says IHsh. (MF, TA.) And one says of a calamity (شِدَّة), on the occasion of its befalling, صَابَتْ بِقُرٍّ, meaning *It became* [or *fell*] *in its* قرار [or *settled* or *fixed place*, or *in the place where it should remain*]. (Ṣ, TA. [See also art. قر.]) — And صاب, aor. as above, (M, TA,) inf. n. صَوْبٌ, (Ḳ, TA,) *It*, or *he, came from a high place*; (Ḳ, TA;) *descended from above*; (M, TA;) as also ▼ تصوّب: (Ḳ, TA:) and (TA) *it*, or *he, descended*; *went down, downwards, down a declivity*, or *from a higher to a lower place* or *position*; or *it sloped down;* syn. اِنْحَدَرَ; and so ▼ تصوّب. (M, TA. [See also 4, first sentence; and see 2, last sentence.]) — [Hence, app.,] صَابُوا بِهِمْ *They fell upon them,* or *assaulted them:* and agreeably with this meaning is expl. the saying of the Hudhalee,

* صَابُوا بِسِتَّةِ أَبْيَاتٍ وَأَرْبَعَةٍ
* حَتَّى كَأَنَّ عَلَيْهِمْ جَابِئًا لُبَدَا

meaning [*They fell upon,* or *assaulted, six tents,* or *dwellings, and four; so that it was as though there were upon them*] *numerous locusts.* (TA.) = صَوْبٌ [app. meaning صَوْبُ مَطَرٍ] signifies also The sky's *bringing rain.* (A, K.) — And The *pouring forth* (A, K, TA) of water [&c.]. (TA.) One says, صاب المَآءَ *He poured forth the water;* as also ▼ صوّبهُ. (M, TA.) = صاب as syn. with أَصَابَ: see the latter in eight places.

2: see above, last sentence but one. — [Hence, app.,] صَوَّبْتُ الفَرَسَ † *I sent forth,* or *started,* or *let go, the horse in running.* (Ṣ, TA.) — And تَصْوِيبٌ is the *contr. of* تَصْعِيدٌ [generally in a trans. sense (though also in an intrans. sense as will be seen below); i. e. it signifies The *making to descend*]. (M, TA.) One says, صوّب رَأْسَهُ *He lowered,* or *depressed, his head.* (Ṣ, A, Mgh, Mṣb, K.) And صَوَّبَ ٱللّٰهُ رَأْسَهُ ‡ [*May God degrade him;* lit.] *may God lower,* or *depress, his head.* (TA.) It is said in a trad., مَنْ قَطَعَ سِدْرَةً صَوَّبَ ٱللّٰهُ رَأْسَهُ فِى النَّارِ, which, accord. to Aboo-Dáwood Es-Sijistánee, is abridged, and means, *Whoso cuts down,* or *lops, a* سدرة [which is a species of lote-tree], in a desert, by the shade whereof the traveller shelters himself, without just cause, *God will,* or *may God, lower his head* [*in the fire* of Hell]. (L, TA.) And one says, صوّب يَدَهُ *He lowered,* or *depressed, his hand,* or *arm.* (L, TA.) And صوّب الإِنَآءَ *He inclined the vessel* (Mgh, Mṣb) *downwards, in order that what was in it might run* [*out*]: (Mgh:) or *he lowered,* or *depressed, the vessel;* and in like manner, رَأْسَ الخَشَبَةِ [*the head of the piece of wood*]. (T, TA.) = And صوّب إِلَيْهِ بَصَرَهُ [*He directed his sight towards him*]. (Mṣb in art. لمح.) [From الصَّوَابُ.] And صَعَّدَ فِى النَّظَرِ وَصَوَّبَهُ: see art. صعد. — And صَوَّبْتُ قَوْلَهُ † *I said that his saying was* صَوَاب [i. e. *right;* or *I pronounced his saying to be right*]. (Mṣb.) And صوّب رَأْيَهُ ‡ [*He pronounced his opinion to be right*]. (A.) And صوّبهُ † *He said to him* أَصَبْتَ [*Thou hast hit the right thing;* or *said,* or *done, right*]. (Ṣ, K.) You say, إِنْ أَخْطَأْتُ فَخَطِّئْنِى وَإِنْ أَصَبْتُ فَصَوِّبْنِى ‡ [*If I do,* or *say, wrong, tell me that I have done so; and if I do,* or *say, right, tell me that I have done so*]. (A, TA.) = [تَصْوِيبٌ is also the *contr. of* تَصْعِيدٌ in an intrans. sense as well as in the trans. sense mentioned above:] one says, طَالَ فِى الأَرْضِ تَصْوِيبِى وَتَصْعِيدِى [*Long have continued my descending,* or *going down, and my ascending,* or *going up, in the land*]. (A in art. صعد.)

4. اصاب, (M, TA,) inf. n. إِصَابَةٌ, (M, K, TA,) *He descended,* or *went down, into a lower land,* or *country; contr. of* أَصْعَدَ. (M, K,* TA. [See also 1 as syn. with 5; and see 2, last sentence.]) = اصاب القِرْطَاسَ, [inf. n. as above,] said of an arrow, [*It hit,* or *struck, the butt,* or *target;* or *went right thereto;*] (Ṣ, TA;) and ▼ صَابَهُ, (Ṣ, TA,) or صاب الهَدَفَ, (M,) aor. يَصِيبُهُ, (Ṣ, M,) inf. n. صَيْبٌ, (Ṣ, TA,) likewise said of an arrow, (Ṣ, M, TA,) signifies the same; (Ṣ, TA;) or صاب said of an arrow is intrans. (M.) And اصاب alone, [as though used elliptically,] (Mṣb, TA,) inf. n. as above; (Mṣb, K;) and ▼ صاب, aor. يَصُوبُ, (Ṣ, Mṣb,) inf. n. صَيْبُوبَةٌ, (Ṣ,) or صَوْبٌ (Mṣb, K;) and ▼ صاب, aor. يَصِيبُ, inf. n. صَيْبٌ; (Mṣb;) likewise said of an arrow, (Ṣ, Mṣb,) *It went right; did not deviate from the right course:* (Ṣ, K,* TA:) or *it reached* [or *hit*] *the object of aim.* (Mṣb.) And ▼ صاب نَحْوَ الرَّمِيَّةِ, (M, A, TA,) aor. يَصُوبُ, (A, TA,) inf. n. صَوْبٌ and صَيْبُوبَةٌ, (M, TA,) said of an arrow, (M, A, TA,) *It went right towards the thing,* or *animal, shot at;* (M, TA;) as also اصاب. (TA.) — Also اصاب فِى القِرْطَاسِ, (Ṣ, TA,) and اصاب القِرْطَاسَ, (TA,) [said of a man, as is indicated by the context in the Ṣ and TA, *He hit the butt,* or *target;*] *he did not miss the butt,* or *target.* (TA.) And اصاب alone is said of an archer or the like [as meaning *He hit the object of his aim*]: (Mṣb:) one says, رَمَى فَأَصَابَ [*He shot,* or *cast, and hit the object of his aim*]. (A.) — [Hence, likening an event, &c., to an arrow,] one says also, اصابهُ أَمْرٌ, inf. n. as above, † [*An event smote him,* or *befell him;*] and ▼ صابهُ, aor. يَصُوبُهُ, inf. n. صَوْبٌ, signifies the same. (Mṣb.) And أَصَابَتْهُ مُصِيبَةٌ † [*An affliction,* or *a calamity,* &c., *smote him,* or *befell him*]. (Ṣ.) And اصابهُ الشَّىْءُ † *The thing reached him* [*so as to take effect upon him*]: (Mgh,* Mṣb:) whence the saying, مِنْ قَوْلِ النَّاسِ مَا أَصَابَهُ † [*There reached him* &c., *of the sayings of the people, what reached him* &c.]. (Mṣb.) [Thus tropically used, اصابهُ may generally be rendered *It hit, struck, smote, wounded, hurt, affected, assailed,* or *befell, him.* One says, اصابهُ مَرَضٌ, and وَجَعٌ, and اصابتهُ رِيحٌ, &c., † *A disease,* and *pain,* and *wind,* &c., *smote, affected,* or *assailed, him.*] And ▼ صَابَهُ المَطَرُ, (Ṣ, Mṣb,) aor. يَصُوبُهُ, inf. n. صَوْبٌ, (Mṣb,) † [*The rain fell,* or *lighted, upon him,* or *it; wetted him,* or *it;*] *he,* or *it, was rained upon.* (Ṣ.) And ▼ صَابَتِ السَّمَآءُ الأَرْضَ i. e. † [*The sky,* or *clouds,* or *rain,*] *watered the earth,* or *land, copiously:* (Lth, M, TA:) or it means أَصَابَتْهَا بِصَوْبٍ [*it smote it with rain;* or *sent rain upon it*]. (M, L, TA.) In the following verse, cited by IAar,

* فَكَيْفَ تُرَجِّى العَاذِلَاتُ تَجَلُّدِى
* وَصَبْرِى إِذَا مَا النَّفْسُ صِيبَ ▼ حَمِيمُهَا

he explains صِيبَ as being like قُصِدَ, and says that it may be of the dial. of him who says صَابَ الشَّهْرَ; but [ISd remarks,] I know not how this is, for صَابَ الشَّهْرَ is not trans.; [though, as shown above, he has mentioned it as being trans.;] and in my opinion, [he says,] صيب here is from the phrase صَابَتِ السَّمَآءُ الأَرْضَ [expl. above; the meaning of the verse being, *But how should the censuring women hope for my constraining myself to behave with hardiness, and for my being patient, when the beloved of the soul has been smitten* by death, or by the decree of death; for ISd adds,] كَأَنَّ المَنِيَّةَ صَابَتِ الحَمِيمَ فَأَصَابَتْهُ بِصَوْبِهَا. (M, TA.*) — [اصاب is also used in many phrases in which its agent is likened to an archer.] One says, اصاب الصَّوَابَ ‡ [*He hit the right thing* or *point,* or *the object,* or *aim, of his words* or *of his actions*]: (A:) and اصاب السَّدَادَ [which means the same]. (Ṣ in art. سد.) And اصاب alone [means thus likewise; or] † *he said,* or *did, that which was right.* (M, K.*) And اصاب فِى قَوْلِهِ وَفِعْلِهِ † *He hit the right thing in his saying and his deed;* (Mṣb;) and so فِى رَأْيِهِ *in his opinion; contr. of* أَخْطَأَ. (A.) And اصاب بُغْيَتَهُ † *He attained,* or *obtained, the thing that he sought,* or *wanted:* whence the saying, اصاب مِنْ زَوْجَتِهِ [and so app. أَصَابَهَا (see سَفَقَ)] † *He obtained his desired enjoyment of his wife:* (Mṣb:) اصاب مِنِّى occurs in a trad., [as a euphemism,] said by the wife of Handhaleh, meaning † *He compressed me:* (Mgh:) and it is said in a trad., كَانَ يُصِيبُ مِنْ رَأْسِ بَعْضِ نِسَائِهِ وَهُوَ صَائِمٌ, meaning † *He used to kiss* [*the head of some one or more of his wives when he was fasting*]. (TA: and the like is said in the Mgh.) And اصاب مِنَ المَالِ وَغَيْرِهِ † *He took,* or *took with his hand, of the property and other things.* (TA.) And اصاب الشَّىْءَ ‡ [*He hit upon,* or *lighted on, the thing;*] *he found the thing.* (Ṣ, M, K,* TA.) And اصابهُ [† *He found it, met with it,* or *experienced it;* namely, a good or an evil event. And † *He found it out,* or *discovered it;* namely, an enigma (see 8 in art. حجو) or the like. And] † *He found it to be right:* and † *he saw it, considered it,* or *held it, to be right.* (TA. [See also 10.]) And † *He aimed at it;* (Aṣ, TA;) ‡ *he desired, wished, willed, intended,* or *meant, it.* (Aṣ, M, A, Mṣb, TA.) One says, أَصَابَ فُلَانٌ الصَّوَابَ فَأَخْطَأَ الجَوَابَ † *Such a one aimed at, and desired,* [to say] *that which was right,* (Aṣ, Mṣb,* TA,) *and failed of giving rightly the reply.* (Aṣ, TA.) And أَيْنَ تُصِيبَانِ † [*Whither do ye two desire to go?*]; a saying of Ru-beh. (TA.) تَجْرِى بِأَمْرِهِ رُخَآءً حَيْثُ أَصَابَ, in the Kur [xxxviii. 35, referring to the wind], has been expl. as meaning † [*Running by his command softly,* or *gently,*] *whithersoever He desireth.* (M,* TA.) And اصاب ٱللّٰهُ الَّذِى أَرَادَ, said in a trad., in reply to a question respecting the interpretation of a text, means † *God desireth,* or *meaneth,* [thereby,] *what He desireth,* or *meaneth.* (TA.) And اصاب ٱللّٰهُ بِكَ خَيْرًا means أَرَادَهُ ‡ [i. e. *May God intend thee good*]. (A.) And اصاب alone † *He desired,* or *intended,* or *meant, that which was right.* (M, K.*) One says also, اصابهُ بِخَيْرٍ † [meaning *He did good to him*]. (El-Muarrij, TA in art. اسو.) [But] اصابهُ بِكَذَا, (M,) inf. n. إِصَابَةٌ, (K,) with which are syn. ▼ مُصَابٌ [in accordance with a usage generally allowable] (Ṣ, TA) and ↑ مُصَابَةٌ, (Ḳ, TA,) † [generally] means *He afflicted him with, or by, such a thing; or gave pain to him thereby.* (M, Ḳ:* in the latter, only the inf. n. of the verb in this sense; and so in other senses.) [Thus one says, اصابهُ بِشَرٍّ † *He afflicted him with evil; or did evil to him:* and اصابهُ بِمَكْرُوهٍ † *He afflicted him with, or did to him, an abominable, or an evil, thing or action:* and اصابهُ بِقَوْلٍ قَبِيحٍ † *He afflicted him with, or said to him, a foul saying:* and اصابهُ بِذَحْلٍ † *He punished him by blood-revenge:* and اصابهُ بِمَرَضٍ † *He,* (i. e. God,) *or it,* (a thing,) *affected him with disease; or rendered him diseased:* and in many similar cases, the phrase may be well rendered with a verb derived from the noun; like phrases in which "affecit" (a Latin equivalent of اصاب) occurs; as in "honore affecit," meaning "honoravit."] El-Ḥárith Ibn-Khuld El-Makhzoomee says,

* أَظُلَيْمُ إِنَّ مُصَابَكُمْ ↑ رَجُلًا *
* أَهْدَى السَّلَامَ تَحِيَّةً ظُلْمُ *

† [*O Dhuleymeh, verily your afflicting a man who has given the salutation of peace, greeting, is tyranny*]: IB says that this verse is not of El-'Arjee, as El-Ḥareeree imagined it to be: the correct reading is أَظُلَيْمُ, as above: ظُلَيْمُ is an apocopated form of ظُلَيْمَةُ; which is the dim. of ظَلُوم: some read أَظَلُومُ: and some, أُسَلَيْمُ: [the verse is cited accord. to this last reading in the Ṣ:] رَجُلًا is governed in the accus. case by مُصَاب [as an inf. n.]: and ظُلْمُ is the enunciative of إِنَّ. (L, TA.) أَصَابَهُمُ الدَّهْرُ بِنُفُوسِهِمْ وَأَمْوَالِهِمْ † means *Time, or fate, afflicted them by destruction, or extirpation, among themselves and their cattle, or possessions.* (M.) [In the Ḳ, الإِصَابَةُ is expl. as signifying الاِخْتِيَاحُ: but the right reading is evidently الاِجْتِيَاحُ, as Ibr D has remarked in the margin of my copy of the TA; so that اصاب signifies † *He destroyed, or extirpated;* agreeably with an explanation in the sentence next preceding above, from the M.] مَنْ يُرِدِ ٱللّٰهُ بِهِ خَيْرًا يُصِبْ مِنْهُ † occurring in a trad., means *Him whom God intendeth good He trieth with afflictions,* that He may recompense him for them. (TA.) And one says, مَا كُنْتُ مُصَابًا وَلَقَدْ أُصِبْتُ † [app. meaning *I was not affected with weakness of intellect, or madness, and I have become affected therewith:* see مُصَاب, below]. (IAạr, TA.)

5. تصوّب [quasi-pass. of 2]: see 1, in three places. — Also *It was, or became, lowered, or depressed;* syn. تَسَفَّلَ. (A.)

[6. تصاوب, accord. to Freytag, signifies *He, or it, was well directed:* but for this he names no authority.]

7: see 1, first sentence.

10. اِسْتَصْوَبَهُ and اِسْتَصَابَهُ signify the same, (Ṣ, M, A, Mṣb, Ḳ,) ‡ *He saw it, considered it, or held it, to be right;* (M, Mṣb, TA;) namely, his deed, (Ṣ, Mṣb,) or his opinion, (M, TA,) or his saying: (A:) Th says, اِسْتَصْبْتُهُ is the regular form; but the Arabs say, اِسْتَصْوَبْتُ رَأْيَكَ. (M, TA. [See also 4, latter half.])

صَابٌ *A certain species of tree, from which, when it is pressed, there issues what resembles milk, a drop of which sometimes spirts into the eye, producing an effect like that of a flame of fire, and in some instances weakening the sight:* (M, TA:) or *a certain kind of bitter tree;* (Aṣ, T, M, Ḳ, TA;) one of which is termed ↑ صَابَةٌ: (M, Ḳ:* [in the latter it is said that صَاب is the pl. of صَابَةٌ; but properly speaking, the former is a coll. gen. n., and the latter is its n. un.:]) or the *expressed juice of a kind of bitter tree:* (Ṣ:) but accord. to the Ḳ, this is a mistake, though it is the saying of leading lexicologists: (TA:) or, as some say, the *expressed juice of the* صَبِر [or *aloes*]. (M.)

صَوْبٌ an inf. n. used as a subst. (Mṣb) meaning *Rain;* (Lth, Mṣb;) and so ↑ صَيِّبٌ, which is originally [صَيْوِبٌ, i. e.] of the measure فَيْعِلٌ from الصَّوْبُ: (Bḍ in ii. 18:) or صَيِّبٌ is an epithet applied to clouds (غَيْمٌ, Sh, O, or سَحَابٌ, Ṣ, Mṣb) meaning *having rain,* (O,) *i. q.* ذُو صَوْبٍ: (Ṣ, Mṣb:) or صَوْبٌ and ↑ صَيِّبٌ and ↑ صَيُّوبٌ [the last of which is written in the CḲ صَيْوُبٌ] all signify the same, (M, Ḳ,) as epithets applied to rain, meaning *pouring forth:* (M:) or ↑ صَيُّوبٌ, which is originally of the measure فَيْعُولٌ, [being altered from صَيْوُوبٌ,] means rain *pouring forth much, or abundantly:* (IDrd, O:) [↑ صَائِبٌ, also, is applied as an epithet to rain, like صَوْبٌ and صَيِّبٌ; and] in the phrase صِيَابُ المَطَرِ, accord. to Abu-l-'Alà, صِيَابٌ is pl. of صَائِبٌ; or it may be an inf. n., like حِرْمَانٌ: and if one say ↑ صَيَبَانٌ, with fet-ḥ, the meaning is, *what has poured forth* of rain, notwithstanding the ى in it, for similar to this are رَيْحَانٌ from الرَّوْحُ and عَيْدَانٌ (meaning "tall" palm-trees) from العَوْدُ. (Ḥam p. 796.) — Also *Course, or tendency;* syn. قَصْدٌ: so in the saying, to one who is traversing a desert in uncertainty and has declined from the right way, أَقِمْ صَوْبَكَ [*Rectify thy course*]: and in the phrase فُلَانٌ مُسْتَقِيمُ الصَّوْبِ [*Such a one is pursuing the right course*], said of a person when he is not declining from his way to the right or left. (TA. [See also another ex. voce أَوْبٌ.]) — And *A place, or point, of tendency or direction or bearing,* syn. جِهَةٌ, (Mṣb, TA,) of a thing; (Mṣb;) and نَاحِيَةٌ [which means the same; and also *a side;* or *a lateral,* or *an adjacent, part* or *tract* of a thing; and in this sense صَوْبٌ is used in the present day]; and جَانِبٌ [which generally has the latter of these meanings]. (TA.) — See also صَوَابٌ, in three places.

صَابَةٌ: see مُصِيبَةٌ. — Also *Weakness, or feebleness, in the intellect;* (M, A, Ḳ;) or *a touch of insanity therein;* (A;) or *somewhat of insanity,* or *of madness produced by diabolical possession.* (Ṣ.) — See also صَابٌ.

صُوبَةٌ *A collection,* (جَمَاعَةٌ, M, or مُجْتَمَعٌ, Ḳ,) or *a collection, or heap, not measured nor weighed,* (صُبْرَةٌ, A) of wheat: (M, A, Ḳ:) *a heap* of wheat, and of dates, and of other things: (M:) *a quantity collected together* of dust or earth: (TA:) or *anything collected together:* (Kr, M, Ḳ:) *a place in which dates are collected and dried* is thus called by the people of El-Felj. (ISk, Ṣ.) One says, دَخَلْتُ عَلَى فُلَانٍ فَإِذَا الدَّنَانِيرُ صُوبَةٌ بَيْنَ يَدَيْهِ i. e. [*I went in to such a one, and lo, the deenárs were*] *a heap poured out without measure before him:* (Ṣ, M,* A:*) or, as some relate the saying, الدِّينَارُ, which is thus used as a gen. n. (M.)

صَيَبَانٌ: see صَوْبٌ.

صَوَابٌ † *A thing that is right,* of what is said and of what is done; [like سَدَادٌ;] (Mṣb;) *contr. of* خَطَأٌ; (Ṣ, M, Mṣb, Ḳ;) as also ↑ صَوْبٌ. (Ṣ, Mṣb, Ḳ.) One says, ↑ دَعْنِى وَعَلَىَّ خَطَئِى وَصَوْبِى i. e. صَوَابِى [meaning † *Leave thou me, and on me be* the consequence of *my wrong saying or deed, and my right*]. (Ṣ.) [And hence the phrase, frequent in some of the lexicons &c., الصَّوَابُ كَذَا meaning † *The right, or correct, word or wording or reading is thus:* and صَوَابُهُ كَذَا † *The right, or correct, writing or wording or reading of it is thus.*] — And one says also ↑ قَوْلٌ صَوْبٌ and صَوَابٌ [meaning † *A right, or correct, saying:* thus using each as an epithet]. (M.)

صَوِيبٌ: see صَائِبٌ, in two places.

صَيُوبٌ: see صَائِبٌ; and see also art. صيب.

صَائِبٌ: see صَوْبٌ. — Also, (Ṣ, M, A, Ḳ,) and ↑ مُصِيبٌ (A) and ↑ صَيُوبٌ and ↑ صَوِيبٌ, (M, Ḳ,) *An arrow going right, or hitting the mark:* (Ṣ, M, A,* Ḳ,* TA:) ↑ the last of these is the only epithet, known to IJ, of the measure فَعِيلٌ having the ف and ل sound and having و for its ع, except عَوِيصٌ and قَوِيمٌ and طَوِيلٌ; for عَوِيصٌ is [held by him to be only] used as a subst.: صُيَّابٌ is pl. of صَائِبٌ, like صُيَّامٌ and قُيَّامٌ pls. of صَائِمٌ and قَائِمٌ; either from صَابَ السَّهْمُ الهَدَفَ or from الصَّوَابُ فِى الرَّمْىِ having يَصِيبُ for its aor. (M.) [See also صَوْبٌ in art. صيب.] One says, إِنَّهُ لَسَهْمٌ صَائِبٌ *Verily it is an arrow that goes right.* (TA.) مَعَ الخَوَاطِئِ سَهْمٌ صَائِبٌ is a prov. [expl. in art. خطأ]. (Ṣ.) — [Hence,] one says also رَأْىٌ صَائِبٌ and ↑ مُصِيبٌ ‡ [*A right opinion*]: (A, TA:) [Mṭr says,] ↑ رَأْىٌ صَيِّبٌ meaning صَائِبٌ I have not found. (Mgh.)

صَيِّبٌ: see صَوْبٌ, in two places: and صَائِبٌ.

صُيَّابٌ: see صُوَّابَةٌ, in two places; and see art. صيب.

صَيُّوبٌ: see صَوْبٌ, in two places.

صُوَّابَةٌ The *choice,* or *best, class* of a people;

(Fr, Ṣ, M, Ḳ;) as also ↓ صُيَّابَةٌ (Fr, Ṣ, Ḳ) and ↓ صُيَّابٌ. (Ḳ.) And ↓ قَوْمٌ صُيَّابٌ *A choice*, or *an excellent, people*. (Ṣ.) And ↓ صُيَّابَةٌ signifies The *choice*, or *best*, of anything. (Ṣ.) [See also art. صيب.] — Also, صُوَّابَةٌ, The *collective body* of a people; (M;) and so ↓ صُيَّابَةٌ. (Kr, M in art. صيب.)

صُيَّابَةٌ: see the next preceding paragraph, in three places; and see art. صيب.

أَصْوَبُ [*More, and most, affected with weakness in the intellect*, or *insanity*, or *madness*: see صَابَةٌ]. When a man says to another أَنْتَ مُصَابٌ [meaning *Thou art affected with weakness in the intellect*, &c.], the latter replies أَنْتَ أَصْوَبُ مِنِّى [*Thou art more affected with weakness in the intellect*, &c., *than I*]. (IAạr, M, TA. [Thus these phrases are used in the present day.])

مَصَابٌ [*A place of pouring forth*: pl. مَصَاوِبُ]. One says, هُوَ مَصَابُ الوَدْقِ [*It is the place of the pouring of rain* in the clouds]: and شِمْتُ مَصَاوِبَ المَطَرِ [*I watched*, or *watched for, the places of the pouring of rain* in the clouds]: and سَقَاهُمْ مَصَاوِبُ السَّمَآءِ [*The places of the pouring of the rain watered them*; or *may the places* &c. *water them*]. (A.)

مُصَابٌ pass. part. n. of 4 [meaning *Hit, struck, smitten, wounded, hurt, affected, assailed, afflicted*, &c.]. (Ṣ, Mṣb, TA.) — *Affected with weakness*, or *feebleness, in the intellect*; (TA;) or *with somewhat of insanity*, or *madness produced by diabolical possession*: (Ṣ, TA:) or *mad*, or *possessed*. (TA.) [See صَابَةٌ; and see also 4, last sentence; and أَصْوَبُ.] ═ Also *Syn. with* إِصَابَةٌ: (Ṣ, TA:) see 4, latter half, in two places. — And *Syn. with* مُصِيبَةٌ, q. v. (A, Mṣb.) ═ Also The *sugar-cane*. (L, TA, and so in a copy of the Ṣ.)

مَصُوبٌ pass. part. n. of صَابَ [q. v.]. (Mṣb.)

مِصْوَبٌ *A ladle*. (IAạr, Ḳ.)

مُصِيبٌ: see صَائِبٌ, in two places.

مُصَابَةٌ *Syn. with* إِصَابَةٌ: (Ḳ, TA:) see 4, latter half. — See also مُصِيبَةٌ. — تَرَكْتُ النَّاسَ عَلَى مُصَابَاتِهِمْ is a saying mentioned by Ibn-Buzurj, as meaning [*I left the people* disposed, or placed,] *according to their classes*, or *ranks*. (TA.)

مَصُوبَةٌ: see the next paragraph.

مُصِيبَةٌ, (Ṣ, M, A, Mṣb, Ḳ,) said by Aḥmad Ibn-Yaḥyà to be originally مُصْوِبَةٌ, (TA,) and ↓ مَصُوبَةٌ (Ṣ, M, Ḳ) and ↓ مُصَابَةٌ (M, Ḳ) and ↓ مُصَابٌ (A, Mṣb) and ↓ صَابَةٌ, (M, Ḳ,) signify the same, (Ṣ, M, A, Mṣb, Ḳ,) *An affliction, a calamity, a misfortune, a disaster*, or *an evil accident*: (M, Mṣb, TA:) it is said in the Towsheeḥ that the primary signification of مُصِيبَةٌ is *a shot with an arrow*: (TA:) the pl. is مَصَائِبُ, (Ṣ, M, A, Mṣb,) the form commonly obtaining, (Mṣb,) but irregular, (M,) the Arabs agreeing in pronouncing it with ء, as though they likened the radical letter to the augmentative, (Ṣ,) or they imagined what is of the measure مُفْعَلَةٌ to be of the measure فَعِيلَةٌ without a radical و or ى, (M,) and it is thought by Aṣ to be of the speech of the people of the cities, (Mṣb,) and مَصَاوِبُ, (M,) which is the original form, (Ṣ,) or is said to be so, (Mṣb,) and is said by Zj to be the form preferred by the grammarians, (TA,) and مُصِيبَاتٌ. (Aṣ, A, Mṣb.)

قَطٌّ مُصَوَّبٌ *A nibbing in which the exterior of the writing-reed is made to extend beyond the pith*: opposed to قَائِمٌ. (TA in art. حرف.)

صوبج

صَوْبَجٌ and صُوبَجٌ, (Ḳ,) the latter the only word of its measure except سُوسَنٌ (AḤei, TA) and كُوسَجٌ, (TA,) *A thing with which bread is made*; (Ḳ;) *a wooden implement with which the makers of bread expand the cake of bread*; (AḤei, TA;) the مِحْوَرٌ *of the maker of bread, with which the dough*, or *bread, is expanded*: (TA in art. لط:) an arabicized word, (Ḳ, TA,) from the Pers. چُوبَهْ [or چُوبَهْ]. (TA.) [See what is said in art. صرج respecting words in which both ص and ج occur.]

صوت

1\. صَاتَ, aor. يَصُوتُ (Ṣ, M, O, Ḳ) and يَصَاتُ, (M, O, Ḳ,) inf. n. صَوْتٌ, (Ṣ, M,) said of a thing (Ṣ, O) [and of a man and of any animal]; and ↓ صَوَّتَ, (Ṣ, M, O, Ḳ,) inf. n. تَصْوِيتٌ, said of a man (Ṣ) [and of any animal &c.]; and ↓ اصات; (M, Ḳ;) *It sounded; it*, or *he, made, produced, emitted, sent forth*, or *uttered, a sound, noise, voice*, or *cry*; (PṢ and KL in explanation of the first, and MA and KL in explanation of the second;) *he raised his voice, voiced, called* or *called out, cried* or *cried out, shouted, clamoured, exclaimed*, or *vociferated*: (M, Ḳ:) صَوْتٌ signifies also the *making lamentation*: (KL:) and صَوَّتَ ↓ بِهِ, (M, TA,) inf. n. as above, (TA,) *he called, hailed*, or *summoned, him; called out, cried out*, or *shouted, to him*. (M,* TA.) It is said in a trad., كَانُوا يَكْرَهُونَ الصَّوْتَ عِنْدَ القِتَالِ [*They used to dislike blustering on the occasion of combat*, or *fight*]: meaning one's calling to another, or doing a deed to be mentioned in after times, and shouting, and making oneself known in a boasting and self-conceited manner. (TA.) [See also صَوْتٌ below.]

2: see above, in two places: ═ and see also 4, likewise in two places.

4: see 1. — اصات signifies also *He became possessed of* صِيت [or *fame*, &c.; i. e. *he became famous*]. (O.) ═ [It is also trans.; as in the phrase] اصات القَوْسَ *He made the bow to sound* [or *twang*]: (M, TA:) [and so is ↓ صَوَّتَ; as in the phrase] صَوَّتَ العِلْكَ [*He caused the* kind of resin called عِلْك *to make a sound*, or *sounds*]. (Ḳ voce أَنْقَضَ.) — [And it is trans. by means of ب; as in the phrase] اصات بِالرَّجُلِ [and in like manner ↓ صَوَّتَ (see جَرَسَ)] *He rendered the man notorious by a thing that he did not desire.* (Ibn-Buzurj, TA.)

7\. انصات بِهِ الزَّمَانُ [*The age resounded with the mention of him*; meaning] *he became famous*, or *celebrated*. (Ḳ.) — And انصات *He answered, and came*, (Ṣ, O, Ḳ,) being called: of the measure انفعل from الصَّوْتُ. (Ṣ, O.) — And *He became straight in stature after having been bent*; (Ṣ, O, Ḳ;) as though his youthful vigour returned to him; (Ṣ, O; [in one of my copies of the former of which, and in the TA, أُقْتِبِلَ شَبَابُهُ is put for أَقْبَلَ شبابه; or the right explanation is, as though he conformed with a prayer that his youthful vigour might be restored to him; for] it is said, by a poet, of Naṣr Ibn-Duhmán, after he had lived a hundred and ninety years, (Ṣ, O,) when, in answer to a prayer of his people, his youthful vigour returned to him and his hair became again black. (O.) — Also *He went away hiding himself*. (Ḳ.)

صَاتٌ: see صِيتٌ: — and see also صَيِّتٌ, in two places.

صَوْتٌ [an inf. n. (see 1): and also a simple subst., signifying] *A sound*, (M, MA, TA, PṢ,) *a noise, a voice, a cry, a shout, an exclamation*, or *a vociferation*; (MA, PṢ;) of a human being and of other things: (ISk, TA:) conventionally, the *sound of speech*: (Mṣb:) [also *a tone*, considered with regard to the degree of elevation or depression of the voice:] and *any sort of singing*: (M, TA:) [and *an air*, or *a song*:] and it is used to signify *a clamour*, or *confused noise*, or *mixture of sounds*, (Ṣ,) and *a cry for aid* or *succour*: (Ṣ, M:) the pl. is أَصْوَاتٌ: (M, Mṣb, TA:) it is masc.: (Ṣ,* M, Mṣb, TA:) in the following verse, (Ṣ, M, Mṣb,) of Ruweyshid Ibn-Ketheer (Ṣ, M) Eṭ-Ṭáïee, (Ṣ,)

* يَا أَيُّهَا الرَّاكِبُ المُزْجِى مَطِيَّتَهُ *
* سَائِلْ بَنِى أَسَدٍ مَا هٰذِهِ الصَّوْتُ *

[*O thou, the rider urging on his beast, ask the sons of Asad what is this clamour?*], (Ṣ, M, Mṣb,) the poet has made الصوت fem. because meaning thereby الضَّوْضَآءُ and الجَلَبَةُ and الاِسْتِغَاثَةُ, (Ṣ,) or he has made it fem. as meaning الصَّيْحَةُ, (M, Mṣb,) or الاِسْتِغَاثَةُ: (M:) the like is often done by the Arabs, when two words, masc. and fem., are syn.: thus they say, أَقْبَلَتِ العِشَآءُ, meaning العَشِيَّةُ; and هٰذَا العَشِيَّةُ, meaning العِشَآءُ: (Mṣb:) but the making a masc. n. fem. for this reason is bad; though the reverse is held to be allowable. (M.) The Arabs say, أَسْمَعُ صَوْتًا وَأَرَى فَوْتًا, meaning *I hear a sound, or voice, but I see not a deed*. (TA.) بِصَوْتِكَ in the Ḳur xvii. 66 is said to mean *With the sounds of* [*thy*] *singing, and musical pipes*. (M, TA.) — اِسْمُ صَوْتٍ is a term applied to *A noun significant of a sound*: nouns of this kind being of two classes; namely, *nouns applied to the purpose of addressing irrational beings, or what are virtually in the predicament of irrational beings, as young infants*; and *onomatopœias*, or *nouns imitative of sounds*: the former class consists of two descriptions of words; namely, *ejaculations used for the purpose of chiding*, as هَلَا (to horses) and عَدَسْ (to mules) and كِخْ كِخْ (to a young infant);

and *ejaculations used for the purpose of calling,* as جِىْءِ (to camels) and تُشَّأْ (to an ass): of the other class are غَاقِ (imitative of the cry of the crow) and طَقْ (imitative of the sound produced by the falling of stones) and قَبْ (imitative of the sound produced by the fall of a sword) &c.: nouns significant of sounds are generally indecl., because they resemble certain particles in neither governing nor being governed; but some of them are occasionally decl. [like other nouns]. (El-Ashmoonee's Expos. of the Alfeeyeh of Ibn-Málik, section اسماء الافعال والاصوات.) — See also the next paragraph, in four places.

صِيتٌ (Ṣ, M, A, Mṣb, Ḳ) and ▼ صَوْتٌ (Ṣ, M, A, Ḳ) and ▼ صَاتٌ (M, Ḳ) and ▼ صِيتَةٌ (Ḳ) *Fame, report, repute,* or *reputation,* whether good or evil: (TA:) or *good fame, good report, good repute* or *reputation,* (Ṣ, M, Mṣb, Ḳ,) *that spreads* (Ṣ) *among the people;* (Ṣ, Mṣb;) so some say; (TA;) not evil: (Ṣ:) [they may often be well rendered *renown*:] صِيتٌ is originally صِوْتٌ; the و being changed into ى on account of the kesreh preceding it: it seems as though they made it to be of the measure فِعْلٌ to distinguish between the صَوْت that is heard and the fame &c. that is known: but sometimes they said, اِنْتَشَرَ صَوْتُهُ ▼ فِى النَّاسِ in the sense of صِيتُهُ [i. e. *His fame* &c., or *good fame* &c., *spread among the people*]: (Ṣ, TA:) and لَهُ صِيتٌ and ▼ صَوْتٌ فِى النَّاسِ [*He has fame* &c., or *good fame* &c., *among the people*]: and ذَهَبَ صِيتُهُ فِيهِمْ [*His fame* &c., or *good fame* &c., *went among them*]. (A.) It is said in a trad., مَا مِنْ عَبْدٍ إِلَّا لَهُ صِيتٌ فِى السَّمَآءِ, meaning [*There is no servant* of God, i. e. *no man, but he has*] *a report by which he is known* [*in Heaven*]; and it may be in respect of good and evil. (TA.) And in another trad., فَصْلُ مَا بَيْنَ الحَلَالِ وَالحَرَامِ الصَّوْتُ ▼ وَالدُّفُّ [*The distinction between the lawful* (i. e. marriage) *and the unlawful* (i. e. fornication) *is the report* that is made in the case of the former, *and the tambourine* that is used in that case], meaning the publication of the marriage, and the going of the report thereof among the people. (TA.) = صِيتٌ also signifies *A blacksmith's hammer.* (Ḳ,* TA.) — And *An artificer,* or *a handicraftsman;* syn. صَانِعٌ: (Ḳ accord. to the TA:) or *a goldsmith;* syn. صَائِغٌ. (So in the CḲ and in my MS. copy of the Ḳ.)

صِيتَةٌ: see the next preceding paragraph.

صَائِتٌ [*Sounding; making, producing, emitting, sending forth,* or *uttering, a sound, noise, voice,* or *cry;* (see its verb, صَاتَ;)] *raising his voice, calling* or *calling out, crying* or *crying out, shouting, exclaiming,* or *vociferating;* (Ṣ, Mṣb, TA;) as also ▼ صَيِّتٌ; the two words being like مَيِّتٌ and مَائِتٌ; the latter originally صَيْوِتٌ. (TA. [But see the next paragraph: and see also مِصْوَاتٌ.])

صَيِّتٌ, applied to a man, (Ṣ, M, A, Mṣb, Ḳ,) and ▼ صَاتٌ, so applied, (Ṣ, M, Ḳ,) and the latter likewise applied to an ass, (Ṣ,) both signify the same, (Ḳ,) *Vehement, strong,* or *loud, of voice:* (Ṣ, M, Mṣb:) ▼ رَجُلٌ صَاتٌ is like رَجُلٌ مَالٌ "a man having much property," and رَجُلٌ نَالٌ "a man who gives much," and كَبْشٌ صَافٌ ["a ram having much wool"], &c., all of these epithets being originally of the measure فَعِلٌ: (Ṣ:) or صَاتٌ may be of the measure فَاعِلٌ from which the medial radical has gone; or it may be [originally صَوِتٌ,] of the measure فَعِلٌ. (M.) One says also صَوْتٌ صَيِّتٌ [*A vehement, strong,* or *loud, voice*]. (A.) See also صَائِتٌ.

صَوَّاتٌ: see مِصْوَاتٌ.

مُصَوِّتٌ: see the next paragraph, in two places.

مِصْوَاتٌ One *who raises his voice, calls* or *calls out, cries* or *cries out, shouts, clamours, exclaims,* or *vociferates;* *i. q.* ▼ مُصَوِّتٌ: (Ḳ, TA:) [or, as also ▼ صَوَّاتٌ, often occurring, *who does so much,* or *is in the habit of doing so;* each being of a measure denoting intensiveness of the signification.] — [Hence,] one says, مَا بِالدَّارِ مِصْوَاتٌ, meaning *There is not in the house any one* (Ḳ, TA) *that raises his voice,* &c.: in some copies of the Ḳ ▼ مُصَوِّتٌ, which has the same meaning. (TA.)

مُنْصَاتٌ *Straight in stature.* (Ṣ.)

صوج

صَوْجَانٌ: see صَوْلَجَانٌ, in art. صولج.

صوح

1. صُحْتُهُ, (Ṣ, Ḳ,) [third pers. صَاحَ, aor. يَصُوحُ,] inf. n. صَوْحٌ, (TḲ,) *I clave, split,* or *slit, it;* (Ṣ, Ḳ;) namely, a thing. (Ṣ.)

2. صَوَّحَتِ البَقْلَ, said of the wind, (الرِّيحُ, Ṣ, A,) and of the heat, (الحَرُّ, A,) and of the sun, (الشَّمْسُ, TA,) inf. n. تَصْوِيحٌ, (Ḳ,) *It dried up,* or *caused to dry up,* (Ṣ, A, Ḳ,) *the herbs,* or *leguminous plants,* (Ṣ, A,) *so that they became much split;* (A;) and so الخَشَبَ [*the wood*]; and the like of these: and صَيَّحَت signifies the same. (TA.) And صَوَّحَ الشَّعَرَ, said of dryness, *It caused the hair to split much, and to fall off, and become scattered.* (L.) = See also 5, in four places. — It is said in a trad., نَهَى عَنْ بَيْعِ النَّخْلِ قَبْلَ أَنْ يُصَوِّحَ, meaning [*He forbade the selling of palm-trees*] *before that the good thereof become distinguishable from the bad:* related by some with ر [i. e. يُصَرِّحَ]: (TA:) but El-Khaṭṭábee says that the right word is يُصَوِّحَ, with و. (TA in art. صرح.)

5. تَصَوَّحَ البَقْلُ *The herbs,* or *leguminous plants, became dried up;* as also ▼ صَوَّحَ: (IB, TA:) or *became completely dried up;* or *became blighted and dried up;* and ▼ صَوَّحَ signifies the same: (L:) or *became dried up in the hot season, not by reason of a blight or the like:* (T, TA:) or *became dried up in the upper part,* (AA, Ṣ, Ḳ,) *yet retaining moisture:* (AA, Ṣ:) or *became dried up and split;* (Aṣ, TA;) and ▼ صَوَّحَ signifies [the same, or] *became dried up and much split:* (A:) or (and so the verb تَصَوَّحَ said of wood, and the like,) *became much split, spontaneously, and parts thereof became scattered:* and تَصَيَّحَ signifies the same. (TA.) It is said in a trad. of 'Alee, فَبَادِرُوا العِلْمَ قَبْلَ تَصْوِيحِ ▼ نَبْتِهِ † [*Therefore hasten ye to obtain knowledge before the drying-up of its plants* for want of mental vigour]. (TA.) — تَصَوَّحَ also signifies *It became much split;* (Ṣ, Ḳ;) said of hair &c.; (Ṣ;) as also ▼ انصاح: (Ḳ: [but this latter is more correctly expl. below:]) [or] said of hair, *it fell off and became scattered;* as also تَصَيَّحَ: (Ḳ:) or *it became much split,* (A, L,) *of itself,* (L,) [or *by reason of dryness,* (see 2,)] *and fell off and became scattered.* (L.)

7. انصاح *It clave, split,* or *slit;* or *became cloven, split,* or *slit.* (Ṣ, Ḳ.) See also 5. — *It* (a mountain) *became much cleft,* or *cracked, and dried, by reason of want of rain.* (TA, from a trad.) — *It* (a garment) *slit,* or *rent, of itself.* (AO, Ṣ.) — ‡ *It* (the moon, Ṣ, Ḳ, and the dawn, and lightning, TA) *showed its light:* (Ṣ, Ḳ, TA:) originally, *became cleft.* (TA.) [See also 7 in art. صيح.]

صُوحٌ: see what next follows.

صَوْحٌ (Ṣ, A, Ḳ) and ▼ صُوحٌ (IAạr, Ḳ) *The wall* (حَائِط) of a valley: (Ṣ, Ḳ:) [app. meaning its *perpendicular side;* for] a valley has صَوْحَانِ, (Ṣ,) which means *the two sides* thereof, *resembling two walls.* (A.) — And *The lower part of a mountain:* (Ḳ:) or the *face of a mountain that stands up* (Ṣ, Ḳ) *appearing* (Ṣ) *as though it were a wall.* (Ṣ, Ḳ.) It is said in a trad., أَلْقَوْهُ بَيْنَ الصَّوْحَيْنِ حَتَّى أَكَلَتْهُ السِّبَاعُ, meaning [*They cast him*] *between the two mountains* [*so that the beasts, or birds, of prey ate him*]. (Ṣ.)

صَاحَةٌ *A plain,* (A,) or *land,* (Ḳ,) *that produces nothing* (A, Ḳ) *ever;* (Ḳ;) i. e., *in which is no good.* (A.)

صُوحَانٌ, with ḍamm [to the ص], *Dry.* (Ḳ.) And نَخْلَةٌ صُوحَانَةٌ *A palm-tree of which the branches with their leaves upon them have become dried up, rigid, and contracted.* (Ḳ, TA.)

صُوَاحٌ *Gypsum.* (Ṣ, Ḳ.) — And † *The sweat of horses:* (Ṣ, Ḳ:) said to be likened to gypsum because of its whiteness. (T, L.) — And † *Milk mixed with water, the latter being the more in quantity.* (Aboo-Sa'eed, Ḳ.) — Also *An elevated piece,* (نَجْوَة, so in the L and CḲ, and in my MS. copy of the Ḳ,) or *such as is soft,* or *yielding,* (رِخْوَة, so in the TA as from the Ḳ,) *of land.* (L, Ḳ.) — And *The spadix* (طَلْع) *of the palm-tree,* (AḤn, Ḳ,) *when it dries up, and falls in pieces and becomes scattered.* (AḤn.)

صُوَاحَةٌ, like رُمَّانَةٌ, [but accord. to analogy it

should be without teshdeed, like سُقَاطَةٌ &c., and so it is written in the L as relating to wool,] *What has become much split*, of hair, and *what has fallen off and become scattered*, thereof, (K,) and so of wool. (L, TA.)

مُنْصَاحٌ *Flowing*, or *flowing copiously, running upon the surface of the ground;* (K, TA;) applied to rain-water. (TA.) — And Herbage *of which the blossoms have appeared.* (TA.) [See a verse cited voce مُرْتَفِقٌ.]

صوح

4. اصاخ لَهُ (Ṣ, A, K, TA) and إِلَيْهِ, (A, TA,) inf. n. إِصَاخَةٌ, (TA,) *He listened to him*, or *it*. (Ṣ, K, TA.) [See a verse of Aboo-Du-ád (cited here as an ex. in the Ṣ and TA) voce نَاشِدٌ.] — And اصاخ signifies also ‡ *He was silent*, or *spake not*, or *ceased from speaking:* so in the saying, أَصَاخَ فُلَانٌ عَلَى حَقِّ فُلَانٍ, meaning ‡ *Such a one was silent respecting the right*, or *due, of such a one, that he might take it away.* (A, TA.) [And it is said that] it signifies thus in the prov., أَصَاخَ إِصَاخَةَ المُنْدِهِ لِلنَّاشِدِ, i. e. *He was silent with the silence of the frequent chider of camels* [or *of him who drives and chides many camels*] *to one making known*, or *giving information of, a thing lost:* applied to him who strives, or labours, in seeking [a thing] and then lacks ability, and desists. (Meyd. [But the verse cited voce نَاشِدٌ suggests another rendering, which I think preferable. In Freytag's "Arab. Prov." i. 718, للناشد is omitted.])

صود

2. صَوَّدَ الصَّادَ, inf. n. تَصْوِيدٌ, *He wrote the* صاد [i. e. the letter ص]. (K.)

صَادْ *The name of one of the letters of the alphabet.* (M, L. [See art. ص.]) — [It is also *The title of a* سُورَة, *the thirty-eighth chapter of the Kur-án.*] If you make it a sign of the سورة, you write it as a single letter, and make it indeclinable with its last letter quiescent [in pronunciation]: if you make it a name for the سورة, you write it as [it is pronounced] in spelling; and say صَادِ, with kesr, because of the concurrence of two quiescent letters [in the former case]; and you may say صَادَ, because this is easier of pronunciation: some make it imperfectly decl., considering it as fem. [and a proper name]: and some make it perfectly decl., considering it as masc.; and say, قَرَأْتُ صَادًا [*I read*, or *recited*, the chapter ص]: and the like is done in the cases of ق [the title of the fiftieth chapter] and ن [the title of the sixty-eighth chapter]. (Mṣb.) — Accord. to ISd, its medial radical letter is originally و: (L:) accord. to IJ, it is ى. (MF.) — See also art. صيد.

صور

1. صَارَهُ, aor. يَصُورُ, (Ṣ, M, K,) inf. n. صَوْرٌ, (M, K,) *He made it* (a thing, M, K, or, as some say, specially the neck, M) *to incline*, or *lean;* (Ṣ, M, K;) as also صاره, aor. يَصِيرُ; (Ṣ;) and ▼ اصارهُ: (Ṣ, M, Mṣb, K:) or *he demolished it, threw it down*, or *pulled it down to the ground;* as also ▼ اصارهُ. (K.) One says, of a man, يَصُورُ عُنُقَهُ إِلَى الشَّىْءِ *He inclines his neck to the thing.* (Lth.) And صُرْتُ إِلَىَّ الشَّىْءَ, and ▼ أَصَرْتُهُ, *I inclined*, or *bent, the thing to*, or *towards, me.* (El-Ahmar.) And صُرْتُ الغُصْنَ لِأَجْتَنِىَ الثَّمَرَ [*I inclined*, or *bent, the branch, that I might pluck*, or *gather, the fruit*]. (A.) And قُلُوبٌ لَا تَصُورُهَا الأَرْحَامُ † [*Hearts which the ties of relationship do not incline*]. (TA, from a trad.) فَصُرْهُنَّ إِلَيْكَ, in the Kur [ii. 262], means *And turn them towards thee;* and so فَصِرْهُنَّ: (Akh, Ṣ, M:) but the former is the more common reading: this is the meaning commonly known, of each reading: though Lh says that the former means as above, and the latter means *cut them*, and *divide them, in pieces;* (M;) and some thus explain the former, making a transposition in the verse, as though the words were thus, فَخُذْ إِلَيْكَ أَرْبَعَةً مِنَ الطَّيْرِ فَصُرْهُنَّ. (Ṣ.) One says also, صُرْ وَجْهَكَ إِلَىَّ, and صُرْ إِلَىَّ, *Turn thou thy face towards me.* (Akh, Ṣ.) And صَارَ وَجْهَهُ, aor. يَصُورُ, (M, K,) and يَصِيرُ, (K,) *He turned his face* towards a person or thing. (M, K.) And هُوَ يَصُورُ مَعْرُوفَهُ إِلَى النَّاسِ ‡ [*He turns his beneficence towards men*]. (TA.) — [Agreeably with a statement cited above, it is said that] صَارَهُ, aor. as above, (Ṣ, K,) and so the inf. n., (TA,) signifies also *He dissected it;* or *cut it*, or *divided it, in pieces.* (Ṣ, K, TA.) — And hence, (TA,) صَارَ الحُكْمَ † *He* (the judge, A, TA) *decided the judgment.* (Ṣ,* A, TA.) — [Freytag states, on the authority of the Kitáb el-Addád, that صار, aor. as above, has two contr. significations: *He separated*, or *dispersed:* — and *He collected.*] — See also 2. — صَارَ also signifies *He* (a man, M) *uttered a cry*, or *sound.* (M, K.) — صَوِرَ, (M, A, K,) [aor. يَصْوَرُ,] inf. n. صَوَرٌ, (Ṣ, M, A,) *He*, (Lth,) or *it*, (a thing, M, Mṣb, K, or a man's neck, M, A,*) *inclined*, or *leaned;* (Lth, Ṣ,* M, A, K;) as also ▼ انصار: (Ṣ, M, Mṣb, K:*) *it bent;* or *was*, or *became, crooked.* (A.) One says, فِى عُنُقِهِ صَوَرٌ *In his neck is an inclining;* and *a bending*, or *crookedness.* (A.) — And صَوَرٌ as an attribute of a man signifies also ‡ *An inclining*, or *inclination;* (Ṣ;) *a desiring*, or *desire.* (Ṣ, Mṣb.)

2. صوّر [inf. n. تَصْوِيرٌ,] *He formed, fashioned, figured, shaped, sculptured*, or *pictured*, him, or it; (Ṣ, M, K;) and ▼ تصوّر signifies the same; (Mṣb, and Bd in iii. 4;) and so does ▼ صار, accord. to Aboo-'Alee, in the saying,

* بَنَاهُ وَصَلَّبَ فِيهِ وَصَارَا *

[*Which* (referring to a church) *he has built, and in which he has made a cross*, or *crosses, and has made sculptured*, or *painted, work*]. (M.) One says, صَوَّرَهُ اللّٰهُ صُورَةً حَسَنَةً [*God formed him a goodly*, or *beautiful, form*]. (Ṣ.) — See also 5, in two places.

4: see 1, in three places.

5. تصوّر *He*, or *it, was*, or *became, formed, fashioned, figured, shaped, sculptured*, or *pictured.* (Ṣ, M, K, TA.) — And [hence,] تصوّر لِى [and ▼ صَوَّرَ لِى, like خُيِّلَ لِى and تَخَيَّلَ لِى,] *It appeared to my mind*, or *imagination*, (Ṣ, Mṣb,) *as an image*, or *a picture.* (Mṣb.) — See also 2. — [Hence,] تصوّر شَيْئًا *He imagined a thing; imaged it in the mind;* as also ▼ صوّرهُ; [like خَيَّلَهُ and تَخَيَّلَهُ;] *he imagined*, or *conceived, the form of the thing.* (Ṣ.) [تَصَوُّرٌ in logic signifies The *forming of an idea; conception, perception*, or *apprehension;* sometimes qualified by the epithet سَاذَجٌ i. e. *simple.*] — Also *He* (being pierced with a spear or the like) *inclined, to fall:* (Ṣ:) or *he* (being struck) *fell:* (M, K:) or *he*, or *it, fell*, or *alighted.* (TA.)

7. انصار: see صَوِرَ. — Also *It* (a thing) *became demolished, and cut*, or *divided, in pieces:* (O:) *it* (a mountain) *became demolished, and fell:* (Ṣgh, TA:) *it cracked*, and *split.* (TA.)

8. اصطارهُ *He doubled it*, or *folded it;* or *he bent it;* syn. ثَنَاهُ. (O.)

صَارٌ: see صَيِّرٌ, below, in two places.

صَوْرٌ *Small palm-trees:* (M, K:) or *a collection of small palm-trees:* (Ṣ, M, K:) a word having no proper sing.: (Ṣ, M:) [but see صَوْرَةٌ:] pl. صِيرَانٌ: (Sh, M, K:) and *other trees:* pl. as above. (Sh, TA.) — Also The *root* of a palm-tree, (M, K,) or of a palm-trunk. (M.) — And The *bank*, or *side*, of a river or rivulet. (M, K.) — And The *side of the neck.* (O,* K,* TA. [In the CK, والليت is erroneously put for وَاللِّيتُ.]) — And The *forelock:* so in the saying of a rájiz,

* كَأَنَّ عُرْفًا مَائِلًا مِنْ صَوْرِهِ *

[*As though a mane inclining from his forelock*]. (Ṣ.)

صُورٌ *A horn:* (Ṣ, M:) and *a horn in which one blows:* (Ṣ, M, K:) so in the Kur [vi. 73, &c.], يَوْمَ يُنْفَخُ فِى الصُّورِ [i. e. *On the day when the horn shall be blown in*]: El-Kelbee says, I know not what is الصور: and it is said to be pl. of صُورَةٌ, like as بُسْرٌ is of بُسْرَةٌ; [or rather a coll. gen. n., of which صُورَةٌ is the n. un.;] i. e., [the phrase means] *when the souls shall be blown into the forms* of the dead: and El-Hasan read فِى الصُّوَرِ: (Ṣ, L, TA:) this is related on the authority of AO; but AHeyth asserts him to have said wrong. (L, TA.)

صَوَرٌ inf. n. of صَوِرَ [q. v.]. (M, A.) — Also *An itching* (أُكَالٌ) *in the head.* (IAar, TA.) [See also صَوْرَةٌ.]

صَارَةٌ The *head*, (O,) or the *upper*, or *uppermost, part*, (K,) of a mountain: (O, K:) and صُوَيْرَةٌ [with ء] has been heard from the Arabs as its dim. (TA.) — See also صِوَارٌ.

صَوْرَةٌ ‡ *An inclination*, or *a desire.* (TA.) You say, أَرَى لَكَ إِلَيْهِ صَوْرَةً ‡ *I see thee to have a loving inclination to him.* (A.) And مَا بِى إِلَيْهَا صَوْرَةٌ ‡ *I have not any inclination to*, or *desire for, her.*

(TA, from a trad.) — And *An itching*, or *itch*, (حِكَّة,) *in the head:* (A:) or *an affection like* حِكَّة *in a man's head, occasioning a desire to be loused.* (Ṣ, M, Ḳ.) [See also صَوَرٌ.] ══ And *A palm-tree.* (IAạr.) [See also صَوْرٌ.]

صُورَةٌ *Form, fashion, figure, shape,* or *semblance;* syn. شَكْلٌ, (M, Ḳ,) and مِثَالٌ; (Mṣb;) the *external state* of a thing; (IAth;) *that whereby a thing is sensibly distinguished by men in general, and even by many other animate beings, from other things;* as the صورة of a man, and of a horse, and of an ass. (B.) — And *An effigy; an image,* or *a statue; a picture; anything that is formed, fashioned, figured,* or *shaped, after the likeness of any of God's creatures, animate* or *inanimate:* it is said that the maker of an effigy, or image, will be punished on the day of resurrection, and will be commanded to put life into it; and that the angels will not enter a house in which is a صورة. (Mgh.) [See also تَصَاوِيرُ.] — [Hence, *A mental image;* or *a resemblance, of any object, formed,* or *conceived, by the mind; an idea:* a meaning of frequent occurrence in philosophical works &c.] — And *Species;* syn. نَوْعٌ. (Ḳ.) — And The *essence* of a thing; *that by being which a thing is what it is;* or the *property,* or *quality,* or the *aggregate of properties* or *qualities, whereby a thing is what it is;* syn. حَقِيقَةٌ: (IAth:) [*specific character;*] *that whereby a thing is mentally distinguished by particular persons, not by the vulgar, from other things;* as the صورة by which a man is specially distinguished, consisting in reason and thought and other distinctive attributes: (B:) *a quality, an attribute, a property;* or *a description,* as meaning the *aggregate of the qualities* or *attributes* or *properties,* of a thing; or the *state, condition,* or *case,* of a thing; syn. صِفَةٌ: (IAth, Mṣb, Ḳ:) as when you say, صُورَةُ الأَمْرِ كَذَا [*The quality, &c., of the thing is of such a kind*]: (IAth, Mṣb:) and صُورَةُ المَسْأَلَةِ كَذَا [*The description, statement,* or *form, of the question is of such a kind*]: (Mṣb:) and so in the saying of the Prophet, أَتَانِى اللَّيْلَةَ رَبِّى فِى أَحْسَنِ صُورَةٍ [*My Lord came to me to-night in a most goodly state*]; or صورة may here refer to the Prophet, and may mean *external state,* or *manner of being,* or *condition.* (IAth.) — And The *mode,* or *manner,* of an action. (IAth.) — The pl. is صُوَرٌ (Ṣ, M, Mṣb, Ḳ) and صِوَرٌ and صُوْرٌ; (Ṣ, M, Ḳ;) the second of which is rare, and by some disallowed. (MF.) — The saying of the Prophet خَلَقَ ٱللّٰهُ آدَمَ عَلَى صُورَتِهِ may mean that *God created Adam in the* صورة [or *form* &c.] *that He,* namely, God, *originated and ordained;* or *in the* صورة *proper to him,* namely, Adam. (M.) — صُورَةٌ signifies also The *face:* so in a trad. cited voce مُحَرَّمٌ; in which it is said that the صورة is pronounced sacred, i. e. that it is not to be slapped: and in another, in which it is said that the Prophet disliked marking the صورة with a hot iron. (TA.)

صُوَارٌ: see the next paragraph, in four places.

صِوَارٌ *A herd* of [wild] bulls or cows; (Ṣ, M, Mṣb, Ḳ;) as also ↓ صُوَارٌ and ↓ صِيَارٌ [the latter in the CḲ written صِيَّار] and ↓ صُوَّارٌ [in some copies of the Ḳ erroneously written صُوَار, which, as observed in the TA, is a repetition]: (M, Ḳ, TA:) pl. of the first (Ṣ, M) and second and third (M) صِيرَانٌ. (Ṣ, M.) ══ Also *A sweet odour;* and so ↓ صُوَارٌ. (M, Ḳ.) — And *A vesicle* (وِعَآء) of musk; (Ṣ, Mṣb;) as also ↓ صُوَارٌ, (Mṣb,) and ↓ صِيَارٌ, (Ṣ,) and ↓ صَارَةٌ [also] signifies [the same, i. e.] *a* فَارَة or فَأْرَة of musk: (O, Ḳ:) or صِوَارٌ and ↓ صُوَارٌ signify *a small quantity* of musk: (M, Ḳ:) or *a piece,* or *portion,* thereof: (M:) and صِوَارٌ signifies also *musk* [itself]: (TA:) pl. أَصْوِرَةٌ. (M, Ḳ.) [Said in the M to be Pers.] ══ الصَّوَارَانِ *The two corners of the mouth;* (O, Ḳ;) called by the vulgar الصَّوَّارَيْنِ, (O, TA,) or الصَّوَارَيْنِ. (O in art. صمغ.)

صِيَارٌ: see the next preceding paragraph, in two places.

صُوَيْرَةٌ [with ء] a dim. of صَارَةٌ [q. v.]. (TA.)

صَيِّرٌ *Goodly in* صُورَة [i. e. *form* &c.]; (Fr, Ṣ, Ḳ;) as also ↓ صَارٌ. (TA in art. شور.) One says رَجُلٌ صَيِّرٌ شَيِّرٌ (Fr, Ṣ) and ↓ صَارٌ شَارٌ (TA ubi suprà) *A man goodly in* صورة [or *form* &c.] *and in* شَارَة [i. e. *appearance* or *apparel* &c.]. (Fr, Ṣ.) [See also شَيِّرٌ in art. شور.]

صَوَّارٌ A sparrow (عُصْفُورٌ) *that answers when called.* (Ṣ, M, Ḳ.*)

صُوَّارٌ: see صِوَارٌ, first sentence.

أَصْوَرُ *Inclining:* (M, Ḳ:) pl. صُورٌ. (M.) One says رَجُلٌ أَصْوَرُ *A man having an inclining,* or *a bending,* or *crooked, neck.* (A.) And هُوَ أَصْوَرُ إِلَى كَذَا *He is inclining his neck and face towards such a thing.* (A.) — [And hence,] † *Having an inclination,* or *a desire,* (Ṣ, M, Mṣb,) to, or for, (إِلَى,) a friend, or an object of love. (M.)

تَصَاوِيرُ [pl. of تَصْوِيرٌ and تَصْوِيرَةٌ] *Effigies, images,* or *statues; pictures;* and *the like.* (Ṣ, Mgh.) [See also صُورَةٌ.]

مُصَوِّرٌ [*A sculptor;* and *a painter,* or *limner,* or *the like*]. المُصَوِّرُ as an epithet of God, *The Former,* or *Fashioner, of all existing things, who hath established them, and given to every one of them a special form and a particular manner of being whereby it is distinguished, with their variety and multitude.* (TA.)

صوع

1. صُعْتُهُ, (O, Ḳ,) [from صَاعٌ,] aor. أَصُوعُهُ, (Ḳ,) inf. n. صَوْعٌ, (TA,) *I measured it with the* صَاع [q. v.]. (O, Ḳ.) One says, هٰذَا طَعَامٌ يُصَاعُ i. e. [*This is wheat*] *that is measured* [*with the* صاع]. (O.) — And † [*I collected it together,* like as the measurer collects the corn &c. in the measure: and the contr., i. e.] *I dispersed it,* or *scattered it;* (Ṣ, O, Ḳ;) in which sense it is [said to be] tropical; (TA;) and صِعْتُهُ, aor. أَصِيعُهُ, (Ḳ in art. صيع,) inf. n. صَيْعٌ, (TA in that art.,) signifies the same. (Ḳ in that art.) One says, صُعْتُ الأَقْرَانَ, and غَيْرَهُمْ, ‡ *I came to the antagonists, and others, from their sides:* (Ḳ, TA:) of a courageous man, or a courageous armed man, one says, يَصُوعُ أَقْرَانَهُ ‡ *He comes to his antagonists from their sides;* (Ṣ, O, TA;) and the like is cited in the T from Lth; or as meaning *he encompasses their sides;* (TA;) or *he collects together his antagonists* (IḲṭṭ, Z, TA) *from every side,* (IḲṭṭ, TA,) like as the measurer collects together that which is measured: (Z, TA:) and of a man, (Ṣ, O,) or a pastor, (Lth, IḲṭṭ, Z,) يَصُوعُ الإِبِلَ, (Ṣ, O,) or مَاشِيَتَهُ, (Lth,) or إِبِلَهُ, (IḲṭṭ, Z,) ‡ *He comes* [*to the camels* or] *to his cattle* [or *to his camels*] *from their sides;* or *he encompasses their sides;* (Lth, TA;) or *he collects them together* (IḲṭṭ, Z, TA) *from every side,* (IḲṭṭ, TA,) like as the measurer collects together that which is measured: (Z, TA:) but Az says that the foregoing explanations by Lth are wrong; that يَصُوعُ أَقْرَانَهُ, said of a courageous man, or a courageous armed man, means *he charges upon his antagonists and disperses them;* and يَصُوعُ إِبِلَهُ, said of a pastor, *he disperses his camels in the place of pasture;* and يَصُوعُ المِعْزَى, said of a he-goat, *he disperses the* [*she-*] *goats;* and صَاعَ الغَنَمَ, aor. as above, and so the inf. n., *he dispersed the sheep* or *goats;* (TA;) and ↓ اصاع الغَنَمَ, inf. n. إِصَاعَةٌ, signifies thus likewise: (Lḥ, TA in art. صيع:) Lḥ also says that صُعْتُ الغَنَمَ, aor. أَصُوعُهَا, inf. n. صَوْعٌ, and صِعْتُهَا, aor. أَصِيعُهَا, inf. n. صَيْعٌ, both signify *I dispersed the sheep* or *goats:* (O in art. صيع:) or, accord. to IḲṭṭ, صاع إِبِلَهُ, said of a pastor, has two contr. meanings; *he collected together his camels from every side;* and also *he dispersed his camels.* (TA.) — Also *I frightened him.* (Ibn-'Abbád,* O,* Ḳ.) — And صُعْتُ القَوْمَ, aor. أَصُوعُهُمْ, (Lḥ, O in art. صيع,) inf. n. صَوْعٌ, (TA in that art.,) *I urged,* or *incited, the people,* or *party;* (Lḥ, O and TA in that art.;) and so صِعْتُ القَوْمَ, (Lḥ, O and Ḳ in that art.,) aor. أَصِيعُهُمْ, (Lḥ, O ibid.,) inf. n. صَيْعٌ. (TA ibid.) — [And صاع الكُرَةَ *He propelled the ball* with the صَوْلَجَان. (See صَاعٌ below, last sentence.)] — And صَاعَتِ النَّحْلُ, (Ḳ,) [app. for صاعت النحل بَعْضُهَا بَعْضًا,] aor. تَصُوعُ, (O,) inf. n. صَوْعٌ, (TA,) *The bees followed* [as though *driving along*] *one another.* (O, Ḳ.) — And صاع الشَّىْءَ, inf. n. صَوْعٌ, *He folded,* or *doubled, the thing; twisted it;* or *bent it.* (IḲṭṭ, TA.)

2. صَوَّعَتْ مَوْضِعًا, (O, Ḳ,) inf. n. تَصْوِيعٌ, (Ḳ,) *She* (a woman) *prepared a place, such as is termed* صَاعَة, (O, Ḳ, TA,) *and made it even,* (TA,) for the separating and loosening of cotton. (O, Ḳ.) — صوّعت الرِّيحُ النَّبَاتَ *The wind dried up,* or *caused to dry up, the plants,* or *herbage;* (O, Ḳ;) as also صَوَّحَتْهُ. (TA.) — صوّع الشَّىْءَ *He made the thing pointed in its head.* (Ibn-'Abbád, O, Ḳ.) — And *He rounded the thing in its*

sides. (O, Ḳ.) —— صوّع, (Ḳ,) inf. n. as above, (O,) said of an ass, [meaning a wild ass,] *He drove his she asses to the right and left:* (O, Ḳ:) so expl. by Ibn-'Abbád. (O.) And, said of a horse, *He went at random, and resisted his owner* [or *rider*]. (TA.) —— صوّع إِلَيْهِ [said of a man, as is indicated in the O,] *He turned about his head towards him:* and *he turned his face towards him.* (O, TA.) —— And صوّع رَأْسَهُ, said of a bird, *It moved,* or *moved about, its head.* (TA.)

4. اصاع الغَنَمَ: see 1, latter half.

5. تصوّع *It became dispersed,* or *scattered;* as also ▼ انصاع. (Ṣ.) You say, تصوّع القَوْمُ *The people,* or *party, became dispersed,* or *scattered, and remote, all of them, one from another.* (O, Ḳ.) —— Also, said of hair, *It became contracted, and much split:* [app. by reason of dryness: like تصوّح:] (Lth, O, Ḳ:) or *it became dispersed,* or *scattered;* (Lḥ, O, Ḳ;) and *it fell off by degrees.* (O, Ḳ.) —— And, said of herbage, *It became dried up;* (Ṣ, O, Ḳ;) like تصوّح; (O;) as also تصيّع. (Ṣ; and O and Ḳ in art. صيع.)

7. انصاع: see 5. —— Also ‡ *He turned away,* or *back, retreating,* or *returning,* (Ṣ, O, Ḳ, TA,) *and went* (Ṣ, TA) *quickly,* or *hastening:* (Ṣ, O, Ḳ, TA:) or you say, انصاع القَوْمُ ‡ *The people,* or *party, went away quickly:* and انصاع مُدْبِرًا ‡ *He went away* [*turning back*] *quickly.* (TA.) [See an ex. voce صَارَةٌ.] —— And † *It* (a bird) *ascended,* or *mounted, into the air, between the earth and sky,* or *into the middle of the sky.* (TA in art. صيع, from the book entitled "Ghareeb el-Ḥamám" by El-Ḥasan Ibn-'Abd-Alláh El-Kátib El-Iṣbahánee.)

صَاعٌ (Ṣ, Mgh, O, Mṣb, Ḳ) and ▼ صُوعٌ and ▼ صَوْعٌ (O, Ḳ) and ▼ صُوَاعٌ (Ṣ, O, Ḳ) and ▼ صِوَاعٌ, (O, Ḳ,) thus accord. to five different readers of the Ḳur in xii. 72, (O, Ḳ,* TA,) *A certain measure used for measuring corn* [&c.], (Ṣ, O, Mṣb, Ḳ,) *and upon which turn* [or *depend*] *the decisions of the Muslims* [*relating to measures of capacity*]: (Ḳ:) or the صاع is *different from the* ▼ صُوَاع; (Ṣ, Ḳ;) the latter being *a certain vessel, in* [or *from*] *which one drinks* [as will be expl. hereafter in this paragraph]: (Ṣ, TA:) the former is *four* أَمْدَاد [pl. of مُدّ]; (Ṣ, O, Mṣb, Ḳ;) i. e. (Mṣb) *five* أَرْطَال [or *pints*] *and a third,* (Mgh, Mṣb, TA,) *by the measure of Baghdád;* (Mṣb;) the مُدّ being a pint and a third: (Ḳ, TA:) so with the people of El-Ḥijáz, (Mgh, TA,) [i. e.] so with the people of the Ḥarameyn, as was proved by a number of specimens of the صاع used in dealings with the Prophet, (Mṣb,) and so accord. to Esh-Sháfi'ee: (TA:) but with the people of El-'Irák it was *eight pints,* (Mgh, Mṣb, TA,) with whom agreed Aboo-Ḥaneefeh; the مُدّ with them being two pints; (Mṣb, TA;) but the addition was made by El-Ḥajjáj; and their صاع was the قَفِيز حَجَّاجِىّ, and was unknown to the people of El-Medeeneh, as is said by Az: (Mṣb:) accord. to Ed-Dáwoodee, its invariable measure is *four times the quantity* [of corn &c.] *that fills the two hands, that are neither large nor small, of a man;* for the صاع of the Prophet is not found in every place; and this (the author of the Ḳ says, TA) I have tried, and found to be correct: (Ḳ, TA:) the word is masc. and fem.: (Zj, Mṣb, Ḳ, TA:) accord. to Fr, the people of El-Ḥijáz make it fem.; and Benoo-Asad, except some of them, make it masc., as do the people of Nejd; and Zj says that the more chaste way is to make it masc.: (Mṣb:) the pl. (of pauc., used by those who make the sing. fem., O, Mṣb) is أَصْوُعٌ, (Ṣ, Mgh, O, Mṣb, Ḳ,) for which one may say أَصْؤُعٌ, (Ṣ, O, Ḳ,*) changing the و into hemzeh, (Ṣ, O,) and accord. to AAF some say آصُعٌ, like آدُرٌ, (Mgh, Mṣb,) a pl. of دَارٌ, (Mgh,) but AḤát says that this is a vulgar mistake, (Mṣb,) and أَصْوَاعٌ, (O, Mṣb, Ḳ,) which is used by those who make the sing. masc., (O, Mṣb,) and [of mult.] صُوعٌ, (Ḳ,) which is app. pl. of ▼ صِوَاعٌ, with kesr, (TA,) and صِيعَانٌ, (Mgh, O, Mṣb, Ḳ,) which is [likewise] a pl. of mult., (Mṣb,) or this last is pl. of ▼ صُوَاعٌ: and this sing. signifies *a* [*vessel of the kind called*] جَام, [app. here used in the sense which this word commonly has in Pers., i. e. as meaning *a cup,*] *in which,* (Ḳ, TA,) or *from which,* (TA,) *one drinks:* (Ḳ, TA:) Sa'eed Ibn-Jubeyr says that the صواع of the king [mentioned in the Ḳur xii. 72] was the *Persian* مَكُّوك, *of which the two extremities* [*are compressed so that they*] *meet together* [app. *in such a manner that the whole vessel resembles a small boat,* the word مكّوك being expl. in several dictionaries as applied to a drinking-vessel of this form, probably from the Pers. مَكُّوك signifying "a shuttle" and used in this sense in modern Arabic]: El-Ḥasan says that *the* صُوَاع *and the* سِقَايَة *are one thing,* as Zj also says; and that the صواع of the king is said to have been of وَرِق [meaning silver], and that they used to measure with it and sometimes they drank with it: Zj says that it is explained as *an oblong vessel, resembling the* مَكُّوك, with which the king used to drink; and said by some to have been of مِسّ [which (as is said in the TA in art. مس) means copper, from the Pers. مِسْ]. (TA.) [See also صَوْغٌ, with غ.] —— صَاعٌ signifies also † The *place* [or *plot*] *in which a* صاع [*of seed*] *is sown:* so in a trad. (TA.) —— And ‡ *A depressed piece of ground;* (Ṣ, O, Ḳ, TA;) as also ▼ صَاعَةٌ; (O, Ḳ, TA;) *like an excavation:* or, as some say, *a depressed place, sloping down from its surrounding borders:* (TA:) or *a narrow, depressed place.* (TA in art. طأ.) —— And † *A place that is swept and in which one then plays:* (Ibn-'Abbád, O, Ḳ:) [see the verse cited in what follows:] and ▼ صَاعَةٌ is said to signify *a piece of ground which a boy sweeps, removing its pebbles, and in which he plays with the ball:* and *a bare place, in which is nothing.* (TA.) —— And The *place of the breast of the ostrich when she puts it upon the ground:* (Ḳ:) or such a place is called صَاعُ جُؤْجُؤِ النَّعَامِ. (IF, O.) And one says, ضَرَبَهُ فِى صَاعِ جُؤْجُؤِهِ and فى صاع صَدْرِهِ meaning ‡ *He struck him in the middle of his breast.* (Z, TA.) —— And it is said that] صَاعٌ also signifies The [*kind of goff-stick called*] صَوْلَجَان. (Ḳ.) In the following verse of El-Museiyab Ibn-'Alas, describing a she-camel,

• مَرِحَتْ يَدَاهَا لِلنَّجَاءِ كَأَنَّمَا •
• تَكْرُو بِكَفَّىْ لَاعِبٍ فِى صَاعِ •

[the most obvious meaning of which is, *Her fore legs moved briskly for the purpose of hastening, as though she were propelling a ball with the hands of a player in a piece of ground cleared for that exercise,*] or, as some relate it, بِكَفَّىْ مَاقِطٍ, meaning *with the hands of a player with the ball,* it is said by some that he means بِصَاعٍ, [though it is not easy to see why, if so, he did not say بِالصَّاعِ,] and that by the صاع he means the صَوْلَجَان, because it is bent (يُعْطَفُ [see 1, last sentence,]) for the purpose of striking with it, that the ball may be propelled (تُصَاعُ) with it. (O.)

صُوعٌ and صَوْعٌ: see صَاعٌ, first sentence. —— The latter is also a pl., (Ḳ, TA,) app. of صِوَاعٌ, with kesr. (TA.)

صَوْعٌ *Portions* of herbage *beginning to dry up.* (Ibn-'Abbád, O, Ḳ.) —— And of the flesh of a horse, *Such as is scattered,* or *sparse; not collected together in one place.* (Ibn-'Abbád, O.)

صَاعَةٌ: see صَاعٌ, latter half, in two places. —— Also ‡ *A place prepared by a woman for the separating and loosening of cotton:* (Lth, O, Ḳ, TA:) and † *a skin, like a* نِطْع, *which a woman sometimes makes,* or *prepares, for the separating and loosening of cotton and of wool upon it.* (ISh, O, TA.) —— And ‡ *A place specially made,* or *prepared, for guests.* (Z, TA.)

صُوَاعٌ and صِوَاعٌ: see صَاعٌ, former half, in five places.

أُصَيْعٌ occurs as a dim. of صِيعَان [or rather of أَصْوُعٌ, pl. of صَاعٌ, regularly formed therefrom]. (IB, TA.)

مُنْصَاعٌ [part. n. of 7] *Turning away* or *back, retreating,* &c. (TA.)

صوغ

1. صَاغَهُ, (Ṣ, MA, O, Mṣb, Ḳ,) aor. يَصُوغُ, (Ṣ, O, Mṣb,) inf. n. صَوْغٌ (Ṣ, MA, O, Mṣb) and صُوَاغٌ (TA) and صِيَاغَةٌ, (MA,) [or the last is a simple subst.,] *He melted it, and poured it forth into a mould;* (TA;) *he cast it, molten, in a mould:* (PṢ:) *he made, formed, fashioned,* or *moulded, it, by the goldsmith's art;* namely, an ornament [and the like]: (MA: [this last is the most usual meaning:]) or *he prepared it,* (Ḳ, TA,) and *cast it,* (TA,) namely, a thing, *after the pattern of a right model.* (Ḳ, TA.) One says of a man, صَاغَ الذَّهَبَ حُلِيًّا [*He cast the gold so as to make of it ornaments;* or *he made, formed, fashioned,* or *moulded, the gold into ornaments*]. (Mṣb.) —— [Hence,] صَاغَهُ اللّٰهُ صِيغَةً حَسَنَةً ‡ *God created him* (Ṣ, O, Ḳ, TA) *in a goodly mode,* or *manner, of creation.* (O, TA.) And صِيغَ عَلَى صِيغَتِهِ ‡ *He*

was created after his [i. e. another's] mode, or manner, of creation. (TA.) — And صاغ شِعْرًا, or كَلَامًا, ‡ He composed, and adjusted, poetry, or speech, discourse, or language. (TA.) — And يَصُوغُونَ الكَلَامَ ‡ They alter speech, [embellish it with lies,] and falsify it, or forge it. (TA.) And فُلَانٌ يَصُوغُ الكَذِبَ, (Ṣ, O, Mṣb,* TA,) inf. n. صَوْغٌ, (Mṣb,) ‡ Such a one forges, or fabricates, that which is false, or untrue: (O, Mṣb:*) a metaphorical phrase. (Ṣ.) And صاغ فُلَانٌ زُورًا and كَذِبًا ‡ Such a one forged, or fabricated, a lie, a falsehood, or an untruth. (TA.) And صَوْغُ اللِّسَانِ means † The lying of the tongue. (Ḥar p. 605.) — صاغ, aor. يَصُوغُ, (O, Ḳ,) inf. n. صَوْغٌ, (O,) also signifies It sank into the ground, said of water; and into the food, said of sauce, or seasoning: (O, Ḳ:) so says ISh. (TA.) — And صاغ لَهُ الشَّرَابُ The beverage, or wine, was easy and agreeable to him to swallow; i. q. ساغ, (Ibn-'Abbád, O, Ḳ,) as a dial. var. (Ibn-'Abbád, O.)

5. تصوّغ: see what next follows.

7. انصاغ quasi-pass. of صَاغَهُ [in all its senses, proper and tropical: meaning It was, or became, melted, and poured forth into a mould; &c.: and in like manner Freytag explains ▼ تصوّغ as used in the book entitled "Les oiseaux et les fleurs," p. 7, meaning "formatus, fictus fuit;" but this is app. post classical]. (O, Ḳ.)

صَوْغٌ inf. n. of صَاغَهُ [q. v.]. (Ṣ &c.) — [In the Ḳur xii. 72,] some read نَفْقِدُ صَوْغَ المَلِكِ [meaning We miss, or see not, or find not, the King's molten vessel, or vessel made of melted metal]: in this instance, صوغ is an inf. n. (O, Ḳ, TA) used as a subst., (O, TA,) in the sense of ▼ المَصُوغ, which means مَا صِيغَ [i. e. the thing that has been melted, and poured forth into a mould; &c.]; like ▼ المُصَاغُ [a pass. part. n. of a verb which is not mentioned]: (TA:) it is like ضَرْبٌ in the phrase هٰذَا دِرْهَمٌ ضَرْبُ الأَمِيرِ, (O, Ḳ,* TA,) meaning مَضْرُوبُهُ: (O, TA:) and Er-Rághib says that it [i. e. the vessel thus termed] is held to have been made of molten gold: (TA:) some read [in the Ḳur xii. 72] ▼ صُوَاغ, as though this also were [originally] an inf. n. (O, Ḳ, TA) from صَاغَ, (O, TA,) like بُوَالٌ and قُوَامٌ (O, Ḳ, TA) from بَالَ and قَامَ. (O, TA.) [See also صَاعٌ, with the unpointed ع.] — One says also, هٰذَا صَوْغُ هٰذَا This is of the measure of this; or is the like in measure of this: [as though of the make, form, fashion, mould, or cast, of this: (see also صِيغَةٌ:)] (Ṣ, O, Mṣb:) and هٰذَا المَآءُ صَوْغُ الإِنَآءِ This water is of the measure of the vessel; or is the like in measure of the vessel: and everything that is the like in measure of another thing is said to be صَوْغُهُ. (O.) — And هُمَا صَوْغَانِ They two are likes: (Ṣ, O, Ḳ:) or they two are coëtaneans; syn. لِدَةٌ [which is properly a sing., though here used as a dual]. (IDrd, O, Ḳ.) — And هُوَ صَوْغُ أَخِيهِ (AA, O, Ḳ) He is he who was born immediately after his brother; and [in like manner, before him, for] he may be above him and he may be below him, (O,) like سَوْغُهُ; as also ▼ صَوْغَةُ أَخِيهِ, (Ḳ, TA, [in the CḲ, erroneously, أُخْتِهِ,]) like سَوْغَةُ أَخِيهِ: (TA:) and هِىَ أُخْتُكَ صَوْغُكَ and ▼ صَوْغَتُكَ [She is thy sister who was born immediately after thee; or before thee]: (O, TA:) the pl. is أَصْوَاغٌ. (TA voce سَوْغ.)

صَوْغَةٌ: see the last sentence here preceding, in two places.

صِيغَةٌ is originally صِوْغَةٌ, (Ṣ, O, Mṣb,) the و being changed into ى because of the kesreh before it: (Ṣ, O:) it is like [illegible]. (Mṣb.) [Its primary signification is A mode, or manner, of صَوْغ i. e. melting, and pouring forth into a mould; &c.: and hence it signifies a make, form, fashion, mould, or cast:] and it is syn. with صِيَاغَةٌ, q. v.: (TA:) and signifies the making [a thing]; and making according to a certain measure or proportion [and the like]. (Mṣb.) One says سِهَامٌ صِيغَةٌ (Ṣ, O, Ḳ) Arrows [one in make;] uniform; (TA;) of the make of one man. (Ṣ, O, Ḳ,* TA.) And صِبْغَةُ ٱللّٰهِ, meaning † The creation of God. (Mṣb.) And هُوَ حَسَنُ الصِّيغَةِ ‡ He is goodly in respect of make and of stature: or this means هُوَ حَسَنُ العَمَلِ [which may in this case be correctly rendered he is goodly in respect of make: and also he is good in respect of work]. (TA.) And هُوَ مِنْ صِيغَةٍ كَرِيمَةٍ ‡ He is of a generous origin. (Ibn-'Abbád, Z, O, Ḳ, TA.) And صِيغَةُ القَوْلِ كَذَا ‡ The mode, manner, fashion, or form, of the saying is thus. (Mṣb.) And صِيغَةُ الأَمْرِ كَذَا وَكَذَا † The shape of the affair, or case, is thus and thus. (TA.)

صَيْغُوغَةٌ: see صِيَاغَةٌ.

صُوَاغٌ: see صَوْغٌ, second sentence.

صِيَاغَةٌ The craft, or art, (Ḳ, TA,) or work, or operation, (Ṣ, O, Mṣb,* TA,) of the صَائِغ [q. v.]; (Ṣ, O, Mṣb, Ḳ, TA;) [generally meaning the craft or art, or the work or operation, of the goldsmith;] the act of melting [gold &c.], and pouring [it] forth into a mould; [&c.; (see 1, first sentence;)] as also ▼ صِيغَةٌ and ▼ صَيْغُوغَةٌ, this last mentioned by Lḥ. (TA.)

صَوَّاغٌ: see the next paragraph, in five places.

صَائِغٌ and ▼ صَوَّاغٌ (Ṣ, MA, O, Mṣb, Ḳ, KL) and ▼ صَيَّاغٌ, (Ṣ, O, Ḳ, KL,) the last of the dial. of El-Ḥijáz, (Ṣ, O,) originally صَيْوَاغٌ, (IJ, O, TA,) thus altered by some, from صَوَّاغٌ to صَيَّاغٌ, because of their disliking the double و, (IJ, TA,) One who practises, or performs, the craft, art, work, or operation, termed صِيَاغَةٌ [or melting gold &c., and pouring it forth into a mould; &c., as expl. in the first sentence of this art.]; (Ṣ, O, Mṣb, Ḳ, TA;) [generally meaning] a goldsmith, or worker in gold: (MA, KL:) the pl. of صَائِغٌ is صَاغَةٌ [originally صَوَغَةٌ] and صُوَّاغٌ and صُيَّاغٌ. (TA.) One says, هُوَ صَوَّاغُ ▼ الحُلِىِّ [and صَائِغُهَا i. e. He is the moulder of ornaments, or of women's ornaments, of gold or of silver &c.]. (TA.) [And hence مِلْحُ الصَّاغَةِ lit. Goldsmiths' salt; meaning chrysocolla, i. e. borax: thus termed in the language of the present day.] Aboo-Ráfi' the صَائِغ is related to have said, كَانَ عُمَرُ يُمَازِحُنِي يَقُولُ أَكْذَبُ النَّاسِ الصَّوَّاغُ ▼ يَقُولُ اليَوْمَ وَغَدًا ['Omar used to jest with me, saying, The most lying of men is the goldsmith, who says, To-day, and To-morrow]. (TA.) And ▼ كَذْبَةٌ كَذَبَهَا الصَّوَّاغُونَ [lit. A lie which the goldsmiths have told] is a saying (of Aboo-Hureyreh, O) occurring in a trad. (Ṣ, O.) — [Hence,] the pl. صَوَّاغٌ means ‡ Persons who alter speech, [embellish it with lies,] and falsify it, or forge it: and ▼ صَوَّاغٌ, ‡ one who moulds speech, and falsifies it, or embellishes it with lies: (TA:) and [in like manner] ▼ صَيِّغٌ, (O, Ḳ, TA,) originally صَيْوِغٌ, (TA,) ‡ one who lies much, and embellishes his speech [with lies]: (Ḳ, O, TA:) the pl. of this last is صَاغَةٌ, like سَادَةٌ pl. of سَيِّدٌ. (TA.) [See also صَبَّاغٌ.]

صَيِّغٌ, originally صَيْوِغٌ: see the next preceding paragraph, last explanation.

صَيِّغَةٌ i. q. ثَرِيدَةٌ [A mess of crumbled bread moistened with broth and piled up in the middle of a bowl]. (Fr, O, Ḳ.)

صَيَّاغٌ, originally صَيْوَاغٌ: see صَائِغٌ.

أَصْيَغُ [as though originally أَصْوَغُ, being mentioned in this art.,] Water such as is common (عَامٌّ) [app. meaning to all who desire to take of it]), and much in quantity. (IAạr, TA.)

مَصَاغٌ, [as a coll. gen. n.,] with fet-ḥ, Moulded ornaments or women's ornaments, of gold or the like; syn. حُلِىٌّ مَصُوغَةٌ. (TA.)

مُصَاغٌ: } see صَوْغٌ, second sentence.
مَصُوغٌ: }

صوف

1. صَافَ, (Ṣ, O, Ḳ,) aor. يَصُوفُ, (Ṣ, O,) inf. n. صَوْفٌ and صُوُوفٌ; and صَوِفَ, (Ṣ, O, Ḳ,) inf. n. صَوَفٌ; (Ṣ;) He (a ram) had much صُوف [or wool], (Ṣ, O, Ḳ,) after having little thereof. (Ṣ, O.) — صاف السَّهْمُ عَنِ الهَدَفِ, aor. يَصُوفُ and يَصِيفُ, (Ṣ, M, O, Mṣb, Ḳ,) inf. n. صَوْفٌ and صَيْفٌ and صَيْفُوفَةٌ, (O and Ḳ in art. صيف,) The arrow turned aside from the butt: (Ṣ, M, O, Mṣb, Ḳ:) like ضاف. (Ṣ and O in art. ضيف.) And صاف عَنِّى وَجْهُهُ His face turned away from me. (Ḳ.) And صاف عَنِّى شَرُّهُ, (Ṣ, M, O,) aor. يَصُوفُ, inf. n. صَوْفٌ, (M,) His (a man's, Ṣ, O) evil, or mischief, turned away from me. (Ṣ,* M, O.*)

2. صوّف الكَرْمُ The grape-vines showed its fruit-stalks [anew] after the cutting off of its fruit. (M.)

4. اصاف ٱللّٰهُ عَنِّى شَرَّهُ God turned away, or

may God turn away, from me his evil, or *mischief.* (Ṣ, Ḳ.) [Mentioned also in art. صيف.]

5. تصوّف *He became a* صُوفِىّ: (Mṣb:) *he devoted himself to religious exercises; or applied himself to devotion:* or *he asserted himself to do so:* (TA:) but it is post-classical. (Mṣb.)

صَافٌ (Ṣ, M, O, Ḳ) and ▼ صَائِفٌ (Ṣ, M, O, Mṣb, Ḳ) and ▼ صَافٍ, (M, O, Ḳ,) which last is formed by transposition [from the second], (M,) and ▼ صَوِفٌ (M, O, Ḳ) and ▼ أَصْوَفُ (Ṣ, M, O, Mṣb, Ḳ) and ▼ صُوفَانٌ (AHeyth, TA) and ▼ صُوفَانِىٌّ, (M, O, Ḳ,) A ram *having much* صُوف [or *wool*]: (Ṣ, M, O, Mṣb, Ḳ:) fem. with ة, (Ḳ, [in which it seems to refer only to the last, i. e.]) the fem. epithet is ▼ صُوفَانِيَّةٌ, (O,) or ▼ صُوفَانَةٌ, (AHeyth, and so in a copy of the M,) and صَافَةٌ also. (M.) — And لِمَّةٌ صَافَةٌ [*A lock of hair hanging down below the lobe of the ear*] *of which the hair is like* صُوف [i. e. *wool*]. (M.) ═ See also صُوفٌ. ═ And see art. صيف.

صَافٍ: see the next preceding paragraph.

صُوفٌ [*Wool;*] *an appertenance of sheep,* (in the Ṣ لِلشَّاةِ, in the M لِلْغَنَمِ, and in the O and Mṣb [more definitely] لِلضَّأْنِ,) *which is to them like* شَعْرٌ *to goats and* وَبَرٌ *to camels:* (M:) [in the Ḳ only said to be well known:] n. un. صُوفَةٌ, (M,) [i. e.] this latter has a more particular signification [meaning *a portion, flock, tuft,* or *wisp, of wool*]: (Ṣ, O, Mṣb, Ḳ:) and sometimes صُوفٌ is used in the sense of the n. un., as mentioned by Sb: (M:) the pl. of صُوفٌ is أَصْوَافٌ [meaning *sorts of wool*]: (M:) and the dim. of the n. un. is ▼ صُوَيْفَةٌ. (TA.) One says خَرْقَآءُ وَجَدَتْ صُوفًا [*An unskilful woman that has found wool*]: (Aṣ, O, Ḳ:) a prov. (Aṣ, O) relating to property possessed by such as does not deserve to have it: (Aṣ, TA:) because the unskilful woman, when she lights upon wool, mars it, (O, Ḳ,) not spinning it well: (O:) applied to the stupid person who finds property and wastes it; (O, Ḳ;) or to him who finds that of which he knows not the value, and wastes it. (Z, TA.) And one says, فُلَانٌ يَلْبَسُ الصُّوفَ وَالقُطْنَ, meaning *Such a one wears what is made of wool and of cotton.* (A, TA.) In the saying of a poet,

• حَلْبَانَةٍ رَكْبَانَةٍ صَفُوفِ •

• تَخْلِطُ بَيْنَ وَبَرٍ وَصُوفِ •

[*Of one that is milked and ridden, that yields a row of bowls of her milk,* (but see صَفُوفٌ, of which other explanations have been given,) *that mingles camels' fur and wool*], the latter hemistich means, as Th says, accord. to IAạr, that is sold, and with the price whereof are purchased camels and sheep: or, accord. to Aṣ, that is quick in her pace; the drawing back of her fore legs being likened to [the motion of] the bow of the نَدَّاف who mixes camels' fur and wool. (M.) One says also, أَخَذْتُ بِصُوفِ رَقَبَتِهِ (Ṣ, M, Ḳ, but in the M أَخَذَ,) and بِصُوفَتِهَا (M, O) and ▼ بِصَافِهَا, (M, Ḳ,) and بِطُوفِ رَقَبَتِهِ and بِطَافِهَا, and بِطُوفِ رَقَبَتِهِ and بِطَافِهَا, and بِقُوفِ رَقَبَتِهِ and بِقَافِهَا, (Ṣ, O,) meaning ‡ [*I laid hold upon*] *the pendent hair in the hollow of the back of his neck:* (IDrd, Ṣ, M, O, Ḳ:) or *the downy hairs upon the back of his neck:* (M, O:) or *the skin of his neck:* (IAạr, Ṣ, O, Ḳ:) or *the back of his neck, altogether:* (Fr, Ṣ, O, Ḳ:) or *I took him by force:* (Abu-l-Ghowth, Ṣ, O, Ḳ:) or *I followed him, thinking that I should not reach him, and overtook him;* and this one says whether he lay hold upon his neck or not. (Abu-s-Semeyda', Ṣ, O, Ḳ.) And أَعْطَاهُ بِصُوفِ رَقَبَتِهِ ‡ [*He gave it altogether*]; like أَعْطَاهُ بِرُمَّتِهِ: or (as expl. by A'Obey[illegible]O) *he gave it gratuitously; not taking a price.* (Ṣ, O, Ḳ.) — صُوفُ البَحْرِ [lit. *The wool of the sea*] is *a thing* [or *substance*] *in the form of the animal* صُوف [i. e., *of wool;* evidently meaning *sea-weed resembling wool;* such as is found in abundance thrown up on the beaches of the Red Sea: and that this is generally, if not in every instance, meant by the identical Hebrew word סוּף, as used in the Bible, has been most satisfactorily shown in art. "Red Sea" (by my deeply-lamented nephew Edward Stanley Poole) in Dr. William Smith's "Dictionary of the Bible"]: it is said in one of the أَبَدِيَّات, [see art. ابد,] لَا آتِيكَ مَا بَلَّ بَحْرٌ صُوفَةً [*I will not come to thee as long as a sea wets a portion of* صُوف], or, as Lḥ relates it, مَا بَلَّ البَحْرُ صُوفَةً [*as long as the sea wets its* صُوف; meaning, *ever*]. (M, TA.)

صَوِفٌ: see صَافٌ.

صُوفَةٌ n. un. of صُوفٌ [q. v.]. (M &c.) — [Also applied by physicians to *A pessary,* or *suppository, of wool, containing a medicament of some kind, to be inserted into the vagina* or *rectum.*] ═ Also *Any of those who had the management of aught of the work of the* بَيْت [meaning the *House of God,* i. e. the *Kaabeh*], and who were called ▼ الصُّوفَانُ: (M:) [accord. to the TA, it is said that الصُّوفَةُ and الصُّوفَانُ are both alike appellations applied to any of such persons:] J and others say that صُوفَةُ was the father of a tribe of Muḍar, who used to serve the Kaabeh, and to return with the pilgrims from 'Arafát, in the Time of Ignorance; and it is implied in the Ṣ [that they were also called آلُ صُوفَانَ, or] that صُوفَة was also called صُوفَان; and in a saying of Z, that آلُ صُوفَانَ and الصُّوفَان were appellations of one and the same people: [hence, app., the applications of صُوفَةٌ and صُوفَانٌ to any servants of the Kaabeh:] but accord. to Ṣgh and the Ḳ, آلُ صُوفَانَ is a mistake for آلُ صَفْوَانَ. (TA.)

صُوفَانٌ, and its fem., with ة: see صَافٌ: ═ and for the former see also صُوفَةٌ. ═ Also [*A species of agaric, i. e., of the kind of fungus thus called;*] *a certain thing* [or *substance*] *that comes forth from the heart of trees, flaccid and dry, in which fire is struck, and which is the best of things for the purpose of those who strike fire.* (TA.)

صُوفَانَةٌ, applied to a ewe, is fem. of صُوفَانٌ: see صَافٌ. (AHeyth, TA.) — Also *A certain herb,* or *leguminous plant,* (بَقْلَةٌ,) *downy,* (M, Ḳ,) *and short,* (Ḳ,) mentioned by Aboo-Naṣr as *of the kind termed* أَحْرَار [pl. of حُرٌّ], but not specifically described by him. (AḤn, M.)

صُوفِىٌّ, a post-classical word, *A man of the people called the* صُوفِيَّة: (Mṣb:) [formerly applied to any *devotee:* afterwards, particularly, to *a mystic; one who seeks to raise himself to a high degree of spiritual excellence by contemplation of divine things so as to elicit the mysteries thereof:*] the صُوفِيَّة may be so called [from the Greek σοφός: or] in relation to the people called آلُ صُوفَان, [see صُوفَةٌ,] as resembling them in the devotion of themselves to religious exercises: or in relation to those called أَهْلُ الصُّفَّةِ, wherefore they are also called الصُّفِّيَّةُ: or in relation to الصُّوف [i. e. wool], which is proper to devotees and recluses: this last is the derivation commonly received. (TA.)

صُوفَانِىٌّ; and its fem., with ة: see صَافٌ.

صُوَيْفَةٌ dim. of صُوفَةٌ, n. un. of صُوفٌ, q. v. (TA.)

صَوَّافٌ *A manufacturer of* صُوف [or *wool,* or *of woollen garments &c.*]. (TA.)

صَائِفٌ: see صَافٌ.

صَيِّفَةٌ, originally صَيْوِفَةٌ, A [garment of the kind called] جُبَّة *having much* صُوف [or *wool*]. (TA.)

أَصْوَفُ: see صَافٌ.

صوك

1. صَاكَ بِهِ, (O, Ḳ,) aor. يَصُوكُ, (O,) inf. n. صَوْكٌ, (Ḳ,) *It stuck,* or *clave, to him,* or *it:* (O, Ḳ;) said of saffron, (Ḳ,) and of blood, and of other things: (TA:) and (O, Ḳ) so صاك به, aor. يَصِيكُ, (Ṣ, O, Ḳ, in art. صيك,) inf. n. صَيْكٌ; (Ḳ;) said of perfume. (Ṣ, O, Ḳ.) See also صَيَّكَ.

5. تصوّك فِى رَجِيعِهِ, (Aṣ, O, Ḳ,) or, accord. to AZ, تَضَوَّكَ, with ض, (O,) or both, (Lḥ, TA in art. صف,) [and تَصَوَّقَ,] *He* (a man, O) *became defiled,* or *befouled, with* [or *in*] *his dung.* (O, Ḳ.)

صَوْكٌ The *seminal fluid* of a man. (Th, Kr, Ḳ.) ═ Also The *first.* (Ḳ.) One says, لَقِيتُهُ أَوَّلَ صَوْكٍ and بَوْكٍ *I met him the first thing.* (Ṣ, O, Ḳ.) And in like manner, اِفْعَلْهُ أَوَّلَ كُلِّ صَوْكٍ and بَوْكٍ [*Do thou it the first of everything*]. (TA.) And خُذْ هٰذَا أَوَّلَ صَوْكٍ: see 1 in art. صك. (O and TA in that art.) ═ Also *Motion:* so in the phrase مَا بِهِ صَوْكٌ and بَوْكٌ [*There is not in him,* or *it, any motion*]. (IDrd, O, Ḳ.)

صَائِكٌ *Sticking,* or *cleaving.* (AA, TA.) — And [app. as an epithet in which the quality of a subst. is predominant] *Sticking blood:* or *blood of the* جَوْف [or *belly,* &c.]. (TA.) — See also art. صاك.

صول

1. صَالَ عَلَيْهِ, [aor. يَصُولُ,] inf. n. صَوْلٌ and

صَوْلَةٌ (Ṣ, O, Ḳ) and صِيَالٌ, (O,) *He leaped*, or *sprang, upon him:* (Ṣ, O, Ḳ:) and (Ḳ) صَالَ عَلَيْهِ, (M, Ḳ,) aor. يَصُولُ, (TA,) inf. n. صَوْلٌ and صِيَالٌ and صُؤُولٌ and صَوَلَانٌ and صَالٌ and مَصَالَةٌ, *he sprang*, or *rushed, upon him; made an assault*, or *attack, upon him;* namely, his adversary, or antagonist; syn. سَطَا; (M, Ḳ, TA;) and حَمَلَ: (TA:) [or *he sprang upon him and seized him violently* or *laid violent hands upon him;* for so سَطَا is said to signify:] and صال عَلَيْهِ ‡ *he overbore him, overpowered him*, or *subdued him;* (Ṣ,* O,* Mṣb,* TA; [a meaning also assigned to سَطَا;]) namely, one man another man. (TA.) [See also 1 in art. صيل.] One says, رُبَّ قَوْلٍ أَشَدُّ مِنْ صَوْلٍ *Many a saying is more severe than a leaping* or *springing* [&c.]. (Ṣ, O.) And it is said in a trad. respecting prayer, بِكَ أَصُولُ, meaning [*By Thee may I*] *spring*, or *rush*, or *assault, and subdue.* (TA.) — صال, aor. as above, inf. n. صَوْلٌ, is also said of a stallion [camel], meaning *He leaped*, or *sprang:* or, accord. to AZ, صال, inf. n. صَوْلٌ and صِيَالٌ, said of a camel, means *he leaped*, or *sprang, upon the* [other] *camels, and fought them:* (Mṣb:) or one says of a stallion, صال عَلَى الإِبِلِ, inf. n. صَوْلٌ, meaning *he fought the* [other] *camels*, (M, Ḳ,) *and sent them on before:* (M:) or, accord. to AZ, one says of a camel, (Ṣ,) or, accord. to Es-Sarakustee, some of the Arabs say of a camel, (Mṣb,) صَؤُلَ, (Ṣ, Mṣb, [in one of my copies of the Ṣ صال, but the former is the right,]) like قَرُبَ, (Mṣb,) with ء, (Ṣ, Mṣb,) inf. n. صَآلَةٌ, meaning *he betook himself to the killing of men, and springing*, or *rushing, upon them:* (Ṣ:) and without ء in speaking of the act of one adversary, or antagonist, against another: (Mṣb:) Ḥamzeh El-Iṣbahánee says, in his "Proverbs," that صال الجَمَلُ means *the camel bit;* but he is alone in saying this. (TA.) One says also, صال العَيْرُ, meaning *The he-ass attacked the she-ass:* (Ṣ, O:) or صال العَيْرُ عَلَى العَانَةِ *the he-ass drove away the she-ass*, or *the herd of wild she-asses*, (M, Ḳ, TA,) *and attacked her* or *them, biting her* or *them with the fore teeth, and kicking her* or *them with the hind leg* or *hind legs.* (TA.) — صال البُرَّ, aor. as above, inf. n. صَوْلٌ, *He swept away*, or *cleared, the wheat from the pieces of stick and of rubbish:* and صَوَّلْنَا ↓ الحِنْطَةَ *we swept the wheat* [*well, and so cleared it from rubbish*]: the teshdeed denotes intensiveness of meaning: (O:) ↓ التَّصْوِيلُ [or تَصْوِيلُ البَيْدَرِ] means *the sweeping of the* بَيْدَر [or *collected wheat* or *grain*, or perhaps the *place in which wheat* or *grain is trodden out*], (O,) or *of the sides thereof* (نَوَاحِى البَيْدَرِ [*to clear it of rubbish*]). (Ḳ.) — صِيلَ: see art. صيل.

2. صَوَّلَ, and its inf. n.: see 1, last sentence but one. — تَصْوِيلٌ also signifies The *extracting a thing by means of water:* (Ḳ, TA: [in the CḲ, بالمالِ is erroneously put for بِالمَآءِ:]) like the extracting a pebble from rice [by washing]. (TA.) [And app. The *soaking* a thing *to extract the juice* or *bitterness* &c.: see مِصْوَلٌ. See also an ex. in De Sacy's Chrest. Arabe, sec. ed., vol. ii. p. 130 of the Ar. text; and see his remarks thereon in p. 335 of the transl. and notes.] — [Also The *mixing, and stirring about, and beating,* a thing.] One says, الجَرَادُ يُصَوَّلُ فِى مِشْوَاهُ [in the CḲ, مَشْواهُ, which is a mistranscription,] *The locusts are mixed, and stirred about, and beaten, in his* مِشْوًى (O, Ḳ) i. e. *frying-pan.* (TḲ.)

3. مُصَاوَلَةٌ and صِيَالٌ and ↓ صِيَالَةٌ [of which the first and second are inf. ns., the third being a quasi-inf. n.,] are *syn. with* مُوَاثَبَةٌ; (Ṣ, O, Ḳ;) صَاوَلَهُ signifying وَاثَبَهُ [i. e. *He leaped*, or *sprang, upon him;* or *he assaulted*, or *assailed, him:* or *he contended with him, each leaping*, or *springing, upon the other*, or *each assaulting*, or *assailing, the other*]. (Ḳ.) [See also 6.]

6. الفَحْلَانِ يَتَصَاوَلَانِ i. q. يَتَوَاثَبَانِ [i. e. *The two stallion-camels leap*, or *spring, upon each other;* or *assault*, or *assail, each other*]. (Ṣ.)

صَوْلَةٌ is an inf. n.: (Ṣ, O, Ḳ: [see 1, first sentence:]) or it signifies *A leap*, or *spring:* (TA:) or *a single act of* a camel's *leaping*, or *springing, upon* [other] *camels, and fighting them;* as also ↓ صِيَالَةٌ: (Mṣb:) [but more commonly, *impetuosity*, of a man, and of a camel or the like.] — [Hence,] ذُو صَوْلَةٍ فِى المِزْوَدِ *One who springs upon the food, and devours it immoderately.* (M, TA.*) — لَقِيتُهُ أَوَّلَ صَوْلَةٍ means أَوَّلَ وَهْلَةٍ [i. e. *I met him the first thing*, or *the first thing that I saw*]. (A, TA.)

صَوْلَةٌ مِنْ حِنْطَةٍ and ↓ حِنْطَةٌ مُصَوَّلَةٌ [signify nearly the same, the former meaning *A heap of wheat*, and the latter *wheat* in general, *cleared from rubbish by means of the implement called* مِصْوَلٌ or مِصْوَلَةٌ]: (O, Ḳ: [these significations are clearly indicated in the Ḳ, and more so in the O, by the context:]) the pl. of صَوْلَةٌ is صُوَلٌ. (O.)

صِيلَةٌ, mentioned here in the Ḳ: see art. صيل.

صَؤُولٌ A camel *that devours his pastor; that springs upon men, and devours them:* (Lth, TA:) a camel *that kills men, and springs*, or *rushes, upon them:* (Ṣ:) or a camel *that leaps*, or *springs, upon the* [other] *camels, and fights them:* (Mṣb:) or a stallion *that fights the* [other] *camels*, (M, Ḳ,) *and sends them on before.* (M.) And † A man *who beats others, and overbears, overpowers*, or *subdues, them.* (TA.) Accord. to Az, it is originally without ء, and is app. pronounced with ء because the و is with ḍamm. (TA.)

صِيَالٌ an inf. n. of 1 [q. v.]. (M, O, Mṣb, Ḳ.) — [And also an inf. n. of 3, q. v.]

صِيَالَةٌ: see 3: and see also صَوْلَةٌ.

أَصْوَلُ مِنْ جَمَلٍ [*More impetuous than a camel;* or *more wont to spring upon others, or to assault, or assail, them, than a camel*]. (TA.)

مِصْوَلٌ *A thing in which colocynths are soaked in order that their bitterness may depart.* (AZ, Ṣ, O, Ḳ.) — And, accord. to Ibn-'Abbád, *An implement with which the ears of corn are swept away*, or *cleared, from the pieces of stick and of rubbish.* (O. [See also what next follows.])

مِصْوَلَةٌ *A broom* (مِكْنَسَةٌ, O, Ḳ) *with which the sides of the* بَيْدَر [or *collected wheat* or *grain*, or perhaps the *place in which wheat* or *grain is trodden out*,] *are swept* [*to clear it of rubbish*]: (O, TA:) so says IAạr. (TA. [See also what next precedes.])

حِنْطَةٌ مُصَوَّلَةٌ: see صَوْلَةٌ مِنْ حِنْطَةٍ.

صولج

صَوْلَجٌ and صَوْلَجَةٌ: see what here follows.

صَوْلَجَانٌ (T, Ṣ, Ḳ) and ↓ صَوْلَجَانَةٌ (Sb, TA) and ↓ صَوْلَجٌ (T, TA) and ↓ صَوْلَجَةٌ, (TA,) as also صَوْجَانٌ, (L in art. صوج,) [*A kind of goff-stick*, or *golf-stick, played with by men on horseback;*] *a stick with a curved*, or *crooked, end;* syn. مِحْجَنٌ; (Ṣ, Ḳ;) [or rather] *a stick of which the end is curved* [*artificially*] *with which a ball is struck by men on horseback:* a stick of which the end curves, or crooks, naturally, on its tree, is called مِحْجَنٌ: (T, TA:) of Pers. origin, (Ṣ,) [i. e. from the Pers. چوگان,] arabicized: (T, Ṣ:) pl. صَوَالِجَةٌ; (Ṣ, Ḳ;) the ة being added in the pl. because of the foreign origin, (Ṣ, M, TA,) as is mostly the case in broken pls. of words of foreign origin. (M, TA.)

صَوْلَجَانَةٌ: see the next paragraph here preceding.

صوم

1. صَامَ, (Ṣ, M, &c.,) aor. يَصُومُ, (Mṣb,) inf. n. صَوْمٌ and صِيَامٌ; (Ṣ, M, Mgh, Mṣb, Ḳ;) and ↓ اِصْطَامَ; (M, Ḳ;) *He abstained*, (Mṣb, TA,) in an absolute sense: (Mṣb:) this is the primary signification: (TA:) [or] this is said to be the signification in the proper language of the Arabs: (Mṣb:) and in the language of the law, (Mṣb, TA,) *he observed a particular kind of abstinence;* (Mṣb;) i. e. (TA) *he abstained from food* (Ṣ, M, Ḳ, TA) *and drink* (M, Ḳ, TA) *and coïtus:* (M, Ḳ:) and (Ṣ,* M, &c.) by a tropical application, (TA,) ‡ *from speech:* (Ṣ,* M, Mgh, Mṣb,* Ḳ, TA:) or صَوْمٌ in the proper language of the Arabs signifies a man's *abstaining from eating:* and by a secondary application, *a particular serving of God* [by fasting]; (Mgh;) [i. e.] the *abstaining from eating and drinking and coïtus from daybreak to sunset:* (KT:) accord. to Kh, it signifies [properly] the *standing without work.* (Ṣ.) صام فِى الشَّهْرِ means صام الشَّهْرَ [*He fasted during the month*]: agreeably with what is said in the Ḳur ii. 181. (TA.) And it is said (Ṣ, M) by I'Ab (Ṣ) that the saying, in the Ḳur [xix. 27], إِنِّى نَذَرْتُ لِلرَّحْمٰنِ صَوْمًا (Ṣ, M,) means † [*Verily I have vowed unto the Compassionate*] *an abstaining from speech.* (Ṣ, M, Mṣb.) One says also, صام الفَرَسُ, inf. n. صَوْمٌ (Ṣ, M) and صِيَامٌ, (M,) † *The horse stood without eating of fodder;* (Ṣ;) or *abstained from the eating of fodder.* (M, A, Mgh.) And صام عَنِ السَّيْرِ ‡ *He abstained from going along*, or *journeying.* (TA.) — [Hence,]

صامت الشمس † *The sun became* [*apparently*] *stationary* [*in the mid-heaven*]: (T, TA:) or *attained its full height.* (M, TA.) — And صام النّهار, (inf. n. صَوْمٌ, Ṣ,) ‡ *The day reached its mid-point.* (Ṣ, M, Mgh, Ḳ, TA.) — And صامت الرِّيحُ, (M, TA,) inf. n. صَوْمٌ, (Ṣ, Ḳ,) ‡ *The wind became still,* or *calm.* (Ṣ, M, Ḳ, TA.) — And صام المَآءُ, [inf. n. صَوْمٌ (see صُلَاقَةٌ) and probably صِيَامٌ also,] † *The water became still,* or *motionless;* syn. قَامَ and دَامَ. (TA.) — And صام النَّعَامُ, (M, Ḳ,) inf. n. صَوْمٌ, (M,) ‡ *The ostrich cast forth its dung;* (M, Ḳ, TA;) and in the same sense the verb is used in relation to the domestic fowl; because each stands still in doing this, or because each becomes tranquil by reason of the passing forth of that which occasions annoyance: and accord. to [some one or more of the copies of] the M, صام النّهار, inf. n. صَوْمٌ, *The* نهار, by which is here meant the *young one of the* كَرَوَان, [or rather *of the bustard called* حُبَارَى,] *cast forth what was in its belly.* (TA.) = صام مَنِيَّتَهُ i. q. ذَاقَهَا [*He tasted,* or *experienced, his death*]. (Ḳ.) = And صَامَ *He* (a man) *shaded himself by means of the tree called* صَوْم. (Ḳ.)

8: see 1, first sentence.

صَوْمٌ an inf. n. of 1 [q. v.]. (Ṣ, M, &c.) — [Hence,] الصَّوْمُ [app. for وَقْتُ الصَّوْمِ] means also ‡ [*The month of*] *Ramadán*: (Ḳ, TA:) whence the saying of Aboo-Zeyd, أَقَمْتُ بِالبَصْرَةِ صَوْمَيْنِ, meaning [*I remained, stayed, dwelt,* or *abode, in El-Baṣrah*] *two Ramadáns.* (TA.) — And [in like manner] صَوْمٌ also means † *A Christian church;* syn. بِيعَةٌ: (Ṣ, Ḳ, TA:) as though for مَحَلُّ الصَّوْمِ i. e. الوُقُوف [*the place of station:* for, as Hooker says, speaking of the ancient usage of the Church, "their manner was to stand at prayer, whereupon their meetings unto that purpose had the names of stations given them"]. (TA.) = See also صَائِمٌ. = Also † The *dung of the ostrich.* (Ṣ, M, Ḳ.) = And, in the dial. of Hudheyl, (Ṣ,) *Certain trees,* (Ṣ, M,) or *a certain tree,* (Ḳ,) [but] the n. un. is with ة, *of the form of the figure of a human being,* (M,) *ugly in appearance,* (M, Ḳ,) *very much so, the fruits of which are called* رُؤُوسُ الشَّيَاطِينِ i. e. [*the heads*] *of the serpents,* [see شَيْطَانٌ and زَقُّومٌ,] *not having leaves:* AḤn says that *they have* [*what are termed*] هَدَب [q. v.], *their branches do not spread forth, they grow in the manner of the* [*species of tamarisk called*] أَثْل, *but are not so tall, and mostly grow in the districts of Benoo-Shebábeh.* (M.)

صَامَةٌ, for صَوْمَةٌ, inf. n. of un. of صَامَ: see a verse cited voce ثَابَ, in art. توب.

صَائِمٌ: see صَوْمَانُ.

أَرْضٌ صَوَامٌ *Dry land* or *ground, in which is no water.* (Ḳ.)

صَوَّامٌ is like صَائِمٌ but having an intensive signification [i. e. meaning *Abstaining,* &c., *much* or *often*]. (Mṣb.) One says رَجُلٌ صَوَّامٌ قَوَّامٌ, meaning *A man who fasts* (يَصُومُ) [*often*] *in the day, and who rises* [*often*] *in the night* ! [*to pray*]. (TA.)

صَائِمٌ *Abstaining,* in an absolute sense: this is said to be the signification in the proper language of the Arabs: and in the language of the law, *observing a particular kind of abstinence;* (Mṣb;) [i. e.] *abstaining from food* (Ṣ, M, Ḳ) *and drink and coïtus:* and, [by a tropical application, (see 1, first sentence,)] ‡ *from speech:* (M, Ḳ:) it is applied to a man: (Ṣ, M, Mṣb:) and ▼ صَوْمَانُ signifies the same, (Ṣ, Ḳ,) so applied; (Ṣ;) as also ▼ صَوْمٌ, (M, Ḳ,) applied to a man, (M,) and to a woman, and to two men, (TA,) and to a pl. number; (M, Ḳ;) being an inf. n. used as an epithet; (TA;) or it is a pl., [or rather quasi-pl. n.,] like زَوْرٌ: (M voce ضَيْفٌ:) or, in the proper language of the Arabs, صَائِمٌ signifies *abstaining from eating:* and by a secondary application, *serving God in a particular manner* [*by fasting:* see again 1, first sentence]: (Mgh:) accord. to AO, it signifies any creature *abstaining from food,* or † *from speech,* or † *from going along* or *journeying:* (Ṣ, Mṣb:) pl. صِيَامٌ and صُوَّمٌ (Ṣ, M, Mgh, Mṣb, Ḳ) and صُيَّمٌ (Ṣ, M, Mṣb, Ḳ) and صِيَّمٌ and صُوَّامٌ and صُيَّامٌ and صَيَامَى, (M, Ḳ,) the last of which [written in the CḲ صُيَامَى] is extr. (M.) — Applied to a horse, † *Standing still* (Ṣ, M, Mṣb) *without eating of fodder* (Ṣ, Mṣb) or *without eating anything:* (M:) or *abstaining from the eating of fodder:* (Mgh:) or *standing upon his four legs.* (Az in art. صون, and TA.) — And بَكْرَةٌ صَائِمَةٌ † *A sheave of a pulley that remains still,* (Mgh, TA,) *that will not revolve.* (Ṣ, Mgh, TA.) — And مَآءٌ صَائِمٌ † *Water that is still,* or *motionless;* syn. قَائِمٌ and دَائِمٌ. (Mgh, TA.)

مَصَامٌ ‡ The *station,* or *standing-place,* of a horse; as also ▼ مَصَامَةٌ. (Ṣ, Ḳ, TA.) — And مَصَامُ النَّجْمِ † *The* [*imaginary*] *place of suspension of the asterism* [meaning the *Pleiades*]. (M.) Imra-el-Ḳeys says,

* كَأَنَّ الثُّرَيَّا عُلِّقَتْ فِى مَصَامِهَا *

* بِأَمْرَاسِ كَتَّانٍ إِلَى صُمِّ جَنْدَلِ *

[*As though the Pleiades were hung, in their place of suspension, by means of ropes of flax, to hard and solid rocks:* i. e. they seemed as though they were stationary: he means that the night was tedious to him]. (Ṣ. [See EM p. 36, where a reading of the former hemistich different from that above is given, with the same and another reading of the latter hemistich.]) — One says also, جِئْتُهُ وَالشَّمْسُ فِى مَصَامِهَا, meaning † [*I came to him when the sun was*] *in the middle of the sky.* (TA.)

مَصَامَةٌ: see the next preceding paragraph.

صون

1. صَانَهُ, (M, Ḳ,) first pers. صُنْتُهُ, (Ṣ, Mṣb,) aor. يَصُونُهُ, (TA,) inf. n. صَوْنٌ and صِيَانٌ and صِيَانَةٌ, (Ṣ, M, Mṣb, Ḳ,) *He preserved it, kept it, laid it up, took care of it,* or *reserved it,* (Mṣb, Ḳ,) *in its repository;* (Mṣb;) and ▼ اصطانهُ signifies the same: (M, Ḳ:) but one should not say اصانهُ, as the vulgar say. (TA.) — And [hence] one says, (M, Mṣb,) by way of comparison, (M,) صان عِرْضَهُ, (M, Mṣb,) inf. n. صَوْنٌ and صِيَانَةٌ, (M,) † [*He preserved his honour,* or *reputation*], عَنِ الدَّنَسِ [*from pollution*]. (Mṣb. [See also 6.]) And فُلَانٌ يَصُونُ دِيبَاجَتَيْهِ i. e. ‡ [*Such a one preserves from disgrace*] *his cheeks;* (A in art. دبج;) or دِيبَاجَتَهُ *his face.* (Ḥar p. 15.) — And صان الفَرَسُ عَدْوَهُ (M, TA) and جَرْيَهُ, (TA,) inf. n. صَوْنٌ, ‡ *The horse reserved somewhat of his running for the time of need.* (M, TA.) And ذُو صَوْنٍ; فَرَسٌ لَهُ صَوْنٌ وَبَذْلٌ; and وَٱبْتِذَالٍ: see 1 in art. بذل. — And صان الفَرَسُ, aor. يَصُونُ, inf. n. صَوْنٌ, means صَفَّ بَيْنَ رِجْلَيْهِ [app. the same as صَفَّ رِجْلَيْهِ *He set his hind legs evenly, side by side*]: (M:) or *he stood upon the extremity of his hoof,* (Ṣ, M, Ḳ,) *by reason of* [*attenuation,* or *abrasion, such as is termed*] حَفًا or وَجًى. (Ṣ, Ḳ.) — And صان, inf. n. صَوْنٌ, *He* (a horse) *limped,* or *halted, much;* (M;) or, as expl. by IB, *slightly.* (TA.) يَصُنَّ المَشْىَ occurs in a verse (Ṣ, M, TA) of En-Nábighah, (M, TA,) [referring to horses,] and J says that Aṣ knew it not, but that others expl. it as meaning *Reserving somewhat of the rate of going,* (TA,) or as meaning *suffering pain in the hoofs from attenuation,* or *abrasion:* (Ṣ:) accord. to IB, it means *limping,* or *halting, and suffering pain in the hoofs, from fatigue.* (TA.)

5: see the next paragraph.

6. تَصَاوَنَ is the *contr. of* اِبْتَذَلَ, (Mṣb,) or of تَبَذَّلَ: (Ṣ and Mṣb in art. بذل:) one says, of a man, تَصَاوَنَ and ▼ تَصَوَّنَ, the latter on the authority of IJ, (M, TA,) and mentioned also by Z, (TA,) † *He preserved himself,* or *his honour,* or *reputation,* (M, TA,) مِنَ المَعَايِبِ [*from the things,* or *actions, for which he should be blamed*]. (TA. [See also 1, second sentence.])

8: see 1, first sentence.

صَوْنٌ an inf. n. of 1 [q. v.]. (Ṣ, M, &c.) See also صِينَةٌ, below. — And see مَصُونٌ.

صَوْنَةٌ [*A receptacle for perfumes &c., such as is commonly called*] an عَتِيدَة. (IAṣr, Ḳ.)

صِينَةٌ [originally صِوْنَةٌ] *i. q.* ▼ صَوْنٌ: one says, هٰذِهِ ثِيَابُ الصِّينَةِ i. e. الصَّوْنِ [*These are the garments of reservation* for wear on extraordinary occasions]: (M, TA:) *contr. of* بِذْلَةٌ. (TA.)

صِوَانٌ and صُوَانٌ (Ṣ, M, Mṣb, Ḳ) and صَوَانٌ (Ḳ) and صِيَانٌ (Ṣ, Mṣb, Ḳ) and صُيَانٌ and صَيَانٌ, (Ḳ,) but the third and the last two are extr., (TA,) *A thing,* (M, Mṣb, Ḳ,) or *receptacle,* (Ṣ,) [or *chest* or *the like,*] *used as a repository* (Ṣ, M, Mṣb, Ḳ) *for a garment,* (Ṣ, Ḳ,) as also ▼ مَصَانٌ, (Skr, cited by Reiske in Abulf. Ann. ii. 614,) [or for clothes,] or *for a thing:* (M, Mṣb:) pl.

أَصْوِنَةٌ: (MA:) or ▼ مَصَانٌ signifies *any place in which one reposits a garment.* (TA in art. خوس.)

صَوَانِىُّ pl. of صِينِىٌّ. (KL.) See art. صين.

صَوَّانٌ [*Flint-stone;* and *flint-stones:* thus in the present day:] *a sort of stones,* (Ṣ, Mṣb,) *in which is hardness;* (Mṣb;) *hard stones,* (M, Ḳ,) *of a certain sort,* (Ḳ,) *with which fire is struck:* or, as some say, *certain black stones which are not hard:* (M:) or *a sort of hard stones, which, when fire smites it, crackles* (يَتَفَقَّعُ) *and cracks, and sometimes fire is struck with it, but it is not fit for* [*making*] *lime, nor for heating for the purpose of roasting thereon:* (Az, TA:) one thereof is called ▼ صَوَّانَةٌ. (Ṣ, M, Mṣb, Ḳ.)

دُبُر الصَّوَّانَة *The* [meaning *anus*]: (Ḳ, TA:) so called because it keeps [from escape] much, or often, what would issue from it. (TA.) ━ See also صَوَّانٌ.

صَيِّنٌ [thus app., like سَيِّدٌ and جَيِّدٌ, written in my copy of the Mṣb صَيِن,] One *who preserves his honour,* or *reputation.* (Mṣb.)

مَصَانٌ : see صِوَانٌ, in two places.

مُصَانٌ : see مِصْوَانٌ.

مَصُونٌ and ▼ مَصْوُونٌ, (Ṣ, M, Mṣb, Ḳ,) like مَدُوفٌ and مَدْوُوفٌ, (Ṣ and Mṣb in art. دوف, q. v.,) the latter of the dial. of Temeem, (M,) *Preserved, kept, laid up, taken care of,* or *reserved;* (Ṣ,* M,* Mṣb, Ḳ;) applied to a garment [&c.]; (Ṣ, M;) as also ▼ صَوْنٌ, which is an inf. n. used as an epithet: (M:) one should not say مُصَانٌ, (Ṣ, TA,) nor مُنْصَانٌ, as the vulgar say. (TA.)

مِصْوَانٌ *A bow-case;* (Ḳ, TA;) as also ▼ مُصَانٌ. (TA.)

مَصْوُونٌ : see مَصُونٌ.

صوى

1. صَوِيَتِ النَّخْلَةُ, (Lth, Az, Ṣ, M, Ḳ,) aor. تَصْوَى, (Ṣ, Ḳ,) inf. n. صُوِىٌّ; (Lth, Az, Ṣ, M, Ḳ;) and صَوِيَت, (Az, M, Ḳ,) which is the form preferred by Az, [aor. تَصْوَى,] inf. n. صَوًى; (TA;) *The palm-tree needed irrigation, and became slender:* (Az, TA:) or *became dry,* or *dried up;* (Ṣ, M, Ḳ;) as also ▼ أَصْوَت, and ▼ صَوَّت: (Ḳ:) and in like manner one says of other trees: and sometimes, of animals. (M.) And صَوِىَ الضَّرْعُ *The udder had no milk remaining in it.* (Ḥam p. 661.) — [Hence,] صَوِيَت الشَّاةُ *The ewe,* or *she-goat, became fat,* (Ṣ, TA,) *in consequence of her udder's having been made to dry up.* (Ṣ.) And صَوِىَ *He became strong.* (Ḳ.)

2. صَوَّى, (M,) inf. n. تَصْوِيَةٌ, (Ḳ,) primarily, (M,) is used in relation to females, meaning *He abstained from milking her, in order that she might become fat,* (M, Ḳ,) *and not be weak.* (M.) You say, صَوَّيْتُ النَّاقَةَ *I abstained from milking the she-camel for some days in order that the milk might collect in her udder so that she might become fat:* or *I made her milk to dry up, that she might become fatter.* (M.) And صَوَّيْتُ الشَّاةَ, inf. n. as above, *I made the udder of the ewe,* or *goat, to become dry, that she might become fatter:* (Ṣ:) or صَوَّيْتُ الغَنَمَ *I made the milk of the ewes,* or *goats, to dry up, purposely, that they might become fatter;* like as one says in relation to camels: the subst. from the verb thus used is ▼ صَوًى; and this is said to mean The *leaving an animal and not milking her.* (M.) Some say that تَصْوِيَةٌ is like تَصْرِيَةٌ; and hence the trad., التَّصْوِيَةُ خِلَابَةٌ [i. e. *The causing the milk to collect in the udder* of an animal *by abstaining from milking* her *for some days,* when one desires to sell her, *is an endeavouring to deceive:* but I think that the right reading in this instance is probably التَّصْرِيَةُ, with ر]. (TA.) — It is also used in relation to a stallion (Ṣ, M, Ḳ) of the camels: (Ṣ:) thus it is used by El-Fak'asee. (M.) One says, صَوَّيْتُ الفَحْلَ, (M,) inf. n. as above, (Ṣ, Ḳ,) *I put no burden upon the stallion* [*camel*], *and did not bind him with a rope, in order that he might become more brisk in covering, and more strong;* (Ṣ,* M, Ḳ;*) thus expl. by El-'Adebbes El-Kinánee: (Ṣ:) or *I exempted him from work, and fed him, until his spirit returned to him, and he became fat.* (M.) And صَوَّيْتُ لِإِبِلِى فَحْلًا *I chose for my camels a stallion, and fed and nourished him for the office of the stallion.* (Ṣ.) ━ See also 1. ━ [And see art. صو.]

4: see 1. — One says also اصوى القَوْمُ, meaning *The people's cattle became lean,* or *emaciated;* like اضوى القوم. (IḲṭṭ, TA.) ━ [See also art. صو.]

صَوًى a subst. from 2, q. v. (M.)

صَوٍ : see its fem., صَوِيَةٌ, voce صَاوٍ. — [Also, app., *Empty* سُنْبُل (or ears of corn): accord. to the TA (on the authority of Az): the word in this sense, and thus applied, is there written with the article, الصوى, without any syll. sign.]

صَوِيَةٌ : see the following paragraph.

صَاوٍ *Dry,* (Ṣ, Ḳ, TA,) by reason of thirst, or want of irrigation, or by reason of leanness, or emaciation. (TA.) You say نَخْلَةٌ صَاوِيَةٌ, (M, Ḳ,) and ▼ صَوِيَةٌ, (M, TA,) [agreeably with rule, as part. n. of صَوِيَت,] or ▼ صَوِيَّةٌ, (so in copies of the Ḳ, [app. a mistranscription,]) *A dry,* or *dried-up, palm-tree:* (M, Ḳ:) and in like manner one terms other trees: and sometimes, animals: thus the poet Sá'ideh applies the epithet صاوية to wild cows or wild oxen (بَقَر وَحْش). (M.) — And *Strong.* (TA.)

صيب

1. صَابَ aor. يَصِيبُ, (Ṣ, M, Mṣb, Ḳ,) inf. n. صَيْبٌ, (Ṣ, Mṣb, Ḳ,) said of an arrow, (Ṣ, M, Mṣb,) i. q. أَصَابَ [expl. in art. صوب]; (Ṣ,* M, Mṣb, Ḳ;) like صاب having for its aor. يَصُوبُ. (Ṣ, M, Mṣb.)

صَيَّابٌ : see صَوْبٌ, in art. صوب.

صُيَّابٌ : see صُيَّابَةٌ.

صَيُوبٌ An arrow *going right,* or *hitting the mark:* pl. صُيُبٌ (M, Ḳ) and صِيَابٌ, (MF, TA,) or the latter is pl. of صَائِبٌ, which signifies the same. (M, in art. صوب.)

صِيَابَةٌ : see صُيَّابَةٌ.

صَيِّبٌ : see art. صوب.

صُيَّابٌ : see صُيَّابَةٌ, in four places.

صَيُّوبٌ : see art. صوب.

صُيَّابَةٌ and ▼ صُيَّابٌ (M, A, Ḳ) and ▼ صِيَابَةٌ and ▼ صُيَابٌ (A, Ḳ) The أَصْل (M, A, Ḳ) [as meaning the *original stock*] of a people, (M,) or [as meaning the *original,* or the *principal,* or *most essential, part,*] of a thing: (A, Ḳ:) and the *purest,* or *choice,* or *best, part* or *portion,* (M,* A, Ḳ,) of a thing (M, Ḳ) of any kind, (M,) or of a people. (A.) One says, هُوَ فِى صُيَّابَةِ قَوْمِهِ and ▼ صُيَّابِهِمْ *He is of the* أَصْل [or *original stock*] *of his people:* (Fr, TA:) and مِنْ صُيَّابَةِ قَوْمِهِ and صُوَّابَة قومه (TA) and ▼ مِنْ صُيَّابِهِمْ (A) *of the purest in race of his people.* (A,* TA.) And ▼ قَوْمٌ صُيَّابٌ *A choice,* or *an excellent, people.* (TA.) — Also the first, The *collective body* of a people; (Kr, M;) and so صُوَّابَةٌ. (M in art. صوب.) — And *A lord, master,* or *chief.* (M, Ḳ.)

Quasi صيت

صِيتٌ and صِيتَةٌ : and صَيِّتٌ : see art. صوت.

صيح

1. صَاحَ, (Ṣ, A, O, Mṣb, &c.,) aor. يَصِيحُ, (Ṣ, O, Mṣb,) inf. n. صِيَاحٌ and صَيْحَةٌ (Ṣ, A,* O, Mṣb, Ḳ*) and صَيْحٌ and صُيَاحٌ and صَيَحَانٌ, (Ṣ, O, Ḳ,*) *He raised his voice, voiced, called* or *called out, cried* or *cried out:* (Ṣ, A, O, Mṣb, Ḳ:) or *did so vehemently, cried aloud, uttered a loud cry* or *crying, shouted, exclaimed,* or *vociferated:* (T, Ṣ,* A,* O,* Mṣb,* TA:) or *did so with his utmost force or power;* (Ḳ, TA;) as also ▼ صَيَّحَ: (A,* TA:) it is said of a man, and of other things: (TA:) or of anything: (T, TA:) originally, of an animal, and often of a bird of the crow-kind, but rarely of a bird unrestrictedly, and sometimes of a spear as being likened to an animal. (Ḥam p. 187.) One says, صَاحَ صَيْحَةً شَدِيدَةً [*He called,* or *cried,* &c., *with a vehement calling* or *crying* &c., or *with a vehement call* or *cry* &c.]. (A.) And صاح بِهِ *He called* or *cried,* or *called out* or *cried out, to it* [or *to him*]. (Mṣb.) And صِحْ لِى بِفُلَانٍ *Call thou to me such a one.* (A, TA.) And ▼ صَايَحَ بِهِ and صَايَحَهُ, (A, TA,) and ▼ صَيَّحَ بِهِ and صَيَّحَهُ, (A,) *He called, hailed,* or *summoned, him; called out, cried out,* or *shouted, to him.* (A, TA.) — And صِيحَ بِهِمْ † *They were*

frightened, or *terrified*. (Ḳ.) And صِيحَ فِيهِمْ † *They perished.* (Ḳ.) — One says also, لَقِيتُهُ قَبْلَ كُلِّ صَيْحٍ وَنَفْرٍ *I met him before every calling*, or *crying*, *and dispersing*; meaning † *I met him before daybreak*: (Ṣ, TA:) so in the Proverbs of Meyd. (TA.) Or أَتَيْتُهُ قَبْلَ صَيْحٍ وَنَفْرٍ ‡ *I came to him before everything.* (A.) And غَضِبَ مِنْ غَيْرِ صَيْحٍ وَلَا نَفْرٍ ‡ *He was angry for neither little nor much*: (ISk, Ṣ, Ḳ:) or *for nothing.* (A.) — And صَاحَتِ الشَّجَرَةُ, (A, Mṣb,) or النَّخْلَةُ, (Ḳ,) ‡ *The tree*, (A, Mṣb,) or *the palm-tree*, (Ḳ,) *became tall.* (A, Mṣb, Ḳ.) And صاح العُنْقُودُ ‡ *The raceme came forth completely from its envelope, and became long, and in a fresh and tender state.* (Ḳ.) And صاح الكَافُورُ ‡ [app. meaning *The spathe of the palm-tree put forth its spadix, or its raceme, to its full length*]. (A.)

2: see 1, in two places. — صَيَّحَتِ البَقْلَ said of the sun, (Ṣ, Ḳ,) and of the wind, (Ṣ,) i. q. صَوَّحَتْهُ [q. v.]. (Ṣ, Ḳ.) — And صَيَّحْتُ الشَّىْءَ *I broke and split the thing much.* (TA in art. صوح.)

3. مُصَايَحَةٌ and ▼ تَصَايُحٌ signify The *calling* or *crying*, or *calling out* or *crying out*, &c., of people, *one to another.* (Ṣ, Ḳ.) One says, صايح القَوْمُ (TḲ) and ▼ تصايحوا *The people*, or *party*, *called* or *cried*, &c., *one to another.* (A, TḲ.) — See also 1.

5. تصيّح البَقْلُ i. q. تصوّح [q. v.]. (Ṣ, Ḳ.) — And تصيّح الشَّعَرُ i. q. تصوّح [q. v.]. (Ḳ in art. صوح.) — And تصيّح الشَّىْءُ *The thing became much broken and cloven* or *split* or *slit.* (TA in this art. and art. صوح.) See also 7.

6: see 3, in two places. — تصايح said of the scabbard, or sheath, of a sword (A, Ḳ, TA) ‡ *It became much split* or *slit*: (Ḳ, TA:) it is like the phrase تَدَاعَى البُنْيَانُ [q. v.]. (A, TA.)

7. انصاح said of a garment, or piece of cloth, *It became slit*, or *rent*, or *much slit* or *rent.* (A, Mṣb. [See also 7 in art. صوح.]) And انصاحت العَصَا *The staff became much split* or *cracked*; as also ▼ تصيّحت. (A.) — [Hence,] انصاح is also said of the dawn and of lightning ‡ [meaning *It showed its light*: originally, *became cleft*: as expl. in art. صوح]. (A.)

صَيْحَةٌ an inf. n. [and also an inf. n. un.] of صَاحَ. (Ṣ, Mṣb, &c.) [Hence,] one says, مَا يَنْتَظِرُونَ إِلَّا مِثْلَ صَيْحَةِ الحُبْلَى [*They expect not, or wait not for, aught but the like of the crying-out, or cry, of the pregnant woman*]; meaning, *evil*, or *mischief*, *that shall come upon them suddenly.* (TA.) — Hence also (Ṣ) *Punishment*, *castigation*, or *chastisement.* (Ṣ, A, Ḳ.) — And *A hostile*, or *predatory*, *incursion*, *by which the tribe are surprised.* (TA.)

صَيْحَانٌ: see what next follows.

صَيْحَانِىٌّ, (T, Ṣ, A, Mgh, Ḳ,) or ▼ صَيْحَانٌ, (Mṣb,) *A sort of dates of El-Medeeneh*, (T, Ṣ, A, Mgh, Mṣb, Ḳ,) *black, and hard to chew*: (T, Mgh, TA:) said to be so called in relation to a certain ram, named صَيْحَانُ, that was tied to a palm-tree, (A, Mṣb, Ḳ,*) which was hence called نَخْلَةٌ صَيْحَانِيَّةٌ: (A, Mṣb:) or the name of the ram was الصَّيَّاحُ, and صَيْحَانِىٌّ is a rel. n. changed from its proper form, like صَنْعَانِىٌّ, (Ḳ, TA,) from صَنْعَآءُ. (TA.)

صَيَّاحٌ A *clamorous* man: and anything *noisy*, or *sounding much.* (The Lexicons passim.) — الصَّيَّاحُ is another name for العَوَّآءُ [i. e. *The constellation Bootes*]. (Ḳzw.) — And ‡ *A certain perfume*, or *fragrant substance*: (Ḳ, TA:) or *a wash for the head*, (A, Ḳ,*) *consisting of* خَلُوق [q. v.], and *the like.* (A, TA.)

صَائِحَةٌ The *crying*, or *clamour*, *of the place of the wailing of women.* (Ḳ.)

صيد

1. صَادَهُ, (Ṣ, M, A, Mgh, Mṣb, Ḳ,) like بَاعَهُ, (MF,) [first pers. صِدْتُ,] aor. يَصِيدُ, (Ṣ, Mṣb, Ḳ,) inf. n. صَيْدٌ; (Ṣ, M, Mgh, Mṣb;) and صَادَهُ, (Ṣ, &c.,) like هَابَهُ, (MF,) [first pers. صِدْتُ, as above, but originally صَيِدْتُ, whereas the first pers. of the former is originally صَيَدْتُ,] aor. يَصَادُ; (IAạr, Ṣ, Mṣb, Ḳ;) and ▼ اصطادهُ, (Ṣ, M, A, L, Mṣb, Ḳ,) also written and pronounced اِصَّادَهُ; (L;) and ▼ تصيّدهُ; (M, A, L;) *He took, captured*, or *caught, it*; (Mgh, L;) [*made it his prey*;] *snared*, or *ensnared, it*; *trapped*, or *entrapped, it*; (MF;) or *sought to take, capture, catch, snare, or trap, it*; *hunted it*, or *chased it*: namely, [game, i. e.] any kind of wild animals, or the like, (L,) fowl, &c., (Mṣb,) and fish. (L.) [And صَادَ, and ▼ اصطاد, and ▼ تصيّد, without the mention of the object, this being understood, *He took, captured, caught, snared* or *ensnared, trapped* or *entrapped, game*, i. e. *any kind of wild animals*, or *the like, fowl, &c.*, or *fish*; or *he sought to take* &c.; *he hunted* or *chased, stalked*, or *lurked for game*; *he fowled*; or *he fished.*] You say, ▼ خَرَجَ يَتَصَيَّدُ [&c., meaning *He went forth to take* &c., or *seeking to take* &c., *game*, or *wild animals* or *the like*; *to hunt* or *chase, to stalk*, or *lurk for game*; *to fowl*; or *to fish*]. (Ṣ, Ḳ.) And خَرَجَ يَتَصَيَّدُ ▼ الوَحْشَ *He went forth* [*to take* &c., or] *seeking to take* &c., *the wild animals.* (L.) And صِدْتُ لَهُ i. q. صِدْتُ فُلَانًا صَيْدًا [*I took* &c., or *sought to take* &c., *for such a one, game*, or *a wild animal*, or *wild animals*, or *the like*]. (M,* Ḳ.) And صاد المَكَانَ, and ▼ اصطادهُ, i. q. صاد فِيهِ [*He took* &c., or *sought to take* &c., *game*, or *wild animals*, or *the like, in the place*]: Sb mentions, as a phrase of the Arabs, صِدْنَا قَنَوَيْنِ meaning صِدْنَا وَحْشَ قَنَوَيْنِ: قَنَوَانِ being the name of a certain land [or of two mountains]. (M.) And الصَّقْرُ يَصِيدُ [*The hawk preys*]. (Mṣb and Ḳ in art. صقر.) ذَوَاتُ الصَّيْدِ is applied to beasts and to birds [*That prey upon others*; *predatory*]. (Ṣ and Ḳ in art. جرح, &c.) — [Hence,] one says, هُوَ يَصِيدُ النَّاسَ بِالمَعْرُوفِ ‡ [*He captivates men by goodness, beneficence*, or *kindness*]. (A.) — And اقْتَصِدْ تَصِدْ ‡ *Aim thou at that which is right and just: thou shalt obtain that which thou wantest.* (A.) — خَرَجْنَا نَصِيدُ بَيْضَ النَّعَامِ ‡ [*We went forth to take*, or *hunt after, the eggs of ostriches*]. (T, TA.) — And صِدْنَا الكَمْأَةَ, (M, A, TA,) a good phrase of the Arabs, mentioned, but not expl., by IAạr; app. meaning ‡ *We drew forth truffles* [*from the ground*] *like as one draws forth wild animals* [*from their lurking-places*]. (M, TA.) — And صِدْنَا مَآءَ السَّمَآءِ ‡ *We took* [or *caught in vessels* or *collected*] *the water of the sky.* (Th, M, A.*) — صَيِدَ, (Lth, Ṣ, M, L,) of the dial. of El-Ḥijáz, aor. يَصْيَدُ, (Lth, L,) inf. n. صَيَدٌ; (Lth, Ṣ, M, L;) and صَادَ, (Lth, M, L,) [aor. يَصَيدُ;] *He* (a camel) *had the disease termed* صَيَدٌ [expl. below]: (Lth, Ṣ, M, L:) the ى in صَيِدَ is preserved unchanged because it is so preserved in the original form, which is ▼ اِصْيَدَّ, (Ṣ,) though they may not have said اِصْيَدَّ; (Sb, M;) and the like is the case in عَوِرَ: (Sb,* Ṣ, M:*) the augmentative letters are rejected for the purpose of alleviation: hence, one does not say, in the case of verbs of this class, مَا أَفْعَلَهُ, [i. e. مَا أَصْيَدَهُ, and مَا أَعْوَرَهُ, and the like,] forming thus verbs of wonder, because the original form is augmented, and a verb of four letters cannot be formed from a verb of four letters, for a measure can only be formed from a measure that is less. (Ṣ.) Also, both verbs, (the former accord. to the Ṣ and M, and ▼ the latter likewise accord. to the M,) † *He* (a man) *was unable to look aside*, (Ṣ, M,) *by reason of disease.* (Ṣ.) And صَيِدَ, inf. n. صَيَدٌ, † *He raised his head, by reason of pride*: and † *he* (a king) *looked not aside, to the right* or *left.* (Ṣ.) And صَيِدَ (Ḳ, TA, in the CḲ [erroneously] صَيَّدَ,) ‡ *He* (a man, TA) *had an inclining*, or *a bending, neck.* (Ḳ, TA.) — And صِدْتُ فُلَانًا ‡ *I made such a one to have an inclining*, or *a bending, neck.* (Ḳ, TA. [See also 4.])

4. اصادهُ *He made him, incited him*, or *induced him, to take* &c., or *to seek to take* &c., *wild animals*, or *the like*, [*fowl*,] or *fish.* (L.) — Also *He*, or *it*, [app. meaning the vein called صَادٌ, or the disease termed صَيَدٌ,] *annoyed*, or *hurt, him*; (Ḳ;) namely, a camel. (TḲ.) — And *He cured him* (i. e. a camel, TḲ) *of the disease termed* صَيَدٌ, (Ḳ, TA,) *by burning with a hot iron.* (TA.) Thus it has two contr. significations. (Ḳ.) — And أَصْيَدَ بَعِيرَهُ *He* (God) *caused his camel to have the disease termed* صَيَدٌ. (M.)

5: see 1, in four places.

8: see 1, in three places.

9: see 1, in the latter half of the paragraph, in two places.

صَادٌ *A certain vein* (M, Ḳ) *between the eyes of a camel*, (Ḳ,) or *between the eye and the nose*; (M;) *whence the disease termed* صَيَدٌ: pl. أَصْيَادٌ and pl. pl. أَصَايِدُ [in the CḲ أَصَائِدُ]. (Ḳ.) — See also صَيْدٌ, in two places. — And see أَصْيَدُ, likewise in two places. — Also *Brass*; syn. صُفْرٌ:

and *copper:* (Ṣ, M, Ḳ:) or *a species thereof:* (Ḳ:) or *cooking-pots made of* صُفْر, (A'Obeyd, TA,) or *of copper:* (A'Obeyd, M, TA:) pl. صِيدَانٌ, (M, TA,) like تِيجَانٌ pl. of تَاجٌ: and some say that † صَيْدَانٌ [q. v., thus written with fet-ḥ to the ص,] signifies *copper.* (TA.) ═ See also art. صود.

صَيْدٌ an instance of فَعْلٌ in the sense of مَفْعُولٌ, (Mṣb,) or an inf. n. used as a subst. [properly so called, and therefore used in a sing. and in a pl. sense], (Mṣb, TA,) [i. e.] an inf. n. used in the place of the objective complement of its verb; (IJ, M;) [*Game, chase, or prey; an object,* or *objects, of the chase* or *the like;*] i. q. † مَصِيدٌ (Ṣ, Mgh, Ḳ, TA) used as a subst.; (TA;) meaning *what is taken, captured,* or *caught;* or *sought to be taken* or *captured* or *caught;* [*by the chase,* or *by means of a snare or trap,* or *by artifice of any kind;*] *of wild animals* or *the like;* (L;) *of fowl &c.;* (Mṣb;) and *of fish:* (L:) or *what is repugnant,* or *difficult of approach,* (Mgh, L, Ḳ,) *wild,* or *shy, by nature, not to be taken but by means of artifice, whatever it be,* (Mgh,) *but lawful to be taken,* (L,) *having no owner:* (L, Ḳ:) or *any wild animal,* or *wild animals, whether, or not, taken* or *sought to be taken:* (IAạr, M:) but this last application of the word is a deviation from general usage: (M:) pl. صُيُودٌ. (Mgh, Mṣb.) [Also The *quarry* of the hawk; the *prey* of any beast or bird &c.] صَيْدَكَ لَا تُحْرَمَهْ (Meyd, A, but in the latter صَيْدَكَ, [for الْزَمْ صَيْدَكَ,]) is a prov. (Meyd, A) inciting one to seize an opportunity, (A,) applied to a man who seeks another to execute blood-revenge upon him, and lights upon him when he is inadvertent; meaning *Thy prey* has become within thy power, therefore *be not thou neglectful of him* [so as to suffer him to escape, or rather *be not thou rendered hopeless of him*]. (Meyd. [See also Freytag's Arab. Prov. i. 712; where تُحْرَمَهْ is put in the place of تُحْرَمَهْ.]) ═ See also صَيَدٌ.

صِيدٌ: see the next paragraph.

صَيَدٌ (Ṣ, M, A, L, Ḳ) and † صِيدٌ, with kesr, (Ḳ,) or † صَيْدٌ, (L,) and † صَادٌ, (M,* L, Ḳ,) *A certain disease in a camel's head, in consequence of which he raises it:* (Ṣ:) *a certain disease which causes a camel to raise his head:* or *a certain disease in a camel's head, which causes his neck to twist:* (M:) or *a certain disease which attacks camels in the head, in consequence of which there flows from their noses what resembles froth, or foam, and they raise their heads:* (ISk, L, Ḳ:*) or *a certain disease in a camel's neck, in consequence of which he is unable to turn his face aside:* it is said that *its cure is burning with a hot iron* (A, TA) *between the eyes:* (TA:) [*for*] *it arises from a vein between the eyes, called* صَادٌ. (Ḳ.) [Hence,] also صَيَدٌ, (M,* A,) and † صَادٌ, (M,) *Fixedness of the face* of a king, *so that it does not turn aside* (M, A) *to the right* or *left, by reason of pride.* (A. [See also صَيِدَ, of which it is the inf. n.]) [And the former, ‡ *An inclination,* or *bending, of the neck:* (see صَيِدَ:) hence,] one says, لَأُقِيمَنَّ صَيَدَكَ ‡ [*I will assuredly straighten the bending of thy neck:* or *I will assuredly rectify thy proud stiffness*]. (A.)

صَيَدٌ: see أَصْيَدُ.

صَادِىٌّ [*Of,* or *made of, brass* or *copper:*] a rel. n. from صَادٌ signifying "brass" and "copper." (Ṣ.)

صَيْدَاءُ *Stones,* (Ṣ, A, L, Ḳ,) or *stone,* (M,) *of a white colour,* (M, L,) *of which cooking-pots are made;* (Ṣ, M, A, L, Ḳ;) as also † صَيْدَانٌ. (A, L.) See also صَيْدَانٌ. — And *Rugged land* or *ground,* (Ṣ, M, K,) *containing stones:* (M:) or *land of which the earth is red, having rough stones even with the ground:* (ISh:) or *even,* or *level, ground, in which are pebbles:* (AA:) or *pebbles* [themselves]. (Aboo-Wejzeh, L.)

صَيْدَانٌ *Copper:* (L, Ḳ: see also صَادٌ:) and *gold:* (Ḳ:) [but this seems to be taken from the following passage in the T:] in the stone-cooking-pot (البُرْمَة) there is sometimes [what is termed] صَيْدَانٌ and † صَيْدَاءُ, in which is an appearance like the glistening of gold and silver; and the best is that which is like gold: so says AA. (T, L.) See also art. صدن. — And *Stone cooking-pots:* (Ṣ, L, Ḳ; and M in art. صدن:) a coll. gen. n.: n. un. with ة. (IB, L.) — See also صَيْدَاءُ. — صَيْدَانُ الحَصَى *Small pebbles.* (L. [See also art. صدن.])

صَيْدَانَةٌ [as a n. un.: see صَيْدَانٌ, above. — Also] *A* [*demon of the kind called*] غُول. (ISk, Ṣ, K.) — And *A woman of evil disposition,* (ISk, Ṣ, Ḳ,) [and] so † صَيُودٌ, (M,) *and of much talk.* (ISk, Ṣ, Ḳ.) — See also art. صدن.

صَيُودٌ: see صَيَّادٌ. — [Hence,] † A woman *who takes, captures,* or *ensnares, something from her husband.* (L, from a trad.) See also صَيْدَانَةٌ.

رَجُلٌ صَيَّادٌ [*A man accustomed to,* or *in the habit of, taking, capturing, catching, snaring,* or *trapping, game,* i. e. *any kind of wild animals,* or *the like, fowl, &c.,* or *fish; a sportsman; a hunter, a fowler,* or *a fisherman:* see 1, second sentence]: (Mṣb:) and † صَيُودٌ signifies the same as صَيَّادٌ: (Ḳ:) you say كَلْبٌ صَيُودٌ [*A dog used for hunting*]: (Ṣ, A:) and صَقْرٌ صَيُودٌ [*A hawk used for catching game*]: and the same epithet is applied to a female: (M:) its pl. is صُيُدٌ (Ṣ, M, A) and صِيدٌ; (Yoo, Sb, Ṣ, M;) the latter of the dial. of those, (Ṣ, M,) namely, the tribe of Temeem, (M,) who say رُسْلٌ [for رُسُلٌ]; (Ṣ, M;) the ص being with kesr in order that the ى may be preserved unchanged. (Ṣ.) — See also أَصْيَدُ, last sentence.

صَائِدٌ, applied to a man, *Practising* الصَّيْد [i. e. *the taking, capturing,* or *catching, &c., of game,* or *any kind of wild animals,* or *the like, fowl, &c.,* or *fish; hunting, fowling,* or *fishing:* see 1, second sentence]. (Mgh, Mṣb.) — الصَّائِدُ in the dial. of El-Yemen signifies *The shank;* syn. السَّاقُ. (M.)

صَيُودٌ, like تَنُّورٌ [in measure], An arrow *going right,* or *hitting the mark.* (Ḳ.)

أَصْيَدُ [*More,* or *most, wont,* or *able, to take,* or *capture,* or *catch, game,* or *prey*]. أَصْيَدُ مِنْ لَيْثِ عِفِرِّينَ وَمِنْ ضَيْوَنٍ [*More wont,* or *able, to capture prey than the lion of 'Ifirreen and than the he-cat*] is a prov. (Meyd.) ═ Also *A camel having the disease termed* صَيَدٌ; (Ṣ, M, A, L;) and so † صَادٌ, for ذُو صَادٍ, (L, Ḳ,) like مَالٌ for ذُو مَالٍ, (L,) or for † صَيِدٌ: (L:) pl. of the first صِيدٌ. (L.) [Hence,] † A man *unable to look aside,* (Ṣ, M,) *by reason of disease.* (Ṣ.) † A man *who raises his head by reason of pride.* (Ṣ.) ‡ A king *who looks not aside,* (M, A,) *to the right or left, by reason of his pride.* (A.) † *A king:* (Ḳ:) originally used in relation to a camel, and a king is so called because he raises his head by reason of pride, or because he does not look to the right or left. (Ṣ.) And A man *having an inclining,* or *a bending, neck.* (Ḳ, TA.) — الأَصْيَدُ † *The lion;* (Ḳ;) because he walks proudly, not looking aside, as though he had the disease termed صَيَد; (TA;) as also † المُصْطَادُ [as act. part. n. of 8]; and † الصَّادُ; (Ḳ, TA;) thus likened to a camel having the disease above mentioned; or, as in some copies of the Ḳ, not الصَّادُ, but † الصَّيَّادُ. (TA.)

مَصَادٌ and † مُصْطَادٌ and † مُتَصَيَّدٌ [*A place of taking, capturing,* or *catching, &c., of game,* or *any kind of wild animals,* or *the like, fowl, &c.,* or *fish; a place of hunting, fowling,* or *fishing*]. (A. [The meaning is there indicated by the context, but not expressed.]) ═ مَصَادٌ also signifies *The upper,* or *highest, part of a mountain.* (MF, from Aboo-'Alee El-Yoosee. [But this, accord. to the Ṣ &c., belongs to art. مصد.])

مِصْيَدَةٌ and مِصْيَدٌ: see مَصْيَدٌ.

مَصِيدٌ pass. part. n. of 1: (Mgh, Mṣb:) see صَيْدٌ.

مَصْيَدَةٌ (Ṣ, M, A, Mṣb, Ḳ) and مَصِيَدَةٌ (M, and so in the handwriting of Az accord. to the L) and † مِصْيَدٌ (Ṣ, L, Mṣb, Ḳ) and † مَصْيَدٌ (so in the handwriting of Az accord. to the L) and † مِصْيَدَةٌ (M, Mṣb, Ḳ) *A thing used for the purpose of* الصَّيْد [or *the taking, capturing,* or *catching, &c., of game,* or *any kind of wild animals,* or *the like, fowl, &c.,* or *fish*]; (T, Ṣ, M, A, Mṣb, Ḳ;) *a snare, trap, gin,* or *net;* (MA in explanation of the first and last;) [the first and third said by Golius, on the authority of Meyd, to be applied peculiarly to *a net;* but all signify also *any kind of trap:* see شَهْرٌ:] pl. مَصَايِدُ, without ء. (L, Mṣb.)

مَصِيَدَةٌ: see the next preceding paragraph.

مُصْطَادٌ: see أَصْيَدُ: — and see also مَصَادٌ.

مُتَصَيَّدٌ: see مَصَادٌ.

صير

1. صَارَ كَذَا, (T, Ṣ, Mṣb,) aor. يَصِيرُ, (Ṣ,) inf. n. صَيْرُورَةٌ (Ṣ, Mṣb) and صَيْرٌ, (Ṣ,) *He,* or *it, attained to the state,* or *condition, of such a thing;* (T;) *became such a thing;* (T, Mṣb;) in which sense the verb is like كَانَ [in meaning, when the latter is non-attributive, and in having its subject

in the nom. case and its predicate in the accus.]. (T.) You say, صَارَ زَيْدٌ رَجُلًا *Zeyd became a man*; or *attained to the state*, or *condition, of a man*. (TA.) And صَارَ زَيْدٌ غَنِيًّا *Zeyd became rich*, not having been so. (Mṣb.) And صَارَ العَصِيرُ خَمْرًا *The expressed juice became wine*. (Mṣb.) [And صَارَ لَا شَىْءَ عِنْدَهُ *He became in a state*, or *condition, in which there was not anything in his possession*. And صَارَ يَفْعَلُ كَذَا *He became in the state*, or *condition, of doing such a thing*; i. e. *he became occupied*, or *engaged, in doing such a thing*; or *he set about, began, commenced, took to*, or *betook himself to, doing such a thing*; like جَعَلَ. And صَارَ لَا يَفْعَلُ شَيْئًا *He became in the state*, or *condition, of not doing anything*; or *he became unoccupied in doing anything*. And صَارَ لَا يَتَكَلَّمُ *He became in the state of not speaking; he became speechless*. And صَارَ يَتَفَكَّرُ فِى كَذَا *He became in a state of reflection upon such a thing; he began to reflect upon such a thing*.] — One says also, صَارَ الأَمْرُ إِلَى كَذَا, (M, A, Mṣb, Ḳ,) aor. as above, (TA,) inf. n. مَصِيرٌ, (Ṣ, M, A, Mṣb, Ḳ,) which is anomalous, being regularly مَصَارٌ, like مَعَاشٌ, (Ṣ,) and صَيْرٌ and صَيْرُورَةٌ, (M, A, Ḳ,) i. e. رَجَعَ إِلَيْهِ: (Mṣb:) [but this is a loose explanation; the meaning being, *The thing*, or *affair*, or *case, came eventually* (see صَيْرٌ) *to such a state*, or *condition*:] the difference between مَصِيرٌ and مَرْجِعٌ is, that the former word necessarily implies a difference [of the latter state or condition] from the former state or condition; but the latter word does not. (Bḍ in iii. 156.) [In this case, the ulterior state or condition is likened to a place: for] — صَارَ also signifies *He*, or *it, attained in respect of place*: so in the saying, صَارَ زَيْدٌ إِلَى عَمْرٍو [*Zeyd came*, or *went*, or *pursued a course that brought him, to 'Amr*]. (TA.) [صِرْتُ إِلَى فُلَانٍ [*I came, &c., to such a one*] is similar to the phrase in the Ḳur [iii. 27] وَإِلَى ٱللّٰهِ ٱلْمَصِيرُ [*And to God, as the ultimate object, is the transition*, or *course*, of every human being]. (Ṣ.) [Hence, أَلَا إِلَى ٱللّٰهِ تَصِيرُ ٱلْأُمُورُ, in the Ḳur xlii. last verse, which Bḍ explains by adding the words بِٱرْتِفَاعِ الوَسَائِطِ وَالتَّعَلُّقَاتِ; the meaning being, *Verily to God are things*, or *events, referrible*, mediately and dependently: in the Expos. of the Jel expl. as meaning تَرْجِعُ.] — [And in like manner one says, صَارَ لَهُ كَذَا *Such a thing came to, betided*, or *befell, him*, or *it*: and hence, *he*, or *it, came to have*, or *became possessed of, such a thing*.] — And صَارَ فِى أَرْضٍ فَلَاةٍ [*He became*, or *came to be*, meaning *he found himself, in a desert*, or *waterless, land*]; *i. q.* وَقَعَ فِيهَا. (Mṣb in art. وقع.) And صَارَ فِى الرَّبِيعِ [*He entered*, lit. *became in, the* season called ربيع]; *i. q.* أَرْبَعَ [which is expl. in the Ṣ as signifying دَخَلَ فِى الرَّبِيعِ]. (Ḳ in art. ربع.) — صَيْرٌ signifies also The *returning* of seekers after herbage *to the watering-places*. (O, Ḳ.) And one says, صَارَ الرَّجُلُ, aor. يَصِيرُ, [inf. n. صَيْرٌ,] *The man stayed*, or *abode, at the water*. (TA.) And صَارَ النَّاسُ المَآءَ *The people stayed*, or *abode, at the water*. (M, Ḳ, TA.) — صَارَهُ, (Ṣ,) first pers. صِرْتُهُ, (M,) aor. as above, (Ṣ,) inf. n. صَيْرٌ, (Ḳ,) a dial. var. of صَارَهُ having for its aor. يَصُورُهُ, [q. v.,] (Ṣ,) *He cut it*; (Ṣ, M, Ḳ;) and *clave it*, or *split it*. (M.) — And in like manner, [i. e. as a dial. var. of صَارَهُ having for its aor. يَصُورُهُ,] *He made it to incline*, or *lean*. (Ṣ.) You say, صَارَ وَجْهَهُ, aor. يَصِيرُ, (M,) as also يَصُورُ, (M and Ḳ in art. صور,) *He turned his face* towards a person or thing. (M.) And صِرْتُ عُنُقَهُ *I twisted his neck*. (M.) [Respecting the phrase فَصِرْهُنَّ إِلَيْكَ in the Ḳur ii. 262, accord. to one reading, see 1 in art. صور.] — صَارَهُ, aor. يَصِيرُ, inf. n. صَيْرٌ, signifies also حَبَسَهُ [*He confined, restricted*, &c., *him*, or *it*]. (Mṣb.)

2. صَيَّرَهُ كَذَا *He made him*, or *it, to be in such a state*, or *condition*; or *he made him*, or *it, to be such a thing*; [as also ↓ أَصَارَهُ;] syn. جَعَلَهُ. (Ṣ.) You say, صَيَّرَنِى لَهُ عَبْدًا and ↓ أَصَارَنِى [*He made me to be to him a slave*]. (A.) — [And صَيَّرَهُ إِلَى كَذَا and ↓ أَصَارَهُ *He*, or *it, made*, or *caused, him*, or *it, to come*, or *to pursue a course that led, to such a state*, or *condition*; *brought*, or *reduced, him*, or *it, thereto*.] 'Omeyleh El-Fezáree said to his paternal uncle Ibn-'Ankà, مَا الَّذِى أَصَارَكَ ↓ إِلَى مَا أَرَى يَا عَمِّ [*What hath made thee to come*, or *brought thee*, or *reduced thee, to the state*, or *condition, that I see, O my paternal uncle?*]. (M.) [In this case, the ulterior state or condition is likened to a place: for] you say, صَيَّرَهُ إِلَيْهِ and ↓ أَصَارَهُ [meaning *He*, or *it, made him to come*, or *brought him, to him*, or *it*; i. e., to a person, or place, or to a state, or condition:] (M, Ḳ:) and صَيَّرَتْنِى إِلَيْهِ الحَاجَةُ and ↓ أَصَارَتْنِى [*Want*, or *need*, or *necessity, made me to come*, or *brought me, to him*, or *it*]. (A.) And [hence,] صَيَّرَ إِلَيْهِ الأَمْرَ *He committed to him the thing*, or *affair*; syn. فَوَّضَهُ اليه. (M in art. فوض.) [And صَيَّرَ لَهُ كَذَا *He made such a thing to come to, betide*, or *befall, him*, or *it*: and consequently, *he made him*, or *it, to have*, or *become possessed of, such a thing*.] — تَصْيِيرٌ is also by word, or covenant, as well as by deed. (Bḍ in ii. 20.) [You say, صَيَّرَهُ كَذَا meaning *He asserted*, or *pronounced, him*, or *it, to be in such a state*, or *condition*; or *to be such a thing*: in which case, also, it is *syn. with* جَعَلَهُ, whereby it is expl. in the Ṣ. And صَيَّرَ لَهُ كَذَا *He asserted*, or *pronounced, such a thing to belong to him*, or *it*; *asserted*, or *pronounced, him*, or *it, to have such a thing*; *attributed to him*, or *it, such a thing*: and *appointed* or *assigned, to him*, or *it, such a thing*.]

4: see 2, in six places.

5. تَصَيَّرَ أَبَاهُ *He became like his father*. (Ṣ, M, Ḳ.)

صِيرٌ: see what next follows.

صَيْرٌ The *ulterior* or *ultimate, latter* or *last, state*, or *condition*; the *end, conclusion, event, issue*, or *result*; of a thing, an affair, or a case; (Ṣ, M, O, Mṣb, Ḳ;) as also ↓ صِيرٌ (O, Ḳ) and ↓ مَصِيرٌ (Ṣ, O, Mṣb, TA) and ↓ مَصِيرَةٌ (TA) and ↓ صَيُّورٌ, (Ṣ, M, Ḳ,) of the measure فَيْعُولٌ, (Ṣ,) and ↓ صَيُّورَةٌ. (Ḳ.) — The *verge, brink*, or *point*, of an affair, or event. (M, Ḳ.) You say, أَنَا عَلَى صِيرٍ مِنْ أَمْرِ كَذَا *I am on the verge of such an affair*, or *event*. (M.) And أَنَا عَلَى صِيرٍ مِنْ حَاجَتِى *I am at the point of* [attaining] *the object of my want*. (M.) And أَنَا عَلَى صِيرٍ مِنْ قَضَآءِ حَاجَتِى *I am at the point of accomplishing my want*. (A.) And فُلَانٌ عَلَى صِيرِ أَمْرٍ *Such a one is at the point of accomplishing an affair*. (Ṣ.) — *A water at which people stay*, or *abide*; (M, O, Ḳ;) as also ↓ صِيرَةٌ. (TA.) — *A crevice* of a door. (Ṣ, M, A, Mṣb, Ḳ.) It is said in a trad., مَنْ نَظَرَ فِى صِيرِ بَابٍ فَفُقِئَتْ عَيْنُهُ فَهِىَ هَدَرٌ [*Whosoever looks into the crevice of a door and has his eye put out, it is a thing for which no mulct is to be exacted*]: (Ṣ, M:) A'Obeyd says that this is the only instance in which the word [in this sense] has been heard. (Ṣ.) — [The *condiment, made of small fish, called*] صِحْنَاة: (Ṣ, M, Ḳ:) or [*a condiment*, or *the like*,] *resembling* صحناة: (M, Ḳ:) or *what is called in Pers.* مَاهِى آوَهْ [*jelly of salted fish*]; as also صِحْنَاةٌ: (Mgh voce صحناة:) and the *small salted fish of which* صحناة *is made*: (Kr, M, Ḳ:) or *the young ones of fish*: [a coll. gen. n.:] n. un. with ة: (Mṣb:) thought by IDrd to be Syriac; (TA;) by IAth, to be Pers., as also صحناة. (TA in art. صحن.) — Also The أُسْقُفّ [properly *bishop*] *of the Jews*. (O, Ḳ.) — See also the next paragraph.

صِيرَةٌ, (Ṣ, M, Mṣb, Ḳ,) accord. to A'Obeyd صَيْرَةٌ, with fet-ḥ, but Az says that this is a mistake, (TA,) *An enclosure* (حَظِيرَة) *for sheep or goats* (Ṣ, M, Mṣb, Ḳ) *and for cows or bulls*, (M, Ḳ,) *constructed of wood and stones* (M, TA) *and of branches of trees*; (TA;) as also ↓ صِيَارَةٌ, (M, Ḳ,) which latter is said by IDrd to be of the dial. of the people of Baghdád: (TA:) pl. of the former صِيَرٌ (Ṣ, M, Mṣb, Ḳ) and [coll. gen. n.] ↓ صِيرٌ. (M, Ḳ.) — See also صِيرٌ.

صِيَارٌ The صَنْج; (O and TA in this art., and TṢ and Ḳ and TA in art. صبر;) i. e. the *stringed instrument thus called*: (TṢ and TA in that art., and O and TA in the present art.:) [this is the right meaning, as is shown by the latter of the two verses cited voce صُبَارَةٌ: but,] accord. to AHeyth, (O,) the *sound of the* صَنْج. (O and Ḳ in the present art.) — See also art. صور.

صِيَارَةٌ: see صِيرَةٌ. — Also *i. q.* صُبَارَةٌ [q. v., signifying *Stones*, &c.]. (M in art. صبر.)

صَيِّرٌ *A grave*. (AA, O, Ḳ. [Perhaps so called as being the ulterior abode.]) One says, هٰذَا صَيِّرُ فُلَانٍ *This is the grave of such a one*. (O.) — And *A company* (جَمَاعَة). (O, Ḳ.) — See also art. صور.

صَيُّورَةٌ *A thing, upon the head of a* قَارَة [or *small isolated mountain* or *the like*], *resembling the* [*heap of stones, piled up as a sign of the way, called*] أَمَرَة, *except that it is cased, and the* امرة *is taller than it, and larger; or* [in my originals "and"] *they are both cased, but the* امرة *is peaked and tall, and the* صيرة *is round and wide, and has angles* [app. at the base]; *and sometimes it is excavated, and gold and silver are found in it: it is of the work of 'Ád and Irem.* (O, TA.)

صَائِرٌ *Staying,* or *abiding, at a water.* (TA.) And ▼ صَائِرَةٌ *A party, or people, staying,* or *abiding, at a water.* (O, TA.) ═ Also *A twister of men's necks.* (TA.) ═ [And The *pivot at the top,* and that *at the heel, of a door; the former of which turns in a socket in the lintel, and the latter in a socket in the threshold:*] see سَاجِفٌ.

صَائِرَةٌ: see the next preceding paragraph. ═ Also *Rain.* (M, TA.) — And *Herbage,* or *pasture.* (M.) See the next paragraph. — Also The *state of dryness to which herbage comes.* (M.)

صَيُّورٌ: see صِيرٌ. — Also *Judgment,* or *opinion,* (Ṣ,) and *understanding,* or *intellect,* or *intelligence;* (Ṣ, M, Ḳ;) as in the saying, مَا لَهُ صَيُّورٌ [*He has not judgment nor understanding*]: (Ṣ, M:) or *a judgment,* or *an opinion, to which one eventually comes;* as in the saying, مَا لَهُ بَدْءٌ وَلَا صَيُّورٌ [*He has not a first, nor a final, idea, thought, judgment,* or *opinion*]. (A.) ═ Also, (O, Ḳ,) as AḤn says, on the authority of Aboo-Ziyád, (O,) and ▼ صَائِرَةٌ, (Ḳ,) *Dry herbage* or *pasture, that is eaten long after its being green:* (O, Ḳ:) and he adds that no herbs have صَيُّور except such as are of the kinds called الثُّغْر and الأَفَانِى. (O, TA.) ═ أَمْرٌ صَيُّورٌ signifies *A confused and dubious affair,* (M, Ḳ,) *through which there is no way of passing;* as in the phrase وَقَعَ فِى أَمْرٍ صَيُّورٍ, mentioned by Yaạḳoob [ISk] in the "Alfádh" [accord. to some of the copies of that work]: originally meaning *a* [*mountain,* or *hill, such as is termed*] هَضْبَة *without a pass:* but it is more probably صَبُور [q. v., in art. صبر]. (M.)

صَيُّورَةٌ: see صِيرٌ, first sentence.

مَصِيرٌ an inf. n. of صَارَ [q. v.]. (Ṣ, M, &c.) ═ [Also *A place,* and hence *a state* or *condition, to which a person,* or *thing, eventually comes: a place of destination.*] See صِيرٌ. — *A place where people alight and abide: a good place where people alight and abide.* (TA.) — *A place to which waters come,* or *take their course:* (M, Ḳ:) [or *a place of herbage,* or *pasture, and of water:*] pl. مَصَايِرُ: so in the saying, خَرَجُوا إِلَى مَصَايِرِهِمْ *They went forth to their places of herbage,* or *pasture, and of water.* (A.) ═ See also art. مصر.

مَصِيرَةٌ: see صِيرٌ, first sentence.

صيص

1. صَاصَتِ النَّخْلَةُ, [aor. تَصِيصُ,] *The palm-tree bore dates which had become such as are termed* صِيص, i. e., شِيص; (Ḳ,* TA;) as also ▼ صَيَّصَت, (Ḳ,) inf. n. تَصْيِيصٌ; (TA;) and ▼ اصاصت, (Ḳ,) inf. n. إِصَاصَةٌ; (TA;) all three on the authority of IAạr, and the first mentioned by Ṣgh, in the O; and صَأْصَأَتْ, from صِئْصَاءٌ [a dial. var. of صِيصَآءٌ, i. q. صِيصٌ]. (TA.)

2: } see the preceding paragraph.
4: }

صِيصٌ, in the dial. of Belḥárith Ibn-Kaạb, The [bad] *kind of dates called* حَشَفٌ; (Ṣ;) *i. q.* شِيصٌ; as also ▼ صِيصَآءٌ; (Ḳ;) صِيص and صِيصَآء being dial. vars. of شِيص and شِيصَآء. (Ṣ.)

صِيصَةٌ: see صِيصِيَةٌ, throughout.

صِيصَآءٌ: see صِيص. [It is also said to signify] *Dates without stones.* (L in art. لقح.) — Also The *pips of a colocynth that have no hearts,* (AḤn, Ṣ, Ḳ,) *being husks only;* (AḤn;) to which a poet likens ticks that have been long left in a desolate place: (AḤn, Ṣ:*) and so, accord. to some, *of anything, such as the melon and the cucumber and the like.* (AḤn.)

صِيصِيَةٌ, (Ṣ, IB, O,) or ▼ صِيصَةٌ, (Ḳ,) thus in all the copies of the Ḳ, but it is a mistake, or a contracted form, (TA,) *The weaver's* [*implement called*] شَوْكَة, *with which he makes the warp and the woof even:* (Ṣ, IB, Ḳ:) but IB says that its last radical letter is ى, not ص; so that it should be mentioned among the class of infirm words: (TA:) pl. صَيَاصِى. (Ṣ.) — Hence, (Ṣ,) The *spur of the cock.* (Ṣ, Ḳ.) — [Hence also,] The *horn of the bull or cow, and of the gazelle:* (Ḳ:) pl. as above, (TA,) signifying the *horns* of bulls or cows; which were sometimes fixed upon spears, instead of the iron heads: (Ṣ:) and to such horns, called by this name, conflict and faction, or sedition, (فِتْنَة,) is likened in a trad., because of its grievousness: some say that the sing. is صِيصَةٌ, [as in the Ḳ,] contracted. (TA.) — And hence, (TA,) *A wooden pin,* or *peg, with which dates are plucked out* [*when they are compacted in a mass, closely adhering together, in the receptacle of woven palm-leaves, or the like, in which they are packed*]: (Ḳ:) likened to the horn of a bull or cow: in this sense, the word is written صِيصَةٌ: and a certain poet changes it to صِيصَجٌ. (TA.) — [Hence also,] *Anything with which one defends himself:* pl. as above, (Ḳ,) [in the CḲ erroneously written صَيَاصِى, as though it had the article ال prefixed to it, or were itself prefixed to another noun, for otherwise it is written and pronounced] with the [final] ى elided. (TA.) — [Hence also,] *A fortress:* (Ḳ:) pl. in this sense as above. (Ṣ, TA.) — [Hence also,] *A pastor who manages* [*and protects*] *well his herds* or *flocks:* (AA, Ḳ:) in this sense also written صِيصَةٌ. (AA, as in the TA.)

صيع

1. صِعْتُ, aor. أَصِيعُ, inf. n. صَيْعٌ: see 1 in art. صوع, in three places.

4. اصاع الغَنَمَ: see 1, in art. صوع, latter half.

5. تصيّع: see 5 in art. صوع, last sentence. — Also, said of water, *It was,* or *became, in a state of commotion upon the surface of the ground:* (IDrd, O, Ḳ,* TA:) but تسيّع is more approved [in this sense, or as meaning "it ran upon the surface of the ground," as expl. in art. سيع]. (TA.)

7. انصاع: see art. صوع. It belongs to this art. and to art. صوع. (Ḳ.)

أَصْيَعُ [an epithet mentioned, but not expl., in the O and TA: it seems to be from صِعْتُهُ "I dispersed it, or scattered it;" and hence to be *syn.* with أَشْيَعُ, signifying *In a state of commotion,* or *of exceeding commotion*]. Rubeh says,

فَظَلَّ يَكْسُوهَا الغُبَارَ الأَصْيَعَا *

[app. meaning *And he passed the day enveloping her,* or *it,* or *them, in the dust in a state of commotion,* or *of exceeding commotion*]. (O, TA.)

صيغ

2. صَيَّغَ طَعَامَهُ, (ISh, O, Ḳ,) inf. n. تَصْيِيغٌ (Ḳ,) *He soaked his food in sauce,* or *seasoning:* (ISh, O, Ḳ:) and صَيَّغَهُ بِالسَّمْنِ *He soaked it with clarified butter.* (ISh, O.) [صَبَّغَهُ has a similar meaning, and is better known.]

صِيغَةٌ and other words in which ى is substituted for و, see in art. صوغ.

صيف

1. صَافَ, (Ṣ, M, O, Mṣb, Ḳ,) aor. يَصِيفُ, inf. n. صَيْفٌ, (TA,) *He,* or *it,* (a company of men, M, Mṣb,) *remained, stayed, dwelt,* or *abode,* (Ṣ, M, O, Mṣb, Ḳ,) *during the* [*season called*] صَيْف, (Ṣ, O,) or *during his,* or *their,* صَيْف, (O, Mṣb,) or *during a* صَيْف, (Ḳ,) بِهِ *in it,* (Ṣ, M, O, Ḳ,) i. e. in a place; (Ṣ, M, O;) as also ▼ اصطاف, (Ṣ, O,* Ḳ,* TA,) and ▼ تصيّف; (Ṣ,* O,* Ḳ,* TA;) and ▼ صَيَّفَ ▼ اصّيّف بِالمَكَانِ is like [probably a mistranscription for تَصَيَّفَ, of which اصّيّف is a var., and of which, together with one of this var., an ex. will be found in what follows]: (TA:) you say, صِفْتُ بِمَكَانِ كَذَا [*I remained during the* صَيْف *in such a place*], and in like manner صَيَّفْتُهُ, and ▼ تَصَيَّفْتُهُ, and ▼ صَيَّفْتُهُ [probably a mistranscription for ▼ اصّيّفتهُ, as seems to be indicated by what here follows]: (M:) a Hudhalee says,

تَصَيَّفْتُ نُعْمَانَ وَاصَّيَّفَتْ *

[*I remained during the* صَيْف *in Noạmán, and she remained during the* صَيْف]. (M, TA.) — And صِيفَتِ الأَرْضُ, (Ṣ, M, O, Ḳ,) a verb of the class of عُنِىَ, (Ḳ,) originally صُيِفَت, (TA,) *The land was rained upon by the rain of the* [*season called*] صَيْف. (Ṣ, M, O.*) And صِفْنَا, of the measure فُعِلْنَا, like خُوِفْنَا and رُبِعْنَا, *We were rained upon by the rain of the* صَيْف: (Ṣ:) and in like manner ▼ صُيِّفْنَا. (M, TA.*) ═ صاف السَّهْمُ عَنِ الهَدَفِ, (Ṣ, M, O, Mṣb,* Ḳ,*) aor. يَصِيفُ, (Ṣ, O, Ḳ,) inf. n. صَيْفٌ (Ṣ, M, O, Mṣb, Ḳ) and صَيْفُوفَةٌ (Ṣ, M, O) and مَصِيفٌ, (M,) *The arrow turned aside from the butt:* (Ṣ, M, O, Mṣb, Ḳ:) a dial. var. of صاف having for its aor. يَصُوفُ and inf. n. صَوْفٌ. (O, Mṣb,* Ḳ.) —— And صاف الفَحْلُ عَنْ طَرُوقَتِهِ *The stallion-camel turned away from covering the female that he had covered.* (M.)

2. صَيَّفَنِى *It* (a thing, Ṣ, O, Ḳ) *sufficed me for my* [*season termed*] صَيْفَة, (Ṣ, O, Ḳ,) or *for my* صَيْف: (Mṣb:) by the "thing" here spoken of is meant food, or a garment, or some other thing. (TA.) —— See also 1, in three places.

3. صَايَفَهُ مُصَايَفَةً عَامَلَهُ (Ṣ, M, O, Mṣb, Ḳ) and صِيَافًا (Lḥ, M) is from الصَّيْف, (M, O, Mṣb,) like مُشَاهَرَة (Ṣ, O, Mṣb, Ḳ) from الشَّهْر, (O, Mṣb,) and مُعَاوَمَة (Ṣ, O) from العَام, (O,) i. e. [*He made an engagement*, or *a contract, with him for work* or *the like*] *for the days of the* صَيْف. (Ṣ.) And in like manner, اِسْتَأْجَرَهُ مُصَايَفَةً and صِيَافًا [*He hired him*, or *took him as a hired man* or *hireling, for the period of the* صَيْف]. (M.)

4. اصافوا *They entered the* [*season called*] صَيْف: (Ṣ, M, O, Mṣb, Ḳ:) like أَشْتَوْا meaning "They entered the [season called] شِتَآء." (TA.) —— And اصافت *She* (a camel) *brought forth in the* صَيْف. (M.) —— [Hence,] اصاف said of a man, ‡ *He had offspring born to him* [*in the summer of his age*, i. e.] *when he was old*, or *advanced in age:* (Ṣ, M, O, Ḳ, TA:) or *he had no offspring born to him until he was advanced in age*, or *old*. (L, TA.) And ‡ *He abstained from women while a young man, and then married when old*, or *advanced in age*. (M, TA.) —— اصاف اللّٰهُ عَنِّى شَرَّ فُلَانٍ *God turned away*, or *may God turn away, from me the evil*, or *mischief, of such a one:* (Ṣ, O, Ḳ:*) belonging to this art. and to art. صوف. (O, TA.)

5. تَصَيَّفَ, and its var. اِصَّيَّفَ: see 1, first sentence, in four places.

8: see 1, first sentence.

صَافٍ: see صَائِفٌ: —— and see also art. صوف.

صَيْفٌ as signifying *A certain portion of the year* is said by ISk to be fem.: (TA, voce شِتَآء; q. v.:) [but by others I find it treated as masc.:] the صَيْف as meaning *one of the seasons* is well known: (M:) Lth says, it is *one of the quarters of the year;* and is applied by the vulgar to *a half of the year* [i. e. to the *half-year commencing at the vernal equinox;* the other half-year being called by them the شِتَآء]: Az says, it is, with the Arabs, the *division which the vulgar in El-'Irák and Khurásán call the* رَبِيع [i. e. the *spring*]; *it consists of three months;* and the division that next follows it is with the Arabs the قَيْظ; and in it is the جَمْرَة [q. v.] of the قَيْظ; then, after this, is the division called the خَرِيف; and then, after this, the division called the شِتَآء: (TA:) [i. e.] it is the *quarter of the year vulgarly called the* رَبِيع, *commencing when the sun enters Aries:* but is applied by the vulgar to the قَيْظ, which is the [*summer*, i. e.] the *quarter commencing when the sun enters Cancer:* (Mṣb in art. زمن; q. v.:) [F says,] the صَيْف is the قَيْظ [i. e. *summer*, or the *hot season*]; or [the *season*] *after the* رَبِيع: (Ḳ:) and [Ṣgh says,] the صَيْف is *one of the divisions of the year; which is after the* رَبِيع: (O:) [but unless this explanation in the O denote only a vulgar meaning, and the latter of the two explanations in the Ḳ be virtually a repetition, we must suppose that, in each of them, by the رَبِيع is meant the season of rain thus termed, which ends in March: (see the latter of the two tables which I have inserted voce زَمَنٌ:) most probably, I think, both have been faultily transcribed from what here follows; for the Ṣ is largely copied in the O, and the Ṣ and O are among the principal sources of the Ḳ, which generally follows the O when it differs (rightly or wrongly) from the Ṣ:] the صَيْف is *one of the divisions of the year; which is after* [*that called*] الرَّبِيعُ الأَوَّلُ *and before* [*that called*] القَيْظ: (Ṣ:) [this admits of two renderings, both of which are correct; namely, the *quarter after the season of two months called* الربيع الاوّل (*which ends in March*) *and before the quarter called* القيظ (*which is summer*); and also the *season of two months after that called* الربيع الاوّل *and before the similar season called* القيظ: (see the former of the two tables to which I have referred above:) but probably the latter only was meant by him who first gave this explanation:] the pl. is أَصْيَافٌ (M, O, Ḳ) and صُيُوفٌ: (M, Mṣb:) ▼ صَيْفَةٌ is a more particular term [app. meaning *A single* صَيْف; (see 2;)]; it is like شَتْوَةٌ [q. v.]; (O, Ḳ;) and its pl. is صِيَفٌ, like بِدَرٌ pl. of بَدْرَةٌ. (Fr, O, Ḳ.) الصَّيْفَ ضَيَّعْتِ اللَّبَنَ is a saying expl. in art. ضيع [q. v.]. (O, Ḳ.) —— الصَّيْفُ also signifies *The rain that comes in the* [*season called*] صَيْف; (Ṣ, O, Mṣb, Ḳ;) [see, again, the second of the tables to which I have referred above, and see also نَوْءٌ;] and (O, Ḳ) so ▼ الصَّيِّفُ; (M, O, Ḳ;) also signifying *the herbage thereof:* (M:) or, (Ḳ,) accord. to Lth, (O,) the latter signifies *the rain that falls after the division* [a mistake for *the rain*] *called the* رَبِيع; (O, Ḳ;) and so the former; (Ḳ;) and it is also called ▼ الصَّيْفِىُّ; (O, Ḳ;) which likewise signifies *the herbage thereof*. (TA.) Hence the prov., relating to the completing of the performance of a needful affair, تَمَامُ الرَّبِيعِ الصَّيْفُ [*The completion of* the rain called *the* رَبِيع *is* that called *the* صيف]: for the rain called the رَبِيع is the first rain, and the صيف is that which is [next] after it. (TA.) —— آيَةُ الصَّيْفِ is [*A verse*] *in the end* (آخِر) *of* سُورَةُ النِّسَآءِ [*the 4th chapter of the Ḳur-án*, but which verse I know not], mentioned in a tradition. (TA.) —— Also The *female of the* بُوم [or *owl*]. (Kr, M.)

صَيْفَةٌ: see the next preceding paragraph, latter half.

صَيْفِىٌّ A thing *of*, or *belonging to, the* [*season called*] صَيْف. (Ṣ, O.) —— A young camel *born in the* صَيْف. (M.) [And in like manner a sheep or goat: see صَفَرِىٌّ.] —— And [hence,] † A son *born to a father* [*in the summer of his age*, i. e.] *old*, or *advanced in age*. (Ṣ, M, O.) [See an ex. in a verse cited voce رِبْعِىٌّ.] —— See also صَيْفٌ, near the end of the paragraph. —— صَيْفِيَّةٌ [used as a subst., or as an epithet in which the quality of a subst. is predominant, for مِيرَةٌ صَيْفِيَّةٌ,] and ▼ صَائِفَةٌ signify The مِيرَة [or *provision of corn &c.*] *in the first part of the* صَيْف [here meaning *spring*]; i. e. the *second* مِيرَة; for the first of the مِيَر is the رِبْعِيَّة, then the صَيْفِيَّة, then the دَفَئِيَّة, and then the رَمَضِيَّة: (M:) or the ▼ صَائِفَة of a people is their مِيرَة *in the* صَيْف. (Ṣ, O, Ḳ.) [See مِيرَةٌ.] —— صَيْفِيَّةٌ is also applied to The *latter*, or *last, season* of the bringing forth of camels: so in an explanation of هُبَعٌ in the Ṣ and TA.]

صَيْفِيَّةٌ [fem. of صَيْفِىٌّ: and also used as a subst., or as an epithet in which the quality of a subst. is predominant: see the latter word].

صَائِفٌ is used as an imitative sequent in the phrase صَيْفٌ صَائِفٌ, (Ṣ, O, Ḳ,) meaning *A warm*, or *hot*, [*spring* or] *summer:* (PṢ:) a phrase like لَيْلٌ لَائِلٌ &c. (Ṣ, O.) And one says يَوْمٌ صَائِفٌ, (Ṣ, M, O, Mṣb, Ḳ,) meaning *A hot day;* (O, Ḳ;) and ▼ يَوْمٌ صَافٍ (Ṣ, O, Ḳ) was sometimes said, meaning صَائِفٌ; like يَوْمٌ رَاحٌ [as meaning رَائِحٌ]: (Ṣ:) and لَيْلَةٌ صَائِفَةٌ [*a hot night*]. (Ṣ, O, Mṣb.) —— And مَطَرٌ صَائِفٌ [app. *Rain coming in the* صَيْف, meaning *spring;* as also ▼ مُصِيفٌ, occurring in a verse cited voce رَسَمٌ, q. v.]. (M.) See also صَابٍ in art. صفو.

صَائِفَةٌ [fem. of صَائِفٌ, q. v. —— Also, as a subst.,] *A warring*, or *warring and plundering, expedition in the* صَيْف [i. e. either *spring* or *summer*]: (M, Mgh, and Ḥam p. 239:) pl. صَوَائِفُ. (Mgh, and Ḥam ib.) And [particularly] (Mgh) *A warring*, or *warring and plundering, expedition against the Greeks* (الرُّوم): because they [i. e. the Arabs] used to go on expeditions of this kind in the صَيْف, (Ṣ, Mgh, O, Ḳ,) and to return in the winter, (Mgh,) on account of the cold and snow. (Ṣ, O, Ḳ.) And they said, وَلِىَ فُلَانٌ الصَّائِفَةَ, meaning *Such a one was commander of the army going on a warring*, or *warring and plundering, expedition in the* صَيْف: (Ḥam ubi suprà:) [but Mṭr says,] he who explains صَائِفَة as meaning the *place* [*of*], or the *army* [*engaged in, such an expedition*], errs: [adding that the Ḥanafee Imám] Mohammad has used the phrase الصَّوَائِفُ وَنَحْوُهَا مِنَ العَسَاكِرِ العِظَامِ either by surmise or by extension of the [proper] meaning. (Mgh.) —— See also صَيْفِىٌّ, in two places. —— Also The *time*, or *season of the* صَيْف. (M, TA.)

الصَّيِّفُ: see صَيْفٌ, last quarter of the paragraph.

صَيِّفَةٌ, originally صَيْوِفَةٌ: see art. صوف.

مَصِيفٌ *A place of remaining, staying, dwelling*, or *abiding, during the* [*season called*] صَيْف; (Ṣ, O, TA;) as also ▼ مُصْطَافٌ (Ṣ, Ḳ, TA) and ▼ مُتَصَيَّفٌ: (TA:) and *a time thereof:* (Sb, M, TA:) pl. مَصَايِفُ. (Mṣb.) —— And *A place in which dates are dried in the* [*season called*] صَيْف.

(Ḥar p. 165.) ═ [Also part. n. of the verb in the phrase صِيفَتِ الأَرْضُ:] you say أَرْضٌ مَصِيفَةٌ and ↑ مَصْيُوفَةٌ Land rained upon by the rain of the [season called] صَيْف. (Ṣ, M, O, Ḳ.) ═ Also, applied to a channel in which water flows, Winding, or tortuous: (Ṣ, M:) from صَافَ, like مَضِيقٌ from ضَاقَ. (Ṣ.) [See an ex. in a verse cited voce كَرِيَّةٌ: and see also مَضِيف.]

مُصِيفٌ: see صَائِفٌ. — Also, (M, O, Ḳ,) and مُصِيفَةٌ, (O, Ḳ,) [in the CḲ, erroneously, مَصِيف and مَصِيفَةٌ,] and ↑ مِصْيَافٌ, (M, O, Ḳ,) applied to a she-camel, (M, O, Ḳ,) That has brought forth in the [season called] صَيْف: (M, L, TA:) or having with her her young one: (O, Ḳ, TA:) pl. of the last مَصَايِيفُ. (TA in art. جمر.) — And [hence,] the first, ‡ A man having a child born to him [in the summer of his age, i. e.] when he is old, or advanced in age. (TA.)

مِصْيَافٌ, applied to land (أَرْضٌ), Having in it abundance of the rain of the [season called] صَيْف. (O, Ḳ.) — And, so applied, Late in producing herbage. (O, Ḳ.) — See also مُصِيف. — [Hence,] ‡ A man who does not take a wife until he has whiteness in the hair of his head mixed with the blackness thereof. (O, Ḳ.)

مَصْيُوفَةٌ: }
مُصْطَافٌ: } see مَصِيف.
مُتَصَيِّفٌ: }

صيك

1. صَاكَ بِهِ, aor. يَصِيكُ, inf. n. صَيْكٌ: see 1 in art. صوك.

3. ظَلَّ يُصَايِكُنِي مُنْذُ اليَوْمِ a dial. var. of يُصَاوِكُنِي. (TA in art. صوك. See 3 in art. صاك.)

صيل

1. صَالَ, aor. يَصِيلُ, i. q. صال having for its aor. يَصُولُ, (Ibn-'Abbád, O, Ḳ,) i. e. He (a man) leaped or sprang [&c.]. (Ibn-'Abbád, O.) ═ صِيلَ لَهُمْ كَذَا, (Ṣ and Ḳ in art. صول,) or لَهُ, (Ibn-'Abbád and O and Ḳ in the present art.,) Such a thing was appointed, or ordained, or prepared, for them, or for him. (Ibn-'Abbád, Ṣ, O, Ḳ.) This is its proper place. (TA.)

صِيلَةٌ The knot of the عَذَبَة [i. e. of the end, or of the suspensory thong, of a whip]. (Ṣ and Ḳ in art. صول, and O in the present art.)

صِيَالٌ and صِيَالَةٌ: see art. صول.

Quasi صيم

صُيَّمٌ and صِيَّمٌ and صُيَّامٌ and صَيَامَى pls. of صَائِمٌ, expl. in art. صوم.

صين

صِينَةٌ [originally صِوْنَةٌ]: see art. صون.

صِينِيٌّ Of, or relating to, الصِّين [i. e. China]. (TA.) [Hence,] أَوَانٍ صِينِيَّةٌ, (Ḳ, TA,) and [the pl.] صَوَانِيُّ, (Ṣ,) Vessels of الصِّين, (Ṣ, Ḳ, TA,) made in the country thus called [i. e. China]. (TA.)

صِينِينٌ A certain drug, [said to be] well known. (TA. [But what it is I have been unable to learn.])

صِيَانٌ and صِيَانَةٌ inf. n. of صَانَ expl. in art. صون. ═ The former, of which صُيَانٌ and صَيَانٌ are said to be vars., is also syn. with صِوَانٌ, likewise expl. in art. صون.

صَيِّنٌ: see art. صون.

End of the Fourth Part of Book I.*